41ST EDITION

KOVELS'

Antiques & Collectibles PRICE GUIDE 2009

Published by
Black Dog & Leventhal Publishers, Inc.
151 W. 19th Street
New York, NY 10011

Distributed by
Workman Publishing Company
225 Varick Street
New York, NY 10014

Designed by Sheila Hart Design, Inc.
Manufactured in the United States of America

ISBN-13: 978-1-57912-785-5
Library of Congress Cataloging-in-Publication Data is available on file at
the offices of the publisher.

Paperback
b d f h g e c a

Front cover photographs, from top to bottom:
American silver coffee set, stenciled Windsor rocking chair,
and Andy Gump cast-iron car.
On the spine: Thistle pattern carnival glass banana boat.
Back cover photographs, from top to bottom:
mother-of-pearl glass vase, Handel lamp with reverse-painted daffodil shade,
and Rookwood wild rose vase.
Author photograph © Daniel Levin.

BOOKS BY RALPH AND TERRY KOVEL

American Country Furniture, 1780–1875

A Directory of American Silver, Pewter, and Silver Plate

Kovels' Advertising Collectibles Price List

Kovels' American Antiques 1750–1900

Kovels' American Art Pottery

Kovels' American Collectibles 1900–2000

Kovels' American Silver Marks, 1650 to the Present

Kovels' Antiques & Collectibles Fix-It Source Book

Kovels' Antiques & Collectibles Price Guide

Kovels' Bid, Buy, and Sell Online

Kovels' Book of Antique Labels

Kovels' Bottles Price List

Kovels' Collector's Guide to American Art Pottery

Kovels' Collectors' Guide to Limited Editions

Kovels' Collectors' Source Book

Kovels' Depression Glass & Dinnerware Price List

Kovels' Dictionary of Marks—Pottery and Porcelain, 1650 to 1850

Kovels' Guide to Selling, Buying, and Fixing Your Antiques and Collectibles

Kovels' Guide to Selling Your Antiques & Collectibles

Kovels' Illustrated Price Guide to Royal Doulton

Kovels' Know Your Antiques

Kovels' Know Your Collectibles

Kovels' New Dictionary of Marks—Pottery and Porcelain, 1850 to the Present

Kovels' Organizer for Collectors

Kovels' Price Guide for Collector Plates, Figurines, Paperweights, and Other Limited Edition Items

Kovels' Quick Tips: 799 Helpful Hints on How to Care for Your Collectibles

Kovels' Yellow Pages: A Resource Guide for Collectors

The Label Made Me Buy It: From Aunt Jemima to Zonkers—The Best-Dressed Boxes, Bottles, and Cans from the Past

INTRODUCTION

This is the forty-first year *Kovels' Antiques & Collectibles Price Guide* has been published. The book is still written by its original authors, Ralph and Terry Kovel, and has the same reliable content. The new format introduced last year, with 2,500 color photographs, 42,000 prices, and dozens of added tips about care and facts of interest, was a welcome improvement. This book has the same features. Each photograph is shown with a complete caption that includes the price. The book is even bigger this year, with 44,000 prices. It has color tabs and color-coded paragraphs that make it easy to find the listings you want. And it has a modern, readable typestyle. There are 700 categories with introductory paragraphs. And, as always, all of the antiques and collectibles priced here were offered for sale during the past year, most of them in the American market.

READ THIS FIRST

This is a book for the collector. We check prices, visit shops, shows, and flea markets, read hundreds of publications and catalogs, check Internet sales and other online services, and decide which antiques and collectibles are of most interest to most collectors. We concentrate on the average pieces in any category. Sometimes high-priced items are included so you will realize that rarities are very valuable.

Examples of furniture, silver, Tiffany, art pottery, and some other items may sell for more than $40,000; we list a few. Most pieces cost less than $10,000. The highest price in this book is $881,000 for a Tiffany Wisteria lamp. The lowest price is 15¢ for a bottle cap. We also include the weird and the wonderful. This year you can find a medical amputation kit for $785, a 46-inch-long wooden leg for $353, a pair of boxes shaped like feet wearing sandals for $196, and a cane with a hidden scalpel and syringe for $750. The smallest item in the book is a ¼-inch mother-of-pearl button. The biggest is a Napoleon III mahogany bookcase, 9 ½ feet high by 9 feet wide.

Although the economy is suffering, housing prices are down, and gas prices are up, the antiques and collectibles market keeps chugging along. As always, the best of the best brings high prices; ordinary collectibles are bargain-priced; useful furniture is selling well, but for moderate prices; and damaged or uninteresting pieces are difficult, often impossible, to sell. Prices are up in some categories: Several important mechanical bank collections were auctioned this year and prices for the best banks were in the tens of thousands of dollars and even higher. A major collection of shaving mugs also set record prices. Modern furniture made from the 1930s to today by known artists still bring very high prices, often six figures. But ordinary fifties pieces that were selling for high prices last year have come down. Doorstops are still going up in price and there is an inexplicable jump in demand for all things iron, including bookends, doorknockers, toy cars, and furniture.

Prices at large, well-advertised auctions look high when compared to presale estimates, but if you take a closer look you'll find that estimates are low to encourage bidders. In general, Internet-only auction prices are still dropping, and many items don't sell. However, many larger auction houses are selling on land and online at the same time, giving them a wider, international customer base and good prices.

When we started collecting we were young, antiques dealers and buyers were "old" (in their late fifties and sixties). By 1967, the year our first price book was published, there was a new group of dealers—free-spirited independent entrepreneurs who were willing to gamble on their own talent and taste. Books that explained or priced antiques were not readily available, so collectors depended on dealers. Today the older dealers have retired, younger (under 40) dealers are appearing at shows, and everyone has access to information on the Internet and in price guides like this one. Prices have become national, even international, and while collectors have an easier time finding rarities, prices are higher. There was a slump in the market in 2007 but by mid 2008 there were many signs that buyers were back in spite of the economy. But antique malls have been closing, shows require more advertising and more creative salesmanship, and online auctions are undergoing major changes. EBay will be out of the live auction business by the end of the year, while others are striving to take over. There are still bargains to be had, but most are in newer categories: modernist jewelry, European art pottery made after 1975, stoneware (an old favorite that's back), plastic furniture and accessories, farm tools, and copper costume jewelry.

This book seems to have gotten younger over the past forty years. Most items in our original book were made before 1860. Today we have pieces made as recently as 2000, and there is great interest in furniture, glass, and ceramics made since 1950.

The book is about 800 pages long, and crammed full of prices and photographs. We try to have a balanced format—not too many glass, pottery, or collectible items; furniture from the eighteenth through the twentieth centuries; and not too many items that sell for over $5,000. We list a few very expensive pieces so you can realize that a great paperweight may cost $9,000 and an average one only $25. Nearly all the prices are from the American market for the American market. Few European sales are reported. We take the editorial privilege of not including prices we think result from "auction fever." There is a computer-generated index. Use it often. It includes categories and much more. For example, there is a category for Celluloid. Most celluloid will be there, but a toy made of celluloid will be listed under Toy and also indexed under Celluloid. There are also cross-references in the listings and in the paragraphs. But some searching must be done. For example, Barbie dolls are in the Doll category; there is no Barbie category. And when you look at "doll, Barbie," you see a note that Barbie is under "doll, Mattel, Barbie" because most dolls are listed by maker. Where possible, we list the maker at the beginning of an entry, and the size and age at the end.

All photographs and prices are new. Antiques and collectibles pictured are items that were offered for sale. Whenever we had extra space on a page, we filled them with new tips about care of collections and other useful information. Don't discard this book. Old Kovels' price guides should be saved for future reference and for tax and appraisal information.

The prices in this book are reports of the general antiques market. Every price in the book is new. We do not estimate or "update" prices. Prices are either realized prices from auctions or completed sales, or asking prices; a buyer may have negotiated an asking price to a lower selling price. But no price is an estimate. We do not pay dealers, collectors, or experts to estimate prices. Experience has shown us that estimated prices are usually high or low, but rarely an accurate report. If a price range is given, at least two identical items were offered for sale at different prices. Price ranges are found only in categories like Pressed Glass, where identical items can be identified. If the price is from an auction, it includes the buyer's premium; but like all the prices, it does not include sales tax. Some prices in *Kovels' Antiques & Collectibles Price Guide* may seem high and some may seem low because of regional variations, but each price is one you could have paid for the object somewhere in the United States. Some Internet prices, carefully edited, are included, but we find prices there can be misleading. Because so many non-collectors sell online but know little about the objects they are describing, there are often inaccuracies in the descriptions.

If you are selling your collection, do not expect to get retail value unless you are a dealer. Wholesale prices for antiques are usually 50 percent of retail prices. The antiques dealer must make a profit or go out of business. Internet auction prices are less predictable—because of an international audience and "auction fever," prices can be higher or lower than retail.

RECORD PRICES

ADVERTISING

Coca-Cola window display: $40,250 for a 1937 Coca-Cola window display, four-piece display of a soda fountain with die-cut pedestrians viewing the soda shop through a revolving glass door from the sidewalk outside, customers inside being waited on by two soda jerks. Marquee reads "The Pleasantest Place in Town," lithograph by Niagara Litho Co., Buffalo, New York, 52 x 46 in.

El-Bart Dry Gin sign: $60,500 for an El-Bart Dry Gin tin advertising sign, made in 1905 for Wilson Distilling Co., by Kaufmann & Strauss Co., Lithographers, of New York.

Sprague salesman sample mower: $16,100 for a brass salesman sample sickle bar mower by Sprague, with wooden bar, side bar cutting mechanism, spoke wheels, formed seat and an adjustable gear mechanism that works sickle bar. Plaque reads "The Sprague Mower, Providence, R.I.," 14 x 14 x 5 in.

UMC shells box: $1,305 for a fully sealed box of UMC (Union Metallic Cartridge Co.) 24-gauge shotgun shells made in the 1920s. (UMC was later bought by Remington.)

BRONZES & SCULPTURES

Bonheur, bronze sculpture: $58,650 for the Isidore Jules Bonheur bronze grizzly bear sculpture, brown patina, inscribed "I. Bonheur," Peyrol Foundry stamp, late 19th to early 20th century, 27 ½ in. h.

CLOCKS & WATCHES

Lantern clock: $286,000 for an English brass lantern clock made by William Bowyer in 1623, engraved "Memento Mori," Latin for "Remember your mortality," scene of skeleton with Biblical reference and Chronos walking with his scythe.

Vintage Vacheron Constantin wristwatch: $457,000 for a vintage Vacheron Constantin wristwatch, Ref. 4293, 18K pink gold, with complications of triple calendar, phases of the moon, and minute-repeating, 1943.

DECOYS

Crowell curlew: $186,500 for an A. Elmer Crowell decorative curlew in running pose, with carved wingtips, painted body, and legs made from umbrella ribs, c.1915, 17 in.

Crowell preening pintail drake decoy: $1,130,000 for a preening pintail drake carved by A. Elmer Crowell, c.1915.

Crowell sleeping Canada goose decoy: $1,130,000 for a sleeping Canada goose decoy carved by A. Elmer Crowell, c.1917.

FURNITURE

American Rococo armchairs: $32,900 for a pair of American Rococo carved and laminated rosewood armchairs, with floral cartouche crests, pierced scroll work, padded shaped arms, serpentine seat, and cabriole legs, attributed to J. & J.W. Meeks, New York, mid 19th century, 45 in. h.

Dining suite by John Bradstreet: $348,000 for a "Jin-di-Sugi" dining suite by John Bradstreet, dining table, 12 chairs, sideboard, and serving table, cypress and chestnut with Jin-di-Sugi finish, chairs have original under-upholstery, later fabric seat covers, sideboard with brass and glazed ceramic hardware, serving table stenciled with the firm's cipher, dated 1910, fifteen pieces plus four extension leaves.

Greene & Greene armchair: $913,600 (second highest price for work by the designers at auction) for a Greene & Greene armchair, c.1908, mahogany with ebony pegs and splines, oak and exotic wood inlay, later fabric upholstery, 33 ⅜ in. h.

Hunzinger armchair: $18,212 for a late 19th-century American Innovative carved walnut armchair by George Hunzinger, crest with finials and floral drops, padded back, scrolled sides, low boss arms, and canted legs with hoof feet, 41 in. h. x 21 in. w.

McIntire sofa: $167,250 for a Salem Federal mahogany sofa by Samuel McIntire, c.1800, carved with a basket of fruit and flowers on a star-punched field, scrolled arms with waterleaf carving and rosettes.

Paul Evans sideboards: $150,000 for a pair of Paul Evans sideboards, from the "Sculpted Front" series, lacquered and gilt steel, wood, slate top, welded signature and date, 1969, 25 x 53 ½ x 22 ½ in.

Philadelphia furniture: $6,761,000 for a Chippendale carved mahogany tea table, round, with piecrust edge and original casters, attributed to the "Garvan carver," Philadelphia, c.1760, 29 ½ x 31 ⅛ in. diam.

GLASS

Biltmore Dairy Farms quart milk bottle: $5,500 for a 1933 quart milk bottle, Tillman's Grocerter 5¢ Store Bottle, Biltmore Dairy Farms, from Asheville, North Carolina. Also: a half-pint Tillman's Grocerter 5¢ Store Bottle, Biltmore Dairy Farms, milk bottle sold for $1,325 on eBay.

Baker's Orange Grove bitters: $17,920 for an emerald green bottle with amber striations, applied top, smooth base, 1860-80, 9 ⅝ in.

Brown's Celebrated Indian Herb bitters: $29,120, for an greenish aqua bottle with sheared lip, 12 ¼ in.

Chalmer's Catawba Wine bitters: $24,600 for an aqua bottle, 12 in.

Dr. Wonser's U.S.A. Indian Root bitters: $25,760 for a yellow variant bottle with a touch of green, applied top, smooth base, 1871-73.

Harrison's Columbia ink: $29,120 for a blue bottle full of bubbles, with applied top, 1850s, 11 ½ in., gallon master ink.

H.P. Herb Wild Cherry bitters: $10,080 for a yellow olive bottle with smooth base, 10 in.

Kelly's Old Cabin bitters: $51,520 for a green bottle with applied top, cabin shape, patented 1863.

National bitters: $16,240 for a light to medium bluish aqua bottle with applied top, 12 ½ in.

Old Sachem Bitters and Wigwam tonic: $20,720 for a mossy green teal bottle with applied top, smooth base, 1860-80, 9 ½ in.

MISCELLANEOUS

Air King 52 radio: $51,000 for an Air King 52 radio, light blue with black knobs, map of the world dial, 1933, 11 ¾ x 8 ¾ x 6 ¾ in. diam.

Blick Electric typewriter: $100,000 for the world's first electric typewriter, the Blick Electric typewriter, 1902, invented by Charles Blickensderfer.

Christ sickles: $3,500 for a pair of iron and wooden sickles from Pennsylvania, one with blade stamped "S. Christ" and handle with hand inscription in ink, "Presented by Dr. Daniel Yoder Catasauque," other blade stamped "D. Christ," 18 ½ x 17 ¾ in., c.1780.

Faberge egg: $18,500,000 for a Faberge translucent pink egg with a miniature clock made of enamel and gold, topped with diamond-encrusted cockerel that pops out every hour, 1902.

First typewriter: $108,000 for the first commercially made typewriter, the "Malling-Hansen Writing Ball," by Danish inventor Rasmus Malling-Hansen, 1867.

Miniature firkin: $8,892 for a miniature firkin (wooden barrel), original Windsor green paint, stamped "C.H." on lid, 2 ½ in. h. x 2 in. diam.

Punch cigar store figure: $542,400 for a carved Punch cigar store figure, polychrome paint, mounted on metal wheeled base, original condition, 19th century, attributed to Samuel Anderson Robb, 66 in. h.

Rolls-Royce/Pre-1905 automobile: $7,220,000 for the world's oldest running Rolls-Royce (1904), small 10-horse-power 2.0-liter engine with a top speed of 39 mph, open-top two-seater with red leather interior, restored in 1950.

Showboat Casino $1 chip: $28,989 for a $1 gambling chip from the Showboat Casino in Las Vegas, Nevada.

Symphony Split Grille radio: $51,000 for the Symphony Split Grille radio, onyx case with emerald green knobs, split grille and handle, 1939, 5 ¾ x 9 x 4 in. diam.

PAINTING & PRINTS

William Michael Harnett painting: $1,008,000 for the 1886 painting by William Michael Harnett, "Still Life with Pewter Candlestick and Clarinet."

PAPER

Charles Schulz original Peanuts strip: $113,525 for the Charles Schulz Peanuts Sunday comic strip original art dated 4-10-55 (United Feature Syndicate, 1955), eight panels, rainy baseball theme featuring Pigpen, Schroeder, and Shermy, 22 ¾ x 15 ¼ in.

Inverted Jenny stamp, single copy: $977,500 for the 1918 24¢ "Inverted Jenny" error stamp depicting an upside-down Curtis JN-4 biplane known as "Jenny."

Italian poster: $20,000 for an Italian poster featuring a pair of Italian motorboats speeding across the water, "Ila Riunione Motonautica," 1931, artist not identified, 55 x 40 in., published by Barbarino & Graeve, Genoa, Italy.

Magna Carta: $21,321,000 for the Magna Carta issued by King Edward I in 1297. The document will be placed back on view at the National Archives in Washington, D.C., where it had been displayed for 22 years. The purchaser considers this a gift to the American people.

Original cover art by Robert Crumb: $101,575 for the original cover art of Mr. Natural by underground comic artist Robert Crumb, ink and Zipatone on paper, pictures Mr. Natural kicking someone's keister. 1970, 10 x 14 in., matted and framed, 15 ½ x 19 ½ in.

Silver Age comic: $227,000 for a 1962 Amazing Fantasy No. 15 comic book, which introduced Spider-Man to the world, art by Jack Kirby and Steve Ditko, near mint condition.

PHOTOGRAPHY

Daguerreotype camera: $792,333 for the world's oldest commercially produced daguerreotype camera by Susse Fréres of France, full plate for 6 ½-x-8 ½ in. exposures, soft wood, stained black, brass fittings, manufacturer's label, 1839.

Leica or any 35 millimeter camera: $492,500 for an 0-series Leica No. 107 camera.

Weston, Edward, "Nautilus" photograph: $1,105,000 for Edward Weston's "Nautilus," 1927, image of a seashell on matte-surface paper, signed and dated by Weston in 1927.

POTTERY & PORCELAIN

Danse Moderne Plate: $67,375 for a Danse Moderne plate designed by Viktor Schreckengost, from his Jazz Series, impressed stamps, 1931, 11 ¼ in.

Nathaniel H. Dixon stoneware jar, 1827–1863: $13,200 for a stoneware jar, stamped "N.H. Dixon," Chatham County, North Carolina, decorated with alkaline glaze drips on the side, two ear handles, 15 ½ in.

Occupational shaving mug: $45,000 for an occupational shaving mug titled "Aeronaut," with original newspaper article, mug picturing a man flying through the air hanging from a parachute, HCL mark on bottom. Earlier at the same auction, an ambulance occupational shaving mug picturing a horse-drawn wagon and driver set the record at $29,000, but was surpassed when the "Aeronaut" shaving mug sold.

Spatterware plate: $37,400 for a three-color rainbow spatter Festoon pattern plate, purple, green, and red swags with purple dots, 10 ¾ in.

SPORTS

Any nineteenth-century bat: $88,125 for a baseball bat said to have been used by Cincinnati Red Stockings shortstop George Wright during the 1869 season.

Any baseball carte-de-visite: $47,000 for the 1864 Brooklyn Resolutes carte-de-visite team card featuring Henry Chadwick, 4 x 2 ½ in.

Color baseball lithograph: $22,325 for a "New York Fashions" full-color baseball lithograph, issued in 1870, picturing six ballplayers in various uniform styles of the period, untrimmed, matted, 19 x 15 in.

Honus Wagner T206 baseball card: $2,800,000 for a T206 Honus Wagner baseball card, PSA 8-graded. In February 2007 SCP Auctions sold a T206 Honus Wagner baseball card, PSA 8-graded, for $2,350,000.

Peters Target 20-gauge shotgun shells: $2,966 for a fully sealed box of Peters Target 20-gauge shotgun shells, end panel reads "Load No. 3738 Chilled – 2 ¼ Drams – 7/8 ounces – No. 8 Shot – Dead – Shot Smokeless."

TOYS, DOLLS & GAMES

Afghanistan Bank: $18,720 for the cast-iron mechanical "Afghanistan Bank," attributed to either Kyser & Rex or Novelty Works, c.1885.

Billy Goat bank: $15,210 for the mechanical "Billy Goat Bank" by J. & E. Stevens Co., Cromwell, Connecticut, Patent No. 965,842, issued July 26, 1910.

Brinks Armored Truck by Arcade: $34,500 for a Brinks Express Co. armored truck by Arcade, with gun turrets, rear opens to cast-iron bed, painted red, gold highlighting, red hubs, white rubber tires, 5 lbs., 12 in.

Chimpanzee mechanical bank: $92,000 for the "Chimpanzee" mechanical bank, cast iron, by Kyser & Rex Co., Philadelphia, c.1880.

Darky Fisherman mechanical bank: $287,500 for the "Darky Fisherman" mechanical bank, lead, by Charles A. Bailey, 1880s.

Disney toy: $151,534 for Mickey and Minnie Mouse giant display dolls by Charlotte Clark, stuffed velveteen with wire inserts for posing, Mickey has four 2-inch natural pearl buttons and is 44 in. tall, Minnie has hundreds of individual eyelashes, wears a silk-like skirt with pantaloons and is 48 in. tall to the top of her flower, each doll with a 32-in. tail. Mickey was introduced in 1930 and Minnie in 1931.

Doll costume: $19,500 for a Blondinette's blue woolen and ivory silk ensemble from Mlle. Bereux in original box, hip-length taffeta jacket with scalloped hem, black velvet buttons and trim over blue woolen skirt with soutache trim overlaid with ivory silk paneled overskirt.

Eagle and Eaglets Bank (American Eagle): $7,605 for the mechanical "Eagle and Eaglets Bank" by J. & E. Stevens Co.

Flip the Frog mechanical bank: $57,500 for the "Flip the Frog" mechanical bank, tin, by Saalheimer & Strauss, Germany, 1920s.

Frog Bank (Two Frogs): $12,870 for the mechanical "Frog Bank," also known as "Two Frogs," by J. & E. Stevens Co., Patent No. 262,361, issued August 8, 1882.

Jonah and the Whale mechanical bank: $414,000 for "Jonah and the Whale/Jonah Emerges" mechanical bank, cast iron, by J. & E. Stevens Co., late 1880s.

Karr toy stove: $6,325 for an enameled Karr toy stove with original box, blue enameled stove trimmed with nickel-plated iron, manufactured by Karr Range Co., Belleville, Illinois, 21 ½ x 13 x 10 in.

Magic Bank: $19,890 for the "Magic Bank" mechanical bank, cast iron, by J. & E. Stevens, patented March 7, 1886.

Mammy Bank, Red Dress: $46,800 for the "Mammy Bank, Red Dress" mechanical bank, cast iron, by Kyser & Rex Co., c.1884.

Mikado mechanical bank: $287,500 for the Mikado illusionist mechanical bank, cast iron, by Kyser & Rex Co., c.1886.

Patronize the Blind mechanical bank: $58,500 for the "Patronize the Blind" mechanical bank, cast iron, by J. & E. Stevens Co., patent date Feb 19, 1878.

Schoenhut Supplee Milk Wagon: $10,350 for a Schoenhut Supplee Milk Wagon with dapple horse on platform, wagon painted white and green with black roof, original figure and case of milk. Marquee reads "Ask for Supplee Ice Cream," back folds down and has three awnings, 13 x 25 in.

Simon & Halbig doll: $25,300 for a Simon & Halbig 1303 Asian woman doll, with olive-tinted bisque head, glass sleep eyes, articulated French wood and composition lady body, exotic costume of fine silks, paisley waist sash, brass coins, blue bead and brass necklace, and long head scarf, original dark human hair wig, incised "S & H Germany, 1303," 10 in.

Speaking Dog—Blue Dress mechanical bank: $63,250 for the "Speaking Dog—Blue Dress" variation mechanical bank, cast iron, by J. & E. Stevens, c.1895.

Steiff Felix on Irish Mail cart: $10,350 for a Steiff Felix the Cat on Irish Mail cart, Felix sitting on bellows seat, pumping and leaning back action as the bellows make a squeaking sound, original script Steiff button, remnants of paper tag, 1920s, 9 ½ in.

Uncle Remus mechanical bank: $39,780 for the "Uncle Remus" mechanical bank, cast iron, by Kyser & Rex Co., 1890s.

Uncle Sam bank: $21,060 for the "Uncle Sam Bank" mechanical bank, cast iron, by Shepard Hardware Co., Buffalo, New York, patented June 8, 1886.

Weeden's Plantation Darkey Savings Bank: $17,550 for the tin, hand-painted, windup "Weeden's Plantation Darkey Savings Bank," by Weedens Manufacturing Co., New Bedford, Massachusetts, patented August 7, 1888.

A NOTE TO COLLECTORS

You already know this is a great overall price guide for antiques and collectibles. Each entry is current, every photograph is new, and all prices are accurate.

There is also another Kovel publication designed to keep you up-to-the-minute in the world of collecting. Things change quickly. Important sales produce new record prices. Fakes appear. Rarities are discovered. To keep up with developments, you can read *Kovels on Antiques and Collectibles,* our monthly newsletter. It is now available by subscription in two forms, a print edition that is mailed and an electronic edition that includes searchable archives. Both have the identical current information on collecting. They are filled with color photographs, about forty per issue. The newsletter reports prices, trends, auction results, Internet sales, and other news for collectors *as it happens.* Join the community of collectors, visit www.Kovels.com to keep up on the buy-sell world of antiques.

HOW TO USE THIS BOOK

There are a few rules for using this book. Each listing is arranged in the following manner: CATEGORY (such as Pressed Glass), OBJECT (such as vase), DESCRIPTION (as much information as possible about size, age, color, and pattern). Some types of glass, pottery, and silver are exceptions to this rule. These are listed CATEGORY, PATTERN, OBJECT, DESCRIPTION. All items are presumed to be in good condition and undamaged, unless otherwise noted. In most sections, if a maker's name is easily recognized, like Gustav Stickley, we include it near the beginning of the entry. If the maker is obscure, the name may be at the end.

Many of the general glass entries are in their own special categories: Glass-Art, Glass-Blown, Glass-Bohemian, Glass-Contemporary, Glass-Midcentury, and Glass-Venetian. Major glass factories are listed under factory names. Well-known types of glass, such as Cut, Pressed, Depression, Carnival, etc., can be found in their own categories. You will find silver flatware in either Silver Flatware Plated or Silver Flatware Sterling. There is also a section for Silver Plate, which includes coffeepots, trays, and other plated pieces. Most solid or sterling silver is listed by country, so look for Silver-American, Silver-Danish, Silver-English, etc. Silver jewelry is listed under Jewelry. Most pottery and porcelain is listed by factory name, such as Weller; by item, such as Calendar Plate; in sections like Dinnerware or Kitchen; or in a special section, such as Pottery-Art, Pottery-Contemporary, Pottery-Midcentury, etc.

Sometimes we make arbitrary decisions. Fishing has its own category, but hunting is part of the larger category called Sports. We have omitted all guns except toys. It is not legal to sell weapons without a special license, so guns are not part of the general antiques market. Airguns, BB guns, rocket guns, and others are listed in the Toy section. Everything is listed according to the computer alphabetizing system. This means words such as "Mt." are alphabetized as "M-T," not as "M-O-U-N-T." All numerals are before all letters; thus "2" comes before "A."

We made several editorial decisions. A butter dish is a "butter." A salt dish is called a "salt" to differentiate it from a saltshaker. It is always "sugar and creamer," never "creamer and sugar." Political collectors often refer to "pinbacks," the round celluloid or tin pins decorated with candidates' names and faces. We use the word "button" instead of "pinback." The word "button" is also used when referring to fasteners on clothing. Where one dimension is given, it is the height; or if the object is round, the dimension is the diameter. The height of a picture is listed before width. Glass is clear unless a color is indicated.

Every entry is listed alphabetically, but idiosyncrasies of language remain. Some antiques terms, such as "Sheffield" or "Pratt," have two meanings. Read the paragraph headings to know the meaning used. All category headings are based on the language of the average person, and we use terms like "mud figures" even if not technically correct.

This book does not include price listings for fine art paintings, antiquities, stamps, coins, or most types of books. Big Little Books and similar children's books are included. Comic books are listed only in special categories like Superman, but original comic art and cels are listed in their own categories.

Prices for items pictured can be found in the appropriate category. Look for the matching entry with the abbreviation "Illus." The picture will be nearby.

Because of the computer, the book can be produced quickly. The last entries are added in June; the book is available in October. But human help finds prices and checks accuracy. We read everything at least three times, sometimes more. We edit more than 55,000 entries down to the approximately 44,000 entries found here. We correct spelling, remove incorrect data, write category paragraphs, and decide on new categories. We proofread copy and prices at least six times, but there will always be some misspelled words and other errors. Information in the paragraphs is updated each year and this year more than forty updates and additions were made.

Prices are reported from all parts of the United States, Canada, and Europe, converted to U.S. dollars at the time of the sale. The average rate of exchange between June 2007 and June 2008 was $1.00 U.S. to about $1.02 Canadian, €.69 (Euro), and £.50 (British Pound). Prices are from auctions, shops, Internet sales, and shows. Every price is checked for accuracy, but we are not responsible for errors.

We cannot answer your letters asking for price information, but please write if you have any requests for categories to be included in future editions or any corrections to the paragraphs or prices.

When you see us at shows and flea markets, stop and say hello. Don't be surprised if we ask for your suggestions. You can write to us at P.O. Box 22200-K, Beachwood, Ohio 44122, or visit us on our website, www.Kovels.com.

RALPH & TERRY KOVEL
July 2008

ACKNOWLEDGMENTS

We give special thanks to those who helped us with photographs and deeds: 20th Century Art & Design, Aberdeen Auctions, Alderfer Auction Co., Aleph-Bet Books, Alex Cooper Auctioneers, Allard Auctions, American Bottle Auctions, American Cut Glass Association, American Political Items Collectors, Anderson Auctions, Andre Ammelounx, Antique Bottle & Glass Collector, Antique Fan Collectors Association, Antique Place, Antique Toy World, Antique Trader, Antiques and The Arts, Antiques Journal, Antiques Marketplace, Auction Action Antique News, Auction Gallery of the Palm Beaches, Auction Team Köln, Aumann Auctions, Austin Auction Co., B.S. Slosberg Auctioneers, BBR Auctions, Be-Hold, Belhorn Auction Services, Bertoia Auctions, Bill Hood & Sons Art & Antique Auctions, Bingham's Antiques, Bonhams & Butterfields, Bottles & Bygones World, Brewery Gems, Brunk Auctions, Burley Auction Group, Canes Through the Ages, Carlton Antique Toys, Christie's, Cincinnati Art Galleries, Clars Auction Gallery, Clearing House Auction Galleries, Cobbs Auctioneers, Collectics, Collectors News, Compact Collectors Club, Conestoga Auction Co., Copake Auction, Cordier Antiques & Fine Art, Cottone Auctions, Cowan's Auctions, Cripple Creek Auctions, CRN Auctions, Crown Jewels of the Wire, Cyr Auction Gallery, Dallas Auction Gallery, Delmarva Acquisitions & Appraisals, Depew Auction Gallery, Dirk Soulis Auctions, Doyle New York, DuMouchelles, Early American History Auctions, Early Auction Co., Eastbourne Auction Rooms, eBay, Ed's Toy Shop, Elegant Extras, Faganarms, Federation of Historical Bottle Collectors, Fellows & Sons Auctioneers, Fenton Art Glass Collectors of America, Fiftys Dish, Flomaton Antique Auction, Fontaine's Auction Gallery, FPS Archives, Frank & Grace Zuest, Frank's Antiques & Auctions, Freeman & Porcelli, Gallery at Knotty Pine, Garth's Auctions, Gisela Antiques, Glass Works Auctions, Grand View Antiques & Auction, Green Valley Auctions, Grey Flannel Auctions, Griswold & Cast Iron Cookware Association, Gus Knapp, Hake's Americana & Collectibles, Hassinger & Courtney Auctioneering, Heisey Collectors of America, Heritage Auction Galleries, Hewletts Antiques, Hi & Lo Modern, Hoosier Peddler, Hummel Collector's Club, Ivey-Selkirk Auctioneers, J.K. Galleries, Jackson's International Auctioneers & Appraisers, James D. Julia Auctioneers, Jane Martin, Jim Wroda Auction Services, Joy Luke, John Toomey Gallery, Just Art Pottery, Just Glass, Kaminski Auctions, Ken Farmer Auctions, Keystone Toy Trader, L.H. Selman, Lang's Sporting Collectables, Larry & Carole Meeker, Last Moving Picture Co., Leland Little Auctions & Estate Sales, Leslie Hindman Auctioneers, Live Free or Die Antique Tool Auctions, Live Auctioneers, Lloyd Ralston Toys, Los Angeles Modern Auctions, Maine Antiques Digest, Manion's International Auction House, Mastro Auctions, McCoy Lovers' NMXpress, McCulloh's Antiques & Collectibles, McMasters Harris Auction Co., McMurray Antiques & Auctions, Michael Ivankovich Antiques & Auction Co., Mod Father, Monsen & Baer, Morphy Auctions, Mother Drucker's, National Association of Aladdin Lamp Collectors, National Association of Avon Collectors, National Association of Breweriana Advertising, National Association of Milk Bottle Collectors, National Cambridge Collectors, Neal Auction Co., Nelson Rarities, New England Antiques Journal, New Orleans Auction Galleries, Noel Barrett Auctions, Norman C. Heckler & Co., Northeast Auctions, Northgate Gallery, O.J. Club, O'Gallerie, Old Sleepy Eye Collectors Club, Old Time Auctions, Our House Antiques, Page Button Auctions, Paper & Advertising Collectors' Marketplace, Past Tyme Pleasures, Patricia Doyle Associates Auction Gallery, PBA Galleries, Pook & Pook, Potteries Specialists Auctions, Priddy's Auction Galleries, Proxibid, R.O. Schmitt Fine Arts, Rachel Davis Fine Arts, Rago Arts & Auction Center, Randy Inman Auctions, Red Baron's Antiques, RGL Antiques, Rich Penn Auctions, Richard D. Hatch & Associates, Richard Norton, Richard Opfer Auctioneering, Robert C. Eldred Co., Robert Edward Auctions, Rose Galleries, Royka's, RSL Auction Co., Ruby Lane, Russ Cochran's Comic Art Auction, Samuel T. Freeman & Co., San Rafael Auction Gallery, Seeck Auctions, Shelley's Auction Gallery, Showplace Antique Center, Showtime Auction Services, Simmons & Co.

Auctioneers, Skinner Inc., Sloans & Kenyon, Smith House Toys & Auction Co., Sotheby's, Southern Folk Pottery Collectors Society, Stair Galleries, Stanton's Auctioneers, Stein Auction Co., Steve Butler, Strawser Auctions, Swann Auction Galleries, Tea Leaf Club International, Team's Tiffany Treasures, Ted Kromer, The Internet Antique Shop, Theriault's, Thomaston Place Auction Galleries, Tom Harris Auctions, Toys of Yesteryear, Trader Fred's Toys of Yore, Tradewinds Auctions, Treadway Gallery, Trocadero, Turkey Creek Auctions, TW Conroy Auctions, Vicki & Bruce Waasdorp, Vintage Jewelry, Waddington's, William J. Jenack Auctioneers & Appraisers, William Morford Auctions, Willis Henry Auctions, Woody Auction Co., Yankee Toys.

Black Dog & Leventhal suggested the redesign of our price guide last year and the resulting book was bigger and better than ever. This book was produced with much less stress and even more improvements. J.P. Leventhal kept a watchful eye and made sure both the book and his marketing department treated it well. Laura Ross was the editor who kept us on track. To both we say thank you. Your influence on the finished book is not always noticed by our readers. Katherine Furman and True Sims were among others who worked on this project at Black Dog whom we thank for their contributions and patience with us. Mary Flower, Wendy Hoke, and Robin Perlow did the tedious job of copyediting and proofreading. We appreciate their work. Going through 45,000 prices is not as easy as checking the content of a novel.

Thanks to Sheila Hart, who conquered the new computer programs and problems and kept all of us on schedule, coordinated all of the parts, and supervised all of the editing, layouts, copyediting, art decisions, and more. And thanks to her interns, Rob Shimits and Mike Levay.

The details and hard work required to record prices, assemble photos and information, check accuracy and spelling, and solve many other problems are all done by our Kovel staff. We thank Carmie Amata, Lisa Bell, Grace DeFrancisco, Marcia Goldberg, Katie Karrick, Kim Kovel, Liz Lillis, Heidi Makela, Mary Ellen Malone, Liz McBean, Tina McBean, Renee McRitchie, Carol Reid, Nancy Saada, Julie Seaman, Nikki Seaman, June Smith, and Cherrie Smrekar. Pictures come from many sources and they were all sized and digitally enhanced by Karen Kneisley, our photo editor. Gay Hunter, book editor, as always worries the most about the book. She kept the records and made sure all of us were on track and on schedule. She read every word, corrected our spelling errors, and solved the problems of changing technology. She read and reread pages of prices and together we solved problems like changing paragraph information when a company closed or was purchased. Thanks to all of them. We have what we are sure is our best book ever. We know that the book is possible only because of the group effort, even though it is our names that appear on the cover.

A. WALTER made pate-de-verre glass under contract at the Daum glassworks from 1908 to 1914. He decorated pottery during his early years in his studio in Sevres, where he also developed his formula for pale, translucent pate-de-verre. He started his own firm in Nancy, France, in 1919. Pieces made before 1914 are signed *Daum, Nancy* with a cross. After 1919 the signature is *A. Walter Nancy*.

Ashtray, Owl, Perched On Oak Bough, Figural, Green, Blue 4750.00
Bowl, Cover, Blue, Green, Flower, Snail, c.1920, 3 3/8 x 4 5/8 In. 5040.00
Bowl, Cover, Gold, Insects, c.1920, 5 x 7 In. 9600.00
Paperweight, Butterfly, Spread Wings, Green Base, Signed, 4 x 3 1/4 In. 3000.00
Paperweight, Crab, Deep Green, Blue, 1 3/4 x 2 1/2 In. 1080.00
Paperweight, Lizard On Rock, Green, c.1920, 3 1/4 x 3 1/4 In. 4560.00
Paperweight, Moth, Black, Brown, Blue, Turquoise Wing Tips, Teal Base, Pate-De-Verre, 3 3/4 In. 420.00
Paperweight, Satyr, Yellow, Green Leaf Headband, Purple Berries, Green Ears, 3 In. 780.00
Paperweight, Scarab, Marked, 1 x 2 In. .... *illus* 468.00
Perfume Bottle, Canopy Of Trees, Irises, Pottery, Marked, 11 3/4 In. .... *illus* 1200.00
Vase, Flowers, Vines, Yellow Ground, Pottery, Marked, 8 5/8 In. .... *illus* 1763.00
Vase, Trees, Flowers, Water, Signed, 12 1/4 In., Pair .... *illus* 1872.00

ABC plates, or children's alphabet plates, were most popular from 1780 to 1860, but are still being made. The letters on the plate were meant as teaching aids for children learning to read. The plates were made of pottery, porcelain, metal, or glass. Mugs and other items were also made with alphabet decorations.

Plate, Aesop's Fables, Fox & The Grapes, 5 1/2 In. 66.00
Plate, Baseball, American Sports, Black Transfer, Running To First Base, 8 In. 550.00
Plate, Birds Of Paradise, Signed, Edge Malkin & Co., 19th Century, 6 In. 90.00
Plate, Child's, Multicolored, Glaze Crazing, Staffordshire, 6 In. 50.00
Plate, Clock, Alphabets, Numbers, Calendar, Blue Transfer, Staffordshire 225.00
Plate, Crusoe Finding Footprints, Alphabet, Staffordshire, 7 1/8 In. 80.00
Plate, Dog, 19th Century, 7 In. 100.00
Plate, Farmer Loading Hay On Wagon, Staffordshire, 6 In. 80.00
Plate, Fox Hunt, White Ground, Blue Transfer, 7 1/4 In. 320.00
Plate, Keep Thy Shop & Thy Shop Will Keep Thee, Staffordshire, 5 1/4 In. 70.00
Plate, Leopard, Alphabet, Staffordshire, 7 1/2 In. 140.00
Plate, N Stands For Nemophilia Lively Of Lue, 19th Century, 6 In. 135.00
Plate, Organ Grinder & Children, Blue Transfer, Staffordshire, 6 3/4 In. 80.00
Plate, School, Clock, Dinner To Bed, Marked LS &, 8 In. .... *illus* 125.00

ABINGDON POTTERY was established in 1908 by Raymond E. Bidwell as the Abingdon Sanitary Manufacturing Company. The company started making art pottery in 1934. The factory ceased production of art pottery in 1950.

Cookie Jar, Daisy Lid, White, Turquoise Daisies, Yellow Center, 8 x 5 7/8 In. 31.00
Cookie Jar, Girl Smiling, Blond Pigtails, c.1950s, 9 1/4 x 6 3/4 In. 95.00
Cookie Jar, Jack-O'-Lantern, Cream, Tan Stripes, Red Eyes, Nose, Mouth 36.00
Cookie Jar, Pelican, Lid Bill Shape, Multicolored, c.1947, 6 1/4 x 7 1/2 In. 760.00
Cookie Jar, Pineapple, c.1950s, 11 In. 129.00
Jam Serving Set, Lids, Jars, Underplates, Sky Blue, White, 8 1/8 & 4 In. 25.00
Planter, Mexican Worker Leaning On Cactus, 7 3/8 x 4 1/4 x 6 3/4 In. 20.00
Vase, Burgundy Purple, Red Glaze, 9 In. 119.00
Vase, Handles, Antique Green, 10 In. 80.00
Vase, Leaves, Turquoise Gloss, Marked, 8 7/8 In. .... *illus* 28.00
Vase, Seahorse, White, Turquoise, Cylindrical, Footed, 8 1/2 x 3 In. 49.00
Vase, Winter White, Flared, Footed, Scrolled, Twisted Handles, 9 x 5 In. 26.00
Vase, Yellow Matte, Handles, Marked, 10 1/4 In. .... *illus* 25.00

ADAMS china was made by William Adams and Sons of Staffordshire, England. The firm was founded in 1769 and became part of the Wedgwood Group in 1966. The name *Adams* appeared on various items through 1998. All types of tablewares and useful wares were made. Other pieces of Adams may be found listed under Flow Blue and Tea Leaf Ironstone.

Bowl, White Ironstone, Interior Panels, Scallops, Oval, c.1915, 8 1/2 x 6 1/2 x 1 3/4 In. 28.00
Butter, White Ironstone 95.00
Creamer, Adams' Rose, Red, Green Leaves, Yellow Spatter, Paneled, 2-Sided, 5 3/4 In. 1320.00
Creamer, Red, Blue, Green Bands, Spatter, Helmet Form, Dolphin Handle, Footed, 4 In. 220.00
Pitcher, Persia, Blue Transfer, 10 1/2 In. 350.00

A.Walter, Paperweight, Scarab, Marked, 1 x 2 In.
$468.00

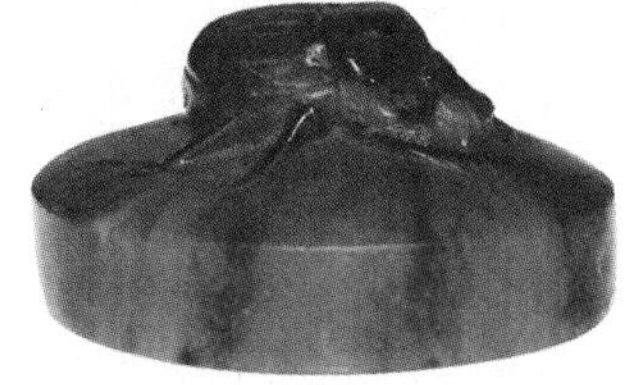

A.Walter, Perfume Bottle, Canopy Of Trees, Irises, Pottery, Marked, 11 3/4 In.
$1200.00

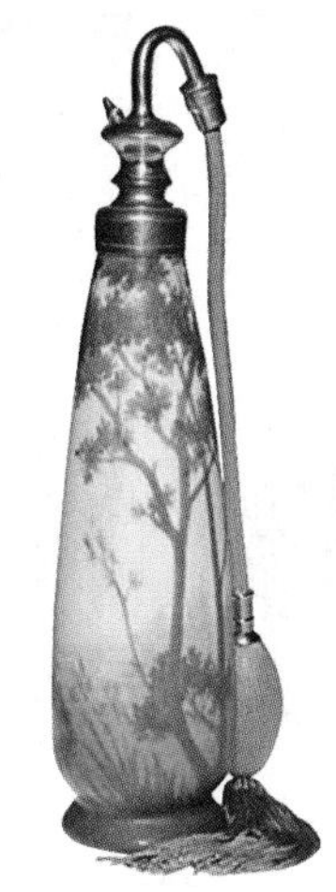

A.Walter, Vase, Flowers, Vines, Yellow Ground, Pottery, Marked, 8 5/8 In.
$1763.00

TIP

Shallow nicks and rough edges on glass can sometimes be smoothed off with fine emery paper.

TIP
If you want to keep your collections free from harm, always clean and dust them yourself.

A.Walter, Vase, Trees, Flowers, Water, Signed, 12 1/4 In., Pair
$1872.00

ABC, Plate, School, Clock, Dinner To Bed, Marked LS &, 8 In.
$125.00

Abingdon, Vase, Leaves, Turquoise Gloss, Marked, 8 7/8 In.
$28.00

Planter, Blue, Wide Mouth, Design Around Rim, 8 x 9 In. 76.00
Plate, Adams' Rose, Blue Spatter, 8 1/2 In. 266.00
Plate, Adams' Rose, Red & Blue, Rainbow, Spatter, 8 1/2 In. 2242.00
Plate, Cyrene, Red Transfer, Ironstone, 14-Sided, c.1850, 10 1/2 In. 65.00
Plate, Green Rings, Scalloped, Red, Blue, Spatter, Impressed Adams, c.1850, 9 In. 144.00
Plate, Monte Video, Connecticut, American Views, c.1835, 6 3/4 In. 85.00
Plate, Red Concentric Rings, Green, Blue, Spatter, Scalloped Edge, 8 In. 358.00
Sugar, Cover, Adams' Rose, Blue, Spatter, 5 x 5 1/8 In. 207.00
Teapot, Ironstone, Hexagonal, Marked, 1950s, 7 1/2 x 9 1/2 x 5 1/2 In. 65.00
Tray, Bridge, Man Fishing, Woman, Dog, Blue, White, Reticulated Rim, 8 x 10 In. 230.00
Tureen, Columbia, Blue Transfer, Scroll Handles, Octagonal, 1850, 10 x 4 In. 125.00
Tureen, Sauce, Undertray, White Ironstone, Scroll Handles, Octagonal, c.1853, 8 In. 250.00

ADVERTISING containers and products sold in the old country store are now all collectibles. These stores, with the crackers in a barrel and a potbellied stove, are a symbol of an earlier, less hectic time. Listed here are many of the advertising items. Other similar pieces may be found under the product name, such as Planters Peanuts. We have tried to list items in the logical places, so large store fixtures will be found under the Architectural category, enameled tin dishes under Graniteware, paper items in the Paper category, etc. Store fixtures, cases, signs, and other items that have no advertising as part of the decoration are listed in the Store category. For more information, see *Kovels' Advertising Collectibles Price List*. The early Dr Pepper logo included a period after "Dr," but it was dropped in 1950. We list all Dr Pepper items without a period so they alphabetize together.

Ad, Magazine, Colgate Dental Cream, With Gardol, Girl & Boy, c.1957, 10 x 14 In. 10.00
Ad, Magazine, Kolynos Dental Cream, Black & White, c.1932, 5 x 14 In. 10.00
Ad, Magazine, Milton Bradley Games, 1905, 2 3/4 x 4 In. 7.00
Ad, Magazine, Squibb Dental Cream, Woman Equestrian, 1940, 5 x 11 In. 10.00
Ad, Magazine, Squibb Dental Cream, Smiling Model, Black & White, c.1938, 8 x 11 In. 10.00
Ad, Magazine, Squibb Dental Cream, Multicolored, c.1940, 5 x 11 In. 10.00
Ad, Magazine, Tin Alpine Express Toy, 1949, 2 1/2 x 5 1/4 In. 7.00
Ad, Magazine, Winchester Roller Skates, 1923, 5 x 8 In. 7.50
Ashtray, American Airlines, Airplane, Embossed Logo, Chrome Finish, 4 x 8 x 8 In. 170.00
Ashtray, Big Boy Restaurant, Red Logo, Round, 3 3/4 In. 18.00
Ashtray, Capital Bread, Rolls, Cakes, Clear, 4 1/4 In. 9.00
Ashtray, Corning Glass Works, Smoky Gray, 1960s, 6 3/4 In. 18.00
Ashtray, Enterprise Ranges, Porcelain, 5 1/2 In. 20.00
Ashtray, H.E. Wagon Drug Stores, Skillet, Greencastle, Fayetteville, 1971 .... 40.00
Ashtray, Reddy Kilowatt, Square, 3 1/2 In. 25.00
Ashtray, Sanka, French Black Glass, Orange Logo, 4 1/2 In. 18.00
Ashtray, Schweppes Soda Water & Ginger Ale, Bottle, Porcelain, Early 1900s, 4 In. 50.00
Ashtray, Smokey Bear, Aluminum, 4 In., 4 Piece 20.00
Ashtray, T.B. Woods Sons Co., Fred 46-84, Cast Iron, Wood Holder 45.00
Ashtray, T.B. Woods Sons Co., Molding Line, Cast Iron, 1975 .... 35.00
Bag Holder, Rempp & Son, Carriage & Wagon Builder, Wood, Wire, 10 x 3 In., Pair 110.00
Banner, Circus, London Punch & Judy, Coney Island, Painted, 1945, 7 x 8 Ft. 2700.00
Banner, Circus, Sideshow, Salome Image, Canvas, Painted, Square 385.00
Banner, J.E. McLeary, Black, Gold Letters, Wood, 2-Sided, 7 x 75 In. 977.00
Banner, Mortar & Pestle, 5 Paper Signs, 8 Ft. 187.00
Banner, Smoke Our Magnet, Attractive 5 Cent Cigar, Red, Yellow, Canvas, 12 x 9 In. 90.00
Banner, Splendid Stewart, Iron Stove, Fuller-Warren Co., 1890s, 84 x 57 In. .... *illus* 2500.00
Bench, Red Goose Shoes, Storefront, 72 x 34 In. 495.00
Bib, Victor's Infants Relief For Teething, Paper, Cloth, Baby, Bottle, 8 x 5 1/2 In. 66.00
Bin, Mistletoe Coffee, Timothy Gay & Co., Children, Harvest, 13 x 20 In. 488.00
Bin, Munsingwear Fashion Books, Woman, Child, Tin Lithograph, 15 x 12 x 15 In. 2200.00
Bin, Waldorf Java Coffee, Embossed Letters, L.F. Hersh & Bros., 20 x 21 In. 480.00
Blotter, Kennywood Park, Pittsburgh's Playground, c.1920, 3 x 7 3/4 In. 100.00
Blotter, Morton Salt, Children On Skates, When It Rains It Pours, Premium, 6 In. 12.00
Blotter, Old Colony Insurance Co., 6 In. 40.00
Blotter, Old Colony Insurance Company, Chambersburg, Pa. 4.00
Blotter, Shredded Wheat, Hot Milk For Work & Play, Premium, Copyright 1916, 6 In. 15.00
Booklet, Gold Dust Twins, Who Are We, Yellow Cover, 1907, 4 1/2 x 6 In., 10 Pages 160.00
Booklet, Management, Rumford Baking Powder, 4 x 7 In., 64 Pages 18.00
Books may be included in the Paper category.
Bottle Holder, Howel's Root Beer, Die Cut, 3-D, 20 x 14 1/2 In. 55.00
Bottle Openers are listed in their own category.
Bottles are listed in their own category.

Box, Adams Gum, Minnie Seligmann, 36 Bars, Cardboard, c.1880, 9¾ x 4 x 1 In. 110.00
Box, Adams' Tutti Frutti Gum, Woman On Cover, June 30, 1885, 9¾ In. 495.00
Box, Bishop's Jelly Joe's, Our Gang, Little Rascals, Paper Labels, 20 x 13½ In. 121.00
Box, Black Eagle Sun Cured Chewing Tobacco, Wood, Unopened, 6 x 6 In. 193.00
Box, Cereal, Kellogg's Corn Flakes, Pep & Krumbles, Red & Black, 1939, 11 In. 65.00
Box, Cereal, Lady Ann, Rolled Oats, Trademark Woman, Cardboard, Lb. 275.00
Box, Cereal, Nebia Rolled Oats, Cardboard, Granger Bros., Graphics, 9½ x 5⅜ In.. .... 330.00
Box, Cereal, Rosemary Rolled Oats, Samuel Kunin & Sons, Cardboard, 20 Oz. 176.00
Box, Certified Aspirin Tablets, 12 Tablets Per Tin, 36 Tins, Unused, c.1940, 7 x 6 x 6 In.. ..... 110.00
Box, Colburn's Mustard, Philadelphia, Wood, Labels, 15 x 20¾ x 10 In. 440.00
Box, Dr. Bovier's Buchu Gin For Kidney & Bladder Troubles, Wood, 17 x 13 x 13 In.. .... 50.00
Box, Dr. Gray's Glycerine Tonic Comp, Wood, Dovetailed, 17 x 13 x 13 In. 61.00
Box, Dr. Hamilton's Butter Milk & Witch Hazel Soap, Wood, 15 x 21 x 8 In.. .... 22.00
Box, Dr. James' Miniature Headache Powders, Wood, 2-Sided, 21 x 13 x 14 In. 22.00
Box, Dr. King's New Discovery For Coughs & Colds, Wood, 22 x 18 x 9 In. 50.00
Box, Dr. S.A. Weaver's Canker & Salt Rheum Syrup, Wood, 14 x 16 x 11 In.. .... 121.00
Box, Dr. S.B. Hartman & Co., Peruna The Great Tonic, 14½ x 11½ x 10 In. 55.00
Box, Dr. Ward's Medical Co., Wood, 15 x 22 x 10½ In. 61.00
Box, Dr. Wilson's Buchu Gin For Kidney Troubles, Wood, 21 x 13 x 14 In. 50.00
Box, Fairbanks Fairy Soap, Brass Bound, Paper Label, 17 x 16 x 8 In. 121.00
Box, Fightin' Marines, Penny Packs, Topps, 1 Cent, 6⅜ x 6½ x 2 In. 572.00
Box, Firemen's Pride Cigar, Fire Station, Fire Wagon, Wood, Paper, 7 x 8 x 5 In. 385.00
Box, Flower Seeds, Oak, Paper Label, 4 x 11 x 7 In. .... *illus* 175.00
Box, Glace Fruit Juice Tablets, Candy, Wood, Paper Label, 9 x 10 x 7 In. 295.00
Box, Ivory Snow, Marilyn Chamber, 1970s, 8 x 6 In. 110.00
Box, Jolly-Washer Soap, It's Kind To Hands & Clothes, Cardboard, 3 x 3½ In.. .... 40.00
Box, Lash's Bitters Tonic Laxative, Wood, Dovetailed, 4-Sided, 13 x 10 x 10 In. 88.00
Box, Milk, Lendenbrook Farms, Insulated, Aluminum, 10 x 12½ x 14 In. 35.00
Box, Pen, Eagle Pencil Company, c.1915. .... 10.00
Box, R. Ovens Bakery, Cakes, Crackers, Biscuits, Buffalo, N.Y. 395.00
Box, Rinso Blue, 24 Paladin Cards, Contents, Late 1950s, 8½ x 6 x 2 In. 5407.00
Box, Robin Brand Starch, Robins, Cardboard, Unopened, 3 x 3½ In.. .... 40.00
Box, Seed, D.M. Ferry & Co., Wood, Girl Holding Melons, 13 x 22 In. 550.00
Box, Vanity Jar Rubbers, Kickbusch, Cardboard, 3⅜ x 3⅜ x 1⅜ In.. .... 176.00
Box, Vet, Peoples Poultry Remedy, Graphics, Portrait Images, 7¾ x 4¾ In. 440.00
Box, Williams Root Beer Extract, Labels, Slide Top, Stenciled, 7 x 10 x 5 In. 600.00
Box, see also Box category.
Brochure, Bonanza Airlines, August 1, 1966 .... 22.00
Broom Holder, Wilbur's Cocoa, Cherub Stirring Cocoa, Tin Litho, 6¾ x 2½ In. 176.00
Brush, Clothes, Nuoffer & Peran Clothing Shoes, Chicago, Germany, 7 In. 20.00
Bucket, Lid, Atmore's Mince Meat, Wood, Yellow Paint, Label, Bail Handle 580.00
Cab Light, Star Brewing Co., Boston, Mass., Gillco 3000.00
Cabinet, Briar Pipes, Oak, Wall Mount, D.T. Sanders & Sons, c.1900, 42 x 25 In. 196.00
Cabinet, Diamond Dyes, Children With Balloon, Tin Lithograph, 24 x 15 x 9 In. .... *illus* 550.00
Cabinet, Diamond Dyes, Court Jester, Tin Panel, 27 x 21 x 10 In.. .... 345.00
Cabinet, Diamond Dyes, Evolution Of Women, Wood, Tin Lithograph, 29 x 22 x 10 In.. ..... 1075.00
Cabinet, Diamond Dyes, Fairy, Vignettes, Wells & Richardson Co., Cherry, 30 x 24 x 10 In.... 1840.00
Cabinet, Dr. Daniels' Veterinary Medicines, Embossed Tin, 21½ x 28¾ In.. .... 460.00
Cabinet, Humphreys' Homeopathic Specifics, Wood, Tin, c.1890, 34 x 21 x 10 In. ..... *illus* 9700.00
Cabinet, Lucky Strike Cigarette Tins, Hanging, Drawers, 16 In. 110.00
Cabinet, Putnam Dye, Revolutionary War Soldier, Redcoats, Tin, 19 x 14¾ In. 180.00
Cabinet, Seed, Store, Sherer, c.1920, 68 x 29 x 33 In. 3295.00
Cabinet, Spool, Chadwick's, Oak, Reverse Painted Glass, 22 x 25 x 18 In. .... *illus* 2000.00
Cabinet, Spool, Clark's Cotton, Oak, Carved, Bird Egg Collection, Drawers 646.00
Cabinet, Spool, Clark's Mile-End Thread, Cherry, 6 Drawers, 22½ x 25¾ x 19½ In. 935.00
Cabinet, Spool, Corticelli, Glass Door, 4 Drawers, 42 x 36 In. 1375.00
Cabinet, Spool, Corticelli Silk, Revolving, 3 Drawers, 28 x 16 In. .... *illus* 3100.00
Cabinet, Spool, J. & P. Coats', Cherry, 2 Drawers, Pillar Corners, 8¾ x 21½ x 17 In. 357.00
Cabinet, Spool, J. & P. Coats', Walnut, 6 Drawers, Embossed, c.1890, 22 x 26 x 19 In .... *illus* 2100.00
Cabinet, Spool, Merrick's, Oak, Pat'd July 20, 1897, 24 x 32 x 18 In. .... *illus* 3100.00
Cabinet, Tintex Dye, Tints As You Rinse, Metal, Counter, 23½ x 17½ In. 121.00
Calendars are listed in their own category.
Can, Baker Castor Oil Co., Contents, Gal. 22.00
Can, Donald Duck Root Beer, Donald On Sides, Amber, Cone Top, 1957, 5¾ In. 85.00
Can, Opaline Motor, Sinclair Refining Co., Race Car, Gal., 8 x 11 In. 920.00
Canisters, see introductory paragraph to Tins in this category.

Abingdon, Vase, Yellow Matte, Handles, Marked, 10¼ In.
$25.00

Advertising, Banner, Splendid Stewart, Iron Stove, Fuller-Warren Co., 1890s, 84 x 57 In.
$2500.00

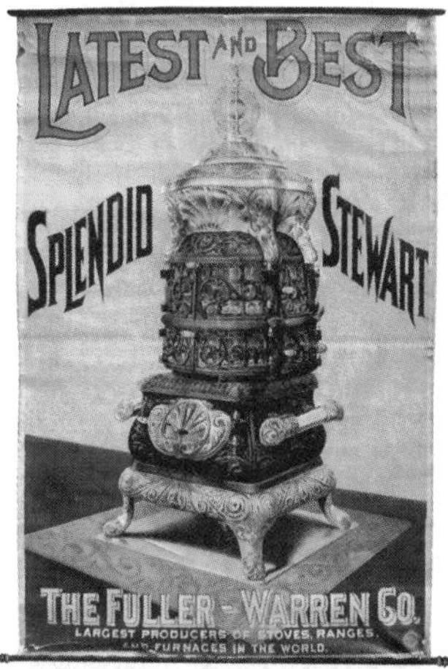

Advertising, Box, Flower Seeds, Oak, Paper Label, 4 x 11 x 7 In.
$175.00

Tin Trays
The tin advertising tray was first used in the 1880s and is still popular.

Advertising, Cabinet, Diamond Dyes, Children With Balloon, Tin Lithograph, 24 x 15 x 9 In.
$550.00

Advertising, Cabinet, Humphreys' Homeopathic Specifics, Wood, Tin, c.1890, 34 x 21 x 10 In.
$9700.00

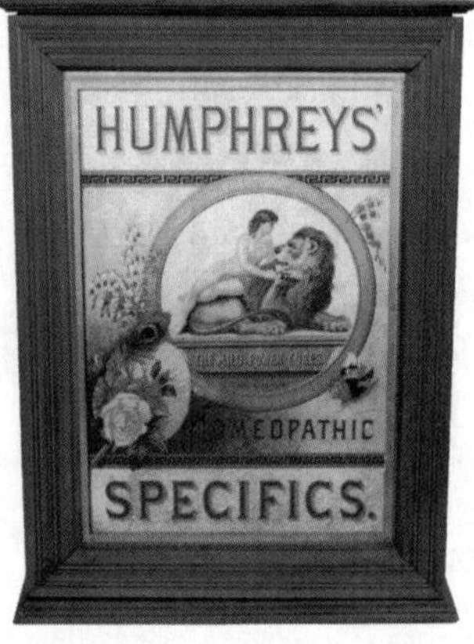

Advertising, Cabinet, Spool, Chadwick's, Oak, Reverse Painted Glass, 22 x 25 x 18 In.
$2000.00

Cards are listed in the Card category.
Carton, Borden's Ice Cream, Elsie The Cow, 1957, Pt. . . . 12.00
Case, Display, Jack-O'-Lantern Hot Peanut, Decal, Countertop . . . 165.00
Case, Display, Pen, A.A. Waterman & Co., Oak, Glass, Blue Velvet . . . 325.00
Case, Haller's Butter Krust Brand, Etched Glass, Shelves, 32 x 24 x 24 In. . . . 770.00
Case, Primley's California Gum, Glass, Wood, 12 x 18 x 9 In. . . . *illus* 345.00
Change Receiver, Andy Gump Cigars, Andy Gump, Wood Base, Glass Dome, 7 x 7 In. . . . 630.00
Change Receiver, Fatima Cigarettes, 12 ¼ x 9 ¾ In. . . . 33.00
Change Receiver, Pointer's Cigar, 5 Cent Cigar, 2 Dogs, Blue, White, Glass . . . 1200.00
Change Receiver, Vicks Cough Drops, Glass, c.1950, 7 x 8 x 2 In. . . . 158.00
Change Receiver, Wrigley's Chewing Sweet Peppermint Flavor, Yellow, Red, Felt, 5 x 8 In. . . . 80.00
Change Receiver, see also Tip Tray in this category.
Charger, Champagne Velvet Beer, 1905, 24 In. . . . 460.00
Charger, Dortmunder, Actien-Bier, Porcelain, 14 ½ In. . . . 45.00
Charger, Miller Brewing Co., Milwaukee, Wis., 24 In. . . . 1403.00
Churn, Borden's, Buttermilk, Enamelware, White & Blue, 12 In. . . . 495.00
Cigar Box, Black Crook, Devil, Dancing Girls, Wood, 6 ½ x 8 x 5 ½ In. . . . 210.00
Cigar Box, Buffalo Bill, Wood, c.1890, 7 x 8 ⅜ x 4 ¾ In. . . . 550.00
Cigar Box, Burl, Front Opening, Brass, Wood Border, Mother-Of-Pearl Inlay, Britain, 1800s, 8 x 12 x 9 In. 630.00
Cigar Cutter, Betsy Ross, 5 Cent Cigars, Iron, 1890, 9 In. . . . 1100.00
Cigar Cutter, Betsy Ross, Iron, 8 ½ x 6 In. . . . 770.00
Cigar Cutter, Dean's Havanas, Iron, Clockwork, W.O. Dean Co., 5 In. . . . *illus* 1150.00
Cigar Cutter, Manhattan Girl, Dome, Crank, W.E. Baker Co., N.Y., 8 ½ x 6 ½ In. . . . 748.00
Cigarette Pack, Home Run Cigarettes, Sealed, Wax Paper, Batter & Catcher, 1917, 3 In. . . . 360.00
Clicker, Columbus Buggy Co., Celluloid, 1 ¼ In. . . . 185.00
Clocks are listed in their own category.
Cloth, Rub No More, Mama Elephant, Baby Elephant Taking Shower, 31 ½ x 30 In. . . . 837.00
Coaster, Knickerbocker, The Beer Drinkers Beer, Metal, c.1965 . . . 6.00
Coaster, Ranier Pale Beer, Mountain Scene, Hand Painted, Germany, 3 In. . . . 45.00
Container, Norris Atlanta Exquisite Candies, 1940s-50s, 4 x 8 In. . . . 25.00
Cooler, Hires Root Beer, Metal, c.1940, 19 x 10 x 16 In. . . . 115.00
Crock, Friend's Brick Oven Baked Beans, Pottery, 2 ¾ In. . . . 26.00
Cup, Tastee Freeze, Elf, 3 ½ In. . . . 35.00
Decal, Ingersoll Watches, 3 Pocket Watches, We Sell, $1.00 To $2.00, 6 ½ x 9 In. . . . 110.00
Dish, Lutted's Cough Drops, Cabin Shape, Glass, Lid, 7 x 7 ¾ x 5 ½ In. . . . 315.00
Dispenser, Allen's Red Tame Cherry, Metal, 18 In. . . . 633.00
Dispenser, Buckeye Root Beer, Metal Spout, Label, Cleveland Fruit Juice Co., 14 In. . . . 675.00
Dispenser, Buckeye Root Beer, Tree Stump Form, Brown, 16 x 7 In. . . . 253.00
Dispenser, Century Electric Co., Hot Drinks, Metal Frame, Panels, Globe, Red Cap . . . 550.00
Dispenser, Cherry Smash Syrup, 5 Cents, 14 In. . . . 9200.00
Dispenser, Concord Ade Syrup, Grape, Frosted Glass, Painted Metal Base, 19 x 7 In. . . . 908.00
Dispenser, Crawford's Cherry Fizz Syrup, Ceramic, c.1920s, 14 In. . . . 10350.00
Dispenser, Hires Root Beer, Drink Hires, It Is Pure, Metal Pump, 14 In. . . . 364.00
Dispenser, Hires Root Beer, Keg, 3 Aluminum Signs, c.1940, 32 In. . . . 259.00
Dispenser, Hires Root Beer, Marble, Salesman Sample, No Case, 12 In. . . . 55000.00
Dispenser, Ma's Root Beer, Plastic, 1940s, 22 In. . . . *illus* 316.00
Dispenser, Middleby Root Beer, Mug, Amber Glass, c.1940, 16 In. . . . *illus* 173.00
Dispenser, Orange Crush, Pump, 10 ½ x 13 ½ In. . . . 8250.00
Dispenser, Orange Julep, Stoneware, Pump, 14 In. . . . 2970.00
Dispenser, Richardson Root Beer, Red, Signs On 3 Sides, c.1940, 18 In. . . . 144.00
Dispenser, Ward's Lemon Crush, 13 x 10 In. . . . 3100.00
Dispenser, Ward's Lime Crush Syrup, 1920s, 14 In. . . . 1840.00 to 3738.00
Dispenser, Ward's Orange Crush Syrup, Figural, Ceramic, 1920s, 14 In. . . . 1035.00
Dispenser, Zipp's Cherri-O Syrup, 5 Cents . . . 8050.00
Display, AAA Root Beer, Redhead Girl Sipping Pop, Yellow, Decal, 1940, 9 x 8 In. . . . 135.00
Display, Amos 'N Andy, Pepsodent Toothpaste, Cardboard, 1930, 22 x 61 In. . . . 460.00
Display, Ardenter Mustard, Dean's Patent, Label, Wood, 16 ¼ x 22 ⅝ x 11 In. . . . 385.00
Display, Avalon Farms, Puts Kinks In Their Tails, Papier-Mache Hog, 31 x 18 In. . . . 1980.00
Display, Bank Note Cigar, Cardboard, 14 x 21 In. . . . 90.00
Display, Bear Brand Hosiery, Papa Mama & Baby Bear, Papier-Mache, 18 ½ In. . . . 1035.00
Display, Big Top Peanut Warmer, Motion Lamp, Tin, Plastic, 120 Volt, 19 ½ x 12 In. . . . 358.00
Display, Blatz, 2 Beermen Holding Flags, Light-Up, 23 In. . . . 225.00
Display, Blatz, Banjo Player, I'm From Milwaukee, 17 In. . . . 135.00
Display, Blue Goose Fruits, Oranges & Grapefruit, Papier-Mache, 24 x 28 In. . . . 440.00
Display, Boot, Plaster, Wall Mounted, 18 x 9 In. . . . 110.00
Display, Bryant Pup, Vet Remedies, Composition, c.1930, 14 x 18 In. . . . *illus* 810.00

Display, California Syrup Of Figs, For Healthy Children, Girl, Boy, Dog, Cardboard, 14 x 18 In. 469.00

Display, Calox Tooth Powder, Your 32 Teeth Are 32 Reasons, Mirrors, 12 x 7 x 4 In. 385.00

Display, Camel, Worumbo Polo Cloth, Papier-Mache, 36 x 30 In. 1540.00

Display, Cigar Indian, Saluting, Figural, Painted, Composition, c.1950, 20 In. 170.00

Display, Colburn's Bag Blue, Wood, Paper Label, 14 x 11¾ x 11¾ In. 469.00

Display, Country Gentlemen Tobacco, 12 Cloth Pouches, Cardboard, 9 x 8 x 5 In. 143.00

Display, Cow-Ease, Spray Your Team Free, Keeps Flies Off, Metal, Wood, 34 In. 2420.00

Display, Dandy Catnip Mouse, Make Kitty Happy, Mouse, Hat, Electric, 34 x 26 x 12 In. 1480.00

Display, Double Barrel Shotgun, F & S, 80 In. 385.00

Display, Edison, Mazda Lamps, Light Bulb, Get Together, Maxfield Parrish, 15 x 23 In. 2300.00

Display, Edison Lamps, Cardboard, Lithograph, Shadowbox, 1920s, 34 x 22 In. 908.00

Display, Edison Light Bulbs, Cardboard, Folding, Shadowbox, 1920s, 26 x 16 In. 2640.00

Display, Ford & Medley, Straight Razor, Oval, 18 x 21 In. 1045.00

Display, Fredelle Footwear, Ladies' Boot, Figural, Flowers, Canada, 11 x 9 x 3 In. 90.00

Display, Grain Belt Beer, Good Luck, Diamond Clear, Perfect Beer, Bubbles, 12 In. 75.00

Display, Greeting Card, Raphael Tuck & Sons, Balloon Shape, Children, c.1900, 15 In. 425.00

Display, Jo-Jo Sodas & Seltzer, Clown, All Flavors, Die Cut, Composition, Stand-Up 90.00

Display, Keenes Glad-Pheet Corn Cure, Plaster, Salve, 15 Cents, 17 x 7 In. 3575.00

Display, Kodak Instamatic X-15 Camera, 24 x 21 In. 330.00

Display, Lehman, For All Dogs, Dog, Boxer, Papier-Mache, 23 x 20 In. 220.00

Display, Majestic Radio Authorized Dealer, Eagle, World, Papier-Mache, 28 x 41 In. 1540.00

Display, Mandrake Compound Liver Pills, c.1916, 2 x ¾ In. 25.00

Display, McGregor's Happy Foot Sock, Face, 16 x 10 In. 660.00

Display, Mohawk Moccasins, Indian, Seated, Holding Sign, 30 In. 880.00

Display, Monkey Grip Tube Repair, Monkey Holding Tube, 22 x 12 In. 660.00

Display, National Biscuit Co., Mickey Mouse Cookies, 1937, 11 x 14 In. 705.00

Display, National Mazda Lamps, 11 Bulbs, Tin Lithograph, 2-Sided, 1920s, 30 In. *illus* 650.00

Display, Nut House, Figural, Mahogany, Embossed Glass Jars, Counter, 18 x 16 In. 480.00

Display, Oscar Mayer Wiener, Blow Up, 14 x 14 In. 25.00

Display, Pig, Hog-Tone, Avalon Farms, Figural, Black, White 6325.00

Display, Pioneer Belts & Suspenders, Conestoga Wagon Shape, Papier-Mache 165.00

Display, Ram, Turnbull's Ceetee, Pure Wool Underwear, Papier-Mache, 23 x 25 In. 990.00

Display, RCA Radiotrons, Tubes Tested Free, Reverse Glass, Metal, Wood, Light-Up. 530.00

Display, RCA Victor Records, Wood, 1940-50, 4 x 3 In. *illus* 75.00

Display, Red Goose Shoes, Bobs, Tin, Windup, 1924, 4½ x 9 In. *illus* 800.00

Display, Red Goose Shoes, Riding Toy, Wood, 17 x 16 In. 2420.00

Display, Red Goose Shoes, Teeter-Totter, 35 x 38 In. *illus* 1500.00

Display, Reddy Kilowatt, Wood, Counter, 19 x 12 In. 358.00

Display, Remington-UMC, Boy, Army Of Rabbits, Cardboard, c.1925, 10 x 14 In. 799.00

Display, Ritz Ice Cream Cone, Bathing Boy, Girl, Composition, Art Deco Base, 22 In. 1035.00

Display, Ruppert Beer-Ale, Foam Scraper Holder, Blue Glass, Bakelite, 6½ x 4¾ In. 358.00

Display, Smith Brothers Cough Drop, Tin, 10½ In. 546.00

Display, Topps Spot, Assorted Flavors Of Gum, 100 Sticks, 5 x 2 In. 90.00

Display, Tray, Clark's Teaberry Gum, Citron, Glass, Embossed, Footed 375.00

Display, Whistle, Bottle, Elf, Die Cut, Cardboard, 1940s *illus* 725.00

Display, Whitman's Chocolate, Lego Stylized Messenger, Counter, 1920s, 18¾ In. 2645.00

Display, World War Gum, Goudey Gum Co., World War Pictures, 1933, 11 x 11 In. 1805.00

Display, Wrigley Man, Die Cut, Metal, 4 Gum Boxes, c.1920, 14 x 14 In. *illus* 950.00

Dolls are listed in their own category.

Door Pull, Buy Anderson's Bread, General Store, Embossed, Enamel, 15 x 29 In. 235.00

Door Pull, Colonial Bread 265.00

Door Pull, Major's Cement, Mends Everything, Blue, White, Oval, Porcelain 495.00

Door Push, Bottle, Korker The OK Refresher, King Size, Yellow, Green, Enamel 90.00

Door Push, Canada Dry Pale Ginger Ale, Embossed, Plate, 3½ x 12 In. 70.00

Door Push, Crescent Flour, Push & Try A Sack, Tin Lithograph, 9⅝ x 3¾ In. 275.00

Door Push, Old Gold Cigarettes, For A Treat, Red, White, Blue, Yellow 300.00 to 405.00

Door Push, Orange Kist, Other Kist Flavors, Red, Black, Orange, Embossed 220.00

Door Push, Senate Beer, Heurick Brewing Co., Washington, Enamel, 3 x 11 In. 120.00

Door Push, Sweet Heart Products, Red, Heart Shape, Wheat Flour, Corn Flour, 5 x 5 In. 440.00

Door Push, Vicks Vaporub, Come In, For All Cold Remedies, Porcelain, 6 x 4 In. 575.00

Door Push, Yeast Foam Makes Good Bread, Brown, Yellow, 5 x 3 In. 550.00

Door Screen, Wilson's Splendid Bread, Cardboard Tobacco Signs, 81 x 32 In. 301.00

Dose Glass, Compliments Of Yuma Drug Co., Embossed, 1 In. 530.00

Dose Glass, Davis & Co., Druggist, Clear, 2 In. 280.00

Dose Glass, Jerome Drug Co., Jerome Drug Co., Clear, 2 In. 1456.00

Dose Glass, Laird & Dines, Arizona, 1 In. 530.00

Advertising, Cabinet, Spool, Corticelli Silk, Revolving, 3 Drawers, 28 x 16 In.
$3100.00

Advertising, Cabinet, Spool, J. & P. Coats', Walnut, 6 Drawers, Embossed, c.1890, 22 x 26 x 19 In.
$2100.00

Advertising, Cabinet, Spool, Merrick's, Oak, Pat'd July 20, 1897, 24 x 32 x 18 In.
$3100.00

Advertising, Case, Primley's California Gum, Glass, Wood, 12 x 18 x 9 In.
$345.00

Advertising, Cigar Cutter, Dean's Havanas, Iron, Clockwork, W.O. Dean Co., 5 In.
$1150.00

Advertising, Dispenser, Ma's Root Beer, Plastic, 1940s, 22 In.
$316.00

Advertising, Dispenser, Middleby Root Beer, Mug, Amber Glass, c.1940, 16 In.
$173.00

Advertising, Display, Bryant Pup, Vet Remedies, Composition, c.1930, 14 x 18 In.
$810.00

Dose Glass, Sanitarium 11th, Kansas City, Mo., Clear, 2 In. ... 101.00

Dose Glass, Santa Rita Drug Store, Graduated Reverse, Acid Etched, 2 ½ In. ... 179.00

Envelope, Allen's Foot Ease, Images, Sealed, Contents, 5 ½ x 3 ⅛ In. ... 17.00

Fan Hanger, Howdy, Don't Say Orange Say Howdy, Cardboard, 2-Sided, 5 x 12 In. ... 60.00

Fan Hanger, Smoke Commander 5 Cent Cigar, Cardboard, 2-Sided, 6 x 8 ½ In. ... 50.00

Fan Pull, Hires Root Beer, Soda Jerk, Die Cut, Cardboard, c.1915, 6 x 7 In. ... 3738.00

Fan Pull, Lifebuoy Soap, Dog, Red, White, Blue, Die Cut. ... 330.00

Fans are listed in their own category.

Figure, Allen's Red Tame Cherry, Boy Eating Cherries, Plaster, 27 In. ... 770.00

Figure, Bulldog Suspenders, Bulldog, Papier-Mache, 16 x 25 In. ... 2310.00

Figure, Dutch Boy, White Lead Paint, Pail, Papier-Mache, 30 In. ... 275.00

Figure, General Electric, Drum Major, Composition, Wood, Cameo Prod., c.1900, 18 ½ In. ... *illus* 650.00

Figure, Lord Calvert Whiskey, Calvert Distillers, N.Y., Plaster, 25 x 8 In. ... 55.00

Figure, Nipper, Gramophone Company, His Master's Voice, Ceramic, 15 In. ... 418.00

Figure, Nipper, RCA Dog, Papier-Mache, c.1920, 11 ½ In. ... 186.00

Figure, Nipper, RCA Dog, Victor, Papier-Mache, 42 In. ... 1375.00

Figure, Oertels Beer, 1940-50, 16 In. ... *illus* 150.00

Figure, Oil Rim Rung, Chalkware, c.1930, 17 In. ... 58.00

Figure, Old Crow Kentucky Bourbon Whiskey, Crow, Composition, 26 x 22 In. ... 425.00

Figure, Pilgrim Rum, Chalkware, c.1930, 17 In. ... 58.00

Figure, Seaforth's, Men, Holding Jug, Talc, Plaster, c.1950 ... 402.00

Figure, Sheikh, Hamburg-American Line Cruise Ship, Plaster, 1920s, 24 x 12 x 30 In. ... 748.00

Figure, Star-Kist, Charlie The Tuna, Bendable, Vinyl, Box, c.1973, 9 ½ In. ... *illus* 160.00

Figure, Woman, Bared Breast, Hole For Beer Tap, Wood, Early 1900s, 48 x 25 In. ... 1380.00

Flue Damper, Round Oaks, Indian, Embossed, Cast Iron, 6 ½ x 4 ½ In. ... 300.00

Hat, H & C Coffee Soda Jerk Grocery Store, 11 x 3 ½ In. ... 9.00

Holder, Western Union, Telegraph Blanks, Wall Mount, Porcelain, Enamel, 6 x 8 In. ... 275.00

Ice Cream Lid, Jean Harlow, Clark Gable, Nelson Eddy, Loretta Young, 4 Piece ... 25.00

Ice Cream Scoop, Tyree Funeral Home, Oak Hill, Va., 1968, 8 In. ... 10.00

Inkwell, Madison Square Theater, Trip To China Town, Hat Lifts, Hoyts, 1890, 6 x 5 x 3 In. ... 90.00

Jar, Bardwell's Root Beer, Die Cut, Cylindrical, Embossed, Blue, 11 x 10 In. ... 715.00

Jar, F. & J. Heinz, Cauliflower, Blue Tint, Paper Label, 11 ¾ In. ... 191.00

Jar, Heinz Horseradish, Pressed Glass, Horse Head Finial, Embossed, 5 x 3 In. ... 2100.00

Jar, Honey-Moon Tobacco, Will Not Bite The Tongue, Paper Label, 5 ¼ x 5 x 5 In. ... 550.00

Jug, Detrick Distilling Co., Dayton, Oh, Motto, Brown, White ... 176.00

Jug, Heinz Pure Cider Vinegar, Die Cut, Paper Label, 9 x 6 ½ In. ... 242.00

Jug, Hires Root Beer, Amber, c.1940, Gal., 12 ½ In. ... 805.00

Knife Stone, Celebrated Hog Powder, Barber Medicine Co., Celluloid, 1 ¾ x 2 ⅞ In. ... 120.00

Label, Cigar Box, Dr. Sun Yat Sen, Chromolithograph, Embossed, c.1910, 6 x 10 In. ... 230.00

Label, Cigar Box, Admiral David Farragut, Lithograph, c.1896, 6 x 8 ¼ In., 2 Piece ... 150.00

Label, Cigar Box, Al Smith, W. Mulford & Son, Unadilla, N.Y., 1920s ... 102.00

Label, Cigar Box, American Beauties, Schmidt & Co., N.Y., 1893, 6 x 8 ½ In. ... 150.00

Label, Cigar Box, American Commerce, Eagle, Morgan Dollar, c.1900, 6 x 10 In. ... 220.00

Label, Cigar Box, American Empire, Deservedly Popular, McKinley, c.1900, 6 x 9 In. ... 90.00

Label, Cigar Box, American Stock, Buffalo, American Flags, Lithograph, c.1898. ... 219.00

Label, Cigar Box, American Twins, American Lithograph Co., 1898, 4 ½ x 4 In. ... 215.00

Label, Cigar Box, Andy Gump, Tops 'Em All, Cut Corners, 1920s, 4 ¾ x 4 ¾ In. ... 102.00

Label, Cigar Box, Black Man Smoking, c.1890, 2 Piece ... 92.00

Label, Cigar Box, Captain January, Chromolithograph, c.1900, 4 ¼ x 4 ¼ In. ... 115.00

Label, Cigar Box, Dante, Profile, Heaven With Angels, c.1900, 6 x 8 ½ In. ... 374.00

Label, Cigar Box, Eddie Cantor, Banjo Eyes, Now 2 Of 5 Cents, 1920s, 7 x 9 In. ... 173.00

Label, Cigar Box, Embossed, Al Smith, 7 x 9 In. ... 12.00

Label, Cigar Box, Greenbacks, Woman Frog Fishing, c.1900, 4 ¾ x 4 In. ... 219.00

Label, Cigar Box, Jack Necker, Famous Sportsman, Embossed, Gilt Edge, 12 x 13 In. ... 50.00

Label, Cigar Box, John Ericsson, Civil War Naval Battle Scene, c.1900, 6 x 7 ½ In. ... 259.00

Label, Cigar Box, Johnny Fresh, Boy In Sailor Suit, c.1885, 5 ½ x 8 In. ... 196.00

Label, Cigar Box, Los Patriotos, Henry Clay, Chromolithograph, c.1900, 6 x 10 In. ... 92.00

Label, Cigar Box, Miss Liberty, Glories Caption, Schmidt & Co., c.1902, 6 x 8 ½ In. ... 374.00

Label, Cigar Box, No Monkeying, 2 Dogs, Monkey Playing Cards, Frame, 10 x 12 In. ... 50.00

Label, Cigar Box, Professor Darwin, International Flags, Chromolithograph, c.1890. ... 460.00

Label, Cigar Box, Spirit Of St. Louis, 5 Cent Cigar, Inner Label, Frame, 12 x 12 In. ... 40.00

Label, Cigar Box, Spirit Of St. Louis, Chromolithograph, c.1927, 9 x 10 In. ... 805.00

Label, Cigar Box, Sunset Club, 6 Giants Of American Industry, c.1895, 6 ¾ x 9 In. ... 127.00

Label, Cigar Box, Warpath, American Indian Warriors On Horses, c.1885, 4 x 4 In. ... 173.00

Label, Cigar Box, White Elephant Tobacco, Frame, 10 x 12 In. ... 50.00

Label, Cigar Box, Woman Whip, Fox Hunting, Chromolithograph, c.1908, 6 x 8 ½ In. ... 316.00

Label, Cigar Box, Yellow Cab, Driver, Passengers, Lithograph, 1930s 150.00
Label, Food, Sunkist Orange, Indian, Spear, Indian Hill Citrus Assoc., Frame 200.00
Label, Tobacco, Covered Wagon, Mat, Frame, 12 x 14 In. 50.00
Label, Tobacco, General Custer, Auer & Co., 6 ½ x 7 ½ In. 50.00
Lamps are listed in the Lamp category.
Letter Opener, Kellogg's, Rooster Head, Celluloid, Germany, 2 x 8 In. 90.00
Letter Opener, Kellogg's, Use Is The Test, Telephone, 9 In. 30.00
Lunch Box, Dixie Queen, Tobacco, Factory No. 2 District Of MD, Tin, c.1920, 4 x 6 In. 100.00
Lunch Box, Just Suits, Tobacco, Gold, Red, Buchanan & Lyall, Tin, 8 x 5 In. 103.00
Lunch Box, Penny Post Cut Plug, Tobacco, Hinged Lid, Strater Brothers, Tin. 185.00
Lunch Box, U.S. Marines, Tobacco, Factory No. 2 District Of MD, Tin, c.1920, 4 x 6 In. 100.00
Lunch Box, Winner Cut Plug Tobacco, Race Cars, Tin Lithograph, 4 x 7 ¾ In. 523.00
Lunch Boxes are also listed in their own category.
Mannequin, Dr. Warner's Health Corset, c.1877, 29 x 16 In. 3750.00
Match Striker, Tylers Sherwood Rangers Cigars, Woman, Tin Lithograph, 10 x 3 In. 470.00
Matchbook, Kessler Brewing Co., Moose Club, Deer Lodge, Montana, 1939 . . . . 10.00
Menu Board, 7Up, Sandwiches Of Day, Red, White Letters, 1940s, 10 x 17 In. 290.00

Advertising mirrors of all sizes are listed here. Pocket mirrors range in size from 1½ to 5 inches in diameter. Most of these mirrors were given away as advertising promotions and include the name of the company in the design.

Mirror, Anthracite Beer Co., Santa On Cover, 2 ⅛ In. 336.00
Mirror, Armstrong Beer & Malt, Wine, Reverse Painted. 115.00
Mirror, Baking Powder, Girl Holding Box, Celluloid, 2 ⅛ In. 1595.00
Mirror, Bastian Bros., Factory, Rochester, N.Y., Celluloid, Oval 410.00
Mirror, Bee Hive Overalls Best Maid, Celluloid, 2 ¾ In. 221.00
Mirror, Bradford Wholesale Furniture Mfg., Stork, Baby, Celluloid, Oval, 2 ¾ In. 605.00
Mirror, Cascarets, Best For The Bowels, Woman Reclining On Moon, Round, 2 ⅛ In. 61.00
Mirror, Coney Island Hotel, Frank F. Clayton, 2 ¾ In. 104.00
Mirror, Dowagiac Drills & Seeders Are The Leaders, 2 ¾ In. 201.00
Mirror, Dr. A.C. Daniels, Animal Medicines, Celluloid, 2 ⅛ In. 98.00
Mirror, Ferner Show, Brunette Woman, 2 ¾ In. 125.00
Mirror, Garrett's XXXX Baker Rye, Nude, Bow & Arrow, Celluloid, 1 ¾ x 2 ¾ In. 90.00
Mirror, Genuine Elephant Brand Gin, J.J. Melcher S.WZ, c.1900, 20 ½ x 24 ¾ In. 550.00
Mirror, Hinga & Wilkins, Woman, Celluloid, 2 ¼ In. 179.00
Mirror, Hires Root Beer, Girl Holding Mug, Celluloid, c.1905, 2 ¾ In. 230.00
Mirror, Lawecki The Druggists, Remember The Name, Round, 2 ⅛ In. 105.00
Mirror, McCormick & Co., Bee Brand, Teas, Spices, Extracts, Drugs, Celluloid, 2 ¾ In. . . *illus* 208.00
Mirror, New King Snuff, Scotch King, Celluloid, 2 ¾ x 1 ¾ In. 50.00
Mirror, Ohio Blue Tip Matches, Celluloid, 3 ½ x ¼ In. 110.00
Mirror, Poet Cigar, Paper Label Under Glass, c.1910, 1 ⅞ In. 97.00
Mirror, R.S. Kiltz, Buggies, Wagons, Deering, Binders, Mowers. 150.00
Mirror, Seager Engine Works, Olds Engine, Celluloid, Round, 2 ½ In. 176.00
Mirror, Use Beautyskin For Health & Beauty, Celluloid, 2 ½ In. 58.00
Mirror, Van & Schenck Club, Celluloid, 1917, 1 ¾ In. . . . . *illus* 107.00
Mirror, W.F. Fairchild & Son Pure Drug Druggist, Round, 2 ⅛ In. 165.00
Mirror, Walkers Saloon, Good For 12 ½ Cent Trade, Woman, Butte, Mont., Round. 3400.00
Mirror, Weaver Jackson Hair Co., Lithograph, Commercial L.A. Surface, 2 x 3 In. 235.00
Mirror, Wilbur's Peppermint Gum, Woman, Low Cut Dress, Celluloid, 2 ¼ In. 400.00
Mirror, Woman, Naughty Metamorphic, Oval, 2 ¼ In. 58.00
Mug, Flaccus Bros., Die Cut, Gray & Blue, Handle, Wheeling, W. Va., 4 ¼ In. 225.00
Mug, Hires Root Beer, Boy, Pointing, Bib, Drink Hires Root Beer, Footed 310.00
Mug, Hires Root Beer, Child At Soda Fountain, Serving Mug Of Hires, Die Cut, 4 ½ In. 475.00
Mug, Hires Root Beer, Ugly Kid, Die Cut, 4 x 3 In. 475.00
Mug, Hires Root Beer, Ugly Kid, Pedestal, c.1900, 4 In. 2185.00
Needle Book, Elsie The Cow, For Borden's, Needles, Package, 5 x 3 In. 15.00
Needle Book, Lipton Tea, Figural, West Germany, 4 x 5 In. 19.00
Notepad, Dental Scotch Snuff, Jokes, American Snuff Co., Memphis 5.00
Notepad, Dental Scotch Snuff, Sweet Vintage, Lined, Facts, Jokes. 5.00
Package, Handy Dyes, Cherubs Dyeing Laundry, 17 x 13 In. 55.00
Pail, California Peanut Co., Peanut Butter, Bail Handle, Tin, Lb., 3 ¾ x 3 ¼ In. 120.00
Pail, Gillies Coffee, Boys Playing Football, Girls At Shore, Victorian, Lb. 415.00
Pail, Stover Candy Co., Seashore, Cartoon Animals, Tin Lithograph, 3 x 3 ⅜ In. 264.00
Pail, Toyland Peanut Butter, Circus Parade, Lid, Handle 275.00
Pails are also listed in the Lunch Box category.
Paper Doll, Fletcher's Castoria, Mammy, 11 ¼ x 14 In. 121.00

Advertising, Display, National Mazda Lamps, 11 Bulbs, Tin Lithograph, 2-Sided, 1920s, 30 In.
$650.00

Advertising, Display, RCA Victor Records, Wood, 1940-50, 4 x 3 In.
$75.00

Advertising, Display, Red Goose Shoes, Bobs, Tin, Windup, 1924, 4 ½ x 9 In.
$800.00

Advertising, Display, Red Goose Shoes, Teeter-Totter, 35 x 38 In.
$1500.00

Advertising, Display, Whistle, Bottle, Elf, Die Cut, Cardboard, 1940s
$725.00

Advertising, Display, Wrigley Man, Die Cut, Metal, 4 Gum Boxes, c.1920, 14 x 14 In.
$950.00

Advertising, Figure, General Electric, Drum Major, Composition, Wood, Cameo Prod., c.1900, 18 ½ In.
$650.00

Advertising, Figure, Oertels Beer, 1940-50, 16 In.
$150.00

Pen, Arpege, My Sin Perfume, Ballpoint, Green, 14K Gold Detail, Eliza Of N.Y. 45.00
Pen, Phillip Morris, Smokers Have Rights Too, Chrome 4.00
Pen, Salem Cigarettes, Sheaffer, Ballpoint, Box, Instructions 9.00
Pendant, Old Dutch Cleaner, Woman, Paper, Gold, Red, 16 x 25 In. 40.00
Pennant, Elk Chocolates, Elk, Red, White, Felt, 13 ½ x 36 In. 80.00
Pin, Anchorage Fur Factory, Honored Guest, Real Fur, Celluloid, 2 ¾ In. 33.00
Pin, Arby's, Promoting B.C. Glasses, 1982, 3 In. 60.00
Pin, Atlanta Watermelon City, Large Slice Removed, c.1930, 1 ⅝ In. 34.00
Pin, Audubon Society, Bastian & Offset Gravure, c.1920, ⅞ In., 7 Piece 152.00
Pin, Austin Ammunition, 3 Dogs, Celluloid, ⅞ In. 250.00
Pin, Ballistite, Only Perfect Dense Smokeless Powder, Red, White, Blue, Celluloid 140.00
Pin, Beech-Nut Chewing Gum, I Am A Beech-Nut, 1 ⅛ In. 10.00
Pin, Bowtie Shape, General Electric, Silver Metal, 2 ¾ In. 19.00
Pin, Ceresota, Best Four Sold, Embossed Tin, Celluloid, 1 ¾ In. 55.00
Pin, Daisy Air Rifles, Boy Holding Rifle, Celluloid, ⅞ In. 825.00
Pin, Daisy Cadet, Shield, Star, Celluloid, 1 ¼ In. 275.00
Pin, Deering Harvester Co., 2 Horses, Farmer, Celluloid, Chicago, U.S.A. 50.00
Pin, Dr Pepper, Fonz On Glass, Thumb Up, 1970s, 4 In. 140.00
Pin, DuPont Smokeless Powders, Bird, Celluloid, 1897, ⅞ In. 50.00
Pin, Esso, Merry Christmas, Santa Claus, Red, White, Gray 55.00
Pin, Experts Use Peters Cartridges, Bullet, Red, Brown, Silver, Celluloid 50.00
Pin, Fly Wein Air Alaska, Goose, Wearing Flying Cap & Goggles, Celluloid, 1 ¼ In. 73.00
Pin, Gimme H-O Oats For Breakfast, Celluloid, 1 ¼ In. 17.00
Pin, Grass Valley Calif., Days Of 49, July 3-5, Miner, Blasting Keg, Celluloid 235.00
Pin, Hercules Powder, Orange, Black, Celluloid, ⅝ In. 90.00
Pin, I Like Skeezix Sweaters, Parisian, 1930s, 1 ¼ In. .... *illus* 40.00
Pin, I'm For Health, St. Louis Area TV Prevention, 1926, ⅞ In. 63.00
Pin, Indian Motorcycle, Gold Filled, Hagerstown, Md., Pre-World War II 100.00
Pin, Indian Motorcycle, Whitehead & Hoag, Back Paper, Celluloid, ⅞ In. 55.00
Pin, J.I. Case Threshing Machine, Corn Palace, Celluloid, 1 ¾ In. 50.00
Pin, Junior Winchester Rifle Corp., Medal, Bronze, Marked, Panikoff, ⅝ In. 50.00
Pin, King Neptune, Atlantic City, Cream Back, c.1900 .... 140.00
Pin, King's Smokeless Powder, Black, Gray, Red, White, Celluloid 875.00
Pin, Laflin & Rand Smokeless Powder, Wreath, Flag, Celluloid, 1 ¼ In. 100.00
Pin, Lee Mfg. Co., Cobalt Blue Enamel, ¾ In. 18.50
Pin, Liberty Flour, Statue Of Liberty, 1903, 1 ¼ In. .... *illus* 138.00
Pin, Macy's, Shari Lewis, Lambchop, Macy's Has A Little Lamb, 2 x 3 In. 17.00
Pin, Manner's Big Boy, Photo Of Big Boy, Hamburger, Employees, 1952, 3 ½ In. 80.00
Pin, N.Y. News, Say Hey, Willie Mays, Mets, 3 In. 58.00
Pin, Newsboy, Evening, American League Of Junior Salesmen, No. 780, 2 ¼ In. 40.00
Pin, Ohio Foods, I Eat & Boost, c.1920, 1 ¼ In. .... *illus* 90.00
Pin, Old Dutch Cleanser, 1 ⅛ In. 25.00
Pin, Peters Patriotic, Stars & Stripes P, Light Blue Ground, Celluloid, ⅞ In. 50.00
Pin, Peters Shells, Steel Where Steel Belongs, Duck In Flight, Celluloid, ⅞ In. 160.00
Pin, Pollyanna Club, Be Glad, Boston Badge, Back Paper, Celluloid, ⅞ In. 10.00
Pin, RCA Victor, Wurlitzer-Cincinnati, His Master's Voice, Celluloid, c.1910, 1 ¼ In. 353.00
Pin, Rockdale Powder, Only Independent Powder & Dynamite Co., Celluloid, 1 ¼ In. 350.00
Pin, Satan-Et, The Drink With A Wink, c.1910-20, ⅞ In. .... *illus* 153.00
Pin, Shoot A Remington, U.M.C., 22 Repeater, 2 Bears, Celluloid, ⅞ In. 50.00
Pin, Shoot DuPont Powders, World's Best Trap Load, Baby Bird, Celluloid, ⅞ In. 250.00
Pin, Shoot Winchester Shotgun Shells Shotguns, Red, White, Blue, Celluloid, ⅞ In. 50.00
Pin, Smokey Bear, Metal, Ceramic, Green Duck Co., 2 In. 15.00
Pin, Steel Where Steel Belongs, Light Blue, White, Red, Celluloid, ⅞ In. 150.00
Pin, Steven Shotguns, Close Shooting Self Pointing, ⅞ In. 616.00
Pin, Use Peters Referee Shells, Celluloid, ⅞ In. 50.00
Pin, Wavy Gravy, Something Good For A Change, 3 In. 17.00
Pin, Webster City Carnival, We Meet, Woman, Clown, Whitehead & Hoag, 1899 .... 85.00
Pin, White Flyer-Shooters Favorite, Celluloid, ⅞ In. 425.00
Pin, Winchester, J.R. Taylor, Rifle, Photo, Bullet, Celluloid 575.00
Pin, Winchester, Leaders At The Trap In 1912, 3 Photos, Celluloid, 1 ¼ In. 2600.00
Pin, Winchester Guns & Cartridges, Wonderful Topperweins, Celluloid, 1 ¼ In. 130.00
Pin, Winchester Leader, W.R. Crosby, Champion Shot, Celluloid, 1 ¼ In. 170.00
Pin, Winchester The Repeater, Celluloid, Whitehead & Hoag, 1 x ⅝ In. 250.00
Pin, Yellow Kid, No. 7, Kid With His Goat 46.00
Pin, Yellow Kid, No. 76, Tiny Cannon, Dagger, Revolver Over Shoulder 139.00
Pin, Yellow Kid, No. 134, Flag Of Uruguay 132.00

Pin Tray, Elko Drug Co., Elko, Nevada, Baby Girl, Aluminum, 3 x 4½ In. 150.00
Plaque, Hercules Powder Co., Shield Shape, Bronze, Box, 1915 2500.00
Plaque, Miller High Life, Bottle, 29 x 8 In. 15.00
Plate, Atlantic City, Woman Diving In 1920's Swimsuit, 6 In. 379.00
Plate, Calvert, Clear Heads Choose, Owl, Taylor, Smith & Taylor, 10 In. 45.00
Plate, Carr China, Reading Nest No. 2, 9 In. 19.00
Platter, Greyhound Bus Lines, Logo In Center, Shenango, China, 1940s, 11¾ In. 210.00
Platter, Let's Go!, U.S.A. Keep 'Em Flying, Airplanes, Red, White, Blue 90.00
Pot Scraper, American-Maid Bread, Yellow, Red & Blue Letters, 1¾ In. 310.00
Pot Scraper, Henkel's Flour, Blue Ground, Red Accents, White Letters, 3 x 2 In. 110.00
Pot Scraper, Kenny Co., Tea, Coffees, Sugars, Embossed, Cast Iron 132.00
Printer's Plate, Chesterfield Cigarettes, Kirk Douglas, Mercersburg Journal, 10 x 6 In. 30.00
Punch Bowl, Bardwell's Root Beer, Die Cut, Greek Key, White's, Utica, c.1890 1840.00
Rack, Baby Ruth, Tin, 10 x 4¼ x 5¼ In., Pair 605.00
Rack, Heinz, Keystone Pickling & Preserving Works, Pittsburgh, Wire, 36 x 51 In. 508.00
Rack, Heinz Ketchup, Metal, Plastic Bottom 5.00
Rack, J. & P. Coats', 24 Compartments, Metal, 14 x 13½ x 7 In. 65.00
Rack, Savage, Stevens, Fox, World Famous Rifles & Shotguns, Wood, 29 x 20 In. 537.00
Rack, Waring Hat Co., Oak, Figural, Embossed, Wall Mount, 16 x 21 In. 259.00
Rack, Watkins Coconut Oil Shampoo, Quality For Over 50 Years, Wood, 10 x 24 x 8 In. 232.00
Rolling Pin, Golden Grain Home Made Bread, Bristol Glaze, Stoneware, Wood, 9 In. 198.00
Salt & Pepper shakers are listed in their own category.
Scales are listed in their own category.
Scoop, Marinique Coffee, Sprague Warner Co., Patented 65.00
Sign, 20 Mule Team Borax, 1920s, 12 x 22 In. 66.00
Sign, A & W Root Beer, Double Bubble, Light-Up, c.1950, 15 In. 230.00
Sign, A. Levy's, Ladies' Coats, Suits, Dresses, Peacock, Metal, 15 In. 230.00
Sign, A.P.W. Satin Tissue Toilet Paper, Maid At Cupboard, Easel, 1920s, 38 x 21 In. 1155.00
Sign, Abbey's Effervescent Salt, Shrink Wrapped, Foam Core Board, 12¾ x 5½ In. 50.00
Sign, Adams Express, Porcelain, 2-Sided, Flange, 11 x 14 In. 1650.00
Sign, Age's Violet Pepsin Chewing Gum, Tin Lithograph, 3 x ⅜ In. 358.00
Sign, Alhambra Cigars, Clock Shape, Hands, Wood, Round, 42 In. 248.00
Sign, All American Cables, Porcelain, 44 x 26 In. 385.00
Sign, All-American Soap Box Derby, Shield, Red, White, Blue, Composition 100.00
Sign, Alley's Hambone 5 Cent Cigars, Cardboard, 2-Sided, Hanging 40.00
Sign, American Cancer Society, Anti-Smoking, Brooks Robinson, 1971, 8 x 12 In. 132.00
Sign, American Express Company, Porcelain, Flange, 1905, 12 x 17 In. 200.00
Sign, American Ingot Iron Road Culverts, Blue, White, Embossed, Tin, 5½ x 20 In. 50.00
Sign, American Mills Coffee, Man Fighting Lion, J.S. Silvers & Bro., 5½ x 4¾ In. 187.00
Sign, Ammo Bath Cleanser, 1919, 12 x 22 In. 55.00
Sign, Andersons, Curved Panel, Painted, Wood, 2-Sided, Iron Brackets 470.00
Sign, Antiques, Wood, Applied Molding, White Lettering, Black Ground, 12 x 26 In. 764.00
Sign, Apple Brandy, Celluloid Over Cardboard, 14 x 10 In. 345.00
Sign, Arcade, Etched, Mirror Back Glass, Scalloped Edge, Metal Bracket, 3⅛ x 9 In. 198.00
Sign, Arden Ice Cream, Red, White, Oval, Porcelain, 23 x 30 In. 325.00
Sign, Ask For Cascade Lager, Union Brewing Co., A Close Game, Tin, 13 x 19 In. 400.00
Sign, Atlantic Coast Line Railroad, Round, 29¾ In. 143.00
Sign, Ayer's Cathartic Pills, Black Doctor, Children, Die Cut, Cardboard, Easel, 12 In. 550.00
Sign, Ayer's Cherry Pectoral, Santa Claus, Holding Bottle, Sleigh, Die Cut, Cardboard, 12 In. 550.00
Sign, Ayer's Hair Vigor, Restores Gray Hair, Woman, Long Curly Hair, Paper, Frame 1350.00
Sign, Aztec Manufacturing Co., Yellow, Brown, Porcelain, 5 x 13 In. 50.00
Sign, B-1 Lemon-Lime Soda, Black, Yellow, Red, Beveled Edge, 3 x 16 In. 40.00
Sign, Baby First Pevely Best Milk, Baby & Bottle, Porcelain, 1930s, 17 x 21 In. 2625.00
Sign, Baby Ruth, Tin Lithograph, 28 x 9⅝ In. 413.00
Sign, Baker's Chocolate, Tin, Wood Frame, c.1900, 23 x 29 In. 403.00
Sign, Barker's Poultry Remedy, Yellow, Black, Red, White, Tin Lithograph, 26 x 18 In. 2640.00
Sign, Beech-Nut, Trolley, 1920s, 21 x 11 In. 55.00
Sign, Beech-Nut Chewing Tobacco, Die Cut, Cardboard, Easel Back, 35¾ x 26 In. 176.00
Sign, Berengaria Steamship, Passenger Steamer, A.F. Bishop, Tin, c.1924, 40 x 30 In. 480.00
Sign, Best Quality Sewing Machine Needles, Washington, Lincoln, Tin, 11 x 16 In. 418.00
Sign, Bicyclettes, Lithograph, Gorrois, A. Dutheil Et Cie Frame, Paris, c.1920, 26 x 39 In. 669.00
Sign, Big Dutchman Poultry Feeder, Red, White, Porcelain, 4 x 5 In. 275.00
Sign, Bixby's Shu-White Shoe Cleaner, Woman, 39½ x 15¼ In. 853.00
Sign, Black Cat Cigarettes, Black, Yellow, Tin Lithograph, Embossed, 23 x 23 In. 605.00
Sign, Blatz Brewing Co., Reverse On Glass, Milwaukee, Wis., 14¼ x 8½ In. 1750.00
Sign, Blatz Brewing Co., Saloon, Gold Leaf, 1898, 30 x 22 In. 625.00

Advertising, Figure, Star-Kist, Charlie The Tuna, Bendable, Vinyl, Box, c.1973, 9½ In.
$160.00

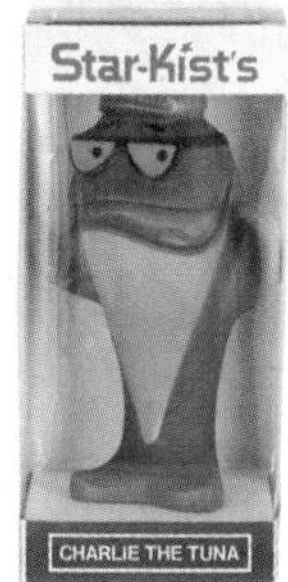

Advertising, Mirror, McCormick & Co., Bee Brand, Teas, Spices, Extracts, Drugs, Celluloid, 2¾ In.
$208.00

Advertising, Mirror, Van & Schenck Club, Celluloid, 1917, 1¾ In.
$107.00

Advertising, Pin, I Like Skeezix Sweaters, Parisian, 1930s, 1¼ In.
$40.00

Advertising, Pin, Liberty Flour, Statue Of Liberty, 1903, 1 ¼ In.
$138.00

Advertising, Pin, Ohio Foods, I Eat & Boost, c.1920, 1 ¼ In.
$90.00

Advertising, Pin, Satan-Et, The Drink With A Wink, c.1910-20, ⅞ In.
$153.00

Advertising, Sign, Chew Paycar Scrap, Embossed, Tin, c.1920, 17 x 13 In.
$403.00

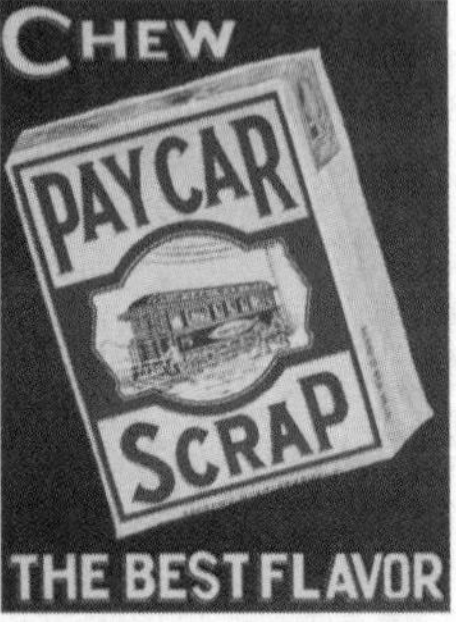

Sign, Blue Bird, Woman, Citrus Products, Cardboard Lithograph, 1920s, 9 x 12 In. 90.00
Sign, Blue Goose, Blue, Gold, Porcelain, 48 x 41 In. 476.00
Sign, Bond Bread, Vitamin D, Yellow, Green, Red, Embossed 198.00
Sign, Boot, Wood, Laminated, Cast Metal Spur, Hanging Loop, 24 In. 1035.00
Sign, Boots Repair, Boot Shape, Wood, Black Paint, Busche Harness Shop, 19 In. 1610.00
Sign, Boston American, Newspaper, Eagle, Shield, Inscription, Painted 7638.00
Sign, Brook Hul Whiskey, Tin Lithograph, 1905, 28 x 38 In. 1093.00
Sign, Buckeye Paint & Varnish, Victorian Woman With Roses, 20 x 26 In. 55.00
Sign, Budweiser, Custer's Last Stand, Cardboard, Frame, 36 x 47 In. 345.00
Sign, Budweiser Beer, Hanging, Revolving, 1950s, 26 x 16 In. 298.00
Sign, Butcher Boy, Black Ground, Reverse Painted On Glass, 1893, 16 x 12 In. 345.00
Sign, Call A Cab, Yellow, Checker, Red, Black, Cardboard 550.00
Sign, Call Again 5 Cent Cigar, Embossed, Tin, Enamel, 14 x 3 In. 67.00
Sign, Camden Woolen Co., White, Black Letters, 2-Sided, 132 x 13 x 2 In. 2530.00
Sign, Cantilevers Brewing Co., Man & Woman On Train, Paper, 23 x 18 In. 160.00
Sign, Carling Beer, Man On High-Wheel Bicycle, Neon, 21 ½ In. 28.00
Sign, Carnation Fresh Milk, Red, White, Yellow, Green, Die Cut 350.00
Sign, Carney Drugs, Painted, Sheet Metal, 2-Sided, Wrought Iron Mounts, 36 x 29 In. 764.00
Sign, Carnival, World's Fair Wonder Show, Masonite, Painted, 144 x 31 In. 1380.00
Sign, Caterpillar, Tractor, Porcelain, 32 x 66 In. 375.00
Sign, Centlivre Tonic, Nurse, Cardboard, String Hanger, 21 x 11 In. 110.00
Sign, Ceresota Prize Bread Flour, Match Holder, Embossed, Die Cut, 2 ½ x 5 ½ In. 325.00
Sign, Cherry Sparkle, Taste Tells The Tale, Boy Holding Bottle, Tin, Cardboard, 6 x 13 In. 1900.00
Sign, Cherry's Motor Boat Supplies, Buy At, Eastport, Maine, Red, White, Cardboard 60.00
Sign, Chesterfield Cigarettes, Girl In Red Sweater, 27 x 22 In. 57.00
Sign, Chesterfield Cigarettes, Men Of America, Construction Workers, 26 x 28 In. 57.00
Sign, Chesterfield Tobacco, Alexis Smith In Montana, 20 x 23 In. 57.00
Sign, Chesterfield Tobacco, Arthur Godfrey, 48 x 26 ½ In. 57.00
Sign, Chesterfield Tobacco, Carole Landis, 21 x 22 In. 57.00
Sign, Chesterfield Tobacco, Perry Como, Jo Stafford, Frame, Glass, 27 x 29 In. 115.00
Sign, Chesterfield Tobacco, Roller Skating Couple, 21 x 22 In. 57.00
Sign, Chew Copenhagen Snuff, Porcelain, 2-Sided, Flange, 20 x 8 In. 121.00
Sign, Chew Mail Pouch & Treat Yourself To The Best, Barn Shape, 52 x 35 In. 154.00
Sign, Chew Paycar Scrap, Embossed, Tin, c.1920, 17 x 13 In. .... *illus* 403.00
Sign, Chew Star Tobacco, Gold Ground, Hugh Star Center, Porcelain, 24 x 12 In. 250.00
Sign, Choctaw Machinery Sales Inc., Porcelain, Red, Black, White, 1950s 476.00
Sign, Cinderella Coal, Girl Sitting By Fire, Porcelain, 21 ½ x 18 In. 1320.00
Sign, Circus, Ringling Brothers, Wood, 1944, 22 x 17 In. 575.00
Sign, Clossman Hardware, Open Touring Car, Bi-Plane, Embossed, Tin, 1920s 403.00
Sign, Colgate Octagon Soap, 1920s, 12 x 22 In. 66.00
Sign, Columbia Records, Record, Great Music, World's Greatest Artists, Metal, 48 x 48 In. 99.00
Sign, Common Sense Rat Exterminator, Rats, Top Hats, Tin On Cardboard, 8 x 6 In. 4180.00
Sign, Continental Insurance Co., Soldier, Tin Lithograph, Self-Framed, 30 x 20 In. 935.00
Sign, Cook's Beer, Spinning, 2-Sided, Curved End Flaps, c.1940s, 29 x 12 In. 403.00
Sign, Cook's Beer T.O.C., Plantation, Black Waiter, Maid, Evansville, Ind. 288.00
Sign, Crane's Philadelphia Ice Cream, Dog, 25 Years, Die Cut, Cardboard, Easel 330.00
Sign, Crane's Philadelphia Ice Cream, Girl, Die Cut, Cardboard, Easel, 14 x 8 In. 495.00
Sign, Crimps Cigarettes, Drunk Woman Smoking, Liggett & Myers, Paper, 18 x 24 In. 1870.00
Sign, Croce's Beverages, Boy Sipping Soda, Porcelain, Asbury Park, N.Y., 1920s 1380.00
Sign, Crystal Dairy Foods, Really Farm Fresh, Yellow Ground, Porcelain, 27 x 17 In. 900.00
Sign, Cunard Line, Deco, Porcelain, Canada, 1930s, 14 ¾ In. 633.00
Sign, C-Y Chocolate Yeast Cakes, 1920s, 12 x 22 In. 55.00
Sign, Dad's Root Beer, Bottle Cap, c.1940, 29 In. 288.00
Sign, Del Monte Food Products, Green, Red, Yellow, Porcelain, 21 x 26 ½ In. 425.00
Sign, DeLaval, We Use The DeLaval, Milker, Embossed, Tin, c.1926, 12 x 16 In. 134.00
Sign, Diamond Edge Tool, Tin, 10 x 27 In. 105.00
Sign, Dingman Soap, Kitty's Bath, Girl, Paper Lithograph, Roll Down, 25 x 14 ½ In. 440.00
Sign, Directional, Boy In Sunday Best, Pointing, White, Black, c.1900, 33 ½ x 19 In. 385.00
Sign, Doctor Woody, Cobalt Blue, White, Porcelain, 10 x 19 In. 150.00
Sign, Donaldsons Cigar, Arthur Donaldson, Die Cut, Cardboard, Easel, c.1905 .... 121.00
Sign, Double Cola, A Mighty Flavor, Bottle, Embossed, Metal, Signed, 65 In .... *illus* 580.00
Sign, Dove Brand, Sugar Cured Family Meats, Tin Lithograph, Frame, 32 x 23 In. 1595.00
Sign, Dove Ice Cream, Where Served, Cones, Soda, Painted, Iron 19550.00
Sign, Dr. Henry Baxter's Mandrake Bitters, Girl, Flower, Tin Lithograph, 19 x 13 In. 1485.00
Sign, Dr. J.R. Miller's Magnetic Balm, Glass, Reverse, Wood Frame, 25 x 7 In. 1595.00
Sign, Dr. Radcliff's Seven Seals, Golden Wonder, Maple Frame, 27 ½ x 20 ½ In. 880.00

Sign, Dr. Scholl's, Zino Pads, Multicolored, Porcelain, 7 ½ x 24 In. 770.00
Sign, Drink Barqs, It's Good, Bottle, Red, White, Blue 240.00
Sign, Drink Brownie, If You Like Chocolate Soda, Frame, 21 ½ x 60 In.. .... 688.00
Sign, Drink Nesbitt's California Orange, 5 Cent, Metal, c.1940s, 13 x 5 In.. .... 230.00
Sign, Drink R-Pep, 5 Cent, Red, Yellow, White, Tin 154.00
Sign, Dutch Baby Condensed Milk, Yellow, Red, Porcelain, 36 x 24 In.. .... 1093.00
Sign, Dyers Pork & Beans, Beveled Edge, Tin On Cardboard, c.1930, 8 x 11 In.. .... 259.00
Sign, Ellis Tiger Co., Fishing Tackle, Embossed, Tin Lithograph, 12 x 36 In. 615.00
Sign, Enjoy Grapette Soda, Stout Sign Co., Embossed, Tin, Enamel, 12 x 8 In. 78.00
Sign, Epco 5 Cent Cigar Tobacco, Best In America, Paper, Frame, 9 x 18 In. 50.00
Sign, Ericsson Steamship, Lord Baltimore, 20 Knot Boat, Tin, Self-Framed, 33 x 23 In. 2875.00
Sign, Euthymol Toothpaste, Parke Davis & Co., Die Cut, Easel Back, 9 ¾ x 5 ½ In. 550.00
Sign, Eveready Flashlight, Batteries, Man, Flashlight, Red, Blue. 450.00
Sign, Eveready Flashlight, Paper, 1930s, 20 x 30 In. 403.00
Sign, Eye-Gene For Your Eyes, Cobalt Blue, White, Porcelain, 5 x 4 In. 200.00
Sign, Fairbanks & Co. Fairy Soap, Girl Holding Flowers, Die Cut, Cardboard, 7 x 5 In. 160.00
Sign, Fairbanks Scales, Black & White Paint, Wood, Marked, Chicago, c.1880 .... 441.00
Sign, Fairmont's Pasteurized Milk Store, Bottle, 20 x 8 In. 550.00
Sign, Farmers & Mechanics National Bank, Die Cut Overlay, Brass, 30 In. 55.00
Sign, Feen-A-Mint, Chewing Laxative, Red, White, Blue, Porcelain. 675.00
Sign, Fehr's Malt Tonic, Seminude Woman, Cherubs, Bottle, Tin, 1905 .... 403.00
Sign, Ferris Waists, Tin, c.1905, 17 x 23 In.. .... 1093.00
Sign, Figaro Cigars, 2 Women, Umbrella, Seidenberg & Co., Die Cut, Easel 2320.00
Sign, First National Bank, Copper, Brass, 24 x 30 In. 402.00
Sign, Fish, Sheet Metal, Die Cut, 33 In. 165.00
Sign, Fish Monger, Cod Fish Shape, Applied Fins, Pressed Metal, Hollow, 8 x 22 In. 660.00
Sign, Fish Monger, Fish, Full-Bodied, Scales, Open Jaws, Gilt 31000.00
Sign, Fleischmann's Fresh Yeast, Eat 3 Cakes Daily, Enamel, 5 ½ x 8 ½ In. 60.00
Sign, Fleischmann's Fresh Yeast, Yellow, Blue, Red, Embossed, Tin 60.00
Sign, Flor De Moss Havana Cigar, Kids, 5 Cent Size, Tin Lithograph, 2-Sided, 4 x 6 In. 176.00
Sign, Foot Rest Hosiery, Tin, 17 ¼ x 11 ¼ In.. .... 275.00
Sign, Forbes Baking Powder, Never Sold In Bulk, 25 Cents, Tin Lithograph, 12 x 8 In. 880.00
Sign, Four Roses Whiskey, Days Hunt, Tin, 35 x 24 In.. .... 100.00
Sign, Franklin's High Class Mineral Waters, Rickmansworth, Porcelain, 24 x 18 In. 160.00
Sign, Fresh Honey, Hand, Pointing Finger, 2 Bumblebees, Beehive, Tin, 2 Piece 795.00
Sign, Fresh Up With 7Up, It Likes You, Cardboard, Man With Gun, Counter, 1950s. 90.00
Sign, Fresh X Foot Cream, 1931, 12 x 22 In. 44.00
Sign, Friskies For Your Dog, Flange, Enamel, 2-Sided, Stout Sign Co., 18 In.. .... 812.00
Sign, Frostie Root Beer, Embossed, Cap, Tin, 1950s, 28 In. .... *illus* 403.00
Sign, G.E., Coil Top Refrigerator, Porcelain, 2-Sided, 36 x 16 In. 3200.00
Sign, Gavel, Turned Wood Shaft, Hollow, Black, Gold Paint, 43 x 17 In.. .... 468.00
Sign, Gem-Nut Margarine, Nut Spread For Bread, Tin Lithograph, 6 ⅛ x 13 ¼ In. 187.00
Sign, Geo. H. Myers Loans & Insurance, Room 202, White, Black, Tin, 14 x 12 In. 22.00
Sign, Gettelman Beer, 2 Bottles, Glass, Tin, Self-Framed, 16 x 19 In. 550.00
Sign, Gillette Super Rapid Razor, Rolled Edge, Tin, 1956, 13 x 13 In.. .... 70.00
Sign, Glazo Nail Polish, 1920s, 12 x 22 In. 22.00
Sign, Globe & Rutgers Fire Insurance, N.Y., Atlas, Globe, Painted, Wood 33.00
Sign, Goetze's Ham, The Great Gildersleeve Show, 1950s, 13 x 13 In.. .... 100.00
Sign, Gold Label Beer, Walter Bros. Brewing Co., Menasha, Wis., Tin, 20 x 28 In. 375.00
Sign, Gold Medal Flour, White, Red, Black, Porcelain, 4 x 24 In. 495.00
Sign, Gold Medal Hosiery, Man, Woman, Fold-Out, Die Cut, Cardboard 469.00
Sign, Gold Medal Salad Dressing, 1929, 12 x 22 In. 50.00
Sign, Golden Light Coffee, Multicolored, Metal Over Cardboard, c.1930, 8 x 15 In.. .... 153.00
Sign, Goodyear, Wingfoot Heels, 12 x 22 In. 44.00
Sign, Grape Sparkle, Snappy Wine Flavor, Girl, Embossed, Tin On Cardboard, 6 x 13 In. 630.00
Sign, Grape-Nuts, There's A Reason, Girl, Dog, Embossed, Tin, 26 x 22 In. 2250.00
Sign, Great American Insurance Co., Reverse On Glass, c.1930s, 19 x 13 In. 115.00
Sign, Green River Whiskey, Black Man & Mule, Metal, 1900, 24 In. Diam.. .... 950.00
Sign, Greensmith's Derby Dog Biscuits, Clowns, Dog, Hoop, Cardboard, 19 x 24 In. 500.00
Sign, Griffins, Locksmiths, Skeleton Key Shape, Painted, Wood, c.1900 .... 375.00
Sign, Griswold, Fine Cooking Utensils Sold Here, 2 Logos, White, Light-Up 55.00
Sign, Gund Brewing Company, Tin, 1904, 17 x 23 In. 1265.00
Sign, H.P. Hood & Sons Ice Cream, Cow, In Pasture, Porcelain, c.1934, 30 In. 3738.00
Sign, Hail Insurance, Chas. W. Bert Jr., Greencastle, Pa., 20 x 13 ¾ In.. .... 145.00
Sign, Hamilton Brown Shoes, Black, Red, White, Embossed, Tin Lithograph. 60.00
Sign, Hart Brand Canned Foods, Fruits & Vegetables, Tin Over Cardboard, 9 x 13 In. 1100.00

Advertising, Sign, Double Cola, A Mighty Flavor, Bottle, Embossed, Metal, Signed, 65 In.
$580.00

Advertising, Sign, Frostie Root Beer, Embossed, Cap, Tin, 1950s, 28 In.
$403.00

Advertising, Sign, Horlacher's Genuine Bock Beer, Die Cut, Cardboard, c.1950, 20 x 21 In.
$115.00

SECURITY TIP

Never run an ad that says "Call after 6 p.m." It is an announcement that you are away from the house during the day.

Advertising, Sign, Ipana, Dentist, Woman, Cutout, Paper, c.1935, 85 x 53 x 20 In.
$403.00

Advertising, Sign, Kerr View's Ice Cream, Porcelain, 2-Sided, 1940s, 54 x 24 In.
$5500.00

Advertising, Sign, Kodak, Tin, 2-Sided, Bracket, c.1930-40, 20 x 30 In.
$800.00

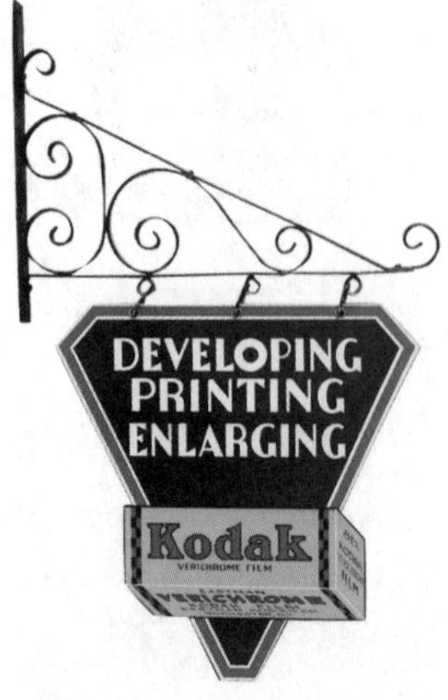

Sign, Hazle Club, Tru-Orange, Tin Lithograph, 20 x 14 In. 187.00
Sign, Heartwellville Inn, Wood, 2-Sided, Gilt Lettering, Black Ground, 24 ½ x 36 In. 999.00
Sign, Helmbold's Fluid Extract, Buchu, Glass, Reverse, Frame, 13 ½ x 7 ½ In. 198.00
Sign, Helmbold's Fluid Extract, Sarsaparilla, Glass, Reverse, Frame, 13 ½ x 7 ½ In. 385.00
Sign, Hires Root Beer, Bottle, Die Cut, Porcelain, 22 x 79 In. 920.00
Sign, Hires Root Beer, Children, Bench, Bats, Cutout, Cardboard 4600.00
Sign, Hires Root Beer, Drink Hires, Delicious Healthful Treat, Cardboard, 11 In. 360.00
Sign, Hires Root Beer, Ugly Kid, Cutout, Cardboard, c.1895, 10 ½ x 14 ½ In. 920.00
Sign, Hires Root Beer, Waitress, Die Cut, Cardboard, Shadowbox, c.1905 10925.00
Sign, Hires Root Beer, Woman Holding Glass, Cutout, Cardboard, c.1940, 32 x 30 In. 3163.00
Sign, Hodson Superior Pork Butcher, Pig, 1880s, 58 x 37 In. 1080.00
Sign, Holbrook Shoes, Winter Scene, Victorian Girls, c.1885, 28 x 16 In. 1150.00
Sign, Holiday Publications, Prang & Co., art Nouveau, Louis J. Rhead, 25 x 20 In. 1265.00
Sign, Honey Moon Tobacco, Pocket, Embossed, Tin Lithograph, Ohio, 6 ¾ x 10 In. 179.00
Sign, Hood's Sarsaparilla, Food For The Wise, Die Cut, Easel, Counter, 6 ¼ x 8 In. 235.00
Sign, Hood's Tire Dealer, Crossing Guard, Lithograph On Sheet Metal, 48 In. 546.00
Sign, Hopkins & Allen Arms Co., Prairie Girl, Cowgirl, Revolver, 10 x 24 In. 1960.00
Sign, Horlacher's Genuine Bock Beer, Die Cut, Cardboard, c.1950, 20 x 21 In. *illus* 115.00
Sign, Hotel St. James, San Diego's Tallest Building, Embossed, Tin, 1930s, 9 x 20 In. 115.00
Sign, Howard Dusters, Colored Graphic Image, Paper Lithograph, 29 ½ x 20 In. 1155.00
Sign, Howel's Rootbeer, Embossed, Tin, 27 ¼ x 19 ½ In. 413.00
Sign, Humboldt Times, Eureka, $6.00 A Year, Blue, White, Porcelain 100.00
Sign, Humphrey's Specific Homeopathic Remedies, Cardboard, Frame, 18 x 14 In. 495.00
Sign, Hunter's Ice Cream, Sidewalk, 2-Sided, Hinged, 1910, 21 x 23 In. 403.00
Sign, IBM Electric Typewriters, Woman, Typewriter, 1954, 13 x 10 In. 8.00
Sign, Ice Cream, Chocolate Milk Shake, Embossed, Enamel, 23 x 48 In. 130.00
Sign, Ilco Lock & Key Products, Key Shape, Fitchburg, Mass., 14 x 32 In. 165.00
Sign, Ipana, Dentist, Woman, Cutout, Paper, c.1935, 85 x 53 x 20 In. *illus* 403.00
Sign, Iroquois Brewing Co., Indian Head, Lithograph, 15 x 12 In. 90.00
Sign, Iroquois Indian Head Beer & Ale, Lithograph, Self-Framed, Oval, 15 x 12 In. 880.00
Sign, It's Cott, 17 Delicious Flavors, Tin, 17 ½ x 54 In. 165.00
Sign, Iver Johnson Revolver, Hammer The Hammer, Tin, 2-Sided, 16 x 12 In. 5750.00
Sign, Job Cigarette Papers, Red-Headed Woman, Cardboard, c.1900, 15 x 20 In. 345.00
Sign, John Barbee Whiskey, Die Cut, c.1905, 38 x 25 In. 863.00
Sign, Johnson & Johnson Baby Department, Glass, Wood Frame, 29 x 7 In. 488.00
Sign, Kellogg's, Campfire Girl, Ready To Serve, Paper, 26 x 21 ¾ In. 520.00
Sign, Kellogg's Corn Flakes, Baby, Wicker Highchair, Tin, 2-Sided, 1910 230.00
Sign, Kentucky Tavern Whiskey, Man Reading Paper In Bar, Cardboard, 24 x 18 In. 80.00
Sign, Kerr View's Ice Cream, Porcelain, 2-Sided, 1940s, 54 x 24 In. *illus* 5500.00
Sign, Kimball's Vanity Fair Cigarettes, Woman Smoking, Frame, 22 x 18 x 10 In. 180.00
Sign, Kist Beverages, Bottle, Red, Orange, Yellow, Embossed 240.00
Sign, Kodak, Tin, 2-Sided, Bracket, c.1930-40, 20 x 30 In. *illus* 800.00
Sign, Kool Cigarettes, NRA, Penguin Smoking, 1940s, 17 ½ x 11 ¾ In. 201.00
Sign, La Vida Lime N' Lemon, Bottle, Black, 19 x 14 In. 140.00
Sign, Lasting Paints, 25 ¾ x 20 ¼ In. 110.00
Sign, Lee Union-Alls, For Comfort, Economy, Safety, Porcelain, 1920-30, 11 x 30 In. 2912.00
Sign, Levi's, Dealers, Wood, 1950s, 11 x 8 In. 80.00
Sign, Lifebuoy, House Maid, Fisherman, Life Preserver, Die Cut, 2-Sided 230.00
Sign, Lifesavers, 1921, 12 x 22 In. 44.00
Sign, Lifesavers, Cryst-O-Mint, 1920s, 12 x 22 In. 77.00
Sign, Lillian Russell Cigars, Woman, Die Cut, Easel Back, 17 ¼ x 9 ½ In. 880.00
Sign, Lipton's Instant Cocoa, Woman, Cup Of Cocoa, Tin Over Cardboard, 9 x 13 In. 201.00
Sign, Little Giant, Muscle Man, Globe, Red, White, Black 80.00
Sign, Locksmiths, Key, Wood, Red Paint, c.1885, 74 ½ In. 2703.00
Sign, Lorillard's Snuff, Won The Only Gold Medal In 1895 Exposition, 20 x 26 In. 625.00
Sign, Lucky Lager, Stout Sign Co., Embossed, Tin, Enamel, 1940s 280.00
Sign, Lucky Strike, 2 Bathing Beauties, Die Cut, c.1930, 51 ½ x 30 ¾ In. 303.00
Sign, Lyons Cocoa, Always The Best, Both Food & Drink, Red, Black, Porcelain 200.00
Sign, Lytle's Mayflower Moving Van, Masonite, Red & Black, 37 x 49 In. 1175.00
Sign, Mail Pouch Tobacco, Mail Carriage, 4 Horses, 6 Sheets, 7 x 6 Ft. 19800.00
Sign, Majestic Electric Radio, New & Mightier, Model 72, Paper, Frame, 10 x 20 In. 89.00
Sign, Man Chasing Pig, Knife Shape, Die cut, Painted, Wood, 1900s, 31 x 40 In. 880.00
Sign, Marconi & Pan-American Cigars, Leading 10 Cent Cigars, Tin, 9 ¾ x 6 ¾ In. 77.00
Sign, Maryland Casualty Com. Insurance, Aluminum, c.1950, 14 x 26 In. 86.00
Sign, Mason's Peaks Coconut & Chocolate Candy, 1920s, 12 x 22 In. 44.00
Sign, Master Big Loaf, Really Big, Really Good, Blue, White, Red 130.00

Sign, Maxwell House Coffee, Mr. Maxwell Drinking Coffee, Cardboard, 50 x 15 In.	700.00
Sign, Mayo's Plug Tobacco, Rooster, Lithograph On Linen, 18 x 30 In.	336.00
Sign, McClure's Office Supplies, Glass, Tin Foil, Frame, Rawson & Evans, 48 x 18 In.	198.00
Sign, Merrell's Female Tonic, Cure For All Diseases, Tin, 9 ½ x 13 ½ In.	42.00
Sign, Milk, Sandwich's, Galvanized Metal, Black & White, Frame, c.1920, 18 x 28 In.	705.00
Sign, Milk Bottle, Still The Milkman, White, Blackwood c.1950	1000.00
Sign, Miller High Life Beer, 14 ½ x 20 In.	185.00
Sign, Minnehaha Beverages, Paper Festoon, Uncut, 50 x 34 In.	950.00
Sign, Monitor Radiator, Living Room, Glowing Heater, Embossed, Tin, 19 x 13 In.	805.00
Sign, Monkey Brand Cleans & Polishes, Monkey, Porcelain, c.1915, 9 x 18 In.	1750.00
Sign, Mortar & Pestle, Zinc, Wood Base, Baluster Shape, Gilt, Hanger, 34 x 23 In.	1045.00
Sign, Mother Gray's Powders For Children, Die Cut, Cardboard, Easel, 19 x 27 ¾ In.	688.00
Sign, Mother Hubbard Flour, Perfect Family Flour, Tin Lithograph, 2-Sided, 12 x 8 In.	99.00
Sign, Moxie, Frank Archer, Cardboard, 2-Sided, c.1920, 16 x 16 In.	115.00
Sign, Moxie, Soda Jerk Holding Bottle, I Want You, Uncle Sam Posing, 27 x 41 In.	1150.00
Sign, Munsingwear, Union Suits, Die Cut, Tin Lithograph, 21 ½ x 21 In.	2640.00
Sign, Munyon's Paw-Paw, Restorative Elixir, 3-D, 1900s, 22 x 33 In.	230.00
Sign, Mutual Orange Distributors Members, Pure Gold, Orange, Black, Round, 12 In.	224.00
Sign, N.Y. State Fair 1911, Anthropomorphic Pumpkin, Cardboard, 11 x 14 In.	194.00
Sign, National Liberty Insurance Co., Reverse On Glass, Frame, c.1940s, 16 x 28 In.	115.00
Sign, Nehi Beverages, Embossed, Tin, 29 ½ x 11 ¼ In.	176.00
Sign, Nehi Quality Beverages, Bottle, Embossed, Tin Lithograph, 20 x 5 ½ In.	110.00
Sign, New Haven Dairy, Ice Cream Cones 5 Cent, Porcelain, 1920s, 21 x 27 In.	775.00
Sign, Odin 5 Cent Cigar, Multicolored, Embossed, Tin Lithograph, 20 x 27 In.	280.00
Sign, Old Coon Sour Mash, Coon Hunters, Tin, Self-Framed, 1900, 23 x 29 In.	1350.00
Sign, Old Dutch Cleaner, Gold, Black Letters, Embossed, Tin, 14 x 7 In.	60.00
Sign, Old Dutch Cleanser, B.S. Co., Chi. & Beaverfalls, Pa., Porcelain, 14 x 20 In.	3024.00
Sign, Old Fort Feeds, Porcelain, 1940s, 40 x 48 In.	575.00
Sign, Old Gold, Carole Lombard, Full Color, 1934, 31 x 42 In.	657.00
Sign, Old Gold, Not A Cough In A Carload, Man, Woman, Cardboard, c.1920	50.00
Sign, Old Monk Mayonnaise, Light-Up, c.1940, 13 ½ In. *illus*	1200.00
Sign, Old Reliable Peg Top, 5 Cents, Yellow, Red, Black, Cardboard	160.00
Sign, Opera House, Figural, Pointing Hand, Black, Red, White	4313.00
Sign, Orange Crush, Kerb Service, Kid In Car, Boy Serving Pop, Cardboard, 8 x 11 In.	130.00
Sign, Orange Crush, Self-Framed, 37 ⅜ x 25 ¾ In.	275.00
Sign, P & G, White Naphtha Soap, Porcelain, Corner, 24 x 20 In.	143.00
Sign, P & H Quality Service, Pawling & Harnisch Feger, 18 In.	30.00
Sign, Pabst, Spanish-American War Generals, 27 x 21 In.	1000.00
Sign, Pall Mall, Sophia Loren, Tin, Frame, 21 ½ x 15 ¾ In.	165.00
Sign, Parrot Crackers, Multicolored, Die Cut, Cardboard, 2-Sided, 12 ¼ x 9 ¼ In.	990.00
Sign, Pears Soap, Woman Washing Boy, Die Cut, Cardboard, 12 ½ x 7 In.	160.00
Sign, Pendelton Shirts, Wood, Cloth, Stand-Up, 24 x 27 x 12 In. *illus*	288.00
Sign, Pens Books, Book Form, Black & Gilt Trim, 19th Century, 18 x 18 In.	4406.00
Sign, Peters Weatherbird Shoes, Uncle Sam, Animals, Frame, c.1900, 21 ½ x 30 In.	144.00
Sign, Pickwick Ale, Draft Horses, Pulling Wagon, Ale That Is Ale, Cardboard, Frame	325.00
Sign, Pippins Cigars, 5 Cents, Trademark Apple, Porcelain, 34 x 24 In.	500.00
Sign, Plee-Zing Food Stores, Porcelain, 3-Piece, 15 x 20 In.	413.00
Sign, Prairie Farmer, Protective Agency Member, Tin, 8 x 12 In.	40.00
Sign, Prang, Easter Cards, Blond Haired Angel, Amid Clouds, c.1885, 22 ½ x 16 In.	288.00
Sign, Prince Albert Tobacco, Chief Many-Horns, Cardboard, Frame, 30 x 23 ½ In.	770.00
Sign, Procter & Gamble's, Soap, R.O.G., Man In Moon, Foil, Mother-Of-Pearl	1668.00
Sign, Pure Maple Syrup, Red, Green, White, Porcelain, 18 x 24 In.	308.00
Sign, Quaker Craft Lace, Porcelain, Wood Frame, Bracket, 28 x 7 In.	110.00
Sign, Quaker Maid Milk, Milk Maid, Red, White, Porcelain, 41 x 24 In.	1250.00
Sign, Quaker Oats, Best Porridge, Multicolored, Porcelain, 18 x 30 In.	1736.00
Sign, R.G. Sullivan's, Cigars, Multicolored, Porcelain, 23 x 10 ½ In.	201.00
Sign, Railway Express Agency, Navy Blue, White, 1930s, 6 In.	575.00
Sign, Ralph McCutcheon Motion Picture Live Stock, Porcelain, c.1945, 12 x 42 In.	750.00
Sign, RC Cola, Lucille Ball, Cardboard Lithograph, 27 ⅞ x 11 In.	248.00
Sign, RCA Victor, Enrico Caruso's Aida, Porcelain, 2-Sided, Hanging, 28 In.	330.00
Sign, RCA Victor, Record, World's Greatest Artists, 47 In. Diam.	523.00
Sign, RCA Victrola, His Master's Voice, Porcelain, 18 x 24 In.	700.00
Sign, Read The Star, Baltimore's Best Evening Paper, Black, White, Tin, 10 x 14 In.	50.00
Sign, Red Goose Shoes, Neon, Porcelain, 1930s, 12 x 24 x 8 In.	4888.00
Sign, Red Indian Cut Plug, Must Have It, Indian, Multicolored, 22 x 28 In.	1792.00
Sign, Red Man Cigar Leaf Tobacco, Fresh, Wax Wrapped, 2 Sizes, Red, Yellow	50.00

Advertising, Sign, Old Monk Mayonnaise, Light-Up, c.1940, 13 ½ In. $1200.00

Advertising, Sign, Pendelton Shirts, Wood, Cloth, Stand-Up, 24 x 27 x 12 In. $288.00

Advertising, Sign, Samoset Chocolates, Indian, Canoe, Chalkware, c.1920, 23 x 22 In. $863.00

Advertising, Sign, Squirt, Boy, Bottle, Porcelain, 1959, 36 x 60 in. $1500.00

TIP
To remove an unwanted gummed price sticker, try heating it with a hair dryer. The glue will melt a bit, and it will be easier to peel off the sticker.

Advertising, Sign, Weco, Dr. West's Tooth Brush, Composition, Stand-Up, 1935, 9 x 6 In.
$1093.00

Advertising, Sign, Yankee Doodle Root Beer, Embossed, Tin, 30 x 11 In.
$230.00

Sign, Remington Kleanshave Razor Blades, Just Try, Red, White, Blue, Paper 50.00
Sign, Remington Knife, Knives That Bite, Radio Electricians, Die Cut, Cardboard, 10 x 7 In. . . 1825.00
Sign, Rex Bitters, Cures Indigestion, Constipation, Nude Woman On Bed, 17 x 14 In. 616.00
Sign, Rexall Drugs, Light-Up, Counter, 37 x 8⅞ In. 248.00
Sign, Rexall Drugs, School Carnival, Folds, 32 x 38¾ In. 55.00
Sign, Rice's Seeds, Gardener, Big Cabbage, Stone Lithograph, c.1890, 22 x 27 In. 1093.00
Sign, Ringling Bros. & Barnum & Bailey, Brunn Juggler Circus, c.1950s, 20 x 26 In. 115.00
Sign, Ringling Brothers Circus, Cardboard, 1944, 22 x 17½ In. 575.00
Sign, Rooster, Die Cut, Sheet Iron, France, Late 19th Century, 64 x 58 In. 2420.00
Sign, Round House, Ladies' & Girls' Ranch Pants, Cardboard, Easel, 22 x 14 In. 50.00
Sign, Roxbury & Highland Co-Operative Banks., Black, Gilt Letters, Wood, 24 x 17 In. 330.00
Sign, Royal Crown Cola, Bottle, Die Cut, Metal, c.1936, 16 x 59 In. 230.00
Sign, Royal Exchange Assurance, Blue, White, Porcelain, Enamel, 13 x 20 In. 120.00
Sign, R-Pep, Bottle, Make It Yours, Prune Juice, Berries, Red 170.00
Sign, Ruff's Beer, Chrysanthemum Girl, Tin, Self-Framed, 1910, 14 x 11 In. 350.00
Sign, S & H Green Stamps Today, Double Stamps, All Day, Tin, 29 x 36 In. 50.00
Sign, Safe Deposit Vaults, Bronze, 6 x 36 In. 82.00
Sign, Samoset Chocolates, Indian, Canoe, Chalkware, c.1920, 23 x 22 In. . . . . *illus* 863.00
Sign, San-Cura Ointment, Keep On Hand, Die Cut, Cardboard, 7 x 8 In. 154.00
Sign, Sandwich Room, White & Black Letters, Red, Wood, 2-Sided, Early 1900s, 12 x 37 In. . . 325.00
Sign, Savage Stevens, Fox, Shotguns, Rifles, Bear 50.00
Sign, Savage Stevens, Nature's Rogues Gallery, Paper, Metal Bands, 18 x 26 In. 120.00
Sign, Sawyers Crystal Blue, Woman, Washboard, Girl, Cardboard, Fold-Out 1100.00
Sign, Schlitz Beer, Nude Woman With Wings, Frame, 28 x 20 In. 485.00
Sign, Schmidt's Brewing, Hunter Enjoying Beer, Tin, Self-Framed, 1910, 23 x 33 In. 1150.00
Sign, Scissors, Die Cut, Sheet Metal, 33 In. 143.00
Sign, Sealtest Ice Cream, Tin, Metal, 2-Sided, Spinning Flange, c.1945 . . . . . 345.00
Sign, Sealy Cotton Mattresses, Blacks, Die Cut, Cardboard, 4-Piece, 60 x 41 In. 2200.00
Sign, Sen-Sen Mints, Fashionably Dressed Woman, Singing, Mums, 12 x 48 In. 518.00
Sign, Sex-Ine Pills, Restore Lost Manhood, Man, Before, During, After 440.00
Sign, Shamrock Smoking Tobacco, Fashion Woman, Linen, Late 1800s, 15 x 20 In. 952.00
Sign, Sherwin-Williams, Cover The Earth Logo, Porcelain, 35 x 63 In. 210.00
Sign, Shoe, Sheet Metal, Glass, 2-Sided, Man In Boot, Light-Up, c.1925, 43 x 8 In. 2233.00
Sign, Silver Spring Brewery Ltd., The Life Saver, Fireman Holding Beer, 18½ In. 135.00
Sign, Sir Walter Raleigh Tobacco, World War II Pilot, Pipe, Cardboard, 12 x 18 In. 153.00
Sign, Skour-Pak Steel Wool, 1920s, 12 x 22 In. 55.00
Sign, Smith Brothers Cough Drops, Brother, Cough Drops, Embossed, Tin, 9½ In. 315.00
Sign, Smithdeal Realty & Insurance Co., Sold, Yellow, Red, Embossed, Tin 40.00
Sign, Snoboy, Picked For Flavor, Fruits, Vegetables, Multicolored, Porcelain 1400.00
Sign, Soda, Phosphate, Soda Water, Coffee, Aluminum, Chain, c.1899, 9 x 10 In. 305.00
Sign, Soft Pretzels, Red, Yellow, Brown, White, Metal 150.00
Sign, Southern Railroad Tickets, Glass Panel, Frame, 36 x 6 In. 77.00
Sign, Spokane Daily Chronicle Sold Here, Red, Black, Tin Over Cardboard, 6 x 13 In. 50.00
Sign, Spratt's Budgerigar & Canary Mixture, Black, White, Porcelain, 12 x 12 In. 157.00
Sign, Spreckels Ice Cream, French Custard, Embossed, Tin, 28 x 20 In. 67.00
Sign, Squirt, Boy, Bottle, Porcelain, 1959, 36 x 60 In. . . . . *illus* 1500.00
Sign, St. Bruno Flake Tobacco, Die Cut, Cardboard, Hanging, 8 x 20 In. 70.00
Sign, Star Soap, Girl, Striped Dress, Paper, Metal Strips, 23 x 15 In. 1320.00
Sign, Star Tobacco, Best For 70 Years, Yellow, Red, Black, Embossed 110.00
Sign, Stone Homestead Tea, Dinners, Sandwiches, Wood, 2-Sided, 22½ x 43 In. 60.00
Sign, Street, Poll-Parrot Shoes For Boys & Girls, 2-Sided, Free Standing, 45 x 20 In. 825.00
Sign, Stroh Brewery, Factory, Glass, Frame, 21½ x 13½ In. 187.00
Sign, Subrikups Plumbing, We Sell 'Em, Celluloid, Tin, Cardboard, 9 x 13 In. 440.00
Sign, Sunbeam Bread, Bread Loaf, Silver Tray, Embossed, Metal, Self-Framed 303.00
Sign, Sunbeam Bread, Girl Holding Bread, Cardboard, Stand-Up, c.1950, 28 x 50 In. 230.00
Sign, Sunlight Soap, Monkey Brand Washing Powder, Lithograph, 14 x 19 In. 230.00
Sign, Sunny Brook Whiskey, Tin, c.1890, 19 x 39 In. 920.00
Sign, Super Peters Shot Shells, Frame, 33 x 43 In. 3190.00
Sign, Sweet Home Soap, Little Girl, Roses, Lithograph, Frame, c.1895 . . . . . 345.00
Sign, Sweet-Orr Overalls, Black, White, Curved Corner, Lithograph, 18 x 14 In. 1610.00
Sign, Swift's Bacon, Die Cut, Cardboard, 21½ x 15½ In. 248.00
Sign, Taka-Kola, Every Hour, Woman, Bottle, Clock, Tin Over Cardboard 580.00
Sign, Tavern, Sheet Metal Cutouts, Rearing Horses, Rossli, 47 x 37 In. 863.00
Sign, Taxidermist, Geo. E. Brown, Preserved To Order, Painted, Wood, 21 x 18 In. 2938.00
Sign, Temperance Hotel, C.C.P. Eldredge, Half-Circle, Wood, 2-Sided, c.1830 . . . . . 3300.00

Sign, Texlite Inc., Makers Of Porcelain, Enamel Signs, Factory, 1930s, 12 In. 160.00
Sign, Thixton Millett & Co., Log Cabin Whiskey Distillery, Tin, c.1904, 22 x 14 In. 1265.00
Sign, Tippecanoe, Best For Bilious Headache, Lithograph, c.1890, 8 x 20 In. 460.00
Sign, Tom Sawyer Root Beer, Bottle Cap, Cutout, Wood, c.1950, 31 x 30 In. 259.00
Sign, True Fruit & Golden Orangeade, Soda Fountain, Cardboard, 13 x 27 In. 805.00
Sign, Uncle Sam Ale, Paper, Frame, 1890s, 35 x 23 In. 316.00
Sign, Uneeda Biscuit, National Biscuit Co., Cardboard Lithograph, 12 x 22 In. 1155.00
Sign, Union Leader Smoking Tobacco, Eagle, Red, Black, Gold, Tin Lithograph 70.00
Sign, US Ammunition, Hits Where You Aim, Cardboard, 12 x 16 In. 100.00
Sign, US Cartridge Co., Self-Cleaning Cartridges, Rabbits, Cardboard, Easel, 19 x 13 In. 80.00
Sign, Van Camp's Soups, Dutch Boy & Girl, Die Cut, Tin Lithograph, 32 x 20¾ In. 5830.00
Sign, Van Houten's Cocoa, Woman With Basket, Cardboard, Frame, 33 x 24½ In. 55.00
Sign, Velvet Tobacco, Pipe, Porcelain, 9 x 5 In. 1100.00
Sign, Victor Burglar Alarms System, Chicago, Porcelain, 4½ x 4¼ In. 180.00
Sign, Virginia Leaf Tobacco, Fine Cut, Woman, Cardboard, Frame, 14¾ x 11¾ In. 330.00
Sign, W. Arthur Boutwell, Memory Of Quality Remains, Wood, 1800s, 18 x 105 In. 475.00
Sign, W.L. McCulloh, New Idea, Farm Equipment, Dealership, c.1955, 33 x 72 In. 150.00
Sign, Walter A. Wood Harvesting Machinery, Paper, Canvas, Frame, 27 x 34 In. 1150.00
Sign, Warner's Lithia Tablets, Accurate, Convenient, Tin Lithograph, 5 x 7½ In. 580.00
Sign, Warning Hargrave Secret Service, Crime Does Not Pay, Porcelain, 5½ x 8 In. 130.00
Sign, Washington National Insurance Co., Washington Silhouette, 2-Sided, 14 x 60 In. 110.00
Sign, Watch Repair, Pocket Watch Shape, Cast & Sheet Iron, 26 x 3½ In. 605.00
Sign, Water Spar Lacquer, Dries In No Time, Pittsburgh Plate Glass Co., 26 x 38 In. 550.00
Sign, We Are Agents For Portland Cement, Cobalt Blue, White, Porcelain, 12 x 21 In. 275.00
Sign, Weco, Dr. West's Tooth Brush, Composition, Stand-Up, 1935, 9 x 6 In. .... *illus* 1093.00
Sign, Wedding Bell Chocolates, St. Nick, Girls Sleeping, Cardboard, 15 x 14¾ In. 440.00
Sign, Wellsboro Cigar Co., Kids, Toys, Child On Pot, Paperboard, 1904 .... 450.00
Sign, Western Ammo, Perfect From Primer To Crimp, Cardboard, 13 x 8 In. 550.00
Sign, Western Union, Porcelain, 2-Sided, Hanging, 15 x 30 In. 88.00
Sign, Western Union, Porcelain, 2-Sided, Hanging, 17 x 30 In. 154.00
Sign, Western Union Telegraph & Cable Office, Porcelain, 2-Sided, 25½ x 12 In. 352.00
Sign, Western Winchester, Frame, 31 x 43 In. 138.00
Sign, Western Winchester, Pheasant In Flight, 1955, 41 x 28 In. 40.00
Sign, Westinghouse Bulb, 18 x 13½ In. 121.00
Sign, White King Washing Machine Soap, Crown Co., Tin Lithograph, 10 x 14 In. 235.00
Sign, White Owl Cigars, Red, Mustard, Black, Silkscreened, 38 x 28 In. 495.00
Sign, Winchester, They Are Hitters, Frame, 23 x 28½ In. 138.00
Sign, Winchester, Wittle Wabbit Chased By Big Mean Hunter, 1955, 26 x 40 In. 67.00
Sign, Wink Soda, Winking Moon, Orange, Black, Embossed, Tin Lithograph 303.00
Sign, Wood, Gilt Numerals, Black & Red, Applied Molding, 1894, 16 x 49 In. 2350.00
Sign, Worcester Salt, 1929, 12 x 22 In. 50.00
Sign, Wright's Little Liver Pills, Sick Headache, Man, Woman, Boat, 25 Cents 470.00
Sign, Wrigley's Gum, 2 Packs Of Gum, Yellow, Porcelain, 36 x 14 In. 840.00
Sign, Wurlitzer, Bubbler Light, Wood, Glass, 19½ x 6½ In. 275.00
Sign, Yankee Doodle Root Beer, Embossed, Tin, 30 x 11 In. .... *illus* 230.00
Sign, Yardley's Old English Lavender, Paper, Cardboard, Lithograph, 28 x 22 In. 805.00
Sign, Zebra Grate Polish, Girl Riding On Zebra Toy, Paper, 15 x 11 In. 495.00
Sign, Green Mountain Balm Of Gilead, Paper, 1868, 17 x 21 In. 115.00
Sign, Home Of Crescent Bicycle, Western Wheel Works, Chicago, Ill., 1896 .... 1650.00
Soap, Yellow Kid, Molded Figure, Partial Box, 3⅞ In. 110.00
Soap, Yellow Kid, Oh But I'm Full Of Lather, David S. Brown Co., Box, c.1905. .... 520.00
Spoon, Sunny Jim, Force Cereal, Wm. Rogers & Son, 1902, 6 In. 18.00
Stained Glass, Winner Rye Whiskey, Pebbled, Red Letters, Milk Glass, 13 x 13 In. 650.00
Stickpin, D & M Sporting Goods, Pointer, Figural, Gold Wash, ⅝ x ¾ In. 308.00
Stickpin, Dominion Cartridge Company, Figural, Gold Wash, Enamel, ½ x 2¼ In. 392.00
Stickpin, Du Pont, Dog, Du Pont On Collar, Figural, ¾ In. 180.00
Stickpin, Duck, Dead Shot, Figural, Gold Flash, 3 x ¾ In. 350.00
Stickpin, Shoot Peters Shells, Brass, Enamel, Stamped, 1¾ x ¾ x ½ In. 50.00
Stickpin, Weatherbird, Iridescent Enamel, 2½ In. 25.00
Stickpin, Winchester Shells, No. 12 Repeater, Brass, Enamel, 1 x 2 In. 392.00
Stove Pipe Flapper, Cherryville, Pa., Cast Iron, Marked, Dieter Foundry, 6 In. 12.00
Strawholder, Hires Root Beer, Blue & Gold Sign, Metal, Tin, c.1910, 9 x 4 In. 3163.00
Strawholder, Hires Root Beer, Metal, c.1910, 9½ In. .... *illus* 2070.00
Strawholder, Welch's, Grape Juice, Grapes, Bottle, Tin Lithograph, 10 x 4 x 5 In. 1650.00
Stringholder, Post Toasties, Improved Corn Flakes, 11½ In. 550.00
Stringholder, Shenandoah Valley Candy Co., Apple Shape, Tin Lithograph, 4 x 4 In. 70.00

Advertising, Strawholder, Hires Root Beer, Metal, c.1910, 9½ In. $2070.00

Advertising, Tin, Biscuit, Huntley & Palmers, Artist Palette, Brushes On Lid, 1900 $345.00

Advertising, Tin, Biscuit, Huntley & Palmers, Grandfather Clock, 1929 $518.00

TIP

When ordering antiques by mail, do not send cash; send a check or charge them. Keep a copy of your order.

Advertising, Tin, Biscuit, William Crawford Bi-Plane, 1926 $3163.00

Advertising, Tin, Dunnsboro Tobacco, Pipe Smoking, Vertical Pocket, 4 x 3 In. $350.00

Advertising, Tin, Epicure Coffee, Marked, S.A. Ilsey, Brooklyn, N.Y., 3 x 11 In. $150.00

TIP

Never wash a tobacco "felt." The small flannel flags and pictures that were packed with cigarettes in the early 1900s lose value if washed.

Syrup Holder, Log Cabin's Wigwam, For Table Use In Restaurants, Glass, 2 ¼ In. 9.00
Tankard, Berry's Root Beer, Silver Plated, 9 In. 173.00
Tankard, Miner's Root Beer, Silver Plated, c.1870, 9 ½ In. 345.00
Tap Handle, Great Divide Brewing Co., Ceramic, Denver, 9 ¼ In. 15.00
Thermometers are listed in their own category.
Thermos, Monarch Coffee 44.00

Advertising tin cans or canisters were first used commercially in the United States in 1819 and were called tins. Today the word *tin* is used by most collectors to describe many types of containers, including food tins, biscuit boxes, roly poly tobacco containers, gunpowder cans, talcum powder sprinkle-top cans, cigarette flat-fifty tins, and more. Beer Cans are listed in their own category. Things made of undecorated tin are listed under Tinware.

Tin, 3 Pirates Condoms, Latex, Ship, Palm Trees, Tin Lithograph, 1 ½ x 9/16 In. 3520.00
Tin, A Delicious Blend Of Choice Coffees, Multicolored, Lb., 6 ½ x 4 ¼ In. 88.00
Tin, Alright Tobacco, Von Eicken, Vertical Pocket, 4 x 2 In. 288.00
Tin, Apache Trail Cigar, Indian On Horse, Coast To Coast, 50 Count, 6 x 6 x 4 In. 1870.00
Tin, Bambino Tobacco, Bailey Bros., Winston-Salem, Vertical Pocket, 4 x 3 In. 1840.00
Tin, Banquet Hall Little Cigars, Man Smoking, 1897 Tax Stamp, 3 x 3 In. 50.00
Tin, Bennett, Sloan & Co., Tea, Elk, c.1880, Lb. 140.00
Tin, Big Ben Tobacco, Imperial Tobacco Co., Canada, Vertical Pocket, 4 x 3 In. 435.00
Tin, Biscuit, Book Stack Shape, Embossed, Huntley & Palmer, 1900s, 6 ¼ x 6 ¼ In. 420.00
Tin, Biscuit, Gray Dunn, Horse Drawn Delivery Van, c.1905 .... 2875.00
Tin, Biscuit, Huntley & Palmers, Artist Palette, Brushes On Lid, Biscuit, 1900 .... *illus* 345.00
Tin, Biscuit, Huntley & Palmers, Grandfather Clock, Biscuit, 1929 .... *illus* 518.00
Tin, Biscuit, William Crawford Bi-Plane, 1926 .... *illus* 3163.00
Tin, Biscuit Carlisle, Hinged Lid, Paper Label, 20 ¼ x 14 x 19 In. 86.00
Tin, Blanke's Coffee, Promoters Of Good Goods, Lb., 6 ¾ x 4 ⅜ In. 110.00
Tin, Blenown Tobacco, Extra High Grade, Daniel Frank Co., Vertical Pocket, 4 x 3 In. 470.00
Tin, Bouquet Roasted Coffee, Red, White, Lb., 6 x 4 In. 120.00
Tin, Brink-Dolan Tobacco, Black & Red, Vertical Pocket, 4 x 3 In. 5750.00
Tin, Buckingham Smoking Tobacco, John J. Bagley & Co., Vertical Pocket, 4 x 3 In. 70.00
Tin, Bulldog Tobacco, Lovell & Buffington Tobacco Co., Vertical Pocket, 4 x 2 In. 201.00
Tin, Bulldog Tobacco, Lovell-Buffington Tobacco Co., Vertical Pocket, 4 x 2 In. 345.00
Tin, Burley Boy Tobacco, Pipe Or Cigarette, Child Boxer, Lunch Box Style, Red, White 2860.00
Tin, Cafe Bustelo Coffee, Yellow, Blue, Red, 3 ¾ x 5 In. 110.00
Tin, Calabash Tobacco, Concave, American Tobacco Co., Vertical Pocket, 3 x 2 In. 518.00
Tin, Cannon's Tobacco, Irish Sliced Plug Flake, Smoking Blend, Aromatic, 4 x 2 In. 121.00
Tin, Capital Peanut Butter, Empire State Nut Co., 10 Lb., 9 ¾ x 8 ⅝ In. 165.00
Tin, Capitol Brand, Peanut Butter, Playing Children, 14 Oz., 3 ¼ x 3 ½ In. 495.00
Tin, Capitol Mills Pure Coffee, Building, Yellow, Black, Lincoln, Seyms & Co. 1320.00
Tin, Checkers Tobacco, Weisert Brothers Tobacco Co., Vertical Pocket, 4 x 3 In. .... 460.00 to 495.00
Tin, Chicago Cubs Chewing Tobacco, Rock City Tobacco Co., Round, 3 x 6 In. 80.00
Tin, Cigar, Nebraska Blossom, Western Cowgirl, Round, 5 ¼ x 5 ½ In. 775.00
Tin, Clarke's Charleton Tobacco, Oval, Vertical Pocket, 3 x 3 In. 460.00
Tin, Cleopatra Rose Talc, White & Black Ground, 2 x 6 In. 45.00
Tin, Colgate's Baby Talc, Baby Holding Talcum Powder, Light Blue, 6 x 2 In. 80.00
Tin, Columbia Biscuit Company, Lady Columbia, Hinged Lid, Orange, 10 x 7 In. 300.00
Tin, Continental Cubes Tobacco, American Tobacco Co., Vertical Pocket, 3 x 2 In. 345.00
Tin, Continental Cubes Tobacco, Multicolored, Lithograph, Cube, 5 In. 420.00
Tin, Convention Hall Coffee, Kansas City Convention Hall, Green, Lb., 6 x 4 In. 880.00
Tin, Darby's Swan Tolu Gum, Cherubs, Swan, Children, Boat, Hinged Lid 264.00
Tin, De Roode Pelikaan Coffee, Scarlet, Canister, Gold Tole, Belgium, 1900s 720.00
Tin, Del-Monte, Coffee, Key Inside, Lb. 22.00
Tin, Dial Smoking Tobacco, Turn To A Real Smoke, Red, Yellow, 4 x 3 In. 50.00
Tin, Dill's Look Out Tobacco, Vertical Pocket, 4 x 2 In. 2645.00
Tin, Dixie Kid Cut Plug, Lunch Box Form, Handle, Hinged Lid, 4 x 7 ⅞ x 5 In. .... 495.00 to 715.00
Tin, Dixie Kid Cut Plug, Lunch Box Form, Nalls & Williams Tob. Co., 3 ¾ x 8 x 5 In. 495.00
Tin, Donald Duck Coffee, Donald, Goyer Coffee Co., Greenville, Miss., Key Wind 259.00
Tin, Dr. Hed Medicated Powder, Red, Orange & Black, 25 Cents, Oval, Contents 85.00
Tin, Dr. J.N. Norwood's Guaranteed Gall Cure, 25 Cents, Image, Round, 3 In. 468.00
Tin, Drummer Coffee, Cup Of Coffee, Lux Merc. Co., 4 x 5 ⅛ In. 232.00
Tin, Dunnsboro Tobacco, Pipe Smoking, Vertical Pocket, 4 x 3 In. .... *illus* 350.00
Tin, Dunnsboro Vertical Pocket Tobacco, 4 ½ x 3 x 1 In. 431.00
Tin, Echo Special Coffee, Brown, Gold Cover, E.C. Harley Co., Dayton, Ohio. 201.00
Tin, Egyptian Talc, Black & Orange, Palmolive Company, 2 x 6 x 1 In. 45.00
Tin, Elephant Java Coffee, African Elephant, Steam Locomotive, 3 Lb. 405.00

Tin, Empress Brand Paprika Spice, Empress Mfg. Co., 1 ½ Oz., 2 ½ x 3 x ¾ In. 40.00
Tin, Empress Paprika, Ship, Red, Yellow, Gold, 1 ½ Oz. 40.00
Tin, Ensign Perfection Cut Tobacco, 3 Flags, Red, Blue, Yellow, Vertical Pocket 990.00
Tin, Epicure Coffee, Marked, S.A. Ilsey, Brooklyn, N.Y., 3 x 11 In. .... *illus* 150.00
Tin, Farmers Pride Brand Coffee, Man, Girl, Paper Label, Lb., 6 x 4 ⅛ In. 357.00
Tin, Fleco Condoms, Luxurious, Transparent, Blue, White, 1 ⅞ x 2 ⅝ x 5/16 In. 745.00
Tin, Forest & Stream Tobacco, Vertical Pocket, 4 x 2 In. 413.00
Tin, Four Roses Smoking Tobacco, Knoll & Williams, Vertical Pocket, 4 x 3 In. 580.00
Tin, Franklin Coffee, Black & Yellow Cover, Columbus, Ohio, Key Wind, 4 x 5 In. 230.00
Tin, Frontier Coffee, Nave-McCord Mercantile Co., Pry Lid, 4 x 5 In. 385.00
Tin, Full Dress Tobacco, Sears Roebuck & Co., Dallas, Vertical Pocket, 4 x 2 In. 690.00
Tin, George Horner Good Sweets, England, 1940s, 6 ½ In. 20.00
Tin, Giant Salted Peanuts, Circus Scene, Bail Handle, 10 Oz., 3 ⅜ x 3 ⅞ In. 620.00
Tin, Golden Rule Tea, Citizens' Wholesale Supply Co., Columbus, Ohio, 5 Lb., 10 ½ In. 50.00
Tin, Golden West Coffee, Cowgirl Drinking Coffee, Red Ground, 1937, 3 Lb. 300.00
Tin, Golden West Coffee, Key Wind, Red Ground, Cowgirl, 1927, Lb. 200.00
Tin, Grand Duchess Tooth Powder, Photo, Bees, 4 x 1 ¾ In. 550.00
Tin, Hall's Cannonite Safety Smokeless Sporting Powder, Lb., 4 ½ x 6 ½ In. 364.00
Tin, Helene Varre No. 60 Face Powder, Woman, Mirror, 1 ¾ x 2 In. 50.00
Tin, Henalfa Hair Restorer, Woman, Seated, Blue, White, B. Clements 50.00
Tin, Hiawatha Tobacco, Hiawatha, Gold Ground, 5 x 3 x 2 In. 45.00
Tin, Hoffman's Old Time Coffee, Woman Holding Cup, Lb., 4 ¼ x 5 ¼ In. 242.00
Tin, Honest Spices, Black Pepper, Gillies, Dog, Paper Label, Lb. 176.00
Tin, Honey Moon Tobacco, Penn Tobacco Co., Wilkes-Barre, Vertical Pocket, 4 x 3 In. 201.00
Tin, Honey Moon Tobacco, Rum Flavored, 10 Cent Version, Vertical Pocket, 4 x 3 In. 320.00
Tin, Hoosier Poet Coffee, White & Red, M. O'Connor & Co., Key Wind, 3 x 5 In. 173.00
Tin, Humpty Dumpty Sitting On Wall, Talcum Powder, McNess Co., 1930s 75.00
Tin, Java & Mocha Coffee, Screenings Compounded, Multicolored, 6 ½ x 3 ¾ x 3 In. 88.00
Tin, Jaynes Opium Pills, Man Passed Out, Wolf, 1 ½ x 2 ½ In. 1980.00
Tin, Jewetts Indian Girl Allspice, Paper Label, 2 Oz., 3 ½ x 2 ½ x 1 In. 40.00
Tin, Kidd Land Candy, Nursery Rhyme Characters, Lid, Handle, 3 x 3 ¼ x 4 ½ In. 550.00
Tin, King George Tobacco, Frishmuth Brothers & Co., Vertical Pocket, 4 x 3 In. 460.00
Tin, Kroger's Grapefruit Juice, Paper Label, Patent Date, 1938, 14 Oz. 15.00
Tin, Lambert's Death To Lice Powder, 50 Cents, Sealed, Round, 7 x 5 In. 95.00
Tin, Lenox Tobacco, L. Warick Brown & Co., Vertical Pocket, 4 x 3 In. 3165.00
Tin, Little Elf Coffee, Elf Carrying Tray, Bursley & Co., Fort Wayne, Lb. 670.00
Tin, Log Cabin Syrup, Frontier Inn, Log Cabin, People, Horses, 6 ½ x 6 ½ x 4 In. 121.00
Tin, Lord Kenyon Tobacco, Toledo, Ohio, Vertical Pocket, 3 x 3 In. .... *illus* 345.00
Tin, Lucky Curved Tobacco, Baseball Logo, 7 x 4 x 4 In. 230.00
Tin, Lutted's S.P. Cough Drop, Hinged Lid, 5 Lb., 6 x 4 x 8 In. 688.00
Tin, Malted Slippery Elm Food, Breakfast Or Dinner For Infants, Lb., 5 x 3 ½ In. 50.00
Tin, Mammy's Favorite Brand Coffee, C.D. Kenny Co., Buffalo, N.Y., 6 x 10 ½ In. 460.00
Tin, Max-I-Mum Peanut Butter, General Foods, Pry Lid, 5 Lb., 5 ½ x 6 ⅛ In. 358.00
Tin, Mayo's Cut Plug Tobacco, Roly Poly, Satisfied Customer, 6 ¾ In. 550.00
Tin, Miro-Dena Talcum Powder, Girl, Flowers In Hair, 4 ½ x 2 ½ x 1 ⅜ In. 176.00
Tin, Monopol Smoking Tobacco, London Club, 2 ½ x 4 ½ x 3 ¼ In. 88.00
Tin, Moshier Bros. Spices, Building, Gilt Edge, Hinged Lid, 11 x 7 ⅝ x 7 ⅝ In. 880.00
Tin, Mrs. Brookes Guest Coffee, Woman, Key Wind, Lb., 4 x 5 ⅛ In. 385.00
Tin, Mrs. Dinsmore's Cough Drops, Yellow, Black, Somers Bros., 8 x 5 x 5 In. 330.00
Tin, Nature's Remedy Laxative, Lewis-Howe Co., 1 ½ x ½ In. 18.00
Tin, Nigger Hair Tobacco, African Woman, Rings Through Nose, Ears, Handle, 7 x 5 In. 358.00
Tin, Norris Atlanta Exquisite Candies, Birds, Pennsylvania German, 1940s, 8 x 4 In. 25.00
Tin, Nylotis Baby Powder, Borated, 3 Babies, 4 ½ x 2 In. 50.00
Tin, Ocean Liner, William Crawford, Biscuit, Hinged Tabs, 14 ¾ In. 805.00
Tin, Oceanic Tobacco, Cut Plug, Scotten Dillon Co., Hinged Lid, 6 x 4 In. 121.00
Tin, Orcico Cigars, 2 For 5 Cents, Indian Scene, 50 Count, 5 x 6 x 4 In. 660.00
Tin, Orcico Cigars, Indian On Cover, Heckan Can Co., 5 x 4 In. 316.00
Tin, Oriental Smokeless Gun Powder, Label, Oriental Powder Mills, 5 x 3 x 1 ¾ In. 275.00
Tin, OXO, Beef Stock Cubes, By Appointment To King George VI, 1950s, 6 ¾ x 5 ⅛ In. 40.00
Tin, Pastime Plug Tobacco, Hunting Scene, Steeplechase, 12 ½ x 9 ⅜ In. 143.00
Tin, Paul Jones Tobacco, Blue, Continental Tobacco Co., Vertical Pocket, 4 x 3 In. 1495.00
Tin, Peaches Condoms, Lithograph, 2 x 2 ⅝ In. 688.00
Tin, Peacock Coffee, Key Wind, 4 x 5 In. .... *illus* 175.00
Tin, Peacock Coffee, Overpacker Coffee Co., Louisville, Key Wind, 4 x 5 In. 201.00
Tin, Peek Frean & Bell, Biscuit, Flowers, Arts & Crafts, c.1904. .... 748.00
Tin, Peter Rabbit Talc, Harrison Cady Scene, Lithograph, 3 ¾ x 4 ¼ In. 198.00

Advertising, Tin, Lord Kenyon Tobacco, Toledo, Ohio, Vertical Pocket, 3 x 3 In.
$345.00

Advertising, Tin, Peacock Coffee, Key Wind, 4 x 5 In.
$175.00

Advertising, Tin, Prince Albert Smoking Tobacco, Patent, 1907, 4 ½ x 3 x 1 In.
$225.00

Advertising, Tin, Thompson's Malted Milk, Canister, 8 ½ In.
$100.00

Tobacco Cans
Tobacco can collectors prefer cans made to hold pipe tobacco. Other tins were made to hold chewing plugs, snuff, cigars, or cigarettes. There were large containers to dispense or display tobacco in stores. Tobacco was sold in cloth or paper bags until about 1880, when tobacco tins were made.

Advertising, Tin, Velvet Tobacco, 3 x 4 In.
$250.00

Advertising, Tin, Violet Talcum, Grand Union Tea Co., 4½ x 2½ x 1 In.
$275.00

Tin, Polly Prim Mop, Self-Feeding, Polish, Wood Handle Mop, 7¼ x 4¾ In. 605.00
Tin, Prince Albert Smoking Tobacco, Patent, 1907, 4½ x 3 x 1 In. . . . . *illus* 225.00
Tin, Prince Albert Tobacco, Crimp Cut, Packed For Panama Railroad Co., 4 x 3 x 1 In. 99.00
Tin, Puritan Coffee, Pilgrim, Hewitt Grocery Co., 4 x 5 In. 466.00
Tin, Puritan Tobacco, Light Gray Letters, Philip Morris Tobacco Co., 4 x 3 In. 316.00
Tin, Rainbow Fishing Line, Silkworm Gut Leader, Trout Chasing Lure, 1 x 3½ In. 165.00
Tin, Rawleigh's Talcum Powder, Circus Characters, 1930s, 7 x 3 x 2 In. . . . . 50.00 to 65.00
Tin, Rawleigh's Talcum Powder, Nursery Rhyme Characters, 1922, 14 Oz., 7 x 3 x 2 In. 50.00
Tin, Reel Man After Shave Talc, Fisherman, Screw-On Lid, 3½ Oz., 5 x 3 x 1 In. 70.00
Tin, Rickseckers Tooth Powder, Woman With Hat, Lithograph, 4 x 1¾ In. 975.00
Tin, Roast Mutton, Range Canning Co., Fort McKavett, Tex., Paper Label, 4 x 4 In. 80.00
Tin, Robin Hood Smokeless Gunpowder, Lithograph, Lb., 4 x 6 In. 504.00
Tin, Robinson Crusoe Peanuts, Crusoe & Dog On Island, 10 Lb. 635.00
Tin, Robinson Crusoe Salted Peanuts, Crusoe & Dog, Yellow, Black, Red, 10 Lb. 630.00
Tin, Runkel Brothers Breakfast Cocoa, Green, Red, Blue, Screw-On Lid, 1 x 1 In. 60.00
Tin, Runkel's Pure Cocoa, Blue Ground, Sample, 1 x 1½ x ½ In. 70.00
Tin, Sandy Andy Toys, Wolverine, c.1928, 6½ x 4½ In. 335.00
Tin, Shogun Mixture Tobacco, Heeken Can Co., Red Lid, 1910, 4½ x 3 In. 8800.00
Tin, Sir Walter Raleigh Tobacco, J.G. Flynt Tobacco Co., Vertical Pocket, 4 x 3 In. 2185.00
Tin, Snap Shot Black Sporting Gunpowder, Duck, Screw-On Lid, ½ Lb., 4 x 3½ In. 50.00
Tin, Soul Kiss Talc, Woman & Angel, Embossed, Lithograph, 4⅝ x 2½ In. 385.00
Tin, Squadron Leader Tobacco, Airplane, 3 x 4 x 1 In. 40.00
Tin, Superior Rifle Gunpowder, Red, Black, Paper Label, 3½ x 2½ In. 60.00
Tin, Sweet Bye & Bye Talcum Powder, Tappan Perfumers Co., 5 x 3 x 1½ In. 385.00
Tin, Sweet Girl Peanut Butter, Lithograph, Bail Handle, Lb., 3¾ x 3¼ In. 960.00
Tin, Sweet Violet Tobacco, Globe Tobacco Co., Detroit, Vertical Pocket, 4 x 3 In. 920.00
Tin, Thedford's Black Draught Stock Medicine, Wraparound Label, Round, 6 x 5 In. 72.00
Tin, Thompson's Malted Milk, Canister, 8½ In. . . . . *illus* 100.00
Tin, Torpedo Tobacco, Destroyer, Rock City Tobacco Co., Vertical Pocket, 4 x 3 In. 1725.00
Tin, Totem Tobacco, Indian Smoking Pipe, Red, c.1910, 4 x 3 In. 2100.00
Tin, Towle's Log Cabin Syrup, Figural, 1914, 3½ x 5½ In. 140.00
Tin, Traveler Coffee, Pale Yellow Cover, Robert E. Lee, 6 x 6 In. 1265.00
Tin, Tripolio Toilet Cleanser, Woman Cleaning Sink, 5½ x 2½ In. 209.00
Tin, Trout Line Smoking Tobacco, Man Fishing, Green, Red, Yellow, 3¾ x 3 x 1 In. 1210.00
Tin, Trout Line Tobacco, Man Catching Fish, Oval, 3 x 2½ In. 252.00
Tin, Union Leader Cut Plug, Milk Can Shape, Eagle, Red, 9 x 5 In. 220.00
Tin, Union Leader Redi Cut Tobacco, Uncle Sam, 1917 Tax Stamp, 4½ x 3 x 1 In. 50.00
Tin, Vaseline Camphor Ice, 3½ In. 24.00
Tin, Velvet Tobacco, 3 x 4 In. . . . . *illus* 250.00
Tin, Veteran Brand Coffee, Lb. 193.00
Tin, Violet Talcum, Grand Union Tea Co., 4½ x 2½ x 1 In. . . . . *illus* 275.00
Tin, Vision Baking Powder, 25 Ounces For 25 Cents, Cherub, Paper Label, 7 x 3 In. 130.00
Tin, W G Y Brand Coffee, Coffeepot Image, Screw Top, 4 x 6 In. 100.00
Tin, Watkins Baking Powder, Woman Holding Tray Of Biscuits, Lb., 5 x 3 In. 60.00
Tin, Winchester After Shave Talc, Hunter, Dog, Screw-On Lid, 3½ Oz., 5 x 3 x 1 In. 160.00
Tin, Winchester After Shave Talc, Hunter & His Dog, 4¾ x 3 In. 308.00
Tin, Zingo Candy, Speeding Race Car, Euclid Candy Co., Cleveland, 20 Lb., 10 x 12 In. 550.00
Tin, Zingo Candy, Speeding Race Car, Euclid Candy Co., Cleveland, 8 x 10 In. 385.00

Advertising tip trays are decorated metal trays less than 5 inches in diameter. They were placed on the table or counter to hold either the bill or the coins that were left as a tip. Change receivers could be made of glass, plastic, or metal. They were kept on the counter near the cash register and held the money passed back and forth by the cashier. Related items may be listed in the Advertising category under Change Receiver.

Tip Tray, Bartholomay Beers, Ales & Porter, Woman On Wings, Lithograph, 4½ In. 160.00
Tip Tray, Brooks Realty Co., Woman, Livingston, Mont., 4 In. 65.00
Tip Tray, Cheon Tea, Geisha Girl Serving Tea, 4 In. 125.00
Tip Tray, DeLaval Cream Separators, World's Standard, Kitchen, 1906, 4¼ In. 160.00
Tip Tray, Home Sewing Machine, Grandma Sewing Pants On Boy, 4 In. 135.00
Tip Tray, Hull's Cream Ale, Export Beer, Woman Holding Glass, 4 In. 65.00
Tip Tray, King's Pure Malt, Panama Pacific International Exposition Winner, 4 x 6 In. 50.00
Tip Tray, Luden's Cough Drops, Give Instant Relief, Tin Lithograph, 3⅝ In. 385.00
Tip Tray, Miller High Life Brewery, 6 x 4 In. 20.00
Tip Tray, Moxie, Delicious Feeds The Nerves, Girl Drinking Beverage, 6 In. 1232.00
Tip Tray, Moxie, I Just Love Moxie, Don't You?, Woman Holding Glass, Ivy Border, 6 In. 820.00

Tip Tray, Mr. Thomas Cigars, Black Cat, None Better, Tin Lithograph, 4 In. 500.00
Tip Tray, Old Reliable Coffee, Woman Holding Cup, 1911, 4 1/4 In. 50.00
Tip Tray, Olympia Brewing Co., Cavalier Holding Bottle, 4 In. 135.00
Tip Tray, Prudential Has The Strength Of Gibraltar, 3 1/2 In. 20.00
Tip Tray, Ranier Pale Beer, Compliments Of The Season, 9 1/4 In. 150.00
Tip Tray, Resinol Soap & Ointment, For All Skin Diseases, Woman, 4 1/4 In. 80.00
Tip Tray, Seal Of Minneapolis Cigars, 10 Cents, Tin Lithograph, 4 1/8 In. 688.00
Tip Tray, Skat Players Dream, Hand Holding Playing Cards, Leisy Brewing Co., 4 In. 675.00
Tip Tray, Smith Otto Drug Co., Only The Best, Woman, Looking To Side, 4 1/2 In. Diam. 50.00
Tip Tray, Telling's Ice Cream, Lithograph On Metal, 1900, 4 In. . . . . *illus* 990.00
Tip Tray, Valley Forge & Rams Head Ale, City Scene, 4 In. 28.00
Tip Tray, White Rock Table Waters, Tin Lithograph, Multicolored, 4 3/8 In. 743.00
Tip Tray, Woman, Pioneer Mercantile Co., Memphis, Tex., 4 In. 55.00
Tobacco Cutter, Drummond Tobacco Co. 121.00
Tobacco Cutter, Harle Hass Co., Council Bluffs, Ia., Iron, Pat. Dec 1, 1914. . . . . 121.00
Tobacco Cutter, Master Mason, Embossed, Painted, Cast Iron, 6 3/4 x 19 x 4 1/2 In. 77.00
Tobacco Cutter, Spear Head, Red Paint, Cast Iron, Patina, 16 1/2 x 4 1/4 x 4 5/8 In. 77.00
Tobacco Pack, Brownie, Seated On Fence, Sealed, Contents, Soft Pack, 4 Oz. 143.00
Tobacco Pack, Long Tom Smoking, Cloth, Paper Label, 1 1/4 Oz., 4 3/4 x 1 1/2 In. 529.00
Tool Carrier, National Manufacturing Builder Hardware, Illinois, 14 x 6 In. 25.00
Toy, Car, Promoting 1939 Rio-Tam Cigar Chevrolet, Steel, 5 In. 460.00
Trash Can, Drive A Buick, Pressed Steel, Blue, White, Lithograph Letters, 1930s 165.00
Tray, Bartlett Spring Mineral Water, San Francisco, Tin, 13 In. 425.00
Tray, Blatz, Milwaukee's Finest Bottled Beer, 13 In. 38.00
Tray, Buffalo Brewing Co., Bohemian Woman, Black Hair, 13 In. 3250.00
Tray, Bulldog Beer, Tin, James Hanley Co., Providence, R.I., 12 In. 150.00
Tray, Coors, Adolph Coors Brewing Co., Golden, Co., 13 In. 10.00
Tray, Dr Pepper, Woman Holding Bottles, You'll Like It Too, 1930s, 13 1/4 x 10 1/2 In. 459.00
Tray, Dr Pepper, You'll Like It Too, 10 1/2 x 13 1/4 In. 459.00
Tray, Eagle Brewing Co., Horses In Stall, Dogs, c.1908, 13 1/4 x 13 1/4 In. 345.00
Tray, Evans & Giehl Brewing Co., Filly & Colt, 13 1/4 x 13 1/4 In. 840.00
Tray, Fehr's Malt-Tonic, Woman, Cherubs, Louisville, Ky., 28 x 22 In. 385.00
Tray, Green River Whiskey, Black Man, Mule, Tin Lithograph, 12 In. 90.00
Tray, Green River Whiskey, Man, Horse, Tin Lithograph, 20th Century, 24 In. . . . . *illus* 147.00
Tray, Hekelnkaemper Bros., Soda Water, Ginger Ale, Asti Lady, Annabelle, 13 In. 134.00
Tray, Hires Root Beer, Josh Slinger Holding A Glass, Tin, c.1915, 13 In. 259.00
Tray, Hires Root Beer, Ugly Kid, Black Ground, Red Trim, Tin Lithograph, c.1905, 13 In. 460.00
Tray, Hyan Dry Ginger Ale, Tin Lithograph, 1930-40 . . . . . *illus* 258.00
Tray, Iroquois Indian Head Beer & Ale, Buffalo, N.Y., 13 1/4 In. 49.00
Tray, J. Leinenkugel Brewing Co., Man, Stein, Chippewa Falls, Wis., Oval. 112.00
Tray, Kaier's Brewing Company, Tin, 1905, 13 x 16 In. 575.00
Tray, Mathie Brewing, Red Ribbon Beer, Old Dutch Lager, Woman, Ukulele, 13 In. 500.00
Tray, Miller High Life, Woman On Half Moon, Milwaukee, Wis., 12 In. 13.00
Tray, Old Pepper Whiskey, Revolutionary War Soldiers, Oval, c.1900, 16 In. 180.00
Tray, Oneida Brewing Co., Indian Chief Shenandoah, Porcelain, Enamel, 12 In. 495.00
Tray, Red Ribbon Beer, Bear Drinking Beer, 13 x 13 In. 550.00
Tray, Ruhstaller's Gilt Edge Lager, Image, Purity, Kauffmann & Strauss, c.1910, 12 In. 90.00
Tray, Sanborn's Laxative Bitters, Tin Lithograph, 12 In. 1210.00
Tray, Tip, see Tip Trays in this category.
Trivet, Ellwood Fences Co., Braided Wire, Tin Lithograph, 6 1/2 In. 121.00
Wallet, Old Judge Coffee, Leather, 1933, 8 1/4 In. 25.00
Whistle, Foremost Dairy, Bugle Boy, Horn Shape, Plastic, Premium, 1950 . . . . . 40.00

AGATA glass was made by Joseph Locke of the New England Glass Company of Cambridge, Massachusetts, after 1885. A metallic stain was applied to New England Peachblow, which the company called Wild Rose, and the mottled design characteristic of agata appeared. There are a few known items made of opaque green with the mottled finish.

Bowl, Crimped Fluted Rim, Pontil, 2 1/2 x 5 In. 520.00
Bowl, Dark Pink, Scalloped Rim, 2 7/8 x 5 1/2 In. 387.00
Bowl, Lavender Stain, Scalloped Rim, 3 1/8 x 8 1/4 In. 480.00
Bowl, Opaque, Green, Optic Ribbed, Staining, 3 In. 489.00
Bowl, Opaque, Green, Gold Staining, 4 In. 748.00
Celery Vase, Square Scalloped Rim, Round Base, 6 1/2 In. 625.00
Cruet, Bulbous Base, Tricornered Rim, Applied Handle, Ball Stopper, 5 1/2 In. 690.00
Cruet, Dark Pink, Light Pink Handle, White Stopper, 5 3/4 In. . . . . *illus* 530.00

Tip Tray, Telling's Ice Cream, Lithograph On Metal, 1900, 4 In.
$990.00

Tray, Green River Whiskey, Man, Horse, Tin Lithograph, 20th Century, 24 In.
$147.00

Advertising, Tray, Hyan Dry Ginger Ale, Tin Lithograph, 1930-40
$258.00

Agata, Cruet, Dark Pink, Light Pink Handle, White Stopper, 5 3/4 In.
$530.00

A

Akro Agate, Vase, Cornucopia, Green, White, Marbleized, Fluted, Wavy Base
$550.00

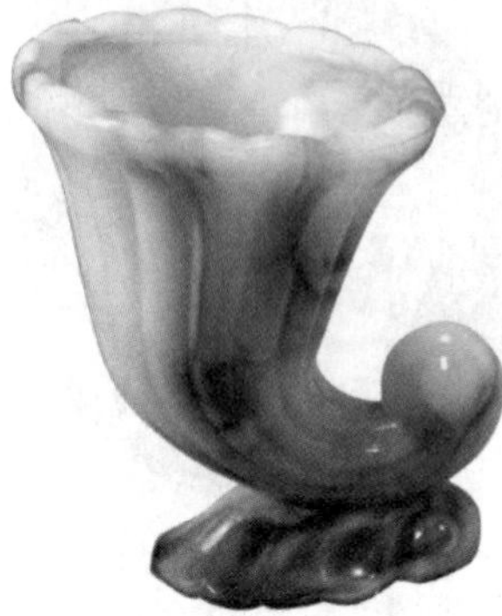

Akro Agate
Glass marbles were made by the Akro Agate Company of Akron, Ohio, founded in 1911. Marbles and toys were the only products the company made until 1932. Then ashtrays, figurines, bowls, garden pots, and other pieces were added to the line. The glass was a mixture of two or more opaque marbleized colors. The factory made children's glass tea sets and glassware after 1942 but went out of business in 1951, and its molds, trademark, and other assets were sold to the Master Glass Company of Clarksburg, West Virginia.

Alabaster, Luminaire, Fruited Vine, Carved, Early 20th Century, 19 In., Pair
$550.00

Finger Bowl, Oil Spots, Ruffled Rim, 5 ¼ x 2 ½ In. 288.00
Pitcher, 8 ¼ In. 5290.00
Tumbler, Purple Spots, 3 ¾ In. 585.00
Vase, Lily, Tricornered Rim, Footed, 8 ¼ In. 1480.00
Vase, Lily, Tricornered Rim, Peachblow, 10 ½ In. 845.00
Vase, Pinched Square Rim Sides, Marbleized, 6 In. 764.00

AKRO AGATE glass was founded in Akron, Ohio, in 1911, and moved to Clarksburg, West Virginia, in 1914. The company made marbles and toys. In the 1930s they began making other products, including vases, lamps, flowerpots, candlesticks, and children's dishes, Most of the glass is marked with a crow flying through the letter *A*. The company was sold to Clarksburg Glass Co. in 1951. Akro Agate marbles are listed in this book in the Marble category.

Ashtray, U.S. Rubber Co., Rubber Tire Rim, Blue Swirl Slag Glass Insert, 6 In. 63.00
Ashtray, White, Blue, Marbleized, Leaf Shape, 4 ¼ x 3 ¼ In. 14.00
Ashtray, White, Oxblood, Marbleized, Tab Handles, 4 In. 13.00
Ashtray, White, Red & Green, Marbleized, 8-Sided, Tab Handles, 1930s 43.00
Bowl, Pumpkin, Marbleized, Fluted, 3-Footed, 1940s, 5 ¼ x 2 ¼ In. 70.00
Flowerpot, Ivory, Oxblood, Marbleized, Fluted Band, 2 ⅝ x 2 ⅜ In. 33.00
Powder Jar, Cover, Guitar Player, Sombrero Cover, Ivory, Orange, Marbleized 30.00
Puff Box, Figural Colonial Woman, Milk Glass, 1940 .... 25.00 to 35.00
Puff Box, Scottie Dogs, Opaque Blue, 6¼ x 4 In. .... 49.00 to 80.00
Smoking Set, White, Oxblood, Marbleized, 1930s, 3-In. Cigarette Jar, 3-In. Ashtrays 49.00
Tea Set, American Maid, Jade, Opaque White, Box, 18 Piece 250.00
Tea Set, American Maid, Lemonade & Oxblood, Marbleized, Octagonal, 18 Piece . 315.00 to 405.00
Tea Set, Concentric Ring, Jade, Closed Handles, 18 Piece 71.00
Tea Set, Interior Panel, Pink, 8 Piece 66.00
Tea Set, Jade Trans Optic, 32 Piece 61.00
Tea Set, Play-Time, Jade, Opaque White, Box, 16 Piece .... 75.00 to 83.00
Tea Set, Stacked Disc, Interior Panel, Green, 16 Piece 250.00
Tea Set, Stippled Band, Green, 21 Piece 101.00
Toothpick, Opaque Cobalt Blue, Marbleized, 8-Sided, 2 ¾ In. 7.50
Vase, Cornucopia, Green, White, Marbleized, Fluted, Wavy Base .... *illus* 15.00
Vase, Urn Shape, Notched Rim, Green, White, Marbleized, Foot 19.00

ALABASTER is a very soft form of gypsum, a stone that resembles marble. It was often carved into vases or statues in Victorian times. There are alabaster carvings being made even today.

Bust, Jeanne D'Arc, In Cap, Pink Bodice, Continental, 19th Century, 13 ½ x 13 In. 470.00
Figurine, Best Friends, Cuddling, Pietro Bazzanti, 19th Century, 18 ½ x 1 ¾ In. 1416.00
Figurine, Buddha, Seated, Burmese, 18th Century, 12 ½ In. 2360.00
Figurine, Head Of Stallion, Black Marble Base, V. Vanni, 20th Century, 12 ½ In. 1298.00
Figurine, Young Musician, Pedestal, Carlo Scheggia, 19th Century, 16 ½ In. 1298.00
Luminaire, Fruited Vine, Carved, Early 20th Century, 19 In., Pair .... *illus* 550.00
Pedestal, Columnar, Ivory Colored, Octagonal Top, Reed Column, 1900s, 24 x 11 In. 403.00
Sculpture, Basket Of Fruit & Flowers, Multicolored, Carved, 35 In. 885.00
Statue, Egyptian Woman, Sitting On Lion, Plinth, Art Nouveau, c.1900, 34 x 18 x 19 In. 15535.00
Statue, Melodic Thought, Woman Sitting On Stone, Italian School, c.1890, 23 In. 1062.00

ALUMINUM was more expensive than gold or silver until the 1850s. Chemists learned how to refine bauxite to get aluminum. Jewelry and other small objects were made of the valuable metal until 1914, when an inexpensive smelting process was invented. The aluminum collected today dates from the 1930s through the 1950s. Hand-hammered pieces are the most popular.

Biscuit Tin, Egg Stand, Huntley & Palmers, Hammered, 1928 .... *illus* 1610.00
Bowl, Blue Green, Anodized, Emalox, 3 x 8 In. 60.00
Bowl, Cover, Wheat Pattern, Anodized Goldtone, Ring Handle, Arthur Amour, 7 In. 65.00
Bowl, Dark Blue, Anodized, Emalox, 1 ½ x 4 In. 40.00
Bowl, Deep Red, Straight Sides, Anodized, Emalox, Marked, Olden 35.00
Bowl, Red, Anodized, Emalox, 2 ½ x 5 ¾ In. 45.00
Can, Ease, Copper, Black Lid, Strainer, Wet Band, 5 In. 15.00
Cocktail Shaker, Cylindrical, Fluted, Signed, Emson Ezee Pour, 12 ½ In. 155.00
Creamer & Sugar, Black Bakelite Handles, Chrome Plated, 1 ¾ x 3 ¼ In. 12.00
Ice Bucket, Chrysanthemum, Continental Silver Co., 12 x 8 In. 170.00
Muffin Pan, Chrome Plated, 6 Cups, Child's, 6 x 4 In. 13.00
Salt & Pepper, Range Set, West Bend, Black Plastic Lid, 4 In. 20.00

Sculpture, Cast, Cactus, Jan De Swart, c.1962, 9 x 6 x 4 In. 1020.00
Sculpture, Polished, Snowflake Image, Claire Falkenstein, c.1975, 24 In. 8400.00
Tray, 3 Horses, Anodized Goldtone, Handles, Arthur Amour, 14 In.......... 100.00
Tray, Condiment, Glass Insert, No. 462, Rodney Kent, 12 x 5 In.......... 90.00
Tray, Nude Women, Hammered, Round, Everted Rim, Art Deco Style, c.1930, 11 In. 1152.00
Tray, Serving, Grasshopper Design, Wendell August Forge, 11 In.......... 220.00
Wastebasket, Embossed World Map, Gold Tint, Oval, Arthur Armour, 10 In. 210.00

AMBER, *see Jewelry category.*

AMBER GLASS is the name of any glassware with the proper yellow-brown shading. It was a popular color just after the Civil War and many pressed glass pieces were made of amber glass. Depression glass of the 1930s–50s was also made in shades of amber glass. Other pieces may be found in the Depression Glass, Pressed Glass, and other glass categories. All types are being reproduced.

Bowl, Fruit, 6-Petal Foot, Viking Glass, 6 x 9 In.......... 35.00
Bowl, Round, 4 Textured Pheasant Feet, Jeannette, 3 x 8 In.......... 24.00
Bowl, Swan Shape, Curved Neck Handle, 6 x 11 In.......... 88.00
Box, Hinged Cover, Enameled Fence & Birds, Square, 4 Ball Feet, 5 In. 1295.00
Candy Dish, Cover, 12 Panels, Flame Finial, Petal Foot, 7 x 5 In.......... 39.00
Candy Jar, Cover, 6-Petal Sides, Dimpled Foot, 1960s, 10 x 5 ½ In. 45.00
Compote, Controlled Bubbles, Deeply Ruffled Rim, Clear Dome Foot, 6 ½ x 16 In.......... 45.00
Compote, Etched Castle, Deer, Dog, Scrolls, Flattened Bowl, Broad Foot, 6 ½ In.......... 195.00
Compote, Teardrop Rim, Fluted Stem, Stepped Foot, 8 ½ x 7 ½ In. 16.00
Console, Etched Greek Figures In Garden, Greek Key Bands, Rolled Rim, 10 In. 50.00
Creamer, Paneled, Wide Shaped Rim, 3 ¾ In. 24.00
Decanter, Beaded Oval Panels, Oval Stopper, Notched Edge, 12 ¾ In. 18.00
Decanter, Embossed Zodiac Symbols, Fluted Cylindrical Neck, Hobnail Stopper, Italy, 13 In. . 25.00
Decanter Set, Enameled, Stylized Propeller Decoration, Black Faceted Stopper, 5 Piece 295.00
Dresser Set, Fluted Sides, Crescent-Shaped Tray & Pin Tray, 13 x 7-In. Tray, 6 Piece.......... 189.00
Elephant, Figural Cover, Co-Operative Flint.......... 895.00
Figurine, Apple, Crackled, 3 In.......... 44.00
Figurine, Bird, Elongated Tail, Ball Knop, Dome Foot, 9 x 2 ½ In.......... 30.00
Goblet, Faceted Sides, Flared Rim, Footed, 6 In., 6 Piece.......... 52.00
Nut Dish, Pinched & Scalloped Sides, 2 x 3 ¼ In., Pair.......... 18.00
Pitcher, Martini, Straight Sides, Applied Handle, 10 x 4 In. 35.00
Pitcher, Red, Pink & Orange Polka Dots, Fluted Handle, 1960s, 9 In. 15.00
Relish, 4 Clover-Leaf Shaped Sections, Center Fan-Shaped Handle, 9 x 7 ½ In.......... 26.00
Shade, Flame Shape, Swirls, Satin Finish, 8 In., 10 Piece.......... 525.00
Shaker Set, Yellow Metal Lids, Salt, Pepper, Cheese, 4 Piece.......... 36.00
Tray, Daisy & Button, Fan Shape,10 ½ x 7 In.......... 12.00
Vase, Bud, 16-Sided Bowl, Long Neck, Shaped Rim, Footed, 15 ¾ In.......... 25.00
Vase, Diamond Optic, Cobalt Blue Base, Original Label, 8 In.......... 145.00
Vase, Handkerchief, Folded Sides, Dimpled Foot, Viking, 7 ¾ x 6 In.......... 15.00

AMBERETTE *pieces are listed in the Pressed Glass category under the pattern name Amberette.*

AMBERINA, a two-toned glassware, was originally made from 1883 to about 1900. It was patented by Joseph Locke of the New England Glass Company, but was also made by other companies and is still being made. The glass shades from red to amber. Similar pieces of glass may be found in the Baccarat, Libbey, Plated Amberina, and other categories. Glass shaded from blue to amber is called Blue Amberina or Bluerina.

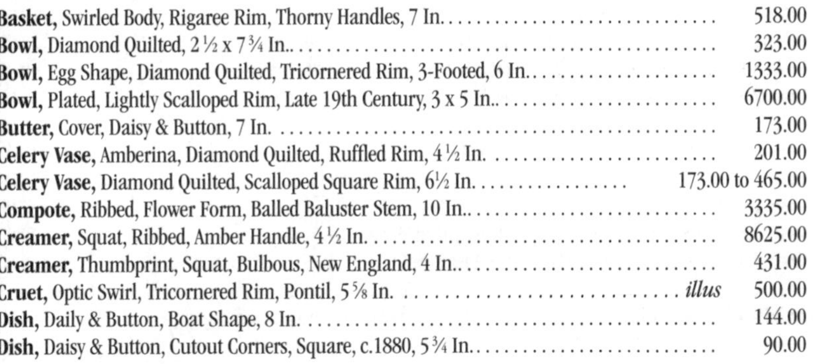

Basket, Swirled Body, Rigaree Rim, Thorny Handles, 7 In.......... 518.00
Bowl, Diamond Quilted, 2 ½ x 7 ¾ In.......... 323.00
Bowl, Egg Shape, Diamond Quilted, Tricornered Rim, 3-Footed, 6 In.......... 1333.00
Bowl, Plated, Lightly Scalloped Rim, Late 19th Century, 3 x 5 In.......... 6700.00
Butter, Cover, Daisy & Button, 7 In. 173.00
Celery Vase, Amberina, Diamond Quilted, Ruffled Rim, 4 ½ In. 201.00
Celery Vase, Diamond Quilted, Scalloped Square Rim, 6½ In. .... 173.00 to 465.00
Compote, Ribbed, Flower Form, Balled Baluster Stem, 10 In.......... 3335.00
Creamer, Squat, Ribbed, Amber Handle, 4 ½ In.......... 8625.00
Creamer, Thumbprint, Squat, Bulbous, New England, 4 In.......... 431.00
Cruet, Optic Swirl, Tricornered Rim, Pontil, 5 ⅝ In. .... *illus* 500.00
Dish, Daily & Button, Boat Shape, 8 In.......... 144.00
Dish, Daisy & Button, Cutout Corners, Square, c.1880, 5 ¾ In.......... 90.00

TIP

You can clean aluminum with silver polishing cream. It's good for the new aluminum wheels on your car, too.

Aluminum, Biscuit Tin, Egg Stand, Huntley & Palmers, Hammered, 1928
$1610.00

Amberina, Cruet, Optic Swirl, Tricornered Rim, Pontil, 5 ⅝ In.
$500.00

Amberina, Muffineer, Inverted Thumbprint, Metal Lid, 5 In.
$1298.00

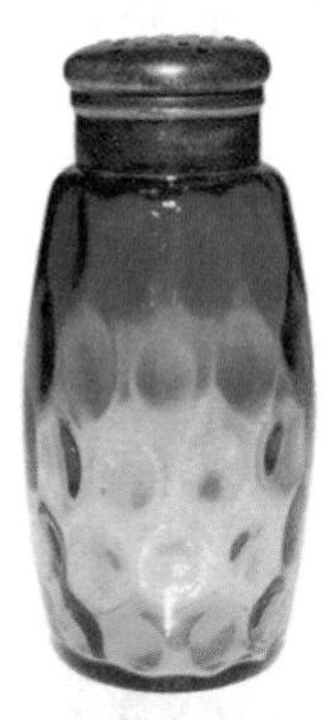

Amberina, Pitcher, Daisy & Button, Straight Sides, 5 In.
$225.00

Amberina, Spooner, Diamond Quilted, Inverted Thumbprint, Square Rim, 4⅞ In.
$170.00

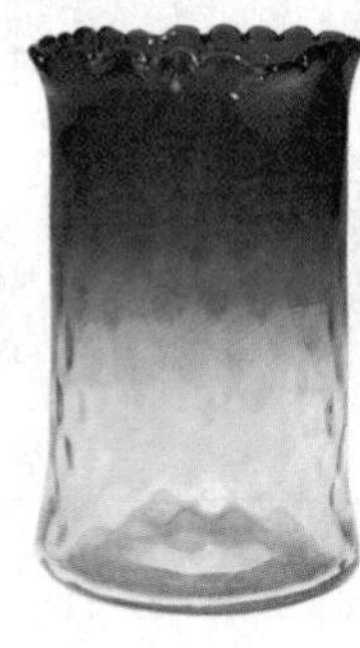

American Encaustic Tiling Company, Tile, Peacock, Parrot, Iridescent Green High Glaze, 11½ x 6 In., Pair
$472.00

Amethyst Glass, Cologne, Figural, Pilgrim, Cork Stopper, 5½ In.
$5.00

Lemonade Set, Inverted Coin spot, 6¾-In., Pitcher, 7 Piece ... 185.00
Muffineer, Inverted Thumbprint, Metal Lid, 5 In. ... *illus* 1298.00
Pitcher, Daisy & Button, Straight Sides, 5 In. ... *illus* 225.00
Pitcher, Thumbprint, Ruffled Rim, 9½ In. ... 201.00
Pitcher, Water, Coin Spot, Square Mouth, Amber Reeded Handle, 8 In. ... 325.00
Pitcher, Water, Inverted Coin Dot, Ruffled Rim, Reed Handle, 8 In. ... 200.00
Punch Cup, Diamond Quilted, Thorn Amber Handle, 2½ In. ... 86.00
Spooner, Diamond Quilted, Inverted Thumbprint, Square Rim, 4⅞ In. ... *illus* 170.00
Spooner, Inverted Thumbprint, Square Ruffled Rim, Round Base, 4½ In. ... 144.00
Toothpick, Tricornered, c.1880, 3 x 2¾ In. ... 240.00
Tumbler, Lemonade, Ribbed, Applied Amber Handle, 5 In. ... 4025.00
Vase, Bud, Bulbous Top, c.1870, 2¾ x 4¼ In. ... 450.00
Vase, Diamond Quilted, Pinched Sides, Oval, Ruffled Rim, Rigaree Collar, 6 In. ... 400.00
Vase, Lily, Optic Ribbed, Tricornered Rim, 10 In. ... 374.00
Vase, Lily, Ruffled Rim, Footed, c.1870, 8 In. ... 285.00
Vase, Square, 9 In., Pair ... 175.00
Vase, Swirled Optic, Pear Shape, Pinched, Flared, Ruffled Rim, 12¾ x 5½ In. ... 358.00
Vase, Trumpet, Swirled Ribs, Applied Amber Edge & Foot, 20 In. ... 518.00

AMERICAN DINNERWARE, *see Dinnerware.*

AMERICAN ENCAUSTIC TILING COMPANY was founded in Zanesville, Ohio, in 1875. The company planned to make a variety of tiles to compete with the English tiles that were selling in the United States for use in fireplaces and other architectural designs. The first glazed tiles were made in 1880, embossed tiles in 1881, faience tiles in the 1920s. The firm closed in 1935 and reopened in 1937 as the Shawnee Pottery.

Border, Stylized Mushroom Design, 1½ x 6 In., 10 Piece ... 85.00
Border, Stylized Wave Design, 2 x 6 In., 8 Piece ... 65.00
Tile, Alhambra, Pink Fleur-De-Lis, c.1920, 6 x 6 In. ... 35.00
Tile, Peacock, Parrot, Iridescent Green High Glaze, 11½ x 6 In., Pair ... *illus* 472.00

AMETHYST GLASS is any of the many glasswares made in the dark purple color of the gemstone amethyst. Included in this category are many pieces made in the nineteenth and twentieth centuries. Very dark pieces are called black amethyst and are listed under that heading.

Ashtray, Rolled Rim, 3 Crimps, 2½ x 4¾ In. ... 14.00
Bowl, Floral, Wide Ruffled Rim, Controlled Bubble Base, 3½ x 7 In. ... 45.00
Candlestick, 6-Sided Cup & Foot, 2½ x 4½ In., Pair ... 95.00
Candlestick, Pulled & Elongated Side, 1950s, 13 x 5½ In. ... 35.00
Cologne, Figural, Pilgrim, Cork Stopper, 5½ In. ... *illus* 5.00
Compote, Clear Twist Stem, 7 x 6 In. ... 60.00
Compote, Flattened Bowl, Baluster Stem, Spread Foot, 4¾ x 9½ In. ... 150.00
Compote, Satin, Wide Rim, Black Enameled, Black Foot, Art Deco, 7 In. ... 175.00
Cordial, Double Knop Stem, 3 In. ... 13.00
Creamer, Swirls, Pear Shape, Pedestal Base, 5 In. ... 39.00
Decanter, Pinched Sides, 8½ In. ... 28.00
Dish, Sweetmeat, Cover, Cut Diamonds, Paneled Cover, Flat Fluted Finial, Footed ... 950.00
Jug, Hobnail, Twisted Neck, Flared Rim, 10½ In. ... 25.00
Lemonade Set, White Enameled Bead, 12 x 5-In. Pitcher, 7 Piece ... 275.00
Pitcher, Crackled, Folded Rim With Ice Lip, Footed, 6¾ In. ... 55.00
Pitcher, Crackled, Wide Flared Rim, 7½ In. ... 125.00
Pitcher, Hobnail, 9 x 5 In. ... 69.00
Pitcher, Melon Ribbed, Flared, Clear Fluted Handle, 3¾ In. ... 18.00
Pitcher, Swirled Top, Diamond Band, Flowers, Clear Scroll Handle, 4½ In. ... 28.00
Punch Cup, Enameled White Flowers, Green Sprigs, Low Handle, 3¼ In. ... 40.00
Rose Bowl, 3-Footed, Clear Flower Frog, Viking Glass, 3 In. ... 50.00
Salt, Scalloped Petal Edge, 1⅛ x 3 In., Pair ... 18.00
Tumbler, Flared, Dark Flattened Ball Foot, 3 In., 6 Piece ... 45.00
Vase, Deep Flutes, Zippered Base, Flared Ruffled Rim, 10¼ In. ... 135.00
Vase, Hyacinth, Squat, 7 In. ... 225.00
Vase, Inverted Strawberry, Hat Shape, Ruffled Rim, 3 x 4½ In. ... 20.00
Vase, Rippled, Bubble Prunts, Clear Base, 11 x 2 In. ... 150.00

ANDIRONS *and related fireplace items are included in the Fireplace category.*

ANIMAL TROPHIES, such as stuffed animals, rugs made of animal skins, and other similar collectibles made from animal, fish, or bird parts are listed in this category. Collectors should be aware of the endangered species laws that make it illegal to buy and sell some of these items. Any eagle feathers, many types of pelts or rugs (such as leopard), ivory, and many forms of tortoiseshell can be confiscated by the government. Related trophies may be found in the Fishing category. Ivory items may be found in the Scrimshaw or Ivory categories.

African Cape Buffalo Head, Mounted, 40 x 34 x 36 In. 643.00
African Nubian Ibex Goat Head, Mounted, 58 x 20 x 26 In. 400.00
African Sable Antelope Head, Mounted, 2 Piece, 53 x 40 In. 938.00
Alaskan Brown Bear Head, Mounted, 18 x 22 In. 410.00
Big Horn Sheep, Half Mount 395.00
Bison, Custer State Park, S.D., Late 20th Century, 42 In. .... *illus* 850.00
Boar, Feral, Mounted To Natural Setting, New Zealand, 40 In. 176.00
Brown Bear Head, 18 x 22 In. 410.00
Cape Buffalo Head, Africa, 40 x 34 In., ... 643.00
Coho Salmon, Skin Mount, 29 ½ In. 140.00
Deer Head, Wall Plaque, Giltwood, Carved, Scroll, Mid 1800s, 15 x 23 In. 1175.00
Eagle Feet, Cast Lead, Painted, Wooden Plaque, 3 ½ x 7 In. 374.00
Elk, Head, Cast Iron, 2 Sections, Mounted On Board, 19th Century, 24 In. 2233.00
Elk Skull, 12-Point Rack, 40 x 32 In. 540.00
Horn, Sword Stand, Wooden Stand, Chrome Mounts, Inscribed, 16 In. 259.00
Horns, Stag, Carved, Stained, Lindenwood Mount, Oak Leaf & Acorn Spray, Germany 720.00
Impala Skull, Horns, Mahogany Backplate, Shield Shape, 23 x 13 In., Pair 480.00
Rocky Mountain Dall Sheep Head, Mounted, 24 x 30 x 16 In. .... 189.00 to 234.00
Rug, Bearskin, Black, Full Head, Open Mouth, Glass Eyes, Claws 750.00
Rug, Brown Bear, 77 x 64 In. 605.00
Steelhead, Skin Mount, 29 ½ In. 140.00
Tuna, Fiberglass, 30 In. .... *illus* 84.00
White Tail Deer Rack, 21 Point 880.00

ANIMATION ART collectibles include cels that are painted drawings on celluloid needed to make animated cartoons shown in movie theaters or on TV. Hundreds of cels were made, then photographed in sequence to make a cartoon showing moving figures. Early examples made by the Walt Disney Studios are popular with collectors today. Original sketches used by the artists are also listed here. Modern animated cartoons are made using computer-generated pictures. Some of these are being produced as cels to be sold to collectors. Other cartoon art is listed in Comic Art and Disneyana.

Cel, 101 Dalmatians, Anita & Perdita, 1961, 15 x 12 ½ In. 418.00
Cel, Alice In Wonderland, Dodo, 1951, 9 ½ x 7 ½ In. 263.00
Cel, Jungle Book, Hand Painted, Baloo The Bear & Mowgli, 1967, 12 x 9 In. 448.00
Cel, Ludwig Von Drake, In Front Of Television Set, Holding Paper, 8 x 10 In. .... *illus* 400.00
Cel, Mad Hatter Animation, Hand Inked, Hand Painted, 11 ½ x 8 ½ In. 120.00
Cel, Mickey Mouse, Pluto, The Pointer, Hunting For Quail, Frame, c.1939, 11 x 8 In. 5676.00
Cel, Rescuers, Orville, Hand Painted, 1977, 15 ½ x 11 ¾ In. 72.00
Cel, Sleeping Beauty, Good Fairy Flora, Hand Inked, Painted, 1959, 11 ½ x 8 ½ In. 179.00
Cel, Snow White & Seven Dwarfs, Disney Production, c.1937, 7 x 6 ½ In. 5079.00
Drawing, Doc & Dopey, Mat, Frame, 1937, 6 ½ x 4 ½ In. 287.00
Drawing, Dognappers, Mickey & Donald In Hot Pursuit, Colored Pencil, 1934 .... 478.00
Drawing, Klondike Kid, Mickey Feeds Minnie Soup, Graphite, 1932, 12 x 10 In. 388.00
Drawing, Mail Pilot, Minnie & Mickey Hoisted Upon Mail Plane, Graphite, 1933 .... 311.00
Drawing, Mellerdrammer, Mickey & Minnie Cut Rug, Graphite, 1933, 12 x 9 ½ In. 299.00
Drawing, Mickey Makes Fresh Coffee, Graphite, 1938, 12 x 10 In. 418.00
Drawing, Mickey Mouse, Mickey's Good Deed, Disney, c.1932, 12 x 10 In. 388.00
Drawing, Mickey Mouse, Steamboat Willie, Disney, c.1928, 12 x 9 ½ In. 359.00
Drawing, Mickey's Elephant, Graphite, Red Pencil, 1936, 12 x 10 In. .... *illus* 448.00
Drawing, Mickey's Fire Brigade, Graphite, 1935, 12 x 9 ½ In. 448.00
Drawing, Mickey's Good Deed, Peering In Window Dressed As Santa, 1932, 12 x 10 In. 329.00
Drawing, Moose Hunters, Graphite, Red & Green Pencil, 1937, 12 x 10 In. 633.00
Drawing, Mother Goose Goes Hollywood, Garbo & Gable, c.1938, 12 x 10 In. 335.00
Drawing, Mother Goose Goes Hollywood, Graphite, Red Pencil, 1938, 12 x 10 In. 777.00
Drawing, Mother Goose Goes Hollywood, Wallace Beery, c.1938, 12 x 10 In. 294.00
Drawing, Pet Store, Mickey & Minnie Walk Arm In Arm, Graphite, 1933, 12 x 10 In. 329.00
Drawing, Pluto, No. 24, Pencil, Gray Cardboard Mat, 1940s, 14 x 16 In. 127.00
Drawing, Puppy Love, Mickey Gives Minnie Candy, Graphite, 1933, 12 x 10 In. 418.00
Drawing, Rumplewatt Has Sneezing Fit, Graphite, 1933, 12 x 9 ½ In. 191.00

Animal Trophy, Bison, Custer State Park, S.D., Late 20th Century, 42 In. $850.00

Animal Trophies, Tuna, Fiberglass, 30 In. $84.00

TIP
Never display a stuffed trophy over a fireplace. The heat will eventually dry the skin and injure the trophy.

Animation Art, Cel, Ludwig Von Drake, In Front Of Television Set, Holding Paper, 8 x 10 In. $400.00

Animation Art, Drawing, Mickey's Elephant, Graphite, Red Pencil, 1936, 12 x 10 In. $448.00

TIP

Cels should be kept away from direct sunlight and high humidity. They should be framed with acid-free mats.

Architectural, Doorknocker, Brass, Butterfly On Sunflower, Painted, 3 ½ x 4 In. $518.00

Architectural, Doorknocker, Butterfly, Waverly Studios, 3 ½ x 2 ¾ In. $495.00

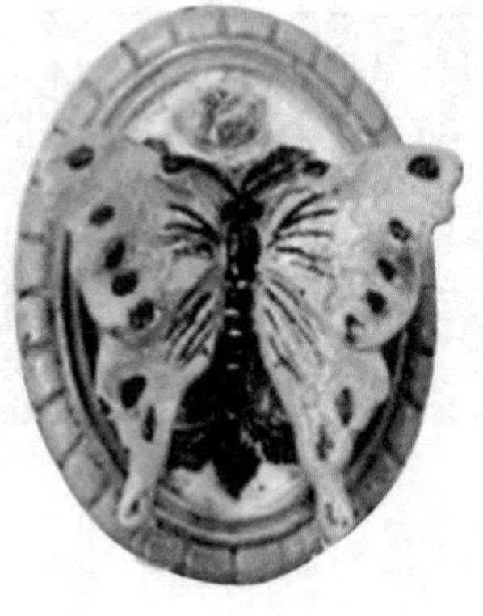

Drawing, Snow White Shares Song With Bird, Graphite, Red Pencil, 1937, 12 x 10 In. 896.00
Drawing, Three Little Wolves, Red & Blue Pencil, 1936, 9 ½ x 12 In. 424.00
Drawing, Thru The Mirror, Drawing No. 69, Pencil, 1936, 10 x 12 In. 115.00

ANNA POTTERY was started in Anna, Illinois, in 1859 by Cornwall and Wallace Kirkpatrick. They made many types of utilitarian wares, bricks, drain tiles, and giftware. The most collectible pieces made by the pottery are the pig-shaped bottles and jugs with special inscriptions, applied animals, and figures. The pottery closed in 1894.

Anna Pottery

Bottle, Figural, Pig, Incised Railroad Map, Brown Glaze, Cairo, St. Louis 4750.00
Bottle, Pig, Molded, Albany Slip, c.1885, 7 ½ In. 18400.00

APPLE PEELERS *are listed in the Kitchen category under Peeler, Apple.*

ARABIA began producing ceramics in 1874. The pottery was established in Helsinki, Finland, by Rörstrand, a Swedish pottery that wanted to export porcelain, earthenware, and other pottery from Finland to Russia. Most of the early workers at Arabia were Swedish. Arabia started producing its own models of tiled stoves, vases and tableware c.1900. Rörstrand sold its interest in Arabia in 1916. By the late 1930s, Arabia was the largest producer of porcelain in Europe. Most of its products were exported. A line of stoneware was introduced in the 1960s. Arabia worked in cooperation with Rörstrand from 1975 to 1977. Arabia was bought by Hackman Group in 1990 and Hackman was bought by Iittala Group in 2004. Arabia is now a brand owned by Iittala Group.

ARABIA FINLAND

Bowl, Black, Pour Spout, Handle, Kaj Franck, 7 ¼ In. 145.00
Cup & Saucer, Ulla Procope, Marked, 12 Piece 200.00
Vase, Charcoal Blue Glaze, Oval, Marked, 5 In. 175.00
Vase, Rice, Star Design, 4-Sided, Marked, 4 x 6 In. 375.00

ARC-EN-CIEL is the French word for rainbow. A pottery factory named Arc-en-ciel was founded in Zanesville, Ohio, in 1903. The company made art pottery for a short time, then became the Brighton Pottery in 1905.

ARC-EN-CIEL POTTERY

Vase, Green Matte Glaze, Raised Organic Design, Baluster Shape, c.1905, 4 ½ In. 175.00

ARCHITECTURAL antiques include a variety of collectibles, usually very large, that have been removed from buildings. Hardware, backbars, doors, paneling, and even old bathtubs are now wanted by collectors. Pieces of the Victorian, Art Nouveau, and Art Deco styles are in greatest demand.

Baluster, Caryatid, Bronze, Patinated, Steel Base, Mounted As Lamp, Italy 1440.00
Baluster, Pine, Carved, Stepped Ends, 19th Century, 26 x 32 In., Pair 550.00
Bracket, Sign, Wrought Iron, Flowers, New Orleans, 20 x 58 In. 432.00
Bracket, Wall, Scrolled, Cast Iron, No. 3, Deitz, New York 198.00
Capital, Corinthian, Terra-Cotta, Plaster, Painted, Early 20th Century, 14 x 17 ½ In. 600.00
Column, Cast Iron, Square Capital, Plinth, Fluted, 150 x 10 In., Pair 390.00
Column, Conifer, Carved Capital, Spiral Turned, 1700s, 77 x 9 In., Pair 374.00
Column, Giltwood, Multicolored, Spiral Twisted, Baldachinno Shape, 12 x 12 In. 1200.00
Corbel, Cast Iron, Painted White, Mid 19th Century, 18 ¾ x 12 In., Pair 58.00
Corbel, Napoleon III, Limestone, Carved, Hunting Dog, Cusped Corona, 15 x 18 In. 2400.00
Cornice, Griffins, Center Cartouche, Wood, Black Forest, Carved, 44 x 12 In. 767.00
Cupola Cover, Directional, Zinc, Sheet Metal, Arrow, Compass, Spear Point Finial 920.00
Doghouse, Chalet Style, Embossed Tin, Painted Bead Board, 1900s, 45 x 38 In. 6300.00
Door, Louis XVI, Carved, Stained, Rubbed, Musical Trophies, 85 x 38 ½ In. 4113.00
Door, Pine, 3 Panels, Leaves, Masks, 100 x 25 In., Pair 1195.00
Door Frame, Cupboard, Provincial, Beechwood, Latch Hook, Continental, 29 x 15 In. 840.00
Door Frame, George III, Stripped Pine, Pewter Mount, 94 x 52 In., Pair 3600.00
Door Hinge, Iron, Scrolls, Flowers, Leaves, Clover, 39 x 23 ½ In. 2185.00
Doorknob, Brass, Tooled, Raised Initials R.E.L., 2 ½ In. 375.00
Doorknob, Bronze, Plinth, High Wheel Bicycle & Rider, Key, 9 ¼ In. 935.00
Doorknob, Gilt Bronze, Fluted, Mushroom Cap Shape, Threaded, Pair 12000.00
Doorknob, Porcelain, Glazed, Adelaide Robineau, 2 ¼ In., 4 Piece 2280.00
Doorknocker, Brass, Dolphin, Cast, Tooled, 18th Century, 7 In. 2013.00
Doorknocker, Brass, Butterfly On Sunflower, Painted, 3 ½ x 4 In. .... *illus* 518.00
Doorknocker, Brass, Neoclassical, Silver, Classical Columns, 4 ½ x 6 In. 5976.00
Doorknocker, Bronze, Snakes, Rosette, 19th Century, 9 x 8 In., Pair 3346.00
Doorknocker, Butterfly, Waverly Studios, 3 ½ x 2 ¾ In. .... *illus* 495.00
Doorknocker, Iron, Bluebirds, Birdhouse, Hubley, 3 ¾ x 1 ¾ In. 920.00
Doorknocker, Iron, Cherub, Holding Roses, Ribbons, No. 616, 4 ¼ x 3 In. 345.00

Doorknocker, Iron, Colonial Man, 4½ x 2⅝ In. 58.00
Doorknocker, Iron, Flower Basket, Oval, Painted, Hubley, Box 260.00
Doorknocker, Iron, Fruit & Leaves, Oval Back, 5¾ x 4 In. 55.00
Doorknocker, Iron, Fruit Basket, Grapes, Gourds Overflowing, 4 x 3 In. 460.00
Doorknocker, Iron, Ivy, Red Basket, Hubley, 4½ x 2 In. 230.00
Doorknocker, Iron, Man, Reading Book, In Chair, Judd Co., 4¼ x 2⅜ In. 575.00
Doorknocker, Iron, Mixed Flowers, Vase, 3¾ x 2¼ In. 29.00 to 115.00
Doorknocker, Iron, Neoclassical, Face, 19th Century, 13½ x 7½ In., Pair 1645.00
Doorknocker, Iron, Owl, On Branch, 4¼ x 3 In. 86.00
Doorknocker, Iron, Parrot, On Branch, Hubley, 4⅝ x 2⅞ In. *illus* 200.00
Doorknocker, Iron, Parrot, On Branch, Looking Over Shoulder, 3¾ x 2⅞ In. 173.00
Doorknocker, Iron, Plymouth Rock, Commemorative, 1620 Pilgrim's Landing 29.00
Doorknocker, Iron, Rooster, Crowing, Ring, 3¼ x 2⅝ In. 201.00
Doorknocker, Iron, Snowy Owl, On Branch, Hubley, 4½ x 2¾ In. 175.00
Doorknocker, Iron, Spider, Catching Fly, 3⅝ x 1¾ In. 1495.00
Doorknocker, Iron, Swing, Black, Hubley 575.00
Doorknocker, Iron, Woodpecker, 3¾ In. 195.00
Doorknocker, Iron, Zinnias, Hubley, 9¾ x 8½ In. 316.00
Downspout, Sheet Iron, Tinned, Eagle, 1876, Painted, Shield 1058.00
Elevator Floor Indicator, 11 Floors, T For Tunnel, Cast Iron 995.00
Fan Light, Wooden, Painted Mustard Yellow, Early 19th Century, 22 x 47½ In. 1293.00
Faucet, Bathroom, Hot & Cold Water, Brass, Nickel Plated, Porcelain, France, c.1920 33.00
Finial, Balustrade, Lion, Cast Iron, Verdigris, Late 1800s, 13 x 9 x 23 In., Pair 1320.00
Finial, Brass, Gilded, Anthemion Shape, Mid 19th Century, 7 In., Pair 300.00
Finial, Fence, Iron, Leaf Shape, 23 In., 12 Piece 440.00
Finial, Gate, Iron, Pineapple, Painted White, Late 19th Century, 24 x 8½ In. 805.00
Finial, Parcel Gilt, Beechwood, Carved, Eagles, Fruit Clusters, Continental 1080.00
Finial, Turret, Galvanized Metal, Aesthetic, Painted Gray, Stylized Flowers, France 840.00
Finial, Zinc, Flame Over Sphere, Square Ribbed Base, 32 x 11 In., Pair 1344.00
Fireplace Surround, Marble, Chippendale Style, Shell & Leaf Carving, 51 x 72 In. 2300.00
Gallery, Wrought Iron, Multicolored, 19th Century, 17½ x 85 In. 7800.00
Gate, Iron, Arch Top, Scroll Design, 32½ In., Pair 82.00
Gate, Wrought Iron, Scroll, Leaves, Edgar Brandt, Marked, c.1930 7200.00
Gate, Wrought Iron, Stylized Flowers, Vines, E. Brandt, Art Deco, 51½ x 31½ In. 6000.00
Hinge, Wrought Iron, Ram's Head, Beveled Edges, 16½ x 7 In., Pair 209.00
Latch, Cast & Wrought Iron, Rooster, Clover, Marked, O'Grady, 12 In. 88.00
Latch, Iron, Thumb, Tulip Shape, 12 In. *illus* 165.00
Mail Boxes, Pine, Green Paint, 19 Slots, Shaped Dividers, 1800s, 30 x 39 x 11 In. 633.00
Mantel, Carrara Marble, Louis XV Style, Serpentine Top, Coquille Crest, 72 x 60 In. 5288.00
Mantel, Federal, Green, Faux Grain, Bowed Top, Shelf, 1800s, 69 x 85 In. 5900.00
Mantel, Maple, Carved, Molded Top, Corbels, c.1910, 47 x 57 In. 420.00
Mantel, Marble, Louis XVI Style, Carved Shell, Pilasters, 50 x 73 In. *illus* 3290.00
Mantel, Oak, Bracketed, Columns, Beveled Mirror, Early 1900s, 79 x 60 In. 125.00
Mantel, Pine, Fluted Columns, 18th Century, 67 x 33 In. 660.00
Mantel, Pine, Ocher, Grain Painted, Applied Molding, Raised Panels, Ohio 230.00
Mantel, Softwood, Faux Marble Paint, Block Panels, Column Stiles, 50 x 62 x 7 In. 825.00
Mantel, Softwood, Reeded & Dentil Moldings, White Paint, Pa., 61 x 67 In. 198.00
Mantel, Stepped & Reeded Molding, Grain Paint, Pa., 59½ x 67 In. 198.00
Mantel, Surround, Mirror Top, Columns, 85 x 61 In. 798.00
Mantel, Teakwood, Carved, Anglo-Indian, 19th Century, 41¾ x 39 In. *illus* 588.00
Mantel, Tiger Oak, Columns, Mirror, Marietta Mantel Co., 1890, 84 x 60 In. 2150.00
Mantel, Walnut, Jacobean Style, Scrolls, Cartouches, Carved Panels 368.00
Mantel, Wood, Mirror, Dentil Border, Rosettes, Fluted Columns, 70 x 74 In. 448.00
Niche, Giltwood, French Gothic Revival, Carved, Decorated Spires, 55 x 12 In. 3290.00
Ornament, Cherub's Head, Winged, Scrolling, Italy, Mid 1800s, 11½ x 28 In. 1440.00
Ornament, Lead, Eagle, Spread Wing, Clutching Orb, Cast Lead, Steel Frame 920.00
Ornament, Temple, Wood, Multicolored, Chinese, 3 Piece 234.00
Overmantel Mirror, Blocked, Cavet To Cornice Over Molded Stiles, c.1830, 26 x 49 In. 1860.00
Overmantel Mirror, Crenelated Crest, Fluted Frieze, 1800s, 63 x 61 In. 1180.00
Overmantel Mirror, Gilt Gesso, Classical, New England, c.1825, 24¾ x 65 In. 1410.00
Overmantel Mirror, Giltwood, 3 Sections, Lions Head, c.1830, 27¼ x 73½ In. 2644.00
Overmantel Mirror, Giltwood, Beaux Arts, Arched Crest, Shell, Ivy, 71 x 59 In. 1838.00
Overmantel Mirror, Giltwood, Belle Epoque, Carved, Basket Of Flowers, 27 x 50 In. 1645.00
Overmantel Mirror, Giltwood, Matte, Federal, Burnished, Triptych Frame, 22 x 64 In. 748.00
Overmantel Mirror, Giltwood, Plaster, Napoleon III, Louis XVI Style, 87 x 44 In. 2160.00
Overmantel Mirror, Giltwood, Victorian, Rounded Top, Molded Frame, 60 x 50 In. 1410.00

Architectural, Doorknocker, Iron, Parrot, On Branch, Hubley, 4⅝ x 2⅞ In.
$200.00

Architectural, Latch, Iron, Thumb, Tulip Shape, 12 In.
$165.00

Architectural, Mantel, Marble, Louis XVI Style, Carved Shell, Pilasters, 50 x 73 In.
$3290.00

Architectural, Teakwood, Carved, Anglo-Indian, 19th Century, 41¾ x 39 In.
$588.00

Architectural, Tub, Oak, Galvanized, Painted, Provincial, Late 19th Century, 28 x 58 x 19 In.
$275.00

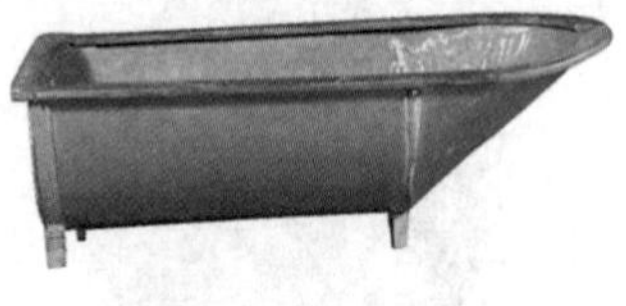

Arequipa Pottery, Bowl, Squeezebag, Trees, Mountains, Clouds, Flared, F. Rhead, 2 ¼ x 6 ¼ In.
$20400.00

Arequipa Pottery, Vase, Green Matte Glaze, Incised Greek Key Design On Shoulder, 4 ¾ x 3 ½ In.
$1440.00

Arita, Bottle, Sake, Flowering Branch, Blue Underglaze, Japan, 19th Century, 16 In.
$441.00

Overmantel Mirror, Gris De Trianon Painted, Louis XVI Style, Pilasters, 70 x 51 In. 1920.00
Overmantel Mirror, Parcel Giltwood, Regency, Painted, Molded Frieze, 31 x 52 In. 3819.00
Overmantel Mirror, Pine, Reverse Painted Tablets, Leaf Swags, 64 x 28 In. 2185.00
Panel, Beechwood, Louis XIV Style, Pendant Flower, Fruit Garlands, 36 x 4 In., Pair 900.00
Panel, Oak, Fretwork, Stick & Ball, c.1900, 30 x 92 In. 531.00
Panel, Oriental, Carved, Animals, Flowers, Multicolored, Red Lacquer 115.00
Panel, Overdoor, Louis XVI Style, Painted White & Blue, Lozenge Shape, 31 x 43 In. 2640.00
Panel, Retablo, Martyrdom Of Saints In Fire, Angel With Water, 1600s, 21 x 16 In. 450.00
Panel, Walnut, Carved, Scrolling Vines, c.1900, 30 x 7 In.. .... 35.00
Panel, Walnut, Wood Carving, Scrolling Acanthus, Relief, Arched Top, Germany, 21 In., Pair. 295.00
Panel, Walnut, Wood Carving, Cherub, Cartouche, Griffin Heads, 10 ½ x 21 ¼ In. 443.00
Panel, Wood, Coromandel, Frame, Chinese, 39 x 13 In. 117.00
Panel, Wood, Watercolor Fresco, Quatrefoil, Multicolored, Continental, 19 x 18 In. 1320.00
Peg Rail, Pine, Green Paint, 9 Hand Hewn Hooks, 4 ½ x 94 In. 173.00
Pilaster, Giltwood, Baroque, Carved, Patinated, Putto Head, Ribbed Scroll 1080.00
Pilaster, Walnut, Mannerist, Carved, Putti, Armorial Shields, 18 x 4 In. 2280.00
Portal, Faux Marble, Parcel Gilt, Molded Cornice, Fluted Pilasters, 47 x 34 In.. .... 431.00
Screen, Oak, Chancel, Late Gothic Style, Crest Rail, Crocket, Heraldic Shield 3600.00
Sink, Conservatory, Wood Frame, Galvanized Metal, England, 35 x 42 In.. .... 1680.00
Sink, Iron, J.W. Fiske Ironworks, New York, c.1855, 35 ½ x 22 In. 1440.00
Tieback, Bronze, Louis XVI Style, Scroll Arms, Acanthus Ends, Marked A.D. 3205, 4 Piece.... 999.00
Tieback, Gilt Bronze, J Shape, Openwork Flowers, Leaves, 9 ½ In., 8 Piece 518.00
Tieback, Gilt Bronze, Swan Shape, Empire Style, Acanthus, 5 x 10 ½ In., 3 Piece 705.00
Tub, Oak, Galvanized, Painted, Provincial, Late 19th Century, 28 x 58 x 19 In. .... *illus* 275.00
Window Fastener, Iron, Double Head, Molding, France, 19th Century, Pair. 250.00

AREQUIPA POTTERY was produced from 1911 to 1918 by the patients of the Arequipa Sanatorium in Marin County, north of San Francisco. The patients were trained by Frederick Hurten Rhead, who had worked at the Roseville Pottery.

Bowl, Green & Brown Mottled Luster Glaze, Incised Quatrefoils, Squat, 3 x 4 In. 1320.00
Bowl, Squeezebag, Trees, Mountains, Clouds, Flared, F. Rhead, 2 ¼ x 6 ¼ In. .... *illus* 20400.00
Vase, Carved Cinquefoils, Dark Green Matte, Marked, 4 ¼ x 6 In. 2400.00
Vase, Floral Band, Blue Gray Frothy Matte Glaze, Stamped, 3 ½ x 3 ¼ In. 960.00
Vase, Frothy Blue & Ivory Matte Glaze, Concave Shoulder, Marked, 1912, 5 x 5 ½ In.. .... 1320.00
Vase, Green Matte Glaze, Incised Greek Key Design On Shoulder, 4 ¾ x 3 ½ In.. .... *illus* 1440.00
Vase, Plum Matte Glaze, Squat Bulbous Organic Shape, Marked, 1912, 2 ¾ x 7 In. 900.00
Vase, Tan & Brown Mottled Semimatte Glaze, Squat, Marked, 3 ¼ x 6 In. 480.00

ARGY-ROUSSEAU, *see G. Argy-Rousseau category.*

ARITA is a port in Japan. Porcelain was made there from about 1616. Many types of decorations were used, including the popular Imari designs, which are listed under Imari in this book.

Bottle, Sake, Flowering Branch, Blue Underglaze, Japan, 19th Century, 16 In. .... *illus* 441.00
Bowl, Blue & White, Man In Boat, Poem On Border, 12 In. 176.00
Bowl, Cover, Orange Flowers In Cartouche, Green Flowers, Blue Ground, Finial, 4 In. 34.00
Charger, Landscape, River, Mountains, Houses, Trees, Blue 275.00
Coffee Set, Man Pulling Woman In Rickshaw, White Ground, Platinum Trim, 17 Piece 125.00
Creamer, Landscape, Black Mountains, Pagoda, Fukagawa 5.00
Tea Set, Silver Gray Dragon Holding Fiery Golden Pearl, 6-In. Teapot, 12 Piece 45.00
Vase, Landscapes, Blue Underglaze, Japan, 18th Century, 11 ¾ In. 294.00

ART DECO, or Art Moderne, a style started at the Paris Exposition of 1925, is characterized by linear, geometric designs. All types of furniture and decorative arts, jewelry, book bindings, and even games were designed in this style. Additional items may be found in the Furniture category or in various glass and pottery categories, etc.

Dresser Jar, Cover, Glass, Circular, Square Base, 7 x 6 ½ In.. .... 58.00
Sculpture, Deer, Wood, Brass, Hagenauer, Austria, 16 x 11 ½ In. 1440.00
Vase, Ceramic, Colorful Glass Face, Italy, 7 ¾ x 4 x 14 ½ In. 240.00
Vase, Landscape Scene, Red, Blue & Yellow, Rich Miller, 10 ¼ In. 180.00

ART GLASS, *see Glass-Art category.*

ART POTTERY *see Pottery-Art*

ARTHUR OSBORNE *plaques are found in the Ivorex category.*

ARTS & CRAFTS was a design style popular in American decorative arts from 1894 to 1923. In the 1970s collectors began to rediscover Mission furniture, art pottery, metalwork, linens, and light fixtures from this period. The interest has continued. Today everything from this era is collectible, including jewelry, graphics, and silverware. Additional items may be found in the Furniture category and other categories.

Jardiniere, Stand, Green Matte Glaze, Bulbous, Scrolled Leaf, Pedestal, 32 x 13 In. 529.00

AURENE glass was made by Frederick Carder of New York about 1904. It is an iridescent gold, blue, green, or red glass, usually marked *Aurene* or *Steuben*. AURENE

Atomizer, Blue, Intaglio Band, Lattice, Flowers, DeVilbiss, 8 ½ In. 920.00
Basket, Blue, Handle, Coiled Prunts, Frilly Ruffled Rim, 12 ½ In. .... *illus* 2242.00
Basket, Blue, Pinched Waist, Loop Handle, Gold Highlights, Signed, 9 In. 1778.00
Basket, Gold, Blue & Purple Highlights, Metal Handle, Flowers, Garland, 9 x 6 In. 1035.00
Basket, Gold, Helmut Shape, Ruffled Edge, Raspberry Prunts, Gold Aurene, 18 In. 4888.00
Basket, Gold, Ruffled Edge, Berry Prunts, 10 x 6 ½ In. 920.00
Bonbon, Gold, Scalloped Rim, 3 Reeded Feet, 5 In. 690.00
Bowl, Blue, Calcite Interior, 9 ¼ In. 403.00
Bowl, Blue, Cobalt Blue Center, Rolled Rim, 4 ½ x 8 In. 805.00
Bowl, Blue, Green, Purple, Ribbed Center, Rolled Rim, Saucer Foot, 12 ½ In. 1150.00
Bowl, Blue, Purple, Cupped Rim, 8 x 4 In. 1610.00
Bowl, Centerpiece, Blue, 9 In. 950.00
Bowl, Centerpiece, Blue Calcite Interior, Low, Rolled Rim, 14 In. 748.00
Bowl, Centerpiece, Gold, Calcite Interior, Pinched Waist, Rolled Rim, 12 In. 518.00
Bowl, Centerpiece, Gold, Red Highlights, 10 ½ In. 546.00
Bowl, Gold, 3-Footed, Tricornered, c.1920, 2 ¼ x 6 In. 179.00
Bowl, Gold, 8 Prunt Flower Holders Around Rim, Signed, 8 ¼ In. 633.00
Bowl, Gold, Blue, Pink, 3-Footed, 8 In. 518.00
Bowl, Gold, Bright Red Highlights, Signed, 8 In. 403.00
Bowl, Gold, Calcite Interior, Rolled Rim, 2 x 10 In. 395.00
Bowl, Gold, Calcite Interior, Oval, Cupped Rim, 7 x 3 ½ In. 200.00
Bowl, Gold, Pinched Rim Forming 8 Bud Vases, Signed, 6 ½ In. 748.00
Bowl, Gold, Pinched Waist, Flared Scalloped Rim, 4 In. 200.00
Bowl, Gold, Purple & Blue Highlights, Scalloped Rim, Signed, 13 In. 2875.00
Bowl, Gold, Red, Blue, Flat Rim, 11 ¼ In. 633.00
Bowl, Gold, Rolled Rim, Waffle Pontil, 4 ¼ x 8 In. 518.00
Candlestick, Blue, Twisted Stem, Spread Foot, Signed, 8 ⅛ In. 588.00
Candlestick, Gold, Blue Highlights, Twisted Stem, Signed, 8 In., Pair 1092.00
Candlestick, Gold, Calcite, Mushroom Shape, Flaring Foot, Rim, 6 ¼ In. 518.00
Candlestick, Gold, Twisted Stem, Signed, 8 In., Pair 1265.00
Compote, Blue, Calcite Interior, Rolled Rim, 6 ¼ In. 633.00
Compote, Blue, Double Banded Ribbing, Signed, 6 ½ In. 2530.00
Compote, Blue, Double Knopped Stem, Twisted Bell Foot, Flared, 7 ¼ In. .... *illus* 1298.00
Compote, Blue, Flared Rim, Signed, 3 ¾ x 8 In. 748.00
Compote, Blue, Twisted Baluster Stem, 4 Cabochons, Stretched Rim, 6 In. 2588.00
Compote, Blue, Twisted Stem, Stretched, Signed, 6 ½ In. 1955.00
Compote, Gold, Calcite Interior, Ribbed, Scalloped Rim, 3 In. 518.00
Compote, Gold, Ruffled Edge, 3 ½ x 5 ½ In. 500.00
Compote, Gold, Twisted Stem, Scalloped Rim, Signed, 7 In. 1495.00
Console Set, Gold, Steuben, 3 x 12-In. Bowl, 5-In. Candlestick, 3 Piece 4200.00
Cordial, Gold, Pinched Waist, 2 ¾ In. 230.00
Cruet, Gold, Gooseneck Spout, 5 In. 1800.00
Cup, Gold, Barrel Shape, 2 x 2 ½ In. 230.00
Cup & Saucer, After Dinner, Blue, Signed, 2 ½ In. 690.00
Decanter, Bulbous, Gold, Pinched Waist, Twist Neck, Teardrop Stopper, 10 ½ In. 3105.00
Dresser Tray, Gold, Applied Handle, 5 ¼ In. 270.00
Finger Bowl, Gold, Underplate, Signed, 6 In. .... *illus* 345.00
Finger Bowl, Underplate, Gold, Flared, Ruffled Edge, Signed, 3 x 5 In. 345.00
Finger Bowl, Underplate, Ribbed, Gold, Calcite Interior, Signed, 6 In. 201.00
Goblet, Gold, Blue, Purple Highlights, 4 ¾ In. 288.00
Goblet, Gold, Magenta Highlights, Coiled Rigaree, Prunts, 5 ⅜ In. .... *illus* 705.00
Goblet, Gold, Twisted Stem, Purple, Blue Highlights, 6 In. 403.00
Nut Dish, Gold, Ruffled Edge, 3 Prunt Feet, Steuben 100.00
Perfume Bottle, Blue, Brass Stopper, 6 In. 510.00
Perfume Bottle, Blue, Footed, Teardrop Stopper, 8 In. 805.00

Aurene, Basket, Blue, Handle, Coiled Prunts, Frilly Ruffled Rim, 12 ½ In.
$2242.00

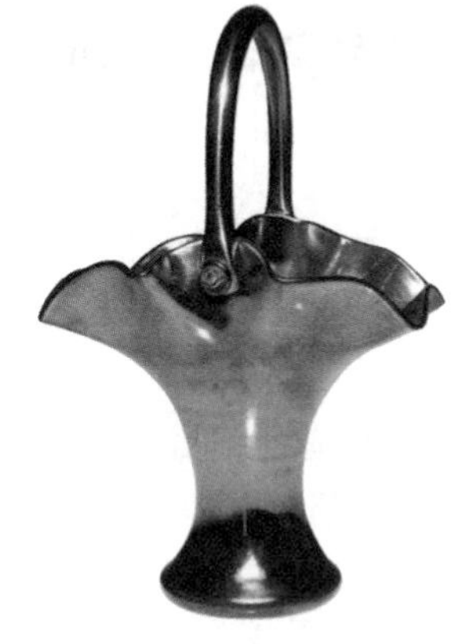

Aurene, Compote, Blue, Double Knopped Stem, Twisted Bell Foot, Flared, 7 ¼ In.
$1298.00

Aurene, Finger Bowl, Gold, Underplate, Signed, 6 In.
$345.00

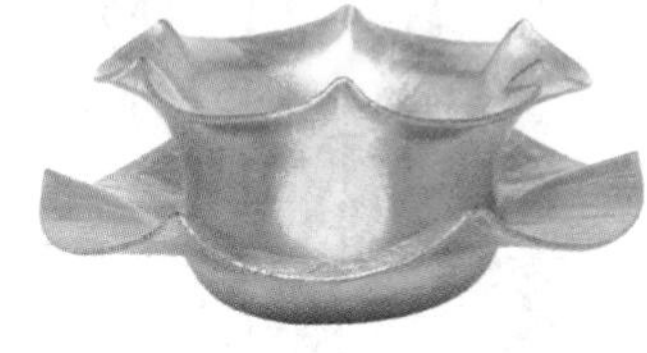

Aurene, Goblet, Gold, Magenta Highlights, Coiled Rigaree, Prunts, 5 ⅜ In.
$705.00

A

Aurene, Salt, Blue Iridescent, Signed, 1 ½ In.
$425.00

Auto, Badge, Radiator, RAC, Chrome Plated, Blue Paint, 5 ½ In.
$66.00

Auto, Bottle, Oil, Embossed, Spout, Carrier, 1920, 10 x 19 x 15 In.
$345.00

Auto, Can, Mobil Freezone, Painted, Tin, Qt.
$40.00

Perfume Bottle, Blue, Intaglio Lattice Band & Foliage, Footed, 10 In. 633.00
Perfume Bottle, Blue, Melon Ribbed, Flame Stopper, 5 ½ In. 660.00
Perfume Bottle, Blue, Urn Shape, Teardrop Stopper, Footed, 7 In. 1265.00
Perfume Bottle, Gold, Dabber, Engraved, 6 ½ In. 960.00
Perfume Bottle, Gold, Stopper, 4 In. 1080.00
Perfume Bottle, Stopper, Signed, 5 ½ In. 1100.00
Potpourri Jar, Gold, Urn Shape, Footed, Domed Cover, 6 ¼ In. 540.00
Ring Tray, Blue, Cupped Rim, Twisted Ring Finial, Signed, 4 In. 748.00
Rose Bowl, Blue, Oval, Scalloped Rim, Pulled Ribs, Signed, 2 ¾ In. 633.00
Salt, Blue Iridescent, Signed, 1 ½ In. .... *illus* 425.00
Salt, Gold, Pedestal Base, Red Highlights, 1 ½ In., Pair 450.00
Shade, Gold, Applied Ribs, Flared Rim, Signed, 4 ½ In., Pair 978.00
Shade, Gold, Pulled Feathers, Lantern Shape, 5 ½ x 5 In. 695.00
Shade, Gold, Ribbed, Scalloped Rim, Signed, 5 ¼ In., 2 Piece 259.00
Shade, Gold, Ribbed, Signed, 5 ½ In., Pair 690.00
Shade, Gold, Scalloped Rim, Signed, 5 ½ In. 489.00
Sherbet, Blue, Signed, 4 In. 345.00
Sherbet, Underplate, Gold, Swirls, 4 ⅜-In. Sherbet 382.00
Shrimp Boat, Gold, Rolled Rim, Central Post, 3-Footed, Signed, 11 In. 2070.00
Sugar & Creamer, Gold, Cabochons, Oval, 4-Footed, 4 In. 1150.00
Sugar & Creamer, Gold, Signed, 2 ½ In. 690.00
Tankard, Gold, Footed, Pontil, c.1905-20, 6 ¼ x 3 ¼ In. 550.00
Tumble-Up, Blue, Oval Pitcher, Applied Handle, Tumbler Cover, 7 In. 1150.00
Urn, Blue, Green, Purple, 3 Coiled Handles, 6 ½ x 7 In. 4140.00
Urn, Gold, Pink, Green, 3 Coiled Handles, Square Shoulder, 6 x 7 In. 3795.00
Vase, Blue, Acid Cut Back, Silver, Flowers, Leaves, Oval 1175.00
Vase, Blue, Dark Blue Foot, Green, Purple Highlights, 11 ¾ In. 1920.00
Vase, Blue, Egg Shape, Coiled Rim, Signed, 5 In. 834.00
Vase, Blue, Platinum Highlights, 10 In. 1610.00
Vase, Blue, Shouldered, Signed, 12 In. .... 1380.00 to 1725.00
Vase, Blue, Silvery Green Highlights, 8 In. 1121.00
Vase, Blue, Tree Trunk, 3-Prong, Signed, 6 In. 1150.00
Vase, Blue, Twisted, 9 ¾ x 7 ¾ In. 3240.00
Vase, Blue, White & Gold Hearts & Vines, 10 ½ x 9 In. 4600.00
Vase, Bud, Gold, Footed, Signed, 8 In. 201.00
Vase, Bud, Gold, Footed, 10 In. 259.00
Vase, Bud, Green & Gold, Ruffled Edge, Signed, 211B, 4 ¾ In. 2100.00
Vase, Fan, Blue, White Applied Heart, Vine, 8 ¾ In. 4600.00
Vase, Fan, Gold, Magenta Highlights, Applied Leaf, Vine, 8 ½ In. 5750.00
Vase, Flower Shape, Blue, Scalloped Rim, Footed, 8 In. 1500.00
Vase, Gold, Bowl, Floral, Coupe, Scalloped Rim, Cascading Bands, 3 x 10 In. 1438.00
Vase, Gold, Bulbous, Shouldered, 10 ¼ x 10 In. 1300.00
Vase, Gold, Egyptian, Bulbous, 2 ½ In. 480.00
Vase, Gold, Fan, Knop Stem, Circular Foot, 8 ½ In. 646.00
Vase, Gold, Flower Shape, Stemmed, Bulbous, Pinched Sides, Quadrafold Rim, 7 In. 978.00
Vase, Gold, Free-Form, Twist Stem, Footed, Ruffled Edge, Signed, 6 ¼ In. 4025.00
Vase, Gold, Oval, Flared Rim, Signed, 3 ½ In. 300.00
Vase, Gold, Pinched Sides, Wide Ruffled Rim, 3 ⅛ In. 240.00
Vase, Gold, Pinched Waist, Flared Scalloped Rim, Signed, 7 In. 662.00
Vase, Gold, Tree Trunk, 3-Prong, 9 In. 400.00
Vase, Gold, Undulating Rim, Double Ribbing, Footed, 6 In. 633.00
Vase, Green Pulled Loops, Gold Border, Brown Pulled Feather, 7 ¼ In. 1725.00
Vase, Jack-In-The-Pulpit, Gold, 6 ½ In. 1150.00
Vase, Stick, Blue, Footed, Signed, c.1910, 8 In. 800.00
Vase, White, Pulled Feathers, Gold, Green, Ruffled Edge, 6 ½ In. 10200.00
Wine, Blue, Signed, 6 In. 1750.00

AUSTRIA *is a collecting term that covers pieces made by a wide variety of factories. They are listed in this book in categories such as Royal Dux or Porcelain.*

AUTO parts and accessories are collectors' items today. Gas pump globes and license plates are part of this specialty. Prices are determined by age, rarity, and condition. Signs and packaging related to automobiles may also be found in the Advertising category. Lalique hood ornaments will be listed in the Lalique category.

Badge, Jaguar, Figural, Racing Car, Green Enamel, 1 ¾ In. 29.00
Badge, Jenney Gasoline & Auto Oils, Cloisonne, Porcelain Insert, 1 ¾ x 2 ¼ In. 1900.00

Badge, Pennzoil, South Penn Oil Co., Bell, Yellow, Red, Black 740.00
Badge, Radiator, RAC, Chrome Plated, Blue Paint, 5 ½ In. . . . . *illus* 66.00
Badge, Sinclair Oil, Five Point Safety Service, Dinosaur, Cloisonne, Porcelain, 1 ¾ x 2 ⅜ In. . . 580.00
Badge, Stag Motor Oil, Deer, Embossed, Inlaid Cloisonne, Enamel, Porcelain. 850.00
Badge, Standard Oil Service, Crown, Red, White, Blue, Cloisonne Inlay. 1150.00
Badge, Union Oil, Service Station Uniform, Inlaid Cloisonne, 1 ¾ x 1 ¾ In. 1200.00
Bottle, Oil, Embossed, Spout, Carrier, 1920, 10 x 19 x 15 In. . . . . *illus* 345.00
Bumper Sign, Police Dept., White Ground, Black Letters, 1950s, 6 ½ x 3 ⅝ In.. . . . . 24.00
Can, Mobil Freezone, Painted, Tin, Qt. . . . . *illus* 40.00
Canister, 8 Bottles, Metal Spouts, Embossed Mobil Oil, 1920s, 10 x 19 x 15 In.. . . . . 345.00
Clock, Round, 8-Day, 20-Size Movement, Waltham Watch Co., Tiffany & Co., Signed. 1435.00
Fob, Magnolia Gasoline, Motor Oil, Red, Blue, Green, White. 420.00
Gas Pump, Flying A, Green, 20 x 72 In. 805.00
Gas Pump, Mobilgas, Pegasus, Red, 25 Cent, 22 x 64 In. 920.00
Gas Pump, Mobilgas, Red, 17 x 72 In. 863.00
Gas Pump, Mobilgas, Red, Blue, 19 x 64 In.. . . . . 690.00
Gas Pump, Mobilgas, Red, Blue, 20 x 63 In.. . . . . 633.00
Gas Pump Globe, Co-Op, Milk Glass, c.1940 . . . . *illus* 250.00
Gas Pump Globe, Dance 92, A Whale Of A Buy, Wide Body, Milk Glass, 1940s, 16 In.. . . . . 316.00
Gas Pump Globe, Dixcel, Milk Glass, Red & Black, 3-Piece 517.00
Gas Pump Globe, Esso, 2 Lenses, Metal Body, 1930s, 16 In.. . . . . 316.00
Gas Pump Globe, Flying A, Milk Glass, 3-Piece, 17 In.. . . . . 805.00
Gas Pump Globe, Frontier, Capco, 1950s, 16 ½ In.. . . . . 690.00
Gas Pump Globe, Frontier Capco, Rarin-To-Go, Red, White, Cowboy On Horse, 1950s 690.00
Gas Pump Globe, Gulf, Orange Globe, 3-Piece, 1950s, 14 ½ In.. . . . . 402.00
Gas Pump Globe, Imperial, Canadian, 3 Red Stars, 3-Piece, 21 In.. . . . . 345.00
Gas Pump Globe, Indian, Red, White & Blue, Milk Glass Body, 3-Piece 575.00
Gas Pump Globe, Kanotex, Bondified, Red, Ripple, 3-Piece, 1940s 747.00
Gas Pump Globe, Kanotex, Bondified, Yellow, Ripple, 3-Piece, 1940s 747.00
Gas Pump Globe, Kanotex, Yellow, Ripple Body, 3-Piece, 1940s. 575.00
Gas Pump Globe, Marathon Mile Maker, Milk Glass, 3-Piece, 1950s, 17 x 7 In.. . . . . 517.00
Gas Pump Globe, Marathon Mile-Maker, Milk Glass, Image Of Runner, 1950s, 17 In. 517.00
Gas Pump Globe, Marathon Super M, 3-Piece, 1950s, 17 ½ In.. . . . . 632.00
Gas Pump Globe, Powermax, Milk Glass, Wide Body, 3-Piece, 1940s, 16 In.. . . . . 345.00
Gas Pump Globe, Red Crown, Wings, Tin, 9 x 2 ½ In. 28.00
Gas Pump Globe, Texaco, Embossed, 1930s, 17½ In. . . . . 972.00 to 1150.00
Gas Pump Globe, Texaco, Screw-On Base, Green T, Red Star, 3-Piece, 1940s 402.00
Gas Pump Globe, Texaco Gasoline, Milk Glass, Aluminum Collar, 1940s, 16 In.. . . . . 575.00
Gas Pump Globe, Tony's Economy Gas & Oil, Bright Red, Black Letter, 1940s, 18 In.. . . . . 402.00
Gas Pump Globe, Tony's Economy Gas & Oil, Red, 1930s, 17 ½ In.. . . . . 402.00
Gas Pump Globe, Vickers, Capco Body, Red & White 316.00
Gas Pump Topper, Phillips 66, Gasoline That Won The West, Indian, Metal, 16 x 15 In. 160.00
Hood Ornament, Eagle Soaring, Bronze, 14 In.. . . . . 410.00
Hood Ornament, Goddess Head, Brass, Gold Patina, 1927 Buick, 3 x 4 In. 910.00
Hood Ornament, Mascot, Policeman, Gesturing, Moustache, Helmet, France 400.00
Hood Ornament, Super Chief, Lights Up, Plastic, Chrome, Box, c.1950 . . . . 470.00
Horn, Brass, Circular, c.1915, 16 In.. . . . . 82.00
License Plate, California, 1915, Porcelain, Yellow, Black Letters, Ing-Rich Mfg. Co. 125.00
License Plate, Indiana, 1968, White, Light Blue Letters 12.00
License Plate, Minnesota, 1949, Minnesota Centennial, Waffled Aluminum 37.50
License Plate, Ohio, 1962, Maroon, White Letters. 19.00
License Plate, Pennsylvania, 1919, Black, Red Letters, Steel 25.00
License Plate, Texas, 1968 . . . . 15.00
License Plate, Texas, 1969 . . . . 17.00
License Plate, Texas, 1970, Blue Numbers, White Ground 15.00
License Plate, Texas, 1971 . . . . 6.00
License Plate, Virginia, 1957, White, Blue Letters 15.00
License Plate, West Virginia, 1973, Orange, Dark Blue Letters, Sticker, 6 x 12 In. 6.00
License Plate Attachment, Harolds Club Or Bust, Covered Wagon, c.1945, 9 x 14 In. 90.00
License Plate Attachment, Kendall's Polly Power, Woman, Car, Metal, 5 x 4 In.. . . . . 120.00
License Plate Attachment, Standard Oil, Research Test Car, Crown, Wings, 5 x 9 In.. . . . . . . 232.00
License Plate Attachment, Tydol, Man, Oil Can, White, Black, Embossed 120.00
License Plate Attachment, Tydol, Man, Oil Can, Yellow, Black, Embossed. 50.00
License Plate Holder, San Francisco Cable Car, Cast Aluminum, 1940, 8 x 16 In.. . . . . 400.00
Map Holder, Service Station, Marathon, Metal, 20 x 11 In. 187.00
Medallion, London Bulldog Society, Bulldog, Red, Silver, Embossed, 3 ¾ In. Diam. 50.00

Road Maps
The first automobile road maps were printed in 1914.

Auto, Gas Pump Globe, Co-Op, Milk Glass, c.1940
$250.00

Auto, Pin, Studebaker, Used The World Over, c.1890, 1 ¼ In.
$133.00

Auto, Pump Plate, Mobilgas Special, Porcelain, 1940s, 13 x 12 In.
$300.00

TIP
Remove small rust spots from old metal with an ink-removing eraser or an old typewriter eraser.

Autumn Leaf, Bowl, Vegetable, 20th Century Shape, 9 In. $118.00

Autumn Leaf, Butter, Cover, Box, 20th Century Shape, Lb., 8¾ In. $225.00

Autumn Leaf, Canister Set, Sugar, Coffee, Tea, Flour, Metal, 4 Piece $175.00

Autumn Leaf, Flour Sifter, Metal, 20th Century Shape, 6¼ In. $225.00

TIP
Don't stack cups. If you must do it, separate the two cups with a piece of paper or felt.

Mileage Route Planner, Shell, Countertop, Plastic, Patina, Yellow, Red . . . 1595.00
Oil Can, Hamilton Beach Motor Oil, Paper Label, 1950s, 4½ In. . . . 25.00
Oil Can, Henley Skate, Stamped Skate Design, 3½ x 2¼ x ½ In. . . . 112.00
Oil Can, Maytag Multi-Motor, Newton, Iowa, Contents, Gal. . . . 44.00
Oil Can, Opaline Motor Oil, Sinclair Refining Co., Race Car Lotto, 8 x 11 In. . . . 920.00
Pin, Now A Cadillac For Only $1345, Red, White, Celluloid, ⅞ In. . . . 17.00
Pin, Studebaker, Used The World Over, c.1890, 1¼ In. . . . *illus* 133.00
Pump Plate, Metro, Green, Red, White Ground, Metal, c.1940 . . . 66.00
Pump Plate, Mobilgas Special, Porcelain, 1940s, 13 x 12 In. . . . *illus* 300.00
Pump Plate, Texaco Diesel Chief, Multicolored, c.1945, 12 x 18 In. . . . 364.00
Pump Plate, Texaco Fire Chief Gasoline, Porcelain, c.1954, 12 x 18 In. . . . 280.00
Radio, Champion Spark Plug, Medallion, 1950s, 14½ In. . . . 185.00
Sign, Auburn Tire, Tin, 17½ x 60 In. . . . 385.00
Sign, Conoco, Porcelain, Die Cut, Green, White, 1940-1950s . . . 112.00
Sign, Englebert Racing Tires, Frame, 1950s, 24 x 20 In. . . . 187.00
Sign, Fire Chief Gasoline, Texaco, White, Red Hat, Porcelain, 1957 . . . 100.00
Sign, Firestone, 1947, 72 In. . . . 185.00
Sign, Goodyear Service Station, Porcelain, c.1920, 24 x 48 In. . . . 575.00
Sign, Gulf Dealer, Station Sign, Porcelain Enamel, 2-Sided, 65½ In. . . . 330.00
Sign, Gulf Oil, Wooden, Graphic, Service Station Attendant, 47½ x 19 In. . . . 1925.00
Sign, Hood Tire Dealer, 2-Sided, Die Cut, Tin, 11½ x 35 In. . . . 24000.00
Sign, Indian Gasoline, Blue, Green, Yellow, Red, White . . . 230.00
Sign, Indian Gasoline, Porcelain Enamel, Curved For Pump, 18 x 10½ In. . . . 165.00
Sign, Kelly Tires, Tin, 2-Sided, Bracket, 1920s, 24 In. Diam. . . . 31200.00
Sign, Kendall Motor Oil, Lollipop, Painted, 47 x 24½ In. . . . 385.00
Sign, Kerosene, Standard Oil Of N.Y., Elephant, Porcelain, 2-Sided, c.1920 . . . 1550.00
Sign, Mobilgas, Flying Red Horse, Shield Form, Porcelain, 13 x 12½ In. . . . 100.00
Sign, Mobiloil, Gargoyle, Porcelain Enamel, 2-Sided, Flange, 16 x 24 In. . . . 193.00
Sign, Mobiloil, Gargoyle, White Ground, Porcelain, 30 x 22 In. . . . 258.00
Sign, Mobiloil, Gargoyle, Arctic, Make The Chart Your Guide, Lubester, Porcelain . . . 440.00
Sign, Sinclair Motor Oil, Porcelain, Trademark Dinosaur, Grommet Holes, 11 In. . . . 825.00
Sign, Standard Oil, Mica Axle Grease, Blue, White, Embossed, 4½ x 19½ In. . . . 275.00
Sign, Standard Polarine Motor Oil, Porcelain Enamel, 2-Sided, Round, 30 In. . . . 220.00
Sign, Texaco Golden Motor Oil, Porcelain Enamel, Flanged, 23 x 18 In. . . . 1155.00
Sign, Texaco Motor Oil, Lubester, Star, T, Red, White . . . 198.00
Sign, Texaco Motor Oil, Stays Full Longer, Porcelain, 1937, 18 x 30 In. . . . 1450.00
Sign, Texaco Oil, Whale Lease, Porcelain, 24 x 36 In. . . . 220.00
Sign, United Motors, Porcelain, Oval, 2-Sided, c.1935, 21 x 36 In. . . . 1955.00
Sign, United Motors Service, Porcelain, Orange Ground, Black Letters, Oval, 2-Sided. . . . 780.00
Sign, Valvoline Racing Oil, Tin, Street Bracket, Original Box, 29½ In. . . . 330.00
Sign, Wesley's Carbon Remover For Automobiles, Car, Red, White, Tin, 5 x 10 In. . . . 196.00
Sign, White Star Gasoline Staroleum, Blue, White, Porcelain, Round, 30 In. . . . 396.00
Toy, Football, Sunoco Gasoline, Black, Multicolored Graphics, Arrow Sign, Embossed . . . 20.00
Traffic Light, Hanging, 1960s . . . 149.00
Watch & Fob, Golden Shell Oil, Lubricated, Cloisonne, 1⅝-In. Watch, 1¼-In. Fob . . . 715.00

AUTUMN LEAF pattern china was made for the Jewel Tea Company beginning in 1933. Hall China Company of East Liverpool, Ohio, Crooksville China Company of Crooksville, Ohio, Harker Potteries of Chester, West Virginia, and Paden City Pottery, Paden City, West Virginia, made dishes with this design. Autumn Leaf has remained popular and was made by Hall China Company until 1978. Some other pieces in the Autumn Leaf pattern are still being made. For more information, see *Kovels' Depression Glass & Dinnerware Price List.*

Baker, French, 3 Pt. . . . 25.00
Bean Pot, Lid, Handle, 20th Century Shape, 2¼ Qt. . . . 224.00
Bean Pot, Lid, Handle, 2¼ Qt., 6¼ In. . . . 130.00
Bowl, Cereal, 6½ In. . . . 10.00
Bowl, Cover, Plastic, 8 Piece . . . 71.00
Bowl, Fruit, 5½ In. . . . 7.00
Bowl, Salad, 9 In. . . . 17.00
Bowl, Vegetable, 20th Century Shape, 9 In. . . . *illus* 118.00
Butter, Cover, ¼ Lb. . . . 165.00
Butter, Cover, Box, 20th Century Shape, Lb., 8¾ In. . . . *illus* 225.00
Butter, Cover, Zephyr Shape, Lb. . . . 266.00
Butter, Wings, ¼ Lb. . . . 1600.00
Cake Plate, 9½ In. . . . 19.00 to 60.00

Cake Plate, Footed, Metal Base, 9 ¼ In. 130.00
Canister Set, Sugar, Coffee, Tea, Flour, Metal, 4 Piece .... *illus* 175.00
Coffeepot, Electric, 8 Cup 250.00
Coffeepot, Metal Dripper, 8 Cup 62.00
Condiment Set 55.00
Cookie Jar, Roll Handles, Eva Zeisel, 8¾ In. .... 142.00 to 155.00
Cup & Saucer 30.00
Dish, Souffle, 7 ¾ In. 25.00
Flour Sifter, Metal, 20th Century Shape, 6 ¼ In. .... *illus* 225.00
Jar, Drip, Cover 19.00
Jug, Ball .... 30.00 to 40.00
Mixing Bowl, 6 In. 12.00
Mixing Bowl, 9 In. 50.00
Mixing Bowl, Nesting, 3 Piece 90.00
Oyster Cup, 20th Century Shape, 2 In. 325.00
Percolator, Electric, 20th Century Shape, 11 ½ In. 225.00
Pitcher, Beer, 80 Oz. 100.00
Pitcher, Jug, Rayed, 2 ½ Pt. 16.00
Plate, Bread & Butter, 6 In. 5.00
Plate, Luncheon, 9 In. 16.00
Salt & Pepper, Handle .... 34.00 to 40.00
Salt & Pepper, Medallion, Scalloped Base 25.00
Saltshaker, Scalloped Edge 8.00
Soup, Cream 60.00
Stack Set, 2 Piece 55.00
Tea Set, Teapot, Underplates, Sugar, Creamer, 5 Piece 106.00
Teapot, Automobile Form, 20th Century Shape, 9 In. .... *illus* 225.00
Teapot, Newport, Reissued, Box, 1978, 7 ½ In. .... *illus* 100.00
Tray, 19 x 11 In. 120.00
Tumbler, 5 ½ In., 6 Piece 120.00
Vase, Bud, Scalloped Rim, 20th Century Shape, 5 ¾ In. 236.00
Warmer, Oval, 3 ½ In. 130.00

AVON *bottles are listed in the Bottle category under Avon.*

AZALEA dinnerware was made for Larkin Company customers from 1918 to 1941. Larkin, the soap company, was in Buffalo, New York. The dishes were made by Noritake China Company of Japan. Each piece of the white china was decorated with pink azaleas.

Berry Bowl, Green M In Wreath Mark, 5 ½ In., Pair 15.00
Butter Chip, c.1933 .... 69.00
Casserole, Cover, Handles, 10 In. 50.00
Creamer, 3 ½ In. .... *illus* 55.00
Nappy, 5 ½ In. 15.00
Plate, Bread & Butter, 6 ¼ In. 9.00
Plate, Dinner, 9 ¾ In. 20.00
Plate, Salad, Green M In Wreath Mark, 7 ½ In., 6 Piece 25.00
Vase, Bud, Fan Shape, Footed, 5 ½ In. 250.00

BACCARAT glass was made in France by La Compagnie des Cristalleries de Baccarat, located 150 miles from Paris. The factory was started in 1765. The firm went bankrupt and began operating again about 1822. Cane and millefiori paperweights were made during the 1845 to 1880 period. The firm is still working near Paris making paperweights and glasswares.

Bowl, Etched Rose, Geometric Design, 8 In. 323.00
Champagne, Genova Pattern, Pair 940.00
Cordial, Silver, Gold Intaglio, Cloverleaf Shape, 4 ¾ In. 100.00
Decanter, Green Cut To Clear, Stopper, 1950s, 15 In. 125.00
Decanter, Red Cut To Clear, Oval Body Panels, Red Stripes, Petal Foot, Stopper, 13 x 5 In. 118.00
Decanter, Remy Martin, 10 In. 88.00
Decanter, Snowflake, Amethyst, Cut To Clear, Steeple Shape, 13 ¼ In. 500.00
Decanter, Whirling Rib, Clear, Stopper, 9 In. 70.00
Figurine, Elephant, Hand Cooler, Clear, 3 In. 94.00
Figurine, Frog, Clear, 4 ½ In. 176.00
Figurine, Polar Bear, Clear, 6 ½ In. 294.00
Figurine, Polar Bear, Clear, Signed, 4 x 6 In. 205.00
Figurine, Porcupine, Clear, 5 In. 147.00

Autumn Leaf, Teapot, Automobile Form, 20th Century Shape, 9 In.
$225.00

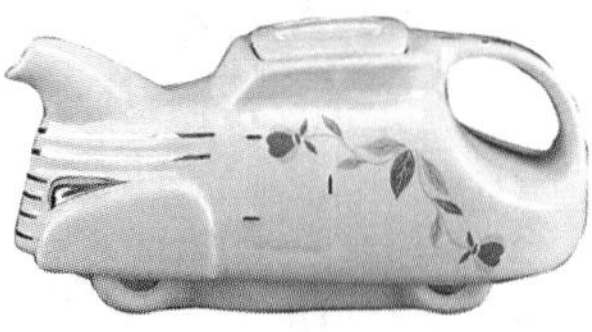

Autumn Leaf, Teapot, Newport, Reissued, Box, 1978, 7 ½ In.
$100.00

Collecting Is Green

Collectors are environmentally friendly. They rescue old pieces that would end up in a landfill. They reuse materials if they're packing and shipping, and they save energy because they often buy at shows, shops, and flea markets where no shipping is necessary. Their homes have better air quality, because old wooden pieces do not emit fumes from new paint or waxes. Next time someone asks why you collect old things, tell them you are saving the environment. Don't mention the gas you used getting to the flea market.

Azalea, Creamer, 3 ½ In.
$55.00

Baccarat, Paperweight, Millefiori, Butterfly, 2 15/16 In.
$7500.00

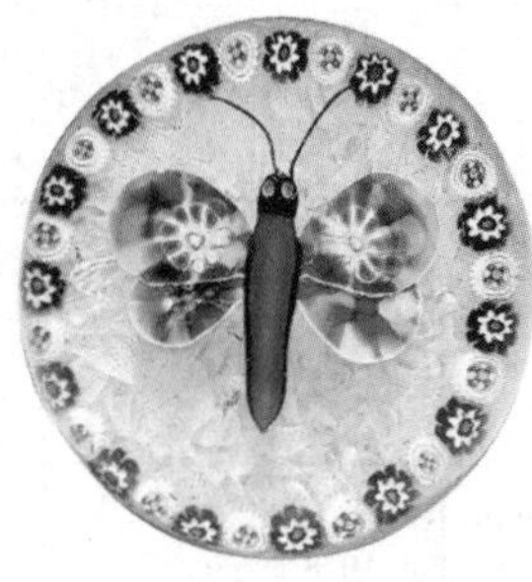

Baccarat, Paperweight, Millefiori, Garlands, Trefoil, Upset Muslin, 3 1/16 In.
$3000.00

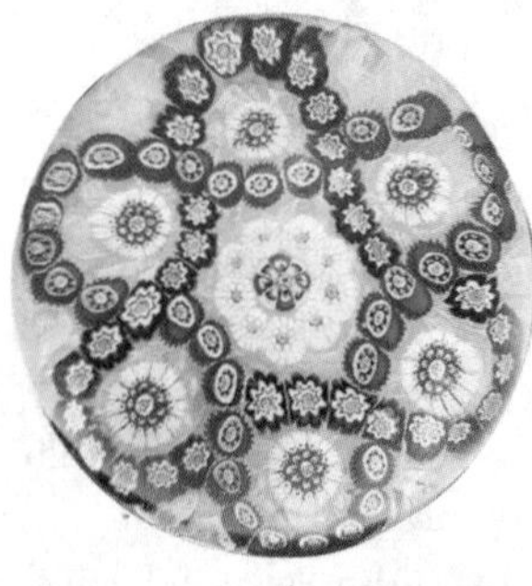

Baccarat, Paperweight, Millefiori, Rose Cane, Close Packed, 2 11/16 In.
$1300.00

Baccarat, Paperweight, Sulphide, Joan Of Arc, Maid Of Orleans, Faceted, 3 1/2 In.
$600.00

Goblet, Cloverleaf Shape, Gold Intaglio Birds, Flower Scrolls, Faceted Stem, 5 In., 4 Piece ... 750.00
Goblet, Water, George V Pattern, Hotel Size, 8 Piece ... 323.00
Obelisk, Clear, Signed, 9 7/8 In. ... 374.00
Orb, Clear, Metal Ring Base, 4 1/4 In. ... 94.00
Paperweight, 6 Faceted Sides, White Bull Center, Blue Ground, Box, 2 1/2 x 1 1/2 x 1 1/2 In. ... 112.00
Paperweight, Bonsai Tree, Red Ground, Signed, 1987, 3 1/4 In. ... 405.00
Paperweight, Clematis, Central Whorl, Star Cane, 2 1/8 x 2 7/8 In. ... 715.00
Paperweight, Faceted, Muslin Ground, Buttercup, 19th Century, 2 7/8 In. ... 2900.00
Paperweight, Flower Chains, Medallion, Concave Base, Red Overlay, Star Cut, 3 In. ... 3500.00
Paperweight, Frog, Green, In Pond, Signed, 1974, 3 In. ... 550.00
Paperweight, Leopard Head, Clear, 4 1/2 In. ... 200.00
Paperweight, Lincoln, Cameo Bust, Blue Base, Franklin Mint, 1977, 1 3/4 x 2 3/4 In. ... 60.00
Paperweight, Millefiori, Animal Canes, Multicolored, White Star Ground, 1848, 3 1/8 In. ... 15800.00
Paperweight, Millefiori, Butterfly, 2 15/16 In. ... *illus* 7500.00
Paperweight, Millefiori, Butterfly, Garland, Blue, Red, White Star Canes, Star Cut, 2 3/8 In. ... 2200.00
Paperweight, Millefiori, Concentric Red, Green, White Arrowhead, 4 Rings, 2 9/16 In. ... 600.00
Paperweight, Millefiori, Deer, Gridel, Silhouette, Signed, 1976, 3 1/4 In. ... 660.00
Paperweight, Millefiori, Garlands, Trefoil, Upset Muslin, 3 1/16 In. ... *illus* 3000.00
Paperweight, Millefiori, Gridel Animal Canes, Scattered, White Upset Muslin, 3 3/16 In. ... 2985.00
Paperweight, Millefiori, Latticinio, Animal Canes, Cane, B, 1848, 2 7/8 In. ... 3150.00
Paperweight, Millefiori, Rose Cane, Close Packed, 2 11/16 In. ... *illus* 1300.00
Paperweight, Millefiori, Scattered, White Upset Muslin, Signed, 1970, 2 15/16 In. ... 605.00
Paperweight, Millefiori, Silhouette Canes, Rooster, Crane, Kangaroo, 1980s, 2 7/8 In. ... 1980.00
Paperweight, Millefiori, Squirrel, Gridel, Silhouette, Concentric, Signed, 1972, 3 1/8 In. ... 495.00
Paperweight, Millefiori, Stars, Animal Canes, Signature Cane, B 1848, 2 3/4 In. ... 3300.00
Paperweight, Millefiori, Stars, Flowers, Signature Cane, B 1847, 3 1/8 In. ... 3900.00
Paperweight, Millefiori, Stars, Arrowheads, Bull's-Eyes, Cogs, Rods, Trefoils, 1 3/4 In. ... 1760.00
Paperweight, Millefiori, Zodiac Canes, Scattered, Yellow Carpet Ground, 1971, 3 In. ... 770.00
Paperweight, Pansy, 19th Century, 2 5/8 In. ... 667.00
Paperweight, Pansy, Purple, Yellow Leaves, Central Whorl, Star Cane, 1 1/2 x 2 1/2 In. ... 605.00
Paperweight, Red & White Primrose, Green Leaves, Star Cut, Faceted, 2 7/8 In. ... 1100.00
Paperweight, Sulphide, Adlai Stevenson, Purple Overlay, Faceted, 1969, 3 1/8 In. ... 355.00
Paperweight, Sulphide, Joan Of Arc, Maid Of Orleans, Faceted, 3 1/2 In. ... *illus* 600.00
Perfume, Bottle, Art Deco, Blue, 3 1/2 x 5 In., Pair ... 235.00
Punch Bowl, Crystal, Bronze, Gold D'Or Maht, c.1860, 17 In. ... 5288.00
Vase, Smokey, Etched, Gold Swallows, Bronze Mount, 9 In., Pair ... 3525.00
Vase, Wisteria, Vines, Cameo, Signed, 13 3/8 In. ... *illus* 1800.00

BADGES have been used since before the Civil War. Collectors search for examples of all types, including law enforcement and company identification badges. Well-known prison or law enforcement badges are most desirable. Most are made of nickel or brass. Many recent reproductions have been made.

AAA Safety Patrol, Massapequa, N.Y., 1960s, 3/4 In. ... 7.00
Baggage, United States Lines, 2 x 2 7/8 In. ... 51.00
Cap, Cycle Touring Club, Sterling Silver, 1894, 1 1/4 In. ... 198.00
Chauffeur, Indiana, 1941, 1 1/4 x 1 In. ... 16.00
Chauffeur, Kansas, Brass, 1949 ... 48.00
Chauffeur, Michigan, 1939, 1 3/8 x 1 3/8 In. ... 16.00
Chauffeur, Missouri, Truck Drivers, Aluminum, Brass Pin, 1941 ... 25.00
Chauffeur, Ohio, 1940s ... 24.00
Commemorative, Russian Boctok Space Flight, April 12th, 1961 ... 32.00
Co-Operative Bus Co., Hatpin, 2 1/4 In. ... 35.00
Employee, Reddy Kilowatt, Arms Outstretched, Blank Area For Name ... 35.00
Employee, Rexall Drugs, Dark Blue, Logo, Tin, Oval, 3 In. ... 20.00
Fat Stock Show & Rodeo, Ft. Worth, Texas, Gold Ribbon ... 250.00
Firefighting, 1 N.Y.F.D./3/Reel Cart, Plated, Number 3 Is In Brass, 1 1/2 In. ... 1680.00
Firefighting, 1 N.Y.F.D./55 Hand Pumper, Brass, Number 55 Is Nickel Plate, 2 1/2 In. ... 505.00
Firefighting, 6 Marine Engineer/Fire Dept New York, Nickel Plated, 2 In. ... 1065.00
Firefighting, Brooklyn Fire Department, No. 290, Nickel Plated, Brass, 2 1/2 In. ... *illus* 1600.00
Firefighting, Fire Patrol, 2-Horse Team Fire Wagon, Fireman Inside, 225, Oval, 2 3/4 In. ... 365.00
Firefighting, Gravesend, Exempt, Volunteer Fireman Assoc., 193, Metal, 2 1/2 In. ... *illus* 600.00
Firefighting, Pilot, Fire Boat, Plated Metal, 2 3/8 x 3 1/8 In. ... 336.00
Firefighting, Rochester Fire Dept, Pa., Stainless Front, Silver Accents, 2 1/2 In. ... 45.00
Fireman, Fabric Fire Hose Co., Hose Around Dog's Head, White Metal, Brass Plated, 1 3/4 In. ... 78.00
Fireman, Housewatchman, Oval, Nickel Plated, 2 x 3 In. ... 34.00 to 45.00

Fireman, New York Fire Department, Brass, Nickel Plated, 2 ¼ In. 3360.00
Fireman, New York Fire Department, Theater Detail, Banner, Metal Plated, 2 ½ In.. .... 134.00
Fireman, Patrol, White Metal, 2 In. 235.00
Hat, British Airlines, Captain, 2 ½ x 2 ½ In. 76.00
Imperial German Crown, Stickpin & Star, Breast, Gold Tone, Berlin, 1 ¼ x 2 ½ In. 165.00
Pinkerton Special Service, Shield, Eagle, New York, 1940s, 3 x 2 In. 55.00
RAF Royal Air Force Cap, Brass, 1 ½ x 1 ⅞ In. 19.00
Sorority, Alpha Gamma Delta, Ohio University, 1936 .... 135.00
St. Louis National Stock Yards, Brass, Purple Ribbon, 1904 .... 165.00
Stewardess Wings, Pan Am Junior Clipper, 2 ¼ In. 12.00
Stock Show, 26th Annual Convention, The Manson, Star Center, Brass, Enamel, 5 In. 150.00
Uniform, Char. H. Sixeas Motor Transit, Mercersburg, Back Patch, 8 x 13 In.. .... 18.00
Union Oil Co., Inlaid Cloisonne, 1 ¾ x 1 ¾ In. 1200.00
Visitor, Mennen Company, Green & White, Copyright 1893, 2 ¼ x 1 ¼ In. 20.00

BANKS of metal have been made since 1868. There are still banks, mechanical banks, and registering banks (those that show the total money deposited on the face of the bank). Many old iron or tin banks have been reproduced since the 1950s in iron or plastic. Some old reproductions marked *Book of Knowledge, John Wright*, or *Capron* are listed. Pottery, glass, and plastic banks are also listed here. Mickey Mouse and other Disneyana banks are listed in Disneyana. We have added the M numbers based on *The Penny Bank Book: Collecting Still Banks* by Andy and Susan Moore and the R numbers based on *Coin Banks by Banthrico* by James L. Redwine.

2-Faced Devil, Red, Iron, A.C. Williams, c.1906, 4 ¼ In. 975.00
3 Wise Monkeys, Cast Iron, Gold Paint, 3 ¼ x 3 ⅝ In. .... *illus* 310.00
Aunt Jemima, No. 168 .... 185.00
Aunt Jemima, Spoon, 5 ⅞ In. 460.00
Baseball, Boston Red Sox, Plastic, Facsimile Autographs, Mark, Fellsway, c.1956, 3 ¼ In. 125.00
Bear Stealing Pig, Cast Iron, Gold Paint, 5 In. .... *illus* 415.00
Birdhouse, Cast Iron, 6 ½ In. 115.00
Book, Brass, 4 ½ x 3 x 1 In. 70.00
Boy Scout, Buckle, Scarf, Cast Iron, Painted, Hubley, c.1912, M 47, 5 ¾ In. .... *illus* 439.00
Bugs Bunny At Tree Trunk, White Metal, Moss, Late 1930s, M 278, 5 ½ x 5 ¾ In.. .... 41.00
Building, Hall's Excelsior, Cast Iron, Painted, White, Red Corners, 5 x 4 In. 173.00
Carnival Glass, Liberty Bell, 4 In.. .... 28.00
Cat, Yellow, Blue, Papier-Mache, Marked, Japan, 4 x 9 ¼ In. 55.00
Chest Of Drawers, c.1890, 6 ½ In. 201.00
City Bank With Chimney, Cast Iron, Thomas Swan, M 1101, 6 ¾ x 4 ¾ x 4 ¾ In. 1170.00
City Bank With Teller, Cast Iron, H.L. Judd, 5 ½ x 3 ¼ x 4 ⅜ In. 1380.00
Clown, Tin Plate, Chein, 5 In. 44.00
Cry Baby, Porcelain, Painted, Stamped, 7696-64, 4 x 3 In. 60.00
Cupola, Bank, Cast Iron, Green, Red, J. & E. Stevens, 3 ¼ x 2 ⅝ x 2 ¼ In.. .... 110.00
Dog, Fido, Cast Iron, Hubley, 5 In. 225.00
Dog At Barrel, Glass, L.E. Smith Co., M 318, 3 In.. .... 59.00
Donkey, Sharecropper, Cast Iron, A.C. Williams, Early 1900s, M 173, 5½ In. .... 201.00 to 230.00
Dutch Boy, Porcelain, Lid, c.1950, 8 ¼ In. 104.00
Edward VII Railway Saloon Car, Tin, England, c.1905, M 1475, 4 ½ x 6 ½ In.. .... 1053.00
Eiffel Tower, Cast Iron, Painted, England .... *illus* 1755.00
Elephant, Jumbo, Mrs. Simms Lucky Jumbo Flavored Syrup, Strawberry, Glass 40.00
Elmer Elephant, Movable Trunk, Bisque, Japan, 1930s, 5 In. 250.00
Fort Mt. Hope, Cast Iron, U.S., M 1189, 2 ⅞ x 2 ¾ In. 702.00
Foxy Grandpa, Cast Iron, 5 ¼ In. 173.00
Galloping Cowboy, Tin, Battery Operated, 6 ⅝ x 7 ⅝ In. 1320.00
Gingerbread House, Cast Iron, France, M 1029, 3 ⅞ x 4 ¼ x 3 In. 995.00
Give Me A Penny, Cast Iron, Screw, 5 ½ In. 403.00
Give Me A Penny, Cast Iron, Turnpin, c.1894, M 167, 5 ⅝ In.. .... 259.00
Globe On Arch, Cast Iron, Grey Iron Casting, c.1905, 5 ½ In. 259.00
Hershey Bar, Vending Machine, 24 Bars, Tin, Plastic, Box, c.1950, 6 x 4 x 4 In. .... *illus* 221.00
House, 2-Story, Cast Iron, Gold, Blue Roof, 3 ⅛ x 2 ¼ x 1 ⅞ In.. .... 110.00
Hunchback, Hand In Mouth, Japanned, Lock On Base, Cast Iron, Ives, 3 In. 2875.00
I Made Chicago Famous, Cast Iron, J.M. Harper, 1902, M 629, 4 ⅛ In.. .... 460.00
Independence Hall Tower, Cast Iron, Enterprise, c.1876, 9 ½ x 3 ⅞ In.. .... 920.00
Indiana Silo, Cast Iron, U.S., M 1247, 3 ½ x 2 In. 1053.00
Jack In The Box, Tin Lithograph, Cragstan, Box, 4 ⅝ In. 495.00
Jug, Fieldman Pottstown Store, Die Cut, 4 ½ In.. .... 316.00
Jug, Pottery, Red, Gold Highlights, 4 ½ In. 44.00

Baccarat, Vase, Wisteria, Vines, Cameo, Signed, 13 ⅜ In.
$1800.00

Badge, Firefighting, Brooklyn Fire Department, No. 290, Nickel Plated, Brass, 2 ½ In.
$1600.00

Badge, Firefighting, Gravesend, Exempt, Volunteer Fireman Assoc., 193, Metal, 2 ½ In.
$600.00

Bank, 3 Wise Monkeys, Cast Iron, Gold Paint, 3¼ x 3⅝ In.
$310.00

Bank, Bear Stealing Pig, Cast Iron, Gold Paint, 5 In.
$415.00

Bank, Boy Scout, Buckle, Scarf, Cast Iron, Painted, Hubley, c.1912, M 47, 5¾ In.
$439.00

Bank, Eiffel Tower, Cast Iron, Painted, England
$1755.00

Bank, Hershey Bar, Vending Machine, 24 Bars, Tin, Plastic, Box, c.1950, 6 x 4 x 4 In.
$221.00

Jug, Stoneware, Blue Sponge, Brown Glaze Drip, 4 In. . . . 440.00

Jukebox, Tin, Windup, Haji, Box, 4⅝ x 3⅞ In. . . . 143.00

Kanter's Baby Bell Telephone, Tin, Kanter, 10 In. . . . 288.00

Key, Cast Iron, 7¾ In. . . . 460.00

Lichfield Cathedral, Cast Iron, England, M 968, 6½ x 2 3/16 x 3½ In. . . . *illus* 556.00

Lion, Tail To Right, Cast Iron, Gold Paint, A.C. Williams, 5⅜ x 6½ In. . . . 33.00

Log Cabin, Pottery, Yellow Clay, Unglazed, Painted, Houghton, 6 x 5 In. . . . 2185.00

Main Street Trolley, Cast Iron, A.C. Williams, 1920s, M 1469, 3 x 6¾ x 1¾ In. . . . 293.00

Mammy, Hands On Hips, Cast Iron, Painted, Hubley, M 176, 5¼ In. . . . 44.00 to 293.00

Man In Barrel, Arms, Cast Iron, J. & E. Stevens, 1890s, M 282, 3½ x 3½ x 3 In. . . . 625.00 to 700.00

Marshall Stove, Cast Iron, U.S., M 1362, 3⅞ x 2⅞ In. . . . 187.00

Mechanical banks were first made about 1870. Any bank with moving parts is considered mechanical. The metal banks made before World War I are the most desirable. Copies and new designs of mechanical banks have been made in metal or plastic since the 1920s. The condition of the paint on the old banks is important. Worn paint can lower a price by 90 percent. Several major collections of mechanical banks were sold this year and we have included some of the higher prices here. These are for very rare banks in very fine condition.

Mechanical, 2 Penny, Brown Lithograph, Germany, c.1900 . . . 1170.00

Mechanical, Acrobat, Lever, Painted, J. & E. Stevens, Pat. 1883 . . . *illus* 2800.00

Mechanical, Afghanistan, Russian Bear, British Lion At Gate Of Heart, c.1885 . . . 18720.00

Mechanical, Artillery, Soldier, Red Tunic, Cast Iron, J. & E. Stevens, 1882, 8 In. . . . 275.00

Mechanical, Artillery Bank, Confederate, J. & E. Stevens, c.1900, 5¾ In. . . . 395.00 to 1315.00

Mechanical, Atlas Bank, Key, Cast Iron Base, Paper Covered Wood Globe, 1890s . . . 48900.00

Mechanical, Automatic Savings, Strong Man, Sailor, Tin, Saalheimer & Strauss, 1920s . . . 28750.00

Mechanical, Bad Accident, Donkey, Cart, Driver, J. & E. Stevens, c.1891, 6 In. . . . 1434.00 to 2070.00

Mechanical, Bill E. Grin, Sticks Out Tongue, Painted, Cast Iron, J. & E. Stevens, 1915 . . . 1495.00

Mechanical, Billy Goat, Painted, J. & E. Stevens, c.1900 . . . *illus* 15210.00

Mechanical, Bird On Roof, Deposits Coin In Chimney, Cast Iron, J. & E. Stevens, 1878 . . . 1955.00

Mechanical, Boy On Trapeze, Blue Pants, J. Barton Smith, c.1888 . . . *illus* 8775.00

Mechanical, Boy Robbing Bird's Nest, J. & E. Stevens, c.1906, 7¼ In. . . . 6395.00 to 11353.00

Mechanical, Boy Scout Camp, Scout Raises Flag, J. & E. Stevens, c.1917, 5¾ In. . . . 4183.00 to 6325.00

Mechanical, Boys Stealing Watermelons, Kyser & Rex, c.1894, 4¼ In. . . . 2868.00 to 8775.00

Mechanical, Bulldog, Pull Tail, Cast Iron, J. & E. Stevens, c.1880, 7¼ In. . . . 460.00 to 1016.00

Mechanical, Bureau, Serrill Patent, c.1870 . . . 644.00

Mechanical, Butting Buffalo, Raccoon, Boy, Kyser & Rex, c.1888, 6 In. . . . 5558.00 to 5975.00

Mechanical, Cabin, Pull Handle Of Tool By Door, c.1885, 3¼ In. . . . 359.00

Mechanical, Calamity, Cast Iron, J. & E. Stevens, Box, c.1905 . . . 69000.00

Mechanical, Chief Big Moon, J. & E. Stevens, c.1899, 5¾ In. . . . 1912.00

Mechanical, Chimpanzee, Monkey Lowers Arm & Head, Kyser & Rex, 1880 Patent, 5 In. . . . 837.00

Mechanical, Chinaman, In Boat, Lead, Multicolored, Charles A. Bailey, 1880s . . . 103500.00

Mechanical, Circus, Cast Iron, Shepard Hardware, c.1888, 7¾ x 7 In. . . . 8775.00

Mechanical, Clown, Harlequin & Columbine, Cast Iron, J. & E. Stevens, c.1907 . . . 103500.00

Mechanical, Clown, Harlequin & Columbine, Second Casting, c.1950 . . . 9360.00

Mechanical, Clown On Globe, Cast Iron, J. & E. Stevens, c.1890, 8¾ In. . . . 1793.00 to 4313.00

Mechanical, Clown, Cart, Pony, Cast Iron, Shepard Hardware, c.1888, 7¾ x 7 In. . . . 115000.00

Mechanical, Coin Registering Painted, Kyser & Rex, c.1890 . . . 8050.00

Mechanical, Confectionery, Woman Gives Candy, Kyser & Rex, c.1881, 7 In. . . . 7768.00 to 15210.00

Mechanical, Creedmoor, Cast Iron, Painted, J. & E. Stevens, 1877 Patent . . . *illus* 1500.00

Mechanical, Cross-Legged Minstrel, Germany, c.1909 . . . 3042.00

Mechanical, Dapper Dan, Tin Lithograph, Louis Marx & Co., 1910 Patent . . . 2875.00

Mechanical, Darktown, Baseball Players, Cast Iron, 1875 . . . 2115.00

Mechanical, Darktown Battery, Cast Iron, Painted, J. & E. Stevens, 1888 Patent . . . 7475.00 to 13145.00

Mechanical, Darky & Watermelon, Football, Cast Iron, J. & E. Stevens, c.1888 . . . 195500.00

Mechanical, Darky Fisherman, Lead, Charles A. Bailey, 1800s . . . 287500.00

Mechanical, Dentist, Cast Iron, J. & E. Stevens, 1880s . . . 40250.00

Mechanical, Dinah, Long Sleeves, Cast Iron, John Harper, c.1911, 6¼ In. . . . 598.00

Mechanical, Dinah, Short Sleeves, Cast Iron, John Harper, c.1822 . . . 316.00 to 805.00

Mechanical, Ding Dong Bell, Tin, Wood, Weeden Mfg. Co., Box, c.1888 . . . 103500.00

Mechanical, Dog On Turntable, Cast Iron, H.L. Judd, c.1895, 4 In. . . . 485.00 to 717.00

Mechanical, Eagle & Eaglets, Cast Iron, J. & E. Stevens, 1883, 5¾ x 6¾ x 4 In. . . . 144.00 to 1793.00

Mechanical, Elephant & 3 Clowns, J. & E. Stevens, c.1882, 5¾ In. . . . 2032.00

Mechanical, Elephant Howdah, Man Pops Out, Enterprise, c.1884, 5¼ In. . . . 777.00 to 2437.00

Mechanical, Flip The Frog, Tin, Saalheimer & Strauss, 1920s . . . 57500.00

Mechanical, Freedman's Bank, Wood, Metal, Cloth, Jerome B. Secor, c.1880 . . . 92000.00

Bank, Lichfield Cathedral, Cast Iron, England, M 968, 6 ½ x 2 3/16 x 3 ½ In.
$556.00

Bank, Mechanical, Boy On Trapeze, Blue Pants, J. Barton Smith, c.1888
$8775.00

Bank, Mechanical, Pig Playing Drum, Schuco, Germany, c.1935
$585.00

Bank, Mechanical, Acrobat, Lever, Painted, J. & E. Stevens, Pat. 1883
$2800.00

Bank, Mechanical, Billy Goat, Painted, J. & E. Stevens, c.1900
$15210.00

Bank, Mechanical, Creedmoor, Cast Iron, Painted, J. & E. Stevens, 1877 Patent
$1500.00

Bank, Mechanical, Lion Hunter, Teddy Roosevelt, J. & E. Stevens, c.1911, 7 In.
$23400.00

Bank, Mechanical, Postman, Burnett Ltd., London, c.1927
$498.00

Bank, Mechanical, Saluting Sailor, Verse, Tin, Painted, Germany, 1915
$2340.00

Bank, Mechanical, Uncle Sam, Cast Iron, Shepard Hardware, Buffalo, N.Y., c.1886, 11 In.
$21060.00

Mechanical, Frog, On Rock, Kilgore, c.1920 . . . . . 1053.00
Mechanical, Frog On Round Base, White Lattice J. & E. Stevens, c.1872, 3¾ In. 2271.00
Mechanical, General Butler, Cast Iron, 6½ In. 1725.00
Mechanical, Germania Exchange, Cast Iron, J. & E. Stevens, 1880s 149500.00
Mechanical, Girl Skipping Rope, Cast Iron, Painted, J. & E. Stevens, c.1890 . . . . . 13800.00 to 92000.00
Mechanical, Goat, Frog, Old Man, Mechanical Novelty Works, c.1880 . . . . . 5558.00
Mechanical, Hall's Excelsior, J. & E. Stevens, c.1869, 5 In.. . . . . . 359.00 to 4972.00
Mechanical, Hall's Liliput, Metal, Painted, c.1875, 4¾ x 3¼ In. 878.00
Mechanical, Hall's Liliput Bank With Tray, J. & E. Stevens, c.1877, 4½ In. 717.00
Mechanical, Hen & Chick, J. & E. Stevens, c.1901, 4½ In. 5975.00
Mechanical, Home Bank, Without Dormers, J. & E. Stevens, c.1872, 5¼ In.. . . . . . 2629.00
Mechanical, Horse Race, Flanged Base, Cast Iron, J. & E. Stevens, c.1871 . . . . . 69000.00
Mechanical, Humpty Dumpty, Cast Iron, Shepard Hardware, c.1884, 7 In. . . . . . 495.00 to 717.00
Mechanical, I Always Did 'Spise A Mule, Bench, White Mule, J. & E. Stevens, c.1890 . . . . . 1170.00
Mechanical, I Always Did 'Spise A Mule, Bench, Yellow Base, J. & E. Stevens, c.1890 . . . . . 1872.00
Mechanical, I Always Did 'Spise A Mule, Jockey, J. & E. Stevens, c.1879 . . . . . 850.00 to 1989.00
Mechanical, Indian Shooting Bear, J. & E. Stevens, c.1900, 7¼ In. 3107.00
Mechanical, Initiating Bank 2nd Degree, George W. Eddy, c.1880, 6¼ In. 5975.00
Mechanical, Japanese Ball Tosser, Tin, Weeden Mfg. Co., Box, c.1888 . . . . . 92000.00
Mechanical, Jolly Joe Clown, Saalheimer & Strauss, Germany, c.1920 . . . . . 1170.00
Mechanical, Jolly Nigger, High Hat, John Harper, c.1900 . . . . . 460.00
Mechanical, Jonah & The Whale, Jonah Emerges, Cast Iron, J. & E. Stevens, 1880s 414000.00
Mechanical, Jonah & The Whale, Shepard Hardware, c.1890, 4¾ In.. . . . . . 1673.00 to 1975.00
Mechanical, Leap Frog, Peter Adams, Shepard Hardware, c.1890, 4¾ In.. . . . . . 1793.00
Mechanical, Lion & 2 Monkeys, Kyser & Rex, c.1883, 9 In. . . . . . 1070.00 to 4780.00
Mechanical, Lion Hunter, Teddy Roosevelt, J. & E. Stevens, c.1911, 7 In. . . . . . *illus* 23400.00
Mechanical, Magician, J. & E. Stevens, c.1901, 7¾ In. 3884.00
Mechanical, Mama Katzenjammer, Cast Iron, Kenton, c.1908 . . . . . 74750.00
Mechanical, Mammy & Child, Red Dress, Cast Iron, Kyser & Rex, c.1884, 7¼ In.. . . . . . 2868.00 to 3250.00
Mechanical, Mammy & Child, Yellow Dress, Cast Iron, Kyser & Rex, c.1884, 7¼ In. 4481.00
Mechanical, Mason Bank, Cast Iron, Shepard Hardware Co., 1887, 7 x 7 In. 2250.00
Mechanical, Mason Bank, Shepard Hardware, c.1887, 7 In. 2868.00
Mechanical, Memorial Money Bank, Cast Iron, Enterprise Label, 6 In.. . . . . . 220.00
Mechanical, Merry-Go-Round, Cast Iron, Kyser & Rex, 1880s 172500.00
Mechanical, Mikado, Cast Iron, Kyser & Rex, c.1886 . . . . . 287500.00
Mechanical, Milking Cow, J. & E. Stevens, c.1888, 5¼ In. . . . . . 7020.00 to 8962.00
Mechanical, Minstrel, Black, Press Lever Lightly, Tin Lithograph, D.R.G.M., c.1925, 7 In.. . . . . . 209.00
Mechanical, Monkey, Hubley Manufacturing, c.1925, 7¾ In. 657.00
Mechanical, Monkey, Moves Arm, Tin Plate, Chein, 1930s, 5 In. 33.00
Mechanical, Monkey, Raises Arms, Opens Mouth, Tin, Germany, 1908 . . . . . 295.00
Mechanical, Monkey & Coconut, J. & E. Stevens, c.1886, 7¾ In. 2390.00
Mechanical, Mule Entering Barn, Cast Iron, J. & E. Stevens, 1880, 5 x 8 x 3 In. 4400.00
Mechanical, Musical Ballerina, Switzerland, c.1940 . . . . . 293.00 to 497.00
Mechanical, New Creedmoor, J. & E. Stevens, c.1877, 10 In.. . . . . . 448.00
Mechanical, North Pole, Flag, Cast Iron, J. & E. Stevens, c.1910 . . . . . 149500.00
Mechanical, Novelty Bank, Swing-Out Cashier, Cast Iron, J. & E. Stevens, 1872, 6¾ x 4¾ In. 660.00
Mechanical, Old Aunt Dina & The Fairy, Lead, c.1881 . . . . . 97750.00
Mechanical, Organ Bank, Boy & Girl, Cast Iron, Kyser & Rex, c.1882, 7¼ In. 1315.00
Mechanical, Organ Bank, Cat & Dog, Kyser & Rex, c.1882, 7¼ In. . . . . . 384.00 to 2032.00
Mechanical, Organ Bank, Monkey, Cast Iron, Painted, Kyser & Rex, Medium . . . . . 373.00 to 439.00
Mechanical, Organ Grinder & Performing Bear, Kyser & Rex, c.1882, 5 In.. . . . . . 2868.00 to 7605.00
Mechanical, Owl, Slot In Book, Cast Iron, Painted, Kilgore, c.1926 . . . . . 115.00 to 258.00
Mechanical, Owl, Slot In Head, Cast Iron, Painted, Kilgore, c.1926 . . . . . 258.00 to 497.00
Mechanical, Owl, Turns Head, Cast Iron, J. & E. Stevens, c.1880, 7 In. . . . . . 316.00 to 657.00
Mechanical, Paddy & The Pig, Cast Iron, Painted, J. & E. Stevens, c.1885, 7¾ In.. . . . . . 717.00 to 1495.00
Mechanical, Patronize The Blindman, J. & E. Stevens, c.1883 . . . . . 6435.00
Mechanical, Peg-Leg Beggar, H. L. Judd, c.1880 . . . . . 2070.00
Mechanical, Pelican, Mammy, Gold Finish, J. & E. Stevens, Trenton Lock Co., c.1878 . . . . . 3393.00
Mechanical, Pelican, Man Thumbs Nose, J. & E. Stevens, Trenton Lock Co., c.1878. . . . . . 1872.00
Mechanical, Penny Pineapple, Hawaiians, Statehood In 1958, John Wright . . . . . 115.00 to 370.00
Mechanical, Picture Gallery, Cast Iron, Shepard Hardware, 1889, 8¼ In. . . . . . 5676.00 to 7020.00
Mechanical, Pig In Highchair, Cast Iron, Nickel Plated, J. & E. Stevens, c.1897 . . . . . 863.00 to 925.00
Mechanical, Pig Playing Drum, Schuco, Germany, c.1935 . . . . . *illus* 585.00
Mechanical, Postman, Burnett Ltd., London, c.1927 . . . . . *illus* 498.00
Mechanical, Postman, Lithograph, Stollwerck, Germany, c.1920 . . . . . 1287.00

Mechanical, Presto, Penny Changes To Quarter, Cast Iron, Henry C. Hart Mfg., c.1884...... 103500.00
Mechanical, Presto, Pull Drawer, Cast Iron, Painted, Kyser & Rex, c.1894 .... 115.00
Mechanical, Pretzel Tree Vending, Blue, Germany, c.1925 .... 644.00
Mechanical, Pretzel Tree Vending, Brown, Orange, Germany, c.1925 .... 878.00
Mechanical, Pretzel Tree Vending, Off-White, Flower On Marquee, Germany.............. 819.00
Mechanical, Professor Pug Frog's Great Bicycle Feat, J. & E. Stevens, c.1886, 7 ½ In......... 103500.00
Mechanical, Punch & Judy, Cast Iron, Shepherd Hardware, 1884............. 863.00 to 1250.00
Mechanical, Rabbit In Cabbage, Kilgore, c.1882, 2½ In..................... 373.00 to 418.00
Mechanical, Reclining Chinaman, J. & E. Stevens, c.1882, 4 In................ 6573.00 to 7020.00
Mechanical, Roller Skating Rink, Cast Iron, Kyser & Rex, 1880s....................... 195500.00
Mechanical, Rooster, Cast Iron, Painted, Kyser & Rex, c.1880, 6 In............. 187.00 to 825.00
Mechanical, Royal Trick Elephant, c.1915 .... 2457.00
Mechanical, Saluting Sailor, Verse, Tin, Painted, Germany, 1915 .... *illus* 2340.00
Mechanical, Santa Claus, Cast Iron, Shepard Hardware, c.1889, 7¾ In......... 2151.00 to 3175.00
Mechanical, Speaking Dog, Blue Dress, Cast Iron, Shepard Hardware, 1885 Patent, 7 ¼ In... 767.00
Mechanical, Speaking Dog, Cast Iron, John Harper, 1902, 7¼ x 7⅛ x 3 In....... 412.00 to 1250.00
Mechanical, Speaking Dog, Red Dress, J. & E. Stevens c.1895, 7 In............ 1434.00 to 2223.00
Mechanical, Sportsman, J. & E. Stevens, 1892 Patent, 9 ⅛ x 3 x 7 ¾ In.................. 4950.00
Mechanical, Squirrel & Tree Stump, Mechanical Novelty Works, c.1881, 4 ½ In........... 2032.00
Mechanical, Stars & 3 Clowns, Germany, c.1925.................................. 878.00
Mechanical, Stump Speaker, Cast Iron, Shepard Hardware, 1886, 9¾ In........ 1850.00 to 2271.00
Mechanical, Tammany, Cast Iron, J. & E. Stevens.................................. 1610.00
Mechanical, Teddy & The Bear, Cast Iron, J. & E. Stevens, c.1907, 7½ In. .... 660.00 to 2390.00
Mechanical, Thing, Addams Family, Battery, Poynter Products, 1964, 5 In................ 1210.00
Mechanical, Toad On Stump, J. & E. Stevens, c.1880, 2 ¾ In........................... 1315.00
Mechanical, Trick Dog, 6-Part Base, Hubley, 1888 Patent.................... 132.00 to 717.00
Mechanical, Trick Pony, Shepard Hardware, c.1885, 5 ¾ In............................ 1135.00
Mechanical, Two Frogs, J. & E. Stevens, c.1882, 4 In................................ 2032.00
Mechanical, Uncle Remus, Cast Iron, Painted, Kyser & Rex, c.1890, 5 In........ 3650.00 to 5676.00
Mechanical, Uncle Sam, Cast Iron, Shepard Hardware, Buffalo, N.Y., c.1886, 11 In. ... *illus* 21060.00
Mechanical, Uncle Sam Bust, Slot In Hat, Cast Iron, Ives, c.1890 .... 920.00
Mechanical, Uncle Wiggly, Chein.. 175.00
Mechanical, Vending, Leo Chocolate Hartwig & Vogel, Germany, c.1925 .... 351.00
Mechanical, Watchdog Safe, Cast Iron, J. & E. Stevens, c.1890, 6 In..................... 633.00
Mechanical, Watchdog Safe, Dog Barks, Cast Iron, Painted, J. & E. Stevens 920.00
Mechanical, Weeden's Plantation Darky Savings, Weeden Mfg. Co., c.1888, 5 ½ In......... 1076.00
Mechanical, White Hen & Chick, J. & E. Stevens, c.1901............................. 7020.00
Mechanical, William Tell, Cast Iron, Painted, J. & E. Stevens, 1896, 6½ x 10½ In. 605.00 to 1195.00
Mechanical, Wireless Bank, Cast Iron, Painted, John Hugo Mfg. Co..................... 69.00
Mechanical, Wood Monkey Cashier, Cast Iron, Hall, 1869 Patent, 5 x 4 x 3 ½ In........... 640.00
Mechanical, World's Fair, J. & E. Stevens, c.1893, 6 In. .... 633.00 to 1315.00
Mechanical, Zoo, Kyser & Rex, 4 x 4 In. .... 1554.00 to 1840.00
Mosque, Cast Iron, Yellow, Red Paint, A.C. Williams, 4 In. .... *illus* 265.00
Mulligan, Policeman, Blue Outfit, Club In Hand, Cast Iron, A.C. Williams, 5 ¾ In. 144.00
Mulligan The Cop, Cast Iron, Painted, Hubley .... *illus* 410.00
Mutt & Jeff, Cast Iron, Painted, A.C. Williams, M 157, 4 ¼ x 3 ½ 263.00
Pagoda, Cast Iron, England, M 1153, 5 x 3 x 3 In...................................... 498.00
Palace, Cast Iron, Ives, c.1885, 7 ½ x 8 x 5 In... 316.00
Parlor Stove, Cast Iron, Black Paint, 7 In.. 143.00
Pear, Pottery, Painted, Yellow, Red, 4 ½ In... 176.00
Pig, Iron, c.1920, 10 ½ In. 175.00
Policeman, Blue Outfit, Embossed, Cast Iron, Arcade, c.1920, M 152, 5 ½ In............ 402.00
Porky Pig, Cast Iron, Hubley, c.1930 .... 210.00
Porky Pig At Barrel, White Metal, Moss, Box, M 265, 4 7/16 x 5 ¾ In...................... 152.00
Professor Pug Frog, Cast Iron, A.C. Williams, c.1905, M 311, 3 ¼ In..................... 86.00
Register, Cash Register Savings Bank, Cast Iron, Paper, Glass, M 1538, 5 ⅝ x 4 ⅝ In........ 1521.00
Register, Prudential Bank Quarters, Cast Iron, 6 In....................................... 585.00
Richmond Ice Cream Freezer, Cast Iron, Grey Iron Casting, c.1910, 4 ¼ x 2 ⅝ In. 263.00
Roof Bank, Painted, Cast Iron, J. & E. Stevens, M 1122.............................. 3042.00
Rose Window, Cast Iron, England, M 1170 .... 702.00
Safe, Junior Safe Deposit, Cast Iron, Painted, American .... *illus* 234.00
Santa Claus, Cast Iron, 6 In.. 575.00
Security Peoples Trust Co., Ceramic, Brown, 3 x 3 ½ x 4 ½ In. 65.00
Security Safe Deposit, Pressed Metal, Safe Shape, Black, Gilt, c.1887, 6 x 4 ¼ In.......... 88.00
Singer Sewing Machine, Tin, Germany, c.1910, 5 ¼ x 4 ½ x 2 ¾ In. 351.00

TIP
If it seems too good to be true, it usually is! Trust your instincts when buying antiques. Experienced collectors notice many little signs of repair or reproduction, often without realizing it.

Bank, Mosque, Cast Iron, Yellow, Red Paint, A.C. Williams, 4 In.
$265.00

Bank, Mulligan The Cop, Cast Iron, Painted, Hubley
$410.00

Bank, Safe, Junior Safe Deposit, Cast Iron, Painted, American
$234.00

Bank, Turkey, Large, Painted, Cast Iron, A.C. Williams, M 585, 4 ¼ x 4 In.
$878.00

Barber, Chair, Walnut, Carved, Koken & Boppert, c.1880, 48 x 26 x 33 In.
$585.00

Sixpenny Piece, Aluminum, England, 1954, 3 x 3 ¼ In. 41.00
Spaniel Begging, Lead, Germany 488.00
Spaniel With Trap, Cast Iron, Hubley, 1930s, 3 ¾ x 6 In. 188.00
St. Bernard With Pack, Cast Iron, A.C. Williams, 5 ½ x 7 ¾ In. 152.00
St. Bernard With Pack, Cast Iron, A.C. Williams, M 439, 3 ⅝ x 5 ½ In. 44.00
Stop Sign, Cast Iron, Dent Hardware, 1920, M 1481, 5 ⅝ x 2 ½ In. 351.00
Tower, Cast Iron, John Harper, Early 1900s, M 1208, 9 ½ In. 316.00
Trolley, Cast Iron, c.1889, 3 15⁄16 x 4 ⅝ In. 425.00
Turkey, Large, Painted, Cast Iron, A.C. Williams, M 585, 4 ¼ x 4 In. . . . . *illus* 878.00
Universal Stoves & Ranges, Spinning Globe, Cribben & Sexton, Tin, 4 In. 1125.00
Victory Ship, World War II Destroyer, Gray, Plaster, Novelty Mfg. Co., Box, 10 ½ In. 144.00
World Globe, Arc Base, Cast Iron, Painted, Grey Iron Casting, 5 ¼ In. 176.00
Yellow Cab, Driver, Cast Iron, Arcade, 8 In. 960.00

BARBER collectibles range from the popular red and white striped pole that used to be found in front of every shop to the small scissors and tools of the trade. Barber chairs are wanted, especially the older models with elaborate iron trim.

Bowl, Flower, Crest, Porcelain, Shell Shape, 14 In. 450.00
Box, Straight Razor, Oak, Lock, Woman Pinup, 3 x 6 x 9 In. 173.00
Chair, Koken Companies, St. Louis 250.00
Chair, Leather, Red, Child's Seat 403.00
Chair, Queen Anne Style, Mahogany, Shaped Seat, Cabriole Legs, 38 x 31 x 25 In. 960.00
Chair, Walnut, Carved, Koken & Boppert, c.1880, 48 x 26 x 33 In. . . . . *illus* 585.00
Chair, Wicker, Revolving, Child's, 41 In. 86.00
Chair, Wood, Leather, Columbia, 50 In. 518.00
Coat Rack, Oak, Hat, Pole, Mirror, 4 Brass Hooks, 33 x 20 In. 173.00
Dispenser, Lather, Electric, Oster, c.1950, 6 x 5 In. 173.00
Pole, Blue, Green, Black, White, Leaded Glass, Globe, 11 In. 1093.00
Pole, Glass Dome, Metal Bar, Electric, 38 In. 288.00
Pole, Pine, Red, White, Blue, c.1900, 72 x 7 ½ In. . . . . *illus* 800.00
Pole, Red, White, Blue, Metal Dome Top, Wall Mounts, Electric, 34 x 16 In. 495.00
Pole, Red, White, Blue, Metal Stand, Tapered, Gold Acorn Finial, 69 ½ In. 1955.00
Pole, Red, White, Porcelain, Globe, Koken, 85 ¾ In. 2090.00
Pole, Silver Top, Bottom, Electric, 26 In. 259.00
Pole, Wood, Red, White, Blue, 19th Century, 65 In. 558.00
Pole, Wood, Red, White, Blue, 19th Century, 85 In. 235.00
Pole, Wood, Red, White, Blue, Ball & Cone Finial, 68 In. 1265.00
Pole, Wood, Red, White, Blue, Late 19th Century, 73 In. 323.00
Pole, Wood, Red, White, Blue, Pine Box Form, Gilt, 72 x 6 In. 4070.00
Pole, Wood, Red, White, Blue, Square Base, Ball Finial, 99 In. 1210.00
Pole, Wood, Red, White, Blue, Turned Ball Ends, Gesso, 26 ½ In. 1208.00
Rack, Shaving Mug, Oak, 5 Rows, 35 Slots, Edwardian, 41 ½ x 8 x 45 In. 1495.00
Rack, Shaving Mug, Renaissance Revival, Walnut, Fox Head, 90 Slots, 74 x 56 x 14 In. 6900.00
Rack, Shaving Mug, Walnut, 8 Rows, 64 Slots, Victorian, 50 x 6 x 54 ½ In. 300.00
Rack, Shaving Mug, Walnut, Crown Molding, Finials, 35 Slots, c.1890, 56 x 28 x 9 In. 1955.00
Rack, Shaving Mug, Walnut, 8 Rows, 72 Slots, Victorian, 43 x 72 In. 4313.00
Razor Set, Days Of Week, Gilt, Homberg Solingen, Box 489.00
Razor Set, Straight, Tobacco, 7 Piece 58.00
Sign, 2 Poles, 21 x 86 In. 385.00
Sign, Barber, Porcelain, 2-Sided, Flange, 24 x 12 In. 173.00
Sign, Look Better, Feel Better, Porcelain, Cylindrical, 49 In. 201.00
Sign, Shaving Saloon, Wood, c.1960, 36 x 24 In. 173.00
Sign, Straight Razor, Pine, Carved, Painted, Black Case, 3 ¾ x 26 In. 660.00
Sterilizer, Hot Towel, Globe, Metal, 56 In. 633.00

BAROMETERS are used to forecast the weather. Antique barometers with elaborate wooden cases and brass trim are the most desirable. Mercury column barometers are also popular with collectors. It is difficult to find someone to repair a broken one, so be sure your barometer is in working condition.

Aneroid, Black Forest, Paper Scale, Intertwined Oak Leaves, Stag Head, 17 In. 147.00
Aneroid, Thermometer, Oak Case, Germany, 21 In. 95.00
Banjo, Burl Mahogany, String Inlaid Edges, Broken Arch Top, 1800s, 39 x 10 In. 750.00
Banjo, Georgian, Inlaid Mahogany, String Borders, Scrolled Arch Pediment, 38 ½ In. 920.00
Banjo, J.J. Lockwood, Mahogany, Preston, Scotland, 19th Century, 37 x 11 In. 688.00
Banjo, Mahogany, Flowers, Mother-Of-Pearl Inlay, Signed, Bon Journo, 39 x 12 In. 575.00
Brass, Coles, Germany, 9 In. . . . . 41.00 to 60.00

Crisscross, Wood, Glass Front, Brass Side Gauge, 19th Century 1200.00
Dickson, Oak, Carved, Scroll, Plaque, Mr. E. Morris Retirement, Nov. 1909, 34 In. 248.00
George III, Mahogany, Flowers, Shells, c.1820, 38 ½ x 10 x 2 ⅛ In. 1320.00
Marine, Thermometer, Adie, Rosewood, Door Concealing Bone Scale, 39 In. 3525.00
Marine, Thermometer, Spencer, Browning & Rust, Mahogany, Bone Scale, 37 In. 4994.00
Nautical, Banjo, Mahogany, Wall, Brass Frame, 44 x 12 ½ x 2 In. 780.00
Nautical, Thermometer, Compass, Ship's Wheel, Anchor, Marble, Brass, 7 x 7 In. 460.00
Nautical, Thermometer, Wall Mounted, Brass, Stick, U.S. Navy, Bracket, 28 ¼ In. 478.00
Riggs & Brother, Brass Case, Late 19th Century, France, 11 ½ x 9 In. 460.00
Stick, Mahogany, Victorian, Twin Wheel-Operated Verniers, Thermometer, 43 In. 1645.00
Stick, Mangavel, Brass Gauge, Turned Stem, 39 In. 1652.00
Stirrup Shape, Bowtie & Ribbon Design, Signed, Veranderlich, 11 ½ x 8 ½ In. 420.00
Thermometer, Banjo, Black, Mother-Of-Pearl Inlay, John Timoney, Blackburn, 37 ½ In. 960.00
Thermometer, Black Forest, Leaves, Swiss, c.1900, 17 In. 59.00
Thermometer, Black Forest, Switzerland, c.1900, 21 In. 148.00
Thermometer, Fagioti & Son, Mahogany, Clerkenwell, c.1800, 45 In. 236.00
Thermometer, J. Hicks, Engraved Bone Scale, Twin Verniers, Key, 40 In. 1763.00
Thermometer, Napoleon III, Giltwood, Carved, Louis XVI Style, Painted, Ivory, 44 x 12 In. 3120.00
Thermometer, Oak, Carved, England, c.1900, 22 In. 48.00
Thermometer, Travel, Silver Plated Brass Case, Asprey, London, c.1920 .... 569.00
Victorian, Rosewood, Convex Mirror, Late 19th Century, 36 x 10 In. 390.00
Wheel, Georgian, Mahogany, Inlay, Swan's Neck Crest, Soldini, Wincanton, 39 In. 646.00
Wheel, Scrolled Arch Top, Brass Finial, Veneer Case, Ivory Knob, 1800s, 38 x 10 In. 800.00

BASALT is a special type of ceramic invented by Josiah Wedgwood in the eighteenth century. It is a fine-grained, unglazed stoneware. Some pieces are listed in that section. The most common type is black, but many other colors were made. It was made by many factories. Some pieces are listed in the Wedgwood section.

Teapot, Black, Rouletted, 19th Century, 6 ¾ x 4 ¼ In. 176.00
Teapot, Roulette Design, Black, Early 19th Century, 6 ⅞ x 4 ¼ In. .... *illus* 193.00

BASEBALL *collectibles are in the Sports category, except for baseball cards, which are listed under Baseball in the Card category.*

BASKETS of all types are popular with collectors. American Indian, Japanese, African, Shaker, and many other kinds of baskets can be found. Of course, baskets are still being made, so the collector must learn to tell the age and style of the basket to determine the value.

Ash, Splint, Bentwood Handle, 2 ¾ x 17 x 10 ½ In. 100.00
Bamboo, Cylindrical, Braided Twigs, Handles, Japan, 20th Century, 17 In. 1763.00
Bamboo, Multilayered Strips, Natural Stems, Dark Brown, Japan, 22 In. 705.00
Bamboo, Wrapped Supports, Footed, Strap, 17 x 9 ¼ In. 270.00
Buttocks, Splint, Bentwood Handle, 9 x 18 ½ In. 144.00
Buttocks, Splint, Fixed Bentwood Handle, Early 20th Century, 26 x 22 In. 86.00
Buttocks, Splint, Oak, Bentwood Handle, God's-Eye Handle Attachment, Gray, 12 x 13 In. 468.00
Buttocks, Splint, Oak, Bentwood Handle, Green, 8 x 11 ½ x 9 In. 88.00
Buttocks, Splint, Oak, Bentwood Handle, White Paint, 17 x 19 In. 198.00
Buttocks, Wicker, Bentwood Handle, Oak Ribs, Patina, 9 x 9 In. 275.00
Cheese, Splint, Round, 6 ½ x 15 x 14 In. 58.00
Coconut Shell, Scrimshaw, Eagle, Banners, Wreath, Leaf Carved Handle, 3 ½ In. 240.00
Coushatta, Timber Bamboo, Round Cover, Loop Handle, c.1890, 28 x 20 In. 353.00
Feather, Cover, Wood Handles, Round Rim, Square Base, Bulging Middle, 23 x 12 In. 288.00
Feather, Splint, Cover, Green Paint, Late 19th Century, 13 ½ In. 940.00
Feather, Splint, Oak, Yellow Paint, c.1940, 26 x 18 In. 58.00
Gathering, Center Handle, Oblong, Curved Sides, Orange, Green, Purple, 12 x 20 x 9 In. 143.00
Gathering, Splint, Oak, Bentwood Handle, 13 x 10 In. 66.00
Gathering, Splint, Oak, Bentwood Handle, Bulbous, Carved Attachments, 11 ½ x 14 In. 176.00
Gathering, Splint, Oak, Bentwood Handle, Red, 12 x 23 ¾ x 14 In. 33.00
Handle, Shells, Wire, Nautical, Sailor Made, 1880, 10 In. 295.00
Ikebana, Horizontal Bamboo Strips, Wide Strips Overlay, Entwined Handle, Japan, 17 In. 330.00
Ikebana, Square, Interwoven Bamboo Strips, Willow Handle, Japan, 16 In. 120.00
Lap Joint Rim, Wrapped Splint Handle, Green Paint, 6 ½ x 6 In. 230.00
Laundry, Hotel, Wicker, Wood Slat Bottom, France, c.1900, 26 ½ x 31 ½ In. 390.00
Laundry, Hotel, Woven Wicker, Pierced Handles, Wood Slat Bottom, 26 x 32 In. 660.00
Leather, Key, Geometric Panels, Handle, S.S. Cottrell & Co., 7 x 8 x 4 In. .... *illus* 1900.00
Market, Splint, Oak, Bentwood Handle, Stained, 11 x 14 ½ x 11 In. 100.00

Barber, Pole, Pine, Red, White, Blue, c.1900, 72 x 7 ½ In.
$800.00

Basalt, Teapot, Roulette Design, Black, Early 19th Century, 6 ⅞ x 4 ¼ In.
$193.00

Basket, Leather, Key, Geometric Panels, Handle, S.S. Cottrell & Co., 7 x 8 x 4 In.
$1900.00

TIP

Never oil a basket. It will attract dirt.

Basket, Slat, Feather, Wire, Metal Bands, Late 19th Century, 30 In. $690.00

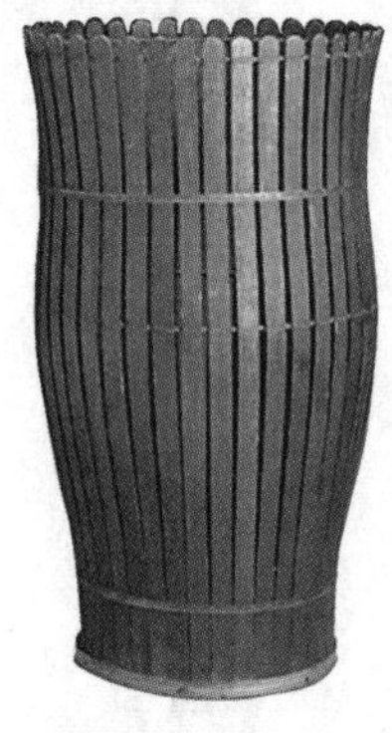

Basket, Splint, Maple, Wood Lid, 2 Bentwood Loops, New England, c.1880, 12 x 15 x 12 In. $145.00

Basket, Splint, Oak, Ash Handle, Carved, Patina, Mid 19th Century, 17 x 15 In. $460.00

Batchelder, Tile, Blue, Green, Black, White, Frame, Marked, 5¾ In. $230.00

Nantucket, Lid, Polymer Whale In Relief, Wood Handle, Signed, Farnum, 11¾ In. 315.00
Nantucket, Lightship, Oval, Rosewood Lid, Handle, Ivory Locking Pin, 9 x 6 x 6 In. 1680.00
Nantucket, Oval, Swing Handle, Mid 20th Century, 5⅜ x 11½ In. 646.00
Nantucket, Oval, Swing Handle, Rosewood Lid, Ivory Sea Gull, 9½ x 6 x 6½ In. 1500.00
Nantucket, Rattan, Wood Base, Inscribed, Frances B. Smith, c.1950, 13 x 11 In. 2465.00
Nantucket, Rattan, Wood Base, Pyrographic Inscriptions, 1950, 13 x 11 In. 2450.00
Nantucket, Round, Carved Swing Handle, Wood Base, R. Folger, c.1900, 9 x 14 In. 3055.00
Nantucket, Round, Swing Handle, Ash, Pine, Brass Pivots, 8¾ x 6¼ In. 1000.00
Nantucket, Round, Swing Handle, Stenciled Bottom, R. Folger, 1879, 5 x 6⅝ In. 896.00
Nantucket, Round, Turned Mahogany Base, Carved Handles, Early 1900s, 2 x 6⅝ In. 1998.00
Nantucket, Splint, Rattan, Round, Swing Handle, Turned Base, c.1940, 7 x 9⅜ In. 1880.00
Nantucket, Swing Handle, Brass Tacks, Walnut Bottom, One-Egg Size, c.1900, 3 x 3 In. 900.00
Nantucket, Wastebasket, Signed, R. Peloso, 14 In. 6750.00
Oval Rim, Rectangular Bottom, Center Handle, Yellow, 8½ x 13½ x 11½ In. 210.00
Picnic, Double Covers, Fixed Handle, 23 x 12 In. 413.00
Potato, Swing Handle, Blue Paint, 14½ In. 110.00
Reed, Round, Wrapped Handle, Rim, 23 In. 58.00
Round, Yellow Band, Blue-Green Design, Potato Stamped, 5 x 13 In. 173.00
Rye Straw, Round, Bail Handle, Late 19th Century, 10½ x 11 In. 121.00
Slat, Feather, Wire, Metal Bands, Late 19th Century, 30 In. *illus* 690.00
Splint, Ash, Carved Rim Notches, D-Shape Lids, 16 x 12½ x 19½ In. 88.00
Splint, Ash, Round, Bentwood Handle, Patina, 8½ x 9 In. 121.00
Splint, Backpack, Oval Rim, Bulging Center, Rectangular Base, 18½ x 12½ x 9 In. 58.00
Splint, Bamboo, Bail Handle, Round Rim, Square Base, Chocolate Brown, 17½ In. 999.00
Splint, Bamboo, Bail Handle, Round Rim, Square Base, Japan, 20th Century, 17 In. 1000.00
Splint, Bamboo, Braided Bail Handle, Chocolate Brown, Japan, 20th Century, 16 In. 470.00
Splint, Bamboo, Braided Foot, Mouth Ring, Jump Handles, Brown, Japan, 10¼ In. 441.00
Splint, Bamboo, Cross Weave, Side Formed Handle, Brown, Japan, 19th Century, 12 In. 1998.00
Splint, Bamboo, Oval, Lateral Panels, Japan, 13 In. 646.00
Splint, Bentwood Handle, Round Rim, Tapered, 2¼ x 5½ x 5 In. 66.00
Splint, Bentwood Handles, Grand Rapids, Michigan, 19 In. 395.00
Splint, Black Ash, Carved Wood Handles, Dome Center, Trim Reinforcement, 18 x 15 In. 259.00
Splint, Bowl Shape, Vegetable Stamped, Red & Blue Bands, 1800s, 5 x 10 In. 235.00
Splint, Cylindrical, Curlicue Top, 7 x 6 In. 230.00
Splint, Grass, Angled Handle, Stepped Back, Ring Hanger, 10 x 10 x 4 In. 230.00
Splint, Green Paint, Early 20th Century, 15 x 8 In. 316.00
Splint, Handle Goes Through Cover, Round, 7 x 8 In. 230.00
Splint, Hickory, Carved Handle, Early 20th Century, 15 In. 35.00
Splint, Kidney Shape, Wide Handle, 20th Century, 4½ x 3½ In. 275.00
Splint, Maple, Wood Lid, 2 Bentwood Loops, New England, c.1880, 12 x 15 x 12 In. *illus* 145.00
Splint, Oak, Ash Handle, Carved, Patina, Mid 19th Century, 17 x 15 In. *illus* 460.00
Splint, Oak, Ash Swing Handle, Double Wrapped Rim, New England, 1800s, 17 In. 460.00
Splint, Oak, Bentwood Carved Handle, Square Base, Gray Enamel, 14½ In. 184.00
Splint, Oak, Bentwood Handle, Round Rim, Square Base, Gray, 20th Century, 14 x 15 In. 187.00
Splint, Oak, Bentwood Handle, Round, Square Base, 16 x 12 In. 77.00
Splint, Oblong, Center Handle, 7 x 34½ x 20 In. 115.00
Splint, Oval Rim, Rectangular Base, Upright Handle, Red Paint, c.1900, 16 In. 529.00
Splint, Red, Green, Lid, 19th Century, 8½ x 11½ In. 441.00
Splint, Round Rim, Square Base, 9 x 21 In. 287.00
Splint, White Oak, Arched Handle, Round Rim, Early 20th Century, 10 x 8 In. 165.00
Splint, White Oak, Flat Arched Handle, Carved Rim, 12 x 12 x 19 In. 209.00
Storage, Rye Straw, White Oak Splints, Coil, Late 19th Century, 10 x 22 In. 121.00
Tapered Rim, Handles, Yellow, Orange, Blue, 14 x 12 In. 173.00
Vendor's, Splint, 2 Handles, Open Side, 10¼ x 41 x 28¼ In. 420.00
Wicker, Japanese, 19¾ x 17 In. 41.00
Wood, Gondola, Half Spindle Ends, Brass Casters, 17¼ x 8 x 6¾ In. 303.00
Work, Hexagonal, 4 x 7 x 8 In. 2574.00
Work, Satinwood, Penwork, Dome Lid, Regency, 6¾ x 7½ x 6½ In. 1200.00

BATCHELDER
LOS ANGELES

BATCHELDER products are made from California clay. Ernest Batchelder established a tile studio in Pasadena, California, in 1909 and expanded until 1916. Then he built a larger factory with a new partner. The Batchelder-Wilson Company made all types of architectural tiles, garden pots, and bookends. The plant closed in 1932. In 1936 Batchelder opened Batchelder Ceramics, also in Pasadena, and made bowls, vases, and earthenware pots. He retired in 1951 and died in 1957. Pieces are marked *Batchelder Pasadena* or *Batchelder Los Angeles.*

Tile, Blue, Green, Black, White, Frame, Marked, 5¾ In. *illus* 230.00

BATMAN and Robin are characters from a comic strip by Bob Kane that started in 1939. In 1966, the characters became part of a popular television series. There have been radio and movie serials that featured the pair. The first full-length movie was made in 1989.

Batmobile, Aluminum, c.1960, 7 In. 97.00
Batmobile, Tin Lithograph, Battery Operated, 1970s, 11 ¾ In. 512.00
Book, Batman Son Of The Demon Graphic Novel, Dust Jacket, c.1987. . . . . . 48.00
Clock, Batman, Batmobile, Skyline, Plastic, c.1974 . . . . . . 75.00
Comic Book, Brave & The Bold, Batman & Plastic Man, No. 76, February-March 1968 . . . . . 10.00
Comic Book, No. 344, February, 1982 . . . . . . 14.00
Comic Book, Sheldon Moldoff Detective Comics, No. 35, 13 ½ x 14 ¼ In. 776.00
Cookie Jar, Batman & Robin, Ceramic, Tin, Vandor, 12 In.. . . . . . 32.00
Model Kit, Batman, No. 467-149, Aurora, c.1964. . . . . . 374.00
Mug, Batman, Fire King Anchor Hocking, D-Handle 35.00
Mug, Batman Forever, Glass, McDonalds, 1995, 8 Oz., 3 ¼ In.. . . . . . 4.00
Mug, Riddler, Glass, McDonalds, 1995, 8 Oz., 3 ¼ In.. . . . . . 5.00
Ornament, Batman, Hallmark, Box, 1994. . . . . . 30.00
Ornament, Batman, Light-Up Bat, Hallmark, Box, 2000, 4 x 3 ½ In.. . . . . . 25.00
PEZ Dispenser, Batman, Turquoise, DC Comics, c.1985 . . . . . . 8.00
Toothbrush, Batman, Battery Operated, Janex Co., Box, 1974 . . . . . . *illus* 84.00
Toy, Batmobile, Red, Batman, Robin, Battery Operated, Tin Lithograph, Box, c.1967 . . . . . . 349.00
View-Master, DC Comics, Booklet, 3 Reel, Box, 1976. . . . . . 22.00
Wastebasket, Batman & Batmobile, Yellow, Metal, Oval, 1989 . . . . . . 25.00

BATTERSEA enamels, which are enamels painted on copper, were made in the Battersea district of London from about 1750 to 1756. Many similar enamels are mistakenly called Battersea.

Box, Red & White Spaniel, Couple Reading, Lid, 1800s, 1 ½ x 1 ¼ In.. . . . . . 1035.00
Candlestick, Brass, Removable Bobeches, Petal Shape Flowers, 9 ⅝ In., Pair . . . . . . *illus* 2350.00
Vase, Potpourri, Metal, Figures, Sheep, Landscape, Turquoise, c.1765, 9 ¼ In. 2703.00

BAUER pottery is a California-made ware. J.A. Bauer bought Paducah Pottery in Paducah, Kentucky, in 1885. He moved the pottery to Los Angeles, California, in 1909. The company made art pottery after 1912 and dinnerwares marked *Bauer* in 1930. The factory went out of business in 1962. See also the Russel Wright category.

Canister, Flour, Oval, White Strawberries, Wood Lid, 1940-50s, 8 x 8 x 6 In. 75.00
Canister, Sugar, Oval, White Strawberries, Wood Lid, 1940-50s, 6 x 6 x 4 In. 75.00
Casserole, Cover, Lemon Yellow, Black Speckle, Metal Frame, 1950s, 3 ¼ x 8 ¼ In. 29.00
Casserole, Cover, Pink Speckle, Metal Frame, Footed, Al Fresco, 1960s 39.00
Casserole, Cover, Turquoise Blue Speckle, Metal Frame, 1 ½ Qt. . . . . . . *illus* 45.00
Casserole, Pink Speckle, French Handle, Brusche, Individual 9.00
Coffee Server, Cobalt Blue, Plainware 100.00
Custard Cup, Jade Green, 3 ½ In. 20.00
Mixing Bowl, No. 12, Jade Green, 4 Wide Bands, 1940s, 9 ½ In. 35.00
Mixing Bowl, No. 18, Black, Plainware, 8 ¼ In.. . . . . . 75.00
Monterey, Pitcher, Burgundy, Ice Lip 250.00
Nut Cup, Cobalt Blue, 4 ¾ In., Pair 20.00
Ring, Charger, Catalina Blue, 31 In. 660.00
Ring, Creamer, Black 75.00
Ring, Dish, Pickle, Chinese Yellow, 9 In. 75.00
Ring, Mixing Bowl, No. 30, Cobalt Blue, 6 In. 24.00
Ring, Pitcher, Blue, 5 In. . . . . . . *illus* 95.00
Ring, Platter, Orange-Red, 9 x 6 In. 22.00
Ring, Platter, Yellow, 12 ¾ x 9 ¼ In.. . . . . . 39.00
Ring, Relish, Orange-Red, Divided, c.1940, 10 ½ In. 79.00
Rose Bowl, Yellow, Fred Johnson, 6 In.. . . . . . 85.00

BAVARIA is a region in Europe where many types of porcelain were made. In the nineteenth century, the mark often included the word *Bavaria.* After 1871, the words *Bavaria, Germany* , were used. Listed here are pieces that include the name *Bavaria* in some form, but major porcelain makers, such as Rosenthal, are listed in their own categories.

Butter Chip, Violet Roses, Green Leaves, Gold Accents, Teardrop Shape, 3 In.. . . . . . 25.00
Cake Plate, Lilies On Pond, Shaded Light Green Border, Pierced Gold Handles, 11 In.. . . . . . 70.00
Celery Dish, Roses, Embossed Shaped Rim, Gold Trim, 10 In. 26.00

Batman, Toothbrush, Batman, Battery Operated, Janex Co., Box, 1974
$84.00

Battersea, Candlestick, Brass, Removable Bobeches, Petal Shape Flowers, 9 ⅝ In., Pair
$2350.00

Bauer, Casserole, Cover, Turquoise Blue Speckle, Metal Frame, 1 ½ Qt.
$45.00

Bauer, Ring, Pitcher, Blue, 5 In.
$95.00

Beatles, Ornaments, Figural, Glass, Box, 7 In., 4 Piece
$220.00

Beehive, Plate, Venus, c.1900, 10 In.
$800.00

Beehive, Vase, Classical Woman, Lavender Ground, Gilt Frame, Wagner, 1800s, 9 ½ In.
$2300.00

Cup & Saucer, Violets, Gold Raised Beaded Band, Gold Handle 25.00
Dessert Set, Forget-Me-Nots, Green Border, Gold Edge, 2-Handled Cake Plate, 5 Piece 75.00
Dish, Basket Of Strawberries Tipped Over, Gold Scalloped Rim, 6 In. 25.00
Eggcup, Gold, Man & Woman In Cartouche, Flared Rim, Pair 24.00
Plate, Dessert, Pink & Peach Cabbage Roses, Gold Beaded & Scalloped Rim, 7 In., 4 Piece . . . 49.00
Plate, Grapes, 2 Bunches, Lavender Shaded To Cream Ground, 10 In. 135.00
Plate, Multicolored Flowers, Raised Gold Scrolls, Scalloped Rim, 7 ½ In. 25.00
Plate, Pink Roses, Buds On Side, Green Leaves, Turquoise Border, 7 ⅝ In. 85.00
Plate, Purple Flowers & Border, Green Leaves, Signed, John Anton Coufall, 7 In. 80.00
Salt & Pepper, Forget-Me-Nots, Gold Painted Top, Scalloped Bottom, 2 ½ In. 46.00
Vase, Pink Flowers, Eggshell Ground, Oval, Notched Rim, Angular Handles, 5 In. 15.00

BEADED BAGS *are included in the Purse category.*

BEATLES collectors search for any items picturing the four members of the famous music group or any of their recordings. Because these items are so new, the condition is very important and top prices are paid only for items in mint condition. The Beatles first appeared on American network television in 1964. The group disbanded in 1971. Ringo Starr and Paul McCartney are still performing. John Lennon died in 1980. George Harrison died in 2001

Clutch, Head Shots, Signatures, Beige, Vinyl, Brass Handle, Dame O, 1960s, 10 x 9 In. 212.00
Lunch Box, George, Paul, John, Ringo, Safety First, Message, Blue, Metal, Aladdin, 6 ⅞ x 8 In. 625.00
Ornaments, Figural, Glass, Box, 7 In., 4 Piece . . . . *illus* 220.00
Paint By Number Kit, Paint Your Own Beatles, Set Of 4, Artistic Creations, 1960 . . . . 580.00
Pin, Free Paul, 1980, 2 ¼ In. 46.00
Pin, John Lennon, Yellow Submarine, Red, Green, Blue, Black, 3 In. 28.00
Pin, The Beatles, 4 Portraits, Black, White, Red, Celluloid, 3 In. . . . . 31.00 to 42.00
Poster, Album Cover, Yesterday & Today, 1966 . . . . 686.00
Poster, Let It Be, Facial Images, 1970, 27 x 41 In. 345.00

BEEHIVE, Austria, or Beehive, Vienna, are terms used in English-speaking countries to refer to the many types of decorated porcelain bearing a mark that looks like a beehive. The mark is actually a shield, viewed upside down. It was first used in 1744 by the Royal Porcelain Manufactory of Vienna. The firm made what collectors call Royal Vienna porcelains until it closed in 1864. Many other German, Austrian, and Japanese factories have reproduced Royal Vienna wares, complete with the original shield or beehive mark. This listing includes the expensive, original Royal Vienna porcelains and many other types of beehive porcelain. The Royal Vienna pieces include that name in the description.

Bowl, Woman, Watering Flowers, Green, Prussia, 10 In. 190.00
Bowl, Woman Pulling Cupid In Chariot, Octagonal, c.1910 . . . . 95.00
Charger, Biblical Scene, Raised Gilt, Portrait Medallions, Jewel Ground 3500.00
Coffeepot, Courting Scenes, Cobalt Blue & Gold, Gilt, 2 Large Medallions, 1800s. 295.00
Cup & Saucer, Cabinet, Bacchanalian Scene, Gilt, Royal Vienna Style, 20th Century 950.00
Ewer, Diana, Huntress, Flower, Iridescent Bronze Ground, Gold Stencil, 10 In. 350.00
Figurine, Mother, Daughters, Late 19th Century, 7 x 5 ¼ In. 400.00
Jar, Cover, Idyllic Scene, 3 People, Man Holding Laurel Wreath 140.00
Jug, Milk, Landscape, Scattered Flowers, Yellow & Ocher Enamel, c.1818 . . . . 500.00
Lamp, Urn Shape, Biblical Scenes, Red Ground, Square Base, Royal Vienna, 15 x 5 In. 819.00
Plaque, Classical Scene, Woman Bathing, Royal Vienna, Aesthetic Movement Frame 11500.00
Plate, Center Portrait, Solitude, Serenity, Daphne, Raised Gold Border, 9 ½ In. 3290.00
Plate, Diana In The Garden, Jewel Ground, 9 ¼ In. 1850.00
Plate, Duck & Grouse, c.1890, 9 ⅝ In. 295.00
Plate, Helen Of Troy, Jewel Ground, 9 ¼ In. 1850.00
Plate, Portrait, Empress Josephine, Letter N, Enameled, 1900, 10 ¾ In. 280.00
Plate, Portrait, Woman, Dark Flowing Hair, Red Dress, Royal Vienna, c.1910, 9 ½ In. 165.00
Plate, Portrait, Woman Holding Flower, Cobalt & Gilt Rim, 10 In. 862.00
Plate, Portrait Medallions, Jewel Ground, Raised Gilt, 10 In. 1850.00
Plate, Venus, c.1900, 10 In. . . . . *illus* 800.00
Saucer, Demitasse, Green Outer Edge, Gold Center, 4 ½ In. 115.00
Urn, Cover, Figures In Landscape, Classical, Stepped Plinth, Royal Vienna, 9 ¼ In., Pair 1351.00
Urn, Mythological Scene, Venus, Cobalt Blue, Gilt, Pedestal Foot, F. Koller, c.1800, 15 In. 660.00
Vase, Classical Woman, Lavender Ground, Gilt Frame, Wagner, 1800s, 9 ½ In. . . . . *illus* 2300.00
Vase, Double Portrait, Nude, Cherubs, Handle, Royal Vienna, 15 ⅝ x 7 ½ In. 699.00
Vase, Royal Vienna, Urn, 2 Handles, c.1900, 12 ¼ x 8 ½ In. 819.00

BEER BOTTLES *are listed in the Bottle category under Beer.*

BEER CANS are a twentieth-century idea. Beer was sold in kegs or returnable bottles until 1934. The first patent for a can was issued to the American Can Company in September of that year, and Gotfried Kruger Brewing Company, Newark, New Jersey, was the first to use the can. The cone-top can was first made in 1935, the aluminum pop-top in 1962. Collectors should look for cans in good condition, with no dents or rust. Serious collectors prefer cans that have been opened from the bottom.

Acme, Flat Top, 1940s.......... 21.00
All-American, Flat Top, Chicago, Ill.......... 83.00
All-American Beer, Atlas Brewing Company.......... 275.00
Alps Brau Beer.......... 275.00
Alt Heidelberg, Guest Beer, Krausenized.......... 950.00
Altes Golden Lager, Cone Top.......... 350.00
Apollo, American Brewing, White, Red, Black, Gold.......... 3601.00
Beverwyck, Famous Beer, Since 1845, Export, Cone Top, Cap.......... 950.00
Billy, 6-Pack.......... 1.00
Billy, Tab Top, Opened, 1978, 12 Oz.......... 9.00
Blackhawk Old Lager, Old Fashioned Flavor, Cone Top, Cap.......... 650.00
Blatz Milwaukee, Cone Top.......... 128.00
Champagne Velvet, Cone Top.......... 47.00
Chief Oshkosh, Supreme Pilsener, Cone Top, Cap.......... 350.00
Copper Club, Cone Top.......... 28.00
Croft Cream Ale, Green, Yellow, Cone Top.......... 3550.00
E & B Light Lager, Cone Top.......... 225.00
Eastside Lager, Pull Tab, White, Red Background, Los Angeles, Calif., 12 Oz.......... 16.00
Erlanger's Pilsner Beer, Green, Yellow, Red, Cone Top.......... 6100.00
Fort Schuyler, Light Ale, Cone Top, Cap.......... 275.00
Golden Old Topper Ale, Man In Top Hat, Cone Top.......... 500.00
Grain Belt Beer, Friendly Beer, Cone Top.......... 350.00
Hanley's Extra Pale Ale, Peerless, Crowntainer, Cap.......... 125.00
Hauenstein, New Ulm Beer, Cone Top.......... 175.00
Hoosier, Quality Beer, Cone Top, Cap.......... 375.00
Iron City, 1979 Super Steelers, Pull Tab, Silver, Pittsburgh Brewing Company.......... 7.00
Iron City, Select Quality, Cone Top, Cap.......... 250.00
Iroquois Indian Head, Cone Top, Cap.......... 750.00
King Cole, Flat Top, Maier Brewing, Los Angeles.......... 233.00
King Cole, Premium Pale Beer.......... 350.00
Kool Beer, Blue, Grace Bros. Brewing, Santa Rosa, Calif.......... 5000.00
McAvoy's Malt Marrow Beer.......... 350.00
Milwaukee Premium, Cone Top.......... 28.00
Narragansett Ale, Flat Top, Opening Instructions.......... 334.00
Old Dutch Premium Lager Beer, Pennsylvania's Best.......... 150.00
Old Gold, Flat Top, St. Claire Brewing.......... 521.00
Old Reading, Flat Top, Pennsylvania Dutch Brewery.......... 6.50
Old Reading Beer, Pilsner, Traditionally Pennsylvania Dutch, Crowntainer.......... 200.00
Olympia Brewing Company, Pale Expert, Pull Tab, It's The Water, 12 Oz.......... 10.50
Pabst Bock Beer, Flat Top, Opening Instructions.......... 260.00
Patrick Henry, Extra Smooth Premium Beer.......... 350.00
Paul Bunyon.......... 450.00
Pilsengold, Flat Top, Opening Instructions, Bottom Opened.......... 16.00
Rheingold Scotch Ale, Flat Top, Liebmann, N.Y.......... 28.00
Richbrau Bock, Flat Top.......... 125.00
Santa Fe Lager, Fully Aged.......... 425.00
Schmidts, Light, Cone Top, Tin, Schmidt & Sons, Phila., 1940s, 12 Oz.......... 103.00
Shopwell Premium, Steel, Red & Gold, Pull Tab, Colonial Brewing Co., 1972, 12 Oz.......... 10.00
Van Merritt, Cone Top, Full.......... 158.00
Weber Waukesha, Cone Top.......... 285.00
White Bear, Strong, Bear With Beer Can.......... 750.00
White Cap, Cone Top.......... 300.00
Yankee Premium Beer, Sailing Ship.......... 175.00

BELL collectors collect all types of bells. Favorites include glass bells, figural bells, school bells, and cowbells. Bells have been made of porcelain, china, or metal through the centuries.

Brass, Beaded Design, c.1760.......... 185.00
Brass, Dolphins, 17 ½ In.......... *illus* 280.00

TIP

To prevent rust, don't store or display beer cans in a damp room. A deteriorating but collectible can is best left as is, although slight dents may be popped out. Some collectors spray cans with wax to keep them looking shiny. Others prefer just to dust.

Bell, Brass, Dolphins, 17 ½ In.
$280.00

Bell, Plantation, Yoke, Rope Pull Wheel, Cast Iron, 26 x 33 In.
$5400.00

Bell, School, Cast Iron, Trestle Foot, Black Paint, No. 4, 1896, 25 x 24 x 17 In.
$425.00

Bell, Turtle, Cast Iron, Painted, Clockwork, Germany, 6 ½ In.
$460.00

TIP
For removing ink prices on matte-finished pottery, try paste silver polish. It is a little abrasive and contains some cleaning chemicals that may help.

Belleek, Basket, Seashell Shape, Green Mark, 3 ¾ In.
$26.00

Belleek, Box, Lid, Basketweave, Relief Molded, 7 ½ In.
$144.00

Belleek, Vase, Triple Hippiritus, Marked, 19th Century, 7 In.
$225.00

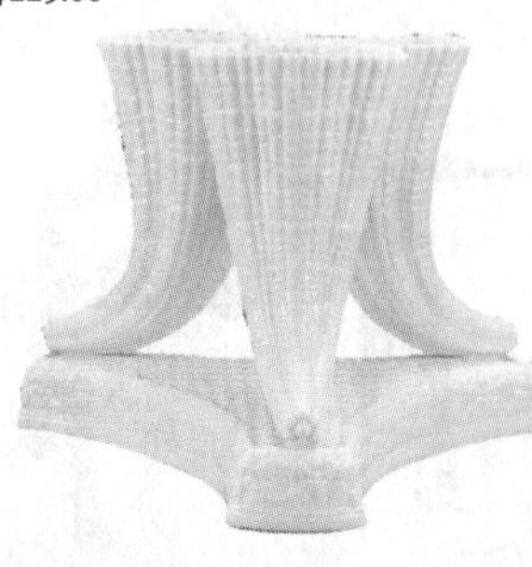

Brass, Gate, Spring Loaded Iron Mount, 9 ½ In. 546.00
Bronze, Dragons, Relief Inscriptions, Hardwood Stand, Chinese, 17 In. 3819.00
Bronze, Frieze, Figures, Putti, Chandeliers, 5 ¾ In. 175.00
Bronze, Liberty Bell Replica, 20th Century, 17 x 12 In. 287.00
Bronze, Shaped Panels, Hydra Finial, 19th Century, 37 In. 5975.00
Bronze, Ship, Wood Stand, 19th Century, 31 x 14 x 17 In. 1434.00
Bronze, Waves, Engraved Inscriptions, Chinese, 11 In. 353.00
Bronze, Wood Frame, Meneely Foundry, c.1883, 38 x 34 In. 3585.00
Call, Glass, Molded, 4-Footed, Embossed Stand, c.1890, 4 In. 324.00
Challis Shape, Leather Strap 11.00
Farm, Cast Iron, Chattanooga, Tenn., 13 x 18 In. 10.00
Front Desk, Silver Plate, 6 x 3 In. 70.00
Gate, Brass, Spring Mounted, Mounting Spike, 19th Century, 7 ½ In. 431.00
Iron, Top Brace, Wheel, 19th Century, 27 x 28 In. 717.00
Iron, Yoke, c.1889, 30 x 28 In. 1016.00
Plantation, Yoke, Rope Pull Wheel, Cast Iron, 26 x 33 In. .... *illus* 5400.00
School, Cast Iron, Trestle Foot, Black Paint, No. 4, 1896, 25 x 24 x 17 In. .... *illus* 425.00
Sleigh, 6 Brass Bells, Leather Strap, 2 ½, 2 ¾, 3-In. Bells, 24 ½-In. Strap 71.00
Sleigh, 23 Bells, Leather Strap, Graduated Sizes No. 2 To No. 12, 90 In. 143.00
Turtle, Cast Iron, Painted, Clockwork, Germany, 6 ½ In. .... *illus* 460.00
Woman In Victorian Coat, Muff & Hat, Legs Are Clapper, Brass, 5 ¼ In. 295.00
Woman In Victorian Dress, Bonnet, Legs Are Clapper, Brass, 3 In. 140.00
Yellow Amber Glass, Applied Threading, Conical, Rigaree, Solid Handle, 1880, 8 In. 56.00

BELLE WARE glass was made in 1903 by Carl V. Helmschmied. In 1904 he started a corporation known as the Helmschmied Manufacturing Company. His factory closed in 1908 and he worked on his own until his death in 1934.

Box, Iris, Beaded Signed, 4 In. 250.00

BELLEEK china was made in Ireland, other European countries, and the United States. The glaze is creamy yellow and appears wet. The first Belleek was made in 1857. All pieces listed here are Irish Belleek. The mark changed through the years. The first mark, black, dates from 1863 to 1890. The second mark, black, dates from 1891 to 1926 and includes the words *Co. Fermanagh, Ireland.* The third mark, black, dates from 1926 to 1946 and has the words *Deanta in Eirinn.* The fourth mark, same as the third mark but green, dates from 1946 to 1955. The fifth mark, green, dates from 1955 to 1965 and has an R in a circle added in the upper right. The sixth mark, green, dates after 1965

Basket, Seashell Shape, Green Mark, 3 ¾ In. .... *illus* 26.00
Basket, Twig, 3-Strand Center, Handles, Openwork Rim, Flowers, Clovers, c.1920, 12 In. 705.00
Biscuit Jar, Clover, White Ground, 6 x 5 ¼ In. 150.00
Box, Lid, Basketweave, Relief Molded, 7 ½ In. .... *illus* 144.00
Chamberstick, Leaves, Basketweave, Green, Gold Mark, 2 ¼ x 6 ¼ In. 22.00
Coffeepot, Raised Coral Handle & Finial, Tridacna, Black Mark 250.00
Flowerpot, Diamond Quilted, Sawtooth Rim, Black Mark, 4 In. 125.00
Goblet, Hand Painted, Man Smoking, 11 ½ In. 308.00
Pitcher, Aberdeen, Off-White, Applied Flowers, 5th Mark, 1955-65, 8 ¾ In. 114.00
Pitcher, Limpet, Ribs, 5 ½ In. 47.00
Pitcher, Milk, Limpet, Green Mark, 1955-65, 5 ½ In. 48.00
Vase, Cornucopia, White, Green Mark, 1955-65, 9 ¼ In. 148.00
Vase, Ribbon, Raised Flowers On Vines, White, Green Mark, 1955-65, 7 ¾ In. 175.00
Vase, Ribbon, Scalloped Edge, 1955-65, 7 ¾ In. 146.00
Vase, Shamrock, Urn Form, 2 Handles, 1955, 8 In. 310.00
Vase, Swirl Form 270.00
Vase, Triple Hippiritus, Marked, 19th Century, 7 In. .... *illus* 225.00

BENNINGTON ware was the product of two factories working in Bennington, Vermont. Both the Norton Company and the Lyman Fenton Company were out of business by 1896. The wares include brown and yellow mottled pottery, Parian, scroddled ware, stoneware, graniteware, yellowware, and Staffordshire-type vases. The name is also a generic term for mottled brownware of the type made in Bennington.

Bottle, Coachman, Albany Slip Glaze, 8 ½ In. 198.00
Bottle, Coachman, Holding Mug, Mottled Brown, Flint Enamel, Marked, 1849. .... 640.00
Bottle, Coachman, Holding Mug, Rockingham Glaze, 1848, 10 In. 615.00
Bottle, Flask, Book, Bennington Battle, Blue, Flint Enamel, 6 In. 546.00

Bottle, Flask, Book, Bennington Battle, Flint Enamel, 6 x 3¾ x 2 In. . . . . 578.00 to 1192.00
Bottle, Flask, Book, Rockingham Glaze, 4⅞ In. 200.00
Candlestick, Flint Enamel, Mottled Green, Ocher & Umber, c.1850, 7 In., Pair . . . . *illus* 978.00
Candlestick, Yellowware, Rockingham Glaze, 7 In., Pair 150.00
Canister, Cover, Blackberries & Leaves, Yellowware, Rockingham Glaze, 8 In. 196.00
Churn, Crossed Birds, Stoneware, J. & E. Norton, Bennington, c.1855, 4 Gal., 17 In. 1650.00
Churn, Flowers, Cobalt Blue, Lug Handles, J. & E. Norton, c.1855, 6 Gal. 9988.00
Churn, Stylized Dotted Leaf, Blue, Handles, E. & L.P. Norton, c.1880, 2 Gal., 14½ In. 1155.00
Coffeepot, Helmet lid, Ocher & Umber Glaze, Flint Enamel, c.1855, 12½ In. . . . . *illus* 805.00
Crock, 2 Benny Birds, Blue, Handles, J. Norton & Co., c.1861, 3 Gal., 9 In. 1430.00
Crock, 2 Bucks, Trees, Cobalt Blue, Salt Glaze, Stoneware, J. & E. Norton, c.1865, 6 Gal. 90000.00
Crock, Bird, Cobalt Blue, Stoneware, E. & L.P. Norton, 4 Gal. 834.00
Crock, Flower Basket, Cobalt Blue, Stoneware, J. & E. Norton, 2 Gal. 275.00
Crock, Flower Basket, Cobalt Blue, Applied Ear Handles, Stoneware, J. & E. Norton, 2 Gal. . . . 475.00
Crock, Flying Hawk, Cobalt Blue, Salt Glaze, Stoneware, J. & E. Norton, c.1855, 3 Gal. 5700.00
Crock, Reclining Stag, Stoneware, Straight-Sided, J. & E. Norton, 3 Gal. 2040.00
Crock, Salt, Peacock & Fountain, Wall Mount, Yellowware, Rockingham Glaze, 6 In. 138.00
Crock, Schoolhouse, Cobalt Blue, Salt Glazed, Stoneware, J. Norton, 1800s, 2 Gal. 24000.00
Crock, Stoneware, Norton & Co., Pecking Chicken, 2 Gal. 1380.00
Crock, Stylized Leaf, Cobalt Blue, Lug Handles, E. & L.P. Norton, c.1885, 4 Gal. 529.00
Jug, Bird, Cobalt Blue, Pulled Strap Handle, J. Norton & Co., Gal., 10¾ In. 764.00
Jug, Bluebird On Branch, Cobalt Blue, Stoneware, J. Norton, Gal., 11½ In. 450.00
Jug, Cobalt Blue Flower, Stoneware, Edward & Luman P. Norton, c.1881, 3 Gal., 15 In. 940.00
Jug, Cobalt Blue Pheasant In Tree, Stoneware, J. & E. Norton, 4 Gal., 17¾ In. 16675.00
Jug, Leaf Design, Blue, E. & L.P. Norton, c.1880, 2 Gal., 13 In. 385.00
Jug, Little Brown Jug, Stoneware, Incised Script, Norton, c.1876, 3 In. 303.00
Jug, Peacock, Blue, J. & E. Norton, c.1855, 2 Gal., 14½ In. 2750.00
Jug, Running Rabbit, Stoneware, Blue Mark, Norton & Fenton, c.1840, 2 Gal., 12 In. 1540.00
Jug, Stylized Dotted Leaf, Blue, J. & E. Norton, c.1855, 13 In. 578.00
Mug, Man On Horse, Yellowware, Rockingham Glaze, 3¼ In. 104.00
Paperweight, Flint Enamel, Mottled, Cone Shape Knop, Lyman Fenton, c.1849, 2 x 5 In. 173.00
Pitcher, Cream, Flint Enamel, Cream, Ocher, Umber, 8 Ribs, Scalloped, 5½ In. 575.00
Pitcher, Flint Enamel, Alternate Rib, C-Scroll Handle, Green, Ocher, Umber, 7 In. 230.00
Pitcher, Flint Enamel, Diamond, Beaded Frame Around, Diamond, 1849, 11 In 1115.00
Pitcher, Peacock, Yellowware, Rockingham Glaze, 8 In. 92.00
Pitcher, Scalloped Rim, 8-Sided, Tan, Brown & Blue Glaze, c.1849, 6½ In. 900.00
Snuff Jar, Cover, Toby, Seated, Impressed, 1849, 3¼ In. 1115.00
Snuff Jar, Toby, Signed, Lyman Fenton, c.1849, 5½ In. 2300.00
Soap Dish, Flint Enamel, 3 Sections, Ogee, Octagonal, Liner, 4 x 4¾ x 4½ In. 230.00
Sugar, Cover, Flint Enamel, Paneled, Octagonal, Acorn Final, Green, Ocher, Umber, 9 In. 2645.00
Teapot, Flint Enamel, Alternate Rib, Acanthus, Blue Green, Ocher, Umber, 7 x 9 In. 207.00
Tiebacks, Flint Enamel, Green Mottled, c.1858, 4½ x 4 In. 460.00
Toby Jug, Man, Seated, Grapevine Handle, Marked, 1849, 6½ In. . . . . *illus* 196.00
Vase, Tulip, Flint Enamel, Green, Ocher, Umber Glaze, Octagonal Foot, 10 In. 431.00
Water Cooler, Barrel Form, Flower, Cobalt Blue, Incised, J. & E. Norton, 5 Gal. . . . . *illus* 1116.00

BERLIN, a German porcelain factory, was started in 1751 by Wilhelm Kaspar Wegely. In 1763, the factory was taken over by Frederick the Great and became the Royal Berlin Porcelain Manufactory. It is still in operation today. Pieces have been marked in a variety of ways.

Portrait, Old Woman, Fur Trimmed Coat, Shawl, Flemish Hood, Frame, 15 x 12 In. 4484.00

BESWICK started making earthenware in Staffordshire, England, in 1936. The company is now part of Royal Doulton Tableware, Ltd. Figurines of animals, especially dogs and horses, Beatrix Potter animals, and other wares are still being made.

Figurine, Adventure, Matte, No. 2876, 1987-89, 4½ In. 28.00
Figurine, Appaloosa, Spotted Walking Pony, No. 1516, 1958-67, 5¼ In. 518.00
Figurine, Bald Eagle, No. 1018, 1945-95, 7¼ In. . . . . 75.00 to 120.00
Figurine, Baltimore Oriole, No. 2183, 1968-73, 3½ In. 288.00
Figurine, Barnacle Goose, No. 1052, 1943-68, 6½ In. 960.00
Figurine, Bison, No. 1019, 1945-73, 5¾ In. 144.00
Figurine, Black Bass, Large Mouth, No. 1266, 1952-68, 6½ In. 360.00
Figurine, Black Beauty, No. 2466, 1974-89, 7¼ In. 59.00
Figurine, Black Labrador, Standing, D 145, 1999-Present, 5 In. 84.00
Figurine, Black-Capped Chickadee, No. 2189, 1968-73, 4½ In. 390.00
Figurine, Bois Roussel Racehorse, White, No. 701, 1952-67, 8 In. 960.00

Bennington, Candlestick, Flint Enamel, Mottled Green, Ocher & Umber, c.1850, 7 In., Pair
$978.00

Bennington, Coffeepot, Helmet Lid, Ocher & Umber Glaze, Flint Enamel, c.1855, 12½ In.
$805.00

Bennington, Toby Jug, Man, Seated, Grapevine Handle, Marked, 1849, 6½ In.
$196.00

Bennington, Water Cooler, Barrel Form, Flower, Cobalt Blue, Incised, J. & E. Norton, 5 Gal.
$1116.00

Beswick, Cat With Mouse, No. 2100, 1967-73, 3 In.
$83.00

Beswick, Figurine, Pheasant, No. 1225B, 1967-77, 7¾ In.
$66.00

Beswick, Figurine, Shire Horse, Brown, No. 2578, 11 In.
$58.00

TIP

Have an emergency plan for your collection. For storms with advance warning, arrange to move the collection or at least pack it and move it to the safest part of the house. Be sure to have packing materials available.

Figurine, Boy On Pony, No. 1500, 1961-76, 5½ In. 570.00
Figurine, Brown Horse, Tail Angled, No. 1549, 1958, 7½ In. 59.00
Figurine, Bull Terrier, White, Gloss, No. 970, 1942-94, 6½ In. 108.00
Figurine, Burnham Beauty, Brown Matte, No. 2309, 1979-82, 10¾ In. 168.00
Figurine, Canadian Mounted Cowboy, No. 1377, 1955-73, 8¾ In. 1800.00
Figurine, Canadian Mountie, No. 1375, 1955-76, 8¼ In. 900.00
Figurine, Cat With Mouse, No. 2100, 1967-73, 3 In. . . . . *illus* 83.00
Figurine, Cedar Waxwing, No. 2184, 1968-73, 4½ In. 300.00
Figurine, Cockatoo, Pink, Gray, No. 1180, 1949-75, 8½ In. 156.00
Figurine, Cocker Spaniel, No. 1754, 1961-96, 3 In. 60.00
Figurine, Dairy Shorthorn Bull, No. 1504, 1957-73, 5 In. 900.00
Figurine, Dairy Shorthorn Calf, No. 1406C, 1956-73, 3 In. 720.00
Figurine, Dog With Toothache, No. 761, 1939-71, 4¼ In. 47.00
Figurine, Duchess With Pie, B P3B, 1979-82, 4 In. 261.00
Figurine, Elephant, Trunk In Salute, No. 1770, 1961-75, 12 In. 144.00
Figurine, English Setter, Large, Speckled Gray, No. 1220, 1951-73, 8 In. 1920.00
Figurine, English Setter, No. 973, 1987-89, 5½ In. 84.00
Figurine, Evening Grosbeak, No. 2190, 1968-73, 4 In. 360.00
Figurine, Foal, Head Down, Chestnut, No. 947, 1958-67, 4½ In. 354.00
Figurine, Foal, Lying, Chestnut, No. 915, 1958-67, 3¼ In. 384.00
Figurine, Fresian Bull, 1439A, 1985-89, 4¾ In. 159.00
Figurine, Ginger, BP 3B, 1976-82, 3¾ In. 432.00
Figurine, Girl On Jumping Horse, No. 939, 1941-65, 9¾ In. 384.00
Figurine, Girl On Pony, No. 1499, 1957-65, 5½ In. 450.00
Figurine, Green Woodpecker, No. 1218B, 1967-89, 9 In. 192.00
Figurine, Guernsey Cow, Horns, No. 1248B, 1985-89, 4¼ In. 216.00
Figurine, Hackney Pony, Brown, A 261, 1999-Present, 6¾ In. 144.00
Figurine, Hereford Calf, No. 1827C, 1987-89, 3 In. 156.00
Figurine, Highland Calf, No. 1827D, 1987-89, 3 In. 93.00
Figurine, Highland Cow, No. 1740, 1961-90, 5¼ In. 187.00
Figurine, Huntsman, Gray, No. 1501, 1962-75, 8¼ In. 960.00
Figurine, Huntsman, On Rearing Horse, Brown, No. 868, 1952-95, 10 In. 280.00
Figurine, Jay, No. 2417, 1972-82, 5 In. 121.00
Figurine, Jemima Puddle-Duck, Foxy Whiskered Gentleman, BP 6B, 1990-99, 4¾ In. 59.00
Figurine, Jersey Bull, No. 1422, 1985-89, 4½ In. 1200.00
Figurine, Leopard, No. 1082, 1946-75, 4¾ In. 108.00
Figurine, Lesser Spotted Woodpecker, No. 2420, 1972-82, 5½ In. 261.00
Figurine, Little Pig Robinson Spying, BP 3C, 1987-93, 3½ In. 71.00
Figurine, Mad Hatter, No. 2479, 1973-83, 4¼ In. 98.00
Figurine, Marlin, No. 1243, 1952-70, 5½ In. 750.00
Figurine, Merino Ram, No. 1917, 1964-67, 4¼ In. 2280.00
Figurine, Miss Moppet, BP 2A, 1954-78, 3 In. 108.00
Figurine, Morgan Stallion, No. 2605, 1979-89, 11½ In. 295.00
Figurine, Mr. Jeremy Fisher, 1st Version, Spotted Legs, BP 2A, 1950-74, 3 In. 75.00
Figurine, Mr. Jeremy Fisher, Marked, F. Warne & Co. Ltd., c.1950, 2¾ In. 165.00
Figurine, Mrs. Rabbit, Umbrella Out, BP 2A, 1951-74, 4¼ In. 132.00
Figurine, Mrs. Tiggy Winkle, BP 2A, 1948-74, 3¼ In. 71.00
Figurine, Norwegian Fjord Horse, No. 2282, 1970-75, 6½ In. 750.00
Figurine, Perch, No. 1875, 1963-71, 6¼ In. 690.00
Figurine, Persian Cat, Blue, Gloss, No. 1898, 1964-66, 5 In. 37.00
Figurine, Persian Cat, Lying, No. 1876, 1963-71, 3½ x 6½ In. 156.00
Figurine, Peter Rabbit, Dark Blue Jacket, 1st Version, BP 2, 1948-80, 4½ In. 56.00
Figurine, Pheasant, No. 1225B, 1967-77, 7¾ In. . . . . *illus* 66.00
Figurine, Pickles, BP 3A, 1971-82, 4½ In. 168.00
Figurine, Pigling Bland, Purple Coat, BP 2A, 1955-74, 4¼ In. 168.00
Figurine, Podgy Pig, 1998, 5¾ In. 83.00
Figurine, Puma On Rock, Tawny Matte, No. 1702, 1970-73, 8½ In. 106.00
Figurine, Quail, No. 2191, 1968-71, 5 In. 990.00
Figurine, Racehorse, Gray, No. 1564, 1959-82, 11¼ In. 192.00
Figurine, Red Setter, Lying, No. 1060, 1946-73, 3 In. 84.00
Figurine, Rupert Bear, No. 2694, 1980-86, 4¼ In. 330.00
Figurine, Rupert With Satchel, Box, No. 4002, 2000, 5 In. 168.00
Figurine, Samuel Whiskers, BP 2, 1948-95, 3¼ In. 144.00
Figurine, Scottish Terrier, No. 3382, 1993-Present, 3 In. 42.00
Figurine, Shire Foal, Gray, Gloss, No. 1053, 1961-73, 5 In. 204.00
Figurine, Shire Horse, Brown, No. 2578, 11 In. . . . . *illus* 58.00

Figurine, Shire Mare, Black, No. 818, 8 ½ In. 1080.00
Figurine, Siamese Cat, No. 1559A, 4 x 7 ¼ In. .... *illus* 36.00
Figurine, Sir Isaac Newton, BP 3A, 1973-84, 3 ¾ In. 187.00
Figurine, Sir Isaac Newton, BP 3B, 1973-84, 3 ¾ In. 204.00
Figurine, Spirit Of Freedom, Brown Matte, No. 2698, 1982-89, 7 In. 65.00
Figurine, Sussex Cockerel, No. 1899, 1963-71, 7 In. 1620.00
Figurine, Tiger, No. 2096, 1967-90, 7 ½ In. 132.00
Figurine, Tom Kitten & Butterfly, BP 3C, 1987-94, 3 ½ In. 149.00
Figurine, Welsh Cob, Palomino, No. 1014, 1961, 10 ¼ In. 540.00
Figurine, Yorkshire Terrier, Gloss, No. 2377, 1971-89, 10 ¼ In. 106.00
Plaque, Horse's Head In Horseshoe, No. 807, 1938-68, 7 ¼ x 6 In. 48.00
Toby Jug, Midshipman, No. 1112, 1948-73, 5 ¼ In. 106.00

BETTY BOOP, the cartoon figure, first appeared on the screen in 1931. Her face was modeled after the famous singer Helen Kane and her body after Mae West. In 1935, a comic strip was started. Her dog was named Bimbo. Although the Betty Boop cartoons ended by 1938, there was a revival of interest in the Betty Boop image in the 1980s and new pieces are being made.

Dish, Betty Boop, Vandor Label, Marked, 1984, 4 ½ In. 3.00
Doll, Red Body Suit, High Heels, 3 Outfits, 1986, 11 ½ In. 76.00
Pencil Holder, Celluloid, Occupied Japan, c.1940, 2 x 5 x 2 In. 460.00
Pendant, Silvertone, Flat, Textured, 2 ½ In. 15.00
Pin, Betty & Scottie Dog, Attached To Chain, Figural, Silver Luster, 1930s, 1 ½ In. 86.00

BICYCLES were invented in 1839. The first manufactured bicycle was made in 1861. Special ladies' bicycles were made after 1874. The modern safety bicycle was not produced until 1885. Collectors search for all types of bicycles and tricycles. Bicycle-related items are also listed here.

Bell, Chain Activated, Rides On Tire 72.00
Certificate, Membership, Boston Cycle Club, March 24, 1919, 12 x 16 In. 28.00
Christy, Saddle, Signed, c.1890 .... 330.00
Colson Commander, Battery Headstock & Badge, Horn, Light, c.1937 .... 2310.00
Display, Boneshaker, Pine, Painted, c.1900, 58 In. .... *illus* 2800.00
Gormully & Jeffrey, Tandem Tricycle, Adult 2-Track, c.1891 .... 25800.00
Henderson Auto Cycle, Block Pedals, Locking Fork, Key, c.1938 .... 660.00
High Wheel, Black Metal Frame, Leather Seat, Brass Handle, 59 x 67 In. 1870.00
High Wheel, Columbia, Drop Handlebars, Dust Shield, Name Plate, 56 In. 6600.00
High Wheel, Columbia, Drop Handlebars, Wood Grips, c.1885, 56 In. 3850.00
High Wheel, Columbia, Pope, Boston, Straight Handlebars, 52-In. Wheel, 61 In. 2468.00
High Wheel, Mixed Wood, Metal Hardware, 40 ¼ x 38 ½ x 15 In. 1045.00
High Wheel, Safety, Star 56, c.1884 .... 4675.00
High Wheel, Star, Safety, c.1884 .... 3850.00 to 4675.00
Horn, Cyclist, Brass, Silver, Henry Keat & Sons, 7 ½ In. 635.00
Huffy, Bendix, 2-Speed, Middle Weight, Power Pak, c.1955 .... 715.00
Imperial, Model 102, Man's, Pneumatic Safety, Ames & Frost, c.1898 .... 770.00
Iver Johnson, Streamline, Boy's, Balloon, Chrome Fenders, c.1937 .... 743.00
Lamp, Carbide, Bracket, Convex Glass Lens, Riemann, Oak Leaf Logo 425.00
Lamp, Kerosene, Bracket, Matthews & Williard Mfg., c.1898 .... 415.00
Lamp, Loop Handles, Slotted Lens Cover, Pedestal Base, T.E. Bladon & Son, 1942, Pair 77.00
Lock, Brass, Key, 19th Century, 4 x 3 In. 165.00
Monark, Silver King, Man's, c.1940 .... 193.00
Motorbike, Rollfast Zep, Hanging Tank, Headlight, c.1937 .... 688.00
Peugeot, Man's, 5-Speed, Generator Lamps, c.1970 .... 28.00
Poster, Cycles Et Motorcycles, Linen Backed, George Penvent, 29 x 20 In. 110.00
Poster, Soldier, Woman, Belgica, Bruxelles, 1898, 60 x 46 In. .... *illus* 365.00
Poster, Tour De France, Multicolored, c.1955 .... 248.00
Quadracycle, Belt Driven, Mobo Of England 105.00
Roadmaster Supreme, Boy's, Art Deco Lines, c.1937 .... 14300.00
Schwinn, Jaguar, Black, 47 x 69 In. .... *illus* 315.00
Schwinn, Mark IV Jaguar, Boy's, Blue, Chrome, Headlights, West Wind Tires, 1960s 735.00
Schwinn, Model B-607, Man's, c.1941 .... 2970.00
Schwinn, Phantom, Saddle, c.1950 .... 55.00
Schwinn, Sting-Ray, Pea Picker, 1960 .... 225.00
Schwinn, Sting-Ray, Stick Shift, 5-Speed, Fastback 248.00
Schwinn, Suburban, Girl's, 10-Speed, Headlamp, c.1960 .... 28.00
Sign, Raleigh Bicycles, Franchised Dealer, 37 ½ x 13 In. 88.00
Singer, Open Head, Fluted Fork, Drop Handlebars, Radial Spokes, c.1885, 54 In. 4400.00

Beswick, Figurine, Siamese Cat, No. 1559A, 4 x 7 ¼ In.
$36.00

Bicycle, Display, Boneshaker, Pine, Painted, c.1900, 58 In.
$2800.00

Bicycle, Poster, Soldier, Woman, Belgica, Bruxelles, 1898, 60 x 46 In.
$365.00

Bicycle, Schwinn, Jaguar, Black, 47 x 69 In.
$315.00

Bing & Grondahl, Figurine, Sparrow & Chick, Hand Painted, Marked, 1 ½ In.
$36.00

Birdcage, Wire, Wood, Apartment House Shape, Feeding Stations, Swing, c.1900, 20 x 20 x 10 In.
$360.00

TIP

Be careful handling birdhouses, birdcages, and bird feeders, old or new. It is possible to catch pigeon fever (psittacosis) through a cut or even from breathing the dust.

Bisque, Figurine, Bronte Peace Blossom Fairy, England, 11 ½ x 6 x 6 In.
$409.00

Sterling, Tandem, Man's, Pneumatic Safety, c.1895 .... 550.00
Tiller, Tricycle, Wooden Spoke Wheels, c.1880, 12-In. Front Wheel.......... 578.00
Tricycle, Child's, Black Metal, Chain & Gear Pedals, Velvet Cushion, 34 x 47 x 27 In. 468.00
Tricycle, Side Car, Strap Steel, Rubber Tires, c.1920, 16 In.. .... 225.00
Tricycle, Sidecar, Strap Steel, c.1920.......... 275.00
Tricycle, Spoke Wheels, Cloth Seat, Back Rest, Cast Iron, Victorian, 45 x 26 x 27 In. 540.00
Velocipede, Buckboard, Foot Steering, Leaf Springs, Wood Seat, c.1880 .... 1210.00
Velocipede, Horse Shape, Painted, Wrought Iron Wheels, France, Late 1800s, 29 In.......... 1763.00

BING & GRONDAHL is a famous Danish factory making fine porcelains from 1853 to the present. Underglaze blue decoration was started in 1886. The annual Christmas plate series was introduced in 1895. Dinnerwares, stoneware, and figurines are still being made today. The firm has used the initials B & G and a stylized castle as part of the mark since 1898. The company became part of Royal Copenhagen in 1987.

B&G KJØBENHAVN MADE IN DENMARK

Dish, Anchor & Rope, White, Blue, No. 2377, 7 ½ In. Diam. 50.00
Figurine, Girl Buttoning Shoe, No. 2317, 4 ¼ x 4 ¾ In.......... 88.00
Figurine, Sea Lion, 7 x 8 x 5 In. 88.00
Figurine, Sparrow & Chick, Hand Painted, Marked, 1 ½ In. .... *illus* 36.00
Vase, Flowers, Leaves, White Shaded To Blue, Bulbous, No. 681, c.1960, 5 In. 55.00

BINOCULARS of all types are wanted by collectors. Those made in the eighteenth and nineteenth centuries are favored by serious collectors. The small, attractive binoculars called opera glasses are listed in their own category.

Chevalier, Field, Leather Case, Paris, 4 ⅛ x 4 In. 55.00
Chevalier Optician Paris, Case.......... 11.00
Lemaire, Brass, 19th Century, 8 In.. .... 431.00
Selsi, 8 x 40, Leather Case, Strap, Japan, 7 x 6 In. 45.00
Sport, 7 x 35, No. 306117, Leather Case, Marked, Holiday.......... 45.00
Sport, National & American Football Conference, Team Helmets, 1970s.......... 10.00
Tasco, 8 x 20, Model No. 502, Field Vision 222 Ft., Leather Case.......... 155.00
Vendome, Military, Leather Covered, Paris, 6 In. 95.00

BIRDCAGES are collected for use as homes for pet birds and as decorative objects of folk art. Elaborate wooden cages of the past centuries can still be found. The brass or wicker cages of the 1930s are popular with bird owners.

Wicker, Stand, Crescent Arch, Tapered Pedestal, 74 x 18 In. 236.00
Wire, Wood, Apartment House Shape, Feeding Stations, Swing, c.1900, 20 x 20 x 10 In. . *illus* 360.00
Wood, Carved, Round, 4 Carved Feet, Brass Hanging Hook, 40 x 21 In. 1120.00
Wood, Metal, Dome Top, 19th Century, 38 x 9 ¼ x 21 In.. .... 468.00
Wood, Metal, Door, 19th Century, 38 x 9 ¼ x 21 In. 468.00

BISQUE is an unglazed baked porcelain. Finished bisque has a slightly sandy texture with a dull finish. Some of it may be decorated with various colors. Bisque gained favor during the late Victorian era when thousands of bisque figurines were made. It is still being made. Additional bisque items may be listed under the factory name.

Basket, Boy & Girl, 10 x 12 In. 132.00
Box, Lovebirds On Cover, 3 ½ x 8 In. 44.00
Figurine, Baby Golden Eagle, Kazmar, 6 x 7 ½ In.. .... 176.00
Figurine, Bathing Beauty, Blue Swimsuit, Red Trim, Marked, Germany, 4 In.. .... 99.00
Figurine, Boy Cobbler, Sitting On Toe Of Shoe, 4 x 5 ¼ In. 44.00
Figurine, Bronte Peace Blossom Fairy, England, 11 ½ x 6 x 6 In.. .... *illus* 409.00
Figurine, Dante, 18 ½ In.. .... 147.00
Figurine, Elephant, Timbo, 34 ½ x 23 In.. .... 5288.00
Figurine, Men At Table, Dog, 9 x 10 In. 150.00
Figurine, Naughty Lady, Reclining, Rubber Bulb On Head, Squirts, Germany, 4 x 2 In. 56.00
Figurine, Polar Bear Cubs, Kazmar, 5 ½ x 8 In. 23.00
Figurine, Raccoon Boy, Bronn, 14 ½ x 16 ½ x 12 In. 643.00
Figurine, Snowshoe Hare, Kazmar, 8 ½ In. 58.00
Figurine, Woman In Bathing Suit, Diving, 15 In. 173.00
Group, People At Table, Dog, 9 x 10 In.. .... 41.00
Pin Tray, Lady On Safety, Germany, 19th Century, 5 x 8 In. 275.00
Plaque, Courting Couple, High Relief, Velvet Matted Frame, Oval, 12 ½ x 10 In.. .... 413.00
Plaque, Imperial, Commemorative House Of Romanov, Russia, 1913, 7 In. 6490.00
Vase, Flowers, Bell Shape, 2 Handles, Art Nouveau, 9 ½ x 6 ¼ In. 58.00

BLACK memorabilia has become an important area of collecting since the 1970s. The best material dates from past centuries, but many recent items are also of interest. *F & F* is the mark used on plastic made by Fiedler & Fiedler Mold & Die Works, Inc. in the 1930s and 1940s. Objects that picture a black person may also be listed in this book under Advertising; Tin; Bank; Bottle Opener; Cookie Jar; Doll; Salt & Pepper; Sheet Music; Toy; etc.

Ashtray, Lighter, Cigarette, Pull Red Tongue, Reveals Lighter, 4 In. 29.00
Ashtray, Musician, Playing Cymbals, Chinese, 1950s, 8 In. .... *illus* 58.00
Ashtray, Nodder, Boy, Metal 86.00
Book, Jumpin' Joe, Jessie Davis, Illustrator John Chase, Signed, J.F. Carter, 1939 .... 250.00
Book, Sambo & Nancy Bell, Crescent Moon Shape, Die Cut, Lewis Novra, c.1890 .... 500.00
Booklet, Story Of Slavery, Booker T. Washington, 1913, 32 Pages 18.00
Bracelet, 6 Black Figures As Slaves, Tied Together, Braided String, 1 ¼ In. 717.00
Broadside, Slaves Wanted, Negro Men, Woman, Clay County, Mo., c.1860, 8 ¾ x 13 In. 5750.00
Dispenser, Unicum Chocolate, Coin-Operated, Gischol & Spenler, Germany, 12 x 36 In. 43700.00
Doll, Alabama Baby, Cloth, Pressed Cloth Face, Painted, Stitch-Jointed, Ella Smith, 23 In. 1232.00
Doll, Babyland Rag, Topsy-Turvy, 2 Heads, Black, White, Muslin, Leather Arms, 12 In. 728.00
Doll, Cloth, Man, Wool Head, Body, Mouth, Button Eyes, Frock Coat, 15 ½ In. 9988.00
Doll, Composition Socket Head, Curly Hair, 5 Piece, 14 In. 1232.00
Doll, Corn Husk, Wood, Oilcloth, Cloth Tape, Hand Sewn, 11 In. 127.00
Doll, Minstrel Man, Stitched, Embroidered Features, c.1900, 24 In. 1760.00
Doll, Slave, Corn Cob, Muslin Head, Hands, Cotton Dress, Belt, Scarf, 10 In. 1016.00
Figurine, Juggler, Hand Carved, 20 In. 288.00
Figurine, Man, Top Hat, Tails, Hand On Hip, Pine, Painted, 1800s, 10 In. 90000.00
Figurine, Policeman, Wearing Tie, Carved, c.1920, 13 In. 526.00
Figurine, Venetian, Multicolored Clothes, Hands Outstretched, 40 x 11 ½ x 19 ¼ In. 4700.00
Game, Target, Jolly Black, McLoughlin Brothers, c.1890, 8 x 14 In. 575.00
Lighter, Cigarette, 4 In. 144.00
Marionette, Wood, Carved, Animal Fur Hair, Corncob Arms 575.00
Menu, Ole Southern Chicken, Mammy, Hotel Westminster, Christmas, 1913, 8 x 6 ¼ In. 45.00
Nodder, Boy With Watermelon, 1895 .... 1150.00
Paperweight, Mammy, Red Dress, White Apron, Blue Bandana, Cast Iron, Hubley, 2 In. 66.00
Postcard, Babies, Children, Higgins Soap, Ayer's Pills, Atwell, Early 1900s, 19 Piece 59.00
Postcard, Novelty, Real Hair, With My Love, Boy Playing Guitar, Early 1900s 153.00
Poster, Hilson's Minstrels, Black Man, Donaldson Litho Co., 19 x 27 In. 115.00
Puppet, Dancing Girl, Lulabelle, Pellam Puppets, c.1950 .... 633.00
Puppet, Hand, Minstrel Makeup, Late 19th Century, 12 In. 316.00
Puppet, Minstrel, Painted, Cloth Clothes, Late 19th Century, 27 In. 6270.00
Smoking Stand, Bellhop, Tack Buttons, Metal Ashtray, 33 ½ In. .... *illus* 209.00
Stringholder, Woman, Bandana, String Hole In Mouth, Chalkware, 8 x 5 ¼ x 3 ¼ In. 121.00
Syrup, Aunt Jemima, Plastic, Marked, F&F Mold & Dieworks, Early 1950s, 5 x 2 ½ In. 25.00
Toy, Man, On Scooter, Tin, Windup, Lehmann, 5 In. 201.00
Toy, Sojourner Truth, Behind Podium, Clockwork, 1880, 4 x 11 x 5 In. 7170.00
Wood Carving, Painted Face, White Hair, Earring, c.1880, 24 x 13 x 8 In. 5500.00

BLACK AMETHYST glass appears black until it is held to the light, then a dark purple can be seen. It has been made in many factories from 1860 to the present.

Basket, Embossed Basket Weave, Handle, 3 ¾ x 2 ¾ In. 22.00
Candlestick, Shaped Cup, Stepped Foot, 1930s, 7 In., Pair 35.00
Coaster, Octagonal, Daisy & Button Base, 3 ½ In., 6 Piece 25.00
Console Set, Shaped Edge, 3-Footed, 8 ½-In. Bowl, 3-In. Candlestick, 3 Piece 35.00
Ginger Jar, Cover, Painted Apple Blossoms, Flame-Shaped Finial, 6 In. 22.00
Muffineer, Acorn, 4 ¼ In. .... *illus* 250.00
Vase, Elongated, Petal Rim, 3 Fluted Bands, Flared Base, 8 In. 13.00
Vase, Shouldered, Elongated Neck, Flared Rim, 13 In. 42.00

BLENKO GLASS COMPANY is the 1930s successor to several glassworks founded by William John Blenko in Milton, West Virginia. In 1933, his son, William H. Blenko Sr., took charge. The company made a line of reproductions for Colonial Williamsburg. They are still in business and are best known today for their decorative wares and stained glass.

Bowl, Opalescent, Jonquil Yellow, Crackle, 3 ¾ x 8 In. 40.00
Bowl, Oval, Green, Crackle, Ruffled Rim 9 x 6 ½ x 4 In. 35.00
Decanter, Blue, Bulbous, Stopper, 1963, 21 x 10 In. 425.00
Decanter, Blue, Flame Stopper, Wayne Husted, 18 ½ In. 250.00

Black, Ashtray, Musician, Playing Cymbals, Chinese, 1950s, 8 In. $58.00

Black, Smoking Stand, Bellhop, Tack Buttons, Metal Ashtray, 33 ½ In. $209.00

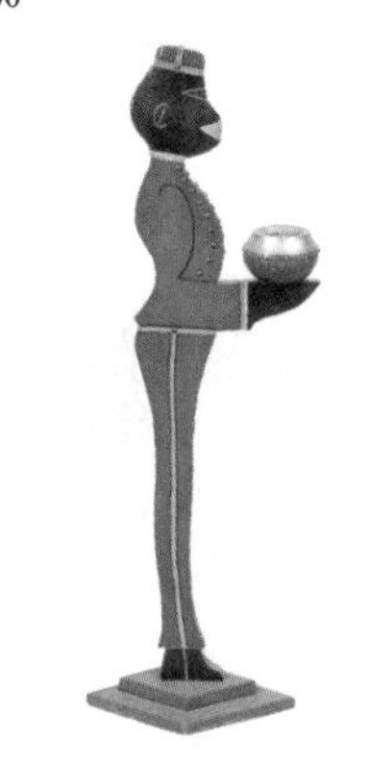

Black Amethyst, Muffineer, Acorn, 4 ¼ In. $250.00

TIP

Scrape your fingernail across the scratch on the glass on your mirror. If it catches, the scratch is too deep to be polished out at home. It requires professional work.

Blenko, Decanter, Orange, Transluscent, Stopper, 29 In.
$495.00

Boch Freres, Vase, Art Deco Flowers, Crackled Enamel, Marked, 11 ⅝ In.
$250.00

Boch Freres, Vase, Art Deco Flowers, Matte Enamel, Marked, Keramis, Delfant, 6 ⅛ In.
$375.00

Decanter, Clear Crackle, Turquoise Rope Trim On Neck, Ruffled Edge, 1968, 12 In. 35.00
Decanter, Dimple, Emerald, Textured, Triangular, Rough Pontil, 14 In. 150.00
Decanter, Dot, Cobalt Blue, Square Base, Hank Adams, 14 In. 175.00
Decanter, Genie, Tangerine, Onion Stopper, 1960, 16 In. 325.00
Decanter, Genie, Turquoise Crackle, 16 ½ In. 200.00
Decanter, Olive, Optic, Stopper, 9 In. 75.00
Decanter, Orange, Translucent, Stopper, 29 In. . . . . *illus* 495.00
Decanter, Undulating Lobes, Amber Yellow, Flat Stopper, Wayne Husted, 1954, 27 In. 650.00
Pitcher, Clear Crackle, Emerald Green Handle, 1960s, 5 ½ In. 45.00
Pitcher, Light Green, Elongated Spout, 1952, 14 In. 56.00
Rose Bowl, Green, Crimped Rim, 5 ¾ x 7 In. 30.00
Vase, Amberina, Dimpled Allover, Crimped Rim, Stamped, 8 In. 90.00
Vase, Amberina, Ribbed, Wayne Husted, 13 In. 185.00
Vase, Blue Spiral, 9 ¼ In. 50.00
Vase, Clear, Turquoise & Olive Green Applied Spirals, 9 ¼ In. 250.00
Vase, Dark Emerald Green, Pinched Sides, c.1951, 6 ½ x 7 In. 55.00
Vase, Flower Shape, Orange, Wide Mouth, 9 In. 35.00
Vase, Hat Shape, Sea Green Seed Glass, Cupped Rim, 9 ¾ x 13 ¾ In. 150.00
Vase, Sea Green, Cone Base, Square Top, Rolled Rim, 1940s, 12 x 11 ¾ In. 95.00

BLOWN GLASS, *see Glass-Blown category.*

BLUE GLASS, *see Cobalt Blue category.*

BLUE ONION, *see Onion category.*

BLUE WILLOW, *see Willow category.*

BOCH FRERES factory was founded in 1841 in La Louviere in eastern Belgium. The wares resemble the work of Villeroy & Boch. The factory is still in business.

BOCH FRERES KERAMIS MADE IN BELGIUM

Charger, Bird Of Paradise, Crackled Enamel, Multicolored, 8 ¼ In. 266.00
Charger, Deer Leaping, Crackled Enamel, Multicolored, 8 ¼ In. 236.00
Charger, Woman Holding Greyhound By Collar, Stoneware, Tan, C. Catteau, 14 In. 10325.00
Pitcher, Nudes, Incised, Green Matte Glaze, Flat Sides, Footed, E. D'Hossche, 11 In. 2124.00
Vase, 3 Colors, Geometric Band Around Middle, 8 In. 767.00
Vase, 3 Stylized Roosters In Cartouches, Green, Yellow, Blue, Swollen Shape, 6 In. 1003.00
Vase, Abstract Flowers, Cuerda Seca, Faceted, Faience, 12 ¾ x 8 In. 2400.00
Vase, Art Deco Flowers, Blue, Yellow Crackle Ground, Tapered, 9 ⅜ In. 1888.00
Vase, Art Deco Flowers, Crackled Enamel, Marked, 11 ⅝ In. . . . . *illus* 250.00
Vase, Art Deco Flowers, Matte Enamel, Marked, Keramis, Delfant, 6 ⅛ In. . . . . *illus* 375.00
Vase, Art Deco Flowers, Matte Enamel, 12 In. 1888.00
Vase, Art Deco Geometrics, Blue, Turquoise, Crackled, 6 Sides, Stepped Handles, 12 ⅜ In. 1770.00
Vase, Black Glaze, Silver Lines, Mottled Orange Uranium Interior, Bulbous, 9 In. 590.00
Vase, Brown Maize, Gray Crackle Ground, 6 ⅝ In. 1062.00
Vase, Deer, Blue, Black, Crackled Ground, Oval, Flared Rim, Keramis, 12 In. 1003.00
Vase, Fauns & Flowers, Multicolored, Crackled Enamel, White Ground, 13 ⅜ In. 4720.00
Vase, Flower Heads, Cobalt Blue, Flared Foot, Gilt Metal Rim, Vase Shape, 19 In., Pair. 1175.00
Vase, Flowers, Brown, Blue, Green, 8 ½ In. 552.00
Vase, Flowers, Crackled Enamel, Multicolored 7 ⅞ In. 266.00
Vase, Flowers, Multicolored, Crackled Enamel, 6 ¼ In. 189.00
Vase, Flowers, Multicolored, Marked, Keramis, 9 ¼ x 6 ½ In. . . . . *illus* 290.00
Vase, Flowers, White, Brown, Repeating Panels, Green & Brown Glaze, 8 ½ In. 708.00
Vase, Leaf Bands, Yellow, Crackle Ground, Black Trim, Bulbous, 14 ½ x 13 In. 3776.00
Vase, Leaves, Brown, Green Mottled Ground, Crystalline Glaze, 9 In. 1062.00
Vase, Oval Peacock Eyes, Blue, Gold, White, Tapered, Footed, C. Catteau, 10 ⅜ In. 3894.00
Vase, Owls, Mottled Brown, Gray & Yellow Glaze, Fold-Out Rim, Keramis, 12 In. 4956.00
Vase, Pastel Flowers, Light Crackle Glaze, 8 ¼ In. 1416.00
Vase, Sea Gulls In Flight, 8 ¼ In. 3186.00
Vase, Squirrels, Black Glaze, Gold Moonlight Ovals, Bulbous, Tapered, 8 ¾ In. 354.00
Vase, Stylized Birds, Flowers, Brown & Yellow, Matte Glaze, Tapered, Flared Rim, 12 In. 1180.00
Vase, Stylized Blue Flowers, Tan & Blue Glaze, Crackle Ground, C. Catteau, 5 ⅜ In. 1180.00
Vase, Stylized Sailboats, Gulls, Crackle Ground, Oval, Cylindrical Neck, 11 ⅝ In. 2714.00
Vase, Stylized White Roses, Brown, Blue & Tan Mottled Ground, Keramis, 8 ½ In. 708.00
Vase, Wading Birds, Flowers, Red Clay Body, Black Trim, Bulbous, Keramis, 9 In. 1416.00
Vase, White Grapes, Green Square Leaves, Green & Black Glaze, Oval, Keramis, 9 In. 560.00

BOEHM is the collector's name for the porcelains of Edward Marshall Boehm. In 1953 the Osso China Company was reorganized as Edward Marshall Boehm, Inc. The company is still working in England and New Jersey. In the early days of the factory, dishes were made, but the elaborate and lifelike bird figurines are the best-known ware. Edward Marshall Boehm, the founder, died in 1969, but the firm has continued to design and produce porcelain. Today, the firm makes both limited and unlimited editions of figurines and plates.

2 Black Grouse, Marked, 15 In. 735.00
African Elephant, Bisque, 8 x 10 In. .... 294.00 to 351.00
American Redstarts, c.1960, 11 ½ In. 300.00
Apple Blossom Cluster, Pink Flowers On Branch, 4 ½ In. .... 58.00 to 160.00
Ashley, Retriever, Bisque, 11 x 10 In. 234.00
Baby Blue Jay, 4 x 3 In. 71.00
Baby Crested Fly Catcher, On Twig, c.1970, 5 x 3 In. 206.00
Bear Cub, 5 x 5 x 5 In. 35.00
Bird Of Paradise, Signed, Helen Boehm, 15 In. 940.00
Black Capped Chickadee, 7 ½ x 6 ¾ In. 94.00
Black Grouse, 15 In. 499.00
Blue Grosbeak, Oak Leaves, Acorns, Marked, c.1967, 11 ¼ In. 515.00
Blue Jay, No. 40218-69, 10 ¾ x 8 ½ In. 470.00
Blue Jay, Raspberries, 18 x 13 In. 936.00
Blue Tits, Apple Blossoms, 9 ¼ In. 1750.00
Bobolink, Cornstalk, 1964, 15 In. .... *illus* 415.00
Boxer, c.1950, 4 ½ x 6 In. 106.00
Broad-Billed Hummingbird, No. 40366-386, 9 x 7 In. 411.00
Brown Pelican, Impressed Mark, 26 In. 5200.00
Brown Thrasher, 8 x 9 ½ In. 411.00
Bust, La Pieta Madonna, c.1953, 6 ½ x 5 ½ In. 40.00
Calliope Hummingbird, 10 x 6 In. 439.00
Cardinal, 8 ½ x 5 ½ x 4 ½ In. 176.00
Catbird, Hyacinths, Marked, 1965, 14 ½ In. 1290.00
Chaffinch, Double Cherries, V Mark, 10 x 13 x 8 In. 615.00
Colt, Lying, 24K Gold, 1978, 4 x 5 In. 264.00
Crested Flycatcher, Marked, 1967, 18½ In. .... 588.00 to 920.00
Cygnet, 7 x 4 In. 117.00
Cygnet, No. 400-46, 4 ½ x 5 In. 323.00
D'Osery's Hermit Hummingbird, 2005, 12 x 6 In. 322.00
Douglas Great Blue Heron, 2004, 16 x 10 x 9 In. 468.00
Downy Woodpeckers, Male, Female, 2 Chicks, Trumpet Vine, 1958, 13 In. 720.00
Eastern Kingbird, 1975, 21 x 11 In. 1872.00
Egret In Flight, Signed, Helen Boehm, 12 x 16 In. 940.00
Fairy Tern, Signed, 1988, 13 x 19 In. 761.00
Falco Sparverius, Kestrel, c.1960, 14 In. 425.00
Fallow Deer, Licking Hind Foot, 6 x 8 In. 70.00
Fifi Chimpanzee, 9 ¼ x 7 ½ x 7 ¾ In. 150.00
Flamingo, Signed, Helen Boehm, 13 x 14 In. 1528.00
Fledgling Blackburnian Warbler, c.1970, 4 x 2 ½ In. 147.00
Fledgling Canadian Warbler, Butterfly, 9 x 8 ½ In. 175.00
Fledgling Great Horned Owl, 7 x 6 In. 206.00
Fledgling Kingfisher, 3 x 2 ½ In. 59.00
Fledgling Kingfisher, On Log, Blue, Orange, Brown, c.1970, 6 x 5 In. 235.00
Fledgling Red Poll, 4 x 4 In. 55.00
Flower, Camellia, 4 x 5 ½ x 8 ¼ In. 235.00
Flower, Hibiscus, Castaways, Bisque, 2004, 5 x 5 In. .... *illus* 146.00
Flower, Iris Bouquet, Bisque, 1993, 20 x 12 In. 410.00
Flower, Nancy Reagan Camellia, 3 ¾ x 8 In. 206.00
Flower, Peach Rose, Bisque, 1989, 4 x 6 In. 117.00
Flower, Pink Cymbidium Orchid, c.1980, 10 x 4 ¾ In. 90.00
Flower, Pink Peony, Bisque, 7 x 21 x 12 In. 1404.00
Flower, Queen Elizabeth Rose, 1986, 10 x 8 In. 351.00
Flower, Rose, Royal Blessing, 1982, 7 x 13 In. 527.00
Flower, Yellow Rose Of Texas With Bluebonnets, Bisque, 1985, 9 x 14 In. 644.00
Giant Panda Cub Reclining, 6 x 7 In. .... 200.00 to 235.00
Goddess Selket, 18 In. 470.00
Golden Crown Kinglets, Poppies, Marked, 1958, 11 In. 575.00
Horned Larks, Grapevines, Signed, Feather Mark, 19 ¼ In. 2100.00

Boch Freres, Vase, Flowers, Multicolored, Marked, Keramis, 9 ¼ x 6 ½ In.
$290.00

Boehm, Bobolink, Cornstalk, 1964, 15 In.
$415.00

Boehm, Flower, Hibiscus, Castaways, Bisque, 2004, 5 x 5 In.
$146.00

B

Boehm, Lapwing & Dandelions, Marked, 16 In.
$1245.00

Boehm, Plate, Bird Of Peace, Mute Swans, 12 ¾ In.
$47.00

Boehm, Wood Thrush, Rhododendron, Marked, 15 ¾ In.
$565.00

Hummingbird, 9 ½ x 4 ⅓ In. 470.00
Hummingbird On Cactus, 8 ½ x 4 ¼ In. 294.00
Hummingbird With Iris, 14 x 4 In. 529.00
Hummingbird With Morning Glory, 11 x 9 In. 470.00
Indigo Bunting, Male, Morning Glories, Marked, c.1970, 10 In. 810.00
Indigo Bunting, Teal Colored, Cherokee Rose Cane, c.1970, 10 ¼ x 5 ½ In. 86.00
Jaguar, 1981, 9 x 17 In. 585.00
Kestrel, 14 x 7 In., Pair 940.00
Kingfisher With Primrose, 9 ½ x 11 x 10 In. 175.00
Koala Cub, 9 x 9 In. 294.00
Lapwing & Dandelions, Marked, 16 In. *illus* 1245.00
Lark Sparrow, Buttercups, 12 ¾ In. 1150.00
Lazuli Bunting, Daisies, Marked, 1973, 13 ¾ In. 2100.00
Lucifer Hummingbird, Bisque, 2002, 12 x 8 In. 439.00
Lucifer Hummingbird With Foxgloves, 1996, 6 x 2 In. 176.00
Macaw, Perched On Stump, 8 In. 2150.00
Mallard Duck, In Flight, 12 In. 80.00
Mourning Doves, 1958, 14 In. 292.00 to 485.00
Myrtle Warblers, Arbutus, 8 ¼ In. 460.00
Orangutan, 7 ½ x 8 ½ In. 353.00
Orchard Orioles, Tulip Poplar Blossoms, Leaves, 11 In. 565.00
Owl, 10 ½ x 6 ½ In. 411.00
Palm Beach Hibiscus, 3 x 4 In. 206.00
Parula Warblers, Flowering Vine, Marked, 15 ½ In. 1290.00
Plate, Bird Of Peace, Mute Swans, 12 ¾ In. *illus* 47.00
Plate, Young America, 1776, 12 ¾ In. 35.00
Polar Bear With Cubs, 6 ½ x 11 In. 382.00
Prothonotary Warbler, Bisque, 6 x 6 In. 82.00
Rabbit, Seated, 4 ½ x 3 ¼ In. 88.00
Racquet Tail Hummingbird, Lily, 11 x 11 In. 529.00
Raised Flowers, Leaves, Melon Shape, Box, 5 ½ x 6 ¼ x 4 ½ In. 147.00
Red Prothonotary Warbler, 6 In. 88.00
Red-Shouldered Hawk, 26 x 17 In. 2633.00
Renaissance Angel, White, Bisque, 1989, 12 x 12 In. 176.00
Robin, No. 400-65, Signed, George Boehm, 1977, 8 ½ x 9 ½ In. 499.00
Robin, Removable Daffodils, Marked, 14 In. 1400.00
Rose, Pink, 1 x 3 In. 82.00
Royal Tern, Signed, 19 x 19 In. 819.00
Sandpipers, 12 x 7 x 4 In. 705.00
Snow Buntings, No. 400-21, 7 ½ x 11 In. 470.00
Song Thrushes, Male Female, Snails, Crabapples, 15 ½ In. 1050.00
Spotted Owl With Young, 23 x 17 In. 2350.00
Sugar Birds, Ferns, Orchids, 1961, 25 In. 4300.00
Sunrise Iris, 5 x 7 ½ x 5 In. 176.00
Sweet Pea In Seashell, 6 ½ x 3 In. 176.00
Thrasher, Male, Brown, Crocus, 7½ In. 411.00 to 475.00
Thrush, 2 Yellow Parrot Tulips, Marked, 18 In. 1600.00
Timeless, 10 x 10 In. 644.00
Tree Creepers, Mistletoe, V Mark, c.1971, 17 In. 1150.00
Tree Sparrow, 7 ½ In. 117.00
Vase, Blue, White Sunflowers, Gold Trim, 12 ½ x 7 In. 118.00
Victorian Child, Amy, c.1986, 9 x 4 In. 35.00
Western Meadowlark, No. 400-95, 13 ½ x 8 ½ In. 705.00
White French Poodle, 3 ½ In. 35.00
White Iris, 5 x 6 In. 94.00
White Stallions, 19 x 17 x 10 In. 1287.00
White Throated Sparrow, 9 ¼ In. 118.00
Wood Thrush, 8 ¼ x 5 ½ x 6 ¼ In. 217.00
Wood Thrush, Rhododendron, Marked, 15 ¾ In. *illus* 565.00
Woodpeckers, White Morning Glories, V Mark, 22 In. 1300.00
Yellowhammers, Hawthorn, V Mark, c.1973, 11 In. 1200.00
Yellow-Shafted Flicker, 13 In. 1645.00
Yellow-Throated Warbler, No. 431, 9 ½ x 4 In. 294.00
Young American Bald Eagle, No. 498, 10 x 5½ In. 125.00 to 147.00
Young Giraffe, No. 20123, 14 ¼ x 7 ¾ In. 353.00

BONE includes those articles made of bone not listed elsewhere in this book.

Bonbon, Mikasa, Eden's Garden, Basket Weave, Gold Gilt, Pink Lily, 7 ¼ x ⅞ In. 25.00
Ditty Box, Ships At Sail, Great Seal Of United States, Dated, 1839 .... 1850.00
Pie Crimper, Whalebone, Baleen, Columnar, Fluted Wheel, Carved, c.1850, 9 In. 10200.00
Triptych, Figural, Carved, Round, Scenes Of Courtly Gentleman, Continental, 7 In. 266.00
Whistle, Carved, Engraved Sailing Ships, Stars, 19th Century, 2 ½ In. 1200.00

BONE DISHES were considered a necessary part of a table setting for the Victorian table. The crescent-shaped dish was kept at the edge of the dinner plate so the bones removed from the fish could be stored away from the uneaten food. Some bone dishes were made in more fanciful shapes and many resemble fish.

Autumn Leaves, Gilt Trim, Crescent, Chadwick 15.00
Crescent, Roses, Pink Luster, Germany 24.00
Kidney, Delicate Flowers & Leaves, Blue Trim, Grindley, 7 In. 20.00
Lavender Flowers, Yellow Centers, Brown Branches, Transfer, Crescent 15.00
Pink Roses, Blue Forget-Me-Nots, Gilt Trim, Crescent, Chadwick 15.00
Rose, Japan, 8 x 3 ½ In. 16.00

BOOKENDS have probably been used since books became inexpensive. Early libraries kept books in cupboards, not on open shelves. By the 1870s bookends appeared, especially homemade fret-carved wooden examples. Most bookends listed in this book date from the twentieth century. Bookends are also listed in other categories by manufacturer or material. All bookends listed here are pairs.

Abraham Lincoln, Bronze, c.1900, 7 ¾ In. .... *illus* 40.00
Abraham Lincoln, Emancipator, Angel, Copper Over Zinc, Pompeian Bronze Co., 5 x 3 ¾ x 2 In. 168.00
Abraham Lincoln, Sitting On Bench, Dark Patina, Felt Bottom, 6 ½ x 6 x 3 ¾ In. 956.00
Antelope, Leaping Over Rock, Art Deco, Pottery, 7 x 7 ½ x 2 In. 168.00
Baseball Player, Safe At First, Cast Iron, 4 ¾ x 6 In. .... *illus* 748.00
Borzoi Dog, Cast Metal, Bronze, Oval Base, c.1930, 8 x 8 In. 350.00
Bronze, Ship, 5 ½ x 8 In. 59.00
Cape Cod Cottage, Shingle Roof, Hollyhocks, Cast Iron, 4 ½ x 5 In. 633.00
Cape Cod Fishermen, Cast Iron, Bronze, Patina, C In Triangle, c.1928, 5 ½ In. 225.00
Cat, Brass, Walter Von Nessen, c.1930, 7 ¼ x 2 ½ x 4 In. 470.00
Cat On Fence, Dog, Painted, Cast Iron, 5 ⅝ x 4 ½ In. .... *illus* 115.00
Cottage, Gardener, Castle Tower, Cast Iron, Bradley & Hubbard, 5 ½ In. 144.00
Dog, Borzoi, Standing, Green, Bronze, Marble Base, Chiparus, 5 ¾ x 5 ½ x 2 ½ In. 478.00
Dog, Scottie, Black Enamel, Cast Iron, 5 ¼ In. 225.00
Dog, Scottie, By Fence, Cast Iron, Hubley, 4 ½ x 4 x 4 ¾ In. 425.00
Dog, Scottie, Cast Iron, Hubley, 5 x 6 ¼ In. .... *illus* 201.00
Dog, Wirehaired Terrier, Cast Iron, Hubley, 5 ¼ x 5 ⅜ In. 230.00
Doorway, Steps, Flower Framed, Painted, Cast Iron, Bradley & Hubbard, 5 ¾ In. 144.00
Elephant, Metal, Bronze Patina, Nuart, c.1931, 6 ¼ x 6 ½ In. 125.00
Figures, Reclining, Brass, Marble, Art Deco, c.1930, 8 x 8 ½ x 3 In. 411.00
Flowers, Urn, Cast Iron, Bradley & Hubbard, 5 ¾ x 4 ⅛ In. 115.00
Foo Dog, Bronze, Chinese, 19th Century, 8 x 2 ⅞ x 5 ¼ In. 616.00
Foo Dogs, Bronze, Rectangular Base, 19th Century, 8 x 2 x 5 In. 550.00
Geisha Girl, Cast Metal, Wood Base, Art Deco Style, 1950-60 .... 79.00
General Motors Building, Blue, Cast Metal, Patina 350.00
Gnomes, Reading, Drinking, Terra-Cotta, Glazed 895.00
Immortals, Boxwood, Rosewood Frame, Chinese, 20th Century, 7 ½ In. 1998.00
Indian, With Headdress, Painted, Green, White, Red, Black, Cast Iron, 6 ½ In. 250.00
Indian Brave, On Horseback, Cast Iron, Hubley, 6 x 5 ¾ In. 633.00
Men, In Boat, With Harpoons, Silver Plate, Jennings Brothers, 7 In. 475.00
Nudes, Stepped Wood Base, Art Deco, 7 ¾ x 6 ¾ In. 350.00
Owl, Marble, White, Abstract, Biomorphic, 5 In. 125.00
Punch & Judy, Seated, Brass, Hollow Back, Early 20th Century, 11 In. 173.00
Raggedy Ann & Andy, Painted, Cast Iron, 1931, 5 ½ x 4 x 2 In. 775.00
Sailboat, Hammered Copper, 6 ¼ x 4 ¾ In. 2160.00
Ship, Cast Iron, Japanned Brass Patina, Bradley & Hubbard, 6 ¼ In. 125.00
Sulgrave Manor, Gold Paint, Cast Iron, 5 ¼ In. 115.00
Sunbonnet Girl, Cast Iron, Marked, National Fdry., 6 x 3 ¾ In. .... *illus* 58.00

Bookends, Abraham Lincoln, Bronze, c.1900, 7 ¾ In.
$40.00

Bookends, Baseball Player, Safe At First, Cast Iron, 4 ¾ x 6 In.
$748.00

Bookends, Cat On Fence, Dog, Painted, Cast Iron, 5 ⅝ x 4 ½ In.
$115.00

Bookends, Dog, Scottie, Cast Iron, Hubley, 5 x 6 ¼ In.
$201.00

Bookends, Sunbonnet Girl, Cast Iron, Marked, National Fdry., 6 x 3 ¾ In.
$58.00

Swan, Cast Iron, Chapman Hardware, Signed, 3¾ x 4⅛ In. 316.00

Woman, Nude, Bronze, Egyptian Style, 7 x 5 In. 1404.00

Wood, Ceramic Inset, Textured Metal Base, Flat Bottom, Marshall Studios, 19¼ In. 220.00

BOOKMARKS were originally made of parchment, cloth, or leather. Soon woven silk ribbon, thin cardboard, celluloid, wood, silver, tortoiseshell, and metals were used. Examples made before 1850 are scarce, but there are many to be found dating before 1920.

Beatrix Potter, Cash's, Woven Silk, 8½ In. 12.00

Bible, 3 Blue Silk Ribbons, Punched Paper Crosses At Ends, Beaded, Late 1880s, 23 In. 65.00

Brookfield Pork Sausage, Swift & Company, Boy In Snow, 1926, 3 In. 28.00

Pig 'N Whistle Candy, Pig Playing Whistle, Ribbon, Paper, 1930s, 5¼ x 1¾ In. 10.00

Religious, 10 Commandments, Celluloid, Late 1800s, 1½ x 4½ In. 15.00

Sterling Silver, Dagger, Silver Sword, 2½ x ½ In. 12.00

Sterling Silver, Hand Holding Cloverleaf, Jade Inserts, Lion Passant, 1928 480.00

Sterling Silver, Heart Shape, Victorian 30.00

Sterling Silver, Laughing Llama Atop, Peru 925, Pointed Saber On Bottom, 3½ In. 45.00

Sterling Silver, Letter Opener, 3 x ¾ In. 26.00

Sterling Silver, Letter Opener, Pumpkin Carriage. 22.00

Sterling Silver, Lunt, Heart Shape 30.00

Sterling Silver, Vintage, 2¼ x ¾ In. 18.00

Stollwerck Gold Brand Chocolate & Cocoa, Celluloid, 5⅝ x ⅝ In. 65.00

BOSSONS character wall masks (heads), plaques, figurines, and other decorative pieces are made by W.H. Bossons, Ltd., of Congleton, England. The company was founded in 1946 and closed in 1996. Dates shown are the date the item was introduced.

Wall Figure, Alsatian, 1967, 4¾ In. 60.00

Wall Figure, Alsatian, 1967, 6¼ In. 60.00

Wall Figure, Blue Tits, 1968, 4¾ In. 68.00

Wall Figure, Cocker Spaniel, 1985, 4½ x 3¾ In. 35.00

Wall Figure, Koalas, 1964-70, 10 In. 45.00

Wall Figure, Pandas, Alice Wilde Brindley, 1979, 8½ In. 135.00

Wall Figure, Raccoon, 1964-82, 12¼ x 4 In. 65.00

Wall Figure, Scottish Terrier, Carnoustie The Dog, 3⅝ In. 65.00

Wall Figure, Terriers, 1962, 4½ In. 66.00

Wall Figure, Woodpeckers, 1968, 12 x 5¼ In. 75.00

Wall Figure, Yorkshire Terrier, 1964, 2½ In. 20.00

Wall Mask, Abdhul, 1965, 7¾ In. 45.00

Wall Mask, Albanian, 5½ In. 100.00

Wall Mask, Bargee, 1988 175.00

Wall Mask, Beefeater, 1966, 8 In. 180.00

Wall Mask, Betsey Trotwood, 1982 85.00

Wall Mask, Bill Sikes, 1981 75.00

Wall Mask, Buccaneer, 1966, 7½ In. 165.00

Wall Mask, Cavalier, 1960, 8 In. 300.00

Wall Mask, Cheyenne, Box, 1970, 11 In. 180.00

Wall Mask, Coolie, 1963, 6½ In. 105.00

Wall Mask, Custer & Sitting Bull, 1990, 8 In. 275.00

Wall Mask, Eskimo, Box, 1969, 8 In. 90.00

Wall Mask, Fagin, 1964 90.00

Wall Mask, Highwayman, 1966, 8 In. 180.00

Wall Mask, Himalayan, 1963, 6½ In. 68.00 to 100.00

Wall Mask, Jock, 1969, 5½ In. 35.00

Wall Mask, Karim, 1972, 8 In. 70.00

Wall Mask, Lichtensteiner, 1962, 5½ x 3½ In. 45.00

Wall Mask, Lords Of The Desert, 1963, 10 In. 135.00

Wall Mask, Mr. Bumble, 1982, 5 In. 130.00

Wall Mask, Mr. Micawber, 1968. 88.00

Wall Mask, Mr. Samuel Pickwick, 1964 90.00

Wall Mask, Old Timer, 1977, 6 In. 59.00

Wall Mask, Old Timer, 1978, 8 In. 250.00

Wall Mask, Paddy, 1969, 5 In. 40.00

Wall Mask, Pancho, 1970, 8 In. 100.00

Wall Mask, Pathan, 1969, 11 In. 70.00

Wall Mask, Persian, 1961, 5 In. 30.00

TIP

If you find an old bottle with an unwanted old cork inside, pour ammonia into the bottle until it covers the cork. The cork will dissolve.

Bottle, Barber, Blue, Stars & Stripes, Hobbs, Brockunier, 7 In.
$120.00

Bottle, Barber, Cranberry Frosted White Enamel Flowers, Fluted Neck, c.1905, 7¾ In.
$815.00

Wall Mask, Pierre, 1980, 5 ½ In. 85.00
Wall Mask, Punjabi, 1984, 7 In. 45.00
Wall Mask, Rawhide, 1967, 6 ½ In. 59.00
Wall Mask, Romany, 1969, 11 ½ In. 200.00
Wall Mask, Saracen, 1960, 7 In. 90.00
Wall Mask, Scrooge, 1982, 5 In. 135.00
Wall Mask, Sea Captain, 1972, 5 ½ In. 70.00
Wall Mask, Sikh, 1963, 6 ½ In. 165.00
Wall Mask, Tecumseh, 8 In. 50.00
Wall Mask, Tibetan, 1959, 5¾ In. . . . . 100.00 to 108.00
Wall Mask, Tony Weller, 1964, 5 ¼ In. 70.00
Wall Mask, Uriah Heap, 1964, 5 ¼ x 3 ⅜ In. 55.00

BOSTON & SANDWICH CO. *pieces may be found in the Lutz and Sandwich Glass categories.*

BOTTLE collecting has become a major American hobby. There are several general categories of bottles, such as historic flasks, bitters, household, and figural. ABM means the bottle was made by an automatic bottle machine after 1903. Pyro is the shortened form of the word *pyroglaze*, an enameled lettering used on bottles after the mid-1930s. This form of decoration is also called ACL or applied color label. For more bottle prices, see the book *Kovels' Bottles Price List* by Ralph and Terry Kovel.

Apothecary, Clear Glass, 3 Cobalt Bands, Domed Lid, c.1850, 11 In. 236.00
Apothecary, Glass, Metal Lid, Red & Black Bordered Gilt Labels, France, 11 x 4 In., Pair. 353.00
Apothecary, Shield-Shaped Label, 19th Century, 13 x 6 ½ In., Pair 470.00

Avon started in 1886 as the California Perfume Company. It was not until 1929 that the name Avon was used. In 1939, it became Avon Products, Inc. Avon has made many figural bottles filled with cosmetic products. Ceramic, plastic, and glass bottles were made in limited editions.

Avon, Alaskan Moose, After-Shave Lotion, 1974 . . . . 15.00
Avon, Decanter, 1910 Firefighter, 1974, 6 Oz. 12.00
Avon, Decanter, Winnebago Motor Home, 1978, 5 Oz. 15.00
Barber, Amethyst, Gold & Yellow Art Nouveau Flowers, Rolled Lip, 7 ¾ In. 179.00
Barber, Amethyst, Grist Mill, White Enamel, Ribs, 7 ⅞ In. 146.00
Barber, Amethyst, Strawberry Diamond Cutting, Faceted Neck, 6 ½ In. 440.00
Barber, Bay Rum, Amethyst, White Enamel Windmill, Ribs, Rolled Lip, 7 ½ In. 112.00
Barber, Bay Rum, Milk Glass, Blue, Label, Victorian Woman, Metal Cap, 11 ¾ In. 295.00
Barber, Bay Rum, Milk Glass, Fiery Opalescent, Enamel Clover, Tooled Lip, 9 ½ In. 146.00
Barber, Blue, Stars & Stripes, Hobbs, Brockunier, 7 In. . . . . *illus* 120.00
Barber, Branches, Bird, Cobalt Blue, Enamel, Squat, White & Gold, 8 In. 220.00
Barber, Cranberry Cut To Clear, Bohemian Glass, 8 In., Pair 144.00
Barber, Cranberry Frosted White Enamel Flowers, Fluted Neck, c.1905, 7 ¾ In. . . . . *illus* 815.00
Barber, Ferns, Blue Opalescent, 7 In. 84.00
Barber, Fiery Opalescent, White Enamel Daisies, Rolled Lip, 8 ½ In. 90.00
Barber, Fiery Opalescent, White Swirled Ribs, Rolled Lip, 9 In. 101.00
Barber, Fiery Opalescent Pink Overlay, Coin Spot, Melon Ribs, Rolled Lip, 8 ½ In. 476.00
Barber, Figural, Clothes Brush, Sweeps Dandruff, 8 ¼ In. 345.00
Barber, Frosted Cranberry, Enamel Flowers, Polished Lip, Finger Grooved Neck, c.1910, 7 ¾ In. 515.00
Barber, Green, Enamel Flowers, 9 In., Pair 104.00
Barber, Green, Enamel Flowers, Christmas Tree, Tooled Lip, c.1900, 3 ¾ In. 2750.00
Barber, Hair Vigor, Phil. Eisemann, Label Under Glass, Applied Lip, Stopper, 8 ¾ x 3 In. 2985.00
Barber, Hobbs, Stars & Stripes, White, Clear, Brockunier, 1886, 7 In. 96.00
Barber, Hobnail, Yellow, Rolled Lip, 7 In. 78.00
Barber, Latticinio, Red, Green & Blue Stripes, Open Pontil, Porcelain Stopper 175.00
Barber, Milk Glass, Blue, Multicolored Enamel Fan, Flowers, Rolled Lip, 8 ¾ In. 123.00
Barber, Milk Glass, Chinese Man, Atomizer . . . . *illus* 230.00
Barber, Milk Glass, Enamel Cherubs Reading Music, Flowers, Tooled Lip, 8 ⅛ In. 146.00
Barber, Milk Glass, Figural, Chinese Man's Head, Atomizer, 1883 . . . . 431.00
Barber, Milk Glass, Opalescent, Cherubs, Flowers, Enamel, Tooled Lip, Pontil, c.1910 . . . . 315.00
Barber, Milk Glass, Opalescent, Hobnail, 7 In. 59.00
Barber, Pink Cased, Round, Elongated Neck, Black & White, Middle Eastern Design, 7 In. . . . 253.00
Barber, Portrait, Basket Cover, Cork Stopper, Chain, 12 ½ In. . . . . *illus* 863.00
Barber, Ruby Red, Thumbprint, Smooth Base, Tooled Lip, Pour Spout, 1900, 5 In. 168.00
Barber, Shampoo, Milk Glass, Fiery Opalescent, Blue Gray, Ski Lodge, 8 ¾ In. 392.00
Barber, Spanish Lace, Red, Opaline Brocade, 9 In. . . . . *illus* 2070.00

Bottle, Barber, Milk Glass, Chinese Man, Atomizer
$230.00

Bottle, Barber, Portrait, Basket Cover, Cork Stopper, Chain, 12 ½ In.
$863.00

Bottle, Barber, Spanish Lace, Red, Opaline Brocade, 9 In.
$2070.00

Bottle, Bitters, Bismarck, C. Lange & Co., Chicago, U.S.A., Amber, c.1900, 8¾ In. $465.00

Bottle, Bitters, Bourbon Whiskey, Barrel, Cherry Puce, Applied Mouth, c.1870, 9 In. $510.00

Bottle, Bitters, Dr. A.S. Hopkins, Union Stomach, Yellow Green, c.1870, 9¾ In. $1695.00

Barber, Spanish Lace, Red Opalescent, Coral Reef, 8 In. 180.00
Barber, Toilet Water, Amethyst, 16 Ribs, Flared Lip, Pontil, Midwestern, 1835, 5 In. 448.00
Barber, Toilet Water, Milk Glass, Fiery Opalescent, Enamel Morning Glory, 8½ In. 190.00
Barber, Topaz, Frosted, White, Green & Gold Art Nouveau Floral Bands, Ribs, 8¼ In. 168.00
Barber, Turquoise, Gold & Yellow Art Nouveau Flowers, Ribs, Rolled Lip, 8 In. 213.00
Barber, Vaseline Opalescent, Coin Spot, Applied Mouth, 10¾ In. 504.00
Barber, Vaseline Opalescent, Hobnail, Pontil, 7 In. 79.00
Barber, Witch Hazel, Fred Dolles, 9 In. 748.00
Barber, Witch Hazel, Milk Glass, Opalescent, Yellow, Green Mums, Tooled Lip, 9 In. 190.00
Barber, Wm. F. Stolte, Hair Tonic, Milk Glass, Blue, Ship, Flowers, Screw Cap, 9½ In. 3080.00
Barber, Woman, Under Glass Label, 8½ In. 300.00
Beer, Anheuser-Busch, Aqua Blue, Eagle, Blob Top, Pony 39.00
Beer, Bohemian Bock Beer, Spokane, Wash., Label, 1947 25.00
Beer, C.C. Haley & Co., Black Glass, Tobacco Amber, Double Collar, October 29, 1870, Qt. 325.00
Beer, Engle Bottling Works, Lancaster, Pa., Embossed, Citron, 9½ In. 89.00
Beer, Foord Bottling Works, Wilmington, Del., Clear, Squat, Blob Top 15.00
Beer, G.B. Seely's Son, New York, Bartender, Filling Glasses, Bottles, Clear, Blob Top, Qt. 559.00
Beer, George Funkler, N.E. Cor. Of 24th & Jefferson, Philada, Clear 15.00
Beer, Golden Age, Spokane, Washington, Amber, Barrel, Embossed, Picnic, ½ Gal., 1935 50.00
Beer, H. Floto's Lager, Reading, Pa., Aqua, Squat 139.00
Beer, Haffenreffer Boylston Lager, Red Amber, Stopper, Pt. 35.00
Beer, Hartmann & Fehrenbach Brewing Co., Winged Horse, Amber, Crown Top, 9½ In. 29.00
Beer, Henry Elias Brewing Co., Attic, Honey Amber, Stopper, Pt. 200.00
Beer, Hoppe & Strub Bottling Co., Toledo, Ohio, Orange Amber, Blob, Qt. 29.00
Beer, John Graf, Milwaukee, Wis., 8-Sided, Amber, Blob Top 10.00
Beer, Joseph Eppig's Brooklyn, N.Y., Brewery, Aqua, Qt. 30.00
Beer, M. Keane, XXX, Cobalt Blue, Applied Sloping Collar, 9⅛ In. 672.00
Beer, Pabst Export, Amber, Blob Top, Labels, 9½ In. 69.00
Beer, Porter, Medium Green, Applied Lip, Open Pontil, 1845, 7½ In. 476.00
Beer, Potosi Wisconsin Brewing Co., Dark Amber, Relief, Wire Closure, 13¾ In. 33.00
Beer, Rainier Bottling Works, Reno, Nev., 1915, 12 Oz. 135.00
Beer, Rolling Rock, Ruby Red, 7 Oz. 364.00
Beer, Rud Wegener Brewing Co., Alexandria, Minn., Amber, Stopper, Qt. 65.00
Beer, Schlitz, Baltimore Branch, Amber, Blob Top 25.00
Beer, Shelby Street Brewery, Louisville, Ky., Golden Amber, Stopper, Qt. 125.00
Beer, Smith's White Root, Salt Glaze Stoneware, Tan, Cobalt Blue, 10⅜ In. 56.00
Beer, Smith's White Root Beer, Stoneware, Salt Glaze, Gray, Cobalt Blue, Blob Top, 10 In. 157.00
Beer, Soda, J. W. Harris Root Beer, Stoneware, Gray, Cobalt Blue, Blob Top, 9⅝ In. 78.00
Beer, Soda, Mattingly's Boston Root Beer, Stoneware, Salt Glaze, Gray, 9¾ In. 112.00
Beer, Swan Brewery Co., XXX Ale, Green, Applied Mouth, 8 In. 2640.00
Beer, Tiffany & Allen, Washington Market, Paterson, N.J., Spruce, Cobalt Blue, Pt., 7⅝ In. 1792.00
Beer, W. Stewart Celebrated Hoxie, Amber, Qt. 125.00
Beer, William Donohue Root Beer, Cream, Black Transfer, Blob Mouth, 10 In. 146.00
Bininger, A.M. & Co., Cannon, Yellow Amber, Sheared Mouth, 12½ In. 728.00
Bininger, A.M. & Co., Old Kentucky Bourbon, 1849 Reserve, Amber, 10 In. 201.00
Bininger, A.M. & Co., Traveler's Guide, Flask, Golden Amber, Applied Mouth, 6½ In. 616.00
Bininger, Knickerbocker, N.Y., Yellow Amber, Sloping Collar, Handle, 6½ In. 1064.00
Bininger, Pink Amethyst, 9¾ In. 1064.00
Bitters, A. Lambert's, Philada, Olive, Amber, Applied Mouth, 11 In. 1456.00
Bitters, Alex Vonhumboldt's Stomach, Olive, Square, Applied Mouth, 10 In. 9520.00
Bitters, Baker's Orange Grove, Puce, Applied Mouth, 9½ In. 3808.00
Bitters, Baker's Orange Grove, Topaz Roped Corners, Applied Top 3740.00
Bitters, Baker's Orange Grove, Yellow Green, Rope Corners, Applied Mouth, 9½ In. 9900.00
Bitters, Barrel, Cobalt Blue, Applied Mouth, 10 In. 4480.00
Bitters, Bell's Cocktail, Copper Puce, Lady's Leg Neck, 10½ In. 476.00
Bitters, Berkshire, Amann & Co., Pig, Pottery, Root Beer Glaze, 10⅜ In. 2240.00
Bitters, Big Bill Best, Light Amber, Tapered, 12 In. 160.00
Bitters, Bismarck, C. Lange & Co., Chicago, U.S.A., Amber, c.1900, 8¾ In. *illus* 465.00
Bitters, Bourbon Whiskey, Barrel, Cherry Puce, Applied Mouth, c.1870, 9 In. *illus* 510.00
Bitters, Bourbon Whiskey, Barrel, Copper Puce, Applied Mouth, 9¼ In. 448.00
Bitters, Brown's Celebrated Indian Herb, Golden Amber, c.1870, 12¼ In. 600.00
Bitters, Brown's Celebrated Indian Herb, Indian Queen, Olive Yellow, 12 In. 2184.00
Bitters, Brown's Celebrated Indian Herb, Patented Feb 11 1868, Amber, 12 In. 952.00
Bitters, C. Gates & Cos., Life Of Man, Aqua, Applied Mouth, Open Pontil, 8 In. 285.00
Bitters, C. Gates & Cos., Life Of Man, Aqua, Rectangular, Embossed, Label, 8 In. 79.00

Bitters, C. Gautier's, Native Wine, Washington, D.C., Olive Yellow, 10 In. 1232.00
Bitters, California Wine, M. Keller, Los Angeles, Monogram, Applied Ring, 1850, 12 In. 12320.00
Bitters, Caracas, Olive Green, Embossed Shoulder & Base, 8 In. 95.00
Bitters, Carmeliter Stomach, Amber, Rectangular, Arched Sides, Embossed, 9 In. 162.00
Bitters, Catawba Wine, Embossed Grapes, Green, Applied Mouth, Pontil, 1860-66, 9½ In. 6720.00
Bitters, Chalmer's Catawba Wine, Embossed Grapes, Amber, Applied Mouth, c.1864, 9½ In. 8400.00
Bitters, Clendenin's Golden Tonic, Stoneware, Salt Glaze, Cream, Jug, Handle, 15¼ In. 308.00
Bitters, Congress, Orange Amber, Rectangular, Applied Mouth, 9¼ In. 275.00
Bitters, Constitution, Seward & Bentley, Buffalo, N.Y., 1864, Golden Amber, Crude Top, 9 In. 5026.00
Bitters, Dingens Bros., Napoleon, Cocktail Banjo, Yellow Amber, Applied Mouth, 10 In. 7280.00
Bitters, Dingens Bros., Napoleon Cocktail, Banjo, Amber, Applied Mouth, 9½ In. 4928.00
Bitters, Dr. A.S. Hopkins, Union Stomach, Yellow Green, c.1870, 9¾ In. *illus* 1695.00
Bitters, Dr. A.W. Coleman's Antidyspeptic & Tonic, Green, Applied Mouth, 1840s, 9½ In. 3808.00
Bitters, Dr. Anthony's, Angostura, Improved, Phila., Pa., U.S.A., Amber, 8⅜ In. *illus* 575.00
Bitters, Dr. B.H. Kauffman's Stomach, Green, Applied Ring Collar, Pontil, 9½ In. 9520.00
Bitters, Dr. Ball's Vegetable Stomachic, Northboro, Mass., Aqua, Open Pontil, 6½ In. 285.00
Bitters, Dr. Baxter's Mandrake, Burlington, Vt., Green, 12-Sided, 6½ In. 48.00
Bitters, Dr. Blake's Aromatic, New York, Aqua, Applied Mouth, 7 In. 258.00
Bitters, Dr. C.W. Roback's Stomach, Barrel, Olive Amber, Sloping Collar, 10 In. 336.00
Bitters, Dr. C.W. Roback's Stomach, Cincinnati, O., Barrel, Amber, Applied Mouth, 10 In. 300.00
Bitters, Dr. C.W. Roback's Stomach, Cincinnati, O., Barrel, Yellow, Applied Mouth, 9⅜ In. 359.00
Bitters, Dr. Caldwell's Great Tonic Herb, Yellow Amber, 12½ In. 280.00
Bitters, Dr. Chandler's, Jamaica Ginger Root, Yellow Shaded To Amber, Barrel, 10 In. 17360.00
Bitters, Dr. Corbett's Renovating, Aqua, Pontil, Applied Ring Collar, 9½ In. 1792.00
Bitters, Dr. D.S. Perry, Excelsior Aromatic, New York, 1800, Semi-Cabin, Amber, 10 In. 2000.00
Bitters, Dr. Flint's Quaker, Aqua, Applied Lip, Rectangular, Beveled, c.1860, 9¼ In. 3450.00
Bitters, Dr. Flint's Quaker, Providence, R.I., Aqua, Label, 9½ In. 1008.00
Bitters, Dr. Harter's Wild Cherry, St. Louis, Amber, Square, 7¾ In. 83.00
Bitters, Dr. Hoofland's German, Liver Complaint, Dyspepsia & C, Blue Aqua, 8 In. 29.00
Bitters, Dr. J. Sweet's Strengthening, Aqua, Applied Mouth, Pontil, 9 In. 420.00
Bitters, Dr. J.G.B. Siegert & Sons, Angostura, Olive, Tooled Lip, 8 In. 35.00
Bitters, Dr. Jacobs, New Haven, Ct., Blue Aqua, Open Pontil, 1840-60, 8½ In. *illus* 375.00
Bitters, Dr. Langley's Root & Herb, Aqua, 6 In. 80.00
Bitters, Dr. Langley's Root & Herb, Aqua, Cylindrical, 8½ In. 69.00
Bitters, Dr. Loew's Celebrated Stomach & Nerve Tonic, Cleveland, Oh., Green, 5 In. 165.00
Bitters, Dr. Loew's Celebrated Stomach & Nerve Tonic, Cleveland, O., Yellow Green, 5 In. 235.00
Bitters, Dr. Loew's Celebrated Stomach & Nerve Tonic, Golden Amber, 3½ In. 385.00
Bitters, Dr. Loew's Celebrated Stomach & Nerve Tonic, Green, Tooled Lip, 9¼ In. 280.00
Bitters, Dr. Mampe's Herb Stomach, Blue Aqua, 6¾ In. 110.00
Bitters, Dr. Manly Hardy's Genuine, Aqua, 7 In. 40.00
Bitters, Dr. Renz's Herb, Olive Yellow, Applied Mouth, c.1860, 10 In. *illus* 1390.00
Bitters, Dr. Soule's Hop, 1872, Semi-Cabin, 9¾ In. 168.00
Bitters, Dr. Soule's Hop, 1872, Semi-Cabin, Apricot, Applied Sloping Collar, 9¼ In. 235.00
Bitters, Dr. Soule's Hop, 1872, Semi-Cabin, Light Green, Applied Sloping Collar, 9¼ In. 728.00
Bitters, Dr. Soule's Hop, 1872, Semi-Cabin, Olive Yellow, 9¼ In. 399.00
Bitters, Dr. Soule's Hop Bitterine, 1872, Hop Flowers, Semi-Cabin, Topaz, 9½ In. 6720.00
Bitters, Dr. W Paetz's Stomach, Orange Amber, Sloping Collar, Iron Pontil, 9⅞ In. 5600.00
Bitters, Dr. Wonser's U.S.A. Indian Root, Yellow, 11½ In. 25760.00
Bitters, Dr. Wood's Sarsaparilla & Wild Cherry, Aqua, Applied Mouth, Pontil, 9 In. 258.00
Bitters, Drake's Plantation, 4 Log, Amber, 10¼ In. 95.00
Bitters, Drake's Plantation, 4 Log, Golden Amber, 10¼ In. 165.00
Bitters, Drake's Plantation, 4 Log, Olive Yellow, Applied Sloping Collar, 1860, 10 In. 2100.00
Bitters, Drake's Plantation, 4 Log, Olive Yellow, Sloping Collar, 10¼ In. 952.00
Bitters, Drake's Plantation, 4 Log, Yellow Gold, 10¼ In. 675.00
Bitters, Drake's Plantation, 5 Log, Chocolate Amber, 9⅞ In. 550.00
Bitters, Drake's Plantation, 6 Log, Cherry Puce, 10 In. 259.00
Bitters, Drake's Plantation, 6 Log, Copper, Sloping Collar Mouth, 10 In. 308.00
Bitters, Drake's Plantation, 6 Log, Light Yellow, Applied Collar, 10 In. 1120.00
Bitters, Drake's Plantation, 6 Log, Olive Yellow To Clear, 1862, 9¾ In. *illus* 5100.00
Bitters, Drake's Plantation, 6 Log, Olive Yellow, 10 In. 1232.00
Bitters, Drake's Plantation, 6 Log, Red Amber, 10 In. 200.00
Bitters, Drake's Plantation, 6 Log, Yellow Amber, Sloping Collar, 9¾ In. 616.00
Bitters, Drake's Plantation, Cabin, Amber, Embossed, Patented 1860, 10 In. 230.00
Bitters, Drake's Plantation, Cherry Puce, Applied Collar, 9½ In. 4928.00
Bitters, Drake's Plantation, Cherry Puce, Smooth Base, Sloping Collar Mouth, 9⅞ In. 476.00

Bottle, Bitters, Dr. Anthony's, Angostura, Improved, Phila., Pa., U.S.A., Amber, 8⅜ In.
$575.00

Bottle, Bitters, Dr. Jacobs, New Haven, Ct., Blue Aqua, Open Pontil, 1840-60, 8½ In.
$375.00

Bottle, Bitters, Dr. Renz's Herb, Olive Yellow, Applied Mouth, c.1860, 10 In.
$1390.00

Bottle, Bitters, Drake's Plantation, 6 Log, Olive Yellow To Clear, 1862, 9¾ In.
$5100.00

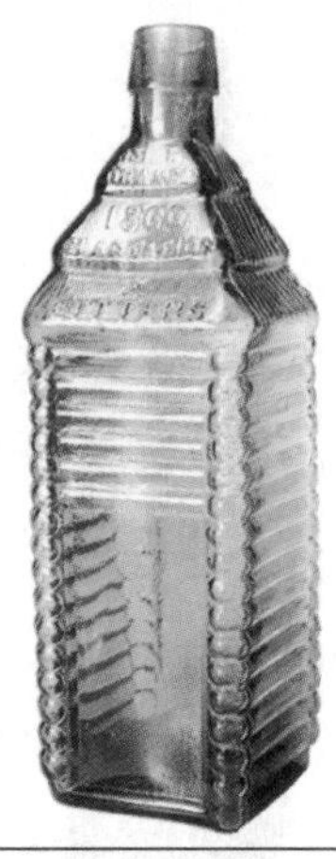

Bottle, Bitters, E.R. Clarke's, Sarsaparilla, Sharon, Mass., Aqua, OP, c.1850, 7⅜ In.
$905.00

Bottle, Bitters, Edwd. Brehm Thuringer Aromatic Stomach, Yellow, OP, c.1855, 8¾ In.
$2100.00

Bitters, Drake's Plantation, Yellow, Green, Applied Collar, 10 In. 10080.00
Bitters, E. Dexter Loveridge, Wahoo, Semi-Cabin, Amber, Applied Mouth, 10 In. 896.00
Bitters, E.R. Clarke's, Sarsaparilla, Sharon, Mass., Aqua, OP, c.1850, 7⅜ In. .... *illus* 905.00
Bitters, Edwd. Brehm Thuringer Aromatic Stomach, Yellow, OP, c.1855, 8¾ In. .... *illus* 2100.00
Bitters, Electric Bitters, H.E. Bucklen & Co., Chicago, Ill., Amber, 8¾ In. 40.00
Bitters, F. Brown Boston Sarsaparilla & Tomato, Aqua, Sloping Double Collar, 9½ In. 364.00
Bitters, Figural, Moses, Hiram Ricker & Sons, Poland Mineral Springs, 7Up Green, 12 In. 55.00
Bitters, Fish, W. H. Ware, Golden Amber, Shaded, Applied Rolled Lip, 11½ In. 476.00
Bitters, Fish, W.H. Ware, Patented 1866, Applied Mouth, Rolled Lip, Green, 12 In. 9990.00
Bitters, Fish, W.H. Ware, Patented 1866, Clear Ice Blue, Applied Mouth, Rolled Lip, 11 In. 16000.00
Bitters, Fish, W.H. Ware, Patented 1866, Golden Amber, Applied Mouth, Rolled Lip, 12 In. 605.00
Bitters, Fish, W.H. Ware, Patented 1866, Green, Applied Lip, 11½ In. 12320.00
Bitters, General Bolivar's, Tooled Lip, 7Up Green, Bulbous, Long Neck, 6¾ In. 280.00
Bitters, Geo. Benz & Sons Apprentine, Tooled Lip, Square Shape, Dark Amber, 8½ In. 448.00
Bitters, Germania, Seated Woman, Milk Glass, Tapered Case, Gin Shape, Labels, 9⅝ In. 6160.00
Bitters, Golden, Geo. C. Hubbel & Co., Aqua, Cabin, Embossed Star, Applied Mouth, 10¼ In. 504.00
Bitters, Greeley's Bourbon, Barrel, Cherry Puce, Applied Sloping Collar, c.1870, 9⅜ In. 850.00
Bitters, Greeley's Bourbon, Barrel, Topaz Olive, 9⅜ In. 5600.00
Bitters, Greeley's Bourbon Whiskey, Barrel, Smoky Pink Puce, Applied Mouth, 9⅜ In. 1456.00
Bitters, H.P. Herb, Wild Cherry, Cabin, Amber, Roped Corners, Tooled Lip, 10 In. 420.00
Bitters, Hall's, E.E. Hall, New Haven, Established 1842, Barrel, Yellow, Applied Mouth, 9 In. 385.00
Bitters, Hall's, E.E. Hall, New Haven, Established 1842, Barrel, Yellow Amber, 9⅛ In. .... *illus* 465.00
Bitters, Hart's Star, 1868 Inside Star, Oval, Clear, Tooled Lip, 9¼ In. 616.00
Bitters, Harvey's Prairie, Tobacco Green, Brickwork Sides, Rounded Shoulders, 9 In. 23000.00
Bitters, Herkules, A.C. Monogram, Green, Tooled Lip, 7 In. 770.00
Bitters, Hertrich's Aesundheits, Olive Green, Applied Mouth, Tooled Lip, 9⅜ In. 168.00
Bitters, Hi-Hi, Citron, Triangular, Smooth Base, Tooled Lip, 9½ In. 364.00
Bitters, Holtzermann's Patent Stomach, Cabin, Amber, Tooled Lip, 9⅞ In. 448.00
Bitters, Indian Queen, Chocolate Amber, Sheared Lip, Smooth Base, 12¼ In. 280.00
Bitters, J.T. Higby Tonic, Milford, Conn., Amber, Square, Applied Mouth, 9½ In. 95.00
Bitters, Jno. Moffat, Phoenix, New York, Yellow, Applied Mouth, c.1840, 5½ In. 750.00
Bitters, John Moffat, Phoenix, New York, $1.00, Emerald Green, 5½ In. 825.00
Bitters, John Moffat, Phoenix, New York, $1.00, Aqua, Applied Mouth, Open Pontil, 5½ In. 220.00
Bitters, John Moffat, Phoenix, New York, Olive Yellow Amber, Sloping Collar, 7 In. 5040.00
Bitters, John Moffat, Phoenix, New York, Olive Yellow, Beveled Corners, c.1840, 5⅜ In. 1064.00
Bitters, John Moffat, Phoenix, New York, Olive Yellow, Pontil, c.1850, 5½ In. 500.00
Bitters, John Roots, Buffalo N.Y., Semi-Cabin, Aqua, Applied Mouth, 10¼ In. 2000.00
Bitters, John Root's, Buffalo N.Y., Semi-Cabin, Emerald, Applied Mouth, 10 In. 4928.00
Bitters, John W. Steele's Niagara, Star, Semi-Cabin, Amber, 10¼ In. 728.00
Bitters, Johnson's Calisaya, Burlington, Vt., Pink, Applied Lip, 10 In. 4650.00
Bitters, Kelly's Old Cabin, Patented 1863, Cabin, Amber, Applied Sloping Collar, 9⅝ In. 1344.00
Bitters, Kelly's Old Cabin, Patented 1863, Cabin, Teal Green, Applied Mouth, 9⅝ In. 52000.00
Bitters, Kelly's Old Cabin, Patented 1863, Cabin, Tobacco Green, Applied Mouth, 9⅝ In. 7250.00
Bitters, Kimball's Jaundice, Purple, Backwards S, Applied Mouth, Pontil, 7 In. 2128.00
Bitters, Lacour's, Sarsapariphere, Green, Round, Applied Mouth, 1866-75, 9 In. 3584.00
Bitters, Lash's Kidney & Liver, Best Cathartic, Blood Purifier, Red Amber, Paneled, 9 In. 476.00
Bitters, Lash's Sample, Medium Amber, Tooled Lip, 4¼ In. 150.00
Bitters, McKeever's Army, Cannon Balls, Drum Base, Amber, Applied Mouth, 10½ In. .... 3530.00 to 3640.00
Bitters, Meredith & Co., 8-Sided, Blue, Aqua, Oval, Embossed, Flared Lip, Open Pontil, 5 In. 48.00
Bitters, Mexican, Henry C. Weaver, ASF5, 1866, Lancaster, O., Amber, 6¼ In. 6720.00
Bitters, Morning, Embossed Star, Amber, Iron Pontil, Sloping Collar, 12¾ In. 308.00
Bitters, Morning, Inceptum 5869, Star, Applied Mouth, Graphite Pontil, 12½ In. 440.00
Bitters, Napoleon, Dingens Brothers, Buffalo, N.Y., 1866, Semi-Cabin, Yellow Amber, 10 In. 6160.00
Bitters, National, Amber, Arched Panels, Dots, Roped Corners, Applied Mouth, 9 In. 7200.00
Bitters, National, Ear Of Corn, Patent 1867, Amber, Applied Mouth, 12¼ In. 504.00
Bitters, National, Ear Of Corn, Patent 1867, Apricot Puce, Applied Mouth, 12⅜ In. 3920.00
Bitters, National, Ear Of Corn, Patent 1897, Olive Yellow, Applied Lip, 12½ In. 2016.00
Bitters, National, Ear Of Corn, Patent, 1867, Amber, 12⅜ In. 560.00
Bitters, National, Light Blue, Arched Panels, Dots, Roped Corners, Applied Mouth, 9 In. 4700.00
Bitters, New York Hop, American Flag, Semi-Cabin, Olive Yellow Green, 9½ In. 5320.00
Bitters, OK Plantation, 1840, Patented 1863, Golden Amber, Applied Mouth, 11 In. 1980.00
Bitters, Old Dr. Goodhue's Root & Herb, Aqua, Rectangular, 9 In. 125.00
Bitters, Old Dr. Townsend's Magic Stomach, New York, Blue Aqua, Applied Mouth, 9⅞ In. 1344.00
Bitters, Old Home, Laughlin & Bushfield, Wheeling, W. Va., Cabin, Amber, 9¾ In. 1780.00
Bitters, Old Homestead Wild Cherry, Cabin, Amber, Applied Sloping Collar, 9⅝ In. 308.00

Bitters, Old Homestead Wild Cherry, Cabin, Yellow Amber, Applied Sloping Collar, 9 ¾ In. 420.00
Bitters, Old Sachem & Wigwam Tonic, Barrel, Apricot, Applied Lip, 9 ½ In.. .... 4190.00
Bitters, Old Sachem & Wigwam Tonic, Barrel, Copper Topaz, 9 ½ In. 532.00
Bitters, Old Sachem & Wigwam Tonic, Barrel, Golden Yellow Amber, Square Collar, 9 ½ In... 448.00
Bitters, Old Sachem & Wigwam Tonic, Barrel, Green, 9 ¼ In.. .... 20720.00
Bitters, Old Sachem & Wigwam Tonic, Barrel, Pink Strawberry Puce, Square Collar, 9 ¼ In. . 1064.00
Bitters, Old Sachem & Wigwam Tonic, Barrel, Purple, Applied Lip, 9 ½ In. 720.00
Bitters, Old Sachem & Wigwam Tonic, Barrel, Yellow Amber, Square Collar, 8 ⅜ In. 280.00
Bitters, Oxygenated, For Dyspepsia Asthma & General Debility, Aqua, Sloping Collar, 7 ½ In. . 78.00
Bitters, Pepsin, Calisaya, Dr. Russell Med. Co., Olive Yellow, Tooled Lip, 8 In. 1792.00
Bitters, Pineapple, Golden Amber, Applied Double Collar, 8 ⅞ In.. .... 532.00
Bitters, Pineapple, Golden Amber, Applied Lip, 9 In. 990.00
Bitters, Pineapple, W & Co., N.Y., Green, Applied Double Collar, Graphite Pontil, 8 ⅞ In. 4640.00
Bitters, Pineapple, Yellow Amber, Applied Double Collar, 8 ⅞ In. 190.00
Bitters, Plow's Sherry, Applied Ring, Bunch Of Grapes, Amber, 1875-85, 8 In.. .... 14000.00
Bitters, Polo Club Stomach, Amber, Square, Applied Mouth, 9 In. 175.00
Bitters, Poor Man's Family Aqua, Contents, Label, 6 ¼ In. 176.00
Bitters, Poor Man's Family Blue Aqua, 6 ¼ In.. .... 59.00
Bitters, Quaker, Aqua, Rectangular, Applied Mouth, 9 ⅛ In. 85.00
Bitters, Reed's, Lady's Leg, Golden Amber, Applied Lip, 12 ½ In. 300.00
Bitters, Romain's Crimean Patented 1863, Amber, Applied Sloping Collar, 10 In.. .... 1344.00
Bitters, Rosenbaum's, San Francisco, Amber, Square, Applied Sloping Collar, c.1865, 9 In.... 672.00
Bitters, Royal, Geo. A. Clement, Niagara Ont., Aqua, Oval, Strap Sides, Double Collar, 8 ¼ In.. 1008.00
Bitters, Royce's Sherry Wine, Aqua 125.00
Bitters, S.C. Brown's, Star, Lime Green, Applied Sloping Collar, 1863-75, 9 ⅝ In. 15120.00
Bitters, S.O. Richardson's, South Reading, Mass., Bitters, Aqua, Applied Lip, 6 ⅞ In. 60.00
Bitters, Sazerac Aromatic, Milk Glass, Lady's Leg, Applied Mouth, 12 ½ In. 202.00
Bitters, Schenk's Pulmonic Syrup, Aqua, OP 130.00
Bitters, Seaworth, Lighthouse, Cape May, N.J., Amber, Tooled Lip, 6 ½ In. 7700.00
Bitters, Seaworth, Lighthouse, Cape May, N.J., Amber, Tooled Lip, 11 ½ In. 17800.00
Bitters, Simon's Centennial, Bust Of George Washington, Amber, 9 ¾ In. 9200.00
Bitters, Simon's Centennial, Bust Of George Washington, Pedestal Base, 10 ½ In. 1232.00
Bitters, Suffolk, Philbrook & Tucker, Boston, Pig, Amber Shaded, 10 ⅛ In. 364.00
Bitters, Suffolk, Philbrook & Tucker, Pig, Yellow, Double Ring, c.1870, 10 ⅛ In. .... *illus* 6100.00
Bitters, Suffolk, Philbrook & Tucker, Pig, Yellow Amber, Double Collar, 10 In. 896.00
Bitters, Suffolk, Philbrook & Tucker, Pig, Yellow Green, Applied Tail, 10 ⅛ In. 5100.00
Bitters, Uncle Tom's, Thomas Foulds & Son, Amber, Square, 10 In.. .... 1195.00
Bitters, Victor Roberg's Prussian, Yellow Amber, Square Case, Yellow Amber, 10 In. 5320.00
Bitters, Wahoo & Calisaya, Jacob Pinkerton, Semi-Cabin, Yellow Amber, 9 ⅝ In. 1008.00
Bitters, Wait's Kidney & Liver, California's Laxative, Blood Purifier, Amber, 8 ¾ In. 90.00
Bitters, Warner's Safe, Rochester, N.Y., Safe, Orange Amber, 9 ½ In.. .... 1680.00
Bitters, Warner's Safe Tonic, Rochester, N.Y., Amber, Applied Double Collar, 9 ⅝ In. 112.00
Bitters, Warner's Safe Tonic, Rochester, N.Y., Safe, Amber, Applied Double Collar, 9½ In. 475.00 to 1120.00
Bitters, William Allen's Congress, Semi-Cabin, Aqua, 7 ¾ In. 245.00
Bitters, William Allen's Congress, Semi-Cabin, Emerald Green, c.1870, 10 ⅜ In. 3000.00
Bitters, William Allen's Congress, Semi-Cabin, Green, Applied Lip, 10 ¼ In. 3300.00
Bitters, William Allen's Congress, Semi-Cabin, Purple Amethyst, Tooled Lip, 7 ¾ In. 364.00
Bitters, Yerba Buena, S.F.Cal., Flask, Amber, Strap Side, Labels, c.1885, 8 ½ In. .... *illus* 935.00
Bitters, Zingari, F. Rahter, Amber, Lady's Leg, Applied Mouth, 12 In. 246.00
Bitters, Zingari, F. Rahter, Golden Amber, Lady's Leg, Applied Mouth, 12 In. 258.00
Bitters, Zingari, F. Rahter, Orange Amber, Lady's Leg, 12 In. .... 269.00 to 349.00
Bitters, Zoeller's Stomach, Golden Amber, Rectangular, 2 Folded Sides, 9 ½ In. 345.00
Black Glass, Cylindrical, Olive Green, Dip Mold, Outward Rolled Lip, c.1790, 6 ¾ In. 246.00
Black Glass, Dutch Onion, Horsehoof, Olive Green, Applied String Lip, Pontil, 1730 .... 90.00
Black Glass, English Mallet, Olive Yellow Green, Applied Lip, Kick-Up, Pontil, 9 ⅝ In. 224.00
Black Glass, English Mallet, Pontil, c.1715-40, Qt. 199.00
Black Glass, Globular, Olive Amber, Outward Rolled Lip, Pontil, Midwestern, 7 ⅞ In. 1568.00
Black Glass, Globular, Olive Yellow Green, Blown, Applied Mouth, c.1790, 11 ⅝ In.. .... 123.00
Black Glass, Olive Amber, Applied Lip, Pontil, 1740, 8 In.. .... 95.00
Black Glass, Onion, Dark Green, String Lip, Pontil, 1740, 6 ¾ In. 90.00
Black Glass, Onion, Horsehoof, Yellow Amber, Applied String Lip, 6 ½ x 4 ⅝ In.. .... 190.00
Black Glass, Onion, Medium Olive Green, Applied String Lip, c.1725, 6 ⅞ x 514 In.. .... 420.00
Black Glass, Wine, Bladder, Olive Green, Kick-Up, Applied String Lip, Pontil, 7 In. 784.00
Black Glass, Wine, Emerald Green, Sheared Mouth, Applied String Lip, c.1795, 10 In. 952.00
Blown, Aqua, Globular, Long Neck, Applied Sloping Collar, Pontil, c.1840, 10 ½ In. 202.00

Bottle, Bitters, Hall's, E.E. Hall, New Haven, Established 1842, Barrel, Yellow Amber, 9 ⅛ In.
$465.00

Bottle, Bitters, Suffolk, Philbrook & Tucker, Pig, Yellow, Double Ring, c.1870, 10 ⅛ In.
$6100.00

Bottle, Bitters, Yerba Buena, S.F.Cal., Flask, Amber, Strap Side, Labels, c.1885, 8 ½ In.
$935.00

TIP

If you collect old bottles that held herb remedies, don't throw out the contents. It adds to the value. But be sure no children will ever open the bottle and taste the herbs.

Bottle, Decanter, Amber, 3-Piece Mold, Tooled Lip, Pontil, c.1825, 7 ⅛ In.
$840.00

Bottle, Decanter, Cobalt Blue, 3-Piece Mold, Tooled Lip, Pontil, c.1825, 9 In.
$1700.00

Whittle Marks
Whittle marks are caused by iron molds that have not been preheated properly. If the glass and the mold are at different temperatures, cooling causes the whittled appearance.

Blown, Carboy, Amber, 24 In. 154.00
Blown, Carboy, Emerald Green, 24 In. 77.00
Blown, Chestnut, Aqua, Applied Collar, Open Pontil, 3 ⅞ In. 150.00
Blown, Chestnut, Olive Amber, Flattened, Applied Lip, 9 ⅜ In. 336.00
Blown, Chestnut, Olive Yellow, Pontil, New England, 5 In. 220.00
Blown, Cylindrical, Blue Green, Outward Rolled Lip, OP, 1780-1810, 6 ⅜ In. 224.00
Blown, Decanter, 3-Piece Mold, Green, Flared Out, Inward Rolled Lip, Pontil, 6 ¾ In. 1036.00
Blown, Decanter, 3-Piece Mold, Flared, Applied Neck Rings, 7 ⅞ In., Pair 784.00
Blown, Gemel, Gourd Shape, 8 Vertical Ribs, 10-Rib Stem, 10 ⅞ In. 99.00
Blown, Globular, 20 Vertical Ribs, Aqua, Sheared Lip, Applied Ring, Continental, c.1790, 6 In. 168.00
Blown, Globular, 24 Ribs, Swirled To Left, Amber, Outward Rolled Lip, 1815-35, 7 ¾ In. 532.00
Blown, Globular, 24 Ribs, Swirled To Left, Yellow Amber, Applied Mouth, c.1820, 8 ½ In. 560.00
Blown, Globular, 24 Ribs, Swirled To Left, Yellow Amber, Outward Rolled Mouth, Pontil, 7 In. 1500.00
Blown, Globular, 24 Ribs, Swirled To Right, Golden Amber, Pontil, 1820-40, 9 ½ In. 1100.00
Blown, Globular, 32 Ribs, Swirled To Left, Aqua, Sloping Collar, Pontil, 1815-1835, 9 ¼ In. 90.00
Blown, Globular, Amber, Flared & Flattened Lip, 4 ⅛ In. 336.00
Blown, Globular, Aqua, Applied Lip, Pontil, 1770-1800, 8 ½ In. 112.00
Blown, Globular, Aqua, Outward Rolled Lip, 9 ¾ In. 246.00
Blown, Globular, Light Green Shaded To Dark Green, Amber Striations, Pontil, c.1830, 7 ⅜ In. 325.00
Blown, Globular, Light Olive Green, Flattened Sides, Applied Lip, OP, 8 ⅛ In. 336.00
Blown, Globular, Light Yellow Green, Free-blown, Tooled Flared Mouth, Pontil, c.1800, 2 ⅝ In. 1300.00
Blown, Globular, Medium Olive Yellow, Pontil, 1780-1830, 10 ¼ In. 850.00
Blown, Globular, Medium Olive Yellow, Sloping Collar, Pontil, c.1805, 10 ⅞ In. 900.00
Blown, Globular, Olive Green, Outward Rolled Lip, Open Pontil, 10 ¼ In. 532.00
Blown, Globular, Olive Yellow, Bulbous, Wide Tooled Lip, Pontil, 1780-1830, 2 ½ In. 3500.00
Blown, Globular, Yellow, Applied Lip, 7 ⅝ In. 1792.00
Blown, Molded, Bulbous, Green, Embossed Hunting Scene 150.00
Carboy, Dark Olive Green, Semi-Kidney Shape, Sheared Lip, Smooth Base, 1800, 17 ¾ In. 190.00
Cognac, Remy Martin Louis XIII, Cut, Stopper, 8 In. 200.00
Cologne, Toilet Water, Blue, Vertical Ribs, 3-Piece Mold, Flared Lip, c.1820, 6 ⅛ In. 134.00
Cologne, Toilet Water, Cobalt Blue, 4-Piece Mold, Embossed, Scrolls, Tooled & Mouth, 6 ⅝ In. 202.00
Cologne, Toilet Water, Cobalt Blue, Vertical Ribs, 3-Piece Mold, Inward Rolled Lip, 5 ¾ In. 420.00
Cologne, Toilet Water, Dark Cobalt Blue, 3-Piece Mold, Ribbed, Swirled Left, 6 In. 392.00
Cordial, Dr. Crook's Wine Of Tar, Citron, Applied Mouth, 8 ⅞ In. 157.00
Cordial, Dr. J.H. McLean's Strengthening & Blood Purifier, Aqua, Tombstone, 8 ¼ In. 35.00
Cordial, Mrs. E. Kidder, Dysentery, Boston, Emerald Green, Oval, OP, 8 ⅝ In. 3080.00
Cordial, Mrs. E. Kidder Dysentery, Apple Green, Applied Sloping Collar, 7 ¾ In. 504.00
Cordial, Wishart's Pine Tree Tar, Phila., Patent 1859, Emerald Green, Embossed Tree, 9 In. 253.00
Cordial, Wishart's Pine Tree Tar, Phila., Patent 1859, Medium Green, Embossed Tree, 7 In. 305.00
Cordial, Wishart's Pine Tree Tar, Pine Tree, Olive Yellow Green, 10 ¼ In. 1344.00
Cosmetic, Ayer's Hair Vigor, Sapphire Blue, Tooled Lip, Glass Stopper, 6 ½ In. 123.00
Cosmetic, Dodge Brothers Hair Tonic, Amethyst, Indented Panels, Double Collar, c.1870, 7 In. 896.00
Cosmetic, Dodge Brothers Melanine Hair Tonic, Puce Amethyst 675.00
Cosmetic, Dr. Tebbetts' Hair Regenerator, Root Beer Amber, Tooled Lip, 7 ⅝ In. 202.00
Cosmetic, Dr. Tebbetts' Physiological Hair Generator, Puce, Rectangular, c.1870, 7 ½ In. 1100.00
Cosmetic, Dr. Tebbetts' Physiological Hair Regenerator, Puce Amber, 7 ½ In. 450.00
Cosmetic, Dr. Tebbetts' Physiological Hair Regenerator, Dark Puce, Tooled Top, 7 ½ In. 168.00
Cosmetic, Madame Girard's Hygienic Hair Restorer, Green, Tooled Top, 7 In. 560.00
Cosmetic, Mrs. H.E. Wilson's Hair Regenerator, Manchester, N.H., Aqua, 8 ¼ In. 90.00
Cosmetic, Mrs. S.A. Allen's World's Hair Restorer, N.Y., Dark Amethyst, 7 ¼ In. 308.00
Cosmetic, Mrs. S.A. Allen's World's Hair Restorer, Purple Amethyst, 7 ¼ In. 202.00
Cosmetic, Newbro's Herpicide Kills The Dandruff Germ, Clear, Square Collar, 9 In. 20.00
Cosmetic, Oldridge's Balm Of Columbia For Restoring Hair, Aqua, Flared Lip, OP, 5 In. 308.00
Cosmetic, Professor Wood's Hair Restorative, Depot, St. Louis, Mo., New York, Teal, 9 In. 532.00
Cosmetic, W.C. Montgomery's Hair Restorer, Philada., Black Amethyst, 7 ½ In. 269.00
Cosmetic, Warner's, Log Cabin, Scalpine, Head & Hair, Pat. Sept 6th, 1887, Amber, Label, 9 In. 4200.00
Cure, Baker's Blood & Liver, Greenville, Tenn., Red Amber, Tooled Lip, 9 ¾ In. 560.00
Cure, Bennett's Hyssop, Stockport, Aqua, Sunken Panel, 5 ½ In. 23.00
Cure, Dr. Agnew's, For The Heart, Light Amethyst, Square Collar, 8 ½ In. 48.00
Cure, Dr. Keeley's For Tobacco Habit, Clear, Tooled Lip, Crimped Spout, 5 ¾ In. 420.00
Cure, Dr. M.M. Fenner's People's Remedies, Amber, Label, 10 In. 242.00
Cure, Dr. Miles' New Heart, Aqua, Label, 8 ¼ In. 330.00
Cure, Dr. Roc's Liver Rheumatic Neuralgic, Knoxville, Tenn., Aqua, 8 In. 68.00
Cure, For Colds, Coughs, Croup, Speedy Cure, Amber, Pumpkinseed Flask, 5 In. 1064.00
Cure, K.K. Cures Bright's Disease & Cystitis, New Jersey, 7 ½ In. 48.00

Cure, Mystic For Rheumatism & Neuralgia, Aqua, Label, Contents, Box, Flyer, 6 In.......... 275.00
Cure, Otto's For The Throat & Lungs, Aqua, Label, Contents, Box, Flyer, 6 In............... 121.00
Cure, Polar Star Cough, Star, Aqua, Tooled Lip, 7 In.................................. 40.00
Cure, Sanford's Radical, Cobalt Blue, Labels, Contents, Box, Booklet, Flyer, 7 1/4 In.......... 715.00
Cure, Spark's Kidney & Liver, Camden, N.J., Perfect Health, Man's Torso, Amber, 9 1/2 In...... 1064.00
Cure, Warner's Safe Diabetes, Melbourne, London, Toronto, Rochester, Amber, 9 1/2 In....... 308.00
Cure, Warner's Safe Diabetes, Olive Yellow, Oval, Applied Blob Top, 9 1/2 In.............. 560.00
Cure, Warner's Safe Kidney & Liver, Red Amber, Oval, Applied Double Collar, 9 5/8 In......... 179.00
Cure, Warner's Safe Kidney & Liver, Rochester, N.Y., Orange Amber, 9 1/2 In................ 20.00
Cure, Warner's Safe London, Amber, Applied Blob Top, 10 3/4 In......................... 1008.00
Cure, Warner's Safe London, Safe, Orange Amber, Blob Top, Qt., 10 3/4 In................. 1344.00
Cure, Warner's Safe London, Yellow Orange, Applied Blob Top, 9 1/2 In.................... 123.00
Cure, Warner's Safe Pressburg, Emerald Green, Applied Blob Top, Germany, 9 1/2 In......... 728.00
Cure, Warner's Safe Rheumatic, Amber, Applied Double Collar, 9 5/8 In.................... 134.00
Cure, Warner's Safe Rheumatic, Orange Amber, Applied Double Collar, 9 1/2 In............. 134.00
Cure, Warner's Safe Rheumatic, Rochester, N.Y., Amber, Applied Mouth, 9 In............... 55.00
Cure, Warner's Safe Yellow Amber, Applied Blob Top, 5 3/8 In........................... 1456.00
Cure, Wm. Radam's Microbe Killer, Man Hitting Skeleton, Yellow Amber, Square, 10 1/2 In.... 168.00
Decanter, Amber, 3-Piece Mold, Tooled Lip, Pontil, c.1825, 7 1/8 In. .... *illus* 840.00
Decanter, Amber Glass, Leaf, Thistle Overlay, Sterling Stopper, Cork Insert, 13 In........... 2588.00
Decanter, Backbar, Buffalo Club, Buffalo, Clear, Corset Waist, Paneled Shoulder, 9 1/4 In..... 1232.00
Decanter, Backbar, Cobalt Blue, Cylindrical, Raised Oval Panel, Ringed Mouth, 11 3/8 In..... 224.00
Decanter, Big Bill's Best Bitters, Fat Man, In Suit, Amber, Tooled Lip, 11 3/4 In............. 258.00
Decanter, Cobalt Blue, 3-Piece Mold, Bulbous, Flared Mouth, Pontil, Stopper, c.1830, Pt..... 4000.00
Decanter, Cobalt Blue, 3-Piece Mold, Tooled Lip, Pontil, c.1825, 9 In. .... *illus* 1700.00
Decanter, Elvis Playing Guitar, Drums, McCormick, Box, 16 1/2 x 8 x 6 In. .... *illus* 25.00
Decanter, Emerald Green, 3-Piece Mold, Tooled Flared Lip, Pontil, Stopper, c.1830, Qt. 1600.00
Decanter, Forest Green, 3-Piece Mold, Applied Sloping Collar, Pontil, Pt., 8 1/2 In........... 1100.00
Decanter, Horn Of Plenty, 3-Piece Mold, Tooled Flared Mouth, Pontil, Stopper, c.1830, Qt.... 550.00
Decanter, Olive Yellow, 3-Piece Mold, Bulbous, Sheared Mouth, Pontil, 1820-40, Pt......... 600.00
Decanter, Olive Yellow, 3-Piece Mold, Flared Mouth, Pontil, Mt. Vernon Glass Works, c.1830, Qt... 3500.00
Decanter, Olive Yellow, 3-Piece Mold, Inverted Cone Shape, Flared, Pontil, Qt............. 2000.00
Decanter, Paneled, Lilac, Josef Hoffman, 8 1/4 x 4 In................................. 2160.00
Decanter, Pillar Mold, Clear, 8 Pillars, Cobalt Blue Edges, Neck Rings, Double Collar, 12 1/2 In. 123.00
Decanter, Pillar Mold, Clear, 8 Pillars, Cobalt Blue, Applied Lip, Pontil, 10 1/4 x 8 In......... 364.00
Decanter, Ship, Green, Pontil, Scotland, c.1830, 7 3/4 x 6 5/8 In.................... *illus* 425.00
Demijohn, Blue Green, Cylindrical, 2 Gal., 17 1/2 In................................. 119.00
Demijohn, Blue Green, Squat, Deep Kick-Up, Applied Mouth, Gal., 12 3/4 In................ 45.00
Demijohn, Citron, Cylindrical, 2-Piece Mold, 1855-1865, Gal., 15 1/2 In................... 39.00
Demijohn, Dark Amber, Stoddard Type, 2-Piece Mold, New England, 14 1/2 In............... 70.00
Demijohn, Free-Blown, Olive Amber, Applied Lip Ring, c.1815, 15 1/4 In.................. 206.00
Demijohn, Green, Sheared Mouth, Applied String Lip, 13 5/8 In.......................... 364.00
Demijohn, Medium Green, Applied Lip, Pontil, 1860, 14 In............................ 56.00
Demijohn, Olive, Free-Blown, Pontil, 1800-20, 18 In................................. 213.00
Demijohn, Olive Yellow, Cylindrical, Open Pontil, 3 Gal., 20 In.......................... 129.00
Demijohn, Yellow Green, Gal., 15 In.. 55.00
Dresser, Emerald Green, Sterling Silver Overlay, Cartouche, Pontil, c.1900, 5 1/2 In.......... 1495.00
Dresser, Sterling Silver Overlay, Monogrammed Cartouche, Smooth Pontil, 4 In........... 144.00
Drug, Chamberlain's Colic, Cholera & Diarrhea Remedy, Embossed, Label, 4 1/2 In.......... 25.00
Figural, Arm, Hand, Holding Dagger, Emerald Green, 14 In........................... 195.00
Figural, Asparagus Stalks, Clear, Frosted Tooled Lip, 12 1/2 In.......................... 78.00
Figural, Bear, Kummel, Black Glass, 11 In...................................... 69.00
Figural, Billy Club, Whiskey, Flask, Tin Screw-On Lid, 10 1/2 x 1 1/4 In. 70.00
Figural, Boar, Pottery, 12 1/2 In... 1265.00
Figural, Cleopatra's Needle, Opaque Blue, Marked, London, 1877, 5 In............. *illus* 546.00
Figural, Family, Milk Glass, Amber Stopper, Lobeco, Italy, 3 Piece .... *illus* 518.00
Figural, Football, Yellow, Pumpkinseed Flask, Tooled Lip, 4 1/2 In...................... 896.00
Figural, Mermaid, Yellowware, Brown Slip Glaze, Sits Flat, 1875, 7 1/2 In................. 336.00
Figural, Monkey On The Pot, Pottery, Rockingham Glaze, 5 1/2 In........................ 55.00
Figural, Pelican Beak, Swallowing, Clear, 15 In.................................. 35.00
Figural, Pig, Corncob In Mouth, Grass, Weeds, Amethyst, 6 1/4 In....................... 295.00
Figural, Pig, Good Old Bourbon In A Hog's, Clear, 7 In. 139.00
Figural, Pig, Something Good In A Hogs, He Won't Squeal, Clear, 4 1/4 In................. 79.00
Figural, Pyramid, Aqua, Rope Twist Corners, Applied Collar, 11 1/8 In.................... 420.00
Figural, Revolver, Amber, Checkered Handle, Metal Cap, 8 In.......................... 79.00

Bottle, Decanter, Elvis Playing Guitar, Drums, McCormick, Box, 16 1/2 x 8 x 6 In.
$25.00

Bottle, Decanter, Ship, Green, Pontil, Scotland, c.1830, 7 3/4 x 6 5/8 In.
$425.00

Bottle, Figural, Cleopatra's Needle, Opaque Blue, Marked, London, 1877, 5 In.
$546.00

Bottle, Figural, Family, Milk Glass, Amber Stopper, Lobeco, Italy, 3 Piece $518.00

B

Bottle, Flask, Corn For The World, Monument, Pink Puce, c.1865, Qt. $6700.00

Bottle, Flask, Cornucopia & Urn, Blue Green, Tooled Lip, Open Pontil, c.1845, ½ Pt. $395.00

Figural, Violin, Amethyst, 10 In. 29.00
Figural, Violin, Yellow Amber, Wood Handle, Strings, Tooled Lip, c.1875, 14½ In. 1232.00
Firefighting, Grenade, Harden's Hand, Star, Turquoise Blue, 6¾ In. 134.00
Firefighting, Grenade, Hayward's Hand, Fire Extinguisher, Amber, Ribs, Sheared Mouth, 5⅝ In. 336.00
Firefighting, Grenade, Hayward's Hand, Fire Extinguisher, Cobalt Blue, Tooled Lip, 5⅞ In. 264.00
Firefighting, Grenade, Hayward's Hand, Fire Extinguisher, Amethyst, Tooled Lip, 6 In. 2688.00
Firefighting, Grenade, Hazelton's High Pressure Chemical Fire Keg, Barrel, Amber, 11 In. 476.00
Firefighting, Grenade, Systeme Labbe, Anchor, Diamond Pattern, Amber, 5¾ In. 308.00
Flask, 16 Ribs, Aqua, Globular, Rolled Lip, Midwest, 8 In. 179.00
Flask, 18 Ribs, Aqua, Sheared Mouth, 1830, 4¾ In. 308.00
Flask, 18 Ribs, Swirled To Right, Dark Cobalt Blue, Tooled Lip, Pontil, 5⅞ In. 336.00
Flask, 18 Vertical Ribs, Light Green, Applied Ring, Pontil, 1835, 7¼ In. 202.00
Flask, 20 Ribs, Swirled To Right, Sapphire Blue, Tooled Flared Lip, Pocket, 3⅞ In. 448.00
Flask, 24 Ribs, Swirled To Right, Golden Amber, Globular, Molded, Outward Rolled Mouth, 8 In. 468.00
Flask, 24 Ribs Swirled To Right, Cornflower Blue, Applied Collar, Iron Pontil, c.1830, 8⅜ In. 1400.00
Flask, 31 Ribs, Vertical, Blue Green, Applied Collar, Pontil, c.1820, 8½ In. 1300.00
Flask, A. Livingston, Carson City, Lavender, Tooled Lip, Pt. 1456.00
Flask, A.M. Smith, Pumpkinseed, Light Purple, Tooled Lip, 1892, 4½ In. 179.00
Flask, Anchor & Phoenix, Resurgam, Yellow Amber, Double Collar, Pt. 784.00
Flask, Aqua, Eagle, c.1875, ½ Pt., 5⅞ In. 86.00
Flask, Barrel, Woman Sitting On Barrel, Drinking, Smokey Gray, ½ Pt. 139.00
Flask, Bill's Place, Indian, Clear, 5 In. 18.00
Flask, Billy Winters Log Cabin, Pumpkinseed, Light Purple, Tooled Lip, Pt. 476.00
Flask, Bird, Flowers, Flared Out Lip, Clear, Painted, 1780-1810, 5¾ In. 190.00
Flask, Blue Green, Half Post, Kick-Up Pontil, France, 10 In. 672.00
Flask, Bryon & Eagle, Amber, Coin Shape, ½ Pt. 728.00
Flask, Byron & Scott, Olive Amber, Tooled Lip, Pontil, 1825-35, ½ Pt. 213.00
Flask, Byron & Scott, Olive Yellow, Tooled Lip, ½ Pt. 308.00
Flask, Calabash, Aqua, Tapered Lip, Iron Pontil, 1865, 9¼ In. 179.00
Flask, Chestnut, 10 Diamond, Sheared Mouth, Amber, Zanesville, 5⅜ In. 1008.00
Flask, Chestnut, 12 Diamond, Blue Green, Sheared Lip, Pontil, 6⅝ In. 213.00
Flask, Chestnut, 16 Ribs, Amethyst, Oval, Sheared Mouth, Round Base, 6¾ x 5¼ In. 154.00
Flask, Chestnut, 24 Ribs, Swirled Right, Blue, Applied Collar, Pontil, c.1830, 8 In. 550.00
Flask, Chestnut, 24 Vertical Ribs, Red Amber, Tooled Lip, Pontil, 5¼ In. 336.00
Flask, Chestnut, Amber, Applied Solid Handle, Pontil, 8 In. 123.00
Flask, Chestnut, Aqua, Applied Tapered Collar, Pontil, 10 In. 134.00
Flask, Chestnut, Aqua, Bulbous Shape, Flared Lip, Pontil, 1810, 3¼ In. 190.00
Flask, Chestnut, Forest Green, Applied Mouth, Bubbles, Pontil, 1780-1820, 8⅛ In. 1400.00
Flask, Chestnut, Olive Amber, Applied Lip, Pontil, 1820, 8¼ In. 308.00
Flask, Chestnut, Olive Green, Applied Lip, Pontil, 1780-1830, 7 In. 280.00
Flask, Chestnut, Olive Green, Applied Lip, Pontil, 5¼ In. 336.00
Flask, Chestnut, Olive Green, c.1820, 5½ In. 485.00
Flask, Chestnut, Olive Yellow, Applied Mouth, Pontil, 1800, 9¾ In. 420.00
Flask, Chestnut, Olive Yellow, Applied String Lip, Pontil, 8 In. 280.00
Flask, Chestnut, Straw Yellow, Sheared Lip, Pontil, 1790, 5 In. 269.00
Flask, Chestnut, Yellow Amber, Flattened, Applied Collar, 8¼ x 5½ In. 385.00
Flask, Clasped Hands & Eagle, Olive Yellow, Applied Ring, Qt. 784.00
Flask, Clyde Glass Works, N.Y., Olive Yellow, Applied Square Collar, 1864-70, Qt. 2750.00
Flask, Cobalt Blue, Sheared Lip, Pontil, 1800-1820, 4 In. 112.00
Flask, Cobalt Blue Man, Holding Glass, German Script, Pewter Mouth, 5⅜ In. 1232.00
Flask, Columbia & Eagle, Aqua, Tooled Lip, Pt. 1344.00
Flask, Concentric Rings Eagle, Yellow Green Amber, Pontil, Pt., 7 In. 33000.00
Flask, Corn For The World, Dark Peacock Blue, Applied Mouth, Qt. 24640.00
Flask, Corn For The World, Monument, Pink Puce, c.1865, Qt. .... *illus* 6700.00
Flask, Corn For The World, Orange Amber, Applied Mouth, Qt. 3300.00
Flask, Corn For The World, Pink Puce, Applied Mouth, 1865-75, Qt. 7280.00
Flask, Cornucopia & Eagle, Olive Amber, Flared Lip, Open Pontil, 1840, 6¾ In. 202.00
Flask, Cornucopia & Medallion, Blue Aqua, Tooled Lip, ½ Pt. 168.00
Flask, Cornucopia & Urn, Aqua, Sheared Lip, Pontil, 1840-50, ½ Pt. 224.00
Flask, Cornucopia & Urn, Aqua, Tooled Lip, ½ Pt. 224.00
Flask, Cornucopia & Urn, Blue Green, Sheared Mouth, Pontil, c.1849, ½ Pt. 728.00
Flask, Cornucopia & Urn, Blue Green, Tooled Lip, Open Pontil, c.1845, ½ Pt. .... *illus* 395.00
Flask, Cornucopia & Urn, Olive Amber, 6½ In. 112.00
Flask, Cornucopia & Urn, Olive Amber, Pt., 6¾ In. 58.00
Flask, Cornucopia & Urn, Olive Green, Sheared Lip, Pontil, 1825-35, ½ Pt. 112.00

Flask, Cornucopia & Urn, Yellow Amber, Pontil, Pt. 198.00
Flask, Diamond Daisy, Amethyst, Flattened, Sheared Mouth, 4⅜ In. 5040.00
Flask, Double Eagle, Amber, Sheared Lip, Pontil, Pt. 242.00
Flask, Double Eagle, Aqua, 8¾ In. 123.00
Flask, Double Eagle, Blue Aqua, Pt. 79.00
Flask, Double Eagle, Blue Aqua, Sheared Lip, Open Pontil, 1835-45, ½ Pt. 213.00
Flask, Double Eagle, Citron, Applied Ring Mouth, Qt. 784.00
Flask, Double Eagle, Clear, Vaseline Tint, Vertical Ribs, Tooled Lip, Pt. 308.00
Flask, Double Eagle, Forest Green, Applied Ring, Pt. 495.00
Flask, Double Eagle, Granite Glass Co., Amber, Pt. 179.00
Flask, Double Eagle, Green, Ribs, Louisville Glassworks, c.1855, 6 In. 3450.00
Flask, Double Eagle, Ice Blue, Applied Ring Mouth, c.1870, Pt. .... *illus* 485.00
Flask, Double Eagle, Olive Amber, Sheared Mouth, Pontil, ½ Pt. 275.00
Flask, Double Eagle, Olive Green, Qt. 784.00
Flask, Double Eagle, Tobacco Amber, Sheared Lip, Pontil, Pt. 358.00
Flask, Double Eagle, Yellow Amber, Sheared Mouth, Pontil, 1845-55, Pt. 179.00
Flask, Double Eagle Head Turned To Right, Aqua, ½ Pt., 6 In. 130.00
Flask, Eagle, Calabash, Green, Applied Mouth, Iron Pontil, Pt. 336.00
Flask, Eagle, Dyottville Glass Works, Aqua, Sheared Lip, Pontil, 8¼ In. 190.00
Flask, Eagle, Pugh & Teater, Blue Green, c.1820, Pt. 4312.00
Flask, Eagle & Anchor, Blue Aqua, Applied Mouth, Iron Pontil, 1845-55, Pt. 202.00
Flask, Eagle & Anchor, Resurgam, Baltimore Glass Works, Yellow, Tooled Lip, 1855, Pt. 1680.00
Flask, Eagle & Coffin, Blue Aqua, Tooled Lip, Open Pontil, Qt. 728.00
Flask, Eagle & Coffin & Hay, Aqua, Sheared Lip, Pontil, 1830-40, ½ Pt. 392.00
Flask, Eagle & Cornucopia, Amber, Sheared Lip, Pontil, Pt. 165.00
Flask, Eagle & Cornucopia, Blue Aqua, Sheared Mouth, Pontil, 1820-30, Pt. 308.00
Flask, Eagle & Cornucopia, Emerald Green, Sheared Lip, Pontil, Pt. 187.00
Flask, Eagle & Cornucopia, Olive Green, Sheared Lip, Pontil, Pt. 187.00
Flask, Eagle & Flag, Calabash, Yellow Green, Applied Mouth, Pontil, c.1855, Qt. .... *illus* 400.00
Flask, Eagle & Morning Glory, Blue Aqua, Tooled Lip, Pontil, Pt. 672.00
Flask, Eagle & Oak Tree, Blue Aqua, Tooled Lip, ½ Pt. 952.00
Flask, Eagle & Prospector, Aqua, Applied Ring Collar, c.1863, Pt. 1000.00
Flask, Eagle & Prospector, Root Beer Amber, 1865-75, Pt. 15680.00
Flask, Eagle & Willington, Light Green, Sheared Lip, Pontil, ½ Pt. 660.00
Flask, Eagle & Willington, Olive Green, Applied Mouth, c.1860, Pt. .... *illus* 275.00
Flask, Eagle & Willington, Olive Green, Applied Sloping Collar, 1855-65, Pt. 308.00
Flask, Eagle & Willington, Olive Green, Tooled Lip, ½ Pt. 560.00
Flask, Eagle & Willington, Shaded Amber, Applied Mouth, c.1860, Pt. .... *illus* 730.00
Flask, Exchange Flood & Barks, Pumpkinseed, Light Purple, Tooled Lip, Pt. 179.00
Flask, For Pike's Peak, Prospector, Aqua, Tooled Lip, ½ Pt. 728.00
Flask, For Pike's Peak, Prospector, Eagle, Aqua, Applied Lip, Pt., 8 In. 134.00
Flask, For Pike's Peak, Prospector, Eagle, Medium Yellow Amber, c.1865, ½ Pt. .... *illus* 1575.00
Flask, For Pike's Peak, Prospector, Hunter, Blue Aqua, 1865, Pt. 364.00
Flask, For Pike's Peak, Prospector, Hunter, Blue Aqua, Applied Ring, ½ Pt. 672.00
Flask, For Pike's Peak, Prospector, Hunter, Olive Yellow, 1865, Pt. .... 1568.00 to 3080.00
Flask, For Pike's Peak, Prospector, Hunter, Orange Amber, 1865, Pt. 1680.00
Flask, Frank Abadie, Eureka, Coffin, Lavender, Tooled Lip 1792.00
Flask, Globular, Aqua, Tooled Lip, Pontil, 1800, 7¾ In. 123.00
Flask, Granite Glass Co., Stoddard, N.H., Yellow Amber, Double Collar, Pt. 840.00
Flask, Grape Amethyst, Baltimore Glass Works, c.1820, ½ Pt. 6900.00
Flask, Haber Macht Ein Wilves, Clear, Painted Horse, 6⅜ In. 190.00
Flask, Highlander, Grapevines, Relief, Cobalt Blue, Pontil. 132.00
Flask, Hunter & Fisherman, Calabash, Strawberry Puce, Applied Mouth, IP, Qt. 896.00
Flask, Hunter & Fisherman, Copper Puce, Calabash, Side Ribs, Applied Mouth, IP, c.1855-65. 575.00
Flask, Hunter & Fisherman, Light Blue Green, Calabash, Qt. 129.00
Flask, Hunter & Stag, Purple Amethyst, 1800s, 5⅜ In. 672.00
Flask, I Got My Fill At Jake's, But Where Did I Eat That Dog, Pumpkinseed, Pt. 660.00
Flask, Isabella & Glasshouse, Green Aqua, Sheared Mouth, Pontil, Qt., 8¾ In. 165.00
Flask, J. Rohrer Liquors, Orange Amber, Strap Side, Embossed, Applied Lip, Qt. 109.00
Flask, J.H. Duker & Bro., Quincy, Ill., Pumpkinseed, Diamond Pattern, Light Amethyst, Pt. 198.00
Flask, Jenny Lind & Glasshouse, Amber, Applied Lip, 1864, 7¼ In. 308.00
Flask, Jenny Lind & Glasshouse, Aqua, 1864, 7¼ In. 146.00
Flask, Jenny Lind & Glasshouse, Calabash, Aqua Blue, Rounded Collar, Pontil, 1855-65, Qt. 224.00
Flask, Jenny Lind & Glasshouse, Calabash, Aqua, Open Pontil, Qt. 119.00
Flask, Jenny Lind & Glasshouse, Calabash, Blue Aqua, 9⅞ In. 448.00
Flask, Jenny Lind & Glasshouse, Calabash, Cornflower Blue, Purple Tint, Sloping Collar, Qt. .. 4400.00

Bottle, Flask, Double Eagle, Ice Blue, Applied Ring Mouth, c.1870, Pt.
$485.00

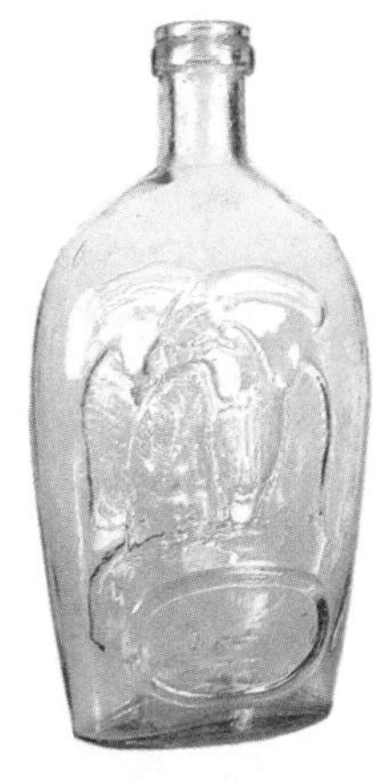

Bottle, Flask, Eagle & Flag, Calabash, Yellow Green, Applied Mouth, Pontil, c.1855, Qt.
$400.00

Bottle, Flask, Eagle & Willington, Olive Green, Applied Mouth, c.1860, Pt.
$275.00

Bottle, Flask, Eagle & Willington, Shaded Amber, Applied Mouth, c.1860, Pt.
$730.00

Bottle, Flask, For Pike's Peak, Prospector, Eagle, Medium Yellow Amber, c.1865, ½ Pt.
$1575.00

Bottle, Flask, Masonic & Eagle, Olive Green, Tooled Lip, Pontil, c.1830, Pt.
$729.00

Flask, Jenny Lind & Glasshouse, Calabash, Light To Medium Blue Green, Pontil, Qt. 952.00
Flask, Jenny Lind & Glasshouse, Calabash, Sapphire Blue, Iron Pontil, 9 ½ In. 4200.00
Flask, Kossuth & Tree, Calabash, Blue Green, Qt. 129.00
Flask, Kossuth & Tree, Calabash, Light Apple Green, Qt., 10 ½ In. 134.00
Flask, Kossuth & Tree, Calabash, Olive Yellow, Applied Mouth, Qt. 1232.00
Flask, Kossuth & Tree, Calabash, Yellow Green, Sloping Collar, Pontil, 1855-65, Qt. 560.00
Flask, Label Under Glass, Clear, Girl, Curly Hair, Blue Scarf, Ground Lip, Handle, 6 In. 258.00
Flask, Label Under Glass, Clear, Merry Christmas, Happy New Year, Pocket, 6 ⅞ In. 672.00
Flask, Lafayette & Clinton, Olive Green, Tooled Lip, Open Pontil, c.1825, ½ Pt. 3920.00
Flask, Lafayette & Clinton, Olive Yellow, Sheared Mouth, c.1824, ½ Pt. 4480.00
Flask, Lafayette & Eagle, Aqua, Tooled Lip, Pontil, c.1825, Pt. 392.00
Flask, Lafayette & Liberty, Olive Yellow Amber, Sheared Mouth, Pontil, ½ Pt. 1210.00
Flask, Larson, 16 Ribs, Swirled, Cobalt Blue, Sheared Lip, Pontil, 6 In. 246.00
Flask, Map, North & South America, Clear, Metal Screw Cap, c.1901, 7 In. 235.00
Flask, Masonic & Eagle, Blue Aqua, Tooled Lip, Pontil, Pt. 1680.00
Flask, Masonic & Eagle, Clear, Smoky Aqua Tint, Tooled Lip, Pt. 1120.00
Flask, Masonic & Eagle, Green, Tooled Lip, Pontil, 1815-30, Pt. 1568.00
Flask, Masonic & Eagle, Light Blue Green, Plain Lip, Pontil, 7 ¼ In. 1175.00
Flask, Masonic & Eagle, Light Blue Green, Sheared Mouth, Pontil, 1820-30, Pt. 1200.00
Flask, Masonic & Eagle, Light Smoky Blue, Tooled Lip, Pontil, Pt. 2352.00
Flask, Masonic & Eagle, Olive Amber, Pontil, Pt., 7 ½ In. 275.00
Flask, Masonic & Eagle, Olive Green, Tooled Lip, Pontil, c.1830, Pt. *illus* 729.00
Flask, Masonic & Eagle, Orange Amber, Tooled Lip, Pontil, 1820-35, Pt. 1680.00
Flask, Masonic & Eagle, Yellow Amber, Tooled Lip, Open Pontil, 1820-30, Pt. 258.00
Flask, Masonic & Seeing Eye, Yellow Amber, Tooled Lip, Pt. 392.00
Flask, McCarty & Torreyson, Yellow Amber, Applied Mouth, Pt. 952.00
Flask, Merry Christmas, Happy New Year, Amber, Half-Barrel, 5 ¾ In. *illus* 690.00
Flask, Merry Christmas, Pumpkinseed, Clear, Wreath, Ribs, Pt. 89.00
Flask, Milk Glass Opalescent Painted Flowers, Birds, Germany, 4 ⅝ In. 235.00
Flask, Monument, A Little More Grape, Apricot Puce, Tooled Lip, OP, ½ Pt. 5320.00
Flask, Olive Amber, Oval, Pinched Sides, Sheared Mouth, Pontil, 1800-30, 3 ⅝ In. 1300.00
Flask, Olive Amber, Sheared Lip, Open Pontil, 1825-30, 7 ¼ In. 1064.00
Flask, Olive Amber, Sheared Lip, Open Pontil, New England, 1835, 6 In. 146.00
Flask, Picnic, Pumpkinseed, Orange Amber, ½ Pt. 69.00
Flask, Pitkin Type, 12 Ribs, Clear, Plain, Lobes, Tooled Lip, c.1770, 4 ⅝ In. 190.00
Flask, Pitkin Type, 32 Ribs, Swirled To Left, Light Green, Tooled Lip, Kick-Up Base, 8 In. 303.00
Flask, Pitkin Type, 32 Ribs, Swirled To Left, Olive Yellow, Tooled Lip, 6 ⅝ In. 728.00
Flask, Pitkin Type, 32 Ribs, Swirled To Right, Green, Pontil, c.1815, 6 In. 1100.00
Flask, Pitkin Type, 32 Ribs, Swirled To Right, Light Olive Yellow Pontil, c.1795, 4 ⅞ In. 950.00
Flask, Pitkin Type, 32 Vertical Ribs, Aqua, Sheared Lip, Open Pontil, 5 In. 448.00
Flask, Pitkin Type, 36 Ribs, Swirled To Left, Olive Yellow, Pontil, c.1795, 6 ⅝ In. 650.00
Flask, Pitkin Type, 36 Ribs, Swirled To Left, Yellow, Sheared Mouth, Pontil, c.1800, 5 In. 800.00
Flask, Pitkin Type, 36 Ribs, Swirled To Right, Olive Yellow, Pontil, 1783-1830, 6 ½ In. 700.00
Flask, Pitkin Type, 36 Ribs, Swirled To Right, Olive Yellow, Tooled Lip, Pontil, 5 ⅜ In. 672.00
Flask, Pitkin Type, 36 Ribs, Swirled, Olive Green, Open Pontil, 5 In. 1129.00
Flask, Pitkin Type, 36 Ribs, Swirled, Olive Green, Sheared Mouth, Pontil, 5 ½ In. 708.00
Flask, Pumpkinseed, A. Colburn Co., Clear, Overall Ribs & Diamonds, ½ Pt. 39.00
Flask, Pumpkinseed, Clear, Clock Face, Spider Web, Pt. 48.00
Flask, Pumpkinseed, Favorite Essence Jamaica Ginger, Swirled Ribs, Clear, Metal Cap, ¼ Pt. 39.00
Flask, Pumpkinseed, Smoke Ambrosia Cigars, ½ Pt. 253.00
Flask, Ribbed, Depressed Ovals, Dots, c.1830, 11 Oz. 9200.00
Flask, S.C. Dispensary Palmetto Tree, Amethyst, Jo-Jo, Pocket, ½ Pt. 79.00
Flask, Scroll, Amber, Applied Mouth, Iron Pontil, 1840-50, Pt. 840.00
Flask, Scroll, Aqua, Stars, Sheared Lip, Pontil, 1860, 6 ½ In. 101.00
Flask, Scroll, Blue Green, Sheared Lip, Open Pontil, Pt. 784.00
Flask, Scroll, Citron, Pontil, Sheared, Tooled Lip, 1840-50, Pt. 1568.00
Flask, Scroll, Dark Olive Amber, Applied Ring Mouth, Qt. 1344.00
Flask, Scroll, Dark Olive Chocolate, Pontil, Applied Ring Mouth, c.1850, Qt. *illus* 2100.00
Flask, Scroll, Grass Green, Sheared Lip, Iron Pontil, 1840-50, Pt. 3360.00
Flask, Scroll, Ice Blue, Open Pontil, 7 In. 175.00
Flask, Scroll, Moonstone, Pink Tone, Rolled Lip, Pontil, Qt. 2016.00
Flask, Scroll, Sapphire Blue, Gray Tint, Stars, Sheared Mouth, 6 ⅞ In. 2310.00
Flask, Scroll, Sapphire Blue, Tooled Lip, Qt. 2240.00
Flask, Scroll, Teal Blue, Sheared Lip, Open Pontil, 1840-50, Pt. 3360.00
Flask, Scroll, Yellow Amber, Sheared Lip, Iron Pontil, 1840-50, Pt. 1792.00

Flask, Scroll, Yellow Amber, Tooled Lip, OP, ½ Pt. 952.00
Flask, Scroll, Yellow Green, Sheared Mouth, Iron Pontil, 1840-50, Pt. 1232.00
Flask, Sheaf Of Grain, Westford Glass Co., Olive Amber, Double Collar, Pt. 202.00
Flask, Sheaf Of Grain & Star, Blue Green, Tooled Lip, Pontil, 1855-65, Pt. 1680.00
Flask, Sheaf Of Grain & Star, Calabash, Blue Aqua, Open Pontil, Qt. 79.00
Flask, Sheaf Of Grain & Star, Calabash, Blue Green, Double Collar, 9 ⅛ In. 476.00
Flask, Sheaf Of Grain & Star, Calabash, Citron, 9 ⅛ In. 392.00
Flask, Sheaf Of Grain & Star, Emerald Green, Tooled Lip, Pontil, ½ Pt. 6720.00
Flask, Sloop & Star, Pale Apple Green, Sheared Lip, 5 ¼ In. 1344.00
Flask, Soldier & Dancer, Olive Yellow, Sheared Lip, Pontil, Pt. 990.00
Flask, Soldier & Eagle, Cobalt Blue, 1840-60, Pt. 308.00
Flask, Soldier & Sunflower, Calabash, Aqua, Applied Mouth, Qt. 364.00
Flask, Spirits, Cobalt Blue, Ribs, Swirled To Right, Tooled Lip, 1770-1800, 6 ⅞ In. 532.00
Flask, Stiegel Type, Amethyst, Flattened, c.1763, Pt. 4600.00
Flask, Success To The Railroad, Blue Aqua, Sheared, Mouth, Pontil, Pt. 616.00
Flask, Success To The Railroad, Dark Yellow Amber, Tooled Lip, Open Pontil, c.1820, Pt. 485.00
Flask, Success To The Railroad, Emerald Green, Tooled Lip, Open Pontil, c.1830, Pt. *illus* 3390.00
Flask, Success To The Railroad, Olive Yellow, Amber, Pontil, 1865-75, Pt. 308.00
Flask, Success To The Railroad, Olive Yellow Green, Applied Mouth, Pontil, c.1825-35, Pt. 1000.00
Flask, Success To The Railroad, Yellow, Amber, Shading, 1825-35, Pt. 560.00
Flask, Success To The Railroad, Yellow, Pontil, c.1830, Pt. 29900.00
Flask, Success To The Railroad, Yellow Amber, Tooled Lip, Pt. 504.00
Flask, Summer & Winter, Blue Aqua, Open Pontil, Qt. 139.00
Flask, Sunburst, Aqua, c.1815, ½ Pt. 3737.00
Flask, Sunburst, Blue Green, Tooled Lip, ½ Pt. 336.00
Flask, Sunburst, Clear Green, Sheared Lip, Pontil, 1815-25, Pt. 134.00
Flask, Sunburst, Clear Green, Tooled Lip, Pontil, c.1820, Pt. *illus* 680.00
Flask, Sunburst, Green, Tooled Lip, Pt. 1064.00
Flask, Sunburst, Light Apple Green, Tooled Lip, Pontil, Pt. 616.00
Flask, Sunburst, Light Olive Yellow Sheared Mouth, Pontil, c.1813, Pt. 1064.00
Flask, Sunburst, Olive Yellow, Tooled Lip, ½ Pt. 952.00
Flask, Sunburst, Olive Yellow, c.1815, Pt. 11500.00
Flask, Sunburst, Olive Yellow, Sheared Mouth, Pontil, 1820-30, ½ Pt. 750.00
Flask, Sunburst, Yellow Grass Green, Sheared Mouth, Pontil, Pt., 8 In. 468.00
Flask, Swirled Ribs, Olive Yellow, Sheared Mouth, c.1783, 6 ½ In. 588.00
Flask, Swirled Ribs, Pale Green, Sheared Mouth, Open Pontil, Pt. 159.00
Flask, Taylor & Monument, Clear, Long Neck, Tooled Lip, Open Pontil, Pt. 336.00
Flask, Traveler's Companion & Star, Amber, Shaded, Sheared Lip, Pontil, 1850, Pt. 616.00
Flask, Traveler's Companion & Star, Applied Lip, c.1860-70, Qt. 59.00
Flask, Union, Clasped Hands & Cannon, Amber, Applied Ring, Pt. 1120.00
Flask, Union, Clasped Hands & Eagle, Calabash, Aqua, Open Pontil, ½ Pt. 48.00
Flask, Union, Clasped Hands & Eagle, Citron, Applied Lip, Smooth Base, 1873, 6 ¼ In. 392.00
Flask, Union, Clasped Hands & Eagle, Cobalt Blue, Applied Ring Mouth, c.1865, Qt. *illus* 3390.00
Flask, Union, Clasped Hands & Eagle, Orange Amber, Sloping Collar, ½ Pt. 329.00
Flask, Union, Clasped Hands & Masonic Tools, H & S, Eagle With Banner, Aqua, OP, ½ Pt. 79.00
Flask, Union, Clasped Hands, Amber, Applied Lip, 1872, 6 In. 123.00
Flask, Union, Clasped Hands, Aqua, Amber Striations, 7 ½ In. 112.00
Flask, Union, Clasped Hands, Yellow Amber, Applied Ring Mouth, 1860-70, Pt. 420.00
Flask, Union, Clasped Hands & Eagle, Aqua, Applied Lip, 1873, 6 In. 67.00
Flask, Union, Clasped Hands & Eagle, Aqua, Applied Lip, 1875, 7 ½ In. 67.00
Flask, Victorian Girl, Clear, Label, Pt. 239.00
Flask, Waldoft & Tavern, Reno, Lavender, Tooled Lip, c.1910, 10 Oz. 235.00
Flask, Warranted, Olive Yellow, Straps, ½ Pt. 48.00
Flask, Washington, Lockport Glass Works, Ice Blue, Pontil, 1843-60, Qt. 2750.00
Flask, Washington & Clay, Taylor, Blue Green, Tooled Lip, Pontil, c.1849, Qt. 952.00
Flask, Washington & Eagle, Adams & Jefferson, Moss Green, Sheared Mouth, Pontil, 7 In. 8250.00
Flask, Washington & Eagle, Blue Aqua, Tooled Lip, Pontil, Pt. *illus* 1590.00
Flask, Washington & Eagle, Clear, Vaseline Tint, Tooled Lip, Pontil, Pt. 3080.00
Flask, Washington & Eagle, Green Aqua, Reversed Letters, 7 In. 440.00
Flask, Washington & Jackson, Amber, Sheared Lip, Pontil, Pt. 468.00
Flask, Washington & Jackson, Yellow Amber, Tooled Lip, c.1830, Pt. 336.00
Flask, Washington & Monument, Clear, Smoky Blue Tint, Tooled Lip, Pontil, Pt. 784.00
Flask, Washington & Taylor, Aqua, Pt. 99.00
Flask, Washington & Taylor, Aqua, Sloping Collar, Pontil, 7 ¼ In. 90.00
Flask, Washington & Taylor, Blue Aqua, Open Pontil, Pt. 39.00
Flask, Washington & Taylor, Blue Aqua, Open Pontil, Qt. 119.00

Bottle, Flask, Merry Christmas, Happy New Year, Amber, Half-Barrel, 5 ¾ In.
$690.00

Bottle, Flask, Scroll, Dark Olive Chocolate, Pontil, Applied Ring Mouth, c.1850, Qt.
$2100.00

Bottle, Flask, Success To The Railroad, Emerald Green, Tooled Lip, Open Pontil, c.1830, Pt.
$3390.00

Bottle, Flask, Sunburst, Clear Green, Tooled Lip, Pontil, c.1820, Pt.
$680.00

Bottle, Flask, Union, Clasped Hands & Eagle, Cobalt Blue, Applied Ring Mouth, c.1865, Qt.
$3390.00

Bottle, Flask, Washington & Eagle, Blue Aqua, Tooled Lip, Pontil, Pt.
$1590.00

Flask, Washington & Taylor, Blue Aqua, Sloping Collar, Open Pontil, Pt. 129.00
Flask, Washington & Taylor, Blue Aqua, Tooled Lip, Pontil, c.1835, Pt. 476.00
Flask, Washington & Taylor, Grass Green, Applied Mouth, Pontil, c.1849, Qt. 1680.00
Flask, Washington & Taylor, Lavender, Tooled Lip, Pontil, c.1849, Qt. 1680.00
Flask, Washington & Taylor, Light Cornflower Blue, Qt. 295.00
Flask, Washington & Taylor, Olive Yellow, Applied Collar, 1849-55, Qt. 1792.00
Flask, Washington & Taylor Never Surrenders, Blue Green, Tooled Lip, Qt. 392.00
Flask, Washington & Tree, Calabash, Cobalt Blue, Applied Collar, Qt. 19040.00
Flask, Wheelman's Favorite, Cushing Process Co., c.1890, 4 In. 165.00
Flask, Willington Glass Works, Olive Green, Smooth Base, 1870, 6 ¼ In. 308.00
Flask, Woman's Boot, White, Blue, Black, Cork Stopper, 4 ¼ x 4 x 1 ¼ In. 50.00
Flask, Zanesville City Glass Works, Yellow Amber, Pt. 728.00
Food, Armours Boullion Cubes, Ground Lid, Yellow Label, Footed, 10 ¼ x 5 ½ In. 232.00
Food, Borden's Malted Milk, Improved, Glass Label, Embossed Metal Lid, 9 x 6 ½ In. 550.00
Food, Candy Bros., Confectioners, St. Louis, Mo., Tooled Top, Glass Insert, 11 ½ In. 175.00
Food, Heinz, Gold Medal Worcestershire Sauce, Embossed, Label, Keystone Stopper, 8 x 2 In. .. 310.00
Food, Heinz's Chow Chow, Keystone, Lid, Paper Label, 11 x 5 ¼ In. 525.00
Food, Mustard, Citron, Embossed, Eagle Insert, Milk Glass Closure, Pt. 151.00
Food, Petal, Olive Green, Shoulder, 10 Flutes, Iron Pontil,, ½ Gal. 2576.00
Food, Royal Salad Dressing, Embossed, Horton-Cato Mfg. Co., Detroit, Patented April 25 1882 12.00
Food, Syrup, Jar, Limon, Pat. Apr 2. 1889, Blue, Label Under Glass, Metal Cap, 10 ⅝ In. . *illus* 378.00
Fruit, Trademark Lighting, Dark Lemon Yellow, Ground Lip, ½ Gal., 10 ¼ In. 288.00
Fruit Jar, A. Stone & Co., Aqua, Embossed, Applied Mouth, Glass Closure, 1860-75, Qt. 1120.00
Fruit Jar, A.B.C., Pat. April 15th 1884, Aqua, Metal Yoke Clamp, Embossed, Qt. 504.00
Fruit Jar, A.B.C., Pat. April 15th 1884, Aqua, Glass Lid, Metal Yoke Clamp, Pt. 476.00
Fruit Jar, Air-Tight, Barrel, Aqua, Wax Seal Groove, c.1850, Pt. 476.00
Fruit Jar, Atherholt, Fisher & Co., Philada., Aqua, Blown Stopper, Qt. 1344.00
Fruit Jar, Ball Perfect Mason, Olive Green, Zinc Lid, Qt. 60.00
Fruit Jar, Baltimore Glass Works, Aqua, Wide Mouth, Qt. 784.00
Fruit Jar, Barrel, Dark Aqua, Iron Pontil, Metal Cap, Qt. 1100.00
Fruit Jar, BBGMCo, Monogram, Facing Right, Porcelain Lined, Aqua, Screw Lid, Midget. 784.00
Fruit Jar, Beaver, Facing Right, Light Green, Ground Lip, Midget. 168.00
Fruit Jar, Beaver, Green, Ground Lip, Screw Lid, Canada, c.1885, Midget .... *illus* 180.00
Fruit Jar, Belle, Pat. Dec. 14th 1869, Domed Lid, Aqua, 3-Footed, Ground Lip, Wire Closure, Qt. 2688.00
Fruit Jar, Best, Patented August 18th 1868, Clear, Screw Lid, Qt. 1792.00
Fruit Jar, Bloeser, Pat. Jan. 12 1886, Aqua, Glass Lid, Metal Closure, Qt. 532.00
Fruit Jar, Bloeser Jar, Pat. Sept 27 1887, Aqua, Glass Lid, Wire & Metal Clamp, ½ Gal. 476.00
Fruit Jar, Blueberry Preserve, Golden Amber, Fluted Shoulders, Cylindrical, 1860-72, 11 In. . 1000.00
Fruit Jar, C.F. Spencer's, Patent Rochester, N.Y., Aqua, Metal Lid, Side Wire Loops, Qt. 1568.00
Fruit Jar, Clarke Fruit Jar Co., Cleveland, O., Pat. M'CH 17 1885, Aqua, Glass Lid, Qt. 448.00
Fruit Jar, Cohansey, Aqua, ½ Pt. 202.00
Fruit Jar, Cohansey, Aqua, Domed Metal Lid, Wax Seal Ring, 1877-80, Qt. 246.00
Fruit Jar, Cohansey, Aqua, Ground Lip, Glass Lid, Wire Closure, 1872-85, Qt. 134.00
Fruit Jar, Daisy Jar, Pat. Jan 3d 88, Clear, Glass Lid, Metal, Closure, ½ Gal. 420.00
Fruit Jar, Dexter, Fruits & Vegetables, Aqua, Midget. 308.00
Fruit Jar, Doolittle Self Sealer, Patented January 1900, Aqua, Glass Lid, Wire Closure, Pt. 202.00
Fruit Jar, E.C. Flaccus Co., Stag's Head, Green, Milk Glass Lid, Metal Band, Pt. 1680.00
Fruit Jar, Eagle, Aqua, Glass Lid, Iron Yoke Clamp, Star Thumbscrew, Qt. 224.00
Fruit Jar, Empire, Feb.13 1886, Aqua, Glass Lid, Metal Clamp, Lever Closure, Qt. 448.00
Fruit Jar, Franklin, R.W. King, 90 Jefferson Ave, Detroit, Mich, Aqua, Glass Lid, Qt. 2800.00
Fruit Jar, Gilberds, Star, Straw Yellow, Glass Lid, Wire Closure, Qt. 416.00
Fruit Jar, Globe, Yellow Amber, Ground Lip, Glass Lid, Metal Closure, ½ Gal. 235.00
Fruit Jar, Hemingray, Sapphire Blue, Metal Lid, Wax Sealer, c.1851, 5 ⅞ In. 4500.00
Fruit Jar, Hero Embossed, Ground Lip, 4 Gal., 17 ¾ In. 3450.00
Fruit Jar, Hoosier Jar, Patd Sept 12th 1882, Aqua, Ground Lip, Screw-On Lid, Qt. 750.00
Fruit Jar, Hoosier Jar, Patd Sept 12th 1882, Green Aqua, Glass Lid, Qt. 896.00
Fruit Jar, Howe Jar, Scranton, Pa., Pat. Feby 28/88, Aqua, Glass Lid, Wire Bail, Pt. 325.00
Fruit Jar, John M. Moore & Co., Blue Aqua, Iron Yoke Clamp, Thumbscrew, Qt. 392.00
Fruit Jar, Joshua Wright, Phila., Blue Aqua, Barrel, ½ Gal. 1120.00
Fruit Jar, King, Pat. Nov 2, 1869, Aqua, Glass Lid, Iron Yoke Clamp, Qt. 190.00
Fruit Jar, Lafayette, Aqua, Cylindrical, Rolled Mouth, Metal Stopper, 1884-90, Qt. 350.00
Fruit Jar, Lafayette, Clear, Metal Closure, Patented Sept. 21, 1884, Qt. 420.00
Fruit Jar, Lightning, Amber, Embossed, Putnam 198, ½ Gal., 10 In. .... *illus* 100.00
Fruit Jar, Lightning, HWP, Putnam 2, Aqua, Pat'd Apr 25, 92, Wire Closure, c.1905, Qt. 350.00
Fruit Jar, Lightning Putnam, Medium Amber, Ground Lip, ½ Gal., 10 In. 115.00
Fruit Jar, Lightning Putnam, Medium Olive Amber, ½ Gal., 10 ¼ In. 86.00

Fruit Jar, Made In Canada, Perfect Seal, Wide Mouth, Adjustable, Olive, c.1915, Pt. . . . . *illus* 115.00
Fruit Jar, Mansfield, Patent Nov. 30th, 1858, N.C.L., Aqua, Zinc Screw-On Lid, c.1880, Midget, Pt. 220.00
Fruit Jar, Mason, Amber, Embossed Mason Fruit Jar On Two Lines, ½ Gal., 9 ½ In. 1035.00
Fruit Jar, Mason's 5 Patent Nov 30th 1858, Cobalt, Qt., 7 ½ In. *illus* 2750.00
Fruit Jar, Mason's CFJCo, Patent Nov 30th 1858, Amber, ½ Gal., 9 ¼ In. 863.00
Fruit Jar, Mason's CFJCo Improved Butter Jar, Aqua, Glass Lid, Screw Band, ½ Gal. 179.00
Fruit Jar, Mason's Patent Nov 30th 1858, Aqua, Ground Lip, Zinc Screw Lid, c.1880, Midget *illus* 240.00
Fruit Jar, Mason's Patent Nov 30th 1858, Aqua, Zinc Screw Lid, Milk Glass Insert, Midget. . . . 90.00
Fruit Jar, Mason's Patent Nov 30th 1858, Aqua, Olive & Amber Striations, Zinc Screw Lid, Qt. 90.00
Fruit Jar, Mason's Patent Nov 30th 1858, Cross, Dark Green, Qt., 7 ½ In. 2185.00
Fruit Jar, Mason's Patent Nov 30th 1858, Cross, Dark Olive Green, Amber Striations, ½ Gal.. . 2850.00
Fruit Jar, Mason's Patent Nov 30th 1858, Cross, Yellow, Ground, Lip, ½ Gal., 9 In. 1150.00
Fruit Jar, Mason's Patent Nov 30th 1858, Dark Amber, Qt., 7 ½ In. 575.00
Fruit Jar, Mason's Patent Nov 30th 1858, Golden Yellow Amber, Ground Lip, Qt. 504.00
Fruit Jar, Mason's Patent Nov 30th 1858, Keystone, Orange Amber, Zinc Lid, ½ Gal. 616.00
Fruit Jar, Mason's Patent Nov 30th 1858, Keystone In Circle, Blue, ½ Gal., 9 In.. . . . . 350.00
Fruit Jar, Mason's Patent Nov 30th 1858, Keystone In Circle, Amber, Embossed, ½ Gal., 9 In.. 805.00
Fruit Jar, Mason's Patent Nov 30th 1858, Keystone In Circle, Olive Amber, Qt., 7 ½ In. 3400.00
Fruit Jar, Mason's Patent Nov 30th 1858, Medium Amber, Ground Lip, Zinc Screw Lid, Qt. . . . 235.00
Fruit Jar, Mason's Patent Nov 30th 1858, Medium Olive Yellow, Ground Lip, Qt., 7 ½ In.. . . . . 345.00
Fruit Jar, Mason's Patent Nov 30th 1858, Medium Orange Amber, ½ Gal., 9 ¼ In. 863.00
Fruit Jar, Mason's Patent Nov 30th 1858, Olive Green, ½ Gal., 9 In. . . . . *illus* 600.00
Fruit Jar, Mason's Patent Nov 30th 1858, Olive Yellow, ½ Gal., 9 ½ In.. . . . . 680.00
Fruit Jar, Mason's Patent Nov 30th 1858, Olive Yellow, Ground Lip, Zinc Screw Lid, Qt.. . . . . . 179.00
Fruit Jar, Mason's Patent Nov 30th 1858, Reversed N's, Dark Amber, Qt., 7 ½ In. 987.00
Fruit Jar, Millville Atmospheric, Aqua, Glass Lid, Cast Iron Yoke, Seal Ring, ½ Pt. 420.00
Fruit Jar, Millville Atmospheric, Clear, Glass Lid, Thumb Screw Closure, Pt.. . . . . 90.00
Fruit Jar, Paragon Valve Jar, Aqua, Ground Lip, Zinc Screw Band, Glass Insert, Qt. 420.00
Fruit Jar, Peerless, Patented Feb 13 1863, Aqua, Glass Lid, Iron Yoke Clamp, Qt. 235.00
Fruit Jar, Potter & Bodine's, Horizontal Ribs, Wax Sealer, c.1855, Qt. 805.00
Fruit Jar, Potter & Bodine's Airtight, Barrel, Applied Pontil, Patented April 13, 1858, Qt.. . . . . 880.00
Fruit Jar, Protector, Blue Aqua, Ground Lip, Metal Lid, Wire Clamp, ½ Gal. 90.00
Fruit Jar, Scranton Jar, Aqua, Applied Lip, Glass Stopper, Qt. 2128.00
Fruit Jar, Scranton Jar, G.H.C., Citron, Aqua Lid, Wood Roller Closure, Qt. 2240.00
Fruit Jar, Sun Trademark, Sun In Circle, Aqua, Glass Lid, Metal Yoke Clamp, Pt.. . . . . 146.00
Fruit Jar, Trademark Lightning, H.W.P. Base, Putnam, Yellow Amber, Qt. 1680.00
Fruit Jar, Trademark Lightning, Olive Yellow, Ground Lip, Glass Lid, ½ Gal., 10 ¼ In. 115.00
Fruit Jar, Trademark Lightning, Yellow, Glass Lid, Wire Bail, Qt. 239.00
Fruit Jar, Trademark Lightning Putnam, Glass Lid, Aqua, Wire Closure, 5 ⅛ In. 258.00
Fruit Jar, Trademark Lightning Putnam, Golden Amber, Numbered Lid, Closure, Qt. 123.00
Fruit Jar, Trademark Lightning Putnam, Olive Yellow, Cover, Qt.. . . . . 258.00
Fruit Jar, Unmarked, Aqua, Cylindrical, Ground Lip, Lid, Metal Yoke Clamp, c.1881, Qt.. . . . . 1456.00
Fruit Jar, Valve Jar Co., Philadelphia, Aqua, Ground Lip, Metal Lid, Wire Closure, Qt. 504.00
Fruit Jar, Valve Jar Co., Philadelphia, Patd Mar 10 1868, Aqua, Glass Lid, Qt.. . . . . 532.00
Fruit Jar, Van Vliet Jar Of 1881, Aqua, Cylindrical, Glass Lid, Metal Yoke Clamp, Pt.. . . . . 2300.00
Fruit Jar, Van Vliet Jar Of 1881, Aqua, Embossed Glass Lid, Iron Yoke Clamp, Pt.. . . . . 3920.00
Fruit Jar, Van Vliet Jar Of 1881, Aqua, Glass Lid, Metal Yoke Clamp, ½ Gal.. . . . . 1792.00
Fruit Jar, Winslow Jar, Patented Nov. 29th 1870, Aqua, Glass Lid, Wire Clamp, ½ Gal. 134.00
Fruit Jar, Wm. L. Haller Carlisle, Pa., Aqua, Qt. 1456.00
Gin, Booth & Sedgwick's, London, Cordial, Emerald, Applied Mouth, IP, 10 In.. . . . . 990.00
Gin, Bouvier's Buchu, For Kidney & Bladder, Flying Bird, Clear, Label, Qt., 11 In.. . . . . 79.00
Gin, Case, Olive Green, Applied Flared Lip, Footed, Pontil, 11 ½ x 3 ¾ In.. . . . . 135.00
Gin, Case, Sea Green, Rectangular, Half Post, Flared Lip, Pontil, Germany, 1780, 10 In.. . . . . . 616.00
Gin, Charles London Cordial, Case, Blue Green, Sloping Collar, 8 In.. 448.00
Gin, J.T. Beuker's Schiedam, Rooster, Olive Yellow, 8 ¼ In.. . . . . 59.00
Gin, London Royal Imperial, Case, Cobalt Blue, 9 ⅞ In.. . . . . 1904.00
Household, Boot Blacking, Blue Green, Open Pontil, c.1850, 4 ⅝ In. . . . . *illus* 345.00
Household, Gum Mastic, Porcelain, Gold Trim, Gold Label, Lid, 10 x 4 ½ In.. . . . . 94.00
Household, Race & Sheldon Boot Polish, Blue Green, 10-Sided, Applied Lip, Pontil, 8 In.. . . . 2128.00
Household, Seabury's Laundry, Bluing, Blue Green, Rolled Lip, Pontil, 3 ⅞ In. 364.00
Ink, 8-Sided, Concave Panels, Cobalt Blue, Tooled Lip, c.1850, 2 ⅜ In. . . . . *illus* 1800.00
Ink, 12-Sided, Olive Yellow Green, Sloping Double Collar, Iron Pontil, Master, ½ Gal., 10 In.. . 6720.00
Ink, 36 Ribs, Swirled, Olive Green, Pontil, East Manchester, Conn., c.1810, 1 ⅝ In. . . . . . *illus* 345.00
Ink, Arrison's Columbian, 8-Sided, Crooked Neck, 2 In.. . . . . 89.00
Ink, Beehive, Apple Green, Sheared Mouth, 2 In. 532.00
Ink, Bertinguiot, Olive Yellow, Sheared Mouth, Pontil, 1845-60, 2 ½ In. 532.00

Bottle, Food, Syrup, Jar, Limon, Pat. Apr 2. 1889, Blue, Label Under Glass, Metal Cap, 10 ⅝ In.
$378.00

Bottle, Fruit Jar, Beaver, Green, Ground Lip, Screw Lid, Canada, c.1885, Midget
$180.00

Bottle, Fruit Jar, Lightning, Amber, Embossed, Putnam 198, ½ Gal., 10 In.
$100.00

Bottle, Fruit Jar, Made In Canada, Perfect Seal, Wide Mouth, Adjustable, Olive, c.1915, Pt.
$115.00

Bottle, Fruit Jar, Mason's 5 Patent Nov 30th 1858, Cobalt, Qt., 7 ½ In.
$2750.00

Bottle, Fruit Jar, Mason's Patent Nov 30th 1858, Aqua, Ground Lip, Zinc Screw Lid, c.1880, Midget
$240.00

Bottle, Fruit Jar, Mason's Patent Nov 30th 1858, Olive Green, ½ Gal., 9 In.
$600.00

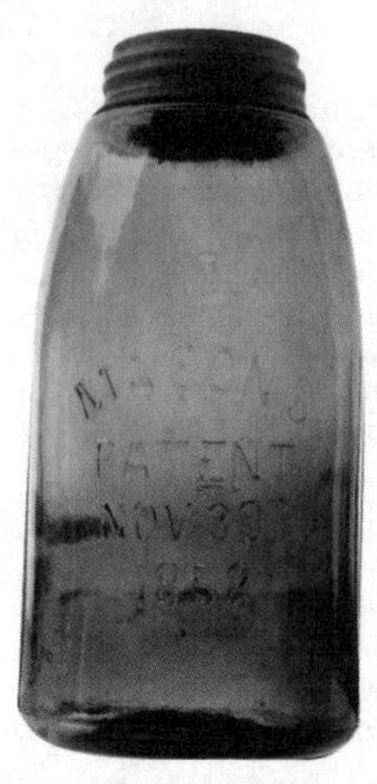

Bottle, Household, Boot Blacking, Blue Green, Open Pontil, c.1850, 4 ⅝ In.
$345.00

Bottle, Ink, 8-Sided, Concave Panels, Cobalt Blue, Tooled Lip, c.1850, 2 ⅜ In.
$1800.00

Bottle, Ink, 36 Ribs, Swirled, Olive Green, Pontil, East Manchester, Conn., c.1810, 1 ⅝ In.
$345.00

Bottle, Ink, Cone, X, Reversed 200, Olive Green, Tooled Lip, Pontil, c.1850, 2 ¼ In.
$795.00

Bottle, Ink, Farley's, 8-Sided, Olive Yellow, Flared Lip, Open Pontil, c.1850, 3 ½ In.
$2800.00

Bottle, Ink, Geometric, Blue, 3-Piece Mold, Mt. Vernon Glassworks, 1 ¾ In.
$6700.00

Ink, Bertinguiot, Sapphire Blue, Sheared Mouth, Pontil, 1845-60, 2 ¾ In. 2128.00
Ink, Butlers, 12-Sided, Clear, Rolled Lip, 2 ¼ In. 302.00
Ink, Carter's, Black Amethyst, Label, c.1865, 2 ⅓ In. 69.00
Ink, Carter's, Blue Green, 8 ½ In. 79.00
Ink, Carter's, Cathedral, Cobalt Blue, Gothic Panels, Embossed, Ca-Rt-Er, c.1925, 8 In. 179.00
Ink, Clark's Patent, Blue Green, May 30, 1845, England, 3 In. 615.00
Ink, Cobalt Blue, Iron Pontil, 7 In. 1495.00
Ink, Collins Ink Co., Applied Mouth, Tooled Pour Spout, Master, 9 ⅞ In. 336.00
Ink, Cone, Draped, Sapphire Blue, Applied Double Collar, Open Pontil, 2 ½ In. 2128.00
Ink, Cone, Draped Light To Medium Green, Inward Rolled Lip, Pontil, 1850-60, 2 ⅛ In. 1100.00
Ink, Cone, Light To Medium Teal Blue, Inward Rolled Lip, 2 ½ In. 448.00
Ink, Cone, R.L. Higgins, Virginia City, Embossed, Light Green, 2 In. 1210.00
Ink, Cone, X, Reversed 200, Olive Green, Tooled Lip, Pontil, c.1850, 2 ¼ In. *illus* 795.00
Ink, Cylindrical, Olive Amber, Flared Lip, Master, 4 ⅜ In. 135.00
Ink, Cylindrical, Olive Green, Free-Blown, Attached Saucer Base, Pontil, c.1825, 2 ½ In. 950.00
Ink, Cylindrical, Olive Yellow, 5 Annular Rings, Sheared Mouth, Pontil, 1783-1830, 2 ¾ In. 1500.00
Ink, Cylindrical, Olive Yellow, Tapered, Ribs, Tooled Disc Mouth, c.1783, 2 ¼ In. 1120.00
Ink, Davids & Black, New York, Blue Green, Sloping Collar, Pontil, 5 In. 101.00
Ink, Emerald Green, Annular Ring, Tooled Lip, Pontil, c.1790-1820 2912.00
Ink, Farley's, 8-Sided, Olive Yellow, Flared Lip, Open Pontil, c.1850, 3 ½ In. *illus* 2800.00
Ink, Geometric, Blue, 3-Piece Mold, Mt. Vernon Glassworks, 1 ¾ In. *illus* 6700.00
Ink, Geometric, Forest Green, Annular Ring, Tooled Disc Mouth, Pontil, 1 ¾ x 2 ⅛ In. 1282.00
Ink, Geometric, Yellow Amber, 3-Piece Mold, Tooled Disc Mouth, Pontil, 1 ½ In. 308.00
Ink, Glass, Geometric, Olive Green, Open Pontil, Coventry Glass, 2 ¼ In. 150.00
Ink, Gross & Robinson's, Blue Aqua, Applied Mouth, Iron Pontil, 5 ⅞ In. 1120.00
Ink, Harrison's Columbian, 8-Sided, Aqua, Crooked Neck, Open Pontil, 2 In. 89.00
Ink, Harrison's Columbian, 8-Sided, Blue Green, Outward Rolled Lip, OP, 1 ⅝ In. 1344.00
Ink, Harrison's Columbian, 8-Sided, Olive Yellow, Inward Rolled Lip, 1 ¾ In. 1232.00
Ink, Harrison's Columbian, 12-Sided, Blue Aqua, Pontil, Applied Lip, Master, 11 ½ In. 3640.00
Ink, Harrison's Columbian, Aqua, Rolled Lip, Open Pontil, 1 ⅝ In. 185.00
Ink, Harrison's Columbian, Cobalt Blue, Gal. 29120.00
Ink, Harrison's Columbian, Cobalt Blue, Rolled Lip, Label, c.1850, 2 In. *illus* 1390.00
Ink, Harrison's Columbian, Cobalt Blue, Rolled Lip, Open Pontil, 2 ¼ In. 1120.00
Ink, Horse, Rider, Diamond, Dark Yellow Amber, Tooled Disc Lip, 1 ⅜ In. 7280.00
Ink, Igloo, Amethyst, Vertical Ribs, Ground Lip, 2 In. 1210.00
Ink, Igloo, Strawberry Puce, Embossed Ribs, Rough, c.1880, 2 ⅛ In. *illus* 2020.00
Ink, J. & I.E.M., Igloo, Emerald Green, Ground Mouth, 1 ⅝ In. 476.00
Ink, J. & I.E.M., Igloo, Olive Yellow, Ground Mouth, 1 ⅝ In. 476.00
Ink, J. & I.E.M., Igloo, Sapphire Blue, Tooled Lip, 1 ¾ In. 1904.00
Ink, J. & I.E.M., Igloo, Yellow, Olive Tint, Tooled Lip, 1 ¾ In. 1232.00
Ink, J. & I.E.M., Igloo, Blue Green, Tooled Lip, 1 ¾ In. 784.00
Ink, J. & I.E.M., Igloo, Aqua, Sheared Lip, 2 ⅛ In. 78.00
Ink, J. & I.E.M., Igloo, Teal, Ground Lip, 2 ⅛ In. 258.00
Ink, J. Raynald, Globe, The World, Aqua, Tooled Lip, Embossed, 2 ¼ In. 134.00
Ink, J. Raynald, Globe, The World, Aqua, Tooled Lip, 1885-95, 2 ¼ In. 392.00
Ink, Locomotive, Trademark, Pat. Oct. 1874, Ground Lip, 2 In. *illus* 1380.00
Ink, Monroe's Patent School Ink, Teakettle, Aqua, 7-Sided, Embossed, 1870, 2 In. 450.00
Ink, Ne Plus Ultra Fluid, Schoolhouse, Blue Aqua, Burst Lip, 2 In. 359.00
Ink, Olive Yellow, Citron, Pt. 39.00
Ink, Olive Yellow, Master, Pt., 7 ½ In. 19.00
Ink, Patterson's Excelsior, 8-Sided, Blue Aqua, Reversed 3X, Inward Rolled Lip, 2 ¾ In. 504.00
Ink, Pitkin Type, 36 Ribs, Swirled To Right, Olive Yellow, Pontil, 2 ⅛ In. 1000.00
Ink, Pitkin Type, Ribs, Olive Yellow, c.1783 5175.00
Ink, R.L. Higgins, Virginia City, Amber, Applied Mouth, Pour Spout, c.1875, 6 In. 13600.00
Ink, S. Fine Black, Aqua, Open Pontil, Sheared Lip, 3 ⅛ In. 246.00
Ink, S.F. Cal Co, House, Amber, Tooled Lip. 2420.00
Ink, S.I., Comp, House, Milk Glass, Applied Lip. 605.00
Ink, Smith's, Perpetual Calendar, Embossed 12 Months, Cone, Blue Aqua, 3 ¼ In. 495.00
Ink, Stafford's, Blue Green, Tooled Spout, 7 ¾ In. 79.00
Ink, Teakettle, 8-Sided, Green Aqua, Double Font, c.1890, 3 ½ In. *illus* 690.00
Ink, Teakettle, Barrel, Amethyst, 2 In. 890.00
Ink, Teakettle, Barrel, Green, Sheared Lip, 2 In. 605.00
Ink, Teakettle, Barrel, Teal, Brass Cap, 2 In. 660.00
Ink, Teakettle, Barrel, Turquoise, Gold Paint, Brass Cap 1560.00
Ink, Teakettle, Beehive, Aqua, Ground Lip, c.1880, 1 ⅛ In. *illus* 295.00
Ink, Teakettle, Blue Clambroth, 2 ½ In. 476.00

Milk Bottles with Messages
Special glass milk bottles with holiday messages are made by dairies and stores for Christmas. Many of the bottles hold eggnog. Bottle collectors are saving the bottles.

Bottle, Ink, Harrison's Columbian, Cobalt Blue, Rolled Lip, Label, c.1850, 2 In.
$1390.00

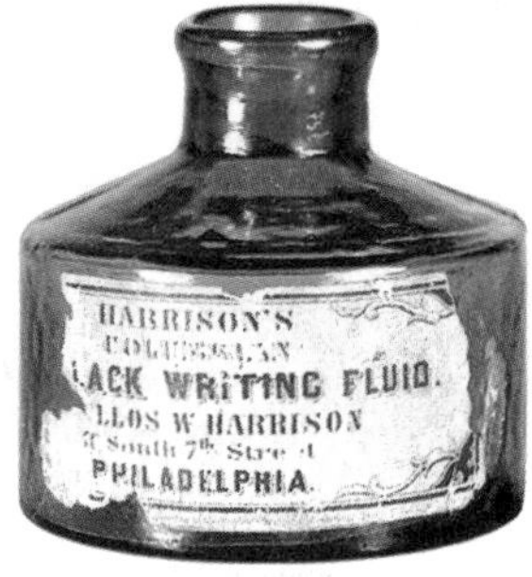

Bottle, Ink, Igloo, Strawberry Puce, Embossed Ribs, Rough, c.1880, 2 ⅛ In.
$2020.00

Bottle, Ink, Locomotive, Trademark, Pat. Oct. 1874, Ground Lip, 2 In.
$1380.00

Bottle, Ink, Teakettle, 8-Sided, Green Aqua, Double Font, c.1890, 3 ½ In.
$690.00

Bottle, Ink, Teakettle, Beehive, Aqua, Ground Lip, c.1880, 1 ⅛ In.
$295.00

Bottle, Ink, Umbrella, 8-Sided, Yellow, Rolled Lip, Open Pontil, c.1850
$910.00

Bottle, Ink, Water's, Troy, N.Y., Umbrella, 6-Sided, Blue Green, c.1850, 2 ¾ In.
$1600.00

Ink, Teakettle, Jade Clambroth, Metal Closure, 2 ½ In. 476.00
Ink, Teakettle, Milk Glass, 2 Tiers, Ground Lip, 2 ¼ In. 308.00
Ink, Teakettle, Sapphire Blue, Sheared Ground Lip, 2 In. 308.00
Ink, Teakettle, Yellow Green, Sheared Lip, 2 ⅛ In. 420.00
Ink, Umbrella, 8-Sided, Citron, Inward Rolled Lip, Open Pontil, 2 ½ In. 1456.00
Ink, Umbrella, 8-Sided, Cobalt Blue, Inward Rolled Lip, 2 ⅝ In. 1568.00
Ink, Umbrella, 8-Sided, Cornflower Blue, Tooled Lip, 2 In. 560.00
Ink, Umbrella, 8-Sided, Purple Amethyst, Inward Rolled Lip, 2 ¾ In. 952.00
Ink, Umbrella, 8-Sided, Red Amber, Tooled Lip, Open Pontil, 2 ½ In. 392.00
Ink, Umbrella, 8-Sided, Sapphire Blue, Inward Rolled Lip, Open Pontil, 2 ⅜ In. 1344.00
Ink, Umbrella, 8-Sided, Shaded Puce, Inward Rolled Lip, Open Pontil, 2 ¾ In. 1064.00
Ink, Umbrella, 8-Sided, Yellow, Rolled Lip, Open Pontil, c.1850 .... *illus* 910.00
Ink, Umbrella, Baltimore Star, 8-Sided, Blue, Rolled Lip, 2 In. 1430.00
Ink, Umbrella, Baltimore Star, 8-Sided, Citron, Rolled Lip, 2 In.. .... 550.00
Ink, Water's, Troy, N.Y., Umbrella, 6-Sided, Blue Green, c.1850, 2 ¾ In. .... *illus* 1600.00
Ink, Wood's Black, Portland, Cone, Amber, Tooled Lip, c.1850, 2 ⅜ In. .... *illus* 3910.00
Jar, Display, Centennial, Pale Aqua, Bell Shape, Crimped Finial, Pontil, 14 ½ In. 224.00
Jar, Olive Amber, 3-Piece Mold, Pontil, c.1830, 8 In. .... *illus* 625.00
Jar, Storage, Apple Green, Dip Mold, Wide Mouth, Flared Outward Rolled Lip, 8 x 5 In. 224.00
Jar, Storage, Black Glass, Emerald Green, Tooled Lip, c.1780, 12 ¾ In.. .... 235.00
Jar, Storage, Cobalt Blue, Applied Mouth, c.1900, 21 ¾ In. 4760.00
Jar, Storage, Olive Yellow Green, Dip Mold, Wide Mouth, Rolled Rim, c.1800, 8 x 4 ¼ In. 364.00
Jar, Storage, Red Amber, Wide Mouth, Flared Lip, 6 ⅜ In. 1904.00
Jar, Utility, Dark Teal Green, Molded Body, Flared Lip, OP, 1800, 13 ¼ In.. .... 1120.00
Jar, Utility, Yellow Green, Tooled Lip, Pontil, 1760-1800, 10 ¼ In. 308.00
Jar, Walla Walla Pepsin Gum, Knoxville, Tenn., Embossed Indian Head, 4-Sided, 11 In.. .... 675.00
Jug, Aqua, 32 Vertical Ribs, Arched Handle, Semi-Oval, 7 In. 5600.00
Medicine, A. Leitch & Co Apothecaries, St. Louis, Aqua, Open Pontil, c.1850, 6 In. .... *illus* 415.00
Medicine, A.M. Cole, Aqua, Applied Lip, c.1780, 8 ½ In.. .... 1064.00
Medicine, Alexander's, Sapphire Blue, Applied Mouth, Open Pontil, 6 ¼ In. 952.00
Medicine, Allan's Anti Fat Botanic Medicine Co., Buffalo, N.Y., Blue, c.1880, 7 ⅝ In. .... *illus* 475.00
Medicine, Apothecary, Ac. Sul, Recessed Lug, Embossed, Label, 8 ½ In. 440.00
Medicine, Apothecary, Amber, Painted, Shield, Pedestal, Domed Lid, Finial, 10 In. 715.00 to 743.00
Medicine, Apothecary, Amber, Tooled Lip, 5 ¾ In. 1232.00
Medicine, Apothecary, Carbonate De Potassium, Peacock Blue, Label, Stopper, Pontil, 8 In... 143.00
Medicine, Apothecary, Clear, Applied Blue Bands, Pontil, Applied Knob, Tooled Rim, c.1845, 9 ⅝ In. 1820.00
Medicine, Apothecary, Clear, Applied Blue Bands, Pontil, Applied Knob, Tooled Rim, c.1845, 12 ¼ In. 920.00
Medicine, Apothecary, Geo. P. Morrill, Applied Mouth, Green, 7 In. 2912.00
Medicine, Apothecary, Hancock's Lozenges, Clear, Glass Label, Stopper, 10 ½ In. 154.00
Medicine, Apothecary, P. Escamon, Embossed, Cobalt Blue, Recessed Lug, 9 ½ In. 303.00
Medicine, Apothecary, P. Subn Bism, Cobalt Blue, Recessed Lug, 9 ½ In. 176.00
Medicine, Apothecary, Peacock Blue, Label, Emetique, Shield, Metal Lid, Pontil, 8 In.. .... 220.00
Medicine, Apothecary, Smooth Base, Tooled Lip, Stopper, 12 In. 190.00
Medicine, Apothecary, Teinture D'Aloes, Peacock Blue, Label, Stopper, Pontil, 8 ¾ In. 221.00
Medicine, Apothecary, Tr. Sanguin, Recessed Lug, Label, 8 ½ In. 165.00
Medicine, Apothecary, W. Campbell & Co., London, Cobalt Blue, Globular, Flared Lip, Seal, 10 In. . 336.00
Medicine, Aqua, Embossed, Smooth Base, Applied & Tooled Lip, 1880, 7 ½ x 7 ½ In., Pair. 56.00
Medicine, B. Denton, Embossed Vine, Auburn, N.Y., Blue Aqua, 6 ⅜ In. 146.00
Medicine, B. F. Shaw, Citrate Of Magnesia, Clear, Tooled Top, 7 ½ In.. .... 672.00
Medicine, Bach's American Compound, Auburn, N.Y., Aqua, Double Collar, OP, 7 ⅝ In. 123.00
Medicine, Bitters, S.B. Goff's, Herb, Camden, N.J.. .... 14.00
Medicine, Blue, Embossed, Tooled Lip, Smooth Base, 1885, 7 ½ In. 246.00
Medicine, C. Brinkerhoff's Health Restorative, Olive Yellow, Sloping Collar, 7 ¼ In. 2240.00
Medicine, C. Heimstreet & Co., Troy, N.Y., Cobalt Blue, 8-Sided, 1865, 6 ¾ In. 146.00
Medicine, C. Heimstreet & Co., Troy, N.Y., Cobalt Blue, 8-Sided, Double Collar, OP, 7 In. 246.00
Medicine, Carter's Spanish Mixture, Cylindrical, Yellow, c.1850, 8 x 3 In. 1120.00
Medicine, Carter's Spanish Mixture, Olive Green, Sloping Double Collar, IP, 8 ½ In. 1232.00
Medicine, Carter's Spanish Mixture, Olive Yellow, Sloping Double Collar, IP, 8 ⅛ In. 672.00
Medicine, Caswell Hazard & Co., Chemists, New York & Newport, R.I., Amber, 7 ½ In. 30.00
Medicine, Centaur Liniment, J.B.R. & Co., New York, Aqua, 4 ¾ In. 30.00
Medicine, Chloride Calcium, St. Catharine's, Canada, Aqua, OP, c.1850, 5 ¾ In. .... *illus* 370.00
Medicine, Connell S. Brahminical, East Indian Remedies, Amber, Double Collar, 8 In. 672.00
Medicine, Cooper's New Discovery, Blue Aqua, Applied Mouth, Smooth Base, 9 ½ In.. .... 269.00
Medicine, Cuticura Treatment, For Affections Of The Skin, Aqua, Square, Labels, 7 ½ In. 35.00
Medicine, Davis' Vegetable Pain Killer, Aqua, Applied Double Collar, OP, 4 ⅝ In. 392.00

Medicine, Dickey Pioneer Chemist, Amber, Embossed Mortar & Pestle, 1850, 5 3/4 In. 112.00
Medicine, Doane's, Aqua, Bulbous, Applied Square Collar, Airtight Cap, 1860-70, Qt. 2750.00
Medicine, Dort & Chandler Druggist, Cylindrical, Yellow Amber, c.1846, 10 x 2 3/4 In. 7840.00
Medicine, Dr. Browder's Compound Syrup Of Indian Turnip, Aqua, Applied Mouth, 7 In. 1008.00
Medicine, Dr. Browder's Compound Syrup Of Indian Turnip, Aqua, Sloping Collar, 7 In. 672.00
Medicine, Dr. C.W. Roback's Scandanavian Blood Purifier, Ice Blue, Oval, IP, 7 3/4 In.. .... 616.00
Medicine, Dr. E.J. Coxe, New Orleans, Southern Cough Syrup, Green, c.1850, 7 3/8 In. ... *illus* 3920.00
Medicine, Dr. G.W. Phillip's Cough Syrup, Cincinnati, O., Aqua, Sloping Collar, IP, 7 1/2 In. ... 224.00
Medicine, Dr. H. James' Cannabis Indica, Aqua, Oval, Tooled Lip, 7 3/4 In. 728.00
Medicine, Dr. Henley's Celery, Beef & Iron, Orange Amber, Kick-Up, Ring Mouth, 11 5/8 In. ... 146.00
Medicine, Dr. Hoofland's Balsamic Cordial, Aqua, Square Collar Mouth, 7 In. 123.00
Medicine, Dr. J.F. Churchill's Specific Remedy For Consumption, Aqua, Sunken Panels, 7 In.. 40.00
Medicine, Dr. J.H. McLean's Liver & Kidney Balm, St. Louis, Label, Contents, Box, Flyer, 8 7/8 In. 440.00
Medicine, Dr. Kilmer's & Co., Cough Cure, Consumption Oil, Catarrh, Indented Lungs, Aqua, 9 In. 940.00
Medicine, Dr. Kilmer's Female Remedy, Aqua, Label, 8 1/2 In. 303.00
Medicine, Dr. Kilmer's Ocean Weed Heart Remedy, Embossed Heart, Aqua, Tooled Lip, 9 In.. . 440.00
Medicine, Dr. Mann's Celebrated Agua Balsam, Galion, Ohio, Aqua, Double Collar, 6 3/4 In.. . 784.00
Medicine, Dr. Miles' Restorative Blood Purifier, Aqua, Label, Contents, Box, 8 1/2 In.. .... 132.00
Medicine, Dr. N. Angell's Rheumatic Gun, Clear, Rectangular, 6 1/2 In.. .... 29.00
Medicine, Dr. Ordway's Celebrated Pain Destroyer, Aqua, Rolled Lip, Open Pontil, 5 In.. .... 80.00
Medicine, Dr. Rose's Magic Liniment, Aqua, Applied Disc Lip, Pontil, 1845-50, 5 1/2 In. 168.00
Medicine, Dr. Rose's Prophylactic Syrup, Aqua, Applied Sloping Collar, 6 7/8 In. 2240.00
Medicine, Dr. S. Hart New York, Vegetable Extract, Aqua, c.1850, 7 1/2 In. .... *illus* 725.00
Medicine, Dr. Sage's Catarrh Remedy, Buffalo, N.Y., Dark Blue Green, Tooled Lip, 2 1/8 In. 190.00
Medicine, Dr. Taylor's Blood Purifier, Aqua, 6 3/4 In.. .... 19.00
Medicine, Dr. Thompson's Eye Water, New London, Conn., Cylindrical, Contents, 4 In. 121.00
Medicine, Dr. W.N. Handy, Easton, N.Y., 12-Sided, Olive, Applied Mouth, 8 3/4 In. .... *illus* 1000.00
Medicine, Dr. Wistar's Balsam Of Wild Cherry, Cincinnati, Ohio, Aqua, 8-Sided, 6 1/2 In. 78.00
Medicine, Dr. Wistar's Balsam Of Wild Cherry, Philada, 8-Sided, Aqua, Embossed, Label, 5 In. 25.00
Medicine, Dr. Wistar's Balsam Of Wild Cherry, Philada., 8-Sided, Aqua, Label, 4 In.. .... 448.00
Medicine, Drs. D. Fahrney & Son, Cleansing The Blood, Boonsboro, Md., c.1860, 9 5/8 In. *illus* 1000.00
Medicine, E. A. Buckhout's Dutch Liniment, Blue Aqua, Inward Rolled Lip, 4 3/4 In. 392.00
Medicine, E.C. Allen, Concentrated Electric Past, Emerald Green, Inward Rolled Lip, 3 In. ... 1344.00
Medicine, Electric Brand, H.E. Bucklen & Co., Chicago, Ill., Amber, Square, 8 In. 29.00
Medicine, Extract Of Butternut, Clear, Gray, Disc Mouth, Pontil, 1850-60, 6 1/4 In. 123.00
Medicine, F.J. Steinmetz Druggist, Carson City, Nev., Clear, 1890s, 7 5/8 In. 125.00
Medicine, Floraplexion, Cures Dyspepsia Liver Complaint & Consumption, Aqua, 6 In. 22.00
Medicine, Follansbee's Elixir Of Health, Blue Aqua, Applied Mouth, 8 3/4 In. 1456.00
Medicine, G.W. Merchant, Chemist, Lockport, N.Y., Blue Aqua, IP, 7 1/4 In. 336.00
Medicine, Gargling Oil, Blue Green, Rectangular, 5 3/4 In.. .... 79.00
Medicine, Gargling Oil, Cobalt Blue, ABM, 5 7/8 In.. .... 146.00
Medicine, Gargling Oil, Emerald Green, 5 5/8 In. 20.00
Medicine, Germ, Bacteria, Or Fungus Destroyer, Amber, Dec. 13, 1887, 10 1/2 In. .... *illus* 520.00
Medicine, H. Lake's Indian Specific, Blue Aqua, Bulbous Neck, Applied Mouth, 8 1/4 In. 280.00
Medicine, Harrison's Tonic Stimulant, Square, Tapered Shoulders, Square Collar, 6 In. 3080.00
Medicine, Healy & Bigelow Indian Sagwa, Aqua, Tooled Lip, 8 In. 157.00
Medicine, Hunt's Liniment, C.O. Stanton, 8-Sided, Blue Green, Inward Rolled Lip, 4 5/8 In. ... 599.00
Medicine, Indian, Clemens Tonic, Standing Indian, Geo. W. House, Aqua, Rolled Lip, 5 In.. . 1008.00
Medicine, Indian Cough Syrup, Warme Springs Oregon, Clear, 7 In. 20.00
Medicine, J.G. Royce's Universal Relief, Blue Aqua, Sloping Collar, Open Pontil, 5 In. 308.00
Medicine, Jelly Of Pomegranate Preparate, By Dr. Gordak Only, Green Aqua, Flared Lip, 7 In. 364.00
Medicine, Keeley Treatment For Inebriety, Tooled Lip, 6 In. 295.00
Medicine, Kilmer's Swamp Root Kidney Liver & Bladder Remedy, Apple Green. 45.00
Medicine, L.P. Dodge, Rheumatic Liniment, Newburg, Yellow Amber, Sloping Collar, OP, 6 In. 2240.00
Medicine, Lindsey's Blood Searcher, Holidaysburg, Aqua, Rectangular, 9 In. 129.00
Medicine, Log Cabin Extract, Rochester, N.Y., Patd Sep 6th 1887, Amber, Box, 8 5/8 In. 448.00
Medicine, Log Cabin Hops & Buchu Remedy, Amber, Applied Lip, Box, 10 In.. .... 2464.00
Medicine, Loomis's Cream Liniment, Green, 6-Sided, Pinch Waist, Flared Mouth, Pontil, 5 In. 3740.00
Medicine, M.D. Dignan Prescription Druggists, Clear, 5 In. 19.00
Medicine, McCulloughs & Sons Pharmacists, Lawrenceburg, In., Lavender, Oval, 7 In.. ..... 168.00
Medicine, Merck, Inverted, Seal, Cork, Label, Contents, 6 1/2 In. 605.00
Medicine, Mexican Mustang Liniment, Blue Aqua, Sloping Collar, Iron Pontil, 7 1/2 In. 112.00
Medicine, Military, Salmon Puce, Sheared Lip, Pontil, 7 1/2 In. 336.00
Medicine, Mitchell's Liniment, Pittsburgh, Pa., Aqua, Double Open Pontil, 4 7/8 In. 202.00
Medicine, Moxie Nerve Food, Denver, Co, Aqua, Applied Mouth, 9 In. 330.00

Bottle, Ink, Wood's Black, Portland, Cone, Amber, Tooled Lip, c.1850, 2 3/8 In.
$3910.00

Bottle, Jar, Olive Amber, 3-Piece Mold, Pontil, c.1830, 8 In.
$625.00

Bottle, Medicine, A. Leitch & Co Apothecaries, St. Louis, Aqua, Open Pontil, c.1850, 6 In.
$415.00

Bottle, Medicine, Allan's Anti Fat Botanic Medicine Co., Buffalo, N.Y., Blue, c.1880, 7⅝ In.
$475.00

Bottle, Medicine, Chloride Calcium, St. Catharine's, Canada, Aqua, OP, c.1850, 5¾ In.
$370.00

Bottle, Medicine, Dr. E.J. Coxe, New Orleans, Southern Cough Syrup, Green, c.1850, 7⅜ In.
$3920.00

Medicine, Murray's Lotion, Clear, Rectangular, Victorian Nurse, Holding Bottle, 4½ In. 48.00
Medicine, Myers' Rock Rose, New Haven, Blue Aqua, Applied Mouth, 8⅞ In. 392.00
Medicine, Old Indian Liver & Kidney Tonic, Paper Label, 5½ x 2 x 1¼ In. 385.00
Medicine, Owl Drug Co., Owl On Mortar & Pestle, Clear, 7 In. 120.00
Medicine, Owl Drug Co., Owl On Mortar & Pestle, Green, 8 In. 3300.00
Medicine, Owl Drug Co., San Francisco, Owl On Mortar & Pestle, Teal, Blob Top, 9½ In. 190.00
Medicine, Pepsinola, Label Under Glass, Metal Cap, 1890-1910, 11 In. ..... *illus* 685.00
Medicine, Pioneer Drug Co., Light Amethyst, Tooled Lip, 6 In. 392.00
Medicine, Procter & Gamble Glycerine, Clear, Applied Lip, 7⅞ In. 532.00
Medicine, Prof. Low's Magnetic Liniment, Philada, Aqua, 6½ In. 19.00
Medicine, Reed, Carnick & Andrus, Pure Cod Liver Oil, Cobalt Blue, Tooled Lip, 9¼ In. 532.00
Medicine, Rees' Remedy For Piles, Aqua, Oval, Open Pontil, Applied Mouth, 7½ In. 1008.00
Medicine, Rheumatic Syrup, R. S. Co., Rochester, N.Y., Amber, Applied Mouth, 9⅝ In. 224.00
Medicine, Roback's Scandanavian Blood Purifier, Aqua, Smooth Base, 9 In. 90.00
Medicine, Roche's Embrocation For Whooping Cough, W. Edwards & Sons, Clear, 5 In. 30.00
Medicine, Rohrer's Expectoral Wild Cherry Tonic, Lancaster, Pa., Amber, Rope Corners, 10 In. 504.00
Medicine, Rohrer's Expectoral Wild Cherry Tonic, Yellow Amber, Roped Corners, 11 In. 840.00
Medicine, Rowand & L. Walton's Panacea, Philad, Aqua, Rectangular, 6½ x 2½ In. 392.00
Medicine, Rumford Chemical Works, Dyspepsia, Green, 8-Sided, Label, 7½ In. 235.00
Medicine, Silver Pine Healing Oil, Clear, Screw Cap, Label, Contents, Box, 7½ In. 143.00
Medicine, Slocum's Oxygenized Pure Cod Liver Oil, New York City, Aqua, 7 In. 35.00
Medicine, Smith's Green Mountain Renovator, Rectangular, Beveled Amber, c.1846, 7 In. 5600.00
Medicine, Smith's Green Mountain Renovator Remedy Co., St. Albans, Vt., Amber, 8¾ In. 59.00
Medicine, St. Andrews Wine Of Life Root, Amber, Rectangular, Embossed, 9 In. 48.00
Medicine, Stearns & Co., 4 Roses, Faceted Stopper, Label, 10 In. 154.00
Medicine, Swaim's Panacea, Philada, Olive Amber, Sloping Double Collar, 8 In. 1064.00
Medicine, Swaim's Panacea, Philada, Olive Green, Sloping Double Collar, 7¾ In. 420.00
Medicine, Swaim's Panacea, Philada., Blue Green, Vertical Panels, 7½ In. 169.00
Medicine, Swaim's Panacea, Philada., Teal Green, Crude Top, 7¾ In. 232.00
Medicine, Swaim's Vermifuge, Dyspepsia, Apple Green, Oval, c.1855, 5⅝ In. 159.00
Medicine, Tarrant & Co., Druggists, New York, Embossed, Label, 5 In. 25.00
Medicine, Tower, Square, Tapered, Dark Amber, c.1870, 9 In. 460.00
Medicine, U.S.A. Hosp. Dept., Cobalt Blue, Oval, Squared Flattened Lip, 3¼ In. 420.00
Medicine, U.S.A. Hosp. Dept., Gasoline Apricot, Applied Mouth, SDS On Base 825.00
Medicine, U.S.A. Hosp. Dept., Light Olive Green, Applied Double Collar, Qt. 2500.00
Medicine, U.S.A. Hosp. Dept., Medium Cobalt Blue, Applied Flared Lip, 4 In. 500.00
Medicine, U.S.A. Hosp. Dept., Medium Cobalt Blue, Applied Flared Lip, 8 In. 1210.00
Medicine, U.S.A. Hosp. Dept., Medium Cobalt Blue, Applied Square Collar, 6 In. 495.00
Medicine, U.S.A. Hosp. Dept., Medium Cobalt Blue, Tooled Flared Lip, 2 In. 405.00
Medicine, U.S.A. Hosp. Dept., Olive Green, Applied Double Collar, Qt., 9½ In. 1120.00
Medicine, U.S.A. Hosp. Dept., Olive Yellow, 6-Pointed Star, Double Collar, 9⅜ In. 2128.00
Medicine, U.S.A. Hosp. Dept., Olive Yellow, Cylindrical, Applied Collar, 1860-70, 9 In. 500.00
Medicine, U.S.A. Hosp. Dept., Olive Yellow, Star On Base, Applied Mouth 1100.00
Medicine, U.S.A. Hosp. Dept., Olive Yellow Amber, Double Collar, 9½ In. 1904.00
Medicine, U.S.A. Hosp. Dept., Orange Puce, Applied Mouth 1540.00
Medicine, U.S.A. Hosp. Dept., Yellow Amber, Olive Tint, Applied Double Collar, Qt., 9¼ In. 1008.00
Medicine, U.S.A. Hosp. Dept., Yellow Amber, Olive Tint, Applied Double Collar, Qt., 9 In. 672.00
Medicine, U.S.A. Hosp. Dept., Yellow Amber, Olive Tint, Double Collar, 9¼ In. 1344.00
Medicine, Udolpho Wolfe's Aromatic Schnapps, Olive Amber, Square, c.1845, 9¾ In. 179.00
Medicine, Vaughn's Vegetable Lithontriptic Mixture, Blue Aqua, Sloping Collar, 7⅝ In. 560.00
Medicine, W.A. Batchelor's Moldavia Cream, Cobalt Blue, Ground Lip, 2⅛ In. 280.00
Medicine, Warner's Safe Nervine, Orange Amber, Smooth Base, Applied Double Collar, 7½ In. 364.00
Medicine, Warner's Safe Tonic, Amber, Applied Double Collar, 9⅝ In. 179.00
Medicine, Whitall Tatum & Co., Applied Ointment, Milk Glass, Embossed, Lid, 5 x 3¾ In. 94.00
Medicine, William's Tonic Expectorant, Aqua, 7½ In. 25.00
Medicine, Wishart's Pine Tree Tar, Blue Aqua, Tapered Collar, 9¾ In. 224.00
Medicine, Wishart's Pine Tree Tar, Emerald Green, Sloping Collar, 9⅝ In. 202.00
Medicine, Wishart's Pine Tree Tar, Yellow Green, Applied Mouth, 1859, 9⅝ In. ..... *illus* 165.00
Medicine, Wishart's Pine Tree Tar, Yellow Green, Sloping Collar, 9⅝ In. 168.00
Medicine, Wm. F. Zoeller Wild Cherry Tonic, Orange Amber, Sloping Double Collar, 10¾ In. 420.00
Milk, Albers Milling Co., Red ACL, Tall, Round, ½ Gal. 65.00
Milk, Alfalfa Farm Dairy, Leipsic, O., Protected For Your Health, Red & Green, ACL, Qt. 560.00
Milk, Alta Crest Farms, Spencer, Mass., Green, Cow's Head, Embossed, Qt. 1100.00
Milk, Alta Crest Farms, Spencer, Mass., Green, Cylindrical, Tapered, Qt. 560.00
Milk, Annapolis Dairy Products Co., Embossed, Cream Top, Pt. 16.00

Milk, Annville Dairy, Embossed, Pt. 350.00
Milk, Antietam Farm, Waynesboro, Pa., Red ACL, Qt. 18.00
Milk, Aristocrat Dairy, Baltimore, Phone LA 3000, Babyface, Painted. 75.00
Milk, Ash Grove Dairy, Kankakee, Ill., Embossed, Round, Qt. 30.00
Milk, Associated Dairy, Buffalo, N.Y., Round, Red ACL, Pt. 20.00
Milk, Athen's Dairy, Athens, Pa., Embossed, Round, Qt. 25.00
Milk, B.C. Lamb & Son, Susquehanna, Pa., Embossed, Round, Qt. 30.00
Milk, Bailey Dairy, East Haven, Conn., Embossed, ½ Pt. 14.00
Milk, Barati Dairy, Broughton, Pa., Embossed, Qt. 12.00
Milk, Beechmont Dairy, Bridgeport, Conn., Square, ACL, Pt. 20.00
Milk, Benson's Dairy, Huntingdon, Pa., Neck Ridges, Round, Qt. 30.00
Milk, Borden's, Elsie, Red, ACL, Qt. 50.00
Milk, Borden's, Embossed, Round, ¼ Pt. 40.00
Milk, Borden's, Malted Milk, Cap, 1930s, 6¾ In. 55.00
Milk, Borden's, Ribs, Embossed, Round, Qt. 30.00
Milk, Borden's, Royal Ruby, Anchor Hocking, Qt. 1800.00
Milk, Boulder Brook Farm, Cow & Farm, Round, Red, ACL, Qt. 45.00
Milk, Bowman Dairy Co., Chicago, Il., Orange ACL, ½ Gal. 25.00
Milk, Bowman Dairy Co., Orange ACL, Tall, Round, ½ Gal. 40.00
Milk, Brookside Dairies, Waterbury, Conn., First National Stores, Embossed, ½ Pt. 14.00
Milk, Brookside Dairy Farm, Henderson, N.C., Babyface, Barn, Red, ACL, Round, Qt. 45.00
Milk, Brown's Dairy, Fairfield, Pa., Embossed, Qt. 95.00
Milk, Candlelight Goat Dairy, New Milford, Conn., Green ACL, Round, Qt. 100.00
Milk, Carrigan's Niagara Dairy Co., Reed, Green ABM, Qt. 672.00
Milk, Central Dairy, 939 Elm St., Reading, Pa., Embossed, Round, Qt. 25.00
Milk, Charles C. Waple Dairy, Tyrone, Pa., Electropure Milk, Embossed, Round, Qt. 30.00
Milk, Charmany Farms Milk, Madison, Wis., Embossed, Round, Qt. 55.00
Milk, Chatfield Dairy, Seymour, Conn., ACL, Qt. 20.00
Milk, Cherry Lane Dairy, Chambersburg, Pa., Red ACL, Qt. 35.00
Milk, Chestnut Farms, Chevy Chase Dairy, Washington, D.C., Long Neck, Square, Qt. 20.00
Milk, Clover Brook Dairy, Embossed, Pt. 340.00
Milk, Cloverleaf Dairy, Sandusky, Oh., Square, ACL, ½ Pt. 15.00
Milk, Cloverleaf Grade A Irradiated Vitamin D Milk, Embossed, Red, Cream Top 65.00
Milk, Creamer, Daricraft, Square, Red ACL 20.00
Milk, Creamer, Fern's Red Letters, Coffee Cup, ¾ Oz., 2 In. 32.00
Milk, Creamer, Old Dominion, Orange ACL, Tall, Round, Pt. 20.00
Milk, Creamer, S.O. Silver Cream, G.F. Soule, Manchester, N.H., Label, Contents, Amber, 3 In. 28.00
Milk, Creamery Pasteurized, Knoxville, Tenn., Embossed, Round, Qt. 175.00
Milk, Crest Haven Farms, Onamia, Minn., Milk, Truck, House, Farm, Red ACL, Qt. 35.00
Milk, D.E. Miller, Embossed, Round, Qt. 280.00
Milk, D.M.D.A. Milk, Duluth, Minn., Embossed, Round, Qt. 20.00
Milk, Dairylea, Embossed, Square, Qt. 10.00
Milk, Delview Dairy, Tuscaloosa, Ala., Fresh Milk, Red ACL, Tall, Round, Qt. 55.00
Milk, Dewhirst Dairy, Bridgeport, Conn., ACL, Cap, ½ Pt. 20.00
Milk, Diamond Dairy Farms, Salem, N.H., ACL, Round, Pt. 15.00 to 22.00
Milk, Eden Plains Dairy Farms, M.W. Showalter & Sons, Hagerstown, Md., Qt. 40.00
Milk, Edgewood Dairy, Braddock, Pa., Embossed, Round, Qt. 30.00
Milk, Eisenhart's Bros., York, Pa., Embossed, Round, Qt. 25.00
Milk, Elm Point Dairy, St. Charles, Missouri., Green ACL, ½ Gal. 15.00
Milk, Embassy Dairy, Washington, D.C., Babyface, Qt. 88.00
Milk, Embossed, Man Milking Cow, Milk Glass & Metal Closure, Pt. 550.00
Milk, Farmers Fairfield Dairy Co., Reading, Pa., Pt. 45.00
Milk, Fawnhoff Goat Farm, Stockton, Reg., Cal., Brown ACL, ½ Gal. 250.00
Milk, Fern's Dairy Jersey Blend, Square, ACL, ½ Gal. 33.00
Milk, Fish Family Farm, Bolton, Conn., Brown ACL, ½ Gal. 14.00
Milk, Fox's Guernsey Dairy, Cow, Round, ACL, ½ Pt. 35.00
Milk, Frey's Farm Dairy, Falling Spring Road, Chambersburg, Pa., Red ACL, ½ Gal. 16.00
Milk, Garden Farm Dairy, Denver, Colo, Polar Bear Ice Cream, Orange Blue ACL, Qt. 50.00 to 60.00
Milk, Gettysburg Ice & Cold Storage Co., Vertical Stripes, 28 On Base, Embossed, Round, Qt. 25.00
Milk, Glendale Dairy Decatur, Registered Jerseys, Cow, Orange ACL, Tall, Round, Qt. 65.00
Milk, Glynwood Farm, Tall, Round, ACL, Qt. 35.00
Milk, Grant's Dairy, Drink Grant's Milk, Eat Aroostook Potatoes, Maine, Red ACL, ½ Pt. 15.00
Milk, Greencastle Sanitary Dairy, Greencastle, Pa., Embossed, Qt. 25.00
Milk, H.J. Culler, Inc., Milk Transportation, McConnellsburg, Pa., 1994, Qt. 16.00
Milk, Harbison Dairy, Registered, Philadelphia, Pa., H's On Neck, Embossed, Round, Qt. 25.00

Bottle, Medicine, Dr. S. Hart New York, Vegetable Extract, Aqua, c.1850, 7½ In.
$725.00

Bottle, Medicine, Dr. W.N. Handy, Easton, N.Y., 12-Sided, Olive, Applied Mouth, 8¾ In.
$1000.00

Bottle, Medicine, Drs. D. Fahrney & Son, Cleansing The Blood, Boonsboro, Md., c.1860, 9⅝ In.
$1000.00

Bottle, Medicine, Germ, Bacteria, Or Fungus Destroyer, Amber, Dec. 13, 1887, 10 ½ In.
$520.00

Bottle, Medicine, Pepsinola, Label Under Glass, Metal Cap, 1890-1910, 11 In.
$685.00

Bottle, Medicine, Wishart's Pine Tree Tar, Yellow Green, Applied Mouth, 1859, 9⅝ In.
$165.00

Milk, Hawthorn Mellody Dairy Farms, Chicago, Embossed, Qt. 25.00
Milk, Hill Top Dairy, Suffield, Conn., Embossed, ½ Pt. 12.00
Milk, Hilltop Dairy, Keep Healthy Use Our Mountain Fresh Milk, Victor, Colo., Red ACL, Qt. 455.00
Milk, Hoard's Dairyman, Fort Atkinson, Wis., Embossed, Round, ¼ Pt. 100.00
Milk, Hoffman Minick, Embossed, Cream Top, Qt. 18.00
Milk, Holbrook Farms Dairy, Hyattsville, Md., Embossed, Round, Qt. 25.00
Milk, Homestead Farm, Round, ACL, Qt. 25.00
Milk, Hull's Dairy, Waynesboro, Pa., Red ACL, Qt. 18.00
Milk, Ideal Dairy, N. Ray, Bradley, Ill., Embossed, Qt. 20.00
Milk, Indiana Co-Op Co., Vertical Stripes, Embossed, Round, Qt. 25.00
Milk, J. Sterling Davis, Wrightstown, N.J., Embossed, Round, ½ Pt. 10.00
Milk, Jacksonville Producers Dairy, Orange ACL, Round, Wire Handle, Gal. 100.00
Milk, James W. Karper, Mercersburg, Pa., K In Circle, Embossed, Qt. 150.00
Milk, Ken's Dairy, K.F. Yager, Eden, N.Y., Embossed, Round, Qt. 30.00
Milk, Klamath Falls Creamery, Round, Qt. 50.00
Milk, Kornely Guernsey Farms Dairy, Manitowoc, Wis., Round, ACL, ½ Pt. 35.00
Milk, Landis Valley Dairy, Pa., Embossed, Round, Qt. 330.00
Milk, Laurens Pasteurizing Plant, Cap, Red ACL, Tall, Round, Qt. 75.00
Milk, Lierman Dairy, Champaign-Urbana, Ill., Yankee Doodle Poem, Round, ACL, Qt. 140.00
Milk, Maple Grove Dairy, Holland, Mich., Red ACL, Round, ½ Pt. 20.00
Milk, Maple Leaf Dairy, Lake Geneva, Wis., 2-Color ACL, Round, ½ Pt. 42.00
Milk, Maplehurst Farm Creamer, Square, Red Letters, ¾ Oz., 1 ¼ x 2 ¼ In. 34.00
Milk, Markel's Glen Rock, Pa., M In Circle, Embossed, Pt. 12.00
Milk, Marland K Dairy, Cambridge, Tall, Round, ACL, Qt. 20.00
Milk, Melrose Dairy, None Better, Ormond, Fla., Blue ACL, Tall, Round, Qt. 65.00
Milk, Merritt's Dairy Farm, Bridgeport, Conn., Embossed, Round, Qt. 12.00
Milk, Meyer's Dairy, Hooversville, Pa., Fluted Neck, Embossed, Round, Qt. 30.00
Milk, Midwest Dairy, Plymouth, Wisconsin, Brown ACL, Tall, Round, Qt. 55.00
Milk, Missouri Pacific Lines, Round, Red ACL, ½ Pt. 15.00
Milk, Moores-Ross Milk Co., Marion, Oh., Embossed, Round, Qt. 25.00
Milk, Naval Academy Dairy, Anchor, Wash & Return, Annapolis, Md., Qt. 566.00
Milk, Nelson-Stearns Dairy, Elkhorn, Wis., War Slogan, Orange ACL, Qt. 50.00
Milk, New Mexico College A & M, Round, Red ACL, ½ Pt. 15.00
Milk, Northern Pacific Yellowstone Line, ½ Pt. 760.00
Milk, Oakdene Goat Dairy, Walnut Creek, Round, Green, Qt. 250.00
Milk, Old Tavern Farm, Portland, Maine, Irradiated, Vitamin D Milk, Red ACL, Tall, Round, 10 Oz. 25.00
Milk, Our Own Dairy Co., Poplar Grove, Il., Embossed, Round, ½ Pt. 32.00
Milk, P.H. Sanger & Sons, Embossed, Round, Qt. 550.00
Milk, Penn-Creek Farm Dairy, Greencastle, Pa., Red ACL, Metal Handle, Gal. 25.00
Milk, Peplau's Dairy, New Britain, Conn., Mother & Babyface, Round, Cap, Pt. 16.00
Milk, Phelps Dairy, Orange ACL, Tall, Round, Qt. 50.00
Milk, Pine Grove Dairy, Chambersburg, Pa., Pine Trees, Orange & Green ACL, Qt. 40.00
Milk, Pine Tree Farms Dairy, McHenry, Il., Embossed, Round, ⅓ Qt. 25.00
Milk, Pleck Dairy, Sturgeon Bay, Door County, Wis., 5 Cent, Embossed, Round, Qt. 40.00
Milk, Quality Dairy, Dutch Girl Carrying Buckets, Orange ACL, Round 45.00
Milk, Reeder Bros. Dairy, Shippensburg, Pa., Embossed, Pt. 35.00
Milk, Ribbon Dairy, Syracuse, N.Y., Blue ACL, Tall, Round, Qt. 60.00
Milk, Rivulet Hurst Dairy, John M. Scholten, Holland, Michigan, Round, ACL, ½ Pt. 20.00
Milk, Saint Paul Milk Company, St. Paul, Minn., Pilgrim Man & Woman, 2-Color ACL, Qt. 100.00
Milk, Sanford's, Oxford, Conn., Round, ACL, Qt. 20.00
Milk, Sangamon Dairy Products Co., Springfield, Ill., Red ACL, Tall, Round, Qt. 65.00
Milk, Sanitary Creamery, Boscobel, Wis., Policeman, Fireman, Milkman, Round, ACL, Qt. 120.00
Milk, Schuchartdt's Dairy, Sheboygan, Wis., Rhyme, Little Jack Horner, Red ACL, Tall, Qt. 85.00
Milk, Scott's Dairy, Winnemucca, Nev., 1910. 250.00
Milk, Shirk Dairy, Map Of U.S.A, Statue Of Liberty, Round, Green, ½ Pt. 15.00
Milk, Shively's Dairy, Chambersburg, Pa., Red ACL, Qt. 16.00
Milk, Sorge's Manitowog Dairy Co., Clear, ABM, Qt. 134.00
Milk, South Dakota State Sanatorium For Tuberculosis, Embossed, ½ Pt. 20.00
Milk, Spring Brook Farm, Newington Jct., Conn., Embossed, ½ Pt. 14.00
Milk, St. Mary's Dairy, Pa., Embossed, Brown ACL, Qt. 35.00
Milk, State Of Connecticut, Orange ACL, Tall, Round, ½ Pt. 30.00
Milk, Stevenson Dairy, Dane, Wis., Round, ACL, Gal. 35.00
Milk, Swan Ponds Dairy, Guernsey Milk, Morganton, N.C., Swan, Green ACL, Round, Qt. 175.00
Milk, Thatcher's Dairy, Man Milking Cow, Embossed, Glass Lid, Metal Closure, Qt. 952.00
Milk, Thompson's Double Malted Milk, Yellow Ground, T Logo 295.00

Milk, Torrington Creamery, Torrington, Conn., Embossed, Cap, ½ Pt. 20.00
Milk, Tumbling Run Park Dairy, ACL, Tall, Round, Qt. 15.00
Milk, Union Grove Creamery, Embossed, Red ACL, Qt. 30.00
Milk, Univ. Of Conn., Embossed, ½ Pt. 25.00
Milk, Univ. Of Rhode Island, U.R.I. Seal, ACL, Qt. 25.00
Milk, University Of Florida, ACL, Qt. 1000.00
Milk, University Of Wisconsin, Archer, Square, Red ACL, ½ Pt. 20.00
Milk, Urbandale Guernsey Dairy, Elkhorn, Wis., 2-Color, ACL, Round, ½ Pt. 42.00
Milk, Valley Dairy Farms, Phone 367, Reno, Yerington, Nevada, Amber ACL, c.1950, Qt. 165.00
Milk, Walnut Dairy Farms, Waterloo, Iowa, Red ACL, Round, Qt. 38.00
Milk, Walnut Tree Hill Farm, Huntington, Conn., ACL, Square, Cap, Qt. 15.00
Milk, White Clover, Embossed, ½ Pt. 290.00
Milk, Willow Farm Dairy, LaGrange, Cow, Square, ACL, Qt. 48.00
Milk, Workman's Dairy, Saxton, Pa., Orange, Yellow, Brown & Green ACL, Qt. 16.00
Mineral Water, A.R. Cox, Norristown, Blue Green, Applied Mouth, IP, 7 ¼ In. 560.00
Mineral Water, Akesion Spring, Sweet Springs Co., Orange Amber, Applied Mouth, Pt., 7 ⅝ In. 420.00
Mineral Water, Avon Spring Water, Blue Aqua, Sloping Double Collar, Qt. 448.00
Mineral Water, B & G, San Francisco, Blue, Applied Mouth, Iron Pontil, 7 ½ In. 476.00
Mineral Water, Blount Springs, Natural Sulphur Water, Blue, Applied Mouth, C.1875, 9 In. 616.00
Mineral Water, Buffum & Co., Sarsaparilla & Lemon, Blue, Ten Pin, Applied Mouth, C.1860, 8 In. 560.00
Mineral Water, C.A. Reiners & Co., Aqua, Moon & Stars, Blob Top, 7 In. 532.00
Mineral Water, Caladonia Spring, Wheelock, Vt., Amber, Swirls, Squat, Qt. 700.00
Mineral Water, Champion Spouting Spring, Saratoga, N.Y., Aqua, Pt. .... *illus* 114.00
Mineral Water, Chase & Co., San Francisco, Green, Applied Mouth, 1850s. 784.00
Mineral Water, Chase & Co., San Francisco, Green, Applied Mouth, Graphite Pontil. 448.00
Mineral Water, Chittenango White Sulphur, Green, Cylindrical, c.1870, Qt. 8000.00
Mineral Water, Clarke & Co., New York, Blue Green, Applied Sloping Double Collar, IP, Pt. 476.00
Mineral Water, Congress & Empire Spring Co., Blue Green, Sloping Double Collar, Pt. 2464.00
Mineral Water, Congress & Empire Spring Co., Hotchkiss' Sons, C, Olive Green, Pt. .. 123.00 to 616.00
Mineral Water, Congress & Empire Spring Co., Olive Yellow, c.1870, Qt. .... *illus* 275.00
Mineral Water, D. Harkins, Richmond, Pa., Slug Plate, Blue Green, Applied Mouth, 7 ¼ In. 896.00
Mineral Water, D.J. Whelan, Troy, N.Y., Aqua, Blob Mouth, 1870-80, Qt. 179.00
Mineral Water, Darien Mineral Springs, Tifft & Perry, Blue Green, c.1870, Pt. .... *illus* 490.00
Mineral Water, Darling & Cobb's, Blue Green, Sloping Collar, Iron Pontil, 1840-60, 6 ⅞ In. 308.00
Mineral Water, Deep Rock Spring, Oswego, N.Y., Aqua, Applied Sloping Double Collar, Qt. 560.00
Mineral Water, Deep Rock Springs, Oswego, N.Y., Teal Blue, Sloping Double Collar, Pt. 784.00
Mineral Water, E-30, Silver Springs Water Company, Triangular, 11 x 4 ¼ In. 110.00
Mineral Water, Eagle, Shield, Crossed Flags, Cobalt Blue, Applied Collar, IP, 7 ½ In. 728.00
Mineral Water, Excelsior Rock Spring, Saratoga, N.Y., Yellow, Olive Tone, Pt., 8 ⅞ In. 952.00
Mineral Water, Excelsior Spring, Saratoga, N.Y., Olive, c.1870, Pt. .... *illus* 310.00
Mineral Water, F. Gleason, Rochester, N.Y., Blue, Green, Applied Collar, Pontil, 1840-60, 7 In. 420.00
Mineral Water, F. Gleason, Sarsaparilla, Blue, 10-Sided, Pontil, c.1850, 7 ½ In. 448.00
Mineral Water, Franklin Spring, Ballston Spa, Olive Yellow, Applied Mouth, Pt., 7 ⅝ In. 616.00
Mineral Water, G.W. Weston & Co., Saratoga, N.Y., Emerald, c.1855, Pt. .... *illus* 270.00
Mineral Water, Gettysburg Katalysine, Yellow Green, Applied Mouth, Qt. 728.00
Mineral Water, Gettysburg Katalysine Water, Golden Yellow Amber, Double Collar, Qt. 1680.00
Mineral Water, Gleason & Cole, Pittsbg., Cobalt Blue, 10-Sided, Applied Mouth, IP, 7 ¾ In. 1344.00
Mineral Water, Haskin's Spring Co., H, Shutesbury, Mass., Blue Green, Sloping Collar, Pt. 3050.00
Mineral Water, Haskin's Spring Co., H, Shutesbury, Mass., Blue Green, Sloping Collar, Qt. 1120.00
Mineral Water, Haskin's Spring Co., H, Shutesbury, Mass., Green, c.1860, 3 Qt. 3450.00
Mineral Water, Henke & Maack, Emerald Green, Torpedo, Applied Mouth, 1855-65, 9 In. 7280.00
Mineral Water, Hennessy & Nolan, Albany, N.Y., Embossed Capitol Bldg, Amber, 6 ¾ In. 15.00
Mineral Water, Highrock Congress Spring, C & W, Rock, Green, Double Collar, Pt. 364.00
Mineral Water, Highrock Congress Spring, C & W, Saratoga, N.Y., Teal, Pt. .... *illus* 525.00
Mineral Water, Highrock Congress Spring, C & W, Saratoga, N.Y., Yellow Amber, Pt. 295.00
Mineral Water, Hopkins Chalybeate, Baltimore, Olive Green, Sloping Collar, IP, Pt. 392.00
Mineral Water, I. Sutton & Co., Covington, Ky., Cobalt Blue, 12-Sided, Applied Mouth, IP, 8 ½ In. 728.00
Mineral Water, Iodine Spring Water, L, South Hero, Vt., Golden Amber, 1860-70, Qt. 1200.00
Mineral Water, J. & H. Casper, Lancaster, Pa., Blue, Arched Slug Plate, Blob Top, 7 In. 280.00
Mineral Water, J. Boardman, New York, Puce, Applied Mouth, Graphite Pontil 7840.00
Mineral Water, J. Tweddle's Celebrated, Courtland Street, 38, New York, Blue, 7 ½ In. 1120.00
Mineral Water, J.B. Edwards, Columbia, Pa., Ice Blue, Applied Mouth, IP, 7 ⅝ In. 784.00
Mineral Water, J.N. Gerdes S.F., Light Green, Applied Mouth, 8 In. 495.00
Mineral Water, John Clarke, New York, Amber, Applied Mouth, Pontil, c.1855, Qt. .... *illus* 180.00
Mineral Water, John Clarke, Olive Yellow, Cylindrical, Sloping Collar, c.1835, Qt. 1904.00

Bottle, Mineral Water, Champion Spouting Spring, Saratoga, N.Y., Aqua, Pt.
$114.00

Bottle, Mineral Water, Congress & Empire Spring Co., Olive Yellow, c.1870, Qt.
$275.00

Bottle, Mineral Water, Darien Mineral Springs, Tifft & Perry, Blue Green, c.1870, Pt.
$490.00

Bottle, Mineral Water, Excelsior Spring, Saratoga, N.Y., Olive, c.1870, Pt.
$310.00

Bottle, Mineral Water, G.W. Weston & Co., Saratoga, N.Y., Emerald, c.1855, Pt.
$270.00

Bottle, Mineral Water, Highrock Congress Spring, C & W, Saratoga, N.Y., Teal, Pt.
$525.00

Mineral Water, John H. Gardner & Son, Sharon Sulphur Springs, N.Y., Blue Green, Pt. 420.00
Mineral Water, Lithia Mineral Spring Co., Gloversville, Aqua, Sloping Double Collar, Pt. 3080.00
Mineral Water, Luke Beard, Blue Green, Ten Pin, Applied Mouth, Pontil, 7 In. 550.00
Mineral Water, Luke Beard, Medium To Dark Green, Ten Pin, Applied Mouth, Pontil, 7 In... 550.00
Mineral Water, Lynch & Clarke, Forest Green, Yellow Tint, Cylindrical, Pontil, c.1840, Pt. ... 2200.00
Mineral Water, Lynch & Clarke, New York, Yellow Amber, Sloping Double Collar, Pontil, Pt. . 672.00
Mineral Water, M.T. Crawford, Springfield, Teal, Paneled Base, Blob Top, IP, 7 ⅝ In.. .... 1232.00
Mineral Water, Magnetic Spring, Cylindrical, Gold Amber, Collared Mouth, c.1860, Qt. 1568.00
Mineral Water, Magnetic Spring, Henniker, N.H., Yellow Amber, Qt. 1008.00
Mineral Water, Massena Spring Water, Monogram, Amber, Tooled Lip, Qt. 280.00
Mineral Water, Massena Spring Water, Monogram, Amethystine Tint, Tooled Lip, Qt.. ...... 308.00
Mineral Water, Middletown Healing Springs, Grays & Clark, Middletown, Vt., Amber, Qt. 224.00
Mineral Water, Minnequa Water, Bradford Co., Pa., Amber, Sloping Double Collar, Pt. 269.00
Mineral Water, Missisquoi, A, Springs, Emerald Green, Sloping Double Collar, Qt. 157.00
Mineral Water, Pavilion & United States Spring Co., Saratoga, N.Y., Blue Green, Pt. 202.00
Mineral Water, Poland Water, H. Ricker & Sons, Moses, Clear, Glass Stopper, 7 In. 79.00
Mineral Water, Poland Water, H. Ricker & Sons, Yellow Amber, c.1865, 10 ¾ In. 850.00
Mineral Water, Polk & Co., Barnum's Building, Balt., Torpedo, Blue, Ten Pin, c.1855, 8 ¾ In. 3920.00
Mineral Water, Ponce DeLeon Water Co., Aqua, Clear Blob Top, ½ Gal., 12 ½ In.. .... 18.00
Mineral Water, Powell's, Burlington, N.J., Sapphire Blue, 8-Sided, IP, c.1850, 7 ⅝ In. .. *illus* 3950.00
Mineral Water, Quaker Springs, I.W. Meader & Co., Saratoga, N.Y., Green, Pt. 3360.00
Mineral Water, Quaker Springs, I.W. Meader & Co., Saratoga, N.Y., Teal Blue, Qt. 952.00
Mineral Water, Rockbridge VA Alum Water, Olive Green, Iron Pontil, c.1850, Pt., 6 ⅞ In. *illus* 16000.00
Mineral Water, S. Keys, Burlington, N.J., Cobalt Blue, Paneled Base, Blob Top, IP, 7 ½ In.. ... 1680.00
Mineral Water, Saratoga A Spring Co., N.Y., Forest Green, Qt. 175.00
Mineral Water, Saratoga Spring Co., Emerald Green, Sloping Collar, c.1860, Qt. 5750.00
Mineral Water, Saratoga Star Springs, N.Y., Olive Green, Sloping Double Collar, Pt. 364.00
Mineral Water, St. Regis Water, Massena Spring, Black Amber, Sloping Double Collar, Pt. ... 504.00
Mineral Water, Syracuse Springs, Excelsior, Dark Amber, Sloping Double Collar, Qt. 336.00
Mineral Water, Syracuse Springs, Excelsior, Yellow, Olive Tint, Double Collar, Qt. 2800.00
Mineral Water, Syracuse Springs, Olive Yellow, Smooth Base, Applied Mouth, 1870-80, Pt. .. 2688.00
Mineral Water, Syracuse Springs, Red Amber, Smooth Base, Applied Mouth, 1870-80, Pt. ... 280.00
Mineral Water, Tahoe Soda Springs, Carson City, Aqua, 1940 .... 25.00
Mineral Water, Teller's, Detroit, Cobalt Blue, Ten Pin, Smooth Base, c.1860, 8 ⅜ In.. .... 364.00
Mineral Water, Vermont Spring, Saxe & Co., Sheldon, Vt., Apricot, Cylindrical, c.1870, Qt.. .. 1400.00
Mineral Water, W. Heiss Jr's, Blue Green, Applied Mouth, 7 In. 476.00
Mineral Water, W. Ryer, Union Glass Works-R, Philada, Cobalt Blue, IP, c.1850, 7 In. .. *illus* 490.00
Mineral Water, Washington Lithia Well, Aqua, Applied Mouth, Pt. 476.00
Mineral Water, Washington Spring Co., Bust Of Washington, Blue Green, Pt. 1232.00
Mineral Water, White Sulfur Springs, Stoneware, Stenciled, Oval 159.00
Mineral Water, White Sulphur Water, Greenbriar, W.Va., Blue Green, Qt., 9 In. 896.00
Mineral Water, Wm. Betz & Co., Pittsbg, Teal Blue, 10-Sided, Iron Pontil. 400.00
Mineral Water, Wm. W. Lappeus, Premium, Albany, Cobalt Blue, 10-Sided, IP, 7 ¼ In. 672.00
Nursing, Tyrian Nipples, 8-Sided, White Letters, 9 ½ x 6 In. 1925.00
Oil, Green, Rounded Base, Reverse Handle, Pour Lip, Pontil, 1880, 3 ¾ In. 34.00
Pepper Sauce, Cathedral, 6-Sided, Blue Green, Applied Double Collar, 10 ½ In.. .... 308.00
Pepper Sauce, Cathedral, Blue Aqua, 3 Panels, 5 Stars, Double Collar, 8 ⅞ In. 258.00
Pepper Sauce, Cathedral, Blue Aqua, Applied Double Collar, Iron Pontil, 8 ⅞ In. 308.00
Pepper Sauce, Hodges & Gross's Yankee Sauce, 8-Sided, Aqua, Applied Mouth, OP, 6 ⅞ In.. .. 134.00
Pepper Sauce, Medium Green, Ribs, 8 ¼ In. 249.00
Pickle, Anchor, Clear, Embossed, Applied Mouth, 7 ½ In.. .... 179.00
Pickle, Barrel, Blue Aqua, Applied Mouth, 10 ½ In. 392.00
Pickle, Blue Aqua, Ribbed, Scalloped, 6 ¼ In.. .... 149.00
Pickle, Cathedral, 4-Sided, Green, Willington Glass Works, 1860-1870, 11 ¾ In.. .... 1345.00
Pickle, Cathedral, 4-Sided, Medium Blue Green, 12 In.. .... 395.00
Pickle, Cathedral, 6-Sided, Blue Aqua, Rolled Lip, 14 ⅛ In.. .... 224.00
Pickle, Cathedral, 6-Sided, Blue, Aqua, 13 In. 295.00
Pickle, Cathedral, 6-Sided, Outward Rolled Lip, 13 In. 230.00
Pickle, Cathedral, Aqua, 13 In. 1650.00
Pickle, Cathedral, Aqua, Applied Mouth, Iron Pontil, 1865, 13 In. 190.00
Pickle, Cathedral, Aqua, Cross Hatching, Applied Lip, Graphite Pontil, 7 ½ In. 616.00
Pickle, Cathedral, Aqua, Open Pontil, 7 ½ In.. .... 295.00
Pickle, Cathedral, Aqua, Square, Arched Panels, Applied Mouth, 9 ⅛ In. 224.00
Pickle, Cathedral, Blue Aqua, Applied Mouth, Iron Pontil, 1850-60, 9 In. 364.00
Pickle, Cathedral, Blue Aqua, Applied Mouth, Iron Pontil, 7 ⅜ In. 308.00

Pickle, Cathedral, Blue Aqua, Arched Panels, Rolled Lip, Iron Pontil, 12 In. 448.00
Pickle, Cathedral, Blue Aqua, Outward Rolled Lip, 12 ¼ In. 146.00
Pickle, Cathedral, Blue Aqua, Outward Rolled Lip, 1860-75, 13 ½ In. 200.00
Pickle, Cathedral, Blue Aqua, Rolled Lip, Open Pontil, 1850-65, 8 ⅝ In. 308.00
Pickle, Cathedral, Blue Green, Applied Mouth, Rolled Lip, 1860-70, 10 ¾ In. 1008.00
Pickle, Cathedral, Blue Green, Arched Panels, Clamshell, 8 ⅝ In. 1344.00
Pickle, Cathedral, Dark Emerald Green, Applied Mouth, 11 ½ In. 2688.00
Pickle, Cathedral, Green, Clamshell, Applied Mouth, 8 ¾ In. 448.00
Pickle, Fern Design, Light Green, Applied Mouth, 13 In. 305.00
Pickle, H.J. Heinz, Clear, 10 Panels, Applied Mouth, Gal., 14 ¼ In. 55.00
Poison, Amber, Embossed Ridges, Label, Cork, 5 ½ In. 55.00
Poison, Bowman's Drug Stores, Dark Cobalt Blue, Embossed, 4 Oz., 5 In. 450.00
Poison, Brewer & Co., Skull & Crossbones, Cobalt Blue, Triangular Grooves, 3 ¾ In. 231.00
Poison, Cobalt Blue, 6-Sided, Broken Ribs, 5 In. 78.00
Poison, Cobalt Blue, Label, Contents, 2 ⅝ In. 33.00
Poison, Cobalt Blue, Triangular, 3 ¼ In. 78.00
Poison, Coffin, Amber, Pointed Diamonds, 5 In. 770.00
Poison, Coffin, Cobalt Blue, Pointed Diamonds, 3 In. 130.00
Poison, Coffin, Medium Cobalt Blue, Tooled Lip, 7 ¼ In. 1232.00
Poison, Coffin, Skull & Crossbones, Cobalt Blue, Tooled Lip, 4 ⅞ In. 3080.00
Poison, Embossed, Skull & Crossbones, 2 Stars, Cobalt Blue, Label, Cork, 2 ¾ In. 231.00
Poison, Embossed, Skull & Crossbones, Pat Appl'd For, Blue, Applied Lip, 3 ½ In. 4650.00
Poison, Embossed, Skull & Crossbones, Stars, Oval, Tooled Lip, 4 ¾ In. 896.00
Poison, Embossed Not To Be Taken, 6-Sided, Tooled Lip, 4 In. 10.00
Poison, Embossed Poison, 7Up Green, 4 Oz., 5 In. 165.00
Poison, F.A. Thompson & Co., Coffin, Yellow Amber, Tooled Lip, 3 ¼ In. 616.00
Poison, Green, 6-Sided, Broken Ribs, 5 In. 154.00
Poison, H.K. Mulford Co., Chemist, Philadelphia, Skull & Crossbones, Amber, 3 ¼ In. 1008.00
Poison, Hobnail, Clear, Tapered Mouth, Pontil, 4 In. 78.00
Poison, Human Skull, Crossbones, Tooled Lip, 4 ¼ In. 3584.00
Poison, KU-21, Warning, Ribs, Crosshatching, Green, 7 In. 300.00
Poison, Martin, KU-20, Tooled Lip, Curved, Ribbed Base. 825.00
Poison, Mulford Laboratories, Skull & Crossbones, Cobalt Blue, Labels, Cork, 3 ¼ In. 88.00
Poison, Not To Be Taken, Amber, 6-Sided, 2 Ribbed Panels, Label, 4 ½ In. 55.00
Poison, Not To Be Taken, Green, Triangular, Round Label Panel, 8 ⅜ In. 1008.00
Poison, Owl Drug Co., Owl On Mortar & Pestle, Cobalt Blue, Triangular, 9 ⅝ In. 1232.00
Poison, Owl Drug Co., Owl On Mortar & Pestle, Embossed, Amber, Rectangular, 6 In. 935.00
Poison, Owl Drug Co., Owl On Mortar & Pestle, Embossed, Blue Striations, 8 In. 220.00
Poison, Poisonous Not To Be Taken, 8 ½ In. 16.00
Poison, Rexall Drug Co., Mercury Bichloride, Cobalt Blue, Label, 3 In. 55.00
Poison, Sharp & Dohme, Amber, Embossed Warning, 2-Sided Label, Contents, 2 ⅞ In. 88.00
Poison, Sharp & Dohme, Lattice, Cobalt Blue, Half Embossed, Label, 2 ¾ In. 264.00
Poison, Strychnia, Tooled Lip, Label, Skull & Crossbones, 2 ½ In. 157.00
Poison, Submarine, Cobalt Blue, Tooled Lip, 4 ¼ In. 2240.00
Poison, Turquoise, 6-Sided, Broken Ribs On 1 Side, 5 In. 605.00
Poison, W.R. Warner, Co., Skull & Crossbones, Cobalt Blue, Mortar, Pestle, Label, Cork, 3 In. . . 33.00
Sarsaparilla, Ayer's, Aqua, Open Pontil, 7 ½ In. 135.00
Sarsaparilla, Ayer's Concentrated, Aqua, Open Pontil 140.00
Sarsaparilla, B.F. Williams, Syrup & Iodide Of Potass, Louisville, Ky., Aqua, 9 ⅞ In. 1120.00
Sarsaparilla, Baldwin's, West Stockbridge, Mass., Aqua, 10-Sided, Tooled Lip, 9 In. 190.00
Sarsaparilla, Beckwith's, Quassia & Wild Cherry, Arched Panels, Aqua, 9 ¼ In. 2128.00
Sarsaparilla, Benjamin Kent, Druggist, Paterson, N.J., Aqua, Tooled Lip, Paneled, 8 ¾ In. 235.00
Sarsaparilla, Bixby's, Bixby's Drug Store, Santa Cruz, Cal., Aqua, Tooled Lip, 8 ⅞ In. 258.00
Sarsaparilla, Bristol's Extract, Buffalo, Aqua, Arched Panels, Sloping Collar, 5 ⅝ In. 134.00
Sarsaparilla, Bristol's Genuine, New York, Aqua, Sloping Collar, 10 In. 560.00
Sarsaparilla, Brown's Sarsaparilla For Kidneys, Aqua, 9 ¼ In. 48.00
Sarsaparilla, Buffum's, Lemon Mineral Water, Cobalt Blue, 10-Sided, 7 ⅛ In. 1120.00
Sarsaparilla, Bush's Smilax, Aqua, Applied Lip, Open Pontil, 9 ⅞ In. 392.00
Sarsaparilla, C.W. Albright's, Camden, N. J., Aqua, Tooled Lip, 8 ¼ In. 616.00
Sarsaparilla, C.W. Brodie, N.Z., Yellow Green, Sloping Collar, 9 ⅝ In. 840.00
Sarsaparilla, Cey & Speed, Stoneware, Salt Glaze, Light Brown, Cobalt Blue Wash, 9 ½ In. . . 560.00
Sarsaparilla, Charles Joly, Philadelphia, Jamaica, Sarsaparilla, Yellow Amber, 9 ⅝ In. 157.00
Sarsaparilla, Colburn's Root, Bark & Herb, Pittsburgh, Pa., Blue Aqua, 8 ⅞ In. 258.00
Sarsaparilla, Crescent Drug Co., Blue Aqua, Tooled Lip, 9 In. 280.00
Sarsaparilla, Dalton's Sarsaparilla & Nerve Tonic, Belfast, Maine, Aqua, 9 ¼ In. 30.00

Bottle, Mineral Water, John Clarke, New York, Amber, Applied Mouth, Pontil, c.1855, Qt.
$180.00

Bottle, Mineral Water, Powell's, Burlington, N.J., Sapphire Blue, 8-Sided, IP, c.1850, 7 ⅝ In.
$3950.00

Bottle, Mineral Water, Rockbridge VA Alum Water, Olive Green, Iron Pontil, c.1850, Pt., 6 ⅞ In.
$16000.00

Bottle, Mineral Water, W. Ryer, Union Glass Works-R, Philada, Cobalt Blue, IP, c.1850, 7 In.
$490.00

Bottle, Sarsaparilla, Dr. Guysott's Compound Extract Of Yellow Dock, Green, c.1860, 9 ¼ In.
$5025.00

Slug Plates

Slug plates were invented in the late nineteenth century. A changeable metal sheet with embossed lettering was made to fit a section of an iron bottle mold. This meant many different customers could have bottles with their own molded name at a lower price. Slug plates leave a round or oval line around the raised lettering in the glass bottle.

Sarsaparilla, Dayton's, Coca Tonic, Blood Remedy, Blue Aqua, 8 ¾ In. 616.00
Sarsaparilla, Dr. Beach's Compound, Dark Blue Aqua, 8 ⅝ In. 280.00
Sarsaparilla, Dr. Cooper's, Woodard, Clarke & Co., Portland, Ore., Aqua, Tooled Lip, 10 In. 258.00
Sarsaparilla, Dr. Cronk's Beer, 8-Sided, Stoneware, Salt Glaze, Light Brown, 9⅝ In. 146.00 to 179.00
Sarsaparilla, Dr. Cummings' Compound Extract, Portland, Me., Blue Aqua, Paneled, 7 In. 896.00
Sarsaparilla, Dr. DeAndries, Yellow Amber, Sloping Collar, 9 ¾ In. 2240.00
Sarsaparilla, Dr. Green's, Aqua, 9 In. 35.00
Sarsaparilla, Dr. Guysott's Compound Extract Of Yellow Dock, Green, c.1860, 9 ¼ In. *illus* 5025.00
Sarsaparilla, Dr. Guysott's Compound, Blue Green, Sloping Collar, Pontil, 9 ⅝ In. 1456.00
Sarsaparilla, Dr. H.K. Root, Clover Blossom, Aqua, Sloping Collar, Open Pontil, 6 ⅛ In. 235.00
Sarsaparilla, Dr. Lameroux's, Crane & Brigham, San Francisco, Blue Green, 9 ⅛ In. 420.00
Sarsaparilla, Dr. M.C. Parker's, Dark Blue Green, Sloping Collar, 9 ⅜ In. 840.00
Sarsaparilla, Dr. Martin's Snake Root, Blue Aqua, Sloping Collar, 8 ¾ In. 3920.00
Sarsaparilla, Dr. Townsend's, Albany, N.Y., Blue Green, Sloping Collar, IP, 9 ⅜ In. 364.00
Sarsaparilla, Dr. Townsend's, Albany, N.Y., Blue Green, Sloping Collar, OP, 9 ¼ In. 1232.00
Sarsaparilla, Dr. Townsend's, Albany, N.Y., Dark Amber, Sloping Collar, 9 ⅛ In. 1680.00
Sarsaparilla, Dr. Townsend's, Albany, N.Y., Medium Blue Green, 9 ⅜ In. 650.00
Sarsaparilla, Dr. Townsend's, Albany, N.Y., Olive Green, Sloping Collar, Pontil, 9 ⅜ In. 420.00
Sarsaparilla, Dr. Townsend's, N.Y., Teal Blue, Square, Iron Pontil, 1845-60, 9 ⅝ In. 2000.00
Sarsaparilla, Dr. Webster's, Ithaca, Blue Aqua, Paneled, Sloping Collar, 6 ½ In. 1120.00
Sarsaparilla, Dr. Wilcox's Compound Extract, Backwards S, Green, IP, 9 ¼ In. 6720.00
Sarsaparilla, Dr. Wynkoop's, Cobalt Blue, Sloping Collar, Open Pontil, 10 ¼ In. 4750.00
Sarsaparilla, E.N. Lightner & Co., Detroit, Mich., Ice Blue, 8 ⅝ In. 235.00
Sarsaparilla, Foley's, Amber, 9 ½ In. 59.00
Sarsaparilla, Foley's, Amber, Rectangular, 9 ½ In. 68.00
Sarsaparilla, Gooch's Extract, Cincinnati, O., Ice Blue, Applied Lip, 9 ¼ In. 330.00
Sarsaparilla, Goodwin's, Clear, Tooled Lip, 9 ½ In. 168.00
Sarsaparilla, Griffith's, Pale Aqua, Tooled Lip, 9 ¾ In. 168.00
Sarsaparilla, Hall's, Shepardson & Gates, S.F., Ice Blue, Arched Panels, 9 ¼ In. 123.00
Sarsaparilla, Indian, J.J. Mack & Co., San Francisco, Cal., Indian, Aqua, Paneled, 9 ⅜ In. 448.00
Sarsaparilla, John Bull Extract, Louisville, Ky., Blue Aqua, Iron Pontil, 9 In. 550.00
Sarsaparilla, John Bull Extract, Louisville, Ky., Blue Aqua, Sloping Collar, 9 In. 392.00
Sarsaparilla, King's Celery Compound, Amber, 2 Panels, Tooled Lip, Labels, 10 In. 258.00
Sarsaparilla, Log Cabin, Rochester, N.Y., Amber, Applied Mouth, Original Label, 9 In. 209.00
Sarsaparilla, Log Cabin, Rochester, N.Y., Golden Amber, Applied Mouth, Label, 9 In. 201.00
Sarsaparilla, M. H. Swift & Co., Stoneware, Salt Glaze, Cream, Cobalt Blue Slip, 10 In. 364.00
Sarsaparilla, Mack & Co., San Francisco, Amber, Sloping Collar, Canted Corners, 9 ⅜ In. 1120.00
Sarsaparilla, Meyer's, Helena, Mont., Aqua, Paneled Sides, Tooled Lip, 9 ¼ In. 728.00
Sarsaparilla, N.A. Gilbert & Co., Enosburgh Falls, Vt., 8-Sided, Yellow Amber, 8 ¾ In. 616.00
Sarsaparilla, Neat Richardson Drug Co., Louisville, Ky., Clear, Tooled Lip, 8 ⅝ In. 246.00
Sarsaparilla, Rackley's, B.F. Rackley Apothecary, Dover, N.H., Aqua, Applied Mouth, 9 In. 504.00
Sarsaparilla, Rush's Sarsaparilla & Iron, A.H. Flanders, N.Y., Amber, c.1880, 9 In. *illus* 210.00
Sarsaparilla, Shepherd's Genuine Preparation, Baltimore, Aqua, OP, 5 ⅞ In. 1904.00
Sarsaparilla, Thos. A. Hurley's Compound Syrup, Amber, Tooled Lip, 9 ⅞ In. 728.00
Sarsaparilla, Turner's, Buffalo, N.Y., Blue Aqua, Sloping Collar, 12 In. 1344.00
Sarsaparilla, W.R. Dickinson Homestake, Lead, So. Dak., Aqua, Tooled Lip, 9 ¼ In. 1904.00
Sarsaparilla, W.S. Green, Stoneware, Albany Brown Glaze, 9 In. 202.00
Sarsaparilla, WC & J. & G. Wilson, Stoneware, Salt Glaze, Gray, Cobalt Blue, 9 ½ In. 235.00
Sarsaparilla, Whipple's, Portland, Me., Aqua, Paneled Sides, Tooled Lip, 9 ⅛ In. 123.00
Sarsaparilla, Wilson's Tonic & Elixir, Blue Aqua, Tooled Lip, 8 ½ In. 157.00
Scent, 2 Men, Canes, Blue, Red, White Swirls, Brass Collar, Hinged, Chain, 2 ⅞ In. 1100.00
Scent, Aqua, Lyre Shape, Flared Lip, 5 ½ In. 39.00
Scent, Bunker Hill Monument, Milk Glass, Tooled Lip, 12 In. 110.00
Scent, Cobalt Blue, Art Nouveau Style, Silver Mount, France, c.1900, 4 ¼ x 2 ½ In. 823.00
Scent, Emerald Green, Silver Overlay, Matching Stopper, 1900, 3 ½ In. 146.00
Scent, Memorial Hall 1876, Clear, Tooled Lip, 6 ¼ In. 336.00
Scent, Milk Glass, Ribs, Swirled To Right, Sheared & Tooled Lip, Pontil, 1840-60, 2 ¾ In. 539.00
Scent, Monument, Milk Glass, Opalescent, Tooled Lip, 8 ¼ In. 168.00
Scent, Porcelain, Silver, Spider Webs, Spiders, Flies, Round, c.1887, 2 x 1 ¾ In. 1314.00
Scent, Porcelain, White & Gold Ground, Gems, Silver Mount, Continental, 5 ¼ In. 177.00
Scent, Purple Amethyst, 6-Sided, Pinched Waist, Tooled Flared Lip, Stopper, 3 ¾ In. 426.00
Scent, Ruby, Flashed, Enameled, Continental, Late 19th Century, 9 In. 118.00
Seal, Saml. Smith 1750, Black Glass, Olive Green, Applied String Lip, Pontil, 8 ¾ In. 5040.00
Seal, W & Co., Cognac, Yellow Amber, Globular, Applied Mouth, Handle, 6 ⅛ In. 784.00
Seal, W.B. Crownell Jr Star Whiskey, Amber, Ribs, Tooled Spout, Handle, 7 ⅞ In. 1456.00
Seal, Wine, G. Forster, Black Glass, Dark Olive Green, Applied Mouth, 14 ⅜ In. 1456.00

Seal, Wine, N. Green, 1724, Black Glass, Onion, High Sides, Dark Olive Green, $7\frac{1}{8}$ In. 6720.00
Seal, Wine, R. Lenox, Black Glass, Dark Olive Amber, Applied Mouth, $11\frac{3}{8}$ In. 560.00
Seltzer, Dr Pepper, Blue, Fluted *illus* 3500.00
Seltzer, Glaser Seattle, USA, Property Of Glaser Beverages Inc., Citron, Stopper, 13 In. 605.00
Seltzer, Green, Safety Rider, Etched, c.1900, $11\frac{1}{4}$ In. 77.00
Seltzer, Roycroft, Clear, c.1920, 12 In. 58.00
Seltzer, Zetz Sparkling Water, New Orleans, La., Amber, Etched, Dr Pepper Stopper, 12 In. 125.00
Shoe Polish, Topsy, Black Girl, Aqua, Paper Label, Applied Lip, $4\frac{3}{4}$ x $1\frac{5}{8}$ x $1\frac{5}{8}$ In. 275.00
Snuff, Agate, Landscape, Red Glass Stopper, $3\frac{1}{2}$ In. 705.00
Snuff, Agate, Leaves, Melon Shape, Coral Stopper, 2 In. 353.00
Snuff, Agate, Lotus Plants, Chinese, 19th Century, 2 In. 176.00
Snuff, Agate, Moss, Lacquered, Inlaid Coral, Brass Stopper, $2\frac{3}{4}$ In. 2938.00
Snuff, Agate, Sage, Carved, Orange Honey, Brown Jasper, Black Jade Cover, $2\frac{1}{2}$ In. 210.00
Snuff, Amber, Gourd Shape, Carved, Chinese, 2 In. 234.00
Snuff, Amethyst, Peach, Child, Bat, Aventurine Stopper, Purple, Chinese, $1\frac{3}{4}$ In. 382.00
Snuff, Black Glass, Olive Yellow, Flared Out Lip, Pontil, c.1820, $4\frac{3}{8}$ In. 258.00
Snuff, Brown, Black Agate, Chinese, $2\frac{1}{2}$ x 2 In. 118.00
Snuff, Buddhist Saints, Relief, Black Ground, 20th Century, $2\frac{3}{4}$ In. 646.00
Snuff, Cinnabar, Carved Figures, Pavilions, Wood Stopper, $3\frac{1}{2}$ In. 646.00
Snuff, Cinnabar, Carved Figures In Landscape, $5\frac{1}{2}$ In. 646.00
Snuff, Cinnabar, Carved Figures On Chariot, Horse, Rock, Spirals, $2\frac{1}{2}$ In. 588.00
Snuff, Cloisonne, Lotus, Red Ground, Chinese, 20th Century 323.00
Snuff, Coral, Goddess With Lute, Dark Red, Japan, 20th Century, 2 In. 411.00
Snuff, Glass, Amber, Glass Stopper, 1800s, $2\frac{1}{4}$ In. 1880.00
Snuff, Glass, Amber, Yellow, Wide Mouth, Open Pontil, 1840, $4\frac{1}{2}$ In. 202.00
Snuff, Glass, E. Roome, Troy, New York, Green, Cork Stopper, Label, 4 In. 1344.00
Snuff, Glass, Leonard Appleby Railroad, Amber, Sheared Flared Out Lip, $4\frac{5}{8}$ In. 420.00
Snuff, Glass, Olive Amber, Rectangular, Tooled & Flared Mouth, c.1850, $4\frac{1}{4}$ In. 177.00
Snuff, Glass, Otto Landberg & Co., Dark Blue, Embossed, $5\frac{1}{4}$ In. 56.00
Snuff, Glass, Ruby Red, Pavilion, Cranes, Clouds, Chinese, 19th Century, 2 In. 529.00
Snuff, Hard Stone, Black, Gray, Chinese, $2\frac{3}{4}$ In. 47.00
Snuff, Ivory, Carved Figures On Horseback, Chinese, 19th Century, $3\frac{1}{2}$ In. 1293.00
Snuff, Ivory, Child Offering Pearl To Dragon, Chinese, 19th Century, $2\frac{1}{4}$ In. 588.00
Snuff, Jade, 2 Figures, Pebble Skin Coral Stopper, Chinese, 19th Century, $2\frac{1}{4}$ In. 5875.00
Snuff, Jade, Celadon, Carved, Tiger, Dragon, Lion Mask Handles, $2\frac{1}{2}$ In. 1116.00
Snuff, Jade, Celadon, Flattened Oval, Chinese 350.00
Snuff, Jade, Green, Lavender, Figures, Tourmaline Stopper, $2\frac{1}{4}$ In. 2115.00
Snuff, Jade, Green, Tan, Coral Stopper, Chinese, 19th Century, $2\frac{3}{4}$ In. 705.00
Snuff, Jade, Grey, Dragon, Phoenix, Flaming Pearl Of Wisdom, Pebble Form, Chinese. 212.00
Snuff, Jade, White, Carved, Crane, Pine Tree, Figures, Rectangular, Flattened Chinese. 1534.00
Snuff, Jade, Yellow, Carved, Foo Dogs, Coral Stopper, 1800s, $2\frac{3}{4}$ In. 7638.00
Snuff, Lapis Lazuli, Chinese, Mid 20th Century, $2\frac{3}{4}$ x 2 In. 118.00
Snuff, Mother-Of-Pearl, Figures, 20th Century, $2\frac{3}{4}$ x $1\frac{3}{4}$ In. 176.00
Snuff, Mother-Of-Pearl, Mango, Coral Stopper, $2\frac{3}{4}$ In. 353.00
Snuff, Mottled Brown & Blue Flint Glaze, Enamel, 1849, $4\frac{1}{2}$ x 4 In. 941.00
Snuff, Obsidian, Carved, Chinese, $3\frac{1}{2}$ x $2\frac{1}{4}$ In. 29.00
Snuff, Opal, Carved, Figures, Chinese, $2\frac{1}{2}$ x $1\frac{1}{2}$ In. 235.00
Snuff, Peking Glass, Amber, Swirls, Melon Shape, Turquoise, Horn Stopper, Chinese, $1\frac{3}{4}$ In. 705.00
Snuff, Peking Glass, Figures Around Censer, Red Carved To Snowflake, $2\frac{1}{4}$ In. 118.00
Snuff, Peking Glass, Figures On Horseback, Red Over White, Chinese, 1800s, $2\frac{1}{2}$ In. 176.00
Snuff, Peking Glass, Foo Dogs, Scrolled Ground, Chinese, 19th Century, $3\frac{1}{2}$ In. 588.00
Snuff, Peking Glass, Green, White, Yellow, 3 In. 176.00
Snuff, Peking Glass, Pomegranate, Bats, Green, Yellow, Blue, Red, $2\frac{1}{2}$ In. 558.00
Snuff, Peking Glass, Red, Chinese, $2\frac{1}{2}$ x 2 In. 206.00
Snuff, Peking Glass, Scholar In Garden, Blue Over White, 3 In. 499.00
Snuff, Porcelain, Blue & White, Figural Landscape, Chinese, c.1840, 3 x 3 In. 176.00
Snuff, Porcelain, Celadon, Blue Top, Chinese, 19th Century, $2\frac{3}{4}$ x $1\frac{3}{4}$ In. 176.00
Snuff, Porcelain, Grasshopper, Painted, Stopper, Chinese, $2\frac{3}{4}$ In. 2520.00
Snuff, Porcelain, Hundred Shou Characters, Blue Underglaze, Chinese, $2\frac{1}{4}$ In. 323.00
Snuff, Porcelain, White, Blue Top, Chinese, 19th Century, 3 x 2 In. 176.00
Snuff, Scotch, Sweetser Brothers, Boston, Mass., Green, Paper Label, OP, 4 In. *illus* 725.00
Snuff, Shadow Agate, Relief Carved Figures, Flattened Oval, Chinese 944.00
Snuff, Silver, Bird, Tibet, Chinese, 3 In. 89.00
Snuff, Silver, Ivory, Turquoise, Carved, Chinese, c.1900, $4\frac{3}{4}$ In., Pair 206.00
Snuff, Tortoiseshell, Basket Weave, Rectangular, Chinese, 3 In. 224.00
Snuff, Turquoise, Carved Figures, Mid 20th Century, $2\frac{1}{2}$ x 3 In. 118.00
Snuff, Whale Tooth Shape, Applied White Metal Cover, Cap, 4 In. 388.00

Bottle, Sarsaparilla, Rush's Sarsaparilla & Iron, A.H. Flanders, N.Y., Amber, c.1880, 9 In.
$210.00

Bottle, Seltzer, Dr Pepper, Blue, Fluted
$3500.00

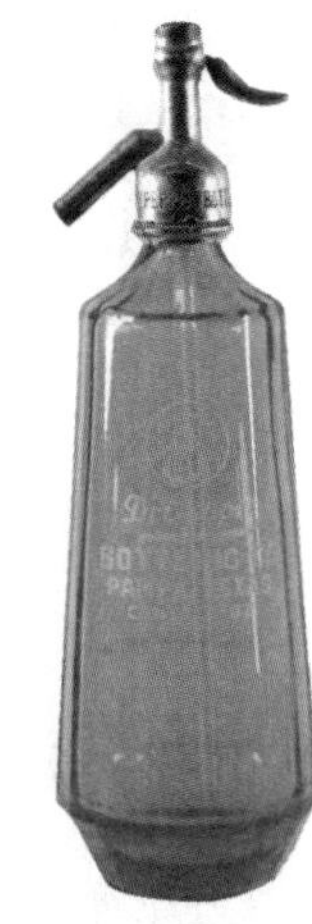

Bottle, Snuff, Scotch, Sweetser Brothers, Boston, Mass., Green, Paper Label, OP, 4 In.
$725.00

TIP

To remove a stubborn stain from the outside of a bottle, try this: Fill a bucket with soft sand. Push the bottle in and out of the sand, rotate it, and try to loosen the stain. Then wash in clean water. To remove a stain inside a bottle, put a handful of gravel in the bottle and shake vigorously.

Bottle, Soda, J. Lake, Schenectady, N.Y., Cobalt, 10 Pin, Iron Pontil, c.1850, 8 In. $1820.00

Bottle, Whiskey, E.G. Booz's Old Cabin, Yellow Amber, Applied Mouth, c.1874, 7⅞ In. $4500.00

Soda, 7Up Salutes Notre Dame Fighting Irish, 16 Oz. 10.00
Soda, A. Hain & Son, Lebanon, Pa., Blue Aqua, Squat, 7¼ In. 48.00
Soda, Abner Royce Co., Pure Fruit Flavors, Cleveland, O., 4⅜ In. 8.00
Soda, Bay City Soda Water Co., S.F., Star, Blob Top 840.00
Soda, Bay City Soda Water Co., S.F., Star, Blue, Blob Top 364.00
Soda, Bay City Soda Water Co., S.F., Star, Green Blue, Blob Top 952.00
Soda, Blanchard & Defreest, Troy, N.Y., Sapphire Blue, Blob Top, IP, 7¾ In. 1008.00
Soda, Bon-Ton, Albany, N.Y., Aqua, Blob Top, 6¾ In. 616.00
Soda, Bremenkampf & Regli, Eureka, Nev., Lime Green .... 225.00 to 750.00
Soda, C. & K. Eagle Works, Sac City, Blue, Blob Top, 1858-66, 7 In. 269.00
Soda, C. & R. Eagle Works, Sac City, 1860, Dark Blue, Blob Top, 7¼ In. 840.00
Soda, C. Alfs, Charleston, S.C., Applied Sloping Collar, Iron Pontil, 8-Sided, 7½ In. 10080.00
Soda, C. Cleminshaw, Troy, N.Y., Sapphire Blue, Applied Mouth, IP, 6¾ In. 672.00
Soda, C. Whittemore, New York, Blue Green, 7½ In. 168.00
Soda, C.W. Rider, Watertown, N.Y., Teal Blue, Hutchinson, 6¾ In. 1120.00
Soda, California Natural Seltzer Water, H & G, Embossed Bear, Hutchinson, 7½ In. 1904.00
Soda, California Soda Works, Eagle, Green, 7 In. 2128.00
Soda, Carpenter & Cobb, Knickerbocker, Saratoga Springs, Blue Green, 10-Sided, 7½ In. 1008.00
Soda, Cassin's English Aerated Waters, Green, Applied Mouth, Holder, 10 In. 475.00
Soda, Cha's Grove, Columbia, Pa., Slug Plate, Blue Green, Applied Collar, IP, 6⅞ In. 952.00
Soda, Circle A, Ginger Ale, Waco, Tex., Crown Top, Metal Stand 224.00
Soda, Cobalt Blue, 8-Sided, Blob Top, Iron Pontil, 7 x⅜ In. 224.00
Soda, Columbia Soda Works, S. F., Seated Liberty, Dark Green, Blob Top, 7¼ In. 364.00
Soda, Crystal Soda Water Co., Patented Nov. 12, 1872, Blue, Blob Top, 7¾ In. 476.00
Soda, Crystal Soda Water Co., Patented Nov. 12, 1872, Dark Green, Blob Top, 7¾ In. 1792.00
Soda, D.J. Whelan, Troy, N.Y, 1881, Tulips, Clear 9.00
Soda, Daniel Ritter, Allentown, Pa., Amber, Hutchinson, Tooled Lip, 6⅜ In. 325.00
Soda, Deri-Del, Clear, Red ACL Label, 10 Oz. 4.00
Soda, Dyottville Glassworks, Philada, Olive Yellow, ½ Pt. 39.00
Soda, E. Bigelow & Co., Springfield, Mass., Emerald Green, IP, 7⅛ In. 504.00
Soda, E. Dean, Cobalt Blue, This Bottle Is Never Sold, Blob Top 250.00
Soda, Eastern Cider Co., Light Amber, Drip Top, 8 In. 358.00
Soda, Empire Soda Works, Frank S. Waldo, San Francisco, Aqua 25.00
Soda, Excelsior, 6-Sided, Green, Applied Mouth, Iron Pontil, 1850s 616.00
Soda, Fairbanks & Beard, Howard St., Boston, F & B, Green, Internal Threads, 7 In. 672.00
Soda, Felix Gingerale, Felix The Cat, Paper Label, c.1920, 9 In. 254.00
Soda, G. Lauter Reading, Pa., Blue Green, Blob Top, 6⅝ In. 119.00
Soda, G.S., Emerald Green, 8-Sided, Blob Top, Pontil, 7¼ In. 896.00
Soda, G.W. Reinke, Plymouth, Wis., Monogram, Aqua 10.00
Soda, Geo W. Hoffman, Allentown, Pa., Teal Blue, 8-Sided, Blob Top, 7¼ In. 300.00
Soda, Geo. Eagle, Blue Green, Diagonal Ribs, Applied Mouth, IP, 7 In. 1344.00
Soda, Geo. Schmuck's Ginger Ale, Cleveland, O., Amber, 12-Sided, Hutchinson, 8 In. 250.00
Soda, Golden Gate, Green, Applied Collar, 7 In. 385.00
Soda, Green, Blob Top, Iron Pontil, 7¼ In. 45.00
Soda, Green, Embossed, Applied Lip, Pontil, 1860, 7 In. 112.00
Soda, Henry Busch, Minnemucca, Nev., Aqua, Hutchinson 1250.00
Soda, Hires Root Beer Extract, Stoneware, White, Brown, c.1900, 7 In. 29.00
Soda, Howell & Smith, Buffalo, Sapphire Blue, Ring & Sloping Collar, 7⅜ In. 258.00
Soda, Hutch, John McMunigal, 1193 Edgemont Ave., Chester, Pa. 10.00
Soda, J. Esposito, Koka Nola, Washington Ave., Philada, Green, Hutchinson 1210.00
Soda, J. Lake, Schenectudy, N.Y., Cobalt, 10 Pin, Iron Puntil, c.1850, 8 In. .... *illus* 1820.00
Soda, J.B. Edwards, Columbia, Pa., Slug Plate, Brown Stout, Green, Squat, 6¼ In. 1232.00
Soda, J.T., Elko, Nev., Blue, Blob Mouth, 1880s, 9 In. 3740.00
Soda, J.W. Harris, Star, New Haven, Conn., Cobalt Blue, 8-Sided, Blob Top, 7½ In. 672.00
Soda, Jacob Schmidt, Pottsville, Pa., Olive Green, Blob Top, Hutchinson, 6¾ In. 616.00
Soda, James Dewar Elko, Nev., Tooled Lip, Hutchinson, 8 In. 2200.00
Soda, John Ryan, Savannah, A., 1859, Sapphire Blue, Iron Pontil, 8 In. 520.00
Soda, Jos. X. Laube, Akron, O., Anisetta, Light Blue, Gravitator, Applied Mouth 190.00
Soda, Keach-Balt., Apricot Puce, Torpedo, Applied Mouth, Holder, 9 In. 17600.00
Soda, Keach-Balt., Green, Torpedo, Applied Mouth, Holder, 9 In. 2860.00
Soda, L. Schmitt, Columbia, Slug Plate, Sapphire Blue, Applied Mouth, IP, 7 In. 672.00
Soda, M. & J. Duffy, Phila, Blue Green, Squat, Double Collar 29.00
Soda, Monroe Bottling Works, Monroe, La., Aqua 12.00
Soda, Mountain Dew, Flask, Label Under Glass, Girl, Screw Cap, Pt. 280.00
Soda, Moxie, Light Green, Tooled Lip, Hutchinson 269.00
Soda, Nome Brewing & Bottling Co., Clear, Tooled Lip, Hutchinson 1344.00
Soda, Orange, Smile, Cap, Contents, Pat. July 11, 1922 .... 440.00

Soda, Owen Casey, Eagle Soda Works, Sac City, Blue Green, Sloping Collar, 7⅜ In. 134.00

Soda, P.J. Serwazi, Manayunk, Pa., Olive Green, Hutchinson, 7⅝ In. 1064.00

Soda, Polk & Co., Barnum's Building, Balt., Ten Pin, Sapphire Blue, Holder 4400.00

Soda, Seitz Bros., Easton, Pa., Cobalt Blue, Applied Mouth, 7⅜ In. 420.00

Soda, Smedley & Brandt, Slug Plate, Emerald Green, Blob Top, IP, 7¼ In. 269.00

Soda, Stephens & Jose, Virginia City, Nevada, Monogram, Blue, Gravitating Stopper, 7 In. 2860.00

Soda, Sun-Drop, Golden Cola, Green ACL, 9 Oz. 10.00

Soda, Upper 10, Green, Nehi Bottling Co., Hagerstown, Md., Red & Yellow ACL, 9 Oz. 10.00

Soda, Vic's, Winnemucca, Nev., Clear, Red & White Label, 1950s 10.00

Soda, W & Co., Burlington, Iowa, Blue 154.00

Soda, Wibles Beverages, Icicles, McConnellsburg Bottling Works, Pa. 12.00

Soda, Williams & Severance, San Francisco, Cal., Cobalt Blue, 8 In. 550.00

Soda, Yerington Ice & Soda Factory, Yerington, Nevada, Crown Top, c.1917 75.00

Target Ball, 7 Embossed Vertical Bands, Amber, 3-Piece Mold, Sheared Mouth, 2⅝ In. 336.00

Target Ball, Agnew & Brown, Pittsburgh Pa., Brown, Embossed Pigeon, 3 In. 28000.00

Target Ball, Amber, 3-Piece Mold, Sheared Mouth, 2⅝ In. 336.00

Target Ball, Amber, Embossed Vertical Bands, 3 In. 775.00

Target Ball, Bogardus, Diamond, Emerald Green, Amethyst Striation, 2¾ In. 3860.00

Target Ball, Bogardus, Pat'd Apr 10 1877, Hobnail, Medium Amber, 3 In. 4700.00

Target Ball, Bogardus, Pat'd Apr 10 1877, Lattice, Amber, 3 In. 6750.00

Target Ball, Bogardus, Pat'd Apr 10 1877, Lattice, Light Blue, Sheared Mouth, 3 In. 3700.00

Target Ball, Bogardus, Pat'd Apr 10 1877, Lattice, Light Purple, Sheared Mouth, 3 In. 4190.00

Target Ball, Bogardus, Pat'd Apr 10 1877, Lattice, Medium Green, 2⅞ In. 4190.00

Target Ball, C.T.H. Graphite, Embossed, Sept 191879, March 91880, 3 In. 375.00

Target Ball, Cobalt Blue, 5-Piece Mold, Sheared Mouth, 2⅝ In. 190.00

Target Ball, Copper Puce, Diamond, Center Band, Ground Lip, 2¾ In. 258.00

Target Ball, Diamond, Van Gutsem, A St Quentin, Blue, Burst Lip, 3 In. 250.00

Target Ball, Diamond, Van Gutsem, A St Quentin, Cobalt Blue, Burst Lip, 3 In. 220.00

Target Ball, G Embossed, Light To Medium Amber, 3 In. 290.00

Target Ball, Gurd & Son, 185 Dundas Street, London, Amber, Sheared Mouth, 3 In. 1390.00

Target Ball, Ira Paine's, Pat. Oct. 23, 1877, Golden Amber, 3-Piece Mold, 3 In. 250.00

Target Ball, Ira Paine's, Pat. Oct. 23, 1877, Medium Amber, 3-Piece Mold, 3 In. 315.00

Target Ball, Lattice, Blue, 3 In. 380.00

Target Ball, Light To Medium Blue, 7 Embossed Horizontal Rings, Sheared Mouth, 3 In. 460.00

Target Ball, Man, Shooting, Round Panel, Diamond, Clear, Sheared Mouth, 2⅝ In. 280.00

Target Ball, Mauritz, Wid'fors, Yellow, Amber Tint, Sheared Mouth, Sweden, 2⅝ In. 1008.00

Target Ball, Sophienhutte In Ilmenau, Lattice, Orange Amber, Germany, 3 In. 1585.00

Target Ball, Stacy Settless London, Lattice, Aqua, Embossed, 3¼ In. 1750.00

Target Ball, Sure Break, Patent App'd For, Golden Yellow, 3 In. 17000.00

Target Ball, W.W. Greener St., London, Lattice, Feathers, Blue, 3 In. 395.00

Target Ball, W.W. Greener St., London, Lattice, Light Plum, 3 In. 725.00

Whiskey, Amber, English Flagon, Applied Silver Neck, Metal Cork, Handle, Qt. 89.00

Whiskey, Backbar, Cobalt Blue, 8 Pillar, Double Collar, Pontil, 1850-60, 11¾ In. 1120.00

Whiskey, Backbar, Ruby Red, Applied Silver Hunter, Dog, Tooled Lip, 1885-1900, 11 In. 258.00

Whiskey, Barry & Patten, 114 & 116 Montgomery St., S.F., Green, c.1850, Fifth 1000.00

Whiskey, Blue Aqua, Pyramid Shape, Roped Corners, Sloping Collar, Open Pontil, 11⅛ In. 560.00

Whiskey, Bulkley Fiske & Co., Brandy, Olive Yellow, Applied Mouth & Handle, IP, 8½ In. 8960.00

Whiskey, Casper's, Made By Honest North Carolina People, Cobalt Blue, 12 In. 952.00

Whiskey, Chestnut Grove, C.W., Yellow Amber, Applied Mouth, Handle, 9 In. 560.00

Whiskey, Chestnut Grove, C.W., Yellow Amber, Chestnut, Applied Ringed Mouth, 9 In. 784.00

Whiskey, Crane & Brigham, San Francisco, Leaf, Yellow Amber, 10¼ In. 952.00

Whiskey, Dog With Bird In Mouth, Olive Green, 8½ In. 48.00

Whiskey, Duffy Malt Whiskey Co., Rochester, N.Y., U.S.A., Medium Amber, Tooled Lip, 4 In. 150.00

Whiskey, Dunbar & Co., Wormwood Cordial, Blue Green, Sloping Collar, 9½ In. 728.00

Whiskey, Dyottville Glassworks, Phila., Olive Yellow, Embossed, 11¾ In. 59.00

Whiskey, E.G. Booz's Old Cabin, 1840, Amber, 7⅝ In. 3920.00

Whiskey, E.G. Booz's Old Cabin, Amber, 1940, 8 In. 134.00

Whiskey, E.G. Booz's Old Cabin, Amber, Applied Sloping Collar Mouth, 7¾ In. 1344.00

Whiskey, E.G. Booz's Old Cabin, Golden Amber, Applied Collar Mouth, c.1860, 7½ In. 3360.00

Whiskey, E.G. Booz's Old Cabin, Yellow Amber, Applied Mouth, c.1874, 7⅞ In. *illus* 4500.00

Whiskey, E.P. Middleton & Bro., 1825 Wheat Whiskey, Gasoline Puce, Squat, Seal, Qt 89.00

Whiskey, Eye, Eye Opener, Milk Glass, Painted, Screw Cap, Nip, 5 In. 476.00

Whiskey, Figural, Clam Shell, Cobalt Blue, Metal Screw Cap, c.1895, 5 In. *illus* 485.00

Whiskey, G. Lewis Liquor Co., Lavender, Flask, Tooled Lip, ½ Pt. 1120.00

Whiskey, Garrett & Co., Eagle & Flags, Norfolk, Va., Fluted Shoulders, 4⅜ In. 25.00

Whiskey, Grapes, On Tree Stump, Amber, Applied Ring Mouth, 9½ In. 2352.00

Whiskey, Greeley's Bourbon, Barrel, Aqua, Horizontal Ribs, c.1860, 9 In. 4600.00

Bottle, Whiskey, Figural, Clam Shell, Cobalt Blue, Metal Screw Cap, c.1895, 5 In.
$485.00

Bottle, Whiskey, J.F.T. & Co., Philad., Medium Amber, Ribs, Applied Handle, Pontil, 7 In.
$660.00

Bottle, Wine, Seal, Sir Will. Strickland, Olive Green, String Lip, Pontil, England, 9 In.
$840.00

TIP
To loosen a perfume bottle stopper, put the bottle upside down in alcohol for a few days. It may help.

Bottle Opener, Cardinal, Cast Iron
$600.00

Bottle Opener, Hires Root Beer, Metal, Lithograph, c.1905-15, 3 ¼ In.
$86.00

Bottle Opener, Mexican Cactus, Souvenir Of Albuquerque, N. Mex., Cast Iron, Wilton Products
$520.00

Whiskey, Greeley's Bourbon, Barrel, Topaz, Applied Mouth, Label, Girl In Field 5600.00
Whiskey, Green River, Old Man, Horse, Label Under Glass, Clear, Cylindrical, Qt. 69.00
Whiskey, Griffith Hyatt & Co., Baltimore, Strawberry Puce, Jug, Handle, 7 ¼ In. 672.00
Whiskey, Griffith Hyatt & Co., Baltimore, Yellow Amber, Jug, Handle, 7 ¼ In. 616.00
Whiskey, Helmet Rye, Figural, Helmet, Redware, Brown & Tan Glaze, 2 ½ In. 78.00
Whiskey, Henry Chapman & Co., Flask, Montreal, Golden Amber, Teardrop, 5 ¾ In. 112.00
Whiskey, Hollander Brothers Drug Co., Clear, ½ Pt. 35.00
Whiskey, I.X.L. Valley Whiskey, E & B Bevan Pittston, Pa., Amber, Embossed Stars, 8 In. 3020.00
Whiskey, J.B., Forest Green, Oval, Embossed, Handle, 1860-70, 11 In. 159.00
Whiskey, J.F.T. & Co., Philad., Medium Amber, Ribs, Applied Handle, Pontil, 7 In. . . . . . . *illus* 660.00
Whiskey, J.F.T. & Co., Philad., Amber, Ribs, Embossed Medallion, Handle, c.1850, 7 In. 325.00
Whiskey, J.H. Cutter Old Bourbon, Golden Amber, Cylindrical, 11 ½ In. 39.00
Whiskey, Macy & Jenkins, New York, Handles, 1860 . . . . 50.00
Whiskey, Milton J. Hardy, Old Bourbon, Louisville, Ky., Yellow Amber, Fifth, 11 ¾ In. 6720.00
Whiskey, Nathans Bros., 1863, Phila, Yellow Amber, Squat, 10 In. 89.00
Whiskey, Old Hettermann Handmade Sour Mash, Man In Suit & Hat, Stoneware, Tan, Qt. . . . 195.00
Whiskey, Old Wheat, Golden Amber, Cylindrical, Iron Pontil, 1835, 12 ¼ In. 425.00
Whiskey, Pig, Drink While It Lasts, From This Hog's, Clear. 165.00
Whiskey, R.B. Cutter, Louisville, Ky., Golden Amber, Pear Shape, Handle, Pontil, 8 ¼ In. 180.00
Whiskey, S. Weinberger, Idaho Springs, Colorado, Flask, Coffin, Pt. 750.00
Whiskey, Sake, Blue & White, 6 ½ x 2 ½ In. 23.00
Whiskey, Senate Saloon, Grand Junction, Colorado, Flask, Ground Lip, Pt. 850.00
Whiskey, Theodore Netter, Cobalt Blue, Barrel, Tooled Lip, 6 In. 157.00
Whiskey, Thurn's Buffet, Leadville, Colo., Figural, Elks Club Tooth, Milk Glass, Label 950.00
Whiskey, Udolpho Wolfe's Aromatic Schnapps, Schiedam, Olive Amber, 9 ¾ In. 175.00
Whiskey, Utah Liquor Company, 223 South Main Street, Salt Lake City, Jug, Redware, Gal. . . . 500.00
Whiskey, W.A. Gaines & Co., Cheyenne, Wyo., Old Crow, Lavender Tint, Screw Top, Pt. 224.00
Whiskey, Wharton's, Chestnut Grove, Sapphire Blue, Pumpkinseed Flask, 5 ¼ In. 616.00
Whiskey, Wilson Fairbanks & Co., Old Bourbon For Medicinal Purposes, Aqua, Embossed, Qt. 128.00
Wine, Dutch Onion, Emerald Green, Applied String Lip, Open Pontil, 6 ⅜ x 5 ¼ In. 90.00
Wine, Dutch Onion, Olive Green, Applied String Lip, 7 ⅜ x 5 ⅝ In. 90.00
Wine, Mallet, Black Glass, Olive Amber, Applied String Lip, Pontil, England, 6 ¾ In. 195.00
Wine, Mallet, Black Glass, Olive Green, Applied String Lip, Pontil, England, 7 ¾ In. 285.00
Wine, Mallet, Black Glass, Olive Green, Applied String Lip, Pontil, England, 8 ¼ In. 565.00
Wine, Mallet, Black Glass, Olive Green, Applied String Lip, Pontil, England, 8 ⅜ In. 410.00
Wine, Onion, Blue Green, Applied String Lip, Open Pontil, 1720-40, 6 ¾ x 5 ⅝ In. 134.00
Wine, Onion, Horse Hoof, Dark Olive Amber, Applied String Lip, 7 ⅞ x 5 ⅝ In. 90.00
Wine, Onion, Olive Amber, Applied String Lip, Pontil, England, c.1710, 5 ¾ x 6 In. 1150.00
Wine, Onion, Olive Green, Applied String Lip, Pontil, England, c.1690, 6 x 5 ½ In. 1290.00
Wine, Onion, Olive Yellow Amber, Applied String Lip, 7 x 5 ½ In. 90.00
Wine, Onion, Squat, Olive Amber, c.1690, 5 x 5 ¾ In. 3450.00
Wine, Pancake Onion, Olive Yellow, Applied String Lip, Pontil, England, c.1700, 5 ⅜ x 6 ¼ In. 880.00
Wine, Rev. John Browder's Bottle, Black Glass, Opalescent Olive Amber, Painted Letters, 9 In. . 112.00
Wine, Seal, Sir Will. Strickland, Olive Green, String Lip, Pontil, England, 9 In. . . . . *illus* 840.00
Zanesville, 24 Ribs, Swirled To Left, Dark Amber, Globular, Outward Rolled Lip, 8 ⅜ In. 1008.00
Zanesville, 24 Ribs, Swirled To Left, Yellow Amber, Globular, Outward Rolled Lip, 8 In. 504.00
Zanesville, 24 Ribs, Swirled To Right, Apple Green, Globular, Outward Rolled Lip, 7 ⅝ In. . . . 2800.00
Zanesville, 24 Ribs, Swirled To Right, Blue Aqua, Globular, Outward Rolled Lip, 8 ¼ In. 392.00
Zanesville, Amber, Swirl Ribbed, Folded Lip, Pontil Scar, c.1840, 8 ¼ In. 472.00
Zanesville, Aquamarine, Rib Swirls, Folded Lip, High Pontil Scar, 7 ¼ In. 472.00

BOTTLE CAPS for milk bottles are the printed cardboard caps used since the 1920s. Crown caps, used after 1892 on soda bottles, are also popular collectibles. Unusual mottoes, graphics, and caps from bottlers that are out of business bring the highest prices.

Dalee Dairy, Concord Grape Drink, 1 ⅝ In. 0.15
H.F. Morrill Milk & Cream Dairy, c.1950, 1 ⅝ In. 0.15
Jersey Parlor Dairy, Whitman Monument, 1 ⅝ In. 0.25
Pure Fresh Milk, Cow, Pull Tab, c.1930, 1 ⅝ In. 0.15
Rushmore Milk, Pasteurized Chocolate Drink, Mt. Rushmore, Custer, S.D., No. 3B. 62.00

BOTTLE OPENERS are needed to open many bottles. As soon as the commercial bottle was invented, the opener to be used with the new types of closures became a necessity. Many types of bottle openers can be found, most dating from the twentieth century. Collectors prize advertising and comic openers.

7Up, Wall Mount, Steel, Enamel, 1940s, 2 ½ x 4 x 2 In. 45.00

Beanie Bert, Cast Iron, Marked, Winter Weekend, L & L Favors 920.00
Beer Drinker, Cast Iron, 5 3/8 In. 259.00
Beer Drinker, Cast Iron, Wall Mount, Sprenger Brewing Co., Pa., 6 In. 160.00
Cardinal, Cast Iron . . . . . *illus* 600.00
Cast Iron, Mexican Cactus, Souvenir Of New Mexico, Wilton Products 520.00
Elephant, Cast Iron, John Wright, 5 In. 144.00
Elephant Head, Gray, Metal, Scott Prod., Newark, N.J., c.1950, 5 1/2 x 4 1/2 In. 60.00
Hires Root Beer, Metal, Lithograph, c.1905-15, 3 1/4 In. . . . . *illus* 86.00
Horse Tail, Cast Iron, Wilton Products, Marked, WO 36, Box, 5 1/8 In. 177.00
Horse's Rear, Brown, White, Black, Metal, Scott Products, N.J., c.1950, 3 x 5 x 2 In. 50.00
Mexican Cactus, Souvenir Of Albuquerque, N. Mex., Cast Iron, Wilton Products . . . . . *illus* 520.00
Palm Tree, Cast Iron, Wilton Products, 5 In. 58.00
Pheasant Head, Green, Yellow, Red, Cast Metal, Rubal, N.Y., c.1950, 4 x 4 1/2 In. 50.00

BOXES of all kinds are collected. They were made of thin strips of inlaid wood, metal, tortoiseshell, embroidery, or other material. Additional boxes may be listed in other sections, such as Advertising, Battersea, Ivory, Shaker, Tinware, and various Porcelain categories. Tea Caddies are listed in their own category.

Apothecary, Mahogany, Drop Handle, Brass Mounted, 2 Hinged Lids, 6 x 12 3/4 x 9 In. 259.00
Art Deco, Porcelain & Bronze, Circular, Hinged Lid, France, c.1930, 4 1/2 x 5 In. 526.00
Arts & Crafts, Applied Metal Design, Green Stones, 9 3/4 x 4 In. 540.00
Ballot, Wood, Dovetailed, Iron Latch, Wire Hinges, Worn Paint, 5 1/4 x 10 x 5 1/4 In. 66.00
Band, Bentwood, Green Over Blue Paint, Tacks, Pine, 3 5/8 x 8 In. 248.00
Band, Bentwood, Painted, Flowers, Children, Swans, GMK, 8 x 18 x 11 In. . . . . *illus* 725.00
Band, Oak, Red Paint, Pine Lid, Tapered Lap Joint, Rope Handle, 8 x 9 1/4 In. 357.00
Band, Oval, Brown Paint, Tapered Lap Joints, 1 3/4 x 5 x 3 3/4 In. 330.00
Band, Oval, Green Over Blue Paint, Tapered Lap Joints, 3 1/2 x 9 1/2 x 6 3/4 In. 660.00
Band, Oval, Green Paint, Tapered Lap Joints, Tack, 1 1/2 x 4 x 2 3/4 In. 385.00
Band, Oval, Lily, Painted, Paper Cover, Diamond Pattern, 1800s, 4 3/4 x 8 1/4 In. 705.00
Band, Oval, Painted Flowers, Children, Swans, Bentwood, Spruce, Laced Joint, 8 x 19 In. 748.00
Band, Oval, Red Paint, Tapered Lap Joints, Tack, Carved, AM, 4 3/8 x 11 1/2 x 8 In. 413.00
Band, Oval, Wallpaper, American, 19th Century, 6 x 9 1/2 x 11 1/2 In. 154.00
Band, Oval, Wallpaper, Flowers, Blue Ground, German Newspaper Lined, 5 x 8 x 6 In. 4125.00
Band, Oval, Wallpaper, Flowers, Geometrics, German Newspaper Lined, 4 x 8 x 5 In. . . . . *illus* 440.00
Band, Oval, Wallpaper, Flowers, Geometrics, Orange, Black, Blue, German Newspaper, 4 x 8 x 5 In. . 770.00
Band, Oval, Wallpaper, Fruit Basket, Leaves, Hannah Davis, N.H., 12 x 18 In. 1645.00
Band, Oval, Wallpaper, Leaves, Green, White, Gray, German Newspaper, 2 1/4 x 4 1/2 x 3 1/4 In. . . 303.00
Band, Oval, Wallpaper, Wooded Landscape, Cardboard, 1800s, 12 x 15 In. 259.00
Band, Oval, Wallpaper, Yellow, Birds, Flowers, Hannah Davis, N.H., 7 x 12 In. 1410.00
Band, Oval, Wood, Tapered Lap Joints, 1 1/2 x 3 1/2 x 2 In. 55.00
Band, Painted, Gray, Carved Wood Hinges, Pine Lid, 7 1/2 x 12 In. 248.00
Band, Painted, Green, Copper Nails, Bail Handle, 7 x 11 1/2 In. 330.00
Band, Pine, Ash, Blue Paint, Stamped, J. Hill, A Sprague, F.H. Market, 3 x 6 3/4 In. 660.00
Band, Pine, Bentwood, Gray Paint, Pegged Fastener, Wood Handle, 6 1/2 x 9 In. 330.00
Band, Poplar, Gray Paint, Handle, 5 1/4 x 7 1/2 In. 467.00
Band, Wallpaper, Animals, Embossed, Gold Flowers, Softwood, Tin Hinges, Lid, 3 x 6 7/8 x 4 In. 110.00
Band, Wallpaper, Building, Flowers, Trees, Red, Green, White Varnish, 1880, 5 3/4 In. 765.00
Band, Wallpaper, Castle Garden, Lid, c.1840, 10 1/2 x 15 1/2 x 11 1/2 In. 696.00
Band, Wallpaper, Castles & Mill, Lid, c.1835, 11 1/2 x 18 1/2 x 16 In. 580.00
Band, Wallpaper, Chicken On Lid, Brown Painted Clay Chicken, Geometrics, 5 x 3 x 3 In. 275.00
Band, Wallpaper, Coach Scene, Yellow, Green, Red Varnish, c.1840, 12 x 17 In. 588.00
Band, Wallpaper, Empire Garden Scene, Lid, 12 1/2 x 16 x 12 3/4 In. 464.00
Band, Wallpaper, Flowers, Geometrics, Blue, Tin Hasp & Hinge, Dome Lid, 6 x 13 x 8 In. 275.00
Band, Wallpaper, Flowers, Partial Bird, Blue Ground, German Newspaper, 4 x 5 3/4 In. 468.00
Band, Wallpaper, Garden Temple & Fountain, Lid, c.1835, 12 x 19 1/2 x 15 1/2 In. 1276.00
Band, Wallpaper, Geometrics, Green & Brown, Woman On Lid, 4 1/4 x 6 3/4 In. 165.00
Band, Wallpaper, Merchant's Exchange, Lid, c.1842, 12 x 18 x 14 In. 290.00
Band, Wallpaper, Purple Flowers, Blue Ground, 5 x 4 1/2 In. 440.00
Band, Wallpaper, Steam Locomotive, Lid, c.1835, 11 1/2 x 17 1/2 x 14 1/4 In. 812.00
Band, Wallpaper, Yellow Bird On Swing, Garlands, Sapphire Paper, Oblong, 17 In. 4200.00
Band, Wood, Oval, Red & Green Pinstripes, 15 x 20 In. 638.00
Basswood, Red Paint, Stenciled, Wallpaper Design, Flowers, Vermont, c.1810, 6 x 14 In. 12000.00
Beekeeper's, Poplar, Slide Lid, Leather Strap, Canisters, Glass Storage Boxes, 4 x 7 x 11 In. . . 88.00
Bentwood, Oval, Pine, Laced, Pinned, Transfer Decorated Top, Tulips, Leaves, 7 x 20 In. 150.00
Bentwood, Pine, Tulip, Dot, Laced, Pinned, Painted, Salmon Ground, 5 x 16 3/4 In. 374.00

Box, Band, Bentwood, Painted, Flowers, Children, Swans, GMK, 8 x 18 x 11 In.
$725.00

Box, Band, Oval, Wallpaper, Flowers, Geometrics, German Newspaper Lined, 4 x 8 x 5 In.
$440.00

Box, Blue Paint, Unicorns, Urn, Flowers, Late 19th Century, 11 x 28 x 13 In.
$115.00

Box, Candle, Pine, Dovetailed, Slide Lid, Mid 19th Century, 5 x 9 x 6 In.
$230.00

SECURITY TIP

The first place a burglar looks for valuables is in the bedroom. A better choice is in your garage or freezer.

Box, Cane, Cut Glass, Cranberry Stained, Gilt Brass Mounted, France, c.1900, 5 x 5 x 3 ½ In.
$1320.00

Box, Cutlery, Pine, Green & Yellow Design, New England, 1800s, 6 x 11 x 9 In.
$625.00

Box, Dovetailed, Smoke Design, Green Ground, Dome Top, 1800s, 10 x 28 x 13 ¾ In.
$510.00

Box, Figural, Sandals, Hardwood, Ivory Soles, Mother-Of-Pearl Inlay, 1800s, 3 x 5 In., Pair
$196.00

TIP

To untie knots in ribbons, shoelaces, or necklaces, sprinkle a little talcum power on them.

Bentwood, Round, Painted, Checkerboard Lid, 19th Century, 5 ½ x 8 In. ... 3000.00
Bible, Brass, Inscribed, A & C, 1733, 18th Century ... 650.00
Bible, Dovetailed, Snipe Hinges, Square Nails, Inlaid Hearts, 18th Century ... 1650.00
Bible, English Oak, 1-Board Lid, Iron Strap Hinges, Fluted Frieze, 1700s, 7 x 20 x 13 In. ... 489.00
Bible, Lift Lid, Bat Wing Brass Escutcheon, 2 Drawers, Yellow Pine, Dovetailed, 12 x 20 In. ... 3220.00
Bible, Red Paint, Snipe Hinges, Rosehead Nails, New England, 8 ½ x 19 In. ... 6670.00
Bird's-Eye Maple, School Girl, Landscape, Shells, Flowers, Beehive, 14 In. ... 928.00
Bird's-Eye Maple, Velvet Top, Floral Theorem, 15 ½ In. ... 406.00
Black Lacquer, Octagonal, Game Pieces, Cards, Trays, Chinese, 5 x 15 x 12 In. ... 1440.00
Blue Paint, Lighthouse, American Flag, Landscape, Oval 4 ½ x 14 In. ... 464.00
Blue Paint, Unicorns, Urn, Flowers, Late 19th Century, 11 x 28 x 13 In. ... *illus* 115.00
Book Shape, Carved, 2 Book Stack, Green Paint, Drilled Hole In Pages, 7 x 11 In. ... 173.00
Boullework, Brass, Tortoiseshell, Arabesque Design, Brass Feet, 1800s, 4 ½ x 7 In. ... 676.00
Brass, Hinged Lid, Applied Chinese Motifs, Handle, 19th Century, 7 ½ x 17 In. ... 6378.00
Bride's, Bentwood, Building, Flowers, Leaves, Continental, 19th Century, 7 x 19 In. ... 800.00
Bronze, Flowers, Wood Interior, Germany, 2 x 3 x 5 In. ... 292.00
Bronze, Silver, Clamshell, Turkey, 3 ¾ x 6 ½ x 2 ½ In. ... 1500.00
Burl, Satinwood, England, 19th Century, 3 ½ x 2 ¼ x 2 In. ... 323.00
Burl, Silver Inlay, Fitted Lid, Round, 2 ⅛ x 4 ¼ In. ... 288.00
Candle, Brass, Lions, Shield, Eagle, Spread Wings, Pressed, Hinged Lid, 8 x 10 x 4 In. ... 230.00
Candle, Carved Finger Pull, Dark Stain, Slide Lid, 3 ¼ x 17 x 3 ⅝ In. ... 33.00
Candle, Curly Maple, Chip Carved Pinwheels, Scrolled Top Edge, 13 x 7 x 5 In. ... 862.00
Candle, Hanging, Pine, Triple Lobed Crest, Chamfered Base, 10 x 13 x 6 In. ... 403.00
Candle, Hanging, Pine, Yellow, Red Grain, Lid, Leather Hinges, 23 x 12 In. ... 11500.00
Candle, Mahogany, Satinwood, Figured, c.1800, 21 ¼ x 7 x 5 In. ... 353.00
Candle, Pine, Black, Red Grain Paint, Dovetailed, Cutout Back, Slant Lid, 14 x 14 x 9 In. ... 460.00
Candle, Pine, Dovetailed, Cut Nail, Slide Lid, 5 ½ x 9 x 6 ¼ In. ... 230.00
Candle, Pine, Dovetailed, Cutout Back, Painted, Black, Red, Slant Lid, 14 x 14 x 9 In. ... 460.00
Candle, Pine, Dovetailed, Slide Lid, Mid 19th Century, 5 x 9 x 6 In. ... *illus* 230.00
Candle, Red Paint, Dovetailed, Gouged Finger Pull, 6 ½ x 14 ½ x 6 ⅞ In. ... 176.00
Candle, Red Paint, Scalloped Top, Early American, 13 In. ... 870.00
Candle, Red Paint, Slide Lid, 19th Century, 4 x 12 In. ... 195.00
Candle, Wood, Grain Paint, Dovetailed, Slide Lid, c.1830, 7 x 10 ¾ In. ... 375.00
Cane, Cut Glass, Cranberry Stained, Gilt Brass Mounted, France, c.1900, 5 x 5 x 3 ½ In. . *illus* 1320.00
Carved, Walnut, Pine, Carved Heart, Diamond Corners, Hinged Beveled Edge Lid, 5 x 13 In. . 144.00
Case A Liqueurs, 4 Hollow Book Stacks Shape, Leather, Glass Decanter, 5 x 7 In. ... 840.00
Chinese, Brass, Enamel, Scenic, 3 Men On Lid, Flower Sides, c.1900, 2 x 4 In. ... 82.00
Cigarette, Brass, Enameled, Signed, c.1960, 1 ¼ x 7 In. ... 23.00
Cigarette, Lute, Red, Brown, Pearly Enamel, Gold Luster, Flip Lid ... 70.00
Coffer, Lockbox, Iron Mounted, Clad, Blue Design, Triple Lock, 22 x 42 In. ... 1380.00
Coffin Shape, School Girl, Brass Handles & Feet, New England, 8 ½ In. ... 232.00
Collar, Elk Lid, Ruby Satin Interior, Celluloid, Embossed, Brass Clasp, 6 x 7 x 8 In. ... 80.00
Collar, Woman, Holding Lamp, Serpentine Front, Fabric Sides, Celluloid, 1890s, 6 x 7 x 7 In.. 475.00
Cosmetic, Tortoiseshell Inset, Jade Panel, Filigree Sides, Chinese, 19th Century, 3 In. ... 705.00
Cutlery, Pine, Green & Yellow Design, New England, 1800s, 6 x 11 x 9 In. ... *illus* 625.00
Cutlery, Pine, Painted, Green & Yellow, New England, 19th Century, 6 ½ x 12 In. ... 633.00
Cutlery, Wood, Ebonized, Carved, Rosette Medallions, Hinged Lid, 5 ½ x 17 In. ... 295.00
Damascus Wood, Mother-Of-Pearl, Medallion Centers, Footed, Hinged Lid, 6 x 10 x 7 In. ... 385.00
Decanter, Mahogany, Brass Mounted, Drop Handles, Hinged Lid, George III, 12 x 16 x 12 In.. 115.00
Desk, Black Lacquer, Gilt, Oblong, Octagonal, Chinese, 8 x 14 ½ x 12 In. ... 900.00
Desk, Bronze, Silver, Gold, Engraved, Clamshell Opening, Turkey, 3 ¾ x 6 ½ x 2 In. ... 1680.00
Desk, Burl, Walnut, Fitted Interior, Glass Inkwells, Hidden Compartment, Victorian ... 440.00
Desk, Burl Walnut, Regency, Ebony Inlaid, Sarcophagus, Handles, Lid, 14 x 10 x 11 In. ... 1058.00
Desk, Lacquer, Gold, Oblong, Lakeside Pavilions, 2 Colors, Gilt, 5 ¼ x 10 x 7 In. ... 1188.00
Desk, Mahogany, Cylinder Roll, Bracket Base, 23 x 7 ¼ x 9 ¼ In. ... 105.00
Desk, Mandarins, Japanned, Decoupaged, Octagonal, Bail Handle, 10 ½ x 16 In. ... 900.00
Desk, Tunbridge, Peasants At Market, Flower Wreath, Victorian, 5 x 16 ¾ x 12 ¼ In. ... 1175.00
Dish, Walnut, Carved, Presentation, Iris, Berry Clusters, Princess Of Wales, c.1875, 4 x 12 In.. 240.00
Ditty, Abalone, Baleen, Inlaid, Diamonds, Stars, Mother-Of-Pearl, Oval, Fitted Lid, 3 x 7 In. .. 3000.00
Document, Black Lacquer, Metal Inlay, Geometrics, Handles, Japan, c.1920, 3 x 11 In. ... 276.00
Document, Brown Hide Covering, Studs, Wallpaper Interior, 6 x 12 x 7 In. ... 230.00
Document, Burl Walnut, Sloped Front, Arched Panel, Fitted Interior, 1800s, 15 In. ... 470.00
Document, Cherry, Oval Inlaid Glass, Squat Ball Feet, Lift Lid, 4 ¾ x 10 ¾ x 10 In. ... 358.00
Document, Curly Maple, Chestnut, Applied Molding, Rhode Island, c.1820, 7 x 13 In. ... 920.00
Document, Curly Maple, Dovetailed, Lock, Key, Brass Ring Pull, Early 1800s, 12 x 7 In. ... 196.00
Document, Hardwood, Carved, Wrought Iron Mounted, Footed, Spanish, 8 x 17 In. ... 240.00

Document, Mahogany, Sarcophagus Shape, Wild Cat Attacking Snake, 18 x 18 In. 2478.00
Document, Oak, Dovetailed, White, Strap Hinges, 18th Century 295.00
Document, Peafowl, Flowers, Lock, Wire Handle, Dome Lid, 9 ¼ x 5 In. 358.00
Document, Pine, Mahogany Grain Paint, Brass Pull, 19th Century, 7 x 15 In. 144.00
Document, Pine, Mustard, Green, Brown, Grain Paint, Banded, Maine, 7 x 18 x 10 In. 288.00
Document, Pine, Poplar, Red & Black Grain Paint, Applied Molding, 15 x 7 In. 173.00
Document, Pinstriped, Asian Figures, Decoupage, Dome Lid, 19th Century, 12 x 8 In. 303.00
Document, Red Paint, Pinwheels, Quarter Round Designs, Brass Rosettes, 13 x 8 x 6 In. 1438.00
Document, Walnut, Brass Handle, Molded Base, Hinged Lid, 6 x 11 x 7 In. 110.00
Document, Walnut, Carved, Europe, 19th Century, 7 ½ x 15 ½ x 9 In. 585.00
Document, Wood, Grain Paint, Brass Hardware, Key, 9 ½ In. 1650.00
Document, Wood, Tiger Maple, Hinged Cover, Dovetailed, Lock, c.1850, 7 ¾ x 10 In. 900.00
Dome Top, Flowers, c.1830, 28 In. 2850.00
Dome Top, Putty Painted, Mustard, Green, Compass Flower, Vermont, 15 x 17 x 17 In. 1528.00
Doves, Micro Mosaic, Ball Feet, 19th Century, 5 ½ In. 2070.00
Dovetailed, Brass Handle, Green Paint, Hinged Cover, 6 x 15 ½ x 6 ¼ In. 230.00
Dovetailed, Iron Mounts, Green Paint, Paper Lined Interior, 9 ½ x 23 In. 104.00
Dovetailed, Red Stain, Paneled, Drawer, Slide Lid, 5 ½ x 11 ⅓ x 6 ¼ In. 385.00
Dovetailed, Smoke Design, Green Ground, Dome Top, 1800s, 10 x 28 x 13 ¾ In. .... *illus* 510.00
Dresser, Blue Glass, Enamel, White Flowers, Swags, Silver Plated Rim, 3 x 4 In. 144.00
Dresser, Lacquer, Black, Brown Ground, Gilt Landscape, Chinese, 4 ½ x 12 x 9 In. 354.00
Dresser, Mahogany, Cock-Beaded Drawer, Bail Pull, England, 6 ¾ x 14 ¼ In. 420.00
Dresser, Malachite, Empire Style, Ormolu Mount, Mirror, Lift Lid, 1800s, 14 In. 5290.00
Dresser, Porcelain, Sevres Style, Courting Couple, Gilt Swags, Cobalt Blue, Oval, 8 In. 353.00
Dressing Table, Burl, Holly Inlay, Mother-Of-Pearl, Paper Lined, 1 ½ x 4 ½ In. 150.00
Enamel, Amalfi Coast Harbor, Fishermen, Temple, Grotto, Seed Pearls, 3 ⅝ x 2 x ⅝ In. 12925.00
Figural, Sandals, Hardwood, Ivory Soles, Mother-Of-Pearl Inlay, 1800s, 3 x 5 In., Pair .. *illus* 196.00
Figural, Snapping Turtle, Cast Iron, 5 ¼ In. 225.00
Games, Black Lacquer, Gilded, Octagonal, 7 Compartments, Chinese, 5 ½ x 15 In. 1440.00
Games, Gilded, Black Lacquer, Red Lacquer Accent, Chinese, 5 x 16 In. 2160.00
Gem Set, 14K Gold, Girl Raising Monkey, Opal, Peridot, Onyx, Amethyst, 3 x 2 x ¾ In. 3055.00
Georgian, Mahogany, 8-Sided, Brass Lock, Handles, Lift Lid, Britain, 1800s, 20 x 21 x 20 In. .. 850.00
Glove, Bird's-Eye Maple, Nickel Mounted, Pietra Dura, Phoenician Purple Lacquer, 3 x 11 In. 390.00
Glove, Flowers, Carved, False Band, Screw Heads, Brass Hinge, Lock, Black, 3 x 11 x 4 In. 11.00
Hanging, Pine, Red Paint, 2 Drawers, Lollipop Handle, 14 x 9 x 8 In. 288.00
Hanging, Softwood, Arched Crest, Red Striping, Olive Ground, 1800s, 8 ¾ x 20 In. 575.00
Hat, New York City Scene, Washington Bridge, Hudson River, Late 1800s, 8 x 20 In. 1500.00
Hide, Lined Interior, Printed Wallpaper, Key, c.1800, 3 x 6 x 4 In. 546.00
Hide, Painted, Traditional Scenes, Hand Stitched, Brass Handles, Chinese, 1800s, 8 x 17 In. .. 450.00
Hinged Lid, Applied Print, Men, Dancing Lady, Art Nouveau, Wood, Gesso 146.00
Honor, Tobacco, Tavern, Brass, Bun Feet, 2 Compartments, Coin Slot, Georgia, 9 x 4 In. 230.00
Incense, Child, Emblems, Famille Rose, Bell Shaped Lid, Chinese, 20th Century 118.00
Incense, Lacquer, Black & Gold, Exotic Fish, Orchids, Japanese, 3 ¾ x 5 ½ In. 150.00
Iron, Arts & Crafts, Incised, Bun Feet, Handle, Samuel Yellin, 1922, 4 ½ x 6 x 4 In. 42920.00
Ivory, Malachite, Wood, Inlaid Chinese Figures, 2 x 5 In. 118.00
Jewel Casket, Mandarin's Garden, Gilded Claret Color, Tray, Velvet Lining, Chinese, 10 x 7 In. 1560.00
Jewelry, Anglo-Indian, Tortoiseshell, Silver Mounted, Navette Shape, Silk Lining, 1 ¼ x 5 In. .. 1920.00
Jewelry, Animals, Geometrics, Inlay, 2 Trays, Turned Feet, c.1875, 7 ¾ x 12 x 8 In. 450.00
Jewelry, Brass, Bronze Patinated, Lindenwood, Oak, Edwardian, Man's, 8 x 12 x 9 In. 1080.00
Jewelry, Brass, Gilt, Beveled Glass, Swinging Mirror, 19th Century, 8 ¾ x 6 In. 231.00
Jewelry, Brass, Mahogany, Moroccan Tray, 3 ½ x 11 x 6 ½ In. 540.00
Jewelry, Brass, Woman's Portrait, Enamel, Wreath, Ball Feet, Hinged Lid, 3 x 7 x 5 In. 690.00
Jewelry, Brass Mounted, Mahogany Inlaid, Drawers, Continental, Man's, 5 x 12 x 8 In. 600.00
Jewelry, French Cut Crystal, Bronze Handle, 5 x 6 x 4 In. 468.00
Jewelry, Glass, Blue, Paneled, Silver Plated, Flowers, Vine, Cover, 4 ½ x 3 ½ In. 448.00
Jewelry, Indo-Persian, Zebra Wood, Drop-In Trays, Ivory Inlaid Lid, 1800s, 6 x 15 In. 500.00
Jewelry, Kingwood, Marquetry, Shaped Sides, Paneled Lid, Gilt Brass Bands & Feet, 5 x 11 In. 900.00
Jewelry, Mahogany, Carved, Applied Flower, Germany, c.1880-90, 3 ½ x 6 x 4 In. 84.00
Jewelry, Mahogany, Piano Form, Carved, England, Late 1800s, 5 x 4 x 9 In. 470.00
Jewelry, Regency, Black & Ivory Penwork, Priest & Vestals, Scrolls, Octagonal, 3 x 8 x 6 In. .. 570.00
Jewelry, Rose Design, Grain Paint, Yellow Pinstripe, Ball Feet, 13 x 8 x 4 In. 230.00
Jewelry, Rosewood, Brass, Chinese, c.1920, 7 x 5 x 1 ½ In. 88.00
Jewelry, Rosewood, Footed, Brass Mounted, Escutcheon, Korea, 9 ¾ x 14 In. 70.00
Jewelry, Rosewood, Walnut, Basswood, Inlaid, Velvet Lined, Mirror, c.1920, 5 x 9 x 5 In. 225.00
Jewelry, Round, Hinges, Scroll Mold, Blue, Yellow, 2 Cherubs, Pink Blossom, 3 x 5 In. 275.00
Jewelry, Sterling Silver, Pincushion, Concave Sides, George III, c.1794, 3 ¼ x 5 In. 764.00

TIP
Keep mousetraps, rat poison, and bug poison in the attic if you store antique furniture or textiles there.

Box, Knife, Georgian, Mahogany, Serpentine Front, Inlaid Stars, 14 x 9 x 10 In.
$345.00

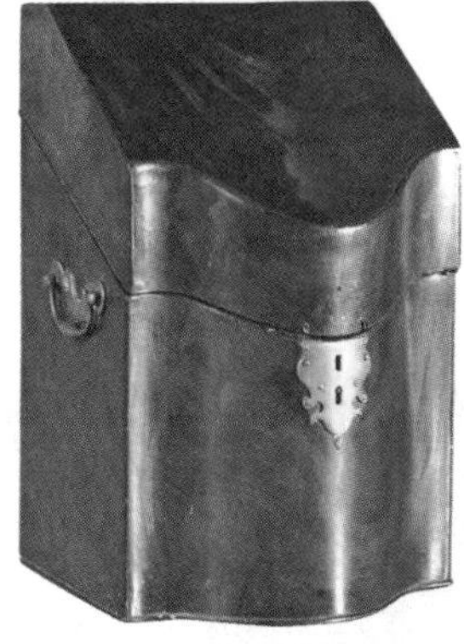

Box, Lacquer, Iron Red & Gilt Exterior, Flowers, Pagodas, Lift Top, Drawer, 5 x 14 In.
$259.00

Box, Needlework, Organic Design, Wood, Inlay, Stand, Galle, 29 x 23 x 12 ½ In.
$4800.00

B

Box, Oak, Lift-Up Lid, Wall, Britain, 19th Century, 16 x 6 x 4 In.
$230.00

Box, Pine, Flowers, Green, White Stripes, 8½ x 13½ x 9½ In.
$518.00

Box, Pine, Grain Paint, Iron Lock, Strap Hinges, c.1910, 12 x 25 x 16 In.
$230.00

Box, Poplar, Dovetailed, Painted, Stars, Lancaster County, 1800-40, 5 x 6¾ x 4 In.
$34000.00

Knife, Cherry, Dovetailed, Splayed Side, Shaped Ends, Arched Divider, Red Wash, 5½ x 12¾ In. 489.00
Knife, Chippendale Style, Federal, Mahogany, Inlaid Leaf, Slant Lid, 1800s, 14 x 9 x 7 In. 517.00
Knife, Crotch Mahogany, Inlaid, Ebony, Serpentine Front, Slant Lid, c.1820, 14 x 11 In. 644.00
Knife, George III, Inlaid Trim, Serpentine Front, Mahogany Veneer, Slant Lid, 8 x 11 In. 575.00
Knife, George III, Mahogany, Band Inlay, Fitted Interior, c.1780, 8¾ x 11 In. 822.00
Knife, George III, Mahogany, Inlaid, Sloped Lid, Fan & Serpentine Front, 14 In. 705.00
Knife, Georgian, Mahogany, Serpentine Front, Inlaid Stars, 14 x 9 x 10 In. *illus* 345.00
Knife, Georgian, Mahogany, Serpentine Front, Satinwood Flowers, 14 x 9 In., Pair 4800.00
Knife, Hepplewhite, Mahogany, Inlaid Conch Shell, Serpentine, c.1800, 14 x 9 x 12 In., Pair 4313.00
Knife, Mahogany, Inlaid, Serpentine, Banding, Salesman's Sample, c.1920, 3 In., Pair 2588.00
Knife, Mahogany, Satinwood, Georgian, c.1800, 14½ x 9 x 10 In. 705.00
Knife, Mahogany Veneer, Inlaid Urn, Star Inlay, Hinged Sloped Lid, 14¼ x 9 In. 282.00
Knife, Pine, Vinegar Grained Paint, Flaring Sides, Shaped Center Divider, 5 x 11 In. 431.00
Knife, Shagreen Exterior, Brass Hardware, England, Late 18th Century, 12¼ In. 1685.00
Knife, Sheraton, Fitted Interior, Inlaid Conch Shell On Lid, c.1820, 15 x 9 In. 770.00
Knife, Sheraton, Fitted Interior, Inlaid Conch Shell On Lid, c.1820, 16 x 10 In. 660.00
Lacquer, 2 Tiers, Fan Shape, Butterfly, Leaves, Hashiji Interior, Japan, 5 x 2¾ In. 561.00
Lacquer, Birds, Flowers, Gold, Rectangular, Inner Tray, Gilt, Japan, 5½ x 8¾ In. 1093.00
Lacquer, Black Ground, Maki-E Decoration, Landscape, Moon, Japan, c.1912, 4 x 4 In. 480.00
Lacquer, Iron Red & Gilt Exterior, Flowers, Pagodas, Lift Top, Drawer, 5 x 14 In. *illus* 259.00
Lacquer, Mandarin's Garden, Lift-Out Tray, 2 Colors, Gilt, Dome Top, 4 x 11 x 5 In. 1452.00
Lacquer, Metallic, Dianthus Flowers, Gold, Black Interior, Japan, 4¼ x 4½ In. 240.00
Leather, Cutouts, Heart, Star, Multicolored, White Stitching, Hinged Lid, 4 x 8 x 5 In. 1175.00
Leather, Painted, Tack Design, Removable Tray, Hinged Lid, 5¼ x 14 In. 546.00
Letter, Brass, Dutch, 5½ x 9 x 3¾ In. 206.00
Letter, Brass Mounted, Serpentine Front, Applied Paw Feet, Early 19th Century, 12 In. 518.00
Letter, Ivory Lacquer, Metal Mounted, France, 4½ x 7½ x 5½ In. 575.00
Letter, Mahogany, Drop Handle, Brass Mounted, Keyhole, Hinged Lid, 5 x 10 x 6 In. 690.00
Letter, Mahogany, Oak, Brass Shield Inlay, Divided, Fall Front Lid, 11 x 15 x 8 In. 184.00
Letter, Persian Inlay Khatam, 17¾ x 12¾ In. 643.00
Liquor, Edwardian, White Brass Mounted, Rosewood, Oblong, 7¼ x 13½ x 7 In. 1452.00
Lock, Continental, Pine, Panels, Handle, Dark Varnish, Red Paint Trim, 13 x 23 x 15 In. 110.00
Louisiana Plantation, Porcelain De Paris, 2 x 4 x 3½ In. 59.00
Mahogany, Chippendale, Inlaid Branches, Herringbone Panel, Fitted, 7 x 12 x 6 In. 3480.00
Mahogany, Maple, Inlay, Hearts, Leaves, Fitted Interior, Ivory Pulls, c.1860, 8 x 17 In. 4800.00
Mahogany, Sea Chest Theme, Brass Butt Hinges, Applied Bracket, 5 x 12 x 6¾ In. 1210.00
Maple, Pine, Green Paint, Star, 2¾ x 5¾ In. 3055.00
Marquetry, Birds, Flowers Inlay, Japan, Late 19th Century, 14 x 11½ In. 323.00
Marquetry, Flowers, 4 Glass Bottles, c.1840, 8½ x 6¾ In. 293.00
Metal, Enameled Ship, Round, Patina, Frank J. Marshall, 4¾ x 2½ In. 1440.00
Mother-Of-Pearl, Inlaid Mahogany, Interior Fabric Liner, 6 x 13 x 9¼ In. 288.00
Notions, Paper Applique Design, Watercolor, Lid, George Lawton, 1800s, 3 x 8 In. 823.00
Needlework, Organic Design, Wood, Inlay, Stand, Galle, 29 x 23, 12½ In. *illus* 4800.00
Oak, Lift-Up Lid, Wall, Britain, 19th Century, 16 x 6 x 4 In. *illus* 230.00
Offering, Lacquer, Gilt, Burma, Early 20th Century, 30 x 13½ In. 472.00
Opaline, Blue, Canted Corners, Scrolled Bronze Rim, Garland Handles, 7 x 6 In. 2703.00
Painted, Brown, Blue Design, Hinged Dome Top, Moses Eaton, Ma., c.1830, 18 x 9 In. 6463.00
Painted, Design, Initials, C.M.C., 6½ x 18¼ In. 1440.00
Painted, Family, Rural Landscape, House, River, Ships, Dome Top, Hinged Lid, 9 x 20 x 10 In. 8225.00
Painted, Multicolored, Green, White Striping, Bail Handle, Dome Top, 8 x 13 In. 518.00
Painted, Potted Plant, Grain Design, Swag, Tassel Border, New England, 24 In. 1508.00
Painted, Smoke Decorated, Fitted Interior, 5 Drawers, Hinged Lid, Early 1800s, 8 x 17 x 8 In. 3819.00
Painted, Unicorns, Pennsylvania Dutch, Flower Urn, Dome Top, 1900s, 11 x 28 In. 115.00
Painter's, Pine, Signs, Portrait, Carnival Figures, Clown, Acrobat, Hinged Lid, 6 x 19 In. 7200.00
Pantry, Baleen, Circular, Pine, Pierced Bottom, Finger Joint, Stars, House, Tree, 4 x 6 In. 500.00
Pantry, Bentwood, Black Over Green Paint, Iron Nails, Round, 1800s, 23 x 9 In. 345.00
Pantry, Bentwood, Blue Paint, Lapped Seams, Iron Tacks, Round, 8⅛ x 4 In. 374.00
Pantry, Bentwood, Blue Paint, Splint Tied, Wood Peg, Lid, Round, 7¼ x 15 In. 198.00
Pantry, Bentwood, Brown Paint, Lapped Seams, Iron Tacks, Round, 1800s, 15 x 7¾ In. 460.00
Pantry, Bentwood, Green Paint, Lapped Seam, Steel Tacks, Round, 7 x 3⅛ In. 374.00
Pantry, Bentwood, Multicolored Scrolling Flowers, Green Ground, Lid, 1871, 16 In. 1652.00
Pantry, Bentwood, Orange Paint, Lapped Seams, Copper Tacks, Round, 1800s, 17 x 8 In. 805.00
Pantry, Bentwood, Red Paint, Lapped Seams, Iron Tacks, Oval, c.1900, 13 x 15 In. 489.00
Pantry, Bentwood, Salmon Paint, Iron Tacks, Square Nails, 1800s, 21¾ x 11½ In. 403.00
Pantry, Blue Paint, Lapped Seams, Copper Nails, 19th Century, 7¾ x 3 In. 690.00
Pantry, Green Paint, Rosewood Nails, Oblong, 18th Century 225.00

Pantry, Pine, Scrimshaw Scenes, Stars, Diamonds, House, Tree, 4 x 5¾ In. 560.00
Peach Shape, Silver, Chased, Repousse, Flying Cranes, Gilt Highlights, Chinese, 3 In........ 649.00
Pencil, Stylized Flowers, Leaves, Carved, Screw Hinge Puzzle Lock Lid, Dovetailed, 2 x 9 x 2 In. 2310.00
Pencil, Wood, Black, Gilt, England, c.1872, 7½ x 2 x 1½ In. 115.00
Pill, Flowers, Leaves, 1½ x 1½ In.. 86.00
Pill, Mosaic, Glass, Goldtone, Flowers, Blue Ground, 2 x ¾ In. 35.00
Pill, Mosaic, Goldtone, Flowers, Black Ground, 1 x ½ In................................ 25.00
Pill, Mosaic, Goldtone, Flowers, Red Ground, 1 x ¾ x ⅝ In............................... 28.00
Pine, Blue Paint, Hinged Lid, 19th Century, 5⅜ x 11⅝ In................................ 235.00
Pine, Brown, Tan Grain Paint, Iron Handles, Paper Lining, Dome Lid, Maine, 22 x 12 x 10 In. 230.00
Pine, Dovetailed, Molded Lid, Green Paint, Brass Pull, Bail, 1800s, 6½ x 12½ In. 460.00
Pine, Dovetailed, Open Till, Lock, Gilt Ornamental Design, c.1820, 14½ x 7 In............. 374.00
Pine, Dovetailed, Painted, Iron Handles, Latch, Early 19th Century, 12¼ x 30 In. 588.00
Pine, Flowers, Green, White Stripes, 8½ x 13½ x 9½ In. .... *illus* 518.00
Pine, Gouge Finger Pull, Patina, Slide Lid, 4¾ x 8¾ x 6¾ In........................... 66.00
Pine, Grain Paint, Iron Lock, Strap Hinges, c.1910, 12 x 25 x 16 In. .... *illus* 230.00
Pine, Gray, Brown Sponge & Feather Design, Dovetailed, Dome Top, 1800s, 9 x 20 x 10 In.... 140.00
Pine, Hide, Leather, Trim, Wrought Nail, Tack Decorated, Hinged Lid, 8 x 15 x 10 In. 633.00
Pine, Hide Cover, Brass Tacks, Nathan Neat, 6¾ x 12 x 8 In. 460.00
Pine, Hide Cover, Leather Trim, Cut Nail, Brass Tacks, Interior Wallpaper, 7 x 12 x 8 In...... 460.00
Pine, Joshua's Box, Gray Paint, Black Letters, Dome Top, New England, 11 x 27 x 13 In...... 2468.00
Pine, Leather, Dome Top, Sarah Gumbell, 18th Century Newspaper Liner, 11 x 6 x 4 In...... 750.00
Pine, Multicolored, Heart & Flower, White Ground, Dome Top, Early 1800s, 6 x 13 In. 294.00
Pine, Nails, Drill Hole Finger Pull, Paneled Slide Lid, 4¾ x 14¼ x 5¾ In. 110.00
Pine, Painted, Cotter Pin Hinges, Lidded Interior Compartments, c.1840, 8 x 14 In.......... 2280.00
Pine, Painted, Seaman, Woman, Martha Cahoon, Signed, 5¾ x 18¾ x 8½ In. 3819.00
Pine, Painted, Trees, Lapped Seam, Round, Lid, Early 1800s, 4 x 9 In.................... 3408.00
Pine, Painted, Tulips, Central Panel Lid, Figures, Scandinavia, 20th Century, 6 x 13 In. 403.00
Pine, Painted Vinegar Design, Square Nails, Dovetailed, Dome Top, 28 x 14 In. 1035.00
Pine, Red Brown Over Mustard, New England, Early 19th Century, 12 x 30 In............... 690.00
Pine, Red Paint, Dovetailed, Applied Molding, Bone Escutcheon, Slant Lid, 16 x 9 In. 633.00
Pine, Red Paint, Hinged Lid, 19th Century, 7¾ x 7¼ x 12¼ In.......................... 323.00
Pine, Smoke Decorated, Dovetailed, Green Ground, Dome Top, 1800s, 10 x 38 In........... 489.00
Pine, Stenciled Design, Blue, Gold, Dovetailed, Hinged, Iron Latch, 1800s, 10 x 28 In........ 600.00
Pine, Yellow, Grain Paint, 2 Drawers, Square Nails, Ogee Bracket Feet, 12 x 8 x 6 In........ 1045.00
Pipe, Mahogany, Figures, Tapered Sides, Scroll Carved, Pierced, Drawer, 16 x 5 In. 8400.00
Pipe, Mahogany, Tapered, Open Top, Footed, Shaped Back, Early 1800s, 16 x 4 In........... 287.00
Pipe, Pine, Drawer, 19th Century, 16½ x 5 x 4¼ In.................................. 2233.00
Pipe, Red & Black Paint, Drawer, New England, 21 In. 20880.00
Pipe, Red Paint, Drawer, 17½ In. 127.00
Pipe, Sheep On Molded Lid, Flower Panels, Base, Brown, Black Forest, 17 x 12 x 6 In........ 385.00
Pipe, Walnut, Scrolled Top, Fan Carved Drawer, c.1800, 18¾ x 4¾ x 4¼ In. 6463.00
Poker Chip, Oak, Insert, Chips, Arts & Crafts, 10 x 7 x 5½ In........................... 240.00
Poplar, Dovetailed, Blue Green Paint, Red Trim, Slide Lid, 6½ x 15 x 9½ In................ 209.00
Poplar, Dovetailed, Painted, Stars, Lancaster County, 1800-40, 5 x 6¾ x 4 In. .... *illus* 34000.00
Poplar, Painted, 6 Boards, Square Nail Construction, Handles, Lift-Off Lid, 11 x 25 In....... 230.00
Poplar, Red Paint, Square Nails, Opaque Finger Pull, Paneled Slide Lid, 5 x 14 x 6 In. 143.00
Porcelain, Sevres Style, Footed, Couple Fishing, Hand Painted, Early 1900, 5 x 9 In......... 588.00
Porcelain, Sevres Style, Painted Scenes, Cobalt Blue, Gilt Borders, Early 1900s, 2 x 4 In. 288.00
Pottery, Loop Handles, Ramona, Geometric Arches, Lid, Marked, 5 x 4 x 5 In. 600.00
Powder, Enamel, Round, Cover, Rustic Landscape, Women Reading Letter, c.1925, 4½ In.... 294.00
Receipts, Cast Iron, National Cash Register, 6½ x 6½ In. 57.00
Regency, Mahogany, Inlaid, Drawer, Splayed Legs, Hinged Cover, 24 x 14 x 11 In........... 940.00
Ring, Crystal, Brass, Footed, France, 2½ x 2 x 3 In.................................... 94.00
Sachet, Coquilla Nut, Reticulated Filigree Top, Screw Lid, India, 2¼ In.................. 525.00
Sachet, Coquilla Nut, Woman's Bust, Flowers, Monk Portraits, Pedestal, c.1800, 5 x 2 In..... 900.00
Saffron, Wood, Turned, Black & Red Paint, 19th Century, 5 x 3⅜ In. .... *illus* 187.00
Salt, Wall, Wood, Red Paint, Dovetailed, Drawer, Hinged Lid, Scroll Design, Ed Scholl, 14 x 11 x 8 In. 330.00
Sardine, Fishing Scenes, Sutherland Lavender Lustre, c.1820, 6 x 4 In. 822.00
School Girl, Painted, New England, 10½ In.. 348.00
Shark Skin, Brass Swan Neck Handle, Blue Silk Cushioned Interior, 4¼ x 16 In. 359.00
Silver, Wang Hing, Writhing Dragon Stamp, Early 20th Century, 6½ In.................... 1116.00
Stenciled Grapevine, Green & Red Paint, New England, 6 x 13½ In..................... 1044.00
Storage, Hoopskirt, Bentwood, Paper Liner, 19th Century, 22½ x 10 In................... 850.00
Storage, Oak, Dovetailed, Pinned, Painted, Green, Landscape, Slide Lid, 4 x 21 x 10 In. 207.00
Storage, Pine, Dome Top, Painted, Fruit, Flowers, Vignettes Of Ships, 9 x 20 x 10 In......... 232.00
Straw, Napoleonic, Sections, c.1790, 2¼ x 7½ x 4¾ In................................ 118.00

Box, Saffron, Wood, Turned, Black & Red Paint, 19th Century, 5 x 3⅜ In.
$187.00

Box, Wall, 8 Drawers, Arched Scrolled Top, Gray Paint, c.1910, 17 x 10 x 5 In.
$330.00

Box, Wall, Poplar, Angled Open Pocket, 11 x 6 x 3 In.
$165.00

Boy Scout, Badge, First National Jamboree, Washington, D.C., 1937, Celluloid, 1 In.
$139.00

Boy Scout, Button, Scoutorama, Ticket Salesman, April 20, 21, 22, c.1930, ⅞ In.
$45.00

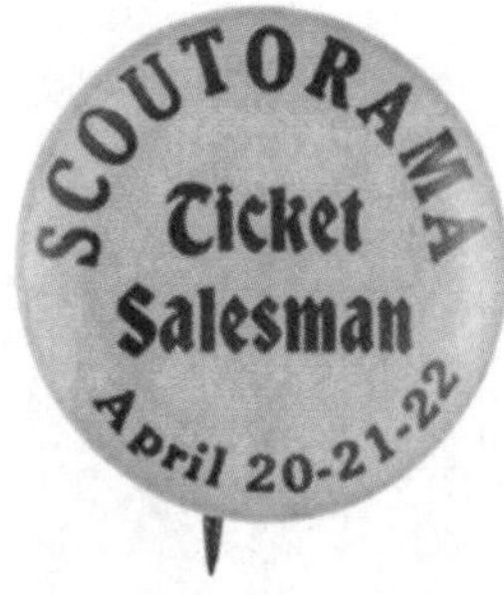

Bradley & Hubbard, Desk Set, Tree Of Life, Brass, Gilt, c.1910, 8 Piece
$125.00

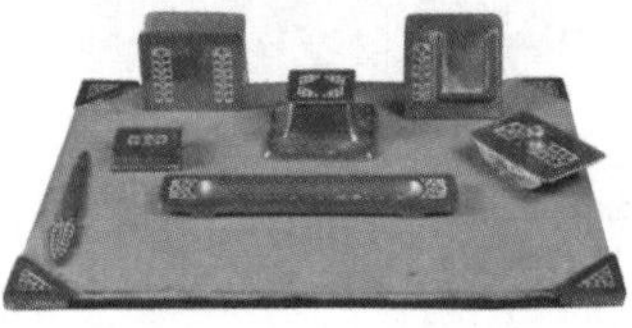

Bradley & Hubbard, Lamp, Leaves, 8 Panels, Painted Satin Glass, Frosted, Relief Molded, 15-In. Shade
$305.00

Tinder, Slanted Lift Lid, Brass Strap, Arts & Crafts, 32 x 18 x 17½ In. 780.00
Tobacco, Brass, Copper, Military Views, Base Stamped, Ember Tongs, 6 In. 232.00
Tobacco, Brass, Double Lids, Engraved, Oval, c.1750, 4 In 5100.00
Tobacco, Brass, Hinges, Compartments, Coin Slot, Plunger, George III, 7 x 9¾ In. 325.00
Tobacco, Brass, Tavern Scenes, Oval, Engraved, 4½ x 1½ In. 470.00
Tobacco, Iron, Chinese Design, Bracket Feet, Wire Inlay Lid, Korea, 3 x 5⅞ x 4 In. 330.00
Tobacco, Punch Design On Lid, c.1760 . . . . 250.00
Tobacco, Salt Glazed, Damper, Leaf Handles, England, 5 x 4½ x 3 In. 1150.00
Top Hat, Furrier & Bean, Belfast, Maine, Blue Paper Covered, Oval, 9 x 13 In. 940.00
Travel Case, Cartier, Blue Leather, Gold Plate Mounted, c.1900, 8 x 20 x 13 In. 1880.00
Travel Case, Walnut, Blue Velvet Liner, England, Mid 1800s, 6 x 8 x 12 In. 705.00
Tunbridge, Marquetry, Cubes, Marbled Paper Interior, Square, Lid, England, 4¾ In. 270.00
Utensil, Softwood, 2 Compartments, Handle, White Ground, Yellow Grain & Comb, 5 x 13 x 8 In. 220.00
Utility, Center Divider Handle, Tapered Sides, 5 x 16 x 9 In. 44.00
Utility, Poplar, Gray Over Red Paint, Arched Sides, Handle Divider, 8½ x 13¾ x 9¾ In. 248.00
Vanity, Burl, Inlaid, Traveling, 2 Drawers, Ivory Knob Pulls, Easel Back Mirror, 10 x 8 In. 531.00
Vanity, Mahogany, Brass, Boulle, c.1840, 4 x 12¾ x 8 In. 88.00
Wagon, Conestoga, Wood, Iron Hardware, J-Shape Hinges, Rose Head Nails, 18 x 17 x 7 In. . . 1100.00
Wagon, Dovetailed, Wrought Iron Hanger, Stamped, A. Bissey, 5⅜ x 15¾ x 7¾ In. 22.00
Wall, 3 Tiers, Small Open Box Over 2 Large, Red Paint, Renfrew County, c.1860. . . . . 5500.00
Wall, 8 Drawers, Arched Scrolled Top, Gray Paint, c.1910, 17 x 10 x 5 In. . . . . *illus* 330.00
Wall, Pine, Dovetailed, Drawer, Shaped Backboard, Slant Lid, 1800s, 14 x 11 x 9 In. 300.00
Wall, Pine, Salmon Paint, Arched Top, 6 x 3½ x 2⅞ In. 220.00
Wall, Pine, Square Nails, 2 Shelves, Scalloped Crest, Yellow, Red Sponge, 18 x 14 x 6 In. 3190.00
Wall, Poplar, Angled Open Pocket, 11 x 6 x 3 In. . . . . *illus* 165.00
Wall, Red Paint, Lollipop Handle, Early American, 14 In. 522.00
Wall, Walnut, Brown Paint, Scroll Cut Top, Brass Hinges, 14 x 8 x 5½ In. 165.00
Walnut, Acorn Finial, Triangular Lid, Turned Feet, Varnish Finish, 4¾ x 5 x 3 In. 110.00
Walnut, Chip Carved, Geometrics, Circles, Brass Hinges, 3½ x 12½ x 5¾ In. 33.00
Walnut, Dovetailed, Center Divider, Molded Top, Base, Slide Lid, 4½ x 11½ x 6 In. 220.00
Walnut, Dovetailed, Peg Construction, Slide Lid, 4¼ x 12 x 5⅞ In. 176.00
Walnut, Dovetailed, Removable Tray, Hinged Lid, 6¾ x 15 x 8½ In. 77.00
Walnut, Green Paint Molding, Herringbone Inlay, Velvet Interior, 1⅝ x 6½ x 3⅜ In. 17.00
Whatnot, Copper, Enamel, Figures, Animals, Landscape, Cobalt Blue Ground, 5 x 5 x 5 In. . . 999.00
Wood, Brass Tooled Strapwork, Diamond Motif, Sliding Lid, India, 19th Century, 5 x 18 In. . . 299.00
Wood, Carved, Coat Of Arms On Sides & Top, c.1900, 9 x 15 x 7 In. 55.00
Wood, Carved, Peafowl Figures, Coffin Shape, Rotating Lid, Peacock, 3⅞ x 6 In. 206.00
Wood, Dome Top, Painted, Birds, Swags, Flowerpot, Tulips, Red, Yellow, Green, 12 x 13 In. . . . 403.00
Wood, Globular Body, Carved, Lotus Leaves, Flowers, Rat Curved In Leaf, Lid, 3 In. 570.00
Wood, Ivory, Malachite, Jade, Mother-Of-Pearl, Teak, Musicians, 2 x 5 x 3 In. 58.00
Wood, Mahogany, Carved Ferns, Sunflowers, Lift Lid, 24½ x 16½ x 16 In. 1320.00
Wood, Slant Side Top, Stylized Birds, Fruit, Flowers, Green Ground, 4½ x 9 x 5 In. 275.00
Wood, Stud Design, Wallpaper Interior, Hinged Lid, 4¾ x 10 x 6¾ In. 92.00
Wood, Water Bird & Pinecone Designs, Bronze Hinged, Austria, 3 x 4¼ In. 495.00
Writing, Brass, England, 3½ x 9 x 4¾ In. 176.00
Writing, Burl, Slant Front, England, 11¾ x 9½ x 6½ In. 212.00
Writing, Ivory, Brass, Pewter Inlay, Double Hinged Lid, Inkwell, Napoleon III, 5 x 9 x 5¼ In. . 863.00
Writing, Pine, Serpentine Front, Forged Hinges, Lift Lid, 19th Century, 10 x 15 In. 950.00
Writing, Queen Anne, Walnut, Slant Front, 8 Drawers, 13¼ x 19¾ x 13¼ In. 3190.00

BOY SCOUT collectibles include any material related to scouting, including patches, manuals, and uniforms. The Boy Scout movement in the United States started in 1910. The first Jamboree was held in 1937. Girl Scout items are listed under their own heading.

Armband, Emergency Service, Explorer, 3 x 5 In. 13.00
Badge, First National Jamboree, Washington, D.C., 1937, Celluloid, 1 In. . . . . *illus* 139.00
Belt Buckle, Brass, Anchor On Back, 1½ x 2¼ In. 35.00
Book, Boy Scouts In The North Sea, Mystery Of A Sub, M.A. Donohue & Co., c.1915. . . . . 7.00
Book, Great Hike, Or Pride Of The Khaki Troop, c.1913 . . . . 18.00
Book, Lucky, The Boy Scout, E. Sherwood, Racine, Wis., c.1916 . . . . 29.00
Book, Merit Badge, My First Stamp Album, Stamp Identifier, 1952. . . . . 19.00
Book, Old Superior Or Tale Of The Pictured Rocks, G. Harvey Ralphson, c.1913. . . . . 17.00
Button, Scoutorama, Ticket Salesman, April 20, 21, 22, c.1930, ⅞ In. . . . . *illus* 45.00
Canteen, Boy Scout, Green Canvas Sack, Emblem, Aluminum. 24.00
Display, Nautical Knot, Frame, 13¾ x 9¾ In. 43.00
Drum, Drumsticks, Scouts Having Rifle Practice, Buglers, Tin, Graphics, Early 1900s. 225.00

First Aid Kit, Tin, Leather Pouch, 1928 .... 55.00
Handbook, c.1948, 568 Pages 125.00
Handbook, Training For Citizenship Through Scouting, c.1970 .... 7.00
Hat, Campaign, Canadian Badge, Beaver Felt, 1950s 63.00
Leaflet, Camp Service & Song Folder, Religious Hymns, 5 ½ x 8 ½ In., 8 Pages 5.00
Marionette, Cub Scout, 14 In. 200.00
Membership Card, Trifold, c.1919, 3 ⅞ x 7 ¼ In. 25.00
Mess Kit, Logo, Heavy Gauge Metal, National Council, New York City 12.00
Mug, Logo, White Ground, c.1991 .... 30.00
Neckerchief, Red, 30 x 30 In. 15.00
Neckerchief Bolo, Blue Enamel, Cub Scout Logo, 1 ½ x 1 ¼ In. 5.00
Paperweight, Brass, Emblem Shape, 4 ¼ x 3 ½ In. 29.00
Patch, 50th Anniversary, National Jamboree, Colorado Springs, 1960, 3 In. 9.00
Patch, St. Louis Council Camporee, c.1941, 3 ¼ x 2 In. 34.00
Photograph, Scouting Troop, Uniform With Knickers, Leggings, c.1921 .... 225.00
Pin, Emblem, Blue Ground, ½ In. 6.00
Pin, Gold Plated, 7/16 x ½ In. 21.00
Plate, Norman Rockwell, Can't Wait, c.1972 .... 35.00
Plate, Norman Rockwell, Tomorrow's Leader, David Grossman Designs, c.1983 .... 35.00
Postcard, Boy In Uniform, Knickers, 1920s 42.00
Postcard, One Kind Act A Day, Artist Phillip Boileau, Reinthal & Newman 45.00
Ring, Cubs BSA, Sterling Silver, Size 4 .... 24.00
Ring Box, Art Deco, Gray, Blue Velvet Lining, 1930s 99.00
Sign, Kellogg's, Boy Scout, First Call For Breakfast, Paper, 26 x 21 ¾ In. 520.00
Sign, Kellogg's Corn Flakes, Boy Scouts Of America, 23 x 30 In. 225.00
Spoon Set, Silver Plated, Case, c.1930, 6 Piece 99.00
Tie Tack, Wolf's Head, Cub Scout, 14K Gold 20.00
Uniform, Badges, Camp Chickagami, 1950s 112.00
View-Master Reels, Boy Scout Jamboree, 1955, 3 Piece 75.00
Whistle, Brass, Chrome Plated, Emblem 23.00

BRADLEY & HUBBARD is a name found on many metal objects. Walter Hubbard and his brother-in-law, Nathaniel Lyman Bradley, started making cast iron clocks, tables, frames, andirons, lamps, chandeliers, sconces, and sewing birds in 1854 in Meriden, Connecticut. The company became Bradley & Hubbard Manufacturing Company in 1875. Charles Parker Company bought the firm in 1940. Their lamps are especially prized by collectors.

Ashtray, Butterfly, Spread Wings, Multicolored, Embossed, Cast Iron, 5 ½ In. 144.00
Desk Set, Inkwell, Pen Tray, Blotter, Letter Holder With Calendar Insert 110.00
Desk Set, Tree Of Life, Brass, Gilt, c.1910, 8 Piece .... *illus* 125.00
Lamp, 8 Panels, Flowers, Reeded Columns, Caramel Slag Glass, Signed, 19 x 14 In. 330.00
Lamp, 8 Panels, Painted Satin Glass, Relief Molded, Patina, 15 In. 330.00
Lamp, Apple Blossom, 20th Century, 22 ½ In. 1200.00
Lamp, Ball Shade, Flowers, Iron Feet & Rim, Brown Metal Body 132.00
Lamp, Electric, Frosted Glass Domed Shade, Bronze Metal Base, 12 x 18 In. 288.00
Lamp, Flowers, Parasol Shade, 8 Panels, Caramel Slag Glass, 23 ½ x 20 In. 2072.00
Lamp, Hanging, Victorian, Milk Glass, Painted Flowers, Brass, 35 x 14 In. 364.00
Lamp, Leaves, 8 Panels, Painted Satin Glass, Frosted, Relief Molded, 15-In. Shade .... *illus* 305.00
Lamp, Mossy Ground, Ivy Band, Arts & Crafts Base, 25 ½ x 18 In., Pair 6000.00
Lamp, Student, 2-Faceted Shades, Green Slag Glass, 16 x 15 ½ In. 2280.00
Lamp, Yellow, Fleur-De-Lis, Kerosene, Brass, Marked, 22 In. .... *illus* 100.00
Sculpture, Sphinx, Egyptian Revival, Bronze, Late 1800s, 5 ¾ x 7 ⅝ In., Pair 588.00

BRASS has been used for decorative pieces and useful tablewares since ancient times. It is an alloy of copper, zinc, and other metals. Additional brass items may be found under Bell, Candlestick, Tool, or Trivet.

Ashtray, Empire State Wine Co., State Seal, Art Nouveau Woman, Grapes, Holder, 5 x 7 x 4 In. 330.00
Bed Warmer, Copper Bottom, 19th Century, 40 In. 117.00
Bed Warmer, Copper Bottom, Chased Flowers, Ring Pull, Maple Handle, 45 x 10 ½ In. 193.00
Bed Warmer, Engraved Birds, Turned Handle, 41 ½ In. 330.00
Bed Warmer, Engraved Star, Turned Giltwood Handle, Early 19th Century, 42 x 10 ¼ In. 230.00
Bed Warmer, Pierced, Bird, Flowers, Engraved Lid, Wrought Iron Handle, 40 x 12 In. 259.00
Bed Warmer, Pierced Star Decoration, Wrought Iron Handle, 1800s, 42 In. 69.00
Bed Warmer, Punched, Black Painted Wood Handle, 19th Century, 40 x 10 ½ In. 99.00
Bed Warmer, Spirals, Medallions, Maple Handle, 19th Century, 44 ½ In. .... *illus* 289.00
Bed Warmer, Swan, Engraved, Hinged Lid, Copper Ring, Maple Handle, 42 x 11 x 3 In. 252.00

Bradley & Hubbard, Lamp, Yellow, Fleur-De-Lis, Kerosene, Brass, Marked, 22 In.
$100.00

Brass, Bed Warmer, Spirals, Medallions, Maple Handle, 19th Century, 44 ½ In.
$289.00

Brass, Jar, Cover, Silver & Patinated Brass, Ivory Finial, Paul Haustein, c.1929, 10 x 8 In.
$8750.00

Brass, Weight, Cherub, Jewels, Lapis Lazuli Ground, Victorian, 6 In. $88.00

Bride's Basket, Cranberry Opalescent, Swirling Maze, Silver Plated Frame, 11 ¼ x 9 ½ In. $121.00

Bride's Bowl, Mother-Of-Pearl, Enamel Flowers, Silver Frame, Meriden, c.1890, 12 ½ In. $1300.00

Bride's Bowl, Peachblow, Chrysanthemums, Gold Wreaths, Plated Frame, 5 ⅜ x 10 In. $1100.00

Bed Warmer, Swan, Maple Handle, 19th Century, 42 x 11 x 3 In. 225.00
Book Stand, Art Nouveau, Woman's Head Ends, Telescoping Base, 4 ½ x 15 In. 58.00
Bowl, Alms, Brass, Repousse Protruding Center, Engraved Designs, 18th Century, 19 In. 236.00
Bucket, Cover, Handles, England, 19th Century, 16 x 10 ½ In. 235.00
Bucket, Embossed, Figures, Handles, Continental, 19th Century 235.00
Bucket, Embossed, Handles, England, 11 ¼ x 11 ¾ x 13 ½ In. 94.00
Bucket, Embossed, Handles, England, 19th Century, 11 x 12 In. 264.00
Candleholder, Cast, Rectangular Column, Scalloped Base, England, 1800s, 7 In., Pair. 2151.00
Candlestand, Engraved Top, Trees & Birds, 19th Century, Miniature, 7 ¼ In. 193.00
Cardholder, Figural, Man, Holding Tray, Wearing Tights, 20th Century, 26 In. 425.00
Chalice, Georgian, c.1800, 4 ½ x 3 ½ In. 176.00
Cigar Cutter, Ship's Telegraph, Full, Half, Slow, Stand By, Stop, Chadburn's, 5 In. 550.00
Coffeepot, Hinged Lid, Teak Handle, Triangular Finial, Marked, Italy, 11 In. 125.00
Comb, Cutout Design, Dark Patina, 14 Tines, 18th Century 210.00
Desk Set, Bulldog's Head, Tray, Inkwell, Letter Opener, Blotter, Austria 837.00
Desk Set, Louis XVI Style, Gilt, White Onyx, Vase Shape Encrier, Ironstone Liner, 4 Piece 300.00
Dog Collar, Adjustable, Round, Padlock, Key, Lead Ring, Inscribed, Britain, 1800s, 6 In. 1195.00
Fire Torch, Parade, Round Font, Turned Shaft, 1845, 58 In., Pair. 4405.00
Flask, Peace, Clasped Hands, War Trophy Shield, Marked, U.S., NP Ames 1838, 9 In. 403.00
Flask, Peace, Shaking Hands, Shield, Marked U.S, N.P. Ames 1838, 11 In. 400.00
Footman, Pierced Design, England, 13 ½ x 12 ½ In. 375.00
Girandole, Prisms, Gilt, Stepped Marble Base, c.1850, 17 ½ In., Pair. 480.00
Jar, Cover, Beehive Form, Wiener Werkstatte, 6 In. 175.00
Jar, Cover, Silver & Patinated Brass, Ivory Finial, Paul Haustein, c.1929, 10 x 8 In. . . . . *illus* 8750.00
Jardiniere, Repousse, Lion's Head Handles, Paw Feet, England, Late 1800s, 7 x 12 In. 245.00
Jug, Milk, Dovetailed, 18th Century 265.00
Letter Holder, Art Nouveau, Patinated, c.1890, 15 ¼ In. 300.00
Pail, Farm, Copper, Pewter, Bail Handle, 19th Century, 14 x 10 In. 82.00
Pipe Tamper, Portrait, Queen Anne, 1704 . . . . . 325.00
Planter, Hammered, 3-Footed, 8 x 10 In. 47.00
Plaque, Hammered, Relief Design, Dutch, c.1950, 22 In. 59.00
Plaque, Victorian, Pietra Dura, Botanicals, Malachite, Oval Frame, 1800s, 7 x 6 In., Pair. . . . 1062.00
Plate, Porcelain Center & Medallions, Spain, 12 In., Pair 205.00
Plate Stand, 3 Dragons, 3 Bells, 6 In. 2390.00
Playing Card Case, Inlaid Exotic Woods, Knights In Battle, c.1914, 9 x 6 x 2 ½ In. 1450.00
Sculpture, Lion, Reclining, Marble Base, Continental, 6 x 10 x 5 In., Pair 920.00
Sculpture, Tigers, Standing On Hind Legs, Red Glass Eyes, India, 7 ½ In., Pair 1315.00
Sculpture, Twisted, Chrome Ball, Polished Granite Base, c. Jere, 1970s, 20 x 37 In. 360.00
Shoehorn, Seamed, Curved Handle, c.1760 . . . . . 195.00
Statue, Classical Figures, Satyr, Holding Child, Leaning On Tree Trunk, 23 ¾ In. 1380.00
Teapot, 18th Century, 7 ½ In. 411.00
Tray, Oval, Silver, Red Wax Inlay, Engraved, Hallmark, Persia, 20 x 15 ½ In. 200.00
Tray, Teakwood Stand, 5 Legs, 25 x 27 In. 82.00
Urn, Art Nouveau, Pierced, Women, Supporting Garlands, Handles, 18 x 16 x 10 ¼ In. 630.00
Urn, Tea, Stand, 18th Century, Holland, 13 x 7 ½ In. 646.00
Weight, Cherub, Jewels, Lapis Lazuli Ground, Victorian, 6 In. . . . . *illus* 88.00

BRASTOFF, *see Sascha Brastoff category.*

BREAD PLATE, *see various silver categories, porcelain factories, and pressed glass patterns.*

BRIDE'S BASKETS OR BRIDE'S BOWLS were usually one-of-a-kind novelties made in American and European glass factories. They were especially popular about 1880 when the decorated basket was often given as a wedding gift. Cut glass baskets were popular after 1890. All bride's baskets lost favor about 1905. Bride's baskets and bride's bowls may also be found in other glass sections. Check the index at the back of the book.

BRIDE'S BASKET

Apricot, Mother-Of-Pearl, Square Ruffled & Crimped Rim, Footed, Silver Plated Frame, 10 ½ In. 400.00
Blue Opalescent, Silver Plated Frame, 13 ½ x 10 In. 117.00
Chartreuse Over Pink, Gold Vines, Silver Mica, Pinch Sides, Ruffled Rim, 9 ½ In. 575.00
Cranberry Opalescent, Swirling Maze, Silver Plated Frame, 11 ¼ x 9 ½ In. . . . . *illus* 121.00
Diamond Quilted, Mother-Of-Pearl, Square Ruffled & Crimped Rim, Silver Plated Frame, 10 ½ In. 500.00
Green Satin, Melon Ribbed, Ruffled Rim, Pierced Silver Plated Frame, 12 In. 288.00
Green Satin, Molded Lattice, Morning Glories, Scalloped Rim, Leaf Handle, 12 In. 345.00
Opal To Green, Flared, Petal Shape, Cupped Rim, Enameled, 11 x 12 In. 250.00

Pink, Cased, Silver Plated Frame, c.1870, 11 ½ In. 175.00
Pink, Crescent Co., Silver Plated Frame, c.1880, 11 In. 117.00
Pink, Ruffled Rim, Electroplated Frame, c.1870, 12 x 12 In. 263.00

BRIDE'S BOWL

Green Satin, Ruffled Rim, Pink Interior, Gold Stemmed Flowers, Figural Holder, 16 In. 1500.00
Melon Ribbed, Fireglow Tan, White Flowers, Gold Leafy Stems, 10 In. 633.00
Mother-Of-Pearl, Enamel Flowers, Silver Frame, Meriden, c.1890, 12 ½ In. *illus* 1300.00
Peachblow, Chrysanthemums, Gold Wreaths, Plated Frame, 5 ⅜ x 10 In. *illus* 1100.00

BRISTOL glass was made in Bristol, England, after the 1700s. The Bristol glass most often seen today is a Victorian, lightweight opaque glass that is often blue. Some of the glass was decorated with enamels.

Urn, Black, Enameled Flowers, Square Foot, c.1870, 11 In., Pair 1521.00 to 1690.00
Vase, Blue, Enameled Flowers, Late 19th Century, 7 ½ In., Pair 47.00
Vase, Blue, White Flowers, Brown Leaves, Scalloped Rim, Late 19th Century, 7 ½ In., Pair 110.00
Vase, Pink, Landscape, 8 In. 35.00
Vase, White, Bird, Flowers, Flared Rim, Footed, c.1870, 14 ½ In. *illus* 60.00
Vase, White, Blue Flowers, Bird, Silver Mount, 18th Century, 3 ½ In. 354.00
Vase, White, Scenic, Birds, Flowers, England, c.1870, 14 ½ In. 70.00

BRITANNIA, *see Pewter category.*

BRONZE is an alloy of copper, tin, and other metals. It is used to make figurines, lamps, and other decorative objects. Bronze lamps are listed in the Lamp category. Pieces listed here date from the eighteenth, nineteenth, and twentieth centuries.

Basin, Animal Shape Feet, 12 ½ In. 1528.00
Basket, Bird, Oval, Handles, Japan, Late 19th Century, 5 In. 201.00
Belt Hook, Gold, Silver Dragons Inlay, Huai Style, 11 ½ In. 6463.00
Bowl, Cover, Animal Finials, Handles, Spiral Covered, Chinese, 7 In. 529.00
Box, Cover, Military Drum, Napoleonic, 3 ¾ x 3 ¾ In. 443.00
Box, Sarcophagus, Fluted Legs, Paw Feet, Lion Masks, 3 Compartments, Handles, 4 x 6 x 3 In. 597.00
Brazier, Medallions, Birds, Flowers, Engraved Scrolling, Japan, 19th Century, 14 In. 1058.00
Brush Holder, Chinese, 6 ½ In. 443.00
Brushpot, Parcel Gilt, Cast, Pierced, Cranes, Clouds, Japan, 19th Century, 5 In. 881.00
Buddha, Gilt, Seated, Abhaya, Dhyana Mudras, Sino-Tibet, 1800s, 10 ½ In. 4140.00
Buddha, Ratnakosin Style, Seated, Bhumisparsa, Double Lotus, Thailand, 24 x 25 In. 805.00
Buddha, Seated, 10 x 8 ¾ In. 409.00
Burner, Pastille, Cluster Of 3 Storks, Dome Base, 1800s, 20 ¾ In., Pair 4113.00
Bust, Abraham Lincoln, Black Marble Base, 5 x 11 ¼ In. 568.00
Bust, Abraham Lincoln, Pompeian Bronze Co., 6 ¾ x 11 In. 388.00
Bust, African Man, 20 x 12 x 15 In. 1062.00
Bust, African Woman, Braided Hair, Benin, 16 x 9 x 11 In. 236.00
Bust, African Woman, Cone Shape Headdress, Benin, 17 x 6 x 6 In. 153.00
Bust, African Woman, Spiked Headdress, 24 x 7 x 9 In. 1062.00
Bust, Buddha, Curled Hair Knots, Flame Finial, Wood Base, Asia, 9 x 2 In. 353.00
Bust, Caruso, Enrico, Laughing Buddha, 1909, 5 ¾ In. 560.00
Bust, Fille De Boheme, Patinated, Emmanuelle Villanis, 20th Century, 23 x 14 In. 2144.00
Bust, Giacomantonio, A.A., Young Girl, Brown Patina, Signed, 12 ½ In. 767.00
Bust, Julius Caesar, Tapered Square Column, Marble Plinth Base, 9 ¼ In. 499.00
Bust, Lehmbruck, Wilhelm, Pensive Woman, 15 ¾ In. 6000.00
Bust, Marioton, Eugene, Suffering Christ, Marble Plinth, 14 ½ In. 708.00
Bust, Napoleon, Gilt, France, 19th Century, 6 In. 118.00
Bust, Old Woman, Brown Patina, Black Granite, Plinth, Signed, 12 ¾ In. 649.00
Bust, Pajou, Agustin, Marie Antoinette, Signed, 33 x 18 x 10 In. 4608.00
Bust, Spanish Military Officer, c.1908, 11 x 7 ¼ x 5 In. 605.00
Bust, Woman, Art Nouveau, Anemone Blossom Hat, Oak Leaf Robe, Alabaster Socle, 16 In. 354.00
Bust, Woman, Bare Shoulders, Wildflowers, Wheat, Marble Socle, France, 16 In. 940.00
Casket, Embossed, Art Nouveau Style, France, 8 x 3 x 5 ½ In. 148.00
Censer, 2 Handles, 3-Footed, Chinese, 5 ½ x 4 ½ In. 420.00
Censer, 2 Handles, Ring Foot, Chinese, 6 x 3 In. 504.00
Censer, Animal Mask Handles, Engraved, Bats, Cylindrical, Chinese, 1800s, 4 ¾ In. 1175.00
Censer, Arabic Calligraphy, Chinese, 19th Century, 3 In. 1645.00
Censer, Archaic Designs, Animal Feet, Swirling Dragon Finials, Handles, 24 In. *illus* 1880.00
Censer, Brown, Swing Bail Handle, Pierced Egret Lid, Late 1800s, 5 ½ x 7 In. 173.00

Bristol, Vase, White, Bird, Flowers, Flared Rim, Footed, c.1870, 14 ½ In.
$60.00

Bronze, Censer, Archaic Designs, Animal Feet, Swirling Dragon Finials, Handles, 24 In.
$1880.00

Bronze, Jardiniere, Chased Mountain Dwellings, Applied Rim, Mums, Gilt, Japan, 18 ½ In.
$944.00

Ever "read" a statue?
Sculptors follow a historic set of rules for making a statue of a rider on horseback. If the horse is standing on all four legs, and the rider mounted, the rider is a national hero. If the horse has three legs on the ground and a mounted rider, the rider died as a result of battle injuries. If the horse has only two legs on the ground, and a mounted rider, the rider died in battle. And if the rider is standing beside the horse, the horse and rider were killed.

Bronze, Sculpture, Barye, Antoine Louis, Stag, Leaping, c.1890, 15 x 15 In. $9300.00

Bronze, Sculpture, Bouret, Eutrope, Maiden Holding Flowers, Signed, 22 ¾ In. $1900.00

Censer, Candle Pricket, Chrysanthemums, Flower Scrolls, Handle, Japan, 19th Century 176.00
Censer, Finial, Elephant Handles, Japan, 19th Century, 9 In. 499.00
Censer, Gold Splashed, Dragons, Long Tail Handles, Chinese, 17th Century, 6 ¾ In. 944.00
Censer, Goose, Blue Glass Eyes, Tail Feathers, Lily Pad, 13 ⅝ x 9 x 7 In. 194.00
Censer, Goose, Glass Eyes, Arched Neck, Lily Pad Base, 13 x 9 x 7 In. 173.00
Censer, Scenic Panels, Figural Handles, Foo Dog Finial, 20th Century, 19 In. 304.00
Censer, Wood, Animal Handles, Jade Finial, 7 ½ In. 999.00
Compote, Louis XV Style, Gilt, Cut Crystal, 3-Footed, Lion's Head, Paw, 14 x 13 In. 1180.00
Cross, Byzantine Style, Relief Design, Wood Panel, Frame, 9 ¾ x 8 ½ In. 146.00
Crucifix, Gilt, Silvered, Round Pedestal Foot, Glass Dome, Wood Base, 20 x 7 ½ In. 382.00
Dice, Man & Woman, Erotic, Grappling, Japan, Mid 19th Century, ¾ x ¾ In. 70.00
Ewer, Baluster, Festive Scene, Grapevines, Scrolled Handle, Plinth, 38 In., Pair 2270.00
Garniture Set Clock, Porcelain Plaques, Courtly Scene, 2 Cupidons, 19 In. 767.00
Hand Mirror, Landscape, Birds, Prunus Blossoms, Chinese, 10 ½ x 6 ¾ In. 118.00
Incense Burner, Chinese, c.1900, 5 x 4 In. 117.00
Incense Burner, Goose, 19th Century, Chinese, 6 ¾ In. 826.00
Jardiniere, Bulbous, Flared Top, Cast Elephant Head Handles, Asia, 1800s, 10 x 16 In. 252.00
Jardiniere, Chased Mountain Dwellings, Applied Rim, Mums, Gilt, Japan, 18 ½ In. ..... *illus* 944.00
Jardiniere, Leaf & Festoon Design, Footed, France, 10 x 26 In. 1170.00
Jardiniere, Louis XVI Style, Wreath Handles, Footed, France, 10 x 26 x 10 ½ In. 810.00
Lock, Key, Sample, Scroll Cut, Engraved, Lever Tumbler, 9 x 7 & 11 x 6 In., Pair 2070.00
Match Holder, 2 Harlequins, Beside Basket, Black Marble Base, 5 ½ x 4 In. 177.00
Orb, Stand, Round, Beaded, Suspension Loop, 12 ¾ In. 266.00
Page Cutter, Beetle Accent, Japan, Early 20th Century, 6 In. 70.00
Pin Tray, Golfer, Hagenauer, Marked, c.1930, 4 ½ x 3 In. 570.00
Plaque, Crest, Baroque, Putti, Horizontal Panel, Scrolls, Flowers, 24 x 130 In. 4113.00
Plaque, Lion's Head, Japan, 14 In. 764.00
Plaque, Luccesi, Bruce, Man & Angel, Relief, Round, Square Marble Base, 10 x 7 In. 748.00
Plaque, Rembrandt, Angels, c.1900, 38 In. 88.00
Plaque, Theodore Roosevelt, Quote, Bas-Relief, 1920, 12 ¾ x 9 ⅞ In. 1116.00
Plaque, Winged Horse, Swirling Birds, Gilt, 10 In. 5288.00
Plaque, Winged Man, Flower Nymph, Art Nouveau, Onyx Mount, Easel Back, 12 x 7 In. 646.00
Plateau, Gilt, Truncated Mirror, 8-Sided, 3 Ornamental Bands, 1800s, 3 x 21 In. 1175.00
Pot, Lid, Footed, Square Handles, Chinese, 11 x 12 ¾ In. 1755.00
Samovar, Silvered, Cone Shape, 2 Panels, Fluted Sides, Gadroon Rim, Russia, 20 x 14 In. 525.00
Sculpture, 2 Irish Setters, Marble Base, 12 ½ x 20 ½ In. 345.00
Sculpture, Aichele, Woman, Nude, Playing Castanets, Green Marble Pedestal, 11 In. 646.00
Sculpture, Akshobya Buddha, Seated In Dhyanasana, Gilt, Tibet, 1800s, 8 In. 384.00
Sculpture, Antoine, Jean, Cupid, Lovebirds At Feet, Marked, 19 In. 2390.00
Sculpture, Arab, Daggers In Belt, Bullet Strap, Turban, 19th Century, 35 x 11 x 10 In. 1344.00
Sculpture, Bacchanal Dancer, French School, c.1850, 16 ¼ In. 1298.00
Sculpture, Bacchante Riding Lion, Holding Wine Horn, Grand Tour, 8 ¾ In. 529.00
Sculpture, Ballerina, Marble Base, 19th Century, 19 ½ In. 2200.00
Sculpture, Barye, Antoine Louis, Stag, Leaping, c.1890, 15 x 15 In. ..... *illus* 9300.00
Sculpture, Barye, Bear, Raiding Bird's Nest, Tree Trunk, Rouge Marble Base, 6 x 4 In. 5581.00
Sculpture, Barye, Dromedary, Standing, Marble Base, Incised Signature, 6 x 7 In. 4700.00
Sculpture, Bauer, M., Bison, Fighting, Brown Patina, Marked, 8 ¼ x 32 x 7 In. 4182.00
Sculpture, Bird, Cardinal, Cold Painted, Signed, Geschutz, c.1920, 3 ½ In. 550.00
Sculpture, Bird, Standing, Cold Painted, Austria, c.1900, 4 ½ x 5 x 4 ½ In. 1760.00
Sculpture, Blacksmith, Bare Chest, Holding Hammer, Shield, Helmet At Feet, 32 In. 1998.00
Sculpture, Bodhisattva, Kneeling On Lotus Plinth, Attributes, Tibet, 1800s, 12 ½ In. 650.00
Sculpture, Bohdisattva, Seated, On Lotus Base, Gilt, Chinese, 6 ½ In. 3304.00
Sculpture, Bonheur, Rosa, Bull, Ivory Horns, France, c.1850, 10 x 6 ½ In. 575.00
Sculpture, Bouret, E., Minerva, Seated, Holding Spear & Shield, c.1890, 13 In. 1140.00
Sculpture, Bouret, Eutrope, Maiden Holding Flowers, Signed, 22 ¾ In. ..... *illus* 1900.00
Sculpture, Boy, Fishing, In Canoe, Loincloth, Hat, Stingray In Net, 6 x 7 ¾ In. 2233.00
Sculpture, Buddha, Seated, Right Hand Raised, Left Hand Open, Cast, 1800s, 15 In. 4608.00
Sculpture, Buddha, Seated On Lotus Throne, Gilt, Tibet, 9 In. 1062.00
Sculpture, Buddha, Seated On Lotus Throne, Holding Bowl, Silver, Tibet, 8 ½ In. 590.00
Sculpture, Bull, Lunging, Rectangular Stone Plinth, 6 ½ In. 478.00
Sculpture, Bull, Reclining, Brown Patina, Oval Base, 4 ½ In. 885.00
Sculpture, Bull, Standing, Brown Patina, 9 ¼ In. 649.00
Sculpture, Capturing The Hen, Auguste Moreau, Signed, France, 10 ½ In. 531.00
Sculpture, Chicken, Head Feathers, Oval Slate Base, 5 ⅞ In. 1116.00
Sculpture, Chicken, In Mid Stride, Asia, 20th Century, 7 ⅞ In. 863.00

Sculpture, Chiparus, Dog, German Shepherd, Marble Base, Marked, 11 x 21 x 8 In. 657.00
Sculpture, Christ Carrying The Cross, Brown Patina, French, 19th Century, 14½ In. 266.00
Sculpture, Clown, With Whip, Pig, Multicolored, 20th Century, 3½ In. 330.00
Sculpture, Coletti, Joseph Arthur, Mare & Stallion, Signed, 15 x 16 x 8 In., Pair 1763.00
Sculpture, Cossack Warrior On Rearing Horse, France, 24 x 8 x 23½ In. 5581.00
Sculpture, Crayfish, Articulated, Japan, 19th Century, 9 In. 2468.00
Sculpture, Csaky, Joseph, The Kiss, Foundry Mark, 1964, 20¾ In. 13750.00
Sculpture, Cupid, Crouching, Holding Rose, Butterfly, Grand Tour, Early 1900s, 9 In. 588.00
Sculpture, Dancer, Exotic Costume, Art Deco, Marble Base, 18¼ x 6 In. 1058.00
Sculpture, Descomps, J.E., Dancer, Holding Drapery, Art Deco, Signed, 19 x 9 x 5 In. 881.00
Sculpture, Diana, The Huntress, Holding Songbird, Bow, Tan Marble Socle, 14½ In. 529.00
Sculpture, Dog, Boxer Head, White Marble Base, 1965, 8 In. 110.00
Sculpture, Dog, Bulldog, Standing, Continental, 20th Century, 12 In. 1673.00
Sculpture, Dog, Greyhound, Hamlet, Reclining, Base, Marked, Lawrie, 5 x 9 x 3 In. 2689.00
Sculpture, Dog, On Hind Legs, Rectangular Base, 32 x 10 In., Pair 858.00
Sculpture, Dog, Setter, On Point, Brown, Green Patina, 7¾ x 18 In. 590.00
Sculpture, Dog, Spaniels, On Pouf Bed, Signed, 20th Century, 18 x 18 x 16 In. 980.00
Sculpture, Dog, Stalking Grouse, 8 In. 1652.00
Sculpture, Dog, Whippet, Leaning On Haunches, Ball, Oval Base, 4⅜ x 6 In. 646.00
Sculpture, Dog, Whippet, Seated, Rectangular Base, 1919, 15¼ x 18½ x 6¼ In. 7050.00
Sculpture, Dogs, German Shepherds, Standing, Reclining, 21 x 16 In. 1888.00
Sculpture, Don, P., Girl, Barefoot, Goose, Black Stone Base, Signed, Early 1900s, 6½ In. 288.00
Sculpture, Eckhardt, Edris, Unicorn, Marble Base, 8 In. . . . . *illus* 1000.00
Sculpture, Elephant, Attacked By Tigers, Wood Base, Japanese, c.1900, 14 x 16 In. 468.00
Sculpture, Elephant, Walking, Black Marble Base, 11¼ x 10½ x 14¼ In. 11740.00
Sculpture, Falconer, Standing, Falcon On Upraised Hand, Oval Base, 33¾ In. 7050.00
Sculpture, Farnese Hercules, Square Black Marble Base, Late 1800s, 14¼ x 5½ In. 600.00
Sculpture, Fayral, Woman, Nude, Gazelle, Art Deco, Black Stone Base, 1920s, 21 x 8 In. 1560.00
Sculpture, Figure, Riding Goat, Wearing Hat, Japan, 19th Century, 7 In. 944.00
Sculpture, Flannagan, John Bernard, Nude, Brown & Green Patina, 10½ In. 2242.00
Sculpture, Fontinelle, L., Dog, Pekingese, Seated, Base, Green, 1800s, 10 x 12 x 7 In. 700.00
Sculpture, Foo Dogs, Male, Female, Mica, Stone Inlay, 1900s, Thailand, 34 x 33 In., Pair. . . . 575.00
Sculpture, Fournier, A., Dog, Pekingese, Playing With Ball, Marble Base, Marked, 5 In. 299.00
Sculpture, Fox, Barking, Austria, 5 x 1¾ In. 1495.00
Sculpture, Fremiet, E., Dog, Stretching Hind Legs, Oval Base, Green Bronze Patina, 4 x 7 In. . 480.00
Sculpture, Frog, 3 In. 27.00
Sculpture, Fuchs, Emil, Dog, Mastiff, Reclining, Rome, Marked, 1893, 5½ In. 1434.00
Sculpture, George Washington, Mahogany Pedestal, 24 In. 11500.00
Sculpture, Girl, In Fan Embroidered Kimono, Tokyo School, Japan, 13 In. 1615.00
Sculpture, Girl, Smiling, Bird On Shoulder, Slate Plinth, France, 19¼ In. 1534.00
Sculpture, Girl, Windy Weather, Base, c.1920, 7 In. 205.00
Sculpture, Giroux, Alph., Bull Mastiff, Chained To Post, Gilt, Paris, c.1880, 6 In. 550.00
Sculpture, Goddess, Rising From Lotus Pond, Dragon, Chinese, 12¾ In. 2115.00
Sculpture, Godet, Henri, Woman, Flowering Bough, France, 42 In. 2415.00
Sculpture, Grachev, Vassili, Man, Standing Next To Seated Lady, c.1880, 12 In. 27140.00
Sculpture, Gypsy Woman, Raised Arm, Smelling Flower, Marble Socle, 13 In. 823.00
Sculpture, Hebald, Milton Elting, 3 Graces, Brown Patina, 1961, 43 In. 11210.00
Sculpture, Henjes, H., Dog, Hunting, On Point, Signed, c.1880, 12 x 3 x 42¼ In. 476.00
Sculpture, Horse, Tang Style, Standing, Allover Gold Chinese Designs, 30 In., Pair 177.00
Sculpture, Horseman, Stallion, Galloping, Russia, 12 x 6 In. 650.00
Sculpture, Indian Chief On Horse, 12½ x 30 x 42 In. 1540.00
Sculpture, Jackson, Harry, The Marshal, Signed, 1970, 30 x 32 x 12 In. . . . . *illus* 18000.00
Sculpture, Janniot, Alfred-Auguste, Antelope, Marked, c.1930, 14 In. 15600.00
Sculpture, Jullien, E., Leda & The Swan, Late 19th Century, 11⅛ In. 1998.00
Sculpture, Knight In Armor, Preparing For Battle, 17 In. 944.00
Sculpture, Lambeaux, Sapphic Lovers, Erotic, Signed, Early 1900s, 3 x 4¾ In. 420.00
Sculpture, Lang, H., Satyr With Pipe, Brown Patina, Signed, 17 In. 1180.00
Sculpture, Lauter, Henri, 3 Dancers, Signed, France, 12½ In. 797.00
Sculpture, Levy, Charles, Laborer, No Shirt Or Shoes, Harvesting Wheat, 9⅝ In. 382.00
Sculpture, Levy, Charles Octave, Girl, Picking Apples, Dark Brown Patina, 20 In. 944.00
Sculpture, Lincoln, Holding Emancipation Proclamation, Gorham Co., 8½ In. 7768.00
Sculpture, Lion, Paw On Ball, Tail, 4¼ x 7½ In. 252.00
Sculpture, Lizard, Cold Paint, Austria, 2¾ x 9¾ In. 1763.00
Sculpture, Lorenzi, Joseph, Dancing Girls, Cold Paint, Marked, 12½ In., Pair 4920.00
Sculpture, Madonna, Grieving, Round Base, Gorham Co., 8 x 2⅜ In. 245.00
Sculpture, Man, Nude, Goat Skin Over Shoulder, Round Base, 8½ In. 550.00

Bronze, Sculpture, Eckhardt, Edris, Unicorn, Marble Base, 8 In.
$1000.00

Bronze, Sculpture, Jackson, Harry, The Marshal, Signed, 1970, 30 x 32 x 12 In.
$18000.00

Bronze, Sculpture, Warbler, Cold Painted, Austria, Late 19th Century, 5½ In.
$400.00

TIP

Outdoor bronze garden figures should be waxed twice a year for protection.

Bronze, Urn, Anthemion, Fluted, Male Masks, Dome Foot, Square Base, Grand Tour, 9 In.
$206.00

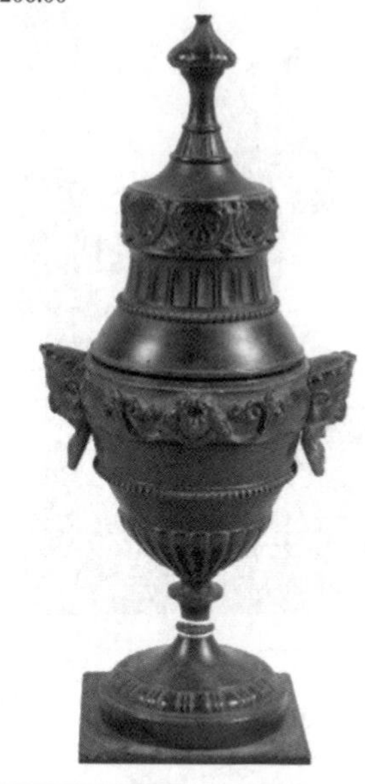

Brownie, Candlestick, Figural, Uncle Sam, Majolica, 9 In.
$230.00

Brownie, Croquet Wicket, Cast Iron, Painted, Signed, G. Freihofer, 16 x 7¾ In., Pair
$978.00

Sculpture, Man, Nude, Roman, Hand On Hip, Italy, c.1920, 13 In. 350.00
Sculpture, Man, Nude, Saluting, Marble Base, Italy, 11½ x 4 x 9⅝ In. 660.00
Sculpture, Man, On Bucking Horse, Wooly Chaps, Marble Base, 13½ In. 140.00
Sculpture, Man, Scholar, Standing, Holding Scroll, Walking Stick, Early 1900s, 15 In. 411.00
Sculpture, Man, Woman, On Knees, Traditional Japanese Costumes, 7 In., Pair 83.00
Sculpture, Marioton, E., Muse De Bois, Blowing Instrument, Brown Patina, 32 In. 4375.00
Sculpture, Marioton, Eugene, Sorrowful Mother, Brown Patina, 19th Century, 7 In. 649.00
Sculpture, Marqueste, Cupid, Kneeling, Bow, Arrow, Brown Patina, France, 17 In. 1080.00
Sculpture, Mars, Seated With Cupid At Feet, Bicolor Marble Base, 1800s, 21 In. 3525.00
Sculpture, Masson, Charles, Lioness, Resting, Brown Patina, 1800s, 7¾ x 14¼ In. 2950.00
Sculpture, Mene, Pierre-Jules, Dog, On Point, Brown Patina, 1800s, 5¼ x 7½ In. 1062.00
Sculpture, Mene, Pierre-Jules, Ewe & Lamb, Dark Brown Patina, 1800s, 5¾ x 8 In. 649.00
Sculpture, Mercury, Flying, Marble Socle, 19th Century, France, 20½ x 35 In. 1792.00
Sculpture, Mercury, Renaissance Style, Green, Brown Patina, Marble Socle, 25 In. 1763.00
Sculpture, Miserendino, Theodore Roosevelt, Aggressive Fight, Marble Base, c.1923, 8 x 11 In. 2032.00
Sculpture, Monk, Standing On Lotus Base, Gilt, Chinese, 8 In. 1645.00
Sculpture, Moreau, 2 Women, Signed, 27½ In. 8125.00
Sculpture, Moreau, Mathurin, Reading Lesson, Brown Patina, 19th Century, 17 In. 2242.00
Sculpture, Mother, Child, Fleeing Storm, Dark Brown Patina, France, 1800s, 16 In. 1239.00
Sculpture, Narcissus, Green Patina, Italy, 24 x 12 x 10 In. 1058.00
Sculpture, Naughty Boys, Erotic, Oval Travertine Base, Continental, 2½ x 2½ In. 84.00
Sculpture, Nereid, Bare Breasted, Hoop Over Head, Oblong Base, 12 x 11 x 4 In. 3432.00
Sculpture, Orpheus, Seminude, Standing Over Cerberus, Harp At Feet, France, 25 In. 4113.00
Sculpture, Owl, Sitting On Books, Tree Stump, Marble Base, 5⅛ x 4¾ In. 325.00
Sculpture, Owl, On Branch, 7 x 4 In. 146.00
Sculpture, Paillet, Ch., Wolfhound & Cat, Reclining, Base, 5¾ x 12½ In. 2988.00
Sculpture, Pan, Instructing Nymph On Flute, Brown, Silver Patina, Spain, 18 x 13 In. 1888.00
Sculpture, Panda Bear, Seated, 27 x 22 x 23 In. 1170.00
Sculpture, Panther, In Tree, Wood base, 15 x 5 x 14 In. 1870.00
Sculpture, Peleschka, Fr., Hoop Dancer, Marked, c.1920, 13¼ In. 1170.00
Sculpture, Pernot, Henri, Big Sister, Holding Little Sister, 16¾ In. 8750.00
Sculpture, Pharaoh, Upraised Hand, Black Marble Base, Egyptian Revival, 30¼ In. 3173.00
Sculpture, Picault, Emile, Draped Nude, Male, Classical Style, c.1900, 66 In. 2645.00
Sculpture, Picault, Pro Jura, Warrior, Shield, Sword, Fallen Roman Standard, 28⅝ In. 4113.00
Sculpture, Poertzel, Otto, Egyptian Lady, Marble Base, c.1925, 18¾ In. 7200.00
Sculpture, Queen, Seated On Throne, Holding Staff, Egyptian Revival, 1800s, 10 In. 588.00
Sculpture, Rabbit, Gold Inlaid Eyes, Signed, Japan, Late 19th Century, 3 In. 2233.00
Sculpture, Rabbit, On Pussy Willows, Cold Paint, c.1900, 4¼ In. 275.00
Sculpture, Race Horse, Standing, Dark Brown Patina, France, 9¾ x 14¾ In. 1770.00
Sculpture, Robin Hood, Bow, Arrow, Dog, Slate Base, France, c.1930, 28 x 29½ In. 1121.00
Sculpture, Romanelli, Raffaello, 3 Horsemen, Signed, 18 In. 2360.00
Sculpture, Rowe, Phil, Giraffe, Wood Base, 1965, 21 In. 270.00
Sculpture, Ruggeri, G., Woman, Classical Clothing, Holding Fruit Harvest, 15½ In. 403.00
Sculpture, Russell, Charles, Last Laugh, Wolf Staring At Human Skull, c.1900, 7 x 6 In. 900.00
Sculpture, Samurai, Armored Warrior, Swords, Spear, Cast, 17 In. 288.00
Sculpture, Satyr, Woman, Nude, Erotic, Detachable To Change Positions, c.1920, 3 x 5½ In. .. 210.00
Sculpture, Sgraffito, S.E., Peasant Woman, Wood Gatherer, Signed, 10½ x 5 In. 252.00
Sculpture, Sika Deer, Antlers, Arched Back, Japan, 18th Century, 19 In. 4182.00
Sculpture, Silenus, Rock Crystal Orb, Serpent Band, Grand Tour, Marble Base, 22 x 7 In. 1058.00
Sculpture, Skeleton, Seated, Thinking Position, Marble Base, Late 20th Century, 10 In. 708.00
Sculpture, Sphinx, English Regency, Gilt Marble Base, Early 19th Century, 6½ x 5½ In 300.00
Sculpture, Stag, Black Marble Base, France, 21¾ x 13⅛ x 4⅞ In. 1293.00
Sculpture, Stallion, Running, Eagle, Signed, 20 x 23½ x 24½ In. 306.00
Sculpture, Swan, Upraised Wings, Oval Gilt Bronze Base, Continental, 3 x 3½ In. 1560.00
Sculpture, Szaboles, Peter, Woman, Seated On Bench, 8½ In. 392.00
Sculpture, Tiger, Burlwood Base, Japan, Late 19th Century, 21 In. 1410.00
Sculpture, Tiger, Glass Eyes, Japan, 19th Century, 8¾ In. 826.00
Sculpture, Valverde, Abstract, Modern, 12¼ x 9 x 9 In. 411.00
Sculpture, Vidal, Louis, Elk, Running, France, 1831-92, 11 x 3 x 10 In. 4400.00
Sculpture, Vienna, Dog, Poodle, Umbrella In Mouth, Black, 1 x 2 In. 325.00
Sculpture, Vienna, Dog, Standing, Red Coat, Painted, 3¾ In. 499.00
Sculpture, Vienna, Eagle, Spread Wings, 3¼ In. 411.00
Sculpture, Warbler, Cold Painted, Austria, Late 19th Century, 5½ In. .... *illus* 400.00
Sculpture, Warrior, Wearing Helmet, Standing Over Fallen Shield, France, 23½ In. 2820.00
Sculpture, Wolf, Stalking, White Marble Base, 8 x 13¾ In. 1293.00
Sculpture, Woman, Carrying Basket Of Lobsters, Brown Patina, 23¾ In. 1534.00

Sculpture, Woman, Hiking Clothes, Hat, Roman Bronzeworks, N.Y., c.1915 . . . 1725.00
Sculpture, Woman, Holding Lockbox, Admiring Necklace, Gothic Costume, 13 x ¾ In. . . . 1062.00
Sculpture, Woman, Nude, Standing, Hands On Hip, Mid 20th Century, 12 ¼ In. . . . 1058.00
Sculpture, Woman, Nude Crouching, Pink Marble Base, 20th Century, 8 ¾ In. . . . 764.00
Sculpture, Woman, Pinning Robe At Shoulder, Marble Base, 14 ⅛ In. . . . 392.00
Sculpture, Woman, Raising Cloak Over Head, Stylized Clouds, Cherub, 17 ⅝ In. . . . 1645.00
Sculpture, Woman & Man, Kissing, Abstract 9 ¼ In. . . . 1652.00
Sculpture, Wounded Stag, Brown Patina, France, 19th Century, 10 ½ x 10 ½ In. . . . 472.00
Tray, Chariot Of Fame, 4 Panthers, Parcel Gilt, Northern Continental, 7 x 10 In. . . . 1320.00
Tray, Leaves, Fruit, Tree Branch Handles, 4 Knob Feet, Cast, Art Nouveau, 13 ½ x 8 In. . . . 690.00
Urn, Anthemion, Fluted, Male Masks, Dome Foot, Square Base, Grand Tour, 9 In. . . . *illus* 206.00
Urn, Classical, Mask Form Handles, Garland, Stepped Marble Bases, 17 ½ x 5 In. . . . 940.00
Urn, Empire, Owl Finial, Swagged Lion Head Masks, 12 ½ In., Pair . . . 826.00
Urn, Neoclassical Style, Fluted Neck, Triton Handles, 29 x 26 x 21 In. . . . 3525.00
Urn, Neoclassical Style, Putti At Play, Handles, Rams Head, Paw Feet, 31 x 29 x 23 In. . . . 2350.00
Urn, Neoclassical Style, Silvered, Masques, Sphinxes, Lion Head, Handles, 24 x 22 In., Pair . . 1763.00
Urn, Rococo Style, Ram Head Handles, 29 x 22 x 19 In. . . . 1528.00
Urn, Roman Figures, Engraved Design, Gilt, Polished Slate Base, 13 ½ In., Pair . . . 1400.00
Vase, Art Deco, Round Base, Flared & Ringed Top, Scroll Handle, Japan, 1900s, 10 x 5 In. . . . 250.00
Vase, Birds, On Lotus Branches, Embossed, Gilt Ground, Japan, 11 ¾ In. . . . 590.00
Vase, Dragon, Fan Shape Reserves, Bird, Flowers, Japan, 35 In. . . . 2360.00
Vase, Fox, Holding Double Gourd, Japan, Late 19th Century, 7 ¼ In. . . . 881.00
Vase, Garniture, Louis Philippe, Gilt Lacquer, Pyriform, Footed, 11 x 5 In., Pair . . . 1200.00
Vase, Oriental, Applied Dragon, Clouds, 20th Century, 10 ½ In. . . . 35.00
Vase, Scenic Panels, Embossed, Handles, Japan, 20th Century, 15 In., Pair . . . 384.00
Vase, Warwick, Vine Handles, Open Bowl, Relief Masks, Continental, c.1885, 5 x 8 In. . . . 551.00

BROWNIES were first drawn in 1883 by Palmer Cox. They are characterized by large round eyes, downturned mouths, and skinny legs. Toys, books, dinnerware, and other objects were made with the Brownies as part of the design.

Book, Brownie At Home, Illustrated, Signed Drawing Included, Century, 1893, 144 Pages. . . . 1100.00
Book, Brownie Yearbook, Illustrated, Chromolithographs, McLoughlin, 1895 . . . 450.00
Book, Brownies Around The World, 1st Ed., 4th Book, Century, 1894, 144 Pages . . . 700.00
Bottle, Figural, Majolica, 7 In. . . . 29.00
Candlestick, Figural, Sailor, Majolica, 9 In. . . . 138.00
Candlestick, Figural, Uncle Sam, Majolica, 9 In. . . . *illus* 230.00
Croquet Wicket, Cast Iron, Painted, Signed, G. Freihofer, 16 x 7 ¾ In., Pair . . . *illus* 978.00
Flatware, Daisy Handle, Leaves, Grass, Malabar Plate, Early 1900s, 7 ¼ & 6 ¼ In. . . . 24.00
Game, Brownie Skeet Ball, 15 Brownies In Actions, Board, M.H. Miller Co., 1920s . . . 305.00
Humidor, Sailor's Head, Defender On Rim Of Hat, Majolica, 6 ¼ In. . . . 161.00
Match Holder, Resting On Stump, Schafer & Vader, Late 1800s, 7 ¼ In. . . . 225.00

BRUSH Pottery was started in 1925. George Brush first worked in 1901 in Zanesville, Ohio. He started his own pottery in 1907, but it burned to the ground soon after. In 1909 he became manager of the J.W. McCoy Pottery. In 1911, Brush and J.W. McCoy formed the Brush-McCoy Pottery Co. After a series of name changes, the company became The Brush Pottery in 1925. It closed in 1982. Old Brush was marked with impressed letters or a palette-shaped mark. Some new pieces are being marked in raised letters or with a raised mark. Collectors favor the figural cookie jars made by this company. Because there was a company named Brush-McCoy, there is great confusion between Brush and Nelson McCoy pieces. See McCoy category for more information.

Cookie Jar, Crock With Bat Finial, Pink, Embossed Cookies . . . 35.00
Cookie Jar, Granny Holding Rolling Pin, Plaid Skirt, 1956 . . . 65.00
Cookie Jar, Hippo, Laughing, Monkey On Back, 1961 . . . *illus* 300.00
Cookie Jar, Humpty Dumpty, Marked, 9 ⅞ In. . . . *illus* 64.00
Cookie Jar, Old Shoe, Shoe-Shaped House, 1959 . . . 65.00
Cookie Jar, Teddy Bear, Feet Together, 1940s, 11 In. . . . 180.00
Vase, Blue Onyx, 6 ⅛ In. . . . *illus* 30.00

BRUSH-MCCOY, *see Brush category and related pieces in McCoy category.*

BUCK ROGERS was the first American science fiction comic strip. It started in 1929 and continued until 1967. Buck has also appeared in comic books, movies, and, in the 1980s, a television series. Any memorabilia connected with the character Buck Rogers is collectible.

Ad, Sylvania Space Ranger Kit, 1950s, 10 ¾ x 8 In. . . . 125.00
Book, Pop-Up, Strange Adventures In The Spider Ship, Pleasure Books, 1935, 9 x 8 In. . . . 115.00

Brush, Cookie Jar, Hippo, Laughing, Monkey On Back, 1961
$300.00

Brush, Cookie Jar, Humpty Dumpty, Marked, 9 ⅞ In.
$64.00

Brush, Vase, Blue Onyx, 6 ⅛ In.
$30.00

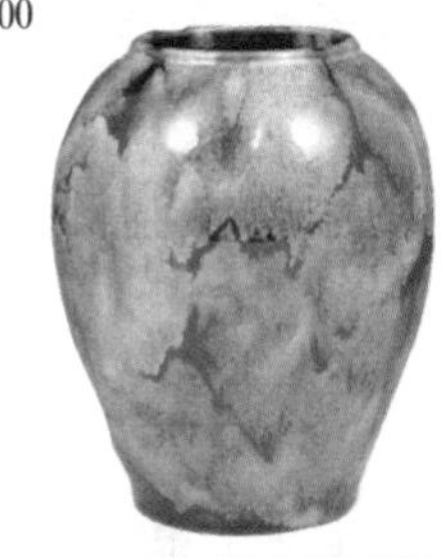

Buck Rogers, Toy, Atomic Pistol, Sparks, Pressed Steel, Comic Book, Daisy, Box, 9 In.
$575.00

Buck Rogers, Toy, Spaceship, Destroyer, Red, Yellow, Tootsietoy, Box, 4 ¾ In.
$1430.00

Comic Book, No. 1, 1940 . . . . 657.00
Pocket Watch, Buck Rogers & Wilma, Comet Man On Back, Silver, Ingraham, 1935 455.00 to 633.00
Squirt Gun, Buck Rogers 25th Century Liquid Helium, Tin Lithograph, Daisy, 6 x 7 In. 388.00
Toy, 25th Century Rocket Police Patrol, Moves, Flashes, Roars, Tin, Windup, Marx, 12 In. 3307.00
Toy, Atomic Pistol, Sparks, Pressed Steel, Comic Book, Daisy, Box, 9 In. . . . . *illus* 575.00
Toy, Battle Cruiser, Die Cast, Yellow, Blue, Tootsietoy 253.00
Toy, Battle Cruiser, White, Blue, Die Cast, Box, Tootsietoy, 4¾ In. 1495.00
Toy, Rocket Police Patrol, Seated, Gun In Hand, Tin, Windup, Marx, 11½ In. 345.00
Toy, Rocket Ship, Detailed Wings, Tin Lithograph, Windup, 12 In. 805.00
Toy, Rocket Ship, Tin Lithograph, Windup, Marx, Patent March 15, 1927, 12½ In. 613.00
Toy, Space Ranger Kit, Sylvania, 1952 . . . . 175.00
Toy, Spaceship, Destroyer, Red, Yellow, Tootsietoy, Box, 4¾ In. . . . . *illus* 1430.00
Toy, Venus Duo Destroyer, Red, Yellow, Die Cast, Tootsietoy, Box, 4¾ In. 1495.00
Toy, Water Pistol, XZ-44 Liquid Helium, Yellow, Red, Steel, Daisy, 1936, 7¼ In. . . . . 388.00 to 506.00

BUFFALO POTTERY was made in Buffalo, New York, after 1902. The company was established by the Larkin Company, famous manufacturers of soap. The wares are marked with a picture of a buffalo and the date of manufacture. Deldare ware is the most famous pottery made at the factory. It has either a khaki-colored or green background with hand-painted transfer designs.

BUFFALO POTTERY

Bowl, Cover, Building, Trees, Blue, White, 1909, 5½ x 11 x 10 In. 55.00
Bowl, Vegetable, Cover, Willow, Blue, 5½ x 8 In. 545.00
Cake Plate, Rose Bouquets, Gilt Border, Light To Dark Green, Handle, 10½ In. 35.00
Canister, Sugar, Marked, 8¼ In. 125.00
Cheese Dish, Cover, Roses At Edges, Gold Rim, Handle, 4 x 7¾ In. 55.00
Dish, Dolly & Donnie Dingle, Child's, 7¾ In. 15.00
Pitcher, Gloriana, Blue Transfer, Enameled, Gilt, 1907, 9 In. 174.00
Pitcher, Pink & Yellow Roses, Marked, 7½ x 7½ In. 100.00
Pitcher, Quotes, Man Handing Over Piece Of Paper, 2 Men Shaking Hands, 1909, 8 In. 595.00
Pitcher, Rip Van Winkle, Transfer, 1907, 5⅞ In. 163.00
Pitcher, Roosevelt Bears, Marked, 1907, 8 In. . . . . *illus* 900.00
Plate, Dinner, Pink Flowers, Scalloped, Metallic Gold Trim. 15.00
Plate, Independence Hall, Philadelphia, Pa., 10 In. 40.00
Platter, La France Rose, White, Blue Flower Sprays, Gold Trim, 15 x 11 In. 34.00
Soap Dish, Indian, Full Headdress, Blue Glaze, High Relief, 4 In. 95.00
Soup, Coupe, Arlington, Green Underglaze, Transfer Print Border, Gold Trim. 12.00
Soup, Dish, Restaurant, Ivory, Impressed Mark, 4 x 2¼ In. 10.00
Vase, Silver Overlay, Daisy Border, Cylindrical, Tapered, 1910, 7¾ In. 493.00
Warming Dish, Bluebirds, Nickel Plated, 9½ In. 47.00

BUFFALO POTTERY DELDARE

Bowl, Fallowfield Hunt, Signed, 1909, 9 In. 395.00
Bowl, Ye Village Tavern, Signed, 1924, 9 x 3¾ In. 495.00
Bowl, Ye Village Tavern, Signed, Marked, 1908, 9 In. 275.00
Charger, An Evening At Ye Lion Inn, Marked, 13¾ In. 1800.00
Charger, Fallowfield Hunt, Breakfast At The 3 Pigeons, c.1908, 12¼ In. 295.00
Cup & Saucer, Ye Olden Days, Marked, 1924, 3½-In. Cup, 2-In. Saucer 195.00
Humidor, Dr. Syntax Returned Home, Emerald, 1911, 7½ In. 275.00
Mug, Dr. Syntax Again Filled Up His Glass, Marked, 1911, 5¼ In. 450.00
Pitcher, Fallowfield Hunt, Breaking Cover, Marked, 1909, 8¾ In. *illus* 110.00
Pitcher, Fallowfield Hunt, The Return, 1908 . . . . 575.00
Plaque, An Evening At Ye Lion Inn, Signed, 1908, 13½ In. 230.00
Plate, At Ye Lion Inn, Signed, J. Gerhardt, 1908 . . . . 110.00
Plate, Dr. Syntax Star Gazing, Signed, M. Gerhardt, c.1911, 9½ In. 695.00
Plate, Ye Village Street, Marked, 7⅜ In. . . . . *illus* 140.00
Tray, Heirlooms, Marked, 1908, 10⅜ x 17⅞ In. . . . . *illus* 250.00

BUNNYKINS, *see Royal Doulton category.*

BURMESE GLASS was developed by Frederick Shirley at the Mt. Washington Glass Works in New Bedford, Massachusetts, in 1885. It is a two-toned glass, shading from peach to yellow. Some pieces have a pattern mold design. A few Burmese pieces were decorated with pictures or applied glass flowers of colored Burmese glass. Other factories made similar glass also called Burmese. Related items may be listed in the Fenton category, the Gundersen category, and under Webb Burmese.

Biscuit Jar, Cover, Enameled White & Yellow Blossoms, 5 x 4 In. 863.00

Buffalo Pottery, Pitcher, Roosevelt Bears, Marked, 1907, 8 In. $900.00

Buffalo Pottery Deldare, Pitcher, Fallowfield Hunt, Breaking Cover, Marked, 1909, 8¾ In. $110.00

Buffalo Pottery Deldare, Plate, Ye Village Street, Marked, 7⅜ In. $140.00

Buffalo Pottery Deldare, Tray, Heirlooms, Marked, 1908, 10⅜ x 17⅞ In. $250.00

Biscuit Jar, Dimpled, Applied Gold Starfish & Jewels, Oval, Embossed Metal Lid, 6 In. 1840.00
Biscuit Jar, Gold Enameled Leaves, Oval, Oval, Marked, 7 In. 635.00
Biscuit Jar, Yellow To Pink, Gold Enameled Leaves, Buds, Egg Shape, 7 In. 633.00
Bowl, 3-Footed, Glossy, 5 x 6 ½ In. 1150.00
Bowl, Applied Rigaree, Scrolls & Bow, Scalloped Rim, 4 ½ In. 2900.00
Bowl, Diamond Quilted, Crimped Scalloped Rim, Glossy, 5 In. 115.00
Bowl, Diamond Quilted, Footed, Ruffled Edge, 6 x 5 ½ In. 3450.00
Bowl, Footed, Crimped Ruffled Edge, Tricornered, 10 In. 664.00
Bowl, Pink Stripes, Fluted, Ruffled Edge, 4 ½ x 9 In. 1600.00
Bowl, Queen's Pattern, Diamond Quilted, Ruffled Edge, 3-Footed, 6 x 5 ½ In. 5175.00
Bowl, Ribbed, Tricornered, Ruffled Edge, 8 ½ In. 275.00
Bowl, Applied Feet, c.1890, 4 In. 200.00
Bowl, Scalloped & Folded Rim, Satin, 4-Footed, 6 ¾ In. 275.00
Bride's Basket, Enameled Red & White Mums, Green Stems, Ruffled Edge, 9 In. 1035.00
Bride's Basket, Ruffled Edge, Rope Handles, 11 x 14 In. 2588.00
Castor, Pickle, Enameled Chrysanthemums, 4-Footed Caddy, Fork, 9 In. 1380.00
Centerpiece, Fairy Lamp, Bud Vases, Bowl, Metal Holder, Pink, 8 ½ In. 748.00
Charger, Flower, Leaves, Stems, Traceries, 12 ¼ In. . . . . 288.00 to 690.00
Charger, White, Yellow Mums, Gold Enameled Rim, 10 ¼ In. 690.00
Condiment Set, Melon Enameled Ribbed Shakers, Cruets, Stoppers, 10 In., 5 Piece 2500.00
Creamer, Enameled Roses, Green Stems, Red Rim, Footed, Handle, 3 ¾ In. 1150.00
Cruet, Ribbed, Enameled Mums, Yellow, White, Ribbed Stopper, 6 ½ In. 2300.00
Cruet, Ribbed Stopper, 6 ¾ In. 725.00
Dish, Tricornered, 3-Footed, 2 ½ In. 83.00
Jack-In-The-Pulpit, Glossy, Crimped Rim, 10 ½ In. 385.00
Lamp Base, Enameled, Ibis In Flight, Pyramids Of Egypt, Metal Base, 10 ¼ x 7 In. 1150.00
Mug, Enameled Amethyst Flowers, Earth Tone Stems, Outlined Rim, Handle, 2 ½ In. 850.00
Perfume Bottle, Gold Enameled Berries, Leaves, Silver Lid, Marked, CM, 1911, 4 In. 1100.00
Pitcher, 8 ¾ In 675.00
Pitcher, Applied Green Vine, Leaves & Reeded Handle, Ruffled Edge, 9 ¼ In. 230.00
Pitcher, Tankard, Enameled Ivy, Green, Brown, Handle, 9 In. 3738.00
Pitcher, Tankard, Enameled Violet, Butterfly, Applied Handle, 9 In. 5175.00
Shade, Hurricane, Glossy, 8 ¼ In. 600.00
Shade, Ruffled Edge, Glossy, 5 ¼ In. 354.00
Sugar, Enameled Flowers, Leaves, Traceries, Applied Foot, 3 x 2 ¼ In. 748.00
Sugar, Queen's Pattern, Applied Foot, 3 ½ x 2 In. 1380.00
Sugar & Creamer, Applied Reeded Handles 850.00
Sugar & Creamer, Beaded Enameling Teardrop & Dot 2600.00
Sugar & Creamer, Diamond, Optic, Glossy, 4 ½ In. 450.00
Toothpick, Enameled Chrysanthemums, Bulbous, Square Mouth, 2 ¾ In. 403.00
Toothpick, Enameled Yellow & White Stemmed Mums, Tricornered, 2 In. 288.00
Tumbler, Queen's Pattern, Green, Yellow, Brown, White, 3 ¾ In. 900.00
Vase, 4 Parts, Urn Form, Handles, Metal Rod, Ruffled Foot, Stopper, 14 In. 375.00
Vase, Bulbous, Tricornered Ruffled Edge, Footed, 12 ½ In. 403.00
Vase, Double Gourd, 6 ¾ In. 400.00
Vase, Egyptian Bottle Shape, Elongated Scroll Handles, 12 In. 500.00
Vase, Enameled Fish, Seaweed, Gold Netting, 7 ½ In. 9775.00
Vase, Enameled Flower, Petticoat Shape, Tricornered Rim, 10 In. 2013.00
Vase, Enameled Hawthorn Flowers, Gourd, 8 In. 805.00
Vase, Enameled Verse, Cowslip Is A Country Lass, Flowers, Vines, Bulbous, 11 ½ In. . . . . . *illus* 2400.00
Vase, Fish, Enameled Gold Fish Net, Underwater Vegetation, 9 ¾ In. 3393.00
Vase, Flowers, Blue & White Blossoms, Bulbous, Long Neck, 10 In. 978.00
Vase, Glossy, Scalloped Rim, Footed, 10 ¼ In. 385.00
Vase, Gold Enameled Flowers, Leaves, Bulbous, Long Neck, 10 In. 518.00
Vase, Gourd, 4 Enameled Swallows, Gold Beading Around Rim, 8 In. 4600.00
Vase, Jack-In-The-Pulpit, Crimped Rim, 10 ¾ In. 400.00
Vase, Jack-In-The-Pulpit, Enameled Flowers, Beading, Crimped Top, 11 ¼ In. 1265.00
Vase, Jack-In-The-Pulpit, Ruffled Edge, 8 In. 345.00
Vase, Jack-In-The-Pulpit, Salmon Pink To Yellow, Ruffled Top, 6 ¾ In. 115.00
Vase, Lily, Footed Tricornered Rim, 8 In. 150.00
Vase, Lily, Glossy, 5 ¾ In. . . . . *illus* 225.00
Vase, Lily, Tricornered Rim, 5 ¾ In. 266.00
Vase, Melon Ribbed, 4 ¼ In. 413.00
Vase, Oval, Scalloped Rim, 4 ¾ In. 140.00
Vase, Pointed Handle, 6 ¾ In. 420.00
Vase, Pouch, Flared Rim, 8 Points, 5 x 5 In. 374.00

Burmese Glass, Bowl, Applied Feet, c.1890, 4 In.
$200.00

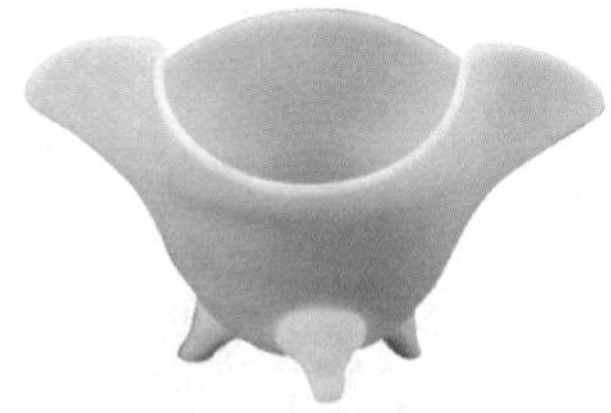

Burmese Glass, Vase, Enameled Verse, Cowslip Is A Country Lass, Flowers, Vines, Bulbous, 11 ½ In.
$2400.00

Burmese Glass, Vase, Lily, Glossy, 5 ¾ In.
$225.00

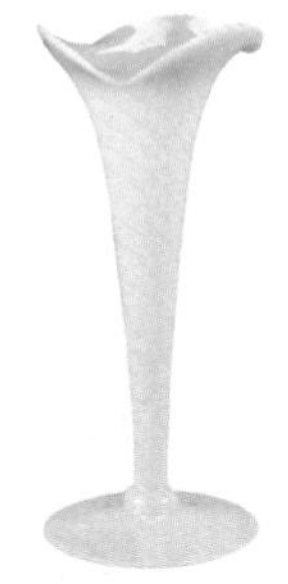

TIP

If you have a small-neck decanter or bottle that doesn't seem to dry after it is washed, try putting a small amount of rubbing alcohol in the bottle. Shake, pour out, and wait for the remaining drops to evaporate.

Buster Brown, Bank, Good Luck, Horse, Gold Horseshoe, Iron, Arcade, 4 ½ x 4 In.
$170.00

Butter Chip, Majolica, 3 Overlapping Leaves, Pink Pebbled Ground, 3 In.
$189.00

Butter Chip, Royal Copenhagen, Basket Weave Border, Flower Bouquet, 3 ¼ In.
$14.00

Bybee Pottery, Vase, Blue, Wheel Thrown, Bulbous, Flared Rim, 5 In.
$49.00

Vase, Queen's Pattern, Applied Handles, Gold Enameling, 5 ½ In. 3450.00
Vase, Reverse Trumpet, Flowers, Gold Scroll, 10 In. 2300.00
Vase, Ruffled Edge, 3 Reeded Feet, 6 ¼ In. 485.00
Vase, Scalloped Rim, 10 In. 413.00
Vase, Stick, Enameled Flowers, Needlepoint Style, Bulbous, Double Loop Handles, 12 In. 3450.00
Vase, Stylized Flowers, Leaves, Berries, Long Neck, Bulbous, 11 ½ In. 1150.00
Vase, Trumpet, Scalloped Rim, 10 In. 345.00
Vase, Verse, Cowslip Is A Country Lass, Flowers, Vines, Bulbous, 11 ½ In. 4200.00

BUSTER BROWN, the comic strip, first appeared in color in 1902. Buster and his dog, Tige, remained a popular comic and soon became even more famous as the emblem for a shoe company, a textile firm, and other companies. The strip was discontinued in 1920. Buster Brown sponsored a radio show from 1943 to 1955 and a TV show from 1950 to 1956. The Buster Brown characters are still used by Brown Shoe Company, Buster Brown Apparel, Inc., and Gateway Hosiery.

Bank, Good Luck, Horse, Gold Horseshoe, Iron, Arcade, 4 ½ x 4 In. .... *illus* 170.00
Button, Blue Ribbon Shoes, ⅞ In. 25.00
Button, Buster Brown Shoes, c.1910, 1 ½ In. 164.00
Card Set, Buster At The Circus, With Yellow Kid, 1904, 40 Piece 379.00
Display, Tige, Tread Straight, Chalkware, Countertop, 16 ½ In. 460.00
Game, Pin-The-Tail Type, Cloth, c.1910 .... 203.00
Laundry Bag, Buster & Tige, Embroidered, Heavy Cloth, c.1904, 20 x 26 In. 115.00
Magazine, First Issue, January, 1906, 32 Pages 316.00
Match Holder, Tige, Friends, Bread, Tin Lithograph, 7 x 2 In. 825.00
Pin, Blue Ribbon Shoes, Brown Paper Back, 1 ¼ In. 14.00
Postcard Set, Buster & Yellow Kid, Numbered, 1903, 3 x 5 ½ In., 10 Piece 172.00
Rug, Store Display, Buster & Tige, Yellow, Navy, Mohawk, 1960s, 52 In. 540.00
Shoetree, Molded Plastic, Adjustable, Package, 1960s, 9 ½ In. 75.00
Wristwatch, Plastic Box, Buster Logo, 1975, 10 In. 115.00

BUTTER CHIPS, or butter pats, were small individual dishes for butter. They were the height of fashion from 1880 to 1910. Earlier as well as later examples are known.

Blue Transfer, Poppies, Ferns, Scalloped Edge, 3 In. 20.00
Brown Transfer, Daffodil, Square, Grindley, c.1992, 3 ⅛ In. 32.00
Brown Transfer, Fern, Butterfly, Patterned Border, 8-Sided, 1878, 3 In. 12.00
Flow Blue, Country Scenes, c.1891, 3 In., Pair 116.00
Flow Blue, Touraine Pattern, Flowers, Henry Alcock, 3 In., 3 Piece 90.00
Flower Border, Gold, Meakin, c.1890, 2 ½ In. 20.00
Franciscan Company, Blue On White, c.1984, 2 ¾ In. 16.00
Green Transfer, Garland Of Flowers, Scalloped Edge, Raised Decoration, 3 In. 18.00
Ironstone, Le Vieux Quebec, Blue, White, 4 ⅜ In. 15.00
Ironstone, Purple Day Lily, Rolled Edge, 3 In. 32.00
Ironstone, White, Scalloped Rim, 3 ¼ In., 4 Piece 45.00
Majolica, 3 Overlapping Leaves, Pink Pebbled Ground, 3 In. .... *illus* 189.00
Noritake, Azalea No. 312, c.1930 .... 69.00
Pink Transfer, Country Scene, Horse & Rider, 3 In. 26.00
Porcelain, Brown Transfer, Vine With Leaves, 3 In. 15.00
Porcelain, Leaf Design, Brown, Pale Blue, 3 ⅛ In. 10.00
Porcelain, S, Green Leaves, Gold Rim, 3 In. 24.00
Royal Copenhagen, Basket Weave Border, Flower Bouquet, 3 ¼ In. .... *illus* 14.00
Violets, Gold Trim, Windsor China, c.1950, 3 ½ In. 20.00
White, Black Leaping Gazelle, Art Deco Style, Bauscher Ivory China, 3 In. 65.00
White, Bluebird, Pink Flowers, 12-Sided, Embossed Edge, 3 ⅜ In. 30.00
White, Green Greek Key Band, Gold Trim, 3 In. 10.00

BUTTER MOLDS *are listed in the Kitchen category under Mold, Butter.*

BUTTON collecting has been popular since the nineteenth century. Buttons have been known throughout the centuries, and there are millions of styles. Gold, silver, or precious stones were used for the best buttons, but most were made of natural materials, like bone or shell, or from inexpensive metals. Only a few types are listed for comparison.

Baby Chicks, Blue, Gold, Card 6.00
Bakelite, Apple Juice, Stippled Leaf Center, Transparent Border, c.1935, 1 ¼ In. 25.00
Bakelite, Cherry Red, 2 Holes, 1 ¼ In. 6.00
Bakelite, Navy Anchor, Embossed, Black, 1940s, 1 ¼ In. 20.00
Brass, Cut Steel, Faceted, Rolled Edge, Brass Shank, Victorian, c.1870, 1 ¼ In. 18.00

Brass, Cut Steel, Water Lilies, Pierced, Wire Shank, Openwork, 1 ¼ In. 15.00
Celluloid, Ear Of Corn, c.1930. .... 15.00
Celluloid, Swirled, Tite Top, 1 ¼ In. 2.00
Cloisonne, Brass Back, Wire Shank, ⅜ In. 49.00
Enamel, 2 Flags, Order Of Catholic Church, Spain, 1 ¼ In. 29.00
Enamel, Paisley Swirls, Brass Base, Loop Shank, Cobalt Blue Ground, Dome, 1 ⅛ In. 38.00
Enamel, Pink, Blue Flowers, France, ⅞ In. 85.00
Glass, Cherub, Stamped, Black, Flower Border, Brass Back, Victorian 35.00
Glass, Peacock Eye, Blue, Green, Brass Loop Shank, 9/16 In. 25.00
Glass, White, Gold Trim, ¾ In. 2.00
Hematite, Beads, 3 Parts, Holes, Hand Wired, Victorian, c.1890, ⅝ x ½ In. 7.00
Jadeite Jade, ⅝ x 1 In. 50.00
Metal, Plastic, Eagle, ¾ In., 2 Piece 1.00
Metal, Windmill, Bronze Color, ¾ In., 5 Piece 10.00
Mother-Of-Pearl, ¼ In. 6.00
Mother-Of-Pearl, Figural, Fish, Self-Carved Shank, ¾ x ½ In. 10.00
Plastic, Basket Shape, Hand Painted Fruit, 1 x ⅞ In. 5.00
Plastic, Horse, White, Original Card, ⅝ x ¾ In., 6 Piece 16.00
Silver, Ships, Orange Enamel Sky, Leather Box, 1 In., 6 Piece 2040.00
U.S. Military, Arrows, Stars, Eagle's Head, ¾ In. 35.00
Wood, Mexican Sombrero, Metal Shank, Green, Orange, Black Stripes 5.00

BUTTONHOOKS have been a popular collectible in England for many years but are now gaining the attention of American collectors. The buttonhooks were made to help fasten the many buttons of the old-fashioned high-button shoes and other items of apparel.

Amber, Celluloid Handle, Silvery Green Layer, Outlined In Black Art Deco, 7 In. 27.00
Bakelite Handle, c.1900, 7 In. 11.00
Bone Handle, Victorian, Doll Size 32.00
Hammered Steel Front, Advertising On Reverse, 1920s, 3 ⅞ In. 15.00
Hunter Bicycles, Dog, Bird, Fulton, N.Y., Celluloid, Metal 275.00
Mother-Of-Pearl, c.1890, 2 ¼ In. 66.00
Steel, Folding Handle, 1920s, 4 ⅝ In. 17.00
Sterling Silver, Amethyst Stone, 6 ⅞ In. 109.00
Sterling Silver, For Gloves, Repousse Design, 3 In. 50.00
Sterling Silver, Hollow Ware, Repousse, 4 ½ In. 125.00
Sterling Silver, Long Handle, Acanthus Knob, Wreath Leaf Design, 8 In. 68.00
Sterling Silver, Unger's, Love's Dream, Art Nouveau, 8 ¾ In. 125.00
Yellow Gold, Eagle's Head, 18K, France, c.1870, 2 ¾ In. 268.00

BYBEE POTTERY was started in 1845 and is still working. The Lexington, Kentucky, firm makes pottery that is sold at the factory. Pieces are marked with the name or with the name enclosed by the outline of the state of Kentucky.

Bank, Pig, Standing, Glossy Gray, 5 ⅝ In. 16.00
Batter Bowl, Brown, 7 ½ In. 18.00
Batter Bowl, Dark Green Glaze, Spout, Loop Handle, 7 ½ In. 18.00
Bowl, Blue, 2 Tab Handles, Marked, 9 In. 15.00
Bowl, Handles, Marked BB, 9 x 2 ¼ In. 15.00
Figurine, Duck, White, 2 ¾ In. 7.00
Figurine, Owl, Blue & Tan, Pierced Eyes, Marked BB, 1 ¼ In. 8.00
Pitcher, Blue, Wheel Thrown, 8 In. 65.00
Strawberry Jar, Blue, Cornelison Bybee Pottery, Incised Stamp, 3 ½ x 5 In. 27.00
Strawberry Jar, Gloss Black, Incised Stamp, Cornelison, Kentucky, 4 x 5 In. 30.00
Vase, Blue, Wheel Thrown, Bulbous, Flared Rim, 5 In. .... *illus* 49.00

CALENDARS made to hang on the wall or to be displayed on a desk top have been popular since the last quarter of the nineteenth century. Many were printed with advertising as part of the artwork and were given away as premiums. Calendars with guns, gunpowder, or Coca-Cola advertising are most prized.

1891, Page, July, Russell & Morgan, US Playing Cards, Cherubs, 7 ½ x 12 In. 78.00
1893, Hires Root Beer, 2 Young Girls With Cat, 1893, 8 x 14 In. 2390.00
1896, Mellwood Distillery Company, 12 x 18 In. .... *illus* 403.00
1899, Cream Of Wheat, Seminude Woman, Frame, 36 x 29 In. 250.00
1900, Antikamnia, 6 Sheet, Clothed Skeletons, 7 x 10 In. 495.00
1901, DuPont Powder Mini, Clabrough Golcher & Co., Lithograph, December, 3 ½ x 6 In. 308.00
1902, Coal Dealer, Woonsocket, Cardboard, Die Cut, Lithograph, Children, 22 x 15 In. 187.00

Calendar, 1896, Mellwood Distillery Company, 12 x 18 In.
$403.00

Calendar, 1903, Indian Maidens, Fan, Syracuse Herald, N.Y., 9 x 14 In.
$472.00

Calendar, 1904, Youth Companion, Edwardian, Fold-Out, 11 In.
$649.00

Potichomania

Potichomania, a type of decoupage, has been popular since the nineteenth century. Victorian women glued small pictures, cigar bands, and paper lace to the back or inside of a piece of glass, then sealed it with shellac or felt. The finished piece had a colorful all-over design that looked like painted porcelain. Today potichomania is easier. Pictures are glued to the back of a clear glass plate, then sealed with a special spray found at craft shops.

Calendar, 1950, Crossroads Of Commerce, Pennsylvania Railroad, Grif Teller, 28 ½ In.
$48.00

Calendar Plate, 1980, Astrological Scenes, Couples, Red, Scalloped Edge, Myott, 9 In.
$10.00

Camark, Figurine, Nude, Flower Holder, Maroon High Glaze, 8 ¾ In.
$82.00

1902, Marlin Fire Arms Co., Wildlife Images, Full Pad, 6 x 3 ½ In. 700.00
1903, DuPont, Generations Have Used DuPont Powder, Man, Boy, Full Pad, 6 x 3 In. 850.00
1903, Globe Saloon, Die Cut, Hoanker & Dasbagh, Canton Mo., 9 ½ x 11 ½ In. 168.00
1903, Indian Maidens, Fan, Syracuse Herald, N.Y., 9 x 14 In. *illus* 472.00
1903, S. Jung & Co., Woman, Lying On Bed, Frame, 14 x 20 In. 350.00
1904, Equitable Insurance, Girls, Maud Humphrey, 6 Pages, 12 ¾ x 10 In. 440.00
1904, Youth Companion, Edwardian, Fold-Out, 11 In. *illus* 649.00
1905, George Miller, Couple Pointing Up To Sign, 8 x 14 In. 575.00
1905, Youth's Companion Magazine, Girl Holding Flowers, Trifold, 11 x 20 In. 110.00
1907, Frank Coe-Mortimer Fertilizers, Farmer, Man In Car, Frame, 16 x 12 In. 1100.00
1908, McCormick, Woman Having Her Palm Read, 20 x 13 In. 500.00
1908, Rice's Seeds, Woman In Rose Garden, Embossed, Cardboard, 20 x 13 In. 357.00
1909, Lakewood Pharmacy, Setting Sun On A Dying Race, Cleveland Ohio, 10 x 15 In. 90.00
1911, Dr. Simmons' Liver Regulator, Woman, Pink & Yellow Dress, 11 x 7 In. 176.00
1914, National Lumber Co., Holtville, Calif., Philip R. Goodwin, Hunting, 22 x 31 In. 123.00
1915, Lambertville Footware, Rubber Boots, Winter, Palmer Cox Brownie, 36 x 24 In. 1155.00
1916, Dr. Le Gear's Veterinary Medicines, Trademark Horse, 15 ¾ In. 187.00
1917, Rock Island Plows, Daddy's Treasures, J.H. Cruise, Earlville, Ill., 7 x 17 In. 56.00
1927, Detmer Woolen Bathing Suits, Bathing Girl, A.C. Silva, 15 x 9 In. 200.00
1928, Goodrich Silvertowns Tires, Tubes, Cowboy, B.E. Needles, Full Pad, 16 x 10 In. 160.00
1929, Sinclair Gasoline, Loves Treasure, Mother & Child, Full Pad, 21 x 11 In. 50.00
1929, US Cartridge, Come On What Ails Yer, William Handen Foster, 16 x 35 In. 700.00
1930, Edison Mazda Lamps, Girl On Rocks, Maxfield Parrish, Frame, 21 x 11 In. 605.00
1931, Mendota Ford Auto Co., Image, We Three, 11 x 14 In. 45.00
1935, Firestone Tires, Art Deco Image, Rome Tire & Battery Service, 21 x 42 In. 288.00
1937, Ready To Go, Pennsylvania Railroad, Trimmed, Grif Teller, 24 x 17 In. 47.00
1938, Utica Club, Brewery, Roosevelt, Cleveland, Fiftieth Anniversary, 34 x 15 In. 343.00
1939, Dangerous Sport, Philip R. Goodwin, 15 x 10 In. 375.00
1943, Wilson's Store, Boy, Holding Rifle, Puppies, Cardboard, 9 ½ x 6 ½ In. 50.00
1948, Charlie Moon, Wagon Train, Dowling, Mich., Full Pad, 12 x 15 In. 50.00
1948, Oyster Shell Products, Frame, 13 ½ x 19 ½ In. 105.00
1950, Crossroads Of Commerce, Pennsylvania Railroad, Grif Teller, 28 ½ In. *illus* 48.00
1953, Maid In Baltimore, Woman In Yellow Bikini, 16 x 33 ½ In. 84.00
1955, Mass Transportation, Army Navy Game, Penn. Railroad, 28 ½ In. 59.00
1958, G.L. Pine, Mercersburg, Pa. 35.00
1965, Marilyn Monroe, Cowgirl Outfit, Topless 86.00

CALENDAR PLATES were very popular in the United States from 1906 to 1929. Since then, plates have been made every year. A calendar and the name of a store, a picture of flowers, a girl, or a scene were featured on the plate.

1909, Calendar Center, Rope Around Calendars, Blue Edges, Signed, 9 ¼ In. 17.00
1909, Wright's Store, Columbus, Kansas, Garland, Embossed, Carnation McNicol 83.00
1910, C.F. Company, Pink Roses, Gold Rim, Marked In Green, 8 ¾ In. 33.00
1910, Horseshoe, Woman, Greyhound Center, H.H. Wiefel Home Bakery, Scalloped 65.00
1910, Peter Wold, Pool Room & Livery, Mercersburg, Pa., 7 ¼ In. 125.00
1911, W.F. Clawson, Fancy Groceries & Meats, Anderson, Indiana, 8 ½ In. 18.00
1912, Hunting Scene, Bird, Man With Gun, Gold Trim, J.R. Dietrich & Co., 8 ¼ In. 20.00
1912, Kitty Hawk Airplane, Compliments C.B. Willis, The Buggy Man, 8 ¼ In. 69.00
1915, Panama Canal, American Flags, Gold Rim, Dresden, 7 ½ In. 31.00
1920, The Great World War, Muskegon Heights Furn. Co., Mich., East Liverpool, 8 In. 35.00
1959, Windmill, Gately's, Floral Border, White, Gilt, Taylor Smith Taylor, 10 In. 13.00
1961, Ivory & Gold, Taylor Smith Taylor, Marked, 10 In. 20.00
1962, God Bless Our House, Mulberry Color, Royal Staffordshire, 9 In. 12.00
1962, Zodiac Signs, Months, Church Center, Brown On White, Gold Trim, 9 ¼ In. 7.00
1967, Dog, Spaniel, Promotional, Walter's Auction Gallery, Pa., Sabina Line 24.00
1972, Astrological Scenes, Farmhouse, Brown, White, Alfred Meakin 10.00
1976, Bicentennial, 200th Anniversary, Eagle, American Shield, Flags 8.00
1977, States, God Bless America, Liberty Bell, Crossed American Flags, 9 ¼ In. 23.00
1979, Fair Store 90th Anniversary, Binghamton, N.Y., Cream Ground 5.50
1980, Astrological Scenes, Couples, Red, Scalloped Edge, Myott, 9 In. *illus* 10.00

CAMARK POTTERY started in 1924 in Camden, Arkansas. Jack Carnes founded the firm and made many types of glazes and wares. The company was bought by Mary Daniel. Production was halted in 1983.

Figurine, Nude, Flower Holder, Maroon High Glaze, 8 ¾ In. *illus* 82.00

Salt & Pepper, Figural, P-Shape, S-Shape, Turquoise, 2¾ In. 14.00
Vase, Cobalt Blue, Gold Crackle, Folded Rim, Marked, 7 x 7⅜ In. .... *illus* 795.00
Vase, Lake Scene, Trees, Iridescent, Marked, Le-Camark, 6 In. .... *illus* 750.00
Vase, Landscape, Opalescent Glaze, Signed, Lessell, 13 x 7 In. .... *illus* 1800.00
Vase, Tapered, Blue Matte, Yellow Drip, Paper Label, 3½ x 6½ In. 259.00

CAMBRIDGE GLASS Company was founded in 1901 in Cambridge, Ohio. The company closed in 1954, reopened briefly, and closed again in 1958. The firm made all types of glass. Their early wares included heavy pressed glass with the mark *Near Cut.* Later wares included Crown Tuscan, etched stemware, and clear and colored glass. The firm used a *C* in a triangle mark after 1920.

Adonis, Bowl, Footed, 12 In. 190.00
Adonis, Dish, Mayonnaise, Underplate, Sections 80.00
Aero Optic, Jug, Ball, Amethyst, Clear Handle, 80 Oz. 95.00
Apple Blossom, Compote, Footed, 5⅜ x 2¾ In. 80.00
Apple Blossom, Decanter, Amber, 28 Oz. 495.00
Apple Blossom, Relish Dish, Handles, 4 Sections, 8¾ x 7¼ x 5 In. 185.00
Arcadia, Candy Dish, Cover, Frosted 60.00
Aurora, Cocktail, Mocha, 3 Oz. 23.00
Aurora, Cordial, Amber, Optic Bowl, Oz. 25.00
Aurora, Cordial, Carmen, Oz. 36.00
Aurora, Cordial, Emerald Green, Optic, Oz. 36.00
Aurora, Cordial, Laurel Wreath Cut, Optic Bowl, Oz. 12.00
Aurora, Goblet, Moonlight Blue, Optic Bowl, 9 Oz. 37.00
Aurora, Goblet, Royal Blue, 9 Oz. 36.00
Ball, Decanter Set, Amber, Clear Stopper, Mushroom Tumblers, 80 Oz., 6 Piece 90.00
Ball, Pitcher, Emerald Green, 8 Oz. .... *illus* 50.00
Ball, Pitcher, Ice Lip, Amber, Clear Handle, 10 In. 95.00
Ball, Pitcher, Moonlight Blue, 80 Oz. 185.00
Barrel, Tumbler, Whiskey, Carmen, 2½ Oz. 11.00
Barrel, Tumbler, Whiskey, Green, 2½ Oz. 6.00
Barrel, Tumbler, Whiskey, Royal Blue, 2 Oz. 11.00
Bashful Charlotte, Flower Frog, 6½ In. 100.00
Bashful Charlotte, Flower Frog, 11½ In. 450.00
Bashful Charlotte, Flower Frog, Amber, 11½ In. 550.00
Bashful Charlotte, Flower Frog, Cobalt Blue, 11½ In. 475.00
Bashful Charlotte, Flower Frog, Frosted, 11½ In. .... 300.00 to 495.00
Bashful Charlotte, Flower Frog, Peach-Blo, 6½ In. .... 225.00 to 300.00
Bashful Charlotte, Flower Frog, Peach-Blo, 11½ In. 595.00
Blossom Time, Bowl, 11 In. 60.00
Blossom Time, Plate, Handles, 8 In. 53.00
Blossom Time, Torte Plate, 13 In. 60.00
Blossom Time, Vase, Footed, Gold Trim On Rim & Foot, 11 In. 145.00
Blossom Time, Vase, Hat Shape, 8¾ x 7 x 4½ In. 165.00
Blue Jay, Flower Frog, 5½ In. 153.00
Blue Willow, Champagne, 5½ Oz., 5½ In. 35.00
Blue Willow, Goblet, 9 Oz., 7 In. 55.00
Blue Willow, Plate, Luncheon, Etched, 9 In. 29.00
Blue Willow, Sandwich Server, Keyhole Handle, 10¾ In. 85.00
Blue Willow, Tumbler, Cone, Footed, 12 Oz., 6 In. 75.00
Bluebell, Atomizer, 7 In. 525.00
Bluebell, Salt & Pepper 72.00
Calla Lily, Candleholder, Pair 48.00
Calla Lily, Candlestick, Emerald Green, 6½ In., Pair 98.00
Calla Lily, Candlestick, Mandarin Gold, 6½ In., Pair 25.00
Candle Base, For Figural Flower Frog, Dianthus Pink 475.00
Candlelight, Relish, Sections, 7 In. 37.00
Caprice, Ashtray, Moonlight Blue, 3-Sided, 4 Piece 43.00
Caprice, Bonbon, Footed, Oval, Moonlight Blue, 6 In. .... 45.00 to 65.00
Caprice, Bonbon, Moonlight Blue, Square, 5 In. 30.00
Caprice, Bowl, Footed, 7 In. 30.00
Caprice, Bowl, Oval, Moonlight Blue, 12 In. 62.00
Caprice, Bowl, Round, Flared, 4-Footed, 10½ In. 25.00
Caprice, Bowl, Shallow, 4-Footed, 13 In. 40.00
Caprice, Candlestick, 3-Light, 6¼ x 10 In., Pair 96.00
Caprice, Candlestick, 3-Light, Cascading, 6½ x 6½ In., Pair .... 55.00 to 100.00

Camark, Vase, Cobalt Blue, Gold Crackle, Folded Rim, Marked, 7 x 7⅜ In.
$795.00

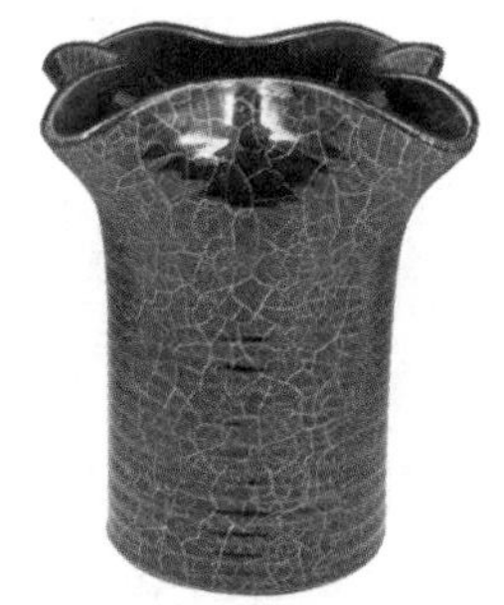

Camark, Vase, Lake Scene, Trees, Iridescent, Marked, Le-Camark, 6 In.
$750.00

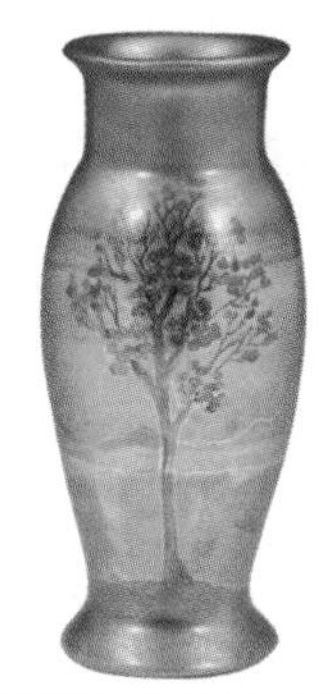

Camark, Vase, Landscape, Opalescent Glaze, Signed, Lessell, 13 x 7 In.
$1800.00

TIP

When you open your windows in warm weather, watch out for blowing curtains. They may hit glass or china displayed nearby and cause damage.

Cambridge, Ball, Pitcher, Emerald Green, 8 Oz.
$50.00

Cambridge, Caprice, Sugar & Creamer, Moonlight Blue
$35.00

Cambridge, Carmen, Cup & Saucer, After Dinner, Gold Trim
$33.00

TIP

To find a small crack in porcelain or glass, try this. Put the piece on a table. Tap it with your fingernail. A cracked piece gives off a dull thud, a perfect piece will "ring." Learn to recognize the sound by practicing on some pieces you know are broken.

Caprice, Candlestick, 3-Light, Cascading, Moonlight Blue, 6 ½ x 6 ½ In., Pair 200.00
Caprice, Candlestick, Moonlight Blue, 7¼ In., Pair . . . . 136.00 to 145.00
Caprice, Candy Dish, Cover, Moonlight Blue, Alpine 225.00
Caprice, Compote, Moonlight Blue, 5 ½ In. 62.00
Caprice, Compote, Moonlight Blue, Low, 7 In. 35.00
Caprice, Cordial, Oz. 40.00
Caprice, Cruet, Oil, Moonlight Blue, 3 Oz. 150.00
Caprice, Cruet, Oil & Vinegar, Tray, Stoppers, 5 Piece 78.00
Caprice, Cup & Saucer 15.00
Caprice, Dish, Lemon, Handles, Moonlight Blue, 6 In. 25.00
Caprice, Dish, Mayonnaise, Underplate, Moonlight Blue, Alpine, 5 ¼ In.. . . . . 110.00
Caprice, Dish, Mayonnaise, Underplate, Moonlight Blue, Ladle, Sections. . . . . 130.00 to 145.00
Caprice, Dish, Pickle, 9 In. 19.00
Caprice, Epergne, 3-Light Candlestick, Bud Vases, Holder, Bobeches 90.00
Caprice, Goblet, Blown, 9 Oz. . . . . 30.00 to 32.00
Caprice, Iced Tea, Moonlight, 12 Oz.. . . . . 68.00
Caprice, Jelly, Handles, Moonlight Blue, 5 In. 30.00
Caprice, Pitcher, Ball, 80 Oz. 225.00
Caprice, Pitcher, Ball, Moonlight, 80 Oz. 450.00
Caprice, Pitcher, Doulton, 80 Oz. 795.00
Caprice, Plate, Salad, Moonlight Blue, 8 ½ In.. . . . . 35.00
Caprice, Relish, 3 Sections, Moonlight Blue, 8 In. 45.00
Caprice, Relish, Cloverleaf, 3 Sections, 8 ½ In.. . . . . 15.00
Caprice, Relish, Sections, Moonlight Blue, 6¾ In. . . . . 35.00 to 45.00
Caprice, Salt & Pepper 42.00
Caprice, Salt & Pepper, Ball Shape. . . . . 125.00 to 140.00
Caprice, Sugar 11.00
Caprice, Sugar & Creamer. 21.00
Caprice, Sugar & Creamer, Gold Krystol. 45.00
Caprice, Sugar & Creamer, Mocha 42.00
Caprice, Sugar & Creamer, Moonlight Blue . . . . *illus* 35.00
Caprice, Sugar & Creamer, Tray 48.00
Caprice, Torte Plate, 4-Footed, 14 In. 35.00
Caprice, Tray, For Sugar & Creamer, Moonlight Blue, 6 In. 35.00
Caprice, Tumbler, Blown, 12 Oz. . . . . 30.00 to 35.00
Caprice, Tumbler, Footed, Alpine, 10 Oz. 20.00
Caprice, Tumbler, Whiskey, Mocha, 2 Oz. 48.00
Carmen, Ashtray, Flat 30.00
Carmen, Candy Dish, Cover, 3 Sections, 6 In.. . . . . 120.00
Carmen, Cigarette Holder, Ashtray Foot. . . . . 78.00 to 90.00
Carmen, Cordial, Oz. 48.00
Carmen, Cup & Saucer, After Dinner, Gold Trim . . . . *illus* 33.00
Carmen, Nut Cup, Footed, 3 In.. . . . . 60.00
Carmen, Pitcher, Ball, 80 Oz. 235.00
Carmen, Plate, Salad, 8 In. 28.00
Carmen, Sugar. 35.00
Carmen, Tumbler, Cordial, Mushroom, Oz. 15.00
Cascade, Bowl, 4-Footed, 10 ½ In.. . . . . 21.00
Century, Cordial, Oz. 11.00
Chantilly, Bell. 125.00
Chantilly, Candy Dish, Cover, 3 Sections, 5 In.. . . . . 135.00
Chantilly, Champagne, 7 Oz., 5 ¾ In. 18.00
Chantilly, Coaster, Sterling Silver Base, Fluted Edge, 3 In. 27.00
Chantilly, Cocktail, 3 Oz. 20.00
Chantilly, Cruet, Sterling Silver Base 250.00
Chantilly, Dish, Mayonnaise, Underplate 135.00
Chantilly, Ice Bucket, Chrome Handle, 5 ¾ In. 95.00
Chantilly, Ice Tub, Tab Handles, Sterling Silver Base, 5 ¼ x 7 In. 210.00
Chantilly, Jug, Martini, Sterling Silver Base, 32 Oz., 9 In. 236.00
Chantilly, Marmalade, Cover, Sterling Silver Foot, 8 Oz., 5 ¼ In. 120.00
Chantilly, Pitcher, Sterling Silver Base, 20 Oz. 235.00
Chantilly, Salt & Pepper, Footed. . . . . 110.00 to 115.00
Chantilly, Salt & Pepper, Sterling-Silver Lids, Applied Handles, 3¾ In. . . . . 55.00 to 60.00
Chantilly, Sugar & Creamer 20.00
Cleo, Candlestick, Light Emerald Green, Decagon, 3 ½ In. 35.00
Cleo, Celery Dish, Oval, Light Emerald Green, 9 In. 50.00

Cleo, Cracker Plate, Peach-Blo, 10½ In.. 40.00
Cleo, Plate, Luncheon, Light Emerald Green, Decagon, 8 In. 17.00
Corinth, Sugar & Creamer 20.00
Crown Tuscan, Bowl, Flared, 4-Footed, Low, 12 In.. 125.00
Crown Tuscan, Bowl, Footed, Deep, 11 In.. 195.00
Crown Tuscan, Bowl, Seashell, 4-Footed, 8 In. 48.00
Crown Tuscan, Cocktail, Seafood, Seashell, 3 Oz. 65.00
Crown Tuscan, Compote, Seashell, Charleston Roses, Gold Trim, Footed, 6 In. 175.00
Crown Tuscan, Compote, Seashell, Footed, 6 In.. 60.00
Crown Tuscan, Lamp, Urn Shape, 11-In. Base 795.00
Crown Tuscan, Nut Dish, Gold Rim, 7½ x 7 In. *illus* 24.00
Crown Tuscan, Urn, Cover, Footed, 12 In., Pair. 295.00
Crown Tuscan, Vase, Cornucopia, 10¼ In. 90.00
Crown Tuscan, Vase, Urn Shape, Keyhole, 9 In. 295.00
Cut Wild Rose, Punch Set, Cups, 17 Piece 650.00
Daffodil, Compote, 3¼ x 6¼ In.. 45.00
Decagon, Creamer, Green 14.00
Decagon, Dish, Almond, Gold Krystol, 2½ In. 20.00
Decagon, Dish, Almond, Light Emerald, 2½ In. 20.00
Decagon, Dish, Almond, Mocha, 2½ In.. 20.00
Decagon, Dish, Almond, Moonlight Blue, 2½ In. 20.00
Decagon, Dish, Mayonnaise, Underplate, Pink 35.00
Decagon, Ice Tub, Amber, 5½ In. 44.00
Decagon, Ice Tub, Light Emerald, 5½ In. 50.00
Decagon, Ice Tub, Pink, 5½ In *illus* 100.00
Decagon, Plate, Bread & Butter, Green, 6¼ In. 11.00
Decagon, Plate, Moonlight Blue, 8½ In. 13.00
Decagon, Relish, Moonlight Blue, Sections, 8½ In.. 42.00
Decagon, Sandwich Server, Amber, Center, 11 In. 45.00
Decagon, Sandwich Server, Center Handle, Pink, 11 In. 50.00
Decagon, Saucer, Green. 8.00
Decagon, Sugar & Creamer, Pink 14.00
Deerfield, Cordial, Oz. 21.00
Diane, Bottle, Bar, Stopper 525.00
Diane, Celery, Relish, 5 Sections, 10 In. 46.00
Diane, Cigarette Holder, Footed 195.00
Diane, Cocktail, Oyster, 4½ Oz.. 32.00
Diane, Cocktail, Oyster, Amber, 4½ Oz.. 65.00
Diane, Cocktail Icer, Insert 59.00
Diane, Compote, 7 x 7½ In.. 49.00
Diane, Dish, Mayonnaise, Underplate, Ladle 145.00
Diane, Finger Bowl. 95.00
Diane, Goblet, 9 Oz. 25.00
Diane, Ice Bucket, Amber, Chrome Handle. 325.00
Diane, Lamp, Carmen, Gold Encrusted, Sterling Silver, Base & Neck, 11 In. 1250.00
Diane, Pitcher, Ball, 80 Oz., 9 In. 175.00 to 375.00
Diane, Platter, Handles, 16 x 11 In.. 52.00
Diane, Relish, 5 Sections, 12 In. 80.00
Diane, Salt & Pepper, Ball. 95.00 to 135.00
Diane, Salt & Pepper, Footed 42.00
Diane, Salt & Pepper, Footed, Sterling Silver Lids 175.00
Diane, Torte Plate, 14 In. 61.00 to 115.00
Diane, Tumbler, 13 Oz.. 95.00
Diane, Tumbler, Iced Tea, Footed, 12 Oz. 25.00 to 50.00
Diane, Tumbler, Whiskey, Sham, 2½ Oz. 100.00
Diane, Urn, Cover. 795.00
Diane, Urn, Cover, Crown Tuscan 795.00
Diane, Vase, Amber, Wide Baluster, 12 In.. 1650.00
Dolphin, Candlestick, Peach-Blo, 9½ In. *illus* 125.00
Doric, Candlestick, Azurite, 9¼ In., Pair 250.00
Draped Lady, Flower Frog, 8½ In. 125.00 to 150.00
Draped Lady, Flower Frog, 12½ In. 180.00 to 425.00
Draped Lady, Flower Frog, Amber, 12½ In. 255.00
Draped Lady, Flower Frog, Amber, 8½ In. 375.00
Draped Lady, Flower Frog, Frosted, 8½ In. 195.00 to 225.00
Draped Lady, Flower Frog, Gold Krystol, 8½ In. 160.00 to 425.00

TIP

Be sure copies of lists of valuables, photographs, and other information can be found in case of an insurance loss. Give copies to a trusted friend. Do not keep them in the house. If you keep them in your safe deposit box, be sure you have a key off site. The key could be lost in a house fire.

Cambridge, Crown Tuscan, Nut Dish, Gold Rim, 7½ x 7 In. $24.00

Cambridge, Decagon, Ice Tub, Pink, 5½ In. $100.00

Cambridge, Dolphin, Candlestick, Peach-Blo, 9 ½ In. $125.00

Cambridge, Everglade, Bowl, Floral, Irises, Moonlight Blue, 14 In. $40.00

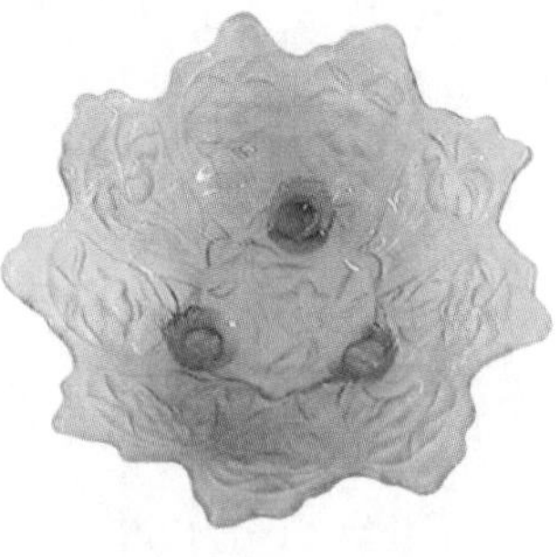

Cambridge Glass Colors
The most popular Cambridge Glass Company colors made during the 1920s and '30s were given special names in the advertising. Look for Amberina (shaded red amber), Carmen (ruby), Crown Tuscan (pink opaque), Ebony, Moonlight Blue, Peach-Blo (pink), Royal Blue, and several shades of Emerald Green.

Draped Lady, Flower Frog, Green, 8 ½ In. 325.00
Draped Lady, Flower Frog, Light Emerald, 8 ½ In. 180.00
Draped Lady, Flower Frog, Light Emerald, 12 ½ In. 390.00
Draped Lady, Flower Frog, Mocha, 12 ½ In. 625.00
Draped Lady, Flower Frog, Moonlight Blue, 12 ½ In. 1125.00
Draped Lady, Flower Frog, Moonlight Blue, 8 ½ In. 250.00
Draped Lady, Flower Frog, Peach-Blo, 12 ½ In. 595.00
Draped Lady, Flower Frog, Peach-Blo, 8½ In. 240.00 to 325.00
Ebony, Cigarette Box, Ashtrays On Cover, 4 Piece 275.00
Ebony, Cigarette Box, Cover 40.00
Elaine, Bowl, Floral, Footed, Handles, 12 In. 135.00
Elaine, Bowl, Handle, 9 ½ In. 65.00
Elaine, Candleholder, Keyhole, 5 In., Pair 69.00
Elaine, Champagne, 6 Oz. 30.00
Elaine, Goblet, 9 Oz. 50.00
Elaine, Ice Bucket, Chrome Handle 84.00
Elaine, Plate, Handles, 8 x 6 ¼ In. 45.00
Elaine, Salt & Pepper 95.00
Elaine, Tumbler, Iced Tea, Footed, 12 Oz. 55.00
Elaine, Vase, Footed, 11 In. 225.00
Everglade, Bowl, Floral, Buffalo & Indians, Moonlight Blue, Low, 16 In. 420.00
Everglade, Bowl, Floral, Irises, Moonlight Blue, 14 In. *illus* 40.00
Everglade, Bowl, Floral, Swans, Mocha, 14 In. 150.00
Everglade, Candlestick, 2-Light, 5 ¼ x 9 ¾ In. 40.00
Everglade, Candlestick, Moonlight Blue, 4 In., Pair 54.00
Everglade, Plate, 16 In. 48.00
Everglade, Sandwich Server, 3-Footed, 15 In. 65.00
Everglade, Sandwich Server, Moonlight Blue, 3-Footed, 13 In. 120.00
Everglade, Vase, Green, Footed, 11 In. 350.00
Figurine, Bridge Hound, Hole For Pencil, Amber, 1 ¾ In. 42.00
Figurine, Bridge Hound, Hole For Pencil, Amethyst, 1¾ In. 20.00 to 42.00
Figurine, Bridge Hound, Hole For Pencil, Crown Tuscan 42.00
Figurine, Bridge Hound, Hole For Pencil, Ebony, 1 ¾ In. 42.00
Figurine, Bridge Hound, Hole For Pencil, Gold Krystol 42.00
Gadroon, Sugar & Creamer 25.00
Geisha, Flower Frog, One Bun, Amber, 12 In. 750.00
Geisha, Flower Frog, One Bun, Peach-Blo, 12 In. 750.00
Geisha, Lamp, One Bun, Amber, 12 In. 1100.00
Gloria, Bowl, Vegetable Handles, 9 ½ In. 95.00
Gloria, Butter, Cover, Amber 425.00
Gloria, Compote, Handles, 6 x 5 In. 50.00
Gloria, Console Set, Silver Overlay, 3 Piece 550.00
Gloria, Tumbler, Whiskey, Footed, 2 ½ Oz. 85.00
Ham Bone, Ashtray, Moonlight Blue, 6 In. 32.00
Heirloom, Sugar & Creamer, Milk Glass 30.00
Heron, Flower Frog, 9 In. 78.00 to 140.00
Keyhole, Bowl, Cereal, Gold Krystol, 6 In. 19.00
Keyhole, Candlestick, 3-Light, 6 ½ x 8 ½ In., Pair 95.00
Keyhole, Candlestick, 3-Light, Pink Frosted, Stems, 6 x 8 ¼ In. 24.00
Keyhole, Cruet, Oil, Stopper 20.00
Keyhole, Cruet, Oil, Stopper, Green 26.00
Keyhole, Cruet Set, Tray, Oil & Vinegar, Mocha 125.00
Keyhole, Cruet Set, Tray, Oil & Vinegar, Royal Blue 98.00
Keyhole, Ivy Ball, 7 In. 72.00
Keyhole, Ivy Ball, Royal Blue, 7 In. 135.00
Keyhole, Platter, Oval, Light Emerald Green, 13 ½ In. 45.00
Keyhole, Vase, Amethyst, Clear Stem & Foot, 13 ¾ In. 95.00
Keyhole, Vase, Gold Krystol, 10 In. 66.00
Keyhole, Vase, Royal Blue, 10 In. 84.00
King Edward, Relish, 5 Sections, 12 In. 41.00
King Edward, Sugar & Creamer, Sterling Silver Base 38.00
Laurel Wreath, Punch Set, Underplate, Ladle, 11 ½-In. Bowl, 15 Piece 395.00
Lucia, Cigarette Holder, Footed 66.00
Magnolia, Candlestick, 2-Light, Prisms, Pair 185.00
Mandolin Lady, Flower Frog, 9 ¼ In. 400.00
Marjorie, Sherbet, Footed, 4 ¾ In., 12 Piece 150.00
Martha, Sugar & Creamer 24.00

Martha, Sugar & Creamer, Tray, Gold Krystol 55.00
Martha Washington, Jar, Pretzel, Cover 150.00
Minerva, Bell 95.00
Mocha, Cordial, Oz. 24.00
Mocha, Tumbler, Cordial, Mushroom, Oz. 8.00
Mt. Vernon, Candy Dish, Cover, Ball Knop, Footed, 8 3/4 In. 22.00
Mt. Vernon, Decanter, 40 Oz. 60.00
Mt. Vernon, Decanter, Carmen, 40 Oz. 175.00
Mt. Vernon, Relish, 5 Sections, 12 In. 50.00
Nautilus, Salt & Pepper, Mocha 54.00
Nautilus, Salt & Pepper, Tray, Amethyst 36.00
Nautilus, Sherry Set, Royal Blue, 28-Oz., Decanter, 5 Piece 171.00
Nautilus, Vase, Ebony, 11 In. 350.00
Near Cut, Bowl, Azurite, 7 1/2 In. 15.00
Near Cut, Cruet, Oil, 6 1/2 In. 40.00
Near Cut, Dish, Sweetmeat, Azurite, 3-Toed, 7 In. 15.00
Near Cut, Saltshaker 30.00
No. 620, Sugar & Creamer, Tray With Center Handle, Amber Glo 60.00
No. 726, Pitcher, Cover, Boudoir, Peach-Blo, 6 1/2 In. 135.00
Nude, Brandy, Amethyst, Frosted Stem & Foot, Oz., 6 1/2 In. 180.00
Nude, Brandy, Gold Krystol, Oz., 6 1/2 In. 125.00
Nude, Brandy, Light Emerald Green, Oz., 6 1/2 In. 72.00
Nude, Brandy, Pistachio, Clear Stem & Foot, Oz., 6 1/2 In. 250.00
Nude, Brandy, Royal Blue, Oz., 6 1/2 In. 250.00
Nude, Brandy, Tahoe Blue, Clear Stem & Foot, Oz., 6 1/2 In. 250.00
Nude, Candlestick, 9 In. 300.00
Nude, Champagne, 6 Oz., 7 In. 200.00
Nude, Champagne, Mocha, 6 Oz., 7 In. 675.00
Nude, Cigarette Box, 9 In. 695.00
Nude, Cigarette Box, Amethyst, 9 In. 1195.00
Nude, Cigarette Box, Cover, Cobalt Blue, 7 3/8 In. . . . . . *illus* 523.00
Nude, Cigarette Box, Light Emerald Green, 9 In. 695.00
Nude, Claret, 4 1/2 Oz., 7 In. 245.00
Nude, Claret, Amber, 4 1/2 Oz., 7 In. . . . . . 132.00 to 235.00
Nude, Claret, Amethyst, 4 1/2 Oz., 7 In. 325.00
Nude, Claret, Carmen, 4 1/2 Oz., 7 In. 240.00
Nude, Claret, Gold Krystol, Optic, 4 1/2 Oz., 7 In. 120.00
Nude, Claret, Royal Blue, 4 1/2 Oz., 7 In. 210.00
Nude, Cocktail, Amber, 3 Oz., 6 1/2 In. 125.00
Nude, Cocktail, Amethyst, Clear Stem & Foot, 3 Oz., 6 1/2 In. 225.00
Nude, Cocktail, Clear Bowl, Amber, Stem & Foot, 3 Oz., 6 1/2 In. 185.00
Nude, Cocktail, Frosted Stem & Foot, 3 Oz., 6 1/2 In. 225.00
Nude, Cocktail, Gold Krystol, Crown Tuscan, Stem & Foot, 3 Oz., 6 1/2 In. 225.00
Nude, Cocktail, Light Emerald Green, Clear Stem & Foot, 3 Oz., 6 1/2 In. 225.00
Nude, Cocktail, Mocha, Clear Stem & Foot, 3 Oz., 6 1/2 In. 495.00
Nude, Cocktail, Moonlight Blue, Clear Stem & Foot, 3 Oz., 6 1/2 In. 265.00
Nude, Cocktail, Peach-Blo, Clear Stem & Foot, 3 Oz., 6 1/2 In. 265.00
Nude, Cocktail, Pistachio, Clear Stem & Foot, 3 Oz., 6 1/2 In. 265.00
Nude, Compote, Carmen, 7 In. 210.00
Nude, Compote, Royal Blue, 7 In. 360.00
Nude, Compote, Seashell, 7 In. 250.00
Nude, Goblet, Roemer, Amethyst, 5 Oz., 6 1/2 In. 795.00
Nude, Ivy Ball, 7 In. . . . . . 192.00 to 295.00
Nude, Mint Dish 650.00
Nude, Vase, Bud, Amethyst, 11 In. 995.00
Nude, Vase, Bud, Royal Blue, 11 In. 1500.00
Nude, Wine, 3 Oz., 6 1/2 In. 235.00
Nude, Wine, Carmen, 3 Oz., 6 1/2 In. 395.00
Peach-Blo, Relish, 5 Sections, 12 1/4 In. 45.00
Plainware, Bowl, Azurite, 10 In. 87.00
Plainware, Creamer, Royal Blue. 45.00
Poppies, Candlestick, Keyhole Stem, 5 In., Pair 43.00
Portia, Bowl, Handles, 9 1/2 In. 65.00
Portia, Bowl, Shaped Pulled & Ruffled Rim, 4-Footed. 99.00
Portia, Cocktail, Oyster, 3 Oz. 18.00
Portia, Cordial, Oz. 54.00

TIP

The way you display your collection on the wall shows you are a serious collector. Hang clothing on padded hangers, don't suspend heavy purses from their handles, keep lunch boxes and fabrics out of the sun, leave space between salt and pepper shakers, hang potato mashers as a border in the kitchen, put bottles on glass shelves in front of windows, and stuff padding in purses, shoes, or hats. You will enjoy the collection and your friends will either agree—or decide you are an individualist with strange taste.

Cambridge, Nude, Cigarette Box, Cover, Cobalt Blue, 7 3/8 In. $523.00

Cambridge, Rose Lady, Flower Frog, Console, Peach-Blo, 8 ½ In, 2 Piece. $350.00

C

TIP

Put together a "flea market transportation kit." Start with a large shopping bag to carry small items or a collapsible shopping cart if you think you'll need it. Include packing materials like newspapers, bubble wrap, boxes, or old blankets. Diapers and plastic-lined bedding pads are good for wrapping breakables. Carry a rope or bungee cords to hold items on top of the car or to secure an open trunk. Don't forget a screwdriver, hammer, and rust-loosening oil in case you have to dismantle a bed or table to fit it in your car. Take a tape measure to check the size of a chair against the size of your car's open door and storage space. We have seen people trying to force a chair into a trunk or backseat by twisting it in every direction.

Portia, Decanter, Footed, Stopper, 29 Oz. 525.00
Portia, Goblet, 9 Oz. 34.00 to 55.00
Portia, Lamp, Hurricane, Dolphin Base 225.00
Portia, Pitcher, Ball, Gold Krystol, Gold Encrusted 330.00
Portia, Plate, Salad, 8 ½ In. 20.00
Portia, Relish, 5 Sections, 12 In. 53.00 to 90.00
Portia, Sherbet, 6 Oz. 34.00
Pristine, Bowl, Gardenia, 13 In. 48.00
Pristine, Bowl, Shallow, 10 ½ In. 48.00
Pristine, Cocktail Shaker, 32 Oz. 35.00
Pristine, Console Set, Mandarin Gold, 3 Piece 146.00
Pristine, Cordial, Oz. 36.00
Pristine, Flower Circle, 7 In. 24.00
Pristine, Flower Frog, 3 ½ In. 10.00
Pristine, Goblet, 11 Oz. 7.00
Pristine, Salt 6.00
Pristine, Salt & Pepper, Tray 20.00
Pristine, Tumbler, Iced Tea, 12 Oz. 7.00
Regency Stradivari, Cordial, Moonlight Blue, Oz. 54.00
Regency Stradivari, Cordial, Pistachio, Oz. 54.00
Rose Lady, Flower Frog, 9 ½ In. 78.00
Rose Lady, Flower Frog, Console, Peach-Blo, 8 ½ In, 2 Piece. *illus* 350.00
Rose Lady, Flower Frog, Frosted, Scalloped Base, 9 ¾ In. 395.00
Rose Lady, Flower Frog, Light Emerald Green, 9 ½ In. 240.00
Rose Point, Bowl, 4-Footed, 10 In. 60.00
Rose Point, Bowl, Crimped, 4-Toed, 12 In. 110.00
Rose Point, Bowl, Footed, 13 In. *illus* 105.00
Rose Point, Bowl, Handles, 9 ½ In. 90.00
Rose Point, Bowl, Oval, Footed, Handles, 12 In. 175.00
Rose Point, Bowl, Round, 2 Open Handles, Footed, 7 ½ In. 75.00
Rose Point, Bowl, Square, Shaped Edges, 4-Footed, 4 x 12 In. 110.00
Rose Point, Candlestick, 2-Light, 6 In. 70.00
Rose Point, Candlestick, 2-Light, 6 In., Pair 85.00
Rose Point, Candlestick, 2-Light, 6 x 5 ¼ In. 165.00
Rose Point, Candlestick, 3-Light, 6 In. 175.00
Rose Point, Candy Dish, Cover, 3-Footed, Rose Finial, 6 In. 450.00
Rose Point, Candy Dish, Cover, 4-Footed, 7 ½ x 6 ½ In. 142.00
Rose Point, Celery Dish, 3 Sections, Footed, 9 In. 53.00
Rose Point, Champagne, 6 Oz., 6 ½ In. 35.00
Rose Point, Cocktail, 3 Oz. 30.00
Rose Point, Cocktail Icer, Insert 65.00
Rose Point, Cocktail Shaker, Sterling Silver Foot, 32 Oz. 175.00
Rose Point, Compote, 9 In. 65.00
Rose Point, Cordial, 6 x 3 In., 6 Piece 130.00
Rose Point, Cordial, Oz. 80.00 to 90.00
Rose Point, Cruet, Vinegar, 6 In. 89.00
Rose Point, Cup & Saucer 35.00
Rose Point, Fruit Cocktail, 4 ½ Oz. 24.00
Rose Point, Goblet, 10 Oz., 8 ¼ In. 35.00 to 55.00
Rose Point, Goblet, Bell Shape, 9 Oz. 47.00
Rose Point, Goblet, Claret, 3 ½ Oz., 6 ¼ In. 118.00
Rose Point, Goblet, Royal Blue, 10 Oz. 100.00
Rose Point, Ice Bucket, 5 ¾ In. 140.00
Rose Point, Lamp, Hurricane, Martha Candlestick Base, 9 ¼ In., Pair 395.00
Rose Point, Marmalade, Cover, 8 Oz. 250.00
Rose Point, Marmalade, Cover, Footed, 7 Oz. 250.00
Rose Point, Plate, Dinner, 10 ½ In. 150.00
Rose Point, Plate, Handles, 8 In. 37.00
Rose Point, Plate, Salad, 7 ½ In. 15.00
Rose Point, Plate, Salad, 8 In. 22.00
Rose Point, Platter, Handles, 11 In. 75.00
Rose Point, Relish, 2 Sections, Handle, 6 In. 150.00
Rose Point, Relish, 3 Sections, 11 In. 85.00
Rose Point, Relish, 3 Sections, 12 x 7 ½ In. 70.00
Rose Point, Relish, 3 Sections, Gold Encrusted, 6 ½ In. 90.00
Rose Point, Relish, 3 Sections, Handles, 4-Footed, 10 In. 65.00

Rose Point, Relish, Divided, 2 Open Handles, 6 In. 40.00
Rose Point, Relish, Oval, 3 Sections, Tab Handles, 11 x 7 In. 75.00
Rose Point, Salt & Pepper, Chrome Lids 40.00 to 90.00
Rose Point, Salt & Pepper, Footed, Large 115.00
Rose Point, Salt & Pepper, Glass Lid, Footed, Large 145.00
Rose Point, Saucer 8.00
Rose Point, Sherbet, 6 Oz. 30.00
Rose Point, Sherbet, 7 Oz. 23.00
Rose Point, Sherbet, Carmen, 7 Oz. 100.00
Rose Point, Sugar & Creamer 46.00 to 65.00
Rose Point, Torte Plate, 4-Toed, 13 In. 115.00
Rose Point, Tray, Rectangular, Handles, 13 x 10 ¾ In. 170.00
Rose Point, Tumbler, Footed, 10 Oz. 35.00 to 40.00
Rose Point, Tumbler, Iced Tea, 12 Oz. 40.00
Rose Point, Tumbler, Juice, Footed, 5 Oz. 25.00
Rose Point, Vase, Bud, 10 In. 70.00
Rose Point, Vase, Keyhole, 10 In. 175.00
Rose Point, Vase, Trumpet, Footed, 6 In. 70.00
Rose Point, Vase, Urn, Crown Tuscan, Keyhole, Gold Encrusted, 11 In. 895.00
Rose Point, Wine, 2 ½ Oz. 55.00
Rose Point, Wine, Mocha, 3 ½ In. 40.00
Roselyn, Candlestick, 2-Light, Keyhole, 6 In., Pair 69.00
Roselyn, Pitcher, 76 Oz. 210.00
Roselyn, Sugar & Creamer 41.00
Rubina, Vase, Sweet Pea 150.00
Square, Ashtray, 3 ½ In. 10.00
Square, Bowl, Oval, Shallow, 10 In. 15.00
Square, Bowl, Oval, Shallow, 12 In. 38.00
Square, Bowl, Salad, 6 ½ In. 18.00
Square, Bowl, Salad, 9 In. 26.00
Square, Candleholder, 2 ¾ In., Pair 36.00
Square, Celery Dish, 11 In. 21.00
Square, Cordial, Oz. 16.00
Square, Cruet, Oil, Stopper 42.00
Square, Cup & Saucer 12.00
Square, Decanter 125.00
Square, Dish, Mayonnaise, Underplate 36.00
Square, Goblet, 10 Oz. 15.00
Square, Relish, Sections, 6 ½ In. 21.00
Square, Rose Bowl, 7 ½ In. 60.00
Square, Salt & Pepper 25.00
Square, Sugar & Creamer, Individual *illus* 23.00
Square, Sugar & Creamer, Tray 41.00
Square, Tumbler, Iced Tea, Footed, 14 Oz. 28.00
Square, Tumbler, Juice, Footed, 5 Oz. 20.00
Square, Vase, Bud, 8 In. 28.00
Square, Wine, 2 ½ Oz. 12.00
Swan, Dish, Amberina, 8 ½ In. 45.00
Swan, Dish, Crown Tuscan, 3 In. 40.00 to 59.00
Swan, Dish, Ebony, 10 In. 495.00
Swan, Dish, Ebony & Clear, 13 In. 895.00
Swan, Dish, Emerald, 6 ½ In. 275.00
Swan, Dish, Frosted, 10 In. 335.00
Swan, Dish, Gold Krystol, Marked, 12 In. *illus* 633.00
Swan, Dish, Red, Carmen, 9 In. 495.00
Swan, Nut Dish, Pink Milk Glass, Crown Tuscan, 3 ½ In. 36.00
Swan, Punch Bowl, 12 Cups 2100.00
Tally-Ho, Beverage Set, Decanter, 11-Oz. Tumbler, 7 Piece 102.00
Tally-Ho, Beverage Set, Decanter, Mug, Amber, 7 Piece 96.00
Tally-Ho, Bowl, Vegetable, Wildflower Etch, Divided, 8 ½ In. 138.00
Tally-Ho, Candleholder, Bobeches, 6 ½ In., Pair 183.00
Tally-Ho, Compote, Low, Carmen, 4 ½ In. 36.00
Tally-Ho, Compote, Tall, 6 ½ In. 24.00
Tally-Ho, Decanter, Green, 34 Oz. 57.00
Tally-Ho, Ice Pail, Green, Chrome Handle 84.00
Tally-Ho, Punch Bowl, Carmen, Clear Ladle, 12 6-Oz. Mugs, 14 Piece 950.00
Tally-Ho, Salt, Handle, Individual 10.00

TIP

Try this to remove the stain from a glass decanter: Put warm water, ½ teaspoon of liquid detergent, and some uncooked rice grains into the decanter. Shake well, then rinse.

Cambridge, Rose Point, Bowl, Footed, 13 In.
$105.00

Cambridge, Square, Sugar & Creamer, Individual
$23.00

Cambridge, Swan, Dish, Gold Krystol, Marked, 12 In.
$633.00

Cambridge, Turkey, Jam Jar, Amber, 8 x 9 In.
$633.00

Cameo Glass, Dresser Set, Red Flower, Green, Gold Enameled, St. Louis, c.1920, 3 Piece
$700.00

Cameo Glass, Vase, Orchids, Leaves, Pale Olive Ground, Flower & Scroll Around Rim, 8 In.
$2300.00

Cameo Glass, Vase, White Vines, Red Ground, Round, Flared Rim, 2½ In.
$1900.00

Tally-Ho, Salt & Pepper, Royal Blue, Glass Lid 90.00
Tally-Ho, Sauce, Carmen, 6 In. 75.00
Tally-Ho, Stein, Mocha, 14 Oz. 48.00
Tally-Ho, Stein, Royal Blue, 14 Oz. 72.00
Tally-Ho, Tumbler, Juice, Willow Blue, 5 Oz. 17.00
Turkey, Jam Jar, Amber, 8 x 9 In. .... *illus* 633.00
Two Kids, Flower Frog, Amber, 9¼ In. 435.00
Two Kids, Flower Frog, Frosted, 9¼ In.. .... 225.00
Two Kids, Flower Frog, Peach-Blo, 9¼ In. 425.00
Valencia, Cigarette Holder, Oval 125.00
Valencia, Dish, Mayonnaise, Underplate 135.00
Valencia, Relish, 3 Sections, Handle, 12 In. 40.00
Valencia, Vase, Bud, 10 In.. .... 150.00
Wheat Sheaf, Sherbet, Footed, 4½ x 4½ In. 14.00
Wildflower, Bonbon, 2 Open Handles, 5½ x 7½ In. 52.00
Wildflower, Bowl, Centerpiece, 4-Footed, 12 In.. .... 75.00
Wildflower, Cake Plate, Footed, 13 In. 200.00
Wildflower, Candlestick, 2-Light, 6¼ x 5¼ In., Pair 125.00
Wildflower, Candlestick, 2-Light, Keyhole Center, Pair 100.00
Wildflower, Candlestick, 5 In., Pair 70.00
Wildflower, Candlestick, Keyhole, 6 In. 145.00
Wildflower, Candy Dish, Cover, 5¾ x 5½ In. 250.00
Wildflower, Champagne 36.00
Wildflower, Compote, Cheese 30.00
Wildflower, Compote, Handles, 6 In. 35.00
Wildflower, Cordial, Oz.. .... 60.00
Wildflower, Dish, Divided, Handles, 8 In. 48.00
Wildflower, Ivy Ball, 5 In. 62.00
Wildflower, Plate, Salad, 7½ In.. .... 33.00
Wildflower, Relish, 5 Sections, 12¼ x 10½ In. 95.00
Wildflower, Relish, Handles, 10 In.. .... 45.00
Wildflower, Sugar & Creamer 34.00
Wildflower, Sugar & Creamer, Gold Encrusted 43.00
Wildflower, Vase, Ebony, Gold Encrusted, Footed, 10 In. 1600.00
Willow, Tray, Center Handle, Oval, Amber, 10 In. 175.00

CAMEO GLASS was made in much the same manner as a cameo in jewelry. Parts of the top layer of glass were cut away to reveal a different colored glass beneath. The most famous cameo glass was made during the nineteenth century. Signed cameo glass pieces are listed under the glasswork's name, such as Daum or Galle.

Atomizer, Enameled Flower, Chipped Ice Texture, c.1900, 5½ In. 325.00
Biscuit Jar, Prussian Blue, Opal Leaves, Scalloped Rim, England, 5¼ In.. .... 800.00
Bowl, Trifold, Prussian Blue, Cascading White Flowers, Low, Tricornered Rim, 5 In. 460.00
Charger, Frosted Citron, Central Medallions, Pomegranates, 12 In.. .... 1035.00
Dish, Sweetmeat, Citron, Cascading Morning Glory, Oval, 4½ In. 748.00
Dresser Set, Red Flower, Green, Gold Enameled, St. Louis, c.1920, 3 Piece .... *illus* 700.00
Jar, Red Thistles, Green Stems, Textured Body, Metal Cover, St. Louis, 4¼ In. 230.00
Perfume Bottle, Oval, Prussian Blue, Flowers, Butterflies, Monogram Lid, 2½ In. 920.00
Pitcher, Rose, Fish Scales, Gold Handle, 3½ In.. .... 201.00
Shade, Thorny Branches, Band Borders, Oval, Frosted, 5 In. 805.00
Spoon, Pictorial Medallion, Yellow, White Flowers, Gold-Washed Metal Bowl, 8 In. 900.00
Sugar Shaker, Prussian Blue, Morning Glories, Barrel Shape, Border, England, 3 In.. .... 315.00
Tumbler, Deep Purple Birds, Scrolling Leaves, France, 4 In.. .... 115.00
Tumbler, Opal Over Green, Grapevine Band, Round Borders, Richardson, 5 In.. .... 374.00
Vase, Amber, Peach, White Morning Glories, Oval, 4¼ In.. .... 460.00
Vase, Berries, Orange Pink, Frosted Ground, Translucent Plum Enamel, 13½ In. 472.00
Vase, Blue Art Deco Design, Textured Pink Body, 15½ In. 1150.00
Vase, Blue Grass, Leaf, Berry, Mottled Lemon, Signed, 5 In. 266.00
Vase, Cherub, Flowering Water Garden, E. Michel, 4¼ In. 650.00
Vase, Citron, Opal Flowering Vine, Butterfly, Bulbous, England, 9½ In.. .... 700.00
Vase, Citron, Opaque Flower, Butterfly, England, 6 In. 600.00
Vase, Clematis Vine, Blossoms, Blue Translucent Over Burgundy, 4 In. 325.00
Vase, Flowers, White Over Blue, Frosted, 6¼ In.. .... 1450.00
Vase, Flowers & Leaves, Blue Frosted Ground, Silver Collar, Theodore B. Starr, 13 In.. .... 1500.00
Vase, Flowers & Leaves, White, Pale Rose Ground, Geometric Bands, 5¼ In.. .... 1400.00
Vase, Green Flowers, Frosted Ground, Signed, Arsall, 4 In. 115.00

Vase, Green Iris, Textured & Frosted Ground, Honesdale, 12 ¼ In. 705.00
Vase, Leafy Flower Buds, Frosted, Arsall, 12 In. 575.00
Vase, Lily & Bee, Leaves, White On Pale Green, Bottle Shape, 13 ¼ In. 4700.00
Vase, Medallion, Greek Life, Textured Red, Burgun Schverer, 9 In. 6325.00
Vase, Morning Glories, Moths, White & Red Over Blue, Tapered, Trumpet Neck, 12 In. 7300.00
Vase, Oak Leaves, Seed Pods, Blossoms, Citron, Triple Stalactite Rim, Bulbous, 4 In. 1093.00
Vase, Orchids, Leaves, Pale Olive Ground, Flower & Scroll Around Rim, 8 In. *illus* 2300.00
Vase, Prussian Blue, Bulbous, Shouldered, Everted Rim, Ferns, England, 6 ½ In. 1400.00
Vase, Purple Morning Glories, Green Stems, Frosted, Arsall, 10 ¼ In. 460.00
Vase, Red, White Leafy Vine, Oval, 6 ¾ In. 705.00
Vase, Red & White Flowers, Frosted Ground, Urn Shape, 4 ¼ In., Pair 1553.00
Vase, Red Iris, Textured Green, Gold Highlights, Bulbous, 9 ¼ In. 575.00
Vase, Stick, Bird Perched In Dogwood Tree, Bulbous Base, Citron, 12 ½ In. 115.00
Vase, Trumpet, Gold Aurene Moon, Sun, Stars, Frosted, Correia, 12 In. 201.00
Vase, Vine & Berry, Green Over Frosted White, Bulbous, Long Neck, 6 In. 180.00
Vase, White & Pink Flowers, Pale Green Ground, Baluster, 6 ¾ In. 7300.00
Vase, White & Pink Flowers & Leaves, Gold Ground, Satin, 6 ¼ In. 2000.00
Vase, White Dancing Nymphs, Amethyst Ground, Signed, Cook, 12 In. 940.00
Vase, White Fuchsias & Leaves, Green Ground, 7 In. 3400.00
Vase, White Over Green ivy, Blue Ground, Green Rim & Foot, Squat, 4 In. 5700.00
Vase, White Vines, Red Ground, Round, Flared Rim, 2 ½ In. *illus* 1900.00

CAMPAIGN *memorabilia is listed in the Political category.*

CAMPBELL KIDS were first used as part of an advertisement for the Campbell Soup Company in 1904. The kids were created by Grace Drayton, a popular illustrator of the day. The kids were used in magazine and newspaper ads until about 1951. They were presented again in 1966; and in 1983, they were redesigned with a slimmer, more contemporary appearance.

Ad, Boy & Girl Skating, Spelling Campbell's, Frame, 1970s, 10 x 8 In. 22.00
Bowl, 1984 Sarajevo Olympic Games, Corelle, Marked, 1 ⅛ x 8 ½ In. 13.00
Bowl, Cover, Marked, 1998, 4 ½ x 5 In. 8.00
Bowl, Spoon, Boy & Girl, Handles, 2001, 2 ½ x 5 In. 15.00
Bridge Tallies, Girl, Boy, Cardboard, Premium Form, 1930s, 2 x 6 ¾ In., 6 Piece 48.00
Cookie Jar, Boy, Chef, 2004, 13 ¾ In. 75.00
Cookie Jar, Boy Holding Can, 2005, 12 ½ In. 75.00
Cup, Girl's Face, Plastic, Melamine, 1970s, 2⅝ x 3¼ In. 6.50 to 8.00
Dish, Child's, Deep, Marked Buffalo Pottery, 7 ½ In. *illus* 96.00
Doll, Bicentennial Boy, Vinyl, Movable Arms, Legs, Colonial Clothing, 10 In. *illus* 115.00
Doll, Bicentennial Boy & Girl, Colonial Clothing, Original Boxes, 1976, 10 In. 175.00
Doll, Girl, Chef, 1950s, 10 ½ In. 135.00
Doll, Girl, Cloth, Printed, Holding Baby Doll, 16 In. 55.00
Doll, Girl, Composition, Jointed, Side-Glancing Eyes, E.L. Horsman Co., 1948, 12 In. 293.00
Doll, Girl, Plastic, Red Skirt, White Sweater, Red Script C, Ideal, 1960s, 8 In. 40.00
Mug, Boy & Girl, Marked, 1998, 3 ⅜ In. 7.00
Paper Doll, Girl, 2 Outfits, Cutout, 1930s. 22.00
Salt & Pepper, Boy, Girl, Chef's Aprons & Hats, Plastic, 4 ¼ In. *illus* 42.00
Salt & Pepper, Campbell Kids In Paper Hats, Metal, 1995, 3 ¾ x 2 ½ In. 15.00
Soup, Dish, Raised Painted Kids' Heads, Nippon, c.1920s, 6 In. 225.00
Spoon, Boy, 6 In. 24.00
Spoon, Girl, 6 In. 24.00
Thimble, Girl, Porcelain 10.00

CAMPHOR GLASS is a cloudy white glass that has been blown or pressed. It was made by many factories in the Midwest during the mid-nineteenth century.

Ashtray, Eagle, 7 Stars, Hammered Silver Rim, 2 x 10 In. 250.00
Candlestick, Scalloped Cup, Flared Fluted Foot, 4 In., Pair 22.00
Decanter, Enameled Forget-Me-Nots, Bulbous Base, Elongated Neck, 7 x 5 ½ In. 135.00

CANDELABRUM refers to a candleholder with more than one arm to hold many candles; a candlestick is designed to hold one candle. The eccentricity of the English language makes the plural of candelabrum into candelabra.

2-Light, Bronze, Aesthetic, Figural, Couple, Stoutenberg & Cox, c.1800, 13 In., Pair 1175.00
2-Light, Bronze, Parcel Gilt, Louis XVI Style, Cherub, Scrolled Arms, 13 In., Pair 940.00
2-Light, Crystal, Fluted, Prisms, c.1900, 22 x 13 In., Pair 585.00
2-Light, Crystal, Spear & Star Finials, Prisms, Bobeche, c.1900, 22 x 13 In., Pair 835.00

Campbell Kids, Doll, Bicentennial Boy, Vinyl, Movable Arms, Legs, Colonial Clothing, 10 In.
$115.00

Campbell Kids, Dish, Child's, Deep, Marked Buffalo Pottery, 7 ½ In.
$96.00

Campbell Kids, Salt & Pepper, Boy, Girl, Chef's Aprons & Hats, Plastic, 4 ¼ In.
$42.00

Candelabrum, 7-Light, Brass, Arts & Crafts, Adjustable, 16 ½ x 16 x 5 In.
$370.00

Candlestick, Amber Glass, Goddess, Winged, Portieux, 10 ¼ In., Pair
$120.00

Candlestick, Brass, Footed, Spain, c.1710, 8 ¼ In., Pair
$345.00

Candlestick, Chamber, Silver, Detachable Lid, Crown Monogram, Russia, 1 ¼ x 3 ½ x 3 In.
$487.00

2-Light, Sheffield Plate, Convertible, Bypass Arms, Reeded, Columnar Stem, 21 In., Pair 823.00
2-Light, Tin, Adjustable, Shades, Conical Snuffer, Bird Finial, c.1870, 25 ½ In.. .... 4800.00
2-Light, U-Shape Arms, Turquoise Stone-Clad Parrot, Castillo, Mexico 646.00
3-Light, Brass Fauns, Urn Sockets, Applied Patina, Pink Marble Base, 13 ¼ In., Pair 546.00
3-Light, Georgian, Sheffield, Hurricane Shades, 31 x 22 In., Pair 3290.00
3-Light, Giltwood, Carved, Vase Shape, Neoclassical Style, Iron Pricket, 22 In., Pair 900.00
3-Light, Silver, Fisher, 12 In. 117.00
3-Light, Silver, George VI, Anglo Irish Style, Saucer Bobeche, Glass Drops, 15 In., Pair 780.00
3-Light, Silver Plate, Baluster Columns, Flowers, Scrolls, Ellis-Barker Silver, 20 In., Pair 303.00
3-Light, Silver Plate, Georgian Style, Trumpet Shape, Round Base, 20 In., Pair 738.00
3-Light, Silver Plate, Trumpet Stem, Bands, Drip Pans, England, 18 x 13 In., Pair 115.00
4-Light, Baccarat, Panel Pressed Glass, Bobeche, Panel & Facet Cut Glass, 22 x 13 In.. .... 780.00
4-Light, Gilt Bronze, Empire, 3 Scrolled Arms, Tripod Base, Stamped, 23 In., Pair 1800.00
4-Light, Gilt Bronze, Enameled, Patinated, Urn Pedestal, Curved Arms, 20 In., Pair 259.00
4-Light, Silver, G. Jensen, Marked, No. 623B, c.1937, 7 ⅝ In., Pair 27000.00
4-Light, Tin, Iron, Green Paint, Mid 19th Century, 34 ½ x 8 ½ In. 546.00
5-Light, Brass, Cherub Pedestal, 19 ¾ x 9 In. 59.00
5-Light, Brass, Teardrop Glass Pendants, Electrified, Early 1900s, 30 ½ In., Pair 633.00
5-Light, Bronze, Marble, France, c.1880, 15 x 6 In., Pair 588.00
5-Light, Bronze, Winged Victory, Gilt, Patinated, Marble Base, 35 x 11 x 9 In., Pair 5288.00
5-Light, Gilt Bronze, Empire Style, Patinated Vines, Griffin Tripod, 25 In., Pair 940.00
5-Light, Gilt Metal, Neoclassical Style, Reed Columnar Shaft, Tripod Base, 36 In. 1888.00
5-Light, Silver, Circular Base, Cluster Shaft, 19th Century, 28 ½ x 18 ½ In. 2115.00
5-Light, Silver, Double C-Scroll Arms, Tulip Shape Sconces, Paneled, Peru, 11 In., Pair 411.00
5-Light, Silver, Fluted, Gadrooned, Bulbous Knop, Domed Foot, England, 28 x 25 In. 9720.00
5-Light, Silver, Gilt Bird, In Tree, Ruby Eyes, Marked Tane, Mexico, 15 x 12 In. 1840.00
5-Light, Silver, Waisted Sconces, Candle Arms, Domed Foot, Mexico, 13 ½ In., Pair 1998.00
5-Light, Silver Plate, Aesthetic, Bell Nozzles, Scrolled Arms, Gorham, 17 ⅝ In. 353.00
5-Light, Silver Plate, Continental, Baluster Stem, 27 x 19 In., Pair 1716.00
5-Light, Silver Plate, Trumpet Stem, Bands, Drip Pan, England, 17 ½ x 14 ¾ In. 403.00
5-Light, Victorian, Gilt, Brass, Satyr's Mask, 23 ⅜ x 13 ½ In., Pair 1645.00
5-Light, Wrought Iron, Twisted Rod Post, 3 Scroll Legs, Early 1900s, 58 ½ In., Pair 748.00
6-Light, Brass, Bobeches, Dovetail Mounting, 18th Century 1200.00
6-Light, Gilt Brass, Glass, 19th Century, 21 ¾ In., Pair 990.00
7-Light, Brass, Altar, 2 Adjustable Arms, Knobbed Swirled Column, Domed Base, 22 In. 118.00
7-Light, Brass, Arts & Crafts, Adjustable, 16 ½ x 16 x 5 In. .... *illus* 370.00
8-Light, Gilt Bronze, Classical Figures, Octagonal Base, 39 ¼ In., Pair 4375.00
8-Light, Iron, Brass Fittings, Jens Quistgaard, Dansk, 7 In.. .... 155.00
Bronze, Thistle, Candles Or Flame Shape, Electric, Jessie Preston, 13 ½ x 10 In.. .... 9600.00
Girandole, 2-Light, Brass Mounted, Regency, c.1825, 14 x 13 In., Pair 4113.00
Girandole, 2-Light, Patinated Bronze, Regency, c.1825, 10 x 4 In., Pair 1200.00
Girandole, 3-Light, Glass, Brass, 18 x 15 In., Pair 234.00

CANDLESTICKS were made of brass, pewter, glass, sterling silver, plated silver, and all types of pottery and porcelain. The earliest candlesticks, dating from the sixteenth century, held the candle on a pricket (sharp pointed spike). These lost favor because in times of strife the large church candlesticks with prickets became formidable weapons, so the socket was mandated. Candlesticks changed in style through the centuries, and designs range from Classical to Rococo to Art Nouveau to Art Deco.

Amber Glass, Goddess, Winged, Portieux, 10 ¼ In., Pair .... *illus* 120.00
Bell Metal, Flared, Ring, Baluster Turned Shaft, Stepped Base, c.1800, 8 ½ In., Pair 403.00
Brass, Baluster Shaft, Round Foot, Continental, 11 ¾ In., Pair 59.00
Brass, Beehive, Push-Up, Square Footed, England, 10 ¾ In., Pair 88.00
Brass, Beehive & Faceted, Marked, England, 9 ¾ In., Pair 55.00
Brass, Bobeche, c.1900, 14 In., Pair 70.00
Brass, Bobeche, c.1900, 14 In. 70.00
Brass, Charles X, Gilt, Chased, Columns, Fluted, Round Base, 10 x 5 In., Pair 960.00
Brass, Chased, Engine Turned, Tapered, Tiered Bobeches, Charles X, 10 In., Pair 1440.00
Brass, Classical, Urn Form, Stop-Fluted Columns, Square Base, c.1780, 11 In., Pair 294.00
Brass, Continental, Square Base, Mid 16th Century, 10 In., Pair 978.00
Brass, English, Circular Drip Pan, Ringed Stem, Domed Base, 5 ⅝ In.. .... 1856.00
Brass, English, Circular Drip Pan, Ringed Stem, Domed Base, 6 ⅞ In., Pair 1160.00
Brass, English, Cylindrical, Ring-Turned Nozzle, Medial Drip Pan, 6 ⅞ In. 580.00
Brass, English, Inverted Pear Stem, Hexagonal Base, Cylindrical Nozzle, 7 In., Pair 754.00
Brass, English, Petal Base, Seamed Construction, c.1740, 8 In. 250.00

Brass, English, Ringed Cylindrical Nozzle, Knopped Stem, Petal Base, 9 In., Pair 1160.00
Brass, Federal, Baluster, Ring Turned, Flared Rim, Square Base, Push-Up, 5 In., Pair 173.00
Brass, Footed, Spain, c.1710, 8 ¼ In., Pair *illus* 345.00
Brass, Georgian, Swirl Base, Glass Hurricane Shades, c.1770 3000.00
Brass, Gothic, Gilt Lacquer, England, 33 In., Pair 2736.00
Brass, Hog Scraper, 18th Century 295.00
Brass, Jarvie, Holder, Marked, 6 x 6 In. 360.00
Brass, Leaf Molded Mount, Opalescent Glass Column, 3 Claw Legs, France, c.1850 2390.00
Brass, Octagonal Base, France, c.1710, 7 ¾ In., Pair 441.00
Brass, Petal Base, England, 18th Century, 8 In., Pair 264.00
Brass, Petal Base, Seamed, England, c.1740, 8 In. 295.00
Brass, Pricket, Engraved Crest, Lions, Flowering Tree, Continental, 16 ½ In., Pair 1438.00
Brass, Queen Anne, Baluster Shape, Petal Base, England, c.1750, Pair 4800.00
Brass, Queen Anne, Petal Base, Mid 18th Century, England, 9 ½ In., Pair 2400.00
Brass, Queen Anne, Stepped Octagonal Base, 8 In., Pair 696.00
Brass, Ringed Baluster Nozzle, Knopped Stem, Square Base, Push-Up, 8 In., Pair 580.00
Brass, Round, Pierced Socket, Swollen Shaft, Round Dish Base, c.1610, 10 In. 881.00
Brass, Scalloped Base, Threaded Post, Seamed, Taper Stick, 7 ¼ & 4 In. 173.00
Brass, Seamed, Scalloped, Petal Bases, Push-Up, Mid 1700s, 8 In., Pair 518.00
Brass, Seamed, Square Base, Scalloped Edge, Early 1700, 8 In., Pair 230.00
Brass, Seamed Stem, Domed Base, 4 ⅜ In. 144.00
Brass, Side Ejectors, Tooled, Stepped Bases, Dutch, c.1800-25, 7 ½ In., Pair 345.00
Brass, Square Base, Stamped, King Of Diamonds, 12 In., Pair 99.00
Brass, Straight Shaft, Cupped Base, Cornelius & Baker, Philadelphia, c.1855, 9 In., Pair 406.00
Brass, Tapered, Square Base, Beaded Border, Push-Up, England, c.1780, 11 ½ In., Pair 235.00
Brass, Trumpet Shape, Gadrooned, Bracket Feet, England, 19th Century, 7 In., Pair 4780.00
Bronze, 2 Oni Figures, Holding Ribbed Goblet Candlecup, 16 ¼ In., Pair 784.00
Bronze, 3 Lions, Tails Form Candlecup Supports, Stepped Tripod Base, 12 ½ In., Pair 858.00
Bronze, Children, Holding Vases, Chinese, 18th Century, 10 ½ In., Pair 1175.00
Bronze, Empire Style, Elephant, Seated, Ivory Tusk, 6 ¾ In., 4 Piece 235.00
Bronze, Jarvie, Alpha Model, Marked, 5 x 11 In., Pair 1320.00
Bronze, Lion's Face, 3-Footed, Italy, 17th Century, 3 ¾ In. 175.00
Bronze, Swirl Form, 10 ½ In., Pair 760.00
Bronze, Wood, Lacquer, Paw Feet, Art Deco, c.1930, 12 In., Pair 495.00
Bronzed Metal, Spiral Stem, Patina, Arts & Crafts, 5 x 12 In., Pair 374.00
Chamber, Brass, Rectangular Base, Conical Snuffer, Shaft, Side Ejector, 5 ½ In. 205.00
Chamber, Brass, Shaft, Side Ejector, Finger Handle, 9 ½ x 8 In., Pair 690.00
Chamber, Copper, Hammered, Footed, Handle, Marked, No. Y1, Gorham, 3 x 4 In. 270.00
Chamber, Copper, Hammered, Handle, Impressed Mark, Gustav Stickley, 9 x 7 In. 1140.00
Chamber, Copper, Hammered, Removable Bobeche, Patina, Signed, Jarvie, 2 ½ x 6 In. 1020.00
Chamber, Silver, Circular Rim, Fluted Nozzle, Snuffer, Henry Wilkinson, 1838, 6 In. 705.00
Chamber, Silver, Detachable Lid, Crown Monogram, Russia, 1 ¼ x 3 ½ x 3 In. *illus* 487.00
Chamber, Silver, Gadroon Border, Snuffer, James Dixon & Sons, England, c.1860, 4 x 7 x 6 In. *illus* 285.00
Chamber, Silver, Round Base, Scrolled Border, Germany, Early 1900s, 4 In. 60.00
Chamber, Silver Plate, Round, Gadroon Border, Snuffer, James Dixon & Sons, 4 x 7 In. 288.00
Chamber, Tin, Saucer Base, Finger Ring, Push-Up, 5 ¾ In. 55.00
Chamber, Tin, Weighted, Push-Up, 9 In., Pair 468.00
Chinese Cloisonne, Brass, 8 ½ In., Pair 117.00
Classical, Bell Metal, Urn Shape Socket, Fluting, Beading, Push-Up, c.1780, 4 In., Pair 173.00
Coiled Wick, Bronze, Miniature, Neoclassical, Chained Snuffer, 3 ½ In. 110.00
Cut Glass, Fluted, Faceted Knob Ray Base, Hollow Stem, 11 ¾ In. 200.00
Flint Glass, Canary Yellow, 8-Sided Base, 9 In., Pair 345.00
Gilt Brass, Altar, Columnar, Tripodal, Neoclassical Style, Portraits, 28 In., Pair 720.00
Gilt Bronze, Brass, Engine Turned, Caryatid, Restauration, 10 In., Pair 1380.00
Gilt Bronze, Figural, Putto, Scroll Base, Pan With Pipes, Rococo Revival, 9 In., Pair 235.00
Gilt Gesso, Pricket, Baluster, Knop Stem, Tripartite Base, Baroque Style, 18 In., Pair 1116.00
Giltwood, Angel, Fluttering Robes, Hand Holds Candle, Polychrome, 17 x 29 In. 5060.00
Giltwood, Pricket, Figural, Gesticulating Robed Angel, Cornucopia, 26 x 16 In. 9900.00
Glass, Enamel, Square Handled Tray, Footed Brass Base, c.1900, 8 In., Pair 294.00
Glass, Ruby Flashed, Panels, Gilt Highlights, 6 In., Pair 475.00
Iron, Ejector, 3-Footed, 19th Century, 11 ½ In., Pair *illus* 495.00
Iron, Hog Scraper, 5 In. *illus* 33.00
Iron, Hog Scraper, Triple Brass Wedding Band, 18th Century 650.00
Mahogany, Brass, Removable Bobeches In Leaf Shell Design, 1700s, 15 In., Pair 575.00
Milk Glass, Goddess, Winged, Blue, 10 ¼ In., Pair *illus* 192.00
Oak, Copper Bobeche, Base, Splayed, Charles Rohlfs, 14 ½ x 7 x 7 In. *illus* 6000.00

Candlestick, Chamber, Silver, Gadroon Border, Snuffer, James Dixon & Sons, England, c.1860, 4 x 7 x 6 In.
$285.00

Candlestick, Iron, Ejector, 3-Footed, 19th Century, 11 ½ In., Pair
$495.00

Candlestick, Iron, Hog Scraper, 5 In.
$33.00

Candlestick, Milk Glass, Goddess, Winged, Blue, 10 ¼ In., Pair
$192.00

Candlestick, Oak, Copper Bobeche, Base, Splayed, Charles Rohlfs, 14 ½ x 7 x 7 In.
$6000.00

Candlestick, Purple Slag, Dolphin Heads, George Davidson, c.1885, 7 In., Pair
$288.00

Candlestick, Silver, Continental, Flower Border, Melon Post, Marked, E, 5 In., Pair
$525.00

Candlestick, Silver Plate, Sheffield, Vines, Stepped Base, Marked, Q JKB, 1800s, 5 ¼ In., Pair
$345.00

Candlestick, Sterling Silver, Lord Roberts, International, 11 In., Pair
$510.00

Pewter, Baluster, Knop, Bobeche Top, 6-Sided Base, 9 ¾ In., Pair 99.00
Pewter, Baluster, Knop, Inscribed, A.S., 9 ¾ In., Pair 187.00
Pressed Glass, Acanthus Leaf, Starch Blue, Clambroth, c.1840, 11 In., Pair 2016.00
Pressed Glass, Boston & Sandwich Cobalt Blue, Hexagonal Socket, Crucifix, 9 In., Pair 812.00
Pressed Glass, Translucent Opaque Green Dolphin, 6-Petal Socket, Square Base, 10 In. 667.00
Purple Slag, Dolphin Heads, George Davidson, c.1885, 7 In., Pair . . . . *illus* 288.00
Satin Brass, D-Shape Handles, Art Deco, Albert Reimann, 6 ½ x 6 ⅛ In., Pair 1020.00
Silver, Baluster, Shaped Cup Rim, Dome Base, R. Wallace & Son, 11 ¼ In, Pair 295.00
Silver, Classical, Octagonal, Fluted Standard, Etched Band, Reed & Barton, 14 In., Pair 316.00
Silver, Continental, Flower Border, Melon Post, Marked, E, 5 In., Pair . . . . *illus* 525.00
Silver, Edwardian, Ribbed Vase Form Stem, Sheffield, England, 1903, 9 ½ In. Pair 850.00
Silver, Figural, Male, Female, Cornucopia, Acanthus, Continental, 12 ¾ In., Pair 540.00
Silver, Flowers & Leaves, Continental, 8 ¼ In., Pair 177.00
Silver, Fluted Columns, Stepped Hexafoil Base, George II, England, c.1758, 9 In., Pair 4370.00
Silver, Footed, Monogram, Engraved, Dominick & Haff, c.1900, 9 In., Pair 470.00
Silver, G. Jensen, Marked, No. 860, c.1938, 5 ⅝ In., Pair 9600.00
Silver, Georgian, 15 In., Pair 3584.00
Silver, Oval, Urn Sockets, Tapered Fluted Columns, England, 1897, 7 ¼ In., Pair 259.00
Silver, Preisner, 11 In., Pair 351.00
Silver, Removable Bobeches, Maker's Marks, c.1735, 8 ¾ In., Pair 3055.00
Silver, Scrolled Base, John Quantock, George III, c.1755, 9 ½ In., Pair 7605.00
Silver, Shaped Centers, Scalloped, Gorham, 1900s, 11 ¼ In., Pair 316.00
Silver, Stepped Square Base, Baluster Stems, J. Steward, George II, England, 6 ¾ In. 6600.00
Silver, Tapered, Bat's Wing Fluting, Gorham, 1923, 12 In., 4 Piece 1880.00
Silver, Tapered, Fluted, Square, Inverted Bell Nozzle, John Green, England, 11 In., Pair 3600.00
Silver, Weighted, 10 In., Pair 117.00
Silver Plate, Altar, Footed, 19th Century, 24 In., Pair 480.00
Silver Plate, Googie, Kidney Shape, 3-Footed, Incised P, Denmark, Pair 55.00
Silver Plate, Neoclassical, Flaring Sconce, Tapering Square Stem, 12 In., 4 Piece 1175.00
Silver Plate, Rococo Style, Rogers Brothers, 11 In., Pair 156.00
Silver Plate, Round, Tapered, Leaves, Dragon & Crown Crest, Sheffield, 13 In., Pair 1955.00
Silver Plate, Rounded Square, Tapered, Gadroon Border, Early 1900s, 12 In., 4 Piece 518.00
Silver Plate, Sheffield, Beaded, Bobeche Over Stop, Fluted Column, 5 ¾ x 3 In., Pair 125.00
Silver Plate, Sheffield, Tapered Columns, Vining Leaves, Stepped Base, 5 In., Pair 345.00
Silver Plate, Sheffield, Vines, Stepped Base, Marked, Q JKB, 1800s, 5 ¼ In., Pair . . . . *illus* 345.00
Silver Plate, Sheffield, Whale Oil Peg Lamps, 2-Tube Burner, 14 ¼ In., Pair 231.00
Spanish Brass, Flattened Ridge Ball Stem, Octagonal Base, c.1680, 5 ¾ In. 575.00
Spanish Brass, Square Base, c.1710, 8 ¼ In. 805.00
Sterling Silver, Bronze, Pine Needle Pattern, Brown Ground, 14 ¼ In., Pair 1560.00
Sterling Silver, Lord Roberts, International, 11 In., Pair . . . . *illus* 510.00
Tin, Pricket, Baroque Style, Vase Shape, Silvered, Saucer Bobeche, 18 x 7 In., Pair 1560.00
Tin, Weighted, Pin Prick Design, Push-Up, Pair 468.00
Walnut, Gothic, Triple Knopped Stems, Capstan Base, 10 x 5 In., Pair 1265.00
Wood, Chamois Under Pine Trees, Black Forest, Carved, 8 ½ In., Pair 325.00
Wood, Pricket, Neoclassical, Vasiform, Silver Leafed, Cut Tin Bobeche, 17 In, Pair 1440.00
Wood, Pricket, Neoclassical Style, Turned, Carved, Paw Feet, Italy, 26 x 7 ½ In., Pair 780.00
Wood, Pricket, Provincial, Turned, Painted, Distressed, Orange Shades, 19 In., Pair 540.00
Wood, Provincial, Turned, Painted Antique White, Distressed, Italy, 29 ½ In., Pair 540.00
Wood, White Paint, Parcel Gilt, Neoclassical, Pricket, 1700s, 29 In., Pair 2160.00

CANDLEWICK *items may be listed in the Imperial Glass and Pressed Glass categories.*

CANDY CONTAINERS have been popular since the late Victorian era. Collectors have long favored the glass containers, but now all types, including tin and papier-mache, are collected. Probably the earliest glass container sold commercially was the Liberty Bell made in 1876 for sale at the Centennial Exposition. Thousands of designs were made until the cost became too high in the 1960s. By the late 1970s, reproductions were being made and sold without the candy. Containers listed here are glass unless otherwise described. A Belsnickle is a nineteenth-century figure of Father Christmas. Some candy containers may be listed in Toy or in other categories.

Baby Chick, Glass 75.00
Barney Google, Hands Out, Base, Glass 250.00
Belsnickle, Green, Blue, Cloth, Hand Painted, Fur Beard, Wood Base, 6 In. . . . . *illus* 1600.00
Camera On Tripod, Glass, Tin, Screw Cap, Embossed, 5 ½ In. 230.00
Cat, Pushing Jack-O'-Lantern, Hard Plastic, Multicolored, Rosbro, 6 ½ x 5 ¼ In. 78.00
Chicken, Dispenses Egg Candy When Body Is Pressed Down, Painted, 3 ½ In. 431.00

Candy Container, Belsnickle, Green, Blue, Cloth, Hand Painted, Fur Beard, Wood Base, 6 In.
$1600.00

Candy Container, Child Holding Snowball, Bisque Head, Papier-Mache, Germany, 7 In.
$500.00

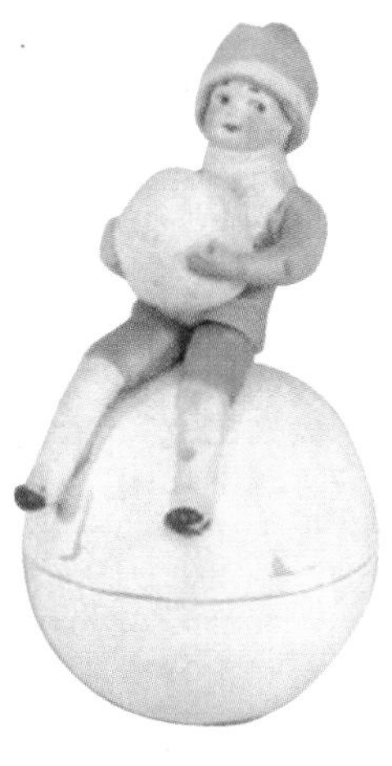

It's Free

Are you or your children looking for free collectibles? Try sugar packets, airline tags, business cards, candy wrappers, apple labels (a collection related to our banana stickers), stamps, license plates, paper bags, matchboxes, beer bottles, invitations, beer mats, bookmarks, shampoo and soap from hotels and ships, and wine memorabilia. Displayed, they are decorative—and you can be proud to be recycling.

Candy Container, Fire Engine, Glass, Tin Wheels, Stough, 1914, 3⅜ x 5 In.
$20.00

Candy Container, Fire Engine, Glass, U.S.A., 3¼ x 5¼ In.
$20.00

Candy Container, Fire Engine, Little Boiler, No. 2, Vaseline Glass, Tin, 3 x 4¾ In.
$20.00

Candy Container, Happy Hooligan, Holding Chicken, Composition, Wood, 8 ½ In.
$200.00

Candy Container, Rabbit, Nodder, Glass Eyes, Composition, Germany, 6¾ In.
$50.00

Candy Container, Toonerville Trolley, Glass, Painted, 3 ¼ In.
$978.00

Chicken On Nest, Wood Composition, Paper. 88.00
Chickens, On Wood Drum, Composition 132.00
Child Holding Snowball, Bisque Head, Papier-Mache, Germany, 7 In. . . . . *illus* 500.00
Clown Face, Red, White, Blue, Composition, 4 ¼ In. 88.00
Easter Rabbit, Pink, Blue Pants, Plastic, 12 ½ In.. . . . . 45.00
Fire Engine, Glass, Tin Wheels, Stough, 1914, 3⅜ x 5 In. . . . . *illus* 20.00
Fire Engine, Glass, U.S.A., 3 ¼ x 5 ¼ In. . . . . *illus* 20.00
Fire Engine, Little Boiler, No. 2, Vaseline Glass, Tin, 3 x 4¾ In. . . . . *illus* 20.00
Fire Engine, Little Boiler, Pressed Glass, 4¾ x 3 ⅛ In. 22.00
Fire Engine, No. 11, Pressed Glass, 4⅞ x 2 ⅛ In.. . . . . 22.00
Fire Engine, Pressed Glass, 5 x 1⅝ In.. . . . . 34.00
Fire Engine, Pressed Glass, Aluminum Wheels, Slide Cap, 5 ⅛ x 3 ¼ In. 22.00
Fire Ladder Truck, Pressed Glass, Tin Wheels, Snap On Lid, 5 x 2 ¼ In.. . . . . 45.00
Flying Reindeer Pulling Santa In Sled, c.1920, 20 In. 1250.00
Girl, Laughing, Pink Egg, Hooded Bunny, Bisque, Germany, 5 In. 588.00
Gun, Checkered Handle, Screw Cap, 8 In. 25.00
Gun, Screw Cap, 4 ½ In. 25.00
Happy Hooligan, Holding Chicken, Composition, Wood, 8 ½ In. . . . . *illus* 200.00
Jack-O'-Lantern, Scarecrow, Checkered Coat, Plastic, Rosbro, 3¾ x 5¾ In. 146.00
Man Riding Rabbit, Composition, Wood, 7 ¼ x 6 ¼ In. 143.00
Ornament, Child, Muff, Bisque, Cotton, Wire, Germany, 3 ½ In. 300.00
Pear, Painted, Yellow, Red, Chalkware, 3 ¼ x 5 ¼ In. 77.00
Peter Rabbit, Hinged Cover, Handle, 1930s, 3¾ x 6 x 3 In. 173.00
PEZ, Casper, Full Display, c.1960, 24 Piece 4780.00
PEZ, Cocoa-Marsh Spaceman, Dome Shape, Austria 95.00
Rabbit, Nodder, Glass Eyes, Composition, Germany, 6 ¾ In. . . . . *illus* 50.00
Rabbit, Seated, Glass, 8 In. 120.00
Revolver, 8-Sided Barrel, Mercury Lined, Molded, Glass, 8 In. 57.00
Rooster, Multicolored, Papier-Mache, Cast Legs, 5 In., Pair 230.00
Santa Claus, Cloth Coat, Pants, Fur Beard, Papier-Mache, Composition, Germany, 10 ¼ In. . . 550.00
Santa Claus, Composition, Hand Painted, Japan, 4 In.. . . . . 40.00
Santa Claus, Felt, Papier-Mache, Fur, Red Jacket, Composition, Germany, 11 ¾ In.. . . . . 1800.00
Santa Claus, Holding Tree, Coat, Pants, Fur Beard, Composition, Germany, 4¾ In. 220.00
Santa Claus, Holding Tree, Coat, Pants, Fur Beard, Papier-Mache, Germany, 12 ¼ In. 825.00
Santa Claus, Holding Tree, Papier-Mache, Cardboard, Germany, 1920s, 4 In. 131.00
Santa Claus, Stuffed Hat, Long Red Felt Coat, White Fur, Composition, 22 In. 4313.00
Santa Claus, Toy Sack, Holding Holly, Painted Plaster, Germany, 4 ½ In. 400.00
Spark Plug, Glass, Embossed, King Features Syndicate, 4 ⅛ In.. . . . . 115.00
Spirit Of Goodwill, Pilot, Embossed Star In Circle, Glass, Painted, 5 In. 316.00
Toonerville Trolley, Glass, Painted, 3 ¼ In. . . . . *illus* 978.00
Tot Telephone, Glass, Paper Dial, Plastic Hand Set, 5 ½ In. 260.00
Ye Olde Oaken Bucket, Milk Glass, Tin Closure, Painted, 2 In.. . . . . 185.00
Zook The Clown, Hard Plastic, Multicolored, Rosbro, 3 x 6 ½ In. 78.00

CANES and walking sticks were used by every well-dressed man in the nineteenth century, but by World War I the style had changed. Today canes are used by few but the infirm. Collectors prize old canes made with special features, like hidden swords, whiskey flasks, or risqué pictures seen through peepholes. Examples with solid gold heads or made from exotic materials are among the higher-priced canes. See also Scrimshaw.

Bamboo, Bulldog's Head, Glass Eyes, 32 ½ In. . . . . *illus* 66.00
Black Horn, Bearded Man, Nude, Steel Collar, Wood Shaft, Brass Ferrule, 1863, 40 In. 575.00
Dagger, Ebony, Ivory, Ring Of Leaves, 36 x 16 ½ In.. . . . . 110.00
Ebony, Porcelain, Gold Collar, Head Of Girl With Flowered Scarf, 11800s, 38 In. 1725.00
Enamel, Mushroom Shape, Hinged, Flower Basket, Ebony Shaft, 35 ½ In. 1725.00
Glass, Paperweight, Brass Ferrule, Embossed Gold Collar, Ebony Shaft, 36 In. 240.00
Hardwood, Patriotic Carving, Outdoor Themes, Steel Ferrule, 36 In. 863.00
Hardwood, Spherical Knob, Coiled Snake, Multicolored, Carved, Painted, 35 ½ In. 259.00
Horn, Horse Head, Glass Eyes, Knotty Wood Shaft, Bone Tip, Carved, 35 ½ In. 33.00
Horn, Rope Twist Shaft, Painted, Red, Yellow, Black, Green, 37 ½ In.. . . . . 230.00
Horse Hair, Braided, Over Wood, Diamond Pattern, American Western, 34 In.. . . . . 2070.00
Ivory, 2 Horse Heads, Carved Tip, Rosewood, Glass Eyes, Brass Ferrule, 37 In.. . . . . 403.00
Ivory, Clenched Fist, Holding Wrapping Serpent, Double Cuff, Wood Shaft, 7 ¼ In. 1210.00
Ivory, Dog Head, Spaniel, Glass Eyes, Gold Plated Collar, Wood Shaft, Horn Ferrule, 35 In. . . . 1035.00
Ivory, Eagle Head, Silver Tone Ferrule, Sterling Collar, Wood Shaft, 34 In. 2250.00
Ivory, Eagle Head, Wood Shaft, Silver Ferrule, Sterling Collar, 34 In. 2250.00

Ivory, Horse Head, Flowing Mane, Ebony Shaft, Silver Collar, 34 In. 336.00
Ivory, Horse Head, Silver Collar, Malacca Shaft, 19th Century, 37 ½ In. 2300.00
Ivory, Monkey, Reading Newspaper, Silver Collar, Malacca Shaft, 38 ¼ In. 5175.00
Ivory, Napoleon's Head, Ebony Shaft, 19th Century, 36 ¾ In. 1380.00
Ivory, Scrolled Silver Collar, Lion, Malacca Shaft, England, 35 ¼ In. 1495.00
Ivory, Silver Collar, Marked, London, 1896, 36 In. .... *illus* 66.00
Ivory, Silver Eyelets, Malacca Shaft, Pomander, England, 35 ¾ In. 4255.00
Ivory, Swan, On Reeds, Malacca Shaft, England, 19th Century, 37 ¾ In. 2875.00
Malacca, Gun, Trigger Button On Collar, Continental, 31 In. 1265.00
Red Coral, Ivory, Leaves & Acorns, Rosewood Shaft, Italy, 36 ¾ In. 2070.00
Scalpel, Syringe, Brass Anchor & Crown, Brass Ferrule, Wood Shaft, 38 In. 750.00
Silver, Monkey Head, Wood Shaft 920.00
Softwood, Vines, Snakes, Tapered Shaft, Brass Ferrule, 37 ½ In. 1955.00
Sword, 32-In. Blade, Silver, Malacca Shaft, England, c.1898, 39 In. 1725.00
Sword, Ivory, Ebony, Brass Pommel, 19th Century, 36 In. 550.00
Sword, Stag, Gilt Flowers, Leaf Engraved Blade, Silver Ring, Wood, 36 x 12 In. 600.00
Tortoiseshell, Ivory Collar, Stork Head, Rosewood Shaft, 36 In. 2875.00
Vine Branch, Climbing Child, Germany, Mid 19th Century, 32 ½ In. 1553.00
Walking Stick, Albatross, Ivory Eyes, Silver Collar, Ebony, Edwardian, 36 In. 1016.00
Walking Stick, Bamboo, Turned, 19th Century, 37 In. 598.00
Walking Stick, Bone, Carved, Knot Finial, Reeded, Spiral, 19th Century, 34 ½ In. 881.00
Walking Stick, Carved, Cross-hatching, Vine, Handcuffs, Pistol, Clasped Hands, 36 In. 1673.00
Walking Stick, Coin & Stamp, Black Painted Shaft, Horn Tip, 37 In. 315.00
Walking Stick, Compass, Black Painted Shaft, Horn Tip, F. Barker & Son, London, 1932, 36 In. 695.00
Walking Stick, Elephant, Bone Eyes, Ebony, Carved, 37 ½ In .... *illus* 51.00
Walking Stick, Flask, Glass, Nickel Plated, Metal Cup, Wood Shaft, Brass Tip, 35 In. 420.00
Walking Stick, Hand, Holding Snake, Apple In Mouth, Angels, Soldiers, 34 In. 2530.00
Walking Stick, Horn, Wood, c.1886, 34 In. 47.00
Walking Stick, Iron, Horse Leg, Iron Foot, Mahogany, England, 19th Century, 37 In. 269.00
Walking Stick, Ivory, Bone, Carved Finial, Spiral Shaft, Mid 1800s, 36 In. 3055.00
Walking Stick, Leather, Wicker, England, 19th Century, 34 In. 837.00
Walking Stick, Man's Head, Glass Eyes, Vine, Engraved, 36 In. 239.00
Walking Stick, Silver, Hound's Head, Turned Foot, Wood, England, 1891, 35 In. 1135.00
Walking Stick, Sterling Silver, Dog's Head, Amber Eyes, Edwardian, c.1903, 33 In. 390.00
Walking Stick, Telescope, 5-Stage, Painted, Horn Tip, Abraham & Co., Liverpool, 35 In. 1300.00
Walking Stick, Telescope, Birch, Brass, Single Draw, Van Cort, 34 In. 264.00
Walking Stick, Wood, Carved, House, Man With Top Hat, Geometric, 1800s, 40 In. 18800.00
Walking Stick, Wood, Gnarled, Ivory Hoof, Metal Foot, England, 19th Century, 33 In. 1554.00
Walking Stick, Wood, Silver Golf Club, Ivory Foot, Edwardian, 34 In. 239.00
Wood, Bird, Multicolored, Black Shaft, 34 In. 55.00
Wood, Cherry, Spherical Knob, Faceted Collar, Tapered Shaft, Coiled Snake, 37 In. 2415.00
Wood, Clenched Fist, Holding Snake, Silver Shield, Thistles, Steeplechase, 36 In. 480.00
Wood, Dog Head, Farm Animals, Leaves, Marked, D.S.R., 34 ¼ In. 523.00
Wood, Dog Head, Irish Setter, Open Mouth, Tongue, Tapered, Horn Ferrule, 36 In. 287.00
Wood, Dog Head, Labrador, T-Shape Handle, Brass Collar, Birch, Bark & Metal Ferrule, 38 In. 345.00
Wood, Entwined Snakes, Vine, Brown & Green Paint, Iron Ferrule, 35 In. 1208.00
Wood, Fist & Scroll, Victorian .... *illus* 161.00
Wood, Ivory, Sterling Silver Band, Horn Tip, 31 In. 44.00
Wood, Man's Head, Bird, Dog, Root Knot Handle, Varnished, 34 ¼ In. 303.00
Wood, Snake, Eagle Head Around Mermaid, Anchor, Whale, U.S. Flag, 40 In. 460.00

CANTON CHINA is blue-and-white ware made near the city of Canton, in China, from about 1785 to 1895. It is hand decorated with Chinese scenes. Canton is part of the group of porcelains known today as Chinese Export Porcelain.

Bowl, Harbor Scene, Fishing Boats, Scalloped Rim, 10 & 8 & 7 In., 3 Piece 1035.00
Bowl, Square Sided, Scalloped Edge, Orange Peel Glaze, 9 x 9 In. 345.00
Bowl, Underplate, Reticulated Sides, Rim, Rain & Cloud Borders, 1800s, 8-In. Bowl 201.00
Candleholder, Tapering, Landscapes, 11 ½ In., Pair 1150.00
Candlestick, Landscape, Lake, 19th Century, 11 ½ In. .... *illus* 1150.00
Dish, Cover, 19th Century, 5 x 8 x 9 ½ In. 529.00
Dish, Cover, Pinecone Knop, Tapered, Notched Corners, 5 ⅞ x 10 In. 144.00
Dish, Landscape, Rain & Cloud Border, Leaf Form, 19th Century, 8 In., Pair .... *illus* 205.00
Dish, Octagonal, Hot Water Base, c.1840, 8 ¾ x 10 In. 470.00
Dish, Vegetable, Cover, Nut Finial, 4 ½ x 8 ½ x 7 In. 289.00
Ewer, Leaf Design, Mid 19th Century, 12 ¼ In. 2013.00

Cane, Bamboo, Bulldog's Head, Glass Eyes, 32 ½ In.
$66.00

Cane, Ivory, Silver Collar, Marked, London, 1896, 36 In.
$66.00

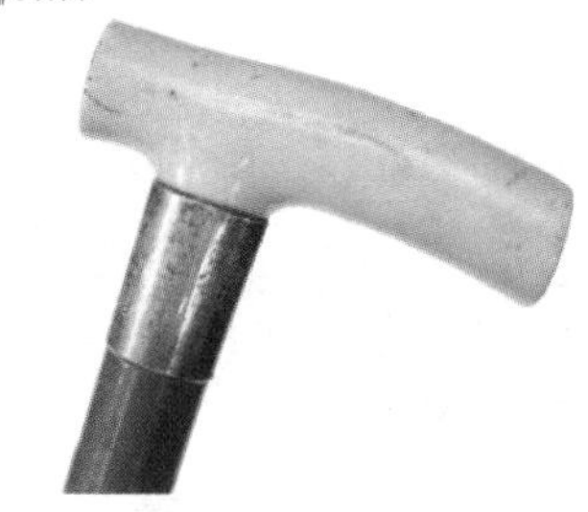

Cane, Walking Stick, Elephant, Bone Eyes, Ebony, Carved, 37 ½ In.
$51.00

Cane, Wood, Fist & Scroll, Victorian
$161.00

C

Canton, Candlestick, Landscape, Lake, 19th Century, 11 ½ In.
$1150.00

Canton, Dish, Landscape, Rain & Cloud Border, Leaf Form, 19th Century, 8 In., Pair
$205.00

Canton, Platter, Harbor Scene, Borders, 8-Sided, Late 19th Century, 19 In.
$490.00

Captain Midnight, Badge, Secret Squadron, Decoder, Revolves, Plastic, Ovaltine, 1945, 2 ½ In.
$190.00

Pitcher, Buildings & Landscape, Early 1800s, 6 ½ & 5 ½ In. 1840.00
Plate, 19th Century, 9 In. 83.00
Plate, Hot Water, Tab Handles, Berry Finial, Round, 11 In. 870.00
Plate, Landscape Scene, c.1850, 8 In., 3 Piece 88.00
Platter, Boats In Harbor, Pagoda, Rain & Cloud Border, 1800s, 18 ¾ & 18 In., 2 Piece 546.00
Platter, Buildings, Water, Bridge, Cut Corner, c.1900, 17 ¼ x 14 ¼ In. 345.00
Platter, Chamfered, Rectangular, 19th Century, 13 ⅝ x 16 ¾ In., 2 Piece 999.00
Platter, Harbor Scene, Borders, 8-Sided, Late 19th Century, 19 In. .... *illus* 490.00
Platter, Houses, Trees, Bridge, Blue & White, 8-Sided, 13 x 10 In. 690.00
Platter, Landscape, Bridge, Water, Mountains, Oval, 16 x 19 ½ In. 1380.00
Teapot, 19th Century, 9 ½ x 9 In. 292.00
Teapot, Building, Landscape, Lighthouse Shape, Strap Handle, 6 In. 1380.00
Teapot, Buildings, Bridge, Water, Tapered, Round, Domed Lid, 6 ½ In. 460.00
Tray, Trees, House, Pheasant, Bridge, Cut Corner, 10 In. 754.00
Tureen, Cover, 10 ½ In. 205.00
Tureen, Cover, Blue & White, Scroll Knop, Tapered, Double Twist Handles, 9 x 13 In. 403.00
Tureen, Landscape, 19th Century, 5 x 8 ¾ x 13 ¾ In. 264.00
Tureen, Landscape Scenes, Animal Mask Handles, 3 x 7 x 4 ½ In. 85.00
Tureen, Oval, Bud Finial, Cover, 14 x 8 ¼ x 11 ½ In. 704.00

CAPO-DI-MONTE porcelain was first made in Naples, Italy, from 1743 to 1759. The factory moved near Madrid, Spain, reopened in 1771, and worked to 1834. Since that time, the Doccia factory of Italy acquired the molds and is using the crown and N mark. Societe Richard Ceramica is a modern-day firm often referred to as Ginori or Capo-di-Monte. This company also uses the crown and N mark.

Box, Cupids Frolicking, Flowers, Brass Rim, Blue Crown Over N, 5 x 11 x 4 In. 730.00
Cachepot, Figural, Woman, Lion's Head, Blue, Gold, 19th Century, 9 x 6 In. 100.00
Cigarette Carousel, Multicolored, Footed, 16 In. 275.00
Cigarette Holder, Carousel Shape, Multicolored, 16 In. 146.00
Compote, Raised Relief Cupids, Pierced Design, c.1950, 8 x 15 In. 47.00
Dresser Box, Bronze, Babies In A Cloud, c.1900, 4 x 6 In. 205.00
Figurine, Angel, Green Marble Base, 8 In. 58.00
Figurine, Cobbler, Il Calzolaio, Wood Base, 8 x 8 ¾ In. 146.00
Figurine, Victorian Couple, 4 In. 17.00
Group, Drunkards, Bisque, G, Armani, 18 In. 150.00
Group, Hobo With Dog, Bisque, G. Armani, 18 In. 250.00
Stein, N With Crown, Porcelain Lid, 1 Liter, 14 In. 362.00
Stein, N With Crown, Porcelain Lid, 2 Liter 1179.00
Teapot, Raised Relief Figures, c.1930, 16 x 12 In. 29.00
Tureen, Footed, Woman With Child On Lid, 2 Handles, 8 ¼ x 10 In. 322.00
Urn, Lidded, Classical Nude Border, Crown Mark, Blue Saxony, 13 ¾ In., Pair 940.00

CAPTAIN MARVEL was introduced in February 1940 in Whiz comic books. An orphan named Billy Batson met the wizard, Shazam, and whenever he said the magic word he was transformed into a superhero. A movie serial was released in 1940. The comic was discontinued in 1954. A second Captain Marvel appeared in 1966, a third in 1967. Only the original was transformed by shouting "Shazam."

Toy, Car, Racing, Lightning, 4 Cars, Tin, Windup, Automatic Toy Co., Box 960.00
Watch, Chromed Metal Case, Blue Band, Full Figure, Fawcett, 1948 .... 885.00

CAPTAIN MIDNIGHT began as a network radio show in September 1940. The first comic book appeared in July 1941. Captain Midnight was really the aviator Captain Albright, who was to defeat the Nazis. A movie serial was made in 1942 and a comic strip was published for a short time. The comic book version of Captain Midnight ended his career in 1948. Radio premiums are the prized collector memorabilia today.

Badge, Secret Squadron, Brass, Photograph, c.1945 .... 115.00
Badge, Secret Squadron, Decoder, Revolves, Plastic, Ovaltine, 1945, 2 ½ In. .... *illus* 190.00
Badge, Secret Squadron, Skelly Oil Company, Brass, Photo, c.1949 .... 115.00
Book, Big Little Book, Secret Squadron, No. 1488, Winterbotham & Hess, c.1941 .... 50.00
Record, Special Squadron Message, Flexi-Disc, Code-O-Graph, c.1962, 7 In. 8.00
Shake-Up Mug, Cover, Plastic, Decal, Ovaltine, Heart Of Hearty Breakfast 100.00
Shake-Up Mug, Ovaltine Premium, Lid, Decal, 1947-49 .... 100.00

CARAMEL SLAG, *see Imperial Glass category.*

CARDS listed here include advertising cards (often called trade cards), baseball cards, playing cards, and others. Color photographs were rare in the nineteenth century, so companies gave away colorful cards with pictures of children, flowers, products, or related scenes that promoted the company name. These were often collected and stored in albums. Baseball cards also date from the nineteenth century when they were used by tobacco companies as giveaways. Gum cards were started in 1933, but it was not until after World War II that the bubble gum cards favored today were produced. Today over 1,000 cards are issued each year by the gum companies. Related items may be found in the Christmas, Halloween, Movie, Paper, and Postcard categories.

Advertising, Arrowhead Hot Springs, California's Ideal Resort, Die Cut, 4 ½ x 3 ½ In. 300.00
Advertising, Border Sheriff, Jack Hoxie, Blue Streak Western, 11 x 14 In. 40.00
Advertising, Gold Dust Washing Powder, 2 Black Boys In Tub, Die Cut, 3 ½ x 3 In. 40.00
Advertising, Gun Code, Tim McCoy, 11 x 14 In. 60.00
Advertising, McCormick Harvesting Machine Co., Grain Reaper, c.1884. . . . . 110.00
Advertising, Pet Cigarettes Are Best, Children, Lamb, Allen & Ginter, Cardboard, c.1890, 8 x 4 In. . . 80.00
Advertising, Phantom Horseman, Jack Hoxie, Universal Attraction, 11 x 14 In. 40.00
Advertising, Thundering Trails, 3 Mesquiteers, Tom Tyler, Bob Steel, 11 x 14 In. 60.00
Advertising, Trick Pony Bank, Shepard Hardware . . . . *illus* 5558.00
Advertising, Watch Dog Safe, J. & E. Stevens, Peabody & Whitney, Boston, Mass. . . . . *illus* 7020.00
Advertising, Wyoming Wildcat, FBO Pictures, Tom Tyler, 1925, 11 x 14 In. 60.00
Baseball, A. Coomb, Athletics, A.L. Rose Company, c.1908. . . . . 472.00
Baseball, A. Wagner, Boston, A.L. Rose Company, c.1908. . . . . 649.00
Baseball, Charles Comiskey, Allen & Ginter's Cigarettes, 1 ½ x 2 ¾ In. 224.00
Baseball, Charlie Gehringer, 1937 . . . . 756.00
Baseball, Eddie Mathews, Rookie, Topps, No. 407, 1952 . . . . 22800.00
Baseball, Henry Aaron, Rookie, Topps, No. 128, 1954 . . . . 19200.00
Baseball, Hugh Duffy, Old Judge Cigarettes, 1887 . . . . 2693.00
Baseball, Jackie Robinson, 1952. . . . . 2384.00
Baseball, Jackie Robinson, Autographed, Topps, No. 50, 1955 . . . . 1931.00
Baseball, Joe DiMaggio, 1938 . . . . 2886.00
Baseball, Joe DiMaggio, Rookie, World Wide Gum, No. 51, 1936 . . . . 36000.00
Baseball, Joe Jackson, Cracker Jack, No. 103, 1915 . . . . 19468.00
Baseball, John Ward, Old Judge Cigarettes, 1887. . . . . 1669.00
Baseball, Kid Nichols, Old Judge Cigarettes, 1887 . . . . 6544.00
Baseball, King Kelly, Old Judge Cigarettes, 1887 . . . . 2225.00
Baseball, Larry Doyle, N.Y. Nationals, White Border, 1909 . . . . 2185.00
Baseball, Lou Gehrig, 1934. . . . . 3493.00
Baseball, Lou Gehrig, Goudey, No. 37, 1934. . . . . 96000.00
Baseball, Lou Gehrig, Rookie, 1925 . . . . 24200.00
Baseball, Mickey Mantle, Rookie, Autographed, No. 253, 1951. . . . . 5975.00
Baseball, Mordecai Brown, Chicago Cubs, White Border, 1909. . . . . 2693.00
Baseball, Satchel Paige, Rookie, Leaf, No. 8, 1948. . . . . 20400.00
Baseball, Topps, Rack Pack, From Santa Claus To, 1952, 12 Packs, 11 x 4 In. . . . . *illus* 1297.00
Baseball, Tris Speaker, Cracker Jack, No. 65, 1915. . . . . 4915.00
Baseball, Ty Cobb, American Caramel, 1909 . . . . 3691.00
Baseball, Ty Cobb, No. 9, 1911 . . . . 21600.00
Basketball, Michael Jordan, Rookie, Fleer, No. 57, 1986-87 . . . . 295.00
Basketball, Pete Maravich, Rookie, Topps, No. 123, 1970. . . . . 18000.00
Football, Joe Namath, Rookie, Topps, No. 122, 1965 . . . . 7919.00
Football, Knute Rockne, National Chicle No. 9, 1935 . . . . 4522.00
Football, Knute Rockne, Topps, No. 16, 1955. . . . . 12000.00
Greeting, Boy With Cat & Flower, Norcross, 7 x 5 In. 22.00
Greeting, Congratulations, Baby, H.J. Heinz, Menu Of Baby Foods On Back, 4 x 5 In. 18.00
Greeting, Valentine, Children In Garden, Fold Down, Die Cut, Germany, c.1900, 9 ½ In. . *illus* 212.00
Greeting, Valentine, Cobweb Center, Cherubs, Swans, Lace Fringe, 1850, 7 x 5 In. 510.00
Greeting, Valentine, Coronation Carriage, Fold-Out, Die Cut, 1800s, 10 x 12 x 4 In. . . . . *illus* 502.00
Greeting, Valentine, Edwardian, Fan, Peacock Feathers, Ladies' Faces, Tuck, c.1908, 8 x 15 In. 561.00
Greeting, Valentine, Embossed, Garden Gate, Children, Fold Down, Germany, c.1900, 9 ½ In. 212.00
Greeting, Valentine, Girl At Flower Stand, Honeycomb, Die Cut, c.1897-1901, 12 x 15 In. *illus* 295.00
Greeting, Valentine, Girl At Vanity, Man's Face Appears In Mirror, Mechanical, Die Cut, 11 x 7 In. . 50.00
Greeting, Valentine, Guitar Shape, With Love & Affection, Silk Covered Cardboard, c. 1910, 19 In. . 295.00
Greeting, Valentine, Paper Lace, Little Girl, Die Cut, Tuck & Brundage, c.1900, 9 ½ In., 2 Piece 295.00
Greeting, Valentine, Paper Lace, Cut, Pin Prick, Esther Howland, 1850s, 8 x 10 In. 177.00
Greeting, Valentine, Ship, Children, Crepe Paper Sails, 3-D, Box, 14 x 13 In. . . . . *illus* 1200.00
Greeting, Valentine, Stylized Cutwork, Poem, Round, Frame, 6 ¾ x 7 ¾ In. 132.00
Greeting, Valentine, Suffrage, Love Me Love My Vote, Clapsaddle, c.1912 . . . . 71.00

Card, Advertising, Trick Pony Bank, Shepard Hardware
$5558.00

Card, Advertising, Watch Dog Safe, J. & E. Stevens, Peabody & Whitney, Boston, Mass.
$7020.00

Card, Baseball, Topps, Rack Pack, From Santa Claus To, 1952, 12 Packs, 11 x 4 In.
$1297.00

Card, Greeting, Valentine, Children In Garden, Fold Down, Die Cut, Germany, c.1900, 9 ½ In.
$212.00

Card, Greeting, Valentine, Coronation Carriage, Fold-Out, Die Cut, 1800s, 10 x 12 x 4 In.
$502.00

Card, Greeting, Valentine, Girl At Flower Stand, Honeycomb, Die Cut, c.1897-1901, 12 x 15 In.
$295.00

Greeting, Valentine, Sweethearts, 6 Blades, Tuck, c.1900, 9 x 12 In. . . . . *illus* 436.00
Greeting, Valentine, To My Valentine, Die Cut, Fold-Out Honeycomb, Brundage, c.1901, 12 x 15 In. 295.00
Greeting, Valentine, Windsor, Lace, 2 Piece, Die Cut, C. King, c.1860, 5 x 7 In. 35.00
Proposal, Marriage, Pin Prick, Silk, Painted, Joseph Mansell, Mid 1800s, 8 x 10 In. . . . . *illus* 177.00

CARDER, *see Aurene and Steuben categories.*

CARLSBAD is a mark found on china made by several factories in Germany, Austria, and Bavaria. Many pieces were exported to the United States. Most of the pieces available today were made after 1891.

Vase, Art Nouveau, Hand Painted, Victoria, Austria, c.1910, 13 ½ In. 146.00

CARLTON WARE was made at the Carlton Works of Stoke-on-Trent, England, beginning about 1890. The firm traded as Wiltshaw & Robinson until 1957. It was renamed Carlton Ware Ltd. in 1958. The company went bankrupt in 1995, but the name is still in use.

Ashtray, Bird, Tree, Green Ground, 4 ¼ x 4 ¼ In. 60.00
Cup & Saucer, Demitasse, Heron, Flowers, Rouge, Gold, Marked . . . . . *illus* 110.00
Cup & Saucer, Heron, Flowers, Gold Trim, Rouge Royal 130.00
Figurine, King George VI 541.00
Ginger Jar, Cover, Cranes, Rain Tree, Gold Trim, Rouge Royal, 7 ¼ In. 142.00
Jug, Insects, Spider Web, Rouge Royale, Gilt, Marked, 7 ¼ In. . . . . *illus* 110.00
Teapot, Moonlight Cameo, Black Matte Glaze, Flame Luster Medallion, Marked, 7 In.. . . . . 300.00
Vase, Birds Of Paradise, 7 In. 48.00
Vase, Bulbous, Persian, Gold Rim, Cream, 6 ½ In. 222.00
Vase, Fish, Seaweed, Cover, 7 In. 354.00
Vase, Ribbed, Pagoda Scene, Yellow Ground, 7 ¼ In. 157.00

CARNIVAL GLASS was an inexpensive, iridescent, pressed glass made from about 1907 to about 1925. More than 1,000 different patterns are known. Carnival glass is currently being reproduced. Additional pieces may be found in the Northwood category.

Acorn Burrs, Punch Bowl, Marigold, 8 Piece 2000.00
Acorn Burrs & Bark pattern is listed here as Acorn Burrs.
African Shield, Vase, Marigold, 3 In. 50.00
Amaryllis pattern is listed here as Tiger Lily.
American Beauty Roses pattern is listed here as Wreath of Roses.
Banded Medallion & Teardrop pattern is listed here as Beaded Bull's-Eye.
Basket, Dish, Handles, Opalescent Aqua, c.1900, 4 ½ In. 118.00
Battenburg Lace No. 1 pattern is listed here as Hearts & Flowers.
Battenburg Lace No. 2 pattern is listed here as Captive Rose.
Battenburg Lace No. 3 pattern is listed here as Fanciful.
Beaded Bull's Eye, Vase, Swung, 12 ½ In. 85.00
Beaded Bull's-Eye, Vase, Marigold, 11 In. 350.00
Beaded Cable, Rose Bowl, Amethyst 85.00
Beaded Cable, Rose Bowl, Aqua Opalescent, 4 In. . . . . *illus* 193.00
Beaded Cable, Rose Bowl, Blue 165.00
Beaded Cable, Rose Bowl, Marigold, 4 In. 44.00
Beaded Star & Snail pattern is listed here as Constellation.
Beads & Flowers, Plate, Peach, 7 In. 15.00
Beauty Bud, Vase, Amethyst, 8 ¾ In. 85.00
Big Thistle, Punchbowl & Base, Radium, Purple 24000.00
Birds & Cherries, Card, Tray, Bonbon Shape, Marigold 40.00
Birds & Cherries, Nappy, Wide Panels, Handles, Blue, Fenton, 7 In. 38.00
Birds on Bough pattern is listed here as Birds & Cherries.
Blackberry, Compote, Marigold, 5 In. 40.00
Blackberry A pattern is listed here as Blackberry.
Blackberry Bramble, Compote, Green, 5 In. . . . . *illus* 85.00
Broken Arches, Punch Bowl, Amethyst 625.00
Bushel Basket pattern is listed here as Basket.
Butterfly, Bonbon, Handles, Amethyst, 8 ¼ In. . . . . *illus* 55.00
Butterfly & Stippled Rays pattern is listed here as Butterfly.
Captive Rose, Bowl, Blue, 9 ¼ In. . . . . *illus* 150.00
Captive Rose, Plate, Blue, 9 In.. . . . . 325.00
Cattails & Fish pattern is listed here as Fisherman's Mug.
Cattails & Water Lily pattern is listed here as Water Lily & Cattails.

Checkerboard, Goblet, Marigold 205.00
Cherries, Plate, Amethyst, 6 In. 200.00
Cherry & Cable, Pitcher, Marigold 525.00
Christmas Cactus pattern is listed here as Thistle.
Chrysanthemum, Bowl, Ruffled Edge, Red, 9 In. 2000.00
Chrysanthemum, Bowl, Scalloped Edge, Footed, Marigold, 9 In. 22.00
Chrysanthemum, Chop Plate, Amethyst 1000.00
Cobblestone, Bowl, Ruffled Edge, Amethyst, 8 ½ In. 250.00
Coin Dot, Bowl, Scalloped Edge, Footed, Green, 8 In. 17.00
Colonial Lady, Vase, Amethyst, 6 In. 600.00
Colonial Lady, Vase, Marigold, 6 In. 145.00
Constellation, Compote, White, 5 ¼ In. 35.00
Constitution pattern is listed here as God & Home.
Coral Medallion pattern is listed here as Mayan.
Cosmos & Cane, Compote, White 700.00
Daisy & Drape, Vase, 3-Footed, Ice Blue, 6 ¼ In. 1800.00
Daisy & Drape, Vase, Aqua Opalescent, 3-Footed, 6 ¼ In. . . . . *illus* 315.00
Dandelion, Mug, Marigold 150.00
Diamond Point, Vase, Blue, 8 In. 105.00
Diamond Point & Daisy pattern is listed here as Cosmos & Cane.
Dogwood & Marsh Lily pattern is listed here as Two Flowers.
Dragon & Lotus, Bowl, Ruffled Edge, Footed, Marigold, 9 In. . . . . 35.00 to 55.00
Dragon & Lotus, Bowl, Ruffled Edge, Vaseline Opalescent, Marigold, 9 In. 385.00
Dragon & Lotus, Bowl, Ruffled Edge, Cobalt Blue, 9 In. 85.00
Dragon & Lotus, Bowl, Scalloped Edge, Blue, 8 In. 99.00
Drapery, Rose Bowl, Aqua Opalescent, 4 x 6 In. 130.00
Drapery, Rose Bowl, Ruffled Edge, Footed, Opalescent Aqua, 3 ½ In. 118.00
Drapery, Vase, White, 8 In. 45.00
Fan & Arch pattern is listed here as Persian Garden.
Fanciful, Bowl, Ruffled Edge, Marigold, 8 ½ In. 30.00
Fanciful, Plate, Ruffled Edge, 9 In. . . . . *illus* 200.00
Fantasy pattern is listed here as Question Marks.
Farmyard, Bowl, Pie Crust Edge, Amethyst, 10 In. 3500.00
Farmyard, Bowl, Ruffled Edge, Square, Amethyst, 10 In. 5500.00
Fenton's Butterfly pattern is listed here as Butterfly.
Fern, Compote, Amethyst, 4 ¾ In. . . . . *illus* 140.00
Fine Rib, Vase, Jack-In-The-Pulpit, Marigold, 5 ½ In. 33.00
Fisherman's Mug, Coffee Mug, Amethyst, Dugan, c.1900, 4 In. . . . . *illus* 59.00
Flowering Almonds pattern is listed here as Peacock Tail.
Flowers & Frames, Bowl, Ruffled Edge, Footed, Peach Opalescent 100.00
Four Flowers, Plate, Satin Marigold Luster, White Opalescent, 6 ¼ In. 27.00
Four Pillars, Vase, Custard, 8 In. 10.00
Four Seventy Four, Pitcher, Milk, Marigold 60.00
Fruits & Flowers, Bowl, Blue, Ruffled, 7 In. 105.00
Garden Path Variant, Bowl, Scalloped Edge, Soda Gold, 9 In. 44.00
Garland, Rose Bowl, Blue, Footed, 4 ¼ In. 55.00
Golden Wedding, Bottle, Marigold, Paper Label 60.00
Good Luck, Bowl, Amethyst, Ruffled Edge, Basketweave Back, 8 ½ In. 249.00
Good Luck, Bowl, Piecrust Edge, Marigold, 8 ½ In. 295.00
Good Luck, Bowl, Piecrust Edge, Ribbed Back, Blue, 8 ½ In. 300.00
Good Luck, Bowl, Ruffled Edge, Marigold, c.1900, 9 In. 118.00
Gothic Arches, Vase, Marigold, 12 In. 250.00
Grape & Cable, Bowl, 3-Footed, Marigold, 10 ½ In. 30.00
Grape & Cable, Bowl, Ruffled Edge, Amethyst, 8 ¾ In. 99.00
Grape & Cable, Bowl, Ruffled Edge, Marigold, 8 ¾ In. 30.00
Grape & Cable, Butter, Cover, Marigold, Thumbprint, 6 In. 49.00
Grape & Cable, Compote, Cover, Amethyst, 9 In. . . . . *illus* 80.00
Grape & Cable, Decanter, Marigold, 6 In. 33.00
Grape & Cable, Hatpin Holder, Amethyst, 6 ⅞ In. 176.00
Grape & Cable, Lamp, Candle, Amethyst 450.00
Grape & Cable, Pitcher, Green 525.00
Grape Leaves, Bowl, Ruffled Edge, Footed, Amethyst, 8 ¾ In. 44.00
Grapevine Diamonds pattern is listed here as Grapevine Lattice.
Grapevine Lattice, Tumbler, White 110.00
Greek Key, Bowl, Amethyst, Northwood, 9 In. . . . . *illus* 165.00

Card, Greeting, Valentine, Ship, Children, Crepe Paper Sails, 3-D, Box, 14 x 13 In.
$1200.00

Card, Greeting, Valentine, Sweethearts, 6 Blades, Tuck, c.1900, 9 x 12 In.
$436.00

Card, Proposal, Marriage, Pin Prick, Silk, Painted, Joseph Mansell, Mid 1800s, 8 x 10 In.
$177.00

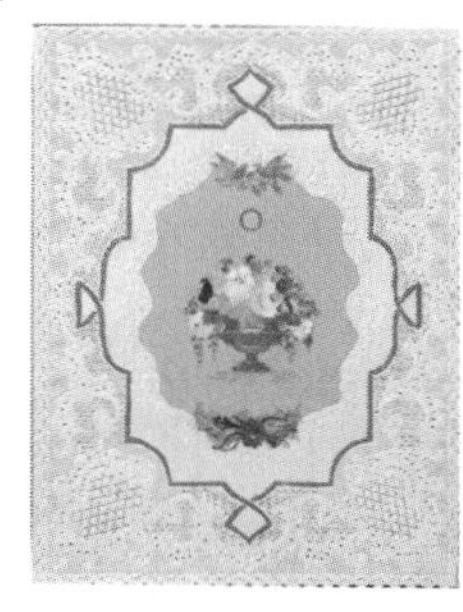

Carlton Ware, Cup & Saucer, Demitasse, Heron, Flowers, Rouge, Gold, Marked
$110.00

Carlton Ware, Jug, Insects, Spider Web, Rouge Royale, Gilt, Marked, 7 ¼ In.
$110.00

Carnival Glass, Beaded Cable, Rose Bowl, Aqua Opalescent, 4 In.
$193.00

Carnival Glass, Blackberry Bramble, Compote, Green, 5 In.
$85.00

Carnival Glass, Butterfly, Bonbon, Handles, Amethyst, 8 ¼ In.
$55.00

Carnival Glass, Captive Rose, Bowl, Blue, 9 ¼ In.
$150.00

Carnival Glass, Daisy & Drape, Vase, Aqua Opalescent, 3-Footed, 6 ¼ In.
$315.00

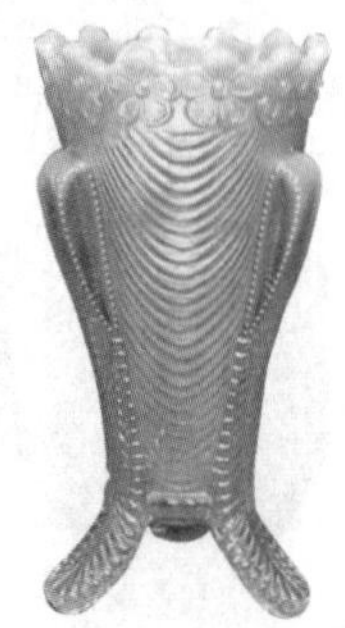

Greek Key, Plate, Marigold, 9 In.. 650.00
Greek Key & Scales, Bowl, Ruffled Edge, Footed, Green, 4 x 8 In. 77.00
Hattie, Bowl, Amethyst, 8 ½ In. 44.00
Heart & Vine, Bowl, Ruffled Edge, Footed, Blue, 7 ½ In. 77.00
Hearts & Flowers, Bowl, Ribbed Back, Lime Green, 8 ½ In. 900.00
Hearts & Flowers, Plate, Amethyst, 9 In. 650.00
Heavy Grape, Berry Bowl, Blue, 8 ½ In. 300.00
Heron, Mug, Amethyst, 4 In. *illus* 118.00
Hobnail pattern is listed in this book as its own category.
Holly, Bowl, Blue, Footed, 8 ½ In. *illus* 66.00
Holly & Berry, Nappy, Ruffled Edge, Handle, Amethyst, 7 In. 44.00
Homestead, Chop Plate, Amethyst 1700.00
Horse Medallions pattern is listed here as Horses' Heads.
Horses' Heads, Bowl, Footed, Scalloped Rim, Marigold, 7 ½ In.. 55.00
Imperial Grape, Bowl, Smoke, Ruffled, Deep 75.00
Inverted Strawberry, Cuspidor, Green 65.00
Inverted Strawberry, Sauce, Round, Amethyst, 4 ½ In.. 35.00
Iris, Compote, Ruffled Edge, Marigold 45.00
Iris, Goblet, Marigold, 6 ½ In. 40.00
Kittens, Bowl, Sides Folded Up, Powder Blue, Marigold Iridescense 175.00
Kittens, Cup & Saucer, Marigold *illus* 145.00
Kittens, Sauceboat, Marigold 4800.00
Labelle Poppy pattern is listed here as Poppy Show.
Labelle Rose pattern is listed here as Rose Show.
Leaf & Beads, Rose Bowl, Sunflower Interior, Amethyst 65.00
Leaf & Daisy, Water Set, 6 Piece 150.00
Lined Lattice, Vase, Peach Opalescent, 5 ½ In. 275.00
Lion, Bowl, Marigold, 6 ¼ x 2 In.. 135.00
Little Flowers, Bowl, Scalloped Edge, Footed, Blue, 9 ½ In. 77.00
Loganberry, Vase, Amber 400.00
Long Thumbprint, Scalloped Rim, Amethyst, 10 ½ In. 44.00
Long Thumbprint, Vase, Swung, Green, 11 In. 55.00
Lotus & Grape, Blue, Ruffled Rim, 8 ½ In. 44.00
Luster Rose, Bowl, Round, Amethyst, 7 ½ In. 105.00
Magnolia & Poinsettia pattern is listed here as Water Lily.
Maple Leaf, Water Set, Amethyst, 7 Piece *illus* 125.00
Melinda pattern is listed here as Wishbone.
Melon Rib, Cuspidor, Marigold 80.00
Memphis, Berry Bowl, Amethyst, 5 In., 8 Piece 375.00
Moonprint, Tumbler, Whiskey, Marigold 105.00
Morning Glory, Vase, Smoke, 7 In.. 55.00
Octagon, Sherbet, Marigold. 50.00
Old Fashion Flag pattern is listed here as Iris.
Open Rose, Plate, Marigold, 9 In. 65.00
Optic & Button, Rose Bowl, Marigold 10.00
Orange Tree, Bowl, Scalloped Edge, Blue, 9 In. 77.00
Orange Tree, Bowl, Scalloped Edge, Marigold, 8 ¼ In. 55.00
Orange Tree, Hatpin Holder, Blue, 6 ½ In. 121.00
Orange Tree, Hatpin Holder, Blue, 6 ¾ In. 99.00
Orange Tree, Hatpin Holder, Marigold, 6 ¾ In. 77.00
Orange Tree, Loving Cup, Blue 250.00
Orange Tree, Mug, Blue 45.00
Orange Tree, Plate, Blue, 9 In. 400.00
Orange Tree & Scroll, Pitcher, Blue 1000.00
Palm Beach, Dish, Butter, Honey Amber 95.00
Pansy, Dish, Pickle, Amethyst 185.00
Panther, Berry Set, Marigold, 3 Piece 55.00
Parlor Panels, Vase, Marigold, 10 In. 50.00
Pastel Swan, Salt, Marigold 45.00
Peacock & Dahlia, Bowl, Footed, Scalloped Edge, Marigold, 6 In.. 55.00
Peacock & Grape, Bowl, Blue, c.1900, 8 In. *illus* 100.00
Peacock & Grape, Bowl, Marigold, 8 ½ In. 33.00
Peacock & Grape, Bowl, Marigold, Scalloped Rim, 9 In. 27.00
Peacock & Urn, Bowl, Ruffled Edge, Blue, 8 ½ In. 2000.00
Peacock & Urn, Compote, Ruffled Edge, Blue 40.00

Carnival Glass, Fanciful, Plate, Ruffled Edge, 9 In.
$200.00

Carnival Glass, Fern, Compote, Amethyst, 4¾ In.
$140.00

Carnival Glass, Fisherman's Mug, Coffee Mug, Amethyst, Dugan, c.1900, 4 In.
$59.00

Carnival Glass, Grape & Cable, Compote, Cover, Amethyst, 9 In.
$80.00

Carnival Glass, Greek Key, Bowl, Amethyst, Northwood, 9 In.
$165.00

Carnival Glass, Heron, Mug, Amethyst, 4 In.
$118.00

Carnival Glass, Holly, Bowl, Blue, Footed, 8½ In.
$66.00

Carnival Glass, Kittens, Cup & Saucer, Marigold
$145.00

Carnival Glass, Maple Leaf, Water Set, Amethyst, 7 Piece
$125.00

Carnival Glass, Peacock & Grape, Bowl, Blue, c.1900, 8 In.
$100.00

C

Carnival Glass, Peacock Tail, Bowl, Ruffled Edge, Green, Delmar Garden, c.1900, 3 In.
$40.00

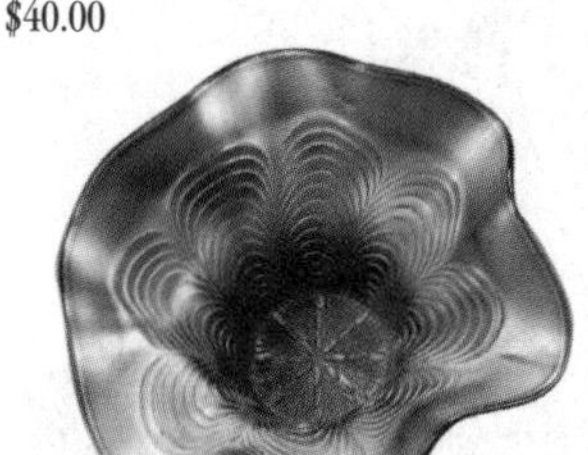

Carnival Glass, Poppy Show, Plate, Footed, Green, 9 ½ In.
$3540.00

Carnival Glass, Thistle, Banana Boat, Cobalt Blue, 10 ½ In.
$145.00

Carnival Glass, Wishbone & Spades, Plate, Amethyst, 6 ½ In.
$165.00

Carnival Glass, Wreath Of Roses, Bonbon, Marigold, 8 In.
$55.00

Peacock & Urn, Plate, Blue, 9 In. 325.00
Peacock At The Fountain, Pitcher, Ice Blue. 2700.00
Peacock On Fence pattern is listed here as Peacocks.
Peacock Tail, Bowl, Ruffled Edge, Green, Delmar Garden, c.1900, 3 In. *illus* 40.00
Peacock Tail, Dish, Green, Advertising, 3 In. 47.00
Peacocks, Plate, Ribbed Back, Amethyst, 9 In. 375.00
Persian Garden, Bowl, Peach, 10 In. 600.00
Persian Medallion, Bonbon, Handles, Amberina, 6 ½ In. 77.00
Persian Medallion, Bowl, Blue, Scalloped Edge, 6 In. 27.00
Persian Medallion, Bowl, Green, Handles, 8 In. 99.00
Persian Medallion, Compote, Scalloped Edge, Blue, 6 In. 132.00
Persian Medallion, Hair Receiver, Marigold. 125.00
Persian Medallion, Plate, Marigold, 6 In. 20.00
Persian Medallion, Rose Bowl, Marigold 32.00
Persian Medallion, Sauce, Ruffled Edge, Blue 40.00
Peter Rabbit, Plate, Blue, 9 In. 3000.00
Plaid, Bowl, Ruffled Edge, Marigold, 9 In. 66.00
Plume Panels, Vase, Cobalt Blue, Ruffled Edge, 11 In. 44.00
Plume Panels, Vase, Swung, Green, 10 In. 71.00
Poinsettia & Lattice, Bowl, Ribbed Back, Ruffled, Footed, Amethyst, 8 ½ In. 325.00
Poppy Show, Plate, Footed, Green, 9 ½ In. *illus* 3540.00
Poppy Show, Plate, Marigold, 9 In. 525.00
Princess Lace pattern is listed here as Octagon.
Question Marks, Bonbon, Black Amethyst, 7 In. 90.00
Question Marks, Bonbon, Marigold, 7 In. 10.00
Question Marks, Bonbon, Peach Opal, 7 In. 15.00
Rainbow, Compote, Ruffled Edge, Amethyst. 10.00
Raspberry, Pitcher, Milk, Lime Green. 1500.00
Rays & Ribbons, Bowl, Green, Cactus Exterior, 9 In. 33.00
Rib & Panel, Cuspidor, Ruffled Edge, Marigold, 6 ¼ In. 143.00
Ripple, Vase, Green, 5 ¾ In. 55.00
Rising Sun, Pitcher, Marigold. 105.00
Rising Sun, Tumbler, Marigold. 45.00
Rococo, Vase, Marigold 25.00
Rose & Ruffles pattern is listed here as Open Rose.
Rose Show, Bowl, Ruffled Edge, Marigold, 8 ¾ In. 325.00
Rose Show, Plate, Blue, 9 In. 900.00
Rosette, Bowl, Footed, Scalloped Edge, Amethyst, 8 In. 77.00
Shriner, Champagne, New Orleans, Marigold 85.00
Singing Birds, Butter, Cover Only, Marigold 10.00
Singing Birds, Water Set, Green, 7 Piece 700.00
Single Flower, Bowl, Footed, Ruffled Edge, Peach Opalescent, 9 In. 27.00
Smooth Ray, Card Tray, Footed, Green, 5 ¾ In. 22.00
Soldiers & Sailors, Plate, Illinois, Blue, 7 In. 1700.00
Soldiers & Sailors, Plate, Illinois, Marigold, 7 ½ In. 1300.00
Stag & Holly, Bowl, Blue, Footed, Marigold Iridescent Finish, c.1900, 10 In. 148.00
Stag & Holly, Bowl, Spatula Footed, Marigold, 8 In. 75.00
Starfish, Compote, 2 Handles, Amethyst, 4 In. 71.00
Stippled Diamond & Flower pattern is listed here as Little Flowers.
Stippled Leaf & Beads pattern is listed here as Leaf & Beads.
Stippled Posy & Pods pattern is listed here as Four Flowers.
Stippled Rays, Bowl, Amethyst, 10 ½ x 3 In. 85.00
Stippled Rays, Bowl, Ruffled Edge, Footed, Green, 11 In. 44.00
Stippled Rays, Compote, Ruffled Edge, Footed, Marigold, 4 ½ In. 25.00
Stippled Ribbons & Rays pattern is listed here as Rays & Ribbons.
Stippled Strawberry, Plate, Green, 9 In. 850.00
Stippled Strawberry, Plate, Ice Blue, 9 In. 16000.00
Stippled Strawberry, Plate, Ribbed Back, Marigold, 9 In. 900.00
Strawberry, Bonbon, Ruffled Edge, Amethyst, 6 In. 66.00
Strawberry, Bowl, Ruffled Edge, Basketweave Back, Green, 8 In. 44.00
Strawberry, Bowl, Ruffled Edge, Green, 8 ½ In. 70.00
Strawberry Intaglio, Bowl, Scalloped Edge, Marigold, 9 ½ In. 44.00
Sunflower pattern is listed here as Dandelion.
Target, Vase, White, 11 In. 75.00
Thistle, Banana Boat, Cobalt Blue, 10 ½ In. *illus* 145.00

Thistle, Bowl, Ruffled Edge, Footed, Marigold, 9 In. .... 30.00 to 33.00
Thistle & Lotus, Bowl, Footed, Stippled Grape Back, Marigold, 7 In. 44.00
Three Fruits, Bowl, Ruffled Edge, Green, 9 In. 60.00
Three Fruits, Plate, Amethyst, 9 In. 106.00
Three Fruits, Plate, Green, 9 In. 65.00
Three Fruits, Plate, Stippled, Ribbed Back, Amethyst, 9 In. 250.00
Three Fruits Medallion, Bowl, Footed, Green, 8¾ x 3¼ In. 115.00
Three Fruits Medallion, Bowl, Ruffled Edge, Spatula Feet, Amethyst, 8 In. 55.00
Tiger Lily, Pitcher, Marigold, 8½ In. 225.00
Tiger Lily, Water Set, Amethyst, 7 Piece 955.00
Tree Of Life, Vase, Marigold, Metal Frame, 7¼ In., Pair 121.00
Tree Trunk, Vase, Ruffled Edge, Footed, Amethyst, 9½ In. .... 35.00 to 44.00
Twig, Vase, Bud, Footed, Amethyst, 9 In. 40.00
Two Flowers, Bowl, Ruffled Edge, Footed, Marigold, 10 In. 27.00
Two Flowers, Bowl, Scalloped Edge, Footed, Marigold, 9½ In. 33.00
Venetian Giant, Rose Bowl, Marigold 900.00
Vintage, Sauce, Blue, 6 In. 47.00
Vintage Leaf, Bowl, Ruffled Edge, Green, 8½ In. 27.00
Water Lily, Berry Bowl, Ruffled Edge, Footed, Opalescent Lime Green 545.00
Water Lily & Cattails, Cuspidor, Hat Shape, Marigold, Rolled Under Edge 775.00
Wild Grapes pattern is listed here as Grape Leaves.
Windmill, Bowl, Moonstone, 8 In. 200.00
Windmill Medallion pattern is listed here as Windmill.
Wishbone, Bowl, Footed, Amethyst, 8 In. 88.00
Wishbone, Bowl, Green, 9½ x 2½ In. 275.00
Wishbone, Plate, Amethyst, 9 In. 1900.00
Wishbone, Plate, Amethyst, Footed, 9 In. 400.00
Wishbone & Spades, Chop Plate, Amethyst 1200.00
Wishbone & Spades, Plate, Amethyst, 6½ In. .... *illus* 165.00
Wreath Of Roses, Bonbon, Marigold, 8 In. .... *illus* 55.00
Wreath Of Roses, Bonbon, Tricornered Rim, Marigold, 5¼ In. 27.00
Wreath Of Roses, Punch Bowl, Persian Medallion Interior, Amethyst 550.00
Wreath Of Roses, Punch Cup, Amethyst, Set Of 3 .... 550.00

CAROUSEL or merry-go-round figures were first carved in the United States in 1867 by Gustav Dentzel. Collectors discovered the charm of the hand-carved figures in the 1970s, and they were soon classed as folk art. Most desirable are the figures other than horses, such as pigs, camels, lions, or dogs. A jumper is a figure that was made to move up and down on a pole; a stander was placed in a stationary position.

Bull, Wood, Carved, Painted, Brass Horns, Glass Eyes, 38 x 63 x 22 In. .... *illus* 1320.00
Giraffe, Carved, Painted, Early 20th Century, 79 x 56 In. 8400.00
Horse, Galloping, Wood, Glass Eyes, Metal, Leather, c.1890, 47 x 52 x 11 In. .... *illus* 1500.00
Horse, Gray, White Sponge, Green, Yellow, Glass Eyes, Iron Base, 46 x 57 x 10 In. 715.00
Horse, Jumping, Carved, Wood, Glass Eyes, Jewels, 40½ x 58 In. .... *illus* 1160.00
Horse, Leaping, Wood, Shields, Painted, Wood, Iron Rocker, 43½ x 89 x 24 In. 2420.00
Horse, Mounted, Gliding Platform, Carved, Multicolored, Early 1900s, 36 x 44 In. 4994.00
Horse, Pine, Marble Eyes, Horsehair Tail, Cast Iron Base, C.W.F. Dare, N.Y., 1800s, 55 x 44 In. .. 7200.00
Horse, Pine, Painted, Marble Eyes, Leather Bridle, Mounted, 55 In. 7200.00
Horse, Raised Leg, Outside Row, Basswood, Gustav Dentzel, 53 x 53 In. 49000.00
Horse, Running, Poplar, Armored, Outside Row, C.W. Parker, c.1918, 54 x 80 In. 11250.00
Horse, Stander, Outside Row, Charles Carmel, Pine, N.Y., Jewels, Tassels, 59 x 62 In. 20000.00
Horse, Stein & Goldstein, The Artistic Carousel Mfg. Co., 58 x 52 In. 5775.00
Rooster, Wood, Brass, Glass Eyes, 32 x 53 In. 2070.00

CARRIAGE means several things, so this category lists baby carriages, buggies for adults, horse-drawn sleighs, and even strollers. Doll-sized carriages are listed in the Toy category.

Baby Buggy, Sleigh Frame, Fringed Top, 2 Large & 2 Small Wheels, 1800s, 41 x 52 In. 350.00
Pram, Canoe, Wooden Wheels, Velvet Interior, 58 x 50 In. .... *illus* 3000.00
Stroller, Wicker, Metal Wheels, Leather Restraints, 34½ x 33½ x 21 In. 77.00
Stroller, Wicker, Metal Wheels, Red Satin Interior, 36½ x 48 x 21½ In. 220.00
Stroller, Wicker, Wood Spoke Wheels, Cushion, Parasol, Heywood, 37 x 45½ x 21 In. 220.00
Stroller, Wood, Leather Canopy, Maroon, Gold & Yellow, Coach Line, Horses, 40 x 56 x 23 In. 495.00

Carousel, Bull, Wood, Carved, Painted, Brass Horns, Glass Eyes, 38 x 63 x 22 In.
$1320.00

Carousel, Horse, Galloping, Wood, Glass Eyes, Metal, Leather, c.1890, 47 x 52 x 11 In.
$1500.00

Carousel, Horse, Jumping, Carved, Wood, Glass Eyes, Jewels, 40½ x 58 In.
$1160.00

Carriage, Pram, Canoe, Wooden Wheels, Velvet Interior, 58 x 50 In.
$3000.00

Cash Register, National, Model 313, 15-Key, Brass, 10 x 16 x 21 In.
$500.00

TIP

Clean brass with commercial brass polish. Wear white cotton gloves. The gloves make the difference.

Castor Jar, Pickle, Cranberry Paneled Spring, New Amsterdam Silver Co., 10¾ In.
$363.00

CASH REGISTERS were invented in 1884 because an eye on the cash was a necessity in stores of the nineteenth century, too. John and James Ritty invented a large model that resembled a clock and kept a record of the dollars and cents exchanged in the store. John Patterson improved the cash register with a paper roll to record the money. By the early 1900s, elaborate brass registers were made. About World War I, the fancy case was exchanged for the more modern types.

Hopkins & Robinson, Victorian Design, Walnut, Carved, c.1890 .... 4400.00
Hough, Security, Oak, Nickel Plated Hardware, Lift Top, Chimes, c.1895, 18 x 10 In. 173.00
National, Model 1, Candy Store Style, Marquee, Time Clock, c.1893 .... 14300.00
National, Model 1, No. 64923, Candy Store Style 14300.00
National, Model 2, Scrolls, 21 x 16 In. 1150.00
National, Model 5, Scrolls, 1 Dollar Ring Up, 22 x 9 In. 1610.00
National, Model 6, Extended Base 3875.00
National, Model 6½ Fleur-De-Lis, Extended Wood Base, c.1901 .... 5720.00
National, Model 7, Clock, 21 x 16 In. 1035.00
National, Model 33, Fleur-De-Lis Cabinet, Ticket Validating Keyboard, c.1896 .... 2475.00
National, Model 47, Renaissance, 21 x 17 In. 518.00
National, Model 51¼, 50 Cent Ring Up, Nickel Plated 863.00
National, Model 92, Serial No. 262534, 19th Century 295.00
National, Model 311, Copper, 1 Dollar Ring Up, 21 x 10 In. 863.00
National, Model 313, 15-Key, Brass, 10 x 16 x 21 In. .... *illus* 500.00
National, Model 442, Brass Plate Over Iron, Oak Base, c.1908, 20 x 20 In. 351.00
National, Model 722934, Wood Grain, Stewart Typewriter, Columbus, Ga., 1944, 17 x 24 x 16 In. .. 75.00
National, Model 5306252, Nickel, Scroll & Flower, Black Glass, 17¾ x 12½ x 16 In. 330.00
Sun Manufacturing, Model 10, Operates With Marbles & Keys, c.1896 .... 4400.00

CASTOR JARS for pickles are glass jars about six inches in height, held in special metal holders. They became a popular dinner table accessory about 1890. Each jar had a top that was usually silver or silver plate. The frame, also of a silver metal, had a handle that arched above the jar and a hook that held a pair of tongs. By 1900, the pickle castor was out of fashion. Many examples found today have reproduced glass jars in old holders. Additional pickle castors may be found in the various Glass categories.

Pickle, Apple Blossom Mold, Blue Opalescent, Daisy, Fern, Northwood 350.00
Pickle, Cranberry, Diamond Quilted, Silver Frame 825.00
Pickle, Cranberry, Inverted Thumbprint, Silver Frame .... 325.00 to 600.00
Pickle, Cranberry, Thumbprint, Toronto Silver Plated Holder, c.1870, 11½ In. 382.00
Pickle, Cranberry Flowers, Silver Frame, Tongs, Cover, Victorian .... 775.00 to 825.00
Pickle, Cranberry Glass, Diamond Quilted, Aurora Frame 825.00
Pickle, Cranberry Glass, Gold Enameled Flowers, Silver Plate Frame, c.1900, 10½ In. 148.00
Pickle, Cranberry Glass, Inverted Thumbprint, Enameled Flowers, Bird Finial, Tongs, 11 In. .. 950.00
Pickle, Cranberry Opalescent Swirl, Cover, Curly Hair, 1880, 11 In. 206.00
Pickle, Cranberry Opalescent Swirl, Electro-Plate Frame, Cover, Tongs, 1880, 11 In. 206.00
Pickle, Cranberry Paneled Spring, New Amsterdam Silver Co., 10¾ In. .... *illus* 363.00
Pickle, Jacob's Ladder, Wilcox Quadruple Plate Stand, 11 x 3⅜ In. .... *illus* 121.00
Pickle, Little River, Meriden, Quadruple Plate Stand, Tongs, 10½ x 4¼ In. .... *illus* 150.00
Pickle, Paneled Button, Meriden, Frame 350.00
Pickle, Quilted Case, Pink, Silver Frame, Tongs, Aurora Mfg. Co., 11¼ In. 795.00
Pickle, Quilted Cased Glass, Pink, Tongs, Silver Plated Frame, Aurora Mfg., 11¼ In. 795.00
Pickle, Seaweed Pattern, Opalescent, Hobbs, Brockunier, Rockford Silverplate Co., Frame ... 1250.00
Pickle, Vaseline, Meriden, Silver-Plated, Frame, 4-Footed, Flowers, Tongs, 13 In. 700.00

CASTOR SETS holding just salt and pepper castors were used in the seventeenth century. The sugar castor, mustard pot, spice dredger, bottles for vinegar and oil, and other spice holders became popular by the eighteenth century. These sets were usually made of sterling silver. The American Victorian castor set, the type most collected today, was made of silver plated Britannia metal. Colored glass bottles were introduced after the Civil War. The sets were out of fashion by World War I. Be careful when buying sets with colored bottles; many are reproductions. Other castor sets may be listed in various porcelain and glass categories in this book.

3 Bottles, Clear Glass, Shakers, Mustard, Ribbed Stoppers, Copper Stand 143.00
3 Bottles, Cut Glass, Boat Shaped Tray, Hester Bateman, England, 1782, 9¾ In. 900.00
4 Bottles, Daisy & Button, Blue, 9 In. .... *illus* 105.00
5 Bottles, Bellflower, Meriden Silver Plated Stand, 12½ In. .... *illus* 423.00
5 Bottles, Pineapple, Reed & Barton Silver Plated Frame, New England, 12½ In. .... *illus* 231.00
6 Bottles, Silver Plated Frame, Sheffield, c.1870, 12 x 7½ In. 293.00

Castor Jar, Pickle, Jacob's Ladder, Wilcox Quadruple Plate Stand, 11 x 3⅜ In.
$121.00

Castor Set, 5 Bottles, Bellflower, Meriden Silver Plated Stand, 12½ In.
$423.00

Castor Jar, Pickle, Little River, Meriden, Quadruple Plate Stand, Tongs, 10½ x 4¼ In.
$150.00

Castor Set, 5 Bottles, Pineapple, Reed & Barton Silver Plated Frame, New England, 12½ In.
$231.00

Castor Set, 4 Bottles, Daisy & Button, Blue, 9 In.
$105.00

It's Pretty, But Is It Old?

Most people know art glass when they see it. Most is colorful, often shaded from one color to another, and embellished with fancy details like ruffles and three-dimensional fruit and flowers. But is it the original old glass? In the 1930s, there was renewed interest in nineteenth-century glass styles. Several factories, including Fenton Art Glass Company, Gunderson Glass Works, and Pairpoint Manufacturing Company, introduced glassware that imitated the styles of the 1880s.

Cauldon, Platter, Wild Turkey, Flow Blue, Marked, 16½ x 19½ In.
$633.00

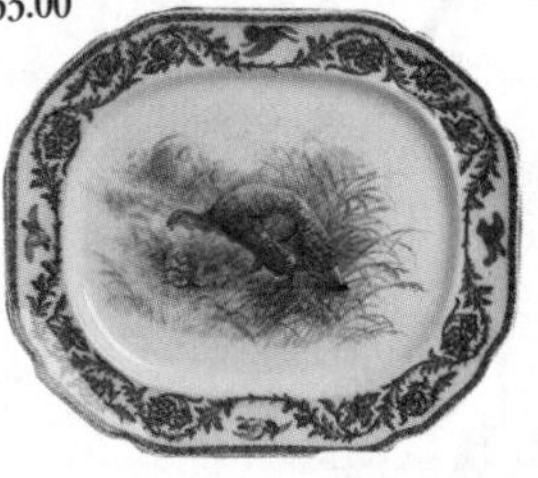

Celluloid, Desk Set, Orange, Stylized Leaves & Berries, Art Deco, Case
$65.00

Celluloid, Shaving Kit, Mug, Brush, Razor, Mirror, 7 x 5 In.
$460.00

Ceramic Arts Studio, Figurine, Couple, Gay '90s, Marked, 6⅝ In., Pair
$30.00

Ceramic Arts Studio, Head Vase, Mei-Ling, Marked, 5 In.
$35.00

CATALOGS *are listed in the Paper category.*

CAULDON Limited worked in Staffordshire, Great Britain, and went through many name changes. John Ridgway made porcelain at Cauldon Place, Hanley, until 1855. The firm of John Ridgway, Bates and Co. of Cauldon Place worked from 1856 to 1859. It became Bates, Brown-Westhead, Moore and Co. from 1859 to 1862. Brown-Westhead, Moore and Co. worked from 1862 to 1904. About 1890, this firm started using the words *Cauldon* or *Cauldon Ware* as part of the mark. Cauldon Ltd. worked from 1905 to 1920, Cauldon Potteries from 1920 to 1962. Related items may be found in the Indian Tree category.

Platter, Wild Turkey, Flow Blue, Marked, 16½ x 19½ In. . . . . *illus* 633.00

CELADON is the name of a velvet-textured green-gray glaze used by Chinese, Japanese, Korean, and other factories. The name refers both to the glaze and to pieces covered with the glaze. It is still being made.

Bottle, Wine, Blue, Green, Tilted Neck, Funnel Shaped Mouth, Korea, 8¾ In. 1293.00
Bowl, Dogwood, Indigo, Bernard Leach, 3¼ x 6 In. 1140.00
Bowl, Lotus, Sea Green Glaze, Cone Shape, 13th Century, Korea, 8 In. 4994.00
Bowl, Semimatte Glaze, Wood Fired, Flared, Mary Roehm, 9 x 21½ In. 1200.00
Bowl, Stoneware, Incised, Leaf Decoration, Korea, 6¾ In. 472.00
Censer, Aqua, Children At Play, Japan, 8 In. 1416.00
Censer, Tripod, Upright Handles, Taotie Mask, 5¼ x 5¼ In. 142.00
Compote, Figures In Landscape, Ormolu Mount, 6 In. 522.00
Cup, Stand, Flower Springs, Engraved, Korea, 13th Century, 5½ In. 1410.00
Dish, Bat & Cloud, Flared, Lobed Body, Engraved Mark, Chinese, 11½ In. 270.00
Figurine, Boy, Jade, Chinese, 19th Century, 2½ In. 531.00
Jar, Crackle Glaze, Gilt, Bronze Mounted, 19th Century, 29½ In. 705.00
Jar, Ribbed, Cone Shape Cover, Chinese, 10 In. 324.00
Planter, Flower Panels, Ming Dynasty, Round, Signed, Chinese, 14 x 20 In. 6800.00
Plate, Chinese, Flower Leaf, Blue, White, 9 In. 70.00
Ruyi, Jade, Russet Inclusions, Chinese, 20th Century, 14 In. 1652.00
Umbrella Stand, Japanese Export, Potted, Glazed, Eagle In Pine Tree, Winter, 24 In. 900.00
Urn, Asia, Signed, 13 x 7½ In. 118.00
Vase, Blue & White, Dragon & Phoenix, Openwork Handles, c.1900, 22¾ In. 460.00
Vase, Harlan House, Dated, 1976, 28 In. 360.00
Vase, Landscape, Ju-I Panels, Flared, Animal Handles, Chinese, 13 In. 4700.00
Vase, Leaves, Crackle Glaze, 13½ In. 472.00

CELLULOID is a trademark for a plastic developed in 1868 by John W. Hyatt. Celluloid Manufacturing Company, the Celluloid Novelty Company, Celluloid Fancy Goods Company, and American Xylonite Company all used celluloid to make jewelry, games, sewing equipment, false teeth, and piano keys. The name *celluloid* was often used to identify any similar plastic. Celluloid toys are listed under Toy.

Comb, Copper, Marked Made In U.S.A., 3 In. 24.00
Comb, Spanish Style, Cream Color, Art Nouveau Pattern, 5⅛ x 2½ In. 29.00
Desk Set, Orange, Stylized Leaves & Berries, Art Deco, Case . . . . *illus* 65.00
Dresser Set, Art Deco, c.1930, 8 In. To 13¼ In., 3 Piece 45.00
Frame, Art Deco Style, Swings On Stand, Ivory, 1920s, 9 x 11 In. 95.00
Shaving Kit, Mug, Brush, Razor, Mirror, 7 x 5 In. . . . . *illus* 460.00

CELS *are listed in this book in the Animation Art category.*

CERAMIC ART COMPANY of Trenton, New Jersey, was established in 1889 by J. Coxon and W. Lenox and was an early producer of American belleek porcelain. It became Lenox, Inc. in 1906. Do not confuse this ware with the pottery made by the Ceramic Arts Studio of Madison, Wisconsin.

Mug, Blue, White, Gilt, Enamel, Belleek, c.1900, 5 In. 35.00

CERAMIC ARTS STUDIO was founded about 1940 in Madison, Wisconsin, by Lawrence Rabbett and Ruben Sand. Their most popular products were expensive molded figurines. The pottery closed in 1955. Do not confuse these products with those of the Ceramic Art Co. of Trenton, New Jersey.

Figurine, Couple, Gay '90s, Marked, 6⅝ In., Pair . . . . *illus* 30.00
Head Vase, Mei-Ling, Marked, 5 In. . . . . *illus* 35.00

Salt & Pepper, Children In Asian Dress, Yellow, Blue, Black, 3 ¼ In. 76.00
Salt & Pepper, Mother Gorilla Holding Baby, 4 In. 35.00

CHALKWARE is really plaster of Paris decorated with watercolors. One type was molded from Staffordshire and other porcelain models and painted and sold as inexpensive decorations in the nineteenth century. This type is very valuable today. Figures of plaster, made from about 1910 to 1940 for use as prizes at carnivals, are also known as chalkware. Kewpie dolls made of chalkware will be found in their own category.

Bank, Pig, Red Ears, Spots, 19th Century, 4 ¾ x 8 ½ In. 81.00
Figurine, Bird On Nest, Yellow, Red, Late 19th Century, 3 ⅞ In. .... *illus* 345.00
Figurine, Cat, Mouse In Mouth, On Pedestal, Red, Black Paint, 3 ⅝ x 4 In. 110.00
Figurine, Cat, Seated, Red, Black, Green Paint, Hollow, 5 ¼ x 3 ½ x 2 ½ In. 440.00
Figurine, Cat, Sleeping, Black, Late 19th Century, 3 ¾ x 9 ½ In. 35.00
Figurine, Deer, Painted, Early 19th Century, 7 ½ In. 115.00
Figurine, Deer, Reclining, Brown, Red, Black Paint, Hollow, 8 x 8 x 3 ½ In., Pair 110.00
Figurine, Dog, King Charles Spaniel, Gray, Black Spots, Late 19th Century, 8 ½ In. 45.00
Figurine, Dog, Poodle, Seated, Basket Hanging From Mouth, Hollow, 6 ½ x 5 x 3 In. 413.00
Figurine, Eagle, Painted, 19th Century, 8 In. 764.00
Figurine, Girl, Praying, Yellow Dress, Black Hair, Green Base, Hollow, 14 x 6 x 6 In. 22.00
Figurine, Parrot, Perched On Pedestal, Painted, Patina, Hollow, 10 x 5 x 3 In. 550.00
Figurine, Rabbit, Seated, Black Spots, Pink, Late 19th Century, 5 ¼ In. .... *illus* 275.00
Figurine, Rabbit, Seated, White, Spots, Late 19th Century, 9 ¼ In. 100.00
Figurine, Squirrel, With Nut, Gray, Brown, Late 19th Century, 6 ½ In. 250.00
Figurine, Swan, Painted, 5 ¾ x 8 ½ In. 115.00
Figurine, Town Crier, Ringing Bell, Reading Proclamation, 19 ¼ x 7 In. 51.00
Nodder, Cat, Hollow, 4 ¼ x 8 x 3 ½ In. .... *illus* 1210.00
Nodder, Cat, White, Hand Painted, Late 19th Century, 4 x 8 In. 325.00
Nodder, Pig, Red, Black, Collar, Face, Hollow, 3 ¾ x 7 ¾ x 3 In. 110.00
Nodder, Rabbit, White, On Red & White Base, Late 19th Century, 2 ½ x 3 ½ In. 100.00
Planter, Gay '90s Woman, J.B. Co., Signed, c.1940, 12 ½ In. 25.00

CHARLIE CHAPLIN, the famous comedian, actor, and filmmaker, lived from 1889 to 1977. He made his first movie in 1913. He did the movie *The Tramp* in 1915. The character of the Tramp has remained famous, and in the 1980s appeared in a series of television commercials for computers. Dolls, candy containers, and all sorts of memorabilia with the image of Charlie's Tramp are collected. Pieces are being made even today.

Condiment Set, Charlie Chaplin, 2 Attached Containers, Germany, 1920s, 5 ½ In. 275.00
Lapel Toy, England, Rubber Band, Pull String, Tips Hat, Tin, 4 In. 322.00
Slate Dancer, Tramp Costume, Tin, Lever Operated, 6 In. 2070.00
Squeeze Toy, Changes Facial Expression, Hat Raises, Wiggles Feet, Tin, 8 In. 554.00
Toy, Charlie Chaplin, Windup, Composition, Lead Feet, 9 ½ In. .... *illus* 403.00
Toy, Charlie Playing Cymbals, Cat, Tin Litho, Distler, Germany, 5 ½ In. .... *illus* 795.00
Toy, Walker, Tin, Clockwork, B&R, USA, Box, 8 ½ In. .... *illus* 1150.00

CHARLIE MCCARTHY was the ventriloquist's dummy used by Edgar Bergen from the 1930s. He was famous for his work in radio, movies, and television. The act was retired in the 1970s.

Bank, Mechanical, Movable Jaw, Metal, c.1938 .... 460.00
Book, A Day With Charlie & Edgar Bergen, No. 770, 8 x 11 In. 149.00
Doll, Charlie McCarthy, Mouth Moves, Effanbee, Box, 20 In. .... *illus* 259.00
Figure, Celluloid, Windup, Moving Mouth & Chin, Box, 1930, 7 In. 575.00
Puppet, Hand, Composition, Monocle, Embossed Back Of Neck, Cloth Body, 11 x 9 In. 100.00
Spoon, Silver Plate, Marked, Duchess, 6 In. 18.00
Toy, Benzine Buggy, Tin, Windup, Marx, c.1930, 6 x 7 x 3 In. .... 750.00 to 850.00
Toy, Celluloid, Charlie, Mouth, Chin Moves, Windup, Box, 1930s 575.00
Toy, Charlie McCarthy, Drummer, Tin Lithograph, Windup, Marx, Box, 8 ½ In. 1610.00
Toy, Charlie McCarthy, Walker, Tin, Windup, Louis Marx, 8 ¼ In. .... *illus* 200.00
Toy, Crazy Car, Mortimer Snerd, Tin, Windup, Marx, 1930s 575.00
Toy, Mortimer Snerd, Drummer, Tin, Windup, Louis Marx, Box, 8 ½ In. .... *illus* 1480.00
Toy, Mortimer Snerd, Private Car, Tin, Windup, Marx, 15 ½ In. 2587.00
Toy, Mortimer Snerd, Shakes, Hat Flips Up, Tin, Windup, Marx, Box, 1939, 8 ¼ In. 748.00
Toy, Mortimer Snerd, Walker, Tin Lithograph, Windup, Marx, 8 ½ In. 173.00
Toy, Strike Up The Band, Drummer, Windup, Marx, 1938, 8 In. .... 750.00 to 850.00

Chalkware, Figurine, Bird On Nest, Yellow, Red, Late 19th Century, 3 ⅞ In.
$345.00

Chalkware, Figurine, Rabbit, Seated, Black Spots, Pink, Late 19th Century, 5 ¼ In.
$275.00

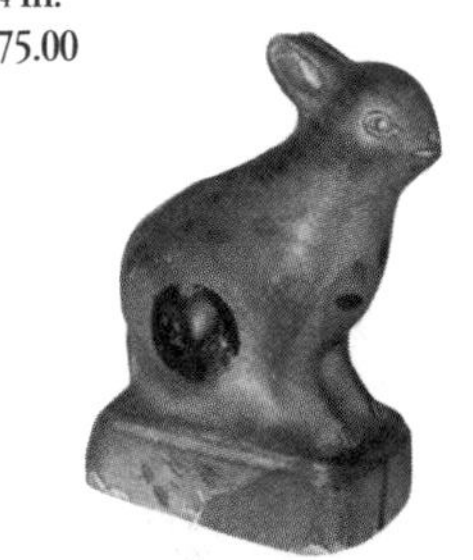

Chalkware, Nodder, Cat, Hollow, 4 ¼ x 8 x 3 ½ In.
$1210.00

Charlie Chaplin, Toy, Charlie Chaplin, Windup, Composition, Lead Feet, 9 ½ In.
$403.00

Charlie Chaplin, Toy, Charlie Playing Cymbals, Cat, Tin Litho, Distler, Germany, 5 ½ In.
$795.00

Charlie Chaplin, Toy, Walker, Tin, Clockwork, B&R, USA, Box, 8 ½ In.
$1150.00

Charlie McCarthy, Doll, Charlie McCarthy, Mouth Moves, Effanbee, Box, 20 In.
$259.00

CHELSEA porcelain was made in the Chelsea area of London from about 1745 to 1769. Some pieces made from 1770 to 1784 are called Chelsea Derby and may include the letter *D* for *Derby* in the mark. Ceramic designs were borrowed from the Meissen models of the day. Pieces were made of soft paste. The gold anchor was used as the mark but it has been copied by many other factories. Recent copies of Chelsea have been made from the original molds. Do not confuse Chelsea porcelain with Chelsea Grape, a white pottery with luster grape decoration.

Dish, Oval, Flower Sprays, Sprigs, Fluted Rim, 8 ½ In., 4 Piece 1920.00
Dish, Sweetmeat, Red Anchor, Grape Leaf, Ladybug, Butterfly, 9 ½ x 7 ¾ In. 840.00
Figurine, Dogs, Seated, Painted, Gold Anchor, 5 ½ x 3 ½ x 2 ¼ In., Pair 523.00
Figurine, Gentleman & Lady, 18th Century Costume, 9 ½ x 10 In., 2 Piece 176.00
Plate, Exotic Birds, Scalloped, Gilt Rim, 9 ½ In., 6 Piece 259.00
Plate, U.S. Dolphin, Wave Band, Cloverleaf, c.1895, 8 ½ In. 609.00
Platter, Tiger, Bamboo Shoot, Chrysanthemum, Peony, Kakiemon, c. 1755, 13 ¾ In. 1440.00
Saucer, Acanthus, Leaf Molded, Flower Bouquet, Sprigs, c.1765, 8 ⅜ In. 960.00
Tea Bowl & Saucer, Pinecone, Gilt Fringed Border, c.1765, 5 In. 1560.00

CHELSEA GRAPE pattern was made before 1840. A small bunch of grapes in a raised design, colored with purple or blue luster, is on the border of the white plate. Most of the pieces are unmarked. The pattern is sometimes called Aynsley or Grandmother. Chelsea Sprig is similar but has a sprig of flowers instead of the bunch of grapes. Chelsea Thistle has a raised thistle pattern. Do not confuse these Chelsea patterns with Chelsea Keramic Art Works, which can be found in the Dedham category, or with Chelsea porcelain, the preceding category.

Cup & Saucer, Raised Grapes 50.00
Pitcher, Raised Grapes, Elongated Spout, Embossed Scrolls, Scalloped Foot, 5 ¾ In. 105.00
Plate, Dessert, Raised Purple Grapes, 6 ¾ In. 25.00
Sugar & Creamer, Lavender Grapes In Relief, Open Sugar 45.00
Teapot, Dome Lid, Paneled Bottom, Shaped Scroll Handle, Octagonal Foot, 10 In. 100.00

CHINESE EXPORT porcelain comprises all the many kinds of porcelain made in China for export to America and Europe in the eighteenth, nineteenth, and twentieth centuries. Other pieces may be listed in this book under Canton, Celadon, Nanking, and Rose Medallion.

Bough Pot, Cover, Mandarin Colors, 2 Handles, Canted, Square, c.1785, 7 ¾ In., Pair 5313.00
Bowl, Blue & White, Flowers, Bats, 5 x 16 In. .... 350.00 to 392.00
Bowl, Blue Flowers, Scalloped Rim, Ribbed Sides, 5 x 12 In. 300.00
Bowl, Butterflies, Insects, Panels, Scalloped Rim, 2 ½ x 10 ½ In. 358.00
Bowl, Copper Red, 3 x 7 ¼ In. 201.00
Bowl, Dragons Chasing Pearl Of Wisdom, Yellow, Green, Scalloped, 5 In., Pair 2242.00
Bowl, Famille Rose, Court Officials, Turquoise Ground, Flared, Scalloped Rim, 3 ½ In. 316.00
Bowl, Famille Rose, Ducks, Aquatic Plants, 6 ¾ In. 5875.00
Bowl, Famille Rose, Flowers, 4 ¾ In., 10 Piece 767.00
Bowl, Famille Rose, Flowers, Armorial Urns, Puce, Enameled, 5 ½ In., Pair 420.00
Bowl, Famille Rose, Interior Diaper Pattern Border, 8 ⅞ x 3 ½ In. 144.00
Bowl, Famille Rose, Peaches On Branch, 2 ½ In. 472.00
Bowl, Famille Rose, Precious Object, Hexagonal, 19th Century, 9 In. 236.00
Bowl, Famille Rose, Riverscape, 1 ½ x 8 In. 148.00
Bowl, Famille Rose, Rose Sprigs, Chrysanthemum, Ribbon, c.1785, 7 ¼ In. 480.00
Bowl, Famille Rose, Roses, Diaper Pattern Border, Orange Peel Glaze, 11 ¼ x 4 ⅝ In. 403.00
Bowl, Famille Verte, Bird, Wave, 3 x 5 ¼ In. 384.00
Bowl, Famille Verte, Flowers, Multicolored, Octagonal, c.1840, 3 ¼ x 7 In. 234.00
Bowl, Fish, Carp, Iron Red, Powder Blue Ground, 18 x 19 ½ In. 354.00
Bowl, Landscape, Flowers, Red Border, Reserve Panels, Multicolored Enamel, 10 ¼ In. 300.00
Bowl, Lotus, Peach Bloom, 1 ½ x 6 ½ In. 2540.00
Bowl, People, Courtyard, Blue Underglaze, Floral Borders, 5 ⅜ x 12 ¾ In. 999.00
Box, Blue & White, Flowers, 3 x 2 ¼ In., Pair 94.00
Box, Cover, Leaves, White Glaze, 5 ¾ In. 1593.00
Box, Famille Rose, Cover, Peaches, 9 ½ In. 236.00
Brush Holder, Blue & White, Flowers, 5 ¾ x 4 In. 230.00
Brush Holder, Blue & White, Rice Pattern, 6 ¼ x 7 In. 826.00
Brush Holder, Famille Rose, 2 Court Women, 4 ¾ x 2 ¼ In. 767.00
Brush Holder, Famille Rose, Court Woman Reading At Table, 5 ½ x 3 ¼ In. 384.00
Brush Washer, Frog, Lotus Leaf Shape, Green Glaze, 6 In. 94.00
Brushpot, Bats In Clouds, Birds In Plum Branches, Celadon Glaze, 5 ½ In. 480.00
Brushpot, Blue & White, Flowers, Leaves, 5 ½ In. 413.00
Butter Tub, Cover, Stand, Lake Landscape, Villas, Figures, Peach Sprig Knop, 5 ½ In. 717.00

Cachepot, Blue & White, 6¾ x 9 In. 176.00
Candleholder, Elephant Base, Trumpet Vase Holder On Back, 8 In., Pair 2640.00
Candleholder, Famille Rose, Elephant Shape, 19th Century, 5 In., Pair 2242.00
Candlestick, Famille Rose, Lady, Wood Stand, c.1780, 11½ In., 6 Piece 31000.00
Charger, Cabbage Leaf, Center Shou Character, Flower Cartouches, 1900s, 15¾ In. 690.00
Charger, Famille Rose, 1000 Flowers, Mid 18th Century, 15¾ In. 1955.00
Charger, Famille Verte, Figures In Garden, 14½ In. 646.00
Charger, Vase, Cover, Blue & White, Flowers, Leaves, Painted, Early 1700s, 12 In., Pair 5312.00
Coffee Service, Armorial, Scholten Van Aschat, Fruit, Flowers, Gilt, c.1770, 16 Piece 4688.00
Condiment Set, Eagle & Shield, Sepia & Gold Border, Teak Stand, 13 In., 9 Piece 1554.00
Creamer, Chinese Family Life, Landscape, Handle, Mid 1700s, 6½ In. *illus* 1093.00
Creamer, Cover, Blue & White, Lake, Landscape, Flower Form Finial, 5½ In. 240.00
Cup, Stem, Blue & White, Duck, Lotus, 3¼ x 3½ In. 165.00
Cup & Saucer, Cyman & Iphigenia, Grisaille, 2½ x 4¾ In. 316.00
Dessert Stand, Famille Rose, Reticulated Border, c.1790, 8 In. 1416.00
Dish, Blue & White, Butterfly, 5¾ In., Pair 413.00
Dish, Blue & White, Figures, 8 In. 153.00
Dish, Bouquet, Reserve Panel Border, Overglaze Enamel, Blue, Red, Gilt, 10⅝ In. 60.00
Dish, Condiment, Famille Verte, Scholar In Pavilion, Square, 8⅝ In. 570.00
Dish, Green & White, Dragon Chasing Pearl Of Wisdom, 7½ In. 1180.00
Dish, Shell, Enameled Flowers, Central Integral Cup, Gilt Border, c.1785, 8¾ In. 264.00
Dish, Sweetmeat, Blue & White, 7 Parts, 12½ In. 472.00
Dish, Sweetmeat, Blue & White, Flowers, 6 Parts, 10 In. 224.00
Dish, Tobacco Leaf, Scalloped, 6¾ In. 719.00
Ewer, Double Gourd, Copper Red, 4½ In. 1239.00
Ewer, Double Gourd, Dragon Handle, 4½ In. 1062.00
Ewer, Flowers, Blue, Copper Red, Green, 7¾ In. 3186.00
Figurine, Buddha, Blue, 5½ In. 165.00
Figurine, Cat, Seated, Green Glaze, 18th Century, 6⅜ In., Pair 4500.00
Figurine, Dog, Seated, Yellow, Black Fur, Collar, 3 Gilt Bells, 6⅛ In., Pair 2400.00
Figurine, Famille Rose, Dog, Hound Seated, Pink Peony Spray, 6¾ In. 5100.00
Figurine, Famille Rose, Immortal, Glazed Robes, Closed Scroll, Leather Shade, 18 In. 720.00
Figurine, Famille Rose, Phoenix, Peonies, Early 1900s, 14¼ In., Pair 690.00
Figurine, Famille Rose, Smiling Man, Yellow & Blue Robes, 25 In. 431.00
Figurine, Famille Verte, Boy, In Manganese Robe, Breeches, 13 In. 3600.00
Figurine, Famille Verte, Dignitary, Seated, 11⅜ In. 3480.00
Figurine, Famille Verte, Horse, Caparisoned, 19th Century, 10½ In. 470.00
Figurine, Horse, Peach Bloom Glaze, 19th Century, 10 In., Pair 3000.00
Figurine, Lion, Open Mouth, Iron Red Whorl Patterned Coats, 9¼ In., Pair 9000.00
Figurine, Musical Instrument, Blue & White, Dragon Head, 29¾ In. 1534.00
Figurine, Ram, Head Turned To Side, Celadon, Chocolate Inclusions, 3½ In. 295.00
Figurine, Recumbent Foo Dog With Sphere, 1¼ x 3 In. 118.00
Figurine, Rooster, White, 10½ In. 118.00
Figurine, Woman Holding Scepter, White, 10⅜ In. 649.00
Flask, Moon, Pilgrim, Dragon Chasing Pearl Of Wisdom, Green, 8¾ In. 325.00
Fruit Bowl, Famille Rose, Undertray, Oval, Reticulated Sides, 12 In. 960.00
Garniture, Blue & White, 3 Vases, Cover, Birds, Peony, Blossoms, 1800s, 19 In. 5938.00
Ginger Jar, Blue & White, Plum Blossoms Clusters, Characters, Blue Ground, 8¾ In. 1728.00
Ginger Jar, Blue & White, Plum Blossoms Clusters, Blue Ground, 18th Century, 10 In. 1440.00
Ginger Jar, Blue & White, Tapered, Scrolled Leaves, Globular Blossoms, 9½ In. 210.00
Ginger Jar, Blue & White, Village, Cover, 7 In. 58.00
Ginger Jar, Famille Verte, Birds, Flowers, Multicolored, Gilt Enamel, 1800s, 9 In., Pair 294.00
Group, Children Playing Musical Instruments, Pine Trees, Redwood Stand, 11 In. 1357.00
Group, Twins, Underglaze Blue, Celadon Glaze, 10⅞ In. 9600.00
Jar, Blue & White, Dragon, 3½ x 2¾ In. 413.00
Jar, Cover, Blue & White, Blossoms, Prunus Branches, Cracked Ice Ground, 16¾ In. 7200.00
Jar, Cover, Blue & White, Prunus Branches, Cracked Ice Ground, 16⅛ In. 4500.00
Jar, Cover, Blue & White, Temple, Flower Head, Scrolling Leaves, 17½ In. 944.00
Jar, Cover, Famille Rose, Flowers, Precious Objects, Molded, 12 In. 1062.00
Jar, Cover, Famille Rose, Baluster Shape, Birds, Branches, Calligraphy, 1800s, 17 In, Pair 295.00
Jar, Cover, Famille Rose, Children At Play, 19th Century, 8 x 9 In. 295.00
Jar, Cover, Famille Rose, Flower Scrolls, Enameled Birds, Flowers, 19th Century, 24 In. 3173.00
Jar, Cover, Leaves, White Glaze, Loop Finial, 4 Handles, 4 In. 531.00
Jar, Cylindrical, Multicolored, c.1800, 4 x 2¾ In. 234.00
Jar, Famille Rose, Cover, c.1840, 8 x 8 In. 585.00
Jar, Tea, Blue, White, c.1800, 7 x 4½ In. 468.00

Charlie McCarthy, Toy, Charlie McCarthy, Walker, Tin, Windup, Louis Marx, 8¼ In.
$200.00

Charlie McCarthy, Toy, Mortimer Snerd, Drummer, Tin, Windup, Louis Marx, Box, 8½ In.
$1480.00

TIP

Most ceramics can be washed with soap or detergent and water but a few things should not be. Any pieces that are repaired, damaged, or with painted decorations should not be soaked in water. Wipe them with a damp cloth after testing a small area. Unglazed pieces should be dusted.

Chinese Export, Creamer, Chinese Family Life, Landscape, Handle, Mid 1700s, 6 ½ In.
$1093.00

Chinese Export, Plate, Famille Rose, Deer, People, 8 ¼ In.
$1416.00

Chinese Export, Platter, Blue & White, Riverscape, Octagonal, c.1780-1800, 15 x 11 ½ In.
$266.00

Chinese Export, Punch Bowl, Eagle, Armorial, Blue Rim, Gilt, Enamel, 1700s, 4 x 11 In.
$1840.00

Jardiniere, Blue & White, 19th Century, 6 ¾ x 7 In. 263.00
Jardiniere, Famille Rose, 4 Reserves, Bamboo Celadon Ground, 7 In.. .... 354.00
Jardiniere, Famille Rose, Flowering Tree, 19th Century, 16 In. 590.00
Jardiniere, Famille Rose, Flowers, Clair-De-Lune Ground, 13 ½ x 15 In.. .... 3540.00
Jardiniere, Gilt Metal Mounts, Cream Ground, Blue Figures, 13 x 13 In. 88.00
Jardiniere, Koi, Fish, Porcelain, Bronze Mounted, 20th Century, 13 x 13 In. 206.00
Jardiniere, Village, Gilt Rim, 11 x 12 In. 47.00
Jug, Famille Rose, Barrel, Twisted Handle, Fitzhugh, 7 ½ In.. .... 863.00
Lamp, Blue & White, Foo Dog Handles, Figural Panels, Wood Base, 18 In. 250.00
Mug, Ale, Landscape, Blue, Red, Folded-In Rim, 2-Strap Handle, 6 ¾ In. 450.00
Mug, Famille Rose, 4 Fish, Sea Plants, Crab, Footed, Baluster, Gold Rim, c.1745, 4 ½ In. 1035.00
Mug, Famille Rose, Armor, Crest, 3 Birds, Armadillos, Fleur-De-Lis, c.1750, 5 In. 2013.00
Mug, Famille Rose, Bowl Of Fruit, Serpent Handle, Late 18th Century, 5 ¾ In. 460.00
Mug, Famille Rose, Crest, 2 Cherubs, Winged Lion's Head, Barrel, c.1785, 4 ¾ In.. .... 4025.00
Mug, Famille Rose, Figures, Landscape, Flowers, Cylindrical, Handle, 5 ¼ In.. .... 780.00
Mug, Famille Rose, Flower Swag, Cylindrical, Strap Handle, 5 ½ In. 510.00
Mug, Famille Rose, Handle, Reserve Panels, Puce Landscape, 6 ⅛ In. 600.00
Mug, Famille Rose, Monogram Roundel, Bamboo, Flower, Gilt, Beaded, Barrel, 6 In.. .... 1035.00
Mug, Flower, Vase, Cylindrical, Rope Handle, 6 In.. .... 440.00
Mug, Flowers, Leaves, Diamond Lattice Band, Red, Gold, Flared Foot, Mid 1700s, 6 In. 1035.00
Mug, Gate, Rockery, Flowers, Multicolored, c.1750, 5 ½ In. 480.00
Mug, Oval Panel, Figures In Garden, Lake, T-Fret Ground, Dragon Handle, 5 In. 270.00
Mug, Trailing Flowers, Iron Red, White, Flared Base, Gilt Strapwork Handle, 6 In.. .... 240.00
Planter, Famille Rose, Birds, Flowers, Lotus Scroll, Lavender Ground, 15 In., Pair. 2585.00
Planter, Famille Rose, Flowers, Pail Shape, Late 1800s, 6 ¼ In., Pair. 353.00
Planter, Famille Rose, Shaped Feet, Enamel, Birds, Trees, Ingot Shape, 11 ½ x 17 In. 1560.00
Plaque, Famille Rose, Figures In Garden, 19th Century, 17 x 6 In., Pair 881.00
Plaque, Famille Rose, Landscape, Rosewood Frame, 15 ½ x 10 In., Pair 2115.00
Plaque, Famille Rose, Riverscape, Round, 10 ¾ In.. .... 590.00
Plaque, Famille Rose, Scholar & Attendant, Rosewood Frame, 15 x 9 ¾ In. 4113.00
Plate, Armorial Crest, 2 Lions, Griffin, Eagles, Double Gilt Leaf Border, 9 ⅛ In.. .... 66.00
Plate, Blue & White, Basket Of Flowers, 8 ¼ In., 6 Piece 2400.00
Plate, Dessert, Butterfly, Blue, Yellow Flowers, 8 ¼ In., 6 Piece 392.00
Plate, Dinner, Blue & White, Birds, Prunus, Peonies, Diaper Border, 1750, 10 In., 12 Piece... 4688.00
Plate, Elephant & Mahout, Indian Market, c.1785, 9 ¼ In., Pair 1200.00
Plate, Famille Rose, Armorial, Crest, Knights, Flower Border, 8-Sided, 8 ¾ In., Pair 1380.00
Plate, Famille Rose, Butterfly, Chestnuts, Chrysanthemums, Reticulated, Gilt, 10 In., Pair ... 2645.00
Plate, Famille Rose, Deer, People, 8 ¼ In. .... *illus* 1416.00
Plate, Famille Rose, Fish, Iron Red, Pink, Leafy Flowers, Flower Rim, c.1745, 9 In., Pair. 2070.00
Plate, Famille Rose, Flowers, Octagonal, 18th Century, 9 In. 147.00
Plate, Famille Rose, Foo Dog, Bat, Flowers, 9 ¼ In., Pair. 354.00
Plate, Fitzhugh, Orange, 19th Century, 9 ¼ In., Pair 489.00
Plate, Judgment Of Paris, Spearhead Border, c.1750-60, 9 In., Pair.. .... 1320.00
Plate, Woman, Boys, Flower Sprays, Ruby Ground Border, c.1730, 11 ½ In., 4 Piece. 6600.00
Platter, Blue, White, Village, 19th Century, 14 x 17 In. 431.00
Platter, Blue & White, Bird, Flowering Tree, 14 ¾ x 11 ¼ In.. .... 472.00
Platter, Blue & White, Landscape, Banded Border, 19th Century, 14 x 18 In.. .... 660.00
Platter, Blue & White, Riverscape, c.1770-90, 11 x 8 ½ In. 212.00
Platter, Blue & White, Riverscape, Octagonal, c.1780-1800, 15 x 11 ½ In.. .... *illus* 266.00
Platter, Famille Rose, Canted Corners, Center Flower Group, Borders, 12 x 15 In. 1440.00
Platter, Famille Rose, Figures Drinking Tea, Garden, Multicolored, 9 In. 2160.00
Platter, Famille Rose, Floral Swags, Exotic Birds, Octagonal, Shaped Rim, 12 x 15 In., Pair.. 3525.00
Platter, Famille Rose, Landscape Rim, Floral Sprays, 1 ½ x 13 ½ x 16 In. 2115.00
Platter, Famille Rose, River, People, Birds, Rectangular, Canted Corners, 13 x 16 In.. .... 1800.00
Platter, Famille Verte, People In Garden, Flower Borders, Celadon Glaze, 16 ½ In.. .... 499.00
Platter, Mandarin Garden, Blue, Orange, Gilt Border, 18th Century, 12 x 15 In.. .... 1610.00
Platter, Shield Crest, Gilt W, Fox & Crown, Blue Enamel Diaper Border, Oval, 16 In. 812.00
Pot-De-Creme, Blue, Iron Red, Gilt, Domed Lid, Berry Knop, 4 In., 4 Piece 227.00
Punch Bowl, 100 Butterflies, 19th Century, 14 ¼ In. 823.00
Punch Bowl, 1000 Figure Pattern, Orange Sepia, Late 19th Century, 5 x 13 In. 1440.00
Punch Bowl, Armorial, Eagle, Spread Winged, Shield Breasted, Footed, 4 ½ x 11 In. 1840.00
Punch Bowl, Blue & White, Birds, Butterflies, Flower Band Border, Gold Trim, 14 In. 837.00
Punch Bowl, Eagle, Armorial, Blue Rim, Gilt, Enamel, 1700s, 4 x 11 In. .... *illus* 1840.00
Punch Bowl, Famille Rose, Butterflies, 11 ¼ In. 1292.00
Punch Bowl, Famille Rose, Peonies, Butterflies, Brown Bird, c.1750, 5 x 10 In. 1320.00
Punch Bowl, People In Pavilions, Flower Ground, Blue, Enamels, 15 ¾ In. 2304.00

Punch Bowl, Pink Lotus, Petals, c.1760, 15¾ In. 5700.00
Punch Bowl, Reserve Panels, People, Feather & Fruit Border, Fleur-De-Lis, 11 In. 1020.00
Salt, Trencher, Flowers, Leaves, Blue, White, 8-Sided, c.1770-90, 1½ In. 330.00
Salt, Trencher, Garland, 8-Sided, Gilt Rim, c.1785-95, 1¾ In. 248.00
Sauceboat, Flame Red, Black, Flowers, Gilding, 1700s, 9½ In., Pair 1800.00
Sauceboat, Fleur-De-Lis, Flower Swag, Shield, 8½ In. 840.00
Saucer, Rooster, Flowers, Gilt, 1700s, 5¼ In., Pair 259.00
Serving Bowl, Flowers, Overglaze Enamels, Fleur-De-Lis Border, 1700s, 9¼ x 11 In. 960.00
Storage Jar, Blue & White, Flowers, Leaves, Waisted Globular, 19th Century, 9 In. 216.00
Tea Bowl & Saucer, New York State Coat Of Arms, Liberty, Justice, 1700s, 2 In. .... *illus* 235.00
Teapot, Blooming Trees, Birds, Multicolored, 5½ In. 359.00
Teapot, Cover, Blue & White, Armorial, Twisted Handle, Strawberry Finial, 6 x 10 In. 345.00
Teapot, Famille Rose, Flowers, Monogrammed, 5½ In. 413.00
Teapot, Famille Verte, Bird Perched On Leaf, 9¾ In. 277.00
Teapot, Famille Verte, Flowers, Birds, 19th Century, 7½ In. 146.00
Teapot, Figures, Double Wire Handle, c.1810, 5 x 7 In. 205.00
Teapot, Flowers, Baskets, Cylindrical, Intertwining Handles, Late 1700s, 5½ In. 115.00
Teapot, People, Landscape, Loop Handle, Paneled Gilt Multicolored, 5½ x 4¼ In. 330.00
Tray, Armorial, Dagger, Scalloped, Oval, Diaper, 16 x 13½ In. 920.00
Tray, Armorial, Pinched Corner, Blue, Gold, 4-Footed, c.1800, 7¾ x 9¾ In. 403.00
Tray, Condiment, Blue & White, Peonies, Buddhist Symbols, Oval, 7 x 11 In., Pair 1440.00
Tray, Famille Rose, Canted Corners, Performers, 11¼ x 15¼ In. 1560.00
Tray, Famille Verte, Mandarin, Servants, Flowers, 7½ x 8½ In. 570.00
Tray, Tobacco Leaf, Rectangular, Rounded, Scalloped, 16 x 13 In. 480.00
Tureen, Armorial, Crest, Bird, Blue Shield, Mushroom Finial, Underplate, 6 x 8 In. 1610.00
Tureen, Characters, Fish, Gilt Painted Scales, Turquoise, Orange, 14 In. 2749.00
Tureen, Cover, Blue & White, Floral Panels, Boar's Head Handles, 8 In. 2151.00
Tureen, Cover, Blue & White, Riverscape, 10 x 9 In. 165.00
Tureen, Cover, Blue & White, Riverscape, Rectangular, Painted, 14¼ In., Pair 6000.00
Tureen, Cover, Stem Handle On Cover, Boar's Head Handles On Bowl, 1800s, 8 x 10 In. 382.00
Tureen, Cover, Undertray, Fish, Flowers, Twisted Handles, c.1800, 8 In. 826.00
Tureen, Dome Cover, Famille Verte, Bombe Shape, c.1810, 6¾ In. 531.00
Tureen, Underplate, Famille Rose, Boar's Head, Bird On Branch, 8 x 12 x 8 & 17 x 13 In. 3850.00
Tureen, Undertray, Flower Sprays, Bamboo, Peony, Scalloped Rim, Celadon Ground, 17 In. 2938.00
Tureen Stand, Couple, Fashionably Dressed, Spearhead Border, c.1780, 14½ In. 1080.00
Undertray, Bather In River, Attendant, Servant, 7 x 8½ In. 1080.00
Urn, Cover, Famille Verte, Potpourri, Pinecone Finial, Bronze Mounted, 18 In. 4406.00
Urn, Cover, Red, Flowers, Cobalt Blue, 14 x 11 In. 205.00
Vase, 3 Foo Dogs, Garlic Form Mouth, Copper Red, White, 7½ In. 142.00
Vase, Blue & White, Flower Head, Scrolling Leaves, 12 In. 266.00
Vase, Blue & White, People, 9½ In. 236.00
Vase, Blue & White, Riverscape, Baluster, Shaped Cartouches, 9½ In., Pair 944.00
Vase, Citrus Fruit, Butterflies, Iron Red, Blue, 7½ In. 177.00
Vase, Cover, Blue & White, Baluster, 18th Century, 13½ In., Pair 9600.00
Vase, Cover, Blue & White, Baluster, Riverscape, 16 In. 8260.00
Vase, Cover, Blue & White, Landscapes, Flowers, Hexagonal, Baluster, 11 In., Pair 10200.00
Vase, Cover, Famille Rose, Birds Perched On Peony Branch, Baluster, 16½ In. 189.00
Vase, Cover, Flowers, Red Overlay, 7½ In. 413.00
Vase, Cover, Gilded Foo Dogs, Dragon, Mandarin, Women, Garden, Fitzhugh, 24 In. 2350.00
Vase, Cylindrical, Green Flower Trim, 19th Century, 6 x 5 In. 146.00
Vase, Double Gourd, Blue, 9 In. 590.00
Vase, Dragon, Carp, Apple Green, 13½ In. 472.00
Vase, Dragon, Green, White, Oval, 12 x 9½ In. 236.00
Vase, Famille Jaune, Dragon, Flowers, 13½ In. 767.00
Vase, Famille Rose, Baluster Shape, Applied Openwork Handles, 17½ In. 150.00
Vase, Famille Rose, Calligraphy, Foo Dog, Ring Handles, 15½ In. 266.00
Vase, Famille Rose, Court Scenes, Robed Judges, Flower Ground, 19¾ In. 1080.00
Vase, Famille Rose, Dignitaries, Under Pine Tree, Playing Children, 18 In. 560.00
Vase, Famille Rose, Dragon, Flower, Squared Sleeve Handles, Pear Shape, 13 In. 236.00
Vase, Famille Rose, Dragon, Phoenix, Gilt Qilins, High Relief, 1800s, 12 In., Pair 1003.00
Vase, Famille Rose, Flattened Quatrefoil Pear Shape, Dragon Handles, 12 In. .... *illus* 633.00
Vase, Famille Rose, Flowers, Painted, Reserves, Iron Red Ground, 8¼ In., Pair 266.00
Vase, Famille Rose, Lion's Head & Ring Handles, 19th Century, 24¾ In. 1380.00
Vase, Famille Rose, Mandarin, Bronze Figural Handles, 24 x 7½ In. 5000.00
Vase, Famille Rose, Molded Fruit, Relief, Robin's-Egg Blue, 8 In. 2596.00
Vase, Famille Rose, Monkey Perched On Flowering Branch, Early 1900s, 11 In. 502.00

Chinese Export, Tea Bowl & Saucer, New York State Coat Of Arms, Liberty, Justice, 1700s, 2 In.
$235.00

Chinese Export, Vase, Famille Rose, Flattened Quatrefoil Pear Shape, Dragon Handles, 12 In.
$633.00

Chinese Export, Vase, Famille Verte, Scrolling Leaves, Ruyi Head, 11 In.
$354.00

Chintz, Flowers, Sugar & Creamer, Royal Winton, Blue Lattice Ground, Ascot Shape
$85.00

Chocolate Glass, Cactus, Salt & Pepper, 2 7/8 In.
$55.00

Chocolate Glass, Cat In Basket, Dish, Cover, 4 3/4 In.
$184.00

Santa's Suit

Santa Claus was often pictured in a mauve or blue suit before 1930. Any Santa toy, postcard, or decoration that is not in a red suit is worth extra money.

Vase, Famille Rose, People, 9 1/2 In. 354.00
Vase, Famille Rose, People, Calligraphy, Square, c.1850, 13 1/2 In.. .... 189.00
Vase, Famille Rose, People, Landscape, Baluster, c.1775, 11 In., Pair 1920.00
Vase, Famille Rose, People, Trumpet Neck, Elephant Head Handles, 16 In., Pair 1560.00
Vase, Famille Rose, Person On Horse, Mountain, Tear Shape, 5 In., Pair 150.00
Vase, Famille Verte, Birds, Flowering Prunus Tree, 12 In. 384.00
Vase, Famille Verte, Dragon Chasing Flaming Pearl Of Wisdom, 1900s, 13 In. 531.00
Vase, Famille Verte, Immortals, Reticulated, Molded Sides, Wood Stand, 1900s, 14 In.. .... 518.00
Vase, Famille Verte, People, 17th Century, 6 1/4 In. 649.00
Vase, Famille Verte, Phoenix, Flowering Branches, 9 1/2 In. 590.00
Vase, Famille Verte, Scrolling Leaves, Ruyi Head, 11 In. .... *illus* 354.00
Vase, Famille Verte, Wood Cover, Blue Ground, 19th Century, 16 In.. .... 649.00
Vase, Flowers, Aubergine, Black, 5 1/2 In. 142.00
Vase, Incised Dragon, Garlic Mouth, Yellow, 6 1/4 In.. .... 708.00
Vase, Leaves, Butterflies, Bottle Shape, Coral, 14 3/4 In.. .... 920.00
Vase, Shouldered, Turquoise Glaze, Grey Metallic, 31 3/8 In.. .... 3000.00
Vase, Tsun, Famille Verte, Birds, Flowers, Butterfly Borders, 19th Century, 18 In. 999.00
Washbasin, Famille Rose, Turned-Out Rim, Center Medallion, Flowers, 11 1/2 In.. .... 450.00

CHINTZ is the name of a group of china patterns featuring an overall design of flowers and leaves. The design became popular with English makers about 1928. A few pieces are still being made. The best known are designs by Royal Winton, James Kent Ltd., Crown Ducal, and Shelley. Crown Ducal and Shelley are listed in their own sections.

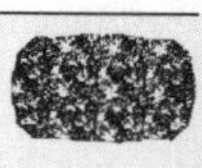

Bedale, Sugar & Creamer, Royal Winton, Hector Shape, Paneled, Open Sugar 155.00
Briar Rose, Trio, Lord Nelson, Cup, Saucer, 8 1/2-In. Square Plate, 3 Piece 125.00
Cynthia, Saucer, Royal Albert 10.00
Daisy, Cup & Saucer, Merit China Co., Marked, Occupied Japan 20.00
Du Barry, Sugar & Creamer, Open, James Kent Ltd. 70.00
Eleanor, Cup & Saucer, Royal Winton 77.00
Eleanor, Pin Dish, Royal Winton, Roses, Gold Trim, Scalloped, Indented Sides, 4 x 3 In.. .... 48.00
Flowers, Plate, James Kent, Pink, Yellow & Blue Gold Trim, 8-Sided, 6 1/4 In.. .... 60.00
Flowers, Sugar & Creamer, Royal Winton, Blue Lattice Ground, Ascot Shape .... *illus* 85.00
June Festival, Nut Dish, Royal Winton, Blue & Lavender Flowers, Burgundy, 5 1/2 In.. .... 35.00
Lorna Doone, Cup & Saucer, Old Royal, Bird, Butterfly, Flowers, England 35.00
Marguerite, Trio, Royal Winton, Daisies, Fluted Sides, Cup, Saucer, 6-In. Plate, 3 Piece 130.00
Marina, Cake Plate, Lord Nelson, 2 Tab Handles, 1937, 10 In. 175.00
Marina, Pitcher, Lord Nelson, 4 7/8 x 4 3/4 In. 199.00
May Blossom, Pitcher, Bourne & Leigh, Blue, White, 5 1/2 In. 105.00
Old Cottage, Cup & Saucer, Royal Winton 50.00
Old Cottage, Tea Set, Royal Winton, 3 Piece 176.00
Old Cottage, Tray, Royal Winton, Gold Trim, Indented Sides, 8 1/4 x 6 3/4 In.. .... 65.00
Old Country Roses, Dessert Set, Royal Albert, 14 Piece 176.00
Old Foley, Sugar & Creamer, James Kent, Open, Hydrangeas 25.00
Pansy, Candy Dish, Royal Albert, Blue Flowers, Gold Trim, 2 Handles, 5 3/4 x 3 3/4 In.. .... 28.00
Pompadour, Lunch Set, Lord Nelson, Cup, Saucer, 8 1/2-In. Plate, 3 Piece 28.00
Primula, Cup, James Kent Ltd. 15.00
Queen Anne, Butter, Cover, Royal Winton, 5 1/4 x 4 1/2 x 3 In.. .... 145.00
Queen Anne, Relish, Royal Winton, Boat Shape, 10 1/2 x 5 In. 80.00
Rapture, Dish, James Kent, Roses, Pink, Green, Ruffled & Fluted Sides, 4 3/4 In. 55.00
Rose, Cup & Saucer, Royal Albert, Pink, Blue, Yellow Flowers, Gold Trim 55.00
Rose Time, Sugar & Creamer, Lord Nelson, Open Sugar 78.00
Royal Brocade, Cup, Lord Nelson, Yellow & Blue Flowers, Burgundy Ground, 4 x 4 In. 20.00
Royal Brocade, Cup & Saucer, After Dinner, Lord Nelson 45.00
Stratford, Butter, Cover, Royal Winton, Tulips, Leaves, Blue Ground, Square, 6 In. 238.00
Summertime, Cup & Saucer, Royal Winton, Green Trim 70.00
Summertime, Dish, Royal Winton, Flared Sides, 2 Flared-Out Handles, 4 x 6 x 2 In. 60.00
Summertime, Teapot, Royal Winton, 2 Cup, 6 In.. .... 200.00
Tea Set, Red & White Apples, British Anchor Pottery, c.1875, Child's, 16 Piece 455.00

CHOCOLATE GLASS, sometimes mistakenly called caramel slag, was made by the Indiana Tumbler and Goblet Company of Greentown, Indiana, from 1900 to 1903. It was also made at other National Glass Company factories. Fenton Art Glass Co. made chocolate glass from about 1907 to 1915. More recent pieces have been made by Imperial and others.

Cactus, Compote, Cover, Greentown, 9 1/2 In. 173.00
Cactus, Plate, Scalloped Edge, 7 1/2 In.. .... 40.00
Cactus, Salt & Pepper, 2 7/8 In. .... *illus* 55.00

Cactus, Water Set, Greentown, Pitcher, 6 Tumblers, 8 In. 95.00
Cat In Basket, Dish, Cover, 4¾ In. .... *illus* 184.00
Leaf Bracket, Butter, Cover, Greentown, 7 In. 58.00
Rabbit, Dish, Cover, Basket Base, Greentown, 4¼ x 5½ In. 480.00

CHRISTMAS collectibles include not only Christmas trees and ornaments listed below, but also Santa Claus figures, special dishes, and even games and wrapping paper. A Belsnickle is a nineteenth-century figure of Father Christmas. A kugel is an early, heavy ornament made of thick blown glass, lined with zinc or lead, and often covered with colored wax. Christmas cards are listed in this section under Greeting Card.Christmas collectibles may also be listed in the Candy Container category. Christmas trees are listed in the section that follows.

Angel, Carved Hair, Face, Detachable Wooden Wings, Decorated Gown, 10¾ In. 1955.00
Bell, Die Cut, Czechoslovakia............ 15.00
Belsnickle, Cardboard, Red Coat, Carrying Basket On Back, Marked, Germany, 8 In. 935.00
Belsnickle, Green, Red, Composition, Feather Tree, Germany, c.1890, 11 In. .... *illus* 1300.00
Belsnickle, Papier-Mache, Blue Coat, Feather Tree, 5¼ In. 935.00
Belsnickle, Papier-Mache, Red Coat, Feather Tree, 10½ In. 523.00
Belsnickle, Papier-Mache, White Coat, Feather Tree, Marked, Germany, 9½ In. 990.00
Belsnickle, Papier-Mache, White Coat, Feather Tree, Marked, Germany, 13¾ In. 1320.00
Belsnickle, Papier-Mache, White Coat, Gold Trim, Feather Tree, 10½ In. 1045.00
Belsnickle, Papier-Mache, Yellow Coat, 13 In. 1650.00
Book, Adventure Of Santa Claus, J.B. Greene, Cloth, Inscribed To Geo. Webster, c.1871 .... 4400.00
Book, All About Santa Claus, Going Down Chimney, Die Cut, McLoughlin, 1896, 6 Pages 500.00
Book, Christmas Greetings From Santa Claus, Die Cut, c.1900, 8 x 5 In., 12 Pages 300.00
Book, Christmas Tales & Christmas Verse, Eugene Field, F. Storer, Green Gilt, Cloth, 1926 .... 75.00
Book, Merry Christmas ABC, McLoughlin, 1900 .... 300.00
Book, Night Before Christmas, Clement Moore, Cloth, Illustrator E. Lupton, c.1905 .... 1000.00
Book, Old Santa Claus, Die Cut, Nister, c.1890 .... 500.00
Book, Santa Claus & His Works, McLoughlin Bros., 1889 .... 450.00
Book, Santa Claus In Toyland, Pop-Up, Movable Spiral Backed Stiff Card Wraps, Color, 1951. 125.00
Book, Santa Claus Picture Book, McLoughlin Bros., 1901, 12 Pages 1250.00
Book, The Night Before Christmas, Fuzzy Fabric, Whitman, 1949 .... 250.00
Book, The Night Before Christmas, Pop-Up, Clement Moore, Random House, c.1960 .... 85.00
Button, Santa Claus, Celluloid, Montreal, Canada, 1¼ In. 19.00
Button, Santa Claus Club, Porteous, Mitchell & Braun, Portland, Me., Celluloid, 1¼ In. 30.00
Candy containers are listed in the Candy Container category.
Candy Mold, Santa, Tin, Continental, 3½ & 5 In., 4 Piece 117.00
Church, Trees, Reindeer, Snowman, Light-Up, Music Box, Homemade, c.1950 .... 79.00
Display, Window, Santa Claus, Elves, Animated, 32 x 48 In. 66.00
Figure, Santa Claus, Animated, 30 In. 23.00
Figure, Santa Claus, Cloth Face, Molded, Silk Suit, Mid 20th Century, 26 In. 188.00
Figure, Santa Claus, In Sleigh, Reindeer, Celluloid, 4½ In. 14.00
Figure, Santa Claus, Walks When Wound, Chein, 1930s 385.00
Lantern, Blue Hood, Papier-Mache, Germany, 6½ In. .... *illus* 1000.00
Mold, Cake, Santa Claus, Standing, Griswold 425.00
Nodder, Santa Claus, Composition, Clockwork, Germany, 1920s, 28 In. .... *illus* 1400.00
Nodder, Santa Claus, Tin, Celluloid, Windup, Box, Prewar Japan, 1940s 150.00
Pail, Candy, Santa Claus, Lid, Handle 475.00
Pin, Father Adelaide Christmas, Santa In Chimney, Australia, c.1917, 1 In. 128.00
Pin, Merry Christmas, Green Duck, Chicago, 1930s, 1⅛ In. 70.00
Pin, Santa, Don't Forget Me, Lithograph, 1930, 1⅛ In. 46.00
Pin, Santa In Airship, Australian Version, c.1915, 1¼ In. 58.00
Pin, Santa Upside Down In Chimney, You Will Find Me At Garver's Strasburg, 1910 .... 538.00
Pin, Santa, Doin' The Twist, New York City, 1960s 83.00
Plate, Christmas Goodies, Blue & White, Gold Edged, 8¼ In. 20.00
Plates that are limited edition are listed in the Collector Plate category or in the correct factory listing.
Platter, Tree, Oval, Chrome, Paper Label, Griswold 50.00
Postcard, Girl's Head, Leaves, Christmas Greetings, Raphael Kirchner .... *illus* 248.00
Postcard, Mechanical, Pink Santa, Pull Tab Changes To Girl Holding Doll, c.1920 .... 142.00
Postcard, Novelty, Fold-Out Christmas Tree Tissue, Early 20th Century 153.00
Postcard, Uncle Sam Holding Tree, A Jolly Christmas To You .... *illus* 1298.00
Postcard, Uncle Sam Santa Claus, Die Cut, Hold To Light, Early 1900s 2360.00
Postcard Set, Santa, Red Silk Applique, Embossed, Langsdorf, Early 1900s, 4 Piece 83.00
Salt & Pepper, Bell Shape, Pearl Luster Finish, Santa's Workshop Scenes 22.00
Salt & Pepper, Figural, Boy & Girl, Red & Green Clothes, Avon, c.1983 .... 12.00

Christmas, Belsnickle, Green, Red, Composition, Feather Tree, Germany, c.1890, 11 In.
$1300.00

Christmas, Lantern, Blue Hood, Papier-Mache, Germany, 6½ In.
$1000.00

Christmas, Nodder, Santa Claus, Composition, Clockwork, Germany, 1920s, 28 In.
$1400.00

Christmas, Postcard, Girl's Head, Leaves, Christmas Greetings, Raphael Kirchner
$248.00

Christmas, Postcard, Uncle Sam Holding Tree, A Jolly Christmas To You
$1298.00

Christmas, Toy, Santee Claus, Tin, Windup, Strauss, Box, 11 In.
$3738.00

Salt & Pepper, Mr. & Mrs. Snowman, Top Hat, Bonnet, Hard Plastic, 3 In. 12.00
Salt & Pepper, Reindeer, Red Hat, Presents, Satin Finish 15.00
Salt & Pepper, Santa & Mrs. Claus Kissing, Japan, 1960s, 3½ In. 12.00
Salt & Pepper, Santa Claus, Ceramic, 3 In. 15.00
Salt & Pepper, Santa Claus Heads, Rosy Cheeks, Spaghetti Trim 15.00
Salt & Pepper, Santa Pepper, Bag Of Presents Salt, 3½ In. 8.00
Snow Globe, Santa Claus, Hard Plastic, Belly Is Globe, Hong Kong, 5 In. 24.00
Toy, Father Christmas, Sleigh, 4 Reindeer, F.A.O. Schwartz, Box, c.1893, 29 In. 8625.00
Toy, Happy Santa, Stands Up, Sits Down, Rings Bell, Battery Operated, Z Co., Box, 10 In. 144.00
Toy, Jolly Santa On Snow, Tin, Fabric, Battery Operated, Remote Control, Alps, 12 In. 250.00
Toy, Rocking Santa, Lighted Silver Tree, Stocking, Bell, Battery Operated, Alps, 21 In. 322.00
Toy, Rudolph The Red Nosed Reindeer, Wood, Metal Bells, Pull Toy, c.1940s, 5 x 8 In. 127.00
Toy, Santa Claus, Fabric Cover, Vinyl Face, Moves, Bell, Battery Operated, 1960s, 13 In. 115.00
Toy, Santa Claus, Plastic, Friction, Pull Reins, Reindeer's Head Bobs, 1960s, 5 x 3 In. 34.00
Toy, Santa Claus, Pulling Sleigh, Composition, Cloth, Fur Beard, Pull, 6 x 8¾ x 2 In. 385.00
Toy, Santa Claus, Roly Poly, Composition, c.1910, 8 In. 495.00
Toy, Santa Claus, Santa Car, Mickey Mouse In Sack, Tree, Windup, Box, Lionel, 1935, 10 In. . . 2875.00
Toy, Santa Claus, Sleigh, Reindeer, Composition, Cloth, Wood, Pull, 4 x 11 x 3 In. 412.00
Toy, Santa Claus, Sleigh, Reindeer, Composition, Cloth, Wood, Pull, Germany, 5 x 10 x 2 In. . . 275.00
Toy, Santa Claus, Squeak, Papier-Mache, F.A.O. Schwarz, Germany, 1900s, 8 In. 345.00
Toy, Santa Claus, Windup, Box Top, Alps Of Japan 114.00
Toy, Santa Claus, Windup, Papier-Mache, Germany, c.1925 . . . . 234.00
Toy, Santa Claus, Windup, Rabbit Fur Beard, Prewar Germany, 6 In. 275.00
Toy, Santa Claus Car, Epoch, Colorful, Santa Driving, Bag Of Toys, Tin, 5½ In. 153.00
Toy, Santa Claus On Skis, Tin, Fabric, Plush, Battery Operated, Alps. 250.00
Toy, Santa Claus Riding Donkey, Nods, Composition, Wood, Cloth, 9 x 8½ In. 825.00
Toy, Santee Claus, Tin, Windup, Strauss, Box, 11 In. . . . . *illus* 3738.00

CHRISTMAS TREES made of feathers and Christmas tree decorations of all types are popular with collectors. The first decorated Christmas tree in America is claimed by many states, including Pennsylvania (1747), Massachusetts (1832), Illinois (1833), Ohio (1838), and Iowa (1845). The first glass ornaments were imported from Germany about 1860. Dresden ornaments were made about 100 years ago of paper and tinsel. Manufacturers in the United States were making ornaments in the early 1870s. Electric lights were first used on a Christmas tree in 1882. Character light bulbs became popular in the 1920s, bubble lights in the 1940s, twinkle bulbs in the 1950s, plastic bulbs by 1955. In this book a Christmas light is a holder for a candle used on the tree. Other forms of lighting include light bulbs. Other Christmas memorabilia is listed in the preceding section.

Feather, 23 In. 180.00
Foil, Green, Electric Stand Turns Tree, Original Box, 8 Ft. 750.00
Kugel, Cobalt Blue, Germany, 7 In. 125.00
Light Set, Bubble, 9 Lights, Noma, Box . . . . *illus* 150.00
Light Set, Mickey & Minnie Mouse, Pluto, 8 Lights, Noma, Box, c.1930. . . . . 330.00
Light Set, Mother Goose, Figural Character, Original Box 144.00
Light Set, Silly Symphony, 8 Bulb Covers, Noma, Box, 1936, 16½ In. 173.00
Ornament, Airplane, Paper Santa, Wire Wheels, Blown Glass, Metal Trim, 7 In. . . . . . *illus* 225.00
Ornament, Angel, On Cloud, Balloon, Wire Wrapped 30.00
Ornament, Angel, On Cloud, Scrap Face, 4½ In.. . . . . 35.00
Ornament, Angel, On Lyre, Scrap 42.00
Ornament, Angel, Scrap, Balloon, Wire Wrapped 38.00
Ornament, Balloon, Wire Covered, Paper Angel, Blown Glass, 5 In. . . . . *illus* 75.00
Ornament, Basket, Wire Handle, Dresden, Germany, 2½ x 4 In. . . . . *illus* 50.00
Ornament, Belsnickle, Feather Sprig, Gold, Hand Painted, Germany, 1910, 4 In.. . . . . 180.00
Ornament, Belsnickle, Red, Brown, Germany, 1910, 2 In. 226.00
Ornament, Boy Clown In Moon, Glass, Germany, 3½ In.. . . . . 127.00
Ornament, Double Balloon, Scrap, Purple Glass, Wire Wrap, 5 In. 128.00
Ornament, Girl's Head, Candle Light, Clip-On, Blown Glass, Painted, Germany . . . . *illus* 275.00
Ornament, Horn Of Plenty, Candy Container, Cardboard, 6 In. 38.00
Ornament, Horn Of Plenty, Hand Blown Glass, Embossed, 4½ In. 80.00
Ornament, Man, Kaiser Wilhelm, Red, Gold Paint, Glass, 3¾ In. . . . . *illus* 200.00
Ornament, Mermaid, Flowing Hair, Forked Tail, Glass, 4 In. . . . . *illus* 325.00
Ornament, Monkey Head, Wearing Hat, Germany, c.1910 . . . . 495.00
Ornament, Pony, Cotton, Glass Eyes, Wooden Legs, Silver Buckle, Germany, 2½ In. 69.00
Ornament, Sailboat, Dresden, Germany, 3¾ x 3 In. . . . . *illus* 750.00
Ornament, Santa Claus, Scrap Face, Sprig Tree, Crepe Paper, Cape, Germany, 6 In. 250.00
Ornament, Santa Claus, Tree, Mushrooms, Composition, Cardboard, Japan, 3½ In.. . . . . 66.00

Christmas Tree, Light Set, Bubble, 9 Lights, Noma, Box
$150.00

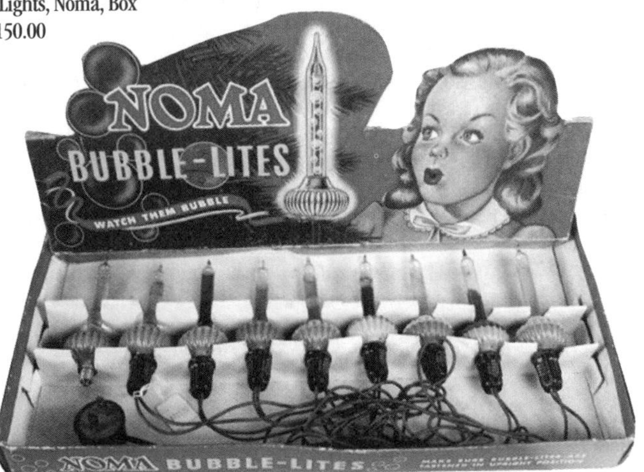

Christmas Tree, Ornament, Airplane, Paper Santa, Wire Wheels, Blown Glass, Metal Trim, 7 In.
$225.00

Christmas Tree, Ornament, Balloon, Wire Covered, Paper Angel, Blown Glass, 5 In.
$75.00

Christmas Tree, Ornament, Basket, Wire Handle, Dresden, Germany, 2 ½ x 4 In.
$50.00

Christmas Tree, Ornament, Girl's Head, Candle Light, Clip-On, Blown Glass, Painted, Germany
$275.00

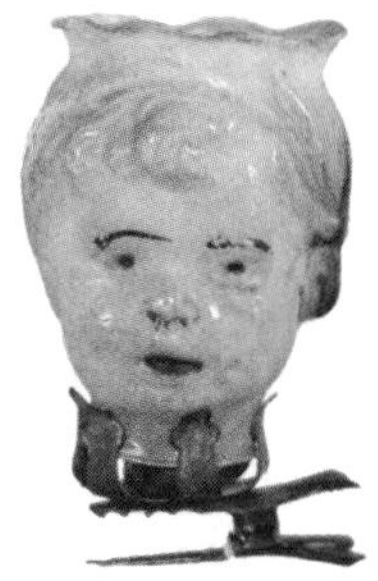

Christmas Tree, Ornament, Man, Kaiser Wilhelm, Red, Gold Paint, Glass, 3 ¾ In.
$200.00

Christmas Tree, Ornament, Mermaid, Flowing Hair, Forked Tail, Glass, 4 In.
$325.00

Christmas Tree, Ornament, Sailboat, Dresden, Germany, 3 ¾ x 3 In.
$750.00

Christmas Tree, Ornament, Santa Head, Blue Hat, Blown Glass, Germany, 6 In.
$150.00

Christmas Tree, Ornament, Zeppelin, Glass Blown, Wire Wrapped, 5 In.
$500.00

Christmas Tree, Stand, Musical, Windup, Germany, 10 In.
$650.00

Cigar Store Figure, Indian, Holding Boxes & Bundles, Pine, Carved, Painted, 1800s, 56 In.
$8050.00

Civil War, Button, Grand Army Of Republic, Welcome Awaits You, 1911, 1½ In.
$155.00

Civil War, Canteen, Bull's-Eye, Brown Cloth, White Paint, Initials, W.H.M.
$230.00

Civil War, Drum, Regimental, Tenor, Eagle, Painted, c.1862, 16 x 17½ In.
$1000.00

Ornament, Santa Head, Blue Hat, Blown Glass, Germany, 6 In. . . . . *illus* 150.00
Ornament, Soldier, Cotton, Composition, Crepe Paper Clothes, Cardboard, 5 In. 25.00
Ornament, Star, Reflector, Plastic, Tinsel Center, 4½ x 4¾ In., 14 Piece 15.00
Ornament, Zeppelin, Glass, Wire Wrapped, Soldiers, Gondola, Germany, 7 In. 431.00
Ornament, Zeppelin, Glass Blown, Wire Wrapped, 5 In. . . . . *illus* 500.00
Stand, Father Christmas, Winter Scene, Cast Iron, Marked, 1919, 12 x 12 In. 1265.00
Stand, Green, Receptacles & Outlets, Cast Iron, Peerless, 1930s 500.00
Stand, Musical, Windup, Germany, 10 In. . . . . *illus* 650.00
Topper, Mazda Star Of Bethlehem, Noma, c.1933 . . . . . 35.00
Tree, Bubble Light, 9 Lights, Base, 19 In. 80.00
Tree, Glo-Lite, Glass Decorations, Base, 17 In. 24.00
Tree, Glo-Lite, Musical Stand, 22 In. 36.00

CHROME items in the Art Deco style became popular in the 1930s. Collectors are most interested in high-style pieces made by the Connecticut firms of Chase Brass & Copper Co. and Manning-Bowman & Co.

Ashtray, Cowboy Hat, Griswold 1800.00
Bell, Black Handle, Chase, 3½ x 2 In. 250.00
Cake Server, Open Filigree, Italy, 10 In. 15.00
Candleholder, Plated, Art Deco Style, 5¼ x 2¼ In. 19.00
Cocktail Set, Shaker, Red Bakelite Handle, Goblets, 13 x 4 In., 6 Piece 35.00
Cocktail Shaker, Butterscotch, Wood Handle, Screw Mount Spout, Lid Finial 125.00
Cocktail Shaker, Butterscotch Bakelite Handle, Incised Lines 75.00
Condiment Set, Hammered Tray, Recessed Inserts, Creamer, Sugar, Holder, 4 Piece 18.00
Dish, Cover, Stamped Plate, Pressed Glass, Bakelite Knob 46.00
Flask, 2-In-1, Screw Lids, Tin Liner, Engraved, Germany, 7½ In, 13 Oz. 85.00
Humidor, Lid, Gold Matte 95.00
Lamp, Desk, Ribbed, Swivel Light Socket, Art Deco, c.1930s, 14½ In. 100.00
Lazy Susan, Crystal Inserts, Bowl, Lid, 13½ In. 35.00
Pitcher, Fruit, Tree, Copper Luster, Flow Blue, Multicolored 311.00
Pour Spout, Cork Seat, 4 x 1½ In. 13.00
Powder Box, Glass, Cover, Bakelite Heart, 1920. . . . . 25.00
Serving Fork, Bakelite, Butterscotch Yellow Handle, 1937, 11 In. 12.00
Spatula, Red Swirls, Bakelite Handle, 1940s, 13¼ x 4¾ In. 28.00
Stopper Set, Ball, Box, Inverted Cone, Rack, 3 Piece, 4 In. 70.00
Sugar & Creamer, Brown Bakelite Handles, Farberware 26.00
Sugar & Creamer, Rosewood Tray, Oval, Handle, Lid, Marked, Lindtofte, Denmark 75.00
Sugar & Creamer, Tray, Irvinware, 9 In. 18.00
Tray, Cutout Edge, Farber Bros, 1940s, 15⅜ In. 25.00
Waffle Iron, Round, Model W36, Winchester, 5 x 9 In. 275.00

CIGAR STORE FIGURES of carved wood or cast iron were used as advertisements in front of the Victorian cigar store. The carved figures are now collected as folk art. They range in size from counter type, about three feet, to over eight feet high.

Indian, Feather Headdress, Pine, Multicolored, c.1885, 48 In. 8050.00
Indian, Headdress, Holding Can Of Cigars, Carved, 20th Century, 72 In. 176.00
Indian, Holding Boxes & Bundles, Pine, Carved, Painted, 1800s, 56 In. . . . . *illus* 8050.00
Indian, Holding Cigars, Carved, Painted, Early 20th Century, 68 x 18 In. 20400.00
Indian, Holding Pipe, Carved, Painted, Wood, Tin, 19th Century, 33 In. 7800.00
Indian, Maiden, Holding Cigar Box, Feather Headdress, Wheels, 85 x 26½ x 23 In. 4950.00
Indian, Papier-Mache, Painted 4500.00
Indian, Princess, Holding Tobacco Leaf, Cast Iron, Painted, 25 In., Pair 13200.00
Indian, Sign, Stand-Up, Cardboard, Lithograph, Easel Back, 12 x 5 In. 1815.00
Indian, Tobacco Leaf Headdress, Skirt, Wood, Carved, Painted, Late 1800s, 50 x 17 In. 2350.00
Indian, Woman, Carved, Painted, Wood Base, Late 1800s, 33 x 11 In. 2820.00
Indian Maiden, Feather Headdress, Cap, Cigars, Carved, 61 In. 4406.00
Jester, Bell, Hearts, Multicolored, Plaster Of Paris, Wood Base, 71 x 21 x 20 In. 1980.00

CINNABAR is a vermilion or red lacquer. Pieces are made with tens to hundreds of thicknesses of the lacquer that is later carved. Most cinnabar was made in the Orient.

Bowl, 20th Century, 4¾ x 2¼ In. 50.00
Box, Cover, Peony, Square, 3¼ x 4½ In. 90.00
Box, Flower, 4 In. 55.00

Box, Flower, Cover, 3 ¼ x 4 ½ In. 90.00
Jar, Cover, 6-Panels, Figures, Building, Flower Base, Chinese, 12 x 5 ½ In., Pair 518.00
Jar, Cover, Green, Blue Enamels, 20th Century 70.00
Plaque, Man & Woman, In Boat, Trees, Mountains, Black, Red Ground, 9 In. 30.00
Snuff Bottle, White Porcelain Shell, Mounted Warrior, Brass Cap Stopper 129.00
Vase, Enamel, Wood Base, 20th Century, 1 ½ In., Pair 270.00
Vase, Oriental, c.1930, 7 ½ x 2 ½ x 3 ¾ In. 115.00

CIVIL WAR mementos are important collectors' items. Most of the pieces are military items used from 1861 to 1865. Be sure to avoid any explosive munitions.

Badge, Press, 5-Point, Engraved, Flowers, Pin Back, Silver Metal, 1 ½ In. 3346.00
Badge, Ribbon, 49th New York Veteran, Gettysburg, Wolf's Hill 100.00
Belt, Bayonet Rig, Rifleman's, Leather Scabbard, Brass Buckle, 34 & 27 In. 25009.00
Belt Plate, Cavalryman's, Virginia, Company D, Cast Brass, Silver Wreath, 3 x 2 In. 896.00
Boots, Leather, Square Headed Nails, Union 538.00
Bucket, Artillery, Hand Forged, 7 ½ x 8 In. 688.00
Buckle, Sash, Eagle, Union Streamer, Liberty & Justice Figures, Gold, 2 x 1 In.. .... 956.00
Bullet Pouch, Leather, Embossed, Brass Ball Frog Closure, Belt Loops, 6 x 5 In. 1052.00
Button, Confederate, CSA, Enlisted, Brass, 12 ⅞ In. 940.00
Button, Grand Army Of Republic, Welcome Awaits You, 1911, 1 ½ In. .... *illus* 155.00
Camp Chair, Oak, Ladder Back, Folding, 14th Conn. Infantry, Gettysburg, 30 In. 346.00
Cane, Pistol Ball Embedded In Knob, Hardwood Branch, Devils Den, c.1863, 31 In.. .... 805.00
Canteen, Bull's-Eye, Brown Cloth, White Paint, Initials, W.H.M. .... *illus* 230.00
Canteen, Confederate, Tin, Soldered, Spout, Stopper, Cotton Strap, 6 ½ x 2 ¼ In. 1076.00
Canteen, Leather Cover, Strap, 7 In. 275.00
Cutlass, Naval, Cup Shape Guard, Sheet Brass, Leather Grip, Ames Mfg., c.1862, 26 In.. .... 1912.00
Discharge Order, Private Adam Shat, Age 19, Co. D, 197th Pennsylvania Volunteers 125.00
Drum, Field, Maple, Red Painted, 100th New York Volunteers, 11 ½ x 1612 In.. .... 3346.00
Drum, Maple, Painted Eagle, 19th Century, 15 ½ x 16 ½ In. 1434.00
Drum, Regimental, Eagle, Label, Alpheus M. Holbrook, 19th Maine Infantry 11241.00
Drum, Regimental, Tenor, Eagle, Painted, c.1862, 16 x 17 ½ In. .... *illus* 1000.00
Drum, Tension Ropes, Tacked Sides, Wood Box, Sticks, Late 19th Century 287.00
Field Orders, Pennsylvania Bucktails, Signed By Thomas Kane, 4 x 6 ½ In.. .... 1265.00
Frock Coat, Union, Medical Officer, Shoulder Boards, Medals, 2 Rows Of 9 Buttons 3346.00
Pin, Confederate Veterans, CSA, Rhinestone, Diamond Shape 359.00
Pin, Navy Button, Confederate, Fouled Anchor, CSN. 568.00
Poster, Wanted 35 Able-Bodied Men, Virginia Brigade, 38 x 24 In. .... *illus* 7100.00
Powder Flask, Brass, Copper, Bag Shape, 6 ½ x 2 In. 85.00
Powder Flask, Leather Horn, Leaf, Geometric, Brass Top, Charger, 6 ½ & 2 ¾ In. 225.00
Ring, 16th New Hampshire Volunteer Infantry, Silver, c.1862. .... 837.00
Saber, Cavalry, Scabbard, N. Starr, c.1821 .... 550.00
Saber, Cavalry, U.S. Military, c.1863, 41 In. 275.00
Sash, Field Officer, Crimson Red, Silk, Brass Frame Belt Buckle, Fringe Tassels 311.00
Sash, Officer's, Confederate, Coarse Silk, Buff Color, Corded Tassels, 90 In. 1793.00
Shell Jacket, U.S. Artillery, Corporal, Coarse Brown Lining, Black Cloth 4631.00
Spurs, Confederate, 12-Point Rowels, Cast Iron, Yorktown, c.1862. .... 777.00
Sword, Calvary, Plain Hilt, Blade, 36-In. Blade, 41 ½ In. 144.00
Sword, Cast Brass, Eagle Hilt, Gilt Cord, Wrapped Leather Handle, Etched Blade 657.00
Sword, Officer's, Brass Fitted Leather Scabbard, c.1864 .... 299.00
Sword, Presentation, Officer's, Gilt Brass, Scabbard, Horstmann & Sons, 40 In. 2629.00

CKAW, *see Dedham category.*

CLARICE CLIFF was a designer who worked in several English factories, including A.J. Wilkinson Ltd., Wilkinson's Royal Staffordshire Pottery, Newport Pottery, and Foley Pottery after the 1920s. She is best known for her brightly colored Art Deco designs, including the Bizarre line. She died in 1972. Reproductions have been made by Wedgwood.

Bizarre, Biscuit Jar, Cover, Multicolored Flowers, Square, 1930, 5 In. 2455.00
Bowl, 2 Parrots Perched On Branch, 8 ¾ In. 165.00
Bowl, Flower, Green Band, 1 ¾ x 6 ¼ In. 29.00
Crocus, Bowl, Low, Yellow Border, Cream Ground, Brown Band, c.1939, 7 ¾ In.. .... 116.00
Crocus, Jardiniere, 3-Footed, Yellow Border, Round, 1939, 8 ½ In. 290.00
Crocus, Jug, Handles, Cream Ground, Yellow Border, Egg Shape, c.1939, 11 ¾ In. 232.00
Crocus, Sugar & Jug, Lotus, Cream Ground, Yellow Border, c.1939, 7 ¾ In. 261.00

Civil War, Poster, Wanted 35 Able-Bodied Men, Virginia Brigade, 38 x 24 In.
$7100.00

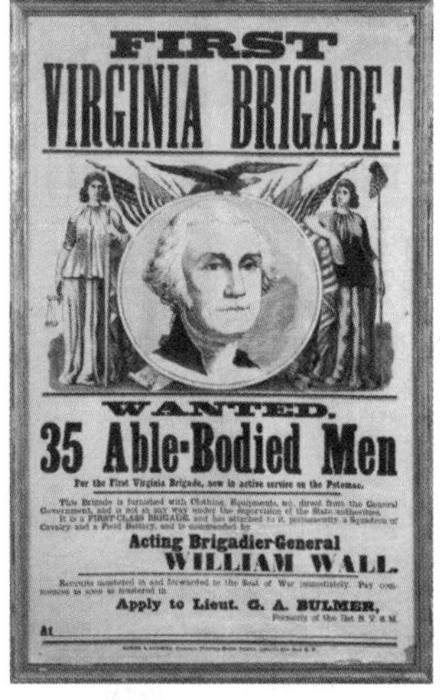

Clarice Cliff, Fantasque, Plate, 8-Sided, 8 ¾ In.
$261.00

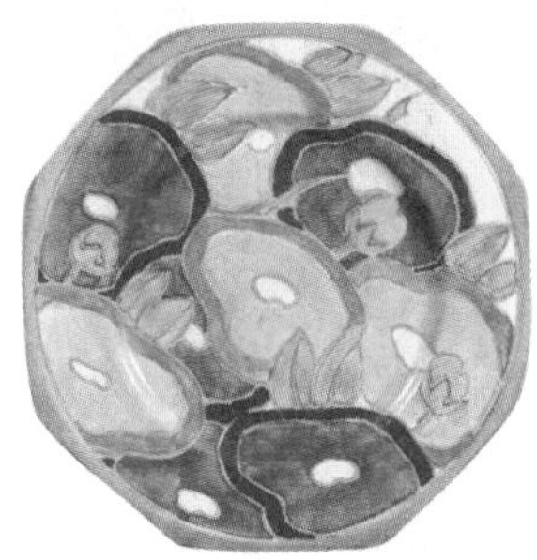

Clarice Cliff, Gayday, Jam Jar, Beehive, Hand Painted, Marked, 3 In.
$265.00

Clarice Cliff, Honolulu, Vase, Marked, 9 ¼ In.
$1500.00

Clarice Cliff, Vase, Relief Molded, Hollyhocks, Marked, 7¾ In.
$250.00

Clewell, Candlestick, Crusty Patina, Marked, 9⅜ In., Pair
$650.00

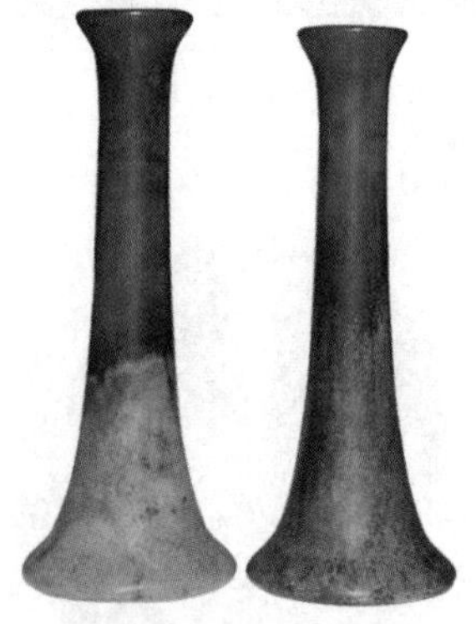

Clewell, Pitcher, Embossed, Arts & Crafts, 5¾ In.
$1015.00

Timepiece or Clock?

In clock collectors' lingo, a timepiece is an instrument that measures time but does not strike. A clock keeps time and has a striking mechanism that sounds on the hour and sometimes the quarter hour.

Crocus, Vase, Lotus, Cream Ground, Yellow Border, Cylindrical, c.1939, 11¾ In. 232.00
Delecia Citrus, Jug, Lotus, Fruit, Leaves, Tapered, Handle, c.1939, 11½ In. 232.00
Fantasque, Plate, 8-Sided, 8¾ In. . . . . *illus* 261.00
Gardenia, Beehive Jar, Bee In Relief On Cover, Multicolored, 3½ In. 552.00
Gayday, Jam Jar, Beehive, Hand Painted, Marked, 3 In. . . . . *illus* 265.00
Globe, Vase, Spherical, Narrow Mouth, Turquoise Glaze, Concentric Rings, 6 In. 139.00
Honolulu, Vase, Marked, 9¼ In. . . . . *illus* 1500.00
Jug, Perched Parrot, Branch, Handle, Ivory Ground, Bulbous, Ribbed, 8½ In. 116.00
Persian, Bowl, Turquoise, Dark Blue, Pink, 9½ In. 565.00
Petunia, Jug, Daisies, Daffodils, Speckled Brown, Tapered, c.1939, 9⅝ In. 116.00
Plate, Dinner, Flowers, Green Band, 9 In. 40.00
Raffia, Bowl, Bizarre, Hand Painted, Marked, 3¼ x 8¼ In. 79.00
Secrets, Sugar Sifter, Cone Shape, Multicolored, Cream Ground, 5½ In. 828.00
Vase, Molded Flowers, Turquoise, Bulbous, Flared Rim, c.1925, 8 In. 100.00
Vase, Relief Molded, Hollyhocks, Marked, 7¾ In. . . . . *illus* 250.00
Viscaria, Jug, Handle, Flowers, Egg Shape, c.1939, 11½ In. 116.00

CLEWELL ware was made in limited quantities by Charles Walter Clewell of Canton, Ohio, from 1902 to 1955. Pottery was covered with a thin coating of bronze, then treated to make the bronze turn different colors. Pieces covered with copper, brass, or silver were also made. Mr. Clewell's secret formula for blue patinated bronze was burned when he died in 1965.

Bowl, Copper Clad, Broad Form, Marked, 384-2-6, 4 x 9½ In. 1050.00
Candlestick, Crusty Patina, Marked, 9⅜ In., Pair . . . . *illus* 650.00
Jar, Lid, Copper Clad, Panels Of Flowers, 6 x 5¼ In. 1020.00
Pitcher, Embossed, Arts & Crafts, 5¾ In. . . . . *illus* 1015.00
Pot, Cover, Copper Clad, Barrel Shape, Rivets, Patina, 4¼ x 6¾ In. 633.00
Urn, Solid Bronze, Verdigris Patina, 9 x 6 In. 2760.00
Vase, Copper, Broad Shouldered, Original Patina, 7½ x 17¼ In. 5100.00
Vase, Copper, Bulbous, Original Patina, 4½ x 6 In. 480.00
Vase, Copper Clad, Arts & Crafts Landscape, Patina, 13½ x 4 In. 3900.00
Vase, Copper Clad, Bulbous, Flared Rim, Original Patina, Marked, 9½ x 4 In. 2200.00
Vase, Copper Clad, Flowers, Patina, 4½ x 3½ In. 360.00
Vase, Copper Clad, Grapes, 4½ x 7 In. 1020.00
Vase, Copper Clad, Organic, Original Patina, 4 x 6½ In. 1320.00
Vase, Copper Clad, Patina, 4½ x 10 In. 1020.00
Vase, Copper Clad, Shouldered, Patina, 4 x 7½ In. 330.00
Vase, Copper Clad, Tapered, Flared Base & Rim, Patina, 13 In. 940.00

CLIFTON POTTERY was founded by William Long in Newark, New Jersey, in 1905. He worked there until 1909 making lines including Crystal Patina and Clifton Indian Ware. Clifton Pottery made art pottery until 1911 and then concentrated on wall and floor tile. By 1914 the name had been changed to Clifton Porcelain and Tile Company. Another firm, Chesapeake Pottery, sold majolica marked *Clifton Ware.*

Vase, Crystal Patina, Flaring Rim, Signed, Dated, 1905, 7¼ x 5¼ In. 270.00
Vase, Geometric, Brown, Tan, Black, Bulbous, Incised Mark, No. 32, 7 x 4½ In. 140.00

CLOCKS of all types have always been popular with collectors. The eighteenth-century tall case, or grandfather's, clock was designed to house a works with a long pendulum. In 1816, Eli Terry patented a new, smaller works for a clock, and the case became smaller. The clock could be kept on a shelf instead of on the floor. By 1840, coiled springs were used and even smaller clocks were made. Battery-powered electric clocks were made in the 1870s. A garniture set can include a clock and other objects displayed on a mantel.

Adams, E.W., William Tell, Mahogany, 8-Day, Brass, c.1830, 36 x 20 In. . . . . *illus* 1100.00
Advertising, Arizona Brewing Co., Phoenix, Ariz., Backbar, Light-Up, 11 x 13 x 6½ In. 960.00
Advertising, Calvert Whiskey, Globe Spins, Tin, Light-Up 358.00
Advertising, Davis Paints, Neon, Octagonal, 18½ In. 297.00
Advertising, Diamond Black Leather Oil, Baird, 31 x 18½ In. . . . . *illus* 1200.00
Advertising, Dr Pepper, Electric, Wall, 20 x 13 In. 72.00
Advertising, Four Roses Whiskey, Light-Up, 4-Sided, 16 In. 95.00
Advertising, Gruen, Steel, Aluminum Case, Electric, c.1939, 15½ In. 77.00
Advertising, Heintz, Alarm, Musical, Battery Operated 19.00
Advertising, Hires Root Beer, Light-Up, Pam, 1950s, 15 In. . . . . *illus* 518.00
Advertising, Ingraham Shop, Oak, Regulator, 8-Day, c.1900, 37 x 16 In. . . . . *illus* 200.00
Advertising, Keen Kutter, Electric, Wood Stand, 19 In. 880.00

Advertising, Monarch Fine Foods, Telechron Pam Clock, Reverse Painted Face, 1950s 380.00
Advertising, Mr. Cola, Aristocrat Of Colas, Glass Dome, c.1950, 10 In. .... *illus* 115.00
Advertising, Old Mr. Boston, Bottle Shape, 8-Day, Gilbert, 1807 .... 110.00
Advertising, Old Overholt Rye, 14 ½ x 8 In. 187.00
Advertising, Pabst Blue Ribbon Beer, What'll You Have?, Light-Up, Electric, Plastic, 13 In.... 176.00
Advertising, Premium Brewing Co., Reading, Pa., Light-Up, 10 ¼ x 10 In. 256.00
Advertising, Red Goose Shoes, Light-Up, Pam Clock Co., 15 In. .... *illus* 550.00
Advertising, Rival Dog Food, Electric, Square, Wall 44.00
Advertising, Royal Crown Cola, 4-Sided, Diamond Shape 200.00
Advertising, Thompson's Wild Cherry Bitters, Ansonia, c.1880, 18 x 16 In. .... *illus* 735.00
Amerden & Forster, Shelf, Louis XVI, Gilt Bronze, Enamel, 19th Century, 21 x 11 In.. .... 990.00
American Clock Co., Burning Building, Iron, Pendulum, 18 x 14 In. 230.00
Animated, Birdcage, c.1930, 11 ¼ In. 390.00
Animated, Pendulette, Little Red Riding Hood, Painted, 30-Hour, Porcelain Dial, c.1930s, 4 In. 138.00
Annular Dial, 3 Graces, Rotating Dial, Bronze, Trefoil Base, France, c.1875, 22 ½ In. 6600.00
Ansonia, Capitol, Oak, Weight Driven, ... 2116.00
Ansonia, Carriage, Gilt Brass, Beveled Glass, Enamel, Paste-Brilliant, 10 ½ x 6 ½ In.. .... 360.00
Ansonia, Crystal Regulator, Brass & Glass Case, Pendulum, 11 In. 259.00
Ansonia, Crystal Regulator, Prism, Brass Case, Porcelain Dial, c.1914, 10 ¾ In.. .... 325.00
Ansonia, Dalton, Pendulum, Key, Alarm 225.00
Ansonia, Figural, Seated Classical Man, Spelter, Late 19th Century, 15 x 16 In. 380.00
Ansonia, Gilt Column, Mahogany Case, 30-Hour, Time & Strike, c.1860, 18 ¾ In. 66.00
Ansonia, Gloria, Ball Swings, Spelter, Brass Top, Bottom Ball, 8-Day, 29 In. .... *illus* 4025.00
Ansonia, Kitchen, Oak, Gingerbread, 8-Day, Time & Strike, c.1894, 21 In. 50.00
Ansonia, La Capelle, Blue Delft, c.1900, 15 In.. .... 935.00
Ansonia, Malta, Cabinet, Oak Case, 8-Day, Gong Strike, c.1900, 12 ¾ In. 495.00
Ansonia, Man Seated, Holding Cup & Book, Spelter, Key, Late 19th Century, 15 x 16 In. 550.00
Ansonia, Mantel, Figural, Mozart, 18 In. 1250.00
Ansonia, Mystery, Gloria Ball Swing, Bronze, Patinated Spelter, c.1900, 29 In. 3190.00
Ansonia, Queen Mab, 8-Day, Time & Gong Strike, c.1904, 36 In. 1265.00
Ansonia, Reflector, Gong Strike, 8-Day, Ebony Finish, c.1885, 35 In. 1155.00
Ansonia, Regulator, Mahogany, 8-Day, Weight Driven, c.1925, 37 In. 1045.00
Ansonia, School, Regulator, Long Drop, Walnut, Walnut Veneer, c.1901, 32 ½ In. 138.00
Ansonia, Shelf, Brass, Cast Iron, Hunting Design, Black Painted Dial, c.1904, 13 ½ In. 413.00
Ansonia, Shelf, Brass, Copper, 1-Day Lever Movement, c.1874, 12 ¼ In. 303.00
Ansonia, Shelf, Cast Iron, Black Enamel Case, Gray Marbleized Columns, 12 In. 177.00
Ansonia, Shelf, Crystal Regulator, Gong Strike, Faux Mercury Pendulum, c.1900, 9 In. 308.00
Ansonia, Shelf, Dakota, Porcelain, White, Green, Flowers, c.1901, 12 In. 138.00
Ansonia, Shelf, Enamel, Gilt, Late 19th Century, 12 In.. .... 411.00
Ansonia, Shelf, Green Onyx Top & Bottom, Glazed Door & Panels, 11 ¾ x 7 ¾ In. 384.00
Ansonia, Shelf, Iron Case, Ormolu Mounts & Feet, 10 ¼ In. 99.00
Ansonia, Shelf, King, Walnut, 8-Day, c.1901, 24 In.. .... 303.00
Ansonia, Shelf, La Orne, Porcelain, White, Blue, c.1901, 11 ½ In. 220.00
Ansonia, Shelf, Mahogany, Steeple, Alarm, c.1850, 20 In. 319.00
Ansonia, Shelf, Oak, c.1880, 17 ½ x 12 ¾ x 5 ½ In. 94.00
Ansonia, Shelf, Porcelain, 4 Different Scenes, 2 Butterflies On Top, c.1905, 12 ½ In. 275.00
Ansonia, Shelf, Porcelain, Lavender Case, Flowers, 8-Day, Gong Strike, c.1901, 11 ¼ In. 550.00
Ansonia, Shelf, Porcelain, Pink, Violet Flowers, 8-Day, Gong Strike, c.1895, 11 ¼ In.. .... 523.00
Ansonia, Shelf, Porcelain, Wabash, Gold Highlights, Red, Flowers, c.1904, 12 ½ In.. .... 275.00
Ansonia, Shelf, Regent, Cast Metal, Open Escapement, Gong Strike, c.1904, 23 In. 1595.00
Ansonia, Shelf, Rosewood Veneer, Stenciled Design, 8-Day, c.1850, 15 ½ In.. .... 275.00
Ansonia, Shelf, Walnut, Silvered Glass Mirrored Pendulum, c.1878, 22 ¾ In.. .... 303.00
Ansonia, Shelf, Walnut, Woman's Head Medallion, Painted Glass, 21 In. .... *illus* 265.00
Ansonia, Shelf, White Onyx, Brass Dial, Marble, 8-Day, c.1895, 12 In. 110.00
Ansonia, Shelf, Wyoming, Cobalt Blue, Movement Is Signed, c.1904, 11 ¾ In. 633.00
Ansonia, Swinging Arm, Maiden, Raised Arm, Socle Base, c.1860, 19 In. 1287.00
Ansonia, Wall, Queen Elizabeth, Oak Case, 8-Day, c.1885, 37 In. 770.00
Ansonia, Wall, Walnut, 8-Day, Cup Hook At Top, c.1906, 32 In. 248.00
Art Deco, Black Wood Spikes, Brass Dial, Colored Hands, George Nelson, 18 ½ In.. .... 360.00
Art Deco, Box, Beveled Glass Panel, 8-Day, Gong Strike, Germany, c.1930, 30 In. 220.00
Art Deco, Box, Westminster Chime, Octagonal, Silvered Dial, Walnut, France, 24 In.. .... 165.00
Art Deco, Oak, Leaded Glass, Westminster, Box, Germany, c.1925, 26 In.. .... 286.00
Art Deco, Oak, Westminster Chime, 8-Day, Spring Driven, Round Top, Germany, c.1920, 28 In. 220.00
Art Deco, World Time, Terrestrial Globe, 30-Hour, Germany, c.1900, 16 ½ In.. .... 1650.00
Art Nouveau, French Style, Walnut Case, Spring Movement, Germany, c.1930, 21 In. 66.00
Atkins, Shelf, Rosewood Veneer, London, 1870, 16 ¾ In. 413.00

Clock, Adams, E.W., William Tell, Mahogany, 8-Day, Brass, c.1830, 36 x 20 In.
$1100.00

Clock, Advertising, Diamond Black Leather Oil, Baird, 31 x 18 ½ In.
$1200.00

Clock, Advertising, Hires Root Beer, Light-Up, Pam, 1950s, 15 In.
$518.00

Clock, Advertising, Ingraham Shop, Oak, Regulator, 8-Day, c.1900, 37 x 16 In.
$200.00

TIP
Cuckoo clocks sometimes need minor first aid or major repair. First try home remedies. If the clock stops, it may be because it is not level. Try shifting the clock a bit. The clock will not run correctly in a draft. Hang the clock so it is flat against the wall. Have the clock oiled every two years and cleaned every four years. Major repairs should be done by a professional.

Austrian, Annular, Cobalt Blue Guilloche Enamel, Over Silver, 7 Cameos, c.1890, 5 In. 4675.00
Bailey, Putnam, Shelf, 30-Hour, Time & Strike, Column & Splat, Goshen, Conn., 34 In. 110.00
Banjo, Federal, Mahogany, Banded Veneer, 8-Day Brass Movement, c.1820, 34 In.. .... 1058.00
Banjo, Federal, Mahogany, Reverse Painted, Brass, Mass., c.1815, 33 In. .... *illus* 4600.00
Banjo, Horace Tifft, Mahogany, 8-Day, Beveled Edge, Weight, c.1840, 33 In. 2750.00
Banjo, Howard, E. & Co., No. 5, Weight Driven, 8-Day, c.1900, 29 In. 6600.00
Banjo, Howard, E. & Co., No. 95, Gold Front, 8-Day, Weight, c.1930, 42 ½ In. 3190.00
Banjo, Howard, No. 1, Cherry, 8-Day, Weight Driven, Regulator Size, c.1900, 50 In. 11100.00
Banjo, Ingraham, Nile, Mahogany, 8-Day, Time & Strike, c.1915, 39 In. 330.00
Banjo, Lyre, 8-Day, Weight Driven, Gilded, Boston, c.1830, 40 In.. .... 3630.00
Banjo, Lyre, Curtis & Dunning, Finial, 37 In.. .... 6500.00
Banjo, Lyre, L. Curtis, 70 Below Howard Signature, 41 In. 2420.00
Banjo, Lyre, Mahogany, Weight Driven, Time Only, Brass Movement, 1900s, 44 x 12 In. 3500.00
Banjo, Mahogany, Paddle Wheeler, Pendulum, c.1825, 32 In. 1880.00
Banjo, Mahogany, Pine, Reverse Painted, Boats, Urn & Flowers, Acorn Finial, 41 x 11 In..... 920.00
Banjo, Mahogany, Pine, Reverse Painted, Ladies In Garden, New England, 31 x 10 In. 863.00
Banjo, Waltham Watch Co., Willard Type, Mahogany Case, Eagle Finial, c.1920, 42 In.. ..... 1485.00
Banjo, Willard, Aaron Jr., Reverse Glass Panel, Gilt Case, Boston, 39 In. 1783.00
Banjo, Willard, Aaron Jr., Mahogany, Iron Dial, 8-Day Brass Timepiece, c.1825, 33 In. 2820.00
Banjo, Willard Type, Mahogany, Battle Of Lake Champlain, Brass Eagle Finial, 23 x 10 In.... 575.00
Becker, Gustav, Shelf, Mahogany, c.1920, 10 x 6 ½ x 19 ¼ In.. .... 146.00
Becker, Gustav, Shelf, Westminster Chime, 8-Day, Germany, c.1911, 12 ¼ In. 220.00
Becker, Gustav, Vienna Regulator, 2-Weight, Gong Strike, Walnut, Carved, c.1870, 49 In. 715.00
Becker, Gustav, Vienna Regulator, 2-Weight, Serial No. 583387, c.1885, 50 In. 660.00
Becker, Gustav, Wall, 8-Day, Oak, Walnut, Serial No. 651092, c.1887, 22 In. 770.00
Becker, Gustav, Art Deco, Grand Sonnerie, 3-Weight, Walnut Case, c.1910, 33 ½ In.. .... 990.00
Benson, J.W. Mahogany, Bezel, England, c.1910, 14 ½ In.. .... 770.00
Birge & Fuller, Steeple On Wheel, Candle Finials, Mahogany Veneer, c.1845, 21 ¾ In.. ...... 5775.00
Birge & Fuller, Wall, Column & Cornice, Puff N Betsy Label, 8-Day, c.1845, 32 ½ In. 1100.00
Boardman, Chauncey, Steeple, Mahogany, Windsor Castle, Double Fusee, 20 In. ..... *illus* 265.00
Boston Clock Co., Shelf, Crystal Regulator, 8-Day, Tandem Wind Lever, c.1890, 9 ¾ In. 523.00
Bottermann, Shelf, Biedermeier, Fruitwood, Onyx, Gilt Metal, Enamel Dial, 22 ¼ In.. .... 2585.00
Boudoir, Bronze, Marble, Fired Enamel Dial, Swiss, c.1900, 7 In. 1815.00
Bracket, Bronze, Louis XVI, 19th Century, 17 ½ x 11 In.. .... 877.00
Bracket, Cast Brass Spandrels, Mahogany Case, Silvered Dial, England, c.1960, 10 ½ In. 330.00
Bracket, Louis XV, Boulle, France, 19th Century, c.1850, 59 x 21 In. 7150.00
Bracket, Mahogany, Brass Mounted, 4-Gong Strike, Domed Top, 25 x 16 ½ x 12 ½ In.. ...... 2938.00
Bracket, Regency, Mahogany, 2 Fusee, Burled Panel, c.1840, 21 ½ In.. .... 1320.00
Bracket, Westminster Chime, Wurttemburg, Germany, c.1900, 15 ¾ In. 358.00
Brass, Alarm, Swinging Bail Handle, Beveled Panels, c.1900, 4 x 2 x 1 ¾ In.. .... 119.00
Brass, Copper Steeple, Monk Rings Bell, Stained Glass Windows, 17 In. 826.00
Brass, Faux Tortoise, 8 In. 70.00
Brass, Gilded, Annular, Open Ended Globe, c.1890, 9 ¾ In.. .... 605.00
Brewster & Ingrahams, Shelf, Gothic, Mahogany Veneer, 4 Columns, 8-Day, c.1850, 20 In. . 1650.00
Brocat, Shelf, Regulator, Jeweled Escapement, 2-Vial Pendulum, France, c.1900, 15 ½ In. ... 825.00
Brown, J.C., Acorn, Shelf, Rosewood, Painted Dial, 8-Day, Time & Strike, 24 x 14 x 5 In.. *illus* 6900.00
Caldwell, J.E., Folding Travel, Quarter Repeater, Maroon Leather Case, 8-Day, 7 x 8 In.. ..... 121.00
Caldwell & Co., Shelf, Slate, Handles, c.1890, 9 ¾ x 11 In. 263.00
Calendar, Perpetual, Single Dial, Moon Phase, Week, Day, Date, Month, France, c.1885, 17 In. 2640.00
Carr, R., Boudoir, Sterling Silver, Ebony, 3 x 2 In. 70.00
Carriage, Brass, Beveled Convex Glass, 17 Jewel, 8-Day Movement, 4 x 2 ¾ In.. .... 210.00
Carriage, Brass, France, 5 ½ x 3 In. 292.00
Carriage, Brass, Key Wind, Open Escapement, Enameled Face, Figures, Chime, 8 ¼ In.. ..... 1840.00
Carriage, Brass, Oval Top Panel, Drop Handle, France, 5 ¼ x 4 In. 230.00
Carriage, Brass Case, Aviary Theme, Ducks In The Marshes, c.1900, 6 ½ In.. .... 2200.00
Carriage, Brass Case, Beveled Glass, Enameled Roman Dial, 4 In.. .... 200.00
Carriage, Brass Case, Time & Strike, Alarm, 8-Day, Beveled Glass, France, c.1900, 5 ½ In.... 1155.00
Carriage, Brass Corniche Case, Time Strike & Repeater, Porcelain Dial, c.1900, 7 In. 688.00
Carriage, Bronze, Gorge Case, Reeded Columns, Roundels, Women's Busts, Ivorine, 4 ½ In. . 1528.00
Carriage, Sonnerie, Brass Case, Alarm, Gilt Case, Leafy Mask, Handle, c.1900, 6 ¼ In.. ...... 2750.00
Cartier, Art Deco, Quartz, Gilt, Enameled, Bronze, Roman Dial, Calendar, 5 ¾ In. 144.00
Cartier, Desk, Silver, Gold Bezel, Marked, c.1930, 4 ½ In. 4800.00
Chelsea Clock Co., Beechwood, Brass Dial, Hour Glass Finial, c.1900, 12 ½ x 7 x 4 In. 1100.00
Chelsea Clock Co., Boudoir, Gothic, Silvered Dial, No. 530, c.1925, 5 ¼ In. 440.00
Chelsea Clock Co., Desk, 8-Day, Silvered Dial, Serial No. 185503, c.1928, 5 In. 385.00
Chelsea Clock Co., Engine Room, White Painted Dial, Serial No. 846884, c.1984, 7 ½ In. ... 330.00

Chelsea Clock Co., Pendulum No. 1, Golden Oak, 8-Day, Weight Driven, c.1908, 34 In. 1595.00
Chelsea Clock Co., Pilot House, U.S. Navy Dial, Nickel Finish, c.1918, 10 ½ In. 1375.00
Chelsea Clock Co., Shelf, Mahogany, Pillar, House Strike, c.1958, 24 ¾ In. 605.00
Chelsea Clock Co., Terry Model, Pillar & Scroll, c.1949, 24 ¾ In. 550.00
Chelsea Clock Co., Ward Room, Composition Case, Bakelite, c.1954, 7 ½ In.. ..... 385.00
Chipperfield, Steeple, 30-Hour, 13 Stars, Crossed Flags, Eagle, c.1848, 20 In.. ..... 220.00
Coffin Style, Willard, Simon, 8-Day, Weight Driven, Mahogany Case, 34 ¾ x 10 ½ In. 14950.00
Cooper, William, Bracket, Brass Double Fusee Works & Face, Scrollwork, 10 ½ x 7 In.. ..... 6325.00
Cottage, 30-Hour, Walnut Case, Seth Thomas Clock Co., c.1880, 9 ¼ In. 110.00
Desk, Crystal Case, Gilt Bronze Mounts, Scrolling Flowers, Ribbon Above Eagle, 10 ½ In. 708.00
Desk, Double Dials, Raised Bronze Numerals, Swiss, c.1905, 6 In. 688.00
Desk, Enamel Dial, Roman Numerals, Guilloche Blue Enamel Case, 2 ¼ x 1 ½ x 1 In. 1998.00
Desk, Gilt Bronze, Blue & White Jasperware Plaque, Early 20th Century, 10 x 6 In. 6463.00
Doepke, Take A Part, Alarm, Wooden, Square, 7 x 6 In.. ..... 95.00
Elliott, F.W., Wall, Double Dial, Chain Fusee, Mahogany, c.1936, 15 ½ In. 770.00
English, Mahogany, Carved, 8-Day, Fusee, c.1900, 17 ¼ In. 396.00
Figural, Flautist, 2 Flutes At Lips, Gilt Lovebirds, Bell Strike, France, c.1890, 11 In. 1320.00
Figural, Mounted Soldier, Dress Uniform, Bronze, Marble Stand, 30-Hour, France, c.1810 ... 660.00
Figural, Russian Clock Peddler, White Metal, 3 Clocks, Painted, Germany, c.1955, 16 In. 385.00
Forestville Mfg., Wall, Column & Cornice, Mahogany, 8-Day, c.1845, 31 In. 358.00
French, Alabaster, Carved, Empire Style, 8-Day, Silk Thread Suspension, c.1840, 14 ½ In.. ..... 330.00
French, Atlas Holding Marble Globe On Shoulders, Bronze, Marble, France, c.1890, 13 In.... 770.00
French, Boulle, Battery, Glass Dome, c.1921, 14 ½ In.. ..... 523.00
French, Cartel, Louis XVI, Gilt Bronze, 8-Day, Sunburst Pendulum, c.1895, 13 ½ In. 660.00
French, Empire, Ebonized, Temple Shape, Griffins, Birds, Snakes, Ball Feet, 19 ¾ In. 588.00
French, Figural, Cherub With Drum & Drum Stick, Marble, Bronze, c.1890, 11 ½ In. 1210.00
French, Figural, Huntress, Arrow, Dead Fowl, Marble, Ormolu, Bell Strike, c.1890, 14 In. 1760.00
French, Globe, Glass Case, Bell Strike, c.1920, 15 ½ In.. ..... 2090.00
French, Louis Philippe, Troubadour, Gilt, Patinated Bronze, c.1845, 18 ¾ x 8 ¾ In. 3750.00
French, Shelf, Architectural, White, Mottled Onyx, Bronze, Gong Strike, c.1900, 11 ¼ In. 110.00
French, Spherical Case, Patinated Bronze, Yellow Marble, 20th Century, 14 x 12 In. 5288.00
French, Swinging Doll, White Alabaster, Original Dome & Base, c.1890, 11 In. 935.00
Furtwangler, Shelf, 30-Hour, Alarm, Painted Dial, c.1920, 13 ½ In. 99.00
Gardener's, Watering, Oak, 4 Faces, c.1900, 25 x 74 In. ..... *illus* 3000.00
Garniture Set, Art Deco, Granite, Rose Striated Marble, White Dial, Ucra, 16 x 4 ½ In. 230.00
Garniture Set, Cavalier, 5-Light Candelabra, Bronze, Black Marble, France, c.1900, 20 In. .. 354.00
German, Box, Edwardian, Oak, Beveled Glass, c.1905, 29 ½ In. 165.00
German, Box, Rod Strike, Walnut Veneer, Leaded Frame, Beveled Glass, c.1900, 34 In. 523.00
German, Dial, Alarm, Wooden Plates, Metal Wheels, Scene In Arch, c.1880, 13 In. 495.00
Gilbert, Banjo, Mahogany, Eagle Finial, Colonial Scene, 8-Day, 30 In.. ..... 44.00
Gilbert, Calendar, Oak, 8-Sided, 8-Day, 27 ¼ In. 165.00
Gilbert, Shelf, Walnut, Gingerbread, 19th Century 28.00
Gilbert, William L., Cottage, Chromo, Broken Arch Scroll Top, 30-Hour, c.1890, 14 ½ In. 55.00
Gilbert, William L., Shelf, Porcelain, Painted, c.1898, 11 In. 39.00
Gilbert Clock Co., Shelf, Curfew, Bell Strike, Black Enameled Wood, c.1915, 17 ½ In. 330.00
Gilbert Clock Co., Shelf, Enameled Wood, c.1914, 17 ¾ In. 275.00
Gilbert Clock Co., Shelf, Pressed Oak, Geranium, c.1910, 24 In. 165.00
Gilbert, W.L., Regulator, Oak, Standard Time, 8-Sided, 28 In.. ..... 110.00
Gilbert, W.L., Regulator No. 2, Rosewood, 8-Day, Weight Driven, c.1875, 33 ½ In.. ..... 2530.00
Goodrich, Steeple, Mahogany, 8-Day, Gong Strike, c.1853, 19 ½ In.. ..... 275.00
Guilment, Shelf, Animated, Lighthouse, Industrial Series, Paris, Brickwork, c.1880, 24 In... 8800.00
Haddon, Animated, No. 30, Home Sweet Home 200.00
Hamburg American Clock Co., School, Walnut Veneer, c.1900, 23 ¾ In. 220.00
Hart & Son, Bracket, 2 Shelf, Regency, 2-Fusee, Bell Strike, Signed, c.1840, 17 ½ In.. ..... 1650.00
Herman Clock Co., Shelf, Battery Operated, Mahogany, Silvered Dial, c.1925, 13 ½ In. 275.00
Hoadley, Silas, Shelf, Ogee Mahogany Veneer Case, Wood Dial, Painted, c.1845, 26 x 16 In. .. 288.00
Howard, E., Regulator, Mahogany, Reverse Painted, Door, Brass Works, Pendulum 2300.00
Howard, E. & Co., No. 123A Gallery, Oak Case, Hinged Bezel, c.1920, 14 In. 1045.00
Howard, E. & Co., Wall, Marble Dial, No. 20, Weight Driven, 8-Day, c.1930, 28 In. 1320.00
Howard, E. & Co., Wall, Regulator No. 10, Figure 8, Walnut, c.1980, 34 In. 1980.00
Howard & Davis, Banjo, Black Gilt Throat, Table Glass, 19th Century, 32 In. 1610.00
Ingraham, Banjo, Nyanza, Mahogany Stained Case, c.1915, 39 In.. ..... 275.00
Ingraham, Banjo, Walnut Color, Wood Side Arms, 8-Day, 35 x 10 x 4 In. ..... *illus* 230.00
Ingraham, E., Oak, 8-Day, Gold Stenciled, Front Glass Door, 1905, 23 In.. ..... 263.00
Ingraham, E., Wall, 8-Day, Metal Dial, Roman Numerals, c.1880, 21 ½ x 13 In. 146.00
Ingraham, E. & Co., Commemorative, Peace, Spanish-American War, 8-Day, 1899, 23 In.... 440.00

Windup Clocks
Twentieth-century windup clocks were made in Art Deco and later styles. Marble, onyx, chrome, brass, copper, Bakelite, Formica, wood, celluloid, and glass were used for clock cases for living room and bedroom clocks. Eight-day windups were sometimes made in unusual modern shapes. Clocks were shaped like airplanes or statues with an added clock face. Clocks with neon trim were fashionable. A windup alarm clock with a cartoon character like Mickey Mouse or Popeye moving its arms to point to the time was made for children's bedrooms.

Clock, Advertising, Mr. Cola, Aristocrat Of Colas, Glass Dome, c.1950, 10 In.
$115.00

Clock, Advertising, Red Goose Shoes, Light-Up, Pam Clock Co., 15 In.
$550.00

Clock, Advertising, Thompson's Wild Cherry Bitters, Ansonia, c.1880, 18 x 16 In. $735.00

Clock, Ansonia, Gloria, Ball Swings, Spelter, Brass Top, Bottom Ball, 8-Day, 29 In. $4025.00

Clock, Ansonia, Shelf, Walnut, Woman's Head Medallion, Painted Glass, 21 In. $265.00

Ingraham, E. & Co., Dew Drop, Calendar, 8-Day, Rosewood Case, c.1909, 23 ½ In. 204.00
Ingraham, E. & Co., Landau, Oak, 8-Day, c.1907, 38 ¼ In. 281.00
Ingraham, E. & Co., Shelf, 8-Day, Time & Strike, Eglomise Panel, c.1880, 21 ½ x 13 In. 146.00
Ingraham, E. & Co., Shelf, Phoenix, 8-Day, Time Strike, Walnut Case, c.1881, 21 In. 132.00
Ingraham, E. & Co., Shelf, Rebus, 8-Day Time & Strike, Hardwood Case, c.1914, 18 In. 77.00
Ingraham, Regulator, c.1900, 36 x 15 In. 263.00
Ingraham, Shelf, Black, Marbleized, Lion's Head, Rings, Metal Feet, 8-Day, 11 In. 44.00
Ingraham, Shelf, Black, Wood Case, Flat Top, 8-Day, 10 In. 22.00
Ingraham, Shelf, Cabinet, Maple, Ebony Accents, c.1889, 17 ½ In. 220.00
Ingraham, Shelf, Pressed Oak, 8-Day, Alarm, c.1891, 23 In. 110.00
Ingraham, Shelf, Rosewood Bull's-Eye, 8-Day, Time & Strike, c.1868 100.00
Ingraham & Co., Kitchen, Walnut, 8-Day, Alligatored Finish, c.1896, 21 ½ In. 165.00
Ingraham & Co., Steeple, Mahogany & Mahogany Veneer, 4 Column, c.1938, 20 In. 550.00
Ithaca Calendar Clock Co., Shelf, Library, No. 8, Double Dial, Walnut, c.1875, 25 In. 715.00
Ithaca Calendar Clock Co., Shelf, Walnut, 8-Day, Time & Strike, 20 x 11 x 6 In. *illus* 6038.00
Jaeger LeCoultre, Atmos, Presentation, Brass, 9 x 8 In. 585.00
Japy Freres, Architectural, Bronze Dore Case, Painted, France, c.1890, 20 In. 2200.00
Japy Freres, Shelf, Bronze, Enamel, c.1900, 20 x 9 x 7 In. 2574.00
Jerome & Co., Ignatz, Flying Pendulum, Oak Case, Paper Dial, c.1885, 11 In. 3080.00
Jerome & Co., Shelf, 2-Weight, 8-Day, Gong Strike, Double Door, Mahogany, c.1870, 30 In. 385.00
Jerome & Co., Shelf, Mahogany, Triple Decker, c.1840 234.00
Junghans, Chimney, Brass Platinum Mechanism, Bell Strike Walnut Case, c.1930 517.00
Junghans, Elephant, Swing Arm, Spelter, 8-Day, Germany, 11 x 7 In. *illus* 748.00
Junghans, Minstrel, Mahogany, Tin, c.1920, 9 In. 292.00
Junghans, Mystery, Swinging Arm, Spelter Statue, Gilt Bronze, 8-Day, c.1910, 15 ¼ In. 1100.00
Junghans, Wall, Gothic, Walnut Veneer, Germany, c.1900, 37 ¼ In. 193.00
Junghans, Wall, Walnut Veneer, Silvered Dial, Beveled Glass, c.1925, 30 In. 143.00
Junghans, Wall Regulator, Keyhole, Eagle, Walnut Veneer, Germany, c.1915, 44 ¼ In. 330.00
Junghans, World Time, Windmill Shape, 8 Subsidiary Dials, c.1900, 22 ½ In. 798.00
Karl Griesbaum Co., Drunk At Lamp Post, Mechanical, Whistling, Key, c.1950, 18 In. 688.00
Kieninger & Obergfell, Dome, Louvre, 400-Day, Germany, c.1950, 16 ½ In. 138.00
Kienzle, World Time, Lever Movement, 8-Day, Germany, c.1859, 5 In. 99.00
Kitchen, Oak, Carved Leaves, 23 x 13 In. 65.00
Kroeber, Cast Iron, 8-Day, Time & Strike, c.1880, 13 x 16 ½ In. *illus* 250.00
Kroeber, F., Shelf, Black Iron, Gold Incised Lines, c.1882, 11 ½ In. 105.00
Kroeber, F., Shelf, Red Paint, Iron, Ormolu Design & Feet, 8-Day, 11 ¼ In. 77.00
Kroeber, Shelf, 8-Day, Walnut, Indicator Pendulum, c.1884, 20 In. 468.00
Kroeber, Shelf, Walnut Case, Burl Panels, 8-Day, Time & Strike, Mirror Side, c.1888, 24 In. 1100.00
L.E. Whiting, Timby Solar, Terrestrial Globe, Saratoga Springs, c.1864, 27 In. 8525.00
Lantern, Wall, Brass Panels, Bell, Wooden Mounting Block, England, 14 In. 1972.00
Lantern, Wall, Mahogany, Porcelain Dial, 30-Day, Weight Driven, c.1830 21275.00
LeCoultre, Atmos, Perpetual Motion, Square Glass Case, Round Face, 9 x 8 In. 580.00
Leroy & Cie., Boudoir, Rosewood Inlay, Portable, 8-Day, Bell Strike, c.1840, 10 ¼ In. 578.00
Liberty & Co., Pewter, Enameled Face, Stamped, 4 ¾ x 3 ¼ x 2 ½ In. 4200.00
Lux, Cottage, Red Bird, Yellow, Green Trim, Composition, Pendulum, 8 In. *illus* 72.00
Lux, Golfers, Green, Tin Lithograph, 7 ⅛ In. *illus* 575.00
Lux, Shmoo, Inserts, Display Card, Plastic, Box, 10 ¼ In. *illus* 175.00
Manross, Elisha, Shelf, Decal Glass, Connecticut State House, c.1845, 19 ¾ In. 231.00
Mantel, Stand, Rococo Style, Green, Scrolls, Painted Flowers, Jacob Petit, 17 x 11 In. 2040.00
Mayer, Animated, 3 Dogs In Basket, Pot Metal Jesters, Germany, c.1875, 7 In. 2035.00
Morez, Wall, Picture Frame, Mother-Of-Pearl, Iron Frame, France, c.1870, 25 In. 193.00
Mueller & Co., Striking, Shelf, 400-Day, Muhlheim, Germany, c.1900, 7 In. 880.00
Muller & Co., Bracket, 3 Train, Chiming, Westminster, Germany, c.1890, 34 ¼ In. 7975.00
Mystery, Flower Girl, Patinated Spelter, Red Marble Base, France, c.1890, 35 In. 3520.00
Mystery, Swinging Youths, c.1885, 33 In. 25300.00
Nelson, George, Ball, No. 4755, 1947, 13 In. 540.00
New Haven, Cottage, Molded Base, Gilt Trim, c.1880, 15 ½ In. 66.00
New Haven, Gothic, Visible Pendulum, Steeple, 30-Hour, Alarm, c.1886, 15 ½ In. 110.00
New Haven, Iron, Brass Women's Heads, Enamel, 10 ½ In. *illus* 179.00
New Haven, Regulator, No. 1, Round, Walnut, Walnut Veneer, c.1880, 32 In. 330.00
New Haven, School, 8-Day, Rosewood Veneer, c.1875, 24 In. 138.00
New Haven, Shelf, Florence, 8-Day, Time & Gong Strike, c.1890, 10 In. 44.00
New Haven, Shelf, French Cathedral Gong Strike, 8-Day, Cabinet No. 10, 16 In. 358.00
New Haven, Shelf, Mahogany Case, 19 x 18 ½ In. 193.00
New Haven, Shelf, Malachite Finish, Enameled Iron, c.1900, 15 In. 176.00
New Haven, Shelf, Oak, Scrolling, Carved Crest, Stepped Base, 22 x 14 In. 110.00

New Haven, Shelf, Porcelain, Cream, Flowers, 8-Day, c.1900, 11 ¼ In. 149.00
New Haven, Shelf, Quincy, Tambour, Mahogany, Porcelain Dial, c.1913, 5 ½ In. 55.00
New Haven, Shelf, Thurston, Crystal, Regulator, Gong Strike, Mahogany, c.1917, 11 ¼ In. 413.00
New Haven, Shelf, Walnut, 8-Day, Strike, Alarm, c.1886, 21 In. 187.00
New Haven, Theone, Inlaid Mahogany, Porcelain Dial, c.1917, 11 ¼ In. 138.00
New Haven, Wall, Regulator, Office No. 1, Weight, Mahogany, Black Flocked, c.1885, 42 In. 1320.00
Oswald, Boston Terrier, Rotating Eyes Show Time, Wood Case, c.1928, 6 In. 633.00
Oswald, Sheik, Rotating Eyes Show Time, 30-Hour Movement, Osuhr, c.1928, 8 In. 605.00
Oswald, Wise Old Owl, Rotating Eyes Show Time, Composition, c.1930, 7 ¼ In. 495.00
Oswald, Yorkshire Terrier, Rotating Eyes Show Time, Composition, c.1935, 6 In. 605.00
Peerless, Shelf, Westminster Chime, Satin Wood, Barrel Movement, c.1900, 15 In. 688.00
Pequegnat Clock Co., Shelf, Oak, 25 ½ x 16 x 7 ½ In. 1170.00
Plato, Brass, Glass, Celluloid Tab Numbers, 6 In. .... *illus* 153.00
Pons, Boudoir, Enameled, Ormolu, Dragon Tongue Mask, Footed, c.1900, 6 ½ In. 770.00
Pons, Shelf, Figural, 2 Boys Chasing A Bird, Marble, Bronze, c.1830, 17 ¾ In. 2310.00
Postal, Mahogany Case, Fusee, England, c.1920, 14 ½ In. 220.00
Raingo Fres A Paris, Base, Flowers, Gilt, Key Wind, Marked, 17 In. 1080.00
Regulator, 4 Glass Sides, Crystal, Brass Case, 8-Day, Gong Strike, France, c.1900, 10 In. 385.00
Regulator, Brass & Glass, Ormolu Dial Overlay, Beveled Glass, France, c.1900, 11 ¼ In. 633.00
Regulator, Crystal, Brass Case, Beveled Glass, Porcelain Dial, 20th Century, 10 In. 143.00
Regulator, Vienna, 1-Weight, Serpentine Case, c.1890, 42 In. 1210.00
Regulator, Vienna, 2-Weight, Rosewood, Silver Inlay, 8-Day, c.1850, 40 In. 3300.00
Regulator, Vienna, 2-Weight, Walnut, Built In Top, Austrian, c.1890, 48 In. 468.00
Regulator, Vienna, 3-Weight, Grand Sonnerie, Walnut, Austrian, c.1875, 56 In. 2750.00
Regulator, Vienna, Biedermeier Case, Silver & Pewter Inlay, 8-Day, c.1850, 38 In. 3190.00
Regulator, Vienna, Wood, Ebonized Borders, Brass Works, Enameled Face, 18 ½ In. 259.00
Regulator, Walnut & Veneers, Keyhole Door, Spring, Germany, c.1905, 44 In. 385.00
Regulator, Walnut Case, Swiss Pinwheel Movement, American Jeweler's, c.1880, 95 In. 1815.00
Regulator, Weight Driven, Gustav Becker, 8 Day Time, Brass Movement, 1800s, 44 x 14 In. 700.00
Regulator, Spring, Ornate Door, Striking Movement, 2 Gongs, Germany, c.1890, 38 In. 330.00
Reisewecker, Model No. 100, Travel Alarm, Lenzkirch, Germany, c.1900, 3 In. 55.00
Rimbault, Stephen, Bracket, George III, Gilt Metal, Mahogany, c.1790, 21 x 13 In. 15000.00
Roy, M.C., Shelf, Vase, Figures, Limoges, Key, Signed, c.1880, 10 x 9 x 4 In. .... *illus* 480.00
Russell, H., Skeleton Timepiece, Fusee, Architectural Frame, England, c.1850, 11 In. 1375.00
S.B. Terry, Cottage, 30-Hour, Printed Paper Veneer, Brass Hands, c.1852, 10 ¼ In. 990.00
School, Oak, c.1910, 33 x 17 In. 82.00
Selsi, Carriage, Plain Case, Beveled Glass Panels, Handle, Repeater, Enamel Dial, 6 In. 236.00
Serin, Edouard, World Time, Terrestrial Globe, 8-Day, Bell Strike, Germany, c.1885, 20 In. 6325.00
Sessions, Aztec, Mission Style, Oak Case, c.1910, 19 In. 32.00
Sessions, Bahama, Mission Style, Oak Case, 8-Day, c.1910 .... 77.00
Sessions, Kitchen, Gingerbread, Oak, 8-Day, 23 In. .... 55.00 to 66.00
Sessions, Panelescent, Red, Trapezoid Shape, Model 34606, c.1960. .... 30.00
Sessions, Ramona, Mission Style, 8-Day, Time & Strike, c.1908, 31 In. 165.00
Sessions, Seneca, Mission Style, 8-Day, Cherry Case, c.1912, 24 In. 22.00
Seth Thomas, Art Deco, Alarm, Wood Case, Rounded Face, Brass Band, 3 ¼ In. 55.00
Seth Thomas, Banjo, Mahogany, c.1970, 28 x 9 ½ In. 47.00
Seth Thomas, Bracket, 8-Day, Flowers On Glass Panels, 2 Key Winds, 17 x 11 In. 234.00
Seth Thomas, Candlestick, Dome, Wood Base, c.1860, 11 ¼ x 8 ¼ In. 499.00
Seth Thomas, Column, Rosewood Case, 2-Weight, 8-Day, c.1875, 25 In. 248.00
Seth Thomas, Octagon Top E, Cottage, 30-Hour, Time Alarm, Mahogany, c.1880, 9 In. 143.00
Seth Thomas, Office Calendar No. 13, Oak, 8-Day, Weight Driven, c.1901, 49 In. 17600.00
Seth Thomas, Parlor Calendar No. 3, Rosewood, Double Dial, 8-Day, c.1875, 26 ¾ In. 1650.00
Seth Thomas, Pillar & Scroll, Mahogany, Masonic Seeing Eye, Moon, Star, 8-Day, 31 In. 1870.00
Seth Thomas, Regulator, Brass, 8-Day, Time & Strike, c.1910, 10 x 6 In. .... *illus* 300.00
Seth Thomas, Regulator No. 2, Mahogany, Painted Dial, c.1890, 36 In. 990.00
Seth Thomas, Regulator No. 20, Mahogany, Single Weight, c.1909, 62 In. 6710.00
Seth Thomas, Shelf, 8-Day, Walnut Veneer, Gong Strike, c.1880, 16 In. 385.00
Seth Thomas, Shelf, 30-Hour, Half Column 60.00
Seth Thomas, Shelf, Arch Top, Burled Walnut Veneer, Alarm, c.1880, 16 In. 468.00
Seth Thomas, Shelf, Arch Top, Rosewood Veneer, 8-Day, c.1880, 16 In. 154.00
Seth Thomas, Shelf, Beulah, Adamantine, 8-Day, Time & Strike, c.1905, 10 ½ In. 220.00
Seth Thomas, Shelf, Chime No. 72, Mahogany, Silvered Dial, c.1920, 14 ¾ In. 303.00
Seth Thomas, Shelf, Empire, Crystal Regulator, Cathedral Gong, c.1911, 10 ¾ In. 176.00
Seth Thomas, Shelf, Eton, Adamantine Mahogany. 395.00
Seth Thomas, Shelf, Figural, Children Playing, Cast Metal Case, No. 8064, c.1875, 19 In. 440.00
Seth Thomas, Shelf, Garfield, 2-Weight, 8-Day, Gong Strike, Walnut, c.1883, 29 In. 770.00

Clock, Banjo, Federal, Mahogany, Reverse Painted, Brass, Mass., c.1815, 33 In.
$4600.00

Clock, Boardman, Chauncey, Steeple, Mahogany, Windsor Castle, Double Fusee, 20 In.
$265.00

Clock, Brown, J.C., Acorn, Shelf, Rosewood, Painted Dial, 8-Day, Time & Strike, 24 x 14 x 5 In.
$6900.00

Clock, Gardeners, Watering, Oak, 4 Faces, c.1900, 25 x 74 In.
$3000.00

Clock, Ingraham, Banjo, Walnut Color, Wood Side Arms, 8-Day, 35 x 10 x 4 In.
$230.00

Clock, Ithaca Calendar Clock Co., Shelf, Walnut, 8-Day, Time & Strike, 20 x 11 x 6 In.
$6038.00

Seth Thomas, Shelf, Lincoln, Walnut, 2-Weight, 8-Day, Nickeled Pendulum, c.1896, 27 In. . . 2420.00
Seth Thomas, Shelf, Mahogany, 13½ x 11 x 7 In. . . . 322.00
Seth Thomas, Shelf, Mahogany, Pillar & Scroll, 30-Hour, 31 In. . . . 1875.00
Seth Thomas, Shelf, Mahogany, Pillar & Scroll, c.1830 . . . 2357.00
Seth Thomas, Shelf, Mahogany, Sonora Chime, c.1900, 14 x 9¾ x 7½ In. . . . 117.00
Seth Thomas, Shelf, Mahogany, Strike Pillar & Scroll, Painted Dial, c.1950, 20 In. . . . 358.00
Seth Thomas, Shelf, Mahogany, Westminster Chime, c.1973, 14¼ In. . . . 77.00
Seth Thomas, Shelf, Metal, Beveled Glass, 15¾ x 8 x 6 In. . . . 292.00
Seth Thomas, Shelf, Modena, 8-Day, Time & Strike, Inlaid Mahogany, c.1913, 12 In. . . . 297.00
Seth Thomas, Shelf, New Orleans, Mahogany, Kroeber Gong Stand, c.1880, 16½ In. . . . 121.00
Seth Thomas, Shelf, Pillar & Scroll, Mahogany, Wood Gears, Eli Terry, 31 x 17½ In. . . . 1610.00
Seth Thomas, Shelf, Pillar & Scroll, Off-Center, 30-Hour,Wooden Works, c.1820, 32 In. . . . 3410.00
Seth Thomas, Shelf, Sonora Chime, Mahogany, Brass, c.1890, 13½ x 6½ x 15 In. . . . 300.00
Seth Thomas, Shelf, Triple Tier, Reverse Painted, 8-Day, Time & Strike, 32 x 16 x 5 In. . *illus* 920.00
Seth Thomas, Shelf, Tudor No. 1, Walnut, 8-Day, Time & Strike, c.1879, 15 In. . . . 66.00
Seth Thomas, Shelf, Walnut, Quarter Strike, 2 Bells, 8-Day, c.1888, 23 In. . . . 1595.00
Seth Thomas, Sonora, Chime Clock No. 14, 8-Day, Quarter Chime, c.1921, 14 In. . . . 413.00
Seth Thomas, Sunflower, 3-Petal Base, Cast Iron, 15½ In. . . . *illus* 720.00
Seth Thomas, Wall, Nickel Plated, Banner Lever, c.1879, 32 In. . . . 193.00
Seth Thomas, Wall, Queen Anne, Walnut, 8-Day, Time & Strike, c.1883, 36 In. . . . 2400.00
Seth Thomas, Wall, Regulator No. 1, Rosewood, Front Pendulum, c.1875, 34 In. . . . 5720.00
Seth Thomas, Wall, Regulator No. 2, Single Weight, Oak, 8-Day, c.1900, 36 In. . . . 2090.00
Seth Thomas, Wall, Rosewood Veneer, 8-Day, Gong Strike, c.1898, 32 In. . . . 275.00
Seth Thomas, Wall, Umbria, 15-Day, Oak, c.1890, 39 In. . . . 1650.00
Seth Thomas, Walnut, 8-Day, Ogee Bracket, 17 x 11 In. . . . 234.00
Shelf, Aesthetic Revival, Faience, ¾ Balustered Gallery, Flowering Branches, 1800s, 12¾ In. . 499.00
Shelf, Allegorical, Shepherd & Shepherdess, Brass Plated, Footed, Italy, 1900s, 17 x 14 In. . . . 176.00
Shelf, Annular Dial, Winged Cherubs, Glass Cylinder, Bell Strike, France, c.1875, 18 In. . . . 8250.00
Shelf, Art Nouveau, 8-Day, Gong Strike, Cast Brass, 4 Glass, France, c.1890, 14½ In. . . . 1100.00
Shelf, Art Nouveau, Westminster Chime, c.1920, 17½ In. . . . 715.00
Shelf, Arts & Crafts, Brass, Green Enamel, Porcelain Dial, Key Wind, 13 x 9½ x 6 In. . . . 1100.00
Shelf, Balloon, Mahogany, Satinwood, Crossbanded Case, Shell Medallion, Bracket Feet, 11 In. 236.00
Shelf, Black Marble, Bronze, 8-Day, Time & Strike, France, c.1890, 15 In. . . . 165.00
Shelf, Bronze, Marble, 2 Female Figures, Gilt Mounts, 19th Century, 25 In. . . . 956.00
Shelf, Bronze, Ormolu, The Fox & The Spoon, Bell Strike, France, c.1875, 10½ In. . . . 2750.00
Shelf, Bronze, Porcelain, Finial, 6-Footed, 19th Century, 19 x 12 x 6 In. . . . 1755.00
Shelf, Bronze, Shields, Axes, Porcelain Dial, T-Shaped Feet, 17 x 10 x 7¼ In. . . . 764.00
Shelf, Bronze, Sienna Marble, Diana, Goddess Of Hunt, Dog, Roman Numerals, 25½ In. . . . 1998.00
Shelf, Bronze, Standing Figure Of Ajax Holding Sword, Gilt, Marked, c.1835, 23 x 16 In. . . . 1440.00
Shelf, Bronze Case, White Globe, 2 Curly Haired Spaniels, France, c.1890, 11½ In. . . . 660.00
Shelf, Bronze Dore, Black Stevedore, Bail Of Cotton, Ebonized Wood Base, 14½ In. . . . 17550.00
Shelf, Bronzed Metal, Cherub Holding Leaf, Scroll Case, 20th Century, 13 In. . . . 176.00
Shelf, Calendar, Gilt Metal, Urn Form, Rectangular Base, 14½ In. . . . 856.00
Shelf, Capitol Building Shape, White Metal, 10 x 4 In. . . . 146.00
Shelf, Carved Split Columns, Stenciled Decoration, 32 x 16 In. . . . 570.00
Shelf, Cathedral, Brass Case, Gilt Trim, 8-Day, Time & Strike, France, 20 x 7 x 4 In. . . . *illus* 3600.00
Shelf, Cathedral Case, Gilt Bronze, Striking Bell Pendulum, France, 21 x 8 x 5 In. . . . 2820.00
Shelf, Cut Crystal Case, 1-Day, Verge Movement, Frances, c.1825, 9¾ In. . . . 1540.00
Shelf, Cut Glass, c.1900, 8 In. . . . 390.00
Shelf, Ebonized Body, Two Kneeling Wood Male Figures, Gilt Highlights, Key Wind, 19 In. . . . 748.00
Shelf, Edwardian, Mother-Of-Pearl, Inlaid Mahogany, ½ Strike Movement, 12 In. . . . 382.00
Shelf, Empire, Round Dial, Gilt Metal Eagle, Marble Columns, Sphinx, 1800s, 24 x 17 In. . . . 588.00
Shelf, Federal, Mahogany, Pillar & Scroll, Eglomise Panel, Mount Vernon, 31 x 17 In. . . . 2760.00
Shelf, Figural, Lady In Hat Giving Dog A Treat, Marble, Ormolu, France, c.1870, 11¾ In. . . . 1485.00
Shelf, French Black Belgian Marble, c.1880, 8½ x 13½ In. . . . 205.00
Shelf, Georgian, Ebonized, Bell Form Top, Silvered Pressed Tin Dial, 1700s, 13¼ In. . . . 588.00
Shelf, Gilt Bronze, Artist, Palette, Paint, Brushes, Cartouche, Masque, 22 x 19 In. . . . 353.00
Shelf, Gilt Bronze, Footed, France, 19th Century, 14 x 10½ In. . . . 2115.00
Shelf, Gilt Bronze, Green Marble, Circular Case, Early 20th Century, 9 x 17½ x 4 In. . . . 4995.00
Shelf, Gilt Bronze Case, France, 19th Century, 13 In. . . . 750.00
Shelf, Gilt Lacquered, Brass Mounted, Ebonized, Fruitwood, 23 x 12 In. . . . 3120.00
Shelf, Giltwood, c.1925, 11 x 14½ x 4 In. . . . 3900.00
Shelf, Girl With Mandolin, Case Metal Case, Marble Base, c.1895, 18¾ In. . . . 385.00
Shelf, Kitchen, Victorian, Walnut, Alarm, 19th Century, 22 In. . . . 83.00
Shelf, Louis XVI, Lyre, Ormolu, Marble, Silk Thread Pendulum, France, c.1790, 22¼ In. . . . 3575.00
Shelf, Louis XVI, Mahogany, Ormolu, France, c.1880, 16 In. . . . 743.00

Clock, Junghans, Elephant, Swing Arm, Spelter, 8-Day, Germany, 11 x 7 In.
$748.00

Clock, Kroeber, Cast Iron, 8-Day, Time & Strike, c.1880, 13 x 16 ½ In.
$250.00

Clock, Lux, Cottage, Red Bird, Yellow, Green Trim, Composition, Pendulum, 8 In.
$72.00

Clock, Lux, Golfers, Green, Tin Lithograph, 7 ⅛ In.
$575.00

Clock, Lux, Shmoo, Inserts, Display Card, Plastic, Box, 10 ¼ In.
$175.00

Clock, New Haven, Iron, Brass Women's Heads, Enamel, 10 ½ In.
$179.00

Clock, Plato, Brass, Glass, Celluloid Tab Numbers, 6 In.
$153.00

Clock, Roy, M.C., Shelf, Vase, Figures, Limoges, Key, Signed, c.1880, 10 x 9 x 4 In.
$480.00

Clock, Seth Thomas, Regulator, Brass, 8-Day, Time & Strike, c.1910, 10 x 6 In.
$300.00

Clock, Seth Thomas, Shelf, Triple Tier, Reverse Painted, 8-Day, Time & Strike, 32 x 16 x 5 In.
$920.00

Shelf, Louis XVI, Marble, Ormolu, Roman Numerals, 8-Day, Strike Movement, 27 ¼ In. 1880.00
Shelf, Louis XVI Style, Gilt Lacquered Brass, Rose Pompadour, Parcel Gilt, 17 x 9 In. 780.00
Shelf, Magnum, Louis Philippe, Shelf, Gilt, Bronze Mounted, Ebonized, 28 ½ x 14 ½ x 8 In... 1320.00
Shelf, Mahogany, House, Park Scene, Wood Dial, Door Panel, 32 x 17 ½ x 4¾ In. 920.00
Shelf, Mahogany, Pillar & Scroll, 30-Hour, East-West Movement, c.1825, 30 x 13 In......... 15275.00
Shelf, Mahogany, Porcelain Dial, Roman Numerals, Brass Feet, c.1825, 19 ¼ x 11 ½ In. 1292.00
Shelf, Mahogany Veneer, 8-Day, Time & Strike, 2-Weight, Top Trim, c.1830, 33 In.. .... 1980.00
Shelf, Majolica, Green, Embossed Floral Motif, 7 In. 75.00
Shelf, Nautical Theme, Rotating Globe, Barometer, Compass, France, c.1880, 14 In. 2420.00
Shelf, Neoclassical, Bronze, Psyche Opening Box, c.1830, 25 x 12 In. 2400.00
Shelf, Patinated Metal, Classically Draped Figure Of Fame, Late 1800s 390.00
Shelf, Porcelain, Blue, White, Germany, c.1895, 13 ½ In. 1870.00
Shelf, Porcelain, Boy By Water Wheel, Germany, c.1930, 10 x 5 In. 29.00
Shelf, Porcelain, Court Figures, Conforming Base, Mid 19th Century, 16 x 16 x 5 In.. .... 3525.00
Shelf, Porcelain, Painted, Pink & White, 8-Day, Time & Strike, France, c.1900, 13 ½ In. 220.00
Shelf, Porcelain, Scrolling Ormolu, 18th Century Couple, Cherub, Flowers, 15 In.. .... 1208.00
Shelf, Porcelain, Urn Shape, Handles, Gilt Ground, Lavender Band, 15 x 6 x 6 In. 1410.00
Shelf, Red & Black Marble, Porcelain Dial, 8-Day, Time & Strike, c.1885, 12 ½ In. 770.00
Shelf, Rosewood Case, Embossed Bronze Handle, Satin Band, Inlay, 19th Century, 8 In. 472.00
Shelf, Slate Base, Gilt Bronze Bust, Woman, Pendulum, Key Wind, 1800s, 17 In. 403.00
Shelf, Spelter, Onyx, Swordsmen, Enamel Dial, Roman Numerals, Dragons, Dome 561.00
Shelf, Spelter, Winged Man In Chariot, 2 Horses, c.1940, 22 x 14 In. 100.00
Shelf, Spelter & Marble, Man On Horse, Early 20th Century, 19 x 10 In. 351.00
Shelf, Steeple, Eglomise Panel, c.1850, 21 x 10 ½ In.. .... 59.00
Shelf, Steeple, Mahogany, 2 Finials, Short Pendulum, Flowers, Key, 4 x 8 ½ In. 121.00
Shelf, Steeple, Mahogany, Bristol, Conn., c.1840 .... 6435.00
Shelf, Steeple, Mahogany & Rosewood Veneer, Tablet, House Of Theodore Terry, c.1845, 20 In. 468.00
Shelf, Steeple, Mahogany Veneers, Painted Dial, c.1840, 19 ¾ x 11 In.. .... 218.00
Shelf, Swinging Doll, White Marble Case, Gilt Brass Trim, Dome, France, c.1890, 9 ½ In. 1320.00
Shelf, Tortoiseshell, Scroll & Engraved Brass, St. Christopher, Boulle, France 900.00
Shelf, Veined Marble Case, 2 Bacchanalian Boys, Bun Feet, 13 x 15 x 5 ½ In. 413.00
Shelf, Warrior Aiming A Bow & Arrow, Naturalistic Base, Gilt Metal. 531.00
Shelf, Wedgwood, Basalt, Flowers, Scrollwork, 19th Century, 7 x 4 x 2 In. 717.00
Shelf, Westminster Chime, Mahogany, Carved Frieze, c.1900, 17 In. 4070.00
Shelf, William IV, Mahogany, Gadrooned, Flowerhead, 2-Train Movement, c.1835, 17 ½ In... 1058.00
Shelf, Woman Holding Rose, Bronze, 8-Day, Strike Movement, France, c.1830, 18 ½ In. 1880.00
Shelf, Gothic, Spires, Carved, Fretwork, Balance Lever, Travel Case, c.1900, 36 In. 880.00
Shelf, Gravity, 30-Hour Movement, Black Painted Case, England, c.1921, 10 In. 248.00
Sperry & Shaw, Shelf, 2-Weight, Mahogany Veneer, Column & Cornice, c.1848, 30 ½ In..... 578.00
Strongwater, Jay, Elephant, Ishmael, Enameled, Jeweled 644.00
Swiss, Musical, Apostle, Gothic, Church, Gingerbread, Bell Towers, 46 x 26 x 13 In.. .... 4256.00
Tall Case, A. Hopkins, Federal, Poplar, Tombstone Door, Painted Dial, c.1815, 82 x 19 In..... 1610.00
Tall Case, Abraham Schwartz, Chippendale, Walnut, Carved, Pennsylvania, 86 x 12 In. 4640.00
Tall Case, Benjamin Witman, Hepplewhite, Cherry, Mahogany, Finials, 8-Day, 99 ½ In.. ..... 25300.00
Tall Case, Boulle, Lacquer, Electric Works, France, c.1890, 90 x 31 In. 3520.00
Tall Case, Bracket, Georgian, Japanned, Brass, Silvered Dial, 8 Chimes, 93 x 21 In.. .... 863.00
Tall Case, Brass Face, Beveled Glass Door, Glass Shelves, 78 x 15 ¼ x 9 ½ In. 1800.00
Tall Case, Brass Movement, Calendar Dial, Arch Bonnet, Eagle, 8-Day, c.1790 .... 12000.00
Tall Case, Cherry, Federal, Scrolling Pediment, Arched Hood, 98 x 19 In. 4366.00
Tall Case, Cherry, Moon Phase, 2-Weight, c.1930, 92 ½ In.. .... 3850.00
Tall Case, Chippendale, Cherry, 8-Day, Time & Strike, Painted Dial, c.1790 .... 7000.00
Tall Case, Chippendale, Mahogany, Brass Spire Finials, Painted Dial, 92 ½ x 14 x 11 In...... 9860.00
Tall Case, Chippendale, Walnut, Tombstone Door, Molded Cornice, c.1780, 102 x 22 In...... 1093.00
Tall Case, Classical Style, Oak, Arched Hood, Oval Crest, Painted Moon Phase, 97 In. 4130.00
Tall Case, Colonial, Acid Etched Brass Face, Weights, Pendulum, 84 ½ x 27 x 14 ¾ In. 6600.00
Tall Case, Daniel Rose, 8-Day, Reading, c.1870 .... 25740.00
Tall Case, Elmer O. Stennes, Westminster Chime, Mahogany, Roxbury, c.1975, 60 In. 3410.00
Tall Case, Federal, Cherry, Arched Bonnet, Rocking Ship Movement, Flag, 89 x 17 x 9 In..... 4888.00
Tall Case, Federal, Cherry, Flowers, Birds, c.1815, 84 In.. .... 3173.00
Tall Case, Federal, Cherry, Fluted Columns, Fretwork, Painted Dial, Ship, 91 x 20 In. 3680.00
Tall Case, Federal, Cherry, Tiger Maple, c.1810, 84 ¼ x 20 ½ x 10 ½ In.. .... 1593.00
Tall Case, Federal, Inlaid Mahogany, Rocking Ship, Mass, c.1810, 96 ½ x 21 In. 19200.00
Tall Case, Federal, Mahogany, Arched Face Door, 88 ½ In. 6573.00
Tall Case, Federal, Mahogany, Inlaid, 92 ½ x 18 ¼ x 9 ½ In.. .... 39400.00
Tall Case, Federal, Mahogany, Painted Dial, Concave Rocking Ship, c.1810, 91 In. 9988.00
Tall Case, Flower Form Inlay, Brass Face, Hardware, 78 ½ x 14 ½ x 8 ¼ In.. .... 7800.00

Tall Case, Flowers, Cranes, Pagodas, Lacquer, Westminster Chimes, 1930s, 68 In. ..... *illus* 450.00
Tall Case, French Provincial, Serpentine Door, Arched Panel, 92 x 18 ½ x 7 ½ In. 826.00
Tall Case, George III, Bonnet Pediment, Arched Door, Brass Spandrels, 83 x 19 x 7 In. 4425.00
Tall Case, George III Marquetry, Mahogany, Dentillated Cornice, Columns, 82 x 22 In...... 10500.00
Tall Case, George III Style, Mahogany, Quarter Chime, Brass Mounted, 1918, 94 In. 5288.00
Tall Case, Georgian Style, Japanned Case, Arched Hood, Brass Dial, 8 Chimes, 93 x 21 In. ... 863.00
Tall Case, Gideon Roberts, Federal, Painted Red, Painted Face, Mass., c.1810, 78 x 17 In.... 3000.00
Tall Case, Grain Painted, Broken Arch Pediment, Rosettes, Dial, c.1830, 100 x 19 In. 3910.00
Tall Case, Gustavian, Neoclassical, Carved, Painted, Parcel Gilt, Late 1700s, 77 x 18 In. 1560.00
Tall Case, Herschede, Mahogany, Chiming, Broken Swan Neck Pediment, 78 In. 1888.00
Tall Case, Ithaca Clock Co., 8-Day, Spring Driven, c.1910, 87 In. 413.00
Tall Case, J. Farrer, Mahogany, Flat Top, 8-Day, 18th Century, 83 x 19 x 9 ½ In. 1100.00
Tall Case, J.C. Jennens & Son, Renaissance Revival, Carved Oak, Brass, Steel Face, 95 In..... 3290.00
Tall Case, Jacob Eby, Cherry, Flat Bonnet, Arched Glazed Door, 89 x 20 In. 1770.00
Tall Case, John Crampton, Trelliswork Blind Fret, Ireland, 85 In. 10575.00
Tall Case, John Fessler, Figured Mahogany, Broken Pediment, Sun & Moon Wheel, 97 In. ... 13225.00
Tall Case, John V. Baird, Mahogany, 2 Ball & Spire Finials, London, 1790, 94 In. 4113.00
Tall Case, Jullion, Federal, Cherry, Mahogany, Scrolled Arch, England, 1730s, 91 x 20 In..... 2530.00
Tall Case, Leroyer, French Provincial, Flat Top, Flowers, Andouille, France, 93 In. 633.00
Tall Case, Louis Phillippe, Paint Decorated, Scalloped Bonnet, Oval Glass Door, 91 x 18 In... 823.00
Tall Case, Mahogany, Animated Nautical Scene, 8-Gong Strike, 60 In. 6272.00
Tall Case, Mahogany, Brass Time, Strike, Calendar, c.1810, 81 x 18 ½ In. .... *illus* 1920.00
Tall Case, Mahogany, Regency Style Hood, Painted Dial, Scotland, c.1810, 81 In. 550.00
Tall Case, Mahogany, Scrolled Arch, Brass Finial, French Feet, 95 x 17 ½ x 10 In. 6600.00
Tall Case, Mahogany, Urn Finial, 8-Day, Time & Strike, Brass Weight, 96 ½ x 20 x 10 In. 6050.00
Tall Case, Mahogany, Weight Driven, Time & Strike, Turned Finials, Ky., c.1800, 103 In...... 8050.00
Tall Case, Maple, Brass Dial, Arched Door, Bracket Feet, c.1740, 91 ¼ In. 81900.00
Tall Case, Marquetry, Sarcophagus Top, 8-Day, Brass-Faced Works, Dutch, 95 In. 23400.00
Tall Case, Oak, Flat Top Hood, Full Columns, Painted Flowers & Birds, 75 ½ In. 885.00
Tall Case, Oak, Gilt Metal Rosettes, Brass Face, Mounts, 89 x 21 x 10 ¼ In................ 3442.00
Tall Case, Oak, Swan's Neck, Brass, 30-Hour, Quarter Columns, 88 ½ In. 660.00
Tall Case, Osborne, Federal, 8-Day, Moon Phase Dial, Swan Neck Crest, c.1810, 95 In. 8050.00
Tall Case, Paul Horti, Roycrofters, c.1906 .... 18000.00
Tall Case, Pine, Scroll-Cut Hood, Skirt & Feet, Brass Movement, c.1825, 83 x 17 In. 920.00
Tall Case, Polychrome, Round Face, Enameled, Lyre Shape, Paneled Base, 83 x 25 In. 4320.00
Tall Case, Riley Whiting, Wooden Works, Painted Clock, Village Landscape, Flowers 550.00
Tall Case, Robert Roskell, Regulator, Astro Dial, Mahogany, 8-Day, c.1830, 78 In. 1750.00
Tall Case, Robert Williams, Georgian, Mahogany, Crest, Lunar Arch, Ogee Feet 8225.00
Tall Case, Stained Poplar, Floral & Geometric Painted Wooden Dial, 88 x 18 ½ In. 920.00
Tall Case, Tiffany & Co., Mahogany, Weight Driven, Brass Movement, 90 x 23 x 14 In. 3920.00
Tall Case, Tiffany & Co., Mahogany, Weight Driven, Brass, 8-Day, 91 x 23 ½ x 15 ½ In. 4480.00
Tall Case, Tobey, Weight Driven, 21 ½ x 17 x 73 ½ In. 2880.00
Tall Case, Tobey Furniture, Wood, Weight-Driven, Signed, 73 x 21 ½ x 17 In. .... *illus* 2800.00
Tall Case, Victorian, Inlaid Mahogany, Crest, Brass, Tombstone Door, Scotland, 83 In. 2468.00
Telechron, Alarm, Electric, Bakelite, c.1940 .... 85.00
Telechron, Alarm, Pharaoh, Mahogany Case, Model 3H151, 1950s 120.00
Telechron, Bakelite, Brown Case, Buzzing Alarm, Electric Switch, 1940s 85.00
Terry, Eli, Mahogany, Maple, Pine, 30-Hour, Pillar & Scroll, c.1820, 30 In. .... *illus* 1020.00
Terry, Eli, Shelf, George Washington, Painted Face, Reverse Painted, Key, 24 x 20 x 5 In. *illus* 520.00
Terry, Eli & Samuel, Shelf, Pillar & Scroll, Mahogany, Painted Dial, Reverse Painted, 31 In.. 1116.00
Terry, Samuel, Shelf, Mahogany, Pillar & Scroll, Reverse Paint On Glass, 29 x 17 x 4 In...... 2200.00
Terry & Sons, Shelf, Mahogany Veneer, Wood Movement, Pillar & Scroll, c.1828, 29 In...... 1320.00
Tiffany & Co., 8-Day, Carriage, Handle, Brass, Glass, 4 ½ In. 201.00
Tiffany & Co., Mantel, 8-Sided, Base, Finial, Bronze, Patina, c.1910, 9 ⅜ x 10 ⅞ x 3 ½ In..... 6600.00
Tiffany & Co., Shelf, Bronze, Arched Top, Ball Feet, Brass Works, Alarm, 9 ¾ In. 1495.00
Tiffany & Co., Shelf, Bronze, Dark Patina, Fruit & Flower Garland, White Dial, 15 x 24 In. .. 1080.00
Tiffany & Co., Travel, 14K Gold, Ribbed Case, Leaf Border, Marked, c.1929. .... 2450.00

Tiffany clocks that are part of desk sets made by Louis Comfort Tiffany are listed in the Tiffany category. Clocks sold by the store, Tiffany & Co., are listed here.

Travel, Pocket Watch Form, Carrying Case, Battery Compartment, 6 ¼ In. 148.00
U.S. Army, Black Thermoplastic, Walnut Carrying Case, 10 ½ x 9 ½ In. 201.00
Upjohn, James, Bracket, George III, Satinwood, Inlaid, Painted, c.1800, 26 In. 37000.00
Vincenti & Cie., Shelf, Black Marble Case, Pink Marble Accents, c.1900, 13 ¼ In. 149.00
Vincenti & Cie., Shelf, Bronze, Marble, France, 17 ½ x 22 x 6 ¾ In. 5850.00
Wag-On-Wall, 2-Train Chiming Movement, Pressed Metal Hood, 1800s, 19 x 14 In. 999.00

Clock, Seth Thomas, Sunflower, 3-Petal Base, Cast Iron, 15 ½ In.
$720.00

Clock, Shelf, Cathedral, Brass Case, Gilt Trim, 8-Day, Time & Strike, France, 20 x 7 x 4 In.
$3600.00

Clock, Tall Case, Flowers, Cranes, Pagodas, Lacquer, Westminster Chimes, 1930s, 68 In.
$450.00

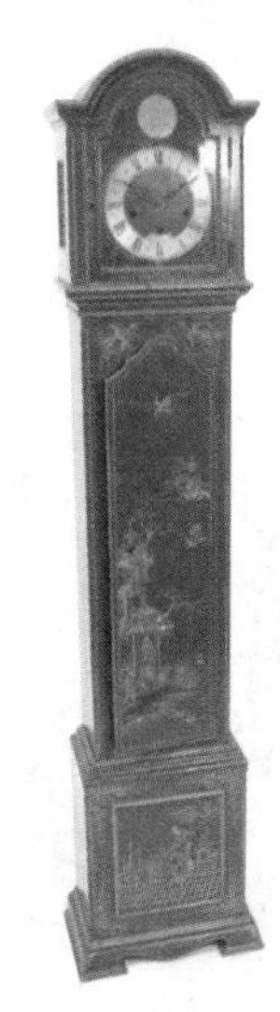

C

Clock, Tall Case, Mahogany, Brass Time, Strike, Calendar, c.1810, 81 x 18½ In.
$1920.00

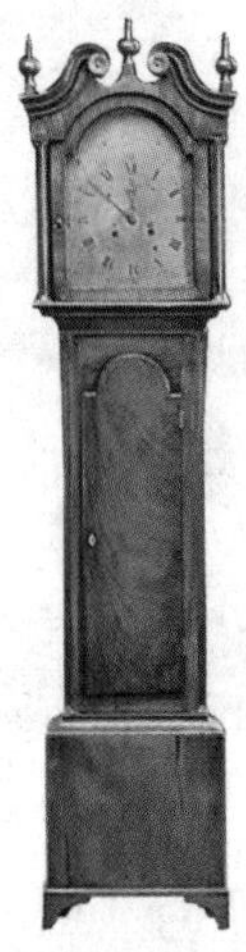

Clock, Tall Case, Tobey Furniture, Wood, Weight-Driven, Signed, 73 x 21½ x 17 In.
$2800.00

Clock, Terry, Eli, Mahogany, Maple, Pine, 30-Hour, Pillar & Scroll, c.1820, 30 In.
$1020.00

Wag-On-Wall, Enamel Floral Lace, Sheet Brass Face, 2-Part Pendulum, 59½ In. 288.00
Wall, Bronze, Louis XVI, 2-Train Movement, Enamel Dial, Swags, 30 In. 1410.00
Wall, Empire, Gallery, Mahogany, 15 In. 110.00
Wall, Floral Engraved Mirrors, France, c.1900, 23½ x 14 x 3½ In. 881.00
Wall, Fusee Postal, Oak, 8-Day, England, c.1900, 15 In. 330.00
Wall, Gilt Bronze, Porcelain, Neoclassical, Urn Finial, Cast Heads, Garlands, 18½ x 16 In. 5520.00
Wall, Oak, Carved, Barometer, France, 28 x 10 In. 175.00
Wall, Office No. 5, Oak, 8-Day, Seth Thomas, c.1895, 22½ In. 331.00
Wall, Regulator, Spring Driven, Bim-Bam, 2-Rod Strike, c.1900, 38 In. 165.00
Wall, Riveted Copper Patchwork, Electric, 20 x 20 x 7 In. 9600.00
Wall, Rosewood, Mirror, Chain Fusee, 8-Day, Reverse Ogee Frame, c.1845, 33½ In. 1870.00
Wall, Round Drop, Mahogany, 8-Day, Fusee, Cast Brass Bezel, c.1890, 18 In. 468.00
Wall, Transfer On Glass Door, Spring, 1-Year Duration, Oak, c.1918, 39¼ In. 3135.00
Wall, Walnut, 8-Day, Gong Strike, Applied Porcelain Numbers, France, c.1880, 24 In. 220.00
Wall, Walnut, Architectural Pediment, Glazed Door, Carved Half Column Pilasters, 44 In. 295.00
Wall, Walnut, Porcelain Dial, Brass Frame, Mid 19th Century, 60 x 19 x 10 In. 5581.00
Waltham Watch Co., Banjo, 8-Day, Car Clock Movement, c.1935, 19 In. 275.00
Waltham Watch Co., Banjo, Antique Green, Yellow Stripe, Willard, c.1930, 42 In. 3410.00
Watchman's, Brass, Ring Carrying Handle, Keys 266.00
Waterbury, Banjo, Willard No. 1, Steel Strap Drive, Oak, Porcelain Dial, c.1910, 43 In. 1045.00
Waterbury, Banjo, Willard No. 4, Oak, 1-Weight, Porcelain Dial, c.1910, 43 In. 1540.00
Waterbury, Bracket, Brass, c.1950, 6 In. 55.00
Waterbury, Brighton, Calendar, 8-Day, Time & Gong Strike, c.1903, 18 In. 138.00
Waterbury, Calendar, Gingerbread, Oak, 8-Day, 27¾ In. 468.00
Waterbury, Galesburg, 8-Day, Viennese Style, c.1906, 52 In. 605.00
Waterbury, School, Oak, c.1900, 24 In. 303.00
Waterbury, Shelf, Black, Marbleized Case, Ormolu Designs, Label, Feet, 8-Day, 12½ In. 66.00
Waterbury, Shelf, Brass Handle, 5 x 3½ x 2½ In. 146.00
Waterbury, Shelf, Cast Metal, Open Escapement, Porcelain Dial, c.1905, 14½ In. 330.00
Waterbury, Shelf, Cherry Case, Mercury Pendulum, Alarm, c.1885, 18½ In. 248.00
Waterbury, Shelf, Kent, Tambour, Mahogany Case, Beveled Glass Door, c.1913, 10¾ In. 248.00
Waterbury, Shelf, Mahogany Veneer, Ogee, Woman Playing Harp, Cherubs, 8-Day, 30¼ In. 88.00
Waterbury, Shelf, Oak, Time & Strike Movement, Alarm 88.00
Waterbury, Shelf, Parlor, Walnut, Incised, c.1900, 22 In. 165.00
Waterbury, Shelf, Surrey, 9-Day, Mahogany, Keyhole Style, c.1913, 14 In. 495.00
Waterbury, Shelf, Sussex, Mahogany, 8-Day, Time & Strike, c.1910, 12½ In. 165.00
Waterbury, Shelf, Tambour, 8-Day, Gong Strike, c.1915, 8 In. 220.00
Waterbury, Victorian, Walnut, Flowers, Leaves, Etched Glass, 8-Day, 23¼ In. 121.00
Welby Corp., Bracket, Mahogany, Germany, 13½ x 10¾ In. 88.00
Welch, E.N., School, Verdi, Rosewood, Long Drop, c.1880, 32 In. 165.00
Welch, E.N., Regulator, Calendar, Rosewood, Double Dial, No. 4 .... 1265.00
Welch Mfg. Co., Wall, Sembrich, Walnut, Calendar, 8-Day, c.1889, 39 In. 1210.00
Welch, Spring & Co., Audran, Perpetual Calendar, Double Dial, Walnut, c.1875, 31½ In. 2860.00
Welch, Spring & Co., Patent Regulator No. 3, Rosewood, Zinc Dial, c.1875, 30 In. 8800.00
Welch, Spring & Co., Shelf, Rosewood, Rosewood Veneer, 8-Day, c.1889, 10½ In. 4180.00
Westclox, Alarm, Curved Case, Cream Color Painted Metal Case, Glass Crystal, c.1952 .... 49.00
Westclox, Plastic, Ball, Hot Pink, White, Black, Manual Wind, Box, 1970s 80.00
Westclox, War Alarm, Pressed Molded Paper, Crinkle Finish, c.1943, 5½ In. 55.00
Whiting, Riley, 30-Hour, Time & Strike, Wood Movement, Winchester, Conn., c.1830, 33 In. 138.00
Whiting, Riley, Shelf, Mahogany, Half Columns, Pineapple Finials, c.1835, 34 x 17 In. 863.00
Willard, Aaron, Shelf, Classical Revival, Mahogany, Mirror, Boston, c.1820, 33 In. 3408.00

CLOISONNE enamel was developed during the tenth century. A glass enamel was applied between small ribbons of metal on a metal base. Most cloisonne is Chinese or Japanese. Pieces marked *China* are twentieth-century examples.

Bowl, Flower Heads, Blue & Red, Brass Lines Rim, 3¼ x 8⅝ In. 236.00
Bowl, Pink & Yellow Moths, Flowers & Vines, Blue Green Ground, 4½ x 8½ In. 384.00
Box, Dragons, Clouds, Turquoise Ground, Chinese, 18th Century, 4 x 3 In. 1293.00
Box, Egg Shape, Ball Feet, 2½ In. 144.00
Box, Gaming, Wood, Green, Gilt, c.1900, 2 x 10 x 13 In. 275.00
Box, Opium, Flowers, Multicolored, Oval, Chinese, c.1760, 2⅛ In. 150.00
Candlestick, Bell Base, Grease Trap, Chinese, c.1900, 28 In., Pair 5079.00
Censer, Bird Mask Handles, Chinese, 19th Century 767.00
Censer, Dragons, Clouds, Turquoise Ground, Leaf Handles, Finial, Japan, 5 In. 1116.00
Censer, Flower Reserves, Teal Ground, Square, Marked, Japan, 20th Century, 3½ In. 646.00

Charger, Blue, Japan, 19th Century, 10⅞ In. 200.00
Cup & Saucer, Turkish, c.1900, 4 In. 1888.00
Egg, Birds, Scrolling Leaves, Stippled, Silver, Gilt, Hinged Lid, Russia, c.1950, 4½ In. .... *illus* 200.00
Ewer, Celadon Jade Plaques, Flowers, Finial, Chinese, 19th Century, 14½ In. 561.00
Figurine, Bird, Chinese, 6 In., Pair 295.00
Figurine, Camel, Chinese, 22½ In., Pair 708.00
Figurine, Phoenixes, Stump, Multicolored, Chinese, 19th Century, 14 In., Pair 3055.00
Ginger Jar, Cover, Peonies, Begonias, Prunus, Fretwork Ground, Chinese, 9½ In., Pair 840.00
Holder, Joss Stick, Gilt Bronze, Lotus, Turquoise Ground, Chinese, 18th Century, ½ In. 1998.00
Incense Burner, Chien Lung Style, Blue Ground, Pierced Cover, 5½ In. 72.00
Incense Burner, Ming Dynasty Style, Lions, Wood Stand, Chinese, 5½ x 6½ In., Pair 270.00
Planter, Masks, Animal Form Feet, Japan, 19th Century, 6 In., Pair 294.00
Plaque, Flowers, Turquoise Ground, Gilt Bronze Mount, Chinese, c.1900, 6¼ In. 1116.00
Plate, Armored Warriors, Japan, 19th Century, 12 In., Pair 1116.00
Plate, Cherry Blossoms, Green Ground, Cobalt Blue Borders, Japan, 9½ In. 353.00
Plate, Flowers, Butterflies, Turquoise Ground, Japan, 19th Century, 12 In. 294.00
Plate, Hawk, Sparrows, Black Ground, Japan, 19th Century, 12 In. 382.00
Pricket Stand, Trumpet Shape Top, Horned Heads On 3-Footed Base, 1800s, 21 In., Pair 259.00
Tea Caddy, Mica Flecks, 19th Century, 4 x 3 In. 351.00
Tea Set, Blue On Brass, Teapot, Sugar, Creamer, 4-In. Teapot, 3 Piece 375.00
Tea Set, Oriental Decoration, Pot, Sugar, Creamer, 4 In. 117.00
Teapot, Cover, Butterflies, 4 In. 288.00
Tray, Flower Branches, Red, Blue, Green, White, c.1890, 7¼ x 7¼ In. 60.00
Tray, Sparrows, Peonies, Bamboo, Blue Ground, 8¾ x 12⅜ In. 600.00
Vase, 6 Panels, Seasonal Flowers, Millefleur, Baluster, 6¼ In., Pair 420.00
Vase, Arabesques, Brown Ground, Chinese, 20th Century, 9 In. 353.00
Vase, Cover, Butterflies, Japan, 4½ In. 288.00
Vase, Double Gourd, Gilt, Reserve Panels, Turquoise, Handles, Chinese, 17 In., Pair 2350.00
Vase, Dragons, Salmon Pink Ground, Phoenixes On Goldtone Ground, Japan, 12 In. 881.00
Vase, Family Crest, Flowers, Dark Green Ground, Trumpet Mouth, Japan, 14½ In., Pair 323.00
Vase, Flora & Fauna, Multicolored, Metal Base Rim, 6 In. 649.00
Vase, Flowers, Multicolored, Shouldered, Paneled, Footed, 12¼ x 5 In. 234.00
Vase, Flowers, Multicolored, White Ground, Scales & Scrolls On Shoulder, 8½ In. 118.00
Vase, Flowers, Turquoise Ground, Japan, 19th Century, 18 In. 1763.00
Vase, Garlic Mouth, Birch Bark, Flowers, Porcelain, 12 In. 646.00
Vase, Lotus, Turquoise Ground, Square, Chinese, 4 In. 4700.00
Vase, Pigeons, Blue Ground, 19th Century, 13 In. 384.00
Vase, Red, White Flowers, c.1950, 10 x 5 In. 175.00
Vase, Roses, Bamboo, Pigeon's Blood Red, Bassetaille Ground, 7¼ In. 353.00
Vase, Tiger Lilies, Slate Blue Ground, Japan, 19th Century, 12 In. 940.00
Vase, Tortoise, Copper, Ring Handles, Wood Base, 16 In. .... *illus* 480.00
Vase, White Birds Flying, Black Enamel Ground, Baluster, 7 In. 140.00

CLOTHING of all types is listed in this category. Dresses, hats, shoes, underwear, and more are found here. Other textiles are to be found in the Coverlet, Movie, Quilt, Textile, and World War I and II categories.

Blouse, Embroidered, Padded Shoulders, Lenvol, Paris, Size 40 .... 45.00
Bolero, Metal Mesh, Paco Rabanne, c.1968 .... 2640.00
Boots, Go-Go, Kickerinos, 1950s 125.00
Boots, Riding, Child's, Pennsylvania 225.00
Chaps, Leather, Fringe, 35½ In. 150.00
Chaps, Leather, Suede, Batwing Style, Longhorn Steer Head Design, 1940s, 31 In. 200.00
Coat, Leopard, Full-Length, ¾ Sleeve, Medium 1450.00
Coat, Ranch Mink, Full-Length, Natural Brown, Shawl Collar, ¾ Sleeves, Medium 700.00
Coat, Wool, White, Plastic Buttons, Knee Length, Pierre Cardin, 1960s, Size 10 .... 2235.00
Costume, Silk, Embroidered Flowers, Red Ground, Chinese, 20th Century 118.00
Dealer's Outfit, Harold's Club, Vest, Pant, Cummerbund, Apron, 1950s, Medium 110.00
Dress, Campbell's Soup Can, Red, Black, White, Paper, Andy Warhol 7000.00
Dress, Evening, Black, Rose Sequins, Silk Lining, Back Zipper, Paris, 42 In. 65.00
Dress, Silk Organza, Velvet, Blue, Pink Flowers, Lace, Underdress, c.1900 .... 130.00
Dress, Victorian, Dark Blue Blouse, Skirt, Lace, c.1900, Petite .... *illus* 50.00
Dress, Victorian, Jacquard Fabric, 1890s, 2 Piece 475.00
Dress Set, Victorian, 2-Piece, Brown Wool, Green Velvet Trim, 1880, Small 55.00
Gauntlets, Quillwork, Beaded, Geometric, Red Field, Multicolored Borders, 13 x 20 In. 805.00
Gloves, Hide, Beaded, Multicolored Flowers, Leaves, 20th Century, 15 In. 259.00

Clock, Terry, Eli, Shelf, George Washington, Painted Face, Reverse Painted, Key, 24 x 20 x 5 In.
$520.00

Cloisonne, Egg, Birds, Scrolling Leaves, Stippled, Silver, Gilt, Hinged Lid, Russia, c.1950, 4½ In.
$200.00

Cloisonne, Vase, Tortoise, Copper, Ring Handles, Wood Base, 16 In.
$480.00

Clothing, Dress, Victorian, Dark Blue Blouse, Skirt, Lace, c.1900, Petite
$50.00

Clothing, Jacket, Sequin, Beads, Hong Kong Labels, Woman's, 1950s
$66.00

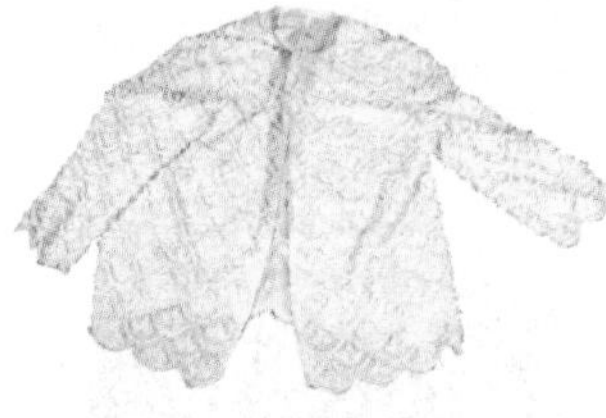

Clothing, Kimono, Bamboo, Flowers, Orange Shaded To Ivory, Silk, Japan, c.1980, 64 In.
$250.00

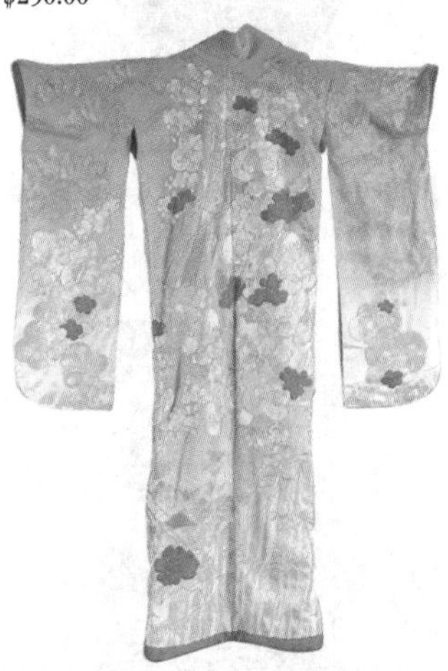

Gloves, Lace, Tan, Bottom Button, Medium, 9 1/4 In. 38.00
Hat, Band, Aqua, Velvet, Netting. 10.00
Hat, Beaded, Aurora Borealis, Black Velvet Bow, Leslie James, Size 22 95.00
Hat, Corona, Black, Rhinestones, Black Satin Ribbon, Braid, Woman's, 7 In. 28.00
Hat, Lavender, Pink Brim Netting, 1960s, 9 3/4 x 6 1/2 In. 18.00
Hat, Mourning, Floppy Box On Side, Jacquard, Paris, Mid 1800s 150.00
Hat, Pillbox, Yellow, Gathered Scarf Sides, Bow In Back, 7 In. 18.00
Hat, Pink Feathers, Beaded, High Dome, 1960s, 8 x 6 1/2 In. 18.00
Hat, Tea, Open Crown, Beige, Green Netting, Roses, 1950s, 10 1/2 In. 30.00
Jacket, Leather, 13 Black Cats, Los Angeles Stunt Circus, Gloves, Cap, Goggles, c.1921 1955.00
Jacket, Leather, Stunt Pilot's, Marked 13 Back Cats, Los Angeles, 1921 1955.00
Jacket, Lounging, Lucille Ball, Royal Blue, Red, White Polka Dots, Size 10 1/2 468.00
Jacket, Metal Mesh, Paco Rabanne, c.1968 4560.00
Jacket, Satin, Birds, Map, Reversible, Korea, 1950s 270.00
Jacket, Sequin, Beads, Hong Kong Labels, Woman's, 1950s *illus* 66.00
Kimono, Bamboo, Flowers, Orange Shaded To Ivory, Silk, Japan, c.1980, 64 In. *illus* 250.00
Kimono, Flowers, Birds, Black, Red Lining, Silk, Cord, Japan, c.1950, Medium To Large 112.00
Pocket, Patchwork, Cotton, Geometric, Calico, Blue Waistband, 1800s, 14 x 9 In. 323.00
Robe, Embroidered Flowers, Blue Ground, Chinese, 20th Century 147.00
Scarf, Silk, Antique Keys, Crimson Ropework & Tassels, Black Ground, Hermes, Box 411.00
Serape, Multicolored, Diamond Center, Wool, Cotton, Mexico, 75 x 40 1/2 In. 35.00
Shawl, Paisley, Black Medallion, Red, Yellow, Turquoise, Wood, 1900s, 138 x 68 In. 502.00
Shawl, Paisley, Red, Olive, Gold Border, Wool, Kashmiri, c.1850, 116 x 57 In. 118.00
Shawl, Scarlet Paisley, Indian Border, c.1885, 66 x 68 In. 300.00
Shirt, Multicolored Beads, Fur, Hair Tassels, Red, Wool, Hand Sewn, 29 x 68 In. 920.00
Shoes, Dr. Lape's Foot EZ High Button, Black Leather, Fabric, Woman's, 8 x 8 1/2 In. 90.00
Shoes, Toinettes, Lame & Rhinestone Heels, Open Toe, Plastic, c.1955, 9 1/2 In. 38.00
Slippers, Wedding, Flowers, Embroidered, Silk, Linen Canvas Uppers, c.1773, 9 1/2 In. 5581.00
Swimsuit, Red, White, Cotton, Canvas, Catalina Surfers, Mid 20th Century, Size 12, 2 Piece 150.00
Underskirt, Quilted, Brown Print, Plaid Inside, Padded, Bone Button, 38 x 50 In. 100.00
Uniform, Red Cross, White Dress, Red Collar, Veil, Blue Cap, c.1975, 27 x 21 In. *illus* 115.00
Vest, Flowers, Beaded Bands, White Leather, 20th Century, 23 x 21 1/2 In. 288.00

CLUTHRA glass is a two-layered glass with small bubbles and powdered glass trapped between the layers. The Steuben Glass Works of Corning, New York, first made it in 1920. Victor Durand of Kimball Glass Company in Vineland, New Jersey, made a similar glass from about 1925. Durand's pieces are listed in the Durand category. Related items are listed in the Steuben category.

Perfume Bottle, White, Blue, Elongated Conical Stopper, Steuben, 7 In. 863.00
Vase, 2-Prong, Green, Clear Base, Steuben, 10 1/2 In. 748.00
Vase, Blue, Oval, Ribbed, Steuben, 8 In. 460.00
Vase, Bubbles, Pink, Flared, Schneider, c.1930, 7 In. *illus* 125.00
Vase, Geometric Shape, Pink & White, Footed, Signed, Steuben, 12 1/2 x 5 1/4 In. 730.00
Vase, Green, Applied Handles, Steuben, 10 In. 1995.00
Vase, Green, Baluster, Steuben, 10 1/2 In. 1438.00
Vase, Green, Signed, Steuben, 10 In. 1955.00
Vase, Opalescent, Bottle Shape, Signed, Bertil Valien Boda, 8 In. 110.00
Vase, Pink, Shouldered, Steuben, 6 1/2 In. 316.00
Vase, Pink, Urn Shape, Mottled Red, Opalescent M-Shape Handles, Steuben, 10 In. 3565.00
Vase, Purple, Oval Shouldered, Rosaline Over Alabaster, Iris, Steuben, 9 1/2 In. 800.00
Vase, Smokestack Shape, White To Green Mottled, Signed, 8 1/2 In. 288.00
Vase, White, Bulbous, Shouldered Shape, 8 1/4 In. 690.00
Vase, White & Green Design, Flattened, Steuben, 7 1/2 x 9 1/2 In. 805.00
Vase, Yellow, Brown, White, Rust, Ground Pontil, Kimball, 12 In. 575.00
Vase, Yellow & Tangerine, Clear Foot, Kimball, 15 In. 780.00

COALPORT ware has been made by the Coalport Porcelain Works of England from 1795 to the present time. Early pieces were unmarked. About 1810–25 the pieces were marked with the name *Coalport* in various forms. Later pieces also had the name *John Rose* in the mark. The crown mark has been used with variations since 1881. The date 1750 is printed in some marks, but it is not the date the factory started. Some pieces are listed in Indian Tree.

Bough Pot, Red, Floral, Paneled, Footed, c.1810, 10 3/4 In. 810.00
Cachepot, Paneled, Green, River Scene, Stand, c.1800, 5 1/2 In. 690.00
Cachepot, Paneled, River Goddess, Stand, c.1800, 4 1/2 In. 2220.00
Cachepot, Paneled, Scenic, Gold Trim, Stand, c.1800, 4 In. 630.00
Dessert Set, Compotes & Plates, Porcelain, Hand Painted, Landscape, c.1830, 22 Piece 2750.00

Dish, Encrusted Flowers, Handle, Blue Mark, Late 1800s, 5 x 12 ½ x 9 ½ In., Pair 530.00
Figurine, Ladies Of Fashion, Hayley, 8 In. 65.00
Figurine, Letter From A Lover, Marked, 7 ¾ In. .... *illus* 22.00
Figurine, Mousey Thompson's Cottage, 8 In. 197.00
Figurine, Running Ostrich, 4 ¼ In. 37.00
Figurine, Skater, Marked, Limited Edition, 7 In. .... *illus* 29.00
Jug, Cabbage Leaf, 19th Century, 7 ½ In. 690.00
Plate, 7 Oval Reserves, Landscapes, Roses, Speckled Blue Ground, Gold Trim, 9 In. 360.00
Platter, Gold & Blue, c.1880, 15 x 12 In. 248.00
Service Plate Set, Tiffany, Raised Gilt, Cobalt Blue Reserves, 10 ⅛ In., 12 Piece 1265.00
Vase, Landscape, 2 Handles, Lid, Ball Finial, 10 In. 1210.00

COBALT BLUE glass was made using oxide of cobalt. The characteristic bright dark blue identifies it for the collector. Most cobalt glass found today was made after the Civil War. There was renewed interest in the dark blue glass in the late 1930s and dinnerwares were made.

Wine Set, Balustrade Decanter, Egg Shape Stopper, 12 Bell Shape Glasses, 13 Piece 176.00

COCA-COLA was first served in 1886 in Atlanta, Georgia. It was advertised through signs, newspaper ads, coupons, bottles, trays, calendars, and even lamps and clocks. Collectors want anything with the word *Coca-Cola*, including a few rare products, like gum wrappers and cigar bands. The famous trademark was patented in 1893, the *Coke* mark in 1945. Many modern items and reproductions are being made.

Advertisement, Boy Scout, Scout Law No. 8, c.1931, 10 ½ x 14 In. 15.00
Bank, Man's Head, Bowtie, Coca-Cola Cap On Head, Cast Metal, Painted, 8 In. .... 175.00 to 190.00
Bicycle, Red Monster Cruiser, 7-Speed, Drum Front Brake 660.00
Bottle, Amber, Cumberland, Maryland, c.1900 .... 250.00
Bottle, Best By Adam Site Coca-Cola Bottling Co., Las Vegas, Nev., Light Green, Aqua 450.00
Bottle, Blue Ridge Bottling Works, Staunton, Va., Aqua, Crown Top 69.00
Bottle, Boise, Idaho, Crown Top, 7 ½ In. 250.00
Bottle, Coca-Cola Bottling Co., Clear, Tooled Top 2464.00
Bottle, Coca-Cola Bottling Works, Pueblo, Co., 7 ½ In. 180.00
Bottle, Colorado Springs, Tooled Crown Top, 9 In. 250.00
Bottle, Commemorative, First Run, Ball Ground, Ga., 1916 .... 200.00
Bottle, Crown Bottling Works, Cheyenne, Wyo. 1000.00
Bottle, Denver, Colo., Tooled Crown Top, 7 ½ In. 120.00
Bottle, Los Angeles, Amber, Tooled Crown Top, 7 ½ In. 240.00
Bottle, Los Angeles, Embossed Around Bottom, 7 In. 180.00
Bottle, Richfield, Utah, 9 In. 180.00
Bottle, Seattle, Tooled Crown Top, 8 In., Pt. 121.00
Bottle, Seltzer, Morgantown, W. Va., Metal Stopper, 12 In. 825.00
Bowl, Metal, Bottle Legs, c.1935, 8 x 4 In. 306.00
Button, Celluloid, 9 In. 165.00
Calendar, 1911, Coca-Cola Girl, Hamilton King, Full Pad, Cardboard, 17 ½ x 10 ½ In. 2050.00
Calendar, 1918, June Caprice, Allison's News Stand, Full Pad, 9 x 5 In. 160.00
Calendar, 1919, Girl With Knitting Bag, Frame, Glass, Metal Strip, 13 x 31 In. 1495.00
Calendar, 1922, Summer Girl, Holding Glass, Mat, Frame, Glass, 12 x 30 ½ In. 403.00
Calendar, 1924, Smiling Girl, Mat, Frame, 11 ½ x 18 ½ In. 920.00
Calendar, 1925, Girl At Party 748.00
Calendar, 1929, Girl With Long String Of Pearls, Mat, Frame, 23 ¾ x 11 ½ In. .... *illus* 3000.00
Calendar, 1939, Girl Pouring Coke, Full Pad, Frame, 33 x 20 ½ In. 248.00
Card, Lillian Nordica, Woman Holding Feather Fan, Coupon, Paper, 1905, 9 ¾ x 6 ½ In. 358.00
Carrier, 6-Pack, Metal, Bail Handle, Drink Coca-Cola 70.00
Cash Register, National, No. 1, 1893 .... 14300.00
Cigarette Case, Frosted Glass, 50th Anniversary, c.1936, 5 ½ In. 345.00
Clock, Dome, Gold Plated, c.1950, 11 ¼ In. 173.00
Clock, Drink Coca-Cola, Metal, Masonite Wings, 1940s, 19 x 36 In. .... *illus* 840.00
Clock, Electric, Exposed Hands, Black Rim, Electric, c.1950, 18 In. 86.00
Clock, Fishtail, Light-Up, Swihart 200.00
Clock, Light-Up, Steel, Painted, c.1950, 47 x 50 In. .... *illus* 810.00
Clock, Pam Square .... 225.00 to 270.00
Cooler, Airline, Red Plated Surface, Side Opener, Latches, Handle, c.1950 .... 230.00
Cooler, Embossed, Handle, 23 ½ In. 77.00
Cooler, Floor, Ideal Dispenser Co., c.1950s, 38 x 20 x 40 In. 403.00
Cooler, Picnic, 1950s, 18 x 9 x 14 In. 201.00
Cooler, Salesman's Sample, Glascock, Bottle Opener, Casters 28600.00

Clothing, Uniform, Red Cross, White Dress, Red Collar, Veil, Blue Cap, c.1975, 27 x 21 In.
$115.00

Cluthtra, Vase, Bubbles, Pink, Flared, Schneider, c.1930, 7 In.
$125.00

Coalport, Figurine, Letter From A Lover, Marked, 7 ¾ In.
$22.00

Coalport, Figurine, Skater, Marked, Limited Edition, 7 In.
$29.00

Coca-Cola, Calendar, 1929, Girl With Long String Of Pearls, Mat, Frame, 23¾ x 11½ In.
$3000.00

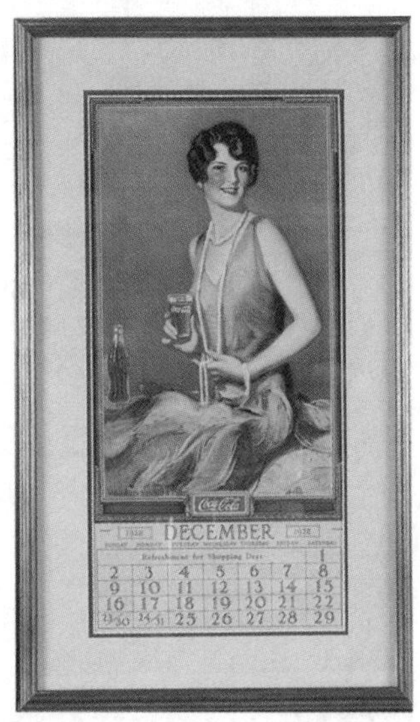

Coca-Cola, Display, Die Cut, Metal, Wood, Kay, 1930s, 20 x 19 In.
$6500.00

Coca-Cola, Pocketknife, Drink Coca-Cola In Bottles, Celluloid, A. Kastor & Bros., c.1920, 3¼ In.
$115.00

Coca-Cola, Clock, Drink Coca-Cola, Metal, Masonite Wings, 1940s, 19 x 36 In.
$840.00

Coca-Cola, Menu Board, Fishtail, Masonite, Wood, 1960s, 30 x 17 In.
$275.00

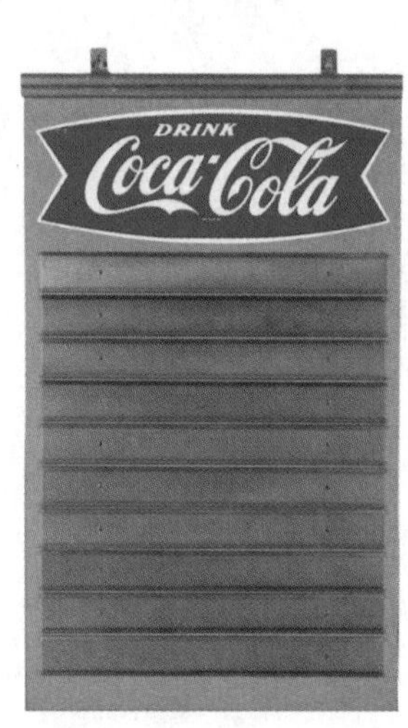

Coca-Cola, Sign, Circus, Cardboard, Frame, 1936, 50 x 30 In.
$3250.00

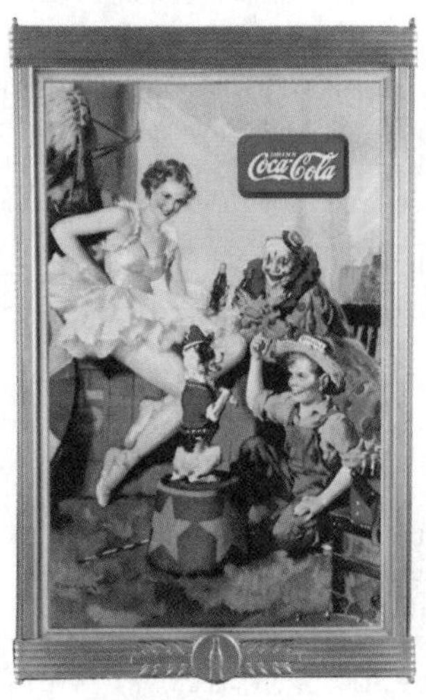

Coca-Cola, Clock, Light-Up, Steel, Painted, c.1950, 47 x 50 In.
$810.00

Coca-Cola, Sign, Coca-Cola, Confectionery, Porcelain, 2-Sided, Pole, Brackets, c.1933, 3 x 5 In.
$1400.00

Crate, Wood, Holds 48 Bottles, 1917, 25 x 18 x 9¾ In. 330.00

Cutout Town, Cardboard, Framed Under Glass, c.1930, 19 In. 288.00

Dispenser, Napkin, Chrome, Sprite Boy, Red, Green, c.1940s, 9¼ In. 518.00

Display, 1932 Olympic Games, Lake Placid, Sports Records On Back, 15 x 10 In. 65.00

Display, Clown With Cups Of Coke, Molded Plastic, 15¼ x 13½ In. 385.00

Display, Die Cut, Metal, Wood, Kay, 1930s, 20 x 19 In. *illus* 6500.00

Display, Lighted, 1930s, 14 x 12½ In. 9350.00

Doll, Buddy Lee, Plastic, White Hat & Uniform With Red Logo, 1950s 690.00

Door Push, Buvez Coca-Cola Glace, Red White & Yellow Letters, France. 100.00

Flashlight, Zippo Flashlight, 2002 Coca-Cola Collectors Club Convention 35.00

Golf Bag, Red & White, Hand Towels 95.00

Hat Rack, Coca-Cola, Wood, 8 x 19 In. 25.00

Ice Pick, Drink Coca-Cola, Delicious & Refreshing, Wood Handle, Box, 1960s, 9 In. 30.00

Jar, Coca-Cola Chewing Gum, Embossed, 4-Sided, 9 In. 1100.00

Menu Board, Fishtail, Masonite, Wood, 1960s, 30 x 17 In. *illus* 275.00

Mirror, Drink Coca-Cola, Girl Holding Glass, Oval, 1906, 2¾ In. 130.00 to 316.00

Mirror, Hand, Brass Tone, Gold Tone Coke Bottle On Back, 1963, 5 In. 125.00

Music Box, Cooler Shape, Red & White Lettering, Mini. 225.00

Napkin, 5 Cents, Matted, Square 13 In. 55.00

Norman Rockwell Art, Cardboard, Boy With Dog, Under Glass, c.1931, 19 x 27 In. 12650.00

Paperweight, Glass, Red, Coke Is Coca-Cola 50.00

Pin Set, Executive, Seoul Olympics, Frame, 1988 120.00

Pin Set, Olympic, Frame, c.1984 90.00

Pocketknife, Drink Coca-Cola In Bottles, Celluloid, A. Kastor & Bros., c.1920, 3¼ In. *illus* 115.00

Poster, Pause For A Coke, Archery, Cardboard, Wood Frame, 1948, 50¼ x 29¾ In. 1100.00

Shade, Leaded Glass, c.1960, 18 In. 4025.00

Shade, Milk Glass, c.1930 748.00

Sign, Advertising, Drink A Bottle, Swastika Motif, Cardboard, 1916, 14 x 11 In. 319.00

Sign, Autumn Girl, Cardboard, Framed Under Glass, c.1941, 16 x 27 In. 1495.00

Sign, Be Refreshed, Woman, In Bathing Suit, 1949, 20 x 36 In. 978.00

Sign, Bottle, 58 Million A Day, Cardboard, c.1957, 20 x 36 In. 300.00

Sign, Bottle, Tin, Self-Framed, 1952, 36 x 18 In. 385.00

Sign, Bottle Cap Shape, 2-Sided, Tin, c.1940, 13 In. 615.00

Sign, Bottle Shape, Embossed Tin, Die Cut, 1933, 12 x 39 In. 1610.00

Sign, Button, Delicious, Refreshing, Celluloid, String Hanger, Easel, 9 In. 198.00

Sign, Button, Plain, Red With White Writing, Tin, 1950, 16 In. 460.00

Sign, Cameo, Enameled Paper On Cardboard, Girl In White Dress, 1904, 8 x 10 In. 5175.00

Sign, Cardboard, Bottle, Drink Coca-Cola, Sparkling Quality, c.1957, 20 x 36 In. 210.00

Sign, Cardboard, Die Cut, Girl Holding Coke, 22¼ x 27 In. 578.00

Sign, Cardboard, Have A Coke, Frame, 1944, 36 x 20 In. 523.00

Sign, Cardboard, He's Coming Home Tomorrow, Woman Shopping, 1944, 27 x 56 In. 403.00

Sign, Cardboard, Lithograph, 3 Woman In WAC Outfits Drinking Coke, 1943, 20 x 36 In. 1083.00

Sign, Cardboard, Seated Girl, Tennis Outfit, Sitting On Cooler, 1948, 16 x 27 In. 518.00

Sign, Circus, Cardboard, Frame, 1936, 50 x 30 In. *illus* 3250.00

Sign, Coca-Cola, Confectionery, Porcelain, 2-Sided, Pole, Brackets, c.1933, 3 x 5 In. *illus* 1400.00

Sign, Declaration Of Independence, Frame, 1942, 34¾ x 28¾ In. 61.00

Sign, Dispenser, Yellow, 2-Sided, Porcelain, 1940, 25 x 26 In. 3163.00

Sign, Drink Coca-Cola, Refresh Yourself, Tin, 1927, 28 x 29 In. 288.00

Sign, Drink Coca-Cola, Tin, Mounting Holes, Dimples, 27 x 19 In. 242.00

Sign, Drink Coca-Cola Ice Cold, 5-Cent Bottle Of Coke, 2-Sided, Hanging, 1941 7475.00

Sign, Drugstore, Drink Coca-Cola, Refreshing, Porcelain, 1930s, 4½ x 8 In. 1495.00

Sign, Drugstore, Neon, Porcelain, 2-Sided, 7 Piece, 63 x 49 In. 1650.00

Sign, Fountain Service, Porcelain, 2 Spigots, Red, Black, White, Yellow, c.1939, 27 x 14 In. 1008.00

Sign, Girl Drinking, Cardboard, 1935, 21 x 15 In. *illus* 125.00

Sign, Girl In White Dress, Soldier On Bicycle, Bottle, 1943, 30 x 50 In. 2305.00

Sign, Ice Cold, Sold Here, Tin, Embossed, c.1910, 20 x 28 In. 3163.00

Sign, Iced Coca-Cola Here, Flange, Canada, 19 x 18 In. 176.00

Sign, Lillian Nordica, Self-Framed, 1905 21600.00

Sign, Mom Knows Her Groceries, Cardboard, Frame, 1946, 30 x 50 In. 863.00

Sign, Pause & Refresh, Waterfall Motion, Light-Up, c.1940, 9 x 19 In. *illus* 1800.00

Sign, Pause That Refreshes, Cardboard, Wood Frame, 1942, 20 x 36 In. 518.00

Sign, Porcelain, 2-Sided, Yellow Buttons, 1941, 60¼ x 50 In., 5 Piece 688.00

Sign, Porcelain, Die Cut, 6 Pack, 13 x 11 In. 935.00

Sign, Porcelain, Enamel, 2-Sided, Rectangular, 1933, 60 x 42 In. 770.00

Sign, Refreshing, Cardboard, Frame, Glass, 1946, 20 x 36 In. 1035.00

Coca-Cola, Sign, Girl Drinking, Cardboard, 1935, 21 x 15 In. $125.00

Coca-Cola, Sign, Pause & Refresh, Waterfall Motion, Light-Up, c.1940, 9 x 19 In. $1800.00

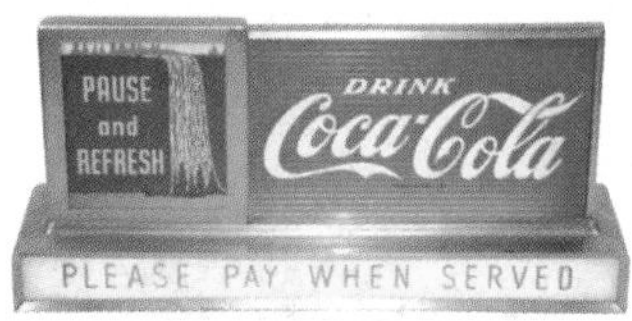

Coca-Cola, Sign, Sprite Boy, Cardboard, 1946, 50 x 30 In. $450.00

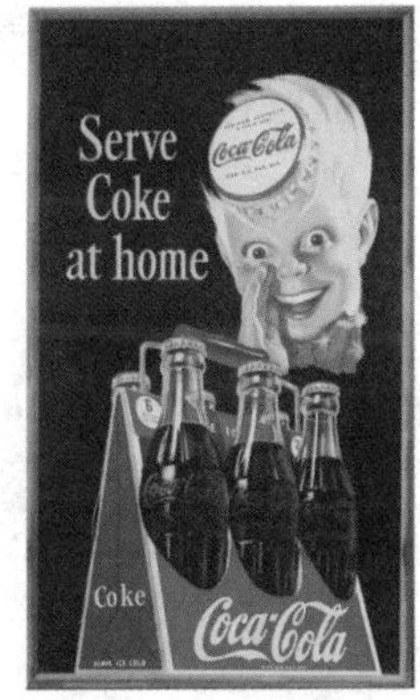

Coca-Cola, Thermometer, Bottles, Embossed, Tin, 1942, 16 x 7 In. $350.00

Coca-Cola, Tip Tray, 1909, Exhibition Girl, 6 ¼ x 4 ½ In. $175.00

Coca-Cola, Tray, 1910, Coca-Cola Girl, 13 ¼ x 10 ½ In. $400.00

Coca-Cola, Tray, 1922, Summer Girl, 13 ¼ In. $405.00

TIP

Most Coca-Cola trays had green or brown borders in the 1920s, red borders in the 1930s.

Sign, Santa, Fold-Out, Die Cut, 1950s, 27 ½ x 20 In. 198.00
Sign, Sidewalk, 2-Sided, Metal Frame, 1946 .... 495.00
Sign, Sprite Boy, Cardboard, 1946, 50 x 30 In. .... *illus* 450.00
Sign, Time Out For Food & Drink, Cardboard, Frame, Plexiglas, 1938, 14 ½ x 32 In. 1150.00
Sign, Tomese Coca-Cola En Botellitas, 6 Cents Plata, Spanish, Tin, c.1908, 12 x 36 In. 1840.00
Sign, Trolley Car, 4 Seasons, Mat, Frame, Glass, Cardboard, 1923, 10 x 19 ¾ In. 2300.00
Tag, Truck, Buddy L, Yellow, Soda Cases, 15 In. 550.00
Tag, Truck, Plastic, Marx, Yellow, c.1950, 11 In., Box 460.00
Thermometer, 2 Bottles, Tin, Embossed, 1941, 16 x 6 ½ In. 316.00
Thermometer, Bottles, Embossed, Tin, 1942, 16 x 7 In. .... *illus* 350.00
Thermometer, Dial, Round, 12 ¼ In. 220.00
Thermometer, Embossed Tin, Cutout Bottle, c.1935, 16 In. 173.00
Thermometer, Enjoy Coca-Cola, Red, White, 12 In. Diam. 130.00
Thermometer, Figural, Bottle, Die Cut, Embossed, 1950s, 17 x 5 In. 67.00
Thermometer, Porcelain, Silhouette Girl, Canada, c.1939, 6 x 18 In. 978.00
Tip Tray, 1903, Hilda Clark, Round, 6 In. 890.00
Tip Tray, 1909, Exhibition Girl, 6 ¼ x 4 ½ In. .... *illus* 175.00
Tip Tray, 1914, Betty, Drink Coca-Cola, Delicious & Refreshing, 6 In. 157.00
Toy, Route Truck, Drink Coca-Cola, Battery Operated, Tin Litho, Box, 1960s, 12 ½ In. 520.00
Toy, Tramway Trolley, Friction, Original Packaging, Payva, Spain, 1960s 60.00
Toy, Truck, 10 Bottles, Metalcraft 275.00
Toy, Truck, 10 Bottles, Metalcraft, Box 1000.00
Toy, Truck, Battery Operated, Metal, Yellow, White, Red, Sanyo, Box, 1950s, 4 ½ x 12 In. 413.00
Toy, Truck, Delicious, Refreshing, 8 Bottles, Hand Cart, Marx, Box, c.1954, 5 x 13 In. 950.00
Toy, Truck, GMC, Buddy L, 1959 .... 295.00
Toy, Truck, Tin Lithograph, Battery Operated, Box, Allen Haddock Co., 1960s 349.00
Trade Card, Woman In Bathtub, Fold-Out, c.1907, 3 ½ x 6 ¼ In. 250.00
Tray, 1905-07, Topless Woman, 12 ¼ In. 4406.00
Tray, 1910, Coca-Cola Girl, 13 ¼ x 10 ½ In. .... *illus* 400.00
Tray, 1913, Hamilton King Girl, Oval, 15 In. 173.00
Tray, 1914, Betty, Passaic Metal Ware, 13¼ x 10½ In. .... 448.00 to 498.00
Tray, 1922, Summer Girl, 13 ¼ In. .... *illus* 405.00
Tray, 1923, Flapper Girl, 13 ¼ x 10 ½ In. 230.00
Tray, 1924, Smiling Girl, 13 ¼ In. .... *illus* 295.00
Tray, 1925, Party Girl, 13¼ x 10½ In. .... 230.00 to 395.00
Tray, 1926, Golfing Couple, American Art Works, 13 ¼ x 10 ½ In. 359.00
Tray, 1927, Curb Service, 10 ½ x 13 ¼ In. .... *illus* 518.00
Tray, 1929, Girl In Yellow Bathing Suit, Bobbed Hair, 13 ⅓ x 10 ½ In. 525.00
Tray, 1930, Meet Me At The Soda Fountain, American Art Works, 13¼ x 10½ In. .... 227.00 to 388.00
Tray, 1931, Barefoot Boy, American Art Works, 13¼ x 10½ In. .... 644.00 to 673.00
Tray, 1932, Girl In Yellow Bathing Suit, Blond, 13 x 10 ½ In. 413.00
Tray, 1934, Maureen O'Sullivan & Johnny Weissmueller, Tin Lithograph, 10 x 13 In. .... 1035.00 to 1380.00
Tray, 1935, Madge Evans, American Art Works, 13 ¼ x 10 ½ In. 343.00
Tray, 1936, Hostess, American Art Works, Inc., 13 ¼ x 10 ½ In. 418.00
Tray, 1937, Running Girl, American Art Works, 13 ¼ x 10 ½ In. 221.00
Tray, 1938, Girl At Shade, 13 x 10 ½ In. 115.00
Tray, 1939, Springboard Girl, 13 ¼ x 10 ½ In. 215.00
Tray, 1940, Sailor Girl, American Art Works, 10½ x 13½ In. .... 190.00 to 260.00
Tray, 1941, Skater Girl, Girl Seated On Log, 10 ½ x 13 ¼ In. 155.00
Tray, 1942, 2 Girls At Car, American Art Works, 13¼ x 10½ In. .... 115.00 to 196.00
Tray, 1953, Menu Girl, Outdoor Activities Border, 13 ¼ x 10 ½ In. 720.00
Tumbler, Bell Shape, 50th Anniversary, Somersworth Bottling Co., c.1966 .... 15.00
Vending Machine, 36 x 24 x 20 In. 825.00
Vending Machine, Model 27 .... 1430.00
Window Display, Edgar Bergen With Charlie McCarthy On CBS Radio, 24 x 11 In. 160.00

COFFEE MILLS are also called coffee grinders, although there is a difference in the way each grinds the coffee. Large floor-standing or counter-model coffee mills were used in the nineteenth-century country store. Small home mills were first made about 1894. They lost favor by the 1930s. The renewed interest in fresh-ground coffee has produced many modern electric mills and hand mills and grinders. Reproductions of the old styles are being made.

Arcade, Crystal, No. 3, Cast Iron, Receiving Cup, 18 ¾ In. 154.00
Arcade, X-Ray, No. 1, Grinder, Wood, Cast Iron, Wall Mount, 13 ½ In. 77.00
Black Hawk, Cast Iron, No. 100, A.H. Patch, Clarksville, Tenn., Late 1800s, 9 x 15 In. 115.00
C. Parker, No. 350, Wood Wall Mount, Cast Iron, Meriden, Ct., 5 ½ x 5 ½ x 3 ½ In. 90.00

C. Parker, No. 555, Rapid Grinding, Drawer, Partial Label, 6¾ x 6¾ x 8½ In.......... 66.00
Cast Iron, Blue Paint, Large Wheel, Wood Handle, Drawer, Made In Spain, 10 x 7 In........ 55.00
Elgin National, Original Paint, Decal, No. 48, Iron, 21 x 11½ x 8½ In.......... 995.00
Enterprise, No. 0, Clamp On, 11½ In.......... 35.00
Enterprise, No. 2, 2 Wheels, Drawer, 8¾-In. Wheel, 10 In.......... 180.00
Enterprise, No. 2, 2 Wheels, Drawer, Red, 10½ In.......... 1320.00
Enterprise, No. 2½, 2 Wheels, Nickel Plated Hopper, 15 In.......... 300.00
Enterprise, No. 3, 2 Wheels, Cast Iron Hopper, 15 x 10 In.......... 300.00
Enterprise, No. 3, 2 Wheels, Drawer, Pat. July 12, 1898, 15 In.......... 595.00 to 1295.00
Enterprise, No. 5, 2 Wheels, Drawer, Red, 12-In. Wheel.......... 500.00
Enterprise, No. 7, 2 Wheels, Cast Iron, Drawer, Red, Black, 17 In.......... 230.00
Enterprise, No. 12½, Cast Iron, Painted, Pat. Oct. 1873, 37 In.......... *illus* 2750.00
Griswold, No. 145, Glass Catcher, Wall Mount.......... 1450.00
Landers & Clark County Store, Pat. Date 1801.......... 450.00
Landers, Frary & Clark, No. 20, Wood Drawer, Painted, 12½ x 11 In.......... 935.00
Landers, Frary & Clark, Universal, No. 14, Cast Iron, Tin Canister, Wall Mount, 13½ In.......... 175.00
Lane Brothers, No. 12, Cast Iron, Single Wheel, Tin Drawer, Red Paint, 15 x 9 x 7 In.......... 525.00
Lane Brothers, Swift Mill, Cast Iron, Painted, 14 In.......... *illus* 450.00
Star, No. 10, Nickel Plated Hopper, 33 In.......... 450.00
Wood, Brass, Raised Relief, Drawer, Moroccan, 8 x 5 In.......... 125.00

COIN-OPERATED MACHINES of all types are collected. The vending machine is an ancient invention dating back to 200 B.C., when holy water was dispensed in a coin-operated vase. Smokers in seventeenth-century England could buy tobacco from a coin-operated box. It was not until after the Civil War that the technology made modern coin-operated games and vending machines plentiful. Slot machines, arcade games, and dispensers are all collected.

Arcade, Clown, Wood, Cast Aluminum Marquee, 33 x 20 x 10½ In.......... 1430.00
Arcade, Pelican Game, Feed Bill, Mechanical Amusement Co., Tonawanda, N.Y.......... 3450.00
Arcade, Photographer, Sitter's Skirt Goes Up, Reveals Bloomers, France, 1800s.......... 6100.00
Arcade, Speedway, Chicago Coin, 1970, 69 x 39¼ x 29½ In.......... 28.00
Fortune Teller, 5 Cent, Oak, Exhibit Supply, 1929, 72 x 22 x 13 In.......... *illus* 18699.00
Fortune Teller, Wizard, 1 Cent, Painted, Paper, Lock, c.1920.......... 1700.00
Graphophone, Hinged Lid, Oak Case, Coin Drawer, Columbia, 1897, 15 In.......... 4113.00
Gum, Cop, Porcelain, Pulver, 21 In.......... 530.00
Gum, D-Lish-Us, 5 Cents, Iron, American Auto Vending, c.1890, 27 x 3¾ In.......... 9775.00
Gum, Double, 5 Cents, Decals, Patriotic, 14¼ In.......... 132.00
Gum, Penny, Columbus, Decal, 14 In.......... 154.00
Gum, Pulver, Clown, 20¾ x 9 In.......... 935.00
Gum, Puritan Baby, 10¼ x 9¼ In.......... 880.00
Gum, Short's, 1 Cent, 2 Columns, Metal, Cast Iron, c.1920, 28 x 8¼ In.......... 198.00
Gum, Zeno, 1 Cent, Key, Oak Case, c.1895.......... 1320.00
Gum, Zeno, Keys, 16½ x 5¾ In.......... 1625.00
Gum, Zeno, Porcelain, Steel Case, Enameled, Yellow, Black, Clockwork, 17 x 7 In.......... 144.00
Gumball, Baker, Pedestal Base, c.1920, 48 In.......... *illus* 3750.00
Gumball, Flavor Of The Month Marquee, Ford, 15¾ In.......... 88.00
Gumball, Jaycees Marquee, Ford, 15¾ In.......... 99.00
Mutoscope, International, Monkey Lift, 5 Cent, 92 x 28 x 36 In.......... 9775.00
Nickelodeon, Pianola-Orchestrion, Drum, Accordion, Brinkerhoff Piano, c.1920.......... *illus* 11706.00
Orpheus, Wood, Ludwig & Co., Germany, 14 Discs, 45 x 31 x 18 In.......... *illus* 2676.00
Peep Show, International Mutoscope, 5 Cent, 1926, 65 x 14 x 18 In.......... 1380.00
Pinball, Humpty Dumpty, Wood, Glass, 66 x 52 x 25 In.......... 1066.00
Pinball, Mata Hari, Bally, 1978.......... 528.00
Pinball, Poker, Play A Hand, Tabletop, 27 x 17¼ In.......... 193.00
Punching Bag, Mutascope, Wood, Cast Iron, 81 x 29½ x 41 In.......... 7150.00
Ride, Elephant, Switch, Coin Slot, 64 x 50 x 36 In.......... 1035.00
Ride, Horse, Big Bronco, Tooled Leather Saddle, 66 x 52 In.......... 4400.00
Ride, Motorcycle, Switch, 55 x 48 x 30 In.......... 1610.00
Ride, Space Ship, Electric, 80 x 52 x 30 In.......... 4600.00
Skill, Challenger, Target, 10 Balls, 1 Cent, 1946, 14 x 110 x 24 In.......... 345.00
Skill, Gambling, Moon Rocket, Triumph Automaten, Germany, c.1930.......... 2341.00
Skill, J.F. Frantz, Kick Catcher, 18 x 13 x 13 In.......... 575.00
Skill, Marvel, Slugger, 5 Cent, 19 x 13 x 13 In.......... 575.00
Skill, Mexican Baseball, 21 x 12 In.......... 403.00
Skill, Mills, Flip Skill, Wood, Gingerbread, 1938, 34 x 16 x 15 In.......... 748.00
Skill, Whiz Ball, 1 Cent, 18 x 8 In.......... 633.00

Coca-Cola, Tray, 1924, Smiling Girl, 13¼ In. $295.00

Coca-Cola, Tray, 1927, Curb Service, 10½ x 13¼ In. $518.00

Coffee Mill, Enterprise, No. 12½, Cast Iron, Painted, Pat. Oct. 1873, 37 In. $2750.00

Coffee Mill, Lane Brothers, Swift Mill, Cast Iron, Painted, 14 In. $450.00

C

Coin-Operated Machine, Fortune Teller, 5 Cent, Oak, Exhibit Supply, 1929, 72 x 22 x 13 In. $18699.00

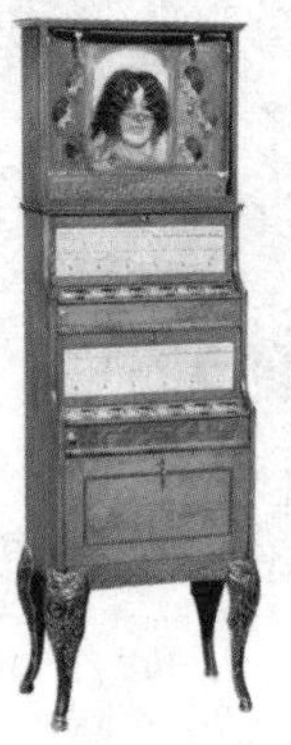

Coin-Operated Machine, Gumball, Baker, Pedestal Base, c.1920, 48 In. $3750.00

Coin-Operated Machine, Nickelodeon, Pianola-Orchestrion, Drum, Accordion, Brinkerhoff Piano, c.1920 $11706.00

Coin-Operated Machine, Orpheus, Wood, Ludwig & Co., Germany, 14 Discs, 45 x 31 x 18 In. $2676.00

Skill, Whiz Bowler, 1, 5, 10 Cents, 10 Balls, Graphics, Playboard, 18 x 12 x 9 In. 633.00
Slot, Bingo, Aristocrat Elite, 25 Cents, 1970s, 16 x 19 x 30¾ In. 495.00
Slot, Cracker Jack, 25 Cents, 2-Sided, Wood Case, Rotawin, 69¾ x 20 In. 385.00
Slot, Gabel's Niagara, Oak, Nickel Mounted, Glass Panel, 72 x 46 In. 4484.00
Slot, Jennings, Club Chief, 10 Cent, Metal, Wood Base, 1946, 33½ x 17 x 17½ In. 2405.00
Slot, Jennings, Star Chief, 10 Cent, 27 x 14 In. 1150.00
Slot, Jennings, Sweepstake Chief, 5 Cent, 27 x 15 In. 2070.00
Slot, Little Duck, 10 Cent, Oak, Cast Metal, 22 x 13 x 11 In. 1792.00
Slot, Mills, Blue Bell, High Top, 26 x 14 x 16 In. 1650.00
Slot, Mills, Vest, 5 Cent, 8 x 7 In. 239.00
Slot, Mills Jockey, 1 Cent, Oak, Copper 12100.00
Slot, Mills Jockey, Fortune Teller, Princess Doraldina, 5 Cent 12100.00
Slot, Mills New Century, Bandit, 3 Reels, 5 Cent, Green & Gold Case, 28 In. 881.00
Slot, Pace, 25 Cent, 1930s .... *illus* 1035.00
Slot, Superior, Triple, 5 Cent, 22 x 14 In. 1265.00
Slot, Wild Deuce, 5 Cent, Cast Metal, Wood, 26¼ x 16 x 15 In. 660.00
Smiley Clown, Pioneer Coin Machine Co., 25 In. 330.00
Strength Tester, El Toro Bull, Zamperia, Inc., 62 In. 440.00
Strength Tester, Shake Hands With Uncle Sam, Howard Mills 26400.00
Trade Simulator, Fortune, Slot, 1 Cent, 8½ x 13 x 9½ In. 230.00
Trade Simulator, Tri-O-Pack, Slot, 12½ x 10½ x 10 In. 518.00
Vending, 7Up, Lift Top, Porcelain, Keys, Ideal, 37¾ x 22 In. 413.00
Vending, Chocolate, Stollwerck, Art Nouveau, 3 Column, c.1900 .... 1672.00
Vending, Matches, 1 Cent, Nickel-Plated, Twin Window, 2 Dolphins, 13 In. 764.00
Vending, Peanut Warmer, Baseball Graphics, 1930, 18 x 19 x 49 In. 7638.00
Vending, Penny Pack, Bandit, 3 Cigarette Packet Reels, Gum Dispenser, Metal Case, 11 In. 264.00
Vending, Pulver's Chocolate, Cocoa & Gum, 1 Cent, Foxy Grandpa, Metal, c.1899, 24 x 10 In. 6325.00
Viewing, Auto-Stereoscope, Rosenfield, Oak Case, Erotic Images, c.1905, 68 In. 6407.00

COLLECTOR PLATES are modern plates produced in limited editions. Some may be found listed under the factory name, such as Bing & Grondahl, Royal Copenhagen, Royal Doulton, and Wedgwood.

Gorham, Mother & Child Of The Apache People 75.00
Gorham, Snowy Owl, No. 680, American Wildlife Heritage 125.00
Knowles, Lazy Morning, 8¼ In. 30.00
Konigszelt, Rumpelstiltskin, 1981 .... 25.00
McClelland, Little Miss Muffet, Mother Goose Series, 1981, 8½ In. 30.00

COMIC ART, or cartoon art, is a relatively new field of collecting. Original comic strips, magazine covers, and even printed strips are collected. The first daily comic strip was printed in 1907. The paintings on celluloid used for movie cartoons are listed in this book under Animation Art.

Cover Art, Adventures Into Unknown, No. 160, Nemesis Tracks Mystery, 1965, 15 x 22 In. 756.00
Cover Art, Adventures Of Tom Sawyer, No. 50, Classic Illustrated, 18 x 26 In. 717.00
Cover Art, Aquaman, Nick Cardy, 1969, 10 x 15 In. 4226.00
Cover Art, Arak, Son Of Thunder, No. 34, Ron Randall, 10 x 15 In. 261.00
Cover Art, Blondie, Dagwood Should Leave Cooking To Blondie, Paul Fung, Jr., 11 x 14 In. 206.00
Cover Art, Dagwood, No. 16, Daisy's Pups Have Dagwood On Run, 1952, 11 x 13¾ In. 178.00
Cover Art, Dagwood, No. 34, Is A Man On The Moon, Paul Fung, Jr., 1953, 9 x 11¼ In. 344.00
Cover Art, Dagwood, No. 48, Dagwood Considering A Diet, 10½ x 12½ In. 220.00
Cover Art, Detective Comics, Alternate Batman, No. 379, 10 x 15 In. 2199.00
Cover Art, Drawing, Disney's Comics & Stories, No. 214, Carl Barks, 10 x 13 In. 18522.00
Cover Art, Gene Autry, No. 78, Arnold Holeywell, 13 x 16 In. 263.00
Cover Art, Jetsons, No. 21, Rosie Lifting George To Vacuum, Gold Key, 1966, 10 x 11 In. 311.00
Cover Art, Mad, No. 70, Alfred E. Neuman Skating, Kelly Freas, 1961, 8¾ x 6 In. 1421.00
Cover Art, Red Ryder Ranch, c.1950, 30 x 25½ In. 1924.00
Cover Art, Roy Rogers, No. 83, Arnold Holeywell, Gouache, 13 x 16 In. 418.00
Cover Art, Tim Holt, No. 21, Horses, Ghost Rider, Split Cover, Frank Frazetta, 13 x 18 In. 13743.00
Cover Art, Unexpected, No. 168, Luis Dominguez, 1975, 10 x 15 In. 845.00
Cover Art, Weird Western Tales, No. 29, Luis Dominguez, 9¾ x 15 In. 1099.00
Cover Painting, Mad, No. 159, Crockwork Lemon, Norman Mingo, c.1973, 24 x 29 In. 11950.00
Drawing, Promotional, Donald's First Birthday, Disney, c.1935, 8 x 7½ In. 3107.00
Page, Amazing Spider Man, No. 23, Page 8, Steve Ditko, Marvel, c.1965, 15 x 22 In. 22705.00
Page, Billy The Kid, No. 10, Page 17, Get Ready For A Necktie Party, 1952, 12 x 18 In. 137.00
Page, Mighty Avengers, No. 97, Godhood's End, J. Buscema, T. Palmer, 1972, 10 x 14 In. 3381.00

Page, Prince Of Peril, Hall Forrest, 13 ½ x 20 ½ In. 301.00
Page, Star Trek, No. 4, Page 4, Captain Kirk, Mr. Spock, Sulu, 1969, 10 ¼ x 15 In. 446.00
Page, Sunday, Li'l Abner, Al Capp, June 30, 1957, 27 ½ x 18 In. 956.00
Page, Sunday, Mutt & Jeff, Al Smith, October 28, 1956, 13 x 19 In. 176.00
Page, Sunday, Mutt & Jeff, Bud Fisher, November 28, 1948, 16 x 24 In. 286.00
Page, Sunday, Superman, Wayne Boring, June 12, 1949, 12 x 19 In. 5676.00
Page, The Spirit, No. 2, Will Eisner, Page 2, c.1967, 12 x 16 In. 1434.00
Page, Uncle Scrooge, No. 62, Carl Banks, Queen Of The Wild Dog Pack, 16 x 23 In. 11950.00
Painting, Production, Cinderella, Fairy Godmother, Mary Blair, Disney, c.1950, 6 x 5 In. 5378.00
Panel, Ballyhoo, John Dempsey, c.1950, 6 x 5 ½ In. 66.00
Panel, Big George, Virgil Partch, August 17th, 7 x 9 In. 34.00
Panel, Dennis The Menace, Hank Ketcham, February 19, 1977, 6 x 8 In. 263.00
Strip, Andy Capp, Reg Smythe, 10 x 8 In. 388.00
Strip, Barney Google & Snuffy Smith, Fred Lasswell, June 10, 1984, 14 x 21 In. 220.00
Strip, Beetle Bailey, Mort Walker, December 26, 1984, 4 x 13 In. 200.00
Strip, Big George, Virgil Partch, August 6, 1969, 10 x 10 In. 55.00
Strip, Brenda Starr, Dale Messick, August 16, 1968, 4 ½ x 15 In. 396.00
Strip, Daily, Toots & Casper, December 16, 1938, 17 ¾ x 4 In. 38.00
Strip, Dennis The Menace, 10 Oct., 1972, 8 x 6 ½ In. 410.00
Strip, Dennis The Menace, Feed The Kitty, Hank Ketcham, c.1979, 6 ½ x 8 In. 388.00
Strip, Donald Duck, Al Taliaferro, November 19, 1957, 19 ½ x 5 ½ In. 448.00
Strip, Li'l Abner, Al Capp, August 17, 1947, 19 x 22 In. 836.00
Strip, Li'l Abner, Al Capp, November 3, 1957, 27 ½ x 18 In. 446.00
Strip, Li'l Abner, Al Capp, September 12, 1951, 22 x 6 In. 448.00
Strip, Peanuts, Charles Schulz, June 30, 1971, 27 ½ x 5 ½ In. 16730.00
Strip, Popeye, Tom Sims, Bill Zaboly, December 23, 1947, Mat, 4 ½ x 17 In. 320.00
Strip, Rube Goldberg, McNaught Syndicate, February 12, 1930, 17 x 5 In. 956.00
Strip, Sad Sack, George Baker, April 13, 1952, 21 ½ x 14 In. 657.00
Strip, Sunday, Dick Tracy, Chester Gould, May 8, 1955, 27 x 18 In. 653.00
Strip, Sunday, Dick Tracy, Chester Gould, September 21, 1947, 27 x 18 In. 584.00
Strip, Sunday, Peanuts, Charles Schulz, March 1, 1959, 22 ½ x 15 In. 77675.00
Strip, Sunday, Pogo, Walt Kelly, March 16, 1952, 23 x 16 In. 1972.00
Strip, Sunday, Popeye, Swee Pea Plans Fun Day, June 1, 1969, 21 ½ x 14 In. 369.00
Strip, Superman, Curt Swan, Al Williamson, No. 409, July 1985, 15 x 10 In. 110.00
Strip, Tiger, Bud Blake, March 9, 1981, 4 ½ x 15 In. 33.00

COMMEMORATIVE items have been made to honor members of royalty and those of great national fame. World's fairs and important historical events are also remembered with commemorative pieces. Related collectibles are listed in the Coronation and World's Fair categories.

Apollo Moon Landing, Astronaut Holding Flag, Metal, Pewter, Franklin Mint, 1976. 55.00
Badge, Queen Victoria 60th Anniversary, Sterling Silver, 1897 261.00
Barometer, Duke Of Wellington, c.1852, 50 In. 8500.00
Bell, Prince Charles & Lady Diana Wedding, Newhall, 1981, 6 In. 14.00
Bonbon, Czar & Czarina Nicolas II, Milk Glass, Tin Cover, 13 In., 2 Piece *illus* 1265.00
Button, Cleveland Brewery, Indian, Cuyahoga County Centennial, Oct., 1910, 1 ½ In. *illus* 136.00
Button, Queen Victoria, In Memoriam, 1901, 1 ¼ In. *illus* 63.00
Jug, Lieutenant General White V.C.G., Portrait, 6 In. *illus* 15.00
Plaque, Louis Pasteur, Laurel Leaf Headdress, Porcelain, 9 ¼ In. 173.00
Plate, Queen Caroline, Flower Border, 19th Century, 7 ½ In. *illus* 72.00
Towel, Queen Elizabeth, 25 Year Reign 1952-77, Buckingham Palace 12.00

COMPACTS hold face powder. A woman did not powder her face in public until after World War I. By 1920, the beauty parlor, permanent waves, and cosmetics had become acceptable. A few companies sold cake face powder in a box with a mirror and a pad or puff. Soon the compact was designed by jewelers and made of gold, silver, and precious materials. Cosmetic companies began to sell powder in attractive compacts of less valuable metal or plastic. Collectors today search for Art Deco designs, commemorative compacts from world's fairs or political events, and unusual examples. Many were made with companion lipsticks and other fittings.

A.L. Siegel Co., Bakelite, Red, 3 ¼ In. 30.00
Avon, Blue & Green Pillow Type Design, Mirror, Oval, 2 ¾ x 2 ¼ In. 7.50
Bakelite, Art Deco 184.00
Black Enamel, Carved Lucite Center, Red Roses, Square Puff, 1960s, 2 ½ In. 34.00
Cartier, 14K Gold, Sterling Silver, Ribbed, Geometric Border, Sapphires, 2 ¼ x 2 In. 646.00
Celluloid, Belle Of The Ball 512.00

Coin-Operated Machine, Slot, Pace, 25 Cent, 1930s
$1035.00

Commemorative, Bonbon, Czar & Czarina Nicolas II, Milk Glass, Tin Cover, 13 In., 2 Piece
$1265.00

Commemorative, Button, Cleveland Brewery, Indian, Cuyahoga County Centennial, Oct., 1910, 1 ½ In.
$136.00

Commemorative, Button, Queen Victoria, In Memoriam, 1901, 1 ¼ In.
$63.00

Commemorative, Jug, Lieutenant General White V.C.G., Portrait, 6 In.
$15.00

Commemorative, Plate, Queen Caroline, Flower Border, 19th Century, 7 ½ In.
$72.00

Compact, Flato, 4-Leaf Clovers, Rhinestones, Goldtone Metal, Hinged, Signed, c.1950, 2 ¾ x 2 ¾ In.
$777.00

Compact, Flato, Rhinestones, Goldtone Metal, Art Deco, Hinged, Signed, c.1930, 2 ½ x 2 ⅓ In.
$448.00

Celluloid, Lady 202.00
Chrome, Flowers 16.00
Chrome Over Brass, Art Deco, England 45.00
Coty, Goldtone Mesh Design, Mirror, Puff, 3 ½ x 2 ¾ In. 65.00
Cuff Bracelet, Hinged, Silver, Rhinestone 255.00
Dorothy Gray, Savoir Faire Mask 99.00
Elgin, E.A.M., Purse, Enamel, Deco 204.00
Estee Lauder, Dolphins 235.00
Estee Lauder, Faux Mother-Of-Pearl Face, Tassle, Mirror, Sun Burnt Powder, 2 ⅜ In. 45.00
Flato, Cat Face, Jeweled Eyes, Box 349.00
Flato, 4-Leaf Clovers, Rhinestones, Goldtone Metal, Hinged, Signed, c.1950, 2 ¾ x 2 ¾ In. *illus* 777.00
Flato, Black Enamel, Goldtone Scrolls, Green Rhinestones, c.1950, 2 ½ x 2 ¼ In.. . . . . 478.00
Flato, Horse & Carriage, Rhinestones, Goldtone Metal, c.1930, 2 ½ x 2 ¼ In. 448.00
Flato, Horseshoe, Clover, Stars, Goldtone Metal, Sleeve, Lipstick Holder, c.1940, 2 ½ In. 538.00
Flato, Leaf Sprig, Goldtone Metal, Pearl Buds, Hinged, c.1940, 2 ½ x 2 ¼ In.. . . . . 508.00
Flato, Rhinestones, Goldtone Metal, Art Deco, Hinged, Signed, c.1930, 2 ½ x 2 ⅓ In. . . . . *illus* 448.00
Flato, Rhinestones, Goldtone Metal, Hinged, Signed, c.1940, 2 ½ x 2 ½ x 5/16 In. . . . . *illus* 777.00
Flato, Scrolls, Blue Rhinestones, Goldtone Metal, Hinged, c.1950, 2 ½ x 2 ¼ In. 508.00
Flato, Seashells, Goldtone Metal, Hinged, Signed, c.1940, 2 ½ x 2 ¼ x ½ In. . . . . *illus* 837.00
Flato, Star, Clovers, Horseshoes, Goldtone Metal, c.1940, 2 ½ x 2 ¼ In. 460.00
Flower & Leaf Design, Etched, Goldtone, Mirror, Puff, 2 ¾ x ⅔ In.. . . . . 40.00
Hat, Big Brim, France 369.00
House Of Westmore, Turquoise, Rouge, Jarol, 1950s, 1 ¼ In. 5.00
Kigu, Playing Cards, Good Luck Symbols 166.00
Lucite Slab, Goldtone Metal, Silver Glitter, Mesh Liner, Puff, 2 ½ x 2 ¾ x ½ In.. . . . . 45.00
Metal, Art Deco, Octagonal, Powder & Rouge Compartments, Polished Metal Mirror, 1 ⅞ In. . 25.00
Molinard, Father, Twist-Up Powder Puff 55.00
Mondaine, Leather, Goldtone Frame, Art Deco Fans, Gold Sparkle, Mirror 35.00
Petite Point Flowers, Ivory Background, Flower Border, Mirror, Puff, Round, 2 ⅝ In. 35.00
Plastic, Acorn Shape, Brown 103.00
Pygmalion Piano, Goldtone Metal, Powder Screen, Mirror, 2¾ In. . . . . . 264.00 to 450.00
Schuco, Cat, Art Deco, Germany, 1926 . . . . . 2334.00
Schuco, Turtle, Plush, Germany, 1929 . . . . . 1499.00
Silver, Enamel, Carved, Ivory 405.00
Silver, Silhouette, Key Ring 50.00
Silvertone Metal, Thistle, Flowers, Scrolls, Mirror, Puff, Rouge. 59.00
Sterling Silver, Turned Pattern, Diamond Shape Grid, Mirrored Lid, c.1944, 2 ¾ In. 84.00
Stratton, Silver Back, Engraved, Spray Of White Flowers, 3 ¼ In. 32.00
Stratton, Pontoon, Playing Cards. 54.00
Super Zell, Automobiles 11.00
Trinity Plate, 2-Sided, Goldtone, Purse 750.00
Van Cleef & Arpels, Enamel, Diamonds, 22K Gold, c.1920, 2 ⅝ x 1 ¾ In. 3107.00
Volupte, Zodiac Hand. 252.00
Wiesner, Rhinestones, Filigree Gold Star, Goldtone Metal, Mirror, Signed Puff, 2 ½ x 2 ¾ In. . 40.00
World War II Sweetheart, Until We Meet Again 125.00
Yellow Gold, Silver, Continental, 20th Century, 3 ½ x 2 ½ In. 4320.00
Zell, Swirl Pattern, Initial Letter Boxes, Dial Wheel, Mirror, Puff, Pink Sleeve 75.00

CONSOLIDATED LAMP AND GLASS COMPANY of Coraopolis, Pennsylvania, was founded in 1894. The company made lamps, tablewares, and art glass. Collectors are particularly interested in the wares made after 1925, including black satin glass, Cosmos, Martele (which resembled Lalique), Ruba Rombic (1928–32 Art Deco line), and colored glasswares. Some Consolidated pieces are very similar to those made by the Phoenix Glass Company. The colors are sometimes different. Consolidated made Martele glass in blue, crystal, green, pink, white, or custard glass with added fired-on color or a satin finish. The company closed for the final time in 1967.

Bonbon, Ruba Rombic, Smoky Topaz, 3 Sections 550.00
Lamp, Dancing Nudes, Frosted, Cobalt Blue Foot & Top, 14 In. 403.00
Pitcher, Ruba Rombic, Smoky Topaz 1450.00
Relish, Ruba Rombic, 2 Sections, Smoky Topaz 875.00
Vase, Bittersweet, Custard, Gold, 12 In. 186.00
Vase, Catalonian, Spanish Knobs, Honey, 6 ½ In. 150.00
Vase, Fern, Light Pink, 7 x 6 In. 153.00
Vase, Sea Gulls, Orange, Green Ground, 11 x 10 In.. . . . . 205.00
Vase, Wild Rose, Red, Opaque Yellow Ground, c.1920, 11 In. . . . . . *illus* 100.00

CONTEMPORARY GLASS, *see Glass-Contemporary.*

COOKBOOKS are collected for various reasons. Some are wanted for the recipes, some for investment, and some as examples of advertising. Cookbooks and recipe pamphlets are included in this category.

Bond Bread, 1933, 22 Pages	5.00
Brer Rabbit Molasses, 1936	18.00
Butter-Krust Bread, 1940s, 8 Pages	7.00
Calumet Baking Powder Recipe Book, 1931, 31 Pages	6.50
Carnation, 1941, 6 ½ x 9 In., 96 Pages	15.00
Chiquita Banana Recipe Book, 1950, 24 Pages	12.00
Davis Gelatine Dainty Dishes Cookbook, Davis Sparkling Gelatine, 48 Pages	8.00
Dr. Price Cookbook, Baking Powder Factory Cook Recipe Book, 1920s, 51 Pages	20.00
Federal Bread The Most Important Food Cookbook, 1925, 24 Pages	12.00
General Electric, The New Art Of Buying, Preserving & Preparing Foods, 1934, 112 Pages	5.00
Honey Recipes, My Favorite Honey Cookbook, 1980s	15.00
Hoover Blenders Cookbook, 5 x 8 In., 67 Pages	15.00
Joan Of Arc Recipe Booklet, Premium, Illinois Canning Co.	7.50
Junket Sherbet Mix Cook Booklet, Fold-Out, 1949, 3 Pages	4.00
KC Baking Powder Cook's Book, 1935, 5 x 7 ½ In., 47 Pages	20.00
Knox Gelatine Cookbook, 1933, 79 Pages	10.00
Knox Gelatine Cookbook, 1943, 40 Pages	12.00
Lea & Perrins Cookbook, Success In Seasoning, 1936, 6 x 7 In., 48 Pages	17.50
Mazola Salad Bowl Cookbook, 1938, 6 x 9 ½ In., 32 Pages	5.00
McNess Cookbook, c.1925, 64 Pages	10.00
Metropolitan Cookbook, 1930s, 64 Pages	10.00
Metropolitan Insurance Recipe Cookbook, 1935, 100 Pages	8.00
Metropolitan Life Insurance Company Cookbook, 1930s, 64 Pages	10.00
Metropolitan Life Insurance Recipe Cookbook, 100 Recipes, 1942, 63 Pages	5.00
My Favorite Honey Cookbook, 1980s, 6 x 9 In., 10 Pages	13.00
One Dish Land O' Lakes Recipes, Healthy Meals, 97 Pages	10.00
Riceland Rice Cookbook, 1952, 30 Pages	12.00
Royal Baking Powder Cookbook, 1932, 45 Pages	6.00
Royal Baking Powder Cookbook Recipes, 100 Recipes, 1932, 5 x 7 ½ In., 31 Pages	5.00
Rumford Baking Powder Cook Booklet, 1913, 12 Pages	45.00
Rumford Common Sense Cookbook, 1900, 7 x 5 In.	17.50
Sealtest Cream Cook Booklet, Tune To Sealtest Village Store, Nib's, 1940s	4.00
Sealtest Food Adviser Cookbook, Dodds Milk, Tune In Rudy Vallee, 1941, 8 Pages	10.00
Sealtest Food Adviser Cookbook, Dodds Sealtest Milk, No. 67, 1947	10.00
Sealtest Food Adviser Cookbook, Holiday 1946, 8 Pages	10.00
Sealtest Food Adviser Cookbook, No. 71, 1948, 8 Pages	10.00
Sealtest Food Adviser Cookbook, No. 75, Dorothy Lamour, 1948	10.00
Sealtest Food Adviser Cookbook, Summer 1940, 8 Pages	10.00
Sealtest Food Adviser Cookbook, Tune In-Village Store Program, No. 71, 1948	10.00
Sealtest Food Adviser Cookbook, Winter 1940, 5 ½ x 7 In., 15 Pages	5.00
Sears Coldspot Freezers Cookbook, 1948, 7 x 10 In., 44 Pages	25.00
Tabasco Sauce Cookbook, 1979, 37 Pages	11.00
The Way To The Heart, Virginia Tested Recipes, Carrie Pickett Moore, 1905, 150 Pages	42.00
White House Cookbook, Mrs. F.l. Gillee & Hugo Zieman, 1894	125.00
Working Wives, Salaried Or Otherwise, Crown Publisher, 1963	70.00

COOKIE JARS with brightly painted designs or amusing figural shapes became popular in the mid-1930s. Many companies made them and collectors search for cookie jars either by design or by maker's name. Listed here are examples by the less common makers. Major factories are listed under their own names in other categories of the book, such as Abingdon, Brush, Hull, McCoy, Metlox, Red Wing, and Shawnee. See also the Disneyana category.

Alice In Wonderland, Queen Of Hearts, Fitz & Floyd, 10 ½ In.	85.00
Bear Beating Drum, Maurice Of California, 10 ½ In.	95.00
Blue Cow, Painted, Flowers, Flair, 12 x 6 In..	48.00
Castle, Sentry Cover Knop, Box, Treasure Craft	33.00
Cat, Painted, N.S. Gustin Co., c.1941, 13 ¾ In.	40.00
Charleton Roses, Forget-me-nots, Tufted Pillow, Consolidated Glass, 6 ½ x 19 ½ In.	85.00
Cheerleaders, Megaphone, Corner Jar, American Bisque	210.00
Cookie Jug, Jug Shape, Cork Insert, Monmouth, 10 x 7 In.	35.00

Compact, Flato, Rhinestones, Goldtone Metal, Hinged, Signed, c.1940, 2 ½ x 2 ½ x 5/16 In.
$777.00

Compact, Flato, Seashells, Goldtone Metal, Hinged, Signed, c.1940, 2 ½ x 2 ¼ x ½ In.
$837.00

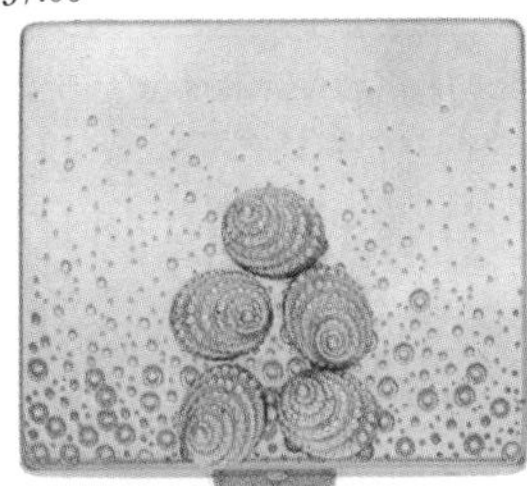

Vanity Cases
A vanity case is a compact plus more. It is a case, perhaps a small purse or box, for a dressing table. It holds rouge, mascara, powder, puff, mirror, lipstick, etc.

Consolidated, Vase, Wild Rose, Red, Opaque Yellow Ground, c.1920, 11 In.
$100.00

Cookie Jar, Cookies, Shaded Mint Green, Ecru Ground, Royal Haeger, c.1957, 11 x 8 In.
$125.00

Cookie Jar, Kitten On Beehive, American Bisque, 11 ¾ In.
$19.00

Cookie Jar, Sandman Cookies, Flasher, Marked, 801, American Bisque, 10 In.
$37.00

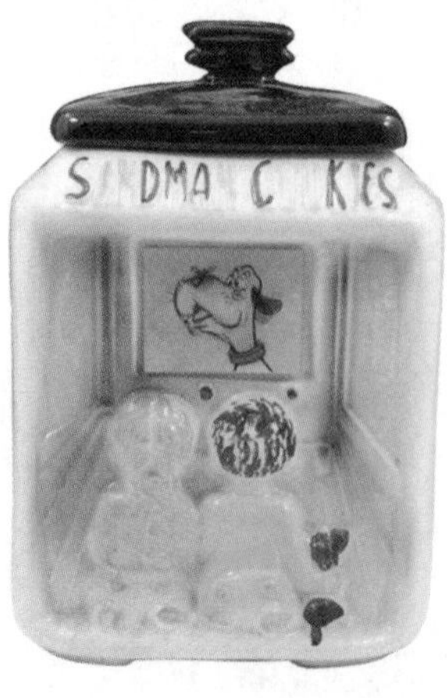

Cookie Sack, Painted, White Ground, Multicolored, Cardinal, 10 In. 75.00
Cookie Shack, Bird In Chimney, Twin Winton, 12 x 7 In. 40.00
Cookie Truck, American Bisque, 13 ¼ In. 25.00
Cookies, Raised Cookies, Walnut Finial, Los Angeles Potteries, 10 In. 55.00
Cookies, Shaded Mint Green, Ecru Ground, Royal Haeger, c.1957, 11 x 8 In. *illus* 125.00
Cooky, Black Chef, Painted, 22K Gold Trim, Peal China Co., 10 ½ x 7 In. 850.00
Country Gourmet, Fitz & Floyd, 10 ¼ x 8 ¾ In. 60.00
Cow Jumped Over The Moon, Yellow, Doranne Of California, 13 ½ In. 275.00
Cowboy Boots, Yellow Star, Embossed Cookies, American Bisque, 12 ½ In. 57.00
Daisy & Dot, Brown Gloss Glaze, Marcrest, 9 ½ x 7 ½ In. 15.00
Dino, Golf Bag, American Bisque, 13 ½ In. 130.00
Dutch Boy, Blue, White, APCO, c.1965, 12 In. 159.00
Dutch Kids, Bartlett Collins, Reverse Painted, Teal, White, 8 x 6 ½ In. 55.00
Friar Tuck Monk, Thou Shalt Not Steal, Ceramic, Japan, 1960s, 12 x 7 In. 56.00
Glass, Chrome Cover, Red Plastic Knob, 6 ¼ x 8 ¼ In. 26.00
Grandma, Basket Of Goodies, White, Green, Orange, Paper Label, Fitz & Floyd, 11 ½ x 7 In. 55.00
Green Cat In The Straw Hat, Japan, 1950s, 10 x 6 In. 55.00
Hansel & Gretel, Pokee, Brown, White, Bartlett Collins, 1960s, 10 x 5 ¼ In. 16.00
Hobbyhorse, Treasure Craft, 12 x 6 In. 65.00
Joyful Noise, Clay Art, c.1999, 10 ½ In. 75.00
Kitten On Beehive, American Bisque, 11 ¾ In. *illus* 19.00
Locomotive, Painted, Green, Black, Maurice Ceramic Of California, 7 ½ x 8 ½ In. 129.00
Mammy, Molded Plastic, Marked F & F Mold & Die Works, Dayton, Ohio, 11 ¾ In. 500.00
Monk, Thou Shalt Not Get Fat, 12 x 5 ¼ In. 285.00
Monkey On Pot, Sierra Vista, 9 ½ x 5 ½ In. 185.00
Mr. & Mrs. Santa Claus, Label, Enesco, c.1987, 10 x 9 In. 24.00
Noah's Art, Animals, Painted, Treasure Craft, 9 x 12 In. 50.00
Nun, Lord Helps Him Who Helps Himself, DeForest Of California, c.1970, 12 ½ In. 125.00
Old Country Roses, Basketweave, Ribbon & Bow, Roses, Gold Trim, Royal Albert, 12 In. 49.00
Old Mother Hubbard Lived In A Shoe, Maurice, Calif., 12 x 11 In. 60.00
Old Woman In The Shoe, Enesco, c.1994 16.00
Oreo Cookie, Chocolate Brown, White, Doranne Of California, 10 ½ x 9 ½ In. 24.00
Oriental Woman, Regal, c.1943, 12 x 9 ½ In. 895.00
Parrot, Painted, Green, Yellow, Red, Spotted, Fitz & Floyd, 8 ½ x 6 In. 85.00
Pennsylvania Dutch, Yellowware, Yellow Slip Glaze, Sun, Flowers, 8 x 7 In. 65.00
Pinky Lee, American Bisque, 10 ½ In. 250.00
Poodle, Wearing Bow, American Bisque, 1960, 10 ½ In. 45.00
Potbellied Stove, Painted, White, Multicolor, Cleminsons Of California, 9 In. 275.00
Puss 'N Boots, Box, Janal 33.00
Quaker Oats, Promotional, 100th Anniversary, Regal China, c.1977 65.00
Rabbit, Carrot, Green Glaze, Yellowware, 1930s, 9 ¾ x 7 ¼ In. 65.00
Rustic, Brown, Decal, Pitcher, Flowers, 1940s, 8 ½ x 6 In. 70.00
Saddle, American Bisque, 12 In. 100.00
Sandman Cookies, Flasher, Marked, 801, American Bisque, 10 In. *illus* 37.00
Santa Claus, Painted, Red, White, Plastic, Empire 21.00
Santa, Plastic, Carolina Enterprises Inc., Empire Crown Mark, 11 ¾ In. 29.00
Sid's Taxi, Signed, Appleman, 15 x 9 ½ In. 600.00
Space Cadet, Laser Gun, Jet Packs, California Originals 125.00
Space Ship, Cookies Out Of This World, American Bisque, 12 ¼ In. 210.00
Squirrel On Log, Using Mallet To Hit Walnut, Brush, c.1961, 10 ½ x 10 ½ In. 145.00
Tole, Flowers, Red Painted Base, Ransburg, 6 ½ x 20 In. 32.00
Tree Log, 3 Bears, Embossed, Cream, Brown, Brock, 10 ½ x 6 In. 25.00
Trolley Car, Brown Matte Finish, Treasure Craft, 10 x 10 In. 55.00
Wagon Wheel Hub, House Of Webster, 7 ½ In. 16.00
Wild West, Boots, Red, Black, White, Yellow, Clay Art, 11 x 9 In. 45.00
Yarn Doll, American Bisque, 12 In. 73.00

COORS ware was made by the Coors Porcelain Company of Golden, Colorado, a company founded with the help of the Coors Brewing Company. Its founder, John Herold, started the Herold China and Pottery Company in 1910. The company name was changed in 1920, when Herold left. Dishes were made from the turn of the century. Coors stopped making nonessential wares at the start of World War II. After the war, the pottery made ovenware, teapots, vases, and a general line of pottery, but no dinnerware—except for special orders. The company is still in business making industrial porcelain. For more information, see *Kovels' Depression Glass & Dinnerware Price List*.

COORS
U.S.A.

Batter Bowl, Rosebud, Blue, Spout, Handle, 8 In. 110.00

Cake Plate, Rosebud, Maroon, Round, 11 In. 121.00
Cake Plate, Thermo-Porcelain, Tulip, Round, 11 In. 85.00
Casserole, Rosebud, Cover, Ivory, 7 In. 150.00
Casserole, Thermo-Porcelain, Open Window, Cover, Indented Handle 95.00
Casserole, Thermo-Porcelain, Tulip, Cover, Indented Handle, 7 In. 95.00
Cookie Jar, Dusty Rose, Flowers, Cover, Flattened Knob, 10 In. 125.00
Cookie Jar, Red, 2 Rope Twist Handles, Cover, 10 In. 75.00
Mixing Bowl, Rosebud, Yellow, 10¼ In. 120.00
Mortar & Pestle, White, Spout, Wood Handle On Pestle, 5-In. Mortar 110.00
Pie Baker, Rosebud, Blue, 11¼ In. 95.00
Pitcher, Thermo-Porcelain, Flowers, 8-Sided, Cover, 7½ In. 169.00
Platter, Rosebud, Yellow, Oval, 2 Handles, 13 In. 69.00
Pudding Bowl, Thermo-Porcelain, Open Window, 8½ In. 95.00
Salt & Pepper, Barley & Hops, Ivory, 4¾ In. 25.00
Vase, Blue Matte Glaze, Stepped Shape, Art Deco, 9 x 6 In. 200.00
Vase, Glossy, Yellow & Satin White, 2 Buttressed Handles, 5 In. 85.00
Vase, Maroon Glaze, White Lion Crest, Decal, Teardrop Shape, 7¾ In. 75.00
Water Jug, Thermo-Porcelain, White, 6-Sided, Shaped Handle, 3¼ Pt. 100.00

COPELAND pieces listed here are those that have a mark including the word *Copeland* used between 1847 and 1976. Marks include *Copeland Spode* and *Copeland & Garrett.* See also Copeland Spode and Royal Worcester.

Bowl, Center, Satyrs Eating Grapes, Impressed Mark, 17 In. 1668.00
Bust, Clytie, Parian, Waisted Round Socle, c.1855, 13¼ In. 411.00
Bust, Mother, Parian, Holding Child, Waisted Round Socle, c.1876, 15 In. 1058.00
Butter Pat, Pansy Flower, Burgundy, Yellow, Cobalt Blue Accent 230.00
Butter Pat, Pansy Flowers, Cobalt Blue & Yellow 230.00
Ewer, Wine, Winged Lady, Serpent, Cobalt Blue Ground, Vine Handle, Grapes, 14 In. 127.00
Figurine, Maidenhood, Gold Trim, Impressed, Parian, c.1861, 22 In. 441.00
Figurine, Sabrina, Parian, W. Calder Marshall, Mid 1800s, 11¾ In. 646.00
Jug Set, Hunting Scene, Embossed, Cream, Tan Ground, Tallest Is 5½ In., 3 Piece 130.00
Pitcher, Baluster, Leaf Molded Spout, Scrolled Handle, Gilt, Columbus & Crew, 7 In. 388.00

COPELAND SPODE appears on some pieces of nineteenth-century English porcelain. Josiah Spode established a pottery at Stoke-on-Trent, England, in 1770. In 1833, the firm was purchased by William Copeland and Thomas Garrett and the mark was changed. In 1847, Copeland became the sole owner and the mark changed again. W.T. Copeland & Sons continued until a 1976 merger when it became Royal Worcester Spode. Pieces are listed in this book under the name that appears in the mark. Copeland Spode, Copeland, and Royal Worcester have separate listings.

Dessert Service, Rust & Gilt Decoration, Square, Lobed, Compotes, Plates, 9 Piece 411.00
Jardiniere, Black & White, Boats On River, 5 x 6 In. 94.00
Pitcher, Chicago Fire, Blue, White, Marked, No. 76, 8¼ In. 345.00
Pitcher, Green, Gold Handle, c.1891, 7 In. 175.00
Platter, Multicolored Turkey, 19th Century, 16¼ x 20½ In. 1293.00

COPPER has been used to make utilitarian items, such as teakettles and cooking pans, since the days of the early American colonists. Copper became a popular metal with the Arts & Crafts makers of the early 1900s, and decorative pieces, like desk sets, were made. Other pieces of copper may be found in the Arts & Crafts, Bradley & Hubbard, Kitchen, Roycroft, and other categories.

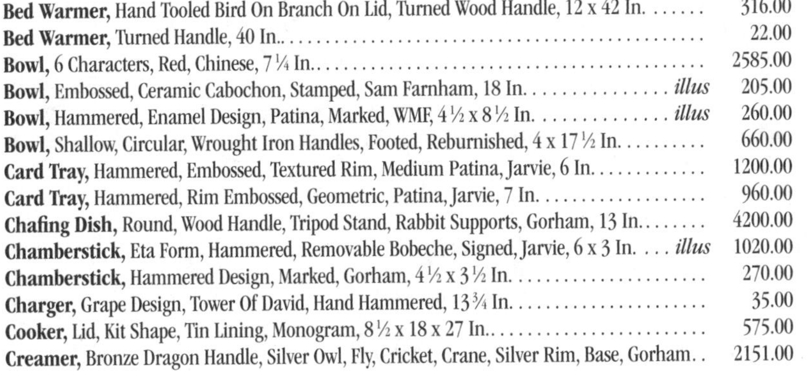

Bed Warmer, Hand Tooled Bird On Branch On Lid, Turned Wood Handle, 12 x 42 In. 316.00
Bed Warmer, Turned Handle, 40 In. 22.00
Bowl, 6 Characters, Red, Chinese, 7¼ In. 2585.00
Bowl, Embossed, Ceramic Cabochon, Stamped, Sam Farnham, 18 In. .... *illus* 205.00
Bowl, Hammered, Enamel Design, Patina, Marked, WMF, 4½ x 8½ In. .... *illus* 260.00
Bowl, Shallow, Circular, Wrought Iron Handles, Footed, Reburnished, 4 x 17½ In. 660.00
Card Tray, Hammered, Embossed, Textured Rim, Medium Patina, Jarvie, 6 In. 1200.00
Card Tray, Hammered, Rim Embossed, Geometric, Patina, Jarvie, 7 In. 960.00
Chafing Dish, Round, Wood Handle, Tripod Stand, Rabbit Supports, Gorham, 13 In. 4200.00
Chamberstick, Eta Form, Hammered, Removable Bobeche, Signed, Jarvie, 6 x 3 In. .... *illus* 1020.00
Chamberstick, Hammered Design, Marked, Gorham, 4½ x 3½ In. 270.00
Charger, Grape Design, Tower Of David, Hand Hammered, 13¾ In. 35.00
Cooker, Lid, Kit Shape, Tin Lining, Monogram, 8½ x 18 x 27 In. 575.00
Creamer, Bronze Dragon Handle, Silver Owl, Fly, Cricket, Crane, Silver Rim, Base, Gorham. . 2151.00

Copper, Bowl, Embossed, Ceramic Cabochon, Stamped, Sam Farnham, 18 In.
$205.00

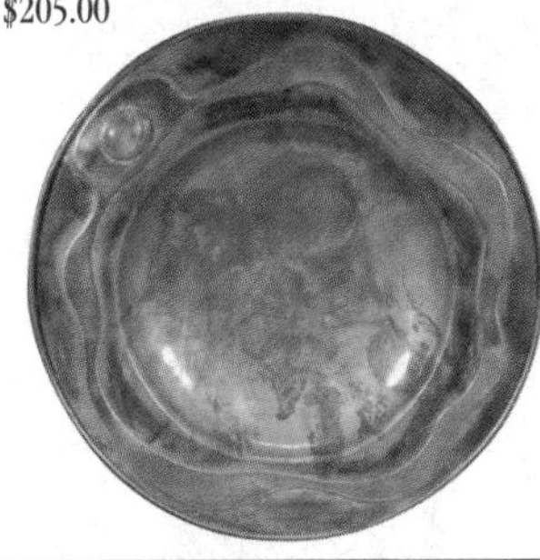

Copper, Bowl, Hammered, Enamel Design, Patina, Marked, WMF, 4½ x 8½ In.
$260.00

Tarnish Prevention
We prefer the modern tarnish-preventing polishes. There is more time between cleanings.

Copper, Chamberstick, Eta Form, Hammered, Removable Bobeche, Signed, Jarvie, 6 x 3 In.
$1020.00

Copper, Plate, Hammered, Inlaid Metal Star, Marked Linossier, 15¾ In.
$920.00

TIP
Don't display copper on bare wooden shelves. The wood should be sealed with varnish to avoid allowing the acids in the wood and the acid vapors to attack the copper.

Copper, Tea Caddy, Applied Silver Snail, Grapes, Bird, Butterflies, Gorham, 1869, 4¼ In.
$1560.00

Copper, Tray, Arts & Crafts, Cutout Handles, Oak Bottom, 4 x 18 x 7½ In.
$525.00

TIP
Polish brass, copper, or pewter only once or twice a year.

Cup, 2 Handles, 18th Century, 5 In. . . . 55.00
Food Warmer, Dome Lid, Acorn Finial, Footed, Gadrooned Border, Sunburst, 12 x 14 In. . . . 500.00
Inkwell, Double, Hand Hammered, Glass Liners, Hinged, Copper Rivet, Signed, Stickley,. . . . 4300.00
Jar, Water, Hammered, Patinated, Flat Everted Lip, Geometric Pattern, Middle East, 13 In. . . . 120.00
Jardiniere, Brass Handles, Owls, Birds Of Paradise, 12 x 13 In. . . . 1200.00
Jardiniere, Hammered, Red Lacquer Finish, Turchin Co., 7 x 13 In. . . . 117.00
Jug, Brass, Hammered, Arts & Crafts, 5 In. . . . 45.00
Kettle, Bail Handle, Marked, Harbeson . . . 9200.00
Kettle, Candy, Canted, Dovetailed Seams, Iron Handles, JM Kavanagh, Balto., 8 x 26 In. . . . 77.00
Kettle, Dovetailed Body, Applied Gooseneck Spout, 14 x 11 In. . . . 4675.00
Kettle, Pewter Lined, Wire Handle, Iron Bolsters, Hudson Bay Copper Trade, 5 x 5 In. . . . 83.00
Kindling Bucket, Brass, Swing Handle, Rivet Bands, Burnished, France, 13 x 16 In. . . . 780.00
Ladle, Hemispheric, Brass Handle, Marked, Paul Beyer, Philadelphia, 21 In., 2 Piece. . . . 253.00
Mirror, Arts & Crafts Style, Hammered, Raised Flower Medallion, Beveled, Square 14 In. . . . 81.00
Mirror, Hammered, Raised Floral Medallion Corner, Beveled Mirror, 14 In. . . . 80.00
Molds are listed in the Kitchen category.
Oil Lamp, Tray, Hammered Design, Marked, Gorham, 5½ x 2½ In. . . . 450.00
Pan, Poaching, Lozenge Form, 2 Handles, France, 10 x 19½ x 26¼ In. . . . 900.00
Pan, Sauce, Long Wrought Iron Handle, Reburnished, France, 9 In. . . . 561.00
Pitcher, Bohemian, Hand Chased Design, Coat Of Arms, Early 1800s, 17½ In. . . . 403.00
Pitcher, Hammered, Original Patina, Stickley Brothers, 14½ x 10 In. . . . 140.00
Pitcher, Riveted Handle, Marked, 14¼ x 7¼ In. . . . 600.00
Pitcher, Tapered, Wide Shoulder, Small Spout, Flat Lid, Ring Finial, Dovetailed, 8½ In. . . . 115.00
Plaque, Relief Allegorical, Austria, Frame, 19th Century, 19 x 10½ In., Pair . . . 1638.00
Plaque, Wall, Repousse, Petrus Paulus Rubens, c.1900, 25½ In. . . . 207.00
Plate, Hammered, Inlaid Metal Star, Marked Linossier, 15¾ In. . . . *illus* 920.00
Plate, Hammered, Inlaid Metal Star Pattern, Copper To Red, Linossier, 15¾ In. . . . 920.00
Pot, 2 Handles, Burnished, Early 20th Century, 6 x 15 In. . . . 360.00
Pot, Brass Handles, Circular, France, 5½ x 18 In. . . . 627.00
Pot, Cooking, Wrought Steel Handle, Reburnished, France, 5¼ x 19¾ In. . . . 462.00
Pot, Cover, Brass Handles, Oval, Reburnished, 5½ x 12 In. . . . 594.00
Pot, Hammered, Dovetailed, Handles, 8½ x 8½ In. . . . 115.00
Pot, Lid, Oval, Iron Swing Handle, Late 19th Century, 13 x 18 In. . . . 960.00
Pot, Wrought Iron Handle, Early 20th Century, 10¾ x 11¾ In. . . . 420.00
Sauce Pot, Brass Handle, Cylindrical, France, 9½ x 9½ In. . . . 360.00
Standish, Brass Footed, Lobed Ends, Ink Bottle Wells, Pen, 1800s, 13 x 8 In. . . . 118.00
Tankard, Repousse, Brass Trim, Marked WMF, 15½ In. . . . 495.00
Tea Caddy, Applied Silver Snail, Grapes, Bird, Butterflies, Gorham, 1869, 4¼ In. . . . *illus* 1560.00
Tea Service, Silver, Hammered, Applied Bunches Of Grain, Birds, Butterflies, 1902, 4 Piece . . 5750.00
Teakettle, Dome Lid, Swing Handle, Short Spout, Dovetailed, 8 x 9½ In. . . . 270.00
Teakettle, Gooseneck, C-Shape Handle, Dome Lid, Brass Finial, Heiss Phila, 11 x 12 x 8 In. . . . 825.00
Teakettle, Gooseneck, Dome Lid, Arched Finial, Stamped, H. De, 13½ x 14½ x 10 In. . . . 330.00
Teakettle, Gooseneck, Dome Lid, Brass Finial, Crown Handle, 11 x 11½ x 8 In. . . . 165.00
Teakettle, Gooseneck, Dome Lid, Crown Handle, American, 1800s, 12½ x 14 x 10 In. . . . 248.00
Teakettle, Marked On Handle, J Scaife, Pittsburgh, 1815-40, 11 In. . . . 2500.00
Teakettle, Swing Handle, Brass Finial, Marked, 5, 1800s, 5 Qt., 11½ In. . . . 360.00
Teapot, Hammered, Flat Double Banded Handle, Brass Mounts, 1800s, 9¾ In. . . . 230.00
Tray, Arts & Crafts, Cutout Handles, Oak Bottom, 4 x 18 x 7½ In. . . . *illus* 525.00
Tray, Haloed Figures, Animals, Relief, 10 x 11 In. . . . 125.00
Tray, Hammered, 2 Handles, Benedict Art Studio, c.1910, 15½ In. . . . 117.00
Tray, Oval, Cutout Handles, Original Patina, Arts & Crafts, 22 x 14 In. . . . 120.00
Tray, Rectangle, Incised Landscape, Silver Bird, Butterflies, Plants, Gorham, 11 x 8 In. . . . 1195.00
Tray, Rectangular, Incurved Edge, Applied Lilies, Leaves, Birds, Gorham, c.1881, 10 In. . . . 2160.00
Tub, Banded, Studded, Patinated, Continental, 20th Century, 16½ x 23 In. . . . 480.00
Tub, Banded, Studded, Patinated, Continental, 20th Century, 22 x 30 In. . . . 960.00
Tub, Banded, Studded, Patinated, Continental, 20th Century, 24 x 32½ In. . . . 960.00
Umbrella Stand, Embossed C Monogram, 24¾ x 14 In. . . . 1800.00
Urn, Hammered, Handles, 17½ x 12 In. . . . 25.00
Vase, 2 Handles, Horse Head, Grapes, Orivit, Marked, 9½ x 10 In. . . . 60.00
Vase, Hammered, Bulbous, Original Patina, Arts & Crafts, 13 x 13 In. . . . 575.00
Vase, Hammered, Silver, Oval, Claudius Linossier, 6¾ x 6¾ In. . . . 9600.00
Wash Tub, ⅔ Hinged Lid, Ring Handle, 15 x 22 x 18 In. . . . 287.00
Watering Can, Engraved Flowers, England, 19th Century . . . 395.00

COPPER LUSTER *items are listed in the Luster category.*

CORALENE glass was made by firing many small colored beads on the outside of glassware. It was made in many patterns in the United States and Europe in the 1880s. Reproductions are made today. Coralene-decorated Japanese pottery is listed in the Japanese Coralene category.

Bowl, Blue Flowers, Mother-Of-Pearl, Herringbone, Amber To Pearl, 3 ½ x 7 ½ In. 575.00
Butter Cover, Domed, Wheat Stalks, Shaded Pink, Ruffled Finial, 7 ½ In. 29.00
Vase, Allover Seaweed, Mother-Of-Pearl, Herringbone, Bottle Shape, 8 ¾ In., 8 ¾ In. 725.00
Vase, Allover Yellow Coral, Light Blue To White, Footed, 4 In. 173.00
Vase, Diamond Quilted, Purple Flowers, Mother-Of-Pearl, Blue To White, 6 In. 945.00
Vase, Pink, Gold Fleur-De-Lis, Diamond Quilted, Mother-Of-Pearl, 7 In. 290.00
Vase, Yellow Flowers, Blue Herringbone, Mother-Of-Pearl, 4-Lobe Shape, 8 ¼ In. 415.00
Vase, Yellow Seaweed, Blue & Cream Alternating Bands, Satin, 9 In. 345.00
Vase, Yellow Seaweed, Pink, Moire Mother-Of-Pearl, 6 ⅞ In. 275.00
Vase, Yellow Stars, Blue Herringbone, Mother-Of-Pearl, 8 In. 350.00
Vase, Yellow Stars, Red To Pink, Herringbone, Mother-Of-Pearl, 8 In. 345.00

CORKSCREWS have been needed since the first bottle was sealed with a cork, probably in the seventeenth century. Today collectors search for the early, unusual patented examples or the figural corkscrews of recent years.

Brass Sailboat Handle, Hanging Loop, England, 1930-40s, 5 ¾ x 2 ⅛ In. 65.00
Bronze, Brass, Wood, Barrel Shape Column, England, 6 ½ In. 359.00
Cat, Metal, 3 Colored Rhinestones, Gloss Finish, Mid Century, 3 x 5 In. 20.00
Chrome Over Iron, Le Presto, France, c.1900, 6 In. 475.00
Clown, Mechanical, Bottle Opener, Metal, 1920-30s, 10 x 4 ¼ In. 326.00
Dog, English Setter, Figural, Brass Handle, England, 1930-40s, 4 ¾ x 3 In. 78.00
Grapes, Vines, Bronze, Steel Helix, 5 In. 75.00
Ivory Brush, Bronze Column Base, 19th Century 956.00
Ivory Handle, Cast Iron Shank, 5 In. 225.00
Kentucky Tavern Whiskey, Opener, 2 In. 5.00
Lady's Leg, Blue & White Stripes, Folding, Germany .... *illus* 165.00
Metal, Fold-Out Lid Lifter, Orange Plastic Case, 4 ¼ In. 15.00
Metal, Wood, Williams, 3 ½ x ¾ In. 29.00
Monkey Head Handle, Carved Tropical Nut, Metal Eyes, Inset Ears, Hat, 4 ¼ x 1 ½ In. 55.00
Olive Wood, Wood, Iron, Double Handle Grip, Italy, 8 In. 2271.00
Pig, Tail, Metal, 1900s. 112.00
Plastic Handle, Green, 5 ¼ In. 10.00
Plastic Handle, Red. 12.00
Pocket Knife, Combination, 14K Gold 175.00
Riding Boot, Sterling Silver, Gorham. 125.00
Sterling Silver, Hammered Funnel, Black Leather Travel Case 350.00
Sterling Silver Handlebar, 2 ¾ x 3 In. 38.00
Vaughans, Opener, 5 ½ In. 4.00
Wood, Steel, Adjustable Compression Spring, c.1920, 6 ½ In. 88.00
Worms, Bells, Waiter, Painted, c.1940-50s 247.00

CORONATION souvenirs have been made since the 1800s. Pottery, glass, tin, silver, and paper objects with a picture of the monarchs and date have been sold at many coronations. The pieces that mention King Edward VIII, the king who was never crowned, are not rare; collectors should be sure to check values before buying. Related pieces are found in the Commemorative category.

Beaker, King Edward VII, Alexandra, Town, Hamlets, Watcombe Torquay, 4 ¼ In. .... *illus* 43.00
Beaker, King Edward VII, Children, Gold Band, Enamel, 1902 .... 75.00
Beaker, King Edward VIII, Triple Reeded Feet, Wedgwood, 1937. .... 130.00
Bottle, Labatts Beer, Queen Elizabeth, Gold Foil Wrapped, 1953, 9 ½ In. 200.00
Bowl, King George V & Queen Mary, Pierced Rim, Porcelain, 1911 .... 55.00
Corkscrew, Key Shape, Queen Elizabeth, 1953, 7 ½ In. 121.00
Corkscrew, Lion, Unicorn, Crown, Rose, Thistle, Daffodil, Shamrock, 1953, 7 ½ In. 121.00
Cup, Nicholas II, Czar, Russia, 1896, 4 In. .... *illus* 600.00
Dish, King George V & Queen Mary, Portraits, Royal Doulton, 1911. .... 55.00
Dish, King George VI & Queen Elizabeth, Square, Scalloped Edge, Aynsley, 1937 .... 15.00
Handkerchief, Edward VIII, 11 x 11 In. 65.00
Humidor, King George V & Queen Mary, Moorcroft, 1911. .... 125.00
Medal, King George VI & Queen Elizabeth, Pin, Ribbon, 1937, 2 ¾ x 1 ¼ In. 46.00
Medallion, King George VI, State Of Victoria, Stokes Of Melbourne, 1937. .... 75.00
Mug, King Edward VII, Coat Of Arms, Flowers Of The Union, Gilded Rim, 1902 .... 65.00

Corkscrew, Lady's Leg, Blue & White Stripes, Folding, Germany
$165.00

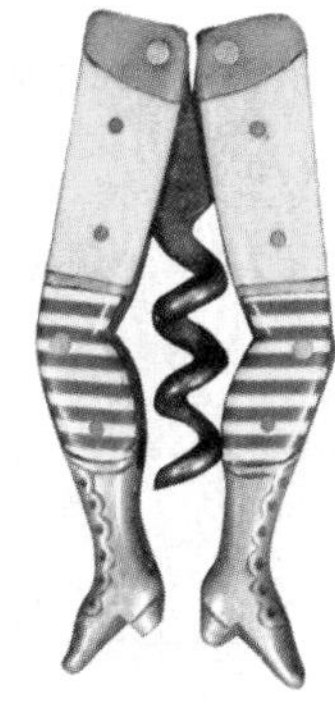

Coronation, Beaker, King Edward VII, Alexandra, Town, Hamlets, Watcombe Torquay, 4 ¼ In.
$43.00

Coronation, Cup, Nicholas II, Czar, Russia, 1896, 4 In.
$600.00

Coronation, Mug, King Edward VIII, Art Deco, 1937
$75.00

CORONATION

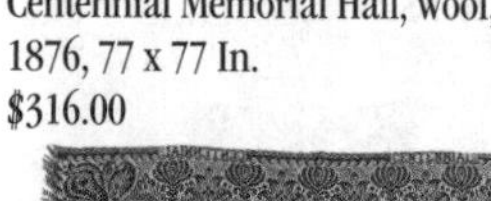

Coverlet, Jacquard, Blue, White, Centennial Memorial Hall, Wool, 1876, 77 x 77 In.
$316.00

Coverlet, Jacquard, Double Roses, Stars, William Stroud, Cadiz, Ohio, 1836, 72 x 79 In.
$748.00

Coverlet, Jacquard, Red, Blue, Green, Flower Border, Wool, David Yingst Lebanon, 1867, 84 x 95 In.
$92.00

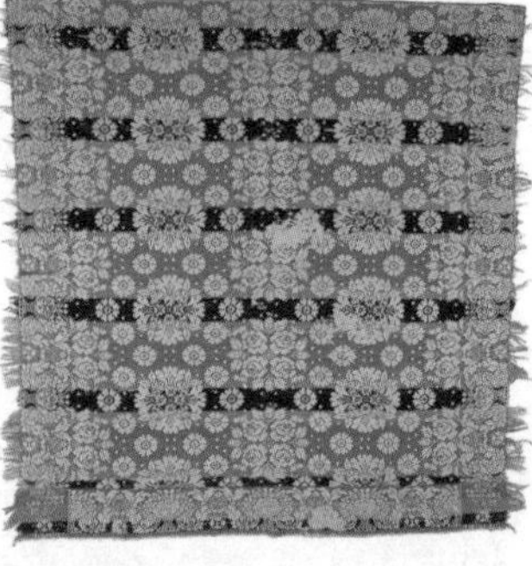

Coverlet, Jacquard, Washington Hall, 3 Fringed Sides, 1869, 76 x 82 In.
$110.00

Mug, King Edward VII, Portraits, Dates, Bone China, 1902 . . . . . 65.00
Mug, King Edward VII & Queen Alexandra, Barrel, Lion, Shield, 1902 . . . . . 50.00
Mug, King Edward VIII, Art Deco, 1937 . . . . . *illus* 75.00
Mug, King George V & Queen Mary, Portraits, Military Scene, Bone China, Aynsley, 1911 . . . . 95.00
Mug, King George V & Queen Mary, Shelley, 1911 . . . . . 45.00
Mug, Queen Elizabeth II, Portrait, Creamware, 1953, 4 x 3 In. 58.00
Mug, Queen Elizabeth II, Rose, Daffodil, Thistle, Shamrock, 1953 . . . . . 30.00
Mug, Queen Victoria In Purple Print, Swansea, 1837-1901 . . . . . 1450.00
Pen Knife, Queen Elizabeth II, Crown, Orb, Scepter, Silver Metal, 1¾ In. 47.00
Pin Tray, King Edward VIII, 12 In. 78.00
Plate, King George V, Royal Worcester, 1911, 10½ In. 95.00
Plate, King George V & Queen Mary, 1911, 5½ In. 35.00
Plate, King George V & Queen Mary, Cetem Ware, 1911 . . . . . 55.00
Plate, Portraits Of King George V & Queen Mary, 1910-36, 5½ In. 35.00
Plate, Queen Elizabeth II, 1953 . . . . . 65.00
Plate, Queen Elizabeth II, Pressed Glass, Beaded Letters, 1953, 10½ In. 60.00
Plate, Queen Elizabeth II, Scalloped Rim, 1953, 5½ In. 35.00
Plate, Queen Victoria, Daisy Border, Luster Trim, Staffordshire, 1838, 6 In. 750.00
Plate, Roasting, King George & Queen Mary, Blue, White, 1911 . . . . . 75.00
Tankard, King George VI, Pewter, 1937, 2¾ In. 69.00
Toffee Tin, Queen Elizabeth & Prince Philip, 4¾ x 4¾ x 3 In. 45.00
Tray, King Edward VIII, Tin, 1937, 12 In. 78.00

COVERLETS were made of linen or wool during the nineteenth century. Most of the coverlets date from 1800 to the 1880s. There was a revival of hand weaving in the 1920s and new coverlets, especially geometric patterns, were made. The earliest coverlets were made on narrow looms, so two woven strips were joined together and a seam can be found. The weave structures of coverlets can include summer and winter, double weave, overshot, and others. Jacquard coverlets have elaborate pictorial patterns that are made on a special loom or with the use of a special attachment. Quilts are listed in this book in their own category.

Central Medallion, Roses, Leaves, Vines, Red, Blue, Green, Fringes, 90 x 96 In. 81.00
Double Weave, Blue & White, Wool & Cotton, Blue, Medallions, 1851, 88 x 76 In. 265.00
Jacquard, 4 Roses, Oval Frame, 8-Point Star, Fruit Basket, 1860, 91 x 86 In. 1265.00
Jacquard, Blue, Orange, Flowers, House, Animals, Jacob Schnell, York County, 1848, 96 x 84 In. 440.00
Jacquard, Blue, White, Centennial Memorial Hall, Wool, 1876, 77 x 77 In. . . . . . *illus* 316.00
Jacquard, Blue & White, Medallion, Baskets Of Flowers, Floral Vine Border, 75 x 90 In. 220.00
Jacquard, Blue & White, Stars, Snowflakes, Bird & Tree Border, c.1855, 70 x 96 In. 176.00
Jacquard, Blue & White, Wool, Cotton, 6 Medallions, Flowers, 1839, 93 x 74 In. 588.00
Jacquard, Blue & White, Wool, Cotton, Flowers, Pineapples, Star, Birds, 1845, 95 x 77 In. 558.00
Jacquard, Blue & White, Wool, Cotton, Medallions, Bird Border, 1838, 94 x 71 In. 825.00
Jacquard, Double Roses, Stars, William Stroud, Cadiz, Ohio, 1836, 72 x 79 In. . . . . . *illus* 748.00
Jacquard, Double Weave, Blue Wool, Eagle On Branch, Peacock Fringe, 1849, 82 x 88 In. . . . 450.00
Jacquard, Double Weave, Blue Wool, Natural Cotton, Harry Tyler, N.Y., c.1858, 80 x 91 In. . . . 1610.00
Jacquard, Double Weave, Blue Wool, Natural Cotton, Rose Center Field, 72 x 80 In. 115.00
Jacquard, Double Weave, Indigo Blue, Natural, Rose Center Field, Wool, Cotton, 76 x 84 In. . 288.00
Jacquard, Flowers, Ribboned Bouquets, Vining Flowers, Craig, c.1843, 83 x 98 In. 518.00
Jacquard, Indigo Blue, Red Wool, Natural Cotton, Isaac Sheaffer, 84 x 90 In. 633.00
Jacquard, Indigo Wool, Double Roses, Eagles, Stars, Fruit Trees, 72 x 79 In. 748.00
Jacquard, Navy Blue, White, Sailboat Corner Blocks, Gilmour Brothers, Ind., 72 x 86 In. 345.00
Jacquard, Red, Blue, Blue Green, Grapevine Borders, Wool, Ardner, Mt. Vernon, 78 x 86 In. . . 920.00
Jacquard, Red, Blue, Green, Flower Border, Wool, David Yingst Lebanon, 1867, 84 x 95 In. *illus* 92.00
Jacquard, Red, Blue, Snowflake, Geometrics, J. Brosey, 1850 For J. Hare, 2 Panel, 80 x 94 In. . 220.00
Jacquard, Red, Blue, Turquoise, White, C. Hefner, Greentown, Ohio, 90 x 74 In. 575.00
Jacquard, Red, Yellow, Blue, Center Medallion, Flowers, Leaves, Fringe, 100 x 90 In. 198.00
Jacquard, Red & White, Floral Center, Cotton & Wool, 19th Century, 90 x 80 In. 470.00
Jacquard, Washington Hall, 3 Fringed Sides, 1869, 76 x 82 In. . . . . . *illus* 110.00
Overshot, Blue & White, Geometric, 2 Panel, 64 x 89 In. 35.00
Overshot, Interlocking Circles, Gold, Indigo Blue, Linen Warp, Wool Weft, c.1875, 61 x 90 In. 540.00
Overshot, Linen Warp, Indigo & Rust Wood Weft, Banded Squares, c.1880, 71 x 94 In. 360.00
Overshot, Summer & Winter, Blue & White, 19th Century 138.00
Overshot, Whig's Retreat, Linen & Indigo Wool Warp, Fringe, c.1875, 72 x 84 In. 390.00
Overshot, Wizard's Rainbow, Summer & Winter, Linen Warp, Blue Wool Weft, 69 x 81 In. . . . 390.00
Snowflakes, Geometric, Pine Tree Border, Fringe, Blue, White, 78 x 84 In. 230.00
Star, Flowers, Geometric Triangles, Fringe, P. Schum, 76 x 80 In. 250.00
Summer & Winter, Blue, White, Indigo Blue Wool, Cotton, Geometric, 80 x 86 In. 173.00
Summer & Winter, Blue & White, Wool, Cotton, Geometric Tree Borders, 1800s, 94 x 76 In. . 295.00

Summer & Winter, Multicolored, Center Star, Flowers, Mid 19th Century, 76 x 80 In. 280.00
Tomato Red, Indigo Blue, Olive Green, Flower Medallions, 88 x 92 In. 288.00
Wool, Bird, Flower Urn, Blue, White, 19th Century, 73 x 78 In. 295.00

COWAN POTTERY made art pottery and wares for florists. Guy Cowan made pottery in Rocky River, Ohio, a suburb of Cleveland, from 1913 to 1931. A stylized mark with the word *Cowan* was used on most pieces. A commercial, mass-produced line was marked *Lakeware*. Collectors today search for the Art Deco pieces by Guy Cowan, Viktor Schreckengost, Waylande Gregory, or Thelma Frazier Winter.

Ashtray, Ram, Egyptian Blue, Marked, Edris Eckhardt, 5⅜ In. .... *illus* 315.00
Bookends, Elephants, Push-Pull, Margaret Postgate, Ivory, 4½ In. 250.00
Bookends, Horse, Kicking, Black Semigloss, Gregory, c.1931, 9 x 6 In. .... *illus* 1695.00
Bookends, Horse, Kicking, Egyptian Blue, Waylande Gregory, 8½ In. 1700.00
Bookends, Polar Bears, Margaret Postgate 6000.00
Bookends, Rams, Charging, Black Glaze, 7½ In. 1500.00
Bookends, Scholar, Antique Green, 6¼ In. 200.00
Candlestick, Rowfant Club, Lion, Book, Pine Green, Frank Wilcox, c.1925, 9¼ In. 1300.00
Console Set, April Green, Marked, 16⅝-In. Bowl, 3 Piece .... *illus* 89.00
Console Set, Copper Luster Glaze, 4 x 11-In. Bowl, 3-In. Candlesticks, 3 Piece .... *illus* 82.00
Decanter, King & Queen, Marked, 11⅞ In. .... *illus* 1150.00
Figurine, Flower Bowl, Saguinay Stag, Green, Mother-Of-Pearl, Marked, 10 x 8 In. ..... *illus* 345.00
Figurine, Head, Girl, Art Deco, Primrose, Waylande Gregory, 16 In. 2700.00
Figurine, Russian Peasant, Accordion Player, Parchment 600.00
Figurine, Russian Peasant, Dancer, Terra-Cotta, Alexander Blazys, c.1927 .... 650.00
Figurine, Russian Peasant, Tambourine Player, Parchment 650.00
Flower Frog, Awakening, Ivory, R.G. Cowan 300.00
Flower Frog, Debutante, Ivory, 14¼ In. 750.00
Flower Frog, Female Figure, White High Glaze, Mark, 4½ x 9¾ In. 431.00
Flower Frog, Flamingo, Oriental Red Glaze, 11½ In. 325.00
Flower Frog, Mayflower Stag, Caramel, 8¼ In. 450.00
Flower Frog, Pavlova, Caramel, Green Overtones, R.G. Cowan, 6¼ In. 500.00
Flower Frog, Swirl Dancer, 10¼ In. 600.00
Lamp, Aztec Man, Holding Jug Over Head, Art Deco, Waylande Gregory 500.00
Lamp, Urn, Black, Gold, Lady Head Handles 325.00
Lamp, Waylande Gregory, Seated Nude Profile, White Glaze, Art Deco 650.00
Lamp, Woodland Nymph, Nude, Seated On Tree Stump, Ivory, Waylande Gregory, 14 In. 3750.00
Plaque, Round, Polo, Ming Green, Viktor Schreckengost, 11½ In. 1400.00
Plate, Sea, Fish In Spiral, Clair De Lune Glaze, Thelma Frazier, 11¼ In. 1528.00
Vase, Logan, Marigold, Handles, Marked, 8⅛ x 7⅛ In. .... *illus* 65.00
Vase, Seahorse, Fan, Verbena, 7 x 6½ In. .... *illus* 77.00
Vase, Squirrel, Crane, Pheasant, Mother-Of-Pearl Glaze, Waylande Gregory, 8¼ In. 1200.00
Vase, Squirrels, Ball Shape, Footed, Mother-Of-Pearl Glaze, Waylande Gregory, 1930, 8 In. 323.00
Vase, Women In Woodland, Abstract, Mottled Multicolored Glaze, 8½ In. 264.00

CRACKER JACK, the molasses-flavored popcorn mixture, was first made in 1896 in Chicago, Illinois. A prize was added to each box in 1912. Collectors search for the old boxes, toys, and advertising materials. Many of the toys are unmarked.

Box, Jack In Black Uniform, Bingo, White, Cardboard, 1915 .... 120.00
Box, More You Eat The More You Want, 5 Cents, Cardboard, 1908, 6 x 3 In. 60.00
Crate, Shipping, 100 Packs, 32¾ x 13¼ x 9¼ In. 660.00
Mirror, Red & White Box, 2¼ In. 253.00
Toy, Car, 1920s Sedan, Metal 45.00
Toy, Cop On Motorcycle, Metal 90.00
Toy, Horse Pulling Wagon, Metal 45.00
Toy, Toonerville Trolley, Tin, 2½ In. 460.00

CRACKLE GLASS was originally made by the Venetians, but most of the ware found today dates from the 1800s. The glass was heated, cooled, and refired so that many small lines appeared inside the glass. It was made in many factories in the United States and Europe.

Basket, Green, Kanawha, 4 x 4⅛ x 3¼ In. 25.00
Basket, Satin, Amber, Kanawha, 4 x 4 x 3¼ In. 25.00
Bowl, Amberina, Ruffled Rim, Kanawha, 3 x 5½ In. 20.00
Bowl, Floral Enameled, Amber, 1960s, 6¼ x 8 In. 35.00
Candy Dish, Heart Shape, Tangerine, Applied Handle, 6½ x 6¾ x 1½ In. 18.00
Candy Jar, Iridescent Body, Smokey Blue Finial Top & Base, 8¼ x 4 In. 70.00

Cowan, Ashtray, Ram, Egyptian Blue, Marked, Edris Eckhardt, 5⅜ In.
$315.00

Cowan, Bookends, Horse, Kicking, Black Semigloss, Gregory, c.1931, 9 x 6 In.
$1695.00

Cowan, Console Set, April Green, Marked, 16⅝-In. Bowl, 3 Piece
$89.00

Cowan, Console Set, Copper Luster Glaze, 4 x 11-In. Bowl, 3-In. Candlesticks, 3 Piece
$82.00

Cowan, Decanter, King & Queen, Marked, 11⅞ In.
$1150.00

Cowan, Figurine, Flower Bowl, Saguinay Stag, Green, Mother-Of-Pearl, Marked, 10 x 8 In.
$345.00

Cowan, Vase, Logan, Marigold, Handles, Marked, 8 ⅛ x 7 ⅛ In.
$65.00

Cowan, Vase, Seahorse, Fan, Verbena, 7 x 6 ½ In.
$77.00

Cranberry, Vase, Portrait, Flowers In Hair, Scalloped Rim, Gilt, 13 x 4 In.
$320.00

Decanter, Stopper, Amberina, Hamon, 9 In. 65.00
Decanter, Stopper, Applied Blue Spiral, Rainbow Glass Co., 12 In. 85.00
Decanter, Stopper, Olive Green, Rainbow Glass Co., 14 ½ In. 60.00
Figurine, Pear, Clear, Applied Green Leaf & Stem, 5 ½ In. 65.00
Jug, Light Cobalt Blue, Clear Handle, Pilgrim, 4 In. 18.00
Patio Light, Ruby Red, Viking, 4 x 4 ¾ In. 36.00
Pitcher, Amberina, Molded Foot, Applied Yellow Handle, 4 ½ In. 22.00
Pitcher, Amethyst, Pilgrim, Handle, 5 In. 38.00
Pitcher, Blue Satin, Applied Blue Handle, Kanawha, 5 ¼ In. 45.00
Pitcher, Cranberry, Applied Clear Handle, Rainbow Glass Co., 5 In. 45.00
Pitcher, Light Cobalt Blue, Applied Handle, Rainbow Glass Co., 5 In. 20.00
Pitcher, Pale Yellow, Applied Handle, Pilgrim, 5 In. 25.00
Pitcher, Pink, Handle, 2 5/16 In. 25.00
Vase, Applied Scrolls, Green, 4 ¾ x 2 ¾ In. 24.00
Vase, Hat Shape, 2 ¾ x 3 ⅝ x 4 ¾ In. 30.00
Vase, Hat Shape, Pale Green, Pilgrim, 2 ½ x 3 ⅝ x 2 ¾ In. 17.00
Vase, Heart Shape, Amber, 5 ⅛ x 3 ½ In. 40.00
Vase, Pinched, Cranberry Flashing, Pilgrim, 5 x 4 ½ In. 50.00
Vase, Pinched, Emerald Green, 1960s, 4 ½ In. 30.00
Vase, Pinched, Emerald Green, Pilgrim, 8 x 6 In. 58.00

CRANBERRY GLASS is an almost transparent yellow-red glass. It resembles the color of cranberry juice. The glass has been made in Europe and America since the Civil War. It is still being made, and reproductions can fool the unwary. Related glass items may be listed in other categories, such as Northwood, Rubina Verde, etc.

Bottle, Dresser, Sterling Overlay, Monogrammed Cartouche, 7 ½ In., Pair 3738.00
Bottle, Stopper, 6 ½ In. 65.00
Compote, Melon Ribbed, Sawtooth Rim, Interior Opalescent Spatter, 5 In. 59.00
Console Set, Candlesticks, White Opalescent Rim, 2 x 12-In. Bowl, 3 Piece 308.00
Decanter, Stopper, Controlled Bubbles, 1960s, 10 In. 30.00
Dresser Box, Fitted Filigree Ormolu, Porcelain Medallion On Cover, c.1900, 3 In. 325.00
Dresser Box, Gold Enameled, Enameled Cupid, Medallion On Cover, c.1900, 4 In. 177.00
Epergne, Flower Stem, Applied Twisted Snake, Victorian, 13 ½ In. 288.00
Lamp, White Enamel, Gold Banding, Burner, 9 ½ In. 86.00
Pitcher, Inverted Thumbprint, Victorian, 7 In. 59.00
Rose Bowl, Inverted Coin Dot 35.00
Sugar Shaker, Inverted Thumbprint 95.00
Syrup, Inverted Thumbprint, Pewter Lip, Hobbs, Brockunier, 1883, 7 ¾ In. 385.00
Tumbler, Enameled Flowers, Victorian, 4 In., 4 Piece 70.00
Vase, Columnar, Victorian, Enameled, 10 ½ In. 82.00
Vase, Opalescent, Applied Detail, Ruffled Edge, Victorian, 9 ¾ In. 146.00
Vase, Opalescent, Narrow Neck, American, c.1880, 7 In. 70.00
Vase, Portrait, Flowers In Hair, Scalloped Rim, Gilt, 13 x 4 In. *illus* 320.00
Water Set, c.1880, 10-In. Pitcher, 5 Piece 263.00

CREAMWARE, or queensware, was developed by Josiah Wedgwood about 1765. It is a cream-colored earthenware that has been copied by many factories. Similar wares may be listed under Pearlware and Wedgwood.

Basket, Lattice Border, Undertray, Twig Handles, Sepia Trim, 19th Century, 10 x 8 In. 270.00
Beaker, Blue, Yellow Crown & Coin, Marked, E.W.B., 4 ¾ In. *illus* 80.00
Bowl, Centerpiece, Cover, Pierced, Handles, England, Late 20th Century, 10 x 10 ½ In. 100.00
Jug, Black Transfer, Constitution, Guerriere, Cyane & Levant, c.1815, 6 ½ In. 2390.00
Jug, Grape, Leaf & Fish Scale Design, Embossed, 5 In. 248.00
Jug, Washington Apotheosis, Harvest Scene, Eagle, Spread Wings, 10 ½ In. 3220.00
Mug, Brown, Green, Marbleized, Incised Band, 3 ⅝ x 2 ¾ In. *illus* 1000.00
Mug, GR Crowned Emblem, Blue, Carried By British Soldier At Saratoga, c.1760, Qt. 850.00
Mug, Sepia Transfer, Eagle, Shield, Verse, England, 1800s, Child's, 2 In. 717.00
Pitcher, America Lamenting The Death Of Her Favorite Son, Transfer, c.1810, 6 In. 2151.00
Pitcher, Black Transfer, Oval, Coat Of Arms, Farmers Arms, Sprig, c.1800, 9 ½ In. 1315.00
Pitcher, Blue, Yellow, Green Flowers, Yellow Band Top, Soft Paste, c.1810, 8 ½ In. 748.00
Pitcher, Bulbous, Blue Flowers, Leaves, 5 ½ In. 115.00
Pitcher, Flowers, Green Woven Band, Early 19th Century, 7 In. 115.00
Pitcher, Free Trade & Sailors Rights, Arms Of The U.S., Eagle, Wreath, 1812, 5 ¾ In. 1837.00
Pitcher, Presentation, Gilt, 3-Masted Ship, Man With Hammer, John Dockity, 8 ¼ In. 2390.00
Pitcher, Sepia Transfer, Cartoon, Caged Napoleon In Boat, Caption, 8 In. 1315.00
Pitcher, Transfer, Memory Of Washington, Success To America, c.1810, 8 ¼ In. 5079.00

Pitcher, Transfer, Washington, Map Of U.S., First In War, Ribbon, Wreath, c.1800, 8 In. 1554.00
Plate, Pierced, Molded Swag & Tassel, Scalloped Rim, England, 9¾ In., 12 Piece 5875.00
Salt, Boat Shape, Divided, Footed, c.1770-80, 2⅝ In. 121.00
Salt, Cobalt Blue Design, Pedestal Base, England, c.1850-60, 1¾ In. 77.00
Teapot, Chintz, Cover, c.1775. .... 4000.00
Teapot, Cover, Aurora In Chariot, Globular, Pierced Gallery, Greatbatch, 5 In. 1293.00
Teapot, Cover, Globular, Lead Glaze, Molded Fruit, Multicolored, Greatbatch, 4¼ In. 705.00
Teapot, Cover, Prodigal Son, Globular, Multicolored, Greatbatch, 5¾ In. 823.00

CREDIT CARDS, credit tokens, metal charge plates, phone cards, and other similar collectibles that replace money are now part of the numismatic collecting hobby.

Bank Of America, Master Charge, Expired September 1980 .... 10.00

CROWN DERBY is the name given to porcelain made in Derby, England, from the 1770s to 1935. Pieces are marked with a crown and the letter *D* or the word *Derby*. The earliest pieces were made by the original Derby factory, while later pieces were made by the King Street Partnerships (1848–1935) or the Derby Crown Porcelain Co. (1876–90). Derby Crown Porcelain Co. became Royal Crown Derby Co. Ltd. in 1890. It is now part of Royal Doulton Tableware Ltd.

Cake Dish, Shell Dish, Blue & Gilt Border, 10½ x 7½ In. & 9½ x 9½ In. 264.00
Urn, Iron Red With Gild Highlights, Lion Rampant Above Seahorse, 10 In. 635.00

CROWN MILANO glass was made by Frederick Shirley at the Mt. Washington Glass Works about 1890. It had a plain biscuit color with a satin finish. It was decorated with flowers and often had large gold scrolls.

Biscuit Jar, Enameled Red Flowers, Gold Lined, Leaves, Oval, 6½ In. 400.00
Biscuit Jar, Garden Of Allah Scene, Marked, 8½ In. 1955.00
Biscuit Jar, Opal, Green Enameled Mottling, Leaves, Oval, 8 In. 1333.00
Card, Tray, Gold Enameled Flowers, 5¼ In. .... *illus* 69.00
Creamer, Enameled Flowers, Netting, Melon Ribbed, 4½ In. 518.00
Jam Jar, Alternating Bands, Mauve Peach, 4½ In. 604.00
Jam Jar, Enameled Floral & Golden Grid, Melon Ribbed, 5 x 3¾ In. 863.00
Jar, Sweetmeat, Starfish, Gold Enameled, Jewels, Silver-Plated Mounts, 6 x 3 In. .... *illus* 1595.00
Jar, Sweetmeat, Swirled, Opal, Sea Scenes, Finial Lid, 5 In. 425.00
Pitcher, Milk, Melon Ribbed, Cream, Mums, Scrolled Rim, 6½ In. 1000.00
Rose Bowl, Amethyst, Purple Pansies, 4½ In. 115.00
Syrup, Melon Ribbed, Enameled Blossoms, Netting, Silver-Plated Spout, Handle, 5½ In. 1610.00
Vase, Bulbous, Green Ferns, Enameled, Gold Dragon, c.1880 .... *illus* 502.00
Vase, Enameled Flowers, Pink, Red, White, Cactus Branches, Oval, 7½ In. 1300.00
Vase, Enameled Garlands, Bird Beak Rim, Serpentine Handles, Square, 8 In. 800.00
Vase, Enameled Pink Amethyst, Blue Blossoms, Ball Cover, Handles, 12½ In. 3220.00
Vase, Enameled Spider Mums, Diamond Quilted, Pink & White, 4½ In. 403.00
Vase, Gold Enameled Thistles, Leaves, Oval, Pierced Top, Handles, Oval, 7½ In. 1600.00
Vase, Oval, Enameled Flower Clusters, Gold Scrolling, 8½ In. 575.00

CROWN TUSCAN *pattern is included in the Cambridge glass category.*

CRUETS of glass or porcelain were made to hold vinegar, oil, and other condiments. They were especially popular during Victorian times and have been made in a variety of styles since the eighteenth century. Additional cruets may be found in the Castor Set category and also in various glass categories.

Blue Satin Glass, Clear Handle, Victorian, 7¾ In., Pair. 99.00
Bohemian Glass, Green, Gold Orchid, Flat Sides, Rope Twist Handle, 8 In. 58.00
Cranberry Glass, Moorish Style, White, Enameled, Clear Foot, Stopper, 9 In. 115.00
Cranberry Glass, Optic Ribbed, Gold Scrolling, Conical, 7 In. 58.00

CUP PLATES are small glass or china plates that held the cup while a diner of the mid-nineteenth century drank coffee or tea from the saucer. The most famous cup plates were made of glass at the Boston and Sandwich factory located in Sandwich, Massachusetts. There have been many new glass cup plates made in recent years for sale to gift shops or limited edition collectors. These are similar to the old plates but can be recognized as new.

8-Sided, Clear, 3⅜ In. .... *illus* 120.00
9 Pairs Of Large Scallops, 4 Smaller Scallops Between, Deep Green, 3½ In. .... *illus* 2010.00

Creamware, Beaker, Blue, Yellow Crown & Coin, Marked, E.W.B., 4¾ In.
$80.00

Creamware, Mug, Brown, Green, Marbleized, Incised Band, 3⅝ x 2¾ In.
$1000.00

Crown Milano, Card, Tray, Gold Enameled Flowers, 5¼ In.
$69.00

Crown Milano, Jar, Sweetmeat, Starfish, Gold Enameled, Jewels, Silver-Plated Mounts, 6 x 3 In.
$1595.00

Crown Milano, Vase, Bulbous, Green Ferns, Enameled, Gold Dragon, c.1880
$502.00

Cup Plate, 8-Sided, Clear, 3 3/8 In.
$120.00

Cup Plate, 9 Pairs Of Large Scallops, 4 Smaller Scallops Between, Deep Green, 3 1/2 In.
$2010.00

Cup Plate, 10-Scallop Rope, Bottle Green, 3 7/16 In.
$575.00

Cup Plate, 24 Scallops, Points Between, Lavender, 2 7/8 In.
$79.00

Cup Plate, 30 Bull's-Eye Scallops, Medium Blue, 3 In.
$1680.00

Cup Plate, 34 Bull's-Eye Scallops, Amethyst, 3 1/2 In.
$1490.00

Cup Plate, 55 Even Scallops, Peacock Blue, 3 3/8 In.
$160.00

Cup Plate, 60 Even Scallops, Cloudy Amber, Black Impurities, 3 1/2 In.
$3020.00

Cup Plates & Labels

The dark areas on some of the pictured cup plates are labels showing they came from the collection of William J. Elsholz, an early cup plate collector. This provenance adds value to the plates.

Cup Plate, 66 Even Scallops, Yellow Green, Dot Center, 3 1/2 In.
$231.00

Cup Plate, Fiery Opalescent Shaded To Clear, Swirled, Plain Rim, 3 5/8 In.
$79.00

Cup Plate, Opaque Powder Blue, Swirled, Periwinkle, Plain Rim, 3 5/8 In.
$1050.00

10-Scallop Rope, Bottle Green, $3\frac{7}{16}$ In. *illus* 575.00
24 Scallops, Points Between, Lavender, $2\frac{7}{8}$ In. *illus* 79.00
30 Bull's-Eye Scallops, Medium Blue, 3 In. *illus* 1680.00
34 Bull's-Eye Scallops, Amethyst, $3\frac{1}{2}$ In. *illus* 1490.00
55 Even Scallops, Peacock Blue, $3\frac{3}{8}$ In. *illus* 160.00
60 Even Scallops, Cloudy Amber, Black Impurities, $3\frac{1}{2}$ In. *illus* 3020.00
64 Even Scallops, Ice Blue Tint, $3\frac{7}{16}$ In. 99.00
66 Even Scallops, Olive Green, $3\frac{5}{16}$ In. 170.00
66 Even Scallops, Yellow Green, Dot Center, $3\frac{1}{2}$ In. *illus* 231.00
Fiery Opalescent Shaded To Clear, Swirled, Plain Rim, $3\frac{5}{8}$ In. *illus* 79.00
Opaque Powder Blue, Swirled, Periwinkle, Plain Rim, $3\frac{5}{8}$ In. *illus* 1050.00
Staffordshire, Historical, Blue, Woodlands, Philadelphia, Eagle Border, $3\frac{1}{8}$ In. 230.00
Staffordshire, Landing Of Gen. Lafayette At Castle Garden, Blue, Clews, c.1830, $3\frac{1}{2}$ In. 329.00
Staffordshire, Picturesque Views-So-Called Fairmount, Black Transfer, Clews, c.1830, $3\frac{3}{4}$ In. 325.00

CURRIER & IVES made the famous American lithographs marked with their name from 1857 to 1907. The mark used on the print included the street address in New York City, and it is possible to date the year of the original issue from this information. Earlier prints were made by N. Currier and use that name from 1835 to 1847. Many reprints of the Currier or Currier & Ives prints have been made. Some collectors buy the insurance calendars that were based on the old prints. The words *large, small,* or *medium folio* refer to size. The original print sizes were very small (up to about 7 x 9 in.), small (8.8 x 12.8 in.), medium (9 x 14 in. to 14 x 20 in.), large (larger than 14 x 20 in.). Other sizes are probably later copies. Other prints by Currier & Ives may be listed in the Card category under Advertising and in the Sheet Music category. Currier & Ives dinnerware patterns may be found in the Adams or Dinnerware categories.

American Country Life, May Morning, c.1855, $21\frac{3}{8}$ x $27\frac{5}{8}$ In. 1528.00
American Country Life, Pleasures Of Winter, Giltwood Frame, c.1855, $21\frac{1}{2}$ x 28 In. 4113.00
American Prize Fruit, Tinted Background, Lithograph, Mat, Frame, 30 x 38 In. 1150.00
Battle Of Gettysburg, Union Soldiers, 1863, $12\frac{1}{4}$ x 16 In. *illus* 374.00
Brush For The Lead, New York Flyers On The Snow, c.1867, $23\frac{3}{4}$ x $33\frac{3}{4}$ In. 1175.00
Buffalo Hunt Under The White Wolf Skin, 15 x $19\frac{5}{8}$ In. 823.00
Camping Out, Some Of The Right Sort, Frame, 1856, $21\frac{1}{2}$ x $30\frac{1}{4}$ In. 4888.00
Cares Of A Family, Frame, 1865, $10\frac{3}{4}$ x 14 In. 230.00
Cavalry Tactics, By The Darktown Horse Guards, $3\frac{1}{2}$ x 5 In. 345.00
Celebrated Clipper Ship, Dreadnought, Frame, 1857-1907, 9 x $12\frac{1}{4}$ In. 323.00
Chicago In Flames, Randolph Street Bridge, Gilt Frame, $11\frac{3}{4}$ x 15 In. 150.00
City Of San Francisco, 23 Landmarks, c.1877, 12 x $16\frac{1}{4}$ In. 2115.00
Coming From The Trot, Sports On The Home Stretch, c.1869, $21\frac{3}{4}$ x $31\frac{1}{4}$ In. 1763.00
Darktown Opera, Lover Leap, 10 In. 115.00
Ethan Allen & Mate & Dexter, Frame, 1867, $22\frac{1}{2}$ x 31 In. 460.00
Falls Of Niagara, From The Canada Side, Frame, $23\frac{1}{2}$ x $31\frac{1}{2}$ In. 345.00
Farm-Yard In Winter, Wood Frame, c.1861, 25 x 31 In. *illus* 2185.00
Flora Temple, Mat, Bird's Eye Maple Frame, 28 x 35 In. 546.00
Four Seasons Of Life, Middle Age, Frame, 1868, $21\frac{1}{2}$ x $29\frac{1}{4}$ In. 1410.00
General Grant & Family, Mat, Frame, 1867, 10 x 14 In. 70.00
Great Fire At St. John, N.B., June 20th 1877, Gilt Frame, 11 x $14\frac{1}{2}$ In. 100.00
Home From The Brook, Lucky Fisherman, c.1867, $20\frac{5}{8}$ x $27\frac{3}{4}$ In. 1175.00
Home In The Wilderness, Frame, 19th Century, $10\frac{1}{4}$ x $13\frac{1}{2}$ In. 575.00
Home Of The Deer, Frame, 19th Century, $13\frac{1}{2}$ x $17\frac{1}{2}$ In. 345.00
Home Of The Deer, Morning In The Adirondacks, c.1862, $22\frac{3}{4}$ x 28 In. 5288.00
Infant Brood, Frame, 1865, 15 x $19\frac{1}{2}$ In. 403.00
Infantry Maneuver, 1887 316.00
Last War-Whoop, Frame, 19th Century, $21\frac{1}{4}$ x $27\frac{1}{2}$ In. 3738.00
Manhattan, Bird's-Eye View, Equitable Life Insurance Building, 1876, $21\frac{3}{4}$ x $34\frac{1}{4}$ In. 2185.00
My Little White Kitties, Playing Dominoes, Frame, 1857-1907, $9\frac{1}{8}$ x 14 In. 940.00
New York Club Regatta, 1869, Large Folio 10440.00
Old Homestead, Frame, 1855, $12\frac{1}{2}$ x $17\frac{1}{2}$ In. 518.00
Old Oaken Bucket, Hand Colored, c.1864, $20\frac{1}{4}$ x $27\frac{1}{8}$ In. 705.00
Presidents Of The United States, Washington To Polk, N. Currier, Frame, 1844, $13\frac{1}{2}$ In. 50.00
Scenery Of The Hudson Near Anthony's Nose, Frame, 1857-1907, $18\frac{7}{8}$ x $23\frac{3}{4}$ In. 1410.00
Star Spangled Banner, Mahogany Veneer Frame, 14 x 10 In. *illus* 881.00
Summer Shades, Frame, 1859, 19 x 26 In. 431.00
The Life Of A Fireman, The Ruins, 19 x 28 In. 170.00
Trotting Cracks At Home, A Model Stable, Frame, 1868, $22\frac{3}{4}$ x $31\frac{7}{8}$ In. 1200.00
Trotting Mare Goldsmith Maid, Signed, J. Cameron, Frame, 29 x 35 In. *illus* 1790.00

Currier & Ives, Battle Of Gettysburg, Union Soldiers, 1863, $12\frac{1}{4}$ x 16 In.
$374.00

Currier & Ives, Farm-Yard In Winter, Wood Frame, c.1861, 25 x 31 In.
$2185.00

Currier & Ives, Star Spangled Banner, Mahogany Veneer Frame, 14 x 10 In.
$881.00

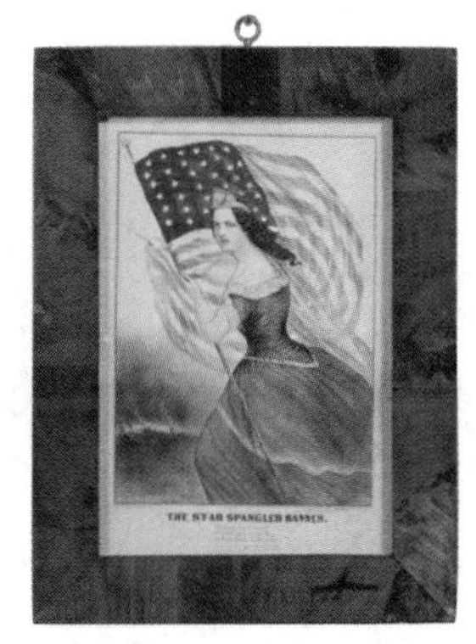

Currier & Ives, Trotting Mare Goldsmith Maid, Signed, J. Cameron, Frame, 29 x 35 In.
$1790.00

Trotting Stallion Phallas, Driven By E.D. Bithers, c.1883, 24 x 31 In. 353.00
Won By A Neck, Lady Thorn, Goldsmith Maid, Frame, 1889, 23 ¾ x 30 ⅞ In. 2160.00
Yacht Squadron At Newport, Frame, 1872, 23 ¼ x 31 ¾ In. 4800.00

CUSTARD GLASS is a slightly yellow opaque glass. It was made in England in the 1880s and was first made in the United States in the 1890s. It has been reproduced. Additional pieces may be found in the Cambridge, Fenton, Heisey, and Northwood categories. Custard glass is called Ivorina Verde by Heisey and other companies.

Argonaut Shell, Butter, Cover, Footed, 8 In. 345.00
Argonaut Shell, Cruet, 7 In. 690.00
Argonaut Shell, Pitcher, 8 ½ In. 460.00
Argonaut Shell, Table Set, Creamer, Covered Sugar, Spooner, 7 In., 3 Piece 518.00
Chrysanthemum Sprig, Spooner, Signed, 4 ½ In. 115.00
Georgia Gem, Salt & Pepper, Green, Squat, c.1904 120.00
Intaglio, Compote, Gold Enameled Flowers, Blue Scrolling, 6 In. 50.00
Intaglio, Water Set, 9 In. Pitcher, 7 Piece 195.00
Little Gem, see Georgia Gem pattern in this category.
Louis XV, Berry Bowl, Master, c.1900, 10 ½ x 7 ¼ In. 150.00
Louis XV, Berry Set, Northwood, 11 In. Footed Master, 6 Piece 259.00
Maize is its own category in this book.
Singing Bird, Mug, Brown Trim, Gold Enameled, 3 ⅝ In. *illus* 33.00

Custard, Singing Bird, Mug, Brown Trim, Gold Enameled, 3 ⅝ In.
$33.00

TIP
Is it cut or pressed glass? Feel the edges of the design of the glass. Cut glass has sharp edges; pressed-glass designs are molded into the glass.

CUT GLASS has been made since ancient times, but the large majority of the pieces now for sale date from the brilliant period of glass design, 1880 to 1905. These pieces have elaborate geometric designs with a deep miter cut. Modern cut glass with a similar appearance is being made in England, Ireland, and the Czech and Slovak republics. Chips and scratches are often difficult to notice but lower the value dramatically. A signature on the glass adds significantly to the value. Other cut glass pieces are listed under factory names.

Atomizer, Crosscut Diamond, Star & Fan, Green To Clear, Pyramid Shape, 7 ¼ In. 140.00
Atomizer, Hobstar, Vesica, Cane & Fan, Lime Green To Clear, 5 In. 200.00
Banana Boat, Hobstar, Cane, Strawberry Diamond, Vesica, American Brilliant, 5 x 12 In. 275.00
Banana Boat, Hobstar Border, Engraved Flowers, American Brilliant, 4 x 11 In. 200.00
Basket, Diamond Cut, Pedestal Base, 6 x 7 In. 350.00
Basket, Engraved, Flowers, Rope Twist Handle, 7 In. 100.00
Basket, Engraved Rose, Double Notched Handle, Step Cut Base, 11 ½ In. 475.00
Basket, Engraved Rose, Rope Twist Handle, 5 In. 75.00
Basket, Harvard, Alternating Hobstar, Twisted Handle, 8-Rayed Star, 6 ¼ In. 100.00
Basket, Hobstar, Vesica, Strawberry Diamond, Vertical Notch, Square, 10 x 8 In. *illus* 200.00
Basket, Hobstar & Fan, Strawberry Diamond, Twist Handle, 3 ½ x 5 In. 175.00
Basket, Ribbed Base, Braided Handle, 17 x 11 ¾ In. 205.00
Biscuit Jar, Starburst, 9 ¼ In. 48.00
Bottle, Silver Mounted, Vertical Prisms, Flared Neck, Globular, c.1897, 8 ⅝ In., Pair 354.00
Bowl, Aurora Borealis, Signed, Pitkin & Brooks, 8 In. 275.00
Bowl, Cane, Bar & Fan, Rayed Center, Green To Clear, 4 x 8 ¼ In. 175.00
Bowl, Canoe Shape, Faceted Rim, Pinwheels, Hobstars, 4 x 9 In. 58.00
Bowl, Centerpiece, Oblong, Scalloped Rim, Flowers, American Brilliant, 5 x 12 ¾ In. 472.00
Bowl, Centerpiece, Ruffled, Engraved Flowers, American Brilliant, 4 ½ x 14 In. 125.00
Bowl, Cornucopia, Bergen, 4 ¾ x 6 ½ In. 2250.00
Bowl, Diamond Crosshatch & Fan, Ormolu Tazza, Empire Tripod Base, 12 In., Pair 1265.00
Bowl, Empire, Blue Twist Handle, Splash Center, Flowers, Cane, American Brilliant, 8 In. 250.00
Bowl, Engraved Flowers, Christofle Base, American Brilliant, 5 ¼ x 8 In. 450.00
Bowl, Engraved Waterlily, 6 x 8 In. 400.00
Bowl, Faceted, Flaring Russian-Cut Rim, American, 19th Century, 10 In. 59.00
Bowl, Flashed Hobstar, Notched Handles, 4 Sections, American Brilliant, 8 In. 125.00
Bowl, Flashed Hobstar Center, Pinwheel Tabs, Amethyst To Clear, 3 ¾ x 7 ½ In. 175.00
Bowl, Floral, Green To Clear, Rococo, Punty, Notched Handles, 5 ¼ x 6 ¼ In. 1200.00
Bowl, Fruit, Crisscross Rim, 19th Century, 9 ½ In. 360.00
Bowl, Greek Key, Gold Intaglio, Edwardian, 13 ½ x 12 ½ In. 510.00
Bowl, Harvard Cut, Hobstar, Square, American Brilliant, 4 ¾ x 9 ¼ In. 275.00
Bowl, Hex Button Center, Green To Clear, Kohinoor Border, Medallions, Gilt, 3 x 10 ¼ In. 225.00
Bowl, Hindoo, American Brilliant, J. Hoare, 7 In. 100.00
Bowl, Hobstar, Cane, Vesica, Strawberry Diamond & Fan, Pitken & Brooks, 2 ¼ x 8 In. 125.00
Bowl, Hobstar, Nailhead Diamond, Vesica, American Brilliant, 9 ¼ In. 200.00
Bowl, Hobstar, Pillar & Prism, Embossed Sterling Border, American Brilliant, 3 ½ x 8 In. 325.00
Bowl, Hobstar, Prism, Pitken & Brooks, 3 ¼ x 7 In. 600.00

Cut Glass, Basket, Hobstar, Vesica, Strawberry Diamond, Vertical Notch, Square, 10 x 8 In.
$200.00

Cut Glass, Bowl, Hobstar & Fern, 5 x 10 In.
$375.00

Bowl, Hobstar, Round Cane, Strawberry Diamond Star, American Brilliant, 3¾ x 8 In. 125.00
Bowl, Hobstar, Split Vesica, Strawberry Diamond, Flower Center, American Brilliant, 10 In. .. 500.00
Bowl, Hobstar, Star & Pinwheel, American Brilliant, 3½ x 8 In. 60.00
Bowl, Hobstar, Strawberry Diamond & Fan, Square, American Brilliant, 3 x 11 In. 225.00
Bowl, Hobstar, Vesica, Harvard, Strawberry Diamond & Fan, American Brilliant, 4 x 9 In. ... 125.00
Bowl, Hobstar & Fern, 5 x 10 In. ...... *illus* 375.00
Bowl, Hobstar Chain, Prism Highlights, Flared, American Brilliant, 2¼ x 8 In. 50.00
Bowl, Hobstar Cluster, Button Border, Sterling Rim, 6 x 11¾ In. 1250.00
Bowl, Hobstars, Cane & Harvard, Deep, 8 In. 83.00
Bowl, Hobstars, Fans, American, 20th Century, 9 In. 147.00
Bowl, Intaglio, Grapes, Pears, Cherries, Geometric, 8 In. 70.00
Bowl, Intaglio Cherries, Flared, American Brilliant, 4½ x 10 In. 175.00
Bowl, Lotus, American Brilliant, Egginton, 4¼ x 9 In. 275.00
Bowl, Nailhead Diamond Bars, Square, 4 x 10 In. 350.00
Bowl, Nailhead Diamond Border, Engraved 3 Fruits, American Brilliant, 2¼ x 9 In. 1200.00
Bowl, Orange To Vaseline To Clear, Silver Threading & Punties, 3¼ x 8 In. 225.00
Bowl, Pedestal Base, Crisscross, 9½ In. 1320.00
Bowl, Pinwheels, Hobstars, 8 x 4 In. 86.00
Bowl, Pinwheels, Hobstars, 9½ In. 132.00
Bowl, Pinwheels, Stars, Sawtooth Border, 8¼ In. 86.00
Bowl, Propeller, Parsche Bros., 8 In. 275.00
Bowl, Punty, Amethyst Cut To Clear, Art Deco, 11 In. 75.00
Bowl, Radiant, 9½ x 3 In. 29.00
Bowl, Red To Clear, Hobstar, Cane & Fan, 3½ x 9½ In. 50.00
Bowl, Rose, Blossom & Thorn Branch, Scalloped, Flowers, Dorflinger, 3 In. 450.00
Bowl, Scalloped Edge, American Brilliant, c.1900, 2¾ x 10½ x 11 In. 234.00
Bowl, Scalloped Rim, Geometric, 3¼ x 8 In. 89.00
Bowl, Scalloped Rim, Spirals, Geometric, 3¼ x 8 In. 59.00
Bowl, Shell Shape, Crosscut Diamond Panel, 9¼ In. 50.00
Bowl, Square, Hobstar, Strawberry Diamond & Fan, American Brilliant, 9½ In. 350.00
Bowl, Star Cut Diamond Lattice, Pillar Corners, Square, 3½ x 7 In. 175.00
Bowl, Star With Fans, Caning, Hobstar Circle, Center Hobstar, 8 In. 225.00
Bowl, Wreath Bishop's Hat, Intaglio Floral, Daisies, 10½ In. 300.00
Box, Cover, Amethyst To Clear, Crosscut Diamond & Star, Round, 4 In. 175.00
Box, Cover, Green To Clear, Fan & Geometric Cut, Round, 4½ In. 250.00
Box, Cranberry To Clear, Bull's-Eye & Notched Panel, Sterling Cover, Dorflinger, 3½ In. 275.00
Box, Jewel, Engraved, Flowers, Round, Hinged Cover, 3½ x 5¼ In. 100.00
Box, Jewel, Hinged Lid, Hobstar & Prism, Cover, Thumbprint Base, Metal Band, 3 x 6 In. 250.00
Butter, Cover, Hobstar, File, Fan, 8-Sided, 6½ x 9 In. 900.00
Candlestick, Hobstar, Strawberry Diamond, Hollow Stem, Skirted Base, 8 In., Pair 1800.00
Candlestick, Prism, Hobstar, 24-Pt., 12 In., Pair 1000.00
Candlestick, Russian Swirl, 5½ x 10¼ In., 1955 ...... 826.00
Celery Dish, Folded Edge, Crosscut Diamond & Fan, American Brilliant, 11½ In. 175.00
Celery Dish, Hobstar, Vesica, Nailhead Diamond, American Brilliant, 11½ In. 110.00
Celery Tray, Carnation, 12 x 5½ In. ...... *illus* 30.00
Celery Tray, Gondola Shape, Crosscut Diamond, Fan, 12½ In. 175.00
Chamberstick, Hobstar, Crosscut Diamond & Fan, 6 In. ...... *illus* 700.00
Champagne, Flute, Princess Pattern, Tiffany & Co., 8½ In. 863.00
Champagne, Panel Cut, 20th Century, 7½ x 2½ In., 10 Piece 360.00
Cheese Dish, Cover, Hobstar, Strawberry Diamond & Fan, American Brilliant, 9 In. 400.00
Cheese Dish, Lobster-Cut Cover, Daisy & Button Fields, Faceted Knob, 8 x 6 In. 212.00
Chip & Dip, Hobstar, Nailhead, 24 Point, 10 x 4 In. 86.00
Cologne Bottle, 15 Ribs, Paneled Neck, Double Step Shoulder, 7½ x 4¼ In. 44.00
Cologne Bottle, Cranberry To Clear, Allover Cane, Matching Stopper, 8½ In. 550.00
Cologne Bottle, Engraved, Flowers, Harvard Band, Ray Base, Faceted Stopper, 6¾ In. 50.00
Cologne Bottle, Green Cut To Yellow, Jewel Top Stopper, Dauber, Enameled, 5¼ In. 325.00
Cologne Bottle, Opaque White To Cranberry, Punties, c.1855, 5¼ In. ...... *illus* 295.00
Cologne Bottle, Sterling Silver Cap, Spherical, Lapidary Cut Stopper, Edwardian, 6 x 4 In. .. 660.00
Compote, Amethyst To Clear, Art Deco, Strawberry Diamond & Flute, 8¼ x 8½ In. 100.00
Compote, Amethyst To Clear, Spiral Air Twist Stem, Hobstar & Diamond, 6½ x 6 In. 325.00
Compote, Bishop's Hat, Diamond, File & Fan, Vaseline Pedestal, Rolled Rim, 5 x 10 In. 375.00
Compote, Cover, 12 Flutes, Thumbprints, Scalloped Rim, Hollow Stem, 15 In. 2970.00
Compote, Cover, Hobstar, Fan, Steeple Finial, Teardrop Stem, 12½ In. 850.00
Compote, Emerald Green To Clear, Pedestal Base, 14 In. 472.00
Compote, Engraved Flowers, Amethyst Rim, Notched Stem, Ray Base, 8¼ x 8½ In. 200.00
Compote, Faceted Stem, Pinwheels, Cut Fans, Sawtooth Rim, 7 In. 690.00

Cut Glass, Celery Tray, Carnation, 12 x 5½ In.
$30.00

Cut Glass, Chamberstick, Hobstar, Crosscut Diamond & Fan, 6 In.
$700.00

Cut Glass, Cologne Bottle, Opaque White To Cranberry, Punties, c.1855, 5¼ In.
$295.00

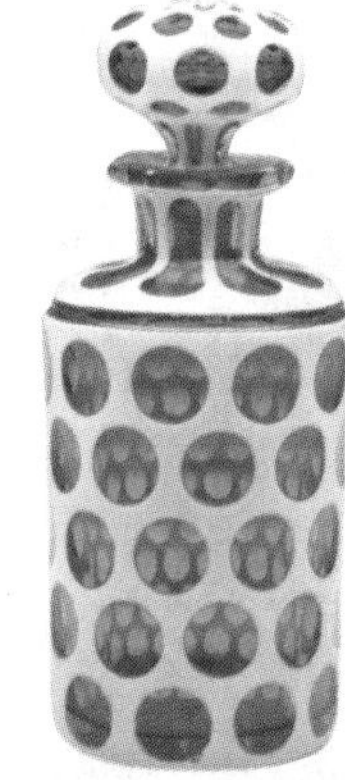

TIP
Never put anything hot in a cut glass bowl. It was not made to withstand heat and will crack.

C

TIP
A signature adds 25 percent to the value of cut glass.

Cut Glass, Dish, Hobstar, Cane & Vesica, Honey Amber, Empire, 6 In.
$200.00

Cut Glass, Epergne, 4-Lily, Engraved Flowers, American Brilliant, 18 In.
$1300.00

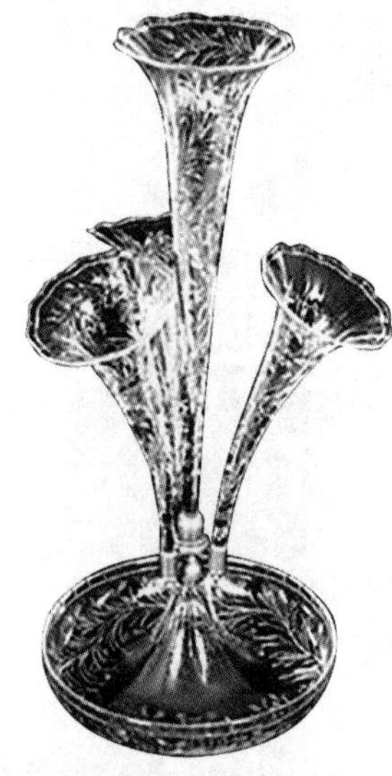

Cut Glass, Humidor, Emerald Green To Clear, Chester Pattern, Dorflinger, 9 In.
$2300.00

Compote, Hobstar, Cane, Teardrop Stem, 7 x 6 In. 175.00
Compote, Hobstar, Cane, Vesica, Red To Clear, Red & White Twist Stem, 8 ¼ x 7 ¼ In. 300.00
Compote, Lozenge Cut, Ice Blue, 20th Century, 8 ¼ x 6 ¾ In. 100.00
Compote, Primrose, Teardrop Stem, Tuthill, Marked, 7 ¾ x 6 ¼ In. 200.00
Compote, Red White & Blue Candy Twist Stem, American Brilliant, 9 x 7 ½ In. 200.00
Compote, Rolled Rim, Scalloped Hobstar Base, American Brilliant, 12 ½ x 9 ½ In. 1200.00
Compote, Russian Pattern, 8 ½ x 3 In. 345.00
Compote, Scalloped Edge, Notched Stem, 24-Point Hobstar Base, 10 ½ x 13 In. 748.00
Compote, Vaseline, Diamond, File & Fan, Rolled Rim, American Brilliant, 3 ½ x 6 ½ In. 300.00
Cordial, Green To Clear, Renaissance, Dorflinger, 3 ¼ In. 250.00
Creamer, Crosscut Diamond Hobstar Border, Prism Cut Body, American Brilliant, 4 ½ In. 100.00
Cruet, Butterfly & Floral Motif, Tricornered Rim, American Brilliant, 6 ½ In. 125.00
Cruet, Hobstar, Strawberry, Diamond, Vesica, Fan, Pedestal Base, Stopper, 8 In. 325.00
Decanter, Blue To Clear, Hobstar, Cane Vesica & Fan, Pedestal Base, 15 In. 400.00
Decanter, Blue To Clear, Steeple Shape, Hobstar, Crosscut Diamond & Fan, Stopper, 14 In. 850.00
Decanter, Bull's-Eye, Notched, Hobstar Base, Stopper, Pinched Waist, 10 ½ In. 300.00
Decanter, Cranberry To Clear, Panel & Bull's-Eye, Clear Foot, 13 ½ In. 350.00
Decanter, Diamond-Cut Panels, Strawberry Diamond, Fans, Stopper, Paneled Handle, 11 In. 175.00
Decanter, Donut Shape, Clear Tusk, Notched Fern, Stopper, 10 In. 650.00
Decanter, Emerald Green To Clear, Geometric, Stopper, 14 In. 150.00
Decanter, Faceted, Fluted, c.1900, 9 In. 147.00
Decanter, Fox & Game Bird Scene, Footed, 10 ½ In. 350.00
Decanter, Geometric, Vaseline, Blue, Stopper, 16 ½ In. 500.00
Decanter, Green To Clear, Oval, Panels, Gold Enameled, Stopper, 9 ½ In. 300.00
Decanter, Hobstar, Bars & Hobstar Squares, Stopper, Hobstar Base, Handle, 12 ½ In. 400.00
Decanter, Hobstar, Fan, Strawberry Diamond, Ferns, Oval, Handle, Stopper, 10 ½ In. 200.00
Decanter, Hobstar, Strawberry Diamond, Prism & Bull's-Eye, Stopper, Handle, 9 In. 325.00
Decanter, Hobstar Fans, Nail Cut, Fluted Neck, Hobstar Base, Notched Handle, 10 In. 125.00
Decanter, Honeycomb, Quatrefoil, Panel Cut Neck, Bar Lip, Pontil, 10 x 3 ¾ In. 44.00
Decanter, Pinched Waist, Stopper, 10 In. 30.00
Decanter, Russian Pattern, Scalloped Pedestal Base, Stopper, Air Trap Handle, 13 In. 600.00
Decanter, Russian Pattern, Star-Cut Buttons, Faceted Ring Neck, Handle, Stopper, 11 In. 300.00
Decanter, Steeple Shape, Engraved Iris, Stopper, 18 In. 475.00
Decanter, Vaseline, Triple Faceted Cut Rings, Medallions, Russia Imperial Era, 14 In. 1800.00
Decanter, Whiskey, Stopper, Engraved Flowers, Grape Cluster, 12 ¾ In. 150.00
Decanter Set, Diamond Shape, Light Green, 9 x 2 ½ x 8 In., 7 Piece 117.00
Decanter Set, Fluted, American Brilliant, 10 In., 5 Piece 350.00
Decanter Set, Green To Clear, Rococo Swirl, Engraved Floral Highlights, 5 ¾ In, 5 Piece 350.00
Dish, Engraved Berries, Handles, 4 Sections, 7 In. 225.00
Dish, Hobstar, Cane & Vesica, Honey Amber, Empire, 6 In. *illus* 200.00
Dish, Ice Cream, Sawtooth Rim, Oval, 20th Century, 14 In. 118.00
Dish, Oval, Harvard, American Brilliant, 7 In. 50.00
Dish, Pineapple Shape, Allover Cane, 12 x 7 In. 150.00
Dish, Shell Shape, Hobstar, Notching, Strawberry Diamond, 6 In. 525.00
Dish, Sweetmeat, Cover, Cut Swag, Rooted Base, Late 18th Century, 8 In. 384.00
Epergne, 4-Lily, Engraved Flowers, American Brilliant, 18 In. *illus* 1300.00
Finger Bowl, Amethyst To Clear, Geometric Cut Border, Ray Center, 4 ¾ In. 40.00
Finger Bowl, England, 19th Century, 4 ½ In., 4 Piece 126.00
Finger Bowl, Hobstar & Fan, American Brilliant 70.00
Finger Bowl, Underplate, Engraved, Chinese Building, Bird, Tree 125.00
Finger Bowl, Underplate, Renaissance Pattern, Apple Green, Dorflinger 50.00
Flask, Cane & Concave Pillar Bands, Sterling Flip Top, 6 In. 425.00
Flask, Cranberry To Clear, Engraved Rabbits, Monogram, Acorns, 7 ½ In. 500.00
Glove Box, Cover, Hobstars & Fans, 10 ⅜ In. 590.00
Glove Box, Cover, Stars, Fans & Hobstar, Vertical Cuttings On Base, 3 ½ x 10 ⅞ In. 826.00
Goblet, Lyric, Stuart, 7 In., 12 Piece 82.00
Goblet, Red To Clear, Notched Stems, 2 ½ x 4 ¾ In., 8 Piece 1150.00
Goblet, Ruby To Clear, Hobstar Foot, Paneled Stem, 11 In. 266.00
Humidor, Emerald Green To Clear, Chester Pattern, Dorflinger, 9 In. *illus* 2300.00
Humidor, Pinwheel, Hobstar, Prism & Fan, American Brilliant, 7 In. 275.00
Ice Bucket, Hobstar, Diamonds, Raised Handles, 6 In. 105.00
Ice Bucket, Honeycomb, 2 Handles, Dorflinger, 4 ¾ x 9 ¼ In. 200.00
Ice Cream Set, Shell, Crosscut Diamond, Strawberry, 11 ¼-In. Tray, 6 Piece 125.00
Jar, Silver Lid, Daisy & Button, Applied 14K Gold, c.1865, 4 x 2 ½ In., Pair 316.00
Jar, Sterling Cover, Gold Washed Interior, Stopper, 6 ¼ x 3 ¼ In. 920.00
Jug, Claret, Stopper, Handle, Crisscross, 19th Century, 18 ½ In. 420.00

Jug, Green, Clear Applied Handle, Engraved, Whiskey, Stopper, 7 ½ In.. .... 100.00
Jug, Green Cut To Clear, Handle, Stopper, Engraved Vine, Blossom & Swirl, 10 ½ In. 900.00
Jug, Green Cut To Clear, Stopper, Vertical Miter, Notched Handle, American Brilliant, 9 In. ... 675.00
Jug, Hobstar, Cane & Fan, Faceted Stopper, 6 ½ In.. .... 100.00
Jug, Hobstar, Prism, Strawberry Diamond, Bull's-Eye, Stopper, Notched Handle, 10 ½ In. 250.00
Jug, Hobstar, Strawberry Diamond, Prism & Bull's-Eye, Stopper, Notched Handle, 9 ½ In. 175.00
Jug, Rum, Flute Pattern, Green Cut To Clear, Strap Handle 1150.00
Jug, Silver, Prism Motif, Handle, Notched Prisms, R. Wallace & Son, Early 1900s, 11 ½ In. ... 325.00
Jug, Squatty, Hobstar Fan, Crosscut, Fluted Neck, Stopper, 8 x 6 In. 150.00
Jug, Strawberry Diamond, Star & Fan, Hobstar Base, Notched Handle, 5 In. 200.00
Jug, Whiskey, Engraved Thistle, Sterling Silver Stopper, American Brilliant, 8 ½ In. 200.00
Jug, Whiskey, Geometric, Crosscut Diamond & Fan, Strap Handle, Stopper, 9 ½ x 6 In. 275.00
Jug, Whiskey, Hobstar, Fan & Can, Notched Handle, Flattened Oval, Fluted Neck, 10 ½ In. 200.00
Knife Rest, Red Cut To Clear, Steel Handle, Engraved Silver, Crosscut Diamond, 17 In.. ...... 700.00
Ladle, Hobstar, Fan, 17 In. 250.00
Ladle, Punch Bowl, Silver Plated, Signed Pairpoint 495.00
Ladle, Sterling Dipper, Flashed Hobstar, Crosscut Diamond, Fan, American Brilliant, 16 In. .. 600.00
Ladle Holder, Hobstar & Vesica, American Brilliant, 5 ½ In.. .... 110.00
Lamp, 4-Sided Base, Ball Shade, Lavender, 10 ¾ In. 1323.00
Lamp, Parlor, Mushroom Shade, Drop Prisms, 19th Century, 21 In. 472.00
Lamp, Table, Mushroom Shade, Deeply Cut Allover, 2 Sockets, 19 In. 805.00
Loving Cup, Prism, 3 Handles, Double Notched, 3 ¼ In.. .... 150.00
Mug, Prisms, Double Notched Handle, Sterling Rim, 4 ½ In. 225.00
Nappy, Cranberry To Clear, Crosscut Diamond, Applied Rigaree, Yellow Trim, 4 ¾ In. 175.00
Nappy, Crosscut Diamond & Fan Motif, American Brilliant, 5 ¾ In., 2 Piece 125.00
Nappy, Harvard, Scalloped Border, Hobstar Center, 6 In. .... *illus* 80.00
Nappy, Hobstar, Cane Vesica, Block, Bull's-Eye, Tricornered Handle, 7 ½ In. 75.00
Nappy, Shell, Hobstar, Handle, 6 In. 20.00
Nappy, Strawberry Diamond, Nailhead & Vesica, Round, 6 In. 100.00
Perfume Bottle, Colonial Pattern, Dorflinger 325.00
Perfume Bottle, Crosscut Diamond & Fan, Orange To Clear, Silver Plated Top, 4 In. 200.00
Perfume Bottle, Harvard Variant, Brass Flip Top, 8 ½ In. 200.00
Pitcher, Amethyst To Clear, Clear Applied Handle, Art Deco, 7 ¼ In.. .... 60.00
Pitcher, Cider, Squat, Hobstar, Prism Cut, Triple Notch Handle, American Brilliant, 7 In. 325.00
Pitcher, Croesus, Green, Gold Trim, 11 ½ In. 150.00
Pitcher, Crosscut Diamond & Fan, American Brilliant, 5 ¼ In.. .... 70.00
Pitcher, Engraved, Tiger Lily, 10 ½ In. 350.00
Pitcher, Fluted, Bulbous, Duckbill Lip, 7 ½ In.. .... 200.00
Pitcher, Geometric & Fan Designs, Pear Shape, 9 ½ In. 177.00
Pitcher, Green To Clear, Crosscut Diamond, File & Fan, Notched Handle, 9 ¼ In.. .... 200.00
Pitcher, Intaglio, Thistle, Squat, Signed, Clark, 7 x 8 In.. .... 180.00
Pitcher, Pinwheel, 9 In. 47.00
Pitcher, Starburst, Silver Hinged Cap, Collar, Lip, S. Kirk & Son, 11 ¼ In. 862.00
Pitcher, Water, Engraved Vintage, American Brilliant, 9 ¼ In. 375.00
Plate, Canape, Hobstar, c.1900, 10 In.. .... 23.00
Plate, Chains Of Cane & Hobstars, 7 In. 225.00
Plate, Chartreuse To Clear, 12-Point Star, 7 ½ In., 8 Piece 80.00
Plate, Cranberry To Vaseline, Hobstar Center, Punty Border, 6 ¼ In. 650.00
Plate, Green To Clear, Cane, Bar & Fan, Ray Center, 11 ½ In. 150.00
Plate, Intaglio Star, Hobstar Border, Rolled Edge, Tuthill, Marked, 9 ¾ In. 875.00
Plate, Prima Donna, Signed, Clark, 9 In. 2000.00
Plate, Ray Center, Hobstar & Cane Border, Square, American Brilliant, 7 In. 25.00
Plate, Seneca, American Brilliant, Empire, 7 In. 250.00
Plate, Star Diamond, Turquoise, Cranberry Flashed, 6 In. .... *illus* 5500.00
Plate, Wine Ringer, Cranberry To Clear, Diamond Band, Miter Details, 4 ¼ x 6 ¾ In. 275.00
Powder Box, Cover, Wild Rose, Pedestal, Tuthill, 4 x 4 ¼ In. 375.00
Punch Bowl, Base, Egg Shape, Scalloped Rim, Hobstars, 19th Century, 15 In. 944.00
Punch Bowl, Base, Hobstar, Cane, Vesica, Zipper, American Brilliant, 11 ¼ x 12 In.. .... 850.00
Punch Bowl, Base, Hobstar & Zipper, 10 ¾ x 12 ¾ In. .... *illus* 1150.00
Punch Bowl, Base, Hobstar Border, Zipper, American Brilliant, 10 ¾ x 12 ¾ In.. .... 1150.00
Punch Bowl, Pedestal Base, Hobstar, 11 In.. .... 575.00
Punch Cup, Dorflinger, Green To Clear, Montrose, 8 Piece 2600.00
Punch Cup, Hobstar & Fan, 5 Piece 50.00
Punch Set, Emerald Green To Clear, Signed, Dorflinger, 14-In. Bowl, 10 Piece 18500.00
Punch Set, Whirling Star, 14 Piece 550.00
Salt, Boat Shape, Stepped Diamond Base, Intaglio, 3 x 4 In., 4 Piece 58.00

Nappy, Harvard, Scalloped Border, Hobstar Center, 6 In.
$80.00

Cut Glass, Plate, Star Diamond, Turquoise, Cranberry Flashed, 6 In.
$5500.00

TIP

When using antiques on a holiday table, be careful. Wax from candles can stain a cloth. Dishes may be stained from cranberry or other fruits. Flower containers are easily water stained. Vases and plants often stain wood; be sure to use a coaster or dish. Greens draped on pictures or marble can stain. Cellophane tape will leave a mark.

Cut Glass, Punch Bowl, Base, Hobstar & Zipper, 10¾ x 12¾ In. $1150.00

Cut Glass, Tray, Vintage, Engraved, Tuthill, 13¾ x 8½ In. $2000.00

TIP

If you live in an earthquake area, a few precautions may help limit damage. Be sure there is a lip on the edge of a shelf that holds dishes and glassware. String a fishing line across the front of a shelf holding baskets or other very light objects to help keep them from falling. Use dental wax to stick the objects to the shelf. Keep cabinet doors locked shut so pieces will not fall out. Magnetic "childproof" locks help some also.

Salt & Pepper, Ridged, Sterling Silver Cap, 1930s, 3⅛ In. 35.00
Saltshaker, Crosscut Diamond & Fan, Silver Plated Top, American Brilliant, 4¼ In. 100.00
Spooner, Russian, Buttons & Engraved Feathers, 8½ In. 550.00
Stringholder, Flower Engraved, 10-Sided, Sterling Base, American Brilliant, 5¼ In. 200.00
Sugar, Handles, Engraved Strawberry, Sterling Cover, American Brilliant 175.00
Sugar & Creamer, Broken Heart, American Brilliant 50.00
Sugar & Creamer, Hobstar, Strawberry Diamond, Fan, Notched Handles 225.00
Tankard, Amethyst To Clear, Flowers, Notched Handle, Sterling Rim, 9¾ In. 750.00
Tankard, Cranberry To Clear, Sterling Silver Spout, American Brilliant, 10½ In. 1700.00
Tankard, Fluted, Hobstar Base, Notched Handle, American Brilliant, 13 In. 350.00
Tankard, Intaglio Pomegranate, Cut Base, Handle, American Brilliant, 14¼ In. 450.00
Tankard, Sunburst, Bull's-Eye, Prism, Hobstar, Notched Handle, 11½ In. 200.00
Tazza, Genoa, Clark 495.00
Tazza, Panel Cut, Engraved Thistle, American Brilliant, 7¾ x 8¾ In. 400.00
Tazza, Rolled Rim, Flashed Hobstar, Strawberry Diamond, 11½ x 9 In. 375.00
Tray, Engraved Briar Rose, American Brilliant, 11¾ In. 1700.00
Tray, Hobstar, Step Cut, Fan, Chartreuse To Clear, 12 In. 125.00
Tray, Hobstars, Vesica, Strawberry Diamond Border, Oval, Sterling Rim, 13 x 9½ In. 250.00
Tray, Ice Cream, Chrysanthemum, American Brilliant, 14¼ x 7¾ In. 550.00
Tray, Ice Cream, Hobstar, Vesica, Fan, 16¼ x 9 In. 350.00
Tray, Ice Cream, Pinwheel & Fan, Diamond Panels, Star Bottom, Marked, 3 x 7 In. 195.00
Tray, Ice Cream, Pinwheel & Fan, Diamond Panels, Star, American Brilliant, 2 x 10 In. 196.00
Tray, Ice Cream, Scalloped Rim, Gundy, Clapperton, c.1900, 14½ In. 236.00
Tray, Square, Modified Hobstar Center, Cane Border, American Brilliant, 5½ In. 110.00
Tray, Vintage, Engraved, Tuthill, 13¾ x 8½ In. . . . . . *illus* 2000.00
Trophy, Chalice Shape, Green, Air Twist Stem, Hobstar Base, Cane & Fan, 13½ In. 850.00
Tumbler, Amethyst To Clear, Crosscut Diamond & Thumbprint, 5½ In. 250.00
Tumbler, Iced Tea, Engraved Dahlia, American Brilliant, 5¾ In. 50.00
Urn, Cover, Intaglio, Swags With Parrots, 8-Sided Base, Handles, 10¼ In. 4800.00
Urn, Engraved Carriage & Hunt Scene, Faceted Waist, Plinth Base, 11 x 8 In., Pair 2233.00
Vase, Allover Diamond, Pinched Waist, 12 In. 70.00
Vase, Art Deco, Amethyst To Clear, 15 In. 350.00
Vase, Art Deco, Swirl, Gold Leaf Rim, Green To Clear, Pinched Waist, 13¼ In. 125.00
Vase, Bud, Engraved Poppy & Leaf, American Brilliant, 9¾ In. 100.00
Vase, Bud, Green To Clear, Rococo Swirl, Engraved Flowers, 13¾ In. 1300.00
Vase, Bud, Rose To Clear, Flower, Diamond & Punty, 1920s, 12 In. 325.00
Vase, Butterfly Engraved, Pinched Waist, 14 In. 325.00
Vase, Diamonds, Fans, Urn Shape, Footed, 20th Century, 12 In. 147.00
Vase, English Trellis, Square Stepped Base, Anglo-Irish Style, 15 x 5½ In., Pair 780.00
Vase, Engraved Poppy, Art Nouveau, 13½ In. 600.00
Vase, Engraving, Geometric, J. Hoare, 17 In. 1450.00
Vase, Fan, Green, To Clear, Geometric, 1960s, 6¼ In. 25.00
Vase, Flowers, Geometric, Flattened, Flared Rim, 7½ x 10 In. 649.00
Vase, Green Threading, Engraved Floral, F. Carder, Pedestal Base, 13¾ In. 750.00
Vase, Green To Clear, Crosscut Diamond, Hobstar, Strawberry Diamond & Fan, 10¼ In. 125.00
Vase, Green To Clear, Engraved Flowers, Oval, 7¼ In. 150.00
Vase, Hobstar, Cane Vesica, Strawberry Diamond, Fan, Pinched Waist, 20 In. 1000.00
Vase, Hobstar, Prism & Fan, American Brilliant, 4 In. 150.00
Vase, Hobstar, Strawberry Diamond, Vesica, Fan, Notched Handles, 8 In. 200.00
Vase, Hobstar, Zipper, Palmate Cluster, 19¾ In. 316.00
Vase, Hobstar & Cane, Sawtooth Lip, Scalloped, Pinched Waist, 8 x 7¼ In. 324.00
Vase, Hobstar Cluster, Cane, Prism, Pinched Waist, American Brilliant, 18 In., Pair 950.00
Vase, Pedestal Base, Monarch Pattern, Scalloped Base, 17½ In. 1200.00
Vase, Prism Cut Body, Strawberry Diamond Rim, Bulbous, 14¾ In. 650.00
Vase, Swans, Eagle, Quail, Trees, Pinched Waist, 6½ In. 425.00
Vase, Trumpet, Green To Clear, Strawberry Diamond, Prism & Punty, American Brilliant, 14 In. 550.00
Vase, Trumpet, Hobstar Base, Tricornered Rim, Elmira, 11¾ In. 225.00
Vase, Trumpet, Hobstars, Scalloped Base, 12 In. 300.00
Vase, Trumpet, Sapphire Blue To Clear, Hobstar, Strawberry Diamond & Fan, 14 In. 400.00
Vase, Tulip Shape, Hobstar, Vesica, Zipper, Strawberry Diamond, American Brilliant, 12 In. . . 375.00
Vase, Urn Shape, Sterling Overlay, Frieze Around Body, Engraved Flowers, 7 x 5 In. 201.00
Water Set, Hindoo, Hobstar & Prism, American Brilliant, 8 In., 7 Piece 475.00
Wine, 6 Panels, Oval, Peacock Green, Applied Foot, 4¾ In. 77.00
Wine, 11 Panels, Oval, Teal, Applied Baluster Stem, 4½ In. 88.00
Wine, Amber To Yellow To Clear, Diamond, Strawberry, Diamond & Fan, 8 In. 300.00
Wine, Apple Green, Apple Core Stem, Base, 6 In., 8 Piece 200.00

Wine, Cranberry To Clear, Swirl Panel, Hex Cut Stem, 5 3/4 In. 25.00
Wine, Cut Panels, Rays, Flared, 3 7/8 In., 6 Piece 230.00
Wine, Green To Clear, Engraved Flower & Feather, Clear Stem, 5 3/4 In., 6 Piece 1600.00
Wine, Rhine, Amber Cut To Clear, Engraved Flowers, Vane, 8 1/4 In. 700.00
Wine, Rhine, Cobalt Blue Cut To Orange Cut To Clear, 7 3/4 In. 1100.00
Wine, Rhine, Flute Pattern, Green Cut To Clear, Apple Core Stem, Gilt Detail, 7 In. 275.00
Wine, Rhine, Green Cut To Clear, Engraved Flowers, Basket Weave, Rope, 8 3/4 In., 8 Piece. ... 1100.00
Wine, Rhine, Green Cut To Vaseline Cut To Clear, Engraved Flowers, 7 3/4 In. 1300.00
Wine, Trumpet Shape, Light Green, Engraved Blossom & Vine, 7 In., 8 Piece 150.00

CYBIS porcelain is a twentieth-century product. Boleslaw Cybis came to the United States from Poland in 1939. He started making porcelains in Long Island, New York, in 1940. He moved to Trenton, New Jersey, in 1942 as one of the founders of Cordey China Co. and started his own Cybis Porcelains about 1950. The firm is still working.

CYBIS

Bust, Eskimo Boy, 10 x 6 In.. .... 205.00
Bust, George Washington, Wood Base, 11 In.. .... 234.00 to 497.00
Egg, Hand Painted, Gilt, Footed, 1984, 6 In. 40.00
Figurine, Baby Boy, 10 In. 234.00
Figurine, Ballerina, 10 x 4 1/2 In. 71.00
Figurine, Ballerina, 1983, 9 In.. .... 146.00
Figurine, Buffalo, 5 1/2 In. 65.00
Figurine, Buffalo, White, 1975, 14 x 18 3/4 In.. .... 1175.00
Figurine, Bust, Guinevere, 12 In. 353.00
Figurine, Calla Lily, 16 x 8 x 7 In. .... 263.00 to 294.00
Figurine, Clematis, Flower, 15 x 8 In. 410.00
Figurine, Colts, Darby & Joan, 1969, 8 1/4 x 9 In. 353.00
Figurine, Columbine, Woman, 15 1/4 x 9 1/4 x 6 1/4 In. 764.00
Figurine, Elizabeth Ann, Girl, Seated Holding Doll, 5 x 3 1/2 In. 82.00
Figurine, Flower, Chinese Maid Pansy, 9 x 5 In.. .... 94.00
Figurine, Funny Face, 1976, 12 In. 205.00
Figurine, Girl With Butterfly In Hair, 7 In.. .... 264.00
Figurine, Great White Heron, 17 1/4 x 8 1/2 In. 646.00
Figurine, Harlequin, 16 x 7 In. 585.00
Figurine, Holding Bouquet, 8 In. 35.00
Figurine, Jamie, Chicks, 7 x 8 In. 82.00
Figurine, Jane Eyre, c.1981, 12 1/2 In. 150.00
Figurine, Juliet, No. 104, 12 x 6 In. .... 250.00 to 468.00
Figurine, Kestrel, 16 x 9 In.. .... 468.00
Figurine, Little Miss Muffet, 6 x 5 In. 3428.00
Figurine, Little Red Riding Hood, 1973, 6 1/2 x 3 In.. .... 29.00
Figurine, Madonna With Wreath Of Roses, 11 x 4 In. 351.00
Figurine, Moses, 20 x 9 In. 380.00
Figurine, Oberon, Woman, 10 1/2 x 3 1/2 x 5 In. 441.00
Figurine, Pandora, Woman Seated, 4 1/2 x 4 In. 88.00
Figurine, Persephone, Woman, 14 1/4 x 9 1/4 x 11 In.. .... 1645.00
Figurine, Pink Dogwood, 8 x 7 In. 322.00
Figurine, Rose With Forsythia, 8 x 10 In.. .... 380.00
Figurine, Unicorn, Lying Down, 4 3/4 x 6 3/4 In. 175.00
Figurine, Unicorn, Striped Horn, No. 64, Wood Base, 13 In. 350.00
Figurine, Water Bird, 8 x 8 In.. .... 234.00
Figurine, Wendy, Girl, Holding Doll, 7 x 3 3/4 In.. .... 59.00

CZECHOSLOVAKIA is a popular term with collectors. The name, first used as a mark after the country was formed in 1918, appears on glass and porcelain and other decorative items. Although Czechoslovakia split into Slovakia and the Czech Republic on January 1, 1993, the name continues to be used in some trademarks.

CZECHOSLOVAKIA GLASS

Cheese Plate, Cover, Cut, 8 1/4 In. 35.00
Panel, Pink, Pair Of Songbirds On Flowering Branch, Riedel, 7 x 10 In. .... *illus* 764.00
Perfume Bottle, Jeweled, Filigree Lid, Marked, 2 1/4 In.. .... 55.00
Perfume Bottle, Malachite, Embossed Roses, Scrolls, Lid, Marked, 6 In. .... *illus* 750.00
Vase, Berry Vines, Green, Yellow Ground, 19 In. .... *illus* 500.00
Vase, Bubble, Leaf, Flower, Applied Blue Iridescent Base, 9 In. 675.00
Vase, Clear, Engraved, Transparent Enameled Figures, 1945-48, 13 1/2 In. 2832.00
Vase, Conch Shell, Light Amber, Pearl Oil Spots, Rainbow Highlights, Wave Base, 9 In. 213.00

Czechoslovakia Glass, Panel, Pink, Pair Of Songbirds On Flowering Branch, Riedel, 7 x 10 In.
$764.00

Czechoslovakia Glass, Perfume Bottle, Malachite, Embossed Roses, Scrolls, Lid, Marked, 6 In.
$750.00

Czechoslovakia Glass, Vase, Berry Vines, Green, Yellow Ground, 19 In.
$500.00

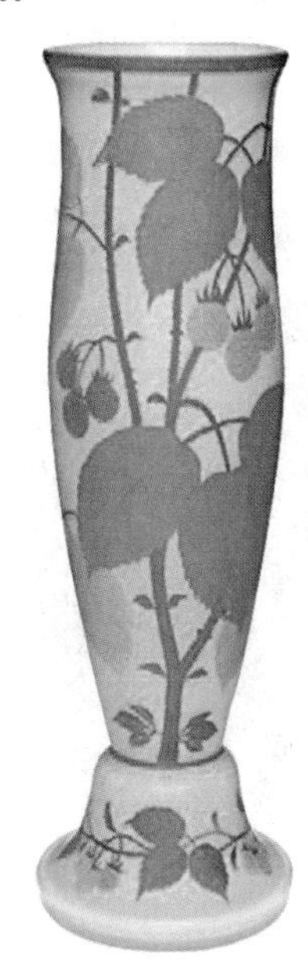

Czechoslovakia Glass, Vase, Fiery Opalescent, Draped Design, 3-Sided, Metal Trim, 9 In. $300.00

Czechoslovakia Pottery, Pitcher, Stylized Fruit, Red, Yellow, Black, Marked, Ditman Urbach, 6 ¾ In. $130.00

Czechoslovakia Pottery, Vase, Woman's Head Medallion, Cobalt Blue Sponge, Marked, 8 ¾ In. $92.00

Vase, Conch Shell, Tendrils, Leaf Pod Base, Gold & Green Iridescent, 10 In. 235.00
Vase, Enameled, Rectangular, Etched, Frosted, c.1935, 10 ¼ In. 590.00
Vase, Fiery Opalescent, Draped Design, 3-Sided, Metal Trim, 9 In. . . . . *illus* 300.00
Vase, Oil Spot, Beaker Shape, 4 Pulled Arms, Flattened Rim, 9 ¾ In. 177.00
Vase, Orange, Amethyst Pulled Up From Base, Bulbous, Marked, 4 ½ In. 44.00
Vase, Orange, Green & Amethyst Spatter Base, Marked, 9 In. 38.00
Vase, Orange & Yellow Spatter, Amethyst Base, Marked, 9 In. 55.00
Vase, Orange Confetti, Swirls, Iridescent, Dimpled, Ruffled Rim, 5 ⅝ In. 265.00
Vase, Yellow, Scrolls, Green, Purple, Red Medallions, Cobalt Blue Rim, Marked 99.00

CZECHOSLOVAKIA POTTERY

Basket, Multicolored Glaze, Marked, 4 ¼ x 5 In. 17.00
Coffee Set, Scenes, Cobalt Blue, Gold Trim, 8 Piece 500.00
Console, Birds & Flowers, 11 ½ In. 69.00
Creamer, Cow, Figural, Marked, 9 In. 44.00
Jardiniere, Flowers, Handles, Marked 4 In. 44.00
Pitcher, Stylized Fruit, Red, Yellow, Black, Marked, Ditman Urbach, 6 ¾ In. . . . . *illus* 130.00
Plate, Scrolling Gilt Border, Flower Spray, 1 ½ In., 9 Piece 189.00
Urn, Classical Scene, 24K Gold Trim, Porcelain, c.1950, 18 In. 234.00
Vase, Figural, Woman Playing Instrument, Dog Under Tree, 13 In. 104.00
Vase, Gourd Shape, Indents At Bottom, 5 ½ x 9 In. 316.00
Vase, Woman's Head Medallion, Cobalt Blue Sponge, Marked, 8 ¾ In. . . . . *illus* 92.00
Wall Pocket, Bird & Birdhouse On Twig, Vibrant Colors, 16 In. 30.00

DANIEL BOONE, a pre–Revolutionary War folk hero, was a surveyor, trapper, and frontiersman. A television series, which ran from 1964 to 1970, was based on his life and starred Fess Parker. All types of Daniel Boone memorabilia are collected.

Button, Daniel Boone, Official Wilderness Scout, 1 ⅛ In. . . . . *illus* 33.00
Comic Book, No. 11, 1967 . . . . . 8.00
Comic Book, Test Of A Leader, No. 14, 1969 . . . . . 15.00
Figure, 1734-1820, Marx, 3 ¼ In. 15.00
Head Ring, Raised Head, Gold, Plastic, 1960s 15.00
Mug, Face, Coonskin Hat, Rockingham Glaze, Harker 48.00
Postcard, Birthplace, Reading, Pa., c.1930-45 . . . . . 2.00
Postcard, Cabin, Baumstown, Pa. 2.00
Postcard, Cave, Chimney Rock, Kentucky, 1950-60 . . . . . 8.00
Postcard, Wagon Train 3.00
Record, Fess Parker, DQ1336 . . . . . 22.00
Record, Tale Spinners For Children, 33 RPM 16.00

D'ARGENTAL is a mark used in France by the Compagnie des Cristalleries de St. Louis. The firm made multilayered, acid-cut cameo glass in the late nineteenth and twentieth centuries. D'Argental is the French name for the city of Munzthal, home of the glassworks. Later they made enameled etched glass.

Vase, Blue, Crimson Sailing Ships, Shoreline, 11 In. 1035.00
Vase, Citrine, Amethyst, Wild Roses, Signed, 7 In. 885.00
Vase, Flowers, Stems, Leaves, Purple, Brown, Blue Frosted Ground, 18 In. 480.00
Vase, Sapphire Blue, Cherries, Leafy Branches, Citron Ground, Swollen, 11 ½ In. 1410.00
Vase, Stick, Ruby Thistle Branches, Leaves, Signed, 12 In. 805.00

DAUM, a glassworks in Nancy, France, was started by Jean Daum in 1875. The company, now called *Cristalleries de Nancy*, is still working. The *Daum Nancy* mark has been used in many variations. The name of the city and the artist are usually both included. The term *martele* is used to describe applied decorations that are carved or etched in the cameo process.

Basket, Flower Buds, Enameled, Signed, c.1910, 7 ¼ x 6 ⅛ In. 7800.00
Bookends, Clear, 5 ¾ x 4 ½ In. 125.00
Bowl, Applied Leaves, Handles, Cameo, Signed, c.1905, 3 ½ x 8 In. 4375.00
Bowl, Centerpiece, Clear, Canoe Shape, Signed, c.1950s, 24 In. 71.00
Bowl, Centerpiece, Flower, Orange, Butterscotch, Olive Green, Brown, Blue, 3 x 14 ¼ In. 3163.00
Bowl, Crimson Flowers, Gold Enameled, Crimped Rim, Cameo, 7 In. 1035.00
Bowl, Floral, Frosted Mottled Blue, Trees, Lake, Shoreline, Footed Coupe, Signed, 4 ½ In. 3163.00
Bowl, Flowers, Leaves, Burnt Yellow To Mauve Ground, Enameled, Cameo, 2 In. 1610.00
Bowl, Flowers, Leaves, Gold Enameled, Squat, Footed, c.1905, 7 ¼ x 11 In. 4560.00
Bowl, Flowers, Leaves, Multicolored, Squat, Footed, Cameo, c.1910, 3 ¾ x 12 In. 7800.00
Bowl, Flowers, Leaves, Purple, Red, Green, Handles, c.1910, 4 x 10 ½ In. 9600.00

Bowl, Flowers, Stems, Leaves, Frosted Green, Chipped Ice Ground, 8 ½ In.. 1035.00
Bowl, Flowers, Violet, Lobed, Enameled, c.1910, 3 In. 4560.00
Bowl, Free-Form Cutting, Ruffled Rim, No. 874, c.1950, 10 In.. 47.00
Bowl, Grape Leaves & Clusters, Mottled Orange, Yellow Ground, Applied Snail, 6 In. 4600.00
Bowl, Heron, Green, Red, Gold Enameled, Cameo, Silver Applied Flowers, c.1885, 5 ¾ In. 6600.00
Bowl, Landscape, Lake, Swan, Trees, Enameled, Handles, c.1910, 3 ⅛ In. 7800.00
Bowl, Landscape, Trees By Lake, Black, Blue, Yellow, Cameo, 1920s, 8 In. 3586.00
Bowl, Leaves, Stems & Berries, Green & Amber, Textured, Cameo, 7 ½ In. 1495.00
Bowl, Mottled Orange, Lavender, Red, Mica Flakes, 3 Pulled Ear Handles, 7 ½ x 8 In.. 425.00
Bowl, Orchid, Yellow, Gold Enameled, 3 Loop Feet, Signed, c.1900, 4 ¼ In. 6000.00
Bowl, Sprigs Of Red Blossoms, Mottled Amber Ground, Enameled, 3 ½ x 8 In. 2280.00
Bowl, Stems, Leaves & Berries, Red Enameled, Yellow & Cream Ground, Cameo, 8 In.. 2070.00
Bowl, Trees, Green, Orange Mottled Sky, Lake Background, 10 ¼ In. 863.00
Bowl, Wheat & Poppy, Handles, Enameled, c.1900, 5 In. 4800.00
Bowl, Winter Scene, Enameled Trees, Yellow To Mottled Orange Ground, Cameo, 5 In. 2415.00
Bowl, Winter Scene, Enameled, Orange & Yellow Ground, Rolled Lip, Cameo, 3 ¼ In. 1150.00
Bowl, Yellow Blossoms, Stems, Multicolored Mottling, Crimped Rim, 2 ½ x 4 In. 2185.00
Box, Cover, Butterfly, Gold, Enameled, c.1895, 3 In. 3840.00
Box, Cover, Enameled Yellow, Orange Leaves, Trees, Round, Leather, Medallion, 6 ½ In.. 1265.00
Box, Cover, Farmhouse Scene, Frosted Ground, Signed, Gold Enameled, 5 In.. 5865.00
Box, Cover, Flowers, White Ground, Border, Gold Enameled, c.1910, 2 ¾ In. 2880.00
Box, Cover, Wheat, Lavender, Gold Enameled, c.1910, 4 ¼ In. 6000.00
Box, Covered, River, Shore, Woods, Mountains, Orange & Yellow Ground, Cameo, 5 ½ In. 1840.00
Box, Dome Cover, Dragonflies, Flowers, Amethyst, Cameo, c.1910, 3 x 5 ½ In. 5760.00
Box, Dome Cover, Wheat & Poppy, c.1900, 2½ In. 3360.00 to 5400.00
Chandelier, 3-Light, Flowers, Leaves, Cameo, c.1900, 25 In.. 11400.00
Cordial, Frosted Purple, Green Stemmed Violets, Cone Shape, Cameo, 2 ¼ In. 1400.00
Cordial, Landscape, Lake, Swan, Enameled, Cameo, c.1910, 1 ⅞ In. 3360.00
Cruet, Flowers, Ribbed, Clear, Flowers, Gold Enameled, Ribbed Handle, Stopper, Cameo, 5 In. 460.00
Decanter, Dutch Landscape, Boats, Lake, Opalescent, Enameled, Stopper, 1890s, 7 In. 2040.00
Decanter, Tulip, Enameled, Multicolored, Stopper, 1890s, 4 ⅝ In. 5760.00
Decanter, Tulip, Enameled, Stopper, 7 ⅛ In.. 6600.00
Ewer, Dutch, Landscape, Windmills, Opalescent, Enameled, 1890s, 8 ¾ In. 3120.00
Ewer, Flower, Pointed Spout, Fire Polished, c.1910, 16 ½ In. 9000.00
Ewer, Landscape, Autumn, Trees, Lake, 6 ¼ In.. 5040.00
Ewer, Pale Blue, Martele, Shaped Handle, Tapered, Footed, Cameo, c.1900, 11 ¾ In. 9000.00
Ewer, Tulip, Multicolored, Handle, Gold Enameled, 1890s, 7 ½ In. 3360.00
Figurine, Elephant, Multicolored, Pate-De-Verre, 8 x 9 ¼ In. 1175.00
Figurine, Elephant Sitting, Trunk Up, Clear, 10 In. 205.00
Figurine, Panther, Multicolored, Pate-De-Verre, 5 ½ x 16 ¾ In.. 1763.00
Figurine, Swan, Pink, 9 ¾ x 18 In. 2350.00
Figurine, Tiger, Amber, 4 x 8 In. 529.00
Figurine, Tiger, Amber, Pate-De-Verre, 4 ¾ x 10 ¾ In. 940.00
Figurine, Turtle, Green, Pate-De-Verre, 2 ½ x 2 ½ In. 235.00
Inkwell, Applied Berries, Indigo Blue, Brown To Green Leaves, Frosted, 3 ¼ x 5 In. 8050.00
Inkwell, Cover, Applied Oak Leaves & Acorns, Signed, c.1900, 4 ¾ In. 4750.00
Inkwell, Cover, Flowers, Leaves, Enameled, Multicolored, 1890s, 5 x 4 ¼ In. 4560.00
Jar, Cover, Orchid, Yellow, Gold Enameled, Gilt, Signed, c.1900, 6 In. 11250.00
Jar, Thistle, Pale Yellow Ground, Enameled, Stopper, c.1900, 3 ½ In. 5040.00
Lamp, Boats, Ocean, Cameo, c.1900, 33 In. 18000.00
Lamp, Flowers, Leaves, Dome Shade, Wrought Iron Base, c.1910, 9 ½ x 9 ½ In.. 7200.00
Lamp, Mottled Pink, Iron Frame, Marble Base, Majorelle, Signed, 28 In. *illus* 4800.00
Lamp, Orchids, Mottled, Signed, c.1900, 24 In. 18000.00
Lamp, Red, Flowers, Leaves, Cameo, Wrought Iron Base, Edgar Brandt, c.1925, 14 ½ In. 4000.00
Lamp, Winter, Trees, Red, Yellow, Green, Enameled, Cameo, c.1905, 14 ½ In. 19200.00
Lamp Base, Autumn Leaves, Seed Pods & Stems, Yellow Orange, Green Ground, 6 ½ In. 1003.00
Lamp Base, Grape, Vine, Yellow & Orange Ground, Applied Grapes, Cameo, 10 ½ In.. 4800.00
Lamp Base, Mottled Yellow, Amethyst, Red Body, Flowers, Green Leaves, 11 ½ In. 518.00
Page Turner, Gold Enameled, 16 In. 5040.00
Perfume Bottle, Amethyst, Flowers, Leaves, Pear Shaped, Enameled, Stopper, 8 ¼ In.. 7800.00
Perfume Bottle, Flowers, White Ground, Stopper, c.1910, 8 ¾ In., Pair 9600.00
Perfume Bottle, Gold Scrolling Vines, Amethyst Ground, Cameo, Stopper, 3 In. 1208.00
Pitcher, Blue, Daffodil, Leaves, Mottled, Cameo, Signed, c.1910, 7 ½ In. 9000.00
Pitcher, Opalescent, Lily-Of-The-Valley, Silver Mounted, Cameo, 4 ¾ In. 1320.00
Pitcher, Violet's, Purple To White Ground, Gold Enameled, 1890s, 5 In. 4200.00

Daniel Boone, Button, Daniel Boone, Official Wilderness Scout, 1 ⅛ In. $33.00

Daum, Lamp, Mottled Pink, Iron Frame, Marble Base, Majorelle, Signed, 28 In. $4800.00

Daum, Plate Set, 4 Seasons, Pate-De-Verre, Box, c.1970, 10 ½ In., 4 Piece $230.00

TIP

You can remove stickers from most things by spraying them with a lubricant.

Daum History
Cut and enameled glass, often with heraldic crests, was made by Daum at first. In 1885 Daum's sons Auguste (1853–1909) and Antonin (1864–1930) introduced Art Nouveau–style pâte-de-verre and cameo glass. Pieces were decorated with flowers, landscapes, and other natural forms. In 1900 Daum joined Emile Gallé and Louis Majorelle to found the École de Nancy. Daum started making free-form clear glass in the 1950s. It reintroduced pâte-de-verre glass in 1966, using contemporary designs. Daum glass is still being made.

Daum, Vase, Flowers, Green, Red, Fuchsia Leaves, Purple Agate, c.1900, 19½ In.
$16730.00

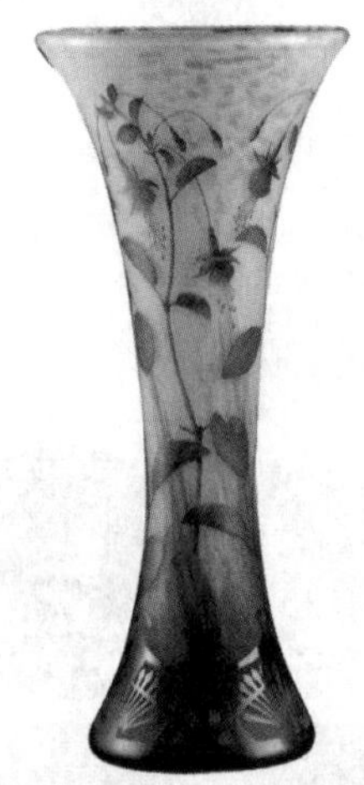

Daum,Vase, Landscape, Rainy, Trees, 2 x 1½ In.
$2640.00

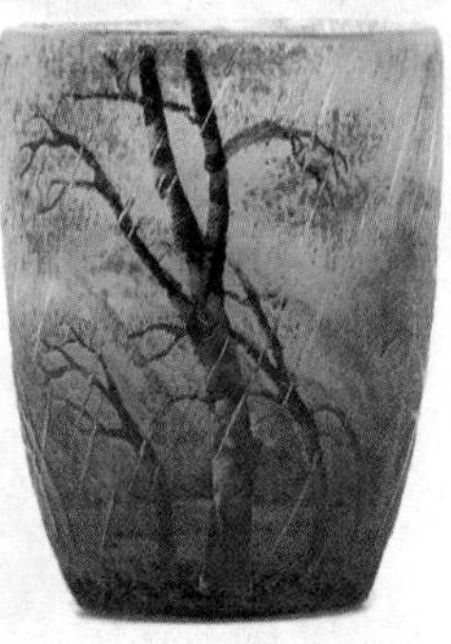

Plate Set, 4 Seasons, Pate-De-Verre, Box, c.1970, 10½ In., 4 Piece .... *illus* 230.00
Rose Bowl, Multicolored, Pate-De-Verre, 4 x 9 In. 823.00
Salt, Amethyst, Amber, Red Sweet Peas, Green Stem, Oval, Cameo, 2 In. 978.00
Salt, Bridge, Mountain Scene, Bucket Shape, Enameled, Textured, Cameo, 1¼ In. 518.00
Salt, Winter Scene, Enameled, Yellow To Orange Ground, Oval, Cameo, 1⅛ x 2 In. 1035.00
Scent Bottle, Gold Enameled, Dandelions, Pink Ground, Cameo, 5½ In. 1668.00
Scent Bottle, Gold Enameled Thistle, Textured, Metal Foot, Collar, Lid, 4½ In. 748.00
Scent Bottle, Opalescent Blue To Purple, Amethyst Flower, Lid, Cameo, 4½ In. 600.00
Scent Bottle, Poppy, Enameled, Mottled Yellow, Shaded To Ecru, Silver Cap, 4¾ In. 1668.00
Shade, Bell, Mottled Yellow & Red, White Trailings, Scalloped Pointed Rim, 5½ In. 173.00
Shade, Mottled Pink, Yellow, Green, Frosted, 5¼ In. 173.00
Tumbler, Mistletoe Stems, Gold & White Enamel, Rose Ground, Gold Rim, Cameo, 5 In. 575.00
Tumbler, Mottled Red, Yellow, Yellow Flowers, Green Stems, Barrel Shape, Signed, 5 In. 1840.00
Tumbler, Mottled Yellow & Orange, Crimson, Yellow Orchids, Signed, 5 In. 1668.00
Tumbler, Rose Hips, Berries, Leaves, Mottled Burnt Yellow Ground, Cameo, 3¼ In. 1265.00
Tumbler, Winter Scene, Enameled, Trees, Orange & Yellow Ground, Cameo, 1¾ In. 920.00
Vase, Amber, Running Gazelles, Landscape, Cameo, Signed, 12¼ In. 316.00
Vase, Amber, Wide Mouth, Tapered, Mottled, Wrought Iron Mount, c.1920, 9¼ In. 5400.00
Vase, Amber Blossom, Sprigs, Yellow & Purple Mottled Ground, Cameo, 3½ x 2 In. 1200.00
Vase, Applied Berries, Leaves, Bulbous Base, Green Tones, Cameo, Signed, c.1910, 12 In. 6000.00
Vase, Applied Roses, Enameled, Signed, c.1910, 10¼ In. 10200.00
Vase, Bellflowers, Leaves, Blue, Shaded, Mottled Blue To Purple, Gold Rim, 4 In. 288.00
Vase, Bellflowers, Leaves, Red, Green, Mottled Yellow To Mauve Ground, 10¼ In. 780.00
Vase, Berries, Yellow, Green Leaves, Mottled, Orange Ground, Shade To Mauve, 10 In. 2358.00
Vase, Birch Trees, Hills, Ribbed Top, Cameo, Marked, 8¾ In. 4313.00
Vase, Blackbirds On Trees, Mottled Blue, White, Irregular Rim, Enameled, Cameo, 6 In. 7200.00
Vase, Black-Eyed Susan, Burnt Salmon, Olive Green Centers, Martele Ground, 8¾ In. 9775.00
Vase, Bleeding Heart, Blue Ground, Verse In Gold, Cameo, 3 In. 1265.00
Vase, Bleeding Heart, Enameled Leaves & Vines, Fall Colors, Diamond Shape, 4½ In. 3600.00
Vase, Blue & Green, Handles, Cone Shape, Martele Ground, Cameo, 10 In. 4080.00
Vase, Blue Cornflower, Pink Shaded To Deep Blue Mottled Ground, Cameo, 3½ In. 1800.00
Vase, Blue Cornflowers, Leaves, Broken Egg Shape, Enameled, Cameo, 3¾ In. 6900.00
Vase, Bud, Wild Orchid, Spider Web, Purple To Green Ground, Cameo, 4 In. 2400.00
Vase, Bulbous Stick, Opalescent Amber, Red Vines, Thistle, Gilt, Cameo, Signed, 9 In. 1610.00
Vase, Butterflies, Enameled, Cameo, Signed, c.1893, 11 In. 24000.00
Vase, Carnations, Frosted Pink To Green Ground, Shaded, Mottled, Gold Rim, 4½ In. 575.00
Vase, Cinnamon Orange, Green Pitted Spatter, Art Deco, 8 In. 575.00
Vase, Circles, Squares, Blue Green, Cameo, Signed, c.1925, 14½ In. 6600.00
Vase, Citron, Bell Flowers, Bulbous, Cameo, 16 In. 1725.00
Vase, Columbine, Wheat, Opal, Peach Striations, Gold Trim, Tricornered Rim, Cameo, 4 In. .. 4115.00
Vase, Crocuses, Red, Clear, Frosted, Martele Ground, Cameo, 5½ In. 3600.00
Vase, Dark Green, Diamonds, Footed, Flared, c.1925, 14¾ In. 7200.00
Vase, Enameled Leaves, Red, Green, Orange Ground, Insects, 24½ In. 8400.00
Vase, Flower, Burgundy To White, Martele, Cameo, c.1910, 7¼ In. 3600.00
Vase, Flower, Lavender, Purple, Goblet Shape, Swollen Stem, Footed, Cameo, c.1925, 10 In. .. 9000.00
Vase, Flower, Pink, Green Stem, White Ground, Cameo, c.1910, 7¼ In. 7200.00
Vase, Flower, Red, Mottled Ground, Cameo, c.1910, 11½ In. 9600.00
Vase, Flowers, Gold, Cameo, Signed, c.1925, 16¾ In. 8400.00
Vase, Flowers, Green, Red, Fuchsia Leaves, Purple Agate, c.1900, 19½ In. .... *illus* 16730.00
Vase, Flowers, Leaves, Agate Ground, Dark Purple, c.1900, 5½ In. 9600.00
Vase, Flowers, Leaves, Gold Enameled, Tapered, Footed, Cameo, c.1895, 20¼ In. 13200.00
Vase, Flowers, Pink, White, Tapered, Spread Foot, Martele, Cameo, c.1900, 9¾ In. 7200.00
Vase, Flowers, Purple, Butterflies, Leaves, White Ground, Cameo, c.1894, 11¼ In. 6600.00
Vase, Flowers, Red, Green, Leaves, Mottled Ground, Cameo, c.1910, 19½ In. 6600.00
Vase, Flowers, Shades Of Red, Yellow Ground, Cameo, 5 x 18½ In. 3900.00
Vase, Flowers, Stems, Leaves, Pink, Cream Ground, Enameled, c.1910, 11 3/4 In. . 2460.00 to 5040.00
Vase, Flowers, Stems, Leaves, Shaded Blue, Tapered, Bulbous, Cameo, c.1900, 12 In. 9600.00
Vase, Flowers, Violet, 3-Footed, Gold Enameled, 1890s, 4 In. 8400.00
Vase, Flowers, White, Brown Stems, Leaves, Mottled White To Blue Ground, 7½ In. 8050.00
Vase, Flowers & Leaves, Textured, Iridescent Gold, Green, Blue, White Beads, Signed, 5 In. 1500.00
Vase, Frosted, Wrought Iron Band, Majorelle, Signed, c.1925, 9¾ In. 3500.00
Vase, Fruit, Brown, Mauve Leaves, Raspberry To Green Mottled Ground, 15½ In. 8050.00
Vase, Fruit, Stems, Leaves, Mottled Yellow, Orange, Raspberry Ground, Cameo, 18¾ In. 3450.00
Vase, Geometric, Yellow, Amber, Brown Mottled, Art Deco, Cameo, 10¾ In. 1150.00
Vase, Golden Blossoms, Mottled Yellow & Purple Frosted Ground, Square, 4½ x 2 In. 1920.00

Vase, Golden Orchids, Mottled Ground, Enameled, Cameo, 3 ½ x 2 ¾ In. 1200.00
Vase, Grapes, Leaves, Multicolored, Applied Snail Handles, Pate-De-Verre, c.1910, 8 ¼ In. 3250.00
Vase, Grapes, Vines, Leaves, Applied Snail, Multicolored, Pate-De-Verre, c.1910, 7 ½ In. 13200.00
Vase, Green, Geometric, Shouldered, Cameo, c.1925, 9¼ In. .... 2640.00 to 5400.00
Vase, Green, Hammered Spiral, Art Deco, Flared, Signed, 10 ½ x 8 In. 1380.00
Vase, Green, Wrought Iron Frame, Gold Foil, Wide Mouth, c.1910, 9 ¼ In. 5040.00
Vase, Green Flowers, Frosted Ground Shaded Green, Swirling Bands, Cameo, 6 ¾ In. 2300.00
Vase, Internal Decoration, Mottled Blue, White & Brown, Orange Ground, c.1960, 13 In. 518.00
Vase, Internal Mottled Green, Orange Ground, Peacock Feather Eyes, 9 ¾ In. 690.00
Vase, Lake Landscape, Sailboats At Dusk, Amber Ground, Cameo, 21 ½ x 6 In. 2520.00
Vase, Landscape, Autumn, Enameled, Cameo, 2 ½ In. 3120.00
Vase, Landscape, Birch Trees, Enameled, Handles, Cameo, 3 ¼ x 5 ¾ In. 3738.00
Vase, Landscape, Birds In Flight, Gray To Pink, 3 Handles, c.1900, 6 ½ In. 7200.00
Vase, Landscape, Boat, Enameled, Green To Frosted Gold, Signed, 4 In. 4025.00
Vase, Landscape, Boats, Rocky Shore, Enameled, Cameo, 12 In. 4715.00
Vase, Landscape, Dutch, Lake, Boats, Trees, Opalescent, Enameled, 1890s, 7 ¾ In. 4560.00
Vase, Landscape, Dutch, Opalescent, Enameled, Long Neck, Bulbous, 1890s, 14 ¾ In. 10800.00
Vase, Landscape, Gray, Lake Scene, Tall Trees, Milk Bottle Shape, Signed, 1 ¼ In. 978.00
Vase, Landscape, Lake, Gingko Leaves, Vines, Shaded Lavender, Frosted, 3 ¼ x 4 ¼ In. 1150.00
Vase, Landscape, Lake, Swan, Trees, Enameled, c.1910, 4 ¾ In. 4560.00
Vase, Landscape, Lake, Swans, Pale Green, Tapered, Cameo, c.1910, 17 ¼ In. 1680.00
Vase, Landscape, Purple Trees, Lake, Blue Sky, Mottled Yellow, Cameo, 7 ½ In. 1800.00
Vase, Landscape, Rainy, Bare Trees Blowing, Enameled, c.1910, 5¾ In. .... 4800.00 to 5760.00
Vase, Landscape, Rainy, Trees, 2 x 1 ½ In. .... *illus* 2640.00
Vase, Landscape, Red Tree, Lake, Burgundy Shore, Citron Ground, Cameo, 8 ½ In. 1610.00
Vase, Landscape, Snow Covered Trees, Bottle Shape, Cameo, 6 ½ In. 2415.00
Vase, Landscape, Summer, Enameled Trees, Mottled Yellow, Frosted Ground, 4 ¾ In. 2875.00
Vase, Landscape, Trees, Grass, Mottled Yellow, Orange Blush, Black, Cameo, 25 In. 2703.00
Vase, Landscape, Trees, Green, Blue, Squat, 4 ¼ In. 5040.00
Vase, Landscape, Winter Scene, Orange, Brown Trees, Gray Forest, Flared Rim, 3 ½ In. 1955.00
Vase, Landscape, Winter Scene, Trees, Orange & Yellow Ground, Cameo, 1 ½ In. 920.00
Vase, Landscape, Winter, Bare Trees, Snow, Tapered, Shouldered, c.1910, 10 ½ In. 10200.00
Vase, Landscape, Winter, Dark, Bare Trees, Snow, Footed, Enameled, c.1910, 6 ¾ In. 9600.00
Vase, Landscape, Winter, Trees, Red, Green, Enameled, Cameo, c.1900, 5 ¾ In. 7800.00
Vase, Landscape, Yellow Berries, Green Leaves, Mottled, Burnt Orange Ground, 3 ¾ In. 1150.00
Vase, Lavender, Triangles, 6 Bands, Cameo, c.1925, 15 ¾ In. 4200.00
Vase, Leaves, Berries, Applied Scarabs & Jewels, Cameo, Signed, 4 ¼ In. 5100.00
Vase, Leaves, Prickly Stems, Textured, 4 Handles, Cameo, 8 ⅝ In. .... *illus* 4600.00
Vase, Leaves, Stems & Berries, Red & Black Shading, Yellow & Cream, Cameo, 5 ½ In. 2185.00
Vase, Leaves, Stems & Flowers, Green To Pink Ground, Gold Band Rim, Cameo, 3 ¼ In. 1323.00
Vase, Leaves, Stems & Pods, Yellow & Cream Ground, Green Foot, Cameo, 14 ¼ In. 2185.00
Vase, Lizards, Figs, Honey Amber, Pate-De-Verre, 8 x 11 In. .... *illus* 1645.00
Vase, Moth, Spider Webs, Leaves, Martele Ground, 11 ½ In. 7763.00
Vase, Mottled, Orange, Green, Geometric, Blown Into Iron Frame, 9 x 9 In. .... 1920.00 to 2520.00
Vase, Mottled Amethyst, White, Purple Stem Irises, Oval, Cameo, Signed, 3 In. 690.00
Vase, Mottled Bright Yellow, Orange & Blue, Blown Into Wrought Iron Frame, 9 ½ x 9 In. 1440.00
Vase, Mottled Moss Green & Purple, Bottle Shape, Signed, 19 ¼ In. 915.00
Vase, Mottled Yellow, Red, Amethyst, Double Gourd, Cameo, Signed, 4 ½ In. 2415.00
Vase, Mushrooms, Brown, Red, Green, Mottled Yellow, Amber, Scalloped Rim, 5 ¼ In. 2012.00
Vase, Nancy Blue, Ribbed, c.1950, 13 ½ In. 702.00
Vase, Oak Leaves, Brown, Gold, Applied Cabochon, Beetle, Acorns, Footed, c.1900, 6 In. 6600.00
Vase, Pansies, Amethyst, Gold Applied, Textured Ground, Metal Foot, 3 ¼ In. 230.00
Vase, Pillow, Flowers, Mottled Red, Amber, Flat Sides, Cameo, 4 ¾ In. 2000.00
Vase, Pillow, Landscape, Spring, Trees, Frosted, Purple To Green Mottled, 4 In. 4313.00
Vase, Pillow, Leaves & Stems, Berries, Textured Ground, Cameo, 1 ½ x 2 ¼ In. 2300.00
Vase, Pillow, Opalescent Pink, Green Trees, Red Forest, Signed, 1 ¾ In. 1150.00
Vase, Pillow, Rose Hip, Berries, Leaves, Mottled, Shaded Burnt Yellow To Purple, 4 ¾ In. 2875.00
Vase, Pillow, Trees & Meadow, Mountains, Blue Ground, 1 ½ x 2 ¼ In. 1898.00
Vase, Pink, Gold Cross Of Lorraine, Gold Trim, Bulbous, Flared Rim, 3 ⅛ In. 646.00
Vase, Pink Crocuses, Frosted Pale Pink Ground, Cupped Rim, Cameo, 5 ¼ In. 11400.00
Vase, Poppy, Buds, Leaves, Gold Enamel, Amethyst Textured Ground, 7 ½ In. 920.00
Vase, Poppy, Leaves, Enameled, Multicolored, Square, c.1910, 3 ¾ In. 2400.00
Vase, Purple, Shaded Orange To Green Ground, Ribbed, Pate-De-Verre, 14 ¼ In. 2300.00
Vase, Red, Stems & Leaves, Light Green Opalescent Ground, Martele, Cameo, 6 ¾ In. 2588.00
Vase, Red Shading To Orange, Melon, Blown Into Wrought Iron Frame, 9 ¼ x 11 In. 1560.00

Daum, Vase, Leaves, Prickly Stems, Textured, 4 Handles, Cameo, 8 ⅝ In.
$4600.00

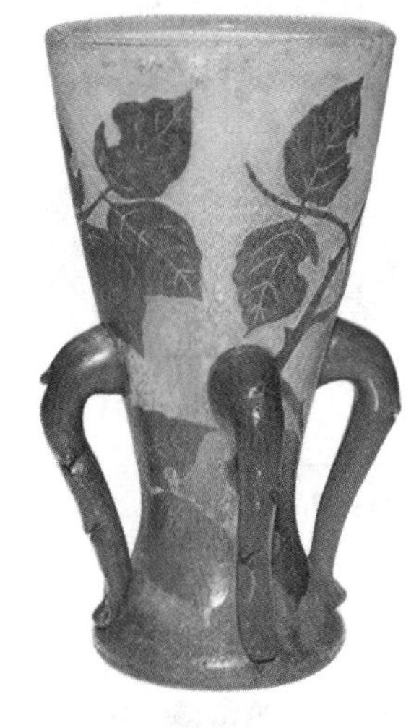

Daum, Vase, Lizards, Figs, Honey Amber, Pate-De-Verre, 8 x 11 In.
$1645.00

Daum, Vase, Stalks, Columbine, Opal & Peach, Cameo, 3 ¾ In.
$3500.00

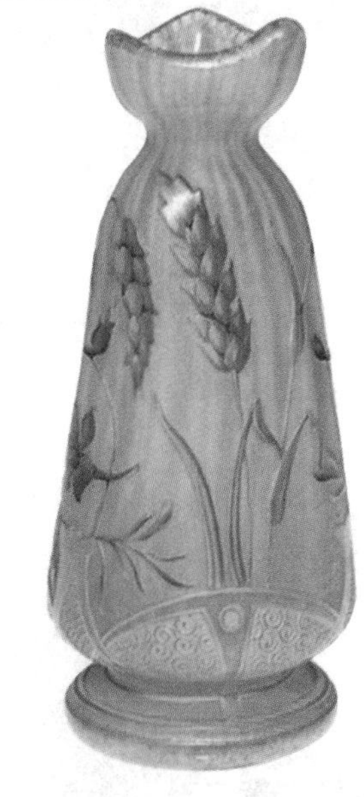

Davenport, Teapot, Cyprus, Black Transfer, Ironstone, Marked, 9 ½ In.
$130.00

Davenport, Teapot, Cyprus, Flow Blue, Marked, 9 ½ In.
$450.00

Davy Crockett, Button, King Of The Frontier, Celluloid, Emress Novelty, 1955, ⅞ In.
$32.00

Davy Crockett, Toy, Alamo Fix-It Stagecoach, Plastic, Ideal, Box
$57.00

Vase, Red Sweet Peas, Enameled, Cameo, 5 ½ In. 2280.00
Vase, Roses, Cranberry, Green Stems, Leaves, Frosted, Textured Ground, Green Foot, 7 In.. . . . 2415.00
Vase, Stalks, Columbine, Opal & Peach, Cameo, 3 ¾ In. . . . . *illus* 3500.00
Vase, Stick, Flowers, Stems, Red, Green Ground, Bulbous, c.1905, 9 ½ In. 4200.00
Vase, Stick, Frosted Amber, Internal Blue Stripes, Bulbous, Cameo, 4 ½ In. 460.00
Vase, Stick, Green Trees, Gray, Purple Ground, Cameo, 2 ½ In. 1035.00
Vase, Stick, Opalescent Amber, Crimson Thistles, Footed, Cameo, 4 ½ In.. . . . . 431.00
Vase, Stick, Spider Webs & Leaves, Red, Black, Gold, Cameo, Signed, 14 ¼ In. 7200.00
Vase, Stick, Textured Amethyst, Flowers, Bulbous, Cameo, 9 In. 690.00
Vase, Stick, Thistle, Blue, Bulbous, Gold Enameled, c.1910, 18 ¾ In. 7800.00
Vase, Stick, Vines, Dragonflies, Flowers, Blue, Bulbous, Cameo, c.1893, 11 In. 4200.00
Vase, Stylized Forest, Blue, Mauve, Yellow, Orange, Black, Art Deco, 17 In.. . . . . 2415.00
Vase, Sunflower, Magenta, Handles, Martele, Cameo, c.1910, 8 ⅜ In. 9600.00
Vase, Sweet Pea Flowers, Leaves, Frosted, Burnt Orange, Enameled, Cameo, 2 ¾ In. 1610.00
Vase, Textured Opalescent Purple Flowers, Gray Stems, Gold Rim, Cameo, 2 ½ In. 2588.00
Vase, Thistle, Burgundy, Gold Enameled, Cameo, c.1905, 5 ¼ In., Pair. 2640.00
Vase, Trumpet, Leafy Branches, Mottled Yellow, Applied Beetles, Cameo, Signed, 20 In. 1700.00
Vase, Tulip, Multicolored, Gold Enameled, c.1910, 8 ⅜ In.. . . . . 4560.00
Vase, Tulip, Multicolored, Square, Enameled, c.1910, 4 ¾ In. 2640.00
Vase, Violet, Purple To White Ground, Enameled, Cameo, 7 ½ In.. . . . . 9600.00
Vase, Yellow, Iris, Bee, Enameled, Mottled, Cameo, c.1900, 10 In.. . . . . 13200.00

DAVENPORT pottery and porcelain were made at the Davenport factory in Longport, Staffordshire, England, from 1793 to 1887. Earthenwares, creamwares, porcelains, ironstone, and other ceramics were made. Most of the pieces are marked with a form of the word *Davenport*.

Cup Plate, Rondeau. 100.00
Pitcher, Washbowl, Benjamin Franklin, Handle, Blue, Hill & Henderson Importers, c.183511 x 13 In. . 2629.00
Platter, Octagonal, Amoy, Blue, Light Glaze Crazing, 14 x 17 In. 275.00
Potty, Fig Cousin. 250.00
Punch Bowl, Franklin Flying Kite, Historic Light Blue, c.1830, 9 In.. . . . . 717.00
Sugar, Cover, Fig Cousin, 2 Loop Handles. 375.00
Teapot, Cyprus, Black Transfer, Ironstone, Marked, 9 ½ In. . . . . *illus* 130.00
Teapot, Cyprus, Flow Blue, Marked, 9 ½ In. . . . . *illus* 450.00
Teapot, Fig Cousin 135.00

DAVY CROCKETT, the American frontiersman, was born in 1786 and died in 1836. The historical character gained new fame in 1954 when the Walt Disney television show ran a series of episodes featuring Fess Parker as Davy Crockett. Coonskin caps and buckskins became popular and hundreds of different Davy Crockett items were made.

Book, Legend Of Davy Crockett, Pop-Up, 3-D Pictures, Mopak, 1955 . . . . 250.00
Button, King Of The Frontier, Celluloid, Emress Novelty, 1955, ⅞ In. . . . . *illus* 32.00
Display Box, Picture Card Bubble Gum, 1 Cent, Bazooka, 8 x 5 ¾ x 3 In. 3944.00
Hat, Indian Fighter Coonskin Hat, Photo Of Fess Parker, Weathermac Corp., 1955. . . . . 253.00
Toy, Alamo Fix-It Stagecoach, Plastic, Ideal, Box . . . . *illus* 57.00
Wristwatch, Davy Crockett Holding Rifle, Powder Horn, Box, US Time, c.1955 . . . . 572.00
Wristwatch, Plastic Powder Horn, Timex, Box, 1950s. 350.00

DE MORGAN art pottery was made in England by William De Morgan from the 1860s to 1907. He is best known for his luster-glazed Moorish-inspired pieces. The pottery used a variety of marks.

Bowl, Ruby Luster, Wedgwood Blank, Bear Cubs, Floral Medallion, c.1885, 11 ¼ In.. . . . . 3525.00

DE VEZ was a signature used on cameo glass after 1910. E. S. Monot founded the glass company near Paris in 1851. The company changed names many times. Mt. Joye, another glass by this factory, is listed in its own category.

deVez

Vase, Blue & Yellow, Lake Scene, Frosted, Signed, 10 In. 805.00
Vase, Lake Scene, Rose, Grape Vines, Frosted Blue, 9 ½ In.. . . . . 1495.00
Vase, Peach, Leafy Branches, Pastoral Scene, Shouldered, 12 In.. . . . . 1898.00
Vase, River Scene, Tree, Golden Yellow, Orange Ground, Cameo, Oval, 6 ⅞ x 4 In.. . . . . 930.00
Vase, Yellow, Cascading Orange, Brown, Mums, 8 ¼ In. 805.00

DECORATED TUMBLERS have been made by Anchor Hocking, Federal, Hazel Atlas, Libbey, and other companies since the 1930s, when the pyroglaze process of printing was introduced. The barware and other glasses feature drinking jokes, characters, or decorative geometric patterns. Swankyswigs are listed in their own category. Decorated tumblers may also be listed in Advertising, Coca-Cola, Pepsi-Cola, and many other categories.

Heinz Tomato Juice, Logo On Front, 5 In. . . . . 8.00 to 10.00
Hires Root Beer, Flared, Etched, c.1910, 4 ¾ In. 259.00
Howard Johnson's Motor Lodge, 4 ½ In. 28.50
Jim's Place Restaurant Bar, Put-In-Bay, Red Letters, 6 ¾ In. 14.00
Mug, Red, Circus Scenes, Milk Glass, Hazel Atlas, c.1950, 3 In. 20.00
Rexall Drug Store Pharmacy, Logo, Gold Rim, 6 ¼ In. 20.00
Smith's Sizzling Steaks, Fulton, Kentucky, 4 In. 14.00
Starkist Tuna, Charlie, Tell 'em Charlie Sent You, 3 ¼ In. 20.00
Swankyswig, Cornflower, Light Blue, Green Leaves, 3 ¼ In. 18.00

DECOYS are carved or turned wooden copies of birds, fish, or animals. The decoy was placed in the water or propped on the shore to lure flying birds to the pond for hunters. Some decoys are handmade; some are commercial products. Today there is a group of artists making modern decoys for display, not for use in a pond.

Black Duck, Carved, Black, White, Gray, James Hammond, Nantucket 224.00
Black Duck, Hollow Carved, Painted, Glass Eyes, Delaware River, 15 In. 2510.00
Black Duck, Hollow Carved, Painted, Tack Eyes, Fluted Tail, Delaware River, 16 In. 896.00
Black Duck, Sleeping, Shang Wheeler, c.1935, 5 ¾ x 16 ½ In. 2400.00
Black Duck, Standard Grade, 7 x 16 In. 125.00
Black Duck, William Stout, Saginaw Bay, Painted, c.1940 . . . . . 112.00
Black-Bellied Plover, Carved Wood, Painted, Black, White, Tan, New England, 10 ¼ In. 881.00
Bluebill, Carved, Painted, Inset Glass Eyes, Mid 20th Century, 7 ¼ x 13 In. 176.00
Bluebill, Mason Factory, Detroit 995.00
Bluebill, Mason's Premier Grade, 15 In. 633.00
Bluebill Drake, Glass Eyes, Painted, Black, Gray, 14 x 7 In. 115.00
Blue-Winged Teal, Glass Eyes, Illinois River School, Early 20th Century, 15 ¼ In. 201.00
Bufflehead, White Pine, Glass Eyes, Jim Van Brunt, c.1950, 9 x 5 In., Pair 374.00
Canada Goose, Canvas, 32 In. 27.00
Canada Goose, Canvas, Wire, Mannie Haywood, North Carolina, 26 In. 173.00
Canada Goose, Carved, Painted, Glass Eyes, Joseph Lincoln, 20th Century, 11 x 24 In. 499.00
Canada Goose, Joseph Lincoln, Early 20th Century, 25 In. 13200.00
Canada Goose, Wood Body, Canvas Open Wings, 37 In. 27.00
Canvasback, Applied Glass Eyes, Feather Decoration, Cast Iron Weights, 9 x 5 ¼ In., Pair 546.00
Canvasback, Chesapeake Bay, Wood, Painted, 14 ¼ In. . . . . *illus* 310.00
Canvasback, Masons, Stamped, Rocke, 17 In. 288.00
Canvasback, Painted Eyes, Chesapeake Bay, 15 ¼ In. 230.00
Canvasback, Tack Eyes, Painted, New York, 1880s, 14 ½ In. 322.00
Common Loon, Black, White, B. Kearns, St. Louis, Mo., 15 ¾ In. 40.00
Coot, Root Head, North Carolina 395.00
Crane, Pine, 3 Parts, Painted, Metal Stand, 29 x 39 In. 230.00
Eider, Black & White, Carved Eyes, Inset Head, Gus Wilson, 19 ¾ x 7 In. 550.00
Eider Drake, Horseshoe Weight, Monhegan Island, Early 20th Century, 17 ½ In. 2640.00
Fish, Blue Herring, Isaac Goulette, Tack Eyes, New Baltimore, Mich., c.1930, 10 In. 476.00
Fish, Brown Trout, Oscar Peterson, Gold, Black, Red Spots, 6 ¾ In. 784.00
Goldeneye Hen, Wildflower Decoy Co., Painted, 2 Piece 252.00
Goose, Tack Eyes, Carved Tail, c.1900, 6 ½ x 30 x 10 In. 448.00
Goose, Wood, Preening Neck, Tack Eyes, 6 ½ x 30 x 10 In. 400.00
Loon, Red Glass Eyes, Painted, Grindstone, Ishmal, Manley Rush, 18 x 9 ½ In. 431.00
Mallard, P.S. Lovejoy, c.1930, 11 In. 2574.00
Merganser Hen, Raised Neck Seam, Pad Weight, Mass., Early 1900s, 19 In. 2880.00
Mourning Dove, Driftwood, Mahogany Base 230.00
Pintail, Wood, Carved, Painted, Glass Eyes, 10 x 19 In. 84.00
Pintail Drake, Joe Lincoln, 17 In. . . . . *illus* 748.00
Pintail Drake, Marked, R Madison Mitchell, c.1976, 18 ¼ In. 575.00
Redhead, Triangular Weight, Oscar Carroll, North Carolina, 17 In. 288.00
Scoter, Inlet Head, Carved, Painted, Gus Wilson, 18 In. 3450.00
Scoter, Sleeping, White, Reddish Brown Head, Bill, 20th Century, 5 ¾ x 12 ½ In. 3840.00
Seagull, Wood, Carved, Painted, Wooden Base, 10 In. . . . . *illus* 144.00

Decoy, Canvasback, Chesapeake Bay, Wood, Painted, 14 ¼ In.
$310.00

Decoy, Pintail Drake, Joe Lincoln, 17 In.
$748.00

Decoy, Seagull, Wood, Carved, Painted, Wooden Base, 10 In.
$144.00

Decoy, Shorebird, Flattened Full-Bodied Figure, Wood Plinth, Early 1800s, 19 ½ In.
$3995.00

TIP
If you discover a cache of very dirty antiques and you are not dressed in work clothes, make yourself a temporary cover-up from a plastic garbage bag.

Shorebird, Flattened Full-Bodied Figure, Wood Plinth, Early 1800s, 19 ½ In. . . . . *illus* 3995.00
Shorebird, Root Head, Carved, Integral Beak, Painted Black, Black Metal Stand, 12 In. 1410.00
Shoveler, Drake, Standing, Tin Feet, Glass Eye 300.00
Snow Goose, Hissing, Long Neck, Hollow, Wing Detail, Bottom Weight, H. Conklin 2875.00

DEDHAM Pottery was started in 1895. Chelsea Keramic Art Works was established in 1872 in Chelsea, Massachusetts, by members of the Robertson family. The factory closed in 1889 and was reorganized as the Chelsea Pottery U.S. in 1891. The firm used the marks *CKAW* and *CPUS*. It became the Dedham Pottery of Dedham, Massachusetts. The factory closed in 1943. It was famous for its crackleware dishes, which picture blue outlines of animals, flowers, and other natural motifs. Pottery by Chelsea Keramic Art Works and Dedham Pottery are listed here.

DEDHAM POTTERY

Ashtray, Nude Carrying Yoke, 4 ⅝ In. 1508.00
Azalea, Cup & Saucer 151.00
Azalea, Dish, 5-Point Star, Marked, 7 ½ In. 336.00
Azalea, Jam Jar, Cover, 4 ¼ In.. . . . . . *illus* 696.00
Azalea, Plate, 9 ¾ In. 221.00
Birds In Orange Tree, Plate, Blue Rabbit Mark, 8 ½ In.. . . . . . 383.00
Birds In Orange Tree, Plate, Raised, 10 ⅛ In.. . . . . . 197.00
Butterfly, Cup & Saucer, Blue Rabbit Mark 290.00
Butterfly, Plate, 10 In.. . . . . . 348.00 to 667.00
Clover, Plate, 10 In. 754.00
Crab, Cup & Saucer 928.00
Crab, Plate, Seaweed, Blue Mark, 8 ¼ In. 406.00
Crab, Plate, Seaweed, Impressed, Blue Rabbit Mark, 8 ⅜ In. 928.00
Crab, Plate, Seaweed, Rabbit Mark, 7 ½ In.. . . . . . 261.00
Day & Night, Pitcher, 5 In. 435.00
Day Lily, Plate, Blue Rabbit Mark, 9 ¾ In.. . . . . . 1392.00
Dolphin, Plate, Blue Rabbit Mark, 7 ½ In. 1740.00
Dolphin, Platter, 12 ⅜ In.. . . . . . 1856.00
Duck, Bowl, 4 ½ In.. . . . . . 174.00
Duck, Plate, 10 ⅛ In.. . . . . . 116.00
Duck, Plate, Blue Rabbit Mark, Maude Davenport, 10 In.. . . . . . 595.00
Duck, Plate, Marked, 6 1/16 In. . . . . . . *illus* 50.00
Duck, Plate, Pond Lily, Marked, 7 ½ In.. . . . . . 162.00
Duck, Plate, Stamped, 8 ¼ In. 104.00
Elephant, Bookends, Raised Trunk, 3 ¼ In. 754.00
Elephant, Bowl, 5⅞ x 11¾ In. . . . . . . 3190.00 to 3700.00
Elephant, Coaster, 3 ⅞ In. 197.00
Elephant, Cup & Saucer, Blue Rabbit Mark 348.00
Elephant, Jam Jar, Cover, 4 ½ In.. . . . . . 2204.00
Elephant, Mug, Child's, 3 ⅜ In. 1624.00
Elephant, Plate, 7⅝ In. . . . . . . 696.00 to 1320.00
Elephant, Plate, Marked, 8 ½ In.. . . . . . 1450.00
Ewer, Baluster Form, Reeded Scroll Handle, Hugh Robertson, c.1880, 10 ¾ In.. . . . . . 8410.00
Fairbanks House, Plate, Rabbit Border, 8 ½ In.. . . . . . 1840.00
Grape, Bowl, Blue Ink Mark, 7 ½ In.. . . . . . 580.00
Grape, Bowl, Marked, 4 In. 232.00
Grape, Bowl, Square, 8 In.. . . . . . 812.00
Grape, Pitcher, Scroll Handle, 4 ¾ In. 238.00
Grape, Plate, Marked, 6 ⅛ In.. . . . . . 169.00
Grape, Tray, Blue Rabbit Mark, 9 ¾ In. 186.00
Grouse, Plate, 9 ⅞ In.. . . . . . 5104.00
Horse Chestnut, Bowl, 5 ¼ In. 174.00
Horse Chestnut, Candlestick, 1 ½ In., Pair 266.00
Horse Chestnut, Cup & Saucer. 232.00
Horse Chestnut, Plate, 9 ½ In. 104.00
Horse Chestnut, Plate, Raised, 8 ½ In.. . . . . . 293.00
Iris, Bowl, Blue Rabbit Mark, 5½ In. . . . . . . 93.00 to 267.00
Iris, Plate, 8 ½ In. 186.00
Lobster, Plate, Blue Rabbit Mark, c.1931, 6 In. 795.00
Lobster, Plate, Seaweed, Blue Rabbit Mark, 7 ⅝ In. 377.00
Lobster, Plate, Seaweed, Blue Rabbit Mark, 8¼ In.. . . . . . 1044.00 to 1160.00
Lotus Petal, Bowl, Blue Ink Mark, 5 ⅛ In. 162.00
Magnolia, Plate, 7 ⅜ In.. . . . . . 158.00

Dedham, Azalea, Jam Jar, Cover, 4 ¼ In.
$696.00

Dedham, Duck, Plate, Marked, 6 1/16 In.
$110.00

Dedham, Rabbit, Bowl, Marked. 7 In.
$110.00

Moth, Plate, 10 ⅛ In. 870.00
Moth, Plate, Raised Repeat, 6 ⅛ In. 319.00
Moth With Flower, Plate, Signed, Maude Davenport, 8 ½ In. 464.00
Mushroom, Plate, 6 In. 232.00
Mushroom, Plate, Blue Rabbit Mark, 8 ½ In. 3712.00
Owl, Plate, Rabbit Mark, 9 ¾ In. 5800.00
Polar Bear, Cup & Saucer 464.00
Polar Bear, Cup & Saucer, Blue Rabbit Mark 580.00
Polar Bear, Plate, 10 ¼ In. 1073.00
Polar Bear, Plate, Band Of Water, Snowy Mountain Peaks, 8 ⅞ In. 1276.00
Polar Bear, Plate, Rabbit Mark, 9 In. 1275.00
Pond Lily, Bowl, 5 ¼ In. 145.00
Poppy, Plate, Marked, 8 ½ In. 267.00
Rabbit, Bowl, 4 ¾ In. 1044.00
Rabbit, Bowl, Marked, 7 In. .... *illus* 110.00
Rabbit, Candle Snuffer, 2 In. 429.00
Rabbit, Chop Plate, 11 ⅞ In. 151.00
Rabbit, Creamer, 2 ¾ In. 121.00
Rabbit, Creamer, 3 ¼ In. 139.00
Rabbit, Dish, Mayonnaise, 5 In. 267.00
Rabbit, Dish, Pickle, Marked, 10 In. 406.00
Rabbit, Eggcup, 2 ⅜ In. 58.00
Rabbit, Fish, Platter, Oval, Blue Rabbit Mark, 13 ¾ In. 696.00
Rabbit, Flower Holder, Marked, 6 ⅛ In. 464.00
Rabbit, Flower Holder, Pierced Base, Marked, 6 ⅛ In. 406.00
Rabbit, Knife Rest, 2 ⅝ In. 464.00
Rabbit, Mug, 2 ¾ In. 522.00
Rabbit, Mug, Incised, Marked, 4 ¼ In. 348.00
Rabbit, Nappy, 6 In. 104.00
Rabbit, Nappy, Marked, 7 ⅜ In. 348.00
Rabbit, Pitcher, Baluster, Angular Handle, 5 In. 209.00
Rabbit, Pitcher, Bulbous, Blue Ink Mark, 6 ½ In. 406.00
Rabbit, Plate, 6 In. 187.00
Rabbit, Plate, Blue Ink Mark, 10 In. 116.00
Rabbit, Plate, Blue Rabbit Mark, 5 ¾ In. 1624.00
Rabbit, Plate, Soup, 8 ⅞ In. 140.00
Rabbit, Platter, Marked, 17 In. 1334.00
Rabbit, Salt & Pepper, Round, Footed, 3 ½ In. 220.00
Rabbit, Spoon, Marked, 4 ½ In. 116.00
Rabbit, Stein, Angular Handle, 5 ¼ In. 203.00
Rabbit, Sugar & Creamer, Marked .... *illus* 235.00
Rabbit, Tea Stand, Blue Rabbit Mark, 6 ⅛ In. 151.00
Rabbit, Teapot, Blue Rabbit Mark, 5 ½ In. 360.00
Rabbit, Teapot, Cover, 8 ½ In. .... *illus* 232.00
Rabbit, Tile, Blue Rabbit Mark, 5 ⅝ x 5 ½ In. 406.00
Rabbit, Toothpick, 4 ½ In. 406.00
Rabbit, Toothpick, Marked, 4 ½ In. 464.00
Scottie Dogs, Bowl, 5 ⅜ In. 4872.00
Scottie Dogs, Bowl, Marked, 5 ⅜ In. 5568.00
Snowtree, Plate, 9 ⅝ In. 174.00
Swan, Ashtray, Blue Rabbit Mark, 4 In. 81.00
Swan, Bowl, 4 ¾ In. 174.00
Swan, Bowl, Blue Ink Stamp, 8 ⅝ In. 261.00
Swan, Cup & Saucer 186.00
Swan, Plate, Marked, 7 ½ In. 302.00
Tapestry Lion, Plate, Marked, 10 In. 1740.00
Turkey, Creamer, 2 In. 139.00
Turkey, Cup & Saucer 406.00
Turkey, Plate, 6 ⅜ In. 377.00
Turkey, Plate, 8 ½ In. 197.00
Turkey, Plate, Blue Rabbit Marked, Maude Davenport, 8 ½ In. 425.00
Turkey, Plate, Raised, Blue Rabbit Mark, 8 ½ In. 319.00
Turtle, Cup & Saucer, Blue Rabbit Mark, 6⅛ In. .... 493.00 to 522.00
Turtle, Plate, Impressed, Blue Rabbit Mark, 8 ½ In. 1740.00
Vase, Amber, Deep Brown Feathered Glaze, Verdigris, Hugh Robertson, 8 x 5 In. 1320.00

Dedham, Rabbit, Sugar & Creamer, Marked
$235.00

D

Dedham, Rabbit, Teapot, Cover, 8 ½ In.
$232.00

TIP

It is easy to glue pieces of broken china. Use a new fast-setting but not instant glue. Position the pieces correctly, then use tape to hold the parts together. If the piece needs special support, lean it in a suitable position in a box filled with sand.

Dedham, Vase, Frothy Ultramarine Beige, Amber Glaze, Hugh Robertson, 9 ½ x 6 ¼ In
$1080.00

Degenhart, Toothpick, Forget-Me-Not, Milk Blue, 2 ½ In.
$38.00

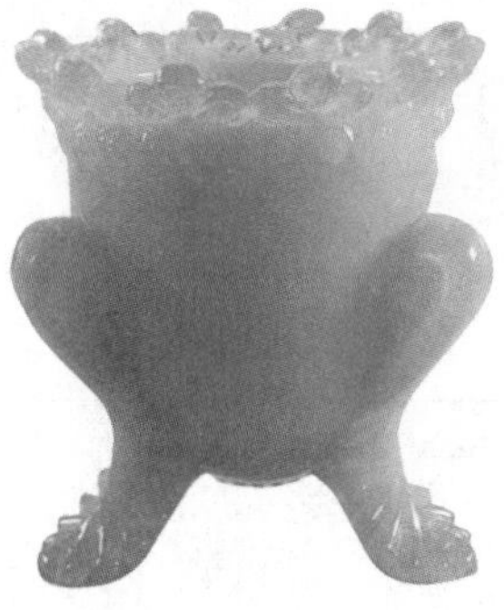

Delft, Bowl, Shaving, Colored, Scalloped Rim, 3 ½ x 10 ½ In.
$300.00

Delft, Charger, Adam & Eve, Serpent, Blue Dash Border, London, c.1660, 13 ½ In.
$10760.00

Delft, Charger, Peacock, Earthenware, Dutch, 18th Century, 13 In.
$360.00

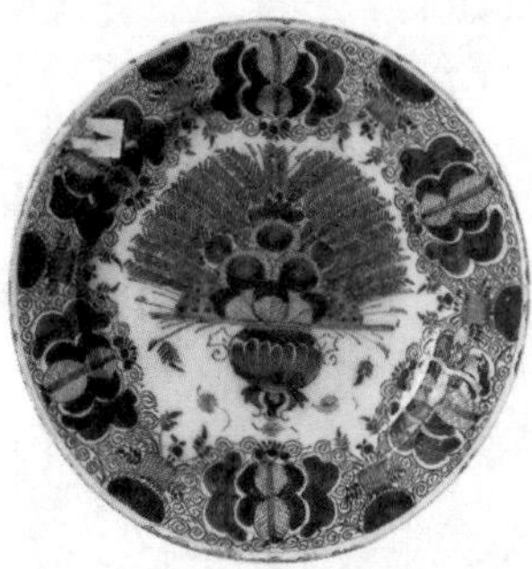

Vase, Blue Gray Oxblood Glaze, Incised, Hugh Robertson, 5 x 4 In. 1080.00
Vase, Bottle Shape, Oxblood Glaze, Stamped, 7 ½ x 3 ½ In. 4800.00
Vase, Frothy Indigo & Amber Drip Glaze, Hugh Robertson, 7 x 3 ½ In. 1440.00
Vase, Frothy Ultramarine Beige, Amber Glaze, Hugh Robertson, 9 ½ x 6 ¼ In. .... *illus* 1080.00
Vase, Gray, Green, Blue, Black Glaze, Swollen, Cylindrical, Narrow Mouth, 1908, 9 In. 2624.00
Vase, Orange Peel Oxblood Glaze, Stamped, 4 ¼ x 3 ½ In. 1200.00
Vase, Oxblood Glaze, Luster, Hugh Robertson, 6 ½ x 2 ¾ In. 2400.00
Vase, Volcanic, Cobalt Blue, Brown, Speckled Ground, Cylindrical, c.1908, 8 ½ In. 522.00
Vase, Volcanic, Green, Brown, Streaks, Cylindrical, c.1908, 7 ¾ In. 464.00
Wild Rose, Plate, Blue Rabbit Mark, 8 ⅜ In. 5104.00

DEGENHART is the name used by collectors for the products of the Crystal Art Glass Company of Cambridge, Ohio. John and Elizabeth Degenhart started the glassworks in 1947. Quality paperweights and other glass objects were made. John died in 1964 and his wife took over management and production ideas. Over 145 colors of glass were made. In 1978, after the death of Mrs. Degenhart, the molds were sold. The *D* in a heart trademark was removed, so collectors can easily recognize the true Degenhart piece.

Toothpick, Forget-Me-Not, Milk Blue, 2 ½ In. .... *illus* 38.00

DEGUE is a signature acid-etched on pieces of French glass made in the early 1900s. Cameo, mold blown, and smooth glass with contrasting colored rims are the types most often found.

Vase, Blown Into, Iron Frame, Art Deco, France, 1926-39, 13 x 9 In. 644.00

DELATTE glass is a French cameo glass made by Andre Delatte. It was first made in Nancy, France, in 1921. Lighting fixtures and opaque glassware in imitation of Bohemian opaline were made. There were many French cameo glassmakers, so be sure to look in other appropriate categories.

Box, Cover, Egg Shape, Red, Flowers, Frosted Yellow Ground, 6 In. 420.00
Vase, Bottle Shape, Footed, Citron & Blue Green, Footed, Signed, 8 ¾ In. 230.00
Vase, Brown, Flowers, Mottled, Yellow Ground, 17 ¾ In. 978.00
Vase, Stick, Mottled Brown, 14 ½ In. 115.00
Vase, Stick, Mottled Sunset Orange & Tan, Brown Speckles, 21 In. 705.00

DELDARE, *see Buffalo Pottery Deldare.*

DELFT is a tin-glazed pottery that has been made since the seventeenth century. Delft was made in England in the eighteenth century. It is decorated with blue on white or with colored decorations. Most of the pieces sold today were made after 1891, and the name *Holland* usually appears with the Delft factory marks. The word *Delft* appears alone on some inexpensive twentieth- and twenty-first-century pottery from Asia and Germany that is also listed here.

Bottle, Flowers, Leaves, Tree, Blue, White, Bulbous, Long Neck, Britain, c.1750, 9 ½ In. 705.00
Bottle, Wine, Blue & White, Globular, Molded Rim, Scroll Handle, England, 5 ¾ In. 4060.00
Bowl, Birds, Flowers, Red Flowers, Blue Scroll Border, Dutch, 1700s, 4 ¾ x 10 ½ In. 1528.00
Bowl, Colander, Blue & White, Rayed, Flowers, Scroll Panel, London, c.1770, 7 ⅝ In. 522.00
Bowl, Flower Stems, 4 Dots, Footed, 5 ⅝ x 10 In. 805.00
Bowl, Rose, Blossoms, Buds, Flowering Stem, Blue & White, London, c.1780, 10 ⅝ In. 348.00
Bowl, Shaving, Colored, Scalloped Rim, 3 ½ x 10 ½ In. .... *illus* 300.00
Bowl, Trees, Pavilions, Pointed Rocks, Flowers, Bristol, Multicolored, c.1730, 8 ¾ In. 1624.00
Canister Set, Dutch Scene, Blue & White, Marked, 8 In., 4 Piece 99.00
Charger, Adam & Eve, Serpent, Blue Dash Border, London, c.1660, 13 ½ In. .... *illus* 10760.00
Charger, Birds, Flowers, Blue, White, Marked, GK, Dutch, c.1645, 15 ½ In., Pair 8225.00
Charger, Figures In Landscapes, Multicolored, Maker's Mark, c.1715, 19 ¾ In. 5581.00
Charger, Flower Vase Design, 14 In. 518.00
Charger, Fruit Basket, Insect & Flower Border, Dutch, 18th Century, 12 ½ In., Pair 999.00
Charger, Hebrew Spies, Grapes, Tulip Border, Yellow, Purple, Dutch, 1700s, 16 ⅝ In. 2585.00
Charger, Peacock, Blue & White, 14 In. 460.00
Charger, Peacock, Earthenware, Dutch, 18th Century, 13 In. .... *illus* 360.00
Charger, Peacock, Stylized Flower Border, Blue, White, Dutch, 18th Century, 12 ¼ In. 235.00
Charger, Taking Of Chagre, Leaf Border, Blue & White, Bristol, c.1745, 13 In. 8400.00
Charger, Tree, Fence, Flowers, Blue & White, Scalloped Rim, Dutch, 1700s, 14 In. 499.00
Charger, White Horse Rearing, 2 Palm Trees, Multicolored Floral Border, 13 ¾ In. 805.00
Charger, Flower Center, Scrolled Leaf Borders, Blue & White, 18th Century, 13 ¾ In. 705.00
Dish, William III, London, Multicolored, Armor, Sword, c.1710, 13 ⅜ In. 4350.00

Figurine, Man Milking Cow, Marked, Jacobus Halder Andriaensz, 6 x 8 x 4 In. *illus* 575.00
Flower Brick, Blue, White, Flowers, Pierced Holes, Scalloped Rim, England, 1700s, 3½ x 6 In. 881.00
Flower Brick, Blue On White, 18th Century, 3 x 5 x 2 In. *illus* 570.00
Flower Brick, Blue, White, Cartouche, Diaper Border, Bristol, c.1740, 2½ x 4⅝ x 2 In. 580.00
Flower Brick, River Landscape, Small Boats, England, Mid 1700s, 4⅝ In., Pair 6600.00
Inkstand, Flowers, Blue, Manganese, Square, Pierced, England, 1700s, 2⅝ x 3½ In. 294.00
Jar, Apothecary, Blue & White, Oval, Leaf, Scroll Surround, 10⅝ x 9½ In. 575.00
Jar, Dome Lid, Flower Urn, Scrolls, Iznik Style, Earthenware, Baluster Shape, 15 In. 470.00
Mug, Bristol, Flowers, Dots, Brush Dabs, Multicolored, Flared, c.1730, 7 In. 928.00
Mug, Buildings, Landscape, Lozenge Reserve, Manganese Ground, c.1735, 5⅛ In. 1528.00
Perfume Bottle, Sailing Ship, Bird, Metal Cork Stopper, 3 In. 33.00
Pitcher, Swirled Ribs, Blue Flowers, Parrot & Peacock, Applied Handle, 8½ In. 230.00
Plaque, Coastal Scene, Multicolored Enamel, Flower Border, Oval, Self-Framed, 12¾ In. 2350.00
Plaque, Horse Drawn Sleigh, Blue & White, Earthenware, Shield Shape, 22 x 15 In. 2233.00
Plaque, Pastoral River Scene, Blue & White, Oval, Enameled, Late 1800s, 23 In. 441.00
Plaque, Sleigh Carriage Ride, Blue & White, Round, 16 In. 47.00
Plate, 2 Birds, Quadruped, Buildings, Multicolored, England, c.1780, 8¾ In., Pair 588.00
Plate, Couple Seated At Ruins, Blue & White, Dutch, c.1780, 9 In. 431.00
Plate, Dutch Inscription, Geometrics & Stylized Flower Border, 18th Century, 8¾ In. 353.00
Plate, Flower Basket, Fruit & Flower Rim, Multicolored, Dutch, 18th Century, 9¼ In. 294.00
Plate, Hound Chasing Stag, Blue & White, c.1750, 9 In., Pair 6000.00
Plate, Oriental Scene, Blue & White, 9 In. 86.00
Plate, Parrot, Flowers, Pinecone & Flower Rim, Multicolored, England, 7½ In., Pair 588.00
Plate, Peacock, Stylized Flower Border, Blue, Yellow Rim, Dutch, 18th Century, 9¼ In. 353.00
Plate, Tulips, Multicolored, 18th Century, 9 In. 460.00
Plate, Windmill, Blue, White, Pierced Border, Marked, 10¾ In. 22.00
Posset Pot, Dome Lid, Flowers, Birds, Blue, White, Handles, Dutch, c.1700, 8⅝ In. 558.00
Posset Pot, Twin Bungalows, Tree, Mountains, Multicolored, Bristol, c.1730, 7¼ In. 9280.00
Pot, Lid, Blue, White, Flowers, Handles, 18th Century, 5¼ In. 294.00
Punch Bowl, Blue, White, Leaf Shaped Panels, Stylized Flower Sprays, c.1740, 11½ In. 2040.00
Punch Bowl, Blue & White, Bristol, Birds, Flowered Sprigs, England, c.1740, 11¾ In. 1856.00
Punch Bowl, Multicolored, House, Landscape Trees, Flowers, London, c.1760, 10¾ In. 464.00
Punch Bowl, Trellis Diaper Border, Blue & White, Cell Border, London, c.1780, 9 In. 3944.00
Puzzle Jug, Toping Verse, Oriental Flowering, Plants, Blue & White, Mid 1700s, 6¾ In. 6600.00
Salt, 3 Upstanding Scrolls On Rim, White Tin Glaze, c.1675, 4½ In. 42000.00
Tankard, Pewter Base Rim, Lid, Flowers, Peacock, Blue, White, Dutch, 1700s, 5 In. 322.00
Tile, Bowl Of Fruit, Vase With Jonquils, Wine Jug, Square, Frame, 4⅝ In. 59.00
Tile, Picture, Children Wading In Ocean, Toy Boat, Blue & White, 6 Tiles, 27 x 18 In. 1410.00
Tile, Plaque, Maritime Scene, 24 x 30¾ In., 20 Piece 885.00
Tile, Scheveningen, Woman Holding Basket, Crystalline Glaze, 5⅞ x 3⅞ In. *illus* 95.00
Tile, White Dove Holding Olive Branch Over World, Banner, Frame, 7¾ x 5½ In. 168.00
Tile, Woman Working In Kitchen, 1944 Winter 1945, Frame, 7¾ x 5½ In. 154.00
Tile Set, Flower Urns, Geometric Corners, Manganese, Dutch, 5⅛ x 5⅛ In., 10 Piece 259.00
Tobacco Jar, Indian, Man, Smoking, Banner, Spaanse, Multicolored, Dutch, Mid 1700s 881.00
Vase, Blue, White, Fluted, Hexagonal, Greek A, 13 x 6 In., Pair 1800.00
Vase, Canal View, 8-Sided, Marked, 12 In. *illus* 73.00
Vase, Cover, Figures, Flowers, Birds, 8-Sided, Bird & Ball Finial, England, 1700s, 15 In. 4700.00
Vase, Cover, Multicolored, Jan Gaal, Dutch, 18 x 8 In. 588.00
Vase, Flowers, Birds, Blue, White, Drilled, Lamp Mounted, Octagonal, 1700s, 14½ In., Pair 7800.00
Vase, Incised Bands, Bronze Enamel, Pale Luster, Dutch, 19th Century, 14¾ In. 1763.00
Vase, Quintal, Figures, Dog, Bridges, Flowers, 5-Socket, 8¼ x 9 x 2½ In. *illus* 230.00
Vase, Teasels, Porcelyne Fles, Marked, Sanders, 5¾ In. *illus* 250.00
Wall Pocket, Cornucopia, Molded Mask, Flowers, Blue, White, England, 1700s, 8½ In. 176.00

DENTAL cabinets, chairs, equipment, and other related items are listed here. Other objects may be found in the Medical category.

Book, Dental Anatomy & Physiology, Russell C. Wheeler, 2nd Ed., 422 Pages, c.1950 15.00
Bottle, Preparation, Caulk Phenol Residue, Porcelain Stopper 50.00
Bracelet, Charm, Tooth Car, Silver, Mouthwash, Tooth, Toothbrush, Floss, Mirror 10.00
Cabinet, 2 Sections, Broken Pediment Crest, Upper Glass Doors, 25⅜ In. 2895.00
Cabinet, Eastlake, Walnut, Marble, Spindles, Burled Panel, Drawers, c.1880, 71 x 28 In. 5950.00
Cabinet, Mahogany, Marble, 25 Drawers, 3 Doors, c.1900, 63 x 40 x 13 In. *illus* 850.00
Cabinet, Mahogany, Textured Glass, 16 Drawers, 1920s 2850.00
Cabinet, Oak, 25 Drawers, 38 x 63 In. 863.00
Chair, Foot Pump, 4 Legs, Ritter Dental Mfg., Rochester, N.Y., 1918-25 500.00

Delft, Figurine, Man Milking Cow, Marked, Jacobus Halder Andriaensz, 6 x 8 x 4 In.
$575.00

Delft, Flower Brick, Blue On White, 18th Century, 3 x 5 x 2 In.
$570.00

Delft, Tile, Scheveningen, Woman Holding Basket, Crystalline Glaze, 5⅞ x 3⅞ In.
$95.00

Delft, Vase, Canal View, 8-Sided, Marked, 12 In.
$73.00

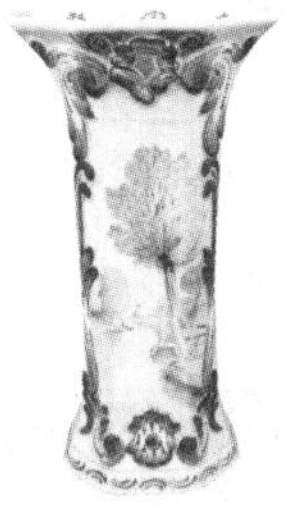

Delft, Vase, Quintal, Figures, Dog, Bridges, Flowers, 5-Socket, 8¼ x 9 x 2½ In.
$230.00

Delft, Vase, Teasels, Porcelyne Fles, Marked, Sanders, 5 ¾ In.
$250.00

Old Delft, New Delft

You can learn to tell old delft from new. Delft crumbles and chips easily, so old delft dishes and tiles should show some signs of wear. The blue decorations on old delft are slightly darker. Old wares are much thicker and heavier than new ones. New pieces have much whiter bodies and much clearer designs. Look at the mark. If the word "Holland" appears, it was made after 1891. If the word "delft" appears, it is probably a twentieth-century piece. But the easiest way to judge whether your delft is old or new is to compare it with a new, fresh-from-the-gift-shop piece of delft.

Dental, Cabinet, Mahogany, Marble, 25 Drawers, 3 Doors, c.1900, 63 x 40 x 13 In.
$850.00

Field Kit, Army, 3 Milk Glass Trays, Numbered Tool Sleeves, Cloth Holder 125.00
Magazine, Dental Students' Magazine, May 1930 .... 12.00
Mirror, Creators Of Oral Art, Boos Dental Labs, Minn., Pocket, c.1902, 3 ½ In. 65.00
Mirror, Drs. V.T. & R.S. Schlosser, Hagerstown, Md., Celluloid 260.00
Pin, Lawton School For Dental Assistants, Gold Filled, Engraved Initials, 1 In. 25.00
Powder, Dental, Colgate's Antiseptic, Colgate & Co., 2 ⅛ x 1 In. 140.00
Tin, Dental Floss, Spool, Cutter, Johnson & Johnson 35.00
Tin, Dental Plate Powder, Dr. Wernets, Box, c.1930s, 2 ⅛ In. 14.00
Tin, Hygienic Pure Latex Dam Box, ½ Yd., Medium, Akron, 6 ½ x 1 ½ In. 10.00
Tin, Tooth Powder, Drucker's Revelation, Cone Top, Yellow, 4 In. 41.00
Tin, Tooth Powder, Pepsodent, Trial Size, 2 ⅛ In. 31.00
Tin, Tooth Powder, Plastic Pull-Off Cap, Norcliff Laboratories, 1960s, 6 In. 12.00
Tool, For False Teeth, Contains 4 Teeth, Letters RU, LL, RL, LU 32.00
Tools, Pliers, Extractors, Tooth Keys, Boil Lance, Wood Box, 19th Century 950.00
Tray, Instrument, Nevamar, Milk Glass, 3 Sections, 3 ⅞ x 8 In. 12.00

DEPRESSION GLASS is an inexpensive glass that was manufactured in large quantities during the 1920s and early 1930s. It was made in many colors and patterns by dozens of factories in the United States. Most patterns were also made in clear glass, which the factories called crystal. If no color is listed here, it is clear. The name Depression glass is a modern one and also refers to machine-made glass of the 1940s through 1970s. For more descriptions, history, pictures, and prices of Depression glass, see the book *Kovels' Depression Glass & American Dinnerware Price List*.

Adam, Bowl, Dessert, Pink, 4 ¾ In. 18.00
Adam, Bowl, Pink, 9 In. 35.00
Adam, Cake Plate, Green, 3-Footed, 10 In. 35.00
Adam, Cup & Saucer, Green 34.00
Adam, Grill Plate, Green, 9 In. 15.00
Adam, Grill Plate, Pink, 9 In. 30.00
Alice, Cup, Jade-Ite, 2 ⅜ x 4 In. 15.00
Alice, Saucer, Jade-Ite 3.00
American Sweetheart, Berry Bowl, Pink, 9 In. 25.00
American Sweetheart, Chop Plate, Monax, 11 In. 18.00
American Sweetheart, Creamer, Cobalt Blue .... *illus* 265.00
American Sweetheart, Cup, Ruby 95.00
American Sweetheart, Cup & Saucer, Monax 15.00
American Sweetheart, Plate, Bread & Butter, Monax, 6 In. 10.00
American Sweetheart, Plate, Dinner, Pink, 9¾ In. .... 30.00 to 37.00
American Sweetheart, Plate, Luncheon, Monax, 9 In. 10.00
American Sweetheart, Plate, Salad, Monax, 8 In. 12.00
American Sweetheart, Plate, Salad, Pink, 8 In. 7.00
American Sweetheart, Sandwich Server, Monax, 12 In. .... 25.00 to 30.00
American Sweetheart, Sandwich Server, Pink, 12 In. .... 20.00 to 27.00
American Sweetheart, Sherbet, Pink, 4 In., Pair 25.00
American Sweetheart, Soup, Flat, Pink, 9 ½ In. 30.00
American Sweetheart, Sugar, Pink 15.00
American Sweetheart, Sugar & Creamer, Monax 32.00
Anniversary, Bowl, Pink, 3-Footed, 5 ½ In. 20.00
Apple Blossom pattern is listed here as Dogwood.
Aunt Polly, Plate, Sherbet, Iridescent, Pair 6.00
Aurora, Creamer, Ritz Blue 25.00
Aurora, Cup & Saucer, Cobalt Blue .... *illus* 22.00
Aurora, Plate, Cobalt Blue, 6 ½ In. 15.00
Ballerina pattern is listed here as Cameo.
Banded Rings pattern is listed here as Ring.
Basket pattern is listed here as No. 615.
Block pattern is listed here as Block Optic.
Block Optic, Bowl, Salad, Green, 7 ¼ In. 121.00
Block Optic, Candy Jar, Cover, Green, Footed, 6 ¼ In. .... *illus* 55.00
Block Optic, Cup & Saucer, Pink 15.00
Block Optic, Dish, Mayonnaise, Green, 5 ⅜ In. 76.00
Block Optic, Ice Tub, Pink, Tab Handles 128.00
Block Optic, Pitcher, Green, 54 Oz., 7 ½ In. 80.00
Block Optic, Sherbet, Green, 3 ¾ In. .... *illus* 7.00
Block Optic, Sugar & Creamer, Green 56.00

Block Optic, Sugar & Creamer, Pink, Footed 40.00
Block Optic, Tumbler, Juice, Green, 3 Oz., 3 ½ In. 25.00
Block Optic, Wine, 4 ⅝ In. 10.00
Bouquet & Lattice pattern is listed here as Normandie.
Bubble, Berry Bowl, Royal Ruby, 4 ½ In. .... *illus* 12.00
Bubble, Berry Bowl, Sapphire Blue, 8 ⅜ In. 23.00
Bubble, Bowl, Cereal, Sapphire Blue, 5 ½ In. 16.00
Bubble, Bowl, Fruit, Sapphire Blue, 4 ½ In. 14.00
Bubble, Bowl, Vegetable, Pink, 8 ½ In. 18.00
Bubble, Candlestick, 2 ¾ x 4 ½ In., Pair 12.00
Bubble, Cup & Saucer, Blue 21.00
Bubble, Cup & Saucer, Forest Green 10.00
Bubble, Cup & Saucer, Sapphire Blue 5.00
Bubble, Goblet, Desert Gold, Clear Foot, 4 Oz. 7.00
Bubble, Pitcher, Water, Ruby Red, 9 In. 65.00
Bubble, Plate, Bread & Butter, Sapphire Blue, 6¾ In. .... 3.00 to 4.00
Bubble, Plate, Dinner, Sapphire Blue, 9 ½ In. 7.00
Bubble, Platter, Sapphire Blue, 11 In. 15.00
Bubble, Sherbet, Forest Green, Gold Rim, Clear Foot, 3 ¾ In., 6 Piece 60.00
Bubble, Soup, Dish, Sapphire Blue, 7 ¾ In. 14.00
Bubble, Tumbler, Lemonade, Royal Ruby, 12 Oz., 6 In. .... 15.00 to 19.00
Bubble, Tumbler, Old Fashioned, 5 Oz., 3 In. 14.00
Bubble, Tumbler, Royal Ruby, 9 Oz., 4 ½ In. 14.00
Bullseye pattern is listed here as Bubble.
Buttons & Bows pattern is listed here as Holiday.
Cabbage Rose pattern is listed here as Sharon.
Cameo, Bowl, Vegetable, Oval, Green, Tab Handles, 10 x 7 In. 37.00
Cameo, Creamer, Green 35.00
Cameo, Dish, Mayonnaise, Green, 5 ⅜ In. 43.00
Cameo, Grill Plate, Green, 3 Sections, 10½ In. .... 20.00 to 22.00
Cameo, Platter, Round, Green, Tab Handles, 12 In. 15.00
Cameo, Soup, Dish, Flat Rim, Green, 9 In. 86.00
Cameo, Sugar, Green 35.00
Cameo, Tumbler, Juice, Green, Footed, 3 Oz., 3 ½ In. 85.00
Candlewick pattern is listed in the Imperial Glass category.
Cape Cod pattern is listed in the Imperial Glass category.
Caprice pattern is included in the Cambridge Glass category.
Cherry, Berry Bowl, Pink, 6 ¼ In. 75.00
Cherry Blossom, Bowl, Cereal, Pink, 5 ¾ In. 52.00
Cherry Blossom, Cake Plate, Delphite, Open Handles, 3 Legs, 10 ¼ In. 25.00
Cherry Blossom, Cake Plate, Green, 3-Footed, 10 ¼ In. 34.00
Cherry Blossom, Cup & Saucer, Child's, Pink .... 45.00 to 48.00
Cherry Blossom, Plate, Dinner, Pink, 9 In. .... 24.00 to 45.00
Cherry Blossom, Platter, Pink, 13 In. .... *illus* 40.00
Cherry Blossom, Sugar, Child's, 2 7⁄16 In. 45.00
Cherry Blossom, Tumbler, Juice, Pink, 4 Oz., 3¾ In. .... 18.00 to 20.00
Chevron, Pitcher, Milk, Ritz Blue, 4 In. 24.00
Chevron, Sugar, Pink 30.00
Chevron, Sugar & Creamer, Cobalt Blue 20.00
Christmas Candy, Creamer, Teal 35.00
Christmas Candy, Cup, Teal 25.00
Christmas Candy, Cup & Saucer, Teal 58.00
Christmas Candy, Plate, Luncheon, Teal, 8 In. 45.00
Christmas Candy, Saucer, Teal 12.00
Circle, Sugar, Footed, Pink 15.00
Cloverleaf, Bowl, Salad, Green, 7 In. 115.00
Cloverleaf, Cup, Pink 8.00
Cloverleaf, Cup & Saucer, Black .... *illus* 25.00
Cloverleaf, Grill Plate, Green 48.00
Cloverleaf, Salt & Pepper, Black, 3 ½ In. 95.00
Cloverleaf, Sherbet, Green, 3 In. .... 10.00 to 15.00
Colonial, Berry Bowl, 4 ½ In., Pair 34.00
Colonial, Berry Bowl, 8 ¾ In. 13.00
Colonial, Pitcher, 68 Oz., 7 ¾ In. 22.00
Colonial, Plate, Dinner, Pink, 10 In. 25.00
Colonial, Wine, 4 ½ In. 7.00

Depression Glass, American Sweetheart, Creamer, Cobalt Blue
$265.00

Depression Glass, Aurora, Cup & Saucer, Cobalt Blue
$22.00

Depression Glass, Block Optic, Candy Jar, Cover, Green, Footed, 6 ¼ In.
$55.00

D

TIP

If two tumblers get stuck when stacked, try putting cold water into the inside glass, then put both into hot water up to the lower rim.

Depression Glass, Block Optic, Sherbet, Green, 3 ¾ In.
$7.00

Depression Glass, Bubble, Berry Bowl, Royal Ruby, 4 ½ In.
$12.00

Depression Glass, Cherry Blossom, Platter, Pink, 13 In.
$40.00

Depression Glass, Cloverleaf, Cup & Saucer, Black
$25.00

Depression Glass, Cubist, Bowl, Pink, 3-Footed, 10 In.
$40.00

Colonial Block, Berry Bowl, Green, 4 In. 16.00
Columbia, Bowl, Ruffled Edge, 10 In. 10.00
Columbia, Butter, Cover 16.00
Columbia, Cake Plate, Pink, 11 In. 25.00
Columbia, Plate, Dessert, Square, Pink, 6 In. 6.00
Constellation, Cake Stand, 7 x 10 In. 99.00
Corded Optic, Tumbler, Water, Green 12.00
Cracked Ice, Sugar, Pink 30.00
Cracked Ice, Sugar & Creamer, Cover, Pink 95.00 to 149.00
Cracked Ice, Tumbler, Footed, Pink 40.00
Cremax, Bowl, Cereal, Castle Decal, 5 ¾ In. 15.00
Cremax, Bowl, Vegetable, Round, Flower Decal, 9 In. 19.00
Cremax, Creamer, Castle Decal 20.00
Cremax, Cup & Saucer, Flower Decal 20.00
Cremax, Plate, 9 ¼ In., Pair 10.00
Cremax, Plate, Dessert, Castle Decal, 6 ¼ In. 10.00
Cremax, Plate, Dinner, Castle Decal, 9 ½ In. 22.00
Cremax, Platter, Fired-On Pink Border, 12 In. 22.00
Cremax, Sandwich Server, Flower Decal, 11 ½ In. 25.00
Criss Cross, Pitcher, Water, Green, 8 In. 35.00
Cube pattern is listed here as Cubist.
Cubist, Bowl, Pink, 3-Footed, 10 In. *illus* 40.00
Cubist, Cake Plate, Pink, 3-Footed, 12 In. 24.00
Cubist, Candy Jar, Cover, Green, 6 ½ In. 24.00
Cubist, Powder Jar, Pink, 4 ¼ x 3 ½ In. 35.00
Cubist, Sherbet, Underplate, Green 10.00
Cubist, Sugar & Creamer 6.00
Cubist, Sugar & Creamer, Pink 20.00 to 22.00
Daisy pattern is listed here as No. 620.
Daisy & Button, Bowl, Marigold, 4 x 4 ¼ In. 24.00
Dancing Girl pattern is listed here as Cameo.
Diamond pattern is listed here as Miss America.
Diana, Bowl, Cereal, Pink, 5 In., 4 Piece 18.00
Diana, Bowl, Fruit, Amber, 11 In. 12.00
Diana, Bowl, Pink, Rolled Edge, Footed, 3 ¾ x 8 ½ In. 50.00
Diana, Bowl, Salad, Pink, 9 In. 18.00
Diana, Bowl, Scalloped Edge, 12 In. 20.00
Diana, Creamer, Amber 10.00
Diana, Cup & Saucer, After Dinner, Pink 12.00
Diana, Plate, Dinner, Pink, 9 ½ In. 12.00
Diana, Sandwich Server, Amber, 11 ¾ In. 7.00
Diana, Sugar, Oval, Pink 15.00
Dogwood, Creamer, Thin, Pink 29.00
Dogwood, Plate, Dinner, Pink, 9 ¼ In. 20.00
Dogwood, Salver, Pink, 12 In. 40.00
Dogwood, Saucer, Pink 14.00
Doric, Berry Bowl, Ultramarine, 5 ½ In. 13.00
Doric, Candy Dish, Blue, Delphite, 3 Sections, 7 x 6 In. 24.00
Doric, Candy Dish, Cover, Pink, 8 In. 38.00
Doric, Pitcher, Green, 32 Oz., 5 ½ In. *illus* 62.00
Doric, Plate, Dinner, Pink, 9 In., 4 Piece 64.00
Doric & Pansy, Plate, Sherbet, Pink, 6 In. 8.00
Double Shield pattern is listed here as Mt. Pleasant.
Dutch Rose pattern is listed here as Rosemary.
Early American Rock Crystal pattern is listed here as Rock Crystal.
Fine Rib, Tumbler, Iced Tea, Cobalt Blue, 5 In. *illus* 50.00
Fire-King, Baker, Milk White, Handles, 1 ⅝ x 6 $\frac{3}{16}$ In. 5.00
Fire-King, Bowl, Chili, Ivory, 5 In. 13.00
Fire-King, Bowl, Chili, Jade-Ite, 5 In. 22.00
Fire-King, Bowl, Fruit, Shell, Jade-Ite, 4 ¾ In. 15.00
Fire-King, Cake Pan, Sapphire Blue, 2 x 6 ½ x 11 ½ In. 25.00
Fire-King, Casserole, Anchor Hocking, 11 x 7 ½ In. 8.00
Fire-King, Casserole, Cover, Peach Blossom, Gay Fad, 1 ½ Qt. 15.00
Fire-King, Casserole, Nature's Bounty Decal, White, 1 ½ Qt. 18.00
Fire-King, Cup & Saucer, St. Denis, Jade-Ite 43.00
Fire-King, Custard Cup, Copper Tint, 6 Oz., 3 ¾ x 2 In., 2 Piece 4.00

Fire-King, Custard Cup, Ivory, 4 In. 8.00
Fire-King, Eggcup, Jade-Ite, 4 x 2¾ In. 48.00
Fire-King, Grill Plate, Turquoise, Blue, 9⅜ In.. .... 16.00
Fire-King, Measuring Cup, Sapphire Blue, 1 Cup 22.00
Fire-King, Mixing Bowl, Gay Fad, 6 In.. .... 13.00
Fire-King, Mug, Turquoise Blue 14.00
Fire-King, Pie Plate, Juice Saver, Sapphire Blue. 133.00
Fire-King, Pie Plate, Sapphire Blue, 4⅛ In. 18.00
Fire-King, Plate, Salad, Shell Shape, Jade-Ite, 7¼ In. 18.00
Fire-King, Refrigerator Dish, Cover, Milk White, 4⅛ x 8½ In. 12.00
Fire-King, Saucer, Jade-Ite. 4.00
Fire-King, Soup, Dish, Jade-Ite, 9¼ In.. .... 90.00
Fire-King, Soup, Dish, Turquoise Blue, 6½ In.. .... 25.00
Fire-King, Trivet, Philbe, Sapphire Blue. 28.00
Fire-King, Vase, Deco, Rainbow Peach 19.00
Fire-King, Loaf Pan, Milk White, Vegetable Decal, 5 x 7 In. 10.00
Fire-King, Loaf Pan, Sapphire, Blue, 9⅛ x 5⅛ In.. .... 18.00
Fire-King, Mixing Bowl, Milk White, Beaded Edge, 5 x 2½ In. 6.00
Fire-King, Mixing Bowl, Swirl, 8 x 3⅞ In. 35.00
Fire-King, Refrigerator Dish, Cover, Jade-Ite, 4¼ x 8¼ In. 85.00
Fire-King, Sugar, Cover, Azurite, Swirl, 4½ x 3¾ In. 29.00
Fleurette, Bowl, Cereal, 6 9/16 In. 28.00
Floragold, Bowl, Ruffled Edge, 9½ In. 8.00
Floragold, Bowl, Salad, Deep, Amber, 9½ In.. .... 45.00
Floragold, Tumbler, Footed, Iridescent, 10 Oz., 4¾ In. 18.00
Floral, Bowl, Vegetable, Pink, Handles, 8 In. .... *illus* 45.00
Floral, Pitcher, Cone, Footed, Pink, 32 Oz., 8 In. 50.00
Floral, Relish, Oval, Sections, Pink, 7 x 4 In. 30.00
Floral, Sherbet, Pink 18.00
Floral, Sugar, Cover, Pink 29.00
Floral, Tumbler, Pink, Footed, 7 Oz., 4¾ In. .... 20.00 to 25.00
Floral & Diamond Band, Pitcher, Green, 42 Oz., 8 In.. .... 140.00
Floral & Diamond Band, Sugar, Green. 22.00
Florentine No. 1, Butter, Cover, Green .... *illus* 165.00
Florentine No. 1, Cup & Saucer, Yellow. 15.00
Florentine No. 1, Pitcher, Green, Footed, 36 Oz., 6½ In. 85.00
Florentine No. 1, Plate, Sherbet, 6 In. 6.00
Florentine No. 1, Sugar, Cover, Green 40.00
Florentine No. 1, Tumbler, Footed, Green, 8 Oz.. .... *illus* 25.00
Florentine No. 2, Bowl, Cereal, Yellow, 6 In. 48.00
Florentine No. 2, Butter, Cover, Green. 100.00
Florentine No. 2, Butter, Cover, Yellow. 125.00
Florentine No. 2, Candlestick, Green, 2¾ In., Pair. 65.00
Florentine No. 2, Candlestick, Yellow, 2¾ In. 39.00
Florentine No. 2, Compote, Pink, Ruffled Edge, 3½ x 5 In. 45.00
Florentine No. 2, Creamer, Green 10.00
Florentine No. 2, Creamer, Pink .... *illus* 45.00
Florentine No. 2, Cup, Green 8.00
Florentine No. 2, Gravy Boat, Underplate, Yellow. 140.00
Florentine No. 2, Grill Plate, Yellow, 10 In. 20.00
Florentine No. 2, Pitcher, Footed, Ice Blue, 28 Oz., 7½ In. .... *illus* 1200.00
Florentine No. 2, Pitcher, Footed, Yellow, 24 Oz., 6¼ In. 175.00
Florentine No. 2, Plate, Dinner, Green, 10 In.. .... 15.00
Florentine No. 2, Relish, 3 Sections, Pink, 10 In. 39.00
Florentine No. 2, Soup, Cream, Green, 4¾ In. 14.00
Florentine No. 2, Soup, Cream, Ruffled Edge, Cobalt Blue, 5 In.. .... 95.00
Florentine No. 2, Soup, Cream, Ruffled Edge, Pink, 5 In. 25.00
Florentine No. 2, Sugar & Creamer, Pink 35.00
Florentine No. 2, Tumbler, Footed, Green, 12 Oz., 5 In. 26.00
Florentine No. 2, Tumbler, Footed, Pink, 9 Oz., 5 In. 22.00
Florentine No. 2, Tumbler, Iced Tea, Green, 12 Oz., 5 In.. .... 60.00
Flower & Leaf Band pattern is listed here as Indiana Custard.
Flower Rim pattern is listed here as Vitrock.
Forest Green, Punch Set, 10-In. Bowl, 7 Piece 39.00
Fruits, Berry Bowl, Green, 8 In. .... *illus* 115.00
Fruits, Cup & Saucer, Green 15.00

Depression Glass, Doric, Pitcher, Green, 32 Oz., 5½ In.
$62.00

Depression Glass, Fine Rib, Tumbler, Iced Tea, Cobalt Blue, 5 In.
$50.00

Depression Glass, Floral, Bowl, Vegetable, Pink, Handles, 8 In.
$45.00

TIP

Sometimes glasses get a cloudy look from the lime deposits in hard water. Cover the cloudy part with wet potato peelings for 24 hours. Rinse and dry.

Depression Glass, Florentine No. 1, Butter, Cover, Green
$165.00

Depression Glass, Florentine No. 1, Tumbler, Footed, Green, 8 Oz.
$25.00

Tumbler Sizes

A tumbler is a drinking glass, usually with a flat base. It never has a stem. Some tumblers are footed. Tumblers in several sizes have special names:

Whiskey or shot
1½–3 ounces, 2–2½ inches

Juice
4–7 ounces, 3¾–4½ inches
often footed

Old-fashioned
8 ounces, 2½ inches

Water
9–10 ounces, 4–5½ inches
often footed

Iced tea
12–16 ounces, 5½–6 inches
often footed

Fruits, Plate, Luncheon, Green, 8 In. . . . 12.00
Fruits, Tumbler, Pink, Combination Fruits, 4 In. . . . 20.00
Georgian Federal, Creamer, Green, Footed . . . 24.00
Georgian Federal, Hot Plate, Green, 5 In. . . . 105.00
Georgian Federal, Plate, Sherbet, Green, 6 In., 4 Piece . . . 32.00
Georgian Federal, Sugar, Green, Footed . . . 12.00
Georgian Federal, Sugar & Creamer, Green, Footed . . . 38.00
Hairpin pattern is listed here as Newport.
Harp, Cake Stand, 9 In. . . . 25.00 to 42.00
Harvest, Candy Box, Marigold, 6¾ In. . . . 35.00
Holiday, Cup & Saucer, Pink . . . 12.00
Holiday, Pitcher, Pink, 52 Oz., 6¾ In. . . . 35.00
Holiday, Plate, Dinner, Pink, 9 In. . . . 20.00
Homespun Look-Alike, Pitcher, Milk, Pink, 20 Oz., 5 In. . . . 65.00
Horizontal Ribbed pattern is listed here as Manhattan.
Horseshoe pattern is listed here as No. 612.
Indiana Custard, Sugar, Cover . . . 21.00
Iris, Bowl, Fruit, Iridescent, Ruffled Edge, 11½ In. . . . 10.00
Iris, Candlestick, 2-Light, 5¼ In., Pair . . . 35.00
Iris, Candy Dish, Cover, Tab Handles, 7 x 6 In. . . . 19.00
Iris, Goblet, Wine, 3 Oz., 4½ In. . . . 12.00
Iris, Pitcher, 48 Oz., 9 In. . . . 50.00
Iris, Pitcher, Footed, 9½ In. . . . 37.00 to 50.00
Iris & Herringbone pattern is listed here as Iris.
Jane Ray, Creamer, Jade-Ite . . . 22.00
Jane Ray, Cup & Saucer, Demitasse, Jade-Ite . . . 62.00
Jane Ray, Cup & Saucer, Jade-Ite . . . 10.00
Jane Ray, Mug, D-Handle, Jade-Ite . . . 19.00
Jane Ray, Platter, Jade-Ite, 12 In. . . . 32.00
Jane Ray, Saucer, Ring, Jade-Ite . . . 6.00
Jane Ray, Sugar & Creamer, Cover, Jade-Ite . . . 38.00
Jubilee, Plate, Luncheon, Yellow, 7 In. . . . 15.00
Knife & Fork pattern is listed here as Colonial.
Lace Edge pattern is listed here as Old Colony.
Landrum, Bowl, Footed, Yellow, 8¼ x 3½ In. . . . 26.00
Line 300 pattern is listed in the Paden City category as Peacock & Wild Rose.
Lorain pattern is listed here as No. 615.
Louisa pattern is listed here as Floragold.
Madrid, Berry Bowl, Amber, 5 In., 6 Piece . . . 42.00
Madrid, Bowl, Salad, Deep, Amber, 9½ In. . . . 40.00
Madrid, Bowl, Vegetable, Oval, Amber, 10 In. . . . 20.00
Madrid, Butter, Cover . . . 14.00 to 22.00
Madrid, Butter, Cover, Amber . . . 50.00
Madrid, Creamer . . . 5.00
Madrid, Jell-O, Amber, 2⅛ In., 6 Piece . . . 94.00
Madrid, Pitcher, Juice, Amber, 36 Oz., 5½ In. . . . *illus* 40.00
Madrid, Plate, Salad, Green, 7½ In. . . . 7.00
Madrid, Plate, Sherbet, Amber, 6 In. . . . 5.00
Madrid, Plate, Sherbet, Green, 6 In. . . . 12.00
Madrid, Saucer, Amber, 5¾ In. . . . 5.00
Madrid, Sherbet, Amber, 3⅞ In., 6 Piece . . . 30.00
Madrid, Sugar & Creamer . . . 20.00
Madrid, Tumbler, Amber, 5 Oz., 3⅞ In. . . . 10.00
Manhattan, Berry Bowl, Handles, 7½ In. . . . 10.00 to 18.00
Manhattan, Candlestick, Square, 4½ In. . . . 14.00
Manhattan, Candy Dish, 3-Footed, Pink, 6½ In. . . . 16.00
Manhattan, Candy Jar, Cover, 7 In. . . . 35.00
Manhattan, Candy Jar, Cover, Pink, 7 In. . . . 63.00
Manhattan, Compote, Pink, 5¼ In. . . . *illus* 50.00
Manhattan, Creamer, Oval . . . 9.00
Manhattan, Creamer, Oval, Pink . . . 15.00
Manhattan, Pitcher, Tilted, 25 Oz. . . . 32.00
Manhattan, Relish, 5 Sections, 14 In. . . . 25.00
Manhattan, Sherbet, 3¾ In. . . . 13.00
Manhattan, Sugar, Oval, Pink . . . 15.00

Manhattan, Sugar & Creamer 15.00
Manhattan, Sugar & Creamer, Pink. 35.00
Manhattan, Tumbler, Footed, 10 Oz., 5 ¼ In. 35.00
Many Windows pattern is listed here as Roulette.
Martha Washington pattern is included in the Cambridge Glass category.
Mayfair, Bowl, Vegetable, Yellow, 10 In. 35.00
Mayfair, Cookie Jar, Cover, Pink 50.00
Mayfair Federal, Plate, Dinner, Amber, 9 ½ In. 15.00
Mayfair Open Rose, Bowl, Handles, Pink, 11 ½ In. 50.00
Mayfair Open Rose, Bowl, Vegetable, Oval, Pink, 9 ½ In. 24.00
Mayfair Open Rose, Grill Plate, Yellow, 9 ½ In. 150.00
Mayfair Open Rose, Plate, Dinner, Blue, 9 ½ In. 85.00
Mayfair Open Rose, Salt & Pepper, 4 ½ In. 49.00
Mayfair Open Rose, Sandwich Server, Green, Center Handle, 11 ½ In. 75.00
Mayfair Open Rose, Sugar & Creamer 74.00
Meadow Wreath, Relish, 3 Sections, 7 ½ In. 30.00
Miss America, Bowl, Cereal, Green, 6 ½ In. 18.00
Miss America, Bowl, Fruit, Deep, Pink, 8 ¾ In. 45.00
Miss America, Candy Jar, Cover, Pink, 11 ½ In. 176.00
Miss America, Candy Jar, No Cover, Pink, 7 In. 50.00
Miss America, Creamer, Pink 35.00
Miss America, Cup. 7.00
Miss America, Pitcher, Ice Lip, Green, 48 Oz., 8 In. 28.00
Miss America, Relish, Pink, 4 Sections, 8 ¾ In. 50.00
Miss America, Sherbet. 10.00
Miss America, Sherbet, Pink. 16.00
Moderntone, Cup, Platonite 5.00
Moderntone, Cup & Saucer, Amethyst 16.00
Moderntone, Cup & Saucer, Cobalt Blue 13.00
Moderntone, Plate, Dinner, Platonite, Fired-On Blue, 8 ⅞ In. 8.00
Moderntone, Plate, Luncheon, Platonite, 7 ¾ In. 6.00
Moderntone, Plate, Luncheon, Platonite, Fired-On Blue, 7 ¾ In. 5.00
Moderntone, Salt & Pepper, Cobalt Blue, 4¼ In. . . . . 24.00 to 40.00
Moderntone, Saucer, Platonite, 5 ½ In. 5.00
Moderntone, Sherbet, Cobalt Blue, 3 In. 14.00
Moderntone, Sherbet, Platonite 5.00
Moderntone, Sherbet, Platonite, Fired-On Blue 5.00
Moderntone, Soup, Cream, Amethyst. 22.00
Moderntone, Soup, Cream, Cobalt Blue. 20.00
Moderntone, Sugar, Cobalt Blue, Metal Cover. 65.00
Moderntone, Sugar & Creamer, Cobalt Blue . . . . . *illus* 20.00
Moderntone, Tumbler, Whiskey, Green, 1 ½ Oz., 2 ¼ In. 30.00
Moon & Star, Candleholder, Blue, 3 ¾ x 4 ½ In. 15.00
Moondrops pattern is listed in the New Martinsville category.
Moonstone, Bowl, Crimped Edge, 9½ In. . . . . 25.00 to 28.00
Moonstone, Goblet, 10 Oz., 5 ½ In. 18.00
Moonstone, Plate, Luncheon, 8 ½ In. 20.00
Moonstone, Relish, Cloverleaf, 3 Sections, 6 ½ In. 20.00
Moonstone, Sandwich Server, 10¾ In. . . . . 25.00 to 32.00
Moonstone, Sherbet, 4 Piece . . . . . *illus* 45.00
Moonstone, Sugar. 15.00
Moonstone, Sugar & Creamer 21.00
Mt. Pleasant, Bowl, 3-Footed, Handles, Black, 6 x 3 In. 22.00
Mt. Pleasant, Cup, Cobalt. 11.00
Mt. Pleasant, Plate, Handles, Cobalt Blue, 8 ½ In. 16.00
Mt. Pleasant, Sherbet, Cobalt, 4 ¼ In. 16.00
Mt. Vernon pattern is included in the Cambridge Glass category.
New Century, Plate, Sherbet, Green, 6 In. 15.00
Newport, Bowl, Cereal, Amethyst, 5 ¼ In. 30.00
Newport, Creamer, Amethyst. 16.00
Newport, Cup, Cobalt Blue 14.00
Newport, Sandwich Server, Amethyst, 11 In. 55.00
Newport, Sherbet, Amethyst . . . . . *illus* 15.00
Newport, Soup, Cream, Cobalt Blue, Handles, 4 ¾ In. 25.00
Newport, Sugar, Amethyst. 14.00

Depression Glass, Florentine No. 2, Creamer, Pink
$45.00

Depression Glass, Florentine No. 2, Pitcher, Footed, Ice Blue, 28 Oz., 7 ½ In.
$1200.00

Depression Glass, Fruits, Berry Bowl, Green, 8 In.
$115.00

Depression Glass, Madrid, Pitcher, Juice, Amber, 36 Oz., 5 ½ In.
$40.00

TIP
Get an automatic dialer on your bedside phone and program the police number so you can simply push a button for help.

Depression Glass, Manhattan, Compote, Pink, 5 ¼ In.
$50.00

Depression Glass, Moderntone, Sugar & Creamer, Cobalt Blue
$20.00

Depression Glass, Moonstone, Sherbet, 4 Piece
$45.00

Depression Glass, Newport, Sherbet, Amethyst
$15.00

No. 610, Bowl, Oval, Yellow, 9 ½ In. 85.00
No. 612, Cup & Saucer, Green 18.00
No. 612, Platter, Oval, 10 ¾ In. 36.00
No. 612, Sugar, Green 20.00
No. 615, Bowl, Vegetable, Oval, Yellow, 9 ¾ In. 85.00
No. 616, Cup & Saucer, Yellow 25.00
No. 616, Plate, Luncheon, Yellow, 8 In. 15.00
No. 616, Saucer, Yellow 6.00
No. 616, Sugar & Creamer, Yellow 60.00
No. 618, Compote, Amber, Diamond Shape, 4 ½ In. 7.00
No. 618, Plate, Dinner, Amber, 9 ¼ In. 15.00
No. 618, Soup, Cream, Amber 20.00
No. 620, Coaster, Green, 3 ¼ In., 6 Piece 80.00
No. 620, Soup, Cream, Amber 9.00
Normandie, Berry Bowl, Pink, 5 In. 9.00
Normandie, Bowl, Cereal, Amber, 6 ½ In. 20.00
Normandie, Bowl, Vegetable, Oval, Amber, 10 In. 25.00
Normandie, Grill Plate, Iridescent, 11 In. 20.00
Normandie, Pitcher, Pink, 80 Oz., 8 In. 235.00
Normandie, Plate, Salad, Pink, 8 ¾ In. 16.00
Normandie, Plate, Sherbet, Pink, 6 In. 8.00
Normandie, Sherbet, Iridescent, 4 Piece 30.00
Normandie, Sugar & Creamer, Iridescent 26.00
Norse, Punch Bowl Set, 7 ½ x 11 ½-In. Bowl, 9 Piece 35.00
Old Cafe, Bowl, Oval, Pink, Handles, 6 ½ In. 12.00
Old Cafe, Plate, Dinner, Pink, 10 In. 70.00
Old Cafe, Relish, Pink, Oval, Scroll Handles, 7 In. 28.00
Old Cafe, Tumbler, Juice, Pink 20.00
Old Colony, Bowl, Salad, Pink, 7 ¾ In. 28.00
Old Colony, Bowl, Salad, Ribbed, Pink, 7 ¾ In. 67.50
Old Colony, Bowl, Vegetable, Pink, 9 ½ In. 38.00
Old Colony, Compote, Pink .... *illus* 35.00
Old Colony, Creamer, Pink 29.00
Old Colony, Plate, Pink, Solid Lace, 13 In. 67.00
Old English, Fruit Stand, Amber, 11 In. 50.00
Old Florentine pattern is listed here as Florentine No. 1.
Open Lace pattern is listed here as Old Colony.
Open Rose pattern is listed here as Mayfair Open Rose.
Optic Design pattern is listed here as Raindrops.
Ovide, Sugar & Creamer, Fired-On Chartreuse 18.00
Oyster & Pearl, Bowl, Heart Shape, Pink, Handle, 5 ¼ In. 22.00
Oyster & Pearl, Candleholder, Ruby, 3 ½ In. .... *illus* 16.00
Oyster & Pearl, Relish, Pink, Sections, Handles, 10½ In. .... 14.00 to 24.00
Panelled Aster pattern is listed here as Primo.
Parrot pattern is listed here as Sylvan.
Patrician, Berry Bowl, Amber, 5 In. 13.00
Patrician, Berry Bowl, Pink, 8 1/2 In. .... 18.00 to 31.00
Patrician, Bowl, Cereal, Pink, 6 In. 36.00
Patrician, Bowl, Vegetable, Oval, Pink, 10 In. 37.00
Patrician, Cup & Saucer, Pink 30.00
Patrician, Pink, Salt & Pepper 120.00
Patrician, Plate, Amber, 6 In. 10.00
Patrician, Plate, Dinner, 10 ½ In. 20.00
Patrician, Plate, Dinner, Amber, 10½ In. .... 12.00 to 23.00
Patrician, Plate, Luncheon, Amber, 9 In. 10.00
Patrician, Plate, Luncheon, Pink, 9 In. .... 15.00 to 23.00
Patrician, Platter, Oval, Pink, 11 ½ In. 37.00
Patrician, Saltshaker, Amber, Metal Top 32.00
Patrician, Sugar, Amber 10.00
Patrician, Sugar & Creamer, Cover, Pink 90.00
Patrician, Tumbler, Amber, 14 Oz., 5 ½ In., 4 Piece 115.00
Patrician, Tumbler, Amber, 5 Oz., 4 In. 33.00
Peacock & Wild Rose pattern is listed in the Paden City category.
Petal Swirl pattern is listed here as Swirl.
Petalware, Cup, Pink 8.00

Petalware, Plate, Dinner, Monax, 9 In., Pair 10.00
Petalware, Plate, Dinner, Pink, 9 In. 20.00
Petalware, Plate, Salad, Pink, 8 In. 7.00
Petalware, Salver, Monax, 11 In. 15.00
Petalware, Soup, Cream, Pink, 4 ½ In. 16.00
Petalware, Sugar, Monax 10.00
Petalware, Sugar & Creamer, Monax 20.00
Pillar Optic, Pitcher, Ice Lip, 80 Oz. 16.00
Pillar Optic, Plate, Luncheon, Green, 8 In., 4 Piece 20.00
Pineapple & Floral pattern is listed here as No. 618.
Pinwheel pattern is listed here as Sierra.
Pioneer, Bowl, Fruit Center, 10 ½ In. 9.00
Pioneer, Plate, Fruit Center, Notched Edge, 12 In. 12.00
Poinsettia pattern is listed here as Floral.
Poppy No. 1 pattern is listed here as Florentine No. 1.
Poppy No. 2 pattern is listed here as Florentine No. 2.
Primo, Cup & Saucer, Yellow 17.00
Primo, Grill Plate, Green, 10 In. 14.00
Primo, Tumbler, Yellow, 5 ¾ In. 30.00
Primrose, Custard Cup, 6 Oz. 3.00
Princess, Bowl, Salad, Octagonal, 9 In. 34.00
Princess, Cake Stand, Silver Overlay, 10 In. 40.00
Princess, Cup, Topaz 9.00
Princess, Grill Plate, Topaz, 10 ½ In. 8.50
Princess, Pitcher, Pink, 6 In. 70.00
Princess, Plate, Dinner, Topaz, 9 ½ In. 14.00
Princess, Salt & Pepper, Green, 6 In. 68.00
Princess, Sandwich Server, Green, Tab Handles, 10 ¼ In. 22.00
Princess, Tumbler, Footed, Topaz, 10 Oz., 5 ¼ In. 17.00
Princess, Tumbler, Juice, 5 Oz., 3 In. 33.00
Princess, Tumbler, Juice, Topaz, 5 Oz., 3 In. 31.00
Prismatic Line pattern is listed here as Queen Mary.
Provincial pattern is listed here as Bubble.
Pyramid pattern is listed here as No. 610.
Queen Mary, Berry Bowl, 8 ½ In. 12.00
Queen Mary, Berry Bowl, Pink, 4 ½ In. 9.00
Queen Mary, Berry Bowl, Pink, 8 ¾ In. 38.00
Queen Mary, Bowl, Cereal, Pink, 6 In. 29.00
Queen Mary, Bowl, Deep, 7 In. 20.00
Queen Mary, Bowl, Handle, Pink, 4 In. ..... 4.00 to 6.00
Queen Mary, Bowl, Handles, Pink, 5 ½ In. 18.00
Queen Mary, Candlestick, 2-Light, 4½ In., Pair ..... 21.00 to 40.00
Queen Mary, Candy Dish, Cover, Pink 81.00
Queen Mary, Compote, 5 ¾ In. 13.00
Queen Mary, Console, 3-Footed, 10 In. 34.00
Queen Mary, Cup, Pink, Large 6.00
Queen Mary, Cup, Pink, Small ..... *illus* 6.00
Queen Mary, Plate, Dinner, Pink, 9 ¾ In. 56.00
Queen Mary, Sherbet, Pink 10.00
Queen Mary, Sugar & Creamer 45.00
Queen Mary, Sugar & Creamer, Pink 25.00
Queen Mary, Tumbler, Pink, 9 Oz., 4 In. 19.00
Rainbow, Jug, Ball, Fired-On Tangerine Red, 80 Oz., 7 ¼ In. 32.00
Raindrops, Cup, Green 7.00
Raindrops, Tumbler, 4 Oz., 3 In. 7.00
Ribbon, Plate, Sherbet, Green, 6 In. 12.00
Ribbon, Salt & Pepper 38.00
Ribbon, Salt & Pepper, Green 38.00
Ring, Plate, Off-Center Ring, Green, 6 ½ In. 5.00
Ring, Tumbler, Iced Tea, Footed, Silver Band, 6 ½ In. 12.00
Rock Crystal, Bowl, Low Footed, 12 ¼ x 2 ¾ In. 55.00
Rock Crystal, Candleholder, 2-Light, 5 ¼ x 6 ½ In., Pair 29.00
Rosemary, Berry Bowl, Amber, 5 In. 7.00
Rosemary, Soup, Cream, Amber, Handles, 5 In. ..... *illus* 26.00
Rosemary, Tumbler, Amber, 9 Oz., 4 ¼ In. 18.00

SECURITY TIP

Use opaque window shades or drapes so the contents of your rooms can't be seen from outside.

Depression Glass, Old Colony, Compote, Pink
$35.00

Depression Glass, Oyster & Pearl, Candleholder, Ruby, 3 ½ In.
$16.00

Depression Glass, Queen Mary, Cup, Pink, Small
$6.00

Pressed Glass Names

Many of the pressed glass pattern names used in books are not the ones originally used by the factory. When old pressed glass became popular in the 1930s, collectors and authors like Ruth Webb Lee and Minnie Watson Kamm gave names to the patterns. Sometimes more than one name is used to identify a pattern.

Depression Glass, Rosemary, Soup, Cream, Amber, Handles, 5 In.
$26.00

Depression Glass, Royal Lace, Platter, Oval, Cobalt Blue, 13 In.
$60.00

Depression Glass, Royal Ruby, Cigarette Box, Clear Base, Sections, 6 ¼ x 4 In.
$59.00

Depression Glass, Sandwich Anchor Hocking, Cup & Saucer, Desert Gold
$20.00

Depression Glass, Sharon, Cup & Saucer, Pink
$19.00

Roulette, Cup & Saucer, Green 8.00
Roulette, Plate, Luncheon, Green, 8 ½ In. 7.00
Roulette, Plate, Sherbet, Green, 6 In. 12.00
Royal Lace, Butter, Cover, Green 345.00
Royal Lace, Butter, Cover, Pink 250.00
Royal Lace, Cookie Jar, Cover, Green 150.00
Royal Lace, Creamer, Cobalt Blue 55.00
Royal Lace, Cup & Saucer, Cobalt Blue 58.00
Royal Lace, Pitcher, Cobalt Blue, Ice Lip, 48 Oz. 220.00
Royal Lace, Platter, Oval, Cobalt Blue, 13 In. . . . . . *illus* 60.00
Royal Lace, Sugar, Cover 35.00
Royal Lace, Tumbler, Green, 9 Oz., 4 In. 36.00
Royal Lace, Tumbler, Juice, Green, 5 Oz., 3 ½ In. 60.00
Royal Ruby, Berry Bowl, Handles, 4 ½ In., 6 Piece 40.00
Royal Ruby, Berry Bowl, Handles, 8 In. 22.00
Royal Ruby, Candy Dish, Folded-Out Sides, Tab Handles, 8 In. 18.00
Royal Ruby, Cigarette Box, Clear Base, Sections, 6 ¼ x 4 In. . . . . . *illus* 59.00
Royal Ruby, Goblet, 9 Oz., 5 ¼ In. 10.00
Royal Ruby, Sugar & Creamer 18.00
Royal Ruby, Nappy, Scrolled Handles, Ribbed, 7 ¾ x 2 ¼ In. 18.00
S Pattern, Tumbler, 3 ½ In., 6 Piece 28.00
S Pattern, Tumbler, 4 In., 6 Piece 25.00
Sailboat pattern is listed here as Sportsman Series.
Sandwich Anchor Hocking, Bowl, Forest Green, 6 ½ In. 95.00
Sandwich Anchor Hocking, Bowl, Vegetable, 8 ¼ In. 14.00
Sandwich Anchor Hocking, Cookie Jar, Cover, 9 ¼ In. 25.00
Sandwich Anchor Hocking, Cup, 4 Piece 18.00
Sandwich Anchor Hocking, Cup & Saucer, Desert Gold . . . . . *illus* 20.00
Sandwich Anchor Hocking, Punch Set, 12 Cups, Stand, 9 ¾-In. Bowl, 14 Piece 55.00
Sandwich Indiana, Tumbler, Footed, Green, 9 Oz., 6 ¼ In. 9.00
Sharon, Berry Bowl, Amber, 8½ In. . . . . . 6.00 to 12.00
Sharon, Berry Bowl, Pink, 5 In. 12.00
Sharon, Berry Bowl, Pink, 8 ½ In. 30.00
Sharon, Bowl, Fruit, Amber, 10 ½ In. 10.00
Sharon, Bowl, Fruit, Pink, 10½ In. . . . . . 34.00 to 39.00
Sharon, Bowl, Vegetable, Oval, Pink, 9½ In. . . . . . 25.00 to 31.00
Sharon, Bowl, Cereal, Pink, 6 In. 25.00
Sharon, Butter, Cover, Pink 99.00
Sharon, Candy Jar, No Cover, Pink, 5 x 5 ¾ In. 12.00
Sharon, Cup, Amber 10.00
Sharon, Cup & Saucer, Pink . . . . . *illus* 19.00
Sharon, Plate, Dinner, Pink, 9½ In. . . . . . 17.00 to 18.00
Sharon, Plate, Salad, Pink, 7 ½ In. 25.00
Sharon, Platter, Oval, Pink, 12 ½ In. 29.00
Sharon, Soup, Cream, Pink, Handles, 5 In. 50.00
Sharon, Soup, Dish, Pink 56.00
Sharon, Sugar & Creamer, Amber 18.00
Sharon, Tumbler, Pink, 9 Oz., 4⅛ In. . . . . . 30.00 to 45.00
Sharon, Tumbler, Pink, 12 Oz., 5 ¼ In. 59.00
Sharon, Tumbler, Pink, Thin, 4 ⅛ In. 30.00
Sierra, Plate, Dinner, Pink, 9 In. 25.00
Sierra, Platter, Oval, Pink, 11 In. 57.00
Sierra, Tray, Handles, Pink 24.00
Soreno, Snack Set, Avocado Green, 9 ¾-In. Plate, 2 Piece 28.00
Spoke pattern is listed here as Patrician.
Sportsman Series, Cocktail Shaker, Cobalt Blue, Windmill 38.00
Sportsman Series, Ice Tub, Cobalt Blue, Windmill, 4 ½ x 4 ⅝ In. 29.00
Sportsman Series, Tumbler, Cobalt Blue, Sailboats, 9 Oz., 3 ¼ In. 30.00
Stippled Rose Band pattern is listed here as S Pattern.
Strawberry, Compote, Pink, 5 ¾ In. 60.00
Sunburst, Bowl, Scalloped Rim, 4 x 10 ½ In. 55.00
Sunflower, Cake Plate, 3-Footed, Pink, 10 In. . . . . . 18.00 to 22.00
Sunflower, Cake Plate, Footed, Green, 10 In. . . . . . *illus* 31.00
Sunflower, Cake Plate, Green, 10 In. 18.00
Sunflower, Cup, Pink 17.00
Sunflower, Sugar, Green 15.00

Swirl, Berry Bowl, Ultramarine, 5 ¼ In. 12.00
Swirl, Bowl, Salad, Ultramarine, 9 In. 20.00
Swirl, Bowl, Vegetable, Footed, Handles, 10 In. 33.00
Swirl, Butter, Cover, Pink 176.00
Swirl, Butter, No Cover, Ultramarine 30.00
Swirl, Candlestick, 2-Light, Ultramarine, Pair 57.00
Swirl, Candy Dish, Cover, Ultramarine 177.00
Swirl, Creamer, Ultramarine 12.00
Swirl, Cup, Ultramarine 14.00
Swirl, Cup & Saucer, Ultramarine 15.00 to 18.00
Swirl, Plate, Dinner, Pink, 9 ¼ In. 15.00
Swirl, Plate, Dinner, Ultramarine, 9 ¼ In. 21.00
Swirl, Plate, Sherbet, Ultramarine, 6 ½ In. 7.00
Swirl, Sherbet, Ultramarine 20.00 to 22.00
Swirl, Soup, Dish, Tab Handles, Ultramarine, 5 In. 50.00
Swirl, Tumbler, Footed, Ultramarine, 9 Oz. 45.00
Swirl, Tumbler, Iced Tea, Cobalt Blue, 12 Oz., 5 In. 12.00
Swirl, Tumbler, Ultramarine, 13 Oz., 5 ⅛ In. 176.00
Swirl, Tumbler, Ultramarine, Footed, 9 Oz., 4 ½ In. 46.00
Swirl, Vase, Footed, Ultramarine, 8 ½ In. 27.00
Sylvan, Bowl, Vegetable, Oval, 10 In. 47.00
Sylvan, Grill Plate, Green, 10 ½ In. 90.00
Sylvan, Plate, Salad, Green, 7 ½ In. 49.00
Sylvan, Platter, Oval, Green, 11 ¼ In. 50.00
Sylvan, Sherbet, Cone, Amber, 3 In. *illus* 32.00
Sylvan, Sugar & Creamer, Green 80.00
Threading pattern is listed here as Old English.
Vernon pattern is listed here as No. 616.
Vertical Ribbed, Mixing Bowl, Clover Foot, 4 x 10 In. 20.00
Vertical Ribbed, Mixing Bowl Set, Nesting, Amber, Clover Foot, 3 Piece 75.00
Vitrock, Bowl, 4½ x 2¼ In. 6.00 to 10.00
Vitrock, Canister, Rice, 6 In. 45.00
Vitrock, Plate, 8⅛ In. 6.00 to 10.00
Vitrock, Salt & Pepper, Red Tulips, Oval, 4 ¼ In. 50.00
Vitrock, Salt & Pepper, Tulip, Square, 3 ¼ In. 45.00
Vitrock, Shaker, Flour, 5 In. 20.00
Vitrock, Shaker, Sugar, 5 In. 20.00
Waffle pattern is listed here as Waterford.
Waterford, Ashtray, 4 In. 8.00
Waterford, Cake Plate, Pink, Handles, 10 In. *illus* 28.00
Waterford, Pitcher, Juice 24.00
Waterford, Pitcher, Tilt, Juice, 42 Oz., 6 In. 25.00
Waterford, Plate, Dinner, 9 ⅝ In. 11.00
Waterford, Plate, Salad, 7 ⅛ In. 13.00
Waterford, Relish, 5 Sections, 13 ¾ In. 48.00
Waterford, Sandwich Server, Round, 13 ¾ In. 14.00
White Ship pattern is listed here as Sportsman Series.
Wild Rose pattern is listed here as Dogwood.
Windmill pattern is listed here as Sportsman Series.
Windsor, Berry Bowl, Pink, 4 ¾ In. 12.00
Windsor, Berry Bowl, Pink, 8 ½ In. 24.00
Windsor, Cake Plate, Pink, Footed, 10 ¾ In. 24.00
Windsor, Candy Jar, Cover, Pink 25.00
Windsor, Creamer, Pink 15.00
Windsor, Cup & Saucer, Pink 12.00
Windsor, Pitcher, Green, 52 Oz., 6 ¾ In. 62.00
Windsor, Pitcher, Pink, 52 Oz., 6 ¾ In. 33.00
Windsor, Plate, Dinner, Pink, 9 In. 21.00
Windsor, Salt & Pepper, Pink 35.00 to 38.00
Windsor, Sandwich Server, Pink, Open Handle, 10 ¼ In. 19.00
Windsor, Sherbet, Pink 13.00
Windsor, Sugar, Cover, Pink 29.00
Windsor, Sugar & Creamer, Pink 24.00
Windsor, Tumbler, Juice, Pink, 5 Oz., 3 ¼ In. 21.00
Windsor, Tumbler, Pink, 9 Oz., 4 In. 19.00
Windsor Diamond pattern is listed here as Windsor.

Depression Glass, Sunflower, Cake Plate, Footed, Green, 10 In. $31.00

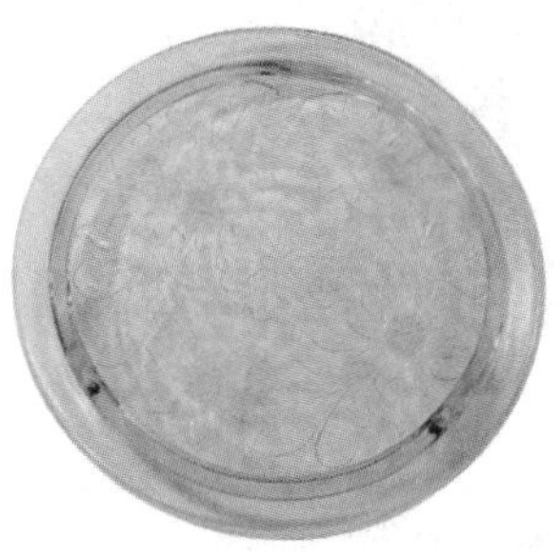

Depression Glass, Sylvan, Sherbet, Cone, Amber, 3 In. $32.00

Depression Glass, Waterford, Cake Plate, Pink, Handles, 10 In. $28.00

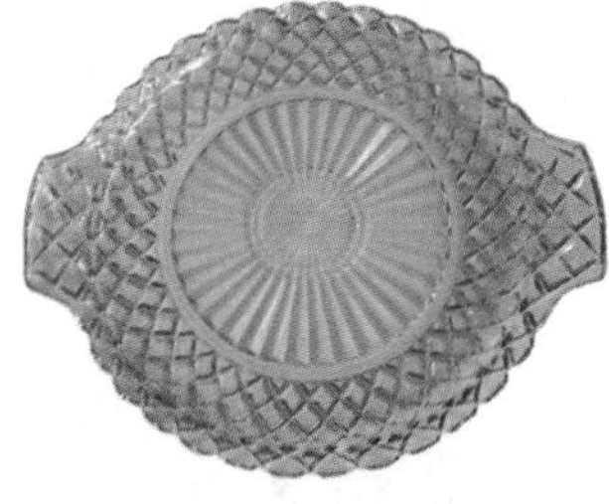

TIP

When the stopper of a glass decanter becomes too tight, a cloth wet with hot water and applied to the neck will cause the glass to expand so that the stopper may be easily removed.

D

Derby, Inkwell, Drum Form, Early 19th Century, 2½ x 6 x 5½ In. $65.00

Dick Tracy, Toy, Squad Car, Green, Windup, Battery Operated Light, Box, 6¾ In. $385.00

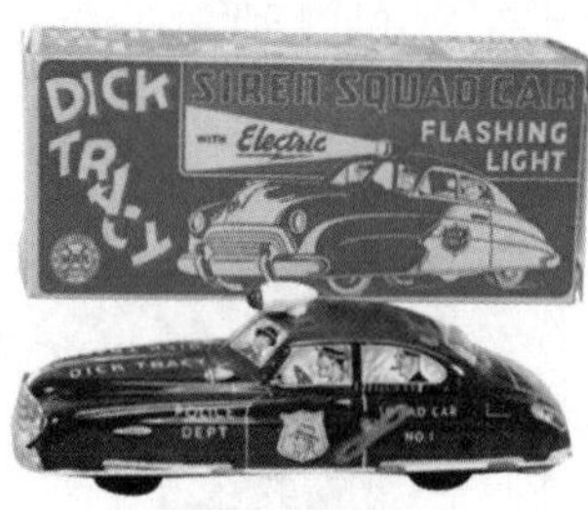

Dinnerware, Apple Trio, Bowl, Vegetable, Round, Blue Ridge, 9¼ In. $28.00

TIP

When stacking dinner plates, put a piece of felt or paper between each plate. Never put more than 24 in one stack.

DERBY has been marked on porcelain made in the city of Derby, England, since about 1748. The original Derby factory closed in 1848, but others opened there and continued to produce quality porcelain. The Crown Derby mark began appearing on Derby wares in the 1770s.

Bowl, Footed, Apricot & Gilt Border, Rectangular, 19th Century, 12 In. 480.00
Bowl, Fruit, Summer Flower Spray, Blue Glaze, Oval, Lobed, c.1780, 9¾ x 12¾ In. 96.00
Butter Tub, Birds, Octagonal, c.1765, 4¾ In. 1170.00
Inkstand, Imari Decoration, Double Lip, 2 Handles, c.1800, 4 x 6½ In. 510.00
Inkwell, Drum Form, Early 19th Century, 2½ x 6 x 5½ In. .... *illus* 65.00
Jam Jar, Cover, Imari Decoration, Gold Loop Finial, 2 Shaped Handles, 4½ x 3 In. 270.00
Plate, Yellow Banded Scenic, Floral, c.1810, 8¼ In. 300.00
Tureen, Sauce, Cover, Flower Cartouches, Blue, White, Gold Trim, 2 Handles, 5 x 7 In., Pair. . 720.00

DICK TRACY, the comic strip, started in 1931. Tracy was also the hero of movies from 1937 to 1947 and again in 1990, and starred in a radio series in the 1940s and a television series in the 1950s. Memorabilia from all these activities are collected.

Button, Dick Tracy Detective, Celluloid, 1¼ In. 46.00
Comic Book, No. 9, 1938 .... 510.00
Lunch Box, City Scene On Both Sides, Steel, Aladdin, Thermos, 1967 .... 132.00
Pin, Dick Tracy Detective, Chicago Tribune, Celluloid, Chester Gould, 1¼ In. 50.00
Toy, Squad Car, Siren, Green, Tin Lithograph, Windup, Marx, 11 In. 316.00
Toy, Water Gun, Submachine, Box, 3¾ x 4 x 12½ In. 348.00
Toy, Squad Car, Green, Windup, Battery Operated Light, Box, 6¾ In. .... *illus* 385.00

DICKENS WARE *pieces are listed in the Royal Doulton and Weller categories.*

DINNERWARE used in the United States from the 1930s through the 1950s is listed here. Most was made in potteries in southern Ohio, West Virginia, and California. A few patterns were made in Japan, England, and other countries. Dishes were sold in gift shops and department stores, or were given away as premiums. Many of these patterns are listed in this book in their own categories, such as Autumn Leaf, Azalea, Coors, Fiesta, Franciscan, Hall, Harker, Harlequin, Red Wing, Riviera, Russel Wright, Vernon Kilns, Watt, and Willow. For more information, see *Kovels' Depression Glass & Dinnerware Price List.*

Abingdon, Sugar, Cover, Skyline Shape, Blue Ridge 18.00
Allegro, Plate, Salad, Homer Laughlin, 8½ In. 9.00
Allegro, Platter, Oval Shape, Rhythm, Homer Laughlin, 13½ x 11 In. 28.00
Amberstone, Plate, Bread & Butter, Homer Laughlin, 6¼ In. 4.00
Amberstone, Platter, Homer Laughlin, 12 In. 20.00
American Beauty, Plate, Bread & Butter, Paden City, 6 In. 4.00
American Beauty, Plate, Dinner, Paden City, 9½ In. 7.50
American Beauty, Soup, Dish, Paden City, 8 In. 7.50
American Rose, Cup & Saucer, Paden City 14.00
American Rose, Plate, Bread & Butter, Paden City, 6⅜ In. 5.00
American Rose, Plate, Dinner, Paden City, 9½ In. .... 8.00 to 10.00
American Rose, Platter, Tab Handles, Paden City, 10⅛ In. 14.00
American Rose, Sugar, Paden City 13.00
Annie Laurie, Berry Bowl, Universal, 5¾ In. 12.00
Apple Blossom, Cup & Saucer, After Dinner, Homer Laughlin 15.00
Apple Blossom, Soup, Dish, Rim, Liberty Shape, Homer Laughlin 9.00
Apple Trio, Bowl, Vegetable, Round, Blue Ridge, 9¼ In. .... *illus* 28.00
Apple Trio, Plate, Dinner, Blue Ridge, 10½ In. 15.00
Applejack, Platter, Oval, Skyline Shape, Blue Ridge, 11½ In. 20.00
Aristocrat, Bowl, Vegetable, Round, Salem China, 9 In. 26.00
Aristocrat, Creamer, Salem China 36.00
Aristocrat, Cup & Saucer, Salem China 8.00
Aristocrat, Plate, Bread & Butter, Eggshell, Nautilus, Homer Laughlin, 6 In. 3.00
Aristocrat, Platter, Eggshell, Nautilus, Homer Laughlin, 11 In. 12.00
Aristocrat, Sugar, Cover, Salem China .... *illus* 46.00
Arlington, Berry Bowl, Harmony House, 5¼ In. 7.00
Arlington, Cup, Harmony House 9.00
Autumn, Plate, Dinner, Ever Yours Shape, Taylor, Smith & Taylor, 10 In. 8.00
Autumn Apple, Sugar, Cover, Colonial Shape, Blue Ridge 20.00
Autumn Delight, Luncheon Set, Johnson Brothers, Cup, 7½ In. Plate, 2 Piece 25.00
Autumn Gold, Bowl, Vegetable, Round, Homer Laughlin, 8¾ In. 20.00

Autumn Harvest, Bowl, Vegetable, Taylor, Smith & Taylor, 8 ¼ In. 19.00
Autumn Harvest, Casserole, Cover, 2 Handles, Taylor, Smith & Taylor, 10 ½ x 7 In. 38.00
Autumn Harvest, Platter, Oval, Taylor, Smith & Taylor, 11 ¼ In. 20.00
Autumn Harvest, Sugar & Creamer, Taylor, Smith & Taylor 11.00
Autumn Leaves, Creamer, Taylor, Smith & Taylor 17.00
Autumn Leaves, Cup & Saucer, Taylor, Smith & Taylor 17.00
Azalea, Cake Plate, Iva-Lure, Crooksville, 12 In. 35.00
Azalea, Plate, Dinner, Crooksville, 10 In. 12.00
Azalea, Plate, Dinner, Johnson Brothers, 10 In. 6.00
Aztec, Plate, Dinner, Impromptu, Ben Seibel, Iroquois, 10 In. 12.00
Bachelor Button, Platter, Oval, Taylor, Smith & Taylor, 13 ½ In. 16.00
Ballerina, Butter, Cover, Rosette, Universal, ½ Lb. 40.00
Ballerina, Cake Plate, Chrysanthemums, Tab Handles, Universal, 12 In. 32.00
Ballerina, Canister Set, Covers, Nesting, Rosette, Universal, Largest 5 x 6 ½ In., 3 Piece 50.00
Ballerina, Chop Plate, Iris, Tab Handles, Universal, 11 ½ In. .... *illus* 22.00
Ballerina, Cup, Iris, Universal 9.00
Ballerina, Pitcher, Ball Shape, Ice Lip, Universal, 7 In. 32.00
Ballerina, Pitcher, Rosette, Universal, 7 In. .... *illus* 22.00
Ballerina, Plate, Bread & Butter, Iris, Universal, 6 ¼ In. 9.00
Ballerina, Salt & Pepper, Rosette, Universal 12.00
Ballerina, Sauce, Iris, Universal 9.00
Ballerina Mist, Mixing Bowl Set, Sea Green, Universal, Largest 4 x 8 ¾ In., 3 Piece 24.00
Baltic Ivy, Creamer, Skyline Shape, Blue Ridge 15.00
Baltic Ivy, Platter, Oval, Skyline Shape, Blue Ridge, 11 ½ In. 10.00
Barnyard King, Cup & Saucer, Johnson Brothers 75.00
Barnyard King, Platter, Turkey, Johnson Brothers, 20 ½ x 16 In. 392.00
Becky, Eggcup, Blue Ridge, 3 ¼ In. 32.00
Beige Rose, Plate, Dinner, Ben Seibel, Iroquois, 10 ½ In. 11.00
Beige Rose, Plate, Salad, Ben Seibel, Iroquois, 8 In. 9.00
Bells Of Ireland, Cup & Saucer, Harmony House 10.00
Bells Of Ireland, Soup, Dish, Harmony House, 7 ¾ In. 5.00
Biscayne, Creamer, Paden City, 1956 .... 17.00
Biscayne, Cup & Saucer, Paden City 15.00
Biscayne, Plate, Dinner, Paden City, 10 ¼ In. 14.00
Biscayne, Plate, Salad, Paden City, 7 ½ In. 9.50
Biscayne, Platter, Oval, Paden City, 14 ¼ x 11 ½ In. 45.00
Biscayne, Relish, Oval, Paden City, 9 ½ x 5 ½ In. 15.00
Biscayne, Sugar & Creamer, Salem China 15.00
Bittersweet, Canister Set, Stacking, Top, Cover, Universal, 9 ¾ In., 3 Piece 50.00
Bittersweet, Mixing Bowl Set, Universal, Largest, 3 ½ x 6 ½ In., 3 Piece 35.00
Bittersweet, Plate, Salad, Blue Ridge, 7 ½ In. 15.00
Black Forest, Cake Plate, Black, Gold Trim, Footed, Paden City, 11 In. 180.00
Blue Duchess, Plate, Bread & Butter, Homer Laughlin, 6 ½ In. 6.00
Blue Holland, Plate, Dessert, Johnson Brothers, 7 In. 35.00
Blue Lace, Bowl, Cereal, Taylor, Smith & Taylor, 6 ½ In. 5.50
Blue Lace, Bowl, Vegetable, Round, Taylor, Smith & Taylor, 9 In. 14.00
Blue Lace, Creamer, Taylor, Smith & Taylor .... *illus* 10.00
Blue Lace, Plate, Bread & Butter, Taylor, Smith & Taylor, 6 ¼ In. 2.50
Blue Lace, Plate, Dinner, Taylor, Smith & Taylor, 10 ⅛ In. 7.00
Blue Mist, Bowl, Vegetable, Taylor, Smith & Taylor, 9 In. 25.00
Blue Mist, Plate, Luncheon, Taylor, Smith & Taylor, 9 ¼ In. 6.75
Bluebell Bouquet, Platter, Oval, Blue Ridge, 13 In. .... *illus* 75.00
Bluebell Bouquet, Serving Bowl, Round, Blue Ridge, 9 In. 55.00
Bluebird, Bowl, Cereal, Taylor, Smith & Taylor, 5 ¼ In. 24.00
Bluebird, Platter, 12-Sided, Tab Handles, Salem China, 13 ½ x 11 In. 175.00
Bluebird, Platter, Oval, Empress Shape, Homer Laughlin, 16 x 10 ¼ In. 160.00
Bountiful, Plate, Bread & Butter, Square, Blue Ridge, 6 In. 20.00
Boutonniere, Berry Bowl, Ever Yours Shape, Taylor, Smith & Taylor, 5 ¼ In. 4.00
Boutonniere, Mug, Taylor, Smith & Taylor 13.00
Boutonniere, Plate, Dessert, Taylor, Smith & Taylor, 6 ¾ In. 5.00
Boutonniere, Plate, Dinner, Ever Yours Shape, Taylor, Smith & Taylor, 10 In. 13.00
Boutonniere, Relish, Divided, Ever Yours Shape, Taylor, Smith & Taylor, 11 In. 13.00
Boutonniere, Sugar, Cover, Taylor, Smith & Taylor, 4 In. 9.00
Bow Knot, Berry Bowl, Colonial Shape, Blue Ridge, 5 ¼ In. 12.00
Bow Knot, Bowl, Cereal, Colonial Shape, Blue Ridge, 6 In. 12.00
Bow Knot, Bowl, Vegetable, Round, Colonial Shape, Blue Ridge, 9 In. 20.00

Dinnerware, Aristocrat, Sugar, Cover, Salem China
$46.00

Dinnerware, Ballerina, Chop Plate, Iris, Tab Handles, Universal, 11 ½ In.
$22.00

Dinnerware, Ballerina, Pitcher, Rosette, Universal, 7 In.
$22.00

Dinnerware, Blue Lace, Creamer, Taylor, Smith & Taylor
$10.00

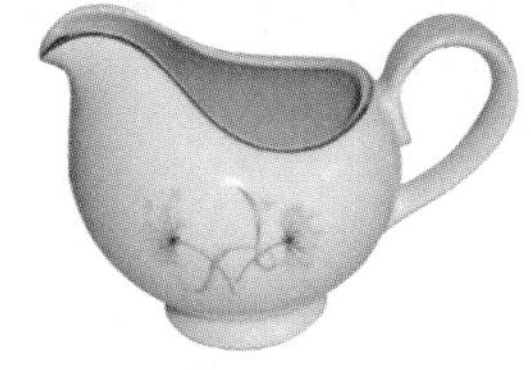

Dinnerware, Bluebell Bouquet, Platter, Oval, Blue Ridge, 13 In.
$75.00

Dinnerware, Cattail, Pitcher, Disc Sides, Cork Stopper, Universal, 7 x 7 ½ In.
$42.00

Dinnerware, Cattail, Pitcher, Milk, Universal, 6 In.
$30.00

Dinnerware, Colonial Kitchen, Platter, Swing Shape, Homer Laughlin, 13 ¼ In.
$52.00

Dinnerware, Country Gentleman, Plate, Bread & Butter, Cow, Bird, Flowers, Salem China, 6 In.
$28.00

D

Bow Knot, Creamer, Blue Ridge 15.00
Bow Knot, Plate, Bread & Butter, Colonial Shape, Blue Ridge, 6 In. 6.00
Bow Knot, Plate, Dinner, Colonial Shape, Blue Ridge, 9 ¼ In. 15.00
Bow Knot, Platter, Oval, Colonial Shape, Blue Ridge, 13 In. 20.00
Bow Knot, Sugar, Cover, Colonial Shape, Blue Ridge 20.00
Breakfast Bar, Bowl, Vegetable, Round, Skyline Shape, Blue Ridge, 9 In. 18.00
Bridal White, Cup & Saucer, Ben Seibel 8.00
Brown Daisy, Bowl, Vegetable, Round, Skyline Shape, Blue Ridge, 9 In. 18.00
Brown Plaid, Cup & Saucer, Blue Ridge 10.00
Brown Tulip, Berry Bowl, Blue Ridge 5.00
Brown Tulip, Cup, Blue Ridge 5.00
Brown Tulip, Cup & Saucer, Skyline Shape, Blue Ridge 12.00
Brown Tulip, Sugar & Creamer, Skyline Shape, Blue Ridge 12.00
Bryn Mawr, Sugar & Creamer, Salem China 40.00
Buttercup, Sugar, Cover, Taylor, Smith & Taylor 10.00
Caliente, Mixing Bowl, Yellow, Paden City, 4 x 8 In. 29.00
Caliente, Platter, Tangerine Orange Oval, Tab Handles, Paden City, 12 In. 10.00
Camwood Ivory, Plate, Salad, Square, Universal, 7 ½ In. 5.00
Camwood Ivory, Water Jug, Disc Sides, Cork Stopper, Universal, 7 ¾ In. 45.00
Cape Cod, Platter, Oval, Ever Yours Shape, Taylor, Smith & Taylor, 13 ½ In. 27.00
Carly's Apple, Plate, Luncheon, Blue Ridge, 9 ½ In. 22.00
Carnival, Butter, Cover, Blue, White, Harmony House 20.00
Carnival, Chop Plate, Harmony House, 12 In. 40.00
Carnival, Coffeepot, Blue, White Cover, Harmony House, 9 In. 30.00
Carnival, Sugar & Creamer, Blue, White Cover, Harmony House, 9 In. 30.00
Cattail, Bowl, Cover, Round, Universal, 3 ¾ x 8 ¼ In. 45.00
Cattail, Casserole, Cover, Round, Universal, 2 Qt. 55.00
Cattail, Pie Baker, Universal, 9 ⅞ In. 32.00
Cattail, Pitcher, Disc Sides, Cork Stopper, Universal, 7 x 7 ½ In. .... *illus* 42.00
Cattail, Pitcher, Milk, Universal, 6 In. .... *illus* 30.00
Cattail, Platter, Oval, Universal, 11 ¾ x 10 ¾ In. 18.00
Center Bouquet, Bowl, Vegetable, Oval, Handles, Taylor, Smith & Taylor, 9 ¼ x 6 ¾ In. 35.00
Center Bouquet, Plate, Luncheon, Taylor, Smith & Taylor, 9 In. 14.00
Center Bouquet, Platter, Oval, Taylor, Smith & Taylor, 11 ½ x 8 ¼ In. 35.00
Century, Plate, Dinner, Cobalt Blue Rim, Salem China, 9 ⅞ In. 7.00
Century, Plate, Salad, Salem China, 7 In. 5.00
Century Riviera, Teapot, Mauve Blue, Homer Laughlin, 8 x 4 ½ In. 135.00
Century Riviera, Tumbler, Juice, Red, 3 ½ In. 83.00
Chateau Buffet, Bowl, Cereal, Taylor, Smith & Taylor, 6 In. 5.00
Chateau Pink, Creamer, Taylor, Smith & Taylor 8.00
Chateau Pink, Cup & Saucer, Taylor, Smith & Taylor 8.00
Chateau Pink, Soup, Dish, Taylor, Smith & Taylor, 7 ¼ In. 5.00
Chelsea, Bowl, Vegetable, Cover, Round, Acacia, Taylor, Smith & Taylor, 9 In. 75.00
Chelsea, Gravy Boat, Acacia, Taylor, Smith & Taylor, 7 ⅝ In. 15.00
Cherry Blossom, Sugar & Creamer, V. Schreckengost, Salem China 95.00
Cherrytone, Salad Fork & Spoon, Universal 18.00
Chicory, Bowl, Vegetable, Round, Colonial Shape, Blue Ridge, 9 ½ In. 15.00
Chintz, Cake Plate, Leaf Shape, Blue Ridge, 10 In. 28.00
Chrysanthemum, Berry Bowl, Blue Ridge, 5 ¼ In. 7.00
Chrysanthemum, Bowl, Vegetable, Oval, Blue Ridge, 9 ¼ x 7 In. 25.00
Chrysanthemum, Creamer, Blue Ridge 19.00
Chrysanthemum, Cup & Saucer, Blue Ridge 13.00
Chrysanthemum, Gravy Boat, Blue Ridge 35.00
Chrysanthemum, Plate, Bread & Butter, Blue Ridge, 6 ¼ In. 6.50
Chrysanthemum, Plate, Dinner, Blue Ridge, 9 ¼ In. 13.00
Chrysanthemum, Platter, Oval, Blue Ridge, 11 ¼ x 9 ½ In. 26.00
Chrysanthemum, Sugar, Cover, Blue Ridge 20.00
Clairmont, Bowl, Vegetable, Round, Laurel Shape, Taylor, Smith & Taylor, 8 ¾ In. 20.00
Clairmont, Creamer, Taylor, Smith & Taylor 16.00
Clairmont, Cup & Saucer, Laurel Shape, Taylor, Smith & Taylor 15.00
Clairmont, Platter, Oval, Handles, Laurel Shape, Taylor, Smith & Taylor, 11 ¾ In. 25.00
Clairmont, Sugar, Cover, Empire Shape, Taylor, Smith & Taylor 29.00
Coaching Scenes, Cup & Saucer, Blue Transfer, Johnson Brothers 12.00
Coaching Scenes, Plate, Dinner, Blue, Johnson Brothers, 10 In. 13.00
Coaching Scenes, Sugar & Creamer, Underplate, Johnson Brothers, Miniature 30.00
Colonial Couple, Bowl, Cereal, Salem China, 6 ¼ In. 8.00

lonial Couple, Creamer, Crooksville 15.00
lonial Kitchen, Bowl, Vegetable, Oval, Swing Shape, Homer Laughlin, 9 In. 35.00
lonial Kitchen, Platter, Swing Shape, Homer Laughlin, 11¼ In. 40.00
lonial Kitchen, Platter, Swing Shape, Homer Laughlin, 13¼ In. . . . . *illus* 52.00
lumbia, Sugar & Creamer, Crooksville. 24.00
rinthian, Bowl, Vegetable, Round, Taylor, Smith & Taylor, 9½ In. 29.00
smos, Salt & Pepper, Shenandoah Ware, Paden City, 3¼ In. 10.00
untry Fair, Plate, Luncheon, Grapes, Colonial Shape, Blue Ridge, 8¼ In. 15.00
untry Fair, Plate, Luncheon, Pears, Colonial Shape, Blue Ridge, 8¼ In. 15.00
untry Gentleman, Plate, Bread & Butter, Cow, Bird, Flowers, Salem China, 6 In. . . . *illus* 28.00
untry Scenes, Baker, Oval, Taylor, Smith & Taylor, 9 In. 15.00
untry Scenes, Bowl, Fruit, Taylor, Smith & Taylor, 5½ In. 7.50
untry Scenes, Celery Dish, Taylor, Smith & Taylor, 10 In. 8.00
untry Scenes, Cup, Taylor, Smith & Taylor 9.00
untry Scenes, Plate, Bread & Butter, Taylor, Smith & Taylor 4.50
untry Scenes, Plate, Dinner, Taylor, Smith & Taylor, 10 In. 10.00
untry Scenes, Platter, Oval, Tab Handles, Taylor, Smith & Taylor, 13 In. 19.00
untry Scenes, Sugar, Cover, Taylor, Smith & Taylor 18.00
untry Time, Coffee Server, Ben Seibel, Pfaltzgraff 65.00
untry Time, Relish, 3 Sections, Ben Seibel, Pfaltzgraff. 25.00
untryside, Platter, Oval, Steubenville, 13¾ x 11¾ In. 21.00
abapple, Plate, Dinner, Blue Ridge, 9½ In. . . . . 14.00 to 15.00
rrier & Ives, Sugar, Franklin's Experiment, Red Transfer, Homer Laughlin. 35.00
ahlia, Plate, Dinner, Candlewick Shape, Blue Ridge, 9¼ In. 15.00
aisy, Grill Plate, Taylor, Smith & Taylor, 10 In. 14.00
aisy Wreath, Platter, Oval, Taylorstone, Taylor, Smith & Taylor, 13½ In. 29.00
arcy, Plate, Salad, Blue Ridge, 7¾ In. . . . . *illus* 16.00
ay In June, Plate, Dinner, Johnson Brothers, 10 In. 25.00
aybreak, Bowl, Vegetable, Dura-Print, Homer Laughlin, 8¼ In. 10.00
aylily, Bowl, Vegetable, Round, Taylor, Smith & Taylor, 9 In. 28.00
elft Rose, Bowl, Vegetable, Round, Colonial Shape, Blue Ridge, 9 In. 25.00
elmar Begonia, Berry Bowl, Crooksville, 5¼ In. 6.50
elmar Begonia, Bowl, Vegetable, Tab Handles, Crooksville, 8½ In. 27.00
elmar Begonia, Creamer, Crooksville 20.00
elmar Begonia, Cup & Saucer, Crooksville. 13.00
elmar Begonia, Plate, Bread & Butter, Crooksville, 6¼ In. 5.00
elmar Begonia, Plate, Luncheon, Crooksville 7.50
elmar Begonia, Platter, Shaped Sides, Crooksville, 11¾ x 9 In. 27.00
elmar Begonia, Sugar, Cover, Crooksville. 27.00
elmar Marie, Berry Bowl, Crooksville, 5¼ In. 6.50
elmar Marie, Plate, Bread & Butter, Crooksville, 6¼ In. 5.00
elmar Marie, Plate, Luncheon, Crooksville, 9½ In. 10.00
ubarry, Berry Bowl, Georgian Shape, Homer Laughlin, 5½ In. 7.00
ubarry, Gravy Boat, Eggshell Nautilus Shape, Homer Laughlin. . . . . *illus* 39.00
ubarry, Salt & Pepper, Eggshell Nautilus Shape, Homer Laughlin 36.00
uchess, Bowl, Vegetable, Oval, Harmony House, 11 In. 18.00
utch Iris, Plate, Pie Crust Edge, Blue Ridge, 9¼ In. 20.00
utch Onion, Plate, Dinner, Taylor, Smith & Taylor, 10 In. 16.00
ggshell Georgian, Cup & Saucer, Ivory, Gold Trim, Homer Laughlin 12.00
l Camino, Cup & Saucer, Ben Seibel, Iroquois. 8.00
l Camino, Plate, Bread & Butter, Ben Seibel, Iroquois, 6½ In. 4.00
l Camino, Plate, Dinner, Ben Seibel, Iroquois, 11 In. 10.00
l Camino, Relish, Ben Seibel, Iroquois. 18.00
l Camino, Sherbet, Ben Seibel, Iroquois. 7.00
l Camino, Sugar, Ben Seibel, Iroquois 11.00
legance, Pitcher, Milk, Milady Shape, Blue Ridge, 8 In. . . . . *illus* 175.00
npire, Teapot, Green Trim, Cavalier Shape, Homer Laughlin, 6¾ In. 85.00
nchanted Garden, Bowl, Vegetable, Oval, Red Transfer, Johnson Brothers, 10 In. 125.00
nchanted Garden, Plate, Salad, Square, Johnson Brothers, 7¾ In. 22.00
nchanted Garden, Sugar, Cover, Johnson Brothers 55.00
nglish Chippendale, Bowl, Vegetable, Red, Johnson Brothers, 9 x 7 In. 40.00
nglish Chippendale, Cup & Saucer, Red, Johnson Brothers, Oversize. 275.00
nglish Chippendale, Plate, Bread & Butter, Red, Johnson Brothers, 6⅜ In. 10.00
nglish Chippendale, Plate, Dinner, Johnson Brothers, 10⅛ In. 24.00
nglish Chippendale, Platter, Shaped Sides, Red, Johnson Brothers, 17 x 14½ In. 195.00
nglish Collection, Pot De Creme, Cover, Salem China, 5½ In. 29.00

Dinnerware, Darcy, Plate, Salad, Blue Ridge, 7¾ In.
$16.00

Dinnerware, Dubarry, Gravy Boat, Eggshell Nautilus Shape, Homer Laughlin
$39.00

Dinnerware, Elegance, Pitcher, Milk, Milady Shape, Blue Ridge, 8 In.
$175.00

SECURITY TIP

Join with your neighbors to keep informed about workmen who might be using a ladder or trying to get into a garage. Call the police if you are suspicious.

SECURITY TIP

Protect your home and antiques from theft. Use a timer on your lights at all times, even when you are at home. This will set a pattern of certain lights going on and off each day. When you are away, the house will appear to have normal activity. If possible, when you are away, park a car near the front of the house. The car will block your driveway so a burglar cannot load up through your garage. Have someone keep your trash cans filled. This will help to make the house look occupied. Keep the grass mowed and the snow shoveled. Stop your mail and paper deliveries.

D

Dinnerware, Flora, Pitcher, Chick Shape, Beak Spout, Blue Ridge, 5½ In. $85.00

English Garden, Platter, Shaped Sides, Red Transfer, Johnson Brothers, 12 x 10 In. 55.0
English Garden, Sugar, Cover, Johnson Brothers 55.0
English Garden, Teapot, Red Transfer, Johnson Brothers, 5 Cup 195.0
English Village, Cup & Saucer, Salem China 14.0
English Village, Plate, Dinner, Salem China, 10 In. 19.0
Evening Flower, Plate, Dessert, Blue Ridge, 7¼ In. 14.0
Fairlane, Cup & Saucer, Steubenville 7.0
Fascination, Platter, Oval, Universal, 14¼ x 13 In. 24.0
Ferndale, Bowl, Vegetable, Round, Harmony House, 9 In. 10.0
Ferndale, Creamer, Harmony House 12.0
Ferndale, Cup & Saucer, Harmony House 10.0
Fjord, Plate, Salad, Ben Seibel, Iroquois, 8 In. 12.0
Flora, Pitcher, Chick Shape, Beak Spout, Blue Ridge, 5½ In. *illus* 85.0
Flower Ring, Creamer, Colonial Shape, Blue Ridge 15.0
Flower Ring, Plate, Salad, Colonial Shape, Blue Ridge, 7 In. 10.0
Flower Ring, Platter, Oval, Colonial Shape, Blue Ridge, 11¾ In. 15.0
Flower Ring, Sugar, Cover, Colonial Shape, Blue Ridge 20.0
Fluffy Rose, Sugar, Cover, Virginia Rose, Homer Laughlin 25.0
Forest Fruit, Berry Bowl, Blue Ridge, 5⅜ In. 7.0
Forget-Me-Not, Bowl, Vegetable, Round, Homer Laughlin, 8½ In. 36.0
Forget-Me-Not, Casserole, Cover, Handles, Eggshell Georgian, Homer Laughlin, 10 In. 99.0
Forget-Me-Not, Plate, Breakfast, Eggshell Georgian, Homer Laughlin, 9 In. 10.0
Fox Fire, Plate, Dinner, Skyline Shape, Blue Ridge, 10¼ In. 19.0
Friendly Village, Coffeepot, Johnson Brothers, 8 In. 99.0
Friendly Village, Mug, Johnson Brothers, 4 In. 20.0
Friendly Village, Plate, Luncheon, Johnson Brothers, 8¾ In. 13.0
Friendly Village, Plate, Salad, Square, Johnson Brothers, 7½ In. 11.0
Friendly Village, Plate, Salad, Willow By The Brook, Johnson Brothers, 7½ In. 11.0
Friendly Village, Soup, Rim, Stone Wall, Johnson Brothers, 8¾ In. 15.0
Game Birds, Platter, Partridge, Johnson Brothers, 11 x 10 In. 45.0
Game Birds, Platter, Wild Turkey, Johnson Brothers, 11 x 10 In. 45.0
Garland, Plate, Bread & Butter, Homer Laughlin, 6¼ In. 8.0
Gloriosa, Plate, Dinner, Skyline Shape, Blue Ridge, 9¼ In. 15.0
Godey Ladies, Charger, Red Rim, Salem China, 11 In. 31.0
Godey Prints, Cup & Saucer, Victory Shape, V. Schreckengost, Salem China 15.0
Godey Prints, Platter, Oval, Victory Shape, V. Schreckengost, Salem China, 11¼ In. 40.0
Gold Crest, Creamer, Harmony House 12.0
Gold Crest, Gravy Boat, Underplate, Harmony House 50.0
Gold Crest, Plate, Dinner, Harmony House, 10 In. 8.0
Gold Crest, Platter, Oval, Harmony House, 16½ In. 50.0
Gold Crest, Sugar, Cover, Harmony House 25.0
Golden Wheat, Gravy Boat, Homer Laughlin 32.0
Golden Wheat, Platter, Oval, Homer Laughlin, 12 In. 22.0
Golden Wheat, Sugar, Cover, Homer Laughlin 18.0
Green Eyes, Bread & Butter, Blue Ridge, 6 In. 10.0
Green Plaid, Sugar & Creamer, Blue Ridge *illus* 36.0
Hacienda, Creamer, Homer Laughlin *illus* 65.0
Harvest, Cup & Saucer, Johnson Brothers 45.0
Harvest, Plate, Buffet, Johnson Brothers, 10¾ In. *illus* 127.0
Harvest Fruit, Plate, Buffet, Johnson Brothers, 10¾ In. 108.0
Harvest Time, Bowl, Vegetable, Ben Seibel, Iroquois, 10 In. 19.0
Harvest Time, Cup, Ben Seibel, Iroquois 6.0
Harvest Time, Cup & Saucer, Johnson Brothers 7.0
Harvest Time, Plate, Bread & Butter, Johnson Brothers, 6¼ In. 9.0
Harvest Time, Plate, Dinner, Ben Seibel, Iroquois, 10 In. 12.0
Harvest Time, Plate, Dinner, Johnson Brothers, 10 In. 8.00 to 9.0
Harvest Time, Plate, Salad, Ben Seibel, Iroquois, 8 In. 4.0
Harvest Time, Platter, Oval, Ben Seibel, Iroquois, 12 x 8¾ In. 15.0
Harvest Time, Platter, Oval, Ben Seibel, Iroquois, 15½ x 10¾ In. 25.0
Harvest Time, Soup, Coupe, Ben Seibel, Iroquois 11.0
Harvest Time, Tidbit, 2-Tier, Johnson Brothers 75.0
Henrietta, Platter, Skyline Shape, Blue Ridge, 11¾ In. 25.0
Hibiscus, Berry Bowl, Gray-Lure, Crooksville, 5¼ In. 5.0
Hibiscus, Plate, Dinner, Gray-Lure, Crooksville, 10¼ In. 5.00 to 8.0
Highland Plaid, Platter, Oval, Dura-Print, Homer Laughlin, 11 x 9 In. 18.0
Highland Plaid, Platter, Oval, Dura-Print, Homer Laughlin, 14 x 11 In. 22.0

Highlander, Coffeepot, Harmony House, 5 Cup . . . 15.00
Hornbeak, Creamer, Blue Ridge . . . 15.00
Ida Rose, Pitcher, Sally, Blue Ridge, 6 ½ In. . . . 59.00
Indian Summer, Cup & Saucer, Ironstone, Taylor, Smith & Taylor . . . 8.50
Inheritance, Berry Bowl, Grecian Gold, 4 ½ In. . . . 13.00
Iona, Casserole, Cover, Taylor, Smith & Taylor . . . 34.00
Iva-Lure, Bowl, Cereal, Bittersweet, Crooksville, 7 In. . . . 12.00
Iva-Lure, Bowl, Dessert, Bittersweet, Crooksville, 5 ½ In. . . . 7.00
Iva-Lure, Bowl, Vegetable, Bittersweet, Crooksville, 9 ½ In. . . . 27.00
Iva-Lure, Chop Plate, Apple Blossom, Crooksville, 12 ¼ In. . . . 12.00
Iva-Lure, Chop Plate, Cars, Crooksville, 12 In. . . . 15.00
Iva-Lure, Chop Plate, Dairy Maid, Crooksville, 12 In. . . . 24.00
Iva-Lure, Creamer, Bittersweet, Crooksville . . . 18.00
Iva-Lure, Cup & Saucer, Bittersweet, Crooksville . . . 15.00
Iva-Lure, Pie Server, Apple Blossom, Crooksville . . . 35.00
Iva-Lure, Plate, Bread & Butter, Bittersweet, Crooksville, 6 ¼ In. . . . 5.00
Iva-Lure, Plate, Dinner, Bittersweet, Crooksville, 10 ¼ In. . . . 15.00
Iva-Lure, Plate, Salad, Apple Blossom, Crooksville, 8 In. . . . 8.00
Iva-Lure, Sugar, Cover, Bittersweet, Crooksville . . . 20.00
Ivora, Berry Bowl, Crooksville, 5 ¼ In. . . . 5.50
Ivora, Cup & Saucer, Crooksville . . . 10.00
Ivora, Plate, Bread & Butter, Crooksville, 6 ¼ In. . . . 3.50
Ivora, Plate, Luncheon, Crooksville, 9 In. . . . 7.50
Ivora, Platter, Oval, Crooksville, 11 ½ In. . . . 25.00
Ivy, Berry Bowl, Paden City, 5 ¼ In. . . . 4.00
Ivy, Celery Dish, Paden City, 9 ¼ x 5 ½ In. . . . 8.00
Ivy, Plate, Bread & Butter, Paden City, 6 ¼ In. . . . 5.00
Ivy, Plate, Dinner, Paden City, 10 In. . . . 7.50
Ivy Twine, Plate, Bread & Butter, Taylor, Smith & Taylor, 6 ¾ In. . . . 2.50
Ivy Twine, Sugar, Cover, Taylor, Smith & Taylor . . . 13.00
Jade Rose, Plate, Dinner, Homer Laughlin, 10 ⅛ In. . . . 12.00
James Riviere, Plate, Dinner, Crooksville, 10 In., 6 In. . . . 8.00
James Riviere, Platter, Oval, Crooksville, 13 ½ In. . . . 25.00
John's Plaid, Plate, Dinner, Woodcrest Shape, Blue Ridge, 10 ¼ In. . . . 13.00
Jonquil, Creamer, Paden City . . . 10.00
Jonquil, Cup & Saucer, Paden City . . . 7.50
Jonquil, Plate, Dinner, Paden City, 9 ½ In. . . . 8.50
Jonquil, Sugar, Cover, Paden City . . . 13.00
Kitchen Kraft, Bowl Set, Nesting, Priscilla, Homer Laughlin, 3 Piece . . . 55.00
Kitchen Kraft, Cake Plate, Priscilla, Homer Laughlin, 11 In. . . . 22.00
Kitchen Kraft, Teapot, Flowers, Gold Trim, Homer Laughlin, 7 ½ In. . . . 60.00
Knollwood, Sugar, Cover, Ben Seibel, Iroquois . . . 15.00
Labelle, Berry Bowl, Harmony House, 5 ½ In. . . . 9.00
Labelle, Bowl, Vegetable, Oval, Harmony House, 10 ¼ In. . . . 18.00
Labelle, Creamer, Harmony House . . . 13.00
Labelle, Plate, Dinner, Harmony House, 10 In. . . . 15.00
Labelle, Sugar, Cover, Harmony House . . . 13.00
Lady Greenbriar, Teapot, Homer Laughlin . . . *illus* 90.00
Lady Stratford, Sugar & Creamer, Homer Laughlin . . . 75.00
Laurel Wreath, Plate, Bread & Butter, Colonial Shape, Blue Ridge, 6 In. . . . 5.00
Laurel Wreath, Plate, Salad, Colonial Shape, Blue Ridge, 7 In. . . . 6.00
Lazy Daisy, Bowl, Cereal, Ben Seibel, Iroquois, 5 ¾ In. . . . 13.00
Lazy Daisy, Bowl, Gravy, Ben Seibel, Iroquois . . . 19.00
Lazy Daisy, Bowl, Vegetable, Round, Taylor, Smith & Taylor, 8 ½ In. . . . 20.00
Lazy Daisy, Creamer, Taylor, Smith & Taylor . . . 13.00
Lazy Daisy, Cup & Saucer, Taylor, Smith & Taylor . . . 15.00
Lazy Daisy, Platter, Oval, Taylor, Smith & Taylor, 13 ½ In. . . . 19.00
Lazy Daisy, Syrup, Taylor, Smith & Taylor, 6 In. . . . 13.00
Leaf Fantasy, Snack Set, Maple, Yellow, Universal, 9 ¾-In. Plate, 4-In. Cup . . . 35.00
Leaf O' Gold, Bowl, Cereal, Taylor, Smith & Taylor, 6 ½ In. . . . 5.00
Leaf O' Gold, Bowl, Vegetable, Round, Taylor, Smith & Taylor, 9 In. . . . 9.95
Leaf O' Gold, Plate, Bread & Butter, Taylor, Smith & Taylor, 6 ½ In. . . . 3.00
Leaf O' Gold, Plate, Dinner, Taylor, Smith & Taylor, 10 ⅛ In. . . . 7.00
Lily Of The Valley, Bowl, Vegetable, Homer Laughlin, 9 In. . . . 45.00
Lily Of The Valley, Plate, Salad, Eggshell Nautilus, Homer Laughlin, 8 In. . . . 7.00
Lily Of The Valley, Soup, Dish, Homer Laughlin, 8 ¼ In. . . . 16.00

Dinnerware, Green Plaid, Sugar & Creamer, Blue Ridge $36.00

Dinnerware, Hacienda, Creamer, Homer Laughlin $65.00

Dinnerware, Harvest, Plate, Buffet, Johnson Brothers, 10 ¾ In. $127.00

Plate Sizes and Shapes

Dessert	6 inches
Bread	7 inches
Salad	7 1/2 inches
Luncheon	8–9 inches
Breakfast	9 inches
Dinner	10 inches
Grill	10 1/2 inches divided into three sections
Sandwich	11–13 inches usually with 2 handles
Chop	13 inches

SECURITY TIP

We like this answering machine message we just heard: "Please leave a message at the beep. The person now at home does not speak English." It is plausible and explains why the house is occupied yet the answering machine is on.

Dinnerware, Lady Greenbriar, Teapot, Homer Laughlin
$90.00

Dinnerware, Lu-Ray, Pitcher, Persian Cream, Taylor, Smith & Taylor
$125.00

Dinnerware, Mount Vernon, Coffeepot, Drip, E Style, Harmony House, 11 In.
$115.00

Lily Of The Valley, Sugar & Creamer, Swing Shape, Homer Laughlin, Individual 47.00
Lorraine, Spoon, Serving, Crooksville, 10 ¾ In. 19.00
Lupine, Platter, Green Band, Eggshell Nautilus, Homer Laughlin, 11 ¾ x 9 ¾ In. 17.00
Lu-Ray, Berry Bowl, Surf Green, Taylor, Smith & Taylor, 5 ½ In. 4.00
Lu-Ray, Coffeepot, Surf Green, Empire Shape, Taylor, Smith & Taylor 90.00
Lu-Ray, Creamer, Windsor Blue, Taylor, Smith & Taylor 16.00
Lu-Ray, Pitcher, Persian Cream, Taylor, Smith & Taylor .... *illus* 125.00
Lu-Ray, Plate, Dinner, Surf Green, Taylor, Smith & Taylor, 10 In. 30.00
Lu-Ray, Plate, Luncheon, Yellow, Taylor, Smith & Taylor, 9 In. 28.00
Lu-Ray, Platter, Oval, Pink, Taylor, Smith & Taylor, 12 x 8 ¼ In. 25.00
Magic Flower, Platter, Candlewick Shape, Blue Ridge, 11 ¾ In. 20.00
Magnolia, Gravy Boat, Eggshell Shape, Homer Laughlin 18.00
Magnolia, Platter, Oval, Eggshell Shape, Homer Laughlin, 13 ½ x 10 ¾ In. 34.00
Mardi Gras, Cup, Blue Ridge 15.00
Marigold, Berry Bowl, Colonial Couple Dancing, Homer Laughlin, 5 ½ In. 9.00
Marigold, Plate, Dinner, Colonial Couple Dancing, Homer Laughlin, 9 ¼ In. 25.00
Marigold, Soup, Dish, Red Rim, Colonial Couple Dancing, Homer Laughlin, 8 ½ In. 12.00
Marilyn, Bowl, Vegetable, Cover, Pink Band, Homer Laughlin, 11 In. 77.00
Marilyn, Creamer, Pink Band, Homer Laughlin 23.00
Marilyn, Cup & Saucer, Blue Band, Eggshell Georgian, Homer Laughlin 10.00
Marilyn, Gravy Boat, Pink Band, Homer Laughlin 34.00
Marsh Violet, Plate, Dinner, Taylor, Smith & Taylor, 10 ¼ In. 22.00
Mary, Bowl, Vegetable, Harmony House, 9 In. 42.00
Mary, Gravy Boat, Underplate, Harmony House 41.00
Mary, Plate, Dinner, Harmony House, 10 ¼ In. 14.00
Mary, Platter, Oval, Harmony House, 12 In. 41.00
Melody, Casserole, Cover, Empire Shape, Taylor, Smith & Taylor 68.00
Mexican, Berry Bowl, Paden City, 5 ¼ In. 9.00
Mexican, Bowl, Vegetable, Paden City, 8 In. 13.00
Mexican, Plate, Salad, Paden City, 7 In. 9.00
Mexican, Platter, Tab Handles, Paden City, 14 ½ In. 40.00
Minuet, Bowl, Vegetable, Harmony House, 10 ½ In. 12.00
Minuet, Cup & Saucer, Harmony House 6.00
Minuet, Plate, Bread & Butter, Harmony House, 6 ¾ In. 7.00
Minuet, Plate, Dinner, Harmony House, 10 ½ In. 10.00
Minuet, Plate, Salad, Harmony House, 7 ½ In. 8.00
Minuet, Sugar, Cover, Harmony House 8.00
Moderne, Cup, Harmony House 5.00
Moderne, Plate, Salad, Harmony House 10.00
Moderne, Sugar & Creamer, Harmony House 28.00
Monticello, Bowl, Vegetable, Oval, Harmony House, 10 ½ In. 18.00
Monticello, Creamer, Footed, Harmony House .... 13.00 to 15.00
Monticello, Cup & Saucer, E Style, Harmony House 13.00
Monticello, Plate, Dinner, Harmony House, 10 In. 15.00
Mosaic, Bowl, Vegetable, Round, Harmony House, 9 In. 12.00
Moss Rose, Bowl, Vegetable, Oval, Wide Rim, 2 Handles, Taylor, Smith & Taylor 15.00
Mount Vernon, Berry Bowl, Harmony House, 5 ¼ In. 7.00
Mount Vernon, Bowl, Cereal, Tab Handles, Harmony House, 7 In. 16.00
Mount Vernon, Bowl, Vegetable, Oval, Harmony House, 9 ¼ x 6 ½ In. 20.00
Mount Vernon, Coffeepot, Drip, E Style, Harmony House, 11 In. .... *illus* 115.00
Mount Vernon, Creamer, Harmony House 15.00
Mount Vernon, Gravy Boat, Underplate, Harmony House 50.00
Mount Vernon, Plate, Dinner, Harmony House, 10 ½ In. 12.00
Mount Vernon, Platter, Harmony House, 13 ¼ x 10 In. 30.00
Mount Vernon, Sugar, Cover, Harmony House 25.00
Mountain Ivy, Berry Bowl, Candlewick Shape, Blue Ridge, 5 ¼ In. 8.00
Mountain Ivy, Plate, Dinner, Blue Ridge, 10 ¼ In. 28.00
Mountain Ivy, Soup, Dish, Blue Ridge, 8 In. 25.00
Niagara, Pitcher, White, Gold Trim, Homer Laughlin, 6 x 7 ½ In. 10.00
Nocturne, Platter, Colonial Shape, Blue Ridge, 15 ½ In. 17.00
Nora, Cup & Saucer, Harmony House 12.00
Nora, Plate, Bread & Butter, Harmony House, 6 ½ In. 3.00
Nora, Platter, Oval, Harmony House, 12 ¼ In. 13.00
Nordic, Cup & Saucer, Johnson Brothers 14.00
North Star, Berry Bowl, Salem China, 5 ¼ In. 9.00
North Star, Pitcher, Salem China, 5 x 4 ¾ In. .... *illus* 35.00
North Star, Sugar & Creamer, Salem China 35.00

Nosegay, Platter, Oval, Candlewick Shape, Blue Ridge, 13 ½ In. 15.00
Nova Rose, Cake Plate, Maple Leaf Shape, Handle, Blue Ridge, 10 In. 60.00
Old Britain Castles, Plate, Dinner, Pink, Johnson Brothers, 10 In. 16.00
Old English Abbey, Gravy Boat, Taylor, Smith & Taylor 40.00
Old English Countryside, Platter, Shaped Sides, Johnson Brothers, 12 In. 28.00
Old Mill, Plate, Salad, Johnson Brothers, 8 In. 25.00
Old Rose, Plate, Dinner, Paden City, 9 ¼ In. 9.00
Opulance, Pitcher, Alice Shape, Blue Ridge, 6 ¼ In. 175.00
Orient, Soup, Dish, Harmony House, 7 ½ In. 12.00
Pantry Bak-In Ware, Platter, Rectangular, Shaped Sides, Flowers, Crooksville, 12 x 9 In. 33.00
Paramount, Platter, Rectangular, Cut Corners, Taylor, Smith & Taylor, 11 In. 25.00
Pastoral, Bowl, Cereal, Homer Laughlin, 5 ¾ In. 5.00
Pebbleford, Berry Bowl, Mint Green, Taylor, Smith & Taylor, 5 ¼ In. 6.95
Pebbleford, Cup & Saucer, Mint Green, Taylor, Smith & Taylor 8.95
Pebbleford, Plate, Bread & Butter, Mint Green, Taylor, Smith & Taylor, 6 ¾ In. 5.95
Pebbleford, Plate, Dinner, Mint Green, Taylor, Smith & Taylor, 10 In. 15.00
Pebbleford, Plate, Dinner, Pink, Taylor, Smith & Taylor, 10 In. 6.00
Pebbleford, Plate, Dinner, Turquoise, Taylor, Smith & Taylor, 10 In. 6.00
Pebbleford, Sugar & Creamer, Mint Green, Taylor, Smith & Taylor 25.00
Petal Point, Platter, Gold Trim, Salem, 11 In. *illus* 25.00
Petit Point Basket, Berry Bowl Set, Century Shape, Salem China, 6-In. Master, 7 Piece 30.00
Petit Point House, Bowl, Bak-In, Crooksville, 6 In. 59.00
Petit Point House, Bowl, Vegetable, Oval, Crooksville, 9 In. 25.00
Petit Point House, Chop Plate, Bak-In, Crooksville, 12 ¼ In. 38.00
Petit Point House, Pitcher, Cover, Bak-In, Crooksville, 6 In. 79.00
Petit Point House, Plate, Dinner, Crooksville, 10 In. 33.00
Petit Point House, Plate, Luncheon, Crooksville, 9 In. 14.00
Petit Point House, Platter, Bak-In, Crooksville, 13 ¼ In. 40.00
Petit Point House, Platter, Crooksville, 11 ¼ In. 29.00
Petit Point Vine, Chop Plate, Crooksville, 12 ¼ In. 15.00
Petit Point Vine, Plate, Salad, Crooksville, 8 In. 8.00
Pinecone, Plate, Bread & Butter, Paden City, 6 ¼ In. 3.00
Pinecone, Plate, Dinner, Paden City, 10 In. 9.50
Pinecone Branch, Creamer, Homer Laughlin 9.00
Pink Dogwood, Bowl, Vegetable, Round, Universal, 9 In. 10.00
Pink Dogwood, Cup & Saucer, Universal 10.00
Pink Dogwood, Plate, Bread & Butter, Universal, 6 ¼ In. 12.00
Pink Petal, Berry Bowl, Homer Laughlin, 5 ½ In. 8.00
Pink Petal, Bowl, Vegetable, Oval, Homer Laughlin, 9 x 7 In. 30.00
Pink Petal, Plate, Bread & Butter, Homer Laughlin, 6 In. 6.00
Pink Petal, Plate, Dinner, Homer Laughlin, 9 ⅞ In. 14.00
Pins & Beads, Cup & Saucer, Ben Seibel, Iroquois 16.00
Pins & Beads, Pitcher, Tall, Ben Seibel, Iroquois 52.00
Plantation Ivy, Platter, Skyline Shape, Blue Ridge, 12 In. 10.00
Platinum Garland, Soup, Rim, Harmony House, 7 ¾ In. 14.00
Poinsettia, Berry Bowl, Colonial Shape, Blue Ridge, 5 ¼ In. 12.00
Poinsettia, Bowl, Vegetable, Oval, Colonial Shape, Blue Ridge, 9 ½ In. 40.00
Poinsettia, Cake Tray, Maple Leaf Shape, Blue Ridge, 9 ½ In. 50.00
Poinsettia, Creamer, Colonial Shape, Blue Ridge 9.00
Poinsettia, Cup, Blue Ridge 10.00
Poinsettia, Cup & Saucer, Blue Ridge 22.00
Poinsettia, Plate, Bread & Butter, Colonial Shape, Blue Ridge, 6 In. 12.00
Poinsettia, Plate, Dinner, Colonial Shape, Blue Ridge, 9 ½ In. 15.00
Poinsettia, Plate, Salad, Colonial Shape, Blue Ridge, 7 In. 12.00
Poinsettia, Plate, Soup, Colonial Shape, Blue Ridge, 8 In. 24.00
Poinsettia, Platter, Oval, Blue Ridge, 13 ½ x 11 ½ In. 25.00
Poinsettia, Saucer, Colonial Shape, Blue Ridge 5.00
Poinsettia, Bowl, Vegetable, Round, Blue Ridge, 10 In. 45.00
Poppy, Bowl, Vegetable, Universal, 8 ¾ In. 11.00
Poppy, Platter, Oval, Universal, 11 ¼ In. 12.00
Poppy Duet, Plate, Bread & Butter, Candlewick Shape, Blue Ridge, 6 In. 20.00
Prairie Rose, Berry Bowl, Colonial Shape, Blue Ridge, 5 ¼ In. 4.00
Primrose, Snack Set, Sugar & Creamer, V. Schrekengost, 24 Piece 115.00
Pyramid, Bowl, Ben Seibel, Iroquois, 9 ½ In. 16.00
Pyramid, Bowl, Ben Seibel, Iroquois, 11 ½ In. 18.00
Pyramid, Creamer, Ben Seibel, Iroquois 10.00
Pyramid, Cup & Saucer, Ben Seibel, Iroquois 9.00

Dinnerware, North Star, Pitcher, Salem China, 5 x 4 ¾ In.
$35.00

Dinnerware, Petal Point, Platter, Gold Trim, Salem, 11 In.
$25.00

TIP

If you have an instant-on television set, beware! The instant-on works because a current is always running through the set, even when it is off. This means more power is used, the set wears out faster, and, most serious for the collector, there is a greater risk of fire. Next time the set needs repair, ask the serviceperson to remove the instant-on feature. If you use a remote unit to turn off the set, the same dangers exist.

Dinnerware, Rose Of Sharon, Snack Tray, Martha, Leaf Shape, 3 Sections, Blue Ridge
$85.00

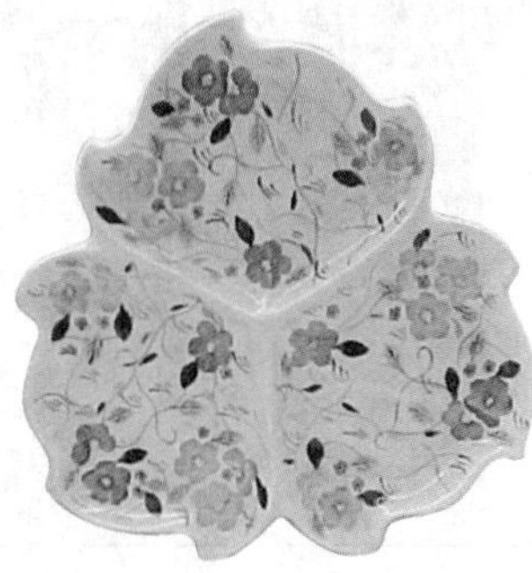

Dinnerware, Rosemary, Creamer, Ben Seibel, Iroquois
$15.00

Dinnerware, Rosemary, Sugar, Cover, Ben Seibel, Iroquois
$15.00

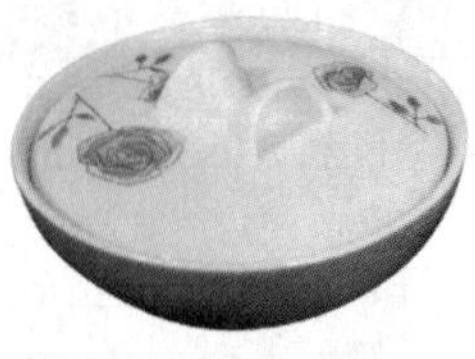

Dinnerware, Sailing, Plate, Tricorn Shape, Don Schreckengost, Salem China, 11½ In.
$45.00

Pyramid, Gravy Boat, Ben Seibel, Iroquois . . . 14.00
Pyramid, Plate, Bread & Butter, Ben Seibel, Iroquois, 6½ In. . . . 6.00
Pyramid, Plate, Dinner, Ben Seibel, Iroquois, 10¼ In. . . . 12.00
Pyramid, Platter, Ben Seibel, Iroquois, 15 In. . . . 24.00
Pyramid, Sherbet, Pedestal Base, Ben Seibel, Iroquois . . . 6.00
Pyramid, Sugar, Cover, Ben Seibel, Iroquois . . . 11.00
Quilted Fruit, Creamer, Woodcrest Shape, Blue Ridge . . . 20.00
Raymond, Gravy Boat, Underplate, Homer Laughlin . . . 50.00
Raymond, Plate, Bread & Butter, Homer Laughlin, 6½ In. . . . 8.00
Raymond, Plate, Dinner, Yellowstone Shape, Homer Laughlin, 10¼ In. . . . 14.00
Raymond, Sugar & Creamer, Yellowstone Shape, Homer Laughlin . . . 50.00
Red Rose, Berry Bowl, Paden City, 5¼ In. . . . 8.00
Red Rose, Bowl, Vegetable, Paden City, 9 In. . . . 30.00
Red Rose, Cup & Saucer, Paden City . . . 16.00
Red Rose, Plate, Luncheon, Paden City, 9¼ In. . . . 9.50
Red Rose, Platter, Paden City, 9¼ x 5¾ In. . . . 15.00
Red Rose, Platter, Paden City, 12 x 8½ In. . . . 30.00
Red Rose, Soup, Dish, Minion Shape, Square, Paden City, 8 In. . . . 8.00
Red Rose, Sugar, Cover, Paden City . . . 27.00
Regal Red, Berry Bowl, Cavalier Shape, Homer Laughlin, 6 In. . . . 7.00
Regal Red, Creamer, Cavalier Shape, Homer Laughlin . . . 15.00
Regal Red, Cup & Saucer, Cavalier Shape, Homer Laughlin . . . 10.00
Regal Red, Soup, Dish, Cavalier Shape, Homer Laughlin, 8 In. . . . 10.00
Regal Red, Sugar, Cover, Cavalier Shape, Homer Laughlin . . . 16.00
Regency, Coffee Set, Leaves & Vines, Monticello, Steubenville, 3 Piece . . . 189.00
Reveille, Bowl, Cereal, Taylor, Smith & Taylor, 6½ In. . . . 7.00
Reveille, Plate, Dinner, Taylor, Smith & Taylor, 10 In. . . . 9.00
Reveille, Platter, Oval, Rooster, Taylor, Smith & Taylor, 13½ In. . . . 17.00
Reveille, Saucer, Taylor, Smith & Taylor, 6⅜ In. . . . 5.00
Ridge Daisy, Plate, Dinner, Colonial Shape, Blue Ridge, 10 In. . . . 20.00
Ridge Daisy, Platter, Oval, Blue Ridge, 11¾ x 9½ In. . . . 39.00
Ridge Rose, Bowl, Salad, Colonial Shape, Blue Ridge, 10½ In. . . . 50.00
Rita, Casserole, Cover, Taylor, Smith & Taylor, 8¼ x 11 In. . . . 35.00
Rita, Creamer, Taylor, Smith & Taylor . . . 15.00
Rita, Cup & Saucer, Taylor, Smith & Taylor . . . 7.50
Rita, Plate, Dinner, Taylor, Smith & Taylor, 9 In. . . . 6.75
Rita, Platter, Rectangular, Cut Corners, Taylor, Smith & Taylor, 13 In. . . . 18.00
Romance, Pitcher, Antique Shape, Blue Ridge, 4⅝ In. . . . 32.00
Rose Band, Plate, Dinner, Crooksville, 10 In. . . . 6.00
Rose Chintz, Bowl, Cereal, Johnson Brothers, 6¼ In. . . . 11.00
Rose Chintz, Eggcup, Johnson Brothers . . . 12.00
Rose Mist, Sugar & Creamer, Taylor, Smith & Taylor . . . 30.00
Rose Of Sharon, Snack Tray, Martha, Leaf Shape, 3 Sections, Blue Ridge . . . *illus* 85.00
Rose Sachet, Console, Taylor, Smith & Taylor, 17 In. . . . 70.00
Rosebud, Cup & Saucer, Harmony House . . . 12.00
Rosebud, Plate, Dinner, Harmony House, 10¼ In. . . . 15.00
Rosedale, Saucer, Harmony House . . . 5.00
Rosedale, Soup, Dish, Harmony House, 8½ In. . . . 18.00
Rosemary, Bowl, Cereal, Ben Seibel, Iroquois . . . 11.00
Rosemary, Bowl, Vegetable, Ben Seibel, Iroquois, 10½ In. . . . 16.00
Rosemary, Creamer, Ben Seibel, Iroquois . . . *illus* 15.00
Rosemary, Soup, Dish, Ben Seibel, Iroquois . . . 8.00
Rosemary, Sugar, Cover, Ben Seibel, Iroquois . . . *illus* 15.00
Rosemont, Berry Bowl, Green Border, Taylor, Smith & Taylor, 5¼ In. . . . 5.50
Rosemont, Berry Bowl, Taylor, Smith & Taylor, 5½ In. . . . 5.50
Rosemont, Creamer, Green Border, Taylor, Smith & Taylor . . . 9.50
Rosemont, Cup & Saucer, Green Border, Taylor, Smith & Taylor . . . 8.00
Rosemont, Plate, Bread & Butter, Taylor, Smith & Taylor, 6⅜ In. . . . 5.00
Rosemont, Plate, Dinner, Green Border, Taylor, Smith & Taylor, 10 In. . . . 10.00
Rosemont, Soup, Dish, Green Border, Taylor, Smith & Taylor, 7¾ In. . . . 13.00
Rosemont, Soup, Dish, Taylor, Smith & Taylor, 8 In. . . . 8.50
Roses, Berry Bowl, Crooksville, 5 In. . . . 5.00
Roses, Bowl, Cereal, Crooksville, 6 In. . . . 5.00
Roses, Chop Plate, Crooksville, 12 In. . . . 10.00
Roses, Plate, Luncheon, Crooksville, 9¼ In. . . . 10.00
Roses, Soup, Dish, Crooksville, 7¼ In. . . . 7.00
Roses & Dots, Candy Box, Cover, Round, Blue Ridge, 6 In. . . . 125.00

Rustic Plaid, Plate, Bread & Butter, Blue Ridge, 6¼ In.	2.50
Rustic Tulip, Pie Baker, Pantry Bak-In Ware, Crooksville, 10 In.	9.00
Sailing, Plate, Tricorn Shape, Don Schreckengost, Salem China, 11½ In. *illus*	45.00
Sally, Berry Bowl, Paden City, 5⅛ In.	3.00
Sally, Cup & Saucer, Paden City	8.00
Sally, Plate, Bread & Butter, Paden City, 6¼ In.	3.00
Sally, Plate, Dessert, Paden City, 7½ In.	5.00
Sally, Plate, Dinner, Paden City, 10¼ In.	8.00
Sally, Soup, Dish, Scalloped Rim, Paden City, 8 In.	6.00
Sandra, Platter, Round, Handles, Steubenville	18.00
Sea Shell, Casserole, Cover, Taylor, Smith & Taylor, 8 In.	50.00
Sea Shell, Plate, Bread & Butter, Taylor, Smith & Taylor, 6¼ In.	5.00
Sea Shell, Plate, Dinner, Taylor, Smith & Taylor, 10¼ In.	11.00
Sea Shell, Plate, Luncheon, Taylor, Smith & Taylor, 8 In.	7.00
Sea Shell, Platter, Rectangular, Taylor, Smith & Taylor, 13½ In.	30.00
Sea Shell, Saucer, Taylor, Smith & Taylor	3.00
Sea Shell, Soup, Dish, Conversation Shape, Taylor, Smith & Taylor, 8 In.	13.00
Serenade, Plate, Dinner, Regency Shape, Homer Laughlin, 10 In.	6.00
Serenade, Platter, Oval, Homer Laughlin, 13 In.	10.00
Shadow Fruit, Creamer, Blue Ridge, 3½ In.	15.00
Shadow Fruit, Sugar & Creamer, Blue Ridge	15.00
Shenandoah, Bowl, Vegetable, Gray, Paden City, 8¾ In.	3.00
Shenandoah, Plate, Dinner, Pink, Paden City, 9½ In.	7.50
Shenandoah, Plate, Dinner, Green, Paden City, 9½ In.	10.00
Shenandoah, Plate, Salad, Chartreuse, Paden City, 8¼ In.	5.00
Shenandoah, Platter, Gray, Paden City, 12¾ In.	3.00
Shenandoah, Platter, Morning Glory, Oval, Paden City, 16 x 13 In.	40.00
Sheraton, Cup & Saucer, Johnson Brothers	28.00
Silver Oak, Chop Plate, Taylor, Smith & Taylor, 12½ In.	29.00
Simplicity, Cup & Saucer, Salem China	4.00
Simplicity, Plate, Dinner, Salem China, 10 In.	5.00
Simplicity, Soup, Coupe, Salem China, 8 In.	3.50
Simplicity, Sugar, Cover, Salem China, 3½ In.	6.00
Skytone, Saucer, Homer Laughlin	5.00
Spring Wreath, Berry Bowl, Virginia Rose, Homer Laughlin, 5¼ In.	10.00
Spring Wreath, Plate, Dinner, Virginia Rose, Homer Laughlin, 9¼ In.	14.00
Spring Wreath, Plate, Salad, Homer Laughlin, 7 In.	9.00
Stanhome Ivy, Cup, Blue Ridge	8.00
Stanhome Ivy, Plate, Bread & Butter, Blue Ridge, 6½ In.	4.00
Stanhome Ivy, Plate, Luncheon, Blue Ridge, 9½ In.	7.50
Star Dust, Platter, Oval, Skytone Shape, Homer Laughlin, 13½ x 10¾ In.	15.00
Starbrite, Berry Bowl, Homer Laughlin, 5½ In.	6.00
Starbrite, Bowl, Vegetable, Homer Laughlin, 8¼ In.	12.00
Starbrite, Sugar & Creamer, Homer Laughlin	45.00
Starlite, Bowl, Vegetable, Regal China, 10¾ In.	34.00
Starlite, Creamer, Regal China	15.00
Starlite, Plate, Bread & Butter, Regal China, 6¼ In.	8.50
Starlite, Platter, Oval, Regal China, 14½ In.	45.00
Stellar, Creamer, Ben Seibel, Iroquois	13.00
Stellar, Cup & Saucer, Ben Seibel, Iroquois	11.00
Summer Rose, Bowl, Vegetable, Taylor, Smith & Taylor, 9 In.	17.00
Summer Rose, Cake Plate, Taylor, Smith & Taylor, 10½ In.	15.00
Summer Rose, Cup & Saucer, Taylor, Smith & Taylor	8.00
Summer Rose, Platter, Oval, Taylor, Smith & Taylor, 13½ In.	17.00
Sunflower, Plate, Dinner, Colonial Shape, Blue Ridge, 9¼ In.	15.00
Sunny Spray, Cup & Saucer, Blue Ridge	11.00
Sunny Spray, Plate, Dinner, Skyline Shape, Blue Ridge, 10½ In.	20.00
Sunny Spray, Plate, Luncheon, Blue Ridge, 9½ In.	11.00
Susannah, Sugar & Creamer, Blue Ridge	48.00
Symphony, Berry Bowl, Turquoise, Harmony House, 5½ In.	12.00
Symphony, Cup & Saucer, Blue, Harmony House	9.50
Symphony, Cup & Saucer, Gray, Harmony House	9.50
Symphony, Plate, Bread & Butter, Chartreuse, Harmony House, 6¼ In.	12.00
Symphony, Plate, Bread & Butter, Pink, Harmony House, 6¼ In.	12.00
Symphony, Plate, Luncheon, Gray, Harmony House, 9¼ In.	7.50
Symphony, Plate, Luncheon, Pink, Harmony House, 9¼ In.	7.50

Dinnerware, Virginia Rose, Bowl, Vegetable, Homer Laughlin, 9¾ In.
$48.00

Dinnerware, Virginia Rose, Bowl, Vegetable, Scalloped Edge, Homer Laughlin, 8 In.
$25.00

Dinnerware, Weathervane, Plate, Dinner, Salem China, 10 In.
$16.00

Dinnerware, Wild Turkeys, Plate, Buffet, Windsor Ware, Johnson Brothers, 10¾ In.
$77.00

DINNERWARE

Dinnerware, Windsor Fruit, Cup & Saucer, Johnson Brothers $28.00

D

Dinnerware, Woodfield, Snack Set, Tropic Green, Leaf Plate, Steubenville, 2 Piece $17.00

Dinnerware, Yellow Nocturne, Cup & Saucer, Blue Ridge $14.00

TIP

Go to antiques shows early; there may be plenty of antiques left at the end of the show, but the dealers are tired and not as eager to talk to the customers.

Tartan, Sugar, Cover, Harmony House 23.00
Taverne, Plate, Bread & Butter, Laurel Shape, Taylor, Smith & Taylor, 6 ¼ In. 12.00
Thistle, Platter, Oval, Scalloped Edge, Taylor, Smith & Taylor, 13 ¼ In. 8.00
Tiger Lily, Dessert Set, Cups, Saucers, Plates, Harmony House, 23 Piece 125.00
Tiger Lily, Dish, Divided, Open Center Handle, Crooksville, 10 ½ x 7 ¼ In. 28.00
Tulip, Cup & Saucer, Shell Crest, Paden City. 12.00
Verna, Cake Plate, Maple Leaf Shape, Handle, Blue Ridge, 10 In. 60.00
Virginia Rose, Bowl, Vegetable, Homer Laughlin, 9 ¾ In. .... *illus* 48.00
Virginia Rose, Bowl, Vegetable, Scalloped Edge, Homer Laughlin, 8 In. .... *illus* 25.00
Virginia Rose, Cup & Saucer, Homer Laughlin 7.50
Virginia Rose, Platter, Homer Laughlin, 13 In. 16.00
Vision, Cruet Set, Oil & Vinegar, Stoppers, Ben Seibel, Iroquois 40.00
Vitrastone, Salt & Pepper, Ben Seibel, Kasuga, Handles 45.00
Vitrastone, Sugar, Cover, Ben Seibel, Kasuga. 55.00
Weathervane, Plate, Dinner, Salem China, 10 In. .... *illus* 16.00
Wheat, Creamer, Salem China 8.00
Whirligig, Platter, Colonial Shape, Blue Ridge, 11 ¾ In. 20.00
White Flower, Tea Set, Tray, Rhythm Shape, Homer Laughlin, 4 Piece 75.00
White Rose, Bowl, Vegetable, Round, Homer Laughlin, 8 ½ In. 25.00
Wild Quince, Creamer, Taylor, Smith & Taylor 18.00
Wild Rose, Cup & Saucer, Paden City 9.00
Wild Rose, Plate, Dinner, Paden City, 9 ½ In. 11.00
Wild Rose, Platter, Oval, Paden City, 11 ¾ In. 12.00
Wild Rose, Platter, Oval, Green Border, Taylor, Smith & Taylor, 12 x 8 ¼ In. 35.00
Wild Strawberry, Creamer, Blue Ridge 10.00
Wild Strawberry, Gravy Boat, Blue Ridge 30.00
Wild Strawberry, Plate, Dinner, Blue Ridge, 10 In. 50.00
Wild Strawberry, Soup, Dish, Colonial Shape, Blue Ridge, 8 In. 8.00
Wild Strawberry, Sugar, Cover, Blue Ridge 15.00
Wild Turkeys, Plate, Buffet, Windsor Ware, Johnson Brothers, 10 ¾ In. .... *illus* 77.00
Wild Turkeys, Platter, Turkey, Windsor Ware, Johnson Brothers, 20 ¼ x 15 ½ In. 425.00
Wildflowers, Berry Bowl, Crooksville, 5 ¼ In. 5.50
Wildflowers, Bowl, Vegetable, Tab Handles, Crooksville, 8 ¾ In. 25.00
Wildflowers, Creamer, Crooksville 12.00
Wildflowers, Cup, Crooksville. 12.00
Wildflowers, Plate, Dinner, Crooksville, 10 ¼ In. 12.00
Wildflowers, Platter, Oval, Crooksville, 13 In. 25.00
Wildflowers, Soup, Dish, Lug Handles, Crooksville, 6 ¼ In. 5.50
Wildflowers, Sugar, Cover, Crooksville, 13 In. 16.00
Willow, Soup, Dish, Rim, Homer Laughlin. 18.00
Winchester, Platter, Oval, Johnson Brothers, 12 In. 77.00
Windblown, Bowl, Vegetable, Iva-Lure, Crooksville, 8 ½ In. 26.00
Windblown, Creamer, Iva-Lure, Crooksville 20.00
Windblown, Plate, Dinner, Iva-Lure, Crooksville, 10 ¼ In. 12.00
Windblown, Sugar, Cover, Iva-Lure, Crooksville 28.00
Windmere, Cup & Saucer, Taylor, Smith & Taylor. 7.50
Windsor Fruit, Cup & Saucer, Johnson Brothers. .... *illus* 28.00
Winnie, Berry Bowl, Skyline Shape, Blue Ridge, 5 ½ In. 5.00
Winnie, Plate, Bread & Butter, Skyline Shape, Blue Ridge, 6 In. 5.00
Winnie, Plate, Dinner, Skyline Shape, Blue Ridge, 10 ½ In. 18.00
Wood Rose, Casserole, Cover, Taylor, Smith & Taylor, 9 In. 19.00
Wood Rose, Gravy Boat, Underplate, Taylor, Smith & Taylor 25.00
Wood Rose, Sugar, Cover, Taylor, Smith & Taylor 23.00
Woodfield, Cup & Saucer, Dove Gray, Steubenville 8.00
Woodfield, Snack Set, Blue, Leaf Plate, Steubenville, 2 Piece 14.00
Woodfield, Snack Set, Salmon Pink, Leaf Plate, Steubenville, 2 Piece 17.00
Woodfield, Snack Set, Tropic Green, Leaf Plate, Steubenville, 2 Piece. .... *illus* 17.00
Woodland, Bowl, Vegetable, Cover, Triumph Shape, Homer Laughlin 41.00
Woodland, Bowl, Vegetable, Triumph Shape, Homer Laughlin, 8 ½ In., Pair 44.00
Woodland, Creamer, Homer Laughlin 12.00
Woodland, Platter, Oval, Homer Laughlin, 11 ½ x 8 ½ In. 23.00
Woodland, Platter, Oval, Homer Laughlin, 13 ½ x 10 ½ In. 19.00
Wrinkled Rose, Bowl, Vegetable, Oval, Colonial Shape, Blue Ridge, 9 ¼ x 7 In. 25.00
Wrinkled Rose, Plate, Bread & Butter, Colonial Shape, Blue Ridge, 6 In. 5.00
Wrinkled Rose, Platter, Oval, Colonial Shape, Blue Ridge, 13 In. 20.00
Yellow Nocturne, Bowl, Vegetable, Colonial Shape, Blue Ridge, 9 ¼ In. 30.00

Yellow Nocturne, Cup & Saucer, Blue Ridge . . . *illus* 14.00
Yellow Nocturne, Plate, Dinner, Colonial Shape, Blue Ridge, 9¼ In. . . . 13.00
Yellow Nocturne, Platter, Oval, Colonial Shape, Blue Ridge, 14 In. . . . 28.00
Yellow Nocturne, Sugar & Creamer, Blue Ridge . . . 25.00

DIONNE QUINTUPLETS were born in Canada on May 28, 1934. The publicity about their birth and their special status as wards of the Canadian government made them famous throughout the world. Visitors could watch the girls play; reporters interviewed the girls and the staff. Thousands of special dolls and souvenirs were made picturing the quints at different ages. Emilie died in 1954, Marie in 1970, Yvonne in 2001. Annette and Cecile still live in Canada.

Ad, Karo Syrup, Food Energy, Children Playing, 1939, 5¼ x 13½ In. . . . 9.00
Calendar, Photos, Quintuplets All Dressed Up, 10 Years Of Age, 1940s . . . 45.00
Dish, Embossed Faces, Names, Metal, Child's, 6 In. . . . 25.00
Doll, Cecile, Composition, Eyes, Oiled, Alexander, 14 In. . . . 525.00
Doll, Toddler, Mohair Wig, Clothing, Bar Name Pin, 1930s, 8 In., 5 Piece . . . 2900.00
Doll, Yvonne, Clothing, Pin, Jointed, Toddler, Composition, Alexander, 7½ In. . . . 299.00
Dolls, Babies, Nurse, Madame Alexander, Composition, Furniture, c.1935 . . . 1550.00
Dolls, Quintuplets, Crib, Bedding, Batiste Nighties, Pink Smocking, 1935, 7½ In. . . . 1650.00
Fan, Advertising, Paper, 8½ x 8 x 14 In. . . . 25.00
Handkerchief, Embroidered Quintuplet Faces, 1940 . . . 45.00
Mug, Crystal Glasbake, Quintuplets . . . 18.00
Postcard, Black & White, N.F.A. Service, 1937, 3½ x 5¼ In. . . . 22.00
Postcard, Dafoe Hospital, Playhouse, Lines Of People Waiting To Visit . . . 13.00

DIRK VAN ERP was born in 1860 and died in 1933. He opened his own studio in 1908 in Oakland, California. He moved his studio to San Francisco in 1909 and the studio remained under the direction of his son until 1977. Van Erp made hammered copper accessories, including vases, desk sets, bookends, candlesticks, jardinieres, and trays, but he is best known for his lamps. The hammered copper lamps often had shades with mica panels.

Ash Pan, Copper, Highly Polished, P Finial, Impressed Mark, 11 x 7 In. . . . 290.00
Basket, Copper, Hammered, Cutouts To Handle, Patina, 11½ x 7½ In. . . . 1800.00
Blotter, Copper, Hammered, Monogram, Patina, Impressed Mark, 2¾ x 5½ In. . . . 120.00
Blotter, Hammered Monogram, Impressed Mark, 5½ x 2¾ In. . . . 120.00
Bowl, Copper, Hammered, Sculpted, Original Patina, Impressed Mark, 3 x 10½ In. . . . 840.00
Cigar Box, Hammered, Hinged Lid, Applied Silver Monogram, OM, 2¾ x 10 x 6 In. . . . 690.00
Fire Tools Set, Stand, Copper, c.1912, 32½ In. . . . 15600.00
Jardiniere, Bulbous, Rolled Rim, Copper, Hammered, Patina, 16 x 7½ In. . . . 6000.00
Jardiniere, Copper, Hammered, Marked, 13 x 14½ In. . . . 3000.00
Lamp, Bean Pot, Copper, Hammered, 4-Panel Mica Shade, 12 x 11¼ In. . . . 6600.00
Lamp, Copper, Hammered Base, Cone Shaped Copper Shade, Marked, 11 In. . . . 3600.00
Lamp, Copper, Hammered, 4-Panel Mica Shade, Bulbous Base, 16 x 14 In. . . . 7800.00
Lamp, Copper, Hammered, Mica & Copper Shade, Cone Shape, 11½ x 11 In. . . . 3600.00
Lamp, Copper, Hammered, Mica Shade, 3-Light, Patina, 18 x 19 In. . . . *illus* 13200.00
Lamp, Copper, Hammered, Mica, 4-Panel Shade, Vented Cap, Stamped, 20 x 17¼ In. . . . 10200.00
Lamp, Copper, Hammered, Mica, Paneled Shade, c.1905, 24 x 24 In. . . . 57600.00
Lamp, Copper, Mica, Shouldered Base, Orange Red Shade, 11½ x 15 In. . . . 16800.00
Lamp, Table, Copper, Hammered, 4-Panel Mica Shade, 2 Sockets, 16½ x 15½ In. . . . 8400.00
Vase, Copper, 2 Handles, Marked, 10¼ In. . . . 6600.00
Vase, Copper, Hammered, Fluted Rim, Cylindrical Base, Patina, 1903, 25½ x 14¼ In. . . . 5300.00

DISNEYANA is a collectors' term. Walt Disney and his company introduced many comic characters to the world. Collectors search for examples of the work of the Disney Studios and the many commercial products modeled after his characters, including Mickey Mouse and Donald Duck, and recent films, like *Beauty and the Beast* and *The Little Mermaid*.

Bank, Donald Duck, Lever, Tin Lithograph, Marx, Box, 1940, 4 In. . . . 454.00
Bank, Mickey Mouse, Jam Jar, Glass, Tin Lid, Embossed, 1930s, 6 In. . . . 86.00
Bank, Mickey Mouse Treasure Chest, Brown, Vinyl, Metal, Zell Products . . . 129.00
Bank, Mickey Mouse Treasure Chest, Green, Vinyl, Metal, Zell Products . . . 129.00
Book, Adventures Of Mickey Mouse, Book 1, Red Cloth, Phil McKay, 1931 . . . 1750.00
Book, Donald Duck, Whitman, 1935, 16 Pages . . . 500.00
Book, Mickey Mouse, Alphabet Book, A To Z, 1936 . . . 500.00
Book, Mickey Mouse, Stories, Verses, Puzzles, Games, Whitman, 1936, 12 x 10 In., 40 Pages . . 1850.00
Book, Pluto, The Pup, 1937, 12 Pages . . . 225.00
Book, Pop-Up, Minnie Mouse, 1933 . . . 150.00 to 175.00

How Bright the Light?
The light from one regular 60-watt light bulb is equal to the light from twenty-five double-wick whale-oil lamps used in the nineteenth century.

D

Dirk Van Erp, Lamp, Copper, Hammered, Mica Shade, 3-Light, Patina, 18 x 19 In.
$13200.00

TIP

Moving is a collector's nightmare. Rolls of paper that schools use to cover lunch tables are best. Cut the paper to different sizes before starting to pack. Put paper plates between plates. Wrap saucers 10 to 15 together at one time. Put paper napkins between the cover of a teapot and the upside down lid. Toilet paper tubes are good holders for mustard spoons or ladles. Disposable diapers are best for large items.

Disneyana, Clock, Alarm, 3 Little Pigs, Big Bad Wolf, Ingersoll, 1934
$633.00

Disneyana, Doll, Mickey & Minnie Mouse, Printed Face, Oilcloth Eyes, 1930s, 13 In., Pair
$700.00

Disneyana, Doll, Snow White, Plastic, Fashion Academy Award, Box, 1952, 14 In.
$1750.00

Disneyana, Doll, Snow White & Seven Dwarfs, Composition, Cloth, Ideal, 21½ In.
$425.00

Bowl, Mickey Mouse, Large, Beetleware, 1930s		65.00
Bracelet, Snow White & Seven Dwarfs, 8 Metal Charms, Enamel Paint, c.1938		40.00
Calendar, Various Characters, Morrell Hames, Smith Market, 1942, 8 x 20 In., 12 Pages		356.00
Candleholder, Mickey Mouse, 5-Light, Cypress Novelty, 1930s		85.00
Candleholder, Mickey Mouse, Unopened, c.1930, 5¾ x 1¼ In., 5 Piece		85.00
Cigarette Case, Mickey Mouse, Steel, 3¾ x 4½ x 1 In.		73.00
Clock, Alarm, 3 Little Pigs, Big Bad Wolf, Ingersoll, 1934	*illus*	633.00
Clock, Alarm, Mickey Mouse, Head Bobs, Metal, 5 In.		186.00
Clock, Alarm, Mickey Mouse, Red Case, Nickel Finish, Bayard, France, Box, 1930s, 4½ In.		143.00
Clock, Alarm, Mickey Mouse, White, Ingersoll, 1947, 4½ In.		144.00
Clock, Mickey Mouse, Yellow, Bakelite, Rounded Top, c.1947, 4½ In.		88.00
Cookie Jar, Bambi, Tree Trunk Form, Enesco		105.00
Costume, Mouseketeers, Western, Cooper-Iskin Inc., c.1955, 4 Piece		140.00
Decanter, Walrus, Removable Head, Goebel, 1950-56, 7 In.		401.00
Desk, Mickey & Minnie Mouse, Kohler, 26 x 27 x 15¾ In., Pair		1210.00
Disneyana, Cel, see Animation Art category		
Doll, Donald Duck, Band Leader, Stuffed, Cloth, Oilcloth Eyes, c.1936, 16 In.		685.00
Doll, Donald Duck, Stuffed, Felt, Corduroy, Hat, Bowtie, Jacket, c.1940, 12 In.		266.00
Doll, Dopey, Stuffed, Musical, Windup, 11 In.		115.00
Doll, Mickey & Minnie Mouse, Printed Face, Oilcloth Eyes, 1930s, 13 In., Pair	*illus*	700.00
Doll, Mickey Mouse, Cloth, Toothy Grin, Felt Hands, Button Eyes, Dean's Rag Book, 8 In.		345.00
Doll, Mickey Mouse, No Tail, Stitched Cloth Shoes, 14 In.		147.00
Doll, Mickey Mouse, Velvet Body, Celluloid Pie Eyes, 4 Fingers, Knickerbocker, 13 In.		632.00
Doll, Mickey Mouse, Velvet, Plush, Steiff, c.1931, 11½ In.		924.00
Doll, Mickey Mouse, Wood, Jointed, Saucer Shaped Handle, 1930, 4½ In.		360.00 to 465.00
Doll, Pinocchio, Wood, Jointed, Krueger, 1939, 16 In.		275.00
Doll, Snow White, Plastic, Fashion Academy Award, Box, 1952, 14 In.	*illus*	425.00
Doll, Snow White & Seven Dwarfs, Composition, Cloth, Ideal, 21½ In.	*illus*	1750.00
Doorstop, Donald Duck, Cast Iron		550.00
Embroidery Set, Disney Characters, Standard Toycraft Prod., Box, 1939		75.00
Figurine, Bashful, Plastic, Box, 8 In.		160.00
Figurine, Donald Duck, Holding Hockey Stick, Ceramic, Marked DIS 123, 4¼ In.		181.00
Figurine, Donald Duck, Long Bill, Plays Violin, Bisque, 4½ In.		278.00
Figurine, Dumbo, Vernon Kilns, 5¼ In.		75.00
Figurine, Mickey Mouse, Bisque, Japan, 1930, 3½ In.		125.00
Figurine, Mickey Mouse, Dipsy Car, Tin, Windup, Box, Linemar		695.00
Figurine, Mickey Mouse, Express Airplane, Tin, Windup, Marx, Box, 8 In.		287.00
Figurine, Mickey Mouse, Playing Violin, Bisque, 1930s, 4 In.		285.00
Figurine, Mickey Mouse, Riding Pluto, Bisque, 1930s		75.00
Figurine, Mickey Mouse, Twirling Tail, Tin, Windup, Linemar, 5⅝ In.		225.00
Figurine, Mickey Mouse, Twirling Tail, Tin, Windup, Linemar, Box, 5⅝ In.		595.00
Figurine, Mickey Mouse, Wood, Jointed, Ball Shape Hands, Painted, c.1930, 9½ In.		431.00
Figurine, Mickey Mouse, Xylophone Player, Marx, Box, 1950s		350.00
Figurine, Mickey Mouse & Betty Boop, Umbrella, Celluloid, Painted, Japan, 5¼ In.		1265.00
Figurine, Minnie Mouse, Bisque, Japan, 1930, 3½ In.		125.00
Figurine, Minnie Mouse, Celluloid, Jointed, Painted, c.1930, 5 In.		115.00
Figurine, Minnie Mouse, Holding American Flag, Carved, Painted		225.00
Figurine, Minnie Mouse, Rocking Chair, Knitting, Tin, Windup, Disney Productions, 7 In.		750.00
Figurine, Pecos Bill & Widowmaker, Bisque, Melody-Time, 10 In.		100.00
Figurine, Sprite, No. 10, Vernon Kilns, 4½ In.		275.00
Figurine Set, 3 Little Pigs, Bisque, Japan, 1930s, 3½ In., 3 Piece		165.00
Figurine Set, Alice In Wonderland, Rabbit, Ceramic, Painted, c.1951, Pair		350.00
Figurine Set, Huey, Dewey, Louie, Baseball Outfits, Ceramic, 1940s, 2½ In., 3 Piece		125.00
Figurine Set, Snow White, Seven Dwarfs, Beswick, 8 Piece		600.00
Figurine Set, Snow White & Seven Dwarfs, 2nd Version, Wade, 8 Piece		707.00
Figurine Set, Snow White & Seven Dwarfs, Bisque, Borgfeldt, 3½ & 2½ In., 8 Piece		173.00
Figurine Set, Snow White & Seven Dwarfs, Hand Colored, Pottery, 6 & 9 In., 8 Piece		368.00
Figurine Set, Tigger, Owl, Kanga, Piglet, Pooh, Eeyore, Beswick, 6 Piece		390.00
Game, Donald Duck, Bean Bag Party Game, Parker Brothers, 1939, 18¼ x 12½ In.		520.00
Game, Mickey Mouse, Target, Cardboard Lithograph, Box, 18 In.	*illus*	345.00
Game, Snow White, Premium, Tek Toothbrush, 1937		22.00
Game, Snow White & Seven Dwarfs, Board, Parker Brothers, Box, 1938		350.00
Game, Snow White & Seven Dwarfs, Walt Disney's Own Game, Parker Bros., 1938		350.00
Hat, Mouseketeer, Wiggle Ears, Club Logo, Welded Plastic Corp., 1950s, 7 x 6½ In.		86.00
Jug, Snow White & Seven Dwarfs, Squirrel On Handle, Musical, Wadeheath, 8¾ In.		588.00
Lamp, Mickey Mouse, Die Cut Lampshade, Pressed Steel, Soreng-Manegold, 1930s, 10 In.		260.00

ımp, Snow White, Motion, Plastic, Lightcraft Co., 1948, 8 3/4 In. 173.00
ıntern, Pluto, Battery Operated, Linemar, Box, 8 In. 450.00
ıntern, Pluto, Glass, Tin, Battery Operated, Linemar, Box, 7 In. 230.00
ınch Box, Mickey & Minnie Mouse, Passing Note, Pink, Plastic, Aladdin 17.00
ınch Box, Mickey Mouse, School, Metal, Aladdin, 1970s, 7 3/4 x 6 In. 35.00
ovie Projector, Mickey & Minnie Mouse, Hand Crank, Keystone, Box, 1936, 12 x 9 x 6 In. 396.00
ug, Epcot Center, Epcot Emblem, Black Metallic Finish 12.00
apkin Ring, Mickey Mouse, Hand Painted, Celluloid 265.00
odder, Donald Duck, Lead Pendulum, Celluloid, Windup, Metal Base, 1930s, 6 In. 885.00 to 990.00
odder, Donald Duck, Long Bill, Celluloid, Rubber Band Driven, Japan, 6 In. 230.00 to 426.00
odder, Mickey Mouse, Holding Guitar, Celluloid, Tin, Painted, 1930, 7 In. 690.00
odder, Tweedledum, China, 1956, 5 In. 299.00
ail, Mickey Mouse, Tin Lithograph, 1930s 374.00
arade Roadster, Tin, Windup, Marx, 11 In. 1000.00
encil Case, Mickey Mouse, Pluto, Blue, c.1930, 5 x 8 In. 275.00
encil Sharpener, Dumbo, Green, Yellow, Plastic, 1 3/4 In. 86.00
encil Sharpener, Ferdinand The Bull, Red, Figural, Catalin, 1930s, 1 3/4 In. *illus* 86.00
encil Sharpener, Mickey Mouse, Brass Rim, Plastic, Catalin, 1930s, 1 1/8 In. *illus* 145.00
encil Sharpener, Peter & The Wolf, Bakelite, Round, c.1946. 125.00
encil Sharpener, Pluto, Dog House, Red, Green, Yellow, Bakelite, Round, 1 1/8 In. 90.00
encil Sharpener, Snow White, Plastic, 1930s 75.00
icnic Basket, Mickey Mouse, Felix The Cat, Die Cut, Tin, Rogelio Sanchez, Spain, 6 In. 6900.00
illow Cover, Mickey & Minnie Mouse, Vogue Needlecraft, c.1931, 16 In. 85.00
in, Mickey Mouse, Courier, Black, White, 1930s, 2 3/16 In. *illus* 316.00
in, Mickey Mouse, Globe Trotters Member, 1 1/4 In. 58.00
in, Minnie Mouse, Good Teeth 230.00
laying Cards, 3 Little Pigs, Pigs Playing & Singing, c.1930, 52-Card Deck 73.00
luto, Running, Tongue Moves In & Out, Tin, 5 In. 475.00
oster, The Little Mermaid, Ariel & Undersea Friends, 13 x 19 In. 3107.00
urse, Minnie Mouse, Mesh, Enameled Metal Frame, 2 1/2 x 3 In. 733.00
adio, Mickey Mouse, Cello, Wood, Emerson, 1934, 7 x 7 x 5 In. 1760.00 to 2303.00
ocking Chair, Mickey Mouse, Shoo-Fly, Painted, 35 x 16 In. 115.00
alt & Pepper, Dumbo, 3 1/4 x 1 1/2 In. 13.00
alt & Pepper, Mickey & Minnie Mouse, Chefs 20.00
alt & Pepper, Mickey Mouse, Black & White, Germany, 1930s, 2 In. 365.00
ovel, Snow, Mickey Mouse & Pluto, Wood Handle, 1930s 590.00
gn, Mickey Mouse, Sport Figures, Trifold, Ingersoll, 1935, 30 1/4 x 42 In. 2310.00
ap, Mickey Mouse, Clarabelle Cow, Pictorial Products, 1930s, 3 Piece 75.00
raw, Donald Duck, Sunshine, Super Long, Paper, Box, 100 Piece 14.00
ble, Minnie Mouse, Wood, Child's, 16 x 27 x 26 In. 528.00
ble Cover, Snow White, Embroidered, Cotton, 30 x 42 In. 73.00
a Set, Mickey & Minnie, Geo. Borgfeldt Corp., Japan, Box, 1930s, 22 Piece *illus* 290.00
a Set, Mickey & Minnie Mouse, Geo. Borgfeldt, Box, c.1930, 28 Piece. 288.00
a Set, Mickey Mouse, Mickey & Minnie On Teapot, Ceramic, Borgfeldt, Box, 11 Piece 369.00
e Rack, Mickey Mouse, Wood, 8 3/4 In. 140.00
n, Mickey & Minnie Mouse, Snow White, Goofy, 3 Little Pigs, 1939, 8 x 12 1/8 In. 160.00
n, Mickey Mouse, c.1935, 7 1/4 x 10 x 8 In. 385.00
n, Snow White & Seven Dwarfs, Snow White, Sleeping, 1939, 8 x 12 1/8 In. 160.00
othbrush Holder, 3 Little Pigs, Painted, Bisque, c.1930, 4 x 4 In. 90.00
othbrush Holder, Donald Duck, Bisque, Japan, Marked Walt E. Disney, 1930s, 5 In. 325.00
othbrush Holder, Donald Duck, Mickey & Minnie, Tray, Bisque, Japan, 1930s, 4 1/2 In. 260.00
othbrush Holder, Donald Duck, Mickey & Minnie, Bisque, Japan, 3 1/2 x 4 1/2 In. 179.00
othbrush Holder, Mickey & Minnie Mouse, Jointed, Painted, Bisque, Japan, 4 In. 460.00
othbrush Holder, Mickey & Minnie Mouse, Pluto, Painted, Japan, 4 x 3 3/4 In. 90.00
othbrush Holder, Mickey & Minnie Mouse On Sofa With Pluto, Bisque 295.00
y, Cinderella, Railcar, Mice, Composition, Tin Lithograph, Windup, Wells-Brimtoy, Box 1955.00
y, Disney, Ferris Wheel, Tin, Windup, Chein, 1950s, 16 In. 550.00
y, Disney, Ferris Wheel, Tin Lithograph, Windup, 16 1/2 In. 448.00
y, Disneyland, Carousel, Happy Birthday, Bells Ring, Tin Lithograph, Ross Products, Box, 9 In. 115.00
y, Disneyland, Carousel, Happy Birthday, Celluloid, Tin, Windup, Borgfeldt, 7 1/4 In. 586.00
y, Disneyland, Melody Player, Music Rolls, Crank, Tin Lithograph, Chein, Box, 6 3/4 x 7 In. 201.00
y, Disneyland, Monorail, Plastic, No.6333G, Schuco, Box, 14 1/2 In. 334.00
y, Disneyland, Van & Trailer, Characters On Truck, Tin, Friction, 12 In. 1380.00
y, Doc, Painted, Rubber, Seiberling, 1940s, 6 In. 95.00
y, Donald Duck, Acrobat, Celluloid, Windup, Linemar 275.00
y, Donald Duck, Carousel, Celluloid, Tin, Windup, Borgfeldt, 6 1/2 In. 380.00

Disneyana, Game, Mickey Mouse, Target, Cardboard Lithograph, Box, 18 In.
$345.00

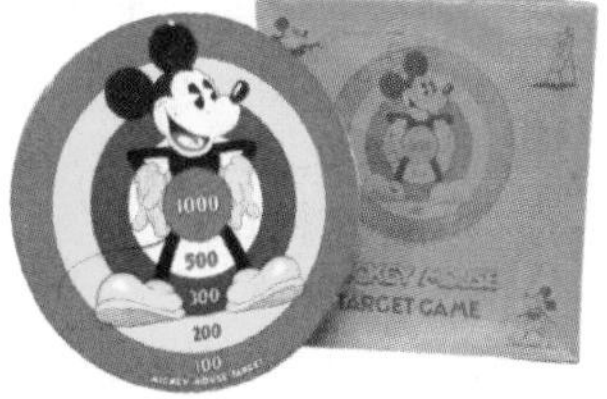

Disneyana, Pencil Sharpener, Ferdinand The Bull, Red, Figural, Catalin, 1930s, 1 3/4 In.
$86.00

Disneyana, Pencil Sharpener, Mickey Mouse, Brass Rim, Plastic, Catalin, 1930s, 1 1/8 In.
$145.00

Disneyana, Pin, Mickey Mouse, Courier, Black, White, 1930s, 2 3/16 In.
$316.00

TIP

Take batteries with you to toy sales if you plan to buy a battery-operated toy. Check to see if the toy really works.

Disneyana, Tea Set, Mickey & Minnie, Geo. Borgfeldt Corp., Japan, Box, 1930s, 22 Piece
$290.00

Disneyana, Toy, Donald Duck, Pluto, Rail Car, Composition, Tin, Clockwork, Lionel, Box, 11 In.
$690.00

Disneyana, Toy, Ferdinand The Bull, Matador, Windup, Marx, Box, 8 In.
$690.00

Disneyana, Toy, Mickey Mouse, Tow Truck, Plastic, Remote Control, Andy Gard, Box, 9 In.
$180.00

Toy, Donald Duck, Carousel, Celluloid, Tin, Windup, Borgfeldt, Box, 10½ In. 3278.0
Toy, Donald Duck, Carousel, Celluloid, Tin, Windup, Borgfeldt, Box, 7½ In. 1293.0
Toy, Donald Duck, Composition, Windup, Walker, Box, 7 In. 748.0
Toy, Donald Duck, Crawler, Long Bill, Head Moves Side To Side, 9¾ In. 735.0
Toy, Donald Duck, Crawler, Short Bill, Head Moves Side To Side, 6¾ In. 396.0
Toy, Donald Duck, Dipsy Car, Tin, Windup, Linemar, Box, 5¾ In. 575.0
Toy, Donald Duck, Driver, Tin, Windup, Marx, Box, 6½ In. 690.0
Toy, Donald Duck, Drummer, Tin Lithograph, Windup, Linemar, 6 In. 316.0
Toy, Donald Duck, Drummer, Tin, Windup, Marx, Box, 6 In. 661.0
Toy, Donald Duck, Fireman, Climbing, Tin, Windup, Linemar, Box, 13½ In. 431.0
Toy, Donald Duck, Goofy, Duet, Tin Litho, Windup, Louis Marx, 1940, 9¾ In. 595.0
Toy, Donald Duck, Long Bill, Walks, Windup, Celluloid, 1930s, 5¼ In. 860.0
Toy, Donald Duck, Long Bill, Pop-Up, Paperboard Jack-In-The-Box, Celluloid, 1930s 485.0
Toy, Donald Duck, Pedaling Cart, Talks, Wood, Pull Toy, Fisher-Price, Box, 8 In. 281.0
Toy, Donald Duck, Pluto, Rail Car, Composition, Tin, Clockwork, Lionel, Box, 11 In. . . . *illus* 690.0
Toy, Donald Duck, Pluto, Rail Car, Orange House, Green Roof, Steel, Windup, Box, Lionel, 10 In. 2588.0
Toy, Donald Duck, Pluto, Rail Car, White House, Green Roof, Steel, Windup, Box, Lionel, 10 In. . . 863.0
Toy, Donald Duck, Pulling Pluto In Cart, Fisher-Price, No. 149, c.1936, 15 In. 920.0
Toy, Donald Duck, Rocking Horse, Windup, Plastic, Illco Toy Co. 15.0
Toy, Donald Duck, Roly Poly, Bell, Celluloid, 4 In. 96.0
Toy, Donald Duck, Skier, Plastic, Windup, Box, Marx, c.1970 . . . . 388.0
Toy, Donald Duck, Straight Shooter, Plastic, Windup, Mavco, Box, 6 In. 488.0
Toy, Donald Duck, Tricycle, Celluloid, Tin, Windup, 4 In. 399.0
Toy, Donald Duck, Tricycle, Tin, Celluloid, Japan, 4 In. 395.0
Toy, Donald Duck, Waddler, Long Bill, Celluloid, Windup, Borgfeldt, Box, 5½ In. 1150.0
Toy, Donald Duck, Walker, Long Bill, Celluloid, Windup, 1930s, 5¼ In. . . . . 860.00 to 895.0
Toy, Donald Duck, Walker, Tin, Celluloid, Windup, Japan, Box, 3 In. 546.0
Toy, Donald Duck, Walker, Windup, Box, 7 In. 400.0
Toy, Donald Duck & Pluto, Handcar, Track, Windup, Lionel, Box, 1930s 1250.0
Toy, Donald Duck & Pluto Handcar, Quacks, Windup, Lionel, 10 In. 230.0
Toy, Donald Duck Racing Kart, Plastic, Marx, 6 In. 345.0
Toy, Dopey, Walker, Tin, Windup, Marx, 8⅛ In. . . . . 345 to 362.0
Toy, Dumbo, Acrobatic Elephant, Flips Over, Tin, Windup, Marx, Box, 4 In. 633.0
Toy, Dumbo, Windup, 1941 . . . . 450.0
Toy, Ferdinand The Bull, Matador, Windup, Marx, Box, 8 In. . . . . *illus* 690.0
Toy, Goofy, Turns In Circles, Tail Spins, Linemar 350.0
Toy, Goofy, Unicycle, Tin, Windup, Linemar, 5¾ In. 759.0
Toy, Jiminy Cricket, Walker, Tin, Windup, Linemar, 7 In. 546.0
Toy, Lady & The Tramp, Bus, Tin, Friction, Japan, 14 In. 225.0
Toy, Merry Makers Band, Conductor, Tin Lithograph, Windup, Marx, Box, 9½ In. 2300.0
Toy, Mickey & Minnie Mouse, Acrobats, Wood, Pull Toy, 1930, 11 x 6 In. 1725.0
Toy, Mickey & Minnie Mouse, Handcar, Steel, Composition, Clockwork, Lionel, 10 In. . . 805.00 to 863.0
Toy, Mickey & Minnie Mouse, Handcar, Steel, Composition, Clockwork, Lionel, 8¾ In. 515.0
Toy, Mickey & Minnie Mouse, Handcar, Steel, Composition, Clockwork, Lionel, Box, 10 In. . . . 1725.0
Toy, Mickey & Minnie Mouse, Organ Grinder, Minnie Dances, Germany, c.1931, 6 In. 3162.0
Toy, Mickey & Minnie Mouse, Riding Elephant, Celluloid, Windup, Japan, 9½ In. 4313.0
Toy, Mickey & Minnie Mouse, Top, Red Ground, 1930s, 7 x 6½ In. 237.0
Toy, Mickey Mouse, Acrobat, Trapeze, Celluloid, Windup, Linemar, Box, 6 In. 288.0
Toy, Mickey Mouse, Blocks, Safety, Wood, Halsam, Box, 1930s, 1¼ In., 20 Piece 110.0
Toy, Mickey Mouse, Convertible, Tin, Celluloid, Friction, Linemar, 4¾ In. 288.0
Toy, Mickey Mouse, Dipsy Car, Tin Lithograph, Windup, Linemar, 5¼ In. 345.0
Toy, Mickey Mouse, Dipsy Car, Tin, Windup, Box, 6 In. 747.0
Toy, Mickey Mouse, Drawing Set, Cowboy, Graphite, Red & Green Pencil, c.1930, 12 x 9½ In. . 263.0
Toy, Mickey Mouse, Driver Car, Windup, US Zone Germany, 4 In. 725.0
Toy, Mickey Mouse, Drum, Tin Lithograph, 1930s, 5¼ x 9 In. 288.0
Toy, Mickey Mouse, Drummer, Plunger, Tin, 6½ In. 989.0
Toy, Mickey Mouse, Pluto, Drum, Wood, Paper, Push Toy, Fisher-Price, 1935, 12 In. 891.0
Toy, Mickey Mouse, Race Car, No. 5, Tin Lithograph, Windup, Lindstrom, 4 In. 230.0
Toy, Mickey Mouse, Rambler, Celluloid, Windup, 1930s, 7¼ In. 1350.0
Toy, Mickey Mouse, Ramblin Mickey, Waddles, Celluloid, Windup, 7½ In. 1017.0
Toy, Mickey Mouse, Riding Horse, Occupied Japan, 6½ x 5½ In. 2200.0
Toy, Mickey Mouse, Riding Pluto, Tin, Windup, Linemar, 7 In. 1035.0
Toy, Mickey Mouse, Roly Poly, Orange, White, Celluloid, Japan, 7⅞ In. 690.0
Toy, Mickey Mouse, Roly Poly, Seated On Pink Ball, Jointed, Japan, 1930s, 3½ In. 201.0
Toy, Mickey Mouse, Scooter Jockey, Head Bobs, Plastic, Windup, Mavco, Box, c.1950, 6 In. . . 150.00 to 175.0
Toy, Mickey Mouse, Sparkler, Die Cut, Tin Lithograph, Chein, 5½ In. 144.0

oy, Mickey Mouse, Sparkler, Plunger, Tin, 5 ½ In. 435.00
oy, Mickey Mouse, Top, Friends, Musical, Tin Lithograph, Chein, Box, 7 In. 144.00
oy, Mickey Mouse, Top, Minnie, Baby Minnie, Donald Duck, Horace Horsecollar, Tin, 7 In. 178.00
oy, Mickey Mouse, Tow Truck, Plastic, Remote Control, Andy Gard, Box, 9 In. *illus* 180.00
oy, Mickey Mouse, Tractor, Rubber, Red, White Wheels, 5 In. 350.00
oy, Mickey Mouse, Tricycle, Celluloid, Wood, Pull Toy, Japan, 3 ¾ In. 373.00
oy, Mickey Mouse, Tricycle, Tin, Celluloid, Linemar, Box, 4 In. 460.00
oy, Mickey Mouse, Tricycle, Tin, Celluloid, Windup, Linemar, Box, c.1955, 3 ½ In. 386.00
oy, Mickey Mouse, Twirling Tail, Plastic, Windup, Box 525.00
oy, Mickey Mouse, Twirling Tail, Plastic, Windup, Marx, Box, 7 ½ In. 287.00
oy, Mickey Mouse, Twirling Tail, Tin, Windup, Linemar, Box, 5 ½ In. 288.00
oy, Mickey Mouse, Typewriter, Mouseketeers, No. 41, 4 ¾ x 10 ⅜ x 7 In. 90.00
oy, Mickey Mouse, Walker, Cloth Outfit, Composition, Windup, Germany, 7 ½ In. 460.00
oy, Mickey Mouse, Walker, Red, White, Black, Celluloid, Windup, Japan, 1934, 8 In. 978.00
oy, Mickey Mouse, Xylophone Player, Tin, Windup, Linemar, 1950s, 6 In. 316.00
oy, Mickey Mouse & Donald Duck, Boat, Celluloid, 1930s 1475.00
oy, Mickey Mouse & Donald Duck, Canoe, Celluloid, Japan, 5 ¾ In. 690.00
oy, Mickey Mouse & Donald Duck, Handcar, Windup, Wells-O-London, Box, 8 In. 1150.00
oy, Mickey Mouse & Pluto, Cart, Celluloid, Tin, Japan, 5 In. 747.00
oy, Mickey Mouse Riding Pluto, Celluloid, 1930s, 3 ¼ In. 125.00
oy, Mickey Mouse Watering Can, Tin Lithograph, 1930s, 6 In. 259.00
oy, Minnie Mouse, Luggage, Felix, Tin Litho, Windup, Rogelio Sanchez, Spain, 6 ⅞ In. 10350.00
oy, Minnie Mouse, Rocking Chair, Knitting, Tin, Linemar, Box, 7 In. *illus* 495.00
oy, Pinocchio, Express, Fisher-Price, Pull Toy, 1930s, 12 x 10 In. 195.00
oy, Pinocchio, Express, Rides Unicycle, Pulling Cart, Wood, Paper, Fisher-Price, 11 In. 368.00
oy, Pinocchio, Pull Toy, Fisher-Price, 1939, 8 ½ In. 395.00
oy, Pinocchio, Waddler, Eyes Move Up & Down, Tin, 8 ½ In. 706.00
oy, Pinocchio, Walker, Buckets In Hand, Tin, Windup, Marx, 1939, 8 ¾ In. 374.00
oy, Pinocchio, Walker, Tin Lithograph, Windup, Linemar, Japan, 6 In. 115.00
oy, Pinocchio, Walker, Windup, Marx, Box, 8 In. 316.00
oy, Pluto, Acrobat, Celluloid, Windup, Linemar, Box, 9 In. 288.00
oy, Pluto, Drum Major, Tin Lithograph, Clockwork, Linemar, Box, 6 ½ In. *illus* 420.00
oy, Pluto, Head Bobs, Tail Spins, Windup, Linemar 350.00
oy, Pluto, Roll Over, Rubber Tail & Ears, Marx, Box, 8 In. 287.00
oy, Pluto, Roll Over, Tin Lithograph, Windup, Marx, Box, 1939, 3 x 8 ¼ In. 747.00
oy, Pluto, Tricycle, Celluloid, Windup, Linemar, Box, 3 ¾ In. 288.00
oy, Pluto, Tricycle, Tin, Celluloid, Windup, Linemar, Box, 3 ¾ In. 625.00
oy, Snow White & Seven Dwarfs, Bisque, Box, 1930s, 5 & 4 In. 550.00
oy, Submarine, 20,000 Leagues Under The Sea, Nautilus, Windup, Steel, Walt Disney 350.00
oy, Tinkerbell, Plays 6 Bells, Tin, Plastic, Peter Puppet Playthings, 1953, 16 In. 184.00
oy, Train, Disneyland Express Casey Jr., Tin, Windup 250.00
oy, Train, Disneyland Express, Tin, Windup, Marx 675.00
oy, Windup, Donald Duck, Marx, Original Box, 1940s 890.00
ain, Mickey Mouse, Melody Railroad, Tin, Plastic, Battery, Frankonia, Box, 1967, 7 In. 235.00
ain, Mickey Mouse, Melody Railroad, Tin, Plastic, Rubber, Battery, Frankonia, Japan, Box, 15 In. 115.00
ain, Mickey Mouse Express, Lionel, Box, 1976, 12 Piece 1500.00
umbler, Horace Horsecollar, c.1938, 4 ¾ x 2 ¾ In. 110.00
mbrella, Mickey Mouse, Donald Duck, Pluto, Donald Duck Handle, Walt Disney Prod. 250.00
atch, Pocket, Mickey Mouse, Box, 1933 *illus* 316.00
ristwatch, 3 Little Pigs, Metal Link Band, c.1934 1020.00
ristwatch, Mickey Mouse, Blue Strap, U.S. Time 118.00
ristwatch, Mickey Mouse, Celluloid, England, 1930s, 1 ¼ In. 2245.00
ristwatch, Mickey Mouse, Leather Strap, Ingersoll Watch Co., c.1930 220.00

OCTOR, *see Dental and Medical categories*

OLL entries are listed by marks printed or incised on the doll, if possible. If there are no marks, e doll is listed by the name of the subject or country or maker. Notice that Barbie is listed nder Mattel. G.I. Joe figures are listed in the Toy section. Eskimo dolls are listed in the Eskimo ction and Indian dolls are listed in the Indian section. Doll clothes and accessories are listed at the end this section. The twentieth-century clothes listed here are in mint condition.

OLL

M., 253, Nobbikid, Bisque, Googly, Mohair Wig, Composition Body, Mark, 6 In. 470.00
M., 323, Bisque Head, Googly Sleep Eyes, Glancing Left, Composition, Jointed, 5 ¾ In. 353.00
M., 324, Bisque Socket Head, Googly Eyes, 5-Piece Composition Body, Toddler, 10 In. 1008.00
M., 327, Bisque Head, Intaglio, Side Glancing Eyes, 5-Piece Composition, Boy, 6 ½ In. 176.00

Disneyana, Toy, Minnie Mouse, Rocking Chair, Knitting, Tin, Linemar, Box, 7 In.
$495.00

Disneyana, Toy, Pluto, Drum Major, Tin Lithograph, Clockwork, Linemar, Box, 6 ½ In.
$420.00

Disneyana, Watch, Pocket, Mickey Mouse, Box, 1933
$316.00

TIP

If your battery-operated toy stops working, try sanding the terminals and the ends of the batteries. There may be slight corrosion that interferes with the battery connections.

Doll, Alabama Baby, Cloth Shoulder Head, Stitched-On Ears, Painted, Canvas, 13 In.
$1058.00

Doll, Amberg, Bisque Head, Sleep Eyes, Cloth Body, Celluloid Hands, 1914, 12 In.
$95.00

Doll, Automaton, Woman Photographer, Bisque, Key Wind, c.1890, 16 x 12 x 7 In.
$25085.00

A.M., 353, Bisque Socket Head, Asian, Sleep Eyes, Composition, Germany, c.1925, 14 In. 1232.0

A.M., 353, Bisque Socket Head, Asian, Sleep Eyes, Composition, Germany, c.1925, 9 In. 785.0

A.M., 353, Bisque Socket Head, Solid Dome, Asian, Sleep Eyes, Composition, Germany, c.1925, 9 In. 560.0

A.M., 400, Bisque, Socket Head, Sleep Eyes, Mohair Wig, Ball Jointed, 20 In. 2300.0

A.M., 1894, Boy, Bisque Head, Mohair Wig, Glass Eyes, Composition Body, 1900s, 14½ In. 294.0

A.M., 401, Flapper, Bisque Socket Head, Sleep Eyes, Mohair, Composition, Wood, 13 In. 2688.0

A.M., Bisque, Socket Head, Googly, Glass Eyes, Mohair Wig, 253, 13 In. 3000.0

A.M., Bisque Head, Brown Glass Sleep Eyes, Open Mouth, Bent Limb Body, Baby, 26 In. 518.0

A.M., Bisque Head, Sleep Eyes, Teeth, Felt Tongue, Jointed Kid Body, 27 In. 147.0

A.M., Bisque Socket Head, Closed Mouth, Glass Eyes, Composition, 10½ In. 460.0

A.M., Blue Glass Googly Sleep Eyes, Button Nose, Closed Mouth, Mohair Wig, 12 In. 1725.0

Advertising, Blue Bonnet Sue, Original Tag, Dakin, 11 In. 19.0

Advertising, Brandy, G.E. Co., Wood, Composition, Red Uniform, Baton 470.0

Advertising, Kellogg's, Snap, Plastic, Painted, 1960s, 7½ In. 30.0

Advertising, McDonald's Hamburglar, Cloth, 16 In. 30.0

Advertising, Radiotron, General Electric Radio, 1930s 848.0

Advertising, Sunbeam Bread, Vinyl, Blond Hair, Blue Dress, White Dots, Horsman 115.0

Alabama Baby, Cloth, Brown Eyes, Closed Mouth, 1919, 30 In. 1232.0

Alabama Baby, Cloth, Pressed, Oil Painted Shoulder Head, Ella Smith, 18 In. 2600.0

Alabama Baby, Cloth, Pressed, Oil Painted, Bobbed Hair, Stitch-Jointed, Ella Smith, 18 In. 1064.0

Alabama Baby, Cloth, Pressed, Oil Painted, Human Hair, Stitch-Jointed, Ella Smith, 30 In. 1232.0

Alabama Baby, Cloth, Pressed, Oil Painted, Pale Complexion, Stitched Ears, Ella Smith, 18 In. 1344.0

Alabama Baby, Cloth, Pressed, Oil Painted, Stitched-On Ears, Ella Smith, 19 In. 1568.0

Alabama Baby, Cloth, Pressed, Oil Painted, Stitch-Jointed, Ella Smith, 22 In. 2128.0

Alabama Baby, Cloth Shoulder Head, Stitched-On Ears, Painted, Canvas, 13 In. *illus* 1058.0

Alabama Baby, Mammy, Cloth, Brown, Painted Features, Shawl, Bandana, 1919, 22 In. 6275.0

Alabama Baby, Pressed, Oil Painted Face, Closed Mouth, Stitch-Jointed, Ella Smith, 24 In. 2912.0

Alexander dolls are listed in this category under Madame Alexander.

Alt Beck & Gottschalck, Turned Shoulder Head, Closed Mouth, Glass Blue Eyes, 19 In. 690.0

Amberg, Bisque Head, Sleep Eyes, Cloth Body, Celluloid Hands, 1914, 12 In. *illus* 95.0

American Character, Betsy McCall, Sleep Eyes, Tosca Wig, 7-Piece Body, 1957, 8 In. 137.0

American Character, Betsy McCall, Vinyl Socket Head, Sleep Eyes, 1958, 24 In. 455.0

Armand Marseille dolls are listed in this category under A.M.

Arranbee, Littlest Angel, Plastic, Blond Wig, Walker, Polka Dot Dress, Box, c.1955, 11 In. 165.0

Arranbee, Nancy Lee, Cinderella, Lavender Taffeta, Leaves & Flowers, 1949, 14 In. 850.0

Arranbee, Nanette, Sleep Eyes, Blond Wig, Plastic, Walker, Dress, 1950s, 14 In. 110.0

Automaton, Bisque, Cork Pate, Glass Eyes, Mohair Wig, Musical, Gustav Vichy, c.1875, 21 In. 23520.0

Automaton, Buffalo Bill, Papier-Mache Head, Paperweight Eyes, Gustav Vichy, 28 In. 67200.0

Automaton, Cyclist, From Gambling Game, High Wheel Bicycle, Spoked Wheels, 10 In. 1410.0

Automaton, Dancer, 3 Musicians, Bisque Heads, Glass Eyes, France, 16 x 11 x 6 In. 5880.0

Automaton, Girl Playing Piano, Bisque, Wood, J.B. Secor, Box 17000.0

Automaton, Harlequin, Bisque Head, Glass Eyes, Mohair, Music Box, c.1905, 17 In. 3808.0

Automaton, Mae West, Frank Dale, Peach Gown, Feather Boa, Hat, 36 In. 6900.0

Automaton, Moroccan Harpist, Papier-Mache Head, Paperweight Eyes, G. Vichy, 19 In. 11750.0

Automaton, Organ Grinder, Monkey, Donkey, Zinner & Sohne, c.1890, 13 In. 2240.0

Automaton, Page Boy, Seated With Violin, Velvet Box, Gustav Vichy, 14 In. 4480.0

Automaton, Winter Girl, Snow Bird, Bisque, Human Hair, Roullet & Decamps, 23 In. 6500.0

Automaton, Woman, Seated, Holding Feathered Fan, Flowers, Turns To Side, Dog, 22 In. 7670.0

Automaton, Woman Photographer, Bisque, Key Wind, c.1890, 16 x 12 x 7 In. *illus* 25085.0

Automaton, Young Girl With Seashell & Flute, Platform, Music Box, Bisque, 20 In. 5250.0

Bahr & Proschild, 2072, Socket Head, Glass Sleep Eyes, Human Hair, c.1915, 14 In. 1300.0

Barbie dolls are listed in this category under Mattel.

Bisque, Chimney Sweep, Black Painted, Carries Ladder, Brush, c.1915, 3½ In. 308.0

Bisque, Glass Eyes, Joined Arms & Legs, Paper Hat, Stick Horse, 20th Century, 4 In. 121.0

Bisque, Glass Inset Eyes, Mohair Wig, Pin Jointed, Twins, 3½ In. 336.0

Bisque, Open Mouth, Sleep Eyes, Shaker Dress, Bonnet, Leather Shoes, 12½ In. 1170.0

Bisque, Swivel Head, Googly, Glass Sleep Eyes, Mohair Wig, c.1915, 7 In. 1300.0

Bisque Head, Brown Sleep Eyes, Painted Lashes, Brows, Jointed, Child, France, 31 In. 690.0

Bisque Head, Mohair Wig, 3-Wheeled Tin Platform, Playing Badminton, c.1875, 13 In. 4480.0

Bisque Socket Head, Enamel Eyes, Mohair Wig, Cork Pate, Composition, c.1878, 16 In. 11200.0

Bisque Socket Head, Mohair Wig, Composition, Jointed Shoulders, c.1914, 22 In. 2400.0

Bisque Socket Head, Sleep Eyes, Mohair Wig, Composition, Ball-Jointed, c.1918, 25 In. 2000.0

Bisque Swivel Head, Blue Googly Eyes, Kid-Lined Body, Jointed, c.1915, 7 In. 896.0

Bisque Swivel Head, Glass Eyes, Mohair Wig, Jointed Arms, Sculpted Smock, 3 In. 450.0

Bisque Swivel Head, Glass Paperweight Eyes, Closed Mouth, Hinged Hips, 21 In. 16800.0

Black dolls are also included in the Black category.

u Jne, Closed Mouth, Blue Paperweight Eyes, Painted Brows, Lashes, Bebe, c.1890, 27 ½ In. 5750.00
uckner, Topsy-Turvy, Cloth, Black, White Painted Faces, Red, White Gingham, 1900, 11 In. 205.00
uno Schmidt, Wendy, Blue Glass Eyes, Painted Lashes, Brows, Dress, c.1910, 13 In. 6038.00
e-Lo, Bisque Head, Blue Glass Sleep Eyes, Molded Painted Hair, 16 ½ In. 230.00
e Lo, Bisque Head, Glass Sleep Eye, Closed Mouth, Cloth Body, Celluloid Hands, 20 In. 345.00
meo, Pete The Pup, Composition Head, Wood, Jointed, 1930s, 9 In. 345.00
meo, Scootles, Plastic, Jointed, Wrist Tag, 15 ½ In. *illus* 80.00
ase, Girl, Blond Bobbed Hair, Painted Face, Bare Feet, c.1917 Dress, 12 ½ In. 1020.00
ase, Painted Eyes, Textured Hair, Cotton Sateen Body, Child, 13 In. 206.00
ina Shoulder Head, Curly Hair, Molded, Painted Face, Cloth Body, China Limbs, 24 In. 460.00
ina Shoulder Head, Painted Eyes, Plaited Bun, Gusseted, Kid Body, 22 ½ In. 9106.00
ina Shoulder Head, Pink Tinted, Painted Eyes, Cloth Body, Kid Hands, Boy, 19 In. 3055.00
oth, Babe Ruth, Composition, N.Y. Yankees Uniform, Hat, 29 In. 2310.00
oth, Notre Dame Fighting Irish, 1950s, 11 In. 45.00
oth, Painted Hair, Sewing Society Of Moravian Church, c.1872, 17 In. 4704.00
oth, Stockinet Mask Face, Oil-Painted Features, Stitch-Jointed, c.1930, 17 In. 235.00
oth, Stuffed Head, Sculpted & Embroidered Features, Individual Fingers, 1800s, 25 In. 132.00
lumbian, Cloth, Flat Face, Seamed Head, Stitch-Jointed, Emma Adams, 15 In. 2016.00
mposition, Socket Head, Marching Man, Holding Baton, Ball-Jointed, c.1930, 18 In. 896.00
nte & Boehme, Porcelain, Sculpted Hair, Standing, Bathing Suit, c.1885, 18 In. 800.00
namur, Blue Glass Eyes, Painted Eyelashes, Brows, Composition Body, Bebe, 24 In. 1560.00
or Of Hope, Manchu Woman, Carved Headdress & Feet, 12 In. 6612.00
or Of Hope, Rice Farmer, Wooden Head, Cloth Body, Grass Shawl, Skirt, Hat, 12 In. 1610.00
essel, Bisque Head, Glass Eyes, Painted Lashes, Open Mouth, 1920s, 24 In. 403.00
essel, Papier-Mache Shoulder Head, Sculpted Hair, Leather, c.1880, 27 In. 550.00
essel, Uncle Sam, Bisque Head, Molded Face, Glass Eyes, Wood, Composition, 14 In. 633.00
fanbee, Baby, Flirty Eyes, Original Clothes, 20 In. 175.00
fanbee, Charlie McCarthy, Composition Head, Hands, Feet, Cloth Body, c.1940, 17 In. 616.00
nco, Bisque Head, Googly, Blue Glass Eyes, Mohair Wig, Jointed, Toddler, Germany, 13 In. 5175.00
shion, Bisque, Blue Glass Eyes, Blond Mohair Wig, Ethnic Costume, 17 ½ In. 2128.00
shion, Bisque Shoulder Head, Closed Mouth, Inset Glass Eyes, Mohair Wig, 18 In. 540.00
shion, Bisque Shoulder Head, Plump Face, Glass Eyes, Mohair, Kid Body, France, 14 In. 2464.00
shion, Bisque Swivel Head, Brown Complexion, Glass Eyes, Fleecy Wig, France, 14 In. 4760.00
shion, Bisque Swivel Head, Flat Cut Neck, Kid Edge, Mohair, Gusset-Jointed, France, 18 In. 7280.00
shion, Bisque Swivel Head, Shoulder Plate, Glass Eyes, Mohair, Wood, Jointed, France, 18 In. 785.00
shion, Bisque Swivel Head, Walnut, Octagon Shadowbox, France, 12 In. 4400.00
shion, Dome Head, Blue Inset Eyes, Closed Mouth, Pierced Ears, Leather Body, 16 In. 288.00
shion, Porcelain, Cork Pate, Mohair Wig, c.1860, 15 In. 2240.00
shion, Swivel Neck, Blue Glass Stationary Eyes, Braided Human Hair, France, 17 In. 2070.00
shion, Turkish Princess, Bisque Swivel Head, Kid Edge, Beauty Marks, France, 18 In. 5600.00
shion, Turned Shoulder Head, Glass Eyes, Closed Mouth, Sheepskin Wig, Germany, 19 In. 403.00
rodora, Bisque Head, Open Mouth, Fixed Eyes, Composition Body, Jointed, 1900s, 19 In. 288.00
rodora, Bisque Socket Head, Composition Body, Ball Jointed, Germany, 17 In. 115.00
anz Schmidt, Blue Glass Sleep Eyes, Open Mouth, Teeth, Sailor Costume, 27 In. 690.00
ench, Bisque Socket Head, Flirty Eyes, Mohair, Composition, Jointed, Legs, 22 In. 2912.00
ench, Bisque Socket Head, Glass Eyes, Human Hair, Composition, Jointed, c.1915, 18 In. 700.00
ench, Bisque Socket Head, Sleep Eyes, Mohair, Composition, Jointed, Bebe, 13 In. 4704.00
ench, Mignonette, Bisque Swivel Head, Mohair Wig, Peg-Jointed, 4 In. 800.00
ench, Papier-Mache, Clown, Bisque Socket Head, Glass Eyes, Jointed, 20 In. 1344.00
ench, Papier-Mache Shoulder Head, Painted Hair, Muslin Body, Storekeeper, 14 In. 952.00
ench, Pressed Bisque Socket Head, Paperweight Eyes, Mohair, Composition, Bebe, 14 In. 7280.00
. Joe figures are listed in the Toy category.
ultier, Bisque Socket Head, Paperweight Eyes, Mohair, Composition, Jointed, 17 In. 3584.00
ultier, Bisque Swivel Head, Closed Mouth, Glass Eyes, Mohair Wig, Fashion, 23 In. 3738.00
ultier, Bisque Swivel Head, Glass Enamel Eyes, Mohair Wig, Cork Pate, Fashion, 15 In. 1900.00
ultier, Bisque Swivel Head, Kid Edge, Glass Eyes, Mustache, Kid Body, Gusset-Jointed, Man, 15 In. 4200.00
ultier, Bisque Swivel Head, Kid Edge, Paperweight Eyes, Mohair, Kid Body, Fashion, 18 In. 4200.00
ultier, Bisque Swivel Head, Kid-Lined Shoulder Plate, Mohair, Wood, Fashion, 18 In. 5040.00
ultier, Bisque Swivel Head, Paperweight Eyes, Human Hair, Gusset-Jointed, 23 In. 3024.00
ultier, Bisque Swivel Head, Shoulder Plate, Glass Eyes, Muslin Body, Kid Arms, Fashion, 12 In. 1680.00
ultier, Blue Glass Paperweight Eyes, Open Mouth, 5 Upper Teeth, Wooden Limbs, 16 In. 1093.00
ultier, Fashion, Bisque Socket Head, Shoulder Plate, Glass Eye, Leather Body, 12 In. 862.00
ultier, Glass Eyes, Open Mouth, Mohair Wig, French Body, Satin Dress, 16 In. 1093.00
bruder Heubach, 6970, Bisque Socket Head, Glass Eyes, Mohair, Composition, 12 In. 1344.00
bruder Heubach, 7246, Bisque Socket Head, Sleep Eyes, Pouty, Composition, 22 In. 3136.00
bruder Heubach, 7407, Bisque Socket Head, Sleep Eyes, Dimples, Mohair, Composition, 15 In. 3248.00

Doll, Cameo, Scootles, Plastic, Jointed, Wrist Tag, 15 ½ In.
$80.00

Doll, Georgene, Girl Scout, Cloth, Original Outfit, Tag, 1930-40, 13 In.
$140.00

Doll, Handwerck, 109, Bisque Head, Sleep Eyes, Composition Jointed Body, 25 In.
$310.00

Doll, Horsman, Composition, Jointed, No. 61X4289, Box, 20 In.
$180.00

Doll, Jumeau, Bisque Head, Composition Jointed Body, Printemps, 25 In.
$1900.00

Doll, Kathe Kruse, Blond, Braids, Winter Outfit, Box, 12 In.
$150.00

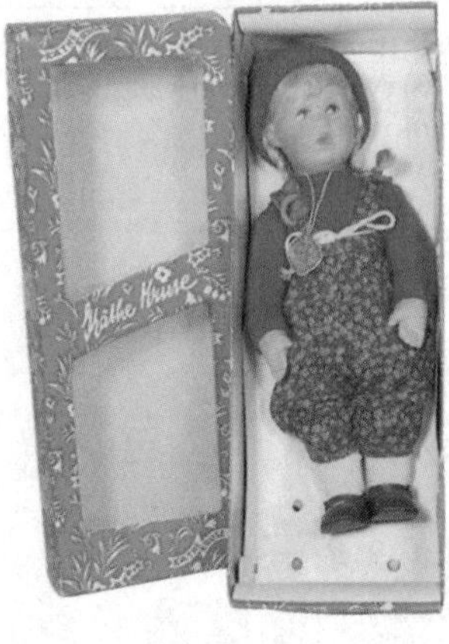

Gebruder Heubach, Baby Stuart, Bisque Socket Head, Intaglio Eyes, Composition, 9 In. . . . . 952.

Gebruder Heubach, Bisque, Googly Eyes, Laughing, Seated Knees Drawn Up, Child, 8 In. . . . 840.

Gebruder Heubach, Bisque, Seated, Legs Crossed, Ladybug On Knee, Baby, 5½ In. . . . . 2016.

Gebruder Heubach, Bisque Socket Head, Sculpted Hair, Composition, Wood, 7 In. . . . . 448.

Gebruder Heubach, Closed Mouth, Pouty, Sleep Eyes, Painted Lashes, 30½ In. . . . . 4888.

Gebruder Heubach, Our Fairy, 1-Piece Head, Googly Eyes, 2 Teeth, Bisque Body, Jointed Arms, 11 In. . . 1955.

Gebruder Heubach dolls may also be listed in this category under Heubach.

Georgene, Bonnie Babe, Socket Head, Glass Eyes, Open Mouth, Composition Body, 31 In. . . . 1150.

Georgene, Girl Scout, Cloth, Original Outfit, Tag, 1930-40, 13 In. . . . . *illus* 140.

German, Admiral Dewey, Bisque Socket Head, Mustache, Papier-Mache, Costume, Epaulets, 12 In. 2464.

German, Amberg, Vanta Baby, Bisque Socket Head, Sculpted Hair, Sleep Eyes, c.1927, 23 In. . 1000.

German, Bisque, Glass Eyes, Painted, Mohair, Poufy Knit Dress, c.1920.5 In. . . . . 616.

German, Bisque, Painted Eyes, Sailor Suit, c.1912, 17 In. . . . . 784.

German, Bisque Shoulder Head, Sculpted Hair, c.1890, 11 In. . . . . 550.

German, Bisque Shoulder Head, Sculpted Hair, Glass Eyes, Muslin, Bisque Limbs, 12 In. . . . . 672.

German, Bisque Shoulder Head, Sculpted, Glass Eyes, Muslin, Stitch-Jointed, 13 In. . . . . 784.

German, Bisque Shoulder Head, Sleep Eyes, Mohair, Kid, Girl Scout Uniform, 13 In. . . . . 1456.

German, Bisque Swivel Head, Kid Lined, Enamel Eyes, Peg-Jointed, Nun Habit, 5 In. . . . . . . 336.

German, Bisque Swivel Head, Weighted Glass Eyes, Mohair, Kid Body, Bisque Arms, 14 In. . . . 294.

German, Celluloid Head, Flanged Neck, Sculpted Hair, Sleep Eyes, Baby, 1935, 18 In. . . . . 336.

German, Fortune Teller, Bisque Shoulder Head, Painted, Muslin, Paper Fortunes, 7 In. . . . . . 560.

German, Modeled Socket Head, Dark Complexion, Rooted Red Hair, 16 In. . . . . 1064.

German, Papier-Mache Shoulder Head, Sculpted Hair, Chignon, c.1840, 17 In. . . . . 4032.

German, Porcelain, Pink Tint, Sculpted Hair, Bathing Beauty, c.1885, 16 In. . . . . 800.

German, Porcelain, Sculpted Curly Hair, Blue Painted Eyes, c.1885, 28 In. . . . . 1200.

German, Spanish Lady, Porcelain, Sculpted Hair, Pincushion Skirt, c.1915, 9 In. . . . . 500.

German, Wax Over Papier-Mache, Glass Sleep Eyes, Mohair Wig, Muslin, 23 In. . . . . 952.

Greiner, Papier-Mache Head, Cloth Body, 19th-Century Child's Clothes, c.1858, 30 In. . . . . . 2530.

Half Dolls are listed in the Pincushion Doll category.

Handwerck, 79, Socket Head, Sleep Eyes, Composition, Ball-Jointed, c.1900, 42 In. . . . . 2400.

Handwerck, 109, Bisque Head, Sleep Eyes, Composition Jointed Body, 25 In. . . . . *illus* 310.

Handwerck, Bisque Head, Weighted Eyes, Mohair, Papier-Mache Body, Ball-Jointed, 25 In. . . 646.

Handwerck, Bisque Socket Head, Glass Sleep Eyes, 42 In. . . . . 2800.

Handwerck, Bisque Socket Head, Sleep Eyes, Human Hair, Composition, Wood, 19 In. . . . . . . 952.

Handwerck, Bisque Socket Head, Sleep Eyes, Mohair Wig, Composition, 29 In. . . . . 2700.

Handwerck, Open Mouth, Upper Teeth, Painted Lashes, Brows, Jointed Body, 7 In. . . . . 1020.

Hasbro, Charlie's Angels, Kate Jackson, Jaclyn Smith & Cheryl Ladd, 1977, 8½ In. . . . . 200.

Hertel Schwab, Bisque Socket Head, Glass Eyes, Mohair Fleecy Wig, Composition, 15 In. . . . 5800.

Hertel Schwab, Bisque Socket Head, Glass Googly Eyes, Mohair Wig, c.1917, 24 In. . . . . 9520.

Heubach, 7404, Bisque Socket Head, Painted Hair & Eyes, Mechanical, 9 In. . . . . 500.

Heubach, 7602, Painted Intaglio Eyes, Molded Hair, Jointed, Boy, 14½ In. . . . . 230.

Heubach, 8191, Bisque Socket Head, Intaglio Googly Eyes, Composition, c.1912, 15 In. . . . . 1568.

Heubach, 10617, Bisque, Socket Head, Sleep Eyes, Mohair Wig, c.1918, 25 In. . . . . 6750.

Heubach, Baby Stuart, Bisque Socket Head, Sculpted Bonnet, Composition, 12 In. . . . . 1700.

Heubach, Bisque, Sculpted Hair, Painted Eyes, Loop-Jointed, c.1916, 8 In. . . . . 800.

Heubach, Bisque, Socket Head, Pouty, Sculpted Hair, Ball-Jointed Body, 14 In. . . . . 750.

Heubach, see also Gebruder Heubach.

Horsman, Composition, Jointed, No. 61X4289, Box, 20 In. . . . . *illus* 180.

Huret, Molded, Painted Features, Gutta-Percha Body, Articulated, Fashion, 19 In. . . . . 8338.

Huret, Porcelain Shoulder Head, Slightly Tinted, Mohair, Wood, Fashion, 17 In. . . . . 16800.

Ideal, Betsy McCall, Soft Head, Head Plastic, Jointed Shoulders & Hips, White Dress, c.1952, 14 In. 55.

Ideal, Jiminy Cricket, Wooden, Painted Face, Segmented Body, 8½ In. 400.

Ideal, Little Miss Revlon, Sleep Eyes, Rooted Hair, Undergarments, Hat, Jewelry, 10 In. . . . . . 150.

Ideal, Pinocchio, Composition, Wood Arms & Legs, c.1940, 19 In. . . . . 900.

Ideal, Toni, Plastic Head, Sleep Eyes, Platinum Hair, Accessories, Box, 1950s, 20 In. . . . . 895.

Ideal, Toni, Plastic Head, Sleep Eyes, Platinum Hair, Accessories, Box, 1952, 14 In. 485

Ideal, Toni, Plastic, Sleep Eyes, Platinum Wig, Striped Dress, c.1952, 15 In. 193

Indian dolls are listed in the Indian category.

J.D.K. dolls are also listed in this category under Kestner.

Jumeau, 3590, Shoulder Plate, Blue Glass Eyes, Open Mouth, Blond Mohair Wig, 13 In. . . . . . 259.

Jumeau, Bisque, Papier-Mache Jointed Body, Bebe, Diplome D'Honneur, 24 In. . . . . 2040.

Jumeau, Bisque, Socket Head, Paperweight Inset Eyes, Mohair Wig, Bebe, c.1888, 19 In. 7580

Jumeau, Bisque Head, Blue Paperweight Eyes, Closed Mouth, Composition, Bebe, 14 In. . . . . 3738.

Jumeau, Bisque Head, Blue Paperweight Eyes, Closed Mouth, Composition, Bebe, 24 In. . . . . 4140.

Jumeau, Bisque Head, Closed Mouth, Brown Paperweight Eyes, Painted Face, Brown Wig, 25 In. . 1495

Jumeau, Bisque Head, Composition Jointed Body, Printemps, 25 In. . . . . *illus* 1900

Jumeau, Bisque Head, Glass Eyes, Pierced Ears, Auburn Wig, Jointed Composition, Bebe, 26 In. 1058.00
Jumeau, Bisque Head, Paperweight Eyes, 6 Upper Teeth, Composition Body, 20 In. 1880.00
Jumeau, Bisque Head, Paperweight Eyes, Mohair, Composition, Box, c.1850, 9 In. 840.00
Jumeau, Bisque Head, Weighted Glass Eyes, Pierced Ears, Wig, Jointed Composition, 26 In. 1058.00
Jumeau, Bisque Shoulder Head, Paperweight Eyes, Human Hair, Composition, Wood, Bebe, 25 In. 3360.00
Jumeau, Bisque Socket Head, Brown, Paperweight Eyes, Mohair, Composition, 24 In. 8400.00
Jumeau, Bisque Socket Head, Clockwork, Brass Key, Bebe, Phonograph, 24 In. 6160.00
Jumeau, Bisque Socket Head, Enamel Eyes, Mohair Wig, Cork Pate, Bebe, 22 In. 9500.00
Jumeau, Bisque Socket Head, Enamel Inset Eyes, Mohair Wig, Composition, c.1878, 13 In. 6720.00
Jumeau, Bisque Socket Head, Paperweight Eyes, Human Hair, Bebe, 21 In. 4200.00
Jumeau, Bisque Socket Head, Paperweight Eyes, Human Hair, Composition, 32 In. 8000.00
Jumeau, Bisque Socket Head, Paperweight Eyes, Mohair, Composition, Wood, 22 In. 4704.00
Jumeau, Bisque Swivel Head, Blue Enamel Eyes, Closed Mouth, Fashion, 1880, 11 In. 1680.00
Jumeau, Bisque Swivel Head, Enamel Eyes, Dowel & Swivel-Jointed, Fashion, 17 In. 5600.00
Jumeau, Bisque Swivel Head, Enamel Eyes, Mohair Wig, Fashion, 15 In. 2016.00
Jumeau, Bisque Swivel Head, Enamel Eyes, Mohair, Gusset-Jointed, Fashion, 17 In. 4144.00
Jumeau, Bisque Swivel Head, Glass Eyes, Mohair, Cork Pate, Fashion, 11 In. 1680.00
Jumeau, Bisque Swivel Head, Paperweight Eyes, Mohair, Kid Body, Fashion, 23 In. 5600.00
Jumeau, Pressed Bisque Socket Head, Paperweight Eyes, Composition, Wood-Jointed, 29 In. 18480.00
Jumeau, Pressed Bisque Socket Head, Paperweight Eyes, Mohair, Composition, Wood, 16 In. 7280.00
Jumeau, Pressed Bisque Socket Head, Paperweight Eyes, Mohair, Composition, Wood, 18 In. 8680.00
K * R, 36, Kaiser Baby, Painted & Molded Features, Lace, Christening Gown, 14 In. 230.00
K * R, 101, Bisque Head, Intaglio Eyes, Mohair, Composition, Ball-Jointed, 17 In. 1058.00
K * R, 114, Bisque Socket Head, Glass Sleep Eyes, Mohair Wig, Composition, c.1912, 12 In. 5264.00
K * R, 114, Bisque Socket Head, Mohair Wig, Composition, Ball-Jointed, c.1910, 7 In. 952.00
K * R, 114, Gretchen, Bisque Head, Pouty Mouth, Blond Mohair, Composition, 12 In. 1293.00
K * R, 115A, Bisque Socket Head, Glass Sleep Eyes, Mohair Wig, Jointed, c.1912, 12 In. 2600.00
K * R, 117, Bisque Head, Intaglio Eyes, Lever Operated, Composition, Ball-Jointed, 21 In. 499.00
K * R, 117, Mein Liebling, Bisque Socket Head, Sleep Eyes, Mohair, Composition, Wood, 18 In. 6440.00
K * R, 117A, Mein Liebling, Bisque Socket Head, Sleep Eyes, Ball-Jointed, c.1912, 21 In. 5200.00
K * R, 122, Bisque Socket Head, Sleep Eyes, Bobbed Mohair, Toddler, c.1915, 14 In. 840.00
K * R, 126, Bisque Head, Flirty Eyes, Composition, Bent Limbs, 21 ½ In. 382.00
K * R, 127, Boy Scout, Bisque, Brown Painted Hair, Blue Gray Glass Eyes, 17 In. 2150.00
K * R, 131, Bisque Socket Head, Googly Sleep Eyes, Mohair, Composition, 14 In. 10080.00
K * R, 131, Bisque Socket Head, Sleep Eyes, Mohair Wig, Composition, c.1916, 15 In. 13440.00
K * R, 728, Celluloid Socket Head, Mohair Lashes, Hair, Composition, Toddler, 17 In. 560.00
K * R, Bisque Socket Head, Sleep Eyes, Mohair Wig, Composition, Ball-Jointed, 36 In. 1600.00
K * R, Bisque Socket Head, Sleep Eyes, Mohair Wig, Composition, Side Hip Jointed, 25 In. 850.00
K * R, Blue Glass Sleep Eyes, Open Mouth, Mohair Wig, Simon & Halbig Head, 11 In. 345.00
K * R, Mein Liebling, Bisque Head, Glass Sleep Eyes, Mohair Wig, Ball-Jointed, 12 In. 3136.00
K * R, Peter, Blue Painted Eyes, Molded Lids, Pouty Mouth, 17 In. 1840.00
Kathe Kruse, Blond, Braids, Winter Outfit, Box, 12 In. *illus* 150.00
Kathe Kruse, Boy, Molded Face, Painted, Cropped Hair, Stitch & Disc-Jointed, 18 In. 336.00
Kathe Kruse, Cloth, Pressed, Oil Painted, Brown Eyes, Infant, 13 In. 4200.00
Kathe Kruse, Du Mein, Molded Head, Painted, Curly Wig, Stockinet Body, 18 In. 616.00
Kathe Kruse, Girl, Sculpted Swivel Head, Painted, Red Hair, Stitch-Jointed, 18 In. 224.00
Kathe Kruse, Hampelchen, Pressed, Oil Painted, Boyish Hair, Muslin Body, Stitch-Jointed, 18 In. 2016.00
Kathe Kruse, Kurti, Brown Eyes & Hair, Wardrobe, Basket, 19 In. 3819.00
Kathe Kruse, Painted, Swivel Head, Blond Wing, Rayon Dress, 1950s, 14 In. 360.00
Kathe Kruse, Sculpted Head, Painted, Curly Hair, Stitch-Jointed, Baby, 1950, 18 In. 1904.00
Kathe Kruse, Sculpted Socket Head, Painted, Green Eyes, Stitch-Jointed, 1962, 18 In. 672.00
Kathe Kruse, Sculpted Swivel Head, Painted, Pigtails, Stitch-Jointed, 1961, 18 In. 280.00
Kathe Kruse, Sleeping, Painted Features, Stockinet, Weighted Sand, Baby, 1945, 20 In. 1904.00
Kathe Kruse, Sober Face, Painted Brown Hair & Eyes, 1927, 14 In. 1116.00
Kathe Kruse, Twin Girls, Molded Swivel Heads, Human Hair, Jointed, 14 In. 1120.00
Kathe Kruse, Weighted Head, Auburn Hair, Intaglio Eyes, c.1914, 16 ½ In. 1645.00
Kestner, 15, Bisque Head, Sleep Eyes, Sheepskin Wig, Composition Body, 1880s, 23 In. 1410.00
Kestner, 128, Bisque Head, Pouty, Papier-Mache Body, Child, 15 ¼ In. 558.00
Kestner, 128, Bisque Socket Head, Sleep Eyes, Mohair Wig, Composition, Jointed, c.1890, 20 In. 2100.00
Kestner, 129, Bisque Head, Glass Eyes, Blond Mohair, Composition, Jointed, 15 In. 235.00
Kestner, 134, Bisque Head, Brown Complexion, Sleep Eyes, Mohair, Ball-Jointed, 9 In. 2900.00
Kestner, 143, Bisque Head, Sleep Eyes, Composition Jointed Body, 10 In. *illus* 515.00
Kestner, 143, Bisque Head, Sleep Eyes, Open Mouth, Composition, c.1910, 25 ½ In. 1265.00
Kestner, 154, Bisque Shoulder Head, Brown Wig, Sleep Eyes, Kid Body, Shaker Dress, 22 In. 702.00
Kestner, 167, Bisque Socket Head, Sleep Eyes, Mohair, Composition, Wood, Child, 13 In. 1064.00
Kestner, 171, Bisque Socket Head, Sleep Eyes, Mohair, Composition, Wood, Child, 15 In. 1064.00

Doll, Kestner, 143, Bisque Head, Sleep Eyes, Composition Jointed Body, 10 In.
$515.00

Doll, Lenci, Girl, Googly Eyes, Swivel Neck, Mohair Wig, 1930s, 18 In.
$1300.00

Doll, Madame Alexander, Amy, Plastic, Blond, Curler Box, Dress Tag, Box, 14 In.
$660.00

D

Doll, Madame Alexander, Little Betty, Washing On Monday, Mohair, Composition, c.1935, 7 In.
$1100.00

Madame Alexander
The Alexander Doll Company was founded in New York City in 1923 by Beatrice Alexander Behrman (1895–1990) and her three sisters. Beatrice trademarked the name Madame Alexander for her dolls in 1928—and used the name for herself, for the rest of her 95 years.

Doll, Mattel, Barbie, No. 850, Red Swirl Ponytail, Wrist Tag, Box
$300.00

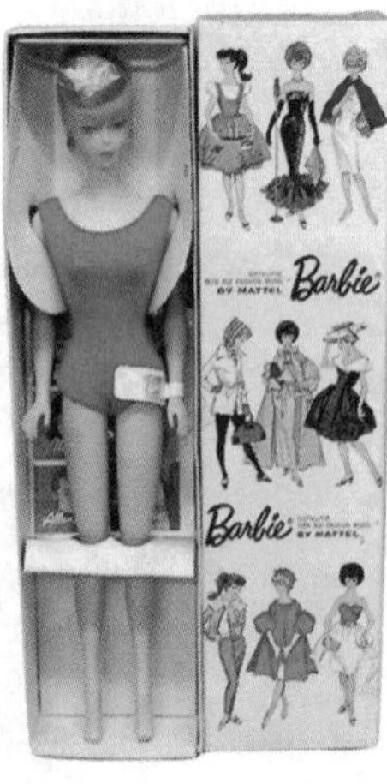

Kestner, 172, Gibson Girl, Bisque Shoulder Head, Sleep Eyes, Kid Body, c.1910, 19 In. 764.00
Kestner, 184, Bisque Socket Head, Painted, Pouty, Composition, Wood, Ball-Jointed, 11 In. . . 2240.00
Kestner, 200, Bisque Head, Sleep Eyes, Mohair Wig, Loop-Jointed, c.1920, 9 In. 500.00
Kestner, 206, Bisque Socket Head, Glass Sleep Eyes, Composition, c.1912, 18 In. 11400.00
Kestner, 221, Bisque Head, Googly, Mohair, Composition, Ball-Jointed, 13 In. 4113.00
Kestner, 221, Bisque Socket Head, Glass Googly Eyes, Mohair Wig, Composition, c.1915 . . . . . 10080.00
Kestner, 243, Chinese Baby, Bisque Socket Head, Sleep Eyes, Composition, 18 In. 5600.00
Kestner, Bisque Head, Brown Sleep Eyes, Painted Lashes, Brows, Teeth, Child, 35 ½ In. 150.00
Kestner, Bisque Head, Closed Mouth, Pouty, Blond Hair, Brown Sleep Eyes, Jointed, 14 In. . . . 1495.00
Kestner, Bisque Head, Glass Sleep Eyes, Hair Wig, Jointed Body, Red Outfit, 14 ¾ In. 7187.00
Kestner, Bisque Head, Oval Face, Brown Sleep Eyes, Closed Mouth, Dress, Hat, Child, 30 ½ In. 2040.00
Kestner, Bisque Socket Head, Brown Sleep Eyes, Porcelain Teeth, 25 In. 2300.00
Kestner, Bisque Socket Head, Glass Eyes, Pierced Ears, Mohair, Toddler, 11 In. 440.00
Kestner, Bisque Socket Head, Googly Eyes, Mohair, Composition, Wood, Toddler, 12 In. 7280.00
Kestner, Bisque Socket Head, Sleep Eyes, Mohair Wig, Composition, c.1890, 28 In. 3800.00
Kestner, Bisque Socket Head, Sleep Eyes, Mohair Wig, Jointed, c.1885, 20 In. 2500.00
Kestner, Bisque Swivel Head, Glass Sleep Eyes, c.1885, 7 In. 616.00
Kestner, Bisque Swivel Head, Weighted Glass Eyes, Mohair, Cloth, Kid Arms, 23 In. 4406.00
Kestner, Chinese Baby, Bisque Socket Head, Solid Dome, Amber Tint, Painted Hair, 16 In. . . . 3640.00
Kestner, Gibson Girl, Bisque Shoulder Head, Weighted Eyes, Cloth, Bisque Arms, Feet, 10 In. . 529.00
Kewpie dolls are listed in the Kewpie category.
Kley & Hahn, 166, Domed Socket Head, Sculpted Hair, Sleep Eyes, c.1912, 10 In. 650.00
Kley & Hahn, 167-2/0, Bisque Head, Mohair Wig, Bent Limb Composition Body, 10 In. 206.00
Kley & Hahn, 549, Bisque Head, Weighted Glass Eyes, Mohair, Composition, 19 In. 4406.00
Kley & Hahn, Bisque Head, Googly Glass Eyes, Blond Mohair, Composition, 10 In. 999.00
Kley & Hahn, Bisque Socket Head, Painted Features, Mohair, Composition, Wood, 19 In. 5264.00
Kling, Bisque Shoulder Head, Molded Hair, Glass Eyes, Pierced Ears, Parian, 19 In. 264.00
Koenig & Wernicke, Blue Sleep Eyes, Brows, Open Mouth, Toddler, c.1910, 24 In. 805.00
Lenci, Bali Dancer, 25 In. 4800.00
Lenci, Felt Swivel Head, Pressed Features, Mohair Wig, 5-Piece Body, Felt Joints, 11 In. 1400.00
Lenci, Girl, Felt, Brown Eyes, Blond Wig, Fur Trim Coat, 1930s, 21 In. 1995.00
Lenci, Girl, Googly Eyes, Swivel Neck, Mohair Wig, 1930s, 18 In. . . . . *illus* 1300.00
Lenci, Girl, Toscana, Felt Swivel Head, Pressed, Painted, Coiled Braids, Jointed, 19 In. 1680.00
Lenci, Italian Girl, Felt Swivel Head, Pressed, Painted, Mohair, 5-Piece Body, 20 In. 4760.00
Lenci, Lucy, Felt Swivel Head, Blond Braids, Green Dress, Sport Series, 1935, 14 In. 2350.00
Lenci, Lucy, Italian Girl, Felt Swivel Head, Pressed, Painted, Coiled Braids, Jointed, 17 In. 952.00
Lenci, Scottish Boy, Felt Swivel Head, Pressed, Painted, Mohair, Jointed, Box, 15 In. 1600.00
Lenci, Scottish Girl, Felt Swivel Head, Pressed, Painted, Googly Eyes, Mohair, Box, 15 In. 1800.00
Lenci, Side-Glancing, Blond Wig, Felt Body, Swivel Limbs, c.1930s, 18 In. 275.00
Lenci-Type, Carmen Miranda, Boudoir, Painted Face, Black Hair, Earrings, 1930s, 25 In. 355.00
Limoges, Blue Glass Sleep Eyes, Painted Lashes, Teeth, Human Hair Wig, 26 In. 403.00
Madame Alexander, Amy, Plastic, Blond, Curler Box, Dress Tag, Box, 14 In. . . . . *illus* 660.00
Madame Alexander, Ballerina, Plastic, Swivel Head, Jointed Knees, Tutu, c.1958, 10 In. 700.00
Madame Alexander, Cynthia, Margaret Face, Black Wig, Sleep Eyes, 5-Piece Body, 1952, 14 In. 935.00
Madame Alexander, Cynthia, Plastic, Brown Complexion, Swivel Head, 14 In. 850.00
Madame Alexander, David Copperfield, Boiled Felt Face, Blond Wig, Cloth, Hat, 1930, 16 In. 510.00
Madame Alexander, Dr. Dafoe, Composition Socket Head, Painted Features, 1936, 6 In. 2300.00
Madame Alexander, Elise, Ballerina, Sleep Eyes, Vinyl, Jointed Ankles, Knees, 11-Piece Body, 1959 . . 358.00
Madame Alexander, Jo, Little Women, Plastic, Maggie Face, Sleep Eyes, Brunette Wig, 1948, 14 In. 402.00
Madame Alexander, Judy, Portrait Series, Composition, Sleep Eyes, Pursed Lips, 1930s, 21 In. 1093.00
Madame Alexander, Little Betty, Washing On Monday, Mohair, Composition, c.1935, 7 In. *illus* 1100.00
Madame Alexander, Little Genius, Vinyl, Fur Wig, Sleep Eyes, Jointed Shoulders, Bottle, Rattle, Box 137.00
Madame Alexander, Little Genius, Vinyl, Fur Wig, Sleep Eyes, Nursing Mouth, c.1960, 8 In. . 165.00
Madame Alexander, Maggie, Brunette, Sleep Eyes, 5-Piece Body, Walker, Flower Skirt, c.1949, 14 In. 402.00
Madame Alexander, Maggie, Platinum Wig, Sleep Eyes, 5-Piece Body, Sweater, Curlers, Box, c.1949, 17 In. 1870.00
Madame Alexander, Marlo Thomas, That Girl, Vinyl, Brown Eyes, Boots, 1966, 17 In. 315.00
Madame Alexander, Marmee, Little Women, Margaret Face, Plastic, Curlers, Box, c.1948, 14 In. 357.00
Madame Alexander, Marybel, Doll That Gets Well, Vinyl, Medical Supplies, 1960s, 16 In. . . . 175.00
Madame Alexander, Marybel, Vinyl Head, Blond, Sleep Eyes, Pajamas, No. 1575, c.1960, 15 In. 85.00
Madame Alexander, Polly Pigtails, Dark Blond Braids, Sleep Eyes, Box, c.1949-51, 20 In. . . . 962.00
Madame Alexander, Prince Charles, Flocked Brown Hair, Bent Legs, Blue Suit, 1958, 8 In. . . 240.00
Madame Alexander, Scarlett O'Hara, Composition, Sleep Eyes, Human Hair, 5-Piece Body, 17 In. 1120.00
Madame Alexander, Shari Lewis, Hard Plastic, 5-Piece Body, Red Dress, 1959, 14 In. 600.00
Madame Alexander, Snow White, Plastic Socket Head, Blue Sleep Eyes, 1952, 15 In. 610.00
Madame Alexander, Wendy, Loves To Waltz, Blond Wig, Sleep Eyes, Walker, c.1955, 8 In. . . . 605.00

Madame Alexander, Wendy, Roller Skating, Tosca Wig, Sleep Eyes, Bent Knee, Walker, 1956, 8 In. 182.00
Madame Alexander, Wendy, Time For School, Blonde, Sleep Eyes, Bent Knee, Walker, c.1956, 8 In.. 402.00
Madame Alexander, Wendy Ann, Composition Socket Head, Sleep Eyes, Human Hair, Lady, 13 In. 616.00
Madame Alexander, Winnie, Blond Wig, Sleep Eyes, Walker, c.1953, 24 In. 110.00
Marotte, Bisque, Glass Eyes, Mohair Wig, Papier-Mache, Maple, Music Box, c.1890, 14 In. 672.00
Marotte, Bisque Shoulder Head, Glass Eyes, Mohair, Ball Shaped Body, Maple, 16 In. 896.00
Mary Hoyer, Composition Socket Head, Sleep Eyes, Mohair, c.1940, 14 In., Pair 1008.00
Mattel, Barbie, Color Magic, Midnight & Ruby Red, Print Swim Suit, 1966, 11 In. 1900.00
Mattel, Barbie, No. 850, Red Swirl Ponytail, Wrist Tag, Box *illus* 300.00
Mattel, Francie, Velvet Gown, Jacket, Black Hair 5880.00
Mattel, Midge, No. 860, Brunette, Shoes, Booklet, Box *illus* 60.00
Mattel, Mrs. Beasley, Vinyl Head, Hands, Glasses, Rooted Hair, Cloth, 1967, 21 In. 55.00
Mattel, Skipper, No. 950, Blond, Liner Stand, Booklet *illus* 190.00
Nancy Ann Storybook, Baby, Hard Plastic, Sleep Eyes, Jointed, c.1945. 38.00
Nancy Ann Storybook, Bride, Hard Plastic, Painted Features, Jointed, Mohair Wig, 5 In. 55.00
Nancy Ann Storybook, Bridesmaid, Hard Plastic, Painted Features, Jointed, Mohair Wig, 5 In. 55.00
Nancy Ann Storybook, Daisy Belle, Bisque, Painted Features, Jointed, Mohair Wig, 5 ½ In. 82.00
Nancy Ann Storybook, Flower Girl, Hard Plastic, Jointed Arms, 4 In. 82.00
Nancy Ann Storybook, Groom, Painted Features, Flocked Brown Hair, Jointed, 6 In. 11.00
Nancy Ann Storybook, Ring Bearer, Hard Plastic, Painted Features, Mohair Wig, 4 ½ In. 55.00
Paper dolls are listed in their own category.
Papier-Mache, Bisque Head, Clown, Glass Eyes, Straw Filled, Muslin, Legs, 23 In. 1008.00
Papier-Mache, Bisque Socket Head, Asian, Inset Eyes, Upswept Hair, c.1900, 15 In. 3024.00
Papier-Mache, Molded Hair, Kid Body, Upper Legs, Carved Arms, Legs, c.1835, 11 ½ In. 382.00
Papier-Mache, Sailor, Ball-Shaped Body, Weighted, Hands On Tummy, c.1910, 11 In. 1120.00
Papier-Mache, Sculpted Hair, Painted Eyes, Wood Limbs, c.1850, 15 In. 784.00
Papier-Mache, Shoulder Head, Glass Eyes, Wooden, Germany, c.1865, 23 In. 2300.00
Papier-Mache, Shoulder Head, Painted Face, Muslin Body, Germany, c.1870, 11 In. 2300.00
Papier-Mache, Solid Dome, Oval Face, Human Hair, Inset Eyes, Kid Body, France, 28 In. 4480.00
Pincushion dolls are listed in their own category.
Puppet, Captain Kangaroo, Fabric Body, Felt Hands, Bowtie, Rushton, 1950s, 10 In. 189.00
Puppet, Cat, Black, Glass Eyes, Button In Ear, Hang Tag, Steiff, 8 ½ In. 66.00
Puppet, Chipmunk, Glass Eyes, Button In Ear, Hang Tag, Steiff, 9 In. 275.00
Puppet, Gnome, Gucki, Button, Steiff, 10 In. *illus* 44.00
Puppet, Hand, Cat, Felix, Black Mohair, Felt Face, Button In Ear, Steiff, c.1925, 9 In. 575.00
Puppet, Hand, The Munsters, 1960s, Set Of 3. 791.00
Puppet, Hedge Hog, Mecki, Glass Eyes, Button, Hang Tag, Steiff, 8 ½ In. 77.00
Puppet, Judy, Punch & Judy, Eyes Move, Peter Puppet, 1950s 65.00
Puppet, Lion Cub, Glass Eyes, Button In Ear, Hang Tag, Steiff, 8 ½ In. 220.00
Puppet, Monkey, Mungo, Glass Eyes, Button In Ear, Hang Tag, Steiff, 9 In. 88.00
Puppet, Our Pet, Bisque, Blue Eyes, Celluloid Hands, Strauss, Seco, Germany, 8 x 7 In. *illus* 120.00
Puppet, Owl, Wittie, Glass Eyes, Button, Steiff, 8 ½ In. *illus* 77.00
Puppet, Rabbit, Glass Eyes, Button In Ear, Hang Tag, Steiff, 11 ½ In. 187.00
Puppet, Squirrel, Possy, Glass Eyes, Button In Ear, Hang Tag, Steiff, 9 In. 220.00
Puppet, Tiger, Glass Eyes, Hang Tag, Button In Ear, Steiff, 8 ½ In. 121.00
Rabery, Delphieu, Closed Mouth, Blue Paperweight Eyes, Hair Wig, Bebe, 29 In. 720.00
Raggedy Ann, Cloth, Painted Features, Shoebutton Eyes, 1915, 15 ½ In. *illus* 600.00
Recknagel, 243, Bisque Socket Head, Solid Dome, Painted Hair, Composition, 7 In. 200.00
Recknagel, Bisque Socket Head, Dimples, Composition, Wood, Ball-Jointed, Boy, 15 In. 2016.00
S & H dolls are also listed here as Simon & Halbig.
S.F.B.J., 60, Bisque, Fixed Eyes, Synthetic Wig, Jointed Composition, Girl, 15 In. 176.00
S.F.B.J., 252, Bisque Head, Sleep Eyes, Mohair, Composition, Toddler, 18 In. 3819.00
S.F.B.J., 252, Bisque Socket Head, Sleep Eyes, Mohair Lashes, Hair, Composition, Wood, 13 In. 4760.00
S.F.B.J., Bisque Head, Molded Features, Glass Eyes, Open Mouth, Painted Hair, Boy, 22 In. 1495.00
S.F.B.J., Bisque Head, Open Mouth, 6 Teeth, Blue Sleep Eyes, Pierced Ears, Child, c.1900, 31 In. 1150.00
Sasha, Gregor, Socket Head, Dark, Blue Eyes, Blond Hair, Pajamas, 16 In. 1232.00
Sasha, Socket Head, Brown Eyes, Cloth Body, Jointed Shoulders, c.1960, 20 In. 4480.00
Sasha, Socket Head, Brown, Brown Eyes, 5-Piece Body, Swiss Studio, 1958, 20 In. 7280.00
Sasha, Socket Head, Full Cheeks, Blue Eyes, Human Hair, 5-Piece Body, 20 In. 4760.00
Sasha, Socket Head, Square Face, Green Eyes, Human Hair Braids, Cloth, Swiss Studio, 20 In. 7840.00
Sasha, Socket Head, Tan Complexion, Waist Length Hair, 5-Piece Body, 1965, 16 In. 1344.00
Schmitt & Fils, Bisque Socket Head, Enamel Eyes, Lamb's Wool Wig, Bebe, c.1882, 14 In. 11200.00
Schoenau & Hoffmeister, Bisque Socket Head, Sleep Eyes, Mohair, Composition, Baby, 13 In. 1680.00
Schoenhut, Max & Moritz, Molded Heads, Jointed Bodies, Wagon, 8 In., 3 Piece *illus* 320.00
Schoenhut, Miss Dolly, Wood, Painted Eyes, Blond Wig, Period Clothing, 21 In. 118.00

Doll, Mattel, Midge, No. 860, Brunette, Shoes, Booklet, Box
$60.00

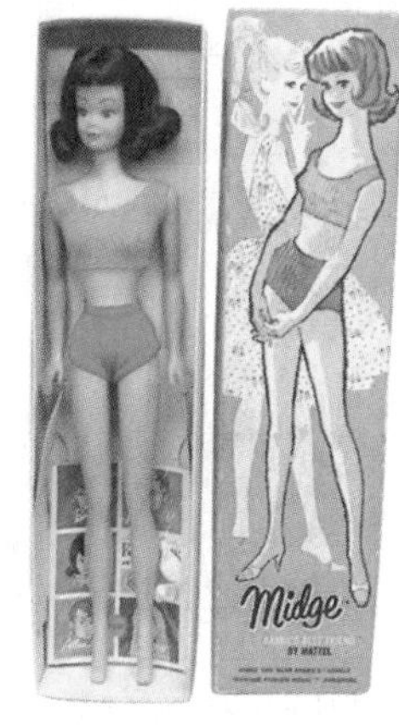

Doll, Mattel, Skipper, No. 950, Blond, Liner Stand, Booklet
$190.00

Doll, Puppet, Gnome, Gucki, Button, Steiff, 10 In.
$44.00

D

Doll, Puppet, Our Pet, Bisque, Blue Eyes, Celluloid Hands, Strauss, Seco, Germany, 8 x 7 In.
$120.00

Doll, Puppet, Owl, Wittie, Glass Eyes, Button, Steiff, 8 ½ In.
$77.00

Doll, Raggedy Ann, Cloth, Painted Features, Shoebutton Eyes, 1915, 15 ½ In.
$600.00

Doll, Schoenhut, Max & Moritz, Molded Heads, Jointed Bodies, Wagon, 8 In., 3 Piece
$320.00

Schoenhut, Painted Features, Wood Limbs, Baby, Grotesque, 8 ¼ In. 4600.00
Schoenhut, Schnickel Fritz, Wood, Jointed Body, Painted Eyes, Teeth, c.1920, 16 In. 705.00
Schoenhut, Wood, Painted Eyes, Mohair Wig, Elastic Strung, 1920s, 14 In. 176.00
Schoenhut, Wood Socket Head, Carved, Bobbed Hair, Spring-Jointed, Girl, 14 In. 1680.00
Schoenhut, Wood Socket Head, Carved, Intaglio Eyes, Spring-Jointed, Boy, 16 In. 1456.00
Schoenhut, Wood Socket Head, Carved, Sculpted Hair, Spring-Jointed, Boy, 14 In. 1680.00
Schoenhut, Wood Socket Head, Intaglio Eyes, Pouty, Bobbed Hair, Spring-Jointed, Girl, 16 In. 1064.00
Schoenhut, Wood Socket Head, Sculpted Hair, Spring-Jointed, c.1912, 15 In. 2240.00
Shirley Temple dolls are included in the Shirley Temple category.
Simon & Halbig, 122, Sleep Eyes, Tongue, Papier-Mache Bent Limbs, Toddler, 15 In. .. *illus* 315.00
Simon & Halbig, 164, Bisque Socket Head, Asian, Sleep Eyes, Mohair, Composition, Child, 13 In. . 1232.00
Simon & Halbig, 886, Bisque Swivel Head, Sleep Eyes, Mohair, Peg-Jointed, 8 In. 1065.00
Simon & Halbig, 939, Bisque Socket Head, Open Mouth, Teeth, 36 In. 3000.00
Simon & Halbig, 939, Bisque Socket Head, Plump Cheeks, Mohair, Composition, 14 In. 5750.00
Simon & Halbig, 939, Paperweight Eyes, Mohair, Jointed Composition, Child, 14 ½ In. 999.00
Simon & Halbig, 1009, Bisque Socket Head, Kid Body, 20 In. .... *illus* 480.00
Simon & Halbig, 1039, Bisque Socket Head, Sleep Eyes, Composition, Ball-Jointed, 28 In. ... 1500.00
Simon & Halbig, 1078, Bisque Socket Head, Sleep Eyes, Mohair Wig, c.1900, 36 In. 2200.00
Simon & Halbig, 1079, Bisque Head, Weighted Eyes, Pierced Ears, 19 In. 206.00
Simon & Halbig, 1079, Bisque Socket Head, Sleep Eyes, Human Wig, c.1900, 33 In. 800.00
Simon & Halbig, 1160, Bisque Head, Glass Eyes, Mohair Wig, Cloth Body, 5 ¾ In. 176.00
Simon & Halbig, 1249, Bisque Socket Head, Sleep Eyes, Composition, Ball-Jointed, 18 In. ... 2016.00
Simon & Halbig, 1269, Bisque Socket Head, Open Mouth, 32 In. 1500.00
Simon & Halbig, 1279, Bisque Socket Head, Sleep Eyes, Composition, Wood, 32 In. 4480.00
Simon & Halbig, 1358, Bisque Socket Head, Brown, Glass Eyes, Composition, 20 In. 6160.00
Simon & Halbig, 1358, Bisque Socket Head, Brown, Sleep Eyes, Composition, 16 In. 5040.00
Simon & Halbig, Bisque Head, Clockwork Flirty Blue Glass Eyes, Bent Limbs, Baby, 25 In. ... 1495.00
Simon & Halbig, Bisque Head, Open Mouth, Blond Wig, Composition, Jointed, 25 In. 546.00
Simon & Halbig, Bisque Head, Sleeping Eyes, Blond Mohair, Composition, 18 In. 235.00
Simon & Halbig, Bisque Shoulder Head, Solid Dome, Glass Eyes, Mohair, Muslin, 10 In. 728.00
Simon & Halbig, Bisque Swivel Head, Glass Eyes, Open Mouth, Teeth, Mignonette, 8 In. 1065.00
Simon & Halbig, Bisque Swivel Head, Glass Eyes, Sheepskin Wig, Kid Body, 12 In. 764.00
Simon & Halbig, Bisque Swivel Head, Solid Dome, Kid Lined, Mohair, Twill Over Wood, 11 In. 4032.00
Simon & Halbig, Schoolboy, Bisque Head, Jointed Papier-Mache Body, 22 In. 1980.00
Sonneberg, Bisque Swivel Head, Glass Eyes, Mohair Wig, Stitch-Jointed, c.1885, 13 In. 1400.00
Steiff, Felt Swivel Head, Glass Eyes, Stitched Ears, Mohair, Jointed, c.1913, 16 In. 1120.00
Steiff, Mountaineer, Black Steel Eyes, Applied Ears, Boots, Steiff, Germany, 1913 .... 2355.00
Steiner, Bebe Gigoteur, Bisque, Glass Eyes, Clockwork, Trunk, Trousseau, 1889, 18 In. 4480.00
Steiner, Bisque Socket Head, Brown, Enamel Eyes, Composition, Jointed, 10 In. 3584.00
Steiner, Bisque Socket Head, Brown, Glass Eyes, Mohair, Composition, Jointed, 16 In. 2800.00
Steiner, Bisque Socket Head, Brown, Mohair, Composition, Jointed, 10 In. 2240.00
Steiner, Bisque Socket Head, Glass Paperweight Eyes, Mohair Wig, Bebe, 17 In. 3584.00
Steiner, Bisque Socket Head, Wire Lever Eyes, Human Hair, Bebe, c.1888, 24 In. 5264.00
Steiner, Gigoteur, Bisque Head, Solid Dome, Mohair, Clockwork Mechanism, Bebe, 13 In. ... 5880.00
Steiner, Gigoteur, Bisque Head, Solid Dome, Paperweight Eyes, Bebe, 18 In. 4480.00
Steiner, Gigoteur, Raises Arm, Turns Head, Moves Legs, Cries, Mechanical Baby, 17 ½ In. 2070.00
Swaine & Co., Lori, Bisque Head, Open Mouth, Baby, 2 Teeth, Molded Hair, 12 In. 403.00
Swaine & Co., Sleep Eyes, Open Mouth, 4 Teeth, Dimple Chin, Mohair Wig, Child, 15 In. 345.00
Vogue, Ginny, Coronation Queen, Plastic, Mohair Wig, Tag, 1954 .... *illus* 180.00
Vogue, Ginny, Lunch At The Plaza, Town & Country Collection, 8 In. 50.00
Vogue, Ginny, Plastic, Straight Leg, 1955, 8 In. 175.00
Vogue, Jan, Vinyl, Socket Head, Brunette Sleep Eyes, Swivel Waist, 1958, 10 In. 175.00
Vogue, Steve & Eve, Brother & Sister, Plastic, Brown Eyes, Plaid Outfits, 1951, 8 In. 1100.00
Wax Head, Glass Eyes, Mohair, Cloth Body, Kid Arms, Hands, Quaker Dress, 19 In. 2350.00
Wax Over Composition, Shoulder Head, Glass Eyes, Mohair, Cloth Limbs, 15 In. 470.00
Wax Shoulder Head, Glass Eyes, Mohair, Muslin, Leather Arms, England, c.1865, 23 In. 1792.00
Wax Shoulder Head, Sleep Eyes, Muslin, Stitch Jointed, Poured Wax Limbs, 26 In. 2128.00
Wax Socket Head, Glass Paperweight Eyes, Human Hair, Mannequin Body, c.1890, 41 In. ... 3200.00
Wood, Carved, Shoulder Head, Muslin, Wooden Limbs, Man, c.1840, 28 In. 4256.00
Wood, Carved, Shoulder Head, Oval Face, Sculpted Hair, Muslin, c.1850, 14 In. 840.00
Wood, Carved, Shoulder Head, Socket Eyes, Muslin, Kid, Germany, c.1840, 24 In. 2128.00
Wood, Enamel Eyes, Human Hair, 18th Century, 26 In. 13000.00
Wood, Human Hair, Dowel-Jointed, Plinth, 18th Century, 12 In. 2100.00
Wood Swivel Head, Carved, Sculpted Features, Dowel-Jointed, Costume, 45 In. 2128.00
Yellow Kid, Composition, Hugh Ears, 2 Teeth, Straw Body, Yellow Cotton Gown, 13 In. 1550.00

DOLL CLOTHES

Alexander-Kins, White Pleated Dress, Red Jacket, Slip, Panties, Hat, Hat Box, Box, 1950s.... 440.00
Betsy McCall, April Showers, White Taffeta Rain Cape, Cap, Beige Boots, No. B-3, Box, 1957 . 82.00
Betsy McCall, Aqua Coat, Black Collar & Hat, No. B-79, Box, 1959 .... 165.00
Betsy McCall, Ballerina Outfit, Red Tutu, Panties, Ballet Slippers, No. B-4, Box, 1957....... 192.00
Betsy McCall, Bar B-Q, Hot Dog Roaster, Hot Dog Buns, No. 9158, c.1960, Bubble Pack 82.00
Betsy McCall, Birthday Party Outfit, Pink Dress, Panties, Straw Hat, Shoes, Box, 1958 ...... 220.00
Betsy McCall, Birthday Party Outfit, Yellow Dress, Panties, Straw Hat, Socks, Shoes, Box, 1958 165.00
Betsy McCall, Bride Outfit, 2-Tier Ruffled Skirt, Satin Bodice, Panties, Slip, Veil, Box 220.00
Betsy McCall, Brunch Outfit, Robe, 2-Piece Pajamas, Sandals, No. B-27, Box, 1957 .... 55.00
Betsy McCall, Farm Girl, Strapless Gown, Taffeta, Stole, Panties, Slippers, c.1960, Bubble Pack 165.00
Betsy McCall, Gray Felt Coat, Pink Hood, Mittens, No. B1, Box, 1957 .... 110.00
Betsy McCall, Happy Birthday, Dress, Lace Overskirt, Panties, Hat, Shoes, Socks, c.1960, Bubble Pack 165.00
Betsy McCall, Holiday Outfit, Pleated Dress, Velvet Jacket, Panties, Hat, Socks, Shoes, Box, 1957 192.00
Betsy McCall, Little Cook, Bubble Pack, 1962-63 .... 110.00
Betsy McCall, Little Cook, Checked Dress, Apron, Socks, Shoes, Pot, Cake Pans, 1962, Bubble Pack 137.00
Betsy McCall, Mommy's Helper, Apron, Pants, Mop, Iron, Sandals, Box 165.00
Betsy McCall, On The Ice, Plaid Skirt, Blue Top, White Top, Beret, Ice Skates, Box, 1957..... 275.00
Betsy McCall, Pony Pals, Brown Jodhpurs, Blouse, Vest, Scarf, Box, 1959 .... 82.00
Betsy McCall, Schoolgirl Outfit, Striped Dress, Apple Applique, Panties, Shoes, Box, 1958.... 137.00
Betsy McCall, Sugar & Spice Outfit, Strapless Gown, Panties, Flowers, Slippers, Box, 1957... 137.00
Betsy McCall, Sunday Best Outfit, White Skirt Pink Slip, Panties, Straw Hat, 1957 .... 292.00
Bonnet, Woven Poplar, Pink Silk Lining & Ribbons, 4 In.. .... 146.00
Caroline, Raspberry Pique Top & Bloomers, Box, 1950s, 14 In. 82.00
Caroline, White, Pink Flowers, No. 49, Box, 1961-62. .... 55.00
Dress, Taffeta, Silk, Green, Fitted Waist, Gored Skirt, Ruffled Hem, Au Nain Bleu, c.1890, 30 In. 1608.00
Harvard Football Player, Celluloid Head, Crimson Uniform, 14 ½ In.. .... 175.00
Little Genius, Organdy Dress, Lace, Pink Crocheted Sweater, Diaper, Spoon, Box, 1950s, 8 In. 330.00
Little Genius, Organdy Dress, Pink Lace, Trim, Bonnet, Slip, Diaper, Box, 1950s 192.00
Madame Alexander, Kelly, Turquoise Dress, Lace Collar, Ribbon Trim, No. 15-25, Box...... 55.00
Madame Alexander, Lissy, Pink Skirt & Blouse, Ribbon Trim, Fur Muff, No. 10-14, Box, 1950s 495.00
Madame Alexander, Rosebud Print Gown, Ribbon Trim, c.1955, For 18 In. Doll 27.00
Raincoat, Purse, Umbrella, Ginny, Off-White, Red Trim 45.00
Shoes, Sporty, Rust, Ties, Toe Decoration, Flat Foot, For Sandra Sue 16.00
Vogue, Ginny, Yellow Knit Skirt, Panties, Shirt, Tam, Shoes, No. 7030, Box, 1957 .... 110.00
Wendy-Kins, Blue Dress, 3 Rows Of Ruffles, Slip, No. 0353, Box 247.00
Wendy-Kins, Pink Organdy Dress, Pinafore, No. 0676, Box, 1950s. 165.00
Wendy-Kins, Red Dress, White Rick-Rack Trim, Panties, No. 0430, Box, 1950s 110.00

DONALD DUCK *items are included in the Disneyana category.*

DOORSTOPS have been made in all types of designs. The vast majority of the doorstops sold today are cast iron and were made from about 1890 to 1930. Most of them are shaped like people, animals, flowers, or ships. Reproductions and newly designed examples are sold in gift shops.

3 Geese, Walking, Cast Iron, Hubley, No. 457, 8 x 8 In.. .... 517.00 to 690.00
Accordion Player, Black, Painted, Cast Iron, Label Spencer, Guilford, Conn., 6⅞ In... 1380.00 to 1725.00
Airplane, Over Treetops, Gold Paint, Iron, 6 x 9¾ In. .... *illus* 920.00
Alligator, Open Mouth, Full Figure, Embossed, Painted, Cast Iron, 12¼ In. 575.00
Banjo Player, Black, Spencer, 6½ In. 3450.00
Banjo Player, Cast Iron, 6¼ In. 920.00
Bellhop, Cast Iron, 9 In.. .... 345.00
Bellhop, Creations Co., 7½ In. 1150.00
Black Boy On Basket, 2-Piece Casting, Cast Iron, 7⅛ In. 8625.00
Black-Eyed Susan, No. 455, Hubley, 17⅞ In. 316.00
Bobby Blake, Holding Teddy Bear, Hubley, 1930s 450.00
Bowl, Marigolds, White, Blue, Cast Iron, Hubley, 7½ x 8 In. 403.00
Calla Lilies, Cast Iron, Hubley, 7⅛ x 5¼ In.. .... 345.00
Cat, Black, Seated, Ribbon, Figural, Cast Iron, 14 x 8 In.. .... 330.00
Cat, Copper, Brass, Art Deco, Chase, 8½ In.. .... 440.00
Cat, Gray, White, Reclining, c.1900, 7 x 13 In. 205.00
Cat, Licking Paw, Seated, Painted, Cast Iron, Waverly Studios, 7⅝ x 4½ In. 230.00
Cat, Puss 'N Boots Cast Iron, Creations Co., 1930, 8¾ In. 805.00
Cat, Seated, Painted, Cast Iron, 10 In. 265.00
Cat, White, Black, Cast Iron, 10⅜ In., Pair 259.00

Doll, Simon & Halbig, 122, Sleep Eyes, Tongue, Papier-Mache Bent Limbs, Toddler, 15 In.
$315.00

Doll, Simon & Halbig, 1009, Bisque Socket Head, Kid Body, 20 In.
$480.00

Doll, Vogue, Ginny, Coronation Queen, Plastic, Mohair Wig, Tag, 1954
$180.00

TIP

Keep dolls away from direct sunlight to avoid fading their hair and clothes.

Doorstop, Airplane, Over Treetops, Gold Paint, Iron, 6 x 9¾ In.
$920.00

Doorstop, Flower Basket, Bow Handle, Multicolored, Judd Co., 8 x 6 In.
$230.00

Doorstop, Lady In Hoop Skirt, Iron, Painted, National Foundry, 6¾ x 5¼ In.
$288.00

Doorstop, Little Red Riding Hood & Wolf, Iron, No. 860, 7 x 9 In.
$630.00

Item	Price
Cat, White, Raised Back, Green Eyes, Long Tail, Cast Iron, 10⅝ x 7½ In.	230.00
Cats, Side-Glancing, Pink, Blue, White, Black, Cast Iron, National Foundry, 7 x 5 In.	115.00
Children, Running, Dog, Green Base, Painted, Cast Iron, 6¾ x 10⅞ In.	4025.00
Clown, Blue Hat, Painted, Cast Iron, 19th Century, 10¼ x 4½ In.	400.00
Conestoga Wagon, Yellow, Black, Red, Cast Iron, 1930, 8 x 12 x 2 In.	350.00
Cornucopias, Cast Iron, Hubley, 8½ x 6 In.	144.00
Cottage, Cape Cod, Cast Iron, No. 211, Hubley, 5¾ x 7½ In.	115.00
Cottage, Cape Cod, Hollyhocks, Painted, Cast Iron, National Foundry, 5¾ x 8¾ In.	325.00
Covered Wagon, 2 Horses, Painted, Hubley, 5⅛ x 9½ In.	230.00
Covered Wagon, 2 Oxen, Cast Iron, Late 1800s, 8 x 12 In.	240.00
Cow, Walking, Brown, White, Full Figure, Cast Iron, 12⅜ x 13½ In.	1035.00
Daisy Bowl, Green Bowl, Cast Iron, Hubley, 6 x 7½ In.	173.00
Dancing Couple, Cast Iron, Painted, Early 20th Century, 8¾ In.	1175.00
Dog, Basset Hound, Cast Iron, 7⅛ x 7¼ In.	4025.00
Dog, Boston Terrier, Black, White, Cast Iron, 19th Century, 8¾ x 8¼ In.	130.00
Dog, Boston Terrier, Cast Iron, 10¾ In.	1500.00
Dog, Boston Terrier, Cast Iron, Rubber Bumpers, Bradley & Hubbard, 9⅝ x 12 In.	805.00
Dog, Boston Terrier, Grass, Embossed, Painted, Cast Iron, Bradley & Hubbard, 10 x 10 In.	373.00
Dog, Boxer, Standing, Brown, Black, White, Full Figure, Cast Iron, Hubley, 8½ x 9 In.	747.00
Dog, Cocker Spaniel, Brown, Tan, White, Full Figure, Cast Iron, Hubley, 11 In.	747.00
Dog, Dachshund, Begging, Black, Tan, Cast Iron, Dick Bros., 11 In.	1955.00
Dog, Dachshund, Standing, Cast Iron, 6¼ x 12¾ In.	173.00
Dog, Doberman Pinscher, Standing, Full Figure, Cast Iron, Hubley, 8 x 8½ In.	1093.00
Dog, English Setter, Pointing, Black, White, Cast Iron, Hubley, 8¾ x 15⅞ In.	431.00
Dog, Fox Terrier, Pointing, Painted, Cast Iron, 8¼ x 10½ In.	5463.00
Dog, Fox Terrier, Seated, Full Figure, Painted, Cast Iron, Hubley, 4¾ In.	173.00
Dog, Irish Setter, Cast Iron, c.1900, 10 x 15 In.	165.00 to 234.00
Dog, Pekingese, Brown, White, Black, Full Figure, Cast Iron, Hubley, 9 x 14½ In.	1955.00
Dog, Scottie, Begging, Full Figure, Marked No. 2, 8 In.	700.00
Dog, Scottie, Black, Standing, Full Figure, Cast Iron, Hubley, 8½ x 10¼ In.	230.00
Dog, Scottie, Black, Tan, Cast Iron, 19th Century, 8¼ x 10½ In.	375.00
Dog, Setter, Full Figure, Hubley, 8 x 15 In.	149.00 to 345.00
Dog, St. Bernard, Standing, Full Figure, Painted, Cast Iron, 7⅛ x 9 In.	1610.00 to 4300.00
Dog, Wolfhound, Cast Iron, 8½ x 9 In.	575.00
Dog, Wolfhound, Standing, Brown, White, Black, Cast Iron, 8½ In.	1035.00
Dog, Bulldog, Iron, Painted Black, 15½ x 25 In.	294.00
Dolphin, Rising From Wave, Brass, 14 x 9¼ x 3 In.	345.00
Duck, In Top Hat, Blue Pants, 2-Sided, Cast Iron, 10½ x 4 In.	115.00
Eagle, On Rocks, Snakes, Cast Iron, English Registry Marks, c.1975, 14 In.	489.00
Eagle & Vase, Black, Cast Iron, England, 11 x 8 In.	180.00
Elephant, G.O.P., 1936 Election, Landon, Copper Flashed, Cast Iron, 8 x 11 x 5 In.	300.00
Elephant, Palm Tree, Wedge Back, Cast Iron, 13¾ x 10¼ In.	345.00
Elephant, Trunk Raised, Full Figure, Cast Iron, 8¼ x 12 In.	201.00
Elephant, White, Cast Iron, 7½ In.	287.00
Fawn, Standing, Gold Paint, No. 6, Marked, Taylor Cook, 1930, 10 x 6 In.	402.00
Flower Basket, Bow Handle, Multicolored, Judd Co., 8 x 6 In. *illus*	230.00
Flower Basket, In Oval, Painted, Cast Iron, 5¾ x 7½ In.	110.00
Flower Vase, Gladiolas, Cast Iron, Hubley Manufacturing Co., 10⅜ x 8 In.	288.00
Flower Vase, Roses, Pink, Green, Urn, Cast Iron, Hubley, 10 x 6 In.	345.00
Frog, Brown, Green, Cast Iron, Early 20th Century, 5½ In.	71.00
Fruit Bowl, Oranges, Plum, Grapes, Green Bowl, Cast Iron, Hubley, 7 In.	230.00
Geese, Iron, Hubley, No. 457, 8 x 8 In.	517.00
Geese, Painted, Cast Iron, Early 20th Century, 8 In.	353.00
Geisha, Playing Mandolin, 6¾ In.	58.00
Girl, Brushing Hair From Face, West Wind, Flowers, Handle, Cast Iron, CJO, 18 x 8 In.	2185.00
Gladiolas, No. 489, Hubley, 10⅜ In.	288.00
Gnome, Barrel On Shoulder, Cup In Hand, Full Figure, Painted, Cast Iron, 11 x 5 In.	575.00
Gnome, Standing, Red Hat, Blue Pants, Brown Coat, Full Figure, Cast Iron, 11 x 6 In.	260.00
Gnome, With Keys, Lantern, Full Figure, Embossed, Painted, Cast Iron, 10 x 5⅜ In.	230.00
Gnome, With Shield, Club, Painted, Cast Iron, Bradley & Hubbard, 13½ In.	1450.00
Golfer, Overhead Swing, A Difficult Lie, Painted, Cast Iron, Hubley, 10 x 7 In.	1035.00
Golfer, Putting, Painted, Cast Iron, Hubley, 8⅜ x 7 In.	546.00
Grapes, Cast Iron, 7⅞ x 6⅝ In.	144.00
Halloween Girl, 17⅜ In.	1265.00
Horse, Cast Iron, Hubley, 8 x 8½ In.	402.00
Horse, Cast Iron, Hubley, 11 x 12¼ In.	460.00

Humpty Dumpty, On Wall, Full Figure, Embossed, Painted, Cast Iron, 4½ x 3⅜ In. 316.00
Indian Chief, Ceremonial Robe, Arms Crossed, Cast Iron, 8⅛ x 3½ In. 749.00
Indian Woman, Cast Iron, John Wright, 8⅝ x 2¾ In. 259.00
Jonquils, Bending In Breeze, Yellow, White, Green, Cast Iron, Hubley, 8 x 7½ In. 230.00
Jungle Boy, Leopard Skin Pelt, Arms Out, Painted, Cast Iron, 12½ In. . . . . 1150.00 to 1380.00
Koala, On Orange Log, Painted, Cast Iron, Taylor Cook, 1930, 7¼ x 5½ In. 201.00
Lady In Hoop Skirt, Iron, Painted, National Foundry, 6¾ x 5¼ In. . . . . *illus* 288.00
Leaf, Ivy, Black, Curled Stems, Wedge Back, Cast Iron, 10 In. 86.00
Lion, Reclining, On Pedestal, Cast Iron, 20th Century, 15 In. 165.00
Little Black Sambo, Signed, Blodgett Studios, Lake Geneva, Wis., 8½ In. 1380.00
Little Miss Muffet, Sewing On Mushroom, Embossed, Painted, Cast Iron, 7¾ In. 230.00
Little Red Riding Hood, Painted, Cast Iron, 19th Century, 9½ x 5 In. 275.00
Little Red Riding Hood & Wolf, Iron, No. 860, 7 x 9 In. . . . . *illus* 630.00
Lobster, Partially Emerged In Base, Painted, Cast Iron, 12 x 6½ In. 431.00
Lovebirds, Nestling, Tropical Foliage, Painted, Cast Iron, No. 600, Marked, 7 x 3¾ In. 258.00
Major Demo, No. 1249, Marked, CJO, 8½ In. 259.00
Mammy, Blue Dress, White Apron, Red Bandanna, Cast Iron, Hubley, 11¾ In. 198.00
Mammy, Red Dress, Blue Scarf, Yellow Headwrap, Iron, Littco, 13 x 8 In. . . . . 373.00 to 518.00
Mammy, Red Polka Dot Bandanna, Cast Iron, Hubley, 9 In. 633.00
Monkey, Seated, Head In Hand, Full Figure, Painted, Cast Iron, 8½ In. 345.00
Old Curiosity Shop Wedge, Painted, Cast Iron, 5 x 6 In. 2588.00
Old Stone House, Brass, Spencer, Marked, State Museum Guilford, 4 x 6 In. 460.00
Organ Grinder, Monkey, Solid Casting, 9 x 6 In. 2588.00
Oriental Girl, Standing, Teal, Gray, Wine, Full Figure, Cast Iron, 8 In. 115.00
Owl, On Branch, Cast Iron, 8⅞ x 5¼ In. 518.00
Owl, On Stump, Iron, CJO, No. 1287, 10 x 6 In. 862.00
Pan, Standing On Mushroom, Playing To Nymph, Painted, Cast Iron, 9¼ x 14 In. 805.00
Pansy Bowl, Blue & Cream Striped Bowl, Iron, Hubley, 7 x 6 In. . . . . *illus* 420.00
Parrot, In Ring, Bradley & Hubbard, 13¾ In. 260.00
Parrot, Multicolored, Cast Iron, 11¾ x 5¼ In. 230.00
Parrot, On Stump, Painted, Cast Iron, Stamped, KS, 7¾ x 6 In. 201.00
Peacock, On Barrel, Painted, Cast Iron, 6⅜ x 6½ In. 115.00
Peacock, Standing On Railing, Urn, Painted, Cast Iron, Hubley, 7½ x 4 In. 173.00
Pelican, On Dock, Cast Iron, Albany Foundry, 8 x 7¼ In. 230.00
Penguin, In Top Hat, Bowtie, Painted, Cast Iron, Hubley, 10½ x 4 In. 201.00
Penguin, Looking Up, Yellow, Red, Black, Cast Iron, Taylor Cook, 9½ x 5¼ In. 4312.00
Penguin With Flask, Cast Iron, 7¾ x 5½ In. 3450.00
Pheasant, Cast Iron, Hubley, 8½ x 7½ In. 575.00
Pheasant, In Underbrush, Painted, Cast Iron, Hubley, 8½ x 7½ In. 747.00
Pheasant, Iron, Hubley, No. 458, 8½ x 7½ In. 575.00
Pilgrim, Brown & White Outfit, Green Base, Cast Iron, CJO, 8¾ x 5⅜ In. 144.00
Pilgrim Boy, Iron, Full Figure, Marked CJO, 9 In. 500.00
Pilgrim With Gun, 10 In. 185.00
Police Boy, In Diaper, Cap, Red Mittens, Dog, Painted, Cast Iron, 10½ x 7¼ In. 460.00
Policeman, Resting On Fire Hydrant, Safety First, Embossed, Cast Iron, 9½ x 5⅜ In. 4313.00
Punch, Cast Iron, Painted, Late 19th Century, 13 In. . . . . *illus* 710.00
Rabbit, On Hind Legs, Embossed, Cast Iron, Bradley & Hubbard, 15 x 8½ In. 1725.00
Rabbit, Pushing Wheelbarrow, Blue Overalls, Green Base, Cast Iron, Littco, 11 x 8½ In. 4600.00
Rabbit, Seated, Painted, Cast Iron, 11½ x 10 In. 198.00
Rooster, Painted, Cast Iron, Late 19th Century, 11½ x 10 In. 390.00
Royal Coach, Driver, 2 Horses, Painted, Cast Iron, Hubley, 5⅞ x 11¼ In. 201.00
Rumba Dancer, Black Woman, Long Ruffled Dress, Yellow Headwrap, Cast Iron, 8 In. 7475.00
Rumba Dancer, Painted, Cast Iron, 11⅛ x 6⅜ In. 1840.00
Sailboat, High Seas, 17⅜ In. 1955.00
Sailor, Hands On Hips, Rope, Barrel, Painted, Cast Iron, 11⅝ x 5 In. 1955.00
Ship, Clipper, Painted, Cast Iron, Early 20th Century, 9¾ x 12 In. 470.00
Snow Owl, On Stump, White, Cast Iron, 10¼ x 6 In. 862.00
Southern Belle, Dress, National Foundry, 11¾ x 6 In. . . . . *illus* 205.00
Spanish Dancer, Red, Black, Gold, White, Cast Iron, Waverly Studios, 9 x 5 In. 345.00
Squirrel, With Nut, Cast Iron, 8 x 5½ In. 345.00
Street Singers, 2 Men, Woman, Painted, Cast Iron, Hubley, 6¼ x 7½ In. . . . . 865.00 to 1840.00
Topsy, Black Girl In Plaid Dress, Striped Socks, Hubley, 6⅛ In. 403.00
Uncle Sam, For The Open Door, Painted, Cast Iron, 12 x 5¼ In. . . . . *illus* 16000.00
Windmill, Cast Iron, National Fdry, 7 x 6⅞ In. 58.00
Woman, With Muff, Victorian Dress, Painted, Cast Iron, Albany Foundry, 9¼ x 5 In. 144.00
Women, Bathing, Holding Umbrella, Cast Iron, c.1920, 11 x 5 x 2 In. 990.00

Doorstop, Pansy Bowl, Blue & Cream Striped Bowl, Iron, Hubley, 7 x 6 In.
$420.00

Doorstop, Punch, Cast Iron, Painted, Late 19th Century, 13 In.
$710.00

Doorstop, Southern Belle, Dress, National Foundry, 11¾ x 6 In.
$205.00

Doorstop, Uncle Sam, For The Open Door, Painted, Cast Iron, 12 x 5¼ In.
$16000.00

Doulton, Teapot, Silicon Ware, Embossed Band, Impressed, Lambeth, 6¼ In.
$204.00

Doulton, Vase, Horses, Incised, Hannah Barlow, Lambeth, 1881, 7½ In.
$950.00

Doulton, Vase, Raised Flowers, Blue, Brown Panels, Lambeth, WR, 10¾ In., Pair
$605.00

TIP

Some disciplined collectors have a rule: Add a new piece to the collection only if you can get rid of a less desirable old one. Most of us just keep adding.

Yawning Child, Full Figure, Signed, MLC NY, c.1931, 8¾ In. 86.00
Zinnias, Cast Iron, Hubley, 7¼ x 7 In. 259.00

DORCHESTER POTTERY was founded by George Henderson in 1895 in Dorchester, Massachusetts. At first, the firm made utilitarian stoneware, but collectors are most interested in the line of decorated blue and white pottery that Dorchester made from 1940 until it went out of business in 1979.

DORCHESTER POTTERY WORKS BOSTON, MASS.

Bowl, Spongeware, 4 x 6¾ In. 15.00
Foot Warmer, Henderson, Stoneware, Stopper, 11 In. 40.00
Plate, Lilies Of The Valley, Blue Trim, Signed N. Ricci & C.A.H., 6¼ In. 75.00

DOULTON pottery and porcelain were made by Doulton and Co. of Burslem, England, after 1882. The name *Royal Doulton* appeared on their wares after 1902. Other pottery by Doulton is listed under Royal Doulton.

Biscuit Jar, Cats, Acanthus Scroll Ground, Beaded, Triangle Bands, Lambeth, 1888, 7 In. 5288.00
Jug, Liquor, For John Dewer, Incised DY, Lambeth, 5½ x 5 In. 168.00
Mug, Tyg, Bicycle, 3 Handles, Lambeth, 6 In. 248.00
Mug, Tyg, Stylized Flowers, Tan, Blue, Green, Footed, 3 Handles, Rosina Brown, 5⅞ In. 189.00
Pitcher, Asa Worthly, Lambeth, 7¼ x 5 In. 112.00
Pitcher, Commemorative, Colombian Exposition, Lambeth, c.1893, 6⅝ In. 335.00
Pitcher, Medallions, Embossed, Lambeth, 6 x 4 In. 56.00
Teapot, Band, Raised Designs, Blue, Gray Green, White, Lock-On Cover, 6¼ In. 201.00
Teapot, Silicon Ware, Embossed Band, Impressed, Lambeth, 6¼ In. *illus* 204.00
Vase, Farmer, Watering Horses At Stream, Sunset Sky, Holbeinware, 11¼ In. 600.00
Vase, Horses, Incised, Hannah Barlow, Lambeth, 1881, 7½ In. *illus* 950.00
Vase, Raised Flowers, Blue, Brown Panels, Lambeth, WR, 10¾ In., Pair *illus* 605.00
Vase, Scrolled Leaf, Ivory, Green, Plum, Green Washed Ground, c.1900, 8¾ In. 382.00

DRESDEN china is any china made in the town of Dresden, Germany. The most famous factory in Dresden is the Meissen factory. Figurines of eighteenth-century ladies and gentlemen, animal groups, or cherubs and other mythological subjects were popular. One special type of figurine was made with skirts of porcelain-dipped lace. Do not make the mistake of thinking that all pieces marked *Dresden* are from the Meissen factory. The Meissen pieces usually have crossed swords marks, and are listed under Meissen. Some recent porcelain from Ireland, called *Irish Dresden*, is not included in this book.

Bracket, Vines, Flowers, Putto, Reticulated Border, Mid 1900s, 8 x 9½ In., Pair 177.00
Centerpiece, 3 Angel Supports, Rose Design, Pierced, Marked, 7¾ x 15 In. 140.00
Centerpiece, 3 Cherub Supports, Polychrome, 7¾ x 15 In. 205.00
Centerpiece, Painted, Flowers, Multicolored, 2 Handles, Schumann, c.1950, 5 x 11 In. 264.00
Chocolate Pot, Flowers, Gilt, Marked, 1286/1, Late 19th Century, 9½ In. 121.00
Figurine, 2 Women, Lacey, c.1940, 7½ x 8 In. 118.00
Figurine, Dancing Ballerina, Marked, Blue Crown, 20th Century, 8 In. 106.00
Figurine, Dancing Lady, Marked, Blue Stamp, 20th Century, 7¾ In. 59.00
Figurine, Man, Woman, Dancing The Minuet, 5 x 5 In. 88.00
Figurine, Man Playing Flute, Woman, Playing Viola, c.1900, 6 x 5 In. 82.00
Figurine, Monkey Orchestra, 18th Century Dress, Instruments, 1900s, 5 In., 10 Piece 823.00
Figurine, Tailor, Holding Shears, Goat Wearing Spectacles, 6¾ x 6 x 2¾ In. 605.00
Figurine, Woman, On Couch With Parrot, c.1930, 4 x 5 x 3 In. 150.00
Figurine, Woman, Wearing White Gown With Flowers, c.1930, 6 x 5 x 4 In. 125.00
Frame, Angels, 20th Century, 11 In. 570.00
Group, 18th Century Couple Playing Music, c.1900, 6 x 5 In. 82.00
Group, Pastoral, 2 Women, Shepherd, c.1950, 9 In. 94.00
Group, Plateau, 2 Women Playing Game, Man Watching, 1950s, 8 x 10 In. 176.00
Plate, Cabinet, Raised Gilt, c.1920, 10½ In., Pair 1116.00
Standish, Cover, Man, Women Playing Chess, Oval Base, 8¾ x 10⅜ In. 118.00
Vase, Colonial Man & Woman Dancing, Blue Aurene Neck, Gold Ground, Handles, 8 In. 382.00
Vase, Gentleman & Woman, Aurene Blue Neck, Stamped, 7¾ In. *illus* 325.00

DUNCAN & MILLER is a term used by collectors when referring to glass made by the George A. Duncan and Sons Company or the Duncan and Miller Glass Company. These companies worked from 1893 to 1955, when the use of the name *Duncan* was discontinued and the firm became part of the United States Glass Company. Early patterns may be listed under Pressed Glass.

American Way, Console Set, Ruby, 3 Piece *illus* 150.00

anterbury, Basket, Blue Opalescent, 4 In. 24.00
anterbury, Condiment Set, Bottles, Salt, Pepper, Tray, 7 Piece 84.00
anterbury, Dish, Mayonnaise, Underplate 27.00
anterbury, Sugar & Creamer, Tray 27.00
hanticleer, Vase, Blue Opalescent 25.00
oronet, Goblet, Low, 6⅜ In., 6 Piece 180.00
estive, Bowl, Salad, 9½ In. 175.00
estive, Creamer, Honey Amber 75.00
estive, Gravy Boat, Honey Amber, Ladle 300.00
estive, Relish, 3 Sections, Metal Handle 375.00
estive, Sugar & Creamer, Cover, Wood Stand, Metal Handle 375.00
irst Love, Bowl, Sterling Silver Base, 3 Sections, 7½ In. 25.00
irst Love, Cordial, Terrace Blank, 1 Oz. 92.00
obnail, Candlestick, Amethyst, 4 x 4½ In., Pair 38.00
obnail, Vase, Pink Opalescent, Ruffled Rim, 7⅝ x 8¼ In. .... *illus* 100.00
esa, Cordial, 1 Oz. 53.00
autical, Berry Bowl, Handles, 9 In. 195.00
andwich, Bowl, Grapefruit, Light Green, 7 x 1½ In. 35.00
andwich, Goblet, Yellow Trim, 9 Oz., 5¾ x 3¼ In. 22.00
andwich, Plate, Salad, Yellow, 8 In. 15.00
andwich, Sherbet, Yellow, 5 Oz., 3¾ x 4¼ In. 20.00
andwich, Sugar & Creamer, Tray .... *illus* 40.00
anibel, Celery Tray, 3 Sections, Yellow Opalescent, 13 x 9 In. 80.00
pring Beauty, Cordial, 1 Oz. 30.00
ear Drop, Relish, 5 Sections, 12 In. 40.00
errain, Cordial, 1 Oz. 44.00

URAND art glass was made from 1924 to 1931. The Vineland Flint Glass Works was established y Victor Durand and Victor Durand Jr. in 1897. In 1924 Martin Bach Jr. and other artisans rom the Quezal glassworks joined them at the Vineland, New Jersey, plant to make Durand art lass. They called their gold iridescent glass Gold Luster.

owl, Translucent Ambergris, Blue Rim, White Pulled Feather, 9 In. 748.00
andlestick, Cranberry, White Pulled Feather, Ambergris Stem, 3 In., Pair 248.00
ompote, Cover, King Tut, Blue, Silver, Gold Luster, Oil Spot Foot, Amber Finial, 10 x 4 In. 2990.00
ompote, Iridescent Green, Bowl Cased In White, Onionskin Rim, Signed, 5½ In. 690.00
ecanter, Green Cut To Clear, Punty & Pillar, 12 In. 800.00
inger Jar, Cover, King Tut, Gold Iridescent, Blue, White, Amber Finial, 7½ In. 4600.00
inger Jar, Cover, Opal, Green, Gold Iridescent, Heart, Vines, Gold Threading, Oval, 7½ In. 3220.00
oblet, Pulled Feather, Ambergris Stemmed, Cobalt Blue, Ruby, 6¾ In., 2 Piece 690.00
amp, Blue, Moorish Crackle, Iridescent Gold, Cone Shape, Bronze Base, 16 In. 300.00
amp, Blue Iridescent, Applied Threading, Shouldered, Bronzed Metal, 6 x 25 In. 345.00
amp, Bronze, Blue, Moorish Crackle, Gold Iridescent, Bronze Base, 16 In. 690.00
amp, Iridescent Green, Gold Pulled Coil, Urn Shape, Metal Fittings, 25 In. 575.00
amp Base, Applied Green Ribs, Gold Interior, Conical, Metal Base, 11½ In. 1265.00
amp Base, Moorish Crackle, Mint Green, Gold & Pearl White Trailings, Metal Base, 9 In. 382.00
amp Base, Opal Blue Pulled Coil, Baluster, 13½ In. 403.00
late, Cup & Saucer, White Pulled Feathers, Ambergris Handle, 8½ & 4 In., 5 piece 920.00
ose Bowl, Gold Iridescent Orange, Yellow Highlights, Gold Luster Foot, 5¼ In. 460.00
ose Bowl, Iridescent Gold Foot, Blue Luster, Oval, Footed, Signed, 5 In. 805.00
hade, Torchere, Lady Gay Rose, Crimson Shaded To Pink, Ribbed, Double Ring, 9½ In. 1400.00
ase, Ambergris, Intaglio Stemmed Thistles, 4 In. 201.00
ase, Ambergris, White Threads & Leaves, Flared Rim & Base, 12¼ In. 558.00
ase, Beehive, Blue Luster, Egg Shape, Beehive, Signed, 8½ In. .... 650.00 to 834.00
ase, Beehive, Gold Luster, Oval, Signed, 10½ In. 1438.00
ase, Blue Iridescent, Flared Rim, Tapered, 8½ In. 470.00
ase, Blue Iridescent, Ribbed, Flared Rim, Long Neck, Bulbous, Signed, 18½ In. 1116.00
ase, Blue Iridescent, Shaded To Amethyst Iridescent, Squat Oval, 1 In. 805.00
ase, Blue Iridescent, White Pulled Heart & Vine, Ambergris Foot, 9 In., Pair 4465.00
ase, Blue Luster, Iridescent Blue, White Pulled Coils, Shouldered, 8½ In. 2530.00
ase, Blue Luster, Iridescent Gold Foot, Signed, 12 In. 850.00
ase, Blue Pulled Heart & Vine, Signed, 9 In. 3450.00
ase, Blue Pulled Heart & Vine, White Ground, Shouldered, 8½ In. 978.00
ase, Blue Pulled Waves, Creamy White Ground, Shouldered, 6½ In. 748.00
ase, Burnt Orange Iridescent, Black Pulled Heart & Vines, 10 In. 900.00
ase, Gold, Green Pulled Heart & Vine, 10¾ In. 1750.00

Fast-Food Glasses

If you collect the decorated glasses from fast-food restaurants, never wash them in the dishwasher. The heat and detergent will change the coloring and lower the value.

Dresden, Vase, Gentleman & Woman, Aurene Blue Neck, Stamped, 7¾ In.
$325.00

Duncan & Miller, American Way, Console Set, Ruby, 3 Piece
$150.00

Duncan & Miller, Hobnail, Vase, Pink Opalescent, Ruffled Rim, 7⅝ x 8¼ In.
$100.00

Duncan & Miller, Sandwich, Sugar & Creamer, Tray
$40.00

D

Durand, Vase, Gold Iridescent, c.1900, 6 In.
$375.00

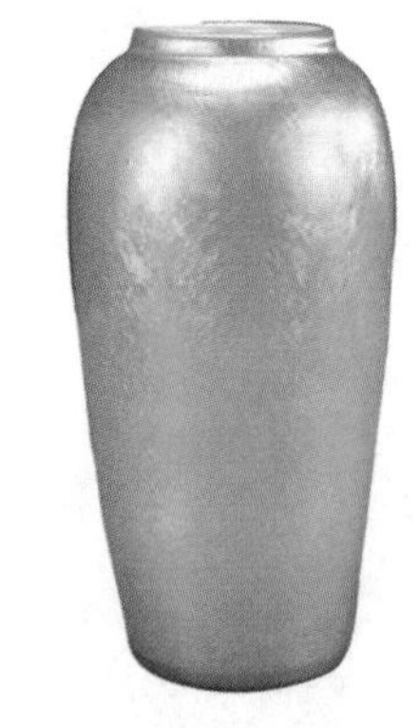

Durand, Vase, King Tut, Blue Iridescent, Purple Highlights, Flared, 7½ x 13 In.
$3000.00

Vase, Moorish Crackle, Green, White, Gold Iridescent, 10 In.
$1200.00

Vase, Gold, Orange Iridescent, Pulled Feather, Blue Tipped, Gold Threading, 9⅝ In. 411.0
Vase, Gold, Orange, Blue, Baluster, Rolled Rim, Signed, 7 In. 650.0
Vase, Gold Iridescent, c.1900, 6 In. . . . . *illus* 375.0
Vase, Gold Iridescent, Flared, Signed, 14 In. 780.0
Vase, Gold Iridescent, Saucer Foot, Flared Rim, 12½ In. 1495.0
Vase, Gold Iridescent, Shouldered, 9¾ x 7 In. 441.0
Vase, Gold Iridescent, Squat, 8 x 9¾ In. 1440.0
Vase, Gold Luster, Oval, Signed, 6½ In. 600.0
Vase, Green, Gold Iridescent Interior, Squat, 7¾ x 10½ In. 2760.0
Vase, Iridescent Blue, Purple Highlights, Squat, 5½ x 6 In. 748.0
Vase, Iridescent Blue, Threading, Gold Highlights, Shouldered, 8 In. 863.0
Vase, Iridescent Blue, Wide Mouth, Signed, 10 In. 748.0
Vase, Iridescent Gold, Blue Highlights, Shouldered, Flared Rim, 8½ In. 575.0
Vase, Iridescent Gold, Orange, Blue Highlights, Baluster, Tapered Rim, 8½ In. 575.0
Vase, Iridescent Marigold, Blue Pulled Feather, Shouldered, 8¼ In. 1840.0
Vase, Iridescent Silver Blue, Cobalt Blue, Shouldered, 9¼ In. 1610.0
Vase, King Tut, Blue Iridescent, Purple Highlights, Flared, 7½ x 13 In. . . . . *illus* 3000.0
Vase, King Tut, Green, Gold Iridescent, Purple, Blue, 10 In. 1150.0
Vase, King Tut, Green, Iridescent Gold, Bulbous, Signed, 6¼ In. . . . . 900.00 to 1725.0
Vase, King Tut, Iridescent Gold & Blue Swirl, Cream Ground, 12 In. 360.0
Vase, King Tut, Opal Blue, Baluster, Signed, 9½ In. 1333.0
Vase, King Tut, White Pearlescent, Blue Iridescent, Shouldered, 9½ In. 1150.0
Vase, King Tut, White, Blue Iridescent Ground, 10 In. 1800.0
Vase, Lady Gay Rose, Coral Red, Gold Iridescent Interior, Squat, 7¾ x 10½ In. 6000.0
Vase, Marigold Luster, Pulled, Coil, Bulbous Urn, Signed, 6 In. 1035.0
Vase, Moorish Crackle, Green, Iridescent Gold Ground, Shoulder, 9½ In. 345.0
Vase, Moorish Crackle, Green, White, Gold Iridescent, 10 In. . . . . *illus* 1200.0
Vase, Moorish Crackle, Iridescent, Gold Luster, Blue, White, 8 In. 1380.0
Vase, Opal, Iridescent Gold Coil, Shouldered, Signed, 4 In. 1035.0
Vase, Ruby Red, Pulled White Feathers, Flared Rim, Cupped Foot, 14 In., Pair 2350.0
Vase, Trumpet, Iridescent Blue, Iridescent Gold Pedestal Foot, 12 In. 805.0
Vase, White, Silvery Gold Iridescent, Bulbous, Long Neck, Flared Rim, 6¾ In. 920.0
Vase, White Hearts & Vines, Yellow Luster, c.1920, 7½ In. 385.0
Vase, Yellow, Iridescent Gold, Applied Gold, Blue Threading, 9¼ In. 230.0
Wine, Translucent Cranberry, White Pulled Feathers, Ambergris Stem, 5 In., Pair 650.0
Wine, Translucent Green Pulled Feathers, Ambergris Stem, Signed, 4¼ In., Pair 700.0

ELVIS PRESLEY, the well-known singer, lived from 1935 to 1977. He became famous by 1956. Elvis appeared on television, starred in twenty-seven movies, and performed in Las Vegas. Memorabilia from any of the Presley shows, his records, and even memorials made after his death are collected.

Bear, Plush, Black Leather Jacket, Dakin Signature, 11 In. 18.0
Bubble Gum Card, Boxcar Collectors, No. 14, 1978 . . . . 3.5
Bubble Gum Card, Boxcar Collectors, No. 20, 1978 . . . . 3.5
Bubble Gum Card, Boxcar Collectors, No. 38, 1978 . . . . 3.5
Bubble Gum Card, Boxcar Collectors, No. 42, 1978 . . . . 3.5
Cookbook, Elvis Presley American Discography, 1976, 224 Pages 24.0
Doll, With Guitar, Black Molded Hair, White Silky Shirt, Gold Tie, Eugene Doll Co., 12 In. 45.0
Magazine, The King's 22 Golden Years Of Glory, 1977 . . . . 12.9
Ornament, Army Dress Uniform, Playing Guitar 28.0
Pencils, Sealed Pack, c.1956, 3 x ¾ x 7½ In., 12 Pencils 287.0
Pendant & Chain, Plastic Photo Of Elvis, Goldtone, 1977, 18 In. 12.5
Photo On Wood, Lacquered, Hand Carved Pinewood Frame, 13 x 11 In. 30.0
Plate, Elvis In Hollywood, Limited Edition, 8½ In. 35.0
Plate, White Jumpsuit, In Vegas, Limited Edition, 8½ In. 46.0
Record, 45 RPM, Can't Help Falling In Love, 1961 . . . . 14.0
Record, 45 RPM, Devil In Disguise 12.0
Record, 45 RPM, Little Sister, Picture Sleeve, 1961 . . . . 15.0
Record, 45 RPM, Rags To Riches, 1971 . . . . 15.0
Record, 78 RPM, On Stage Album, Orange Label, 1970 . . . . 15.0
Record Player, Manual, Wood, Plastic Handle, Model 7-EP-45, 12 x 12½ x 7 In. 633.0
Scarf, I Want You I Need You, Image Of Elvis, 1956, 29 x 31 In. 150.0
Sheet Music, Love Me Tender, 1956 . . . . 25.0
TV Guide, Vol. 49-No. 2, January 13, 2001 . . . . 16.0

Umbrella & Tote Bag Set, Elvis In Front, Silver Glitter, Blue Microfiber, 12 x 13 In. 32.00
Wall Clock, High Gloss Laminated Picture Of Elvis, Brass Numbers, 1970s, 11 x 9 In. 21.00
Wallet, Image Of Elvis Playing Guitar, Record In Background, White Plastic, 1956 .... 200.00

ENAMELS listed here are made of glass particles and other materials heated and fused to metal. In the eighteenth and nineteenth centuries, workmen from Russia, France, England, and other countries made small boxes and table pieces of enamel on metal. One form of English enamel is called *Battersea* and is listed under that name. There was a revival of interest in enameling in the 1930s and a new style evolved. There is now renewed interest in the artistic enameled plaques, vases, ashtrays, and jewelry. Enamels made since the 1930s are usually on copper or steel, although silver was often used for jewelry. Graniteware is a separate category and enameled metal kitchen pieces may be included in the Kitchen category.

Ashtray, Copper, Flowers, Turquoise, White, Gold Leaves, Dots, 8 In. 40.00
Bowl, Abstract, Blue, Green, Thick, Translucent, 6 x 8 ½ In. 100.00
Bowl, Abstract, Textured, Chartreuse, Turquoise, Blue, Black, Vallenti, 1 ½ x 6 ½ In. 95.00
Bowl, Abstract, Textured, Chartreuse, Turquoise, Blue, Black, Vallenti, 1 ¼ x 8 ½ In. 135.00
Bowl, Turquoise & Orange Flame, Gold Green Ground, 3-Sided, Kareka, 1 ½ x 6 ½ In. 45.00
Creamer, Silver, Jeweled, Blue, St. Petersburg, Russia, 2 x 2 x 4 In. 3159.00
Cup, Abstract, Textured, Chartreuse, Turquoise, Cobalt Blue, Black, Signed, Vallenti, 4 In. ... 45.00
Desk Set, Champleve, Rococo Style, Brass Encrier, Blotter 207.00
Dish, Blue Flower, Buds, Signed, Edward Winter, 6 ½ In. 125.00
Dish, Noah's Ark, Multicolored, Signed, Annemarie Davidson, 7 ½ In. 45.00
Egg, Guilloche, Gilt, Silver Base, Dmitrii Nikolaveich Nikolaev, c.1900, 2 ½ In. 3900.00
On Board, Going Home, New York Countryside In Autumn, F. Carder, 18 x 22 In. 920.00
Placecard Holder Set, Figural, Ladies, 19th Century Fashion, 1 ⅜ In., 15 Piece 354.00
Plate, Abstract, Brown, Beige, Yellow, Signed, Vallenti, 8 ½ In. 135.00
Plate, Multicolored, Edward Star For Gumps, 8 ¼ In. 125.00
Pot, Cover, Enamel Over Cast Iron, Red, Handles, Copco, Michael Lax, 9 ½ In. 125.00
Toilette Service, Sterling Silver, Pink Guillochem, D & S, England, 1935, 6 Piece ..... *illus* 515.00
Vase, Overlapping Red Petals, White Circles, Rolled Silver Rim, Flared, Limoges, C. Faure, 10 In. 10350.00
Vase, Green, Orange Foil-Like Ground, Drips, Metal Rim, Silver Footed, C. Faure, 5 ½ In. 920.00
Vase, Limoges, Camille Faure, Hummingbird, Flowers, Silver Blue Ground, 8 In. 354.00
Vase, Limoges, Swirls, Pinwheels, Red, White, Black Enamel, Silver Foot, C. Faure, 11 x 12 In. 13200.00
Vase, Pink & White Petals, Beading, Foil Ground, Brass Base, Rim, Limoges, C. Faure, 5 In. .. 5175.00
Young Woman, Renaissance Clothes, Portrait On Copper, Louis XVI Frame, 7 x 5 In. 235.00

ERPHILA is a mark found on Czechoslovakian and other pottery and porcelain made after 1920. This mark was used on items imported by Ebeling & Reuss, Philadelphia, a giftware firm that is still operating in Pennsylvania. The mark is a combination of the letters *E* and *R* (Ebeling & Reuss) and the first letters of the city, Phila(delphia). Many whimsical figural pitchers and creamers, figurines, platters, and other giftwares carry this mark.

Ashtray, Topped With Figure Of Black Boy Stacking 2 Large Dice, Germany, 4 x 4 In. 20.00
Bust, Washington, Germany, 5 In. .... *illus* 25.00
Figurine, 2 Foals, Tan & Brown, Base With Impressed Grass, Marked, Germany, 8 x 11 In. 80.00
Pitcher, Toucan, Red & Black, Ditmar Urbach, Czechoslovakia, 9 x 7 ½ In. .... *illus* 475.00
Powder Box, Woman Holding Flowers, Nancy Pert Dresser Doll, Germany, 1920s, 7 ½ x 6 In. .. 100.00
Vase, Flared, 2 Rows Of Tapered Spheres, White, Stamped, Czechoslovakia, 8 x 12 x 4 In. 45.00
Vase, Calla Lilies, Black Ground, Germany, 7 ½ x 5 In. 35.00
Vase, Nude Dancer, Robes Trailing, 3 Tree Trunk Vases, White, Germany, 5 x 4 ¾ x 2 In. 55.00

ES GERMANY porcelain was made at the factory of Erdmann Schlegelmilch from 1861 to 1937 in Suhl, Germany. The porcelain, marked *ES Germany* or *ES Suhl*, was sold decorated or undecorated. Other pieces were made at a factory in Saxony, Prussia, and are marked *ES Prussia*. Reinhold Schlegelmilch made the famous wares marked RS Germany.

Cake Plate, 2 Handles, Hand Painted, c.1920, 10 In. 165.00
Candy Dish, 2 Birds On Flowered Branch, Open Molded Handle, Scalloped Rim 35.00
Plate, Fuchsia & Green On Border, Lady, Lady In Waiting, Gentleman, Wreath, 7 ½ In. 23.00

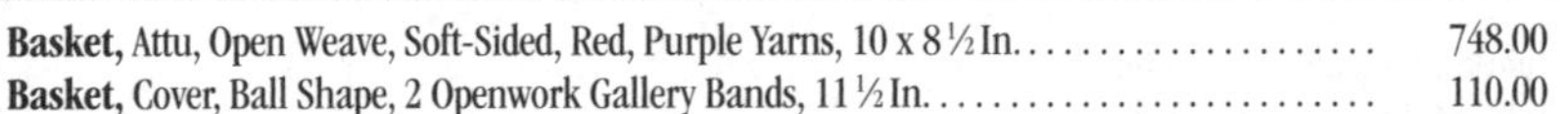

ESKIMO artifacts of all types are collected. Carvings of whale or walrus teeth are listed under Scrimshaw. Baskets are in the Basket category. All other types of Eskimo art are listed here. In Canada and some other areas, the term *Inuit* is used instead of Eskimo.

Basket, Attu, Open Weave, Soft-Sided, Red, Purple Yarns, 10 x 8 ½ In. 748.00
Basket, Cover, Ball Shape, 2 Openwork Gallery Bands, 11 ½ In. 110.00

Enamel, Toilette Service, Sterling Silver, Pink Guillochem, D & S, England, 1935, 6 Piece
$515.00

Erphila, Bust, Washington, Germany, 5 In.
$25.00

Erphila, Pitcher, Toucan, Red & Black, Ditmar Urbach, Czechoslovakia, 9 x 7 ½ In.
$475.00

TIP
Glue broken china with an invisible mending cement that is waterproof.

Faberge, Kovsh, Silver, Scrolling Leaves, Rope Rim, 12 In.
$68000.00

Faberge, Powder Box, Hinged Cover, Red Enamel, 1908-17, 1¾ In.
$12000.00

Faience, Plate, Putti On Griffin, Blue Ground, Marked, Italy, 6¼ In.
$145.00

TIP

Look in your hardware store for the new glues that can fix almost anything. Buy the proper one to fix transparent glass, porous pottery, or nonporous metals. There will be one that will work.

Basket, Cover, Flowers, Handles, 10½ x 12 In. 950.00
Basket, Lid, Double Handle, Multicolored Flowers, 12 x 10 In. 1140.00
Basket, Squares, Banded, 8 x 3¾ In. 44.00
Doll, Wood, Carved, Period Clothes, Leather, Sealskin, c.1900, 15 In. 325.00
Figure, Walrus, Black, Soapstone, 13 x 18 In. 220.00
Scoop, Bone, Alaska, 14 In. 138.00
Sculpture, Adult & Child Hunting Seal, Soapstone, Carved, 8 x 8½ In. 200.00
Sculpture, Fisherman, Seated, Holding Catch, Dark Soapstone, 13 In. 475.00
Sculpture, Hunters On Polar Bear-Shaped Ice Sheet, Ivory, Carved 2¼ x 10 In. 650.00
Sculpture, Stone, Whale On Pedestal, Alaskan, 13 In. 165.00
Storage Basket, Stone Duck Handle On Lid, 21¼ x 8½ In. 495.00
Whalebone Carving, Dog, S. Weyiouanna, Signed 1650.00

FABERGE was a firm of jewelers and goldsmiths founded in St. Petersburg, Russia, in 1842, by Gustav Faberge. Peter Carl Faberge, his son, was jeweler to the Russian Imperial Court from about 1870 to 1914. The rare Imperial Easter eggs, jewelry, and decorative items are very expensive today.

ФАБЕРЖЕ
КФ

Bowl, Cut Glass, Feather & Arch, Hobstar, Silver Ribbon Rim, 1917, 8¾ In. 14160.00
Box, Silver, Hinged Cover, Egg Shape, Cloisonne, Inset Stones, Feodor Rucket, 2¾ x 4 In. 2415.00
Box, Silver, Oval Domed Cover, Scroll, Shell, Flowers, Cattails, Reed Rim, 1895, 6¼ x 5 In. 27140.00
Box, Silver, Yellow Enamel, Flower Border, Gilt, Oval, 1¼ x 3½ In. 460.00
Candy Dish, Cut Glass, Oval, Cut Flying Birds, Tropical Trees, Sunset, Silver Banded, 10½ In. 15340.00
Case, Salmon Enamel, Guilloche Ground, Gold Ribbon, 1917, 4½ In. 70800.00
Cigarette Case, Blue Enamel, Sunburst, Diamond Set, 1917, 3¾ In. 30680.00
Cigarette Case, Gold, Ribbed, Imperial Eagle, Diamonds, Sapphire Cabochon, 1908, 3 In. 21240.00
Cigarette Case, Pink & White Enamel, Guilloche Waves, Gold Palmette Bands, 3½ In. 56640.00
Cigarette Case, Pink Enamel, Guilloche, Reeds, Pellets, Gem Set Crown, 3½ In. 64900.00
Console, Cut Glass, Star Facets, Large Center Star, Silver Ribbon Rim, 1917, 14½ In. 20060.00
Creamer, Silver, Chased With Scrolls, Shellwork, Flowers, Gilt Interior, 1917, 5¼ In. 22420.00
Cup, Earthenware, Green Glaze, Silver Reeded Rim, Flower Swags, 1908, 2¼ In. 18880.00
Kovsh, Silver, 8 Lobed Panels, Gilt Interior, Circular Foot, Ornate Handle, 1896, 8¼ In. 28320.00
Kovsh, Silver, Double Engraved Band, Hook Handle, Circular Raised Foot, 1917, 4½ In. 12980.00
Kovsh, Silver, Scrolling Leaves, Rope Rim, 12 In. *illus* 68000.00
Kovsh, Silver, Tea Glass, Banded Reed, Laurel Swags, Stylized Handle, 1908, 2¾ In. 7080.00
Page Turner, Landscape, Sterling Silver, Pink Stone Cabochons, 7½ x 1¼ In. 5676.00
Plateau, Mirrored Centerpiece, Rococo Scrolls, Baluster Railing, 1908, 13¼ In. 22420.00
Powder Box, Hinged Cover, Red Enamel, 1908-17, 1¾ In. *illus* 12000.00
Powder Box, Hinged Cover, Strawberry Red Enamel, Guilloche Waves, 1¾ In. 14160.00

FAIENCE refers to tin-glazed earthenware, especially the wares made in France, Germany, and Scandinavia. It is also correct to say that faience is the same as majolica or Delft, although usually the term refers only to the tin-glazed pottery of the three regions mentioned.

Bowl, Barber, Flowers, Insects, Multicolored, France, 18th Century, 3 x 11¼ In. 176.00
Bowl, Blue Leafy Design, Cream Glaze, Hanging Hole, 19th Century, 12¾ x 3 In. 805.00
Bowl, Hen Shape, Applied Flowers, Pastel Glazes, 12¼ x 16½ x 8½ In. 3360.00
Centerpiece, Oval, Pedestal, Griffin Handles, Multicolored, Dragon, Crowns, 8 x 18 In. 605.00
Figurine, Madonna, Gown, Crown, 18th Century, 10 In. 250.00
Gravy Boat, Side Handles, Flowers, Butterflies, Tray, 4 x 9 In. 35.00
Plate, Dinner, Flowers, Rouen, France, 10 In., Pair 180.00
Plate, Putti On Griffin, Blue Ground, Marked, Italy, 6¼ In. *illus* 145.00
Plate, Renaissance Decoration, Scalloped Borders, Rooster Mark, 1800s, 8¾ In., 6 Piece 575.00
Platter, Flowers, Blue & White, Oval, Continental, 18th Century, 13½ x 18⅝ In. 353.00
Salt, Dragonfly Center, Flowers, Scalloped Base, c.1780-1810, 1½ In. 77.00
Salt, Flowers, 8-Sided, Rouen, Normandy, c.1750-69, 1¾ In. 77.00
Tankard, Painted, Blue Underglaze, Couple In Garden, Pewter Hinged Cover, 11 In. 413.00
Tankard, Painted, Castle, Medallion, Blue Ground, Pewter Base, Hinged Cover, 11 In. 384.00
Urn, Multicolored, Older Man, Lady, Flowers, Leaves, 18th Century, 6½ x 5 In. 1100.00
Vase, French Aesthetic, Gilt Decorated, c.1878, 14¾ x 7 In., Pair 11456.00

FAIRINGS are small souvenir boxes and figurines that were sold at country fairs during the nineteenth century. Most were made in Germany. Reproductions of fairings are being made, especially of the famous *Twelve Months after Marriage* series.

Trinket Box, Boy On Dresser, 4¼ In. 44.00
Trinket Box, Brass, Swirl Legs, 4¼ x 3 In. 18.00

Trinket Box, Child In Bed, Curtains, Flower Cover, Cat, Marked, 4 ¼ In. 88.00
Trinket Box, Child On Chair, Gold Trim, 4 In. 140.00
Trinket Box, Girl On Dresser, 4½ In. .... 44.00 to 77.00
Trinket Box, Hatching Angel, 4 ½ In. 77.00
Trinket Box, Maple, Pine, Painted Scenes, Cut Nails, Lift Lid, 7 Drawers, 7 ½ x 10 ¾ In. 2185.00
Trinket Box, Mosaic, Flowers, Goldtone Metal, Stamped Designs, 1 ⅛ x 1 ⅝ In. 10.00

FAIRYLAND LUSTER *pieces are included in the Wedgwood category.*

FAMILLE ROSE, *see Chinese Export category.*

FANS have been used for cooling since the days of the ancients. By the eighteenth century, the fan was an accessory for the lady of fashion and very elaborate and expensive fans were made. Sticks were made of ivory or wood, set with jewels or carved. The fans were made of painted silk or paper. Inexpensive paper fans printed with advertising were giveaways in the late nineteenth and early twentieth centuries. Electric fans were introduced in 1882.

Advertising, Huylers Ice Cream, Polar Bear, Chocolate Ice Cream Soda, Paperboard, 1910 .. 75.00
Advertising, International Ice Cream, Child, Cart, Rooster, Cardboard, Wood Handle....... 80.00
Advertising, Moxie Soda, Folding, Celluloid, c.1900, 6 ½ In. 58.00
Advertising, Sleepy Eye Flour, Indian, Die Cut, Cardboard, 13 ⅝ x 6 In. 275.00
Bamboo, Paper, Bird Under Pine Tree, Calligraphy, Chinese, 12 In. 531.00
Electric, Edison Bi-Polar, No. 7009, Twin Coils, 4 Blades, Brass Cage, 10 In. 3055.00
Electric, Metal, 2 Blades, Wood Base, Label, Trico Vacuum Fan, Pat. No. 745, 117, 6 ¾ In. 290.00
Electric, Universal, Hurricane, Eck, 4 Blades, Brass Cage, 13 In. 940.00
Feather, Brown, White, Red Handle, 12 x 8 In. 82.00
Ivory Sticks, Gold Lacquer, Village Scene, Henoki Wood Box, Japan, 19th Century 1293.00
Lace, Ivory, France, Frame, c.1900, 21 In. 88.00
Lithograph, 2 Men, 3 Women, Dog, Multicolored Sticks, 25 ½ x 15 ½ x 2 In., Pair 840.00
Metal, Gilt, Figures, Instruments, Flowers, Continental, 4 In. .... *illus* 17.00
Mother-Of-Pearl, Gilt, Carved, Painted, Figures In Landscape, Gilt Frame, 21 x 25 In. 575.00
Paper, Figures, Birds, Hand Painted, England, Frame, 19th Century, 14 x 24 In. 79.00
Paper, Sandalwood Stays, Figures, Ivory Faces, Brocade Gowns, Frame, Chinese, 19th Century 441.00
Sandalwood, Carved, Chinese, Box, 8 In. 60.00
Silk, 2 Women, Red Dress, Blue Dress, Hand Painted, Frame, c.1900, 24 In. 150.00
Silk, Embroidered, Flowers, Victorian, Frame, 14 x 24 In. 59.00
Silk, Flowers, Bone Sticks, Ebony, Chinese, Frame, 19th Century, 26 In. .... *illus* 65.00
Silk, Hand Painted, 19th Century, Chinese Frame, 7 x 21 In., Pair 176.00
Silk, Hand Painted, Carved, Gilt Wood, Bird, Flowers, Lace Border, Shadowbox, 32 x 19 In.... 206.00
Silk, Hand Painted, Embroidered, Late 19th Century, 18 x 31 In. .... *illus* 175.00
Silk, Hand Painted, Frame, Late 19th Century, 21 In. 88.00
Silk, Trees, Stream, Pearl Sticks, Ebony & Gilt Frame, 19th Century, 26 In. .... *illus* 65.00
Silver, Cast, Filigree, Blue, Green Enamel, 7 ½ In. 1998.00
Tortoiseshell, Carved, Pierced Figures, Garden Pavilions, 7 ½ In. 1880.00
Tortoiseshell, Figures, Garden Scene, Painted Flowers, Chinese, Lacquered Box, 19 Century. 1645.00

FAST FOOD COLLECTIBLES *may be included in several categories, such as Advertising, Coca-Cola, Toy, etc.*

FEDERZEICHNUNG, *see Loetz category.*

FENTON Art Glass Company, founded in Martins Ferry, Ohio, by Frank L. Fenton, is now located in Williamstown, West Virginia. It is noted for early carnival glass produced between 1907 and 1920. Some of these pieces are listed in the Carnival Glass category. Many other types of glass were also made. Spanish Lace in this section refers to the pattern made by Fenton. The pottery closed in 2007.

Aqua Crest, Basket, Ruffled Edge, 5 In. 70.00
Aqua Crest, Jug, 6 In. 30.00
Aqua Crest, Vase, Footed, Ruffled Edge, 6 In. 48.00
Atlantis, Vase, Red Carnival, 6 ½ In. 54.00
Bicentennial, Plate, Red Slag, Daniel Webster Quote, 8 In. 65.00
Black Rose Crest, Basket, Low, Black Handle, 1950s, Low, 7 In. 85.00
Burmese, Basket, 5 In. 125.00
Burmese, Basket, Beaded Melon 75.00
Burmese, Cruet, Glossy, Stopper, 7 In. 30.00
Burmese, Dresser Set, Flowers, Coralene, Signed, T. Deuley, 3 Piece .... *illus* 115.00

TIP
Folding fans should be stored closed.

Fan, Metal, Gilt, Figures, Instruments, Flowers, Continental, 4 In.
$17.00

Fan, Silk, Flowers, Bone Sticks, Ebony, Chinese, Frame, 19th Century, 26 In.
$65.00

Fan, Silk, Hand Painted, Embroidered, Late 19th Century, 18 x 31 In.
$175.00

Fan, Silk, Trees, Stream, Pearl Sticks, Ebony & Gilt Frame, 19th Century, 26 In.
$65.00

Fenton, Burmese, Dresser Set, Flowers, Coralene, Signed, T. Deuley, 3 Piece
$115.00

F

Fenton, Coin Dot, Pitcher, Blue Opalescent, 9 ½ In.
$92.00

Fenton, Hobnail, Basket, Green Opalescent, Footed, 6 In.
$180.00

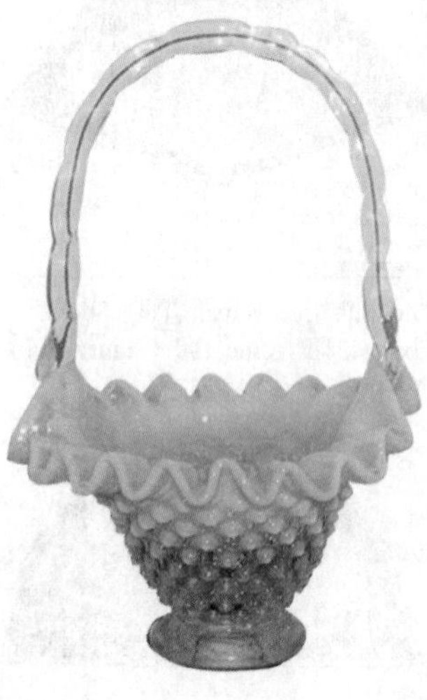

Burmese, Vase, Tricornered, 7 In. . . . 45.00
Butterfly, Ring Holder, Pink Iridescent . . . 20.00
Butterfly & Grape, Bowl, Footed, Golden, c.1918, 5 In. . . . 35.00
Coin Dot, Bowl, Honeysuckle, Opalescent, 7 In. . . . 45.00
Coin Dot, Creamer, Hurricane, Blue Opalescent . . . 46.00
Coin Dot, Lamp, Hurricane, Blue Opalescent . . . 135.00
Coin Dot, Pitcher, Blue Opalescent, 9 ½ In. . . . *illus* 92.00
Coin Dot, Vase, Cranberry Opalescent, 6 x 7 In. . . . 185.00
Coin Dot, Vase, Cranberry Opalescent, Handles, Ruffled Edge, 8 In. . . . 250.00
Crystal Velvet, Basket, Water Lily, 7 In. . . . 35.00
Crystal Velvet, Figurine, Butterfly On Stand . . . 50.00
Crystal Velvet, Rose Bowl, Water Lily . . . 25.00
Daffodil, Vase, Blue Burmese, 5 In. . . . 25.00
Daisy & Button, Basket, Handles, Milk Glass, 1936, 5 ½ In. . . . 20.00
Daisy & Button, Shoe, Milk Glass, Marked . . . 5.00
Daisy & Button, Vase, Hat, Blue Opalescent, 5 In. . . . 22.00
Diamond Optic, Ginger Jar, Cover, Burmese . . . 198.00
Diamond Optic, Vase, Cranberry Opalescent, Signed, Bill Fenton, 13 In. . . . 55.00
Dogwood, Bell, Blue Cameo . . . 45.00
Dogwood, Vase, Dusty Rose, 1984-85, 8 In. . . . 25.00
Fern, Barber Bottle, Cranberry Opalescent . . . 65.00
Fern, Sugar Shaker, Blue Opalescent . . . 65.00
Fern, Tumbler, Topaz Opalescent . . . 10.00
Figurine, Alley Cat, Black Satin, 10 ½ In. . . . 165.00
Figurine, Alley Cat, Chocolate, 10 ½ In. . . . 65.00
Figurine, Alley Cat, Periwinkle Blue, 10 ½ In. . . . 50.00
Figurine, Alley Cat, Purple Slag, 10 ½ In. . . . 360.00
Figurine, Bear, Reclining, Cameo Satin, Hearts & Flowers, 4 In. . . . 29.00
Figurine, Bear, Reclining, Happy Anniversary, Pink Flowers, Gold Features & Paws, 4 In. . . . 49.00
Figurine, Bear, Sitting, Empress Rose, 1900s, 3 ½ In. . . . 20.00
Figurine, Bear, Sitting, Morning Mist, 1990s, 3 ½ In. . . . 25.00
Figurine, Bear, Sitting, Emerald Green, 3 ½ In. . . . 59.00
Figurine, Bird, Cameo Satin, Daisies, 4 In. . . . 25.00
Figurine, Bird, Rosalene, 4 In. . . . 25.00
Figurine, Bird, White Carnival, 4 In. . . . 25.00
Figurine, Bunny, French Opalescent, 3 ½ In. . . . 20.00
Figurine, Cat, Aquamarine, 5 In. . . . 20.00
Figurine, Cat, Blue, 3 ¼ In. . . . 20.00
Figurine, Cat, Empress Rose, 1990s, 3 ¾ In. . . . 35.00
Figurine, Cat, Empress Rose, Daisy, 1990s, 3 ¾ In. . . . 45.00
Figurine, Cat, Martha's Rose Opalescent, 1990s, 3¾ In. . . . 25.00 to 40.00
Figurine, Elephant, Cobalt, Marigold Carnival, 3 ½ In. . . . 29.00
Figurine, Fawn, Ruby, Roses . . . 70.00
Figurine, Fox, Red Carnival . . . 35.00
Figurine, Frog, Rosalene . . . 69.00
Figurine, Girl, Holding Hat, Burmese, Flowers, 8 In. . . . 55.00
Figurine, Happiness Bird, Blue Satin, 6 In. . . . 25.00
Figurine, Happiness Bird, Cameo Satin, Daisies, 6 In. . . . 25.00
Figurine, Happiness Bird, Custard, Daisies, 6 In. . . . 30.00 to 45.00
Figurine, Happiness Bird, Rosalene, 6 In. . . . 25.00
Figurine, Happiness Bird, White Satin, Pink Blossom, 6 In. . . . 45.00
Figurine, Mouse, Spruce, Gold Trim, 3 In. . . . 25.00
Figurine, Swan, Cameo Satin, Daisies . . . 35.00
Fine Rib, Vase, Red, Scalloped Edge, 12 In. . . . 190.00
Florentine Green, Candy Jar, Lid, c.1921, 8 In. . . . 89.00
Hanging Hearts, Vase, Amethyst, White, 1981, 7 In. . . . 145.00
Hanging Vine, Console Set, Bowl, Footed, Candlesticks, Turquoise, Red Leaves, 3 Piece . . . 3163.00
Heart Optic, Basket, Cranberry Opalescent, 1990s, 4 In. . . . 55.00
Heart Optic, Puff Box, Cover, Cranberry, 1990s, 4 In. . . . 95.00
Hobnail, Basket, Blue Opalescent, Handle, Ruffled Edge, c.1950, 4 ½ In. . . . 40.00
Hobnail, Basket, Blue Opalescent, 10 In. . . . 150.00
Hobnail, Basket, Cranberry Opalescent, 4 ½ In. . . . 50.00
Hobnail, Basket, Cranberry Opalescent, 10 In. . . . 75.00
Hobnail, Basket, Green Opalescent, Footed, 6 In. . . . *illus* 180.00
Hobnail, Bowl, Plum Opalescent, Ruffled & Crimped Edge, 10 In. . . . *illus* 345.00

Hobnail, Candy Dish, Center Handle, Ruby Overlay, 7 ½ In. 30.00
Hobnail, Candy Dish, Milk Glass, Center Handle, Marked, 7 ½ In. 12.00
Hobnail, Cruet, Stopper, Cranberry Opalescent 185.00
Hobnail, Fairy Lamp, Colonial Blue 20.00
Hobnail, Jug, Cranberry Opalescent, Handle, 80 Oz. 350.00
Hobnail, Lamp, Courting, Colonial Green 45.00
Hobnail, Sugar & Creamer, Blue Opalescent, c.1950 .... 215.00
Hobnail, Toothpick, Hat, Blue 10.00
Hobnail, Vase, Bud, Green Opalescent, c.1960, 8 In., Pair 38.00
Hobnail, Vase, Cranberry, 4 ½ In. 40.00
Hobnail, Vase, Cranberry, 5 In. 25.00
Hobnail, Vase, Cranberry, 8 In. 35.00
Hobnail, Vase, Jack-In-The-Pulpit, Cranberry Opalescent, Signed, Pre 1970, 11 In. 150.00
Hobnail, Water Set, Blue Opalescent, 80-Oz. Pitcher, 9 Piece 500.00
Hobnail, Water Set, Cranberry Opalescent, 80-Oz. Pitcher, 7 Piece 650.00
Iris, Basket, Bone White, 8 ¼ In. 60.00
Ivy Ball, Green, Ribbed, Optic 50.00
Magnolia, Candy Box, 10 ½ In. 95.00
Mandarin Red, Basket 185.00
Mandarin Red, Bowl, Cupped, 6 In. 85.00
Mandarin Red, Bowl, Flared, 7 ½ In. 90.00
Mandarin Red, Bowl, Oval, 12 In. 135.00
Mandarin Red, Vase, Crimped, 6 In. 85.00
Melon, Jug, Rose Overlay, 1940s, 9 In. 70.00
Ming, Bowl, Cupped, Footed 35.00
Ming, Bowl, Tulip, 10 ½ In. 65.00
Ming, Ginger Jar, Cover, White, 6 In. 115.00
Ming, Tumbler, White, 5 In. 25.00
Ming, Vase, 11 In. 135.00
Moon & Star, Bowl, Green Opalescent, Beaded 45.00
Mosaic, Vase, Amethyst, Spattered Red, Yellow Threading, Blue, Oval, Shoulders, 5 In. 1333.00
Mulberry Overlay, Cruet, Stopper, 1942 .... 69.00
Orange Tree, Candlestick, Favrene, 1990s, Pair 135.00
Owl, Fairy Light, Blue Satin, 2 Piece 25.00
Peach Crest, Basket, Hobnail, 10 In. 160.00
Peach Crest, Bowl, 10 In. 30.00
Peach Crest, Bowl, Ruffled Edge, 7 In. 42.00
Peach Crest, Candlestick, No. 7270, 5 In., Pair 87.00
Peach Crest, Creamer, 4 In. 30.00
Peach Crest, Pitcher, Ivy & Small Flowers, Ruffled Edge, 9 In. 125.00
Peach Crest, Vase, Hat, Ruffled Edge, 4 In. 35.00
Peach Crest, Vase, Ruffled Edge, 9 In. .... *illus* 181.00
Peacock, Bookend, Black Satin, c.1935 .... 260.00
Persian Medallion, Plate, Blue, 9 In. 71.00
Persian Pearl, Bowl, Swan, 1993 .... 85.00
Persian Pearl, Epergne, 3-Lily, 1993 .... 155.00
Poppy, Basket, Rose Satin, 10 In. 75.00
Poppy, Basket, Rose Satin, 11 In. 33.00
Provincial Bouquet, Vase, 1978-88, 13 In. 105.00
Rib Optic, Vase, Blue, Ruffled Edge, Signed, 11 In. 35.00
Rose Crest, Vase, 3 ½ In. 100.00
Rose Crest, Vase, 5 In. 75.00
Rose Crest, Vase, 6 In. 120.00
Rose Crest, Vase, 9 In. 140.00
Rose Garden, Bell, 6 ½ In. 30.00
Rose Overlay, Basket, Handle, Ruffled Edge, 7 In. 75.00
Silver Crest, Basket, 7 In. 65.00
Silver Crest, Bowl, 7 In. 55.00
Silver Crest, Bowl, Sections, 1956 .... 30.00
Silver Crest, Candy Dish, Cover, Finial, Footed, 9½ In. .... 75.00 to 80.00
Silver Crest, Epergne, 3-Lily, 9 ½ In. 185.00
Silver Crest, Epergne, 5-Lily, 14 In. 235.00
Silver Crest, Tidbit, 2 Tiers 55.00
Silver Crest, Vase, 4 In. 30.00
Silver Crest, Vase, 12 ¾ In. 55.00

Fenton, Hobnail, Bowl,
Plum Opalescent,
Ruffled & Crimped Edge, 10 In.
$345.00

Fenton, Peach Crest, Vase,
Ruffled Edge, 9 In.
$181.00

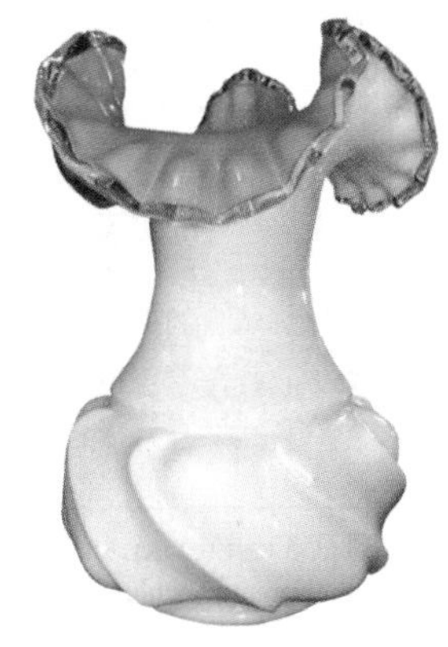

Fenton, Spanish Lace, Rose Bowl,
Cranberry Opalescent
$65.00

TIP

Keep your collection of glassware away from the speakers of your sound system. Heavy bass and high-pitched sounds can crack the glass.

Fenton, Vasa Murrhina, Vase, Rose, Crimped Rim, 4 In..
$65.00

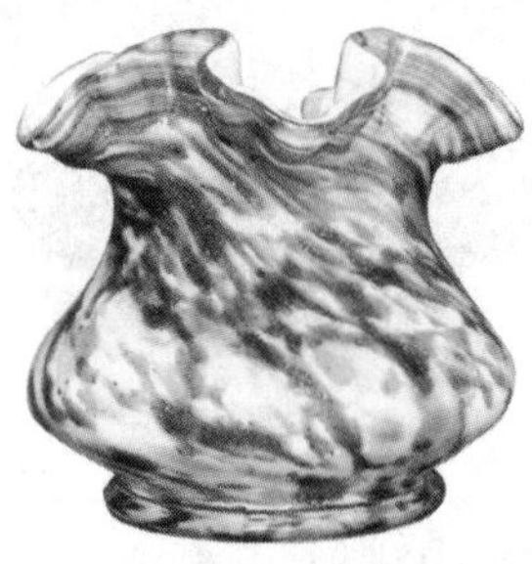

Fiesta, Chartreuse, Cup & Saucer, Rings, Homer Laughlin
$50.00

Fiesta, Cobalt Blue, Creamer, Rings, Ring Handle, Homer Laughlin
$40.00

Fiesta, Cobalt Blue, Pitcher, Syrup, Drip Top
$330.00

Silvertone, Console Set, 3 Piece ... 150.00
Sophisticated Ladies, Vase, Art Deco Style, Ball Shape, Black, 1982, 8 In. ... 375.00
Spanish Lace, Rose Bowl, Cranberry Opalescent ... *illus* 65.00
Spiral Optic, Basket, Cranberry Opalescent, 11 In. ... 95.00
Spiral Optic, Epergne, 1-Lily, Rosalene Satin, 9 ½ In. ... 125.00
Stretch Glass, Bowl, Green Russet, 4 ½ x 9 ¼ In. ... 45.00
Stretch Glass, Sherbet, Celeste Blue, 3 In. ... 20.00
Stretch Glass, Tumbler, Vaseline, Cobalt Blue Handle, 4 ¾ In. ... 67.00
Thumbprint, Creamer, Blue Marble Slag, 4 In. ... 35.00
Thumbprint, Lavabo, Milk Glass, Olde Virginia, 1956 ... 60.00
Vasa Murrhina, Vase, Autumn ... 25.00
Vasa Murrhina, Vase, Rose, Crimped Rim, 4 In.. ... *illus* 65.00
Vase, Hobnail, Jack-In-The-Pulpit, Cranberry Opalescent, c.1970, 11 In.. ... 150.00
Water Lilies & Cattails, Bowl, French Opalescent ... 45.00
Water Lily, Bowl, 9 In. ... 35.00
Water Lily, Candlestick, White Satin, Pair ... 30.00
Water Lily, Pitcher, Blue Satin, 8 In.. ... 25.00
Water Lily, Pitcher, Custard Satin, 8 In. ... 20.00
Water Lily, Vase, Bud, Lime Sherbet ... 35.00
Wheat, Vase, Dust Rose Overlay, 1984-85, 8 In. ... 25.00
Wheat, Vase, Petite Fleur, c.1984 ... 40.00
Wheat, Vase, Powder Blue Overlay, c.1961 ... 40.00
Yellow Overlay, Basket, Ruffled Edge, Label, 11 In.. ... 42.00

FIESTA, the colorful dinnerware, was introduced in 1936 by the Homer Laughlin China Co., redesigned in 1969, and withdrawn in 1973. It was reissued again in 1986 in different colors and is still being made. New colors, including some that are similar to old colors, are introduced regularly. The simple design was characterized by a band of concentric circles, beginning at the rim. Cups had full-circle handles until 1969, when partial-circle handles were made. Harlequin and Riviera were related wares. For more information about Fiesta, its colors and prices, and prices of American dinnerware, see the book *Kovels' Depression Glass & Dinnerware Price List*.

Fiesta

Chartreuse, Casserole ... 92.00
Chartreuse, Chop Plate, 15 In. ... 61.00
Chartreuse, Coffeepot, Cover ... 275.00
Chartreuse, Cup & Saucer, After Dinner ... 200.00
Chartreuse, Cup & Saucer, Rings, Homer Laughlin ... *illus* 50.00
Chartreuse, Eggcup ... 66.00
Chartreuse, Pitcher, Disk ... 45.00
Chartreuse, Plate, Compartment, 10 ½ In. ... 58.00
Chartreuse, Plate, Compartment, 12 In. ... 55.00
Chartreuse, Sugar & Creamer ... 33.00
Chartreuse, Teapot, 6 Cup ... 190.00
Cobalt Blue, Candleholder, Bulb, Pair ... 55.00
Cobalt Blue, Candleholder, Tripod ... 83.00
Cobalt Blue, Carafe ... 175.00
Cobalt Blue, Casserole ... 75.00
Cobalt Blue, Chop Plate, 15 In. ... 27.00
Cobalt Blue, Coffeepot, Cover ... 55.00
Cobalt Blue, Compote, Sweets ... 93.00
Cobalt Blue, Creamer, Rings, Ring Handle, Homer Laughlin ... *illus* 40.00
Cobalt Blue, Eggcup, Homer Laughlin ... 65.00
Cobalt Blue, Mixing Bowl, Cover, No. 4 ... 355.00
Cobalt Blue, Mixing Bowl, No. 1 ... 205.00
Cobalt Blue, Mixing Bowl, No. 2 ... 65.00
Cobalt Blue, Mixing Bowl, No. 3 ... 68.00
Cobalt Blue, Mixing Bowl, No. 4 ... 60.00
Cobalt Blue, Mixing Bowl, No. 5 ... 30.00
Cobalt Blue, Mixing Bowl, No. 6 ... 135.00
Cobalt Blue, Mixing Bowl, No. 7 ... 490.00
Cobalt Blue, Pitcher, Disk ... 55.00
Cobalt Blue, Pitcher, Syrup, Drip Top ... *illus* 330.00
Cobalt Blue, Relish Tray ... 125.00
Cobalt Blue, Sugar & Creamer ... 33.00
Cobalt Blue, Teapot, 8 Cup ... 132.00

Forest Green, Chop Plate, 15 In. 66.00
Forest Green, Coffeepot, Cover 275.00
Forest Green, Cup & Saucer, After Dinner 200.00
Forest Green, Eggcup *illus* 77.00
Forest Green, Jug, 2 Pt. 88.00
Forest Green, Pitcher, Disk 79.00
Forest Green, Sugar & Creamer 49.00
Gray, Casserole 92.00
Gray, Chop Plate, 15 In. 66.00
Gray, Coffeepot, Cover 110.00
Gray, Eggcup 103.00
Gray, Pitcher, Disk *illus* 79.00
Gray, Pitcher, Juice 132.00
Gray, Sugar & Creamer 27.00
Ivory, Bowl, Fruit, 11 3/4 In. 92.00
Ivory, Bowl, Salad, Footed 140.00
Ivory, Candleholder, Bulb, Pair 55.00
Ivory, Carafe 132.00
Ivory, Casserole 110.00
Ivory, Coffeepot, Cover 132.00
Ivory, Compote, Sweets 93.00
Ivory, Creamer, Stick 28.00
Ivory, Eggcup, Pair 60.00
Ivory, Mixing Bowl, No. 1 150.00
Ivory, Mixing Bowl, No. 2 65.00
Ivory, Mixing Bowl, No. 3 40.00
Ivory, Mixing Bowl, No. 4 40.00
Ivory, Mixing Bowl, No. 5 90.00
Ivory, Mixing Bowl, No. 6 185.00
Ivory, Mixing Bowl, No. 7 105.00
Ivory, Pitcher, Disk 50.00
Ivory, Pitcher, Ice Lip 105.00
Ivory, Pitcher, Syrup, Drip Top 275.00
Ivory, Soup, Onion, Cover 330.00
Ivory, Sugar & Creamer 44.00
Ivory, Teapot, 6 Cup *illus* 100.00
Ivory, Vase, 10 In. 330.00
Ivory, Vase, 12 In. 450.00
Light Green, Candleholder, Bulb, Pair 55.00
Light Green, Carafe 143.00
Light Green, Casserole 88.00
Light Green, Coffeepot, After Dinner *illus* 335.00
Light Green, Coffeepot, Cover 88.00
Light Green, Compote, 12 In. 77.00
Light Green, Compote, Sweets 88.00
Light Green, Creamer, Stick 28.00
Light Green, Mixing Bowl, No. 1 170.00
Light Green, Mixing Bowl, No. 2 60.00
Light Green, Mixing Bowl, No. 3 55.00
Light Green, Mixing Bowl, No. 4 50.00
Light Green, Mixing Bowl, No. 5 70.00
Light Green, Mixing Bowl, No. 6 70.00
Light Green, Mixing Bowl, No. 7 200.00
Light Green, Pitcher, Disk 45.00
Light Green, Pitcher, Ice Lip 60.00
Light Green, Pitcher, Syrup, Drip Top 120.00
Light Green, Soup, Onion, Cover 445.00
Light Green, Sugar & Creamer 32.00
Light Green, Vase, 8 In. 270.00
Medium Green, Ashtray 88.00
Medium Green, Bowl, Dessert, 6 In. 210.00
Medium Green, Bowl, Fruit, 4 3/4 In. 225.00
Medium Green, Bowl, Salad 82.00
Medium Green, Casserole 550.00 to 575.00
Medium Green, Chop Plate, 13 In. 160.00

Fiesta, Forest Green, Eggcup
$77.00

Fiesta, Gray, Pitcher, Disk
$79.00

Fiesta, Ivory, Teapot, 6 Cup
$100.00

Fiesta, Light Green, Coffeepot, After Dinner
$335.00

Fiesta, Medium Green, Sauceboat
$132.00

F

Fiesta, Red, Carafe
$120.00

Fiesta, Rose, Sugar & Creamer
$38.00

Fiesta, Turquoise, Salt & Pepper
$26.00

Fiesta, Yellow, Plate, Homer Laughlin, 9 In.
$15.00

Fiesta, Yellow, Sugar, Cover
$18.00

Medium Green, Mug, Tom & Jerry .... 45.00 to 60.00
Medium Green, Nappy, 8 ½ In. 57.00
Medium Green, Pitcher, Disk. .... 385.00 to 403.00
Medium Green, Platter, Oval, 12 In. 145.00
Medium Green, Salt & Pepper 40.00
Medium Green, Sauceboat .... *illus* 132.00
Medium Green, Sugar & Creamer 129.00
Medium Green, Teapot, 6 Cup. .... 830.00 to 2000.00
Red, Bowl, Salad 69.00
Red, Bowl, Salad, Footed 330.00
Red, Candleholder, Bulb, Pair 50.00
Red, Carafe .... *illus* 120.00
Red, Casserole 120.00
Red, Chop Plate, 15 In. 27.00
Red, Coffeepot, After Dinner .... 550.00 to 575.00
Red, Coffeepot, Cover 143.00
Red, Compote, Sweets 110.00
Red, Creamer, Stick 38.00
Red, Eggcup 55.00
Red, Mixing Bowl, Cover, No. 4 .... 395.00
Red, Mixing Bowl, No. 1 .... 175.00
Red, Mixing Bowl, No. 2 .... 40.00
Red, Mixing Bowl, No. 3 .... 35.00
Red, Mixing Bowl, No. 4 .... 45.00
Red, Mixing Bowl, No. 5 .... 40.00
Red, Mixing Bowl, No. 6 .... 55.00
Red, Mustard 310.00
Red, Pitcher, Disk. .... 86.00 to 210.00
Red, Pitcher, Ice Lip 73.00
Red, Pitcher, Syrup, Drip Top 350.00
Red, Relish Tray, Multicolored Inserts .... 175.00 to 184.00
Red, Soup, Onion, Cover 375.00
Red, Sugar & Creamer 88.00
Red, Teapot, 8 Cup 110.00
Red, Vase, 10 In. 660.00
Red, Vase, Bud 55.00
Rose, Chop Plate, 15 In. 50.00
Rose, Coffeepot, Cover 132.00
Rose, Eggcup 72.00
Rose, Jug, 2 Pt. 86.00
Rose, Pitcher, Disk 55.00
Rose, Sugar & Creamer .... *illus* 38.00
Turquoise, Bowl, Salad 35.00
Turquoise, Candleholder, Bulb, Pair 60.00
Turquoise, Candleholder, Tripod, Pair 176.00
Turquoise, Carafe .... 165.00 to 173.00
Turquoise, Casserole 75.00
Turquoise, Chop Plate, 15 In. 23.00
Turquoise, Coffeepot, Cover 121.00
Turquoise, Compote, Sweets 88.00
Turquoise, Creamer, Stick 40.00
Turquoise, Marmalade 245.00
Turquoise, Mixing Bowl, No. 1 .... 175.00
Turquoise, Mixing Bowl, No. 2 .... 65.00
Turquoise, Mixing Bowl, No. 3 .... 88.00
Turquoise, Mixing Bowl, No. 4 .... 70.00
Turquoise, Mixing Bowl, No. 5 .... 50.00
Turquoise, Mixing Bowl, No. 6 .... 120.00
Turquoise, Mixing Bowl, No. 7 .... 210.00
Turquoise, Pitcher, Disk 40.00
Turquoise, Pitcher, Ice Lip 90.00
Turquoise, Pitcher, Syrup, Drip Top 145.00
Turquoise, Salt & Pepper, 2 ½ In. .... *illus* 26.00
Turquoise, Sugar & Creamer 22.00
Turquoise, Teapot, 6 Cup 88.00

Turquoise, Vase, 8 In. 345.00
Yellow, Bowl, Fruit, 11 ¾ In. 99.00
Yellow, Bowl, Salad 50.00 to 105.00
Yellow, Cake Plate 385.00
Yellow, Calendar Plate, 1955 55.00
Yellow, Candleholder, Bulb, Pair 55.00
Yellow, Carafe 154.00
Yellow, Casserole 140.00
Yellow, Chop Plate, Metal Handle, 13 In. 44.00
Yellow, Coffeepot, After Dinner 230.00
Yellow, Coffeepot, Cover 77.00
Yellow, Compote, 12 In. 72.00
Yellow, Compote, Sweets 72.00
Yellow, Creamer, Stick 22.00
Yellow, Cup & Saucer, After Dinner 42.00
Yellow, Mixing Bowl, No. 1 92.00
Yellow, Mixing Bowl, No. 2 35.00
Yellow, Mixing Bowl, No. 3 35.00
Yellow, Mixing Bowl, No. 4 45.00
Yellow, Mixing Bowl, No. 5 80.00
Yellow, Mixing Bowl, No. 6 110.00
Yellow, Mixing Bowl, No. 7 132.00
Yellow, Mustard 120.00
Yellow, Pitcher, Disk 50.00
Yellow, Pitcher, Syrup, Drip Top 275.00
Yellow, Plate, 9 In. *illus* 15.00
Yellow, Relish Tray 154.00
Yellow, Soup, Onion, Cover 345.00
Yellow, Sugar, Cover *illus* 18.00
Yellow, Sugar & Creamer 27.00
Yellow, Teapot, 6 Cup 50.00
Yellow, Vase, 10 In. 250.00
Yellow, Vase, 12 In. 290.00

FINCH, *see Kay Finch category.*

FINDLAY ONYX AND FLORADINE are two similar types of glass made by Dalzell, Gilmore and Leighton Co. of Findlay, Ohio, about 1889. Onyx is a patented yellowish white opaque glass with raised silver daisy decorations. A few rare pieces were made of rose, amber, orange, or purple glass. Floradine is made of cranberry-colored glass with an opalescent white raised floral pattern and a satin finish. The same molds were used for both types of glass.

Creamer, Oval, Opal, Silver Flowers, Handles, 4 ¾ In. 288.00
Muffineer, Opal, Platinum Flowers, 5 In. *illus* 170.00
Shaker, Opal, Silver Flowers, 5 ½ In. 288.00
Syrup, Opal, Flowers, Applied Opal Handle, 7 In. *illus* 475.00

FIREFIGHTING equipment of all types is wanted, from fire marks to uniforms to toy fire trucks. It is said that every little boy wanted to be a fireman or a train engineer 75 years ago and the collectors today reflect this interest.

Alarm, Pedestal, Keyless Door, Police Box, Citizen Key, Gamewell, 81 In. 3080.00
Alarm, Watchman's, Metal, Wire Handle, 2 ½ In. 45.00
Alarm Box, Gamewell, Cast Aluminum, 17 x 12 ½ In. 115.00
Alarm Box, Harrington Seaberg, Cast Aluminum, 17 x 12 ½ In. 303.00
Alarm Box, Holtzer Cabot, ½ In. Tape 132.00
Alarm Box, No. 7, Cole Key Guard, Instructional Door, 17 In. 303.00
Alarm Box, No. 27, Self Starting, Keyless Door 523.00
Alarm Box, No. 39, Gamewell, Cast Aluminum, 17 x 12 x 6 In. *illus* 115.00
Alarm Box, No. 123, Slant, Telegraph Station, Keyless Door, Gamewell 725.00
Alarm Box, No. 631, Self Start, Keyless Door, 17 x 12 ½ In. 1100.00
Alarm Box, Pedestal, Helmet, Trumpet, Red, Fluted, 73 ½ In. 1155.00
Alarm Box, Quick Action Door, Universal Tool, Cast Aluminum, 18 x 13 ¼ In. 210.00
Alarm Box, Western Electric Tel. Co., 11 x 32 x 13 In. 1265.00
Alarm Pull, Schoolhouse, Boston 55.00
Banner, Horse Drawn Fire Pumper, West Side Hose Co., No. 3, Steelton, Pa., Cloth 935.00
Bell, Brass, Clapper, Cast Iron, Lanyard Ring, Wood Handle, 4 ¾ In. 224.00

Findlay Onyx, Muffineer, Opal, Platinum Flowers, 5 In.
$170.00

Findlay Onyx, Syrup, Opal, Flowers, Applied Opal Handle, 7 In.
$475.00

TIP
Every collection as well as every collector should have a smoke detector and fire extinguisher nearby.

Firefighting, Alarm Box, No. 39, Gamewell, Cast Aluminum, 17 x 12 x 6 In.
$115.00

Firefighting, Bucket, Leather, Mousan, Yellow, Red, Cast Iron Handle Rings, 11 ½ In.
$800.00

Firefighting, Fire Mark, Aetna, Gold Letters, Black Ground, Tin, 2⅜ x 6 ½ In.
$30.00

Firefighting, Fire Mark, Fire Hydrant, FA, Raised, Cast Iron, 11 ¾ x 7 ½ In.
$70.00

Firefighting, Fire Mark, Horseshoe, Phenix, Brass, Raised Letters, 3⅝ x 3⅞ In.
$750.00

Bell, Indicator, Pull Handles, Oak Case, Gamewell, 36 x 13 In. 5720.00
Bell, Slate Base, Toronto Tapper, 6 In. 193.00
Belt Buckle, Fire Department City Of New York, Brass, Blue & Red Enamel, 3 In. 35.00
Belt Buckle, New York Fire Department, Brass, Blue, Red, 3 In. 35.00
Bucket, Leather, C.F.S. No. 2, Jonathan Fise, Heart, Wings, Banner, Hands, 1825, 12 In. 2185.00
Bucket, Leather, Cast Iron Ring Handles, 11 ½ In. 308.00
Bucket, Leather, D.M. Owen, Green, Black, Yellow, White, Early 19th Century, 12 ½ In. 460.00
Bucket, Leather, G.K. Haswell, Federal Fire, Society, No. 2, Yellow, Black, Red, c.1789 5616.00
Bucket, Leather, Mousan, Yellow, Red, Cast Iron Handle Rings, 11 ½ In. *illus* 800.00
Bucket, Leather, Multicolored, Mercury Blowing Trumpet, 1824, 11 In. 2700.00
Bucket, Leather, Painted, First Church Chancy-Place, Gilt Letters, 1821, 13 x 19 In. 475.00
Bucket, Leather, Painted, I.H. Bartlett, Green, Mustard Letters, 1829, 13 In. 633.00
Bucket, Leather, Painted, E.P. Pike, W.F. Club, Eagle, Oak Leaves, Red, Oval,1829 748.00
Bucket, Leather, Painted, E.T. Rumery, No. 1, Green, Mustard Letters, 13 ½ In. 863.00
Bucket, Leather, Painted, Augusta B. Tappan, Green, Mustard, Black, Red,1827, 12 In. 920.00
Bucket, Leather, Painted, Boston Street Fire Club, Salem, F. Carelton, 1826, 12 ¾ In. 1725.00
Bucket, Leather, Painted, Boston Ward 11 Fire-Man No. 3, Green, 1826, 12 ½ In. 1725.00
Bucket, Leather, Painted, J.H. Russell, WSFS, 1842 1416.00
Bucket, Leather, Painted, John J. Linzee, No. 3, Multicolored, c.1807, 13 In. 2938.00
Bucket, Leather, Painted, Bodwell, Spread Wing Eagle, No. 1, No. 2, 15 In., Pair 8225.00
Bucket, Leather, Royal Coat Of Arms, Black Ground, Multicolored, Gilt, 13 x 11 In. 374.00
Bucket, Leather, Salvatore Divitiarun, Richard Chamberlain, Heart, Hands, 12 In. 1495.00
Bucket, Leather, W. & S. Pattin, Green, White Design, c.1800, 13 x 18 In. 600.00
Call Box, Blue Citizen Key, Cast Iron, Finial, Gamewell, 84 x 18 In. 1705.00
Call Box, Cast Iron, Fluted Ribbed Pedestal, Red Light, 1913-14, 82 In. 1980.00
Call Box, No. 236, Gamewell, 16 x 11 In. 330.00
Certificate, Veteran Firemen's Asso., To Joe McCormick, Dec. 28th, 1897 220.00
Circuit Board, Alarm, Molded Edge, 37 ¼ x 11 ¾ In. 3900.00
Door Opener, Oak, Case, Spring Operated, 22 ½ x 15 In. 963.00
Door Opener, Oak, Case, Weight Driven, 11 x 31 ½ In. 495.00
Fire Hose & Rack, Cast Iron, Brass Nozzle 1200.00
Fire Mark, 4 Clasped Hands, No. 906, Embossed, Iron, 10⅝ x 7 ¼ In. 44.00
Fire Mark, Aetna, Gold Letters, Black Ground, Tin, 2⅜ x 6 ½ In. *illus* 30.00
Fire Mark, Aetna, Insured, Raised Letters, Tin, 4 x 7 ¼ In. 157.00
Fire Mark, Eagle, Spread Wings, Hobnail Border, Oval, Embossed, Iron, 7 ¾ x 11 In. 22.00
Fire Mark, Fire Hydrant, FA, Raised, Cast Iron, 11 ¾ x 7 ½ In. *illus* 70.00
Fire Mark, Fire Hydrant, Water Gushing From Hose, Oval, Embossed., Iron, 11 x 7 In. 22.00
Fire Mark, Fireman With Trumpet, Oval, Cast Iron, 11 ¾ x 9 ¼ In. 672.00
Fire Mark, Home, New York, Raised Letters, 3 ⅛ x 6 ¼ In. 101.00
Fire Mark, Horseshoe, Phenix, Brass, Raised Letters, 3⅝ x 3⅞ In. *illus* 750.00
Fire Mark, L.I.C.O., Log Border, Square, Cast Iron, 9 ¼ In. 179.00
Fire Mark, Ohio Farmers, Black Ground, Gold Letters, Tin, 2 ¾ x 3 ¼ In. 34.00
Fire Mark, Raised Tree, Oval, Cast Iron, 8 ¼ x 8 ½ In. 134.00
Fire Mark, Steam Fire Engine, Beveled Edge, Black Paint, Oval, Embossed, Iron, 9 x 11 In. 22.00
Fire Mark, Sun Face, 16 Rays, Lead, 6⅝ x 6 ½ In. 123.00
Fire Mark, Tree, Embossed, Squat, Oval, Iron, 8 ¼ x 8 ½ In. 22.00
Fire Mark, U Steam Fire Engine F, Oval, Cast Iron, 9⅜ x 12 In. 202.00
Fire Mark, United Firemen's Ins. Co., Steam Engine, Cast Iron, 11 ½ In. 896.00
Globe, Glass, Blue, Police, 5 ¾ x 10 In. 33.00
Globe, Glass, Red, 6 x 10 In. 132.00
Globe, Glass, Red, Cast Iron Collar, 10 In. 187.00
Gong, Banjo Form, Gamewell, 22 In. 2090.00
Gong, Banjo Form, Gamewell, 24 In. 2585.00
Gong, Flat Top, Gamewell Excelsior, 33 x 17 ½ In. 4400.00
Gong, Oak, Arched Crest, Ball Finials, Gamewell, 36 x 18 In. 5170.00
Gong, Oak, Flat Top, Mechanism, Gamewell, 33 x 19 In. 2970.00
Gong, Oak, Gamewell, Excelsior, 16 x 9 ½ In. 1100.00
Gong, Oak, Gamewell, 22 x 10 ½ In. 1980.00
Gong, Oak, U.S. Fire & Police Co., 5/28/1891, 18 x 9 ¼ In. 1650.00
Gong, Viaduct, Encased, 17 x 27 In. 2090.00
Gong, Walnut, Ahlstrom Mechanism, 45 x 17 ½ In. 8250.00
Grenade, Babcock Hand, Non-Freezing, Blue, Plug, Contents, c.1890, 7 ½ In. *illus* 1800.00
Grenade, Harden, Star, Cobalt, No. 60064, Metal Pull Ring, Contents, 17 ¾ In. *illus* 1300.00
Grenade, Harden's, Clear, Sheared, Ground Lip, Contents, c.1885-95, 6⅝ In. 2464.00
Grenade, Harden's, Star, Clear, Tubular, Tooled Lip, Cast Iron Mounts, c.1885, 17 ¾ In. 1232.00
Grenade, Harden's Hand, Fire Extinguisher, Turquoise Blue, Footed, Ground Lip, 6 ½ In. 180.00
Grenade, Harden's Hand, Fire Extinguisher, Blue, Footed, 5 In. 200.00

irefighting, Grenade, Babcock Hand, lon-Freezing, Blue, Plug, Contents, .1890, 7½ In.
1800.00

irefighting, Grenade, Harden, Star, Cobalt, o. 60064, Metal Pull Ring, Contents, 17¾ In.
1300.00

irefighting, Grenade, Hayward's Hand, mber, Diamond Panels, Patent Aug. 8, 871, 6 In.
425.00

Firefighting, Grenade, Hayward's Hand, Turquoise, Aug. 8, 1871, Seal, Contents, 6 In.
$425.00

Firefighting, Grenade, Hayward's Hand, Yellow Green, c.1877-95, 6 In.
$900.00

Firefighting, Grenade, Kalamazoo Hand, Cobalt Blue, c.1880-95, 11 In.
$700.00

Firefighting, Helmet, New York, Bowery, 135, Leather, White, Whipple Steam Co., 1872
$4500.00

Firefighting, Parade Hat, America, Eagle, J.H. Jr. In Wreath, Leather, c.1850, 7½ x 6¾ In.
$27500.00

Fire Buckets

Leather fire buckets painted or stamped with the name of the firehouse, the city, or its insignia were used in America from the seventeenth century. Some were decorated with elaborate paintings of arms, eagles, and figures. The leather bucket was used in larger cities until the 1840s and in rural areas for many years after that. Old painted leather buckets sell for hundreds of dollars each.

Leather was used to make fire buckets because metal buckets would get too hot, and wooden buckets leaked if they dried out.

FIREFIGHTING

TIP

Never unplug an electrical cord by pulling the cord. Always hold the plastic part of the plug. Weak cords cause fires.

F

Firefighting, Rattle, Watchman's, Reeded, Wood, Brass, Impressed, City 384, 8 In.
$210.00

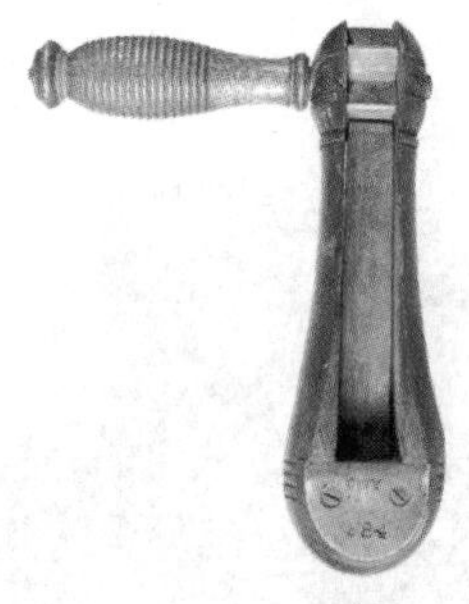

Fireplace, Andirons, Brass, Empire, Beehive Finial, Ball Feet, c.1840, 17 x 18 In.
$345.00

TIP

The most important rule for fire safety is get out of the house immediately. Don't try to save pets or belongings. Draw up an escape route and plan a place to meet to be sure everyone is out and safe.

Grenade, Hayward's Hand, Amber, Diamond Panels, Patent Aug. 8, 1871, 6 In. *illus* 425.00
Grenade, Hayward's Hand, Cobalt Blue, Tooled Lip, Pleated, 1877-95, 6 In. 336.00
Grenade, Hayward's Hand, Medium Lime Green, Tooled Lip, Metal Neck, 1871, 6 In. 532.00
Grenade, Hayward's Hand, Pale Aqua, Tooled Lip, Metal Neck Foil, c.1877, 7⅝ In. 392.00
Grenade, Hayward's Hand, Turquoise, Aug. 8, 1871, Seal, Contents, 6 In. *illus* 425.00
Grenade, Hayward's Hand, Yellow Green, c.1877-95, 6 In. *illus* 900.00
Grenade, HNS, Light Amber, Panels, 7 In. 250.00
Grenade, Kalamazoo Hand, Cobalt Blue, c.1880-95, 11 In. *illus* 700.00
Grenade, Rockford, Hand, Automatic, Cobalt Blue, Tooled Lip, c.1880-95, 11⅛ In. 840.00
Grenade, Turquoise Blue, Footed, Rough Sheared, Ground Lip, c.1885-1900, 5⅛ In. 213.00
Helmet, Leather, White Paint, Embossed Fire Hydrants, Shield, Brass Plaque 1680.00
Helmet, New York, Bowery, 135, Leather, White, Whipple Steam Co., 1872 *illus* 4500.00
Helmet, New York, Bowery, 135, Crossed Ladder & Pike, Leather, 7¼ In. 476.00
Helmet, New York, Bowery, 178, Leather, Wooden Case, 7¾ In. 1232.00
Helmet, Presentation, White Leather, Metal Disc, Brass Plaque 3920.00
Horn, Copper, Gamewell, 30½ In. 550.00
Lantern, Brass, Loop Handle, Clear Globe, Embossed Thumb Screw, 17½ In. 952.00
Lantern, Fire Department, Etched Leaves, Howard & Morse, 10 In. 406.00
Lantern, Metal, 3-Sided, Clear Globe, Loop Handle, 7½ In. 235.00
Light, Alarm, Localite, 12 In. 77.00
Paperweight, Union Engine Co., No. 3, 4 Firemen Fighting Fire, 8-Sided, 2⅞ In. 112.00
Parade Hat, America, Eagle, J.H. Jr. In Wreath, Leather, c.1850, 7½ x 6¾ In. *illus* 27500.00
Parade Hat, Ceremonial, Painted, Eagle, Columbia Hose Company, c.1850, 7 x 14 In. 8400.00
Parade Torch, Morrisville, NJ, Tin, Swivel Bracket, Black Paint, c.1877, 53 In. 259.00
Pedestal, Cast Iron, Finial, Police Box, 79 x 15 In., 2 Piece 1320.00
Rack, Wire, 3 Grenade Holders, Handle, 15½ In. 123.00
Rattle, Watchman's, Reeded, Wood, Brass, Impressed, City 384, 8 In. *illus* 210.00
Rattle, Watchman's, Wood, Single Reed, 10 In. 45.00
Rattle, Watchman's, Wood, Iron Weight, Double Reed, 8 In. 235.00
Register, Glass Cover, Frederick Pearce, 6 x 9 x 12 In. 1430.00
Siren, Fireboat, Sparton, Bronze Bullet Case, 6 Volt Motor, Model 203, 8 x 8 In. 100.00
Stamp, Time, Clock, Month, Day, Gamewell, 8½ x 6¼ x 6¼ In. 550.00
Status Board, Eng. 36, Pegs, Numbered, 33½ x 30½ In. 880.00
Torch, Brass, 11¾ In. 101.00
Torch, Parade, Tin, Soldered, Wood Handle, Copper Burner, Double Swing, 43 In. 67.00
Torch, Tin, Soldered, Swing Handle, Screw-On Burner, 4¼ In. 34.00
Torch, Tin, Soldered, Swing Handle, Screw-On Burner, 7½ In. 34.00
Transmitter, 50 Code Wheels, Flat Top, Oak Case, Gamewell Excelsior, 32 x 19 In. 3850.00
Transmitter, 100 Code Wheels, Flat Top, Oak Case, Gamewell, 39 x 21½ In. 3410.00
Trough, Fire Horse Comfort Feed Pot, Cast Iron, Embossed, 2¾ x 18 x 25 In. 146.00
Trumpet, Silver Plated, Etched Flowers, Eagle Ring Holder, Silk Loop, 19 In. 1293.00

FIREGLOW glass is attributed to the Boston and Sandwich Glass Company. The light-tan-colored glass appears reddish brown when held to the light. Most fireglow has an acid finish and enamel decoration, although it was also made with a satin finish.

Sugar & Creamer, Stemmed Flowers, Ruffled Rims, 3½ In. 50.00

FIREPLACES were used to cook food and to heat the American home in past centuries. Many types of tools and equipment were used. Andirons held the logs in place, firebacks reflected the heat into the room, and tongs were used to move either fuel or food. Many types of spits and roasting jacks were made and may be listed in the Kitchen category.

Andirons, Bell Metal, Federal, Double Urn, Arched Spurred Legs, Slipper Feet, 22¾ In. 1437.00
Andirons, Brass, Ball Top, Pierced Baluster, 17 x 16¼ x 8½ In. 118.00
Andirons, Brass, Ball Top, Spiral, 29½ x 12 In. 146.00
Andirons, Brass, Ball Top, Hourglass, Snake Feet, 18th Century, 24 x 12½ x 17 In. 700.00
Andirons, Brass, Ball Top, Baluster Finial, Log Holder, 20½ x 10 x 19½ In. 1150.00
Andirons, Brass, Baluster, Urn, 21 In. 47.00
Andirons, Brass, Baroque Revival, Turned Finials, Gadrooned Mid Knop, 1800s, 14 In. 264.00
Andirons, Brass, Beehive, Finials, Arched Legs, Spurs, Ball Feet, 17 x 11 x 16½ In. 852.00
Andirons, Brass, Chippendale, Snake Foot, Double Hour Glass, 24 x 12½ x 18 In. 784.00
Andirons, Brass, Classical, Funnel Shape Feet, Mid 19th Century, 19 In. 403.00
Andirons, Brass, Double Lemon, Top, Hexagonal Stem, 8¾ x 8½ x 16½ In. 489.00
Andirons, Brass, Elongated Acorn Finials, England, 22 In. 380.00

Andirons, Brass, Empire, Beehive Finial, Ball Feet, c.1840, 17 x 18 In. .... *illus* 345.00
Andirons, Brass, Empire Style, Ball Top, Turned Columns, Spurred Legs, 1900s, 18 In....... 115.00
Andirons, Brass, Federal, Turned Posts, Ball Finials, Ball Feet, Early 1800s, 19 ¼ In......... 489.00
Andirons, Brass, Federal, Double Lemon Finials, Spurred, Arches, Ball Feet, c.1825, 20 In.... 518.00
Andirons, Brass, Federal, Steeple Top, Ball Feet, Early 19th Century, 19 In. 570.00
Andirons, Brass, Federal, Lemon Finials, Beehive Baluster Post, 19th Century, 19 In.... *illus* 575.00
Andirons, Brass, Federal, Iron, Belted Ball Tops, Urn & Ball Finials, 22 x 11 ¼ In........... 764.00
Andirons, Brass, Flame Finials, Cornucopia, Dog Log Stops, 27 x 11 x 23 ½ In............. 280.00
Andirons, Brass, Georgian Style, Knop Stems, Scrolled Feet, 21 In....................... 235.00
Andirons, Brass, Gilt, Edwardian, Oval Shield, Flowers, Leaves, Steeple Finial, 18 x 8 In. 240.00
Andirons, Brass, Iron, Wrought, Ball Finials, Slipper Feet, Early 1800s, 15 x 21 In.......... 144.00
Andirons, Brass, Iron, Tapered Shaft, Spiral Leaf, Mounted Rings, 29 x 14 In.............. 150.00
Andirons, Brass, Iron, Leaves, Flowers, Arts & Crafts, 19 x 24 x 12 In..................... 270.00
Andirons, Brass, Iron, Ball Top, Log Holder Stop, Snake Foot, 14 x 18 In.................. 330.00
Andirons, Brass, Iron, Wrought, Steeple Finials, Arched, Spurred Legs, 14 x 16 ½ x 6 In...... 825.00
Andirons, Brass, Iron, Chamfered & Flame Finials, Flat Post, Penny Feet, 19 ½ In. 990.00
Andirons, Brass, Iron, Ball Top, Baluster Finials, Claw & Ball Feet, 20 x 14 x 23 In.......... 1116.00
Andirons, Brass, Iron, Urn Top, Claw & Ball Feet, c.1800, 24 ½ In....................... 2350.00
Andirons, Brass, Iron, Urn, Column, Cabriole Legs, Willow Tree, Philadelphia, 28 In........ 3173.00
Andirons, Brass, Neoclassical, Urn, Cup Flame Finials, Baluster, 12 x 14 In. 299.00
Andirons, Brass, Spur Arches, Nipple Finials, Slipper Feet, Early 1800s, 17 ¾ In. 201.00
Andirons, Brass, Stepped Ring Finials, Early 20th Century, 19 In........................ 490.00
Andirons, Brass, G. Stickley, Ball Over Ring, Curved Feet, Marked, 10 x 22 x 20 In...... *illus* 15600.00
Andirons, Bronze, French Empire Style, Winged Griffin, Paw Feet, 23 x 12 In.............. 770.00
Andirons, Bronze, Nickel, Snarling Lions Heads, 14 ½ In.............................. 325.00
Andirons, Bronze, Renaissance Revival, Flower Finials, Scroll Work, 1800s, 22 In. 382.00
Andirons, Federal, Steeple Top, Ball Feet, Early 19th Century, 19 In...................... 570.00
Andirons, Federal, Stepped Beehive Baluster Posts, Lemon Finials, Ball Feet, 1800s, 19 In.... 575.00
Andirons, Figural, George Washington, Standing, Hand On Hip, Paint, 15 In.............. 431.00
Andirons, Iron, Bell Metal, Urn Top, Acorn Finials, Cabriole Legs, Slipper Feet, 15 x 17 In.... 558.00
Andirons, Iron, Bolted Billet Bars, Early 20th Century, 20 x 22 In. 230.00
Andirons, Iron, Brass, Queen Anne Style, 20th Century, 20 ½ x 20 In. .... *illus* 403.00
Andirons, Iron, Cannonball Top, Spiral Column, Stepped Billet Bars, 26 ¾ x 12 ¾ In........ 920.00
Andirons, Iron, Cast, Owl, 14 ½ In.. 460.00
Andirons, Iron, Cast, Owl, 15 ¼ In.. 143.00
Andirons, Iron, Cast, Hessian Soldier, Moving Forward, Half-Round, 17 In................ 480.00
Andirons, Iron, Cast, Lion, Standing, 18 ⅜ In.. 805.00
Andirons, Iron, Cast, Fat Geese, 14 ½ x 24 In. 33000.00
Andirons, Iron, Cat, Green Marble, Early 20th Century, 15 ¾ x 18 In. .... *illus* 460.00
Andirons, Iron, Curved, Medallion Finials, Tooled Foot, 20th Century, 19 In.............. 92.00
Andirons, Iron, George Washington, Standing, Right Arm Behind Back, 1850, 7 x 15 In..... 945.00
Andirons, Iron, Heart Design, Loop Top, 3-Footed, 9 In................................ 165.00
Andirons, Iron, Stylized Flame, Raymond Subes, 15 ¾ x 9 x 15 ¾ In..................... 9000.00
Andirons, Iron, Wolf, Large Eyes, Marked, 1887, 15 ¼ In.............................. 145.00
Andirons, Iron, Wrought, Brass Ball Tops, Footed, 19 In................................ 27.00
Andirons, Iron, Wrought, Heart & Loop Finials, Early American, 19 In.................... 319.00
Andirons, Iron, Wrought, Indian, Arts & Crafts, 25 x 6 In.............................. 330.00
Andirons, Iron, Wrought, Knob Finials, Trammel Hooks, 28 ½ In......................... 330.00
Andirons, Iron, Wrought, Openwork Finials, Twisted Rings, Penny Feet, Arts & Crafts, 30 In.. 374.00
Andirons, Iron, Wrought, Arts & Crafts, Twisted, Curled, Patina, 30 x 26 x 12 In........... 570.00
Andirons, Iron, Wrought, Arts & Crafts, Curled, Crossbar, Patina, 27 x 46 x 25 In.......... 960.00
Andirons, Iron, Wrought, Arts & Crafts, Scroll Form, Twisted Shaft, 40 In................. 1116.00
Andirons, Iron, Wrought, Gothic, Continental, 32 x 10 ½ In............................ 2645.00
Andirons, Iron, Wrought, Arrow Shape, Openwork, 21 In............................... 2700.00
Andirons, Iron, Wrought, Cast, Tweedledee & Tweedledum, 20 In. 7200.00
Andirons, Swag Chain Rings, Ball Tops, 20 ½ x 14 x 24 In.............................. 9600.00
Andirons & Fender, Brass, Federal, Urn Top, D-Shape Fire, Early 1800s, 45-In. Fender 2400.00
Andirons & Fender, Brass, Louis XVI, 20th Century, 21-In. Andiron 705.00
Bellows, Black & Gold Design, Chinoiserie, 19th Century, 6 x 15 In...................... 17.00
Bellows, Flowers, Gold Stencil, Green Ground, Brass Nozzles, 16 ⅝ In. 58.00
Bellows, Flowers, Orange, Teardrop Form, Leather, Tacked, Brass Nozzle, 11 ½ x 4 ½ In...... 198.00
Bellows, Flowers, Painted, Teardrop Form, Leather, Tacked, Brass Nozzle, 17 ½ x 8 ½ In...... 176.00
Bellows, Flowers, Yellow, Teardrop Form, Leather, Tacked, Brass Nozzle, 17 ½ x 7 In......... 165.00
Bellows, Fruit, Leaves, Red, Green, Gilt, Yellow, Wood, Leather, 17 ¾ In. 294.00
Bellows, Gold Flower, Red Ground, Leather, Brass Tacks, 1900, 21 In..................... 175.00
Bellows, North Wind Face, Leather, Wood, Carved, Iron Nozzle, W.R. Pries, N.Y., 30 In. 6463.00

Fireplace, Andirons, Brass, Federal, Lemon Finials, Beehive Baluster Post, 19th Century, 19 In.
$575.00

Fireplace, Andirons, Brass, G. Stickley, Ball Over Ring, Curved Feet, Marked, 10 x 22 x 20 In.
$15600.00

Fireplace, Andirons, Iron, Brass, Queen Anne Style, 20th Century, 20 ½ x 20 In.
$460.00

Fireplace, Andirons, Iron, Cat, Green Marble, Early 20th Century, 15 ¾ x 18 In.
$403.00

Fireplace, Fender, Brass, Openwork, Neptune, Dolphins, Britain, 1800s, 9 x 47 x 11 In.
$4495.00

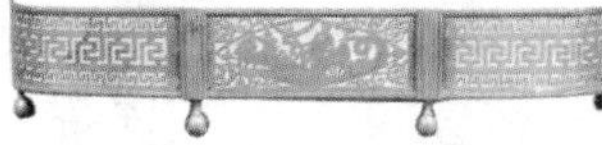

Fireplace, Fireback, Iron, Puddle Cast, Scrollwork, Black Paint, 18th Century, 24 x 18 In.
$690.00

Fireplace, Fireplace, Montgomery Ward, Metal, Orange Enamel, Free Standing, 1960s, 75 x 30 In.
$1090.00

Bellows, Turtle Back, Cornucopia, Fruit, Red Ground, 19th Century, 17 In. ... 345.00
Bellows, Turtle Back, Red Pear, Apples, Mustard Ground, Brass Nozzle, 16 ¾ In. ... 288.00
Broom, Horsehair, White, Black Smoke Design, Flowers, Red & Black Band, 27 x 7 In. ... 413.00
Bucket, Kindling, Mahogany, Turned, Brass Handle, Liner, Early 1800s, 11 x 12 In. ... 660.00
Bucket, Leather, Painted, Strap Handle, 12 ½ x 7 In. ... 770.00
Chenet, Andirons, Bronze, Scrolls, Fans, Fruit, 20th Century, 20 ¾ In. ... 345.00
Chenet, Andirons, Iron, Wrought, Bronze, Spain, 19th Century, 46 x 20 x 22 In. ... 1715.00
Coal Bin, George IV, Iron, Patina, Ringed Lion Masque Handles, 18 x 18 ½ x 11 In. ... 2160.00
Coal Scuttle, Brass, Copper, Applied Detail, Handles, Crests, 11 x 19 In. ... 288.00
Coal Scuttle, Brass, Hammered, Helmet Shape, 16 x 17 In. ... 351.00
Coal Scuttle, Copper, Hammered, Arts & Crafts, Curled Edges, 14 x 18 x 25 In. ... 330.00
Coal Scuttle, Mahogany, Brass Handle, Scoop, Late 19th Century, 15 x 13 x 20 In. ... 110.00
Coal Scuttle, Walnut, Brass Scoop, England, c.1840, 13 x 17 In. ... 205.00
Fender, Brass, 19th Century, 9 ½ x 37 x 4 In. ... 205.00
Fender, Brass, Crest, Rope Design, Arts & Crafts, 12 x 47 x 13 In. ... 375.00
Fender, Brass, Cutout Design, 20th Century, 41 In. ... 70.00
Fender, Brass, D-Shape, Grill Top, 19th Century, 6 x 48 x 11 In. ... 144.00
Fender, Brass, Fan Shape, 8 Panels, Gilt, 25 ½ x 37 x 3 In. ... 472.00
Fender, Brass, Flower & Scroll, Arts & Crafts, Claw Feet, 11 x 42 x 15 In. ... 375.00
Fender, Brass, Openwork, Neptune, Dolphins, Britain, 1800s, 9 x 47 x 11 In. ... *illus* 4495.00
Fender, Brass, Pierced, Victorian, 53 In. ... 110.00
Fender, Brass, Pierced Leaves, Reeded Bun Feet, D-Shape, 1800s, 10 x 47 x 11 In. ... 490.00
Fender, Brass, Regency, Molding Center, Lozenge, Reticulated, c.1830, 34 In. ... 240.00
Fender, Brass, Rope Twisted Crest Rail, Finials, 8 x 59 x 12 In. ... 140.00
Fender, Brass, Serpentine, Openwork, Paw Feet, 20th Century, 8 x 55 x 16 In. ... 575.00
Fender, Brass, Tufted Leather Seat, Victorian, 18 ½ x 61 x 13 In. ... 649.00
Fender, Brass, U-Shape, Openwork, Fluted, Scrolled Leaf, Paw Feet, Victorian, 10 ½ In. ... 235.00
Fender, Brass, Wirework, Kidney, 8 ½ x 34 In. ... 489.00
Fender, Brass, Wirework, 3 Finials, c.1820, 14 ¾ x 50 ¾ In. ... 881.00
Fender, Brass, Wirework, Swags & Scrolls, c.1800, 24 x 39 In. ... 2703.00
Fender, Federal, Brass Mounted, Wirework, 12 ½ x 42 ¼ x 9 ½ In. ... 633.00
Fender, Footman, Brass, Wrought Iron, Turned Handle, Openwork, 1800s, 12 In. ... 235.00
Fender, Iron, Brass, Serpentine, Urn Finials, Rail Over Wires, Scrolls, 58 In. ... 2820.00
Fender, Iron, Twist Top Rail, Finials, Bull's-Eye, Dividers, 45 x 9 x 1 In. ... 280.00
Fender, Steel, Phoenixes, Flowers, Scrolls, Pierced, Frieze Early 1800s, 6 ½ x 62 In. ... 345.00
Fender, U-Shape, Twisted Band, Openwork, Brass, Victorian, 1800s, 50 ½ In. ... 470.00
Fender, Wirework, Federal, Serpentine, Urn Finials, Paw Feet, 1800s, 16 x 50 x 12 In. ... 1700.00
Fender, Wrought Iron, Twist Top, Scrolls, Mounted Balls, Scroll Feet, c.1900, 20 x 40 In. ... 800.00
Fire Grate, Brass, Steel, Federal, Husk Swags, Oval Fans, Leaf Stems, 33 x 31x 14 In. ... 1035.00
Fire Grate, Cast Iron, Gilt Brass, Edwardian, Relief, Backplate, 31 x 26 x 14 In. ... 900.00
Fireback, Cast Iron, Mother Holding Several Small Children, Beaded Edge ... 600.00
Fireback, Cast Iron, Arched Top, Serpents, Man, Potted Tulips, c.1767, 30 x 21 In. ... 1058.00
Fireback, Iron, Puddle Cast, Scrollwork, Black Paint, 18th Century, 24 x 18 In. ... *illus* 690.00
Firedogs, Cast Iron, Dachshunds, c.1900, 7 x 21 In. ... 380.00
Firedogs, Iron, Brass, Scroll Legs, Urn Shape Finials, Victorian, 12 x 9 ½ In. ... 147.00
Fireplace, Montgomery Ward, Metal, Orange Enamel, Free Standing, 1960s, 75 x 30 In. *illus* 1090.00
Log Holder, Scroll Type, Iron, Brass Ball Finials, 20th Century, 20 x 22 x 21 In. ... 165.00
Mantel is listed in the Architectural category.
Peel, Iron, Wrought, Curved Blade, 6-Sided Knob End, 45 In. ... 86.00
Screen, Aesthetic Movement, Bird, Fish, Leaded, Painted Glass, Brass, 33 x 27 In. ... *illus* 2840.00
Screen, Aesthetic Movement, Walnut, Carved, Center Pivots, 4 Brass Feet, 1885, 46 x 32 In. ... 795.00
Screen, Arts & Crafts, Brass, Glass, Caned Beveled Panels, 1900s, 31 ½ x 21 ¼ In. ... 176.00
Screen, Arts & Crafts, Oak, Embroidered, Silk, 49 x 35 In. ... 345.00
Screen, Arts & Crafts, Owl, Oak Frame, Silk Embroidery, 48 ½ x 34 x 11 ¾ In. ... *illus* 365.00
Screen, Arts & Crafts, Wrought Iron, Scrolled Panel, 33 x 37 ½ x 12 In. ... 944.00
Screen, Brass, Butterfly Shape, Iron Mounts, Britain, Early 1800s, 18 x 22 In. ... 370.00
Screen, Brass, Fan Shape, Scalloped Edge, c.1920, 25 x 36 In. ... 115.00
Screen, Brass, Wirework, Diamond Woven, 19th Century, 28 x 39 ½ x 12 In. ... 357.00
Screen, Butterflies, Pressed Fern Fronds, 3-Footed, Mahogany Base, 56 In. ... 259.00
Screen, Cast Iron, Wire Mesh, Patina, France, 23 ½ x 27 In. ... 840.00
Screen, Copper, Peacock On A Branch, 28 x 18 In. ... 1440.00
Screen, Ebonized, Painted Flower, Fluted, Block Uprights, Peg Feet, 40 ½ x 30 ½ In. ... 1440.00
Screen, Gilt, Rococo, C & S Scrolls, Scrolled Legs, 30 x 22 ¼ In. ... 411.00
Screen, Jacobean Revival, Mahogany, Anthemion Crest, Needlepoint Panel, 53 x 31 In. ... 588.00
Screen, Louis XV Style, Fruitwood, Acanthus, Tapestry Panel, 43 x 30 x 16 In. ... 529.00
Screen, Louis XV Style, Giltwood, Tapestry, Landscape, Splayed Feet, 42 x 26 In. ... 840.00

Screen, Louis XV Style, Ormolu, Mesh, Rococo, Lovebirds, Vines, 32 x 26 In. 764.00

Screen, Louis XVI Style, Fan Shape, Carved, Giltwood, 35¾ x 47¾ In.. .... 4375.00

Screen, Napoleon III, Ebonized, Pierced Scrolled Crest, 52 x 33 x 13½ In. 390.00

Screen, Napoleon III, Ebonized, Giltwood, Chinoiserie Style, Needlework, 40 x 22 In. 1680.00

Screen, Oak, Applied Brass Egyptian Design, Arts & Crafts, 24 x 16½ x 5½ In. 270.00

Screen, Papier-Mache, Flowers, Painted, Black Lacquer, Wood Base, 42 x 24 In. 550.00

Screen, Pole, Cherry, Turned, Grooved, Needlepoint, 55 In. 115.00

Screen, Pole, George III, Mahogany, Shield, Rolled Paper Framing, Oval Portrait, 1700s 3040.00

Screen, Pole, Regency Style, Mahogany, Shield, Needlework, Baluster, Tripod, c.1890, 56 x 13 x 9 In., Pair 465.00

Screen, Walnut, Renaissance, Angel Of Sleep, Mid 19th Century, 39 x 27 x 19 In. 1880.00

Stand, Kettle, Iron, Grid Shelf, Penny Feet, Brass Pierced Apron, c.1843, 18 x 13 In. 230.00

Stand, Wrought Iron, 2 Hooks, 3-Footed, Penny Feet, 36½ In. 55.00

Stand, Kettle, Round, Dish Top, Turned Stem, Spiral Twist Base, Tripod Legs, 28 x 11 In. 2468.00

Surround, Cast Iron, Tile, Brass, Flower, Tiles, 20th Century, 33 x 35 x 28 In. 336.00

Surround, Louis XV, Mahogany, Serpentine, Carved Foliage, 47¾ x 72½ x 22¼ In.. .... 2640.00

Tinder Pistol, Strike-A-Light, Steel, Walnut, Mid 18th Century, Dutch, 8 x 4 In.. .... 863.00

Tongs, Iron, Ember, 14½ In. 30.00

Tongs, Wrought Iron, Ember, Round Handle, Finial, 19th Century, 20½ In. 11.00

Tongs, Wrought Iron, Ember, Devil Tail End, 19½ In. 440.00

Trammel, Iron, Bird Finial, c.1720 .... 1650.00

Trammel, Wrought Iron, 4-Footed, Penny Feet, 41½ In.. .... 135.00

FISCHER porcelain was made in Herend, Hungary, by Moritz Fischer. The factory was founded in 1839 and continued working into the twentieth century. The wares are sometimes referred to as Herend porcelain.

Candelabrum, 2-Light, Rothschild Bird, 8½ x 5¼ In., Pair 411.00

Figurine, Ducks, Green Fishscale Design, Gilt, Herend, 1900s, 3 In.. .... 72.00

Figurine, Rabbit, Seated, Red, White, Gilt, Herend, 12¼ In. 690.00

Platter, Chinese Bouquet, Rust, 12 x 10 In. 205.00

Tray, Rothschild Bird, Rounded Corners, 7 In. 118.00

FISHING reels of brass or nickel were made in the United States by 1810. Bamboo fly rods were sold by 1860, often marked with the maker's name. Lures made of metal, or metal and wood, were made in the nineteenth century. Plastic lures were made by the 1930s. All fishing material is collected today and even equipment of the past thirty years is of interest if in good condition with original box.

Casting Line, Bullfrog Silk, R.J. Hillinger & Co., Box 60.00

Catalog, Heddon's Rods, Minnows, Color, c.1911, 38 Pages. 1960.00

Catalog, Milam's Frankfort Kentucky Fishing Reels, c.1892, 5⅝ In. 504.00

Creel, Fine Weave, Mahogany Lid, Bottom, 11 x 7 x 9 In. 672.00

Creel, Joseph Schnell, Leather Trim, Split Willow, c.1940, 15 x 9 x 8 In. .... *illus* 952.00

Creel, Low Boy, Whole, Split Reed, Harness, 17 x 8 x 8 In. 172.00

Display, Heddon, River Runt Spook Lures, Largest Bass, Walleye, c.1938, 18 x 20 In. 345.00

Fish Gig, 3 Prongs, Wood Handle, Hand Forged 94.00

Flies, Superior Bass, King Of Waters, Winchester, No. 3266 .... 80.00

Flies, Superior Trout, Brownhackle, Winchester, No. 3201 .... 45.00

Fly Chest, 8 Drawers, Mixed Woods, 17⅝ x 13½ x 11 In. 224.00

Harpoon, 2 Flue Toggle, Smith & Sons, 19th Century, 21¼ In. .... 510.00 to 588.00

Kit, Ocean City Reels, Let's Go Fishing, Photo Of Man Fishing, Complete, 4 In. 260.00

License, Hunting, Fishing, Holder, 1926-27 .... 95.00

License, Pennsylvania Resident, Round, Green, 1935 .... 14.00

Line Spool, Heddon Black Gold, 50 Yd., 12 Lb., Japan Silk 252.00

Line Winder, Double, Wooden, Adjustable, 40 In. 532.00

Lure, Creek Chub, Crawdad, No. 331, Rainbow Fire Finish 168.00

Lure, Creek Chub Weed Bug, Yellow, Gold, Black, Bead Eyes, Weed Guard, Wire Leader 336.00

Lure, Ed Slominski, Musky, 2 Sections, Green, Gold Spots, 5¼ In. 201.00

Lure, Gen-Shaw, Painted Eyes, Lip, Kankakee, Ill. 112.00

Lure, Heddon, Aluminum, Spinner, Brass Rudder, c.1904, 3 In. 3220.00

Lure, Heddon, Bucktail Minnow 345.00

Lure, Heddon, Bucktail Minnow, No. 402, Yellow, c.1908. .... 448.00

Lure, Heddon, Crab Wiggler, No. 1800, Glass Eyes, Box 570.00

Lure, Heddon, Crazy Crawler, Wood, Green Top, Red & Yellow, 2½ In. 55.00

Lure, Heddon, Dowagic Crab Wiggler, Yellow, c.1916, 4 In. 60.00

Lure, Heddon, Fly Rod, Wiggler, 1½ In.. .... 112.00

Lure, Heddon, Fly Rod, Peet's Choice 196.00

Lure, Heddon, Fly Rod, Bass Bug, Green, White, 1¾ In.. .... 720.00

Fireplace, Screen, Aesthetic Movement, Bird, Fish, Leaded, Painted Glass, Brass, 33 x 27 In.
$2840.00

Fireplace, Screen, Arts & Crafts, Owl, Oak Frame, Silk Embroidery, 48½ x 34 x 11¾ In.
$365.00

Fishing, Creel, Joseph Schnell, Leather Trim, Split Willow, c.1940, 15 x 9 x 8 In.
$52.00

Fishing, Lure, Heddon, Night Radiant Minnow, Glass Eyes, Belly Weights, Spinners, 4⅝ In.
$13500.00

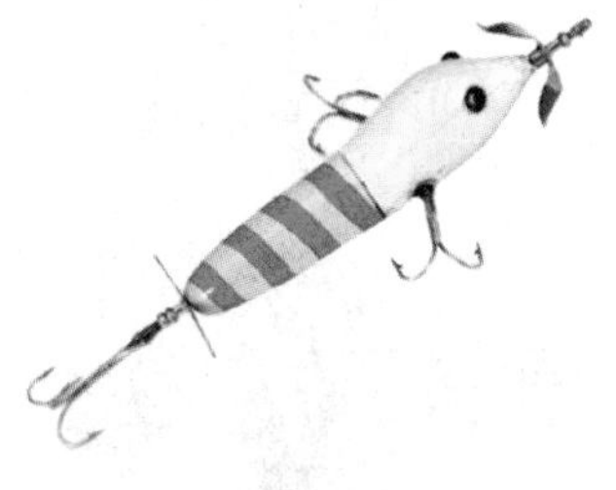

Fishing, Lure, Shakespeare, Frog, Mechanical, Rubber, Box
1568.00

Fishing, Reel, Pflueger, Line Drying, Trout Size, Thumb Activated, Green Finish, c.1896
$504.00

Flash Gordon, Toy, Rocket Fighter, Windup, Tin Lithograph, Marx, 12 In.
$520.00

Florence Ceramics, Figurine, Delia, Olive Green Coat, Muff, Gold Mesh Overlay, Blond Hair, 8 In.
$145.00

Lure, Heddon, Gamefisher, Rubber Frog Legs, Metal Flange, Treble Hook 2040.00
Lure, Heddon, King Zig Wag, Glass Eyes, No. 8359 PLXR, 5 In. 168.00
Lure, Heddon, Lucky 13, Wood, Glass Eyes, Red Head, 3 Treble Hooks, 1940s, 4 In. 54.00 to 65.00
Lure, Heddon, Night Radiant Minnow, Glass Eyes, Belly Weights, Spinners, 4⅝ In. . . . . . *illus* 13500.00
Lure, Heddon, No. 490NP, Single Hook, Box 224.00
Lure, Heddon, Spinner Blade, Feathered Treble Hook, Belly Weights 115.00
Lure, Heddon, Underwater Minnow, Brass Hardware, Internal Belly Weights, c.1904 . . . . 720.00
Lure, Jim Donaly, Redfin Floater, Black, Yellow Accents, No. 2, 2¼ In. 224.00
Lure, K&K, Minnow, Green Over Gold, Glass Eyes, Chin Weight, c.1907, 3⅞ In. 420.00
Lure, Pflueger, Floater Frog, Wood Eyes, 2⅛ In. 364.00
Lure, Shakespeare, Frog, Mechanical, Rubber, Box . . . . *illus* 1568.00
Lure, South Bend, Minnow, Salt Water, Yellow, Red, Belly Cup Rig Treble Hook, No. 999 . . . . . 240.00
Lure, South Bend, Whirl-Oreno, Black & Yellow, Backlit, 1932, 3 In. 85.00
Lure, Surface Bait, Blue Head, 2 Pin Collar, c.1910, Box 728.00
Lure, Winchester, Multi Wobbler, Red, Orange, Black 644.00
Minnow Bucket, Copper, Torpedo Shape, Tow Behind, 12 In. 460.00
Minnow Bucket, Floating, Aluminum, Ribbed, Smith Co., 9 x 17 In. 28.00
Minnow Bucket, Green, Floating, Supplee-Biddle Hardware Co., 11½ x 5 x 10½ In.. . . . . 532.00
Minnow Bucket, Lucas, Stenciled Leaping Pike, 11 x 5½ x 10 In.. . . . . 140.00
Minnow Plug, Winchester, No. 2001 . . . . 50.00
Minnow Trap, Green Glass, 3 Holes, Tin Lid, Bail Handle, Rectangular, 14 x 7 x 6 In.. . . . . 1904.00
Net, Carl Christiansen, Trout Carved Handle, 24 In.. . . . . 280.00
Net, Raymond Ferland, Y Shape, 20 In.. . . . . 168.00
Reel, Airex Corp., Spinning, Bache Brown, Metal Line Clips, Master, No. 3. . . . . 25.00
Reel, Ambassadeur 600, Case. 60.00
Reel, Brass, Wood Handle, Inscribed T. Blundel, c.1820-30, 4½ In. 1673.00
Reel, Cow & Son, Brass, Bone Handle, Maker's Mark, c.1850, 4 In.. . . . . 2032.00
Reel, Heddon, Casting, Sapphire Jeweled Bearings, No. 18, c.1920 . . . . 392.00
Reel, Jack Welch, Silver, Aluminum, Casting, No. 0153, Box 2016.00
Reel, Mitchell, Spinning, Gold Finish Parts, Spare Spool, No. 279 . . . . 300.00
Reel, Nottingham, Mahogany, Brass Star Back, Bone Handles, 3 In. 140.00
Reel, Pflueger, Line Drying, Trout Size, Thumb Activated, Green Finish, c.1896. . . . . *illus* 504.00
Reel, Shakespeare, Fly, Model 1821, Silent Winding, Original Box, 1950s 38.00
Reel, South Bend, No. 550 . . . . 5.00
Reel, Winchester, No. 1118. . . . . 150.00
Reel, Winchester, No. 2291. . . . . 140.00
Reel, Winchester, No. 2342. . . . . 80.00
Reel, Winchester, No. 2393. . . . . 100.00
Reel, Winchester, No. 4252. . . . . 100.00
Reel, Winchester, No. 4253. . . . . 90.00
Reel, Winchester, No. 4256. . . . . 50.00
Reel, Winchester, No. 6015, Bamboo 35.00
Reel, Wm. H. Talbot Co., German Silver, S Handle, 1½-In. Spool, No. 3708. . . . . 600.00
Reel Box, The Milam, Size 4, Paper Label, Slide Top 840.00
Reel Can, Simmons Hardware, No. S-100 . . . . 130.00
Rod, Abercrombie & Fitch, 3 Piece, 2 Tips, Nickel Silver Reel Seat, No. A510, Sack 460.00
Rod, Gary Howells, Trout, 3 Sections, 2 Tips, Durabronze Ferrules, No. 4431, Bag, Tube 1904.00
Rod, Jim Payne, Bass, 1 Tip, Chrome Guides, 9½ Ft. 336.00
Rod, Jim Payne, Trout, 2 Tip, c.1955 . . . . 3360.00
Rod, Kosmic, Fly, Ivoroid Reel Seat, 2 Tips, Canvas Sack, Leather Case, c.1890 . . . . 397.00
Rod, Leonard, Salmon, Double Handle, Pinched Snake Guides, Aluminum Tube, Sack 112.00
Rod, Winchester, Metal, No. 5430, Bag 50.00
Rod, Wright & McGill Co., Fly, Eagle Claw, Dr. Lurie, 1950s, 8 Ft. 113.00
Spear, Cal Deming, 7 Tines, Wood Handle 118.00
Spinner, Chapman, Son & Co., Brass, Feather, Marked. 168.00
Tackle Box, Leather, Brass Name Plate, Metal Trays, Brass Feet, Lock, 9⅛ x 7⅝ In. 1008.00
Trap, S.W. Evans, Eagle Claw, Brass, Marked, 2½ In. 540.00
Trophy, Sawfish Rostrum, Mounted Upright, Steel Display Stand, Rusted Finish, 48 In. 720.00

FLAGS *are included in the Textile category.*

FLASH GORDON appeared in the Sunday comics in 1934. The daily strip started in 1940. The hero was also in comic books from 1930 to 1970, in books from 1936, in movies from 1938, on the radio in the 1930s and 1940s, and on television from 1953 to 1954. All sorts of memorabilia are collected, but the ray guns and rocket ships are the most popular.

Costume, Space Outfit, Esquire Novelty, Box, 1952 . . . . 179.00

oy, Click Pistol, Radio Repeater, Tin, Marx, 1930s, 10 In. 242.00
oy, Rocket Fighter, Windup, Tin Lithograph, Marx, 12 In. *illus* 520.00
oy, Signal Pistol, Light Green, Pressed Steel, Marx, 7 In. 144.00
oy, Rocket Fighter, Moves, Makes Noise, Sparks, Tin, Windup, Marx, 12 In. 437.00

LORENCE CERAMICS were made in Pasadena, California, from World War II to 1977. lorence Ward created many colorful figurines, boxes, candleholders, and other items for ne gift shop trade. Each piece was marked with an ink stamp that included the name *lorence Ceramics Co*. The company was sold in 1964 and although the name remained the same, the roducts were very different. Mugs, cups, and trays were made.

hip & Dip, White, Leaf Form, 14 x 9¾ In. 18.00
igurine, Abigail, Blue Gray Gown, White Collar, Hat, Gold Trim, 8½ In. 175.00
igurine, Abigail, Gray Victorian Outfit, Burgundy & Gold Trim, 1940s, 8 In. 50.00
igurine, Camille, Blue Green Coat, Magenta Bow, Hat, Blond Hair, Gold Trim, 8½ In. 169.00
igurine, Charmaine, Parasol, White Lace Dress, Gold Trim, 8½ In. 95.00 to 125.00
igurine, Clarissa, Rose Gown, Ermine Trim, Godey, 7¾ In. 165.00
igurine, Delia, Olive Green Coat, Muff, Gold Mesh Overlay, Blond Hair, 8 In. *illus* 145.00
igurine, Elaine, 1950s, 6 In. 38.00
igurine, Elizabeth, Seated On Chair, Blue Dress, White Lace, Gold Trim, 7 x 8 In. 385.00
igurine, Irene, Cream Dress & Coat, Gold Trim, 6 In. 65.00
igurine, Irene, Green Dress & Coat, Gold Trim, 7 In. 60.00
igurine, Irene, Pink Dress & Coat, Brown Hair, White Bonnet, 7 In. 60.00
igurine, Linda Lou, Rose Gown, Gold Trim, 7¾ In. 180.00
igurine, Marilyn, Pink Dress, Carrying Hat Box, 8¼ In. 500.00
igurine, Matilda, Blue Gray Dress, Brown Hair, 1940s, 8½ In. 45.00
igurine, Melanie, Green Skirt & Coat, White Blouse, Brown Hair, 8½ In. 105.00
igurine, Memories, Grandmother, On Chair, Photo Album, Pink Dress, Shawl, 6¾ In. 695.00
igurine, Nita, Royal Red Gown, Blond Hair, Lace Trim, 1940s, 8 In. 225.00
igurine, Oriental Girl, White Dress, Flower, Blue Pants, Collar, 8¼ In. 30.00
igurine, Priscilla, Blue Dress, White Apron, Bonnet, 1940s, 7¾ In. 95.00
igurine, Rhett, White Tux, Top Hat, Gold Trim, 9 In. 225.00
igurine, Scarlett, Beige Dress, Green Hat, Brown Hair, Gold Trim, Stamped No. 2, 9 In. 145.00
igurine, Scarlett, Blue Outfit, Magenta Hat, Muff, Parasol, Gold Trim, 8¾ In. 425.00
igurine, Sue, Aqua Dress, White Bonnet, Gold Trim, 5¾ In. 110.00
igurine, Sue Ellen, Muff, Blue Dress, White Bonnet, Gold Trim, 8¼ In. 225.00
igurine, Victor, Green Tux & Tails, White Top Hat, 1940s, 9¼ In. 100.00
igurine, Woman, Carrying Basket, Roses, White Dress, Pink Hat, Brown Hair, 9 In. 149.00
rame, Pink Roses, Green Leaves, Cream Ground, Gold Trim, 8 x 5½ In. 35.00

LOW BLUE was made in England and other countries about 1830 to 1900. The dishes were rinted with designs using a cobalt blue coloring. The color flowed from the design to the hite body so that the finished piece has a smeared blue design. The dishes were usually ade of ironstone china. More Flow Blue may be found under the name of the manufacturer.

owl, Lugano, Gold Trim, 9½ In. 66.00
owl, Oriental, Footed, 5¾ x 10 In. *illus* 130.00
owl, Vegetable, Cover, Amoy, 8-Sided, 7 x 10 In. *illus* 250.00
owl, Vegetable, Cover, Formosa, 9 x 12 In. 325.00
utter, Cover, Normandy, 4 x 7¾ In., 3 Piece 385.00
oot Bath, Scalloped Edge, Checkered & Flower Border, 19th Century 200.00
ıg, Toby, Twig Handle, Glaze Crazing, 19th Century, 5½ x 6 In. 100.00
itcher, Luster Embossed, Stags & Dogs, Vines, Epsom Cup, 7½ In. 50.00
itcher, Sinde, Footed, Large Handle, Marked, Oriental Stone, 12½ In. 120.00
late, Luncheon, Formosa, T.J. & J. Mayer, 7¾ In., 8 Piece 250.00
late, Manilla, Marked P.W. & Co., 9½ In. 110.00
latter, Formosa, 19th Century, 14 x 19 In. 750.00
latter, Formosa, T.J. & J. Mayer, 15½ x 12 In. 375.00
latter, Gothic, Buildings, Trees, 6-Sided, Marked, J.F. & Co., 16 x 12½ In. 115.00
latter, Japan Tree, 15½ x 19¾ In. 431.00
latter, Landscape, Cobalt Blue, 8-Sided, T. Furnival, c.1820, 17 x 12 In. *illus* 431.00
latter, Madras, Oval, Blue, White, Marked, 19th Century, 21 In. 213.00
latter, Oriental, Octagonal, Fluted, Cobalt Blue, 16 x 11 In. 431.00
latter, Scinde, Scalloped, Oriental, 18½ x 14½ In. 250.00
latter, Tonquin, J.H. Eath, 13¾ x 10¼ In. *illus* 250.00
ugar, 2 Handles, Footed, Cover, 19th Century, 4½ x 2½ In. 125.00

Flow Blue, Bowl, Oriental, Footed, 5¾ x 10 In.
$130.00

Flow Blue, Bowl, Vegetable, Cover, Amoy, 8-Sided, 7 x 10 In.
$250.00

Flow Blue, Platter, Landscape, Cobalt Blue, 8-Sided, T. Furnival, c.1820, 17 x 12 In.
$431.00

Flow Blue, Platter, Tonquin, J.H. Eath, 13¾ x 10¼ In.
$250.00

TIP

Rinse food off plates as soon after use as possible to avoid stains.

Tea Set, Formosa, T.J. & J. Mayer, Teapot, Waste Bowl, Sugar, Lid, Creamer 450.00
Teapot, Metal Pumper, Brass Lid, Gilt, c.1890, 8 In. 322.00
Teapot, Normandy, Marked, Johnson Brothers, 7 ½ In. 1760.00

FLYING PHOENIX, *see Phoenix Bird category.*

FOLK ART is also listed in many categories of this book under the actual name of the object. See categories such as Box, Cigar Store Figure, Paper, Weather Vane, Wooden, etc.

Decorating Goes Big

Perhaps it started because the walls are full of paintings or the tables are covered with small collectibles, but the newest look, according to the fashionistas, is large sculptures inside the house. Folk art collectors have displayed carousel horses, cigar store Indians, and huge advertising signs for years.

Bank, House, Peaked Roofs, Wood Strips, Coin Slots, Glass Panes, c.1904, 12 x 14 In. 144.00
Basket, Bottle Caps, Snake Form, 7 ½ In. 30.00
Bird, Black, Orange Wings, Crest, Yellow Bill, Glass Eyes, Wire Legs, Carved, 5 ½ x 8 In. 77.00
Bird, In Cage, Wood, Carved, Wire Bars, Painted, Signed, June Walter 88, 14 x 6 In. 209.00
Bird Tree, 3 Birds, Stick Tree, Tiered Chip Carved Base, Painted, D & D Strawser, 20 In. 121.00
Bird Tree, 4 Birds, Bentwood Tree, Log Base, DDS 89, Strawser, 17 ½ x 10 In. 209.00
Bird Tree, 5 Birds, Carved, Painted, Wood Base, Finch Norton No. 13 Bananiquit, 31 In. 1035.00
Bird Tree, 6 Birds, Natural Branch, Wood Base, Wire Legs, Late 1800s, 24 In. 1495.00
Bird Tree, 6 Carved & Painted Birds On Branches, Bead Eyes, Wire Feet, 23 In. 1725.00
Bird Tree, 9 Birds, Yellow, White, Black Eyes, 51 ½ x 18 In. 1344.00
Bird Tree, Various Birds, Multiple Branches, White Picket Fence Base, Carved, 29 In. 8500.00
Bookends, Cat, White, Arched Back, Black Base, Wood, 12 x 6 ½ In. 125.00
Bookends, Horse, Black, Yellow, Red, Front & Rear, Wood, 7 x 4 ½ In. 125.00
Bookshelf, Carved, 5 Tiers, 19th Century, 33 x 63 In. 743.00
Cage, Squirrel, Tin, Wire, Pine, Rotates, Punched Star, c.1890, 29 x 28 x 13 In. . . . . *illus* 315.00
Cage, Squirrel, Wood, Metal, Painted, Green, Yellow, Grain Painted Roof, 1800s, 15 x 8 In. . . . 235.00
Cat Carrier, Wood, Mustard Paint, Metal Bars, Handle, c.1890, 12 x 13 In. 1400.00
Chain, Prisoner Art, Oak, 100s Of Interlocking Dagger Shape Pieces, Early 1900s, 74 In. 230.00
Chain, Wood, Padlock, 2 Links, Carved Cages, Free Moving Balls, 1800s, 10 Ft. 8 In. 294.00
Chicken, Pottery, Reggie Meaders, 13 ¾ In. . . . . *illus* 440.00
Cow, Holstein, Painted, Tack Eyes, Wood Carving, Early 20th Century, 17 ⅝ x 25 ¾ In. 353.00
Dragon & Car, Fanciful, Watercolor & Ink, On Paper, Frame, c.1820, 7 x 10 In. 646.00
Eagle, Spread Wings, Wood, Carved, Painted, Signed, Perry County, Pa.,1996, 19 In. 2530.00
Figure, Chained Slave, Carved, Studded Yoke, Cuffed To Block, 14 In. 203.00
Figure, Napoleon, Sitting On White Horse, Wood, Carved, 1832, 11 x 10 In. 259.00
Figurehead, Mermaid, Relief Carving, Shield Crest, Weathered, c.1877, 30 x 13 In. 1610.00
Fish, Carved, Red & White Paint, Applied Copper Fins & Tail, Mounted On Base, 22 x 29 In. . . 403.00
House, Cream, Blue, Cutout Windows, Wood, 18 x 14 x 18 In. 475.00
Palette, Artist's, Terrier's Head, Hand Painted, Signed, MT, 10 ½ x 15 In. 478.00
Peacock, Wood Carving, Tin Legs, Sheet Iron Comb, Bent Wire Loop, Painted, 26 x 6 In. 690.00
Pig, Black, White Highlights, Green Base, Wood Carving, 4 ¼ x 6 In. 660.00
Pilothouse Eagle, Carved, Gilded, Carved Wooden Base Painted To Resemble Rock, 24 In. . . 4600.00
Plate, Wood, Painted, Great Dane, c.1900, 14 In. 475.00
Plate, Wood, Painted, Great White Pelican, Clifford A. Reynolds, c.1900, 14 In. 500.00
Rooster, Multicolored Paint, Carved, Signed, LB 72, 6 ½ x 6 x 2 In. 412.00
Rooster, Pine, Painted Red & Black, Yellow Feet, W. Schimmel, Cumberland Cty., Pa., 7 In. . . 999.00
Shelf, Willow Tree Form, Tulip Top, Green, Yellow Highlights, D.Y. Ellinger, 16 x 9 ¾ x 8 In. . . 412.00
Shelf, Wood, Carved, Scrolls, Stars, Heart, Green Gray, Rounded Corners, 5 x 18 x 5 In. 29.00
Skeleton Bust, Papier-Mache, Wood, Articulated Jaw, Painted, 13 ½ In. 230.00
Snake, Diamond Back Rattler, Wood, Carved, Oscar Spence, 31 In. 316.00
Stone Fruit, Wire Basket, 19th Century, 6 ¼ In., 20 Piece . . . . *illus* 955.00
Toy, Articulated Figures, Dance, Play Castanets, Lower Sleeve Moves Up & Down 2500.00
Vase, Bottle Caps, Glass Insert, Handles, 4 In. 50.00
Whirligig, 2 Sailors, In Rowboat, Painted, Wood, 25 In. 230.00
Whirligig, Figural, Indian Chief In Canoe, Paddle Arms, 20th Century, 6 x 16 x 6 In. 250.00
Whirligig, Fish, Wood, Carved, Painted, Propeller Opens Fish's Mouth, Stand, 22 x 33 In. . . . 2233.00
Whirligig, Grenadier Soldier, 19th Century, 22 ¼ In. 1528.00
Whirligig, Indian, Carved, Painted Red, Black, White, Rotating Hatchet Paddles, 55 In. 646.00
Whirligig, Musician, Seated, Dancer, Wood, 17 ⅜ In. 345.00
Whirligig, Roman Centurion, Paddle Arms, Plumed Helmet, Breast Plate, Painted, 17 In. . . . 805.00
Whirligig, Sailor, Blue Pants, White Shirt, Red Collar, Tin Rim On Hat, Nantucket, 15 In. . . . 460.00
Whirligig, Sailor, Carved, Painted, Paddle Hand Blades, 1800s, 17 x 5 In. 10800.00
Whirligig, Sailor, Dewey Boy, Carved, Painted, Stand, Early 20th Century, 16 ½ In. 1410.00
Whirligig, Soldier, Carved, Painted, Extended Arm Blades, 1800s, 43 x 9 ½ In. 21600.00
Whirligig, Soldier, Carved Wood, Red & White Paint, Paddle Arms, c.1890, 20 In. 2350.00
Whirligig, Soldier, Wood, Leather Hat, Wood Brim, Early 20th Century, 19 ¼ In. 441.00

Folk Art, Cage, Squirrel, Tin, Wire, Pine, Rotates, Punched Star, c.1890, 29 x 28 x 13 In.
$315.00

Folk Art, Chicken, Pottery, Reggie Meaders, 13 ¾ In.
$440.00

Folk art, Stone Fruit, Wire Basket, 19th Century, 6 ¼ In., 20 Piece
$955.00

Whirligig, Soldier, Wood, Carved, Gray Uniform, Black Boots, Paddle Hands, Base, 20 In. 805.00
Whirligig, Wood, Man At Pump Well, White Horse, American Indian, 1930s, 17 x 19 In. 1725.00
Wood Cannon Model, Iron Rimmed Wheels 110.00

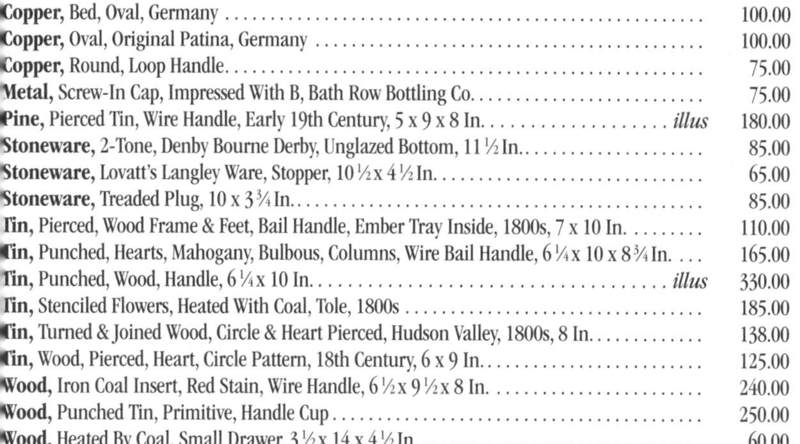

FOOT WARMERS solved the problem of cold feet in past generations. Some warmers held charcoal, others held hot water. Pottery, tin, and soapstone were the favored materials to conduct the heat. The warmer was kept under the feet, then the legs and feet were tucked into a blanket, providing welcome warmth in a cold carriage or church.

Copper, Bed, Oval, Germany 100.00
Copper, Oval, Original Patina, Germany 100.00
Copper, Round, Loop Handle 75.00
Metal, Screw-In Cap, Impressed With B, Bath Row Bottling Co. 75.00
Pine, Pierced Tin, Wire Handle, Early 19th Century, 5 x 9 x 8 In. *illus* 180.00
Stoneware, 2-Tone, Denby Bourne Derby, Unglazed Bottom, 11½ In. 85.00
Stoneware, Lovatt's Langley Ware, Stopper, 10½ x 4½ In. 65.00
Stoneware, Treaded Plug, 10 x 3¾ In. 85.00
Tin, Pierced, Wood Frame & Feet, Bail Handle, Ember Tray Inside, 1800s, 7 x 10 In. 110.00
Tin, Punched, Hearts, Mahogany, Bulbous, Columns, Wire Bail Handle, 6¼ x 10 x 8¾ In. 165.00
Tin, Punched, Wood, Handle, 6¼ x 10 In. *illus* 330.00
Tin, Stenciled Flowers, Heated With Coal, Tole, 1800s 185.00
Tin, Turned & Joined Wood, Circle & Heart Pierced, Hudson Valley, 1800s, 8 In. 138.00
Tin, Wood, Pierced, Heart, Circle Pattern, 18th Century, 6 x 9 In. 125.00
Wood, Iron Coal Insert, Red Stain, Wire Handle, 6½ x 9½ x 8 In. 240.00
Wood, Punched Tin, Primitive, Handle Cup 250.00
Wood, Heated By Coal, Small Drawer, 3½ x 14 x 4½ In. 60.00

FOOTBALL *collectibles may be found in the Card and the Sports categories.*

FOSTORIA glass was made in Fostoria, Ohio, from 1887 to 1891. The factory was moved to Moundsville, West Virginia, and most of the glass seen in shops today is a twentieth-century product. The company was sold in 1983; new items will be easily identifiable, according to the new owner, Lancaster Colony Corporation. Additional Fostoria items may be listed in the Milk Glass category.

American, Bonbon, 3-Footed, 2¼ x 7 In. 30.00
American, Bowl, Vegetable, Oval, Divided, 10 x 7 In. 35.00
American, Butter, Cover 145.00
American, Cake Plate, 3-Footed, 14 In. 45.00
American, Cake Stand, 7 x 10 In. *illus* 125.00
American, Cake Stand, Square, 10 In. 176.00
American, Candleholder, 1-Light, 4½ x 3 In., Pair 18.00
American, Candleholder, 2 x 4½ In. 60.00
American, Candlestick, Octagonal Foot, 6 In., Pair 45.00
American, Candy Jar, Cover, Hexagonal Foot, 7¼ In. 45.00
American, Cigarette Box, Cover, 4¾ x 3½ In. 100.00
American, Creamer, 4¼ x 3½ In. 15.00
American, Cup, Flared 12.00
American, Dish, Jelly, Footed, 4¼ In. 25.00
American, Dish, Mayonnaise, Divided, 6¼ In. 20.00
American, Dish, Sundae, Footed, 3 x 4 In. 12.00
American, Nappy, Flared, Handles, 1¾ x 5¼ In. 24.00
American, Salt, 2 In. 12.00
American, Sandwich Server, Open Center Handle, 12 In. 45.00
American, Straw Jar, Cover, Footed, 12½ In. 350.00
American, Sugar, Cover, 6¼ In. 60.00
American, Sugar, Individual 15.00
American, Tumbler, Footed, 3 Oz., 2⅞ In. 13.00
American, Vase, Bud, Footed, 6 In. 20.00
American, Whiskey, 2 Oz., 2½ In. 8.00
American, Nut Cup, Amber, Footed 8.00
American, Nut Cup, Green, Footed 20.00
Animal, Deer, Reclining, 2⅜ In. 32.00
Animal, Deer, Reclining, Milk Glass, 2⅜ In. 32.00
Animal, Deer, Standing, Crystal, 4¼ In. 32.00
Animal, Deer, Standing, Milk Glass, 4¼ In. 32.00
Animal, Duck, Mama, Cobalt Blue, 4 In. 36.00

Foot Warmer, Pine, Pierced Tin, Wire Handle, Early 19th Century, 5 x 9 x 8 In.
$180.00

Foot Warmer, Tin, Punched, Wood, Handle, 6¼ x 10 In.
$330.00

TIP
Never use hot or cold water on glass. Use dishwashing liquid, a soft toothbrush, and warm water. Rinse, then dry with a terrycloth towel.

Fostoria, American, Cake Stand, 7 x 10 In.
$125.00

Fostoria, Bookends, Horse, Rearing, 7⅜ x 5¼ In.
$125.00

Fostoria, Coin, Urn, Cover, Footed, Amber, 12¾ In.
$160.00

Fostoria, Colony, Candlestick, 7 In., Pair
$55.00

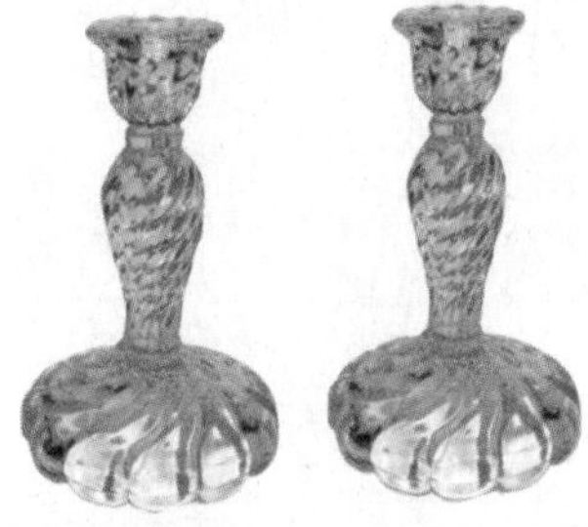

Fostoria, Heirloom, Epergne, Blue Opalescent, 9 x 15¾ In.
$145.00

Animal, Duckling, Head Back, Cobalt Blue, 2½ In. 40.00
Animal, Duckling, Walking, Amber, 2⅜ In. 14.00
Animal, Duckling, Walking, Cobalt Blue, 2⅜ In. 24.00
Animal, Owl, Green, 2½ In. 30.00
Animal, Polar Bear, Silver Mist, 4⅝ In. 92.00
Animal, Rabbit, Mama, Canary, 2⅛ In. 38.00
Animal, Squirrel, Running, Green 24.00
Animal, Squirrel, Running, Cobalt Blue 42.00
Animal, Squirrel, Sitting, Green 24.00
Animal, Squirrel, Sitting 38.00
Art Glass, Vase, Gold Iridescent, Amethyst Hearts & VIne, Cylindrical, Rolled Rim, 12 In. 575.00
Baroque, Bowl, Flared, 12 In. 30.00
Baroque, Candlestick, 2-Light, 8¼ x 5½ In., Pair 125.00
Baroque, Candlestick, Chintz Etch, 4 In., Pair 60.00
Baroque, Cup & Saucer, Chintz Etch 30.00
Baroque, Relish, 3 Sections, 10 In. 30.00
Baroque, Salt & Pepper, Individual 49.00
Baroque, Sugar & Creamer, Tray 24.00
Baroque, Sugar & Creamer, Tray, Azure 85.00
Bookends, Horse, Rearing, 7⅜ x 5¼ In. .... *illus* 125.00
Bookends, Lyre, 7 In. 65.00
Bookends, Plume, Ebony 204.00
Bridal Wreath, Cordial 7.00
Brocade, Vase, Fan, Oakleaf, Pink 650.00
Brocade, Vase, Oakleaf, Ruffled Edge, 8 In. 265.00
Brocade, Vase, Oakleaf, Pink, Ruffled Edge, 8 In. 325.00
Brocaded Grape, Bowl, Centerpiece, Flower Holder, Orchid, 3 Piece, 13-In. Bowl 120.00
Brocaded Grape, Compote, Orchid, 11 In. 180.00
Brocaded Grape, Vase, 6 In, Blue 102.00
Brocaded Summer Gardens, Sandwich Server, Center Handle, White 75.00
Buttercup, Dish, Mayonnaise, Underplate 52.00
Celestial, Celery Vase, Green, 7½ In. 30.00
Century, Bowl, Oval, Handles, Heather Etch, 10 x 6½ In. 38.00
Century, Candleholder, 4½ In., Pair 38.00
Century, Candlestick, 2-Light, 7 In., Pair 54.00
Century, Pitcher, Water, 7 In. .... 78.00 to 110.00
Century, Plate, Salad, Crescent Shape 32.00
Century, Platter, Oval, 12 In. 40.00
Century, Relish, 3 Sections, 11 In. 33.00
Century, Salt & Pepper, Heather Etch 16.00
Century, Sugar & Creamer, Tray 30.00
Chalice, Cordial, Oz. 12.00
Chintz, Bonbon, 3-Footed, 7 In. 25.00
Chintz, Bowl, Tricornered, Handle, 4½ In. .... 20.00 to 35.00
Chintz, Candlestick, 2-Light, 4½ x 8 In. 50.00
Chintz, Candlestick, 3-Light, Pair 175.00
Chintz, Creamer 15.00
Chintz, Goblet, 9 Oz., 6⅛ In. 35.00
Chintz, Goblet, 9 Oz., 7¾ In. 50.00
Chintz, Goblet, Cocktail, 4 Oz., 5 In. 30.00
Chintz, Goblet, Low, 9 Oz., 6⅛ In. 40.00
Chintz, Jug 525.00
Chintz, Mayonnaise Set, 3 Piece 155.00
Chintz, Plate, Salad, 7½ In. 18.00
Chintz, Salt & Pepper, Individual, Pair 95.00
Chintz, Sandwich Server, Center Handle 85.00
Chintz, Sherbet, Low, 5 Oz., 4⅜ In. 22.00
Chintz, Sherbet, Tall, 6 Oz., 5½ In. 28.00
Chintz, Sugar 15.00
Chintz, Sugar & Creamer .... 32.00 to 55.00
Chintz, Tidbit, 3-Footed, 8¼ In. 48.00
Chintz, Tumbler, Iced Tea, Footed, 9 Oz., 6⅛ In. 68.00
Chintz, Tumbler, Juice, Footed, 5 Oz., 4¾ In. 26.00
Coin, Bowl, Oval, Amber, 9 In. 55.00
Coin, Candlestick, 4½ In., Pair 35.00
Coin, Candlestick, Crystal, Frosted Coins, 4½ In. 35.00

oin, Candy Box, Cover, Blue, 6 ¼ In. 90.00
oin, Cigarette Urn, Ashtray, Amber 45.00
oin, Cigarette Urn, Ruby 36.00
oin, Compote, 6 ½ x 8 ½ In. 55.00
oin, Compote, Amber, 6 ½ x 8 ½ In. 48.00
oin, Cruet, Amber 95.00
oin, Lamp, Coach, Oil, Blue 265.00
oin, Nappy, Amber, Frosted Coins, Handle, 5 In. 28.00
oin, Salt & Pepper, Amber 27.00
oin, Salt & Pepper, Blue 47.00
oin, Salt & Pepper, Ruby 47.00
oin, Sugar & Creamer, Cover 55.00
oin, Urn, Cover, Footed, Amber, 12 ¾ In. *illus* 160.00
oin, Wedding Bowl, Cover, Amber, 8 In. 80.00
olony, Candlestick, 2-Light, 6 ¼ In. 30.00
olony, Candlestick, 3 In., Pair 25.00
olony, Candlestick, 7 In., Pair. *illus* 55.00
olony, Goblet, Water, 9 Oz., 5 ¼ In. 9.00
olony, Goblet, Wine, 3 ¼ Oz., 4 ¼ In. 14.00
olony, Salt & Pepper, Tray, 3 Piece. 45.00
olony, Sandwich Server, Center Handle, 11 In. 32.00
olony, Sherbet, Footed, 5 Oz., 3 ½ In. 5.00
olony, Sugar & Creamer, Individual 24.00
ontour, Cordial, Oz. 20.00
ontour, Sugar & Creamer, Pine Cutting 45.00
ontour, Sugar & Creamer, Wedding Ring Decoration 27.00
orsage, Goblet, 9 Oz., 7 ½ In. 40.00
orsage, Oyster Cocktail, 4 Oz., 3 ¾ In. 20.00
orsage, Plate, Salad, 7 In. 18.00
orsage, Relish, 3 Sections, Handles, 12 ¼ In. 45.00
orsage, Vase, Flared, Footed, 10 In. 250.00
ynthia, Goblet, 9 Oz., 7 ½ In. 28.00
airfax, Ashtray, Rose. 14.00
airfax, Bowl, Icer, Rose 23.00
airfax, Candlestick, Rose, 3 ¼ In. 35.00
airfax, Candy Dish, Cover, Rose, 5 x 7 In. 70.00
airfax, Cup, After Dinner, Rose, Footed 15.00
airfax, Cup, Rose, Footed 6.00
airfax, Flower Holder, Window Box, Silver Deposit, Rose, Large 204.00
airfax, Pitcher, Azure, 9 ½ In. 295.00
airfax, Salt & Pepper 71.00
airfax, Salt & Pepper, Ebony 125.00
airfax, Sugar, Amber 10.00
airfax, Sugar, Cover, Rose 50.00
airfax, Sugar, Rose, Individual 15.00
airfax, Sugar & Creamer, Ebony 46.00
airfax, Sugar & Creamer, Individual, Ebony 38.00
airfax, Sugar & Creamer, Individual, Rose. 45.00
airfax, Sugar & Creamer, Individual, Topaz. 28.00
airfax, Sugar & Creamer, Topaz 45.00
airfax, Window Box, Azure 96.00
igurine, Madonna, Satin Mist, 10 In. 110.00
uchsia, Goblet, Water, 9 Oz., 7 ¼ In. 45.00
rape Leaf, Dish, Almond, Green, Individual 9.00
eirloom, Bonbon, White Opalescent, Folded-Up Handle, 6 ½ In. 34.00
eirloom, Candlestick, Rose, 3 ½ In., Pair 48.00
eirloom, Epergne, Blue Opalescent, 9 x 15 ¾ In. *illus* 145.00
eirloom, Plate, Blue Opalescent, 9 ¼ In. 35.00
eirloom, Plate, Green Opalescent, 10 ¼ In. 38.00
eirloom, Vase, Bud, Green Opalescent, 6 In. 23.00
eirloom, Vase, Bud, White Opalescent, 6 In. 23.00
eirloom, Vase, Bud, White Opalescent, 12 In. 45.00
eirloom, Vase, Pink Opalescent, 12 In. 24.00
amestown, Goblet, Water, Ruby, 9 ½ Oz., 5 ¾ In. *illus* 16.00
une, Candlestick, Blue, Scroll, 5 In. 70.00
une, Candy Dish, Folded-Up Sides, Tab Handles, 2 ½ x 7 x 5 ½ In. 25.00

Fostoria, Jamestown, Goblet, Water, Ruby, 9 ½ Oz., 5 ¾ In.
$16.00

TIP

What to do when the power fails? If only a few rooms are affected, the problem may be an overloaded circuit. Turn off major appliances and the light switches and replace any burned-out fuses or reset the circuit breaker. When you turn appliances and lights back on, if the power fails again, call an electrician. An electrical fire is dangerous to you and your collection. If the neighborhood is blacked out, it is probably a problem with the electric power company. Turn off major appliances to avoid an overload on circuits when the power comes back. If the power fails in freezing weather, open the faucets to keep the pipes from freezing and to prevent water damage to your collection.

Fostoria, Lido, Cup & Saucer.
$8.00

Fostoria, Mayfair, Cruet, Green, Stopper, 7 ½ In.
$130.00

TIP

Glassware, old or new, requires careful handling. Stand each piece upright, not touching another. Never nest pieces. Wash in moderately hot water and mild detergent. Avoid wiping gold- or platinum-banded pieces while glasses are hot. Never use scouring pads or silver polish on glass. When using an automatic dishwasher, be sure the water temperature is under 140 degrees.

June, Celery Dish, 11 ½ In. 34.00
June, Celery Dish, Topaz, 11 ½ In. 35.00
June, Champagne, 6 Oz., 6 In. 38.00
June, Champagne, Hollow Stem, 6 Oz., 6 In. 355.00
June, Cup & Saucer 30.00
June, Cup & Saucer, Topaz 28.00
June, Goblet, 9 Oz., 8 ¼ In. 70.00
June, Goblet, Azure, 9 Oz., 8 ¼ In. 105.00
June, Goblet, Claret, 4 Oz., 6 Oz. 110.00
June, Goblet, Rose, 9 Oz., 8 ¼ In. 110.00
June, Goblet, Topaz, 9 Oz., 8 ¼ In. 70.00
June, Goblet, Wine, 2 ½ Oz., 5 ⅜ In. 45.00
June, Goblet, Wine, Rose, 2 ½ Oz., 5 ⅜ In. 80.00
June, Ice Bucket 85.00
June, Oyster Cocktail, Topaz, 3 Oz. 35.00
June, Pitcher 495.00
June, Pitcher, Azure 995.00
June, Pitcher, Rose 1055.00
June, Plate, Bread & Butter, Topaz, 6 In. 11.00
June, Plate, Dinner, Topaz, 10 ¼ In. 120.00
June, Plate, Luncheon, Topaz, 8 ½ In. 22.00
June, Plate, Salad, Topaz, 7 ½ In. 15.00
June, Sherbet, High, Topaz, 6 Oz., 6 In. 42.00
June, Sherbet, Low, Rose, 6 Oz., 4 ⅛ In. 40.00
June, Torte Plate, Rose, 14 In. 175.00
June, Tumbler, Iced Tea, 6 In. 50.00
June, Tumbler, Water, Footed, 5 ¼ In. 30.00
June, Whiskey, Footed, 3 In. 35.00
Kashmir, Berry Bowl, Topaz, 5 In. 28.00
Kashmir, Bottle, Dressing, Flat, Topaz 650.00
Kashmir, Bowl, Cereal, Topaz, 6 In. 45.00
Kashmir, Gravy Boat, Underplate, Topaz 185.00
Kashmir, Grill Plate, 10 ½ In. 55.00
Kashmir, Relish, 8 In. 45.00
Kashmir, Relish, Topaz, 11 In. 55.00
Kashmir, Sherbet, Tall, Topaz, 6 Oz., 6 ⅛ In. 35.00
Lafayette, Relish, Wisteria, 3 Sections, 3 Tab Handles, 7 ¼ In. 65.00
Lafayette, Sugar & Creamer, Tray, Rose 74.00
Lido, Cup & Saucer .... *illus* 8.00
Lido, Plate, Salad, 7 In. 18.00
Mademoiselle, Cordial, Oz., 3 ⅝ In. 7.00
Manor, Sherbet, Wisteria Stem, 5 ½ Oz., 5 ⅜ In. 45.00
Mayfair, Cruet, Green, Stopper, 7 ½ In. .... *illus* 130.00
Mayfair, Sugar & Creamer, Footed, Rose 44.00
Mayfair, Sugar & Creamer, Tray, Topaz 60.00
Mayflower, Salt & Pepper, Footed 125.00
Mayflower, Torte Plate, 14 In. 80.00
Meadow Rose, Cake Plate, Handles, 10 In. 70.00
Meadow Rose, Cheese & Cracker, 2 Piece 125.00
Meadow Rose, Claret, 6 ½ Oz., 6 ¼ In. 60.00
Meadow Rose, Compote, 5 ½ In. 25.00
Meadow Rose, Compote, 6 ½ In. 50.00
Meadow Rose, Dish, Mayonnaise, Underplate 39.00
Meadow Rose, Dish, Mayonnaise, Underplate, Ladle 165.00
Meadow Rose, Goblet, 10 Oz., 7 ⅝ In. 55.00
Meadow Rose, Goblet, Azure, 10 Oz., 7 ⅝ In. 60.00
Meadow Rose, Goblet, Wine, 3 ¼ Oz., 5 ¼ In. 46.00
Meadow Rose, Oyster Cocktail, 4 Oz., 3 ⅝ In. 45.00
Meadow Rose, Pitcher 550.00
Meadow Rose, Plate, Salad, 7 In. 18.00
Meadow Rose, Relish, 3 Sections, 10 x 7 ½ In. 85.00
Meadow Rose, Relish, 5 Sections, 13 ¼ In. 65.00
Meadow Rose, Salt & Pepper, Individual 95.00
Meadow Rose, Sandwich Server, Fleur-De-Lis Center Handle, 11 In. 55.00
Meadow Rose, Sherbet, Tall, 6 Oz., 5 ⅝ In. 32.00

Item	Price
Meadow Rose, Tumbler, Iced Tea, Footed, 13 Oz., 5⅞ In.	65.00
Meadow Rose, Vase, 9½ In.	325.00
Melrose, Oyster Cocktail, 4 Oz., 3⅝ In.	16.00
Melrose, Parfait, 5½ Oz., 6 In.	15.00
Midnight Rose, Cake Plate, Handle, 10½ In.	65.00
Midnight Rose, Celery Dish	50.00
Morning Glory, Mayonnaise Set, 3 Piece	39.00
Navarre, Bell, Dinner, Blue, 4⅞ In.	85.00
Navarre, Bowl, Crown, Gold Trim, 9 In.	66.00
Navarre, Bowl, Handles, 10½ In.	105.00
Navarre, Champagne, Saucer, 6 Oz., 5⅝ In.	35.00
Navarre, Champagne, Saucer, Blue, 6 Oz., 5⅝ In.	60.00
Navarre, Claret, Blue, 4½ Oz., 6 In.	85.00
Navarre, Cocktail, 3½ Oz., 5¼ In.	35.00
Navarre, Cordial, ¾ Oz., 3⅞ In.	85.00
Navarre, Goblet, 10 Oz., 7⅝ In.	55.00
Navarre, Goblet, Blue, 10 Oz., 7⅝ In.	85.00
Navarre, Goblet, Wine, Blue Bowl, Clear Stem & Foot, 3¼ Oz., 5¼ In.	44.00
Navarre, Goblet, Wine, 3¼ Oz., 5¼ In.	45.00
Navarre, Ice Bucket, No Handle	175.00
Navarre, Magnum, 16 Oz., 7¼ In.	235.00
Navarre, Mayonnaise Set, 3 Piece	165.00
Navarre, Oyster Cocktail, 4 Oz., 3⅝ In.	45.00
Navarre, Plate, Bread & Butter, 6 In.	15.00
Navarre, Plate, Salad, 7 In.	18.00 to 23.00
Navarre, Relish, 3 Sections, 10 In.	85.00
Navarre, Relish, Square, 2 Sections, 6 In.	45.00
Navarre, Salt & Pepper	110.00
Navarre, Salt & Pepper, Footed	195.00
Navarre, Sherbet, Low, 6 Oz., 4⅜ In.	35.00
Navarre, Sugar & Creamer	32.00 to 62.00
Navarre, Sugar & Creamer, Individual	32.00
Navarre, Tumbler, Footed, 10 Oz., 5⅜ In.	40.00
Navarre, Tumbler, Iced Tea, Footed, 13 Oz., 5⅞ In.	68.00
Navarre, Tumbler, Iced Tea, Blue, Footed, 13 Oz., 5⅞ In.	85.00
Navarre, Tumbler, Juice, Footed, 5 Oz., 4⅝ In.	45.00
Navarre, Vase, 5 In.	195.00
Navarre, Vase, 9½ In.	250.00
Neo Classic, Cordial, 1 Oz., 3¼ In.	10.00
New Century, Candlestick, 2-Light, 7 x 6½ In.	35.00
No. 2380, Candy Jar, Cover, Azure, Flattened Knob Finial	75.00
No. 2666, Sugar & Creamer, Platinum Band	35.00
No. 4040, Goblet, Water, Green, Square Foot, 9 Oz., 5¾ In.	23.00
Oakleaf, Dish, Lemon	58.00
Oakwood, Bonbon, Blue, Folded-Up Sides, Handles, 6½ In.	45.00
Oakwood, Pail, Whipped Cream, Azure	177.00
Paradise, Ice Bucket, Green	114.00
Paradise, Pail, Whipped Cream, Amber	80.00
Paradise, Pail, Whipped Cream, Azure	41.00
Paradise, Pail, Whipped Cream, Green	50.00
Pebble Beach, Relish, Lemon Twist, 3 Sections, 10 In.	65.00
Priscilla, Sugar & Creamer, Tray, Amber	27.00
Queen Anne, Candelabrum, 2-Light, Amber, Clear Arms, 17 In. *illus*	695.00
Raleigh, Sugar & Creamer, Tray	30.00
Rambler, Sugar & Creamer	36.00
Scepter, Sherbet, High, Gold Tint Bowl, 6 Oz., 5½ In.	13.00
Seascape, Bowl, Square, Blue, 8¾ In.	51.00
Serenity, Goblet, Yellow Bowl, Clear Stem & Foot, 12 Oz., 7⅜ In.	50.00
Sonata, Sandwich Server, Center Handle, Holly Etch, 4¾ x 11¼ In.	45.00
Sprite, Candlestick, 3-Light, 7¾ x 7½ In., Pair	180.00
Sunburst, Pitcher, 7¾ In.	80.00
Sunray, Coaster	3.00
Sunray, Goblet, Water, 9 Oz., 5¾ In.	15.00
Sunray, Sherbet, Footed, 5½ Oz., 3½ In.	10.00
Table Charms Set, Trindle Candlearm, 3 Peg Vases, 3 Bowls, 10 x 9 In.	156.00

"Elegant" Glass

Glass collectors use the term ***elegant*** to refer to American hand-pressed items made from about 1925 to 1955. Even though the glassware was produced in large quantities, the "elegant" factories used higher-quality raw materials and employed skilled glassmakers. Several companies, including Heisey and Fostoria, called their glassware ***American crystal.***

Fostoria, Queen Anne, Candelabrum, 2-Light, Amber, Clear Arms, 17 In. $695.00

Fostoria, Versailles, Ice Bucket, Green $285.00

F

TIP

To remove a price tag without damaging the collectible, be careful. Liquid solvents are usually safe to use to remove tags on nonporous items like glass or ceramics. Porous materials like leather, paper, and wood must be tested. Vegetable oil will sometimes remove paper or grease-pen prices. Never pull a label off a piece of paper or cardboard. It will probably tear the paper.

Franciscan, Apple, Cup & Saucer
$40.00

Franciscan, Autumn, Pitcher, 1960s, 6 In.
$13.00

Trojan, Goblet, Topaz, 9 Oz., 8 1/4 In. 75.00
Versailles, Bowl, Bow Handles, Topaz, 10 In. 135.00
Versailles, Bowl, Topaz, 7 In. 125.00
Versailles, Bowl, Vegetable, Oval, Topaz, 9 In. 145.00
Versailles, Candy Dish, Cover, 3 Sections, Green 325.00
Versailles, Cocktail, Green Bowl, 3 Oz., 5 1/8 In. 58.00
Versailles, Cocktail, Topaz Bowl, 3 Oz., 5 1/8 In. 28.00
Versailles, Creamer, Rose Bowl, Individual 85.00
Versailles, Cup & Saucer, Footed, Topaz 28.00
Versailles, Cup & Saucer, Footed, Green 35.00
Versailles, Cup & Saucer, Footed, Rose 35.00
Versailles, Cup & Saucer, Green 25.00
Versailles, Goblet, Azure Bowl, 9 Oz., 8 1/4 In. 115.00
Versailles, Goblet, Green Bowl, 9 Oz., 8 1/4 In. .... 58.00 to 125.00
Versailles, Goblet, Rose Bowl, 9 Oz., 8 1/4 In. 97.00
Versailles, Goblet, Topaz Bowl, 9 Oz., 8 1/4 In. 68.00
Versailles, Ice Bucket, Green .... *illus* 285.00
Versailles, Oil, Handle, Footed, Topaz 495.00
Versailles, Pitcher, Azure 925.00
Versailles, Pitcher, Green 995.00
Versailles, Pitcher, Rose 695.00
Versailles, Plate, Dinner, Topaz, 9 In. 120.00
Versailles, Relish, 2 Sections, Green, 8 1/2 In. 62.00
Versailles, Salt & Pepper, Footed, Rose 295.00
Versailles, Sandwich Server, Center Handle, Green 145.00
Versailles, Sherbet, Low, Rose, 6 Oz., 4 1/8 In. 40.00
Versailles, Sherbet, Low, Green, 6 Oz., 4 1/8 In. 52.00
Versailles, Sherbet, Tall, Rose, 6 Oz., 6 In. 45.00
Versailles, Sherbet, Tall, Green, 6 Oz., 6 In. 75.00
Versailles, Sugar & Creamer, Green 95.00
Versailles, Sugar & Creamer, Yellow, Individual 95.00
Versailles, Torte Plate, Rose, 14 In. 125.00
Versailles, Tumbler, Iced Tea, Footed, Rose, 12 Oz., 5 7/8 In. 75.00
Versailles, Vase, Flip, Green, 8 In. 495.00
Westchester, Brandy, Ruby, Oz., 4 In. 44.00
Westchester, Brandy, Watercress Etch, Oz., 4 In. 33.00
Westchester, Claret, Ruby, 4 1/2 Oz., 5 3/4 In. 30.00
Westchester, Cordial, Oz., 3 1/2 In. 10.00
Westchester, Cordial, Ruby, Oz., 3 1/2 In. 48.00
Willowmere, Bowl, Handle, 9 In. 85.00
Willowmere, Cocktail, 3 1/2 Oz., 4 3/4 In. 27.00
Willowmere, Goblet, 10 Oz., 7 1/8 In. 45.00
Willowmere, Salt & Pepper, Individual 95.00
Woodlands, Goblet, 9 Oz., 7 In. 45.00

FOVAL, *see Fry category.*

FRAMES *are included in the Furniture category under Frame.*

FRANCISCAN is a trademark that appears on pottery. Gladding, McBean and Company started in 1875. The company grew and acquired other potteries. They made sewer pipes, floor tiles, dinnerwares, and art pottery with a variety of trademarks. In 1934, dinnerware and art pottery were sold under the name Franciscan Ware. They made china and cream-colored, decorated earthenware. Desert Rose, Apple, El Patio, and Coronado were best-sellers. The company became Interpace Corporation and in 1979 was purchased by Josiah Wedgwood & Sons. The plant was closed in 1984 but a few of the patterns are still being made. For more information, see *Kovels Depression Glass & Dinnerware Price List.*

Apple, Bowl, Salad, 10 1/4 In. 75.00
Apple, Bowl, Vegetable, Divided, Oval, 10 3/4 In. 25.00
Apple, Bowl, Vegetable, 8 1/4 In. 25.00
Apple, Bowl, Vegetable, Cover, Handles, 10 In. 50.00
Apple, Casserole, Individual, Branch Handle 37.00
Apple, Chop Plate, 12 In. .... 22.00 to 50.00
Apple, Coffeepot, Cover, Twig Handle 119.00
Apple, Compote, 3 1/2 x 8 In. 65.00

Apple, Creamer . . . 6.00
Apple, Cup & Saucer . . . *illus* 40.00
Apple, Gravy Boat, Attached Underplate, 8 ½ In. . . . 25.00
Apple, Mixing Bowl, 4 ½ x 7 ¼ In. . . . 79.00
Apple, Pitcher, Water, 8¾ In. . . . 90.00 to 125.00
Apple, Plate, Dinner, 10 ⅝ In. . . . 24.00
Apple, Platter, Oval, Handles, 19 In. . . . 220.00
Apple, Relish, 3 Sections, Handles, 11 ¾ x 9 ½ In. . . . 44.00
Apple, Salt & Pepper, 2 In. . . . 49.00
Apple, Teabag Holder . . . 35.00
Apple, Tidbit, 2 Tiers, 10 ½ In. . . . 185.00
Apple, Trivet, Tea Tile, 8-Sided, 6 In. . . . 190.00
Apple, Tumbler, 5 ¼ In. . . . 23.00
Apple, Tureen, Cover, Leaf Handles, 11 In. . . . 270.00
Apple, Tureen, No Cover, Leaf Handles, 7 ½ In. . . . 135.00
Autumn, Berry Bowl, 4 Piece . . . 19.00
Autumn, Bowl, Cereal, Lug Handle . . . 9.00
Autumn, Bowl, Salad, 11 ½ In. . . . 38.00
Autumn, Bowl, Vegetable, Divided, Lug Handles, 13¾ x 6½ In. . . . 17.00 to 25.00
Autumn, Bowl, Vegetable, 9 ¼ In. . . . 25.00
Autumn, Pitcher, 1960s, 6 In. . . . *illus* 13.00
Autumn, Platter, Oval, 13 ¾ x 10 ½ In. . . . 40.00
Autumn, Platter, Oval, 16 ½ x 12 ½ In. . . . 38.00
Cafe Royal, Canister, Tea, 5 ¾ In. . . . 45.00
Coronado, Bowl, Vegetable, Satin Ivory, 7 ½ In. . . . 20.00
Coronado, Chop Plate, Satin Coral, 11 ¾ In. . . . 19.00
Coronado, Chop Plate, Satin Turquoise, 13 ⅝ In. . . . 45.00
Coronado, Gravy Boat, Underplate, Satin Ivory, 2 Spouts . . . 24.00
Coronado, Plate, Dessert, Satin Coral, 6 ⅜ In. . . . 12.00
Coronado, Plate, Dinner, Turquoise Gloss, 10 ½ In. . . . 10.00
Coronado, Plate, Dinner, Satin Coral, 10 ½ In. . . . 12.00
Dawn, Plate, Dinner, Green Blue, 10 ½ In. . . . 26.00
Desert Rose, Baker, 9 ½ x 8 ½ In. . . . 145.00
Desert Rose, Berry Bowl, 5 In. . . . 10.00
Desert Rose, Butter, Cover . . . 30.00
Desert Rose, Dish, 3 Sections . . . 110.00
Desert Rose, Pitcher, Milk, 6½ In. . . . 45.00 to 115.00
Desert Rose, Plate, Dessert . . . *illus* 8.00
Desert Rose, Plate, Snake, Oval, 13 ¾ x 8 In. . . . 150.00
Desert Rose, Platter, Oval, 14 ½ In. . . . 45.00
Desert Rose, Platter, Oval, 19 ½ In. . . . 425.00
Desert Rose, Relish, 11 x 4 ½ In. . . . 45.00
Desert Rose, Salt & Pepper, 3 In. . . . 15.00
Desert Rose, Sugar & Creamer . . . 50.00
Desert Rose, Teapot . . . 90.00 to 124.00
Duet, Pitcher, 1950s, 7 In. . . . *illus* 28.00
El Patio, Creamer, Turquoise . . . 18.00
El Patio, Gravy Boat, Stand, Turquoise . . . 55.00
El Patio, Punch Bowl, 6 ⅜ x 11 ¾ In. . . . 95.00
El Patio, Salt & Pepper, Turquoise . . . 20.00
Ivy, Chop Plate, 14 In. . . . 80.00
Ivy, Plate, Dinner, 10 ⅜ In. . . . 25.00
Madiera, Coffeepot, Brown, 12 ¼ In. . . . 24.00
Madiera, Salt & Pepper, Brown . . . 10.00
Maytime, Platter, 13 ¼ x 8 ½ In. . . . 18.00
Meadow Rose, Candleholder, 3 In. . . . 31.00
Montecito, Bowl, Vegetable, 7 ½ In. . . . 25.00
Montecito, Sugar & Creamer, Coral Gloss . . . 39.00
Poppy, Chop Plate, 12 In. . . . 78.00
Sandalwood, Cup & Saucer . . . 14.00
Starburst, Bowl, Cereal, 7 In. . . . 15.00
Starburst, Cup . . . 7.00
Starburst, Cup & Saucer . . . 12.00
Starburst, Plate, Bread & Butter, 6 In. . . . 9.00
Starburst, Salt & Pepper, 6 In. . . . 89.00

Franciscan, Desert Rose, Plate, Dessert
$8.00

Franciscan, Duet, Pitcher, 1950s, 7 In.
$28.00

Franciscan, Sunburst, Bowl, Vegetable, Oval
$85.00

TIP

If the glaze on your dishes is crazed, covered with small lines and cracks, don't use them to serve greasy food like butter or cream or bright-colored food like beets. The foods will stain the ceramic under the crazed glaze.

Franciscan, Wheat, Sugar & Creamer
$35.00

Frankart, Lamp, Nude, Silhouette, Against Frosted Glass Panel, c.1931, 10 In.
$950.00

Frankoma, Ashtray, Fish Shape, Prairie Green, 7 ½ x 4 ¼ In.
$17.00

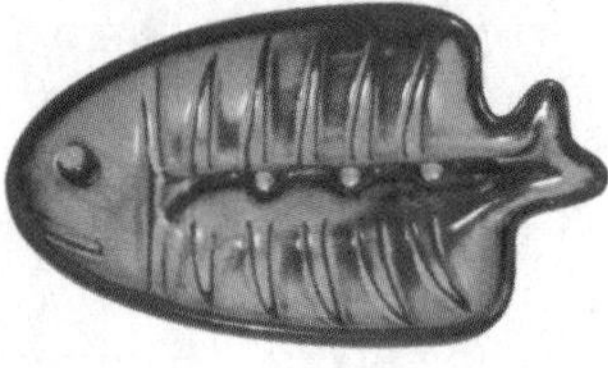

Frankoma, Canteen, Thunderbird, 7 x 6 ½ In.
$28.00

Sunburst, Bowl, Vegetable, Oval ... *illus* 85.00
Topaz, Bowl, Dessert, 5 In. ... 20.00
Topaz, Plate, Bread & Butter, 6 ¼ In. ... 5.00
Twilight Rose, Trivet, 6 ½ In. ... 125.00
Westwood, Bowl, Dessert, 6 ¼ In. ... 10.00
Westwood, Creamer ... 9.00
Westwood, Plate, Bread & Butter, 6 ⅜ In. ... 6.00
Westwood, Salt & Pepper ... 24.00
Wheat, Sugar & Creamer ... *illus* 35.00
Wildflower, Cup & Saucer ... 125.00
Willow, Bowl, Dessert, 6 ¼ In. ... 25.00
Winsome, Creamer ... 10.00

FRANKART, Inc., New York, New York, mass-produced nude *dancing lady* lamps, ashtrays, and other decorative Art Deco items in the 1920s and 1930s. They were made of white lead composition and spray-painted. *Frankart Inc.* and the patent number and year were stamped on the base.

Bookends, Nudes, Playing Peek-A-Boo, 8 In. ... 700.00
Bookends, Scottie, Rhinestone Eyes, Bronze Finish, Spelter, 5 x 7 In. ... 75.00
Bookends, Woman's Head, Art Deco, Bronze, Felt Bottom, Signed, 6 ¾ In. ... 285.00
Figure, Nude, Green, Jadite Ashtray Ball, Art Deco, 10 In. ... 1100.00
Lamp, Eagle, Gray, Metal, Pen Tray, Art Deco, 13 ½ x 10 In. ... 350.00
Lamp, Elephant, Green Shade, Bronze Finial, Patina, Art Deco, 1930s, 20 In. ... 210.00
Lamp, Nude, Green, Amber Globe, Crackle Finish, Metal, Art Deco, 1930s, 11 x 8 In. ... 695.00
Lamp, Nude, Silhouette, Against Frosted Glass Panel, c.1931, 10 In. ... *illus* 950.00
Plaque, Man, Woman, Oxidized Gold, Art Deco, 8 ½ In. ... 125.00

FRANKOMA POTTERY was originally known as The Frank Potteries when John F. Frank opened shop in 1933. The factory is now working in Sapulpa, Oklahoma. Early wares were made from a light cream-colored clay from Ada, Oklahoma, but in 1956 the company switched to a red burning clay from Sapulpa. The firm made dinnerwares, utilitarian and decorative kitchenwares, figurines, flowerpots, and limited edition and commemorative pieces. John Frank died in 1973 and his daughter, Joniece, inherited the business. Frankoma went bankrupt in 1990. It was bought by Richard Bernstein in 1991 and closed in 2004. The pottery was bought by H.B. "Det" and Crystal Merryman in 2005 and is in business as Frankoma, Inc.

ORIGINAL CREATION by FRANKOMA

Ashtray, Arrowhead, Woodland Moss, 4 ¼ In. ... 18.00
Ashtray, Brown Satin, Round ... 10.00
Ashtray, Covered Wagon Shape, Prairie Green, Divided, 6 ¼ x 4 ½ In. ... 15.00
Ashtray, Fish Shape, Prairie Green, 7 ½ x 4 ¼ In. ... *illus* 17.00
Ashtray, Kansas Shape, Sunflower State, Brown Glaze, Red Clay, 7 x 3 ¾ In. ... 24.00
Ashtray, Oklahoma Shape, Raised Letters, Yellow Glaze, 5 In. ... 18.00
Baker, Cover, Westwind, Brown Satin, Sapulpa Clay, 9 ¼ In. ... 59.00
Baker, Wagon Wheel, Cover, Desert Gold, Handles, Individual, 1942 ... 25.00
Bank, Owl, Desert Gold, 6 ⅞ x 4 In. ... 35.00
Bean Pot, Cover, Lazybones, Desert Gold, Sapulpa Clay, 6 ½ x 8 In. ... 25.00
Bowl, Cereal, Lazybones, Brown Satin, Folded Out Handle ... 13.00
Bowl, Lazybones, Cup Shape, Desert Gold, Square Handle, 2 ½ x 5 In. ... 12.00
Bowl, Vegetable, Lazybones, Divided, Satin, Brown, 11 x 6 In. ... 24.00
Canteen, Thunderbird, 7 x 6 ½ In. ... *illus* 28.00
Carafe, Desert Gold, 7 ¾ x 6 In. ... 38.00
Casserole, Cover, Mayan-Aztec, Desert Gold, 4 ¾ x 10 ½ In. ... 62.00
Casserole, Cover, Plainsman, Prairie Green, 4 ½ x 10 ½ In. ... 62.00
Charger, Plainsman, 14 ¾ In. ... *illus* 60.00
Creamer, Lazybones, Prairie Green ... 20.00
Cup & Saucer, Plainsman, Desert Gold, After Dinner, Ada Clay ... 18.00
Cup & Saucer, Wagon Wheel, Desert Gold ... 20.00
Decanter, Mayan-Aztec, Off-White ... 125.00
Decanter Set, Prairie Green, 6 Cups, 1976, 7 Piece ... 110.00
Dish, Leaf Shape, Black, Gloss, 9 ¼ x 4 ¼ In. ... 12.00
Dish, Leaf Shape, Desert Gold, 4 ⅜ In. ... 15.00
Dish, Magnolia Shape, Black, Gloss, 6 ½ x 5 In. ... 16.00
Honey Jar, Mayan-Aztec, Prairie Green, 9 In. ... 25.00
Honey Pot, Cover, Beehive Shape, Brown Satin, Bee Finial, 4 ¾ In. ... 32.00

Honey Pot, Cover, Beehive Shape, White Sand, Bee Finial, 4¾ In. 55.00
Mug, Flame Red Gloss, Pedestal Base, 4¼ In. 25.00
Mug, Political, Donkey, Carter, Mondale, Pink Glaze, 1972 30.00
Mug, Political, Elephant, Red Flame Glaze, 1976. 10.00
Mug, Political, Elephant, Blue, 1982 28.00
Mug, Woodland Moss, Footed, 4¼ In. 11.00
Pin Tray, Dogwood Blossom, Flame, 6 x 4½ In. 25.00
Pitcher, Ball Shape, Brown Satin Speckled Drip, 2½ In. 22.00
Pitcher, Desert Gold, Ada Clay, 9 In. 55.00
Pitcher, Mayan-Aztec, Prairie Green, 2 Qt. 55.00
Pitcher, Wagon Wheel, Desert Gold, 7 In. 8.00
Planter, Duck, Brown Satin, 6 x 12 In. 30.00
Planter, Green Glaze, Brown, Folded Sides, 4 x 7 x 4 In. 20.00
Planter, Mallard Duck, Brown Satin, 11½ In. 55.00
Plate, Bicentennial Celebration, John Adams, Paul Revere, 1972, 8 In. 15.00
Plate, Bread & Butter, Plainsman, Woodland Moss, 6 In. 8.00
Plate, Christmas, 1966, Joy To The World, 8½ In. 65.00
Plate, Christmas, 1968, Flight Into Egypt, 8½ In. 25.00
Plate, Christmas, 1969, Laid In A Manger, 8½ In. 20.00
Plate, Christmas, 1971, No Room At The Inn, 8½ In. 24.00
Plate, Christmas, 1972, Seeking The Christ Child, 8½ In. 20.00
Plate, Christmas, 1974, She Loved & Cared, 8½ In. 20.00
Plate, Christmas, 1976, Gift Of Love, 8½ In. 22.00
Plate, Christmas, 1978, All Nature Rejoice, 8½ In. 24.00
Plate, Christmas, 1979, Star Of Hope, 8½ In. 22.00
Plate, Dinner, Lazybones, Cinnamon, 10 In. 16.00
Plate, Dinner, Wagon Wheel, Prairie Gold, 10½ In. 9.00
Platter, Lazybones, Prairie Green, Sapulpa Clay, 1970-80, 8½ x 15 In. *illus* 12.00
Platter, Lazybones, Prairie Green, 15 x 8½ In. 20.00
Platter, Plainsman, Brown Satin, 9¾ x 6 In. 12.00
Relish, Leaf Shape, Prairie Green, 3 Sections, 12 x 6½ In. 38.00
Salt & Pepper, Oil Derrick, Rust Red, Desert Gold, Sapulpa Clay, 3¼ In. 24.00
Salt & Pepper, Wagon Wheel, Prairie Green 22.00
Salt & Pepper, Wheat, Ada Clay, 2¾ In. 37.00
Spoon Rest, Lazybones, Desert Gold. 15.00
Sugar, Cover, Plainsman, Brown Satin 15.00
Sugar & Creamer, Plainsman, Brown Satin, Sapulpa Clay 45.00
Sugar, Cover, Mayan-Aztec, Desert Gold 28.00
Teapot, Wagon Wheel, Prairie Green, 2 Cup. 55.00
Teapot, Wagon Wheel, Prairie Green, 6 Cup. 95.00
Teapot, Westwind, Deep Blue, 4½ x 7¼ In. *illus* 14.00
Teapot, Westwind, White Sand Glaze, 6½ In. 29.00
Trivet, Butterfly On Flower, Desert Gold, 6 In. 32.00
Tumbler, Plainsman, Woodland Moss, 12 Oz. 15.00
Vase, Cornucopia, Prairie Green, Sapulpa Clay, 6¼ x 7½ In. 35.00
Vase, Cowboy Boot, White Sand, Sapulpa Clay, 4½ x 5¾ In. 40.00
Vase, Crescent Shape, Prairie Green, 12½ x 5½ In. 17.00
Vase, Crocus, Brown Satin, Elongated, Footed, 8 In. 22.00
Vase, Crocus, Sunflower Yellow, Elongated, Footed, 8 In. 20.00 to 35.00
Wall Pocket, Billiken, Prairie Green, Ada Clay, 1954, 7 In. 85.00
Wall Pocket, Phoebe, 1948, 7 In. 285.00
Water Set, Mayan-Aztec, Desert Gold, Sapulpa Clay, 6 Cups, 2-Qt. Pitcher 85.00

FRATERNAL objects that are related to the many different fraternal organizations in the United States are listed in this category. The Elks, Masons, Odd Fellows, and others are included. Also included are service organizations, like the American Legion, Kiwanis, and Lions Club. Furniture is listed in the Furniture category. Shaving mugs decorated with fraternal crests are included in the Shaving Mug category.

4-H, Pin, Square, Canted Corners, Gold Tone, ½ x ½ In. 5.00
4-H, Pin, Sterling Silver, Enamel, Green 4-Leaf Clover, Blue Leaf Border, ⅜ In. 11.00
American Legion, Drum, Leedy, 8¾ x 13¾ In. 59.00
American Legion, Gavel, Covered Wagon Design, Bristol, R.I., c.1925, 19 x 46 In. 403.00
American Legion, Token, Armistice Day, 20th Anniversary, 1918-1938 10.00
Antediluvian Royal Order Of Buffaloes, Medal, Brass, Blue Enamel, 3 In. 50.00

Frankoma, Charger, Plainsman, 14¾ In. $60.00

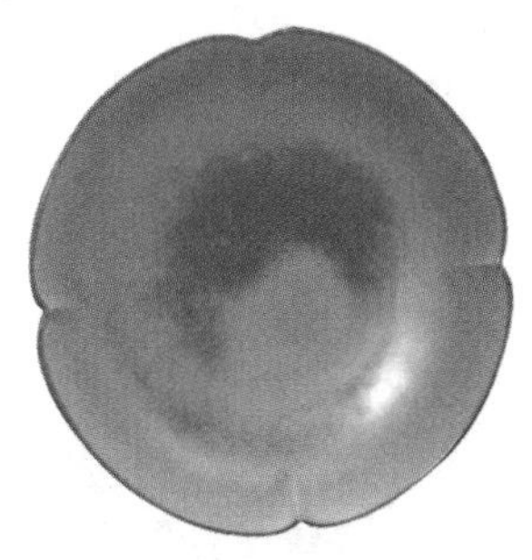

Frankoma, Platter, Lazybones, Prairie Green, Sapulpa Clay, 1970-80, 8½ x 15 In. $12.00

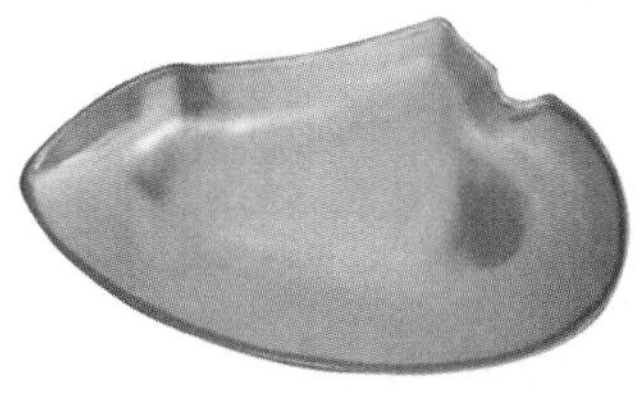

Frankoma, Teapot, Westwind, Deep Blue, 4½ x 7¼ In. $14.00

Fraternal, Knights Templar, Pin, York, Cross Of Honor, 14K Gold, Jewels, c.1914, 6 x 2 In. $1725.00

F

Fraternal, Masonic, Apron, King Solomon's Temple, Watercolor On Silk, c.1800, 18 x 22 In.
$978.00

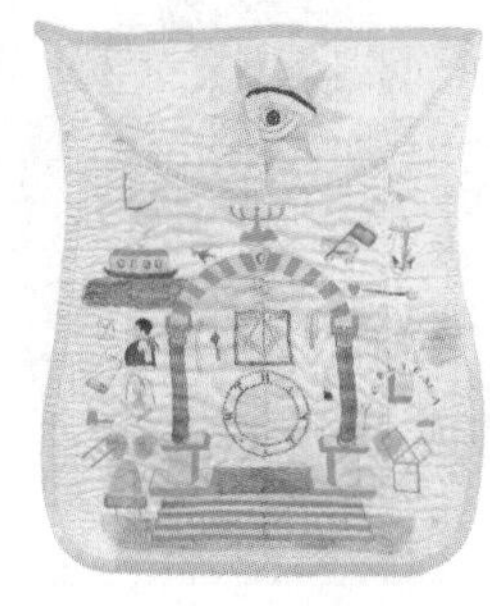

Fraternal, Masonic, Pendant, 6 Minecut Diamonds, 14K Gold, Dec. 1922, Ribbon
$432.00

Fraternal, Masonic, Pendant, Silver Gilt, Enamel, Kent, Box
$44.00

Fraternal, Shriner, Button, Minneapolis, Bridge, Convention, Washington D.C., 1900, 2 In.
$230.00

Eagles, ID Card Holder, Toledo Aerie No. 197, Leatherette, 3-Fold, c.1907 . . . . . 5.00
Eagles, Pendant, Crystal Heart, 2-Headed Eagle, No. 32, Chain 30.00
Eagles, Pin, 30 Years, Enamel, 10K Gold Filled, Push Pin Style, Clutch Holder, ½ In. 7.00
Eagles, Pin, Enamel, Red White & Blue Shield, Screw Back, ⅜ In. 3.00
Eagles, Pin, Ladies Auxiliary, Bow, F.O.E. Emblem, Brass, Open C-Clasp, 1½ In. 15.00
Eagles, Pin, Patron, Gold Tone, Blue Enamel, Tack Back, ½ In. 5.00
Eagles, Pin, Red Rhinestones, Gold Tone Metal, Applied Enamel Emblem, 1⅞ In. 5.00
Eagles, Sauceboat, White Ground, Liberty Truth Justice Equality, Greek Key Design, 9 x 3 In.. 15.00
Eagles, Tumbler, Waynesboro, Lodge 1758, Red Enamel Decoration 4.00
Eastern Star, Bracelet, Hinged, 5 Color Enamel 27.00
Eastern Star, Buzza Motto, Star Cutout, Gold Foil Background, Frame, 6½ x 7½ In. 30.00
Eastern Star, Cocktail Fork, Fantasy, Emblem, Carlton, Silver Plate, 6 In. 10.00
Eastern Star, Picture, Emblems, Angel Hair Backing, Dried Flowers, 5¾ x 5¾ In., Pair 30.00
Eastern Star, Pill Box, Porcelain, Oval, Trim, 3 Gold Legs, 2¼ x 1¾ In. 10.00
Eastern Star, Sewing Kit, Aluminum, White Cross, Blue Enamel, c.1937, 2¼ x ¾ In.. . . . . 38.00
Eastern Star, Spoon, Sterling, Emblem, Applied Enamel, c.1900, 4 In.. . . . . 95.00
Eastern Star, Toothpick Holder, Lincoln Park Chapter No. 479, c.1973, 2½ x 1½ In. 20.00
Eastern Star, Wall Hanging, Emblem, Multicolored, White Satin, Frame, 22 x 18 In. 70.00
Elks, Ashtray, Embossed, BPOE On Rim, Western Stoneware Pottery Co., 4¼ In.. . . . . 26.00
Elks, Decanter, Pottery, Star, Centennial Celebration, 1868-1968 . . . . . 44.00
Elks, Flask, Figural, Tooth, Porcelain, Elk, Clock, Portland, c.1912, 4½ x 2⅜ In. 575.00
Elks, Match Case, 14K Yellow Gold, 11th Hour Emblem, Elk, Ruby Eyes, 2¼ x 1¼ In. 725.00
Elks, Money Clip, Watch Fob, Gold Tone Metal, Emblem 63.00
Elks, Pin, Enamel, Push Pin Back, ¾ In. 4.00
Elks, Plate, Grand Lodge Reunion, Phila., Metal, Gilt Border, c.1907 . . . . . 165.00
Elks, Shaving Mug, Star & Mountains, R.O. Bowman, Signed, C.P. Pain, 3¾ In. 55.00
International Brotherhood Of Electrical Workers, Coaster, Brass, 3⅜ In., Pair. 24.00
Kiwanis, Cuff Links, 2-Tone Enamel, Blue & White, 1 In. 28.00
Knights Of Columbus, Matchbook Holder, Brass, 2 Shields, c.1919 . . . . . 75.00
Knights Of Pythias, Badge, Ribbon, 29th Annual Convention, Dayton, c.1898, 5 x 2 In. 25.00
Knights Of Pythias, Pin, S.S. Davis, Supreme Lodge, S.C., 2¾ x 2 In.. . . . . 20.00
Knights Of Pythias, Badge, Ribbon, Watch Fob, 9 x 2½ In. 25.00
Knights Of St. George, Sword, Ceremonial, Scabbard, Scrollwork, 34½ In.. . . . . 65.00
Knights Templar, Medal, Hexagonal, Raised Relief, Blue & White Ribbon, 4½ x 2 In. 155.00
Knights Templar, Pin, York, Cross Of Honor, 14K Gold, Jewels, c.1914, 6 x 2 In. . . . . . *illus* 1725.00
Lions Club, Pin, Gold, Blue Enamel, Bow Shape, 1½ x 2½ In.. . . . . 25.00
Lions Club, Pin, Statue Of Liberty, New York, Dist. 20, Dallas, c.1975, 2½ In. 3.00
Lions Club, Tie Tack, Round, Gold Tone, Enamel, ½ In. 4.00
Masonic, Apron, King Solomon's Temple, Watercolor On Silk, c.1800, 18 x 22 In. . . . . . *illus* 978.00
Masonic, Apron, Leather, 3 Blue Silk Circles, Silver Bars, Tassels, Snake Fastener 100.00
Masonic, Apron, Leather, White, Red, Blue, Gilt Bars, Tassels, Embroidered 100.00
Masonic, Apron, Watercolor On Silk, Green, Symbols, 18½ x 22½ In.. . . . . 978.00
Masonic, Ashtray, Ceramic, Emblem, White Ground, Blue & Gold, c.1954, 6¼ x 6¼ In. 18.00
Masonic, Ashtray, Monmouth, Western Stoneware Co., Symbol, 4 In. 24.00
Masonic, Button, In Hoc Signo Vinces, Waterbury, 1 In. 9.00
Masonic, Card Case, Metal, Emblem, Fineberg Mfg. Co., 1¾ x 1¼ In. 85.00
Masonic, Fan, Silk, Multiple Emblems 50.00
Masonic, Fez, Mosiah, Wool, Burgundy, Rhinestones, Case, c.1963, Size 6¾ In. 69.00
Masonic, Medal, 32nd Degree, Cairo Temple, Rutland, Vt., c.1908. . . . . . 84.00
Masonic, Mug, Aluminum, Clear Bottom, Ismaillia Temple, c.1974, 4½ x 3 In., Pair 10.00
Masonic, Mug, Black Transfer, Early 19th Century, 4¾ In. 323.00
Masonic, Pendant, 6 Minecut Diamonds, 14K Gold, Dec. 1922, Ribbon . . . . . *illus* 432.00
Masonic, Pendant, Silver Gilt, Enamel, Kent, Box . . . . . *illus* 44.00
Masonic, Pin, 25 Year, Blue & White Enamel. 27.00
Masonic, Pin, Emblem, 14K White Gold, Blue Enamel, Screw Back, ¼ x ¼ In.. . . . . 28.00
Masonic, Pin, Heart, Dangling Charm, Silver Tone, Rhinestones, ORA, 1½ x 1½ In. 24.00
Masonic, Postcard, Grand Master, Cawston Ostrich Farm, 3½ x 5½ In.. . . . . 67.00
Masonic, Rainbow Girls, Compact, Pouch, Mirror, Emblem, Elgin American Co., 3 In. 62.00
Masonic, Rainbow Girls, Medal, Service, 14 Bars, Pot Of Gold, Wreath, Enameled, 7 In. 25.00
Masonic, Sash, Embroidered, Gold & Silver Metallic Thread, 100 In. 295.00
Masonic, Sash, Silk, Blue, Red, Gilt Thread, Fringe. 25.00
Masonic, Watch Key, Engraved Symbols, Devices, Gold Filled, 2 In. 205.00
Masonic, Badge, 47th Annual Convention, New Jersey, 1915 . . . . . 10.00
Moose, Bookends, Cast Iron, Bronze Finish, Emblem, Deco Style, 4 x 5¼ In. 65.00
Moose, Pin, Enamel, Red, Gold Plate, Moose Figure, FCH, Screw Fastener, 1½ x ½ In. 20.00
Odd Fellows, Badge, Memoriam, Silk, 2-Sided, Lodge 585, Bemus Point, c.1893, 9 x 2 In. . . . 35.00
Odd Fellows, Badge, Montana, 7¼ In. 22.00
Odd Fellows, Book, Rules & Regulations, 7th Edition, Grand Lodge, Okla., 4 x 5 In. 10.00

Odd Fellows, Clock, Presentation, Marble Dial, E. Howard & Co., c.1874, 29 In. 3410.00
Odd Fellows, Lodge Staff, Heart In Hand, Painted, c.1900, 62 ½ In. 3737.00
Odd Fellows, Medallion, 1921 Annual Session, Toronto, Gold Tone, FLT, Beehive, 3 x ½ In. ... 55.00
Odd Fellows, Pin, Blue Enamel, FLT Symbol, ⅝ In. 10.00
Odd Fellows, Pin, Service, Marcasite 8.00
Odd Fellows, Rebekah, Pin, Enamel, White Green, Blue, Silver Moon, Stars, ⅝ In. 12.00
Odd Fellows, Ribbon, Memorial, No. 216, Black, Silver Printing, Ashtabula, Ohio, 1890s 49.00
Odd Fellows, Wall Pocket, Jigsaw Cut Panel, Applied Burl Wood Symbols, 24 x 10 In. 1840.00
Odd Fellows, Badge, Lodge 585, 2-Sided, 1893 .... 35.00
Patriotic Order Of Americans, Pin, Ribbon, Pennsylvania Camp, 1 ⅝ x 5 ⅞ In. 14.00
Patriotic Order Sons Of America, Plate, White, Brown Transfer, Gold, 1884-1909 .... 39.00
Patrons Of Husbandry, Pin, Bristol Grange No. 116, Conn., Celluloid, Blue, Gold, 1890s ... 32.00
Rotary Club, Songbook, 100 Songs, Soft Cover, Staple Bound, c.1940, Pocket Size 5.00
Shepherds Of Bethlehem, Pin, Gold Tone, Enameled, White, Blue, ½ In. 10.00
Shriner, Belt Buckle, Pewter 25.00
Shriner, Book Rack, Folding, Camels, Cast Iron, Brass Plated, 1920s, 13 x 6 ¾ x 5 ¼ In. 195.00
Shriner, Button, Minneapolis, Bridge, Convention, Washington D.C., 1900, 2 In. .... *illus* 230.00
Shriner, Goblet, Westmoreland, Ruby Flash, St. Paul Minn., Convention, 1908, 5 ⅛ x 5 In. ... 36.00
Shriner, Medal, Imperial Council, Harold Lloyd, Green, Yellow, Red Ribbon, c.1950 .... 13.00
Shriner, Money Clip, Enameled 28.00
Shriner, Paperweight, Metal Emblem, Controlled Bubble, Polished Bottom, 3 ¼ In. 35.00
Shriner, Pin, Rhinestones, Scimitar, Crescent Moon, 2 ¾ x 1 In. 24.00
Shriner, Planter, Fez Shape, Red, Gold Emblem, Black Tassel, Klay Draft, 4 In. 30.00
Shriner, Pocket Mirror, Celluloid, Convention, Cawston Ostrich Farm, 1 ¾ x 2 ¾ In. 179.00
Shriner, Postcard, Shriner Hospital For Crippled Children, Phila., Color Tinted, 1950s 6.00
Shriner, Tie Tack, Red Enamel, Al Bahr, ⅜ In. 5.00
Shriner, Tie Tack, Silver Tone, Oval, Crescent & Scimitar, ½ x ⅜ In. 10.00
United Workman, Shadowbox, Fabric Background, AOUW Emblem, 16 x 17 ½ In. 48.00
VFW, Ladies Auxiliary, Cup & Saucer, White, Blue & Gold Emblem, 2 ¼ x 5 ½ In. 14.00
Woodmen Of The World, Florist's Form, Wire, Mallet, Ax, Wedge, Log, c.1910, 20 x 20 In. .. 395.00
YWCA, Saucer, White, Rolled Edge, Decorated, Underglaze Blue Bands, Logo, Pair 4.00

FRY GLASS was made by the H.C. Fry Glass Company of Rochester, Pennsylvania. The company, founded in 1901, first made cut glass and other types of fine glasswares. In 1922 it patented a heat-resistant glass called Pearl Ovenglass. For two years, 1926–1927, the company made Fry Foval, an opal ware decorated with colored trim. Reproductions of this glass have been made. Depression glass patterns made by Fry may be listed in the Depression Glass category. Some pieces of cut glass may also be included in the Cut Glass category.

FRY GLASS

Candlestick, Blue, Blue Spiral Threading, Flared Cup, Spread Foot, 10 ⅜ In., Pair. 705.00
Vase, Chicago Pattern, Marked, 16 ½ In. 1400.00

FRY FOVAL

Bowl, Fruit, Delft Blue, Opalescent, Foot, 7 ¼ x 12 In. .... *illus* 450.00
Candlestick, Opalescent, Jade Green Threading, Trim, 12 In. 275.00
Casserole, Cover, Metal Holder, 3 ¾ x 11 In. .... *illus* 65.00
Casserole, Cover, Vine & Flower Cutting, Pearl Oven Ware, 1932-38, 8 In. 35.00
Centerpiece, Opalescent, Footed, c.1920, 5 ½ x 12 In. 292.00
Cup & Saucer, Opalescent, Delft Blue Handle. .... 65.00 to 86.00
Custard Cup, Opalescent, c.1927, 4 Oz., 2 ¼ x 3 ¼ In. 8.00
Custard Cup, Opalescent, c.1936, 6 Oz., 2¼ x 4 In. .... 10.00 to 12.00
Perfume Bottle, Opaline, Blue Foot, Floral Engraving, Dabber, 5 ½ In. 420.00

FULPER Pottery Company was incorporated in 1899 in Flemington, New Jersey. They made art pottery from 1909 to 1929. The firm had been making bottles, jugs, and housewares from 1805. Doll heads were made about 1928. The firm became Stangl Pottery in 1929. Stangl Pottery is listed in its own category in this book.

Bookends, Books, Open Pages, c.1930, 4 ¾ x 4 ¾ x 2 ¾ In. 351.00
Bowl, Brown & Yellow Flambe Glaze, 12 In. 240.00
Bowl, Bulb, Sea Green Flambe, Caramel, Lobed, Swirl, 1 ½ x 12 ¾ In. 176.00
Bowl, Bulb, Sea Green Glaze Crystalline Structure, Low Lobed, 13 x 2 ½ In. 415.00
Bowl, Cafe Au Lait Over Mustard Matte, 6 ½ x 14 ½ In. 2040.00
Bowl, Inverted Rim, Blue Flambe Glaze, Gray & Caramel, 13 ½ x 5 In. 207.00
Bowl, Swirl Design, Lobed, Sea Green Flambe To Carmel, Footed, 1 ½ x 12 ¾ In. 176.00
Candlestick, Chamber, Blue-Green Flambe Glaze, Marked, c.1920, 4 ½ In. 88.00

Tax Donations

If you plan to give your collection to a museum and get a tax deduction, you must find the proper museum. Your gift must fit into the museum's collection and be displayed most of the time. Museums want pieces that fill gaps in their collections and are given without too many restrictions. But you might want to set rules for any future sale of the items. Perhaps ask that the money from a sale be used to purchase another item for the same collection.

Fry Foval, Bowl, Fruit, Delft Blue, Opalescent, Foot, 7 ¼ x 12 In.
$450.00

Fry Foval, Casserole, Cover, Metal Holder, 3 ¾ x 11 In.
$65.00

TIP

Do not light a cabinet filled with glass with light bulbs over 25 watts. Stronger bulbs generate too much heat. Some new types of bulbs are brighter and give off less heat.

Fulper, Perfume Lamp, Girl, Peach & White Matte Glaze, Impressed, 6 In.
$120.00

Fulper, Vase, Green & Rose Glaze, Ring Handles, Marked, 12¾ In.
$525.00

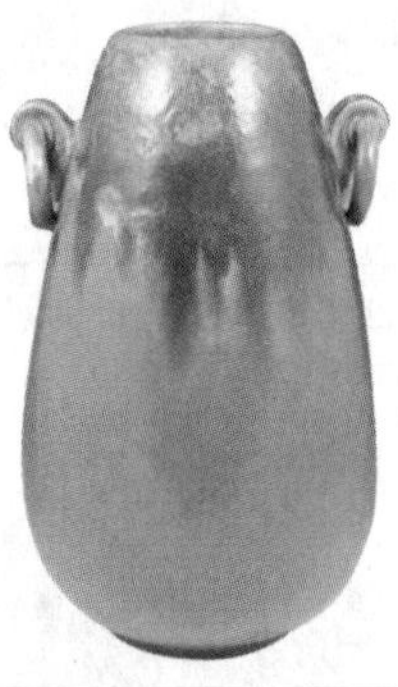

Fulper, Wall Pocket, Mottled Blue Matte Glaze, Marked, 10¼ In.
$231.00

Fulper, Wall Pocket, Mottled Blue, Green, Mahogany, Geometrics, 7½ x 4¾ In., Pair
$115.00

Flower Frog, Multitoned Blue Crystalline Glaze, Stamped, 5½ x 8 In. 86.00
Flowerpot, Cobalt Blue Brushed Flowers, 7½ x 6 In. 210.00
Humidor, Black Mirror Glaze, Silver Crystals, Flattened Finial, 6 In. 165.00
Jar, Cover, Copper Dust Crystalline Glaze, 2 Handles, 1925 .... 384.00
Lamp, Mushroom, Black To Mahogany Mirror Flambe Glaze, No. L24, 10¼ x 14 In. 6000.00
Lamp, Mushroom Shade, Glass Inserts, Cat's-Eye, Vasekraft, 21 x 16 In. 16800.00
Lamp Base, Blue Flambe Glaze, Inverted Rim, Swollen Cylinder, Ring Handles, 13 In. 294.00
Perfume Lamp, Girl, Peach & White Matte Glaze, Impressed, 6 In. .... *illus* 120.00
Urn, Blue & Amber Flambe Glaze, 2 Handles, Hammered Texture, 12½ x 12 In. 840.00
Urn, Leopard Skin Crystalline Glaze, 12 x 11½ In. 1080.00
Vase, Black & Blue Flambe Glaze, Shouldered, Marked, Label, 6 x 9½ In. 288.00
Vase, Black Mirror Glaze, Bulbous Footed, 6½ x 8 In. 840.00
Vase, Black Mirror Glaze, Flambe, Dripping Blue To Pink, 8 In. 470.00
Vase, Black Mirror Glaze, Shape No. 579, 2 Handles, 9 x 9 In. 1080.00
Vase, Blue Crystalline Glaze, Egg Shape, Green Drip Rim, 4 Green Loop Handles, 13 In. 1058.00
Vase, Blue Glaze, Black Highlights, 2 Handles, 9 In. 345.00
Vase, Blue Glaze, Signed, 7½ In. 117.00
Vase, Blue Snowflake Crystals In Flambe Glaze, 2 Squared Handles, 8⅞ In. 558.00
Vase, Brown, Black, Green Flambe Glaze, 2 Handles, Marked, 5½ x 7½ In. 259.00
Vase, Brown, Blue, Yellow Flambe Glaze, Cylindrical, Vertical Ink Mark, 4 x 5 In. 345.00
Vase, Brown, Flemington Green Glaze, Buttressed Shape, 8 x 10½ In. 1320.00
Vase, Brown Crystalline Glaze, Mustard Matte, Squat, 8 x 10 In. 1920.00
Vase, Brown Crystalline Glaze Over Mustard Matte, Squat, 8 x 10 In. 2160.00
Vase, Brown Matte Glaze, Geometric Design, Low, 6½ x 4½ In. 259.00
Vase, Chinese Blue Glaze, Flambe, Vertical Ink Mark, 10½ x 10½ In. 1020.00
Vase, Chinese Blue To Flemington Green Glaze, Shape No. 647, 7 x 13½ In. 1200.00
Vase, Copper Dust Crystalline, Black Mirror Flambe Glaze, 2 Handles, 9¾ x 7 In. 540.00
Vase, Copper Dust Crystalline Glaze, Green Flambe, Pinched Waist, 2 Handles, 9 x 7 In. 360.00
Vase, Copper Dust Over Flemington Green, Tapered, Squared Handles, 9½ In. 499.00
Vase, Cream To Gray Flambe Glaze, Flared, c.1920, 10 In. 470.00
Vase, Crystalline, Olive, Carmel, Aqua Blue Ground, Oval, 9¼ In. 203.00
Vase, Cucumber Crystalline Glaze, Shape No. 452, 2 Handles, 6 x 5 In. 2040.00
Vase, Cucumber Matte Glaze, Squat, 2 Handles, Scalloped Rim, Marked, 9¼ x 11 In. 660.00
Vase, Drippy Cucumber Crystalline Glaze, Baluster Shape, 16¾ In. 264.00
Vase, Green & Brown Crystalline Glaze, 3 Handles, Stamped, 4 x 6½ In. 431.00
Vase, Green & Rose Glaze, Ring Handles, Marked, 12¾ In. .... *illus* 525.00
Vase, Green Crystalline Glaze, Shouldered, Handles, Impressed, 10 x 6 In. 690.00
Vase, Green Crystalline Glaze, Tapering, 8 In. 510.00
Vase, Green Flambe Glaze, Feathering To Blue, Tapered Base, Early 1900s, 14¾ In. 1410.00
Vase, Leopard Skin Crystalline Glaze, Shape No. 27, 2 Handles, 5 x 11 In. 1200.00
Vase, Leopard Skin Crystalline Glaze, Shape No. 490, 2 Handles, 12 x 12 In. 720.00
Vase, Leopard Skin Glaze, Coiled Design, 2 Handles, 17½ In. 780.00
Vase, Leopard Skin Glaze, Handles, Marked, 4¾ x 6 In. 300.00
Vase, Mahogany To Ivory Flambe Glaze, Shape No. 55, 7½ x 13 In. 840.00
Vase, Mirror Flambe Glaze On Neck & Shoulder, Dripping Blue To Pink, Marked, 8 In. 470.00
Vase, Pink & Green Crystalline Glaze, Shouldered Form, 2 Handles, Marked, 6 In. 300.00
Vase, Pink & Green Flambe Glaze, Ribbed Shouldered, 7 x 11¼ In. 374.00
Vase, Thick Green Flambe Glaze Over Mottled Gray, Bulbous, Stand-Up Rim, 5 In. 823.00
Vase, Turquoise Mottled Glaze, Green Rim, 7½ In. 117.00
Vase, Wisteria Glaze, Oval, Slightly Flared Rim, 11⅜ In. 499.00
Wall Pocket, Mottled Blue, Green, Mahogany, Geometrics, 7½ x 4¾ In., Pair .... *illus* 231.00
Wall Pocket, Mottled Blue Matte Glaze, Marked, 10¼ In. .... *illus* 115.00

FURNITURE of all types is listed in this category. Examples dating from the seventeenth century to the 1970s are included. Prices for furniture vary in different parts of the country. Oak furniture is most expensive in the West; large pieces over eight feet high are sold for the most money in the South, where high ceilings are found in the old homes. Condition is very important when determining prices. These are NOT average prices but rather reports of unique sales. If the description includes the word *style*, the piece resembles the old furniture style but was made at a later time. It is not a period piece. Garden furniture is listed in the Garden Furnishings category. Related items may be found in the Architectural, Brass, and Store categories.

Armchairs are listed under Chair in this category.
Armoire, Charles X, Burl Walnut, Flared Molded Cornice, Plain Frieze, 88 x 46 In. 2585.00
Armoire, Eastlake, Walnut, Flower Carved Frieze, c.1875, 94 x 64 x 24 In. 3120.00
Armoire, Egyptian, Mahogany, Trapezoid Feet, c.1820, 90 x 69 x 29 In. 5288.00

Armoire, Elm, Maison Desny, Marked, c.1930, 69 x 52 x 24¾ In. 3600.00
Armoire, Empire, Mahogany, Double Paneled Doors, Shelves, Plinth Base, 86 x 59 x 23 In. 1770.00
Armoire, Faux Bamboo, Mirrored Door, France, Late 19th Century, 93 x 40 x 19 In. 2100.00
Armoire, Federal, Mahogany, Cuban, 3 Shelves, c.1810, 90 x 55 x 22 In. 6463.00
Armoire, Louis XV, Fruitwood, Provincial, Paneled, Shelves, 90½ x 67 x 27 In. 1771.00
Armoire, Louis XV Style, Fruitwood, Molded, Domed Cornice, 2-Panel Doors, 103 In. 6600.00
Armoire, Louis XVI Style, Walnut, Carved, Arched Crest, Mirror Doors, 99 x 70 In. 960.00
Armoire, Mahogany, Arched Acanthus, Paneled Doors, Flower Carving, 101 x 58 In. 7638.00
Armoire, Mahogany, Paneled Doors, Center Stile, Divided Interior, 84 x 72 x 27 In. 1763.00
Armoire, Mirrored Door, Glass Window, Oak, Copper, 63¾ x 35¾ x 18 In. 1381.00
Armoire, Neoclassical, Mahogany, Child's, 35 x 26¾ x 13 In. 4800.00
Armoire, Neoclassical, Mahogany, Molded Cornice, Interior Drawers, 85 x 55 In. 8813.00
Armoire, Neoclassical, Mahogany, Projecting Cornice, Brass Ball Feet, 94 x 75 In. 9900.00
Armoire, Oak, Carved Pediment Crest, Double Finials, 2 Doors, France, 116 x 88 In. 6435.00
Armoire, Provincial, Burl Elm, Oak, Pansy Relief, c.1850, 85 x 53 x 20 In. *illus* 5500.00
Armoire, Provincial, Pine, 2 Doors, Carved Crest, Pegged, France, c.1800, 90 x 60 In. 2640.00
Armoire, Provincial Louis Philippe, Walnut, Figured, Ogee, 3-Panel Doors, 95 x 64 In. 4560.00
Armoire, Provincial Louis XV Style, 2 Scroll Panel Doors, Birds, Wheat, 90 x 52 In. 5280.00
Armoire, Provincial Louis XV Style, Fruitwood, Paneled Frieze, 2 Doors, 95 x 64 In. 3600.00
Armoire, Provincial Louis XV Style, Pine, Carved Crest, Panels, c.1850, 95 x 54 In. 4800.00
Armoire, Provincial Style, Oak, Sections, Acanthus, Glass Panel Doors, France, 67 x 19 In. 1380.00
Armoire, R.J. Horner & Co., Faux Bamboo, Figured Maple, c.1890, 90 x 40 In. 8400.00
Armoire, Restauration, Mahogany, Drawer, 2-Panel Door, 104 x 69 x 28 In. 7200.00
Armoire, Rococo Revival, Walnut, Carved Crest, Projecting Cornice, 107 x 68 In. 4080.00
Armoire, Rosewood, Drawers, Blocked Plinth, 94 x 66 x 25 In. 1763.00
Armoire, Tiger Maple, Mid Atlantic, c.1830, 76 x 54½ x 20 In. 3055.00
Armoire, Tiger Maple, Paneled Doors, c.1830, 76 x 54½ x 20 In. 3055.00
Armoire, Victorian, Mahogany, Divided, Scalloped Base, Drawers, 96 x 64 x 24 In. 2350.00
Armoire, Walnut, 2-Panel Doors, Recessed Side Panels, France, 90 x 64 x 20 In. 3300.00
Armoire, Walnut, Beveled Glass, Flower Festoon, France, c.1890, 96 x 57 x 20 In. *illus* 605.00
Armoire, Walnut, Flared Cornice, Paneled Door, Scalloped Base, 76 x 45 In. 3819.00
Banquette, Rosewood, George IV, Padded Cushion, 16 x 64 x 23½ In. 944.00 to 1121.00
Bar, Adirondack, Marquetry, Lift Top, 62 x 19 x 29½ In. 385.00
Bar, Cedar, Poplar, Birch, Carved, Caesar Series, c.1928, 33⅝ x 36⅝ x 18 In. 2400.00
Bar, G. Nakashima, Walnut, Wall Hanging, Glass Shelves, Illuminated, 18 x 60 x 8 In. 4200.00
Bar, Tiki, Pine, Carved, 2 Stools, Witco Co., 42 x 67 In., 3 Piece *illus* 550.00
Barstool, Bamboo & Brass, Upholstered, Karl Springer, 1970s, 18 x 20 x 17 In., Pair 1100.00
Bed, Arts & Crafts, Oak, Straight Crest Rails, Vertical Slats, Side Rails, 42 x 57 x 75 In. 823.00
Bed, Baby, Victorian, Walnut, c.1860, 48 x 57 In. 605.00
Bed, Baby, Victorian, Walnut, Folding, 50 x 51 In. 715.00
Bed, Baker Furniture, Teak, Maple, Slated Headboard, Marked, 31½ x 57 x 88 In. 2040.00
Bed, Brass, Art Nouveau, Bronze Cherub Medallions, c.1900, 42 x 78 In. 220.00
Bed, Brass, Head & Footboard, Reeded, Geometric, Ball Feet, 37½ x 53 x 75½ In. 1000.00
Bed, Cast Iron, Victorian, Triple Arched, 52 x 80 x 56 In. 175.00
Bed, Chippendale, Claw & Ball, Domed Canopy, Ribbed Posts, 58 In. 1150.00
Bed, Curly Maple, Cherry Head & Footboard, Walnut Rails, Rope, 50½ x 53½ In. 460.00
Bed, Curly Maple, Pencil Post, Paneled Tapered Posts, Shaped Headboard, 82 x 66 In. 748.00
Bed, Eastlake, Walnut, Burl, Scrolled Leaf, Flowers, Crown, Footboard, c.1890, 72 x 62 x 80 In. 700.00
Bed, Eastlake, Walnut, Headboard, Paneled, Arched Footboard, 78 x 57 In. 353.00
Bed, Eastlake, Walnut, Veneer, Sawtooth Carved Cornice, Flowers, Leaves, 50 In. 705.00
Bed, Empire, Mahogany, Gilt Bronze, c.1840, 56½ x 79½ x 47 In. 3900.00
Bed, Empire, Walnut, Gilt Mounted, Rollover Head, Foot, 1800s, 44 x 52 In. 2596.00
Bed, Empire Style, Mahogany, Parquetry, Bronze Mounted, 1900, 59 x 83 x 58 In. 384.00
Bed, Federal, Tiger Maple, Turned, Pineapple Finials, 49½ x 58 In. 6600.00
Bed, Four-Poster, Allard, Mahogany, Tapered Cluster Columns, c.1885, 94 x 75 x 84 In. 1610.00
Bed, Four-Poster, Cannonball, Scalloped Head, Footboard, Ring, 46 x 56 In. 184.00
Bed, Four-Poster, Canopy, Cherry, Slatted Top, Brass Hinged Center, 73 x 81¾ x 40 In. 476.00
Bed, Four-Poster, Carved, Mahogany, 19th Century, 98 x 74 x 60 In. 6463.00
Bed, Four-Poster, Cherry, Faux Bamboo, Finials, Padded Headboard, 94 x 58 x 78 In. 1225.00
Bed, Four-Poster, Curly Maple, Cherry, Finials, Blanket Rail, Rope, 52 x 49 In. 161.00
Bed, Four-Poster, Federal, Mahogany, Pineapple Finials, 82 x 72 x 60 In. 2128.00
Bed, Four-Poster, Federal, Pencil, Maple, 75 x 61 x 81 In. 633.00
Bed, Four-Poster, Federal, Tiger Maple, Early 19th Century, 87 x 81 In. *illus* 3285.00
Bed, Four-Poster, Federal, Tiger Maple, Cherry Headboard, Canopy Frame, 87 x 82 In. 3335.00
Bed, Four-Poster, George III, Mahogany, Square, Arched Headpost, 1890s, 96 x 60 In. 3150.00
Bed, Four-Poster, Mahogany, Scroll Headboard, Urn Finials, West Indies, 86 x 52 x 77 In. 4113.00

Furniture, Armoire, Provincial, Burl Elm, Oak, Pansy Relief, c.1850, 85 x 53 x 20 In. $5500.00

Furniture, Armoire, Walnut, Beveled Glass, Flower Festoon, France, c.1890, 96 x 57 x 20 In. $605.00

Furniture, Bar, Tiki, Pine, Carved, 2 Stools, Witco Co., 42 x 67 In., 3 Piece $550.00

Furniture, Bed, Four-Poster, Federal, Tiger Maple, Early 19th Century, 87 x 81 In. $3285.00

Twin Beds

Twin beds were designed by Sheraton in England in the eighteenth century, but they did not become popular or even acceptable until the twentieth century. The Hays Code covering morals in movies ruled in 1934 that married couples could only be pictured in twin beds about a foot apart. It became stylish. In 1959 Doris Day played a decorator in the movie *Pillow Talk* and designed a bedroom with a double bed, challenging the ruling.

Furniture, Bed, Four-Poster, Yellow Paint, Early 1900s, 69 x 36 x 77 In., Pair
$575.00

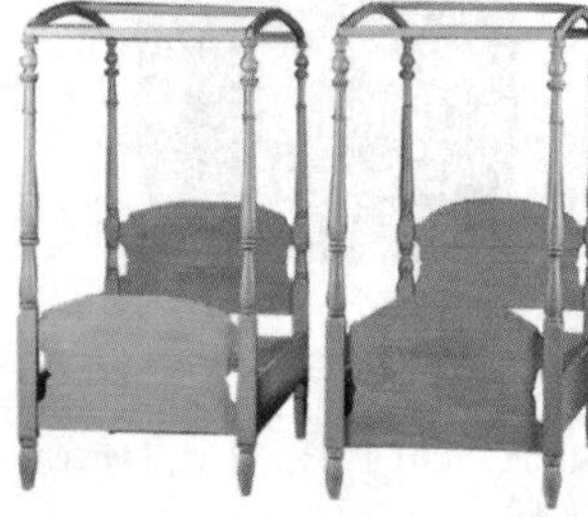

Furniture, Bed, G. Nelson, Birch, Cane, Steel Legs, Herman Miller, 1960s, 36 x 54 x 79 In.
$5010.00

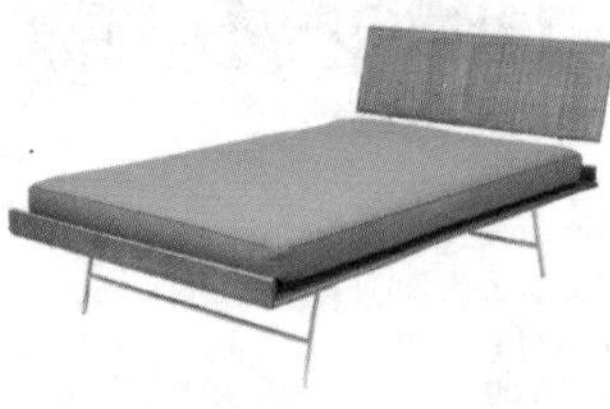

Furniture, Bed, G. Stickley, No. 912, Paneled, Signed, 51 x 79 x 58 In.
$3900.00

Bed, Four-Poster, Mallard, Mahogany, Tapered Columns, Shell Pediment, 94 x 75 In. 1610.00
Bed, Four-Poster, Maple, Cherry Stained Pine, Head & Footboards, Rope, 45 x 20 In. 201.00
Bed, Four-Poster, Mississippi River Valley Gros Rouge, Faceted Posts, 90 x 87 In. 2820.00
Bed, Four-Poster, Neoclassical, Egyptian Revival, Carved, Mahogany, Walnut, 58 x 72 In. 2115.00
Bed, Four-Poster, New Lebanon, Shaker, Maple, Pine Head & Footboard, Rails, 37 x 52 In. ... 234.00
Bed, Four-Poster, Ohio Valley, Curly Maple, Headboard, Footboard, 49 x 51 x 76 In. 518.00
Bed, Four-Poster, Red Over Salmon Paint, Shaped Headboard, Rope, 1800s, 48 x 52 In. 144.00
Bed, Four-Poster, Rococo Revival, Rosewood, Carved Crest, 106 x 61 In. 5040.00
Bed, Four-Poster, Rococo Revival, Walnut, 10 x 55 ½ In. 1920.00
Bed, Four-Poster, Scrolled Headboard, Acorns, Double Finials, Rope, 1880s, 48 x 54 In. 575.00
Bed, Four-Poster, Sheraton, Cherry, Arched Canopy Frame, Pa., 84 x 55 x 79 In. 2320.00
Bed, Four-Poster, Sheraton, Mahogany, Iron Box Spring Holders, 87 x 81 x 52 In. 1210.00
Bed, Four-Poster, Sheraton, Mahogany, Ring-Turned Posts, Louisiana, 70 x 94 In. 9300.00
Bed, Four-Poster, Trundle, Scalloped Head, Footboard, Ball Finials, c.1830, 80 x 55 In. 1150.00
Bed, Four-Poster, Turned, Paneled, Blanket Rail, Rope Knobs, 63 x 45 x 69 ½ In. 132.00
Bed, Four-Poster, Yellow Paint, Early 1900s, 69 x 36 x 77 In., Pair .... *illus* 575.00
Bed, G. Nakashima, Walnut, Spindles, Headboard, c.1957, 36 x 81 In. 2880.00
Bed, G. Nakashima, Walnut, c.1962, 32 ⅛ x 55 ¼ x 89 ¼ In. 5100.00
Bed, G. Nelson, Birch, Cane, Steel Legs, Herman Miller, 1960s, 36 x 54 x 79 In. .... *illus* 5010.00
Bed, G. Stickley, No. 912, Paneled, Signed, 51 x 79 x 58 In. .... *illus* 3900.00
Bed, G. Stickley, Single, Pencil Post, Side Rails, 46 x 39 x 78 In. 1320.00
Bed, Half-Tester, P. Mallard, Rosewood, c.1850 .... 18700.00
Bed, Half-Tester, Rococo, Rosewood, Finials, Scalloped Headboard, 122 x 78 x 66 In. 7344.00
Bed, Half-Tester, Rococo, Mahogany, Scalloped Rails, 108 x 72 x 72 In. 11400.00
Bed, Half-Tester, Walnut, Rosewood, Paneled Head, Footboards, 130 x 55 x 75 In. 3525.00
Bed, Jean Palardy, Pine, Shaped Headboard, Carved Oval, Doves, Initials, Twin Size. 150.00
Bed, Jenny Lind, Machine Turned Spools, Green Paint, Twin Size. 550.00
Bed, Jenny Lind, Oak, Spindle, Headboard & Footboard, c.1890, 43 x 50 ½ In. 90.00
Bed, Jenny Lind, Walnut, Spool Turned, Scalloped Headboard, 41 ½ x 51 In. 118.00
Bed, Late Victorian, Mahogany, Acanthus & Shell Crests, c.1890, 80 x 84 In. 3740.00
Bed, Louis Philippe, Rosewood, Tall Headboard, c.1840, 68 x 62 x 75 In. 3120.00
Bed, Louis XVI Style, Cane Panel, Swags, Crest, Painted, c.1880, 72 x 69 x 86 In. ...... *illus* 3000.00
Bed, Louis XVI Style, Mahogany, Early 20th Century, 61 x 60 In. .... *illus* 225.00
Bed, Louis XVI Style, Walnut, Carved Crest, Side Rails, c.1900, 58 x 81 In. 148.00
Bed, Mahogany, Bell & Ball, Shaped Head & Footboards, 54 x 74 x 48 In. 288.00
Bed, Maple, Faux Bamboo, Pyramid Finial Post, Paneled Head, Footboard, 78 x 61 In. 3525.00
Bed, Maple, New England, Fluted, Pencil Post, 85 x 77 x 55 In. 8700.00
Bed, Mitchell & Rammelsberg, High Back, Signed, c.1850, 11 ½ Ft. Headboard. 9900.00
Bed, Napoleon III, Rosewood, Paneled Headboard, Footboard, 63 x 76 x 53 In. 1763.00
Bed, Oak, High Back, Carved Leaf, Crest, Columns, Footboard, c.1900, 81 x 58 In. 220.00
Bed, Old Hickory Style, Woven Headboard, Footboard, 34 x 58 x 80 In. .... *illus* 240.00
Bed, Plantation, Mahogany, Post, Figures, Late 19th Century, 105 x 65 x 79 In. .... *illus* 4800.00
Bed, Renaissance Revival, Burl Walnut, Bronze Mounted, c.1865, 86 x 59 x 77 In. 6169.00
Bed, Renaissance Revival, Burl Walnut, Carved Crest, Finials, c.1870, 99 x 82 In. 3025.00
Bed, Renaissance Revival, Rosewood, Veneers, Carved Putto Masque, 69 x 60 x 62 In. 1800.00
Bed, Renaissance Revival, Walnut, Conforming Footboard, Rails, c.1865, 79 x 63 x 76 In. ... 3600.00
Bed, Rococo, Rosewood, Carved, Flower & Leaf Arched Crest, Victorian, c.1850. .... 990.00
Bed, Rococo, Rosewood, Carved, Victorian, c.1860, 93 x 63 In. 1485.00
Bed, Rococo, Walnut, Carved, High Back, Victorian, c.1860, 99 x 62 In. 1760.00
Bed, Rococo, Walnut, High Back, Double Oval Panels, Carved Crest, c.1870, 94 x 64 In. 2200.00
Bed, Rococo Revival, Mahogany, Paneled, Carved, 19th Century, 55 x 55 x 77 In. 1140.00
Bed, Rococo Revival, Walnut, Arched Headboard, Carved, Shell & Serpent, 87 x 57 In. 266.00
Bed, Rococo Revival, Walnut, Carved, Fruit, Leafy Crest, Arched, 1800s, 98 x 60 In. 266.00
Bed, Rococo Revival, Walnut, Leafy Crest, Shield Medallion, Arched, 76 x 54 In. 325.00
Bed, Sheraton, Mahogany, Rolled & Turned Posts, Pineapple Tops, 46 x 72 x 50 In. 403.00
Bed, Sleigh, Mahogany, Scrolled, Paneled Headboard, Shaped Rails, 39 x 67 In. 470.00
Bed, Sleigh, Mahogany, 19th Century, 41 x 73 x 57 In. 1838.00
Bed, Sleigh, Mahogany, Figured, Paneled, American Restauration, 40 x 60 x 83 In. 2280.00
Bed, Trundle, D-End Mattress Platform, Ring-Turned Legs, c.1850, 72 x 61 In. 720.00
Bed, Trundle, Rope, Beaded Edges, Red Paint, 18 ½ x 26 x 73 In. .... *illus* 88.00
Bed, Trundle, Rope, Cherry, Mushroom Finials, Modified Rails, 18 ½ x 44 In. 144.00
Bed, Venetian, Painted, Arched Headboard, Fruit Basket Center, 1800, 39 In., Pair 2465.00
Bed, Victorian, Walnut, Carved Headboard, 10 Ft. 11000.00
Bed, Walnut, Carved Headboard, Leaf, Leg, Footboard, Scrolled Toe, 63 x 57 x 79 In. 561.00
Bed, Walnut, Scalloped Crest, Late 20th Century, 64 x 48 In. 88.00
Bed, Zoar, Cherry, Turned Post, Panel Head & Footboards, Rolled Tops, 38 x 39 In. 403.00

Bed Steps, Mahogany, Folding Top, Red Leather, Peg Feet, 18 x 17 x 20 In.. 646.00
Bed Steps, Pine, Graduated, Rabbit Joints, 18 x 17 x 12½ In. *illus* 275.00
Bed Steps, Regency, Mahogany, Leather Inset, Paneled Cupboard, 28 x 32 x 18 In. 1560.00
Bed Steps, Regency, Mahogany, Tooled Leather Treads, Turned Legs, 27 x 16 In. 1586.00
Bed Steps, William IV, Mahogany, Needlepoint Lift Top, 1800s, 24 x 17 x 27 In. 470.00
Bedroom Set, Mahogany, Acanthus Carved, Dresser, Bed, Chest 1870.00
Bedroom Set, Mahogany, Bombe Shape, Mirror Chest, Dresser, Vanity, Bed, c.1890. 4620.00
Bedroom Set, Oak, Acanthus Carved Crests, Bed, Dresser, Washstand, c.1900 2200.00
Bedroom Set, R.J. Horner, Faux Bamboo, Mirrored Chest, Dresser, Bed, c.1890, 3 Piece 7700.00
Bedroom Set, T. Brooks, Victorian, Walnut, 3 Piece 15400.00
Bedroom Set, Venetian Style, Cream Paint, Scalloped Ribbon Swags, 5 Piece 1763.00
Bedroom Set, Victorian, Drape Carving, Coral Colored Marble, 3 Piece 15400.00
Bedroom Set, Victorian, Mahogany, Bed, Chest, Mirror, Carved Leaf, Crest, c.1910 500.00
Bedroom Set, Victorian, Walnut, Carved, Bird & Squirrel Crown, 3 Piece. 19800.00
Bedroom Set, Walnut, Wardrobe, Vanity, Bed, Stand, Animal Feet, c.1920 177.00
Bench, Arts & Crafts, Keyed Construction, Leather Seat, c.1910 1650.00
Bench, Beech, Beaded Apron & Stretchers, Chinese, 1700s, 20 x 45 In. 590.00
Bench, Birch, Pine, 32-Spoke Back, Carved Seat, New Hampshire, c.1840, 33 In. 9360.00
Bench, Bucket, 2 Tiers, Mortised, 19th Century, 36 x 12 x 34 In. 523.00
Bench, Bucket, Blue Paint, 2 Shelves, Bracket Feet, Square Nails, 11 x 15 x 7 In. 357.00
Bench, Bucket, Green Over Red Paint, Canted Legs, 28 x 46 x 17 In. *illus* 176.00
Bench, Bucket, Mortise & Tenon, Paint, Lancet Arched Ends, Early 1900s, 95 x 12 In. 403.00
Bench, Bucket, Painted, Applied Skirt, Cutout Ends, Medial Shelf, c.1815, 29 x 42 In. 999.00
Bench, Bucket, Pine, Red Paint, 2 Shelves, Cross Brace, 29 x 26¼ In. 460.00
Bench, Bucket, Poplar, Yellow Paint, 2 Shelves, Scalloped Galleries, 39 x 42 In. 546.00
Bench, Bucket, Poplar, Brown Paint, Cutout Ends, Medial Shelf, c.1925, 30 x 62 In. 1175.00
Bench, Bucket, Red, Arched Cutout Feet, Back Supports, Patina, 55 x 54 x 14½ In. 2970.00
Bench, Bucket, Yellow Pine, 2 Shelves, Shaped Ends, Blue Paint, 21½ x 37 In.. 575.00
Bench, Carved, 5-Plank Top, Squatting Male Supports, Africa, 22 x 60 x 17 In. 1224.00
Bench, Chippendale, Mahogany, Upholstered, Cabriole Legs, Claw Feet, 17 In. 570.00
Bench, Deacon's, Back Crest Rail, 1-Board, Yellow Ocher, c.1830, 34½ x 77 x 20 In. 523.00
Bench, Deacon's, Shaped Spindle Back, Continuous Arms, Slat Rail, Painted, 33 x 90 In. 392.00
Bench, Deacon's, Stenciled, 8 Spindle Legs, Mustard Paint, 1800s, 96 x 31 In. 1700.00
Bench, Deacon's, Tablet Crest, Scroll Arms, Painted, Pa., c.1850, 35 x 85 In. *illus* 1210.00
Bench, Directoire, Mahogany, Curule, Early 19th Century, 23 x 26 x 15 In. 1058.00
Bench, Elm, Bamboo, Square Feet, Chinese, 19¼ x 64 x 21 In. 792.00
Bench, Empire Style, Padded, Shell Carved Curule Base, Stretcher, 16 x 49 x 21½ In. 1121.00
Bench, Fireside, William & Mary Style, Mahogany, Gold Velvet, Stretcher, 21 x 52 In. 1763.00
Bench, Folding, 2-Section Body, Hinged Legs, Ebonized Head & Footboard, 41 x 54 In. 35.00
Bench, French, Splayed, Turned Legs, Cross Stretcher, 7¼ x 19½ In., Pair 83.00
Bench, Fruitwood, Inlaid Ivory, Marquetry, Crest, Hunting Scenes, c.1880, 58 In.. 3878.00
Bench, G. Nelson, Birch, Cane Top, Steel Legs, Herman Miller, 48 x 18 x 41 In. 600.00
Bench, G. Nelson, Birch, Platform, Herman Miller, 1950s, 72 x 18 x 14 In. 1440.00
Bench, G. Nelson, Platform, Birch Top, Wood Legs, 72½ x 18½ x 14 In. 1800.00
Bench, G. Nelson, Platform, Birch Top, Wood Legs, 102½ x 18½ x 14 In. 1920.00
Bench, G. Stickley, Trestle, Keyed-Through Stretchers, 15 x 36 x 15 In., Pair 3900.00
Bench, Geo. B. Gruber, Softwood, Beaded Skirt, V-Notched Legs, Perry, Pa., 19 x 72 x 10 In. 495.00
Bench, Georgian, Mahogany, Saddle Seat, Marlboro Legs, 17 x 21 x 18 In. 2006.00
Bench, Hall, G. Stickley, Leather Seat & Back, No. 162, 50½ x 24½ x 36 In. 7800.00
Bench, Hall, R.J. Horner, Mahogany, Figural, New York. 6900.00
Bench, Hall, Renaissance, Oak, Carved, Lift Seat, Paw Feet, 53 x 60 x 21 In.. 1762.00
Bench, Irish Chippendale, Cabriole Legs, Paw Feet, Needlework Seat, 18 x 51 In. 2070.00
Bench, Louis XV, Walnut, Floral Carved Cabriole Legs, 17 x 42 x 30 In. 1880.00
Bench, Louis XV Style, Fruitwood, Carved Leaved, Cabriole Legs, 21 x 87 In.. 3360.00
Bench, Louis XVI Style, Gilt, Carved, Elliptical Top, Ribbon Border, 20 x 40 In.. 999.00
Bench, Maitland-Smith, Mahogany, Cane Seat, Acanthus, Parcel Gilt, 24 x 32 In. 259.00
Bench, Mammy, Mixed Woods, Stenciled, Bamboo Spindles, c.1820, 34 x 60 In. *illus* 1495.00
Bench, Music, Eastlake, Mahogany, Half Round Frame, Arched Legs, 20 x 20 In. 86.00
Bench, Neoclassical, Carved, Gilt, Scroll Arms, Curved Seat, Paw Feet, 34 x 32 In. 1762.00
Bench, Neoclassical, Curule, Upholstered, Dolphin Feet, Pair. 2115.00
Bench, Neoclassical, Mahogany, Serpentine Back, Carved, Upholstery, 39 x 42 In. 480.00
Bench, Neoclassical Style, Carved, Paint, Silver, Dolphin Supports, 20 x 38 In., Pair 1410.00
Bench, Neoclassical Style, Gilt, Needlework Upholstery, Early 1900s, 17 x 18 In. 472.00
Bench, Oak, 3 Reticulated Arches, Trefoil Finials, Paneled Back, 1800s, 48 x 72 In. 1762.00
Bench, Oak, England, 19th Century, 28 x 60 x 16¾ In. 15000.00
Bench, Oak, Paneled, Pegged, 20th Century, 59 In. 630.00

Furniture, Bed, Louis XVI Style, Cane Panel, Swags, Crest, Painted, c.1880, 72 x 69 x 86 In.
$3000.00

Furniture, Bed, Louis XVI Style, Mahogany, Early 20th Century, 61 x 60 In.
$225.00

Furniture, Bed, Old Hickory Style, Woven Headboard, Footboard, 34 x 58 x 80 In.
$240.00

Furniture, Bed, Plantation, Mahogany, Post, Figures, Late 19th Century, 105 x 65 x 79 In.
$4800.00

Furniture, Bed, Trundle, Rope, Beaded Edges, Red Paint, 18½ x 26 x 73 In.
$88.00

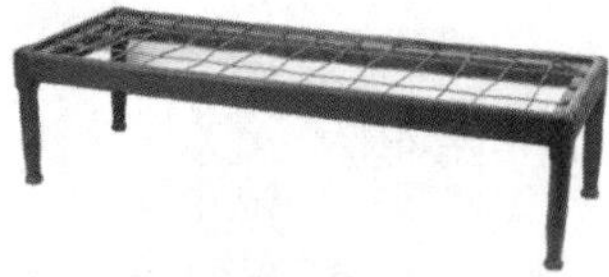

Bed Sizes
Old beds were not made in standard sizes. A double bed may be the size of a modern queen-size bed or up to 6 inches narrower than a queen.

Furniture, Bed Steps, Pine, Graduated, Rabbit Joints, 18 x 17 x 12½ In.
$275.00

Furniture, Bench, Bucket, Green Over Red Paint, Canted Legs, 28 x 46 x 17 In.
$176.00

Furniture, Bench, Deacon's, Tablet Crest, Scroll Arms, Painted, Pa., c.1850, 35 x 85 In.
$1210.00

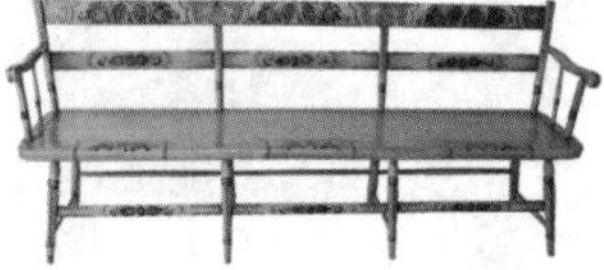

Bench, Piano, Walnut, Burled, Hinged Seat, c.1890, 29 x 24 x 17 In., Pair 8108.00
Bench, Pine, 3 Scalloped Pedestals, 19th Century, 19 x 125 In. 147.00
Bench, Pine, Bootjack Ends, Red Paint, Mortised, 18½ x 12 x 58 In. 316.00
Bench, Pine, Bootjack Ends, Half Circle Through Mortise, 17½ x 40 x 9 In. 3744.00
Bench, Pine, Curved Arms, Arched Cutout Feet, 22 x 18 x 11 In. .... *illus* 165.00
Bench, Queen Anne Style, Mahogany, Upholstered, Cabriole Legs, Pad Feet, 43 In. 189.00
Bench, Refectory, English Oak, Ash, Scalloped Back, Tudor Rose Crest, 42 x 40 In. 470.00
Bench, Refectory, Jacobean Revival, Oak, High Shaped Back, Scroll Arms, 62 x 46 In. 411.00
Bench, Regency, Ivory, Ebonized, Parcel Gilt, X-Shape Frame, 20 x 42 In., Pair 73000.00
Bench, Regency, Mahogany, Slip Seat, Turned Legs, Casters, 18 x 42 x 18 In. 1410.00
Bench, Regency, Oak, Provincial, Cane Seat, Lion's Head Armrests, c.1850, 20 x 40 In. 1320.00
Bench, Regency Style, Frieze, Applied Flowers, Gilt, 20 x 47 x 18 In., Pair .... *illus* 2000.00
Bench, Renaissance Revival, Walnut, Carved, Armorial Carved Crest, 52 In. 1058.00
Bench, Rosewood, Sycamore, Upholstered, c.1932, 13¼ x 25½ x 13½ In. 9600.00
Bench, Roycroft, Ali Baba, Plank Seat, Bark On Underside, Splayed Legs, 42 x 19 In. 11400.00
Bench, Savonarola Persian Design, Bone Inlay, c.1880, 25 x 21 In. 280.00
Bench, Slatted Back, Plank Seat, Scroll Arms, 19th Century, 35 x 85 x 19½ In. 1100.00
Bench, Softwood, Green Paint, Mortised, Cutout Legs, Skirt, 18 x 72 x 12½ In. 358.00
Bench, Stainless Steel, Curved Top, 15¼ x 47½ x 15¾ In. 14400.00
Bench, Standing Bear Sides, Open Carved Back, Black Forest, c.1885 .... 5175.00
Bench, Stickley, Rectangular Top, Splayed Legs, 48 x 15 x 16 In. 3900.00
Bench, Trestle, Georgian, Fruitwood, Yew Top, H-Stretcher, 10½ x 81 In. 2990.00
Bench, Trestle, Pine, Molding, 1-Board Seat, Arms, Mortise & Peg, c.1840, 8 Ft. 1872.00
Bench, Vanity, Rohde, Birch Frame, Striped Velvet, No. 4141, 19 x 19 x 22 In. 780.00
Bench, Wagon Seat, 2 Horizontal Slat Backs, Turned Posts, Woven Seat, 31 x 15 In. 230.00
Bench, Walnut, Seat Slabs, Paired Supports, Tuscan Half Columns, 19 x 93 In., Pair 3643.00
Bench, Window, English Oak, Ebonized, Carved Leaves, Armrest, Late 1800s, 25 x 36 In. 900.00
Bench, Window, William & Mary, Mahogany, Upholstered Top, Turned Legs, 18 x 49 In. 560.00
Bench, Windsor, Poplar, Cherry Finish, Oak Spindles, Red Cushion, 74 x 39 In. 1725.00
Bench, Windsor, Poplar, Grain Paint, Arrow Back Spindles, Faux Bamboo, 34 x 79 In. 4600.00
Bench, Wood Carved Bear Support, Glass Eyes, Music Box, c.1880, 20 x 6 x 10 In. 4348.00
Bench Bed, Provincial, Pine, Hinged Seat, Fold-Out, 36 x 76 x 18 In. .... *illus* 600.00
Book Trough, Arts & Crafts, V-Trough, Open Shelf, Slab Sides, Carved, 33 x 24 x 9 In. 345.00
Bookcase, 3 Sections, Stacking, Oak, 20th Century, 46 x 34 In. 265.00
Bookcase, Aesthetic Revival, Walnut, 3 Doors, Gallery, Egg Shape Molding, 67 x 70 In. 1760.00
Bookcase, Aesthetic Revival, Walnut, Mirrored Gallery, Step Back, 61 x 46 In. 1815.00
Bookcase, Arts & Crafts, Oak, 3 Shelves, Cutouts, 20th Century, 51 x 43 x 13 In. 302.00
Bookcase, Breakfront, Sheraton, Mahogany, Pullout Central Interior, 86 x 60 In. 2585.00
Bookcase, Chest, George III, Mahogany, T. Wilson, 91 x 38 x 19 In. 7200.00
Bookcase, Chippendale, Walnut, Paneled Doors, Shelves, Drawers, 80 x 38 x 20 In. 2415.00
Bookcase, Empire, Flame Mahogany, Step Back, c.1840 .... 880.00
Bookcase, Empire Style, Mahogany, Gilt Bronze, 2 Doors, Drawers, France, 82 x 72 In. 7500.00
Bookcase, Federal, Mahogany, 2 Parts, Glazed Doors, Kneehole, 82 x 49 x 24 In. 8050.00
Bookcase, G. Stickley, 2 Doors, Gallery Top, Fixed Shelves, 56 x 54 x 13 In. 1560.00
Bookcase, G. Stickley, 2 Doors, Iron Hardware, Glass Doors, No. 523, 39 x 12 x 45 In. 6600.00
Bookcase, G. Stickley, Door, 16 Panes, Tenon Construction, 36 x 13 x 56 In. 4800.00
Bookcase, G. Stickley, Double Door, Gallery Top, Six Shelves, 56 x 42 x 13 In. 5700.00
Bookcase, G. Stickley, Oak, 2 Doors, 12 Panes, Sideboard, c.1912, 56 x 61 x 13 In. 5875.00
Bookcase, G. Stickley, Single Door, 3 Shelves, 56 x 35 x 13 In. 4500.00
Bookcase, G. Stickley, Single Door, Mitered Mullions, 1902, 55½ x 31 x 12¼ In. 9600.00
Bookcase, George II, Mahogany, 2 Sections, Glazed Doors, Shelves, 92 x 57 In. 31000.00
Bookcase, George III, Fruitwood, 4 Doors, 10 Shelves, 2-Piece, c.1800, 81 In. 6325.00
Bookcase, George III Style, Mahogany, Glazed Doors, 82½ x 51 x 18 In. 1528.00
Bookcase, George III Style, Mahogany, Glazed Doors, Faux Drawer Doors, 81 x 53 In. 3360.00
Bookcase, George III Style, Mahogany, Drop Leaf, Drawers, Cubbyholes, 104 x 127 In. 20160.00
Bookcase, George III Style, Provincial, Oak, Pine, Glazed Doors, 43¾ x 53 x 12 In. 1920.00
Bookcase, Georgian Style, Mahogany, Curved Molding, French Feet, 82 x 48 x 13 In. 3819.00
Bookcase, Globe-Wernicke Co., Oak, Stacking, c.1900, 79 x 34 x 12 In. .... *illus* 1200.00
Bookcase, Gothic, Rosewood, Walnut, Fleur-De-Lis Finials, Doors, c.1835, 95 x 48 In. 4113.00
Bookcase, Hepplewhite, Mahogany, Step Back, 3 Parts, 109 x 61 x 23 In. 4025.00
Bookcase, Jacobean Style, Oak, Shelves, Carved Pilasters, 45 x 73 x 17 In. 1440.00
Bookcase, Lawyer's, Arts & Crafts, Oak, 3 Stacked Cases, Leaded Glass, 51 x 34 In. 633.00
Bookcase, Lifetime, 3 Doors, Divided Glass, 56½ x 13½ x 55½ In. 2040.00
Bookcase, Limbert, 2 Doors, Copper Hardware, 32 x 11 x 46 In. 2040.00
Bookcase, Limbert, 2 Doors, Single Vertical Mullion, 6 Shelves, 48 x 15 x 57 In. 2640.00
Bookcase, Louis Philippe, Mahogany, Glazed Doors, 19th Century, 79½ x 37 In. 1058.00

Bookcase, Mahogany, 3 Doors, Acanthus, Lion, Paw Feet, c.1890, 62 x 71 In.. 990.00
Bookcase, Mahogany, 3 Sections, Beveled Glass Doors, Shelves, 70 x 66 In. 2500.00
Bookcase, Mahogany, 4 Doors, Bracket Feet, 18th Century, 94 x 43 x 18 In. 1792.00
Bookcase, Mahogany, 4 Sections, Glass Lift Doors, 59 x 34 x 11 In. 560.00
Bookcase, Mahogany, Scroll Spindle Sides, Rectangular, 19th Century, 10 x 9 x 12 In. 822.00
Bookcase, Mahogany, Step Back Upper Section, Carved Gilt Leaf, 91 x 39 x 24 In. 1652.00
Bookcase, Napoleon III, Mahogany, 4 Doors, Beveled Glass, 111 x 107 x 21 In. *illus* 5000.00
Bookcase, Neoclassical, Mahogany, Cyma Cornice, Glazed Panel Doors, 73 x 55 In. 960.00
Bookcase, Neoclassical, Mahogany, Cornice, Arched Frieze, Glazed Doors, 80 x 64 In.. 1920.00
Bookcase, Oak, Beveled Glass Doors, Turned Rail, Cane Band, 77 x 83 x 16 In. 1232.00
Bookcase, Oak, Door, Carved Rope Trim, Key, c.1920, 25 x 49 x 12 In. 575.00
Bookcase, Oak, Revolving, Barley Twist Columns, Cane Panels, 32 In. 935.00
Bookcase, Oak, Revolving, Shelves, Drawers, Beaded, c.1910, 48 x 22 In. 324.00
Bookcase, Open Shelves, Ogee Molding, Bracket Feet, c.1900, 81 x 39 x 13 In. 425.00
Bookcase, Regency, Mahogany, Ebony Inlay, Geometric Glazed Doors, 95 x 60 x 15 In.. 5288.00
Bookcase, Regency, Mahogany, Geometric Glazed Doors, Drawers, 88 x 47 x 11 In.. 4935.00
Bookcase, Regency Style, Mahogany, 2 Sections, Grillwork, 1800s, 93 x 54 In. 1840.00
Bookcase, Regency Style, Mahogany, England, 19th Century, 92 x 54 x 16 In. *illus* 1800.00
Bookcase, Renaissance Revival, Circassian Burl, Walnut Panels, Minerva Crest 17930.00
Bookcase, Renaissance Revival, Mahogany, Carved, 19th Century, 92 ½ x 21 In. 9988.00
Bookcase, Renaissance Revival, Oak, Carved, Vines, Glass Doors, Shelves, 65 x 76 In. 8225.00
Bookcase, Renaissance Revival, Walnut, 3 Doors, Raised Panels, c.1860, 78 x 82 In.. 1540.00
Bookcase, Renaissance Revival, Walnut, Doors, Crest, Raised Panels, c.1860, 105 x 70 In. 4950.00
Bookcase, Rhododendron, Laurel Roots, Crackled Paint, c.1910, 59 x 36 In. *illus* 2400.00
Bookcase, Stand, Georgian Style, Mahogany, Greek Key Cornice, 80 x 44 x 15 In. 2585.00
Bookcase, Stickley Bros., 2 Doors, Paneled Ends, 20th Century, 55 x 49 x 12 In. 1650.00
Bookcase, Transitional, Walnut, Turned Finials, Gallery Top, c.1870, 90 x 54 In.. 1980.00
Bookcase, Walnut, Flared Ogee Cornice, Glazed Doors, Drawers, c.1830, 88 x 48 x 21 In. 1960.00
Bookcase, Walnut, Incised Decoration, 2 Drawers, Glazed Doors, 84 x 50 x 19 In. 767.00
Bookcase, Walnut, Victorian, 4 Doors Over Drawer, 74 x 44 x 20 In. 767.00
Bookcase-Cabinet, George III, Chippendale Style, Arched Astragals, 93 x 93 In. 46000.00
Bookcase-Chest, Mahogany, H.F. Co. Ld., 19th Century, 84 x 49 x 23 In. *illus* 735.00
Bookrack, Arts & Crafts, Mahogany, 4 Shelves, Shoefoot Base, 36 x 17 ½ x 56 In.. 390.00
Bookrack, G. Stickley, Oak, c.1902, 30 ¾ x 32 ¾ x 10 In. 1320.00
Bookrack, Marquetry, Woman & Young Girl Kneeling, 6 ¼ x 13 ¾ In. 58.00
Bookrack, Oak, Expanding, Fretwork Back, Sides, Scrolls, Late 1800s, 10 x 23 In. 403.00
Bookstand, Arts & Crafts, Octagonal Top, Carved, Barley Twist Legs, 24 x 24 x 26 In. 570.00
Bookstand, Biedermeier, Fruitwood, Lyriform, Dolphins, Putto, Austria, 23 ½ x 15 In. 1560.00
Bookstand, Burl, Rococo Style, Scroll, Sawn, Adjustable Easel Back, 9 x 14 x 11 In. 2448.00
Bookstand, G. Stickley, 3 Shelves, Slab Cutout Sides, 1904, 30 x 38 In. 4875.00
Bookstand, Italian Baroque, Walnut, Collapsing X-Shape, Scalloped Supports, 53 x 21 In. 863.00
Bookstand, Limbert, Inset Cane Sides, 2 Shelves, Arched Toeboard, 18 x 11 x 32 In. 1200.00
Bookstand, Mahogany, Adjustable Back, Round Base, Mid 19th Century, 13 x 10 x 6 ½ In. 1058.00
Bookstand, Oak, Gothic Style, Hinged Easel, Fleur-De-Lis, 22 x 16 In. 432.00
Bookstand, Peg Leg Base, 29 In. 72.00
Bookstand, Pierced Carved Scroll, Ratched Holder, Geometric Feet, 7 x 14 x 13 In. 343.00
Bookstand, Renaissance Style, Gilded Walnut, Swan Leaves, Eagle, c.1890, 13 x 19 In. 2400.00
Bookstand, Roycroft, Little Journeys, Oak, 2 Shelves, 26 x 14 x 26 In.. 900.00
Bottle Carrier, George III, Brass, Mahogany, Sliding Panels, Bail Handle, 13 x 11 In.. 7500.00
Bracket, Gilt, Scalloped Plinth, Scrolled Leafy Sprays, Italy, 1900s, 12 x 5 In. 129.00
Bracket, Wall, Renaissance, Carved Walnut, Lion's Head, c.1875, 11 x 11 ¾ In., Pair 705.00
Breakfront, Chippendale Style, Mahogany, S. Hille & Co., London, c.1900, 81 x 75 x 16 In. *illus* 1900.00
Breakfront, George III Style, Mahogany, 4 Glazed Doors, Shelves, 86 x 82 x 20 In. 1645.00
Breakfront, George III Style, Mahogany, 6 Doors, Shelves, Plinth, 80 x 60 x 22 In. 2832.00
Breakfront, George III Style, Mahogany, Inlay, 2 Sections, Glazed Doors, 96 x 96 x 21 In. 6300.00
Breakfront, Renaissance Revival, Walnut, Swags, Figures, Fruit Basket, c.1850, 123 x 80 In. *illus* 12000.00
Breakfront, William IV, Mahogany, Molded Cornice, Shelves, 89 x 106 In. 2938.00
Breakfront-Bookcase, George III Style, Pine, Panel Doors, Drawers, 96 x 140 In. 4320.00
Breakfront-Bookcase, Georgian Style, Pine, Glazed Door, Shelves, Drawer, 80 x 48 In. 590.00
Breakfront-Bookcase, Regency Style, Walnut, Drop Front, Grill Doors, 85 x 74 In. 6000.00
Buffet, French Provincial, Drawers, 2 Doors, Stars, Floral Sprays, 39 ¾ x 74 ¾ x 18 In. 940.00
Buffet, French Provincial, Fruitwood, Drawers, Cupboard Doors, Medallion, 40 x 23 In. 3360.00
Buffet, French Provincial, Oak, Diamond Pattern Drawers, Cupboard, 49 x 64 In.. 2880.00
Buffet, Louis XVI, Oak, Marble Top, Late 18th Century, 42 ½ x 58 x 27 In. 2644.00
Buffet, Louis XVI Style, Mottled Marble Slab, Porcelain Appliques, 1900s, 38 x 84 In. 767.00
Buffet, Neoclassical Revival, Mahogany, Satinwood, Dutch, 33 ½ x 36 x 21 ½ In. 2950.00

Furniture, Bench, Mammy, Mixed Woods, Stenciled, Bamboo Spindles, c.1820, 34 x 60 In.
$1495.00

Furniture, Bench, Pine, Curved Arms, Arched Cutout Feet, 22 x 18 x 11 In.
$165.00

Furniture, Bench, Regency Style, Frieze, Applied Flowers, Gilt, 20 x 47 x 18 In., Pair
$2000.00

Furniture, Bench Bed, Provincial, Pine, Hinged Seat, Fold-Out, 36 x 76 x 18 In.
$600.00

Furniture, Bookcase, Globe-Wernicke Co., Oak, Stacking, c.1900, 79 x 34 x 12 In.
$1200.00

Furniture, Bookcase, Napoleon III, Mahogany, 4 Doors, Beveled Glass, 111 x 107 x 21 In.
$5000.00

Furniture, Bookcase, Regency Style, Mahogany, England, 19th Century, 92 x 54 x 16 In.
$1800.00

Furniture, Bookcase, Rhododendron, Laurel Roots, Crackled Paint, c.1910, 59 x 36 In.
$2400.00

Furniture, Bookcase-Chest, Mahogany, H.F. Co. Ld., 19th Century, 84 x 49 x 23 In.
$735.00

Buffet, Oak, Carved, 2 Drawers Over Paneled Doors, Continental, 39¾ x 55 x 22 In. 1200.00

Buffet, Provincial, Louis XV, Fruitwood, 3 Drawers, Paneled Doors, 40 x 61 In. 10200.00

Buffet, Provincial, Louis XV Style, Fruitwood, Drawers, Cupboards, 1800s, 38 x 40 In. 2880.00

Buffet, Provincial, Louis XV Style, Pine, Turreted Corners, Panel Drawers, 41 x 51 In. 3120.00

Buffet, Provincial, Mahogany, 2 Doors, Diamond Inset, Continental, 45 x 64 x 25 In. 3360.00

Buffet, Provincial, Oak, Molded Edge, Cupboard Doors, Scrolling Panels, 38 x 76 In. 3360.00

Buffet, Provincial, Louis XV Style, Oak, Plank Top, 3 Panel Drawers, Doors, 34 x 75 In. 5520.00

Bureau, Bombe, Chippendale, Mahogany, Slant Front, Stepped Drawers, 42 x 41 In. 2006.00

Bureau, Chippendale, Kneehole Front, 9 Drawers, Paneled Door, Mass., 30 x 35 In. 2760.00

Bureau, Dressing, Rococo Revival, Mahogany, Mirror, Carved Leaf, Drawers, 79 x 42 In. 600.00

Bureau, Edwardian, Mahogany, Louis XVI Style, Tambour, Leather Surface, 34 x 29 In. 2640.00

Bureau, Faux, Bamboo, Maple, Mirror, 3 Drawers, Casters, 1910, 31 x 44 x 21 In. 4405.00

Bureau, Federal, Mahogany, Bowfront, 4 Drawers, c.1800, 36 x 42 x 21 In. 2820.00

Bureau, Federal, Maple, Wavy Birch Veneer, Swellfront, c.1815, 38 x 40 In. 3819.00

Bureau, Federal, Pine, Painted, 4¾ x 2¾ In. 3600.00

Bureau, Figures, Flowers, Ebonized, Porcelain, Meissen, c.1890, 52 x 43 In. *illus* 61200.00

Bureau, George III, Mahogany, Walnut, Slant Front, Leather, Cubbyholes, 41 x 38 In. 3840.00

Bureau, George III, Walnut, Slant Front, 3 Drawers, Herringbone Banding, 38 x 28 In. 2640.00

Bureau, Mahogany, Slant Front, Fitted Interior, 42 x 40 x 21 In. 1880.00

Bureau, Northern Italian, Walnut, Slant Front, Fitted Interior, c.1780, 42 x 36 x 23 In. 4113.00

Bureau, Provincial, Cherry, Slant Front, Drawers, Cubbyholes, 44 x 51 x 23 In. 2730.00

Bureau, Renaissance Revival, Oak, Candlestands, Handkerchief Boxes, 33 x 43 x 20 In. 660.00

Bureau, Shaker, Cherry, Casters, 19th Century, 45½ x 34 x 18 In. *illus* 2000.00

Bureau, Shaker, Cherry, Poplar, 2-Door Top, Arcaded Interior, 45 x 34 In. 2070.00

Bureau, Sheraton, 5 Drawers, Reeded Pilasters, American Eagle Brasses, 40 x 43 In. 460.00

Bureau, Sheraton, Bowfront, Mahogany, Reeded Columns, c.1800, 40 x 43 x 22 In. 747.00

Bureau, Sheraton, Cherry, 5 Drawers, 19th Century, 43½ x 40½ In. 690.00

Bureau, Victorian, Rosewood, Marble Top, Arched Mirror, Shelves, 89 x 51 x 25 In. 3231.00

Bureau-Bookcase, Georgian, Walnut, Leather Writing Surface, 86 x 43 x 24 In. 13512.00

Cabinet, Art Nouveau, Fruitwood, Devil Finial, Flowers, Leaves, Dragon, 35 x 26 In. 2415.00

Cabinet, Arts & Crafts, 3 Drawers, Wood Knobs, 17 x 17 x 27 In. 270.00

Cabinet, Arts & Crafts, Oak, 3 Doors, Religious Figures, Lock, 43 x 63 x 20 In. 1568.00

Cabinet, Arts & Crafts, Oak, Door, Pierced Gothic Circle & Arch Design, 56 x 47 In. 2160.00

Cabinet, Arts & Crafts, Oak, Landscape, Pyrography, Iron Hinges, 58 x 25 x 16 In. *illus* 1285.00

Cabinet, Barber, 5 Drawers, Bakelite Handles, 46 x 13 x 18 In. 201.00

Cabinet, Barber, Chestnut, Shaving Mug Display, Marble Top, 3 Mirrors, 86 x 94 In. 575.00

Cabinet, Barber, Chestnut, Walnut, Poplar, Dovetailed Drawer, Razor Slots, 13 x 10 In. 575.00

Cabinet, Barber, Oak, Shaving Mug Display, 2 Glass Doors, 75 x 96 In. 4888.00

Cabinet, Bedside, Mahogany, Rectangular, Pierced, Drawer, Apron, 34 x 22 x 21 In. 1175.00

Cabinet, Beech, Lacquered, 2 Drawers, Chinese, 51½ x 32 x 15 In., Pair 1534.00

Cabinet, Biedermeier, Fruitwood, Drawer, 2 Doors, Boat-Shape Cutout, 60 x 36 In. 1560.00

Cabinet, Biedermeier, Mahogany, Marble Top, Round, Fluted, Door, 29 x 16 In. 984.00

Cabinet, Black Lacquer, Grillwork Doors, Asian, 43½ x 27 x 20 In. *illus* 485.00

Cabinet, C. Boulle, Bronze Mounts, c.1880, 40 x 33 In. 2310.00

Cabinet, Carved Wood, Flower Hearts, Scrolling Leaves, India, 39½ x 51½ x 23 In. 325.00

Cabinet, China, 2 Doors, Removable Shelves, 55 x 46 x 15 In. 1920.00

Cabinet, China, Arts & Crafts, Door, Divided Glass Panels, 3 Shelves, 49 x 15 x 56 In. 960.00

Cabinet, China, Empire Revival, Mahogany, Bow Front, Paw Feet, c.1900, 69 x 48 In. 5390.00

Cabinet, China, G. Stickley, 2 Doors, 3 Shelves, 70 x 50 x 17¼ In. 10800.00

Cabinet, China, G. Stickley, 2 Doors, Glass Panes, Copper, No. 815, 42 x 15 x 65 In. 6600.00

Cabinet, China, G. Stickley, 2 Glass Doors, 2 Cabinet Doors, 2 Shelves, 40 x 14 x 60 In. 960.00

Cabinet, China, G. Stickley, Door, Gallery Top, 58 x 36 x 13 In. 3240.00

Cabinet, China, G. Stickley, Oak, 2 8-Pane Doors, Red Decal, c.1904, 63½ In. 8125.00

Cabinet, China, L. & J.G. Stickley, 2 Doors, Copper, Arched Toe Board, 44 x 16 x 62 In. 9600.00

Cabinet, China, L. & J.G. Stickley, 2 Doors, Fixed Shelves, 62¾ x 42 x 15 In. 3120.00

Cabinet, China, Limbert, 3 Doors, 3 Shelves, 62¾ x 64½ x 18¼ In. 6600.00

Cabinet, China, Mission Style, Oak, Glazed Panel Door, Post Feet, 69 x 46 x 18 In. 944.00

Cabinet, China, Oak, Curved Glass, Claw Feet, 68 x 50 x 20 In. 649.00

Cabinet, China, Oak, Griffin, Bowed Glass, Canopy Top, Mirrored Back, c.1890, 85 x 51 In. 5775.00

Cabinet, China, Sectional, Kingwood, Satinwood Veneer, Crossband, 71 x 72 x 25 In. 590.00

Cabinet, China, Stickley Bros., Oak, 2 Doors, Hardware, Shelves, 56 x 37 x 14 In. 1528.00

Cabinet, Chinese, Red Lacquer, Mortised Construction, 2 Blind Doors, Brass, 45 x 22 In. 180.00

Cabinet, Chinese, Walnut, Red Lacquer, Drawer, 2 Doors, Openwork, 1700s, 28 x 32 In. 826.00

Cabinet, Chippendale Style, Mahogany, Broken Arch Crest, c.1900, 71 x 33 In. 1763.00

Cabinet, Corner, Biedermeier, Mahogany, 2 Sections, Paneled Door, Drawer, 81 x 42 In. 646.00

Cabinet, Corner, Centennial, Mahogany, Scrolled Pediment, Flame Finials, 91 x 43 In. 1650.00

Cabinet, Corner, Chippendale, Cherry, 12-Pane Door, H-Hinges, 80 x 42½ x 20 In. 4025.00
Cabinet, Corner, Continental Rococo, Fruitwood, c.1790, 30 x 27 x 20 In. 470.00
Cabinet, Corner, Federal, Mahogany, Glazed Door, 2 Piece, 78¼ x 38½ x 21 In. 2300.00
Cabinet, Corner, Federal, Pine, Stained, 4 Shelves, 2 Doors, Bracket Feet, 83 x 56 In. 3163.00
Cabinet, Corner, Federal, Mahogany, 2 Parts, Glazed Doors, Shelves, 89¼ x 47 x 23 In. 5175.00
Cabinet, Corner, Flowers, Painted, Pa., Late 18th Century, 90 x 52 x 17 In. .... *illus* 1980.00
Cabinet, Corner, French Provincial, Fruitwood, Triangular Top, Drawer, 37 x 26 In. 646.00
Cabinet, Corner, Georgian, Oak, Arched Paneled Door, 3 Shelves, Mid 1700s, 42 x 31 In. 531.00
Cabinet, Corner, Georgian Style, Pine, Hanging, Arched Door, 36½ x 22 x 15 In. 390.00
Cabinet, Corner, Hanging, Mahogany, Astragal Glazed Door, 44½ In. 1035.00
Cabinet, Corner, Louis Philippe, Mahogany, 19th Century, 37 x 23 x 16½ In., Pair 2233.00
Cabinet, Corner, Oak, Double Curved Glass, 59 In. 1395.00
Cabinet, Corner, Oak, 3 Drawers, Wavy Glass, 2 Piece, 103 x 55 In. 1495.00
Cabinet, Corner, Satinwood, Arched Mullioned Doors, Pediment Top, c.1865 .... 3737.00
Cabinet, Corner, Walnut, 3 Graduating Open Shelves, 2 Doors, 1800s, 32 x 20 In. 177.00
Cabinet, Corner, Walnut, 2 Sections, Raised Panel Doors, c.1830, 84 x 56 In. 1870.00
Cabinet, Display, Aesthetic Revival, Marquetry, Rosewood, Walnut, c.1880, 72 x 58 In. 48000.00
Cabinet, Display, Arts & Crafts, Oak, Faceted Posts, Leaded Glass, Shelves, 63 x 38 In. 800.00
Cabinet, Display, Chinese, Hong Mu, Shelves, Doors, Openwork Scenes, 77 x 37 x 15 In. 4406.00
Cabinet, Display, Chinese, Rosewood, Carved, Pierced, 2 Doors, Shelves, 38 x 39 x 14 In. 3055.00
Cabinet, Display, Chinese, Rosewood, Carved Flowers, c.1880, 61 x 34 x 15 In. 3408.00
Cabinet, Display, Chinese, Wood, Painted, Drawers, Ring Handles, 80 x 61 x 15 In. 1296.00
Cabinet, Display, Edwardian, Fruitwood, Mother-Of-Pearl, Glass Doors, 73 x 46 x 16 In. 646.00
Cabinet, Display, Flowers, Lacquered Panels, Ivory Inset, Mother-Of-Pearl, 82 x 51 x 15 In. .. 1410.00
Cabinet, Display, G. Nelson, Birch, Glass Doors, Shelf, 34 x 12 x 24 In. 270.00
Cabinet, Display, Gothic Revival, Ebonized, Spire Finials, Frieze, Quatrefoils, 55 x 29 In. 1116.00
Cabinet, Display, Louis Phillippe, Mahogany, Stepped Cornice, Glazed Door, 84 x 42 In. 1645.00
Cabinet, Display, Louis XV, Parquetry, Bronze Accents, 19th Century, 67 x 50 In. 495.00
Cabinet, Display, Louis XV Style, Mahogany, Glass Door, Ormolu Banding, 66 x 27 In. 460.00
Cabinet, Display, Mediterranean Revival, Pine, 4 Carved Doors, 104 x 102 x 17 In. 478.00
Cabinet, Display, Oak, Glass, 3 Shelves, 20th Century, 42 x 20 x 14 In. 325.00
Cabinet, Display, Regency, Mahogany, Arched Figured Doors, 22 x 20 In. 852.00
Cabinet, Display, Victorian, Rosewood, Hanging, 45 x 28 In. 550.00
Cabinet, Door, Silver Pull, Green Key Pattern, Shelf, 32 x 30½ x 15¼ In., Pair 12000.00
Cabinet, Dutch Marquetry, Light, Flower & Bird Inlay, Late 19th Century, 22 x 50 In. 288.00
Cabinet, Ebonized, Mirrored, Glass Top, 27¾ x 25 x 15¾ In., Pair 3120.00
Cabinet, Edwardian, Mahogany, Bowfront, Raised Back Panel, Glazed Doors, 32 x 34 In. 472.00
Cabinet, Edwardian, Satinwood, Corner, Broken Arch, 48 x 18 x 10 In., Pair .... *illus* 6000.00
Cabinet, Empire, Mahogany, Mint Julep, Mirrored Door, Scroll Feet, c.1830, 41 x 37 In. 5610.00
Cabinet, Empire, Walnut, Pedestal, Round Top, Turned Knop, Shelves, 1800s, 33 x 18 In. 764.00
Cabinet, Empire Revival, Mahogany, Leaded Glass, 61 x 39 In. 1925.00
Cabinet, F. Knoll, Walnut, Shallow Case, 2 Sliding Doors, Tapered Legs, 40 x 12 x 29 In. 390.00
Cabinet, Faux Bamboo, Black Paint, Drawer, Cupboard Doors, 63 x 42 In. 470.00
Cabinet, Federal, Inlaid Mahogany, 2 Doors, False Drawer Front, Shelves, 29 x 30 In. 1495.00
Cabinet, French Gothic, Oak, Carved, Removable Cornice, Door, Drawer, 96 x 37 In. 1840.00
Cabinet, G. Nakashima, Walnut, 2 Sliding Doors, 4 Drawers, 2 Shelves, 32 x 50 x 20 In. 7800.00
Cabinet, Galvanized Metal, 2 Glazed Doors, Square Legs, 48 x 30 In., Pair 1200.00
Cabinet, Galvanized Metal, Square, Cupboard Door, Square Legs, 26 x 18 x 16 In., Pair 780.00
Cabinet, George III Regency, Mahogany, Shelves, Drawers, 2 Doors, 65 x 35 x 18 In. 2478.00
Cabinet, George III Style, Beech, Molded Cornice, Fitted Case Doors, 90 x 46 In. 960.00
Cabinet, George III Style, Pine, 2 Parts, Egg & Dart Molding, 90 x 60 x 28 In. .... *illus* 3200.00
Cabinet, Georgian, Inlaid Mahogany, Mullion Glazed Doors, 2 Drawers, 83 x 44 In. 3335.00
Cabinet, H. Probber, Drop Front, Mahogany, Lower Shelf, 42 x 18 x 43¾ In. 900.00
Cabinet, Hanging, G. Nakashima, Walnut, Sliding Doors, Shelves, 14 x 72 x 14 In. 14400.00
Cabinet, Hanging, Rosewood, 2 Doors, Bas Relief, Moorish Couple, 24 x 29 x 5 In. 858.00
Cabinet, Hanging, Victorian, Faux Bamboo, Grill Inset, Drawer, Shelves, 33 x 21 In. 705.00
Cabinet, Hanging, Walnut, 5 Drawers, c.1962, 108⅝ x 17¼ In. 11400.00
Cabinet, Italian Baroque, Oak, Shaped Top, Door, Bracket Feet, c.1720, 35 x 28 In. 3981.00
Cabinet, Italian Baroque, Walnut, Carved, Marble Top, Paneled, Dog Feet, 41 x 39 In. 2875.00
Cabinet, Italian Baroque, Walnut, Frieze Drawer, 2 Doors, Shelves, Paw Feet, 35 x 35 In. 3450.00
Cabinet, Italian Baroque, Walnut, Carved, 2 Drawers Over Doors, Paw Feet, 35 x 44 In. 4600.00
Cabinet, Italian Renaissance Revival, Ivory, Stone Inset, Ebonized, c.1880, 76 x 48 In. 4700.00
Cabinet, Jewelry, Gilt, Black Lacquer, Mandarin's Garden, Chinese Export, 19 x 16 In. 1560.00
Cabinet, Jules Leleu, Bar, Mahogany, Parquetry, Brass, c.1940, 51½ x 33 x 16 In. 4800.00
Cabinet, L. & J.G. Stickley, 2 Doors Over Doors, 12 Panes, 70 x 17 x 50 In. .... *illus* 15800.00
Cabinet, Lacquered, Red, Landscape, Cupboard Doors, Asia, 39 x 28 In. 30.00

Furniture, Breakfront, Chippendale Style, Mahogany, S. Hille & Co., London, c.1900, 81 x 75 x 16 In.
$1900.00

Furniture, Breakfront, Renaissance Revival, Walnut, Swags, Figures, Fruit Basket, c.1850, 123 x 80 In.
$12000.00

Furniture, Bureau, Figures, Flowers, Ebonized, Porcelain, Meissen, c.1890, 52 x 43 In.
$61200.00

Furniture, Bureau, Shaker, Cherry, Casters, 19th Century, 45½ x 34 x 18 In.
$2000.00

F

Furniture, Cabinet, Arts & Crafts, Oak, Landscape, Pyrography, Iron Hinges, 58 x 25 x 16 In.
$1285.00

Furniture, Cabinet, Black Lacquer, Grillwork Doors, Asian, 43 ½ x 27 x 20 In.
$485.00

Furniture, Cabinet, Corner, Flowers, Painted, Pa., Late 18th Century, 90 x 52 x 17 In.
$1980.00

Cabinet, Lawyer's, Walnut, Revolving, Drawers, 2 Doors, Shelves, 48 x 25 x 25 In. 2115.00
Cabinet, Library, Ash, Oak, Card Catalog, 24 Drawers, Mid 1900s, 68 x 40 In. 796.00
Cabinet, Lifetime, Overhanging Top, Drawer, Shoefoot Base, 44 x 18 x 30 In. 3000.00
Cabinet, Loewy, 6 Drawers, Door, Red, Orange, 60 ¾ x 21 ¾ x 29 ¾ In. 2160.00
Cabinet, Louis XVI, Carved, Gilt, 2 Doors Open To Side, Fluted Legs, 60 x 43 x 16 In. 5581.00
Cabinet, Louis XVI, Fruitwood, Sham Front Drawers, Door, Shelves, 54 x 42 x 16 In. 705.00
Cabinet, Louis XVI Style, Drawer Over Door, Inlaid, Ormolu Mounts, 1900s, 39 x 36 In. 590.00
Cabinet, Louis XVI Style, Kingwood, Gilt, Bronze, Marble Top, 44 x 46 x 19 In. .... *illus* 1400.00
Cabinet, Louis XVI Style, Mahogany, Marble Top, 2 Glazed Doors, 44 ¼ x 39 x 15 In. 2700.00
Cabinet, Louis XVI Style, Marble Top, Parquetry Veneers, Bronze Mounts, 30 x 22 In. 460.00
Cabinet, Louis XVI Style, Parquetry Veneer, Marble, France, 30 x 22 x 13 In. .... *illus* 465.00
Cabinet, Louis XVI Style, Polychrome, Parcel Gilt, Molded Cornice, 89 x 47 In., Pair 4800.00
Cabinet, Mahogany, 2 Doors, 4 Drawers, Ole Wanscher, c.1940, 63 ¼ x 48 x 16 In. 8400.00
Cabinet, Mahogany, Fitted Pedestal, Molded Top, Paneled Sides, Drawers, 38 x 27 In. 705.00
Cabinet, Mahogany, Frieze Drawers, Gothic Panels, Saber Legs, 47 x 18 x 24 In., Pair 2467.00
Cabinet, Mahogany, Lacquered Parchment, 4 Drawers, 2 Doors, c.1940, 71 ½ x 39 In. 9600.00
Cabinet, Mahogany, Marble Top, Cylindrical, Door, 19th Century, 28 x 15 In. 489.00
Cabinet, Mahogany, Mid 19th Century, 65 ½ x 32 x 17 ½ In. 2350.00
Cabinet, Mahogany, Round, Mid 19th Century, 14 In. Diam. 510.00
Cabinet, Mirror, Napoleon III, Gilt, Marble Top, Trisected Mirror, 41 x 48 In. 5520.00
Cabinet, Moorish Revival, Hardwood, Mother-Of-Pearl, Geometrics, 87 x 55 x 17 In. 3884.00
Cabinet, Music, G. Stickley, Amber Glass Door, 4 Shelves, 47 ¼ x 20 x 16 In. 9000.00
Cabinet, Music, Louis XV Style, Mahogany, 19th Century, 33 ½ x 25 In. 1528.00
Cabinet, Music, Louis XVI Style, Gilt, Painted, Scroll Backsplash, 48 x 21 In. 353.00
Cabinet, Music, Marble Top, Marquetry, Scrolls, Carved, Paw Feet, 44 x 23 x 16 In. 8050.00
Cabinet, Music, Verni Martin, Marble Top, Gallery Top, Bronze Trim, c.1880, 56 x 23 In. 880.00
Cabinet, Neoclassical, Door, Inlaid Coat Of Arms, Banded Surrounds, 30 x 21 In. 1725.00
Cabinet, Neoclassical, Dutch, Mahogany, Landscape, 33 ½ x 30 x 18 ½ In. 2350.00
Cabinet, Oak, Built-In, Wainscot Back, Drawers, 2 Doors, 50 x 15 x 88 In. 2495.00
Cabinet, Oak, Glass Doors, 4 Shelves, 2 Drawers, Carved, Frieze, c.1900, 84 x 50 x 18 In. 400.00
Cabinet, Pedestal, Frieze Drawer, Door, Interior Shelf, Half Columns, 33 ⅝ x 22 In. 411.00
Cabinet, Pedestal, Regency, Backsplash, Frieze Drawer, Door, 43 ½ x 17 ½ In. 1645.00
Cabinet, Pine, 8-Sided, Drawers, Porcelain Pulls, 30 x 21 In. .... *illus* 1500.00
Cabinet, Pine, Painted, Flowers, Plank Top, 2 Doors, 3 Drawers, Iron Pulls, Tibet, 40 x 44 In. 600.00
Cabinet, Pine, Red Paint, 2-Panel Doors, 58 ½ x 45 ½ x 19 In. 1410.00
Cabinet, Print, Mahogany, Hinged Top, Folding Front, Dividers, Shoefoot Base, 42 x 17 In. 4700.00
Cabinet, Provincial, Walnut, Drawer, Cupboard, Paneled Door, Italy, 38 x 37 x 17 In. 1660.00
Cabinet, Provincial Louis XV Style, Ivory Paint, Paneled Door, Green Scrolls, 51 x 40 In. 2880.00
Cabinet, Provincial Neoclassical, Painted, Molded Cornice, Doors, 99 x 90 In. 12000.00
Cabinet, Queen Anne Style, Entertainment, Cherry, Late 20th Century, 78 x 61 In. 531.00
Cabinet, Red Lacquer, 2 Doors, Shelf, Birds, Flowers, Branches, Chinese, 43 x 31 In. 443.00
Cabinet, Red Lacquer, 2 Doors, 2 Shelves, Chinese, 71 x 44 x 30 In. 1003.00
Cabinet, Red Lacquer, 2 Drawers Over Doors, Brass Hardware, Chinese, 34 x 35 In. 748.00
Cabinet, Red Lacquer, Japanned, 4 Legs, 69 x 43 x 15 ½ In. 2032.00
Cabinet, Regency, Mahogany, Ormolu, Patinated Bronze, Jasper, c.1810, 36 x 47 In. 61000.00
Cabinet, Regency Style, Ormolu Mounted Mahogany, Bowed Top, Slide Doors, 35 x 37 In. 2880.00
Cabinet, Renaissance Revival, Ebonized, Ivory Inlaid, Paneled Door, 43 x 33 x 17 In. 1770.00
Cabinet, Renaissance Revival, Walnut, Inlaid, Ebonized, c.1890, 45 x 49 x 19 In. .... *illus* 2640.00
Cabinet, Renaissance Style, Burl, Mask, Leaf Carving, Italy, c.1880, 36 x 30 x 13 In. .... *illus* 2000.00
Cabinet, Renaissance Style, Walnut, Carved, Animals, Figures, Breakfront, 54 x 82 In. 11750.00
Cabinet, Rococo Style, Walnut, Panel Door, Cabriole Legs, Italy, 31 x 33 x 10 ½ In. 1121.00
Cabinet, Secretary, Victorian, Rosewood, Spiral Legs, Mid 19th Century, 74 x 36 In. .... *illus* 847.00
Cabinet, Sewing, Singer, Notions, Pincushion, 14 ¾ x 4 ¾ In. 73.00
Cabinet, Shaker, Pine, Door, 32 x 31 x 9 In. 780.00
Cabinet, Side, 4 Grilled Doors Over Solid Doors, Iron Ring Pulls, 41 x 56 x 18 In. 600.00
Cabinet, Side, Regency, Inlaid Mahogany, Crossbanded, Paneled Doors, 47 x 45 x 24 In. 470.00
Cabinet, Side, Regency, Rosewood, Lacquered, Gilt Metal Mount, 46 x 56 In. 9000.00
Cabinet, Sino-Tibetan, Polychrome, 2 Hinged Doors, Shaped Apron, 35 x 71 In. 1320.00
Cabinet, Sino-Tibetan, Polychrome, Red & Black, Shaped Borders, 35 x 75 In. 2040.00
Cabinet, Specimen, Inlaid Rosewood, Walnut, 7 Drawers, 2-Sided, 1800s, 27 x 19 In. 5980.00
Cabinet, Spice, Chippendale, Walnut, Single Door, Fitted Interior, Pa., 22 x 16 x 10 In. 4350.00
Cabinet, Spice, Walnut, 6 Drawers, Late 19th Century, 16 x 15 x 8 In. .... *illus* 269.00
Cabinet, Spice, Walnut, 8 Drawers, Wall Mounted, Curved Top, Turned Pulls, 18 x 10 In. 71.00
Cabinet, Spice, Wood, 6 Drawers, Tin Drawer Liner, Porcelain Pulls, 15 x 7 ½ In. 44.00
Cabinet, Step, Express Wood, Japan, 19th Century, 100 x 77 In. 2115.00
Cabinet, Storage, Chinese, Distressed, Black Paint, 2 Doors, Shaped Apron, 87 x 31 In. 2400.00

Cabinet, Storage, Chinese, Pine, 2 Double Doors Over 3 Drawers, 37 x 63 x 17¾ In. 1440.00
Cabinet, Storage, Chinese, Wood, Lacquered, Painted, 2 Doors, 37½ x 36½ x 21 In. 2376.00
Cabinet, Storage, Oak, Tambour Front, Hinged Fall Front, 56½ x 26 x 15 In. 1003.00
Cabinet, Storage, Wood, Red Paint, 2 Doors, Drawer, Tibet, 1800s, 35 x 51 x 16½ In. 1368.00
Cabinet, Valet, Loewy, Wood, Laminated, Red Fronts, Hinged Top, 20 x 20 x 39½ In. 1800.00
Cabinet, Victorian, Ebonized, Ormolu Mounted, Curved Glazed Doors, 38 x 60 x 15 In. 840.00
Cabinet, Victorian, Pillar & Scroll Style, Astragal Shape Top, Scroll Feet, 64 x 45 In. 189.00
Cabinet, Walnut, 3 Drawers, Recessed Handles, Interwoven Sliding Doors, 38 x 62 In. 4888.00
Cabinet, Walnut, Angled Doors, Shelves, Singer Label, c.1952, 38 x 40 x 18 In. 2400.00
Cabinet, Walnut, Double Door, 2 Raised Arch Paneled Doors, Continental, 29 x 12 In. 201.00
Cabinet, Walnut, Ebonized Serpentine, Drawer, Door, 61 x 29 x 17 In. 1175.00
Cabinet, Wedding, Chinese, Red Lacquer, Carved Doors, 1800s, 52 x 34 In. 400.00
Cabinet, Wormley, Walnut, 2 Bifold Doors, Carved Pulls, 32 x 20 x 29¼ In. 420.00
Cabinet, Yellow Pine, Cypress, White Pine, 4 Glazed Cupboards, Drawers, 93 x 83 In. 2880.00
Cabinet-On-Cabinet, Chinese, Carved, Painted, 2 Doors, Drawers, Footed, 55 x 25 In. 478.00
Cabinet-On-Stand, Chinese Chippendale Style, Mahogany, Marlboro Legs, 67 x 26 In. 2242.00
Cabinet-On-Stand, Chinoiserie Lacquer, England, 18th Century, 46 x 41 x 20 In. 2400.00
Cabinet-On-Stand, Dutch Colonial, Rosewood, Molding Cornice, Paneled Doors, 61 x 42 In. 2040.00
Candlestand, 2-Light, Iron, Steel, Spiral Twist, Arched Tripod Legs, 52 In. 7656.00
Candlestand, 2-Light, Wooden, Adjustable, Round Turned Base, Splayed Legs, 38 In. 1210.00
Candlestand, 2-Light, Wooden, Adjustable, Snake Foot, Tripod Base, 43 In. 1430.00
Candlestand, 2-Light, Wrought Iron, Adjustable, Nut Finial, Penny Feet, 51 In. 440.00
Candlestand, 3-Light, Wrought Iron, Handle, 56½ In. 110.00
Candlestand, Adjustable, Arm, Round Tabletop, T Base, Splayed Legs. 358.00
Candlestand, Adjustable, Pair Brass Bobeches, Oval Tray, Square Shaft, Brass Fixture 165.00
Candlestand, Adjustable, Round Base, Peg Legs, Old Green Paint, 34 In. 660.00
Candlestand, Apple Green Paint, Square Top, Tripod Base, New England, 26 x 16 In. 1528.00
Candlestand, Baronial Style, Wrought Iron, Turned Standard, Dome Legs, Spain, 50 x 14 In. 600.00
Candlestand, Birch, Maple, Cusped Corners, Urn & Baluster Support, c.1815, 27 x 15 In. 7480.00
Candlestand, Cherry, Dish Top, Tripod Base, Birdcage Support, c.1760. 6435.00
Candlestand, Cherry, Octagonal, String Inlay, Snake Foot Base, 25 x 15 In. 800.00
Candlestand, Cherry, Paint, Tray Top, Baluster Post, Cabriole Legs, Snake Feet, 14 x 14 In. 863.00
Candlestand, Cherry, Square Top, Snake Foot, Early 19th Century, 26¾ x 17¾ In. 495.00
Candlestand, Cherry, Square Tray Top, Slender Urn Post, Cabriole Legs, 18 x 27 In. 1265.00
Candlestand, Chippendale, Mahogany, c.1800, 29 x 17 In. 358.00
Candlestand, Chippendale, Mahogany, Tilt Top, Beaded Edge, Snake Feet, 26 x 21½ In. 633.00
Candlestand, Chippendale, Mahogany, Pie Crust, Tilt, Carved Legs, c.1780, 27 x 22 In. 1540.00
Candlestand, Country, Maple, Round Top, Faceted Shaft, T-Shape Base, 27 x 17½ In. 300.00
Candlestand, Dish Top, 2 Candlecups, Threaded Shaft, c.1790, 37 x 21 x 20 In. *illus* 1800.00
Candlestand, Federal, Cherry, Octagonal Tray Top, Early 19th Century, 27¾ x 16½ In. 470.00
Candlestand, Federal, Cherry, Octagonal Top, Vase & Ring-Turned Post, c.1810, 29 x 18 In. 470.00
Candlestand, Federal, Cherry, Inlaid, Square Top, Tripod Base, Maine, c.1810, 26 x 25 In. 3408.00
Candlestand, Federal, Maple, Oval Top, New England, Early 19th Century, 28 x 14 In. 441.00
Candlestand, Federal, Maple, Vase & Ring-Turned, Cabriole Legs, c.1790, 26 x 14 In. 940.00
Candlestand, Federal, Pine, Maple, Tilt Top, Black Over Green Paint, 20 x 19 In. 920.00
Candlestand, Federal, Walnut, Inlay, 29 x 14½ x 21¾ In. 4375.00
Candlestand, Federal Style, Tilt Top, Round Dish Top, Turned Standard, 30 x 19 In. 323.00
Candlestand, Fruitwood, Lathe Turned, Adjustable, Late 18th Century, 8 x 6 In., Pair. 920.00
Candlestand, Hardwoods, Dish Top, 2 Candleholder, Adjustable, Late 1800s, 39 In. 978.00
Candlestand, Hepplewhite, Walnut, Cherry, Drawer, Baluster Shaft, Tripod Base, 29 x 18 In. 663.00
Candlestand, Hooded, Adjustable, Tiger Maple Drawer, Tripod Base, Pad Feet 2970.00
Candlestand, Hooded Backsplash, Urn Turned Shaft, Tripod Base, Snake Feet. 1320.00
Candlestand, Mahogany, Molded Top, Vase & Ring Post, Tapered Legs, c.1820, 28 x 16 x 21 In. 470.00
Candlestand, Mahogany, Round Top, Turned Column, Snake Feet, 27 x 14 In. 1265.00
Candlestand, Mahogany, Square Top, Turned Pedestal, Snake Feet, 25 x 17 x 17 In. 632.00
Candlestand, Mahogany, Swivel Top, Box Mechanism, Carved, c.1780, 28 x 20 In. 633.00
Candlestand, Maple, Adjustable, Lathe Turned, Late 18th Century, 18 x 15 In. *illus* 431.00
Candlestand, Maple, Octagonal Top, Turned Shaft, Cruciform Base, New Eng., 14 x 11 In. 2185.00
Candlestand, Maple, Yellow Paint, Decorated, New England, c.1780, 27 x 15 In. 26400.00
Candlestand, Nutting, Windsor, Tripod 330.00
Candlestand, Peg Leg, Adjustable, Splayed Legs, 18¼ In. 330.00
Candlestand, Queen Anne, Birch, Tripod Feet, New England, c.1800, 25½ x 18½ In. 960.00
Candlestand, Queen Anne, Birchwood, c.1800, 25½ x 18½ In. 960.00
Candlestand, Queen Anne, Cherry, Square Top, Snake Feet, 27 x 16 x 16 In. 464.00
Candlestand, Queen Anne, Mahogany, Cherry Pedestal, Snake Feet, 27 x 16 x 17 In. 300.00
Candlestand, Queen Anne, Mahogany, Circular Top, Vase Shape Pedestal, 27 x 17 In. 345.00

Furniture, Cabinet, Edwardian, Satinwood, Corner, Broken Arch, 48 x 18 x 10 In., Pair
$6000.00

Furniture, Cabinet, George III Style, Pine, 2 Parts, Egg & Dart Molding, 90 x 60 x 28 In.
$3200.00

Furniture, Cabinet, L. & J.G. Stickley, 2 Doors Over Doors, 12 Panes, 70 x 17 x 50 In.
$15800.00

Handles
Many Victorian chests had mushroom-turned wooden knobs. But by the later part of the Victorian era, the leaf-carved handle or the molded, mass-produced leaf handle was used.

Furniture, Cabinet, Louis XVI Style, Kingwood, Gilt, Bronze, Marble Top, 44 x 46 x 19 In.
$1400.00

Furniture, Cabinet, Louis XVI Style, Parquetry Veneer, Marble, France, 30 x 22 x 13 In.
$465.00

Furniture, Cabinet, Pine, 8-Sided, Drawers, Porcelain Pulls, 30 x 21 In.
$1500.00

Furniture, Cabinet, Renaissance Revival, Walnut, Inlaid, Ebonized, c.1890, 45 x 49 x 19 In.
$2640.00

F

Candlestand, Queen Anne, Mahogany, Round Top, Cabriole Legs, c.1760, 19 3/8 In. 4183.00
Candlestand, Queen Anne, Mixed Woods, Rectangular Top, 25 x 15 x 16 In. . . . . *illus* 240.00
Candlestand, Queen Anne, Tilt Top, Walnut, Birdcage, Ring & Ball Shaft, 26 x 21 In. 2530.00
Candlestand, Sheet Iron, Red Paint, Adjustable, Conical, Sand Ballasted Base, 41 x 8 In. 633.00
Candlestand, Tilt Top, Birch, Scalloped Corners, Pedestal, Tripod, 30 x 18 x 19 In. 209.00
Candlestand, Tilt Top, Cherry, Octagonal, Spider Base, 18th Century, 29 x 21 x 14 In. 575.00
Candlestand, Tilt Top, Chippendale, Walnut, Round Dish Top, Late 1700s, 28 x 20 In. 382.00
Candlestand, Tilt Top, Federal, Inlaid Mahogany, Oval Top, Burl, 28 x 24 x 17 In. 230.00
Candlestand, Tilt Top, Federal, Cherry, Tripod Base, Fluted Rim, 28 x 23 In. 316.00
Candlestand, Tilt Top, Federal, Cherry, Oval, Inlay, Urn & Baluster Shaft, 29 x 16 In. 374.00
Candlestand, Tilt Top, Federal, Mahogany, Tripod, 29 1/4 x 24 x 19 1/4 In. 633.00
Candlestand, Tilt Top, Federal, Cherry, Inlay, Turned Post, Cabriole Legs, 29 x 23 In. 646.00
Candlestand, Tilt Top, Hepplewhite, Mahogany, Spurred Feet, c.1810, 29 x 26 In. . . . . . *illus* 403.00
Candlestand, Tilt Top, Oak, Round Top, Pedestal, Late 18th Century, 27 x 30 In. 220.00
Candlestand, Tilt Top, Papier-Mache Top, Black Lacquer, Painted Classical Ruins, 39 In. 633.00
Candlestand, Tilt Top, Queen Anne, Cherry, Snake Feet, Pennsylvania, 27 x 17 In. 754.00
Candlestand, Tilt Top, Queen Anne, Mahogany, Dish Top, 28 1/2 x 20 In. 4200.00
Candlestand, Tilt Top, Tripod, 19th Century, 28 1/2 x 22 x 16 In. 175.00
Candlestand, Tilt Top, Walnut, Oval, 19th Century, 24 x 18 x 28 In. 275.00
Candlestand, Walnut, Rotating Top, Turned Birdcage, Tripod, N.C., c.1830, 27 x 18 In. 4113.00
Candlestand, Windsor, Mixed Wood, Adjustable, Bamboo Legs, Stretcher, 42 In. 518.00
Candlestand, Wood, Adjustable, Tripod Stretcher Base, 30 In. 50.00
Candlestand, Wood, Adjustable, 2-Light, Turned Legs, 28 1/2 In. 578.00
Candlestand, Wood, Adjustable, Primitive Peg Legs, 32 In. 605.00
Candlestand, Wood, Primitive, Double Top, Pole Shaft, Oval Base, Red Patina, 44 1/2 In. 440.00
Candlestand, Wood, Turned Shaft, Tripod, 55 In. 33.00
Candlestand, Wrought & Cast Iron, 4 Curved Legs, Acorn Finial, 40 In. 862.00
Candlestand, Wrought Iron, 2-Light, Tripod, Penny Feet, 35 In. 110.00
Candlestand, Wrought Iron, Adjustable, Swing-Out Extension, Tripod, 45 1/2 In. 165.00
Candlestand, Wrought Iron, Adjustable, Swing-Out Extension, Urn Finial, 52 In. 385.00
Candlestand, Wrought Iron, Adjustable, Tripod, 48 1/2 In. 275.00
Candlestand, Wrought Iron, Tripod, 45 In. 39.00
Canterbury, Anglo-Indian, Bamboo, Compartments, Lacquer, c.1890, 35 x 22 x 15 In. . *illus* 600.00
Canterbury, Cherry, Burl, Rosewood, Drawer, 19th Century. 925.00
Canterbury, Continental, Bamboo Turned, Spindles, Turned Feet, 17 x 21 x 10 In. 240.00
Canterbury, Federal Style, Inlaid Mahogany, Dovetailed, Banded Drawer, 19 x 17 1/2 In. 546.00
Canterbury, Federal Style, Mahogany, Cypress, Ash, Inlaid Legs, c.1890, 19 x 17 x 13 In. *illus* 525.00
Canterbury, Mahogany Stain, Drawer, 23 x 21 3/4 x 17 1/2 In. 230.00
Canterbury, Regency, Mahogany, Drawer, Turned Legs, Brass Ferrules, 19 1/2 x 20 x 14 In. . . . 1320.00
Canterbury, Regency, Mahogany, 2 Tiers, 2 Drawers, Turned Legs, 41 x 22 x 22 In. 2937.00
Canterbury, Victorian, Mahogany, Openwork Scrolls, Flower Heads, c.1880, 18 x 22 In. 470.00
Canterbury, Victorian, Mahogany, Compartments, Drawer, Bulbous Feet, 21 x 21 In. 1320.00
Canterbury, Victorian, Walnut, Shelves, Drawer, Shaped Gallery, Finials, 17 x 19 x 13 In. . . . 173.00
Case, Display, Museum, Chinese Chippendale, Carved Stand, Glaze Top, Locks, 74 x 39 In. . . . 1062.00
Cellarette, Adam Style, Mahogany, Ram's Head Bronze Mounts, Hoof Feet, 29 x 20 In. 2415.00
Cellarette, Arts & Crafts, Drawers, Strap Hinges, Arched Toe Board, Shelf, 18 x 13 x 46 In. . . . 660.00
Cellarette, Arts & Crafts, Panel Door, Divided Interior, Sliding Tray, 20 x 14 1/2 x 38 In. 570.00
Cellarette, Federal, Walnut, Inlay, Bellflower Inlaid Legs, c.1825, 38 x 21 x 16 In. 3420.00
Cellarette, George III, Fruitwood, Square, Tapered Legs, 27 1/2 x 16 1/2 x 16 1/2 In. 1080.00
Cellarette, Hepplewhite, Cherry, Drawer, Mixing Slide, Stand, 39 x 16 x 15 In. 2990.00
Cellarette, Lakeside Craftshop, Flip Top, Slatted Door, Leaded Glass, Pipe Holders, 34 x 14 x 14 In. . 725.00
Cellarette, Limbert, Door, Oval Cutout, Recoated Finish, 34 x 14 x 36 In. 1800.00
Cellarette, Mahogany, Lead Lined, Brass Hardware, 19th Century, 22 x 32 x 19 In. 2990.00
Cellarette, Regency, Mahogany, Octagonal, Brass Banding, 27 1/8 x 18 1/8 In. 2468.00
Cellarette, Walnut, Pine, Flat Top, 4 Square Tapered Legs, 33 x 26 x 16 1/2 In. 18400.00
Chair, Adam, Satinwood, Arched Crest, Cane Seat, Scroll Arms, 37 In. 1410.00
Chair, Adam Style, Satinwood, Painted, Britain, c.1890, 39 x 22 x 21 In., Pair . . . . *illus* 835.00
Chair, Adam Style, Satinwood, Shield Back, Arms, Velvet Upholstery, 39 x 22 In., Pair 863.00
Chair, Aesthetic Revival, Beast-Head Finials, Arms, 1875, 18 In. 2585.00
Chair, Aesthetic Revival, Gilt Bronze, Rosewood, Tufted Back, Upholstered, c.1865, 17 In. 353.00
Chair, Aesthetic Revival, Openwork Backrest, Twig Spindles, Upholstered Seat, 35 x 19 In. . . . 1416.00
Chair, Art Deco, Brown Leather, Arched Crest, Wood Feet, Early 1900s, 32 x 29 In., Pair 3105.00
Chair, Arts & Crafts, Oak, Shaped Crest Rail, 2 Slats, Spring Cushion, Arms, 40 x 27 In. 206.00
Chair, Arts & Crafts, Oak, Carved Back, Posts, Rush Seat, Shaped Arms, c.1900, 38 x 33 In. . . . 748.00
Chair, Arts & Crafts, Wicker, Braided Crest, Upholstered, Pillow Cushion, Arms, 40 x 31 In. . . . 235.00
Chair, Arts & Crafts, Wood, Adjustable Back, Leather Seat & Back, 36 x 29 x 32 In. 900.00

Chair, Banister, Red Paint, Shaped Crest Rail, Flattened Ball Finials, 40 x 16½ In., Pair 863.00
Chair, Banister Back, Carved Crest, Rush Seat, Box Stretcher, Sloping Arms, 1700s, 46 In. 920.00
Chair, Banister Back, Mixed Woods, 4 Banisters, Acorn Finials, 1700s, 17½ x 43 In.......... 345.00
Chair, Banister Back, Paint, Rush Seat, Double Box Stretcher, Sausage Churn Front Legs, 42 x 16½ In. . 115.00
Chair, Banister Back, Paint, Double Box Stretcher, Splint Seat, 18th Century, 43 In. 201.00
Chair, Banister Back, Paint, Shaped Crest, Turned Finials, Splint Seat, Yellow, 40 In......... 402.00
Chair, Banister Back, Paint, Carved Crest, Spurs, Splint Seat, Turned Stretchers, 39 In....... 420.00
Chair, Barcelona, Leather, Chrome, 30 x 30 x 30 In. .... *illus* 2275.00
Chair, Baroque, Leather Seat, Back, Carved Finials, Stretchers, 39 x 20 In., Pair 863.00
Chair, Baroque Style, Diana, Huntress, Needlepoint, Spanish Feet, 47 x 27 In. 1058.00
Chair, Baroque Style, Oak, Carved Leaves, Barley Twist, Plank Seat, 18 In., Pair........... 235.00
Chair, Barrel Back, Turned Legs, Leather, Scroll Arms, 1800, 33 x 25 x 24 In............... 1760.00
Chair, Belter, Oak, Laminated, Arms, Fountain Elms.................................. 16854.00
Chair, Belter, Rococo Revival, Rosewood, Laminated, Ribbon Pattern, Arms, 42 In.......... 2640.00
Chair, Belter, Rosewood, Carved Crest, Back, Needlework Upholstered Seat, 40 x 18 In....... 2070.00
Chair, Belter, Rosewood, Fountain Elms 8050.00
Chair, Belter, Rosewood Laminate, Rosalie Without Grapes Pattern, 38 x 18 In............ 1265.00
Chair, Belter, Spingmeyer, Laminated, Plaid Upholstery 1654.00
Chair, Bergere, Biedermeier, Fruitwood, Double Arch Crest, Closed Arms, 35 x 24 In., Pair ... 767.00
Chair, Bergere, Louis Philippe Style, Mahogany, Arched Crests, Closed Arms, 37 In., Pair 1225.00
Chair, Bergere, Louis XV Style, Fruitwood, Padded Back, Closed Arms, 38 In. 600.00
Chair, Bergere, Louis XV Style, Molded Edge, Upholstered, Closed Arms, 32 x 26 x 21 In., Pair 1003.00
Chair, Bergere, Louis XV Style, Fruitwood, Carved, Padded, Arched Back, Closed Arms, 41 In., Pair 2160.00
Chair, Bergere, Louis XVI Style, Multicolored Cane, Seat, Closed Arms, 32 In............... 480.00
Chair, Bergere, Louis XVI Style, Petite, Music, Closed Arms, 1800s, 32 x 29 In. 590.00
Chair, Bergere, Louis XVI Style, Polychrome, Domed Back, Closed Arms, 40 In. 1080.00
Chair, Bergere, Louis XVI Style, Painted, Carved, Cane Backs, Seats, Closed Arms, 34 x 22 In., Pair 2350.00
Chair, Bergere, Louis XVI Style, Walnut, Domed, Padded, Floral Carved Crest, 39 In., Pair.... 4800.00
Chair, Bergere, Provincial Louis XV Style, Fruitwood, Leather, Closed Arms, 46 In........... 4560.00
Chair, Bergere, Regency, Rosewood Grained, Leather, Closed Arms, 19th Century, 31 In...... 2585.00
Chair, Bergere, Regency, Mahogany, Cane, Brass Caps, Casters, Closed Arms, 41 In.......... 3120.00
Chair, Bergere, Regency, Mahogany, Cane, Leather, Tapered Legs, Closed Arms, 33 In., Pair .. 5875.00
Chair, Bergere, Regency Style, Beech, Cane, Leather Cushion, Closed Arms, 22 In., Pair 3231.00
Chair, Bergere, Restauration, Blond Mahogany, Padded Back, Crest, Closed Arms, 36 In. 780.00
Chair, Bergere, Rococo, Rosewood, Crest Carved, Closed Arms, c.1850, 45 In.............. 4994.00
Chair, Bergere, Rococo Style, Marquetry, Closed Arms, c.1910, 36 x 29 In., Pair 826.00
Chair, Bishop's, Elizabethan Style, Barley Twist, Late 19th Century, 36 In. .... *illus* 650.00
Chair, Boardwalk Rolling Wicker, Leather Canopy, Windows, 68 x 45 x 61 In. 2300.00
Chair, Borge Mogensen, Oak, Leather, Arms, c.1950, 26½ In............................ 8400.00
Chair, Boudoir, Victorian, Mahogany, Chenille Upholstery, Turned Legs, 29 In............. 780.00
Chair, Burl Walnut, Woman's Mask, Carved Crest, Upholstered, c.1890, 43 In. .... *illus* 1970.00
Chair, Butterfly, Wrought Iron, Leather Sling Seat, Argentina, 1938, 33 x 30 x 36 In......... 360.00
Chair, Byzantine, Multicolored, Late 19th Century 4700.00
Chair, Caribbean, Hardwood, Cane Planters, Sling Back, 19th Century, 36 x 62 In. 2233.00
Chair, Carlo Mollino, Steel, Cutouts, Enamel, Upholstered, 38 x 13 x 20 In., Pair ...... *illus* 8400.00
Chair, Carved, Ivory & Gilt Paint, Upholstered Back, Seat, c.1850, 34 In................... 120.00
Chair, Carved, Painted, Italian Neoclassical, 18th Century, 41½ x 20 x 18 In............... 1880.00
Chair, Charles II, Walnut, Pierced Crest, Putti, England, 46½ x 19½ x 16 In.............. 1888.00
Chair, Chesterfield Style, Nailed Leather, Loose Cushion, Arms, 30 x 29 x 26 In., Pair 2124.00
Chair, Chinese, Carved, Rolling Wave Splat, Dragon Head Arms, c.1900, 35 x 26 In., Pair.... 468.00
Chair, Chinese, Elm Root, Intertwined Roots, Pair 177.00
Chair, Chinese, Huali Wood, Yoke Back, Splat, 18th Century 4406.00
Chair, Chinese, Natural Root Form, Plank Seat, Arms, 37 x 29 x 30 In., Pair 920.00
Chair, Chinese, Rosewood, 3 Drawers, Scrolled Feet, 32 x 48 x 21 In...................... 472.00
Chair, Chinese, Rosewood, Lacquer, Horseshoe Shape, Curved Splat, Spindles, 37 In., Pair ... 960.00
Chair, Chinese, Rosewood, Carved, Rose Medallion Plaques, 19th Century 2468.00
Chair, Chinese, Walnut, Lacquered, Square Back, 18th Century, 43 x 21 x 17 In. 531.00
Chair, Chinese, Wood, Carved, Dragon Back, Head, Arms, Cabriole Legs, 25 x 18 x 34 In. 112.00
Chair, Chinese, Wood, Open Back, Solid Seat, Stretcher, 1800s, 44 x 25 In., Pair........... 660.00
Chair, Chinese, Yoke Crest, Serpentine Pierced Vertical Splat, Decorated, 47 x 26 In......... 472.00
Chair, Chinese Export, Rosewood, Carved Back, Plank Seats, 38 x 25 In., Pair 900.00
Chair, Chinese Export, Rosewood, Flowers Back, Stone Insert, 39 x 25 In., Pair 1200.00
Chair, Chippendale, Acanthus Knees, Skirt, Paw Feet, Arms, Ireland, 1800s, 43 x 29 In...... 550.00
Chair, Chippendale, Carved Crest Rail, Pierced Gothic Splat, Slip Seat, c.1780, 38½ In...... 1840.00
Chair, Chippendale, Chestnut, Open Splat, Scrolled Crest Rail, Ears, c.1780, 16 In., Pair..... 633.00
Chair, Chippendale, Curly Maple, Heart Cutouts, Crest, Rush Seat, Square Legs, 40 In. 540.00

Furniture, Cabinet, Renaissance Style, Burl, Mask, Leaf Carving, Italy, c.1880, 36 x 30 x 13 In.
$2000.00

Furniture, Cabinet, Secretary, Victorian, Rosewood, Spiral Legs, Mid 19th Century, 74 x 36 In.
$847.00

Furniture, Cabinet, Spice, Walnut, 6 Drawers, Late 19th Century, 16 x 15 x 8 In.
$269.00

Furniture, Candlestand, Dish Top, 2 Candlecups, Threaded Shaft, c.1790, 37 x 21 x 20 In.
$1800.00

Furniture, Candlestand, Maple, Adjustable, Lathe Turned, Late 18th Century, 18 x 15 In.
$431.00

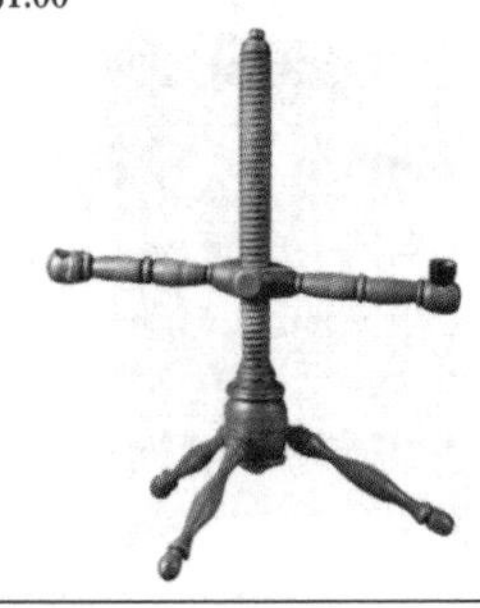

F

Furniture, Candlestand, Queen Anne, Mixed Woods, Rectangular Top, 25 x 15 x 16 In.
$240.00

Furniture, Candlestand, Tilt Top, Hepplewhite, Mahogany, Spurred Feet, c.1810, 29 x 26 In.
$403.00

Furniture, Canterbury, Anglo-Indian, Bamboo, Compartments, Lacquer, c.1890, 35 x 22 x 15 In.
$600.00

Chair, Chippendale, Mahogany, Ladder Back, 3 Carved Slats, Slip Seat, Stretcher, 37 In...... 345.00
Chair, Chippendale, Mahogany, Leaf & Rosette Carved Crest, Pierced Splat, 36 In........... 489.00
Chair, Chippendale, Mahogany, Ribbon Back, H-Stretcher, Pierced Crest Rail............. 598.00
Chair, Chippendale, Mahogany, Open Arms, Griffin Knees, Ireland, c.1870, 40 x 28 In....... 605.00
Chair, Chippendale, Mahogany, Voluted Ears, Pierced Splat, Upholstered 632.00
Chair, Chippendale, Mahogany, Carved, Leafy Pierced Crest, Splat, New Eng., c.1790, Pair ... 646.00
Chair, Chippendale, Mahogany, Flowers, Scrolls, Seat Rail, Claw & Ball Feet, 1770 .... 820.00
Chair, Chippendale, Mahogany, Tassel Back, Britain, 18th Century, 38 x 23 x 18 In..... *illus* 830.00
Chair, Chippendale, Mahogany, Shaped Splat, Scroll Arms, Lamb's Tongue, 36 x 28 x 21 In. . 990.00
Chair, Chippendale, Mahogany, Oak, Gothic Splat, Britain, c.1790, 38 x 25 x 18 In..... *illus* 1300.00
Chair, Chippendale, Mahogany, Shaped Crest Rail, Pierced Splat, Slip Seat, Child's, c.1770... 1380.00
Chair, Chippendale, Mahogany, Shell Carved Crest, Pierced Splat, 38 x 22 In., Pair 1380.00
Chair, Chippendale, Mahogany, Carved, Serpentine Crest, Owl Splat, c.1775, 37 In.......... 1528.00
Chair, Chippendale, Mahogany, Serpentine Crest, Fan, Pierced Owl Splat, Mass., 37 In....... 3770.00
Chair, Chippendale, Mahogany, Pierced Splat, Upholstered Seat, Arms, c.1790, 38 In........ 4560.00
Chair, Chippendale, Mahogany, Scrolled Terminals, Pierced Splat, c.1775 .... 4700.00
Chair, Chippendale, Mahogany, Shell Carved, Upholstered Seat, c.1765, 40 3/4 In............ 5875.00
Chair, Chippendale, Mahogany, Drop-In Seat, Cabriole Legs, Claw, Ball Feet, 40 x 24 In., Pair 8625.00
Chair, Chippendale, Mahogany, Upholstered, Cabriole Legs, Carved Crest, 37 1/2 In. 9600.00
Chair, Chippendale, Mahogany, Serpentine Crest Rail, Scrolled Ears, c.1760, 38 x 22 In...... 18000.00
Chair, Chippendale, Mahogany, Leaf Knees, Pierced Splat, c.1755, 39 In., Pair............. 90000.00
Chair, Chippendale, Maple, Pierced Splat, Spanish Feet, Mass., c.1790, 40 1/2 In............ 529.00
Chair, Chippendale, Mixed Wood, Outcurved Ears, Lyre Form Splat, 37 x 21 x 17 In......... 354.00
Chair, Chippendale, Pierced Serpentine Ribbon Back, 3 Slats, 37 In., Pair 1740.00
Chair, Chippendale, Pierced Splat, England, c.1780, 43 x 22 In., Pair 1320.00
Chair, Chippendale, Walnut, Carved Crest, Pierced Splat, Pad Feet, 1700s, 38 1/2 In. 1725.00
Chair, Chippendale, Walnut, Crest, Ears, Pierced Splat, Claw & Ball Feet, 39 In............ 2530.00
Chair, Chippendale, Walnut, Carved, Scroll Pierced Splat, c.1755, 41 In.................. 3840.00
Chair, Chippendale, Walnut, Yoke Crest Rail, Pierced Urn Shaped Splat, c.1750............ 9560.00
Chair, Chippendale, Wing, Mahogany, Straight Molded, Upholstered, 44 x 27 x 25 In........ 2970.00
Chair, Chippendale Style, Georgian, Upholstered, Arms, 36 1/2 x 26 In., Pair............... 1239.00
Chair, Chippendale Style, Mahogany, Reticulated Splat, Upholstered, Scroll Arms, 38 In. 382.00
Chair, Chippendale Style, Mahogany, Pierced Splat, Claw & Ball Feet, Arms, 40 In., Pair..... 489.00
Chair, Chippendale Style, Ribbon Back, Brown Finish, Cane Slip Seat, 17 1/2 x 38 In., Pair.... 58.00
Chair, Chippendale Style, Upholstered, Claw & Ball Feet, 44 1/2 x 31 x 34 In. 605.00
Chair, Chippendale Style, Wing, c.1920, 44 x 26 In., Pair 440.00
Chair, Club, Art Deco, Leather Upholstery, Reclines To Single Bed, 36 x 27 In. 748.00
Chair, Club, Frank Lloyd Wright, Upholstery, Loose Cushions, Taliesin Legs, 27 In. 575.00
Chair, Club, Off-White Wool, Chrome Plated Platform Base, 33 x 33 x 25 In., Pair.......... 420.00
Chair, Club, Old Hickory, Woven Arms, Spindles, Cushion Seat, Marked, 30 x 39 x 36 In...... 1440.00
Chair, Cock Fighting, Georgian Style, Mahogany, Leather, Britain, c.1890, 32 x 22 x 18 In. *illus* 1015.00
Chair, Corner, 3 Spindles, Edwardian, Fruitwood, Half Moon Back, 29 x 22 x 22 In......... 168.00
Chair, Corner, Chippendale, Comb Back, Beech, Pierced Splats, Slip Seat, 47 x 27 In. 1035.00
Chair, Corner, Chippendale, Walnut, Shaped Splat, Carved, Shell, Bellflower, 34 x 30 In...... 5750.00
Chair, Corner, Chippendale, Cherry, Carved, Cushion, c.1770, 33 1/2 In. 12000.00
Chair, Corner, Chippendale, Mahogany, Raised Crest, Curved Back, Upholstered 2300.00
Chair, Corner, Chippendale Style, Shaped Crest, Cabriole Legs, 32 x 22 x 29 1/2 In. 316.00
Chair, Corner, Georgian, Oak, Vase Shape Splats, Provincial, c.1820, 32 1/8 In.............. 529.00
Chair, Corner, Georgian, Mahogany, Upholstery, Curved Railing, 29 x 28 In. 1320.00
Chair, Corner, Mahogany, Square Seat, Scroll Arms, 18th Century, 31 x 29 x 26 In.......... 2115.00
Chair, Corner, Mahogany, Upholstered Seat, 18th Century, 31 1/2 x 17 In.................. 3525.00
Chair, Corner, Maple, Mixed Wood, Red Paint, Pillow Crest, Rush Seat, Country, 31 In....... 345.00
Chair, Corner, Maple, Turned, New England, Mid 18th Century, 29 3/4 In................... 881.00
Chair, Corner, Queen Anne, Splint Seat, Shaped & Molded Rail, 31 x 27 In. 240.00
Chair, Corner, Queen Anne, Cherry, Chamber, New England, Mid 1700s, 33 In. 2155.00
Chair, Corner, Queen Anne, Maple, Rush Seat, Arm, c.1760, 31 In. 2160.00
Chair, Corner, Queen Anne, Commode, Walnut, Stepped Pillow Crest, 2 Vase Splats......... 3480.00
Chair, Corner, William & Mary, Cushion Crest, Shaped Arms, Turned Supports 3016.00
Chair, Corner, William & Mary, Curved, Shaped Crest Rail, Upholstered, 30 x 17 In. 3776.00
Chair, Directoire Style, Mahogany, Rectangular Crest, Tapered Legs, Padded, 34 In., Pair 600.00
Chair, Directoire Style, Multicolored Padded Back, Seat, Arms, 34 1/2 In., Pair 2880.00
Chair, Donald Knorr, Steel, Red Enamel, Knoll, c.1950, 28 x 22 x 18 In. .... *illus* 1400.00
Chair, Eames, La Chase, Fiberglass, Chromed Steel, Oak Organic Form, 1948, 34 In......... 3835.00
Chair, Eames, Lounge, Ottoman, High Back, Headrest, Herman Miller, 21 x 21 x 18 In...... 1020.00
Chair, Eames, Shell, Orange, Fiberglass, Steel, Herman Miller, 1950s, 33 x 25 x 23 In. . . *illus* 180.00
Chair, Easy, Federal, Mahogany, Upholstered, c.1820, 45 1/2 In.......................... 6463.00

Chair, Edwardian, Mahogany, Regency Style, Padded Backs, Arms, Early 1900s, 34 In., Pair . . 823.00
Chair, Edwardian Style, Stenciled, Gilt, Carved Legs, 39 In., Pair . . . . *illus* 260.00
Chair, Egyptian Revival, Rosewood, Gilt Incised, Bronze Mounted, Oval Back. 940.00
Chair, Empire Style, Mahogany, Gilt, Carved Backrest, Scrolled, Slip Seat, 18 In., Pair. 499.00
Chair, Empire Style, Mahogany, Tub, Ormolu Mounted, Lyre Form Splat, 33 In.. . . . . 960.00
Chair, Empire Style, Mahogany, Gilt Bronze, Leather, 30 x 48 x 22 In.. . . . . 3750.00
Chair, Ernest Race, Flamingo, Upholstered, Wood, Plastic Glides, 33 x 28 x 36 In., Pair 2400.00
Chair, Fan Back, Wicker, Child's, 37 In.. . . . . 177.00
Chair, Federal, Inlaid Mahogany, Square Seat, Saber Legs, c.1790, 34½ In. 3055.00
Chair, Federal, Mahogany, Carved, Upholstered, c.1800, 42½ In. 1920.00
Chair, Federal, Mahogany, Barrel Back, Wing, Arms, 49 x 33 In. 2185.00
Chair, Federal, Mahogany, Inlay, Pierced Leaf & Drapery Splat, Arms, 35 In. 3016.00
Chair, Federal Style, Mahogany, Molded Edge Back, Upholstered, 35 x 20 x 17¾ In. 177.00
Chair, Flemish Baroque, H-Stretchers, Upholstered, Open Scroll Arms, 45 x 28 In.. . . . . . . 1093.00
Chair, Folding, Syrian, Carved & Inlaid, Mother-Of-Pearl, 40 In. 400.00
Chair, Franco Albini, Walnut, Leather Upholstery, A. Dassi & Figli, c.1931, 37 In.. . . . . . . 8750.00
Chair, Frank L. Wright, Upholstered, Heritage Henredon, Arms, 27 x 32 x 34 In.. . . . . *illus* 2700.00
Chair, French Baroque, Walnut, Carved Finials, Upholstery, c.1750, 45 x 27 In., Pair. 1380.00
Chair, French Provincial, Fruitwood, Lyre Back, Rush Seat, Rails, 1800s, 36 x 23 In.. . . . . . 590.00
Chair, Fritz Henningsen, Teak, Leather, Arms, c.1930, 34½ In.. . . . . 11400.00
Chair, G. Nakashima, Captain's, 9 Spindles, Poplar, Saddle Seat, c.1958, 26½ x 24 In.. . . . . 3525.00
Chair, G. Nakashima, Walnut, Arms, 1970, 39 x 25 x 21 In. 7800.00
Chair, G. Nelson, Pretzel, Oak Plywood Frame, Upholstered, Arms, 26 x 19 x 30 In. 1800.00
Chair, G. Stickley, 3 Vertical Slats To Back, Arms, 26½ x 23½ x 38½ In. 450.00
Chair, G. Stickley, 4 Vertical Slats, Rush Seat, 17 x 16 x 35 In. 420.00
Chair, G. Stickley, 4-Rung Ladder Back, 18 x 16 x 37 In.. . . . . 420.00
Chair, G. Stickley, 5 Vertical Slats, Cushion Seat, 19½ x 19 x 36½ In. 180.00
Chair, G. Stickley, 5 Vertical Slats Under Arms, 29 x 30 x 39½ In.. . . . . 2160.00
Chair, G. Stickley, Ash, Notched Peaked Top Rail, Drop-In Cushion, 19 x 18 x 37 In. 570.00
Chair, G. Stickley, Bungalow, Hump Top, Vertical Slats, 18 x 18 x 37½ In.. . . . . 780.00
Chair, G. Stickley, Cube, Slatted, Drop-In Spring Seat, 29 x 25¾ x 27¾ In.. . . . . 4200.00
Chair, G. Stickley, Desk, Oak, Vertical Slats, Leather Seat, 37 x 16 x 15 In.. . . . . 198.00
Chair, G. Stickley, Desk, Chatlet, Single Horizontal Board, 16 x 16 x 29½ In. 330.00
Chair, G. Stickley, Desk, H-Back, 16½ x 16 x 33 In. 600.00
Chair, G. Stickley, Ladder Back, Corbels Under Arms, 24½ x 21 x 36 In. 510.00
Chair, G. Stickley, Loose Seat Cushion, Cotton Upholstery, Arms, 38½ x 32 x 29 In. 1200.00
Chair, G. Stickley, Oak, Leather Seat, Harvey Ellis Decal, Arms, c.1903. . . . . 24000.00
Chair, G. Stickley, Rabbit Ear, Slatted, Through Tenon, 19 x 15 x 38 In. 3600.00
Chair, G. Stickley, Side, Oak, 3 Slats, Angled Supports At Base, 19 x 34½ x 19 In.. . . . . . 840.00
Chair, G. Stickley, Slatted Sides, Burgundy Leather, Arms, 39¼ x 29 x 29½ In.. . . . . 1560.00
Chair, G. Stickley, Slatted Sides, Loose Cushion, Arms, 1902, 39½ x 28¾ x 29 In.. . . . . . . 1800.00
Chair, G. Stickley, Vertical Slats, Recovered Seat, 17½ x 18 x 38½ In. 150.00
Chair, Gent's, Victorian, Walnut, Carved, Upholstered, Front Casters, 45 x 35 In. 112.00
Chair, George I, Walnut, Carved, Carved Top Rail, Drop-In Seat, c.1720, 40 In., Pair 16250.00
Chair, George II, Mahogany, Canted Square Back, Upholstered, Open Arms, 35 In. 1093.00
Chair, George II Style, Mahogany, Carved Knees, Arm Supports, Upholstered, Pair. 8125.00
Chair, George II Style, Mahogany, Claw Feet, Arms, Upholstered, 43 In., Pair 16250.00
Chair, George II Style, Walnut, Scalloped Seat, Cabriole Legs, Claw, Ball Feet, 43 In., Pair. . . . 4080.00
Chair, George III, Carved Mahogany, Open Baluster Splat, Needlepoint, 18 In., Pair 1175.00
Chair, George III, Chippendale, Mahogany, Upholstered, Marlboro Legs, 37 In. 561.00
Chair, George III, Leather Upholstered, U-Shape Back, Drawer, c.1790 . . . . 11875.00
Chair, George III, Mahogany, Arched Top, 3 Carved Slats, Slip Seat, Arms, 17 In. 294.00
Chair, George III, Mahogany, Scalloped Crest, Scrolled Ears, 41½ In., Pair. 1293.00
Chair, George III, Mahogany, Upholstered, Padded, Cushion, 49 x 33 x 21 In. 1410.00
Chair, George III, Mahogany, Leather Caster, Arms, c.1770. . . . . 2400.00
Chair, George III, Mahogany, Upholstered Seat, Arms, 1800, 18 x 39½ In., Pair 3105.00
Chair, George III, Regency, Mahogany, Shield Back, Upholstered, Arms, 35 x 23 x 20 In.. . . . . 1003.00
Chair, George III, Upholstered, Scrolled Wings, Rolled Arms, 18 x 49 In.. . . . . 1955.00
Chair, George III, Wheel Back, Tapered Legs, Spade Feet, Shaped Arms, 37 In., Pair. 633.00
Chair, George III Style, Barrel Back, Green Tufted Leather, Serpentine Seat, 1900s, 20 In.. . . . 1763.00
Chair, George III Style, Floral Carved, Ivory & Rose Striped, c.1900, 43½ In. 940.00
Chair, George III Style, Mahogany, Carved, Yoke Crest, Pierced Floral Splat, 37 In. 294.00
Chair, George III Style, Mahogany, Carved, Yoke Crest, Pierced Splat, Arms, 40 In.. . . . . . . 470.00
Chair, George III Style, Mahogany, Upholstered, 41 x 30 x 27 In. 590.00
Chair, Gothic Revival, Walnut, Serpentine Rails, Cabriole Legs, Upholstered, 36 In.. . . . . . . 3456.00
Chair, Great, Pilgrim, Ash, Maple, Slat Back, New England. 9860.00

Furniture, Canterbury, Federal Style, Mahogany, Cypress, Ash, Inlaid Legs, c.1890, 19 x 17 x 13 In.
$525.00

Furniture, Chair, Adam Style, Satinwood, Painted, Britain, c.1890, 39 x 22 x 21 In., Pair
$835.00

Furniture, Chair, Barcelona, Leather, Chrome, 30 x 30 x 30 In.
$2275.00

Furniture, Chair, Bishop's, Elizabethan Style, Barley Twist, Late 19th Century, 36 In.
$650.00

Furniture, Chair, Burl Walnut, Woman's Mask, Carved Crest, Upholstered, c.1890, 43 In.
$1970.00

Furniture, Chair, Carlo Mollino, Steel, Cutouts, Enamel, Upholstered, 38 x 13 x 20 In., Pair
$8400.00

Furniture, Chair, Chippendale, Mahogany, Oak, Gothic Splat, Britain, c.1790, 38 x 25 x 18 In.
$1300.00

Furniture, Chair, Chippendale, Mahogany, Tassel Back, Britain, 18th Century, 38 x 23 x 18 In.
$830.00

Chair, H. Probber, Silk Upholstery, 38 x 29 x 32 In. . . . *illus* 30.00
Chair, H. Wegner, Teak, Upholstered, Arms, c.1950 . . . 4320.00
Chair, Hall, Arts & Crafts, Cutout Back, Plank Seat, 16 x 21 x 41 In. . . . 330.00
Chair, Hall, Arts & Crafts, Shoefoot Form, Drop-In Cushion, 18 x 19 x 39 In. . . . 330.00
Chair, Hall, Belter, Rosewood, Laminated, Carved, Pierced Back, Upholstered. . . . 3450.00
Chair, Hall, G. Stickley, Oak, Upholstered, No. 180, c.1902, 36 x 41 x 21½ In. . . . 6600.00
Chair, Hall, Gothic, Spool Turned, Carved, c.1850, 40 x 19 In. . . . 110.00
Chair, Hall, Limbert, Cutout, Flared Legs, Signed, 24 x 25 x 18 In. . . . *illus* 7100.00
Chair, Hall, Limbert, Square Cutouts On Sides, Flared Legs, 25 x 18 x 24 In.. . . . 7800.00
Chair, Hall, Mahogany, Inlay, Ebonized, Scrolling Leaf Crest, Putti, Italy, 23½ In. . . . 2640.00
Chair, Hall, Walnut, Leather, Sea Serpents, Scrolls, Brass Tacks, 19th Century . . . 176.00
Chair, Hall, Walnut, High Back, Hinged Seat, Turned Legs, c.1860, 61 x 24½ x 21 In. . . . 940.00
Chair, Hall, William IV, Mahogany, Rounded Back, Leaf Carving, Ball Feet, 35 In. . . . 720.00
Chair, Hall, William IV, Mahogany, Rounded Top, Scroll Crest, Shield Back, 34 In., Pair . . . 720.00
Chair, Hall, William IV, Mahogany, Leaf Carving, Wooden Seat, Ball Feet, 34½ In., Pair . . . 960.00
Chair, Hepplewhite, Mahogany, Oval Back, Pierced Splats, Tapered Legs, 37 In., Pair. . . . 345.00
Chair, Hepplewhite, Mahogany, Carved Drapery Backs, Stretchers, c.1800, 37 In., Pair . . . 863.00
Chair, Horn, Arched Back & Arms, Brown, Black & White Hide, 41½ In. . . . 575.00
Chair, Horn, Steer, Leopard Fur Upholstered Seat, Inscription, 1800s . . . 4025.00
Chair, Invalid, Reclining, William IV, Mahogany, 49½ In. . . . *illus* 900.00
Chair, Irish, Mahogany, Carved, 19th Century, 40 x 37 In. . . . 495.00
Chair, Italian, Walnut, Needlepoint Seat, Cabriole Legs, c.1840, Pair. . . . 1410.00
Chair, J.M. Young, Morris, Slats, Cushion, Flat Arms, 39 x 32 x 36 In. . . . *illus* 5010.00
Chair, Jacobean Style, Carved, Scrolled Crest, Trapezoid Seat, 51 x 20 In. . . . 354.00
Chair, Jacobean Style, Mahogany, Cane Seat, Block Legs, Peg Feet, Arms, 49½ In. . . . 684.00
Chair, Jocko Johnson, Walnut, Heart, c.1978, 34 x 16 x 24 In. . . . 2160.00
Chair, Jules Leleu, Art Deco, Beech, Tropical Hardwood, Faux Ostrich Leather, Pair . . . 5520.00
Chair, Ladder Back, Arched, Woven Splint Seat, Blue Paint, Child's, 33 In. . . . 358.00
Chair, Ladder Back, Federal, Tiger Maple, Rush Seat, Turned Legs, 45¾ x 18 In. . . . 3450.00
Chair, Ladder Back, Mixed Wood, Rush Seat, Folk Art, c.1900, 19 In.. . . . 173.00
Chair, Ladder Back, Mixed Wood, 4 Arched Slats, Red Paint, c.1800, 44 In.. . . . 403.00
Chair, Ladder Back, Rush Seat, Red Stain, Arms . . . 72.00
Chair, Ladder Back, Rush Seat, Shaped Stiles, Arms, 19th Century . . . 201.00
Chair, Ladislas Medgyes, Lucite, Upholstered, 39 x 20 x 25 In. . . . 9000.00
Chair, Library Steps, English Arts & Crafts, 1800s, 34 x 17 In. . . . 1652.00
Chair, Limbert, Desk, Oak, Ebony Inlay, Branded Signature, 16 x 18 x 36 In. . . . 1560.00
Chair, Limbert, Tall Back, Cutouts, Leather Cushion, Arms, 25 x 24 x 42 In.. . . . 1140.00
Chair, Lolling, Federal, Mahogany, Inlaid Arms, Casters, Upholstered, 42 x 26 x 24 In. . . . 1760.00
Chair, Lolling, Federal, Mahogany, Upholstered. . . . 1800.00
Chair, Lolling, Federal, Mahogany, Serpentine Arms, Lemuel Churchill, c.1810, 43 In. . . . 24000.00
Chair, Lolling, George III Style, Mahogany, Upholstered Back, Arched Rail, Arms, 38 In.. . . . 780.00
Chair, Lolling, Mahogany, Poplar, Cabriole Legs, Claw & Ball Feet, c.1790, 43 x 29 In.. . . . 7480.00
Chair, Louis Philippe, Mahogany, Carved, Turned Stiles, Upholstered, Arms, c.1820. . . . 450.00
Chair, Louis Philippe Style, Ebonized Boulle, Inlay, Cabriole Legs, Arms, 40 x 25 x 23 In. . . . 2124.00
Chair, Louis Philippe Style, Yellow Plaid Upholstery, Cartouche Back, Arms, 39½ In.. . . . 207.00
Chair, Louis XIV Style, Beech, Padded Back, Leafy Crest, Stretcher, Arms, 42 In.. . . . 1920.00
Chair, Louis XIV Style, Walnut, Carved, Inlaid Needlework, Arms, 19 x 26 x 25 In. . . . 885.00
Chair, Louis XV, Beech, Carved, Open Arms, France, c.1780, 36 x 24 In.. . . . 688.00
Chair, Louis XV, Beech, Cabriole Legs, Upholstered, Padded Arms, 37 x 26½ In., Pair. . . . 8400.00
Chair, Louis XV, Carved, Armrest, c.1840, 26½ x 20½ In., Pair . . . 3600.00
Chair, Louis XV, Gilt, Shell Carved Arms, 19th Century, 44 x 28 In.. . . . 1320.00
Chair, Louis XV, Needlepoint Upholstery, Open Arms, Early 19th Century, 34 x 26 In.. . . . 385.00
Chair, Louis XV, Provincial, Walnut, Domed, Padded Back, Seat, Scroll Arms, 37 In. . . . 3120.00
Chair, Louis XV, Walnut, Stretcher Base, Cane Back, Seat, Open Arms, c.1900, 52 x 27 In., Pair. 825.00
Chair, Louis XV, Walnut, Scalloped Molded Back, Seat Rail, Cabriole Legs, Arms, 38 x 26 x 26 In. 3525.00
Chair, Louis XV, Walnut, Upholstered, Cabriole Legs, Padded Arms, 36 x 26 In., Pair . . . 9000.00
Chair, Louis XV Style, Flat Back, Beech, Carved Frame, Serpentine Seat, Upholstered, Arms, 18 In. . 470.00
Chair, Louis XV Style, Gilt, Padded, Flower Carved Crest, Arms, 35½ In., Pair . . . 1560.00
Chair, Louis XV Style, Oak, Carved, Cane, Arms, 36 x 23 In., Pair. . . . 2350.00
Chair, Louis XV Style, Walnut, Carved Crests, Garland, Arms, 41 In., Pair. . . . 1704.00
Chair, Louis XVI, Curved Back, Arms, Medallion Back, Ball Feet, Upholstered, Scroll Arms, 34 x 24 In. 826.00
Chair, Louis XVI, Fruitwood, Carved, Oval Back, Fluted Supports, Padded Arms, 34 In., Pair. . 1998.00
Chair, Louis XVI Style, Carved, Needlepoint Upholstery, Guilloche Molding, Arms, 38 In., Pair 480.00
Chair, Louis XVI Style, Provincial, Polychrome, Domed, Padded Back, Arms, 40 In.. . . . 1440.00
Chair, Louis XVI Style, Urn Shape Splat, Baluster Arms, Shell Detail, Upholstered, 17½ x 36 In. 58.00
Chair, Louis XVI Style, Walnut, Carved, Nailed Needlework, Continental, Arms, 46 x 25 In. . . . 944.00

Chair, Lounge, G. Nakashima, Walnut, Writing Arm, Marked, 33 x 33x 27 In. 10200.00
Chair, Lounge, Modern, Geometric, Orange Wool Upholstery, Metal Legs, 33 x 33 x 33 In., Pair. 1800.00
Chair, Lounge, Risom, Walnut, Upholstered, Foam Cushion, Denmark, c.1955, Pair 705.00
Chair, Lounge, Robsjohn-Gibbings, Mahogany, Upholstered, Widdicomb, 31 x 28 In. .... *illus* 2500.00
Chair, Lounge, Rosewood, Black Leather Seat, Jean Gillon, Brazil, 34 x 35 x 28 ½ In......... 1440.00
Chair, Mahogany, Arched Crest, Bowed Splat, Early 19th Century, 35 ½ In., Pair............ 5581.00
Chair, Mahogany, Arched Crest, Upholstered, c.1900, 53 In. .... *illus* 240.00
Chair, Mahogany, Cabriole Legs, Trifid Foot, Beige, Upholstered......................... 2200.00
Chair, Mahogany, Ladder Back, Rush Seat, Mackmurdo Foot, 18 x 18 x 36 In.............. 330.00
Chair, Mahogany, Parquetry, Shaped Crest Rail, Gilt Bronze, Arms, 31 x 22 x 17 In. 118.00
Chair, Mahogany, Reading Rest, Balloon Shaped Cane Seat, Candle Arms 6000.00
Chair, Mahogany, Rosette Inner Border, Late 19th Century, 34 ½ In...................... 823.00
Chair, Mahogany, Side, Acanthus Carved Crests, Slip Seats, Saber Legs, 1840, Pair.......... 414.00
Chair, Mahogany, Tufted Seat Back & Arms, Scroll Legs, c.1885, 36 In.................... 210.00
Chair, Maple, Banister Back, Woven Seat, Turned Legs, 43 ¾ x 26 ½ In.................... 489.00
Chair, Maple, Saber Leg, Crest Rail, Eagle, Upholstered, 33 ½ x 17 ½ x 18 In. 275.00
Chair, Maple, Slat Back, Turned Finials, Arms, Tapered Legs, Stretcher, Early 18th Century, 21 x 6 In. 470.00
Chair, Marcel Breuer, Wassily, Tan Leather, Knoll International, 27 ¼ x 30 ¼ In.. .... 316.00
Chair, Marco Zanuso, Wool Upholstery, Brass Legs, 31 x 32 x 31 In.. .... 1800.00
Chair, Milo Baughman, Chrome, Geometric Upholstered, T. Coggin, 1987, 29 x 23 x 26 In., Pair.. 1800.00
Chair, Mirror, Pier, Federal, Gilt, Molded Cornice, Drop Acorn Pendants, c.1815, 43 x 25 In... 460.00
Chair, Moderne, Club, Half Round Back, Lucite Feet, Mohair Upholstery, 28 x 32 In., Pair ... 518.00
Chair, Moravian, Oak, Half-Crescent Top, Cutout Sides, Mortised Legs 1100.00
Chair, Morris, G. Stickley, Rope Seat, Bow Arm Form, 31 x 37 x 38 In.................... 9600.00
Chair, Morris, Oak, Spool Spindle, Slat Back, Shaped Arms, c.1900, 38 x 30 x 34 In., Pair.... 275.00
Chair, Morris, Oak, Carved Lion, 39 x 31 In.. .... 550.00
Chair, Musical, Wood, Folding, Velvet Upholstery, France, Child's. c.1870, 29 In. 616.00
Chair, N. Cherner, Walnut Plywood Seat, Tubular Steel Frame, Arms, 22 ¾ x 20 ½ x 32 In.. .... 240.00
Chair, Napoleon III, Multicolored, Spindle Back, Leafy Carved Crest, Padded Seat, 31 In. 480.00
Chair, Neoclassical, Mahogany, Brass Inlaid Legs, Russia, 19th Century, 37 In. 2400.00
Chair, Neoclassical, Mahogany, Swan Arm Supports, c.1840, 41 ½ In. 823.00
Chair, Neoclassical, Mahogany, Trapezoid Slip Seat, c.1840, Pair....................... 1103.00
Chair, Neoclassical Style, Fruitwood, Carved, Leafy Cartouche, H-Stretcher, Italy, Pair....... 588.00
Chair, Neoclassical Style, Sphinx Arm Supports, Paw Feet, Silk Upholstery, 36 x 24 In., Pair.. 805.00
Chair, Nutting, Chippendale, No. 334, Carved, Paper Label, Philadelphia 825.00
Chair, Nutting, Windsor, No. 301, Bow Back, Side, Turnings & Pieced Seat, Paper Label 220.00
Chair, Nutting, Windsor, No. 401, New England Turnings, Arms........................ 468.00
Chair, Oak, Bow Back, Cane Seat, Turned Back Spindles, 24 In......................... 71.00
Chair, Oak, Carved Crown Top, Double Griffins, Hairy Paw Feet, c.1837 .... 1600.00
Chair, Oak, Lincoln, Washington Carved Backs, Plank Type Seat, Turned Legs, 1909, Pair ... 1715.00
Chair, Oak, Woven Straw, Barrel Shape Back, Flat Arms, Northern Scotland, 42 ¼ In. 3120.00
Chair, Old Hickory, Y-Back, Twigs, Stool, 32 x 28 x 27-In. Chair, 2 Piece .... *illus* 145.00
Chair, Ottoman, Arne Norell, Scandinavian Modern, Leather, Steel, 30 x 26 & 15 x 26 In..... 2006.00
Chair, Ottoman, Baker, Tightly Upholstered, Box Seat Cushion, Skirt, 34 x 35 In.. .... 590.00
Chair, Ottoman, Eames, Walnut, Leather, Aluminum, Herman Miller, c.2000, 32 x 33 In. *illus* 1900.00
Chair, Ottoman, Eames, Rosewood, Black Leather, c.1956, 31 x 36 In.. .... 3120.00
Chair, Ottoman, George III Style, Mahogany, Padded, Tufted, Wing, 43 ½ In. 2160.00
Chair, Ottoman, Jean Gillon, Rosewood, c.1965, 32 ½ x 43 x 35 In. 3900.00
Chair, Ottoman, Ralph Lauren, Leather, Brass Nail Trim, Cushion, 36 x 40 x 31 In.. .... 2124.00
Chair, Painted, Gilt, Turned, Crest Rail, English Script, c.1760, 44 ¼ x 16 ½ In.. .... 3173.00
Chair, Painted, Gilt Urn Of Flowers, Multicolored, Maryland, c.1830, 30 In. 353.00
Chair, Painted, Stenciled Fruit, c.1830, 17 x 8 ¾ In...................................... 764.00
Chair, Parcel Gilt, Mother-Of-Pearl Inlay, Arms, France, 19th Century, 40 In.............. 2160.00
Chair, Paul Laszlo, Steel Frame, 2 Backrests, c.1954, 29 x 20 x 22 In. 9600.00
Chair, Piano, Regency, Gadrooned Molding, c.1810, 33 ½ x 14 x 14 In.................... 940.00
Chair, Pierced Arrow, Slats At Back & Sides, Leather Cushion, Arms, 26 x 24 x 35 In......... 3480.00
Chair, Pilgrim, Banister Back, Carved Crest, Ram's Head, Brown Paint, Arms............... 2900.00
Chair, Planter's, Hardwood, Saber Legs, Canvas Sling Seat, West Indies, 33 x 25 x 24 In...... 764.00
Chair, Planter's, Walnut, Broad Arms, Leather Upholstery, 19th Century, 35 x 26 In. 1175.00
Chair, Portuguese, Carved, Gilt Walnut, Serpent Heads, Claw Feet, Open Arms, 45 x 34 In. ... 523.00
Chair, Portuguese, Walnut, Carved, Open Arms, 18th Century, 51 x 29 In. 4070.00
Chair, Pottier & Stymus, Aesthetic Revival, Gilt, Ebonized Mahogany, Raked Backrest....... 1998.00
Chair, Provincial, Elm, Spindle Back Windsor, Plank Seat, Arms 323.00
Chair, Provincial, Fruitwood, Ladder Back, Circular Legs, Arms, c.1850, 45 ¼ In. 330.00
Chair, Provincial, Fruitwood, Shaped Crest, Vase Splat, Rush Seats, Cabriole Legs, 40 In. 1440.00
Chair, Provincial, George III Style, Elm, Ears, Scalloped Crest, Pierced Splat, 35 In., Pair 600.00

Furniture, Chair, Cock Fighting, Georgian Style, Mahogany, Leather, Britain, c.1890, 32 x 22 x 18 In.
$1015.00

Furniture, Chair, Donald Knorr, Steel, Red Enamel, Knoll, c.1950, 28 x 22 x 18 In.
$1400.00

Furniture, Chair, Eames, Shell, Orange, Fiberglass, Steel, Herman Miller, 1950s, 33 x 25 x 23 In.
$180.00

Furniture, Chair, Edwardian Style, Stenciled, Gilt, Carved Legs, 39 In., Pair
$260.00

F

Furniture, Chair, Frank L. Wright, Upholstered, Heritage Henredon, Arms, 27 x 32 x 34 In.
$2700.00

Furniture, Chair, H. Probber, Silk Upholstery, 38 x 29 x 32 In.
$30.00

Furniture, Chair, Hall, Limbert, Cutout, Flared Legs, Signed, 24 x 25 x 18 In.
$7100.00

Furniture, Chair, Invalid, Reclining, William IV, Mahogany, 49 ½ In.
$900.00

Chair, Provincial, Louis XIII Style, Mahogany, Domed, Padded Back, Arms, 45 In. 1800.00
Chair, Provincial, Louis XV, Fruitwood, Padded Back, Seat, Arms, 37 In., Pair 4080.00
Chair, Provincial, Louis XV Style, Fruitwood, Double Cane Back, Reeded Arms, 33 In. 1140.00
Chair, Provincial, Louis XV Style, Multicolored, Cane Back, Carved Crest, Arms, 37 In. 1920.00
Chair, Provincial, Mahogany, Painted, Oval, Bird Scene, Wood Saddle Seat, 36 In., Pair 2640.00
Chair, Queen Anne, Birch, Shaped Yoke Crest, 41 ¼ x 19 x 18 In. 300.00
Chair, Queen Anne, Birchwood, Carved, Padded Seat, Scroll Arms, c.1730, 40 ¾ In. 31000.00
Chair, Queen Anne, Cherry, Shaped Crest, Lathrop Shops, Norwich, c.1750, 43 In. 19200.00
Chair, Queen Anne, Curved Vase Back, Rush Seat, Block & Turned Legs, Tiger Maple Stretchers 1150.00
Chair, Queen Anne, Elm, Open Backrest, Splat, Arms, Country, 1700s, 16 ½ In. 764.00
Chair, Queen Anne, Figured Maple, Vase Splat, Canted Rear Legs, New England, 39 In. 6380.00
Chair, Queen Anne, Fruitwood, Cabriole Legs, Scroll Arms, Tapestry Upholstered 705.00
Chair, Queen Anne, Hardwood, Rush Seats, Baluster, Trumpet Legs, Arms, 17 x 41 ½ In., Pair 2185.00
Chair, Queen Anne, Mahogany, 39 ½ In. *illus* 880.00
Chair, Queen Anne, Mahogany, Shaped Splat, Front Rail, Turned Stretchers, Pad Seat, 44 In. 360.00
Chair, Queen Anne, Mahogany, Wing, c.1760, 46 x 30 In. 1650.00
Chair, Queen Anne, Mahogany, Wing, Cabriole Legs, Pad Feet, Upholstered, 47 x 34 x 25 In. 7700.00
Chair, Queen Anne, Rush Seat, 18th Century, 38 In. 165.00
Chair, Queen Anne, Side, Mahogany, Shaped Yoke Crest Rail, Horseshoe Seat, 39 x 18 In. 4313.00
Chair, Queen Anne, Vase Splat, Rush Seat, Yoke Top, Block & Vase Legs, Bulbous Stretcher, 39 In. 575.00
Chair, Queen Anne, Walnut, 18th Century, 40 x 21 In. 220.00
Chair, Queen Anne, Walnut, Arched & Carved Crest Rail, Rush Woven Seat, 45 In., Pair 1840.00
Chair, Queen Anne, Walnut, Arched & Carved, Pierced Crest Rail, Scrolls 2151.00
Chair, Queen Anne, Walnut, Balloon Seat, Stocking Trifid Feet 19500.00
Chair, Queen Anne, Walnut, Cabriole Legs, Pad Feet, Gold Upholstery, Arms, 39 ½ In. 441.00
Chair, Queen Anne, Walnut, Scroll Ear Crest, Vase Splat, Arms, Philadelphia, 42 x 24 In. 588.00
Chair, Queen Anne, Walnut, Slip Seats, Cabriole Legs, 39 ½ x 17 ½ In. 2185.00
Chair, Queen Anne, Walnut, Vase Splat, Balloon Slip Seat, Philadelphia, 40 In. 6960.00
Chair, Queen Anne, Yew, Vase Splat, Cabriole Legs, Pad Feet, Pair 449.00
Chair, Queen Anne, Yoke Back, Black Paint, Vase Splat, c.1785, 41 ½ In. 1058.00
Chair, Queen Anne Style, Mahogany, Cabriole Leg, Leather Upholstery, Scroll Arms, 43 In. 646.00
Chair, Queen Anne Style, Rush Seat, Vase Splat, Turned Supports, Pad Feet, 40 In. 303.00
Chair, Queen Anne Style, Vase Splat, Upholstered, Japanned, 40 ½ In., Pair 354.00
Chair, Red, 4 Slats, Plain Stiles, Ball Finials, Stretchers, Rush Seat, 1800s, 39 ½ In. 173.00
Chair, Regency, Fruitwood, Domed, Padded Back, Scrolled Down Arms, 45 ¼ In. 1188.00
Chair, Regency, Mahogany, Acanthus, 36 In., Pair. *illus* 232.00
Chair, Regency, Mahogany, Inlaid Leaves, Scroll Downswept Arms, Dutch, 35 In. 600.00
Chair, Regency, Tub, Mahogany, Scrolled Crest, Cane Back, Seat, 33 ½ In. 1872.00
Chair, Regency, Walnut, Ring-Turned Circular Back, Shaped Saddle Seats, 19th Century 3819.00
Chair, Regency Revival, Oak, Carved, Strapwork Shield Back, Trapezoid Seat, 35 In., Pair 245.00
Chair, Regency Style, Ebonized, Cane Seat, Saber Legs, 33 ½ x 21 x 16 ½ In. 1003.00
Chair, Regency Style, Fruitwood, Carved, Tapestry, Velvet Upholstery, 43 x 21 x 18 In. 443.00
Chair, Regency Style, Painted Palmetto, Cane Back, Seat, Top-Shaped Feet, 36 In. 1440.00
Chair, Renaissance Revival, Brass, Steel, Cannon Ball Finials, Leather, Arms, 40 x 28 x 17 In. 502.00
Chair, Renaissance Revival, Carved, Ebonized, Breasts, Paterae, U-Shape Padded Armrest, 13 In. 323.00
Chair, Renaissance Revival, Gilt, Incised, Bronze Mounted, Burl Walnut, Arms, 40 In., Pair 1200.00
Chair, Renaissance Revival, Walnut, Carved, Upholstered Backrest, Seat, c.1880, 17 ½ In. 705.00
Chair, Renaissance Revival, Walnut, Drape, Tassel Carved, Open Arm, c.1870, 41 In., Pair 605.00
Chair, Renaissance Revival, Walnut, Short Armrest, c.1860, 38 x 25 In., Pair 550.00
Chair, Renaissance Style, Applied Fleur-De-Lis, Tooled Leather Panel, Brass, 20 In. 235.00
Chair, Renaissance Style, Walnut, Leather Upholstery, Brass Studs, 19 ¼ In., Pair 500.00
Chair, Rene Herbst, Bakelite, Chrome, Arms, c.1947, 33 ¼ In. 1080.00
Chair, Restauration, Mahogany, Flat Crest, Padded Back, Reeded Downswept Arms, 36 In., Pair 2280.00
Chair, Restauration, Walnut, Padded Back, Seat, Plain Crest, Downswept Arms, 36 In. 1800.00
Chair, Restauration Style, Fruitwood, Padded, Saber Legs, Scrolled Arms, 35 In., Pair 2400.00
Chair, Roche Bobois, Leather, Loose Seat & Back Cushions, 25 x 29 ½ In. 472.00
Chair, Rococo, Mahogany, Carved, Upholstery, Cabriole Legs, c.1850, 45 In. 300.00
Chair, Rococo, Mahogany, Shaped Carved Back Support, Scroll Arms, 38 x 24 In., Pair 1528.00
Chair, Rococo, Rosewood, Child's, c.1850, 38 ½ x 17 x 14 In. 588.00
Chair, Rococo, Rosewood, Laminated, Arms, Mid 19th Century 1763.00
Chair, Rococo, Rosewood, Flowered Crest, Scroll Stiles, c.1850, 48 In. 2350.00
Chair, Rococo, Rosewood, Floral Carved Crest, c.1850, 38 In. 5581.00
Chair, Rococo, Rosewood, Floral Crest, Rosalie With Grapes, c.1860, 43 In. 5581.00
Chair, Rococo, Rosewood, Laminated, Pierced Back, Carved Crest, 43 x 44 In., Pair 8813.00
Chair, Rococo, Rosewood, Carved, Laminated, Scrolled Crest, Cabriole Legs 9988.00
Chair, Rococo, Walnut, Needlepoint Seat, Back, c.1870, 43 x 26 In. 413.00

Chair, Rococo Revival, Mahogany, Carved, Gentleman's, Lady's, Silk Upholstery, 40 In., Pair . 240.00
Chair, Rococo Revival, Rosewood, Serpentine Sides, Upholstered, 14 x 19½ x 16 In. 840.00
Chair, Rococo Revival, Rosewood, Laminated, Concave, Serpentine Seat, Arms, 40½ In. 1680.00
Chair, Rococo Revival, Rosewood, Walnut, Quilled Birch Bark Panels, 37 x 18¾ In. 1998.00
Chair, Rococo Style, Beech, Carved, Cherub, Harp, Serpentine Seat, Continental, 19 In. 588.00
Chair, Rococo Style, Beech, Grotto, Carved, Painted Standing Bird, 15 In.. . . . . 1998.00
Chair, Rosewood, Carved Crest, Vase Splat, Leather Upholstery, Portugal, 42 In.. . . . . 325.00
Chair, Rosewood, Hoop Shape, Padded Back, Oval Medallion Crest, 1800s, 36 In., Pair 236.00
Chair, Rosewood, Laminated, Heart Shaped Back, Ram's Horn, Carved, c.1860 . . . . 1045.00
Chair, Rush Seat, Banister Back, Rising Sun Crest, Arms, Rhode Island, c.1780 . . . . 11700.00
Chair, Satinwood, Diamond Inlaid Crest, Padded Seat, Saber Legs, Continental, 30 In., Pair . 720.00
Chair, Savonarola, Walnut, Hoof Feet, Italy, Late 18th Century, 32 In. . . . . *illus* 800.00
Chair, Savonarola, Walnut, Studded Tooled Leather Back, Seat, Scrolled Arms, 35 x 26 In.. . . . 2938.00
Chair, Sergio Radrigues, Rosewood, Leather, c.1963, 32 x 39 x 36 In. 7500.00
Chair, Shaker, Invalid, Hardwoods, Turned, Pinned, Braced Ladder Back, Cane Seat, 45 x 17 In. 805.00
Chair, Shaker, Ladder Back, 4 Slats, Acorn Finials, Tape Seat, Arms, Stamped, c.1890, 41 In. . 1989.00
Chair, Shaker, Maple, Blue & Black Tape Seat & Back, Arms, Mt. Lebanon, c.1870, 38 In. 1170.00
Chair, Shaker, Tilters, Maple & Cherry, Rush Seat, 1870, 28 x 16 In., Pair. 4700.00
Chair, Shaker, Weaver's, Maple & Oak, 2 Slats, Tape Seat, Mt. Lebanon, 1835, 42 In. 1325.00
Chair, Sheraton, Country, c.1820, 33 x 21 In., Pair 110.00
Chair, Sheraton Style, Ash, Oak, Bamboo, Rush Seat, 35 In.. . . . . 359.00
Chair, Sheraton Style, Mahogany, Vase Splats, Plumes, Spandrels, 36 x 21 In., 6 Piece 1840.00
Chair, Sheraton Style, Painted Flowers, c.1900, 40 x 24 x 19 In. *illus* 695.00
Chair, Shiro Kuramata, How High The Moon, Nickel Plated Wire Mesh, 28 x 27 x 33 In.. . . . . 11400.00
Chair, Shop Of The Crafters, Tacked On Leather Seat, Arms, 47¾ x 27½ x 23 In.. . . . . 1800.00
Chair, Slipper, Neogrecque, Round Seat, Late 19th Century, 30 In.. . . . . 5288.00
Chair, Slipper, Queen Anne, Walnut, Rhode Island, c.1770, 34¾ In. 3125.00
Chair, Slipper, Rococo Revival, Laminated Rosewood, Concave Back, Leaves, 37 In., Pair 2880.00
Chair, Spratling, Leather Sling, Tacks, Arched Legs, Curved Frame, 18½ x 24 In.. . . . . 1150.00
Chair, Spratling, Wood, Leather, Scoop Seat, Tacks, Curule Legs, Stretchers, 27 x 18 In. 1840.00
Chair, Stickley Bros., Desk, Low Back, Single Slat, Saddle Seat, 14 x 15 In.. . . . . 360.00
Chair, Stone Veneered, Applied Variegated Green & Black, Upholstered Seat, 37 In., Pair. 1150.00
Chair, Teak, Carved, Krishna, Floral Scrolls, Anglo-Indian, 19th Century, Pair. 940.00
Chair, Theater Seat, Art Deco, 1930s, 34 x 42 In., Pair . . . . *illus* 350.00
Chair, Thonet, Bentwood, Vinyl, 31 x 36 x 28 In., Pair . . . . *illus* 720.00
Chair, Tub, Provincial Italian, Walnut, Domed Back, Seat, Arms, Early 1800s, 34 In.. . . . . 1320.00
Chair, Upholstered, Pony Shape, Orange Velour, 35¼ x 24½ x 40 In.. . . . . 3000.00
Chair, Upholstered, Wooden Border, Inlaid Flowers, Mother-Of-Pearl, 26 x 31 In. 207.00
Chair, V. Panton, Wire Cone, Blue Cushion, c.1958, Pair. 1620.00
Chair, Venetian, Walnut, Carved, c.1780, 28 x 18 In., Pair 385.00
Chair, Victorian, Mahogany, Balloon Back, Leaf & Scroll Arms, 38 x 29 In.. . . . . 168.00
Chair, Victorian, Mahogany, Campaign Style, Leather Back, Sling Seat, c.1880, 33 In., Pair . . 1680.00
Chair, Victorian, Rosewood, Balloon Back, Tufted Upholstery, 38 In.. 193.00
Chair, Victorian, Walnut, Balloon Back, Carved Crest, Arms, c.1880, 46 x 25½ x 24 In.. . . . . . . 220.00
Chair, Victorian, Walnut, Carved, Oval Cane Back, Seat, 45 x 26 In.. 252.00
Chair, Victorian, Walnut, Medallion Back, Carved, Upholstered, Open Arms, c.1879, 40 x 25 In. 358.00
Chair, W. Platner, Chrome Plate, Mohair, c.1966, 30 x 35½ x 26 In.. 3900.00
Chair, Walnut, Fluted Crest Rail, Lotus Carved Splat, Turned Finials, 19th Century 558.00
Chair, Walnut, Padded, Garland Carved Apron, Arms, Italy, 19th Century, 42 In. 420.00
Chair, Walnut, Satinwood Back, Scalloped Seat, Inlaid Frieze, 18th Century, 44 x 23 In.. . . . . 1180.00
Chair, Walnut, Sculptured Back, Arms, Leather Strap Seat, c.1951, 28 x 23 x 21 In.. . . . . 19200.00
Chair, Walnut, Serpentine Crest, Carved Shell, Pierced Splat, Claw & Ball Foot, c.1760 . . . . . . 6500.00
Chair, William & Mary, Cane, Cabriole Legs, Japanned, Upholstered, 43 x 24 x 17 In. 561.00
Chair, William & Mary, Maple, Black Paint, Carved Crest Rail, Cane Back, Seat, c.1740, 46 In. 345.00
Chair, William IV, Mahogany, Round Crest, Medial Splat, Scroll Arms, c.1840, Pair 1058.00
Chair, Windsor, 6 Spindles, Black Paint, Sack Back, Arms, New England, 37 In.. . . . . 928.00
Chair, Windsor, 7 Spindles, Serpentine Crest Rail, White Paint. 200.00
Chair, Windsor, 7 Spindles, Black Paint, Sack Back, Arched Crest, Arms, 35 In.. . . . . 348.00
Chair, Windsor, 7 Spindles, Turned Center Spindle, Shaped Crest, Carved Ears, Pa., 40 In. . . . 13800.00
Chair, Windsor, 9 Spindles, Bamboo Turned, Painted, Downswept Arms, 37 x 17 In. 412.00
Chair, Windsor, 9 Spindles, Bamboo, Saddle Seat, H-Stretcher, Arms, 39½ In.. . . . . 523.00
Chair, Windsor, Arrow Back, Plank Seat, 19th Century, Pair 55.00
Chair, Windsor, Beech, Elm Shaped Seat, England, c.1800, 31 In. 1315.00
Chair, Windsor, Birdcage, Bamboo Turned, c.1810 . . . . 220.00
Chair, Windsor, Bow Back, Oak, Cane Seat, 24 In.. . . . . *illus* 60.00
Chair, Windsor, Bow Back, 8 Spindles, c.1800 . . . . 247.00

Furniture, Chair, J.M. Young, Morris, Slats, Cushion, Flat Arms, 39 x 32 x 36 In.
$5010.00

Furniture, Chair, Lounge, Robsjohn-Gibbings, Mahogany, Upholstered, Widdicomb,
31 x 28 In.
$2500.00

Furniture, Chair, Mahogany, Arched Crest, Upholstered, c.1900, 53 In.
$240.00

Furniture, Chair, Old Hickory, Y-Back, Twigs, Stool,
32 x 28 x 27-In. Chair, 2 Piece
$145.00

Furniture, Chair, Ottoman, Eames, Walnut, Leather, Aluminum, Herman Miller, c.2000, 32 x 33 In. $1900.00

Furniture, Chair, Queen Anne, Mahogany, 39½ In. $880.00

Furniture, Chair, Regency, Mahogany, Acanthus, 36 In., Pair. $232.00

Furniture, Chair, Savonarola, Walnut, Hoof Feet, Italy, Late 18th Century, 32 In. $800.00

Chair, Windsor, Bow Back, Hartford, c.1800, 36 In. 345.00
Chair, Windsor, Bow Back, 9 Spindles, Turned H-Stretcher, Saddle Seat, Blue, Child's, 23 In.. .... 495.00
Chair, Windsor, Bow Back, Green Gray Paint, Arms, Early 1800s, 44 x 17½ In.. .... 588.00
Chair, Windsor, Bow Back, Painted, 35 In. .... *illus* 660.00
Chair, Windsor, Bow Back, Blue Paint, New England, c.1810, 36½ x 16½ In., Pair 1880.00
Chair, Windsor, Bow Back, Blue Paint, c.1810, 36½ In., Pair 1880.00
Chair, Windsor, Brace Back, 11 Spindles, Turned Legs, Green Paint, Connecticut, 35 In., Pair. 2990.00
Chair, Windsor, Colonial Revival, Pine, 35 In. 411.00
Chair, Windsor, Comb Back, Arms, Phoenix Chair Company 850.00
Chair, Windsor, Comb Back, Splayed Legs, Arrow Feet, H-Stretcher, Paint, Lancaster, Pa., 15 In. 935.00
Chair, Windsor, Comb Back, Mixed Woods, Painted, Knuckled Arms, c.1780, 47 In. 3220.00
Chair, Windsor, Comb Back, 9 Spindles, U-Shape Arm, Scrolled Knuckles, 46¾ x 27 In. 4025.00
Chair, Windsor, Comb Back, Green Paint, Knuckle Arms, c.1780, 42 In. 45000.00
Chair, Windsor, Commode, 5 Bamboo Spindles, Mixed Woods, Shaped Skirt, 37 In. 115.00
Chair, Windsor, Continuous Arm, Black Over Red & Green Paint, 35 In. 1763.00
Chair, Windsor, Continuous Arm, 11 Spindles, Turned Legs, c.1800, 37 x 21 In. 2300.00
Chair, Windsor, Continuous Arm, 9 Spindles, Ring Turned, Saddle Seat, Arms, 1789 .... 4310.00
Chair, Windsor, Continuous Arm, Black Paint, Parcel Gilt, Rhode Island, 36 In., Pair 18000.00
Chair, Windsor, English Yew, Spindle Inset Backrest, U-Shape Arms, Saddle Seat, 18 In. 558.00
Chair, Windsor, Fanback, 7 Spindles, Black, Saddle Seat, Bamboo Turnings, 19th Century, 35 In. 173.00
Chair, Windsor, Fanback, Shaped Crest, 7 Spindles, H-Stretcher, E. Tracy, c.1790, 35 In. 270.00
Chair, Windsor, Fanback, Swivel Base, Arms 316.00
Chair, Windsor, Fanback, 6 Spindles, Shaped Crest Rail, Bamboo Turned, Stretchers, 23 In... 660.00
Chair, Windsor, Fanback, Brown Paint, New England, Late 18th Century, 36 In.. .... 764.00
Chair, Windsor, Fanback, 7 Spindles, Scrolled Ears, 18th Century 920.00
Chair, Windsor, Fanback, 7 Spindles, Mixed Woods, Baluster Turned Stiles, 40 In. 1150.00
Chair, Windsor, Fanback, 6 Spindles, Painted, Serpentine Crest, Child's, c.1880, 34 In. 2585.00
Chair, Windsor, Fanback, Painted, 35 x 16 In. 3525.00
Chair, Windsor, Half Arrow Back, Mixed Wood, Crossed Splat, Red, Gold Striping, 35 In., Pair 230.00
Chair, Windsor, High Back, Curved Crest Rail, Spindles, Plank Seat, 43 x 18 x 16 In. 100.00
Chair, Windsor, High Back, 6 Spindles, Plank Seat, 43½ x 18½ x 16¾ In.. .... 112.00
Chair, Windsor, Hoop Back, 7 Spindles, Plank Seat, 19th Century, 37 In.. .... 83.00
Chair, Windsor, Hoop Back, Yew, Bentwood, Spindles, Arms, 18th Century 1300.00
Chair, Windsor, Low Back, Ball Feet, Green Paint, 27½ In. .... *illus* 3300.00
Chair, Windsor, Rod Back, Red Paint, New England, c.1825, 35 In. 600.00
Chair, Windsor, Sack Back, Plank Seat, Turned Legs, Arms, New England, 34½ In. 210.00
Chair, Windsor, Sack Back, 7 Spindles, Painted, Bulbous Stretchers, 1700s, 33½ In. 460.00
Chair, Windsor, Sack Back, Red Paint, Arms, New England, 38 In. 580.00
Chair, Windsor, Sack Back, Green Paint, Arms, c.1790, 37 In.. .... 600.00
Chair, Windsor, Sack Back, Metal, Black, Red Paint, Arms, Ohio, Early 1900s, 35½ In. 863.00
Chair, Windsor, Sack Back, Red Paint, New England, c.1800, 38 In.. .... 1080.00
Chair, Windsor, Sack Back, Painted, c.1800, 37½ In.. .... 1200.00
Chair, Windsor, Sack Back, 6 Flared Spindles, Black Paint, Arched Crest, Arms, 38 In. 1624.00
Chair, Windsor, Sack Back, Mixed Wood, Stout Baluster Turned Legs, c.1800, 16¾ In.. .... 2070.00
Chair, Windsor, Sack Back, Poplar, Baluster Supports, Knuckle Arms, c.1780, 37 In. 2330.00
Chair, Windsor, Sack Back, Black Paint, 38½ In. 2640.00
Chair, Windsor, Sack Back, Maroon Paint, Arms, New England, c.1800, 39 In. 3600.00
Chair, Windsor, Sack Back, Black Paint, Arms, Rhode Island, c.1790, 38½ In. 5700.00
Chair, Windsor, Sack Back, Blue Over Green Paint, Knuckle Arms, Philadelphia 7605.00
Chair, Windsor, Sack Back, Lancaster County, c.1766 .... 10530.00
Chair, Windsor, Sack Back, 6 Spindles, Yellow Paint, Knuckle Arms, New England, 36 In. 10575.00
Chair, Windsor, Slat Back, Yellow Ground, Green, Black Design, c.1845, 15 x 29 In., Pair 173.00
Chair, Windsor, Writing Arm, 5 Spindles, Drawer, 19th Century 467.00
Chair, Windsor, Writing Arm, Slat Back, Grain Paint, Yellow, Gilt, c.1840, 47 In.. .... 863.00
Chair, Windsor, Writing Arm, Poplar Seat, Drawer, Upholstered, 47 x 37 In. 2875.00
Chair, Windsor, Writing Arm, Bottle Green Paint, Stamped, C.C. Clark, c.1750 .... 10500.00
Chair, Windsor Style, Comb Back, Paint, Stamped, D.R. Dimes, 44 In. .... *illus* 550.00
Chair, Wing, Arched Crest, Curved Seat Rail, Loose Cushion, Flared Arms, 47 x 19 In. 633.00
Chair, Wing, Carved, Walnut Legs, Upholstered, Scrolled Arms, 1800s, 41 x 33 In. 500.00
Chair, Wing, Chippendale, Mahogany, England, Early 18th Century, 44 In. .... *illus* 5175.00
Chair, Wing, Chippendale, Mahogany, Cabriole Legs, Ireland, 47 x 34 x 26 In. .... *illus* 1350.00
Chair, Wing, Chippendale, Mahogany, Marlboro Legs, Stretcher, Damask Upholstery, 43 x 32 In. 280.00
Chair, Wing, Chippendale, Mahogany, Shell Carved, Upholstery, Ireland, 48 x 34 In. 1380.00
Chair, Wing, Chippendale Style, Mahogany, Red Upholstery, Claw & Ball Feet, 43 In. 115.00
Chair, Wing, Chippendale Style, Shaped Back, Upholstered, Scroll Arms, 43 x 32 In. 150.00
Chair, Wing, Chippendale Style, Tiger Maple, Lamb's Tongue, Upholstered, Scroll Arms 468.00

Chair, Wing, Chippendale Style, Leather, Brass Tacks, Cabriole Front Legs, 42 In., Pair 1150.00
Chair, Wing, Georgian, Crewelwork, Cabriole Legs, Paw Feet, Upholstered, 20 In.. . . . . 2115.00
Chair, Wing, Queen Anne, Walnut, Cabriole Legs, Trefoil Feet, Upholstered, 44 ½ In. 4025.00
Chair, Wing, Serpentine Crest, Seat Cushion, Box Stretchers, Casters, 48 x 17 ½ In. 3105.00
Chair, Winged Griffin, Carved, Fabric, 47 x 41 x 43 In. . . . . *illus* 1800.00
Chair, Wood, Carved, 3 Monkeys Eating Fruit, In Tree, Dragon Shape Armrests, 48 x 28 In. . . 30.00
Chair, Wormley, Executive, Black Leather, Walnut & Steel Base, 27 ½ x 28 x 41 In.. . . . . 660.00
Chair, Wormley, Walnut, Loose Cushions, Leather Webbing, Arms, 16 ½ x 28 ½ In.. . . . . 58.00
Chair, Zoar, Cherry, Laminated, Balloon Back, Hexagonal, Ohio, c.1835, 38 In. 633.00
Chair Set, Anthony Quervelle, Neoclassical, Mahogany, Slip Seat, c.1825, 6 . . . . 7800.00
Chair Set, Balloon Back, Mixed Woods, Poplar, Painted Decoration, Stenciled, 34 In., 6 . . . . . 489.00
Chair Set, Biedermeier, Maple, Ebonized, C-Shape Crest, Upholstered Seat, 19 In., 6. . . . . 881.00
Chair Set, Charles X, Mahogany, 3 Slats, Slip Seat, Saber Legs, 18 ½ In., 6 . . . . 2115.00
Chair Set, Chippendale, Gothic Pierced Splat, H-Stretchers, Leather Seat, 39 In., 6 . . . . 1955.00
Chair Set, Chippendale Style, Mahogany, Carved, Pierced Splat, Silk Upholstery, 37 In., Pair . 518.00
Chair Set, Country, Rails, Rush Woven Seats, 43 x 17 ½ x 19 In., 6 . . . . 295.00
Chair Set, Eames, DCM, Plywood, Chrome, Herman Miller, 19 x 21 In., 4. . . . . 1020.00
Chair Set, Eames, Orange Fiberglass, Eiffel Tower Base, Herman Miller, 1958, 6 . . . . 840.00
Chair Set, English Regency, Mahogany, Carved, Reeded Top Rail, Rope Twist Slat, 18 In., 4 . . 823.00
Chair Set, Fan Shaped, Cane Splat, Seat, Circular Legs, Raised, 35 In., 4 . . . . 3744.00
Chair Set, Federal, Mahogany, Ball Applied Cross Splat, Drop-In Seat, 2 Armchairs, 10. . . . . . 9775.00
Chair Set, Federal Shield, Flower Carved, Molded Crest Rail, 38 ½ x 20 x 17 ½ In., 4 . . . . 1652.00
Chair Set, Federal Style, Shield Back, Bellflowers, Wheat Sheaves, 37 In., 6 . . . . 590.00
Chair Set, Folding, Yellow Polypropylene Seat & Back, G. Piretti, 18 x 20 x 30 In., 4 . . . . 120.00
Chair Set, Fruitwood, Cartouche Shape Back, Carved Crest, Upholstered, Padded Arms, 4 . . . 460.00
Chair Set, G. Nakashima, Walnut, 7 Spindles, 36 ½ x 19 x 18 ½ In., 4 . . . . 6600.00
Chair Set, George II Style, Walnut, Rope Carved Crest, Vase Shape Splat, 39 ½ In., 6 . . . . 1440.00
Chair Set, George III, Mahogany, Gothic Chippendale Style, 2 Armchairs, 41 In., 10. . . . . 4080.00
Chair Set, George III, Mahogany, Carved, Chippendale Style, Earred Crest, 40 In., 8 . . . . 5280.00
Chair Set, George III Style, Mahogany, Shaped & Earred Crest, Padded Seat, 37 In., 6. . . . . . . 840.00
Chair Set, George III Style, Mahogany, Dome Crest, Sheaf Splat, 36 In., 8 . . . . 2400.00
Chair Set, George III Style, Mahogany, Domed, Shell Carved Crest, Saddle Seat, 38 ½ In., 8 . . 4320.00
Chair Set, Gondola, Beech, Renaissance Style Inlay, Bellflowers, 38 x 18 In., 4 . . . . 920.00
Chair Set, Gothic Revival, Upholstered, New York City, c.1850, 33 ½ In., 8. . . . . 7638.00
Chair Set, H. Bertoia, Chrome Wire, Gray Wool Seat Pads, 21 x 22 x 30 ½ In., 12. . . . . 3240.00
Chair Set, H. Bertoia, Knoll, Fabric Pad Seats, White Vinyl Coated Steel, 30 x 22 In., 8 . . . . . . 3335.00
Chair Set, Hepplewhite, Mahogany, Pierced Scalloped Crests, 38 x 25 In., 6. . . . . 1763.00
Chair Set, Hepplewhite Style, Mahogany, Shield Back, Lotus Splats, Padded Seat, 38 In., 10. . 9000.00
Chair Set, Industrial Design, Steel, Domed Back, Rectangular Splat, Splayed Legs, 33 In., 6 . 2640.00
Chair Set, Jacobean Style, Oak, Carved, Barley Twist Supports, 2 Armchairs, 18 ½ In., 8 . . . . . 1880.00
Chair Set, Kaare Klint, Mahogany, Leather Upholstery, Tacks, R. Rasmussen, 33 In., 8 . . . . . . 22500.00
Chair Set, Ladder Back, 3 Shaped Slats, Rush Seat, Turned Stretcher, Square Legs, 39 In., 10 2280.00
Chair Set, Ladder Back, Black Paint, 4 Arched Slats, Turned Stiles, Rush Seats, 43 In., 6 . . . . 1495.00
Chair Set, Louis XV Style, Beech, Rectangular Seat & Back, Padded, Scroll Arms, 40 In., 8 . . . 6600.00
Chair Set, Louis XVI Style, Mahogany, Cane Back, Bulbous Feet, 38 In., 8 . . . . *illus* 360.00
Chair Set, Mahogany, Leaf Carving, 2 Armchairs, c.1835, 18 In., 8 . . . . 3819.00
Chair Set, Mahogany, Peaked Crest, Tapered Legs, Padded Seats, 4 . . . . 10755.00
Chair Set, Napoleon III, Gilt, Louis XVI Style, Oval Back, Seat, Fluted Legs, 29 In., 4. . . . . 2400.00
Chair Set, Neoclassical, Curly Maple, Carved Tablet Top, Turned Legs, Cane Seat, 33 ½ In., 6 . 2070.00
Chair Set, Neoclassical, Mahogany, Carved, Padded Seat, New York, c.1820, 33 In., 4 . . . . 1875.00
Chair Set, Neoclassical, Mahogany, Gondola Shape, Leaf Carving, Crest, 36 In., 8. . . . . 2880.00
Chair Set, Neoclassical, Paint Decorated, Urn Crest, Diamond Panel, Molded Rail, 4 . . . . 1528.00
Chair Set, Neoclassical Style, Medallion Back, Painted, Overstuffed Seats, 36 ¼ In., 4 . . . . 2124.00
Chair Set, Oak, Carved, Historical Figures, Arched Crest, Barley Twist Stiles, 14. . . . . 4994.00
Chair Set, Oak, Larkin, Pressed Backs, Pressed Leather Seats, c.1900, 41 In., 6 . . . . 280.00
Chair Set, Parlor, Belter, Rosewood, Laminated, c.1850, 34 x 18 In., 4 . . . . 3190.00
Chair Set, Patio, Rattan Seat, Metal Legs, 3 Stools, Plywood, Metal, Denmark, 1950s, 5 . *illus* 270.00
Chair Set, Provincial, Oak, Scalloped Shell Crest, Rush Seat, Cabriole Legs, 36 ¼ In., 6. . . . . . 1920.00
Chair Set, Provincial Louis XV Style, Fruitwood, Domed Crest, Shell, Padded, 41 In., 8 . . . . . . 1560.00
Chair Set, Queen Anne, Black Lacquer, Vase Splat, Gilt Oriental Design, 43 In., 8 . . . . 10200.00
Chair Set, Queen Anne, Walnut, Walnut, 4 . . . . 4800.00
Chair Set, Queen Anne Style, Mixed Woods, Scrolled Crest, Cabriole Legs, 2 Armchairs, 12 . . . 4025.00
Chair Set, Regency, Mahogany, Cane Back, Rolled Arms, Turned Legs, 35 In., 4. . . . . 3910.00
Chair Set, Regency, Upholstered Slip Seat, Turned Front Legs, England, 33 x 18 x 15 In. 472.00
Chair Set, Regency Style, Mahogany, Concave Rail, Pierced Splat, 35 In., 6 . . . . 590.00
Chair Set, Regency Style, Mahogany, Satinwood, Ebony Band, Paneled Crest Rail, Arms, 4. . . 769.00

Furniture, Chair, Sheraton Style, Painted Flowers, c.1900, 40 x 24 x 19 In.
$695.00

Furniture, Chair, Theater Seat, Art Deco, 1930s, 34 x 42 In., Pair
$350.00

Furniture, Chair, Thonet, Bentwood, Vinyl, 31 x 36 x 28 In., Pair
$720.00

Furniture, Chair, Windsor, Bow Back, Oak, Cane Seat, 24 In.
$60.00

F

Furniture, Chair, Windsor, Bow Back, Painted, 35 In.
$660.00

Furniture, Chair, Windsor, Low Back, Ball Feet, Green Paint, 27 ½ In.
$3300.00

Furniture, Chair, Windsor Style, Comb Back, Paint, Stamped, D.R. Dimes, 44 In.
$550.00

Furniture, Chair, Wing, Chippendale, Mahogany, Cabriole Legs, Ireland, 47 x 34 x 26 In.
$1350.00

Chair Set, Renaissance Revival, Oak, Beast, Leaf Carving, Twist Legs, 18 In., 8 . . . . 1175.00
Chair Set, Renaissance Revival, Upholstered Back, Seat, Mahogany, 2 Armchairs, 41 In., 6 . . 518.00
Chair Set, Renaissance Revival, Walnut, Carved Shell, Incised, Turned Legs, 1870, 36 In., 4. . 225.00
Chair Set, Risom, Walnut, Cane Back, Black Vinyl Seat, 20 x 21 x 32 In., 6 . . . . 780.00
Chair Set, Roycroft, Spanish Mission Style, Oak, Upholstered, Arts & Crafts, 37 In., 6 . . . . 650.00
Chair Set, Shaker, Ladder Back, 3 Slats, Maple, Tape Seats, Mt. Lebanon, c.1925, 40 ½ In., 6 . 4680.00
Chair Set, Sheraton, Mahogany, Padded Seat, 2 Armchairs, 33 In., 10 . . . . 8000.00
Chair Set, Sheraton, Yellow, Balloon Rush Seat, Grape & Leaf Crest Rail, 33 In., 8 . . . . 2300.00
Chair Set, Sheraton Style, Mahogany, Straight Top Rails, 37 In., 10 . . . . 1180.00
Chair Set, Sheraton Style, Mahogany, Padded Leather Seat, Arm, 34 ½ In., 7 . . . . 3168.00
Chair Set, Victorian, Renaissance, Walnut, Carved, c.1870, 31 x 22 In., 6. . . . . 825.00
Chair Set, Victorian, Walnut, 36 x 14 In., 12 . . . . 2090.00
Chair Set, Victorian Style, Wrought Metal, Scrolled Back, Strapwork Seat, 40 In., 6. . . . . 3600.00
Chair Set, W. McArthur, Aluminum, Green Vinyl Upholstery, 17 x 16 ½ x 33 ½ In., 4 . . . . 1200.00
Chair Set, Wicker, Hooped Back, Rattan, Cushion, 41 x 24 x 23 In., 4. 252.00
Chair Set, William & Mary, Ox Yoke Crest Rail, Rush Woven Seat, 17 x 42 In., 6 . . . . 2100.00
Chair Set, William IV Style, Mahogany, Upholstered, Casters, 43 In., 7 . . . . *illus* 2700.00
Chair Set, Windsor, Birdcage, Black Paint, 7 Bamboo Spindles, Stretcher, 33 In., 4 . . . . 1150.00
Chair Set, Windsor, Bow Back, Saddle Seats, Black Paint, 2 Armchairs, 37 ½ In., 6 . . . . 1150.00
Chair Set, Windsor, Bow Back, Painted, H-Stretcher, Boston, Early 1800s, 37 In., 4 . . . . 4406.00
Chair Set, Windsor, Decorated, Mixed Woods, Bamboo Turned Legs, Stretchers, 34 In., 6 . . . . 3738.00
Chair Set, Windsor, Rabbit Ear, Plank Seat, Yellow, Fruit Design, 4 . . . . 632.00
Chair Set, Windsor, Rod Back, Black Paint, c.1820, 35 In., 4 . . . . 840.00
Chair Set, Windsor, Rod Back, Red, Brown, Nova Scotia, 1825, 6. . . . . 4988.00
Chair Set, Windsor, Step-Down, Red, 4. . . . . 862.00
Chair Set, Windsor, Thumb Back, Yellow Paint, Design On Backs, 6 . . . . 2588.00
Chair Set, Windsor, Thumb Back, Yellow Paint, 5 . . . . 2900.00
Chair, Hall, Oak, Slats, Solid Seat, Derby & Co., 41 x 16 x 17 In.. . . . . 302.00
Chair, Rocker, is listed under Rocker in this category.
Chair-Table, 2-Board Top, Mustard Yellow, 43 In.. . . . . 3975.00
Chair-Table, 2-Board Top, Oval, 53 x 42 ½ In.. . . . . 25000.00
Chair-Table, Chestnut, Lift Top Seat, Hinges, 19th Century, 30 x 47 ½ x 33 ¾ In. 330.00
Chair-Table, Green Paint, Shoefoot, New England, c.1800, 27 x 46 In.. . . . . 1175.00
Chair-Table, Hudson Valley, 3-Board Scrubbed Top, Shoefoot Base, 48 x 27 In.. . . . . 2090.00
Chair-Table, Pine, Maple, Round Top, Spanish Brown Paint, 30 x 48 In.. . . . . 6960.00
Chair-Table, Pine, Poplar, 3-Board Top, Lidded Seat, Brown Paint, 29 x 35 In. 1610.00
Chair-Table, Pine, Scrubbed Top, Round Lift Seat, Red Paint, 56 ½ x 29 In.. . . . . 1380.00
Chair-Table, Pine, Shoe Foot, 2 Drawers, Red Paint, Late 18th Century, 29 ½ x 51 ¾ In. 8225.00
Chaise Longue, Anglo-Indian Style, Hardwood, Cane, 20th Century, 96 In.. . . . . 3750.00
Chaise Longue, Barrel Back, Tufted Velvet Upholstery, Fluted Legs, c.1940, 32 x 77 In.. . . . . . . 400.00
Chaise Longue, French Style, 2 Sections, Ivory Finish, High Back, Loose Cushion, 29 x 16 In. 690.00
Chaise Longue, Louis XV, Gilt, Scrolled Supports, Upholstered, 39 ½ x 64 ½ In.. . . . . 7200.00
Chaise Longue, Louis XV Style, Beech, Cane Back, Cushion Seat, 37 x 56 In.. . . . . 1320.00
Chaise Longue, Louis XVI, Walnut, Curved Back & Foot, Beaded Molding, 36 x 72 x 26 In. . . 1527.00
Chaise Longue, V. Kagan, Channeled Back, Curved Arms, Lucite Leg, 28 x 31 x 66 In. . . *illus* 1600.00
Chaise Longue, Walnut, Damask Upholstery, Eastlake, Late 19th Century, 24 x 76 In. . . *illus* 200.00
Cheese Trolley, Regency, Mahogany, Brass Casters, England, c.1820, 7 x 15 x 7 In.. . . . . 695.00
Chest, 6-Board, Blue Paint, Bootjack Ends, 32 x 56 In.. . . . . 1495.00
Chest, American Empire, Mahogany, Projecting Drawer, 2 Recessed Drawers, 13 x 13 In. 294.00
Chest, Applied Molding, String Inlay, 4 Graduated Drawers, Southern, 39 x 37 In.. . . . . 1495.00
Chest, Bachelor's, Chippendale, Mahogany, 4 Drawers, Bracket Feet, Britain, c.1780, 33 x 37 x 18 In. 3000.00
Chest, Bachelor's, Edwardian, Mahogany, 4 Graduated Drawers, 32 ½ x 22 ¼ x 15 ¾ In.. . . . . 1584.00
Chest, Bachelor's, George III, Mahogany, 4 Drawers, 31 ½ x 31 x 16 ½ In.. . . . . 1410.00
Chest, Bachelor's, George III Style, Mahogany, 2 Short Over 3 Long Drawers, 30 x 28 In., Pair 1680.00
Chest, Bachelor's, George III Style, Mahogany, Canted Corners, 4 Drawers, 29 x 24 In., Pair. . 4080.00
Chest, Baker Furniture, Bowfront, Cock-Beaded Drawers, Apron, Splayed Feet, 30 x 28 In. . . . 679.00
Chest, Baker Furniture, Georgian Style, Bowfront, 4 Graduated Drawers, 32 x 34 In.. . . . . 1003.00
Chest, Biedermeier, Curly Maple, 4 Drawers, Ebonized Columns, 36 x 35 In., Pair 3480.00
Chest, Biedermeier, Satinwood, Bowfront, 4 Long Drawers, Continental, 32 x 29 In. 2703.00
Chest, Biedermeier, Walnut, Inlay, Burl, Boxwood, Ebony Borders, 10 x 9 In. 1763.00
Chest, Biedermeier, Walnut, Marble Top, 3 Drawers, Shaped Base, 34 x 43 x 17 In. 1293.00
Chest, Bird's-Eye Maple, 4-Stepped Back, 10 Drawers, Mahogany Pulls, 51 x 40 x 18 In.. . . . . 1650.00
Chest, Blanket, 2 Drawers, Dovetailed, 28 x 21 x 51 In.. . . . . 2185.00
Chest, Blanket, 2 Drawers, Red Paint, 18th Century 2850.00
Chest, Blanket, 6-Board, Blue Paint, Flowers, J.G., Schoharie County, N.Y., 1815, 22 x 44 In.. . 1725.00
Chest, Blanket, 6-Board, Smoke & Paint Decorated, Lift Top, New England, 28 x 50 In.. . . . . . 3173.00

Furniture, Chair, Wing, Chippendale, Mahogany, England, Early 18th Century, 44 In.
$5175.00

Furniture, Chair, Winged Griffin, Carved, Fabric, 47 x 41 x 43 In.
$1800.00

Furniture, Chair Set, Louis XVI Style, Mahogany, Cane Back, Bulbous Feet, 38 In., 8
$360.00

Furniture, Chair Set, Patio, Rattan Seat, Metal Legs, 3 Stools, Plywood, Metal, Denmark, 1950s, 5
$270.00

Furniture, Chair Set, William IV Style, Mahogany, Upholstered, Casters, 43 In., 7
$2700.00

Furniture, Chaise Longue, V. Kagan, Channeled Back, Curved Arms, Lucite Leg, 28 x 31 x 66 In.
$1600.00

Furniture, Chaise Longue, Walnut, Damask Upholstery, Eastlake, Late 19th Century, 24 x 76 In.
$200.00

Furniture, Chest, Blanket, Cherry, Birch, Ocher & Yellow Sponge, 24 x 44 x 19 In.
$1100.00

Furniture, Chest, Federal, Walnut, Pine, 2 Drawers, Iron Strap Hinges, c.1885, 27 x 47 x 18 In.
$2600.00

Furniture, Chest, Mahogany, Bowfront, England, 40 x 45 x 21 In.
$1100.00

Furniture, Chest, Blanket, Poplar, Painted, Initials, Werrey, 1882, 28 x 48 x 23 In.
$11500.00

Furniture, Chest, George III, Mahogany, Molded Edge, Ogee Bracket Feet, 35 x 33 x 18 In.
$2000.00

Furniture, Chest, Mule, Mahogany, Oak, Columns, Inlaid, England, 41 x 62 x 22 In.
$3105.00

Furniture, Chest, Bombe, Louis XV Style, Burl Veneers, Late 19th Century, 54 x 23 x 11 ½ In.
$650.00

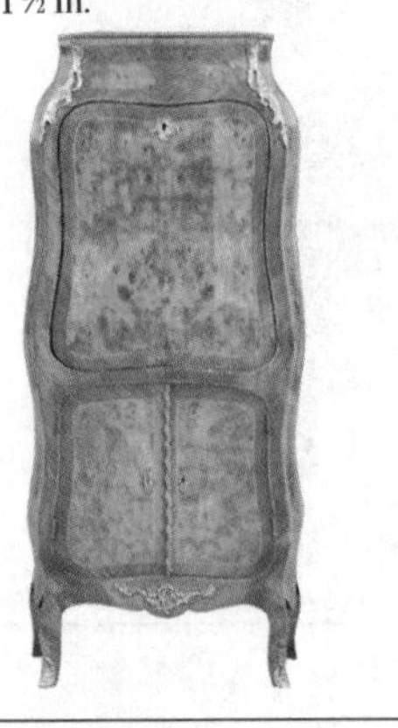

Furniture, Chest, Georgian, Walnut, String Inlay, Cock-Beaded, 31 x 74 x 23 In.
$5250.00

Furniture, Chest, Mule, Pine, New England, 44 x 41 ½ x 18 In.
$715.00

Furniture, Chest, Cottage, Fold-Out Writing Surface, Painted, Italy, c.1950, 82 x 30 x 17 In.
$475.00

Furniture, Chest, Heywood-Wakefield, Symphonic, Wheat Finish, 1958, 44 x 34 x 18 In.
$300.00

Furniture, Chest, Neoclassical, Cherry, Maple, c.1825-35, 57 ½ x 43 ½ x 18 In.
$1093.00

Chest, Blanket, 6-Board, Decorated, Poplar, Interior Till, Dovetailed, Late 1700s, 19 x 41 In. . 5462.00
Chest, Blanket, Arts & Crafts, Lift Top, Cedar Lined, 2 Drawers, 46 x 20 x 38 In. 1140.00
Chest, Blanket, Blue Paint, Dovetailed, Molded Base, 43 In. 464.00
Chest, Blanket, Bullnose Edge, Breadboard Ends, Strap Handles, 1800s, 24 x 61 ½ In. 224.00
Chest, Blanket, Carved, Stubby Feet, 19th Century, 36 x 13 x 17 In. 413.00
Chest, Blanket, Cherry, Birch, Ocher & Yellow Sponge, 24 x 44 x 19 In. . . . . *illus* 1100.00
Chest, Blanket, Chestnut, Lid, Till, Iron Hinges, 2 Drawers, Bun Feet, Pa., 29 x 55 x 22 In. . . . 3574.00
Chest, Blanket, Chippendale, Pine, Red Brown Paint, Bracket Base, Dovetailed, 22 x 45 x 22 In. 150.00
Chest, Blanket, Chippendale, Pine, 2 Drawers, Lift Top, Bracket, 34 x 18 ½ x 36 In. 330.00
Chest, Blanket, Chippendale, Country Pine, False Drawer Top, Drawers, Pulls, 37 x 38 x 18 In. 350.00
Chest, Blanket, Chippendale, Paint Decorated, Lift Top, 18th Century, 30 x 49 In. 980.00
Chest, Blanket, Chippendale, Poplar, Painted, 2 Drawers, 42 x 38 x 17 ½ In. 1044.00
Chest, Blanket, Chippendale, Maple, 3 Drawers, Molded Edge, Bracket Base, 46 x 38 x 18 In. . 1380.00
Chest, Blanket, Chippendale, Walnut, Poplar, Breadboard Lid, c.1774, 29 ¾ x 52 ½ In. 2875.00
Chest, Blanket, Dovetailed, Red Design, Yellow Round, Heart Center, Turned Feet, 1810 . . . . . 6355.00
Chest, Blanket, Federal, Cherry, Figured Maple, Hinged Top, Drawers, 41 x 38 x 19 In. 345.00
Chest, Blanket, Federal, Tiger Maple, Hinged Top, 24 x 43 ½ x 19 In. 1380.00
Chest, Blanket, Federal, Pine, Red, Brown Paint, Bootjack Ends, c.1810, 25 x 25 In. 4200.00
Chest, Blanket, Federal, Blue Paint, c.1825, 19 ¾ x 43 ¼ x 17 ¼ In. 6000.00
Chest, Blanket, Federal, Inlaid Walnut, Pennsylvania, c.1820, 17 x 21 ½ In. 7500.00
Chest, Blanket, Grain Paint, Dovetailed, Molded Lid, Bracket Feet, Pa., 20 ½ x 38 x 19 In. 165.00
Chest, Blanket, Green Paint, 6-Board, Lift Top, Shaped Legs, N.H., 7 x 10 x 5 In. 1645.00
Chest, Blanket, Italian, Baroque, Walnut, Hinged Top, 19th Century, 22 x 60 x 21 In. 1880.00
Chest, Blanket, Lift Top, 2 False Drawers, 38 x 39 x 18 In. 595.00
Chest, Blanket, Lift Top, Arts & Crafts, Oak, Panels, 42 x 19 ¾ x 23 In. 728.00
Chest, Blanket, Lift Top, Red Paint, Drawer, Bootjack Ends, c.1800, 42 ½ x 20 ¼ In. 805.00
Chest, Blanket, Lift Top, Red Paint, Till, Turned Ball Feet, Lanc. Cty., 11 x 13 x 8 In. 1880.00
Chest, Blanket, Molded Edge, Open Case, Bracket Feet, Painted, 20 x 25 In. 259.00
Chest, Blanket, Mustard & Brown Grain Paint, 2 Drawers, Sponge Design, c.1820, 41 x 42 x 21 In. . 1553.00
Chest, Blanket, Painted, Dark Blue, Compass Rose, Nautical, Dovetailed, 14 x 32 x 17 In. 690.00
Chest, Blanket, Pine, Dovetailed, Wrought Nails, Lidded Till, Molding, 19 ½ x 39 In. 138.00
Chest, Blanket, Pine, Brown Paint, Till, Bootjack Ends, Snipe Hinges, 1800s, 25 x 49 In. 250.00
Chest, Blanket, Pine, Dovetailed, Iron Side Handles, 21 ½ x 43 x 20 ½ In. 275.00
Chest, Blanket, Pine, 6-Board, Salmon, Wavy Lines, Circles, Iron Handles, Pa., 14 x 34 In. . . . 288.00
Chest, Blanket, Pine, Lift Top, Applied Bracket Base, Handles, 21 ½ x 43 ½ x 20 ½ In. 308.00
Chest, Blanket, Pine, Red & Blue Paint, Hinged Lid, Inset Panels, 19th Century, 25 x 42 x 21 In. 345.00
Chest, Blanket, Pine, Lift Top, Base, Drawer, Bootjack, 19th Century 425.00
Chest, Blanket, Pine, Red Paint, Black Trim, Reeded Lid, Turned Feet, 19 ½ x 36 In. 460.00
Chest, Blanket, Pine, Cotter Hinges, 2 Drawers, Oval Brass Pulls, 38 x 34 x 18 In. 546.00
Chest, Blanket, Pine, Drawer, Ball Feet, Batwing Brasses, Snipe Hinges, 1800s, 33 x 39 In. . . . 550.00
Chest, Blanket, Pine, Lift Top, 2 Drawers, Shaped Apron, 43 x 50 x 19 In. 550.00
Chest, Blanket, Pine, Decorated, Turned Feet, Interior Till, Drawers, 24 x 40 In. 748.00
Chest, Blanket, Pine, 6-Board, Blue, Red Stripes, Flower Panels, Bracket Base, 18th Century, 25 x 54 ½ In. 805.00
Chest, Blanket, Pine, Drawer, Iron Strap Hinges, Milk Glass Knobs, 34 x 49 x 20 In. 977.00
Chest, Blanket, Pine, Grain Painted, Yellow & Red, Till, Turned Feet, Pa., 44 x 22 x 25 In. 1208.00
Chest, Blanket, Pine, Paneled Case, Square Feet, 19th Century, 26 x 43 x 19 In. 1320.00
Chest, Blanket, Pine, 6-Board, Red & Yellow Paint, Dovetailed, Interior Till, 15 x 39 In. 1380.00
Chest, Blanket, Pine, Blue Gray, Paint, Dovetailed, Strap Hinges, Lock, Till, 49 x 22 In. 1380.00
Chest, Blanket, Pine, Poplar, Lift Top, Yellow, Red Grain Paint, 3 Drawers, 29 ½ x 49 In. 1840.00
Chest, Blanket, Pine, Red Paint, Arched Molding, Bootjack Ends, Child's, 18 x 28 In. 1856.00
Chest, Blanket, Pine, 6-Board, Green Paint, Thumbnail Top, Bootjack Ends, 21 x 43 In. 2050.00
Chest, Blanket, Pine, 6-Board, Hinged Top, Vinegar Paint, N.H., 22 x 39 In. 2233.00
Chest, Blanket, Pine, Painted, Red & Black, Scalloped Apron, 29 x 37 x 16 In. 2900.00
Chest, Blanket, Poplar, Pine, Painted, Interior Till, c.1829, 26 x 50 In. 518.00
Chest, Blanket, Poplar, 6-Board, Blue Paint, Wrought Iron Strap Hinges, 40 x 16 ½ In. 546.00
Chest, Blanket, Poplar, Pine, Paint, Reeded Molding, 2 Drawers, Bracket Base, 24 x 40 x 18 In. 1093.00
Chest, Blanket, Poplar, Painted, Initials, Werrey, 1882, 28 x 48 x 23 In. . . . . *illus* 11500.00
Chest, Blanket, Poplar, Gold Stenciled Flowers, Turned Feet, 28 x 48 x 23 In. 11500.00
Chest, Blanket, Rag Paint, Brown Over Tan, Trim, Turned Feet, Pa., 1843, 26 x 47 x 20 In. . . . 468.00
Chest, Blanket, Grain Paint, Iron Hinges, Jaw Lock, Ring Turned Feet, Pa., 26 x 49 x 23 In. . . 440.00
Chest, Blanket, Red Brown Paint, Cutout Half-Moon Sides, 2 Tills, Drawers, 27 x 49 x 19 In. . 288.00
Chest, Blanket, Red Over Yellow Paint, Ball Feet, Lock, Lancaster Co., Pa., 26 x 49 x 22 In. . . . 1953.00
Chest, Blanket, Red Paint, Arched End, Rosehead Nails, New England, 26 x 41 In. 232.00
Chest, Blanket, Red Paint, Interior Till, Bracket Feet, 25 ½ x 50 ¼ x 23 In. 275.00
Chest, Blanket, Red Paint, Double Arch Molding, New England, 38 x 35 ½ In. 7540.00
Chest, Blanket, Sheraton, Cherry, Paneled Front, Sides, Blunt Arrow Feet, 24 x 36 x 19 In. . . . 154.00

Furniture, Chest, Nutting, Oak, Sunflower, 40 ½ x 45 In.
$6600.00

Furniture, Chest, Roycroft, Arts & Crafts, Oak, 4 Drawers, Stamped, Early 20th Century, 36 x 42 x 26 In.
$1694.00

Furniture, Chest, William IV, Walnut, Molded Edge, Early 19th Century, 40 x 45 x 24 In.
$1200.00

Scalloped and Peg

One type of joint often found on drawers in Victorian furniture is called the "scalloped and peg" type. It was invented in 1867 by Charles Knapp, who made a machine that could cut the semicircular holes and other parts. He eventually sold his patented machine to a group of inventors.

Furniture, Coat Rack, 4 Dogs At Base, Cutout, Wood, Early 20th Century, 49 In.
$96.00

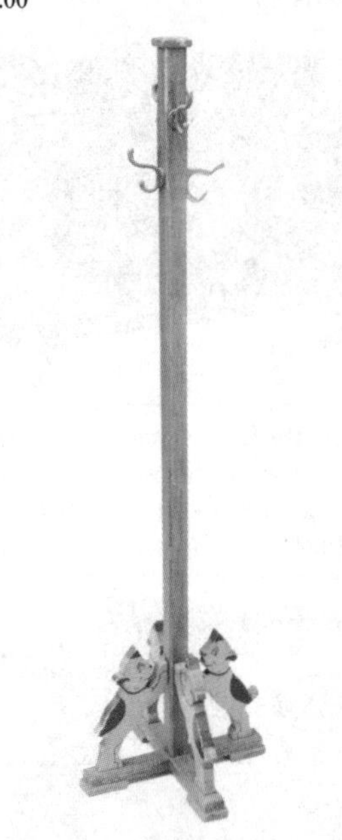

Furniture, Coat Rack, Cherry, Stained, Fleur-De-Lis, Cast Iron, 13 x 41½ x 1 In.
$175.00

Furniture, Coat Rack, Costumer, G. Stickley, Tenon Construction, 72 x 12 x 22 In.
$2800.00

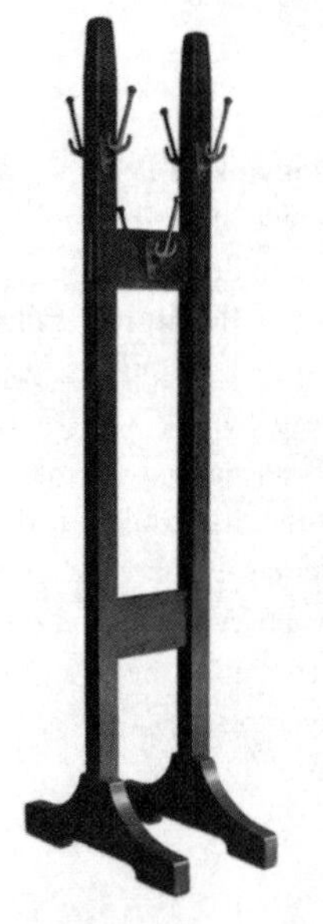

Chest, Blanket, Soap Hollow, Pine, Red Paint, Stenciled, A.E. 1843, 47 x 22½ In. 4313.00
Chest, Blanket, Softwood, Grain Brown Over Yellow, Bracket Feet, Pa., 25 x 44 x 21 In. 330.00
Chest, Blanket, Stand, Red Paint, New England, 52½ x 36½ In. 6960.00
Chest, Blanket, Tiger Maple, Lift Top, Square Legs, Turned Feet, 18 x 36 x 16 In. 1495.00
Chest, Blanket, Walnut, Inlaid IVG, Bear Trap Lock, Turned Legs, Pa., 24 x 43 x 21 In. 431.00
Chest, Blanket, Walnut, Red, Mustard Graining, Hinges, 19½ x 34 x 16½ In. 633.00
Chest, Blanket, Walnut, Molded Lid, Turned Feet, Inlaid, A.E., c.1790, 24 x 47 x 23 In. 935.00
Chest, Blanket, Walnut, Bracket Feet, Dovetailed, 3 Drawers, 18th Century, 30 x 52 x 23 In. .. 4600.00
Chest, Blanket, White, Blue Highlights, Dovetailed, Cutout Bracket Feet, 24 x 49 x 21 In. 990.00
Chest, Blanket, Yellow Pine, Iron Strap Hinges, 19th Century, 21 x 46 x 22 In. 470.00
Chest, Bombe, Louis XV Style, Burl Veneers, Late 19th Century, 54 x 23 x 11½ In. ..... *illus* 650.00
Chest, Bonnet, Federal, Walnut, 5 Drawers, Bracket Feet, 42½ x 38¼ In. 1998.00
Chest, Bonnet, Painted, 19th Century, 49½ x 20½ x 49½ In. 990.00
Chest, Bonnet, Sheraton, Cherry, Projecting Drawer Over 3 Graduated, 47 x 43 In. 960.00
Chest, Campaign, Contemporary, Mahogany, Brass Hardware, 22 x 22 In. 77.00
Chest, Campaign, English Walnut, 2 Over 3 Drawers, Brass Handles, 38½ x 36 x 18 In. 784.00
Chest, Campaign, Mahogany, 2 Sections, Brass Handles, 37 x 28 x 14 In. 3737.00
Chest, Campaign, Mahogany, Oak, Brass, 2 Parts, 5 Drawers, 38¾ x 41 x 17½ In. 3738.00
Chest, Campaign, Regency, Mahogany, 5 Drawers, Turnip Feet, 40¾ x 39 x 18 In. 3900.00
Chest, Campaign, Victorian, Mahogany, 2 Short Over 3 Long Drawers, 39 x 30 x 17 In. 3120.00
Chest, Campaign, Walnut, 5 Drawer, Key, Dovetailed, 38½ x 36 x 17 In. 700.00
Chest, Camphorwood, Brass, Paneled Lid, c.1850, 19 x 39 In. 777.00
Chest, Camphorwood, Brass Mounts, Iron Handles, Chinese, 16 x 34 x 17 In. 460.00
Chest, Camphorwood, Lift Top, Carved Landscape, Figures, 19½ x 41½ x 20½ In. 345.00
Chest, Carved, Applied Molding, Dentil Frieze, Figures, 3 Drawers, Italy, 34½ x 35 In. 518.00
Chest, Cherry, 2 Over 4 Scratch Beaded Drawers, Scalloped Skirt, c.1820, 46 x 46 In. 1093.00
Chest, Cherry, 5 Drawers, Fluted Quarter Columns, Ogee Base, c.1800, 40 x 36 x 18 In. 1323.00
Chest, Cherry, Bird's-Eye Maple, Drawers, 2 Doors, Ogee Bracket Feet, 42 x 35½ x 18 In. 431.00
Chest, Cherry, Hinged Lid, Dovetailed Case, Lock, 7 x 8 x 10¾ In. 880.00
Chest, Cherry, Paneled Sides, Frame & Panel Back, 3 Drawers, Kentucky, 13½ x 16 In. 5750.00
Chest, Cherry, Southern Piedmont, Outset Over 3 Graduated Drawers, c.1840, 44 x 45 In. ... 1800.00
Chest, Cherry, Tiger Maple, 4 Drawers, Cut Glass Handles, Turned Feet, 46 x 41 x 18 In. 448.00
Chest, Cherry, Walnut, Poplar, Graduated Drawers, 27 x 23 x 16½ In. 1093.00
Chest, Chinese, Ivory Inlay, Dome Top, Mahogany, Ebony, Ivory, 1800s, 23 x 34 In. 633.00
Chest, Chinese, Storage, Painted, Lift Top Sections, Divided Interior, 37 x 67 In. 1058.00
Chest, Chippendale, 4 Drawers, Overhang Top, Maine, c.1790, 34 x 36 x 17 In. 2358.00
Chest, Chippendale, 7 Drawers, Brass Key Escutcheons, Brass Handles, 60 x 41 x 20 In. 1265.00
Chest, Chippendale, Birch, Pine, Red Paint Trace, Molded Edge Top, 4 Drawers, 33 x 35 In. .. 2645.00
Chest, Chippendale, Burl Walnut, 6 Over 3 Drawers, 71 x 41 In. 9440.00
Chest, Chippendale, Cherry, Pine, 4 Drawers, Brass Drop Handle, Pilasters, 38 x 40 x 24 In. .. 173.00
Chest, Chippendale, Cherry, 5 Drawers, Shaped Feet, 18th Century, 36 x 17 x 41 In. 578.00
Chest, Chippendale, Cherry, Pine, 4 Drawers, Brass Drop Handle, 38 x 40 x 24 In. 805.00
Chest, Chippendale, Cherry, 7 Graduated Drawers, 18th Century, 60 x 36 x 17 In. 3360.00
Chest, Chippendale, Cherry, Poplar, Pine, Cove Molded Cornice, 3 Over 2 Drawers, 69 x 40 In. 5175.00
Chest, Chippendale, Cherry, Reverse Serpentine, c.1790, 33½ x 42¼ In. 15600.00
Chest, Chippendale, Curly Maple, Pine, 2 Faux Fronts, c.1800, 36½ x 41 In. 1410.00
Chest, Chippendale, Figured Walnut, 2 Over 3 Graduated Drawers, Pa., 39 x 37 In. 2415.00
Chest, Chippendale, Figured Walnut, 3 Faux Over 2 Short Over 5 Drawers, Pa., 68 x 39 In. ... 25520.00
Chest, Chippendale, Mahogany, Oak, Pullout Writing Surface, 40 x 36 x 20 In. 1725.00
Chest, Chippendale, Mahogany, Pullout Writing Surface, 4 Drawers, 31 x 28 x 18 In. 1725.00
Chest, Chippendale, Mahogany, Bowfront, 4 Drawers, Dovetailed, 18th Century 2000.00
Chest, Chippendale, Mahogany, 5 Drawers, Bail Handles, Cutout Base, 41 x 43 x 22 In. 2200.00
Chest, Chippendale, Mahogany, 2 Over 3 Drawers, Brass Handles, 41½ x 43 x 22 In. 2464.00
Chest, Chippendale, Mahogany, Carved, Figured, Serpentine Chest, c.1780, 35 x 40 In. 10000.00
Chest, Chippendale, Mahogany, 4 Graduated Drawers, Ogee Bracket Feet, Pa., 32 x 36 In. ... 10350.00
Chest, Chippendale, Mahogany, Serpentine Front, Mass., c.1790, 32 x 38 In. 14400.00
Chest, Chippendale, Mahogany, Block Front, Thumb-Molded Edge, c.1780, 32 x 33 In. 24675.00
Chest, Chippendale, Mahogany, 4 Drawers, Overhang Top, c.1780, 31¾ x 38 In. 73000.00
Chest, Chippendale, Maple, 4 Drawers, Brass Drop Handle, 34¼ x 40 x 18½ In. 805.00
Chest, Chippendale, Maple, 6 Drawers, Molded Cornice, 18th Century, 58 x 39 x 19 In. 2760.00
Chest, Chippendale, Maple, 6 Drawers, Late 18th Century, 56 x 36 In. 5875.00
Chest, Chippendale, Maple, Carved, Block Front, 7 Drawers, c.1765, 85 x 45 In. 27600.00
Chest, Chippendale, Maple, Chestnut & White Pine, Bracket Feet, 1700s, 44½ x 36 In. 920.00
Chest, Chippendale, Maple, Chestnut, Pine, Decorated, 2 Over 4 Drawers, 47 x 38 In. 6325.00
Chest, Chippendale, Maple, Molded Top, Fitted Case, 4 Drawers, 36 x 38½ x 21 In. 2784.00
Chest, Chippendale, Maple, Pine, 4 Graduated Drawers, Scroll Bracket Feet, 36 x 40 In. 12000.00

Chest, Chippendale, Pine, Reeded Molded Top, Thumb-Molded Drawers, 48 x 44 In. 588.00
Chest, Chippendale, Pine, 4 Drawers, Bracket Feet, New England, c.1800, 38 x 38 In. 1495.00
Chest, Chippendale, Pine, Birch, Grain Paint, String Inlay, Late 1700s, 52 x 36 In. 7050.00
Chest, Chippendale, Semi-Tall, Cherry & Ash, 3 Drawers, 44 x 38 x 21 In. 3800.00
Chest, Chippendale, Walnut, Poplar, Paneled Door, Bracket Feet, 20 x 16 In. 5750.00
Chest, Chippendale, Walnut, 4 Drawers, Fluted Columns, Ogee Bracket Feet, 40 x 42 In. 6960.00
Chest, Chippendale Style, Mahogany, Bowfront, Veneer, Satinwood, Inlay, 31 x 34 x 18 In. 460.00
Chest, Chippendale Style, Maple, Drawers, Bracket Base, New England, 49 x 36 In. 800.00
Chest, Cottage, Fold-Out Writing Surface, Painted, Italy, c.1950, 82 x 30 x 17 In. *illus* 475.00
Chest, Cottage, Pine, Mirror, Brown & Amber Grain Paint, Shaped Crest, 73 x 29 In. 450.00
Chest, Curly Maple, Backsplash, Overhanging Cock-Beaded Drawer, c.1825, 46 x 43 In. 1265.00
Chest, Document, Chippendale, Slant Front Drawer, 3 Graduated Drawers, 32 x 40 In. 1645.00
Chest, Dower, 2 Painted Hearts, 2 Drawers, c.1790, 48 ¾ In. 44500.00
Chest, Dower, 3 Panels, Unicorns, Lions, Tulip Pots, Orange Ground, 18th Century 22230.00
Chest, Dower, Continental, Wrought Iron Mounts, Walnut, Hearts, Flower, 11 x 30 In. 840.00
Chest, Dower, Oak, Carved, Panel Front, Molded Edge, 17th Century, 28 x 48 In. 1008.00
Chest, Dower, Pine, Lift Top, 2 Drawers, Dovetailed, 30 x 48 ½ x 23 ½ In. 1925.00
Chest, Dower, Pine, Paint Decorated, Repeating Putty Heart, Late 1700s, 26 x 48 In. 3819.00
Chest, Dower, Spanish Provincial, Carved, Wrought Iron Mounts, 12 x 19 In. 510.00
Chest, Dower, Stylized Hearts, Stippled Ground, 2 Drawers, 18th Century 25740.00
Chest, Dressing, Gentleman's, Neoclassical, Mahogany, Shaped Backsplash, 2 Drawers, 53 x 45 In. 1293.00
Chest, Dressing, Gentleman's, Neoclassical, Mahogany, Drawers, Reeded Columns, 41 x 43 In. 1410.00
Chest, Dressing, Gentleman's, Mahogany, Molded Mirror, Drawers, 71 x 38 ½ x 25 In. 1763.00
Chest, Dunlap School, Maple, Bonnet Drawer, Skirt Drop, Bracket Feet, 54 x 40 In. 690.00
Chest, Empire, Bird's-Eye Maple, Mahogany, Drawers, Side Columns, c.1840, 47 x 43 x 19 In. 402.00
Chest, Empire, Cherry, Walnut, 7 Drawers, Split Columns, 49 ½ x 42 ½ In. 2300.00
Chest, Empire, Curly & Bird's-Eye Maple, Cherry, 6 Drawers, 26 x 23 x 11 In. 2990.00
Chest, Empire, Mahogany, 4 Drawers, Carved Pilasters, Paw Feet, 46 x 47 x 21 In. 295.00
Chest, Empire, Mahogany, Shaped Backsplash, Glove Drawers, 49 ½ x 43 ½ x 21 In. 413.00
Chest, Empire, Mahogany, 4 Drawers, c.1840, 46 x 42 In. 440.00
Chest, Empire, Mahogany, 3 Drawers, Step Back Top, Paw Feet, Carved 600.00
Chest, Empire Style, Mahogany, 2 Over 3 Drawers, Mirror, c.1825, 70 x 36 x 20 In. 476.00
Chest, English Oak, Carved, Paneled Front, Inlaid Diamond Paneled Sides, 25 x 45 In. 1265.00
Chest, English Oak, Lift Top, 3 Floral Carved Panels, Paneled Back, 25 x 52 x 23 In. 978.00
Chest, Federal, Birch, Bird's-Eye Maple, Mahogany, Inlay, 6 Drawers, c.1810, 40 x 40 In. 2820.00
Chest, Federal, Bird's-Eye Maple, Backsplash, Drawers, Glass Pulls, Columns 800.00
Chest, Federal, Bird's-Eye Maple, Cherry, Pine, 2 Over 3 Drawers, 53 ¾ x 47 x 19 In. 896.00
Chest, Federal, Bird's-Eye Maple, Cherry Veneer, 4 Drawers, Cutout Feet, Vermont, 37 x 38 In. 3408.00
Chest, Federal, Cherry, Poplar, 4 Drawers, Turned Legs, Glass Pulls, 1800s, 43 x 45 In. 403.00
Chest, Federal, Cherry, 4 Drawers, Brass Pulls, Ships, Cutout Base, 39 ¾ In. 700.00
Chest, Federal, Cherry, 2 Short Over 3 Long Drawers, Splayed Bracket Feet, 37 x 42 x 21 In. 978.00
Chest, Federal, Cherry, 4 Graduated Drawers, Paneled Sides, Tennessee, 1800s, 45 x 40 In. 1150.00
Chest, Federal, Cherry, Tiger Maple, Bowfront, Reeded Top, 4 Drawers, 40 x 41 In. 1410.00
Chest, Federal, Cherry, Inlaid, String Inlay, Graduated Drawers, 42 x 41 In. 2938.00
Chest, Federal, Cherry, Pine, Cornice, Reeded Columns, Applied Beading, Pa., 62 x 40 In. 6325.00
Chest, Federal, Faux Grain Paint, Scrolled Backsplash, 4 Drawers, 1800s, 42 x 43 In. 748.00
Chest, Federal, Figured Mahogany, 2 Over 4 Drawers, New England, c.1820, 43 x 39 In. 690.00
Chest, Federal, Grain Paint, Hinged Lid, 2 Drawers, Ringed Columns & Legs, 36 x 48 x 19 In. 5288.00
Chest, Federal, Mahogany, 4 Drawers, Bracket Feet, 39 ½ x 43 x 19 ½ In. 460.00
Chest, Federal, Mahogany, Bowfront, 36 ½ x 37 x 21 ½ In. 1593.00
Chest, Federal, Mahogany, Bowfront, 4 Drawers, Turned Legs, c.1815, 39 x 44 In. 1920.00
Chest, Federal, Mahogany, Bowfront, Graduated Drawers, c.1800, 44 x 42 ½ In. 2160.00
Chest, Federal, Mahogany, Outset Corners, Reeded Edge, Scrolled Skirt, 41 x 43 In. 2300.00
Chest, Federal, Mahogany, Serpentine Front, Inlaid Top, Splay Feet, c.1790, 39 x 48 In. 2640.00
Chest, Federal, Mahogany, Inlay, 4 Beaded Drawers, Brass Handles, 40 x 37 x 21 In. 2645.00
Chest, Federal, Mahogany, Marquetry, 4 Long Drawers, Scalloped Apron, c.1800, 48 x 37 In. 2880.00
Chest, Federal, Mahogany, Inlay, Bowfront, Drawers, Panels, c.1825, 41 x 42 x 25 In. 2938.00
Chest, Federal, Mahogany, Veneer, Bowfront, North Shore, Mass., c.1820, 40 x 38 In. 3055.00
Chest, Federal, Mahogany, 19th Century, 40 x 43 ¾ x 24 ½ In. 3878.00
Chest, Federal, Mahogany, Bowfront, 4 Graduated Drawers, Splayed Feet, 41 x 45 x 25 In. 5760.00
Chest, Federal, Mahogany, Bowfront, c.1800, 40 ¼ x 43 x 22 ½ In. 6048.00
Chest, Federal, Mahogany, Flame Birch, Serpentine Front, 4 Drawers, c.1815, 38 x 41 In. 11400.00
Chest, Federal, Maple, Pine, 4 Drawers, Bail Brasses, Bracket Feet, Late 1700s, 29 x 40 In. 546.00
Chest, Federal, Pine, Overhanging Top, Graduated Drawers, Early 1800s, 32 x 31 In. 411.00
Chest, Federal, Red Wash, 6 Drawers, Bracket Base, c.1800, 55 x 36 x 19 In. 4025.00
Chest, Federal, Tiger Maple, Cherry, 6 Drawers, c.1810, 63 ½ x 39 ¾ In. 6463.00

Furniture, Commode, Biedermeier Style, 3 Drawers, Baker Label, 32 x 33 x 19 In.
$920.00

Furniture, Commode, Bombe, Louis XV Style, Geometric Inlay, Scroll & Leaf Mounts, c.1780, 36 x 31 x 14 In.
$675.00

Furniture, Commode, Provincial, Louis XV Style, Pierced Apron, Painted, 32 x 42 x 19 In., Pair
$1000.00

Furniture, Cradle, Chippendale, Walnut, Dovetailed, Handles, c.1790, 28 x 44 x 24 ½ In.
$300.00

F

Furniture, Cradle, Hanging, Walnut, Shaped Crest, Spindles, Casters, c.1890, 41 x 26 In.
$115.00

F

Furniture, Cradle, Walnut, Dovetailed, Cutout Handles, c.1780, 24 x 37 x 20 In.
$140.00

Furniture, Cradle, Walnut, Oak, Swings, Runner Feet, Early 19th Century, 39 x 42 x 28 In.
$200.00

Furniture, Crib, Walnut, Spool Turned, Mid 19th Century, 39 x 39 x 21 In.
$190.00

Chest, Federal, Walnut, Popular, 4 Graduated Dovetailed Drawers, c.1810, 14 x 13 In. 920.00
Chest, Federal, Walnut, Pine, 2 Drawers, Iron Strap Hinges, c.1885, 27 x 47 x 18 In. . . . *illus* 2600.00
Chest, Federal, Yellow Pine, Figured Birch, 3 Over 4 Drawers, Early 1800s, 46 x 40½ In. 4600.00
Chest, G. Nakashima, Walnut, 3 Drawers, Signed, 1957, 32 x 36 x 20 In. 2500.00
Chest, G. Nakashima, Walnut, 3 Drawers, c.1965, 32¾ x 36 x 23½ In. 19200.00
Chest, G. Stickley, 2 Over 3 Drawers, Round Knobs, Paneled Sides, 42 x 37 x 19 In. 2880.00
Chest, G. Stickley, 2 Over 3 Drawers, Paneled Sides, 42 x 37 x 19½ In. 4200.00
Chest, G. Stickley, Ash, Paneled, Arched Corbel Design, 2 Trays, 24 x 12 x 15 In. 16800.00
Chest, G. Stickley, Maple, 3 Drawers, Arched Toe Board, 42 x 20 x 42 In. 6600.00
Chest, George III, Burl Walnut, 6 Drawers, Cabriole Legs, Claw Feet, 69 x 46 x 23 In. 3884.00
Chest, George III, Mahogany, 2 Over 3 Drawers, Scalloped Apron, 46 x 38 x 18 In. 1175.00
Chest, George III, Mahogany, 5 Graduated Drawers, Bracket Feet, 31 x 32 In. 1560.00
Chest, George III, Mahogany, 5 Drawers, Ivory Escutcheons, 1800s, 42 x 42 In. 1800.00
Chest, George III, Mahogany, Frieze Drawer, 2 Over 3 Drawers, 41 x 47 In. 1800.00
Chest, George III, Mahogany, 3 Graduated Drawers, Bracket Feet, 32½ x 32 x 18 In. 1980.00
Chest, George III, Mahogany, Molded Edge, Ogee Bracket Feet, 35 x 33 x 18 In. . . . . *illus* 2000.00
Chest, George III, Mahogany, Molded Edge, 2 Over 3 Drawers, 1800s, 38 x 43 In. 2040.00
Chest, George III, Mahogany, Oak, Molded Edge, Bracket Base, 4 Drawers, 32 x 21 In. 2070.00
Chest, George III, Mahogany, Bowfront, Graduated Drawers, Bracket Feet, 36½ x 40 x 20 In. . 2115.00
Chest, George III, Mahogany, Bowfront, Satinwood Banding, 2 Over 3 Drawers, 41 x 40 In. . . 2160.00
Chest, George III, Mahogany, String Inlaid Edge, 5 Drawers, Ivory Escutcheons, 40 x 36 In. . . 2280.00
Chest, George III, Mahogany, Serpentine, 4 Drawers, c.1770, 31 x 26½ In. 4375.00
Chest, George III, Mahogany Veneer, Oak, Pine, Bowfront, 5 Drawers, c.1820, 42 x 42 In. 863.00
Chest, George III, Walnut, Banded Top, 3 Short Over 3 Long Drawers, 39 x 38 In. 3360.00
Chest, George III Style, Mahogany, Molded Edge, 5 Drawers, 1800s, 36 x 37 In. 1200.00
Chest, George III Style, Mahogany, Canted, Molded Edge, 5 Drawers, c.1880, 36 x 40 In. 1440.00
Chest, George III Style, Mahogany, 2 Over 3 Drawers, 44 x 42 x 19½ In. 1680.00
Chest, George III Style, Mahogany, Inlaid Looped Stringing, 2 Over 3 Drawers, 44 x 42 In. . . . 1920.00
Chest, George III Style, Mahogany, Molded Edge, 4 Graduated Drawers, 33 x 33 In. 1920.00
Chest, George III Style, Walnut, Banded, Inlaid Star, 2 Short Over 3 Drawers, 38 x 44 In. 3360.00
Chest, Georgian, 2 Case Construction, Inlaid, Figured Mahogany Veneers, 1800s, 75 x 44 In. . 1265.00
Chest, Georgian, Figured Mahogany, Cedar, 2 Over 3 Drawers, Ebony Pulls, 15½ x 14½ In. . . 1380.00
Chest, Georgian, Hepplewhite Style, Faded Mahogany, 2 Over 3 Drawers, 42 x 39 In. 1293.00
Chest, Georgian, Mahogany, 2 Over 3 Drawers, Bracket Feet, England, 39 x 40 x 20 In. 590.00
Chest, Georgian, Mahogany, 2 Case Construction, 3 Drawers, 19th Century, 54 x 44 In. 690.00
Chest, Georgian, Mahogany, Pine, 3 Dovetailed Drawers, Bracket Feet, 1800s, 37 x 43 In. 805.00
Chest, Georgian, Mahogany, 5 Drawers, Pine, Bracket Feet, 38 x 43 In. 978.00
Chest, Georgian, Mahogany, 5 Drawers, Dovetailed, 1800s, 41½ x 48 In. 1150.00
Chest, Georgian, Mahogany, Bowfront, Graduated Cock-Beaded Drawers, c.1800, 34 x 32 In. . 1998.00
Chest, Georgian, Mahogany, Oak, 2 Over 6 Drawers, Dentil Cornice, c.1800, 68 x 42 In. 3335.00
Chest, Georgian, Walnut, String Inlay, Cock-Beaded, 31 x 74 x 23 In. . . . . *illus* 5250.00
Chest, Georgian Style, Mahogany, 5 Long Drawers, c.1875, 41 x 41 In. 1440.00
Chest, Georgian Style, Nahon, Serpentine Case, Molded Top, Drawers, 33 x 39 In. 1416.00
Chest, Green Paint, Pinstripes, 3 Drawers, 19th Century, 11 x 7½ In. 1440.00
Chest, Hardwood, Bowfront, Parquetry, 8 x 6¾ x 4½ In. 1265.00
Chest, Hepplewhite, 4 Drawers, Footed, 36 x 40 In. 1450.00
Chest, Hepplewhite, Bowfront, Mahogany, Pine, 4 Graduated Drawers, c.1820, 39 x 42 In. . . . 1495.00
Chest, Hepplewhite, Bowfront, Mahogany, 4 Drawers, Flared Feet, c.1800, 36 x 41 x 22 In. . . . 3105.00
Chest, Hepplewhite, Cherry, Banded Diamond & String Inlay, 2 Over 3 Drawers, 43 x 42 In. . . 805.00
Chest, Hepplewhite, Cherry, Mahogany Veneer, Curved Skirt, String Inlay, c.1800, 46 x 41 In. . 1093.00
Chest, Hepplewhite, Cherry, 4 Graduated Drawers, Fluted Quarter Columns, 38 x 38 In. 2204.00
Chest, Hepplewhite, Cherry, 4 Drawers, c.1800, 35 x 40 x 22 In. 2805.00
Chest, Hepplewhite, Cherry, 4 Drawers, Oval Brass Handles, French Feet, 36 x 39 x 18 In. 2990.00
Chest, Hepplewhite, Mahogany, Oak, 2 Over 2 Drawers, England, 32 x 35½ x 18½ In. 575.00
Chest, Hepplewhite, Mahogany, 2 Over 3 Drawers, French Foot, 38 x 19 x 38 In. 1150.00
Chest, Hepplewhite, Mahogany, Inlay, Dovetailed, 5 Drawers, French Feet, 1800s, 42 x 40 In. . 1265.00
Chest, Hepplewhite, Mahogany, Crossbanded Top, 2 Short Over 3 Long Drawers, 35 x 38 x 20 In. . . 1495.00
Chest, Hepplewhite, Mahogany, Bowfront, 4 Drawers, Cutout Feet, Apron, 37 x 38 x 17 In. . . . 1725.00
Chest, Heywood-Wakefield, Symphonic, Wheat Finish, 1958, 44 x 34 x 18 In. . . . . *illus* 300.00
Chest, High, 2 Sections, 2 Over 3 Drawers, 3 Lower Drawers, Turned Legs, Stretcher, c.1730 . . 9360.00
Chest, Jacobean, Oak, 4 Drawers, Geometric Panels, Bracket Foot Base, 36 x 35 In. 1293.00
Chest, Jacobean Style, Oak, 2 Short Over 3 Long Paneled Drawers, Bracket Feet, 39 x 38 In. . . 881.00
Chest, Jewelry, Black Forest, Walnut, Carved Flowers, 2 Bird Finials, 23 x 15 x 9 In. 3776.00
Chest, Korean, Wood, Brass Mounts, Rosette Corner Protectors, 19th Century, 45 x 18 x 18 In. 2233.00
Chest, L. & J.G. Stickley, 2 Over 3 Drawers, Round Wood Knobs, 38 x 48 x 22¼ In. 2880.00
Chest, Lift Top, Heart & Flower Painted Decoration, Regina Pschoppn, 1808, 25 x 51 In. 1100.00

Chest, Lift Top, Inlaid Walnut, Tapered Feet, Southern, 21 ¾ x 47 ¼ x 18 ¼ In. 1265.00
Chest, Lift Top, Mahogany, File Cabinet, 32 x 35 In. 767.00
Chest, Lift Top, Oak, Dark Finish, 2 Drawers, Footed, England, Early 18th Century, 51 In. 1195.00
Chest, Linen, Louis XVI Style, Marble Top, Gilt Bronze Mounts, 2 Doors, 50 x 40 In. 518.00
Chest, Lingerie, Louis XV Style, Marble Top, Bombe Case, Bronze Mount, 39 x 16 In., Pair 633.00
Chest, Louis XV Provincial, Mixed Wood, Paneled Doors, Scalloped Apron, 53 x 24 In. 748.00
Chest, Louis XV Style, Kingwood, Tulipwood, Marble Top, 2 Drawers, 33 x 27 x 16 In. 1058.00
Chest, Louis XVI, Fruitwood, Marble Top, 3 Drawers, Square Legs, 33 x 52 x 23 In. 3055.00
Chest, Louis XVI Style, Mahogany, Gilt, Brass, Marble Top, 6 Drawers, 55 x 33 x 15 ½ In. 1680.00
Chest, Mahogany, 2 Over 3 Drawers, Brass Rings, Shaped Feet, c.1840, 12 x 14 x 7 In. 2860.00
Chest, Mahogany, 2 Over 4 Graduated Drawers, Turned Feet, 1800s, 11 In. 1150.00
Chest, Mahogany, 3 Over 2 Drawers, England, 19th Century, 38 x 39 x 18 In. 3776.00
Chest, Mahogany, 5 Drawers, Inlaid, Beaded Edge, Bracket Base, England, c.1775, 39 x 42 x 20 In. 747.00
Chest, Mahogany, 6 Drawers, Beaded Edge, Leaf Apron, Scroll Backsplash, 47 x 45 x 21 In. 2645.00
Chest, Mahogany, Bowfront, England, 40 x 45 x 21 In. .... *illus* 1100.00
Chest, Mahogany, Bowfront, 4 Graduated Drawers, Fan Inlay, Bracket Feet, 34 x 39 ½ x 21 In. 1610.00
Chest, Mahogany, Bowfront, 2 Short & 3 Long Drawers, Turned Legs, 51 ½ x 58 In. 1770.00
Chest, Mahogany, Bowfront, Plain Top, 2 Short & 3 Long Cock-Beaded Drawers, 45 x 46 In. 3068.00
Chest, Mahogany, Hinged Top, Backsplash, 5 Drawers, 40 x 62 x 22 In. 3105.00
Chest, Mahogany Veneer, Pine, Brass Pulls, 4 Graduated Drawers, c.1790, 41 x 36 In. 500.00
Chest, Maple, Backsplash, 5 Drawers, Turned Pilasters, Wood Pulls, 47 x 46 x 23 In. 360.00
Chest, Mule, Cherry, Inlay, Overlapping Molded Edge, 5 Graduated Drawers, 41 x 43 In. 863.00
Chest, Mule, Mahogany, Oak, Columns, Inlaid, England, 41 x 62 x 22 In. .... *illus* 3105.00
Chest, Mule, Oak, 2 Drawers, Bracket Feet, 18th Century, 25 x 43 x 21 In. 825.00
Chest, Mule, Pine, Green Paint, Applied Molding, Cotter Pin Hinges, 47 x 18 In. 489.00
Chest, Mule, Pine, New England, 44 x 41 ½ x 18 In. .... *illus* 715.00
Chest, Mule, Pine, Swirl Painted, 2 Drawers, Inlaid Banding, Cutout Feet, 18 x 41 In. 920.00
Chest, Neoclassical, Cherry, Maple, c.1825-35, 57 ½ x 43 ½ x 18 In. .... *illus* 1093.00
Chest, Neoclassical Revival, 1 Over 3 Long Drawers, Spiral Pilasters, 50 x 44 In. 295.00
Chest, Nutting, Oak, Sunflower, 40 ½ x 45 In. .... *illus* 6600.00
Chest, Oak, 6-Board, Hand Wrought Hardware, 19 x 43 x 16 In. 325.00
Chest, Oak, Pine, Jointed, Late 17th Century, 23 ½ x 41 ¼ x 17 In. 16450.00
Chest, Painted, Country Pine, Shaped Apron, 4 Drawers, 38 ½ x 38 ½ x 20 In. 100.00
Chest, Pine, Grain Paint, 6-Board, New England, c.1800, 20 ¾ x 30 ¾ In. 764.00
Chest, Pine, Oak, Painted, 4 Drawers, c.1700, 38 x 39 ½ x 19 In. 7200.00
Chest, Pine, Over 2 Drawers, Hinged Lift Top, Cutout Feet, 1835, 31 x 48 x 20 In. 1765.00
Chest, Pine, Painted, Strawberries, Linear Borders, Late 19th Century, 20 x 14 ½ In. 1410.00
Chest, Pine, Red Paint, 4 Drawers, Molded Base, Bun Feet, New England, 72 x 39 In. 7540.00
Chest, Pine, Salmon Pink, Hinged, 2 Short Drawers, 1850s, 41 x 40 In. 3290.00
Chest, Pine, Spanish Brown Paint, Wrought T-Head Nails, 21 x 43 In. 575.00
Chest, Pine, Square Nails, Scalloped Backboard, Cutout Base, Reeded Drawer, 14 x 10 x 5 In. 998.00
Chest, Poplar, 3 Drawers, Wood Pulls, New England, c.1800, 44 x 39 ½ In. 823.00
Chest, Poplar, Red Stain, Ring Turned Legs, c.1800, 53 x 37 x 17 In. 2115.00
Chest, Queen Anne, Cedar, Carved, Bermuda, Mid 18th Century, 68 x 35 ¾ x 19 In. 18800.00
Chest, Queen Anne, Cherry, Maple, Fan Carved Drawer, Cabriole Legs, 1700s, 74 x 39 In. 5750.00
Chest, Queen Anne, Deerfield, Frame, 4 Drawers, Scalloped Apron, Slipper Feet, 36 x 30 In. 522.00
Chest, Queen Anne, Maple, 6 Drawers, Cabriole Legs, New Hampshire, 58 x 38 x 19 In. 1972.00
Chest, Queen Anne, Maple, Pine, 6 Graduated Drawers, Scrolled Skirt, c.1770, 48 x 39 In. 2185.00
Chest, Queen Anne, Maple, 2 Sections, 7 Drawers, Scroll Apron, 75 x 39 x 19 In. 4600.00
Chest, Queen Anne, Maple, Fan Carved, Massachusetts, c.1760, 75 x 38 In. 12925.00
Chest, Queen Anne Style, Burl Walnut, Banded Top, Drawers, Bun Feet, 30 x 29 ½ In. 2400.00
Chest, Raised Paneled Sides, 2 Over 2 Drawers, Pegged Mortise, 36 x 45 ½ x 28 In. 495.00
Chest, Regency, Bowfront, Mahogany, Banded Top, 2 Over 3 Drawers, Splayed Feet, 44 x 41 In. 1800.00
Chest, Regency, Mahogany, Bowfront, 2 Short Over 3 Long Drawers, c.1810, 41 x 42 In. 1800.00
Chest, Regency, Mahogany, Bowfront, 4 Graduated Drawers, Bracket Feet, 39 x 43 In. 1800.00
Chest, Regency, Mahogany, 5 Drawers, Bracket Feet, 32 ½ x 31 ½ x 17 In. 1888.00
Chest, Regency, Mahogany, Bowfront, 5 Drawers, Ebonized Stringing, 42 x 42 In. 1920.00
Chest, Regency, Mahogany, Bowfront, Bowed Top, 5 Drawers, 1800s, 40 x 41 In. 1920.00
Chest, Regency, Mahogany, Bowfront, Inlaid String Banding, Reeded, 5 Drawers, 43 x 43 In. 1920.00
Chest, Regency, Mahogany, Bowfront, Banded, Bowed Top, 4 Graduated Drawers, 40 x 39 In. 2280.00
Chest, Regency, Mahogany, Bowfront, Inlaid Ebonized Stringing & Fleur-De-Lis, 41 x 41 In. 2280.00
Chest, Regency, Mahogany, Bowfront, Rosewood Banding, 5 Drawers, 42 x 42 In. 3120.00
Chest, Regency Style, Mahogany, Satinwood, Bowfront, 2 Over 3 Drawers, 42 x 41 x 21 In. 1800.00
Chest, Regency Style, Mahogany, Bowfront, 2 Over 3 Drawers, 20 x 43 x 20 In. 1920.00
Chest, Regency Style, Mahogany, Veneer, Bowfront, 5 Drawers, 41 x 40 ½ x 20 ½ In. 2040.00
Chest, Rococo, Walnut, Bowfront, Crossbands, Cabriole Legs, 2 Drawers, 31 x 52 x 26 In. 4700.00

Furniture, Cupboard, Bonnetiere, French Provincial, Beech, Glass Vitrine, 72 x 27 x 16 In.
$1300.00

Furniture, Cupboard, Corner, 2 Sections, Grain Paint, 78 ½ x 36 x 21 In.
$4100.00

Furniture, Cupboard, Corner, Walnut, 2 Sections, Ohio Valley, c.1840, 88 x 53 x 33 In.
$1840.00

Furniture, Cupboard, Corner, Walnut, Pine, 4 Doors, Drawer, Va., c.1850, 78 ½ x 38 ½ x 26 In.
$792.00

Furniture, Cupboard, Corner, Yellow Pine, Piedmont, 19th Century, 88 x 49 x 23 In.
$3600.00

Furniture, Cupboard, Drawers, Glass Doors, Grain Paint, 92 x 52 x 28 In.
$12100.00

Chest, Roycroft, Arts & Crafts, Oak, 4 Drawers, Stamped, Early 20th Century, 36 x 42 x 26 In. *illus* 1694.00
Chest, Shaker, Cherry, Walnut, 2 Over 4 Drawers, Dovetailed, O.H., c.1835, 47 x 39 In. 3510.00
Chest, Sheraton, 4 Drawers, Ring Turned Columns, 19th Century, 8 ¾ x 9 In. 2415.00
Chest, Sheraton, Bowfront, 4 Drawers, Dovetailed, Turned Feet, c.1810, 42 x 42 x 23 In. 2620.00
Chest, Sheraton, Cherry, Poplar, 3 Graduated Drawers, Ohio Valley, c.1830, 47 x 41 x 21 In. . . 460.00
Chest, Sheraton, Mahogany, 2 Over 3 Drawers, Splayed Feet, 42 x 36 In. 550.00
Chest, Sheraton, Mahogany, Bowfront, 4 Drawers, Backsplash, Turned Posts, 43 x 40 In. 450.00
Chest, Sheraton, Mahogany, Bowfront, Inlaid, 4 Drawers, Columns, Britain, c.1810, 42 x 44 x 19 In. 4100.00
Chest, Sheraton, Maple, 4 Drawers, Oval Top, Flame Birch Panels, 42 x 43 In. 4500.00
Chest, Slant Front, Oak, Pine, Inlaid Mahogany, 5 Drawers, Paneled Back, 53 x 23 In. 374.00
Chest, Spice, 9 Drawers, 18 ¼ x 12 ½ x 16 In. 358.00
Chest, Spice, Wood, Red Stain, 6 Short Over 1 Long Drawers, Brass Knobs, 12 x 15 ½ In. 823.00
Chest, Storage, Paint, Trim, Yellow Stencil, Leaves, Flowers, Bail Handles, 24 x 10 x 10 In. . . . 460.00
Chest, Sugar, Chippendale, Cherry, c.1820 . . . . 12500.00
Chest, Sugar, Federal, Walnut, Lift Top, c.1810, 38 ½ x 29 x 19 ½ In. 5700.00
Chest, Sugar, Hinged Top, Divided Interior, Panel Front, Drawer, 1800s, 30 x 36 In. 1770.00
Chest, Sugar, Sheraton, Cherry, Poplar, Hinge Lid, 2 Drawers, Button Feet, 33 x 38 x 18 In. . . 3450.00
Chest, Sugar, Southern Walnut, Hinged Top, Tapered Legs, 19th Century, 28 x 27 x 22 In. . . . 4830.00
Chest, Teakwood, Lift Top, Iron Strap Mounted, Wrought Handles, Wood Wheels, 38 x 61 In. . 173.00
Chest, Tiger Maple, Shaped Apron, Bracket Feet, New England, 39 x 45 x 21 In. 1610.00
Chest, Tiger Maple, White Pine, 5 Graduated Drawers, Cabriole Legs, New England, 65 x 40 In. 2990.00
Chest, Twig, 2 Drawers, Nail Construction, Chip Carved, Miniature, 14 In. 230.00
Chest, Victorian, Burl Walnut, 6 Drawers, Reeded Sides, Lock, 54 x 40 In. 1120.00
Chest, Victorian, Mahogany, Canted Corners, 5 Drawers, Plinth Base, Late 1800s, 48 x 48 In. . 900.00
Chest, Victorian, Mahogany, Carved, 6 Drawers, Pilasters, 50 x 53 In. 441.00
Chest, Victorian, Renaissance, Walnut, Side Locking, Carved, 60 x 41 In. 1980.00
Chest, Victorian, Walnut, 4 Carved Drawer Fronts, 41 x 40 x 20 In. 384.00
Chest, Victorian, Walnut, Burl, 6 Drawers, Side Locking, 19th Century, 36 x 22 x 59 In. 578.00
Chest, Walnut, 4 Graduated Drawers, Turned & Ebonized Feet, 41 x 41 x 19 In. 4140.00
Chest, Walnut, 5 Short Over 3 Graduated Drawers, 48 ½ x 45 ¼ x 23 In. 115.00
Chest, Walnut, Bird's-Eye Maple, 5 Graduated Drawers, French Feet, c.1775, 43 x 45 In. 5500.00
Chest, Walnut, Frieze Drawer, 3 Long Drawers, Columnar Pilasters, Tuned Feet, 48 x 43 In. . . 826.00
Chest, Walnut, Lift Top, Drawers, Beveled Front, North Carolina, 1771, 32 x 50 x 22 In. 1000.00
Chest, Walnut, Striped, Figured, Carved Front, Crest, c.1930, 62 x 36 x 18 In. 325.00
Chest, Walnut, Yellow Pine, Poplar, 4 Drawers, Wood Pulls, 41 x 40 x 21 In. 1725.00
Chest, Wellington, Aesthetic Revival, Walnut, Carved, 4 Drawers, Carved Vines, 41 x 34 In. . . . 529.00
Chest, William & Mary Style, Walnut, Veneered, 5 Drawers, Banding, Bun Feet, 39 x 37 In. . . . 4080.00
Chest, William IV, Walnut, Molded Edge, Early 19th Century, 40 x 45 x 24 In. . . . . *illus* 1200.00
Chest-On-Chest, Chinese, Camphorwood, 54 x 38 In. 1904.00
Chest-On-Chest, George I, Burl Walnut, Inlaid, 2 Sections, Drawer, 72 x 43 ¼ In. 11400.00
Chest-On-Chest, George II, Walnut, Inlaid, 77 x 42 ½ x 22 In. 5000.00
Chest-On-Chest, George III, Inlaid Mahogany, 2 Short Over 3 Graduated Drawers, 77 x 44 In. 4800.00
Chest-On-Chest, George III, Inlaid Mahogany, 76 x 43 ¾ In. 7200.00
Chest-On-Chest, Georgian, Mahogany, 2 Case, Drawers, 74 x 45 In. 1725.00
Chest-On-Chest, Georgian, Mahogany, Bowfront, c.1790, 79 x 42 x 19 In. 1880.00
Chest-On-Chest, Mahogany, 2 Case, Drawers, 1800s, 66 x 47 In. 1610.00
Chest-On-Chest, Mahogany, Molded Top, 2 Short & 3 Long Drawers, 76 x 44 x 22 In. 2478.00
Chest-On-Frame, Inlaid, Mother-Of-Pearl, Black Lacquer, 5 Doors, Korea, 36 x 11 In. 472.00
Chest-On-Frame, Mahogany, Breakfront Top, Plain Frieze, 5 Graduated Drawers, 54 x 50 In. 2006.00
Chest-On-Frame, Oak, 3 Short & 3 Long Drawers, Inverted Cup Feet, 49 x 41 In. 531.00
Chiffonier, George III Style, Mahogany, Serpentine Shelved Backsplash, 53 x 28 In. 1175.00
Chiffonier, George IV, Rosewood, Gilt-Metal Mounted, Gilt Inset, Lined Doors, 60 x 48 In. . . . 6000.00
Chiffonier, Regency, Mahogany, Brass Inlay, Tier, Drawers, 2 Doors, 49 ½ x 35 ⅜ x 13 In. 3819.00
Chiffonier, Regency, Rosewood, Marquetry, Mirrored Back, Beaded Molding, 56 x 25 x 13 In. 1410.00
Chiffonier, Regency, Rosewood, Marquetry, 19th Century, 56 ½ x 25 x 13 In. 1528.00
China Press, Federal, Cherry, Glazed Doors, Shelved Interior, Panel Doors, 90 x 40 In. 5980.00
Coat Rack, 4 Dogs At Base, Cutout, Wood, Early 20th Century, 49 In. . . . . *illus* 96.00
Coat Rack, Black Forest, Carved Gnome, 2 Hooks 632.00
Coat Rack, Cherry, Stained, Fleur-De-Lis, Cast Iron, 13 x 41 ½ x 1 In. . . . . *illus* 175.00
Coat Rack, Costumer, G. Stickley, Tenon Construction, 72 x 12 x 22 In. . . . . *illus* 2800.00
Coat Rack, Wood, Enameled Porcelain Feet, Nickel-Plated Iron Hooks, White Paint, 74 In. . . 575.00
Coat Tree, Mahogany, Brass Hooks, Mushroom Ball Top Finial, Claw Feet, 69 x 24 In. 248.00
Coffer, 3-Panel Top, Hinged, Leaf Dome Carved, Continental, 30 x 50 x 25 In. 1440.00
Coffer, Continental, Oak, Lift Top, 2 Drawers, Raised Panel Front, 1700s, 32 x 56 In. 392.00
Coffer, English Walnut, Pine, Planked, 16th Century, 62 ½ In. 9500.00
Coffer, Walnut, Burl Walnut Front Panel, Draped Women, Continental, 59 x 23 In. 1955.00

Column, Louis XVI Style, Golden Scagliola, White Marble Base, 47 x 15 In. 1200.00
Commode, Adam Style, Demilune, Satinwood, Inlaid Top, Swag, Bellflower, 36 x 45 In. 1150.00
Commode, Adam Style, Satinwood, Inlaid Patera & Bands, 2 Drawers, 30 x 23 In., Pair 1920.00
Commode, Biedermeier, 3 Drawers, Baker, 32 x 33 ½ In. 920.00
Commode, Biedermeier, Fruitwood, Applied Sloping Edge, 3 Long Drawers, 33 x 49 In. 5280.00
Commode, Biedermeier Style, 3 Drawers, Baker Label, 32 x 33 x 19 In. . . . . *illus* 920.00
Commode, Bombe, Louis XV, Kingwood, Mahogany, Marble Top, Ormolu, 37 x 51 In. 1920.00
Commode, Bombe, Louis XV Style, Geometric Inlay, Scroll & Leaf Mounts, c.1780, 36 x 31 x 14 In. *illus* 675.00
Commode, Bombe, Louis XV Style, Drawers, Cabriole Legs, 36 x 39 x 20 In. 1062.00
Commode, Bombe, Louis XV Style, Polychrome, Marble Top, 32 x 38 In. 7800.00
Commode, Bombe, Regency Style, Bronze Mounted, Faux Inlay, Drawers, 34 x 56 In. 2115.00
Commode, Bombe, Venetian Rococo Style, Faux Painted, Early 1900s, 32 x 26 In.. . . . . 1840.00
Commode, Continental, Mahogany, Elm, 19th Century, 30 x 26 ½ x 18 In. 1293.00
Commode, Demilune, Mahogany, Marble, c.1940, 34 x 32 x 15 In. 468.00
Commode, Directoire, Inlaid Satinwood, Late 18th Century, 31 x 46 x 24 In. 5875.00
Commode, Dutch Neoclassical, Mahogany, Banded Frieze, 3 Long Drawers, 35 x 45 In. 9000.00
Commode, Empire, Fruitwood, White Marble Top, 2 Drawers, Brass Band Panels, 42 x 23 In. 1880.00
Commode, Empire Style, Figured Mahogany, Drawers, Caryatid Pilasters, 31 x 33 In., Pair . . 1880.00
Commode, Empire Style, Mahogany, Marble Top, 1 Over 3 Drawers, 37 x 49 x 22 In. 7920.00
Commode, Exotic Wood, Marble Top, Italy, 19th Century, 35 x 51 x 22 ½ In.. . . . . 4700.00
Commode, Floral Swags, Italy, 19th Century, 39 x 49 ½ x 23 ½ In. 1998.00
Commode, George III, Mahogany, 18th Century, 30 ¾ x 21 ½ x 18 In. 1175.00
Commode, George III, Mahogany, Tambour Door, 2 Drawers, Gallery Top, 32 ½ x 21 ½ In. . . . 1175.00
Commode, George III, Mahogany, Tambour Cupboard, Drawer, 31 x 21 x 19 In. 1368.00
Commode, George III, Mahogany, Raised Gallery, 2 Doors Over Drawer, 31 x 22 x 20 In. 1420.00
Commode, Georgian, Mahogany, Bowfront, Step, Embossed Leather, c.1830, 55 x 18 x 28 In. 960.00
Commode, Georgian Style, Inlaid Mahogany, Bronze Mount, 32 x 29 x 16 In., Pair 1528.00
Commode, Kidney Shape, 2 Drawers, Marquetry Top, Brass Gallery, 1900s, 31 x 24 In., Pair . 863.00
Commode, Kingwood, Satinwood Parquetry, Marble Top, Cabriole Legs, 33 ⅛ x 29 ½ In. 5700.00
Commode, Lacquered Wood, 3 Drawer, Mirror, Bracket Feet, 31 x 38 x 19 In.. . . . . 287.00
Commode, Louis Philippe, Burl Walnut, Marble Top, Canted Corners, 4 Drawers, 38 x 47 In.. 2280.00
Commode, Louis Philippe, Mahogany, Marble Top, 37 ½ x 50 x 21 ½ In. 2244.00
Commode, Louis XV, Marble Top, Brass Gallery, 2 Drawers, Cabriole Legs, 30 x 11 In., 2 Piece 690.00
Commode, Louis XV, Provincial Fruitwood, 3 Drawers, Mid 1700s, 33 x 51 In. 8813.00
Commode, Louis XV, Walnut, Carved, 18th Century, 34 x 49 x 24 ½ In. 3525.00
Commode, Louis XV Style, 3 Drawers, Variegated Red & White Marble Top, 34 x 31 In. 863.00
Commode, Louis XV Style, Art Deco, Burl, 4 Long Drawers, Cabriole Legs, 36 x 42 In. 3360.00
Commode, Louis XV Style, Green Marble Top, 2 Drawers, Parquetry Veneers, 1900s, 36 x 50 In. 1093.00
Commode, Louis XV Style, Kidney Shape Marble Top, 1900s, 31 x 24 In.. . . . . 375.00
Commode, Louis XV Style, Marble Top, Parquetry, Bronze Mounts, Drawers, 35 x 34 In. 575.00
Commode, Louis XV Style, Red Lacquer, Gilt Flowers, 2 Over 2 Drawers, 34 x 35 x 22 In. 4080.00
Commode, Louis XVI, Marquetry, Variegated Red & Brown Marble Top, Drawers, 34 x 37 In. . 1150.00
Commode, Louis XVI, Walnut, Scalloped Base, Late 18th Century, 35 x 50 x 24 In. 3819.00
Commode, Louis XVI Style, Bronze Mounted, White Marble Top, 37 x 57 In. 2056.00
Commode, Louis XVI Style, Fruitwood, Marble Top, 3 Drawers, Lower Shelf, 1800s, 31 x 15 In. 2040.00
Commode, Louis XVI Style, Fruitwood, 3 Drawers, Fluted Posts, Gray Marble Top, 32 x 48 In. 2600.00
Commode, Louis XVI Style, Inlaid Kingwood Bronze, Marble Top, 36 x 46 x 20 ½ In. 2350.00
Commode, Louis XVI Style, Mahogany, Parquetry, 2 Drawers, 34 x 39 ½ x 19 ½ In. 2640.00
Commode, Louis XVI Style, Marquetry, Ivory Marble Top, 3 Drawers, 33 ½ x 53 In. 2185.00
Commode, Mahogany, Burl, Serpentine Front, Banded, Inset Burled Panel, 32 x 46 In. 4080.00
Commode, Mahogany, Cylinder, White Marble Top, 29 x 18 ½ In., Pair 1763.00
Commode, Mahogany, Serpentine Top, Drawer, Paneled Doors, 31 x 34 In., Pair 4700.00
Commode, Neapolitan, Oak, Multicolored, 19th Century, 39 x 55 x 20 ½ In.. . . . . 7344.00
Commode, Neoclassical, Demilune, Inlaid Mahogany, Egyptian Black Marble Top, 38 x 50 In. 858.00
Commode, Neoclassical, Mahogany, Marble, 3 Drawers, Ormolu Mounted, 36 x 48 x 17 In. . . 5040.00
Commode, Neoclassical, Walnut, 32 ½ x 40 x 17 ½ In.. . . . . 3000.00
Commode, Neoclassical, Walnut, Marquetry, Leaf Sprays, Figures, 37 x 41 ½ x 21 In. 6600.00
Commode, Neoclassical Style, Walnut, Decorative Inlay, Drawer, 33 x 46 In. 2350.00
Commode, Pedestal, Rococo, Rosewood, Mid 19th Century, 29 x 16 x 16 In.. . . . . 2350.00
Commode, Provincial, Directoire, Fruitwood, 3 Raised Edges, Inlay, Cabriole Leg, 28 x 16 In. 1800.00
Commode, Provincial, Empire, Fruitwood, Raised Edge, 3 Drawers, Lower Shelf, 31 x 18 In. . 2280.00
Commode, Provincial, Fruitwood, Molded Edge, 3 Drawers, Mid 19th Century, 28 x 19 In. . . . 660.00
Commode, Provincial, Louis XV Style, Pierced Apron, Painted, 32 x 42 x 19 In., Pair . . . *illus* 1000.00
Commode, Regency, Kingwood, 4 Drawers, Bronze Scroll Feet, 5 ½ x 11 x 5 ¼ In.. . . . . 508.00
Commode, Regency, Mahogany, Bedside, 32 x 17 x 21 In., Pair 1880.00
Commode, Regency Style, Mahogany, Door, Shelf, 28 x 15 In. 325.00

Furniture, Cupboard, Hanging, Cherry, Beaded Molding, c.1800, 58 x 33 x 24 In.
$4600.00

Furniture, Cupboard, Hanging, Pine, Green Paint, American, 19th Century, 26 x 22 x 7 In.
$235.00

Furniture, Cupboard, Napoleon III, Kingwood, Marble, Book Spines, c.1850, 42 x 30 x 15 In.
$1400.00

Furniture, Cupboard, Poplar, 4 Shelves, Plate Rail, Bootjack Ends, c.1850, 76 x 36 x 8 In.
$605.00

Furniture, Cupboard, Yellow Pine, Blue Paint, Georgia, Late 18th Century, 93 x 53 x 24 In.
$1290.00

TIP

If you find mold on your furniture, wipe the spot with a very diluted solution of bleach and warm water, one tablespoon bleach to a quart of water. It should kill the mold.

Commode, Rococo Revival, Walnut, Marble Top, Cabriole Legs, Door, Cupids, 49 x 17 In. 590.00
Commode, Venetian, Paint, Marble Top, 34 ½ x 59 In. 2938.00
Commode, Venetian Style, Paint, Octagonal Plinth, 32 x 16 In., Pair 1998.00
Commode, Victorian, Paint, Serpentine Marble Top, Drawer, Cupboard, 32 x 17 In. 940.00
Commode, Walnut, 3 Graduated Drawers, Serpentine Top, 33 x 39 ½ x 21 In. 1410.00
Commode, Walnut, Backsplash, Molded Top, Drawer, c.1890, 35 x 29 In. 250.00
Commode, Walnut, Shaped, 3 Drawers, Bedside, Italy, 25 ½ x 24 ¾ x 14 In., Pair 5760.00
Cradle, Chippendale, Walnut, Dovetailed, Handles, c.1790, 28 x 44 x 24 ½ In. .... *illus* 300.00
Cradle, Curly Maple, 4-Board, Arched, Curved Ends, Wrought Iron Heart Handles, 36 x 20 In. 288.00
Cradle, Hanging, Mahogany & Pine, 4 Interior Stiles, Knob Finials, 1810, 16 x 15 x 34 In. 510.00
Cradle, Hanging, Walnut, Shaped Crest, Spindles, Casters, c.1890, 41 x 26 In. .... *illus* 115.00
Cradle, Mahogany, Hooded, Veneers, Brass Handles, Silk Liner, 44 x 39 In. 4704.00
Cradle, Pine, Arched Head, Footboard, Heart Handholds, Corner Posts, 23 x 40 In. 144.00
Cradle, Pine, Hooded, Red Stain, Rockers, Dovetailed, Rosehead Nails, 1800s, 25 x 39 In. 425.00
Cradle, Pine, Hooded, Green Paint, Dovetailed, 38 In. 464.00
Cradle, Polychrome, Arched End Panels, Rockers, c.1900, 31 In. 147.00
Cradle, Poplar, Pine, Red Wash, Square Nail Construction, Rounded Ends, 1800s, 38 x 24 In. 201.00
Cradle, Slave, Canoe Shape, Suspended From Bentwood Frame, 1876, 49 x 26 x 24 In. 405.00
Cradle, Softwood, Cheese Cutter Rockers, Scrolled Cutouts, Pa., 23 x 41 ½ x 26 In. 110.00
Cradle, Walnut, Dovetailed, Cutout Handles, c.1780, 24 x 37 x 20 In. .... *illus* 140.00
Cradle, Walnut, Oak, Swings, Runner Feet, Early 19th Century, 39 x 42 x 28 In. .... *illus* 200.00
Cradle, Walnut, Rockers, Turned Finials, Paneled Sides, Cutouts, Pa., 23 x 39 x 26 In. 413.00
Cradle, Windsor, Hickory, Blue Paint, Tiger Maple Rockers, Maple Spindles, 41 x 18 In. 10800.00
Credenza, 4 Drawers, Cream, Blue, 38 ½ x 80 ½ x 18 ½ In. 5288.00
Credenza, Aesthetic Revival, Inlaid, Serpentine Ends, Glass Curios, c.1870, 50 x 83 In. 3410.00
Credenza, H. Probber, Rosewood, Walnut, 4 Drawers, 2 Doors, 6 Legs, 34 x 77 x 18 In. 2350.00
Credenza, Neoclassical Style, Marble Top, Ebonized Hardwood, Scrolled Legs, 66 x 17 In. 920.00
Credenza, Renaissance Revival, Inlaid, Ebonized, Incised Carving, c.1850, 95 x 48 In. 7425.00
Credenza, Walnut, 2 Doors, 2 Drawers, Paw Feet, 19th Century, 46 x 62 x 21 ½ In. 5875.00
Crib, Walnut, Spool Turned, Mid 19th Century, 39 x 39 x 21 In. .... *illus* 190.00
Cupboard, 2 Doors, Green Paint, 19th Century, 39 x 14 ½ x 33 In. 1155.00
Cupboard, 2 Doors, Raised Panels, Blue Green Paint, Cutout Bootjack Ends, 52 x 72 In. 3737.00
Cupboard, 4 Doors, Drawer, Reeded Cornice Molding, 18th Century, 80 x 30 x 18 In. 1035.00
Cupboard, Arts & Crafts, 2-Door Glass Case, 2 Drawers, Carved Heart, 48 x 20 x 84 In. 780.00
Cupboard, Backsplash, Drawer, Paneled Doors, Canada, 4739 ½ x 18 In. 480.00
Cupboard, Baroque Style, Walnut, 2 Doors, Caryatid Supports, Flemish, 69 x 54 In. 944.00
Cupboard, Biedermeier, Bird's-Eye Maple, Cylindrical, Door, Shelves, Bun Feet, 26 x 15 In. 1080.00
Cupboard, Bonnetiere, French Provincial, Beech, Glass Vitrine, 72 x 27 x 16 In. .... *illus* 1300.00
Cupboard, Bonnetiere, French Provincial, Fruitwood, 2 Arched Panel Doors, Drawer, 84 x 35 x 22 In. 4320.00
Cupboard, Butternut, Step Back, Cove Molding, Paneled Doors, 85 x 70 In. 3750.00
Cupboard, Cherry, 2 Sections, Raised Panel Doors, Adjustable Shelves, 84 x 54 In. 1725.00
Cupboard, Chestnut, Blue Paint, 2 Sections, 2 Over 2 Flat Panel Doors, Pa., 79 x 47 In. 3838.00
Cupboard, Chimney, Pine, H-Hinges, New England, 19 x 16 ½ x 9 ¼ In. 2088.00
Cupboard, Chimney, Walnut, 2 Paneled Doors, Shaped Bracket Base, 1800s, 81 x 25 In. 1035.00
Cupboard, Chippendale, Cherry, 4 Doors, 2 Drawers, c.1830, 86 In. 14500.00
Cupboard, Chippendale, Gumwood, Arched Door, Glazed Lancet Arches, 90 x 46 In. 5220.00
Cupboard, Corner, 2 Sections, Grain Paint, 78 ½ x 36 x 21 In. .... *illus* 4100.00
Cupboard, Corner, Cherry, Poplar, Blind Door, Stepped Cornice, Paneled Doors, 88 x 54 In. 1380.00
Cupboard, Corner, Cherry, 2-Pane Doors, 2 Paneled Doors, Scalloped Bracket, 88 x 52 In. 1725.00
Cupboard, Corner, Cherry, 12-Pane Door, Paneled Door, Drawer Below, 43 x 92 In. 3163.00
Cupboard, Corner, Chippendale, Pine, Pennsylvania, Early 1800s, 84 x 44 ¼ In. 1200.00
Cupboard, Corner, Chippendale, Mahogany, Glazed Door, 80 x 35 x 18 In. 1955.00
Cupboard, Corner, Chippendale, Walnut, 8-Pane Doors, 2 Drawers, 93 x 52 x 22 In. 3300.00
Cupboard, Corner, Chippendale, Mahogany, 2 Parts, 89 ½ x 56 ½ In. 5175.00
Cupboard, Corner, Federal, Pine, Glazed Door, 84 x 46 In. 863.00
Cupboard, Corner, George III Style, Chinoiserie, Decorated, Paneled Door, 39 ½ x 27 In. 705.00
Cupboard, Corner, Hanging, Georgian, Oak, Molded Cornice, Paneled Door, 41 x 34 In. 748.00
Cupboard, Corner, Hanging, Cherry, Pendant Shelf, Beaded Molding, c.1800, 58 x 33 x 24 In. 4600.00
Cupboard, Corner, Hanging, Mahogany, England, 19th Century, 32 x 26 x 14 In. 295.00
Cupboard, Corner, Mahogany, Dentil Molding, Gothic Arch, Glazed Door, 82 x 36 In. 767.00
Cupboard, Corner, Pine, Molded Cornice, Paneled Doors, Scalloped Shelves, c.1800, 75 x 45 In. 748.00
Cupboard, Corner, Pine, 4 Paneled Doors, 19th Century, 64 x 43 x 26 In. 1003.00
Cupboard, Corner, Pine, 2 Scrolled Open Shelves, Drawer Over Paneled Door, 74 x 34 In. 1495.00
Cupboard, Corner, Pine, 8-Pane Door, Canted Corners, Scalloped Shelves, 82 x 29 In. 1840.00
Cupboard, Corner, Pine, 12-Pane Door, 2 Lower Paneled Doors, Cream Paint, 86 x 42 In. 4370.00
Cupboard, Corner, Pine, Red Paint, Scalloped Shelves, New England, 79 x 37 In. 6264.00

Cupboard, Corner, Poplar, 2 Doors, 3 Shelves, 60 x 38 ½ x 28 In. . . . 522.00
Cupboard, Corner, Red Paint, Raised Panel, Shaped Shelves, 36 In. . . . 15000.00
Cupboard, Corner, Red Stain, Glass Door, 2 Drawers, 2 Doors, 93 x 43 x 20 ½ In. . . . 2530.00
Cupboard, Corner, Walnut, Pine, 4 Doors, Drawer, Va., c.1850, 78 ½ x 38 ½ x 26 In. . . . *illus* 792.00
Cupboard, Corner, Walnut, Poplar, Step Back, Raised Panels, Interior Shelves, 85 x 44 In. . . . 1150.00
Cupboard, Corner, Walnut, 4 Doors, Shelves, Virginia, 81 ½ x 48 x 23 In. . . . 1180.00
Cupboard, Corner, Walnut, 2 Sections, Ohio Valley, c.1840, 88 x 53 x 33 In. . . . *illus* 1840.00
Cupboard, Corner, Walnut, Poplar, 2 Sections, 2 Blind Doors, 87 ¾ x 53 x 33 In. . . . 1840.00
Cupboard, Corner, Walnut, Yellow Pine, Scrolled Pediment, Paneled Doors, 86 x 50 In. . . . 1840.00
Cupboard, Corner, Walnut, Blue Paint, 2 Paneled Doors, 3 Inside Shelves, 80 ½ x 32 In. . . . 4313.00
Cupboard, Corner, Walnut, 16-Pane, Shelves, Bracket Feet, c.1800, 87 x 33 In. . . . 8050.00
Cupboard, Corner, Walnut, Arched Doors, Pennsylvania, c.1730 . . . 15800.00
Cupboard, Corner, Yellow Pine, Piedmont, 19th Century, 88 x 49 x 23 In. . . . *illus* 3600.00
Cupboard, Curly Maple, Step Back, 2 Sections, 2 6-Pane Doors, Paneled Doors, 1800s, 85 x 51 In. 3910.00
Cupboard, Drawers, Glass Doors, Grain Paint, 92 x 52 x 28 In. . . . *illus* 12100.00
Cupboard, Elm, 2 Doors, Open Shelf, Carved Leaves, 19th Century, 55 x 40 In. . . . 230.00
Cupboard, English Oak, Fitted Case, 2 Doors, Carved Panels, Shelves, 63 x 36 In. . . . 1200.00
Cupboard, Federal, Maple, Pine, Blue Paint, Salmon Interior, 2 Doors, c.1830, 48 x 43 In. . . . 10800.00
Cupboard, Federal, Pine, Poplar, Painted, 3 Shelves, Early 1800s, 88 x 44 In. . . . 1763.00
Cupboard, Federal, Pine, Step Back, Glazed, Shelves, Spoon Holes, Early 1800s, 88 x 56 In. . . 2350.00
Cupboard, Federal, Pine, Carved, Reeded, Oval Reserves, New Jersey, 87 x 53 In. . . . 10575.00
Cupboard, Federal, Poplar, Salmon Glaze, 2 Sections, New Jersey, 1800s, 81 x 56 In. . . . 2468.00
Cupboard, Federal, Walnut, 2 Sections, 2 Doors, 2 Drawers, Dutch, 83 ½ x 64 x 19 In. . . . 4400.00
Cupboard, Federal Style, Mahogany, 2 Glass Doors, 2-Door Base, 79 ¼ x 39 ¾ x 26 In. . . . 1568.00
Cupboard, French Provincial, Pine, 2 Sections, Shelves, 2 Drawers Over Doors, 82 x 47 x 22 In. 470.00
Cupboard, Georgian, Hanging, Barrel Back, Cornice, Paneled Doors, Painted, 1800s, 49 x 32 In. . 748.00
Cupboard, Gray Green, Paneled Door, Shelves, Butt Hinges, Reeded Edge, c.1875, 42 x 28 x 15 In. 1495.00
Cupboard, Hanging, Cherry, Red Paint, 2 Paneled Doors, Adjustable Shelves, 39 x 34 In. . . . 345.00
Cupboard, Hanging, Cherry, Beaded Molding, c.1800, 58 x 33 x 24 In. . . . *illus* 4600.00
Cupboard, Hanging, Edwardian, Satinwood, George III Style, Bowfront Doors, Shelf, 25 x 13 In. . 780.00
Cupboard, Hanging, Georgian, Oak, Dentil Molded Cornice, Paneled Door, 41 ½ x 29 In. . . . 390.00
Cupboard, Hanging, Germanic, Pine, Dovetailed Case, Pediment, Paneled Door, 26 x 20 In. . 633.00
Cupboard, Hanging, Oak, Molded & Ebonized Doors, Fitted Interior, 10 Drawers, 30 x 31 In. . 2185.00
Cupboard, Hanging, Pine, Green Paint, American, 19th Century, 26 x 22 x 7 In. . . . *illus* 235.00
Cupboard, Hanging, Pine, 3 Shelves, Early 19th Century, 39 x 30 x 9 In. . . . 990.00
Cupboard, Hanging, Pine, Yellow, Black, Green, Red, 18 x 18 ¼ x 10 ½ In. . . . 6000.00
Cupboard, Hanging, Walnut, Poplar, Canted Corners, Paneled Door, Zanesville, 39 x 30 In. . . 920.00
Cupboard, Hardwood, 2 Sections, 4-Pane Doors, 63 x 45 In. . . . 200.00
Cupboard, Hudson Valley, Pewter Hutch, 5 Gallery Drawers, Shoefoot Base, 1900s, 23 x 18 In. 1150.00
Cupboard, Jelly, 2 Drawers, Door, Paint, Shoefoot Base, 11 x 11 x 8 In. . . . 2750.00
Cupboard, Jelly, Poplar, White, Drawer, Recessed Panel Drawers, 47 x 43 In. . . . 500.00
Cupboard, Jelly, Poplar, 2 Drawers, 2 Doors, Mid 19th Century, 47 x 43 x 20 In. . . . 1210.00
Cupboard, Jelly, Walnut, Block Feet, Mid 19th Century, 49 x 45 x 22 In. . . . 1058.00
Cupboard, Jelly, Yellow Pine, 2 Dovetailed Drawers, Paneled Doors, 38 x 38 In. . . . 518.00
Cupboard, Kitchen, Open Shelves, Bone White Paint, 38 ½ x 19 x 34 In. . . . 1430.00
Cupboard, Linen, 2 Doors, Pullout Interior Shelves, 42 x 17 ½ x 39 ¼ In. . . . 1320.00
Cupboard, Louis XV Style, Kingwood, 2 Doors, Drawer, Flower Spray, 30 x 19 x 14 In. . . . 3456.00
Cupboard, Mahogany, Flower, Bird Inlay, Drawer, 26 x 19 ¼ x 11 ¾ In. . . . 1080.00
Cupboard, Mahogany, Walnut, Door Of 5 Faux Bookshelves, Plinth Base, 50 x 13 In. . . . 3600.00
Cupboard, Mixed Wood, Stepped Cornice, Open Shelves, Sponged, Stippled Paint, 85 x 47 In. 406.00
Cupboard, Molded Breakfront Cornice, Carved Fan Form Spandrels, 82 ½ x 58 ½ In. . . . 3068.00
Cupboard, Napoleon III, Kingwood, Marble, Book Spines, c.1850, 42 x 30 x 15 In. . . . *illus* 1400.00
Cupboard, Oak, Gothic Carved, 2 Doors, Drawer, 4 Shelves, 69 x 28 x 17 In. . . . 826.00
Cupboard, Orange Wash Stain, Drawers, Paneled Doors, Shelves, 51 x 42 In. . . . 384.00
Cupboard, Paint, Sponge, Comb Grain, 2 Paneled Doors, 3 Drawers, Shelves, 30 x 23 x 11 In. 248.00
Cupboard, Paneled Door, Red Paint, Molded Flat Top, Beveled Corners, c.1800, 68 x 46 x 17 In. 1610.00
Cupboard, Pie, Walnut, Glazed Doors, Shelves, Tin Panels, 85 x 44 x 17 In. . . . 2070.00
Cupboard, Pine, 2 Doors, 2 Drawers, Red Paint, c.1800, 40 x 42 x 12 In. . . . 420.00
Cupboard, Pine, 2 Sections, 2 Doors, Drawers, Cornice Top, 87 x 48 In. . . . 2360.00
Cupboard, Pine, 2 Shelf Open Top Over Doors, Yellow Paint, Maine, 38 x 20 x 76 In. . . . 2875.00
Cupboard, Pine, Chrome Yellow Paint, Drawer, New England, c.1840, 45 x 35 In. . . . 2233.00
Cupboard, Pine, Grain Paint, Mustard & Cream, Scalloped Gallery, Door, 46 x 29 In. . . . 690.00
Cupboard, Pine, Open Shelves, Plate Rails, 2 Doors, 45 ½ x 72 ½ x 19 ½ In. . . . 1680.00
Cupboard, Pine, Painted, Raised Paneled Door, 4 Interior Shelves, Bootjack Ends, 63 x 33 In. 2530.00
Cupboard, Pine, Paneled Door, Molded Top, Interior Shelves, 19th Century, 25 x 46 In. . . . 259.00
Cupboard, Pine, Picture Frame Molding Front, Paneled Doors, 1700s, 82 x 44 In. . . . 750.00

Furniture, Daybed, Com-Packt Furniture Co., Slated Headrest, Cushion, 26 x 30 x 80 In.
$600.00

Furniture, Daybed, G. Nelson, Birch, Zinc Plated Legs, Herman Miller, 1950s, 23 x 75 x 34 In.
$1200.00

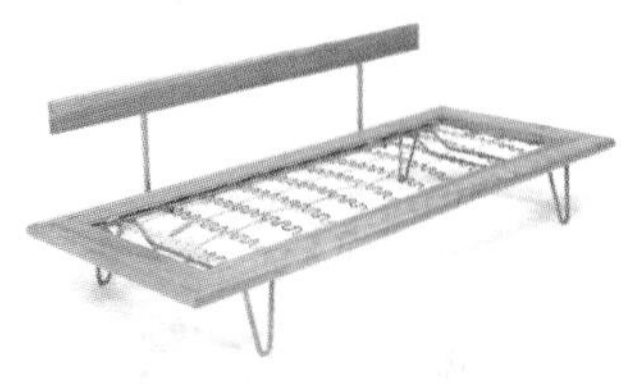

Furniture, Daybed, Pine, Yellow & Black Paint, Hinged Seat, Drawer, c.1850, 32 x 70 x 21 In.
$1285.00

Furniture, Desk, Bamboo, Lift Top, 3 Drawers, Birds, Flowers, Lacquer, 44 x 24 x 20 In.
$230.00

Furniture, Desk, Chippendale, Mahogany, Drawers, Claw & Ball Feet, c.1780, 43 x 44 x 24 In.
$2995.00

Furniture, Desk, Federal, Slant Front, Mahogany, Birch Veneer, Tenn., c.1890, 40 x 24 x 20 In.
$5100.00

Furniture, Desk, French Provincial, Slant Front, Cabriole Legs, 40 x 48 x 23 In.
$3400.00

Furniture, Desk, Pedestal, Georgian, Mahogany, Britain, 19th Century, 31 x 48 x 23 In.
$510.00

Cupboard, Pine, Red Paint, Canted Back, Stepped Cornice, 79 x 35 In. 1495.00
Cupboard, Pine, Shelves, Lamb's Tongue, Paneled Door, 84 x 36 ½ x 14 ½ In. 550.00
Cupboard, Pine, Step Back, Painted, 4 Shelves, Pie Shelf, 2 Doors, Ireland, 87 x 45 In. 805.00
Cupboard, Pine, Step Back, 4 Beadboard Doors, Drawers, Iron, c.1860, 79 x 48 In. 1008.00
Cupboard, Pine, Step Back, 2 Cases, Arched Raised Doors, 3 Drawers, 84 x 59 In. 1840.00
Cupboard, Pine, Step Back, Gray, Paneled Doors, Brass Pulls, 83 ½ x 39 x 16 ½ In. 2310.00
Cupboard, Pine, Step Back, Drawers, Pulls, Latches, 74 x 62 x 20 In. 5500.00
Cupboard, Poplar, 2 Drawers, 2 Doors, Red Paint, Hudson River Valley, c.1840, 50 x 45 In. .. 2300.00
Cupboard, Poplar, 4 Shelves, Plate Rail, Bootjack Ends, c.1850, 76 x 36 x 8 In. .... *illus* 605.00
Cupboard, Poplar, Pewter, 3 Shelves, 2 Doors, 19th Century, 61 x 37 x 18 In. 1210.00
Cupboard, Provincial, Oak, Leaf Carving, Cornice, Panels, Continental, 54 x 25 ½ x 11 In. 660.00
Cupboard, Secretary, Lift Cover, Fitted Interior, 22 x 21 ½ x 53 ½ In. 523.00
Cupboard, Shaker, Pine, Molding, Raised Panels, 6 Interior Shelves, Watervliet, N.Y., c.1825 . 2340.00
Cupboard, Shaker, Pine, Poplar, 4-Panel Door, 6 Interior Shelves, Mt. Lebanon, 70 x 38 x 17 In. . 2925.00
Cupboard, Step Back, Painted, Distressed Blue Paint, Shaped Shelves, Open Top, 74 x 36 In. . 1840.00
Cupboard, Step Back, Pine, Shelves, Plate Rails, 2 Doors, 19th Century 1500.00
Cupboard, Step Back, Pine, Old Red & Blue Paint, 3 Shelves, Raised Panel Door, 80 x 49 In. . 4485.00
Cupboard, Step Back, Poplar, Pine, Panel Doors, Cutout Feet, Shelves, c.1900, 85 x 62 In. 1725.00
Cupboard, Step Back, Redwood, 2 Lower Doors, Interior Shelves, Late 1800s, 72 x 50 In. 715.00
Cupboard, Step Back, Tiger Maple, Scroll Cut Backsplash, 4 Drawers, 2 Doors. 3250.00
Cupboard, Step Back, Walnut, Flat Cornice, Raised Panel Doors, Overhang Shelf, 79 x 52 In. 1763.00
Cupboard, Step Back Bucket, 6 Shelves, Mixed Woods, 1850s, 76 x 39 x 15 In. 1610.00
Cupboard, Twin Paneled Doors, Matching Sides, 19th Century, 53 ½ x 22 x 43 In. 495.00
Cupboard, Walnut, Poplar, Step Back, Chamfered Paneled Doors, 77 x 17 In. 489.00
Cupboard, Walnut, Poplar, 2 Glazed Doors, 2 Panes, Drawer, 79 ½ x 40 x 16 In. 748.00
Cupboard, Walnut, Poplar, Dovetailed Case, Drawer, Paneled Door, Ohio, 64 x 47 In. 1035.00
Cupboard, Walnut, Poplar, Crown Molding, 8-Pane Doors, 2 Recessed Panel Doors, 88 x 21 In. 1495.00
Cupboard, Walnut, Yellow Pine, Corner, 4 Paneled Doors, Shelved Interior, 95 x 52 In. 1495.00
Cupboard, Welsh, Fruitwood, 3 Dovetailed Drawers, Iron Pulls, 1930s, 31 x 17 In. 1300.00
Cupboard, Welsh, Oak, Open Shelves, Painted, 3-Drawer Base, 82 ½ x 72 x 20 In. 1792.00
Cupboard, William & Mary, Red Paint, 55 ⅜ x 40 ¾ x 17 ½ In. 6000.00
Cupboard, Yellow Pine, Blue Paint, Georgia, Late 18th Century, 93 x 53 x 24 In. .... *illus* 1290.00
Cupboard, Zoar, Cherry, Walnut, 2 Paneled Doors, 2 Lower Drawers, Ohio, c.1882, 39 x 33 In. 2415.00
Daybed, Cherry, Poplar, Scrolled Ends, Stretchers, Scalloped Rail, 72 x 30 ½ In. 374.00
Daybed, Chippendale, Cherry, Carved Crest, Cabriole Legs, Padded, 36 x 63 x 23 In. 6600.00
Daybed, Com-Packt Furniture Co., Slated Headrest, Cushion, 26 x 30 x 80 In. .... *illus* 600.00
Daybed, French Empire, Mahogany, Wreath Shape Ormolu Mounts, Gilt, 43 x 77 In. 1380.00
Daybed, G. Nelson, Birch, Zinc Plated Legs, Herman Miller, 1950s, 23 x 75 x 34 In. .... *illus* 1200.00
Daybed, G. Nelson, Birch Frame, Floating Backrest, Upholstered Seat, 75 x 36 x 24 In. 1140.00
Daybed, L. & J.G. Stickley, 4 Wide Vertical Slats, Tapered Posts, 80 x 30 x 28 In. 3200.00
Daybed, Louis XVI Style, Oak, Scrolled Shell Carved Head Rail, Rounded Stiles, 32 x 81 In. .. 1320.00
Daybed, Pine, Yellow & Black Paint, Hinged Seat, Drawer, c.1850, 32 x 70 x 21 In. .... *illus* 1285.00
Daybed, Provincial, Louis XV Style, Fruitwood, Domed Ends, Padded, Cushion, Crests, 36 x 78 In. . 4080.00
Daybed, Regency, Ebonized, Ivory, Scrolled Sides, Transforms To Tester, 51 x 106 In. 10625.00
Daybed, Restauration, Mahogany, Swan Carved Scroll Ends, 1800s, 35 x 30 In. 2400.00
Daybed, Restauration, Walnut, Padded Seat, Paneled, Bracket Feet, 31 x 78 x 27 ½ In. 1680.00
Daybed, Slanted Headrest, 4 Vertical Slats At Each End, 72 ½ x 28 x 25 In. 1020.00
Daybed, Stainless Steel, Black Leather, 12 x 74 x 31 In. 13200.00
Daybed, Tasseled Headboard, Arched, Gold Stenciled, Victorian Beauties, Footboard, 54 x 74 In. 1103.00
Desk, Aesthetic Revival, Drop Front, Burl Veneer, Mahogany, Black Lacquer, 39 x 33 In. 700.00
Desk, Art Deco, Padded Writing Surface, 3 Over 4 Drawers, 30 x 54 x 29 ⅝ In. 483.00
Desk, Arts & Crafts, Drop Front, Oak, Drawer, Shelf, Slatted 302.00
Desk, Arts & Crafts, Drop Front, Open Storage, Leaded Glass Doors, 34 x 16 x 48 In. 960.00
Desk, Bamboo, Lift Top, 3 Drawers, Birds, Flowers, Lacquer, 44 x 24 x 20 In. .... *illus* 230.00
Desk, Biomorphic, Mahogany Top, 3 Drawers, Brass Pulls, 1950, 48 x 26 ½ x 29 ½ In. 510.00
Desk, Bookcase, Slant Front, Inlaid Cherry, Paneled Doors, Interior Shelves, 1800s, 86 x 44 In. . 7480.00
Desk, Burl, Kneehole, Leather, 6 Drawers, Brass Bail Handles, 29 x 40 x 19 In. 1200.00
Desk, Butler's, Empire, Mahogany, Swirl Carved Column, Bun Feet, c.1840, 46 x 44 In. 825.00
Desk, Butler's, Neoclassical, Inlaid Mahogany, Escritoire Drawer, c.1835, 53 x 44 In. 1580.00
Desk, Campaign, Slant Front, Mahogany, Brassbound, Victorian, 20 x 7 In. 148.00
Desk, Chinese, Red Lacquer, Painted, Carved Flowers, Drawers, 1800s, 35 x 37 In. 660.00
Desk, Chippendale, Drop Front, Tiger Maple, Ogee Bracket Base, 36 x 17 x 42 In. 2300.00
Desk, Chippendale, Mahogany, Drawers, Claw & Ball Feet, c.1780, 43 x 44 x 24 In. .... *illus* 2995.00
Desk, Chippendale, Slant Front, Walnut, 4 Drawers, Bracket Feet, 41 x 38 x 20 In. 825.00
Desk, Chippendale, Slant Front, Figured Mahogany, Fitted Interior, 4 Drawers, 42 x 38 In. 920.00
Desk, Chippendale, Slant Front, Walnut, Bracket Feet, Shell Carved, 39 x 21 x 33 In. 1056.00

Desk, Chippendale, Slant Front, Cherry, 4 Drawers, Brass Drop Handles, 40 x 37 x 20 In. 1150.00
Desk, Chippendale, Slant Front, Mahogany, Poplar, Pine, Fitted Interior, R.I., 43 x 36 In. 1265.00
Desk, Chippendale, Slant Front, Birch, Wavy Birch, Graduated Drawers, 43 x 36 x 19 In. 1610.00
Desk, Chippendale, Slant Front, Maple, Pigeonholes, 3 Drawers, c.1785, 29 x 24 x 13 In. 1645.00
Desk, Chippendale, Slant Front, Mahogany, Fitted Interior, Dovetailed, 1800, 20 x 19 In. 1840.00
Desk, Chippendale, Slant Front, Mahogany, Yellow Pine, Fitted Interior, 43 x 42 In.. .... 1840.00
Desk, Chippendale, Slant Front, Tiger Maple, Bird's-Eye Maple, 4 Drawers, 48 In. 2310.00
Desk, Chippendale, Slant Front, Mahogany, 4 Drawers, Inlaid, Bracket Feet, c.1775, 43 x 39 x 20 In. 2400.00
Desk, Chippendale, Slant Front, Dovetailed Case, 4 Graduated Drawers, 44 x 37 In.. .... 2990.00
Desk, Chippendale, Slant Front, Maple, Rhode Island, Late 18th Century, 42 x 36 In. 3819.00
Desk, Chippendale, Slant Front, Mahogany, Rhode Island, c.1800, 41 ½ x 40 ½ In.. .... 3840.00
Desk, Chippendale, Slant Front, Maple, Drawers, Bracket Base, Drop Apron, 42 x 36 x 19 In. . 4140.00
Desk, Chippendale, Slant Front, Curly Maple, Pigeonholes, 8 Drawers, 1700, 42 x 36 x 18 In.. 5460.00
Desk, Chippendale, Slant Front, Curly Maple, Pigeonholes, c.1770, 42 x 36 x 18 In.. .... 5462.00
Desk, Chippendale, Slant Front, Cherry, Pine, Pigeonholes, 9 Drawers, c.1800, 44 x 40 In. ... 5463.00
Desk, Chippendale, Slant Front, Cherry, Birch, Late 18th Century, 42 x 37 In.. .... 33000.00
Desk, Chippendale Style, Drop Front, Gallery, Low Shelf, Claw Feet 1035.00
Desk, Chippendale Style, Mahogany, Tooled Leather, Paneled Doors, 64 x 30 x 48 In. 2644.00
Desk, Colonial Revival, Mahogany, Serpentine Front, Bowed Ends, Scroll, c.1900, 31 x 46 x 23 In.. 225.00
Desk, Compass, Oak, Steel, Curved, c.1953, 29 x 70 ½ x 28 ¼ In.. .... 6600.00
Desk, Country Sheraton, Walnut, Poplar, Dovetailed Gallery, Hinged Lid, 41 x 23 In.. .... 460.00
Desk, Davenport, Lift Top, Carved Gallery, Fitted Interior, England, c.1800, 34 x 24 In. 825.00
Desk, Davenport, Renaissance Revival, Walnut, Gallery, Leather, Drawers, England, 37 x 22 In. 590.00
Desk, Davenport, Slant Front, Burl Walnut, Carved, Fitted Drawers, England, 33 x 29 In. 264.00
Desk, Davenport, Slant Front, Faux Bamboo, Bird's Eye Maple, 1800s, 33 x 24 In. 529.00
Desk, Drop Front, Oak, Mirror, Griffin Heads, Glass Doors, Key. 1695.00
Desk, Drop Front, Reverse Painted, Mirror, Flowers, Scroll, Green, Gold, 48 x 31 x 16 In.. .... 1800.00
Desk, Drop Front, Walnut, Center Door, 4 Drawers, Leather Interior, c.1700, 36 x 33 x 18 In. . 5676.00
Desk, Edwardian, Satinwood, Paint Decorated, Leather Inset, Carlton House, 36 x 41 In. 5875.00
Desk, Escritoire, Rococo, Rosewood, Mid 19th Century, 75 x 64 x 19 In. 5875.00
Desk, Executive, Mahogany, Double Bank, Drawers, Central Drawer, 31 x 65 x 35 ½ In.. ..... 330.00
Desk, Federal, Lady's, Inlaid Mahogany, Mass., c.1810, 49 ¾ x 42 ¼ In. 4560.00
Desk, Federal, Mahogany, Bird's-Eye Maple, Inlaid, Blind Door, c.1800, 46 ¾ x 41 In. 823.00
Desk, Federal, Slant Front, Cherry, Butternut, 4 Drawers, Fitted Interior, 44 x 38 In. 863.00
Desk, Federal, Slant Front, Walnut, Early 19th Century, 41 ½ x 42 x 21 In. 3185.00
Desk, Federal, Slant Front, Mahogany, Birch Veneer, Tenn., c.1890, 40 x 24 x 20 In. .... *illus* 5100.00
Desk, Florence Knoll, Rectangular, Rosewood Veneer, Chrome Base, 72 x 38 x 29 In.. .... 900.00
Desk, French Provincial, Slant Front, Cabriole Legs, 40 x 48 x 23 In. .... *illus* 3400.00
Desk, G. Nakashima, Walnut, Single Pedestal, Turned Leg Supports, 1956, 29 x 54 x 26 In. .. 7800.00
Desk, G. Nelson, Walnut, 3 Drawers, Sliding Door, Herman Miller, 72 x 84 In. 1440.00
Desk, G. Stickley, 2 Drawers, Strap Hardware, Lower Shelf, 36 ½ x 30 ½ x 34 In. 1800.00
Desk, G. Stickley, 2 Drawers, Copper Hardware, No. 453, 39 ½ x 22 x 36 In.. .... 1800.00
Desk, G. Stickley, 2 Drawers, Copper Hardware, Arched Apron, 37 ½ x 23 x 38 In.. .... 2160.00
Desk, G. Stickley, Drop Front, 2 Over 3 Drawers, Gallery Interior, 45 x 36 ¼ x 15 In.. .... 3120.00
Desk, G. Stickley, Drop Front, Mahogany, Copper Hinges, Shelf, 32 x 12 x 46 In.. .... 4800.00
Desk, G. Stickley, Drop Front, Paneled Front, Drawer, Open Shelf, 26 x 15 x 47 In.. .... 5100.00
Desk, G. Stickley, Kneehole, 5 Drawers, 29 ½ x 36 ½ x 24 ¼ In. 1560.00
Desk, George II Style, Molded Top, Leather, Mid 18th Century, 30 x 39 x 22 In.. .... 2233.00
Desk, George III, Mahogany, 5 Drawers, Hinged Top, Tooled Leather, 38 ½ x 49 x 27 In. 5581.00
Desk, George III, Mahogany, Pedestal, Leather Inset, 7 Drawers, c.1780, 31 x 53 In.. .... 15000.00
Desk, George III, Slant Front, Walnut, 3 Drawers, 42 ¾ x 47 x 20 ½ In. 1880.00
Desk, George III Style, Mahogany, Tooled Leather, Drawers, Carved Corners, 30 x 57 x 38 In.. 266.00
Desk, George III Style, Walnut, 3 Drawers Each Side, 2 Pedestals, 31 x 72 x 52 In. 4080.00
Desk, Georgian, Slant Front, Mahogany, Fitted Interior, 4 Graduated Drawers, 41 x 41 In. ... 690.00
Desk, Georgian, Slant Front, Mahogany, 4 Drawers, Britain, c.1850, 43 x 21 x 43 ½ In. 1900.00
Desk, Gothic Revival, Oak, Brass Mounted, Late 1800s, 37 x 24 In. 4800.00
Desk, Hepplewhite, Cherry, Inlaid, 2 Tambour Doors, 4 Drawers, Fitted Interior, 48 x 39 In. .. 3450.00
Desk, Hepplewhite, Mahogany, Lift Top, Masonic Symbols, Stars, Eagle, 38 x 43 In. 38000.00
Desk, Hepplewhite, Slant Front, Cherry, Drawers, Cock-Beaded, Bracket Feet, 43 x 43 x 20 In. 715.00
Desk, Hepplewhite, Slant Front, Cherry, Inlaid, 3 Drawers, Carved Apron, 42 x 42 x 18 ½ In. .. 1725.00
Desk, Herter Bros., Drop Front, Open Compartments, 54 ⅝ x 31 ¼ In. 10856.00
Desk, Kittinger, Mahogany, Leather, Gilt Trim, Maroon Leather, 5 Drawers, 31 x 60 In. 1416.00
Desk, L. & J.G. Stickley, Postcard, Round Wood Knobs, 36 ¾ x 40 x 22 In. 1020.00
Desk, Larkin, Drop Front, Oak, Shelf, Mirror, c.1900, 62 x 30 x 12 In. 200.00
Desk, Library, L. & J.G. Stickley, Drawers, Shelves, Signed, 48 x 28 x 30 In. 2040.00
Desk, Library, Mahogany, Cherry, Baize Surface, 8 Drawers, 2 Doors, 1878, 69 x 48 x 31 In. .. 2938.00

Furniture, Desk, Plantation, Walnut, Drawer, 19th Century, 91 ½ x 47 ½ x 23 ½ In. $1700.00

Furniture, Desk, Roll Top, Oak, No. 4, W.J. Heath, N.H., Salesman Sample, c.1900, 15 x 18 x 9 In. $735.00

Furniture, Desk, Slant Front, Arts & Crafts, Oak, Joerms Bros., Early 20th Century, 41 x 32 x 14 In. $335.00

TIP

Have an extra key made to fit doors and drawers in old furniture. Stick it to the bottom of the piece with a wad of gum or tape.

Furniture, Desk, Slant Front, Cherry, Poplar, Kentucky, c.1825, 43 x 38 x 22 In.
$14950.00

Furniture, Desk, Slant Front, Curly Maple, c.1750-70, 41 x 36 x 19 In.
$7475.00

Furniture, Desk, Slant Front, Walnut, Countertop, c.1885, 21½ x 17 x 18 In.
$460.00

Furniture, Desk, Victorian, Mahogany, Inlaid Tambour, Cylinder Roll, 47 x 31½ x 20 In.
$1200.00

Desk, Loewy, Wood, Laminate, Orange, Red, Slide Top, 41 x 20 x 30½ In. 1440.00
Desk, Louis Philippe, Mahogany, Leather Surface, 6 Over 4 Drawers, Turned Legs, 39 x 50 In. 1200.00
Desk, Louis XV, Lady's, Fruitwood, Floral Inlays, 18th Century, 31 In. 2495.00
Desk, Louis XVI, Fruitwood, Inset Leather, Trisected Top, Central Drawer, 30½ x 63 In. 924.00
Desk, Louis XVI, Mahogany, Marble Top, Brass Mounted, Fluted Legs, 45¾ x 40½ x 20 In. 2112.00
Desk, Louis XVI Style, Ebonized, Gilt, Inset Leather Top, 3 Drawers, Square Legs, 29 x 63 In. 2880.00
Desk, Louis XVI Style, Fruitwood, Leather Surface, 5 Drawers, 31 x 63 In. 1080.00
Desk, Louis XVI Style, Lady's, Marquetry, Urn, Vines, Drop Leaves, Brass, 29 x 30 In. 2990.00
Desk, Mahogany, Block Front, Kneehole, c.1700, 29¾ x 33¾ In. 35100.00
Desk, Mahogany, Brass, 4 Drawers, Josef Frank, c.1930, 28¼ x 51 x 24⅞ In. 9000.00
Desk, Mahogany, Maple, Leather Inlay, 2 Drawers, France, 31 x 48¾ x 27 In. 476.00
Desk, Mahogany, Raised Backsplash, Letter Boxes, Flat Top, Molded Edge, c.1920, 36 x 53 In. 325.00
Desk, Mahogany, Slant Front, Fitted Interior, 3 Long & 2 Short Drawers, 42 x 38 In. 588.00
Desk, Mahogany, Tooled Leather, 3 Over 3 Drawers, c.1920, 31 x 50 x 26 In. 364.00
Desk, Mahogany Veneer, Pine, Oak, Paneled Pedestal, Inkwell, 24 x 18 In. 316.00
Desk, Maple, Slant Front, 10 Drawers, 10 Pigeonholes, Scrolled Base, 43 x 40 x 18 In. 5175.00
Desk, Neoclassical, Lift Top, Tiger Satinwood, Fitted Interior, Painted Scene, Inlay, c.1820 4200.00
Desk, Neoclassical, Mahogany, Fitted Interior, Drawers, Rope Twist Columns, 46 x 42 In. 1645.00
Desk, Neoclassical Style, Walnut, Satinwood Inlay, Banded Edge, Drawers, 32 x 50 In. 2056.00
Desk, Oak, Carved, 3 Over 6 Drawers, Brass Drop Pulls, c.1900, 31 x 51 x 23 In. 476.00
Desk, Oak, Rectangular Plinth, 2 Drawers, Tapered Legs, 19th Century, 30 x 59 x 29 In. 478.00
Desk, Oak, Slant Front, Victorian, Paneled, 2 Pedestals, Spindle Gallery, 37 x 50 x 25 In. 295.00
Desk, Partners, George III, Mahogany, Inlay, Drawers, Cupboards, c.1800, 29 x 60 In. 15000.00
Desk, Partners, Limbert, 4 Drawers, Corbels, Lower Shelf, 29¼ x 60 x 39¾ In. 9000.00
Desk, Partners, Mahogany, Green Tooled Leather Top, Twin Tower Supports, 31 x 67 x 36 In. 826.00
Desk, Partners, Mahogany, Standing Lions, R.J. Horner 5692.00
Desk, Partners, Oak, Lion's Heads, North Wind Faces, Paw Feet, Paine Furniture Co., 54 In. 4795.00
Desk, Partners, Rosewood, 12 Drawers, Pullout Shelves, 27 x 67 x 34 In. 4200.00
Desk, Partners, William IV, Mahogany, Inset Green Leather Top, Pedestal Drawers 1175.00
Desk, Pedestal, Georgian, Mahogany, Britain, 19th Century, 31 x 48 x 23 In. *illus* 510.00
Desk, Pedestal, Victorian, Ebonized, Faux Bamboo, Plinth Base, 31¼ x 47 x 24 In. 2640.00
Desk, Pedestal, Walnut, 7 Drawers, Inlaid Leather, Block Front, 30 x 61 x 30 In. 4182.00
Desk, Pine, Bleached Mahogany, Leather Top, 10 Drawers, Brass Pulls, 31 x 72 x 53 In. 1075.00
Desk, Plantation, Cherry, Poplar, 2 Parts, 2 Inset Paneled Blind Doors, 74 x 29 x 38 In. 1320.00
Desk, Plantation, Pine, Red Brown Paint, Crown Molding, 2 Parts, 71 x 36 In. 2300.00
Desk, Plantation, Sheraton, Mahogany, Recessed Panel, Pigeonholes, 58 x 32 In. 600.00
Desk, Plantation, Walnut, 2 Glazed Doors, Adjustable Shelves, Drawer, Southern, 92 x 48 In. 1955.00
Desk, Plantation, Walnut, Drawer, 19th Century, 91½ x 47½ x 23½ In. *illus* 1700.00
Desk, Plantation Style, Walnut, 2 Doors, Worktable, 73 x 43 In. 767.00
Desk, Prouve, Oak, Lacquered Steel, c.1950, 29 x 49⅜ x 25⅝ In. 7200.00
Desk, Queen Anne, Slant Front, Pine, Oak, 2 Drawers, Interior Pigeonholes, 41 x 34 In. 633.00
Desk, Queen Anne, Slant Front, Walnut, Maple, 4 Drawers, 43 x 35 x 18½ In. 4060.00
Desk, Queen Anne Style, Slant Front, Walnut, 2 Drawers, Child's, c.1910, 33 x 21 x 17½ In. 400.00
Desk, Regency, Inlaid Mahogany, Decoupage, Lithograph, 19th Century, 4 x 12 x 10 In. 570.00
Desk, Regency Style, Mahogany, Inlay, Drawers, 32 x 54 x 29½ In. 384.00
Desk, Renaissance Revival, Walnut, Felt Writing Surface, Scroll Carved Base, c.1870, 29 x 61 In. 1320.00
Desk, Roll Top, C Roll, Tiger Oak, Golden, 42 x 66 x 33¾ In. 850.00
Desk, Roll Top, Oak, Chair, Child's, 32 x 22 x 16 In. 50.00
Desk, Roll Top, Oak, No. 4, W.J. Heath, N.H., Salesman Sample, c.1900, 15 x 18 x 9 In. *illus* 735.00
Desk, Roll Top, Oak, Walnut, 6 Drawers, 60 In. 1375.00
Desk, Roll Top, S Roll, Oak, Paneled Sides, Early 1900s, 44 x 48 x 30 In. 450.00
Desk, Rosewood, Rectangular, Gallery Top, Half Circle, Lovig, 63 x 31 x 33 In. 2160.00
Desk, School, Prairie, Paneled, 2 Hidden Drawers, 55 x 17¾ x 30 In. 660.00
Desk, Schoolmaster's, Pine, Turned Legs, 36 x 36 x 24 In. 207.00
Desk, Schoolmaster's, Pine, Blue Paint, New England, c.1840, 42 x 34 In. 960.00
Desk, Shaker, Slant Front, Pine, Fitted Interior, Drawer, Mt. Lebanon, c.1840, 20 x 13 In. 4095.00
Desk, Sheraton, Slant Front, Cherry, Pine, Dovetailed Case, 35 x 28 x 23 In. 1150.00
Desk, Sheraton, Slant Front, Tiger Maple, 10 Drawers, Octagonal Turned Legs 4312.00
Desk, Sheraton Revival, Mahogany, Bird's-Eye Maple, Pigeonholes, 46 x 36 x 18 In. 1016.00
Desk, Ship Captain's, Slant Front, Yellow Pine, 4 Over 1 Drawer, 1800s, 46 x 38 In. 546.00
Desk, Slant Front, Arts & Crafts, Oak, Joerms Bros., Early 20th Century, 41 x 32 x 14 In. *illus* 335.00
Desk, Slant Front, Cherry, Ash, Ball Feet, Drawers, 18th Century 3250.00
Desk, Slant Front, Cherry, Poplar, Kentucky, c.1825, 43 x 38 x 22 In. *illus* 14950.00
Desk, Slant Front, Curly Maple, 8-Sided Turned Legs, c.1840, 37 x 37 x 20 In. 4313.00
Desk, Slant Front, Curly Maple, c.1750-70, 41 x 36 x 19 In. *illus* 7475.00
Desk, Slant Front, Federal, Inlaid Mahogany, Drawers, Cubbyholes, 45 x 42 x 22¾ In. 6325.00

Desk, Slant Front, Fruitwood, Marquetry, Mahogany Bombe Base, 6 Drawers, 55 x 39 x 22 In. 3055.00
Desk, Slant Front, Mahogany, 2 Inlaid 6-Point Compass-Like Stars, 5 Drawers 1416.00
Desk, Slant Front, Mahogany, Carved Shell, Applied Leaves, Pigeonholes, 39 x 31 x 20 In. 590.00
Desk, Slant Front, Mahogany, Serpentine, 4 Drawers, Cutout Bracket Base, 48 x 43½ x 23 In. 4600.00
Desk, Slant Front, Oak, Banded Edge, 4 Graduated Drawers, Bracket Base, 42 x 39 x 19½ In. 288.00
Desk, Slant Front, Oak, Carved Drawers, Leaves, God Is Love, 43 x 37 x 21 In. 823.00
Desk, Slant Front, Pine, Ivory Paint, 3 Sections, Lift Top, Mid 19th Century, 48 x 30 x 22 In. 168.00
Desk, Slant Front, Pine, Sections, Open Back, Tapered Legs, 48 x 29 x 22 In. 150.00
Desk, Slant Front, Quartersawn Oak, Griffin, Carved, Winged Maiden, c.1880, 40 x 37 In. 7700.00
Desk, Slant Front, Walnut, Countertop, c.1885, 21½ x 17 x 18 In. *illus* 460.00
Desk, Spinet, William & Mary, Fold-Up Top, Scalloped, Turned Legs, Mid 1900s, 34 x 48 x 23 In. 175.00
Desk, Stand, Hinged Top, Decoupage, Drawer, Shelf, 33 x 14 In. 179.00
Desk, Stand, Slant Front, Mahogany, Leather, Squared Legs, Drawer, 48 x 36 x 28 In. 717.00
Desk, Table Top, Walnut, Carved, Figures, Heads, Drawer Over Door, Shelf, Lift Top, 24 x 27 In. 1495.00
Desk, Traveling, Burl Walnut, Storage Compartments, 5½ x 10½ x 15 In. 110.00
Desk, Victorian, Mahogany, Inlaid Tambour, Cylinder Roll, 47 x 31½ x 20 In. *illus* 1200.00
Desk, Walnut, Bank, 4 Drawers, Finger Pulls, c.1860, 30 x 42 x 26½ In. 275.00
Desk, Wooten, Gilt, Burl, Bird's-Eye Maple, 1874, 74 x 41 x 29 In. *illus* 19800.00
Desk, Wormley, Mahogany, Inset Leather Top, 8 Drawers, 1940, 43¾ x 24 x 30½ In. 240.00
Desk-Bookcase, Cherry, Double Arched Bonnet Top, Inlay, Secret Drawers, c.1745, 93 In. 32760.00
Desk-Bookcase, Curly Maple, Cherry Interior, 3-Drawer Base, Shelves, 75 x 43 In. 3450.00
Desk-Bookcase, Kittinger, Chippendale Style, Mahogany, 82 x 39 x 22 In. *illus* 4960.00
Dining Set, Chromed Metal, Leather Top, 2 Upholstered Chairs, Andre Sornay, c.1929 4000.00
Dining Set, Drop Leaf Table, 4 Chairs, Conant Ball, 1950s *illus* 300.00
Dining Set, K. Christensen, Brazilian Rosewood, 6 Chairs, Denmark, 29 x 78 x 49 In. 3408.00
Dining Set, Round Table, 6 Vertical Back Chairs, Stickley Bros., 48 In. 2900.00
Dining Set, Wrought Iron, Mirrored Glass Top, 6 Chairs, Upholstered, Rene Drouet, c.1940 25000.00
Dog Bed, Mirror, Cane Back, Upholstered Pad, Dolphin Mounts, Maitland-Smith, 16 x 31 In. 920.00
Dresser, Burl Walnut, 18 Drawers, Burl Veneer, Cock-Beaded, 74 x 22 x 31 In. 1298.00
Dresser, Cherry, Panel-End, c.1850, 50½ x 39½ In. 1700.00
Dresser, Chippendale, Walnut, 18th Century, 33½ x 38 x 21 In. 6463.00
Dresser, Chippendale, Walnut, 4 Drawers, 18th Century, 33½ x 37 x 21 In. 7638.00
Dresser, English Oak, Dentilated Cornice, Open Shelves, Frieze Drawers, 50 x 67 In. 2040.00
Dresser, Federal, 6 Drawers, Bracket Feet, Oliver Parsell, 49 x 44 In. 19890.00
Dresser, G. Nakashima, Cherry, 4 Drawers, Free Edge Top, 32 x 36 x 21 In. 10800.00
Dresser, G. Nakashima, Walnut, 4 Drawers, 32 x 36 x 20 In. 9600.00
Dresser, G. Nelson, Walnut, 5 Drawers, Tapered Legs, 24 x 18½ x 39½ In. 330.00
Dresser, G. Nelson, Walnut, Door, 4 Drawers, Tapered Legs, 56½ x 18½ x 29¾ In. 780.00
Dresser, G. Stickley, 2 Half Drawers, 3 Full Drawers, 36½ x 20½ x 42 In. 9600.00
Dresser, G. Stickley, Mirror, 4 Drawers, Arched Front, Copper Hardware, 48 x 22 x 66 In. 3600.00
Dresser, Henredon, 2 Doors, Drawer, Shelf, Brass Hinges, Stylized, 39 x 31 In., Pair 532.00
Dresser, Herts Brothers, Mahogany, Marble Top, Panel Door, Open Display, 28 x 48 In. 531.00
Dresser, Leather Patchwork Covered Drawers, Serpentine Front, S. Marx, 36 x 38 x 22 In. 7800.00
Dresser, Loewy, Wood, Laminate, Orange, Red, 4 Drawers, 41 x 19¾ x 29¾ In. 1560.00
Dresser, Louis XVI Style, Satinwood, Kingwood, Drawers, A. Krieger, 54 x 47 x 22 In. 8135.00
Dresser, Mahogany, 6 Drawers, Black Stain, Polish Finish, Ribbed, 31 x 72 x 18 In. 19200.00
Dresser, Mahogany, Acanthus, Lyres, Mirror, Winged Paw Feet, c.1890, 61 x 50 x 25 In. *illus* 1300.00
Dresser, Mahogany, Cornice, Pierced, Shaped Apron, Open Shelves, Wales, 89 x 68 In. 5040.00
Dresser, Mahogany, Kneehole, Molded Edge, England, c.1730, 30 x 26 x 13 In. *illus* 2990.00
Dresser, Mirror, 3 Drawers, Painted Decoration, Child's, c.1870, 45 x 23 In. 354.00
Dresser, Neogrecque, Burl Walnut, Mirror, Candle Shelves, Marble Top, 97 x 52 In. 2115.00
Dresser, Nutting, No. 942, Pine, 75 x 50 x 18½ In. 3190.00
Dresser, Oak, 3 Shelves, Drawers, Paneled Doors, Bracket Feet, England, 81 x 67 x 18 In. 8640.00
Dresser, Oak, Doghouse, Plate Rail, Cup Hooks, Welsh, c.1800, 84 x 65 x 18 In. *illus* 3800.00
Dresser, Oak, Drawers, Cupboards, Plate Racks, Wales, 73 x 19 In. 4700.00
Dresser, Paul McCobb, Mahogany, 4 Drawers, Brass Pulls, 35 x 19 x 35 In. 900.00
Dresser, Renaissance, Burl Walnut, Mirror Back, c.1865, 94 x 52 x 21 In. 1470.00
Dresser, Tiger & Bird's-Eye Maple, Frieze Drawers, Brass Pulls, Reeded, 42 x 45 x 21 In. 2185.00
Dresser, Tiger Maple, 4 Graduated Drawers, Bowfront, 40 x 40¾ x 22½ In. 2820.00
Dresser, Victorian, Pine, Beveled Mirror, Drawers, England, c.1900, 65 x 36 x 17 In. 210.00
Dresser, Victorian, Walnut, 4 Drawers, 19th Century, 90 x 46 In. 354.00
Dresser, Victorian, Walnut, Marble Top, Arched Mirror, 3 Drawers, 1880s, 87 In. 635.00
Dresser, Victorian, Walnut, Marble Top, Carved Crest, Arched Mirror, 3 Drawers, 1880, 87 In. 635.00
Dresser, Walnut, 4 Drawers, Turned Feet, 19th Century, 53 x 43 x 20 In. 770.00
Dresser, Walnut, 4 Drawers, Singer Label, 36 x 47 x 20 In. 13200.00
Dresser, Welsh, Inlaid Oak, Deep Drawers, Mid 18th Century, 78½ x 71 x 20 In. 7931.00

Furniture, Desk, Wooten, Gilt, Burl, Bird's-Eye Maple, 1874, 74 x 41 x 29 In.
$19800.00

Furniture, Desk-Bookcase, Kittinger, Chippendale Style, Mahogany, 82 x 39 x 22 In.
$4960.00

Furniture, Dining Set, Drop Leaf Table, 4 Chairs, Conant Ball, 1950s
$300.00

Furniture, Dresser, Mahogany, Acanthus, Lyres, Mirror, Winged Paw Feet, c.1890, 61 x 50 x 25 In.
$1300.00

Furniture, Dresser, Mahogany, Kneehole, Molded Edge, England, c.1730, 30 x 26 x 13 In.
$2990.00

Furniture, Dresser, Oak, Doghouse, Plate Rail, Cup Hooks, Welsh, c.1800, 84 x 65 x 18 In.
$3800.00

Furniture, Dry Sink, Red Paint, Drawer, 2 Doors, Turned Feet, 36 x 44 x 19 In.
$1650.00

Furniture, Dumbwaiter, Mahogany, 3 Tiers, Leather Casters, Britain, c.1810, 44 x 26 In.
$730.00

Dresser, Welsh, Oak, Elm, 3 Shelves & 2 Banded Cupboards Over 3 Drawers, 79 x 66 In. 3360.00
Dresser, Welsh, Oak, Enclosed Base, 3 Drawers, 2 Cupboards, c.1800, 65 x 18 x 84 In. 4484.00
Dresser, Wyburd, Mirror, 2 Over 3 Drawers, 61 x 38 x 20½ In. 1920.00
Dresser, Roycroft, Oak, 4 Drawers, Backsplash, Mackmurdo Feet, 36 x 41 x 25 In. 1540.00
Dry Sink, Amish, Pine, Poplar, 3 Upper Drawers, Paneled Doors, 44 x 49 In. 4313.00
Dry Sink, Drawer, Scalloped Backsplash, 2 Doors, Paint, Brown Grain, 46 x 44 x 20 In. 440.00
Dry Sink, Maple, Lift Top, 2 Drawers, 2 Doors, 46½ x 20 x 37 In. 115.00
Dry Sink, Old Red Paint, 2 Doors, Side Drawer, Turned Feet, 36 x 44 x 19 In. 1650.00
Dry Sink, Pine, 2 Doors, Shaped Bracket Base, Gallery Back, 39 x 42 In. 336.00
Dry Sink, Pine, 3 Drawers, Door, Copper, Bootjack Base, 40 x 51 x 18 In. 550.00
Dry Sink, Pine, Backsplash, 3 Drawers, Panels, Copper Lined, 40 x 51 x 18 In. 616.00
Dry Sink, Pine, Drawer, 2 Doors, Late 19th Century, 32 x 58 x 19 In. 467.00
Dry Sink, Poplar, Apple Green, Rectangular Top, Drawer, Hinged Door, 1880, 34 In. 1295.00
Dry Sink, Red Paint, Drawer, 2 Doors, Turned Feet, 36 x 44 x 19 In. . . . . . . *illus* 1650.00
Dumbwaiter, Black Lacquer, Papier-Mache, Gilt, Chinese Style, Gallery, Oval, 31 x 24 In. . . . 1920.00
Dumbwaiter, Burl Walnut, Ebonized Telescoping, 3 Tiers, Carved Legs, 38 x 26 x 17 In. 998.00
Dumbwaiter, Federal, Mahogany, Door, Rotating Platform, Reeded, 35 x 24½ In. 7480.00
Dumbwaiter, George III, Mahogany, 3 Graduated Round Shelves, 43 x 25 In. 633.00
Dumbwaiter, George III, Mahogany, Dished Shelves, Reeded Supports, Cabriole Legs, 42 x 23 In.. 1440.00
Dumbwaiter, Georgian, 3 Graduated Tiers, Dished Mahogany Tops, 44 x 26 In. 748.00
Dumbwaiter, Georgian, Mahogany, Dished Swivel Tops, Vase-Form Stems, 41 x 24 In. 1116.00
Dumbwaiter, Mahogany, 3 Tiers, Leather Casters, Britain, c.1810, 44 x 26 In. . . . . . . *illus* 730.00
Dumbwaiter, Mahogany, 3 Tiers, Dish Top, Tripod Base, Slipper Feet, 45½ In. 977.00
Dumbwaiter, Mahogany, England, Mid 19th Century, 47½ x 36 x 18 In. 1410.00
Dumbwaiter, Regency, 3 Tiers, Baluster Standard, Tapered Legs, England, 42 x 25 In. 885.00
Dumbwaiter, William IV, Mahogany, 3 Tiers, Block Spindles, Casters, 1860, 30 x 21 x 10 In. . 940.00
Easel, Aesthetic Revival, Painted, Floral Garland, Mortised Splat, 80 x 26 x 15 In. 2585.00
Easel, Arts & Crafts, Wrought Iron, Sculpted Rose At Top, Patina, 11 x 21 In. 540.00
Easel, Baroque Style, Fruitwood, Leaf Carving, Base, Gargoyle Finial, Italy, 78 In. 1440.00
Easel, Bentwood, Brass Fittings, Scrolled Crest, Fold-Out Legs, Late 1800s, 66 x 22 In. 470.00
Easel, Brass, Dragon Decoration, 17 x 30 In. 303.00
Easel, Chinese, Hardwood, Undulating Frame, Confronting Dragons, Snakes, 48 x 20 In. 431.00
Easel, Eastlake, Walnut, Incised Sunflower Band, Adjustable Shelf, 79 x 24 In. 1116.00
Easel, Louis XVI Style, Gilt, Laurel Wreath Festoon, 1900s, 69 x 22 In. 649.00
Easel, Scrolled Feet, Tripod Base, Wrought Iron, 60 x 20 In. 275.00
Easel, Victorian, Mahogany, Brass Support, Hinged Case, c.1880, 72½ In x 22 In. 3600.00
Easel, Wood, Cane, Acorn Form Finials, Scrolling Columns, 75 In. 2151.00
Etagere, Belter, Gothic Revival, Mahogany, Marble Top, c.1850 . . . . 7370.00
Etagere, Chinoiserie, Gilt, Patinated Iron, 32 x 25 x 12¾ In., Pair. 2057.00
Etagere, Directoire Style, Metal X-Shaped Sides, 3 Lacquered Shelves, Birds, 32 x 25 In., Pair 4800.00
Etagere, Federal, Mahogany, Four Shelves, 19th Century, 60 x 25½ x 12½ In. 2880.00
Etagere, Herter Brothers, Table, Center, Rosewood, Inlaid, c.1870, 4 In. 11000.00
Etagere, Louis Philippe, Rosewood, Gilt Bronze, 19th Century, 57½ x 16 x 13 In. 1293.00
Etagere, Louis XVI, Walnut, Ebonized, Mid 19th Century, 42½ x 29 x 15½ In. 1410.00
Etagere, Mahogany, Carved, Serpentine Base, Mirrored Back, c.1860, 83 x 55 In. 2475.00
Etagere, Mahogany, Pagoda Style, Drawer, Paw Feet, 68 x 20 x 20 In., Pair . . . . *illus* 1700.00
Etagere, Meeks, Victorian, Rosewood, Marble Top, c.1865, 96 In. 22000.00
Etagere, Meeks, Walnut, Burl Trim 3740.00
Etagere, Regency, Rosewood, Gallery Top, c.1820, 42½ x 18 x 14¾ In. 2350.00
Etagere, Regency Style, Mahogany, 3 Shelves, Turned Supports, Footed, 41 x 46 In. 345.00
Etagere, Rococo, Carved, Victorian, c.1850, 66 x 39 In. 660.00
Etagere, Rococo, Rosewood, Carved, Reticulated Crest & Scroll Supports, 69 x 32 In. 940.00
Etagere, Rococo, Rosewood, Domed Shell, Mid 19th Century, 95½ x 50 x 20 In. 7050.00
Etagere, Victorian, Rosewood, Marble Top, c.1860. . . . . . . 7700.00
Etagere, Wood, 3 Shelves, Leafy Openwork Sides, India, 19th Century, 32 x 36 In. 649.00
Food Safe, Door, 2 Shelves, 16 Tins, Punched Geometric Pattern, 55 x 51 x 27 In. 1495.00
Footlocker, Industrial Design, Galvanized Metal, 4 Doors, Lattice Pierced Panels, 79 x 65 In. 1560.00
Footlocker, Industrial Design, Galvanized Steel, Hinged Lid, Lift Out Tray, Stand, 24 x 31 In.. 720.00
Footlocker, Industrial Design, Steel, Green Paint, Door Pairs, 68 x 37 In., Pair 2400.00
Footstool, Art Deco, Green Upholstery, Lucite Square Frame, Modern, 26 x 19 x 17 In. 240.00
Footstool, Arts & Crafts, Leather Cushion, Inverted V-Rail, Tenon Construction, 16 x 19 x 15 In. 360.00
Footstool, Arts & Crafts, Wood, Leather Top, 15 x 16 x 16 In. 150.00
Footstool, Chestnut, Poplar, Painted, Applied Diamonds, Scalloped Skirt, 8¾ x 18 In. 201.00
Footstool, Directoire, Fruitwood, Curule, 19th Century, 15½ x 19 x 16 In., Pair. 858.00
Footstool, Fruitwood, Ball, Bobbin Turned Legs, H-Form Stretcher, Upholstered, 14 x 15 x 15 In. . 443.00
Footstool, G. Stickley, Hard Leather Top, Tacks, 20 x 16½ x 15 In. 1080.00
Footstool, G. Stickley, Rush Seat, Shortened Legs, 20 x 15½ x 13 In. 210.00

Furniture, Etagere, Mahogany, Pagoda Style, Drawer, Paw Feet, 68 x 20 x 20 In., Pair
$1700.00

Furniture, Footstool, Mahogany, Fretted Frame, Piercework, c.1750-55, 17½ x 19 x 15 In.
$3450.00

Furniture, Hall Stand, Anglo-American, Bamboo, Mirror, Flower Panel, c.1900, 78 x 29 x 9 In.
$175.00

Furniture, Hat Rack, Table, Twig, Applied Hearts, Seed Pods, Hooks, Mirror, Virginia, c.1910, 66 x 29 In.
$185.00

Furniture, Huntboard, Yellow Pine, Drawers, Glass Pulls, Georgia, 19th Century, 42 x 57 x 18 In.
$11150.00

Furniture, Iron Safe, Pedestal, Key, c.1900
$350.00

Furniture, Love Seat, Mahogany, Cornucopia Rolled Arms, Paw Feet, c.1850, 35 x 58 x 27 In.
$1490.00

Coat Racks

Coat racks are an ignored furniture form. The oak coat rack once favored by offices can still be found in antiques shops. Less common but more unusual are the coat racks designed by Eames, Sottsass, and other Twentieth-century designers. These often look more like sculpture than furniture.

Furniture, Map Case, Oak, 3 Sections, 26 Drawers, c.1900, 48 x 26 x 33 In.
$1416.00

Furniture, Mirror, Castle Scene, Reverse Painted, Gilt, Eglomise, 19th Century, 34 x 18 In.
$475.00

Furniture, Mirror, Children, Giltwood, Reverse Painted, Molded Frame, 33 x 17 In.
$1150.00

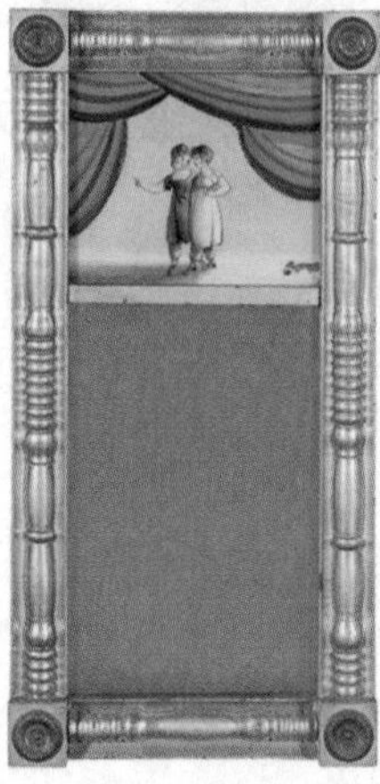

Footstool, G. Stickley, Rush Seat, Tapered Legs, 20 x 16 x 17½ In. 330.00
Footstool, George II, Mahogany, Carved Chinoiserie, Upholstered, 8 x 15 x 15 In. 561.00
Footstool, George III, Mahogany, Beaded Edges, Chamfered Legs, Upholstered, 17 x 22 x 18 In. 690.00
Footstool, Harden, Slatted, Tenon Construction, Leather Cushion, 20 x 14 x 17 In. 900.00
Footstool, Horn, 3 Legs, Upholstered, Green Velvet, Fringe Trim, 11 In. 144.00
Footstool, L. & J.G. Stickley, Leather Top, Arched Side Rails, Handcraft Decal, 16 x 19 x 15 In. 600.00
Footstool, Leather, Green, 20th Century, 21 In. 198.00
Footstool, Mahogany, Fretted Frame, Piercework, c.1750-55, 17½ x 19 x 15 In. *illus* 3450.00
Footstool, Mahogany, Gilt Rosettes, Horsehair Upholstery, c.1815, 13 x 20 x 11 In. 345.00
Footstool, Mahogany, Kittinger, Stylized Cabriole Legs, Upholstered, 16 x 22 x 16 In. 115.00
Footstool, Mahogany, Needlepoint, Concave, Upholstered, 5 x 15 x 12½ In., Pair 325.00
Footstool, Mahogany, Scrolled Legs, Needlepoint Top, c.1925, 14½ x 9 x 7 In. 300.00
Footstool, Mustard Paint, Scrolled Edge Top, Cutout Feet, Sides, 8 x 12¾ In. 230.00
Footstool, Neoclassical, Rosewood, Curule Shape, Upholstered, c.1830, 16 x 21 In., Pair 9600.00
Footstool, Pine, Red Stain, Openwork Compass Star On Top, Shaped Sides, 1883, 6 x 11 In. 288.00
Footstool, Queen Anne, Walnut, Slip Seat Cover, Flower Needlepoint, 16 x 15 x 17 In. 3738.00
Footstool, Restauration Style, Fruitwood, Ebonized, France, 13 x 16 x 9½ In. 1140.00
Footstool, Rococo, Rosewood, Cabriole Legs, Mid 19th Century, 8 x 12 x 9 In. 1175.00
Footstool, Rosewood, Carved, Octagonal, Leather, Turtle Feet, Continental, 5½ x 16 In., Pair. 240.00
Footstool, Shaker, Wood, Old Black Paint, 7 x 12 x 11½ In. 180.00
Footstool, Upholstered Top, Cabriole Legs, Japanned, Black, Gold, Red, 11 x 16 x 13 In. 115.00
Footstool, Victorian, Mahogany, Velvet Cover, Late 19th Century, 10½ x 16 In. 81.00
Footstool, Walnut, Carved, Turned Spindles, Tapestry Upholstery, 10¾ x 17 x 7 In., Pair 60.00
Footstool, Walnut, Marquetry, Flower, Trifid Feet, Upholstered, Dutch, 7 x 12 x 10½ In. 960.00
Footstool, Walnut, Needlepoint, Louisiana, Early 19th Century, 7½ x 14 x 9 In. 1645.00
Footstool, Walnut, Splayed Scalloped Ends, Stretcher, Early 19th Century, 7¾ x 14 In. 138.00
Footstool, Windsor, Pine, Maple, Stretchers, Black & Red Grain, Faux Bamboo, 15 x 10½ In. 690.00
Footstool, Wood, Compass Star, Inlaid, Oval, Early 19th Century, 7 x 7½ x 15 In. 940.00
Footstool, Wood, Gray Paint, Scrubbed, Half Moon Cutout Legs, 12½ x 19 x 10 In. 259.00
Frame, Arts & Crafts, Carved Roses, c.1940, 23 x 12 In. 390.00
Frame, Barbizon Style, Giltwood, Plaster, Carved, France, Late 1800s, 56¾ x 50 In. 1680.00
Frame, Baroque, Giltwood, Carved, Acanthus Leaves, c.1800, 17¾ In. 388.00
Frame, Black Forest, Walnut, Carved, 23 x 19 In., Pair 558.00
Frame, French Style, Gilt, Painted Wood, Composition, Cartouches, Flower Scroll, 37 x 32 In. 633.00
Frame, Giltwood, Composition, Pastiche Plate, Chain & Ball Edge, Flames, 53 x 63 In. 1265.00
Frame, Hudson River Style, Giltwood, Composition, Garland, 1800s, 24 x 18 In. 1093.00
Frame, Louis XV Style, Giltwood, Composition, Shell, Scroll, Acanthus, 1800s, 19 x 12 In. 460.00
Frame, Louis XVI Style, Bronze, Enamel, Wreath, Rose, Trophy Crest, Frame, 20 x 15 In. 4700.00
Frame, Rococo, Giltwood, Molded, Scroll Embossed, Beaded, Flowers, c.1850, 60 x 41 In. 529.00
Frame, Softwood, Brown Ground, Dark Brown Highlights, Crotched Mahogany Design, 15 x 12 In. 248.00
Frame, Wood, Softwood, Red Brown Highlights, 16¼ x 12½ In. 198.00
Girandole, George III, Carved, Gilt, c.1810, 42 x 13½ In., Pair 8225.00
Girandole, Patinated Brass, Centurion, c.1845, 15 x 4¾ x 4¾ In., Pair. 240.00
Glider, Rohde, Tubular Chrome, Burgundy Upholstery, 1930, 39 x 32 In. 5400.00
Gun Box, Stand, Campaign, Mahogany, Brass Trim, Engraved Mr. Johan Cohen, 22 x 35 In. 1020.00
Hall Seat, G. Stickley, Oak, Hinged Seat, c.1909, 41¾ x 47½ In. 3000.00
Hall Stand, Aesthetic Revival, Bamboo, Pediment Crest, Diamond Shape Mirror, 82 x 31 In. 823.00
Hall Stand, Anglo-American, Bamboo, Mirror, Flower Panel, c.1900, 78 x 29 x 9 In. *illus* 175.00
Hall Stand, Bamboo, Rack, Hooks, Mirror, 84 x 33 x 10 In. 690.00
Hall Stand, Bronze, Bear, Holding Branch, Baby Bear, 69 x 29 x 17½ In. 1880.00
Hall Stand, Fruitwood, Ivory Marquetry, Grotesque Hooks, Mirror, 1800s, 96 x 51 In. 3819.00
Hall Stand, Mahogany, Broken-Arch Crest, Panels, Spindle, Mirror, 36 x 84 x 13 In. 560.00
Hall Stand, Mahogany, Scrolled Flat Arms, Mirror, Iron Shell Drip Pan, 91 x 41 x 16 In. 1645.00
Hall Stand, Rococo, Iron, Scrolled Back, Mirror, Umbrella Rack, Drip Pan, 76 x 27 x 16 In. 2350.00
Hall Stand, Victorian, Oak, Carved, Rope Turned, Seat, Beveled Mirror, Green Man, 84 x 47 In. 805.00
Hall Stand, Victorian, Walnut, 6 Turned Pegs, Oval Mirror, Drawer, c.1880, 85 x 32 In. 550.00
Hall Stand, Victorian, Walnut, Oval Mirror, Shaped Cutouts, Umbrella Holder, 84 x 32 In. 336.00
Hall Tree, Black Forest, Full-Figured Bears, 2 Cubs, Carved, 19th Century, 84 x 27 In. 6875.00
Hall Tree, G. Stickley, 2 Posts, Through Tenon, Hangers On Both Sides, No. 53, 12 x 22 x 72 In. 2880.00
Hall Tree, Lifetime, 4 Flared Feet, Iron Hooks, 68 x 24 In. 630.00
Hall Tree, Pine, Lift Seat, Mid 1900s, 75 x 28 x 16 In. 175.00
Hall Tree, Renaissance Revival, Walnut, Arched Cornice, Garment Hooks, Bowed Top, 90 x 51 In. 2400.00
Hall Tree, Shaker, Pine Post, Gray Paint, 16 Graduated Pegs, Crossed Shoe Foot Base, 74½ In. 633.00
Hall Tree, Victorian, Oak, Carved, Old Man Of The North, Pediment, Tin Drip Pans, 96 x 44 In. 978.00
Hall Tree, Walnut, Marble Top, Burled Panels, Umbrella Pans, 19th Century, 88 x 36 In. 590.00
Hat Rack, Table, Twig, Applied Hearts, Seed Pods, Hooks, Mirror, Virginia, c.1910, 66 x 29 In. *illus* 185.00

Hat Rack, Walnut, Porcelain Knobs, 7 Pegs, Expandable, 23 x 10 In. 6.00
Hat Rack, Wood, Chamois Head, Leaves, Branches, Hooks, Black Forest, Carved, 17 x 8 In. .. 295.00
Highboy, Chippendale, Cherry, 2 Sections, Carved Fans, Rosettes, Connecticut, 93 x 41 In. ... 8625.00
Highboy, Chippendale, Mahogany, Queen Anne, Bonnet Top, 77 x 38 x 18 In. 2552.00
Highboy, Georgian, Oak, Pine, 2 Over 3 Drawers, Lower 1 Over 2 Drawers, 65 x 40 In. 805.00
Highboy, Maple, 2 Parts, Fan Carved Apron, 6 Drawers, Cabriole Legs, 68 x 38 x 21 In. 4887.00
Highboy, Maple, Flat Top, Slipper Feet, New England 12500.00
Highboy, Queen Anne, Cherry, Inlaid, 10 Drawers, 8-Point Stars, Cabriole Legs, 71 x 20 In. .. 5290.00
Highboy, Queen Anne, Cherry, Wood Pulls, c.1760, 73 x 38 x 20¾ In. 11750.00
Highboy, Queen Anne, Mahogany Veneers, Broken-Arch Top, 7 Drawers, 74 x 38 x 20 In. 1610.00
Highboy, Queen Anne, Maple, Crown Molding, 4 Long Over 4 Short Drawers, 70 x 40 In. 6900.00
Highboy, Queen Anne, Tiger Maple, 36 x 17 x 74 In. 4600.00
Highboy, Queen Anne, Walnut, Scroll, 9 Drawers, c.1740, 82½ x 40 x 21 In. 28200.00
Highboy, Queen Anne, Walnut, 2 Sections, 12 Drawers, Cabriole Legs, 71 x 40 In. 37120.00
Highboy, Queen Anne Style, Poplar, Green Over Red Paint, 2 Sections, 76 x 22 In. 3737.00
Highchair, Canted, Sausage Turnings, 3-Slat Back, Rush Seat, Front Step 1725.00
Highchair, Ladder Back, Arched Slats, Blue Paint, Splint Seat, 35 x 21 In. 201.00
Highchair, Ladder Back, Red Paint, Arms, 17½ x 35½ In. 193.00
Highchair, Ladder Back, Rush Seat, Old Surface, 19th Century, 18½ x 33 In. 165.00
Highchair, Mixed Wood, Decorated, 2-Slat Back, Rush Seat, Turned Legs, c.1840, 22 x 34 In.. 431.00
Highchair, Shaker, Maple, 2-Slat Back, Tape Seat, Footrest, Mt. Lebanon, N.Y., c.1880, 33 In. . 4095.00
Highchair, Splayed Legs, Slat Back, Sausage Turned, Pilgrim, New England 4640.00
Highchair, Windsor, Green Paint, Bent Press, Plank Seat, Turned Splayed Legs, Foot Rest, 29 In.. 345.00
Highchair, Windsor, Painted, Continuous Arm, c.1800, 36 In. 5288.00
Highchair, Windsor, Rod Back, Bamboo Turnings, Green Paint, Splayed Legs, 21 x 34 In. ... 345.00
Highchair, Windsor, Sack Back, 19th Century, 34½ In. 523.00
Humidor, Wegner, Teak, Oak, c.1960, 19½ x 19⅝ x 20½ In. 7200.00
Huntboard, Cherry, Arched Backsplash, Central Door, Drawers, 54 x 60 x 19¼ In. 4320.00
Huntboard, Federal, Yellow Pine, 3 Dovetailed Drawers, Tapered Square Legs, 40 x 53 In. ... 1725.00
Huntboard, Federal Style, Yellow Pine, Red Paint, Backsplash, Drawers, 50 x 55 In. 460.00
Huntboard, Hepplewhite, Walnut, Inlay, 2 Drawers, 2 Doors, Great Seal Brasses, Va., 40 x 57 In. 16240.00
Huntboard, Pine, 2 Short & 1 Long Drawer, Turned Legs, Button Feet, 37 x 41 In. 674.00
Huntboard, Victorian, Renaissance, Walnut, D-Shape Base, Griffin, Shell Crest, 111 x 79 In.. 6050.00
Huntboard, Victorian, White Marble Top, Silverware Drawers, 2 Doors, 64 x 84 x 24 In. 767.00
Huntboard, Yellow Pine, Drawers, Glass Pulls, Georgia, 19th Century, 42 x 57 x 18 In. . *illus* 11150.00
Hutch, Ethan Allen, Walnut, 4 Doors, 3 Drawers, 2 Shelves, 2 Sections, 79 x 65 In. 265.00
Hutch, Victorian, Mahogany, Arched Crest, 3 Shaped Shelves, 1800s, 82 x 43 In. 472.00
Iron Safe, Pedestal, Key, c.1900 .... *illus* 350.00
Jardiniere, Fruitwood Parquet, Bucket Shape, Pedestal, Brass Liner, Handle, 1800s, 14½ In.. 750.00
Jardiniere, George III, Mahogany, Oval, Plank Construction, Brass, Tin Liner, 6½ x 20⅝ In.. 940.00
Jardiniere, George III Style, Mahogany, Inlay, Cover, 12-Sided, Acorn Knop, 28 x 9 In. 1725.00
Jardiniere, Walnut, Carved, Panels, Metal Liner, Cabriole Legs, 25 x 14 x 14 In., Pair 1800.00
Kas, Dutch Baroque, Oak, Part Ebonized, Molded Cornice, Lion Masks, Panel Doors 2350.00
Kneeler, Prie-Dieu, Louis XV, Gilt, Padded, Floral Carved Frieze, Cabriole Toes, 7 x 48 In. 900.00
Kneeler, Prie-Dieu, Napoleon III, Oak, Rococo, Leaf & Scroll Carved, Upholstered, 34½ In. .. 720.00
Kneeler, Shaker, Pine, Red Paint, Beveled Board Top, Dovetailed, 3¼ x 24½ In. 585.00
Knife Box, Urn, Federal Style, Acorn Finial, Early 20th Century, 24½ In., Pair 2070.00
Lap Desk, Brass Mounted, Inlaid, Brass Handles, 19th Century, 5 x 15 x 10¾ In. 316.00
Lap Desk, Federal, Maple, Mahogany, Inlaid Stars, Fans, Drawer, Newport, c.1810, 7 x 20 x 11 In.. 3525.00
Lap Desk, Lacquered Wood, Chinese, 19th Century, 6½ x 18 x 9¾ In. 702.00
Lap Desk, Mahogany, Inlay, Flared Sides, Domed Cover, Florentine Paper Lining, 9 x 8 In. ... 840.00
Lap Desk, Pine, Black On Cream Smoke Paint, Curved Back, New England, 10 x 21 In. 1093.00
Lap Desk, Pine, Divided Interior, 7½ x 21½ x 15 In. 115.00
Lap Desk, Rosewood, c.1840, 6 x 11¾ x 8½ In. 300.00
Lap Desk, Rosewood, Inlay, Penwork, Warrior, Chariot, Putto, Loop Border, 13 x 11 In. 720.00
Lap Desk, Sarcophagus, Mahogany, Inlaid Shell, Flower Basket, Rondels, Brass Paw Feet, 9 x 8 In. 1200.00
Lap Desk, Stand, Colonial, Oak, 19th Century, 21 x 22 x 13 In. 2585.00
Lap Desk, Stand, Rosewood, Leather Liner, Britain, 19th Century, 24 x 21 x 10¾ In. 2200.00
Lap Desk, Tortoiseshell, Bone Edges, Green Baize Lining, Ebonized Wood Pen Tray, 3 x 11 x 9 In.. 2640.00
Lap Desk, Walnut, Brassbound, Ebony Highlights, Leather Surface, 1800s, 8 x 16 In. 885.00
Lectern, Georgian, Mahogany, Candle Slides, Tripod Base, Britain, c.1750, 29 x 24 x 19 In. .. 1800.00
Lectern, Gothic, Mahogany, Swivel Bookrests, Faceted Pedestal, Stepped Base, c.1885, 52 In. . 353.00
Lectern, Pine, Eagle, Spread Wings, Articulated Feathers, Early 1900s, 20 x 16 In. 345.00
Lectern, Walnut, Incised Decoration, c.1885, 35 x 20 In. 129.00
Lectern, Wood, Eagle, Angle Wings, Back Shelf, Marked, Chapman, Spain, 19½ x 16 In. 575.00
Letter Rack, G. Stickley, Wood, Revolving, 4 Compartments, Cutout Handle, Red Mark, 9 x 12 In. . 1300.00

TIP
Gilt frames can be cleaned with beer.

Furniture, Mirror, Chippendale Style, Mahogany, Phoenix, Gilt, c.1890, 60 x 29 x 2 In.
$1600.00

Furniture, Mirror, Eastlake, Stick & Ball, Shelves, Painted, Late 19th Century, 39 x 56 x 10 In.
$720.00

Furniture, Mirror, Gothic Revival, Columns, Carved, Gilt, American, c.1850, 66 x 76 In.
$4500.00

Furniture, Mirror, Pine, Mortised, Arched Crest, Thumb-Molded Edge, Otsego County, c.1800, 12 x 14 In.
$1035.00

Furniture, Mirror, Shaving, Federal, Mahogany, Satinwood Inlay, 19 x 17 x 6 In.
$150.00

TIP
Old glass in a mirror reflects with an off-white tone. Hold the edge of a white card against the glass. If it has a white reflection that matches the color of the card, it is probably late Victorian or newer. The card reflection will be more yellow or gray if the glass was made before 1850.

Library Catalog, Oak, Card Bin, 4 Sections, 68 x 33 In. 550.00
Library Ladder, Folding, Rounded Posts, Grooved Channel, Oak Rungs, Early 1800s, 98 x 13 In. 2040.00
Library Ladder, Oak, Faux Bamboo Stiles, 77½ x 46 In. 600.00
Library Ladder, Provincial, Oak, Hinged, Graduated, 9 Rungs Each Side, 105 In. 960.00
Library Steps, Victorian, Pine, Side Handrail, Block Legs, 6 Steps, 80 In. 1200.00
Linen Press, Chippendale, Mahogany, Figured, Dentil Molding, 2 Doors, 2 Drawers, 84 x 54 In. 1150.00
Linen Press, Chippendale, Molded Cornice, Recessed Panel Doors, 4 Drawers, 75 x 50 In. 4600.00
Linen Press, Federal, Cherry, Molded Pediment, Frieze, Paneled Doors, 57 x 52 In. 1410.00
Linen Press, Federal, Cherry, Paneled Doors, 4 Drawers, 78 x 43 x 19 In. 3173.00
Linen Press, Federal, Cherry, 2 Doors, 4 Graduated Drawers, 80½ x 48 x 20 In. 3369.00
Linen Press, George II, Mahogany, 5 Drawers, c.1800, 87 x 49½ In. 4130.00
Linen Press, George III, Mahogany, 3 Drawers, 4 Shelves, Scalloped Molding, 77 x 49 x 22 In. 1175.00
Linen Press, George III, Mahogany, Paneled Doors, 4 Graduated Drawers, 78 x 45 In. 3240.00
Linen Press, George III, Mahogany, Inlay, Paneled Doors, Sliding Shelves, 84 x 49 x 21 In. 3290.00
Linen Press, George III, Mahogany, Paneled Doors, Bracket Feet, 78¾ x 50¾ x 24 In. 4488.00
Linen Press, Georgian, Figured Mahogany, 2 Doors, 4 Lower Drawers, 1800s, 78 x 50 In. 2415.00
Linen Press, Hepplewhite Style, Mahogany, Inlaid Doors, 6 Bowfront Drawers, 83 x 50 In. 1380.00
Linen Press, Irish Regency, Mahogany, Satinwood, Crossbanded Doors, 1800s, 83 x 48 In. 2832.00
Linen Press, Mahogany, Flat Top, 2 Doors, Cock-Beaded Drawers, 76 x 60 In. 1062.00
Linen Press, Regency, Mahogany, Molded Cornice, 2 Doors, Drawers, 84 x 50 x 24 In. 2640.00
Linen Press, Regency, Satinwood, Inlaid Mahogany, Paneled Doors, Shelves, 79 x 50 x 24 In. 3408.00
Linen Press, Walnut, 4 Drawers, Arched Paneled Doors, Carved Pediment 6600.00
Linen Press, William IV, Mahogany, 2 Arched Panel Doors, 2 Over 2 Drawers, 84 x 49 In. 2280.00
Linen Press, William IV, Mahogany, 2 Doors, Shelves, 2 Over 2 Drawers, 92 x 57 x 24 In. 3120.00
Linen Press, William IV, Mahogany, Paneled Doors, Drawers, Ball Feet, 83 x 52 x 25 In. 3819.00
Linen Press, William IV, Mahogany, Paneled Doors, Pilasters, 83 x 70 x 24 In. 8644.00
Love Seat, Art Nouveau, Carved, Floral Crest, Acanthus Arms, Paw Feet, c.1880, 47 x 65 In. 2090.00
Love Seat, Chippendale, Mahogany, Upholstered, Humpback, Cabriole Legs, Claw Feet 950.00
Love Seat, Mahogany, Cornucopia Rolled Arms, Paw Feet, c.1850, 35 x 58 x 27 In. .... *illus* 1490.00
Love Seat, Meeks, Rosewood, Laminated, Hawkins 9200.00
Lowboy, Colonial, Cherry, Queen Anne Style, Drawers, Mid 1700s, 34 x 39 In. 1020.00
Lowboy, George I Style, Walnut, Banded, Frieze Drawer, 3 Drawers, 28 x 32 In. 840.00
Lowboy, George II, Walnut, Burl Walnut, 1 Over 2 Drawers, 27½ x 30 x 19¼ In. 2596.00
Lowboy, George III, Mahogany, 3 Drawers, Scrolled Kneehole, 29 x 32 x 20 In. 1175.00
Lowboy, George III Style, Mahogany, Inlay, Drawers, Cabriole Legs, 29 x 30 x 21 In. 147.00
Lowboy, Mahogany, Hooded Knees, Pad Feet, Ireland, c.1780, 28 x 30 In. 2310.00
Lowboy, Queen Anne, 4 Drawers, Kneehole, Scalloped, Cabriole Legs, 28 x 30 x 20 In. 6325.00
Lowboy, Queen Anne, Mahogany, 5 Drawers, Scrolled Skirt, Bandy Legs, 34 In. 375.00
Lowboy, Queen Anne, Mahogany, Pine, Cabriole Legs, Acorn Drops, Drawers, 32 x 17 In. 805.00
Lowboy, Queen Anne, Tiger Maple, Drawers, Shaped Apron, c.1920, 32 x 35 x 20 In. 3150.00
Lowboy, Queen Anne, Walnut, 3 Drawers, Pad Feet, Britain, 18th Century, 28 x 29 x 21 In. 1750.00
Lowboy, Queen Anne Style, Tiger Maple, 3 Drawers, c.1920, 32 x 35 x 20 In. 3528.00
Lowboy, William & Mary, H-Stretcher, Turned Legs, Shaped Apron, Early 1700s, 30 x 35 In. 1760.00
Map Case, Oak, 3 Sections, 26 Drawers, c.1900, 48 x 26 x 33 In. .... *illus* 1416.00
Map Case, Oak, 5 Drawers, 27 x 29 x 32 In. 675.00
Mirror, 3 Panels, Leaf, Scrolls, Mantel, c.1920, 29 x 59 x 2 In. 336.00
Mirror, Adam Style, Giltwood, Oval Frame, 47 x 27 In. 411.00
Mirror, Aesthetic Revival, Framed Panel, Beveled, Carved, Flowers, Dragonflies, 46 x 41 In. 2415.00
Mirror, Anglo-Indian, Ivory Veneer, Silver Mounted, Vizagapatam, c.1790, 28 x 21 In. 6875.00
Mirror, Argente, Rectangular Plate, Canted Silvered Metal Frame, 44 x 31½ x 3¾ In. 288.00
Mirror, Arts & Crafts, Pyrographic & Inlaid Dragons, Diamond Shaped, 30 x 29 In. 780.00
Mirror, Baluster, Black Paint, Gilt, Fruit Basket, c.1830, 24 x 11 In. 705.00
Mirror, Baroque, Cartouche Shape, Walnut Veneer, Gilt Bronze, Late 1800s, 28 x 20 In., Pair. 403.00
Mirror, Baroque Style, Ebonized, Metal Mounted, Beveled Glass, 1800s, 50 In. 1058.00
Mirror, Beaux Arts, Cushion Back, Rocaille & Guilloche Crest, 19th Century, 69 x 41½ In. 3408.00
Mirror, Beech, Parcel Gilt, Polychrome, Scallop Shell, Leafy Scrolls, 45 x 32 In. 1920.00
Mirror, Beveled, Columns, Flowers, Mantel, 19th Century, 27 x 56 In. 440.00
Mirror, Biedermeier, Arched Pediment, Frieze, Geometric Inlay, 34 x 13½ In. 266.00
Mirror, Biedermeier, Mahogany, Geometric Inlay, 33½ x 13½ In. 236.00
Mirror, Biedermeier, Mahogany, Mid 19th Century, 56 x 25¾ In. 840.00
Mirror, Bocage, Porcelain, Sockets, Germany, Late 19th Century, 31 x 17 x 8 In. 3525.00
Mirror, Carved, Painted, Urn & Vine Pierced Crest, Sides, Gold, Silver, Asian, 46 x 36 In. 115.00
Mirror, Castle Scene, Reverse Painted, Gilt, Eglomise, 19th Century, 34 x 18 In. .... *illus* 475.00
Mirror, Cherry, Reverse Painted Landscape, Reeded Column, Cornice, c.1830, 32 x 17 In. 115.00
Mirror, Cheval, Bamboo Maple, c.1880 .... 1150.00
Mirror, Cheval, Chippendale Style, Mahogany, Oval, Floral, Leaf Carving, 1900s, 75 x 35 In. 1495.00

Mirror, Cheval, Empire, Mahogany, Ormolu Urns, Fluted Supports, 77 ½ x 34 x 25 In. 1980.00
Mirror, Cheval, Empire Style, Mahogany, Urn Form Finials, Trestle Base, 62 x 25 ½ In. 558.00
Mirror, Cheval, Mahogany, Arched Scalloped Crest, Lobed Finials, 74 x 42 x 27 In. 1102.00
Mirror, Cheval, Mahogany, Mid 19th Century, 64 ½ x 36 ½ x 28 In. 1410.00
Mirror, Cheval, McHugh, Shoefoot Base, Marked, 36 x 21 x 82 In. 3600.00
Mirror, Cheval, R.J. Horner, Mahogany, Carved 2358.00
Mirror, Cheval, Regency, Mahogany, 19th Century, 63 x 26 In. 715.00
Mirror, Cheval, William IV, Mahogany, Gadroon Carved, Scroll Feet, 61 x 38 In. 1800.00
Mirror, Children, Giltwood, Reverse Painted, Molded Frame, 33 x 17 In. .... *illus* 1150.00
Mirror, Chinese, Lacquer, Parcel Gilt Frame, 18th Century, 11 x 13 In., Pair 28000.00
Mirror, Chinoiserie, Beveled Glass, Painted Landscape, 42 x 28 In. 293.00
Mirror, Chip Carved, Corner Fans, Roundels, Hand & Heart, Stained, 20 x 20 In. 173.00
Mirror, Chippendale, Bleached Walnut, 35 x 18 In. 1150.00
Mirror, Chippendale, Gilt Eagle Crest, Late 19th Century, 49 x 22 In. 1950.00
Mirror, Chippendale, Inlaid Mahogany, Scrolled Crest, c.1780, 41 x 22 In. 928.00
Mirror, Chippendale, Mahogany, Parcel Gilt, Plaster Prince Of Wales Feathers, 72 ½ In. 120.00
Mirror, Chippendale, Mahogany, Parcel Gilt, Beveled Plate, Phoenix, 42 ½ x 23 ½ In. 230.00
Mirror, Chippendale, Mahogany, Gilt Bronze Eagle, 18 x 30 In. 575.00
Mirror, Chippendale, Mahogany, Carved Shell, Eagle, Gilt Bezel, 36 x 20 In. 805.00
Mirror, Chippendale, Mahogany, Pine, Wood Inlay, Figural, c.1775-90, 45 x 22 In. 1155.00
Mirror, Chippendale, Mahogany, Gilt Gesso, Eagle Crest, New England, Late 1700s, 31 x 18 In. 1763.00
Mirror, Chippendale, Mahogany, Cutout Crest, Ears, Scrolled Skirt, 18 x 11 ½ In. 3575.00
Mirror, Chippendale, Mahogany, Shaped Outline, Scrolled Ears, c.1770, 23 x 13 In. 3900.00
Mirror, Chippendale, Mahogany Veneer, Pine, Scalloped Crests, Reeded Frame, 27 x 15 In. .. 259.00
Mirror, Chippendale, Poplar, Stained, Gold Painted Highlights, 20 x 15 ¾ In. 374.00
Mirror, Chippendale, Tiger Maple, Top Crest, Corner Ears, 39 ¼ x 20 ¼ In. 600.00
Mirror, Chippendale Style, Curly Maple, Scrolled Ears, Crest, Base, Late 1800s, 41 x 20 In. ... 403.00
Mirror, Chippendale Style, Giltwood, Winged Phoenix Finial, 58 x 32 In. 1150.00
Mirror, Chippendale Style, Inlaid Mahogany, Parcel Gilt, Swan's-Neck Crest, 64 x 25 In. 1058.00
Mirror, Chippendale Style, Mahogany, Scroll, Turned Finial, 45 x 22 In. 39.00
Mirror, Chippendale Style, Mahogany, Giltwood, Scroll, Broken-Arch Pediment, 48 x 25 In. .. 115.00
Mirror, Chippendale Style, Mahogany, Parcel Gilt, Eagle, 42 x 20 In. 460.00
Mirror, Chippendale Style, Mahogany, Phoenix, Gilt, c.1890, 60 x 29 x 2 In. .... *illus* 1600.00
Mirror, Chippendale Style, Mahogany, Gilt Eagle Crest, c.1880, 49 x 22 In. 1950.00
Mirror, Commemorative, Spanish-American War, Pressed Copper, Portraits, 26 x 26 In. 235.00
Mirror, Courting, Flowers, Painted Panel, 16 In. 348.00
Mirror, Courting, Paint Decorated Frame, Sarcophagus Top, Flower Basket, 13 x 18 In. 805.00
Mirror, Dieppe, Masque Bone Appliques, Oval Plate, Beveled, 32 ½ x 20 In. 5808.00
Mirror, Directoire Style, Giltwood, Sunburst, Carved Rays & Curls, Italy, 23 In. 1200.00
Mirror, Directoire Style, Oak, Trumeau, Carved Musical Trophy, 82 x 22 In. 1440.00
Mirror, Directoire Style, Sunburst, Giltwood, Carved, Gilt, 32 ½ In. 330.00
Mirror, Dresden Style, Porcelain, c.1950, 18 x 12 ½ In. 234.00
Mirror, Dressing, Federal Style, Mahogany, Tapered Supports, Finials, 20 x 18 In. 118.00
Mirror, Dressing, Georgian Style, Inlaid Mahogany, Tapered Supports, Drawers, 25 x 19 In. .. 150.00
Mirror, Dressing, Mahogany, 3 String Inlaid Drawers, 17 ½ x 19 ½ x 9 ¼ In. 413.00
Mirror, Dutch, Walnut, Beveled Plate, Molded, Gadroon Carved Frame, 28 x 19 In. 270.00
Mirror, Eastlake, Square Fretwork, Flowers, Geometrics, 1800s, 22 ¼ x 20 x ¾ In. 472.00
Mirror, Eastlake, Stick & Ball, Shelves, Painted, Late 19th Century, 39 x 56 x 10 In. ..... *illus* 720.00
Mirror, Ebonized, Carved, 19th Century, 74 x 44 In. 1348.00
Mirror, Eglomise Panel, Steamship, Black & Gilt Frame, New England, c.1830, 29 x 13 In. .. 6463.00
Mirror, Empire, Giltwood, Flower Medallion Corner Blocks, Split Spindles, 23 x 16 In. 189.00
Mirror, Empire, Giltwood, Temple Shape Top, Sunburst & Gilt Frieze, 77 x 29 In. 4370.00
Mirror, Empire, Mahogany, Reverse Painted, Ship With Flag, 44 x 21 x 1 ¾ In. 600.00
Mirror, Empire, Reverse Painted, Tablet, Federal Home, Mid 19th Century, 18 ½ x 11 In. 374.00
Mirror, Federal, 2 Panels, Reverse Painted, Flowers, Landscape With House, 41 In. 275.00
Mirror, Federal, 2 Panels, Gilt, Molded Crest, Fluted Columns, 42 x 26 In. 450.00
Mirror, Federal, 2 Panels, Molded Crest, Picture Panel, Ruins, Castle, Ship, 40 x 24 In. 550.00
Mirror, Federal, Convex, Wood, Gold Painted, Gesso, Ebonized, c.1800, 27 In. 978.00
Mirror, Federal, Giltwood, Ring-Turned Column, 3 Schooners, Flag, 25 x 12 x 2 In. 400.00
Mirror, Federal, Giltwood, Reverse Painted Panel, Lady Liberty At Washington's Tomb, 42 In. 2070.00
Mirror, Federal, Giltwood, Composition, Rosette Mounted Frieze, 62 x 37 x 6 ¼ In. 2478.00
Mirror, Federal, Giltwood, Pier, 72 x 40 In. 2875.00
Mirror, Federal, Giltwood Gesso, Columns, Reverse Painted Panel, Mother Reading To Child, 44 In. 1645.00
Mirror, Federal, Mahogany, Paddleboat Scene, Mold Cornice, Reeded, G. Jackson, 22 x 13 In. 303.00
Mirror, Federal, Mahogany, American Eagle On Perch, Stars, 19th Century, 27 x 14 In. 1410.00
Mirror, Federal, Parcel Gilt, Marble, Bilboa, c.1805, 50 x 22 ¾ In. 8400.00

Is It a Marriage?
If you have a two-part piece of furniture like a highboy or secretary-desk, the two parts should match in every way: wood grain, dovetailing, and other construction details. If they do not, it is possible that the piece is a "marriage." The parts originally came from two different pieces later joined together by a dealer. Recently we saw a "divorce"—a Victorian dresser split into a mirror and two small chests of drawers.

Furniture, Parlor Set, Art Deco Style, Faux Suede, 2 Armchairs, 32 x 88 x 32 In. Sofa, 3 Piece
$1300.00

Furniture, Parlor Set, Walnut, Woman's Bust On Arm, Crest, Armchair, 41 x 62 In., 2 Piece
$1100.00

TIP
When replacing old upholstery, look at the marks left by the tacks. Round tack holes indicate a date after 1880.

Furniture, Pedestal, Bombe, Burl, Marble Top, Brass, 46 x 14 x 14 In.
$480.00

Furniture, Pedestal, Mahogany, Man, Garland, 6-Sided Burl Veneer Top, Bird, c.1890, 33 x 18 In.
$1500.00

Furniture, Pedestal, Quartersawn Oak, Column, Wreath Ring, c.1900, 34 ½ x 15 In.
$325.00

F

Mirror, Federal, Reverse Painted Panel, Gold Leaf, Ball Finials, c.1816, 22 x 15 In. 224.00
Mirror, Federal, Reverse Painted Top Panel, Coastal Scene, Corner Blocks, 32 x 15 In. 150.00
Mirror, Federal, Tabernacle, Mansion, Lake, Reverse Painted, Gilt, John Reeves, 31 x 18 In... 475.00
Mirror, Federal Style, Giltwood, Urn Filled Crest, Pier, 57 x 23 In., Pair.................. 2415.00
Mirror, Federal Style, Mahogany, Scalloped Crest, Projecting Ears, c.1900, 33 x 18 In. 266.00
Mirror, Federal Style, Patriotic Tablet, Reverse Painted, Eagle, Shield, 50 x 26 In........... 748.00
Mirror, Federal Style, Reverse Painted, Gilt, 3 Parts, Figures, Cottage, Columns, 24 ¼ x 48 In. 1800.00
Mirror, Florentine, Relief Carved, Gesso Scrolled Flowers, Leaves, Gilt, 19th Century, 38 x 34 In. 6098.00
Mirror, Frame, Curly Maple, Square Nails, Split Turnings, Corner Blocks, 16 ½ x 12 ½ In..... 690.00
Mirror, G. Stickley, Maple, Peaked Top, 30 x 24 ½ In.................................. 1080.00
Mirror, G. Stickley, Oak, 4 Iron Hooks, c.1915, 36 x 26 ¾ In........................... 875.00
Mirror, George II Style, Gilt Frame, Egg & Dart, Bead & Reel, Sand Panel, 35 x 29 In........ 354.00
Mirror, George III, Giltwood, Leafy Shield Crest, Pierced Scrolling, 50 x 31 In............. 960.00
Mirror, George III Style, Giltwood, Oval, Shell Crest, Molded, 49 x 34 In. 1080.00
Mirror, George IV, Giltwood, Convex, Leaf Carving, Crest, Eagle, c.1820, 57 x 37 In. 10000.00
Mirror, Georgian, Carved Floral, Gilt, Molded, Shells, c.1820, 40 x 25 ½ In. 1058.00
Mirror, Georgian, Trumeau, Mahogany, Gilt, Paneled, 82 x 48 In........................ 5288.00
Mirror, Gilt Plaster, Wood Eagle, Round Convex, c.1920, 33 x 25 In..................... 800.00
Mirror, Giltwood, Carved, Gesso, Grapevines, Cherub Head, Easel Back, 20 x 19 In.......... 374.00
Mirror, Giltwood, Carved, Frame, 39 x 27 In... 570.00
Mirror, Giltwood, Carved, Sunburst, Convex, Italy, 14 ¼ In. 1008.00
Mirror, Giltwood, Carved, Octagonal, Italy, c.1750, 13 x 12 In.......................... 1320.00
Mirror, Giltwood, Carved, Mirror Strip Inlay, Cushion Shape, 36 x 24 In.................. 2160.00
Mirror, Giltwood, Iron Wall Mounts, 19th Century, 29 ½ x 59 In......................... 200.00
Mirror, Giltwood, Napoleon III, Lion Mask, 104 x 68 ½ In.............................. 2938.00
Mirror, Giltwood, Oval, Reeded, Beehive Crossed Crest, 50 x 36 ½ In..................... 9775.00
Mirror, Giltwood, Pediment, Tapestry Style Fabric Cartouche, Bow & Swag, 65 x 33 In...... 546.00
Mirror, Giltwood, Polychrome, Guilloche Carved, Scrolling Crest, 51 x 29 In. 4560.00
Mirror, Giltwood, Reverse Painted, Sailboat, Early 1900s.............................. 440.00
Mirror, Giltwood, Teardrop Shape, Pierced, Leaves, Scrolls, 1800s, 21 x 14 In............. 354.00
Mirror, Girandole, Gilt, Eagle Crest Over Acanthus Leaf Carvings, c.1825................ 3450.00
Mirror, Gold Painted Gesso, Flower & Scroll, Bow Crest, c.1910, 30 x 39 In............... 50.00
Mirror, Gothic Revival, Columns, Carved, Gilt, American, c.1850, 66 x 76 In. .... *illus* 4500.00
Mirror, Hall, Arts & Crafts, Beveled Glass, 4 Coat Hooks, 34 x 22 In. 540.00
Mirror, Hall, Carved, Scrolling Leaf Crest, Gadrooned Framing, 67 x 24 In................ 472.00
Mirror, Hall, Giltwood, Eagle Carved Crest, Arched Frame, Medallions, Scrolls, 70 x 36 ½ In. . 1528.00
Mirror, Hand, Willow Strip, Black, 18th Century...................................... 395.00
Mirror, Hepplewhite, Giltwood, Carved, 18th Century, 32 x 18 In. 605.00
Mirror, Howard Miller, Hexagonal, Walnut, Round Cutouts, 33 x 28½ In. .... 540.00 to 1320.00
Mirror, Inlaid Mahogany, Parcel Gilt, Ebonized, Inlay, Eagle, Oval Medallion, 51 ½ x 22 In... 863.00
Mirror, Italian Rococo, Giltwood, 41 x 24 In... 354.00
Mirror, Italian Rococo, Giltwood, Carved, Arched Frames, 41 ½ x 30 In., Pair 2398.00
Mirror, Louis Philippe, Giltwood, Plaster, Ivory, Flower, Shell, 19th Century, 41 x 30 In...... 840.00
Mirror, Louis Philippe, Giltwood, Molded, Corner & Side Patera, 46 x 31 In. 1080.00
Mirror, Louis Philippe, Giltwood, Paneled, Palmetto Corner Accents, 29 x 22 In............ 1200.00
Mirror, Louis Philippe, Giltwood, Shield Shape, Rocaille Crest, Scrolled Leaves, 37 x 31 In. .. 1200.00
Mirror, Louis Philippe, Silver Gilt, Molded, Round Corners, Beaded, c.1850, 53 x 37 In...... 1410.00
Mirror, Louis Philippe Style, Giltwood, Carved, Laurel Wreath, Palmetto, Beaded, 36 x 28 In.. 960.00
Mirror, Louis XIV Style, Multicolored, Leafy Crest, Continental, 48 x 30 In................ 1080.00
Mirror, Louis XV Style, Giltwood, Carved, Beveled Oval Plate, Ribbon Crest, 36 x 25 In....... 1320.00
Mirror, Louis XV Style, Giltwood, Double Dome, Floral Carved Crest, 67 x 35 In. 1800.00
Mirror, Louis XV Style, Oak, Carved, Scrolled Crest, Courting Couple, Beveled, 79 x 41 In. ... 1058.00
Mirror, Louis XV Style, White Pickled Carved Wood, Plaster, France, 24 x 22 In............. 600.00
Mirror, Louis XVI, Flower & Urn Carved Crest, Molded Frame, Mid 1800s, 71 x 43 In........ 960.00
Mirror, Louis XVI, Giltwood, Chinoiserie, Urn, Laurel Leaf Garland Crest, 55 ½ x 33 In. 1848.00
Mirror, Louis XVI, Giltwood, Carved, Ribbon Trim, 58 In............................... 2937.00
Mirror, Louis XVI, Multicolored, Beveled, Oval Plate, Carved Frame, 37 ½ x 31 ½ In. 792.00
Mirror, Louis XVI Style, Giltwood, Floral Crest, Birds, Oval, Ogee Frame, 60 x 31 In. 1645.00
Mirror, Louis XVI Style, Giltwood, Domed Cornice, Torchere, Flower Crest, 77 x 46 In. 6600.00
Mirror, Louis XVI Style, Giltwood, Leafy Urn, Bellflower Swags, 82 x 36 In., Pair 8700.00
Mirror, Louis XVI Style, Multicolored, Scrolling Floral Urn Crest, 44 x 28 In.............. 540.00
Mirror, Louis XVI Style, Napoleon III, Giltwood, Floral Shell Crest, 1800s, 50 x 28 In........ 3600.00
Mirror, Louis XVI Style, Napoleon III, Giltwood, Beveled Oval, Swag Crest, 52 x 34 In....... 4560.00
Mirror, Louis XVI Style, Paint Decorated, Carved, Gilt, Verde Antico, Urn Crest, 68 x 33 In.... 1998.00
Mirror, Louis XVI Style, Paint Decorated, Gilt, Crest, 62 x 33 In........................ 2585.00
Mirror, Louis XVI Style, Square Frame, 40 ½ x 32 In., Pair............................ 1410.00

Mirror, Mahogany, Crest, Molded, Gesso, Pierced, Carved, 1800s, 15 x 9¼ In. 173.00
Mirror, Mahogany, Scroll Arm, 3 Drawers, 19th Century, 25 x 24 x 8 In. 632.00
Mirror, Meridian Series, Hexagonal, Walnut, Round Cutouts, Marked, 33 x 28 In. 1440.00
Mirror, Napoleon III, Giltwood, Beveled Plate, Molded Frame, Flowers, 38½ x 30 In. 840.00
Mirror, Napoleon III, Giltwood, Carved Leaf, Frame, Corner Scrolling, 31 x 27 In. 960.00
Mirror, Napoleon III, Giltwood, Piecrust, Rope Twist, Carved, 48½ x 35½ In. 1800.00
Mirror, Napoleon III, Giltwood, Painted, Arched, Carved Leaf, Beaded, 47 x 30 In. 1920.00
Mirror, Napoleon III, Giltwood, Molded, Rosettes, 75 x 47 In. 3120.00
Mirror, Napoleon III, Louis XVI, Carved, Parcel Gilt, Blanc De Trianon, 71 x 49 In. 2400.00
Mirror, Napoleon III, Polychrome, Pierced Scrolling, Floral Crest, 66 x 40 In. 840.00
Mirror, Neoclassical, Gilt Gesso, Baluster, Black Paint, Reverse Painted, 34 x 15½ In. 177.00
Mirror, Neoclassical, Gilt Gesso, Shell & Floral Decoration, New England, c.1825, 47 x 22 In. 764.00
Mirror, Neoclassical, Giltwood, Composition, Carved Borders, Urn Finial, Flowers, 34 x 18 In. 147.00
Mirror, Neoclassical, Giltwood, Ogee Molded, Mid 1800s, 43 x 29 In. 823.00
Mirror, Neoclassical, Giltwood, Carved, Shell, Leaf Crest, Oval, Star Surround, 38 x 31 In. 863.00
Mirror, Neoclassical, Giltwood, Oval, 32 x 18¼ In., Pair 12500.00
Mirror, Neoclassical, Parcel Gilt, Mahogany, Eagle Crest, Beaded, Continental, 46 x 24 In. 881.00
Mirror, Neoclassical Style, Black, Stenciled Flowers, Rosettes, New England, c.1825, 27 x 14 In. 2585.00
Mirror, Neoclassical Style, Giltwood, Reeded Edge, 1900s, 46 x 36 In. 165.00
Mirror, Neoclassical Style, Giltwood, Relief Carved, Corners Rosettes, Italy, 26 x 21 In. 900.00
Mirror, Neoclassical Style, Giltwood, Bead & Reel Surround, 52½ x 42 In. 1380.00
Mirror, Nutting, Chippendale, Inlaid Mahogany, Gold Eagle, 52 x 23 In. 1760.00
Mirror, Nutting, Queen Anne, Gold Intaglio Bird, 41 x 23 In. 2310.00
Mirror, Oak, Turned Columns, Shelves, Carved Crest, Mantel, 32 x 60 x 7 In. 90.00
Mirror, Ogee Style, Mahogany, c.1900, 23½ x 35½ In. 29.00
Mirror, Oval, Etched, Italy, 29 x 44 In. 165.00
Mirror, Painted Gesso, Multicolored, Wood Frame, Mythological Figures, Flowers, 17 x 15 In. 235.00
Mirror, Parlor, Adams Style, Gilt, Rose Garlands, Early 20th Century, 33 x 12 In. 275.00
Mirror, Pier, Federal, Giltwood, Gilt Columns, Carved, Early 1800s, 55 x 36 In. 2070.00
Mirror, Pier, George III, Giltwood, Reverse Painted Panel, Cherubs, Corn, c.1800, 59 x 30 In.. 5313.00
Mirror, Pier, Georgian, Giltwood, Beveled Mirror, c.1900, 56½ x 27½ In. 588.00
Mirror, Pier, Giltwood, Composition Rosettes, Paneled Back, 1800s, 93 x 70 In. 1380.00
Mirror, Pier, Louis XV Style, Leaf Carving, Reserve, Landscape, 71 x 52 In. 1998.00
Mirror, Pier, Louis XVI Style, Beech, Parcel Gilt, 79 x 52 In. 1680.00
Mirror, Pier, Neoclassical, Giltwood, Painted, Turned Rice-Carved Stiles, c.1820, 36 In. 480.00
Mirror, Pier, Neoclassical, Mahogany, 19th Century, 47 x 25½ In. 674.00
Mirror, Pier, Neogrecque, Carved, Giltwood, Mantel, 19th Century, 105 x 30 In. 1763.00
Mirror, Pine, Mortised, Thumb-Molded Edge, Otsego County, c.1800, 12 x 14 In. .... *illus* 1035.00
Mirror, Pine, Painted, Gilt, Brass Rosettes, Performer On Stage, 27 x 13 In. 412.00
Mirror, Pine, Reverse Painted, Striped Surround, Fruit Crest, Early 1800s, 16½ x 11¼ In. 920.00
Mirror, Plateau, French Style, Silver Plated, 20th Century 175.00
Mirror, Queen Anne, Chippendale, Mahogany, Pierced Gilt Plume Crest, 38 x 19 In. 200.00
Mirror, Queen Anne, Mahogany, Carved, Gilt Shell, 64 x 26½ In. 3450.00
Mirror, Queen Anne, Mahogany Veneer, Molded Frame, Applied Gesso, 24 x 13 In. 431.00
Mirror, Queen Anne, Rosewood Grained, Chinoiserie, Cushion Back, Shaped Crest, 17 In. 580.00
Mirror, Queen Anne, Scalloped Crest, 19 x 10¼ In. 14896.00
Mirror, Queen Anne, Veneered Courting, Painted, Hunting Scene, 20 In. 812.00
Mirror, Queen Anne, Walnut, Bent Back Top, Gilt Embellishments, 33 x 13 In. 450.00
Mirror, Queen Anne, Walnut, 2 Parts, Beveled Edge, Molded Frame, 18th Century, 39 x 17 In. 1495.00
Mirror, Queen Anne Style, Red Japanned, 2-Panels, Etched, Beveled Plate, 49 x 20 In. 633.00
Mirror, Regency, Carved, Gilt, Parcel Ebonized, Convex, England, 27 In. 1320.00
Mirror, Regency, Carved, Gilt, Eagle Top, Convex, 19th Century, 54 x 31 In. 6463.00
Mirror, Regency, Giltwood, Parcel Ebonized, Beaded, Spiral Ribbon Trim, Convex, 23 In. 1920.00
Mirror, Regency, Giltwood, Parcel Ebonized Inner Rim & Spheres, Convex, 25 In. 2160.00
Mirror, Regency, Girandole, Giltwood, Eagle, Spread Wings, Candle Arms, 43½ In. 588.00
Mirror, Regency, Pine, Waxed, Eagle Top, Leaf Spray Bottom, 36 Beads, Convex, 42 x 26 In... 2280.00
Mirror, Regency Style, Faux Bamboo Frame, Convex, England, 31 In. Diam. 1560.00
Mirror, Regency Style, Giltwood, Ebonized Frame, Floral Border, 56 x 34 In. 108.00
Mirror, Regency Style, Mahogany, Parcel Gilt, Oval, Eagle Form Crest, 34½ x 24 In. 500.00
Mirror, Regency Style, Satinwood, Mahogany, String Inlay, 48 x 31 In. 288.00
Mirror, Regency Style, Waxed Wood, Reeded Slip, Molded Frame, 23 In. Diam. 1020.00
Mirror, Restauration, Carved, Ivory Enameled, Wood, Composition, 53 x 35 In. 960.00
Mirror, Reverse Painted, Classical Woman & Child, Ebonized, Gilt Split Column, 31 In. 403.00
Mirror, Reverse Painted, Tablet, Children, Molded, Wood, Gilt, 33 x 17 In. 1150.00
Mirror, Rococo, 3 Arms, Brass, Oval, Scrolling Frame, 19th Century, 17 In. 717.00
Mirror, Rococo, Gilt Gesso, Beveled Glass, Relief Bow, Ribbons, Flowers, 1800s, 33 In. 900.00

Furniture, Pie Safe, Poplar, Blue, Tulip & Heart Punched Tin, 49 x 39 x 17 In. $4400.00

Furniture, Pie Safe, Poplar, Blue Paint, Pierced Tin, 19th Century, 56 x 42 x 17 In. $1680.00

Furniture, Rack, Magazine, Robsjohn-Gibbings, Mahogany, Birch, 23 x 29 x 24 In. $960.00

TIP

Cigarette burns on wooden furniture are difficult to conceal. Rub the burn with scratch-cover polish. If that does not help, rub the burn with a paste of rottenstone (found in most hardware stores) and linseed oil.

Furniture, Rocker, 4 Slats, Maple, Woven Seat, Delaware Valley, c.1790, 39 x 20 x 31 In.
$230.00

TIP
Glue weather stripping to the bottom of a chair rocker to protect the floor.

Furniture, Rocker, Lifetime, Wood, Slats, Signed, 32 x 28 x 32 In.
$2420.00

Furniture, Rocker, Windsor, Stenciled, Spindles, Plank Seat, Marked, Raymond, c.1860, 31 x 16 In.
$345.00

Mirror, Rococo, Giltwood, Gesso, Openwork Crest, Flower Basket, Scrolls, 41 x 21 In. 646.00
Mirror, Rococo, Giltwood, Carved, Tall Crest, Mid 19th Century, 86 x 34 In. 1763.00
Mirror, Rococo, Limewood, Carved, Cartouche Shape, Leaf Scroll Crest, 1700s, 48 x 30 In.. . . 1800.00
Mirror, Rococo, Porcelain, White, Floral Bouquets, 30 x 18½ In., Pair 588.00
Mirror, Rococo Revival Style, Oak, Flower, Acanthus, Victorian, 58 x 44 In. 1560.00
Mirror, Rococo Style, Carved Leaf, Scrolls, Acanthus, Italy, 19th Century, 65 x 53 In.. . . . . 3894.00
Mirror, Rococo Style, Gilt Walnut, Carved, Shell Crest, Brackets, 33 x 18 In., Pair 2468.00
Mirror, Rococo Style, Giltwood, Faux Wedgwood, Carved, Scrolled Crest, 60 x 28 In. 764.00
Mirror, Rococo Style, Giltwood, Carved, Reticulated Crest, Scroll & Leaf, 43 x 29 In. 1100.00
Mirror, Rococo Style, Painted Gesso, Scroll & Leaf Borders, Continental Scenes, 57 x 33 In. . . 1495.00
Mirror, Rococo Style, Venetian, Multicolored, Cartouche Shape, Openwork, 29 In. 823.00
Mirror, Rococo Style, Venetian, Giltwood, Carved, Italy, Early 1900s, 35 x 18 In., Pair. 3360.00
Mirror, Shaving, Federal, Mahogany, Satinwood Inlay, 19 x 17 x 6 In. . . . . *illus* 150.00
Mirror, Shaving, Federal, Mahogany, Tilt Mirror, Turned Posts, 2 Drawers, Bowfront, 19 x 17 In. 150.00
Mirror, Shaving, Mahogany, Drawer, Bowfront, Mushroom Pulls, Bun Feet, 16 x 14 x 7 In. . . 150.00
Mirror, Shaving, Mahogany Veneer, Pine, Ebonized Trim, Bowfront, Drawers, 20 x 20 In.. . . . 201.00
Mirror, Shaving, Oval, Wood, Pedestal Base, 25 In. 66.00
Mirror, Shaving, Regency, Satinwood Veneer, Cross Band & Inlay, 3 Drawers, 23 x 10 In. 374.00
Mirror, Sheraton, Giltwood, Beveled Glass, Reverse Painted Panel, Military Band, 40 x 24 In. 2013.00
Mirror, Softwood, Tan Grain Ground, Brown Highlights, Tiger Maple Design, 17 x 13¾ In. . . 275.00
Mirror, Split Column, Fruit Basket In Top Panel, Rosette Corners, 38½ x 18 In. 230.00
Mirror, Stickley Bros., Hooks, Through Tenon, 29½ x 5 x 22½ In.. . . . . 840.00
Mirror, Sunburst, Carved, Alternating Small & Large Giltwood Leaves, Italy, 28 In.. . . . . 1122.00
Mirror, Sunburst, Gilt Metal, Round Plate, 3 Tiers Of Graduated Pendants, Early 1900s, 26 In. 1140.00
Mirror, Tabernacle, Federal, Gilt, Carved Eagle, Sheaf Of Wheat, Rope Turned Columns, 39 In. 350.00
Mirror, Table, Cornucopia, Crest Of Swans, Continental, 23 x 21 In. 823.00
Mirror, Trumeau, Louis XVI, Egg & Dart Cornice, Oval Reserve, 107½ x 45½ In.. . . . . 5288.00
Mirror, Trumeau, Louis XVI Style, Beechwood, Painted, Scallop Shell, 64 x 61 In.. . . . . 2640.00
Mirror, Trumeau, Louis XVI Style, Gilded, Leafy Shield Crest, Paneled Frame, Garland 3840.00
Mirror, Trumeau, Scenic Panel, Harvest Setting, Skaters, Bird Pediments, 24 In., Pair 1840.00
Mirror, Vanity, Rococo, Gilt Bronze, Scroll & Leaf Designs, Beveled Glass, 17 x 11½ In., Pair . 411.00
Mirror, Walnut, Lion Carvings, c.1875 . . . . 805.00
Mirror, Walnut, Twist Carved Columns, Twisted Spindles, Late 20th Century, 57 x 24 In. 265.00
Mirror, Woman On Each Side, American Flag, 16 Stars, Iron, c.1850, 15 In. 880.00
Mirror, Wood, Flowers, Black Ground, Stepped Scroll Crest, 19 x 8½ In.. . . . . 173.00
Mirror, Wood, Flowers, Beveled, Black Forest, Germany, 18 x 15 In.. . . . . 230.00
Mirror, Wood, Frame, Leaf & Flower Detail, Black Forest, 18 x 15 In. 293.00
Mirror, Wood, Octagonal, Deep Outer Molding, 19th Century, 35 x 35 In.. . . . . 168.00
Mirror, Wood, Softwood, Red Grain Ground, Black Highlights, 16 x 12 In.. . . . . 154.00
Mirror & Console, Neoclassical Style, Carved, Gilt, Divided Plate, 91 x 48 In. 2585.00
Muffineer, Wood, 3 Tiers, Carved, Inlaid Band, Round Top Hub, 3 Square Supports, 35½ x 12 In.. 290.00
Muffineer, Wood, 3 Tiers, Turned Legs, Early 20th Century, 31 x 28 In.. . . . . 489.00
Ottoman, Centennial Chippendale, Carved Skirt, Claw & Ball Feet, c.1870, 20 x 26 In.. . . . . . . 715.00
Overmantel Mirror, see Architectural category.
Parlor Set, Art Deco Style, Faux Suede, 2 Armchairs, 32 x 88 x 32 In. Sofa, 3 Piece . . . . *illus* 1300.00
Parlor Set, Biedermeier, Walnut, Settee, 2 Armchairs, Scroll Crest, Ends, 42 x 66 In.. . . . . 4320.00
Parlor Set, Mahogany, Griffin Carved, Settee, Rocker, Chair 1430.00
Parlor Set, Walnut, Woman's Bust On Arm, Crest, Armchair, 41 x 62 In., 2 Piece . . . . . . *illus* 1100.00
Pedestal, Aesthetic Revival, Carved Gilt, Marble Top Stand, Molded Frame, Tripod Base, 32 x 16 In. 900.00
Pedestal, Art Nouveau, Walnut, Inlaid Dragonflies, Shelf, 52 x 16 x 16 In., Pair 2016.00
Pedestal, Bombe, Burl, Marble Top, Brass, 46 x 14 x 14 In. . . . . *illus* 480.00
Pedestal, Bronze, Octagonal Top, Bird, Flared Center, 36 x 13¾ In.. . . . . 840.00
Pedestal, Carved, Gilt, Flared Top, Scroll Feet, 18th Century, 50 x 14 In.. . . . . 1410.00
Pedestal, Directoire Style, Gilt, Round, X-Shaped Sides, 3-Part Base, 35 x 19 In. 1260.00
Pedestal, Exotic Woods, Veneer, Inlaid, Drawer, 33 x 23 x 13½ In., Pair 4500.00
Pedestal, Gilt, Cast Iron, Square Top, 4-Footed Base, Medallion, Flowers, 45 x 12 In.. . . . . 400.00
Pedestal, Gothic Revival, Oak, Leather Inset, Paneled Frieze, Cluster Column, 39 x 18 In. . . . 588.00
Pedestal, Ionic, Tapered, Fluted, Scrolled Capitals, Painted White, 39 x 9½ In. 403.00
Pedestal, Louis XVI, Sienna, Marble, Gilt Leaf Band, Plinth Base, 47 x 16 x 16 In., Pair 1800.00
Pedestal, Louis XVI Style, St. Anne Des Pyrenees, Marble, Doric Shape, 44 x 19 In. 1800.00
Pedestal, Mahogany, Geometric Inlay, Dish Top, Pierced Frieze, Canted Base, N. Africa, 51 In. 600.00
Pedestal, Mahogany, Man, Garland, 6-Sided Burl Veneer Top, Bird, c.1890, 33 x 18 In. . *illus* 1500.00
Pedestal, Mahogany, Round Top, 3 Legs, Reeded Column, Claw & Ball Feet, 50 x 11¾ In. . . . 230.00
Pedestal, Marble, Gray, Curved, Fluted, Hairy Paw Feet, 32 x 13 In.. . . . . 5520.00
Pedestal, Marble, Green, Square Top, Notched Corners, Turned Columns, 39 x 9 In., Pair . . . 633.00
Pedestal, Marble, Red, Black, Rotating Square Top, Wood Base, 43 x 15 In. 575.00

Pedestal, Marble, Round Column, 20th Century, 47 ½ In. . . . 4320.00
Pedestal, Marble, White, Gray Striations, Rope Twist Column, Urn Shape Base, 10 x 41 In. . . 288.00
Pedestal, Marble, Square Top, Round Base, 27 ½ x 13 ¼ In. . . . 353.00
Pedestal, Neoclassical, Carved, Gilt, Figural Support, Marble Top, 37 x 12 In. . . . 1380.00
Pedestal, Neoclassical, Oak, Octagonal, Fluted, Rosettes, Scrolling Leaves, 47 x 12 x 12 In. . . 502.00
Pedestal, Neoclassical, Painted, Gilt, Garland, Ribbon, Applied Shell, 1900s, 41 x 12 In. . . . 431.00
Pedestal, Neoclassical, Terra-Cotta, 4 Ringed Lion Masques, France, 31 ½ x 13 ¼ In. . . . 1254.00
Pedestal, Onyx, Bronze Mounted, Revolving, Pair . . . 2588.00
Pedestal, Painted, Octagonal, Paneled, Plinth Base, England, Late 19th Century, 44 x 17 In. . 2280.00
Pedestal, Quartersawn Oak, Column, Wreath Ring, c.1900, 34 ½ x 15 In. . . . *illus* 325.00
Pedestal, Regency, Mahogany, Frieze Drawer, Arched Door, Early 1800s, 44 x 18 In. . . . 3055.00
Pedestal, Renaissance, Walnut, Burl, Ebonized, Geometric Skirt, c.1870, 35 x 12 ½ In. . . . 470.00
Pedestal, Renaissance Revival, Walnut, Marble Top, c.1875-85, 32 x 18 In. . . . 470.00
Pedestal, Verde Antico Marble, Round Top, Twist Fluted Standard, Octagonal Base, 44 x 13 In. . 705.00
Pedestal, Victorian, Ebonized, Incised Carved, 40 x 15 In. . . . 330.00
Pedestal, White Marble, Black Grain, 32 In. . . . 59.00
Pew, Church, Renaissance, Paneled Backrest, Scrolled Ends, Plank Seat, Trestle Legs, 88 In. . 118.00
Pie Safe, 2 Doors, 12 Punched Tin Panels, 61 x 36 x 15 In. . . . 150.00
Pie Safe, Hinged Drop Door, 2 Double Doors, Pierced Tin Panels, 55 x 39 In. . . . 1315.00
Pie Safe, Pine, 2 Drawers, 2 Doors . . . 110.00
Pie Safe, Pine, Punched Tin Face, 2 Sections, 4 Doors, 19th Century, 69 x 53 x 24 In. . . . 5175.00
Pie Safe, Poplar, Blue, Tulip & Heart Punched Tin, 49 x 39 x 17 In. . . . *illus* 4400.00
Pie Safe, Poplar, Blue Paint, Pierced Tin, 19th Century, 56 x 42 x 17 In. . . . *illus* 1680.00
Pie Safe, Poplar, Paint, Pierced Tin Doors, 2 Interior Shelves, Drawer, Southern, 56 x 42 In. . 1610.00
Pie Safe, Softwood, Punched Tin Panel, Tapered Legs, 59 x 42 x 17 In. . . . 850.00
Pie Safe, Walnut, 2 Doors, 2 Drawers, Pierced Tin Panels, 55 x 39 x 18 In. . . . 6050.00
Pie Safe, Walnut, Arched Backsplash, Dovetailed Drawer, 2 Doors, Punched Tins, 60 x 40 In. . 748.00
Pie Safe, Walnut, Pine, 8 Tins, Swastika, Green Paint, Ohio, 67 x 40 In. . . . 1610.00
Pie Stand, Arts & Crafts, 3 Shelves, 8-Sided, Splayed Legs, Cutout, 34 x 13 x 13 In. . . . 150.00
Pipe Rack, Wavy Birch, Scrolled Sides, Bone Knobs, 18th Century, 28 ½ In. . . . 825.00
Planter, Art Deco, Metal, 17 ½ x 17 ¾ In., Pair . . . 165.00
Planter, Victorian, Twist Turned Legs, Slate Gray Paint, 32 ½ In. . . . 121.00
Plate Rail, G. Stickley, Peaked Top, Chamfered Board Back, 59 ½ x 5 ½ x 27 In. . . . 3900.00
Plateau, Mirror, Embossed Flowers, Victorian, 12 In. . . . 177.00
Potty Chair, Renaissance Revival, Walnut, Carved Columns, c.1875 . . . 2587.00
Rack, Backbar, Heine & Kogel, Walnut, Marble Top, 2 Piece, 47 x 15 x 102 In. . . . 3335.00
Rack, Baking, Brass, Iron, Corner, 3 Shelves, Late 19th Century, 83 x 25 x 22 In. . . . 580.00
Rack, Baking, Brass, Iron, 3 Shelves, Scroll & Wheat Sheaf Crest, France, c.1880, 79 x 41 x 20 In. . 1820.00
Rack, Barber Bottle, Mahogany, 3 Shelves, 3 Slots, 30 x 10 x 52 ½ In. . . . 35.00
Rack, Blanket, Walnut, Carved, 31 x 15 x 35 ½ In. . . . 540.00
Rack, Bread, Provincial Louis XV Style, Fruitwood, Domed Top, 5 Turned Finials, 42 x 31 In. . 1200.00
Rack, Bread, Provincial Louis XV Style, Fruitwood, Domed Cornice, Turned Finials, 36 x 33 In. 3120.00
Rack, Clothes, Federal, Mahogany, Salem, c.1800, 72 ¼ In. . . . 5875.00
Rack, Drying, 2 Panels, Hinged, Mixed Wood, Mortised, 49 x 30 & 57 x 47 In., 2 Piece . . . 138.00
Rack, Drying, Poplar, Pine, Red Paint, Mortised, Pegged Shoe Feet, 1800s, 48 x 47 ½ In. . . . 259.00
Rack, Luggage, Roycroft, Slatted Top, Carved Orb & Cross Mark, 25 ¾ x 30 x 18 In. . . . 1440.00
Rack, Magazine, Arts & Crafts, Oak, Hinges, Geometric Cutouts, Slats, Wall, 17 x 20 In. . . . 147.00
Rack, Magazine, Robsjohn-Gibbings, Mahogany, Birch, 23 x 29 x 24 In. . . . *illus* 960.00
Rack, Magazine, Wire, Red, White, Yellow, Black, Handle, France, 1950s, 18 x 14 x 7 In. . . . 165.00
Rack, Plate, Oak, Hanging, Shelves, Plate Rails, England, 19th Century, 17 ½ x 63 In. . . . 470.00
Rack, Plate, Pine, Pegged Mortise & Tenon, 2 Size Plate Holders, Hanging, 29 x 39 In. . . . 460.00
Rack, Pool Cue, Brunswick, Balke, Mahogany, 36 x 64 In. . . . 863.00
Rack, Quilt, Blue Paint, 3 Bars, Chamfered Uprights, Arched Shoe Feet, 49 x 70 In. . . . 201.00
Recamier, Belter, Rococo Revival, Rosewood, Laminated, Henry Clay, c.1880, 38 x 39 In. . . . 5775.00
Recamier, Empire, Mahogany, Scrolled Ends, Rectangular Backrest, 1840, 72 In. . . . 2115.00
Recamier, Federal, Applied Rosette, Carved Dolphin, Arm, Velvet Upholstery, 35 x 25 x 80 In. . 1375.00
Recamier, Mahogany, Block Feet, Mid 19th Century, 37 x 81 x 25 In. . . . 950.00
Recamier, Mahogany, Grecian Form, Bolster Ends, Casters, France, 32 x 64 x 23 In. . . . 4720.00
Recamier, Neoclassical, Mahogany, Scrolled Head, Foot, Scalloped Splat, Rush Seat, 31 x 73 In. 9106.00
Recamier, Regency Style, Ebonized, Padded, Scrolled Side, Bolster, Reeded Frame, 38 x 78 x 28 In. 2160.00
Reflector, Regency Style, Ebonized Surround, Wood, Gesso, Convex, 8 ½ In., Pair . . . 288.00
Rocker, 4 Slats, Bentwood Arms, Woven Oak Split Seat, Tennessee, 41 x 22 In. . . . 1035.00
Rocker, 4 Slats, Maple, Woven Seat, Delaware Valley, c.1790, 39 x 20 x 31 In. . . . *illus* 230.00
Rocker, 5 Vertical Back Slats, 4 Arm Slats, No. 518, 27 x 33 x 34 ½ In. . . . 660.00
Rocker, Arrow Back, Decorated, Plank Seat, 19th Century . . . 61.00
Rocker, Art Deco, Tubular Metal, Red, Green, c.1920, 30 x 21 x 44 In., Pair . . . 3000.00

Furniture, Schrank, Pine, Poplar, Wood Grain Paint Over Yellow, Late 19th Century, 83 x 63 x 24 In. $2400.00

Furniture, Screen, 3-Panel, Sunburst, Dowels, 1950s, 86 x 26 In. $1350.00

TIP

If the veneer on old furniture is just loose, make a small slit in the wood with the grain of the wood. Use this as a way to apply the glue under the veneer. If the veneer is bubbled up and loose, place a piece of cardboard on the wood and press with an iron set at medium heat. The heat should soften the glue and you will be able to feel the wood give a little. Press down and weight the spot until the glue has redried.

F

Furniture, Screen, 4-Panel, Farm House, Landscape, Paper On Linen, France, c.1895, 67 x 110 In.
$2840.00

Furniture, Screen, Arts & Crafts, Owls, Vines, Flowers, Oak, Glass Eyes, 33 x 26 x 5 In.
$1096.00

Furniture, Screen, Table, Stylized Leaves, 8-Sided, England, Early 19th Century, 12 In.
$230.

TIP
Sticking drawers? Try using some plastic weather stripping on the bottom edge of the drawer and the top of the case hole.

Rocker, Boston, Black Paint, 6 Curved Back Spindles, Scroll Arms, Plank Seat, 40 x 15 In.... 115.00
Rocker, Comb Top, Arrow Spindles, Scroll Arms, 19th Century, 43 x 16 In. 330.00
Rocker, Edler's, Ladder Back, Maple & Cherry, 4 Slats, Green Tape Seat, c.1830 14627.00
Rocker, G. Stickley, Back Slats, Leather Seat, 26 x 27 x 38 In.. 510.00
Rocker, G. Stickley, Cutout To Back, Vertical Slats, Worn Cushion, 20 x 30 x 28½ In.. 840.00
Rocker, G. Stickley, Horizontal Slats To Back, Rush Seat, 21 x 25 x 33 In.. 3600.00
Rocker, G. Stickley, Oak, Leather, Paper Label, c.1900, 24 In. 118.00
Rocker, G. Stickley, Oak, Curved Back, 11 Square Spindles, 9 Side Spindles, Double Slat Skirt 644.00
Rocker, G. Stickley, Oak, Upholstered, c.1905, 45 In. 3840.00
Rocker, G. Stickley, Sewing, Thornden, 2 Horizontal Slats, 18 x 22 x 31 In. 330.00
Rocker, G. Stickley, Sewing, Slat Back, Leather Seat, 17 x 24 x 32 In.. 450.00
Rocker, George Hunzinger, Walnut, Turned, Padded Back, Spindles, c.1870 588.00
Rocker, L. & J.G. Stickley, High Slatted Back, Oilcloth Seat, 40 x 27½ x 22 In., Pair 2400.00
Rocker, L. & J.G. Stickley, Slat Back, Slat Arm Supports, Leather Upholstery, 36 x 32 In. 1300.00
Rocker, Ladder Back, Arched, Turned Arms, Oval Finials, Black Paint, Woven Seat, Child's, 25 In. 275.00
Rocker, Ladder Back, Figured Maple Posts, 4 Slats, Oak Split Seat, 41 In. 115.00
Rocker, Ladder Back, Grain Paint, Acorn Finials, Mushroom Arms, Woven Splint Seat, 41 In. 165.00
Rocker, Ladder Back, Maple, Mixed Woods, Painted, Arms, Splint Seat, 46 x 27 In. 60.00
Rocker, Ladder Back, Maple, Ebony Finish, Green & Black Tape Seat, Shawl Bar, Child's 1053.00
Rocker, Lifetime, Slat Sides & Back, Drop-In Spring Seat, 36½ x 30½ x 31 In.. 2520.00
Rocker, Lifetime, Wood, Slats, Signed, 32 x 28 x 32 In. *illus* 2420.00
Rocker, Limbert, Curved Front Rail, Recovered Leather Cushions, 33 x 36 x 32 In. 6600.00
Rocker, Limbert, Oak, 4 Vertical Slats, Shaped Arms, Leather Seat, Spring Cushion, 35⅝ In. 586.00
Rocker, Lincoln Style, Walnut, Grape & Leaf Crest, c.1890, 36 x 22 In. 75.00
Rocker, Lincoln Style, Walnut, Carved Shell Crest, Upholstered, 40 x 22 In. 300.00
Rocker, Mahogany, Dolphin Carved, 34 x 25 In. 990.00
Rocker, Mahogany, Leafy Crest Rail, Scroll Arms, Silk Upholstery, 38½ In. 4043.00
Rocker, Nutting, Continuous Arm, Brace Back, 37 x 21 In.. 600.00
Rocker, Queen Anne, Salmon Paint, 4 Graduated Arched Slats, Turned Stiles, Splint Seat, 46 In. 288.00
Rocker, R.J. Horner, Faux Bamboo, c.1890, 36 x 20 In. 413.00
Rocker, Rococo, Mahogany, Carved, Padded Arms, Upholstered, c.1850, 40 In.. 450.00
Rocker, Rococo Revival, Rosewood, Carved, Openwork Curved Backrest, Scrolled Vines 823.00
Rocker, Shaker, 3 Arched Slats, Paper Rush Seat, Stamped 4, Armless, 34½ In. 230.00
Rocker, Shaker, Maple, Acorn Finials, 3 Slats, Tape Seat, Mt. Lebanon, Decal, 32 In. 263.00
Rocker, Shaker, Maple, 3 Graduated Slats, Cane Seat, Harvard, Ma., c.1840, 37 In. 645.00
Rocker, Shaker, Maple, 4 Slats, Oak Shawl Bar, Rush Seat, Mt. Lebanon, c.1870, 44 In.. 1755.00
Rocker, Shaker, No. 1, Decal On Back Splat, Arms, Woven Tape Seat, Child's, 10½ In. 558.00
Rocker, Shaker, No. 6, Slat Back, Turned Finials, Tape Seat, Stenciled, Mt. Lebanon, Arms, 42 In. 2070.00
Rocker, Sleigh, Walnut, Renaissance, c.1880 2012.00
Rocker, Stickley, Sewing, Arched Top, Vertical Slats, Drop-In Cushion, 18 x 26 x 33 In. 150.00
Rocker, Twig, Red Paint, Silver Highlights, Child's, Mid 20th Century, 19 x 20 In. 92.00
Rocker, Windsor, 5-Spindle Comb, Birdcage Crest, Red Paint, Plank Seat, 19th Century, 41x 23 In. 130.00
Rocker, Windsor, Arrow Back, Step-Down Comb & Crest, Painted, 1800s, 38 In.. 100.00
Rocker, Windsor, Arrow Back, Plank Seat, Kentucky, 19th Century, 45 x 24 x 18 In.. 360.00
Rocker, Windsor, Comb Back, Spindles, Stenciled, Plank Seat, Child's, 17½ In. 138.00
Rocker, Windsor, Comb Back, Black, Gold Decorations, c.1810 287.00
Rocker, Windsor, Firehouse Type, Comb Back, Turned Spindles, Child's, 1850, 17 In. 155.00
Rocker, Windsor, Green Paint, G. Brown, Mass., c.1840, 28 x 16 x 17 In.. 230.00
Rocker, Windsor, Green Paint, New England, c.1820, 28 In. 470.00
Rocker, Windsor, Stenciled, Spindles, Plank Seat, Marked, Raymond, c.1860, 31 x 16 In. *illus* 345.00
Rocker, Shaker, No. 6, 4 Slats, Ladder Back, Rush Seat, Double Box Stretcher, Marked, 41 x 17 In. 260.00
Safe, Egyptian Revival, Figural Legs, Iron, Henry, Farrel & Sherman, c.1870 4312.00
Schrank, Pine, Poplar, Wood Grain Paint Over Yellow, Late 19th Century, 83 x 63 x 24 In. *illus* 2400.00
Screen, 2-Panel, Lacquer, Red, Dragon Border, Pagoda, Figural, 75 x 34 In.. 649.00
Screen, 3-Panel, A Belle Epoque, Gilt, Carved, Painted, Flowers, Seed Pods, 74 x 60 In. 4465.00
Screen, 3-Panel, Aesthetic Revival, Painted, Leather, 20th Century, 66½ x 20 In. 3120.00
Screen, 3-Panel, Arts & Crafts, Cutout Top, Tapestry Panels, Flowers, 19 x 68 In. 420.00
Screen, 3-Panel, Folding, Copper Tact Trim, Painted Romantic Scenes, 60 x 68 In. 288.00
Screen, 3-Panel, Folding, Canvas, Painted, Leather, Flowers, Scrolls, c.1900, 75 x 24 In. 1232.00
Screen, 3-Panel, Folding, Paper, Block Printed Grisaille Landscapes, 85 x 74 In., Pair 6900.00
Screen, 3-Panel, Genre Scenes, Rice Paper, 19th Century, 67 x 24½ In. 132.00
Screen, 3-Panel, Gilt, Beveled Grass Mirror, Romantic Prints, Silk Brocade, 65 In. 489.00
Screen, 3-Panel, Louis XV Style, Giltwood, Architectural Ruins, 59 x 20 x 1½ In.. 2832.00
Screen, 3-Panel, Mahogany, Glass, 60 x 63 In.. 717.00
Screen, 3-Panel, Rococo, Leather, Trompe L'Oeil, Embossed, Ships, c.1750, 73 x 68 In. 7344.00
Screen, 3-Panel, Sunburst, Dowels, 1950s, 86 x 26 In. *illus* 1350.00

creen, 3-Panel, Victorian, Painted, Flowers, Folding, c.1875, 69 x 21 In. 2350.00
creen, 4-Panel, Chinese, Landscapes, Children Playing, 19th Century, 21 x 15 In. 2585.00
creen, 4-Panel, Chinoiserie Scenes, 18th Century, 68 ½ x 96 In. 7050.00
creen, 4-Panel, Continental, Italian Harbor, 18th Century, 67 ½ x 42 In. 3819.00
creen, 4-Panel, Courtesans, Garden, Pavilions, Red Lacquer, Chinese, 72 x 72 In. 576.00
creen, 4-Panel, Ebonized, Decoupaged Leather, Floral Urn Panels, 1800s, 69 x 88 In. 1920.00
creen, 4-Panel, Farm House, Landscape, Paper On Linen, France, c.1895, 67 x 110 In. *illus* 2840.00
creen, 4-Panel, Figures In Palace, Landscape, Coromandel, Chinese, 19th Century, 72 x 76 In. 294.00
creen, 4-Panel, Folding, Village Sunset, 43 x 102 In. 994.00
creen, 4-Panel, Folding, Buildings, Water, Landscape, Gold, Black, 60 ⅝ x 80 In. 1008.00
creen, 4-Panel, Landscape, Birds, River, Hand Painted, c.1930 250.00
creen, 4-Panel, Latticework, Bird, Mountain Scene, 69 x 20 ⅝ In. 590.00
creen, 4-Panel, Leather, Chinoiserie, Pagodas, Figures, Cranes, Scenery, 73 x 76 In. 2880.00
creen, 4-Panel, Oriental, Black Lacquer Ground, Landscape, Gold, Silver, 1900s, 18 x 72 In. 115.00
creen, 4-Panel, Painted, Fruit, Mottled Ground, 1900s, 71 x 16 In. 266.00
creen, 4-Panel, Paper, Gouache, Oxidized Metallic Leaf, Court Figures, Japan, 48 x 97 In. 2640.00
creen, 4-Panel, Riverscape, Marble, Famille Verte, 14 x 4 ½ In. 236.00
creen, 4-Panel, Teakwood, Dragons, Figures, Flowers Scrolls, Carved, Pierced, 74 x 82 In. 646.00
creen, 4-Panel, Walnut, Floral Crest, Inset Fabric, C-Scroll Carved Feet, France, 67 x 89 In. 980.00
creen, 4-Panel, Walnut, Carved, Florentine, Feet, Scrolls, c.1900, 75 x 100 In. 2200.00
creen, 4-Panel, Wood, City View, c.1950, 81 ½ x 80 In. 13200.00
creen, 5-Panel, Oil On Panel, Harbor Scene, Bjorn Wiinblad, Signed, c.1980, 96 x 196 In. 7767.00
creen, 6-Panel, Birds, Shrubs, Flowers, Black Frame, Gilt, Chinese, 71 ¾ x 99 In. 2160.00
creen, 6-Panel, Famille Rose Panels, Animals, Birds, Hardwood Frame, 33 ¼ x 42 ½ In. 8400.00
creen, 6-Panel, Japanese, Folding, Landscape, Birds, c.1912, 67 x 148 In. 4080.00
creen, 8-Panel, Porcelain, Teakwood, 19th Century, 34 ¼ x 7 In. 6463.00
creen, Arts & Crafts, Owls, Vines, Flowers, Oak, Glass Eyes, 33 x 26 x 5 In. *illus* 1096.00
creen, Rosewood, Ivory Inlay, People In Palace, 72 x 60 In. 2115.00
creen, Table, Chinese, Jade, Carved, High Relief, Confronting Dragons, Flaming Pearl, 17 In. 1320.00
creen, Table, Famille Rose, People, Landscape, Wood Mounts, 37 x 22 x 15 In. 708.00
creen, Table, Folding, Chinese, 18 x 24 In. 18.00
creen, Table, Goddess Of Mercy On Elephant, White Jade, Frame, Stand, 19 ¾ x 12 ½ In. 1298.00
creen, Table, Regency, Gilt, Penwork, Octagonal, Leaves, 19th Century, 12 In. 230.00
creen, Table, Stylized Leaves, 8-Sided, England, Early 19th Century, 12 In. *illus* 230.00
creen, Walnut, Multicolored Glass Discs, 48 x 94 ½ In. 10200.00
creen, Window, Pine, Geometric, Chinese, 56 ½ x 46 ½ In. 2160.00
eat, Chinese, Marble Top, Drum Shape, 21 x 21 In., Pair 1944.00
ecretary, Biedermeier, Drop Front, Mahogany, Pediment, Cupboard, Drawers, 82 x 42 In. 1920.00
ecretary, Butternut, 2 Sections, 2 Doors, 5 Drawers, 33 x 18 x 72 In. 1650.00
ecretary, Chippendale, Cherry, Paneled Doors, Fitted Interior, c.1780, 88 x 40 In. 1840.00
ecretary, Chippendale, Cherry, Slant Front, c.1750-80, 88 x 40 x 20 In. 1920.00
ecretary, Chippendale, Mahogany, Block Front, 13-Pane Doors, Drawers, 87 x 39 In. 3680.00
ecretary, Chippendale, Walnut, Blind Door, Swan's Neck Pediment, c.1780, 94 x 41 In. 6875.00
ecretary, Chippendale, Walnut, Mahogany, 2 Doors, 4 Drawers, 86 x 38 x 22 In. 8700.00
ecretary, Drop Front, Curly Maple Veneers, 14 Drawers, Mirrored Doors, 56 x 46 x 20 In. 4025.00
ecretary, Drop Front, Walnut, 2 Doors, 6 Drawers, Pigeonholes, 73 x 17 x 42 In. 384.00
ecretary, Drop Front, Walnut, Desk, 3 Long Drawers, Shaped Block Feet, 54 x 45 x 15 In. 940.00
ecretary, Drop Front, Walnut, 2 Doors, 3 Drawers, 78 ½ x 38 x 16 ½ In. 990.00
ecretary, Drop Front, Walnut, Poplar, Ash, American, 96 x 63 x 15 ½ In. *illus* 1360.00
ecretary, Empire, Mahogany, 75 x 46 In. 770.00
ecretary, Flemish Style, Slant Front, Mahogany, Marquetry, Scalloped Doors, 8 x 48 In. 4700.00
ecretary, French Empire, Fruitwood, Marble Top, Gilt Mounted, 50 x 25 x 15 In. 6136.00
ecretary, George III, Mahogany, Cornice, Astragal Glazed Doors, 89 x 47 In. 2640.00
ecretary, George III, Mahogany, c.1780, 96 x 42 x 21 ½ In. 2938.00
ecretary, George III, Mahogany, 2 Gothic Doors, Writing Drawer, 85 x 38 x 21 In. 6463.00
ecretary, George III, Mahogany, Glazed Doors, Slant Front, 95 x 45 In. 13800.00
ecretary, George III, Slant Drop Front, Oak, Paneled Doors, 4 Drawers, 87 x 40 x 21 In. 1645.00
ecretary, Georgian, Satinwood Inlay, Mahogany, 2 Doors, Shelves, Sliding Drawer, 43 x 22 In. 940.00
ecretary, Georgian, Slant Front, Mahogany, Glazed Doors, Shelves, 86 x 38 x 20 ½ In. 8260.00
ecretary, Hepplewhite, Mahogany, Tambour, Pullout, A.W. Clark, N.Y., 38 x 49 In. 5750.00
ecretary, Louis XV Style, Drop Front, Kingwood, Rosewood Marquetry, Leather, 57 x 29 x 16 In. 510.00
ecretary, Louis XV Style, Drop Front, Bombe, Burl Veneer, Interior Drawers, 54 x 23 In. 748.00
ecretary, Louis XVI, Drop Front, Floral Inlay, Marble Top, Drawer, Early 1900s, 56 x 26 In. 1093.00
ecretary, Mahogany, Glazed Doors, Writing Surface, Pigeonholes, 88 x 46 x 22 In. 2233.00
ecretary, Mahogany, Inlay, Sliding Shelves, c.1800, 90 x 46 x 23 In. *illus* 2400.00
ecretary, Mahogany, Late 19th Century, 68 x 64 ½ x 17 In. 2100.00

Furniture, Secretary, Drop Front, Walnut, Poplar, Ash, American, 96 x 63 x 15 ½ In.
$1360.00

Furniture, Secretary, Mahogany, Inlay, Sliding Shelves, c.1800, 90 x 46 x 23 In.
$2400.00

Furniture, Secretary, Oak, Glass Door, c.1900, 74 x 38 In.
$750.00

F

TIP
New research suggests that you should never use silicone-based furniture polish or feed the wood with oils. Just dust with a soft cloth.

F

Furniture, Secretary, Queen Anne Style, Drop Front, Japanned, c.1950, 84 x 34 x 21 In. $1600.00

Furniture, Semainier, Oak, 7 Banded Drawers, Bracket Feet, 51 x 20 x 19 In. $750.00

Secretary, Mahogany, Scroll Top, Brass Finial, Rosettes, c.1830, 65 x 40 In. ... 1540.00
Secretary, Mahogany, Shelves, Pigeonholes, Drawers, 76 x 39 x 21 In. ... 3850.00
Secretary, Mitchell & Rammelsberg, Rosewood, Mechanical, Dome Top, c.1850, 108 In. ... 6930.00
Secretary, Neoclassical, Mahogany, Gilt Metal Finials, Astragal Doors, 71 x 40 In. ... 1180.00
Secretary, Oak, Glass Door, c.1900, 74 x 38 In. ... *illus* 750.00
Secretary, Oak, Slant Front, Glass Panel Doors, Painted, England, 77 x 36 In. ... 330.00
Secretary, Queen Anne Style, Drop Front, Japanned, c.1950, 84 x 34 x 21 In. ... *illus* 1600.00
Secretary, Regency, Mahogany, 4 Drawers, 19th Century, 88 x 47 In. ... 8400.00
Secretary, Restauration, Drop Front, Burl Walnut, Marble Top, 60 x 38 x 15 ½ In. ... 3120.00
Secretary, Rococo, Rosewood, Mid 19th Century, 80 ½ x 35 x 19 In. ... 14100.00
Secretary, Sheraton Style, Mahogany, Inlay, Glass Paned Doors, Fitted Interior, 34 ¾ x 17 In. 1725.00
Secretary, Slant Front, Walnut, Paneled Doors, Drawers, 84 x 39 x 22 ¼ In. ... 3600.00
Secretary, Victorian, Drop Front, Walnut, Burl, Drawer Panels, 84 x 39 x 21 In. ... 472.00
Secretary, William IV, Drop Front, Mullioned Doors, c.1840 ... 4125.00
Secretary, William IV, Mahogany, Acanthus Brackets, c.1830, 92 x 52 In. ... 4406.00
Secretary Chest, Napoleon III, Kingwood, Ormolu Mounted, Marble Top, 37 x 37 In. ... 2400.00
Semainier, Empire Style, Mahogany, 7 Cock-Beaded Drawers, 57 x 28 x 17 In. ... 705.00
Semainier, Louis Philippe, Fruitwood, Marble Top, Fitted Case, 7 Drawers, 55 x 36 In. ... 4800.00
Semainier, Louis XVI Style, Brass Mounted, Marble Top, 7 Drawers, 57 x 29 ½ In. ... 1058.00
Semainier, Louis XVI, Kingwood, Marble Top, Gilt Metal, 7 Drawers, 54 x 23 x 14 ¾ In. ... 885.00
Semainier, Oak, 7 Banded Drawers, Bracket Feet, 51 x 20 x 19 In. ... *illus* 750.00
Server, Arts & Crafts, 2 Drawers, Arched Apron, Iron Hardware, 42 x 18 x 41 In. ... 660.00
Server, Arts & Crafts, Mahogany, 2 Drawers, Inlaid Gallery, 36 x 17 x 35 ½ In. ... 240.00
Server, Arts & Crafts, Mahogany, 2 Drawers, Inlaid Gallery, 39 x 17 x 38 In. ... 240.00
Server, Chinese, Pine, 10 Drawers, 2 Doors, Brass Fittings, 36 ½ x 70 x 20 In. ... 960.00
Server, Edwardian, Mahogany, Poplar, Hand Dovetailed Drawers, 33 ½ x 47 ¼ In. ... 1380.00
Server, Edwardian, Mahogany, Adam Style, Demilune Top, Tambour Cupboards, 39 x 48 In. ... 3840.00
Server, G. Stickley, 2 Drawers, Copper Hardware, Open Shelves, 48 x 22 x 49 In. ... 1520.00
Server, G. Stickley, 3 Drawers, 2 Doors, 46 x 49 x 18 In. ... *illus* 1050.00
Server, G. Stickley, 3 Drawers, 2 Doors, Open Storage, Plate Rack, 49 x 18 x 46 In. ... 1140.00
Server, G. Stickley, 3 Drawers, Plate Rail, 43 ½ x 48 x 20 ¼ In. ... 1440.00
Server, G. Stickley, Gallery To Back, Arched Rail, Lower Stretcher, 54 x 21 x 43 In. ... 5100.00
Server, G. Stickley, Leather Lining, 2 Drawers, 43 x 53 ¼ x 21 In. ... 4500.00
Server, G. Stickley, Slatted Plate Rail, 2 Drawers, Copper Strap, 54 x 21 x 47 In. ... 6600.00
Server, Inlaid Mahogany, Serpentine Front, 2 Drawers, 2 Doors, 35 x 36 In. ... 1293.00
Server, Louis XVI Style, 2 Tiers, Oval Variegated Cream Marble Top, Parquetry, 36 x 32 In. ... 316.00
Server, Mahogany, 3 Tiers, Urn Finials, Baluster & Ring Turned Supports, Mid 1800s, 57 x 46 In. ... 633.00
Server, Mahogany, Pedestal, 3 Drawers, Bowed, Ogee Molding, 19th Century ... 1800.00
Server, North Shore, Mahogany, Semicircular Plateau, c.1815, 47 ½ x 23 In. ... 550.00
Server, Pine, Backsplash, Drawers, Brass, Dovetailed, Square Legs, 44 x 29 x 21 In. ... 150.00
Server, Pine, Corner Backsplash, 2 Drawers, Brass Pulls, 44 ½ x 29 ½ x 21 ½ In. ... 168.00
Server, Quartersawn Oak, Acanthus Carved Backsplash, Drawers, Columns, 45 x 47 In. ... 605.00
Server, Regency, Mahogany, Gallery Top, Mid 19th Century, 47 x 54 x 20 In. ... 1058.00
Server, Sheraton, Maple, 5 Drawers, 2 Doors, Brass Pulls, Turned Legs, 42 x 42 x 19 In. ... 5750.00
Server, Side, Painted Wood, 5 Drawers, Iron Ring Handles, 35 ½ x 103 In. ... 900.00
Server, Walnut, Pine, Scalloped Gallery, Carved Brackets, Fluted Legs, 33 x 41 In. ... 288.00
Server, William & Mary, Cherry, Lower Shelf, 2 Drawers, 29 x 47 ½ x 16 In. ... 115.00
Server, William & Mary, Oak, Carved Leaf, Drawer, Shelf, Barley Twist Legs, 34 x 54 x 18 In. ... 235.00
Serving Cart, Walnut Flip Top, 2 Drawers, White Laminate Shelf, Casters, 40 x 17 x 29 ¾ In. ... 1200.00
Settee, Baroque, Fruitwood, Padded, Brass Tacks, Cushions, Italy, 39 ¼ x 80 x 30 ½ In. ... 16560.00
Settee, Cast Iron, Twigs, Branches, Leaves, 32 x 29 x 23 In. ... 1060.00
Settee, Edwardian, Mahogany, Cane Double Backs, Putti, Cane Seats, 38 ½ x 45 x 26 In. ... 2643.00
Settee, Federal, Mahogany, Shaped Back, High Shaped Arms, Early 1800s, 37 x 55 In. ... 7200.00
Settee, G. Nakashima, Walnut, Slat Back, 30 ½ x 72 x 31 In. ... 5100.00
Settee, G. Stickley, Cane Seat, 84 x 35 x 37 In. ... 24000.00
Settee, George II, Walnut, Double Chair Back, Shepherd Crook Arms, Britain, 38 x 54 x 21 In. 5300.00
Settee, George III, Mahogany, Padded, Molded Frame, 19th Century, 38 x 77 x 27 ½ In. ... 1920.00
Settee, George III Style, Serpentine Crest, Gilt, Velvet Upholstery, 75 In. ... 3750.00
Settee, Hepplewhite, Mahogany, Scroll Sloped Arms, Damask Upholstery, c.1785, 78 In. ... 3525.00
Settee, Irish Chippendale, Triple Back, Shell Carved Crest, Pierced Slats, 1700s, 39 x 67 In. ... 4600.00
Settee, Louis XV Style, Beech, Scalloped Back, Closed Arms, 35 x 60 In. ... 1680.00
Settee, Louis XV Style, Beech, Domed Padded Back, Downswept Arms, 35 x 83 In. ... 3360.00
Settee, Louis XVI, Fruitwood, Padded Back, Wreath Crest, Scrolling Arms, Damask, 41 x 64 In. 2040.00
Settee, Louis XVI Style, Beech, Padded Back, Molded Frame, Top Shaped Feet, 35 x 68 In. ... 1020.00
Settee, Louis XVI Style, Carved Frame, Ivory Paint, Gray Upholstery, 75 x 27 In. ... 374.00
Settee, Louis XVI Style, Gilt, Ribbon Crest, 40 x 54 x 24 In. ... *illus* 500.00

Settee, Mahogany, Carved Crest, Inlaid Putti & Leaves, Pierced, Downswept Arms, 33 x 37 In. 3600.00
Settee, Mahogany Veneer, Cherry, Scrolled Arms, 19th Century, 37 x 43 x 23 In. . . . . *illus* 245.00
Settee, Meridienne, Empire Style, Mahogany, Gilt Bronze Mounted, Sloped Back, 35 x 60 In. . 3290.00
Settee, Meridienne, Louis Philippe, Mahogany, Sloping Arm, Rocaille Feet, c.1840, 36 x 50 In., Pair 3185.00
Settee, Neoclassical, Mahogany, Baluster & Ring Turned, Scroll Arms, 37 x 44 In. 230.00
Settee, Neoclassical, Mahogany, Cornucopia Faces, Hairy Paw Feet, c.1850, 35 x 72 x 27 In. *illus* 850.00
Settee, Neoclassical, Mahogany, Eagle Carved Back, Rolled Arms, Paw Feet, 35 x 58 x 27 In. . 1495.00
Settee, Neoclassical, Mahogany, Flat Crest, Scroll Arms, Continental, 37 x 59 In. 1680.00
Settee, Neoclassical, Mahogany, Carved, Padded Back, Reeded Frame, Continental, 37 x 63 In. 3600.00
Settee, Neoclassical, Mahogany, Carved, Philadelphia, c.1830, 37 x 68 In. 9600.00
Settee, Neoclassical, Slat Back, Beaded Accents, Padded Arms, Bulbous Legs, 36 x 70 x 28 In.. 2880.00
Settee, Neoclassical Revival, Mahogany, Rolling Crest, Scrolls, Leaves, Arms, 36 x 85 In.. . . . . 1652.00
Settee, Nutting, Windsor, Comb Back, 10 Legs, Knuckle Arms, Carved Ears. 715.00
Settee, Provincial, Louis XV Style, Fruitwood, Domed Padded Back, Seat, 43 x 53 In.. . . . . 2400.00
Settee, Regency, Mahogany, Shaped & Padded Back, Outscrolled Arms, Early 1800, 37 x 84 In. 2160.00
Settee, Regency Style, Mahogany, Triple Back, Reeded Crest, Padded, 36½ x 54 x 24 In. 1440.00
Settee, Renaissance Revival, Walnut, Upholstered, Pillows, 66 x 41 In. 1400.00
Settee, Rococo, Mahogany, Carved, Crest, Serpentine Seat & Back, c.1850, 36 x 65 In., Pair . . 1320.00
Settee, Rococo Revival, Rosewood, Laminated, Serpentine Seat, Closed Arms, 42 x 52 x 32 In. 3840.00
Settee, Rococo Revival, Rosewood, Belter Style, Red Brocade Upholstery, 44 x 44 In., Pair . . . 7800.00
Settee, Rosewood, Carved, Serpentine & Rocaille Crest, Acanthus Scrolls, 46 x 71 In. 429.00
Settee, Spanish Colonial, Walnut, Late 18th Century, 46 x 50 x 17½ In. 1998.00
Settee, Thonet, Bentwood, Open Scroll Back, Arms, Cane Kidney Shape Seat, c.1890, 37 x 56 In. 1850.00
Settee, Victorian, Cane Walnut, Parish Hadley Upholstery, c.1880, 28 x 45 In. 3900.00
Settee, Victorian, Mahogany, Serpentine Crest Rail, Bracket Feet, 39 x 40 x 18 In. 529.00
Settee, Victorian, Mahogany, Scooped Back, Paw Feet, Upholstered, 30 x 83 x 45½ In. 2242.00
Settee, Victorian, Rosewood, Oval Back, Carved Crest, Hip Rest, Cabriole Legs, c.1870, 38 x 49 In. . 385.00
Settee, Victorian, Rosewood, Triple Back, Tufted Back, Carved Crests, c.1870, 39 x 66 In. 770.00
Settee, Walnut, Cameo Back, Carved Crest, Ivory Upholstery, c.1890, 38 x 70 In. 400.00
Settee, Walnut, Marquetry Bone Inlay, Arched Backrest, Trelliswork, 78½ x 19 In.. . . . . 2938.00
Settee, Walnut, Plain Serpentine Top Rail, Carved Scrolling Rail, 40 x 82 In.. . . . . 590.00
Settee, Windsor, Bamboo, Shaped Seat, Turned Arms, 35¾ x 76 x 19¼ In. 550.00
Settee, Windsor, Bamboo Spindles, Serpentine Seat, Tidewater, c.1800, 81 x 23 x 30 In. . *illus* 7187.00
Settee, Windsor, Square Back, Double Bow Crest, Rush Seat, Early 1800s, 35 x 68 In. 1534.00
Settle, 3 Recessed Panels, Red Brown Finish, Curved Sloping Arms, 37 x 70 x 23 In.. . . . . 2875.00
Settle, 10-Panel Back, Shelf, Wing Sides, 3 Doors, Paint, Scroll Arms, England, 54 x 71 x 20 In. 4313.00
Settle, Arts & Crafts, Oak, Crest Rail, Vertical, Side Slats, Shaped Arms, 39 x 50 x 25 In. 470.00
Settle, Arts & Crafts, Pyradmidal Accents To Top, Recovered Seat, 76 x 31 x 34 In.. . . . . 2640.00
Settle, Belter, Meridienne, Rosewood, Carved, 42 x 74 In. 4400.00
Settle, G. Stickley, Low Form, Cushions, 78 x 33 x 28 In.. . . . . 6600.00
Settle, G. Stickley, No. 216, Oak, Leather Cushion, Red Decal, c.1904, 29¾ x 80 In. 2375.00
Settle, G. Stickley, Wide Board Back, Foam Cushion, Even Arm, 28 x 60 x 31 In. 3900.00
Settle, Meridienne, Neoclassical, Mahogany, Carved, c.1845, 37 x 78 x 26 In.. . . . . 5581.00
Settle, Pine, Barrel Back, Shaped Sides, Plank Seat, 66 x 61 In.. . . . . 336.00
Settle, Pine, Paneled Back, Plank Seat, Wing Shape Ends, Scroll Arms, 73 x 52 In. 805.00
Settle, Pine, Raised Panel Back, Lift Seat, Rolled Arms, 1800s, 52 x 72 In. 308.00
Settle, Queen Anne Style, Oak, Arched Raised Panels, Scroll Arms, Plank Seat, 40 x 74 In. . . . 1763.00
Settle, Spring Back, Lift Plank Seat, Pegged Mortise, Tenon, 37 x 62 x 23 In. 2200.00
Settle, Windsor Style, Ebonized, Stencil Decorated, Flowers, Horizontal Splat, 32 x 84 In.. . . . . 590.00
Shadowbox, Schooner, 3 Masts, Sails, Figures, c.1900 . . . . 450.00
Shadowbox, Victorian, Walnut, Gilt Oval Windows, 23 x 21 In., Pair 470.00
Shadowbox, Walnut, Oval, Molded Edges, White, Gilt Liners, 22 x 19 In., Pair. 302.00
Shelf, Cherry, Brown Stain, New England, Early 19th Century, 50½ x 55½ In.. . . . . 2468.00
Shelf, Clock, Dentil Work Border, Blue Paint, Quebec, 10 x 30½ In.. . . . . 1430.00
Shelf, Clock, Louis XVI, Gilt, Carved, Cartel, Acanthus, Flowerhead Terminal, 12 x 21 In. 2400.00
Shelf, Clock, Wood, Drawer, Painted, Hanging, Early 19th Century, 35 x 19 x 7 In. . . . . . *illus* 895.00
Shelf, Corner, Hanging, Pine, Lobed Back, 2 Open Shelves, Hinged Compartment, 20 x 16 In. 201.00
Shelf, Hanging, 2 Shelves, Carved, Owl & Bird Supports, Late 1800s, 32½ x 36 In.. . . . . 1150.00
Shelf, Hanging, 4 Serpentine Shelves, Finialed Stiles, Panels, c.1830, 41½ x 8 In. 4112.00
Shelf, Hanging, Corner, Painted, Scalloped Edge, Early 1800s, 13½ x 15½ In.. . . . . 2880.00
Shelf, Hanging, Cutout Shelf, Olive Brown, Scrolled Brackets, 26 x 11½ In. 58.00
Shelf, Hanging, Pierced Carvings, Pinwheels, Scalloped Edge, Brackets, 24 x 8 In.. . . . . 173.00
Shelf, Hanging, Pine, Green Paint, Scalloped Back Board, 10 x 5½ In. 81.00
Shelf, Hanging, Pine, Green Paint, Scroll Cut Ends, 16 x 21½ In. 489.00
Shelf, Hanging, Pine, Red Finish, 3 Shelves, 52 x 60 In. 862.00
Shelf, Hanging, Pine, Old Brown Paint, 2 Drawers, New England, Early 1800s, 32 x 26 In. . . . 1528.00

Furniture, Server, G. Stickley, 3 Drawers, 2 Doors, 46 x 49 x 18 In.
$1050.00

Furniture, Settee, Louis XVI Style, Gilt, Ribbon Crest, 40 x 54 x 24 In.
$500.00

Furniture, Settee, Mahogany Veneer, Cherry, Scrolled Arms, 19th Century, 37 x 43 x 23 In.
$245.00

Furniture, Settee, Neoclassical, Mahogany, Cornucopia Faces, Hairy Paw Feet, c.1850, 35 x 72 x 27 In.
$850.00

Furniture, Settee, Windsor, Bamboo Spindles, Serpentine Seat, Tidewater, c.1800, 81 x 23 x 30 In.
$7187.00

Furniture, Shelf, Clock, Wood, Drawer, Painted, Hanging, Early 19th Century, 35 x 19 x 7 In.
$895.00

Furniture, Shelf, Hanging, Walnut, Drawers, Lewis Spohn & Son, Ohio, 4 x 34 x 8 In.
$660.00

Furniture, Sideboard, Eastlake, Walnut, Marble, Columns, Late 19th Century, 87 x 45 x 22 In.
$1420.00

Shelf, Hanging, Provincial, Fruitwood, Scalloped Back, Chamfered Open Sides, 36 x 32 In. . . . 123.00
Shelf, Hanging, Walnut, Drawers, Lewis Spohn & Son, Ohio, 4 x 34 x 8 In. . . . . *illus* 660.00
Shelf, Hanging, Walnut, 4 Drawers, c.1950, 81¾ x 14 x 5¾ In. 1320.00
Shelf, Louis XVI, Mahogany, Gilt Metal, Pierced Brass Gallery, 24 x 10 In., Pair 3600.00
Shelf, Neoclassical, Mahogany, Whale End, Concentric Roundels, c.1825, 35 x 28 In. 1410.00
Shelf, Pine, 5 Shelves, Square Nails, Shaped Ends, Center Brace, Metal Brackets, 41 x 58 In. . 1035.00
Shelf, Pine, Blue Paint, Rectangular Molded, Paneled Bracket, 19th Century, 6 x 26 In. 353.00
Shelf, Pine, Green Paint, 4 Shelves, Scroll-Cut Sides, 64 x 39 x 9 In. 460.00
Shelf, Pine, Red Paint, 3 Mortised Shelves, Shaped Ends, 61 x 30 In.. 1035.00
Shelf, Red Brown Paint, Black, Yellow Design, 3 Drawers, Dovetailed, Scroll Top, Base, 24 x 13 x 6 In. 495.00
Shelf, Renaissance, Walnut, Lion's Head, Bracket, c.1875, 18½ x 17¼ In.. . . . . 558.00
Shelf, Rococo Style, Parcel Gilt, Carved, Bracket, Northern Italy, Early 1900s, 5 x 6 In., Pair. . 660.00
Shelf, Walnut, Compartments, Mid 19th Century, 50 x 31½ In. 1410.00
Shelf, Shaker, Pine, Birch, Painted, 2 Shaped Vertical Hangers, 22½ In. 3510.00
Sideboard, Alexander Roux, Victorian, Walnut, Marble Top, Carved, Mirror, Shelf, c.1860 . . . 20350.00
Sideboard, Arts & Crafts, Oak, Mirror, Shelf, Drawers, 52 x 60 x 23 In. 1880.00
Sideboard, Arts & Crafts, Paneled Doors, Brass Hardware, 72 x 26 x 51½ In. 1800.00
Sideboard, Black Lacquered, 4 Drawers, Shelves, 31 x 72 x 18 In.. . . . . 7800.00
Sideboard, Butler's, Hepplewhite, Mahogany, Desk Interior, Salem, Mass., 58 x 42 In.. . . . . . . 2300.00
Sideboard, Charleston, Mahogany, Figured Veneer, Inlay, Early 1800s, 52 x 69 In. 7480.00
Sideboard, Chinese, Elm, Green, 2 Doors, 2 Sliding Doors, 34 x 76 In. 1180.00
Sideboard, Chippendale, Mahogany, Backsplash, Footed, c.1830, 45 x 91 In.. . . . . 1210.00
Sideboard, Corner, Hepplewhite, Mahogany, Demilune, Fluted Legs, c.1790, 33 x 66 In.. . . . . 2090.00
Sideboard, Eastlake, Walnut, Marble, Columns, Late 19th Century, 87 x 45 x 22 In. . . . *illus* 1420.00
Sideboard, Edwardian, Fruitwood, Inlaid Mahogany, 3 Drawers, 2 Doors, 37 x 66 x 24 In.. . . 1528.00
Sideboard, Edwardian, Mahogany, George III Style, Cutlery Drawer, c.1900, 36 x 53 In.. . . . . 1680.00
Sideboard, Edwardian, Mahogany, George III Style, Bowed, String Banding, c.1900, 35 x 71 In. 2040.00
Sideboard, Edwardian, Mahogany, Inlaid Serpentine, 19th Century, 42 x 96 x 34 In. 6169.00
Sideboard, Edwardian, Walnut, Burl, Rosettes, Mirror, Paneled Base, 10 x 85 x 28 In. . . *illus* 1400.00
Sideboard, Empire, Flame Mahogany, Display Cabinet Top, c.1830, 96 x 52 In.. . . . . 2750.00
Sideboard, Empire, Mahogany Veneer, Pine, Carved Backsplash, 19th Century, 58 x 56 x 22 In. 690.00
Sideboard, Federal, 3 Drawers, 2 Doors, Turned Feet, 50 x 82 x 21 In. . . . . *illus* 3575.00
Sideboard, Federal, Hepplewhite, Mahogany, Inlay, c.1795, 40 x 73 x 20½ In. . . . . *illus* 4887.00
Sideboard, Federal, Mahogany, Gilt Metal, Drawers, Cellarettes, 58 x 59½ x 22 In. 1610.00
Sideboard, Federal, Mahogany, Serpentine Front, Salesman's Sample, c.1920, 14 x 8 In. 3450.00
Sideboard, Federal, Mahogany, Inlay, 29¾ x 65¾ x 24½ In. 4750.00
Sideboard, Federal, Mahogany, Brass Gallery, 19th Century, 52 x 72½ x 26 In. 5581.00
Sideboard, Federal, Reeded, 3 Drawers, 3 Doors, Dovetailed, Turned Feet, 50 x 82 x 21 In. . . . 3575.00
Sideboard, Federal Style, Mahogany, 2 Doors, 3 Drawers, 41 x 71 x 27½ In. 1380.00
Sideboard, Federal Style, Mahogany, Bellflower Inlay, 20th Century, 38 x 58 x 24 In. . . . *illus* 2900.00
Sideboard, Federal Style, Mahogany, 3 Drawers,4 Doors, Quarter Fans, c.1890, 40 x 73 x 26 In. 5000.00
Sideboard, G. Stickley, 2 Doors, Hammered Copper Hinges, 2 Half Drawers, 66 x 23 x 38 In. . 1800.00
Sideboard, G. Stickley, 3 Drawers Over Full Drawer, No. 819, 48 x 20 x 39½ In.. . . . . 6000.00
Sideboard, G. Stickley, Oak, Long Center Drawer, 2 Cabinet Doors, 46 x 50 x 22 In.. . . . . 1380.00
Sideboard, G. Stickley, Plate Rack, 2 Doors, 3 Drawers, Copper Hardware, 1912, 66 In.. . . . . . 5280.00
Sideboard, G. Stickley, Series Of Drawers & Cabinets, 66 x 22 x 48 In. 3600.00
Sideboard, George III, Hepplewhite, Bowfront, Oval Flower Inlays, Drawers, c.1790, 37 x 78 x 32 In. . 4313.00
Sideboard, George III, Inlaid Mahogany, Brass Mounted, 39 x 63 In. 10000.00
Sideboard, George III, Mahogany, Bowfront, Banded Bowed Top, Cutlery Drawer, 36 x 71 In. 1920.00
Sideboard, George III, Mahogany, Serpentine Front, Frieze Drawer, c.1790, 37 x 72 In. 3750.00
Sideboard, George III, Mahogany, Inlay, Bowfront, 3 Drawers, Tambour Door, 35 x 48 x 21 In. 3819.00
Sideboard, George III, Mahogany, Inlay, Frieze Drawer, 4 Drawers, 37½ x 77 In.. . . . . 10000.00
Sideboard, George III, Mahogany, Inlay, 2 Drawers, Metal Lined, c.1780, 37 x 72 In. 12500.00
Sideboard, George III, Regency, Mahogany, Serpentine Top, Drawer, 36 x 70 x 21 In.. . . . . 3658.00
Sideboard, George III Style, Mahogany, Bowed Top, Inlaid Banding, Early 1900s, 36 x 43 In. 540.00
Sideboard, George III Style, Mahogany, Bowed Top, Drawers, Square Legs, 36 x 66 x 26 In.. . . 4896.00
Sideboard, George IV, Inlaid Mahogany, Bowfront, c.1820, 36 x 48 x 22¾ In. 9600.00
Sideboard, George IV, Mahogany, Demilune Top, Arched Drawer, Bottle Door, 36 x 72 x 28 In. 3819.00
Sideboard, Georgian, Mahogany, Serpentine, Drawer, 2 Doors, Tapered Legs, 36 x 53 x 22 In. 940.00
Sideboard, Hepplewhite, Inlaid Mahogany, c.1800, 41 x 72 In. 2750.00
Sideboard, Hepplewhite, Mahogany, Stretcher Tray Base, 19th Century, 39 x 15 x 34 In. 2035.00
Sideboard, Herter Bros., Gothic Revival, Walnut, c.1875, 54 x 62 In.. 5760.00
Sideboard, Kittinger, Rosewood, Mahogany, Reeded, Ribbed Feet, c.1950, 35 x 56 x 19 In. *illus* 295.00
Sideboard, Kittinger, Tudor Style, Ebonized, Stained Wood, Panel Drawers, 35 x 83 In.. . . . . . 767.00
Sideboard, L. & J.G. Stickley, Drawers, Cabinet Doors, Strap Hardware, 56 x 23 x 46 In. 9000.00
Sideboard, Mahogany, 2 Doors, Drawer, 41 x 63 x 22 In. 8625.00

Sideboard, Mahogany, 3 Drawers, Lattice Doors, Leather Slide, 36 x 68 x 19 In. 460.00
Sideboard, Mahogany, 3 Drawers, 4 Doors, Serving Slides, 74 x 24 x 37 ½ In. 805.00
Sideboard, Mahogany, 3 Panel Drawers, Ivory Key Escutcheons, 11 x 12 ½ x 6 In.......... 2035.00
Sideboard, Mahogany, 5 Frieze Drawers Over Covered Drawers, 2 Doors, 44 x 75 x 26 In..... 1380.00
Sideboard, Mahogany, Bowfront, Brass Back Rail, Satinwood Crossbanded Top, 35 x 60 In.. . 826.00
Sideboard, Mahogany, Bowfront, Carved, 19th Century, 39 ¾ x 98 x 32 In.................. 2100.00
Sideboard, Mahogany, Bowfront, 2 Doors, Drawers, c.1795 .... 15210.00
Sideboard, Mahogany, Demilune, Single Frieze Drawer, 38 ½ x 75 ½ x 29 In................ 1770.00
Sideboard, Mahogany, Ebony Inlay, Scotland, c.1840, 44 x 85 x 24 In..................... 3525.00
Sideboard, Mahogany, Pedimented Backsplash, Paneled Doors, Paw Feet, 49 x 60 x 24 In. .. 4700.00
Sideboard, Mahogany, Scalloped Backsplash, c.1830, 59 x 51 x 22 ½ In. 1763.00
Sideboard, Mirrored Back, Branded, Limbert, 52 ½ x 54 x 21 ½ In....................... 2880.00
Sideboard, Neoclassical, Mahogany, Backsplash, 45 x 75 x 23 In. .... *illus* 480.00
Sideboard, Neoclassical, Mahogany, Molded Backsplash, 3 Drawers, Paneled Doors, 56 x 72 In. 2115.00
Sideboard, Neoclassical, Mahogany, 3 Drawers, Paneled Doors, Columns, 43 ½ x 70 x 24 In.. 2160.00
Sideboard, Neoclassical, Mahogany, Carved, Raised Plinths, Beaded Pediment, 56 x 72 In. .. 7963.00
Sideboard, Neoclassical Revival, Mahogany, Cornucopias, Pineapples, 40 x 72 x 24 In. 1500.00
Sideboard, Oak, Marble Top, 6 Drawers, Burl Panels, Late 19th Century, 36 x 70 x 23 In..... 660.00
Sideboard, Oak, Sliding Doors, End Cabinets, Tile Insets, 43 x 90 ¼ x 19 ½ In............. 8400.00
Sideboard, Pollard Oak, Oak, Paneled, Drawer, Edwards & Roberts, 1800s, 37 x 90 In....... 4406.00
Sideboard, Queen Anne Style, Walnut, Drawers, Panels, Cabriole Legs, c.1900, 44 x 60 x 23 In. 225.00
Sideboard, Regency, Mahogany, Arched Skirt, c.1820, 37 x 74 x 28 ½ In. 2938.00
Sideboard, Regency, Mahogany, Scrolled Splash Panel, Drawer, Paneled Doors, 43 x 91 In... 3105.00
Sideboard, Regency Style, Figured Mahogany Veneer, Bellflower Swag, 1800s, 38 x 85 In. ... 230.00
Sideboard, Regency Style, Mahogany, Canted Side, 3-Drawer Center Section, 83 x 46 In..... 1035.00
Sideboard, Renaissance Revival, Walnut, Marble Top, Drawers, 2 Doors, Shelf, 83 x 54 x 21 In. 1920.00
Sideboard, Renaissance Revival, Walnut, Marble, Glass, Brass, 3 Doors, 120 x 80 x 26 In. ... 5975.00
Sideboard, Rosewood, Inlay, Arches, 3 Drawers, England, c.1880, 41 x 66 x 17 In...... *illus* 795.00
Sideboard, Sheraton, Mahogany, Bowfront, Drawers, 2 Doors 2000.00
Sideboard, Sheraton, Mahogany, Drawers, 2 Doors, 48 x 77 x 23 In..................... 2240.00
Sideboard, Sheraton, Turkey Breast Center Doors, 3 Drawers, 6-Footed, 44 x 74 In. 10500.00
Sideboard, Slatted Gallery, Cabinet Doors, Copper Overlay, 70 x 22 ½ x 65 In. 4800.00
Sideboard, Veneer, Yellow Pine, Drawers, 2 Doors, Wilmington, N.C., 55 x 71 x 22 In. .. *illus* 2410.00
Sideboard, Victorian, Rococo, Mahogany, Carved, Mirrored Back, Griffins, c.1880, 82 x 73 In. 2475.00
Sideboard, Victorian, Walnut, Figured Walnut Veneer, Interior Compartment, 13 ½ x 8 ½ In.. 575.00
Sideboard, Walnut, 3 Doors, Shelves, Drawers, M. Singer, 37 ½ x 71 x 17 ½ In............ 16800.00
Sideboard, Walnut, Inlay, Yellow Pine, Drawers, Paneled Doors, 1800s, 41 x 55 In.......... 1955.00
Sideboard, Wegner, Rosewood, Drawers, Shelves, 2 Piece, 1950s, 68 x 79 x 19 In. 6600.00
Sideboard, Welsh Type, Fruitwood, 3 Dovetailed Drawers, Pierced Iron Pulls, 1930s........ 1300.00
Sideboard, William IV, Mahogany, Early 19th Century, 50 x 75 x 26 In.................. 1175.00
Silver Chest, Oak, 5-Finger Jointed, Graduated Drawers, Brass Handles, Early 1900, 15 x 23 In. 403.00
Smoking Stand, Pelican, Stylized, Iron, Painted, 25 ⅝ x 10 In. .... *illus* 978.00
Sofa, Art Nouveau, Mahogany, Figural, Carved, Serpentine Front, Caryatids, c.1880, 35 x 82 In. 4950.00
Sofa, Baker Furniture Co., Mahogany, Cutouts, Upholstered, 1960s, 26 x 89 x 32 In. ... *illus* 1640.00
Sofa, Belter, Rococo Revival, Rosewood, Laminated, Rosalie With Grapes, 39 x 73 In........ 10200.00
Sofa, Belter, Rosewood Laminate, Pattern, c.1850, 72 In. 19250.00
Sofa, Belter, Victorian, Rosewood, Solid Back, Green Upholstery, c.1845 .... 9350.00
Sofa, Camelback, Square Tapered Legs, 32 x 57 In.................................. 920.00
Sofa, Camelback, Tapered Reeded Legs, c.1800, 79 x 19 In. 3300.00
Sofa, Chesterfield, Edwardian, Brown Tufted Leather, Casters, Early 1900s, 78 In. 2350.00
Sofa, Chesterfield, Leather Upholstery, Tufted, Brass Tacks, 1950s, 28 x 84 In. 1456.00
Sofa, Chesterfield, Tufted Back, Arms, Loose Leather Seat Cushions, 30 x 63 In............ 1058.00
Sofa, Chinese, Chippendale Style, Camelback, Green Damask Upholstery, 34 x 76 In. 944.00
Sofa, Chippendale, Camelback, Mahogany Leg Base, Lace, 34 x 70 x 28 In. 800.00
Sofa, Chippendale, Camelback, Mahogany, Rolled Arms, Upholstered, 36 x 76 x 31 In....... 1000.00
Sofa, Chippendale, Camelback, Mahogany, Serpentine Crest, Rolled Arms, 42 x 94 In. 48000.00
Sofa, Chippendale Style, Camelback, Mahogany, Upholstered, 34 ½ x 75 x 30 In............ 1045.00
Sofa, Chippendale Style, Cherry, Marlboro Legs, Damask Upholstery, 72 x 35 In. 975.00
Sofa, Chippendale Style, Silk Upholstery, 38 ½ x 97 In. 15600.00
Sofa, Curved, Slopping Back, Tufted Buttons, Mohair Upholstery, 102 x 30 x 30 In.......... 1140.00
Sofa, Eames, Aluminum, Model 3743, Slab Seat, Black Leather, Herman Miller, 73 x 26 x 33 In. 3960.00
Sofa, Edwardian, Mahogany, Russet Leather Upholstery, Scroll Arms, 34 x 84 In............ 1200.00
Sofa, Empire, Flame Mahogany, Scroll Carved Ends, Footed, c.1840, 31 x 73 x 27 In. 880.00
Sofa, Empire, Mahogany, Box Shape, Backswept Crest, Upholstered, 38 x 83 In............. 1180.00
Sofa, Federal, Flame, Mahogany, Scroll Arms, Cornucopia, Fruit, Paw Feet, Philad., 1840, 35 x 90 x 25 In. 650.00
Sofa, Federal, Mahogany, 4-Section Crest Rail, Curved Arms, Leaf Carving 650.00

Furniture, Sideboard, Edwardian, Walnut, Burl, Rosettes, Mirror, Paneled Base, 10 x 85 x 28 In.
$1400.00

Furniture, Sideboard, Federal, 3 Drawers, 2 Doors, Turned Feet, 50 x 82 x 21 In.
$3575.00

Furniture, Sideboard, Federal, Hepplewhite, Mahogany, Inlay, c.1795, 40 x 73 x 20 ½ In.
$4887.00

Furniture, Sideboard, Federal Style, Mahogany, Bellflower Inlay, 20th Century, 38 x 58 x 24 In.
$2900.00

F

Furniture, Sideboard, Kittinger, Rosewood, Mahogany, Reeded, Ribbed Feet, c.1950, 35 x 56 x 19 In.
$295.00

Furniture, Sideboard, Neoclassical, Mahogany, Backsplash, 45 x 75 x 23 In.
$480.00

Furniture, Sideboard, Rosewood, Inlay, Arches, 3 Drawers, England, c.1880, 41 x 66 x 17 In.
$795.00

Furniture, Sideboard, Veneer, Yellow Pine, Drawers, 2 Doors, Wilmington, N.C., 55 x 71 x 22 In.
$2410.00

Sofa, Federal, Mahogany, Scrolled Arms, Reeded Arm Supports, Legs, Upholstered, 38 x 72 In. 1035.00
Sofa, Federal, Mahogany, Crest Rail, Turned Arm Support, Upholstered, c.1810, 36 x 79 In. . . 1064.00
Sofa, Federal, Mahogany, Reeded Supports, Silk Upholstery, Down Cushion, 79 x 34 In. 2760.00
Sofa, Federal, Mahogany, Straight Back, High Arms, N.Y., c.1810, 35 x 76½ In. 4800.00
Sofa, Federal, Transitional, Mahogany, Bowed Crest, Upholstered, 79 x 27 In.. . . . . 2875.00
Sofa, Footstool, Queen Anne Style, Wingback, Muslin Cover, 60 x 46 & 15 x 21 In., 3 Piece . . . 1840.00
Sofa, G. Nakashima, Cherry, Slat Back, 30½ x 72 x 31 In.. . . . . 7200.00
Sofa, G. Nakashima, Walnut, Cushion, Single Arm, c.1962, 32¾ x 95½ x 26 In.. . . . . 15600.00
Sofa, G. Nelson, Sling, Leather, Chrome, c.1964, 29 x 80 x 32 In.. . . . . 3600.00
Sofa, G. Nelson, Wool, 6 Square Legs, 90 x 31 x 27 In.. . . . . 1680.00
Sofa, George III Style, Mahogany, Padded & Domed Back, Outscrolled Arms, 42 x 77 In.. . . . . 1140.00
Sofa, George IV, Rosewood, Carved Leaf, Molded Seat Rail, c.1825, 29 x 77 In., Pair. 34000.00
Sofa, Grecian, Neoclassical, Mahogany, Bolster, Scrolled Crest Rail, Scroll Arms, 30 x 76 In. . . 4560.00
Sofa, Half Spindles, Stretcher Base, Arms, 76 x 29 x 32 In. 605.00
Sofa, Jeliff, Walnut, Maiden Heads, Triple Back 2645.00
Sofa, Louis XV Style, Walnut, Carved, Scalloped Back & Seat Rail, 39 x 79 In.. . . . . 3055.00
Sofa, Low Back, Swept Arms, Ball Feet, Upholstered, Down Filled Cushions, 29 x 76 In. 275.00
Sofa, Mahogany, Arched Crest Rail, Paw Feet, Upholstered, 36 x 75 In. 1434.00
Sofa, Mahogany, Bronze Mounts, Box Shape, Chamfered Rail, Scrolls, Blocked, 36 x 79 x 29 In. 3760.00
Sofa, Mahogany, Cornucopia, Ribbons, 19th Century, 33 x 87 x 28 In. 5875.00
Sofa, Mahogany, Cornucopia Carved Crest, Early 19th Century, 28 x 94 x 22½ In.. . . . . 7050.00
Sofa, McCobb, Wood Legs, Brass Stretcher, Calvin, 31 x 77 x 35 In. . . . . *illus* 1400.00
Sofa, Meeks, Rosewood Laminate, Stanton Hall Pattern, Pair. 7370.00
Sofa, Modern, Geometric, Metal Legs, Wool Upholstery, 84 x 32 x 32 In. 1320.00
Sofa, Neoclassical, Empire, Veneer, Scrolled Back, Paw Feet, Cornucopia Arms, 83 x 18 In. . . . 489.00
Sofa, Neoclassical, Flame Mahogany, Crest Rail, Scroll Arms, Velvet Upholstery, 36 x 80 In. . . 1410.00
Sofa, Neoclassical, Mahogany, Box Shape, Molded Crest Rail, Scroll Brackets, 32 x 85 In.. . . . . 1440.00
Sofa, Neoclassical, Mahogany, Carved, Scrolled, Paneled Crest Rail, Scroll Arms 1528.00
Sofa, Neoclassical, Mahogany, Carved, Acanthus, c.1815, 90 x 22 x 19 In. . . . . *illus* 1680.00
Sofa, Neoclassical, Mahogany, Paw Feet, Bolster Cushions, Outscrolled Arms, 90 x 22 x 19 In. 1680.00
Sofa, Neoclassical, Mahogany, Duncan Phyfe, Figured Crest Rail, Scroll Arms, 1800s, 31 x 84 In.. . 2040.00
Sofa, Neoclassical, Mahogany, Carved, Scrolled Crest, Arms, Silk Upholstery, c.1840, 93 x 27 In. 4406.00
Sofa, Neoclassical, Mahogany, Box Shape, Bronze Mounts, Panel Crest Rail, Upholstered, 34 x 78 In. 19200.00
Sofa, R.J. Horner, Neoclassical, Mahogany, Griffin Carved, Carved Crest Rail, c.1880, 42 x 79 In. 3850.00
Sofa, Renaissance Revival, Ebonized, Parquetry, Porcelain Mounts, 36 In.. . . . . 4375.00
Sofa, Renaissance Revival, Walnut, Maiden's Heads, Center Medallion, c.1860, 41 x 29 In. . . . 880.00
Sofa, Rococo, Rosewood, Triple Back, c.1850, 45 x 74 x 23½ In. 1880.00
Sofa, Sergio Radrigues, Rosewood, Leather, c.1963, 33 x 73 x 37 In. 4800.00
Sofa, Shiro Kuramata, Steel Mesh, Chrome, 1986, 28½ x 38 x 32 In.. 7500.00
Sofa, Upholstered, Embossed Circle, Flower, Head Rest, 4 Square Legs, 27 x 81 x 24 In.. . . . . . . 358.00
Sofa, Victorian, Walnut, Open End, Carved, Tufted Upholstery, 39 x 68 In. 500.00
Sofa, Victorian, White Wicker, Rolled Arms, Stick & Ball Decoration, 37 x 50 In. 1232.00
Sofa, Wormley, Walnut, Gondola, Upholstered, Removable Cushions, 111 x 31½ x 27 In. 5400.00
Sofa, Wormley, Wool Upholstery, Mahogany Supports & Legs, 84 x 24 x 30 In.. . . . . 2760.00
Stand, 4 Drawers, R.M. Schindler, c.1933, 27 x 22 x 22 In.. . . . . 6000.00
Stand, Adirondack, Twig, 8-Sided Top, Black Paint, 28 x 14 In. . . . . *illus* 575.00
Stand, Aesthetic Revival, Mahogany, Round Marble Top, Baton Shape Legs, c.1875, 30 x 14 In. 323.00
Stand, Arts & Crafts, Mahogany, 3 Shelves, 3 Vertical Slats On Sides, 19 x 12 x 32 In. 390.00
Stand, Arts & Crafts Style, Brown Paint, Door, 24 x 24 x 16 In. *illus* 220.00
Stand, Black Forest, Egg & Dart, Oval Scalloped Top, Twisted Standard, Austria, 32 x 23 In. . . 826.00
Stand, Bronze, Dragon, Birds, Monkey, Rat, Square Frame Base, 19th Century, 8 x 8 x 8 In. . . 198.00
Stand, Butler's, Mahogany, Turned Legs, Frame, 3 Tiered Shelves, 37 x 18 x 12 In. 633.00
Stand, Cherry, Applied Scalloped Molding, Dovetailed & Nailed Drawers, 25 x 23 In.. . . . . 575.00
Stand, Cherry, Dovetailed Drawer, Tapered Square Legs, Kentucky, 1800s, 28 x 16 In. 1035.00
Stand, Cherry, Drawer, Tapered Legs, 19th Century, 19 x 16 x 28 In. 880.00
Stand, Cherry, Grain Painted, 2-Board Overhanging Top, Turned Legs, 28 x 17 In. 518.00
Stand, Cherry, Tiger Maple, Drawer, Turned Legs, 30¼ x 21½ x 20¾ In.. . . . . 198.00
Stand, Cherry, Tiger Maple, Dovetailed Drawer, Pencil Post Legs, 30 x 26 x 27 In. 385.00
Stand, Chinese, Carved Legs, Bamboo & Leaf, Marble Top, Stretcher, c.1880, 36 x 14 In.. . . . . 168.00
Stand, Chinese, Rosewood, Marble Inset, 7½ x 6 In.. . . . . 248.00
Stand, Chinese, Rosewood, Marble Mounted, 32 x 11½ In., Pair 443.00
Stand, Chinese, Rosewood, Octagonal, Pierced Openwork, X-Stretcher, 1900s, 24 In., Pair . . . 633.00
Stand, Corner, Oak, Canted Corner, Pilasters, Shelves, England, 41 x 28 x 19 In.. . . . . 472.00
Stand, Dressing, Silver Plate, Oval Mirror, 2 Galleried Tiers, Marble Base, 65 x 15 In. 999.00
Stand, Drop Leaf, Drawer, Rounded Corners, Turned & Block Legs, N.Y., 29 x 21 x 35 In. 201.00
Stand, Drop Leaf, Mahogany, 3 Curved Drawers, Carved Leaf, Claw Feet, c.1810, 29 x 16 x 16 In. 345.00

tand, Edgar Brandt, Mahogany, Oval Top, 3-Footed, 20 x 14 In. 47.00
tand, Empire, Cherry, Overhanging Top, ½ Spindle Columns, Kentucky, c.1840, 29 x 28 In. 575.00
tand, Empire, Walnut, Pine, Carved, Spiral Turned Legs, Plinth, 29½ x 21 x 16 In. 840.00
tand, Empire Style, Mahogany, Parquetry, Green Marble Top, 40 x 15 x 18 In. 266.00
tand, Federal, Cherry, Inlay, 28½ x 22¼ In. 5000.00
tand, Federal, Inlaid Tiger Maple, Drawer, New England, c.1810, 26 x 20 In. 22800.00
tand, Federal, Poplar, 2 Drawers, Dovetailed Construction, 29 x 16 x 16 In. 748.00
tand, Federal, Softwood, Dovetailed Drawer, Turned Legs, Sandwich Glass Pull, 29 x 21 x 18 In. 187.00
tand, Federal, Stained, Drawer, Ceramic Pull, 28¼ x 18½ x 18¼ In. 288.00
tand, Federal, Tiger Maple, Carved, Splayed Leg, Drawer, c.1790, 27½ x 15 In. 1528.00
tand, Federal, Tiger Maple, Figured, 2 Drawers, Wood Knobs, 1800s, 29 x 20 In. 1840.00
tand, Federal, Yellow, Black & Tan Banding, Overhanging Top, Drawer, c.1810, 29 x 15 In. 15275.00
tand, Fern, Aesthetic, Square, Brass, 4 Bracket Supports, American, 1880, 32 In. 1415.00
tand, Fern, Aesthetic Revival, Walnut, Ebonized Carving, c.1870, 36 x 16 In. 460.00
tand, Fern, Aesthetic, Square, Brass, 4 Bracket Supports, American, 1880, 32 In. 1415.00
tand, Fern, Oak, Marble Top, 8-Sided *illus* 325.00
tand, Fern, Stone Inset, Square Top, Drawer, Display Shelf, Asian, 37 x 15½ In. 413.00
tand, Fern, Tiger Maple, 19th Century, 31 x 10 In. 24.00
tand, Frankl, Limed Mahogany, Drawer, Brown Saltman, 24 x 20 x 13 In. *illus* 145.00
tand, French Style, Mahogany, Kidney Shape Top, Ormolu Mount, Brass Gallery, 31 x 25 In. 316.00
tand, Fruitwood, Walnut, Marquetry, Marble Top, 31¾ x 20½ In. 411.00
tand, G. Stickley, 4 Legs, Round Top, c.1903 6325.00
tand, Glass Tray, Removable, Chinoiserie, Painted, Wheel Supports, 28 x 26 x 17½ In. 561.00
tand, Hat, Mahogany, Carved, Flame Finial, Twist Turned Shaft, 77½ x 30 In. 529.00
tand, Hepplewhite, Cherry, Drawer, Splayed & Tapered Legs, 26 x 17 In. 546.00
tand, Hepplewhite, Cherry, Drawer, Tapered Legs, c.1800, 17 x 17½ x 28 In. 550.00
tand, Hepplewhite, Curly Maple, Scrub Top, Drawer, Red Stain Base, 27 x 19 x 16 In. 288.00
tand, Hepplewhite, Mahogany, Drawer, Brass Pull & Casters, 29 x 18 x 18 In. 660.00
tand, Hepplewhite, Mixed Wood, Tapered Legs, Red Paint, c.1825, 28½ x 19 In. 230.00
tand, Hepplewhite, Pine, Tapered Legs, Red, Black Paint, c.1820, 27 x 19 In. 1035.00
tand, Hepplewhite, Tiger Maple, Drawer, Square Tapered Legs, Late 1790s, 28 x 27 x 18 In. 4889.00
tand, Hitchcock, Fruit Stencil, Green Paint, 4-Footed, 21 x 14 In. 85.00
tand, Kettle, George III Style, Mahogany, Full Gallery, Frieze, Square Legs, 25 x 11 In. 646.00
tand, Lamp, Oak, Wicker, Cross Stretchers, 30 x 28 x 24 In. 231.00
tand, Magazine, Arts & Crafts, Rectangular Top, 3 Shelves, 18 x 14 x 37 In. 390.00
tand, Magazine, G. Stickley, 4 Shelves, 14 x 14 x 42 In. 840.00
tand, Magazine, G. Stickley, V-Trough, Cutout Pulls, 30¾ x 32 x 10 In. 1200.00
tand, Magazine, G. Stickley, 4 Shelves, Slab Sides, Cutouts, 14 x 10 x 40 In. 1440.00
tand, Magazine, G. Stickley, 3 Lower Shelves, Arched Rail, 21½ x 13 x 42 In. 1440.00
tand, Magazine, G. Stickley, 4 Shelves, 3 Slats At Each Side, 21 x 12 x 42 In. 1800.00
tand, Magazine, G. Stickley, 3 Shelves, Arched Rail, 21½ x 13 x 42 In. 2160.00
tand, Magazine, Mahogany, Birch, c.1950, 29 x 23 x 23 In. 960.00
tand, Magazine, Roycroft, 3 Shelves, Arched Top, 18 x 15½ x 38 In. 4800.00
tand, Magazine, Roycroft, 3 Shelves, Signed, 38 x 18 x 15 In. *illus* 4800.00
tand, Magazine, V. Kagan, Walnut, c.1950, 20 x 20½ x 30 In. *illus* 3900.00
tand, Mahogany, 3-Footed, Round Top, Center Column, Scroll Legs, 30½ In. 100.00
tand, Mahogany, Kidney Shape, Rosewood Inlay, 2 Tiers, c.1900, 27 x 26 x 16 In. 224.00
tand, Mahogany, Muffin, 3 Tiers, Early 20th Century, 35¾ x 10¼ In. 29.00
tand, Mahogany, Piecrust Edge, Snake Feet, c.1770, 29 x 22 In. *illus* 978.00
and, Mahogany, Pine, Poplar, Figured Veneer, 2 Drawers, Shaped Shelf, 29 x 24 In. 374.00
and, Mahogany, Tray Top, Turned Pedestal, Adjustable, 1800s, 5¾ x 7½ In. 431.00
and, Mahogany, Turret, Canted Corners, 2 Drawers, New England, c.1810 975.00
and, Music, Duet, Victorian, Fruitwood, 4 Brass Candle Arms, Scroll Legs, 13 x 18 In. 1062.00
and, Music, George III, Mahogany, Bronze Candle Arms, Spider Legs, 40 x 20 In. 470.00
and, Music, Italy, 3-Footed, Iron, 18th Century, 73½ In. 1434.00
and, Music, Maple, 3 Slat Shelves, Stick & Ball, c.1900, 38 In. 47.00
and, Music, Regency Style, Mahogany, Melon Finial, 5 Stiles, Stepped Plinth, 55 x 23 In. 1528.00
and, Neoclassical, Drop Leaf, Curly & Bird's-Eye Maple, Cherry, Curved Drawers, 29 x 20 In. 518.00
and, Neoclassical Style, Figural, Man Holding Tray, Carved, Multicolored, 41 x 14 In. 165.00
and, Oak, Wicker, Reed Fiber, Ionic, Mich., Early 20th Century, 30 x 28 x 24 In. *illus* 253.00
and, Pine, Tapered Legs, Drawer, Gallery, Faux Paint, Marble Top, 25 x 18 In. 863.00
and, Plant, Art & Crafts, Pierced & Carved Top, Shelf, 42 x 13 x 13 In. 150.00
and, Plant, Chinese, Ju Wood, Square Top, Inset Panel, Beaded Edge, Carved Apron, 30 x 15 In. 390.00
and, Plant, Cottage, Round Top, Lower Shelf, Spool Legs, 18 x 21½ In. 1020.00
and, Plant, First Empire Style, Mahogany, Marble, Tapered, 41 x 13 In. 1080.00
and, Plant, G. Stickley, Square, Cut Corners, Splayed Legs, 18 x 17 x 20 In. 1080.00

Furniture, Smoking Stand, Pelican, Stylized, Iron, Painted, 25⅝ x 10 In. $978.00

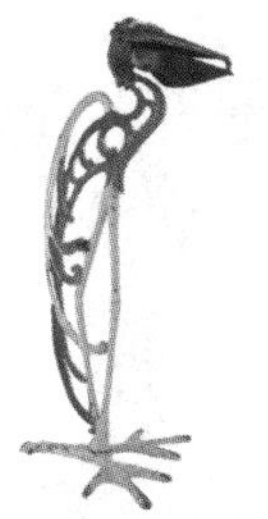

Furniture, Sofa, Baker Furniture Co., Mahogany, Cutouts, Upholstered, 1960s, 26 x 89 x 32 In. $1640.00

Furniture, Sofa, McCobb, Wood Legs, Brass Stretcher, Calvin, 31 x 77 x 35 In. $1400.00

Furniture, Sofa, Neoclassical, Mahogany, Carved, Acanthus, c.1815, 90 x 22 x 19 In. $1680.00

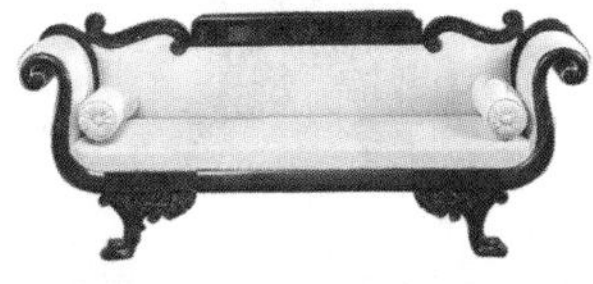

TIP

Never push antique furniture across the floor. Pick it up. Old furniture may have weak glue joints and may be damaged.

Furniture, Stand, Adirondack, Twig, 8-Sided Top, Black Paint, 28 x 14 In.
$575.00

Furniture, Stand, Arts & Crafts Style, Brown Paint, Door, 24 x 24 x 16 In.
$220.00

Furniture, Stand, Fern, Oak, Marble Top, 8-Sided
$325.00

Priscilla

The "Priscilla" is a stand with a slanted top that can be opened on both sides. There is a handle so it can be carried. It is a type of sewing cabinet named for a popular treadle sewing machine made in the early Twentieth-century. There was also a sewing magazine called *Modern Priscilla.*

Stand, Plant, G. Stickley, Oak, Paper Label, c.1907, 20 x 18 In. 1440.00
Stand, Plant, G. Stickley, Oak, Tile, Paper Label, c.1902, 22 x 17 In. 7800.00
Stand, Plant, Rosewood, Marble Insets, Carved Flower Apron, Cabriole Legs, 27 In., Pair 648.00
Stand, Plant, Wicker, Arched Support, Liner, White, Early 20th Century, 64 x 29 In.. .... 177.00
Stand, Portfolio, American Renaissance, Walnut, Carved, Adjustable Frame, 46 x 31 In.. .... 4994.00
Stand, Portfolio, Walnut, Slats, Adjustable Arms, Scrolled Legs, 47 x 30 x 21 In. 2937.00
Stand, R.J. Horner, Aesthetic Revival, Faux Bamboo, 33 x 18 In. 2200.00
Stand, Reading, William IV, Mahogany, Carter's Patent Library Machine, 32 In. 1410.00
Stand, Regency Style, Cast Iron, Brass, Marble Top, France, 24 x 16 x 16 In.. .... 236.00
Stand, Renaissance Revival, Walnut, Marble Top, Drawer, Door, 30 x 18 x 17 In. 600.00
Stand, Rosewood, Square Top, Beaded, Carved Skirt, Dragons, 34 x 11 In., Pair. 260.00
Stand, Shaker, Butternut, Pine, Painted, Drawer, Tapered Legs, Canterbury, c.1845, 18 x 18 In. 1521.00
Stand, Shaker, Cherry, Round, Birdcage Support, Tapered Post, Tripod, c.1830, 24 x 21 In.. .. 22325.00
Stand, Shaker, Mahogany, Drawer, Tapered Legs, 28 x 18½ x 17 In. 740.00
Stand, Shaker, Walnut, Turned Legs, Hancock Community, 27 x 18 x 17 In.. .... 960.00
Stand, Shaving, Georgian, Mahogany, England, 23 x 15¾ x 7½ In.. .... 207.00
Stand, Shaving, Late Neoclassical, Rosewood, Serpentine Marble Top, Drawer, 28 x 16 In. ... 184.00
Stand, Shaving, Louis XVI Style, Mahogany, Ormolu Mounted, Marble Top 354.00
Stand, Shaving, Mirror, Gilt Striping, Dots, Fretwork Frame, Scalloped Drawers, 26 x 21 In.. . 431.00
Stand, Shaving, Renaissance, Walnut, Mirror, Burled Frame, Arched Crest, Drawers, 78 x 20 In. 2640.00
Stand, Shaving, Sheraton, Tiger Maple, Swivel Mirror, Drawer, 21 x 17 x 11 In. .... *illus* 495.00
Stand, Shaving, Walnut, Cushion Mirror, Mid 19th Century, 61½ x 14 x 14 In. 1293.00
Stand, Shaving, William IV, Mahogany, Scrolled Mirror Supports, 3 Drawers, c.1825, 25 In.. . 300.00
Stand, Sheet Iron, Tin, Black Paint, Continental, 19th Century, 9 In. 81.00
Stand, Sheraton, Birch, 2 Drawers, Red Paint, Square Top, Turned Legs, 28 x 17 x 17 In. 464.00
Stand, Sheraton, Cherry, Painted, Drawer, Overhanging Top, 28 x 16 x 14¾ In.. .... 130.00
Stand, Sheraton, Cherry, Turned Legs, Glass Knob, Drawer, 29½ x 19 x 18½ In. 259.00
Stand, Sheraton, Cherry, Drawer, 1-Board Top, Ky, c.1830, 29 x 24 x 20½ In. 390.00
Stand, Sheraton, Cherry, Walnut, Drawer, Turned Legs, Michigan, c.1850, 29 x 18 In. 403.00
Stand, Sheraton, Cherry, 2 Drawers, Turned Legs, c.1840, 28¾ x 20 In. 805.00
Stand, Sheraton, Curly Maple, Poplar, 2 Drawers, Turned Legs, c.1830, 29 x 20 In. 1610.00
Stand, Sheraton, Curly Maple, Drawer, Turned Legs, Mushroom Feet, Early 1800s, 28 x 21 In. 1725.00
Stand, Sheraton, Mahogany, Cookie Corner Top, Tapered Legs, 28½ x 20 x 18 In. 495.00
Stand, Sheraton, Mahogany, Tiger Maple Front, 2 Drawers, Legs, Sides, 28 x 21 x 19 In. 1760.00
Stand, Sheraton, Maple, Birch, Drop Leaf, 2 Drawers, Wooden Pulls, c.1820, 29 x 17 x 19 In.. 413.00
Stand, Sheraton, Maple & Curly Maple, Drop Leaf, 2 Drawers, Maine, c.1810, 28 x 18 x 17 In. 1150.00
Stand, Sheraton, Tiger Maple, Drawer, Turned Legs, c.1820, 28½ x 20 x 18 In.. .... 800.00
Stand, Sheraton, Tiger Maple, 2 Drawers, Turned Leg, 28½ x 20½ x 17 In.. .... 1120.00
Stand, Smoking, Arts & Crafts, Copper Top, Shelf, Corbelled Supports, Door, 28 x 16 x 9 In.. . 475.00
Stand, Smoking, Arts & Crafts, Door, Copper Hinges, Original Pull, 16 x 14 x 26 In. 540.00
Stand, Smoking, Arts & Crafts, Oak, Copper, Slag Glass Details 750.00
Stand, Smoking, Black Forest, Wooden, Bear, Holding Table Top, 3 Bear On Top, 34 x 17 In. . 1323.00
Stand, Smoking, Bronze, Horse Heads On Sides, Seahorse Finial, Oscar Bach, 39 x 10 In.. ... 302.00
Stand, Smoking, Renaissance Style, Gilt, Patinated Bronze, Beast, Satyrs, 15 In., Pair. 1410.00
Stand, Smoking, Wood, Train Porter, Tack Buttons, Big Shoes, Metal Ashtray, Painted, 36 In.. 330.00
Stand, Smoking, Wood, Jiggs, Butler Outfit, Slotted Rectangular Base, Painted, Early 1900s, 31 In. 33.00
Stand, Smoking, Wood, Lady Bell Hop, Holding Heart-Shaped Tray, Blue Uniform, 39¼ In.. . 77.00
Stand, Step Back, Sheraton, Pine, 3 Drawers, Tapered Turned Legs, 36 x 33 x 15 In. 345.00
Stand, Telephone, Laminate, Enameled Steel, Casters, Elliot Noyes, c.1957, 15 x 13 x 22 In.. . 780.00
Stand, Telephone, Teak, Black Formica Top, 2 Sliding Trays, Drawer, 1958, 22 In. 710.00
Stand, Tiger Maple, Dovetailed Drawer, Tapered Legs, 28¾ x 12⅝ x 13⅝ In. 495.00
Stand, Tiger Maple, Tiered, Scroll Legs 875.00
Stand, Tilt Top, Cherry, Oval Top, Spider Legs, Turned Pedestal, 29 x 21 In. 207.00
Stand, Tilt Top, Mahogany, Round Top, 3 String Inlaid Circles, Turned Post, 3 Legs, 29 x 20 In. 115.00
Stand, Tilt Top, Mahogany, Dish Top, Birdcage Support, Turned Shaft, Snake Feet, 29 x 26 x 25 In. 420.00
Stand, Tree Of Life, 4 Shelves, Carved Organic, Leather Facings, 14 x 14 x 44 In. 2880.00
Stand, Victorian, Gilt Paint, Mirrored, 2 Round Tiers, Beveled Glass, 1800s, 31 x 20 In.. ..... 264.00
Stand, Walnut, 2 Drawers, Molded Top, Turned & Block Legs, N.Y., 27 x 19½ x 19½ In.. ..... 58.00
Stand, Walnut, Butternut, Drop Leaf, Red Wash, 2 Drawers, 29 x 20 In. 460.00
Stand, Walnut, Drawer, Dovetailed, Beaded Skirt, Tapered Legs, 26 x 16 x 14 In. 1210.00
Stand, Walnut, Drop Front, Modern, 1950s, 25 x 22 x 17 In., Pair .... *illus* 120.00
Stand, Wood, Painted, Stenciled, Shaped Back Rail, Drawer, Tapered Legs, c.1840, 32 In. 1315.00
Stand, Writing, Regency, Mahogany, Inlay, Upholstered, Britain, 19th Century, 45½ x 22 x 3 In.. 240.00
Stand, Shaker, Butternut, Pine, Square Top, 2 Dovetailed Drawers, Snake Legs, 28 x 21 In. .. 3510.00
Stationery Rack, Georgian, Mahogany, 7 Compartments, Early 19th Century, 7½ x 11 In.. . 300.00
Steps, Shaker, Pine, 3 Steps, Arched Sides, Mortise & Peg, New Lebanon, c.1840, 30 x 19 x 21 In. 7020.00

Stool, Anglo-Indian, Bamboo, Octagonal Seat, Splayed Legs, X-Stretchers, 17 x 15 In. 360.00
Stool, Arts & Crafts, Leatherette Top, Tacks, Slab Sides, Cutout Details, 18 x 12 x 12 In....... 150.00
Stool, Arts & Crafts, Oak, Rails, Tapestry, 11 x 37 ½ x 15 In. 302.00
Stool, Arts & Crafts, Splayed Slab, Cutouts, Recovered Seat, 18 ½ x 11 x 17 In. 510.00
Stool, Bar, Leather, Gilt Bronze, c.1950, 32 x 14 x 14 In. 3600.00
Stool, Black Paint, Turned, Providence, Early 19th Century, 19 In. 1200.00
Stool, Chinese, Bamboo, Shaped Seat, X-Shape Braces, 19 x 16 x 11 In. 780.00
Stool, Chinese, Elm, Square Top, Beaded Skirt, Rectangular Legs, 20 x 17 In., Pair 1003.00
Stool, Chinese, Red Lacquer, Octagonal, Leaf Decoration, 20 In., Pair 944.00
Stool, Chippendale Style, Mahogany, Upholstered Rail, Claw & Ball Feet, c.1890, 19 x 18 x 14 In. . 725.00
Stool, Drawer, Lock, Dutch, c.1740, 10 ½ x 11 x 10 In. 33.00
Stool, Ebonized, Parcel Gilt, Padded, Upholstered Seat, 17 x 14 In. 295.00
Stool, Empire, Mahogany, X-Form Legs, Medial Stretcher, Upholstered, 16 x 18 x 16 In. 413.00
Stool, George III, Mahogany, Carved Legs, Serpentine Crest, Upholstered, c.1760, Pair 37000.00
Stool, Georgian, Leather, Acanthus Carved Cabriole Legs, Upholstered, 19 x 7 x 17 In. 797.00
Stool, Gout, Regency, Mahogany, Adjustable, Early 19th Century, 15 x 13 x 23 In. 969.00
Stool, Jacobean, Oak Joint, Block & Ring Turned Legs, 23 x 18 ½ In. 294.00
Stool, Limbert, Cricket, Splayed Sides, Cutout Design, 20 x 12 x 12 In. 900.00
Stool, Louis XV, Walnut, Scalloped Frame, Cabriole Legs, Upholstered, 18 x 20 x 18 In. 294.00
Stool, Louis XV Style, Gilt, Padded, Shell Carved Apron, 16 x 19 x 17 In. 960.00
Stool, Louis XV Style, Gilt, Padded Top, Concave Sides, Leaf Frieze, Damask, 16 x 30 In. 1680.00
Stool, Louis XV Style, Gilt, Padded, Square, Cabriole Legs, 19 x 16 x 16 In. 1800.00
Stool, Louis XVI Style, Gilt, Padded Top, Laurel Leaf Frieze, Scroll, Fluted, 16 x 18 In. 1560.00
Stool, Lucite, Brown, Steven Chase, c.1980, 19 x 31 x 14 In. 1080.00
Stool, Lucite, Green Seat, Charles Hollis Jones, c.1985, 19 x 14 In. 1560.00
Stool, Milk, Round, Primitive, 11 In. 27.00
Stool, Monk, G. Stickley, Low Form, Leather Seat, Flared Feet, 5 x 12½ x 12½ In... 410.00 to 780.00
Stool, Oak, Crossed Legs, Beige Wool Upholsterey, Jean-Michel Frank, 1930s, 18 In. 6250.00
Stool, Oak, Iron, Telescoping, Adjustable, Box Form Base, 25 In., 6 Piece 1872.00
Stool, Oak, Joint, Turned Splayed Legs, Box Stretcher, Molded Edge, 18th Century, 18 x 16 x 10 In. 2300.00
Stool, Piano, Mahogany, Adjustable, Rope Twist Urn Pedestal, Platform Base, 20 x 17 In. 275.00
Stool, Piano, Neoclassical, Mahogany, Adjustable, Carved, c.1830, 20 x 13 In. 764.00
Stool, Piano, Tufted Leather, Nailed Seat, Adjustable, Steinway & Sons, 20 x 20 x 17 In. 472.00
Stool, Pine, Windsor, Rocker, Mustard & Red Paint, New York, c.1850, 18 In. 1440.00
Stool, Plank Top, Splayed Sides, Arched Cutout Feet, Compton Village, N.H., Oct. 1894, 6 x 24 x 6 In. 110.00
Stool, Pouf, Upholstered, Fringe, 17 x 37 In. .... *illus* 206.00
Stool, Regency, Polychrome, Klismos, Padded Seat, X-Stretcher, 16 x 24 In., Pair 3600.00
Stool, Regency, Walnut, Tapestry Top, Scrolled Feet On Balls, 19 ¾ x 24 ½ x 16 ½ In. 2376.00
Stool, Rococo Revival, Mahogany, Serpentine Apron, Cabriole Legs, 14 x 18 x 18 In. 6600.00
Stool, Thebes, Arts & Crafts, Curved Seat, Turned Legs, Spindle Detail, 14 x 17 x 17 In. 390.00
Stool, Victorian, Iron, Pierced Apron, Cabriole Legs, 8 x 15 ½ x 12 In. 115.00
Stool, Victorian, Mahogany, Square, Bobbin-Turned Legs, Needlework Top, Padded, 19 x 19 In. 2160.00
Stool, Victorian, Reticulated Flowers, Lattice, Cast Iron, Upholstered, 9 ½ x 13 In. 141.00
Stool, Walnut, Jocko Johnson, c.1976, 17 x 21 x 21 In. 2280.00
Stool, Walnut, Needlepoint, Flowers, Green Ground, 3-Footed, 10 x 18 x 12 In. 47.00
Stool, Walnut, Square Seat, Turned Legs, X-Stretchers, Upholstered, 18 x 18 In., Pair 1058.00
Stool, William & Mary Style, Walnut, Turned Legs, Stretcher, Leather Upholstery, 18 In., Pair 881.00
Stool, Windsor, Pine Top, Splayed Bamboo Turned Legs, 18th Century, 12 x 13 In. 224.00
Stool, Work, Chip Carved Platform, Black Paint, 18 x 14 In. 138.00
Stool, Wormley, Vanity, Mahogany, Swiveling Seat, Tan Vinyl, 1940, 20 x 20 x 29 ½ In. 720.00
Stool Set, Ebonized Mahogany, 3 Legs, Round Seat, Perriand, 13 x 15 ¾ In., 4 .... 4800.00
Stool Set, Metal, Polished, Rounded Square Seat, Tapered Legs, Early 1900s, 17 ½ In., 6 ..... 930.00
Table, 2-Board Top, 2 Drawers, Stretcher Base, Turned Legs, Lancaster, Pa., 30 x 65 x 37 In. . 4400.00
Table, Adam Style, Satinwood, Extension, Burl Veneer, Carved Legs, Irwin, 29 x 68 In. 1265.00
Table, Adirondack, Twig, 19 ½ x 14 ½ x 31 In. 171.00
Table, Adirondack, Twig, Horseshoes, Hearts, Gold, White 525.00
Table, Aesthetic Revival, Inlaid Mahogany, Marble Top, Frieze, Leaves, c.1880, 31 x 26 In. 646.00
Table, Anglo-Indian, Rosewood, Marble Top, Molded Skirt, Stepped Paneled Stem, 28 x 33 In. 1880.00
Table, Art Deco Style, Mahogany, 3 Shaped Supports, Stepped Base, 25 ½ x 26 ½ In. 792.00
Table, Art Moderne, Gilt Metal, Brass, Circular Dish, Tubular Supports, Legs, 30 ½ x 13 In. 720.00
Table, Art Nouveau, Kingwood, Round Top, Sunburst Veneer, 3 Splayed Legs, 24 x 20 In. 1320.00
Table, Arts & Crafts, Oak, Round, Square Legs, Shelf, 20th Century 154.00
Table, Arts & Crafts, Round Top, Shelf, Reticulated Flowers, Rose Valley Style, 17 x 24 In. 600.00
Table, Arts & Crafts, Serving, Oak, 3-Board Top, Round Legs, 20th Century 275.00
Table, Arts & Crafts Style, California Tile Insert Top, Spool Legs, Square Top, 18 x 18 x 18 In.. 510.00
Table, Asian, Round, Ebonized Top, Shaped Apron, 6 Round Legs, Stretcher, 35 x 47 In. 59.00

Furniture, Stand, Frankl, Limed Mahogany, Drawer, Brown Saltman, 24 x 20 x 13 In.
$145.00

Furniture, Stand, Magazine, Roycroft, 3 Shelves, Signed, 38 x 18 x 15 In.
$4800.00

Stand, Magazine, V. Kagan, Walnut, c.1950, 20 x 20 ½ x 30 In.
$3900.00

Furniture, Stand, Mahogany, Piecrust Edge, Snake Feet, c.1770, 29 x 22 In.
$978.00

Furniture, Stand, Oak, Wicker, Reed Fiber, Ionic, Mich., Early 20th Century, 30 x 28 x 24 In.
$253.00

Furniture, Stand, Shaving, Sheraton, Tiger Maple, Swivel Mirror, Drawer, 21 x 17 x 11 In.
$495.00

Furniture, Stand, Walnut, Drop Front, Modern, 1950s, 25 x 22 x 17 In., Pair
$120.00

Furniture, Stool, Pouf, Upholstered, Fringe, 17 x 37 In.
$206.00

Table, Baker Furniture, Figured Walnut, Parquetry Veneers, 5 Drawers, 29 x 60 In. 978.00
Table, Baroque, Marble, Lapis, Sienna, Malachite, Flowers, 28 ¾ x 70 x 36 ¼ In. 7050.00
Table, Baroque, Walnut, Heart & Carved Leaf, Drawers, Skirt, Baluster Legs, 30 x 56 In. 7480.00
Table, Baroque, Walnut, 1-Board Top, Baluster Turned Supports, Tenon Stretcher Base, 31 x 6 In. 8050.00
Table, Biedermeier, Bird's-Eye Maple, 4-Sided Standard, Stepped, Square Base, 31 x 44 In.... 3456.00
Table, Bistro, Napoleon III, Wrought Iron, Marble Top, 3 Shaped Supports, 29 x 23 ¾ In. 1920.00
Table, Black Walnut, Frieze Drawer, Square Legs, Pegged Construction, 32 x 27 x 25 In. 1410.00
Table, Blackamoor, Ebonized, Polychromed, Round Top, 3 Splayed Legs, Italy, 31 x 13 In. 2880.00
Table, Bouillotte, Louis XVI Style, Mahogany, Gilt, Brass, Marble Top, 28 ¾ x 24 In. 1560.00
Table, Brazilian Bamboo, Geometric, Leaves, Square, 15 ½ x 41 ½ x 41 ½ In. 224.00
Table, Bronze, Glass Top, Tree Shape Base, 5 Support Branches, 46 x 29 In. 1568.00
Table, Bronze, Swan Shape, Glass Top, Round Beveled Glass Top, Mid 1900s, 31 x 60 In. 575.00
Table, Brooks, Round Top, Open Base, Limbert Style, 28 ¼ x 18 In. 2400.00
Table, Burl, Cherry, Rustic, 20th Century, 24 ½ x 45 In. 2185.00
Table, Butcher Block, Maple, Thick Block Top, Square To Round Legs, c.1920, 33 x 30 In. 748.00
Table, Butterfly, Maple, Pine, Drawer, Baluster Legs, Ball Feet, Stretcher, 26 x 16 In. 2185.00
Table, Card, Centennial Hepplewhite, Mahogany, Swing Leg, String Inlay. 650.00
Table, Card, Chippendale, Mahogany, Back Swing Leg, Flip Top, Square Legs, 29 x 34 x 16 In. 300.00
Table, Card, Federal, Mahogany, Figured Mahogany Veneer, Philadelphia, c.1820, 30 x 38 In. 1150.00
Table, Card, Federal, Inlaid, Shaped Top, Birch Panel, Tapered Square Legs, c.1820, 29 x 36 x 18 In. 1410.00
Table, Card, Federal, Inlaid Mahogany, Mass., c.1810, 28 ¾ x 36 In. 1800.00
Table, Card, Federal, Mahogany, Rectangular Top, String Inlay, Banded Skirt, c.1800 .... 2233.00
Table, Card, Federal, Mahogany, Carved, Inlay, Massachusetts, Early 1800s, 31 x 38 In. 2820.00
Table, Card, Federal, Serpentine Sides, 36 In. 5900.00
Table, Card, Federal, Mahogany, Inlay, Massachusetts, c.1790, 29 ¾ x 34 ½ In. 7638.00
Table, Card, Federal Style, Mahogany, 30 x 36 x 17 ½ In. 1840.00
Table, Card, Flip Top, Drawer, Cabriole Legs, c.1765, 27 ¾ x 30 In. 5382.00
Table, Card, George II, Mahogany, Needlepoint, Drawer, 18th Century, 33 x 34 In. 7670.00
Table, Card, George III, Mahogany, Inlaid Top, Playing Card Needlework, 31 x 34 x 18 In. 862.00
Table, Card, George III, Mahogany, Inlay, D-Form Gaming Top, 29 x 36 x 18 In., Pair 6490.00
Table, Card, Hepplewhite, Mahogany, Fan Inlay, Drawer, Swing Leg, 29 x 35 x 17 In. 550.00
Table, Card, Hepplewhite, Mahogany, Vase, Inlay, Swing Legs, Britain, c.1790, 28 x 36 x 18 In. 920.00
Table, Card, Hepplewhite, Mahogany, D-Form Flip Top, Tapered Legs, 1800, 27 x 36 x 17 In. . 1495.00
Table, Card, Hepplewhite, Mahogany, Flip Top, Square Top, Oval Corners, 30 x 36 x 17 In. 2860.00
Table, Card, Hepplewhite, Mahogany, Panels, String Inlay, 35 x 17 ½ x 30 In. 3450.00
Table, Card, Hepplewhite, Mahogany, Eagle & Bellflower Inlay, 36 x 17 x 30 In. 5150.00
Table, Card, Hepplewhite Style, Mahogany, Swing Leg, Brass Hinges, 36 ½ x 30 x 17 In. 728.00
Table, Card, Inlaid Mahogany, Extension, Drop Legs, 3 Leaves, 20th Century 55.00
Table, Card, Mahogany, Demilune, Inlay, Flowers, 29 ¾ x 36 ¾ x 18 ½ In. 598.00
Table, Card, Mahogany, Demilune, Early 19th Century, 30 x 36 x 18 In. 2938.00
Table, Card, Mahogany, Square Legs, Gadroon Trim, Drawer, c.1780, 30 x 35 x 18 In. 3737.00
Table, Card, Mahogany, Shaped Top, 4 Colonnettes, Plinth Base, Philadelphia, 30 x 19 In. 8120.00
Table, Card, Neoclassical, Mahogany, Gilt Stenciled, Swivel Top, c.1830, 29 x 35 In. 4700.00
Table, Card, Sheraton, Mahogany, Flip Top, Leaf, Star Punch Back, Bell, c.1810, 29 x 36 x 17 In.... 575.00
Table, Card, Sheraton, Mahogany, Cherry, Bowfront, Tapered Legs, Reeded, 29 x 36 x 17 In... 633.00
Table, Card, Sheraton, Mahogany, Inlaid Band, Flip Top, Frieze, Reeded Legs, 29 x 35 x 34 In. 1783.00
Table, Card, Sheraton Style, Mahogany, Serpentine Flip Top, 29 x 36 In. 259.00
Table, Cast Iron, Round Top, Cabriole Legs, Britannia Bust, Shield Embossed, 30 x 24 In. ... 1293.00
Table, Center, Aesthetic Revival, Lacquer, Painted, Brass, Tooled Leather, c.1880, 30 x 29 In.. . 1528.00
Table, Center, Chinese, Hardwood, Travertine Top, 26 x 61 In. 587.00
Table, Center, Dutch Neoclassical, Mahogany, Satinwood, Oval Top, 24 x 40 In. 2640.00
Table, Center, Eastlake, Brown Marble Top, Reeded Skirt, Open Pedestal, Late 1800s, 29 x 30 x 20 In. 150.00
Table, Center, Ebonized Wood, Carved Dragon, Beast Heads, Cabriole Legs, 30 x 35 x 23 In. .. 597.00
Table, Center, Empire, Bronze Mounts, 32 x 40 ½ In. 1645.00
Table, Center, Empire, Marble Top, Double Pedestal, Carved Skirt, c.1830, 29 ½ x 49 In. 1760.00
Table, Center, Georgian, Carved, Gilt, Cabriole Legs, 32 ½ x 44 ½ In. 3675.00
Table, Center, Gothic, Mahogany, c.1860, 30 x 43 In. 1980.00
Table, Center, Gothic, Mahogany, Octagonal, Trefoil Drops, c.1840, 28 x 36 In. 4800.00
Table, Center, Heywood & Wakefield, Aesthetic Revival, Oak, Wicker, 29 x 28 In. 2040.00
Table, Center, Italian Walnut, Octagonal Top, Inlaid Star, 3 Shaped Splayed Legs, 30 x 28 In.. 2400.00
Table, Center, Louis XV, Checkerboard Inlays, Cabriole Legs, 36 ½ x 21 ¾ In. 2467.00
Table, Center, Louis XV Style, Rosewood, Carved Skirt, Drawers, 30 x 51 In. 1320.00
Table, Center, Louis XV Style, Mahogany, Gilt, Brass Mounts, Flower Spray, 28 ½ x 31 In. 2640.00
Table, Center, Louis XV Style, French Provincial, Walnut, Carved, Marble Top, 31 x 33 In. 3525.00
Table, Center, Mahogany, Marble Top, Square Pedestal, c.1830, 29 x 36 x 36 In. 940.00
Table, Center, Mahogany, Inlay, Round, Lyres, Butterfly, Flower, Bulbous Pedestal, Dutch, 30 x 37 In. 1320.00

able, Center, Mahogany, Marble Top, Pedestal, Scrolled Feet, 30 x 33 In. 1837.00
able, Center, Mahogany, Figured Top, Molded Skirt, Triangular Stem, Plinth, 28 x 37 In. 5580.00
able, Center, Meeks, Rosewood, Pierce Carved, Marble Top, Bird Pattern, c.1850, 49 In. 30250.00
able, Center, Miniature, Circular Top, Mid 19th Century, 10 x 11 ½ In. 646.00
able, Center, Neoclassical, Mahogany, Carved, Round, Winged Paw Feet, c.1825, 30 ½ In. 480.00
able, Center, Neoclassical, Rosewood, Veneered Center, 31 x 43 ½ In. 1680.00
able, Center, Neoclassical, Mahogany, Serpentine Marble Top, S-Scrolls, 31 x 33 In. 2350.00
able, Center, Neoclassical, Mahogany, Oval Top, Russia, 30 x 49 x 31 In. 2400.00
able, Center, Neoclassical, Restauration Style, Mahogany, Egyptian Marble Top, 31 x 36 In. 6169.00
able, Center, Neoclassical Empire, Rosewood, Stenciled, Bronze Mount, c.1820, 30 x 38 In. 2530.00
able, Center, Oak, Turned Legs, Shelf Stretcher, c.1900, 27 x 20 x 20 In. 45.00
able, Center, Oak, Reeded Edge, Turned, Tapered, Bulbous Base, Splayed Legs, 30 x 52 In. 1560.00
able, Center, Oval Flower Medallion, Line, Geometric Medallions, 18 x 46 x 33 In. 826.00
able, Center, Pedestal Base, Square Top, Banded Inlay Top, c.1830, 28 x 36 In. 300.00
able, Center, Polychrome, Painted Flowers, Glass Top, Mid 20th Century, 20 x 29 In. 35.00
able, Center, Polychrome Japanned, Parcel Gilt, Bird, Butterflies, Tree, England, 31 x 36 In. 5312.00
able, Center, Regency Style, Mahogany, Satinwood, Reeded, Splayed Legs, 29 x 60 In. 1920.00
able, Center, Renaissance, Walnut, Marble Top, Carved Skirt, Bulbous Legs, 28 x 40 In. 1705.00
able, Center, Renaissance Revival, Walnut, Marble Top, 28 x 33 In. 472.00
able, Center, Renaissance Revival, Rosewood, Marquetry, Victorian 6900.00
able, Center, Rococo, Carved Rosewood, Marble Top, 19th Century, 29 x 40 x 29 In. 1763.00
able, Center, Rococo Revival, Rosewood, Marble Top, Tortoise Form, 30 x 43 x 32 In. 1680.00
able, Center, Rococo Revival, Mahogany, Marble Top, Flower Carved, 30 x 31 x 41 In. 2280.00
able, Center, Rosewood, Marble Top, Carved Skirt, Cabriole Legs, c.1850, 31 x 41 In. 935.00
able, Center, Rosewood, Mahogany, Burl, Rosettes, Flowers, 30 x 26 x 27 In. 1116.00
able, Center, Scalloped Gilt Stenciled Top, Painted, Shoeing Of Bay Mare, 31 x 32 In. 4700.00
able, Center, Silvered Metal, Glass Top, Scrolled Base, Continental, 29 x 45 In. 3360.00
able, Center, Tilt Top, Oak, Burl Walnut, Inlaid Compass Star, Octagonal, 30 x 40 ½ In. 2700.00
able, Center, Tobey, Circular, Mahogany Top, Carved & Scrolled Cabriole Legs, 29 x 32 In. 590.00
able, Center, Victorian, Walnut, Drop Finials, Turned Legs, Scroll Feet, 19th Century, 29 x 24 In. 175.00
able, Center, Victorian, Mahogany, Cartouche Shape, Marble Top, Carved, 30 x 33 In. 288.00
able, Center, Victorian, Mahogany, Acanthus Carved, Round, Gadrooned Edge, 29 x 40 In. 660.00
able, Center, Victorian, Walnut, Inlay, Carved, Serpentine Top, 30 x 32 x 31 ½ In. 823.00
able, Center, Walnut Marquetry, Shaped Top, Medallion, Goats, 29 x 20 x 27 In. 1410.00
able, Chalet, G. Stickley, Chestnut, c.1900 6900.00
able, Charles II, Oak, Drawer, Turned Legs, Box Stretcher, Late 1600s, 29 x 41 In. 2415.00
able, Chart, William IV, Mahogany, Leather Top, Paneled Frieze, c.1835, 31 x 105 In. 5288.00
able, Chinese, Altar, Red, Black Lacquer, 2 Drawers, Carved Ducks, Buddhist Symbols, 37 x 70 In. 805.00
able, Chinese, Altar, Wood, 3-Board Top, Upturned Ends, Fretwork Apron, 37 x 101 x 16 In. 1728.00
able, Chinese, Altar, Provincial, Painted, Inset Panel, Iron Ring Handles, 34 x 64 In. 1920.00
able, Chinese, Demilune, Ju Mu Wood, 19th Century, 35 x 63 x 21 In., Pair 2880.00
able, Chinese, Elm, Square Top, Green Stone Inset, Circular Legs, 22 x 32 In. 826.00
able, Chinese, Elm, Lacquer, Rectangular Top, Drawer, Shell, 36 x 18 In., Pair 1426.00
able, Chinese, Elm Root, Intertwined, Barrel Shape 59.00
able, Chinese, Marble Top, Carved Apron, Legs, Bamboo, Claw Feet, 24 x 14 In. 196.00
able, Chinese, Red Lacquer, Painted Panels, Boats On Lake, Scrolling Lotus, 32 x 49 In. 575.00
able, Chinese, Rosewood, Soapstone Scene, Octagonal, Tilt Top, Cabriole Legs, 27 x 23 In. 392.00
able, Chinese, Rosewood, Open Skirt, Square Legs, Carved Feet, 13 x 35 In. 1175.00
able, Chinese, Rosewood, Shaped Skirt, Rectangular Legs, 33 x 53 x 32 ½ In. 2478.00
able, Chinese, Wood, Marble Inset, Painted, Horse Hoof Feet, 19 ¾ x 35 ½ In. 570.00
able, Chippendale, Mahogany, Swing Leg, 44 x 20 x 28 In. 450.00
able, Chippendale Style, Mahogany, Cabriole Legs, Council Craftsman, 24 x 24 x 26 In. 201.00
able, Chrome Plate, Walnut, Glass, W. Platner, c.1966, 19 x 26 In. 1920.00
able, Coaching, Charles II, Oak, Cleated Square Tilt Top, 28 ¼ x 28 ½ In. 7200.00
able, Coffee, 1-Piece Aluminum Propeller Base, Round Glass Top, Hesterberg, 43 x 18 In. 3120.00
able, Coffee, 2-Piece Frame, Teak Supports, Elliptical Glass, 59 x 19 ½ x 16 In. 1020.00
able, Coffee, 4 Horn Shaped Legs, Square Base, Round Beveled Glass Top, 36 x 16 In. 420.00
able, Coffee, Art Deco, Mirrored, Wood, c.1930, 33 ¼ x 16 x 26 ⅛ In. 646.00
able, Coffee, Brass, Directoire, Inset Mirrored Glass, Stretchers, 21 x 38 In. 1920.00
able, Coffee, Cherry Frame, Wood Starburst, Inset Glass Top, Frosted, 60 x 26 ½ x 14 ½ In. 420.00
able, Coffee, Chinese, Elm Root, Intertwined, Pierced All Around Apron, 19 x 40 In. 59.00
able, Coffee, Ebonized Wood, Lobed Square Top, Bamboo Turned Legs, 17 ½ In. 4360.00
able, Coffee, Eero Saarinen, Rosewood, Oval, c.1956, 15 x 36 x 55 ½ In. 1800.00
able, Coffee, F. Henningsen, Oak, Trestle, Basket-Like Holder Under Top, c.1953, 21 x 47 In. 2500.00
able, Coffee, Free-Form, Open Top, Linked Sides, Chris Lauterbach, c.1960, 15 x 63 In. 11400.00
able, Coffee, Fruitwood, Bone Inlay, Medallion, Vine Borders, North Africa, 24 x 24 In. 1440.00

Furniture, Table, Console, Baroque Style, Walnut Inlay, Drawer, Italy, 19th Century, 30 x 34 x 15 In. $1900.00

Furniture, Table, Console, McCobb, Bleached Mahogany, Drawers, Brass Frame, 30 x 48 x 19 In. $1200.00

Table Measures

When buying a dining room table, remember you need at least 24 inches for each person. It is better to allow 30 inches. So a 10-foot-long table could seat four on the side comfortably, five if you don't mind close quarters. You need an extra foot at the ends to seat an extra person there. Watch out for the apron or top. Antique tables were 27 to 28 inches from the floor. Today the table is 29 to 30 inches tall. Try sitting on a dining room chair with your legs under the table before you buy.

Furniture, Table, Console, Provincial, Branch & Carved Leaf, Apron, Painted, 32 x 62 x 14 In.
$7250.00

Furniture, Table, Dining, Drop Leaf, Duncan Phyfe, Mahogany, Hairy Paw Feet, 29 x 39 x 24 In.
$9400.00

Furniture, Table, Dining, Drop Leaf, Federal, D-Shape Top, Reeded Legs, c.1890, 29 x 41 x 42 In., 2 Piece
$1475.00

Furniture, Table, Dining, Limbert, No. 409, Flared Column, Signed, 31 x 54 In.
$2620.00

Table, Coffee, G. Nakashima, Walnut, c.1950, 13¼ x 59 x 51¼ In. 20400.0
Table, Coffee, G. Nelson, Laminate, Steel Frame, 48 x 17 x 16 In. 180.0
Table, Coffee, G. Nelson, White Laminate, Birch Trim, 1950, 40 x 15½ In. 480.0
Table, Coffee, Glass Top, Wood Plant Stand Base, Whitewash, 27½ x 43 In. 1560.0
Table, Coffee, Glass Top, Cast Bronze Base, Wishbone Shape, Silas Seandel, 16 x 41 In. 4200.0
Table, Coffee, H. Probber, Travertine Top, Mahogany Legs, 42 x 18 x 15 In. 960.0
Table, Coffee, I. Noguchi, Birch Base, Green Glass, Herman Miller, 1950s, 50 x 36 In. 2640.0
Table, Coffee, LaVerne, Brass, Pewter Inlay, Multicolored Chinoiserie Top, 17 x 60 x 50 In. . . . 8625.0
Table, Coffee, Louis XVI Style, Gilt Metal, Glass, Brass Frame, Tubular Supports, 17 x 46 In. . . 2040.0
Table, Coffee, Mahogany Base, Round Glass Top, Half Barrel, 26½ x 17¼ In. 1080.0
Table, Coffee, Mid Century Modern, Rosewood, Tapered Legs, Denmark, 20 x 61 In. 600.0
Table, Coffee, Oak Legs, Round Glass Top, 16 x 41 In. 7200.0
Table, Coffee, Ox Art, Teak, Tile, 57 In. 300.0
Table, Coffee, P. Evans, Steel, Plate Glass, 17 x 48 x 24 In. 7200.0
Table, Coffee, Painted Checkerboard, 19th Century, 20 x 35 x 20 In. 302.0
Table, Coffee, Patinated Welded Pipe Base, Plate Glass, 16 x 42 x 42 In. 3600.0
Table, Coffee, Paul Laszlo, Teak, Inlaid Capis Shell Top, 2 Base Legs, c.1954, 14 x 46 x 27 In. . 21600.0
Table, Coffee, Redwood, Square Brass Legs, Free-Form Redwood Slab, 51 x 43 x 15 In. 960.0
Table, Coffee, Robsjohn-Gibbings, Biomorphic Wood Top, 3 Tapered Legs, 71 x 42 x 21 In. . . . 1080.0
Table, Coffee, Rosewood, Tray Style Top, Handles, 17 x 59 x 23 In. 3000.0
Table, Coffee, Round, Lazy Susan, Old Hickory, Marked, 48 x 16 In. 180.0
Table, Coffee, Round, Italian Marble Top, Nickel Plated Wire Base, 38 x 15½ In. 780.0
Table, Coffee, Square Glass Top, Chromed Steel Legs, Zanuso, 35½ x 35½ x 15½ In. 1320.0
Table, Coffee, V. Kagan, Mahogany, 15 x 60 x 21½ In. 1920.0
Table, Coffee, Walnut, Plank Legs, John Kael, Label, 16 x 67 x 24 In. 900.0
Table, Coffee, Walnut, Tray Top, Man On Horse, Dogs, Hunting Scene, 31 x 23 In. 1210.0
Table, Coffee, Walnut, Painted, Gilt Chiseled Glass, Fontana Arte, 15 x 50 x 20 In. 10800.0
Table, Coffee, White Marble, Black Wood Base, 4 Splayed Legs, 60 x 28½ x 15 In. 450.0
Table, Coffee, Wormley, Walnut, 4-Board Top, Drawer, Bentwood Legs, 11½ x 84 x 19¼ In. . . 1440.0
Table, Coffee, Wormley, Glass, Rosewood, Brass, c.1960, 16½ x 57 In. 10200.0
Table, Cone, V. Panton, Round, Laminate Top, Metal Cone, 3-Point Base, Black, 32 x 16 In. . . 390.0
Table, Conservatory, Victorian, Cast Iron, Marble Top, Vase-Form Splat, 30 x 40 x 20 In. 1200.0
Table, Conservatory, Victorian, Cast Iron, Marble Top, 30¼ x 27½ x 18¾ In. 2880.0
Table, Console, Art Nouveau Style, Mahogany, Carved, Figural Legs, Tauber Brothers, 24 x 12 In. . 288.0
Table, Console, Baroque Style, Walnut Inlay, Drawer, Italy, 19th Century, 30 x 34 x 15 In. *illus* 1900.0
Table, Console, Baroque Style, Marble Top, Carved, Gilt, Satyr Mask, 35 x 46½ x 22 In. 2056.0
Table, Console, Continental, Drawer, Marble, Carved Fruit & Flowers, Paw Feet, 37 x 63 x 20 In. 4182.0
Table, Console, Empire, Black Marble Top, Frieze Drawer, Turned Legs, Low Shelf, 31 x 39 In. 2450.0
Table, Console, Faux Marble, Carved, Molded Top, Drawers, Paneled Doors, 36 x 40 In. 1293.0
Table, Console, Federal, Chestnut, Serpentine Top, Beaded Legs, Tapered, c.1800, 30 x 34 x 18 In. . 353.0
Table, Console, George III Style, Painted, Marble Top, Carved, Fluted Panels, 34 x 42 In., Pair 3600.0
Table, Console, George III Style, Gilt, Carved, D-Shape, Marble Top, 33 x 36 x 16 In. 3738.0
Table, Console, Georgian Style, Burl Walnut, Japanned, Openwork Frieze, 32 x 48 In. 1645.0
Table, Console, Italian Rococo, Gilt, Variegated Gray, Ivory, Rose Marble Top, 1800s, 34 x 35 In. 2300.0
Table, Console, Louis Philippe, Mahogany, Early 19th Century, 36½ x 59 x 20 In. 6110.0
Table, Console, Louis XV, Layered Gilt, Rococo Scrolls, Faux Marble Top, 1700s 3900.0
Table, Console, Louis XV, Painted, Shaped Marble Top, Pierced Frieze, Garlands, 1700s, 34 x 53 In. 8800.0
Table, Console, Louis XV Style, Gilt, Marble Top, Scrolled Leaves, 39 x 34 x 19 In. 2520.0
Table, Console, Louis XV Style, Gilt, Marble Top, Frieze Pierced, Acanthus Scrolls, 33 x 47 In. . 6900.0
Table, Console, Louis XVI, Gilt, Marble, Mask Carving, Mid 1800s, 36 x 51 In. 18600.0
Table, Console, Mahogany, Black Marble Top, Frieze Drawer, Gilt Bronze Mount, 36 x 37 x 17 In. . 2938.0
Table, Console, Marble Top, Quartersawn, 38 x 32 In. 330.0
Table, Console, McCobb, Bleached Mahogany, Drawers, Brass Frame, 30 x 48 x 19 In. . . *illus* 1200.0
Table, Console, Multicolored Paint, Deep Drawer, Italy30½ x 50 x 22½ In. 2703.0
Table, Console, Neoclassical, Painted, Parcel Gilt, Marble Top, Italy, 1800s, 39 x 59 In. 3186.0
Table, Console, Neoclassical Style, Faux Marble Top, Blue & Gilt Decorated Skirt, Base, 29 x 26 In. 546.0
Table, Console, Oak, Carved Front Legs, Turned Knuckle, 29 x 43 x 17 In. 140.0
Table, Console, P. Evans, Wall, Patchwork Squares, Olive Burl Veneer, 42 x 12 x 8 In. 960.0
Table, Console, Polished Steel, Woven Cane Top, Glass Cover, 28 x 60 x 19 In. 1200.0
Table, Console, Portuguese Rococo, Mahogany, Marble Top, Acanthus Frieze, 53 x 24 In. 5287.0
Table, Console, Provincial, Branch & Carved Leaf, Apron, Painted, 32 x 62 x 14 In. . . . . *illus* 7250.0
Table, Console, Regency, Gilt, Carved, 32 x 22 In., Pair 2540.0
Table, Console, Regency, Polychrome, Marble Top, Annulated Frieze, Gilt Carving, 36 x 70 In. 4800.0
Table, Console, Regency Style, Mahogany, Gilt, Yellow Faux Marble Top, Stretcher, 28 x 36 In. 540.0
Table, Console, Regency Style, Gilt, Marble Top, 28 x 31 x 11½ In., Pair 3600.0
Table, Console, Renaissance Revival, Walnut, Gilt Bronze, Marble Top, Stretchers, 35 x 42 In., Pair 881.0

Table, Console, Restauration, Mahogany, Marble Top, Blind Drawer, c.1840, 33 ½ x 38 x 19 In. 1765.00
Table, Console, Restauration, Rosewood, Marble Top, Cushion Frieze, Turreted Feet, 34 x 28 In. 1800.00
Table, Console, Rococo, Marble Top, Drawer, Green Flowers, 36 ½ x 49 ½ x 22 ½ In. 1880.00
Table, Console, Tiger Maple, 2 Drawers, Eldred Wheeler, 30 x 45 x 16 ¾ In. 632.00
Table, Contemporary, Burl Redwood, 16 x 84 In. 1320.00
Table, Continental, 2-Board Top, Drawers, Frieze, Iron Cross Support, c.1740, 31 x 67 x 29 In. 5750.00
Table, Continental, Fruitwood, Moorish Style, Scalloped Square Top, Ebonized, 27 x 16 In. .. 360.00
Table, Continental, Marble, Iron, Splatter Paint, 35 x 26 x 26 In. 515.00
Table, Continental Provincial, Walnut, Rectangular, Shaped Top, Scalloped Apron, 24 x 38 In. . 1800.00
Table, Country, Pine, Demilune, Blue Over Mustard, Triangular Apron, 3 Legs, 36 x 18 In. ... 748.00
Table, Country, Pine, Turned Mahogany Legs, 29 x 60 x 47 In. 805.00
Table, Cubist, Lacquered Wood, Multicolored, Schroeder, G. Rietveld, 19 ¾ x 20 x 24 In. 660.00
Table, Cypress, Square Legs, Pegged, Mortised, 30 x 62 x 44 In. 2644.00
Table, Danish Modern, Rosewood, Tapered Legs, Mid 20th Century, 17 ½ x 19 ½ In., Pair 1320.00
Table, Demilune, Cherry, Molded Legs, Carved Corner Brackets, Kentucky, 1800s, 29 x 48 In. . 2300.00
Table, Demilune, Pine, Chestnut, Square Legs, Stretchers, Red Wash, 28 ½ x 37 In. 431.00
Table, Dinette, Eero Saarinen, Round, White Laminate Top, Metal Base, 42 x 28 ½ In. 510.00
Table, Dinette, W. McArthur, Lacquered Wood Top, Aluminum Frame, 36 x 36 x 29 ¼ In. 480.00
Table, Dining, Art Deco, Walnut, Pedestals, Platform Stretcher, Fluted Scroll Legs, 1930, 29 x 67 x 46 In. . 900.00
Table, Dining, Art Deco, Teak, Rectangular Banded Top, Slab Legs, 31 x 83 In. 1020.00
Table, Dining, Arts & Crafts, Trestle, Shoefoot, Upended Stretcher, 29 ½ x 96 x 36 In. 5700.00
Table, Dining, Baroque Style, Walnut, Guilloche-Carved Frieze, Flemish, 25 x 60 In. 944.00
Table, Dining, Burnished Metal, Square Legs, 31 x 60 In. 3744.00
Table, Dining, Chippendale, Satinwood, Salesman's Sample, 3 Pedestals, 6 Chairs, c.1920 ... 6613.00
Table, Dining, Chippendale Style, Walnut, 3 Leaves, Flower Heads, 30 x 44 x 140 In. 881.00
Table, Dining, Chippendale Style, Mahogany, Round Top, Carved Urn Pedestal, 30 x 84 In. .. 5520.00
Table, Dining, Danish, Teak Top, Oak Legs, 2 Leaves, 60 x 39 ½ x 28 ¾ In. 1680.00
Table, Dining, Drop Leaf, Hepplewhite, Mahogany, Hinged Leaves, 2 Gatelegs, 29 x 17 In. 230.00
Table, Dining, Drop Leaf, Walnut, Turned Leg, Casters, 19th Century, 30 x 40 In. 590.00
Table, Dining, Drop Leaf, Hepplewhite, Mahogany, Swing Leg, c.1920, 30 x 42 In. 700.00
Table, Dining, Drop Leaf, Gateleg, Birch, Swing Legs, c.1950, 40 x 18 ½ x 30 In. 720.00
Table, Dining, Drop Leaf, Chippendale, Mahogany, Claw & Ball Feet, Swing Legs, 29 x 48 x 40 In. 920.00
Table, Dining, Drop Leaf, Duncan Phyfe, Mahogany, Hairy Paw Feet, 29 x 39 x 24 In. .. *illus* 9400.00
Table, Dining, Drop Leaf, Federal, D-Shape Top, Reeded Legs, c.1890, 29 x 41 x 42 In., 2 Piece *illus* 1475.00
Table, Dining, Drop Leaf, Mahogany, Spiral Legs, c.1830, 29 x 47 x 60 In. 3120.00
Table, Dining, Drop Leaf, Sheraton, Mahogany, 2 Sections, D-Shape Ends, 29 x 45 x 86 In. .. 3450.00
Table, Dining, Drop Leaf, Louis Philippe, Fruitwood, 1800s, 39 x 52 In. 3600.00
Table, Dining, Federal, Mahogany, Carved, Thomas Seymour, c.1812, 29 x 46 In. 11163.00
Table, Dining, Federal, Figured Maple, Inlay, 3 Sections, c.1800, 28 x 48 In. 12000.00
Table, Dining, Florence Knoll, Walnut Top, 2 Leaves, 66 x 46 x 29 In. 1440.00
Table, Dining, G. Nelson, Lazy Susan, Round, Plywood, White, Steel, 4-Point Base, 47 ¾ x 29 In.. 390.00
Table, Dining, G. Stickley, Circular Top, 2 Leaves, 29 x 54 In. 1140.00
Table, Dining, G. Stickley, Circular Top, Corbel Supports, No Leaves, 48 x 30 In. 1440.00
Table, Dining, G. Stickley, Circular Top, 5 Legs, Cross Stretcher Base, 54 x 30 In. 2400.00
Table, Dining, G. Stickley, 5 Legs, 6 Leaves, 30 x 54 In. 2640.00
Table, Dining, G. Stickley, Circular Top, 5 Legs, 3 Leaves, 1902, 31 x 48 In. 2760.00
Table, Dining, George III, Mahogany, 2 Pedestals, Reeded Edge, Leaves, 101 x 50 In. 4700.00
Table, Dining, George III, Mahogany, 2 Pedestals, 2 Leaves, 29 ½ x 115 In. 7500.00
Table, Dining, George III, Mahogany, 3 Pedestals, 2 Leaves, c.1770, 191 In. 46800.00
Table, Dining, George III Style, Blond Wood Banding, Pedestals, Baluster Standard, 30 x 48 In. 2880.00
Table, Dining, George III Style, Mahogany, 3 Pedestals, Splayed Legs, 31 x 54 x 126 In. 5040.00
Table, Dining, George III Style, Mahogany, 2 Pedestals, 3 Splayed Legs, Casters, 31 x 48 In. .. 5760.00
Table, Dining, George III Style, Mahogany, Reeded Edge, 3 Pedestals, 2 Leaves, 31 x 54 In. ... 9000.00
Table, Dining, George IV, Mahogany, 2 Leaves, c.1820, 27 x 108 In. 31000.00
Table, Dining, Georgian Style, Double Pedestal, Crossbanded Mahogany Top, 29 x 46 In. 354.00
Table, Dining, Kaare Klint, Mahogany, Extension, R. Rasmussen, 1930s, 54 x 36 In. 4000.00
Table, Dining, Lifetime, Circular Top, Octagonal Pedestal, 1 Leaf, 48 x 28 ½ In. 600.00
Table, Dining, Limbert, Arts & Crafts, Oak, Round, Pedestal Base, 1910, 28 In. 1050.00
Table, Dining, Limbert, No. 409, Flared Column, Signed, 31 x 54 In. .... *illus* 2620.00
Table, Dining, Limbert, Circular Top, Splayed Leg Base, 2 Leaves, 48 x 30 In. 5700.00
Table, Dining, Louis XV Style, Fruitwood, Draw Ends, Scalloped Frieze, 30 x 42 x 60 In. 2640.00
Table, Dining, Louis XVI Style, Mahogany, Oval, Ormolu Banded Frieze, 30 x 45 In. 6600.00
Table, Dining, Mahogany, Duncan Phyfe Style Pedestals, c.1930, 29 ½ x 42 x 62 In. 330.00
Table, Dining, Padouk, Circular, Husks, Beading, Tripod, Leaf Spray, 30 x 76 In. 5875.00
Table, Dining, Regency, Mahogany, 2 Pedestals, 29 ½ x 45 ½ x 47 In. 1888.00
Table, Dining, Regency, 2 Pedestals, Reeded Edge, Extension Leaves, c.1875, 29 x 49 In. 10800.00

Furniture, Table, Dining, Vico Magistretti, Tessera-Mezza-Tessera, Plastic, Artemide, Italy, 28 x 46 In.
$935.00

Furniture, Table, Drafting, Georgian, Mahogany, Adjustable, Brass Casters, c.1790, 32 x 34 x 21 In.
$1570.00

Furniture, Table, Drafting, Wood, Steel, Enamel, Adjustable, Friso Kramer, Dutch, 29 x 41 x 32 In.
$2100.00

Furniture, Table, Dressing, Queen Anne, Walnut, Drawers, c.1750, 28 x 33 x 19 In.
$900.00

Furniture, Table, Drop Leaf, Drawer, Dovetailed, 29 x 44 x 30 In.
$715.00

Furniture, Table, Drop Leaf, L. & J.G. Stickley, Shoefoot Base, No. 509, 24 x 24 x 24 In.
$2600.00

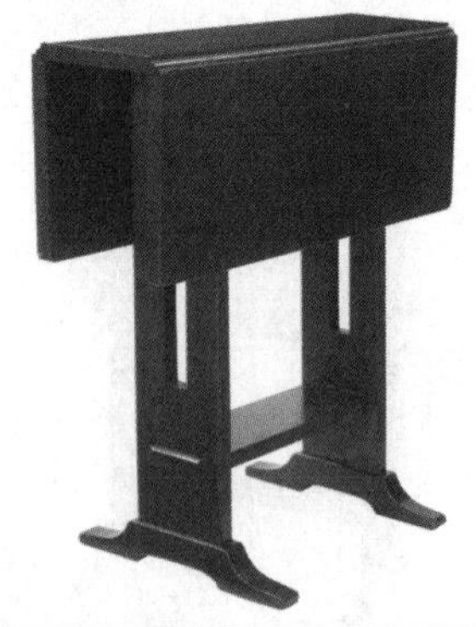

Furniture, Table, Drop Leaf, Mahogany, Brass & Bone Vine Inlay, 19th Century, 29 x 24 x 41 In.
$1690.00

Furniture, Table, Drop Leaf, Queen Anne, Mahogany, Pad Feet, Britain, 1700s, 28 x 16 x 40 In.
$1600.00

Table, Dining, Regency Style, Mahogany, Fruitwood, Circular Top, 2 Leaves, Pedestal, 30 x 60 In. . 3360.00
Table, Dining, Rococo, Walnut, Carved, Extension, Scalloped Top, Turned Pedestal, 30 x 43 In. 960.00
Table, Dining, Rococo Style, Painted, Cabriole Legs, Scroll Feet, Frieze, Legs, Gilt, 31 x 81 In.. 4140.00
Table, Dining, Spanish Style, Mahogany, Extension, Provincial, Scrolling Supports, 31 x 142 In. 5760.00
Table, Dining, Stickley Bros., Round Top, 5 Legs, Cross Stretchers, 30 x 54 In. 2280.00
Table, Dining, Textured, Stapled, Steel, Lacquered Patchwork, 30 x 72 x 40 In. 2520.00
Table, Dining, Vico Magistretti, Tessera-Mezza-Tessera, Plastic, Artemide, Italy, 28 x 46 In. *illus* 935.00
Table, Dining, Walnut, Wrought Iron Trestle, Scrolls, 17th Century, 30 x 79 x 42 In. 472.00
Table, Dining, Walnut, Shaped Turtle 2-Board Top, Scalloped Apron, 1800s, 31 x 45 In. 489.00
Table, Dining, Wegner, Teak, Leaves, 27 ½ x 55 x 43 In. 1440.00
Table, Dining, Wegner, Oak Base Supports, Teak Top, 2 Leaves, 63 x 39 ½ x 28 ¼ In. 1800.00
Table, Dining, William & Mary, Maple, Gateleg, Ring Turned Legs, c.1750, 29 x 56 In. 16450.00
Table, Dining, William IV, Mahogany, 2 Leaves, Carved, Reeded Legs, Turned Feet, 29 x 49 In. 575.00
Table, Dining, William IV, Mahogany, 2 Pedestals, Bulbous Standard, Splayed Legs, 29 x 52 In. . 5040.00
Table, Directoire, Mahogany, Brass, Inset Leather Surface, Frieze Drawer, Lower Shelf, 23 x 16 In.. 330.00
Table, Directoire Style, Brushed Metal, Gilt, Glass Top, X-Stretcher, 17 x 19 In., Pair 1440.00
Table, Drafting, Georgian, Mahogany, Adjustable, Brass Casters, c.1790, 32 x 34 x 21 In. *illus* 1570.00
Table, Drafting, Herman Miller, Mahogany, Steel, Adjustable Leaf, Trestle Legs, 48 x 20 In. . . . 2820.00
Table, Drafting, Mahogany, Trestle, Baluster Turned Stand, England, 33 x 35 x 20 In. 1473.00
Table, Drafting, Mahogany, Hinge, Drawer, Candle Slides, Millar & Beatty, Dublin, 29 x 35 x 35 In.. 3450.00
Table, Drafting, Wood, Steel, Enamel, Adjustable, Friso Kramer, Dutch, 29 x 41 x 32 In. . *illus* 2100.00
Table, Drawer, Embossed Leather Top, Faux Paint, Maitland-Smith, 1900s, 26 x 25 In. 403.00
Table, Drawing, Mahogany, Lift Top, Baise Covered Surface, Writing Slide, c.1800, 36 x 42 In. 2415.00
Table, Dressing, Biedermeier, Maple, Hinged Top, Scrolled Trestle, 31 x 29 x 19 In. 353.00
Table, Dressing, Chippendale, Mahogany, Fluted Columns, Carved Legs, 29 x 21 In. 9200.00
Table, Dressing, Chippendale, Walnut, 3 Drawers, Claw & Ball Feet, c.1800, 30 x 37 In. 38400.00
Table, Dressing, Chippendale Revival, Mahogany, Dolphin Carved Mirror Supports, 66 x 48 In. 440.00
Table, Dressing, Chippendale Style, Hinged Top, Drawers, 31 x 36 x 21 ½ In. 384.00
Table, Dressing, Chippendale Style, Maple, 3 Short, 1 Long Drawer, Cabriole Legs, 31 In. 2151.00
Table, Dressing, Federal, Mahogany Veneer, Mirror, Boston, c.1817, 71 ½ x 38 In. 38400.00
Table, Dressing, French Empire, Mahogany, Ormolu, Arched Mirror, Drawers, 61 x 32 x 19 In. 6463.00
Table, Dressing, George III, Oak, Pine, 2 Drawers, Square Legs, c.1820, 28 x 30 In. 575.00
Table, Dressing, George III, Mahogany, Oak, Drawer, Shaped Skirt, England, 28 x 26 In. 863.00
Table, Dressing, George III Style, Mahogany, Mirror, Basket, Fluted, Bellflowers, 66 x 32 In. . . 960.00
Table, Dressing, Gothic, Rosewood, Marble Top, Caryatid Supports, Mallard, c.1850, 61 x 43 In. 3300.00
Table, Dressing, Grain Painted, Scrolled Backsplash, Turned Legs, c.1840, 34 x 32 In. 336.00
Table, Dressing, Mahogany, Mirror, Marble Topped Pedestals, 2 Doors, 70 ¾ x 49 x 14 In. 561.00
Table, Dressing, Mahogany, Mirror, Molded Frame, Columns, Drawers, 77 x 39 x 21 In. 1800.00
Table, Dressing, Napoleon III, Gilt Bamboo, Lacquer, Hinged Top, Mirror, 29 x 20 x 13 In. . . . 3784.00
Table, Dressing, Pine, Curly Maple Drawer, Scrolled Gallery, Tapered Legs, 32 x 27 x 14 In. . . 201.00
Table, Dressing, Pine, Drawer, Reverse Heart Apron, Pegged, Dovetailed, 29 x 33 x 17 In. 500.00
Table, Dressing, Pine, Yellow Paint, Decorated, 2 Graduated Drawers, Shaped Top, 39 x 36 In. 2645.00
Table, Dressing, Queen Anne, Cherry, 4 Drawers, Erastus Grant, c.1740, 30 x 32 In. 60000.00
Table, Dressing, Queen Anne, Cherry, Carved, C-Scroll Knees, c.1775, 31 x 36 In. 25000.00
Table, Dressing, Queen Anne, Cherry, Fan Carved Drawer, Mid 1700s, 31 x 36 In. 39000.00
Table, Dressing, Queen Anne, Cherry, Pine, Overhang Top, Drawers, c.1750, 32 x 30 In. 5720.00
Table, Dressing, Queen Anne, Walnut, Drawers, c.1750, 28 x 33 x 19 In. . . . . *illus* 900.00
Table, Dressing, Queen Anne, Walnut, 3 Cock-Beaded Drawers, Scalloped Apron, 33 x 28 ½ In. 1062.00
Table, Dressing, Queen Anne, Walnut, 4 Drawers, Cabriole Legs, Pad Feet, c.1780, 31 x 33 x 20 In.. 3900.00
Table, Dressing, Queen Anne, Walnut, Arched Apron, Cabriole Legs, 30 x 32 ¾ x 22 In. 9860.00
Table, Dressing, Queen Anne, Walnut, c.1760, 29 x 34 In. 48000.00
Table, Dressing, Queen Anne, Walnut, Shell Carved Knees, Trifid Feet, c.1750, 29 x 33 In. 19975.00
Table, Dressing, Rococo Revival, Mahogany, Shield Shape Mirror Frame, Carved Crest, 68 x 40 In. 3360.00
Table, Dressing, Victorian, Mahogany, Shaped Mirror, Scroll Supports, Drawers, 68 x 44 In. . . 588.00
Table, Dressing, William & Mary, Walnut, Overhanging Top, Arched Apron, 28 x 28 In. 17400.00
Table, Dressing, Yellow Paint, Flowers, Fruit, Shells, D-Shape Box On Top, Maine, 36 x 36 In. 3525.00
Table, Drop Leaf, Cherry, Turned Legs, Brass Bucket Casters, 28 x 42 x 22 ½ In. 460.00
Table, Drop Leaf, Cherry, Gateleg Leaf Support, Square, 29 x 47 ½ x 20 In. 840.00
Table, Drop Leaf, Chippendale, Walnut, Claw & Ball Carved Feet, 18th Century, 29 x 19 In. . . . 690.00
Table, Drop Leaf, Chippendale, Mahogany, Shaped Skirts, Cabriole Legs, 29 x 53 In. 748.00
Table, Drop Leaf, Chippendale, Mahogany, Oval, Swing Leg, Cabriole Legs, 28 x 38 x 18 In. . . 1320.00
Table, Drop Leaf, Chippendale, Mahogany, Oval Top, Cabriole Legs, 28 x 37 In. 1380.00
Table, Drop Leaf, Chippendale, Walnut, Pine, Double Swing Leg, 28 x 50 x 23 ½ In. 1624.00
Table, Drop Leaf, Chippendale, Cherry, Cut Corners, Square Legs, 27 x 16 In. 1840.00
Table, Drop Leaf, Chippendale, Figured Maple, Massachusetts, c.1790, 30 x 14 In. 2880.00
Table, Drop Leaf, Chippendale, Walnut, c.1770, 28 x 16 x 48 ½ In. 3900.00

Table, Drop Leaf, Chippendale, Figured Maple, c.1770, 28 ½ x 19 ½ x 49 ½ In.. 7800.00
Table, Drop Leaf, Chippendale, Mahogany, Claw & Ball Feet, c.1790, 29 x 19 In. 8400.00
Table, Drop Leaf, Chippendale, Mahogany, Cabriole Legs, c.1770, 29 x 45 In. 15600.00
Table, Drop Leaf, Colonial Revival, Walnut, Double Reeded Top, Stretchers, 28 x 27 In.. 206.00
Table, Drop Leaf, Country Sheraton, Bird, 1-Board Top, Red Paint 29 x 21 In. 200.00
Table, Drop Leaf, Drawer, Dovetailed, 29 x 44 x 30 In. *illus* 715.00
Table, Drop Leaf, Edwardian, Polychrome, Oval, Gesso, Gilt, Oriental Landscape, 24 x 29 In. 840.00
Table, Drop Leaf, Edwardian, Satinwood, Painted, Flowers, Leaves, 29 x 64 x 46 In.. 2115.00
Table, Drop Leaf, Edwardian, Satinwood, Painted, Drawers, 30 x 49 x 32 In. 2703.00
Table, Drop Leaf, Federal, Mahogany, Mahogany Veneer, Carved, Turned Pulls, c.1820, 29 x 21 In. 1528.00
Table, Drop Leaf, Federal, Pembroke, Mahogany, Maple, Pine, Shaped Leaves, c.1810, 30 x 21 In. 1840.00
Table, Drop Leaf, Federal, Mahogany, 28 ⅜ x 21 ¼ x 42 In. 3750.00
Table, Drop Leaf, G. Stickley, Round Top, Shoe Feet, 30 x 32 In. 1800.00
Table, Drop Leaf, Gateleg, George I, Mahogany, Oval Top, Cabriole Legs, 29 x 16 In. 826.00
Table, Drop Leaf, Gateleg, Corbel, 40 x 30 x 16 In.. 900.00
Table, Drop Leaf, Georgian, Chippendale, Demilune, Claw & Ball Feet, 22 x 48 x 18 In.. 3716.00
Table, Drop Leaf, Georgian Style, Mahogany, Carved, 2 Drawers, 30 x 48 In.. 940.00
Table, Drop Leaf, Hepplewhite, Curly Maple, Scrub Top, Red Finish, Tapered Legs, 28 x 36 x 32 In. 690.00
Table, Drop Leaf, Hepplewhite, Mahogany, Square Legs, 26 x 18 x 37 In.. 1430.00
Table, Drop Leaf, Hepplewhite Style, Burl, Oval Top, 20th Century, 29 x 23 In. 345.00
Table, Drop Leaf, Kittinger, Chippendale Style, Mahogany, Swing Leg, Oval, 28 x 34 In.. 360.00
Table, Drop Leaf, L. & J.G. Stickley, Gateleg, Circular Top, 30 x 41 ½ x 15 ¼ In. 1920.00
Table, Drop Leaf, L. & J.G. Stickley, Shoefoot Base, No. 509, 24 x 24 x 24 In. *illus* 2600.00
Table, Drop Leaf, Mahogany, Swing Leg, Tapered Molded Legs, Casters, 46 x 18 x 28 In. 193.00
Table, Drop Leaf, Mahogany, Reeded, Paw Form Casters, 28 ½ x 66 In. 575.00
Table, Drop Leaf, Mahogany, Inlay, Concave Base, Splayed Legs, Dutch, 30 x 49 In. 1440.00
Table, Drop Leaf, Mahogany, Brass & Bone Vine Inlay, 19th Century, 29 x 24 x 41 In. *illus* 1690.00
Table, Drop Leaf, Mahogany, Pine, Cabriole Legs, Claw & Ball Feet, 29 x 44 x 21 In. 1725.00
Table, Drop Leaf, Neoclassical, Mahogany, Frieze Drawer, Saber Legs, 30 x 44 In.. 1645.00
Table, Drop Leaf, Neoclassical, Mahogany, c.1820, 28 ¾ x 21 ¾ x 43 ¾ In. 24675.00
Table, Drop Leaf, New England, Cherry, Drawer, Turned Legs, 29 x 42 x 17 In. 190.00
Table, Drop Leaf, Oak, Molded Rim, Barley Twist Supports, 28 ½ x 12 x 24 In. 502.00
Table, Drop Leaf, Pine, Drawer, Turned Legs, c.1830, 28 ½ x 40 x 21 In.. 600.00
Table, Drop Leaf, Queen Anne, Mahogany, Pad Feet, Britain, 1700s, 28 x 16 x 40 In. *illus* 489.00
Table, Drop Leaf, Queen Anne, Mahogany, Pad Feet, Britain, c.1795, 27 x 11 x 22 In. *illus* 1600.00
Table, Drop Leaf, Queen Anne, Mahogany, Drawer, Carved Frieze, c.1760, 28 x 45 x 57 In. 575.00
Table, Drop Leaf, Queen Anne, Mahogany, Oval Top, Turned Legs, Pad Feet, 1700s, 27 x 39 In. 863.00
Table, Drop Leaf, Queen Anne, Mahogany, Oval Top, Turned Legs, Pad Feet, 1700s, 28 x 16 In. 489.00
Table, Drop Leaf, Queen Anne, Mahogany, Tapered Legs, Pad Feet, 1800s, 27 x 11 In. 1610.00
Table, Drop Leaf, Queen Anne, Maple, Arched Skirts, Cabriole Legs, Pad Feet, 27 x 43 In. 546.00
Table, Drop Leaf, Queen Anne, Walnut, Cylindrical Legs, 28 x 54 x 16 In. 580.00
Table, Drop Leaf, Queen Anne, Walnut, Oval, Scrolled Skirt, Delaware Valley, 28 x 53 In.. 978.00
Table, Drop Leaf, Queen Anne, Cherry, Pad Foot, 39 x 15 x 28 In.. 3738.00
Table, Drop Leaf, Queen Anne, Red Paint, Round, Cabriole Legs, Pad Feet, c.1760, 26 x 9 x 38 In. 8625.00
Table, Drop Leaf, Queen Anne, Walnut, New England, c.1760, 25 x 31 In. 11400.00
Table, Drop Leaf, Queen Anne Style, Mahogany, Round Top, Drop Leaves, 30 x 50 In. 1320.00
Table, Drop Leaf, Regency, Mahogany, Drawers, c.1820, 28 x 21 x 20 In. *illus* 425.00
Table, Drop Leaf, Regency, Pembroke, Inlaid Mahogany, Crossbanded, 29 x 43 In.. 940.00
Table, Drop Leaf, Regency, Pedestal Base, Sweeping Legs, Casters, Early 1800s, 29 x 43 In. 1120.00
Table, Drop Leaf, Regency, Mahogany, 2 Dovetailed Drawers, 28 ¼ x 37 x 24 In.. 2645.00
Table, Drop Leaf, Renaissance Style, Oak, Gateleg, Stretcher, 28 x 27 ½ In. 354.00
Table, Drop Leaf, Sheraton, Mahogany, Rope Turned Legs, 29 ½ x 48 x 18 ⅜ In. 100.00
Table, Drop Leaf, Sheraton, Mahogany, Spiral Carved Legs, 28 x 17 x 36 In. 230.00
Table, Drop Leaf, Sheraton, Reeded & Turned Legs, c.1830, 30 x 40 In. 303.00
Table, Drop Leaf, Sheraton, 2 Leaves, Gateleg, Ohio Valley, 31 x 43 In.. 374.00
Table, Drop Leaf, Sheraton, Cherry, Gateleg, Ball-Turned Legs, 29 x 42 x 62 In. 402.00
Table, Drop Leaf, Sheraton, Skirt Drawer, Turned Legs, Paint, Bennington Pull, 29 x 32 x 21 In. 467.00
Table, Drop Leaf, Sheraton, Mahogany, Drawer, 4 Spiral Turned Legs, c.1820, 29 x 42 x 45 In. 575.00
Table, Drop Leaf, Sheraton, Pembroke, Cherry, Drawer, New England, c.1820, 28 x 36 x 40 In. 633.00
Table, Drop Leaf, Sheraton, Cherry, D-Shape End, Reeded Legs, 29 x 46 In. 978.00
Table, Drop Leaf, Sheraton, Curly Maple, 8 Turned Legs, 2 Swing Legs, c.1840, 29 x 51 In. 1610.00
Table, Drop Leaf, Sheraton, Curly & Bird's-Eye Maple, 3 Drawers, Portsmouth, N.H., 18 x 28 In. 2300.00
Table, Drop Leaf, Stickley, Prairie School, Shoefoot Base, 24 ½ x 24 x 24 In. 2760.00
Table, Drop Leaf, Sunderland, Late Neoclassical, Mahogany, Center Support, Paw Feet, 32 x 36 In. 646.00
Table, Drop Leaf, V. Kagan, Rosewood, Formica, Plexiglas, 29 x 31 x 54 In.. 10800.00
Table, Drop Leaf, Walnut, D-Shape, Turned Legs, c.1750, 28 x 35 ¾ In. 345.00

Furniture, Table, Drop Leaf, Queen Anne, Mahogany, Pad Feet, Britain, c.1795, 27 x 11 x 22 In.
$489.00

Furniture, Table, Drop Leaf, Regency, Mahogany, Drawers, c.1820, 28 x 21 x 20 In.
$425.00

Furniture, Table, Drop Leaf, Walnut, Pad Feet, c.1750, 28 x 36 x 15 ½ In.
$360.00

Furniture, Table, Fornasetti, Sun, White Lacquer, Wood, Metal Legs, Milano, Italy, 21 ½ x 4 In.
$750.00

Furniture, Table, G. Stickley, 6-Sided, Leather, Tacks, No. 624, 30 x 48 In.
$15000.00

Furniture, Table, Game, Federal Style, Mahogany, Flip Top, Charak Furniture Co., 1931, 31 x 36 x 18 In.
$710.00

Furniture, Table, Game, Walnut, Inlay, Drawer, 19th Century, 30 x 19 In.
$325.00

Furniture, Table, George III Style, Mahogany, Brass, Casters, 29 x 52 x 182 In.
$5250.00

Table, Drop Leaf, Walnut, Pad Feet, c.1750, 28 x 36 x 15½ In. . . . *illus* 360.00
Table, Drop Leaf, Walnut, Gateleg, Oval Top, Box Stretcher, Carved Skirt, 28 x 46 x 54½ In. . . 1552.00
Table, Drop Leaf, Walnut, Oval Top, Square Legs, Brass Caps & Casters, 29 x 50 x 61 In. . . . 1762.00
Table, Drop Leaf, William & Mary, Maple, Butterfly, 27¾ x 14½ x 37½ In. . . . 3000.00
Table, Drop Leaf, William & Mary Style, Oak, D-Shape Leaves, Turned Legs, 29 x 45 x 48 In. . 705.00
Table, Drum, George III, Pine, Round Top, Frieze, 4 Drawers, Paneled Standard, 28 x 24 In. . 1680.00
Table, Drum, George III, Mahogany, Leather Inset, 12 Drawers, Inlaid Ivory, 29½ x 42 In. . . . 13200.00
Table, Drum, George III Style, Mahogany, Circular, Gilt Tooled Leather Insert, Drawers, 27 x 48 In. 5040.00
Table, Drum, Neoclassical, Mahogany, Carved, Figured, Phila., c.1830, 28 x 28 In. . . . 3000.00
Table, Duncan Phyfe, Mahogany, Turned Posts, Hairy Paws Feet, 29 x 39 In. . . . 9775.00
Table, Dutch Neoclassical, Bowed Top, Matchbook Veneer, Tambour Cupboards, 30 x 33 In. . . 2640.00
Table, Edwardian, French Chippendale Style, Mahogany, Parcel Gilt, Dish Top, 28 x 20 In. . . . 660.00
Table, Edwardian, Mahogany, George III Style, Bowed Top, Drawer, c.1900, 35 x 42 In. . . . 1200.00
Table, Edwardian, Mahogany, Flip Top, Drawer, Folding Mirror, 31 x 29 x 17 In. . . . 1469.00
Table, Egyptian Revival, Mahogany, Marble Top, 8 Columnar Legs, Sphinx-Form Feet, 34 x 33 In.. 5800.00
Table, Empire, Bronze Beaded Frame, Gray Marble Top, Shelf, 3 Ram's Head Legs, 27 x 29 In. 4320.00
Table, Empire, Burl, Leather, 3 Drawers, Egyptian Revival Style Mounts, 32 x 61 In. . . . 3220.00
Table, Empire, Cherry, Lift Top, 3 Compartments, Turned Legs, Peg Feet, 29 x 22 x 17 In. . . . 201.00
Table, Empire, Mahogany, Marble Top, Trestle Base, Inverted Lyre Supports, 29 x 43 In. . . . 940.00
Table, Empire, Ormolu Mounted, Marble Top, Circular Top, 29½ x 14¾ In., Pair . . . 4752.00
Table, Empire Revival, Mahogany, Marble Top, Petticoat, Scroll Ends, c.1880, 37 x 48 In. . . . 1540.00
Table, Empire Style, Bronze, 3 Shelves, Embossed Greek Key, 35¾ x 25 x 19 In. . . . 4320.00
Table, Empire Style, Mahogany, Brass Inlay, Frieze Drawer, Stretcher, 30 x 29 In., Pair . . . 2400.00
Table, Encyclopedia, G. Stickley, Square Top, 2 Shelves, 27 x 27 x 29 In. . . . 7200.00 to 10800.00
Table, English Oak, Fruitwood, 2 Drawers, Paneled Round Legs, Late 1800s, 30 x 54½ In. . . . 900.00
Table, Farm, Benchmade, Drawer On Side, 2 Leaves, 72 x 36 x 30 In. . . . 935.00
Table, Farm, Country, Scrubbed Top, Red Surface, Tapered Leg, 45 x 29 x 28¾ In.. . . . 523.00
Table, Farm, French Provincial, Fruitwood, Frieze, Pullout Slide, Drawer, 30 x 81 In. . . . 2880.00
Table, Farm, Pine, 3-Board Top, Turned Legs, Green Paint, 30½ x 92 In. . . . 2070.00
Table, Farm, Poplar, 2-Board Top, Turned Legs, Green Paint, Holmes County, 30 x 71 In. . . . 1495.00
Table, Farm, Provincial, Oak, 2 Drawers Tapered Square Legs, 30 x 36 In. . . . 840.00
Table, Farm, Provincial Louis XV Style, Oak, Scalloped Frieze, 31 x 96 x 40 In.. . . . 1140.00
Table, Faux Bamboo, Bird's-Eye Maple, Round Top, Turned Stem, X-Shape Base, 33 x 17 In. . 1645.00
Table, Federal, Mahogany, Pine, Demilune, Inlaid Banding, 29 x 48 In., Pair. . . . 1035.00
Table, Federal, Mahogany, Figured, c.1800, 29½ x 18 x 15¾ In.. . . . 3300.00
Table, Federal, Mahogany, Acanthus Carved Base, Feather Carved Feet, 12 Ft. . . . 12100.00
Table, Federal, Poplar, Drawer, Turned Legs, Glass Pulls, Tennessee, 1800s, 28 x 29 In. . . . 259.00
Table, Federal, Walnut, 2-Board Top, Scrolled Bracket Returns, Tapered Legs, 28 x 29 In. . . . 920.00
Table, Federal Style, Poplar, Painted, Tapered Splayed Legs, Dovetailed Drawer, 29 x 24 In. . . 259.00
Table, Fornasetti, Circular Top, Black & White Figures, Black Ground, 20¾ x 23¼ In. . . . 898.00
Table, Fornasetti, Sun, White Lacquer, Wood, Metal Legs, Milano, Italy, 21½ x 4 In. . . . *illus* 750.00
Table, Frank Lloyd Wright, Double V Base, 64 x 42 x 29 In.. . . . 3840.00
Table, Frank Lloyd Wright Design, Mahogany, Circular, Extension, X-Base, Copper Edge, 29 x 48 In. 1380.00
Table, French Provincial, Cherry, Pegged, Shaped Apron, Cabriole Legs, 30 x 32 In.. . . . 2115.00
Table, French Provincial, Walnut, Drawer, Square Legs, 30 x 71 x 32 In.. . . . 2040.00
Table, Fruitwood, Octagonal Top, Lyre Form Support, 29¾ x 17¼ In. . . . 924.00
Table, G. Nakashima, Rosewood, Bottom Shelf, 21¾ x 46 x 20¼ In. . . . 16800.00
Table, G. Nakashima, Triangular, Cherry Top, 3 Legs, 23 x 26½ x 21½ In. . . . 1440.00
Table, G. Nakashima, Triangular, 3 Legs, Walnut, c.1963, 20¾ x 26½ x 23 In. . . . 3300.00
Table, G. Nelson, Walnut & Leather, Drawer, Copper Planter, 19 x 30 In., Pair . . . 6600.00
Table, G. Stickley, 6-Sided, Leather, Tacks, No. 624, 30 x 48 In. . . . *illus* 15000.00
Table, G. Stickley, Circular Top, Lower Shelf, 29 x 24 In. . . . 2280.00
Table, G. Stickley, Cut Corner Top, Lower Shelf, Arched Stretchers, 24 x 24 x 29 In. . . . 2520.00
Table, G. Stickley, Hexagonal, 6 Legs, Leather Top With Tacks, 48 x 48 x 30 In.. . . . 15600.00
Table, G. Stickley, Round Top, Arched Stretchers, 24 x 30 In. . . . 1200.00
Table, Galle, 2 Tiers, Marquetry, c.1900, 29 x 29⅞ x 19¾ In. . . . 2880.00
Table, Galle, Organic Carvings, Exotic Leaf Marquetry, c.1900, 22 x 24 In. . . . 1760.00
Table, Galle, Scalloped Top, Lower Shelf, Wild Flowers, Butterflies, 28 x 34 x 24 In. . . . 5400.00
Table, Game, Anglo-Chinese, Inlaid, Huang Hua Li, Early 19th Century, 29 x 28½ In. . . . 16250.00
Table, Game, Chippendale, Mahogany, Drawer, Philadelphia, c.1780, 34¼ x 18 In. . . . 2233.00
Table, Game, Chippendale Style, Mahogany, Fret Skirt, Acanthus Carved Knees, 1930s . . . 460.00
Table, Game, Duncan Phyfe Style, Mahogany, Shaped Flip Top, Turned Support, 1800s . . . 1033.00
Table, Game, Empire, Parquetry, Brass Mounted, Flip Top, Inlay, Early 1800s, 30 x 30 In. . . . 1175.00
Table, Game, Empire, Mahogany, Early 19th Century, 30½ x 38 x 19 In., Pair . . . 1528.00
Table, Game, Federal, Mahogany, D-Form Flip Top, Flower Carved Pedestal, 28 x 36 x 18 In. . 590.00

Table, Game, Federal, Inlaid Mahogany, Cherry, Pine, Flip Top Top, False Drawer, 24 x 30 In. 978.00
Table, Game, Federal, Flip Top, Rose Twist Legs, Peg Feet, 30 x 35 x 18 In. 1041.00
Table, Game, Federal, Mahogany, Trefoil Top, Beaded, Reeded, Thimble Casters, 30 x 36 x 18 In. 1265.00
Table, Game, Federal, Mahogany, Late 18th Century, 30½ x 37¾ x 18½ In. 1763.00
Table, Game, Federal, Mahogany, Early 19th Century, 29 x 38 x 18½ In. 1998.00
Table, Game, Federal, Inlaid Mahogany, Reeded Legs, c.1800, 28¾ x 36 x 17 In. 2468.00
Table, Game, Federal, Bird's-Eye Maple, D-Shape, Convex Skirt, Turned Legs, Vermont, 29 x 36 In. 2820.00
Table, Game, Federal Style, Inlaid Mahogany, Flip Top, Medallion, 29 x 36 x 18 In. 575.00
Table, Game, Federal Style, Mahogany, Flip Top, Charak Furniture Co., 1931, 31 x 36 x 18 In. *illus* 710.00
Table, Game, Fruitwood, Marquetry, Mahogany, Jeux De Precision, c.1880, 31 x 75 In. 2703.00
Table, Game, George II, Mahogany, Flip Top, Leather Inset, c.1750, 28 x 34 In. 10625.00
Table, Game, George III, Mahogany, Demilune Top, Flip Top, Late 1700s, 29 x 36 In. 540.00
Table, Game, George III, Satinwood, Crossbanded Mahogany, Felt Lined, 29 x 24 In. 764.00
Table, Game, George III, Mahogany, Satinwood Top Panel, Square Legs, 29 x 40 x 16 In. 1057.00
Table, Game, George III, Mahogany, Inlaid Satinwood, c.1790, 30 x 36 x 18 In., Pair 6463.00
Table, Game, George III Style, Mahogany, Banded Demilune Top, Flip Top, 30 x 40 In. 1200.00
Table, Game, George III Style, Polychrome, Japonesque Style, Mythical Animals, 30 x 32 In. 4800.00
Table, Game, Hardwood, Geometric Inlay, Bone, Mother-Of-Pearl, Shaped Legs, N. Africa, 32 In. 780.00
Table, Game, Inlaid, Flip Top, Drawer, Gold Embossed Leather Surface, Early 19th Century, 35 In. 1800.00
Table, Game, Inset Specimen Top, Round, Slate, Incised Borders, 4 Reserves, 24½ x 29 In. 3105.00
Table, Game, Louis Philippe, Mahogany, Flip Top, Sliding Tapered Skirt, 29 x 33 In. 1293.00
Table, Game, Louis XVI Style, Satinwood, Inlaid Chessboard, Corner Wells, 29 x 34 In. 2400.00
Table, Game, Mahogany, Inlaid Leaves, Cherubs & Birds, Square Legs, Dutch, 31 x 32 In. 1200.00
Table, Game, Mahogany, Swivel Top, Reeded Edge, Carved Legs, c.1820, 29½ x 35 x 11¾ In. 1528.00
Table, Game, Maple, Mahogany, Inlaid Panels, Reeded Legs, c.1790 5500.00
Table, Game, Marquetry, Flower Inlay, 2 Removable Tops, Italy, 30 x 32 In. 324.00
Table, Game, Neoclassical, Mahogany, Scroll Feet, Casters, D-End Top, Boston, c.1830, 28 x 36 In. 360.00
Table, Game, Neoclassical, Mahogany, Flip Top, Veneered Frieze, Acanthus Pedestal, 30 x 36 In. 510.00
Table, Game, Neoclassical, Mahogany, Figured, Reeded Legs, c.1830, 29 x 38 In. 748.00
Table, Game, Neoclassical, Mahogany, Gilt Stenciled, c.1830, 29 x 36 x 18 In. 2880.00
Table, Game, Neoclassical, Mahogany, Carved, Figured, Philadelphia, c.1820, 29 x 36 In. 8750.00
Table, Game, Queen Anne, Burl, Candle Corners, Cabriole Legs, Britain, 28 x 33 x 31 In. 1790.00
Table, Game, Queen Anne, Mahogany, Demilune, Tapered Legs, Pad Feet, 27 x 27 x 13 In. 1800.00
Table, Game, Rococo, Rosewood, Carved, Serpentine Top, Leather Surface, 31½ x 34 x 17 In. 1645.00
Table, Game, Rococo, Victorian, Rosewood, Shell Carved Skirt, Knees, c.1870, 30 x 33 In. 2420.00
Table, Game, Rosewood, Flip Top, Volute Terminals, Scrollwork Legs, c.1850, 30 x 38 In. 1680.00
Table, Game, Vine Carved Frieze, Swinging Leg, 29 x 34½ x 15 In. 330.00
Table, Game, Walnut, Oak, Checkerboard Top, Geometric Inlay, Early 1900s, 29 x 26 In. 225.00
Table, Game, Walnut, Inlay, Drawer, 19th Century, 30 x 19 In. *illus* 325.00
Table, Game, Walnut, Checkerboard Top, Tapered Pedestal, Drawer, 30 x 19 In. 383.00
Table, Game, Walnut, Suede Top, 4 Pullout Glass Holders, Andre Arbus, 1940s, 29 x 30 In. 6250.00
Table, George II, Mahogany, Tripod, Circular Tilt Top, Scalloped Edge, Birdcage, 28 x 31 In. 5625.00
Table, George II, Mahogany, Gateleg, Oval Top, 2 Flaps, 27 x 50 In. 6000.00
Table, George II, Mahogany, Chippendale Style, Carved, c.1755, 32 x 66 In. 17500.00
Table, George III, Figured Mahogany, Inset Leather Top, Swivel, Folding, Drawer, 29 x 19 In. 690.00
Table, George III, Mahogany, Circular Top, Piecrust Edge, Tripod, Splayed Legs, 25 x 24 In. 1680.00
Table, George III, Satinwood, Figured Rosewood, Inlay, c.1815, 29 x 36 In. 7500.00
Table, George III Style, Mahogany, Brass, Casters, 29 x 52 x 182 In. *illus* 5250.00
Table, George III Style, Mahogany, Oval, 3 Pedestals, Casters, 30½ x 53½ x 105 In. 6840.00
Table, George III Style, Walnut, Fruitwood, Banded Drawers, Cabriole Legs, 30 x 39 In. 1920.00
Table, Georgian Style, Victorian, Mahogany, Vase-Form Splat, Splayed Legs, 28 x 45 x 36 In. 1440.00
Table, Gilt Brass Bamboo Frame, Mirrored Glass Top & Shelf, Maison Bagues, 25 x 19 In., Pair 7200.00
Table, Gueridon, Bronze, Steel, Dish Top, Salmon Paint, Scrolled Border, Baltic, 27 x 24 In. 5288.00
Table, Gueridon, Directoire, Gilt, Rouge Marble Top, 19th Century, 30 x 36 In. 2644.00
Table, Gueridon, Louis XVI, Gilt Bronze, Marble Top, 27½ x 20¼ In., Pair 5700.00
Table, Gueridon, Neoclassical, Gilt Bronze, Marble, 3 Legs, Casters, 29½ x 27½ In. 2115.00
Table, Gueridon, Neoclassical, Dore Bronze, Circular, Marble Top, 29 x 32 In., Pair 5581.00
Table, Gueridon, Neogrecque, Multicolored, Late 19th Century, 28 x 27 In. 7344.00
Table, Gueridon, Rococo, Painted, Wrought Iron, 30 x 36 x 30½ In., Pair 1528.00
Table, Hall, Chippendale Style, Mahogany, Drawer, Cabriole Legs, Claw Feet, 27 x 42 x 17 In. 502.00
Table, Hall, Georgian, Mahogany, Carved, Inlaid Corners, c.1800, 31 x 60 In. 1880.00
Table, Hall, Neoclassical, Bowfront, Mid 19th Century, 27½ x 43½ x 23 In. 823.00
Table, Hans Bellman, Birch, Folding Legs, Knoll, 1950s, 19½ x 24 In. *illus* 660.00
Table, Hardwood, Bone Inlay, Leafy Scrolls, Octagonal, Arched Friezes, N. Africa, 19 x 18 In. 1440.00
Table, Hardwood, Inlaid Star & Bands, Octagonal, Arched Friezes, North Africa, 20 x 20 x 20 In. 960.00

Gateleg Table
The gateleg table was a seventeenth-century form. Usually the more legs on a gateleg table, the more expensive the table.

Furniture, Table, Hans Bellman, Birch, Folding Legs, Knoll, 1950s, 19½ x 24 In.
$660.00

Furniture, Table, Library, Renaissance Revival, Oak, Drawer, Sypher & Co., c.1890, 31 x 45 x 28 In.
$1500.00

Furniture, Table, Mahogany, 12-Sided Skirt, Marble Top, Mid 19th Century, 30 x 36 In.
$1900.00

F

Furniture, Table, Mahogany, Pedestal, Drawer, Baltimore, 19th Century, 30 x 23½ x 44 in.
$750.00

Furniture, Table, Mahogany, Turned Legs, Mid 19th Century, 30 x 28 x 16 In.
$350.00

Furniture, Table, P. Evans, Chrome & Brass Patchwork, Cantilevered Form, Signed, 20 x 30 x 12 In.
$980.00

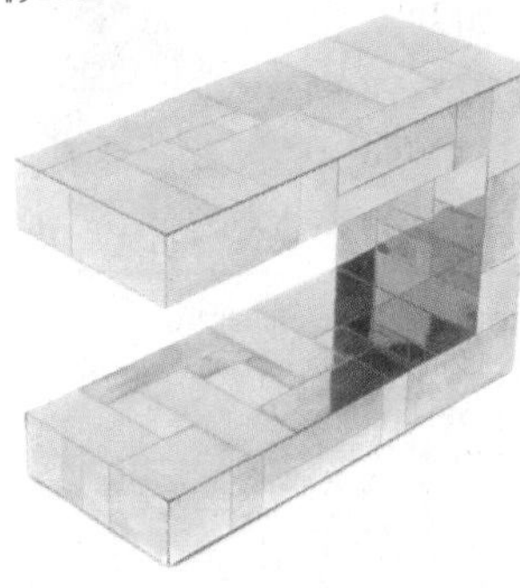

Furniture, Table, Pembroke, Federal, Walnut, Tapered Legs, 19th Century, 29 x 34 x 20 In.
$685.00

Table, Hardwood, Octagonal, Scrolling Leaf Brass Inlay, Arched Shape, North Africa, 25 x 24 In. 1080.00
Table, Harvest, Drop Leaf, Softwood, Drawer, Turnip Feet, 1700s, 28 x 53 In. 2535.00
Table, Harvest, Hepplewhite, Red Paint, Scrubbed Top, 72 x 24 x 29 In. 2300.00
Table, Harvest, Pine, Multiboard Top, Breadboard Ends, 19th Century, 30 x 84 x 33 In. 1320.00
Table, Harvest, Pine, Maple Drop Sides, Red Stain, Turned Legs, 72 In. 5712.00
Table, Harvest, Southern Yellow Pine, Drawer, Red Paint, 19th Century, 30 x 60 In. 748.00
Table, Hepplewhite, 2-Board Overhang Top, Drawer, Tapered Legs, Maine, c.1800, 28 x 36 x 25 In. 748.00
Table, Hepplewhite Style, Fan Inlay, Gallery Top, Maitland-Smith, 1900s, 29 x 24 In. 431.00
Table, Herman Miller, Mahogany, Race Track Top, Mirror Chromed, Pedestals, 28 x 72 x 42 In. 295.00
Table, Hunt, Gateleg Supports, George III, Mahogany, Oval Flip Top, 29 x 108 x 20 In. 10200.00
Table, Indian Teak, Planked, Pegged, Carved Floral Frieze, Leaf Carved Edge, 1800s, 23 x 69 In. 720.00
Table, Industrial Design, Galvanized Metal, Round Legs, c.1950, 29 x 43 In. 780.00
Table, Inlaid Hardwood, Octagonal Top, Banded, Bone Inlay, North Africa, 18 x 17 In. 360.00
Table, Iron, Glass, Knoll International, Round, c.1966, 24 In. 1260.00
Table, Italian, Walnut, Carved Skirt, Paw Feet, 31 x 47 x 22¾ In. 980.00
Table, Italian Baroque, Walnut, Carved, 2 Dovetailed Drawers, Wrought Iron, 29 x 37 In. 3105.00
Table, Italian Renaissance Style, Octagonal Top, Paneled Support, Scrollwork, 28 x 34 In. 1725.00
Table, Jacobean, Gateleg, Mahogany, Oval, 2 Drawers, Rope Trim, 29 x 41 x 21 In. 1673.00
Table, Jardiniere, Walnut, Carved, Painted, Figures, Leaves, Trestle Base, 33 x 36 x 15 In. 1880.00
Table, Jules Leleu, Mahogany Column, Tripod Base, Glass Top, Round, J. Leleu, c.1935, 21 x 20 In., Pair 5000.00
Table, Kitchen, Cypress, Rectangular Plank, Block Legs, Weathered, 30½ x 45 x 26 In. 660.00
Table, Lacquered Wood, John Dickinson, c.1975, 27¾ x 34 In. 12000.00
Table, Lamp, Art Deco, Hexagonal Top, Oak Center, Rosewood Inlay, Birch Edge 1440.00
Table, Lazy Susan, Pine, Round Top, Block Legs, X-Stretcher, 30⅝ x 46 In. 764.00
Table, Library, Arts & Crafts, Rectangular, Shelf, Tenon Construction, 44 x 26 x 32 In. 360.00
Table, Library, Arts & Crafts, 2 Vertical Slats On Sides, Lower Board Support, 36 x 24 x 28 In. 420.00
Table, Library, Drop Leaf, Figured Veneer, Mahogany, Oak, Band Inlaid Top, 28 x 22 In. 920.00
Table, Library, Empire, Mahogany, Black Marble Top, Shaped Trestle, Scrolls, 30 x 39 In. 2703.00
Table, Library, G. Stickley, Drawer, Iron Pull, 36 x 24 x 29 In. 600.00
Table, Library, G. Stickley, Oak, 2 Drawers, 20th Century, 30 x 54 x 32 In. 715.00
Table, Library, G. Stickley, 3 Vertical Slats On Sides, 42 x 28 x 30 In. 1020.00
Table, Library, G. Stickley, 2 Blind Drawers, Lower Shelf, 36 x 24 x 29½ In. 1200.00
Table, Library, G. Stickley, Rectangular Top, 2 Drawers, Shelf, 42 x 29½ x 29½ In. 1200.00
Table, Library, G. Stickley, Single Drawer, 29 x 36 x 24 In. 1680.00
Table, Library, G. Stickley, Oak, 2 Drawers, Lower Median Shelf, 29 x 48 x 30¼ In. 1795.00
Table, Library, G. Stickley, 2 Drawers, Wood Knobs, 36 x 24 x 30 In. 2400.00
Table, Library, G. Stickley, Drawer, Iron Hardware, 29 x 36 x 24 In. 2500.00
Table, Library, G. Stickley, Oak, 3 Drawers, c.1909, 29 x 53½ x 32 In. 3840.00
Table, Library, Heywood & Wakefield, Aesthetic Revival Style, Oak, Wicker, 29 x 37 In. 2040.00
Table, Library, Inlaid Mahogany, 5-Sided Top, Ormolu Mounts, Cabriole Legs, 29 x 29 In. 450.00
Table, Library, Jacobean Style, 2-Board Plank Top, Trestle Base, Early 1900s, 29 x 71 In. 502.00
Table, Library, Kittinger, Mahogany, Molded Edge Top, Square Legs, 2 Drawers, 30 X50 In. 489.00
Table, Library, L. & J.G. Stickley, Rectangular, Stretcher, Through Tenon, Shoefoot, 30 x 48 x 28 In. 890.00
Table, Library, Limbert, Drawers At End, 48 x 34 x 29½ In. 2760.00
Table, Library, Limbert, Turtle Top, Drawer, Slab Sides, 48 x 30 x 29 In. 4440.00
Table, Library, Mahogany, Molded Top, Flower Carved Frieze, Shell Form Medallion, 30 x 60 In. 708.00
Table, Library, Mahogany, Shaped Top, Claw & Ball Feet, England, 74 x 42 x 31 In. 2185.00
Table, Library, Regency Style, Mahogany, Inset Leather Top, Reeded Curule Legs, 30 x 66 In. 7800.00
Table, Library, Renaissance Revival, Carved Frieze, Drawer, Stretcher, Dolphin Feet, 31 x 45 In. 1495.00
Table, Library, Renaissance Revival, Oak, Drawer, Sypher & Co., c.1890, 31 x 45 x 28 In. *illus* 1500.00
Table, Library, Renaissance Revival, Walnut, Carved, Leather Top, Stretcher 3162.00
Table, Library, Rosewood, Gadrooned, Mid 19th Century, 30½ x 48 x 25½ In. 2880.00
Table, Library, Roycroft, Arrow Shape Stretchers, Carved, Orb Mark, 30¼ x 42 x 30 In. 1440.00
Table, Library, Walnut, Carved, Trestle Base, Continental, 32½ x 36 x 67¾ In. 660.00
Table, Library, Walnut, Inset Gilt Tooled Leather, Scrolling Sides, Stretcher, Paw Feet, 30 x 37 In. 2640.00
Table, Library, William IV, Mahogany, Tooled Leather Surface, Drawers, Casters, 30 x 60 In. 3063.00
Table, Library, William IV, Rosewood, Figured, 2 Drawers, Column Supports, Bun Feet, 29 x 49 In. 4320.00
Table, Library, William IV, Mahogany, Inset Leather Top, 3 Frieze Drawers, 30 x 78 In. 5875.00
Table, Limbert, Circular, Tapered Legs, Lower Cross Stretcher, 29 x 24⅛ In. 828.00
Table, Limbert, Mouse Hole, Rectangular, Double Key & Tenon, 42 x 30 x 29 In. 3600.00
Table, Limbert, Oak, Oval Top, Cutout Trestles, Lower Shelf, 45 In. 4100.00
Table, Limbert, Octagonal, Cutout Slab Legs, Key & Tenon, 30 x 30 x 30 In. 2640.00
Table, Limbert, Oval, Lower Shelf, Cutout On Sides, 29 x 45 x 30 In. 2400.00
Table, Limbert, Oval Top, Cutout Sides, Branded, 45 x 30 x 29 In. 3360.00
Table, Limbert, Square Top, Rounded Corners, Open Shelf, Signed, 30 x 20 x 20 In. 2600.00

Table, Louis XV, Carved Oak Center, Molded Edge, Projecting Corners, 30 x 44 ½ x 32 In. 3168.00
Table, Louis XV, Mahogany, Candle Slide, Drawer, Tapered Curved Legs, 28 x 14 x 10 In..... 836.00
Table, Louis XV, Oak, Parquetry, Banded Top, Diamond Inlay, Carved Apron, 30 x 68 x 39 In.. 2376.00
Table, Louis XV Style, Beech, Carved, Cabriole Legs, 30 x 36 x 30 In.................... 118.00
Table, Louis XV Style, Crossbanded Burl, Inlay, Tulipwood, Kidney Shape, 25 x 28 In........ 235.00
Table, Louis XV Style, Gilt, Marble Top, Projecting Corners, Cabriole Legs, 27 x 32 In........ 1440.00
Table, Louis XV Style, Kingwood, Inset Onyx Surface, Frieze, Drawer, Shelf, 27 x 8 ½ In. 780.00
Table, Louis XV Style, Kingwood, Gilt Leather Surface, Ormolu Mount, 31 x 70 In. 4080.00
Table, Louis XV Style, Mahogany, Marble Top, Kidney Shape, Pierced Brass Gallery, 31 x 27 In. 2880.00
Table, Louis XV Style, Mahogany, Round Inset Marble Top, Garlands, 30 x 17 ½ In.......... 6900.00
Table, Louis XV Style, Marble Top, Parquetry, Bronze Mounts, c.1910, 31 x 71 In. 1430.00
Table, Louis XV Style, Oak, Provincial, Drawer, Cabriole Legs, Peg Feet, 27 x 31 x 26 In. 1920.00
Table, Louis XV Style, Silk Damask Top Panel, Painted, Gilt, 19th Century, 29 x 45 In........ 295.00
Table, Louis XV, Chestnut, Scalloped Skirt, Cabriole Legs, 26 x 37 x 27 In. 1645.00
Table, Louis XVI, Gilt Metal, Inset Leather Surface, Lower Shelf, Pineapple Finials, 22 x 14 In. 600.00
Table, Louis XVI, Gilt Metal, Mirrored Glass, Corner Patera Finials, X-Stretcher, 21 x 17 In., Pair 3840.00
Table, Louis XVI, Gilt Metal, Leather Inset Top, Lower Shelf, Early 1900s, 25 x 18 ½ In., Pair.. 4800.00
Table, Louis XVI, Mahogany, Gilt Brass Mount, Marble Top, Brass Gallery, 31 x 24 In........ 2400.00
Table, Louis XVI, Multicolored, Marble Top, Leaf Panel, Fluted Legs, 30 x 33 x 18 In., Pair ... 5040.00
Table, Louis XVI, Parquetry, Tooled Leather Top, 3 Drawers, 29 x 58 In. 1763.00
Table, Louis XVI Style, Gilt Metal, Ebonized Glass, Reeded Legs, X-Stretcher, 18 x 24 In., Pair. 2040.00
Table, Louis XVI Style, Leather, Gilt Metal, Finials, Brass Casters, 23 x 22 x 18 In. 4080.00
Table, Louis XVI Style, Mahogany, Marble Top, Brass Banding, Shelf, 24 x 22 In., Pair....... 2640.00
Table, Louis XVI Style, Mahogany, Round Marble Top, 2 Drawers, Candle Slides, 30 x 26 In... 6900.00
Table, Louis XVI Style, Oak, French Provincial, Carved, 24 ¾ x 24 In..................... 1410.00
Table, Louis XVI Style, Oval Glass Top, Pinecone Finials, 20 ½ x 17 ½ x 13 ½ In. 660.00
Table, Louis XVI Style, Polychrome, Marble Top, Molded Frieze, X-Stretcher, 31 x 21 In., Pair. 6000.00
Table, Louis XVI Style, Shelf, Carved Hearts, Apron, Drawer, Cabriole Legs, 27 x 17 ½ In...... 1293.00
Table, Low, Marble, Gilt Bronze, Columnar Supports, Round, 19 x 36 In.................. 3525.00
Table, Low, Oak, Round, 4 Square Posts, Shaped Lower Shelf, c.1925, 17 ⅜ x 35 ½ In........ 3750.00
Table, Mahogany, 12-Sided Skirt, Marble Top, Mid 19th Century, 30 x 36 In. .... *illus* 1900.00
Table, Mahogany, Bone Inlay, Paneled, Arched Sides, North Africa, 20 ¼ x 20 x 20 In........ 720.00
Table, Mahogany, Brass Pulls & Feet, 32 x 37 In...................................... 2650.00
Table, Mahogany, Cane, 2 Shelves, Bulbous Feet, Brass Caps, 29 x 21 x 16 In.............. 1080.00
Table, Mahogany, Dish Marble Top, Bulbous Standard, Scroll Legs, France, 1820, 29 x 33 In.. 5760.00
Table, Mahogany, Griffin, Winged, Tabletop Head, c.1920, 19 x 12 In.................... 235.00
Table, Mahogany, Oak, 1-Board Top, Rounded Corners, Divided Drawer, Brass, 29 x 29 In.... 1035.00
Table, Mahogany, Oval, Twin Flap Top, 2 Frieze Drawers, Splayed Legs, 28 ½ x 39 x 24 In.... 531.00
Table, Mahogany, Pedestal, Drawer, Baltimore, 19th Century, 30 x 23 ½ x 44 In. .... *illus* 750.00
Table, Mahogany, Turned Legs, Mid 19th Century, 30 x 28 x 16 In. .... *illus* 350.00
Table, Maple, Drawer, c.1950, 21 ½ In., Pair... 810.00
Table, Maple, Painted, Drawer, Canted Skirt, Ring Turned Tapered Legs, c.1850, 26 x 19 In... 10575.00
Table, Maple, Pegged, Pine Stretcher, c.1940, 35 x 60 In. 485.00
Table, Maple, Pine Breadboard Top, Drawer, Wooden Pull, Square Legs, 27 x 43 x 27 In...... 2070.00
Table, Marble Top, Cast Iron Base, Openwork Ends, Steer & Ram Heads, White, 70 x 24 In. .. 1150.00
Table, Marble Top, Lions' Heads, George Henkel, Philadelphia......................... 2645.00
Table, Marble Top, Scroll Iron Legs, Box Stretcher, Peg Feet, Victorian, 31 x 51 x 31 In....... 2640.00
Table, Marquetry, Marble, Octagonal Top, Cream Color, Violet Veining, Brass, 26 x 26 In..... 575.00
Table, McCobb, Mahogany, Square Top, 2 Cane Shelves, Drawer, 20 x 24 x 19 In.......... 60.00
Table, McCobb, Rectangular Top, Drawer, Lower Shelf, 19 x 26 x 20 In. 60.00
Table, Metal, Zigzag Form, Linen Finish, Chromed Cross Bars, 29 x 16 x 24 In. 390.00
Table, Mixing, Georgian, Marble Top, 18th Century, 28 ½ x 24 x 24 In. 1528.00
Table, Mixing, Mahogany, Sliding Tray, Early 19th Century, 38 ½ x 38 x 19 In............. 5581.00
Table, Mixing, Mahogany, Marble Top, Early 19th Century, 30 x 26 x 25 In................ 9400.00
Table, Moorish, Octagonal, Geometric Inlay, Scalloped Sides, Low Shelf, 30 x 28 In., Pair.... 2160.00
Table, Napoleon III, Ebonized, Brass Mounted, Serpentine Top, Drawer, 28 x 50 In.......... 2400.00
Table, Napoleon III, Gilt Metal, Circular Top, Leather Insert, Bamboo Legs, 19 x 20 In....... 1980.00
Table, Napoleon III, Walnut, Oak, Marble Top, Drawer, Top-Shaped Feet, 30 x 36 x 23 In.... 1800.00
Table, Natural Finish, Lacquer, Painted, Scrolling Brackets, Asia, 74 x 14 In............... 177.00
Table, Neoclassical, Birch, Pine, Marble Top, White Marble Top, Backsplash, 36 x 44 In...... 460.00
Table, Neoclassical, Hardwood, Urn, In Wreath, Raised Edge, Fluted Standard, 27 x 18 In.... 900.00
Table, Neoclassical, Mahogany, Turned Pedestal, Acorn Drop Finials, 31 x 24 In........... 748.00
Table, Neoclassical, Mahogany, Empire Period, 3-Footed 1250.00
Table, Neoclassical, Mahogany, Veneer, 3 Parts, c.1825, 28 x 43 x 103 ½ In. 2233.00
Table, Neoclassical, Mahogany, 19th Century, 40 In.................................. 8225.00

Furniture, Table, Pembroke, Mahogany, Drawer, Reeded Legs, c.1810, 29 ½ x 21 x 32 In.
$1600.00

Furniture, Table, Pembroke, Walnut, Drawer, 28 x 33 ½ x 37 In.
$523.00

Furniture, Table, Pub, Drop Leaf, Oak, Britain, 19th Century, 28 x 28 In.
$920.00

TIP

Never use spray polish on antique furniture. It will leave a gray haze and attracts dirt.

F

Furniture, Table, Regency Style, Mahogany, Lion Legs, 34 x 61 x 18 In. $1000.00

Furniture, Table, Rococo Revival, Mahogany, Lift Top, Drawer, c.1890, 30 x 20 x 20 In. $200.00

Furniture, Table, Rococo Revival, Mahogany, Tortoise Top, c.1890, 29 x 38 x 27 In. $225.00

Furniture, Table, Sawbuck, Pine, Pegged Base, New England, Mid 19th Century, 26½ x 42 x 19 In. $513.00

Table, Neoclassical, Walnut, Marble, Plain Frieze, U-Shape Molding, Italy, 1700s, 26 x 20 In. 885.00

Table, Neoclassical Style, Gilt, Painted, Tooled, Applied Molding, Glass Top, Italy, 25 x 18 In. 805.00

Table, Neoclassical Style, Marble Top, 3-Part Supports, Paw Feet, 27 x 18 In., Pair 8125.00

Table, Neogrecque, Gilt, Lapis Lazuli Top, Tripod, Russia, 30 x 28 In. 6600.00

Table, Nesting, Chinese, Rosewood, 22 x 22 In. 266.00

Table, Nesting, Directoire Style, Gilt Metal, Mirrored, Reeded Tubular Legs, 16 x 22 In. 1440.00

Table, Nesting, Directoire Style, Smoked Glass Top, Brass Frame, Largest 16 x 21 In., 3 Piece. 1440.00

Table, Nesting, Glass, Gilt Metal, Mirrored Banding, 17 x 19½ x 14 In. 1800.00

Table, Nesting, Regency Style, Black & Red Lacquer, Gilt Pheasants, Flowers, 26 x 24 In., 4 Piece. 1140.00

Table, Oak, 1-Board Top, Scalloped Apron, Stretcher Base, Turned Legs, 27½ x 17½ In. 431.00

Table, Oak, Banded Top, Molded Edge, 28 x 33½ x 22½ In. 1254.00

Table, Oak, Lacquered Steel, Jean Prouve, c.1945, 28¾ x 78½ x 35⅜ In. 24000.00

Table, Oak, Oval Leaves, Bulbous Legs, Ball Feet, England, 30 x 41 x 48 In. 1440.00

Table, Oak, Pegged Construction, Dovetailed Stretcher, c.1900, 28 x 48 In. 470.00

Table, P. Evans, Chrome & Brass Patchwork, Cantilevered Form, Signed, 20 x 30 x 12 In. *illus* 980.00

Table, Painted, Carved, Glass Top, Inset Silk Damask, Molded Edge, Drawers, 31 x 54 In. 1593.00

Table, Painted, Circular Top, Inset Meissen Style Plaques, Baluster, 27 x 18½ In., Pair 1058.00

Table, Papier-Mache, Chinoiserie, Circular Top, Scalloped Edge, 20 x 25 In. 1416.00

Table, Paul Laszlo, Mahogany, Round, Inset Glass Top, 25 x 24½ In. 510.00

Table, Pedestal, Aesthetic Revival, Cherry, c.1880, 34 x 16 x 13 In. 3525.00

Table, Pedestal, Eero Saarinen, Marble Top, Metal Base, Black, 22 x 15 x 20 In. 900.00

Table, Pedestal, G. Nakashima, Walnut, 28 x 42 In. 9000.00

Table, Pedestal, George III, Mahogany, Circular Top, 20th Century, 36 In. 570.00

Table, Pedestal, Neogrecque, Ebonized, Gilt, c.1870, 41½ x 12 x 12 In. 11456.00

Table, Pembroke, Cherry, Straight Legs, Cross Stretcher, 18th Century, 28 x 21 x 30 In. 977.00

Table, Pembroke, Drop Leaf, Mahogany, Twin Tapered Square Legs, 27 x 20 In. 295.00

Table, Pembroke, Drop Leaf, Mahogany, Cross Stretcher, Drop Leaves, Drawer, 27 x 27 x 15 In. 431.00

Table, Pembroke, Drop Leaf, Chippendale, Walnut, Drawer, Marlboro Legs, 28 x 33 x 37 In. 523.00

Table, Pembroke, Drop Leaf, Hepplewhite, Mahogany, Inlay, Tapered Legs, c.1820, 28 x 35 x 23 In. 835.00

Table, Pembroke, Drop Leaf, Federal, Marquetry, Line Strung Mahogany, Drawer, 28 x 32 In. 1200.00

Table, Pembroke, Drop Leaf, Mahogany, Relief Carved, 28 x 22 x 33 In. 1348.00

Table, Pembroke, Drop Leaf, Hepplewhite, Tapered Legs, Dovetailed, 29 x 37 x 17 In. 1400.00

Table, Pembroke, Drop Leaf, Federal, Mahogany, Inlay, Square Legs, c.1800, 28 x 20 x 40 In. 1970.00

Table, Pembroke, Drop Leaf, Federal, Mahogany, Reeded, Brass Cup Casters, 28¾ x 20½ In. 2300.00

Table, Pembroke, Drop Leaf, Regency, Mahogany, Frieze Drawer, 29 x 21 In. 2640.00

Table, Pembroke, Drop Leaf, Rosewood, Drawer, Square Tapered Legs, 27 x 39 x 33 In. 2640.00

Table, Pembroke, Drop Leaf, Rosewood, Satinwood Banded Top, Drawer, 28 x 17 x 31 In. 3055.00

Table, Pembroke, Drop Leaf, Federal, Mahogany, Scalloped Drop Leaves, c.1810, 29¼ x 21 In. 3290.00

Table, Pembroke, Drop Leaf, Federal, Mahogany, Drawer, Icicle Inlay, c.1800, 28 x 21 x 43 In. 6150.00

Table, Pembroke, Drop Leaf, Mahogany, Late 18th Century, 28 x 27½ x 34¾ In. 7050.00

Table, Pembroke, Federal, Walnut, Tapered Legs, 19th Century, 29 x 34 x 20 In. *illus* 685.00

Table, Pembroke, Federal, Walnut, Tapered Legs, Beaded Corners, Drawer, 29 x 35 In. 690.00

Table, Pembroke, Federal, Mahogany, Inlay, New England, c.1800 705.00

Table, Pembroke, Federal, Mahogany, Inlay, 29½ x 19½ In. 4000.00

Table, Pembroke, Federal, Mahogany, Drawer, Casters, New York, c.1810, 30 x 20 In., Pair 5040.00

Table, Pembroke, Federal, Inlaid Mahogany, Ash, Charleston, c.1810, 27 x 29 In. 10350.00

Table, Pembroke, George III, Mahogany, Pine, Drawer, Tapered Legs, 28 x 15 In. 288.00

Table, Pembroke, George III, Satinwood, Checker, Mahogany, Drawer, 29 x 33 In. 588.00

Table, Pembroke, Hepplewhite, Walnut, Pine, 2-Board Top, Swing Arms, 29 x 33 In. 201.00

Table, Pembroke, Hepplewhite, Mahogany, Oval Inlays, Drawer, 27 x 32 x 34 In. 1495.00

Table, Pembroke, Mahogany, 2 Leaves, Square, Legs, Brass Wheels, England, c.1820, 28 x 60 In. 777.00

Table, Pembroke, Mahogany, Drawer, Reeded Legs, c.1810, 29½ x 21 x 32 In. *illus* 1600.00

Table, Pembroke, Mahogany, Serpentine Leaves, Tapered Legs, X-Stretcher, 28 x 34 x 39 In. 2390.00

Table, Pembroke, Regency, Mahogany, Satinwood, c.1800, 29 x 42 x 26 In. 8400.00

Table, Pembroke, Sheraton, Maple, Curly Maple, Drop Leaves, 30 x 18 x 43 In. 460.00

Table, Pembroke, Vine & Ribbon Painted Banding, Dovetailed Drawer, 28½ x 20 x 30 In. 1093.00

Table, Pembroke, Walnut, Drawer, 28 x 33½ x 37 In. *illus* 523.00

Table, Pickled Wood Top, Steel X-Shaped Supports, 29 x 71 x 19 In. 1320.00

Table, Pier, Continental, Gilt, Early 19th Century, 32 x 31 x 13½ In. 3290.00

Table, Pier, French Restauration, Mahogany, Frieze Drawer, Scroll Supports, 32 x 34 In., Pair 1645.00

Table, Pier, George II, Mahogany, Carved, Scalloped Shell, Marble Top, c.1750, 31 x 52 In. 43000.00

Table, Pier, George III, Satinwood, Inlay, Tulipwood, Demilune Top, c.1780, 37 x 40 In. 5000.00

Table, Pier, George III Style, Satinwood, Tulipwood, Hardwood, 32 x 49 In., Pair 37000.00

Table, Pier, George V, Mahogany, Bronze Mount, 36 x 60 x 16½ In. 4113.00

Table, Pier, Mahogany, White Marble Top, Mirrored Back, c.1830, 37 x 42 x 21 In. 1293.00

Table, Pier, Mahogany, Marble Top, Molded Apron, c.1840, 37 x 42 x 19 In. 3525.00
Table, Pier, Neoclassical, Mahogany, S-Scroll Columns, Serpentine Lower Shelf, 36 x 38 In. . . 660.00
Table, Pier, Neoclassical, Mahogany, Marble Top, Cyma Molded Frieze, Columns, 37 x 38 In. . 2400.00
Table, Pier, Neoclassical, Mahogany, Marble Top, Frieze Drawer, Column Supports, 35 x 33 In. . 3055.00
Table, Pier, Rosewood, Bronze Mounted, White Marble Top, c.1825, 37 x 42 x 18 In. 5581.00
Table, Pine, 4 End Drawers, 6 Legs, Stretchers, 132 x 30 x 30 In. 1870.00
Table, Pine, Amber Graining, 2-Board Top, Tapered Legs, 99 x 28 ½ In.. . . . . 2300.00
Table, Pine, Drawer, Turned Legs, c.1800, 27 ½ x 41 ½ x 23 ½ In. 1080.00
Table, Pine, Paint Decorated, Yellow Ground, Ivy, Berries, Diamonds, New England, 30 x 18 In. 748.00
Table, Pine, Square, Reeded Legs, Skirt, 26 x 26 ¾ x 20 In. 385.00
Table, Planters, Chinese, Lacquer, Wood, Stone, Hoof Feet, Mottled Green Stone, 32 x 96 In. . . 1320.00
Table, Provincial, Anglo-Colonial, Multicolored,Sliding Compartments, Bulbous Legs, 31 x 81 In.. 960.00
Table, Provincial, Fruitwood, Oak, Planked, Canted Blocked Legs, H-Shaped Stretcher, 29 x 21 In. 1320.00
Table, Provincial, Fruitwood, Carved Edge, Drawer, Turned, Fluted Bulbous Legs, 30 x 38 In. . 2640.00
Table, Provincial, Louis Philippe, Fruitwood, Draw End, Turned Legs, 1800s, 31 x 78 In.. . . . . 4080.00
Table, Provincial, Louis XV, Walnut, Scalloped Drawer, Cabriole Legs, Late 1700s, 28 x 36 In. . 2640.00
Table, Provincial, Louis XV Style, Fruitwood, Shaped Gallery, Shelf, Drawer, 35 x 18 In. 1320.00
Table, Provincial, Louis XV Style, Fruitwood, Draw End, Scalloped Frieze, 32 x 42 In. 3840.00
Table, Provincial, Oak, Drawer, Turned, Incised Circular Legs, 28 ½ x 30 ½ x 19 ½ In. 1224.00
Table, Provincial, Oak, Side Frieze Drawer, End Drawer, Square Legs, 30 x 78 x 33 In.. . . . . . . 11880.00
Table, Provincial, Planks, Drawer, Shaped End Supports, Stretcher, Mid 1800s, 31 x 44 In. . . . 2400.00
Table, Provincial, Spanish Style, Hardwood, Iron, Planked Top, Scrolled Supports, 30 x 87 x 38 In.. 2016.00
Table, Provincial Country, Oak, Plank Board, Trestle Form Base, 30 x 82 ½ x 20 In.. . . . . 885.00
Table, Pub, Drop Leaf, Oak, Britain, 19th Century, 28 x 28 In. . . . . *illus* 920.00
Table, Pub, English Oak, Rectangular Top, Square Legs, Stretchers, 29 x 51 ½ In. 325.00
Table, Queen Anne, Drop Leaf, Curly Maple, Cabriole Maple Legs, Pad Feet, 28 x 46 In.. . . . . . 1380.00
Table, Queen Anne, Flip Top, Mahogany, Oak, Pine, Swing-Out Drawers, 1800s, 29 x 28 In. . . 575.00
Table, Queen Anne, Pine, Maple, Stretcher Base, Scalloped Aprons, c.1740, 29 x 24 In. 1380.00
Table, Queen Anne, Walnut, Marble Top, Gothic Arch Frieze, Drake's Feet, 28 x 37 x 18 In. . . . 812.00
Table, Queen Anne, Walnut, Paint, 2-Board Top, 2 Drawers, Turned Legs, Pad Feet, 29 x 46 x 31 In. 1100.00
Table, Queen Anne Style, Black Lacquer, Gilt Landscape, Drawers, 29 x 36 x 21 ½ In.. . . . . 3600.00
Table, Reading, Victorian, Mahogany, Cantilevered Top, Hinged Flap, 26 ½ x 33 ¾ x 18 In. . . . 546.00
Table, Refectory, Continental Renaissance, Walnut, 19th Century, 30 x 78 x 43 In. 4994.00
Table, Refectory, Elm, Baluster Supports, Plank Top, 31 ½ x 93 ½ x 33 In.. . . . . 2585.00
Table, Refectory, Italian Baroque, Walnut, Thick Plank Top, 32 x 108 ½ x 29 In. 4994.00
Table, Refectory, Jacobean, English Oak, Pegged, 3-Board Top, Breadboard Ends, 32 x 82 x 30 In. . 1430.00
Table, Refectory, Provincial, Oak, Plank Top, Turned Legs, H-Shape Stretcher, 20 x 34 In.. . . . 1560.00
Table, Refectory, Renaissance Style, Elm, Column Pedestals, Trestle, 29 x 91 In. 4994.00
Table, Refectory, Spanish Baroque, Walnut, Urn Form Trestle, Scroll Feet, 29 x 115 x 31 In. . . 21150.00
Table, Regency, Anglo-Indian, Mid 19th Century, 31 ½ x 22 ½ x 22 ½ In., Pair. 3600.00
Table, Regency, Inlaid Mahogany, Banded Top, Drawers, Trestle Base, 28 x 42 In. 2938.00
Table, Regency, Mahogany, Gallery Top, 3 Drawers, c.1830, 33 ½ x 42 x 20 ½ In. 2468.00
Table, Regency, Mahogany, Rectangular D-End Top, 4 Drawers, Reed Corners, 28 x 23 x 17 In. 2585.00
Table, Regency, Mahogany, Drawers, Reeded Saber Legs, Paw Feet, 29 x 37 x 23 In.. . . . . 3231.00
Table, Regency, Mahogany, Tilt Top, Oval, Banded, Turned Column, 4 Splayed Legs, 27 x 67 In. 3600.00
Table, Regency, Mahogany, Rosewood, Spindle Supports, Gillows, c.1818, 29 x 38 In. 10625.00
Table, Regency, Rosewood, Tilt Top, Rounded Rectangle, Tripod Base, Bun Feet, 27 x 18 x 14 In. 960.00
Table, Regency, Rosewood, Mahogany, Carved, Turned Stretcher, c.1815, 29 x 24 In. 5625.00
Table, Regency, Rosewood, Tilt Top, Inset Leather, 3-Part Base, 29 x 53 In. 18000.00
Table, Regency Calamander, Rosewood, Crossbanded, Tilt Top, 30 x 51 ½ In. 1880.00
Table, Regency Style, Faux Bois, Molded Gilt Edge, Lower Shelf, Early 1900s, 24 x 18 In.. . . . . 1080.00
Table, Regency Style, Mahogany, Lion Legs, 34 x 61 x 18 In. . . . . *illus* 1000.00
Table, Regency Style, Mahogany, Banded Top, Turned Support, Casters, 28 x 62 In.. . . . . 2875.00
Table, Regency Style, Rosewood, Figured Top, Beaded Edge, Drop End Leaves, 28 x 53 In.. . . . 2880.00
Table, Regency Style, Oak, Oval, Stretcher Shelf, Splayed Legs, Casters, 29 x 63 x 44 In. 1200.00
Table, Renaissance Revival, Marquetry, Gilt Bronze Mount, Ebonized, 31 x 23 In. 2468.00
Table, Renaissance Revival, Polished Steel, C-Scrolls, Trelliswork, Tripod Base, 30 x 15 In. . . 646.00
Table, Renaissance Style, Walnut, Carved Leaf Drawers, Portugal, 36 x 64 x 32 In. 3900.00
Table, Rent, William IV, Rosewood, Inset Leather Top, Cased, 4 Drawers, Scroll Feet, 29 x 43 In. 3525.00
Table, Restauration, Mahogany, Tilt Dish Top, Reeded Bulbous Standard, 28 x 32 In. 2880.00
Table, Rococo, Rosewood, Marble Top, Fruit Basket, Alexander Roux 17250.00
Table, Rococo, Walnut, Portugal, Late 18th Century, 37 ½ x 32 ½ x 21 ½ In. 2350.00
Table, Rococo Revival, Mahogany, Lift Top, Drawer, c.1890, 30 x 20 x 20 In. . . . . *illus* 200.00
Table, Rococo Revival, Mahogany, Tortoise Top, c.1890, 29 x 38 x 27 In. . . . . *illus* 225.00

Furniture, Table, Scrolled Supports, Black Egyptian Marble, 19th Century, 30 x 38 x 22 In.
$1100.00

Furniture, Table, Side, Oak, Fluted, Tapered Square Legs, Late 19th Century, 28 x 20 x 15 In.
$600.00

Furniture, Table, Spanish Baroque Style, Iron Mounts, 2 Drawers, c.1880, 29 x 55 x 25 In.
$6500.00

Furniture, Table, Stickley & Brandt Co., Shelf, Cross Stretchers, 29 x 30 In.
$1050.00

F

Furniture, Table, Tavern, Curly Maple, Late 18th Century, 24 x 41 x 24 In.
$1380.00

Furniture, Table, Tavern, Oval, Painted, 24 x 27 x 21 In.
$1650.00

Furniture, Table, Tavern, Pine, 1-Board Top, American, 19th Century, 36 x 38 x 28 In.
$910.00

Furniture, Table, Tavern, Queen Anne, Maple, 2-Board, Pine Drawer, Oval, 1700s, 27 x 33 x 27 In.
$905.00

Table, Rococo Revival, Rosewood, Marble Top, Scroll Carved Sides, 29 x 37 x 18 In. 2820.00
Table, Rosewood, Regency, D-Shape Ends, 2 Drawers, 28 ½ x 23 x 46 In. 3776.00
Table, Salon, Louis XVI Style, Mahogany, Gilt, Brass Mount, 30 ½ x 16 In. 840.00
Table, Sawbuck, 2-Board Top, Breadboard Ends, Mortise & Tenon, Green Paint, 27 x 37 In. .. 4025.00
Table, Sawbuck, Breadboard Top, Grain Painted Base, Dowel Stretcher, Maine, 29 x 34 In. ... 1763.00
Table, Sawbuck, Pine, 1-Board Top, Nailed & Pegged Base, 26 x 42 x 19 In. 467.00
Table, Sawbuck, Pine, Pegged Base, New England, Mid 19th Century, 26 ½ x 42 x 19 In. . *illus* 513.00
Table, Sawbuck, Pine, Painted, 1-Board Top, Diagonal Stretchers, 45 x 24 In. 1645.00
Table, Sawbuck, Scrubbed Pine, 1-Board Top, Red Paint Base, 24 ½ x 33 ½ In. 546.00
Table, Scrolled Supports, Black Egyptian Marble, 19th Century, 30 x 38 x 22 In. ...... *illus* 1100.00
Table, Seashells, Acorn, Seeds, Glass, Paper, 2 Lovebirds, Nova Scotia, c.1900, 32 x 26 In. 2415.00
Table, Serving, Edwardian, Mahogany, Diamond Pattern Banding, 3 Drawers, c.1900, 34 x 67 In. . 420.00
Table, Serving, George III, Mahogany, Blind Fretwork Frieze, 1700s, 36 x 78 In. 12925.00
Table, Serving, Limbert, Drawer, 2 Shelves, 42 x 19 x 43 In. 5400.00
Table, Settee, Pine, Stained, 3 Plank Top, Folds Back, 2 Drawers, 29 x 60 x 40 ½ In. 460.00
Table, Sewing, 2-Board, Pine Top, Walnut Skirt, Cherry Legs, Red Wash, Overhang, 29 x 29 In. 1150.00
Table, Sewing, Biedermeier, Satinwood, Inlaid String Banding, Drawer, 27 x 24 In. 2880.00
Table, Sewing, Black Lacquer, Lift Top, Bird, Flowers, 24 x 14 ½ x 10 ¼ In. 385.00
Table, Sewing, Cherry, 2 Drawers, Square, Sandwich Glass Pulls, 28 ½ x 20 ¾ x 21 In. 825.00
Table, Sewing, Chinoiserie, Gilt Figures, Claw Feet, c.1850 .... 1700.00
Table, Sewing, Drop Leaf, Mahogany, 3 Short Drawers, Cabriole Legs, 1800s, 28 x 16 In. 354.00
Table, Sewing, Drop Leaf, Neoclassical, Mahogany, Molded Drawers, Pedestal, 29 x 17 In. ... 411.00
Table, Sewing, Drop Leaf, Empire, 2 Drawers, Turned Pedestal, Claw Feet, 28 x 19 x 19 In. ... 885.00
Table, Sewing, Drop Leaf, Federal, Mahogany, c.1825, 29 ½ x 35 ½ x 21 In. 999.00
Table, Sewing, Drop Leaf, Neoclassical, Mahogany, 2 Drawers, Sliding Basket, 1800s, 29 x 21 In. 1058.00
Table, Sewing, Drop Leaf, Mother-Of-Pearl Inlay, c.1920, 27 ½ x 22 x 18 In. 1800.00
Table, Sewing, Drop Leaf, Mahogany, Finials, Acanthus Carved Pedestal, 29 x 39 x 24 In. 2160.00
Table, Sewing, Drop Leaf, G. Stickley, 2 Drawers, Copper Hardware, No. 630, 19 x 18 x 28 In. . 2520.00
Table, Sewing, Drop Leaf, Gateleg, Pine, Drawers, Red Wash, 1700s, 30 x 38 In. 2875.00
Table, Sewing, Federal, Mahogany, Figured Birch, Drawer, 31 x 25 ¾ x 14 In. 403.00
Table, Sewing, Federal, Mahogany, Veneer, Carved, 2 Drawers, New York, c.1820, 29 x 19 ½ In. 411.00
Table, Sewing, Federal, Rosewood, Mahogany, Pedestal Base, Cock-Beaded Drawers, 32 x 21 x 14 In. 413.00
Table, Sewing, Federal, Mahogany, 2 Drawers, Dovetailed, Early 19th Century, 28 x 19 x 18 In. 1520.00
Table, Sewing, Federal, Cherry, Square Top, Frieze Drawers, Ringed Legs, 29 x 21 In. 1880.00
Table, Sewing, Federal, Pine, Red & Black, Decorated, New England, c.1835, 20 x 21 In. 3900.00
Table, Sewing, Federal, Mahogany, Hinged Top, Writing Panel, Silk Basket, 30 x 24 x 12 In. .. 4025.00
Table, Sewing, Federal, Bird's-Eye Maple Veneer, 2 Drawers, Turned Legs, 29 x 21 x 17 In. ... 11163.00
Table, Sewing, Federal Style, Mahogany, Flame Birch, 8-Sided Top, c.1900, 28 x 21 x 14 In. .. 720.00
Table, Sewing, Footed Drawer Cabinet, Pincushion, 6-Peg Spool Holder, 10 x 4 x 4 In. 154.00
Table, Sewing, Louis XV Style, Inlaid Kingwood, Tulipwood, Parquetry, 29 x 23 In. 1058.00
Table, Sewing, Louis XVI Style, Tulipwood, Bronze Mount, Hinged Top, 31 x 18 x 16 In. 1293.00
Table, Sewing, Mahogany, Split Center, 9 Compartments, c.1850, 29 x 18 x 15 ½ In. 165.00
Table, Sewing, Mahogany, Drawers, Reeded Glass Pulls, Saber Legs, 27 ½ x 35 x 21 In. 236.00
Table, Sewing, Mahogany, c.1825, 33 x 30 x 15 ½ In. 999.00
Table, Sewing, Mahogany, Leaves Over Drawers, Paw Feet, 28 x 33 x 19 In. 1020.00
Table, Sewing, Mahogany, Drawers, Acanthus Carved Columns, Paw Feet, 19 x 21 x 20 In. 1200.00
Table, Sewing, Mahogany, Lift Top, Compartment, Drawer, c.1820, 30 x 22 x 15 ½ In. 1584.00
Table, Sewing, Neoclassical, Mahogany, Inlay, 2 Drawers, Work Basket, 29 x 16 x 13 In. 353.00
Table, Sewing, Neoclassical, Cherry, Bird's-Eye Maple, Sheraton Style, 28 x 22 In. 390.00
Table, Sewing, Neoclassical, Mahogany, 1 Over 2 Drawers, 27 x 21 x 17 In. 411.00
Table, Sewing, Neoclassical, Mahogany, 2 Drawers, Lyre Shaped Ends, 29 x 28 x 29 In. 440.00
Table, Sewing, Neoclassical, Mahogany, Reeded Edge Top, Drawers, Turned Stem, 28 x 20 In. 1175.00
Table, Sewing, Neoclassical, Mahogany, 19th Century, 32 x 24 x 20 ¾ In. 5700.00
Table, Sewing, Plank Top, Mortised Joint, Drawer, Square Legs, Cut Corners. 1100.00
Table, Sewing, Queen Anne, Walnut, Lift Top, 2 Drawers, 18th Century, 29 x 54 x 32 In. 1200.00
Table, Sewing, Regency, Rosewood, Brass Inlay, Lift Top, Fabric Lined Interior, 29 x 18 ½ In. . 353.00
Table, Sewing, Rococo, Rosewood, Sarcophagus Form, Rose Carved, 32 x 22 x 17 In. 2350.00
Table, Sewing, Rococo Revival, Rosewood, Lift Top, Hidden Compartment, 1800s, 32 x 21 In.. 1080.00
Table, Sewing, Scrubbed Top, Red Paint, Square Legs, Casters, c.1800, 29 x 43 x 25 In. 1495.00
Table, Sewing, Sheraton, Tiger Maple, 15 ½ x 21 x 28 ½ In. 1500.00
Table, Sewing, Sheraton, Mahogany, Figured Top, Oval Corners, Frieze, Bag Drawer, 28 x 21 In. 2880.00
Table, Sewing, Southern Yellow Pine, Drawer, Tapered Legs, c.1790, 27 x 22 In. 248.00
Table, Sewing, Tulipwood Crossbanded, Trays, Sewing Basket, 31 x 19 ½ x 15 In. 1265.00
Table, Sewing, Victorian, Ebonized, Painted, Sliding Basket, Stretchers, 29 x 18 In. 646.00
Table, Sewing, Walnut, Drawer, Turned Legs, 29 x 28 In. 147.00

Table, Sewing, William IV, Mahogany, 2 Drawers, c.1835, 27 x 14¾ x 17¾ In. 705.00
Table, Shaker, Maple, Quartersawn Oak, Tongue & Groove, Drawer, Mt. Lebanon, c.1860, 40 x 30 In. 3217.00
Table, Side, Art Deco, Burl Yew, Satinwood, Circular, Shelves, 23 x 32½ In. 1348.00
Table, Side, Biedermeier, Burl Walnut, Door, Continental, 28½ x 16¼ x 12½ In. 767.00
Table, Side, Chippendale, Walnut, Drawer, Late 18th Century, 28 x 22 x 36 In. 220.00
Table, Side, Continental, Fruitwood, Drawer, 19th Century, 28 x 33 x 22 In. 1998.00
Table, Side, Demilune, Marble Top, 2 Lyre Form Supports, 31 x 39 x 20 In., Pair 4080.00
Table, Side, Federal, Tiger Maple, Drawer, 27½ x 21 x 19½ In. 316.00
Table, Side, Federal, Drawer, S-Scroll Legs, Wavy Stretcher, 28½ x 24½ x 15 In., Pair 748.00
Table, Side, Federal, Mahogany, c.1820, 28¾ x 22¼ x 16½ In. 2938.00
Table, Side, Florence Knoll, Walnut Top, Chrome Legs, Label 350.00
Table, Side, G. Nelson/Raymor, Black Ceramic Top, Impressed, Walnut Base, 14 x 20 In. 1560.00
Table, Side, George III, Mahogany, Bowed Top, Frieze, 2 Drawers, 29¾ x 36 x 21½ In. 1320.00
Table, Side, George III, Mahogany, D-Form Top, Satinwood Banding, 32 x 36 x 17½ In., Pair 1980.00
Table, Side, Gilt Bronze, Pierced Filigree, Glass Stretcher, 33 x 14 x 14 In. 748.00
Table, Side, Limbert, Oak, Marked, c.1910, 24½ x 17 In. 1560.00
Table, Side, Louis XV, Oak, Serpentine Apron, Cabriole Legs, 30 x 70½ x 28 In. 1528.00
Table, Side, Louis XV, Kingwood, Rosewood, Drawer, Stretcher Shelves, 21 x 14 x 12 In. 3290.00
Table, Side, Louis XVI, Mahogany, Bronze Mounted, 30 x 32 x 20 In. 1645.00
Table, Side, Louis XVI, Gilt, 19th Century, 28½ x 33½ x 17½ In. 2350.00
Table, Side, Louis XVI, Mahogany, Scalloped Top, Cabriole Legs, Shoefoot, 30 x 20 x 20 In. 2937.00
Table, Side, Louis XVI Style, 2 Drawers, Marble Top, Fluted Legs, 26 x 15 x 10 In., Pair 230.00
Table, Side, Mahogany, Brass, Sunflower Braid Skirt, c.1890, 30 x 23 x 17 In. 1763.00
Table, Side, Mahogany, Fruitwood, Drawer, Square Legs, 19th Century, 28 x 35 x 22 In. 1880.00
Table, Side, Mahogany, Carved Skirt, Scallop Shell, Leaf, Cabriole Legs, c.1800, 29 x 50 x 24 In. 2128.00
Table, Side, Neoclassical, Fruitwood, Frieze Drawer, Oval, Italy, 28 x 25 x 19 In. 823.00
Table, Side, Oak, Fluted, Tapered Square Legs, Late 19th Century, 28 x 20 x 15 In. *illus* 600.00
Table, Side, Pine, Shaped Backboard, 2 Drawers, Side Panels, 42 x 44 x 19½ In. 6573.00
Table, Side, Queen Anne, Walnut, Thumb-Molded, Shaped Apron, Cabriole Legs, 30 x 35 x 25 In. 2233.00
Table, Side, Renaissance Style, Walnut, Carved, 32½ x 65 x 29¾ In. 2233.00
Table, Side, Shaker, Cherry, 2 Drawers, Hood Pulls, Square Tapered Legs, 18 x 37 x 21 In. 3105.00
Table, Side, Tulipwood, Parquetry, Drawer, Cabriole Legs, Shelf Stretcher, 28 x 20 x 13 In. 264.00
Table, Side, Tulipwood, Marquetry, Flower, Urn, Scrolls, Italy, 30¾ x 23 x 18½ In. 1410.00
Table, Side, Walnut, Marble, Round, 2 Shelves, Wood Base, c.1950, 26 x 36 In. 2400.00
Table, Side, Walnut, Maple, 23 x 23 x 29 In. 2800.00
Table, Side, Walnut, 3 Legs, Natzler Tile Top, Blue, Green, 23 x 15 x 15 In. 16800.00
Table, Slab, Free-Form, Red Oak Top, Burl, Black Metal Legs, Penny Feet, 1900s, 18 x 68 In. 978.00
Table, Softwood, Mahogany Grain Paint, Dovetailed Drawer, Turned Legs, 20¼ x 20½ x 21 In. 220.00
Table, Spanish Baroque Style, Iron Mounts, 2 Drawers, c.1880, 29 x 55 x 25 In. *illus* 6500.00
Table, Spanish Style, Oak, Wrought Iron, Shaped Pierced Supports, 30 x 71 In. 2400.00
Table, Stickley, Circular Top, Wide Apron, Arched Cross Stretchers, 18 x 28½ In. 2160.00
Table, Stickley, Circular Top, Stacked Crossed Stretcher Base, Through Post, 30 x 28 In. 2640.00
Table, Stickley, Circular Top, Lower Shelf, No. 542, 36 x 30 In. 3360.00
Table, Stickley & Brandt Co., Shelf, Cross Stretchers, 29 x 30 In. *illus* 1050.00
Table, Sunderland, Cherry, Bamboo, Late 19th Century, 26 x 24½ x 27½ In. 881.00
Table, Sweden, Round, Beveled Edge, Tapered Legs, Elias Svedberg, 26 x 20 In. 120.00
Table, Sycamore, Patinated Metal, Circular, 3 Legs, c.1940, 23¾ x 27¾ In. 1800.00
Table, Tap, Oval, 4-Splayed Square Tapered Legs, 1777, 27 x 23¼ x 33½ In. 1208.00
Table, Tavern, Black Paint, Mid 18th Century, 24½ x 33¼ x 21¾ In. 4406.00
Table, Tavern, Breadboard Ends, Hourglass Legs, Pine, 26¼ x 40 x 27½ In. 300.00
Table, Tavern, Breadboard Ends, Windsor Turnings, Box Stretcher, c.1750, 25 x 42 x 28 In. 1610.00
Table, Tavern, Chippendale, Figured Maple, c.1780, 26 x 36 In. 625.00
Table, Tavern, Chippendale, Tiger Maple, Breadboard Top, Cut Corners, 28 x 51 x 27 In. 1955.00
Table, Tavern, Chippendale, Figured Maple, c.1780, 25½ x 34¾ x 25¼ In. 7200.00
Table, Tavern, Country, Queen Anne, Maple, Shaped Top, Pegged, 29 x 18 In. 1265.00
Table, Tavern, Curly Maple, Late 18th Century, 24 x 41 x 24 In. *illus* 1380.00
Table, Tavern, Drawer, Tapered Legs, Red Paint Traces, 41¾ x 26¾ x 28½ In. 633.00
Table, Tavern, Drawer, Dovetailed, Breadboard Ends, Fluted, Carved, Square Legs, 27 x 42 x 26 In. 1150.00
Table, Tavern, Hepplewhite, Walnut, 3-Board Scrubbed Top, c.1820, 27¾ x 36 In. 316.00
Table, Tavern, Maple, Pine, Breadboard Top, Drawer, Turned Legs, 18th Century, 26 x 35 x 22 In. 425.00
Table, Tavern, Maple, Pine, Overhanging Top, Breadboard Ends, Drawer, Pad Feet, 28 x 46 In. 3290.00
Table, Tavern, Maple, Pine, Breadboard Ends, Block-Turned Legs, c.1880, 55 x 29 In. 3819.00
Table, Tavern, New England, Inset Corners, Drawer, 27 x 30½ x 20 In. 232.00
Table, Tavern, Nutting, No. 613, Ball Turned, Maple, Paper Label 385.00
Table, Tavern, Nutting, Maple, Drawer, Turned Legs, Stretcher, Signed, 36 x 27 In. 900.00

Furniture, Table, Tavern, Queen Anne, Walnut, Poplar, 18th Century, 30 x 57 x 43 In.
$1700.00

Furniture, Table, Tavern, William & Mary, Poplar, Red Brown Paint, 18th Century, 26 x 38 x 27 In.
$910.00

Furniture, Table, Tray, Butler's, Mahogany, Cutout Handles, Dovetailed, 19th Century, 15½ x 25½ In.
$181.00

Furniture, Table, Victorian, Mahogany, Marble, 3-Footed, 92 x 44½ In.
$2200.00

Furniture, Table, Writing, Poplar, Pine, Oak, 2 Doors Over Drawer, c.1890, 40 x 39 x 22 In.
$260.00

Furniture, Table Set, Frank Lloyd Wright, 6 Stools, Heritage Henredon, 17 x 48 In. Table, 7 Piece
$8900.00

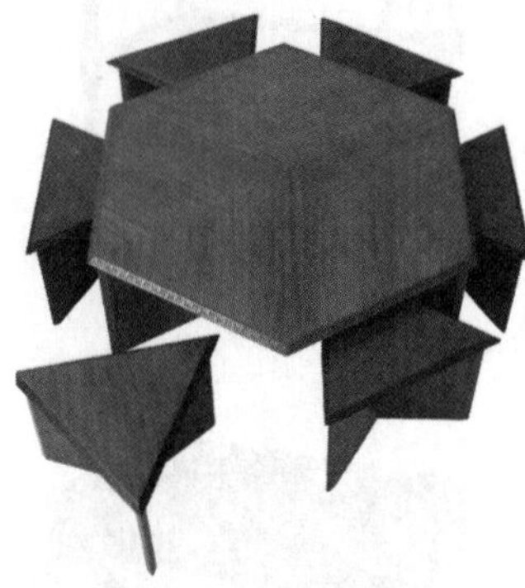

Furniture, Tea Cart, Mahogany, Butler's Tray, Late 20th Century, 30 In.
$100.00

Furniture, Tea Cart, Regency Style, Mahogany, 2 Tiers, Drawers, Casters, 38½ x 39 x 18½ In.
$450.00

Table, Tavern, Oval, Painted, 24 x 27 x 21 In. *illus* 1650.00
Table, Tavern, Oval Top, Single Drawer, 18th Century, 29½ x 25 In. 1320.00
Table, Tavern, Pilgrim, Maple, Pine, Painted, Splayed Leg, 25 x 34 x 26 In. 7540.00
Table, Tavern, Pine, Circular, Tapered Square Pedestal, Scroll Feet, Wood Peg, 28¾ x 31 In. 143.00
Table, Tavern, Pine, 1-Board Top, American, 19th Century, 36 x 38 x 28 In. *illus* 910.00
Table, Tavern, Queen Anne, Curly Maple Top, Red Painted Apron, Oval, 20 x 25 In. 460.00
Table, Tavern, Queen Anne, Pine, Tapered Legs, Pad Feet, 26½ x 30 x 21 In. 518.00
Table, Tavern, Queen Anne, Maple, 2-Board, Pine Drawer, Oval, 1700s, 27 x 33 x 27 In. *illus* 905.00
Table, Tavern, Queen Anne, Walnut, Poplar, 18th Century, 30 x 57 x 43 In. *illus* 1700.00
Table, Tavern, Queen Anne, Walnut, Poplar, Removable Top, 18th Century, 31 x 57 In. 1725.00
Table, Tavern, Queen Anne, Black Paint, Button Feet, N.H., c.1810, 27 x 30 In. 3300.00
Table, Tavern, Queen Anne, Maple, 1-Board Top, Grain Painted, Button Feet, 27 x 23 In. 4140.00
Table, Tavern, Queen Anne, Maple, Oval, Overhanging Top, Pad Feet, Mid 1700s, 27 x 38 In. 11400.00
Table, Tavern, Queen Anne, Green Paint, Breadboard Ends, Drawer, c.1850, 43 x 24 In. 16450.00
Table, Tavern, Red Brown Grain Paint, Ring & Baluster Legs, Stretcher Base, 28 x 50 In. 518.00
Table, Tavern, Red Paint, 1-Board Top, Rounded Corners, Turned Legs, Stretcher, 25 x 18 In. 392.00
Table, Tavern, Shaped Top, Skirt, Stretcher Base, 18th Century, 26¾ x 24 x 17½ In. 1300.00
Table, Tavern, Sliding Top, Block Legs, Stretchers, Button Feet, 25½ x 31¼ x 23¾ In. 4025.00
Table, Tavern, Walnut, Poplar, 2-Board, Drawers, Turned Legs, c.1800, 30 x 59 In. 978.00
Table, Tavern, Walnut, 2 Drawers, Removable Top, Box Stretcher, Ball Feet, Pa., 31 x 45 x 30 In. 1208.00
Table, Tavern, Walnut, Rectangular Top, Turned Legs, Box Stretchers, c.1770, 28 x 30 In. 18720.00
Table, Tavern, William & Mary, Poplar, Red Brown Paint, 18th Century, 26 x 38 x 27 In. *illus* 910.00
Table, Tavern, William & Mary, Pine, Birch, Straight Apron, Turned & Blocked Legs, 26 x 27 In. 1276.00
Table, Tavern, William & Mary, Pine, Maple, Drawer, Mid 18th Century, 25 x 39 In. 2585.00
Table, Tavern, William & Mary, Scrubbed Top, Brown Paint, 26 x 37½ x 24 In. 4930.00
Table, Tavern, William & Mary, Maple, Pine, Drawer, Red Paint, c.1740, 25 x 40 In. 8400.00
Table, Tavern, William & Mary, Maple, Pine, Black, Newport, c.1720, 22½ x 22 N. 27000.00
Table, Tea, Chippendale, Tilt Top, Mahogany, Box Support, Tripod Base, 29 x 35 In. 345.00
Table, Tea, Chippendale, Tilt Top, Mahogany, Birdcage, Dish Top, Slipper Feet, 12 In. 633.00
Table, Tea, Chippendale, Dish Top, Mahogany, Inlay, Beaded Edge, Tripod Base, 28 x 22 In. 690.00
Table, Tea, Chippendale, Walnut, Carved, Tilt Top, Claw & Ball Feet, Late 1700s, 26½ x 32 In. 940.00
Table, Tea, Chippendale, Mahogany, Pierced Frieze, Turned Legs, Stretcher, 29 x 29 In., Pair 2040.00
Table, Tea, Chippendale, 3-Board Top, Beaded Legs, Oval, Maine, 22 x 27 x 26 In. 2300.00
Table, Tea, Chippendale, Mahogany, Piecrust, Tilt Top, Tapered Column, London, 27 x 32 In. 2875.00
Table, Tea, Chippendale, Mahogany, Carved, Circular Top, Cabriole Legs, 18th Century, 28 x 32 In. 2938.00
Table, Tea, Chippendale Style, Mahogany, Gallery, Birdcage, 29 x 25 In. 551.00
Table, Tea, Circular, Arched Apron, Square Legs, 2 Bentwood Supports, 29½ x 20 In. 310.00
Table, Tea, Ebonized, Dish Top, Flower Bouquet, Abalone Highlights, 22 x 16 In. 207.00
Table, Tea, Federal, Pine, Maple, Red Paint, New England, c.1800, 26 x 36 In. 1920.00
Table, Tea, G. Stickley, Circular, Notched Cross Stretcher, 20 x 26 In. 1080.00
Table, Tea, George II, Mahogany, Ireland, Mid 18th Century, 28 x 31¾ In. 11250.00
Table, Tea, George III, Mahogany, 8-Sided Top, Inlaid, Bellflowers, Tripod, Slipper Feet, 29 x 36 In. 4250.00
Table, Tea, Mahogany, Pie Crust, Carved Gallery Top, Reeded Baluster Column, 29 x 27 In. 468.00
Table, Tea, Mahogany, Cherry, Tilt Top, Late 18th Century, 28 x 26½ In. 1175.00
Table, Tea, Oval, Ring-Turned Splayed Legs, Red Stain, Beaded Apron, c.1810, 33 x 21 In. 4700.00
Table, Tea, Porcelain Top, Removable Tray, Cast Metal Handles, Shelf, 28 x 25 In. 650.00
Table, Tea, Queen Anne, Cherry, Column, 3-Footed, Cabriole Legs, 18th Century, 30 x 27 In. 200.00
Table, Tea, Queen Anne, Mahogany, Carved, Tilt Top, 19th Century, 29 x 24 In. 617.00
Table, Tea, Queen Anne, Pine, Maple, Porringer Top, Scalloped Apron, Splayed Legs, 25 x 18 x 26 In. 920.00
Table, Tea, Queen Anne, Mahogany, Dish Tilt Top, Rhode Island, c.1780, 28 x 34 In. 2585.00
Table, Tea, Queen Anne, Mahogany, Circular Dish, Tilt Top, Cabriole Legs, 24 In. 5079.00
Table, Tea, Queen Anne, Maple, Tilt Top, New England, c.1780, 27 x 30½ In. 5100.00
Table, Tea, Queen Anne, Maple, Long Drawer, Incised Edges, Cabriole Legs, 28 x 34 In. 8410.00
Table, Tea, Queen Anne, Maple, Oval Overhanging Top, Canted Skirt, Splayed Legs, 25 x 35 In. 9988.00
Table, Tea, Tilt Top, Regency, Mahogany, 28 x 21 x 25 In. 495.00
Table, Tea, Tilt Top, Queen Anne, Mahogany, Birdcage Support, 29½ x 32½ In. 728.00
Table, Tea, Tilt Top, Mahogany, Urn Turned Support, Tripod Base, Claw & Ball Feet, 29 x 40 In. 805.00
Table, Tea, Tilt Top, Queen Anne, Mahogany, c.1780-90, 29 x 32 In. 880.00
Table, Tea, Tilt Top, Birdcage, Mahogany, Piecrust Top, Reeded Column, 29 x 27 In. 978.00
Table, Tea, Tilt Top, Queen Anne, Mahogany, Piecrust Edge, Urn Form Shaft, 3 Snake Legs, Pad Feet, 29 x 29 In. 1150.00
Table, Tea, Tilt Top, Queen Anne, Maple, Red Paint, 36 x 29 In. 1150.00
Table, Tea, Tilt Top, Maple, Paint, Dish Rim Top, Birdcage, 3 Legs, Claw Feet, c.1880, 29 x 31 In. 1150.00
Table, Tea, Tilt Top, Chippendale, Mahogany, Gallery Top, Britain, 18th Century, 30 x 31 x 29 In. 1600.00
Table, Tea, Tilt Top, Birdcage, Turned Post, Carved Scroll & Leaf, Claw & Ball Feet, 29 x 32 In. 1955.00
Table, Tea, Tilt Top, Chippendale, Mahogany, Leaf, Tripod, Britain, 18th Century, 29 x 27 x 27 In. 2450.00

Table, Tea, Tilt Top, Chippendale, Walnut, Birdcage, Circular, Cabriole Legs, 1700s, 29 x 31 In. . 2938.00
Table, Tea, Tilt Top, Walnut, Figured, Birdcage, Ring & Baluster Support, 30 x 30 In. 6900.00
Table, Tea, Tilt Top, Queen Anne, Mahogany, Tilt Top, Bullnose, Turned Pedestal, c.1750, 27 x 21 In. 550.00
Table, Tea, Tip Top, Queen Anne, Mahogany, Cut Corners, Tripod Base, 28 x 32 x 31 In. 345.00
Table, Tilt Top, Breakfast, Regency, Mahogany, Burl Walnut, Inlay, 29 x 62 x 43 In. 1528.00
Table, Tilt Top, Federal, Pine, Tripod Base, 28 ⅛ x 19 ⅞ x 21 ⅞ In. 235.00
Table, Tilt Top, George III, Mahogany, Columnar Pedestal, Tripod, Snake Feet, 27 x 35 In. . . . 690.00
Table, Tilt Top, George III, Mahogany, Piecrust, Turned Pedestal, 3 Legs, 27 ½ In. 4248.00
Table, Tilt Top, Mahogany, 3-Footed, Early 20th Century, 29 x 26 In. 110.00
Table, Tilt Top, Mahogany, Baluster Shaft, Acanthus Carved, Paw Feet, 29 x 34 ½ In. 705.00
Table, Tilt Top, Papier-Mache, Mother-Of-Pearl Inlay, Scalloped Rim, Britain, c.1870, 29 x 22 In. . 1350.00
Table, Tilt Top, Queen Anne, Birch, Turned Post, Snake Foot Legs, Pad Feet, c.1800, 26 x 32 In. 86.00
Table, Tilt Top, Queen Anne, Walnut, Turned Pedestal, Cabriole Legs, 29 x 34 ¼ In. 495.00
Table, Tilt Top, Round, Inlaid Grapevine, Barley Twist Stem, Concave 3-Part Base, 29 In. 1200.00
Table, Tilt Top, Victorian, Rosewood, Circular, 19th Century, 29 x 52 In. 3000.00
Table, Tilt Top, William IV, Mahogany, Pedestal, Scrolled Feet, Brass Casters, 29 x 57 x 51 In. . 1320.00
Table, Tray, Butler's, Mahogany, Cutout Handles, Dovetailed, 19th Century, 15 ½ x 25 ½ In. *illus* 181.00
Table, Tray, Butler's, Georgian, Mahogany, Dovetailed, X-Shape Folding Stand, c.1810, 39 x 31 In. . 518.00
Table, Tray, Butler's, Oak, Cutout Handles, Rectangular, 39 x 30 x 22 In. 1080.00
Table, Tray, George III, Satinwood, Oval Top, Floral Inlay Medallion, 29 ¼ x 23 In. 2115.00
Table, Tray, Georgian, Pine, Stained, Mahogany Stand, Stretcher, 25 x 24 In., Pair 1200.00
Table, Tray, Mahogany, Handles, Folding Stand, 19th Century, 15 ½ x 25 ½ In. 165.00
Table, Tray, Mahogany, Divided, Carved Handles, H-Stretcher, Stand, 24 x 20 x 16 In. 470.00
Table, Tray, Mahogany, Fitzhugh Platter, Flared Legs, 18 ½ x 15 In. 1150.00
Table, Tray, Oak, Folding Stand, 32 x 15 In. 82.00
Table, Tray, On Stand, Lacquer, Chinese Figures, Heron, River, Mid 1800s, 22 x 31 In. 532.00
Table, Tray, Stand, Queen Anne Style, Burl Walnut, Gallery, Handles, Cabriole Legs, 23 x 29 x 17 In. 823.00
Table, Trestle, Arts & Crafts, Mahogany, 3 Butterfly Inlays, Early 1900s, 31 x 72 In. 2300.00
Table, Trestle, Baroque, Scrolled, Gadrooned, Panels, Italy, 32 ¾ x 69 ¾ In. 5581.00
Table, Trestle, Pine, 3-Board Top, Breadboard Ends, Solid Battens, Scalloped Legs, 74 x 33 In. 863.00
Table, Trestle, Stickley Bros., Rectangular, Slab Sides, Shoefoot Base, Metal Tag, 30 x 54 x 30 In. 2000.00
Table, Trestle, Walnut, Wrought Iron, Plank Top, Splayed Legs, Spain, 28 ¾ In. 2938.00
Table, Victorian, Ebonized, Black Lacquer, Gilt, Gesso, Polychrome, Oriental Scene, 27 x 15 In. 840.00
Table, Victorian, Gothic, Cast Iron, Marble Top, Pendant Frieze, Iron Base, 33 x 38 In. 1920.00
Table, Victorian, Mahogany, Marble, 3-Footed, 92 x 44 ½ In. . . . . *illus* 2200.00
Table, Victorian, Marble Top, Oval, Molded Skirt, c.1860, 30 x 40 In. 1495.00
Table, Victorian, Wedgwood Jasperware Inlay, Brass, Shaped Apron, Fluted Legs, 32 x 30 x 18 In. 1116.00
Table, W. Platner, Nickel Plated, Wire Base, Inset Glass Top, 18 x 16 In. 570.00
Table, Walnut, 2-Board Top, Shaped End Legs, Wrought Iron Trestle, 31 x 51 In. 2000.00
Table, Walnut, Beige, White, Black Marble Top, 4 Legs, c.1870, 28 ¾ x 31 x 22 In. 275.00
Table, Walnut, Carved, Banded, Cabriole Legs, Bellflower, Italy, 19 x 24 x 18 ½ In. 2880.00
Table, Walnut, Drawer, Square Legs, 19th Century, 30 x 60 x 41 In. 385.00
Table, Walnut, Drawers, Tapered Turned Legs, Spoon Feet, 63 x 35 In. 3422.00
Table, Walnut, Drop Leaf, Claw & Ball Feet, c.1800, 29 x 45 In. 743.00
Table, Walnut, Enameled Copper Insert, Brown Saltman, 18 x 18 x 15 ¼ In. 60.00
Table, Walnut, Gateleg, Middle Atlantic States, Late 18th Century, 28 x 36 In. 705.00
Table, Walnut, Oval, Burl Top, Crossbanded, Pedestal Support, Figure Carved Legs, 28 x 45 In. . 531.00
Table, Walnut, Pine, Drawer, Overhanging Top, Missouri, c.1860, 31 x 72 In. 1093.00
Table, Walnut, Serpentine Front & Sides, Beaded Edge, Dovetailed, 22 x 15 x 24 In. 100.00
Table, Walnut, Tilt Top, Marquetry, Tripod, Oval Top, 29 ½ x 22 In. 1003.00
Table, Warren McArthur, Circular, Light Blue Laminate Top, Aluminum Frame, 24 x 26 In. . . 270.00
Table, William & Mary, Gateleg, Walnut, Turned Legs, 3-Board Top, 30 x 80 In. 1725.00
Table, William & Mary, Tiger Maple, Butterfly, Early 1700s, 23 ½ x 35 ½ In. 4406.00
Table, William & Mary Style, Burl Walnut, Drawer, Drop Pulls, 1800s, 29 x 36 In. 1298.00
Table, William & Mary Style, Walnut, Shaped Frieze, Banded Drawer, Turned Legs, 30 x 32 In. 300.00
Table, William IV, Rosewood, 3-Part Base, 8-Sided Marble Game Board Top, 29 x 22 In. 2640.00
Table, Wine, French Provincial, Pine, Tilt Top, Planks, Oval Top, Swinging Support, 28 x 55 In. 720.00
Table, Wine, Louis XVI, Fruitwood, Marble Top, Bottle Inserts, 19th Century, 27 x 16 x 16 In. . 1998.00
Table, Wine, Queen Anne, Pad Feet, 18th Century, 27 x 22 In. 330.00
Table, Wine Tasting, Contemporary, Tilt Top, Lyre Shape Support, 29 x 38 In. 504.00
Table, Wood, Glass, Pedestal, Green Paint, c.1960, 26 ⅝ x 21 In. 7800.00
Table, Writing, Chippendale, Mahogany, Pierced Carved Gallery, Drawers, c.1770, 35 x 28 In. 2255.00
Table, Writing, Edwardian, Mahogany, Inset Leather, 31 x 59 x 33 In. 2056.00
Table, Writing, Federal, Mahogany, Philadelphia, c.1815, 28 x 54 x 29 In. 11353.00
Table, Writing, George III Style, Mahogany, Provincial, Inset Leather Surface, 31 x 60 In. 2640.00

Furniture, Umbrella Stand, Arts & Crafts, Wood, Cutouts, Drip Pan, 32 x 11 x 11 In.
$620.00

Furniture, Vitrine, Louis XV Style, Mahogany, Shell & Flower, Mirror, 71 x 23 x 14 In.
$375.00

Furniture, Vitrine, Louis XVI Style, Mahogany, Gilt Brass Ormolu, 67 x 30 x 20 In.
$480.00

Furniture, Wall Unit, G. Nelson, CSS, 3 Bays, 6 Shelves, Cabinets, Herman Miller, 1950s, 96 x 97 In.
$3600.00

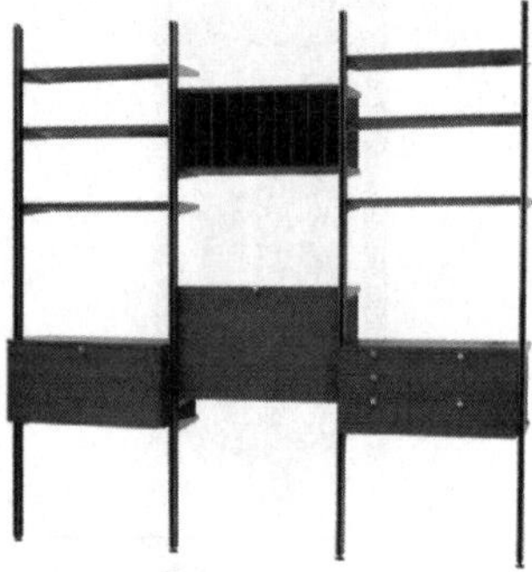

Furniture, Wardrobe, Blue Paint, 2 Doors, Pa., 18th Century, 78 x 58 x 22 In.
$6600.00

Furniture, Washstand, Corner, Federal, Mahogany, Drawer, Boston, 42 x 25 x 17 In.
$547.00

Table, Writing, Louis XV, Kingwood, Tulipwood, 27¾ x 24¾ x 16¾ In. 4200.00
Table, Writing, Louis XV, Kingwood, Ormolu Mounts, 27¾ x 29 x 18½ In. 6000.00
Table, Writing, Louis XV, Tulipwood, Satinwood, Cabriole Legs, 28 x 14½ x 17 In. 7800.00
Table, Writing, Louis XV Style, Fruitwood, Inlaid Kingwood, 36 x 29 In. 235.00
Table, Writing, Louis XV Style, Gilt Metal Mounted, Rosewood, Slant Front, 34 x 36 In. 705.00
Table, Writing, Louis XVI, Mahogany, Casters, 28½ x 37¾ x 21¾ In. 7200.00
Table, Writing, Louis XVI Style, 5 Drawers, Fluted Legs, Brass Mount, 31 x 55 x 28 In. 353.00
Table, Writing, Louis XVI Style, Mahogany, Leather Top, Drawers, Maitland-Smith 1880.00
Table, Writing, Mahogany, Inset Leather, Bulbous Legs, 29 x 32 x 18¾ In. 1452.00
Table, Writing, Mahogany, 2 Drawers, Leather, Turned Legs, Casters, c.1850, 31 x 72 x 46 In. . 1912.00
Table, Writing, Partners, British Colonial, Calamander, 3 Paneled Frieze Drawers, 31 x 61 In. 2115.00
Table, Writing, Poplar, Pine, Oak, 2 Doors Over Drawer, c.1890, 40 x 39 x 22 In. ...... *illus* 260.00
Table, Writing, Provincial, Oak, Paneled Drawer, Mid 19th Century, 31 x 45 In. 3600.00
Table, Writing, Walnut, 2 Drawers, Mid 19th Century, 30 x 54 x 30½ In. 2233.00
Table, Writing, William IV Style, Mahogany, Leather Inset, 3 Drawers, 30½ x 59 x 38 In. 2220.00
Table, Yellow Pine, Blue Paint, Dovetailed Drawer, Southern, 1800s, 28½ x 31 In. 978.00
Table Base, Cast Iron, Scrolling Vine Legs, Twisted Stretchers, Late 1800s, 31 x 72 In. 368.00
Table Set, Frank Lloyd Wright, 6 Stools, Heritage Henredon, 17 x 48 In. Table, 7 Piece . . *illus* 8900.00
Table Set, Kitchen, Chrome, Laminate, Gold Starburst, Silver Studs, Leaves, 4 Chairs, 1950s . 825.00
Table Set, Nesting, Oak, Slat Stretcher Base, Splayed Spindle Legs, 20 x 25 In., 4 Piece 168.00
Table Set, Pine, Painted Checkerboard, Silver, c.1900, 4 Chairs 715.00
Table, Pembroke, Hepplewhite, Maple, Pine, Drawer, Tapered Legs, c.1810, 28 x 16½ In. 382.00
Table, Sewing, Federal, Mahogany, Veneer, Drawer, Spiral Turned Legs, 1800s, 31 x 22 In. ... 1265.00
Table, Sewing, Lacquerware, Compartmented Interior Fitted, Carved Ivory Utensils, 28 x 25 In. 940.00
Table, Sewing, Mahogany, 2 Drawers, Ribbed Legs, Sewing Slide, Basket, 29 x 19 x 13 In. 489.00
Table, Sewing, Victorian, Rosewood, Lift Top, Fitted Interior, Drawer, c.1850, 31 x 23 In. 633.00
Table, Shaker, Tailoring, Maple, Pine, Mt. Lebanon, Mid 19th Century, 30½ x 94½ x 40 In. .. 4914.00
Table, Writing, Mahogany, Drawer, Ebonized Turned Pulls, Saber Legs, 29 x 33 x 16 In. 502.00
Tabouret, Arts & Crafts, Cut Corner Top, Corbel Supports, Gothic Cutouts, 13 x 13 x 19 In. .. 540.00
Tabouret, Arts & Crafts, Hexagonal Top, 4 Splayed Legs, 14 x 14 x 18 In. 210.00
Tabouret, Arts & Crafts, Hexagonal Top, Pyrographic Poppy, 12 x 14 x 17 In. 480.00
Tabouret, Arts & Crafts, Mahogany, Hexagon Top, Inlaid Design, 15 x 17 x 20 In. 480.00
Tabouret, Arts & Crafts, Octagonal Top, Flared Base, 16 x 16 x 16 In. 270.00
Tabouret, Arts & Crafts, Octagonal Top, Slab Sides, Bull's-Eye Detail, 14 x 15 x 18½ In. 450.00
Tabouret, Arts & Crafts, Round Top, Notched Cross Stretcher Base, 16 x 18 In. 240.00
Tabouret, G. Stickley, Round Top, Cross Stretcher Base, No. 603, 18 x 20 In. 1320.00
Tabouret, Stickley Bros., Flared Legs, Cross Stretcher Base, Signed, Metal Tag, 19 x 12 x 12 In. 395.00
Tabouret, Stickley Bros., Square Top, Signed, 18 x 12 x 12 In. 330.00
Tea Cart, Drinks, Gilt Metal, 3 Mirrored Trays, Scrolling End Supports, 28½ x 26 In. 780.00
Tea Cart, Mahogany, Butler's Tray, Late 20th Century, 30 In. .... *illus* 100.00
Tea Cart, Regency Style, Mahogany, 2 Tiers, Drawers, Casters, 38½ x 39 x 18½ In. .... *illus* 450.00
Umbrella Stand, Arts & Crafts, Center Slab, Cutout Club, Peaked Top, 11 x 11 x 32 In. 660.00
Umbrella Stand, Arts & Crafts, Green Matte Glaze, Cylinder, Flower Petal Border, 20 In. 705.00
Umbrella Stand, Arts & Crafts, Slats, Brass Corner Bracket, Drip Pan, 27 x 10 x 10 In. 290.00
Umbrella Stand, Arts & Crafts, Wood, 21 Compartments, Drip Pan, 31 x 16 x 31 In. 200.00
Umbrella Stand, Arts & Crafts, Wood, Cutouts, Drip Pan, 32 x 11 x 11 In. .... *illus* 620.00
Umbrella Stand, Brass, Flared Top, Early 20th Century, 23 x 11¼ In. 35.00
Umbrella Stand, Bronze, Lion's Head Handles, Early 20th Century, 27 x 12 In. 177.00
Umbrella Stand, Cast Iron, Child, Holding Serpent, Drip Pan, Coalbrookdale Works, 33 x 18 In. . 4080.00
Umbrella Stand, Fornasetti, Cylindrical, Colorful Necktie Design, 10½ x 22½ In. 780.00
Umbrella Stand, G. Stickley, 3 Compartments, Tapered Posts, 21 x 11 x 34 In. 960.00
Umbrella Stand, G. Stickley, 3 Compartments, Drip Pan, 21 x 12 x 33 In. 1150.00
Umbrella Stand, G. Stickley, 6-Sided, Hammered Copper, 8½ x 26½ In. 840.00
Umbrella Stand, G. Stickley, Copper, Repousse Design, 12 x 27 In. 3480.00
Umbrella Stand, G. Stickley, Oak, Silver Painted Drip Pan, Brass Tag, 30½ x 50½ In. 1955.00
Umbrella Stand, G. Stickley, Tapered, Slats, No. 100, 12 x 14 In. 1440.00
Umbrella Stand, Iron, White Paint, 19th Century, 28 In. 1315.00
Umbrella Stand, Metal, Doberman, 34¼ x 17½ In. 1020.00
Umbrella Stand, William IV, Mahogany, Ring Tuned Bulbous Supports, 33 x 36 In. 780.00
Valet, Maple, Brass, Finial, Hook, Hanger, Casters, 56½ x 18 x 15 In. 5400.00
Vanity, Bird's-Eye Maple, Scrolled Mirror Supports, 2 Drawers, Queen Anne Legs, 59 In. 118.00
Vanity, Empire, Mahogany, Mirror, American, 19th Century, 36½ In. 690.00
Vanity, Louis XV, Lift Top, Mirror, Bombe, Cabriole Legs, 28 x 17 x 14 In. 2868.00
Vanity, Ormolu & Painted Porcelain, Gilt Bronze Castings, Flowers, Birds, 52 x 27 In. 11500.00
Vanity, Victorian, Faux Bamboo, Bird's-Eye Maple, Mirror, Shelves, Pedestals, c.1880, 32 x 64 In. 3173.00

Vitrine, Chippendale, Mahogany, Gadroons, Carved Legs, 64 x 46 x 15 ½ In. 3290.00
Vitrine, Louis XV, French Style, Mahogany, Ormolu Rim, Diamond Shape, 19 x 21 In. 288.00
Vitrine, Louis XV Style, Fruitwood, Leafy Carved Cornice, 74 x 55 In. 2880.00
Vitrine, Louis XV Style, Kingwood, Rosewood, Marquetry, Glass Shelves, 74 x 31 x 15 In. 1763.00
Vitrine, Louis XV Style, Mahogany, Shell & Flower, Mirror, 71 x 23 x 14 In. *illus* 375.00
Vitrine, Louis XV Style, White & Gray Marble Top, Glazed Doors, Painted Scenes, 63 x 44 In. 633.00
Vitrine, Louis XVI, Mahogany, Lift Top, Gilt Bronze, 30 x 25 x 18 ½ In. 1058.00
Vitrine, Louis XVI Style, Mahogany, Gilt Brass Ormolu, 67 x 30 x 20 In. *illus* 480.00
Vitrine, Louis XVI Style, Mahogany, Ormolu Mounted, Marble Top, Glass Panels, 42 x 50 In. 7050.00
Vitrine, Mahogany, Hinged Glazed Top, Tapered Square Legs, Spade Feet, 26 x 13 ¾ In. 561.00
Vitrine, Mahogany, Octagonal, Drawers, Tapered Square Legs, 33 x 18 x 12 In. 1762.00
Vitrine, Renaissance Revival, Rosewood, c.1870, 67 ½ x 36 x 17 ½ In. 7638.00
Vitrine, Rosewood, Glass Top, 2 Drawers, Silk Lined, 48 x 22 x 29 In. 823.00
Vitrine, Trefoil, Shaped Glass Lift Lid, Curved Sides, Gilt Flowers, Lower Shelf, 29 x 22 In. 518.00
Vitrine, Walnut, Mirrored Glass, 2 Drawers, Late 20th Century, 62 x 28 x 13 In. 295.00
Vitrine, William & Mary Style, Burl Walnut, Linenfold, c.1900, 72 x 34 In. 881.00
Wall Unit, G. Nelson, CSS, 3 Bays, 6 Shelves, Cabinets, Herman Miller, 1950s, 96 x 97 In. *illus* 3600.00
Wardrobe, American Gothic, Knock Down Style, Walnut, Poplar, Panel Doors, 85 x 66 In. 3220.00
Wardrobe, Biedermeier, Mahogany, Maple, Paneled, 86 x 43 x 21 In. 875.00
Wardrobe, Blue Paint, 2 Doors, Pa., 18th Century, 78 x 58 x 22 In. *illus* 6600.00
Wardrobe, Copper Repousse Of Sailboats, 70 x 25 x 86 In. 2400.00
Wardrobe, Eastlake, Walnut, Vertically Partitioned, Mirrored Door, Early 1900s, 78 x 46 In. 236.00
Wardrobe, Empire, Mahogany, Arched Pediment, Paneled Doors, 87 x 79 x 25 In. 885.00
Wardrobe, Empire, Mirrored Door, Picture Frame, Drawer Base, 81 x 41 In. 375.00
Wardrobe, Louis XVI, Walnut, Cabriole Legs, Beveled Glass Door, c.1900, 94 x 48 x 18 In. 708.00
Wardrobe, Louis XVI Style, Walnut, Cabriole Legs, Glass Door, c.1900, 94 x 48 x 18 In. 472.00
Wardrobe, Neoclassical, Empire, Mahogany, Carved & Gilt, Stencil, 2 Doors, Columns 2588.00
Wardrobe, Pine, Door, Mortise & Tenon Jointed, Beveled Panels, Drawer, 1950 3250.00
Wardrobe, Renaissance Revival, Walnut, Raised Panels, Arched Crest, c.1870, 106 x 63 In. 2475.00
Wardrobe, Rosewood, Bird's-Eye Maple Interior, Mirror Door, Carved, c.1875 3850.00
Wardrobe, Victorian, Mahogany, 2 Mirrored Doors, Carved Crest, Finials, c.1860, 102 x 71 In. 1210.00
Wardrobe, Victorian, Rococo, Rosewood, Mirrored Door, Alexander Roux, c.1860, 93 x 40 In. 7425.00
Wardrobe, Victorian, Rosewood, Burl Yew, Arched Crest, Mirror, c.1840, 92 x 43 In. 1410.00
Wardrobe, Walnut, Burl Veneer, 2 Doors, Drawers, Applied Moldings, 88 x 58 In. 500.00
Wardrobe, Walnut, Molded Cornice, Panel Doors, Drawer, Shaped Apron, 86 x 53 In. 118.00
Wardrobe, William IV, Mahogany, Double Paneled Doors, 87 x 57 x 28 ½ In. 5875.00
Wardrobe, Wyburd, Mirror, Single Door, Open Interior, 81 x 37 x 18 ½ In. 2520.00
Washstand, Aesthetic Revival, Walnut, Fable Tile Plaques, Splashboard, Drawers, 28 x 36 In. 705.00
Washstand, Chippendale, George III, Cutout Handles, Drawer, 31 x 20 x 17 In. 1127.00
Washstand, Corner, Federal, Mahogany, Nathaniel Hyde Style, c.1810, 42 x 25 In. 546.00
Washstand, Corner, Federal, Mahogany, Drawer, Boston, 42 x 25 x 17 In. *illus* 547.00
Washstand, Country Sheraton, Grain Painted, Fruit Stenciled, Drawer 252.00
Washstand, Empire, Mahogany, Veneer, Carved, Marble Top, 35 x 25 x 17 In. 1645.00
Washstand, Federal, Mahogany, Scrolled Backsplash, Drawer, Shelf, 36 x 25 In. 1410.00
Washstand, G. Stickley, Strap Hinges, 46 x 41 x 23 In. *illus* 6200.00
Washstand, George III, Backboard, Scalloped Apron, Drawer, Splayed Legs, 23 x 44 x 15 In. 472.00
Washstand, Gothic Revival, Walnut, Marble Top, France, 38 x 17 In. *illus* 175.00
Washstand, Hepplewhite, Pine, Yellow Paint, Stenciled, c.1800, 35 x 18 x 15 In. *illus* 978.00
Washstand, Mahogany, c.1830, 36 x 20 x 17 ½ In. 3055.00
Washstand, Mahogany, Cabriole Legs, 2 Drawers, Brass Basin, 32 ½ In., 2 Piece 287.00
Washstand, Mahogany, Fold-Out Top, Lift Up Mirror, 2 Drawers, Door, England, 34 x 17 x 18 In. 1380.00
Washstand, Mahogany, Marble Top, Drawer, Shaped Stretcher, c.1830, 27 x 22 In. 1645.00
Washstand, Mahogany, Marble Top, c.1820, 37 x 29 ½ x 19 ½ In. 2940.00
Washstand, Pine, Gallery Top Drawer, Low Shelf, Turned Supports, 1800s, 33 x 18 In. 558.00
Washstand, Pine, Lower Tier Shelf, Square Tapered Legs, 32 ½ x 8 ½ x 14 In. 100.00
Washstand, Pine, Yellow Paint, Stenciled Fruits, Striping, Dovetailed Gallery, 39 x 18 In. 863.00
Washstand, Provincial, Pine, Drawer, Mid 19th Century, 31 x 17 x 15 In. *illus* 175.00
Washstand, Regency, Mahogany, Hinged Lid, Mirror, False Drawer Over Drawer, 34 x 18 x 19 In. 520.00
Washstand, Regency, Mahogany, Drawer, c.1800, 29 x 22 In. 767.00
Washstand, Rococo Revival, Rosewood, Marble Top, 3 Drawers, 86 x 35 x 23 ¾ In. 1020.00
Washstand, Scalloped Backsplash, Drawer, Tapered Legs, 19th Century, 39 x 24 x 16 In. 822.00
Washstand, Sheraton, 2 Tiers, Scrolled Backsplash, Drawer, Mustard, Fruit, Leaf, 38 x 18 x 14 In. 385.00
Washstand, Sheraton, Cherry, Poplar, Gallery, Basin Cutout, Shelf, Drawer, 31 x 17 In. 288.00
Washstand, Sheraton, Cherry, Drawers, 18 x 18 x 38 In. 403.00
Washstand, Sheraton, High Back, 2 Shelves, Drawer, Spiral Legs, 41 x 33 x 18 In. 546.00

Furniture, Washstand, G. Stickley, Strap Hinges, 46 x 41 x 23 In.
$6200.00

Furniture, Washstand, Gothic Revival, Walnut, Marble Top, France, 38 x 17 In.
$175.00

Furniture, Washstand, Hepplewhite, Pine, Yellow Paint, Stenciled, c.1800, 35 x 18 x 15 In.
$978.00

Big Is Better

Extra-tall cupboards and highboys, large dining room tables, and other huge pieces of furniture are no longer sold at bargain prices. New homes with cathedral ceilings and large rooms have space for these large antique pieces, so prices are high.

Furniture, Washstand, Provincial, Pine, Drawer, Mid 19th Century, 31 x 17 x 15 In.
$175.00

Furniture, Washstand, Walnut, Curly Maple, Bull's-Eye Medallion, Ohio Valley, c.1880, 39 x 27 x 17 In.
$920.00

Furniture, Window Seat, Gilt, Dolphin Frame, Frieze, Paw Feet, 31 x 85 x 25 In.
$4800.00

Furniture, Window Seat, Painted, Gilt, Turned Armrest, Lotus Panel, 25 x 47 x 18 In.
$375.00

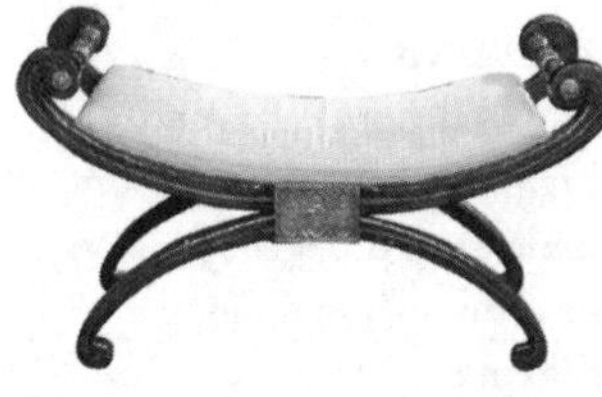

Washstand, Sheraton, Mahogany, Bowfront, Shaped Backsplash, Drawer, 42 x 23 x 16 In. . . . 198.00
Washstand, Sheraton, Maple, Drawer, Shelf, Late 19th Century, 35 x 31 x 18 In. . . . 440.00
Washstand, Softwood, Drawer, Backsplash, Turned Legs, Scroll Cut Shelf, 35 x 22 x 16 In. . . . 88.00
Washstand, Victorian, Faux Bamboo, Bird's-Eye Maple, Mirror, Splashboard, Child's, 23 x 23 In. 881.00
Washstand, Victorian, Mahogany, Divided, Basin Ring, Shelf, Drawer, 32 x 20 x 20 In. . . . 235.00
Washstand, Victorian, Walnut, Marble Top, Skirt, Backsplash, England, c.1880, 40 x 48 x 22 In. 200.00
Washstand, Walnut, Curly Maple, Bull's-Eye Medallion, Ohio Valley, c.1880, 39 x 27 x 17 In. *illus* 920.00
Wastebasket, G. Stickley, Slats, 14 x 12 In. . . . 1800.00
Wastebasket, G. Stickley, Slats, Tapered, 12 x 24 In. . . . 2880.00
Wastebasket, Roycroft, Slats, Orb & Cross Mark, 16 x 14 In. . . . 2040.00
Wastebasket, Stickley Bros., Arched Rails, Hand Hold Cutouts, Twist Posts, 12 x 12 x 18 In. . . 510.00
Wastebasket, Stickley Bros., Cane Panels, Shoefoot Base, 14 x 13 x 18 In. . . . 1140.00
Whatnot, Napoleon III, Marquetry, Brass Mount, 3 Tiers, Kidney Shape, 33 x 19 In. . . . 147.00
Whatnot, Regency, Mahogany, Carved, Molded Shelves, Beehive Supports, 52 x 15 In. . . . 960.00
Whatnot, Regency, Mahogany, Drawer, 4 Tiers, Turned Uprights, c.1825, 52 x 19 In. . . . 2400.00
Window Seat, George III, Gilt, White Paint, Carved, Scrolled Ends, 29 x 58 In. . . . 8125.00
Window Seat, George III, Mahogany, Tapered Legs, Padded Seat, 30 x 49 x 14 In. . . . 3120.00
Window Seat, Gilt, Dolphin Frame, Frieze, Paw Feet, 31 x 85 x 25 In. . . . *illus* 4800.00
Window Seat, Louis XVI Style, Beech, Carved Leaf, Fluted Arms, Legs, 16 x 24 In. . . . 646.00
Window Seat, Painted, Gilt, Turned Armrest, Lotus Panel, 25 x 47 x 18 In. . . . *illus* 375.00
Wine Cooler, George III, Mahogany, Brass Bound, Oval, Lead Lined, Ireland, 20 x 32 In. . . . 7638.00
Wine Rack, 6 Bottle, Circles, Teak, 14 x 13 x 9 In. . . . 150.00
Workbench, Shaker, Pine, Slide Top, Dovetailed Drawer, Bootjack Ends, c.1820, 21 x 30 In. . . 585.00

FURSTENBERG Porcelain Works was started in Furstenberg, Germany, in 1747. It is still working. Many of the modern products are made in the old molds.

Bowl, Pierced, Open, Flowers, 20th Century, 3 ½ x 8 In. . . . 71.00

G. ARGY-ROUSSEAU is the impressed mark used on a variety of objects in the Art Deco style. Gabriel Argy-Rousseau, born in 1885, was a French glass artist. In 1921, he formed a partnership that made pate-de-verre and other glass. He worked until 1952 and died in 1953.

Box, Cover, Gold, Red Mask, Pate-De-Verre, c.1923, 3 ½ x 6 In. . . . 5040.00
Box, Purple Hydrangea Blossoms, White, Black Centers, Pate-De-Verre, 3 ¾ In. . . . 5750.00
Box, Cover, Amber, Brown, Ibis On Lid, Signed, Pate-De-Verre, 5 In. . . . 5175.00
Box, Cover, Brown, Roping, Bird Handle, Pate-De-Verre, Signed, c.1923 . . . 10800.00
Jar, Honesty Leaves, Pate-De-Verre, 3 ¼ x 3 ½ In. . . . 4200.00
Lamp, Dome Shade, Pink, Purple, Acanthus Leaf, Hammered, Pate-De-Verre, 14 In. . . . 34500.00
Paperweight, 2 Butterflies, Amber Cube, Pate-De-Verre, Signed, 2 ¼ x 1 ¾ In. . . . 3000.00
Pendant, Burgundy Butterfly, Pate-De-Verre, Gold Silk Cord, 2 ¼ In. . . . 920.00
Pendant, Green Parrot With Red Beak, Pate-De-Verre, Round, Signed, 4 In. . . . 2070.00
Pendant, Peony Blossom, White, Brown, 0Pate-De-Verre, Silk Cord, 2 ½ In. . . . 1560.00
Sconce, Egg Shape, Pate-De-Verre, Signed, c.1925, 4 Piece . . . 26400.00
Shade, Garland Of Roses, Purple, Pate-De-Verre, Signed, 6 x 3 ¼ In. . . . 5700.00
Shade, Roses, Green, Incised, Pate-De-Verre, 6 x 3 ¼ In. . . . 5100.00
Vase, 2 Masks, Ivy Leaves, Incised, Pate-De-Verre, 4 x 2 ¾ In. . . . 3240.00
Vase, Bud, Ribs, Eagles, Raspberry Ribbons, Purple Border, Pate-De-Verre, 5 ¼ In. . . . 4025.00
Vase, Geometric, Yellow, Brown, Frosted Pate-De-Verre, Ram's Horn Handles, 8 x 7 ½ In. . . . 2750.00
Vase, Loups Et Eventails, Masks, Fans, Pink, Purple, Cream, Pate-De-Verre, c.1925, 5 ¼ In. . . . 7200.00
Vase, Mottled Blue, Amethyst, Papyrus, Pate-De-Verre, 10 ½ In. . . . 12650.00
Vase, Papillons, 4 Butterflies, Green, Orange, Purple & White Ground, Pate-De-Verre, c.1915, 3 In. . . 6000.00
Vase, Purple, Dancer, Pate-De-Verre, c.1923, 11 ⅝ In. . . . 9600.00
Vase, Purple, Gray, Black, Molded Flowers, Leaves, Rolled Rim, Pate-De-Verre, 5 In. . . . 7800.00
Vase, Stacked Triangles, Greens Purples, Pate-De-Verre, 8 ½ x 5 In. . . . 12000.00

GALLE was a designer who made glass, pottery, furniture, and other Art Nouveau items. Emile Galle founded his factory in France in 1874. After Galle's death in 1904, the firm continued to make glass and furniture until 1931. The name *Galle* was used as a mark, but it was often hidden in the design of the object. Galle glass is listed here. Pottery is in the next section. His furniture is listed in the Furniture category.

Atomizer, Cranberry Red, Flowering Branch, Slender Neck, Signed, c.1900, 4 ½ In. . . . 370.00
Atomizer, Ivory, Red Leaves, Signed, c.1900, 6 In. . . . 510.00
Atomizer, Landscape, Purple Trees, Blue Mountains, Green Lake, Frosted, Cameo, 5 ½ In. . . . 1840.00
Biscuit Jar, Flowers, Vines, Leaves, Tangerine To Clambroth, Metal Handle, 9 ¾ In. . . . 1610.00

Bowl, Clematis, Vines, Lavender, Blue, Gray, Blue Ground, 4-Lobed Mouth, Cameo, 3 In.. . . . . 1035.00
Bowl, Green Brown, Leaves, Signed, 6 ¼ x 4 In. 3163.00
Bowl, Purple Blossoms, Frosted Ground, Oval, Cameo, 4 ¼ x 11 In. 1200.00
Box, Cover, Enameled, Gold, Blue Flowers, c.1910, 3 ¾ x 6 ½ In.. . . . . 5040.00
Chandelier, Magnolia, Red, Pink, Brown, Yellow, Gilt Bronze, Cameo, c.1900, 18 In. Diam. . . 42000.00
Dish, Purple Dragonflies Lily Pads, Frosted, Boat Shape, Signed, 3 x 7 In.. . . . . 525.00
Ewer, Enameled, Man Playing Bagpipes, Outdoors, Blue Green & Bronze, 8 x 6 In. 900.00
Ewer, Gold Inclusions, Signed, c.1900, 8 ⅜ In. 8400.00
Lamp, Domed Shade, 3 Butterflies, 3-Arm Black Wrought Iron Base, 4 In. 978.00
Lamp Base, Citron Ground, Turquoise Grapes, Vines, Mold Blown, Signed, 12 In. 2760.00
Perfume Bottle, Pink, Amethyst & Green Flowers, Egg Shape, Teardrop Stopper, 4 In. 460.00
Pitcher, Flowers, Enameled, Clear Ground, Applied Handle, 7 ½ In. 2990.00
Pitcher, Flowers, Fruit, Smoky Yellow, Geometric, Applied Handle, 7 ¾ In. 2760.00
Plate, Pink Flower, Enameled, Pinched Rim, Applied Cabochon Center, 6 ¼ In. 863.00
Powder Jar, Cover, Cherries, Leaves & Stems, Light Yellow Ground, Cameo, 4 In.. . . . . 1610.00
Powder Jar, Cover, Orange, Flowers, Stems & Leaves, Cameo, 4 In. 1093.00
Scent Bottle, Verre Parlant, Pink, Black Handles, Intaglio, Heart Shape, c.1900, 5 ¾ In.. . . . . 10200.00
Tumbler, Poppies, Yellow To Burnt Orange Mottled Ground, Gold Foot Rim, 5 In. 2070.00
Vase, 3 Colors, Canoe Shape, Citron, Pond Scene, Crimson, Yellow, Cameo, 15 In. 2990.00
Vase, Amber, Enameled, Swirl, Ruffled Edge, Flattened Ruffled Foot, c.1900, 8 In. 702.00
Vase, Amber Clematis Branches, Yellow Shaded Ground, Mold Blown, 9 ½ x 6 ¾ In.. . . . . 8400.00
Vase, Banjo, Allover Ferns, Brown & Green, Frosted Ground, Signed, 7 ½ In.. . . . . 480.00
Vase, Banjo, Bending Flowerheads, Frosted Pink Ground, Cameo, 7 ¾ In.. . . . . 325.00
Vase, Banjo, Brick Red Cameo Leaves & Stems, Frosted Yellow Ground, Cameo, 7 In.. . . . . 1035.00
Vase, Banjo, Brown Red, Fiddlehead Fern, Yellow & Green Ground, Cameo, 6 ¼ In. 480.00
Vase, Banjo, Columbine, Lilac, Gray Green, Frosted, Cameo, 6 ½ In. 1060.00
Vase, Banjo, Yellow & Orange Nasturtiums, Frosted Ground, 6 ⅛ In. 355.00
Vase, Berries, Leaves, Brown, Pink & Green Ground, Cameo, 3 ¼ In. . . . . *illus* 475.00
Vase, Berry Pods, Vines, Leaves, Ivory Yellow Ground, Red Strands Pulled Through, 12 In. . . . 1888.00
Vase, Bleeding Heart Branches, Pale Green, Gold, Enameled, Cameo, Signed, c.1895, 13 In. . . 6000.00
Vase, Blossoms & Leaves, Orange Frosted Ground, Tapered, Cameo, Signed, 6 ½ x 2 In.. . . . . . 850.00
Vase, Blue & Purple Blossoms, Blue & Yellow Ground, Cameo, 10 ¾ x 3 In.. . . . . 1920.00
Vase, Blue Lake Scene, Mountains, Amber Cylindrical Body, Rolled Rim, Cameo, 10 In. 2760.00
Vase, Brown Columbine, On Gold To Tan Ground, Cameo, Signed, 6 In. 646.00
Vase, Bud, Green Hibiscus, White Ground, Yellow & Pink Frosted, Cameo, 6 ¾ In. 1300.00
Vase, Bud, Purple Blossoms, Amber Ground, Cameo, 8 ¾ x 3 ¾ In.. . . . . 1920.00
Vase, Bud, Red Carnations, Yellow Ground, Cameo, 8 x 2 In. 1680.00
Vase, Butterflies, Leaves, Lavender, Green To Frosted To Green Ground, Cameo, 22 In.. . . . . . . 4025.00
Vase, Citron, Crimson Leafy Vines, Footed, Elongated Urn, Signed, 15 In. 4600.00
Vase, Citron, Royal Blue Flowers, Leaves, Squat, Bulbous, Cameo, Signed, 3 ¼ In. 2530.00
Vase, Cone, Flared Rim, Brown Forest Over Green Lake, Cameo, Signed, 6 ½ In.. . . . . 1150.00
Vase, Cover, Blue Cameo Mountains, Trees, Cabin, Yellow, Frosted, Egg Shape, 8 In.. . . . . 4140.00
Vase, Cranberry Flowers, Leaves, Opal Ground, Striping, Bottle Shape, Fire Polished, 9 In. . . . 1320.00
Vase, Cranberry Flowers, Leaves, Pale Green Ground, Double Gourd, Fire Polished, 9 In. 2280.00
Vase, Crocus, Pale Blue, Lavender, Petals, Shaded Amber Ground, Mold Blown, Cameo, 8 In. . 6000.00
Vase, Dark Flowers, Blue To Gold Ground, Signed, 7 In. 977.00
Vase, Dragonfly, Water Lilies, Tangerine, Frosted, Shaded To Blue, Handles, Cameo, 8 In. 6325.00
Vase, Enameled, Ferns, Flowers, Optic Ribbed, Bulbous, Applied Handles, 7 ½ In.. . . . . 5290.00
Vase, Enameled, Man On Horse, Silver, Black, Signed, c.1890, 5 In. 4800.00
Vase, Enameled, Vines, Flowers, Signed, c.1895, 8 In. 7800.00
Vase, Flatted Base, White Ground, Brown Leaves, Carved, Cameo, 13 ½ In. 936.00
Vase, Flowered Sprigs, Leaves, Amber, Dimpled Sides, c.1900, 8 In.. . . . . 702.00
Vase, Flowering Branches, Yellow, Brown, Blue, Green, Black Foot, Cameo, c.1900, 21 In. 10200.00
Vase, Flowers, Colorless, Amber, Cameo Cut Amethyst, 3 ⅛ In., Pair 1728.00
Vase, Flowers, Leaves, Mauve, Brown, Yellow Ground, Cameo, 9 In. 1560.00
Vase, Flowers, Leaves, Pale Green Ground, Enameled, Cameo, 3 ½ In. 2160.00
Vase, Flowers, Multiple Shades Of Purple, Yellow Ground, Cameo, 3 x 8 ½ In.. . . . . 1080.00
Vase, Flowers, Orange, Frosted, Leafy Stems, Bulbous, Cameo, Signed, 9 ½ In. 1100.00
Vase, Flowers, Red, Pink, Frosted Yellow, Cameo, Signed, 11 ½ x 5 ½ In. . . . . *illus* 9600.00
Vase, Fougeres, Ferns, Yellow Shaded To Green, Bowl Shape, Signed, 2 x 3 In. 510.00
Vase, Frosted Amethyst To Pink, Green Stemmed Purple Flowers, Cylindrical, Footed, 13 In. . . 2250.00
Vase, Frosted Blue, Carved Pond Lily, Green Highlights, Egg Shape, Signed, 4 In. 633.00
Vase, Frosted Citron, Red Branches, Orange Clusters, White Flowers, Oval, Footed, 14 In. 3500.00
Vase, Frosted Peach, Lake Scene, Bottle Shape, Cameo, Signed, 8 In. 1668.00
Vase, Frosted Pink, Amethyst & Green Flowers, Cameo, Signed, 12 ½ In. 1208.00
Vase, Frosted Pink, Trees, Lake Scene, Island, Oval, Shouldered, Signed, 10 ½ In.. . . . . 2530.00
Vase, Frosted Yellow, Amethyst, Wisteria, Cameo, Signed, 12 In. 1438.00
Vase, Frosted Yellow, Amethyst, Tapered Body, Flowers, Leaves, Cameo, Signed, 8 In. 1265.00

Galle, Vase, Berries, Leaves, Brown, Pink & Green Ground, Cameo, 3¼ In.
$475

Galle, Vase, Flowers, Red, Pink, Frosted Yellow, Cameo, Signed, 11 ½ x 5 ½ In.
$9600.00

G

Galle, Vase, Gloxinias, Leaves, Golden Amber, Chartreuse Ground, Cameo, Signed, 10 In.
$1645.00

TIP

Use coasters under glasses and flower vases on marble-topped tables. Marble can stain easily.

Game, Board, Checkers, Poplar, Painted, On Walnut Stand, 19th Century, 29 x 24 x 24 In.
$325.00

Game, Board, Checkers, Red & Black, Pine, c.1880, 15 ½ x 27 In.
$290.00

Game, Croquet Set, Edwardian, 4 Players, Ball, Early 20th Century, 10 x 42 x 11 In.
$100.00

TIP
Missing part of a jigsaw puzzle? Make a color photocopy of the picture of the puzzle on the box. Enlarge or shrink the copy to exactly the size of the puzzle. Then cut it to make the missing piece. It will be an almost perfect match.

Vase, Frosted Yellow, Green, Amethyst Leaves, Berries, Oval, Bottle Shape, Cameo, 5 ½ In. 604.00
Vase, Frosted Yellow, Purple Wisteria, Cylindrical, Signed, 10 In. 863.00
Vase, Frosted Yellow, Trees, Lake, Castle, Mountains, Shore, Birds, Cameo, 10 ½ In. 7000.00
Vase, Fruit, Burnt Orange, Sienna, Brown Leaves, Amber Ground, Cameo, 15 In. 5750.00
Vase, Fruit & Branches, Red, Pink, White, Signed, 10 ⅜ In. 12000.00
Vase, Fuchsia, Amethyst, Mauve, Squat, Cameo, Signed, 3 In. 390.00
Vase, Fuchsia Berries On Vine, Frosted Ground, Round Base, Straight Neck, 6 In. 705.00
Vase, Gloxinias, Leaves, Golden Amber, Chartreuse Ground, Cameo, Signed, 10 In. .... *illus* 1645.00
Vase, Green Vine, Leaves, Frosted & Pink Ground, Tapered, Squat Base, 13 In. 1175.00
Vase, Hydrangea, Leaves, Lilac, Green, Frosted, Pink Highlights, Flared, 9 ⅝ In. 1763.00
Vase, Irises, Lavender, Brown, Leaves, Shaded Amber To Frosted Green, Cameo, 14 In. 7762.00
Vase, Irises, Purple Leaves, Frosted Ground, Cameo, 10 In. 4025.00
Vase, Landscape, Boats On Pond, Frosted Ground, Cameo, 4 ¼ x 3 In. 840.00
Vase, Landscape, Lake, Boats, Trees, c.1890, 21 In. 1715.00
Vase, Landscape, Purple Trees, Blue Lake, Sky, Mottled Yellow, Cameo, 7 ½ In. 1800.00
Vase, Landscape, Purple Trees, Rocks, Blue Mountains, Frosted Ground, 10 ¼ In. 5400.00
Vase, Landscape, River, Deep Burgundy, Mottled Amber, Cameo, 23 ¾ x 6 ½ In. 2640.00
Vase, Landscape, Trees, Forest, Shoreline, Frosted Green, Cylindrical, Crimson Rim, 14 In. 5000.00
Vase, Lavender Hyacinth, Green Leaves, Yellow Ground, Mold Blown, Cameo, c.1900, 12 In. 9600.00
Vase, Leaf, Multiple Shades Of Purple, Yellow & Frosted Ground, Cameo, 5 x 12 ¼ In. 600.00
Vase, Leaves & Blossoms, Brown, Yellow-Green Frosted Ground, Tapered, Cameo, 5 ½ x 2 In. 850.00
Vase, Light Red Cyclamen Flowers, Amber Ground, Wheel Polished, Cameo, 4 ¾ In. 1560.00
Vase, Long Stem Flowers, Pond Scene, Footed, Cameo, 13 In. 1725.00
Vase, Mauve Cameo Sailing Ships, Harbor, Stone Arch, Trees, Full Moon, Light Pink, 14 In. 1955.00
Vase, Mountain Lake Scene, Frosted, Cameo, Signed, 6 ¾ In. 460.00
Vase, Oak Leaf With Acorn, Green To White, Cameo, 5 ½ In. 588.00
Vase, Olive Green Teasel Silhouettes, Frosted Pink To Green, Footed, Cameo, 16 ½ In. 1765.00
Vase, Orange Nasturtiums, Leaves, Frosted Ground, Tapered, Cameo, 3 ¾ In. 383.00
Vase, Orange Poppies, Frosted Ground, Cameo, 4 ½ x 5 ½ In. 960.00
Vase, Pillow, Purple Leaves, Caramel Ground, Funnel Neck, 6 ⅝ In. 967.00
Vase, Pink Frosted, Amethyst Stemmed Flowers, Heart Shape, Signed, 5 ¼ In. 863.00
Vase, Pink Hyacinth, Red Leaves, Yellow Ground, Mold Blown, Cameo, Signed, c.1900, 12 In. 9600.00
Vase, Pods Of Berries Above Leaves, Brown Against Pink & Green Ground, Cameo, 3 ¼ In. 561.00
Vase, Poppies, Serpentine Stems, Leaves, Orange On Frosty Ground, Cameo, 17 ¼ In. 1534.00
Vase, Purple, Flowers, Leaves, Signed, Cameo, c.1900, 8 In. 3000.00
Vase, Raisin Brown Flowers, Chartreuse Ground, Bulbous, Wide Mouth, Cameo, 4 ⅛ In. 590.00
Vase, Raspberries, Bushes, Leaves, Dark Amber, Yellow Ground, Mold Blown, Cameo, 10 In. 3450.00
Vase, Red & Orange, Flowers, Leaves, Oval, Cameo, Signed, 7 ¾ In. 805.00
Vase, Red Crocus, Amber Shading, Frosted Yellow Ground, Mold Blown, Cameo, 8 ¼ In. 4830.00
Vase, Red Leafy Berries, Yellow Ground, Cameo, Signed, 4 In. 115.00
Vase, Red Wisteria Pods On Vine, Citron Ground, Tapered, Cameo, 6 ¾ In. 765.00
Vase, Roses, Amber Ground, Cameo, 12 ½ In. 7200.00
Vase, Salmon, Deep Amber, Grapevine, Cameo, c.1900, 6 ¼ In. 354.00
Vase, Sprigs, Red & Green Berries, Leaves, Peach Ground, Cameo, 19 x 5 ¼ In. 8400.00
Vase, Stick, Brown Stemmed Flowers, Frosted Yellow Ground, Cameo, Signed, 6 ¾ In. 2645.00
Vase, Stick, Ginkgo Stems, Ferns, Green, Frosted, Bulbous Base, Cameo, Signed, 9 ¾ In. 690.00
Vase, Stick, Pink Frosted, Green, Purple Flower Clusters, Bulbous Base, Signed, 6 In. 489.00
Vase, Stick, Red, Yellow, Frosted Glass, Berries, Leaves, Bulbous Base, Cameo, Signed, 13 In. 1150.00
Vase, Stick, Yellow, Blue Flowers, Olive Green Leaves, Bulbous Base, Flared Rim, Cameo, 5 In. 646.00
Vase, Sunflowers, Red, Pink, Green, Fire Polished, Cameo, Signed, c.1900, 4 ¾ In. 4500.00
Vase, Sunset, Footed, Wide Mouth, Signed, c.1900, 8 ½ In. 4560.00
Vase, Tan & Pink Poppy Buds & Flowers, Frosted To Sky Blue Ground, Cameo, 10 ½ In. 1380.00
Vase, Trees, River, Brown Landscape, Shade Rose To Frosted To Green, 9 In. 1650.00
Vase, Water Lily, Green, White, Blue Rim, Shouldered, Mold Blown, Cameo, c.1910, 10 In. 27000.00
Vase, Wisteria, Frosted Rose Ground, Lavender, Green, Baluster, Wide Foot, c.1900, 8 ¾ In. 956.00
Vase, Wisteria, Vine, Frosted Saffron & Amethyst Ground, Spreading Foot, 17 ¼ In. 1880.00
Vase, Yellow, Brown Stemmed Garden, Bulbous, Cameo, 3 ¾ In. 460.00
Vase, Yellow Orange, Leaves, Blossoms, Handles, Frosted Ground, Cameo, 5 ¼ x 5 In. 1400.00
Vine, Seed Pods, Pumpkin & Frosted Ground, Bulbous, Flared, Frosted Handles, Cameo, 5 In. 1180.00

GAME collectors like all types of games. Of special interest are any board games or card games. Transogram and other company names are included in the description when known. Other games may be found listed under Card, Toy, or the name of the character or celebrity featured in the game.

Across The Continent, Parker Brothers, Tootsietoy Zephyr Markers, Board, 1952. .... 85.00
Board, Buffalo Bill, Parker Brothers, Salem, Mass., Copyright 1898, 9 x 15 In. 717.00
Board, Checkers, 2 Pine Boards, Brass, Painted, Nova Scotia, c.1900. .... 840.00

Board, Checkers, 2-Sided, Painted, Herringbone Inlay, Wood, Varnish Finish, 15 In. 275.00

Board, Checkers, Black & White Squares, Green Border, Black Molding, 1800s, 11 x 10 In. 3173.00

Board, Checkers, Gray, Black, Painted, 15½ x 25 In. 403.00

Board, Checkers, Hex Sign, 2-Sided, Brown, Yellow, Green, 14 x 13½ In. 6000.00

Board, Checkers, Inlaid, Sliding Compartments, 18 x 28 In. 230.00

Board, Checkers, Laminated Maple, Applied Rim, Black Squares, 26½ x 18¾ In. 224.00

Board, Checkers, Maple, Laminated, 19th Century, 26½ x 18¾ In. 200.00

Board, Checkers, Mustard & Black Diamonds, Breadboard Ends, 18¾ x 24½ x 1 In. 4675.00

Board, Checkers, Painted, Multicolored, Dots, Fleur-De-Lis, Stenciled Borders, 15 x 18 In. 1175.00

Board, Checkers, Painted, Black & Cream, Red Outlines, Red Diamond Border, 16 x 15 In. 2703.00

Board, Checkers, Pine, Red & Black, Flourishes, Stenciled, Flowerhead, 26 x 25 In. 10800.00

Board, Checkers, Poplar, Painted, On Walnut Stand, 19th Century, 29 x 24 x 24 In. *illus* 325.00

Board, Checkers, Red, Black, 2-Board Backboard, 1800s, 16 x 26 In. 201.00

Board, Checkers, Red & Black, Pine, c.1880, 15½ x 27 In. *illus* 290.00

Board, Checkers, Red & Black Paint, Trays & Molded Raised Edge, c.1900, 29 x 18½ In. 160.00

Board, Checkers, Salmon, Yellow Painted, 16 x 30 In. 1725.00

Board, Checkers, Softwood, 2-Board, Black Paint, 25½ x 24 In. 187.00

Board, Checkers, Stars & Circles, Quebec, c.1900, 29 x 19¾ In. 5830.00

Board, Checkers, White, Brown, Grained Border, 16 x 16 In. 633.00

Board, Checkers, Wood, Trays, Inlaid Hearts & Clubs, Painted, 1800s, 26 x 21 In. 150.00

Board, Checkers, Wood, Painted, Black, Red, Applied Molding, 19th Century, 19 x 27 In. 235.00

Board, Checkers, Wood, Painted, Red, Yellow, Blue Game Piece Compartments, 17 x 26 In. 353.00

Board, Checkers, Wood, Painted, Gray, Blue, Geometric Verso, Early 1900s, 26½ x 17 In. 805.00

Board, Checkers, Wood, Painted, Green, Black, Applied Molding, 1800s, 16¾ x 24¾ In. 940.00

Board, Checkers, Wood, Painted, Red & Black, Tray Edge, 19⅛ x 19¼ In. 450.00

Board, Checkers, Wood, Painted, Red & Yellow, Square, c.1875, 14¾ x 14½ In. 1880.00

Board, Checkers, Yellow & Black, Yellow End Reserves, Early 1900s, 18 x 30 In. 9600.00

Board, Checkers, Yellow & Black Squares, Red, Black & Green Borders, 14⅜ x 17¼ In. 4700.00

Board, Checkers & Backgammon, Black & Red, 1880, 14 x 17 In. 1645.00

Board, Checkers & Backgammon, Painted, Red, Blue, Black, 18 x 16 In. 2585.00

Board, Checkers & Parcheesi, Painted, Black Ground, Red Molding, 20⅜ x 28 In. 5288.00

Board, Checkers & Parcheesi, Pine, Painted, White Stars, 17 x 17 In. 3600.00

Board, Checkers & Parcheesi, Raised Edges, Church, Indian, Teepees, 16½ x 24¾ In. 110.00

Board, Chess, Chinoiserie, Gold, Lacquered, Backgammon, Gold, Red, Victorian, 20 x 2 In. 173.00

Board, Chinese Checkers, Red, Yellow, Green, Dovetailed, Patina, Octagonal, 28 In. 350.00

Board, Cribbage, Brass, Scalloped Edge, England, 4 x 9 In. 94.00

Board, Cribbage & Chess, Marquetry Compass Star, Mahogany, Beechwood, 13 x 13 In. 480.00

Board, Folding, Green Felt, 7 Wood Balls, Ivory Markers, 19th Century, 37 In. 11950.00

Board, Mickey Mantle's Big League Baseball, Gardner, 1958 210.00

Board, Painted, Red, Blue, Inlaid Veneer Field, Black Borders, Applied Molded Edges, 12 x 12 In. 588.00

Board, Paper, Pine, Funhouse, 2-Sided, McLoughlin Bros., N.Y., c.1930, 16 x 16 In. 5700.00

Board, Parcheesi, Painted, Mahogany, Shamrocks, Crackling, 19th Century, 14 x 14 In. 403.00

Board, Parcheesi, Pine, Applied Sides, Multicolored Paint, Inscribed Lines, 211/2 x 17 In. 3300.00

Board, Parcheesi, Pine, Painted, Home, Red & Black, Yellow Stripes, Early 1900s, 22 x 22 In. 8400.00

Board, Parcheesi, Pine, Painted, Green, Yellow, Orange, Red, Early 1900s, 21 x 20½ In. 10200.00

Board, Parcheesi, Red, White, Blue Paint, 24 x 24 In. 4600.00

Board, Parcheesi, Red, Black, Green, Mustard, Cream Breadboard Ends, 20 x 28 In. 7638.00

Board, Parcheesi, Wood, Painted, Red, Blue, Green, Yellow, Black, c.1880, 10 x 20 In. 5875.00

Board, Wheeling, Jacques & Son, c.1895, 15 x 30 In. 275.00

Branded, Western Themes, Milton Bradley, Board, Spinner, 1966, 9 x 19 In. 195.00

Bulls & Bears, Charles Darrow, Parker Brothers, Board, 1936, 13½ In. 348.00

Carpet Ball, Red Sponge, Cogwheel Design, 3¼ In. 66.00

Chance, Rotating Wheel, Metal, Jockeys, Racehorses, Mason & Co., N.J., c.1910, 93 In. 2468.00

Chess, Dominoes, Cards, Backgammon, Mahogany, Domed Hinged Lid, 8 x 13 x 11 In. 748.00

Chess Set, Ivory, Carved, Hand Painted, Contemporary, 2¾ To 5¼ In., 32 Piece 224.00

Chess Set, Ivory, Neutral, Red Pieces, Gutta Percha Box, c. 1880 329.00

Chess Set, Silver, Silver Gilt, Germany, c. 1840 4500.00

Croquet Set, Edwardian, 4 Players, Ball, Early 20th Century, 10 x 42 x 11 In. *illus* 100.00

Dexterity Puzzle, Cats & Mice, Germany, Prewar 35.00

Dexterity Puzzle, Woman, Eyeglasses, Mirror Back, D.R.G.M., Germany, 2¼ In. 140.00

Dominoes, Bone, 2 Ivory Veneered Counters, 19th Century 956.00

Dominoes, Box, Carved, Sliding Cover, Dice, Game Pieces, 5 In. 5676.00

Game Of The North Pole, Spear, Board, 1910, 8 x 12 In. 115.00

Gizz, Put & Take, Plastic, Hand Held, Box 60.00

Green Ghost, Glows In The Dark, Transogram, Board, Box, 1965 200.00

Game, Jigsaw Puzzle, Horse Drawn Fire Pumper, Cardboard, McLoughlin Bros., 9 x 12 In.
$320.00

Game, Man In The Moon, No Pieces, McLoughlin Bros, 1912, 14 x 15 In.
$850.00

Game, Mother Goose, Figures Pop Up, Knobs, Paper On Wood, 19 In.
$735.00

Game, Rival Doctors, Box Lid & Board Only, McLoughlin Brothers, 1893, 10 In.
$425.00

Game, Train For Boston, Wood Pieces, Spinner, Parker Brothers, c.1900, 14 x 16 In.
$845.00

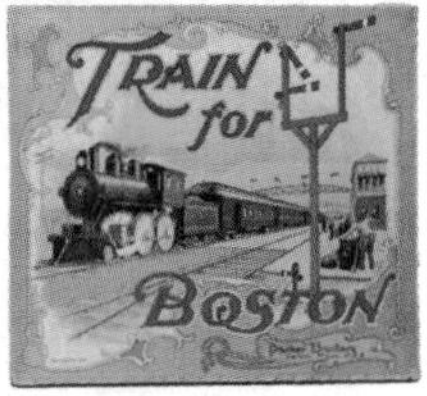

Game, Wheel, Gambling, Carnival, Metal Stand, 26 In.
$460.00

Game, Zeppelin, Cannon Shoots Sticks At Soldiers, Wood, Germany, Box, 10 x 10 In.
$1495.00

TIP
Printed game boards from the 1940s–60s fade very quickly. Older printing seems to be damaged less by exposure to ultraviolet light.

Game Plate, Fish, Platter, 6 Plates, Limoges, 11½ In. Platter, 8½ In. Plate, 7 Piece
$440.00

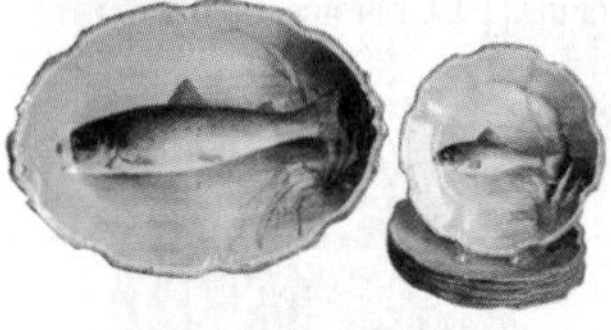

Honey West, Girl Private Eye, Ideal, Board, 1965 ..... 200.00
Improved Game, Fish Pond, Cardboard, Wood, McLoughlin Bros., Board, 1890, 12 x 18 In. 115.00
Jackie Gleason Story Stage Set Game, Cardboard, VIP Corp, 1955 ..... 30.00
Jigsaw Puzzle, Brave Cowboy Bill, Little Golden, 1950 ..... 125.00
Jigsaw Puzzle, Cocomalt Flying Family, 1932, 6 x 10 In. 25.00
Jigsaw Puzzle, Farm Yard, Scroll, McLoughlin Bros., c.1894, 12 x 24 In. 246.00
Jigsaw Puzzle, Fire Engine, Fire Pumper Scene, McLoughlin Bros., 9 x 12 In. 316.00
Jigsaw Puzzle, Horse Drawn Fire Pumper, Cardboard, McLoughlin Bros., 9 x 12 In. ..... *illus* 320.00
Jigsaw Puzzle, Horse Drawn Hose Wagon Rushing To Fire, People Watching, 11 x 17 In. 45.00
Jigsaw Puzzle, Horse Pulling Pumper From The B.F.D. 11, 28 x 18 In. 224.00
Jigsaw Puzzle, Jolly Barnyard, Little Golden, 1950 ..... 125.00
Jigsaw Puzzle, Poky Little Puppy, Little Golden, 1942 ..... 150.00
Jigsaw Puzzle, Quick Be Quick, Pumper, Fireman, Building, 12 x 12 In. 190.00
Jigsaw Puzzle, Tally-Ho Scroll, McLoughlin Brothers, c.1894, 12½ x 24 In. 1540.00
Jigsaw Puzzle, Tootle, Little Golden, 1946 ..... 125.00
Jigsaw Puzzle, White Squadron, Ship, Paper On Wood, McLoughlin Brothers, 40 Piece, 1892 388.00
Jigsaw Puzzle, Wonderful House, Little Golden, 1942 ..... 125.00
Lottery, Roulette Wheel, Prizes, Dolls, Carriage, Furniture, France, 18 x 14 In. 920.00
Man In The Moon, No Pieces, McLoughlin Bros., Board, 1912, 14 x 15 In. ..... *illus* 850.00
Mansion Of Happiness, Parker Brothers, Board, 1894, 21 x 14 In. 310.00
Mother Goose, Figures Pop Up, Knobs, Paper On Wood, 19 In. ..... *illus* 735.00
Motor Cycle, Cyclists On Early 1905 Cycles, Milton Bradley, Board, 9 In. 425.00
National Game Of The Star Spangled Banner, Folding, L.I. Cohen, c.1844, 20 x 16 In. 4113.00
Parcel Post Toy Town, Bradley, 1910 ..... 195.00
Parlor, Theater, Paper Board, Folding, Orchestra, Silhouettes On Stage, France, 19 x 13 In. 896.00
Parlor Football, McLoughlin Brothers, Board, 1890s 575.00
Pope Joan, Chinoiserie, Flowering Wisteria, Papier-Mache, Japan, Board, c.1880, 12 In. 294.00
Puzzle, Aunt Louisa's Cube Puzzle, Jack & The Bean Stalk, McLoughlin Bros., c.1890 ..... 143.00
Puzzle, Hood's, Factory, Plexiglas, 2-Sided, Frame, United States 121.00
Puzzle, Knights Life Insurance, Paper, 4 Piece, Original Envelope 18.00
Puzzle, Rough Riders, McLoughlin Bros., 1898, 18 x 13½ x 1¼ In. 1135.00
Puzzle, Sliding Tile, Casper, 5 x 6 In. 86.00
Puzzle, Sliding Tile, Flintstones, 5 x 6 In. 144.00
Puzzle, Sliding Tile, Huckleberry Hound, 5 x 6 In. 86.00
Rival Doctors, Box Lid & Board Only, McLoughlin Brothers, 1893, 10 In. ..... *illus* 425.00
Robinson Crusoe & His Man Friday, Instructions, Box, 30 Cards, 3¼ x 2¼ In. 538.00
Rough Riders, Teddy Roosevelt, Parker Brothers, 10¼ x 20 In. 345.00
Round The World With Nellie Bly, McLaughlin Brothers, Board, c.1890 ..... 360.00
Scarlett O'Hara, Gone With The Wind, Marble, c.1939 ..... 195.00
Shoot-A-Plane, Box, Abbo-Craft, 9 x 15 In. 86.00
Skee-Ball, Marble, Pressed Steel, Wyandotte, 20 In. 33.00
Snakes & Ladders, Applied Breadboard Ends, Red, Blue, Black, Board, 24 x 18 In. 64625.00
Snapshot, Parker Brothers, Board, 1972 ..... 11.00
Snooker, Scorekeeping Device, Early 19th Century 45.00
Target, Bear Target Game, Shoot Bear, Eyes Light-Up, Tin, Battery, Masudaya, Box, 9 In. 195.00
Target, Little Black Sambo, Wyandotte, Box 325.00
Target, Man From U.N.C.L.E., Ideal Toy Co., 1965, 16½ x 12 In. 472.00
Target, National Defense, Gun On Stand, Tin Lithograph, Metal, Paper, Marx, 12 x 20 In. 201.00
Target, Space Shooting Range, Tin, Windup, Graphics, 19¼ x 13⅞ x 7⅛ In. 248.00
Target Shooting, Playing Cards, Target Blocks, Crossbow, Arrow, Box, 14 x 14 In. 728.00
Tarzan, Parker Brothers, Board, Box, 1939 ..... 489.00
Teddy's Bear Hunt, Theodore Roosevelt, Bowers & Hard, Bridgeport, Board, 18 x 12 In. 836.00
Train For Boston, Wood Pieces, Spinner, Parker Brothers, c.1900, 14 x 16 In. ..... *illus* 845.00
Uncle Sam, John Bull, Chromolithographed Cutouts, Wood, Clay Marbles, 15¼ x 20 In. 633.00
Uncle Wiggily, Parker Brothers, Board, 1979 ..... 12.00
Wheel, Carnival, Horse Racing, Reverse Glass Panel, Brass Cover, 39 x 24 In. 935.00
Wheel, Chance, Dominoes, St. Louis Carnival Supply Co. 770.00
Wheel, Chance, Pine, Sheet Steel, Iron, Round Dial, Horses, Dogs, c.1910, 14¾ In. 978.00
Wheel, Eagle In Center, Poland, 37 In., Diam. 145.00
Wheel, Gambling, Carnival, Metal Stand, 26 In. ..... *illus* 460.00
Wheel, Gambling, Wood, Red & Black Paint, 5 Holes In Wheel, 20¼ In. 495.00
Whist Counter, Hedgehog, Cast Iron, Metal Pins, John Gill Mfg., c.1865 ..... 475.00
Who's Afraid Of The Big Bad Wolf, Marx Brothers, Disney Enterprises, Board 60.00
Wild West Game, McLoughlin Brothers, Board, 1905, 19½ x 19½ x 1½ In. 658.00
Zeppelin, Cannon Shoots Sticks At Soldiers, Wood, Germany, Box, 10 x 10 In. ..... *illus* 1495.00

GAME PLATES are plates of any make decorated with pictures of birds, animals, or fish. The game plates usually came in sets consisting of twelve dishes and a serving platter. These sets were most popular during the 1880s.

Black Grouse, Flowers, Leaves, Pine Branches, Gold Rim, Marked, Fraureuth, 9 ½ In. 69.00
Brooke Trout, Waterfall, Painted, Coin Gold, Limoges, c.1900, 9 ¼ In. 213.00
Buck, 2 Deer, Forest, Ironstone, 12 ½ In. 65.00
Fish, Bottom Of Sea, Scalloped Rim, Flambeau China, Signed, Levy, Late 1800s, 9 ⅞ In. 135.00
Fish, Flowers, Gold Rim, Scalloped, H&B Limoges, 9 ⅛ In. 92.00
Fish, Pink Ground, Green Seaweed, Gold Accents, Signed, Lea, 8 ½ In. 65.00
Fish, Platter, 6 Plates, Limoges, 11 ½-In. Platter, 8 ½-In. Plate, 7 Piece .... *illus* 440.00
Golden Hooded Pheasant, Turquoise, Yellow, Red, Gold Beaded Rim, Borgfeldt, 10 ½ In. 175.00
Grouse Flying, Flower Border, Brown Transfer, Gold Rim, Royal Worcester, 1888, 9 ¼ In. 150.00
Mallard Duck, 2 Drakes, Green & Gold Bands, Schwartzenhammer, Germany, 9 ½ In. 22.00
Mallard Duck At Sunrise, Gold Scrolled Rim, Limoges, c.1900, 9 ½ In. 385.00
Mallard Duck Flying, Purple Iris, Waterfall, Gold Rim, Limoges, 1890s, 10 ¾ In. 795.00
Partridge Flying, Gold Scrolled Rim, Limoges, c.1900, 10 In. 597.00
Pheasant, Signed, Limoges, 10 In. 125.00
Pheasant Flying, Signed, Duval, c.1910, 8 ¾ In. 100.00
Quail, Flying, Transfer, Taylor, Smith & Taylor, Signed, R.K. Beck, 1908-15. .... 98.00
Quail, Gliding, Brown, Beige, Blue, Scrolled Rim, Flambeau Limoges, c.1900, 10 In. 597.00
Rooster, Beading, Scalloped Rim, Laviolette, Flambeau, Limoges, France, c.1890, 8 ½ In. ... 125.00
Turkey, Transferware, Johnson Bros., 11 In. 50.00
Woodcock, Wildflowers, Blue Sky, Gold Rim, Signed, Luz, c.1900, 10 ¾ In. 210.00

GARDEN FURNISHINGS have been popular for centuries. The stone or metal statues, wire, iron, or rustic furniture, urns and fountains, sundials, and small figurines are included in this category. Many of the metal pieces have been made continuously for years.

Arch, Lattice, Geometric, Shield, Pine, White Paint, Mid 19th Century, 121 x 74 In. 6600.00
Armchair Set, Regency, Dolphin Crests, 19th Century, 4 Piece 2350.00
Armillary, Sphere, Rings, Copper, Painted, Iron, Aluminum, Marble Base, 28 x 28 In. 345.00
Bench, Arched, Lattice, Cast Metal Back, Wood Slat Seat, 31 x 50 In. 45.00
Bench, Baroque, Wood, Ivory Paint, England, 38 x 97 x 26 In. .... *illus* 1700.00
Bench, Concrete, Curved, 15 x 40 In., Pair 75.00
Bench, Leaves, Geometric, Scroll Arms, 3 Arch Back, Cast Iron, 33 x 54 ½ x 20 In. 2011.00
Bench, Neoclassical Style, Urn, Swag, Paneled Rods, Curule Base, Cast Iron, 30 x 47 x 21 In. . 2400.00
Bench, Queen Anne Style, Slat Back, Scalloped Skirt, Pine, Painted White, 39 x 78 In. 2040.00
Bench, Root & Branch Back, Slat Seat, Late 19th Century, 39 x 69 x 36 In. .... *illus* 1200.00
Bench, Rustic, Bronze, 33 x 63 ½ x 23 In., Pair 3525.00
Bench, Slatted Seat, Shaped Arms, Metal, Multicolor, France, 39 x 60 x 25 In. 2160.00
Birdbath, Round, Petal Carved Font, Banded, Fluted, Gypsum Marble, Indian, 42 x 28 In. 5520.00
Birdbath, Winged Putto, Raised Arms, Holding Clamshell, Lead, 32 ½ x 15 ¼ In. 1380.00
Birdhouse, 4 Rooms, Green, Tan, Wood, 20th Century, 30 ¾ x 30 ¾ In. 420.00
Birdhouse, Martin, Painted, Wood, Lead, Hexagonal, Arched Openings, Shelf, 51 x 27 In. 1200.00
Birdhouse, Painted, 4 Entry Holes, Wood, Glass Windows, c.1950, 15 x 22 x 13 In. 431.00
Birdhouse, Turret, Half Round, White, Wood, Shingle Roof, 7 Openings, c.1950, 51 x 43 In. . . 1840.00
Boot Scraper, Dachshund Shape, c.1900, 12 In. 205.00
Boot Scraper, Cast Iron, Cat Shape, Glass Eye, 11 x 10 ½ In. 121.00
Boot Scraper, Cast Iron, Gothic Style, H-Shape, Stone Base, Victorian, 15 x 20 x 8 In. 1020.00
Boot Scraper, Cast Iron, Oval Tray, 7 ½ x 11 In. 58.00
Boot Scraper, Cast Iron, Oval Tray Base, 7 ½ x 11 ½ In. 58.00
Boot Scraper, Cast Iron, Scrolled, 19th Century, 15 ¾ x 10 In. 764.00
Bucket, Flower Vendor's, Galvanized Metal, France, Mid 1900s, 13 x 9 ¾ In., 3 Piece 480.00
Chair, Morning Glory, Concave Back, Vines, Leaves, Cast Iron, 33 In., Pair 576.00
Chair, Openwork, Cast Iron, Atlanta Stove Works, c.1890, 31 x 15 x 14 In., Pair .... *illus* 395.00
Chair, Slatted, Scroll Arms, Hardwood, Iron, 35 In., Pair 864.00
Chair Set, Folding, Slatted, Hardwood, Iron, 32 In., 6 Piece 864.00
Chaise Longue, Wicker, White, Roll Arms & Back, Bar Harbor Style, 34 x 63 x 35 In. 50.00
Figure, Cherub, Atop Ball On Square Plinth, Lead, 16 x 8 x 8 In., Pair 705.00
Figure, Pineapple, Plinth Base, Cast Iron, White Paint, 19 x 8 In., Pair 176.00
Figure, Squirrel, Eating Acorn, Cast Iron, 19th Century, 10 ½ In., Pair .... *illus* 748.00
Figure, Woman, With Grapes, Concrete, White Paint, 48 x 19 In. 575.00
Flowerpot, Attached Saucer, Tinware, Late 19th Century, 5 ½ x 5 In. 77.00
Fountain, 3 Tiers, 9-Light, Cherubs, Swans, Water Nozzles, Footed, Copper, 32 x 26 In. 1610.00
Fountain, Boy, Playing Pipes, Cement, 30 In. 527.00

TIP

Outdoor stonework and statues, even if made of granite, can be damaged by acid rain, frost, and plants like ivy. Put garden statues on stands to keep the moisture from the grass away from the statue. Wash with a hose and a soft brush.

Garden, Bench, Root & Branch Back, Slat Seat, Late 19th Century, 39 x 69 x 36 In.
$1200.00

Garden, Bench, Baroque, Wood, Ivory Paint, England, 38 x 97 x 26 In.
$1700.00

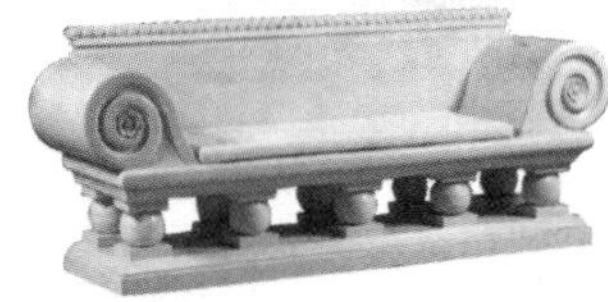

TIP

Some types of stone and metal remain free of organic stains if they're left in partial sunlight and heat, but not if in deep shade.

GARDEN

Garden, Chair, Openwork, Cast Iron, Atlanta Stove Works, c.1890, 31 x 15 x 14 In., Pair
$395.00

Garden, Figure, Squirrel, Eating Acorn, Cast Iron, 19th Century, 10 ½ In., Pair
$748.00

Garden, Fountain, Putti, Urn, Bird, Beaver, Lead, c.1890, 28 x 12 x 12 In.
$1795.00

Garden, Gnome, Carrying Sprinkler Can, Cast Iron, 28 In.
$685.00

Garden, Lawn Sprinkler, Arrow, Red, Embossed, Cast Iron, 10 x 12 In.
$690.00

Garden, Lawn Sprinkler, Mallard Duck, Cast Iron, 13 In.
$345.00

untain, Boy, Rock, With Umbrella, Cast Zinc, Painted, J.W. Fiske Iron Works, 27 In. 935.00
untain, Boy & Girl, Under Umbrella, Lead, Zinc, 19th Century, 60 x 60 In. 3107.00
untain, Cupid, Trumpets, Horn Spouts, Bronze, 29 x 21 In. 1041.00
untain, Frog, Brass, Green, 5¼ x 12 x 11½ In. 248.00
untain, Girl, Nude, Butterfly, Bronze, Rachel Marshall, Early 1900s, 36 x 21 In. 12600.00
untain, Goose, Lead, c.1920, 22 In. 322.00
untain, Lion Face, Lead, 12½ x 11½ In. 173.00
untain, Man, Mustache, Open Mouth, Marble, 1900s, 14 x 14 In. 633.00
untain, Putti, Urn, Bird, Beaver, Lead, c.1890, 28 x 12 x 12 In. *illus* 1795.00
untain, Wall, Baroque Style, Marble, Scrolling Backsplash, Lion's Head Mask, 73 x 63 In. 13200.00
zebo, Neoclassical, Domed, Gilding, Ornamentation, Cast & Wrought Iron, 237 x 135 In. 16450.00
ome, Carrying Sprinkler Can, Cast Iron, 28 In. *illus* 685.00
tching Post, Cannonball Finial, 13 In. 83.00
tching Post, Horse, Iron, Shape, c.1900, 56 In. 1093.00
tching Post, Horse Head, Cast Iron, Late 19th Century, 14¼ In. 147.00
tching Post, Jockey, Arm Extended With Lantern, Concrete, Painted, 27 In. 60.00
wn Sprinkler, 2 Arms Spin, Brass, Steel, Rain King, Model D, Sunbeam Corp., c.1925 45.00
wn Sprinkler, Alligator, Head Up, Heart Shape Sprinkler Head, Cast Iron, 9 x 10 In. 144.00
wn Sprinkler, Arrow, Embossed, Red Paint, Cast Iron, W.D. Allen, Chicago, 10½ x 12 In. 690.00
wn Sprinkler, Arrow, Red, Embossed, Cast Iron, 10 x 12 In. *illus* 690.00
wn Sprinkler, Elephant, White, On Wheels, Cast Iron, 34 x 25 In. 4600.00
wn Sprinkler, Frog, Molded Hose Attachment, Cast Iron, 4¼ x 4¼ In. 201.00
wn Sprinkler, Frog, Seated, Open, Mouth, On Ball, Cast Iron, 8½ In. 320.00
wn Sprinkler, Mallard Duck, Cast Iron, 13 In. *illus* 345.00
wn Sprinkler, Mallard Duck, Multicolored, Cast Iron, Stained, Nuydea, 13¼ In. 978.00
wn Sprinkler, Mermaid, Holding Sprinkler Head, 2-Sided, Green, White, Red, Cast Iron, 14 In. 1043.00
wn Sprinkler, Squirrel, Holding Nut, Zinc Alloy, 7½ x 7 In. *illus* 115.00
wn Sprinkler, Turtle, Cast Iron, 8½ x 9¾ In. 201.00
wn Sprinkler, Turtle, Head Up, Mouth, Spout, Painted, Black, Red, Cast Iron, 9 In. 805.00
wn Sprinkler, Walking, Silver Painted Spoke Wheels, Cast Iron, Green, Brass Spout, 16½ In. 86.00
nament, Acanthus, Pedestal Base, Cement, Cast Mold, 20¼ In., Pair 55.00
neapple, Cast Iron, White Paint, Late 19th Century, 24 x 8½ In., Pair *illus* 805.00
ant Stand, see Furniture, Stand, Plant
anter, Gilt Cast Iron, Scrolling Flowers Borders, Leaves, c.1920, 29 x 33 In. 325.00
anter, Louis XVI Style, Cast Stone, Square, France, 10 x 12 In. 570.00
anter, Marble, Slant Sides, Relief Carved, Birds On Branches, White, 11 x 28 x 13 In. 518.00
anter, Stand, Iron, Figural Supports, Tripod Base, 19 In. 275.00
anter, Wrought Iron, 3 Legs, Copper Insert, Arts & Crafts, 14 x 28 In. 510.00
at, Arts & Crafts, Octagonal, Cutout Base, Curved Sides, 16 x 16 X17 In. 660.00
at, Attendants, Birds, Flowers, Butterflies, Chinese, c.1860, 19 x 14 In. 4510.00
at, Blue & White, Birds, Blossoms, Barrel Shape, Bosses, 1800s, 19 In., Pair 5625.00
at, Blue & White, Porcelain, c.1850, 18½ x 12 In. 351.00
at, Burl Root, Chinese, 18½ In. 4560.00
at, Famille Jaune, Calligraphy, Bat, Flowers, Yellow Ground, 19 x 13 In. 2124.00
at, Famille Rose, Chinese, Ducks, Lotus Blossoms, Lily Pads, Multicolored, 18 x 13 In., Pair 7150.00
at, Gnarled Tree Trunk Root, Applied Seat, Foot Plates, Chinese, 19½ x 15 x 13 In. 2640.00
at, Wood, Allover Relief Carved Vines & Bands, Barrel Shape, Chinese, 20 In. 1020.00
ool, Blue & White, Hexagonal, Flowers, Leaves, 18½ x 12 In. 105.00
ndial, Arrow, Scroll, Bronze, Patina, 10 x 14 In. 139.00
ndial, Bobby Jones, Bronze, Signed, E.E. Codman, 18½ In. *illus* 3540.00
ndial, Copper Hemisphere, Cobalt Glazed, Ceramic Stand, 5⅞ x 5½ In. 1554.00
ndial, Cast Iron, 11 In. 58.00
ndial, Sculpture, Brown Patina, Blue Green, Edwin E. Codman, 18½ In. 3540.00
ble, Figural, Putti, Picking Fruit, Oval Top, Cast Stone, Italy, 30¼ x 55 x 39 In. 7260.00
ble, Napoleon III Style, Limestone Top, Iron Scroll Base, Brass Rondels, 30 x 37 In. 4080.00
ble, White Marble Top, Cast Iron Cheval Base, Spindle Gallery, Victorian, 28 x 36 x 18 In. 840.00
piary, Obelisk, Iron, Burnished Gilt, Latticework, Ball Feet, 78 x 19 In., Pair 294.00
ough, Down Spout Drain, Hand Carved, Sandstone, 6 x 13 x 22½ In. 1045.00
ough, Empire Style, Rounded Body, Ring Handles, Carrara Marble, Late 1800s, 22 x 71 In. 7500.00
ough, Pump, Round, Center Hole, Raised Lip, Spill Slot, Carved, Sandstone, 9½ x 21 In. 1430.00
ough, Victorian Style, Oval, Leaf Scrolled, Ring Handles, Scroll Legs, Cast Iron, 19 x 49 In. 1320.00
n, Basket, Cherubs, On Drum, Leaf & Berry Border, Metal, c.1890, 59 x 30 In., Pair *illus* 1800.00
n, Cast Iron, Flared Lobed Rim, Leaf Waist, Plinth Base, 17 x 18½ In., Pair 1103.00
n, Cover, Edwardian, Fluted, Cast Iron, 22 x 12½ In. 3840.00
n, Neoclassical, Flared Lip, Fluted Waist, Square Base, White Marble, 26¾ In., Pair 1440.00

Garden, Lawn Sprinkler, Squirrel, Holding Nut, Zinc Alloy, 7½ x 7 In.
$115.00

Garden, Pineapple, Cast Iron, White Paint, Late 19th Century, 24 x 8½ In., Pair
$805.00

Garden, Sundial, Bobby Jones, Bronze, Signed, E.E. Codman, 18½ In.
$3540.00

Garden, Urn, Basket, Cherubs, On Drum, Leaf & Berry Border, Metal, c.1890, 59 x 30 In., Pair
$1800.00

GAUDY DUTCH

Gaudy Dutch, Plate, Zinnia, Vine Border, Impressed, Riley, 8 ⅜ In.
$4500.00

Gaudy Dutch, Teapot, Carnation, Blue Vine, 6 ¼ x 10 ¼ In.
$2200.00

Dating by Color

Colors can help date your Twentieth-century antiques and collectibles. Lavender and violet were popular in 1910. Red, green, and beige were favored in the '30s, especially in the kitchen. Pink, black, and turquoise were '50s colors; and chrome, copper, and yellow were popular in the '60s. And who can forget the avocado and harvest gold refrigerators and matching fabrics of the 1970s. The '80s brought bright hues, including teal and mauve; and the '90s, rich tones of red violet, magenta, and plum. Appliances, meanwhile, became black or stainless steel.

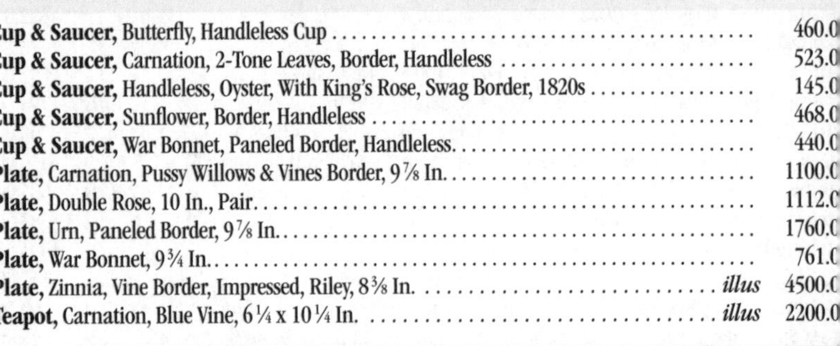

GAUDY DUTCH pottery was made in England for the American market from about 1810 to 1820. It is a white earthenware with Imari-style decorations of red, blue, green, yellow, and black. Only sixteen patterns of Gaudy Dutch were made: Butterfly, Carnation, Dahlia, Double Rose, Dove, Grape, Leaf, Oyster, Primrose, Single Rose, Strawflower, Sunflower, Urn, War Bonnet, Zinnia, and No Name. Other similar wares are called Gaudy Ironstone and Gaudy Welsh.

Cup & Saucer, Butterfly, Handleless Cup 460.0
Cup & Saucer, Carnation, 2-Tone Leaves, Border, Handleless 523.0
Cup & Saucer, Handleless, Oyster, With King's Rose, Swag Border, 1820s 145.0
Cup & Saucer, Sunflower, Border, Handleless 468.0
Cup & Saucer, War Bonnet, Paneled Border, Handleless 440.0
Plate, Carnation, Pussy Willows & Vines Border, 9 ⅞ In. 1100.0
Plate, Double Rose, 10 In., Pair 1112.0
Plate, Urn, Paneled Border, 9 ⅞ In. 1760.0
Plate, War Bonnet, 9 ¾ In. 761.0
Plate, Zinnia, Vine Border, Impressed, Riley, 8 ⅜ In. .... *illus* 4500.0
Teapot, Carnation, Blue Vine, 6 ¼ x 10 ¼ In. .... *illus* 2200.0

GAUDY IRONSTONE is the collector's name for the ironstone wares with the bright patterns similar to Gaudy Dutch. It was made in England for the American market after 1850. There may be other examples found in the listing for Ironstone or under the name of the ceramic factory.

Bowl, Ribbed, Red, Blue, Green, Gold Flowers, 6 In. 40.0
Pitcher, Water, Blue, White, Red Flowers & Leaves, 1890s, 12 In. 165.0
Plate, Old Japan Vase, Flowers Marked, G. Ashworth, c.1862, 10 In. 280.0
Plate, Strawberry, Paneled, 10 ½ In. 275.0
Platter, Flowers, Blue, Red, Gold Overlay, Copeland & Garrett, c.1840, 11 x 14 In. 295.0
Platter, Flowers, Tree, Birds, 22 In. 300.0

GAUDY WELSH is an Imari-decorated earthenware with red, blue, green, and gold decorations. Most Gaudy Welsh was made in England for the American market. It was made from 1820 to about 1860.

Jug, Marigold, 4 ½ In. 350.0
Jug, Sunflower, Scalloped Rim, Octagonal Base, Snake Handle, 5 ½ In. .... 235.
Pitcher, Bulbous, Flowers, Multicolored, 5 ¾ In. .... 517.
Pitcher, Flowers, Leaves, Snake Handle, Scalloped Rim, 6 ½ In. 77.0
Plate, Columbine, Cobalt Blue, Cartouche, 7 ¼ In. 50.0
Teapot, Scalloped Edge Around Top, 7 In. .... 65.
Vase, Spill, Blue Underglaze, Orange, Pink & Copper Luster, 3 ¼ x 2 ½ In. 550.0

GEISHA GIRL porcelain was made for export in the late nineteenth century in Japan. It was an inexpensive porcelain often sold in dime stores or used as free premiums. Pieces are sometimes marked with the name of a store. Japanese ladies in kimonos are pictured on the dishes. There are over 125 recorded patterns. Borders of red, blue, green, gold, brown, or several of these colors were used. Modern reproductions are being made.

Bowl, Portrait, Flowers, Blue Ground, Gold Trim, 10 ¾ In. .... 157.
Cake Plate, Cobalt Blue, Hand Painted, Scalloped Edge, Gold Trim, 2 Handles, 11 In. 50.0
Chocolate Pot, 10 In. .... 97.
Chocolate Pot Set, Cobalt Blue, Gold Rim, 9 ¾-In. Pot, 13 Piece .... 100.
Cup, Geisha, In Garden, Flowers, Lanterns, Japan, 1930s, 10 Piece .... 35.
Cup & Saucer, Stamped, Mori China, Japan 40.0
Demitasse Set, Hand Painted, Marked, 4 ½ x 2 ⅛ In., 8 Piece .... 25.
Figurine, Yellow Robe, Pink Fan, Stamped Japan, 7 ¼ In. .... 15.
Pitcher, Cobalt Blue, Blue Rim, Gold Liner, 5 In. .... 15.
Plate, Dessert, 7 In., 6 Piece .... 30.
Plate, Dessert, Hand Painted, Marked, Japan, 1940s, 9 In. .... 18.
Sake Set, Decanter, Cups, Japan, 5 Piece .... 24.
Sauce Set, Scalloped Edge Dish, Hand Painted, Gold, 6-In. Dish, 6-In. Pitcher .... 30.
Vase, Bulbous, Off-White, Orange Red At Neck, 4 x 3 ½ In. .... 20.

GENE AUTRY was born in 1907. He began his career as the "Singing Cowboy" in 1928. His first movie appearance was in 1934, his last in 1958. His likeness and that of the Wonder Horse, Champion, were used on toys, books, lunch boxes, and advertisements.

Book, Gene Autry & The Badmen Of Broken Bow, 1951 .... 32.
Box, Belt, 1930s, 11 x 6 In. .... 65.

Cap Gun, Cast Iron, Nickel Finish, Orange Grip, Kenton, 6½ In. 109.00
Comic Book, Saddle Tramp, Dell, 1957 23.00
Guitar, Melody Ranch 248.00
Postcard, Home Of Gene Autry, North Hollywood, California, 1950s, 5½ x 3½ In. 14.00

GIBSON GIRL black-and-blue decorated plates were made in the early 1900s. Twenty-four different 10 ½-inch plates were made by the Royal Doulton pottery at Lambeth, England. These pictured scenes from the book *A Widow and Her Friends* by Charles Dana Gibson. Another set of twelve 9-inch plates featuring pictures of the heads of Gibson Girls had all-blue decoration. Many other items also pictured the famous Gibson Girl.

Box, Portrait, Book Shape, Wood, Carved Pages, Flowers, 1920s, 9¼ x 7½ x 3¼ In. 40.00
Dress, Brown, Grosgrain Ribbon Trim, Size 36-26-36 225.00
Hankie Holder, Pyrography, Cut Velvet, Ribbon Trim, Pink Satin Interior, 6½ x 6½ In. 65.00
Paper Dolls, Tom Tierney, Color, 7 Dolls, 29 Costumes, c.1985, 31 Pages 18.00
Pattern, Doll Clothes, Kestner, No. 172, Nora Outfit 20.00
Plate, Gibson Girl & Her Arab Horse, Flow Blue, Gilt, c.1925, 8½ In. 143.00
Plate, Quiet Dinner With Dr. Bottles, c.1904, 10½ In. 265.00
Plate, Some Think She Has Remained In Retirement Too Long, c.1904, 10½ In. 265.00
Postcard, Miss Camille Clifford, Hat, England, c.1904 8.00
Postcard, Studies In Expression, c.1907 24.00
Postcard, Turning Of The Tide, c.1905 30.00
Postcard, Valentine, Inclination Caught Her Eye, Ostrich Plume Hat, Putti, c.1909 20.00
Print, His Christmas Gift, Life Publishing Co., c.1901, 17¼ x 11¼ In. 55.00
Print, New Year's Resolution, Cupid Whispering, Moffat Yard & Co., c.1906, 20 x 16 In. 325.00
Tin, Cigarette, 50 Gold Tipped Cigarettes, Manoli, Berlin, Germany, c.1910, 4¼ x 3 In. 130.00

GILLINDER pressed glass was first made by William T. Gillinder of Philadelphia in 1863. The company had a working factory on the grounds at the Centennial and made small, marked pieces of glass for sale as souvenirs. They made a variety of decorative glass pieces and tablewares.

GILLINDER

Figurine, Buddha, c.1930, 4½ In. 176.00
Paperweight, Lion, Alexandrite, Satin, 2¾ x 2½ In. 27.00
Paperweight, Lion, Pink, Satin, 2¾ x 2½ In. 25.00
Salt, Liberty Bell 1776, Oval, 1876, 2¼ x 1½ In. 75.00
Salt, Swan, Milk Glass, Late 1880s, 5½ In. 85.00

GIRL SCOUT collectors search for anything pertaining to the Girl Scouts, including uniforms, publications, and old cookie boxes. The Girl Scout movement started in 1912, two years after the Boy Scouts. It began under Juliette Gordon Low of Savannah, Georgia. The first Girl Scout cookies were sold in 1928.

Bracelet, Charm, Spells Brownie, Gold Tone, 6 In. 25.00
Coin, 50th Anniversary, 1912-1962, 1 In. 8.00
Doll, Ginny, Green Chintz Outfit, Purse, Beaded Bracelet, Walker, Straight Leg 225.00
Doll, Janie, Uniform, Blond, Vinyl Head, Blue Sleep Eyes 65.00
Doll, Uniform, Brown Curly Hair, Painted Face, Jointed, Effanbee 38.00
Flashlight, Green, Red, Emblem On Sides, 1950 12.00
Handbook, Brownie Scout, Hardbound, 1960 10.00
Handbook, Hardbound, Dust Jacket, 1940 15.00
Lunch Box, Hinged Top, Tin, c.1920, 6 x 3¾ In. 125.00
Pin, Lt. Colonel, Sterling Silver, Safety Clasp, 1¼ x 1 In. 8.00
Pocketknife, 4 Fold-Out Tools, Metal Loop Handle, Green Celluloid Case, 3½ In. 21.00
Pocketknife, Official Deluxe, Green Celluloid Handle, Utica Kutmaster, 1940s, 3 7/16 In. 35.00
Sash, Nassau Council 14, 2 Stars, Wing Badge, First Aid, Skating, Treasure Chest, 1960s 24.00

GLASS-ART. Art glass means any of the many forms of glassware made during the late nineteenth or early twentieth century. These wares were expensive and production was limited. Art glass is not the typical commercial glass that was made in large quantities, and most of the art glass was produced by hand methods. Later twentieth-century glass is listed under Glass-Contemporary, Glass-Midcentury, or Glass-Venetian. Even more art glass may be found in categories such as Burmese, Cameo Glass, Tiffany, and other factory names.

Bowl, Amber, Pink, Striated, Crimped Top, Leafy Stemmed Flowers, Egret, 7 In. 3700.00
Bowl, Centerpiece, Orange & Gray Green Rays, Silver Webbing, Orange Rim, WMF, 13 In. 235.00
Bowl, Dimpled Peach Interior, Cream Exterior, Ruffled Rim, Glossy, 5⅛ x 9¾ In. 115.00
Bowl, Engraved, Art Deco, Footed, Continental, 8¾ x 10¼ In. 1320.00
Bowl, Iridescent Gold, Scalloped Rim, 3¾ x 10 In. 994.00

Glass-Art, Dresser Box, Boy Holding Ball, Etling, Opalescent, France, c.1930, 3½ In.
$489.00

Glass-Art, Epergne, 1-Lily, Baskets, Clear Twist Arms, Green-Yellow Opalescent, England, 17 In.
$478.00

Glass-Art, Epergne, 4-Lily, Cobalt Blue Threads, England, Late 19th Century, 20 x 12 In.
$450.00

Glass-Art, Vase, Enameled Red, Black, Silver, Bruno Mauder, c.1922, 11½ In.
$9375.00

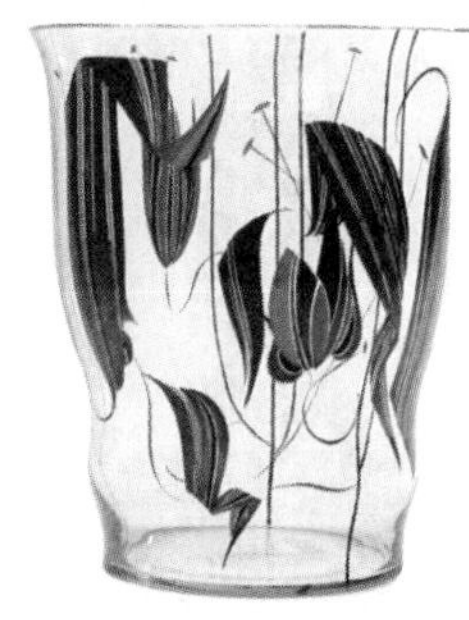

TIP
Spray the inside of a glass flower vase with a nonstick product made to keep food from sticking to cooking pots. This will keep the vase from staining if water is left in too long.

G

Glass-Art, Vase, Irises, Emerald Green, Frosty Textured Ground, Stamped, Honesdale, 12 In.
$600.00

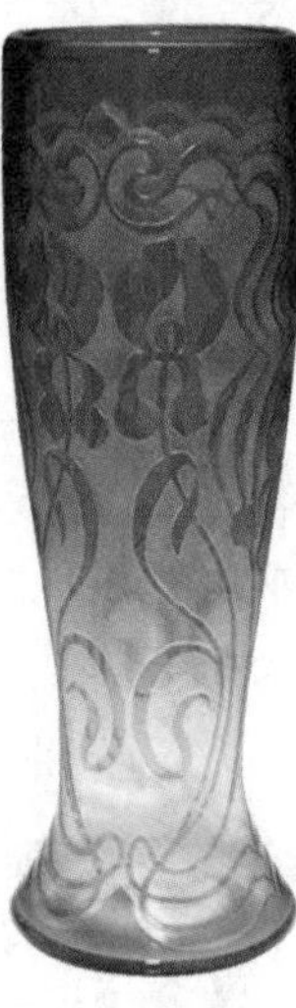

Glass-Blown, Cordial, Green, Solid Stem & Foot, Sheared Rim, England, 18th Century, 4 ⅞ In.
$2740.00

Bowl, Silver Mica Air Traps, Mustard & Yellow Tangles, Flared, Monart, 3 ½ x 9 In. 295.00
Bowl, Venetian Pattern, White Swags, Red Threading, Hobbs, Brockunier, 5 In. 173.00
Compote, Intaglio Flowers, Blue, Red, Amethyst, Green Leaves, Stuart, 5 ½ In.. .... 1150.00
Compote, Translucent Vaseline Opalescent, Melon Ribbed, Footed, Powell, 5 ½ In. 201.00
Decanter, Tumble-Up, Cranberry, Flowers, Aventurine, A. De Carazna, 7 ½ In. 1150.00
Dresser Box, Boy Holding Ball, Etling, Opalescent, France, c.1930, 3 ½ In. .... *illus* 489.00
Epergne, 1-Lily, Baskets, Clear Twist Arms, Green Yellow Opalescent, England, 17 In. .. *illus* 478.00
Epergne, 1-Lily, Blue, Opalescent, Victorian, 7 x 8 ¼ In. 117.00
Epergne, 1-Lily, Blue, Metal Feet, c.1860, 11 x 6 In.. .... 468.00
Epergne, 3-Lily, Cranberry, c.1870, 15 x 11 In.. .... 351.00
Epergne, 4-Lily, 3 Hanging Baskets, Cranberry, c.1880, 20 x 9 In. 175.00
Epergne, 4-Lily, Cobalt Blue Threads, England, Late 19th Century, 20 x 12 In. .... *illus* 450.00
Epergne, 4-Lily, Cranberry, c.1870, 20 x 10 ½ In.. .... 146.00
Epergne, 5-Lily, Clear, Green Fluted Edges, c.1870, 18 x 10 In.. .... 70.00
Ewer, Green, Blue Iridescent, Vine Handle, Silver Plated Mount, c.1900, 12 In.. .... 354.00
Figurine, Nude Woman, Frosted Opalescent, Chrome Base, Etling, c.1925, 9 ¾ In.. .... 3840.00
Figurine, Woman, Wearing Cape, Apron, Round, Opaque Base, 11 ½ In.. .... 705.00
Jar, Sweetmeat, Ribbed Frosted Body, Horizontal Opal & Blue Decoration, 4 ½ In. 115.00
Pitcher, Opalescent, Cranberry, Candy Stripe Swirl, 7 ¾ In. 146.00
Pitcher, Rose, Satin, Enameled Flowers, England, c.1885, 9 ½ x 7 In. 306.00
Pitcher, Water, Blue Satin, Enameled, Red, White, Flowers, Leaves, Bulbous, 8 In. 144.00
Pitcher, Water, Yellow, Silver Aventurine, Ruffled Edge, Reeded Handle, 9 In. 230.00
Rose Bowl, Tortoiseshell, Enameled Blue & White Blossoms, Crimped Top, 4 ½ In. 978.00
Shade, Gold Iridescent, Purple & Blue Highlights, Pulled Fishnet, Ribbed, 5 ¾ x 2 ¼ In. 300.00
Shade, Green, White Pulled Feather, Gold Iridescent, White Ground, 4 ½ x 7 In., 4 Piece. 1380.00
Sugar, Opaque Green, Applied Handles, 3 ½ In. 489.00
Vase, Blue Opalescent, Tulip Shape, Silver Plated Base, c.1900, 12 ¼ In. 82.00
Vase, Bud, Gold Iridescent, Waves, Polished Pontil, 6 ¼ In. 1519.00
Vase, Clear, Red & Blue Pulled Design, Signed, Labino, c.1970, 14 ½ In. 345.00
Vase, Clear, White, Leaves, Vines, Flowers, Ruffled Edge, Victorian, 7 x 3 ¾ In. 1150.00
Vase, Enameled, Etched Hydrangea, France, c.1900, 6 ¼ x 2 ¾ In. 674.00
Vase, Enameled Red, Black, Silver, Bruno Mauder, c.1922, 11 ½ In. .... *illus* 9375.00
Vase, Etched Johnny Appleseed, Footed, c.1942, 11 In.. .... 526.00
Vase, Faceted, Variegated Gray, Green, Friedrich Egerman Lithyalin, 11 In.. .... 2300.00
Vase, Federzeichnung, Mother-Of-Pearl, Oval, Square Rim, Gold Scrolling, 6 ¼ In. 1725.00
Vase, Frosted Glass, Colored Inclusions, Bronzed Metal Holder, France, 9 ½ In.. .... 460.00
Vase, Green, Bulbous, Trailing Prunts, Overlaid Silver Metal On Rim, 5 In.. .... 310.00
Vase, Green, Tree Forest In Relief, Deep Plate Etched, 10 x 8 In. 176.00
Vase, Green Iridescent, Flared, Squat Bulbous Base, Applied Lobes, 4 ½ x 6 In. 100.00
Vase, Green Iridescent Ground, 6 Gold Iridescent Plants, Pontil, 6 In. 588.00
Vase, Green Vines On Iridescent Gold, Pink Ground, 9 In.. .... 1150.00
Vase, Intaglio, Pink, Crimson Band, Shouldered, Optic Ribbed, Richardson, 9 In. 2070.00
Vase, Iridescent, Tulip Shape, Cutout Handles, 9 ¾ x 9 ½ In.. .... 70.00
Vase, Irises, Emerald Green, Frosty Textured Ground, Stamped, Honesdale, 12 In. ..... *illus* 600.00
Vase, Mottled Pink To Green, Allover Gold Flecks, Monart, 8 In. 173.00
Vase, Poppies, Multicolored Mottled Ground, Gold Border, 16 In. 2070.00
Vase, Purple Iridescent, Metal Overlay, Irises, 5 ⅝ In.. .... 207.00
Vase, Red, White Flowers, Shouldered, Florentine, 6 In.. .... 144.00
Vase, Red Ground, Applied Marquetry Flowers, Bulbous, Amethyst Loop Handles, 8 In. 115.00
Vase, Red Interior, Blue Iridescent Draped Design, 3 Stylized Flowers, 5 In.. .... 2072.00
Vase, Silver Overlay, Purple, Iridescent, Australia, c.1900, 5 In. 444.00
Vase, Trumpet, Mottled Purple, Orange, Pink, Flared, Round Flat Base, 16 x 7 In. 400.00
Vase, Trumpet, Willow, Opal Footed, Pulled Feathers, Lundberg, 12 In. 259.00
Vase, White Interior, Rose Colored Leaves, Vines, Flowers, Gold Outlines, 7 x 3 ¾ In. 518.00
Vase, Yellow Spider Mums, Clear To Amethyst, Optic Ribbed, Ruffled Edge, St. Louis, 12 In. .. 235.00

GLASS-BLOWN. Blown glass was formed by forcing air through a rod into molten glass. Early glass and some forms of art glass were hand blown. Other types of glass were molded or pressed.

Bell Jar, 15 ½ In.. .... 657.00
Bell Jar, Amethyst, Applied Beaded Prunt Finial, France, 14 x 12 In., Pair. 900.00
Bird Feeder, Aqua, Sunburst Star, Rough Mouth, Cage Opening, 4 ⅛ x 2 ¼ In.. .... 121.00
Biscuit Jar, Blue Enamel, Silver Rim, Handle, Germany, 8 In. 176.00
Bowl, Aqua, 6 Panels, Pattern Mold, Flared Rim, Pontil, 1840-60, 5 ½ In. 532.00
Bowl, Aqua, 12 Ribs, Mold Pattern, Cobalt Trailing, Funnel Foot, Pontil Base, 7 x 11 ½ In. ... 336.00

Glass-Blown, Decanter, Cobalt Blue, Ribbed, Pontil, 6 ⅜ In.
$130.00

Glass-Blown, Mug, Amethyst, Applied Handle, Pontil, Mid 19th Century, 2 x 2 In.
$650.00

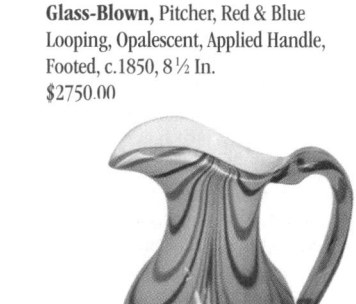

Glass-Blown, Sugar, Cover, White, Cranberry, Pontil, Pittsburgh, c.1860, 13 In.
$5100.00

Glass-Blown, Decanter, Pale Green Aqua, 3-Piece Mold, c.1820-40, 6 ¾ In.
$1450.00

Glass-Blown, Pitcher, Red & Blue Looping, Opalescent, Applied Handle, Footed, c.1850, 8 ½ In.
$2750.00

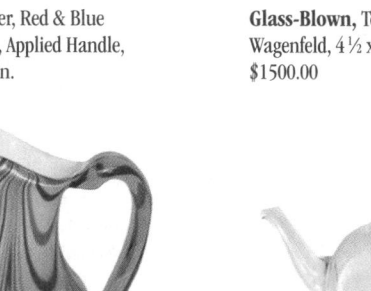

Glass-Blown, Teapot, Jenaer, Wilhelm Wagenfeld, 4 ½ x 10 x 6 In.
$1500.00

Glass-Blown, Jug, Olive Green, Ribbed, Applied Handle, Crimped, Pontil, c.1830, 3 ½ x 2 In.
$3600.00

Glass-Blown, Toilet Water Bottle, Cobalt Blue, Ribbed, Tam-O'-Shanter Stopper, Pontil, c.1830, 6 ¼ Ir
$160.00

Glass-Blown, Darning Egg, Peachblow, Glossy, Pontil, 5 ½ In.
$175.00

TIP
Don't use ammonia on glasses with gold or silver decorations.

Glass-Bohemian, Dresser Box, Cranberry, Gold Enameled, Cherub Medallion, 3-Footed, Metal, 5 In.
$316.00

Glass-Bohemian, Goblet, Toasting, Coat Of Arms, Applied Amber Prunts, Early 1900s, 10 In., Pair
$350.00

Ultraviolet
To tell where your old European glass was made, use an ultraviolet (black) light. The short explanation is that under the light, Bohemian glass is yellow, yellow-green, green, or orange; Venetian glass is pale yellow to yellow-green; and lead crystal is white-yellow to white.

Bowl, Blue Green, Heavy Folded Rim, 1830-60, 5 ¼ x 7 In. 1064.00
Bowl, Utility, Purple Amethyst, Folded Rim, Pontil, 1850, 2 ¾ x 9 In. 560.00
Bowl, Yellow Olive Amber, Flared, Rolled Lip, c.1830, 13 In. 2128.00
Candleholder, Cobalt Blue, Inward Folded Rim, Double Knop Baluster, 4 ½ In. 504.00
Candlestick, 15 Ribs, Sea Green, Applied Socket, Rigaree, Prunts, Footed, 4 In. 672.00
Celery Vase, Heart & Diamond, Tooled Rim, Circular Foot, 3-Piece Mold, 1840, 7 ¾ In. 213.00
Compote, Aqua, 16 Rib, S Pattern Mold, Folded Rim, Drawn Foot, Mold, 1890, 3 x 12 In. 56.00
Compote, Cover, 8 Ribs, Clear, Folded Rim, Baluster Stem, Sloping Foot, 9 ¾ x 6 ¾ In. 523.00
Compote, Cover, 8 Ribs, Clear, Folded Rim, Baluster Stem, Sloping Foot, 12 ½ x 7 ⅜ In. 880.00
Compote, Opaque Blue, Scalloped Rim, Baluster Stem, 1865, 4 ¼ In. 112.00
Compote, Sea Green, Scalloped Rim, 1865, 5 x 10 ¾ In. 179.00
Cordial, Cotton Twist Stem, Engraved Sunflowers, 18th Century, 5 ½ In., Pair 978.00
Cordial, Green, Solid Stem & Foot, Sheared Rim, England, 18th Century, 4 ⅞ In. *illus* 2740.00
Creamer, Aqua To Clear, Opalescent Looping, Footed, Applied Handle, 4 ¼ In. 767.00
Creamer, Cobalt Blue, Bulbous, Threading On Neck, Handle, 1855, 5 ¼ In. 336.00
Cruet, 15 Ribs, Hollow Handle, Footed, Pittsburgh, 1850, 6 ¾ In. 168.00
Cruet, 15 Ribs, Tapered Neck, Hollow Handle, 9 In. 55.00
Cruet, 16 Ribs, Clear, Applied Handle, 7 ¾ In. 168.00
Cruet, 16 Ribs, Swirled To Right, Teal Green, Tooled Rim, Domed Base, Pontil, 5 ½ In. 330.00
Cruet, 24 Ribs, Swirled To Left, Blue, Folded Rim, Domed Base, Pontil, 4 ⅞ In. 154.00
Cruet, Cobalt Blue, Ribs Above Ring Base, Tam-O-Shanter Stopper, Rayed Base, 6 ⅛ In. 165.00
Cruet, Pale Amethyst, 8 Ribs, Hollow Handle, Pontil, 1855, 7 ¾ In. 168.00
Cruet, Satin, Amberina Shading, Stopper, 19th Century, 7 ¾ In. 146.00
Cuspidor, Cobalt Blue, Bulbous, Flared & Folded Rim, Handle, 1875, 3 ½ In. 78.00
Cuspidor, Yellow Amber, Bulbous, Flared Rim, 4 ½ In. 325.00
Darning Egg, Whimsy, Blue Aurene, Steuben, 6 ½ In. 470.00
Darning Egg, Peachblow, Glossy, Pontil, 5 ½ In. *illus* 175.00
Decanter, 8 Ribs, Amethyst, Bar Lip, Neck Ring, Pewter Pour Stopper, Triangular, 12 In. 1430.00
Decanter, 8 Ribs, Green, Panel Cut Neck, Stopper, 1214 In. 176.00
Decanter, 24 Ribs, Swirled To Right, Cobalt Blue, Pinched Sides, Pewter Collar, Screw Cap, 8 ⅞ In. 495.00
Decanter, Amethyst, 3 Neck Rings, 19th Century, 9 ¾ In., Pair 940.00
Decanter, Amethyst, Folded Rim, Molded Neck Ring, ½ Pt. 77.00
Decanter, Aqua, Pinched Sides, Flared Lip, Pontil, 1830, 6 ½ In. 168.00
Decanter, Clear, 9 Molded Panels, Pattern Mold, Bar Lip, Double Border, 9 ¾ x 3 ¾ In. 77.00
Decanter, Clear, Folded Rim, Ringed Base, Pontil, 3 ⅝ x 2 ¾ In. 253.00
Decanter, Clear, Green Tint, Tooled Rim, Molded Neck Ring, Ringed Base, 5 ⅜ In. 66.00
Decanter, Cobalt Blue, Opaque Gray, White Threading, Kick Up Base, 8 ¼ x 2 ¾ In. 303.00
Decanter, Cobalt Blue, Ribbed, Pontil, 6 ⅜ In. *illus* 130.00
Decanter, Cobalt Blue, Silver Plated, Cork Cap, Label, 13 ½ x 2 ⅞ In., Pair 176.00
Decanter, Emerald Green, Flared Lip, Pontil, Britannia, Pour Stopper, 11 ½ In. 176.00
Decanter, Green, Enameled, Verse, Pewter Lid, Embossed Crosses, 9 In. 182.00
Decanter, Light Green, 13 Panels, Applied Ring, Silver Plated, Pour Stopper, 13 In., Pair 77.00
Decanter, Pale Green Aqua, 3-Piece Mold, c.1820-40, 6 ¾ In. *illus* 1450.00
Decanter, Pineapple, Neck Rings, Bulbous, Stopper, c.1820, Qt. 1232.00
Decanter, Ruby Cased, Applied Ring, Britannia & Marble Pour Stopper, Qt., 13 ½ In. 176.00
Decanter, Yellow Olive, Bulbous, Pontil, 3-Piece Mold, c.1840, 7 ¼ In. 531.00
Dish, Clear, Folded Rim, Rayed Base, Pontil, 1 ⅜ x 6 In. 66.00
Eggcup, Teal Green, 20 Ribs, Circular Foot, 1840, 3 In. 67.00
Fishbowl, Clear, Rolled Rim, Trumpet Foot, 13 ¼ x 6 ¾ In. 550.00
Flycatcher, Stopper, 3 Applied Tooled Feet, 19th Century, 9 x 7 In. 353.00
Goblet, Amber, Enameled Crest, 9 ½ In. 201.00
Goblet, Rhine, Amethyst, Clear Stem, 5 ½ In., 11 Piece 23.00
Hat, Amber, New England, 3 In. 170.00
Hat, Clear, Inward Folded Rim, Rayed Base, Iron Pontil, 2 ⅛ x 2 ⅜ In. 66.00
Jar, 16 Ribs, Cobalt Blue, Pattern Mold, Kick Up Base, Pontil, 4 ⅛ x 3 ½ In. 33.00
Jar, Medium Green, Wide Flared Lip, Pinched, Pinched Waist, Pontil, 1860, 10 In. 476.00
Jug, 9 Ribs, Swirled To Right, Clear, Tooled Rim, 2 Rings, Serrated Foot, 7 ½ In. 2750.00
Jug, 16 Ribs, Cobalt Blue, Pear Shape, Applied Handle, Flared Foot, 3 ¾ In. 550.00
Jug, Amber, Globular, Tapered Neck, Plain Rim, Applied Solid Handle, Crimped Foot, Qt. 22.00
Jug, Clear, 3 Rings, Applied Handle, Medial Ribs, Rayed Base, 6 ½ In. 1430.00
Jug, Olive Green, Ribbed, Applied Handle, Crimped, Pontil, c.1830, 3 ½ x 2 In. *illus* 3600.00
Mug, Amethyst, Applied Handle, Pontil, Mid 19th Century, 2 x 2 In. *illus* 650.00
Nappy, Clear, Folded Rim, Rayed, Ringed Base, 1 ⅛ x 4 In. 77.00
Pan, Aqua, Folded Rim, Pour Spout, Pontil, 20 ½ x 4 In. 1568.00
Pan, Yellow, Green, Folded Rim, Pontil, 3 x 8 In. 22.00
Pan, Yellow Amber, Flared Lip, Folded Rim, Pontil, 1845, 2 ¼ x 8 ¼ In. 420.00

ipe, Whimsy, Internally Decorated, Multicolor Spatterware, Steuben, 10 In. 230.00
ipe, Whimsy, Light Blue Jade, Steuben, 10 In. 575.00
itcher, Aqua Green, Flared Rim, Applied Scroll Handle, Footed, 7 ¼ In. 1888.00
itcher, Purple, 3-Piece Mold, 19th Century, 8 In. 292.00
itcher, Red & Blue Looping, Opalescent, Applied Handle, Footed, c.1850, 8 ½ In. . . . . . *illus* 2750.00
alt, Diamond Quilted, Footed, c.1770, 2 ⅞ In. 177.00
alt, Opalescent To Opaque Blue, Ribbed, Rolled Rim, 3 ½ x 3 In. 121.00
alt, Sapphire Blue, Round, Tooled Rim, Drawn Foot, Pontil, 1820-40, 2 ½ In. 1100.00
hade, Hurricane, 19th Century, 22 In. 720.00
hade, Hurricane, Tapered Baluster, Basal Rim, 19th Century, 23 x 8 In., Pair. 2415.00
hade, Hurricane, Waisted Baluster, Basal Rim, 19th Century, 18 x 6 In. 230.00
ugar, Cover, White, Cranberry, Pontil, Pittsburgh, c.1860, 13 In. . . . . *illus* 5100.00
ugar, Dome Cover, Spire Finial, Inward Folded Foot, 7 In. 1120.00
ugar, Flattened Dome Cover, Cobalt Blue, Peafowl Finial, Footed, 4 ½ x 5 In. 303.00
ugar & Creamer, Opalescent, Baluster, Applied Handle, 5 ¼ x 2 ⅛ In. 187.00
yrup, 8 Panels, Amethyst, Tapered, Molded Neck Ring, 9 ½ x 3 ½ In. 1430.00
yrup, 8 Ribs, Clear, Concave Neck Ring, Applied Solid Handle, Pewter Cap, 9 ½ In. 209.00
yrup, 10 Panels, Canary, Waisted, Applied Neck Rings, Pewter Cap, 10 ½ x 4 ⅝ In. 935.00
yrup, Amber, Swirled Rib Optic, Pattern Mold, Applied Neck Ring, 11 ¼ In. 33.00
yrup, Tin Hinged Lid, Clear, Ribbed, Globular, 3 Fans, Applied Hollow Handle, 7 ¼ In. 110.00
eapot, Jenaer, Wilhelm Wagenfeld, 4 ½ x 10 x 6 In. . . . . *illus* 1500.00
oilet Water Bottle, Cobalt Blue, Tam-O'-Shanter Stopper, Pontil, c.1830, 6 ¼ In. . . . . *illus* 160.00
umbler, Ribs, Swirled To Right, Clear, Applied Sapphire Blue Rim, 3 ¼ x 3 In. 468.00
ase, 8 Ribs, Pillar Mold, Flared Rim, Clear Double Knop Stem, Cranberry, 9 ½ In. 1430.00
ase, 15 Ribs, Broken Swirl, Medium Sapphire Blue, Open Pontil, 9 x 7 In. 308.00
ase, Aqua, Handles, Rigaree, Sheared, Fire Polished Lip, Pontil, c.1800, 6 In. 420.00
ase, Arch, Pattern-Molded, Sapphire Blue, Ruffled Edge, Pontil, c.1840, 11 ¼ In. 1680.00
ase, Ball Cover, Cobalt Blue, Drawn Body & Foot, Pontil, 1860, 7 ¾ In. 420.00
ase, Blue, Gold Accents, Folded Rim, Hand-Like Base, c.1900, 11 In. 146.00
ase, Clear, White Dragged Loops, Scalloped Rim, Baluster Stem, 1855-70, 9 ½ In., Pair. 224.00
ase, Emerald Green, Baluster, Footed, Polished Pontil, 8 ¾ In., Pair. 308.00
ase, Light Amber, Polished Pontil, 8-Pillar Mold, 1850, 10 In. 672.00
ase, Trumpet, Amethyst, Applied Baluster Stem, Sloping Foot, 11 ¾ In. 165.00
ase, Trumpet, Citron, Inward Folded Rim, Knop Stem, Sloping Foot, 9 ¼ x 3 ½ In. 1540.00
Vhimsy, Cobalt Blue, Flared, Pontil Base, 7-Panel Mold, 1835-50, 5 In. 616.00
Vhimsy, Powder Horn, Cobalt Blue, Cranberry Swirls, White Looping, 12 ¾ In. 316.00
Vine, Air Twist Stem, Round Base, Tapered Sides, 18th Century, 4 ¾ In. 220.00
Vine, Blue Green, Oval, Applied Folded Foot, 3 ⅝ In. 231.00
Vine, White Air Twist Stem, Paneled Sides, 18th Century, 4 ⅜ In. 180.00
Vitch's Ball, Milk Glass, Amethyst Tint, Trumpet Stand, Cranberry Opalescent, 14 In. 1680.00
Vitch's Ball, Opaque Blue, Open Pontil, 1885, 4 ¾ In. 213.00
Vitch's Ball, Pale Aqua, Opaque, Amber Swirling, Open Pontil, 1840-70, 3 ¾ In. 112.00
Vitch's Ball, Ruby, Open Pontil, 1840-70, 5 In. 190.00
Vitch's Ball, Sapphire Blue, Open Pontil, 1840-70, 4 ½ In. 224.00
Vitch's Ball, Stand, Clear, Paper Butterflies, Chalk Filled, Pontil, c.1890, 16 ⅝ In. 800.00
Vitch's Ball, Stand, Cobalt Blue, Bulbous, Circular Foot, Pontil, 1840-60, 7 ½ In. 364.00
Vitch's Ball, White, Yellow, Blue, Gray Stand, 1840-70, 3 ½ In. 112.00

LASS-BOHEMIAN. Bohemian glass is an ornate overlay or flashed glass made during the ictorian era. It has been reproduced in Bohemia, which is now a part of the Czech Republic. lass made from 1875 to 1900 is preferred by collectors.

eaker, Amethyst, Enameled Stags, Hounds, Paneled Oval, Footed, 5 ⅜ In. 441.00
eaker, Cut, Parcel Satine Amber Overlay, Gold, Sepia, Landscape, 6 ¼ x 3 ½ In., Pair 960.00
eaker, Hunting Scene, Wild Boar, Dog, Yellow Amber, Faceted Base, 5 ¼ In. 470.00
iscuit Jar, Green Iridescent, Amethyst Threading, Flat Sided, 8 In. 230.00
owl, Green, Ruffled Edge, 8 In. 30.00
owl, Iridescent, Oil Spot Opal, Triple Foldover Cut Rim, Oil Spot Opal, 10 In. 201.00
owl, Iridescent Amethyst, Rolled Rim, Bronze Threading, Pallme-Koenig, 9 In. 115.00
ompote, Cobalt Blue, Gold & White Enameled Scrolls & Flowers, 6 ½ x 6 In. 82.00
ompote, Cranberry, Gold Leaves, Baluster Stem, Flared Rim, 8 ½ In. 86.00
ecanter, Amethyst, Silver Overlay, Flowers, Square, Stopper, 8 ¾ In. 502.00
ish, Nautilus Shape, Engraved Man, Dogs, Deer, Rabbit, Footed, 5 In. 325.00
ish, Sweetmeat, Green Iridescent, Mottled Amethyst, Pulled Feathers, 5 In. 125.00
resser Box, Cranberry, Gold Enameled, Cherub Medallion, 3-Footed, Metal, 5 In. . . . . *illus* 316.00
oblet, Rhine, Trumpet Shape, Ruby, Yellow, Clear, Cut Designs, 8 ½ In. 250.00

Glass-Bohemian, Urn, Aqua, Enameled Wreath Of Oranges, Blue & Yellow Stripes, Fritz Heckert, 5 In.
$705.00

Glass-Bohemian, Vase, Malachite, Embossed Apples, Early 20th Century, 10 In.
$275.00

Glass-Bohemian, Vase, Marquetry, Beige Ground, Red, Blue, Purple, Kralik, 6 ¾ In.
$425.00

Glass-Bohemian, Vase, Ox Blood, Blue Iridescent Spirals, Swollen Neck, Ruffled Edge, Rindskopf, 13 In.
$823.00

Glass-Bohemian, Vase, Red, Threaded, Pinched Waist, Kralik, 7¾ In. $140.00

Glass-Contemporary, Sculpture, Honey Amber, Metallic Veins, Harvey Littleton, 1972, 5⅞ x 4 In. $1700.00

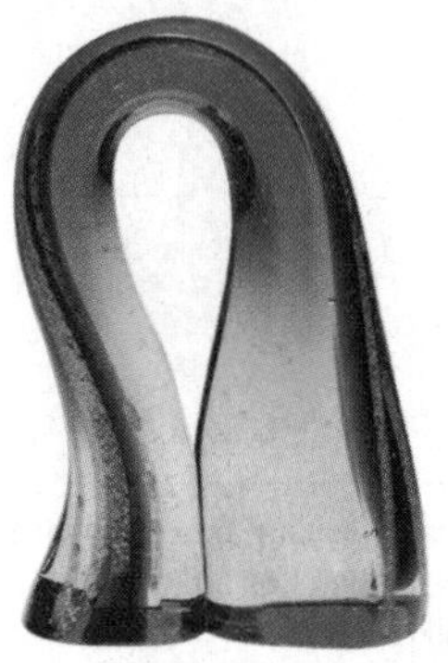

Glass-Contemporary, Vase, Orange, Coral Red, Black Patches, Bubbly Texture, 7¼ x 8¼ In. $500.00

TIP
Wipe glass dry with newspapers for a special shine.

Goblet, Toasting, Coat Of Arms, Applied Amber Prunts, Early 1900s, 10 In., Pair ...... *illus* 350.00
Jar, Ruby Flashed, Engraved Washington Capitol, 10½ In. 6750.00
Perfume Bottle, Red Lithyalin, Faceted Sides, Stopper, c.1820, 6 In. 144.00
Pitcher, Green, Enameled, Pewter Lid, V. Hauten, 11 In. 449.00
Plate, Amber Cut To Clear, Engraved, Birds, Nest, Blossom, Branch, 9¾ In. 375.00
Plate, Bathing Woman, Terrace, Cherubs, Marked, Monole, 10¼ In. 2000.00
Pokal, Engraved Hunters & Bear, Footed, 19th Century, 10½ In. 590.00
Pokal, Ruby Overlay, Intaglio Cut To Clear, Stags In Forest, 16 In. 3738.00
Pokal, Ruby Overlay, Oval Panel, Intaglio Cut Stags, Trees, 14 In. 1725.00
Rose Bowl, Tricornered Rim, Salmon Rose Body, Amethyst Threading, Pallme-Koenig, 3 In. .. 115.00
Scent Bottle, Malachite Green, Embossed Roses, Scrolls, Metal Mounts, Dauber, 6 In. 882.00
Scent Bottle, Ruby Red, Enameled Cream, Gold Enameled Persian Design, 5½ In., Pair 210.00
Tumbler, Cranberry, Gold Rim, c.1890, 4¼ In. 35.00
Tumbler, Intaglio, Emerald Green, Clear, Stag, Doe, Cameo, 6¼ In. 148.00
Urn, Aqua, Enameled Wreath Of Oranges, Blue & Yellow Stripes, Fritz Heckert, 5 In. .... *illus* 705.00
Urn, Cover, Amethyst Faceted, Gold Hunting Scene, 19th Century, 13 In. 708.00
Vase, Amethyst Cut To Clear, Punty & Column, c.1950, 7 In. 50.00
Vase, Burgundy, Millefiori Canes, Double Gourd, Flared Rim, Kralik, 10 In. 355.00
Vase, Cobalt Cut To Clear, Medallion, Pheasant, Landscape, 9½ x 7½ In. 354.00
Vase, Enameled, Green, c.1930, 17 In. 94.00
Vase, Fiery Opalescent, Drapes, Metal Mount, 9 In. 353.00
Vase, Green, Ruffled Edge, Applied Platinum Tendrils, Ribs, 5½ In. 115.00
Vase, Intaglio, Red Flower, Green Leaf Stems, Gold Gingko, Harrach, 9 In. 2300.00
Vase, Iridescent Blue, Gold, Green, Purple, Art Nouveau Frame, Metal, Kralik, 23 In. 2300.00
Vase, Iridescent Green, Enameled, Medallions, Picture, Verses, Squat, Fritz Heckert, 5½ In. .. 288.00
Vase, Iridescent Green, Rose, Blue, Silver Metal Mount, 10½ In. 431.00
Vase, Iridescent Pink, Pinched Waist, Flared 5-Sided Rim, Wilhelm Kralik, 7¼ In. 500.00
Vase, Malachite, Embossed Apples, Early 20th Century, 10 In. .... *illus* 275.00
Vase, Marquetry, Beige Ground, Red, Blue, Purple, Kralik, 6¾ In. .... *illus* 425.00
Vase, Ox Blood, Blue Iridescent Spirals, Swollen Neck, Ruffled Edge, Rindskopf, 13 In. .. *illus* 823.00
Vase, Raindrop, Mother-Of-Pearl, Apricot Gold, White, Columbines, Harrach, 8¼ In. 395.00
Vase, Red, Threaded, Pinched Waist, Kralik, 7¾ In. .... *illus* 140.00
Vase, Rubina Verde, Optic Ribbed, Gold Stemmed Flowers, 8½ In., Pair 144.00
Vase, Ruby Flashed, Scalloped Rim, 5½ In. 41.00
Vase, Sapphire Blue, Ribbed, Gold Waves, Swollen Neck, Rindskopf, 6 In. 141.00
Wine, Amber Stem, Oval Bowl, Enameled, 7⅛ In., 8 Piece 294.00

GLASS-CONTEMPORARY includes pieces by glass artists working after 1970. Many of these pieces are free-form, one-of-a-kind sculptures. Paperweights by contemporary artists are listed in the Paperweight category. Earlier studio glass may be found listed under Glass-Midcentury or Glass-Venetian.

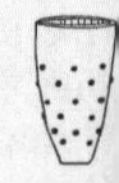

Basket, Platinum Iridescent, Ribs, Blue, Yellow Stripes, Chihuly, 9 x 8½ In. 4600.00
Bowl, Paperweight Base, Daffodils, Aqua, Swirl-Cut, Scalloped Edge, Ayotte, 2000, 9 In. 5000.00
Candleholder, Bluenique, 6-Petal Base, Viking Glass Co., c.1970 .... 30.00
Decanter, Pale Green, Pour Spout, K. Blomberg, 6½ In. 225.00
Dish, Blue, Gold Circles, Delphinium, 4½ In. 75.00
Figurine, Resting Deer, Pilgrim Glass Co., c.1980, 4½ x 3 In. 23.00
Sculpture, Bent, Amber, Harvey Littleton, 1971, 4¼ x 5 In. 3480.00
Sculpture, Egg Shape, 2 Moons & Waves At Night, J. Lewis, 1974, 4¾ In. 764.00
Sculpture, Honey Amber, Metallic Veins, Harvey Littleton, 1972, 5⅞ x 4 In. .... *illus* 1700.00
Tray, Smoke Glass, Vermillion & White Bird, Sun, Gold Detailing, 9 x 7 In. 110.00
Vase, Amber, Pink & Yellow, White, Maroon Lines, Asymmetrical, Chihuly, 9 x 8¾ In. 4700.00
Vase, Amber, Translucent, Spatter, Iridescent Oil Spots, Charles Lotton, c.1974, 7½ In. 316.00
Vase, Amethyst, Orange, White Plume, Dominick Labino, c.1977, 6 In. 510.00
Vase, Blue, Yellow, Turquoise, Clear Cased, Kent Ipsen, c.1977 .... 210.00
Vase, Blue Iridescent, Feathers, Hooked Tips, Flared, Footed, Orient & Flume, 7 In. 235.00
Vase, Blue Iridescent Lava, Cypriot Ground, Oval, c. Lotton, 6 In. 882.00
Vase, Bottle Shape, Cranberry, White & Pink Hearts, Blue Vines, John Lotton, 1992, 6 In. 863.00
Vase, Bottle Shape, Translucent, Opalescent Bubbles, Signed, Bertil Valien Boda, 8 In. 118.00
Vase, Bud, Cranberry, Twist Optic, c.1980, 7¼ In. 35.00
Vase, Bud, Gold Iridescent, Red Heart, Vines, Lundberg Studios, 13½ In. 259.00
Vase, Bulbous, Opal, Cobalt Blue, White Coil, Signed, Charles Lotton, c.1977, 5¾ In. 546.00
Vase, Clear, Transparent Brown, Flared Rim, Tapered Flared Neck, Scandinavia, 7½ In. 59.00
Vase, Cobalt Blue, Brown, Applied Band Of Mineral Salts, Kent Ipsen, 1976, 8 x 7½ In. 180.00
Vase, Cypriot, Lava, Cylindrical, Opal, Green, Blue, Iridescent Blue, Gold, c.1979, 5¼ In. 460.00

se, Ebb Tide, Blue & Gray Base, Purple, Khaki, Red Swirls At Top, Peter Layton, 11 In...... 650.00
se, Free-Form, Periwinkle, Opalescent Supports, 16 ¼ x 8 ¼ In........................ 2880.00
se, Garnet Red, Band Of White Millefiori Flowers, Round, Squat, R. Satava, 4 In.......... 383.00
se, Gold Iridescent Lava, Cypriot Body, Bulbous, C. Lotton, 1986, 4 ¾ In................ 765.00
se, Green Drapery, Metallic Zipped Design, Charles Lotton, c.1977, 8 In................. 633.00
se, Iridescent, Blue Wisteria Flume, Oval, Charles Lotton, Signed, 1982, 6 In............ 460.00
se, Iridescent, Red Abstract Design, Eickholt, 6 ¼ In................................ 70.00
se, Iridescent Gold, Lemon Yellow Heart, Vines, Pinched Waist, Donald Carlson, 9 ½ In.... 201.00
se, Long Neck, Green, Applied Decorations, Dominick Labino, 11 ½ In................. 360.00
se, Orange, Coral Red, Black Patches, Bubbly Texture, 7 ¼ x 8 ¼ In. .... *illus* 500.00
se, Paperweight, Amber To Clear, 10 x 3 ½ In.................................... 47.00
se, Paperweight, Blue, Internal Pink Flowers, Blue Vines, Squat, 7 In.................. 230.00
se, Peacock Eyes, Pulled Feathers, Purple, Green, Ocher Ground, Lundberg, 3 In. 294.00
se, Pink Flowers, Green Ground, Aventurine, Signed, C. Lotton, 1985, 9 In.......... *illus* 950.00
se, Platinum, Blue, Tapestry, Charles Lotton, c.1976, 4 ½ In.......................... 805.00
se, Purple Glass, 3 Orange Intarsia Fish, Dominick Labino, c.1977, 6 In. 480.00
se, Red, Applied White & Orange Bands, Dominick Labino, c.1972, 4 In................ 450.00
se, Red, Blue Rim, Orange Base, Flared, Monson II, 15 ½ In......................... 650.00
se, Red Cased, Multicolored Ribbons, Luster, Oval, Flared, M. Cohn, 1975, 5 ½ In. 176.00
se, Red Leaves, Blue Aurene, Engraved, Carlson, 1983, 5 ¾ In. .... *illus* 200.00
se, Scarlet, Moon Through Blue Tree, Gold Speckles, Oval, R. Satava, 10 In.............. 705.00
se, Swirls, Pulled Feathers & Combs, Earth Tones, Swollen, Orient & Flume, 6 In. 295.00
se, Teal, Clear Bottom, Scandinavian, 10 In. 75.00
se, White, Brown Interwoven Vines, Oval, Flared Rim, Petite Nourot, 3 ¾ In. 59.00
se, White & Blue, Nailsea, Dominick Labino, c.1973, 4 In. 450.00
se, Whooper, Blue, Pink Trim, Dante Marioni, 23 ¼ x 9 In........................... 5400.00
se, Whooper, Frosted, Blue Glass, Orange Trim, Dante Marioni, 25 ½ x 9 In............. 5400.00
se, Woman In Boat, Kisslinger, c.1989, 6 In...................................... 70.00

ASS-CUT, *see Cut Glass category.*

ASS-DEPRESSION, *see Depression Glass category.*

ASS-MIDCENTURY refers to art glass made from the 1940s to the early 1970s. Some glass tories, such as Baccarat or Orrefors, are listed under their own categories. Earlier glass may be ted in the Glass-Art and Glass-Contemporary categories. Italian glass may be found in ass-Venetian.

htray, Patchwork, Green, Blue & Turquoise Rectangles, Higgins 125.00
wl, Daisies, Fused, Slumped, Sydenstricker Glass Co., c.1960, 6 ¾ In. 20.00
wl, Pansies, Fused, Slumped, Sydenstricker Glass Co., c.1960, 6 ½ In.................. 20.00
ndy Dish, Cover, Leaf, Viking Glass Co., c.1960, 6 ¼ x 5 ½ In......................... 35.00
mpote, Cranberry, Overlay, Clear Pedestal, Irena Crystal, 10 x 11 In. 146.00
canter, Blue, Clear Crown Stopper, Holmegaard, 10 ½ In. 60.00
canter, Smoky Gray, Etched, Rooster Stopper, 1960 .... 785.00
sh, 3 Sections, Abstract Gold, Narrowed Center, Briard 8 ¼ x 18 ½ In. 85.00
ephant, Green, Flower Frog Cover, Co-Operative Flint, Small 395.00
Bowl, Irregular Shape, Tapio Wirkkala, 10 x 2 In.................................. 175.00
ay, Basket Weave, Purple, Pink, Blue, Yellow, Higgins, 14 x 14 In...................... 300.00
ay, Smoked Glass, Sections, Double, Gold Leaves & Bugs, Briard, 8 ½ x 14 ½ In........... 75.00
se, Amber Bark, Dark Green Base, Whitefriars, 8 ½ In. 135.00
se, Amethyst, Controlled Bubbles, Cylinder, Nanny Still, 1960s, 11 In. 150.00
se, Amethyst, Iridescent, Hula Dancers, Wide Mouth, Bulbous, 11 ½ In................. 207.00
se, Angel Fish Swimming, Air Trapped, Aqua, Signed, Labino, 1968, 5 In. .... *illus* 275.00
se, Blue, Basket Weave, Slab, Whitefriars, 10 ⅛ In. .... *illus* 176.00
se, Blue, Holmegaard, 5 x 15 ¼ In.. 180.00
se, Bud, Turquoise, Gold, Marked, Medina, 7 ½ In. .... *illus* 43.00
se, Dropout, Clear, Light Blue Decoration, Higgins, 4 In............................ 270.00
se, Dropout, Purple, Blue, Green, Fused, Gold Veins, Signed, Higgins, 6 ¾ In. .... *illus* 600.00
se, Egg Shape, Teal, Holmegaard, 9 ½ In.. 145.00
se, Goblet Shape, Smoky Glass, Swedish, 5 ¼ In. 50.00
se, Green, Round, Ingeborg Lundin, 1957, 16 ½ x 14 In.............................. 5400.00
se, Sage Green, Riihmaki, 11 In. .... *illus* 40.00
se, Savoy, Signed, Alvar Aalto, 6 ¼ In. .... *illus* 58.00
se, Textured, Clear Base, Whitefriars, 4 x 2 In.................................... 135.00
se, Trumpet, Tulpenglass, Rose, Nils Landberg, 1957, 17 In.......................... 1920.00

Glass-Contemporary, Vase,
Pink Flowers, Green Ground, Aventurine,
Signed, c. Lotton, 1985, 9 In.
$950.00

Glass-Contemporary, Vase,
Red Leaves, Blue Aurene, Engraved,
Carlson, 1983, 5 ¾ In.
$200.00

Glass-Midcentury, Vase,
Angel Fish Swimming, Air Trapped,
Aqua, Signed, Labino, 1968, 5 In.
$275.00

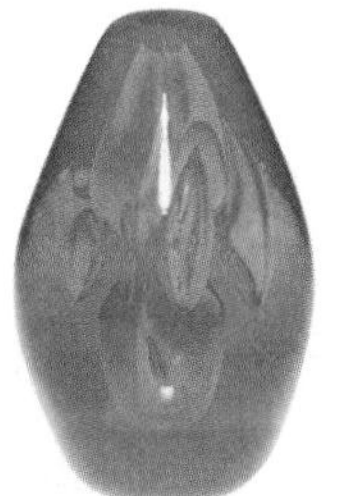

Tapio Wirkkala

Tapio Wirkkala (1915–85) was a Finnish designer of glassware, silver, ceramics, stoneware, cutlery, wooden ware, furniture, jewelry, textiles, and even banknotes. He was chief designer at Iittala glassworks from 1946 until 1985. He also designed for the German firm Rosenthal and Venini glassworks in Murano. His simple, flowing, organic shapes were often inspired by nature—leaves, seashells, birds, and fish.

GLASS-MIDCENTURY

Glass-Midcentury, Vase, Blue, Basket Weave, Slab, Whitefriars, 10 ⅛ In.
$176.00

Glass-Midcentury, Vase, Bud, Turquoise, Gold, Marked, Medina, 7 ½ In.
$43.00

Glass-Midcentury, Vase, Dropout, Purple, Blue, Green, Fused, Gold Veins, Signed, Higgins, 6 ¾ In.
$600.00

Glass-Midcentury, Vase, Savoy, Signed, Alvar Aalto, 6 ¼ In.
$58.00

G

GLASS-PRESSED, *see Pressed Glass category.*

GLASS-VENETIAN. Venetian glass has been made near Venice, Italy, since the thirteenth century. Thin, colored glass with applied decoration is favored, although many other types have been made. Collectors have recently become interested in the Art Deco and fifties designs. Glass was made on the Venetian island of Murano from 1291. The output dwindled in the late seventeen century but began to flourish again in the 1850s. Some of the old techniques of glassmaking were revive and firms today make traditional designs and original modern glass. Since 1981, the name *Murano* may only be used on glass made on Murano Island. Other pieces of Italian glass may be found in the Glass-Contemporary and Glass-Midcentury categories of this book.

Bottle, Pezzato, Multicolored & Patchwork, Signed, Venini, 14 In. 10925.
Bowl, Black, White, Murrine, Signed, Venini Murano, 2 x 8 In. 1800.
Bowl, Center, Amethyst, Shell Shape, Murano, 5 ¾ x 12 In. 94.
Bowl, Corroso, Pink, Rough Texture, Cenedese, 14 x 12 In. 500.
Bowl, Engraved, Blue, Gondola Scene, Scrolling Vine, 1800s, 5 ½ x 14 ½ In. 112.
Bowl, Gold Aventurine, Clear & Green, c.1960, 7 x 3 In. 400.
Bowl, Green, Light Green Interior, Murano, Venini, 9 x 10 In. 80.
Bowl, Latticinio, Murano, 3 x 4 In. 82.
Bowl, Opalescent, Art Deco, Red Geometric, Barovier & Toso, 11 x 4 ½ In. 2640.
Bowl, Opalescent White, Aventurine Flecks, Pink Swirl, Scalloped Edge, c.1960 750.
Bowl, Owl, Green & Red Details, Polished Pontil, Murano, 5 ¾ x 2 ⅜ In. 350.
Bowl, White & Blue Cased, Copper Flecks, Ruffled Tricornered Rim, c.1950, 7 x 6 In. 55.
Bust, Girl, Blond Bun, Venini, c.1962, 13 In. 16100.
Bust, Girl, Red Ponytail, Venini, c.1962, 11 ¼ In. 17250.
Candlestick, 2-Light, Pezzato, Supported By Human Figure, Venini, 9 ½ In. 18400.
Candlestick, Optic Ribbed Canary Yellow, Gold Aventurine, 4 In., Pair 58.
Champagne, Dolphin, Green, Gold Dust Design, 6 In. 121.
Compote, Squared Orange Flowers, Spiked Leaves, 4 ¼ In. 885.
Cup & Saucer, Ruby, Gold Enamel, Clear Handle & Foot, 3 ½ x 5 ½ In. 175.
Dish, Mermaid, Stylized Features, Green Body, Blond Hair, Pontil, 6 x 6 In. 125.
Ewer, Cushioned Base, Domino Flowers Hanging On Vines, Orange, Yellow, 12 In. 1888.
Figurine, Bandstand Acrobat, Venini, 15 ¼ In. 16100.
Figurine, Bird, Pink, Amber, Clear, Curling Tail, Ribbed, Swirled Pedestal, 14 ½ In. 173.
Figurine, Bird, Purple, Ruby, Clear Base, Alfredo Barbini, Murano, 11 ½ In., Pair 354.
Figurine, Bird, Red, Purple, Blue, White, Pink, Long Tail, Hand Blown, 14 In., Pair 350.
Figurine, Bird, Shades Of Green, Clear Base, 14 x 7 In. 175.
Figurine, Cat, Pink, Gold Inclusions, Alfredo Barbini, Murano, 6 In. 180.
Figurine, Chicken, Yellow, Red Beak, Eyes, Comb, Thick Walled, Open Base, Murano, 16 In. 750.
Figurine, Clown, Pink, Blue, Black Shoes, Murano, 9 In. 110.
Figurine, Clown, Yellow Body, Black Shoes, Hat, Green Collar, Murano, 8 In. 120.
Figurine, Crane Standing In Green Leaves, Murano, c.1950, 14 In. 150.
Figurine, Guitar Player, Venini, 11 ½ In. 13800.
Figurine, Iridato Fish, Venini, 14 x 11 In. 5175.
Figurine, Man, Carrying Tray With Fish, Multicolored, Italy, 12 ¼ In. 147.
Figurine, Rooster & Hen, Latticinio Bodies, Multicolored, Venini, 6 ¾ In. 11500.
Jar, Cover, Copper Particles, Clear, White Ground, Ormolu Mounts, Murano, 4 ¼ x 4 ¾ In. 147.
Lamp, Hanging, Applied Orange Canes, Semiopaque, Venini, Murano, 21 x 16 In. *illus* 2400.
Lamp, Hanging, White, Blue, Red Green, Vistosi, Italy, c.1960, 24 ½ In., 7 Piece *illus* 2900.
Paperweight, Millefiori, Satino, Handle, Murano, Fratelli Toso, c.1930, 5 x 3 In. 325.
Paperweight, Twisted Cane, Footed, Murano, Fratelli Toso, c.1950, 5 x 3 In. 225.
Platter, Brown, Red Speckles, Oval, Murano, c.1950, 22 In. 198.
Tile, Girl's Face, Blond, Millefiori In Hair, Beveled Edge, c.1950, 4 x 3 In. 175.
Urn, Pedestal, Cobalt Blue, Mythological Venus, 19th Century, 15 In. 708.
Vase, Amber, Black & White Pulled Design, Signed, Barovier & Toso, 6 ½ x 6 In. *illus* 2000.
Vase, Amber & Blue Fused With Central Band, Paper Label, Venini, 11 ¼ In. 10350.
Vase, Amethyst, Swirls, Gold Inclusions, Clear Scroll Handles & Foot, 1940s, 7 ¾ In. 457.
Vase, Balloon Capsules, Arrow Head Leaves, Orange & Brown, Purple Ground, 7 ⅝ In. 885.
Vase, Bell Flowers, Scrolling Foliage, Cameo, Brown Over Red & Yellow, Squat, 5 ¾ In. 767.
Vase, Blue & Gold Foil Inclusions, Turquoise Ground, 8 ¾ In. 177.
Vase, Blue Interior, Nude, Venini, 1934, 9 ¼ In. 14375.
Vase, Bottle, Black & White Diagonal Design, Mezza Filigrana, 11 In. 825.
Vase, Cannette, Dark Amber Body, Draped With Orange Canes, Signed, Venini, 12 In. 5175.
Vase, Clear, Applied Band, Signed, Venini, 12 ½ In. 13225.
Vase, Clear Ball, Prunts, Signed, Venini, 8 In. 12650.
Vase, Cornucopia, Winged Dragon, Blue Swirl, Scalloped, Footed, 8 In. 198.

lass-Midcentury, Vase,
age Green, Riihmaki, 11 In.
40.00

Glass-Venetian, Lamp, Hanging, White, Blue, Red Green, Vistosi, Italy, c.1960, 24 ½ In., 7 Piece
$2900.00

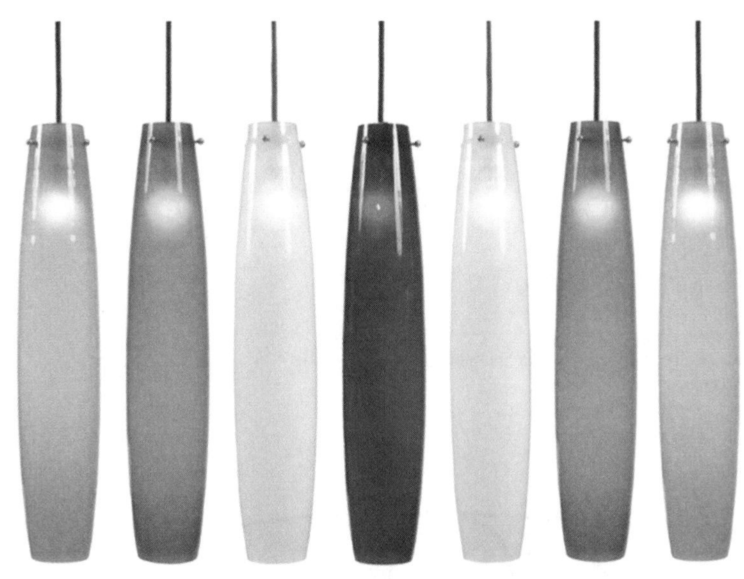

enetian Glass

The glass-blowing traditions of Venice were revitalized in the 1850s. It is said that 80 percent of the Venetian glass made from 1855 to 1914 was purchased by Americans traveling in Italy.

Glass-Venetian, Vase, Amber, Black & White Pulled Design, Signed, Barovier & Toso, 6 ½ x 6 In.
$2000.00

lass-Venetian, Lamp, Hanging,
pplied Orange Canes, Semiopaque, Venini,
Murano, 21 x 16 In.
2400.00

Glass-Venetian, Vase, Fazzoletto, Handkerchief, Yellow, White, Latticinio, Venini Murano, 10 x 11 In.
$550.00

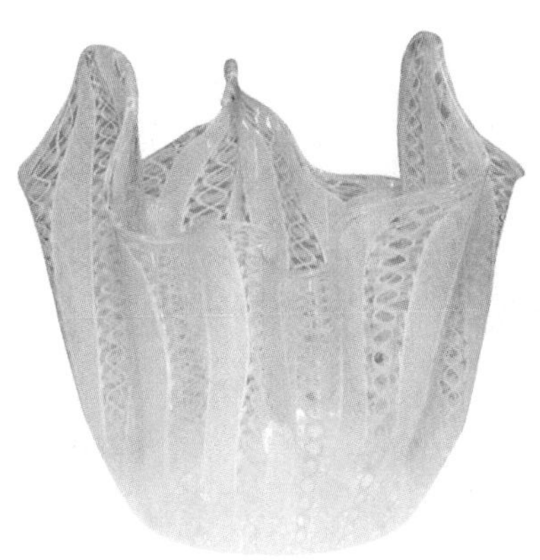

G

Glasses, Scissors Frame, Gilt Metal, Acanthus Scrolls, France, 19th Century, 4 3/8 In.
$495.00

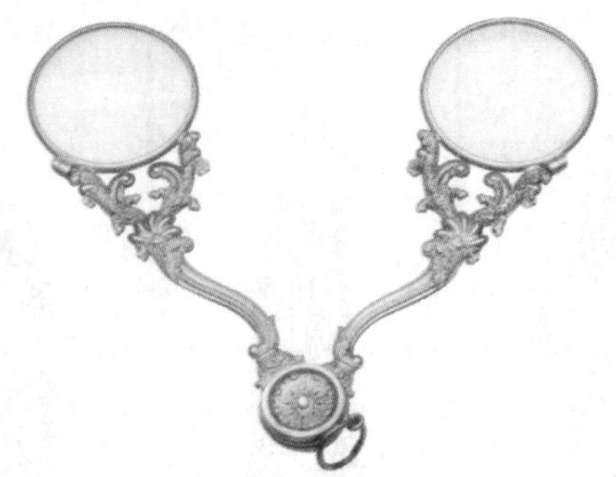

Glasses, Spectacles, Silver, Coin, Stamped, Caldwell, Case, c.1850, 5 x 4 In.
$259.00

Glasses, Steel, Round, Double Hinged, Wood Case, Late 18th Century, 1 7/8 x 5 In.
$460.00

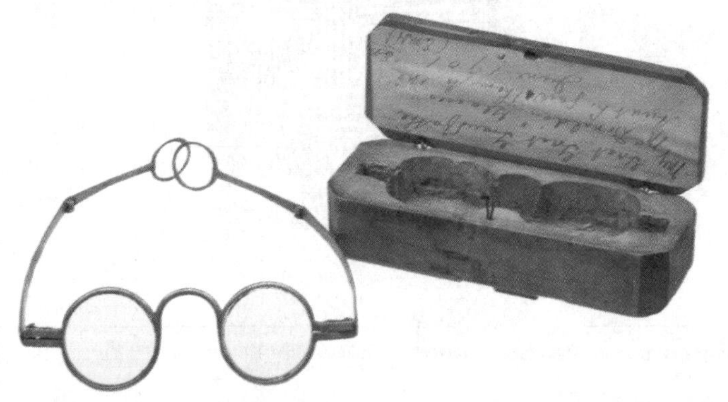

Glasses, Wood, Folding, Black Lacquer, Brass Mounts, Chinese, Case, 2-In. Lenses
$121.00

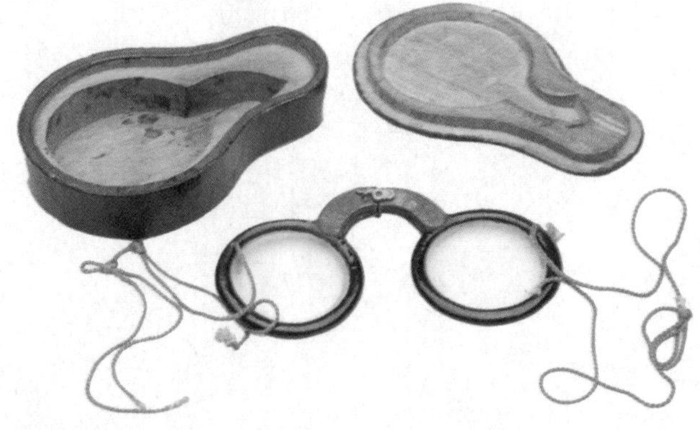

Glidden, Tray, Poodle, Cream Ground, Yellow Rim, 5 1/2 In.
$75.00

Goebel, Finger Bowl, Friar Tuck, Marked, 2 1/2 x 3 1/4 In.
$24.00

Goebel, Mask, Woman, Art Deco, Marked, 8 1/4 In.
$160.00

ase, Fasce Orrizontali, Torso Shaped, Clear, Multicolored Band, Venini, 14 In. 25300.00
ase, Fazzoletto, Handkerchief, Red & White Stripes, Murano, Venini, 8 x 4 In. 90.00
ase, Fazzoletto, Handkerchief, Yellow, White, Latticinio, Venini Murano, 10 x 11 In. .... *illus* 550.00
ase, Flowers & Leaves, Orange & Blue, Egg Yellow Ground, 7 In. 1062.00
ase, Gourd Shape, Clear, Violet Swirls, Marked, F. Bianconi, c.1950, 10 1/8 In.. .... 24000.00
ase, Large Raspberries & Stems, Green, Citron Yellow Ground, 19 1/4 In. 590.00
ase, Multicolored, Rippled Edge, Latticinio, 3 1/2 In. 47.00
ase, Murrine Hat, Bull's-Eye, Fratelli Toso, 4 x 4 In.. .... 292.00
ase, Natural Leaves, Blue Green, Foggy Look, Brown Ground, Square, 4 1/2 In.. .... 944.00
ase, Purple Brown Berries & Green Leaves Around Base, Pale Yellow Ground, 4 1/2 In. 2950.00
ase, Red & Orange Swirls, Ruffled Base, Rough Pontil, Fratelli Toso, 11 In. 225.00
ase, Reddish Orange Poppies, Yellow Ground, Pebbles & Buds, Cameo, 4 1/2 x 7 In. 944.00
ase, Ruby, Dolphin Handles, Ruffled Rim, 11 In. 53.00
ase, Smoky, Folded Lip, Timo Sarpaneva, c.1957, 8 1/2 x 5 3/4 In.. .... 240.00
ase, Sommerso, Blue, Green & Yellow, Flavio Polio, 10 1/2 In., Pair 625.00
ase, Yellow, Brown Stripes, 4 1/2 x 4 1/2 In. 1440.00

LASSES for the eyes, or spectacles, were mentioned in a manuscript in 1289 and have een used ever since. The first eyeglasses with rigid side pieces were made in London in 727. Bifocals were invented by Benjamin Franklin in 1785. Lorgnettes were popular in late Victorian mes. Opera Glasses are listed in their own category.

oin Silver, Jay Cadwell, Leather Case, Philadelphia, c.1850, 5 x 4 In. 489.00
orgnette, Art Deco, 14K Gold, Case, Green Velvet Lining 525.00
lastic, Black & White Laminated, Frame Only, Marked F.G. USA. 13.00
eading, Lenses Fold Into Handle, Golden Bronze, Iridescent, Rhinestones, 7 x 3 In. 58.00
cissors Frame, Gilt Metal, Acanthus Scrolls, France, 19th Century, 4 3/8 In. .... *illus* 495.00
pectacles, 14K Gold Frame, Bifocal, Folding, 4 1/2 In. 22.00
pectacles, Silver, Coin, Stamped, Caldwell, Case, c.1850, 5 x 4 In. .... *illus* 259.00
pectacles, Telescoping Temples, Marked C. Peck, 4 1/2 In. 259.00
teel, Round, Double Hinged, Wood Case, Late 18th Century, 1 7/8 x 5 In. .... *illus* 460.00
ood, Folding, Black Lacquer, Brass Mounts, Chinese, Case, 2-In. Lenses .... *illus* 121.00

LIDDEN Pottery worked in Alfred, New York, from 1940 to 1957. The pottery made stoneware, innerware, and art objects.

ray, Poodle, Cream Ground, Yellow Rim, 5 1/2 In. .... *illus* 75.00

OEBEL is the mark used by W. Goebel Porzellanfabrik of Oeslau, Germany, now Rodental, ermany. Many types of figurines and dishes have been made. The firm is still working. The ieces marked *Goebel Hummel* are listed under Hummel in this book.

igurine, Bald Eagle Landing On Branch, No. 76/200, 1976, 24 x 22 1/2 In.. .... 643.00
inger Bowl, Friar Tuck, Marked, 2 1/2 x 3 1/4 In. .... *illus* 24.00
ask, Woman, Art Deco, Marked, 8 1/4 In. .... *illus* 160.00
erfume Bottle, Figural, Geisha, Crown Mark, c.1923 .... 178.00
ugar & Creamer, Salt & Pepper, 2 Trays, Friar Tuck, Brown Robe, 6 Piece 80.00
ugar & Creamer, Santa Claus, Full Bee Mark, Germany, c.1956, 5 x 4 1/4 In. 295.00

OLDSCHEIDER has made porcelains in three places. The family left Vienna in 1938 nd started factories in England and in Trenton, New Jersey. The New Jersey factory tarted in 1940 as Goldscheider-U.S.A. In 1941 it became Goldscheider-Everlast orporation. From 1947 to 1953 it was Goldcrest Ceramics Corporation. In 1950 the Vienna plant was eturned to Mr. Goldscheider and the company continues in business. The Trenton, New Jersey, business, alled Goldscheider of Vienna, imports all of the pieces.

igurine, Bust Of Woman, Curly Hair, Alabaster, c.1900, 4 1/4 In. 225.00
igurine, Bust Of Woman, Praying, Blue, Black, Gray, White, Lorenzo, 6 1/8 In. .... *illus* 150.00
igurine, Dog, Borzoi, Reclining, 6 1/2 x 13 In. 295.00
igurine, Dutch Boy, Hands On Knees, Signed, Gloria Drew, 7 1/2 x 4 In. 25.00
igurine, Dutch Girl, Bowing, Holding Skirt, Signed, Gloria Drew, 7 1/2 x 4 3/4 In. 75.00
igurine, Judith, Holding Sword Behind Back, Terra-Cotta, Wood Base, c.1920, 25 In. 2200.00
igurine, Madonna, Marked, 5 x 4 In. 60.00
igurine, Man, Evening Clothes, Red Cape, 1950s, 9 x 6 1/2 In. 53.00
igurine, Medieval Woman, Lute, Mid 1940s, 8 1/4 In. 70.00
igurine, Moorish Merchant, Jug, Shoulder Bag, Terra-Cotta, Marked, 33 1/2 x 16 In.. .... 8500.00

Goldscheider, Figurine, Bust Of Woman, Praying, Blue, Black, Gray, White, Lorenzo, 6 1/8 In.
$150.00

Goldscheider, Figurine, Woman, Purple Robe, Marked, No. 8451, 18 In.
$1237.00

TIP

Several types of glue are needed to repair broken pottery and porcelain. Commercial glues found in a local hardware store are often satisfactory. Read the labels. Some types work only with pieces that are porous, others only with pieces that are not porous. Instant glue is difficult to use if the break is complicated.

G

Goofus Glass, Narcissus Spray, Bowl, 1908-20, 9 In.
$34.00

Gouda, Candlestick, Princess, Marked, 10 In., Pair
$200.00

Gouda, Clock, Birds, Flowers, Marked, Zuid-Holland Gouda, c.1905, 11 ½ In.
$1300.00

Graniteware, Bucket, Hanging, Red Roses, White, Budafok, Hungary, 16 x 9 ½ In.
$75.00

Figurine, Nude Woman, Feeding Deer, Marked, No. 8439, 7 x 5 In. 750.0
Figurine, Nude Woman & Wolfhound, Art Deco, 16 x 10 In. 4250.0
Figurine, Venetian Party Girl, Mask, Fan, Burgundy Dress, Marked, No. 7966, 10 ½ In. 1000.0
Figurine, Woman, Harem Dancer, Gold Top, Pedestal Lights Up, 1930s, 23 x 15 In. 2500.0
Figurine, Woman, Purple Robe, Marked, No. 8451, 18 In. .... *illus* 1237.0
Figurine, Woman, Red Hair, Pink & Green Outfit, Muff, 1950s, 8 ¼ x 5 In. 55.0

GOLF, *see Sports category.*

GONDER Ceramic Arts, Inc., was opened by Lawton Gonder in 1941 in Zanesville, Ohio. Gonder made high-grade pottery decorated with flambe, drip, gold crackle, and Chinese crackle glazes. The factory closed in 1957. From 1946 to 1954, Gonder also operated the Elgee Pottery, which made ceramic lamp bases.

Ewer, Blue Matte, Handle, 6 In. 24.0

GOOFUS GLASS was made from about 1900 to 1920 by many American factories. It was originally painted gold, red, green, bronze, pink, purple, or other bright colors. Many pieces are found today with flaking paint, and this lowers the value.

Blossoms & Palms, Bowl, Opalescent, Ruffled & Crimped Edge, 8 ¾ In. 75.0
Butterflies, Plate, Red & Gold, 12 Panels, 11 In. 30.0
Carnation, Bowl, 9 In. 55.0
Galleon At Sea, Vase, Indiana, c.1925, 9 ½ In. 42.0
Iris, Bowl, Ruffled Edge, 9 In. 30.0
La Belle Rose, Plate, Red, Gold, 11 In. 35.0
Narcissus Spray, Bowl, 1908-20, 9 In. .... *illus* 34.0
Peacock, Vase, 10 ½ In. 50.0
Puffy Grape, Vase, Red, Gold, 7 ½ In. 40.0
Puffy Poppy, Vase, Red, Gold, 7 In. 40.0
Red Roses, Platter, 10 ¾ In. 29.0
Roses, Plate, Red, Gold, 10 ¾ In. 43.0
Roses In Snow, Vase, Blue, Gold, Red, 10 In., Pair 110.0
Single Rose, Vase, 4-Sided, 10 ½ In. 55.0
Tree Rose, Vase, Green, Gold, Red, 12 ½ In. 95.0

GOSS china has been made since 1858. English potter William Henry Goss first made it at the Falcon Pottery in Stoke-on-Trent. The factory name was changed to Goss China Company in 1934 when it was taken over by Cauldon Potteries. Production ceased in 1940. Goss China resembles Irish Belleek in both body and glaze. The company also made popular souvenir china, usually marked with local crests and names.

Bust, Hope, Staffordshire, Waisted Round Socle, Parian, Late 1800s, 11 In. 206.0
Jug, Southend-On-Sea, England, 2 ¾ In. 83.0

GOUDA, Holland, has been a pottery center since the seventeenth century. Two firms, the Zenith pottery, established in the eighteenth century, and the Zuid-Hollandsche pottery, made the brightly colored art pottery marked *Gouda* from 1898 to about 1964. Other factories followed. Many pieces featured Art Nouveau or Art Deco designs. Pattern names in Dutch, listed here, seem strange to English-speaking collectors.

Bowl, Bird & Flowers, 20th Century, 5 ¼ In. 24.0
Bowl, Flowers, Moth, Multicolored, White Ground, Flared Rim, 3 ⅛ In. 235.0
Butter, Bowl, Underplate, Appei, 20th Century, 6 ¾ In. 71.0
Candlestick, Princess, Marked, 10 In., Pair .... *illus* 200.0
Chamberstick, Flowers, Multicolored Crystalline Glaze, W. Rhodian, 3 In. 82.0
Charger, Flowers, Red, Green, 20th Century, 11 In. 118.0
Clock, Birds, Flowers, Marked, Zuid-Holland Gouda, c.1905, 11 ½ In. .... *illus* 1300.0
Inkwell, Cover, Kelk Pattern, 20th Century, 3 ¾ In., 3 Piece 165.0
Jardiniere, Favorite, Abstract Flowers, Multicolored, 9 ¾ In. 203.0
Nappy, Ronny, Handle, Regina Holland, 20th Century, 7 In. 71.0
Pitcher, Scrolls, Orange, Red, 20th Century, 6 ½ In. 71.0
Planter, Crocus, 20th Century, 4 ½ In. 35.0
Sconce, Handle, Emmy, 7 ½ In. 189.0
Vase, Abstract, Flower Stems, Multicolored, Bulbous, 1920s, 10 In. 261.0
Vase, Abstract, Flowers, Pods, Stems, Pea Green Ground, Bulbous, Tapered, c.1910, 12 In. 232.0
Vase, Art Nouveau, Flowers, Black Ground, Squat, 20th Century, 4 x 6 ¾ In. 110.0
Vase, Averil, Flowers, Leafy Stems, Ivory Ground, Cylindrical, Tapered, 10 ½ In. 162.0

Vase, Ellipses, Wing Like, c.1928, 9 ¼ In.. . . . . 236.00
Vase, Flowers, Green, Squat, 4 ½ In. 88.00
Vase, Glory, Multicolored, Cylindrical, Signed, 9 ¼ In. 232.00
Vase, Ivora Bird, Songbird, Leafy Branch, Oval, Short Neck, Handles, 7 In. 174.00
Vase, Nipo, Stylized, 20th Century, 9 ½ In. 236.00
Vase, Purdah, Swirls, Turquoise, Red, Green, Brown Matte Glaze, Flared, Footed, 12 ⅝ In.. . . . . 382.00

GRANITEWARE is an enameled tinware that has been used in the kitchen from the late nineteenth century to the present. Earlier graniteware was green or turquoise blue, with white spatters. The later ware was gray with white spatters. Reproductions are being made in all colors.

Bucket, Hanging, Red Roses, White, Budafok, Hungary, 16 x 9 ½ In. . . . . . *illus* 75.00
Chamber Pot, Blue & White, Lid, Handle, 6 x 9 In.. . . . . 70.00
Coffee Boiler, Blue & White Swirl. 55.00
Coffee Broiler, Gray, Graniteware Handle At Bottom, Bail Handle, 11 x 9¾ In. 65.00
Coffeepot, Cobalt Blue, Hinged Lid, 19th Century, 11 In. 88.00
Coffeepot, Flowers, Pewter Trim, White, 11 In. 155.00
Kettle, Blue, Lid, Graniteware Handle & Bail Handle, 13 ½ x 10 In. 50.00
Ladle, Gray, Hooked Handle, 12 ½ In. 10.00
Lunch Box, Brown, White, Aluminum Insert, France, 5 ½ x 6 ¼ In. 95.00
Milk Can, Blue, White, 9 ¼ x 5 In. . . . . . *illus* 94.00
Mug, Mush, Brown, White Lid, 3 x 2 ½ In. . . . . . *illus* 325.00
Pan, White, Green, Lid, Wood Finial, 3 Qt., 4 ½ x 8 In. . . . . . *illus* 34.00
Plate, Blue & White Swirl, 9 In.. . . . . 5.00
Plate, Dinner, Blue & White Swirl, 9 In. 15.00
Pot, Gray, Lid, 2 Handles, 8 ½ x 12 In.. . . . . 25.00
Teapot, Gray, L & G Mfg. Co., 10 In.. . . . . 75.00
Teapot, Pewter Trim, White Enamel, Stork, 10 In. 185.00

GREENTOWN glass was made by the Indiana Tumbler and Goblet Company of Greentown, Indiana, from 1894 to 1903. In 1899, the factory became part of National Glass Company. A variety of pressed glass was made. Additional pieces may be found in other categories, such as Chocolate Glass, Holly Amber, Milk Glass, and Pressed Glass.

Cactus, Bowl, Footed, Scalloped Rim, 7 ¼ In.. . . . . 55.00
Golden Agate, Shelf Support, Whimsy, 9 In. . . . . . *illus* 8250.00

GRUEBY Faience Company of Boston, Massachusetts, was incorporated in 1897 by William H. Grueby. Garden statuary, art pottery, and architectural tiles were made until 1920. The company developed a green matte glaze that was so popular it was copied by many other factories making a less expensive type of pottery. This eventually led to the financial problems of the pottery.

Bowl, Green Matte, Carved & Applied Leaves, 4-Sided, Marked, 3 x 6 ½ In. . . . . . *illus* 660.00
Jar, Cover, Brown Glaze, Bulbous, 3 Handles, 7 ¼ x 5 ¾ In. 2040.00
Paperweight, Scarab, Blue Gray Matte, Stamped, Grueby Faience, 2 x 4 x 2¾ In. . . . . . *illus* 1050.00
Paperweight, Scarab, Green Glaze, Impressed, Grueby Faience, c.1910, 1 ½ x 4 In. 275.00
Tile, Chamberstick, Green, Yellow, Arts & Crafts Frame, 4 ½ x 6 In. 3840.00
Tile, Cherub Playing Cymbals, Green, 6 In. . . . . . *illus* 345.00
Tile, Horse Procession, Cuenca, Arts & Crafts Frame, 6 In., 2 Piece 7200.00
Tile, Houses On Hill, Seashore, Stamped, 4 In. 2880.00
Tile, Pegasus, Hammered Copper, Footed, Signed, 6 In. 3900.00
Tile, Ship, Multicolored Glaze, Oak Frame, 6 In. 2880.00
Tile, St. George & Dragon, Matte Glaze, 8 x 8 In. 10800.00
Tile, Stylized Tree, Blue Ground, 6 x 6 In. 5400.00
Tile, The Pines, Cuenca, 6 x 6 In.. . . . . 2520.00
Tile, Tulip, Brown, Green Ground, Signed, 6 In. 1920.00
Tile, Water Lily, Green Matte Glaze, Flower Petals, 1907, 6 In.. . . . . 1645.00
Tile, Wood Scene, Blue, Green Matte Glaze, 6 x 6 In. 1800.00
Tile, Yellow Tulip, Green Leaves, Green Matte Ground, 6 In. 1800.00
Vase, Blue Matte Glaze, Carved Leaves, Stems, Buds, 5 x 7 ½ In. 1680.00
Vase, Frothy Green Matte Glaze, Bulbous, Buds, Curled Leaves, 7 ½ x 4 ½ In. 2640.00
Vase, Frothy Green Matte Glaze, Full-Height Carved Leaves, 8 x 4 ½ In.. . . . . 2280.00
Vase, Green Matte Glaze, Applied Leaves, Bulbous, 7 x 4 ½ In. 1800.00
Vase, Green Matte Glaze, Broad Leaves, Marked, 5 ½ x 8 ½ In. 2585.00
Vase, Green Matte Glaze, Bulbous, Flared Neck, 11 x 7 ½ In.. . . . . 2160.00
Vase, Green Matte Glaze, Cylindrical Neck, Wide Mouth, Bulbous, 12⅜ In.. . . . . 5523.00

Graniteware, Milk Can, Blue, White, 9 ¼ x 5 In.
$94.00

Graniteware, Mug, Mush, Brown, White Lid, 3 x 2 ½ In.
$325.00

Graniteware, Pan, White, Green, Lid, Wood Finial, 3 Qt., 4 ½ x 8 In.
$34.00

Greentown, Golden Agate, Shelf Support, Whimsy, 9 In.
$8250.00

Grueby, Bowl, Green Matte, Carved & Applied Leaves, 4-Sided, Marked, 3 x 6½ In.
$660.00

Grueby, Paperweight, Scarab, Blue Gray Matte, Stamped, Grueby Faience, 2 x 4 x 2¾ In.
$1050.00

Grueby, Tile, Cherub Playing Cymbals, Green, 6 In.
$345.00

Haeger, Vase, Earthwrap, Cylindrical, Marked, 12 x 4⅜ In.
$35.00

Vase, Green Matte Glaze, Full-Height Leaves, Buds, 7¾ x 4¼ In. 2040.00
Vase, Green Matte Glaze, Razor Clam Leaves, Squat, Bulbous, 7½ x 8 In. 8400.00
Vase, Green Matte Glaze, Ribbed Loops Below Neck, Marked, 16¾ In. 5100.00
Vase, Green Matte Glaze, Rows Of Curled Leaves, Squat, 6 x 8 In. 6000.00
Vase, Green Matte Glaze, Rows Of Leaves, Marked, Wilhelmina Post, 8 x 5½ In. 3240.00
Vase, Green Matte Glaze, Stacked Leaves, Squat, Marked, 1906, 4½ x 5¼ In. 1320.00
Vase, Green Matte Glaze, Tapered, Stamped, 8 x 3¾ In. 840.00
Vase, Green Matte Glaze, Tooled Panels, Bulbous, Cylindrical Neck, 7 In. 1410.00
Vase, Leathery Green Matte Glaze, Applied Leaves, 6 x 6½ In. 2280.00
Vase, Yellow Buds, 3 Full-Height Leaves, 8½ x 5 In. 6600.00
Vase, Yellow Matte Glaze, Shouldered, 9½ x 15½ In. 6000.00

GUSTAVSBERG ceramics factory was founded in 1827 near Stockholm, Sweden. It is best known to collectors for its twentieth-century artwares, especially Argenta, a green stoneware with silver inlay.

Gustafsberg

Bowl, Geometric, Mottled Turquoise Glaze, Silver Inlay, Handles, 6 x 10 In. 173.00
Bowl, Turquoise Glaze, Recessed Center, 4-Sided, Argenta, Wilhelm Kage, c.1960, 8 In. 146.00
Ewer, Green, Brown Luster Glaze, Gilt, Handles, Josef Ekberg, 5 In. 225.00
Figurine, Norseman, On Ship Deck, Parian, c.1880, 21 In. 441.00
Pin Tray, Terra-Cotta, Rectangular, Signed, Stig Lindberg, 6 x 4 In. 185.00
Plate, Rim, Lisa Larsen, 6 In. 150.00
Tray, Hand Painted, Terra-Cotta, Stig Lindberg, 3 x 6 In. 185.00
Vase, Cylindrical, Red, Iridescent, 18 x 7 In. 322.00
Vase, Fish, Bubbles, Mottled Turquoise Glaze, Silver Inlay, 5 In. 345.00

HAEGER Potteries, Inc., Dundee, Illinois, started making commercial artwares in 1914. Early pieces were marked with the name *Haeger* written over an *H*. About 1938, the mark *Royal Haeger* was used in honor of Royal Hickman, a designer at the factory. The firm is still making florist wares and lamp bases. See also the Royal Hickman category.

Haeger

Ashtray, Free-Form, Turquoise, 12¼ x 9 In. 40.00
Ashtray, Leaf Form, Scalloped Edge, c.1950, 13½ x 7½ In. 18.00
Bowl, Bulb Pink, Footed, 9 In. 7.00
Bowl, Scroll, Leaf, Ecru Matte Glaze, Relief, No. 102, Marked 15.00
Bust, Horse Head, Hollow, No. 614, 11 x 7½ In. 319.00
Casserole, Cover, Flowers, Lug Handles, 8 In. 38.00
Console, Leaf, White, Robin's-Egg Blue Interior 15.00
Figurine, Deer, Standing, Gray, 14½ In. 55.00
Figurine, Fish, Tail Up, 1986, 18½ x 10 In. 275.00
Figurine, Peacock, White, 7 x 11¾ In. 37.00
Figurine, Woman, Art Deco, 1986, 24 In. 250.00
Head Vase, Madonna, White Matte Glaze, 14 x 10 In. 95.00
Mixing Bowl, Tan, Cream, Raised Designs, No. 102, 8 x 3½ In. 15.00
Planter, Aqua Matte Glaze, 11¾ x 3¾ In. 36.00
Planter, Candleholder, Double, White, c.1941, 8 x 7 x 4 In. 45.00
Planter, Console, Pedestal, Chinese Red, Drip Glaze, Foil Label, 1950s, 12 x 4½ In. 45.00
Planter, Madonna, White Matte, 6 In. 40.00
Planter, Ruffled Rim, Gold, Marked, 5 x 8 In. 11.00
Planter, Stork, With Diaper, Pink, c.1925 . . . . 16.00
Plate, Mother's Day, Blue, 1979 . . . . 15.00
Vase, 3 Plumes, Round, No. R281, 10½ In. 125.00
Vase, Art Deco, Brown Drip Glaze, c.1930, 10 x 11 In. 100.00
Vase, Bottle Shape, Orange Peel, 1976, 9½ In. 110.00
Vase, Boy & Bear, Mint Green, c.1930 . . . . 35.00
Vase, Bud, Urn Shape, Blue Glaze, Handles, Stamped 8.50
Vase, Double Shell Center, Mauve Agate Cream Interior, No. R322, 6½ In. 50.00
Vase, Earthwrap, Cylindrical, Marked, 12 x 4⅜ In. . . . . *illus* 35.00
Vase, Green, Square, Flared Neck, c.1990, 16 In. 30.00
Vase, Ivory, No. 263, 10 In. 75.00
Vase, Leaf Form, Turquoise, 12 In. 55.00
Vase, Leaf Shape, Pink, Blue, No. R460, 12 x 5⅓ x 3½ In. 75.00
Vase, Mottled Green, Blue High Gloss, Marked, 14½ In. . . . . *illus* 40.00
Vase, Swan, Mauve Agate, Closed Loop Neck, No. R285, 8½ x 5½ In. 45.00
Vase, Yellow Green Glaze, Modern Art, 1940s 110.00
Wall Pocket, Fish, Yellow, Reddish Brown Sprayed Accents, 16¾ In. 98.00

HALF-DOLL, *see Pincushion Doll category.*

HALL CHINA Company started in East Liverpool, Ohio, in 1903. The firm made many types of wares. Collectors search for the Hall teapots made from the 1920s to the 1950s. The dinnerwares of the same period, especially Autumn Leaf pattern, are also popular. The Hall China Company is still working. For more information, see *Kovels' Depression Glass & Dinnerware Price List*. Autumn Leaf pattern dishes are listed in their own category in this book.

Arizona, Bowl, Fruit, Eva Zeisel, 5¾ In. 9.00
Arizona, Bowl, Vegetable, Lug Handles, Eva Zeisel 28.00
Arizona, Gravy Boat, Eva Zeisel 35.00
Arizona, Plate, Dinner, Eva Zeisel, 11 In. 11.00
Bouquet, Bowl, Vegetable, Square, Eva Zeisel, 9 In. 30.00
Bouquet, Creamer, Eva Zeisel 22.00
Bouquet, Plate, Dinner, Eva Zeisel, 11 In. 13.00
Bouquet, Sugar, Eva Zeisel 27.00
Caprice, Ashtray, Eva Zeisel 18.00
Caprice, Casserole, Cover, Eva Zeisel, 8¼ In. 72.00
Caprice, Creamer, Eva Zeisel 40.00
Caprice, Gravy Boat, Eva Zeisel 38.00
Fantasy, Berry Bowl, Eva Zeisel, 6 In. 15.00
Fantasy, Bowl, Cereal, Square, Eva Zeisel, 6 In. 24.00
Fantasy, Bowl, Fruit, Eva Zeisel, 11½ In. 48.00
Fantasy, Candlestick, Eva Zeisel, 4½ In. 37.00
Fantasy, Creamer, Eva Zeisel 40.00
Fantasy, Gravy Boat, Eva Zeisel 33.00
Fantasy, Plate, Dinner, Eva Zeisel, 11 In. 24.00
Fantasy, Platter, Eva Zeisel, 13 In. 40.00
Fantasy, Platter, Eva Zeisel, 15 In. 60.00
Fantasy, Sugar, Eva Zeisel 40.00
Football, Teapot, 1995 80.00
Fort, Baker, Oval, 8 Oz., 1995 25.00
Harlequin, Gravy Boat, Eva Zeisel 66.00
Harlequin, Platter, Eva Zeisel, 15 In. 49.00
Lyric, Plate, Dinner, Eva Zeisel, 11 In. 12.00
Lyric, Platter, Eva Zeisel, 17 In. 46.00
Pepper Shaker, Red, Range Size, 4¾ In. 26.00
Pine Cone, Cruet Set, Oil & Vinegar, Eva Zeisel 66.00
Poppy, Bowl, Salad, 9 In. 22.00
Red Poppy, Bowl, Salad, 9 In. 22.00
Refrigerator Ware, Westinghouse, Butter, Cover, Garden Green, U-shape, Ribbed, 7 x 4 x 3¾ In. 50.00
Refrigerator Ware, Westinghouse, Leftover, White, Oval, 7 x 4 x 4½ In. 24.00
Refrigerator Ware, Westinghouse, Leftover, Yellow, 9 x 5 x 5½ In. 37.00
Refrigerator Ware, Westinghouse, Water Server, Delphinium Blue, 4½ x 5 x 11 In. 126.00
Rose Parade, Drip Jar, Cadet Blue, Wild Rose Transfer On White Handles, 1940s 39.00
Royal Rose, Casserole, Cadet Blue Body, White Lid, Pink Rose Decals, Silver Trim, 1940s, 4 x 8 In. 25.00
Soup, Onion, Cover, Ribbed, 2 Piece 100.00
Springtime, Mixing Bowl, Flower Decal, 6½ In. 12.00
Teapot, Cameo Rose, Elongated Handle, 8 Cup 115.00
Teapot, Medallion, Green Lettuce, Circle Mark, 40 Oz. 225.00
Teapot, The Cube, 2 Cup 50.00
Teapot, Black, 5½ In., 6 Cup 15.00
Tritone, Jar, Mustard, Cover, Eva Zeisel 180.00
Tulip, Bowl, Salad, Cook Coffee Premium, 3 x 9 In. 34.00
Tulip, Gravy Boat, Tulips & Leaves, Platinum Trim, 2¾ x 9 x 3 In. 35.00
Vase, Bud, Flat Base, 1995 39.00

HALLOWEEN is an ancient holiday that has changed in the last 200 years. The jack-o'-lantern, witches on broomsticks, and orange decorations seem to be twentieth-century creations. Collectors started to become serious about collecting Halloween-related items in the late 1970s. The papier-mache decorations, now replaced by plastic, and old costumes are in demand.

Cat, Black, Papier-Mache, Head, Looking Over Fence, Wire Bail, 5½ x 7½ In. 179.00
Coffin, Pine, Odd Fellow, Papier-Mache Skeleton, Barnet, Vt., 19th Century, 69 x 18 x 13 In. 700.00
Costume, JFK, Mr. President, Molded Plastic Mask 172.00
Costume, Land Of The Lost, Ben Cooper, Box, 1975, Medium 135.00
Costume, Moe, Three Stooges, Ben Cooper, Box, 1960, Medium 350.00
Costume, Paladin, Mask, Black Pants, White Logo, Ben Cooper, Box, 1958 380.00

Haeger, Vase, Mottled Green, Blue High Gloss, Marked, 14½ In.
$40.00

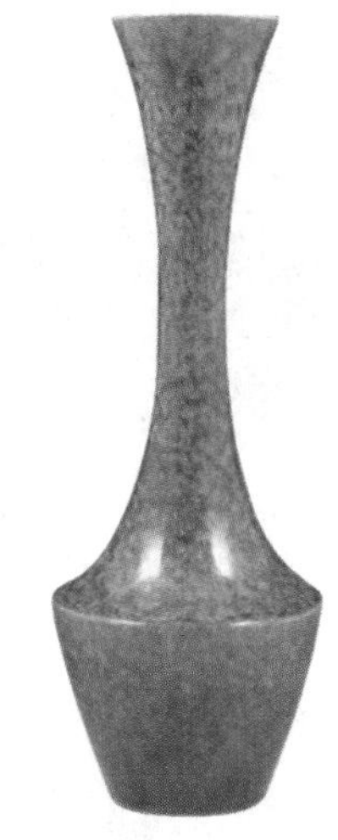

Halloween, Figure, Krampus, Chain, Composition Head, Fur, Wicker Basket, 8¾ In.
$250.00

Halloween, Lantern, Devil's Head, Mustache, Paper Eyes, Mouth, Wire Handle, 4½ In.
$700.00

H

Halloween, Lantern, Witches, Devils, Owls, Cats, Bats, Pumpkins, Germany, 9 In.
$288.00

Halloween, Postcard, Woman Seated On Pumpkin Man's Lap, Schmucker Winsch
$118.00

Halloween, Vase, Devil's Head, Chalkware, Marked, 6 x 4 In.
$250.00

Hampshire, Vase, Green Drip Over Brick Red, High Gloss, Marked, 6 ¼ In.
$215.00

Figure, Krampus, Chain, Composition Head, Fur, Wicker Basket, 8 ¾ In. . . . . *illus* 250.00
Jack-O'-Lantern, Papier-Mache, Candleholder, Pulp Reproduction Co., 1930s 127.00
Lantern, Devil Bat With Wings, Red, Black Shading, Candle In Head, 6 ¾ In. 2185.00
Lantern, Devil's Head, Mustache, Paper Eyes, Mouth, Wire Handle, 4 ½ In. . . . . *illus* 700.00
Lantern, Witches, Devils, Owls, Cats, Bats, Pumpkins, Germany, 9 In. . . . . *illus* 288.00
Light, Jack-O'-Lantern, Plastic, Battery Operated, 1950s, 5 x 16 In. 44.00
Mask Set, Wizard Of Oz, Dorothy, Scarecrow, Tin Man, Lion, Wizard, Einson-Freeman, Lowe's, 1939 310.00
Noisemaker, Devil, Squatting, Germany, 1930s 98.00
Postcard, A Thrilling Halloween, Shrouded Figure, Jack-O'-Lantern Head, Clapsaddle 201.00
Postcard, Black Cat On Jack-O'-Lantern, Unused, 1909, 3 ½ x 5 ½ In. 75.00
Postcard, Children, Pumpkins, Clapsaddle, Series Number 31, Wolf Co., c.1910, 2 Piece. 130.00
Postcard, Woman Seated On Pumpkin Man's Lap, Schmucker Winsch . . . . *illus* 118.00
Postcard Set, Happy Jack-O'-Lantern Head Children, Witch Hats, Whitney, 5 Piece. 142.00
Postcard Set, Orange, Black Cat, White, Metropolitan News, Series No. 1134, 6 Piece 142.00
Toy, Sam The Strolling Skeleton, Tin, Windup, Waddles, Arms Swing, Japan, 1960, 5 In. 160.00
Toy, Witch On Motorcycle, White Witch, Orange Hair & Dress, Plastic, 5 x 6 In. 1236.00
Train Set, Tracks, Tunnel, Dragons, Goblins, Witches, Screaming People, 1950s 855.00
Vase, Devil's Head, Chalkware, Marked, 6 x 4 In. . . . . *illus* 250.00

HAMPSHIRE pottery was made in Keene, New Hampshire, between 1871 and 1923. Hampshire developed a line of colored glazed wares as early as 1883, including a Royal Worcester–type pink, olive green, blue, and mahogany. Pieces are marked with the printed mark or the impressed name *Hampshire Pottery* or *J.S.T. & Co., Keene, N.H.* Many pieces were marked with city names and sold as souvenirs.

Bowl, Artichoke, Green Matte Glaze, 1916, 2 ¾ In. 223.00
Bowl, Carved Design, Blue Matte Glaze, Marked, 5 ½ x 2 ½ In. 115.00
Bowl, Incised Indian Designs On Shoulder, Gray Matte Glaze, Squat, 2 x 5 ¾ In. 264.00
Bowl, Organic Shape, Green Matte Glaze, 5 x 2 ½ In. 240.00
Ewer, Incurved Neck, Pinched Rim, Scroll Handle, Brown Glaze Shading, 6 ¼ In. 174.00
Lamp, Fairy, Flat Spherical, Circular Base, Handle, Green Glaze, c.1905, 3 ⅛ In. 116.00
Lamp Base, Oil, Tulip Stems, Leaves, 3-Footed, Leaded Glass Shade, c.1905, 5 ¾ In. 2320.00
Lamp Base, Water Lilies, 4-Footed, Green Glaze, Leaded Glass Shade, c.1905, 7 ¼ In. 928.00
Pitcher, Cylindrical Flared, Undulating Base, Leaf Tips, Green, c.1905, 11 ¼ In. 174.00
Pitcher, Green Matte Glaze, White Clay Body, Marked, c.1885, 11 ½ In. 353.00
Pitcher, Pinched Spout, Circular Foot, C-Scroll Handle, Egg Shape, 6 ⅝ In. 174.00
Vase, Blue Green Mottled Glaze, Relief Arches, Impressed, 7 In. 748.00
Vase, Blue Mottled Glaze, Bulbous, Flared Neck, 5 In. 470.00
Vase, Green Drip Over Brick Red, High Gloss, Marked, 6 ¼ In. . . . . *illus* 215.00
Vase, Green Matte Glaze, White Body, Marked, Early 20th Century, 6 ½ In. 294.00
Vase, Handle, Leaf & Berry Design, Green Matte Glaze, Marked, 5 x 7 ½ In. 173.00
Vase, Leaves & Buds, Green Matte Glaze, Tapered, Marked, 6 ¾ x 4 In. 605.00
Vase, Molded Acanthus Leaves, Blue Green Crystalline Glaze, Arts & Crafts, Emoretta, 7 In. . . 1116.00
Vase, Mottled Blue, Green Glaze, Arches, 7 In. . . . . *illus* 650.00
Vase, Poppy, Leaves & Flowers, Green Matte Glaze, 5 x 6 In. 660.00
Vase, Raised Design, Corn, Green Matte Glaze, Marked, 6 x 5 ½ In. 403.00
Vase, Tapered, Green Mottled & Brown Matte Glaze, Marked, 4 ½ x 7 In. 460.00
Vase, Urn Form, Buttressed Handles, Leaves, Green Glaze, c.1905, 5 ½ In. 145.00
Vase, Vertical Leaf, Blue & Green Matte Glaze, 4 ½ x 9 In. 660.00
Vase, Water Lily, Green Matte Glaze, Shouldered, Tapered Body, Footed, 1900s, 15 In. 823.00

HANDEL glass was made by Philip Handel working in Meriden, Connecticut, from 1885 and in New York City from 1893 to 1933. The firm made art glass and other types of lamps. Handel shades were made not only of leaded glass in a style reminiscent of Tiffany but also of reverse painted glass. Handel also made vases and other glass objects.

Chandelier, 3-Light, Metal Overlay, Grapevine, Purple, Green, Yellow, White, 13 x 22 In. 1750.00
Chandelier, 5-Light, Leaded Glass, Brass Plate, 5 ½-In. Shades 9000.00
Humidor, Lobed, Mottled Brown, Metal Cover, Figural Pipe, Finial, 5 ½ x 4 ½ In. 360.00
Lamp, 2-Light, Chipped Ice Shades, T Base, Bronze Patina, 55 ½ x 33 In. 3600.00
Lamp, 3 Panels, Metal Overlay, Landscape, Slag Glass, Tree Trunk Base, 18 x 18 x 23 In. 3900.00
Lamp, 4 Panels, Metal Overlay, Ivy Leaves, Red Berries, Caramel Slag Glass, 19 ½ In. 1035.00
Lamp, 6 Panels, Chipped Ice, Stylized Flowers, Signed, 22 x 15 In. 3173.00
Lamp, 6 Panels, Metal Overlay, Palm Tree, Sunset, Green Slag Glass, Tree Trunk Base, 15 In. . 2070.00
Lamp, 6 Panels, Metal Overlay, Rose Trellis, Slag Glass, Bronzed Base, Patina, Signed, 22 In. . 2200.00
Lamp, 6 Panels, Metal Overlay, Landscape, Bronzed Base, Patina, Signed, 20 ½ x 17 In. 2520.00
Lamp, 6 Panels, Metal Overlay, Grape Leaves, Vines, Caramel Slag, Acorn Pulls, 16 In. 2875.00

Lamp, 6 Panels, Metal Overlay, Landscape, Slag Glass, Patina, Signed, 22 x 18 In. 2900.00
Lamp, 6 Panels, Metal Overlay, Queen Anne's Lace, Green, Caramel, Bronzed Base, 24½ In. .. 3120.00
Lamp, 6 Panels, Metal Overlay, Oak Leaves, Grillwork, Carmel Slag Glass, 21½ In. 3680.00
Lamp, 7 Panels, Metal Overlay, Stylized Flowers, Leaves, Stems, White, 22 In. 4025.00
Lamp, 8 Panels, Chipped Ice Shade, Roses, 7 x 15½ x 9 In. .... *illus* 1400.00
Lamp, 8 Panels, Metal Overlay, Fish Scale, Yellow, Gold, White, Cat's Paw Texture, 22 In. 2520.00
Lamp, 8 Panels, Metal Overlay, Oak Trees, Green, Caramel Slag Glass, 21 x 18 In. 4487.00
Lamp, 8 Panels, Metal Overlay, Tropical Scene, Multicolored Slag, 20 x 25 In. 6558.00
Lamp, Band Of Leaves, Yellow & Green Ground, Bronzed Base, Pierced Foot, 23 In. 2350.00
Lamp, Basket Weave Molded Shade, Flower Border, Pink & Yellow, Reverse Painted, 14 In. ... 1495.00
Lamp, Bell Shade, Chipped Ice, Oak Leaves & Acorns, 23½ x 18 In. 10800.00
Lamp, Chipped Ice Shade, Autumn Mountain Landscape, Henri Bedigie, 23 x 18 In. 9000.00
Lamp, Chipped Ice Shade, Flower Border, Orange Ground, Metal Rim, 20½ In. 2760.00
Lamp, Chipped Ice Shade, Lakeside At Dusk, Lobed, Shade, 23½ x 18 In. 10200.00
Lamp, Chipped Ice Shade, Moonlit Landscape, Signed, 23½ x 18 In. 7200.00
Lamp, Chipped Ice Shade, Wreath Of Leaves, Sulfur Yellow, Bronze Base, 23 In. .... *illus* 2000.00
Lamp, Chipped Ice Shade, Yellow Daffodils, Signed, 24¼ x 18 In. 13200.00
Lamp, Domed Shade, Brown Chipped Ice, Bronzed Base, Signed, 57 x 10 In. 1320.00
Lamp, Domed Shade, Daffodils, Bronzed Base, Signed, 24 x 17 In. .... *illus* 8950.00
Lamp, Domed Shade, Landscape, Bronzed Base, 22 x 15 In. 1080.00
Lamp, Domed Shade, Landscape, Bronzed Base, Patina, Signed, 14½ In. 3200.00
Lamp, Domed Shade, Landscape, Bronzed Base, Patina, 14 x 7 In. 3600.00
Lamp, Domed Shade, Peacock, Bronzed Base, Patina, Signed, 23 x 18 In. 22550.00
Lamp, Domed Shade, Persian Design, Bronzed Base, Patina, Signed, 24 x 18 In. 3990.00
Lamp, Domed Shade, Stylized Roses, Bronzed Base, Signed, 22 x 14 In. 870.00
Lamp, Domed Shade, Trees, Yellow Ground, 24 In. 2875.00
Lamp, Domed Shade, Tulips, Patina, Etched, Teroma, 18½ x 16 In. 16800.00
Lamp, Dropped Apron Shade, Parrot On Branch, Blue, Tree Trunk Base, Patina, Signed, 14½ In. . 3900.00
Lamp, Exterior Painted Shade, Daffodils, Yellow, Green, Patinated Base, 14¾ x 18 In. 6600.00
Lamp, Exterior Painted Shade, Landscape, 2 Sockets, Fluted Base, 22 x 16 In. 4560.00
Lamp, Exterior Painted Shade, Landscape, Bronzed Base, 18 x 26 In. 6600.00
Lamp, Hanging, Art Glass Shade, Geometric, 5½ x 33½ In. 2760.00
Lamp, Leaded Glass Shade, Lily, White & Green Slag, Lily Pad Base, 7 x 10 x 14 In. 1440.00
Lamp, Leaded Glass Shade, Tulip, Bronzed Base, 16 In. 5462.00
Lamp, Mushroom Shade, Green Leaves, Yellow Ground, 19 x 11 In. 7200.00
Lamp, Piano, Caramel Slag Glass Shade, Adjustable, Bronzed Base, 14 x 10 In. 840.00
Lamp, Piano, Mosserine Shade, Lily Pad Base, Curved Arm, 13 In. 780.00
Lamp, Shade, Blue Macaw On Branch, Jungle Foliage, Metal, 14½ In. 3055.00
Lamp, Shade, Cone Shape, Stylized Tulips, Hammered Copper, 14 x 8¼ In. 9000.00
Lamp, Shade, Desert Sunset, Camels, Arabs, Oasis Of Trees, Ferns, 16 In. 4313.00
Lamp, Shade, Flowers, Cast Metal Base, Signed, 14½ In. .... *illus* 945.00
Lamp, Shade, Nordic, Evergreens, Tree Trunk Base, Bronzed Base, 15 x 7 In. 6000.00
Lamp, Shade, Ribbed, Landscape At Dusk, 3 Sockets, Bronzed Base, 22½ x 15½ In. 4200.00
Lamp, Shade, Venetian Harbor, 7 In. 2875.00
Lamp, Student, 2-Light, Metal Overlay, Palm Tree, Red & Orange Slag Glass, 25 In. 3105.00
Lamp, Student, Chipped Ice Shade, Peacocks, Gold Painted Base, 14 x 11 x 12½ In. 2400.00
Lamp, Tulip Shade, Metal Overlay, Flowers, Slag Glass, Signed, 8½ x 13½ In. 1200.00
Lamp Base, Disk, Twisted Base, Bronze, 25¾ In. 1243.00
Sconce, Tulip Shade, Yellow Slag Glass, Opalescent Glass, 4 In., Pair 1495.00
Shade, 6 Panels, Metal Overlay, Leaf, Vine, Gold Patina, 6 In., Pair 978.00
Shade, Chipped Ice, Forest Scene, Brown, Green, White, Yellow, Gold, Signed, 10 In. 4800.00
Shade, Tam O'Shanter, Flowers, Yellow, Green, Signed, 6½ x 12 In. 960.00
Vase, Chipped Ice, Forest Scene, Flowering Tree, Teroma, Signed, John Bailey, 7½ In. 1610.00
Vase, Chipped Ice, Mountainscape, Teroma, 9¾ In. 1657.00
Vase, Opal, Painted Flowers, Signed, Weruden Jr., 4¾ In. 518.00

HARDWARE, *see Architectural category.*

HARKER Pottery Company of East Liverpool, Ohio, was incorporated in 1890 in East Liverpool, Ohio. The Harker family had been making pottery in the area since 1840. The company made many types of pottery but by the Civil War was making quantities of yellowware from native clays. They also made Rockingham-type brown-glazed pottery and whiteware. The plant was moved to Chester, West Virginia, in 1931. Dinnerwares were made and sold nationally. In 1971 the company was sold to Jeannette Glass Company and all operations ceased in 1972. For more information, see *Kovels' Depression Glass & Dinnerware Price List*.

Amy, Rolling Pin, 13 In. 99.00

Hampshire, Vase, Mottled Blue, Green Glaze, Arches, 7 In.
$650.00

Handel, Lamp, 8 Panels, Chipped Ice Shade, Roses, 7 x 15½ x 9 In.
$1400.00

Handel, Lamp, Chipped Ice Shade, Wreath Of Leaves, Sulfur Yellow, Bronze Base, 23 In.
$2000.00

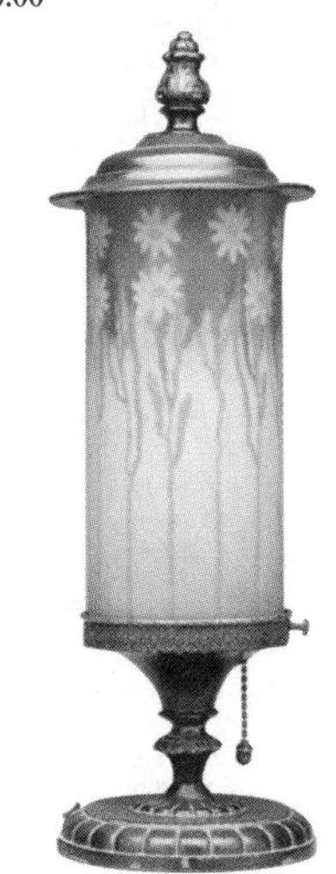

Handel, Lamp, Domed Shade, Daffodils, Bronzed Base, Signed, 24 x 17 In. $8950.00

Handel, Lamp, Shade, Flowers, Cast Metal Base, Signed, 14 ½ In. $945.00

Harker, Godey, Plate, Dessert, Gold Rim, 6 ¼ In. $5.00

Harker, Royal Gadroon, Saucer, Violets, 6 ½ In. $10.00

Cameoware, Dessert Set, Snowleaf, Turquoise, Cup & Saucer, 7 ¼-In. Plate, 3 Piece 18.00
Cameoware, Tidbit, Rose, 10 In. 14.00
Chesterton, Bowl, Vegetable, Round, Gray, 9 In. 18.00
Chesterton, Gravy Boat, Gray 25.00
Chesterton, Pie Server, Gray, 9 ¾ In. 12.00
Compass Rose, Creamer 7.00
Dainty Flower, Platter, Blue, Cameoware, 12 x 9 In. 25.00
Daniel Boone, Mug, Rockingham Glaze, Indian On Handle, 4 ¼ x 5 In. 48.00
Deco Dahlia, Pie Server, 9 ¼ In. 18.00
Emmy, Rolling Pin, 14 ½ In. 99.00
English Garden, Pitcher, Arched Panels, Flowers, 5 ½ x 7 ¾ In. 28.00
Godey, Creamer, Colonial Couple Dancing, Platinum Trim, 3 ¼ x 5 ¼ In. 26.00
Godey, Plate, Dessert, Gold Rim, 6 ¼ In. .... *illus* 5.00
Intaglio, Creamer, Green 2.50
Intaglio, Cup 3.00
Intaglio, Plate, Bread & Butter, 6 In. 3.00
Macaw, Trivet, 8-Sided, 1950s, 6 ¼ In. 28.00
Mallow, Rolling Pin, 15 In. 99.00
Mallow, Sugar Scoop, 5 ⅞ In. 35.00
Modern Tulip, Bowl, 4 ½ x 9 In. 12.00
Modern Tulip, Bowl, Cereal, 6 In. 8.75
Modern Tulip, Cake Plate, Metal Handle 13.00
Modern Tulip, Custard Cup, Modern Age Shape 6.25
Modern Tulip, Plate, Bread & Butter, 6 ½ In. 8.25
Modern Tulip, Plate, Dinner, 9 ½ In. 8.75
Old Rose, Sugar & Creamer, Gadroon Rim, Gold Trim 25.00
Old Rose, Tureen, Cover, Gadroon Rim, Gold Trim, 2 Tab Handles 30.00
Pate-Sur-Pate, Creamer, Teal 23.00
Pate-Sur-Pate, Luncheon Set, Blue, Cream, Cup, 8 ½-In. Plate, 4 Sets 50.00
Persian Key, Platter, Oval, 11 ½ x 9 ¾ In. 18.00
Persian Key, Platter, Oval, 13 ½ x 11 ¼ In. 20.00
Petit Point, Bowl, HotOven, 6 ¾ In. 8.00
Petit Point, Plate, Dinner, 9 ¼ In. 9.50
Petit Point, Rolling Pin, 15 In. 50.00
Pink Poppy, Casserole, Cover, HotOven, 8 ½ In. 33.00
Pitcher, Refrigerator, Cover, Apple, Pear, Square 75.00
Provincial Tulip, Plate, Dinner, Green, 10 ¼ In. 16.00
Royal Gadroon, Plate, Dinner, Red Rose, Dew, 10 ¼ In. 22.00
Royal Gadroon, Saucer, Violets, 6 ½ In. .... *illus* 10.00
Shell Pink, Bowl, Cereal, Gray, Speckled Pink Interior, 6 ½ In. 16.00
Shell Pink, Cup & Saucer 15.00
Shell Pink, Plate, Salad, 1950s, 7 ¾ In. 11.00
Snow Leaf, Luncheon Set, Turquoise, White Leaves, 7 ¼-In. Plate, 3 Piece 18.00
Spring Time, Cake Plate, Lug Handles, 11 ¼ In. 20.00
Spring Time, Plate, Bread & Butter, 6 ½ In. 6.00
Spring Time, Soup, Dish 7.50
Sun-Glo, Tidbit, Yellow, Center Handle, 10 In. 12.00
Vintage, Tidbit, Cameo Rose, Center Handle, Single Tier, 10 In. 14.00
Wild Rose, Pie Server, 9 ¼ In. 28.00

HARLEQUIN dinnerware was produced by the Homer Laughlin Company from 1938 to 1964, and sold without trademark by the F. W. Woolworth Co. It has a concentric ring design like Fiesta, but the rings are separated from the rim by a plain margin. Cup handles are triangular in shape. Seven different novelty animal figurines were introduced in 1939. For more information on Harlequin dinnerware, see *Kovels' Depression Glass & Dinnerware Price List.*

Chartreuse, Cup & Saucer 20.00
Chartreuse, Plate, 9 In. 12.00
Coral, Pitcher, Water 27.00
Coral, Plate, Deep, 8 In. 9.00
Gray, Eggcup, Double 43.00
Gray, Nappy, 9 In. 13.00
Gray, Plate, Salad, 7 ¼ In. 18.00
Green, Bowl, Deep, 5 In. 40.00
Green, Bowl, Oatmeal, 36s, 6 ½ In. 28.00
Green, Plate, Deep, 8 In. 9.00

Green, Plate, Luncheon, 9 In. 12.00
Mauve Blue, Plate, Bread & Butter, 6 ¼ In. 5.00
Mauve Blue, Saltshaker 13.00
Medium Green, Cup 15.00
Medium Green, Plate, Salad, 7 ½ In. 15.00
Red, Creamer 25.00
Red, Eggcup, Double 25.00
Red, Gravy Boat 25.00
Red, Pitcher, Ball 60.00
Red, Plate, Luncheon, 9 In. 13.00
Red, Sugar, Cover 16.00
Rose, Bowl, Cereal 7.00
Rose, Bowl, Salad, Individual, 7 ½ In. 15.00
Rose, Eggcup, Double 23.00
Rose, Pitcher, Ball 75.00
Rose, Plate, Luncheon, 9 In. 12.00
Rose, Sugar, Cover 25.00
Spruce Green, Pitcher, Water, 7 ½ In. 105.00
Spruce Green, Soup, Rim 23.00
Turquoise, Baker, Oval, 9 In. 15.00
Turquoise, Bowl, Cereal 7.00
Turquoise, Bowl, Salad, 7 ½ In. 20.00
Turquoise, Creamer 10.00
Turquoise, Cup, After Dinner, 2 ⅛ In. 24.00
Turquoise, Cup & Saucer 13.00
Turquoise, Nappy, 9 In. 28.00
Turquoise, Plate, Bread & Butter, 6 ¼ In. 9.00
Turquoise, Plate, Salad, 7 ¼ In. 7.00
Turquoise, Sugar, Cover 5.00
Turquoise, Tea Set, Teapot, Sugar, Creamer .... *illus* 62.00
Yellow, Bowl, Oatmeal, 36s, 6 ½ In. 20.00
Yellow, Cup 8.00
Yellow, Cup & Saucer 24.00
Yellow, Figurine, Cat, 1 ¾ x 2 ¾ In. .... *illus* 110.00
Yellow, Gravy Boat 16.00
Yellow, Pitcher, Ball .... 55.00 to 125.00
Yellow, Pitcher, Water, 7 ½ In. 75.00
Yellow, Plate, Deep, 8 In. 10.00
Yellow, Plate, Dinner, 10 In. 20.00
Yellow, Sugar 9.00
Yellow, Teacup 6.50
Yellow, Teapot, 5 ½ In. 75.00
Yellow, Tumbler, 4 ¼ In. 45.00

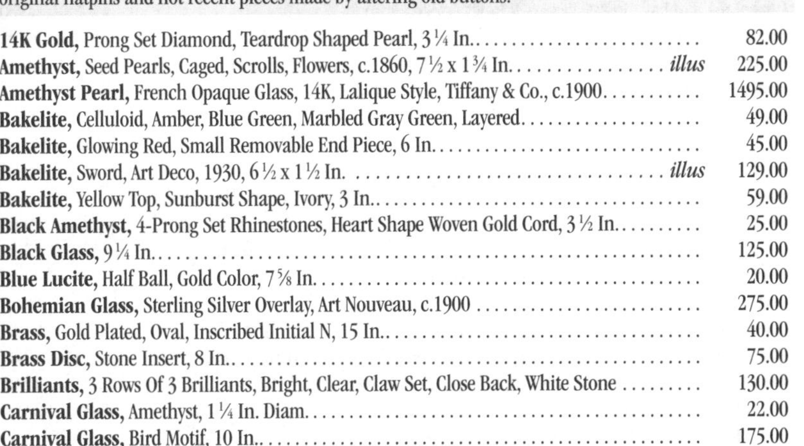

HATPIN collectors search for pins popular from 1860 to 1920. The long pin, often over four inches, was used to hold the hat in place on the hair. The tops of the pins were made of all materials, from solid gold and real gemstones to ceramics and glass. Be careful to buy original hatpins and not recent pieces made by altering old buttons.

14K Gold, Prong Set Diamond, Teardrop Shaped Pearl, 3 ¼ In. 82.00
Amethyst, Seed Pearls, Caged, Scrolls, Flowers, c.1860, 7 ½ x 1 ¾ In. .... *illus* 225.00
Amethyst Pearl, French Opaque Glass, 14K, Lalique Style, Tiffany & Co., c.1900 .... 1495.00
Bakelite, Celluloid, Amber, Blue Green, Marbled Gray Green, Layered 49.00
Bakelite, Glowing Red, Small Removable End Piece, 6 In. 45.00
Bakelite, Sword, Art Deco, 1930, 6 ½ x 1 ½ In. .... *illus* 129.00
Bakelite, Yellow Top, Sunburst Shape, Ivory, 3 In. 59.00
Black Amethyst, 4-Prong Set Rhinestones, Heart Shape Woven Gold Cord, 3 ½ In. 25.00
Black Glass, 9 ¼ In. 125.00
Blue Lucite, Half Ball, Gold Color, 7 ⅝ In. 20.00
Bohemian Glass, Sterling Silver Overlay, Art Nouveau, c.1900 .... 275.00
Brass, Gold Plated, Oval, Inscribed Initial N, 15 In. 40.00
Brass Disc, Stone Insert, 8 In. 75.00
Brilliants, 3 Rows Of 3 Brilliants, Bright, Clear, Claw Set, Close Back, White Stone 130.00
Carnival Glass, Amethyst, 1 ¼ In. Diam. 22.00
Carnival Glass, Bird Motif, 10 In. 175.00
Coin Cluster, 1 ¾ x 1 ¾ x 6 ½ In. 55.00
Faux Topaz Thistle, Sterling Whiplash, Charles Horner, Arts & Crafts, 9 ½ In. 225.00

Harlequin, Turquoise, Tea Set, Teapot, Sugar, Creamer
$62.00

Harlequin, Yellow, Figurine, Cat, 1 ¾ x 2 ¾ In.
$110.00

Hatpin, Amethyst, Seed Pearls, Caged, Scrolls, Flowers, c.1860, 7 ½ x 1 ¾ In.
$225.00

Hatpin, Bakelite, Sword, Art Deco, 1930, 6 ½ x 1 ½ In.
$129.00

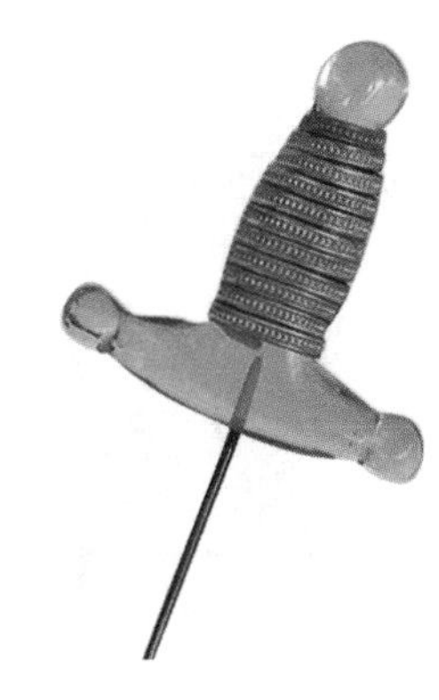

H

TIP
Moving your own belongings? Be careful about insurance. Rental trucks or your car may have coverage for antiques that is too low. Your homeowner's policy probably does not cover damage from poor packing. Check with your agent before you move!

Hatpin, Green Rhinestone, Moonstone, 4 In.
$22.00

Hatpin Holder, Porcelain, Lady, Pink, White, 7 In.
$33.00

Filigree, Double Hearts, Goldtone, 3 In. . . . 9.00
Filigree, Scrolling Heart, Rhinestones, 6 ⅝ x ½ In. . . . 28.00
Glass, Peacock Eye, Bohemian, Art Nouveau, c.1900 . . . 275.00
Glass Seed Beads, 11 In.. . . . 15.00
Gold Chased, Ball Finial, Attached Chain To Hairpin, 3 ½ x 9 ⅜ In. . . . 125.00
Gold Tone, Double Button, Gold, 9 ½ In. . . . 15.00
Gold Tone, Wave Shape, 12 White Beads, Signed, Boucher, 7 ½ In. . . . 55.00
Green Rhinestone, Moonstone, 4 In. . . . *illus* 22.00
Ivory, Pierced Carved Flower, Reticulated, Chinese, 9 In. . . . 120.00
Jet Glass, Faceted Carved Jet Bead, Steel Shaft, 7 In. . . . 45.00
Lucite White Button, Silver Filigree Snowflake Base, 9 In. . . . 20.00
Micro Mosaic, Goldstone, ¾ x 1 ⅜ x 8 ¼ In. . . . 65.00
Moonstone, Gray, Silver Filigree Square, 4 In.. . . . 45.00
Mother-Of-Pearl, Flower, Carved, 7 In. . . . 48.00
Porcelain, Bead, Lavender, 9 In. . . . 6.00
Porcelain, Brown, Gold, 9 In. . . . 6.00
Porcelain, Purple Swirl, 9 In. . . . 6.00
Porcelain, Satsuma, Butterflies, Japanese, 5 ¾ In. . . . 225.00
Purple Amethyst Glass, Victorian, 11 Stones, 1900s, 11 ⅜ In.. . . . 95.00
Purple Glass Stone, Gold Metal Filigree, 12 In. . . . 135.00
Repousse Setting, Jade Cabochon, Art Nouveau, c.1900 . . . 275.00
Rose Gold, Center Turquoise Bead, Steel Shaft, Edwardian, 6 ¾ In.. . . . 210.00
Silver, Charles Horner, Art Nouveau, 9 In., c.1900 . . . 195.00
Silver, Charles Horner, Art Nouveau, 11 ½ In. . . . 145.00
Silver Ball, Flowers, Rhinestones, 6 ⅝ In. . . . 28.00
Sterling Silver, Repousse, Charles Horner, Arts & Crafts, c.1911, 11 In. . . . 195.00
Sterling Silver, Tubular Finding, 10 ¼ In.. . . . 185.00
Stone, Multicolored, Gold Gilt, Steel Shank, 8 ½ In. . . . 195.00
Straw, Fan Shape, Jet Faceted Stones, Brass Setting, 7 In. . . . 35.00
Topaz, Oval, Faceted, Art Nouveau, c.1910, 12 ½ In. . . . 225.00
Topaz, Oval, Victorian, Brass, Bezel Set, 12 ½ In. . . . 225.00

HATPIN HOLDERS were needed when hatpins were fashionable from 1860 to 1920. The large, heavy hat required special long-shanked pins to hold it in place. The hatpin holder resembles a large saltshaker, but it often has no opening at the bottom as a shaker does. Hatpin holders were made of all types of ceramics and metal. Look for other pieces under the names of specific manufacturers.

Bronze, Bear, Holding Lantern, Red Glass Cabochon, Black Base, 24 Holes, 5 ½ In. . . . 197.00
Ebony, Sterling Silver, Hallmark, England, c.1909 . . . 175.00
Figural, Child In Pierrot Costume, Dog, Germany, No. 3489, 7 ⅛ In. . . . 400.00
Glass, Sterling Silver Top, Cherubs, c.1908 . . . 215.00
Gold Beading, Fluted, Scalloped Rim, Embossed, Purple Violets, 4 ¾ In. . . . 35.00
Jasperware, Egyptian Queen, Schafer & Vater, Pink, 5 ¾ In. . . . 165.00
Porcelain, 6-Sided, Cream Tea Rose, Leaves, Blue, Ocher Highlights, R.S. Prussia, Art Deco. . 75.00
Porcelain, Baby Roses, Leaves, 9 Holes, 4 ½ x 3 ¾ In. . . . 20.00
Porcelain, Blue, Tapered, Scalloped Base, Painted, Gold Leaf, Art Nouveau, c.1930, 5 In. . . . 75.00
Porcelain, Blue Flowers, Blue To Rose Beige Base, Signed, c.1912, 4 ¾ In. . . . 62.00
Porcelain, Cabbage Roses, Leaves, 9 Holes, 4 ½ x 3 ¾ In. . . . 30.00
Porcelain, Cobalt Blue, Gold Rim, Metal Mouth, Jewel Cluster, 4 ⅛ In. . . . 40.00
Porcelain, Figural, Bird, Sitting On Branch, 4 Hatpin Holes, Germany, 6 In. . . . 49.00
Porcelain, Flower, Dark Ground, Silver Rim, Scalloped Base, 4 ¾ In. . . . 66.00
Porcelain, Flowers, 6-Sided, Embossed, R.S. Prussia . . . 100.00
Porcelain, Flowers, Bavaria, 5 In.. . . . 113.00
Porcelain, Flowers, Geometric Border, Nippon, c.1921, 4 ¼ In. . . . 100.00
Porcelain, Flowers, Pastel, Pink, Green, Peach Ground, R.S. Prussia, Art Nouveau, 4 In. . . . 80.00
Porcelain, Flowers, Swirl Ribbed, Ruffle Rim, Nippon, Art Nouveau, c.1921 . . . 89.00
Porcelain, Green, Pink, Gold, Gold Trim, Dish Base, Holds 10 Hatpins, 6 In. . . . 25.00
Porcelain, Green, Pink, Gold, Gold Trim, Holds 10 Hatpins, 6 In. . . . 28.00
Porcelain, Hand Painted, Nippon, 5 x 2 ¼ In. . . . 89.00
Porcelain, Hand Painted, Nippon, Art Deco, 5 In. . . . 95.00
Porcelain, High Button Shoe Shape, Flowers, Green, Pink, Gold Trim, 6 In.. . . . 18.00
Porcelain, Iris, Blue, White, Gold Trim, Holds 10 Hatpins, 6 In.. . . . 22.00
Porcelain, Lady, Pink, White, 7 In. . . . *illus* 33.00
Porcelain, Multicolored Flowers, Rosenthal, 5 ¼ In.. . . . 117.00
Porcelain, Pastel Pink, Butterfly, Blossom Flowers, Noritake, 5 In. . . . 65.00
Porcelain, Pink Flower, Peach To Blue Ground, Gilt, 12 Holes, Rosenthal, 5 In.. . . . 35.00

Porcelain, Pink Flowers, Dish Base, 6 In. 35.00
Porcelain, Pink Flowers, Handles, 21 Hatpin Holes, 5 x 2 ½ In. 35.00
Porcelain, Pink Ribbon & Flower Design, Limoges, 5 ½ In. 32.00
Porcelain, Pink Roses, Double Handles, R.S. Prussia, c.1890, 5 x 4 ½ In. 495.00
Porcelain, Pink Roses, Green Leaves, Trailing Stems, Blue Ground, Bavaria 95.00
Porcelain, Pink Top, Saucer Base, Pink, Purple Roses, Gold Painted Rim, 1950s, 5 In. 45.00
Porcelain, Poppies, Gilt, Gold Beading, Iridescent Lavender, Blue, Footed, R.S. Prussia. 325.00
Porcelain, Poppies, White Pearl, Royal Bayreuth, c.1887, 4 ½ In. 475.00
Porcelain, Purple Flowers, Limoges 65.00
Porcelain, Raised Swirl, Double Line Gold Leaf, Nippon, Art Nouveau, c.1921, 4 ¼ In. 125.00
Porcelain, Red & Pink Roses, Cobalt Blue, Gold Trim, Limoges, 5 ½ x 3 ½ In. 25.00
Porcelain, Red Cabbage Roses, Embossed Vine, 22K Gold Trim, 9 Holes, 4 ½ x 3 ¾ In. 30.00
Porcelain, Red Roses, Leaves, Gold Trim, Holds 9 Hatpins, 4 ½ In. 24.00
Porcelain, Ring Tray, 12 Hatpin Holes, Pickard Style, Roses, 5 x 4 In. 30.00
Porcelain, Ringed Neck, Bulbous Body Tapered To Base, Art Nouveau, c.1921, 4 ½ In. 100.00
Porcelain, Scalloped, Pink Roses, Buds, 6-Footed, Royal Vienna, R.S. Prussia, 5 In. 225.00
Porcelain, Scenic, Cottage, Pond, Swan, Cherry Tree, Nippon, 11 Openings, 5 ½ In. 64.00
Porcelain, Souvenir, Victoria Porcelain Factory, Stara Role, Czechoslovakia, c.1920 .... 100.00
Porcelain, Strawberry Buds, Fruit, Signed, M. Hense, c.1930, 4 ¾ In. 125.00
Porcelain, Swirl Ribbed, White, Stylized Flowers, Tangerine, Rose, Japan, 1920s, 5 In. 125.00
Porcelain, Water Scene, Swan, Aqua Ground, Gold Trim, Fluted Sides, Bell Shape, 5 In. 148.00
Porcelain, White Ground, Gold Design, Royal Nippon 14.00
Porcelain, White Ground, Gold Leaf Border, Pattern, Pedestal Base, Bavaria, 4 ¼ In. 129.00
Porcelain, White Pearlized Luster, Pink, Green, Yellow, Blue, Limoges, c.1930, 4 ¼ In. 129.00
Porcelain, Wild Rose, Hand Painted, Pink, Bavaria, 4 ¾ In. 95.00
Porcelain, Yellow, Orange, Apricot Flowers, Beyer & Bock, Royal Rudolstadt, c.1905 .... 125.00
Red Clay, Square, Rounded Corners, Domed Top, Brown Glaze, Greek Key, Flowers, 5 In. 55.00

HAVILAND china has been made in Limoges, France, since 1842. The factory was started by the Haviland Brothers of New York City. Pieces are marked *H & Co., Haviland & Co.*, or *Theodore Haviland*. It is possible to match existing sets of dishes through dealers who specialize in Haviland china. Other factories worked in the town of Limoges making a similar chinaware. These porcelains are listed in this book under Limoges.

HAVILAND & CO.

Butter, Pierced Insert, Lid, Pink Flowers, Scalloped Base, Theodore Haviland, 3 x 7 ½ In. 40.00
Cup & Saucer, Butterfly Handle, Butterfly & Flower Decoration, Haviland & Co. 35.00
Cup & Saucer, Chocolate, 3 & 5 In., 14 Piece 83.00
Cup & Saucer, Dynasty, 2 x 5 In. 94.00
Cup & Saucer, Dynasty, Applied 14K Gold Design. .... 75.00 to 100.00
Cup & Saucer, Dynasty, Flowers, Scrolls, Gold, 3 & 5½ In. .... 118.00 to 235.00
Fish Platter, Flower Bouquets, c.1876, 27 In. 292.00
Pancake Server, Pierced Cover, Pink Flowers, Gilt Rim, Gilt Handle, 9 ½ In. 170.00
Pitcher, Pink Flowers, Scalloped Rim & Base, 7 In. 160.00
Plate, Scene From Lohengrin, Scalloped Border, Gilt Trim, A. Soustre, 9 In. 1000.00
Platter, Pink Flowers, Gilt Trim, Round, Theodore Haviland, 13 ¼ In. 20.00
Tray, Plates, Butterfly Design, 24 x 9 In. 358.00
Tureen, Soup, Gold & Cobalt Blue Trim, Pedestal Base, 2 Handles, 9 ½ x 11 In. 170.00
Vase, Cherry Blossoms, Blue Ground, 8 ¾ In. 1298.00
Vase, Planter, Roses, Blue Ground, Oval, Footed, Impressed, 5 ⅝ x 10 In. .... *illus* 750.00

HAVILAND POTTERY began in 1872, when Charles Haviland decided to make art pottery. He worked with the famous artists of the day and made pottery with slip glazed decorations. Production stopped in 1885. Haviland Pottery is marked with the letters *H & Co*. The Haviland name is better known today for its porcelain.

Vase, Cottage In Garden, Wide Mouth Flask Form, Footed, 2 Handles, 9 ½ In. 1500.00
Vase, Mottled Green, Pink Flowers, 10 ½ x 6 In. 1495.00

HAWKES cut glass was made by T. G. Hawkes & Company of Corning, New York, founded in 1880. The firm cut glass blanks made at other glassworks until 1962. Many pieces are marked with the trademark, a trefoil ring enclosing a fleur-de-lis and two hawks. Cut glass by other manufacturers is listed under either the factory name or in the general Cut Glass category.

Bowl, Centerpiece, Starburst, 7 x 6 In. 201.00
Bowl, Chrysanthemum, Variation, 4-Sided, 7 In. 400.00
Bowl, Hobstars, Diamonds, Fans, Signed, 1930s, 8 In. 225.00
Candelabrum, 5-Light, Marked, 21 In., Pair 13000.00

Haviland, Vase, Planter, Roses, Blue Ground, Oval, Footed, Impressed, 5 ⅝ x 10 In.
$750.00

TIP

The handle on a glass jug is a clue to the jug's age. About 1860 handles were applied at the bottom first, creating a thick blob, then drawn to the top and affixed to the edge. Before 1860 the handles were applied at the top

Hawkes, Pitcher, Amber, Flowers, Vines, Shell Reed Handle, 11 ¼ In.
$250.00

Hawkes, Vase, Zippered Panels, Fan Border, Signed, 9 ½ In.
$310.00

H

Head Vase, Mary Lou, Black Hat, Yellow Ruffled Dress, Marked, Betty Lou Nichols, 7 ¾ In.
$255.00

Head Vase, Teen, Blond, Bonnet, Hand With Bouquet, Relpo, 5 ¾ In.
$80.00

Head Vase, Woman, Blond, Pink, Lashes, Earrings, Inarco, 4 ½ In.
$70.00

Head Vase, Woman, Brown Hair, Blue Glove Hand, Lashes, Earrings, Label, Napcoware, 7 In.
$129.00

Carafe, Brunswick, Honeycomb Neck, Marked, 7 In. 350.00
Cologne Bottle, Gravic, Chrysanthemum & Leaves, Signed, 6 x 5 In. 275.00
Cologne Bottle, Grecian Pattern, Ball Stopper, 6 ½ In. 400.00
Finger Bowl, Underplate, Engraved Carnation, Signed, 6 Piece 225.00
Pitcher, Amber, Flowers, Vines, Shell Reed Handle, 11 ¼ In. *illus* 250.00
Plate, Intaglio Cherries, American Brilliant, Signed, 8 ½ In. 800.00
Plate, Kensington Pattern, Signed, 7 In. 700.00
Plate, Poppy & Engraved Floral Vesica, Signed, Hawkes Gravic Glass, 7 In. 350.00
Plate, Portland, Signed, 7 In. 125.00
Sandwich Server, Green, Star Medallions, Vertical Stripe, Signed, 11 In. 225.00
Sherbet, 3 Fruits, Engraved, Signed, 5 In., 6 Piece 275.00
Soup, Coupe, Neoclassical Style, Signed, 9 In. 420.00
Tobacco Jar, Signed, 6 x 5 ½ In. 1300.00
Tumbler, Pedestal Base, 2 Women In Forest, 5 ¼ In. 400.00
Vase, Intaglio Flowers, Pedestal Base, Ruffled Rim, Signed, Gravic, 8 ¾ In. 200.00
Vase, Pedestal Base, Hobstar, Step-Cut Body, Marked, 10 ¼ In. 250.00
Vase, Queen's Pattern, Flared, Footed, 5 x 12 In. 460.00
Vase, Trumpet, Queen?s Pattern, Faceted Knob, Hobstar Base, Marked, 12 In. 900.00
Vase, Zippered Panels, Fan Border, Signed, 9 ½ In. *illus* 310.00
Water Set, Decanter, Bulbous, Goblets, 9 ½ In., 7 Piece 350.00
Wine Set, Leaf & Berry, 6 Piece 59.00

HEAD VASES, generally showing a woman from the shoulders up, were used by florists primarily in the 1950s and 1960s. Made in a variety of sizes and often decorated with imitation jewelry and other lifelike accessories, the vases were manufactured in Japan and the U.S.A. Less elaborate examples were made as early as the 1930s. Religious themes, babies, and animals are also common subjects. Other head vases are listed under manufacturers' names and can be located through the index in the back of this book.

Carol Channing, Christmas Carol, Hat, Glove, Marked, No. K800, Rubens, 6 In. 375.00
Doris Day, Blue Bow, White Ruffled Collar, Inarco, 8 In. 620.00
Edith, Cowgirl, Blond Hair, Black Shirt 45.00
Girl, Black, Wide Brim Hat, 9 In. 85.00
Girl, Blue Bonnet, Artmark Originals, Japan, 1950s, 5 In. 95.00
Girl, Pony Tail, Bird Perched On Hat, 5 In. 16.00
Girl, Umbrella Brown Braids, Yellow Hat, Black Bow, Japan, 4 ½ In. 60.00
Grace Kelly, Pearl Necklace, Earrings, Black Glove, C5035C, Napco, 1960, 6 In. 430.00
Madonna, Brown Hair, Enesco, 1950s, 5 ½ x 3 ½ In. 36.00
Margo, Ruffled Pink Hat, Ceramic Arts, 1940s, 6 In. 42.00
Mary Lou, Black Hat, Yellow Ruffled Dress, Marked, Betty Lou Nichols, 7 ¾ In. *illus* 255.00
Miss Boston, Blond, Pearls, Earrings, Black, White Outfit, Marked, No. 11308, 5 ¾ In. 350.00
Miss Holland, Blond, Pearl Earrings, Bracelet, C1611, Inarco, 1964, 5 ¾ In. 1295.00
Mitzi Gaynor, E2968, Inarco, 1960s, 7 ½ In. 1475.00
Pearly Girl, Brown Hair, Aqua Strap, Pearl Earrings, Flowers, Netting, Enesco, 8 In. 525.00
Queen, Blond, Fanned Collar, Gold & White Choker, 1950s, 6 ¼ In. 58.00
Red Cross Nurse, Blond, Enesco, 5 ¾ In. 395.00
Rudolph, Red-Nosed Reindeer, Stamped, Napcoware, 5 ¼ x 4 ⅛ In. 15.00
Teen, Ash Blond, Purple Lined Raincoat, Pearl Earrings, No. 4187, Rubens, 7 In. 790.00
Teen, Ash Blond, Side Head Scarf, Pearl Necklace, Earrings, Relpo, 1941, 7 ¼ In. 1995.00
Teen, Ash Blond, Turquoise Dress, Pearl Earrings, Necklace, Floppy Hat, Relpo, 7 In. 350.00
Teen, Blond, Bonnet, Hand With Bouquet, Relpo, 5 ¾ In. *illus* 80.00
Teen, Blond, Pearl Earrings, Newsboy Cap, No. 7245, 1960s, 7 ¼ In. 550.00
Teen, Blue Dress, Buttercup In Hair, No. E3157, Inarco, 6 In. 139.00
Teen, Brown Braids, Pearl Necklace, Earrings, Beret, No. 7333, Lego, 1960s, 7 ½ In. 1690.00
Teen, Brown Hair, Flower Bonnet, Green Dress, Relpo, Japan, 7 In. 1195.00
Veronica Lake, Hair Pulled To One Side, Pink Scarf, 5 In. 70.00
Woman, Ash Blond, Green Dress, Pearl Necklace, Puffy Sleeves, No. 2036, Relpo, 5 ½ In. 115.00
Woman, Black Beauty, Kindell, 5 ½ In. 50.00
Woman, Blond, Blue Dress, Aqua Hat, Marked, No. 484, 5 ¾ In. 190.00
Woman, Blond, Bristle Eyelashes, Green Cape, White Flowers, Ucagco, 5 ½ In. 110.00
Woman, Blond, Pink, Lashes, Earrings, Inarco, 4 ½ In. *illus* 70.00
Woman, Bobbed Hair, Finger-To-Chain Pose, Trimont Ware, 7 In. 166.00
Woman, Brown Hair, Blue Glove Hand, Lashes, Earrings, Label, Napcoware, 7 In. *illus* 129.00
Woman, Gay Nineties, Green Striped Ribbon, Napco, 6 ¼ In. 250.00
Woman, Holding Her Hand, Red Fingernail Polish, Inarco, 1961, 6 In. 45.00
Woman, Pink Dress, Roses On Hat, Lee Wards, 1940s, 5 ¾ In. 64.00

Woman, Turquoise Hat & Dress, Necklace, Earring, Big Lashes, Blond, Napco, 1958 . . . . 60.00
Woman, Wide Ruffled Bonnet, Applied Flowers, Bows, Yellow Bodice, Inarco 225.00
Woman, Winking, Blond, Fan, Turquoise Feathered Hat, Hair, 6 In. 75.00

HEDI SCHOOP Art Creations, North Hollywood, California, started about 1945 and was working until 1954. Schoop made ceramic figurines, lamps, planters, and tablewares.

Hedi Schoop S

Bowl, Butterfly, Gold, Multicolored Rim, 8 In. 35.00
Bowl, Seashell Form, Ruffled Rim, Gold Overlay, 11 In. 22.00
Bowl, Woman, Billowing Skirt, Pink, Gold Trim, 14 x 10 In.. . . . . 50.00
Box, Butterfly, Pink, Gold Trim, 2¾ x 6½ In. 36.00
Console Set, Duck, Candleholders, Bowl, Signed, 6¾ x 13 In. 120.00
Figurine, Dancing Ladies, White Dress, Gold Accents, 12 & 13 In., Pair. 150.00
Figurine, Dancing Lady, Black & Gold Billowing Dress, 9 In. 110.00
Figurine, Dancing Lady, Pink & Gold Dress, Brown Ponytail, 9½ In. 110.00
Figurine, Dutch Boy & Girl, My Sister & I, c.1940, 11½ In., Pair 125.00
Figurine, Exotic Lady, Green Dress, Gold Accents, c.1945, 12½ In. . . . . 95.00 to 125.00
Figurine, Girl, Holding Blue Buckets, White Dress, Blue Flowers, 13½ In. 125.00
Figurine, Hungarian Man & Woman, 10½ & 10 In., Pair 150.00
Figurine, Man, Woman, With Buckets, White, Green, 10¼ & 9¾ In.. . . . . 85.00
Figurine, Mother & Daughter, Father & Son, 1900s Costumes 190.00
Figurine, Oriental Man, 12½ In. 58.00
Figurine, Oriental Man, Green Coat, White Hat, Signed, c.1950, 15 In. 75.00
Figurine, Oriental Man, Shoulder Yoke, Lilac & White, 12 In. 40.00
Figurine, Rooster, Green, Brown, 13 In. 125.00
Figurine, Sailor, Oriental, Signed, 15 In. 75.00
Figurine, Woman, Blond, 2 Pink Flower Holders, c.1940, 13 In. 75.00
Figurine, Woman, Kneeling, Bowl In Lap, Green Glaze, 1940s, 11½ In. 165.00
Figurine, Women With Umbrellas, Oriental Dresses, 11 In., Pair. 220.00
Planter, Book Lady, 9 In. 58.00
Planter, Bowl, Candleholders, Double Ducks, 1942, 4 Piece 119.00
Planter, Chicken, Cranberry Pink, Gold Accents, 5½ In.. . . . . 15.00
Planter, Dancing Lady, Holding Out Apron, Pink & Gray Dress, 7½ In., Pair 100.00
Planter, Dutch Girl, Holding Apron, 11 In.. . . . . 45.00
Planter, Horse, Pink & White, Green Saddle, 9¾ x 10½ In. 75.00
Planter, Tyrolean Girl, Billowing Skirt, 11 In. 75.00
Tray, Butterfly, Pink, White, Gold Accents, c.1942. . . . . 42.00
Vase, Fan, Pink, Beige, Gold Trim, 12 x 7 In. 100.00
Vase, Woman, Blond, 2 Flower Holders, 13 In. . . . . *illus* 75.00

HEINTZ ART Metal Shop used the letters *HAMS* in a diamond as a mark. Otto Heintz took over the Arts & Crafts Company in Buffalo, New York, in 1903. By 1906 it had become the Heintz Art Metal Shop. It remained in business until 1930. The company made ashtrays, bookends, boxes, bowls, desk sets, vases, trophies, and smoking sets. The best-known pieces are made of copper, brass, and bronze with silver overlay. Similar pieces were made by Smith Metal Arts and were marked *Silver Crest*. Some pieces by both companies are unmarked.

HAMS

Bowl, Applied Leaf Designs, Sterling On Bronze, Green Patina, Marked, 8 x 4 In. 201.00
Bowl, Leaves, Sterling On Bronze, Patina, 4 x 8 In. . . . . *illus* 720.00
Box, 2-Sided, Hinged Lids, Applied Arrow, Sterling On Bronze, Green Patina, 8 x 4½ In. 144.00
Candlestick, Applied Design, Sterling On Bronze, Patina, 5 x 12 In., Pair. 480.00
Candlestick, Applied Organic Design, Sterling On Bronze, Patina, 4¼ x 12 In. 201.00
Candlestick, Applied Organic Design, Sterling On Bronze, Patina, 5 x 14 In. 201.00
Compote, Sterling On Bronze, Applied Flowers, Patina, Marked, 4 x 7 In. . . . . *illus* 120.00
Compote, Sterling On Bronze, Organic Design, Marked, 6½ x 6½ In.. . . . . 390.00
Desk Set, Bronze, Silver Overlay, Pen Tray, Blotter Corners, Calendar Holder, Letter Holder . . 206.00
Frame, Applied Designs, Silver, 14½ x 11½ In. 240.00
Frame, Applied Tree Mill, Sterling On Bronze, Original Patina, 6 x 9 In. 660.00
Inkwell, Sterling On Bronze, 4½ x 2½ x 3½ In. 144.00
Lamp, Applied Bird & Branch, Sterling On Bronze, Patina, 8 x 10½ In. 450.00
Lamp, Applied Flowers, Sterling On Bronze, Green Patina, White Globe Shade, 4 x 10 In. 330.00
Lamp, Applied Flowers, Sterling On Bronze, Silver Patina, Cutout Shade, Mica Liner, 12 x 16 In. . 1440.00
Lamp, Applied Geometric Design, Sterling On Bronze, Geometric Cutout Shade, 9 x 10 In. . . 4200.00
Lamp, Flowered Base, Sterling On Bronze, Cutout Flowered Shade, Mica Panels, 8 x 15 In. . . 1800.00
Lamp, Grape Leaf, Sterling On Bronze, Shade With Cutout Grapevines, 8½ x 10 In. 840.00
Lamp, Organic Design, Sterling On Bronze, Patina, 7 x 11½ In. 390.00

Hedi Schoop, Vase, Woman, Blond, 2 Flower Holders, 13 In.
$75.00

H

California Potteries
In the early twentieth century, California potteries were making dinnerware and kitchen pieces, glazed tiles, garden ware, and terra-cotta building tiles. Tiles marked with the name "California" were being made by 1911. Solid-color California dinnerware, like Franciscan and Bauer, was popular in the 1930s, and by 1950 about 600 potteries used the word "California" as part of the company mark. Many firms made inexpensive dinnerware, vases, and figurines that were like the traditional pottery and porcelain made in England, Asia, Ohio, or along the East Coast of the United States. California wares were inspired by Mexican and Asian ideas, Art Deco and modern designs, plus some of the unusual "looks" that were pure West Coast. Easily recognized California items include round-faced, costumed figurines often decorated in pink, blue, and other pastels.

Heintz Art, Bowl, Leaves, Sterling On Bronze, Patina, 4 x 8 In.
$720.00

Heintz Art, Compote, Sterling On Bronze, Applied Flowers, Patina, Marked, 4 x 7 In.
$120.00

Heintz Art, Vase, Applied Flower, Sterling On Bronze, Patina, Marked, 6 x 2 In.
$270.00

Heisey, Animal, Plug Horse, Sparky, 4¼ x 3½ In.
$75.00

Lamp, Sterling On Bronze, Shade With Cutout Birds, Patina, 11½ x 17½ In. 1920.00
Letter Holder, Sterling On Bronze, 2 Sections, Early 20th Century, 4¼ x 7½ In. 225.00
Necklace, Bell, Sterling On Bronze, Patina, 1½-In. Pendant, 18-In. Chain. 725.00
Necklace, Geometric Design, Sterling On Bronze, Patina, 2-In. Pendant, 17-In. Chain 330.00
Vase, Applied Butterfly, Sterling On Bronze, Patina, Marked, 3 x 4½ In. 230.00 to 510.00
Vase, Applied Design, Sterling On Bronze, Patina, Marked, 11 x 4 In. 450.00
Vase, Applied Flower, Sterling On Bronze, Patina, 3 x 4½ In. 259.00
Vase, Applied Flower, Sterling On Bronze, Silver Patina, Mark, 5 x 5 In. 173.00
Vase, Applied Flower, Sterling On Bronze, Patina, 4½ x 3 In. 240.00
Vase, Applied Flower, Sterling On Bronze, Patina, Marked, 6 x 2 In. *illus* 270.00
Vase, Applied Flower, Sterling On Bronze, Green Patina, 4½ x 10 In. 360.00
Vase, Applied Flowers, Bronze, Impressed, 4½ In. 720.00
Vase, Applied Flowers, Sterling On Bronze, Flared, Patina, Marked, 12 x 4½ In. 720.00
Vase, Applied Flowers, Sterling On Bronze, Patina, 1920, 4 x 14½ In. 270.00
Vase, Applied Flowers, Sterling On Bronze, Flared, Footed, Patina, Marked, 15 x 5 In. 960.00
Vase, Applied Hollies, Sterling On Bronze, Original Patina, 5 x 10 In. 300.00
Vase, Applied Organic Design, Sterling On Bronze, Handles, Trophy Form, 15½ x 9½ In. 600.00
Vase, Applied Pansy, Sterling On Bronze, Green Patina, 3 x 3½ In. 390.00
Vase, Applied Pinecone, Sterling On Bronze, Patina, Marked, 4 x 7½ In. 230.00
Vase, Applied Rose, Sterling On Bronze, Patina, 3 x 5 In. 240.00
Vase, Cover, Dog By Tree, Sterling On Bronze, Cylindrical, 3½ x 6½ In. 300.00
Vase, Cylindrical, Applied Daffodil, Sterling On Bronze, Green Patina, 5 x 12 In. 840.00
Vase, Cylindrical, Applied Tree, Silver On Bronze, Patina, 3 x 8 In. 2400.00
Vase, Daffodil, Sterling On Bronze, Green Patina, 3½ x 8 In. 510.00
Vase, Daffodil, Sterling On Bronze, Green Patina, 3 x 6 In. 420.00
Vase, Flaring, Applied Flowers, Sterling On Bronze, Patina, Mark, 3½ x 6½ In. 230.00
Vase, Flaring, Footed, Flowers, Sterling On Bronze, Patina, 4 x 10 In. 210.00
Vase, Flowers, Sterling On Bronze, Patina, 4½ x 12 In. 540.00
Vase, Flowers, Sterling On Bronze, Patina, 5 x 5 In. 270.00
Vase, House & Ducks, Sterling On Bronze, Patina, 3 x 9½ In. 600.00
Vase, Poppies, Sterling On Bronze, Marked, 12¼ x 5 In. 540.00
Vase, Rose Design, Sterling On Bronze, Bulbous, Patina, 6 x 5 In. 240.00
Vase, Slender, Tapered, Applied Ship, Sterling On Bronze, Patina, Mark, 2 x 6 In. 86.00
Vase, Tapered, Applied Flowers, Sterling On Bronze, Original Patina, 3½ x 7½ In. 300.00
Vase, Bud, Applied Leaf & Berry Design, Crest, Sterling On Bronze, Patina, 4 x 11½ In. 173.00
Watch Fob, Dutch Woman, Sterling Silver On Bronze, Patina, 4-In. Pendant. 315.00

HEISEY glass was made from 1896 to 1957 in Newark, Ohio, by A. H. Heisey and Co., Inc. The Imperial Glass Company of Bellaire, Ohio, bought some of the molds and the rights to the trademark. Some Heisey patterns have been made by Imperial since 1960. After 1968, they stopped using the *H* trademark. Heisey used romantic names for colors, such as Sahara. Do not confuse color and pattern names. The Custard Glass and Ruby Glass categories may also include some Heisey pieces.

H

Animal, Giraffe, Head Turned To Right, 11 In. 115.00
Animal, Plug Horse, Sparky, 4¼ x 3½ In. *illus* 75.00
Aristocrat, Candy Jar, Cover, Sahara. 1100.00
Barbara Fritchie, Cordial, 1 Oz., 6 In. 125.00
Beaded Swag, Toothpick, Ruby Stain, Engraved Mane, 1903. 55.00
Bethel, Decanter, Nimrod Etch 170.00
Cathedral, Vase, Cobalt, 8 In. 825.00
Cathedral, Vase, Sahara, Flared, Footed, 7¾ x 9 In. 160.00
Charter Oak, Compote, Hawthorne, 7 In. 125.00
Colonial, Dessert Cup, Footed, 3 Oz. 12.00
Colonial, Wine, 2 Oz. 5.00
Crystolite, Basket, Floral Cutting, 15 In. 118.00
Crystolite, Compote, 5 In. 4.00
Crystolite, Mustard, Cover. 6.00
Crystolite, Sugar & Creamer, Tray, 5½ In. 19.00
Double Rib & Panel, Basket, Flamingo, 8¼ x 6⅛ In. *illus* 235.00
Duck, Flower Frog, Flamingo, 5 x 5¼ In. *illus* 299.00
Empress, Bowl, Lion Footed, Moongleam, 4 x 10½ In. *illus* 1195.00
Empress, Ice Tub, Dolphin Footed 30.00
Empress, Plate, Tangerine, 7 In. 75.00
Empress, Relish, Alexandrite, 3 Sections, 7 In. 205.00
Empress, Sugar & Creamer. 9.00

Engraved Flowers, Mustard, 6-Sided, Sterling Cover, Signed, 5 In.	100.00
Fairacre, Cologne Bottle, Flamingo, Paper Label	195.00
Fancy Loop, Bottle, Water	55.00
Fancy Loop, Butter, Cover	10.00
Fandango, Banana Boat	30.00
Fandango, Sugar & Creamer, Individual	70.00
Fern, Dish, Mayonnaise, Underplate, Ladle, Zircon	225.00
Greek Key, Hair Receiver	165.00
Greek Key, Horseradish Jar, Cover	65.00
Greek Key, Oil Jar, 4 Oz.	45.00
Greek Key, Oil Jar, 6 Oz.	50.00
Hi Lo, Vase, Sahara, 8 In.	315.00
Horse's Head, Cigarette Box	65.00
Ivy, Vase, Tangerine	170.00
Narrow Flute, Tumbler, Enameled	160.00
Octagon, Bonbon, 7 In.	35.00
Old Sandwich, Bottle, Ketchup, Stopper, Moongleam, 8 Oz.	350.00
Old Sandwich, Console Set, Cobalt Blue, 3 Piece	695.00
Old Sandwich, Tumbler, 10 Oz.	6.00
Paneled Cane, Spooner	25.00
Pineapple & Fan, Pitcher, Emerald	275.00
Pineapple & Fan, Vase, 8 In.	30.00
Pineapple & Fan, Vase, 10 In.	35.00
Plaid, Vase, 7 In.	65.00
Plantation, Bowl, 7 ½ In.	45.00
Plantation, Cruet, 3 Oz.	175.00
Plantation, Dish, Jelly, 5 In.	30.00
Plantation, Punch Bowl, 8 Cups	600.00
Plantation, Relish, Ivy Etched, 3 Sections, 7 In.	90.00
Plantation, Salt & Pepper	80.00
Plantation, Sherbet, 6 Oz.	10.00
Plantation, Vase, Footed, 5 In.	150.00
Pleat & Panel, Champagne, Flamingo, 6 Oz.	18.00
Pleat & Panel, Plate, Flamingo, 8 In.	20.00
Punty & Diamond Point, Vase, 6 In.	30.00
Quator, Sugar & Creamer, Flower Etch	60.00
Rearing Horse, Bookends, 8 In.	41.00
Recessed Panel, Candy Jar, Cover, Etched, 1 Lb.	50.00
Revere, Dish, French Dressing, Underplate, Moongleam *illus*	120.00
Ridgeleigh, Dish, Jelly, Handle, 6 In.	15.00
Ridgeleigh, Nappy, 4-Sided, 5 In.	20.00
Ridgeleigh, Relish, Star, 5 Sections, 10 In.	80.00
Ridgeleigh, Salt	15.00
Ridgeleigh, Vase, Zircon, 8 In.	425.00
Ring Band, Butter, Cover, 5 ½ x 7 ⅜ In. *illus*	80.00
Ring Band, Table Set, Ivorina Verde, Flowers, 4 Piece	175.00
Rose, Salt & Pepper, Footed	125.00
Sunburst, Compote, 6 In.	135.00
Sunburst, Pitcher, Straight Sides	75.00
Town & Country, Bowl, Salad, 11 In.	325.00
Town & Country, Sandwich Server, 14 ¼ In.	250.00
Trident, Candlestick, 2-Light, Sahara *illus*	203.00
Triplex, Candlestick, 3-Light, Sahara	600.00
Tudric, Bottle, Oil, Stopper, 4 Oz.	30.00
Twist, Mustard, Underplate, Ladle, Moongleam	125.00
Warwick, Candlestick, Cobalt Blue, 3 In.	120.00
Warwick, Match Holder, Sahara	85.00
Whirlpool, Cream & Sugar	35.00
Winged Scroll, Condiment Set, Ivorina Verde, 4 Piece	325.00
Winged Scroll, Ring Holder, Emerald	875.00
Winged Scroll, Spooner, Ivorina Verde, 3 ½ In. *illus*	50.00
Yeoman, Oil Jar, Sahara, 4 Oz.	65.00
Yeoman, Plate, Coupe, Vaseline	50.00
Yeoman, Soup, Cream, Hawthorne	30.00

HEREND, *see Fischer category.*

Heisey, Double Rib & Panel, Basket, Flamingo, 8 ¼ x 6 ⅛ In.
$235.00

Heisey, Duck, Flower Frog, Flamingo, 5 x 5 ¼ In.
$299.00

Heisey, Empress, Bowl, Lion Footed, Moongleam, 4 x 10 ½ In.
$1195.00

Heisey, Revere, Dish, French Dressing, Underplate, Moongleam
$120.00

Heisey, Ring Band, Butter, Cover, 5 ½ x 7 ⅜ In.
$80.00

Heisey, Trident, Candlestick, 2-Light, Sahara
$203.00

Heisey, Winged Scroll, Spooner, Ivorina Verde, 3 ½ In.
$50.00

TIP
Have an inventory of your collections and adequate insurance.

Holly Amber, Sauce, 1 ¾ x 4 ¼ In.
$154.00

HEUBACH is the collector's name for Gebruder Heubach, a firm working in Lichten, Germany, from 1840 to 1925. It is best known for bisque dolls and doll heads, their principal products. They also manufactured bisque figurines, including piano babies, beginning in the 1880s, and glazed figurines in the 1900s. Piano Babies are listed in their own category. Dolls are included in the Doll category under Gebruder Heubach and Heubach. Another factory, Ernst Heubach, working in Koppelsdorf, Germany, also made porcelain and dolls. These will also be found in the Doll category under *Heubach Koppelsdorf*.

Figurine, Boy With Cigar, Seated, Side-Glancing Eyes, Spectacles, Fez, 16 ¾ In. 499.00
Figurine, Girls Sitting In Dresses, Bisque, 3 ¾ In. 65.00
Vase, Pillow, Female Polar Bear, 2 Cubs, Snowy Domain, c.1910, 4 ½ In.. .... 118.00

HISTORIC BLUE, *see factory names, such as Adams, Ridgway, and Staffordshire.*

HOBNAIL glass is a style of glass with bumps all over. Dozens of hobnail patterns and variants have been made. Clear, colored, and opalescent hobnail have been made and are being reproduced. Other pieces of hobnail may also be listed in the Duncan & Miller and Fenton categories.

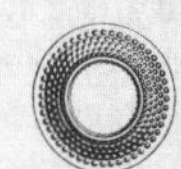

Pitcher, Cranberry, Victorian, 8 In. 115.00
Pitcher, Yellow, Corset Shape, Ruffled Powder Blue Edge, Orange Interior, 9 In.. .... 460.00
Vase, Opalescent, Ruffled Rim, 10 In. 35.00

HOLLY AMBER, or golden agate, glass was made by the Indiana Tumbler and Goblet Company of Greentown, Indiana, from January 1, 1903, to June 13, 1903. It is a pressed glass pattern featuring holly leaves in the amber-shaded glass. The glass was made with shadings that range from creamy opalescent to brown-amber.

Berry Set, Large Bowl 8 ½ In., 5 Piece 413.00
Butter, Cover, 6 In. 1580.00
Compote, Cover, 7 ½ In.. .... 1203.00
Sauce, 1 ¾ x 4 ¼ In. .... *illus* 154.00
Toothpick, 2 ½ In. 250.00
Tray, Pickle, 9 In. 173.00
Tumbler, 3 ½ In.. .... 3600.00

HOLT-HOWARD was an importer that started working in 1949 in Stamford, Connecticut. The company sold many types of table accessories, such as condiment jars, decanters, spoon holders, and saltshakers. The figures shown on some of its pieces had a cartoon-like quality. The company was bought out by General Housewares Corporation in 1969. Holt-Howard pieces are often marked with the name and the year or *HH* and the year stamped in black. The *HH* mark was used until 1974. There was also a black and silver label. Production of Holt-Howard ceased in 1990. Similar pieces by the same Holt-Howard designer are being made today and are marked *GHA*.

Ashtray, Cozy Kitten, Cat Head, Plunger, Ceramic, 1940s-50s 39.00
Beer Mug, Fire Wagon, Stoneware, Black Transfer, Horses, 2 Riders 35.00
Candle Ring, Holder, Jolly Holly Mouse, White, Gold Sticker, 1958, 2 Piece. 15.00
Candleholder, 2 Mice, Riding Train, White Dress, Red Trim, Gold Trim Hat. 30.00
Candleholder, Angel, Holding Bell, Mitten Hands, White Dress, Porcelain, 1964 .... 30.00
Candleholder, Ballerina, 1958, 4 In. 95.00
Candleholder, Coq Rouge, Rooster, 1960s, 4 ⅜ In., 2 Piece 30.00
Candleholder, Double, 2 Angels, 1 With Violin, Other With Banjo. 30.00
Candleholder, Goofy Santa, Wide Eyes, Open Mouth, Mitten Hands, Spaghetti Trim 18.00
Candleholder, Santa Claus, 1960s, 3 ¾ In., Pair 12.00
Candleholder, Santa Claus, Japan, Box, 1950s 28.00
Candleholder, Santa Claus, Open Arms, Belly Holds Candle, 1960s, 4 ½ x 3 In. 10.00
Candleholder, Santa Claus Head, Handle, 5 ¼ In.. .... 16.00
Candleholder, Spaghetti Art, Scalloped Edges, Gold Gilt Trim, c.1958, 1 ¼ x 4 In. 20.00
Candleholder, Wise Man, Bell, Crown, Red Robe, 1960 .... 20.00
Candlestick, Snow Babies Igloo, Red, Gold Foil Label, 1959, 2 ½ In., Pair 60.00
Candy Container, Santa Claus, Just Take 1, Japan 95.00
Chocolate Pot, Holly & Berry, White Fluted, Matte Glaze, 1959 .... 18.00
Christmas Bell, Ornament, Holly Berries, 1960s, 3 ½ In. 10.00
Cigarette Holder, Coq Rouge, Rooster, Box 75.00
Creamer, Coq Rouge, Rooster, 1960 .... 10.00
Cup, Coq Rouge, Rooster, 1960s, 6 Piece. 30.00
Cup, Winking Santa, Hand Painted, Box, 6 Piece 18.00
Dish, Tree, 3 Sections, Gold Star, 13 x 10 In. .... *illus* 18.00
Eggcup, Coq Rouge, Rooster, Red & Yellow Raised Image, Paper Sticker, 1961, 4 ¾ In. 25.00

Eggcup, Figural, Man's Head, Removable Hat 75.00
Eggcup, Man's Head, Salt Shaker Hat, 6 In., 2 Piece 75.00
Figurine, Angel, Plays Harp, Bisque Head, Feather Dress, Chenille Arms, Tulle Wings 20.00
Figurine, Choir Boy, Felt, Porcelain, Cardboard 15.00
Figurine, Feathered Angel, Tulle, Ceramic Heads, Chenille Arms, 4 ¾ & 2 ¾ In., 3 Piece 30.00
Figurine, Santa Claus, Sack, Holding Bell, Raised Arm, Pair 29.00
Head Vase, Rose Bush Hair, Ball Earrings, Pearl Necklace, 4 ¼ In. .... *illus* 225.00
Head Vase, Woman, Holly Leaf & Berry Hair, Label, 3 ¾ In. .... *illus* 50.00
Jar, Jam 'n Jelly, Pixie 125.00
Jar, Ketchup, Cover, Spoon, Coq Rouge, Rooster, Red & Yellow, Red Band, 4 ¼ In. 63.00
Jar, Onions, Pixie, 1958 .... 335.00
Letter Holder, Cozy Kitten, 6 In. .... *illus* 21.00
Mug, Brown Drip, 2-Tone, Marked, 4 x 3 ½ In. 12.00
Mug, Elf, 1967, 4 Piece 58.00
Mustard, Pixie, 1958 .... 145.00
Napkin Holder, Coq Rouge, Red Rooster, Porcelain 32.00
Napkin Holder, Santa Claus, Blue Eyes, Red Cheeks 19.00
Ornament, Honeycomb, Green, Gold Glitter 10.00
Ornament, Santa, Chenille Body, Beard, Fur, Spun Cotton Face, Flocked Hat, Glass Beads 16.00
Pencil Letter Holder, Cozy Kitten, Black, Gold Tag, 6 In. 24.00
Picks, Santa Claus, 12 Piece 12.00
Pitcher, Lid, Coq Rouge, Rooster 45.00
Pitcher, Orange, Orange Blossom, 7 ⅞ In. 33.00
Place Card Set, Name Cards, Porcelain, Figural, Japan, 8 Piece 40.00
Planter, Pumpkin, Scared, 5 ⅜ In. 8.00
Plate, Santa Claus, 10 In. 26.00
Salt & Pepper, Banana Head, Green Suits, Red Bowties, Cork Stoppers, Japan 25.00
Salt & Pepper, Bell, Christmas, Holly, c.1964, 3 In., 3 Piece 18.00
Salt & Pepper, Chicks, Labels, Noise Makers, c.1950s 35.00
Salt & Pepper, Cozy Kitten, 1958, 4 ¼ In. 12.50
Salt & Pepper, Cozy Kitten, 2 ½ In. 67.00
Salt & Pepper, Cozy Kitten, Asian Eyed, Foil Stickers, 4 ½ In. 45.00
Salt & Pepper, Figural, Coq Rouge, Rooster 18.00
Salt & Pepper, Hippie Beatnik, Peace Sign Necklace, Guitar, 3 ½ In. 22.00
Salt & Pepper, Merry Mouse, c.1958, 4 ½ In. .... *illus* 42.00
Shaker, Winking Santa Claus, c.1960, 5 In. .... 6.00 to 12.00
Spoon Rest, Coq Rouge, Rooster, 1960s 25.00
Stringholder, Cozy Kitten, Holds Scissors, 1958, 4¾ In. .... 46.00 to 78.00
Stringholder, Cozy Kitten, Stamped, 1958, 5 x 3 In. .... 44.00 to 70.00
Sugar & Creamer, Coq Rouge, Rooster 55.00
Tray, Coq Rouge, Rooster, Enamelware, Double Handles, 10 x 1 ½ In. 40.00
Tree Topper, Angel, Porcelain, Gold Tinsel Fringe, Paper Dress 24.00
Trivet, Coq Rouge, Rooster, 1960s, Japan, 10 x 5 In. 25.00
Tumbler, Yellow, Bottom Marked, 1962, 3 ½ In., 3 Piece 16.00
Wall Pocket, Cozy Kitten 60.00
Wall Pocket, Smiley Flower Face, Largest 8 x 5 ½ In., Smallest 5 x 4 In., 3 Piece 70.00

HOPALONG CASSIDY was a character in a series of twenty-eight books written by Clarence E. Milford, first published in 1907. Movies and television shows were made based on the character. The best-known actor playing Hopalong Cassidy was William Lawrence Boyd. His first movie appearance was in 1919, but the first Hopalong Cassidy film was not until 1934. Sixty-six films were made. In 1948, William Boyd purchased the television rights to the movies, then later made fifty-two new programs. In the 1950s, Hopalong Cassidy and his horse, named Topper, were seen in comics, records, toys, and other products. Boyd died in 1972.

Card, Riders Of The Deadline, William Boyd, United Artists, 1943, 11 x 14 In. 50.00
Game, Shooting Gallery, Tin, Windup, Automatic Toy Co., Box, 18 In. 144.00
Holster Set, 2 Guns, White Grips, Hoppy Bust, Schmidt 338.00
Lamp, Ranch House, Alacite, Electric, Aladdin, Marked, 7 ½ In. .... *illus* 365.00
Lamp, Revolving, Bar-20 Ranch, Red, 9 ½ x 6 In. 215.00
Lunch Box, Blue, Metal, Thermos, Aladdin, 1950, 7 ½ x 8 ½ x 3 ½ In. 295.00
Pen, Ballpoint, Box, c.1950, 1 ½ x 8 ¼ x ¾ In. 285.00
Pocket Knife, Hopalong, Topper, Can Opener, Screwdriver, Plastic, 1950, 3 ½ In. .... *illus* 107.00
Radio, Hopalong Riding Topper, Metal, Silver, Red, Arvin, 1950, 5 x 8 x 4 In. 478.00
Rocking Horse, Topper, Plastic Head, Wood Legs, Rockers, Rich Toys, 22 ½ x 29 ½ In. 155.00
Toy, Hopalong Cassidy, Boots, Black, White Paint, Leather, Child's 155.00
Wristwatch, Hopalong Cassidy, Round Bezel, Leather Strap, Timex, 7 ½ In. 58.00

Holt-Howard, Dish, Tree, 3 Sections, Gold Star, 13 x 10 In.
$18.00

Holt-Howard, Head Vase, Rose Bush Hair, Ball Earrings, Pearl Necklace, 4 ¼ In.
$225.00

Holt-Howard, Head Vase, Woman, Holly Leaf & Berry Hair, Label, 3 ¾ In.
$50.00

Holt-Howard, Letter Holder, Cozy Kitten, 6 In.
$21.00

Holt-Howard, Salt & Pepper, Merry Mouse, c.1958, 4½ In.
$42.00

Hopalong Cassidy, Lamp, Ranch House, Alacite, Electric, Aladdin, Marked, 7½ In.
$365.00

Hopalong Cassidy, Pocket Knife, Hopalong, Topper, Can Opener, Screwdriver, Plastic, 1950, 3½ In.
$107.00

Old Wallpaper

Old houses often have layers of wallpaper, one on top of another. That was the inexpensive, easy way to repaper a room. Today we are advised to strip off old paper before putting up new paper, because bugs may like to eat old wallpaper paste. When restoring an old home, try shopping for original wallpaper patterns. Many are being copied and are available.

HORN was used to make many types of boxes, furniture inlays, jewelry, and whimsies.

Cup, Libation, Rhinoceros, Branches, Fruit, Fluted Lip, 18th Century, 5 x 4 x 2½ In. . . . 22000.00
Cup, Libation, Rhinoceros, Carved, Chinese, 18th Century, 27 In. . . . 50150.00
Cup, Silver Rim, Sheffield Mark, Shield Emblem, c.1882, 4¾ x 3¼ In. . . . 224.00
Figurine, Goddess Of Mercy, Buffalo Horn, Chinese, 19th Century, 5 In. . . . 705.00
Figurine, Stag, Carved, Frogs, Lizards, Insects, Flowers, Japan, 19th Century, 6 In. . . . 323.00
Mug, Antler Handle, Silver Mount, Swag, Arts & Crafts, 19th Century, 8 x 2¾ In. . . . 476.00
Pleasure Boat, Wave Shaped Base, Buffalo Horn, Chinese, Late 1800s, 15¼ In. . . . 353.00
Spoon, Spanish Colonial, Inscribed, Alifonso Santos, 19th Century, 15 In. . . . 177.00

HOWARD PIERCE began working in Southern California in 1936. In 1945, he opened a pottery in Claremont. He moved to Joshua Tree in 1968 and continued making pottery until 1991. His contemporary-looking figurines are popular with collectors. Though most pieces are marked with his name, smaller items from his sets often were not marked.

Figurine, 3 Parakeets On Branch, 6½ In. . . . 60.00
Figurine, Bird, Head Up, Brown, Light Breast, 2¾ In. . . . 25.00
Figurine, Deer, Resting, Brown Gloss Finish, Marked, 5½ In. . . . 70.00
Figurine, Dogs, Droopy Ears, 8 & 6 In., Pair . . . 150.00
Figurine, Ducklings, Pair . . . 25.00
Figurine, Girl With Basket Of Flowers, Marked, 9 In. . . . 70.00
Figurine, Goose, White Gloss, Set Of 3 . . . 40.00
Figurine, Madonna & Child, Gold Leaf Finish, 13½ In. . . . 85.00
Figurine, Native People, Black & White Matte Glaze, Male & Female, 7¾ In. . . . 75.00
Figurine, Quail, 2½ In., Pair . . . 50.00
Figurine, Quail, Tree Branch, Marked, 7 x 6½ In. . . . 35.00
Figurine, Road Runner, Male, Stamped, 12 In. . . . 100.00
Figurine, Seal, Brown, 7¼ In. . . . 10.00
Planter, Shadowbox Charcoal, Deer & Tree In Planter, 4½ x 9½ In. . . . 85.00

HOWDY DOODY and Buffalo Bob were the main characters in a children's series televised from 1947 to 1960. Howdy was a redheaded puppet. The series became popular with college students in the late 1970s when Buffalo Bob began to lecture on campuses.

Alarm Clock, Howdy Doody's Face, Steel, Plastic, Brass, Westclox, 3½ In. . . . 75.00
Bank, Howdy Doody Bust, Ceramic, 1950s, 8¼ In. . . . 190.00
Bank, Howdy Doody Riding Pig, Shawnee, 6¾ In. . . . 98.00
Camera Outfit, Sun-Ray, Kagran, Box, 1950s . . . 202.00
Cookie Jar, Purinton, 1950s, 9 In. . . . 184.00
Doll, Blinking Eyes, Bisque Head & Hands, Leather Belt, Shoes, Effanbee, Box, 20 In. . . . 406.00
Doll, Blinking Eyes, Plastic, Cloth Clothes, Beehler Arts, Box, 7½ In. . . . 110.00
Doll, Dressed In Western Costume, Vinyl, Squeaks, Stahlwood Toy, 13 In. . . . 75.00
Doll, Princess Summerfall-Winterspring, Stuffed, Painted Eyes, Ahmco Prod., Box, 18 In. . . . 133.00
Doll, Wood, Composition, Jointed, Painted, Noma, Cameo, 12¾ In. . . . 167.00
Lamp, Howdy Doody & Santa Claus, Plastic, Royal Electric, Box, 14 x 10¼ In. . . . 189.00
Lamp, Howdy Doody Magic Twinkle Doll, Plastic, Wood, Electric, Ahmco Prod., 6¼ In. . . . 189.00
Lamp, Pinup, Howdy Doody, Clarabell, Western Theme, Cloth Shade, Box, 10 In. . . . 234.00
Lunch Box, Howdy, Indian Girl, Covered Wagon, Steel, Adco-Liberty Mfg., Thermos . . . 934.00
Marionette, Clarabell, Composition Head, Plastic Hands, Peter Puppet Playthings, Box, 15 In. . . 123.00
Marionette, Composition Head, Googly Eyes, Peter Puppet Playthings, 1950s, 16 In. . . . 325.00
Marionette, Dilly-Dally, Peter Puppet Playthings, Box, 14 In. . . . 333.00
Marionette, Flub-A-Dub, Peter Puppet Playthings, Cloth, 1950s, 10 In. . . . 287.00
Marionette, Flub-A-Dub, Peter Puppet Playthings, Box, 12 In. . . . 333.00
Marionette, Heidi Doody, Mixed Materials, Box . . . 625.00
Marionette, Howdy Doody, Peter Puppet Playthings, Box, 20½ In. . . . 201.00
Marionette, Mr. Bluster, Pocket Watch, Peter Puppet Playthings, Box, 15 In. . . . 322.00
Marionette, Princess Summerfall-Winterspring, Peter Puppet Playthings, Box, 14 In. . . . 173.00
Night-Light, Howdy Doody's Face, Glass, Leco, Box, 2½ In. . . . 75.00
Paint Set, Milton Bradley, 1950s . . . 115.00
Photo, Buffalo Bob Smith, Remember It's Howdy Doody Time . . . 660.00
Pin, Howdy Doody Talks, Plastic, Chelsey Novelty, Card, 3½ In. . . . 98.00
Record Player, Phono Doodle, Plastic, Shura-Tone Products, Box, 9 x 12½ In. . . . 170.00
Ring, Flashlight, Premium, Battery . . . 195.00
Toy, Air-O-Doodle Circus Train, Plastic, Plasticraft, Box, 17 In. . . . 690.00
Toy, Band, Buffalo Bob Plays Piano, Tin, Windup, Unique Art, Box, 8 In. . . . 951.00 to 1926.00

Toy, Band, Buffalo Bob Plays Piano, Tin, Windup, Unique Art Mfg., 5 In. . . . . *illus* 1150.00
Toy, Band, Clarabell Plays Piano, Howdy Dances, Tin, Windup, Linemar, 5¾ In. 2300.00
Toy, Bubble Pipes, Howdy & Clarabell Pipes, Dish, Soap, Plastic, Lido, Box 86.00
Toy, Clarabell, Hops, Squeaks, Tin, Remote Control, Linemar, Box, 6½ In. 805.00
Toy, Clarabell, Walks On Hands, Tin, Windup, Linemar, 5 In. 260.00
Toy, Clock-A-Doodle, Tin, Windup, Bandai, Box, 9½ In. 3225.00
Toy, Fire Engine, Squeeze, Spunky, 1950s, 4 x 7 x 5 In. 221.00
Toy, Howdy Doody & Friends Color Television Set, Kagran, 1950s, 6 x 9 x 12 In. 163.00
Toy, Howdy Doody Delivery, Rides Bike, Pulls Cart, Tin, Celluloid, Friction, Linemar, 6 In.. . . . 863.00
Toy, Hurdy Gurdy, Clarabell, It's Howdy Doody Time, Cardboard, Plastic, E.B.A., 11 x 7 x 4 In. 662.00
Toy, Magic Piano & Xylo-Doodle, Plastic, Harmony Toy Co., Box, 14 x 9 In. 184.00
Toy, Magic Puzzle Ball, Plastic, Jolly Blinker Co., Card, 4 In.. . . . . 260.00
Toy, Puppet, Push Button, Wood, Plastic, Kohner Bros., Box, 5½ In. 58.00
Toy, Put-In-Head, Make 100 Different Faces, Tee-Vee Toys, Box. 75.00
Toy, Soap Dish, Floating, Howdy On Raft, Squeeze, Spunky, 1950, 4 x 7 In. 465.00
TV Viewer, Plus Film Discs, Plastic Television Set, Brown, 2 x 2 In. 45.00
Wristwatch, Chrome, Red Plastic Band, Ideal Watch Co., Box, 1950s 1265.00
Wristwatch, It's Howdy Doody Time, National Broadcasting Co., 1971 . . . . 115.00

Howdy Doody, Toy, Band, Buffalo Bob Plays Piano, Tin, Windup, Unique Art Mfg., 5 In.
$1150.00

HULL pottery was made in Crooksville, Ohio, from 1905. Addis E. Hull bought the Acme Pottery Company and started making ceramic wares. In 1917, A. E. Hull Pottery began making art pottery as well as the commercial wares. For a short time, 1921 to 1929, the firm also sold pottery imported from Europe. The dinnerwares of the 1940s (including the Little Red Riding Hood line), the high gloss artwares of the 1950s, and the matte wares of the 1940s are all popular with collectors. The firm officially closed in March 1986.

Hull U.S.A.

Bird In Flight, Flower Frog, Gold Trim, 10½ In.. . . . . 88.00
Blossom Flite, Pitcher, Metallic, Green Inside, Twisted Rope Handle, 8½ In.. . . . . 550.00
Blossom Flite, Tea Set, Pink, Gray, Gold Trim, Marked, 3 Piece . . . . *illus* 49.00
Bow Knot, Basket, Blue, Turquoise, Marked, 10½ In.. . . . . 412.00
Bow Knot, Basket, Blue, Pink, 12 In.. . . . . 935.00 to 1045.00
Bow Knot, Console Set, Pink, Turquoise, Scalloped Rim, Bowl, Candlesticks, 3 Piece 236.00
Bow Knot, Pitcher, Pink, Blue, Original Label, 13½ In. 522.00
Bow Knot, Pitcher, Turquoise, Blue, 13½ In.. . . . . 412.00
Bow Knot, Plaque, Blue Border, 10 In.. . . . . 242.00
Bow Knot, Plaque, Pink Border, 10 In.. . . . . 110.00
Bow Knot, Vase, Pink, Blue, 12½ In. 440.00
Bow Knot, Wall Pocket, Broom, Blue, Marked, 8 In. 104.00
Bow Knot, Wall Pocket, Cup & Saucer, Blue, Turquoise, 6 In.. . . . . 99.00
Bow Knot, Wall Pocket, Cup & Saucer, Pink, Blue, 6 In.. . . . . 99.00
Bow Knot, Wall Pocket, Iron, Blue, Turquoise, 6⅛ In. . . . . *illus* 135.00
Bow Knot, Wall Pocket, Whisk Broom, 1949, 8 In. 150.00
Butterfly, Bowl, Fruit, Gold Trim, Folded Sides, 4¾ x 10½ In.. . . . . 55.00
Butterfly, Tea Set, Gold Trim, 3 Piece . . . . 143.00 to 253.00
Butterfly, Teapot, 8½ In.. . . . . 33.00
Butterfly, Vase, Cornucopia, 10½ In. 55.00
Butterfly, Vase, Pitcher, Turquoise Interior, 8¾ In.. . . . . 49.00
Calla Lily, Candlestick, Turquoise, Pink, Handle, 2¼ In., Pair 132.00
Calla Lily, Vase, Blue, Handles, 13 In.. . . . . 104.00
Calla Lily, Vase, Turquoise, Cinnamon, Handles, 8 In.. . . . . 88.00
Camellia, Basket, Pink, Blue, Scalloped Edge, 6¼ In.. . . . . 110.00
Camellia, Console Set, Blue, Pink, Dove Handles, 12-In. Bowl, 3 Piece. . . . . 220.00 to 275.00
Camellia, Ewer, White, Elongated Handle & Spout, 13¼ In.. . . . . 220.00
Camellia, Vase, Cornucopia, Pink, Blue, Marked, 8½ In. . . . . *illus* 54.00
Camellia, Vase, Oil Lamp Form, Blue, Pink, 10½ In. 187.00
Camellia, Vase, Pink, Blue, Flared, Scalloped Edge, Scroll Handles, Footed, 12 In.. . . . . 209.00
Capri, Planter, Llama, Pulling Cart, Tan Glaze, 11½ In.. . . . . 143.00 to 154.00
Capri, Planter, Swan, Double, Green, 10½ In.. . . . . 71.00
Cat, Vase, Sitting, Persimmon Glaze, 11 In. 132.00
Chinese Sage Mask, Wall Pocket, Glossy Black, 8 In.. . . . . 60.00
Continental, Basket, Evergreen, Gold Trim, 12¾ In. 132.00
Continental, Basket, Mountain Blue, 12¾ In.. . . . . 358.00
Continental, Basket, Persimmon, 12¾ In. 77.00
Continental, Compote, Mountain Blue, Footed, 5½ x 6¾ In. 165.00
Continental, Flower Bowl, Mountain Blue, Gold Trim, Boat Shape, 4¾ x 15½ In. 104.00
Continental, Pitcher, Evergreen, 12½ In. 27.00

Hull, Blossom Flite, Tea Set, Pink, Gray, Gold Trim, Marked, 3 Piece
$49.00

Hull, Bow Knot, Wall Pocket, Iron, Blue, Turquoise, 6⅛ In.
$135.00

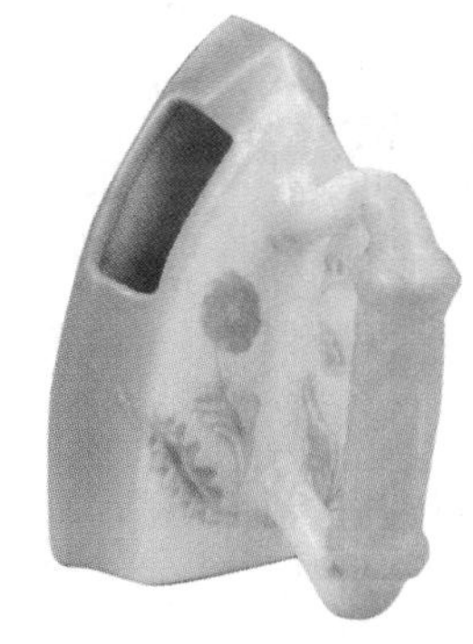

Hull, Camellia, Vase, Cornucopia, Pink, Blue, Marked, 8½ In.
$54.00

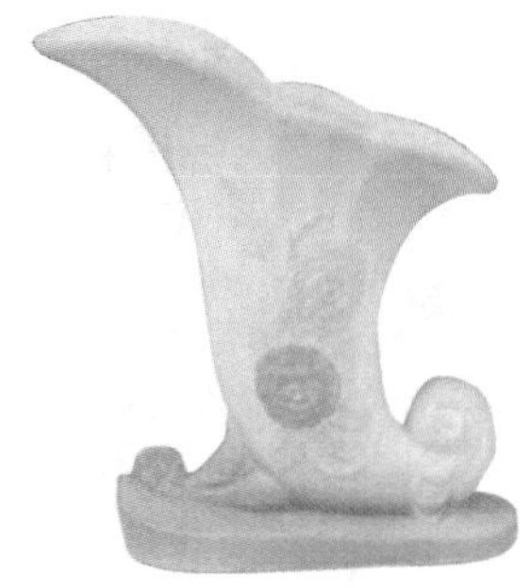

Hull, Cookie Jar, Gingerbread Man, Mirror Brown, 11⅝ In.
$155.00

Hull, Corky Pig, Bank, Blue, Pink, Gold Trim, Marked, 5 x 7½ In.
$270.00

Hull, Ebb Tide, Console Set, Pink, Turquoise, 15½-In. Bowl, 3 Piece
$135.00

Hull, Little Red Riding Hood, Cookie Jar, Poinsettia, 13 In.
$358.00

Continental, Pitcher, Mountain Blue, 12½ In. 165.00
Continental, Planter, Open Front, 14½ In. 17.00
Continental, Planter, Open Front, Mountain Blue, 10 In. 104.00
Continental, Vase, Bud, Mountain Blue, Footed, 9½ In. 55.00
Continental, Vase, Evergreen, Pedestal Base, 15 In. 99.00
Continental, Vase, Mountain Blue, Egg Shape, Deep V Rim, 8½ In. 132.00
Continental, Vase, Mountain Blue, Footed, 11½ In. 154.00
Continental, Vase, Mountain Blue, Waisted, Pulled Rim, 13¾ In. 198.00
Continental, Vase, Persimmon, Flared Top, Flared Pedestal Base, 15 In. 55.00
Cookie Jar, Gingerbread Man, Gray, White Trim, 11½ In. 121.00 to 165.00
Cookie Jar, Gingerbread Man, Mirror Brown, 11⅝ In. *illus* 155.00
Cookie Jar, Gingerbread Man, Tan, White, 11½ In. 550.00
Cookie Jar, Little Boy Blue, Seated, Red Shirt, Blue Pants, Hat, 12½ In. 165.00
Corky Pig, Bank, Blue, Pink, Gold Trim, Marked, 5 x 7½ In. *illus* 270.00
Corky Pig, Bank, Cream, Pink, Green, Marked, 5 In. 121.00
Corky Pig, Bank, Dime, Lime Green, 3½ In. 77.00
Corky Pig, Bank, Dime, Cream, Pink, Blue, Marked, 3½ In. 198.00
Corky Pig, Bank, Dime, Cream, Pink, Blue, 1996 Commemorative, 3½ In. 330.00
Corky Pig, Bank, Flint, White Foam Trim, Marked 715.00
Corky Pig, Bank, Seated, Mirror, Brown & Turquoise Drip Glaze, Marked 55.00 to 60.00
Corky Pig, Bank, Yellow, Blue, Pink, Marked, 5 In. 110.00
Crab Apple, Flowerpot, Attached Saucer, Yellow, Green, 6½ In. 38.00
Crab Apple, Vase, Pinched Waist, Yellow, Green, Pink, 5 In. 88.00
Dogwood, Basket, Cream, Circular Handle Around Basket, 7½ In. 99.00
Dogwood, Ewer, Cream, Pink, Shaped & Scalloped Edge, 13½ In. 297.00
Dogwood, Window Box, Cream, Scalloped Edge, 10½ In. 44.00
Dogwood, Window Box, Cream, Blue, Scalloped Edge, 10½ In. 66.00
Ebb Tide, Ashtray, Mermaid, Chartreuse, Wine, 5 In. 66.00
Ebb Tide, Basket, Chartreuse, Wine, 16½ In. 88.00
Ebb Tide, Console Set, Pink, Turquoise, 15½-In. Bowl, 3 Piece *illus* 135.00
Ebb Tide, Cornucopia, Mermaid, Pink, Turquoise, 7½ In. 55.00
Ebb Tide, Pitcher, Pink, Turquoise, Gold Trim, 14 In. 110.00
Ebb Tide, Pitcher, Wine, Chartreuse, 14 In. 71.00
Ebb Tide, Tea Set, Wine, Chartreuse, Gold Trim, 6½-In. Teapot, 3 Piece 154.00 to 176.00
Ebb Tide, Vase, Angel Fish, Pink, Turquoise, 9¼ In. 77.00
Ebb Tide, Vase, Angel Fish, Wine, Chartreuse, Gold Trim, 9¼ In. 110.00
Ebb Tide, Vase, Pitcher, 8¼ In. 135.00
Fiesta, Vase, Fan, Deer, Gold Trim, Scalloped Rim, Footed, 9 In. 88.00
Figurine, Dancing Girl, Pink Dress, 7½ In. 20.00
Gingerbread Man, Spoon Rest, Mirror Brown, Crooksville Bank 33.00
Granada, Basket, Cream, Mauve, 8 In. 38.00
Granada, Teapot, Cream, Mauve, No Cover, 5½ In. 11.00
Imperial, Basket, Embossed Strawberries, Mirror Brown, White Foam Trim, 7 x 7 In. 82.00
Imperial, Planter, Frog, Mirror Brown, 6½ x 7 In. 60.00
Imperial, Vase, Mountain Blue, Flared, Footed, Marked, 9½ In. 165.00
Iris, Ewer, Cream, Mauve, 8 In. 77.00
Iris, Vase, Cream, Mauve, Long Handles, Shaped Rim, 7 In. 55.00
Lamp, Planter, Cat, Label, Marked, No. 61 38.00
Little Red Riding Hood, Bank, Standing, 7 In. 412.00
Little Red Riding Hood, Basket, Cookie Jar, 13 In. 395.00
Little Red Riding Hood, Biscuit Jar, 8 In. 357.00
Little Red Riding Hood, Butter, Cover 143.00
Little Red Riding Hood, Cookie Jar, Flower Border, Open Basket, 13 In. 90.00 to 177.00
Little Red Riding Hood, Cookie Jar, Poinsettia, 13 In. *illus* 358.00
Little Red Riding Hood, Creamer, Side Pour 77.00 to 99.00
Little Red Riding Hood, Creamer, Tab Handle 187.00
Little Red Riding Hood, Dresser Jar, Black Trim 198.00
Little Red Riding Hood, Feeding Dish, 3 Sections, Child's 1595.00
Little Red Riding Hood, Grease Jar, Cover, White 104.00
Little Red Riding Hood, Grease Jar, Cover, 8½ In. 220.00
Little Red Riding Hood, Grease Jar, Wolf, 6¼ In. 469.00
Little Red Riding Hood, Mustard, 2¼ In. 154.00
Little Red Riding Hood, Pitcher, Batter, 6¾ In. 165.00
Little Red Riding Hood, Pitcher, Milk, 8 In. 104.00
Little Red Riding Hood, Plaque, Commemorative, 1995, House, 8 In. 440.00

Little Red Riding Hood, Salt & Pepper .... 38.00 to 77.00
Little Red Riding Hood, Saltshaker, 4 ½ In. 104.00
Little Red Riding Hood, Sugar, Crawling 198.00
Little Red Riding Hood, Sugar, Side Pour .... 77.00 to 99.00
Little Red Riding Hood, Teapot .... 132.00 to 165.00
Little Red Riding Hood, Wall Pocket, c.1957 .... 285.00
Little Texan, Bank, Save At Graham Chevrolet, Marked, 1972, 9 ½ In. 357.00
Morning Glory, Basket, Ivory Matte, 8 In. 77.00
Orchid, Bookends, Pink, Blue, 7 In. 605.00
Orchid, Bowl, Bulb, Cream, Mauve, 7 In. 44.00
Orchid, Vase, Pink, Blue, Arched Handles, Footed, 8 In. 60.00
Parchment & Pine, Basket, Green, Gold Trim, 16 ½ In.. .... 38.00
Parchment & Pine, Coffee Server, Green, 8 In.. .... 154.00
Parchment & Pine, Ewer, Green, Elongated Spout, Shaped Handle, 14 ¼ In. 49.00
Parchment & Pine, Tea Set, Green, 6-In. Teapot, 3 Piece 99.00
Parchment & Pine, Vase, Cornucopia, Green, Gold Trim, 10 ½ In. 38.00
Planter, Cactus Cat, White, 2 ¾ In. 60.00
Planter, Cat, Wearing Hat, Matte Blue, Yellow, Pink, 6 ¼ In.. .... 55.00
Planter, Cherubs, White, Blue, 7 In. 38.00
Planter, Child's Head, 6 In. 60.00
Planter, Chinese Chicken, Oriental Symbols, Brown, 9 ½ In. 121.00
Planter, Clown, Glossy Black, White Trim, Gold Trim, 6 ¼ In. 440.00
Planter, Crazy Horse, Cream, Brown, 5 In.. .... 154.00
Planter, Donkey, 6 In. 412.00
Planter, Elephant, White, 5 ¼ In. 22.00
Planter, Giraffe, Gold Trim, Marked, 8 In. 49.00
Planter, Hand Holding Telephone, Pink, Gray, Marked, 9 In. 22.00
Planter, Kitten, Pink, 6 ¼ In.. .... 33.00
Planter, Knight On Horseback, Mirror Black, Wine, Chartreuse, 8 ½ In.. .... *illus* 60.00
Planter, Llama & Cart, White, Glossy Green, 9 ¼ x 11 ½ In. 232.00
Planter, Monkey, Scratching Head, Green, 6 In.. .... 297.00
Planter, Pig, Flower In Hair, Blue, Yellow, Pink, 6 ¼ In. 88.00
Planter, Poodle, Wearing Hat, Blue, Pink, Yellow, 6 ¼ In. 55.00
Planter, Rooster, Gold Trim, 7 ¾ x 8 In. 165.00
Planter, Rooster, Golden Mist, 1967, 7 ¾ x 8 In.. .... 88.00
Planter, Rooster, White, Matte, 7 In. 66.00
Planter, Scaredy Cat, Blue, 4 ⅞ In. 22.00
Planter, Siamese Cat, 12 In. 83.00
Planter, Siamese Cat & Kitten, No. 63. .... *illus* 77.00
Poppy, Basket, Cream, Pink, Marked, 9 In. 440.00
Poppy, Ewer, Cream, Pink, 13 ½ In.. .... 220.00
Poppy, Wall Pocket, Cornucopia, Blue, Pink, Handles, 9 ½ In. 104.00
Primrose, Pitcher, Gray, Blue, Experimental Glaze, Marked, 6 In.. .... 66.00
Rabbit, Cotton Dispenser, Pink, 6 In. 38.00
Rosella, Lamp Base, Peach, White Flowers, 6 In. 71.00
Rosella, Vase, Gold Trim, Iridescent Glaze, 8 ½ In. 99.00
Serenade, Pitcher, Blue, Gold Trim, Marked, 6 ⅝ In. .... *illus* 60.00
Serenade, Teapot, Yellow, 6 Cup 38.00
Serenade, Vase, Bud, Trial Glaze, Marked, 6 ½ In.. .... 60.00
Stoneware, Bowl, Blue, Rose, Flared Rim, 8 In.. .... 253.00
Stoneware, Flowerpot, Attached Saucer, No. 540-6, 5 ¼ x 6 ⅝ In. .... *illus* 54.00
Stoneware, Jardinere, Elephant Band, Pink 121.00
Sun Glow, Bell, Pink, Twisted Loop Handle, 6 ½ In.. .... 33.00
Sun Glow, Bell, Yellow, Pink Flowers, Twisted Loop Handle, 6 ½ In.. .... 55.00
Supreme, Basket, Brown, Experimental, 8 ¾ In. 220.00
Supreme, Compote, Green, Footed, 4 ½ x 7 ¾ In. 132.00
Supreme, Vase, Green, Bulbous, Flared Neck, 8 In. 121.00
Thistle, Vase, Light Blue, Angular Handles, 6 ½ In. 49.00
Thistle, Vase, Turquoise, Angular Handles, 6 ½ In. 77.00
Tokay, Basket, 12 In. .... 104.00 to 232.00
Tokay, Candy Dish, Cover, Gold Trim, Pedestal Base, 8 ½ In.. .... 38.00
Tokay, Ewer, Pink, White, Green, Marked, 12 In. 143.00
Tokay, Ewer, White, 12 In. 143.00
Tokay, Tea Set, White, Pink, Green, 7½-In. Teapot, 3 Piece .... 176.00 to 232.00
Tokay, Vase, Pink, Green, Pedestal Base, 15 In.. .... 66.00

Hull, Planter, Knight On Horseback, Mirror Black, Wine, Chartreuse, 8 ½ In
$60.00

Hull, Planter, Siamese Cat & Kitten, No. 63
$77.00

Hull, Serenade, Pitcher, Blue, Gold Trim, Marked, 6 ⅝ In.
$60.00

Hull, Stoneware, Flowerpot, Attached Saucer, No. 540-6, 5 ¼ x 6 ⅝ In.
$54.00

Hummel, Figurine, No. 20, Pray Before Battle, Crown Mark $105.00

Hummel VB Marks

Here are the "VB" Hummel Marks that confuse collectors the most.

Full Bee (Trademark-2) 1950-1959

Stylized Bee (Trademark-3) 1958-1972

Three Line Mark (Trademark-4) 1964-1979

Last Bee Mark (Trademark-5) 1972-1979

Hummel, Figurine, No. 6/0, Sensitive Hunter, Missing Bee, 4¾ In. $205.00

Tokay, Vase, Pink, Branch Handles, Marked, 10 In. 77.00
Tokay, Vase, Pink, White, Green, Branch Handles, Marked, 10 In. 110.00
Tokay, Vase, White, Marked, Pedestal Base, 15 In. 60.00
Tokay, Vase, White, Branch Handles, Marked, 10 In. 77.00
Tropicana, Ashtray, Caribbean Musician, Kidney Shape, Marked, 10 In. 176.00
Tropicana, Basket, Caribbean Man, Bird, Crimped Handle, Marked, 12¾ In. 825.00
Tropicana, Ewer, Caribbean Man, Holding Spear, 12½ In. 770.00
Tropicana, Flower Bowl, Caribbean Swimmer, Fish, Boat Shape, Marked, 15½ In. 469.00
Tropicana, Planter, Caribbean Musician, Open Front, Pulled Side, 14½ In. 797.00
Tropicana, Vase, Caribbean Drummer, Flattened Sides, V-Shaped Rim, 8½ In. 469.00
Tulip, Ewer, Cream, Blue, 13 In. 154.00
Tulip, Flowerpot, Attached Saucer, Cream, Blue, 4¼ In. 100.00
Tulip, Vase, Cream, Blue, Oval, Footed, Handles, 6 In. 60.00
Tulip, Vase, Cream, Blue, 2-Ring Handles, Cutout Rim, Footed, 9 In. 66.00
Tulip, Vase, Pink, Blue, Straight Handles, 6½ In. 132.00
Water Lily, Console Set, Pink, Green, Marked, 3 Piece 104.00
Wildflower, Basket, Pink, Tan, 10½ In. 743.00
Wildflower, Console Set, Pink, Blue, Marked, 3 Piece 232.00
Wildflower, Pitcher, Pink, Blue, Marked, 8½ In. 82.00
Wildflower, Pitcher, Pink, Blue, Marked, 13½ In. 302.00
Wildflower, Pitcher, Yellow, Turquoise, 13½ In. 209.00
Wildflower, Teapot, 1940s, 8 In. 750.00
Woodland, Console Set, Chartreuse, Green, Matte, 14-In. Bowl, 3 Piece 132.00
Woodland, Jardiniere, White, Gold Trim, Handles, Glossy, 9½ In. 412.00
Woodland, Lamp, Cream, Pink & Yellow Flowers, Handles, 14 In. 187.00
Woodland, Tea Set, Chartreuse, Pink, Glossy, Marked, 3 Piece 220.00
Woodland, Vase, Double Cornucopia, Green Experimental Glaze 38.00
Woodland, Vase, White, Gold Trim, Scalloped Rim, Handles, 10½ In. 232.00

HUMMEL figurines, based on the drawings of the nun M.I. Hummel (Berta Hummel) are made by the W. Goebel Porzellanfabrik of Oeslau, Germany, now Rodenthal, Germany. They were first made in 1935. The *Crown* mark was used from 1935 to 1949. The company added the *bee* marks in 1950. The *full bee* with variations was used from 1950 to 1959; *stylized bee,* 1957 to 1972; *three line mark,* 1964 to 1972; *last bee*, sometimes called *vee over gee,* 1972 to 1979. In 1979 the V bee symbol was removed from the mark. *U.S. Zone* was part of the mark from 1946 to 1948; *W. Germany* was part of the mark from 1960 to 1990. The *Goebel, W. Germany* mark, called the *missing bee* mark, was used from 1979 to 1990; *Goebel, Germany* with the crown and *WG,* originally called the *new mark,* was used from 1991 through part of 1999. The newest version of the bee mark includes the word *Goebel.* It was adopted in 2000 and is called the *current mark* or *Goebel with full bee*. A special *Year 2000* backstamp was also introduced. Porcelain figures inspired by Berta Hummel's drawings were introduced in 1997. These are marked *BH* followed by a number. They are made in the Far East, not Germany. Other decorative items and plates that feature Hummel drawings have been made by Schmid Brothers, Inc., since 1971.

Bank, No. 118, Little Thrifty, Full Bee, 5 In. 46.00
Candleholder, Silent Night, Stylized Bee, 3½ In. 115.00
Clock, No. 441, Call To Worship, 13 In. 400.00
Figurine, No. 2/11, Little Fiddler, Three Line Mark, 12 In. 660.00
Figurine, No. 3/1, Book Worm, Full Bee, 5½ In. 316.00
Figurine, No. 3/111, Book Worm, Stylized Bee, 10 In. 489.00
Figurine, No. 5, Strolling Along, Full Bee, 5 In. 109.00
Figurine, No. 6/0, Sensitive Hunter, Missing Bee, 4¾ In. . . . . *illus* 205.00
Figurine, No. 6/11, Sensitive Hunter, Full Bee, 7½ In. 230.00
Figurine, No. 7/11, Merry Wander, Full Bee, 10 In. 633.00
Figurine, No. 9, Begging His Share, Missing Bee, 6 In. 127.00
Figurine, No. 10/1, Flower Madonna, Child, Full Bee, 8¼ x 5¾ In. 69.00
Figurine, No. 10/1, Flower Madonna, Child, Full Bee, 8¼ x 5¾ In. 173.00
Figurine, No. 13/11, Meditation, Full Bee, 7 In. 1380.00
Figurine, No. 15/0, Hear Ye, Hear Ye, Full Bee, 5 In. 85.00
Figurine, No. 19, Doll Bath, Stylized Bee, 5 In. 115.00
Figurine, No. 20, Pray Before Battle, Crown Mark . . . . . *illus* 105.00
Figurine, No. 23/1, Adoration, Full Bee, 7 In. 109.00
Figurine, No. 28/11, Wayside Devotion, Full Bee, 7 In. 201.00
Figurine, No. 42/0, Good Shepherd, Vee Over Gee, 6½ In. 104.00
Figurine, No. 42/1, Good Shepherd, Full Bee, 7½ In. 633.00
Figurine, No. 47/11, Goose Girl, Vee Over Gee, 7½ In. 190.00
Figurine, No. 52, Going To Grandma's, Crown Mark, 6½ In. 374.00

igurine, No. 55, St. George, Vee Over Bee, 6¾ In. 115.00
igurine, No. 56/A, Culprit, Full Bee, 6¾ In. 98.00
igurine, No. 67, Doll Mother, Missing Bee, 4¾ In. 92.00
igurine, No. 69, Happy Pastime, Full Bee, 3½ In. 117.00
igurine, No. 71, Stormy Weather, Missing Bee, 6 In. 230.00
igurine, No. 83, Angel Serenade With Lamb, Missing Bee, 5½ In. 115.00
igurine, No. 88/11, Heavenly Protection, Full Bee, 9 In. 288.00
igurine, No. 112, Just Resting, Full Bee, 5 In. 115.00
igurine, No. 136/5, Friends, Stylized Bee, 10¾ In. .... 690.00 to 850.00
igurine, No. 141/3/0, Apple Tree Girl, Full Bee, 6 In. 110.00
igurine, No. 151, Madonna Holding Child, Blue, Full Bee, 12½ In. 1668.00
igurine, No. 152/A, Umbrella Boy, Full Bee, 8 In. 604.00
igurine, No. 152/B, Umbrella Girl, Full Bee, 8 In. 604.00
igurine, No. 163, Whitsuntide, Missing Bee, 7 In. 155.00
igurine, No. 172, Festival Harmony, Angel With Mandolin, Stylized Bee, 10¾ In. 450.00
igurine, No. 173, Festival Harmony, Angel With Flute, Stylized Bee, 11 In. 450.00
igurine, No. 173, Festival Harmony, Angel With Flute, Full Bee, 11 In. 413.00
igurine, No. 177, School Girls, Full Bee, 9½ In. 403.00
igurine, No. 178, Photographer, Missing Bee, 5 In. 303.00
igurine, No. 183, Forest Shrine, Full Bee, 9 In. 260.00
igurine, No. 201, Retreat To Safety, Full Bee, 5½ In. 425.00
igurine, No. 218/0, Birthday Serenade, Three Line Mark, 5 In. 167.00
igurine, No. 226, The Mail Is Here, Full Bee, 6½ In. 345.00
igurine, No. 256, Knitting Lesson, 3 Line Mark, 7½ In. .... 161.00 to 350.00
igurine, No. 348, Ring Around The Rosie, Stylized Bee, 7 In. 1150.00
igurine, No. 353/1, Spring Dance, 3 Line Mark, 6½ In. 144.00
igurine, No. 374, Lost Stocking, Vee Over Gee, 4½ In. 431.00
igurine, No. 406, Pleasant Journey, 6 In. 820.00
ativity Scene, Musical, Burro Stall, Hay, 19 Figurines, Marked, 39-In. Stable .... *illus* 700.00

UTSCHENREUTHER Porcelain Factory was founded by Carolus Magnus in Hohenburg, avaria in 1814. A second factory was established in Selb, Germany, in 1857. The company nade fine quality porcelain dinnerwares and figurines. The mark changed through the ears, but the name and the lion insignia appear in most versions. Hutschenreuther bacame part of the osenthal division of the Waterford Wedgwood Group in 2000 and the mark is still being used.

LORENZ HUTSCHEN REUTER GERMANY

igurine, 2 Herons, Blue, Nest, Eggs, Limited Edition, Gunther Ganget, 23¼ In. 2900.00
igurine, Bluebird, 5 In. 129.00
igurine, Cybis, White Heron, No. 105, 17 In. 1050.00
igurine, Eagle, Spread Wings, 15 In. 205.00
igurine, Heading South, Limited Edition, 14½ x 18 In. 2633.00
igurine, Ring Around The Rosie, c.1940, 8 x 9 In. .... 275.00 to 351.00
roup, Disdain, Screech Owl, Black-Capped Chicks, Limited Edition, 9 In. 900.00
roup, Friendly Enemies, 2 Nuthatches, Woodpecker, Limited Edition, 10½ In. 1150.00
roup, Heading South, Canadian Geese, Limited Edition, 16½ x 19½ x 12½ In. 1050.00
roup, Take Cover, 2 Pheasants, Chicks, 14½ x 25½ x 9¾ In. 1800.00
late, Gold Encrusted Rim, Center Multicolored, Bouquet, 10¼ In. 59.00
late, Heading South, Geese, Swans, 1979, 8 In. 75.00

CONS, special, revered pictures of Jesus, Mary, or a saint, are usually Russian or Byzantine. he small icons collected today are made of wood and tin or precious metals. Many modern opies have been made in the old style and are being sold to tourists in Russia and Europe and t shops in the United States. Rare, old icons have sold for over $50,000. Some religious statues re also included here.

ngel, Metal, Sculpted In Full Round, Bronzed, 22¼ In. 236.00
lessed Silence, Overlaid Silver Repousse Riza, Russia, 1816, 12½ x 10½ In. 3068.00
ogoliubskaya Mother Of God, Multicolored, Painted, 19th Century, 14 x 12 In. 2832.00
hrist On Way To Calvary, Oil On Canvas, Spanish Colonial, 18th Century, 38 x 27 In. 1770.00
ntrance Into The Temple, Overlaid Repousse Silver Gilt, Chased Riza, 12 x 10 In. 1888.00
azan Mother Of God, Tempera, Gesso, Wood, Pavel Fedorovich Sazikov, 8 x 10 In. 1357.00
ord Almighty, Overlaid Silver Gilt Repousse Riza, Russia, 19th Century, 13 x 10¾ In. 4720.00
adonna & Child, Brass, Porcelain, Embossed Table Top Frame, 10 In. 690.00
adonna & Child, Painting, Wood Panel, Bejeweled Metal Overlay, 43 x 30 x 1½ In. 1116.00
adonna & Child, Relief Plaque, Bronze, Germany, 1920s, 22 In. 207.00
rocessional Cross, Painted Iconographic Images, Hinged Doors, Bronze, 16 In. 384.00
rophet Elias, After Gracanica Yugoslavia Fresco, Tempera, Wood, c.1970, 11 x 11½ In. 236.00

Hummel, Nativity Scene, Musical, Burro Stall, Hay, 19 Figurines, Marked, 39 In. Stable
$700.00

TIP

Never throw out your limited edition plate's original box or papers. They add to the resale value. Your homeowner's insurance doesn't cover your plates or figurines. You will need a fine art's policy with a breakage clause.

Icon, St. George, Russia, Late 19th Century, 28 x 21 In.
$800.00

Icon, Tikhvin Mother Of God, Russia, c.1800, 24 x 18 In.
$1300.00

TIP
The best place to store paintings is in a closet with no exterior walls. The temperature and humidity levels will be the best in your house.

Imari, Bowl, Bands Over Dragons & Phoenix, Red, Fukagawa, 1800s, 7 x 12 In.
$795.00

Imari, Coffeepot, Blue Chrysanthemums, Tapered, Domed Lid, Acorn Finial, 8 In.
$690.00

Protecting Veil Of The Holy Mother, St. Andrew In Constantinople, Gesso, Wood, 16 x 14 In. . . 944.00
Sacred Heart, Plaque, Bronze, Wood Base, c.1920, 14 In. . . . 413.00
Sacred Heart, Statue, Multicolored Cast Plaster, Glass Eyes, c.1920, 64 In. . . . 413.00
Saint Lucy, Statue, Multicolored Cast Plaster, Glass Eyes, 61 In. . . . 354.00
Saint Nicholas Of Mozhaisk, Russia, 18th Century, 12 x 10¾ In. . . . 2596.00
Saint Roch, Statue, Multicolored Cast Plaster, Glass Eyes, c.1920, 61 In. . . . 325.00
Saint Thomas Aquinas, Statue, Multicolored Cast Plaster, Glass Eyes, c.1920, 64 In. . . . 413.00
Sorrowful Madonna, Statue, Multicolored Cast Plaster, Glass Eyes, c.1920, 61 In. . . . 354.00
St. Alexander Nevskiy, St. Olga, Christ Delivering Blessing, Repousse Silver, 8¼ x 6 In. . . . 1770.00
St. George, Russia, Late 19th Century, 28 x 21 In. . . . *illus* 800.00
The Annunciation, Oil On Canvas, Italian School, c.1750, 34¼ x 29 In. . . . 1180.00
Tikhvin Mother Of God, Russia, c.1800, 24 x 18 In. . . . *illus* 1300.00
Vladimir Mother Of God, Gold Letters On Christ's Garment, 18th Century, 12 x 10 In. . . . 2596.00
Vladimir Mother Of God, Painted, Overlaid Gilt Repousse Riza, 1795, 12 x 10 In. . . . 3540.00

IMARI porcelain was made in Japan and China beginning in the seventeenth century. In the eighteenth century and later, it was copied by porcelain factories in Germany, France, England, and the United States. It was especially popular in the nineteenth century and is still being made. Imari is characteristically decorated with stylized bamboo, floral, and geometric designs in orange, red, green, and blue. The name comes from the Japanese port of Imari, which exported the ware made nearby in a factory at Arita. Imari is now a general term for any pattern of this type.

Bottle, Blue, Gilt Flowers, 9½ In. . . . 2478.00
Bowl, 19th Century, 4 x 9¾ In. . . . 294.00
Bowl, 4 Panels, Birds, Flowers, Blue, Rust, Scalloped Rim, 4½ x 10 In. . . . 173.00
Bowl, Bands Over Dragons & Phoenix, Red, Fukagawa, 1800s, 7 x 12 In. . . . *illus* 795.00
Bowl, Birds In Fenced Garden, Peonies, Morning Glory Border, Scalloped Edge, 3 x 7 In. . . . 270.00
Bowl, Dragon & Phoenix, Pattern Bands, Iron Red Ground, Fukagawa, 7½ x 12 In. . . . 805.00
Bowl, Fat Old Man In Red Robe, Blue Drip Rim, c.1820, 2 x 6 In. . . . 125.00
Bowl, Flowers, Birds, Scalloped Rim, 4¼ x 16 In. . . . 1495.00
Bowl, Fruit Basket, Vertical Ribs, Scalloped Rim, Enamel, Japanese Export, 12 In. . . . 300.00
Bowl, Reserve Panels, Chrysanthemums, Asters, Brocade, Scalloped Edge, Wood Stand, 10 In. 360.00
Candleholder, Flowers, Leaves, Blue, Red, Octagonal Foot, 7½ In. . . . 662.00
Charger, Birds, Flowers, Scalloped Edge, Blue, Rust, Gold, 24¼ In. . . . 920.00
Charger, Blue & White, Flowers, Japan, 25 In. . . . 590.00
Charger, Blue & White, Landscape, 18 In., Pair . . . 117.00
Charger, Crane & Riverscape, Japan, 22 In. . . . 590.00
Charger, Flower Border, Central Basket, Late 19th Century, 3 x 14 In. . . . 1404.00
Coffeepot, Blue Chrysanthemums, Tapered, Domed Lid, Acorn Finial, 8 In. . . . *illus* 690.00
Dish, Samurai & Lady Playing Koto, Fish Shape, Marked, 1800s, 14¼ x 9 In. . . . *illus* 1150.00
Ginger Jar, Multicolored, Early 20th Century, 15½ x 8 In. . . . 118.00
Jar, Flowers, Screens, Seated People, Gilt Bronze Base, Japan, 18th Century, 14 In., Pair . . . 1293.00
Mug, Fitted Cover, Metal Hinged, Flower Sprays, Baluster, 7 In. . . . 1652.00
Platter, Flowers, Scalloped Rim, Oval, c.1840, 10 x 13 In. . . . 264.00
Punch Bowl, Geometric Design, Multicolored, 6 x 14½ In. . . . 1762.00
Sake Bottle, Plum Blossoms, Leaves, Fretwork Border, Blue, Red, Hexagonal, 6 In. . . . 210.00
Tobacco Jar, Gilt, Multicolored, Late 19th Century, 5½ x 4¼ In. . . . 143.00
Tureen, Red, Cobalt Blue, Gilt, Marked, 20th Century, 12 x 15¾ x 10 In. . . . *illus* 615.00
Tureen, Red, Cobalt Blue, Gilt Highlights, Cobalt Blue Knop, Handles, 12½ x 15¾ In. . . . 633.00
Umbrella Stand, Flowers, Multicolored, 23½ x 8¾ In. . . . 470.00
Vase, Bottle, Floral Panels, Stylized Bamboo Ground, Elongated Meiping Shape, 7 In., Pair . . . 390.00
Vase, Cover, Pheasants, Flowers, Ormolu Mounted, c.1730, 21 In., Pair . . . 11250.00
Vase, Flared Mouth, 25 x 11½ In., Pair . . . 468.00
Vase, Flowers, Baluster, Everted Lip Rim, Underglaze Blue, 13¼ In. . . . 396.00
Vase, Flowers, Baluster Shape, Flared Lip, Blue, Iron Red, Panels, Japan, 1800s, 23 In., Pair . . . 1680.00
Vase, Red Flowers, Birds, Blue Underglaze, Japan, 12¾ In. . . . 235.00

IMPERIAL GLASS Corporation was founded in Bellaire, Ohio, in 1901. It became a subsidiary of Lenox, Inc., in 1973 and was sold to Arthur R. Lorch in 1981. It was sold again in 1982, and went bankrupt in 1984. In 1985, the molds and some assets were sold. The Imperial glass preferred by the collector is freehand art glass, carnival glass, slag glass, stretch glass, and other top-quality tablewares. Tablewares and animals are listed here. The others may be found in the appropriate sections.

Animal, Bunny, Head Up, Milk Glass. . . . 24.00
Animal, Chick, Milk Glass . . . 15.00
Animal, Dog, Airedale, Schnauzer, Carmel Slag, 6 In. . . . *illus* 235.00

Animal, Dog, Scottie, Ritz Blue 54.00
Animal, Dog, Scottie, Carmel Slag 70.00
Animal, Donkey, Caramel Slag 48.00
Animal, Elephant, Caramel Slag, Medium 48.00
Animal, Elephant, Pink Satin, Small 48.00
Animal, Elephant, Ritz Blue, Medium 48.00
Animal, Parlour Pup, Bulldog, Amber 40.00
Animal, Parlour Pup, Scottie, Caramel Slag 45.00
Animal, Piglet, Sitting, Amber 25.00
Animal, Piglet, Standing, Ritz Blue 25.00
Animal, Plughorse, Carmel Slag 40.00
Animal, Rabbit Family, Milk Glass, Mama, Head Up Bunny, Head Down Bunny 120.00
Animal, Woodchuck, Amber 42.00
Animal, Woodchuck, Ritz Blue 42.00
Animal Dish, Rabbit, Cover, On Lacy Base, Purple Slag, 7¾ In. .... *illus* 480.00
Art Glass, Candlestick, Orange Iridescent, Elongated, White Cased Interior, 10 In. 58.00
Art Glass, Vase, Blue, White Marbleized, Blue Interior, Cylindrical, 11½ In. 316.00
Art Glass, Vase, Blue Swags, Iridescent Foot, Blue Lip, Triple Bulbous, 11 In. 300.00
Art Glass, Vase, Bud, Orange Iridescent, c.1920, 10 In. .... *illus* 100.00
Art Glass, Vase, Cobalt Blue, Orange Hearts & Vines, White Lip Wrap, Label, 6 In. 805.00
Art Glass, Vase, Cobalt Blue, White Pulled Leaf & Vines, 11½ x 5 In. .... *illus* 1320.00
Art Glass, Vase, Iridescent Cream, Applied Cobalt Blue Handles, Lip, Foot, 6¾ In. 633.00
Art Glass, Vase, Iridescent Green, Blue Hearts & Vines, Cylindrical, 9 In. 460.00
Art Glass, Vase, Iridescent Marigold, Blue Luster Draped Swags, Baluster, 11 In. 978.00
Art Glass, Vase, Iridescent Marigold, Cobalt Blue Stem, Lip Wrap, Footed, 7½ In. 460.00
Art Glass, Vase, Iridescent Marigold, Green Hearts & Vines, Shouldered, 6½ In. 460.00
Art Glass, Vase, Iridized Body, Hearts & Vines, c.1923, 8¼ In. 288.00
Art Glass, Vase, Mirror Black, Orange Interior, Pinched Waist, 10½ In. 201.00
Art Glass, Vase, Mirror Black, Orange Interior, Shouldered, 7 In. 144.00
Art Glass, Vase, Opal, Blue Heart & Vines, Shouldered, 8 In. 575.00
Art Glass, Vase, Opalescent, Pink & Green Pulled Leaf & Vine, 11 In. .... *illus* 1800.00
Art Glass, Vase, Orange Hearts & Vines, Dark Amethyst, Baluster, 9 In. 805.00
Art Glass, Vase, Oval, Shouldered, Cobalt Blue, White Heart, Vines, 6 In. 345.00
Art Glass, Vase, Red Iridescent, Gold Veins, Bulbous, Pinched, 7½ x 6 In. .... *illus* 240.00
Art Glass, Vase, Shouldered, Cobalt Blue, White Swags, 8 In. 460.00
Art Glass, Vase, Swirled Agate, Iridescent, 7 In. 115.00
Art Glass, Vase, Translucent, White Hearts & Vines, Blue Lip Wrap, Bulbous, 8½ In. 288.00
Art Glass, Vase, Tricornered Rim, Orange Iridescent, Blue Hearts, Vines, Oval, 7 In. 460.00
Art Glass, Vase, Yellow Drag Loop, Purple Iridescent Ground, 9¾ In. 180.00
Beaded Block, Plate, Green, Square, 8¾ In. 19.00
Big Shot, Pitcher, Magnum, Green, 40 Oz. 90.00
Big Shot, Tumbler, Big Shot, Green, 14 Oz. 22.00
Big Shot, Tumbler, Half Shot, Green, 5 Oz. 22.00
Big Shot, Tumbler, Little Shot, Green, 2½ Oz. 18.00
Candlewick, Ashtray, 4 In. 4.00
Candlewick, Ashtray, Heart, Caramel Slag, 6½ In. 198.00
Candlewick, Ashtray Set, Nested, Square, 3 Piece .... 119.00 to 168.00
Candlewick, Basket, Beaded Handle, 5 In. 156.00
Candlewick, Bell, Beaded Handle, 5 In. 59.00
Candlewick, Bonbon, Cupped Base, Center Handle 145.00
Candlewick, Bonbon, Heart, Handle, 6 In. 12.00
Candlewick, Bonbon, Heart, Handle, Ruby, 5 In. 360.00
Candlewick, Bowl, 3-Toed, 6 In. 66.00
Candlewick, Bowl, 3-Toed, 10 In. 128.00
Candlewick, Bowl, 3-Toed, Caramel Slag, 8½ In. 480.00
Candlewick, Bowl, 4-Toed, Square, Crimped 69.00
Candlewick, Bowl, 4-Toed, Ribbed, Round, Ruby, 8½ In. 350.00
Candlewick, Bowl, Centerpiece, Rolled Rim, 13 In. 48.00
Candlewick, Bowl, Centerpiece, 11 In. 50.00
Candlewick, Bowl, Float, 13 In. 210.00
Candlewick, Bowl, Fluted, 5½ In. 70.00
Candlewick, Bowl, Fruit, 6 In. 9.00
Candlewick, Bowl, Fruit, Ribbed, Dome Foot, 9 In. .... 110.00 to 118.00
Candlewick, Bowl, Fruit, Beaded Stem, Footed, 10 In. 270.00
Candlewick, Bowl, Handles, 8½ In. 14.00
Candlewick, Bowl, Ivy, Footed, Black, 7 In. 510.00

Imari, Dish, Samurai & Lady Playing Koto, Fish Shape, Marked, 1800s, 14¼ x 9 In.
$1150.00

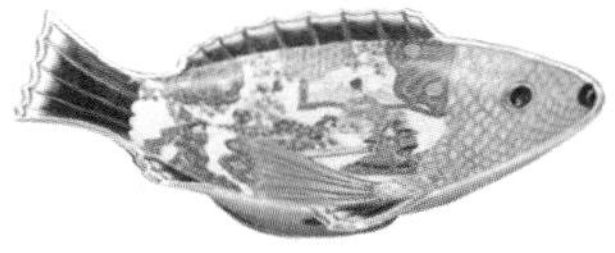

Imari, Tureen, Red, Cobalt Blue, Gilt, Marked, 20th Century, 12 x 15¾ x 10 In.
$615.00

Imperial, Animal, Dog, Airedale, Schnauzer, Carmel Slag, 6 In.
$235.00

Imperial, Animal Dish, Rabbit, Cover, On Lacy Base, Purple Slag, 7¾ In.
$480.00

I

Imperial, Art Glass, Vase, Bud, Orange Iridescent, c.1920, 10 In. $100.00

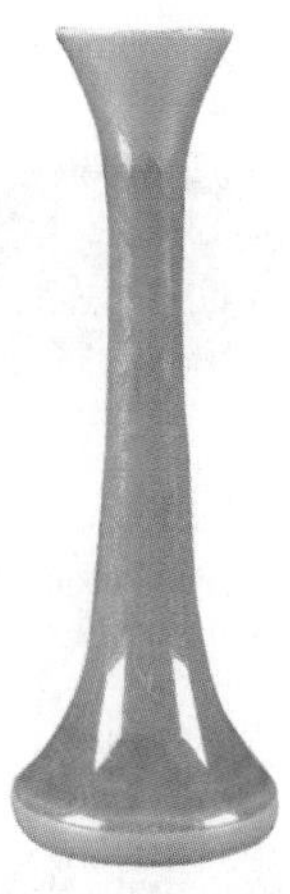

Imperial, Art Glass, Vase, Cobalt Blue, White Pulled Leaf & Vines, 11 ½ x 5 In. $1320.00

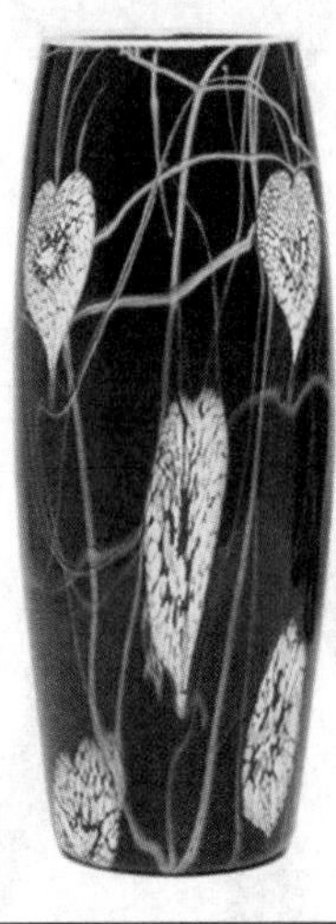

Imperial, Art Glass, Vase, Opalescent, Pink & Green Pulled Leaf & Vine, 11 In. $1800.00

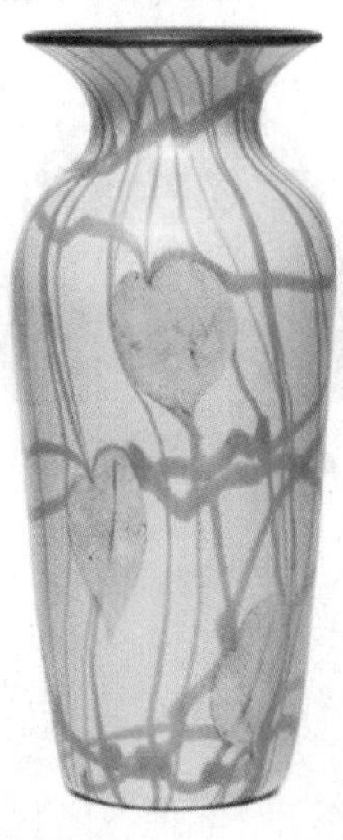

Candlewick, Bowl, Lily, 7 In. 95.00
Candlewick, Bowl, Oval, 14 In. 310.00
Candlewick, Bowl, Oval, Sections, 11 In. 480.00
Candlewick, Bowl, Ruby, Handles, 7 In. 114.00
Candlewick, Bowl, Vegetable, Divided, 2 Handles, 8 ½ In. 72.00
Candlewick, Butter, Cover, ¼ Lb. 23.00
Candlewick, Butter, Cover, Round, 5 ½ In. 26.00
Candlewick, Butter, Cover, No Beads, California 81.00 to 135.00
Candlewick, Cake Plate, Birthday, 72 Candle Holes, 13 In. 500.00
Candlewick, Cake Plate, Mallards Cutting, 12 In. 75.00
Candlewick, Calendar, Beaded Edge, Rectangular, Easel Back 250.00
Candlewick, Canape Set, 2 Piece 23.00
Candlewick, Candleholder, 3 ½ In., Pair 22.00
Candlewick, Candleholder, Heart, Pair 180.00
Candlewick, Candleholder, Saucer Base, Pair 95.00
Candlewick, Candlestick, Flower, Crimped Rim, 5 In. 24.00
Candlewick, Candlestick, Flower, 9 In. 96.00
Candlewick, Candlestick, Flower, Square Rim, 6 ½ In., Pair 106.00
Candlewick, Candlestick, Flower, 4 ½ In., Pair 212.00
Candlewick, Candlestick, Prisms, Pair 630.00
Candlewick, Candlestick, Round, 6 In., Pair 45.00
Candlewick, Candlestick, Urn, 6 In., Pair 360.00
Candlewick, Candy Box, Cover, 5 ½ In. 47.00
Candlewick, Candy Box, Cover, Shallow, 7 In. 64.00
Candlewick, Candy Box, Cover, Deep, 7 In. 114.00
Candlewick, Candy Box, Cover, Section, 7 In. 145.00
Candlewick, Candy Box, Cover, Plain Foot, 1-Bead Stem 165.00
Candlewick, Candy Box, Cover, Beaded Foot, 1-Bead Stem 1400.00
Candlewick, Card Tray, Handle, 6 In. 171.00
Candlewick, Celery Boat, Oval, 11 In. 59.00
Candlewick, Celery Tray, Open Handled, 13 ½ In. 21.00
Candlewick, Chamberstick, Handle 40.00
Candlewick, Chamberstick, Mushroom, Viennese Blue, Pair 96.00
Candlewick, Cigarette Box, Cover 30.00
Candlewick, Cigarette Holder, Footed, 3 In. 45.00
Candlewick, Clock, Boudoir, 4 In. 450.00
Candlewick, Coaster, 10-Spoke Base 6.00
Candlewick, Cocktail, 2-Bead Stem, Ruby 30.00
Candlewick, Cocktail, 3 ½ Oz. 58.00
Candlewick, Cocktail Mixer, Stirrer, 40 Oz. 345.00
Candlewick, Cocktail Stirrer, 12 In. 35.00
Candlewick, Cologne Bottle 50.00
Candlewick, Compote, 2-Bead Stem, 5 ½ In. 14.00
Candlewick, Compote, 4 ½ In. 15.00
Candlewick, Compote, 4-Bead Stem, 5½ In. 21.00 to 40.00
Candlewick, Compote, Cheese, Cover, 4 ¾ In. 65.00
Candlewick, Compote, Crimped, 10 In. 136.00
Candlewick, Compote, Plain Stem, 5 ½ In. 14.00
Candlewick, Condiment Set, 7 Piece 385.00
Candlewick, Cordial, 1 Oz. 24.00 to 89.00
Candlewick, Cruet, Handle, 4 Oz. 105.00
Candlewick, Cruet, Oil, Stopper, No Handle, 4 Oz. 54.00
Candlewick, Cruet, Oil & Vinegar, Tray 156.00
Candlewick, Cruet, Stopper, Cornflower Cutting, 6 Oz. 23.00
Candlewick, Cup, Bouillon, Handles 35.00
Candlewick, Cup & Saucer, After Dinner 16.00
Candlewick, Dish, Baked Apple, 6 ½ In. 22.00
Candlewick, Dish, Jelly, Cover, Footed, Beaded Base 34.00 to 50.00
Candlewick, Dish, Mayonnaise, Underplate, Ladle 29.00
Candlewick, Dish, Mayonnaise, Sections, Gold Trim, 6 ½ In. 120.00
Candlewick, Dish, Mayonnaise, Heart, Underplate, Ladle 510.00
Candlewick, Dish, Pickle, 7 ½ In. 22.00
Candlewick, Dish, Toast, Cover, Round, 7 ¾ In. 350.00
Candlewick, Dish, Pickle, 8 ½ In. 14.00
Candlewick, Dish, Pickle, Oval, 10 In. 19.00

Candlewick, Eggcup 58.00
Candlewick, Epergne, 1-Lily 132.00 to 167.00
Candlewick, Fork, Salad, Viennese 50.00
Candlewick, Fork & Spoon, Salad 16.00 to 21.00
Candlewick, Goblet 20.00
Candlewick, Heart, Handle, 5½ In. 74.00 to 80.00
Candlewick, Hostess Helper, 13-In. Bowl, Sauce Dish, Toothpick Cups, 5 Piece... 480.00 to 600.00
Candlewick, Ice Tub, 5 ½ In. 78.00
Candlewick, Ice Tub, 7 In. 228.00
Candlewick, Icer, Seafood, 2 Piece 65.00 to 75.00
Candlewick, Knife, Butter 500.00
Candlewick, Lamp, Hurricane, Candle, 2 Piece 68.00
Candlewick, Lamp, Hurricane, Candle, 3 Piece 200.00
Candlewick, Lamp, Hurricane, Oil 1500.00
Candlewick, Lamp Adapter 64.00
Candlewick, Lazy Susan Base, 5 In. 50.00
Candlewick, Marmalade, Underplate, Spoon *illus* 55.00
Candlewick, Mirror, Round, Beaded Edge, 2-Footed, Easel Back, Handle, 4 ½ In. 91.00
Candlewick, Muddler 24.00
Candlewick, Mustard & Catsup Set, Jars, Covers, Spoons, Tray 116.00
Candlewick, Nappy, 3-Toed, 4 ½ In. 55.00
Candlewick, Nappy, 4¾ In. 8.00 to 15.00
Candlewick, Nappy, Flat Peg, 7 In. 35.00
Candlewick, Nappy, Square, 6 In. 110.00
Candlewick, Nut Dish, 18 Bead 18.00
Candlewick, Oyster Cocktail, 4 Oz. 14.00 to 17.00
Candlewick, Oyster Cocktail, Underplate, 4 Oz. 29.00 to 75.00
Candlewick, Party Set, 9-In. Off-Center Seat Plate, Coffee Cup 27.00
Candlewick, Pitcher, Beaded Base, 80 Oz. 225.00
Candlewick, Pitcher, Lilliputian, 16 Oz. 240.00 to 261.00
Candlewick, Pitcher, Plain Base, 80 Oz. 110.00
Candlewick, Plate, 4 ½ In. 7.50
Candlewick, Plate, Bread & Butter, 6 In. 6.00
Candlewick, Plate, Crimped, Handles, 10 In. 36.00
Candlewick, Plate, Deviled Egg, Center Handle, 11 ½ In. 130.00
Candlewick, Plate, Dinner, 10 In. 30.00
Candlewick, Plate, Handles, 7 ½ In. 11.00
Candlewick, Plate, Handles, 8 ½ In. 8.00
Candlewick, Plate, Handles, 10 In. 15.00
Candlewick, Plate, Handles, 14 In. 50.00
Candlewick, Plate, Luncheon, 9 In. 11.00
Candlewick, Plate, Salad, 7 In. 8.00
Candlewick, Plate, Salad, Crescent Shape, 8 ½ In. 52.00
Candlewick, Plate, Snack, Ring, 7 In. 9.00
Candlewick, Plate, Snack, Off-Center Ring, 6 In. 11.00
Candlewick, Plate, Snack, Off-Center Ring, 9 In. 12.00
Candlewick, Plate, Snack, Ring, 8 In. 12.00
Candlewick, Plate, Viennese Blue, 4 ½ In. 30.00
Candlewick, Platter, Oval, 13 In. 55.00
Candlewick, Platter, Oval, 16 In. 125.00
Candlewick, Puff Jar, Cover 155.00
Candlewick, Punch Bowl, Base, 12 Cups, Ladle 280.00
Candlewick, Relish, 2 Sections, Handles, 6 ½ In. 8.00
Candlewick, Relish, 2 Sections, Square, 7 In. 110.00
Candlewick, Relish, 3-Toed, 3 Sections, 10 In. 67.00
Candlewick, Relish, 4 Sections, 4 Handles, 8 ½ In. 20.00
Candlewick, Relish, 5 Sections, 13 In. 75.00
Candlewick, Relish, Cover, 3 Sections, 10 In. 600.00
Candlewick, Relish, Cover, No Divider 1050.00
Candlewick, Relish, Oval, Sections, 10 In. 14.00
Candlewick, Rose Bowl, Flower Frog, Cover, 6 In. 475.00
Candlewick, Rose Bowl, Footed, 7 In. 570.00
Candlewick, Salt, Beaded Rim, 2 In. 10.00
Candlewick, Salt & Pepper, Ball 14.00
Candlewick, Salt & Pepper, Beaded Stem, Footed 40.00

Imperial, Art Glass, Vase, Red Iridescent, Gold Veins, Bulbous, Pinched, 7 ½ x 6 In.
$240.00

Imperial, Candlewick, Marmalade, Underplate, Spoon
$55.00

Imperial, Diamond Quilted, Sugar & Creamer, Pink
$35.00

Imperial, Empire Dolphin, Candlestick, Cobalt Blue, 9 In., Pair
$50.00

Imitation—The Sincerest Form of Flattery
Almost every known type of glassware—pressed, blown, colored, clear—has been reproduced or reissued since the nineteenth century. Some reissues are from original molds, which makes identification difficult but not impossible. Some repros have fake marks.

Imperial, Twisted Optic, Vase, Pink, Handles, Footed, 8 In.
$30.00

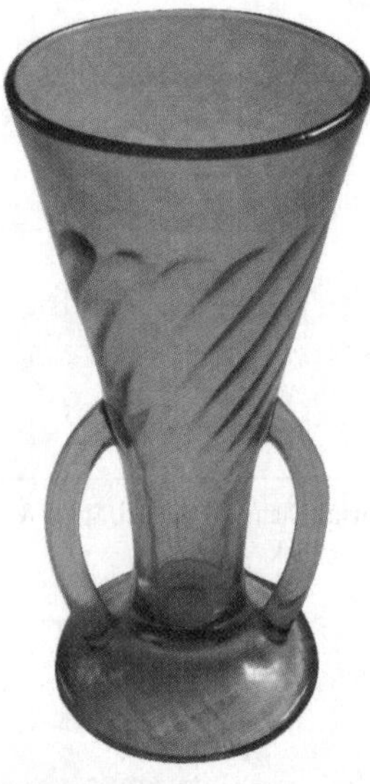

TIP
Mother was right: Have a place for everything and everything in its place. Don't stack old dishes or crowd vases on a shelf. Proper spacing prevents nicks and breaks in pottery or porcelain.

Candlewick, Salt & Pepper, Green 160.0
Candlewick, Salt & Pepper, Straight Sides 14.00 to 16.0
Candlewick, Salt Spoon 30.0
Candlewick, Sauce, 5 ½ In. 55.0
Candlewick, Sauceboat, Underplate 90.0
Candlewick, Sherbet, 2-Bead, Ruby, 6 Oz. 90.0
Candlewick, Sherbet, 6 Oz. 42.0
Candlewick, Sign, Imperial, Oval, Frosted 110.0
Candlewick, Sign, Imperial, Black, Bent Glass 180.0
Candlewick, Soup, Dish, Cream, 5 In. 51.0
Candlewick, Spoon, Salad, Yellow 50.0
Candlewick, Sugar & Creamer, Beaded Foot 30.0
Candlewick, Sugar & Creamer, Beaded Handle 135.0
Candlewick, Sugar & Creamer, Domed Foot 270.0
Candlewick, Tray, 2 Seats, Oblong, 6 ½ In. 60.0
Candlewick, Tray, 5 In. 16.0
Candlewick, Tray, Condiment, Oval, 9 In. 19.0
Candlewick, Tray, Condiment, 8 In. 25.0
Candlewick, Tray, Crimped, 6 ¾ In. 28.0
Candlewick, Tray, Folded, Handles, 7 In. 25.0
Candlewick, Tray, Fruit, Center Handle, 10 ½ In. 200.0
Candlewick, Tray, Lemon, Center Handle, 5 ½ In. 37.0
Candlewick, Tray, Mint, Center Handle, 9 In. 18.0
Candlewick, Tray, Oval, 6 ½ x 3 ¾ In. 18.0
Candlewick, Tray, Oval, Farberware Liner, 9 In. 60.0
Candlewick, Tray, Round, Mirrored, 10 In. 67.0
Candlewick, Tray, Wafer, Center Handle, Gold Beads, 6 In. 24.0
Candlewick, Tumbler, 1-Bead Stem, Ruby, 9 Oz. 60.0
Candlewick, Tumbler, Iced Tea, 14 Oz., 6 In. 27.0
Candlewick, Tumbler, Iced Tea, 12 Oz. 58.0
Candlewick, Tumbler, Juice, 5 Oz. 78.0
Candlewick, Tumbler, Mallard Cutting, 3 ½ Oz. 26.0
Candlewick, Vase, 1-Bead Stem, Footed, 6 In. 110.0
Candlewick, Vase, 7 In. 290.0
Candlewick, Vase, Beaded Edge, 8 ½ In. 225.0
Candlewick, Vase, Bud, Flared Rim, 4 In. 51.0
Candlewick, Vase, Bud, Footed, 5 ¾ In. 56.0
Candlewick, Vase, Bud, Footed, 8 ½ In. 66.0
Candlewick, Vase, Fan, 6 In. 58.0
Candlewick, Vase, Flip, Crimped, 8 In. 75.0
Candlewick, Vase, Flip, Straight Sides, 8 In. 320.0
Candlewick, Vase, Rolled Top, 7 In. 45.0
Candlewick, Wine, 4-Bead Stem, 4 Oz. 15.0
Candlewick, Wine, Hollow Stem, 2 Oz. 161.00 to 240.0
Cape Cod, Cake Plate, Birthday, 72 Candle Holes, 13 In. 270.0
Cape Cod, Salt & Pepper 35.0
Cape Cod, Tumbler, Old Fashioned, 8 Oz., 3 ½ In. 10.0
Daisy, Basket, Marigold, 10 In. 20.0
Diamond Quilted, Candlestick, Green, 8 In., Pair 80.0
Diamond Quilted, Sugar & Creamer, Pink. *illus* 35.0
Empire Dolphin, Candlestick, Cobalt Blue, 9 In., Pair *illus* 50.0
PairGrape, Decanter, Amethyst, 12 In., Pair. 106.0
Grape, Salt & Pepper, Milk Glass 25.0
Laced Edge, Bowl, c.1970, 3 ⅝ x 7 ¼ In. 30.0
Reeded, Beverage Set, 5 Piece 48.0
Reeded, Candleholder, Insert, Pair 72.0
Reeded, Rose Bowl, Ritz Blue, 6 In. 42.0
Reeded, Rose Bowl, Ruby, Footed 132.0
Square, Sugar & Creamer, Ruby 24.0
Tradition, Bowl, Cereal, Pink, 6 In. 24.0
Tradition, Cake Plate, Birthday, 72 Candle Holes, 13 In. 145.00 to 175.0
Tradition, Plate, Salad, Pink, 8 In. 20.0
Tradition, Sherbet, Pink, 3 ½ In. 15.0
Twist, Candleholder, Footed, 3 In., Pair. 17.0
Twisted Optic, Vase, Pink, Handles, Footed, 8 In. *illus* 30.0

NDIAN art from North America has attracted the collector for many years. Each tribe has ts own distinctive designs and techniques. Baskets, jewelry, pottery, and leatherwork are of reatest collector interest. Eskimo art is listed under Eskimo in this book.

rmband, Cheyenne, Beadwork, Buffalo Hide, Sewn With Sinew, 1900s, 2 x 8 In., Pair...... 350.00
aby Carrier, Klamath, Pomo, Woven, Curved, Handle, Patina, 6 ½ x 25 x 11 In........... 633.00
ag, Bandolier, Great Lakes, Beaded, Pocket, Vine & Flowers, White Ground, 37 x 13 In...... 1093.00
ag, Bandolier, Woodlands, Strap, Flowers, Purple Wool Fringe, c.1900, 44 x 15 In.......... 1495.00
ag, Central Plains, Beaded, Buffalo Hide, Multicolored, Barrel Ground, 22 x 15 ½ In....... 4700.00
ag, Corn Husk, Arrow Design, Woven Star, c.1900, 8 x 9 In. 357.00
ag, Cree, Hide, 2 Flowers, Long Flap, Fringe, Strap, 8 x 12 In........................... 225.00
ag, Dance, Cree, Flower, Flap, Czech Seed Beads, 4 ¾ x 4 ½ In.......................... 3450.00
ag, Dance, Cree, Beaded Strap, Fringe, Buckskin Back, Canvas, 10 ½ x 4 ½ In............. 8625.00
ag, Document, Crow, Beaded, Fringe, Tin Design, Abalone Discs, c.1900, 18 x 6 In......... 230.00
ag, Drawstring, Apache, Beaded Front, Back, Early 20th Century, 14 In.................. 495.00
ag, Drawstring, Athabascan, Beaded, c.1900, 7 ¼ In................................. 66.00
ag, Navajo, Yakima Full Beaded, Flat, Image Of Woman Holding Baby In Cradle, 13 x 9 In.. 425.00
ag, Nez Perce, Elk Dreamer, Contour, Beaded, 11 x 14 In............................ 219.00
ag, Octopus, Northwest, Beaded, Cloth, 8 Tabs, Multicolored Flowers, Tassels, 14 In........ 705.00
ag, Arapaho, Coin Basket, Fringed Leather, Beaded, Sweet Grass, 2 ½ x 3 In............... 316.00
andolier, Chippewa, Beaded Flowers, Trade Bead, Hackle Drops, c.1900s, 18 x 17 x 52 In... 316.00
andolier, Chippewa, Beaded Flowers, Tassels, Early 1900s, 22-In. Bag, 44-In. Strap 1500.00
andolier, Great Lakes, Beaded, Pocket, Vine & Flowers, Fringe, 37 x 12 In................ 950.00
andolier, Ojibwa, Beaded, Multicolored Geometric, Trade Cloth, Tassels, 38 In............ 1410.00
asket, Aleut, Cover, Banded Animal Track Pattern, c.1950, 8 ½ x 5 ½ In................. 110.00
asket, Apache, Jicarilla, Cylinder, Handles, Zigzag Motif, 4 Colors, 13 x 11 ½ In. 374.00
asket, Apache, Lightning Design, Dog, 1900s, 3 ½ x 15 In............................ 748.00
asket, Apache, Multicolored, Oval, Devil's Claw, Yucca Root, 3 ¼ x 13 ¼ In. 1150.00
asket, Athabascan, Round, Deep, White Birch Bark, Plaited Triangular Design, 8 x 5 In. ... 110.00
Basket, Burden, Washo, Miniature Form, Multicolored Geometric Design, 6 x 5 ½ In........ 300.00
Basket, Chemehuevi, Olla, Coiled, 2 Diamond Borders, Southwest, 7 x 8 In............... 5645.00
Basket, Cherokee, River Cane, 2-Tone Brown, Orange, Bentwood Handle, 12 ½ In. 374.00
Basket, Cherokee, River Cane, Serrated Diamond Bands, c.1900, 13 In.............. *illus* 420.00
Basket, Cherokee, River Cane, Square To Round Design, Brown & Orange Dyed, 10 In. 431.00
Basket, Cherokee, River Cane, Walnut, Bloodroot, Bentwood Handle, Early 1900s, 9 In...... 460.00
Basket, Cherokee, River Cane, Diagonal Bands, X's, Square To Round, 14 In............... 633.00
Basket, Cherokee, River Cane, Rowena Bradley, Square To Round, Butternut, 14 In......... 690.00
Basket, Cherokee, River Cane, Square To Round, Tied Stretcher Sticks, 1970s, 15 x 14 In. ... 978.00
Basket, Cherokee, Utility, Vegetable Dyed River Cane, c.1910, 16 x 12 In. 1200.00
Basket, Cover, Thompson River North West, Handles, Geometric, 10 ½ x 18 x 10 In......... 385.00
Basket, Cowlitz, Berry, Multicolored, Chevron, c.1900, 11 x 13 In....................... 460.00
Basket, Hava Supai, Standing Dogs, 3 x 4 ¼ In....................................... 920.00
Basket, Hopi, Coiled, Center Bands, Stylized Trees, 1900s, 4 ½ x 14 In. 2090.00
Basket, Hupa, Bowl, Geometric Design, Brown, Reddish Brown, Twisted Overlay, 5 x 7 In. ... 431.00
Basket, Hupa, Cover, Acorn, 2 Colors, Imbricated Designs, 3 x 4 ¾ In.................... 127.00
Basket, Hupa, Geometrics, Brown, Black, 4 ½ x 6 In.................................. 300.00
Basket, Hupa, Multicolored Geometric Design, Red & Black, 6 x 4 ½ In.................. 330.00
Basket, Hupa, Trinket, Bolts Of Lightning, Lid, 8 x 6 In................................ 3450.00
Basket, Iroquois, Birch Bark, Quill Cover, Flower, 1900s, 2 ¾ x 6 In..................... 86.00
Basket, Iroquois, Birch Bark, Quill Cover, Wooden Bottom, Woodlands, 3 ¾ x 5 In.......... 316.00
Basket, Iroquois, Birch Bark, Incised Flowers, Rectangular, Oval Rim, 11 x 15 In........... 325.00
Basket, Karok, Stepped Diamond Pattern, Openwork Rim, 3 x 3 ½ In. 275.00
Basket, Kawaiisu, Zigzags, Blocks, 5 ½ x 5 ½ In. 1150.00
Basket, Klickitat, Hard-Sided, Burden, Berry, Stairstep Design, 1902, 12 x 10 x 8 In......... 316.00
Basket, Klickitat, Hard-Sided, Burden, Berry, Imbricated Designs, 13 x 12 x 10 In.......... 3450.00
Basket, Klickitat, Multicolored, Imbricated, 11 x 14 ½ In.............................. 82.00
Basket, Maidu, Coil Woven, Man & Horse Figures, Early 1900s, 10 x 2 In................. 1568.00
Basket, Melon, Ash, Handle, 10 x 13 x 5 ¼ In.. 144.00
Basket, Menominee, Splint, Oval, Red On Tan Geometric Design, Loop Handle, 11 ¾ In...... 138.00
Basket, Navajo, Geometric & Figural Design, 21 In. 3400.00
Basket, New England, Swing Handle, Oak, Splint, 19th Century, 13 x 9 ½ In............... 99.00
Basket, Northern California, Geometrics, Devil's Claw, Open Weave Bands, 8 x 9 In......... 900.00
Basket, Ohio Oak, Splint, Handle, 12 ½ x 13 ¾ x 7 ½ In................................ 82.00
Basket, Oval, Pitt River, Geometrics, 7 ½ x 13 x 10 ⅛ In.............................. 1045.00
Basket, Papago, Bulbous, Cat Figures & Checkered Triangles, 1940s, 9 ⅜ x 13 In........... 275.00
Basket, Papago, Cover, Multicolored Geometric Design, 6 ½ x 4 ½ In..................... 55.00

Indian, Basket, Cherokee, River Cane, Serrated Diamond Bands, c.1900, 13 In.
$420.00

Indian, Basket, Pima, Martyina, Willow Body, 12 ¼ In.
$990.00

Indian, Belt, Navajo, 8 Conchas, Tooled, Embossed Design, Buckle, Leather Strap, 37 In.
$915.00

Indian, Bowl, Pima, Early 20th Century, 5 x 7 ¼ In.
$150.00

I

TIP
Leather that crumbles to red powder has "red rot." It is caused by absorption of sulfur dioxide and cannot be stopped.

Indian, Jar, Casa Grande, Raised Face, Pierced Rim, Arizona, 6½ In.
$800.00

Indian, Kachina, Hopi, Cottonwood, Painted, Carved, 9 In.
$1450.00

TIP
Let your baskets share the bathroom with you when you take a shower. The hot, moist air is good for the basket. Then let it dry.

Basket, Papago, Handle, Flying Bird, 12¾ x 9 In. 137.00
Basket, Pima, Black Whirling Center, 4-Sided Geometric Design, 1930, 3⅜ x 10 In. 300.00
Basket, Pima, Coiled, Bowl, Geometric, Southwestern, 3 x 15¾ In. 878.00
Basket, Pima, Duck Wing Design, c.1930, 7 In. 80.00
Basket, Pima, Flared, Flat Base, Stepped Geometrics, 5½ x 13 In. 316.00
Basket, Pima, Human Friendship Motif, 7 x 3 In. 403.00
Basket, Pima, Martyina, Willow Body, 12¼ In. .... *illus* 990.00
Basket, Piute, Butterfly, 8½ x 5½ In. 220.00
Basket, Pomo, Clam Shell Beads, Lightning Bolts, 5 x 13 In. 4600.00
Basket, Pomo, Oval, Single Rod, Tsai, 2 x 6 In. 840.00
Basket, Santo Domingo, Painted Organic Design, 4 x 4 In. 140.00
Basket, Shoshoni, Cover, Stepped Geometrics, Yellow, Black, 5½ x 8¾ In. 1900.00
Basket, Shoshoni, Cover, Multicolored Stepped Geometric Design, 8½ In. 2280.00
Basket, Shoshoni, Multicolored Geometric Design, Red & Black, 13 x 9 In. 3480.00
Basket, Southwest Papago, Geometric Design, Deer, Dogs, c.1925 .... 3600.00
Basket, Tlingit, Geometrics, Black, Red, Yellow, Devil's Claw, 6 x 8 In. 2500.00
Basket, Tohono O'Odham, Central Eagle, Checker Design, 1900s, 2½ x 11 In. 207.00
Basket, Trinket, Karok, Stepped Triangle, 8½ x 5¼ In. 403.00
Basket, Wedding, Navajo, 3 Colors, Woven, Central Star, 2 x 16 In. 403.00
Basket, Wine, Pima, Squares, 8½ x 14 In. 330.00
Basket, Yokuts, Double Rattlesnake Pattern, 11 x 21 In. 5500.00
Belt, Concha, Silver Tanned Leather, c.1920, 25½ In. 28.00
Belt, Concha, Turquoise, 9 Domed Sterling Silver Conchas, Black Leather, Signed, 46 In. 805.00
Belt, Navajo, 5 Embossed, Conchas, Tooled Silver, Turquoise Cabochons, 3 x 47½ In. 805.00
Belt, Navajo, 8 Conchas, Tooled, Embossed Design, Buckle, Leather Strap, 37 In. .... *illus* 915.00
Belt, Navajo, Concha, Silver, 36 Spiny Oyster Shell Cabochons, Signed, 1990, 49 In. 475.00
Belt, Navajo, Silver, 7 Center Conchas, Scalloped, Stamped, c.1900, 42 x 3⅞ In. 8225.00
Belt, Plains, Beaded, c.1890, 41 In. 1100.00
Belt, Woodlands, Beaded, Turquoise, Flowers, c.1920, 39 In. 110.00
Blanket, Chimayo, Fringed Ends, Lozenge, Azure Blue Ground, 76 x 51 In. 69.00
Blanket, Navajo, Chief, Anline Dyes, 9 Spot Design, 58 x 58 In. 1955.00
Blanket, Navajo, Chinle, Dupont Dyes, Blue & Red, 80 x 53 In. 632.00
Blanket, Navajo, Saddle, Red, Tan, White, 20 x 34 In. 75.00
Blanket, Navajo, Stacked Diamonds, Red Ground, 48 x 30 In. 1725.00
Blanket, Navajo, Stripe, Interlocking Bands, Multicolored, 49 x 82 In. 863.00
Blanket, Navajo, Stripes, 60 x 84 In. 275.00
Blanket, Saddle, Navajo, Striped, Diamond Details In Red & Gray, c.1940, 32 x 37 In. 275.00
Bolo, Appaloosa Horse, Jet, Abalone, Matching Tips, 2¾ x 3¼ In. 517.00
Bolo, Navajo, Eagle Dancer, Silver, Turquoise, 5 x 5¾ In. 110.00
Bolo, Silver Slide, Bird, Shell, Mother-Of-Pearl, Jet Inlay, Incised Feathers, 3 x 2 In. 316.00
Bolo, Starry Night, Turquoise, Jet, Coral, Mother-Of-Pearl, 3 In. 2415.00
Bolo, Zuni, Sterling Silver, Bird, Cactus, Sawtooth Border, Coral, Turquoise, Jet, 2¼ In. 374.00
Bonnet, Beaded Cloth, Lined, Flowers, 20th Century, 8 x 10½ In. 275.00
Bonnet, Child's, Woven, Quilled, Trade Cloth Lining, 11 In. 193.00
Bonnet, Sioux, Buffalo Fur, Split Horns, Beaded Brow Band, Hawk Bells, Fur Streamers 500.00
Bottle, Paiute, Basketry, Stopper, Geometric Designs, 11 x 5 In. 345.00
Bottle, Washo, Paiute, Basket Covered, Multicolored Design, 3½ x 7½ In. 780.00
Bow, Wooden, Leather Wrapped, Matching Quiver, Deer Hide, Beaded, 47 In. 748.00
Bowl, Acoma, Pottery, White, Prehistoric Human Figures All Around, 1972, 3⅜ x 5½ In. 325.00
Bowl, Anasazi, Multicolored, Bird, 10 x 4½ In. 1035.00
Bowl, Anasazi, Pottery, Black On White, Interior Bands, 5 x 10 In. 225.00
Bowl, Anasazi, Pottery, Multicolored Interior, Exterior, 6½ x 13 In. 489.00
Bowl, Anasazi, Pottery, Black, White On Red, 5¾ x 13¾ In. 1955.00
Bowl, Dough, Santo Domingo, Pottery, 2 Deer, Yucca Plant, 7 x 12 In. 225.00
Bowl, Dough, Santo Domingo, Pottery, Bird, Branch, Mid 1900s, 6 x 14½ In. 325.00
Bowl, Hopi, Pottery, Interior Multicolored Wave Design, Flattened, 1940s, 2 x 8 In. 275.00
Bowl, Hopi, Woven, Flared, Geometric Bands, 4 Kachina Heads, 15½ x 16 In. 999.00
Bowl, Mission, Woven, 2 Serpents, Insect, Band Of Geometrics, 4 x 15 In. 27500.00
Bowl, Mission, Woven, Multicolored Double Serpent & Insect Design, 15 x 4 In. 30000.00
Bowl, Panamint, Woven, Flat Bottom, Flared Sides, Stylized Bird, 6 Perched Birds, 3 x 6 In. 2938.00
Bowl, Papago, Woven, Corn, Bee & Diamond Designs, Flared, Flat Bottom, 4¾ x 9 In. 200.00
Bowl, Pima, Early 20th Century, 5 x 7¼ In. .... *illus* 150.00
Bowl, Pima, Woven, Flat Bottom, Flared Sides, 16 Human Figures, c.1900, 5 x 19 In. 411.00
Bowl, Pima, Woven, Radiating Stairstep Design, 3½ x 12½ In. 500.00
Bowl, Pima, Woven, Flared, 4-Section Pattern, c.1900, 4 x 15¼ In. 529.00

Bowl, Pima, Woven, Multicolored, Geometric Design, 17 ½ In. 748.00
Bowl, Pueblo, Blackware, Oval, Tapered Neck, Avanyu, Madaline Nampeyo, 5 ½ x 6 In. 353.00
Bowl, Rattlesnake, Yokuts, Red & Light Stitches, 7 x 16 ½ In. 2760.00
Bowl, San Ildefonso, Blackware, Bear Paw Impressions, Marie & Julian, 1940s, 5 x 9 In. 5000.00
Bowl, Santa Clara, Blackware, Carved With Avanyu Design, 1900s, 4 x 7 In. 275.00
Bowl, Santa Clara, Redware, Carved Geometric Design, 3 ½ x 5 In. 546.00
Bowl, Southwest, San Ildefonso, Round Bottom, Sloped Side, Black Glaze, c. 1950, 3 x 4 In. 330.00
Bowl, Zuni, Pottery, Fetishes, Prayer Bundles, Turquoise Encrusted, 3 ½ x 5 In. 700.00
Bowl, Zuni, Pottery, Multicolored, Figures, 1800s, 8 ½ x 16 ½ In. 805.00
Box, Cover, Navajo, Silver, Horned Face, Turquoise Features, 2 ¾ x 1 ½ In. 1645.00
Box, Northwest Coast, Cedar, Copper Cover, Symmetrical Designs, 13 ¾ x 24 x 14 In. 150.00
Bracelet, Hopi, Charles Loloma, Silver, Cast, Open Bangle, Signed, 2 ½ x 1 ¾ In. 3450.00
Bracelet, Navajo, Cuff, Sterling Silver, File Work, Turquoise Mosaic Inlay, c.1970, 2 x 6 In. 110.00
Bracelet, Navajo, Silver, Turquoise, Bands, Twisted Wire Center, Spider Web Settings, 2 ¾ In. 1645.00
Bracelet, Navajo, Sterling Silver, 3 Bands, Braided, Twisted, 6 x 1 In. 130.00
Bracelet, Zuni, Silver, 4 Rows Of Square Turquoise Stones, c.1980s. 184.00
Bracelet, Zuni, Silver, Turquoise, Cluster, Split Band, Round Center, 2 ¾ In. 529.00
Breastplate, Cheyenne, Bone Pipe, Bead, Mirror, Elk Tooth, Girl's, 5 ½ x 24 In. 805.00
Cane, Chief's, Stag Grip, Leather Quill, Tin Cone, Red Horse Hair, Pewter Tip, c.1890, 34 In. 319.00
Cane, Plains, Forked Branch, Eagle Head Handle, Tack Eyes, 31 ¼ In. 489.00
Cane, Plateau, Bentwood, 3 Parts, Beaded Bands, Mid 1900s, 30 In. 575.00
Canoe, Model, Bark, Woven Maple Split Rim, Paddle, Painted, Walpole Island, 1902, 31 In. 374.00
Canoe, Model, Northwest Coast, Carved, Painted, Cedar, Flag, Seats, Paddles, 18 x 5 x 26 In. 259.00
Canteen, Acoma, Pottery, Black, Red, White, Stylized Parrot Design, Twisted Handles, 10 In. 250.00
Canteen, Navajo, Silver Shell, Turquoise, Silver Beads, 3 x 3 ½ In. 489.00
Canteen, Santo Domingo, Pottery, Antelope, Branch, 6 x 7 In. 450.00
Cape, Chippewa, Flower, Beaded, Black Velvet, Chain Beaded Fringe, 21 x 24 In. 138.00
Case, Fiddle, Sioux, Beaded, American Flags, Redd Haas, Rosebud, 1889, 31 ½ In. 660.00
Case, Knife, Blackfoot, Rawhide Cutouts, Brass Tack Design, 1960, 10 x 4 In. 225.00
Case, Knife, Chippewa, Tanned Buckskin, Beaded In Floral Pattern, 1920, 11 ½ x 6 In. 275.00
Charger, San Ildefonso, Ayanu Design, Carved, Turquoise Beads, John Gonzalez, 14 In. 750.00
Club, Catlinite, Double Pointed, Pipe Bowl, Hide Covered Wood Handle, 21 In. 523.00
Club, Plains, Double Pointed, Engraved Catlinite Head, Hide Wrapped Handle, 7 In. 201.00
Club, Plains, Double Pointed, Engraved Catlinite Head, Hide Wrapped Handle, 22 In. 440.00
Club, Tlingit, Whale Shape, Whalebone, Carved, Flattened, Inlaid Abalone Eyes, 21 In. 275.00
Club, Woodlands, Wood, Carved Knot, Indian Head, Teepee & Diamond Design, 1930, 23 x 6 In. 200.00
Cradle, Kootenai, Geometric, Horseshoe Top, Center Strap, Toy, 27 x 5 In. 184.00
Cradle, Paiute, Tanned Hide, Beads, Wood Frame, Willow Sunshade, c.1900, 12 x 36 In. 2040.00
Cradle, Plains, Multicolored, Beaded, 2 Applied Umbilical Fetishes, Hide, 16 x 44 ½ In. 6900.00
Dish, San Ildefonso, Effigy, Pottery, Bird Shape, Black Matte, Rose Gonzales, 3 x 6 In. 650.00
Doll, Braided Hair, Beaded Dress, Facial Features, 20th Century, 11 In. 143.00
Doll, Cochiti, Storyteller, Pottery, 3 Children On Lap, Painted, 9 ½ x 6 ½ In. 422.00
Doll, Hopi, Mudhead, With Basket Of Corn, 1970, 19 In. 225.00
Doll, Skookum, Cradleboard, c.1920, 12 ¾ In. 88.00
Doll, Skookum, Squaw, Papoose, c.1930, 10 ½ In. 138.00
Dress, Apache, 2 Piece, Beaded, Tin Cone, Fringe, 29 x 17 & 32 x 21 In. 518.00
Dress, Chippewa, Jingle, Red Cloth, Beaded, Tin Cones, Snuff Can Lids, 1900s, 47 x 48 In. 403.00
Dress, Crow, Buckskin, Lazy Stitch Beaded Trim, Red Ocher Yoke, Fringe, 39 ½ x 33 In. 173.00
Dress, Hide, Sinew Sewn, Beaded Yoke, Sleeves, Front, Back Panels, White Ground, 58 In. 460.00
Dress, Navajo, Leather, Beaded, Sewn Panels, Hide Fringe, Tassels, Mounted, 47 x 27 In. 518.00
Dress, Nez Perce, Beaded Yoke, Multicolored, Geometric, Deer Tail, Fringe, 52 In. 7050.00
Dress, Plains, Girl's, Buckskin, Fringed Cut, Beaded Front Yoke, 26 x 27 In. 489.00
Dress, Sioux, Tan Leather, Beaded, Hourglass Design, Multicolored, Hide Fringes 9560.00
Dress, Southern Plains, Kiowa, Beaded Hide, Fringe, Yellow, Green, c.1900, 50 In. 8225.00
Dress, Yakima, Buckskin, Fringe, Beaded Yoke & Arms, American Flags, Flower, 1920, 45 In. 1800.00
Drum, Chippewa, Blue, Red Stroud Aprons, Beaded Panels, 4 Horse Supports, 20 x 12 In. 316.00
Drum, Kwakiutl, Northwest Coast, Totemic Images, Trade Wool, 13 x 3 In. 345.00
Drum, Powwow, Chippewa, Hand Carved, Wooden, Rawhide Heads, Beaded, Brass, 3 ¼ In. 316.00
Drum, Pueblo, Cottonwood Trunk, Stretched Rawhide, 2 Beaters, 17 ½ x 20 ½ In. 161.00
Drum, Woodlands, Stretched Rawhide, Bark Tree, Painted Shield, 1900s, 4 ½ x 16 In. 288.00
Earrings, Necklace, Navajo, Silver, Turquoise Cluster, c.1990s, 20 In. 138.00
Earrings, Necklace, Navajo, Silver, 12 Squash Blossoms, Coral, 15 In. 382.00
Fetish, Crow, Turtle, Beaded, Tin Tinkers, 20th Century, 6 In. 220.00
Figurine, Owl, Acoma, Pottery, Black, Red, White, Eva Histia, 1980s, 8 x 9 In. 325.00
Garter, Pottawattamie, Loom Beaded, Wool Fringe, 1880, 36 In., Pair. 330.00

Indian, Knife Sheath, Plains, Beaded, Blue, White, Red, Yellow, 1879, 9 ¾ In.
$2420.00

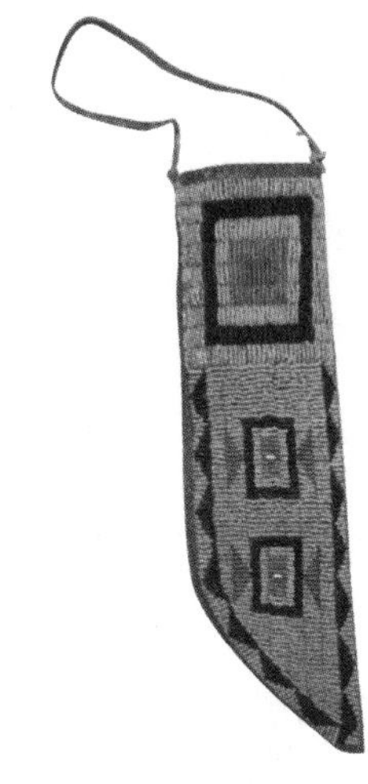

Indian, Leggings, Sioux, Fully Beaded, Sinew, Buffalo Hide, c.1890, Mounted, 15 ½ In.
$3250.00

Indian, Moccasins, Northern Plains, Beaded, Sinew Sewn, c.1900, 11 In.
$475.00

Indian, Necklace, Navajo, 12 Blossoms, Orange Coral Cabochons, Silver, 27 ½ In.
$520.00

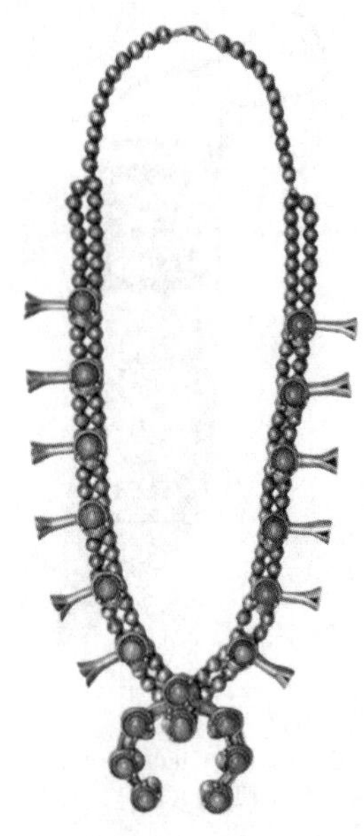

Indian, Necklace, Squash Blossom, Naja, Turquoise, Sterling Silver, 20th Century, 29 ½ In.
$290.00

TIP
Always use your hair spray or perfume before you put on your jewelry. Both products damage some metals and stones.

Gauntlets, Hidatsa, Beaded, Flower, B.J. Youngblood, Signed, 20th Century 165.00
Gloves, Plateau, Tanned Buckskin Gauntlets, Beaded Flowers & 2 American Flags, 1920 . . . . 300.00
Gorget, Oval, Logan, Oh., 4 ¾ In. 132.00
Hat, Basketry, Stepped Geometrics, Tan, Black, 4 x 6 ½ In. 700.00
Hat, Red Beaver, Concha Hat Band, Plume, Man's, Size 6 ⅞ In., Display Cabinet, 15 x 11 In. . . 575.00
Headdress, Chippewa, Old Man's Turkey Feather War Bonnet, 1920s 370.00
Headdress, Hopi, Carved Maskette, Tabletta, 23 x 25 In. 489.00
Headdress, Northwest Coast, Carved, Painted, Wrapped Strip Cedar, Points, 13 x 7 ½ In. 150.00
Headdress, Northwest Coast, Deer, Abalone Eyes, Antlers, Ears, Cedar, 15 x 8 x 11 ¾ In. 184.00
Headdress, Northwest Coast, Raven Mask, Beak, Horsehair, Carved, Painted, 20 ½ x 7 ½ x 6 ½ In. . 150.00
Headdress, Plains, Turkey Feathers, Ermine Drops, Beaded, Brow Band, 1900s, 27 x 15 In. . . 633.00
Hide Scraper, Plains, Antler, Wrought Iron Blade, 1880, 12 ½ In. 316.00
Jar, Acoma, Black, White, Orange, Signed, Sara Garcia, c.1900, 9 ¼ x 6 ⅜ In. 550.00
Jar, Acoma, Geometric Design, 2 Handles, 8 x 10 In. 1080.00
Jar, Acoma, Greenware Pottery, Black Matte On Red, Designs, 1900, 14 ½ x 15 In. 127.00
Jar, Acoma, Greenware Pottery, Black Matte, Red On White, Designs, 13 ¼ x 14 ½ In. 161.00
Jar, Acoma, Orange, Black, Southwest, Sarah Garcia, 7 ⅞ x 7 In. 440.00
Jar, Acoma, Orange, Black, White, 20th Century, 9 ⅜ x 7 In. 440.00
Jar, Casa Grande, Raised Face, Pierced Rim, Arizona, 6 ½ In. . . . . . *illus* 800.00
Jar, Casas Grandes, Blackware, Arrows, Square Notched Rim, 7 x 7 ½ In. 170.00
Jar, Mata Ortiz, Redware, Sgraffito Butterflies & Bees, Squat, Lupe Soto, 7 x 14 In. 140.00
Jar, San Juan Pottery, 20th Century, 8 ⅝ x 5 ½ In. 11.00
Jar, Seed, Hopi, Bulbous, Tan Slip, Geometric Design, Black & Red, 9 x 6 In. 1320.00
Jar, Storage, Nahua, Handles, Painted, Men, Women, Animals, Alligators, c. 1890, 29 In. . 3800.00 to 5500.00
Jar, Water, Hopi, Painted Design In Black & Red, Frog Woman, 13 ½ In. 5400.00
Kachina, Hopi, Ahote, Cottonwood Root, Painted, With Bow & Rattle, 14 In. 225.00
Kachina, Hopi, Cottonwood, Painted, Carved, 9 In. . . . . . *illus* 1450.00
Kachina, Hopi, Cottonwood Root, Tabletta, 1900s, 8 In. 3163.00
Kachina, Hopi, Koshare Clown, Cottonwood Root, Painted, Watermelon, Drum, 17 In. 275.00
Kachina, Hopi, Morning Kachina, Cottonwood Root, 1970, 18 In. 200.00
Kachina, Hopi, White Wolf, Rattle Bow, 1976, 17 x 10 In. 300.00
Kachina, Hopi, Wuyak-Kuita, Cottonwood Root, Long Beard, Horns, Feathers, 14 In. 275.00
Kaibabs, Pueblo, Native Tanned Painted Buckskin, Silver Buttons, c.1910, 10 In. 120.00
Knife & Sheath, Cree, Thread Sewn Beadwork, Tanned Buffalo Hide, 5 Tepees, 12 In. 863.00
Knife & Sheath, Plains, Rawhide, Beaded, Blue, Red, Amber, Tassels, 8 ¼ x 2 ½ In. 364.00
Knife & Sheath, Sioux, Lazy Stitch Beaded, Sinew Sewn, Rawhide, 7 x 2 ½ & 10 In. 316.00
Knife & Sheath, Sioux, Parfleche Backed, Sinew Beaded Hide, Drop, Knife, 2 ½ x 9 In. 127.00
Knife Sheath, Cheyenne, Lazy Stitch Beaded, Sinew Sewn, Multicolored, 10 ½ x 3 In. 518.00
Knife Sheath, Cree, Beaded, Flowers, Fringe Tin Cone, 7 ½ x 3 In. 374.00
Knife Sheath, Plains, Beaded, Blue, White, Red, Yellow, 1879, 9 ¾ In. . . . . . *illus* 2420.00
Lacrosse Stick, Iroquois, Leather, Twine, 24 In., Pair 150.00
Ladle, Great Lakes, Horse Head Handle, 4 ⅞ x 8 ⅜ In. 330.00
Leggings, Central Plains, Beaded Hide, Multicolored, Cheyenne Bar, Girl's, 17 In. 2350.00
Leggings, Sioux, Buckskin, Cloth Uppers, Sinew Sewn, Beaded, Man's, 19 x 8 In. 288.00
Leggings, Sioux, Fully Beaded, Sinew, Buffalo Hide, c.1890, Mounted, 15 ½ In. . . . . . *illus* 3250.00
Mask, Cherokee, Goat, Horns, Painted Eyes & Nose, c.1973, 14 ½ x 6 ½ In. 110.00
Mask, Iroquois, Carved, Painted Red, Horsehair, Tin Eyes, 11 x 7 In. 575.00
Mask, Iroquois, Carved, Booger, Protruding Features, Corn Husk Mane, 1900s, 11 x 7 In. 1495.00
Mask, Iroquois, Corn Husk, 20th Century, 3 x 4 In. 66.00
Mask, Iroquois, Corn Husk, False, 12 In. 138.00
Mask, Iroquois, Corn Husk, Protruding Facial Features & Hair, 1900s, 12 x 13 In. 200.00
Mask, Iroquois, False Face, Broken Nose Design, Horsehair Mane, Copper Eyes, 1980s, 12 x 8 In. 225.00
Mask, Iroquois, False Face, Horsehair Scalp, Metal Eyes, Stones, Wooden, 13 ½ In. 633.00
Mask, Iroquois, False Face, Horsehair Scalp, Metal Eyes, Stones, Wooden, 9 ½ In. 690.00
Mask, Kwakiutl, Moon, Carved, Painted, Wolves, Humans, 1900s, 23 In. 259.00
Mask, Kwakiutl, Moon, Carved, Painted, Alert Bay, British Columbia, 22 x 24 In. 325.00
Mask, Kwakiutl, Raven, Carved, Painted, 1900s, 29 In. 1840.00
Mask, Kwakuitl, Sisutl, Sea Monster, Yellow Cedar, Carved, 23 In. 633.00
Mask, Northwest Coast, Shooting Star, Cedar, Painted, Human Hair, P. Carroll, 11 x 9 In. 350.00
Mat, Navajo, Interlocking Crosses, Red, Tan & Brown, Cream Ground, 1910, 32 x 50 In. 505.00
Mat, Navajo, Woven, Diamonds, Lightning, Red, Tan, Brown, c.1920, 32 x 60 In. 504.00
Mat, Navajo, Woven, Interlocking Crosses, Red, Tan, Brown, c.1910, 32 x 50 In. 504.00
Moccasins, Arapaho, Sinew Sewn, Lazy Stitch Beaded, Chevron Toes, Buffalo Soles, 10 In. . . . 1840.00
Moccasins, Assiniboine, Fully Beaded, Man's, c.1890, 10 In. 1400.00
Moccasins, Beaded, Blue, American Eagle, 4 ½ x 10 ¾ In. 275.00

Moccasins, Beaded, Early 20th Century, 6 ½ In. 138.00
Moccasins, Beaded, Geometrics, Blue, White, Yellow, Leather, c.1890, 4 x 11 In.. .... 500.00
Moccasins, Beaded, Man's, 20th Century, 10 In. 137.00
Moccasins, Beaded, Sinew & Thread Sewn, Red & Green Geometric, White, 10 ½ In.. .... 345.00
Moccasins, Blackfoot, Tanned Buckskin, Beaded, Geometric Designs, c.1940, 11 In. 250.00
Moccasins, Central Plains, Beaded, Hide, Hard Sole, Crossed American Flags, 9 ½ In. 411.00
Moccasins, Central Plains, High Top, Beaded, Hide, Multicolored, Woman's, 18 x 9 In.. .... 7638.00
Moccasins, Cheyenne, Beaded, Red Flowers, Blue Ground, Buffalo Soles, c.1900, 10 In. 275.00
Moccasins, Cheyenne, Beaded, Sinew Sewn, Buffalo Hide, Rawhide Soles, 10 ½ In. 460.00
Moccasins, Cree, Moosehide Mukluks, Flower Beaded, Braided Wool Ties, Drops, 13 x 15 In. . 1495.00
Moccasins, Crow, Tanned, High Top, Buckskin, Flowers, Beadwork, Lacing, 9 ½ x 11 In.. .... 920.00
Moccasins, Northern Plains, Beaded, Sinew Sewn, c.1900, 11 In. .... *illus* 475.00
Moccasins, Plains, Beaded, Buffalo Soles, Valero, Star, Sinew Sewn, 1800s, 11 In. 1610.00
Moccasins, Plains, Sinew Sewn, Beaded, Rawhide Soles, 1900s, 11 In. 1380.00
Moccasins, Plateau, Lazy Stitch, Beaded Sinew Sewn, Buckskin, Double Hard Soles, 11 In. .. 374.00
Moccasins, Sioux, Beaded, Geometric, Brain Tanned Hide, Early 20th Century, 10 ½ In.. .... 403.00
Moccasins, Sioux, Buffalo Soles, Red Cloth, Lazy Stitch Beading, 1800s, 10 In. 546.00
Moccasins, Sioux, Ceremonial, Buffalo Hide, Sinew Sewn, Beading, 1800s, 10 In.. .... 633.00
Moccasins, Sioux, Rawhide Soles, Red, White, Blue, Green Beads, c.1890, 10 In. 460.00
Moccasins, Sioux Plains, Beaded, Red, Blue, Green, 4 ⅜ x 11 ¼ In. 1650.00
Moccasins, Southern Arapaho, Woman's High Top, Tanned Hide, Glass Beads, 1915 .... 1440.00
Moccasins, Ute, Beaded, Sinew Sewn, Buffalo Hide, Soles, 1880s, 11 In. 690.00
Moccasins, Zuni, High Top, Painted Leather, Hard Soles, Beaded Strip, 9 x 12 In. 805.00
Necklace, Cheyenne, Beaded Buckskin, Pouches, Arrowheads, Fingers, 24 In. 546.00
Necklace, Earrings, Navajo, Squash Blossom, Bezel, Silver Beads, Turquoise, 29 In. 633.00
Necklace, Earrings, Navajo, Squash Blossom, Mold Pawn, Silver, Turquoise, 28 In. 633.00
Necklace, Earrings, Pueblo, Old Santo Domingo, Thunderbird, Stone, Turquoise, 15 In. 1265.00
Necklace, Heshi, Turquoise, Rolled Beads, Graduated, 5 Turquoise Drops, 30 In. 110.00
Necklace, Hopi, Silver Overlay, 3 Sections, Turquoise Spider Web Drop, 16 In. 275.00
Necklace, Layered Pendant, Applied Leaf, Bead, Turquoise, Julian Lovato, c.1978, 19 In. 1955.00
Necklace, Milagro, 4 Strands, Silver, White Heart Beads, Crosses, Beads, c.1890, 33 In. 4313.00
Necklace, Navajo, 3 Strands, Turquoise Nugget, 26 In. 690.00
Necklace, Navajo, 12 Blossoms, Orange Coral Cabochons, Silver, 27 ½ In. .... *illus* 520.00
Necklace, Navajo, Pendant, Teardrop, Sterling Silver, 2 Turquoise Stones, 26 In.. .... 120.00
Necklace, Navajo, Silver, 14 Squash Blossoms, Turquoise Stone, 2 Strands, 13 ½ In. 1880.00
Necklace, Navajo, Silver Squash Blossom, Turquoise Stones, Silver Leaves, 1980, 4 ¼ x 4 ½ In. 350.00
Necklace, Navajo, Sleeping Beauty, 10 Strands Turquoise, Silver, 24 In. 403.00
Necklace, Navajo, Squash, 6 Parts, Spider Matrix, Turquoise, Coral, Bear Claws, 27 x 3 x 3 In. 345.00
Necklace, Navajo, Squash Blossoms, Silver, Stone, 18 In. 470.00
Necklace, Plains, Yellow Cornaline D'Aleppo, Brass Beads, 7-Layer Chevron Head, 33 In. 3163.00
Necklace, Pueblo, 3 Strands, Turquoise Heshi, Sterling Cones, 17 In. 69.00
Necklace, Pueblo, 4 Strands, Oxblood Coral, Shell Heshi, 4 Turquoise Fetishes, 24 In.. .... 374.00
Necklace, Pueblo, 18 Strands, Oyster Shell Heshi, Sterling Cones, 24 In.. .... 259.00
Necklace, Pueblo, Shell & Turquoise Beads, Shell Pendant, Turquoise Overlay, 22 ½ In. 200.00
Necklace, Pueblo, Shell Pendant, Mosaic Inlay, Coral Beads, 31 In.. .... 130.00
Necklace, Shell Disk Beads, Glass, Pipestone, 34 In. 33.00
Necklace, Southwestern, 34 Cast Silver Crosses, Hollow Round Beads, 28 In. 1093.00
Necklace, Squash Blossom, 36 Blossoms, 3 Rows Of Lenticular Beads, Turquoise, 32 In.. .... 460.00
Necklace, Squash Blossom, Naja, Turquoise, Sterling Silver, 20th Century, 29 ½ In. .... *illus* 290.00
Necklace, Zuni, 5 Strands, Silver, Turquoise, Coral, Shell, Jet Inlay, Wing Dancer, 3 x 3 In. ... 230.00
Necklace, Zuni, Inlaid Owl Squash Blossom, Inlaid Turquoise, Coral, Shell & Jet, 1990, 26 In. 300.00
Olla, Acoma, Greenware, Black, White, 9 x 12 In.. .... 4025.00
Olla, Acoma, Shouldered Form, White, Painted Birds, Black & Red, Signed, 9 In. 660.00
Olla, Apache, Broad Form, Multicolored Figural Design Of Deer, 11 x 12 In.. .... 18000.00
Olla, Apache, Crucifix Designs, Wide Form, Early 1900s, 20 x 15 ½ In. 12500.00
Olla, Apache, Deer Figures, Geometrics, Broad Form, 12 x 11 In. .... *illus* 15000.00
Olla, Apache, Multicolored Crucifix Design, 1930s, 15 ½ x 20 In. 15000.00
Olla, Jemez, Mica Clay, Painted, Cornstalk, Stylized Birds, Juanita Fragua, 9 x 13 In. 300.00
Olla, Laguna, Pottery, Red & Black, Abstract Triangles, Birds, Orange Base, c.1880, 10 x 14 In. 2750.00
Olla, Panamint, Multicolored Geometric Design, 5 ¾ In. .... *illus* 11400.00
Olla, San Ildefonso, Squat Form, Red, Painted Complex Design In Black, 6 x 4 ½ In.. .... 450.00
Olla, Santa Clara, Blackware, Swollen, Margaret Tafoya, Mid 1900s, 14 x 13 In. 4500.00
Olla, Santa Clara, Flaring Shape, Carved Avanyu Design, 5 x 5 In.. .... 960.00
Olla, Yokuts, Flat Shoulder, Rattlesnake Bands, Red Cloth Feathers, 4 x 6 ½ In. 115.00
Olla, Zuni, Deer, Birds, Cream Ground, 19th Century, 9 ½ x 14 In. 9400.00
Ornament, Sioux Beaded, Hair Drop, Tin Cones, Horsehair Decorations, 9 In.. .... 330.00

Indian, Olla, Apache, Deer Figures, Geometrics, Broad Form, 12 x 11 In.
$15000.00

Indian, Olla, Panamint, Multicolored Geometric Design, 5 ¾ In.
$11400.00

Indian, Pipe Bag, Cheyenne, Sinew Sewn, Beaded, Brine Tanned Hide, Yellow Ocher, 27 In.
$780.00

TIP

Don't shake dirt out of a small rug. The whipping action will break small fibers and loosen the knots.

Indian, Rug, Navajo, Crystal, Geometric Medallion, Hook Border, 20th Century, 43 x 67 In.
$345.00

Skookum

Skookum Indian dolls can be dated by the material used for the parts. The earliest dolls from the mid to late 1910s had apple heads, no feet and a block of wood for a body. In the early 1920s, some apple-head dolls had composition shoes. In the 1930s, the feet were leather-over-wood moccasins. From the 1910s to the 1940s, dolls had composition masks, some marked "Germany." In the 1940s, plastic masks were used.

Outfit, Sioux, Man's, Beaded Harness, Belt, Breech Clout, Armbands, 1970, 9 Piece 350.00
Parfleche, Case, Sioux, Rawhide, Mineral Painted Eye, Hide Lacing, Ties, 18 x 13 In. 325.00
Pendant, Adena, Concave, Convex, Williams Co., Ohio, 4¾ In. 605.00
Pendant, Eagle Dancer, Silver, Turquoise, Jet, Coral, Shell, Chain, 3½ x 3½ In. 374.00
Pendant, Zuni, Butterfly, Inlay, Turquoise, Coral, Jet, Shell, Silver, Chain, 2¾ x 3 In. 184.00
Pillow, Iroquois, Beaded, Eagle & Flag Design, 7½ x 9½ In. 44.00
Pillow, Navajo, Geometric Design, Green, Red, Beige, Germantown Wool, c.1890, 17 In. 375.00
Pin, Navajo, 18 Clustered Turquoise Stones, Round Silver Mount, E. Yazzie, 3 In. 160.00
Pin, Zuni, Covered Wagon, Silver, Turquoise Channel Work, 1⅜ In. 170.00
Pipe, Catlinite, 20th Century, 4 x 3 In. 220.00
Pipe, Catlinite, Bird Effigy, 4 In. 660.00
Pipe, Plains, Ash, Stone, Tapered Stem, T Bowl, 19th Century, 28 In. 940.00
Pipe, Plains, Catlinite Bowl, Quill Wrapped Stem, 31 In. 1265.00
Pipe Bag, Arapaho, Antelope Hide, Beaded, Red, Yellow Ocher, Fringe, 15 x 4½ In. 374.00
Pipe Bag, Central Plains, Beaded, Quilled Hide, Feather, Blue Ground, c.1870, 37 In. 4700.00
Pipe Bag, Cheyenne, Sinew Sewn, Beaded, Red Quilled Slats, Tin Cone, 16½ x 7¾ In. 374.00
Pipe Bag, Cheyenne, Sinew Sewn, Beaded, Brine Tanned Hide, Yellow Ocher, 27 In. ..... *illus* 780.00
Pipe Bag, Chippewa, Fringed Hide, Flower, Beaded Panels, Tab Top, 1900s, 7 x 28 In. 207.00
Pipe Bag, Northern Arapaho, Sinew Sewn, Antelope Hide, Fringe, c.1880, 5½ x 29 In. 288.00
Pipe Bag, Northern Plains, Beaded Hide, Blackfoot Design, Fringe, 31 In. 1528.00
Pipe Bag, Sioux, Beaded, Quilled, Red, White, Green, White Panel, 19 In. 1650.00
Pipe Tomahawk, Plains, Brass Head, Steel Insert Blade, Wood Stem, Beaded, 17½ In. 173.00
Pipe Tomahawk, Plains, Wood Stem, Tack Decorations, 8½ x 22½ In. 259.00
Pipe Tomahawk, Plains, Wood Stem, Tack Decorations, 11 x 24 In. 282.00
Pipe Tomahawk, Plains, Wood Stem, Tack Decorations, 13 In. 770.00
Pitcher, Acoma, Geometrics, Black, White, 9 x 9 In. 700.00
Pitcher, Santo Domingo, Central Handle, Black, Red, Brown Flower, Cream Slip, 8 In. 206.00
Pitcher, Santo Domingo, Organic Design, Black, Brown, Tan Ground, Pottery, 7½ In. 175.00
Plaque, Hopi, Basketry, Squash Blossom Design, Round, 11½ In. 325.00
Plaque, Hopi, Basketry, Coiled, 3rd Mesa, Kachina, Bird, Corn, Round, 21 In. 1100.00
Plate, San Ildefonso, Pablita, Black On Black, Oval, Spread Wing Bird, 6½ In. 411.00
Plate, San Ildefonso, Redware, Flared, Marie & Santana, Mid 1900s, 6½ In. 900.00
Pot, Casas Grandes, Polished Black, Black Matte, Snake, 4½ x 6½ In. 90.00
Pot, Santa Clara, Carved Avanyu Design, Polished Red Finish, Apple Blossom, 7 x 3½ In. 2040.00
Pouch, Apache, Medicine, Beaded, Yellow, Red, Blue Cross, Brass Cones, c.1890, 4½ In. 345.00
Pouch, Athabascan, Beaded, Cloth, Lined, Fringe, Wool Tassels, Multicolored Flowers, 12 In. . 999.00
Quiver, Arapaho, Buffalo Hide, Beadwork, Fringed Hide Strap, 5 x 23 In. 1300.00
Quiver, Case, Sioux, Quilled Hide, Fringe, Bow, Sinew Strings, 42 In. 431.00
Rattle, Crow, Doughnut Shape, Ocher Hide, Horsehair Covered Handle & Trim, 5 x 12 In. ... 235.00
Rattle, Kiowa, Peyote, Carved, Beaded, Twisted Buckskin Fringe, Early 1900s, 21 In. 250.00
Rattle, Kwakiutl, Salmon, Cedar, Carved, 22 In. 374.00
Rattle, Plains, Buffalo Hide, Red Trade Cloth On Handle, 8 In. 430.00
Rattle, Southern Plains, Gourd, Beaded Handle, Fringe, 24 In. 110.00
Rattle, Tortoiseshell 385.00
Rifle Case, Cree, Moosehide, Beaded Red Felt, Flowers & Fringe, c.1900, 49 x 7 In. 475.00
Ring, Sonwai, Inlaid Silver, Turquoise, Sugilite, Coral, Ironwood Inlay, Size 7 In. 1265.00
Ring, Zuni, Turquoise Inlaid Blue Jay, Turquoise Inlay Surrounding, Man's, 1990, Size 11 ... 180.00
Rug, Navaho, Cornstalk Design, Gray Field, c.1940, 34 x 69 In. 1560.00
Rug, Navajo, 9 Blue Head Dancers, Woven, Mid 1900s, 41 x 57 In. 650.00
Rug, Navajo, Crystal, Geometric Medallion, Hook Border, 20th Century, 43 x 67 In. ..... *illus* 345.00
Rug, Navajo, Diamond Design, Red, Brown, Gray & Cream, c.1920, 38 x 50 In. 254.00
Rug, Navajo, Diamond, Orange & Red, Gray Field, 36 x 72 In. 540.00
Rug, Navajo, Diamond, Red, Brown, Gray Field, 53 x 88 In. 960.00
Rug, Navajo, Eagle & Thunderbird Design, Woven, 1968, 61 x 46 In. 350.00
Rug, Navajo, Eastern Reservation, Central Diamond, Forked Border, 71½ x 39 In. 920.00
Rug, Navajo, Geometric, Serrated Diamond Design, Beige Field, Stepped Border, 68 x 52 In. . 518.00
Rug, Navajo, Geometric, Red, Purple, Gray, Brown, Cream Ground, c.1930, 39 x 68 In. 770.00
Rug, Navajo, Geometric, 42 x 72 In. 660.00
Rug, Navajo, Geometric, Flowers, Brown, Cream Field, 36 x 76 In. 840.00
Rug, Navajo, Geometric, Orange, Brown, Gray, Cream Field, 43 x 72 In. 720.00
Rug, Navajo, Geometric, Red, Cream, Gray Field, 36 x 60 In. 1020.00
Rug, Navajo, Gray & Beige, Pyramid Design At Border, c.1930, 48 x 96 In. 1440.00
Rug, Navajo, Interlocking Terraced, Russet, Natural, Tan, Black, c.1930, 41 x 68 In. 633.00
Rug, Navajo, Lozenges, Cream, Caramel, Red, Gray, Gray Border, 74 x 50 In. 1175.00
Rug, Navajo, Pictorial, Corn Plate, 5 Yei Figures, Wool, Mid 20th Century, 40 x 59 In. 805.00
Rug, Navajo, Pictorial, Stylized Diamond, Whirling Log Design, Gray, 1910, 44 x 56 In. 1200.00
Rug, Navajo, Repeating Serrated Diamond Design, Tumbling Log Design, 60 x 45 In. 403.00

Rug, Navajo, Sand Painting, Rainbow God, 4 Yei Figures With Arrows, Woven, 49 x 40 In. . . . 425.00
Rug, Navajo, Serrated, Diamonds, 60 x 43 In. . . . . *illus* 2300.00
Rug, Navajo, Storm Pattern, Whirling Logs, Stepped Border, 89 x 55 In. 1725.00
Rug, Navajo, Stylized Diamonds, Red, Orange & Purple, Beige Field, c.1890, 32 x 40 In. 780.00
Rug, Navajo, Transitional, Serrated Diamonds, Crosses, Blue, Black, Salmon Ground, 60 x 56 In. 1093.00
Rug, Navajo, Two Grey Hills, Woven, Stacked Diamonds, Interlocking Terraced Border, 24 x 48 In. . 420.00
Rug, Navajo, Two Grey Hills, Black Border, Bessie ManyGoats, 1960s, 40 x 25½ In. 600.00
Rug, Navajo, Two Grey Hills, Cross, Valero Stars, Gray Ground, 1920s, 74 x 45 In. 950.00
Rug, Navajo, Two Grey Hills, Woven, Storm Pattern, 93 x 67 In. 2185.00
Rug, Navajo, Wool, Rectangular Shapes, Gray Ground, Red & Black Design, 1930s, 31 x 58 In. 345.00
Rug, Navajo, Zigzag, Brown, Cream & Red, c.1930, 42 x 72 In. 510.00
Rug, Rio Grande, Woven, Center Medallion, Stepped Borders, Arrow, Tumbling Logs, 81 x 62 In. 345.00
Saddle, Crow, Double Horn, Beadwork Stirrups, Child's, 15 x 16 In. 2000.00
Scabbard, Nez Perce, Plateau, Rifle, Leather, Beaded, Trade Cloth, Fringe, 44 x 6 In. 4000.00
Scabbard, North Plains, Hide, Trade Cloth Strip, 50 In. 5581.00
Sculpture, Northwest Coast, Walrus, Soapstone, 10½ x 6 In. 259.00
Sculpture, Sioux, Horned Bison, Inset Buffalo Warrior On Reverse, Soapstone, 14¾ In. 400.00
Sculpture, Sioux, Stylized Figure, Claw Necklace, Floral Garment, Soapstone, 14 x 14 In. . . . 140.00
Seed Pot, Acoma, Deer, Butterfly, Green Lines & Swirls, 1¼ x 3 In. 100.00
Seed Pot, Acoma, Pear Shape, Black & White Segmented Circles, 2½ x 2¼ In. 60.00
Serape, Navajo, Wool, Floating Serrated Pattern, Red Ground, 67½ x 51 In. 4994.00
Shield, Sioux, Dance, Hide, Painted Celestial, Buffalo Images, Brass Bells, 16 In. 431.00
Shirt, Arapaho, Ghost Dance, Muslin, Star, Moon, Bird, Figures, 29 x 49 In. 546.00
Shirt, Great Lakes, Leather, Beaded, Hand Stitching, Vine & Leaf, 31 x 59 In. 259.00
Shirt, Navajo, Purple Velvet, Silver, Turquoise Points, Silver Buttons, 25 x 52 In. 690.00
Spear, Plains, Ceremonial, Stone Point, Wood Handle, Braided Tassels, Strap, 19 In. 300.00
Squaw Ax, Hide Handle, Beads, Copper Wire, Buffalo Hair, 8 x 3¼ In. 825.00
Stool, Iroquois, Floral Beaded Cushion Top, 4 Legged, 19th Century, 4¾ x 11 In. 200.00
Storage Jar, Anasazi, Handles, 14 x 11 In. 880.00
Strap, Chippewa, Beaded, Flowers, Bandolier, 32 x 3¾ In. 259.00
Tomahawk, Brass Pipe, Brass Tacked Stem, 20th Century, 20⅜ In. 770.00
Tomahawk, Plains, Pipe, Wood Stem, Tack Design, 24½ x 11 In. 225.00
Tomahawk, Plains, Pipe, Wood Stem, Tacks On Upper & Lower Stem, 13½ In. 700.00
Totem Pole, Inuit, Stone Carved, Signed, Manno Bay, 12½ In. 330.00
Totem Pole, Kwakiutl, Human, Salmon, Eagle, Carved, 1900s, 26 In. 633.00
Totem Pole, Northwest Coast, 3 Figures, Cedar Pole, Hand Carved, 49 x 7 x 28 In. 690.00
Totem Pole, Northwest Coast, 5 Figures, Removable Wings, Carved, Painted, Patina, 32 In. . . 316.00
Totem Pole, Northwest Coast, Stacked Figures, Raven, Clan Figure, Bear, Frog, Painted, 17 In. 8625.00
Totem Pole, Tlingit, Carved, Painted, Inset Abalone Shell Eyes, Alaska, c.1900, 5 x 5 x 9 In. . 259.00
Trade Beads, Chevron, Yellow, Green, 6 Layers, 34 In. 259.00
Tray, Apache, Basket, Coiled, Pinwheel Pattern, 3½ x 16¾ In. 2468.00
Tray, Apache, Yucca Root Figures, Star Flower, 12¾ x 3¼ In. 862.00
Tray, Cherokee, River Cane, Double Woven, Eva Wolfe, 4 x 15 In. 460.00
Tray, Hopi, Kachina, Basket, Coiled, 9¾ In. 90.00
Tray, Hopi, Woven, Butterfly Kachina, Coiled, 11½ In. Diam. 210.00
Tray, Hopi, Woven, Brown, Tan, Orange, Spiral, 13 In. 220.00
Tray, Pima, Basket, Men In Whirlwind Pattern, Round, 16 In. 1300.00
Tray, Washo, Paiute, Winnowing, 4 Bands, 3 x 10 x 10½ In. 425.00
Trinket Box, Navajo, Sterling, Triangular Turquoise Repousse, 2½ x 2¾ In. 633.00
Vase, Acoma, Birds, Black, Red, White Ground, Shouldered, Rachel Aragon, 7½ x 9 In. 550.00
Vase, Acoma, Black & White Feathers, Red Triangles, Pottery, Chino, 11¼ x 9 In. . . . . . . *illus* 2925.00
Vase, Acoma, Geometrics, Red, Black, Tan Matte Ground, Shouldered, 8½ x 10 In. 958.00
Vase, Acoma, Painted Design In Black & Red, Pottery, 14 x 14 In. 2160.00
Vase, Acoma, Red & Black Designs, Bulbous, Pottery, Barbara & Joseph Cerno, 14 x 14 In. . . . 1800.00
Vase, Acoma, Tan Matte Glaze, Painted Geometric Design, Red & Black, 10 In. 1140.00
Vase, Acoma, White With Stylized Feather Design, Black & Red, Pottery, 9 x 11 In. 3000.00
Vase, Hopi, Broad Shape, Painted Design In Brown & Red, Pottery, 11 x 5 In. 1440.00
Vase, Hopi, Brown & Red Designs, Tan Ground, Broad Shape, Pottery, Mark Tahbo, 5½ x 11½ In. . . 1200.00
Vase, Hopi, Faces, Geometrics, Tan Slip, Black, Red Brown, Tapered, 12 x 5½ In. 1000.00
Vase, Hopi, Painted, Geometric Design, Pottery, 6 x 3 In. 58.00
Vase, Hopi, Tan Slip, Black & Red Designs, Bulbous, Les Namingha, 4 x 6½ In. 800.00
Vase, Jemez, Polished Red, Painted, Brown, Tan, Red, B.J. Fragua, Pottery, 6 x 6¼ In. 282.00
Vase, Navajo, Black On Black, Squat, Turtle Shape, 4 In. 60.00
Vase, Navajo, Flaring, Incised Geometric, Design, Blue, Green, Brown, Pottery, 10 x 5 In. 140.00
Vase, Pueblo, Bulbous Form, 3 Carved Figures, Geometric, Red & Brown, 7 x 7 In. 440.00
Vase, San Ildefonso, Round, Polished Black, Stylized Design, 4½ In. 1320.00
Vase, Santa Clara, Wedding, Blackware, Carved, Serpent Avenyu, 2 Spouts, 8½ x 6 In. 330.00

Indian, Rug, Navajo, Serrated, Diamonds, 60 x 43 In.
$2300.00

TIP
Always put a pad under a carpet or rug used on a hard floor surface.

Indian, Vase, Acoma, Black & White Feathers, Red Triangles, Pottery, Chino, 11¼ x 9 In.
$2925.00

Indian, Vest, Plains, Beaded Geometric Design On Fabric, Blue Ground, Child's, 11 x 11 In.
$1020.00

Inkstand, Brass, Enamel, Inkwell, Woman, Cupid, Reverse Painted, Dragons, 4 x 5 In.
$270.00

Inkstand, Redware, 2 Wells, Brown Glaze, 3 Sections, c.1870, 2 3/8 x 6 x 4 3/4 In.
$210.00

Inkstand, Silver Plate, Glass Liner, Art Nouveau, Marked, Kayser, 10 1/4 In.
$55.00

Inkwell, Cut Glass, Amethyst, Flowers, Sterling Silver Neck Lid, c.1900, 2 3/4 x 3 1/2 In.
$1700.00

Inkwell, Glass, Yellow Amber, 3 Fonts, c.1880-95, 2 3/4 x 5 3/4 x 3 In.
$405.00

Vase, Santo Domingo, Large Form, Red, Geometric Design In Black & White, 14 In. 3000.00
Vase, Santo Domingo, Painted, Bird & Flowers, Black, Red, 9 x 6 1/2 In. 1265.00
Vase, Zia, Flattened Shape, Painted, Signed, Claudina Lomakema, 5 1/2 x 2 In. 58.00
Vase, Zuni, Long Neck, Flared Rim, Frog Handles, 2 Colors, Geometric, Deer, 8 x 6 1/2 In. 823.00
Vest, Chimayo, Wool, Chevron Designs, Leather Buttons, c.1950 .... 259.00
Vest, Plains, Beaded Geometric Design On Fabric, Blue Ground, Child's, 11 x 11 In. ..... *illus* 1020.00
Vest, Plateau, Beaded, Buckskin, Deer, Elk, Grass, Trees, Flowers, 24 x 18 In. 374.00
Vest, Plateau, Beaded, Flowers, Buckskin Fringe, Late 1800s, 21 1/2 x 17 In. 3163.00
Vest, Sioux, Beaded, Red, Green, Yellow, Blue, Pink, Rust & Metallic Gold Beads, 1880 .... 3735.00
Vest, Sioux, Beaded Design On Canvas, Ribbon Accents, Child's, c.1915, 13 x 13 In. 2400.00
Vest, Sioux, Buffalo Hide, Sinew Sewn Beadwork, Boy's, 14 x 15 1/2 In. 374.00
Wall Hanging, Pima, Multicolored Geometric Design, 7 1/2 In. 330.00
Wand, Dance, Blackfoot, Beaded Handle, Attached Buffalo Horns, Hawk Bells, 1900, 27 x 8 In. 350.00
Wand, Sioux, Dance, Lakota Ghost, Horsehair Horn Head, c.1890, 11 x 24 In. 374.00
War Skirt, Blackfoot, Elk Hide, 24-In. Fringe, Roundels, Matching Leggings, 1800 .... 9000.00
Weaving, Navajo, Ganado Style, Gray, Black, Red, White, 1900s, 58 x 62 In. 210.00
Weaving, Navajo, Graphic X, Red, Black, Tan Center Diamonds, 32 x 59 In. 230.00
Weaving, Navajo, Multicolored, Banded, Serrated Diamonds, 54 x 31 In. 6900.00
Weaving, Navajo, Red, Blue, Orange, Indigo Blue, White, Half Chevrons, 52 x 33 In. 4025.00
Weaving, Navajo, Tree Of Life, Birds From The Gap Trading Post, 1970, 39 x 26 In. 900.00
Weaving, Navajo, Yei, Figural, Green, Orange, Red, Natural, Black, 52 x 71 In. 748.00
Weaving, Storm Pattern, Water Bug, Triangle, Gray Ground, 55 x 37 In. 150.00
Winnowing Tray, Washo, Paiute, Multicolored Design, 10 x 10 In. 510.00
Yoke, Dance, Chippewa, Man's, Beaded, Floral Beaded Drops, c.1910, 8 x 20 In. 850.00

INKSTANDS were made to be placed on a desk. They held some type of container for ink, and possibly a sander, a pen tray, a pen, a holder for pounce, and even a candle to melt the sealing wax. Inkstands date to the eighteenth century and have been made of silver, copper, ceramics, and glass. Additional inkstands may be found in these and other related categories.

Bisque, Plinth Shape, Classical Scenes, 3 Open Wells, Sander, Slides, KPM, 3 1/2 In. 118.00
Brass, 2 Wells, Center Handle, 18th Century, 6 x 4 1/4 x 10 1/4 In. 470.00
Brass, Enamel, Inkwell, Cupid, Reverse Painted, Dragons, 4 x 5 In. .... *illus* 270.00
Bronze, Sea Nymphs, Bernard, France, c.1900, 11 In. 690.00
Copper, Glass, 2 Wells, Wood Base, Corber & Oliver, Marked, 7 1/2 x 3 In. 120.00
Copper, Silver, 2 Square Wells, Pen Tray, Oak Base, 4 x 6 x 10 In. 605.00
Ivory, Ebony, 2 Square Wells, Covers, Pen Tray, 9 1/8 In. 470.00
Mahogany, Scale, Early 20th Century, England, 6 1/4 x 12 x 10 In. 235.00
Marble, Square, Bronze Pot, Theatrical Masks, Channeled Edges, Button Feet, 8 In. 735.00
Nickeled Metal, Pen Tray, Stamped, Emmy Roth Workshop, Berlin, c.1930, 10 x 3 1/2 In. 1250.00
Notched Edge, Center Fill Hole, 3 Pen Holes, Cobalt Blue, Stoneware, 1 1/4 x 3 1/4 In. 1210.00
Pewter, Porcelain Liner, Quill Holder, Tin Sander, 2 7/8 x 4 5/8 In. 248.00
Redware, 2 Wells, Brown Glaze, 3 Sections, c.1870, 2 3/8 x 6 x 4 3/4 In. .... *illus* 210.00
Scribe Lines, 3 Ink Holes, Stoneware, Mark, M. Tyler, Albany, c.1840, 2 x 4 3/4 In. 4070.00
Silver, Rococo, 2 Cut Glass Pots, Fountain Pen, Continental, c.1900 .... 800.00
Silver, Winged Lion's Paw Feet, Pen Tray, Glass Bottles, George IV, 8 3/4 x 5 3/4 In. 2400.00
Silver Plate, Glass Liner, Art Nouveau, Marked, Kayser, 10 1/4 In. .... *illus* 55.00
Soapstone, Carved, Brass Mount, Carnelian Finial, Footed 264.00
Tortoiseshell, Bronze Mount, Boulle, France, c.1869, 3 1/2 x 9 1/2 x 7 In. 1775.00
Wood, Penholder, Bear, Figural, Black Forest, 7 1/2 In. 595.00

INKWELLS, of course, held ink. Ready-made ink was first made about 1836 and was sold in bottles. The desk inkwell had a narrow hole so the pen would not slip inside. Inkwells were made of many materials, such as pottery, glass, pewter, and silver. Look in these categories for more listings of inkwells.

Boat, Metal Lid, 1870 .... 336.00
Brass, Bell, White Porcelain Center, Continental, 19th Century 2510.00
Brass, Dragon 71.00
Brass, Lapis Mounts, Globe-Shaped Top Surrounded By Snake, Glass Set, c.1900, 7 In. 288.00
Brass, Scrolls, Cartouche Decoration, 6 1/2 x 13 In. 60.00
Brass, Sphinx, Reclining, Hinged Lid, Draped Base, Cherub, Porcelain Insert, 5 x 7 In. 403.00
Bronze, Bird On Leaf, Continental, c.1920 .... 29.00
Bronze, Cover, France, c.1930, 9 x 8 In. 264.00
Bronze, Foot, 19th Century, 3 1/2 In. 540.00
Bronzed Metal, Embossed Hops & Leaves, 4 1/4 x 3 1/4 In. 120.00
Cut Glass, Amethyst, Flowers, Sterling Silver Neck Lid, c.1900, 2 3/4 x 3 1/2 In. .... *illus* 1700.00

Cut Glass, Bird's Nest Shape, Bronze, Twig Legs, Chicks, Tiffany & Co., c.1910, 7 x 8 In. 2350.00
Cut Glass, Crosscut Diamond, Fan, 3 ½ In. 50.00
Cut Glass, Hinged Lid, Clear, Ruby Red, Brass Neck Ring, c.1910, 3 ⅝ x 4 ¾ In. 850.00
Cut Glass, Hinged Lid, Silver Plated, Ribbed, Bulbous, Tiffany & Co., 3 ⅜ x 5 ½ In. 238.00
Cut Glass, Hinged Lid, Turquoise Blue, Metal Neck Ring, c.1900, 3 ⅜ x 3 In. 175.00
Cut Glass, Hinged Mushroom Lid, Clear, 4-Sided, Crosshatch Pattern, c.1910, 4 ½ In. 142.00
Devil's Fire, Stopper, 9 In. 2128.00
Gilt Bronze, Art Nouveau, Draped Nude Woman, Leaves, Lily Pad, 10 x 5 ½ In. 300.00
Gilt Bronze, Neoclassical, Patinated, Lion Finial, Caryatid Supports, 8 ½ x 8 In. 1645.00
Gilt Bronze, Saddle, 19th Century, 3 In. 480.00
Glass, Clear, Disc Type Lip, Pontil, 1820, 1 ½ x 2 ¼ In. 146.00
Glass, Inkwell, Olive Green, Pontil, 1 ⅞ x 2 ¼ In. 143.00
Glass, Rococo Swirl, Green Cut To Clear, Engraved Flowers, Squat Shape, 4 x 5 In. 2400.00
Glass, Salamander, Bumble Bee, Berries, Mottled Amber & Green, Lid, 4 In. 6400.00
Glass, Yellow Amber, 3 Fonts, c.1880-95, 2 ¾ x 5 ¾ x 3 In. *illus* 405.00
Graniteware, Phrenology Head, White, Black & Blue Markings, F. Bridges, c.1860, 5 ⅜ In. 900.00
Marble, Brass Trim, Vienna, c.1890, 5 x 9 ¾ In. 248.00
Metal, Camel, Cold Painted, White Metal, Early 20th Century, 9 x 5 ½ In. 316.00
Metal, Parrot, White, Painted, Green, Red, Blue, Porcelain Insert, 4 In. 495.00
Milk Glass, Phrenology Head, Iron, Embossed, Pat. Dec. 11, 1855, 6 ½ In. *illus* 4025.00
Olive Amber, 3-Piece Mold, Diamonds, 1 ½ In. 118.00
Pear, Leaves, Stem, Opalescent, Tooled Mouth, 2 x 3 ¾ In. 504.00
Phrenology Head, Sectional Skull, Blue Scroll Work, Porcelain, 6 In. 388.00
Porcelain, Children, Dog, Baby In Cradle, 2 Pots, Plinth Base, c.1850, 5 x 6 In. 1456.00
Pottery, Shepherdess, Sleeping, Brown Glaze, Larkin Bros., E. Liverpool, c.1850, 3 x 5 In. 132.00
Pottery, Tan, Red, Green, Blue Glaze, Wood Cover, Marked, Dalpayrat, 4 x 2 ½ In. 360.00
Pressed Glass, Johnstons Pepsin Gum, Eagle & Flag, Puppies, Cherubs, 3 x 3 x 3 In. 2200.00
Pressed Glass, Woman, Outstretched Arms, Cast Bronze Mount, Art Nouveau, 4 x 5 ½ In. 99.00
Redware, Round, Flared Rim, Mottled, Tan & Black, 1 ½ x 2 ½ In. 165.00
Silver, Cover, Squat Lobed, Leaf Tip Band, Central Hole, England, 2 ½ x 4 ⅛ In. 316.00
Spelter, Cycle Riders, Crossed Flags, Victory Wreath, Wheelmen, 9 x 10 In. 550.00
Stoneware, Brushed Wagon Wheel, Cobalt Blue, Molded Upper Rim, 1 ¼ x 3 In. 1210.00
Stoneware, Incised Lines, Blue, 3 Ink Holes, M. Tyler, Albany, c.1840, 2 x 4 ¾ In. 4070.00
Wood, Devil's Head, Red Face, Black Beard, Yellow Glass Eyes, Black Forest, c.1890, 3 ¾ In. 850.00

INSULATORS of glass or pottery have been made for use on telegraph or telephone poles since 1844. Thousands of different styles of insulators have been made. Most common are those of clear or aqua glass; most desirable are the threadless types made from 1850 to 1870.

AM Insulator Co., N.Y., Double Petticoat, Pat'd Sept. 131881, Nov. 131883, Green 495.00
AM. Tel. & Tel., No. 100, Jade Green, Milk Glass 5.00
American, No. 020, Aqua, Milky Swirls 45.00
American, No. 020, Backwards R, Aqua 5.00
Armstrong, No. 030, Cobalt Blue, Red, Milky Base 430.00
B.T. Co. Of Can., No. 080, Royal Purple 45.00
Brookfield, Aqua, 3-Piece Mold, Embossed Dome 20.00
Brookfield, Embossing, Aqua 15.00
Brookfield, No. 010, Dark Aqua 3.00
Brookfield, No. 010, Green, Amber Swirls 5.00
Brookfield, No. 015, Aqua 4.00
Brookfield, No. 020, Apple Green 2.00
Brookfield, No. 080, Wire Ridge, Round Dome, Olive Green 30.00
Brookfield, No. 150, Aqua 10.00
Brookfield, No. 180, Yellow Green, Olive, Aqua 20.00
Brookfield, No. 430, Lime Green 90.00
Brookfield, Pat. Oct. 8, 1907, Aqua 275.00
Cal. Electric Works, No. 005, Embossed, Wire Groove, Concave Skirt, Aqua 352.00
California, No. 010, Purple, Ghost Embossing 27.00
California, No. 010, Sage Green 5.00
Canada, No. 010, Ice Aqua 1.00
Canadian Pacific, No. 010, Blue 1.00
Canadian Pacific, No. 050, Swirls, Purple, Gray 235.00
Canadian Pacific, No. 170, Aqua, Embossed 1.00
Canadian Pacific, No. 170, Light Aqua, Large Embossing 2.00
Canadian Pacific, No. 170, Steel Gray, Purple, Amber Swirls 100.00
Columbia, Dark Aqua, Pat'd May 23, 1891 302.00
Corning Pyrex, Made In U.S.A., 271, Carnival Glass 220.00

TIP

Clean a glass inkwell carefully. The old ink may cover a crack. Wash in warm water with mild dishwashing liquid or soap, never dishwasher detergent. Don't use ammonia if the glass is decorated or iridescent.

Inkwell, Milk Glass, Phrenology Head, Iron, Embossed, Pat. Dec. 11, 1855, 6 ½ In. $4025.00

TIP

It is possible to clean a glass insulator. Mix a third of a can of Bar Keeper's Friend (found in most grocery stores) with a gallon of water in a non-metal bucket. Put the insulator in the mixture, but be sure the water and the insulator are at the same temperature to avoid stressing the glass. Soak for 12 hours. Scrub the insulator with a nylon pad. Repeat if the insulator does not seem clean.

Iron, Cuspidor, Figural, Dragon, Marked No. 3612, 12 In.
$750.00

Iron, Lamp, Sticking Tommy, Loop Terminal, 12½ In.
$154.00

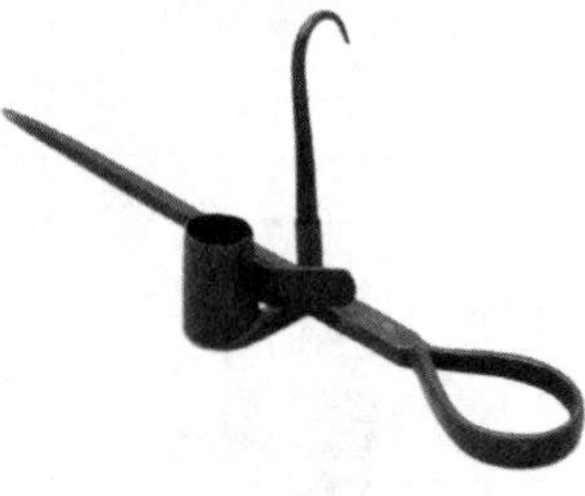

Iron, Shoe Rest, Shoeshine, Horse, Black Paint, 7 In.
$115.00

TIP

Remove the rust from iron by soaking the piece in kerosene for 24 hours, or use any one of several commercial preparations made for the removal of rust. Wash, dry, and coat the piece with a light oil to protect it.

Diamond, No. 050, Dark Straw 2.00
Diamond, No. 060, Mustard Olive Green 60.00
Dominion, No. 020, Yellow Dome, Clear Skirt 175.00
Dominion, No. 040, Light Peach 1.00
E.C. & M Co., No. 060, H-Mold, Aqua 225.00
E.C. & M. Co., Aqua 195.00
E.C. & M. Co., Deep Teal Blue, Olive Streak, Dot On Reverse, 4 In. 495.00
F.F.C.C.N De M, Dark Yellow Green 275.00
FT. W.E. Co., No. 030, Aqua 80.00
G.T.P., No. 010, Emerald Green, Olive Green, Amber Swirls 25.00
G.T.P., No. 080, Gray-Blue, Milk Glass Swirls 20.00
Gayner, No. 020, Blue Aqua 1.00
H.G. Co., No. 020, Jade Green, Milk Glass 1.00
H.G. Co., No. 070, Ice Aqua 5.00
H.G. Co., No. 130, Ice Blue 1.00
H.G. Co., No. 140, Sky Blue, Bubbles 20.00
H.G. Co., Patent May 21893, R-Skirt, Petticoat, Orange Amber 250.00
Hemingray, No. 020, Yellow Tint, Metal Insert 10.00
Hemingray, No. 030, 7Up Green 20.00
Hemingray, No. 080, Transition Embossing, Aqua .... 10.00 to 30.00
Hemingray, No. 110, Carnival Glass, Metal Insert 50.00
Hemingray, No. 250, Jade Green, Milk Glass, Dome Bubble 5.00
K.C.G.W., Ice Blue 100.00
K.C.G.W., No. 010, Ice Green 35.00
L.G.T. & Co., Aqua, Graphite Swirls In Dome, Skirt 65.00
L.G.T. & Co., No. 010, Swirl To Threads, Aqua 135.00
Lynchburg, No. 080, Drip Points, Yellow, Olive Green 40.00
Lynchburg, No. 090, Aqua 1.00
Lynchburg, No. 090, Green, Straw Tint 1.00
Manhattan, No. 10, Blue Aqua 5.00
McLaughlin, No. 010, 7Up Green 35.00
McLaughlin, No. 010, Light Green, Amber Swirls, Wire Groove 1425.00
McLaughlin, No. 010, Yellow Green 285.00
McLaughlin, No. 030, Cornflower Blue 10.00
McLaughlin, No. 030, Ice Green, Large Embossing 2.00
McLaughlin, No. 030, Ice Green, Large Drip Points 3.00
McLaughlin, No. 050, Lime Green 5.00
McLaughlin, No. 060, Dark Aqua 1.00
McLaughlin, No. 060, Light Green 1.00
McLaughlin, No. 160, Light Green 1.00
Montreal Telegraph, No. 010, Blue, Milk Stringers 50.00
O.V.G., No. 010, Aqua 2.00
O.V.G., No. 010, Blue 5.00
O.V.G., No. 010, Celery Green 5.00
Postal, No. 010, Dark Aqua, Light Amber Swirls 1.00
Postal, No. 010, Sage Green 3.00
Prism, No. 010, Aqua 15.00
Santa Ana, Olive Green, Amber 248.00
Standard, No. 010, Royal Purple 75.00
Star, No. 010, Bright Blue 2.00
Star, No. 030, Wire Ridge, Aqua 55.00
Tel. Fed. Mex, Milky Swirls, Teal Green 150.00
W.E. Mfg., No. 040, Light Green 35.00
W.F.G., No. 010, Steel Blue, Graphite Steam 1.00
W.F.G. Co., No. 010, Gray Blue, Swirls 30.00
W.F.G. Co., No. 010, Sage Green 35.00
Whitall Tatum, No. 010, Dark Purple 40.00

IRISH BELLEEK, *see Belleek category.*

IRON is a metal that has been used by man since prehistoric times. It is a popular metal for tools and decorative items like doorstops that need as much weight as possible. Items are listed here or under other appropriate headings, such as Bookends, Doorstop, Kitchen, Match Holder, or Tool. The tool that is used for ironing clothes, an iron, is listed in the Kitchen category under Iron and Sadiron.

Ashtray, Drunk By Signpost, 5 In. 86.00

Ashtray, Griswold, Square 30.00
Ashtray, T.B. Woods Sons Co. 35.00
Ashtray, Wagner Ware, Frying Pan 14.00
Ball & Chain, Leg Shackle, Colorado Territorial Prison 220.00
Bell, Plantation, Cast Frame, Clapper, 19th Century, 14 ½ x 17 In. 1440.00
Bootjack, Naughty Nellie, 9 In. 60.00
Bootjack, Naughty Nellie, Figural, Painted, 10 x 5 x 3 In. 275.00
Bust, Female, Classical Style, Plinth Base, 24 x 20 x 14 In., Pair 1175.00
Cachepot, Napoleon III, Neoclassical, Ribbed, 2 Handles, White, 16 x 19 In., Pair 1440.00
Candleholder, 3-Footed, 61 In., Pair 140.00
Cap Bomb, Figural, Admiral Dewey, Ives, Nickel Plated, Early 1900s, 2 x 2 ½ x 1 In. 101.00
Cigar Cutter, Boy Thumbing Nose, 17 ½ In. 144.00
Cigar Cutter, Indian, Leans Back To Open Lid, Lion's Head, Monroe Mfg. Co., 10 In. 4300.00
Cuspidor, Figural, Dragon, Marked No. 3612, 12 In. .... *illus* 750.00
Dispenser, Cigarette, Elephant, Art Deco, Mechanical, Landon-Springer, 1890, 6 x 8 In. 175.00
Door Mat, Heart Shape Links, 24 Conjoined Rows, Pennsylvania, 1800s, 36 x 21 In. 1320.00
Figure, British, Unicorn, Single Side, Hollow, Painted, 19th Century, 17 x 26 In. 357.00
Figure, Eagle, 12 x 9 In. 115.00
Figure, Eagle, Gold Paint, 19th Century, 7 ¾ x 15 ¼ In. 264.00
Figure, Eagle, Mounting Holes, Painted Wooden Board, 10 ¼ In. 403.00
Figure, Eagle, Spread Wings, Fluted & Gilt Mahogany Pedestal, c.1900, 58 x 46 x 24 In. 2415.00
Figure, Eagle, Spread Wings, Mahogany Base, Gilt, 22 x 48 x 25 In. 4700.00
Figure, Lion, Lying Down, Flat Back, Black Matte Finish, Late 1800s, 13 ½ x 27 ½ In. 1020.00
Figure, Rabbit, Seated, Painted White, 20th Century, 11 ½ In., Pair 646.00
Figure, Shooting Gallery, Duck, Black Over White, 8 x 5 ½ In. 67.00
Figure, Showgirl, Saluting, Light Blue Outfit, Gold Highlights, Base, 23 x 7 In. 6325.00
Flint Striker, Basket Shape, 4 In. 38.00
Flint Striker, Birds Kissing, 4 x 3 In. 82.00
Flint Striker, Dog, 5 In. 60.00
Flint Striker, Lion, 5 In. 66.00
Flint Striker, Snake, 5 In. 110.00
Flower Tree, Cut Tin, Painted, 5 Flowers, Round Base, 19th Century, 16 x 14 In. 9600.00
Frog, Green Paint, 5 In. 60.00
Halbard, 22 In. 61.00
Horseshoe, Silver & White Paint, 17 ½ In. 201.00
Lamp, Sticking Tommy, Loop Terminal, 12 ½ In. .... *illus* 154.00
Mask, Smiling Man, Laborer's Cap, 12 ½ x 9 In. 1057.00
Meat Rack, Wrought, Pine Board, 13 Hooks, Hanging Brackets, 19th Century, 8 x 52 In. 230.00
Mold, Clay Pipes, Late 18th Century 185.00
Paperweight, Dolly Dimple, Painted, Cast, Hubley, 2 ⅝ In. 92.00
Paperweight, George Washington, Bust, Cast, Painted, 4 In. 88.00
Paperweight, Lincoln, On Bench, Cut Corners, Kraeuter & Co., 4 ½ x 3 ¼ In. 90.00
Pipe Kiln, Footed, Loop Handle, 13 In. 165.00
Plaque, Tavern Scene, Embossed, B & H 1814, 8 x 10 ¼ In. 550.00
Safe, Alpine Safe & Lock Co., A.P. Little, Landscape Scene, Cincinnati, Oh. 950.00
Safe, National Security, Shelves, 1500 Lb. 2530.00
Safe, Security, Cast Iron, Nickel Plated, 1887, 4 x 3 x 2 In. 40.00
Sculpture, Prophet, Holding Staff, Finger Pointing Upward, Stone Base, 28 x 13 In. 1195.00
Shield, Battle Scene, Bronzed Finish, 19th Century, 25 x 17 In. 168.00
Shoe Rest, Shoeshine, Horse, Black Paint, 7 In. .... *illus* 115.00
Shooting Gallery Target, Dog, Leaping, Yellow, Stand, 19th Century, 12 ¼ x 26 In. .... *illus* 11162.00
Shooting Gallery Target, Donkey, Bull's-Eye, Display Stand, 19th Century, 18 x 20 In. 1495.00
Shooting Gallery Target, Eagle, Disk Gong, Metal Stand, W. Wurfflein, Phila'd'a., 33 In. .... *illus* 8225.00
Shooting Gallery Target, Flying Duck, Cast 523.00
Shooting Gallery Target, Indian In Canoe, Cast 468.00
Shooting Gallery Target, Man, Wiggly Derriere, Cast 248.00
Shooting Gallery Target, Man In Top Hat, Cast 495.00
Shooting Gallery Target, Monkey, Standing, Side View, Cast 688.00
Soap Dish, Mammy, Basket On Head, Hubley, c.1930, 5 ½ In. 316.00
Strongbox, Lift-Out Tray, Initials RB On Top, Lock & Key, c.1900, 11 x 16 x 12 In. 633.00
Tongs, Wrought, Scissor Handles, 19 x 2 ⅝ In. 22.00
Tractor Seat, Cutout Sections, Walter A. Wood 95.00
Windmill Weight, Horse, Bobtail, Cast, Dempster Mill Mfg. Co., Wooden Base, 16 ½ In. 288.00
Windmill Weight, Horse, Bobtail, Dempster Mill Mfg. Co., c.1930, 16 ½ x 17 In. .... *illus* 360.00

Iron Hardware
The iron hardware used on platform rockers is often referred to as Lowentraut for Peter Lowentraut, who owned half the patent rights given to George Hall in 1887 for his invention of a swing mechanism at the base of a glider-rocker. Although the patent applied only to the hardware, not the chair, it was copied by many, and the name Lowentraut is sometimes used for any glider-rocker. The hardware design is still in use and replacements can be bought today.

I

Iron, Shooting Gallery Target, Dog, Leaping, Yellow, Stand, 19th Century, 12 ¼ x 26 In.
$11162.00

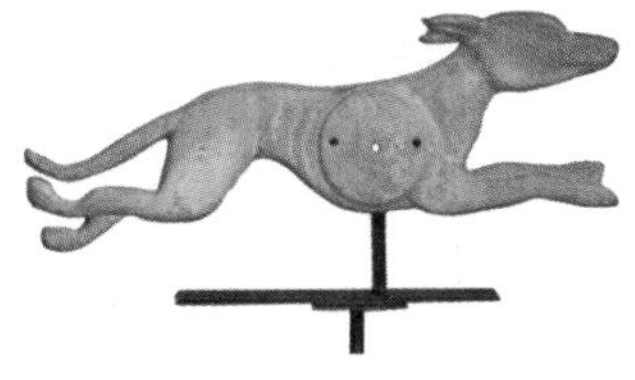

Iron, Shooting Gallery Target, Eagle, Disk Gong, Metal Stand, W. Wurfflein, Phila'd'a., 33 In.
$8225.00

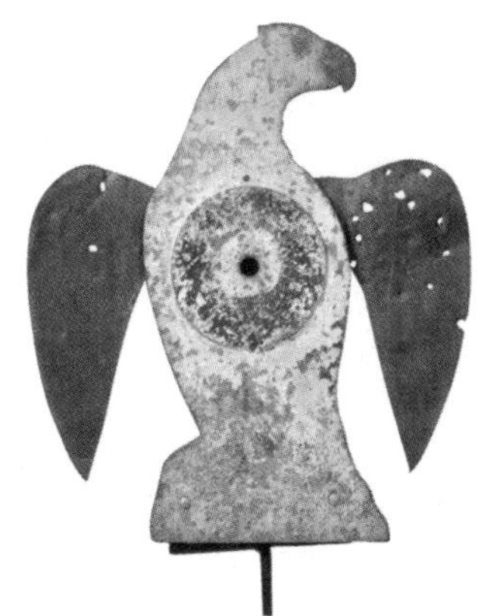

Iron, Windmill Weight, Horse, Bobtail, Dempster Mill Mfg. Co., c.1930, 16 ½ x 17 In.
$360.00

Ironstone, Coffeepot, Cable & Wheat, Marked, 10 ½ In.
$475.00

Ironstone, Relish, Grape & Leaf, Signed, Royal Ironstone, 8 ⅞ x 7 ⅜ In.
$50.00

Ironstone, Tureen, Cover, Lily-Of-The-Valley, Undertray, Ladle, Marked, 7 ½ In.
$110.00

Windmill Weight, Horse, Bobtail, Wire Bridle, Dempster Mill Mfg., c.1940, 17 x 16 In. 374.00
Windmill Weight, Horse, Docked Tail, Dempster Mill Mfg. Co., 17 x 18 In. 489.00
Windmill Weight, Rooster, Elgin Wind Power & Pump Co., 1900s, 9 In. 825.00

IRONSTONE china was first made in 1813. It gained its greatest popularity during the mid-nineteenth century. The heavy, durable, off-white pottery was made in white or was decorated with any of hundreds of patterns. Much flow blue pottery was made of ironstone. Some of the decorations were raised. Many pieces of ironstone are unmarked, but some English and American factories included the word *Ironstone* in their marks. Additional pieces may be listed in other categories, such as Chelsea Grape, Chelsea Sprig, Flow Blue, Gaudy Ironstone, Mason's Ironstone, Moss Rose, Staffordshire, and Tea Leaf Ironstone.

Bottle, Lid, Square, Black Ground, Stylized Flower Design, Gilt, 10 ¼ x 4 ¼ In., Pair 382.00
Coffeepot, Cable & Wheat, Marked, 10 ½ In. ...... *illus* 475.00
Cup, Man On Boneshaker, Woman On Tricycle, c.1870, 3 In. 220.00
Footbath, Geometric Design, Applied Handles, Multicolored, 8 ¾ x 18 In. 316.00
Pitcher, Multicolored, Jesters & Flowers, Blue Trim, White Ground, 8 ½ In. 100.00
Plate, Luncheon, Chinese Style, Gilt Highlights, England, c.1870, 9 In., 9 Piece 411.00
Platter, Challinor, Oval, 16 ½ In. 11.00
Platter, Imari Colors, Black & White Floral Panel Border, Ashworth, 16 x 20 In. 353.00
Platter, Multicolored, Flowers, Exotic Bird, c.1830 ...... 353.00
Platter, White Ground, Blue & Red Flowers, c.1850, 16 ¾ x 21 ½ In. 380.00
Platter, Wilder & Walker, Flower Border, Center Village Scene, 18 x 14 In. 30.00
Relish, Grape & Leaf, Signed, Royal Ironstone, 8 ⅞ x 7 ⅜ In. ...... *illus* 50.00
Sugar, Dome Lid, Bulbous, Eagle Above Banner, Blue, c.1868, 7 ½ In. 388.00
Tureen, Cover, Lily-Of-The-Valley, Undertray, Ladle, Marked, 7 ½ In. ...... *illus* 110.00
Urn, Cover, Victorian, Flowers, Grisaille Vine Border, Rim, Handles, 18 x 11 In. 294.00
Vase, Bottle Shape, Turkish Style, Blue Transfer, Iron Red & Green, Marked, 1 ½ In., Pair 748.00

ISPANKY figurines were designed by Laszlo Ispanky, who began his American career as a designer for Cybis Porcelains. In 1966, he established his own studio in Pennington, New Jersey; since 1976, he has worked for Goebel of North America. He works in stone, wood, or metal, as well as porcelain. The first limited edition figurines were issued in 1966.

Bust, Rosh Hashana, Bearded Man In Robe, Blowing Horn, 10 In. 250.00
Figurine, Dog Chasing Cat, Up Tree Stump, Parian, White, 9 ½ In. 46.00
Figurine, Miner, 12 x 5 In. 88.00
Figurine, Seminude Girl, Seated In Shell, 13 ¼ In. 130.00
Figurine, Storm, Bisque, Signed, 13 In. ...... *illus* 150.00
Figurine, Storm, White, Bisque, 13 In. 177.00

IVORY from the tusk of an elephant is thought by many to be the only true ivory. To most collectors, the term *ivory* also includes such natural materials as walrus, hippopotamus, or whale teeth or tusks, and some of the vegetable materials that are of similar texture and density. Other ivory items may be found in the Scrimshaw and Netsuke categories. Collectors should be aware of the recent laws limiting the buying and selling of elephant ivory and scrimshaw.

Apple, Pierced, Village Scene, Removable Stem, 5 In. 403.00
Boat, Chinese, Flags, Passengers, Carved Wood Stand, 19th Century, 14 ¼ In. 1553.00
Box, Birds, Flowers, Coral, Mother-Of-Pearl, Horn, Lacquer, Japan, 6 x 6 x 2 ½ In. 1880.00
Box, Carved, Flowers, Japan, 19th Century, 3 ½ In. 411.00
Box, Dragons, Vines & Flowers, 2 ¼ x 4 In. 450.00
Box, Flowers, Dragons, Chinese Export, 19th Century, 6 ¾ In. 1175.00
Box, Indian, Carved, Village Scene, Round, 5 x 6 In. 702.00
Box, Mother-Of-Pearl Inlay, Flowers, 1 x 1 ⅞ x 3 ⅜ In. 345.00
Box, Multicolored, Hinged Cover, Hand Painted Garden Scenes, 3 ½ x 2 ⅜ x 1 ⅛ In. 384.00
Box, Relief Carved, 2 Tigers Attacking Elephant, Cylindrical, Tiger Finial, Japan, 5 x 4 In. 540.00
Brushpot, Carved, Pierced, Dragons, Clouds, Cash Coin Ground, Chinese, 1800s, 8 In. 470.00
Brushpot, Dragons, Clouds, Chinese, 19th Century, 5 ¼ In. 529.00
Brushpot, Figural Scene, Cylindrical, c.1820, 4 In. 885.00
Case, Tubular, Threaded Cap, Carved Basket Weave, Braided Band, 4 ½ In. 115.00
Cigarette Holder, Art Deco Style, Roses, Daisies & Leaves, 1920s, 7 In. 49.00
Crucifix, Black Ground, Frame, Continental, 5 ½ x 4 ¼ In. 1053.00
Doctor's Doll, Carved, Chinese, Early 20th Century, 14 ¾ In. 353.00
Doctor's Doll, Carved, Head Resting On Pillow, Flower In Hair, Chinese, 5 In. 499.00
Doctor's Doll, Carved, Nude Woman Lying Down, Wood Base, Chinese, 12 In. 600.00

Doctor's Doll, Chinese, 4 ½ In. 351.00
Doctor's Doll, Chinese, Reclining, 8 In. 468.00
Fetish, Man, Seated, Holding Legs, Carved, 3 ½ In. 350.00
Figurine, 2 Parading Attendants, Oriental, Tree, 20th Century, 11 In. 944.00
Figurine, Archangel Michael, 19th Century, 8 ½ In. 384.00
Figurine, Asian Warrior, With Sword, Black Base, Chinese, 12 In. 325.00
Figurine, Bird, Hatching, Carved, Continental, Wooden Base, 2 In. 88.00
Figurine, Bishop In Miter, Rubies & Sapphires Adorned, Cloak, 13 ½ In.. .... 4248.00
Figurine, Boy, Exercising On Silver Bench, 2 In. 679.00
Figurine, Boy, Playing Game, c.1890, 2 ⅛ In.. .... 266.00
Figurine, Buddha, Seated, Wood Base, Chinese, 5 ½ In. 211.00
Figurine, Crusader, Flowing Hair, Robes, France, 19th Century, 7 In. 826.00
Figurine, Dog, Bird Pillow With Mallard In Its Mouth, Brown Glass Eyes, 1860, 6 In. 1800.00
Figurine, Elder, Mid 20th Century, 4 In. 118.00
Figurine, Elephant, Defending Himself Against Tigers, 18 ¼ In.. .... 3186.00
Figurine, Elephant, Trunk Raised Above Tusks, Carved Ebony Hardwood Base, 2 ½ In. 767.00
Figurine, Emperor, 19th Century, Chinese, 7 In. 387.00
Figurine, Emperor, Seated In Dragon Armchair, 5 In.. .... 224.00
Figurine, Exotic Bird, Mid 20th Century, 9 ¾ In. 1232.00
Figurine, Farmer, Holding Sheaf Of Rice, Japan, 19th Century, 8 In. 646.00
Figurine, Fisherman, Hauling Net, Ivory Handled Iron, Japan, 19th Century, 6 In. 705.00
Figurine, Fisherman, Japan, Mid 20th Century, 5 ½ In. 176.00
Figurine, Fisherman, With Net, Japan, 7 In.. .... 700.00
Figurine, Girl, Resting On Gilt Silver Bench, 1 ⅝ x 2 ⅜ In. 620.00
Figurine, Goddess Meditating, Carved, Chinese, Mid 20th Century, 8 In. 235.00
Figurine, Goddess Of Mercy, Lotus Blossom Over Shoulder & Male Attendant, 10 ⅜ In. 1888.00
Figurine, Horse, Running, Black Stand, Mid 20th Century, 2 ½ x 4 In. 340.00
Figurine, Japanese Woman, Lily Decorated Kimono, Fan, Wood Base, Oriental, 9 ¾ In.. .... 575.00
Figurine, John The Baptist, Flowing Hair, Wooden Plinth, 17 In. 4720.00
Figurine, Landscape, Pierced, Rocky Cliff, Willow Tree, Men With Scroll, 8 In.. .... 210.00
Figurine, Madonna, Pregnant, Spain, 15th Century, 5 ¾ In.. .... 1800.00
Figurine, Madonna & Child, Deep Folds, Wooden Plinth, 18 ½ In.. .... 4956.00
Figurine, Madonna & Child, Wood Plinth, Multicolored, 17 ½ In. 2124.00
Figurine, Man, Carrying Child On Back, On Rock, Japan, Late 19th Century, 4 ½ In.. .... 308.00
Figurine, Man, Kneeling On Platform On Oversized Basket, 10 In. 1180.00
Figurine, Man, Playing Flute On Barrel, 19th Century, 6 ½ In.. .... 112.00
Figurine, Man, Rooster, On Base, 12 In. 205.00
Figurine, Man, Seated With Fish Basket, Wood Base, Chinese, 3 x 4 In. 644.00
Figurine, Man, Supporting Basket Of Vegetables, Digging Tool In Hand, 13 ½ In. 1888.00
Figurine, Man, With Lantern, Japan, 6 ½ In. 205.00
Figurine, Man, Woman, Child, Chinese, 7 In. 439.00
Figurine, Mask Maker, Kneeling On Long Table, Surrounded By Artwork, 3 ⅝ x 7 ¼ In. 767.00
Figurine, Meiren, Holding Flowering Branch, Chinese, 15 ¾ In., Pair 1888.00
Figurine, Mother, Multicolored, Japan, Mid 20th Century, 7 In. 118.00
Figurine, Mother & Child, Multicolored, Japan, Mid 20th Century, 7 ¼ In. 118.00
Figurine, Mountain Goat, Bearded, Continental, 2 ½ In. 118.00
Figurine, Musician, Standing On Wooden Barrel, Playing Flute, c.1890, 6 ¼ In. 443.00
Figurine, Mythological Figure, Flowing Water, Holding Sword, Dwarf, Oriental, 11 ¼ In. 374.00
Figurine, Nobleman, Chinese, Early 20th Century, 8 In.. .... 176.00
Figurine, Oriental Maiden, Basket Of Yarn Swinging From Arm, 20 ⅛ In.. .... 1888.00
Figurine, Owl, Antoghame, 3 ½ In. 199.00
Figurine, Peasant, With Wine Goblet, Wooden Baluster Base, c.1890, 5 In.. .... 413.00
Figurine, Peking Opera Warrior, Holding Flag, Beard, Sword, Chinese, 10 In. 708.00
Figurine, Praying Nun, Clasped Hands, 17th Century, 4 ⅜ In. 375.00
Figurine, Pumpkin, Figures, Wood Base, 21/2 x 4 In. 205.00
Figurine, Quan Yin & Elephant, Seated On Lotus Throne, Holding Vase, 5 ¼ x 3 ¼ In. 644.00
Figurine, Quan Yin, Attendants, Carved Wood Base, Chinese, 20th Century, 10 In.. .... 649.00
Figurine, Quan Yin, Holding Orchid, Fan, Chinese, 19 ¾ In. 1998.00
Figurine, Quan Yin, Holding Sprig, Wood Base, 9 ¾ In. .... *illus* 600.00
Figurine, Quan Yin, Wood Base, 37 In. 5265.00
Figurine, Reindeer, Carved, Stylized Round Designs, Rock Base, Continental, 6 In. 411.00
Figurine, Sage, With Staff, Redwood Base, Chinese, 12 x 13 In. 468.00
Figurine, Samurai, Fly Whisk, Signed, Leaf Symbol, 10 In. 546.00
Figurine, Sea Dragon, Fighting Demonic Man, Inked, Red Eyes, 10 ¼ In.. .... 780.00
Figurine, Shao Lao, Chinese, 19th Century, 6 ½ In.. .... 147.00

Ispanky, Figurine, Storm, Bisque, Signed, 13 In.
$150.00

Ivory, Figurine, Quan Yin, Holding Sprig, Wood Base, 9 ¾ In.
$600.00

Ivory, Okimono, Carved Figure, Samurai, Japan, 8 In.
$885.00

Ivory, Puzzle Ball, Pierced Flower Heads, Chain, 3 ½ In.
$265.00

I

TIP
Moths will attack ivory and bone and make small "pinholes" when the larvae hatch. Don't wash the ivory. To kill the moth larvae, put the ivory in the freezer for a few hours.

Ivory, Rattle, Whalebone, Pierced, Metal Bell, New England, 19th Century, 6 In.
$2400.00

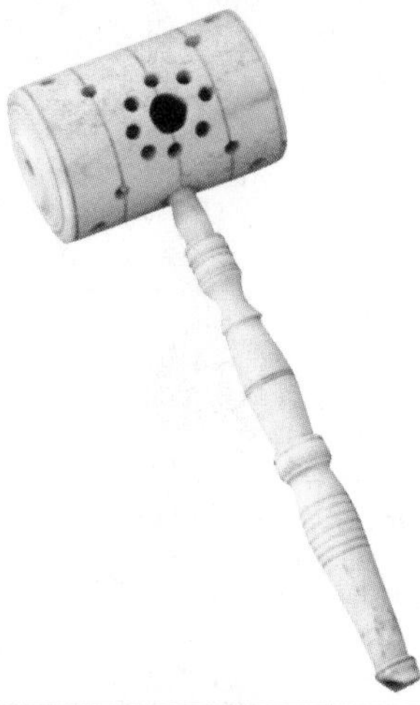

Ivory, Screen, Table, Riverscape, Foo Dog, Rectangular Plaque, Chinese, 10½ x 5¼ In.
$1298.00

Figurine, Sleeping Man, Wood Base, Chinese, 4 In. 211.00
Figurine, Swan, Base, Continental, 19th Century, 4 x 5½ In. 1000.00
Figurine, Taoist Worthies, Phoenixes, 6¾ In. 944.00
Figurine, Warrior, With Sword, Spear, Japan, 19th Century, 6¼ In. 499.00
Figurine, Woman, Chinese, 20th Century, 14 In. 470.00
Figurine, Woman, Holding Chrysanthemum, Multicolored, Chinese, 13½ x 3½ In. 570.00
Figurine, Woman, Holding Flowers, Quan Yin, Oriental, Stand, 14 In. 633.00
Figurine, Woman, Holding Grapes, Chinese, 19th Century, 12½ In. 2585.00
Figurine, Woman, Nude, Classical Style, Venus, Draped Urn, Wooden Base, 7 In. 633.00
Figurine, Woman, With Flowers, Multicolored, c.1900, 14 In. 2006.00
Figurine, Young Woman, Tending To Baby In Her Arms & Toddler At Her Feet, 4⅝ In. 767.00
Figurine, Goddess Lakshmi, Inlaid Hardwood Stand, India, 19th Century, 18 In. 6463.00
Figurine, Goddess Saravati, Inlaid Hardwood Stand, India, Late 19th Century, 18 In. 8225.00
Figurine, Woman, Standing, Mughal Court Costume, Stand, India, 1800s, 11 In., Pair 2350.00
Foo Dog, Male, Female, Octagonal Plinth, Wearing Tasseled Collar, Chinese, 5 In. 420.00
Gavel, Whalebone, Cylindrical, Tapered Shaft, 19th Century 700.00
Group, 2 Men, Staves, Mushrooms, Toads, Signed, 11⅝ In. 316.00
Group, 6 People, Around Covered Bridge, Pine Tree, 25¼ In. 920.00
Group, 6 Wolves Pursuing Ram, Mastodon Ivory, 11½ In. 288.00
Group, Buddha, Children Playing, Chinese, 9 In. 708.00
Group, Man, Bird, Children At Play, Chinese, 13½ In. 1770.00
Jar, Carved, Mid 20th Century, 4¼ x 2½ In., Pair 235.00
Jar, Cover, Court Scene, Lotus Bud Finial, Chinese, 20th Century, 9 In. 1180.00
Jar, Cover, Court Scene, High Relief, Lotus Bud Finial, Chinese, Early 20th Century, 9 In. 2242.00
Jar, Cover, Multicolored, Chinese, Mid 20th Century, 2⅞ x 1½ In. 88.00
Letter Opener, French Dieppe, c.1850, 9 x 1 In. 595.00
Okimono, Carved Figure, Fisherman, Broad Brimmed Hat, Pole, Basket, 8 In. 767.00
Okimono, Carved Figure, Fisherman, Holding Bamboo, Japan, 6½ In. 354.00
Okimono, Carved Figure, Hunter Capturing Eagle, 1800s, 7½ x 5 In. 2500.00
Okimono, Carved Figure, Man & Boy Waving, Japan, 20th Century, 6¾ In. 590.00
Okimono, Carved Figure, Man Carrying Lunch Pail, 1868-1912, 6½ x 2½ x 3 In. 748.00
Okimono, Carved Figure, Monkeys, Peaches, Japan, 19th Century, 2 In. 353.00
Okimono, Carved Figure, Samurai, Japan, 8 In. *illus* 885.00
Page Turner, Elephant, Flowers, Art Nouveau, Silver, Women, c.1890, 10 In. 100.00
Picture, Mythological Scene, Zeus & Ganymedes, Eagle, Nude Woman, 2⅝ In. 764.00
Pie Crimper, Carved, Reeding & Baleen Inlaid Dots, Tortoiseshell Ring, 1¼ x 8¼ In. 2070.00
Pipe, Opium, Fist Holding Opium Head, Bamboo Shaft, Chinese, 19th Century, 15 In. 657.00
Plaque, Carved, Openwork, Phoenix, Dragon, Vining Roses, Crosshatch Border, 4 x 11 In. 720.00
Plaque, Hunting Scene, Continental, 19th Century, 3 x 4¼ In. 325.00
Portrait, Royal Figure, Long Wig, Classical Dress, Carved, Oval, Continental, 2⅜ In. 382.00
Puzzle Ball, Carved, Pierced, Round, Dragon Pedestal Stand, c.1950, 7 x 2½ In. 264.00
Puzzle Ball, Pierced Flower Heads, Chain, 3½ In. *illus* 265.00
Puzzle Ball, Stand, Concentric Balls, Dragons, Flowers, Prancing Horses, 4⅞ In. 518.00
Rattle, Whalebone, Pierced, Metal Bell, New England, 19th Century, 6 In. *illus* 2400.00
Screen, Table, Mother-Of-Pearl, Lacquer, Shibiyama, Japan, c.1900, 16 x 13 In. 470.00
Screen, Table, Riverscape, Foo Dog, Rectangular Plaque, Chinese, 10½ x 5¼ In. *illus* 1298.00
Shoehorn, Shell, Eagle & Shield, Inscribed Lt. McBride, 1789 1100.00
Sphere, Hinged, Carved 18th Century Garden Scene, 19th Century, 2¼ x 4 In. 1416.00
Tankard, 6 Panels, Kings, Gilt Panels, Carved, 1800s, 8½ In., 1 Liter 11213.00
Tankard, Cherub Warriors, Silver Mounts, Chain On Thumblift, Late 1800s, 10 In., 1 Liter 2760.00
Tankard, Festive Scene, Silver Base & Lid, Mother & Child Finial, Marked, 800, 17½ In. 14375.00
Tankard, Hunting Scenes, 3 Cherubs On Lid, 1800s, 8 In., ⅓ Liter 5175.00
Tankard, Scene, Brass Lining, Silver Mounted Top, Hinged Cover, 8¾ In. 3776.00
Trumpet, Side Blown, Stylized Head, Carved, Africa, 18½ In. 646.00
Tusk, Carved, Figures In Garden, Chinese, 19th Century, 18 In. 1763.00
Tusk, Carved, Pierced, Buddha Images, Leaf Scrolls, Burma, Early 19th Century, 56¾ In. 1410.00
Tusk, Carved, Scholars, Mountain Landscape, Chinese, 9½ In. 294.00
Tusk, Kongo, Carved Spiral Scene, Men, Women, Africa, 12½ In. 353.00
Tusk, Pagoda, Pine Tree, Figures, Boats, Mountain Landscape, Chinese, Early 1900s, 48 In. 4720.00
Tusk, Walrus, 19th Century, 22¼ x 2¾ x 1¾ In. 400.00
Urn, Cover, Carved, 2 Handles, Chinese, Mid 20th Century, 14 x 10 In. 176.00
Urn, Cover, Carved, Black Base, Mid 20th Century, 8 x 2¾ In. 176.00
Vase, Cover, Warriors, Chinese, 27 In., Pair 2006.00
Vase, Figural Foo Dogs Cover, Dragon Scene In Relief, 2 Handles, 13½ x 16¼ In. 2596.00

Wax Stamp, Seal, Hollow Eyes, Hooked Nose.. 295.00
Wrist Support, Pavilion, Figures Under Pine Trees, Leaf Finial, Chinese 826.00

JACK-IN-THE-PULPIT vases, shaped like trumpets, resemble the wild flower named jack-in-the-pulpit. The design originated in the late Victorian years. Vases in the jack-in-the-pulpit shape were made of ceramic or glass, and the complete list of page references can be found in the index.

Vase, Pansies, Amberina, Coralene, 3 Crystal Branch Feet, 12 In.......................... 1060.00
Vase, Pink, White, Isle Of Wight Alum Bay, Label, 11 ½ In......................... *illus* 29.00
Vase, Vaseline, Optic Ribbed, Enameled Flowers, Footed, 15 In. 177.00

JADE is the name for two different minerals, nephrite and jadeite. Nephrite is the mineral used for most early Oriental carvings. Jade is a very tough stone that is found in many colors from dark green to pale lavender. Jade carvings are still being made in the old styles, so collectors must be careful not to be fooled by recent pieces. Jade jewelry is found in this book under Jewelry.

Bowl, Stand, Chinese, c.1920, 2 ½ x 5 In. 147.00
Bowl, Swirling Dragons, Clouds, Spinach Green, Chinese, 11 In......................... 3408.00
Box, Diamonds, Lid, 3 ½ x 2 ½ In. 3163.00
Brush Holder, Birds, Flowering Trees, Carved, Celadon, Chinese, 5 ¼ In. 7638.00
Brush Washer, Fruit Vine, Egg Shape Bowl, 1 ⅞ x 4 ¾ In. 885.00
Buckle, Dragon, Pine Tree, Ice Green, Chinese, 19th Century, 2 ¾ x 2 ¼ In. 823.00
Buckle, Dragons, Green, White, 19th Century, 3 ½ In. 764.00
Censer, Bosses, Foo Dog Finial, Handles, Animal Mask Feet, Chinese...................... 5900.00
Censer, Ogre Heads, 3-Footed, Foo Dog On Cover, 5 ¼ In. 3658.00
Cup, Landscape, Translucent Celadon, Flowering Branch Handle, Hardwood Stand, Chinese, 4 In. 2350.00
Figurine, 8 Precious Things, Pale Green, Hardwood Stand, Chinese, 19th Century, 17 x 5 In.. 6463.00
Figurine, Birds On Cherry Blossom Branch, Translucent Amber, Crimson, Opal Jade, 5 ¾ In.. 354.00
Figurine, Buddha, Jadite, Wood Base, Chinese, 9 ½ In. 146.00
Figurine, Buddha, Meditating, Lotus Position, Overlapped Leaf Base, 7 In.................. 502.00
Figurine, Chicken, Dark Green, 2 ½ x 3 In. 117.00
Figurine, Courting Couple, Early 20th Century, 10 In. 55.00
Figurine, Dog, Reclining, Chinese, c.1900, 1 x 2 In., 2 Piece 117.00
Figurine, Duck, White, Chinese, 1 ¾ x 2 In. 1062.00
Figurine, Goddess Holding Peony, Gray, Green, Chinese, Early 20th Century, 9 ¼ In. 705.00
Figurine, Herons, Flowering Tree, Veined 2-Tone, Green, 20th Century, 16 ½ In. 819.00
Figurine, Man, Celadon, Chocolate Inclusions, Chinese, 9 ½ In. 885.00
Figurine, Mythical Animal, Wood Base, Chinese, 5 x 9 ½ In............................. 643.00
Figurine, Mythical Animal, Yellow, Green, Tan, Russet, 5 ½ In........................... 2938.00
Figurine, Pavilion, Person Under Pine Tree, White, Chinese, 4 ¾ In...................... 1888.00
Figurine, Peacock, Pierced Tail, Green, Wood Base, 13 ½ In. .... *illus* 200.00
Figurine, Phoenix, Peony, Pale Green, Apple Green, 9 ½ In............................. 705.00
Figurine, Quan Yin, Holding Lotus Pod, 13 ¼ In.. .... 1180.00
Figurine, Woman, Fan, Flowers, Celadon Stone, Chinese, 10 In. 823.00
Figurine, Woman, Hoisting Tray With Large Fruit, 9 ¾ In............................... 266.00
Figurine, Buddha, Robed, Holding Chinese Scepter, Nephrite, 8 ⅛ In. 115.00
Figurine, Buddha, Sitting, Green, 2 In.. .... 345.00
Group, Man With Double Gourd, Ram, Child, White, Chinese, Late 1700s, 4 In............. 3835.00
Group, Mountain, Liu Hai, Teasing Toad, Cresting Waves, Chinese, 6 ¼ x 6 In.............. 210.00
Hairpin, Chinese, 19th Century, 8 In. 1293.00
Inkwell, Foo Dog Heads With Loose Rings On Sides, Spinach Green, 4 ¾ In. 6490.00
Letter Knife, Gilded Metal, Floral Engraved Blade, 9 ½ In. 364.00
Pendant, Dragons, Multicolored, Chinese, 3 ¼ In. 944.00
Pendant, Mythical Animal, Calligraphy Reverse, Chinese, 20th Century, 2 x 1 ¼ In. 531.00
Pendant, Peach, White, Chinese, 2 ¾ In. 236.00
Scepter, Branch, Gray, Green, 13 In.. .... 1880.00
Screen, Carved Fruit, Ink, Rosewood Inset, Oval Panels, Chinese, 19th Century, 14 x 7 ½ In. . 1763.00
Screen, Table, Celadon Panel, Seal Character, Rosewood Frame, Chinese, 14 ½ x 12 In. 1880.00
Sculpture, 3 Rams, Celadon Green Stone, 18th Century.................................. 705.00
Sculpture, Crane, Pine Tree, Gray Stone, 11 ½ In.. .... 531.00
Teapot, Carved, Green, Chinese, 4 x 6 In. 3744.00
Urn, Carved, Teakwood Base, 8 In. 235.00
Vase, Cover, Celadon, Chinese, 5 In.. .... 4720.00
Vase, Flowering Lotus, Elephant Head, Loose Ring Handles, Apple......................... 944.00

Jack-In-The-Pulpit, Vase, Pink, White, Isle Of Wight Alum Bay, Label, 11 ½ In.
$29.00

Jade, Figurine, Peacock, Pierced Tail, Green, Wood Base, 13 ½ In.
$200.00

TIP

To test a piece of jade to see if it is real, use a small penknife. Rub the tip of the knife across the bottom of the piece until there is a mark. A white line means the knife scratched the stone and it is not jade. A black line means the stone scratched the blade and it is probably jade.

Jasperware, Pancake Server, White Sprigs, Mocha Ground, 19th Century, 10 In.
$225.00

Jewelry, Bracelet, Bakelite, Philadelphia, Laminated, Green, Amber, Butterscotch, 1½ In.
$3890.00

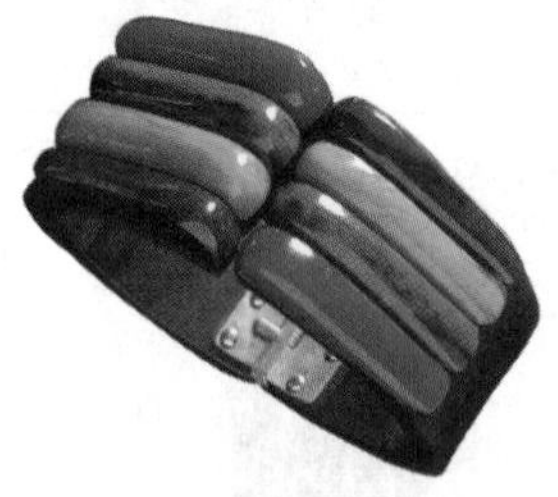

Jewelry, Bracelet, Brass, Green Enamel Inlay, Art Deco, 7¾ x 1¾ In.
$367.00

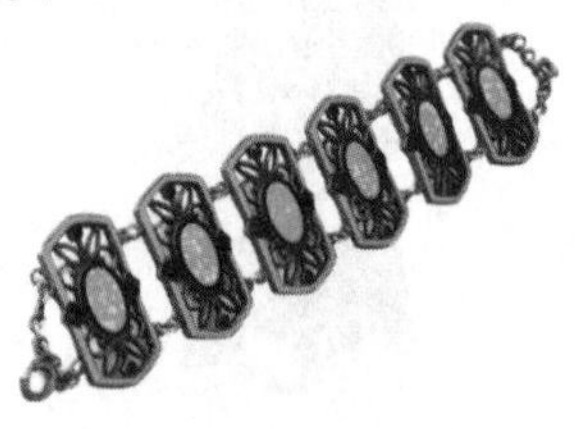

Jewelry, Bracelet, Sterling Silver, Link, Concave Shape, Polished, Marked, Mexico
$175.00

Jewelry, Bracelet, Cameo, Shell, Malachite, Mother-Of-Pearl, Coral, 14K Gold, 7¼ x ¾ In.
$1195.00

JAPANESE WOODBLOCK PRINTS *are listed in this book in the Print category under Japanese.*

JASPERWARE can be made in different ways. Some pieces are made from a solid-colored clay with applied raised designs of a contrasting colored clay. Other pieces are made entirely of one color clay with raised decorations that are glazed with a contrasting color. Additional pieces of jasperware may also be listed in the Wedgwood category or under various art potteries.

Pancake Server, White Sprigs, Mocha Ground, 19th Century, 10 In. . . . . *illus* 225.00
Pitcher, Bulbous, Molded Spout, Grape Leaf Band, Great Seal Of U.S., Brown, 7 In. 657.00

JEWELRY, whether made from gold and precious gems or plastic and colored glass, is popular with collectors. Values are determined by the intrinsic value of the stones and metal and by the skill of the craftsmen and designers. Victorian and older jewelry have been collected since the 1950s. More recent interests are Art Deco and Edwardian styles, Mexican and Danish silver jewelry, and beads of all kinds. Copies of almost all styles are being made. American Indian jewelry is listed in the Indian category. Tiffany jewelry is listed here.

Belt Buckle, Silver, Cartouche Shape, Niello Design, Sword Latch, Russia, 1880s, 28 In. 690.00
Bracelet, 3 Onyx Intaglios, Bezel Set, Rectangular Plaques, Beads, Bjarne Art Silver Shop, 7 In. . . 646.00
Bracelet, 7 Emeralds, Full Cut Diamonds, Platinum, c.1960, 7½ In. 8225.00
Bracelet, 7 Gold Coins, Liberty Head, Suspended, 14K Gold, 8 In. 1880.00
Bracelet, 14K Bicolor Gold, Faceted Domes Joined By Links, Flower Clasp, 1775, 6 In. 353.00
Bracelet, 18K Yellow Gold, Greek Style, Ram's Head Terminal 708.00
Bracelet, 18K Yellow Gold, Rectangular Links, Peruvian Herders & Farm Scene 1180.00
Bracelet, 93 Diamonds, 18K White Gold, Cartier 7434.00
Bracelet, Amethyst, 14K Gold, David Yurman, 7 In. 881.00
Bracelet, Bakelite, Bangle, Butterscotch, 1 x 3 In. 115.00
Bracelet, Bakelite, Philadelphia, Laminated, Green, Amber, Butterscotch, 1½ In. . . . . . . *illus* 3890.00
Bracelet, Bangle, 14K Yellow Gold, Engraved, Inset Coral. 413.00
Bracelet, Bangle, 18K Yellow Gold, Round Scrolls, Blue Enamel Starburst, Beads 2360.00
Bracelet, Bangle, 34 Diamonds, 14K White Gold, Tiffany & Co. 1888.00
Bracelet, Bangle, Bakelite, Marbleized, Butterscotch, Olive, Amber, Orange, 1¼ In. 489.00
Bracelet, Bangle, Blue Topaz, Sterling Silver, 14K Gold, David Yurman, 6¼ In. 441.00
Bracelet, Bangle, Blue Topaz, Sterling Silver Cables, David Yurman, 7 x ¾ In. 598.00
Bracelet, Bangle, Chains, Snake, Expandable, Gold, Forstner, 7½ x ¾ In. 1434.00
Bracelet, Bangle, Diamond Bands, 18K Gold, Ribbed, Amethyst, Peridot, Bulgari, 6 In. 3408.00
Bracelet, Bangle, Diamonds, Sterling Silver, 18K White Gold, David Yurman, 6¼ In. 1175.00
Bracelet, Bangle, Diamonds, Blue Enamel, 18K Gold, Tiffany & Co., 6½ In. 2271.00
Bracelet, Bangle, Diamonds, Graduated, Mine Cut, Opals, 18K Gold, Hinged 3565.00
Bracelet, Bangle, Emerald, Gypsy Set, Diamonds, 14K Gold, Tiffany & Co., 6⅝ In. 881.00
Bracelet, Bangle, Garnets, Bezel Set, 14K Gold, Riker Brothers, 6 In. 3819.00
Bracelet, Bangle, Gold, Multicolored, Enamel, Elephant Terminals, India, 6¼ In. 823.00
Bracelet, Bangle, Hinged, Horses, Diamond Eyes, 18K Gold, Carrera Y Carrera, 7 x ½ In. 1838.00
Bracelet, Bangle, Hinged, Beaded Wirework Accents, Etruscan Revival, 7⅛ In. 3290.00
Bracelet, Bangle, Hinged, Plaque, Full Diamonds, 14K Gold, c.1970, 6 In. 3760.00
Bracelet, Bangle, Onyx Cabochons, Faux Pearls, Flowers, Stanley Hagler, c.1945. . . . . 390.00
Bracelet, Bangle, Sterling Silver, Hans Hansen 174.00
Bracelet, Bangle, Tricolor 18K Gold, Panther Head Terminals, Cartier, 6⅝ In. 3819.00
Bracelet, Black Enamel Center Circles, Diamonds, Red Stones, Seed Pearls 345.00
Bracelet, Bow, Hairwork, Blond, Diamond Ribbon, Pearls, Gold, Victorian, 7 In. 823.00
Bracelet, Brass, Green Enamel Inlay, Art Deco, 7¾ x 1¾ In. . . . . *illus* 367.00
Bracelet, Cameo, Lava, 6 Plaques, Hermes, Diana, Classical Figures, 10K Gold, 7 In. 1058.00
Bracelet, Cameo, Shell, Malachite, Mother-Of-Pearl, Coral, 14K Gold, 7¼ x ¾ In. . . . . . . *illus* 1195.00
Bracelet, Cameo Slide, Multicolored Gemstone, 14K Gold 944.00
Bracelet, Charm, 14K Gold, Triple Figure 8 Shaped Links, Chain, 5 Charms, 7½ In. 230.00
Bracelet, Charm, 14K Gold Chain, 9 Charms, Locket, Cameo, Seals, Bee. 1150.00
Bracelet, Charm, 18K Gold, Hearts, Sterling Silver, Diamonds, J. Ripka, 8¼ In. 823.00
Bracelet, Charm, Spanish Silver, Coins Dated 1768, 1774, 1799, 1807, 1808, Link Chain, 7 In. 59.00
Bracelet, Coral, Reclining Cherubs, Flowing Garments, 14K Gold, Hinged, 5⅝ In. 1998.00
Bracelet, Coral, Red, 25 Strands, 14K Gold, Cartier, 9 In. 3480.00
Bracelet, Coral Beads, Orange, 3 Strands, 14K Gold, Applied Wirework, 7 In. 1175.00
Bracelet, Cuff, Copper, Brass, Patinated, Oval Aperture, Wirework, Art Smith 1410.00
Bracelet, Cuff, Copper, Patinated, Brass Wire, Marked, Art Smith. 2703.00
Bracelet, Cuff, Hinged, Sterling Silver, Curled Feather, Mexico, c.1980, Pair 510.00
Bracelet, Cuff, Hinged, Ram's Head, 18K Gold, Ruby & Sapphire, Zolotas, 7 In. 3173.00
Bracelet, Cuff, Hinged, 9 Leaves, Textured Surface, 18K Gold, Buccellati, ¾ In. 5288.00
Bracelet, Cuff, Red Lizard Skin, Gold Tone Metal Mount, Marked, Hermes 270.00

Bracelet, Cuff, Ribbed, Flexible, 14K Gold, Signed, Forstner, 6½ In. 588.00
Bracelet, Cuff, Serpent, Links, Gold Tone Metal, Pearls, Glass, Beads, Miriam Haskell, c.1960 300.00
Bracelet, Cuff, Sterling Silver, Amber, Textured, Oxidized, Geometric Pattern, 3 x 2¼ In. 225.00
Bracelet, Cuff, Sterling Silver, Hammered, Turquoise, Bezel Set, Art Silver Shop, Chicago 294.00
Bracelet, Diamond, Cultured Pearl, 18K Gold, Signed, Tiffany & Co., 7⅜ In. 2468.00
Bracelet, Diamonds, 18K Gold, Hammerman Brothers, 7 In. 1645.00
Bracelet, Emerald, Prong Set, Diamond Melee, 18K Gold, Tiffany & Co., 7¾ In. 2115.00
Bracelet, Etoile, Star Design, 18K Bicolor Gold, Rope Twist Border, Buccellati, 7⅜ In. 4230.00
Bracelet, Flexible, 3 Sections, Rhinestone Clusters, Marquise & Round Cut, c.1955 150.00
Bracelet, Flowers & Leaves, Link, Blue Stone, 18K Gold, Georg Jensen, 7½ In. 2468.00
Bracelet, Free-Form, Single Cut Diamond Set Arches, Ribbon, Gold, c.1960, 7 x ⅞ In. 900.00
Bracelet, Glass, Links, Green, Cylindrical, Stepped Terminals, Stretch, Lalique 3643.00
Bracelet, Glass Discs, Frosted, Striated, Beaded Edges, Rondeles Plates, Lalique, 1927 1880.00
Bracelet, Green, Brown Glass, Silver, Copper, Gold, Leaf Clasp, Arts & Crafts, H. French 2115.00
Bracelet, Lady Godiva, Glass Lampwork Beads, Quartz, Rock Crystal, 8 In. 96.00
Bracelet, Leaf Link, 10K Gold, Late 20th Century 264.00
Bracelet, Link, 18K Gold, Ribbed Bars, Black Enamel, Art Deco, France, 7¼ In. 764.00
Bracelet, Link, 18K Gold, Orange, Coral & Umber Stones, Tiffany & Co., 7¾ In. 3120.00
Bracelet, Link, 18K Pink Gold, c.1940, 7½ x 1⁵⁄₁₆ In. *illus* 2151.00
Bracelet, Link, 22K Gold, Flower Form, Diamonds, Sapphire, Ron Rizzo, 7½ x ⅝ In. 1793.00
Bracelet, Link, Arched, Pierced, Flowers, Hammered, Sterling Silver, Georg Jensen 764.00
Bracelet, Link, Bird & Leaf, Labradorites, Cabochon, Bezel Set, Georg Jensen, 7⅜ In. 1175.00
Bracelet, Link, Box Shaped, 18K Yellow Gold, Amethyst, Retro, c.1940 1440.00
Bracelet, Link, Brickwork, Buckle, Diamonds, 18K Gold, Adjustable, Retro, 7¾ In. 1528.00
Bracelet, Link, Diamond, Panels, Pierced, Beaded, 14K Gold, Art Deco, 7 In. 1560.00
Bracelet, Link, Diamond Melee, Curb, 18K Gold, Tiffany & Co., c.1970, 7½ In. 4348.00
Bracelet, Link, Flexible, Multicolored, Rhinestones, Brown, Orange, Green, White, c.1960 180.00
Bracelet, Link, Mesh, Diamond Terminals, Clasp, 14K, Art Deco, Box, c.1980, 7 In. 3120.00
Bracelet, Link, Oval, Double, Sterling Silver, Nanna Ditzel, Georg Jensen, 7⅛ In. 1175.00
Bracelet, Link, Reeded, 14K Gold, Tourmalines, c.1930, 7 In. 5581.00
Bracelet, Link, Sailing Ships, 18K Yellow Gold, Cartier, Box 502.00
Bracelet, Link, Sterling Silver, Scrolls, Amethysts, Beads, Murrle Bennett & Co., 7⅝ In. 529.00
Bracelet, Link, Sterling Silver, Oval, Birds, Leaves, Buds, Georg Jensen, 7 In. 999.00
Bracelet, Link, Swirls, Geometric Border, Red Line, 18K Gold, Art Deco, 7½ In. 805.00
Bracelet, Malachite, 2½ In. 35.00
Bracelet, Medallion, Stylized Flowers, Round & Triangular Cut Rhinestones, c.1950 30.00
Bracelet, Micro Mosaic, Flowers, Yellow & Green Tiles, Gold Tone Metal, 6½ In. 14.00
Bracelet, Millefiori Beads, 18K, 6 Round Links, Rope Twist Border, Etruscan Revival 11750.00
Bracelet, Onyx, Pearls, Garnet, Pink Tourmaline, Citrine, Sapphire, Peridot, 1935, 7 In. 6169.00
Bracelet, Pearls, Diamonds, 18K White Gold Rondels, 18K Gold Clasp, Cartier, 8¼ In. 5676.00
Bracelet, Pietra Dura, 6 Plaques, Flower Shape, Rope Twist Frames, 18K Gold, 7 In. 6169.00
Bracelet, Plaques, Hercules & His Labors, Gold, Alfonso Germano, c.1962, 6⅞ In. 2820.00
Bracelet, Plastic, Red, Gold, Spring Hinge, 2½ In. 35.00
Bracelet, Platinum, 18K Gold, Diamonds, David Webb, 7⅛ In. 6169.00
Bracelet, Platinum, Aquamarine Beads, Leaf Spacers, Diamonds, Waterman, 6⅝ In. 2938.00
Bracelet, Platinum, Emerald Cut Aquamarines, Art Deco, 7½ In. 4200.00
Bracelet, Platinum, Sapphires, Diamonds, Straight Line, Sophia D., 7¼ In. 8365.00
Bracelet, Ribbon, Adjustable, Shaded Enameled Pods, 14K Gold, c.1960, ¾ x 9¼ In. 1200.00
Bracelet, Scarabs, Lapis, Carved, Split Pearl, Gold Mount, Edward Oakes, c.1929, 7½ In. 9988.00
Bracelet, Sea Glass, Green & Brown, Mixed Metal, Arts & Crafts, Hazel French 2115.00
Bracelet, Shells, Sterling Silver, Georg Jensen, 7¼ In. 529.00
Bracelet, Snake, Double Chain, Suspended Joker Charm, 14K Gold, Forstner, 7¼ In. 1058.00
Bracelet, Sterling Silver, Arched Oval Links, Pearl Clasp, Georg Jensen, 7⅜ In. 940.00
Bracelet, Sterling Silver, Colorless Stone Accents, Hermes, 7¾ In. 1293.00
Bracelet, Sterling Silver, Flower-Shaped Links, Hammered, Pierced, Georg Jensen 764.00
Bracelet, Sterling Silver, Hammered, Claire Falkenstein, 2 x 2⅞ In. *illus* 900.00
Bracelet, Sterling Silver, Heart Form Clasp, 18K Gold, Scott Kay, 7¾ In. 441.00
Bracelet, Sterling Silver, Landers Blue Turquoise 900.00
Bracelet, Sterling Silver, Link, Concave Shape, Polished, Marked, Mexico *illus* 175.00
Bracelet, Sterling Silver, Spratling, 1940s, 2¼ x 2½ In. *illus* 1300.00
Bracelet, Turquoise Beads, 18K Gold Link Chain, Box Clasp, Tiffany & Co., 7½ In. 1554.00
Bracelet, Turquoise Nugget, Sterling Silver 358.00
Bracelet, Wheat Design, 18K Gold, France, c.1960, 7¾ x 11/16 In. *illus* 1075.00
Bracelet & Earrings, Sterling, Leaf & Berry Links, Oval Spacers, Kalo Shop 881.00
Bracelet & Pin, Flower, Lily Pad, Sterling Silver, Turquoise, M. Gage, 3-In. Pin, 7-In. Bracelet 382.00
Bracelet Set, Bakelite, Zigzag, Yellow, Red, Butterscotch, Nesting, 1⅝ In., 5 Piece *illus* 588.00

Jewelry, Bracelet, Link, 18K Pink Gold, c.1940, 7½ x 1⁵⁄₁₆ In.
$2151.00

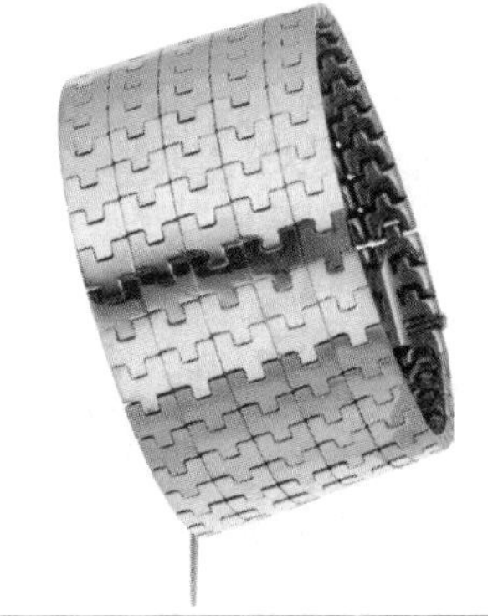

Jewelry, Bracelet, Sterling Silver, Hammered, Claire Falkenstein, 2 x 2⅞ In.
$900.00

Jewelry, Bracelet, Sterling Silver, Spratling, 1940s, 2¼ x 2½ In.
$1300.00

Jewelry, Bracelet, Wheat Design, 18K Gold, France, c.1960, 7¾ x 11/16 In.
$1075.00

Jewelry, Bracelet Set, Bakelite, Zigzag, Yellow, Red, Butterscotch, Nesting, 1⅝ In., 5 Piece
$588.00

Jewelry, Chatelaine, Sterling, Repousse, 5 Accessories, England, 1890, 11 In.
$465.00

Jewelry, Cuff Links, Sterling Silver, Marked, Margaret De Patta, ¾ In.
$980.00

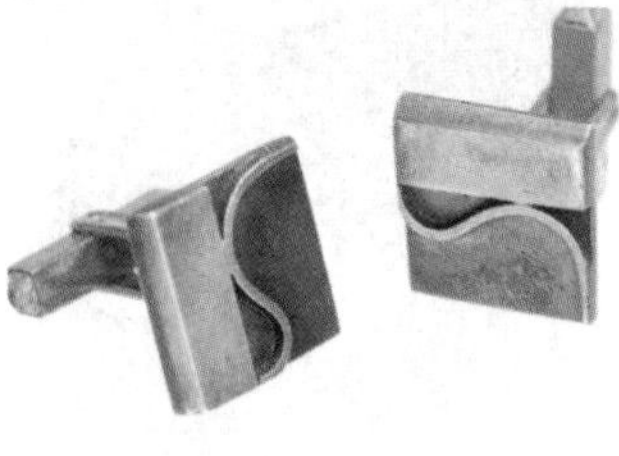

Jewelry, Earrings, Diamonds, Seed Pearls, Silver Plate, Gold, 3 In.
$1700.00

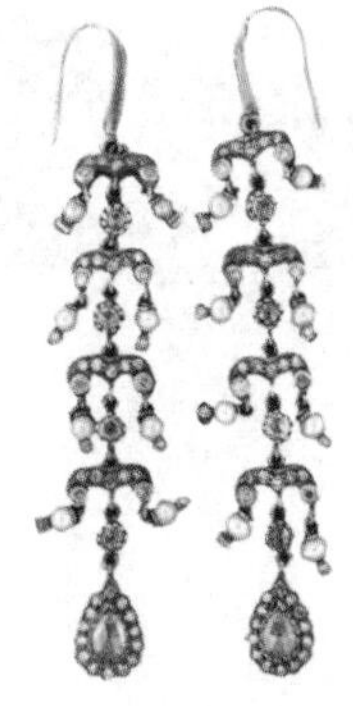

Charm, Frog Prince, Sterling Silver, Ivory Enamel, Inscription, ¾ x ¾ In. 23.00
Charm, Lobster Cage, Sterling Silver, c.1960, ¾ x ½ In. 20.00
Charm, Mousetrap, Sterling Silver, 1 x ¼ In. 75.00
Chatelaine, Silver Plate, Aide Memoire, Sheath, Pencil, Pincushion, Thimble, 11 In. 1400.00
Chatelaine, Sterling, Repousse, 5 Accessories, England, 1890, 11 In. . . . . *illus* 465.00
Cigarette Case, Silver, Watrous Mfg. Co., c.1950, 4 In. 88.00
Cigarette Holder, Trumpet Shape, 14K Gold, Cartier, 4⅝ In. 598.00
Clip, 3 Pearls, Diamonds, Arrow Shaped, Stylized Bow Top, Platinum, 1939, 2 In., Pair 3290.00
Cuff Links, 18K Gold, Double Links, Onyx, Hematite, Angela Cummings, Marked, ⅝ In. 1998.00
Cuff Links, 18K Gold, Sapphire, Arched, Tiffany & Co. 1645.00
Cuff Links, Alfred E. Neuman, Mad Magazine, c.1994. . . . . 358.00
Cuff Links, American Flag, Red Enamel Stripes, Oval, 18K Gold 2640.00
Cuff Links, Blue Flower Tiles, Gold, Marked, Royal Copenhagen, 1 In. 65.00
Cuff Links, Blue Sapphire, Diamond, Platinum, 14K Yellow Gold, Tiffany & Co., c.1910 . . . . . 1120.00
Cuff Links, Champleve Enamel, Red, Turquoise, Purple, Round, 18K Gold, Fouquet 5758.00
Cuff Links, Coral, Rosewood Batons, Rope Twist Band, 18K Gold, Van Cleef & Arpels. 1586.00
Cuff Links, Disc Shape, Diamonds, Blue Enamel, 14K Gold, Beaded, Edwardian, ⅝ In. 2468.00
Cuff Links, Fox, Stags, Mountain Goat, Reverse Painted, Gold, Continental Hallmarks 1880.00
Cuff Links, Jadeite Cabochon, 14K Gold, Silver Buds & Tendrils, Double Link, F.G. Hale 1528.00
Cuff Links, Lapis, 18K Gold, Schlumberger, Tiffany & Co., 1⅜ In. 1880.00
Cuff Links, Lion's Head, Green Stone Eyes, 14K Gold, Art Nouveau, 9/16 In.. . . . . 690.00
Cuff Links, Mosaic, Onyx, Neoclassical Style, 18K Gold, c.1890, ½ In. 357.00
Cuff Links, Rope Twist Batons, Sapphire Cabochon Ends, 18K, Boucheron, Paris 1763.00
Cuff Links, Sapphires, Cabochons, Pyramid Shape, Arched Link, 18K Gold, Cartier. 1955.00
Cuff Links, Sterling Silver, Marked, Margaret De Patta, ¾ In. . . . . *illus* 980.00
Cuff Links, Tube Shape, 14K Bicolor Gold, Cartier, Retro 2115.00
Cuff Links, Turquoise, Cabochons, Triangular, Sterling Silver, Macciarini, 1 In. 235.00
Cuff Links, Wood, Semicircular, Bead, Tapered Bar, Ball End, 18K Gold, Marked, Sophia Vari. . 470.00
Cuff Links, Zigzag, Double Square Links, Platinum, 18K Gold, Art Deco, 7/16 In. 764.00
Earrings, 14K White Gold, Baroque Pearls, Diamonds, Clip-On, Tiffany & Co. 1020.00
Earrings, 18K Gold, Geometric Squares, Lapis, Tiffany & Co., ¾ In. 2468.00
Earrings, 18K Yellow Gold, Pierced, Polished, Swirl, Clip-On, Angela Cummings. 561.00
Earrings, 18K Yellow Gold, Polished Swirl, Pierced, Michael Goode. 1003.00
Earrings, 2 South Sea Pearls, Citrine, Cushion Shape, 18K, Seaman Schepps, ⅞ In. 1528.00
Earrings, 4-Leaf Clover, Enamel, Seed Pearl Center, 14K, Clip-On, Krementz & Co., 1 In. 646.00
Earrings, Acorn Drops, 18K Gold, Mahmoud Muhawish, 1¼ In. 1293.00
Earrings, Angel, Pearls, Freshwater, Sapphire, 14K Gold, Ruser, 1 x ¾ In. 598.00
Earrings, Art Deco, Round, Domed, 18K White Gold, Sapphires, Garnets, Diamonds, 1 In. . . . 2688.00
Earrings, Asian Man's Face, Jurojin, God Of Long Life, White Beard, Screwback, Arita, 1 In. . . 63.00
Earrings, Brass, Double Hoop, Art Smith 1410.00
Earrings, Cheetah, Enameled, Ruby Eyes, Cabochon, 18K Gold, David Webb, 1⅛ In. 3995.00
Earrings, Chinese Character, Carved Leaf, Suspended Cabochon, Gourd, 2½ In. 1645.00
Earrings, Citrines, Quartz, Yellow Tourmalines, 18K, Clip-on, Marilyn Cooperman, 1¼ In.. . . 5288.00
Earrings, Classical Figures, Glass, Intaglio, Pearls, 18K Gold, 1⅛ In.. . . . . 1880.00
Earrings, Diamonds, Double Heart, 18K White Gold, Bulgari, 1 x ¾ In.. . . . . 1793.00
Earrings, Diamonds, Seed Pearls, Silver Plate, Gold, 3 In. . . . . *illus* 1700.00
Earrings, Diamonds, Yellow Sapphire, Amethyst, 18K Gold, Aletto Bros., 1¼ x 1¼ In. 403.00
Earrings, Dove, 18K Gold, Paloma Picasso, 1 1/16 In.. . . . . 823.00
Earrings, Drop, 3 Tiers, Leaf-Shaped Links, Feathered Top, Rhinestones, Boucher, c.1960 . . . 120.00
Earrings, Drop, Micro Mosaic, Glass, Brass Filigree, Screwback, Italy, 1930s, 2½ In. 35.00
Earrings, Drop, Rhinestone, Onyx Spheres, Glass Cabonchon, Haskell, c.1945. . . . . 96.00
Earrings, Drop, Stylized Flower, Teardrop Shaped, Faux Onyx, White Rhinestones, c.1950 . . . 36.00
Earrings, Fan, Wirework, 18K Gold, Clip-On, Schlumberger, Tiffany & Co., 1¼ In.. . . . . 1763.00
Earrings, Faux Pearl, Victorian Style, Gold Tone Metal, Hoop, c.1940 . . . . 96.00
Earrings, Flame, Rock Crystal, Yellow Sapphires, 18K White Gold, Seaman Schepps, 1 In. . . . 3408.00
Earrings, Flower, Stapelia, Ruby Center, Black, White Enamel, 18K Gold, Otto Jakob, ⅝ In.. . . 1410.00
Earrings, Flower, Turquoise Cabochons, Ruby & Diamond, 18K Gold, Aletto Bros., 1 In.. . . . . 4700.00
Earrings, Flowers, Carnelian, Agate, Onyx, Lapis, Arched 18K Gold Wire, Bulgari 2233.00
Earrings, Flowers, Opal, Diamonds, Suspended Opal, 14K Gold, c.1960, 1¼ In. 960.00
Earrings, Flowers, Pink & Blue, Filigree Edge, Clip-On, Oval, c.1950s, 1 x 1 In. 30.00
Earrings, Flowers, Ruby, Diamond, Rock Crystal, Quartz, Aletto Bros., 1¼ In. 4063.00
Earrings, Garnet, 18K Gold Mount, Marina B., ⅞ In.. . . . . 1175.00
Earrings, Half Moon, Sapphire Cabochon, 14K White Gold, Marked, Seaman Schepps 1998.00
Earrings, Harlequin, Copper, Renoir, 1⅛ x ⅞ In. . . . . *illus* 28.00
Earrings, Hawaii, Cascade, Wirework Rings, 18K Gold, Buccellati, 2⅝ In.. . . . . 2820.00
Earrings, Heart, Puffed, 18K Gold, Kieselstein-Cord, ⅞ In. 999.00

Earrings, Hoop, 18K Yellow Gold, Heart Shape Drops, Marina B. 708.00
Earrings, Hoop, Faux Pearl, Flower Top, Rhinestone, Gold Tone Metal, c.1945 150.00
Earrings, Hoop, Ribbed Scrolls, 18K Gold, Otto Jakob, 7/8 In. 1645.00
Earrings, Horses, Multicolored, Enamel, Gold Mount, Hermes, 1 In. 118.00
Earrings, Kinetic, Domed Shape, Flexible Rods, 18K Gold, Pol Bury, 5/8 In. 6756.00
Earrings, Leaf, Berry, Green Stone Bead, 18K Gold, Buccellati, 7/8 In. 2468.00
Earrings, Leaf, Rhinestone Flowers, Frosted Glass, Faux Moonstone, c.1950 54.00
Earrings, Leaf Garland, Round, Faux White Coral, Tubular Beads, Stanley Hagler, c.1950 84.00
Earrings, Lily Of The Valley, Pearls, 18K White Gold Stem, Seaman Schepps, 1 1/2 In. 1175.00
Earrings, Mabe Pearl, 6-Diamond Melee, 18K Gold Mount, Bulgari, 7/8 In. 1116.00
Earrings, Micro Mosaic, Rose, Wave Border, Clip-On, c.1945, 3/4 In. 24.00
Earrings, Mosaic, White Daisy, Gold Filigree Frame, Clip-On, 1970s 10.00
Earrings, Pearl, Cultured, Bead Set, Full Cut Diamond Melee, 14K Gold, Mikimoto, 7/8 In. 2738.00
Earrings, Pearls Cross Of 4 Diamonds, Cone Shaped Mount, 18K Gold, 1989, 1 1/2 In. 3120.00
Earrings, Pendant, Blue Chalcedony, Sterling, 14K Gold, D. Yurman, 1 1/2 & 3/4 In. 999.00
Earrings, Pendant, Diamonds, Enamel, 14K Yellow Gold, c.1870 1680.00
Earrings, Pendant, Rubellites, Peridot, Diamond, 18K Gold, Laura Munder, 2 3/8 In. 2938.00
Earrings, Pendant, Sapphire, Pear Shape, Curb Link Chain, Greek Coin, 18K, 1 1/2 In. 2233.00
Earrings, Pink Tourmaline, Carved, Diamond Centers, 18K, 1983, 7/8 x 5/8 In. 3120.00
Earrings, Platinum, Ruby, Diamond, Marked, Tiffany & Co., 3/8 In. 1998.00
Earrings, Portrait, Enamel, Seed Pearls, Green Glass, Rope Bezel, 14K Gold *illus* 353.00
Earrings, Red Jasper, Wirework, Caged, 18K Gold, Clip-On, Seaman Schepps, 7/8 In. 1645.00
Earrings, Rhinestone, Cluster, Blue, Oval Cut, Bezel Set, White Rhinestone, c.1950 72.00
Earrings, Rhinestones, Paste, Multicolored, Silver Metal, Clip-On, Yves St. Laurent, 2 In. 71.00
Earrings, Rubellites, Circular Cut, 18K Gold, Clip-On, Laura Munder, 3/4 In. 3819.00
Earrings, Ruby Melee, Swirls, 14K Gold, Clip-On, Retro, 1 1/4 In. 588.00
Earrings, Sapphires, 18K Gold, Hammered, Fringe, Lunia, 2 1/3 x 3/4 In. 926.00
Earrings, Shells, Rosewood, 18K Gold Wirework, Seaman Schepps, 1 1/4 In. 1528.00
Earrings, Sugar Loaf Sapphire, Octagonal, Diamonds, Clip-On, Art Deco 1440.00
Earrings, Trefoil Knot, Multicolor Coral Beads, 18K Gold, Clip-On, Seaman Schepps, 7/8 In. 1998.00
Earrings, White Rhinestone, Pear Cut, Round Rhinestone Surround, Clip-On, c.1950 120.00
Earrings, Yellow Rhinestone, Aurora Borealis Crystals, Multicolored Rhinestones, c.1950 48.00
Hat Ornament, Black, Rhinestones, Fleur-De-Lis Finials, Early 1900s, 5 In. 25.00
Hatpins are listed in this book in the Hatpin category.
Lavaliere, Pear Shaped, Heart, Peridots, Enamel, 14K, Link Chain, Art Nouveau, 14 1/2 In. 940.00
Lavaliere, Seed Pearls, Diamonds, Platinum, Scrolls, Beaded Edge, Chain, Art Deco, 14 In. 823.00
Locket, 14K Gold, Diamonds, Emeralds, Rubies, Crystals, Victorian *illus* 270.00
Locket, 14K Gold, Rhodolite Garnet, Fleur-De-Lis, Scroll, Art Nouveau, 1 1/8 In. *illus* 323.00
Locket, 18K Gold, Diamond Melee, Rope Twist Borders, French, 7/8 In. 1410.00
Locket, Brass Suspension Loop, Geometric Border, Photograph, Thermoplastic Case, 1860s 60.00
Locket, Pendant, Hinged, Garland, Beaded, Wirework, Etruscan Revival, 2 5/8 In. 705.00
Locket, Vine, Quilloche, Enamel, Diamonds, Rope Cord, Art Deco, 2 3/4 In. *illus* 2233.00
Lorgnette, Rose Cut Diamond Melee, Platinum, Scroll Handle, Art Deco, 4 In. 2703.00
Money Clip, Ten Dollar Gold Piece, c.1907 633.00
Mourning Set, Black Glass, Seed Pearls, Locket, Earrings, 14K Gold, Victorian *illus* 232.00
Necessaire, Bird, Scissors, Pencil Holder, Knife, Toothpick, Staffordshire, c.1765, 3 7/8 In. 1920.00
Necessaire, Birds, Wasp, Embossed, Enameled, Staffordshire, c.1765, 3 7/8 In. 2640.00
Necessaire, Double Book Form, Landscapes, Silver, Staffordshire, c.1775, 3 3/8 In. 3000.00
Necessaire, Hebe, Mercury, Putto, Doves, Enameled Staffordshire, c.1765, 4 5/8 In. 1560.00
Necessaire, Landscapes, Bird-Shaped Stoppers, Staffordshire, c.1770, 2 7/8 In. 6600.00
Necessaire, Shepherdess, Couple Embracing, Birds, Fruit, Staffordshire, c.1765, 3 7/8 In. 3600.00
Necklace, 3 Strands, Aquamarine Beads, Diamonds, 18K, Tiffany & Co., c.1990, 16 In. 5400.00
Necklace, 4 Strands, Shaped Slide, Enamel, Seed Pearl Accents, 14K Gold, 14 1/4 In. 1763.00
Necklace, 4-Color Poured Glass, Interlocking C Logo Center, Gold Chain, Chanel 470.00
Necklace, 18K Gold, Lady With Emerald & Diamond Melee Flower In Hair, 17 3/4 In. 940.00
Necklace, 18K Yellow Gold, Etruscan Style, Cushion Shape Cabochon Onyx, Diamonds 1003.00
Necklace, 24 Beads, Seed Pearls, Carved Flower Plaque Clasp, 14K Gold, 16 In. 2585.00
Necklace, 25 Pearls, Diamond Melee, 18K White Gold, Gypsy Set Clasp, 17 In. 3525.00
Necklace, 27 Pearls, Platinum Wirework Clasp, Baroque, 22 In. 353.00
Necklace, 33 Pearls, South Sea, Tahitian, Graduated, Seaman Schepps, 20 In. 10575.00
Necklace, 50 Coral Beads, Carved, Black Bead Spacers, China, 1930s, 33 In. 764.00
Necklace, Alhambra Clover, Bezel Set Lapis, Trace Link Chain, 18K Gold, 32 In. 9400.00
Necklace, Aquamarine, Coiled Link Spacers, Toggle Closure, 18K, Tiffany & Co., 15 In. 1293.00
Necklace, Bakelite, 7 Charms, Brown Celluloid Chain, Martha Sleeper, 16 1/2 In. *illus* 265.00
Necklace, Bakelite, 11 Teeth, Celluloid Chain, 17 1/2 In. *illus* 302.00
Necklace, Beads, 2 Strands, Faceted Green & Blue Glass, Miriam Haskell, c.1955 120.00

Orphan Earrings
Wonder what to do with an orphan earring? Wear it as a clip on a collar, a pendant on a chain, or a zipper pull; or put it on a charm bracelet. Big earrings make unusual Christmas tree ornaments. And, of course, you can always wear just one earring.

Jewelry, Earrings, Harlequin, Copper, Renoir, 1 1/8 x 7/8 In.
$28.00

Jewelry, Earrings, Portrait, Enamel, Seed Pearls, Green Glass, Rope Bezel, 14K Gold
$353.00

Jewelry, Locket, 14K Gold, Diamonds, Emeralds, Rubies, Crystals, Victorian
$270.00

Jewelry, Locket, 14K Gold, Rhodolite Garnet, Fleur-De-Lis, Scroll, Art Nouveau, 1 ⅛ In.
$323.00

Jewelry, Locket, Vine, Quilloche, Enamel, Diamonds, Rope Cord, Art Deco, 2 ¾ In.
$2233.00

Jewelry, Mourning Set, Black Glass, Seed Pearls, Locket, Earrings, 14K Gold, Victorian
$232.00

Jewelry, Necklace, Bakelite, 7 Charms, Brown Celluloid Chain, Martha Sleeper, 16 ½ In.
$265.00

Necklace, Beads, 2 Strands, Faux Agate, Faux Pearl, Faux Coral, Faux Goldstone, c.1960 .... 240.00
Necklace, Beads, 2 Strands, Faux Pearl, Pink, Lavender, Flower Drop, M. Haskell, c.1950 .... 270.00
Necklace, Beads, 12 Strands, Platinum Buckle Clasp, Onyx, Tiffany & Co., 16 In. 705.00
Necklace, Beads, Amber, Faceted Sterling Silver, Seed Pearl Clasp, Marsh's, 16 In. 264.00
Necklace, Cameo, Malachite, Cupid, 14K Gold, Wirework Frames, 17½ In. 2468.00
Necklace, Chain, 18K, Enamel Horseshoe, Cowboy Hats, Boots, Round Links, 35 In. 1116.00
Necklace, Chain, 18K Gold, Rope Twist Links, Pendant, Liberty Head Coin, 25 In. 2820.00
Necklace, Chain, 18K Gold, Engraved Links, Van Cleef & Arpels, 30¼ In. 3055.00
Necklace, Chain, Box Links, 18K Gold, Corset Hook Closure, Cartier, 16½ In. 4465.00
Necklace, Chain, Double Interlocking Links, 18K, Italy, Box, Tiffany & Co., c.1950, 16 In. *illus* 2832.00
Necklace, Chain, H Form, Round Links, 18K Gold, David Webb, 35¼ In. 5288.00
Necklace, Chain, Link, 18K Yellow Gold, 8 Bezel Set Cabochons, Bulgaria, 20 In. 3776.00
Necklace, Chain, Lozenge Links, Gold Tone Metal, Faux Amethysts, c.1950 .... 180.00
Necklace, Chain, Sterling Silver, Oval Malachite, Enameled Feathers, Arts & Crafts, 61 In. 1058.00
Necklace, Choker, Leather, White, Blue Paste Stones, France, c.1910, 10¾ In. 500.00
Necklace, Coin, 1880 5-Dollar Liberty Head, Prong Set, Diamond Melee, Chain, David Webb. 1763.00
Necklace, Collar, Sterling Silver, Asymmetrical, Twisted Link Chain, Art Smith, 14¾ In. 3643.00
Necklace, Diamonds, Sapphire Cabochons, Ruby, 14K Yellow Gold, c.1980. .... 1200.00
Necklace, Festoon, 12 Oval Amethysts, 14K Gold Trace Link Chain, Art Nouveau, 18¾ In. 529.00
Necklace, Festoon, Amethysts, 6 Foxtail Chain Swags, Sterling Silver, John Hardy, 16 In. 1175.00
Necklace, Flower, Bronze, Claude Lalanne 9500.00
Necklace, Fringe, Diamonds, Circles, Rope Twist, 15K, Etruscan Revival, 16 In. 5875.00
Necklace, Fringe, Silver, Quatrefoil Links, Cherubs & Beads, Renaissance Revival, 17 In. 1293.00
Necklace, Graduated Beads, Green Glass Spacers, Barrel Clasp, 20 In. 35.00
Necklace, Heart, Crystal, Diamonds, Pearls, Platinum, Trace Link Chain, Edwardian, 27 In. . 7931.00
Necklace, Lariat, 6 Strands, Blue Glass, Rhinestones, Gold Tone Metal Clip, c.1950 .... 72.00
Necklace, Lariat, Triple Rope Twist, Jade Terminals, 2 Pearl Tassels, c.1910, 33 In. 2040.00
Necklace, Link, 14K Yellow Gold, Neiman Marcus, 15½ In. 944.00
Necklace, Link, Bird & Leaf Shape, Sterling Silver, Lapis Accents, Georg Jensen, 18¾ In. 2468.00
Necklace, Link, Curb, Leaf Design, 6-Diamond Melee, 18K Gold, Gubelin, 26½ In. 3231.00
Necklace, Link, Entwined Spirals, 18K Gold, 20th Century, 18 In. 330.00
Necklace, Link, Roman, Textured, 18K Gold, Lobster Clasp, Box, Cartier, 28 In. 1793.00
Necklace, Link, Spiral, Entwined, 14K Gold, 20th Century, 30¼ In. 825.00
Necklace, Mesh, 14K Gold, 20th Century, 22 In. 330.00
Necklace, Onyx, Intaglio, Classical Man, Sterling Plaques, Flowers, Arts & Crafts, 17 In. 411.00
Necklace, Onyx Beads, 4 Strands, Diamond, Pearl Flower Clasp, 14K Gold, c.1950, 15 In. 2040.00
Necklace, Paste Cabochons, Multicolored, Gold Metal, Marked, Yves St. Laurent, 16 In. 411.00
Necklace, Pearls, 2 Strands, Faux Turquoise, Twigs, c.1950 .... 150.00
Necklace, Pearls, 3 Knotted Strands, Silver, Clasp, Mikimoto, 22 In. 1225.00
Necklace, Pearls, 3 Strands, Graduated, Diamond & Jade Clasp, 14K Gold, c.1950, 21 In. 1200.00
Necklace, Pearls, 45 Black Graduated, Diamonds, 18K White Gold Clasp, Mikimoto, 17 In. .. 5581.00
Necklace, Pearls, Baroque, Graduated, Gold Metal Spacers, Bow-Shaped Drop, M. Haskell, c.1950 . 240.00
Necklace, Pearls, Cultured, Rose Tint, Seed Pearl Clasp, 14K White Gold, Mikimoto 1763.00
Necklace, Pearls, Gray, 4 Strands, 18K Gold Buckle Clasp, Paloma Picasso, 16¼ In. 558.00
Necklace, Pearls, Single Strand, 83 Round, Oval Plaque, Haskell, c.1945 .... 120.00
Necklace, Pendant, 3 Faux Baroque Pearl Drops, 2 Strands, Rhinestones, Haskell, c.1955 ... 390.00
Necklace, Pendant, Amethyst, 6 Oval Amethysts, 14K Gold, c.1930, 30 In. 1440.00
Necklace, Pendant, Chrysacolla, Scrolled Frame, 18K, Rope Twist Chain, Emma Heintz, c.1910 1763.00
Necklace, Pendant, Hair, 14K Gold Mount, 20th Century, 16 In. 132.00
Necklace, Pendant, Hotei, Ivory, Diamonds, Gold, Frame, Stuart Moore, c.1985, 19 In. 764.00
Necklace, Pendant, Lantern Tassel, 14K Gold, Edward Oakes, c.1924, 18½ In. 4700.00
Necklace, Pendant, Man Riding On Dolphin, Shell Link Chain, 18K Gold, S. Dali, 25 In. 2820.00
Necklace, Pendant, Pate-De-Verre, Insect, Cord, Amber Bead, G. Argy-Rousseau, 3½ In. 1880.00
Necklace, Pendant, Puffed Heart, Tapered Bar Link Chain, Georg Jensen 705.00
Necklace, Pendant, Sterling, Shaped, Pearl, Paper Clip Chain, Georg Jensen, 19 In. 1410.00
Necklace, Pendant, Teardrop, Diamonds, Platinum, Art Deco, 2-In. Pendant, 15-In. Chain .. *illus* 2629.00
Necklace, Pendant, Wasp, Glass, Blue, Grape, Vine Beads, Cord, Lalique, c.1920, 28 In. 7050.00
Necklace, Plaque, Fish, Nickel-Plated Silver, Crescent-Shaped Bands, Nepal, 13 x 12 In. 660.00
Necklace, Sapphire, Openwork, Honeycomb Links, 14K Gold, Ruser, 15 In. 1838.00
Necklace, Sapphires, Round & Pear Shape Pearls, 14K Gold, Jugendstil, 18 In. 529.00
Necklace, Scarab, Glass, Iridescent, Shaped Plaques, Gold Link Chain, 18 In. 2350.00
Necklace, Scarf, 18K Yellow Gold, Tiffany & Co., 26½ In. 1997.00
Necklace, Snake, 14K Gold, Pave Set Turquoise Head, Ruby & Diamond, 15¼ In. 5405.00
Necklace, Sterling, 3 Shaped Plaques, Leaves, Carnelians, Art Silver Shop, Chicago, 16 In. ... 1410.00
Necklace, Sterling, Leaf & Bud-Shaped Links, Marked, Georg Jensen, 16¾ In. 2703.00
Necklace, Sterling, Links, Abstract-Shaped, Henning Koppel, Georg Jensen, 16 In. 2468.00

Necklace, Sterling Silver, Oval-Shaped Discs, Marked, Georg Jensen, 15¾ In. 823.00
Necklace, Strap, 18K Gold, Hermes, 17 In. 9988.00
Necklace, Tassel, Seed Pearl Fringe, Openwork, Rope, Diamond Clasp, Art Deco, 21 In.. . . . . . 7344.00
Necklace, Tassel, Seed Pearl Fringe, Pink Tourmaline, Emerald, Rope, Edwardian, 42 In. . . . 3173.00
Necklace, Turquoise, Cabochons, Silver Latticework Links, c.1900, 13 In.. . . . . 705.00
Necklace & Bracelet, Faux Pearls, Faux Coral, Gold Toned Spacers, Haskell, c.1945 . . . . 150.00
Necklace & Earrings, 14K White Gold, Iolites, Sapphires, Empire Style, 17-In. Chain . . *illus* 900.00
Necklace & Earrings, Beads, Turquoise, Faux White Coral, Miriam Haskell, c.1945 . . . . 96.00
Necklace & Earrings, Pendant, Pink Quartz, Diamonds, Judith Ripka 1293.00
Necklace & Earrings, Pink Tourmaline, Bezel Set, Gold Leaf, Marsh's, 2-In. Pendant 8813.00
Necklace & Earrings, Rhinestones, 12 Strands, Pearls, Art Deco Style, M. Haskell, c.1938 . . . 600.00
Necklace Set, Bracelet, Earrings, Japanned Metal, Gray & Silver Stones, Schreiner. 451.00
Necklace Set, Flowers, Blue & Green Rhinestones, Crystals, Navettes, Juliana, 4 Piece 600.00
Pendant, 22K Gold Krugerrand, 14K Gold Bamboo-Style Frame, Chain, 1976 . . . . 1058.00
Pendant, Anchor, 14K Gold, 20th Century 143.00
Pendant, Blue Chalcedony Cabochon, Diamonds, Sterling Silver, Cable, David Yurman, 2 x 1 In. . . 1135.00
Pendant, Book, Old Testament, Bronze, Gold, Gold Nugget Chain, c.1955, 1 x 6 In.. . . . . 4200.00
Pendant, Buddha, Angelskin, Coral, Seed Pearl Accents, Applied Beads, c.1910, 2 In. 4230.00
Pendant, Clown, Movable Limbs, Glass Compartment, Bezel Set Diamond Melee, 18K Gold . . 1763.00
Pendant, Coin, U.S., $5, 13 Faceted Rubies, Polished Gold Frame, c.1910. . . . . 354.00
Pendant, Cross, 11 Brilliant Cut Diamonds, Platinum, Rope Chain, Tiffany & Co., 16 In. 2950.00
Pendant, Cross, Yellow Gold, Flowers, Satin Rope Twist Edge, c.1880, 2½ In. 384.00
Pendant, Diamond Melee, Trace Link Chain, 18K White Gold, Tiffany & Co., 16 In.. . . . . 823.00
Pendant, Emeralds, Old Mine, Rose Cut Diamonds, Enamel, Gold Mount, 3 In.. . . . . 2820.00
Pendant, Figure, Stippled, Diamond Accent, 18K Gold, Art Nouveau, 1⅛ In.. . . . . 1175.00
Pendant, Flower, Ivory, Carved, Silver, Enamel, Marcasites, Velvet Ribbon, Fahrner. 640.00
Pendant, G.A.R., Shield Shape, Eagle, Ribbon, Star, Red, White, Blue Enamel, c.1860, 1 In. . . 60.00
Pendant, Golden Fleece, 18K Gold, Cartier, 1½ In. 940.00
Pendant, Grape Cluster, Amber, Enamel Leaves, Scrolling Tendrils, 18K, Otto Jakob, 2 In. . . . 705.00
Pendant, Heart, Diamonds, Pin Fitting, Chain, 14K Yellow Gold, c.1980, 18 In. 900.00
Pendant, Jade, Carved Mutton, Diamonds, 18K Gold, Chinese, c.1890, 2 In. 672.00
Pendant, Maltese Cross, Smoky Quartz, Gold Mount, 1⅝ In. 1528.00
Pendant, Masks, Tragedy & Comedy, 18K Gold, Alfonso Germano, c.1960s, 1½ In.. . . . . 382.00
Pendant, Plique-A-Jour, Flower, Enamel Petals, Peridot, Pearl Accents, 10K, 1½ In.. . . . . 1175.00
Pendant, Satyr Mask, Sterling Silver, Buccellati, 2 In.. . . . . 294.00
Pendant, Silver, Green & Blue Enamel, Art Nouveau, 1½ In. . . . . *illus* 80.00
Pendant, Sterling Silver, 2 Enameled Medallions, Hinged, Chain, 1905, 4¾ x 1¼ In. 3000.00
Pendant, Watch, Guitar, Link Chain, Scrolling Flowered Chatelaine Hook, Gems, 5 In.. . . . . . 2938.00
Pendant, Woman, Draped, Blue, 47 Rose-Cut Diamonds, 15K, 2 x 1¼ In. . . . . *illus* 1495.00
Pin, 2 Butterflies, Sterling Silver, Georg Jensen, 2⅛ In. . . . . *illus* 175.00
Pin, 2 Doves, Wheat, Sterling Silver, Square, c.1930. . . . . 630.00
Pin, 2 Palm Trees, Enamel, Plastic, Blue, Green, Brown, Art Deco, 1930s, 2½ In. 25.00
Pin, 3 Embossed Roses, Green Leaves, Goofus Glass, ½ x 1⅝ In. 48.00
Pin, Abstract Bird Shape, 18K Gold, Abalone & Pearl Accents, Gubelin, 2½ In. 2350.00
Pin, Alligator, Emerald Melee Eyes, 18K Gold, Kieselstein-Cord, 1½ In. 764.00
Pin, Amethyst, 3 Full Cut Diamonds, Abstract Shape, Arthur King, 2¾ x 1⅜ In.. . . . . 558.00
Pin, Aquamarine, Bezel Set, Seed Pearls, Applied Beads, Rope Twist, 14K, 2 In.. . . . . 1645.00
Pin, Aquamarines, 28-Diamond Melee, Beaded & Engraved Accents, Art Deco, 2¼ In. 5288.00
Pin, Astronaut Sitting On Moon, Holding Flag, Enamel, 18K Gold, 2 In. 1293.00
Pin, Azure Malachite, Bezel Set, Oval Cabochon, 14K Gold, Frame, Arts & Crafts, 2 In.. . . . . . . 1293.00
Pin, Bakelite, Airplane, Butterscotch, Red Tail, Wings, Propellor Moves, Paint, 4 In. . . . . *illus* 3360.00
Pin, Bakelite, Flamingo, Yellow, Glass Eye, 4½ In. . . . . *illus* 323.00
Pin, Bakelite, Hand, Butterscotch, Chain Bracelet, 4½ In. . . . . *illus* 588.00
Pin, Bakelite, Heart, Cherry Red, Faceted, Cutout Center Key Hole, 2 x 2¼ In. 518.00
Pin, Bakelite, MacArthur Heart, Key Over Heart, Red, World War II 2500.00
Pin, Bakelite, Mexican Man, Sombrero, Butterscotch, Painted Details, 2½ In.. . . . . 1035.00
Pin, Bakelite, Swan, Red, Wood Beak, Glass Eye, 3½ In. . . . . *illus* 177.00
Pin, Bar, 12 Diamonds, 7 Round Sapphires, Platinum, Edwardian, 2¼ In. 1121.00
Pin, Bar, Diamonds, 14K White Gold, 20th Century, 2¾ In. 154.00
Pin, Bar, Diamonds, 11 Old Mine Cut, Platinum Mount, Beaded Edge, Art Deco, 3 In. 1410.00
Pin, Bar, Diamonds, Ruby & Diamond Melee, Art Deco, Marcus & Co., 2¾ In.. . . . . 4406.00
Pin, Bar, Flowers, Prong Set Diamond Melee, 18K Gold, Georg Jensen, 2⅝ In. 1293.00
Pin, Bar, Flowers, 3 Lapis Cabochons, Gold Mount, Arts & Crafts, Tiffany & Co., 2 In. 6463.00
Pin, Bar, Gold, Coiled Snake, Ball Terminals, Victorian, 2¼ x 1 In. 300.00
Pin, Bar, Leaves, 3 Oval Chalcedony, Sterling Silver Mount, Arts & Crafts, 2⅛ In. 470.00
Pin, Bar, Sapphires, Black, White Enameled Triangles, 18K, Carlo Giuliano, 2 In. 4994.00

Gold Jewelry
We've heard a theory that yellow gold jewelry was popular in the days of gaslights. When electric lights came into general use about 1900, white gold became popular. Whatever the reason, white gold and platinum were not often used on fine jewelry before 1900.

Jewelry, Necklace, Bakelite, 11 Teeth, Celluloid Chain, 17½ In.
$302.00

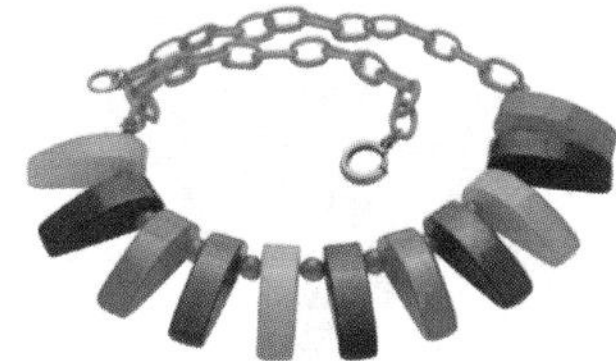

Jewelry, Necklace, Chain, Double Interlocking Links, 18K, Italy, Box, Tiffany & Co., c.1950, 16 In.
$2832.00

Jewelry, Necklace, Pendant, Teardrop, Diamonds, Platinum, Art Deco, 2-In. Pendant, 15-In. Chain
$2629.00

Jewelry, Necklace & Earrings, 14K White Gold, Iolites, Sapphires, Empire Style, 17-In. Chain
$900.00

Jewelry, Pendant, Silver, Green & Blue Enamel, Art Nouveau, 1 ½ In.
$80.00

Jewelry, Pendant, Woman, Draped, Blue, 47 Rose-Cut Diamonds, 15K, 2 x 1 ¼ In.
$1495.00

Jewelry, Pin, 2 Butterflies, Sterling Silver, Georg Jensen, 2 ⅛ In.
$175.00

Pin, Bar, Tapered, Platinum, Diamonds, Baguettes, Sapphires, Art Deco, 3 In. 2160.00
Pin, Bee, Opal Cabochon, Diamond Melee Body & Wings, Silver, 18K Gold, France. 3290.00
Pin, Bee, Ruby, Rose-Cut Diamonds, Silver On 14K Gold, 1½ In. *illus* 1293.00
Pin, Bicolor 18K Gold, Diamond Melee Accents, Hammerman Brothers, 2⅛ In. 764.00
Pin, Bird, Milk Chalcedony, Sapphire Eye, Coral Tail, Diamonds, 18K, Cartier, 1½ In. 4700.00
Pin, Bird, Sterling, Leafy Rectangular Mount, Beaded Corners, Georg Jensen, 1 In. 382.00
Pin, Blackamoor, 18K Gold, Enamel, Coral & Diamond Accents On Turban, Cartier, 1 In. 7931.00
Pin, Bouquet Of Violets, Enamel, 14K Gold, Italy, Tiffany & Co., 1⅞ In. 999.00
Pin, Bow, Diamond, 14K Gold, Retro, Marked, Cartier, 2 In. 470.00
Pin, Bow, Diamond, European Cut, Diamonds, Longated Ends, Tiffany & Co., 2⅝ In. 9400.00
Pin, Bow, Diamond Melee, Silver Washed Gold Mount, 1930s, 2¼ In. 1058.00
Pin, Bow, Diamond Melee, Onyx Accents, Platinum Mount, Art Deco, Dreicer & Co., 2 In. 6463.00
Pin, Bow, Diamonds, Platinum, Tiffany & Co., ⅜ x 2⅛ In. 3884.00
Pin, Bow, Diamonds, Platinum, Openwork, Beaded Edge, Art Deco, 1¾ In., Pair 6169.00
Pin, Bow, Diamonds, Emerald Accents, Platinum, Art Deco, 2 In. 6580.00
Pin, Bow, Gem Set, Emerald, Turquoise, Diamonds, Seed Pearl Fringe, 2 In. 499.00
Pin, Bow, Green Stones, Pearls, Silver Washed Gold, Spain, Foil Back 2 x 2½ In. 264.00
Pin, Bow, Ribboned, 2 Flowers, Diamonds, Brilliant Cut, Platinum Mount 10800.00
Pin, Bow, Rock Crystal, Frosted, Onyx, Diamonds, Seed Pearls, Platinum, Art Deco, 2½ In. 7344.00
Pin, Butterfly, Diamond Wing, Ruby Glass Eyes, 15K Yellow Gold, 1912, 1¾ x 3 In. 3600.00
Pin, Butterfly, Diamonds, Garnets, Red Stone Eyes, Gold Washed, Edwardian, 2 In. 3055.00
Pin, Butterfly, Plique-A-Jour, 800 Silver Filigree, Gold Vermeil, 2 x 1¼ In. 55.00
Pin, Cameo, 2 Women, Bridge, Stream, Trees, 18K Gold, c.1890, 2 x 1½ In. *illus* 197.00
Pin, Cameo, Athena, Onyx, Bezel Set, 18K Gold, Etruscan Revival, 2¾ x ⅞ In. *illus* 897.00
Pin, Cameo, Carved, Gold Mount, Victorian *illus* 125.00
Pin, Cameo, Lady With Hair Comb, Wearing Necklace, Diamond Chip, Silver Mount 179.00
Pin, Cameo, Man & Woman, Feeding Birds, Tree, Gold Mount, 3⅝ In. *illus* 300.00
Pin, Cameo, Medusa, Carnelian, Carved, Variegated Colors, Gold Mount, Gilt Stem 8813.00
Pin, Cameo, Opal, Carved, 14K Gold, Laurel Leaf Border, 19th Century, 1¾ x 1¼ In. 805.00
Pin, Cameo, Venus & Diana, Dove, Owl, Shell, Seed Pearl Frame, Gold Mount, 1¾ In. 1058.00
Pin, Cameo, Woman, Hardstone, Seed Pearl Frame, 14K Gold Mount, 1¼ In. 705.00
Pin, Carnelian, Nestled In Flowers, Diamonds, Heart Shape, 18K Gold, Tiffany, 1½ In. 1293.00
Pin, Cat, Sterling Silver, Green Onyx Cabochon Eye, Henning & Koppel, Georg Jensen 764.00
Pin, Cat's Eye, Chrysoberyl, Diamond, Platinum, Art Deco, c.1930, 2½ x 1 In. 9560.00
Pin, Christmas Tree, Plique-A-Jour, Gold Tone Metal, 3½ In. 46.00
Pin, Circle, Sapphires, Square Cut, Seed Pearls, 14K Gold, Krementz & Co., 1¼ In. 940.00
Pin, Citrine, Intaglio Cut Woman, Silver Grillwork, 18K Frame, Tiffany & Co., 3 In. 17625.00
Pin, Clip, Citrine, 14K Gold, Scrolling Mount, Silver Flowers, Arts & Crafts, 1⅝ In. 705.00
Pin, Cluster Of Coral Beads, Star Set Rose Cut Diamonds, 14K Gold Mount, 1¾ In. 2233.00
Pin, Copper, Tooled, Stylized Figure, Patina, Arts & Crafts, 1¼ x 1½ In. 270.00
Pin, Crescents, 3 Sapphires, 14K Gold, 1½ In. *illus* 820.00
Pin, Crescents, Diamonds, 22 Old European Cut, Bead & Bezel Set, Edwardian, 3 In. 1763.00
Pin, Cross, Maltese, Diamonds, Old Mine Cut, c.1870, 2¼ In. 10575.00
Pin, Crossed Oars, Wreath, Dolphins, Red Enamel, Argonaut, On Back, 1870, 2¼ In. 1725.00
Pin, Diamond Melee, Seed Pearls, Platinum, Edwardian, 1 In. 646.00
Pin, Diamonds, 7 Mine Cut, Opals, Pearl, 18K, Art Nouveau, 2 x 1 In. 3680.00
Pin, Diamonds, European & Single Cut, Caliber Cut Onyx, Platinum, Art Deco 7050.00
Pin, Diamonds, European Cut, Platinum, Art Deco, 1⅞ In. 3055.00
Pin, Diamonds, Full & Single Cut, Baguettes, Platinum, c.1950s, 1⅜ In. 4406.00
Pin, Diamonds, Old European Cut, 4 Sapphires, Shaped Platinum Mount, Art Deco, 2 In. 2938.00
Pin, Diamonds, Rose Cut, 14K White Gold Mount, Art Deco, 2 In. 1175.00
Pin, Diamonds, Sapphires, Platinum, Filigree, Openwork, c.1925, 2 In. *illus* 1300.00
Pin, Dragon On Leaf, Plique-A-Jour, Blue, Flowers, 3¼ In. 50.00
Pin, Dragonfly, Blue Topaz, Single Cut Diamonds, 14K White Gold, 1¾ x 2¼ In. 748.00
Pin, Dragonfly, Diamonds, Ruby, Plique-A-Jour Enamel, 18K Yellow Gold Mount, 2 x 3 In. 2100.00
Pin, Dragonfly, Plique-A-Jour, 14K Pink Gold, Guilloche Green Eyes, 3⅞ x 3⅛ In. 3250.00
Pin, Eagle, Plique-A-Jour, Sterling Silver, c.1890, 1½ In. 500.00
Pin, Elephant, Raised Trunk, Enamel, Ruby, 18K Gold, David Webb, 2⅛ x 2 In. 5288.00
Pin, Emerald, Square Cut, 16 Round Brilliant Cut Diamonds, Bicolor Gold, 2½ In. 708.00
Pin, Emerald & Diamond Blossoms, Movable Diamond Wheels, 18K, c.1960s, 1 In. 3525.00
Pin, Enamel, Raised Glass Prunts, Oval, 2 In. 15.00
Pin, Fishing Rod, Reel, Enameled Swordfish, Pearl Body, Ruby Eye, 14K Gold, c.1930, 4 In. 840.00
Pin, Flower, 2 Sapphires, Scrolls, 14K Gold, No. 36, Georg Jensen, 2 In. 1175.00
Pin, Flower, 6 Petals, White & Yellow Rhinestones, White Metal Frame, c.1945 48.00
Pin, Flower, Aquamarine Petals, Sapphires, 14K Leaves, Stem, Tiffany & Co., 3 In. 1175.00

Jewelry, Pin, Bakelite, Airplane, Butterscotch, Red Tail, Wings, Propellor Moves, Paint, 4 In.
$3360.00

Jewelry, Pin, Bakelite, Flamingo, Yellow, Glass Eye, 4 ½ In.
$323.00

Jewelry, Pin, Bakelite, Hand, Butterscotch, Chain Bracelet, 4 ½ In.
$588.00

Jewelry, Pin, Bakelite, Swan, Red, Wood Beak, Glass Eye, 3 ½ In.
$177.00

Jewelry, Pin, Bee, Ruby, Rose-Cut Diamonds, Silver On 14K Gold, 1 ½ In.
$1293.00

Jewelry, Pin, Cameo, 2 Women, Bridge, Stream, Trees, 18K Gold, c.1890, 2 x 1 ½ In.
$197.00

Jewelry, Pin, Cameo, Athena, Onyx, Bezel Set, 18K Gold, Etruscan Revival, 2 ¾ x ⅞ In.
$897.00

Jewelry, Pin, Cameo, Carved, Gold Mount, Victorian
$125.00

Jewelry, Pin, Cameo, Man & Woman, Feeding Birds, Tree, Gold Mount, 3 ⅝ In.
$300.00

Jewelry, Pin, Crescents, 3 Sapphires, 14K Gold, 1 ½ In.
$820.00

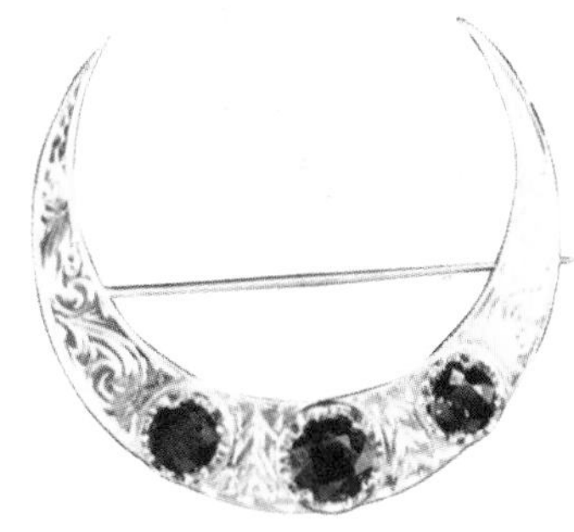

Dating Cameo

We have spoken to many jewelry dealers lately and are convinced that cameos made with a small diamond drop on a tiny chain at the carving's neck were made between about 1910 and 1920. These cameos are almost always set in white-gold filigree mounts (habillé), which were widely used during that decade. New versions of this type of cameo are being made of shell and even plastic.

Jewelry, Pin, Diamonds, Sapphires, Platinum, Filigree, Openwork, c.1925, 2 In.
$1300.00

Jewelry, Pin, Rubies, Emerald, Diamonds, Gold, c.1950
$700.00

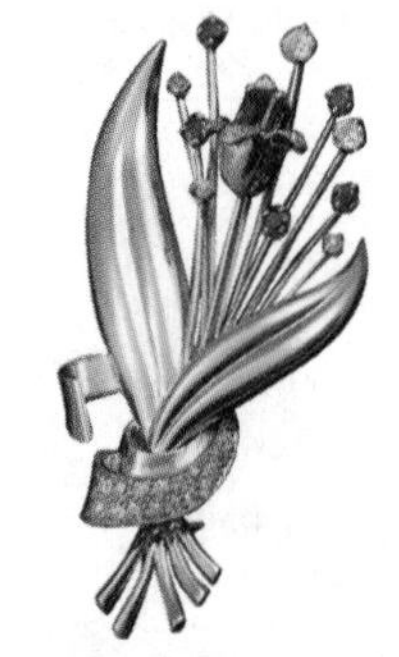

Jewelry, Pin, Seahorse, Sterling Silver, Marked, Cini, 3 x 1¾ In.
$600.00

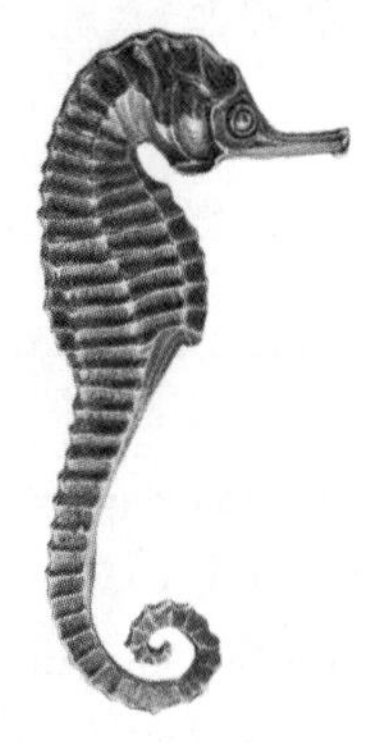

Jewelry, Pin, Snake, Diamonds, Rubies, Coral, Silver On Gold, Victorian, 2 x ⅝ In.
$568.00

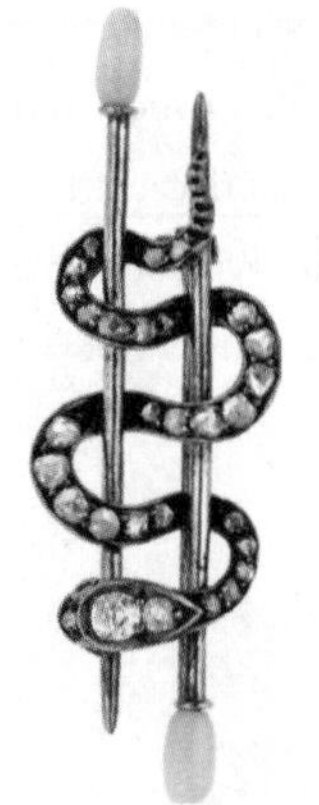

Pin, Flower, Bicolor 14K Gold, Ruby, Marked, Tiffany & Co., 3 In. 1293.00
Pin, Flower, Enamel, Seed Pearl Center, Heart Shaped Frame, Carter, Howe & Co., 1 In. 823.00
Pin, Flower, Freshwater Pearl, Emerald Stalk, Rose Cut Diamond, Platinum, 2 In. 2468.00
Pin, Flower, Kunzite, Square, Step Cut, Diamond, 14K, Tiffany & Co., 1⅝ In. 4113.00
Pin, Flower, Pearls, Sapphires, 14K Gold, 20th Century, 1½ In. 220.00
Pin, Flower, Peridot, Prong Set, 14K Gold, Retro, Tiffany & Co., 2¼ In. 823.00
Pin, Flower Spray, Moonstones, Sapphires, 14K Bicolor Gold Bow, Retro, 2¾ In. 1000.00
Pin, Flowers, Pink, Diamonds, Platinum, Marked, Van Clef & Arpel, 1 x 1¾ In. 2300.00
Pin, Flowers, Silver, Gold Washed Frame, Beaded Edge, Art Nouveau, 1½ In. 823.00
Pin, Free-Form, 18K Yellow Gold, Diamonds, Satin, Angela Cummings, c.1988 .... 1652.00
Pin, Free-Form, Sterling Silver, Nanna Bitzel, Georg Jensen, 1½ x 2 In. 175.00
Pin, Frog, Nephrite Jade Leaf, Diamond Eyes, 14K Yellow Gold, 1⅝ x 1⅜ In. 950.00
Pin, Garnet Cabochon, Heart Shape, Freshwater Pearls, Edwardian, 14K Gold 1058.00
Pin, Giraffe, 18K Gold, Enameled, Ruby Eye, Diamond Melee Accents, 3 In. 705.00
Pin, Glass, Daisy, Blue, Foil Ground, Gilt Frame, Lalique, c.1920, 1⅝ In. 1880.00
Pin, Glass, Flowers, Green, Foiled Ground, Gilt Frame, Lalique, 1⅝ In. 1880.00
Pin, Glass, Grotesque Mask, Rose Foil, Gilt Frame, Lalique, c.1920, 1⅝ In. 2468.00
Pin, Gold Plate, Cutout Designs, Amethyst Stones, Arts & Crafts, 1 x 1¾ In. 360.00
Pin, Gorgon, Entwined Snakes, Rubies, Seed Pearls, Diamonds, 18K, Art Nouveau, 1 In. 1528.00
Pin, Horse & Carriage, Goofus Glass, 1¾ In. 85.00
Pin, Iris, Enamel, Garnet, Diamonds, 14K Gold Scrolls, Art Nouveau, 1¾ In. 940.00
Pin, Ivory, Carved, Shell Ginger, Honolulu, Sterling Silver Mount, 20th Century, 3¾ In. 590.00
Pin, Knight Of Momus, Above The Clouds, Carnival Ball, Mardi Gras, New Orleans, c.1913 .... 1116.00
Pin, Krewe Of Proteus, Adventures Of Telemachus, Carnival Ball, Mardi Gras, c.1913 .... 646.00
Pin, Laurel Branch, Bee, 22 Rose Cut Diamonds, 2 Rubies, Sapphire, Bicolor Gold, 2 In. 207.00
Pin, Leaf, Branch, 18K Bicolor Gold, M. Buccellati, Italy, 2⅛ In. 3643.00
Pin, Leaf, Diamond Cluster, 18K Gold, Andrew Grima, London, 3¼ In. 2233.00
Pin, Leaf, Full Cut Diamond Melee, Prong Set, Rope Twist Borders, 18K Gold, 1⅞ In. 1763.00
Pin, Leaf, Pearls, 14K White Gold, 20th Century 231.00
Pin, Leaf, Plique-A-Jour, 3¼ In. 145.00
Pin, Leaf, Silver, 18K Gold, M. Buccellati, 2 In. 823.00
Pin, Leaves, Silver Tone Metal, 5 Simulated Pearls, Sarah Coventry, c.1971, 3 In. 20.00
Pin, Leopard, Plique-A-Jour, Sterling Silver Marcasite, Art Deco, 4½ In. 305.00
Pin, Les Mysterieuses, Carnival Ball, Mardi Gras, New Orleans 646.00
Pin, Lily Of The Valley, Pearls, Enamel, Diamond Stem, Marcus & Co., c.1950, 3 In. 4230.00
Pin, Lion, 18K Bicolor Gold, Diamond & Emerald, Rubies, Hammerman Bros., 2⅜ In. 2115.00
Pin, Lion, Diamond Melee, Green & Red Stone Eyes & Nose, 18K Gold, 1⅝ In. 470.00
Pin, Lion, Rampant, 18K Gold, Full Cut Diamond Melee, 2¼ In. 881.00
Pin, Lover's Eye, Watercolor On Ivory, Blue Iris, Beaded, Border, Gold, c.1815, ½ x 1 In. 3408.00
Pin, Lover's Eye, Watercolor On Ivory, Brown Iris, Hair, Beaded, c.1815, ½ x ⅞ In. 3525.00
Pin, Maltese Cross, Garnet, Bezel Set, Applied Beads, 14K Gold, 1¾ In. 940.00
Pin, Maple Leaves, Faux Pearl, Rhinestone, Cloth Back, Braided, c.1945 .... 240.00
Pin, Marlin, 18K Gold, Multicolored Enamel, Diamond Melee, Ruby Eye, 2 In. 1528.00
Pin, Martini Glass, Fruit Slice, Cherry, Umbrella, Rhinestones, Butler & Wilson 177.00
Pin, Micro Mosaic, Ancient City Scene, Onyx, Oval 266.00
Pin, Micro Mosaic, Daisy Bouquet, Blue Ground, Silver Mount, c.1875, 2½ x 1½ In. 550.00
Pin, Micro Mosaic, Flower Bouquet, 18K Gold, Etruscan Revival, 2½ x 2¼ In. 5875.00
Pin, Micro Mosaic, Landscape, Oval, Black Onyx Border, 1½ x 1¼ In. 725.00
Pin, Micro Mosaic, Rose, Red, Turquoise, Cobalt Blue, White, Italy, c.1900, 1½ x ⅝ In. 26.00
Pin, Mosaic, Flowers, Oval, Early 20th Century, 1 x 2 In. 40.00
Pin, Mosaic, Geometric Design, Brass Mount, C-Clasp, Italy, 1½ x ½ In. 24.00
Pin, Nike, 18K Gold, Capped Tassel, Bead, Palmette, Drops, C-Clasp, Etruscan Revival 13513.00
Pin, Opals, 14K Gold, Can Be Converted To Pendant, 19th Century 385.00
Pin, Pansy, Sterling Silver, Garnet, No. 113, Georg Jensen, 1⅝ In. 441.00
Pin, Pansy, Sterling Silver, Silver Pearl, Georg Jensen, Denmark 323.00
Pin, Parrot, Sterling Silver, Amethyst Cabochon Eyes, Hector Aguilar, 2½ In. 1320.00
Pin, Pendant, Bird On Flowering Branch, 18K Bicolor Gold, Tiffany & Co., 1½ In. 11750.00
Pin, Pendant, Cameo, Woman, Flowers In Upswept Hair, Pearl Border 1528.00
Pin, Pendant, Cupid, Black Opal, Enamel Peacock Feather, Gold Mount, 2¼ In. 1645.00
Pin, Pendant, European Cut Diamonds, Platinum Topped Gold, Edwardian, 2 x 2 In. 3525.00
Pin, Pendant, Opals, Fire White & Crystal, Gold Mount, Arts & Crafts, 2⅞ In. 646.00
Pin, Pink Tourmaline, Round Cut Peridot Center, 18K Gold, 1983, 1¼ x 1⅜ In. 2760.00
Pin, Plique-A-Jour Enamel, Flowers, Diamonds, 18K, Platinum, Oval, Blue, Rose, Art Nouveau 10200.00
Pin, Porcelain, Mother & Child, Blue Enamel Frame, 2 x 1¾ In. 823.00
Pin, Portrait, Woman, Draped Red Hood, Scrolled Silver Mount, c.1900, 1¾ x 1½ In. 207.00

Pin, Rose, Titanium, Diamond, Vera Wang, 2 In. 4406.00
Pin, Round Cut Diamonds, Pear Shape Amethysts, Platinum, 18K Gold, 2¾ x 1¼ In. 748.00
Pin, Rubies, Emerald, Diamonds, Gold, c.1950 *illus* 700.00
Pin, Ruby & Diamond Melee, 18K Gold, Retro, 3¾ In. 3525.00
Pin, Sapphires, Diamonds, Freshwater Pearls, Gold Mount, Egyptian Revival, 2½ In. 881.00
Pin, Scarab, Sapphires, Ruby Eyes, Pearls, Diamonds, 18K, Egyptian Revival, c.1900, 2 In. 3408.00
Pin, Scarecrow, Diamonds, Textured 18K Bicolor Gold, 2¼ In. 633.00
Pin, Seahorse, Sterling Silver, Marked, Cini, 3 x 1¾ In. *illus* 600.00
Pin, Seed Pearls, Turquoise Cabochons, Pave Set, Diamond Accents, 14K Gold, 1 In. 1116.00
Pin, Shell, 18K Yellow Gold, 3 Silver Baroque Pearls, Marked, Fluhler, 2 x 1⅝ In. 2000.00
Pin, Snake, Diamonds, Rubies, Coral, Silver On Gold, Victorian, 2 x ⅝ In. *illus* 568.00
Pin, Spoon, Sterling Silver, Tara Pattern, Reed & Barton, c.1955 14.00
Pin, Staff Of Music, Sterling Silver, Marked, Cini, 2¾ In. 206.00
Pin, Sterling Silver, 3 Flowers, Hammered, 3 Green Onyx Cabochons, Georg Jensen, 2 In. 470.00
Pin, Sterling Silver, Abstract Design, Torun Bulow Hube, Georg Jensen, 2⅝ x 2 In. 1058.00
Pin, Sterling Silver, Abstract Shape, Patinated, Pearl, Ed Wiener, c.1950, 4 In. 1058.00
Pin, Sterling Silver, Bellflowers, Amber Cabochons, Georg Jensen, c.1909, 3 x 3 In. 11163.00
Pin, Sterling Silver, Bird In Leaves, No. 209, Georg Jensen, 1¾ In. 323.00
Pin, Sterling Silver, Blue Cabochons, Art Nouveau Style, Georg Jensen 600.00
Pin, Sterling Silver, Flower, Leaf, Vine, Garnet, No. 138, Georg Jensen, 1½ In. 764.00
Pin, Sterling Silver, Intertwined Stick & Ball Design, Art Smith, 2¾ In. 1175.00
Pin, Sterling Silver, Purple Stone, Marked, Carence Crafters, 1½ In. *illus* 720.00
Pin, Strawberries, Coral, 18K Gold Leaves, Victorian, $2\frac{3}{16}$ x 2 In. *illus* 478.00
Pin, Stylized Sunflowers, Split Pearls, Garnets, Diamonds, Round, Edward Oakes, 1½ In. 3525.00
Pin, Sunburst, Lapis, Turquoise Surround, Diamonds, 18K, Andrew Grima, 3 In. 9988.00
Pin, Swordfish, 14K Gold, 2½ x 1⅛ In. 254.00
Pin, Toucan, Multicolored Enamel, Diamond Melee, 18K Gold, 1½ In. 2938.00
Pin, Trefoil, Rose Cut Diamonds, Guilloche Enamel Ground, Silver, 1 x 1¾ In. 470.00
Pin, Triangular, Hammered, Tooled, Silver, Inset Abalone, Arts & Crafts 180.00
Pin, Violin, Suspended From Bow, Diamonds, Enamel, 18K Bicolor Gold, Amati, 2¾ In. 1763.00
Pin, Wood Bars Swiveling On Gold Rod, Silver Frame, Betty Cooke, 3⅛ In. 1880.00
Pin & Bracelet, Bar, Etruscan Revival Style, 12K Gold, Applied Leaves, ¾-In. Pin 633.00
Pin & Earrings, 14K Gold, Wirework, Geometric Design, Victorian 550.00
Pin & Earrings, Abstract Shape, 18K Gold, Gubelin, 2-In. Pin 1998.00
Pin & Earrings, Gold Metal, Oak Leaves, Faux Pearls, Rhinestone, M. Haskell, c.1940 1800.00
Ring, 2 Blue Stones, Prong Set, Scalloped, 18K Gold, Georg Jensen, Size 6 705.00
Ring, 2 Graduated Spheres, 18K Gold, Cartier, c.1970, Size 5½ 999.00
Ring, 14K Yellow Gold, Nugget Style, Marquise Diamonds 1416.00
Ring, 22K Gold, Bezel Set, Scrolling Shoulders, Helen Woodhull, Size 6 11750.00
Ring, Amethyst, Bezel Set, Sterling Silver Mount, Incised Geometrics, Kalo Shop 705.00
Ring, Amethyst, Oval, Citrines, 14K Gold Leafy Mount, Arts & Crafts 382.00
Ring, Amethysts & Citrines, Diamond Border, 18K Gold, Cellino, Size 6½ 1058.00
Ring, Ballerina, 14K Gold, 16 Round & 32 Baguette Cut Diamonds 413.00
Ring, Blossoms, Mother-Of-Pearl Branch Shaped Mount, 18K Gold, Stephen Dweck 588.00
Ring, Blue Topaz, Oval, Rose Cut Diamonds, 18K Scrolling, Otto Jakob 2468.00
Ring, Cameo, Classical Man, Blue Hardstone 18K Gold Mount, Ed Wiener 1293.00
Ring, Carnelian, Crowned Escutcheon, Regina & Rampant Lion, Gold Mount, Size 8¾ 1998.00
Ring, Cat's-Eye Chrysoberyl, Rubies, Diamonds, Bombe Shape, 18K, Oscar Heyman, c.1950 6756.00
Ring, Citrine, Gypsy Set, Sterling Silver Mount, Hermes, Size 6 294.00
Ring, Diamond, Brilliant Cut Sapphire, Diamond Surround, 14K Gold Mount, c.1950, Size 5½ 540.00
Ring, Diamond, Loop Design, Mauboussin, France, Size 5½ 1195.00
Ring, Diamond, Pave Set, Platinum Mount, Bombe Form, Van Cleef & Arpels 7768.00
Ring, Diamond, Platinum, Art Deco, c.1935, Size 4 6274.00
Ring, Diamond, Rose Cut, Surrounded By Rose Cut Diamonds, Gold 823.00
Ring, Diamond, Ruby, Platinum Mount, Black, Starr & Frost, Art Deco, c.1920 8573.00
Ring, Diamond Solitaire, 18K Gold Mount, Jabel, Size 4¾ 2580.00
Ring, Diamond Solitaire, Platinum, Marcus & Co., Size 5½ 11750.00
Ring, Diamond Solitaire, Prong Set, Diamond Shoulders, Platinum, Art Deco 2703.00
Ring, Diamonds, 2 Pear Shape, Rose Cut, Platinum Mount, Navette Shape, Edwardian 1763.00
Ring, Diamonds, 5 Bezel Set, Brilliant Cut Diamonds, 18K, Elsa Peretti 1116.00
Ring, Diamonds, Baguettes, Opal, Platinum Mount, Art Deco 4700.00
Ring, Diamonds, European Cut, Prong Set, Textured Mount, 18K Gold, David Webb 1058.00
Ring, Diamonds, Rubies, Platinum, Art Deco, Marked, Black, Starr & Frost, c.1920 *illus* 6573.00
Ring, Emerald, 20 Mine Cut Diamonds, Enameled Gold Mount, 1930s 1770.00
Ring, Emerald, Diamond, Gold, c.1930 *illus* 1500.00

Jewelry, Pin, Sterling Silver, Purple Stone, Marked, Carence Crafters, 1½ In.
$720.00

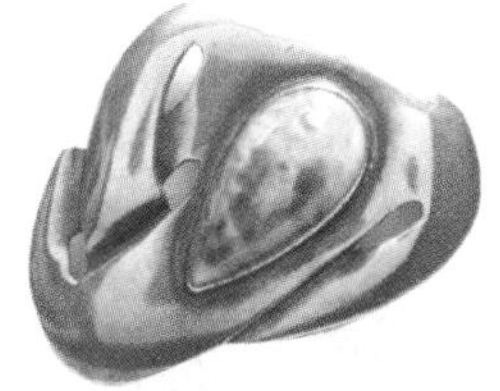

Jewelry, Pin, Strawberries, Coral, 18K Gold Leaves, Victorian, $2\frac{3}{16}$ x 2 In.
$478.00

Jewelry, Ring, 22K, Prince Albert Of Wales Coronation, Gold, Poison Compartment, Box
$2629.00

Jewelry, Ring, Diamonds, Rubies, Platinum, Art Deco, Marked, Black, Starr & Frost, c.1920
$6573.00

Jewelry, Ring, Emerald, Diamond, Gold, c.1930
$1500.00

Jewelry, Ring, Pearl, Diamonds, Navette Shape, Silver On 14K Gold Mount, 1 x ½ In.
$717.00

Jewelry, Ring, Scarab, Blue Favrile Glass, Embossed Heiroglyphics, 18K Gold, Tiffany
$382.00

Jewelry, Ring, Seal, Pivots, Hardstone, Gold, Victorian
$175.00

Jewelry, Stickpin, Diamonds, Mine Cut, Openwork, Platinum, 14K, Edwardian, 3 x ½ In.
$263.00

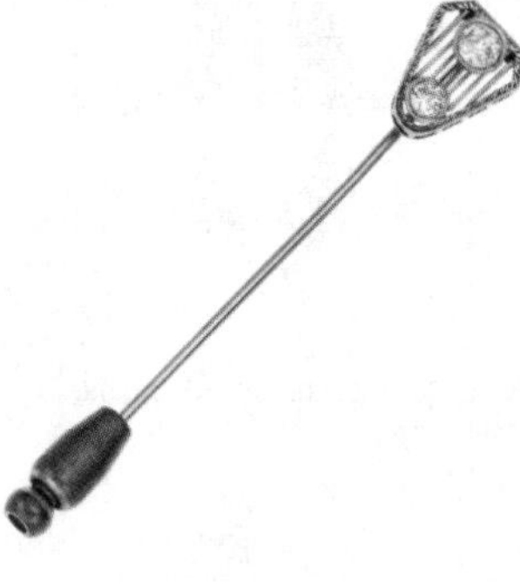

Ring, Emerald, Diamond, Openwork Gallery, Platinum, Art Deco, Size 6 .... 2200.00
Ring, Emerald Cabochon, Wide 18K Gold Ribbed Mount, Bulgari, Size 5¾.......... 1880.00
Ring, Enamel, Multicolored, Hinged Compartment, Renaissance Revival.......... 1998.00
Ring, Eternity Band, Diamond, Platinum, Beaded Accents, c.1930, Size 11.......... 3000.00
Ring, Figure 8 Shape, Circular Cut Diamond, Square Cut Diamond, 14K Gold, c.1950 .... 600.00
Ring, Flower, Diamond, Prong Set, 18K Gold, Georg Jensen, Size 5¾.......... 705.00
Ring, Green Onyx, 18K Gold, Tiffany & Co., c.1970, Size 6¾.......... 1293.00
Ring, Intertwined Loops, 18K White Gold, Mauboussin, Size 7½.......... 359.00
Ring, Kinetic, Dome Shape, Flexible Rods, 18K Gold, Pol Bury, Size 5½ 5405.00
Ring, Knotted Rope Form, Naturalistic, 22K Gold, Lina Fanourakis, Size 6½.......... 353.00
Ring, Kunzite, Cushion Cut Diamonds, 18K, Rope Twist Mount, Schlumberger 3480.00
Ring, Lapis Cabochon, Sterling Silver Geometric Mount, Arts & Crafts, Kalo Shop.......... 264.00
Ring, Lover's Eye, Watercolor On Ivory, Gray Iris, Gold, Black Enamel, Box, Lynstone, Victorian 3173.00
Ring, Moss Agate, 10K Gold, 20th Century 99.00
Ring, Opal, 16 Oval Cut Diamonds, 14K Yellow Gold, c.1955, Size 8½.......... 960.00
Ring, Opal Cabochon, Oval, Diamond, Platinum Mount, Toni Cavelti, Size 7½.......... 4465.00
Ring, Pearl, Diamonds, Navette Shape, Silver On 14K Gold Mount, 1 x ½ In. .... *illus* 717.00
Ring, Peridot, Oval, Baguette Diamonds, Bezel Set, 18K Gold, Cartier, Size 6.......... 1920.00
Ring, Pink Sapphire, European Cut Diamonds Surround, Edwardian, 18K.......... 6463.00
Ring, Pink Tourmaline, 18K Gold, Angela Cummings, Size 5¾ 1410.00
Ring, Pink Tourmaline, Diamond, 18K White Gold, Mauboussin, Size 6 .... 1225.00
Ring, Platinum, 3 European Cut Diamonds, 8 Smaller Round Diamonds, Edwardian.......... 2242.00
Ring, Platinum, Engraved Shoulders, Mine Cut Diamond, Art Deco 1534.00
Ring, Platinum, European Cut Diamond, Openwork Shoulders, Edwardian.......... 619.00
Ring, Platinum, European Cut Diamond, Diamond Melee, Art Deco, Size 8 .... 1175.00
Ring, Prince Albert Of Wales Coronation, 22K Gold, Poison Compartment, Box .... *illus* 2629.00
Ring, Pyramid, Sterling Silver, Hermes, France, Size 5¼ 118.00
Ring, Ruby, Diamonds, 18K Gold, Rope Twist Accent, Elizabeth Gage, Size 6.......... 1912.00
Ring, Ruby, Oval, Faceted, Quatrefoil Diamond Ground, 14K Gold, Art Deco.......... 3600.00
Ring, Ruby, Square Cut Diamonds, 18K Gold, Oscar Heyman, Size 6¼ 4406.00
Ring, Saddle, Jadeite, White Edges, 14K Yellow Gold, Size 6 .... 316.00
Ring, Sapphire, Cushion Cut, 2 Round Diamonds, Platinum, c.1910, Size 8.......... 8960.00
Ring, Sapphire, Diamond, Platinum Topped, 18K Gold, Retro, c.1940.......... 956.00
Ring, Sapphire, Diamond, Half Moon Shape, Platinum, Heyman Brothers, Size 6 .... 6463.00
Ring, Sapphire, Oval Cut, Old Mine Cut Diamonds, Beaded Trim, Edwardian.......... 4113.00
Ring, Scarab, Blue Favrile Glass, Embossed Hieroglyphics, 18K Gold, Tiffany .... *illus* 382.00
Ring, Scarab, Lapis, Flower Hinged Shoulders, Gold Mount, Size 4¼ 646.00
Ring, Seal, Pivots, Hardstone, Gold, Victorian .... *illus* 175.00
Ring, Snake, Gold, Turquoise, Cabochon, Diamond Melee Eyes, Bezel Set, 18K Gold 353.00
Ring, Snake, Round Brilliant Cut Diamonds, Ruby Eyes, 14K Gold, Man's, Size 11.......... 863.00
Ring, South Sea White Pearl, Blue Sapphires, Diamonds, 18K Gold, Size 7½ 1200.00
Ring, Square Glazed Compartment, Diamond, 16 Full Cut Diamonds, Chopard, 18K 1080.00
Ring, Star Sapphire, Bezel Set, Triangular Cut Sapphires, 18K Gold, Kurt Wayne.......... 499.00
Ring, Star Sapphire, Diamond Trillion Shoulders, Platinum, Marcus & Co.......... 2468.00
Ring, Topaz, Marquise Cut, Prong Set, Diamond Baguettes, 14K Gold Mount, Tiffany & Co... 3643.00
Ring, Trinity, Rolling, 32 Round Brilliant Cut Diamonds, 18K White Gold, Cartier.......... 2596.00
Ring, Yellow Paste, Full Cut Diamond Melee, 18K Gold, Misani, Size 6¾.......... 588.00
Ring Set, Platinum, Diamond, White Rose Pattern, Art Deco, Size 6 & 5½.......... 490.00
Stickpin, Bakelite, Knot, Orange, 3⅛ In.......... 19.00
Stickpin, Blue Glass Stone, Round, Faux Tortoise Enamel, Brass Mount, 2¾ In. 5.00
Stickpin, Bow, Silver Plate, Openwork, Script Initials, Victorian, ½ x 2⅝ In. 20.00
Stickpin, Citrine, Oval Cut, 14K Flower Mount, Marked, Kalo Shop.......... 823.00
Stickpin, Clover Leaf, Old Mine Cut Diamonds, 2½ In.......... 7050.00
Stickpin, Diamonds, Mine Cut, Openwork, Platinum, 14K, Edwardian, 3 x ½ In. .... *illus* 263.00
Stickpin, Diamonds, Rose Cut, Platinum, 2 Teardrops, Beaded Edge, Marked, Cartier.......... 499.00
Stickpin, Figure Wearing Plumed Helmet, Maltese Cross On Breastplate, 14K 940.00
Stickpin, Hound In Grassy Landscape, Crystal, Reverse Painted, 14K, Marcus & Co. 1880.00
Stickpin, Jade Cabochon, Oval, Gold Plated Mount, 2 In.......... 8.00
Stickpin, Orange Stone, Brass Mount, 2¼ In.......... 11.00
Stickpin, Rhinestones, Royal Blue, White, Gold Plated Setting, 2¾ In. 11.00
Stickpin, Ruby, Diamond Frame, Surrounded By Ruby Melee, 18K, Tiffany & Co. 2233.00
Stickpin, Scarab, Red Iridescent Enamel, Sterling, c.1910, Tiffany & Co., ⅝ In. 470.00
Stickpin, Sunstone, Copper, Filigree Mount, 3 In.......... 9.00
Stickpin, Turquoise Stone, Round, 3 In.......... 10.00
Tiara, Cameo, Animal, 18K Gold, 7¾ x 1½ In. 3750.00
Tiara, Jeweled, Bird Shape, Upright Wings, Brass Frame, Multicolored Stones, 8 x 7 In.......... 920.00
Tie Tack, Thespian Society, Blue Enamel, Gold, Shield, Chain, 1950s, ½ In. 12.00

Vatch Clip, Woman's 18K, Onyx, Ruby, Arabic Numerals, Retro, Trabert & Hoeffer, $1\frac{3}{4}$ In.... 1058.00
Vatches are listed in their own category.
Vristwatches are listed in their own category.

OHN ROGERS statues were made from 1859 to 1892. The originals were bronze, but the housands of copies made by the Rogers factory were of painted plaster. Eighty different figures vere created. Similar painted plaster figures were produced by some other factories. Rights to he figures were sold in 1893, and the figures were manufactured for several more years by the Rogers Statuette Co. Never repaint a Rogers figure because this lowers the value to collectors.

Group, Coming To The Parson, Sitting At Desk, Couple Standing, Bronze, 22 x $18\frac{1}{2}$ In. 500.00

OSEF ORIGINALS ceramics were designed by Muriel Joseph George. The first pieces were nade in California from 1945 to 1962. They were then manufactured in Japan. The company vas sold to George Good in 1982 and he continued to make Josef Originals until 1985. The ompany was then sold to Southland Corporation. The name is now owned by Applause, and the irthday Girl series is still being made.

igurine, Angel, Christmas, Holding Red Stocking, Gold Wings.......... 15.00
igurine, Angel, Valentine's Day, No. 7699, Marked.......... 12.00
igurine, Bear, White, Christmas Hat, Bow, Lollipop, $3\frac{1}{2}$ In.......... 13.00
igurine, Ding Dong Belle, California, Marked, $3\frac{1}{4}$ In.......... 41.00
igurine, Dog Series, Dalmatian, Paper In Mouth, c.1980, $4\frac{1}{4}$ In.......... 30.00
igurine, Doll Of The Month, Cone, October, Gold Shawl, Marked.......... 45.00
igurine, Doll Of The Month, February, Flowers, Purple.......... 52.00
igurine, Elephant, Flower In Trunk, Marked, $4\frac{1}{2}$ In.......... 45.00
igurine, Elf, Green Frog, Marked, 3 x 2 In.......... 25.00
igurine, Girl, Pink Dress, Blue Flowered Apron, $3\frac{3}{4}$ In.......... 65.00
igurine, Himalayan Cat, Blue Eyes, Marked, 5 In.......... 40.00
igurine, International, Girl, Greece, Apron With Gold & Pink Roses, Belt, Shawl, 4 In. 65.00
igurine, International, Girl, Ireland, Green Dress, Gold Flowers, $3\frac{5}{8}$ In.......... 65.00
igurine, Musical, Girl Playing Lute.......... 80.00
igurine, Owl, Wide-Eyed, Marked, $3\frac{3}{4}$ x $2\frac{1}{2}$ In.......... 9.00
igurine, Sunbather Girl, Diaper Bikini, Sunglasses, $4\frac{3}{4}$ In.......... 345.00
igurine, Sweet 16, Gold Tip Wings, Bouquet Of Roses, 6 x $5\frac{1}{2}$ In.......... 60.00
igurine, Zodiac, Boy, Leo Symbol, $5\frac{1}{2}$ In.......... *illus* 14.00
alt & Pepper, Puppies, White, Gray, $3\frac{1}{4}$ In., Pair.......... *illus* 20.00
oup, Dish, Girl's Face, Blue, Yellow, Marked, $6\frac{1}{2}$ In.......... 75.00

UDAICA is any memorabilia that refers to the Jews or the Jewish religion. Interests range from ewspaper clippings that mention eighteenth- and nineteenth-century Jewish Americans to eligious objects, such as menorahs or spice boxes. Age, condition, and the intrinsic value of ne material, as well as the historic and artistic importance, determine the value.

mulet, Kamea, Necklace, Silver Case, Raised Leafy Design, $3\frac{1}{4}$ In.......... 50.00
ookends, Blowing Shofar, Patinated Bronze, Mottled Green, Israel, Mid 1900s, 5 In.......... 50.00
ottle, Ribbed Glass, Cork Stopper, L'Chaim To Life, Arched, Star Of David.......... 85.00
ox, Porcelain, Star Of David, Flowers, 4-Footed.......... 50.00
racelet, Charm, Sterling, Blue Enamel, Mother-Of-Pearl, Lobster Claw Clasp, Italy, 8 In. ... 113.00
andlestick, Sabbath, 2-Light, Brass, Patinated, Gilded, Hexagonal Base, 1960s, 8 x 11 In. .. 50.00
andlestick, Sabbath, Silver Plate, Fraget N. Plaque, 14 In., Pair.......... 2950.00
harm, Tribal, Tribe Of Issachar Emblem, Donkey, Twisted Rope Loop, 10K Gold.......... 90.00
up, Kiddush, Becha, Silver, Gilt Wash, Engraved, Russia, Late 1800s, 2 In. 100.00
up, Kiddush, Sterling Silver, Engraved, Scrolling Zigzag.......... 160.00
resser Box, Porcelain, Star Of David, Flowers, Gilded, Scalloped Edge, 4-Footed.......... 50.00
reeting Card, Bar Mitzvah, Collage.......... 18.00
reeting Card, Wedding, Pop-Up, Pull-Out, Die Cut, Embossed, Germany, c.1900.......... 75.00
anukkah Lamp, Art Deco, Silver Plate, $10\frac{1}{4}$ x $8\frac{1}{4}$ In.......... 877.00
nife, Shabbot, Challah, Kodesh, Brass Handle, Stainless Steel, Serrated, 12 In.......... 18.00
ithograph, Kabbala, Flowers, Fruit, Lions, Gold Leaf, Frame, 16 x $11\frac{1}{2}$ In.......... 350.00
ap, Old Palestine, Lithograph, c.1902, $9\frac{1}{2}$ x $15\frac{1}{2}$ In.......... 28.00
enorah, Black, Gold Metal Accents, Crown Shape, 6 x 8 In.......... 41.00
enorah, Brass, Classic Shape, Scrolling, Leafy Vines, $8\frac{1}{2}$ x 10 In.......... 200.00
enorah, Brass, Letters, O'je, $5\frac{3}{4}$ In.......... 35.00
enorah, Brass, Oil, Folding, 5 x $4\frac{1}{4}$ In.......... 250.00
enorah, Musicians, 9 Players, Brass, Swirl Pattern, 10 In.......... 30.00
ecklace, Chai, Round Disc, Enameled, White Crystals, 20 In.......... 28.00

TIP

When washing Hummel or other small figurines cover the small air holes. The holes may be near the bottom but are often hidden near branches or arms. It is very difficult to get water out of a figurine.

Josef Originals, Figurine, Zodiac, Boy, Leo Symbol, $5\frac{1}{2}$ In.
$14.00

Josef Originals, Salt & Pepper, Puppies, White, Gray, $3\frac{1}{4}$ In., Pair
$20.00

J

Jugtown, Vase, Sloped, Foamy White Glaze, Blue Interior, Marked, Jugtown Ware, 7 ½ In.
$490.00

Jukebox, Seeburg, Model SP32, 160 Sections, c. 1973, 54 In.
$710.00

Kate Greenaway, Napkin Ring, Silver Plate, Figural, Girl, Dog, Tufts, 7 x 4½ In.
$485.00

Paperweight, Millefiori, Whitefriars, Blue & White Star Of David, c.1978, 3 In. 500.00
Paperweight, Star Of David, Shalom, Rectangular, Crystal Block, Laser Etching, 3 In. 195.00
Paperweight, Star Of David, White, Cobalt Blue, Spaced Bubbles, Caithness, 3¼ In. 110.00
Paperweight, Star Of David, White, Cobalt Blue, Pink Canes, Peter McDougall, 2⅝ In. 155.00
Pen, Sterling Silver, Scrollwork, Inscription, Israel, 1950s 44.00
Photograph, Jewish Synagogue, Nagyvarad, Hungary, 5¾ x 3½ In. 42.00
Pin, Silver, Oval, Blue Cut Gemstone, Hebrew Letter Shin, Signed, Bezalel, c.1950 . . . . 500.00
Plate, Seder, Embossed Grapes, Brass, Turquoise Enamel, 9½ In. 25.00
Plate, Wedgwood, Blue & White, Center Menorah Design, Israel Independence, c.1973 . . . . . . 20.00
Postcard, Bethlehem, Panoramic View, Leporello, Wien 36.00
Postcard, Jewish Book Against Starry Background, Williamsburg Art Co., N.Y., c.1915 . . . . . . 36.00
Spice Box, Silvered Brass, Domed Foot, Domed Foot, Pierced, Hexagonal Reverse Dome, 6⅜ In. 500.00
Spoon, Birth Of Israel, Litvin, Silver Plate, c.1948 . . . . 38.00
Tablecloth, 6 Napkins, Lion Of Judah, Embroidered, Palestine, 27 x 27 In.. . . . . 95.00
Torah Mantle, Lion Of Judah, Luchot Ha Brit, Embroidered, Green Velvet, Bezalel Era, 26 In. 500.00
Torah Pointer, Blown Glass, Amethyst Glass Crown, Beads, Twist Stem, Eng., 1920s, 5 In. . . . 175.00
Torah Pointer, Ribbon Pattern, Silver, Ivory, c.1889. . . . . 695.00
Torah Shield, Arched Back Panel, Applied Crown, Columns, Sterling Silver, 13 x 10½ In.. . . . 259.00
Tray, Latke, Man & Wife Figures, Apple Dish, Ceramic, Box, Lotus International, 5 & 12 In. . . 85.00
Tzedakah Box, Mailbox Shape, Rubber Stopper, 6¼ x 3½ In.. . . . . 18.00

JUGTOWN Pottery refers to pottery made in North Carolina as far back as the 1750s. In 1915, Juliana and Jacques Busbee set up a training and sales organization for what they named Jugtown Pottery. In 1921, they built a shop at Jugtown, North Carolina, and hired Ben Owen as a potter in 1923. The Busbees moved the village store where the pottery was sold to New York City. Juliana Busbee sold the New York store in 1926 and moved into a log cabin near the Jugtown Pottery. The pottery closed in 1959. It reopened in 1960 and is still working near Seagrove, North Carolina.

Pitcher, Turquoise & Red Glaze, Marked, 9½ In. 3290.00
Rose Bowl, Foamy White Glaze, Impressed, 4½ x 7 In. 345.00
Urn, 2 Handles, Ridged, Mirror Black Glaze, 9½ x 7 In.. . . . . 600.00
Vase, Egg Shape, Foamy White Glaze, Impressed, 5⅞ & 6 In., Pair 460.00
Vase, Oval, Tuquoise Glaze, Red Blush Marks, Impressed, 6 In. 470.00
Vase, Sloped, Foamy White Glaze, Blue Interior, Marked, Jugtown Ware, 7½ In. . . . . *illus* 490.00
Vase, Turquoise Glaze Red, Oval, 6 In. 470.00
Vase, White Chinese Style Glaze, Red Earthenware, Marked, c.1923, 5½ x 7½ In. 382.00

JUKEBOXES play records. The first coin-operated phonograph was demonstrated in 1889. In 1906 the Automatic Entertainer appeared, the first coin-operated phonograph to offer several different selections of music. The first electrically powered jukebox was introduced in 1927. Collectors search for jukeboxes of all ages, especially those with flashing lights and unusual design and graphics.

AMI, Wall Unit, 120 Selections, 14½ x 11 In.. . . . . 66.00
Rock-Ola, Commando, Model, 1420. . . . . 23100.00
Rock-Ola, Model 1454, Hi Fidelity, Chrome Plate Front, 120 Selections, c.1955 . . . . 4683.00
Seeburg, Model SP32, 160 Sections, c. 1973, 54 In. . . . . *illus* 710.00
Seeburg, Symphonola, Regal, 1938, 54 In. 1320.00
Wurlitzer, Model 1015, Revolving Color Tube, Bubble System, 78 RPM, c.1946, 60 In. 7150.00 to 7800.00
Wurlitzer, Model 400, Remote Speaker, Light, Oval, 30¼ x 22½ x 11 In. 2750.00
Wurlitzer, Model 4005A, Remote Speaker, 16¼ In. 220.00
Wurlitzer, Model P-10, 1934, 49⅛ x 32 x 24 In.. . . . . 1650.00
Wurlitzer, Multi-Selector Phonograph, Tiger Maple, Walnut, Tubes, 24 Track, 59 x 33 x 23 In. . . 5200.00
Wurlitzer, Remote Wall Speaker, 17⅞ x 17¾ In. 385.00

KATE GREENAWAY, who was a famous illustrator of children's books, drew pictures of children in high-waisted Empire dresses. She lived from 1846 to 1901. Her designs appear on china, glass, and other pieces.

Napkin Ring, Silver Plate, Figural, Boy & Dog Balance 143.00
Napkin Ring, Silver Plate, Figural, Boy, Girl On Teeter-Totter 747.00
Napkin Ring, Silver Plate, Figural, Boy, Riding Wheeled Ring. 3737.00
Napkin Ring, Silver Plate, Figural, Boy, Ruffled Collar, Rogers & Bros.,1865-95 . . . . 58.00
Napkin Ring, Silver Plate, Figural, Boy, Sitting On Fence,1875-1900 . . . . 460.00
Napkin Ring, Silver Plate, Figural, Boy, With Hat, Coat 57.00
Napkin Ring, Silver Plate, Figural, Girl, 3 Owls, Barrel Shape. 1725.00
Napkin Ring, Silver Plate, Figural, Girl, Dog, Tufts, 7 x 4½ in. . . . . *illus* 485.00

Napkin Ring, Silver Plate, Figural, Girl, Emerges From Figure 115.00
Napkin Ring, Silver Plate, Figural, Girl, Parasol, Boy, Hoop, James Tufts,1875-1915 .... 1495.00
Napkin Ring, Silver Plate, Figural, Girl, Pug Dog, Marked, FB Rogers Silver Co. 747.00
Napkin Ring, Silver Plate, Figural, Girl, Pushes Figure 86.00
Napkin Ring, Silver Plate, Figural, Girl, Teaching Poodle 5750.00
Napkin Ring, Silver Plate, Figural, Girl, With Rifle, Simpson, Hall, Miller & Co.,3 In. 316.00
Napkin Ring, Silver Plate, Figural, Girl, With Stick, Crying Boy With Hoop, Meriden Silver Plate 4312.00
Napkin Ring, Silver Plate, Figural, Infant In Chair, Middletown Plate Co. .... *illus* 2588.00
Napkin Ring, Silver Plate, Figural, Lady On Toboggan, Wilcox Silver Plate Co. 2300.00
Napkin Ring, Silver Plate, Figural, Little Sister & Dog, Derby Silver Co. 258.00

KAY FINCH Ceramics were made in Corona Del Mar, California, from 1935 to 1963. The hand-decorated pieces often depicted whimsical animals and people. Pastel colors were used.

Kay Finch CALIFORNIA

Bowl, Egg Shape, White Matte Finish, 11 x 5 In. 45.00
Bowl, Shell, 3½ x 4½ In. 19.00
Candleholder, Scandie, 5¼ In. 75.00
Dish, White Matte Finish, Scalloped Edges, Signed, 14 x 9 In. 65.00
Figurine, Angel, Blessing, 4¼ x 2¾ In. 28.00
Figurine, Angel, Praying, 4 1/4 x 2 3/4 In. .... 28.00 to 32.00
Figurine, Bird, Gold, Freeman McFarlin, 4½ In. 24.00
Figurine, Bird, Gold, Freeman McFarlin, 4 In., Pair 80.00
Figurine, Cat, Hear No Evil, 3¼ In. 65.00
Figurine, Cat, Jezebel, 9 In. .... *illus* 2100.00
Figurine, Cat, Puff, 3 In. 41.00
Figurine, Choir Boy, Kneeling, Blond, 5½ In. 65.00
Figurine, Choir Boy, Kneeling, Brunette, 5½ In. 65.00
Figurine, Duck, Peep, 4 In. 65.00
Figurine, Duckling, Marching, 1⁷⁄₁₆ In. 55.00
Figurine, Elephant, Peanuts, 8⅜ In. 248.00
Figurine, Folk Art Woman, 5 In. 27.00
Figurine, Girl, Scandie, 5 In. 52.00
Figurine, Godey, Man & Woman, 9½ In., Pair 120.00
Figurine, Godey Lady, Applied Roses On Hat, Shoulder, 9 In. 75.00
Figurine, Kangaroo, 9 x 8⅞ In. 199.00
Figurine, Lamb, Kneeling, 2 x 2½ In. 84.00
Figurine, Mama Duck, 4⅕ In. 199.00
Figurine, Mr. & Mrs. Bird, 4½ & 3 In., Pair 175.00
Figurine, Owl, Hoot, Freeman McFarlin, 8¾ In. .... 75.00 to 82.00
Figurine, Owl, Toot, Freeman McFarlin, 5¾ In. 75.00
Figurine, Owl, Tootsie, 3¾ In. .... 38.00 to 55.00
Figurine, Peasants, Black Haired, 6½ In., Pair 126.00
Figurine, Penguin, Pee Wee, 3¼ In. .... 65.00 to 75.00
Figurine, Pig, 3⅝ In. 105.00
Figurine, Playful Poodle, Gold Leaf, 10 x 10½ In. 225.00
Figurine, Rooster, 7 In. 21.00
Figurine, Rooster & Hen, Butch & Biddy, 8 & 5¼ In., Pair 175.00
Figurine, Squirrel, Mama & Papa, Pair 100.00
Flower Bowl, Swan, 6½ x 9 x 8 In. .... *illus* 125.00
Plate, Santa Claus, 6½ In. 95.00
Window Box Planter, Off-White, Gold Leafs, 14 x 5 In. 65.00

KAYSERZINN, *see Pewter category.*

KELVA glassware was made by the C. F. Monroe Company of Meriden, Connecticut, about 1904. It is a pale, pastel-painted glass decorated with flowers, designs, or scenes. Kelva resembles Nakara and Wave Crest, two other glasswares made by the same company.

KELVA

Box, Pink Roses, Leafy Ground, Beaded, 3½ x 8 In. .... *illus* 650.00

KENTON HILLS Pottery in Erlanger, Kentucky, made artwares, including vases and figurines that resembled Rookwood, probably because so many of the original artists and workmen had worked at the Rookwood plant. Kenton Hills opened in 1939 and closed during World War II.

Bowl, Leaves, Brown, Indigo, Hemispherical, 5 x 6 In. 570.00
Figurine, Madonna Holding Infant, White High Glaze, Marked, 13¾ In. 359.00

Kate Greenaway, Napkin Ring, Silver Plate, Figural, Infant In Chair, Middletown Plate Co. $2588.00

Kay Finch, Figurine, Cat, Jezebel, 9 In. $2100.00

Kay Finch, Flower Bowl, Swan, 6½ x 9 x 8 In. $125.00

Kelva, Box, Pink Roses, Leafy Ground, Beaded, 3½ x 8 In. $650.00

K

Kew Blas, Tumbler, Gold Iridescent, 4 Dimples, Engraved, 4 In.
$225.00

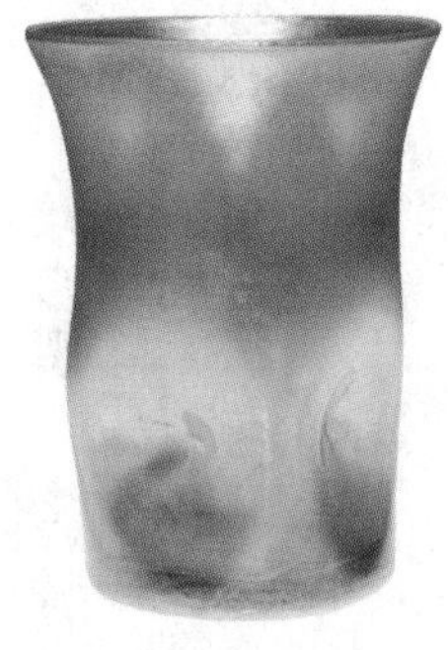

Kewpie, Planter, Kewpie With Mandolin, Spotted Doodle Dog, 3½ In.
$1150.00

Kewpie, Plastic, Jointed, Painted Features, 12 In.
$135.00

Kewpie, Sign, McCann's Ice Cream, Tin, H.D. Beach Co., 27¾ x 20 In.
$275.00

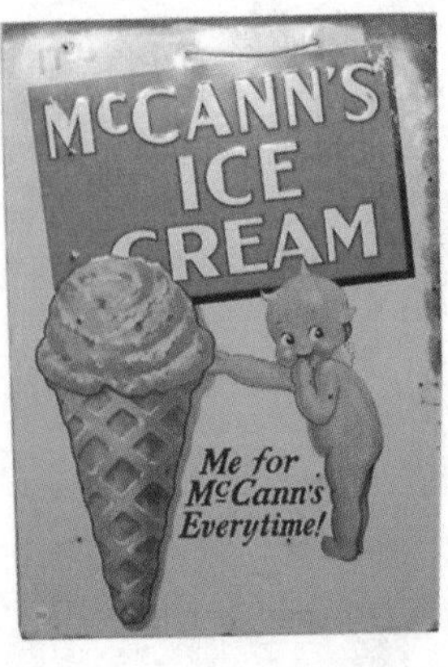

Vase, Golden Irises, Base Drilled For Lamp, 12½ x 5¼ In. 600.00
Vase, Pink Blossoms, Pearl Gray Ground, 12½ x 5½ In. 600.00
Vase, Unica, Blossoms, Brown Butterfat Glaze, White Ground, 8¼ x 4¼ In. 360.00

KEW BLAS is the name used by the Union Glass Company of Somerville, Massachusetts. The name refers to an iridescent golden glass made from the 1890s to 1924. The iridescent glass was reminiscent of the Tiffany glass of the period.

Bowl, Underplate, Iridescent Gold, Ruffled Rim, 6¼-In. Plate 431.00
Cup & Saucer, Opal, Green Pulled Feathers, Iridescent Gold Tips, 6 In. 350.00
Goblet, Iridescent Gold, Optic Ribs, Signed, 6¼ In. 144.00
Nut Dish, Ruffled Edge, Royal Teal, Signed, 4 In. 115.00
Tumbler, Gold Iridescent, 4 Dimples, Engraved, 4 In. .... *illus* 225.00
Vase, Gold Iridescent, Light Orange Ground, Bulbous, 4 In. 323.00
Vase, Gold Pulled Feather, Gold Iridescent Ground, Marked, 5 In. 499.00
Vase, Green Pulled Feather Tipped In Gold, Opal, Gold Interior, Signed, 9¼ In. 460.00
Vase, Iridescent Gold, Fishnet, Cream Ground, Marked, 5½ In. 316.00
Vase, Iridescent Green, Gold Pulled Feathers, Cream Ground, Ruffled Edge, 5 x 6 In. 460.00
Vase, Iridescent Marigold, Green, Gold Pulled Feathers, Signed, 3½ In. 350.00
Vase, Iridescent Opal, Green Pulled Feathers, Gold Tips, Signed, 8 In. 400.00
Vase, Opal, Green Undulating Bands, Fluted, Flaring Rim, Signed, 8½ In. 748.00
Vase, Opal, Iridescent, Gold Zigzag Bands, Signed, 5 In. 450.00
Vase, Opal, Caramel, Iridescent Gold, Pulled Feathers, Corset Shape, Signed, 6 In. 650.00

KEWPIES, designed by Rose O'Neill, were first pictured in the *Ladies' Home Journal*. The figures, which are similar to pixies, were a success, and Kewpie dolls and figurines started appearing in 1911. Kewpie pictures and other items soon followed. Collectors search for all items that picture the little winged people.

Ashtray, Individual, Marked Royal Rudolstadt 60.00
Bisque, Aqua Dress, Lace, Jesco, Box, c.1980, 12 In. 75.00
Bisque, Bewildered, Lefton, 3 In. 20.00
Bisque, Bride & Groom, Loop Jointed, Side-Glancing Eyes, 12 In. 2800.00
Bisque, Emerging From Washtub, Towel Draped Over Side 20.00
Bisque, Germany, 2 In. 175.00
Bisque, Graduation Cap, Diploma, Enesco, Box, c.1993, 4½ In. 65.00
Bisque, Knitted Suit, Kestner, Heart Label, 4 In. 450.00
Bisque, Lying On Stomach, Winking, Lefton 13.00
Bisque, Praying With Teddy Bear, Enesco, Box, c.1991, 3½ In. 50.00
Bisque, Right-Glancing Eyes, Jointed At Shoulders, Pink Sash, c.1920, 4½ In. 456.00
Bisque, Sitting, Holding Jack-O'-Lantern 395.00
Bisque, Sitting, Holding Mandolin, Leaning Against Books, 2 In. 275.00
Bisque, Sitting, Holding Rattle, Enesco, c.1992, 3½ In. 55.00
Bisque, Sitting, In Wicker Chair, Arms & Ankles Crossed, c.1912, 3¾ In. 375.00
Bisque, Socket Head, Side-Glancing Eyes, Composition, Jointed, Toddler, 13 In. 5040.00
Bisque, Standing, Jointed Shoulders, Homespun Hat, Right-Glancing Eyes, c.1917, 4 In. 457.00
Bisque, Stars & Stripes, Jointed Arms, Blue Wings, Extended Arms, Germany, 10½ In. 450.00
Bisque, Sucking Thumb, Big Eyes, Lefton, 4¾ In. 14.00
Celluloid, Jointed Arms, Hollow, Carnival, Occupied Japan, 5 In. 16.00
Celluloid, Sleep Eyes, Jointed Head, Arms & Legs, c.1950, 13 In. 450.00
Chalk, Hands On Chin, Smiling, 5½ In. 45.00
Chalk, WWI Soldier, Jointed, Victory On Base, Movable Arms, c.1918, 14 In. 345.00
Composition, Jointed, Side-Glancing, Eyes, Topknot, Cotton Sun Suit, c.1920, 13 In. 169.00
Composition, Jointed Arms & Legs, Molded Hair, Head Turns, c.1910, 12½ In. 50.00
Composition, Side-Glancing Eyes, 13 In. 75.00
Creamer, Blue Sky Meadow Pattern, Stamped, Rudolstadt, 4 In. 385.00
Glass, Cobalt Blue, V In Circle, Marked, 4½ In. 20.00
Glass, White Carnival, V In Circle, Marked, 4½ In. 20.00
Perfume, Crown Top, Germany 49, 2⅞ In. 195.00
Pincushion, Pink Satin, Green & Brown Trim, Plastic Doll In Center 32.00
Planter, Choirboy Holding Candle, Gold Halo, Red Bow, Harp 24.00
Planter, Kewpie With Mandolin, Spotted Doodle Dog, 3½ In. .... *illus* 1150.00
Plastic, Jointed, Painted Features, 12 In. .... *illus* 135.00
Plate, Christmas, Santa Hat, 1973, 10½ In. 5.00
Postcard, Holding Tennis Racket, c.1976 .... 7.00
Postcard, Suffrage, Votes For Women, Do I Get Your Vote, Klever Kard, Rose O'Neill, c.1914. .... 130.00
Postcard, Wearing Hat, Sash Of Flowers, Greetings From Leipzig, Germany, c.1923 .... 18.00

'oster, Miscellaneous Dolls, Kewpie, World's Favorite Since 1913, 8 x 11 In.. 10.00
uilt Square, Running With Chick, 3 x 5 In. 9.00
ubber, Squeak, Blue Wings, Black Eyes, Red Mouth, Signed, 5½ In. 45.00
ign, McCann's Ice Cream, Tin, H.D. Beach Co., 27¾ x 20 In. *illus* 275.00
oap, Bar, Box, c.1917, 4⅝ In. 125.00
oap, Figural, R.O. Wilson, Box, 1918, 4¼ In. *illus* 104.00
obacco Flannel, 2 Kewpies Playing Leap Frog, c.1914, 5¾ x 4¾ In.. 40.00
rinket Box, Sitting On Lid, Japan, 4 x 2½ In. 45.00

ING'S ROSE, *see Soft Paste category.*

ITCHEN utensils of all types, from eggbeaters to bowls, are collected today. Handmade wooden and metal items, like ladles and apple peelers, were made in the early nineteenth entury. Mass-produced pieces, like iron apple peelers and graniteware, were made in the ineteenth century. Also included in this category are utensils used for other household hores, such as laundry and cleaning. Other kitchen wares are listed under manufacturers' names or nder Advertising, Iron, Tool, or Wooden.

sparagus Buncher, Cast Iron, 6⅛ x 4⅛ In. 80.00
acon Press, Wagner 140.00
aking Pan, Golf Ball, Griswold, No. 19, 966, Iron, 6 Cup 110.00
ar Set, Stainless Steel, Kalmar, Italy, Box, 5 Piece 85.00
aster, Dutch Oven, 3-Footed, Bailed, Lid, Griswold 100.00
athtub, Traveling, Zinc, Grain Painted, Capt. A.C. Cheney, Handle, 15 x 32 In.. 280.00
in, Poplar Wide Boards, Square Nails, Dough Board Lid, Zoar, 1800s, 27½ x 22 In. 144.00
iscuit, Brass, Tiger Maple Handle, 19th Century 350.00
lade, Chopping, Iron, Figural, Bathing Beauty, Incised, Fan Shape, 1900s, 12½ In. 115.00
oard, Cutting, Mahogany, Marked, Nime, 11 x 21½ In. 86.00
oard, Cutting, Bird's-Eye Maple, Carved, Game Bird, Rabbit, Knife, Fork, 19 In.. 259.00
oard, Cutting, Carved Words Health & Happiness, Bells, Horseshoe, c.1890, 11½ In. 275.00
oard, Cutting, Painted, Breadboard Ends, Pricked Design, 18 x 23½ In. 150.00
oard, Dough, Lollipop Handle, Round, 22½ In. 99.00
oard, Slaw, Softwood, Heart Shape Cutout, Iron Blade, Red Paint, 21½ x 7 In.. 385.00
oard, Slaw, Walnut, Heart Shape Cutout, Iron Blade, Lollipop End, Patina, 28 x 8 In. 468.00
oard, Slaw, Wood, Cutout Heart, Wrought Wing Nut & Blade, J Pa, 21 x 6½ In. 99.00
ottle Opener, Iron, Amish Man, Wall Mount, 3½ x 4⅜ In. 1265.00
owl, Burl, Round, Turned, Raised Collar, Early 19th Century, 6 x 14 In. 3995.00
owl, Chopping, Wood, Turned, Incised Bands, Red Paint, 19th Century, 6 x 18 In. 200.00
owl, Dough, Terra-Cotta, French Provincial, 25 In. 60.00
owl, Dough, Wood, Carved, Dark Blue Exterior, Rectangle, 4 x 12 x 20 In. 1058.00
owl, Dough, Wood, Provincial, Mid 19th Century, 12 x 21 x 9 In.. 390.00
owl, Lunch, Cover, Tupperware, 3 Compartments, Green, White Lid, 9½ x 10½ In. 8.00
owl, Stainless Steel, Marked, Gabis, Sweden, 1½ x 7¾ In. 45.00
owl, Tiger Maple, Round, Raised Collar, Painted Exterior, Early 19th Century, 7 x 22 In.. 2468.00
ox, Sugar, Gros Rouge, Hinged Lid, Mid 19th Century, 10 x 16 In. 969.00
read Pan, Griswold, No. 24, 12½ x 7½ In. 900.00
roiler, Cast Iron, Rotating, 26 In. 193.00
roiler, Dutch, Footed, Cast Iron, 20 In.. 110.00
roiler, Meat, Rotating, Cast Iron, 11 In. 495.00
utcher's Block, Maple, Brass Bull's Head, Continental, 1800s, 50 x 64 x 25 In. *illus* 950.00
utcher's Block, Wood, 3 Legs, Cross Cut, Turned, 1800s, 31 x 29 In. 138.00
utter Mold, look under Mold, Butter in this category.
utter Paddle, Ash Burl, Hook Handle, Patina, 19th Century, 5½ x 9¼ In. 173.00
utter Paddle, Burl Maple, 5 x 10½ In. 248.00
utter Paddle, Burl Maple, Carved, Oval Handle, 6½ x 10 In. 385.00
utter Paddle, Poplar, Carved, C-Shape Handle, 4¾ x 8 In. 22.00
utter Roller, Elm Leaf, c.1860, 5 In. 400.00
utter Stamp, Acorn, Poplar, Turned, Round, Handle, 5 x 4 In. 110.00
utter Stamp, Alphabet, Numbers, Carved, Lollipop Shape, 10 In. 735.00
utter Stamp, Clover, Poplar, Round, 1 x 3½ In.. 176.00
utter Stamp, Compass Star, Poplar, 6-Sided, Crosshatched, Turned, 5½ x 4½ In.. 220.00
utter Stamp, Cow, Leaves, Poplar, Serrated Border, Handle, Round, 3 x 4½ In. 330.00
utter Stamp, Elm Leaves, 19th Century, 4¾ x 4 In.. 225.00
utter Stamp, Fern, Star, Plunger & Cylinder, c.1900, 4½ x 3¾ In. 50.00
utter Stamp, Flower, Wreath, Poplar, Round, Handle, 3 x 4 In. 1110.00
utter Stamp, Flowers, Plants, Pennsylvania Dutch, 2-Sided, c.1850, ¾ x 3½ In.. 300.00
utter Stamp, Freeman, Pineapple, c.1900, 4 x 4½ In. 175.00

Kewpie, Soap, Figural, R.O. Wilson, Box, 1918, 4¼ In.
$104.00

TIP
Oil your butcher-block table to keep it from splitting at the seams. Use cooking oil if you plan to cut food on the block, mineral oil if it will be used only as a table. You must oil it at least once a month.

Kitchen, Butcher's Block, Maple, Brass Bull's Head, Continental, 1800s, 50 x 64 x 25 In.
$950.00

Kitchen, Cheese, Strainer, Punched Tin, Heart Shape, 3 Round Feet, 3¼ x 6 x 5⅝ In.
$248.00

K

Kitchen, Churn, Dazey, No. 4, Red Handle
$60.00

Kitchen, Churn, Green Paint, Stenciled, B. Rockwood Jr., 24 x 16 x 16 In.
$55.00

Kitchen, Churn, Wood, Crank, Cylindrical, Blue Paint, Tapered Legs, 39 x 27 x 20 In.
$230.00

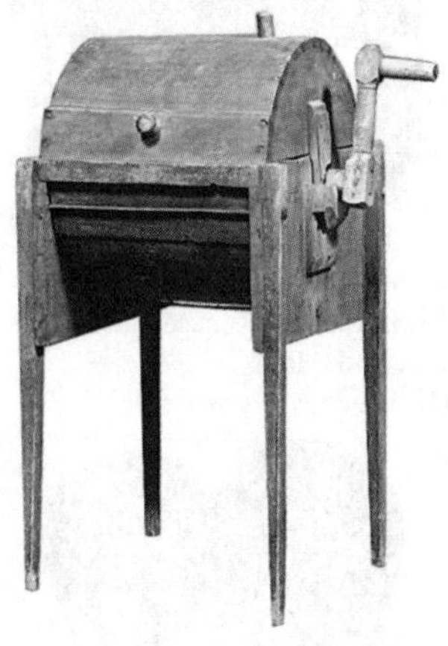

K

Butter Stamp, Heart, Oak, Turned Baluster Handle, Serrated Edge, Initials, E.B., 4½ In. 1540.00
Butter Stamp, Heart, Star, Carved, Oval, Maple, 5½ x 3¼ In. 1540.00
Butter Stamp, Heart, Tulip, Pine, Serrated Edges, Patina, Lancaster Co., Pa., 3¼ x 6 In. 1760.00
Butter Stamp, Leaf, Carved, Poplar, 1⅜ x 4⅛ In. 55.00
Butter Stamp, Leaf, Carved, Pine, 4¾ In. 110.00
Butter Stamp, Lollipop, Eagle, Star, Heart Center, Carved, Coggled Edge, 8¾ x 4½ In. 955.00
Butter Stamp, Lollipop, Tulip, Heart, Swirls, Stars, Pennsylvania Dutch, 7 x 3⅜ In. 1250.00
Butter Stamp, Pineapple, Leaves, Pine, Serrated Border, Carved, Shellac Finish, 4 In. 440.00
Butter Stamp, Pinwheel, Friction Handle, c.1860, 3 x 4 In. 600.00
Butter Stamp, Pomegranate, Poplar, Carved, Serrated Border, Handle, 5 x 4¼ In. 330.00
Butter Stamp, Rose, Leaves, Poplar, Carved, Round Handle, Serrated, 3½ x 2¾ In. 55.00
Butter Stamp, Rosette, Poplar, Carved, Sawtooth Border, Handle, 2¼ x 3⅛ In. 176.00
Butter Stamp, Songbird, Leaves, Pine, Round, Handle, 2¾ x 3½ In. 385.00
Butter Stamp, Star, Pine, Carved, 6-Sided, 4½ In. 220.00
Butter Stamp, Star, Poplar, Round, 3½ In. 121.00
Butter Stamp, Strawberry, Leaf, Plunger, 5½ x 3¾ In. 50.00
Butter Stamp, Thistle, Poplar, Serrated Border, Half Round, Handle, 4 x 7 x 3½ In. 440.00
Butter Stamp, Tree, Flowers, Poplar, Carved, Oval, Gouge Grip Handle, 4 x 3½ In. 715.00
Butter Stamp, Tulip, Arrows, Poplar, Serrated Border, Handle, 4 In. 121.00
Butter Stamp, Tulip, Pine, Carved, Serrated Border, Center County, Pa., 3¾ x 4¼ In. 715.00
Butter Stamp, Tulip, Pine, Serrated Border, Round, 3¾ In. 330.00
Butter Stamp, Tulip, Wood, Patina, Round, 1¼ x 4 In. 99.00
Butter Stamp, Wheat Sheaves, Incised, Wood, Poplar, Round, Handle, 3 x 3½ In. 33.00
Cabbage Cutter, Curly Maple, Figured, Hole In Handle, Amish, Ohio, 14½ x 5¾ In. 201.00
Cake Box, Lustro Ware, Graphic, Columbus Plastic Products, 4¼ x 2¾ In. 10.00
Candy Board, Maple Sugar, Fish, Birds, Animals, Flowers, 8 x 4¾ In. 143.00
Canister, Lid, Rosewood, Marked, Dansk Designs, Denmark, 1960s, 6 x 4 In. 400.00
Carving Set, Boda Nova, Stainless Steel, Mikael Bjornstjerna, Box, 2 Piece 125.00
Casserole, Cover, Wagner Ware, No. 4054, Magnalite, Round, Press, 2 Qt. 20.00
Casserole, Porcelain, Red, Cream, Long, Griswold 100.00
Cheese Cutter, Wrought Iron Frame, Adjustable Handle, Early 1800s, 23 x 17 In. 175.00
Cheese Press, Oak, Maple, Hemp Rope Cords, Crank, Enfield, c.1870, 33 x 26 In. 59.00
Cheese Strainer, Tin, Heart Shape, Punched, Applied Handle, 4½ x 4¾ x 5¾ In. 176.00
Cheese Strainer, Tin, Heart Shape, Punched, 3-Footed, 3¼ x 5½ x 5⅝ In. .... *illus* 248.00
Cheese Strainer, Tin, Punched, 3 Applied Ring Feet, C-Shape Handle, 3¾ x 5¼ In. 33.00
Cheese Strainer, Tin, Punched, 3 Applied Ring Feet, C-Shape Handle, 4½ x 7¼ In. 55.00
Cherry Pitter, Enterprise 13.00
Cherry Pitter, Footed 45.00
Cherry Pitter, No. 16, Enterprise Mfg. Co. 68.00
Churn, Alkaline Glaze, Pottery, Randolph County, Alabama, 19 x 10 In. 550.00
Churn, Countertop, Wood, Painted, Blue Green, DeWolf & Co., Portland, Maine, 24 In. 395.00
Churn, Crank, Tin, Vertical, Wood Paddles, Triumph Model, c.1927, 5 Gal. 175.00
Churn, Crank Handle, Blue Buttermilk Paint, Cylinder, 39 x 27 In. 230.00
Churn, Dazey, No. 4, Red Handle .... *illus* 60.00
Churn, Green Paint, Stenciled, B. Rockwood Jr., 24 x 16 x 16 In. .... *illus* 55.00
Churn, Improved Union, No. 1, 3 Legs, Stencil, Pat. Dec. 20, 1964, Tiffin Union Churn Co. 300.00
Churn, Metal, Crank, White Cedar, Wooden Handle, Tin Bands, Paddles, 9½ x 15¼ In. 388.00
Churn, Rocking, Pine, Red Paint, 37½ x 16 In. 201.00
Churn, Softwood, Red Paint, Iron Handle, Arched Cutout Feet, 32 x 25 x 18 In. 55.00
Churn, Staves, Dasher, 3 Bands, Red Paint, Inset Lid, Ohio, 22 x 14 In. 546.00
Churn, Wood, Crank, Cylindrical, Blue Paint, Tapered Legs, 39 x 27 x 20 In. .... *illus* 230.00
Churn, Wood, Dark Green Paint, 26 In. 247.00
Churn, Wood Slats, Blue Paint, 21 In. 175.00
Coffee Grinders are listed in the Coffee Mill category.
Coffee Mills are listed in their own category.
Coffee Roaster, Cylinder, Sheet Metal, Iron Base, Oval Fire Box, Kingery Mfg., 19 x 9 In. 144.00
Coffeepot, Colonial, Wagner, No. 192, 2 Qt. 25.00
Coffeepot, Griswold, A133, Aluminum 75.00
Coffeepot, Wagner, No. 186, Glass Top, Aluminum 95.00
Coffeepot, Wagner, No. 187, 3 Qt. 95.00
Condiment Set, Salt & Pepper, Mustard, Holder, Chrome, 3¾ x 6 x 2½ In. 12.00
Cooker, Ideal, Oak, Lift Top, 3 Compartments, Pans, Heating Stones, 1900s, 18 x 42 In. 403.00
Cookie Board, King & Queen, 14 x 4¾ In. 55.00
Cookie Cutter, Acrobat, Mounted, Tin, 6 x 4 In. 77.00
Cookie Cutter, Deer, With Antlers, Mounted, Tin, 5⅞ x 4¾ In. .... *illus* 248.00
Cookie Cutter, Hatchet, Tin, Flat Plate, 8½ x 5 In. 77.00

Item		Price
ookie Cutter, Horse, Mounted, Tin, 6½ x 7½ In.		275.00
ookie Cutter, Horse, Standing, Tin, Flat Plate, 6 x 7½ In.		825.00
ookie Cutter, Lady, Hat, Dress, Tin, Flat Plate, 6¾ x 6 In.		187.00
ookie Cutter, Lady, On Chamber Pot, Tin, Flat Plate, 8 x 5 In.	*illus*	385.00
ookie Cutter, Man, Standing, Tin, Flat Plate, Strap Handle, 13¾ x 6 In.		1320.00
ookie Cutter, Man In The Moon, Mounted, Tin, 5 x 3¼ In.		110.00
ookie Cutter, Pig, Tin, 9½ In.		125.00
ookie Cutter, Rabbit, Leaping, Tin, Flat Plate, 4 x 6½ In.		55.00
ookie Sheet, Griswold, No. 18		80.00 to 90.00
orer, Apple, Silver, Faceted Handle, Self Storing Blade, c.1841, 5 In.		299.00
orn Slicer, Cast Iron, Table Clamp, 3 Blades, New Lebanon, N.Y., Pre 1840, 8 In.		585.00
utlery Tray, Cherry, Tulipwood, Center Handle Divider, Dovetailed, 10 x 16 x 12 In.		3450.00
utlery Tray, Mahogany, Center Handle, 12¾ x 8 In.		345.00
eep Fryer, Basket, Griswold		45.00
eep Fryer, Basket, Wagner Ware		33.00
ipper, Ash Burl Bowl, Iron Handle, c.1840, 29 In.		18500.00
ipper, Wrought Iron, Flat Handle, Center Rod, 3-Turned Rings, Hook, 18½ x 6¼ In.		173.00
ouble Broiler, Griswold		145.00
ough Box, Cover, Pine, Dovetailed, Slanted Sides, ½ Round Handles, 1800s, 13 x 38 In.		190.00
ough Box, Mahogany, Stand, Drop Down Door, Flowers, 38 x 43½ x 19 In.	*illus*	480.00
ough Box, Pine, 4-Footed, Late 19th Century, 30 x 20 x 16 In.		83.00
ough Box, Poplar, Cut Nails, Splayed Sides, Shaped Battens, 9 x 30 In.		138.00
ough Box, Slant Side, Lid, Arched Bootjack Cutout Ends, Tongue & Groove, 33 x 49 In.		196.00
ough Box, Stand, Dovetailed, Tapered Sides, Skirt, Turned Feet, 29 x 42 x 19½ In.		660.00
ough Box, Stand, Stenciled, Medallion, Tulips, Swags, Pennsylvania Dutch, 31 x 32 In.		250.00
ough Scraper, Iron Blade, Brass Turned Handle, 2½ x 4 In.		187.00
utch Oven, Griswold, No. 8, Trivet, No. 206, 4 x 10-In. Oven	*illus*	35.00
utch Oven, Griswold, No. 67, Porcelain, Red, Cream		40.00
utch Oven, Lid, Griswold, No. 6, 2606C/2605		140.00
utch Oven, Smooth Cover, High Dome, Black Iron, Griswold		25.00
utch Oven, Tite-Top, Handle, Griswold, No. 8, 1278A		20.00
gg Carrier, 4 Tiers, Wire & Cloth Racks, Wood, Marvin Egg Saver Co., 15 x 15 In.		495.00
gg Crate, Humpty Dumpty, Wooden, 6 Stacking Tiers, Sliding Cover, Owosso Mfg. Co.		85.00
gg Pan, Shirred, Aluminum, Wagner, No. 311		150.00
gg Poacher, 7 Removable Cups, Insert, Lid, Cast Aluminum		120.00
gg Poacher, Griswold, No. 32, 9¼ x 13⅞ In.	*illus*	12.00
gg Scale, Brass Tag, Wooden Mount, Reliable		40.00
gg Scale, Jiffy Way, Egg Grader, 1940s		40.00
gg Timer, Flip The Frog, Ceramic, Marked, RD758233, Ceramic, 4 In.		181.00
gg Timer, Humpty Dumpty, Cast Iron, 3½ In.		250.00
ggbeater, Dover, Patd. Nov. 24th 1891		50.00
ggbeater, Metal, Wood Knob, Marked, Mammoth Dover Egg Beater, 16 In.		495.00
ggbeater, Red Handle, Knob, United Royalties, c.1928, 11¾ In.		11.00
at Collector, Deer Shape, Wrought Iron, 15½ x 29 In.		740.00
latiron, Embossed, Eagle, Arrow		55.00
latiron, Imperial, Gas, Self-Heating, Chicago		35.00
latiron, Single Post, Front Mounted Handle, 2 Lbs.		85.00
latiron, Teardrop Shape, Decorative Edge, No. 10		55.00
latiron, Teardrop Shape, Solid Bodied, Brass Cap, Wooden Handle, 7½ x 4½ In.		225.00
ondue Pot, Wagner, No. 3000, 2 Piece		1100.00
ondue Set, Pot, Lid, Stand, Warmer, Cover, Flower Opening, Cast Iron, 5 Piece		150.00
ood Carrier, Regal Ware, Aluminum, 5 Stack, Bail Handle, Skillet Handle		32.00
ood Chopper, Black, 2 Handles, Germany, 9 In.		45.00
ood Chopper, Griswold, No. 2, Box		13.00
ood Chopper, Rollman, No. 11, 6 In.		25.00
ood Chopper, Sausage Stuffer, Mounted, Wood Bench		45.00
ood Grinder, Winchester, No. W12		15.00
ood Grinder, Winchester, No. W32		28.00
ood Saw, Bakelite Handle, Rensch's Harrison & Makoti, 1960s, 9 x 5¾ In.		35.00
ood Saw, Meat, Bakelite, 1960s, 9 In.		34.00
ork, 2-Tine, Round Shaft, Flat Handle, Hook, Iron, 15¾ In.		44.00
ork, Wrought Iron, 3-Tine, Twisted & Block Turned, Loop Handle, 14 In.		143.00
ork, Wrought Iron, Rattail End, Flat Handle, Stamped, P.E. Will, 14½ x 1⅝ In.		66.00
unnel, Wagner, Aluminum, Qt.		55.00
rain Bin, Lift Lid, 3 Bins, Drawer Over 2 Paneled Doors, Painted, 1800s, 39 x 40 In.		400.00
rater, Flowers, Tin, Punched, Lid, 6¾ x 2½ x 1¼ In.		44.00

Kitchen, Cookie Cutter, Deer, With Antlers, Mounted, Tin, 5⅞ x 4¾ In. $248.00

Kitchen, Cookie Cutter, Lady, On Chamber Pot, Tin, Flat Plate, 8 x 5 In. $385.00

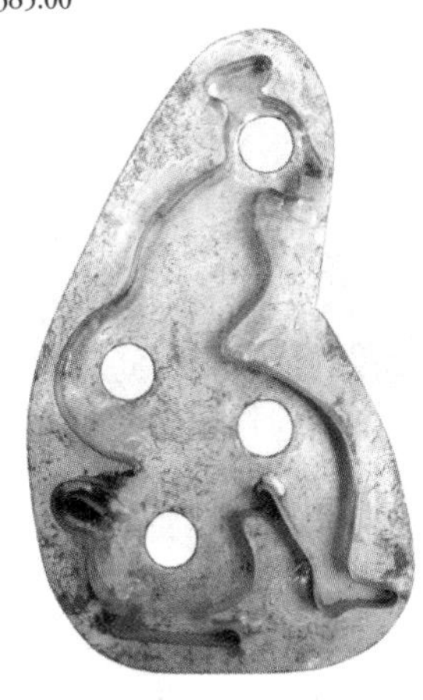

K

TIP

Tin cookie cutters can be dated by the construction method. Old ones are soldered in spots, not a long thin solder joint. If the solder joins the cutting-edge piece to the back by a thin, barely visible line, it is less than 50 years old.

Kitchen, Dough Box, Mahogany, Stand, Drop Down Door, Flowers, 38 x 43½ x 19 In.
$480.00

Kitchen, Dutch Oven, Griswold, No. 8, Trivet, No. 206, 4 x 10 In. Oven
$35.00

Kitchen, Egg Poacher, Griswold, No. 32, 9¼ x 13⅞ In.
$12.00

Kitchen, Grater, Nutmeg, Iron, Wood, Marked, Edgar Mfg. Co., 4¾ x 5½ In.
$115.00

Grater, Nutmeg, Iron, Wood, Marked, Edgar Mfg. Co., 4¾ x 5½ In. . . . . . *illus* 115.0
Griddle, 8 Rods, 4-Footed, Square, Hanging Hole, 25¼ x 9½ In. 58.0
Griddle, Cast Iron, Reeded Handle, Openwork Heart, Round, 3-Footed, 23 x 12½ In. 22.0
Griddle, Erie Diamond, No. 7, 737 . . . . . . 45.0
Griddle, Flop, Stuart Peterson & Co., Pat. Aug. 27, 1867 . . . . . . 60.0
Griddle, Griswold, Cast Iron, No. 7. . . . . . 28.00 to 65.0
Griddle, Griswold, Double Bail Handle 25.0
Griddle, Griswold, No. 7, Rectangular. 100.0
Griddle, Griswold, No. 8, 613, Rectangular, Wood Handle, Chrome 25.0
Griddle, Griswold, No. 9, 746B. 30.0
Griddle, Griswold, No. 10, Bail Handle 25.0
Griddle, Griswold, No. 12, 741A, Bail Handle 75.0
Griddle, Wagner, No. 16, Bail Handle 55.0
Griddle, Wapak, No. 8 . . . . . . 5.0
Griddle, Wrought Iron, Rotating, Round, 3-Footed, 23 x 9½ In. 173.0
Grill, Iron, 4 Slats, 4-Footed, 6¾ In. 550.0
Grill, Roasting, Wrought Iron, Footed, Handle, 8 x 15½ x 10 In. 110.0
Grinder, Nut, Dandy, No. 25. . . . . . 30.0
Herb Chest, Cherry, Dovetailed, 10 Graduated Drawers, c.1835, 16 x 14 x 10 In. 1228.0
Herb Grinder, Grinding Wheel, Cast Iron, 17 In. . . . . . *illus* 385.0
Hot Plate, Gas, 2-Burner, Griswold, No. 32, 1171. . . . . . 55.0
Hot Plate, Gas, Griswold, No. 201 . . . . . . 35.0
Ice Bucket, Domemaster, Top Slides Open, Plastic, Colony, Angelakos, 9½ In. 100.0
Ice Bucket, Orange, Plastic, Heller, Sergio Asti, 8 In. 60.0
Ice Bucket, Smoke Plastic, Teak Lid, 4-Sided, Metal, Atapco Siamese Teak, Hong Kong, 6½ In. 55.0
Ice Bucket, Westbend, Stainless Steel, Teakwood Handle, Thermal, 12 In. 75.0
Ice Chest, Oak, Egg & Dart Trim, Wood Lined, Segal-Cooper Co., 50 x 20 In. 1295.0
Ice Cream Maker, Wood Barrel, Triple Motion, Crank Handle, White Mountain 100.0
Ice Cream Mold, Aluminum, Wagner, Qt. 150.0
Ice Cream Mold, Lily Shape, Cast Metal, Early 20th Century, 4 x 4 In. 118.0
Ice Crusher, Bucketeer, Wall Bracket, Ice-O-Matic, Pink, Chrome, Rival, 1960s. 24.0
Ice Scoop, Wagner, No. 932, Aluminum 15.0
Ice Shave, Gilchrist, No. 78, 5½ x 1¾ In. 45.0
Ice Snow Cone Maker, Shaved, Artic, No. 25 . . . . . . 25.0
Icebox, Oak, 3 Drawers, c.1900, 47 x 35 In. 324.0
Icebox, Pine, Gray Paint, 3 Recessed Panel Doors, Cast Brass Hardware, 48 x 43 In. 425.0
Icebox, Oak, Cold Storage Refrigerator Co., Eau Claire, Wisc., 50 In. . . . . . *illus* 605.0
Iron, Cap, Oval, French, 3³⁄₁₆ In. 500.0
Iron, Charcoal, Brass, Iron Inlay, Hook Locking Mechanism 1900.0
Iron, Charcoal, Cast Iron, Cummings & Bless 75.0
Iron, Charcoal, Combination, Fluter, Revolving Damper, Trivet, Aug. 14, 1888. . . . . . 295.0
Iron, Charcoal, Combination, Fluter, Trivet, Rocker, Ideal, New York Pressing Iron Co., c.1916 325.0
Iron, Charcoal, Combination, Fluter, Geo. Wallace Edmond, Okla. 395.0
Iron, Charcoal, Embossed Stars, Lever Activated Holes, George Finn Patent, 1932 . . . . . . 125.0
Iron, Charcoal, Figural Damper Latch, Cummings & Bless 95.0
Iron, Charcoal, Lion's Head Lock Mechanism, Decorated Handle Top & Sides 750.0
Iron, Charcoal, Wood Handle, Locking Mechanism, Burnot Fuel Co. 500.0
Iron, Coleman, No. 609, Black, Instant Lite Fuel, Enamel. 35.0
Iron, Coleman, No. 609, Black, Trivet, Original Box 80.0
Iron, Combination, Polisher, Revolving Handle. 325.0
Iron, Electric, Sleeve, Chrome, Removable Handle, The Pluto, Cutler-Hammer, 1907 . . . . . . 600.0
Iron, Fluter, Brass Rollers, Patented 1875. . . . . . 80.0
Iron, Fluter, Crown Jewel, Scalloped Base, Black Japanning, Stencil . . . . . . 110.00 to 125.0
Iron, Fluter, Penn Machine, Hand Crank, Patented, Penn. 90.0
Iron, Fuel, Marvel, Horizontal Tank, Milwaukee 125.0
Iron, Fuel, Wooden Handle, Graniteware Finish, Sears 55.0
Iron, Gas, Coleman, Magic, No. 10, Instant Lite, Painted Green Handle & Tank 75.0
Iron, Gas, Enamel, Radiation Rhythm, Black Handle, 1925-45 . . . . . . 75.0
Iron, Gas, Gem, Brite Lite. 45.0
Iron, Gas, Humphrey, No. 2, Natural Gas, Wooden Handle, Milwaukee Gas Spec. Co. 55.0
Iron, Gas, Ideal Sad Iron, FG Co., 1901. . . . . . 35.0
Iron, Gas, Imperial, Tailor's. 250.0
Iron, Gas, Imperial Brass Mfg., Front Mounted Fuel Tank, Lamb, Chicago 75.0
Iron, Gas, Leeds & London, Ornate Base Heater. 1050.0
Iron, Gas, Silent Glorex, Gray-Speckled, Graniteware, Black Handle 525.0
Iron, Gas, Sun Mfg. Co., Horizontal Tank, Iron That Sizzles, Cylindrical Tank, South Bend. . . 125.0

Iron, Gas, Tailor's, Side Tank, Wooden Handle 145.00
Iron, Goffering, 4 Intertwining Serpents, Heater 12000.00
Iron, Harper, Double Pointed, Removable Handle, Nickel Plated, Chicago 75.00
Iron, Hatters, Shackle, Wide Face, Large Handle, Curve Bottom Groove 50.00
Iron, Hatters, Shackle, Movable Front 150.00
Iron, Hatters, Shackle, Mechanical, Thumb Lever 200.00
Iron, Hatters, Shackle, Double, Movable, RC & Co., N.Y. 250.00
Iron, Hatters, Tolliker, Crescent Shape, Flat Bottom 50.00
Iron, Hatters, Tolliker, Gem, Ridge Bottom 100.00
Iron, Krumkake, Nordicware, Flip Over Mechanism, Aluminum 10.00
Iron, Monitor, No. 8, Turned Up Points, Late 1800s 195.00
Iron, Natural Gas, Wright, c.1911, 7 In. 55.00
Iron, Ober No. 1, Sleeve, Child's, 4½ In. 115.00
Iron, Polishing, Gleason's, Heat Shield, Ribbed Edge, c.1870 .... 32.00
Iron, Polishing, Kenrick Manufacturer 37.00
Iron, Polishing, Tailor's, Mahoney, No. 8, Waffle Bottom 23.00
Iron, Sleeve, Bless & Drake, 8 In. 15.00
Iron, Sleeve, Colebrookdale, No. 2, Nickel Plated, 7¾ In. 20.00
Iron, Sleeve, G.H. Ober, Detachable Handle, Chagrin Falls, Oh., c.1890 .... 50.00
Iron, Sleeve, Grand Union Tea Co., Patented, c.1889 .... 50.00
Iron, Sleeve, Long Handle, Bullock & Co. 55.00
Iron, Slug, Brass, Ox Tongue, Lion's Head Post, Wood Handle 1700.00
Iron, Slug, Brass, Scotland, 3½ In. 5700.00
Iron, Slug, Combination, Fluter, Dean Co. 825.00
Iron, Slug, Curly Q Handle, Lift Gate Handle, France, 8 x 4½ In. 595.00
Iron, Slug, Heart Latch, Spade Shape 195.00
Iron, Slug, Iron & Brass, Teardrop Shape, S-Shaped Uprights, Wood Handle, c.1850, 6 In. 2700.00
Iron, Slug, Porcelain Handle, Cherubs, Ox Tongue Shape, Nickel Plated, Germany 1495.00
Iron, Slug, Round Back, Round Lift Gate, Decorative Handle Uprights, Continental, 5 In. 395.00
Iron, Slug, Round Nose, Brass, Bronze, Iron, Hinged Rear Gate, Denmark, 5 x 6½ In. 895.00
Iron, Smoothing Board, Maple, Horse Handle, 19th Century, 30 x 5½ In. .... *illus* 150.00
Iron, Tailor's, Charcoal, Removable Chimney, 10½ x 10 In. 65.00
Iron, Tailor's, Chrome, Brown Bros., 3 In. 1500.00
Iron, Tailor's, Ober Mfg. Co., Chagrin Falls, Ohio, 8 In. 24.00
Iron, Tailor's, Sensible, Detachable Handle, Nelson Streeter, Groton, N.Y., Late 1800s, 8 In. 175.00
Juicer, Acme Supreme, Electric, Painted Metal Base, White, Gray, c.1959 .... 55.00
Kettle, Brass, Iron, Copper, Peter Derr, c.1850 .... 11115.00
Kettle, Brass, Marked, Trade, Pat. 1869, 14 In. 61.00
Kettle, Brass, Waterbury Brass Co., c.1851 .... 45.00
Kettle, Copper, Brass, Oval, Curved Spout, Domed Lid, Acorn Finial, c.1880, 9¼ x 10 In. 350.00
Kettle, Copper, Dovetail, 17 In. 94.00
Kettle, Copper, Dovetail, Brass Finial, A & J Sheriff, Pittsburgh, c.1815, 7 In. .... *illus* 489.00
Kettle, Copper, Wrought Iron, Swing Handle, France, 11 x 18 In. 540.00
Kettle, Flat Bottom, Wagner, No. 7, Iron, Sidney, Oh., c.1940 .... 40.00
Kettle, Handles, 3-Footed, Iron, Pocasset Iron Factory, 19th Century, 16 x 24 In. 240.00
Kettle, Maslin, No. 2, Wagner Ware, c.1900 .... 55.00
Kettle, Sugar, Cast Iron, Columbus Iron Works Co., 19th Century, 18 x 56 In. 2400.00
Kettle, Syrup, Cast Iron, 40 In. 20.00
Kettle, Syrup, Rim, 16-In. Pulley Wheel, 19th Century, 17 x 54 In. 250.00
Kettle, Tripod Legs, Griddle, Sheet Iron, Hanging Loop, 1700s, 9½ x 10 In. 127.00
Kettle Stand, Brass, Shaped Apron, Pierced Hearts, Cabriole Legs, Handles, 12 x 17 In. 489.00
Kettle Stand, Victorian, Gilt Brass, Wrought Iron, Heraldic Pattern, 16 x 24 In. 180.00
Ladle, Brass, Chrome Plated, Italy, 11½ In. 10.00
Ladle, Brass Bowl, Iron, Round & Flat Handle, Hook, 22¼ In. 55.00
Ladle, Burl, 14 x 8 In. 99.00
Ladle, Iron, Brass, Inlaid, Folded Hanger, 4 Rivet Clasp, 19½ In. 33.00
Ladle, Iron, Brass, Inlaid, Folded Rattail Hanger, 2 Rivet Clasp, 19½ In. 33.00
Ladle, Iron, Brass, Inlaid, Hanger, J. Dubs, 22½ x 6¼ In. 440.00
Ladle, Mayonnaise, Cambridge Glass, Dianthus Pink 31.00
Ladle, Mayonnaise, Cambridge Glass, Moonlight Blue 36.00
Ladle, Wagner, No. 717, Aluminum 28.00
Ladle, Wood, Burl, Etched, Scalloped Design On Rim, 7 x 3¼ In. 132.00
Laundry Basket, Chain Link, Strap Metal, Handles, Wood Bottom, c.1900, 24 x 32 In., Pair 660.00
Lazy Susan, Teak, Marked, Digsmed Danmark, 12 In. 100.00
Lemon Squeezer, c.1885 .... 10.00
Lid, Roaster, Griswold, No. 9, Oval 18.00

Kitchen, Herb Grinder, Grinding Wheel, Cast Iron, 17 In.
$385.00

Kitchen, Icebox, Oak, Cold Storage Refrigerator Co., Eau Claire, Wisc., 50 In.
$605.00

Kitchen, Iron, Smoothing Board, Maple, Horse Handle, 19th Century, 30 x 5 ½ In.
$150.00

Kitchen, Kettle, Copper, Dovetail, Brass Finial, A & J Sheriff, Pittsburgh, c.1815, 7 In.
$489.00

K

Kitchen, Meal Bin, Poplar, Blue Paint, Hinged Lid, 19th Century, 32 x 55 x 19 In.
$725.00

Mold, Cake, Rabbit, Griswold, No. 862, 10 x 11 x 4 In.
$170.00

Kitchen, Mortar & Pestle, Black Walnut, Bands, 19th Century, 8 x 8 In.
$316.00

Kitchen, Roaster, Wagner, No. 7, Oval, Stylized Logo, 17 3/8 x 11 In.
$152.00

Lid, Skillet, High Dome, Griswold, No. 8 . . . . . 23.00
Lid, Skillet, High Dome, Griswold, No. 6, Logo 75.00
Lid, Skillet, Low Dome, Griswold, No. 9 . . . . . 40.00
Lid, Skillet, Low Dome, Griswold, No. 11 . . . . . 270.00
Lid, Skillet, Low Dome, Griswold, No. 12 . . . . . 160.00
Lid, Skillet, Low Dome, Griswold, No. 14 . . . . . 250.00
Match Holders can be found in their own category.
Match Safes can be found in their own category.
Meal Bin, Poplar, Blue Paint, Hinged Lid, 19th Century, 32 x 55 x 19 In. . . . . . *illus* 725.00
Measure, Copper, Handle, England, 19th Century, Pt. 165.00
Meat Grinder, Keen Kutter, No. 22, Wood Handle, E.C. Simmons, c.1906 . . . . . 50.00
Meat Tenderizer, Yellowware, Salt Glazed Stoneware, c.1877 . . . . . 295.00
Mixer, Malt, Triple Head, Hamilton Beach, Includes Glassware, Mixers, Spoons 550.00
Mixing Bowl, Fired-On White, Glass, Federal, 8 In. 15.00
Mixing Bowl, Pottery, Provincial, Ocher Gloss Glaze, 2 Handles, Pouring Lip, 11 x 22 In. 570.00
Mold, 6 Tiers, Swirl Design, Copper, 5 In. 365.00
Mold, Butter, 3 Leaves, Plunger & Cylinder, c.1860, 3½ x 3½ In. 750.00
Mold, Butter, Acorn, Plunger & Cylinder, c.1900, 4½ x 3½ In. 145.00
Mold, Butter, Double, Wood, Czech 32.00
Mold, Butter, Eagle, Wood, 19th Century, 3½ In. 411.00
Mold, Butter, Maple, Blue, Pineapple, 19th Century, 5 x 5 In. 110.00
Mold, Butter, Pineapple, 2 Sections, c.1900, 6 x 3½ In. 75.00
Mold, Butter, Rooster, Block, 2 Sections, 4½ x 6¼ In. 325.00
Mold, Butter, Swan, Plunger & Cylinder, c.1900, 4¼ x 4¼ In. 150.00
Mold, Butter, Thistle & Leaf, Handles, c.1900, 2 x 3 In. 100.00
Mold, Cake, Frank Hay, Griswold, c.1891, 9½ x 4½ In. 100.00
Mold, Cake, Lamb, Griswold, No. 866, Sidney O, Box, 13 In. 160.00
Mold, Cake, Rabbit, Griswold, No. 862, 10 x 11 x 4 In. . . . . . *illus* 170.00
Mold, Cake, Santa Claus, Griswold, No. 897, 12⅛ x 6⅞ x 4⅝ In. 300.00
Mold, Candy, Wood, Brass Hooks, 5½ x 6 x 2¼ In. 44.00
Mold, Cheese, Tin, C-Shape Handle, Perforated Side & Bottom, 4⅛ x 7 x 5¼ In. 77.00
Mold, Cheese, Tin, Heart Shape, C-Shape Handle, Perforated, 3-Footed, 3⅜ x 4¾ x 5 In. 66.00
Mold, Cheese, Tin, Punched Heart, 3-Footed, Wire Hanger, 3¼ x 4¾ x 4⅜ In. 187.00
Mold, Chocolate, Father Christmas, Tin, Jabaug Brothers, N.Y.C., 8¼ In. 325.00
Mold, Chocolate, Fire Engine Shape, Pewter, 2 Piece, 3 x 4½ In. 179.00
Mold, Chocolate, Turkey, 3 Sections, 6 x 6 x 4 In. 112.00
Mold, Cookie, Lion, With Mane, Man On Horse, 19th Century, 10½ x 8 In. 400.00
Mold, Cookie, Round, Pine, New England, 5 In. 125.00
Mold, Copper, 5-Turret Design, Hole Down Center, Marked No. 393, Letter C, 5¾ In. 395.00
Mold, Copper, Arch & Swirl Design, Marked No. 214, 6¾ In. 395.00
Mold, Food, Fish, Bead & Rope Bands, Orange, 4-Footed, 2¾ x 12 x 5 In. 66.00
Mold, Food, Fish, Brown Glaze, Black Spatter, 2-Footed, Redware, 2 x 12 x 4 In. 330.00
Mold, Ice Cream, Bunny, In Car, Pewter, Marked, E. & Co., N.Y., 3½ In. 88.00
Mold, Ice Cream, Cat, E. & Co., N.Y., 5 In. 100.00
Mold, Ice Cream, Indian Chief, Pewter, Marked, Des Corp'd, 1896, 5⅜ In. 138.00
Mold, Jelly, Wagner, No. 424 . . . . . 35.00
Mold, Melon, Tin, Copper, 5½ In. 125.00
Mold, Pastry, Dog, Man With Cane, Turkey, Wood, Patina, 4½ x 11¾ In. 154.00
Mold, Pastry, Dog, Rabbit, Bird, Wheat, Wood, Carved, 12 In. 77.00
Mold, Pastry, Rabbits, Horse, Glove, Wood, Carved, Patina, 3¼ x 12 In. 99.00
Mold, Patty, Griswold, No. 1, Scalloped, Concentric Circles, Recipes, Box 30.00
Mold, Patty, Griswold, No. 2, Heart, Circle, Recipes, Box 20.00
Mold, Wagner, No. 5, Gelatin, Aluminum 60.00
Mold, Wagner, No. 425, Gelatin, Aluminum 60.00
Mold, Candle, see Tinware category.
Molds may also be found in the Pewter and Tinware categories.
Mortar, Footed, Flared Rim, Griswold, 2 Qt. 275.00
Mortar, Griswold, Iron, c.1895, Pt. 135.00
Mortar & Pestle, Black Walnut, Bands, 19th Century, 8 x 8 In. . . . . . *illus* 316.00
Mortar & Pestle, Black Walnut, Maple, Decorative Bands, 8½ x 7¾ In. 316.00
Mortar & Pestle, Brass, Loop Handles, Linear Decoration, England, 3½ & 8 In. 295.00
Mortar & Pestle, Burl, Curly Maple, 6 x 5 In. 288.00
Mortar & Pestle, Burl, Turned, 19th Century, 4¾ x 7½ In. 176.00
Mortar & Pestle, Maple, Baluster Shape, Turned Raised Bands, 1800s, 22 x 6½ In. 748.00
Mortar & Pestle, Maple, Yellow Floral Spray, Blue Ground, 19th Century, 8 x 5 In. 161.00

Mortar & Pestle, Wood, Red Paint, Incised Band, Tapered, Footed, 6 x 4¼ In. 303.00
Pail, Brass, Iron Bail, c.1850, 14 In. 125.00
Pan, Brass, Scalloped Rim, England, 19 In. 850.00
Pan, Bread, Loaf, Black Iron, 4-Footed 175.00
Pan, Bread, Vienna Roll, Griswold, No. 6, Var. 4, 6 Sticks 120.00
Pan, Bridge, Wagner, 1340, Little Slam, Solid 35.00
Pan, Cast Iron, Lid, Marked 4 In 1, 10 In. 45.00
Pan, Copper, Iron Handle, 17 x 9 In. 59.00
Pan, Corn Stick, Griswold, A8283, Aluminum 45.00
Pan, Corn Stick, Griswold, No. 21, 961, 7 Cup 60.00
Pan, Corn Stick, Griswold, No. 22, 954 . . . . . . 65.00
Pan, Corn Stick, Griswold, No. 22, 954F 10.00
Pan, Corn Stick, Griswold, No. 262, Crispy Corn, Wheat Stick 75.00
Pan, Corn Stick, Griswold, No. 273, 930, 7 Sticks 5.00
Pan, Corn Stick, Griswold, No. 283 . . . . . . 70.00
Pan, Corn Stick, Griswold, No. 632, 2700 . . . . . . 200.00
Pan, Corn Stick, Wagner, No. 459, Aluminum, Tea Size 30.00
Pan, Corn Stick, Wagner Ware, No. 1319, Junior Krusty Korn Kobs 40.00
Pan, Danish Cake, Griswold, Size No. 32, No. 692 . . . . . . 45.00
Pan, Gem, 9 Hearts, Handles, Cast Iron, Late 19th Century, 9½ x 7½ In. 1965.00
Pan, Gem, G.F. Filley, No. 3, 8 Cup 75.00
Pan, Gem, Griswold, No. 10, Iron, 11 Cup 40.00
Pan, Gem, Griswold, No. 11, Iron, 12 Cup 15.00
Pan, Gem, Wagner Ware, 8 Cup 20.00
Pan, Gem, Wagner Ware, Turk's Head, Iron, 12 Cup 50.00
Pan, Muffin, Chiltonware, Aluminum, 11 x 7¾ In. 7.00
Pan, Muffin, Gem, Griswold, No. 11 . . . . . . 35.00
Pan, Muffin, Gem, Wagner Ware, U-Style, No. 1339, Turk's Head, Solid Frame, 6 Cup 120.00
Pan, Muffin, Gem, Griswold, No. 12, 11 Cup 300.00
Pan, Muffin, Gem, Star & Heart, Griswold, No. 100 . . . . . . 325.00
Pan, Muffin, Griswold, No. 8, 8 Cup 45.00
Pan, Muffin, Griswold, No. 16, 6 Cup 225.00
Pan, Muffin, Griswold, No. 17, Aluminum, 6 Cup 90.00
Pan, Muffin, Griswold, No. 18, 6 Cup . . . . . . 18.00 to 33.00
Pan, Muffin, Popover, Griswold, No. 10, 948, 11 Cup 15.00
Pan, Muffin, Popover, Griswold, No. 10, 948B, 11 Cup 85.00
Pan, Muffin, Popover, Griswold, No. 10, 949C, 11 Cup 17.00
Pan, Plett, Griswold, No. 34, 9½ In. 18.00
Pan, Poaching, Copper, Rectangular, Raised Brass Handles, Prunier, 6 x 21 x 16 In. 420.00
Pan, Popover, Piqua Ware, 9 Deep Cups, Black Iron, 10½ x 10½ In. 170.00
Pan, Preserving, Wrought Iron, Swing Handle, Continental, 19th Century, 7 x 11 In. 150.00
Pan, Tart, W.C. Davis, 7 Cup 120.00
Pan, Tart, W.C. Davis, 13 Cup 55.00
Pan, Vienna Roll, Wagner Ware, H Gem, 4 Rolls 170.00
Pan, Wheat & Corn Stick, Griswold, No. 2700, 7 Sticks 110.00
Pan, Wheat Stick, Griswold, No. 262 . . . . . . 25.00 to 45.00
Patty Bowl, Griswold, No. 871, 7½ x 3⅛ In. 50.00
Peel, Bell Shape Blade, Round Shaft, Flat Handle, Hanger, Iron, 27⅜ In. 11.00
Peel, Bread, Wood, 50 In. 44.00
Peel, Cast Iron, Clamp On, Wood Handle, Goodell Co. 59.00
Peel, Wrought Iron, Doughnut Hanger, 30 In. 72.00
Peel, Wrought Iron, Scrolled Terminal Handle, 19th Century, 47 In. 115.00
Peeler, Apple, Green, White Mountain 20.00
Peeler, Apple, Pine, Turned Handle, Leather Belt, 2-Tine Fork, c.1840, 15 x 29 In. 350.00
Peeler, Apple, Stamped, Goodell Co., Antrim, N.H. 149.00
Peeler, Apple, White Mountain Model, Cast Iron, Clamp On, Wood Handle, Goodell Co. 59.00
Pepper Grinder, Tapered, Wood, Marked, Peugeot Freres, 12½ In. 175.00
Pepper Shaker, Modern Tulip, Anchor Hocking 14.00
Percolator, Coffee, Bakelite Hand Grip, Chrome, Art Deco 195.00
Percolator, Sunbeam, Model, AP10A, c.1955, 6 Cup 85.00
Pie Box, Lustro Ware, Graphic Pie, No. B 40, Columbus Plastic Products, 4½ x 5 In. 10.00
Pie Crimper, Coggle Wheel, Banded Design, Crescent Stamp Terminal, Iron, 6½ In. 110.00
Pie Crimper, Curved Handle, Scrolling, 19th Century, 4¾ In. 1344.00
Pie Crimper, Ivory, Wood Spacer, Tapered 1120.00
Pie Crimper, Whale Ivory, Curved Handle, Scrolling, Flowers, 4¾ In. 1200.00

TIP

Clean a very dirty cast-iron pot the old-fashioned way. Put it in a hot wood fire in a fireplace or barbecue pit for several hours. After it is cool, wash with hot water, soap, and a stiff scrubbing brush. Then season with oil.

Kitchen, Spice Box, Pine, Alligatored Oxblood Paint, c.1850, 22 x 14 x 6 In.
$660.00

Refinishing Kitchenware

Kitchenware, metal or wooden, should never, never be repainted, refinished, or restored if you want it because of its value as an antique. If you plan to use the piece, refinishing or restoring might add to its usefulness but will detract from its value to the serious collector. Rusty iron can be cleaned, but don't repaint the piece.

TIP
All Pyrex, old or new, is safe to use in the microwave.

Kitchen, Spoon Rack, Hanging, Pine, Painted, 19 x 26 In.
$1080.00

Kitchen, Sugar Cutter, Iron, Crescent Terminals, Impressed, Timmins, 9 ½ In.
$77.00

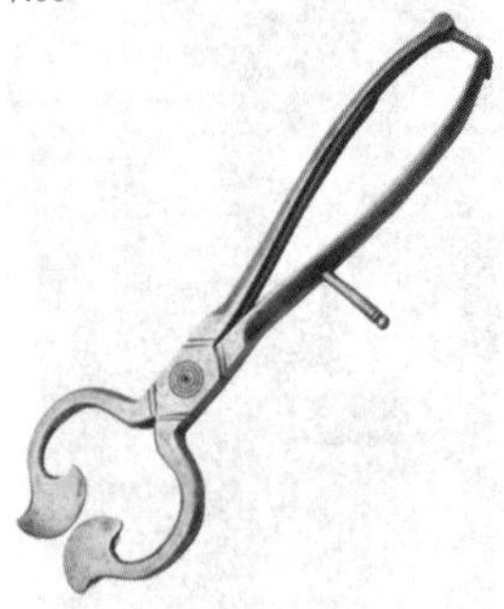

TIP
Caution! We bought an old potato masher with a bright-green painted wooden handle. We put it in the dishwasher. Result: a clean masher with a pale blue painted handle. Never wash kitchenware with painted wooden handles in the hot, hot water of a dishwasher.

Pitcher, Batter, Stoneware, Blue Accents, Bail Handle, Tin Lid, 9 In. 230.00
Pitcher, Griswold, Aluminum, c.1920, 7¾ In. 100.00
Pitcher, Wagner Ware, No. 411, Aluminum, Wood Handle 55.00
Pitcher, Water, Wagner, No. 409, Aluminum 75.00
Platter, Steak, Griswold, No. 848, Aluminum 55.00
Pot, Brass Bell Metal, Posnet Coxtaunton III, 15½ In. 440.00
Pot, Cast Iron, Extended Legs, Marked, 10 Gall's, 14 x 18 In. 40.00
Pot, Cast Iron, Footed, Straight Sides, 12 x 19 In. 25.00
Pot, Cast Iron, Footed, 16 x 21 In. 80.00
Pot, Cast Iron, Footed, Handles, 13 x 17 In. 80.00
Pot, Cast Iron, Footed, 15 x 20 In. 90.00
Pot, Cast Iron, Short Legs, Rings, Savery & Co., Philadelphia, 13 x 22 In. 25.00
Pot, Cast Iron, Short Legs, Thin Handles, 14 x 20 In. 50.00
Pot, Cast Iron, Straight Sides, Handle, 11 x 19 In. 40.00
Pot, Cast Iron, Swing Handle, 3-Footed, 19th Century, 8 x 15¼ In. 35.00
Pot, Copper, Cover, Handles, Brass Inverted Acorn Grip, France, 3½ x 6½ In. 108.00
Pot, Copper, Cover, Wrought Steel Handle, Graduated, France, 5 To 9 In., 7 Piece 1800.00
Pot, Copper, Cylindrical, Cover, Burnished, France, 18½ x 21 In. 1440.00
Pot, Copper, Lighthouse Shape, Brass Handles, Dome Cover, 13 In. 120.00
Pot, Copper, Long Handle, Rolled Rim, Russia, Late 1800s, 3½ x 4 x 6 In. 175.00
Pot, Copper, Round, Curved Handle, Handmade Nails, Early 1800s, 7⅝ x 3¾ In. 125.00
Pot, Copper, Wrought Iron Handle, Graduated, 8 Piece 3456.00
Pot, Copper, Wrought Iron Handles, France, 13 x 15 In. 360.00
Pot, Tin, Cover, C-Scroll Handle, Inverted Spouts, Vented Lower Door, 19th Century 30.00
Rack, Oak, Hanging, Turned Ends, Baluster Supports, 1800s, 23 x 99 In. 138.00
Rack, Pie, Wireware, 6 Tiers, Triangular Shape, Green Paint 95.00
Rack, Pot, Iron Plate, Tripartite, 9 Graduated Shelves, 82½ x 19 In. 2304.00
Rack, Pot, Penny Feet, Wrought Iron, 19th Century, 21 x 37 x 16¾ In. 455.00
Rack, Utensil, Bird Design, 5 Hooks, 10 x 11 In. 137.00
Rack, Utensil, Iron, 3 Hooks, Geometric & Arched Back, 7 In. 220.00
Rack, Utensil, Iron, 3 Hooks 83.00
Rack, Utensil, Iron, 6 Hooks, 26 In. 110.00
Rack, Utensil, Iron, S-Hooks, Rolled 3-Footed Base, Acorn Finial, 26 In. 110.00
Raisin Seeder, Star, Patented 45.00
Reamers are listed in their own category.
Refrigerator, General Electric, Top Mounted Condenser, 1900s, 64 x 29 x 23 In. 550.00
Refrigerator Dish, Cover, Delphite, Glass, 2 x 8½ x 3 In. 75.00
Refrigerator Dish, Cover, Glass, Fruit On Cover, Fluted Base, 5 x 4 In. 12.00
Roaster, Coffee, Sheet Iron, Turned Wooden Handle, 34 x 6 In. 58.00
Roaster, Cover, Griswold, No. 3, Aluminum, Oval 50.00
Roaster, Cover, Wagner Ware, No. 4263, Magnalite, Oval, Trivet 23.00
Roaster, Cover, Wagner Ware, No. 4265, Magnalite, Oval, Trivet 35.00
Roaster, Cover, Wagner Ware, No. 4267, Magnalite, Oval, Trivet 50.00
Roaster, Drip Drop, Dome Lid, Raised Letters, Wagner Ware, No. 1266, Trivet, 2½ Qt. 70.00
Roaster, Montgomery, No. 3, Oval, Cover 95.00
Roaster, Wagner, No. 7, Oval, Stylized Logo, 17⅜ x 11 In. .... *illus* 152.00
Roaster, Wrought Iron, Adjustable, Rolled 3-Footed Base, 30 In. 250.00
Roasting Oven, 4-Footed, Rotating Handle, Drain Spout, Tin, 19th Century, 15 x 19 x 9 In. 143.00
Roasting Rack, Wrought Iron, Adjustable Mounting Fork, Tripod Base, 1800s, 23¾ In. 1380.00
Rolling Pin, Blown Glass, End Of Day, 14 In. 173.00
Rolling Pin, Glass, 1879, 20 In. 115.00
Rolling Pin, Glass, Amethyst, 15½ In. 63.00
Rolling Pin, Maple, Mid 19th Century, 20 x 2 In. 224.00
Rolling Pin, Maple, Ring Incised Handles, 19th Century, 20 x 2 In. 200.00
Rolling Pin, Milk Glass, 1 Open Pontil End, Ground Lip, 1880, 14¾ In. 45.00
Rolling Pin, Milk Glass, Imperial Mfg. Co., 18 In. 144.00
Rolling Pin, Tiger Maple, 19th Century 210.00
Rolling Pin, Tiger Maple, Acorn Knop, 19th Century 225.00
Rolling Pin, Wood, 14 In. 17.00
Rolling Pin, Wood, Carved, 16 In. 29.00
Rolling Pin, Yellowware, 15 In. 380.00
Rotisserie, Clockwork, Tin, Iron Case, Paw Feet, Brass Gears, Chime, 8½ x 10½ In. 460.00
Sadiron, Double Point, Liberty Head, 3⅞ In. 13.00
Sadiron, Double Point, Detachable Handle, Pat. May 9, 1899 .... 40.00
Sadiron, Flat, Rolled Strap Handle, Marked RM, 5 In. 18.00

Sadiron, Ideal Sad Iron Mfg. Co., Cleveland, Patent Date Mar. 5, 1901 .... 35.00
Sadiron, Swan Shape, Brass, Handle Connects Head & Tail, England, 3¼ In. 350.00
Sadiron, Wapak, No. 2, c.1900, 4 1/16 In. 23.00
Safety Cooker, Cover, Griswold, No. 8, 858 .... 110.00
Salt & Pepper Shakers are listed in their own category.
Sausage Stuffer, 4-Footed, Crank Handle 35.00
Scoop, Aluminum, Wagner 5.00
Scoop, Confectionary, Aluminum 5.00
Scoop, Ice Cream Double Action, Dover Mfg., 11 In. 95.00
Scoop, Maple, Shaped Handle, 6¼ x 14 In. 86.00
Scoop, Rectangular Bowl, Short Handle, Light Gray Paint, Wood, 15¾ x 7¾ In. 144.00
Scotch Bowl, Griswold, No. 5 .... 55.00
Sieve, Iron, Brass, Inlaid, Hanger, J. Dubs, 22½ In. 385.00
Sifter, Flour, Measuring, Tin, Green Wooden Handle, Bromwell's 10.00
Skewer Holder, Heart Shape, Punched, 4 Skewers, Cast Iron, Mid 19th Century, 15 In. 480.00
Skillet, Colonial Breakfast, Griswold, No. 666 .... 23.00 to 60.00
Skillet, Egg, Griswold, No. 129A, Square 28.00
Skillet, Erie, No. 9, 730, 3 Hole Handle, Outside Smoke Ring .... 110.00 to 120.00
Skillet, Erie, No. 10 .... 70.00
Skillet, Fry, Square, Griswold, No. 768 .... 28.00
Skillet, Fry, Square, Griswold, No. 768, 769, Iron Cover 235.00
Skillet, Grand Union Tea Co., Coil Handle 25.00
Skillet, Griswold, No. 0, 562 .... 55.00
Skillet, Griswold, No. 2, Chrome 220.00
Skillet, Griswold, No. 2, 703, Nickel Plated 395.00
Skillet, Griswold, No. 2, 703, Heat Ring, Aluminum 860.00
Skillet, Griswold, No. 3, 703B, Chrome 22.50
Skillet, Griswold, No. 3, 703B 35.00
Skillet, Griswold, No. 3, Porcelain, Red, Beige 70.00
Skillet, Griswold, No. 3, High Dome Smooth Cover 125.00
Skillet, Griswold, No. 8, No Smoke Ring 38.00
Skillet, Griswold, No. 8, 704N 45.00
Skillet, Griswold, No. 10, 716, Low Dome Cover 80.00
Skillet, Griswold, No. 12, 719, Heat Ring, Low Chrome Cover 140.00
Skillet, Griswold, No. 14, 694, Bail Handle 1825.00
Skillet, Griswold, No. A20, Aluminum, Miniature 175.00
Skillet, LE, Griswold, No. 11, 717, Smoke Ring 120.00
Skillet, LE, Griswold, No. 12, 719, Smoke Ring 110.00
Skillet, LE, Griswold, No. 15, 1013, Oval 300.00
Skillet, Lodge, No. 4 .... 25.00
Skillet, Otter River, Square, 4 Sections 55.00
Skillet, Piqua Ware, No. 7, Smoke Ring, Iron 23.00
Skillet, Spider, 3 Leg, Child's 15.00
Skillet, Wagner, Sidney O 90.00
Skillet, Wapak, No. 7 .... 32.00
Skillet, Wapak, No. 9, Indian Head 150.00
Skimmer, Brass, 17 In. 61.00
Skimmer, Brass, Punched Holes, Hole In Handle, Richard Lee, Vermont, c.1815, 16 In. 3016.00
Skimmer, Brass Bowl, Iron, Flat Handle, Hook, 18¾ In. 33.00
Skimmer, Geometric, Punched, Tooled, Incised Line, Iron, Hook, 19⅜ In. 11.00
Skimmer, Geometric & Sunburst, Punch Tooled, Iron, 18½ In. 11.00
Skimmer, Star Punched, Round Bowl, Rod Handle, Flat End Hanging Hole, 33½ In. 115.00
Skimmer, Wrought Iron, Copper, Flat Handle, Rattail End, Etched, 25 x 5½ In. 33.00
Skimmer, Wrought Iron, Rattail End, Flat Handle, Stamped, P.E. Will, 18½ x 5½ In. 143.00
Spatula, Iron, Ball Shape, Round Shaft, Flat Handle, Hook, 15⅛ In. 22.00
Spatula, Wrought Iron, Flat Handle, Rattail End, Applied Keyhole Shape, 15½ x 3 In. 33.00
Spatula, Wrought Iron, Flat Handle, Lollipop End, Cutwork, 15 x 3 In. 77.00
Spatula, Wrought Iron, Raised Band, Hooked End, Keyhole Shape Blade, 16¾ x 3 In. 165.00
Spatula, Wrought Iron, Round Shaft, Flat Handle, Rattail End, 17¾ x 2¼ In. 22.00
Spatula, Wrought Iron, Tapered Blade, Flat Rod Handle, Loop Hanging End, 16¾ In. 115.00
Spice Box, Brass, Double Lid, 19th Century 325.00
Spice Box, Cherry, Dovetailed, 6 Compartments, Slide Lid, 1800s, 2¾ x 4¼ x 8 In. 220.00
Spice Box, Cherry, Pine, Pencil Inscriptions, Signed LB, Enfield, 1868, 14 x 11 x 6 In. 1872.00
Spice Box, Pine, Alligatored Oxblood Paint, c.1850, 22 x 14 x 6 In. .... *illus* 660.00
Spice Box, Pine, Cut Nail, Gabled Roof, Cast Iron Pulls, 22½ x 14¼ x 6¼ In. 660.00

Two-in-One Appliances
Some odd combination appliances were invented during the twentieth century. The Perc-O-Toaster, introduced by Armstrong in 1918, made coffee while it also toasted bread or waffles. In the 1930s, Merit-Made used the same idea to make a "moderne" coffeemaker-toaster. Ronson introduced a Cook 'n Stir in 1965 that blended and cooked simultaneously.

Kitchen, Toaster, Toastrite, Blue Willow, Porcelain, Pan Electric Mfg., c.1928
$552.00

Kitchen, Toasting Rack, Hinged, Penny Feet, Wrought Iron, American, 19 x 13 x 8 In.
$415.00

Kitchen, Toasting Rack, Rotating, Iron, 18th Century, 24 x 15½ In.
$330.00

Kitchen, Waffle Iron, Griswold, No. 8, Ball Hinge, 7⅝ x 15¼ In.
$28.00

Kitchen, Wringer, Household, Wood, Metal, 28 x 14 x 11 In.
$150.00

K

TIP
To remove the scale build-up inside a teakettle, put ½ cup of vinegar in the kettle, fill with water, and boil for ten minutes at least once a week.

Kosta, Urn, Rampant Lion, 6-Sided, 1940s, Bergh, 3¾ x 2½ In.
$26.00

Spice Box, Poplar, Leaves, Fruit, Flowers, Salmon Ground, Finial, Joseph Lehn, 5 x 2¾ In.... 413.00
Spice Box, Slide Lid, Mixed Wood, Dovetailed, 4 Compartments, Compass Circle, 2 x 8 x 5 In. 275.00
Spice Box, Wood, 8 Wood Spice Jars, Tin Trim, Round, Patina, 2¾ In.. 198.00
Spice Box, Wood, Tin Trim Patina, 2¾ In. 198.00
Spice Rack, Wood, 8 2¼-In. Jars, 8½ x 9 x 4¾ In. 132.00
Spit, Fireplace, Wrought Iron, Spit Dogs, 3 Scrolled Support Hooks, Swan's Neck Terminals, 21 x 15 In. 230.00
Spit, Iron, 3-Footed Base, Adjustable, 23 In. 520.00
Spoon, Flat, Wagner, No. 709, Aluminum, 11 In. 8.00
Spoon Rack, Hanging, Pine, Painted, 19 x 26 In. *illus* 1080.00
Spoon Rack, Wood, Blue Paint, Star Design, 27 x 9½ In. 32000.00
Stand, Utensil, Iron, 3 Penny Feet, 51½ In.. 400.00
Stand, Wine Bottle, Lucite, Abstract, 9½ In. 75.00
Stove Damper, Griswold, 5½ In. 25.00
Stove Damper, Griswold, 12 In.. 23.00 to 30.00
Stove Damper, Griswold, No. 1487, Oval, 7 In. 28.00
Stringholder, Blown Glass, Applied Violet Rim, Pittsburgh, 5¼ x 6 In. 345.00
Sugar Cutter, Iron, Crescent Terminals, Impressed, Timmins, 9½ In.. *illus* 77.00
Sugar Cutter, Iron, Crescent Terminals, Tooled Shaft, 10 In.. 88.00
Sugar Nippers, Steel, Swivel Joint, Lock Clasp, 19th Century, 9 In. 99.00
Table, Baker's, Cast Iron, Marble Top, Rocaille Fan, Leaf Scrolls, Flowers, 30 x 57 x 25 In. ... 3055.00
Teakettle, Colonial, Griswold, Aluminum, 4 Qt.. 10.00
Teakettle, Griswold, 4544, Cast Aluminum, Wood Handle, 4 Qt.. 40.00
Teakettle, Perfection, Pat., No. 7, Lid Handle Closer, July 13, 1884. 160.00
Teakettle, Wagner Ware, No. 8, Metal Handle 30.00
Teakettle, Wagner Ware, No. 1362, Child's 20.00
Teapot, Cast Iron, Phillips & Buttorff Mfg. Co., Nashville, 6½ In. 25.00
Teapot, Cast Iron, Phillips & Buttorff Mfg. Co., Nashville, Tenn., 7 In. 40.00
Toaster, Revolving, Single Slot, Canted Ends, 3-Footed, Loop Hanger, Iron, 19 x 16 In. 173.00
Toaster, Revolving, Wrought Iron, 16¾ In.. 135.00
Toaster, Sandwich, Wagner, No. 1455, 6 x 6 In. 170.00
Toaster, Swivel, Twisted Supports, 3-Footed, Raised Flat Handle, Iron, 7¾ x 17¾ In. 66.00
Toaster, Toastrite, Blue Willow, Porcelain, Pan Electric Mfg., c.1928 *illus* 552.00
Toasting Rack, Hinged, Penny Feet, Wrought Iron, American, 19 x 13 x 8 In. *illus* 415.00
Toasting Rack, Iron, Adjustable, Penny Feet, 18 x 12 In. 300.00
Toasting Rack, Rotating, Iron, Arched Cages, Tripod, Penny Feet, 1700s, 24 x 15½ In. 316.00
Toasting Rack, Rotating, Iron, 18th Century, 24 x 15½ In. *illus* 330.00
Trivet, see Trivet category.
Wafer Iron, Eagle, Holding Olive Branch, Arrow, E Pluribus Unum, 16 Stars, 28 In. 1495.00
Wafer Iron, Square & Diamond Design, Rectangular, Rod Handle, Iron, 24 In.. 87.00
Waffle Iron, Cast Iron, Signed, Chatham. 80.00
Waffle Iron, Electric, Winchester, No. W36, Cord. 450.00
Waffle Iron, Flip Over, Griswold No. 8, Cast Iron. 20.00
Waffle Iron, Flip Over, Wagner, Aluminum 50.00
Waffle Iron, Good Health, Low Base, Griswold American, No. 8, 395, Bail Handle 30.00
Waffle Iron, Griswold, No. 8, Ball Hinge, 7⅝ x 15¼ In. *illus* 28.00
Waffle Iron, Heart, Low Base, Griswold, No. 981, 988 5.00
Waffle Iron, Heart & Star, High Base, Griswold, No. 18, 920. 130.00
Waffle Iron, Heart Shape, Flip Over, Alfred Andersen 50.00
Waffle Iron, High Base, Griswold American, No. 8 90.00
Waffle Iron, High Base, Griswold American, No.11, 987 45.00
Waffle Iron, High Base, Wagner Ware, No. 1408 25.00
Waffle Iron, High Base, Wagner Ware, No. 8 25.00
Waffle Iron, I.A. Sheppare & Co. 7 & 8 Baltimore 55.00
Waffle Iron, Low Base, E.C. Simmons 140.00
Waffle Iron, Low Base, Griswold, No. 7, 308, 309. 40.00
Waffle Iron, Low Base, Griswold, No. 8, 977, Ball Hinge 35.00
Waffle Iron, Ornate, Buck & Wright, No. 7. 180.00
Waffle Iron, Proctor & Schwartz Electric Co., Model 1510, 1930s 75.00
Waffle Iron, Wagner Ware, No. 0, Child's, Nickel 90.00 to 110.00
Waffle Iron, Wapak, Indian Head. 50.00
Wash Board, Sycamore, Carved, Ribbed, Fluted Flowerhead, French Provincial, 22 x 7 In. .. 108.00
Wash Stick, Wood, Chip Carved, 31 In.. 99.00
Washtub, Wooden, Red Paint, Stave Construction, Iron Bands, Piggin Handles, 11 x 18 In... 288.00
Water Server, Refrigerator, Cover, Cobalt Blue, Westinghouse, Universal, 8½ In. 49.00
Wringer, Household, Wood, Metal, 28 x 14 x 11 In. *illus* 150.00

KNIFE collectors usually specialize in a single type. In the 1960s, the United States government passed a law that required knife manufacturers to mark their knives with the country of origin. This seemed to encourage the collectors, and knife collecting became an interest of a large group of people. All types of knives are collected, from top quality twentieth-century examples to old bone- or pearl-handled knives in excellent condition.

Bowie, Bone Handle, Crosshatch Decoration, Cross Guard, Scabbard, 17¼ In. 1380.00
Bowie, Checkered Rosewood Handle, Gold, Leather Scabbard, 12 In. 358.00
Bowie, Display, Inscribed, Gold Seeker's Protector, Wood Handle, Scabbard, 18 In. 3680.00
Crooked, Carved, Handle, 9½ In. 650.00
Dagger, Metal Scabbard, Leather Hanger, Germany, 16 In. 104.00
Dagger, SS, World War II, Sheath 1775.00
Dagger, World War II, Officer, Straps, Knots 449.00
Fascine, Civil War, Iron, 20¾ In. 200.00
Hunting, German, Stag Handle, Rabbit Hanging From Tree, 12¾ In. 400.00
Hunting, No. 13, Marble's 100.00
Hunting, Sheath, Boker Tree Brand 45.00
Multi Use, 50 Blade, German, Mother-Of-Pearl Handle 1485.00
Paper, Whale Ivory, Tortoiseshell 165.00
Pocket, 2 Blades, Winchester, No. 2703 .... 170.00
Pocket, 2 Blades, Winchester, No. 2874 .... 110.00
Pocket, 2 Blades, Winchester, No. 2914 .... 90.00
Pocket, 3 Blades, Winchester, No. 3005 .... 240.00
Pocket, 3 Blades, Winchester, No. 3906 .... 625.00
Pocket, Brass, Road Racer, Rugby Players, 3⅞ In. 83.00
Pocket, Silver, Mother-Of-Pearl, Sheffield, c.1880, 6 In. 225.00
Spear Point, Hand Forged, Horn Handle, 11¼ In. 94.00

KNOWLES, TAYLOR & KNOWLES *items may be found in the KTK and Lotus Ware categories.*

KOREAN WARE, *see Sumida.*

KOSTA, the oldest Swedish glass factory, was founded in 1742. During the 1920s through the 1950s, many pieces of original design were made at the factory. Kosta and Boda merged with Afors in 1964 and created the Afors Group in 1971. In 1976, the name Kosta Boda was adopted. The company merged with Orrefors in 1990 and is still working.

KOSTA

Decanter, Figural, Bird, Clear, Stopper, Vicke Lindstrand, 8 x 7 In. 550.00
Urn, Rampant Lion, 6-Sided, 1940s, Bergh, 3¾ x 2½ In. .... *illus* 26.00

KPM refers to Berlin porcelain, but the same initials were used alone and in combination with other symbols by several German porcelain makers. They include the Konigliche Porzellan Manufaktur of Berlin, initials used in mark, 1823–1847; Meissen, 1723–1724 only; Krister Porzellan Manufaktur in Waldenburg, after 1831; Kranichfelder Porzellan Manufaktur in Kranichfeld, after 1903; and the Krister Porzellan Manufaktur in Scheibe, after 1838.

K.P.M

Figurine, Coach & 4 Horses, Blue & White, 6 x 13 In. 117.00
Figurine, Cupid Pulling Shoe Chariot, Blue Mark, 5¼ In. .... *illus* 115.00
Group, Power Of Love, Woman Holding Key, Child, Flowers, Blue Scepter Mark, 11 In. 570.00
Lithophane, see also Lithophane category.
Plaque, Loreley, Woman, Seated, Porcelain, Gorner, Signed, 21½ x 16 In. 13800.00
Plaque, The Virgin, Child, St. John, Red Velvet Lined Gilt Wood Frame, c.1800, 5 x 4 In. 980.00
Teapot, Hallesche, Gilt Silver, Marguerite Friedlander-Wildenhain, c.1930, 3½ In. .... *illus* 10625.00
Tray, Round, Pierced Handles, Painted Flowers, Gilt Vines, Late 1800s, 9½ In. 71.00
Vase, Cupid, Companion, Cobalt Blue, Ground, Gilt Scrolls, Footed, 6 In. 1180.00

KTK are the initials of the Knowles, Taylor & Knowles Company of East Liverpool, Ohio, founded by Isaac W. Knowles in 1853. The company made many types of utilitarian wares, hotel china, and dinnerwares. They made the fine bone china known as Lotus Ware from 1891 to 1896. The company merged with American Ceramic Corporation in 1928. It closed in 1934. Lotus Ware is listed in its own category in this book.

K.T.&K.
CHINA

Bowl, Applied Blossoms & Leaves, Milky White, 4¼ x 5½ In. 650.00
Planter, Art Deco, Green & Tan, Raised Leaf, 5 x 5½ In. 85.00
Tray, Shell Shape, Berries & Leaves, Lotus Ware Mark, Signed W.W., 1890s, 8½ x 8¾ In. 500.00
Vase, Lily, White, Pink Leaves On Base, c.1892, 8¾ In. 1200.00

TIP

Use denture cleaning tablets to remove a stain from a ceramic teapot. Follow the directions for use with false teeth.

KPM, Figurine, Cupid Pulling Shoe Chariot, Blue Mark, 5¼ In.
$115.00

KPM, Teapot, Hallesche, Gilt Silver, Marguerite Friedlander-Wildenhain, c.1930, 3½ In.
$10625.00

Kutani, Plate, Reserves, Figures, Poetry, Gilt, Embossed, Yoshida, c.1875, 9½ In., Pair
$230.00

Lacquer, Box, Flowers, Pagodas, Iron Red, Gilt, Chinese, 19th Century, 4¾ x 14 x 9 In.
$265.00

Lacquer, Dish, Coat Of Arms, Fide, Fleices, Facti, 6½ x 11 x 9½ In.
$1090.00

TIP
Lalique fakes have long been a problem. We have seen examples with a raised mark (the thick base was sandblasted away to leave the raised letters) or an acid-etched mark. Many pieces are marked with the old signature form, "R. Lalique." Become familiar with real Lalique shapes and finishes, because often the false signatures are put on Czechoslovakian glass that does not look like Lalique. One clue: The vase with the eight standing nudes is by Lalique. If there are seven or nine nudes, the piece is a fake.

KUTANI porcelain was made in Japan after the mid-seventeenth century. Most of the pieces found today are nineteenth-century. Collectors often use the term *Kutani* to refer to just the later, colorful pieces decorated with red, gold, and black pictures of warriors, animals, and birds.

Figurine, Buddhist Lion, Shishi, Chrysanthemum, Stoneware, Japan, 19th Century, 22 In. . . . 3819.00
Plate, Reserves, Figures, Poetry, Gilt, Embossed, Yoshida, c.1875, 9½ In., Pair . . . *illus* 230.00
Rose Jar, Lid, Flowers, Woman At Table, 3 Panels, 3-Footed, 5¾ x 4½ In. . . . 115.00
Vase, Double Gourd Form, Japan, 19th Century, 9¾ In. . . . 118.00
Vase, Red, Courtiers In Garden, Crackled Gray Ground, Japan, 19th Century, 12¼ In. . . . 294.00
Vase, Red, Phoenix Rondels, Brocade Ground, Japan, 19th Century, 6 In. . . . 646.00
Vase, Winter Landscape, Red, Slightly Graduated, Cylindrical, 13 In., Pair . . . 823.00

L.G. WRIGHT Glass Company of New Martinsville, West Virginia, started selling glassware in 1937. Founder "Si" Wright contracted with Ohio and West Virginia glass factories to reproduce popular pressed glass patterns, like Rose & Snow, Baltimore Pear, and Three Face, and opalescent patterns, like Daisy & Fern and Swirl. Collectors can tell the difference between the original glasswares and L.G. Wright reproductions because of colors and differences in production techniques. Some L.G. Wright items are marked with an underlined W in a circle. Items that were made from old Northwood molds have an altered Northwood mark—an angled line was added to the N to make it look like a W. Collectors refer to this mark as "the wobbly W." The L.G. Wright factory was closed and the existing molds sold in 1999.

Apothecary Jar, White Satin, Red Roses. . . . 350.00
Barber Bottle, Daisy & Fern, Cranberry Opalescent, Stopper . . . 375.00
Candy, Cover, Amber Overlay, Candy, Cover, Corn Finial . . . 300.00

LACQUER is a type of varnish. Collectors are most interested in the Chinese and Japanese lacquer wares made from the Japanese varnish tree. Lacquer wares are made from wood with many coats of lacquer. Sometimes the piece is carved or decorated with ivory or metal inlay.

Box, Boy & Girl On Log, Painted Scene, Wood, Marked, Russia, 3¾ x 5¾ x 3¾ In. . . . 55.00
Box, Carved Mother Of Pearl, 20 x 36 In. . . . 250.00
Box, Cosmetics, Gold, Silver Flowers, Mirror Stand, Copper Mounts, Japan . . . 411.00
Box, Flowers, Bird, Mottled Cover, 20th Century, 7 x 4 x 3 In. . . . 34.00
Box, Flowers, Metallic Flakes, Compartment, 4 Tiers, Japan, 1800s, 15 x 9½ x 9 In. . . . 4406.00
Box, Flowers, Pagodas, Iron Red, Gilt, Chinese, 19th Century, 4¾ x 14 x 9 In. . . . *illus* 265.00
Box, Game, Circular, Reed, Concentric Circles, 7 x 4 In. . . . 75.00
Box, Metallic Flakes, Japan, 19th Century, 10 x 8¾ x 8 In. . . . 499.00
Box, Paper, Irises, Multicolor, Divider Tray, 10 x 8 x 1½ In. . . . 125.00
Box, Pumpkins, Leaves, Orange, Olive Green, 12 x 10¾ In. . . . 588.00
Box, Ribs, Tripod Feet, Gold Mons, Cylindrical, Japan, 19th Century, 17 x 15 In. . . . 235.00
Box, Russian Village, Cylindrical, 7 In. . . . 580.00
Dish, Coat Of Arms, Fide, Fleices, Facti, 6½ x 11 x 9½ In. . . . *illus* 1090.00
Dresser Box, Round, Flowers, 4 In. Diam. . . . 10.00
Plaque, Japanese, Hand Painted, 12½ x 3½ In., Pair . . . 47.00
Plaque, Rickshaw, Coolies, Wood, Oval, Ivory, Mother-Of-Pearl, 20 x 16 In. . . . 235.00
Screen, 6 Panel, Bamboo Rock Garden, Birds, Flowers, 83½ x 96 In. . . . 1150.00
Tray, Autumn Flowers, Metallic Flakes, Mother-Of-Pearl, Coral Inlay, 23 x 17 In. . . . 4466.00
Tray, Bird, Flowers, Raised Edge, Gold Trim, 10 x 10 In. . . . 28.00
Tray, Birds, Grasses, Gold, c.1900, 8½ In. . . . 125.00
Tray, Black, Gold Flowers, Metallic Flakes, 30¾ x 17 In. . . . 764.00
Tray, Black, Papier-Mache, Parcel Gilt, English Town Scene, Oval, 31 x 24 In. . . . 2400.00
Tray, Crumb, Variegated Design, Flower Handles, 19th Century, 9 x 8 In. . . . 25.00
Tray, Red, Gilt Oriental Figures, Trees, Plants, Papier-Mache, 22 x 29 In. . . . 960.00
Vase, Leaves, Bird, Red, Gold, Silver, 11½ x 6 In. . . . 200.00
Writer's Box, Cloud, Moon, Gold, 8 x 5½ x 1¼ In. . . . 300.00

LADY HEAD VASE, *see Head Vase.*

R.LALIQUE

LALIQUE glass was made by Rene Lalique in Paris, France, between the 1890s and his death in 1945. The glass was molded, pressed, and engraved in Art Nouveau and Art Deco styles. Pieces were marked with the signature *R. Lalique*. Lalique glass is still being made. Pieces made after 1945 bear the mark *Lalique*. Some pieces that are advertised as ring dishes or pin dishes were listed as ashtrays in the Lalique factory catalog and are listed as ashtrays here. Jewelry made by Rene Lalique is listed in the Jewelry category.

Ashtray, Bears, Signed, 3½ x 4 In. . . . 59.00
Ashtray, Concarneau, Fish, Bubbles, Frosted, 6¼ In. . . . 88.00
Ashtray, Cugne, Swan, Signed, 3 x 4 In. . . . 71.00

Ashtray, Dindon, Turkey, Opalescent Green, Engraved, c.1925, 2½ In. . . . 1020.00
Ashtray, Statuette De La Fontaine, Frosted & Clear, c.1925, 4¾ In. . . . 2360.00
Ashtray, Thalie, Dove, Signed, 4 x 4 In. . . . 70.00
Berry Set, Coquilles, Bowl, 6 Small Bowls, Underplate, 9½ & 5 & 12 In. . . . 1610.00
Bookends, Hirondelles, Swallows, Birds Leaning Forward, Signed, 6¼ In. . . . 630.00
Bottle, Epines, Thornes, Blue Patination, Matching Stopper, 3¼ In. . . . 633.00
Bowl, Anges, Pairs Of Praying Children, Center Star, Blue Opalescent, 3¾ x 14½ In. . . . 2300.00
Bowl, Charme, Raised Leaves, Brown Patina, Square, Signed, 2 x 9¼ x 9¼ In. . . . 800.00
Bowl, Coquilles, Overlapping Shells, Clear, 8¼ In. . . . 460.00
Bowl, Cremieu, Opalescent Glass, Sawtooth Border, Internal Fluting, 3¾ x 12 In. . . . 633.00
Bowl, Honfleur, Flowering Leaf Handles, Marked, c.1945, 5½ In., 4 Piece . . . 150.00
Bowl, Houppes, Molded Pompoms, Amber, Frosted Ground, Rose Bowl, 5 x 7½ In. . . . 1265.00
Bowl, Nemours, Stylized Flowers, Black Enameled Centers, Brown Patina, 10 In. . . . 978.00
Bowl, Nogent, Frosted Birds Base, Clear Bowl, 3¼ x 5½ In. . . . 205.00
Bowl, Phalenes, Opalescent Moths, Stylized Flowers, 15⅛ In. . . . 6000.00
Bowl, Poissons, Fish, Opalescent, c.1930, 8 In. . . . 630.00
Bowl, Roscoff, Fish, Bubbles, Clear, 2¾ x 13¾ In. . . . 708.00
Box, Enfants, Children, Frosted Cover, Signed, c.1931, 4 x 3 In. . . . 1380.00
Box, Fontainebleau, Rabbits & Birds On Cover, Round, Frosted, 3½ In. . . . 540.00
Box, Roger, Birds & Cabochons, Olive Green, 1¾ x 5¼ In. . . . *illus* 500.00
Candleholder, Dahlia, Frosted, Molded, c.1921, 5½ x 12 In. . . . 2400.00
Chandelier, Trevise, Ribbed Leaf, Frosted Dome, Brass Fleur-De-Lis Hanger, 16 x 12 In. . . . 2875.00
Clock, Dahlia, Frosted, Black Enamel, 5-Sided, Windup, ATO, 1926, 6¾ In. . . . 3736.00
Clock, Marly, Lily Of The Valley, Opalescent, White Enamel, 1931, 6¾ In. . . . 3736.00
Clock, Moineaux, Birds, Flowers, Limbs, House, Frosted, ATO, 6½ x 8½ In. . . . 2070.00
Coupe, Igor, 3 Frosted Dolphins On Base, Clear Bowl, 10 In. . . . 590.00
Decanter, Masques, Concave Front, Back, Amber Brown Patina, 10 In. . . . 2300.00
Decanter, Satyre, Frosted, Sepia Patina, Silvered Port Tag, c.1923, 9¾ In. . . . 3000.00
Dish, 8 Cherub Faces Around Rim, Frosted, 2 x 4 In. . . . 135.00
Figurine, Bear, Frosted, 7 1/2 In. . . . 215.00 to 413.00
Figurine, Cerf, Stag, Frosted, Clear, Polished Base, Marc Lalique, c.1958, 10¼ x 8¼ In. . . . 805.00
Figurine, Chat Assis, Cat, Seated, Frosted, Etched Lalique France, 8 x 4 x 6 In. . . . 585.00 to 646.00
Figurine, Chat Couche, Cat, Crouching, Etched In Script Lalique France, 1970s, 4 x 9 In. . . . 439.00 to 633.00
Figurine, Chat Couche, Cat, Crouching, Frosted, c.1932, 4½ x 9¼ In. . . . 3600.00
Figurine, Chrysis, Kneeling Female Nude, Rises, From Plinth, Frosted, 6¼ In. . . . 384.00
Figurine, Coq Nain, Rooster, Frosted, 8¼ In. . . . 472.00
Figurine, Danseuse, Bra Leves, Dancer, Arms Up, 9 x 4½ x 3 In. . . . 380.00
Figurine, Fairy Crystaidel, 9 In. . . . 646.00
Figurine, Moineau, Sparrow, Head Down, 3½ x 4½ In. . . . 147.00
Figurine, Moineau, Sparrow, Head Up, 3¾ x 4 In. . . . 176.00
Figurine, Owl, Signed, c.1993, 2½ x 2 In. . . . 120.00
Figurine, Panthere, Panther, Crouching, 14 In. . . . 1410.00
Figurine, Polar Bear, Standing, Clear & Frosted, 6 x 6 In. . . . 646.00
Figurine, Seahorse, 3⅞ In. . . . 112.00
Figurine, Sirene, Mermaid, Opalescent, c.1920, 4 In. . . . 3360.00
Figurine, Suzanne Au Bain, Blue Opalescent, Nude, Outstretched Arms, Electrified Bronze Base, 10 In. 18800.00
Figurine, Tete D'Aigle, Eagle Head, Clear, 5½ In. . . . 823.00
Figurine, Tete De Coq, Rooster Head, Clear & Frosted, 7¾ x 6½ In. . . . 323.00
Figurine, Vierge A L'Enfant, Virgin & Child, Frosted, Wood Base, 15 In. . . . 1200.00
Figurine, Woman, Suzanne, Opalescent Amber, Flowing Drape, Marked, c.1925, 9 In. . . . 14700.00
Goblet, Angel, Wine, Clear, Caved, Angel, c.1970, 8 x 3 In., 6 Piece . . . 527.00
Hood Ornament, Saint Christophe, Carries Child, Clear & Frosted, Silver Mount, 6 x 4 x ⅝ In. 1540.00
Inkwell, Cernay, Blackberry Leaves & Berries, Frosted, Green Patina, c.1924, 6 In. . . . 1680.00
Inkwell, Escargots, Snails, Frosted, Sepia & Gray Patina, Engraved, c.1920, 6⅜ In. . . . 7800.00
Inkwell, Mures, Blackberry Thorns & Berries, Opalescent, Blue Patina, c.1920, 2 x 6¼ In. . . . 4200.00
Inkwell, Quatre Sirenes, 4 Mermaids, Blown, Molded, Blue, Cover, Signed, 6 x 2 In. . . . 2587.00
Inkwell, Serpents, Snakes, Opalescent Dark Amber, R. Lalique, c.1920, 6 1/4 In. . . . 4200.00 to 5100.00
Jar, Cover, Cariatides, Stylized Nudes, Ribs, Frosted Smoky Gray, 8 In. . . . 2875.00
Jardiniere, St. Hubert, Gazelles Leaping Handles, Clear, Frosted, Boat Shape, c.1927, 5 x 18 In. 1912.00
Luminaire, Fish, Bronze Base, c.1922, Marked, 15 In. . . . 6600.00
Menu Holder, Faun Head, Clear, Frosted, Sepia Patina, c.1928, 5½ In. . . . 840.00
Menu Plaque, Raisin Muscat, Grapes, Clear, Frosted, c.1924, 6 In. . . . 270.00
Paperweight, Chouette, Owl, Frosted, Engraved, Lalique France, 3¾ In. . . . *illus* 87.00
Paperweight, Daim, Deer, Dark Gray, c.1926, 3 In. . . . 720.00
Paperweight, Tete D'Aigle, Eagle Head, Frosted, Molded, 1928, 4½ In. . . . 413.00
Perfume Bottle, Dancing Nude Maidens, Blossoms On Stopper, 4¾ In. . . . 1380.00

Lalique, Box, Roger, Birds & Cabochons, Olive Green, 1¾ x 5¼ In.
$500.00

Lalique, Paperweight, Chouette, Owl, Frosted, Engraved, Lalique France, 3¾ In.
$87.00

Lalique, Perfume Bottle, Nina Ricci, L'Air Du Temps, Contents, Sealed, Box, 4 In.
$375.00

Lalique, Perfume Bottle, Worth, Sans Adieu, Tiered, Stopper, Emerald Green, Marked, 4 3/8 In.
$275.00

Lalique, Vase, Antinea, Clear Bowl, Female Figure Base, Green Opalescent, Signed, c.1995, 8 x 10 In.
$1400

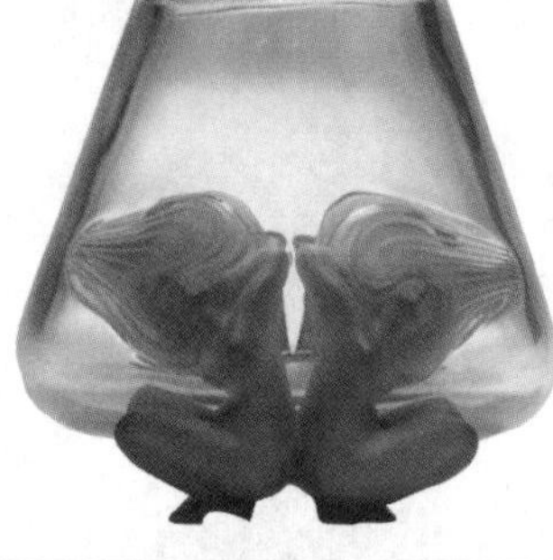

Lalique, Vase, Avallon, Birds & Grapes, Opalescent, Green Patina, c.1927, 5 3/4 In.
$3480.00

TIP

Lalique glass made before 1945 will fluoresce yellow under a black light. Glass made after 1945 does not.

Perfume Bottle, D'Orsay, Le Lys, Display, Molded Flowers, Frosted, Stopper, c.1922, 8½ In. . . . 900.00
Perfume Bottle, Enfants, Embossed, Cover, 1980s, 4¼ In. . . . 270.00
Perfume Bottle, Fleurettes, Frosted, Vertical Bands Of Florets, Gray Patination, 7¾ In. . . . 259.00
Perfume Bottle, Lucien Lelong, Skyscraper, Black Enamel, Chrome Box, c.1929, 4¾ In. . . . 5400.00
Perfume Bottle, Nenuphar, Water Lilies, Frosted, Green Patina, c.1911, 4½ In. . . . 3900.00
Perfume Bottle, Nina Ricci, Coeur Joie, Heart Shape, Screw Cap, 1950s, 4¾ In. . . . 161.00
Perfume Bottle, Nina Ricci, L'Air Du Temps, Contents, Sealed, Box, 4 In. . . . *illus* 375.00
Perfume Bottle, Nina Ricci, L'Air Du Temps, Nina Ricci, Metal Frame, Box, 4 In. . . . 441.00
Perfume Bottle, Phalene, Nude With Butterfly Wings, Red, Amber, c.1925, 3¾ In. . . . 7200.00
Perfume Bottle, Worth, Dans La Nuit, Flask, Blue, Stopper, Crescent Moon & Stars, 9 In. . . . 575.00
Perfume Bottle, Worth, Sans Adieu, Tiered, Stopper, Emerald Green, Marked, 4⅜ In. . . *illus* 275.00
Perfume Burner, Papillons, Butterflies, Opalescent, Blue Green Patina, 1920, 7½ In. . . . 2291.00
Perfume Burner, Papillons, Butterflies, Amber, White Patina, 1920, 7½ In. . . . 2806.00
Placecard Holder, Baskets Of Fruit & Flowers, Frosted, Signed, 1½ x 2 In., 4 Piece . . . 550.00
Plate, Algues, Black, Seaweed, c.1933, 7¾ In. . . . 117.00
Platter, Nippon, Concentric Bubbles, c.1940, 13¾ In. . . . 585.00
Powder Box, Vaucluse, Birds & Ferns, Frosted, Sepia Patina, c.1924, 2¾ In. . . . 1200.00
Powder Jar, Art Nouveau Lady On Cover With Flowing Gown, Frosted, Flowering Bands, 3½ In. 460.00
Sculpture, Fish, Scales & Curving Fins, Clear, Signed On Foot, 12¼ x 16 In. . . . 1140.00
Sparrow, Wings Out, 3¼ x 5¼ In. . . . 176.00
Vase, Ajaccio, Sleeping, Gazelles, Starlit Sky, Frosted White & Clear, Marked, 7 In. . . . 1020.00
Vase, Antinea, Clear Bowl, Female Figure Base, Green Opalescent, Signed, c.1995, 8 x 10 In. *illus* 1400.00
Vase, Archers, Nude Male Archers, Swooping Birds, Amber, White Patina, c.1921, 10¼ In. . . . 14400.00
Vase, Avallon, Birds & Grapes, Deep Blue Patina, 5½ In. . . . 2185.00
Vase, Avallon, Birds & Grapes, Cobalt Blue, Signed, 5¾ In. . . . 2530.00
Vase, Avallon, Birds & Grapes, Opalescent, Green Patina, c.1927, 5¾ In. . . . *illus* 3480.00
Vase, Bacchantes, Frieze Of Female Nudes, Frosted, Marked, 9¾ In. . . . *illus* 4800.00
Vase, Bacchus, Impressed Satyrs, Frosted, Gray Patina, c.1938, 6 1/2 In. . . . 2300.00 to 2760.00
Vase, Bacchus, Impressed Satyrs, Reddish Brown Patina, Clear, Top, c.1938, 7 In. . . . 3600.00
Vase, Bagatelle, 12 Molded Birds, Leaves, Frosted, Gray Patina, Clear, 6¾ In. . . . 1437.00
Vase, Biches, Does, Turquoise, Barrel Shape, 7 x 3½ In. . . . 643.00
Vase, Borneo, Birds & Leaves, Frosted, Green Enamel, c.1930, 9¼ In. . . . 2040.00
Vase, Borneo, Birds & Leaves, Clear & Frosted, Green Enamel Birds, c.1930, 9¼ In. . . . 3360.00
Vase, Bresse, Swirling Feathers, Amber, Cream Patina, c.1932, 3¾ In. . . . 1006.00
Vase, Bresse, Swirling Feathers, Cased Opalescent Turquoise, c.1932, 3½ In. . . . 3600.00
Vase, Canards, Ducks, Cased Opalescent, Butterscotch, White Patina, c.1927, 5½ In. . . . 4200.00
Vase, Ceylan, 4 Pair Parakeets On Branches, Opalescent, Blue Patina, c.1924, 9 In. . . . 7800.00
Vase, Ceylan, 4 Pair Parakeets On Branches, Frosted, Brown Patina, c.1924, 9 In. . . . 9000.00
Vase, Chardons, Teasel, Frosted, Brown, Prickly Leaves, c.1922, 8 1/4 In. . . . 750.00 to 1003.00
Vase, Charmarande, Wild Rose, Handles, Smoky Brown, Polished, Frosted, c.1926, 7½ In. . . . 480.00
Vase, Charmilles, Overlapping Leaves, Oval, Gray, c.1926, 14 In. . . . 2990.00
Vase, Coqs Et Plumes, 12 Strutting Roosters, Frosted, Blue Patina, c.1928, 6 1/4 In. 1610.00 to 2040.00
Vase, Courlis, Curlews, Deep Green, Whitish Patina, c.1931, 6½ In. . . . 8400.00
Vase, Dahlias, Overlapping Flower Heads, Black Centers, Round, c.1923, 7 x 4 In. . . . 500.00
Vase, Dampierre, Protruding Birds, Flared, Footed, 5 x 4 1/2 In. . . . 353.00 to 411.00
Vase, Danaides, Nudes Pouring Water From Urns, Opalescent, R. Lalique, c.1926, 7 In. . . . 1500.00
Vase, Domremy, Thistles, Amber, c.1926, 8 In. . . . 4800.00
Vase, Domremy, Thistles, Emerald Green, c.1926, 8 In. . . . 7200.00
Vase, Druide, Mistletoe, Double Cased Opalescent, Jade Green, c.1924, 7 In. . . . 5100.00
Vase, Epis, Leaves & Flared Ribs, Blue Patina, Polished Border, 6½ In. . . . 1150.00
Vase, Farandole, Cherubs Dancing On Lower Body, Flared Rim, c.1930, 7 x 10¼ In. . . . 3450.00
Vase, Faune, Figural Base, Flarred Top, Frosted, Gray Patina, c.1931, 12½ In. . . . 5700.00
Vase, Formose, Swirling Carp, Molded, Opalescent, Mid 20th Century, 7 x 6½ In. . . . 588.00
Vase, Fougeres, 4 Rows Of Stylized Molded Leaves, Stems, Flowers, Blue Patina, c.1912, 6 In. . 3600.00
Vase, Grenade, Black, White Patina, c.1930, 4¼ In. . . . 3900.00
Vase, Gui, Mistletoe & Berries, Deep Teal Green, Molded, c.1920, 7 In. . . . 3900.00
Vase, Gui, Mistletoe & Berries, Green, c.1920, 6½ In. . . . 4800.00
Vase, Languedoc, Aloe Leaves, Molded & Frosted, Gray, Sepia Patina, c.1929, 8½ In. . . . 4800.00
Vase, Le Mans, Overall Roosters, Opalescent Turquoise, c.1931, 3¾ In. . . . 3600.00
Vase, Malesherbes, Loquat Leaves, Amber, c.1927, 9¼ In. . . . 5100.00
Vase, Malines, Vertical Bands Of Pointed Leaves, Frosted, Blue Patina, c.1924, 4¾ In. . . . 1320.00
Vase, Marguerites, Daisies, Descending From Neck, Frosted Ground, c.1914, 8 In. . . . 1840.00
Vase, Marguerites, Daisies, Descending From Neck, Frosted, Sepia Patina, c.1914, 9 In. . . . 8400.00
Vase, Moissac, Overlapping Raised Leaves, Deep Amber, c.1927, 5⅛ In. . . . 2160.00
Vase, Moissac, Overlapping Raised Leaves, Yellow, c.1927, 4½ In. . . . 3360.00
Vase, Monnaie Du Pape, Money Plant, Leaves, Deep Amber, Orange, Signed, c.1914, 9 In. . . . 8400.00

Vase, Monnaie Du Pape, Money Plant, Plum, c.1914, 9¼ In.. 9600.00
Vase, Narcisse, Abstract Swirl, Clear & Frosted, c.1970, 10½ In.. 700.00
Vase, Nefliers, Molded Flowers, Feathery Leaves, Frosted Ground, Blue Patina, 5½ In. 1380.00
Vase, Oleron, Little Fish, Mold Blown Fish, Signed, c.1927, 4 In.. 748.00
Vase, Oran, Large Dahlias, Opalescent, Molded, 10¼ In. 28800.00
Vase, Orchid, Clear, Protruding Opalescent Orchids, c.1970, 6½ x 8 In. 1053.00
Vase, Ormeaux, Overlapping Elm Leaves, Signed, c.1926, 6½ In. 690.00
Vase, Ormeaux, Overlapping Elm Leaves, Smoky Gray, c.1926, 6½ In. 1140.00
Vase, Ornis, Clear, Opalescent Bird, Handles, Footed, c.1926, 7¼ In.. 4600.00
Vase, Ornis, Topaz, Bird Handles, Footed, c.1926, 7½ In. 1440.00
Vase, Palissy, Snail Shells, Cased Opalescent, Blue Patina, c.1926, 6½ In. 2760.00
Vase, Perruches, Parakeets, Cased Opalescent, c.1919, 10¼ x 9½ In. 3900.00
Vase, Perruches, Parakeets, Smoky Blue, Gray Patina, Signed, c.1919, 10 In. 6900.00
Vase, Pierrefonds, Volute Handles, Wheel Carved, Frosted, c.1926, 6 In. 7200.00
Vase, Piriac, Fish & Waves At Base, Flared Top, Frosted, Blue Patina, c.1930, 7 x 8 In. 1920.00
Vase, Quatre Tetes Femmes Et Raisins, Women's Faces, Grapes, Flared Rim, c.1939, 5 In. 2280.00
Vase, Raisins, Grapes & Vines, Frosted, Sepia Patina, 1928, 6¼ In. 2448.00
Vase, Rampillon, Cabochons & Flowers, Opalescent, c.1927, 4½ In. 3120.00
Vase, Ricquewihr, Ridged Bands, Grapes & Leaves, Green Patina, R. Lalique, 5 In. *illus* 767.00
Vase, Ronces, Thorns, Dark Amber, c.1921, 9½ In. 5400.00
Vase, Saint Tropez, Stems & Berries, Opalescent, Signed, c.1937, 7 In. 2300.00
Vase, Saint-Francois, Finches On Branches, Opalescent, Blue Patina, c.1930, 6½ In. 2875.00
Vase, Saint-Francois, Finches On Branches, Opalescent, c.1930, 6½ In. 3000.00
Vase, Sauge, Sage Leaves, Frosted, Green Patina, c.1927, 9⅛ In. 2160.00
Vase, Sirenes Avec Bouchon Figurine, Mermaids, Figural Stopper, Clear, Frosted, c.1920, 14 In. 13200.00
Vase, Soudan, 3 Bands Of Running Gazelles, Opalescent, Blue Patina, Engraved, c.1928, 7 In. 4200.00
Vase, Spirales, Spirals, Zipper Edge, Peach Patina, c.1930, 6½ In. 4800.00
Vase, Tournesols, Sunflowers, Electric Blue, c.1927, 4½ In. 3120.00
Vase, Tulipes, High Relief Tulips, Clear, Blue Patina, c.1927, 8¼ In. 2243.00

LAMPS of every type, from the early oil-burning Betty and Phoebe lamps to the recent electric lamps with glass or beaded shades, interest collectors. Fuels used in lamps changed through the years; whale oil (1800–1840), camphene (1828), Argand (1830), lard (1833–1863), turpentine and alcohol (1840s), gas (1850–1879), kerosene (1860), and electricity (1879) are the most common. Other lamps are listed by manufacturer or type of material.

Aladdin, B-27, Alacite, Gold Luster, Table Lamp, Kerosene 175.00
Aladdin, B-29, Simplicity, Green, Table Lamp, Kerosene 200.00
Aladdin, B-30, Simplicity, White, Table Lamp, Kerosene 155.00
Aladdin, B-41, Washington Drape, Amber Crystal, Burner, Kerosene 115.00
Aladdin, B-48, Washington Drape, Green Crystal Bell Stem, Kerosene 230.00
Aladdin, B-53, Washington Drape, Clear, Blue Tint, Kerosene 130.00
Aladdin, B-53P, Washington Drape, Pink Tint, Table Lamp, Kerosene 290.00
Aladdin, B-60, Short Lincoln Drape, Alacite, Kerosene 360.00
Aladdin, B-70, Solitaire, White Moonstone, Kerosene 1100.00
Aladdin, B-75, Alacite, Table Lamp, Scalloped Foot, Kerosene 275.00
Aladdin, B-83, Beehive, Red, Kerosene 260.00
Aladdin, B-86, Quilt, Green Moonstone, Burner, Kerosene 260.00
Aladdin, B-88, Vertique, Yellow Moonstone, Burner, Table Lamp, Kerosene 425.00
Aladdin, B-95, Queen, White Moonstone, Table Lamp, Kerosene 230.00
Aladdin, B-105, Corinthian, Clear, Green, Kerosene 120.00
Aladdin, B-111, Cathedral, Green Moonstone, Burner, Kerosene 195.00
Aladdin, B-116, Corinthian, Rose Moonstone, Kerosene 140.00
Aladdin, B-121, Majestic, Rose Moonstone, Table Lamp, Burner, Kerosene 350.00
Aladdin, B-124, Moonstone & Black Corinthian, Model B Burner, T.R. Pod. 110.00
Aladdin, B-132, Orientale, Rose Gold, No Burner, Kerosene 65.00
Aladdin, G-163, Double Nude, Crystal Wreath, Electric 1625.00
Aladdin, G-187, Alacite, Short Harp, Night-Light, Electric. 45.00
Aladdin, G-298D, Alacite, Floral, Scroll Finial, Electric 115.00
Aladdin, G-355C, Gun, Hoppy Holster, Decal, Electric. 110.00 to 275.00
Aladdin, G-375, Dancing Ladies Urn, Lid 600.00
Altar, 5-Light, Giltwood, Carved, Neoclassical, Sacred Heart, Leaf Scrolls, Italy, 15 x 46 In. 1920.00
Argand, 2-Light, Cast Iron, England, 23 x 17 x 6 In., Pair 2185.00
Argand, 2-Light, Gilt Bronze, Cast Brass, Urn Shape Font, Bud Finials, 19 x 17 In., Pair 2415.00
Argand, 2-Light, Regency, Patinated Bronze, c.1805, 21 x 16 x 6 In. 1880.00
Argand, 3-Light, Gilt Bronze, Anthemion Ring, Frosted Globes, Prisms, 44 x 16 In. 12600.00

Lalique, Vase, Bacchantes, Frieze Of Female Nudes, Frosted, Marked, 9¾ In.
$4800.00

Lalique, Vase, Ricquewihr, Ridged Bands, Grapes & Leaves, Green Patina, R. Lalique, 5 In.
$767.00

Lamp, Astral, Gilt Bronze Base, Marble Platform, Cut Shade, 19¾ In.
$465.00

Lamp, Betty, Iron, Brass, Ball Finial, 6½ In.
$550.00

L

TIP
Chandeliers can be cleaned in place with a new spray cleaner made for that purpose. Cover the floor with paper or cloth to catch the drips. Then spray the chandelier. It will clean and drip dry.

Lamp, Chandelier, 15-Light, 2 Tiers, Crystal Chain Swags, 20th Century, 31 x 30 In.
$230

Lamp, Electric, 3-Light, Leaded Glass, Wood, No. 152, Shop Of The Crafters, 72 x 23 x 23 In.
$2900.00

Argand, Sheffield, Blue & White Jasperware Cylinder, Reservoir, 1800, 16½ In. . . . 7800.00
Argand, Silver Plate, Sheffield, 3-Light, Fluted Pilaster, Paw Feet, Lion Masks, 1800, 23½ In. . 9600.00
Astral, Bronze, Glass, Gothic Shape, Signed Cornelius, c.1850 . . . 1375.00
Astral, Cut Glass Shaft, Font, 19th Century, Electrified, c.1870, 19 x 9 In. . . . 660.00
Astral, Gilt Brass, Cut Glass Shades, Prisms, Baluster Standard, Marble Base, 21 x 8 In., Pair. 1440.00
Astral, Gilt Bronze Base, Marble Platform, Cut Shade, 19¾ In. . . . *illus* 465.00
Barber, Milk Glass, Square, Red, White, Blue, Cast Iron, Wall Mount. . . . 2760.00
Betty, Copper, 18th Century . . . 250.00
Betty, Double, Whale Oil, Hanger, 4-In. Reservoirs, 11 In. . . . 120.00
Betty, Iron, Brass, Ball Finial, 6½ In. . . . *illus* 550.00
Betty, Iron, Brass, Peter Derr, c.1851 . . . 8190.00
Betty, Iron, Spike, Heart Shape, 5 In., Pair . . . 6.00
Betty, Iron, Wood Base, 30 In. . . . 92.00
Bouillotte, 2-Light, Silver Plate, Round Dish Base, Sailing Ship On Side, 21 In. . . . 368.00
Bouillotte, 3-Light, Gilt Brass, 24 x 13¼ In., Pair . . . 1200.00
Bouillotte, 3-Light, Restauration Style, Brass, Tole Shades, France, 14½ In. . . . 1872.00
Bouillotte, Empire Style, Brass, Adjustable Candles, Tole Shade, 24 In. . . . 489.00
Bouillotte, Gilt Brass, Red Tole Shade, 3 Scrolled Arms, 25½ x 16½ In., Pair . . . 1175.00
Bouillotte, Silver Plate, Adjustable Shades, England, 18th Century, 19¾ x 13 In., Pair . . . 3819.00
Bradley & Hubbard lamps are included in the Bradley & Hubbard category.
Camphene, Glass, Peacock Blue, Bell Shape, Applied Handle, Brass Burner, 1800s, 5 In. . . . 1175.00
Candle, Silver Plate, 4-Sided, Sliding Scroll Holders, Cone Shape Shades, 24 In., Pair . . . 2183.00
Candle, Tin, Frosted Star Lens, 17½ In. . . . 138.00
Candle, Tin, Repousse, Drip Spout, Handle, Weighted, 18 In. . . . 127.00
Chandelier, 3-Light, Baroque Style, Brass, Putto, Candle Arms, Continental, 26 x 26 In. . . . 660.00
Chandelier, 3-Light, Consular Style, Gilt Brass, Vase Shape, Cornucopia Arms, 15 x 15 In. . . . 1200.00
Chandelier, 3-Light, Gothic Style, Bronze, Reticulated Leaves, Chains, 25 x 29 In. . . . 1528.00
Chandelier, 4-Light, Black Forest, Bears Holding Wicker Shades . . . 7500.00
Chandelier, 4-Light, Regency Style, Brass, Tiered, Cut Glass, Jewel Chains, 38 x 22 In. . . . 2160.00
Chandelier, 4-Light, Restauration Style, Bronze, Parcel Gilt, 33 x 26 In. . . . 1140.00
Chandelier, 4-Light, Solar, Bronze, Petal Shape Corona, Twisted Rods, Lion Masks, 41 x 28 In. 2205.00
Chandelier, 5-Light, Art Glass Shades, 20th Century, 19 x 16 In. . . . 248.00
Chandelier, 5-Light, Empire Revival, Bronze, Crystal Teardrop Pendants, 39 In. . . . 1180.00
Chandelier, 5-Light, Louis XVI Style, Gilt Brass, Blue & Cut Glass, Flower Heads, 23 x 14 In. . 840.00
Chandelier, 6-Light, Art Deco, Bronze Patinated Brass, Ivory Opal Glass, 31 x 30 In. . . . 2280.00
Chandelier, 6-Light, Brass, Candle Arms, Teardrop Finial, c.1900, 17 x 20 In. . . . 115.00
Chandelier, 6-Light, Brass, Scrolled Arms, Prisms, Brass Collar, c.1920, 28 x 18 In. . . . 2016.00
Chandelier, 6-Light, Bronze, Acanthus Leaf Arms, 35 x 24 In. . . . 2000.00
Chandelier, 6-Light, Bronze, Cut Glass, Candle Cups, Swags, Rosettes, 35 x 32 In. . . . 5100.00
Chandelier, 6-Light, Empire Style, Painted Black Urn, Scroll & Leaf Pediment, 23 x 25 In. . . 863.00
Chandelier, 6-Light, Giltwood, Wreath Carving, Scroll Arms, 4 Supports, France, 63 x 30 In. . 1872.00
Chandelier, 6-Light, Louis XIV Style, Giltwood, Carved, Faux Candles, Silk Shade, 54 x 33 In. 4560.00
Chandelier, 6-Light, Louis XV, Gilt Brass, Cut Glass Beading, Amethyst Drops, 26 x 16 In. . . . 1920.00
Chandelier, 6-Light, Louis XVI, Gilt Brass, Cut Glass Swags, Teardrops, Prisms, 30 x 19 In. . . 2880.00
Chandelier, 6-Light, Louis XVI Style, Beechwood, Stained, Turned, Carved, Scrolls, 34 x 36 In. . 960.00
Chandelier, 6-Light, Louis XVI Style, Gilt Brass, Cage Shape, Cut Glass, Faceted Drops, 24 x 21 In. 1200.00
Chandelier, 6-Light, Louis XVI Style, Gilt Bronze, Vase Shape, Enameled, c.1900, 36 x 18 In. . 2820.00
Chandelier, 6-Light, Napoleon III, Lily, Gilt Brass, Matte, 26½ In. . . . 4080.00
Chandelier, 6-Light, Regency Style, Brass, 4 Tiers, Cut Glass Chains, Pendants, 37 x 20 In. . . 3600.00
Chandelier, 6-Light, Restauration Style, Gilt Brass, Orb, Opal Glass Candles, 30 x 14 In. . . . 2160.00
Chandelier, 6-Light, Silver Plated Bronze, Vase Standard, Bead Scroll Arms, France, 25 x 22 In. . . 4800.00
Chandelier, 7-Light, Copper, Glass, Lantern Style, G. Stickley, 49 x 102 In. . . . 33600.00
Chandelier, 8-Light, Brass, Central Urn, 20th Century, 28 x 27 In. . . . 978.00
Chandelier, 8-Light, Continental, Blackened Wrought Iron, Open Ribbed Finial, 57 x 44 In. . 1800.00
Chandelier, 8-Light, Cut Glass, Shepherd Crook Corona, Tiers, Prisms, Garlands, 54 x 36 In. . 2938.00
Chandelier, 8-Light, Dresden, Flowers, Mid 20th Century . . . 59.00
Chandelier, 8-Light, Gilt Brass, Opaline Glass, Elliptical, Faceted Glass Drops, 30 x 21 In. . . . 1680.00
Chandelier, 8-Light, Gilt Brass, Vase Shape, 24 x 28 In. . . . 2904.00
Chandelier, 8-Light, Louis XV Style, Gilt Brass, Cage Shape, Cut Glass Teardrops, 33 x 23 In. . 1440.00
Chandelier, 8-Light, Louis XVI, Gilt Brass, Cage Shape, Tiers, Albert Spears, 27 x 21 In. . . . 1200.00
Chandelier, 8-Light, Louis XVI Style, Cage Shape, Cut Glass Pendants, Swags, 41 x 22 In. . . . 1440.00
Chandelier, 8-Light, Louis XVI Style, Gilt, Bronze, France, c.1890, 31 x 26 In. . . . 6250.00
Chandelier, 8-Light, Maria Theresa Style, Cut Glass Chains & Pendants, 40 x 28 In. . . . 2280.00
Chandelier, 8-Light, Neoclassical, Iron, Parcel Gilt, Cerulean Paint, 54 x 33 In. . . . 2400.00
Chandelier, 8-Light, Neoclassical Style, Silvered Brass, c.1900, 32 x 25 In. . . . 1200.00
Chandelier, 8-Light, Rococo Style, Brass, Parcel Gilt, Bronze Patina, Tiers, 22 x 17 In. . . . 1440.00

Chandelier, 9-Light, Art Nouveau, Gilt Bronze, Scrolled Straps, Dolphins, 42 x 26 In. 1880.00
Chandelier, 9-Light, Louis XVI, Gilt Brass, Jewel Cut Chains, Drops, Spears, 36 x 32 In. 1440.00
Chandelier, 9-Light, Louis XVI Style, Open Cage, Pendant Drops, c.1900s, 35 x 25 In. 2360.00
Chandelier, 9-Light, Venetian, Iridescent Caramel Glass, 37 x 20 In. 431.00
Chandelier, 9-Light, Wrought Iron, Birds In Tree, Scandinavia, 20th Century, 34 In. 246.00
Chandelier, 10-Light, Louis XV Style, Amber, Gilt Brass, Rose & Amethyst Glass Drops, 39 x 30 In. . 1800.00
Chandelier, 12-Light, Louis XVI Style, Gilt Brass, Cut Glass, Faux Candles, 44 x 26 In. 5520.00
Chandelier, 12-Light, Provincial, Wrought Iron, 2 Tiers, Painted, Pendants, 38 x 42 In. 1470.00
Chandelier, 12-Light, Renaissance Revival, Gilt Bronze, 9 Arms, 35 x 22 In. 1763.00
Chandelier, 12-Light, Wood, Iron, Blue, 19th Century, 36 x 20 In. 2200.00
Chandelier, 14-Light, Neoclassical Style, Gilt Brass, Cut Glass, Tiers, 28 x 23 In. 2280.00
Chandelier, 15-Light, 2 Tiers, Crystal Chain Swags, 20th Century, 31 x 30 In. . . . . *illus* 230.00
Chandelier, 16-Light, Empire Style, Coronet Shape Canopy, Athena Masks, 53 x 43 In. 7500.00
Chandelier, 16-Light, Gothic Style, Wrought Iron, Quatrefoil, Crown Canopy, 62 x 45 In. 5280.00
Chandelier, 16-Light, Napoleon III, Gilt Bronze, Cut Glass, Scroll Arms, Electrified, 27 x 34 In. 4560.00
Chandelier, 16-Light, Provincial, Painted, Tiered, Wrought Tin Bobeches, Italy, 47 x 43 In. . . 3120.00
Chandelier, 16-Light, Renaissance Revival, Wrought Iron, Painted, Pierced Gallery, 37 In. . . 881.00
Chandelier, 17-Light, Wood, Tin, 19th Century, 28½ In., Pair 2040.00
Chandelier, 18-Light, Faux Candle Sleeves, Grape Cluster Drops, 44 x 26 In. 1416.00
Chandelier, 18-Light, Gilt Brass, Embossed, Cut Glass Prisms, Electrified, 38 x 31 In. 3120.00
Chandelier, 19-Light, Louis XV Style, 12 Arms, Crystal Pendants, Prism Spears, 45 x 32 In., Pair 6463.00
Chandelier, 20-Light, French Provincial, Wrought Iron, 2 Tiers, Balloon Shape, 65 x 51 In. . 780.00
Chandelier, 20-Light, Louis XVI, Bronze Dore, Triangular Prisms, 53 x 32 In. 3819.00
Chandelier, Arts & Crafts, Amber Slag Glass, 4 Lantern Drops, 31 x 18 In. 1920.00
Chandelier, Arts & Crafts, Caramel Slag Glass, Metal Frame, 60 x 20 In. 960.00
Chandelier, Arts & Crafts, Iron, 6-Candle, Chain, Ceiling Cap, 55 x 30 In. 660.00
Chandelier, Patinated Copper, Silvered Brass, Engraved, Shallow Basin, 32 x 35 In. 2280.00
Chandelier, Victorian, Ornate Brass Frame, Electrified, c.1880, 27 x 15 In. 275.00
Electric, 2-Light, Billiard, Brass, Turquoise Glass Shades, Acanthus Ceiling Rose, 32 x 60 In. . 1880.00
Electric, 3-Light, Leaded Glass, Wood, No. 152, Shop Of The Crafters, 72 x 23 x 23 In. . . *illus* 2900.00
Electric, 4-Light, Leaded Glass, Patinated Bronze, Tree Base, Green, Orange, Yellow, 30 x 24 In. 4594.00
Electric, 4-Light, Silver Plated Bronze Pedestal, Marble Base, 64 In. 1265.00
Electric, 8-Light, Wrought Iron, Gold Stippled, Silk Shade, 4-Footed, 79 x 21½ In. 11400.00
Electric, Alabaster, Figural, Medieval Figures, 26 x 9 In. 605.00
Electric, Arab Merchant, Cold Painted White Metal, Red & Green Glass Panels, c.1925, 13 In. 748.00
Electric, Art Deco, 1930s Period Woman, Spelter, Globe Shade, 17 x 7 In. 275.00
Electric, Art Deco, Gilt Brass, 3-Step Base, Cut Glass, Glass Terminals, 11 In. 96.00
Electric, Art Deco, Peacock, Bronze, Beaded, Czechoslovakia, 13 x 9 In. 1500.00
Electric, Art Deco, Tan Leather, Metal Trim, Pull Cord, Le Tanneur, 16 In. 270.00
Electric, Art Moderne, Floor, Mahogany, Brass, Adjustable, Bulbous Standard, Mid 1900s, 68 In. . . . 1080.00
Electric, Art Nouveau, Cold Painted Metal, Patina, Scroll Border, Slag Glass, c.1910, 22 In. . . 354.00
Electric, Art Nouveau, Leaded Glass Shade, Flowers, Column Base, 18½ x 25 In. 2400.00
Electric, Arteluce, 3-Light, c.1953, 84 In. 6600.00
Electric, Arts & Crafts, Bronzed Base, Enameled, Mesh Panel Shade, 16 x 23 In. 1140.00
Electric, Arts & Crafts, Caramel Slag Glass, Pyramid Shade, Single Post Base, 15 x 15 x 24 In. 780.00
Electric, Arts & Crafts, Carmel Slag Glass, Metal Bands, 2 Sockets, 22 x 15½ In. 1440.00
Electric, Arts & Crafts, Circular, Brass, Cutout Grapevine, Hanging, 16 Sockets, 29 x 25 In. . . 1080.00
Electric, Arts & Crafts, Emeralite, Brass, c.1920, 20 In. 600.00
Electric, Arts & Crafts, Grapevine, Patinated Metal, Green Slag Glass, 22½ In. 3712.00
Electric, Arts & Crafts, Green Slag Glass, Paneled Shade, Oak Base, 24 x 18 In. 1680.00
Electric, Arts & Crafts, Green Slag Glass, Pyramid Shade, Oak Base, 14 x 14 x 20 In. 510.00
Electric, Arts & Crafts, Hammered Copper, Patina, Cone Shape Shade, Mica Panels, 22 x 21½ In. 1020.00
Electric, Arts & Crafts, Hanging, Pink & Green Slag Glass, Flowers, 4-Sided 270.00
Electric, Arts & Crafts, Hanging, Green & Caramel Glass, Geometric, 6-Sided. 390.00
Electric, Arts & Crafts, Landscape Scene, Tulip Stems, E.M. & Co., 16¼ In. 1856.00
Electric, Arts & Crafts, Leaded Glass, 6 Panels, Geometric, Iron Base, 57 x 16 x 14 In. . . *illus* 990.00
Electric, Arts & Crafts, Leaded Glass Pyramid Shade, Wood Base, 3 Sockets, 23 x 23 x 72 In. . 3000.00
Electric, Arts & Crafts, Leaded Glass Shade, 2 Sockets, Oak Base, Square, 25 x 19 In. 480.00
Electric, Arts & Crafts, Leaded Glass Shade, Flowers, Scalloped Edge, 18 x 22 In. 1800.00
Electric, Arts & Crafts, Reverse Painted Shade, Green Leaves, Grassy Border, c.1899, 23½ In. . 232.00
Electric, Arts & Crafts, Wood, Copper, Etched Magnolia, 6-Sided Shade, 23 x 22 In. 1800.00
Electric, Astral, Rococo Style, Brass, Etched Shade, 19th Century, 35 x 8 In. 3173.00
Electric, Aurora Studios, Hammered Copper Base, Cone Shape Shade, 15½ x 13½ In. 2280.00
Electric, Baluster Shape, Turned, Carved, Painted White, Linen Drum Shade, Italy, 18 x 13 In., Pair 780.00
Electric, Bamboo Reeds, Wood Base, Paper Diffuser, 2 Layers, Signed, Japan, 1950s, 10 x 9 In. *illus* 430.00
Electric, Banquet, Brass, Leaf Pattern Font, Rope Twist Column, Paw Feet, c.1890, 30 In. 500.00

Lamp, Electric, Arts & Crafts, Leaded Glass, 6 Panels, Geometric, Iron Base, 57 x 16 x 14 In.
$990.00

Lamp, Electric, Bamboo Reeds, Wood Base, Paper Diffuser, 2 Layers, Signed, Japan, 1950s, 10 x 9 In.
$430.00

Lamp, Electric, Concentric Rings, Enamel, Moon Light, Panton, Poulson, Denmark, 1960s, 14 x 14 In.
$320.00

Lamp, Electric, Duffner & Kimberly, Leaded Glass, Flowers, Bronze Base, 22 x 18 In.
$3400.00

Lamp, Electric, Hanging, Etched Glass, Cast Iron, Gilt Frame, 14 In.
$250.00

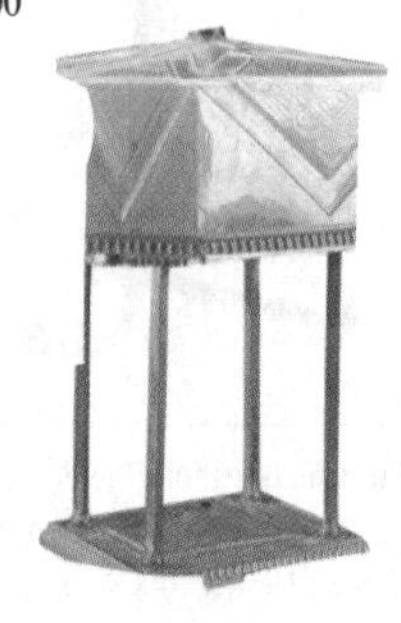

Lamp, Electric, J.H. Whaley, Wisteria, Bronze Base, 21 In.
$9200.00

TIP
Hold glass shades carefully when you remove a light bulb from an old lamp. The Tiffany lily-shaped shade and others like it are held in place by the screwed-in bulb.

L

Electric, Baroque Style, Wood, Lacquer, Multicolored, Parcel Gilt, 55 x 21 In., Pair 4800.00
Electric, Black Enameled Metal, Perforated Shade, 12 x 12½ x 7 In. 1440.00
Electric, Bronze, Columnar, Square Base, 2 Sockets, Oscar Bach, 5½ x 5½ In. 840.00
Electric, Bronze, Glass Mosaic Shade, Green, Pink, Red 20th Century, 28 x 18 In.. . . . . 1057.00
Electric, Bronze, Leaded Glass Shade, Panels, Marble Base, c.1910, 39 In. 1980.00
Electric, Bronze Base, 3-Light Cluster, 4 Serpentine Legs, Paw Feet, 30½ In.. . . . . 920.00
Electric, Bronzed Metal Base, Patinated Support, Leaded Glass Shade, Pink Flowers, 16 x 23 In. . . . 1440.00
Electric, Burmese Glass, Stamp, Webb, 11½ x 4⅜ In.. . . . . 2300.00
Electric, Butter Churn Design, Copper Straps, Old Hickory, 11 x 66 In. 30.00
Electric, Campana Form, Cattail Leaf Pedestal, Drum Shape Shade, France, 28 x 13 In.. . . . . 330.00
Electric, Ceramic, Celadon, Lily Pads, Wood Stand, Shade, Bird Finial, Chinese, 31 In. 112.00
Electric, Ceramic, Painted, Cow Horn, Teardrop Shape, Fluted, Bjorn Wiinblad, 33 In. 956.00
Electric, Ceramic, Sculptured Faces, Pewter Glaze, Shades, Jean Marais, 16 x 5 In., Pair. 4200.00
Electric, Chrome, Black, Marianne Brandt, Brevete, Germany, c.1938, 15 In.. . . . . 1560.00
Electric, Chromed Metal, Interlocking Sections, Black Wood Base, Floor, 35 x 10 In.. . . . . 660.00
Electric, Concentric Rings, Enamel, Moon Light, Panton, Poulson, Denmark, 1960s, 14 x 14 In. *illus* 320.00
Electric, Cork, Teak, Urn Shape, Wood Finial, No Shade, 23½ In., Pair 550.00
Electric, Cranberry Opalescent Glass, Handle, 19th Century, 9 In., Pair 402.00
Electric, D. Martens, Filigrana Glass, White, Black, Aventurine Canes, Shades, 13½ In., Pair . 600.00
Electric, Desk, Emeralite, Adjustable Arm, Spool Edge, Emerald Cased Shade, 13 x 9 x 7 In.. . 392.00
Electric, Desk, Girl In Bonnet, Yellow, Blue, Wave Crest, 17 In.. . . . . 700.00
Electric, Desk, Green & White Cased Glass Shade, Brass Base, Emeralite, 14 x 9 In.. . . . . 270.00
Electric, Desk, Green & White Cased Glass Shade, Brass Base, Tapered Square Post, Emeralite, 18 In. . 288.00
Electric, Dolly Dimple, Iron, Hubley, 13 In. 259.00
Electric, Dresden Style, Porcelain, 4 Dancing Figures Around Tree, Porcelain Shade, 25 In. . . 489.00
Electric, Duffner & Kimberly, Leaded Glass, Flowers, Bronze Base, 22 x 18 In. . . . . *illus* 3400.00
Electric, Duffner & Kimberly, Leaded Glass Heraldic Design, Blue Bows, Scalloped Base 8050.00
Electric, Duffner & Kimberly, Pink Pond Lilies, Green Pads, 4-Light, Brown Patina, 24 In. . . . 5750.00
Electric, Figural, Camel's Head, Gilt Metal, Triangular Silk Shade, 22¾ In. 413.00
Electric, Figural, Diana, Quiver & Bow, Amphitrite, Draped In Net, Bronze, Wood Base, 20 x 6 In., Pair 780.00
Electric, Figural, Knight Holding Torch, Star Shape Shade, Orange To Amber, 19th Century . 2016.00
Electric, Figures Holding Lamps, Brass Fittings, Milk Glass Globes, 34 In., Pair 288.00
Electric, G. Nakashima, French Olive, Burl Walnut, Holly, Fiberglass Shade, 1978, 28 In. 5400.00
Electric, G. Stickley, Hammered Copper, Wicker, c.1912, 26¾ x 22⅜ In.. . . . . 26400.00
Electric, Galvanized Steel Shade, Plaster Tree Trunk, J. Dickinson, No. 105, 1975, 32 In.. . . . . 12500.00
Electric, George IV, Blue John Stone, Turned, Black Marble, Alabaster, Plinth, c.1825, 12 In., Pair. 17500.00
Electric, George V, Black Lacquer, Turned, Candlestick Shape, Geisha, 18 In.. . . . . 390.00
Electric, Gilt Metal, Ivory Mount, Cylindrical, Japanese Woman, Landscape, Leafy Base, 28 In. . 59.00
Electric, Ginger Jar, Cover, Lake, Landscape, Blue Underglaze, Canton, 8 x 19 In. 690.00
Electric, Glass, Blue, Lavender, Barbini, 18 x 7 In.. . . . . 1680.00
Electric, Glass, Fasce Verticale, 34 x 7 In., Pair 2400.00
Electric, Glass, Fish, Sea Plants, Ebonized Wood Base, 14½ x 6 In. 1020.00
Electric, Glass, Painted, House, Landscape, Czechoslovakia, c.1930, Pair 485.00
Electric, Glass Shade, Shepherd, Sheep, 19 x 14 In.. . . . . 325.00
Electric, Green Onyx, Brass Fittings, Verdigris, 66 In. 406.00
Electric, Hanging, 6 Multicolored Shades, Italy, c.1956 . . . . 1320.00
Electric, Hanging, Arts & Crafts, Brass, Carmel Slag Glass Panels, Pull Down, c.1900, 32 x 6 In. 196.00
Electric, Hanging, Asian, Brass, Pierced, Globular, Figures, Flowers, Dragon's Mouth, 45 In. . 354.00
Electric, Hanging, Etched Glass, Cast Iron, Gilt Frame, 14 In. . . . . *illus* 250.00
Electric, Hanging, Octagonal, Tapered, Pierced Scrolls, Greek Key, Demilune Cover, 21 In. . . . 30.00
Electric, Hanging, Stained Glass, Red, Amber, Marbleized Cream, 16 In.. . . . . 100.00
Electric, Hanging, A. Jacobsen, Gray Enamel, White Interior, 4 Bulbs, 20 x 10 In. 210.00
Electric, Hermes, Leather, Cylindrical, Parchment Shade, c.1927, 18½ In., Pair. 73000.00
Electric, Imari Style, Porcelain, Vase Shape, Stylized Birds, Butterflies, 20th Century, 7 In. . . . 24.00
Electric, Italian, Carved Giltwood, Baluster, Square Stepped Base, 24 x 6 x 3 In. 1452.00
Electric, Italian Baroque Style, Carved Giltwood, Early 20th Century, 22¾ In., Pair. 1725.00
Electric, J. Adnet, Stacked Graduated Glass Balls, Chromed Metal, Shade, c.1930, 18½ In. . . . 7500.00
Electric, J. Adnet, Leather, Steel, c.1935, 11¼ x 10¾ In.. . . . . 1200.00
Electric, J.H. Whaley, Wisteria, Bronze Base, 21 In. . . . . *illus* 9200.00
Electric, Jefferson, Reverse Painted Shade, Chipped Ice, Flowers, 1899, 18 x 24 In. 2520.00
Electric, Landscape Shade, Hand Painted, Panels, Brass Collar & Base, Fluted, 16 x 10 In. . . . 224.00
Electric, Leaded Glass, Caramel Slag, Flowers, Tree Trunk Base, Chicago Mosaic, 22 x 18 In. *illus* 1150.00
Electric, Leaded Glass, Dogwood, Flowers, Amber, Purple, Handel Base, 21 In.. . . . . 1380.00
Electric, Leaded Glass, Water Lilies, Acanthus Base, Wilkinson, 21½ x 16 In. . . . . *illus* 3300.00
Electric, Lundberg, Green Splash Glass, Iridescent Green Domed Shade, Wisteria, Metal, 8 x 15 In. 403.00
Electric, Mahogany, Carved Leaves, Turned Base, Single Socket, 57½ In. 86.00

Lamp, Electric, Leaded Glass,
Caramel Slag, Flowers, Tree Trunk Base, Chicago Mosaic, 22 x 18 In.
$1150.00

Lamp, Electric, Moon Crest, Brushed Aluminum, Marked, 1930s, 16 x 13 In.
$170.00

Lamp, Electric, Leaded Glass, Water Lilies, Acanthus Base,
Wilkinson, 21 ½ x 16 In.
$3300.00

Lamp, Electric, Pottery, Lions, Green Matte Glaze, Embossed,
Leaded Glass Shade, Stroble, 23 In.
$4300.00

Lamp, Electric, Moe Bridges, Reverse Painted Shade, Bird Of Paradise,
Butterflies, Urn Base, 23 In.
$6500.00

Lamp, Electric, Stickley Bros., Slag Glass, 4 Panels, Copper Overlay,
21 x 16 ½ In.
$4800.00

TIP
Reverse-painted lamps should never be washed. Just dust them.

Lamp, Electric, Suesse, Scarab, Leaded Glass, Bronze Base, 21 In.
$8050.00

Lamp, Electric, Wicker, Varnish, Heywood-Wakefield, 20th Century, 25 In.
$275.00

Lamp, Electric, Wilkinson, Flowers, Metal Scroll Base, 24 In.
$3450.00

Electric, Mahogany, Spiral Staircase, Octagonal Base, 69 x 11½ In.. . . . . 2880.00
Electric, Marble, The Birth Of Venus, U. Stiaccini, c.1900, 24 In. 3068.00
Electric, Meissen Porcelain, Cobalt Blue, Snake Handles, 24 x 7 In. 330.00
Electric, Metal, Tapered Cylindrical Column, Glass Shade, Jean Perzel, 1935, 29 In. 7500.00
Electric, Michael Ashford, Hammered Copper Base, Cone Shape Shade, 18 x 18 In.. . . . . 2760.00
Electric, Millefiori Glass, Mushroom Shade, Multicolored, 17 In. 526.00
Electric, Miller, Reverse Painted Shade, Paneled, Landscape Scene, c.1920, 21 x 20 In.. . . . . . 1375.00
Electric, Modern, Square Black Base, 6 Chrome Ball Shades, 22 In. 29.00
Electric, Moe Bridges, Reverse Painted Shade, Bird Of Paradise, Butterflies, Urn Base, 23 In. *illus* 6500.00
Electric, Moe Bridges, Reverse Painted Shade, Scenic, 18 In. 2875.00
Electric, Moon Crest, Brushed Aluminum, Marked, 1930s, 16 x 13 In. . . . . *illus* 170.00
Electric, Mosaic, Leaded Glass Shade, Cast Metal Base, Patina, 18 x 20 In. 1320.00
Electric, Murano Glass, Male Figure, Colonial Costume, Red, Gold, Rigaree, Barovier, 24 x 12 In. 600.00
Electric, Neoclassical Style, Gilt Base, Columns, Urns, Arabesques, Putti, 33 x 14 In.. . . . . 411.00
Electric, Newel Post, Art Deco, Painted, Figure, Arched Back, Multicolored Ball On Knee, c.1930, 33 In. 588.00
Electric, Newel Post, Egyptian Revival, White Metal, Woman In Egyptian Dress, Crocodile, 40 In. 881.00
Electric, Pansy, Ceramic, c.1980, 24½ In.. . . . . 33.00
Electric, Parlor, Cherub, Ribbons, Roses, Bell Shade, Metal Base, Footed, 22 In.. . . . . 77.00
Electric, Parlor, Daisies, Chrysanthemums, Yellow, Globe Shade, Openwork Feet & Rim, 22 In. 132.00
Electric, Parlor, Globe Shade, Red Iris, Marked, Made In U.S. Of America, 20 In. 110.00
Electric, Peacock Eye, Domed Shade, Scalloped Rim, Blue To Magenta, Charles Lotton, 27 In. 4600.00
Electric, Pendant, Satin Glass, Blue, Green, White, Italy 330.00
Electric, Phoenix, Reverse Painted Shade, Scenic, c.1920, 22 x 18 In.. 715.00
Electric, Phoenix, Reverse Painted Shade, Landscape, Cottage, Lake, Mountains, Green, Brown, 24 In. 1150.00
Electric, Phoenix, Reverse Painted Shade, Cabin, Trees, Orange, Brown, 2-Socket Base, 24 In. 1725.00
Electric, Piano, Arts & Crafts, Wrought Iron, Hammered, Patina, 12 x 18 In.. . . . . 201.00
Electric, Piano, Brass, Open Leafy Scrolls, Hoof Feet, Chimney, Globe Shade 374.00
Electric, Piano, Pittsburgh, Reverse Painted, Nighttime Scene, Full Moon, Ocean Waves, 12 In. 1380.00
Electric, Pink Murano Glass, Controlled Bubbles, Vase Shape, Brass Base, 20th Century, 20 In. 750.00
Electric, Pittsburgh, Obverse Painted Shade, Forest Scene, 2 Sockets, Art Nouveau Base, 23 In. 575.00
Electric, Pittsburgh, Reverse Painted Shade, Windmill Scene, c.1930, 21 x 18 In. 1100.00
Electric, Pole, Giltwood, Carved Anthemion, Finial, Stepped Base, 25 In., Pair. 1320.00
Electric, Porcelain, Painted, Urn Shape, Ram's Head Bronze Mount, Meissen, 21 In.. . . . . 200.00
Electric, Porcelain, Painted Panels, Figures In Landscape, Encrusted Flowers, Germany, 23 In. 104.00
Electric, Porcelain, Sang De Boeuf Glaze, Gilt Bronze Base, 29 In., Pair 7500.00
Electric, Porcelain, Vase Shape, Eggshell, Hand Painted, Carved Wood Base, Chinese, 9 In. . . 94.00
Electric, Post Modern Style, Polished Nickel, Baluster Shape, Domed Base, France, 19 x 15 In., Pair 180.00
Electric, Pottery Discs, Concentric Rings, Red, Yellow & Black Glaze, 18 x 6 x 19 In., Pair . . . 1080.00
Electric, Pottery, Lions, Green Matte Glaze, Embossed, Leaded Glass Shade, Stroble, 23 In. *illus* 4300.00
Electric, Rumford, Tole Shade, Painted Green, Gilt Design, Malabert, 19th Century, 13 In.. . . 489.00
Electric, Semi-Clad Woman, 3 Trumpet Shape Shades, Paris Foundry, 25 x 14 In.. . . . . 380.00
Electric, Sewing, Cranberry Glass, Diamond Quilted, Veritas, 21 In. 275.00
Electric, Ship, Hand Carved, 12 x 18 In.. . . . . 57.00
Electric, Sinumbra, Patinated Bronze, Gilt, England, c.1840, 36 In. 3369.00
Electric, Slag Glass, Domed Top, Panels, 23 x 14½ In.. . . . . 660.00
Electric, Slag Glass Panels, 31 x 17 In.. . . . . 358.00
Electric, Slag Glass Panels, Dome Top, 26 x 20 In. 770.00
Electric, Smoker's, Victorian, Gilt, Marquetry, Walnut, Octagonal Shelf, c.1860, 31 In., Pair. . 11250.00
Electric, Snake, Frank Gehry, Papier-Mache, No. 44, Marked, c.1989, 66 In.. . . . . 19200.00
Electric, Solar, Gilt Brass, Prisms, Textured, Flowers, Leaves, c.1850, 26 x 8 In. 3525.00
Electric, Steel, Mahogany, Brass Mount, Tripod Base, Silver Shade, Continental, 73 In.. . . . . . 1560.00
Electric, Steel Plated, Half Dome Base, Movable Arm, Shaded Globe, Desk, Continental, 19 In. 504.00
Electric, Steel Plated, Domed Base, Adjustable Shade, Desk, Continental, 15 x 5¼ In., Pair. . . 1008.00
Electric, Stickley, Hammered Copper, 6-Sided Shade, Slag Glass, 21 x 22 In. 3000.00
Electric, Stickley Bros., Slag Glass, 4 Panels, Copper Overlay, 21 x 16½ In. . . . . *illus* 4800.00
Electric, Student, Adjustable, Tole Shade, Drip Base, 20 In. 660.00
Electric, Student, Brass, 2-light, Urn Fuel Tank, Cased Glass Shades, 24 x 26 In. 1008.00
Electric, Student, Carnival Glass, Swirled Ribs, High Domed Shade, c.1900, 10 x 6 In. 2500.00
Electric, Student, 2-Light, Iron Base, Snuffer, 22 In. 330.00
Electric, Suesse, Scarab, Leaded Glass, Bronze Base, 21 In. . . . . *illus* 8050.00
Electric, Table, Arts & Crafts, Pyramid Shade, Green Slag Glass, Mahogany Base, 15 x 26 In.. 600.00
Electric, Table, Arts & Crafts, Pyramid Shade, Slag Glass, 17 x 17 x 28 In. 660.00
Electric, Table, Bronzed Metal, Painted Glass, c.1930, 23½ x 16½ In. 1763.00
Electric, Table, Glass Shade, Transfer, Shepherd With Sheep, Cast Iron Base, 19 x 14 In.. . . . . 364.00
Electric, Tiffany Style, Mushroom Shade, Reverse Painted Glass, Ribbed, 22 In.. . . . . 1150.00

Electric, Tiffany Style, Stained Glass, Openwork Cast Metal Frame, Birds, Vines, 26 In. 1150.00
Electric, Tiles, Landscape, Blue, Green, Yellow, Black, Walnut Base, Harris Strong 1200.00
Electric, Uranium Glass Base, Draped Nude Woman, On Rocks, Torch Shade, 7 x 6 In. 595.00
Electric, Urn Shape, Gilt Bronze, Marble, Festoons, 20 In., Pair 1463.00
Electric, V. Panton, Moon, Concentric White Enameled Rings, 1960, 14 x 14 In. 360.00
Electric, Victorian, Dog Scenes, 22 In. 472.00
Electric, Water Lily, Tulips, 6 Light Sockets, Whaley, 24 x 70 In. 8050.00
Electric, Wicker, Heywood-Wakefield, Woven Base, Paper Label, 20th Century, 25 In. 324.00
Electric, Wicker, Varnish, Heywood-Wakefield, 20th Century, 25 In. *illus* 275.00
Electric, Wilkinson, Flowers, Metal Scroll Base, 24 In. *illus* 3450.00
Electric, Wilkinson, Mosaic Shade, Flowers Border, Bronze Base, 18 x 26 In. 3360.00
Electric, Wilkinson, Tulips, Geometric Panels, Yellow, Orange, Lavender, Green Leaves, 21 In. 2990.00
Electric, Willets, Yellow & Pink Roses, Leaves, c.1900, 30 In. 1280.00
Electric, Wire Cage Top, Cut Glass Prisms, Ruby Red Glass & Metal Base, 19 In., Pair 144.00
Electric, Wood, Turned Baluster, Matte White, Linen Cone Shape Shade, 17 x 14 In., Pair 480.00
Fairy, Burmese Glass, Domed Shade, Ruffled Rim Base, Webb, 6 In. 748.00
Fairy, Burmese Glass, Peach To Yellow, Clear Base, Marked, S. Clarke Fairy Pyramid, 3½ In. 115.00
Fairy, Frosted White Glass, Swirl & Drape, Clear Base, Marked, S. Clarke Fairy Lamp, 4¾ In. 140.00
Fairy, Irish Waterford Pattern, Honey Amber, Westmoreland, 7 In. 60.00
Fairy, Mother-Of-Pearl Glass, Yellow To White, Swirls, 4½ In. 86.00
Fairy, Pink Satin Glass, Wheat Stalk Coralene, Ruffled Base, 4¾ In. 495.00
Fairy, Satin Glass, Butterscotch, Opalescent Stripes, 4½ In. 230.00
Fairy, Spatter Glass, Cranberry, White Flecks, Melon Ribbed, 4½ In. 230.00
Fluid, Amethyst Glass, Molded, Drop-In Burner, Simons, c.1845, 3 In. 705.00
Fluid, Brass, Inverted Urn Shape, Threaded Cap, 4 Interior Wicks, Early 1800s, 13 In. 115.00
Fluid, Pressed Glass, Loop & Leaf, Honey Amber, Wafer, Pewter Collar, 9¼ x 4⅜ In. *illus* 2200.00
Fluid, Tin, Brass, Crimped Mid Drip Plate, Brass Extension, 11 In. 94.00
Gas, Arts & Crafts, Panels, c.1900 995.00
Gas, Coleman, Chrome Plated, c.1919, 19 x 8 In. 295.00
Gas, Gasolier, 6-Light, Bronze, Cut Glass Shades, Electrified, Victorian, c.1870, 30 x 25 In. 660.00
Gas, Gasolier, Bronze, Hand Chased, Cranberry Glass Shades, c.1880, 72 x 53 In. 7150.00
Handel lamps are included in the Handel category.
Kerosene, Artichoke, Purple, White, Green, 7¾ In. *illus* 120.00
Kerosene, Arts & Crafts, Wooden, 4 Slag Glass Panels, Green & White, 14 x 23 In. 300.00
Kerosene, Banquet, Clear Glass, Medial Sleeve, Joined, 17½ x 7¾ In. 248.00
Kerosene, Blown Glass, Brass Pedestal, Square Marble Base, 9½ In. 80.00
Kerosene, Blown Glass, Canary Yellow Frosted, Coralene Fern, Cylindrical, Burner, 7½ In. 86.00
Kerosene, Blown Glass, Opal, Font Stand, Brass Stem, Slate Base, 9½ x 4⅜ In. 77.00
Kerosene, Blown Glass, Translucent Blue, Pear Shape, Opaque Base, 12 x 5 In. 248.00
Kerosene, Blue Opalescent Glass, Coin Dot, Clear Base, Hobbs, Taplin Brown, 7 x 4 In. 413.00
Kerosene, Brass, Globular Chimney, 19th Century 50.00
Kerosene, Brass, White Paint, Drop-In Font, Opaque Glass Domed Shade, 7 In. 121.00
Kerosene, Brass, Colonial Library, Brass, Opaque White, Ribbed Shade, Plume & Atwood, 8 x 10 In. 55.00
Kerosene, Bronze Dore, Urn Shape, Floral Swags, Cupids, Instruments, 17 In., Pair 748.00
Kerosene, Clear Glass, Amber Stain, Engraved, Picket Stand, 9 x 5¼ In. 330.00
Kerosene, Clear Glass, Buckle Font, Metal Cherub Base, 12½ x 4¾ In. 107.00
Kerosene, Clear Glass, Multicolored Flowers, Turkey Foot, 9 x 5 In. 110.00
Kerosene, Cranberry Opalescent Glass, Reverse Swirl, Brass Tree Trunk, 11 x 5 In. 383.00
Kerosene, Cranberry Opalescent Glass, Snowflake, Screw Connector, 8½ x 5 In. 495.00
Kerosene, Cut Glass, Engraved Flowers, American Brilliant, 12¾ In. 300.00
Kerosene, Cut Glass, Hobstar, Zipper & Fan, Mushroom Shade, American Brilliant, 19 x 13 In. 600.00
Kerosene, Cut Glass, Ruby to Clear, Bronze Base, 30 In., Pair 413.00
Kerosene, Cut Glass, Ruby To Clear, Brass Stem, Marble Base, Spring Burner, Lip Chimney, 9 x 4 In. 715.00
Kerosene, Cut Glass, Ruby To Clear, Crimped Rim, Leaves, 6½ x 3 In. 825.00
Kerosene, Cut Glass, White To Ruby, Punty, Oval Stand, Brass, 13 x 6 In. 660.00
Kerosene, Cut Glass, Cobalt Blue To Clear, Brass Stem, Marble Base, 8¼ x 3¾ In. 660.00
Kerosene, Cut Glass, Opaque To Ruby, Fluted Stem, Brass Collar, 12 x 4¼ In. 605.00
Kerosene, Finger, Amethyst Glass, Swirls, Vines, Ribs, 3 x 2⅝ In. 176.00
Kerosene, Finger, Custard Glass, Multicolored, Heart Footed, Taplin Brown Collar, 4¼ x 3¾ In. 176.00
Kerosene, Finger, Green, Fern Foot, Riverside, 5¼ x 4¼ In. 132.00
Kerosene, Finger, Opalescent Glass, Thumbprint, Taplin-Brown, 4 x 3 In. 248.00
Kerosene, Finger, Opalescent Stripes, Swirl Band, Markham, 3½ x 3½ In. 248.00
Kerosene, Gold Indian Princess Stem, Clear Font, Flowers, Black Soapstone Base, 13¼ x 5 In. 187.00
Kerosene, Gone With The Wind, 2 Maidens Joining Hands, Gowns Shape Of Continents, 9 In. 590.00
Kerosene, Gone With The Wind, Beaded Drape, Pink Over White, 9 In. 236.00

Lamp, Fluid, Pressed Glass, Loop & Leaf, Honey Amber, Wafer, Pewter Collar, 9¼ x 4⅜ In.
$2200.00

Lamp, Kerosene, Artichoke, Purple, White, Green, 7¾ In.
$120.00

Lamp, Kerosene, Gone With The Wind, Pink, Beaded Drape, White Casing, 9⅛ In.
$200.00

Lamp, Kerosene, Pink Cased Glass, White Leaf Swags, c.1890, 9 In.
$100.00

Lamp, Kerosene, Pressed Glass, Cosmos, Flowers, c.1900, 17 In.
$125.00

Lamp, Oil, Winter Farm, Milk Glass, Boston & Sandwich
$228.00

Kerosene, Gone With The Wind, Delft, Sailing Vessels, Coastal Windmill, 8⅜ In. 354.00
Kerosene, Gone With The Wind, Eagle, Spread Wings, Flowers, Leaves, Yellow Ground, 7 In. . 153.00
Kerosene, Gone With The Wind, Florette, Pink Shade, Pierced Metal Trim, 7 In. 1062.00
Kerosene, Gone With The Wind, Flowers, White Satin, Victorian 99.00
Kerosene, Gone With The Wind, Lion's Head, Red Satin, Consolidated Glass Co., 22 In. 1265.00
Kerosene, Gone With The Wind, Pink, Beaded Drape, White Casing, 9⅛ In. . . . . *illus* 200.00
Kerosene, Goofus Glass, Opalescent, Primrose, Burner, Chimney, 9¾ x 6 In. 303.00
Kerosene, H.N. Hooper, Patinated Bronze, Single Arm, Urn Shape Font, Chimney, 13 x 9 In., Pair. . 1265.00
Kerosene, Hanging, Cranberry Glass, Inverted Thumbprint, Coralene, c.1900, 17 x 5 In. 2000.00
Kerosene, Hanging, Opaque White Umbrella Shade, Flowers, Brass Base, 14 In. 121.00
Kerosene, Hanging, Swirled Cranberry Glass Shade, Brass Ceiling Mount, Chain, 7 x 7 In. . . 448.00
Kerosene, Juno, Opaque Ruffled Shade, Nickel Plate, Footed, Finger, 4½ x 4 In.. . . . . 132.00
Kerosene, Lowell Loop, Yellow Green, Taplin Brown, 6 x 5 In. 110.00
Kerosene, Milk Glass, Hobnail, Marble Base, Brass Fittings, 1950s, 22½ In. 60.00
Kerosene, Milk Glass, Painted Flowers, Round, Rococo Base, c.1890, 30 x 10 In. 118.00
Kerosene, Milk Glass, World Globe Shade, Brass Fittings, 7½ x 8 In. 1064.00
Kerosene, Mother-Of-Pearl Glass, Blue Opalescent, Sunburst, Diamond Quilted Shade, Silver, 13¾ In. 1660.00
Kerosene, Mother-Of-Pearl Glass, Peach, Melon Ribbed, Draped Swags On Shade, 11 In. 425.00
Kerosene, Opalescent Glass, Clear Base, Ribbed Pillar, Taplin Brown Collar, 9 x 5 In. 275.00
Kerosene, Opalescent Glass, Polka Dot, Swirled Rib Base, 11½ x 5¾ In. 130.00
Kerosene, Parlor, Milk Glass, Scrolls, Marked, Made In U.S.A., Phoenix, 20½ In. 165.00
Kerosene, Parlor, Mother-Of-Pearl Glass, Diamond Quilted, Rainbow, Melon Ribbed, Brass, 19 In.. 3105.00
Kerosene, Parlor, Napoleon III, Gilt Brass, Bronze, Tripod, Electrified, 35 x 9 In., Pair 4560.00
Kerosene, Pink Cased Glass, White Leaf Swags, c.1890, 9 In. . . . . *illus* 100.00
Kerosene, Pottery, Blue Celeste, Urn Shape, Romantic Couples, Bronze Mount, Sevres, 30 In. 646.00
Kerosene, Pottery, Brass, Caramel Glaze, Concave Sides, Swallows, Rookwood, 1883, 11 In. . . 323.00
Kerosene, Pressed Glass, Burner, Chimney, 8 x 4¼ In. 77.00
Kerosene, Pressed Glass, Prince Edward, Opaque Light Green, 9½ x 6½ In. 209.00
Kerosene, Pressed Glass, Princess Feather, Opaque Light Blue, 9½ x 5¾ In. 187.00
Kerosene, Pressed Glass, Princess Feather, Ruby Flowers, Gilt Base, 9½ x 5¾ In. 71.00
Kerosene, Pressed Glass, Bull's-Eye, Clear Font, Jade Green Alabaster Base, Brass Fittings, 11 x 4¼ In. 248.00
Kerosene, Pressed Glass, Bull's-Eye, Hairpin Stand, Clear, Green Alabaster, Brass, 7¾ x 3½ . . 165.00
Kerosene, Pressed Glass, Bull's-Eye, Opaque Pale Blue, Buckle Font, Taplin Brown Collar, 11 x 6 In. 443.00
Kerosene, Pressed Glass, Chieftain, Opaque White Baroque Base, Brass Connector, 14 x 5 In. 66.00
Kerosene, Pressed Glass, Blue, Coolidge Drape Stand, Frosted, Flowers, Taplin Brown Collar, 9 x 6 In. 220.00
Kerosene, Pressed Glass, Cosmos, Flowers, c.1900, 17 In. . . . . *illus* 125.00
Kerosene, Pressed Glass, Moon, Star, Blue, Brass, 12 x 5½ In. 165.00
Kerosene, Pressed Glass, Moorish Windows, Opaque White, Brass Connector, 9¾ In.. . . . . 303.00
Kerosene, Pressed Glass, Petal Ribbed, Clear Font, Opaque White Base, Brass Connector, 14 x 5¾ In. 77.00
Kerosene, Pressed Glass, Princess Feather, Pink, Clear Base, 9¾ x 5 In.. . . . . 468.00
Kerosene, Pressed Glass, Reed Oval, Cobalt Blue, Opaque White Base, Brass Connector, 7¼ x 3¼ In. 413.00
Kerosene, Pressed Glass, Rib Optic, Cranberry Font, Cylindrical Stem, 11 x 5 In.. . . . . 176.00
Kerosene, Pressed Glass, Sheldon Swirl, Amber, Black Base, 8¼ x 4¾ In. 143.00
Kerosene, Pressed Glass, Sheldon Swirl, Clear, Black Base, 8¼ x 5 In. 59.00
Kerosene, Pressed Glass, Stars, Drape, Tassel, 8¾ x 4½ In. 88.00
Kerosene, Red Glass, White Flowers, Globe Shade, Marked, Patent Date 1893, 20 In.. . . . . 137.00
Kerosene, Satin Glass, Pink, Metal Peg, Brass Candlestick, 3½ In. 154.00
Kerosene, Spatter Glass Font, Opaque White, Pink, Clear Base, 8¾ x 5 In. 220.00
Kerosene, Stand, 3 Panels, Burner, Chimney, 8½ x 4¾ In. 66.00
Kerosene, Stand, Amber Glass, Thumbprint, Fine Tooth Panels, Drip Catcher, 9 x 5 In. 176.00
Kerosene, Stand, Clear Glass, Wreath, Torch, Riverside, 7½ x 4½ In. 55.00
Kerosene, Wall & Stand Combination, Brass, Hinged, Opal Shade, Miller Burner, 11 In.. . . . . 440.00
Oil, 2-Light, Bronze, Blackamoor, Patinated, Gilt, Louis XVI Style, 12 x 14 In., Pair 6900.00
Oil, 2-Light, Silvered Brass, Cut Glass Drops, Louis XVI, 12 x 12 In., Pair. 6900.00
Oil, 3-Light, Gilt Bronze, Leaves, France, Late 19th Century, 26 x 16 In., Pair 3120.00
Oil, Amethyst Glass, Enameled Flowers, Gold Trim, Hornet Burner, 9 In.. . . . . 69.00
Oil, Art Glass, Daisy Shade 2530.00
Oil, Beveled Glass Lenses, Pierced Metal, Swing Handle, Gothic Style, 11 In. 138.00
Oil, Blown Glass, 16 Ribs, Tin & Cork Burner, Applied Handle, Mantua Glass Works, 3 In. . . . 764.00
Oil, Blown Glass, Bell Shape, Bronze Collar, Flower Chains, Hanging, 10 x 7 x 25 In.. . . . . . . 1430.00
Oil, Blown Glass, Flowers, Stamped Brass Bands, Smoke Bell, 1800s, 12 x 8 In. 259.00
Oil, Blue Glass, Globe Shade, 12½ In. 248.00
Oil, Blue Milk Glass, Green & White Birch Trees, Orange Mushrooms, 9⅜ In. 575.00
Oil, Brass, Figural, Hand Holding Snake, Urn Shape Knops, 19th Century, 22 In. 175.00
Oil, Bronze, 3 Sections, Beast Head Handles, Dragons, Buddhist Lion Supports, 65 In.. . . . . . . 1150.00
Oil, Bronze, Figural, Youth Resting On Knee, Ear To Shell, Patinated, 15 x 8 In.. . . . . 748.00

Entry	Price
Oil, Clear Glass, Drapery, Austria, 1980s, 16½ In.	30.00
Oil, Cut Glass, Pink To Clear, Flame Facets, Bronze, Electrified, Bohemian, c.1885, 18 In., Pair.	646.00
Oil, Finger, Cobalt Blue Glass, Hornet Burner, 8 In.	29.00
Oil, Finger, Flowers, Brass Collar & Burner, 1871, 3⅛ In.	878.00
Oil, Finger, Satin Glass, Chartreuse To White, Reeded Handle, Stevens & Williams, 4 In.	58.00
Oil, Green Glass Base, Shade, Hornet Burner, 8¾ In.	161.00
Oil, Hanging, Iron, Hinged Font, Bird, Hand Forged Hanger, 23 x 5 In.	518.00
Oil, Hurricane, Cast Stone, Blown Glass Shades, Inverted Bell Shape, Provincial, 21 x 13 In.	540.00
Oil, Lighthouse, Pierced Brass, Strap Handle, Plate, 19th Century, 27½ In.	5378.00
Oil, Marble, Ormolu Mount, Gilt Metal Band, Relief Cupids, Openwork Handles, 19 In., Pair	920.00
Oil, Marble, Urn Shape, Bronze Mounts, Female Heads, Flower Swags, 18 x 33 In., Pair	978.00
Oil, Milk Glass, Amethyst, Tulip Font, Brass Connectors, c.1870, 12½ In., Pair	460.00
Oil, Milk Glass, Block & Dot Pattern, 8½ In.	58.00
Oil, Milk Glass, Blue Paint, Flowers, Melon Ribbed Shade & Base, 8 In.	58.00
Oil, Milk Glass, Embossed Design, Flowers, Gilt Trim, 8 In.	115.00
Oil, Milk Glass, Flowers, Fired-On Yellow Paint, 9½ In.	115.00
Oil, Milk Glass, Green Paint, Chimney, 8 In.	150.00
Oil, Milk Glass, Multicolored Flower Panels, Dresden Mark, Acorn Burner, 10 In.	403.00
Oil, Milk Glass, Multicolored Globe, USS Maine, U.S. Flag, Cast Iron Base, 24 x 9½ In.	660.00
Oil, Milk Glass, Owl, Black Paint, Gray, Orange Eyes, 8 In.	518.00
Oil, Milk Glass, Painted Green Bands, Pink Flowers, Yellow Centers, 8½ In.	127.00
Oil, Milk Glass, Ribs, Swirls, Pink Decoration, Acanthus, 8 In.	69.00
Oil, Milk Glass, Scenic, Blue Windmills, Boats, Ruffled Feet, Acorn Burner, 8¼ In.	805.00
Oil, Milk Glass, Swirls, Pink & Yellow Flowers, Chrysanthemums, 9 In.	173.00
Oil, Milk Glass Base, Clear Shade, Painted White, Frosted Pink, Flowers, 9 In.	58.00
Oil, Milk Glass Shade, Painted, Cut Prisms, Brass Frame, Hanging, 29 x 14 In.	476.00
Oil, Opalescent Glass, Bell Shape Shade, Pull Down, Hanging, Victorian, 33 x 8 In.	196.00
Oil, Opaline Glass, French Blue, Ormolu, Balustrade Shape, Flower Base, 11 In., Pair	353.00
Oil, Pink Cased Glass, Embossed Design, 8½ In.	1093.00
Oil, Pink Cased Glass, Embossed Design, Basketweave, Consolidated Lamp Co., 7½ In.	403.00
Oil, Pink Cased Satin Glass, Diamond Quilted, 8 In.	345.00
Oil, Pink Cased Satin Glass, Melon Ribbed Base, Pansy Ball Shade, Acorn Burner, 7 In.	316.00
Oil, Porcelain Base, Milk Glass Shade, Flowers, Green Trim, 9 In.	403.00
Oil, Pressed Glass, Beaded Swirl, Milk Glass, Hornet Burner, 8½ In.	40.00
Oil, Pressed Glass, Billowing Drapes, Scalloped Base, Brass Collar, 9¼ x 5¾ In., Pair	168.00
Oil, Pressed Glass, Drape, Red Satin, Acorn Burner, 10 In.	173.00
Oil, Pressed Glass, Leaf Swag, Pink, Victorian, c.1890, 9 In.	118.00
Oil, Pressed Glass, Tulip & Star Font, Hexagonal Baluster Base, Brass Collar, 9½ In.	115.00
Oil, Pressed Glass, Hearts & Stars, Burner No. 1, Sucony, 8¾ In.	33.00
Oil, Pressed Glass, Moon & Star, Green, L.E. Smith, 1960s, 12 In.	65.00
Oil, Red Satin Glass, Brass Collar, Pull Down, Hanging, Victorian, 10 x 10 In.	280.00
Oil, Royal Blue Glass, Clear Chimney, c.1870, 19½ In.	88.00
Oil, Ruby Glass, Brass, Hanging, Late 19th Century, 31 x 11 In.	605.00
Oil, Satin Glass, Yellow Shaded To White, White Enamel Flowers, Brass Base, 11 In.	1035.00
Oil, Student, 2 Adjustable Arms, Weighted Dish Base, Green Tole Shades, 21 x 14 In.	978.00
Oil, Student, Milk Glass Shade, Brass Base, German Student Lamp Co., c.1875, 20 In.	165.00
Oil, Time Displayed As Oil Is Used Up, Pride Of America Time & Light, Novelty, c.1890, 7 In.	385.00
Oil, Time Lamp, Embossed, Grand Val's Perfect Time Indicator, Ruby Beehive Shade, 7 In.	127.00
Oil, Torchere, Mahogany, Round Top, Fishscales, Leaf, Flowers, Tripod Legs, 48 x 12 In.	1470.00
Oil, Twinkle, Amethyst, Acorn Burner, 7 In.	138.00
Oil, Vaseline Glass, Thumbprint, Brass Frame, Hanging, 40 In.	275.00
Oil, White Satin Glass, Ribs, Flowers, 7½ In.	115.00
Oil, Winter Farm, Milk Glass, Boston & Sandwich *illus*	228.00
Oil, Carcel, Porcelain, Blue, Classical Busts, Glass Shades, Greek Key, 26 x 7 In., Pair	1410.00
Onyx Base, Petal Shade, Slag Glass Panels, 63 x 19 In.	220.00
Pairpoint lamps are in the Pairpoint category.	
Rush Holder, Heart Shape Base, Iron, 9 In. *illus*	440.00
Rush Holder, Iron, 3-Footed, 30 In.	230.00
Rush Holder, Wrought Iron, 3-Footed, 31 x 11 In.	2940.00
Rush Holder, Wrought Iron, Compressed Ball Finial, Tripod Base, Penny Feet, 48 In.	770.00
Rush Holder, Wrought Iron, Tripod Base, Penny Feet, 11 In.	193.00
Sconce, 2-Light, Arts & Crafts, Polished Nickel, Hammered, Ripple Border, 2 Bobeches	2160.00
Sconce, 2-Light, Federal Style, Carved Eagle, Oval Gilt Framed Mirror, 30 x 15 In., Pair	1495.00
Sconce, 2-Light, Louis XVI, Bronze Dore, Vase Stem, Bacchic Mask, 13 x 11 In., Pair	1531.00
Sconce, 2-Light, Rococo Style, Mirror, Porcelain Mount, Silver Metal, 25 x 13 In., Pair	780.00
Sconce, 3-Light, Brass, Scroll Arms, Prisms, Pair, 17 In.	330.00

TIP

To protect your investment in household furnishings, rewire any lamps in your home that are 15 or more years old. Cords crack and are a fire hazard.

Lamp, Rush Holder, Heart Shape Base, Iron, 9 In.
$440.00

Lamp, Torchere, Bronzed Metal, Patina, Signed, Samuel Yellin, 1925, 54 x 17 In.
$10100.00

Lamp, Whale Oil, Peg, Acorn Fonts, Double Wick, Sheffield Silver Plate, 19th Century, 9 In., Pair
$374.00

Lantern, Dietz, No. 60, Tin, Cone Shaped Reflector, 22 In.
$303.00

Lantern, Footman's, Oil, Tin, Green & Red Paint, 19th Century, 6 x 8 x 5½ In.
$805.00

Lantern, Papier-Mache, Moon Shape, Face, Silk Eyes & Mouth, Candleholder, Early 1900s, 16 In.
$4406.00

TIP

Be careful when cleaning bronze figurines, lamp bases, bowls, etc. Never use steel wool, stiff brushes, or chemicals.

Sconce, 3-Light, Bronze, Blue Aqua, Scroll Arms, Trefoil Ends, 16 In., Pair 705.00
Sconce, 3-Light, Louis XV Style, Bronze, Glass, Trefoil Ends, Scroll Arms, 16 In., Pair 705.00
Sconce, 3-Light, Louis XVI Style, Bronze Dore, France, 19th Century, 17 In., Pair 708.00
Sconce, 4-Light, Giltwood, 20th Century, 25½ In. 348.00
Sconce, 5-Light, Gilt Bronze, Enameled Flower, 23½ x 20 In., Pair 2350.00
Sconce, 6-Light, 5 Movable Arms, 4¼ x 12 x 6 In., Pair. 374.00
Sconce, 6-Light, Bronze, 5 Movable Arms, 13 x 21 In., Pair 374.00
Sconce, 6-Light, Rococo Style, Gilt Bronze, Elongated, Oval Back, Prisms, 15 x 16 In.. . . . . . 529.00
Sconce, Adam Style, Giltwood, Iron Support, Carved, Bellflower & Flame, 38 x 16 In., Pair . . 1150.00
Sconce, Brass, Shield Shape, Acorn Drop Finials, Glass Globe, 13 x 17 In., Pair 1150.00
Sconce, Bronze, France, c.1835, 12 In., Pair 7700.00
Sconce, Copper, Hammered, Candle, Dark Patina, Arts & Crafts, 20½ x 10½ In. 780.00
Sconce, Copper, Hammered, Stylized Flowers, Patina, Arts & Crafts, 5½ x 13 In.. . . . . . 840.00
Sconce, Glass, Brass, Rectangular, Ribbed, Venetian, c.1950, 8 x 17 x 4 In.. . . . . . 3600.00
Sconce, Louis XVI Style, Bronze, 5 Scroll Arms, 47 x 24 x 14 In., Pair 2350.00
Sconce, Mirrored, 2 Arms, Rosette Center, Prisms, 19th Century, 13 x 7 In., Pair 392.00
Sconce, Square, Pierced Shade, Rectangular Wall Plate, Scrolls, Egg & Dart, 45 In. 30.00
Sconce, Tin, Embossed Lines, Crimped Top, 13½ In. 248.00
Solar, Brass, Marble, Frosted Shade, Cornelius & Co., c.1839, 16 In. 374.00
Solar, Gilt Brass, Column, Stems, Etched Globe, Shields, Prisms, Cornelius & Co., 25 In.. . . . . 638.00
Solar, Gilt Brass, Column Standard, Corinthian Capital, Marble Base, c.1848, 24 x 8 In.. . . . . 1116.00
Solar, Gilt Bronze, Caryatid Standard, Etched Globe, Prisms, Marble Base, Dietz & Co., 26 In. 464.00
Solar, Gilt Bronze, Tapered, Leaf Tips, Etched Globe, Trellis, Prisms, Cornelius & Co., 33 In. . . 928.00
Tiffany lamps are listed in the Tiffany category.
Torchere, Blackamoor, Ebonized, Multicolored, Feathered Bowl, Italy, c.1900, 80 x 26 In. . . . 3840.00
Torchere, Bronzed Metal, Patina, Signed, Samuel Yellin, 1925, 54 x 17 In. . . . . . *illus* 10100.00
Torchere, Directoire Style, Mahogany, Round Marble Top, X Supports, 1900s, 47 x 15 In.. . . . 353.00
Torchere, Mahogany, Rosewood, Octagonal Top, Barley Twist Stand, Italy, 51 x 10 In., Pair. . 8400.00
Torchere, Marble, Carved, Flower Shape Top, Turned Finial, 3-Section Column, 8 In.. . . . . . 863.00
Torchere, Neoclassical, Parcel Gilt, Carved, Swags, Tassels, Acanthus, 113 x 27 In., Pair. . . . 9988.00
Torchere, Renaissance Revival, Iron, Acanthus, Gilt, 67¾ In., Pair 499.00
Whale Oil, Blown Glass, Bulbous Font, Rigaree, Baluster Shaft, Tin Tube Drop Burner, 1800s, 9 In. 382.00
Whale Oil, Blown Glass, Aqua Tint, Bulbous Font, Drip Pan, Ribbed Shaft, Early 1800s, 10 In. 353.00
Whale Oil, Blown Glass, Burners, 6¼ In. 2450.00
Whale Oil, Blown Glass, Cobalt Blue, Wick, Cork, 3½ In. 5288.00
Whale Oil, Blown Glass, Opaque White, Hexagonal, Corset Waist, c.1840, 7½ In. 418.00
Whale Oil, Blown Glass, Sparking, Round Base, Early 19th Century, 3 In. 150.00
Whale Oil, Blown Glass, Sparking, 3-Petaled Base, Early 19th Century, 4 In. 170.00
Whale Oil, Brass, Beehive Base, 19th Century, 8 In. 55.00
Whale Oil, Brass, Glass Egg Shape Font, Stamped, Webb, Mid 19th Century, 9½ In. 1610.00
Whale Oil, Cone Shape Font, Round Domed Base, Rufus Dunham, c.1861, 6½ In., Pair. 558.00
Whale Oil, Cut Glass, Faceted Stem, Font, Brass Collar, Square Base, 9 In. 29.00
Whale Oil, Molded Glass, Purple Blue, Hexagonal Base, Ribbed Cone Shape Font, c.1850, 7 In. 1175.00
Whale Oil, Molded Glass, Spiral Rib, Tapered Font, c.1810, 8¼ In.. . . . . . 206.00
Whale Oil, Peg, Acorn Fonts, Double Wick, Sheffield Silver Plate, 19th Century, 9 In., Pair *illus* 374.00
Whale Oil, Pressed Glass, Engraved Grapevines, 4-Tier Base, c.1835, 10 In., Pair. 382.00
Whale Oil, Pressed Glass, Three Printie, Peacock Blue, Square Base, Camphor Burner, 1840, 11 In. 2945.00
Whale Oil, Pressed Glass, Pressed Loop, Canary Yellow, Hexagonal Base, 8¼ In., Pair 441.00
Whale Oil, Tin, Glass Font, 10½ In.. . . . . . 138.00
Whale Oil, Wooden, Adjustable, 2 Clear Glass Fonts, 26 In. 440.00

LAMPSHADE

Art Glass, Iridescent, Multicolored, 8¼ In. 88.00
Fairy, Burmese Glass, Cream To Pink, Dome Shape, 6 Piece 633.00
Hurricane, Blown Glass, Etched, Grapevines, Leaves, Fruit, 19th Century, 20 In. 864.00
Hurricane, Blown Glass, Etched, 22 In., Pair. 5378.00
Stained Glass, Dome Shape, Portland, Maine, 28 In. 2352.00
Tin, Mica, Hexagonal, Arts & Crafts, c.1920, 14 x 22 x 23 In. 748.00

LANTERNS are a special type of lighting device. They have a light source, usually a candle, totally hidden inside the walls of the lantern. Light is seen through holes or glass sections.

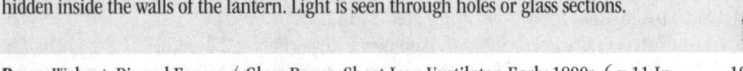

Barn, Walnut, Pinned Frame, 4 Glass Panes, Sheet Iron Ventilator, Early 1800s, 6 x 11 In. . . . 1035.00
Barn, Wood, Round, Early 19th Century, 8½ x 11¼ In. 374.00
Brass, 4-Light, Hammered Hook Ends, Arts & Crafts, c.1900, 18 x 11 In.. . . . . . 1064.00
Brass, Copper, Caryatids, Angels, 20th Century, 35 In. 920.00

Brass, Frosted Glass Bowl, Flower Panels, Vinework, 22 x 11 In. . . . 2990.00
Brass, Lighthouse, Glass Chimney, 19th Century, 27½ In. . . . 5378.00
Brass, Oil, Boat, Flat Back, Davey & Co., 16 In., Pair . . . 633.00
Brass, Repousse Design, Dome Top, 10½ In. . . . 495.00
Brass, Reticulated, Inverted Cloche, Masques, Glass Panels, Louis XVI Style, 37 x 19 In. . . . 2280.00
Brass, Swing Handle, Caged Clear Globe, Marked, Hall Mfg., 19th Century, 35 In. . . . 200.00
Bronze, Aesthetic Movement, Stained & Jeweled Glass Panels, Rewired, 1892, 7 x 32 In. . . . 2375.00
Bronze, Brackets, Pointed Lappets, Blue Etched Glass, Gothic Revival, 19½ x 27 In., Pair . . . 881.00
Bronze, Pagoda Shape, Chinese, 19 x 9½ In. . . . 234.00
Bronze, Patinated, Etched Glass, 30 x 13 In., Pair . . . 1410.00
Candle, 2-light, Punched Tin, Signed, 19th Century, 20 In. . . . 495.00
Candle, Brass, Flowers, Blown Glass Lens, 5¼ In. . . . 182.00
Candle, Brass, Heart & Flower Cutouts, 4½ In. . . . 209.00
Candle, Brass, Octagonal, Pinprick Design, 16½ In. . . . 28.00
Candle, Brass, Pierced Design, 16½ In. . . . 330.00
Candle, Hanging, Brown, Clear Glass Shade, 17½ In. . . . 523.00
Candle, Old Green Paint, Footed, 19 In. . . . 475.00
Candle, Punched Tin, Cylindrical, Cone Top, Ring Handle, 10⅝ In. . . . 413.00
Candle, Tin, Wavy Line Design, Green Paint, Ring Handle, 7 In. . . . 154.00
Candle, Triangular, Old Red Paint, 15 In. . . . 83.00
Candle, Wood, Salmon Paint, Wire Bail Handle, Glass Panels, 10 x 6 x 6 In. . . . 154.00
Carriage, Gilt Brass, Shield, Horse's Head, Frosted Glass, Napoleon III, 23 x 5 In., Pair . . . 1200.00
Carriage, Tin, Kerosene, Cylindrical Smoke Chamber, Wooden Swing Handle, 29 In. . . . 50.00
Copper, Octagonal, Dome Top, Openwork, 15 In. . . . 209.00
Dietz, Little Wizard, Syracuse, 1920-30 . . . 48.00
Dietz, Little Wizard, Red Globe, U.S. Army . . . 40.00
Dietz, No. 60, Tin, Cone Shaped Reflector, 22 In. . . . *illus* 303.00
Footman's, Oil, Tin, Green & Red Paint, 19th Century, 6 x 8 x 5½ In. . . . *illus* 805.00
Gilt Brass, Belle Epoque, Frosted Glass, Inverted Cloche, Sunbursts, 30 x 15 In., Pair . . . 5400.00
Hall, Bronze, Verdigris Patina, Hinged Panel, 26½ x 13 In. . . . 235.00
Hanging, Brass, Hexagonal, Opaque White Glass Panels, Ceiling Mount, 43 In., Pair . . . 110.00
Hanging, Bronze, Pagoda Shape, Square Roof, Pierced Hourglass Body, Asian, 18 x 11 In. . . . 325.00
Hanging, Leaded Glass Panels, Square Top, Arts & Crafts, 14½ x 9½ In. . . . 1560.00
Hanging, Metal Overlay, Slag Glass, Dutch Landscape, Arts & Crafts, 9 x 12 In. . . . 480.00
Iron, Scrolling Brackets, Acanthus, Renaissance Style, Electrified, 42 x 14 In. . . . 1763.00
Leaded Glass, Caramel, Pink Blossoms, Arts & Crafts, 25 x 10 In. . . . 1320.00
Papier-Mache, Moon Shape, Face, Silk Eyes & Mouth, Candleholder, Early 1900s, 16 In. *illus* 4406.00
Tin, 2 Oil Burners, Demilune Reflector, Curved Handle, 16½ x 12 x 7 In. . . . 90.00
Tin, Candle, Outside Grille, 17½ In. . . . 83.00
Tin, Oil, Lens Cover, 1878, 9 In. . . . 165.00
Tin, Onion Globe, Wire Cage, Cone Top, Pierced Stars, Diamonds, Ring Handle, 16 In. . . . 248.00
Tin, Painted, Red, Reticulated Gallery, Glass Panels, c.1860, 18 In., Pair . . . 840.00
Tin, Punched, 2-Light, 29 In. . . . 523.00
Tin, Punched, Half Circle, Loop Handle, Mid 19th Century, 14 x 5 In. . . . 231.00
Tin, Punched, Old Green Paint, 21½ In. . . . 935.00
Tin, Wooden Swing Handle, Tin Strap Handle, Smoke Chamber, Hinged, 13 x 7½ x 9 In. . . . 56.00
Wall, Gothic Revival, Gilt Metal, Rectangular, Pointed Roof Cornice, Acanthus, 1800s, 25 In., Pair . . . 764.00
Wall, Metal, Single Light, Glass Panels, Electrified, Georgian Revival, 36 x 16½ In. . . . 1058.00
Whale Oil, S. Sargent's Patent, Molded Ribbed Globe, Ring Handle, Tin Font, c.1861, 17 In. . 588.00
Wrought Iron, Tin, Tole, Hexagonal, Acanthus Crown, Amber Glass, Louis XV, 33 In. . . . 1170.00

LE VERRE FRANCAIS is one of the many types of cameo glass made by the Schneider Glassworks in France. The glass was made by the C. Schneider factory in Epinay-sur-Seine from 1918 to 1933. It is a mottled glass, usually decorated with floral designs, and bears the incised signature *Le Verre Francais*.

Le Verre Français

Lamp, Fougeres Pattern, Mottled Orange, Green, Cream Ground, 10 In. . . . 4600.00
Vase, Algues Pattern, Orange Shaded Mottled Algae, White Mottled Ground, 7 In. . . . 1560.00
Vase, Azurettes Pattern, Blue, Bright Blue Mottled Ground, 6¾ In. . . . 1440.00
Vase, Cerises Pattern, Orange, Violet, Mauve Ground, Mottled, 17 In. . . . 4140.00
Vase, Dahlia, Leaves, Shaded Lavender To Pink Mottled Ground, 13 In. . . . 2760.00
Vase, Eglantine Pattern, Shaded, Mottled Lavender Ground, Amber, 16¼ In. . . . 2760.00
Vase, Fish, Orange Mottled, Orange, Green Algae, Frosted, Blue Ground, 9½ In. . . . 2875.00
Vase, Flowers, Orange, Leaves, Cobalt Blue, Yellow, Pebbled, Signed, 7 In. . . . *illus* 900.00
Vase, Frosted, Clear, Purple, c.1925, 21⅜ In. . . . 4560.00
Vase, Frosted Yellow, Red Art Deco Flowers, Footed, Cameo, 12¼ In. . . . 1495.00

TIP

To ship small pieces of glass, try this trick: Put the glass in a Styrofoam cup, then wrap in bubble wrap or several layers of paper. Stuff sides and bottom of a large box with Styrofoam trays. Then put the antiques on the trays. Pack more Styrofoam around them. Maybe you can get extra trays at your grocery store.

Le Verre Francais, Vase, Flowers, Orange, Leaves, Cobalt Blue, Yellow, Pebbled, Signed, 7 In.
$900.00

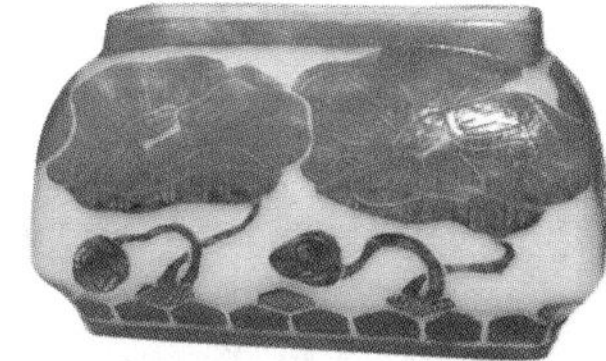

Le Verre Francais, Vase, Poppies, Red, Yellow Ground, 4-Sided, Signed, Ovington, 4 x 7½ In.
$800.00

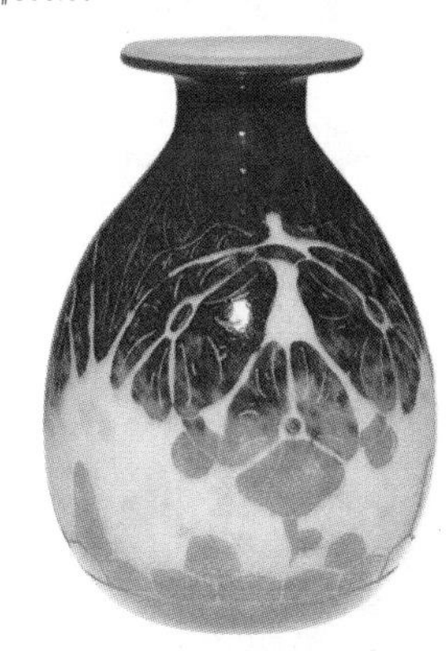

Leeds, Plate, Eagle & Shield, Green Feather Edge, 8 In.
$800.00

Leeds, Plate, Flower Basket, Green Feather Edge, 8 ⅛ In.
$2900.00

Leeds, Plate, House, Blue Feathered Scalloped Edge, Pearlware, c.1810, 9 In.
$345.00

Leeds, Plate, Pomegranate Flower, Blue Feather Edge, Impressed, S. Tams, 10 In.
$8000.00

Vase, Orange, Black, Footed, c.1920, 12½ In. 2880.00
Vase, Philodendrons, Pink To Magenta Flowers, White & Salmon Ground, 15 In.. . . . . . 2520.00
Vase, Poppies, Red, Yellow Ground, 4-Sided, Signed, Ovington, 4 x 7½ In. . . . . . *illus* 800.00
Vase, Red Roses, Mottled Yellow Ground, Green Base, Signed, 12 x 8 In. 4800.00
Vase, Stick, Mottled Red, Art Deco Roses, Bulbous, Cameo, Signed, 11 In. 575.00

LEATHER is tanned animal hide and it has been used to make decorative and useful objects for centuries. Leather objects must be carefully preserved with proper humidity and oiling or the leather will deteriorate and crack. This damage cannot be repaired.

Backpack, Brown, Zippered, Chanel Logo, 10½ In. 105.00
Briefcase, Brass Mounts, Flower Panel, Accordion Filing Pouch, Victorian, 11 x 10 In.. . . . . . 370.00
Cattle Whip, Rawhide, Silver Handle, Metal Balls Marked 800, Argentina 138.00
Cowboy Riata, Braided, 40 Ft. 248.00
Dog Collar, Alligator Skin, Brass Mount, Griffins, Plaques, Padlock, Late 1700s, 2¾ In. 470.00
Key Basket, Star, Tooled Tulip & Geometric Design, Applied Handle, 8 x 6 x 9 In. 6037.00

LEEDS pottery was made at Leeds, Yorkshire, England, from 1774 to 1878. Most Leeds ware was not marked. Early Leeds pieces had distinctive twisted handles with a greenish glaze on part of the creamy ware. Later ware often had blue borders on the creamy pottery. A Chicago company named Leeds made many Disney-inspired figurines. They are listed in the Disneyana category.

LEEDS POTTERY.

Cup & Saucer, Fern Leaf, 4 Colors, Blue Chain Link Border, Soft Paste, Handleless 770.00
Cup & Saucer, Flowers & Leaves, 5 Colors, Soft Paste, Handleless 248.00
Cup & Saucer, Flowers & Leaves, Scalloped Edge, Soft Paste, Handleless 385.00
Cup & Saucer, Flowers & Leaves, Soft Paste, Handleless . . . . . . 440.00 to 770.00
Keg, Brandy, Flowers, Leaves, Vines, 5 Colors, Ribbed Borders, Soft Paste, 3¾ x 3 In. 1870.00
Pepper Pot, Soft Paste, Flower Petal Top, Blue Band, Domed, Footed Base, 4⅜ In.. . . . . . 350.00
Plate, Dahlia, Acorns, Yellow, Brown, Green Feathered & Scalloped Edge, 7¾ In. 633.00
Plate, Eagle & Shield, Green Feather Edge, 8 In. . . . . . *illus* 800.00
Plate, Flower Basket, Green Feather Edge, 8⅛ In. . . . . . *illus* 2900.00
Plate, House, Blue Feathered Scalloped Edge, Pearlware, c.1810, 9 In. . . . . . *illus* 345.00
Plate, Peafowl, On Leafy Branch, 5 Colors, Soft Paste, 9¾ In. 1210.00
Plate, Pearlware, Chinoiserie, Blue Feathered Scalloped Edge, c.1810, 9¼ In.. . . . . . 345.00
Plate, Pomegranate Flower, Blue Feather Edge, Impressed, S. Tams, 10 In. . . . . . *illus* 8000.00
Sugar, Cover, Flower & Fern, 5 Colors, Open Handles, Soft Paste, 4¼ x 4⅜ In.. . . . . . 523.00
Sugar, Cover, Sunflower, Ferns, Acorn Finial, Shell Handles, Vines, Soft Paste, 6 x 5 In.. . . . . . 413.00
Tea Set, Pearlware, Swan Finials, Flowers, Teapot, Sugar, Creamer, Cups & Saucers, Pair. . . . 1150.00
Toddy Plate, Peafowl, On Leafy Branch, 5 Color, Green Feather Edge, 8-Sided, 6⅛ In.. . . . . . 303.00

LEFTON is a mark found on pottery, porcelain, glass, and other wares imported by the Geo. Zoltan Lefton Company. The company began in 1941 and is still in business. It was restructured in 2002 and is now called The Lefton Company. The company mark has changed through the years, but because marks have been used for long periods of time, they are of little help in dating an object.

Lefton China Hand Painted MADE IN JAPAN

Figurine, Ballerina, 1989, 5 In. . . . . . *illus* 16.00
Figurine, Birthday Angel, January, 3¾ In. . . . . . *illus* 15.00
Figurine, Kissing Kids, Label, 5 In. . . . . . *illus* 21.00
Head Vase, Long Flip Hair Style, Gold Flowers On Hat, Closed Eyes, Gloved Hand On Chin . . . 75.00
Head Vase, Woman, Exotic, Gold Highlights, Signed, 1950s 65.00
Salt & Pepper, Dogs, Jeweled Eye, Label . . . . . . *illus* 11.00
Salt & Pepper, Mice, Boy With Flower, Girl With Hair Bow, Japan, 4 In. 12.00
Salt & Pepper, Poinsettia Pattern, Foil Label, 2½ In.. . . . . . 8.00

LEGRAS was founded in 1864 by Auguste Legras at St. Denis, France. It is best known for cameo glass and enamel-decorated glass with Art Nouveau designs. Legras merged with Pantin in 1920 and became the Verreries et Cristalleries de St. Denis et de Pantin Reunies.

LEGRAS

Bowl, Berries, Purple, Enameled Leaves, Textured Salmon Ground, 5¾ x 7¾ In. 115.00
Bowl, Poppies, Orange, Green Leaves, Frosted, Textured Ground, 3¾ x 1½ In. 2300.00
Vase, Amethyst, Flowers, Gold Trim, Pinched Sides, Cameo, 8 x 4½In.. . . . . . 780.00
Vase, Birds In Flight, Light Mauve Stain, 16 In. 660.00
Vase, Camel, Variegated, Leaves, Enameled, Plum, Green, Signed, Cameo, 8 In. 295.00
Vase, Chinese Pheasant, Leaves, Frosted Ground, Enameled, 12 In. 259.00
Vase, Flower Baskets, 3 Oval Panels, Yellow Textured Ground, Cameo, 9½ In. 403.00
Vase, Flowered Band Center, Bright Maroon, Enamel, Salmon Ground, Cameo, 16 In.. . . . . . 2875.00

Vase, Frosted, Peach, Grapevines, Translucent Plum Enamel, Signed, Cameo, 6 In. 295.00
Vase, Green & Gold Grapes & Leaves, Enameled, Chipped Ice Ground, Cameo, 7¾ In. 230.00
Vase, Green & Orange, Blossoms & Leaves, Gold Enameled Rim, Cameo, 3½ x 4½ In. 1495.00
Vase, House, Trees, Water, Mottled Pink Shaded To Blue Ground, Cameo, 2¼ x 2½ In. 900.00
Vase, Landscape, Trees, Meadow, Building, Mottled Orange, Yellow, Green, 2½ x 2½ In. 1150.00
Vase, Landscape, Winter, Birds, Tree, Orange Sky, Enameled, Ruffled Rim, 10½ In. ...... *illus* 550.00
Vase, Leaves, Stems & Berries, Enameled, Yellow & Frosted Ground, 23¾ In. 863.00
Vase, Peacock, White Flower Spray, Green Frosted Ground, Cameo, 12¾ In. 345.00
Vase, Purple Wisteria Pods, Green Leaves, Mottled Sky Blue Ground, Cameo, 9 In. 940.00
Vase, Red, Mottled Brown, Orange Double Arch Band, Oval, Tapered, 8½ In. 560.00
Vase, Seeds, Strawberries, Scrolls, Beige, Orange & Burgundy Swirls, Long Neck, Cameo, 8 In. 383.00

LENOX is the name of a porcelain maker. Walter Scott Lenox and Jonathan Coxon Sr. founded the Ceramic Art Company in Trenton, New Jersey, in 1889. In 1906, Lenox left and started his own company called Lenox. The company makes a porcelain that is similar to Irish Belleek. Lenox was bought by Department 56 in 2005. The marks used by the firm have changed through the years and collectors prefer the earlier examples. Related pieces may also be listed in the Ceramic Art Co. category.

Boullion, Reticulated Silver, Urn Pattern, Gilt Border, c.1900, 12 Piece 1960.00
Candleholder, Porcelain, Angel Figurine, 10 x 3 In., Pair 146.00
Dinner Set, Weatherly, Porcelain, Dinner, Salad, Bread, Cup & Saucer, 60 Piece 1045.00
Dish, Shell, Mid 20th Century, 2¼ x 6 In., Pair 12.00
Perfume Bottle, Figural Cat Stopper, 3¾ In. 219.00
Pitcher, Patriots, White Bisque, Blue Acanthus Leaves, Laszlo Ispanky, Handle, 9 In. 83.00
Plate, Boehm Bird, 2 Meadowlarks, Flowers, 24K Gold 54.00
Stein, Monk Holding Glass Of Wine, 14½ In. 92.00
Vase, Trumpet, Fluted, White, Footed, Mid 20th Century, 8¾ In., Pair 130.00

LETTER OPENERS have been used since the eighteenth century. Ivory and silver were favored by the well-to-do. In the late nineteenth century, the letter opener was popular as an advertising giveaway and many were made of metal or celluloid. Brass openers with figural handles were also popular.

Abe Lincoln, Brass, England, c.1930, 7 In. 90.00
Beetle, Bronze, Feather Texture, Curled Handle, Japan, Early 20th Century, 6 In. 115.00
Crowned King, Possibly George V, Gold Metal, 1910, 10 In. 75.00
Lizard, Bronze, Art Nouveau, 1½ x 11½ In. 600.00
Nude With Deer, Silver, Art Deco, 10 In. 60.00
Parrot, Metal, France, c.1900, 8 In. 100.00
Polar Bears, Brass, Art Deco, c.1940, 9 In. 60.00
Stag's Head, Brass, c.1920, 10 In. 100.00
Sterling & Ivory, Georg Jensen, c.1945, 10⅝ In. 499.00
William Howard Taft Commemorative, Eagle, Cornucopia, Bronze, Ohio Society Of N.Y., Dec. 16, 1908 400.00
Women's Suffrage, Votes For Women, Composition, Woman Handle, 5¾ In. 1315.00

LIBBEY Glass Company has made many types of glass since 1888, including the cut glass and tablewares that are collected today. The stemwares of the 1930s and 1940s are once again in style. The Toledo, Ohio, firm was purchased by Owens-Illinois in 1935 and is still working under the name Libbey Inc. Maize is listed in its own category.

Bowl, Amberina, Flared Ruffled Rim, 1⅝ x 7⅛ In. 294.00
Bowl, Amberina, Ribbed, Scalloped Edge, Marked, 1⅝ x 7⅛ In. .... *illus* 250.00
Bowl, Centerpiece, Empress Cutting, 10 In. 950.00
Bowl, Empress Cutting, Low, 8 In. 125.00
Bowl, Engraved Flower Panels, Zipper Highlights, Signed, 8 In. 125.00
Bowl, Fruit, Ripple, Diamond Cutting, Aqua, 5 In. 20.00
Bowl, Glenda Cutting, Signed, 7 In. .... 225.00 to 300.00
Bowl, Green, Cut To Clear, Fleur-De-Lis, Heart, Pedestal, Signed, 3½ x 10 In. 175.00
Bowl, Salad, Ripple, Diamond Cutting, Gold, 5¾ In. 45.00
Cologne, Itaglio Cut, Pomegranates, Signed, 7 x 4 In. 1000.00
Compote, Amberina, Optic Ribbed, Scalloped Rim, 4 In. 891.00
Compote, Opaline Bowl, Pink Pulled Feathers, Signed, 12 In. 518.00
Cordial, Amethyst, Red, Blue, Tadpoles, Signed, 3 In., 4 Piece 170.00
Decanter, Imperial Cutting, 12 In. 500.00
Dish, Oval, Sawtooth Rim, 5¼ x 8¼ In. 52.00
Finger Bowl, Amberina, Ribbed, Ruffled Edge, 2½ x 5 In. 235.00

Lefton, Figurine, Ballerina, 1989, 5 In.
$16.00

Lefton, Figurine, Birthday Angel, January, 3¾ In.
$15.00

Lefton, Figurine, Kissing Kids, Label, 5 In.
$21.00

Lefton, Salt & Pepper, Dogs, Jeweled Eye, Label
$11.00

L

Legras, Vase, Landscape, Winter, Birds, Tree, Orange Sky, Enameled, Ruffled Rim, 10½ In.
$550.00

Libbey, Bowl, Amberina, Ribbed, Scalloped Edge, Marked, 1⅝ x 7⅛ In.
$250.00

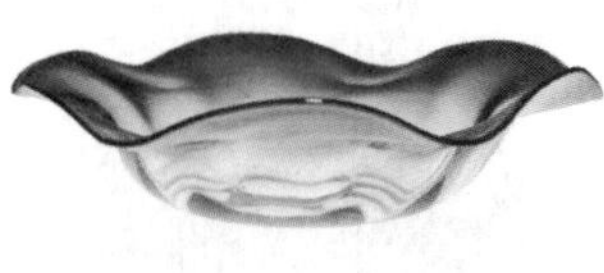

Libbey, Vase, Jack-In-The-Pulpit, Amberina, 7⅛ In.
$323.00

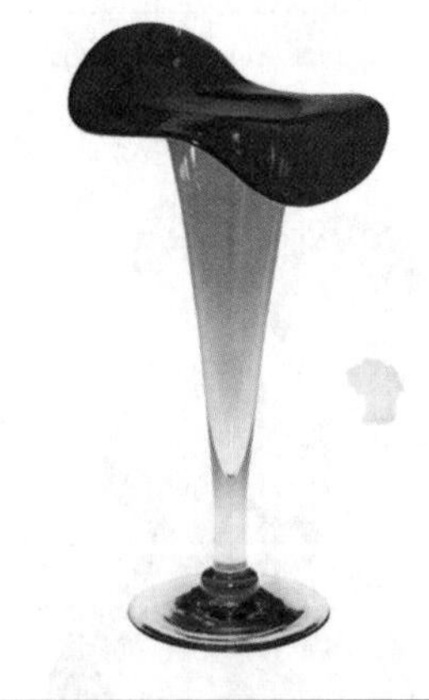

Lighter, Compass Center, Geometrics, Sterling, Guadalajara, Mexico, 2½ x 1½ In.
$73.00

Finger Bowl, Imperial Cutting, Signed, 4¾ In. 125.00
Goblet, Fleur-De-Lis Cutting, 9 Oz. 125.00
Plate, Ice Cream, Aztec Cutting, Signed, 7 In. 275.00
Punch Bowl, Geometric Cutting, Scalloped Rim, Pedestal, 9 x 9 In. 590.00
Tumbler, Iced Tea, Ripple, Diamond Cutting, Gold, 5½ In. 15.00
Tumbler, Iced Tea, Ripple, Diamond Cutting, Aqua, Footed, 6¾ In. 18.00
Tumbler, Juice, Ripple, Diamond Cutting, Gold, 3 1/2 In. . . . . 10.00 to 15.00
Vase, Amberina, Footed, 11 In. . . . . 633.00 to 1092.00
Vase, Amberina, Optic Ribbed, Baluster, Footed, Signed, 8 In. 1093.00
Vase, Amberina, Optic Ribbed, Flared Rim, Footed, 13½ In. 940.00
Vase, Amberina, Optic Ribbed, Red Flared Rim, Footed, 11½ In. 633.00
Vase, Amberina, Ribbed, Footed, Rolled Flared Rim, 8 In. 633.00
Vase, Bud, Amberina, Optic Ribbed, Signed, 9 In. 1325.00
Vase, Jack-In-The-Pulpit, Amberina, 7⅛ In. . . . . *illus* 323.00
Vase, Trumpet, Amberina, Ruffled Edge, Footed, 10¾ In. 1240.00
Vase, Trumpet, Chintz, Clear Optic Ribbed, Green Zipper Pattern, Footed, 9¾ In. 288.00

LIGHTERS for cigarettes and cigars are collectible. Cigarettes became popular in the late nineteenth century, and with the cigarette came matches and cigarette lighters. All types of lighters are collected, from solid gold to the first of the recent disposable lighters. Most examples found were made after 1940. Some lighters may be found in the Jewelry category in this book.

Ace Of Spades, Japan, 1 In. 10.00
Art Deco, Musical, Chrome, Bakelite, Switzerland, c.1940, 4½ x 3½ In. 195.00
Berkeley, Ribbed, Chrome, Austria, c.1950. . . . . 10.00
Bomart, Camel, Flat, Snuffer Cap 10.00
Champ, Trimlite, Austria 30.00
Cheshire, Square, Red Petal Flowers, Black Ground, Cover, c.1953, 4½ In. 20.00
Chrome Plated, Knight, Music Box Base, c.1950, 8½ In. 165.00
Cigar, Fish, Sterling Silver, U.S. Tobacco 6038.00
Cigar, Horse, Painted, Metal, Cloth Covered Electrical Cord, Patina, 3 x 2¼ In. 176.00
Compass Center, Geometrics, Sterling, Guadalajara, Mexico, 2½ x 1½ In. . . . . *illus* 73.00
Cream Glass, Gold Wheat, Japan, Table 20.00
Cricket, Budweiser Can Form, 4½ In. 20.00
Dunhill, 9K Gold, Marked, c.1925. . . . . 850.00
Dunhill, Aquarium, Oval, Lucite, Carved, Foil, Coral, Shells, Sea Grass, 3 x 4 In. 1998.00
Egg Shape, Cream, Blue Sailing Ships, Pedestal Base, c.1950, Table 35.00
Evans, Goldfish, Ceramic, Black, Gray, Polished Brass, 4½ In. 20.00
Evans, Henny Penny, Lucite, 3 1/2 In. . . . . 68.00 to 75.00
Gun Form, Mother-Of-Pearl Handle, Key Chain, Japan, 3 x 1 In. 30.00
Holder, Coors Beer Can, 2¾ x 2 In. 8.00
Horse Head, Ceramic, 3½ In. 13.00
Lefton, White China, Wheat, c.1946, 3 In. 20.00
Mesh Covered, Lift-Arm Mechanism, Japan, c.1940, ⅞ In. 35.00
Model Car, Cigarette, Sedan Roof Opens, Match Holder In Rear Bumper, 1940s, 9 In. 748.00
Neon Rose, Butane, 2¾ In. 2.00
Nude Woman, Silver Plate, Japan, 1¼ x 3 In. 32.00
Octagon, Tubular, Tassel, Japan, 2¼ In. 25.00
Onyx Cube Base, Marbled, 3 x 3 In. 20.00
Oriental Sea Serpent, Sterling, Amfarco, Siam, 2¼ x 1½ In. . . . . *illus* 55.00
Orion, Camera, Tripod, Japan 25.00
Paris, Eiffel Tower, Cigarette Form, Gold Filter Tip, 2½ In. 15.00
Pearl In Shell, Lucite, 4 x 2 In. 20.00
Peppermill Shape, Wood, Brass Legs, 6 In. 37.00
Pigeon, Mother-Of-Pearl, Map Of Ireland. 15.00
Pistol, Tinder, Steel, Walnut, Dutch, Early 18th Century, 8 x 4 In. . . . . *illus* 900.00
Queen Of Hearts, Butane, 1½ x 2½ In. 10.00
Rogers, Chrome, Man Golfer Swinging, Man & Woman Watching, Metal Trim 23.00
Ronson, Cigarette Case, Chrome, 4 x 3 In. 60.00
Ronson, Leather Covered Chrome, Monogram Plaque, 2 x 1 In. 12.00
Ronson, Leona, Brass, Table 33.00
Ronson, Pheasant In Flight, Minton, Marked 82.00
Ronson, Silver Plate, Bulbous Shape, c.1940, Table 34.00
Royal, Holder, Box, 4¼ x 3 In. 35.00
Royal Haeger, Aqua, Flared Top & Bottom, Art Nouveau, No. 813H, 10½ x 4 In. 65.00
Scripto, Trojan Horse, U.S. Pat. No. 2, c.1960. . . . . 19.00

able, Francis I, Gilt Silver, Reed & Barton, 1907, 3 x 3½ In. 116.00
iara, Gold, Frosted, Table, c.1960 .... 35.00
iffany & Co., Owl, Standing, 18K Gold, Stamped, 2½ In. 2950.00
Veston, Tube, Dixie Oils Gasoline 20.00
-16, Blue, 50th Anniversary World War II Midway 10.00
ippo, Camel, Silver Tone Metal 39.00
ippo, Cowboy On Bucking Bronco, Brass 39.00
ippo, Silver, G. Zippo VII 12.00
ippo, Willie Wirehand, Plastic Case 90.00

IGHTNING RODS AND LIGHTNING ROD BALLS are collected. The glass balls were at the enter of the rod that was attached to the roof of a house or barn to avoid lightning damage.

IGHTNING ROD & BALL

opper, Twisted, 63 In. 146.00
mber Glass Ball & Pennant, Hammered Iron & Copper Rod, 30 In. 178.00
ilk Glass Ball, Adjustable Rod, Tripod Legs, Marked, Nation, 24½ In. 65.00
ilk Glass Ball, Twisted Copper Rod, Tripod Stand, Wood Base, 63 In. 146.00

IGHTNING ROD BALL

obalt Blue Glass, Marked, Shinn-System, 4¼ In. 80.00
obalt Blue Glass, Ribbed, 4¼ In. 80.00
awkeye, Milk Glass, 4 x 4¼ In. 82.00
ight Blue Milk Glass, Octagonal, 5 x 3¾ In. 35.00
ight Purple Milk Glass, 5 x 5 In. 45.00
ilk Glass, Electra Embossed, Lightning Bolt 50.00
ilk White Opaque Glass 50.00
urple Milk Glass, 5 x 5 In. 45.00
ed Iridized Glass, 5 x 4¼ In. 220.00
uby Red Glass, 4½ In. 60.00

IMOGES porcelain has been made in Limoges, France, since the mid-nineteenth century. ine porcelains were made by many factories, including Haviland, Ahrenfeldt, Guerin, Pouyat, lite, and others. Modern porcelains are being made at Limoges and the word *Limoges* as art of the mark is not an indication of age. Haviland, one of the Limoges factories, is listed as a separate ategory in this book.

asket, R. Delinieres, Pink, Gold Trim, Marked, c.1890, 4¼ x 5½ In. 58.00
owl & Pitcher, Painted, Hydrangeas, Gilt Highlights, 9¾ & 4¾ x 15 In. 201.00
ox, Blue, Lady & Cupid, Gold Rim, 6¼ x 3 In. 2300.00
ox, Blue Enamel, Cupids, 9 x 2 In. 2588.00
ox, Grandfather Clock, 4½ In. 53.00
ox, Woman, Hand Painted, Enamel Accents, 3 x 3¾ x 5½ In. 323.00
hocolate Pot, Blue, Pink, Flowers, Signed, E. Miller, 1904, 12 In. 325.00
ish, Lobster, Marked, M.I.R. 84, Late 19th Century, 4¼ x 11½ x 10 In. .... *illus* 100.00
resser Set, Pink Summer Roses, Tray, Hair Receiver, Hatpin Holder, c.1900, 3 Piece 684.00
rdiniere, Roses, Leaves, Gold Rim, c.1900, 6¾ x 9¼ In. 88.00
wel Casket, Enamel, Couple Looking In Stream, Cupid Bathing, 1900s, 6 In. 588.00
yster Plate, Oyster Shell, Yellow Ground, Red, Green, 8¾ In., 6 Piece 1150.00
ill Box, Heart Shape, Gold Clasp, Pink & Purple Flowers, 3 In. 35.00
itcher, Cider, Hand Painted, White Ground, Scalloped Rim, Jean Pouyet, c.1910, 6 In. 88.00
itcher, Hand Painted, Signed, M. Brown, 1908, 15 In. 2359.00
itcher, Holly & Berries, Painted, Double Spout, Handles, c.1900, 5 In. 400.00
itcher, Painted Fruit, 15 x 17 In. 351.00
laque, St. Thomas, Enameled Copper, Nouailher, c.1750, 6¾ x 5½ In. 863.00
late, 2 Women In Field, Gold Border, Blakeman & Henderson, 8½ In. 80.00
late, Dinner, Summer Flowers, Royal Blue & Gilt Bands, Vignaud, 10¾ In., 12 Piece 1020.00
late, Evening Prayer, Angelus, Cobalt Blue Border, Gold Trim, 1896, 9 In. 590.00
late, Strawberry Pattern, c. 1900, 13 In. 64.00
late Set, Fish, Green Fish Scale Border, Scalloped Gold Rim, c.1900, 9 In., 6 Piece 588.00
late Set, Fruit Cluster, Gold Border, Scalloped Rim, Signed, J. Pierre, 8½ In., 12 Piece 805.00
late Set, Scenic, Birds, In Natural Setting, Painted, Gold Trim, c.1890, 8½ In., 16 Piece 881.00
latter, Game, 2 Pheasants, Signed, Valentin, 18½ In. 400.00
latter, Game, Bird In Flight, Hand Painted, Oval, c.1900, 12 x 18 In. 294.00
latter, Pink Rose Buds, Ahrenfeldt, c.1910, 12 x 17 In. 58.00

Lighter, Oriental Sea Serpent, Sterling, Amfarco, Siam, 2¼ x 1½ In.
$55.00

Lighter, Pistol, Tinder, Steel, Walnut, Dutch, Early 18th Century, 8 x 4 In.
$900.00

Zippo First

Recent research by Zippo Manufacturing Company confirms that the first Zippo windproof lighter was not actually made until 1933, although it was designed and planned for in 1932. The lighter was an improved version of an Austrian design. Today the company makes 80,000 lighters a day and says one-third sell to collectors.

Limoges, Dish, Lobster, Marked, M.I.R. 84, Late 19th Century, 4¼ x 11½ x 10 In.
$100.00

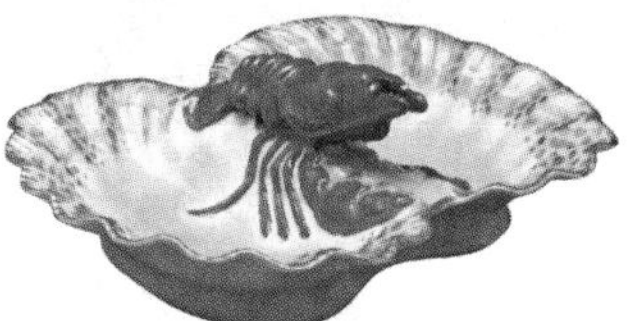

Limoges, Vanity Set, Tray, Powder Jar, Hair Receiver, Marked, W & G Co., 3 Piece
$105.00

Felix Flies
Did you know Charles Lindbergh took his Felix the Cat toy with him on his solo flight across the Atlantic?

Liverpool, Jug, Arms Of Johnston, Ship, Black Transfer, Creamware, c.1790, 11¾ In.
$3500.00

Lladro, Figurine, Litter Of Fun, No. 5364, 1985, 9 In.
$225.00

Shaving Mug, Marked, D & C France, 3¾ In. 170.00
Sugar & Creamer, Dome Lid, Hand Painted, Multicolored 118.00
Tray, Dresser, Roses, Scalloped Edge, c.1890, 16 x 15 In. 70.00
Tray, Flowers, White, Yellow, Pink, Gold Rim, 18½ x 14½ In. 150.00
Urn, Lid, Tavern Scenes, Swags, Lion Masks, Flared Foot, G. Borgfeldt, c.1920, 30 In. 6136.00
Vanity Set, Tray, Powder Jar, Hair Receiver, Marked, W & G Co., 3 Piece . . . . . . *illus* 105.00
Vase, Blue, Green, Pink, Red, Gold, Tapered, Metal Base, C. Faure, 9¼ In. 5750.00
Vase, D'Ore, Bronze Mount, 13½ x 4 In., Pair 1410.00
Vase, Flowers, Multicolored, Foil Ground, Red To Orange, Copper Base, Rim, C. Faure, 10 In. . 3450.00
Vase, Orange Poppies, Stems, Buds, Leaves, Orange Ground, 11¼ In. 240.00
Vase, Pink & Burgundy Roses, Gold Scroll Handles, Vienna, 10 x 8 In. 1235.00
Vase, Rose, Dark Green, Pink, Squat, 4½ x 7½ In. 100.00
Vase, White & Red Blossoms, Brown Green Ground, Oval, Foot Ring, 5¼ In. 2415.00
Vase, Woman At Stream, Angel, Garland Of Flowers, 2 Handles, 11 In. 288.00
Vase, Woman In Blue Flowers, Monogram, c.1900, 5¾ In. 590.00
Vase, Woman In Blue Gown, Portrait, Enameled, c.1900, 4 In. 472.00

LINDBERGH was a national hero. In 1927, Charles Lindbergh, the aviator, became the first man to make a nonstop solo flight across the Atlantic Ocean. In 1932, his son was kidnapped and murdered, and Lindbergh was again the center of public interest. He died in 1974. All types of Lindbergh memorabilia are collected.

Bookends, Spirit Of St. Louis, Bronze, Inscription, 1st Nonstop Flight, c.1927 . . . . . . 58.00
Button, Celluloid, Lindbergh, Spirit Of St. Louis In Background, 1920s, 1¼ In. 8.00
Label, TWA, Lindbergh Line Luggage Label, Gum Backing, c.1937, 3½ x 4 In. 22.00
Medal, Profile Bust, Torch Of Liberty, Spirit Of St. Louis, Bronze, M. Teterger, E. Blin 420.00
Record, Lucky Lindy, Lindbergh Eagle Of U.S.A., 78 RPM, Jack Kaufman, 1920s, 10 In. 4.00
Tapestry, Portrait, Scenes Of New York & Paris, Spirit Of St. Louis, 1927, 20 x 56 In. 34.00
Tie Tack, Spirit Of St. Louis Airplane, Pewter, Plastic Case, 2 In. 6.00
Watch Fob, New York, Paris, Statue Of Liberty, Eiffel Tower, Leather Strap, ¾ x 1¼ In. 90.00

LITHOPHANES are porcelain pictures made by casting clay in layers of various thicknesses. When a piece is held to the light, a picture of light and shadow is seen through it. Most lithophanes date from the 1825–75 period. A few are still being made. Many lithophanes sold today were originally panels for lampshades.

2 Lovers, Crossing Stream, Signed, PR, Sickle, No. 1299, 4⅜ x 5³⁄₁₆ In. 130.00
2 Lovers, Escaping Storm, Marked PR, Sickle, No. 1484, 4¼ x 5³⁄₁₆ In. 200.00
Children, Dog, Stone Fence In Mountains, Marked, EDS&C 78, c.1880, 5½ x 3½ In. 125.00
Coronation, King George V, Coat Of Arms, Altringham, Marked, Crown, GRV, c.1911 . . . . . . 148.00
Cup, King Edward VII, Coronation, Preston Guild, c.1902 . . . . . . 110.00
Cup & Saucer, Custom House, Boston, Delft, Blue, Germany 140.00
Impressed PPM, Stained Glass Border, Frame, Germany, Late 1800, 16 x 14 In. 147.00
Maiden, Cherubs, Signed, PR, Sickle, No. 1586, 4⅜ x 5¼ In. 130.00
Maiden Praying, Signed, PPM 95, 5¼ x 6½ In. 395.00
Panel, 2 Men Engaging In Transaction, Signed, PPM 591, 5¾ x 6½ In. 275.00
Panel, Girl, With Dog & Puppies, Signed, Arrow DPM No. 294 Z, 4⅞ x 6½ In. 295.00
Panel, Woman Being Dressed, Signed, Scepter KPM 306N, 4⅝ x 6 In. 340.00

LIVERPOOL, England, has been the site of many pottery and porcelain factories since the eighteenth century. Color-decorated porcelains, transfer-printed earthenware, stoneware, basalt, figurines, and other wares were made. Sadler and Green made print-decorated wares from 1756. Many of the pieces were made for the American market and feature patriotic emblems, such as eagles, flags, and other special-interest motifs. Liverpool pitchers are always called Liverpool jugs by collectors.

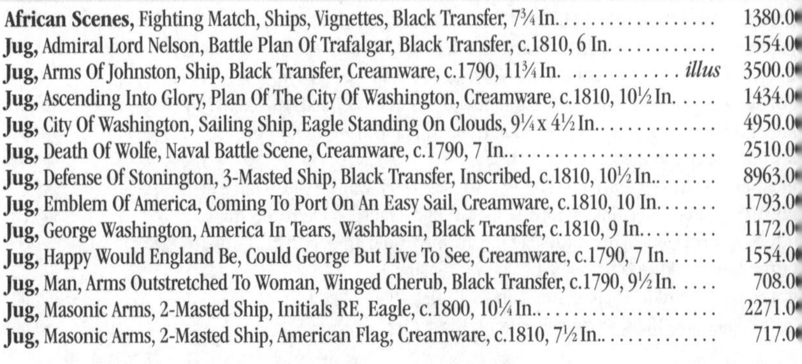

African Scenes, Fighting Match, Ships, Vignettes, Black Transfer, 7¾ In. 1380.00
Jug, Admiral Lord Nelson, Battle Plan Of Trafalgar, Black Transfer, c.1810, 6 In. 1554.00
Jug, Arms Of Johnston, Ship, Black Transfer, Creamware, c.1790, 11¾ In. . . . . . *illus* 3500.00
Jug, Ascending Into Glory, Plan Of The City Of Washington, Creamware, c.1810, 10½ In. 1434.00
Jug, City Of Washington, Sailing Ship, Eagle Standing On Clouds, 9¼ x 4½ In. 4950.00
Jug, Death Of Wolfe, Naval Battle Scene, Creamware, c.1790, 7 In. 2510.00
Jug, Defense Of Stonington, 3-Masted Ship, Black Transfer, Inscribed, c.1810, 10½ In. 8963.00
Jug, Emblem Of America, Coming To Port On An Easy Sail, Creamware, c.1810, 10 In. 1793.00
Jug, George Washington, America In Tears, Washbasin, Black Transfer, c.1810, 9 In. 1172.00
Jug, Happy Would England Be, Could George But Live To See, Creamware, c.1790, 7 In. 1554.00
Jug, Man, Arms Outstretched To Woman, Winged Cherub, Black Transfer, c.1790, 9½ In. 708.00
Jug, Masonic Arms, 2-Masted Ship, Initials RE, Eagle, c.1800, 10¼ In. 2271.00
Jug, Masonic Arms, 2-Masted Ship, American Flag, Creamware, c.1810, 7½ In. 717.00

ug, Washington Bust, Figures, Cherub, Reuben & Charlotte Ross, Black Transfer, c.1810, 9 In. . . 1554.00
ug, Washington Crowned By Liberty, F. Morris Shelton, Black Transfer, c.1810, 13 In. 4183.00
ug, Washington In Glory, Emblem Of America, Creamware, Early 19th Century, 12 In. 2390.00
lug, America Declared Independent, July 4, 1776, 4⅞ In. 5079.00
lug, Oh Liberty Thou Goddess, Ribbon Border, 16 States, Creamware, 6¼ In. 1673.00
lug, Peace, Plenty & Independence, Black Transfer, c.1810, 6 In. 2151.00
lug, Privateering, Inscribed, True Blooded Yankee, Black Transfer, c.1810, 6¼ In. 1315.00
itcher, Susan's Farewell, Gun Ship, Black Transfer, Applied Handle, Creamware, 10 In. 978.00

LADRO is a Spanish porcelain. Juan, Jose, and Vicente Lladro opened a ceramics workshop Almacera in 1951. They soon began making figurines in a distinctive, elongated style. n 1958 the factory moved to Tabernes Blanques, Spain. The company makes stoneware and porcelain gurines and vases in limited and unlimited editions. Dates given are first and last years of production.

LLADRÓ®

igurine, 3 Angels, No. 4542, 7 In. . . . . 82.00 to 118.00
igurine, A Mile Of Stile, No. 6507, 1998, 14 In. 295.00
igurine, Angel With Clarinet, No. 1232, 1972, 9½ In. 189.00
igurine, Bedtime Story, No. 5457, 10½ In. 234.00
igurine, Blushing Bride, No. 6329, 14 In. . . . . 206.00 to 263.00
igurine, Boy, Naughty Dog, No. 4982, 7¾ In. 146.00
igurine, By My Side, No. 7645, 6¼ In. 275.00
igurine, Cat & Mouse, No. 5236, 3 In. 147.00
igurine, Children's Games, No. 5379, 8 1/2 In. . . . . 450.00 to 468.00
igurine, Christ Child, Nativity, No. 5745, 3¼ In. 88.00
igurine, Clown, No. 4618, 6½ In. 205.00
igurine, Doctor, No. 4602, 15¾ In. 147.00
igurine, Duck, No. 1056, 4 In. 147.00
igurine, Ducklings, No. 4895, 2 In. 59.00
igurine, Fairy, No. 4595, 11 In. 93.00
igurine, Family Roots, No. 5371, 11 In. 643.00
igurine, Father Time, No. 6696, 1999, 11 In. 236.00
igurine, Flowers Of The Season, No. 1454, 1983, 12 In. 885.00
igurine, Girl, Seated, Holding Doll, No. 1083, 7 In. 200.00
igurine, Girl Holding Slippers, No. 4523, 5½ In. 71.00
igurine, Golfer, No. 4824, 10½ In. 117.00
igurine, Graceful White, Swan, No. 5230, 8 In. 94.00
igurine, Graceful White, Swans, No. 6175, 4 In. 82.00
igurine, Graduation Dance, No. 5459, 14¼ In. 263.00
igurine, Harmony, No. 5159, 12¼ In. 351.00
igurine, King Balthazar, No. 1425, 13 3/4 In. . . . . 380.00 to 868.00
igurine, King Balthazar On Horse, No. 1020, 15¾ In. 660.00
igurine, King Balthazar Page, No. 1516, 13¾ In. 577.00
igurine, Litter Of Fun, No. 5364, 1985, 9 In. . . . . *illus* 225.00
igurine, Little Fisherman, 6½ In. 118.00
igurine, Mother Duck, Ducklings, No. 4895, 2 In. 88.00
igurine, My Little Explorers, No. 6640 . . . . 325.00
igurine, Noisy Friend, No. 2253, 9¼ In. 146.00
igurine, Puppy Parade, No. 6784, 10 In. . . . . *illus* 350.00
igurine, Ready To Go, No. 2388, 11 In. 125.00
igurine, School Chums, No. 5237, 8½ In. 292.00
igurine, Seesaw, No. 4867, 7¾ In. 205.00
igurine, Serious Clown, No. 4923, 13 In. 221.00
igurine, Sharia, No. 6180, 11½ In. 234.00
igurine, Traveling In Style, No. 5680, 1999, 6½ In. . . . . *illus* 200.00
igurine, Unicorn, No. 7697, 2002, 9 In. 213.00
igurine, Wedding Day, Bride & Groom, No. 5274, 11 In. 345.00
igurine, Woman, Sewing A Trousseau, No. 5126, 11½ In. 205.00
ve Nest, No. 6291, 9 In. 146.00

OETZ glass was made in many varieties. Johann Loetz bought a glassworks in Austria in 340. He died in 1848 and his widow ran the company; then in 1879, his grandson took er. Most collectors recognize the iridescent gold glass similar to Tiffany, but many other pes were made. The firm closed during World War II.

Loetz Austria

asket, Iridescent Green, Blue Highlights, Ruffled Rim, Applied Clear Handle, 13 In. . . 144.00 to 273.00
asket, Olympia, Iridescent Olive Green, Flared Rim, Pulled Handles, 1890s, 9⅝ x 10 In. 188.00
owl, Centerpiece, Creta Papillon, Iridescent Blue, Ruffled Edge, 9 In. 115.00

TIP

If the name "England" (or that of some other country) appears, the dish was probably made after 1891, but it may have been made as early as 1887. The words "made in England" (or some other country) indicate the piece was made after 1914.

Lladro, Figurine, Puppy Parade, No. 6784, 10 In.
$350.00

Lladro, Figurine, Traveling In Style, No. 5680, 1999, 6½ In.
$200.00

L

Loetz, Bowl, Turquoise, Frosted, Handles, Footed, 4 x 9 In.
$320.00

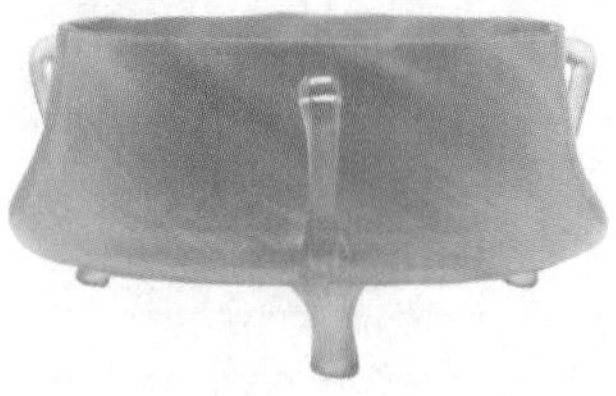

Loetz, Vase, Oil Spot, Cobalt Blue, Pewter Branches, Marked, 4⅝ In.
$540.00

Loetz, Vase, Flower Shape, Medici, Yellow, Green, 9½ x 4½ In.
$960.00

Loetz, Vase, Medici, Blue Green, Gold Over Fuchsia, Twisted, Flared, 5½ In.
$1528.00

Bowl, Centerpiece, Cut Platinum Design, Green Ground, 3¾ x 9 In. 1020.0

Bowl, Iridescent Blue, Oval, Pinched Square Rim, 4½ In. 575.0

Bowl, Oil Spot, Blue, Gold, Handles, Maria Licarz, 10 x 11½ In. 1680.0

Bowl, Olive Green, Threading, Art Nouveau Bronze Frame, 8½ In. 443.0

Bowl, Pale Green, Rose Oil Spots, Amethyst Drippings, Tricornered Rim, 3½ x 7 In. 480.0

Bowl, Turquoise, Frosted, Handles, Footed, 4 x 9 In. .... *illus* 320.0

Conch Shell, Amber, Multicolored Overshot, Ocean Wave Base, 4¾ x 9 In. 529.0

Conch Shell, Iridescent Gold, Green Iridescent, 4¾ In. 690.0

Conch Shell, Oil Spot, Blue, Iridescent Gold, Applied Clear Foot, 8 x 6½ In. 1150.0

Lamp, Amber Dome Shade, Iridescent, Green, Blue, Red, Serpent-Footed Base, 16½ In. 2300.0

Rose Bowl, Platinum, Thumbprint, Scalloped Rim, 4 In. 660.0

Vase, Apple, Leaves, Feather Decoration, Iridescent, Signed, 3⅜ In. 288.0

Vase, Blue, Pulled Feather, Amber Ground, Platinum Iridescent, 8¾ In. 2013.0

Vase, Blue & Opal, Pulled Leaf, Burgundy Red Ground, Twisted Body, 12⅞ In. 531.0

Vase, Bud, 2 Stemmed, Clear Holders, Iridescent Gold Leaf, Scallop Base, 5½ In. 201.0

Vase, Candia Silberiris, Elongated Neck, Pinched, 6¼ In. 270.0

Vase, Creta Papillon, Green Ground, Platinum, Urn Shape, 6 x 6½ In. 230.0

Vase, Cytisus, Bulbous, Squared Rim, Green Combed Threading, Yellow Top, 3 x 5 In. 2520.0

Vase, Federzeichnung, Mother-Of-Pearl, Gold Tracery, Egg Shape, 6 In. 1320.0

Vase, Federzeichnung, Mother-Of-Pearl, Bulbous, Stickneck, Gold Tracery, Pinched, 10 In. 2588.0

Vase, Flower Shape, Medici, Yellow, Green, 9½ x 4½ In. .... *illus* 960.0

Vase, Formosa, Green, 7 x 3½ In. 240.0

Vase, Gold, Allover Combed Threading, Inverted Ribbing, 5⅜ In. 944.0

Vase, Gold, Iridescent Blue, c.1900, 9½ In. 1560.0

Vase, Green, Amber, Blue, Applied Gold & Orange, Twisted Prunts, Tricorner Rim, 5 In. 2300.0

Vase, Green, Amber To Brown, Silver, Iridescent Blue, Tricornered Rim, 3 In. 2875.0

Vase, Green, Bottle Shape, 7¼ x 4½ In. 495.0

Vase, Green, Silvery Blue, Textured Pulled Prunts, Swollen, Footed, 10 In. 823.0

Vase, Green & Pink, Diamond Quilted, White Interior, Exterior Clear Casing, 5½ In. 460.0

Vase, Green To Silver Gray, Pinched Waist, Silver Overlay Scrolling, 5¼ In. 1840.0

Vase, Iridescent Amber, Gathered Neck, 4 In. 117.0

Vase, Iridescent Blue, Bulbous, Oil Spot, Flared Rim, 5½ In. 300.0

Vase, Iridescent Blue, Cobalt Blue, Freeform Panels, Bulbous, Pinched Sides, 9 In. 1208.0

Vase, Iridescent Blue, Silver Overlay, Stemmed Morning Glories, Art Nouveau, 5½ In. 719.0

Vase, Iridescent Gold, Blue Highlights, Silver Overlay, Leaves & Blossoms, 5 In. 1495.0

Vase, Iridescent Gold, Pinched Waist, Amber, Gold, Enameled Art Nouveau Flower, 7½ In. 259.0

Vase, Iridescent Gold, Purple, Silver Overlay, 5 In. 300.0

Vase, Iridescent Green, Pinched Sides, Footed, Silver Rim, Dragonflies, 6 In., Pair 345.0

Vase, King Tut, Cobalt Blue, Flared Neck, Rolled, Pinched Rim, Squat, 4¼ In. 920.0

Vase, Klava, Swirl Body, Green With Rose, Trailing Handles, Square Rim, 7 In. 210.0

Vase, Medici, Blue Green, Gold Over Fuchsia, Twisted, Flared, 5½ In. .... *illus* 1528.0

Vase, Medici, Bronze, Purple Iridescent, Platinum, 6½ In. 748.0

Vase, Medici, Earthen Ground, Platinum, Pinched Waist, Silver Flower Overlay, 6 In. 3738.0

Vase, Moss Green Looped Through Iridescent Silver, Free-Form, 9¾ In. 354.0

Vase, Mottled Blue, Applied Tendrils, Green, Tapered, 4 x 5¾ In. 431.0

Vase, Oil Spot, Amethyst Iridescent, Yellow Ground, Long Neck, Bulbous, 14½ In. 575.0

Vase, Oil Spot, Blue, White, Green Peacock Feather Eye, Art Nouveau, 13 In. 1093.0

Vase, Oil Spot, Blue Iridescent, Freeform, Gold Squares, Purple, Amber Ground, 9 In. 8050.0

Vase, Oil Spot, Cobalt Blue, Pewter Branches, Marked, 4⅝ In. .... *illus* 540.0

Vase, Oil Spot, Cobalt Blue, Clear, 6 Applied Handles, Crown Shape, 8 x 12 In. 4800.0

Vase, Oil Spot, Green, Iridescent Blue, Pinched Sides, Tricornered Rim, Silver Overlay, 5 In. 1438.0

Vase, Oil Spot, Green, Amber, Iridescent Blue, Waves, Rondels, Brass Mount, 10 In. 7638.0

Vase, Oil Spot, Iridescent Blue, Amber, Handles, 5 In. 575.0

Vase, Oil Spot, Iridescent Blue, Silver Blue, Pinched Sides, 4¼ In. 575.0

Vase, Oil Spot, Iridescent Blue, Purple, Green, Sterling Silver Vines, Leaf Overlay, 5½ In. 1438.0

Vase, Oil Spot, Red, Silvery Ribbons, Gourd Shape, Pinched, Dimples, 6½ In. 561.0

Vase, Oil Spot, Red, Purple, Platinum, Yellow Ground, Silver Overlay, 7 In. 4313.0

Vase, Papillon, Amber, Baluster, Copper Overlay Nosegay & V-Shaped Bands, 4 In. 295.0

Vase, Papillon, Blue & Green, Sterling Silver Overlay, 4 x 7½ In. 2520.0

Vase, Papillon, Gold, Large & Small Dimples, Flared Rim, 7¾ In. 411.0

Vase, Pearl Ground, Gold Combed Threading, 7¼ In. 1003.0

Vase, Phanomen, Cobalt Blue, 6 x 10½ In. 1920.0

Vase, Phanomen, Gold, Pearl Ground, Stamped, Czechoslovakia, 7 In. .... *illus* 850.0

Vase, Phanomen, Green Oil Spot, Amethyst, Blue Pulled Heart, Oval, Shouldered, 3½ In. 978.0

Vase, Phanomen, Iridescent, Waisted 4¾ x 3½ In. .... *illus* 600.0

Vase, Phanomen, Iridescent, Cinnamon Peach, Blue Coin Spot, Bulbous, 4½ In. 805.0

Vase, Phanomen, Peach Iridescent Ground, Platinum Feather, Tendrils, 6 In. 7800.0

ase, Phanomen Gre, Vaseline Ground, Platinum, Applied Silver Tendrils, 9½ In. 2300.00
ase, Purple Tree Scene, Cylindrical, Larochere, Footed, Signed, 20th Century, 14 In. 118.00
ase, Prussian Green, Iridescent Blue Pulled Feather, E Shape Handles, 7¼ In. 1035.00
ase, Silberiris, Gold, Dimples, 3 Clear Handles, 5 In. 295.00
ase, Stick, Diaspora, Gold Iridescent, Bulbous, Free-Form Folded Rim, 11 In.............. 690.00
ase, Stick, Paperweight, Iridescent Green, Jewel, Bulbous, Silver Overlay, 10½ In........... 3738.00
ase, Titania, Flower Garden, Green, Orange, Silver Overlay Draping Shoulder, 4½ In. 3600.00
ase, Titania, Fuchsia, Silver Pulled Decoration, Bubbles, Black Rim, Footed, 9¾ In......... 7640.00
ase, Titania, Leaves, Pink, Silver, 5¾ In. .... *illus* 2800.00
ase, Verre-De-Soie, Optic Ribbed, 3 Green Tadpoles, Tricornered Rim, 5½ In. 173.00
ase, Wellenoptisch, Oil Spot, Iridescent Green, Medium Green, 3½ In.................... 29.00
ase, Yellow, Blue, Kolomon Moser, c.1902, 8⅛ In.................................... 4800.00

ONE RANGER, a fictional character, was introduced on the radio in 1932. Over three ousand shows were produced before the series ended in 1954. In 1938, the first Lone anger movie was made. Television shows were started in 1949 and are still seen on some ations. The Lone Ranger appears on many products and was even the name of a restaurant chain for veral years.

ction Figure, Lone Ranger, Tonto, Silver, Scout, Hartland Plastics, c.1961, 5 x 5 In. 125.00
utograph, Clayton Moore, Black & White Glossy Photo, 8 x 10 In. 120.00
adge, Brass, Webber's Safety Kit, T.L.R. Inc., c.1933, 1¼ In.......................... 38.00
adge, Member's, Brass, Premium Of Silvercup Bread, 1934, 1¾ In...................... 173.00
adge, Secret Compartment, Brass, Members Serial Number, 1949, 2 In. 152.00
adge, Webber's Safety Kit, Copyright T.L.R. Inc. 1933, 1½ In. 29.00
elt Buckle, Brass Luster, Embossed Image Of Lone Ranger On Silver, 1 x 2 In. 90.00
ook, Better Little Book, The Lone Ranger Follows Through, 424 Pages 20.00
ook, Big Little Book, Lone Ranger Outwits Crazy Cougar, 248 Pages, 5 x 3½ In........... 15.00
ook, Desert Storm, Whitman Books, Revena, Wenzel, c.1957, 6½ x 5½ In................ 25.00
ook, Lone Ranger & The Warhorse, 1951, 24 Pages...................................... 30.00
oloring Book, Tonto, 1953, Whitman Publishing Co...................................... 12.00
omic Book, Dell, Vol. 1, No. 73, July 1954 .... 44.00
omic Book, Hi-Yo Silver, Dell, No. 4, Oct.-Nov. 1952 .... 54.00
omic Book, No. 19, 1955.. 12.00
omic Book, No. 72, June 1954 .... 35.00
oll, Tonto, Buckskin, Fringe, War Painted Face, Jointed, c.1973, 10 In. 70.00
oll, Tonto, Composition, Fabric, Holster, Rubber Knife, Dollcraft Novelty, 1938, 20 In...... 750.00
oll, Tonto, The Lone Ranger's Pal, Composition, Cloth, 1938, 20 In. 753.00
igurine, Lone Ranger On Silver, Chalkware, 1930s, 11 x 9 In................ 115.00 to 125.00
ilm Strip Ring, 1949.. 175.00
lashlight Ring, Premium 145.00
rontier Town, Premium Of Cheerios, 1948... 1725.00
ame, Lone Ranger & The Silver Bullets, Lisbeth Whiting, Box 98.00
ame, Parker Brothers, Board, 1938.. 20.00
armonica, 4½ In. 65.00
orseshoe, Rubber 34.50
gsaw Puzzle, Lone Ranger, Tonto, Red Dog Saloon, Box, c.1947, 14 x 22 In............... 36.00
gsaw Puzzle, The Legend Of The Lone Ranger, 250 Pieces, Copyright 1980, 19 x 13 In. 6.00
nife, Pocket, Folding, By Camco, Pearl-Like Handle 50.00
odel, Kit, Aurora, Box Unopened, 1974, 4½ x 8 x 10 In. 155.00
odel, Tonto, Aurora Comic Scenes, Copyright 1974, 7 In................................. 50.00
rnament, Lunch Box, Hi-Yo Silver, Hallmark, 1997...................... 7.00 to 30.00
utfit, Belt Keys, Badge, Mask, Esquire Novelty, c.1950 .... 209.00
edometer, Aluminum Front 68.00
in, Lone Ranger Every Day, Boston American, Yellow, Black, Red, ⅞ In.................. 39.00
late, Lone Ranger & Tonto, Hamilton Collection, Limited Edition, c.1990, 8½ In. 55.00
ing, 6-Gun, Sparks, Gray, Plastic, Brass, Kix Cereal Premium, 1947 .... *illus* 86.00
ing, Kix Bomb, Premium, Brass, Image Of Lone Ranger, 1947............................ 145.00
ing, Saddle, Cheerios, Premium 225.00
ing, Weather Forecasting, Original Mailer, General Mills, 4 x 5½ In.................... 194.00
alt & Pepper, Coffeepot & Mug Shapes, Vandor, Original Box, 4 x 3½ In. 18.00
heet Music, Clayton Moore, Jay Silverheels, Signed, c.1938, 9 x 12 In., 6 Pages 316.00
hoe Brush, Hi-Yo Silver, T.L.K. Inc., c.1939, 4½ x 2¼ In................................ 35.00
ign, Merita Bread, Embossed, Tin, 1954, 36 x 24 In. .... *illus* 1600.00
ilver Bullet, Steel Marbles, Original Package, 4 x 5¾ In. 24.00
now Globe, Skill Toy, Put Lasso Over Calf's Head, Yellow Base, Driss Co., 4 In............ 165.00
oy, Decoder, Cryptograph, Weber's Bread Premium, Cardboard, c.1943 .... 145.00

Loetz, Vase, Phanomen, Iridescent, Waisted 4¾ x 3½ In.
$600.00

Loetz, Vase, Phanomen, Gold, Pearl Ground, Stamped, Czechoslovakia, 7 In.
$850.00

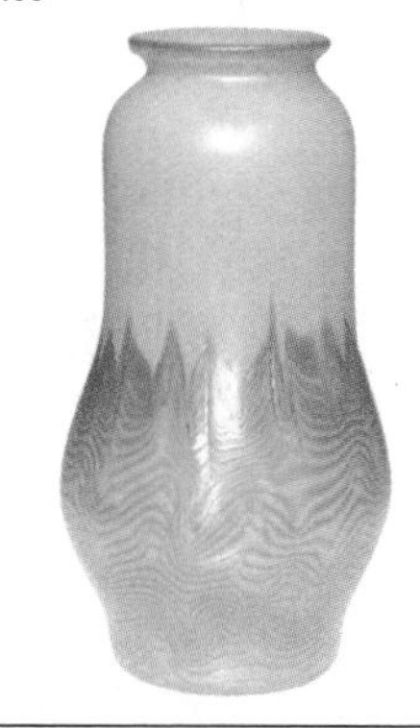

Loetz, Vase, Titania, Leaves, Pink, Silver, 5¾ In.
$2800.00

Lone Ranger, Ring, 6-Gun, Sparks, Gray, Plastic, Brass, Kix Cereal Premium, 1947
$86.00

L

LONE RANGER

Lone Ranger, Sign, Merita Bread, Embossed, Tin, 1954, 36 x 24 In.
$1600.00

Longwy, Box, Tobacco, Flowers, Stepped, Signed, 6¼ x 9¼ In.
$770.00

TIP

To remove sediment in the bottom of a vase or pitcher, put salt and crushed ice into the vase and stir. The friction will remove the stain.

Losanti, Vase, Lilies, Green Stems, Leaves, Blue & White, Carved, Signed, 8 In.
$18000.00

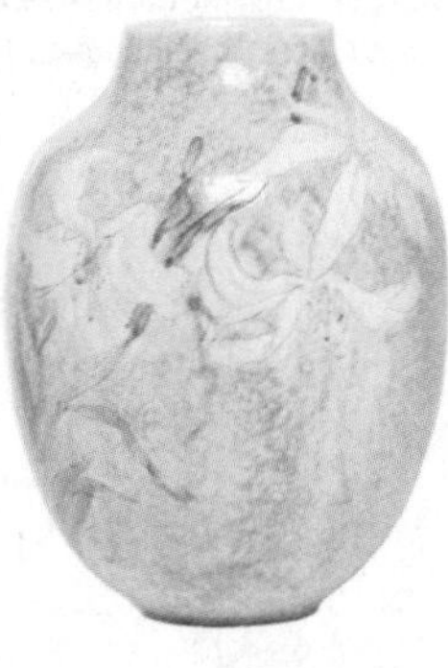

Toy, Lone Ranger Twirling Lasso, Tin, Windup, Marx, Box 585.00
View-Master Set, Mystery Rustler, 3 Reels, Story Booklet, GAF Corp., c.1956 . . . . 20.00

LONGWY Workshop of Longwy, France, first made ceramic wares in 1798. The workshop is still in business. Most of the ceramic pieces found today are glazed with many colors to resemble cloisonne or other enameled metal. Many pieces were made with stylized figures and Art Deco designs. The factory used a variety of marks.

Bowl, Flowers, Oval, 11 In. 150.00
Box, Tobacco, Flowers, Stepped, Signed, 6¼ x 9¼ In. . . . . *illus* 770.00
Cake Stand, Art Deco, Berry & Leaf Design, 11 In. 138.00
Candlestick, Enamel, Brass, Turquoise, Green & Pink Flowers, c.1880, 8½ In., Pair 59.00
Charger, Dragon, Multicolored Crackle Glaze, 8¾ In. 325.00
Jar, Cover, Flowers, Acorn Finial Handle, Shape No. 1320, 6 In. 374.00
Jardiniere, Flowers, Yellow, 14 x 8 In., Pair 3910.00
Lamp, Dragon & Flowers, Brass Base, 12 In. 460.00
Shoes, Dutch, 6 In., Pair 150.00
Tile, Birds, Palm Trees, 3-Light Brass Wall Candelabra Frame, Tiffany & Co., 17 x 11 In. 489.00
Tile, Tea, Coastal Village, Mountain, Crackle Glaze, Flower Border. 201.00
Tobacco Jar, Stepped Shape, Flowers, Marked, 9¼ x 6¼ In. 780.00
Vase, Birds, Butterflies, Flowers, Paneled, Cylindrical Neck, Flared Rim, 9 In., Pair 826.00
Vase, Bud, Flowers, Bulbous, 9 In., Pair 345.00
Vase, Flowers, Pink Ground, 9½ In., Pair 690.00
Vase, Nude Woman Picking Fruit, Full Moon, Blue Ground, 10¼ In. 1180.00
Vase, Primavera, Bulbous, Blue, Black Designs, Marked, Paper Label, No. 17, 10 x 11 In. 780.00

LONHUDA Pottery Company of Steubenville, Ohio, was organized in 1892 by William Long, W. H. Hunter, and Alfred Day. Brown underglaze slip-decorated pottery was made. The firm closed in 1896. The company used many marks; the earliest included the letters *LPCO*.

Vase, Cowboys By Stream, Native Americans, Egg Shape, Stamped, 9 x 5½ In. 5400.00

LOSANTI was made by Mary Louise McLaughlin in Cincinnati, Ohio, about 1899. It was a hard paste decorative porcelain. She stopped making it in 1906.

Vase, Lilies, Green Stems, Leaves, Blue & White, Carved, Signed, 8 In. . . . . *illus* 18000.00

LOTUS WARE was made by the Knowles, Taylor & Knowles Company of East Liverpool, Ohio, from 1890 to 1900. Lotus Ware, a thin porcelain that resembles Belleek, was sometimes decorated outside the factory. .

Bowl, Applied Flowers & Leaves, Beaded Trim, 4¼ x 5½ In. 722.00
Creamer, White, Pink Roses, Buds, Blue Flowers, Gold Fishnet, 3¼ x 4½ In. 350.00
Jar, Diagonal Leaf, Lady Finger Pattern, Knowles Taylor & Knowles, c.1894, 5 x 5 In. 450.00
Sugar & Creamer, Valenciennes, Gold Dotted Fishnet, Pink Flowers 600.00
Syrup, Blue Flowers, Green & Gold Stems, Marked, 5 In. 350.00
Tray, Shell, Berries, Leaves, c.1890, 8¾ x 8½ In. 499.00
Vase, Lily, c.1892, 8¾ In. 1200.00

LOWESTOFT was a factory in Suffolk, England, which from 1757 to 1802 made many commemorative gift pieces and small, dated, inscribed pieces of soft paste porcelain. Related items may be found in the Chinese Export category.

Bowl, Exotic Birds, Flowers, Blue Painted Ground, 3½ x 8¼ In. 316.00

LOY-NEL-ART, *see McCoy category.*

LUNCH BOXES and lunch pails have been used to carry lunches to school or work since the nineteenth century. Today, most collectors want either early tobacco advertising boxes or children's lunch boxes made since the 1930s. These boxes are made of metal or plastic. Boxes listed here include the original Thermos bottle inside the box unless otherwise indicated. Movie, television, and cartoon characters may be found in their own categories. Tobacco tin pails and lunch boxes are listed in the Advertising category.

ABC TV Wide World Of Sports, Yellow, Sports Pictures, c.1976, 13¼ In. 65.00
Astronaut, Dome, American Thermos Co., 1960 . . . . 235.00
Banana Splits, White, Vinyl, Hanna-Barbera, King Seeley, 1969 . . . . 250.00
Beatles, Aladdin, 1965 . . . . 450.00
Bread Loaf, Dome Top, Metal, Graphics, Aladdin, 1968 . . . . 300.00
Bullwinkle, Vinyl, King Seeley, 1963. . . . . 517.00

abbage Patch Kids, Plastic, King Seeley, c.1983 .... 15.00
ampbell Kids, Metal, Ohio Art, 1975 .... 200.00
asper The Friendly Ghost, Vinyl, King Seeley, 1966 .... 287.00
huck Wagon, Dome Top, Steel, Aladdin, 1958-60 .... 351.00
awn, White, Vinyl, Aladdin, 1970 .... 35.00
utch Cottage, Domed, Steel, American Thermos Products, 1958 .... 475.00
ynomutt, Metal, King Seeley, 1976 .... 20.00
.T., Metal, Aladdin, 1982 .... 95.00
mpire Strikes Back, King Seeley, 1980 .... 13.00
all Guy, Metal, Aladdin, 1981 .... 33.00
lintstone, Black Cup, Aladdin, 1971 .... 13.00
lying Nun, Blue, Vinyl, No Thermos, Aladdin, 1968 .... 166.00
rontier Days, Pony Express, Metal, Ohio Art, 1957 .... 126.00
reen Hornet, King Seeley Thermos Co., 1967 .... 230.00
rizzly Adams, Dome, Metal, Aladdin, 1977 .... 75.00
appy Days, King Seeley, 1976 .... 140.00
olly Hobbie, Metal, Aladdin, 1981 .... 45.00
et Petrol, Vinyl, Aladdin, 1957 .... 144.00
etsons, Dome Cover, Metal, Aladdin, 1963 .... 403.00
unior Miss, Metal, Aladdin, 1960s 20.00
id Power Wee Pals, Metal, King Seeley, 1974 .... 30.00
ost In Space, Dome, Metal, Thermos, King Seeley, 1967 .... 410.00
Ir. Merlin, Metal, King Seeley, 1981 .... 30.00
Iunsters, Riding In Car, King Seeley, 1965 .... 840.00
Iy Little Pony, Pink, Plastic, Aladdin, 1986 .... 15.00
athfinder, Metal, Universal, 1959 .... 184.00
eanuts, Thermos Bottle No. 2868, United Features Syndicate, c.1959 .... 35.00
ink Panther & Sons, Metal, King Seeley, 1986 .... 20.00
aggedy Ann & Andy, Metal, Aladdin, 1973 .... 75.00
oad Runner, King Seeley, 1970 .... 50.00
ecret Wars, King Seeley, 1977 .... 65.00
esame Street, Aladdin, 1979 .... 35.00
pace: 1999, Metal, King Seeley, 1975 .... 60.00
tewardess, Airplane, Vinyl, Aladdin, 1962 .... 265.00
trawberry Shortcake, Metal, Aladdin, 1981 .... 45.00
rain, Oval, Painted, Patriotic, Tin, Decoware, 8½ x 5½ In. 38.00
Valtons, Aladdin, 1973 .... 150.00

UNCH BOX THERMOS

londie, King Features, c.1969 .... 50.00
ireball XL5, Independent Television Corp., c.1964 .... 50.00
lipper, 1966 .... 55.00
reyhound Bus, Drink Up America, Red, White, Blue, King Seeley, 1970s 20.00
orse Farm Scene, King Seeley, c.1962 .... 25.00
aser Tag, Worlds Of Wonder, c.1986 .... 11.00
Iunsters, Kayro-Vue Prod., c.1965 .... 100.00
ecret Agent T, King Seeley, c.1968 .... 50.00

UNEVILLE, a French faience factory, was established about 1730 by Jacques Chambrette. is best known for its fine biscuit figures and groups and for large faience dogs and lions. he early pieces were unmarked. The firm was acquired by Keller and Guerin and is still orking.

K G Luneville

sparagus Set, Platter, Cradle Server, 12 9-In. Plates, 14 Piece 1035.00
late, Asparagus, 8½ In. 115.00
ase, Dragonfly, Irises, Metallic Glaze, Marked, K & G Luneville, 3¾ In. .... *illus* 472.00

USTER glaze was meant to resemble copper, silver, or gold. The term *luster* includes any ece with some luster trim. It has been used since the sixteenth century. Some of the luster und today was made during the nineteenth century. The metallic glazes are applied on ottery. The finished color depends on the combination of the clay color and the glaze. Blue, orange, old, and pearlized luster decorations were used by Japanese and German firms in the early 1900s. Tea eaf pieces have their own category.

opper, Bowl, Woman & Animals, 3 x 6 In. 40.00
opper, Goblet, Luster Band, Early 19th Century, 4¼ x 3¼ In. .... *illus* 84.00
opper, Pitcher, Canary, Black Transfer, Lafayette Crowned In Glory, Cornwallis, 4 In. 448.00
opper, Pitcher, Pink Flowers, Green Leaves, Blue Decoration, c.1881, 9 In. 50.00
opper, Pitcher, Raised Figures Of Victoria & Albert, 4½ In. 150.00

Lunch Boxes
About 650 different children's metal lunch box designs have been made in the United States. The first, a Hopalong Cassidy lunch box, was made in 1951; and the last, a Rambo box, dates from 1985. Now children's lunch boxes are plastic.

Luneville, Vase, Dragonfly, Irises, Metallic Glaze, Marked, K & G Luneville, 3¾ In.
$472.00

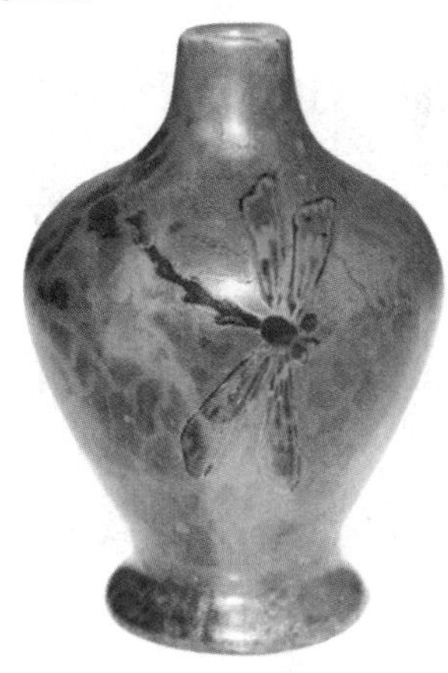

Luster, Copper, Goblet, Sunderland Luster Band, Early 19th Century, 4¼ x 3¼ In.
$84.00

TIP
Never use bleach on luster-decorated pottery. It will destroy the luster effect.

Lustres, Cranberry Glass, Prisms, Late 19th Century, 16½ In., Pair
$1500.00

Lustres, Ruby Glass, Gold, White Dots, Enamel, Prisms, 16 x 7¼ In., Pair
$850.00

Maize, Muffineer, Custard, , 5 3/16 In.
$290.00

TIP
Most old majolica pieces have a colored bottom. The newer pieces have white bottoms.

Copper, Pitcher, Relief Flowers, 19th Century, 7¼ In. 115.00
Copper, Salt, Red & Blue Decorations, Blue Ground, England, c.1875, 2 In. 44.00
Fairyland Luster is included in the Wedgwood category.
Gold, Shade, Gold Ribbing, c.1930, 5½ x 2⅛ In. 100.00
Pink, Creamer, Black Transfer, Fulton Steamer, Cadmus, Eagle, Vine Border, c.1830 .... 120.00
Pink, Creamer, Black Transfer, Enterprise & Boxer, U.S. & Macedonian, 4½ In. 896.00
Pink, Cup & Saucer, Handleless, Pink & Green Design, 2½ In. 30.00
Silver, Pitcher, Water, Resist, Signed Claire, England, c.1969, 9 In.. .... 82.00
Silver, Teapot, S-Handle, Beaded Shoulder & Body, Ribbed Neck, Early 1800s, 10 In. 92.00
Sunderland luster pieces are in the Sunderland category.
Tea Leaf luster pieces are listed in the Tea Leaf Ironstone category.

LUSTRE ART GLASS Company was founded in Long Island, New York, in 1920 by Conrad Vahlsing and Paul Frank. The company made lampshades and globes that are almost indistinguishable from those made by Quezal. Most of the shades made by the company were unmarked.

Vase, Iridescent Blue, Gold, Applied Pedestal Foot, 7¼ x 5¾ In.. .... 920.00

LUSTRES are mantel decorations or pedestal vases with many hanging glass prisms. The name really refers to the prisms, and it is proper to refer to a single glass prism as a lustre. Either spelling, luster or lustre, is correct.

Bristol Glass, Portrait Decoration, c.1880, 12 x 5 In. 468.00
Clambroth Opaline, Blue Bands, Scalloped Edge, 8 Prism Drops, 11 x 5 In. 47.00
Cranberry Glass, Baluster, 8 Prisms, Footed, 19th Century, 13 In. 59.00
Cranberry Glass, Prisms, Late 19th Century, 16½ In., Pair .... *illus* 1500.00
Cut Glass, Diamond & Oval, Panels, 12½ In. 920.00
Cut Glass, White To Green, Xs & Ovals, Painted Flowers, Prisms, 12 In., Pair 588.00
Cut Glass, Cobalt Cut To Clear, Enameled, Bohemian, 23½ In. 5025.00
Lavender Cased Glass, Bohemian, 12 x 8 In., Pair 322.00
Opaque Green, c.1880, 10 In., Pair 234.00
Pink Cased Glass, Gold Trim, Scalloped, Spear Prisms, Victorian, England, 14 In., Pair. 406.00
Ruby Glass, Enameled, Clear Prisms, 14 In., Pair. 585.00
Ruby Glass, Gold, White Dots, Enamel, Prisms, 16 x 7¼ In., Pair .... *illus* 850.00
Ruby Glass, Cut To Clear, Gold Highlights, Bohemian, 7-In. Prisms, 14¼ In. 1093.00
Satin Glass, Pink, Cut Glass Prisms, 10 In., Pair. 263.00

MAASTRICHT, Holland, was the city where Petrus Regout established the De Sphinx pottery in 1836. The firm was noted for its transfer-printed earthenware. Many factories in Maastricht are still making ceramics.

Plate, U.S. Soldier, First Liberated City Of Holland, Blue Transfer. 33.00

MACINTYRE, *see Moorcroft category.*

MAIZE glass was made by W.L. Libbey & Son Company of Toledo, Ohio, after 1889. The glass resembled an ear of corn. The leaves were usually green, but some pieces were made with blue or red leaves. The kernels of corn were light yellow, white, or light green.

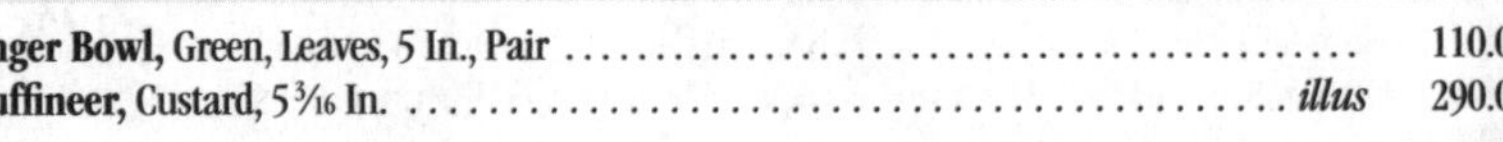

Finger Bowl, Green, Leaves, 5 In., Pair 110.00
Muffineer, Custard, 5 3/16 In. .... *illus* 290.00

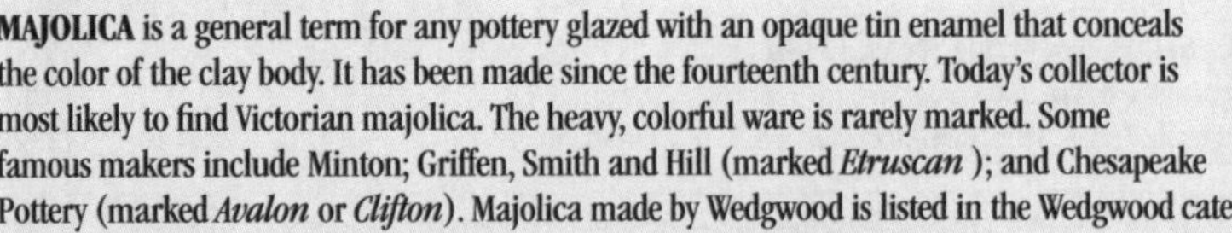

MAJOLICA is a general term for any pottery glazed with an opaque tin enamel that conceals the color of the clay body. It has been made since the fourteenth century. Today's collector is most likely to find Victorian majolica. The heavy, colorful ware is rarely marked. Some famous makers include Minton; Griffen, Smith and Hill (marked *Etruscan*); and Chesapeake Pottery (marked *Avalon* or *Clifton*). Majolica made by Wedgwood is listed in the Wedgwood category.

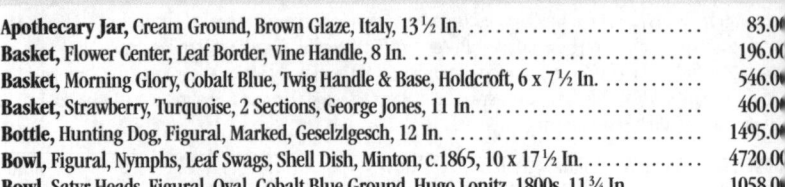

Apothecary Jar, Cream Ground, Brown Glaze, Italy, 13½ In. 83.00
Basket, Flower Center, Leaf Border, Vine Handle, 8 In. 196.00
Basket, Morning Glory, Cobalt Blue, Twig Handle & Base, Holdcroft, 6 x 7½ In. 546.00
Basket, Strawberry, Turquoise, 2 Sections, George Jones, 11 In. 460.00
Bottle, Hunting Dog, Figural, Marked, Geselzlgesch, 12 In. 1495.00
Bowl, Figural, Nymphs, Leaf Swags, Shell Dish, Minton, c.1865, 10 x 17½ In. 4720.00
Bowl, Satyr Heads, Figural, Oval, Cobalt Blue Ground, Hugo Lonitz, 1800s, 11¾ In. 1058.00
Bowl, Shell Shape, 3 Shell Feet, Holdcroft, 11 In.. .... 127.00
Box, Cover, Snakes, Frogs, Shells, Thomas Sargent Tours, 1890, 5⅞ In. 413.00
Bread Tray, Clematis, Cobalt Blue, Ocher, Green, Twisted Twig Handles, 11 x 8 In. 690.00

Bread Tray, Grape Leaf, Vine Border, Beige Ground, 11 ½ x 8 ¾ In. 259.00
Bread Tray, Wheat, Berries, Blossoms, Ribbon Handles, George Jones, c.1880, 13 In. 2585.00
Butter Pat, Begonia Leaf, Brown, Green Accents 345.00
Butter Pat, Begonia Leaf, Green Center, Yellow Border, Pink Accents 288.00
Butter Pat, Begonia Leaf, Green Shaded To Dark Green, Etruscan 184.00
Butter Pat, Begonia Leaf, Pink Basket Weave 92.00
Butter Pat, Butterfly & Bamboo, White Ground, Bamboo Border, Fielding 196.00
Butter Pat, Flowers, Green, Turquoise Center, Holdcroft 127.00
Butter Pat, Geranium, Green, Cobalt Blue Rim, Etruscan 92.00
Butter Pat, Geranium, Green, Yellow Rim, Etruscan 92.00
Butter Pat, Leaf Shape, Dark Green, 6 Piece 161.00
Butter Pat, Leaf Shape, Mottled, Cobalt Blue 92.00
Butter Pat, Pansy, Multicolored, Etruscan 104.00
Butter Pat, Wheat, Daisy, Ribbon & Bow, Turquoise Pebble Ground, Fielding 219.00
Cachepot, Cloven Hoof, Wyvern Handle, Minton, c.1864, 17 x 18 In. 720.00
Cake Set, Classical, Cake Stand, Plates, Etruscan, 8-In. Plates, 6 Piece 58.00
Cake Stand, Maple Leaves, Pink Ground, Etruscan, 9 In. 138.00
Cake Stand, Morning Glory, Cobalt Blue, Etruscan, 8 In. 150.00
Candleholder, Flowers, Wall, Cobalt Blue Center, Eichwald, 12 ½ In. 69.00
Candleholder, Lily, Leaf Shape Base, Minton, 12 ½ In., Pair 10350.00
Charger, Deer Crossing Creek, Spain, 19 ¼ In. 292.00
Charger, Justice, Cherubs, Masks, Grotesques, Italy, 15 In. 411.00
Charger, Seaside Scene, 3 Women, Man, Beach, Ship, Italy, 19 In. 58.00
Cheese Keeper, Blackberry, c.1890, 8 ¾ x 11 ½ In. 865.00
Cheese Keeper, Flowers, Leaves, Mottled Light Blue, Twig Handle, George Jones, 10 In. 4406.00
Cheese Keeper, Picket Fence, Apple Blossom, George Jones, 10 In. 2070.00
Cheese Keeper, Stand, Lobster, Vegetation, Basket Weave, Handles, George Jones, 9 In. 4406.00
Coal Scuttle, Lid, Acorns, Leaves, Bamboo Trim, 16 ½ x 15 x 9 ½ In. 468.00
Compote, Dolphin, Mottled, Footed, 7 ½ In. *illus* 219.00
Compote, Maple Leaves, Open, Etruscan, 9 ¾ x 7 ½ In. 173.00
Compote, Pink Strawberry Blossom, George Jones, 9 ½ x 4 In. 633.00
Compote, Shell, Fishnet, Fielding, 9 ½ x 4 In. 288.00
Compote, Sunflower, Urn, Lavender Border, Samuel Lear, 9 x 5 In. 170.00
Compote, Tobacco Leaf & Roses, Holdcroft, 8 ½ In. 104.00
Creamer, Bamboo & Fern, Wardle, 4 In. 81.00
Creamer, Shell & Seaweed, Etruscan, 3½ In. 58.00 to 92.00
Cup & Saucer, Flowers, Cobalt Blue, Bud Handle, George Jones 1208.00
Cup & Saucer, Pineapple 92.00
Cup & Saucer, Wicker, Yellow, Flowers 81.00
Cuspidor, Berries, Pink, Purple, 7 ½ x 6 In. 146.00
Cuspidor, Oak Leaf, 4 x 8 ½ In. 140.00
Dish, Begonia, Etruscan, 9 In., 4 Piece 546.00
Dish, Mythological Figures, Multicolored, Copper Luster, Footed, 11 In. 382.00
Dish, Pickle, Daisy, Oval, Etruscan, 8 ½ In. 196.00
Dish, Toad, Fly, Shells, Flowers, Leaves, Geoffrey Luff, Palissy Ware, 6 ¾ In. 431.00
Egg Tray, 6 Eggs With Chicks, Corn & Wheat Ground, France, 8 In. 288.00
Eggcup Holder, Basket Weave, Ivy, 3 Eggcups, 4 ½ In. 104.00
Ewer, Satyr's Head, Cobalt Blue Glaze, Serpent Handle, 19th Century, 20 In. 885.00
Figurine, Boy, Holding Plate, Bread, 20th Century, 22 ¼ In. 374.00
Figurine, Elephant, Jumbo, Green, Brown, Ocher, 11 ½ In. 863.00
Figurine, Goose, Stretched Neck, 3 In. 49.00
Figurine, Guinea Fowl, Perched On Knoll, 9 x 6 In. 1020.00
Figurine, Putto, Winged, Depicting Artist Drawing, Holdcroft, 10 ½ In. 58.00
Figurine, Wishing Well, Birds, Flowers, Continental, 13 In. 805.00
Humidor, Figural, Basket Of Fish, 4 ½ In. 138.00
Humidor, Figural, Blackamoor, With Fez, St. Clement, 8 In. 138.00
Humidor, Figural, Cat, With Fish, 7 In. 489.00
Humidor, Figural, Dog's Head, Green Hat, 5 ½ In. 196.00
Humidor, Figural, Indian Chief, Full Headdress, 8 In. 92.00
Humidor, Figural, Man, Beret, 4 ¾ In. 29.00
Humidor, Figural, Man, Straw Hat & Pipe, Terra-Cotta, 5 In. 58.00
Humidor, Figural, Man's Head, Art Nouveau, 4 ¾ In. 29.00
Humidor, Figural, Monk's Head, 6 ½ In. 50.00
Humidor, Figural, Potbellied Man, Black Top Hat, 7 In. 69.00
Humidor, Figural, Scotsman, Blue Cap, Pipe, 4 ¼ In. 58.00
Humidor, Figural, Scotsman, Green Hat With Feather, 9 In. 150.00

TIP
Old majolica pitchers have a glazed interior. Many reproduction majolica pitchers have bisque interiors.

Majolica, Compote, Dolphin, Mottled, Footed, 7 ½ In.
$219.00

Majolica, Jug, Flowers, Leaves, 9 ½ In.
$62.00

Majolica, Pitcher, Chestnut, Twig Feet, Pink, Lavender, Branch Handle, George Jones, 10 In.
$8625.00

M

Majolica, Pitcher, Sunflower, Etruscan, Griffin, Smith & Hill, 6 In.
$330.00

Majolica, Plate, Clematis, Twig Handles, c.1890, 11¾ x 8 In.
$690.00

Majolica, Platter, Apple & Cherry, Vine Handles, Mottled Center, 12 In.
$374.00

Majolica, Sardine Box, Dragonflies, Water Lilies, Bird Knop, Relief Molded, 8½ In.
$117.00

Majolica, Teapot, Cauliflower, Etruscan, Griffin, Smith & Hill, 5½ In.
$230.00

Humidor, Figural, Stag, 6½ In. . . . 35.00
Jardiniere, Bacchanalian Scene, Goat Head Handles, Cobalt Blue, England, 12 x 9 In. . . . 1150.00
Jardiniere, Calla Lily, Bird, George Jones, 22 x 18½ In. . . . 7763.00
Jardiniere, Cobalt Blue, Handles, Mythological Figures, Animals, Leaves, Minton . . . 4025.00
Jardiniere, Continents, Women, Panels, Cobalt Blue, Minton, 17 In. . . . 805.00
Jardiniere, Magnolia, Fly, Bamboo Feet, Rim, George Jones, 10½ In. . . . 1333.00
Jardiniere, Stand, Dragon, Purple, Green, Orange, 24 x 11 In. . . . 472.00
Jardiniere, Stand, Trelliswork, Flower Swags, Blue Ground, England, c.1880, 11 In. . . . 1763.00
Jardiniere, Winged Women, Masks, George Jones, 12 x 14 In. . . . 1495.00
Jug, Flowers, Leaves, 9½ In. . . . *illus* 62.00
Match Striker, Blackamoor Man, With Vase, Melons, 8½ In. . . . 104.00
Match Striker, Man, With Mandolin, 5 In. . . . 115.00
Matchbox, Bird & Fan, Wardle, 4 In. . . . 115.00
Mug, Branch Handle, Fielding . . . 81.00
Mug, Flowers, Basket Weave, 3 In. . . . 69.00
Mug, Oak Leaf, Acorn, Basket Weave, Etruscan, 3½ In. . . . 150.00
Mug, Water Lily, Etruscan, 3¼ In. . . . 115.00
Mustache Cup, Saucer, Fan & Scroll, Fielding . . . 115.00
Oyster Plate, Shells, Basket Weave, Cream, Green, Brown Rope Trim, 1880, 6 Piece . . . 1000.00
Pedestal, Dolphin, Shells, Cobalt Blue, Marble Top, 22 In. . . . 518.00
Pedestal, Musical Instruments, Embossed, Schiller & Son, Continental, 44 x 12 In., Pair . . . 1410.00
Pitcher, Bamboo, Basket Weave, 4-Sided, Cobalt Blue, 9 In. . . . 374.00
Pitcher, Bear, Drum On Back, Figural, Holdcroft, 8½ In. . . . 978.00
Pitcher, Chestnut, Twig Feet, Pink, Lavender, Branch Handle, George Jones, 10 In. . . . *illus* 8625.00
Pitcher, Chickens, In Barnyard, 8 In. . . . 196.00
Pitcher, Corn, 6 In. . . . 161.00
Pitcher, Corn, 9½ In. . . . 259.00
Pitcher, Eagle, Flags, Tobacco Plant, c.1876, 10¾ x 6 In. . . . 770.00
Pitcher, Fan, Fish, Flowers, Bulbous, Fielding, 8½ In. . . . 230.00
Pitcher, Figural, Shell, On Waves, Fielding, 7½ In. . . . 431.00
Pitcher, Fish, 4-Sided, Fish Handle, 9½ In. . . . 259.00
Pitcher, Fish, Cobalt Blue, Fish Handle, 8 In. . . . 288.00
Pitcher, Fishnet, George Jones, England, 19th Century, 4¼ In. . . . 118.00
Pitcher, Flowers, Ribbon & Bow, Bamboo Handle, 9½ In. . . . 173.00
Pitcher, Honey Bear, Seated, Figural, 8½ In. . . . 173.00
Pitcher, Lady, Portrait, England, 6½ In. . . . 138.00
Pitcher, Lily Of The Valley, Brown, 6 In. . . . 150.00
Pitcher, Orchid, Leaf Handle, George Jones, 6 In. . . . 489.00
Pitcher, Parrot, Figural, 11 In. . . . 180.00
Pitcher, Shell, Figural, Fielding, 8 In. . . . 431.00
Pitcher, Shell & Seaweed, Etruscan, 5 In. . . . 288.00
Pitcher, Sunflower, Etruscan, Griffin, Smith & Hill, 6 In. . . . *illus* 330.00
Pitcher, Washington, Lincoln, Ribbon Swags, Flared Spout, Oval, c.1876, 5 In. . . . 418.00
Pitcher, Water Lily, Iris, Turquoise Ground, George Jones, 8¼ In. . . . 2415.00
Pitcher, Water Lily, Turquoise, Lear, 6 In. . . . 127.00
Pitcher, Water Lily, Turquoise, Holdcroft, 6 In. . . . 207.00
Planter, Flowers, Hanging, Minton, c.1865, 14 In. . . . 403.00
Planter, Laurel Wreath Handles, Ribbon Ties, Key, Scrollwork, Minton, 12¾ In. . . . 3408.00
Plaque, Fish, Snake, Frog, Leaves, Sea Life, Blue Ground, Palissy Ware, 9½ In. . . . 1495.00
Plaque, Lizards, Flies, Frog, Flowers, Leaves, Ferns, Geoffrey Luff, Palissy, 12 In. . . . 690.00
Plaque, Snake, Lizards, Frog, Sea Creatures, Heavy Grass Ground, Palissy, 12 In. . . . 633.00
Plate, Asparagus, Artichoke, France, 9 In., Pair . . . 138.00
Plate, Asparagus, Basket Weave, France, 9 In., Pair . . . 184.00
Plate, Asparagus, Leaf Attached, Tray, France, 15 In. . . . 230.00
Plate, Asparagus, Luneville, France, 9 In. . . . 104.00
Plate, Bellflower, Leaf, Cobalt Blue, 8 In. . . . 230.00
Plate, Bird In Flight, Flowers, Pebble Ground, Holdcroft, 8½ In. . . . 69.00
Plate, Clematis, Twig Handles, c.1890, 11¾ x 8 In. . . . *illus* 690.00
Plate, Crab, Seaweed, Seashells, Sable Ground, Palissy, Portugal, Early 1900, 8½ In. . . . 378.00
Plate, Cup & Saucer, Albino Shell, Seaweed, Etruscan, 7 In. . . . 184.00
Plate, Fish, Daisy, Turquoise, Holdcroft, 8½ In. . . . 230.00
Plate, Fruit, Plums, Strawberries, Grapes, Cherries, Peaches, Gold Ground, 12 In. . . . 41.00
Plate, Fruit, Yellow Leaves, 12 In. . . . 110.00
Plate, Napkin & Strawberry, Minton, 11½ In. . . . 316.00
Plate, Pond Lily, George Jones, 8 In. . . . 196.00
Plate, Shell Shape, Mottled, 9 In., Pair . . . 150.00

Plate Set, Asparagus, 4 Piece. 196.00
Platter, Apple & Cherry, Vine Handles, Mottled Center, 12 In. . . . . *illus* 374.00
Platter, Cobalt Blue, Leaves, Fern, 12 In. 374.00
Platter, Dog, Doghouse, 11 In. 173.00
Platter, Fan & Scroll, Fielding, 13 In. 150.00
Platter, Mythological Figures Around Border, Palissy, Minton, 14 In.. . . . . 748.00
Rooster, White Body, Red Comb, Wattle, On Branch, 1900s, 18 ¼ x 14 In.. . . . . 206.00
Sardine Box, Dragonflies, Water Lilies, Bird Knop, Relief Molded, 8 ½ In. . . . . *illus* 117.00
Sardine Box, Pink Pointed Leaves, Overlapping Fish, George Jones 1035.00
Sardine Box, Seaweed, Cobalt Blue, Fish Finial, Attached Undertray 489.00
Sauce, Shell & Seaweed, Scalloped Edge, Etruscan, 3 Piece 207.00
Server, Chestnut, Minton, 11 In. 489.00
Server, Sugar & Creamer, Strawberry, Basket Weave, George Jones, 9 In.. . . . . 2415.00
Server Set, Strawberry, Bird, 2 Bowls, Spoon, Sauce, Ladles, George Jones, 1870, 7 Piece 1410.00
Smoke Set, Tray, Matchbox, Striker, Humidor, Cigarette Jar, Gerbing & Stephan 207.00
Spoon, Strawberry, Turquoise Ribbon Handle, Pierced Bowl, George Jones. 288.00
Syrup, Coral, Pewter Top, Etruscan, 6 In. 316.00
Syrup, Morning Glory, Basket Weave, Pewter Top, 4 ¼ In.. . . . . 127.00
Tazza, Fern & Leaf, Lavender Ground, 4 ½ x 8 ¾ In. 330.00
Tea Set, Bamboo & Fern, Wardle. 184.00
Tea Set, Cauliflower, Teapot, Sugar, Creamer, Waste Bowl, Cup, Saucer, Etruscan, 6 Piece. . . . 184.00
Tea Set, Cottage, c.1890, 6 ¾-In. Teapot . . . . . *illus* 748.00
Tea Set, Shell & Seaweed, Teapot, Sugar, Creamer, Spooner, Etruscan, 4 Piece. 403.00
Tea Set, Wild Rose, Rope Trim, Turquoise, 3 Piece. 115.00
Teapot, Bamboo, Basket Weave, Banks & Thorley, 6 ½ In.. . . . . 196.00
Teapot, Cauliflower, Etruscan, Griffin, Smith & Hill, 5 ½ In. . . . . *illus* 230.00
Toothpick, Deer In Woods, Cobalt Blue, W.S. & S., 2 In. 81.00
Tray, Butterflies, Tropical Plants, Textured Ground, George Jones, c.1875, 11 In. 3819.00
Tray, Fox, Cobalt Blue Ground, Green Leaves, Ivy, 12 In. 920.00
Tray, Mermaid, Riding Fish, Shell Corners, Sea Life Border, France, 21 ½ In. 3335.00
Tureen, Cover, Fish, On Bed Of Leaves, Ferns, Basket Weave Base, George Jones, 15 In. 1553.00
Tureen, Cover, Wicker, Pigeon Finial, 3 Pigeon Feet, Oak Leaf, 1864, 9 ½ In. 9988.00
Tureen Set, Mussel & Scallop Shell Form, Ladle, Coral End, B. Pinheiro, Portugal, 4 Piece . . 780.00
Umbrella Stand, Brown, Green, Ocher Glaze, England, 17 ¾ In.. . . . . 236.00
Umbrella Stand, Flowers, Mottled Glaze, 20 In. 81.00
Umbrella Stand, Greek Key Design, Blue, Gold, Green, c.1910, 20 x 10 In.. . . . . 450.00
Umbrella Stand, Herons & Cattails, Sky Blue, Signed, 1890, 8 ½ x 21 In.. . . . . 840.00
Umbrella Stand, Owl, Marked, Betry, 24 In. 2860.00
Umbrella Stand, Tobacco Leaf, 3-Sided, 21 ½ In. 3105.00
Urn, Cover, Harebill & Leaf, Scroll Handles, 33 In.. . . . . 2013.00
Vase, Bird On Branch, Applied, 5 In. 127.00
Vase, Blackamoor, Boy, Girl, Applied, 12 In., Pair. 345.00
Vase, Lion, Cobalt Blue, Footed, Etruscan, 7 In. 460.00
Vase, Monkey & Pineapple, Applied, 7 In. 690.00
Vase, Snowdrop, Cobalt Blue Ground, Flower, Leaf, Acorn Feet, Minton, c.1880, 7 In. 1763.00
Vase, Spill, Rooster, Trunk Shape Base, 20 x 14 x 8 In. 300.00
Vase, Swan & Bulrush, Applied, Adams & Bromley, 11 In. 1610.00
Vase, Winged Putti, Musical Instruments, Lion Head, Cobalt Blue, Palissy, 13 ½ In., Pair 345.00
Vase, Winged Putto, Applied, Cornucopia, England, 14 ½ x 13 In. 690.00
Waste Bowl, Wild Rose, Etruscan, 5 ½ In. 150.00
Wine Cooler, Putti Gathering Grapes, Turquoise, Scalloped, Oval, Minton, 22 x 11 In. 3910.00

MALACHITE is a green stone with unusual layers or rings of darker green shades. It is often polished and used for decorative objects. Most malachite comes from Siberia or Australia.

Box, Gold Metal Rings, 6 ¼ x 2 ½ In. 695.00
Casket, Dore Bronze, Tahan, 19th Century, France, 10 ½ x 5 ½ In.. . . . . 3295.00
Postal Scale, Decorated, Stamped Weights, ½ Oz., 1 Oz., 4 Oz., Mordan, 8 x 5 In. 2200.00
Stamp Box, Vermeil Armorial Crest, Red Silk Lining, Key. 595.00

MAPS of all types have been collected for centuries. The earliest known printed maps were made in 1478. The first printed street map showed London in 1559. The first road maps for use by drivers of automobiles were made in 1901. Collectors buy maps that were pages of old books, as well as the multifolded road maps popular in this century.

Atlas, Butler County, Pictorial Review, Repugnicon Publishing Co., Leather, c.1914. . . . . 270.00
Atlas, Washington County, Ohio, Blind Stamped, Cloth Binding, Various Views, c.1875 . . . . . 242.00

Majolica, Tea Set, Cottage, c.1890, 6 ¾ In. Teapot $748.00

Map, Globe, Celestial, Mahogany Mount, T.M. Bardin, London, c.1850, 23 x 12 In. $2800.00

Map, New Map Of America, John Senex, Engraved, J. Harris, London, 1721, 18 ½ x 22 In. $1870.00

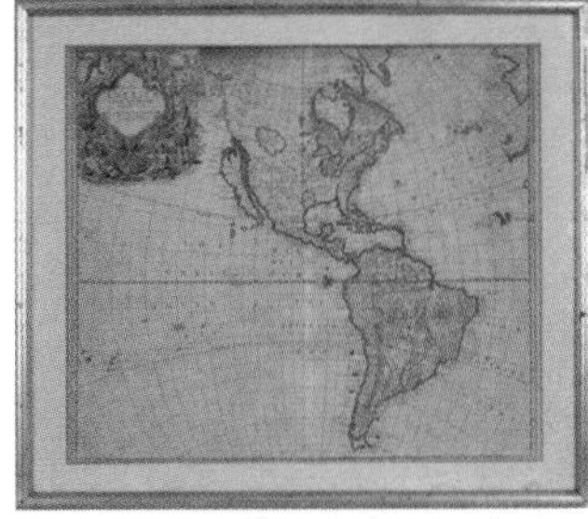

TIP

Do not use transparent tape or other sticky tapes on paper. Even if the tape is removed, the paper will eventually discolor from the contact with the glue.

TIP
It is best to wash marble with distilled water. Any trace of acid or iron in the water will cause deterioration or stains. Use soft soap, a bit of ammonia, and a plastic container.

Bootlegger's, U.S., For Light Medium & Heavy Tipplers, Edward McCandlish, c.1925 .... 1344.00
British Plantations, Canada, Florida, Engraving, London, c.1747, 10 x 10 In. 201.00
Cary's Twelve Miles 'Round London, Gilt Ebonized Frame, 1829, 36 x 43 ½ In. 1920.00
Chicago Harbor, Plan, Captain Thomas Jefferson Cram, c.1839 .... 2352.00
Colorado, Topographical, Louis Nell, c.1906 .... 1120.00
France, Ancient, Charles Knight, London, 1852, 16 x 13 ½ In. 93.00
Globe, Celestial, Constellations, Brass Pins, Painted, Wood Base, c.1940, 5 In. 323.00
Globe, Celestial, Mahogany Mount, T.M. Bardin, London, c.1850, 23 x 12 In. .... *illus* 2800.00
Globe, Lunar, 12 Photos, Landings By Ranger & Apollo Missions, Replogle, 1960s, 12 In. 176.00
Globe, Milk Glass, Black, Red & White, 2-Sided, 1930s, 10 In. 1610.00
Globe, Terrestrial, 12 Engraved Gores, Mahogany Legs, W. Cary Strand, Nov. 1820, 15 In. 6463.00
Globe, Terrestrial, 12 Gores, Arctic Hour Ring, Antarctic Calotte, Plaster, Holbrook, 15 In. ... 940.00
Globe, Terrestrial, Brass Meridian, Turned Mahogany Stand, Mid 19th Century, 14 ¼ In. 1410.00
Globe, Terrestrial, Iron Meridian, Base, Brass Paw Feet, Weber Costello, 39 x 24 In. 2070.00
Globe, Terrestrial, Metal Adjustable Stand, Physical Globe, W. & A.K. Jonson, 16 x 48 In. 450.00
Kentucky, Adjoining Territories, Hand Colored, Russell, Frame, c.1794, 21 x 17 In. 1495.00
Kentucky, Tennessee Government, Indian Villages, Cyrus Harris, Frame, c.1796, 19 x 16 In. . 805.00
Kingdom Of Ireland, 2-Sheet, Elaborate Cartouche, 1780, 50 x 39 In. 470.00
New Map Of America, John Senex, Engraved, J. Harris, London, 1721, 18 ½ x 22 In. ... *illus* 1870.00
North America, Engraved, Thomas Bankes, New System Of Geography, c.1790, 12 x 18 In. .. 374.00
North America, Roll-Up, Wood Hanger, Monk, Jacob, Baltimore, 1854, 60 x 60 In. 1035.00
Ohio, Robert Thomas Anderson, Hand Colored, Gilt Stamped Cover, c.1828, 15 x 13 In. 2990.00
Ohio, Washington County, Tits Simmons & Titus, Frame, c.1875, 16 x 26 In. 144.00
Russian, D'Anville's, Outline Color, 1780, 21 x 51 In. 353.00
United States, According To Treaty Of Paris, Engraving, 9 Maps, John Reid, N.Y., c.1783 .... 863.00
United States, Vignettes, Geo. Washington, Capitol, Case Tiffany & Co., c.1851, 24 x 24 In. .. 1150.00
Virginia, Hand Colored Copper Engraved, Frame, c.1750, 11 ¾ x 13 ¾ In. 187.00
Willis' Plans Of The Cities Of London & Westminster, Ebonized Frame, 1797, 32 x 55 In. 1140.00

MARBLE collectors pay highest prices for glass and sulphide marbles. The game of marbles has been popular since the days of the ancient Romans. American children were able to buy marbles by the mid-eighteenth century. Dutch glazed clay marbles were least expensive. Glazed pottery marbles, attributed to the Bennington potteries in Vermont, were of a better quality. Marbles made of pink marble were also available by the 1830s. Glass marbles seem to have been made later. By 1880, Samuel C. Dyke of South Akron, Ohio, was making clay marbles and The National Onyx Marble Company was making marbles of onyx. The Navarre Glass Marble Company of Navarre, Ohio, and M. B. Mishler of Ravenna, Ohio, made the glass marbles. Ohio remained the center of the marble industry, and the Akron-made Akro Agate brand became nationally known. Other pieces made by Akro Agate are listed in this book in the Akro Agate category. Sulphides are glass marbles with frosted white figures in the center.

Clambroth, Blue, White, 11/16 In. .... *illus* 175.00
Latticinio, 3 Stage White, Yellow, Bands Of Red, Green, Blue & Pink, 2 1/16 In. 575.00
Latticinio, 4 Stage, White, Blue, Yellow, Red, 2 7/32 In. 747.00
Latticinio, Blue, Green, Red, White, 1 15/16 In. .... *illus* 50.00
Latticinio, Blue, White, Brown, Yellow Outer Bands, 13/16 In. 143.00
Latticinio, Blue Core, 4 Stage, White, Yellow & Red Bands, 7/8 In. 402.00
Latticinio, Blue Swirl, White Outer Bands, 11/16 In. 230.00
Latticinio, Clambroth, 3 Stage Yellow & Red Swirl, 5/8 In. 690.00
Latticinio, Cobalt Blue White, 2 7/32 In. 316.00
Latticinio, Core Swirl, Red, White, Blue, Green, Pontil, 1 ¾ In. 66.00
Latticinio, Core Swirl, Red, White, Blue, Pontil, 2 1/8 In. 154.00
Latticinio, Coreless Double, 2 Stages Of Alternating Blue Lines, 1 1/32 In. 3450.00
Latticinio, Cyan Blue, White Outer Bands, 1 5/16 In. 2185.00
Latticinio, Green, White, Early 20th Century, 1 ¾ In. 165.00
Latticinio, Outer Bands Brown, White, Blue, 2 5/32 In. 920.00
Latticinio, Purple, 2 Stage, 11/16 In. 575.00
Latticinio, Red & White Bands, Green, Red & White Outer Bands, 7/8 In. 517.00
Latticinio, Solid Core, Yellow, Green, Red, 2 1/32 In. 402.00
Latticinio, Swirl, Ribbons, Red, Yellow, Blue & Turquoise Bands, 2 1/16 In. 460.00
Latticinio, White, Red, Yellow, Outer Bands, 13/16 In. 750.00
Latticinio, White Core, Tornado, Red, Aqua, 13/16 In. 86.00
Latticinio, White Core, Yellow, Green, Red, White, 2 3/32 In. 230.00
Latticinio, White Swirl, Brown Bands, 2 5/32 In. 920.00
Lutz, Red Ribbon, White Bands, 7/8 In. 977.00
Marble Set, No. 250, 52 Multicolored, Multi-Sized, Sack, Box, Akro Agate, 9 ½ x 5 In. 1000.00

Marble, Clambroth, Blue, White, 11/16 In. $175.00

Marble, Latticino, Blue, Green, Red, White, 1 15/16 In. $50.00

Marble, Onionskin, White, Red, Green, Yellow, Pontil, 1 ¾ In. $748.00

nionskin, 2 Panel, Red, White, Yellow, Blue, 1 15/16 In. 517.00

nionskin, End-Of-Day, Green & Yellow Streaks, Red, 2 3/16 In. 1150.00

nionskin, End-Of-Day, Lobes, Pink, Blue, White, Yellow Swirls, Pontils, 2 1/2 In. 825.00

nionskin, End-Of-Day, Red, White, Blue, Mica Flecks, Pontils, 1 3/4 In. 275.00

nionskin, Lobes, Green, White, Pink, Blue, White & Blue Panels, 2 5/16 In. 632.00

nionskin, Lutz, Blue, White, Red, 7/8 In. 1092.00

nionskin, Mica, 13 Lobes, 2 3/8 In. 1265.00

nionskin, Orange, Yellow, Green, Pontil, Flecks, 2 3/8 In. 4025.00

nionskin, Pink, White & Blue, Streaks, 1 13/16 In. 747.00

nionskin, White, Red, Green, Yellow, Pontil, 1 3/4 In. *illus* 748.00

eppermint Swirl, Blue Bands, Mica, 29/32 In. 2070.00

ottery, Amethyst, Speckled Glaze, 1 3/4 In. 55.00

ottery, Blue Bennington Style Glaze, 1 3/4 In. 88.00

olid Core, Blue & White Fins, Green & White, Outer Bands, 11/16 In. 143.00

olid Core, Yellow Over Bands, 1 7/16 In. 345.00

toneware, Blue Sponge, Salt Glaze, Mid 19th Century, 1 3/4 In. 330.00

ulphide, Frog, Pontil, 2 In. 305.00

ulphide, Rabbit, Running, Early 20th Century, 1 3/4 In. 165.00

ulphide, Santa Claus, 1 5/8 In. *illus* 460.00

wirl, 3 Stage, White Bands, Red With Blue Tip Bands, 7/8 In. 287.00

wirl, Alternating Red, White, Blue, Green & Yellow Bands, 11/16 In. 517.00

wirl, Alternating Red, Yellow, Green & White Ribbons, 21/32 In. 230.00

wirl, Banded Joseph, Clematis With Orange, Lime, Red & Blue Lines, 11 7/32 In. 1150.00

wirl, Broken Core, Red, Green, White, Yellow, Alternating Bands, 2 1/2 In. 86.00

wirl, Divided Core, Green Ribbon With 3 Yellow Lines, Red, White & Blue Outer Lines, 2 11/32 In. 632.00

wirl, Double Core, Red, White & Blue Lines, 2 Yellow Latticinio, Red, Yellow & White, 1 5/8 In. 805.00

wirl, Double Ribbon, White Base, Transparent Pink, Yellow & Orange Lines, Cobalt Cap, 2 5/16 In. 860.00

wirl, Half & Half Naked Ribbon, Yellow, Blue, Red & White, Clear On 1 Side, 7/8 In. 1380.00

wirl, Naked, Divided Core, Red, White, Blue & Yellow Ribbons, 1 3/4 In. 690.00

wirl, Naked Double Ribbon, Red, White & Blue, Red, Green & Yellow, 5/8 In. 172.00

wirl, Red, 11/16 In. 690.00

wirl, Red, Green, Yellow, Blue, White, 11/16 In. 402.00

wirl, Red, White & Blue, Pink With Green Center Ribbon, 7/8 In. 747.00

wirl, Red, Yellow & Green, Red, White & Blue, 2 1/16 In. 1380.00

wirl, Ribbon Core, Yellow & White Outer Bands, 13/16 In. 287.00

wirl, Strands Of Red, Lime, Blue & White, 1 1/2 In. 402.00

wirl, Yellow, Multicolored Core, Outer Pontil, 1 3/4 In. 66.00

wirl, Yellow, Red Caps On Each Fin, 2 1/16 In. 1495.00

/hite Core, Red, White, Blue, Green Outside Swirls, Pontil, 1 3/4 In. 66.00

/hite Core, Yellow & Red Swirl, Pontil, 1 1/4 In. 110.00

IARBLE CARVINGS, such as large or small figurines, groups of people or animals, and rchitectural decorations, have been a special art form since the time of the ancient Greeks. eproductions, especially of large Victorian groups, are being made of a mixture using marble ust. These are very difficult to detect and collectors should be careful. Other carvings are sted under Alabaster.

asin, Half-Shell, Scalloped Rim, Variegated, Drain Hole, 28 x 57 In. 1912.00

owl, Console, Shallow, Cast Bronze Figure, Fighting Cock, Pine Branch, 12 x 9 1/2 In. 489.00

ust, Classical Figure, Flowing Hair, Gazing To His Left, 23 1/2 In. 472.00

ust, Dante, Italy, Early 20th Century, 8 1/4 In. 944.00

ust, Evangeline, Wearing Peasant Blouse, Cross Pendant, Flared Socle, F. Saul, 23 In. 3173.00

ust, Jeanne D'Arc, Carved, Signed, G. Bessi, 13 3/4 In. *illus* 400.00

ust, Julius Caesar, Black Socle, Italy, Late 19th Century, 13 In. 705.00

ust, Julius Caesar, Young, Giuseppe Carnevale, 19th Century, 21 In. 1888.00

ust, Ludwig Van Beethoven, Socle, Continental, Late 1800s, 27 1/2 x 19 In. 235.00

ust, Madame Recamier, Wood Pedestal, 25 In. 4700.00

ust, Maiden, Holding Diaphanous Wrap Against Chest, Italy, 1800s, 20 1/4 In. 1763.00

ust, Napoleon, Socle Base, 19th Century, 24 x 14 x 12 In. 2820.00

ust, Nobleman, 17th Century, Armored, Bewigged, Block Base, 69 x 23 In. 3360.00

ust, Noblewoman, Flower Filled Hair, Pendant Around Neck, 34 In. 708.00

ust, Woman, Lace Bonnet, Flowers, Carved, 18 1/2 In. 1062.00

ust, Woman, Renaissance Dress, Pearl Necklace, Monogram SWS, c.1869, 16 x 11 In. 5500.00

iana, Hanging Cloak, Arm Covers Top, Italian School, 25 1/2 In. 885.00

roup, Three Putti Playing With A Goat, 19th Century, 20 x 20 x 7 In. 3231.00

a Siesta, Man Seated, Black, Polished, F. Castaneda, 1976, 12 In. 8640.00

TIP
Marble will scorch. A marble statue very close to the heat of a 100-watt light bulb may be damaged.

Marble, Sulphide, Santa Claus, 1 5/8 In.
$460.00

Marble Carving, Bust, Jeanne D'Arc, Carved, Signed, G. Bessi, 13 3/4 In.
$400.00

M

TIP
Where to put a marble bust? Not near a window—the outdoor pollutants will discolor it. Not near a fireplace—the smoke will be absorbed. Not near a hot radiator or vent—it may scorch or crack. And not in too damp an environment.

TIP

A good way to remove rings and stains from a white marble top is to mix TSP (trisodiumphosphate, found in paint stores), water, and scouring powder. Rub on the spots. Too much rubbing may remove some of the polish, so be careful.

Marblehead, Pedestal, Rouge, Bronze, Tapered Supports, Paw Feet, 45 x 18 In., Pair
$4113.00

Marblehead, Plate, 3 Wise Men, Camels, Impressed, Child's, 7⅜ In.
$225.00

Marblehead, Vase, Organic, Green Matte Glaze, Handles, Incised, Marked, 2 In.
$600.00

Lions, Mane, Lying, Plinth, 24 x 46 x 17 In., Pair 13145.00
Pedestal, Black, White & Brown Veins, Square Top, Columnar Shape, 35 x 13¾ In. 767.00
Pedestal, Dolphins, Intertwined, Renaissance Style, 42 x 12 In. 1020.00
Pedestal, Green, Round Top, Column Shape, Spiral, Octagonal Base, Late 1800s, 43 x 13 In., Pair. 2415.00
Pedestal, Medallions, Leaves, Canted Corners, c.1865, 34 In., Pair 8962.00
Pedestal, Rectangular Top, Spiral & Turned Support, Octagonal Base, 43 x 24 x 17 In. 443.00
Pedestal, Rouge, Bronze, Tapered Supports, Paw Feet, 45 x 18 In., Pair . . . . . . *illus* 4113.00
Pedestal, Square Top, Turned Plain Columnar Support, Square Base, 36 x 14 In. 620.00
Pedestal, White, 4 Sections, Greek Key Band, Flared, 6-Sided, Top, 10¼ x 42 In. 748.00
Statue, 2 Cherubs Wrestling Over Heart, Quiver & Bow, 18 In. 3186.00
Statue, Allegory Of Charity, Woman, Infant, 19th Century, 42 In. 7050.00
Statue, Aphrodite, Kneeling In Shell, 1876, 18 In. 3819.00
Statue, Baby's New Discovery, Cat By Leg, Italian School, 32½ In. 3540.00
Statue, Boy, Holding Bird, Antonio Argenti, 36½ In. 9375.00
Statue, Carved, Female Nude Holding Clothing, Fruit, Stippled Ground, 19¼ In. 1380.00
Statue, Child, Sleeping, Linen Covered Ground, Quiver, Bow, Carrara, c.1880, 22 In. 1116.00
Statue, Crouching Venus, Nude, Carved, After Roman Antique, Raised Hand, 34 In. 28200.00
Statue, Cupid, Holding Arrow, Roses, 14½ In. 1298.00
Statue, Cupid & Psyche, Antonio Canova, 19th Century, 25 x 25 In. 2360.00
Statue, Nude Man, Draped Woman, Classical, Pedestal, Carrara, 74 x 21 x 18 In. 6000.00
Statue, Nude Woman, Pink, Gray, Wood Base, 20 x 23 In. 230.00
Statue, Nude Woman On Rock, Jane Botsford Armstrong, c.1970, 21 x 8¼ In. 1320.00
Statue, Nymph, Diana's Hunting Dog, Continental, 20th Century, 72 x 28 In. 7638.00
Statue, Putti, Writing, Reading, 29½ x 12½ & 27 x 12 In., Pair 3525.00
Statue, Putto, Seated On Sphere, Carrara, Italy, 19th Century, 23 In. 5310.00
Statue, Rebecca At The Well, Chauncey Bradley Ives, c.1855, 40 In. 11700.00
Statue, Romeo & Juliet, Alabaster, Mounted As A Lamp, 31 In. 2048.00
Statue, Seated Bodhisattva, Lotus Blossom, Guardian Lion, 29th Century, 39½ In. 708.00
Statue, Winged Griffin, Base, 21 In. 3300.00
Statue, Woman, Flowing Hair, Leaf, Ribbon Cartouche, Column Support, 59 In. 2832.00
Statue, Woman, Hand To Breast, Carved, c.1853, 36 In. 1410.00
Statue, Woman, Long Braids, Flowered Dress, Bouquet, White, 15½ In. 295.00
Statue, Woman, Renaissance Bodice, Hair In Bun, 1877, 24 In. 1925.00
Tazza, Sarrancolin, Low, Footed, Round, Early 20th Century, 9½ In. 120.00
Urn, Black Veneer, Parcel Gilt Rim, Water Leaf Base, 18 x 23 In., Pair 460.00
Urn, Dore Bronze, French Veined, c.1880, 24 x 10 In. 2047.00
Urn, Louis XVI, Gilt Bronze, 19th Century, 23 x 8 x 5½ In. 1410.00
Urn, Pedestal, 12 x 5½ In. 88.00
Vase, George III, White, Ormolu Mounted, Blue John, Matthew Boulton, c.1775, 8 In., Pair . . 5200.00

MARBLEHEAD Pottery was founded in 1905 by Dr. J. Hall as a rehabilitative program for the patients of a Marblehead, Massachusetts, sanitarium. Two years later it was separated from the sanitarium and it continued operations until 1936. Many of the pieces were decorated with marine motifs.

Candlestick, Round Base, Green Glaze, Speckled, Cylindrical, 6¾ In., Pair 812.00
Candlestick, Tan Matte Glaze, Slender Shape, Marked, 6¾ x 3½ In. 395.00
Plate, 3 Wise Men, Camels, Impressed, Child's, 7⅜ In. . . . . *illus* 225.00
Tile, Flower Basket, Blue Ground, Frame, Impressed Mark, 6 In. 1560.00
Tile, Sailing Ship, White On Blue Ground, 4¾ x 4¾ In. 354.00
Trivet, Brown Rooster, Red Comb, Tan Feet, Gray Ground, Round, 5 In. 1058.00
Vase, 5 Fruit Trees, Symmetrical, 6⅞ In. 1888.00
Vase, Blue Flower Stalks, Pebble Gray Ground, 8½ x 4 In. 6000.00
Vase, Blue Matte, Tapered, 5 x 8½ In. 600.00
Vase, Blue Matte Glaze, Oval, Flared Rim, 8 In. 499.00
Vase, Blue Matte Glaze, Tapered, Bulbous, Marked, 5½ x 9 In. 660.00
Vase, Blue Stippled Ground, Blue Grape Leaves, Red Fruit Border, Cylindrical, c.1912, 5½ In. 881.00
Vase, Brown, Pea Green Ground, Geometric, 5 x 4¾ In. 13200.00
Vase, Brown Oak Leaves, Acorns, Mustard Ground, Egg Shape, 7 x 4 In. 3900.00
Vase, Brown Pine Boughs, Green Speckled Ground, 12 x 4½ In. 8400.00
Vase, Fruit Trees, Orange, Green, Gray Ground, Tapered, 3½ x 4¼ In. 1920.00
Vase, Grapevines, Grapes, Slate Blue Ground, Cylindrical, Rolled Rim, 8½ In. 5104.00
Vase, Green, Speckled, Bulbous, Impressed, 3¼ In. 406.00
Vase, Green Leaves, Brown Ground, Speckled, Tapered, 6 x 4¼ In. 3900.00
Vase, Multicolored Gray Ground, Organic Decorations, 4¼ x 7 In. 6600.00
Vase, Organic, Green Matte Glaze, Handles, Incised, Marked, 2 In. . . . . *illus* 600.00

Vase, Pink Glaze, High Shoulders, Tapered, Impressed, 3 5/8 In. 580.00
Vase, Purple Matte Glaze, Bulbous, Marked, 5 x 6 1/4 In. 720.00
Vase, Purple Matte Glaze, Tapered, Marked, 8 1/4 x 4 In. 1080.00
Vase, Rose Semimatte Glaze, Bulbous, Wide Mouth, 4 1/4 In. 264.00
Vase, Stylized Flowers, Green Speckled, Barrel Shape, 9 1/2 x 5 1/4 In. 3120.00
Vase, Stylized Leaves, 2 1/4 x 3 1/4 In. 270.00
Vase, Terminals, Blue Glaze, 3 Handles, High Shoulders, Impressed, 1906, 6 1/4 In. 2900.00
Vase, Yellow & Blue Flowers, Gray Ground, Squat, Bulbous, 3 1/2 x 5 In. 3240.00
Vase, Yellow Blossoms, Blue Gray Leaves, Gray Speckled, 4 1/4 x 5 In. 2400.00
Vase, Yellow Blossoms, Brown Leaves, 3 1/2 x 3 In. 1440.00
Vase, Yellow Matte Glaze, Bulbous, Cover, 5 x 6 1/2 In. 660.00

MARTIN BROTHERS of Middlesex, England, made Martinware, a salt-glazed stoneware, between 1873 and 1915. Many figural jugs and vases were made by the three brothers. Of special interest are the fanciful birds, usually made with removable heads. Most pieces have the incised name of the artists plus other information on the bottom.

Pitcher, Incised Sea Creatures, 4-Sided, Stoneware, 1895, 7 1/4 x 6 In. 3480.00
Vase, Crabs, Anemones, 1903, 8 3/4 x 4 In. 6000.00
Vase, Dragons, Stoneware, 11 1/2 x 3 3/4 In. 3600.00
Vase, Dragons, Thistles, Incised, London, 1894, 7 3/8 In. .... *illus* 7250.00
Vase, Fish & Sea Life, 1891, 8 1/2 x 5 1/2 In. 7200.00
Vase, Grotesque Fish & Sea Life, 1913, 6 x 3 In. 4500.00
Vase, Grotesque Sea Life, Stoneware, 7 1/4 x 6 In. 3120.00
Vase, Incised Chrysanthemums, Blue, Gray Ground, Round, Flattened Rim, 6 In. 8555.00
Vase, Incised Thistle, Amber Ground, Stoneware, Signed, 10 1/4 x 5 In. 2880.00

MARY GREGORY is the name used for a type of glass that is easily identified. White figures were painted on clear or colored glass as the decoration. The figures chosen were usually children at play. The first glass known as Mary Gregory was made about 1870. Similar glass is made even today. The traditional story has been that the glass was made at the Sandwich Glass works in Boston by a woman named Mary Gregory. Recent research suggests that it is possible that none was made at Sandwich. In general, all-white figures were used in the United States, tinted faces were probably used in Bohemia, France, Italy, Germany, Switzerland, and England. Children standing, not playing, were pictured after the 1950s.

Bottle, Barber, Girl, Holding Butterfly, Twigs, Emerald Green, Ribs, Rolled Lip, 8 In. 179.00
Bottle, Barber, Girl, With Flower, Turquoise Blue, Ribs, Rolled Lip, 7 3/4 In. 190.00
Bottle, Barber, Woman Standing, Amethyst, Ribs, Rolled Lip, 8 7/8 In. 420.00
Bottle, Barber, Woman's Cameo Head, Clear, Amber Flashed, Coin Spot, 8 1/2 In. 235.00
Plate, Girl, Pulling Sled, Dog, Black Amethyst, Openwork, Signed, E.B. Brown, 1973, 8 1/2 In. .. 55.00
Plate, Girl, Skating, Dog, Black Amethyst, Openwork, Signed, E.B. Brown, 1973, 8 1/2 In. 55.00
Tankard, Girl With Bird On Finger, Sapphire Blue, Rows Of Thumbprint, 11 1/2 In. 264.00
Toothpick, Girl With Flower, Amberina, Red To Gold, Scalloped Rim, Bulbous, 3-Footed, 3 In. .. 202.00
Vase, Cranberry Glass, White Design, Lady In 18th Century Costume, 1900s, 9 x 6 1/2 In. 117.00
Vase, White Cupid, Green, Late 19th Century, 6 3/4 In. 29.00
Vase, Woman & Bird, Ruby Glass, Early 20th Century, 11 In., Pair .... *illus* 250.00

MASONIC, *see Fraternal category.*

MASON'S IRONSTONE was made by the English pottery of Charles J. Mason after 1813. Mason, of Lane Delph, was given a patent for this improved earthenware. He usually called it Mason's Patent Ironstone China. It resisted chipping and breaking so it became popular for dinnerwares and other table service dishes. Vases and other decorative pieces were also made. The ironstone was decorated with orange, blue, gold, and other colors, often in Japanese inspired designs. The firm had financial difficulties but the molds and the name Mason were used by many owners through the years, including Francis Morley, Taylor Ashworth, George L. Ashworth, and John Shaw. Mason's joined the Wedgwood group in 1973 and the name is still found on dinnerwares.

Bowl, Footed, Brown, 10 1/2 In. 72.00
Jardiniere, 2 Handles, Red, Mandalay, 7 1/2 In. 35.00
Jug, Multicolored, Japan Pattern, Marked, 19th Century, 9 3/4 x 7 1/2 In. 330.00
Mug, Chinese Figures In Landscape, 4 In. 58.00
Platter, Multicolored, Anglo-Indian, Flowers, Green Border, Gilt, 19 x 15 In. 360.00
Platter, Multicolored, Japan Pattern, 19th Century, 11 1/4 x 14 1/2 In. 302.00
Vase, Cover, Hexagonal, Gilt Edge, Painted Figures, Scenic, 31 1/2 In., Pair 3125.00

TIP
To remove stains from a glass vase, fill it with warm water and drop in a denture-cleaning tablet.

Martin Brothers, Vase, Dragons, Thistles, Incised, London, 1894, 7 3/8 In.
$7250.00

Mary Gregory, Vase, Woman & Bird, Ruby Glass, Early 20th Century, 11 In., Pair
$250.00

Dinnerware in the Early 1900s
Dinnerware in the average American home in the early 1900s was usually English ironstone or American whiteware for everyday and porcelain from Limoges, France, especially Haviland, for "good" dishes.

M

Massier, Bowl, Ribbons, Art Deco, Metallic Glaze, Marked, C.M. Golfe-Juan, 3 x 7⅝ In.
$300.00

Massier, Vase, Shamrocks, Metallic Glaze, Silver Rim, Marked, C.M. Golfe-Juan, 3½ In.
$375.00

Match Holder, Guessing Man, Seated, White Metal, Gold Finish, 5⅝ In.
$115.00

TIP
The value of a match cover is lowered by writing or marks, scraps or gouge marks from a carelessly removed staple, or a damaged or missing striker.

MASSIER, a French art pottery, was made by brothers Jerome, Delphin, and Clement Massier in Vallauris and Golfe-Juan, France, in the late nineteenth and early twentieth centuries. It has an iridescent metallic luster glaze that resembles the Weller Sicardo pottery glaze. Most pieces are marked *J. Massier*. Massier may also be listed in the Majolica category.

Bowl, Ribbons, Art Deco, Metallic Glaze, Marked, C.M. Golfe-Juan, 3 x 7⅝ In. . . . . *illus* 300.00
Candleholder, Trumpet Shape, Purple & Yellow, Clear Glaze, Handle, 13¼ In. 130.00
Charger, Fish, Waves, Metallic Glaze, Green, Brown, Jerome Massier, 9½ In. 374.00
Compote, Cerulean Glazed, Dolphin, Scallop Shell, 13¼ x 9 In. 1254.00
Pitcher, Poppies, Metallic Glaze, Figural Woman Handle On Shoulder, 12½ In. 590.00
Pitcher, Poppies, Metallic Glaze, Figural Woman Handle, D.M., 17 In. 3540.00
Planter, Figural, Birds & Wishing Well, 9 In. 489.00
Vase, 5-Sided Top Over Cylindrical Body, Leaves, Colorful Metallic Glaze, 2¼ x 4½ In. 480.00
Vase, Butterflies, Moths, Metallic Glaze, Oval, Tapered, 17⅝ In. 3658.00
Vase, Double Gourd, Organic Design, Multicolored Metallic Glaze, 3 x 4½ In. 600.00
Vase, Figural, Rooster, Standing Beside Tree Trunk, Black, Tan, Red, c.1875, 17½ In. 1898.00
Vase, Green, Brown Iridescent, Etched Birds, Waves, Fishtail Handles, Signed, 8½ x 4¾ In. . . 990.00
Vase, Indented Shape, Leaf Impressions, Colorful Metallic Glaze, 3 x 4 In. 480.00
Vase, Pinched, Mottled Tan To Green Glaze, Dragonfly & Cattails, 5 x 7½ In. 1800.00
Vase, Shamrocks, Metallic Glaze, Silver Rim, Marked, C.M. Golfe-Juan, 3½ In. . . . . *illus* 375.00
Vase, Shouldered, Metallic & Crystalline Glaze, Textured Drip, 4½ x 10 In. 1320.00
Vase, Shouldered, Metallic Glaze, Etched Leaves, 3½ x 8¾ In. 1020.00
Vase, Swollen, Leaf Designs, Colorful Metallic Glaze, 3 x 6¼ In. 570.00
Vase, Twisted Bud, Silver Peapod Vine, Signed, 6 x 2¼ In. 1080.00

MATCH HOLDERS were made to hold the large wooden matches that were used in the nineteenth and twentieth centuries for a variety of purposes. The kitchen stove and the fireplace or furnace had to be lit regularly. One type of match holder was made to hang on the wall, another was designed to be kept on a tabletop. Of special interest today are match holders that have advertisements as part of the design.

3 White Mice, Figural, 4 In. 90.00
Acorn, On Stand, Mechanical, 1862, 4⅝ In. 115.00
Bird, On Trough, Pine, Wire Legs, Black Paint, Patina, Carved, 4 x 7 In. 770.00
Bliss Native Herbs, Great Blood Purifier, Tin Lithograph, Wall 154.00
Boy On Bucket, Marble Base, Brass Plate, Late 1800s, 5¾ In. 103.00
Boydell Bros. Paints, Best Paint On Earth, Calendar, Tin Lithograph, 1907, 7⅞ x 5 In. 385.00
Bryant & Hays, Donkey, Walking, Embossed, 5½ In. 103.00
Ceresota, Prize Bread Flour Of The World, Boy, Barrel, Tin Lithograph, 51/4 x 21/4 In. . 154.00 to 209.00
Ceresota Flour, Farmer Boy, Cutting Bread, Tin Lithograph, Die Cut, Embossed, 2 x 5 In. . . . 224.00
Chicago Boys Clothier, Turtle Form, Cast Iron, Hinged Lid, 1¼ x 5¼ x 3 In. 176.00
Chief Cigars, Figural, Indian Head Base, Embossed, Cast Iron, 2¼ x 4 In. 358.00
Crystal Spring Brewing Co., Blue, Salt Glaze, Stoneware, Syracuse, N.Y., 5 In. 220.00
DeLaval Separator Co., Separator Shape, Tin Lithograph, 6¼ x 3½ In. 209.00
Elephant In Suit, Bronze, Signed, Stevens, 4½ In. 460.00
Fly, Figural, Cast Iron, Embossed Silver Lettering, Hinged Lift Up Wing, 2 x 4¾ In. 660.00
General Gordon, Bust, Cast Iron, 5 In. 115.00
Green's August Flower, Black Man, Cardboard, 5 x 8 In. 230.00
Guessing Man, Seated, White Metal, Gold Finish, 5⅝ In. . . . . *illus* 115.00
Guiness Is Good For You, Barrel, Brown, Black, White, Porcelain, 4 x 5 In. 40.00
Juicy Fruit, The Man, Wm. Wrigley, Tin Lithograph, 5 x 3¼ x 1 In. 235.00
Kellogg & Curtis, Boy & Girl By Well, Cardboard, 7⅜ x 5 In. 735.00
Lemon, On Leaves, Yellow, Green, Brown, Cold Paint, Terra-Cotta, Marked, 70, 2¾ x 5½ In. . 165.00
Lighter, Black Man Sitting, Copper, White Metal, 6 In. 29.00
Man, Smoking Pipe, Rosewood, Ivory, China, c.1930, 7 In. 200.00
Old Hickory Wagons, Wagon, Tin Lithograph, 3½ In. 415.00
Old Judson, J.C. Stevens, Man, Woman, Child, Tin Lithograph, Kansas City, Mo., 5 x 3¼ x 1 In. 330.00
Oriental Woman, Baskets, Majolica, 9 In. 184.00
Perpetual Calendar, Lusitania, Sinking, Porcelain, Wlm. Livesey, Eng., 1915, 7½ In. . . *illus* 150.00
Saloon Bell, Brass Tray, Lever Style, Ribbed, Late 1800s, 6½ In. 144.00
Sarcophagus, Hieroglyphics, Brass, 4 In. 173.00
Sheffield Milling Co., Fly, Cast Iron, 2 x 4¾ x 2 In. 240.00
Striker, Blue Glaze, Porcelain, 4 In. 44.00
Striker, Devil's Head, Cast Iron, 6 In. 295.00
Stylized Birds, Gouged Feathers, Geometrics, Slide Lid, Tapered, Wood, Carved, 4¾ x 8 x 2 In. 330.00
Turtle, Old Connecticut Fire Hartford, Cast Iron, Embossed, 5¼ In. 230.00

MATCH SAFES were designed to be carried in the pocket. Early matches were made with phosphorus and could ignite unexpectedly. The matches were safely stored in the tightly closed container. Match safes were made in sterling silver, plated silver, or other metals. The English call these "vesta boxes."

Comic Man, Removable Hat, Iron Art, 4 ¼ In. . . . *illus* 198.00
Drunkard, Painted, Silvered Brass, Early 1900s, 2 ½ In. . . . *illus* 570.00
Home Insurance Company, N.Y., 2 Firemen, Hose, Silver Plated, 2 ½ In. . . . *illus* 400.00
Indian Head, Wood, Wall Mount, 8 ¾ In. . . . 83.00
Sharples Cream Separators, Celluloid, Metal, 3 x ⅕ In. . . . 385.00
Sharples Separator Co., Tubular Cream Separator, Tin Lithograph, 2 In. . . . 275.00
Silver, Monogrammed D, c.1908, 2 In. . . . 82.00
Silver Wax, Annual Dinner, Vesta Embossed, Feb. 12, 1909 . . . 325.00
Tree Trunk, Relief, Painted, Stoneware, c.1880, 2 ½ In. . . . 176.00

MATT MORGAN, an English artist, was making pottery in Cincinnati, Ohio, by 1883. His pieces were decorated to resemble Moorish wares. Incised designs and colors were applied to raised panels on the pottery. Shiny or matte glazes were used. The company lasted less than two years.

Bowl, Pumpkin Color, Sparrows, Bamboo, Gilt Trim, Signed Matt Daly, 6 In. . . . 345.00
Vase, Pillow, Bees Flying Around Pink Roses, Fired-On Gold, 14 ⅜ In. . . . 1610.00
Vase, Squat, Orange, Bird, Stalk Of Leaves, Sponged Gold, 2 ½ x 4 ¾ In. . . . 161.00

McCOY pottery was made in Roseville, Ohio. Nelson McCoy and J.W. McCoy established the Nelson McCoy Sanitary and Stoneware Company in Roseville, Ohio, in 1910. The firm made art pottery after 1926. In 1933 it became the Nelson McCoy Pottery Company. Pieces marked *McCoy* were made by the Nelson McCoy Pottery Company. Cookie jars were made from about 1940 until December 1990, when the McCoy factory closed. Since 1991 pottery with the McCoy mark has been made by firms unrelated to the original company. Because there was a company named Brush-McCoy, there is great confusion between Brush and Nelson McCoy pieces. See Brush category for more information.

McCoy

Bank, Woodsy Owl, Marked, Box, 1974, 8 ⅜ In. . . . *illus* 43.00
Bean Pot, Amber Ware, Marked, No. 2, 6 ⅝ In. . . . *illus* 7.00
Bookends, Violin, Aqua, 9 ¼ In. . . . 65.00
Bowl, Shell, Green, Footed, 6 ¼ In. . . . 15.00
Candy Dish, Leaf, Green . . . 15.00
Coffee Server, El Rancho, Metal Stand, 9 ½ In. . . . *illus* 99.00
Cookie Jar, Boy On A Baseball, 1983 . . . 275.00
Cookie Jar, Chipmunk, 1960-61 . . . 50.00
Cookie Jar, Clown, Bust, 10 In. . . . 15.00
Cookie Jar, Coalby Cat, 1967 . . . 175.00 to 185.00
Cookie Jar, Cookie Cabin, 1956-60 . . . 15.00
Cookie Jar, Cookie House, 1958-60 . . . 30.00
Cookie Jar, Covered Wagon, 7 ¼ In. . . . 35.00
Cookie Jar, Have A Happy Day, Yellow, 11 In. . . . 15.00
Cookie Jar, Hobby Horse . . . 525.00
Cookie Jar, Honey Bear, 1953-55, 8 ½ In. . . . 25.00
Cookie Jar, Indian Head, 1954-56, 11 In. . . . 200.00
Cookie Jar, Kissing Penguins, 1940-43, 8 ¾ In. . . . 25.00
Cookie Jar, Kitten On Coal Bucket, 1983, 10 In. . . . 130.00
Cookie Jar, Mac Dog, 1967-68, 11 ¼ In. . . . 50.00
Cookie Jar, Puppy, Holding Sign, 1961-62, 9 ½ In. . . . 30.00
Cookie Jar, Snoopy, Marked, 11 In. . . . *illus* 50.00
Cookie Jar, Teapot, Slant Lid, 1956-59 . . . 140.00
Cookie Jar, Thinking Puppy, Marked, 10 ½ In. . . . *illus* 20.00
Cookie Jar, Timmy Tortoise, 1977-80, 9 ½ In. . . . 13.00
Cookie Jar, W.C. Fields, c.1972, 10 ½ In. . . . 225.00
Cookie Jar, Woodsy Owl, 1973-74, 9 ½ In. . . . 95.00
Dish, Leaf, Blue . . . 825.00
Dish, Lily Bud, Turquoise Matte Glaze, 1940s, 7 ¾ x 6 In. . . . 65.00
Flower Holder, Praying Hands, 1940s, 3 In. . . . 95.00
Flowerpot, Buff Color, Black Stripes, c.1929 . . . 85.00
Jardiniere, Basketweave, Brown & Green, 16 In. . . . 65.00
Jardiniere, Butterfly, Aqua, With Pot & Saucer, 7 In. . . . 50.00
Jardiniere, Rustic Pine Cone, 4 In. . . . 50.00

Match Holder, Perpetual Calendar, Lusitania, Sinking, Porcelain, Wlm. Livesey, Eng., 1915, 7 ½ In.
$150.00

Match Safe, Comic Man, Removable Hat, Iron Art, 4 ¼ In.
$198.00

Match Safe, Drunkard, Painted, Silvered Brass,Early 1900's, 2 ½ In.
$570.00

Match Safe, Home Insurance Company, N.Y., 2 Firemen, Hose, Silver Plated, 2 ½ In.
$400.00

McCoy, Bank, Woodsy Owl, Marked, Box, 1974, 8⅜ In.
$43.00

McCoy, Bean Pot, Amber Ware, Marked, No. 2, 6⅝ In.
$7.00

McCoy, Coffee Server, El Rancho, Metal Stand, 9½ In.
$99.00

McCoy, Cookie Jar, Snoopy, Marked, 11 In.
$50.00

McCoy, Cookie Jar, Thinking Puppy, Marked, 10½ In.
$20.00

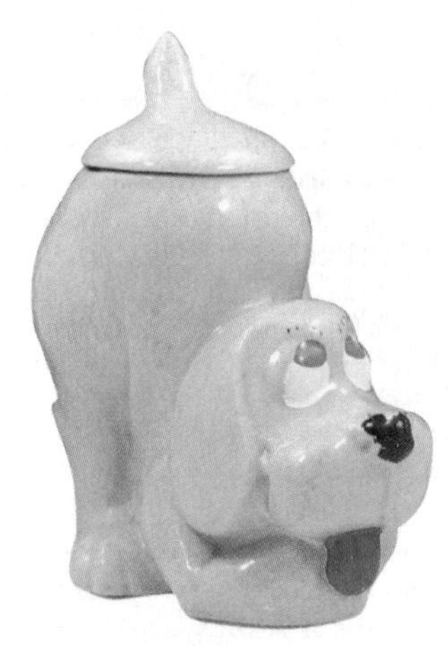

McCoy, Planter, Train, 6 x 10 In.
$25.00

Jardiniere, Woodland, Ivory 55.00
Jug, Brown Neck, Stoneware, No. 2, Marked, 2 Gal. 50.00
Pedestal, Diamond Pattern, Green, Yellow, Art Deco, Signed, c.1930, 13 x 9 In., Pair 175.00
Planter, Bird Dog, No Hunting, 1950s, 61/2 In.. .... 50.00 to 105.00
Planter, Pear, 1950s, 6 ½ In. 25.00
Planter, Pussy At The Well, 1957, 7 In. 73.00
Planter, Train, 6 x 10 In. .... *illus* 25.00
Planter, Triple Fawn, 1954, 12 In.. .... 145.00
Planter, Zebra, 1950s, 8 ½ In. 1000.00
Vase, Crackled Pink Ground, Applied Crimson Flower, Footed, Paneled, Flared, 5 ¾ In. 45.00
Vase, Lily, White, 8 In.. .... 55.00
Vase, White, 15 In. 65.00
Wall Pocket, Apples, 7 x 6 In., Pair 70.00
Wall Pocket, Bellows, Brown, 1956, 9 ½ In. 35.00
Wall Pocket, Berry & Leaf, Pink, 7 ½ In. 90.00
Wall Pocket, Dog Head, Yellow, 1950, 6 In. 30.00
Wall Pocket, Fan, Pink, 1960s, 8 ½ In., Pair 60.00
Wall Pocket, Grapes, Marked, 7 ¼ x 6 ¼ In. .... *illus* 48.00
Wall Pocket, Lady In Bonnet, 1940s, 8 In. 70.00
Wall Pocket, Violin, Brown 30.00
Wall Pocket, Violin, White, Pair 65.00

McKEE is a name associated with various glass enterprises in the United States since 1836, including J. & F. McKee (1850), Bryce, McKee & Co. (1850 to 1854), McKee and Brothers (1865), and National Glass Co. (1899). In 1903, the McKee Glass Company was formed in Jeannette, Pennsylvania. It became McKee Division of the Thatcher Glass Co. in 1951 and was bought out by the Jeannette Corporation in 1961. Pressed glass, kitchenwares, and tablewares were produced. Jeannette Corporation closed in the early 1980s. Additional pieces may be included in the Custard Glass and Depression Glass categories.

McKee

Clock, Shelf, Pressed Glass, Daisy & Button, Tambour, c.1930, 6 ¼ In.. .... 165.00
Dish, Elephant Cover, Split Ribbed Base, Milk Glass, Signed, 5 In. .... *illus* 1680.00
Dish, Frog Cover, Split Ribbed Base, Milk Glass, Signed, 4 ½ In. .... *illus* 690.00
Salt & Pepper, Glass, Swan, 3 In. 55.00
Salt & Pepper, Glass Delphite, Foil Label, Euclid Coffee Co., Cleveland, 6 ¼ In. 32.00
Salt & Pepper, Ships Decal, Roman Arch, Milk Glass, Black Bakelite Lids, 4 In.. .... 49.00
Spice Set, Roman Arches, Jade Green, 4 In., 14 Piece 140.00

MECHANICAL BANKS *are listed in the Bank category.*

MEDICAL office furniture, operating tools, microscopes, thermometers, and other paraphernalia used by doctors are included in this category. Veterinary collectibles are also included here. Medicine bottles are listed in the Bottle category. There are related collectibles listed under Dental.

Amputation Kit, Field, Saw, Touniquet, Cauterizing Tool, Knives, Civil War, 21 In. 798.00
Atomizer, Spray, Electric Motor, Nickel Plated Flywheel, C.M. Sorensen, c.1910, 45 In. 118.00
Bag, Doctor's, Black Leather, Brass Fittings, Miss Liberty Head Latch, Civil War, 13 In. 470.00
Bleeding Bowl, Tin, Embossed With Floral Figures, 11 In.. .... 575.00
Blood Transfusion Apparatus, Needle, Bone Handle, Brass Cylinder, Weiss, 10 In. 118.00
Box, Traveling, Mahogany, Hinged Lid, False Drawer, 16 Potion Bottles, c.1840, 10 x 10 In.. .... 538.00
Bullet Probe, Silvered Steel, Ebony Handle, Schlotterbeck & Co., Civil War, 12 ⅜ In. 425.00
Cabinet, Apothecary, 8 Drawers, 40 ½ x 22 x 33 ¾ In. 825.00
Cabinet, Apothecary, 24 Drawers, Paneled Sides, 70 x 23 x 32 In. 1155.00
Cabinet, Apothecary, 45 Dovetailed Drawers, Paper Labels, Chinese, 1900s, 46 x 24 In.. .... 2530.00
Cabinet, Apothecary, Curly Maple, Poplar, Drawers, Paneled Doors, 35 x 30 In. 1840.00
Cabinet, Apothecary, Mahogany, 6 Drawers, 28 x 11 x 28 ½ In. 83.00
Cabinet, Apothecary, Mahogany, 44 Small Drawers, 18 Large Drawers, 46 x 89 In. 9400.00
Cabinet, Apothecary, Pine, 2 Sections, Scalloped Facing, 24 Cubbyholes, 65 x 49 In. 1380.00
Cabinet, Apothecary, Pine, Red Traces, 14 Drawers, Brass Knobs, 37 x 10 In. 1175.00
Chest, Apothecary, Pine, Red Paint, 30 Drawers, Brass Pulls, 30 x 25 x 7 In. 2585.00
Chest, Apothecary, Pine, Black, Yellow Letters, 9 Drawers, Brass Pulls, 24 x 34 x 13 In. 3173.00
Chest, Apothecary, Traveling, Pine, Slant Top, 37 Bottles, Stoppers, 10 x 20 In.. .... 600.00
Chest, Medicine, Art Deco, Mirrored, Ivory, Black Paint, Glass Shelves, 28 x 23 In. 275.00
Chest, Medicine, Homoeopathic, Bottles, Wood Box, Zahn & Seeger, Germany, 6 x 3 In.. .... 217.00
Chest, Traveling, 3 Drawers, Hinged Top, Bail Handle, Brass Ring Pulls, 16 x 15 x 9 In. 299.00
Coffin, Salesman's Sample, Wood, Inlay Design, Silk Lining, Skeleton, 4 ½ x 1312 In.. .... 1430.00
Cork Press, Pharmacy, Cast Iron, 19th Century 100.00

McCoy, Wall Pocket, Grapes, Marked, 7 ¼ x 6 ¼ In.
$48.00

McKee, Dish, Elephant Cover, Split Ribbed Base, Milk Glass, Signed, 5 In.
$1680.00

McKee, Dish, Frog Cover, Split Ribbed Base, Milk Glass, Signed, 4 ½ In.
$690.00

TIP

If you have unopened bottles of drugs or other pharmaceuticals, be sure to check for ether or picric acid. These can explode spontaneously and are dangerous to keep.

TIP
Keep a "mystery disaster" box. If you find a piece of veneer, an old screw, or even a porcelain rosebud, put it into the box until you are able to make the necessary repairs.

Meissen, Figurine, Pagoda, Movable Head, Hands, Tongue, Crossed Swords, 7 In.
$9565.00

Meissen, Group, Lovers, Harlequin, Woman, Cupid, Amorous Suitor, c.1741-43, 7 ¼ In.
$2160.00

Cupboard, Apothecary, Painted, 19th Century, 72 x 12 x 24 In. 2310.00
Dose Glass, Monogram, Mortar & Pestle, Embossed, Acadia Drug Co., Ltd., La., 1 In. 358.00
Enema Kit, Brass Pump, Bone Fittings, Tube, Angled Nozzles, Mahogany Case, 9 In.. . . . . 353.00
Forceps, Cuts Umbilical Cord, Stork Shape, Beak Forming Grips, Silver, 3 ¾ In.. . . . . 441.00
Head, Phrenology, Porcelain, Sectional Skull, England, c.1875, 8 In. 508.00
Heartometer, Round Paper, Wood, Cameron Heartometer Co., c,1935, 9 x 8 In. 572.00
Leech Jar, Baked Clay, 18th Century, 2 In. 323.00
Leg, Wooden, Leather Covered Support, Civil War Era, 46 In. 353.00
Lens Case, Ophthalmological Trial, 135 Lenses, Brass, 3 Frames, Oak, c.1900, 16 x 14 In. . . . 241.00
Machine, Quack, Magneto-Electric, Compound, Hand-Cranked, Patd. 1859, 10 In.. . . . . 118.00
Microscope, Traveling, Scale, Monoscope, Brass, Dr. Thomas Frye, c.1850s 450.00
Quack Device, Nervous Disorders, Belt, Tin Paddles, Mahogany Case, c.1854, 4 x 10 In.. . . . . 550.00
Saw, Amputation, Pre-Sterilization, Ebony Handle, Caduceus Symbol, 10 In.. . . . . 50.00
Saw, Bow, Surgical, 8-Sided, Faceted, Ebony Handle, Civil War Era, 9 ½ In.. . . . . 264.00
Saw, Metacarpal, Surgeon's, W.F. Fori, N.Y., 7 In. 121.00
Scalpels, Ivory, Celluloid, Wooden Case, Fitted, Blue Velvet Lining, Early 1900s, 7 In. 95.00
Showglobe, Acorn Shape, Glass, Etched, Cast Iron, Stopper, Parke-Davis 880.00
Specimen, Primate, Vertebrae, Mounted, Wrought Iron Stand, Ivory, Patinated 35 x 9 In. . . . 360.00
Stethoscope, Ivory, Mahogany, Pug, 19th Century, 8 x 1 ¾ In.. . . . . 4000.00
Surgeon's Kit, Fitted Mahogany Box, Brass Trim, Dr. Thomas Frye, c.1860, 5 x 16 In.. . . . . 6500.00
Surgeon's Kit, Original Leather Case, Philadelphia, c.1860 . . . . . 2750.00
Surgical Set, Bone Handles, Rosewood Case, Tiemann, New York, Civil War, 12 In.. . . . . 9988.00
Syringe, Case, Lacquered Brass, Wire End Cups, Ferrie & Co., Liverpool, 1800s, 9 In.. . . . . 85.00
Syringe, Glass, Wood Stopper, Cork, Box, Batting Lining, Victorian, 9 ¼ In. 50.00
Table, Wake, Drop Leaf, Queen Anne Style, Mahogany, Drop Leaves, Oval Top, 32 x 88 In.. . . . 1840.00
Urinal, Salesman's Sample, Handles, China, Crown Trademark, 19th Century, 3 ½ In. 264.00
Vampire Killing Kit, Pistol, Flask, Bullets, Stake, Cross, Vials, Case, c.1910, 2 x 17 x 8 In. . . . 4313.00
Vaporizer, Universal Multi-Nebular, Glass Reservoir, Patd. 1892, Oak Base, 12 In.. . . . . 499.00

MEISSEN is a town in Germany where porcelain has been made since 1710. Any china made in the town can be called Meissen, although the famous Meissen factory made the finest porcelains of the area. The crossed swords mark of the great Meissen factory has been copied by many other firms in Germany and other parts of the world. Pieces of Meissen dinnerware in the Onion pattern are listed in their own category in this book.

Basket, Fruit, Applied Flower Handles, Blue Underglaze, 9 In., Pair. 236.00
Bowl, Basket Form, Cobalt Blue, Leaves, Flowers, 10 ½ x 16 x 8 ½ In. 600.00
Bowl, Cobalt Blue, Gold Leaf, Painted Flower Interior, Basket Shape, 10 x 16 x 8 In. 672.00
Bowl, Cover, Bacchus Riding Chariot, Ariadne Seated, Attended By Satyr, c.1725, 5 In. 9600.00
Bowl, Flowers, Insects, Gilt, Crossed Swords Mark, 19th Century, 14 In.. . . . . 415.00
Bowl, Fruit, Cobalt Blue, Gilt, Rococo, Crossed Swords, 12 In. 1020.00
Bowl, Fruit, Embossed Grape Leaf, Blue Underglaze, Crossed Swords, 14 In.. . . . . 148.00
Bowl, Fruit, Vintage Pattern, Reticulated, Oval, Crossed Swords, 12 ¾ x 8 ½ In. 180.00
Bowl, Reticulated, Flowers, Gilt, Footed, Crossed Swords Mark, 7 ¾ x 12 x 8 In. 525.00
Bowl, Rococo Scrolls, Oakleaf Tendrils, Oakleaves In Well, White & Blue, 1850, 11 ½ In.. . . . 165.00
Bowl, Shaped Border, Rococo Scrolls, Oakleaf, Cobalt Blue Glaze, c.1870, 2 ⅛ x 11 ½ In. . . . 165.00
Box, Cover, Cartouche Shape, Flowers, Gilt, Blue Crossed Swords, c.1790, 5 x 10 x 5 In.. . . . . 465.00
Butter Tub, Cover, Blue Underglaze, Crossed Swords, Mid 18th Century, 4 ⅞ In. 2160.00
Candelabrum, Man, Woman Holding Branches, Candle Sockets, Pair 8 In.. . . . . 1534.00
Centerpiece, Figural, Porcelain, Reticulated, Rococo, Couple, Around Tree, 19 In. 1200.00
Charger, Flowers, 13 ½ In.. . . . . 499.00
Compote, Figural, Flowers, Multicolored 1404.00
Creamer, Cover, Turquoise Ground, Oval, 3-Footed, c.1740, 5 ⅝ In.. . . . . 2400.00
Cup & Saucer, Birds In Flight, Gilt Leaf Border, Cobalt Blue Ground, c.1770, 5 ¼ In. 960.00
Cup & Saucer, Flower Heads, Leaves, Twig Handles, Schneeballen, c.1945-50, 5 ⅜ In. 1800.00
Dish, Gilt Rim, Lattice Edge, Oval, Hand Painted, 6 ⅝ x 7 ⅝ In., Pair. 499.00
Dish, Leaf Form, Flowers, 6 ¼ x 7 ¼ In.. . . . . 499.00
Figurine, 2 Figures, Angel, Marked, 12 ¾ x 13 In. 4973.00
Figurine, Angel, Cornucopia, Fame, Blue Crossed Swords Mark, 6 ½ In. 805.00
Figurine, Boy With Carrier Pigeon, Lamb, Blue Crossed Sword Mark, c.1810, 7 ½ In. 2200.00
Figurine, Children Sitting, Late 19th Century, 7 ¾ x 8 ¾ In.. . . . . 1400.00
Figurine, Cockatoo, Blue Crossed Swords Mark, 8 ¾ In. 1093.00
Figurine, Columbine, Malabar, Gilt Rouge De Fer, Porcelain, c.1890, 13 x 14 In., Pair 2640.00
Figurine, Fisherman, Holding Net With Fish, Flowers, Leaves, c.1745-50, 7 ½ In.. . . . . 3000.00
Figurine, Girl, 4 ½ In. 176.00
Figurine, Goat, Straddling Overturned Basket Of Flowers, Oval Base, 5 ¾ In. 1116.00

Figurine, Harlequin, Playing Bagpipes, c.1745, 5¾ In. . . . 2700.00
Figurine, Lady Dancing, Purple Skirt, Short Black Cape, Early 1900s, 5¼ In. . . . 470.00
Figurine, Man, Pitcher, Garden Fountain, Applied, Painted Flowers, Rococo Base, 14 In. . . . 236.00
Figurine, Man, With Fish Basket, 18th Century, 6½ In. . . . 1652.00
Figurine, Musician, Flowers, Leaves, Applied Base, c.1745-50, 8⅛ In. . . . 4800.00
Figurine, Pagoda, Movable Head, Hands, Tongue, Crossed Swords, 7 In. . . . *illus* 9565.00
Figurine, Pan, Blowing Pipe, Child In Cradle, Blue Crossed Swords, Mark, W, 6½ In. . . . 748.00
Figurine, Satyr, Playing Pan Flute, Infant In Cradle, Blue Underglaze, 6½ In. . . . 826.00
Figurine, Woman, Holding Book, At Spinning Wheel, 6½ In. . . . 950.00
Figurine, Woman, Resting, Blue Underglaze, 7¼ In. . . . 1180.00
Group, 3 Fruit Pickers, Apple Tree, Crossed Swords Mark, 11 In. . . . 1888.00
Group, Allegorical, 2 Women, Cherub, Porcelain, 12¾ x 13 In. . . . 4973.00
Group, Apple Harvest, Boy, On Ladder Picking Apples, Boys, Woman At Base, 12 In. . . . 944.00
Group, Bacchus, Nymph, Putti, Early 20th Century, 12 In. . . . 177.00
Group, Betrothal, Man Greeting Woman, Putto, c.1750, 5⅞ In. . . . 3300.00
Group, Birds, 2 Thrushes On Leaf, 19th Century, 7 In. . . . 325.00
Group, Children, Goat, Blue Crossed Swords Mark, 1800s, 6¼ In. . . . 748.00
Group, Courting Couple, Flower Garlands, Late 1800s, Marked, 8½ x 7 In. . . . 2400.00
Group, Courting Couple, Tree, Lamb, Bocage, 1800s, 10 x 9½ In. . . . 840.00
Group, Dancers, Man In Pink Suit, Embracing Woman, c.1760, 7½ In. . . . 960.00
Group, Family, Seated, 19th Century, 9 x 7 In. . . . 1638.00
Group, Lovers, Harlequin, Woman, Cupid, Amorous Suitor, c.1741-43, 7¼ In. . . . *illus* 2160.00
Group, Man, Woman, Seated Below Apple Tree, Girl Standing Behind, 10½ x 6 In. . . . 1840.00
Group, Nymph, Satyr, Kissing, Obelisk, c.1770, 10¼ In., Pair . . . 3600.00
Group, Rococo Musician, Woman, Blue Glaze, Crossed Swords, Mounted As Lamp, 6 In. . . . 300.00
Group, Shepherd Standing, Knitting, 3 Sheep, Oval Base, 14⅜ x 17½ In. . . . 1058.00
Group, Sight For The Senses, Blue Crossed Swords, 19th Century, 11 x 7 x 5 In. . . . *illus* 2160.00
Group, Woman, Holding Arm Of Man, Crossed Swords Mark, 7½ In. . . . 730.00
Group, Woman, Monkey On Plinth, Putto, Footed Base, 11½ x 7 In. . . . 2400.00
Group, Woman, Looking Through Telescope, Putto With Lantern, Eagle, 11¼ x 7 In. . . . 2160.00
Lamp, Ram's Head Bronze Mounts, Electric, 21 In. . . . 200.00
Perfume Bottle, Figural, Boy Pruning Tree, Blue Crossed Swords, Mark, c.1890, 5 In. . . . 510.00
Plate, Bird Center, Basket Weave Border With Insects, Crossed Swords Mark, 10 In., Pair . . . 173.00
Plate, Bouquets, Gilt Border, Blue Crossed Swords Mark, 8¼ In., 11 Piece . . . 316.00
Plate, Cherub Design, Gilt, 9 In. . . . 350.00
Plate, Dinner, Flowers, 9¾ In., 12 Piece . . . *illus* 494.00
Plate, Flowers, Multicolored, Gilt Rim, 19th Century, 11 In. . . . 150.00
Plate, Luncheon, Flowers, 8¼ In., 12 Piece . . . 440.00
Plate, Luncheon, Flowers, Lattice Rim, Gilt Edge, 8 In., 8 Piece . . . 820.00
Plate, Salad, Gilt Rim, Flowers, 7¾ In., 12 Piece . . . 999.00
Plate, Scenic, Hunters In Wooded Landscape, Flower Sprigs, Late 1800s, 9½ In. . . . 118.00
Plate, Service, Painted Bouquets, Basket Weave Border, Gilt Rim, 10 In., 12 Piece . . . 748.00
Platter, Flower, Hand Painted, Oval, 13¼ x 18¾ In. . . . 470.00
Platter, Painted Flowers, White Field, 19¼ In. . . . 431.00
Salt, Basket, Woman Holding Flower, Man With Flowers, 4¾ x 5½ x 3 In., Pair . . . 1064.00
Salt, Circular Basket, Women Busts, Footed, Handles, c.1736, 4 In., Pair . . . 2160.00
Sconce, Mirrored, Cherub Holding Floral Swag, Applied Flowers, 17½ x 11 In. . . . 1057.00
Soup, Dish, Rimmed, Flowers, 9¼ In., 12 Piece . . . 646.00
Spoon Tray, Miners, Wheelbarrow Filled With Ore, c.1740, 6 In. . . . 2700.00
Sugar, Cover, Flowering Branches, Birds, Insects, Butterflies, Oval, c.1725-30, 4¾ In. . . . 1440.00
Tea Service, Pitcher, Sugar, Creamer, Flowers, 3 Piece . . . 382.00
Teakettle, Globular, Figures, Landscape, Bronze Supports, Porcelain Handle, c.1850, 10 In. . . . 1792.00
Tray, Scalloped, Center Portrait, Victorian Man, Women, Flowers, Marked, 10¾ In. . . . 395.00
Tureen, Cover, Footed U-Form, Women's Head Handles, Flower Sprays, c.1730, 12 In. . . . 3900.00
Tureen, Cover, White, Painted Lilies, Scroll Handles & Finial, 10 x 14 In. . . . 411.00
Urn, Blue, Pastel Flowers, Pierced Side Handles, Gilt Trim, Footed, c.1960, 10 In. . . . 175.00
Urn, Double Snake Handle, Floral Bouquet, Gilt Highlights, Marked, 19 In. . . . 300.00
Vase, Amphora Shape, Reeded, Fluted Foot, Coiled Snake Handles, c.1910, 15 In., Pair . . . 1888.00
Vase, Art Nouveau, Floriform, Pierced Top, Blue Decoration, Early 1900s, 7¾ In. . . . 991.00
Vase, Baluster, 2 Handles, Hand Painted Flowers, White Ground, Footed, 11⅜ In. . . . 118.00
Vase, Cobalt Blue Ground, Flower Reserve, Snake Handles, Fluted Foot, 10¾ In. . . . 588.00
Vase, Figural, Bearded Man With Dragon, Blue Underglaze, Blanc De Chine, 5¾ In. . . . 384.00
Vase, Leaves, Teal Ground, Orchids, 5½ x 2¾ In. . . . 412.00
Vase, Pate-Sur-Pate, Mauve, Gray, Gilt Leaves, Medallion, 1800s, 5½ In. . . . 3408.00
Vase, Snake Handles, Blue Underglaze, Pommeled Swords Mark, 11 In. . . . 472.00

Meissen, Group, Sight For The Senses, Blue Crossed Swords, 19th Century, 11 x 7 x 5 In.
$2160.00

Meissen, Plate, Dinner, Flowers, 9¾ In., 12 Piece
$494.00

TIP

Cleaning a lot of small figurines or other collectibles? Line the sink with a towel. Put the pieces in the sink. Spray them with window cleaner. Move them to another towel on the counter to air dry.

TIP

Sweet Annie (Ardemisia annua) *is a fragrant herb that can help remove odors from antiques. Put some fresh sprigs inside the drawer or box or book that needs deodorizing and in a few days the smell will be gone. Be sure the many plant seeds do not become embedded in fabrics or corners.*

Metlox, Cookie Jar, Teddy Bear, 11 ½ In.
$101.00

Metlox, Homestead Provincial, Pitcher, 16 Oz.
$120.00

MERCURY GLASS, or silvered glass, was first made in the 1850s. It lost favor for a while but became popular again about 1910. It looks like a piece of silver.

Salt, Engraved Leaves, New England, 3 ⅛ In., Pair. 147.00

MERRIMAC POTTERY Company was founded by Thomas Nickerson in Newburyport, Massachusetts, in 1902. The company made art pottery, garden pottery, and reproductions of Roman pottery. The pottery burned to the ground in 1908.

Vase, 2 Handles, Green Semimatte Glaze, Marked, 4 x 4 ¼ In. 840.00

METLOX POTTERIES was founded in 1927 in Manhattan Beach, California. Dinnerware was made beginning in 1931. Evan K Shaw purchased the company in 1946 and expanded the number of patterns. Poppytrail (1946-1989) and Vernonware (1958-1980) were divisions of Metlox under E.K. Shaw's direction. The factory closed in 1989.

Antique Grape, Bowl, Vegetable, Cover, 10 In. 105.00
Antique Grape, Salt & Pepper. 36.00
Aztec, Salt & Pepper 35.00
California Apple, Gravy Boat, 4 x 10 ½ In. 28.00
Cookie Jar, Humpty Dumpty, 11 In. 362.00
Cookie Jar, Lion, 12 In. 157.00
Cookie Jar, Mammy, White Dress, Yellow Polka Dot 568.00
Cookie Jar, Slenderella Pig, 13 In. 215.00
Cookie Jar, Squirrel, On Pinecone, 12 In. 165.00
Cookie Jar, Teddy Bear, 11 ½ In. . . . . *illus* 101.00
Cookie Jar, Topsy, 10 ½ In. 605.00
Della Robbia, Bowl, Vegetable, Cover, 10 In. 105.00
Fruit Traditional, Canister Set, Covers, Poppy Trail, 4 Piece 171.00
Homestead Provincial, Bean Pot, Handle, 7 ¾ In. 154.00
Homestead Provincial, Pitcher, 16 Oz. . . . . *illus* 120.00
Navajo, Teapot, Rattan Handle 138.00
Red Rooster, Bowl, Vegetable, Cover, Qt., 10 In. 102.00
Red Rooster, Bread Plate, 9 In. 103.00
Red Rooster, Canister Set, Cover, 4 Piece 265.00
Red Rooster, Carafe, Warmer, 6 Cup, 4 Piece. 143.00
Red Rooster, Dish, Cover, 6 ½ In. 122.00
Tickled Pink, Bowl, Vegetable, 9 ¼ In. 19.00
Tickled Pink, Coffeepot, 11 In. 55.00
Tickled Pink, Gravy Boat 11.00

METTLACH, Germany, is a city where the Villeroy and Boch factories worked. Steins from the firm are marked with the word *Mettlach* or the castle mark. They date from about 1842. *PUG* means painted under glaze. The steins can be dated from the marks on the bottom, which include a date-number code. Other pieces may be listed in the Villeroy & Boch category.

Beaker, No. 2327-1134, ¼ Liter, PUG. 92.00
Beaker, No. 2327-1137, ¼ Liter, Girl With Pitcher, PUG. 81.00
Beaker, No. 2327-1302, ¼ Liter, American Eagle, PUG. 81.00
Box, No. 7028, Lid, Phanolith, 4 Scenes, Stahl, 6 In. 754.00
Butter, No. 1207, Silver Plated Lid, 5 In. 145.00
Butter, No. 2116, Man Milking Cow, Mosaic, 5 In. 242.00
Compote, No. 3340, Flowers, 6 x 6 ½ In. 480.00
Cup, No. 3481, Berries, Footed, Etched, Wekara, 2 ¾ In. 61.00
Ewer, No. 2486, Swans In Stream, Etched, Otto Eckman, 7 ½ In. 475.00
Honey Jar, No. 1208, Barrel Form, Glazed Relief, Silver Plated Lid, 3 ½ In. 95.00
Planter, No. 2208-001, Mosaic, 10 x 12 ½ In. 483.00
Plaque, No. 220-1044, Burghof Der Wartburg, PUG, 12 In. 207.00
Plaque, No. 1044, Cherubs, PUG, 12 In. 193.00
Plaque, No. 1044-94, Altes Stadtthor Cochem, PUG, 12 In. 212.00
Plaque, No. 1044-158, Remagen, PUG, 12 In. 217.00
Plaque, No. 1044-169, Dresden Altstadt, PUG, 12 In. 78.00
Plaque, No. 1044-204, Estate House Scene, PUG, Erbach, 12 In. 173.00
Plaque, No. 1044-5078, City Scene, Blue, White, Delft, PUG, 17 ½ In. 2875.00
Plaque, No. 1044-5418, Girl Feeding Chicks, Gilt, Delft, 12 In. 242.00
Plaque, No. 1044-9022, Wild Boar, Gold Rim, 17 ½ In. 403.00

Plaque, No. 1044-9027, Fox, 14 In. 460.00
Plaque, No. 1244-1044, 2 Girls, Dog, PUG, 17 In. 574.00
Plaque, No. 2079, Soldiers Riding Horses On Beach, 15 ⅛ In. 1121.00
Plaque, No. 2081, Soldier On Horse, Beach, Etched, 15 ⅛ In. 805.00
Plaque, No. 2147, Horses Pulling Cannon, Etched, 15 ⅛ In. 1323.00
Plaque, No. 2546, Woman, Flowers, Lizard, Etched, 9 ½ x 15 ⅛ In. 1610.00
Plaque, No. 2564, Bike Riders, Etched, 17 ½ In. 3650.00
Plaque, No. 2698, Troll Under Mushroom, Butterflies, Etched, 17 In. 6900.00
Plaque, No. 2739, Munchen, Buildings, Etched, 19 In. 2760.00
Plaque, No. 2898, Landscape, Woman, Prunus, Etched, 17 In. 1323.00
Plaque, No. 3225-1290, Munchen, PUG, 16 x 13 In. 604.00
Plaque, No. 5036, Hannover, Delft, 17 ½ In. 432.00
Plaque, No. 7055, Phanolith, White Figures, Blue Ground, 9 x 7 ½ In. 311.00
Punch Bowl, No. 1859, Tavern Scene, Underplate, Lid, Etched, C. Warth, 9 Liter 518.00
Punch Bowl, No. 2088, Courting Couple, Cherub, Underplate, Lid, H. Schlitt, 9 Liter 1691.00
Stein, No. 24, 1 Liter, Scenes Of People, 4 Panels, Relief, Inlaid Lid 207.00
Stein, No. 280, ½ Liter, Eagle, Pewter Lid 299.00
Stein, No. 280, ½ Liter, Crest, Relief, Pewter Lid 362.00
Stein, No. 280, ½ Liter, Corpus Juris, Brass Lid 423.00
Stein, No. 485, ½ Liter, Warriors Fighting, White, Relief, Inlaid Lid, Gnome Finial 250.00
Stein, No. 812, 1 Liter, Hunting Scenes, Relief, Pewter Lid 276.00
Stein, No. 1005, 1 Liter, Tavern Scene, Relief, Inlaid Lid .... 127.00 to 308.00
Stein, No. 1028, ½ Liter, Man, Woman, With Harvest, Relief, Inlaid Lid 75.00
Stein, No. 1120, 3 ¼ Liter, Repeat Design, Mosaic, Pewter Lid 538.00
Stein, No. 1132, ½ Liter, Man Playing Violin, Crocodile, Inlaid Lid 435.00
Stein, No. 1190, ½ Liter, Mosaic, Etched, Pewter Lid 187.00
Stein, No. 1284, 3 Liter, Mosaic, Inlaid Lid 242.00
Stein, No. 1288, ½ Liter, Leaf & Acorn, Mosaic, Inlaid Lid 544.00
Stein, No. 1288, ½ Liter, Mosaic, Footed, Inlaid Lid 345.00
Stein, No. 1379, ½ Liter, Man In Archway, Etched, Pewter Lid 420.00
Stein, No. 1396, ½ Liter, Nymph Drinking, Etched, Silver Plated Lid, C. Warth 207.00
Stein, No. 1431, ½ Liter, Student Society Teutonia U. Budissa Sei's Panier, c.1890 .... 305.00
Stein, No. 1452, ¼ Liter, Flowers, Mosaic, Inlaid Lid 161.00
Stein, No. 1453, ½ Liter, Dwarf, Sitting In Nest, Etched, Inlaid Lid 472.00
Stein, No. 1467, ½ Liter, 4 Harvest Scenes, Relief, Inlaid Lid 98.00
Stein, No. 1526, 1 Liter, Berliner Unions Brauerei, Transfer, Pewter Lid 332.00
Stein, No. 1526, 1 Liter, Gasthaus, Hand Painted, Pewter Lid 483.00
Stein, No. 1526-599, 1 Liter, Soldier Blowing Trumpet, PUG, Pewter Lid 237.00
Stein, No. 1526-702, 3 Liter, Beer Parade, PUG, Pewter Lid 345.00
Stein, No. 1526-1076, ½ Liter, Man Holding Cane, Relief, PUG, Eagle Finial, Lid, H. Schlitt 177.00
Stein, No. 1526-1078, ½ Liter, Man Smiling, PUG, Pewter Lid, H. Schlitt 155.00
Stein, No. 1570, ½ Liter, Leaf Design, Mosaic, Inlaid Lid 292.00
Stein, No. 1642, 1 Liter, Man Drinking, Tapestry, Pewter Lid 293.00
Stein, No. 1648, ½ Liter, Man Holding Open Stein, Tapestry, Pewter Lid 288.00
Stein, No. 1655, ½ Liter, Men, Women Dancing, Pewter Lid 362.00
Stein, No. 1656, ½ Liter, Men, Women Dancing, Pewter Lid, Etched 92.00
Stein, No. 1725, ¼ Liter, Man & Woman, Etched, Inlaid Lid, C. Warth .... *illus* 230.00
Stein, No. 1758, 1 Liter, Man Drinking, Verse, Relief, Tapestry, Pewter Lid 288.00
Stein, No. 1786, ½ Liter, St. Florian, Village Scene, Dragon Handle, Etched .... *illus* 735.00
Stein, No. 1789, ½ Liter, Flowers, Mosaic, Inlaid Lid 345.00
Stein, No. 1851, 3 Liter, Gut Heil, Etched, Pewter Lid 1932.00
Stein, No. 1909-1042, ½ Liter, Man, Woman Holding Key, PUG, Pewter Lid 345.00
Stein, No. 1914, ½ Liter, Man Holding Flag, Etched, Inlaid Lid 399.00
Stein, No. 1917, ¼ Liter, Mosaic Leaf, Flower, Green Ground, Pewter Lid, Pair 224.00
Stein, No. 1932, ½ Liter, Cavaliers Drinking, Etched, Pewter Lid, C. Warth 504.00
Stein, No. 1940, 3 Liter, Keeper Of Wine Cellar, C. Warth 1120.00
Stein, No. 1979, ½ Liter, Man, Fur Hat, Drinking, Etched, Inlaid Lid 529.00
Stein, No. 1997, ½ Liter, Bearded Man, Etched, PUG, Inlaid Lid 236.00
Stein, No. 2001, ½ Liter, Cornell University, Books, Song, Relief, Inlaid Lid 4715.00
Stein, No. 2001A, ½ Liter, Law, Etched, Relief, Inlaid Lid 513.00
Stein, No. 2001C, ½ Liter, Books, Etched, Relief, Inlaid Lid 725.00
Stein, No. 2003, ½ Liter, Cavalier, Etched, Inlaid Lid 420.00
Stein, No. 2005, ½ Liter, 4 People Having Dinner, Etched, Inlaid Lid 472.00
Stein, No. 2007, ½ Liter, Black Cat, Hiddigeigei, Etched, Inlaid Lid, F. Stuck .... 661.00 to 674.00
Stein, No. 2009, ½ Liter, Man & Woman Dancing, Etched, Inlaid Lid 462.00

Mettlach, Stein, No. 1725, ¼ Liter, Man & Woman, Etched, Inlaid Lid, C. Warth
$230.00

Mettlach, Stein, No. 1786, ½ Liter, St. Florian, Village Scene, Dragon Handle, Etched
$735.00

Mettlach, Stein, No. 2809, ½ Liter, Der Getrelle Eckart, Etched, Inlaid Lid, F. Guidenus
$310.00

TIP

If the hinge that holds the lid on a stein or other metal object is balky, try lubricating it.

Milk Glass, Dish, Dog Cover, 5 ½ In.
$74.00

Milk Glass, Dish, Duck Cover, Green, Applied Glass Eyes, Challinor, Taylor & Co., 8 In.
$2070.00

Milk Glass, Dish, Duck Cover, Nest, Base, Applied Eyes, Painted, Challinor, Taylor & Co., c.1890, 8 In.
$184.00

Milk Glass, Dish, Monkey Cover, Scroll & Flower Base, Flaccus, 5 ½ In.
$1265.00

Milk Glass, Dish, Swan Cover, Christmas Tree Base, Challinor, Taylor & Co., 7 In.
$748.00

Stein, No. 2024, ½ Liter, Coat Of Arms, Etched, Inlaid Lid, Pewter Strap 569.00
Stein, No. 2034, ⅓ Liter, Repeating Design, Mosaic, Inlaid Lid 217.00
Stein, No. 2035, ½ Liter, Festive Scene, Etched, Inlaid Lid 403.00
Stein, No. 2043, ⅔ Liter, Mosaic, Flowers, Etched, Pewter Lid 604.00
Stein, No. 2049, ½ Liter, Chessboard, Etched, Pewter Lid 1202.00
Stein, No. 2065, 2 ½ Liter, Man & Barmaid, Etched, Inlaid Lid, H. Schlitt 828.00
Stein, No. 2069, ½ Liter, Monkey, Holding Fish, Stoneware 1668.00
Stein, No. 2076, 2 Liter, Coat Of Arms, Relief, Inlaid Lid 240.00
Stein, No. 2092, ½ Liter, Dwarf Adjusting Clock, Etched, Inlaid Lid, H. Schlitt .... 460.00 to 662.00
Stein, No. 2093, ½ Liter, Cards, Etched, Inlaid Lid .... 362.00 to 633.00
Stein, No. 2097, ½ Liter, Music, Etched, Inlaid Lid 104.00
Stein, No. 2100, ⅓ Liter, Germans Meeting Romans, Etched, Inlaid Lid 483.00
Stein, No. 2106, ⅓ Liter, Monkeys In Cage, Monkey Handle, Etched, Relief, Inlaid Lid 2760.00
Stein, No. 2107, 3 Liter, Men Dancing, PUG, Pewter Lid 403.00
Stein, No. 2140-745, ½ Liter, Garde-Grenadier-Regt. Nr. 91, PUG, Pewter Lid 604.00
Stein, No. 2140-764, ½ Liter, Ulanen-Regt. Nr. 16, PUG, Pewter Lid 259.00
Stein, No. 2140-799, ½ Liter, Pionier-Bataillon Nr. 4, PUG, Pewter Lid 544.00
Stein, No. 2140-942, ½ Liter, Deinbier, PUG, Pewter Lid 230.00
Stein, No. 2141, ½ Liter, Tubingen, Etched, Pewter Lid 3278.00
Stein, No. 2182, ½ Liter, Bowling Scene, Relief, Inlaid Lid 138.00
Stein, No. 2222, ½ Liter, Signatures, PUG, Inlaid Lid 423.00
Stein, No. 2271-1020, ½ Liter, Barmaid Speaking To Crowd, PUG, Pewter Lid 161.00
Stein, No. 2277, ½ Liter, Burg Nurnberg, Figural Lion, Etched, Inlaid Lid 725.00
Stein, No. 2278, ½ Liter, Soldiers, Relief, Pewter Lid 230.00
Stein, No. 2382, ½ Liter, Thirsty Rider, Etched, Inlaid Lid, H. Schlitt 460.00
Stein, No. 2388, ½ Liter, Pretzels, Inlaid Lid 230.00
Stein, No. 2403, ½ Liter, Castle, Etched, Inlaid Lid 672.00
Stein, No. 2419, 4 Liter, Men Drinking, PUG, Pewter Lid, H. Schlitt 1323.00
Stein, No. 2430, 3 Liter, Cavalier, Etched, Pewter Lid 644.00
Stein, No. 2556, ½ Liter, Drinking Scene, Relief, Pewter Lid 200.00
Stein, No. 2580, 1 Liter, Die Kannenburg, Etched, Inlaid Lid, H. Schlitt 690.00
Stein, No. 2632, ½ Liter, Men Seated At Tables, Etched, Inlaid Lid 483.00
Stein, No. 2652, ½ Liter, Man Kneeling, Man Seated, Pewter Lid 230.00
Stein, No. 2716, ½ Liter, Waitress, Men, Etched, Inlaid Lid, F. Quidenus 676.00
Stein, No. 2716-954, 2 Liter, Drinking Scenes, PUG, Pewter Lid, H. Schlitt 820.00
Stein, No. 2724, ½ Liter, Mason, Etched, Inlaid Lid 716.00
Stein, No. 2765, 1 Liter, Knight, White Horse, Etched, Inlaid Lid, H. Schlitt ...... 799.00 to 2116.00
Stein, No. 2766, ½ Liter, Man Drinking, Etched, Inlaid Lid 604.00
Stein, No. 2778, 1 Liter, Tavern Scene, Etched, Inlaid Lid, H. Schlitt 1472.00
Stein, No. 2780, 1 Liter, Lovers, Etched, Inlaid Lid 178.00
Stein, No. 2796, 3 Liter, Heidelberg, Etched, Inlaid Lid 1035.00
Stein, No. 2809, ½ Liter, Der Getrelle Eckart, Etched, Inlaid Lid, F. Guidenus .... *illus* 310.00
Stein, No. 2829, 1 Liter, Rodenstine, Etched, Relief, Inlaid Lid 1323.00
Stein, No. 2871, 1 Liter, Cornell University, Etched, Inlaid Lid 700.00
Stein, No. 2878, 1 Liter, Women, Tapestry, Pewter Lid 245.00
Stein, No. 2934, ½ Liter, Wheat, Leaves, Etched, Inlaid Lid 759.00
Stein, No. 2939, ½ Liter, Barmaid Holding Steins, Etched, Inlaid Lid 574.00
Stein, No. 3003, ½ Liter, Man Holding Paper, Art Nouveau, Etched, Pewter Lid, F. Ringer 262.00
Stein, No. 3043, ½ Liter, Knight, Holding Shields, Etched, Pewter Lid 575.00
Stein, No. 3078-421, ½ Liter, Red Flower Wreath, Enamel, Inlaid Lid, Marked, Bavaria 242.00
Stein, No. 3087, 1 Liter, Woman With Stein Of Beer, Etched, Pewter Lid 785.00
Stein, No. 3099, 3 Liter, Bearded Man Sitting In Barrel, Etched, Inlaid Lid, H. Schlitt 2013.00
Stein, No. 3202, ½ Liter, Man & Woman In Car, Etched, Inlaid Lid 1610.00
Stein, No. 5020, 3 Liter, Munchen, Faience, Pewter Lid 777.00
Stein, No. 5023, 1 Liter, Prussian Eagle, Faience, Pewter Lid 2415.00
Stein, No. 5188, ½ Liter, Cavalier, Delft, Pewter Lid 308.00
Tobacco Jar, No. 4505, Tabac, Man, Etched, 5 ¼ In. 546.00
Toothpick, No. 1440, Flowers, Relief, 2 ½ In. 104.00
Vase, No. 1317, Flowers, Mosaic, Etched, 3 ½ In. 129.00
Vase, No. 1623, Mosaic, Deep Blue, 3-Footed, 5 ¾ In. 311.00
Vase, No. 1728, Peacock, Etched, Brown, Blue, 7 In. 228.00
Vase, No. 1808, Geometric, Brown, Tan, Mosaic, 10 In. 230.00
Vase, No. 2416, Art Nouveau, Flowers, 6 Handles, Etched, Hein, 16 In. 690.00
Vase, No. 2434, Flowers, Red, Blue Ground, Ruffled Rim, Etched, 7 In. 489.00

M

Vase, No. 2461, Cameo, Figures, Gray, White, Handles, Footed, 8¾ In. 334.00
Vase, No. 2905, Art Nouveau, White, Blue, Handles, 9¼ In. 311.00
Vase, No. 2910, Flowers, Art Nouveau, Etched, Marked, 6 x 16 In. 840.00
Vase, No. 5029, Flowers, Entwined Handles, 4 In. 92.00

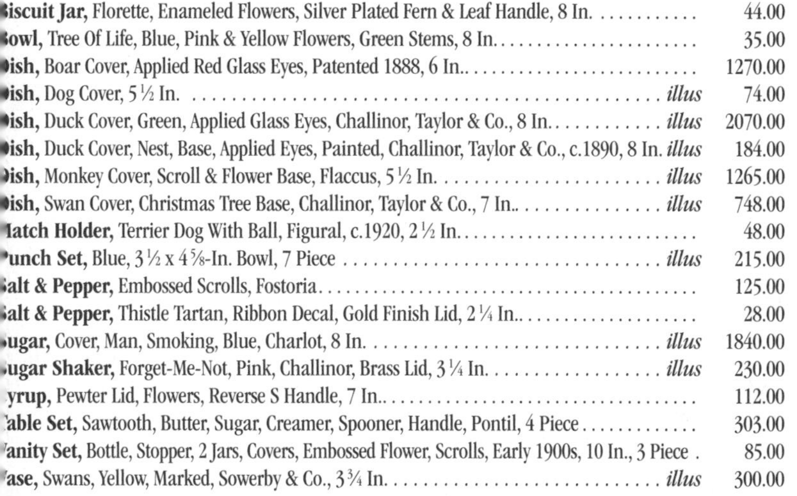

MILK GLASS was named for its milky white color. It was first made in England during the 1700s. The height of its popularity in the United States was from 1870 to 1880. It is now correct to refer to some colored glass as blue milk glass, black milk glass, etc. Reproductions of milk glass are being made and sold in many stores. Related pieces may be listed in the Cosmos, Fallerysthal, and Westmoreland categories.

Biscuit Jar, Florette, Enameled Flowers, Silver Plated Fern & Leaf Handle, 8 In. 44.00
Bowl, Tree Of Life, Blue, Pink & Yellow Flowers, Green Stems, 8 In. 35.00
Dish, Boar Cover, Applied Red Glass Eyes, Patented 1888, 6 In. 1270.00
Dish, Dog Cover, 5½ In. *illus* 74.00
Dish, Duck Cover, Green, Applied Glass Eyes, Challinor, Taylor & Co., 8 In. *illus* 2070.00
Dish, Duck Cover, Nest, Base, Applied Eyes, Painted, Challinor, Taylor & Co., c.1890, 8 In. *illus* 184.00
Dish, Monkey Cover, Scroll & Flower Base, Flaccus, 5½ In. *illus* 1265.00
Dish, Swan Cover, Christmas Tree Base, Challinor, Taylor & Co., 7 In. *illus* 748.00
Match Holder, Terrier Dog With Ball, Figural, c.1920, 2½ In. 48.00
Punch Set, Blue, 3½ x 4⅝-In. Bowl, 7 Piece *illus* 215.00
Salt & Pepper, Embossed Scrolls, Fostoria 125.00
Salt & Pepper, Thistle Tartan, Ribbon Decal, Gold Finish Lid, 2¼ In. 28.00
Sugar, Cover, Man, Smoking, Blue, Charlot, 8 In. *illus* 1840.00
Sugar Shaker, Forget-Me-Not, Pink, Challinor, Brass Lid, 3¼ In. *illus* 230.00
Syrup, Pewter Lid, Flowers, Reverse S Handle, 7 In. 112.00
Table Set, Sawtooth, Butter, Sugar, Creamer, Spooner, Handle, Pontil, 4 Piece 303.00
Vanity Set, Bottle, Stopper, 2 Jars, Covers, Embossed Flower, Scrolls, Early 1900s, 10 In., 3 Piece 85.00
Vase, Swans, Yellow, Marked, Sowerby & Co., 3¾ In. *illus* 300.00

MINTON china has been made in the Staffordshire region of England from 1793 to the present. The firm became part of the Royal Doulton Tableware Group in 1968, but the wares continued to be marked *Minton*. Many marks have been used. The word *England* was added in 1891. Minton majolica is listed in this book in the Majolica category.

Charger, Woman Being Protected By Angry Dog, Painted, Multicolored, 1878, 15⅜ In. 353.00
Coffee Set, Blue, Floral, 6 Cups, 6 Saucers, Coffeepot, Creamer, 15 Piece 72.00
Creamer, Cobalt Blue, Flowers, Snail Feet, Twig Handle, 1871, 5 In. 1035.00
Figurine, Dorthea, Seated On Rock, Parian, 13¾ In. 353.00 to 558.00
Figurine, Miranda, John Bell, Parian, c.1851, 15 In. 558.00
Figurine, Rooster & Hen, 1866, 6 In. 1438.00
Figurine, Solitude, J. Lawlor, Art Union Of London, Parian, c.1852, 19¼ In. 411.00
Figurine, William Shakespeare, John Bell, Parian, c.1851, 17¾ In. 499.00
Garden Seat, Cobalt Blue, Passion Flower, Drum Form 2415.00
Jardiniere, Chartreuse & White Water Lily, Footed, High Relief, 25 In. 316.00
Jardiniere, Malachite Lions' Heads, Paw Feet, 18 In. 690.00
Jardiniere, Monumental, Mosaic Design, 14 x 10½ In. 360.00
Jardiniere, Stand, Relief Flowers, Leaves, Blue Ground, Bamboo Handles, Rim, c.1856, 15 In. 2703.00
Oyster Plate, 9 Well, Majolica, Seamist Green Wells, c.1868, 10 In. 1093.00
Pitcher, Earthenware, Gray Provincial Scene, Flowers, Late 19th Century, 8½ x 8½ In. 88.00
Pitcher, Earthenware, Green Transfer Leaves, Village View, 19th Century, 8½ x 8½ In. 88.00
Plate, Dinner, Pomegranate, Parcel Gilt, Burnt Orange, Ivory, 10 In., 12 Piece 600.00
Plate, Turquoise Ribbon Band, Gilt Medallion, 9¼ In., 6 Piece 144.00
Plate Set, Scenic, Pink, Gilt Borders, 12 9¼-In. Plates, Footed Serving Dish, 2½ x 9¼ In. 431.00
Salt, Figural, Shell On Shells & Seaweed, 1876, 3 In. 1093.00
Tazza, White Ground, Ruins Landscape, Gilt, Cobalt Blue Bands, 2½ x 9¼ In., Pair 147.00
Tile, Man Leaning On Wall, Ruined Building In Background, 6 x 12 In. 188.00
Tile, Sailing Ships, 6 x 6 In., 4 Piece 353.00
Tray, Figural, Oak Leaf, Blue Titmouse Sitting On Edge, 1868, 8 In. 207.00
Tureen, Cover, Rabbit, Duck, Quail, Oakleaves & Acorns On Basket Weave Base, 12 In. 2128.00
Urn, Cover, Haldes, Yellow, Peach, Green Ground, Bird In Flight, Gold Trim, 7¼ In. 100.00
Vase, Bluebird, Red Ground, Flat Sides, Gilt Rim, Footed, Signed, Mintons, 6¼ In. *illus* 275.00
Vase, Exotic Bird, Chrysanthemums, Butterflies, Blue Ground, Pink Interior, Marked, 14 In. 632.00
Vase, Grapes, Bluebird, Red Ground, High Glaze, Round, Flat Sides, Gold Rim, 54 In. 325.00
Vase, Queen, Cat Head, Branch Handles, Ivy Relief, Green, Yellow, 27 In. 7480.00

Milk Glass, Punch Set, Blue, 3½ x 4⅝-In. Bowl, 7 Piece
$215.00

Milk Glass, Sugar, Cover, Man, Smoking, Blue, Charlot, 8 In.
$1840.00

Milk Glass, Sugar Shaker, Forget-Me-Not, Pink, Challinor, Brass Lid, 3¼ In.
$230.00

Milk Glass, Vase, Swans, Yellow, Marked, Sowerby & Co., 3¾ In.
$300.00

Minton, Vase, Bluebird, Red Ground, Flat Sides, Gilt Rim, Footed, Signed, Mintons, 6¼ In.
$275.00

M

Mocha, Mug, Brown, Yellow Sponge, Blue Rim, 3¾ x 4½ In.
$160.00

Mocha, Mug, Earthworm, Cat's-Eye, Brown, Blue, Black, Early 19th Century, 6 In.
$3737.00

Mocha, Pitcher, Earthworm, Pale Blue, Wavy White Lines, Applied Handle, c.1885, 6⅞ In.
$3050.00

TIP

Cups are best stored by hanging them on cup hooks. Stacking cups inside each other can cause chipping.

MOCHA pottery is an English-made product that was sold in America during the early 1800s. It is a heavy pottery with pale coffee-and-cream coloring. Designs of blue, brown, green, orange, black, or white were added to the pottery and given fanciful names, such as Tree, Snail Trail, or Moss. Mocha designs are sometimes found on pearlware. A few pieces of mocha ware were made in France, the United States, and other countries.

Basin, Earthworm, Blue, Looping, 3¾ x 10¾ In. . . . 7050.00
Bough Pot, Encrusted Agate, Blue Slip Bands, Circular Apertures, 3¼ x 5½ In. . . . 406.00
Bowl, 2-Color Slip Splashed Design, Salmon Band, Engine Turned Band, 5¾ In. . . . 325.00
Bowl, Brown Bands, Pearlware, Engine Turned, Dotted Central Band, 7½ In. . . . 210.00
Bowl, Cat's-Eye, Salmon, White & Brown Alternating Bands, Top Green Band, 5⅝ In. . . . 350.00
Bowl, Earthworm, Cat's-Eye, Sienna Band, Rouletted Rim, 3¾ x 7½ In. . . . 1045.00
Bowl, Earthworm, London Shape, Brown Bands, Ocher Band, 4 x 7 In. . . . 440.00
Bowl, Earthworm, London Shape, Bands, Brown, Ocher, Brown, White, Blue, 3¾ x 7¼ In. . . . 441.00
Bowl, Earthworm, Orange Ground, Brown Bands, 5¼ In. . . . 180.00
Bowl, Earthworm, Sand Ground, Blue Bands, 5½ In. . . . 210.00
Bowl, Earthworm, Sand Ground, Double Brown Bands, 3½ x 6⅜ In. . . . 250.00
Bowl, Earthworm, Slate Blue & Brown On White Ground, 3 Rust Bands, Pearlware, 5½ In. . . . 325.00
Bowl, Earthworm, White On Gray, Brown & Rust Band, Blue Border, c.1820, 5½ In. . . . 406.00
Bowl, Earthworm, Yellow, Blue Green Field, Footed, 3½ In. . . . 375.00
Bowl, Marbleized, Salmon Ground, Slip Splashed Design, Turned Engine Turned Rim, 6½ In. 1200.00
Bowl, Sea Worm, Seaweed, Cobalt Band, Yellowware, 2½ x 5¼ In. . . . 431.00
Bowl, Seaweed, Black, Rust Ground, Blue Band On Rim, Creamware, 6¼ In. . . . 220.00
Bowl, Seaweed, Brown Band, Putty Slip Ground, 4¼ In. . . . 240.00
Bowl, Seaweed, Butterscotch Ground, Blue Bands, 7⅜ In. . . . 210.00
Bowl, Seaweed, Butterscotch Ground, Blue Band, 7 In. . . . 300.00
Bowl, Seaweed, Green Rolled Rim, Tan Band, Mid 19th Century, 7¼ x 3½ In. . . . 345.00
Bowl, Seaweed, Hemispherical, Slate Blue Band, Mustard Field, Green Border, c.1800, 6 In. . . . 1073.00
Bowl, Snail Trail, Wide Brown Band Under Rust Band, Pearlware, 4½ In. . . . 200.00
Chamber Pot, Earthworm, Looping, Blue, Green, 8½ In. . . . 2938.00
Chamber Pot, Earthworm, Medial Band, Blue, White, Brown Wavy, 5⅛ In. . . . 940.00
Creamer, Cat's-Eye, Brown Band, Tooled Green Band, Leaf Molded Handle, 3½ In. . . . 460.00
Creamer, Bands, Barrel Form, 3 Rows Of Engine Turned Design, Pumpkin Bands, 3½ In. . . . 200.00
Creamer, Seaweed, Ocher & Brown Band, Barrel Form, 4 In. . . . 300.00
Creamer, Seaweed, Yellow Ground, Creamware, 5½ In. . . . 600.00
Jug, Bands, Baluster, Turned, C-Scroll Handles, Sky Blue, Mustard, 19th Century, 5 In. . . . 406.00
Jug, Bands, Barrel Shape, White, Ocher, Brown, Wavy Blue, Blue Sun, 8¼ In. . . . 2938.00
Jug, Cat's-Eye, Empire Bulge Form, Blue, Brown, Pumpkin Field, c.1820, 7¼ In. . . . 13340.00
Jug, Dark Brown & Cinnamon, Barrel Form, Creamware, c.1830, 6¾ In. . . . 3364.00
Jug, Milk, Earthworm, Barrel, Green Beaded Border, c.1820, 3¾ In. . . . 1740.00
Jug, Rust Slip Field, Leafy Terminal Handle, c.1800, 7½ In. . . . 1218.00
Loving Cup, Marbleized Agate, 3 Green Roulette Bands, 2 Handles, Pedestal, Creamware, 4¾ In. 2200.00
Mug, Brown, Yellow Sponge, Blue Rim, 3¾ x 4½ In. . . . *illus* 160.00
Mug, Cat's-Eye, Multicolored, Sienna Band, Leaves, 5½ x 4½ In. . . . 467.00
Mug, Cat's-Eye, Sand Colored Band, Brown & Blue Bands, Pearlware, 3¾ In. . . . 275.00
Mug, Checkered Band, Surface Agate, Black, Brown, Pumpkin Buff, c.1785, 3½ In. . . . 551.00
Mug, Earthworm, Brown & White, Butterscotch Band, 3¾ In. . . . 230.00
Mug, Earthworm, Brown Stripes, Orange Band, Applied Leaf Handle, Mid 19th Century, 6⅝ In. 920.00
Mug, Earthworm, Cat's-Eye, White & Rust, Black & White, 1850s, 5¾ In. . . . 5580.00
Mug, Earthworm, Cat's-Eye, Brown, Blue, Black, Early 19th Century, 6 In. . . . *illus* 3737.00
Mug, Earthworm, Ocher Ground, Brown Band, 2½ In. . . . 450.00
Mug, Earthworm, Yellow, Blue Green Field, Marked L & T Mont, 2½ In. . . . 325.00
Mug, Marbleized, Agate, Gold Trim, 4½ In. . . . 130.00
Mug, Marbleized, Agate, Yellow Ground, White Beaded Bands Top & Bottom, 2¼ In. . . . 170.00
Mug, Marbleized, Center Band, Yellow Ground, White Beaded Bands, 2¼ In. . . . 170.00
Mug, Marbleized, Combed Body, Green Band, Pearlware Handle, 5⅛ In. . . . 750.00
Mug, Slip Filled Lines, Vertical Dashes, Pumpkin Bands, c.1800, 4¾ In. . . . 3480.00
Mustard Pot, Cover, Seaweed, Bands, Yellowware, 2½ x 3 In. . . . 690.00
Mustard Pot, Cylindrical, Bell Shaped Cover, Zigzag Border, c.1790, 4½ In. . . . 1218.00
Open Salt, Earthworm, Wide Blue Band, Blue Band On Pedestal, Pearlware, 2 In. . . . 400.00
Pepper Pot, Center Black Vine Slip, Ocher Bands, Mustard Ground, 4¼ In. . . . 375.00
Pepper Pot, Earthworm, Blue, Brown, White, Blue Bands, Pedestal Base, Pearlware, 4¾ In. . . 750.00
Pitcher, Earthworm, Blue & White, Blue Gray Ground, Brown & Blue Bands, Bulbous, 5¼ In. 303.00
Pitcher, Earthworm, Bulbous, Mustard Band, Handle, Pearlware, 5⅛ In. . . . 1400.00
Pitcher, Earthworm, Bulbous, Green Bands, 19th Century, 7¾ x 6 In. . . . 2640.00
Pitcher, Earthworm, Center Lavender Band, Brown, White & Blue, Pearlware, 6 In. . . . 1400.00

'itcher, Earthworm, Pale Blue, Wavy White Lines, Applied Handle, c.1885, $6\frac{7}{8}$ In. .... *illus* 3050.00
'itcher, Earthworm, Slate Blue Ground, Brown Band, 2 Blue Bands, Barrel Form, $5\frac{3}{4}$ In.... 500.00
'itcher, Earthworm, Tooled Green, Brown Band, Applied Leaf Handle, Late 19th Century, 6 In. 1955.00
'itcher, Earthworm, Tooled Green Band, Gray, Brown, Applied Leaf Handle, Mid 19th Century, $7\frac{3}{4}$ In. 3738.00
'itcher, Earthworm, Tricolor, Sand Ground, Brown Bands, Barrel Form, Creamware, 5 In. .. 500.00
'itcher, Earthworm, Wavy White Stripes, Brown, Blue, Applied Leaf Handle, Mid 19th Century, $6\frac{7}{8}$ In... 3105.00
'itcher, Seaweed, Creamware Bolster, Tree, Gray Ground, 5 In. 650.00
'itcher, Seaweed, Green, White & Brown Bands, Yellowware, 19th Century, $7\frac{5}{8}$ In. 425.00
'itcher, Seaweed, Tooled Green Bands, Slate, Black Stripes, Brown, Leaf Handle, 1800s, $9\frac{3}{8}$ In. 4313.00
'orringer, Bands, Brown, Pumpkin, Blue, White Lines & Dashes, c.1800, $4\frac{3}{4}$ In. 2436.00
alt, Footed, Earthworm, Cat's-Eye, Butterscotch Ground, Brown Bands, 3 In. 700.00
haker, Pepper, Marblehead, Baluster, c.1820, $4\frac{3}{4}$ In. 928.00
ankard, Marbleized Agate, Brown Band, Pearlware, 6 In. 1500.00
ankard, Marbleized Agate, Green Rouletted Band, 6 In. 1300.00
ankard, Seaweed, Butterscotch Band, 2 Blue Bands, Creamware, $5\frac{3}{4}$ In. 500.00
ase, Waisted, Marbleized, Dark Brown, White, Pumpkin, Green Trim, c.1775, 3 In. 870.00

IONMOUTH Pottery Company started working in Monmouth, Illinois, in 1892. The pottery nade a variety of utilitarian wares. It became part of Western Stoneware Company in 1906. he maple leaf mark was used until 1930. If *Co.* appears as part of the mark, the piece was nade before 1906.

'asket, Blue, Handle, $7\frac{1}{2}$ x $6\frac{1}{8}$ x $4\frac{3}{8}$ In. 34.00
'owl, Banded, Logo, 3 x 5 In. 6.00
asserole, Cover, Dark Tan, Deep Burgundy Spatterware, c.1967, 6 x $8\frac{1}{2}$ In. 79.00
asserole, Cover, Green, Mustard Yellow Glaze, Leaf Logo, 2 Handles 48.00
ookie Jar, Jug, Maple Leaf Logo, Lid, Gal., 10 In. 35.00
'ookie Jar, Jug Shape, Cork, Western Stoneware, White, 11 x 7 In. 29.00
ookie Jar, Maple Leaf On Bottom, 1930s, 7 x $5\frac{3}{4}$ In. 65.00
ookie Jar, Scroll Design, Embossed Cookies On Front, Green Glaze, 7 x $6\frac{1}{2}$ In. 32.00
rock, Cover, Metal Handle, Dark Brown, Glossy Brown Glaze, 7 In. 42.00
'ecanter, Weir Formed, Blue, Stopper, 8 In. 125.00
lowerpot, Vase Planter, 2 Handles, Yellow, $4\frac{1}{4}$ x $5\frac{3}{8}$ In. 25.00
ardiniere, Flowerpot, White, Horizontal Ribbed, Hanging Leaves, $5\frac{1}{8}$ x $4\frac{3}{4}$ In. 30.00
ug, Mofavi, Cover, Rust Color, 11 In. 79.00
'itcher, Blue Glazed Ring, Handle, $5\frac{1}{2}$ x $7\frac{1}{2}$ In. 40.00
'itcher, Brown Drip, Handle, $10\frac{1}{2}$ x 6 x 3 In. 40.00
late, Brown Daisy & Dot, Chocolate Brown, 1950s, $9\frac{3}{4}$ In. 10.00
ase, Acanthus, $6\frac{3}{4}$ x $2\frac{3}{4}$ In. 22.00
ase, Bud, Pink Matte, Lightly Speckled, 1941, $6\frac{1}{4}$ In. 25.00
ase, Design Around Shoulder, 1920s, 16 In. 350.00
ase, Mirror Black, 1940s, 12 In. 24.00

IONT JOYE, *see Mt. Joye category.*

IOORCROFT pottery was first made in Burslem, England, in 1913. William Moorcroft had nanaged the art pottery department for James Macintyre & Company of England from 898 to 1913. The Moorcroft pottery continues today, although William Moorcroft died in 945. The earlier wares are similar to the modern ones, but color and marking will help indicate the age.

iscuit Barrel, Cover, Macintyre, Red Poppies, Kerchief Border, Yellow Flowers 1770.00
iscuit Barrel, Wisteria, Silver Rim, 7 In. 531.00
owl, Claremont, Burslem, 1914, 3 x $8\frac{1}{2}$ In. 1888.00
owl, Cover, Cobalt Blue, Green, Flowers, Multicolored, 20th Century, $3\frac{3}{4}$ x 6 In. 143.00
owl, Footed, Anemone, $6\frac{1}{4}$ In. 122.00
owl, Leaf & Berry, 1998, $2\frac{3}{4}$ x $6\frac{1}{4}$ In. 118.00
owl, Pomegranate, 2 Handles, $3\frac{3}{4}$ x $8\frac{3}{8}$ In. 767.00
owl, Pomegranate, Blue Ground, c.1920, $1\frac{1}{4}$ x $8\frac{1}{2}$ In. 266.00
owl, Temptation Design, Apples, Blossoms, $10\frac{1}{2}$ In. 300.00
ox, Cover, Flambe, Orchids, Impressed Mark, c.1940, $4\frac{1}{2}$ x $3\frac{1}{2}$ In. 360.00
andleholder, Roundel Design, Red High Glaze, $5\frac{3}{4}$ In., Pair 354.00
andlestick, Green, Weeping Willow, Paper Label, c.1930, 3 In., Pair 3960.00
andy Dish, Pomegranate, c.1914, 5 x $9\frac{1}{2}$ In. 2280.00
ompote, Anemone, c.1955, $6\frac{1}{2}$ In. 126.00
ompote, Burslem, Pomegranate In Center, Wreath Of Berries On Side, $5\frac{1}{8}$ x $6\frac{3}{8}$ In. 708.00
ompote, Pedestal, Red & Blue Anemones Encircling Body, c.1950, $3\frac{1}{2}$ x $4\frac{1}{4}$ In. ...... *illus* 177.00
up & Saucer, Cream Ground, Grape & Leaf, c.1930 .... 294.00

Moorcroft, Compote, Pedestal, Red & Blue Anemones Encircling Body, c.1950, $3\frac{1}{2}$ x $4\frac{1}{4}$ In.
$77.00

Moorcroft, Pin Tray, Florian, Red Flower, $4\frac{1}{2}$ In.
$25.00

Moorcroft, Vase, Florian, Yellow Tulips, Jas Macintyre & Co., 11 In.
$7800.00

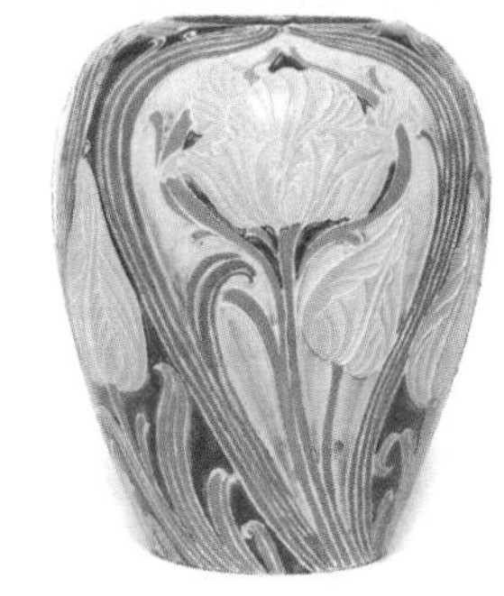

Moorcroft, Vase, Landscape, Blue, Green, Double Gourd, Macintyre, 13 In.
$7200.00

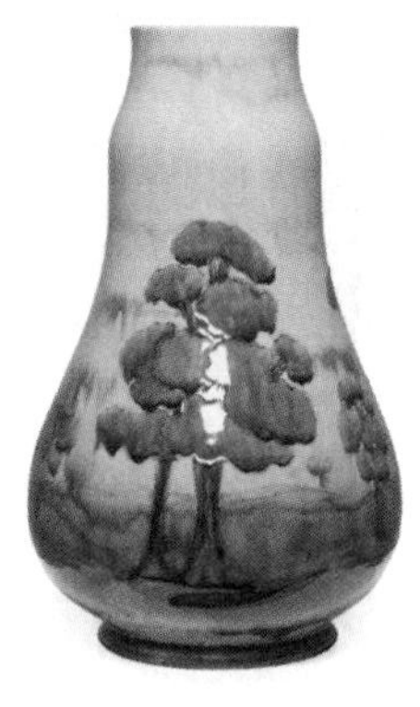

Moorcroft, Vase, Moonlit Blue, Landscape, Impressed, 3 ½ x 2 In.
$2640.00

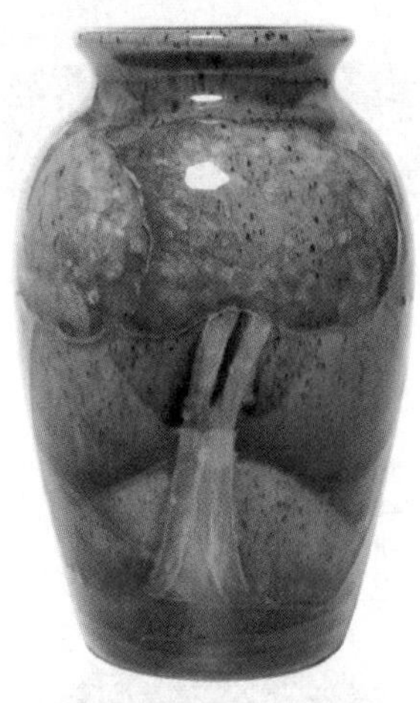

Moorcroft, Vase, Ruby Luster Landscape, Liberty & Co., c.1908, 6 ¼ In.
$1416.00

Moorcroft, Vase, Tropical Flowers, Marked, 8 In.
$250.00

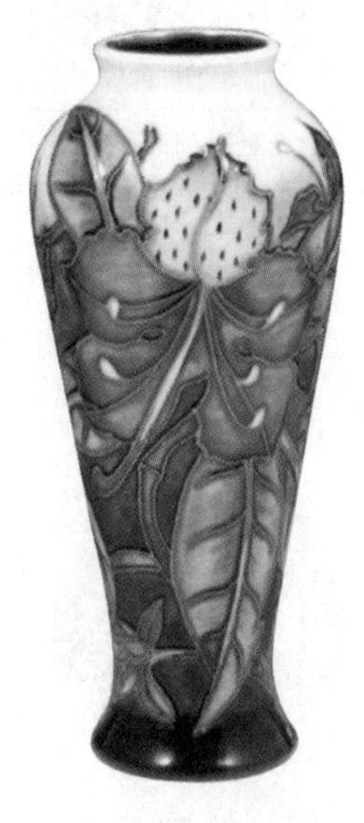

Item	Price
Dish, Anemone, Blue Ground, 2 Handles	112.0
Dish, Magnolias, Blue Ground, 2 Handles	74.0
Ginger Jar, Blue, Banded Fern, Cover, Impressed Mark, c.1926, 5 ¾ In.	510.0
Ginger Jar, Cover, Anemone, Blue Ground	261.0
Ginger Jar, Hibiscus, Dark Blue Ground	260.0
Inkwell, Moonlit Blue, Cover, Impressed Mark, c.1925, 3 In.	9600.0
Inkwell, Pansy On Each Side, 4 Corner Openings, c.1922, 2 ⅛ x 3 In.	295.0
Jar, Canning, Pomegranate, Silver Plated Mounts, c.1914, 5 ¾ In.	324.0
Jar, Cover, Ginger, Flowers, Labours, 2002, 6 ¾ In.	512.0
Jardiniere, Green, Floral, Signed, Dated 1914, 11 ¾ In.	8400.0
Jug, Burslem, Blue & Red Poppies, 6 ¼ In.	561.0
Jug, Pomegranate, 7 In.	1096.0
Lamp, Leaf & Berry, Flambe Glaze, Pierced Metal Base, c.1935, 12 ½ In.	885.0
Lamp, Pomegranate, Scalloped Wood Base, 11 ¼ In.	767.0
Lamp, White Ground, Hibiscus, Bulbous, c.1960, 24 In.	222.0
Lamp Base, Lily, Ivory Ground, 7 In.	80.0
Pin Tray, Florian, Red Flower, 4 ½ In. *illus*	25.0
Pitcher, Florian Ware, Kimberly, Macintyre, 6 In.	325.0
Pitcher, Handle, Squat, Claremont Decoration, Signed, 4 ½ x 2 ¾ In.	1955.0
Plate, Cobalt Blue, Pansies, Impressed Mark, c.1925, Square, 10 ¼ In.	444.0
Plate, Flambe, School Of Minnows Taking Shelter, Green & Blue, c.1935, 8 ⅛ In.	1416.0
Plate, Orange Ground, Trees, Impressed Mark, c.1925, 8 ½ In.	2100.0
Plate, Pomegranate, Blue Ground, 8 ½ In.	377.0
Salt & Pepper, Wisteria, 3 ½ In.	590.0
Sugar Basket, Floral, Macintyre, c.1910, 5 In.	3720.0
Tea Set, Orchids, Light Green Ground, Cobalt Blue, Handle & Foot, 6-In. Teapot, 3 Piece	649.0
Teapot, Lid, Florian, c.1898, 5 ¾ In.	690.0
Tobacco Container, Cover, Moonlit Blue, c.1925, 5 ½ In.	2360.0
Tobacco Container, Forget-Me-Nots On Shoulder, Blue Poppies, Macintyre, 3 ⅜ In.	531.0
Vase, 4 Feathery Plumes, Banded Surface, Blue, Gray & Cream, 7 ⅛ In.	885.0
Vase, Anemone, Blue Ground, 10 ½ In.	268.0
Vase, Anemone, Cobalt Blue Ground, Shouldered, Flared Rim, 8 ¼ In.	384.0
Vase, Anemone, Light Blue Ground, Bulbous, Flared Rim, 5 In.	188.0
Vase, Anemone, Wide Mouth, Impressed Mark, c.1945, 8 In.	660.0
Vase, Aurelian Ware, Blue & Orange Flowers, Macintyre, c.1898, 5 ¼ In.	561.0
Vase, Bands Enclose Wreath Of Pomegranates, c.1927, 7 In.	1062.0
Vase, Brown, Red Stylized Leaves & Panels, Bulbous, Rolled Out Rim, Bernard Moore, 7 In.	353.0
Vase, Bulbous, Blue & White Drip Glaze, 5 ½ x 10 ½ In.	240.0
Vase, Bulbous, Hazelton Decoration, Signed, 4 ½ x 3 ¾ In.	518.0
Vase, Bulbous, Pomegranates, 2 Handles, 8 x 7 ½ In.	1200.0
Vase, Bulbous, Wide Mouth, Red & Green Flowers, Blue Centers, Leaves, 10 ½ In.	622.0
Vase, Cherries, Blossoms, 6 ¼ In.	354.0
Vase, Claremont, Multicolored, Green Ground, c.1905, 5 ½ In.	826.0
Vase, Clematis, Mauve, Purple, Green To Blue Ground, 5 In.	176.0
Vase, Cobalt Blue, Orchids, Impressed Mark, c.1930, 5 ½ In.	480.0
Vase, Cobalt Blue, Pansy, Signed, Impressed Mark, c.1920, 7 ½ In.	3480.0
Vase, Cornflower, Shades Of Blue, c.1920, 18 In.	2360.0
Vase, Double Gourd Shape, Landscape Design, Blue, Green, Macintyre, 13 In.	6900.0
Vase, Double Handled, Pomegranate Decoration, Blue, Green Ground, 7 x 8 ½ In.	1380.0
Vase, Egg Shape, Lamia With Bulrushes, 16 In.	473.0
Vase, Evening Sky, Trees, Swollen Neck, 5 ½ In.	353.0
Vase, Eventide, Summer Foliage Trees, Hills & Dales, c.1925, 6 ⅛ In.	3776.0
Vase, Finches Eating Apples & Berries, Blue Ground, 11 In.	425.0
Vase, Flambe, Anemone, Elongated Neck, 4 In.	450.0
Vase, Flambe, Cover, 11 In.	660.0
Vase, Flambe, Leaves & Berries, Pinched Neck, 5 ¾ In.	663.0
Vase, Flambe, Leaves & Berries, 6 ⅛ In.	885.0
Vase, Flambe, Leaves & Berries, 7 ½ In.	1106.0
Vase, Flambe, Orchid On Front & Back, 3 ¼ In.	266.0
Vase, Florian, Black-Eyed Susans, Stamped, c.1902, 10 x 7 ¼ In.	4500.0
Vase, Florian, Golden Tulips, Green Ground, c.1903, 8 ½ In.	561.0
Vase, Florian, Peacocks, 2 Handles, Green & Blue, Cream Ground, Macintyre, 5 In.	826.0
Vase, Florian, Sponged, Balloon Honesty Plant Flowers, Macintyre, c.1903, 8 ½ In.	1770.0
Vase, Florian, Violets, Yellow, Green, Blue, White, Handles, 10 In.	9000.0
Vase, Florian, Yellow Tulips, Jas Macintyre & Co., 11 In. *illus*	7800.0
Vase, Flying Geese, Black Ground, Marked, 5 In.	591.0

Vase, Flying Geese, Globular, 5 ½ In. 473.00
Vase, Foxglove, 7 ¾ In. 223.00
Vase, Green, Floral, Bulbous, Impressed Mark, c.1925, 6 In. 1740.00
Vase, Green, Gold, Flowers, Macintyre, 10 In. 926.00
Vase, Hazeldene, Blue, Green, Bulbous, Stamped, 5 x 3 ¾ In. 4800.00
Vase, Hibiscus, Blue Ground, Squat, 4 ¼ In. 355.00
Vase, Hibiscus, Cream Ground, 3 ½ In., Pair. 142.00
Vase, Hibiscus, Green Ground, 8 In. 212.00
Vase, Landscape, Blue, Green, Double Gourd, Macintyre, 13 In. *illus* 7200.00
Vase, Landscape & Tree, Turquoise Sky, 10 ¼ In. 353.00
Vase, Leaves, Fruit, 13 x 8 ¼ In. 3600.00
Vase, Moonlit Blue, Impressed Mark, c.1925, 5 In. 1620.00
Vase, Moonlit Blue, Landscape, Impressed, 3 ½ x 2 In. *illus* 2640.00
Vase, Orchid, Bulbous, Straight Neck, Tube Lined, Cobalt Blue Ground, 1930s, 4 ⅞ In. 208.00
Vase, Orchids, 5 ½ In. 98.00
Vase, Pansies, Blue Ground, 7 ¼ In. 414.00
Vase, Pansies, Blue Ground, 8 ¼ In. 609.00
Vase, Pansies, Squatty Body, 3 In. 531.00
Vase, Pomegranate, Footed, Black Ground, 6 In. 568.00
Vase, Pomegranate, Swollen Body, Blue Ground, c.1920, 6 ½ In. 384.00
Vase, Pomegranate, Trumpet, 3 ½ In. 355.00
Vase, Pomegranate & Berries, Cobalt Blue, Green Bands, c.1928, 6 ⅜ In. 708.00
Vase, Poppy, Impressed Mark, c.1920, 6 In. 3000.00
Vase, Poppy Decoration, Red Ground, Signed, 8 x 13 In. 1725.00
Vase, Red Flowers, Cobalt Blue Ground, Blue Inscribed Mark, 4 In. 460.00
Vase, Ruby Luster Landscape, Liberty & Co., c.1908, 6 ¼ In. *illus* 1416.00
Vase, Salt Glazed, Leaf, Berry, Light Blue Ground, 6 ¼ In. 755.00
Vase, Tapered Shape, Pomegranate Decoration, Signed, 5 x 12 ½ In. 1380.00
Vase, Torridon, Duck, Fish, 8 ¼ In. 487.00
Vase, Tropical Flowers, Marked, 8 In. *illus* 250.00
Vase, Turtle Doves, 10 ½ In. 609.00
Vase, White Ground, Magnolia, Impressed Mark, Dated 1980, 14 In. 390.00
Vase, Wisteria, Miniature, 1920s, 3 ⅛ In. 236.00

MORGANTOWN GLASS WORKS operated in Morgantown, West Virginia, from 1900 to 1974. Some of their wares are marked with an adhesive label that says *Old Morgantown Glass*.

Adams, Vase, Green, Slant, 12 In. 75.00
Bristol Yellow, Vase, 10 In. 150.00
Chanticleer, Cocktail, Amber, 3 ½ Oz., 4 ⅛ In. 42.00
Chanticleer, Cocktail, Amethyst, 3 ½ Oz., 4 ⅛ In. 42.00
Chanticleer, Cocktail, Anna Rose, 3 ½ Oz., 4 ⅛ In. 42.00
Chanticleer, Cocktail, Copen Blue, 3 ½ Oz., 4 ⅛ In. 42.00
Chanticleer, Cocktail, Shamrock, 3 ½ Oz., 4 ⅛ In. 42.00
Chanticleer, Cocktail, Smoke, 3 ½ Oz., 4 ⅛ In. 42.00
Crinkle, Pitcher, Green, Ockner, 50 Oz., 8 x 5 ½ In. *illus* 49.00
Crinkle, Vase, Snowball, Amethyst, 7 In. 200.00
Electra, Vase, Ritz Blue, Clear Handles, 9 ¾ In. 795.00
Filament, Cocktail, Red, 3 ½ Oz. 49.00
Filament, Cordial, Green, Oz. 11.00
Golf Ball, Cocktail, Cobalt Blue, 3 ½ Oz., 4 ⅛ In. 36.00
Golf Ball, Cordial, Cobalt Blue, 1 ½ Oz., 3 ½ In. 47.00
Golf Ball, Cordial, Green Stem & Foot, Optic Bowl, 1 ½ Oz., 3 ½ In. 11.00
Golf Ball, Cordial, Peach, 1 ½ Oz., 3 ½ In. 32.00
Golf Ball, Cordial, Spanish Red, 1 ½ Oz., 3 ½ In. *illus* 35.00
Golf Ball, Goblet, Cobalt Blue, 9 Oz., 6 ¾ In. 47.00
Golf Ball, Ivy Ball, Red, Flared Rim, 6 ¾ In. 72.00
Golf Ball, Sherbet, Cobalt Blue, 6 Oz. 29.00
Golf Ball, Sherry, Cobalt Blue, 2 ½ Oz., 4 ⅝ In. 47.00
Golf Ball, Sherry, Gloria Blue, 2 ½ Oz., 4 ⅝ In. 32.00
Golf Ball, Sherry, Peach, 2 ½ Oz., 4 ⅝ In. 32.00
Golf Ball, Sherry, Shamrock, 2 ½ Oz., 4 ⅝ In. 32.00
Golf Ball, Sherry, Smoke, 2 ½ Oz., 4 ⅝ In. 32.00
Golf Ball, Sherry, Yellow, 2 ½ Oz., 4 ⅝ In. 32.00
Gypsy Fire, Console Set, 3 Piece *illus* 100.00
Laura, Vase, Smoke, 10 In. 30.00
Patio, Candle Vase, Smoky Gray, 8 ½ In., Pair *illus* 45.00

Morgantown, Crinkle, Pitcher, Green, Ockner, 50 Oz., 8 x 5 ½ In.
$49.00

Morgantown, Golf Ball, Cordial, Spanish Red, 1 ½ Oz., 3 ½ In.
$35.00

Morgantown, Gypsy Fire, Console Set, 3 Piece
$100.00

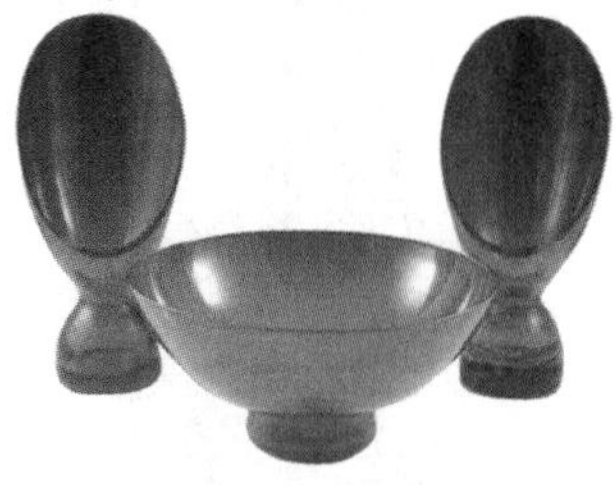

Morgantown, Patio, Candle Vase, Smoky Gray, 8 ½ In., Pair
$45.00

Mosaic Tile Company, Tile, Harbor Scene, Venice, 4 Tiles, Frame, Overall 12 x 24 In.
$4838.00

TIP
Want to remove a bottle stopper that is stuck? Mix a teaspoon of rubbing alcohol with a half-teaspoon of glycerin and a half-teaspoon of salt. Pour the liquid around the stopper; let it seep in. Try removing the stopper after 24 hours.

Moser, Cologne, Women Warriors, Gilt Intaglio Band, Amethyst, Mushroom Stopper, 5¾ In.
$558.00

MORIAGE is a special type of raised decoration used on some Japanese pottery. Sometimes pieces of clay were shaped by hand and applied to the item; sometimes the clay was squeezed from a tube in the way we apply cake frosting. One type of moriage is called Dragonware by collectors.

Ashtray, Flowers, Birds, Orange, Black Border, 5⅜ In. 45.00
Bowl, Handles, 3-Footed, Brown 135.00
Bowl, Serving, Marked, Numbered, 1970, 8¼ x 3⅜ In. 145.00
Bowl, Swan On Lake, Nippon, c.1911, 7¼ In. 95.00
Bowl, Trees, Lake & Church, Tricornered, No. 47, Nippon, 7 x 7½ x 2½ In. 85.00
Celery Dish, Gilded Gold, Hand Painted Roses, Scalloped, Pierced Handles, 11¼ x 5 In. 100.00
Dish, Trinket, Diamond, Hand Painted Roses, Cobalt Blue & Gold, 5 x 1¼ In. 55.00
Dresser Jar, Mt. Fuji, Hand Painted, 4⅞ x 3 In. 75.00
Hair Receiver, Tripod, Nippon, c.1921, 3½ x 4¼ In. 56.00
Incense Burner, Dragonware, Black & Gray Glaze, Foo Dog Handles, 3¼ x 3 In. 24.00
Jar, Cover, Vantine's, c.1920, 6 x 5½ In. 50.00
Mustard Pot, Cover, Scalloped, Rose Insert On Sides, 3½ x 4½ In. 125.00
Plate, Flowers, 2 Children, Scalloped, Gold Trim, 7½ In. 30.00
Relish, Nippon, 7½ x 4½ In. 27.00
Salt & Pepper, Dragon, Washington D.C., Gray, Gold Trim, 2½ In. 22.00
Teapot, Roses, Gold Filigree, Embossed, Green & Brown Glaze, Nippon, 6½ In. 65.00
Trinket Box, Limoges, Gold Gilt Metal Trim, Bow Closure, 5⅛ x 3 x 2½ In. 68.00
Vase, Blooming Iris, Scalloped Base, 2 Handles, 9 x 6½ In. 895.00
Vase, Figures, Bat Handles, Blue Underglaze, Puffed Up, 12 In. 695.00
Vase, Flowers, Applied Leaves, Dark Blue Gray, 3 Handles, 15 x 9 In. 150.00
Vase, Green, Applied Leaf Slipwork, Hexagonal Quilted, Nippon, 4⅝ x 6⅜ In. 210.00
Vase, Pillow, Pink & Yellow Roses, Leaves, Custard Yellow Ground, 6¾ x 6½ In. 225.00

MOSAIC TILE COMPANY of Zanesville, Ohio, was started by Karl Langerbeck and Herman Mueller in 1894. Many types of plain and ornamental tiles were made until 1959. The company closed in 1967. The company also made some ashtrays, bookends, and related giftwares. Most pieces are marked with the entwined *MTC* monogram.

Coaster, Swan, Round, Transfer, Blue, Black, Red, c.1960, 3 In., 3 Piece 20.00
Dish, Horse Head, Diamond Shape, Yellow, Blue, c.1950, 5½ x 3⅜ In., 4 Piece. 35.00
Medallion, Advertising, Hexagonal, Unglazed White Porcelain, c.1930, 2¼ In. 70.00
Paperweight, Abe Lincoln Profile, Blue Ground, White Relief, 3 x 3½ In. 20.00
Paperweight, Bethesda Hospital, Blue Transfer, Cream Body, c.1965, 3 In. 15.00
Paperweight, Commemorative, 250 Years, Robert Treat, c.1916, 3½ In. 135.00
Paperweight, Indian, Feathered Headdress, Round, Matte Glaze, c.1940, 3 In. 35.00
Tile, Checkerboard, Blue, Gold, Semimatte Glaze, 2 x 2 In., 2 Piece 50.00
Tile, Flower Buds, White Ground, Cobalt Blue, Gold, c.1930, 6 x 6 In. 30.00
Tile, Flowers, Cuerda Seca, Center Hole, Red Clay Base, c.1930, 4⅝ In. 55.00
Tile, Harbor Scene, Venice, 4 Tiles, Frame, Overall 12 x 24 In. . . . . . *illus* 4838.00
Tile, Rope Border, Green Semimatte Glaze, c.1920, 6 In. 15.00
Tile, Ship, Blue & White, c.1940, 4¼ x 4¼ In. 35.00
Tile, Woodpecker, Cuerda Seca, Matte Glaze, Frame, c.1935, 4¼ x 4¼ In. 245.00
Trivet, Birds, Audubon, Summer Tanager, Decal, Low Molded Feet, c.1970, 6 x 6 In. 10.00

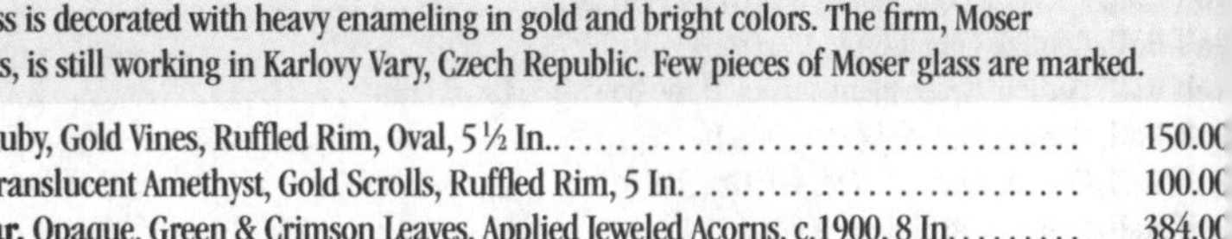

MOSER glass is made by a Bohemian (Czech) glasshouse founded by Ludwig Moser in 1857. Art Nouveau-type glassware and iridescent glassware were made. The most famous Moser glass is decorated with heavy enameling in gold and bright colors. The firm, Moser Glassworks, is still working in Karlovy Vary, Czech Republic. Few pieces of Moser glass are marked.

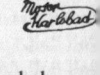

Basket, Ruby, Gold Vines, Ruffled Rim, Oval, 5½ In. 150.00
Basket, Translucent Amethyst, Gold Scrolls, Ruffled Rim, 5 In. 100.00
Biscuit Jar, Opaque, Green & Crimson Leaves, Applied Jeweled Acorns, c.1900, 8 In. 384.00
Bowl, Butterfly Center, Bumble Bee, Crimped, Gold Enameled Rigaree Rim, 5¼ In. 805.00
Bowl, Centerpiece, Flowers, Cranberry Padding, Cut Petals, Allover Engraving, 4¼ In. 2070.00
Bowl, Clear, Faceted, 5 x 16 In. 1200.00
Box, Cover, Cranberry, Flowers, Gold Scrolling, c.1900, 2 In. 266.00
Box, Domed Cover, Ruby, Gilt, Enameled, Footed, 7½ x 6½ In. 1840.00
Candlestick, Double Arm, Spanish Canine Pattern, Enameled, 11¼ In. 230.00
Cologne, Women Warriors, Gilt Intaglio Band, Amethyst, Mushroom Stopper, 5¾ In. . . . *illus* 558.00
Compote, Clear, Gold Clouds, Robin, Optic Ribbed, Gilt Rim, 6 x 5 In. 450.00
Cup, Ruby, Bee, Acorn Jewels, Oval, Amber Handle, Rigaree Feet, 3½ In. 400.00
Cup & Saucer, Cranberry, Shell Shape, Gold Medallions, Scrolling, 3½ In. 425.00
Decanter, Cranberry, Gold Coralene Leaves, Blue Stamens, White Branches, Flat, Oval, 10 In. 1093.00

Decanter, Faceted Stopper, Red Padded Art Leaves, Intaglio Gold Thistles, Long Neck, 18 In. . . 1725.00
Decanter Set, Gold & Brown Leaves, Berries, Insects, Stopper, 13 In., 9 Piece. . . 1560.00
Dresser Box, Amber, Multicolored Enamel, 4-Footed Bronze Mask, 5 In. . . 350.00
Dresser Box, Opaque Green, Bird On Raspberry Bush, Footed Metal Stand, 3 In. . . 50.00
Dresser Box, Red, Silver, Medallions, Gold Leaves, Rectangular, Rope Twist Handles, 4 In. . . 633.00
Ewer, Bumblebee, Butterflies, Scrolling, Applied Blue Handle, 6 ½ In. . . 780.00
Ewer, Cobalt Blue, Blue Medallions, Pink Flowers, Footed, Gilt, Bulbous, 13 ½ In. . . 259.00
Finger Bowl, Underplate, Cranberry, White, Green, Blue, Applied Cobalt Blue, 5 In. . . 250.00
Goblet, Alexandrite, Faceted, Signed, 7 ½ In. . . 240.00
Goblet, Cranberry, Gilt, Faceted Stem, 8 In. . . 633.00
Goblet, Gold Cabochons, Green, Red Jewels, Grape Leaves, Baluster Twisted Stem, 7 In. . . 920.00
Goblet, Green, Blue, Pink Stylized Horns Of Plenty, Baluster Stem, 7 ½ In. . . 350.00
Goblet, Green, Gilt Wheat, Grape Leaves, Multicolored Jewels, Baluster Stem, 7 ½ In. . . 400.00
Goblet, Green, Multicolored Leaves, Gold Stems, Jeweled Grape Clusters, Baluster Stem, 8 In. 450.00
Goblet, Stag's Head, Gilt Intaglio, Gold Grape Vines, Fruit, Leaves, Baluster Form, 8 In. . . 350.00
Goblet, Translucent, Flowers, Scrolling, 4 Enameled Cabochons, 7 In. . . 518.00
Jewelry Box, Flowers, Leaves, Birds, Brass Mounts, Ball Feet, Hinged Cover, 4 ½ x 4 In. . . 1528.00
Mug, Beer, Gold Acanthus Scroll, 7 In. . . 200.00
Perfume Bottle, Multicolored Enameled Oak Leaves, Oval Stopper, 3 In. . . 230.00
Pitcher, Creamer, Cranberry, Gilt Frame Window Panes, Enameled Scrolling, 6 In. . . 460.00
Pitcher, Flowers, Vines, Bird, Insects, Light Blue, Opalescent Rim, Spout, 6 ¾ In. . . 2243.00
Pitcher, Peacock, Butterfly, Chinese Garden, Enameled, c.1900, 9 In. . . *illus* 1117.00
Pitcher, Peacock Blue, Amber, Enameled Flowers, c.1900, 9 In. . . 702.00
Pitcher, Prussian Blue, Gold Scrolling, Multicolored Flowers, Clear Handle, 7 ½ In. . . 1725.00
Salt, Cranberry, Multicolored Acanthus Scrolls, Gilt Rim, Peacock Eyes, Footed, 3 In., Pair. . . 375.00
Tankard, Clear, Pink Flowers, Gold Scrolls, Amber Gilt Handle, 8 In. . . 125.00
Tankard, Multicolored Scrolling, Beer Handle, Gnome, 13 ½ In. . . 1380.00
Tumbler, Cranberry, Gilt, Multicolored Butterflies, Flowers, Reeded Handle, Panels, 3 ¼ In. . . 403.00
Tumbler, Grape Leaves, Insects, Amber, Gold Stems, Tendrils, 4 ¾ In. . . 270.00
Tumbler Set, Flowers, Multicolored, Box, 3 ¾-In. Tumbler, 12 Piece . . . *illus* 600.00
Urn, Black, Bird, Insects, Flowers, Gold Edges, Footed, Faceted Sides, 11 In. . . 1610.00
Vase, Amber, Paneled, Gold Mottled, Enamel, c.1900, 16 ½ In., Pair. . . 410.00
Vase, Aqua, Stylized Birds, Leaves, Leaves, Etched, Flared Wide Mouth, 6 ¼ In. . . 1410.00
Vase, Black Amethyst, Gilt Intaglio Band, Women Warriors, 12 Panels, Flared, Footed, 8 In. . . 470.00
Vase, Clear Shaded To Amethyst, Raised Enamel Hunting Dog, Green, Brown, 5 In. . . 2350.00
Vase, Clear To Blue, Intaglio, Vines, Blooming Flowers, Faceted, 16 In. . . 1000.00
Vase, Coralene Flowers, Peach Ground, White Cased, Applied Handles, 5 ½ In. . . 805.00
Vase, Cranberry, Gold Coralene Flowers, Blue Stamens, White Branches, Shouldered, 10 In. . . 690.00
Vase, Cranberry, Gold Scrolling, Applied Acorns, 7 In. . . 431.00
Vase, Exotic Birds, Aqua, Cameo, Signed, 6 ¼ In. . . *illus* 1200.00
Vase, Ice Blue, Enameled Butterfly, Flowers, Applied Amber Handles, 8 ½ In. . . 350.00
Vase, Moon & Clouds On Lily Pond, Frosted Green, Cameo, Egg Shape, 5 ¼ In. . . 920.00
Vase, Multicolored, Leaves, Gold Scrolls, 4 Amber Ring Handles, 8 In. . . 600.00
Vase, Prussian Blue, Flowers, Egg Shape, Sawtooth Rim, Amber Feet, c.1900, 8 In. . . *illus* 1121.00
Vase, Rubina, Optic Ribbed, Chrysanthemums, Crimped Rim, 11 x 4 ¾ In., Pair . . . 840.00
Vase, Spider Mums, Gold Stalks, Cranberry, 4-Sided, 6 ¾ In. . . 411.00
Vase, Translucent Clear, Green Stem Flowers, Marquetry, Footed, 14 ¼ In. . . 1500.00
Vase, Translucent Green, Enameled Flowers, Lily Pad, Dragonflies, Gold Fish, 9 ½ In., Pair . . 1265.00
Vase, Trumpet, Cranberry, Yellow & Blue Flowers, Gold, Enameled, 13 In. . . 345.00
Vase, Turkeys, Blue To Yellow, Translucent, Cobalt Blue, 10 ¼ In. . . 800.00
Vase, Urn, Cranberry, Multicolored Branches, Leaves, Insects, Acorns, 11 In. . . 1898.00
Vase, Yellow, Elephants In Palm Tree Oasis, Gilt, Intaglio, 11 ½ In. . . 1900.00

MOSS ROSE china was made by many firms from 1808 to 1900. It has a typical moss rose pictured as the design. The plant is not as popular now as it was in Victorian gardens, so the fuzz-covered bud is unfamiliar to most collectors. The dishes were usually decorated with pink and green flowers.

Ashtray, Rectangular, Fluted Edge, Gold Trim, 3 ½ x 2 ½ In., 4 Piece. . . 12.00
Ashtray, Round, Reticulated Border, Lefton, 4 ⅛ In. . . 9.00
Berry Bowl, Bavarian, Scalloped Border, Gold Trim, 5 ¼ In. . . 9.00
Berry Bowl, Gold Trim, Diamond China, Japan, 5 ½ In., 6 Piece. . . 12.00
Biscuit Jar, Ironstone, Brown Transfer, Knopped Lid, 7 x 7 ¾ In. . . 62.00
Bowl, Dessert, Gold Trim, 5 ¼ In. . . 18.00
Bowl, Fruit, Gold Trim, Scalloped, 5 ⅛ In. . . 9.00
Bowl, Vegetable, Oval, Haviland, Gold Rim, 10 ¾ x 7 ¾ In. . . 60.00
Bread & Butter, Luster Ware, Pearlized, Gold Trim, Japan, c.1960, 2 ½ x 3 ¾ In. . . 4.00

Moser, Pitcher, Peacock, Butterfly, Chinese Garden, Enameled, c.1900, 9 In.
$1117.00

Moser, Tumbler Set, Flowers, Multicolored, Box, 3 ¾-In. Tumbler, 12 Piece
$600.00

Moser, Vase, Exotic Birds, Aqua, Cameo, Signed, 6 ¼ In.
$1200.00

Moser, Vase, Prussian Blue, Flowers, Egg Shape, Sawtooth Rim, Amber Feet, c.1900, 8 In.
$1121.00

TIP
Tea stains can be dramatically lightened if they're treated with a mixture of equal parts lemon juice and water. Apply the mixture with a cotton swab, then rinse with cool water.

Moss Rose, Coffeepot, Haviland, c.1880, 9 ¼ In.
$225.00

Moss Rose, Cuspidor, Haviland, Transfer, c.1880, 6 x 7 In.
$350.00

Moss Rose, Vase, Finger, 13 Holes, Gold Sponged Trim, Pedestal Base, 6 In.
$60.00

Candleholder, Cornucopia, Transfer Pattern, 4 In., Pair 20.00
Celery Dish, Edwardian, Limoges 145.00
Cigarette Set, Royal Sealy, Tray, Holder, Ashtrays, Japan, 6 Piece 10.00
Coffeepot, Haviland, c.1880, 9 ¼ In. . . . . . *illus* 225.00
Coffeepot, Sugar & Creamer 30.00
Creamer, Scrolling Gold Gilded Handle, Embossed Rim Design, 1950s 6.00
Cup & Saucer, Demitasse, 41/4 x 13/4 In. . . . . . 18.00 to 20.00
Cup & Saucer, Footed Cup, Raised Handle, Scalloped Saucer, 12 Piece 72.00
Cup & Saucer, Gold Trim, Scalloped, Embossed, Haviland, 6 ⅛ x 3 ¾ In. 25.00
Cup & Saucer, Luster Ware, Pearlized, Gold Trim, Japan, c.1960, 2 ½ x 3 ¾ In. 6.00
Cup & Saucer, Royal Chelsea, Scalloped Edge, Gold Trim 24.00
Cuspidor, 19th Century, 5 x 7 In. 80.00
Cuspidor, Haviland, Transfer, c.1880, 6 x 7 In. . . . . . *illus* 350.00
Dish, Sweetmeat, Octagonal Shape, Scalloped Edges, Roslyn China, England 15.00
Dresser Set, Cologne Bottles, Mirror, Covered Dish, Tray, Japan 55.00
Egg Coddler, Clip, 3 ¾ x 2 ½ In. 13.00
Eggcup, Pedestal, Japan, 2 ⅜ x 1 ¾ In. 28.00
Eggcup, Wavy Top Edge, Gold Trim, Japan, 2 ¼ x 1 ⅞ In., 6 Piece 20.00
Gravy Boat, Underplate, Bavarian, 8 In. 45.00
Jam Jar, Figural Rose Finial 24.00
Lamp, Genie, Electric, 7 x 5 ¼ In. 28.00
Lamp, Oil, Aladdin Style, 6 In. . . . . . 10.00 to 20.00
Lighter, Table, 1960s, 2 ¾ x 2 ½ In. 12.00
Night-Light, Domed Shade, 7-Watt Bulb, In Line Switch, 1950s 27.00
Pitcher, Wash, Haviland, c.1876, 12 In. 600.00
Plate, Bread & Butter, Gold Trim, Scalloped, Embossed Edge, Haviland, 6 ⅛ In. 9.00
Plate, Bread & Butter, Haviland, 6 ¼ In. 5.00
Plate, Dinner, Fuzzy, Haviland, c.1880, 3 Piece 25.00
Plate, Dinner, Gold Trim, Scalloped, Embossed, Haviland, 10 In. 25.00
Plate, Dinner, Luster Ware, Pearlized, Gold Trim, Japan, c.1960, 10 ½ In. 8.00
Plate, Salad, Gold Trim, Haviland, 7 ¼ In. 18.00
Plate, Square, Gold Coast China, Japan, 7 In. 48.00
Plate, Transferware, Staffordshire, A.J. Wilkinson, c.1930 . . . . . 20.00
Platter, East End Pottery, Liverpool, c.1885, 13 x 9 ⅝ In. 35.00
Platter, Oval, Japan, 16 In. 27.00
Platter, Rosenthal, Sterling Silver Rim, 12 In. 135.00
Powder Jar, 3-Footed 16.00
Salt & Pepper, Silver Top, Stopper, 2 ½ In. 22.00
Saucer, Embossed, Scalloped Edge, Japan 5.00
Saucer, Japan, 1950s 5.00
Saucer, Pompadour, Rosenthal 8.00
Serving Bowl, Sterling Silver Base, Aida Shape, 4 ⅛ x 9 ½ In. 165.00
Serving Dish, Cover, Haviland 230.00
Snack Set, Shell Edge, Gold Trim, Lefton, c.1955, 8 ½ In., 2 Piece 45.00
Soup, Dish, Fuzzy, Haviland, c.1880 . . . . . 25.00
Soup, Dish, Scalloped Border, Gold Trim, 9 ⅝ In. 18.00
Sugar, Luster Ware, Pearlized, Gold Trim, Japan, c.1960, 3 ½ In. 10.00
Sugar & Creamer, Ribbed Melon Shape, Gold Handles 26.00
Sugar & Creamer, Royal Albert, Open Sugar, 2 ¼ & 3 ½ In. 28.00
Syrup, Pewter Lid, Staffordshire, c.1878, 7 ¾ x 5 ¼ In. 400.00
Teapot, Bulbous, Knopped Lid, Scalloped Apron Foot 55.00
Teapot, Electric, Japan, 7 In. 12.00
Teapot, Lid, 6 In. 55.00
Teapot, Sugar & Creamer 69.00
Teapot, Warming, Electric, 4 Cup Capacity, Japan, 6 ½ In. 13.00
Tray, Dresser, Scalloped Rim, 6 x 3 ¼ In. 24.00
Trinket Box, Golden Crown, Lid, 2 ½ x 3 In. 22.00
Vase, Finger, 13 Holes, Gold Sponged Trim, Pedestal Base, 6 In. . . . . . *illus* 60.00

MOTHER-OF-PEARL GLASS, or pearl satin glass, was first made in the 1850s in England and in Massachusetts. It was a special type of mold-blown satin glass with air bubbles in the glass, giving it a pearlized color. It has been reproduced. Mother-of-pearl shell objects are listed under Pearl.

Basket, Herringbone, Peach, Fan Shaped, Ruffled Rim, Twisted Handle, 9 In. 200.00
Basket, Moire, White Over Cranberry, Thorn Handles, Crimped Rim, 3 ¾ x 8 ½ In. 180.00

Biscuit Jar, Diamond Quilted, Red To Pink, Enameled Flowers, Leaves, Silver Plated Lid, 7 ¼ In. 795.00
Biscuit Jar, Herringbone, Blue, Lid, Frosted Glass Finial, 8 In. 415.00
Biscuit Jar, Raindrop, Rainbow, Purple Flower, Leaves, Silver Plated Lid, Handle, 8 ½ In. 6500.00
Bowl, Diamond Quilted, Amber, Yellow, Pearl, Scalloped Rim, 2 ¾ x 5 ¼ In. 288.00
Bowl, Diamond Quilted, Apricot, Rolled Ruffled Rim, Clear Feet, Marked, Patent, 3 x 6 ½ In. 850.00
Bowl, Diamond Quilted, Apricot Border, Pink Base, Crimped Rim, 3 ¾ x 7 ¾ In. 385.00
Bowl, Diamond Quilted, Canary Yellow, Scalloped Rim, 4 ½ x 8 ½ In. 490.00
Bowl, Diamond Quilted, Cranberry, Lobed, Scalloped Rim, 4 ¾ x 9 ¾ In. 750.00
Bowl, Diamond Quilted, Cranberry Over Pale Yellow, Foot Ring, 2 ½ x 4 ¼ In. 495.00
Bowl, Diamond Quilted, Rainbow, Scalloped Rim, 3 ¾ x 10 In. 675.00
Bowl, Diamond Quilted, Rainbow, Tricornered, 3 Frosted Feet, 4 ¼ x 7 ½ In. 1400.00
Bowl, Flower & Acorn, Butterscotch, Ruffled, Rigaree Rim, 6 In. 450.00
Bowl, Flower & Acorn, Cranberry Interior, White Ground, Satin, 2 ½ x 9 ¾ In. 790.00
Bowl, Raindrop, Cranberry Border, 3 Clear Twig Feet, 4 ½ x 6 ½ In. 490.00
Bowl, Raindrop, Yellow, Blue Interior, Ruffled Rim, 5 Frosted Petal Feet, 4 ¾ In. 420.00
Bowl, Saucer, Swag, Cranberry, 2 ⅝-In. Bowl 405.00
Butter, Dome Cover, Diamond Quilted, Pink, Frosted Finial, 5 ¾ x 7 ¾ In. 315.00
Candlestick, Raindrop, Green, White Interior, Flowers & Leaves, 8 In., Pair 2900.00
Condiment Jar, Herringbone, White Dogwoods, Gold Branches, Spoon, Lid, 5 In. 403.00
Cruet, Coin Spot, Blue, Faceted Camphor Stopper, 7 In. 515.00
Cruet, Diamond Quilted, Cranberry, Clear Handle, 4 ½ In. 435.00
Cup & Saucer, Raindrop, Cranberry To Pearl, Frosted Handle, Gold Enameled 345.00
Ewer, Diamond Quilted, Pink, Melon Ribbed, Ruffled Rim, Handles, 7 ¼ In. 200.00
Ewer, Diamond Quilted, Yellow To Pearl, Frosted Thorn Handle, 13 ¼ In. *illus* 289.00
Ewer, Herringbone, Rainbow, Frosted Thorn Handle, 12 In. 1060.00
Finger Bowl, Underplate, Pompeian Swirl, Teal Interior, Ruffled Rim, 4 ¼ In. 920.00
Pail, Diamond Quilted, Pink & Pearl, Silver-Plated Handle, 9 In. 400.00
Pitcher, Diamond Quilted, Blue, Clear Twig Handle, 8 ½ In. 1750.00
Pitcher, Diamond Quilted, Rainbow, Clear Handle & Foot Ring, 6 ¾ In. 690.00
Pitcher, Diamond Quilted, Rainbow, Frosted Handle, 5 In. *illus* 2500.00
Pitcher, Herringbone, Canary Yellow, Frosted Handle, 5 ¾ In. 475.00
Pitcher, Raindrop, Rainbow, Frosted Handle, Tricornered Rim, 10 ½ In. 530.00
Plate, Diamond Quilted, Chartreuse, Scalloped Rim, 6 ¼ In. 415.00
Rose Bowl, Peacock Eye, Blue, Green Over Yellow, Enameled Flowers, Leaves, 5 ⅛ In. 4500.00
Rose Bowl, Rainbow, Diamond Quilted, 3-Footed, Broken Egg Shape, 10 In. 1725.00
Saltshaker, Coin Spot, Peach, Blue, Enameled Flowers, 3 ¼ In., Pair 950.00
Sugar Shaker, Raindrop, Apricot To Opal, 5 ¼ In. 1150.00
Tumbler, Herringbone, Pink, Flowers, Leaves, Gold Enameled, 3 ¾ In. 315.00
Urn, Diamond Quilted, Beaded Gold, Enameled Flowers, Apricot, Handles, 5 ½ In. 735.00
Urn, Diamond Quilted, Yellow, Gold Flower & Leaf, 5 In. 420.00
Urn, Herringbone, Birds, Apricot To Pink, Crimped Rim, Frosted Handles, 8 ¼ In. 690.00
Urn, Herringbone, Red To Pearl, Amber Thorn Handles & Rim, Satin, 10 In. 1400.00
Vase, Coin Spot, Alternating Blue & Red, Pinched Sides, c.1890, 9 In. *illus* 125.00
Vase, Coin Spot, Blue & Red, Bulbous, Pinched Stick Neck, c.1890, 9 In. 148.00
Vase, Coin Spot, Pink, Bulbous Base, Stick Neck, Pinched Side, 13 In., Pair 431.00
Vase, Diamond Quilted, Amethyst, Handles, 6 ¼ In. 290.00
Vase, Diamond Quilted, Blue, Ruffled Rim, 8 ¼ In. 145.00
Vase, Diamond Quilted, Blue, Ruffled Rim, 9 ½ In. 295.00
Vase, Diamond Quilted, Cranberry, Crimped Rim, Frosted Feet, 5 x 7 ¼ In. 690.00
Vase, Diamond Quilted, Rainbow, Flared Rim, 5 In. 360.00
Vase, Diamond Quilted, Rainbow, Applied Yellow Rim & Feet, 4 In. 725.00
Vase, Diamond Quilted, Rainbow, Scalloped & Crimped Rim, Oval, 3 Clear Feet, 7 In. 1150.00
Vase, Diamond Quilted, Red, White, Flowers, Leaves, Elongated Neck, 11 ½ In. 1990.00
Vase, Diamond Quilted, Yellow Green, Thorn Handles, Folded Ruffled, 10 ¼ In, Pair 920.00
Vase, Fern, Cranberry, Crimped Rim, 5 ⅜ In. 720.00
Vase, Flower & Acorn, Canary Yellow, Pinched Top, ½ In. 810.00
Vase, Herringbone, Blue, Ribbed, Bottle Shape, 7 ½ In. 290.00
Vase, Herringbone, Butterscotch, Gourd Shape, Thorn Camphor Handles, 8 In. 173.00
Vase, Herringbone, Pink, Spiral Threading, Satin, Elongated Neck, 8 In. 840.00
Vase, Herringbone, Rainbow, Bulbous Base, Stick Neck, Folded Rim, 8 In. 575.00
Vase, Herringbone, Rainbow, Melon Ribbed, Oval, Ruffled Rim, 6 In. 748.00
Vase, Hobnail, Apricot, Amber Shaded To Pale Gold, Folded Rim, 5 ¾ In. 260.00
Vase, Hobnail, Blue, White Interior, Ruffled Rim, 9 ¼ In. 495.00
Vase, Moire, Apricot, Crimped Rim, 3 Reeded Feet, 7 ¼ In. 520.00
Vase, Moire, Cranberry, 6 ½ In. 320.00
Vase, Rainbow, Diamond Quilted, Fluted & Crimped Rim, Marked, Patent, 5 In. 460.00

Mother-Of-Pearl, Ewer, Diamond Quilted, Yellow To Pearl, Frosted Thorn Handle, 13 ¼ In.
$289.00

Mother-Of-Pearl, Pitcher, Diamond Quilted, Rainbow, Frosted Handle, 5 In.
$2500.00

Mother-Of-Pearl, Vase, Coin Spot, Alternating Blue & Red, Pinched Sides, c.1890, 9 In.
$125.00

Mother-Of-Pearl, Vase, Ray, Pink & Lavender, Frosted Applied Rose & Briar, Ruffled Rim, 12 ½ In.
$790.00

Mother-Of-Pearl Glass, Vase, Teardrop, Pink On Blue, White Interior, Oval, Ruffled Rim, 10 ⅛ In.
$2730.00

Motorcycle, Pin, Harley-Davidson, U.A.W. FOA Local 209, c.1940, 1 ¼ In.
$197.00

Vase, Raindrop, Green, Vertically Indented, Crimped Rim, Satin, 8 ¾ In. 400.00
Vase, Raindrop, Pale Amber, Camphor Rim, 8 ¾ In. 210.00
Vase, Raindrop, Yellow Green To Pearl, Enameled Flowers, Vines, Ruffled Rim, 10 In. 620.00
Vase, Raised Diamond & Drop, Rainbow, Bulbous, Scalloped Rim, Looped, Frosted Base, 4 ½ In. 535.00
Vase, Raised Raindrop, Blue, Folded Rim, 5 ¾ In. 378.00
Vase, Ray, Pink & Lavender, Frosted Applied Rose & Briar, Ruffled Rim, 12 ½ In. *illus* 790.00
Vase, Swirl, Blue, 6-Lobes, 8 ¾ In. 475.00
Vase, Swirl, Cranberry, Shaped Neck, 7 ¼ In. 345.00
Vase, Teardrop, Blue & Pink Rainbow, Oval, Tapered Neck, 12 ½ In. 315.00
Vase, Teardrop, Blue To White, Oval, Tapered Neck, 12 ½ In. 372.00
Vase, Teardrop, Pink On Blue, White Interior, Oval, Ruffled Rim, 10 ⅛ In. *illus* 2730.00
Vase, Teardrop, Rainbow, Yellow Ruffled Rim, Looped Brass Wire Mount, 4 In. 230.00
Vase, Zipper, Apricot, Pink Interior, Swirled, Folded Rim, 5 ¾ In. 960.00
Vase, Zipper, Brown, Pink Interior, Ribbed, Swirled, Frosted Petal Rim, 9 In. 1350.00
Vase, Zipper, Cranberry, Round Base, Squared Rim, 4 ¾ In. 345.00
Vase, Zipper, Ribbed, Swirled, Brown, Pink Interior, Crimped Rim, 7 ½ In. 850.00
Vase, Zipper, Yellow Green To Pearl, Globular, Pink Interior, Crimped Rim, Ribbed, 6 ½ In. 490.00
Vase, Zipper, Yellow-Green, Ribbed, Swirl, Bulbous, Ruffled Rim, 7 ½ In. 530.00
Vase, Bud, Diamond Quilted, Rainbow Neck, White Base, 6 In. 675.00

MOTORCYCLES and motorcycle accessories of all types are being collected today. Examples can be found that date back to the early twentieth century. Toy motorcycles are listed in the Toy category.

Oil Can, Harley-Davidson Motorcycle Oil, Orange, Black, Label, Contents, Qt. 120.00
Pin, Harley-Davidson, U.A.W. FOA Local 209, c.1940, 1 ¼ In. *illus* 197.00
Pin, Indian Motorcycle, Pre World War II, Gold Filled, 1937 100.00
Pin, Live To Ride, Ride To Live, Eagle Spirit, Mirror, Gold Filled, c.1937 100.00

MOUNT WASHINGTON, *see Mt. Washington category.*

MOVIE memorabilia of all types is collected. Animation Art, Games, Sheet Music, Toys, and some celebrity items are listed in their own section. A lobby card is 11 by 14 inches. A set of lobby cards includes seven scene cards and one title card. A one sheet, the standard movie poster, is 27 by 41 inches. A three sheet is 81 by 40 inches. A half sheet is 22 by 28 inches. A window card, made of cardboard, is 14 by 22 inches. An insert is 14 by 36 inches. A herald is a promotional item handed out to patrons. Press books, sent to exhibitors to promote a movie, contain ads & lists of what is available for advertising, i.e., posters, lobby cards. Press kits, sent to the media, contain photos and details about the movie, i.e., stars' biographies & interviews.

Bank Check, Marilyn Monroe, Signed, 1958, 6 ½ x 2 ⅞ In. 1986.00
Costume, Detroit Tigers Cap, Cobb, Tommy Lee Jones, 1994 520.00
Herald, A Clockwork Orange, Stanley Kubrick, 1992 6.50
Herald, The Gumball Rally, Gary Busey, 1976 5.50
Lobby Card, Ever Since Eve, Anny Savage, Ross Hunter, 1944 37.50
Lobby Card, G-Men, James Cagney, 1964 21.00
Lobby Card, Gone With The Wind, Burning Of Atlanta, 1968 22.50
Lobby Card, Holiday In Havana, Desi Arnaz, 1949, Title Card 110.00
Lobby Card, Island In The Sky, John Wayne, 1953 11.00
Lobby Card, Lassie Come Home, Roddy McDowell, 1943 16.00
Lobby Card, The Day The Earth Stood Still, Michael Rennie, 1951 3575.00
Lobby Card, The Misfits, Marilyn Monroe, Clark Gable, 1961 82.00
Lobby Card, The Reformer And The Redhead, June Allyson, 1950, Pair 21.00
Lobby Card, Through The Back Door, Mary Pickford, 1921 215.00
Megaphone, Rudy Valle's, Autographed, World War II, 1942-44 145.00
Photo, Billie Burke, 1912, 9 x 13 In. 131.45
Photo, Dennis Morgan, Merle Oberon, 1944, 10 x 13 In. 13.00
Photo, Gary Cooper & Frank Capra, 1936, 8 x 10 In. 145.00
Photo, Ingrid Bergman, 1945, 11 x 14 In. 468.00
Photo, Jeanne Cagney, 1942, 8 x 10 In. 12.00
Photo, John Lennon, Yoko Ono, 1970, 8 x 10 In. 14.50
Photo, Martin Scorsese, Robert DeNiro, 1976, 8 x 10 In. 10.00
Pin, Metro-Goldwyn Pictures, Train, 1 In. 25.00
Pin, Warner Bros., Knute Rockne, Gold, Black, Pudlin, Back Paper 43.00
Poster, An American In Paris, Gene Kelly, 1951, Half Sheet 179.00
Poster, Body & Soul, John Garfield, 1947, 1 Sheet 119.00

'**oster,** Bonnie & Clyde, Waren Beatty, Faye Dunaway, 1967, Insert 179.25
oster, Call Me Madam, Ethel Merman, 1953, Window Card 10.00
oster, Mighty Mouse & Terry Toon, Cartoon Art, 1955, 1 Sheet...... 425.00
'**oster,** Mummy's Curse, Lon Chaney, 1944, Linen Backed, 1 Sheet 2900.00
'**oster,** On Top Of Old Smokey, Gene Autry, 1952, 1 Sheet...... 85.00
'**oster,** Panama Lady, Lucille Ball, 1939, Linen Backed, 1 Sheet...... 165.00
'**oster,** Sundown On The Prairie, Tex Ritter, 1939, 1 Sheet...... 425.00
oster, Taxi Driver, Robert DeNiro, 1976, 1 Sheet 185.00
'**oster,** The Big Street, Lucille Ball, Henry Fonda, 1942, 1 Sheet...... 578.00
'**oster,** The Eagle, Rudolph Valentino, 1925, Linen Backed, 1 Sheet 38837.50
oster, The Man With The Golden Arm, Saul Bass, c.1955, 35 x 25 In. 2040.00
oster, The Spy Who Loved Me, Roger Moore, 1977, 1 Sheet...... 119.00
oster, Two Gun Justice, Tim McCoy, 1936, 1 Sheet...... 425.00
ress Book, Lola Montez, Peter Ustinov, Martine Carol, 1968 ...... 7.50
ress Book, The Uninhibited, Melina Mercouri, James Mason, 1967...... 10.50
ress Kit, Black Eye, Fred Williamson, 1974 ...... 7.00
ress Kit, King Ralph, John Goodman, 1990...... 8.50
rogram, Superman, Christopher Reeve, 1978...... 14.50

IT. JOYE is an enameled cameo glass made in the late nineteenth and twentieth centuries by aint-Hilaire Touvier de Varraux and Co. of Pantin, France. This same company made De Vez 'ass. Pieces were usually decorated with enameling. Most pieces are not marked.

owl, Cyclamen Flowers, Gold Enameled Leaves & Stems, Frosted Textured Ground, 4 In. ... 480.00
owl, Honey Amber, White Opaque Overlay, Enameled Flower, Oval, $4\frac{1}{4}$ In...... 175.00
ase, Acorns, Flared, Green, Gold, Enameled, 13 In. 950.00
ase, Amethyst Enameled Flower Blossoms, Green Chipped Ice Ground, $7\frac{1}{4}$ In...... 840.00
ase, Flower Blossoms, Green Leaves, Raisin Colored, Gold Enameled Band, $7\frac{3}{4}$ In. 660.00
ase, Gold Chrysanthemums, Textured Green Body, Inverted Baluster Shape, 6 In. 325.00
ase, Golden Mums, Green Textured Ground, Gold Enameled, Cameo, $5\frac{7}{8}$ In. ...... *illus* 275.00
ase, Green, Thistles, Leaves, Carved, 26 In...... 3360.00
ase, Irises, Enameled, Purple, White & Mauve, 12 In. 480.00

IT. WASHINGTON Glass Works started in 1837 in South Boston, Massachusetts. In 1870 the mpany moved to New Bedford, Massachusetts. Many types of art glass were made there until 394, when the company merged with Pairpoint Manufacturing Co. Amberina, Burmese, Crown ilano, Cut Glass, and Peachblow are each listed in their own category.

iscuit Jar, Napoli, Palmer Cox Brownies & Duck, Gold Webbing, Signed, 8 x 6 In...... 5460.00
iscuit Jar, White Opal, Gold Enameled Flowers, Green Ground, Melon Ribbed, 9 In...... 173.00
ride's Basket, Enameled Mums, Ruffled Edge, Holder, Handles, 11 x 14 In...... 3721.00
ride's Basket, Oval Bowl, Yellow, Cut Top, Gold Flowers, Footed Stand, 11 In. 978.00
ride's Bowl, White On Pink, Griffins, Urns, Cameo, Rogers Bros., Frame, 10 In. 7188.00
ard Tray, Colonial Ware, Blue Hydrangeas, Glossy Opal, Shell Shape, 7 In. 144.00
ondiment Set, Ribbed Barrel Shape, Enameled Flowers, Pairpoint Caddy, 7 In., 3 Piece. ... 345.00
reamer, Colonial Ware, Violets, Ferns, Cream Ground, Marked, $5\frac{7}{8}$ In. ...... *illus* 118.00
reamer, Cream, Blue, Orange & Yellow Flowers, Ribbed, Silver Spout, 4 In...... 236.00
ish, Napoli, Palmer Cox Brownies Marching, Black Cat, Gold Web, Cut Rim, 6 In...... 2530.00
ish, Sweetmeat, Egg Shape, Opal, Blue, White Daisies, Gold Blue Border, $4\frac{1}{2}$ In...... 345.00
arniture, Blue, Rose, Shaded Light To Dark, Ruffled Edge, 9 x 6 In., Pair 411.00
umidor, Cigar, Opal, Yellow Enamel Leaves, Acorns, Script Cigars, 6 In...... 748.00
m Jar, Opal, Enameled Crimson Flowers, Stems, Flip Lid, No. 4158/221, 4 In...... 200.00
r, Sweetmeat, Opal Body, Leaves, Acorns, Metal Lid, $6\frac{1}{2}$ In...... 288.00
rdiniere, Cream Ground, Red, White Roses, Gold Enameled Scrolling Lattice Rim, 7 In.... 805.00
amp, Flowers, Sky Blue Ground, Raised Gold Work, Gold Tracery, 18 In...... 546.00
uffineer, Pineapple & Fan Cutting, Original Lid, $4\frac{1}{8}$ In...... 531.00
ustard, Ribbed Pillar, Blue Flowers, Flip Lid, 3 In...... 144.00
itcher, Tankard, Inverted Thumbprint, Amberina, Reeded Handle, 9 In...... 288.00
ose Bowl, Enameled Spider Mums, Crimped Edge, Marked, 616, 4 In. 110.00
alt & Pepper, Bark Texture, Rose To Clear, Blue To Clear, Gold, 3 In., Pair ...... *illus* 1155.00
alt & Pepper, Ribbed Pillar, Amber To Peach Body, Meriden, Caddy, 7 In...... 201.00
alt & Pepper, Tomato Shape, Amethyst Flowers, Leaf Gold Embossed Metal, Caddy, 6 In. ... 518.00
cent Bottle, Flowers, Yellow, Opal, Bulbous, Mold Blown Leaves, 8 In. 750.00
ugar Shaker, Fig, Enameled Blue, Pink Flowers, Gold Lines, 4 In. 863.00
ugar Shaker, Fig, Opalescent Blue, Pansies, $4\frac{1}{4}$ In...... 1265.00
ugar Shaker, Fig, Pale Yellow, Enameled Flowers, Metal Lid, 4 In. 1116.00

Mt. Joye, Vase, Golden Mums, Green Textured Ground, Gold Enameled, Cameo, $5\frac{7}{8}$ In.
$275.00

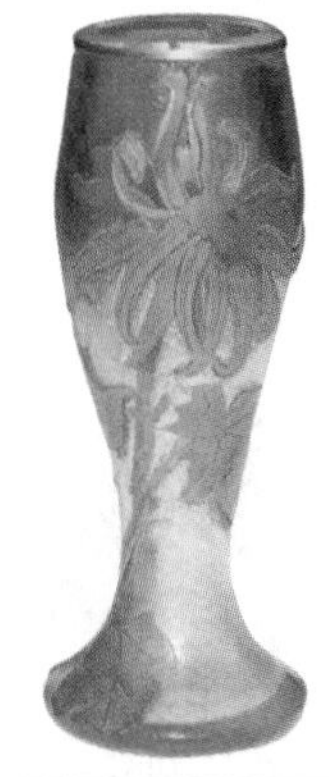

Mt. Washington, Creamer, Colonial Ware, Violets, Ferns, Cream Ground, Marked, $5\frac{7}{8}$ In.
$118.00

M

Mt. Washington, Salt & Pepper, Bark Texture, Rose To Clear, Blue To Clear, Gold, 3 In., Pair
$1155.00

TIP

Metal saltshaker tops can be kept from rusting or oxidizing if they are cleaned or sprayed with a silicone product. Wax will also help.

Music, Guitar, Gibson, No. 93456005, Hummingbird Model, Spruce, Mahogany, Mother-Of-Pearl Inlay
$820.00

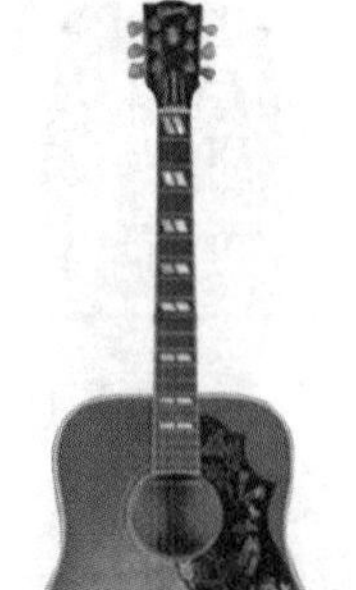

Music, Harp, Empire Style, Satinwood, Pine, 7 Pedals, 43 Strings, Sebastian Erard, c.1800, 67 x 31 In.
$5175.00

Music, Mandolin, Gibson, Case
$350.00

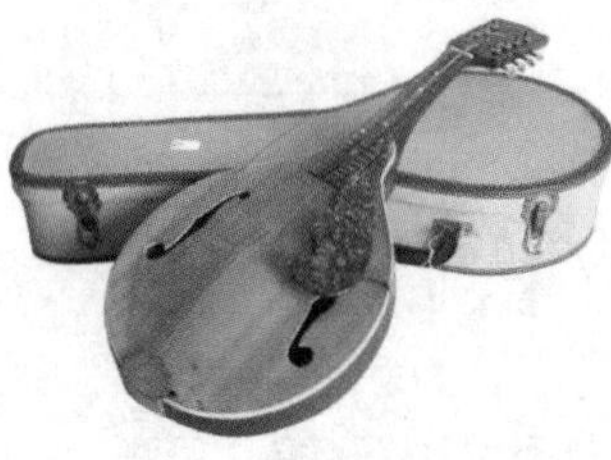

Sugar Shaker, Melon Ribbed, Enameled Flowers, 2 ½ In. 29.0
Sugar Shaker, Molded Panels, Enameled Pink & Blue Flowers, Cream Ground, 2 ⅜ In. 236.0
Sugar Shaker, Pillar, Opal, Blue Pastel Flowers, 4 In., Pair 50.0
Syrup, Enameled Pink Daisies, Flip Lid, 8 In.. . . . . 125.0
Syrup, Pineapple & Fan Cutting, Metal Thump Lift Lid, Side Handle, 5 ⅜ In. 590.0
Toothpick, Chartreuse Ground, Enameled Spring Flowers, 1 ½ In. 374.0
Toothpick, Finger-Cut Rim, Enameled, Beige, 2 ½ x 2 ½ In.. . . . . 373.0
Toothpick, Lava, Multicolored Shards, Gold Highlights, Square Top, Bulbous, 2 In. 5750.0
Toothpick, Shouldered, Enameled Autumn Leaves, Blueberries, 2 ½ In. 345.0
Tumbler, Lava Glass, Multicolored Shards, Raspberry Ground, Gold Enameled, 3 In. 6038.0
Urn, Egyptian, Spring Garden, Handles, Footed, 10 ½ In. 4500.0
Vase, Clear, Frosted, Enameled Pansies, Applied Handle, Signed, 5 ¾ In. 920.0
Vase, Clear, Ribbed, Reverse Painted, Spider Mums, Amethyst, Teal, Brown, 18 ¼ In. 288.0
Vase, Colonial Ware, Opal, Enameled, Louis XVI Portrait, Gold Highlights, 11 ½ In.. . . . . 2300.0
Vase, Jack-In-The-Pulpit, Opal, Applied Pedestal Foot, Swirled Ribs, 12 ¼ In. 600.0
Vase, Lava, Black Ground, Applied Reeded Handles, Multicolored Shards, 3 ¾ In.. . . . . 1265.0
Vase, Lava, Pink, Blue & White Shards, Black Ground, Handles, 3 ¾ x 3 ½ In.. . . . . 4025.0
Vase, Melon Ribbed, Tricornered Rim, Stippled Flowers, Gold Medallions, 8 In. 1150.0
Vase, Multicolored Shards, Lava Black Ground, Gold, Enameled, 3 ¾ In.. . . . . 5175.0
Vase, Pear Shape, Flying Ducks, Gold Clouds, Moon, Rolled Rim, c.1893, 7 ¼ In. 1434.0
Vase, Spider Web & Spiky Leaf, Pink Thistle, Slender Neck, Ruffled Edge, 14 ¼ In. 575.0
Vase, Stick, Gourd Base, Enameled Flowers, Gold Stems, 8 In. 1898.0
Vase, Stick, Lava, Amethyst, Multicolored Shards, 10 ¼ In. 8050.0

MULBERRY ware was made in the Staffordshire district of England from about 1850 to 1860. The dishes were decorated with a reddish brown transfer design, now called mulberry. Many of the patterns are similar to those used for flow blue and other Staffordshire transfer wares.

Plate, Battle Scene, Staffordshire, 7 ½ In.. . . . . 388.0

MULLER FRERES, French for Muller Brothers, made cameo and other glass from about 1895 to 1933. Their factory was first located in Luneville, then in nearby Croismare, France. Pieces were usually marked with the company name.

Vase, Dragonflies, Lake Landscape, Enameled, Flattened Oval, 6 ½ x 3 ½ In.. . . . . 2040.0
Vase, Egg Shape, Shouldered, Leaves, Pods Over Crimson, Frosted, 5 In. 345.0
Vase, Egg Shape, Trees, Mountain Lane, Broken Pine, Chateau, Flared, 15 ¾ In. 4720.0
Vase, Flared Rim, Mottled Blue & Orange, Art Deco, 10 In. 1105.0
Vase, Landscape, Trees, Blue, Amethyst Lake, Mountains, Shoreline, Cameo, 7 ½ In. 4000.0
Vase, Mottled Orange, Crimson Outlined Blue Pinwheels, Signed, 6 ½ In. 374.0
Vase, Mottled Yellow, Blue, Green, Butterflies, Cameo, Signed, 9 ½ In. 3738.0
Vase, Panthers, Blue, Geometric, Frosted, Silver Foil, Art Deco, 9 ½ In.. . . . . 4200.0
Vase, Pink, Gray, Enameled Rain Scene, Cameo, Signed, 3 In. 518.0
Vase, Winter Trees, Mottled Purple To Yellow, 2 Horses, Riders, Hunting Dogs, Cameo, 8 In. . . 978.0

MUNCIE Clay Products Company was established by Charles Benham in Muncie, Indiana, in 1922. The company made pottery for the florist and giftshop trade. The company closed by 1939. Pieces are marked with the name *Muncie* or just with a system of numbers and letters, like *1A*

Pitcher, Terra-Cotta Matte Glaze, Jade Green Drip Glaze, 7 In. 175.0
Vase, Green Matte Over Lilac, 9 ⅛ In. 177.0
Vase, Ruba Rombic, Black High Glaze, 6 x 4 In.. . . . . 115.0

MURANO, *see Glass-Venetian category.*

MUSIC boxes and musical instruments are listed here. Phonograph records, jukeboxes, phonographs, and sheet music are listed in other categories in this book.

Accordion, Hohner, Regina Style, c.1930, 8 ½ x 10 In. . . . . 35.
Banjo, Bacon & Day, Style 1, Tenor, c.1930, 11 In.. . . . . 1293.
Banjo, Fairbanks & Cole, 5-String, Stamped, c.1895, 11 In. . . . . 646.
Banjo, Vega No. 2, 5-String, Rosewood, Mother-Of-Pearl Inlays, Resonator. . . . . 2185.
Bow, Otto Hoyer, Octagonal Stick, Silver Mounted, 55 Grams . . . . 999.
Bow, Violin, Eugene Cuniot, Ebony Frog, Nickel & Ebony Adjuster, c.1900, 58 Grams. . . . . 1880.
Bow, Violin, G.A. Pfretzschner, Octagonal Stick, Silver Adjuster, 62 Grams. . . . . 1410.
Bow, Violin, JTL, Ebony Frog, Pearl Eye, Nickel Ebony Adjuster, c.1920, 63 Grams . . . . 2468.
Bow, Violin, Larry Thibouville, Nickel Mounted, 62 Grams . . . . 499.

M

Bow, Violin, Louis Bazin, Ebony Frog, Pearl Eye, Nickel Adjuster, c.1935, 61 Grams 2115.00
Bow, Violin, Otto Hoyer, Silver & Ebony Adjuster, Pearl Eye, 53 Grams 1175.00
Bow, Violoncello, Silver Mounted, Ebony Frog, Pearl Eye, Silver Adjuster, 80 Grams 4230.00
Box, 12 Tunes, Swiss Cylinder, Wood, Applied Design 725.00
Box, Coin-Operated, Teutonic Style, Walnut, Fidelio, Finials, Bells, c.1907, 80 x 30 x 15 In.... 10640.00
Box, Coin-Operated, Walnut, Columned Door, Fretwork, 39 Notes, Germany, c.1900, 35 x 24 x 15 In. 8400.00
Box, Criterion, Mixed Hardwoods, Walnut, Crank Mechanism, 11 ½ x 23 In.. .... 3910.00
Box, Cylinder, Allard, Lever Wind, Grained Case, Tune Sheet, Inlay, 13 ½ In.. .... 823.00
Box, Cylinder, Cuendet, American Market, Grained Case, Transfer On Lid, 18 In. 470.00
Box, Cylinder, Henriot, 4 Tunes, 8 In. 1116.00
Box, Cylinder, Inlaid, Rosewood, Mahogany, 6 Tunes, 4 ½ x 12 x 6 ½ In. 330.00
Box, Cylinder, M.J. Paillard & Co., Model 22, Style M, Rosewood Case, 8 Tunes, 15 x 36 In. ... 3800.00
Box, Cylinder, Mermod Freres, Crank Wind, 10 Tunes, 6 In. 353.00
Box, Cylinder, Mermod Freres, Nickel Plated, Crank Wind, 12 Tunes, 13 In. 705.00
Box, Cylinder, Nicole Freres, Key Wind, 8 Tunes 1998.00
Box, Cylinder, Nicole Freres, Lever Wind, 8 Tunes. 940.00
Box, Cylinder, Rosewood, Flower Inlay, c.1880 .... 4312.00
Box, Cylinder, Rosewood Inlaid Lid, Winding Lever, 13 ½ In.. .... 1058.00
Box, Cylinder, Snare Drum, 6 Decorated Bells, Castanets, 18-Note Organ, Inlaid Case, 12 x 25 In.. 3450.00
Box, Federalist Style, Wood Case, Glass Door, 78 In.. .... 11200.00
Box, Figural, Woman, Peasant Dress, Porcelain, 10 In.. .... 176.00
Box, Fruitwood, 12 Tunes, Swiss, c.1896, 20 x 7 x 10 In. 3360.00
Box, Gilt, Limoges, Metal, Paneled Sides, 4 x 4 ½ In. 175.00
Box, LeCoultre Freres, Walnut Case, Key Wind, 4 Tunes 382.00
Box, Lyon Stealy, Empress, Mahogany, Interior Crank, 12-In. Metal Discs, 1905, 10 ½ x 19 x 17 In... 1430.00
Box, Mandolin, Paillard Vaucher Fils, Lever Wind, Zither, Case, 22 In.. .... 764.00
Box, Mira, Double Comb, Oak Case, 10 12-In. Discs, 20 ½ In.. .... 1293.00
Box, Monopol, Floor, Disc, 76 Teeth, Steel Comb, 26 Discs, Oak Case, Sweden, 23 x 14 ½ In. .. 4014.00
Box, Nicole Freres, Lever Wind, Grained Case, Rosewood, Inlay, 21 In.. .... 1058.00
Box, Orpheus, Disc, Coin-Operated, 110 Teeth, Duplex Comb, Wood Case, Ludwig, c.1900, 31 x 18 In. 2676.00
Box, Painted, Roses, Pink, 2 ¼ x 4 ¾ x 6 In. 47.00
Box, Polyphon, Single Comb, Wind Motor, Walnut Case, Cherubs, 7 Discs, 12 In.. .... 411.00
Box, Regina, Double Comb, Celluloid Plaque, Mahogany Case, 1800s, 22 In. 2350.00
Box, Regina, Double Comb, Mahogany Case, 10 Discs, 1897, 15 ½ x 20 In.. .... 2938.00
Box, Regina, Mahogany Case, Serpentine, 50 15 ½-In. Discs, 13 x 22 x 19 ½ In.. .... 6050.00
Box, Regina, Walnut, Soundboard, Windup, 5 15 ½-In. Discs, 11 x 21 ½ x 19 ½ In. 2900.00
Box, Singing Bird, Bobbing, Fluttering, Domed Cage, Cylinder, 10 ¾ In. 235.00
Box, Singing Bird, Bontems, 2 Birds, Brass Cage, Barrel Movement, 19 In. 2468.00
Box, Singing Bird, Brass Wire Cage, Wood Base, Gesso Bands, Early 1900s,11 x 20 In.. .... 1380.00
Box, Singing Bird, German Brass, Early 20th Century, 11 ½ x 6 In. 234.00
Box, Singing Bird, Mechanical, Leather Case, Silver Plated, Embossed, Germany, 4 x 2 ¼ In. . 4480.00
Box, Singing Bird, Moves Head, Beak, Tail, Brass Cage, Coin Operated, 21 In.. .... 1175.00
Box, Singing Bird, Red, Black, Moving Heads, Beaks, Tails, Germany, 16 In. 411.00
Box, Singing Birds, 2 Birds, Mechanical, Brass, Ironwork Cage, 21 In.. .... 1610.00
Box, Singing Birds, Enameled Case, Gilt Brass Trim, Painted, Griesbaum, 1900s, 2 x 4 In. ... 3300.00
Box, Sorrento, Exotic Wood Inlay, Meekins Music Box Co., 6 Porter Discs, 11 ½ x 24 In. 4950.00
Box, Stella, Double Comb, Mahogany Case, 10 17 ¼-In. Discs, 28 ½ In.. .... 3819.00
Box, Sublime Harmonic Cartel, Reuge, No. 1068, Double Comb, Rosewood Veneered Case, 20 In.... 1410.00
Box, Trunk Shape, Drawer, Flip-Up Top, Pop-Up Bird, Gilt Bronze, Key Wind, 3 x 4 ⅜ In.. .... 767.00
Box, Fruitwood, 6 Airs, 8 Cylinders, Hinged Lid, Wind Lever, Swiss, c.1860, 16 ½ In.. .... 385.00
Box, Single Comb, Lithograph On Lid, Wind Lever, Polyphon, Germany, c.1904, 12 In. 880.00
Bugle, Brass & Silver, Oval Bell Mouth, Henry Keat, 7 ½ In. 633.00
Clarinet, Basswood, Ivory, Brass, 1820s 685.00
Concertina, Pearl Queen, Abalone, Figured Wood Inlay, Bone Buttons, 1920s, 10 x 18 In. ... 288.00
Decanter, Wood, Carved, Figural, Old German Man & Woman, 10 In., 2 Piece. 205.00
Drum, Marching, Cowes Unit, Naval Insignia 165.00
Drum, Marching, Wood, Banded, Brass Rivets, Painted Red, Rope Strap, 1800s, 25 x 24 ½ In. 1344.00
Drum, Military, Brass, Wooden Bands, Rawhide Heads, Cast Brass Eagle Hanger, Ohio, 15 x 8 In. 374.00
Flute, Buffet & Crampon, Silver, Case, c.1920. .... 764.00
Flute, Ebonized Wood, Case, J.C. Haynes & Co. 649.00
Guitar, C.F. Martin, Nazareth, Model 000-21, Case, 1953, 19 ⅜ In. 7050.00
Guitar, C.F. Martin, Nazareth, Model 000-42, Case, 1995, 19 ⅜ In. 7050.00
Guitar, Epiphone, Emperor, No. 55637, Flower Pearl Inlay, Case, 1946, 20 9/16 In. 4700.00
Guitar, Fender, Jazzmaster, Fullerton, Electric, Stamped 126751, Case, 1966, 17 ⅜ In. 7050.00
Guitar, Gibson, No. 93456005, Hummingbird Model, Spruce, Mahogany, Mother-Of-Pearl Inlay .. *illus* 820.00

TIP
Never put a stringed instrument near a window, a heat duct, or an air-conditioning outlet. Temperature changes and sunlight dry out the wood and can warp or crack the instrument.

Music, Nickelodeon, Oak, Leaded, Stained Glass, Stool, Ragola Co., 55 x 61 x 27 In.
$6325.00

Music, Piano, Baby Grand, Steinway, Walnut, Model M, Bench, 1953, 38 x 57 x 61 In.
$9000.00

TIP
Heat can affect a piano's sound. Do not put an antique or new piano in direct sunlight or near a heat or air-conditioning vent. An interior wall is best.

M

TIP
Never stop a music box in the middle of a tune. If the box is later moved, there is more likely to be damage to the spikes on the cylinder if it is not at the end of a song.

Music, Stand, Lyre Form, Black, Gilt, c.1815-30, 43 x 26 x 14 In.
$1140.00

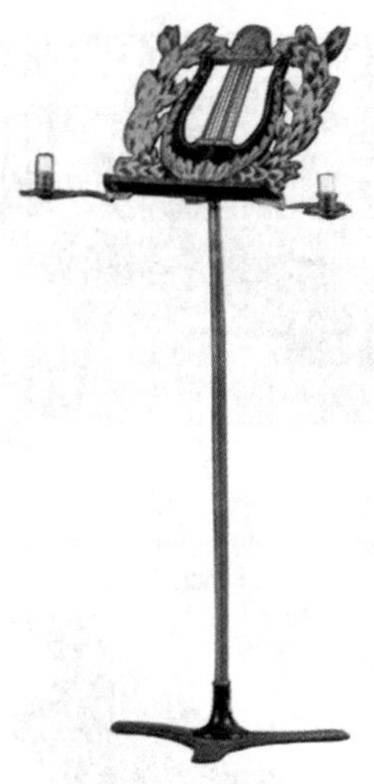

Stradivarius
The label of Antonius Stradivarius has been forged and appears in many Nineteenth- and Twentieth-century violins of low value. One type of labeled violin was originally offered in the Sears catalog for $7.

Guitar, Gibson Les Paul Jr., Original Pots, 1954 . . . . 9350.00
Guitar, Rosewood, One Piece Back & Sides, Spruce Top, Slotted Peghead, John c. Haynes 517.00
Harmonica, 2-Sided, Beaver Brand, Key Of E, University Chimes, Box, Germany, 3 x 9 In. 110.00
Harp, Empire Style, Satinwood, Pine, 7 Pedals, 43 Strings, Sebastian Erard, c.1800, 67 x 31 In. *illus* 5175.00
Harp, Lap Top, Hardwood, Decals, 2 x 13 x 19 In. 23.00
Harp, Lyon & Healy, 45 Strings, 6 Pedals, Carved, Gilt, 68 In. 4406.00
Harp, Maple, Gilded, Sebastian Erard, 66 ½ x 32 In. 5280.00
Mandolin, C.F. Martin & Co., Style C, Stamped 10831, Case, 1924, 11 ⅛ In. 940.00
Mandolin, Gibson, Case . . . . *illus* 350.00
Mandolin, Lyon & Healy, Style A, No. 1256, Case, c.1920, 12 ⅞ In. 2703.00
Mandolin, Tortoiseshell, Mother-Of-Pearl, Ivory, 19th Century, 4 ½ In. 35.00
Nickelodeon, Oak, Leaded, Stained Glass, Stool, Ragola Co., 55 x 61 x 27 In. . . . . *illus* 6325.00
Organ, Concert Roller Wooden Pin Cylinder, Crank, Oak, 12 ½ x 18 x 15 In. 460.00
Organ, Lap Top, Burl Mahogany, Ivory, Ebony, Carrying Case, L.H. Jones, 8 x 28 x 11 In. 600.00
Organ, Pump, W.W. Kimball, Chicago, Victorian, 75 x 41 In. 900.00
Organ, Walnut, Renaissance Revival, Pierced Carved Doors, Crest, c.1875 . . . . 43125.00
Organette, Celestina, 20 Note Paper Roll Organ, Mechanical Orguinette Co. 948.00
Pianette Tabletop Barrel Piano, Mahogany, Hand Cranked, 6 Tunes, 22 Notes, 37 x 16 x 14 In. 920.00
Piano, Baby Grand, Dark Brown, Square Legs, Spade Feet, Brambach, 59 In. 1840.00
Piano, Baby Grand, Steinway, Walnut, Model M, Bench, 1953, 38 x 57 x 61 In. . . . . *illus* 9000.00
Piano, Baby Grand, Weber, Black Lacquered, Neoclassical Style, 39 ½ x 61 x 57 In. 2360.00
Piano, Classical, Mahogany, Mahogany Veneer, Robert & William Nunns, New York, 37 x 31 In. 575.00
Piano, Concert, Lochmann, Coin-Operated, No. 100, Discs, c.1900, 33 x 29 In. 20068.00
Piano, Grand, Ebonized, C. Bechstein, Model M/P 192, c.1890, 39 x 57 In. 4800.00
Piano, Grand, Howard, Ebonized, Bench, 40 ¼ x 62 x 57 ½ In. 1180.00
Piano, Grand, Pleyel, Rosewood, Carved, Brass, Inlay, Louis Grunewald, c.1855, 36 x 51 x 85 In. . 6900.00
Piano, Grand, Steinway, Mahogany, c.1927 . . . . 7700.00
Piano, Grand, Steinway & Sons, Model B, Ser. No. 409352, Ebonized Case, Bench, 1968, 7 Ft. . 14900.00
Piano, Player, Manufactured By Stafford Nickelodeon Co., Pat.1919 . . . . 4400.00
Piano Hammer, Rosewood Handle, 3 Original Heads, German Silver Ferrule, 11 In. 143.00
Pianoforte, M. Clementi & Co., Mahogany, 73 Notes, Ivory Keys, 35 x 71 x 29 In. 2006.00
Record Cleaner, Cello, Nipper, c.1930, 3 ½ In. 76.00
Saxophone, Tenor, Henri Selmer, Mark VI, Case, 1973 . . . . 4113.00
Stand, Lyre Form, Black, Gilt, c.1815-30, 43 x 26 x 14 In. . . . . *illus* 1140.00
Symphonion, Falstaff, Coin-Operated, 84 Teeth, Duplex Comb, 10 Discs, 43 ½ In. 14717.00
Trumpet, Vincent Bach, 15 ⅜ In. 1528.00
Violin, Emile Germain, Case, 1907, 13 ⅞ In. 9988.00
Violin, Emile Laurent, 1923, 14 In. 9400.00
Violin, Francois Barzoni, 2 Bows, 22 In. 935.00
Violin, Giuseppe Ornati, 1911, 14 1/16 In. 1645.00
Violin, Helen Huxtable, Boxton, 1948, 13 15/16 In. 499.00
Violin, Honore Derazey, Branded Internally, 14 ⅛ In. 3055.00
Violin, Nicolaus Amatus Cremone, 2 Bows, 23 In. 330.00
Violin, P.C. Paulsen, Single Board, Curly Maple, Box, Case, c.1919, 23 ¾ x 7 ½ In. 345.00
Violin, Sebastian Klozin Mittenwald, Tiger Back, Gold Mounted Lupot Bow, Case, 1700s 350.00
Violin, Tiger Stripe Maple, Germany, 24 x 8 In. 330.00
Violin Case, Wood, Carved Fish On Lid, Black Paint, 1860-70 . . . . 1850.00
Zither, Menzenhauer, No. 2, Panama Model 1915, c.1894, 19 ½ x 13 In. 225.00
Zither, Spruce Backboard, Oval Sound Hole, White, Plastic Perfing, Case, 23 x 14 x 2 In. 60.00

MUSTACHE CUPS were popular from 1850 to 1900 when the large, flowing mustache was in style. A ledge of china or silver held the hair out of the liquid in the cup. This kept the mustache tidy and also kept the mustache wax from melting. Left-handed mustache cups are rare but are being reproduced.

Bird On Berry Tree Limb, Painted, Sculptured Base, Finger Handle, 3 ¾ x 3 ½ In. 235.00
Blue Birds & Leaves, Transfer, J.C. Moreland, 3 ¾ In. 315.00
Colonel Ichabod Conk, Handle, 4 x 3 ½ In. 10.00
Decal Roses, Gold Rim, White Embossed Ground, Short & Wide, 3 x 3 ½ In. 39.00
Eagle, Flowers, Transfer, William Schaefer, 3 ¾ x 3 ½ In. 235.00
Gay Nineties Design, Enesco, 4 x 3 ¾ In. 68.00
Hand Painted Flowers, Light Blue, Gold Trim, Right Handed, Victorian, 3 ¼ x 3 ½ In. 35.00
Owl Sitting On Tree Limb, Transfer, Coson H. Adams, 3 ½ x 3 ½ In. 285.00
Papa In Raised Gold Lettering, Smooth Ridges, Gold Trim, Handle 50.00
Pink & White, Lusterware, Branch Of Gold Berries, 3 ½ x 4 ¼ In. 25.00

nk Dogwood Flowers & Leaves, Peachy Orange, Scrolled Handle, Nippon, 3 ½ x 4 In. 30.00
nk Flowers, Gold Centers, Gold Trim, White China, Handle, 3 ½ x 5 In. 22.00
nk Flowers & Green Leaves, Ornate Handle, Nippon, 3 ½ x 3 ¼ In................... 30.00
ose, Hand Painted, Germany.. 5.00
calloped Insert, Scroll Pattern, Mold, Gold Trim 9.00
king Surrounded By Beads, Milk Glass, Hobbs, Bruckunier, 1867.................... 295.00
hite Ground, Dark Pink Border, Handle, 3 ¼ x 4 In................................ 22.00
llow Violets, Metallic Gold Detailing, Hand Painted, Handle, 3 ⅜ x 3 ¼ In.............. 75.00

Z AUSTRIA is the wording on a mark used by Moritz Zdekauer on porcelains made at s works in Altrolau, Austria, from 1884 to 1909. The mark was changed to *MZ Altrolau* 1909, when the firm was purchased by C.M. Hutschenreuther. The firm operated under the name rolau Porcelain Factories from 1909 to 1945. It was nationalized after World War II. The pieces were corated with lavish floral patterns and overglaze gold decoration. Full sets of dishes were made as well vases, toilet sets, and other wares.

MZ Austria

wl, Footed, Inward Folding Shape, Gold Edges, Scalloped Border, Roses, 4 x 8 x 7 In. 199.00
wl, Vegetable, Gold Trim, Handles, Cover, Finial, 12 ¼ x 6 ½ x 5 ¼ In.................. 36.00
ke Plate, Art Nouveau, Gilded Handles, 1900.. 72.00
ke Plate, Poppies, Thorny Vines, Multicolored Scalloped Rim, Handles, 10 In. 105.00
arger, Grapes, Art Nouveau, Signed, c.1884, 13 In.................................. 185.00
ug, Cherries, Gold Trim, 4 ½ In. .... *illus* 40.00
ate, Dessert, Berries, Marked, c.1884, 6 In.. 10.00
ate, Gold Trim, Handles, Pastels, 6 ½ In... 32.50
ate, Pink Roses, Leaves, Scalloped Edges, 6 In...................................... 20.00
ate, Poppies, Scalloped Edge, Gold Medallions, 7 In. 30.00
ate, Yellow Roses, Marked, 91/2 In.. .... 8.50 to 9.00
atter, Arts & Crafts, Marked, c.1919, 11 ¾ x 8 In................................... 135.00
atter, Pansies, Purple, Scalloped Gold Rim, c.1884, 13 x 9 In. 75.00
atter, Scalloped Pointed Edge, Flowers, Pink, White, Leaves, c.1900, 7 ¾ In. 25.00
lt Dip, 3-Footed, Enameled Pink & White Flowers, Gilt Rim, c.1900 .... 20.00
gar & Creamer, Art Nouveau, Green, Taupe, Aqua, c.1884 .... 112.00
gar & Creamer, Flowers, Marked, c.1800 .... 95.00
ay, Dresser, Art Deco, Aqua, Green, Coral, Marked, 12 ½ x 8 ¼ In...................... 75.00
ay, Dresser, Flowers, Art Nouveau, Pink, White, Marked, 12 x 8 In...................... 85.00
io, White & Pink Roses 55.00
se, Art Deco, Luster, Handles, 6 ¼ In.. *illus* 125.00
se, Cornflowers, Egg Shape, Handles, Marked, 7 ¼ In................................. 225.00
se, Iris, Cylindrical, Marked, c.1913, 9 ½ x 2 ¾ In.................................. 245.00

ILSEA glass was made in the Bristol district in England from 1788 to 1873. It was made by any different factories, not just the Nailsea Glass House. Many pieces were made with loopings either white or colored glass as decoration.

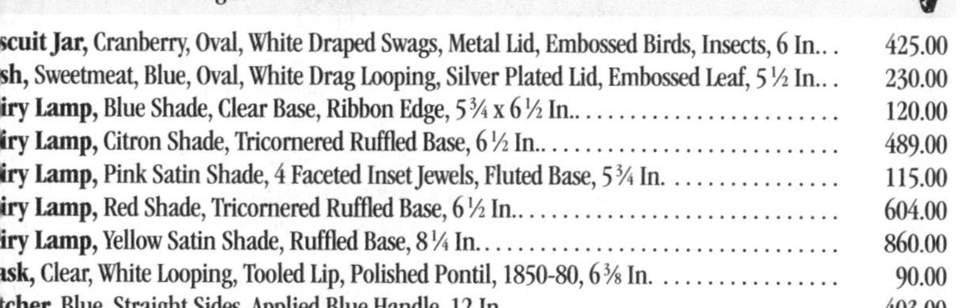

scuit Jar, Cranberry, Oval, White Draped Swags, Metal Lid, Embossed Birds, Insects, 6 In.. . 425.00
sh, Sweetmeat, Blue, Oval, White Drag Looping, Silver Plated Lid, Embossed Leaf, 5 ½ In.. . 230.00
iry Lamp, Blue Shade, Clear Base, Ribbon Edge, 5 ¾ x 6 ½ In.......................... 120.00
iry Lamp, Citron Shade, Tricornered Ruffled Base, 6 ½ In.............................. 489.00
iry Lamp, Pink Satin Shade, 4 Faceted Inset Jewels, Fluted Base, 5 ¾ In. 115.00
iry Lamp, Red Shade, Tricornered Ruffled Base, 6 ½ In................................ 604.00
iry Lamp, Yellow Satin Shade, Ruffled Base, 8 ¼ In.................................. 860.00
ask, Clear, White Looping, Tooled Lip, Polished Pontil, 1850-80, 6 ⅜ In. 90.00
tcher, Blue, Straight Sides, Applied Blue Handle, 12 In................................ 403.00
tcher, Olive, White Splotches, Applied Handle, Pontil, c.1875, 6 In. 364.00
tch's Ball, Cobalt Blue, White, Open Pontil, 4 In..................................... 280.00

KARA is a trade name for a white glassware made about 1900 by the C. F. Monroe mpany of Meriden, Connecticut. It was decorated in pastel colors. The glass was very nilar to another glass, called Wave Crest, made by the company. The company closed in 1916. Boxes for use a dressing table are the most commonly found Nakara pieces. The mark is not found on every piece.

NAKARA

x, Blue, Flowers, Footed, 4 In. 300.00
x, Pink Roses, Green Ground, Metal Feet, Marked, 3 ¾ In. .... *illus* 325.00
x, Ring, Green, Pink Flowers, Flip Lid, Signed, 2 ½ In.. .... 546.00
esser Box, Amber To Pink, Gray Flowers, Marked, 4 ½ In. 230.00
esser Box, Blue, Red Flowers, Signed, C.F. Monroe, 4 ½ In.. .... 144.00
esser Box, Olive Green, Shield Medallion, Cherubs, Pink Flowers, 8 In. 1150.00

MZ Austria, Mug, Cherries, Gold Trim, 4 ½ In.
$40.00

MZ Austria, Vase, Art Deco, Luster, Handles, 6 ¼ In.
$125.00

Nakara, Box, Pink Roses, Green Ground, Metal Feet, Marked, 3 ¾ In.
$325.00

TIP

Don't store a diamond with other jewelry. It may scratch the other stones.

Napkin Ring, Silver Plate, Figural, Angel, Sitting, Legs Crossed, Pairpoint Mfg. Co., 3 ½ In.
$1380.00

Napkin Ring, Silver Plate, Figural, Crossed Rifles
$144.00

TIP

Clean silver with any acceptable commercial polish. Don't use household scouring powder on silver, no matter how stubborn the spot may be. Use a tarnish-retarding silver polish to keep your silver clean. It will not harm old solid or plated wares. Do not use "instant" silver polishes.

NANKING is a type of blue-and-white porcelain made in Canton, China, since the late eighteenth century. It is very similar to Canton, which is listed under its own name in this book. Both Nanking and Canton are part of a larger group now called Chinese export porcelain. Nanking has a spear-and-post border and may have gold decoration.

Bowl, Fitted Wire Edge, Footed Base, Blue & White, 3 x 7 ¾ In. 264.0
Cann, Blue & White, c.1765, 6 x 7 ¼ In. 400.0
Garniture Vase, Cover, River Scene, Blue & White, c.1760, 11 ½ In. 500.0
Platter, Architectural, Lake, Landscape, Underglaze Blue, Dagger Border, 17 x 15 In. 632.0
Platter, Blue & White, Dagger Border, Lake, 17 x 15 In. 632.0
Platter, Cover, Blue & White, 11¼ x 4½ In. . . . . . 125.00 to 200.0
Soup, Dish, Blue & White, Gold Rim, 19th Century, 10 x 2 In. 345.0
Strainer, Pierced, Blue & White, 13 ¼ x 10 ¼ In. 747.0
Tureen, Cover, Stand, Blue & White, Butterfly Border, Strapwork Handles, 5 In. 448.0

NAPKIN RINGS were in fashion from 1869 to about 1900. They were made of silver, porcelain, wood, and other materials. They are still being made today. The most popular rings with collectors are the silver plated figural examples. Small, realistic figures were made to hold the ring. Good and poor reproductions of the more expensive rings are now being made and collectors must be very careful.

Silver, Flared, Pine Branch Decor, Applied Green & Yellow Stones, Germany, 1 ½ x 2 In., Pair. 431.0
Silver Plate, Figural, 2 Eagles, Rogers Smith & Co., Victorian 57.0
Silver Plate, Figural, 2 Fans, Butterfly, Rogers Smith & Co. 57.0
Silver Plate, Figural, 2 Pheasants, Meriden Silver Plate 258.0
Silver Plate, Figural, Angel, Carrying Holder On Back, Meriden-Britannia Co. . . . . . . 86.
Silver Plate, Figural, Angel, Sitting, Legs Crossed, Pairpoint Mfg. Co., 3 ½ In. . . . . . *illus* 1380.
Silver Plate, Figural, Antelope, Standing, Meriden-Britannia Co. . . . . . . 690.
Silver Plate, Figural, Baby, In Rocking Cradle, James Tufts, 4 ½ In. 230.0
Silver Plate, Figural, Bashful Angel, Round Base, James Tufts. 316.0
Silver Plate, Figural, Bird, On Branch . . . . . . 86.
Silver Plate, Figural, Bird, Bud Vase, Leaves, Acme Silver Co. . . . . . . 115.
Silver Plate, Figural, Bird, Ivy, 4 Toupee Feet, c.1860-70, 3 In. . . . . . . 770.
Silver Plate, Figural, Bird, Embossed, Wheels, Prancing Horse, Meriden-Britannia, 2 ¾ In. . . 441.
Silver Plate, Figural, Bird & Horseshoe, Pairpoint Mfg., Co. 115.0
Silver Plate, Figural, Boy, Removable Napkin Ring, James Tufts 29.0
Silver Plate, Figural, Boy, Feeding Dog, Meriden-Britannia Co. . . . . . . 115.
Silver Plate, Figural, Boy, Lying On Stars & Stripes Base, Wilcox Silver Plate Co. . . . . . . 143.
Silver Plate, Figural, Boy, Riding Turtle, Pairpoint . . . . . . 403.
Silver Plate, Figural, Bull, Knickerbocker Silver Co. . . . . . . 258.
Silver Plate, Figural, Cat, On Hind Legs 172.0
Silver Plate, Figural, Cat, Seated, Glass Eyes, Bird Engraving On Holder 230.0
Silver Plate, Figural, Cat, Sheet Music, Over The Garden Wall, James Tufts . . . . . . 805.
Silver Plate, Figural, Cherub, Riding Swan, Acme Silver Co. . . . . . . 115.
Silver Plate, Figural, Cherub, Draped, Holding Cup, Donut, Rat, Middletown Plate Co. . . . . . 143.
Silver Plate, Figural, Cherub, Winged, Pulling Figure On Sled . . . . . . 258.
Silver Plate, Figural, Cherub, Winged, Large Bird, Rockford Silver Plate Co. . . . . . . 690.
Silver Plate, Figural, Cherub, Draped, Bud Vase, Reed & Barton, c.1880, 5 In. 1050.0
Silver Plate, Figural, Cherub, Draped, Riding Bicycle, Adelphi Silver Plate Co. . . . . . . 1840.
Silver Plate, Figural, Child, Kneeling, In Top Hat . . . . . . 145.
Silver Plate, Figural, Child & Dachshund, Van Berg Silver Plate Co. . . . . . . 172.
Silver Plate, Figural, Cow, By Wheat Sheaf, Wilcox . . . . . . 230.
Silver Plate, Figural, Cow, By Milk Bucket . . . . . . 258.
Silver Plate, Figural, Crossed Rifles . . . . . . *illus* 144.
Silver Plate, Figural, Deer, Standing, Meriden-Britannia Co. . . . . . . *illus* 690.
Silver Plate, Figural, Dog, With Wishbone, Derby Siner Co. . . . . . . 115.
Silver Plate, Figural, Dog, On Hind Legs, Stars & Stripes Base, Wilcox Silver Plate Co. . . . . . . 143.
Silver Plate, Figural, Dog, Pug, Glass Eyes . . . . . . 230.
Silver Plate, Figural, Dog, With Bucket, Seated, Barrel Shape, James W. Tufts . . . . . . 345.
Silver Plate, Figural, Dog, Pulling Holder On Sled, Meriden-Britannia Co. . . . . . . 402.
Silver Plate, Figural, Dog, Hunting, Crouching, Simpson, Hall, Miller & Co. . . . . . . 460.
Silver Plate, Figural, Dog, Hunting & Pheasant, Toronto Silver Plate Co. . . . . . . 632.
Silver Plate, Figural, Dog, Bulldog, Doghouse, Simpson, Hall, Miller & Co. . . . . . . 2587.
Silver Plate, Figural, Dog & Cat, Fighting, Charles W. Hammel & Co. . . . . . . 172.

lver Plate, Figural, Dog Pulling Holder On Wheels, American Silver Co. *illus* 805.00
lver Plate, Figural, Eagle, Meriden-Britannia Co. *illus* 288.00
lver Plate, Figural, Emu, Kangaroo, Boomerang, Australia, 2 ½ In., 6 Piece 1540.00
lver Plate, Figural, Fan, Oriental, Long Tailed Bird, Derby Silver Co. 86.00
lver Plate, Figural, Fans, Oriental, Crossed, Derby Silver Co. 143.00
lver Plate, Figural, Fawn, Peers Over Fence, 1880-1910 632.00
lver Plate, Figural, Fox, Bird In Tree, Reed & Barton 58.00
lver Plate, Figural, Fox, Running, William Rogers Mfg. Co. 1150.00
lver Plate, Figural, Giraffe, Eating Leaves, Rogers & Bros. 1380.00
lver Plate, Figural, Girl, Long Braid, Pushing Ring, Middletown Plate Co. 287.00
lver Plate, Figural, Girl, With Basket, Reed & Barton, 1840-1900 575.00
lver Plate, Figural, Girl, Reading Book, Sitting On Snail 575.00
lver Plate, Figural, Goat, Knickerbocker Silver Co. 58.00
lver Plate, Figural, Goat, Pulls Ring, Wheels, Meriden-Britannia, 1880s, 2 ¾ x 4 ½ In. 173.00
lver Plate, Figural, Gold Miner, On Rock, Rogers & Bros. 805.00
lver Plate, Figural, Grapes & Barrel, Acme Silver Co. 57.00
lver Plate, Figural, Hen, Sitting, Rogers & Bros. 316.00
lver Plate, Figural, Horse, Pulls Ring, Wheels, Rogers & Brothers, c.1820-60 173.00
lver Plate, Figural, Hummingbird In Flight, Taunton, 1880-95 258.00
lver Plate, Figural, Lion, Rampant, Meriden & Co., 1868-1900 258.00
lver Plate, Figural, Man, With Barrel On Back, James Tufts 173.00
lver Plate, Figural, Monkey, Playing Violin, 1880-1900 402.00
lver Plate, Figural, Monkey, With Cane, Middletown, Victorian, 3 ¾ In. 518.00
lver Plate, Figural, Nude Child, Bud Vase, West Silver Co. 143.00
lver Plate, Figural, Owl, Glass Eyes, Moon & Stars Engraved On Holder 575.00
lver Plate, Figural, Owl, 2 Baby Owls In Branches, Simpson, Hall, Miller & Co., 1871-97 805.00
lver Plate, Figural, Parakeet, On Barrel, Simpson, Hall, Miller & Co. 115.00
lver Plate, Figural, Pear & Leaf, Hartford Silver Plate Co., 1882-94 58.00
lver Plate, Figural, Pig, Hammered, Reed & Barton, c.1941, 2 ¼ In. 119.00
lver Plate, Figural, Rabbit, Seated, Pairpoint Mfg. Co. 115.00 to 143.00
lver Plate, Figural, Rabbit, Crouching By Log, Simpson, Hall, Miller & Co. 575.00
lver Plate, Figural, Rabbit, Rogers Smith & Co. 690.00
lver Plate, Figural, Rabbit, On Short Pedestal 805.00
lver Plate, Figural, Rabbit & 3 Bunnies, Victor Silver Co. 86.00
lver Plate, Figural, Red Riding Hood, Reed & Barton, 1840-1900 575.00 to 1035.00
lver Plate, Figural, Rooster, With Shovel, Meriden-Britannia Co. 690.00
lver Plate, Figural, Sailor, Bud Vase, Holding Rope To Anchor, Reed & Barton, 1840-67 173.00
lver Plate, Figural, Sailor, Anchor, Simpson, Hall & Miller, 1871-97 480.00
lver Plate, Figural, Squirrel, Bud Vase, Wilcox Silver Plate Co. 29.00
lver Plate, Figural, Swords, Hunting Horns, Meriden Co. 403.00
lver Plate, Figural, Tennis Player, Male, Rogers Smith & Co. 2588.00
lver Plate, Figural, Tom Sawyer, Hands In Pocket, Barbour, 1892-1925 230.00
lver Plate, Figural, Triton, Rogers & Bros. 978.00
lver Plate, Figural, Turtle, Holder On Back, Pairpoint Mfg. Co. 518.00
lver Plate, Figural, Woman, Badminton Racquet, Rogers & Brother 29.00
lver Plate, Figural, Woman, Badminton Player, Reed & Barton 690.00
lver Plate, Figural, Woman, Draped, Bud Vase, Holding Mirror, Rockford Silver Co. 115.00
lver Plate, Figural, Woman, Dog, Reed & Barton, Victorian 748.00
lver Plate, Figural, Woman, Tennis Racquet, Meriden-Britannia Co., Victorian 2530.00
lver Plate, Figural, Workman, Carrying Barrel, On Back, Simpson, Hall, Miller & Co. 200.00
terling Silver, Birds, Bamboo, Scalloped, Square, Gorham, c.1870-80, 2 In. 358.00
terling Silver, Fish, Engraved Seaweed, Square, c.1880, 1 ¼ x 1 ½ x In. 478.00
terling Silver, Gilt, Scrolling Acanthus, Grape Clusters, 1900s, 2 In., 8 Piece 450.00

ASH glass was made in Corona, New York, from about 1928 to 1931. A. Douglas Nash ought the Corona glassworks from Louis C. Tiffany in 1928 and founded the A. Douglas ash Corporation with support from his father, Arthur J. Nash. Arthur had worked at the Webb factory in ngland and for the Tiffany Glassworks in Corona.

NASH

late, Translucent Green, Marked, 8 ¼ In. 288.00
umbler, Chintz, Green & Amethyst Stripes, Signed, 1930, 6 ½ In. 175.00
ase, Impressed Flowers, Long Slender Neck, Flaring Rim, Gold Iridescent, 8 In. 1140.00
ase, Iridescent Blue, Optic Ribs, Footed, Signed, 5 ½ In. 633.00
ase, Iridescent Gold, Molded Tree Bark Neck, Footed, Signed, 5 ½ In. 518.00

TIP

To remove a sticky label on silver, try heating it with a hair dryer to soften the adhesive. Any remaining glue could be removed with isopropyl alcohol. If the silver is discolored, clean it with silver polish.

Napkin Ring, Silver Plate, Figural, Deer, Standing, Meriden Britannia Co. $690.00

Napkin Ring, Silver Plate, Figural, Dog Pulling Holder On Wheels, American Silver Co. $805.00

Napkin Ring, Silver Plate, Figural, Eagle, Meriden-Britannia Co. $288.00

N

Nautical, Diorama, Frigate, Conway, Full Sail, Mixed Wood, Folk Art, 19th Century, 21 x 34 In.
$863.00

Nautical, Figurehead, Algerine, Carved, Painted, Mid 19th Century, 68 x 18 x 21 In.
$16000.00

N

TIP

Dust mites are the subject of many articles today. The more humid the environment, the more quickly they multiply. Dust mites eat dust particles, then will turn to paints and glazing materials on wooden pieces. The only way to avoid damage is to clean regularly.

NAUTICAL antiques are listed in this category. Any of the many objects that were made or used by the seafaring trade, including ship parts, models, and tools, are included. Other pieces may be found listed under Scrimshaw.

Anchor, Brass, Double Hook, 2 Piece 131.0
Anchor, Brass, Double Hook, Chain, Log Wheel, Rope, 2 Handles Rod 215.0
Anchor, Iron, Bull Ring Top, Spade Shape Flukes, Wooden Cross Arm, 1800s, 63 x 27 In. 252.0
Anchor Light, Metal, Gray, 13 In. 57.0
Binnacle, Brass, Deck Mounted, Compass, Lift Top, 2 Lights, Pedestal, Japan, 44 x 31 x 15 In. 1232.0
Binnacle, Brass, Deck Mounted, Compass, Side Lights, Spheres, No. 4010, 44 x 31 x 15 In. 1100.0
Binnacle, Brass, Deck Mounted, Wood, Cast Iron Balls, 55 x 32 In. 1650.0
Binnacle, Brass Hood, Mahogany Pedestal, Rectangular Plinth, Cast Iron 1315.0
Box, Cover, Ivory Inlaid Walnut, Dovetailed, Sailor Made, 10 x 7 x $4\frac{1}{2}$ In. 365.0
Buoy Beacon, Copper, Brass, Fresnel Lens, Hinged Top, 34 x 15 In. 2760.0
Canoe Seat, Old Town, Folding, Oak, Cane Seat & Back, Marked 86.0
Chest, Seaman's, Green Paint, Handles, Rope Beckets, Lift Top, 2 Drawers, $43\frac{1}{2}$ x $21\frac{1}{2}$ In. 715.0
Chest, Seaman's, Hearts, Blue Paint, Becket Handles, Nail Construction, 1800s, 17 x 37 In. 448.0
Chest, Seaman's, Painted, Rope Decorated, Rectangular Lid, 49 In. 1673.0
Chest, Seaman's, Pine, Slant Front, Dovetailed, Interior Ditty Box, c.1840, 16 x 46 In. 168.0
Chest, Seaman's, Pine, Hinged Lid, Painted 3-Masted Vessel On Lid Interior, 17 x 38 In. 3900.0
Chronometer, Mahogany Case, Gimbal, Japan, 5 In. 1195.0
Chronometer, Thomas Mercer, Ltd., Gimbal, Mahogany Case, Box, England, $4\frac{1}{2}$ In. 1195.0
Chronometer, Vacheron & Constantin, Nickel Plated Case, Mahogany Box, c.1900 6355.0
Chronometer, Waltham, Gimbal, Mahogany, Brass Bound Case, Instructions, $3\frac{1}{2}$ In. 1076.0
Chronometer, Widenham & Adams, Second Dial, Brass Bowl Case, c.1840 4828.0
Clock, Brass, Ship Wheel, Hinged Bezel, Waterbury Jeweled Movement, 8 x 6 x $3\frac{1}{2}$ In. 230.0
Clock, Chelsea, Ship's Bell, Yacht Wheel, Nickel Finish, c.1938, $8\frac{1}{4}$ In. 495.0
Clock, Compass, Barometer, Crossed Oars, Anchor, Wood Base 2070.0
Clock, Radio Room, Seth Thomas, Secondary Hour Hand, c.1944, $7\frac{3}{4}$ In. 275.0
Clock, Seth Thomas, Ship's, Black Dial & Case, Mark I-Deck Clock, U.S. Navy, 1942, 7 In. 173.0
Clock, Seth Thomas, Ship's Bell, Wall, Outside, Brass Case, Silvered Dial, c.1935, $10\frac{1}{2}$ In. 193.0
Clock, Seth Thomas, Ship's Bell, 30-Hour, Nickel Plated Case, c.1884, $10\frac{1}{2}$ In. 303.0
Clock, Ship's Bell, Chelsea Clock Co., 8-Day, Brass, Screw Bezel, Mahogany Base, c.1968, 8 In. 413.0
Clock, Ship's Bell, Chelsea Clock Co., Commander, Cast Brass, Mahogany Base, c.1913, 8 In. 468.0
Clock, Ship's Bell, Chelsea Clock Co., Pilot, Brass Case, Silvered Dial, 8-Day, c.1922, 12 In. 578.0
Clock, Ship's Bell, Chelsea Clock Co., Wooden Stand, Red Brass, c.1975, 13 In. 1870.0
Clock, Ship's Bell, Mahogany Base, Brass Case, Silvered Dial, c.1990, $7\frac{1}{4}$ In. 385.0
Clock, Ship's Bell, Seth Thomas, Wall, Nickel, Outside Bell, c.1900, $10\frac{1}{2}$ In. 248.0
Compass, Anshutz & Co., Gyro Compass, Heavy Brass Case, c.1960, 10 In. 117.0
Compass, Binnacle, Floating Dial, Bergen, Brass Case, 9 In. 176.0
Compass, Joseph Halsey, Wood, Directional Star, Leather Pocket, Tripod, $5\frac{1}{2}$-In. Compass 2070.0
Compass, Ship's, Hagger & Brother, Floating Paper Dial, Baltimore, 10 In. 235.0
Diorama, Frigate, Conway, Full Sail, Mixed Wood, Folk Art, 19th Century, 21 x 34 In. *illus* 863.0
Diorama, Schooner, 2-Masted, 4 Wood Sails, Ocean Liner, Early c.1900, 14 x $22\frac{1}{2}$ In. 863.0
Diorama, Ship, 2-Masted, Italy, Green & White, 12 Men, U.S. Flag, Light-Up, 27 x 43 x 12 In. 575.0
Drafting Set, Navigational, Ivory Rules, Sector Type, Sharkskin, 7 In. 297.0
Figurehead, Algerine, Carved, Painted, Mid 19th Century, 68 x 18 x 21 In. *illus* 16000.0
Flow Meter, J. Hicks, Brass, Miles & Feet Scales, Mahogany Box, London, c.1875 448.0
Fog Horn, Brass, Cylinder, Wood Handle, $14\frac{3}{4}$ In. 215.0
Half-Model, Sailboat, Keel, Rudder, Mahogany Backboard, Gilt Edge, 30 x 8 x 5 In. 1100.0
Half-Model, Sailing Ship, Wood, 11 Lifts, Mid 19th Century, 30 In. 495.0
Half-Model, Wood, Painted, Black, Green, Mahogany Plaque, Early 1900s, 10 x 40 In. 2468.0
Lamp, Signal, Marine Boat, Fluid, Convex Glass, Handles, Clip, Victorian, $8\frac{3}{4}$ x $6\frac{3}{4}$ In. 55.0
Lamp, Starboard, Port, Clear Glass, Copper, Pair, $13\frac{3}{4}$ In. 329.0
Lantern, Perkins Marine Lamps, Brass, Clear Lens, Brooklyn, 17 x 10 In. 224.0
Life Ring, Andrea Doria, Red, White, $30\frac{1}{2}$ In. 13200.0
Light, Companionway, Brass, Glass Globe, Pair 316.0
Memento, Sailor's Farewell, Needlework, Silk, Embroidered, Applique, $10\frac{1}{2}$ x $20\frac{1}{4}$ In. 2300.0
Model, Battleship, Chinese, Dragon Junk, Cast Iron, Wood, Acrylic Glass Case, $4\frac{1}{2}$ In. 850.0
Model, Battleship, Wood, Metal, Plastic, On Deck, Base Simulating Ocean, 12 x 57 In. 110.0
Model, Boat, Brown, Green Painted, White Cabin, Lobster Traps, Buoys, Buckets, 1112 In. 165.0
Model, Chinese Junk, Mast, Woven Reed Canopy, Carved Galley, c.1900, 24 x 29 In. 1000.0
Model, Clipper Ship, Sea Witch, Wood, Red, White, Black, Full Rigging, 24 x 13 In. 201.0
Model, Fishing Trawler, Wood Hull, Deck, Nets, Glass Windows, Painted, 25 x 21 In. 201.0
Model, Greek Galley, Single Mast, Oars, White, Wood, Carved, $16\frac{5}{8}$ x $15\frac{3}{4}$ In. 75.0
Model, Mayflower, 4-Masted, Wood, Carved, Painted, 23 x $24\frac{1}{2}$ In. 82.0
Model, Merchant, 3-Masted, Wood, Carved, After 15th Century, $22\frac{3}{4}$ x $20\frac{1}{2}$ In. 55.0

Model, Ocean Liner, Marklin, Augusta Victoria, 1910-20, 29 In. 16100.00
Model, Santa Maria, Columbus, 2-Masted, Flagship, Carved, Wood, Green, Red, 23 x 24 In. . . 165.00
Model, Ship, 2-Masted, Wood, Carved Hull, 1 Board Deck, Cotton Sails, Painted, 38 x 40 In. . . 345.00
Model, Ship, 2-Masted, Wood, Green, Black Hull, Movable Keel, 1800s, 26 x 5 ½ x 25 In. 600.00
Model, Ship, 3-Masted, White, Red Hull, Lifeboats, Anchor, Rigging, Wood, Stand, 20 x 60 x 6 In. 173.00
Model, Ship, 3-Masted, Carved Hull, Deck Fixtures, 32 x 39 x 8 In. 880.00
Model, Ship, 3-Masted, Aurora Borealis, Full Rigging, Union Jack, Glass Case, 31 x 21 In. . . . 891.00
Model, Ship, Baltimore Clipper, Encased, 20 ½ x 25 ½ x 9 ½ In. 351.00
Model, Ship, Hollander, Black & Green Hull, Full Rig, Base, 26 x 36 x 11 In. 690.00
Model, Ship, Medieval, Single Mast, Oars, Wood, Carved, 22 ½ x 18 ¾ In. 60.00
Model, Ship, Schooner, 3-Masted, Rigged, Lifeboats, Stairs, Cabin, c.1920, 17 x 22 x 7 In. 110.00
Model, Ship, Wood, Carved Hull, Painted, Lead Keep, Metal, Plastic, 1940s, 19 x 49 In. 115.00
Model, Spanish Frigate, Masts, Standing & Running Rigging, Planked Hull, 28 In. 117.00
Model, Tug, City Of New York, Painted, 20 In. 598.00
Octant, R. Imme, Lacquered Brass, Signed, Bone Scales, c.1860 . . . . . . 2174.00
Pond Boat, Yacht, Plant On Frame, White, Green, Early 1900s, 13 ¾ x 84 ½ In. 1880.00
Pond Yacht, Edwardian, Brass Mount, Hardwood, Display Stand, Early 1900s, 60 x 46 In. . . . 3120.00
Pressure Gauge, Steam, Steel, Walnut Case 203.00
Quadrant, Rosewood Frame, Boxwood Scales, Whale Ivory Inlay, Made For M. Joseph White. 8500.00
Sailor's Valentine, Hearts, Geometric, Inlay, Wood Box, Cape Cod, 12 ¼ x 7 In. 3500.00
Sailor's Valentine, Shellwork, Present From Barbados, Heart, Rose, Octagonal, 9 x 2 ½ In. . . 3920.00
Seam Rubber, Sail Maker's, Carved, Heart, Geometric Finial, 6 In. 308.00
Sextant, Adams London, Brass, Wood Case, 10 x 10 In. . . . . . *illus* 863.00
Sextant, Berge, Brass, Double Frame, Silver Scale, Mahogany Grip, London, c.1810 . . . . . . 3846.00
Sextant, Double Frame, Position Finder, World War II, G. L'E Turner, c.1940 . . . . . . 241.00
Sextant, John Stancliffe, Brass, Angled & Silvered Scale, Index Arm Adjustable, c.1810. . . . . . 8362.00
Sextant, Jones Gray & Keen, Brass, Ebony, Ivory, Tiger Maple, Mahogany, 12 x 5 In. 900.00
Ship In Bottle, 2-Masted, Full Sails, Jib Sails, Wood, Painted Stand, 24 x 25 x 4 In. 385.00
Ship In Bottle, 3-Masted, American Flag, Rigged, Building, Lighthouse, 13 x 5 In. 330.00
Ship In Bottle, 3-Masted, c.1920, 10 In. 220.00
Ship Model, see Nautical, Model.
Ship's Bell, Bronze, Engraved, Verdigris Patina, Yarmouth, c.1887, 12 x 14 In. 1232.00
Ship's Bell, Chelsea Clock Co., Hinged Bezel, Button Latch, c.1940, 7 ½ In. 550.00
Ship's Log, Thos. Walker & Son., Electric, Trident, Mark III, Brass, Bronze, c.1930 . . . . . . 241.00
Ship's Telegraph, Brass Pedestal, 46 In. 846.00
Ship's Telegraph, White Face, Black Letters, Brass Pedestal, 19 In. 227.00
Ship's Wheel, 8 Spokes, Handles, Brass Center, 30 x 2 ½ In. 700.00
Ship's Wheel, Cast Brass Hub, Mahogany, 8 Turned Spokes, 19th Century, 48 In. 250.00
Ship's Wheel, Walnut, 44 In. . . . . . *illus* 330.00
Ship's Wheel, Wood, 32 In. 248.00
Stadimeter, Telescopic, Oak Case, U.S. Maritime Commission, 1942 . . . . . . *illus* 210.00
Steering Wheel, Yacht, Walnut, Brass, 22 In. 896.00
Stern Board Eagle, Gilded, Wood, 6 Ft. 10 In. 97750.00

NETSUKES are small ivory, wood, metal, or porcelain pieces used as toggles on the end of the cord that held a Japanese money pouch or inro. The earliest date from the sixteenth century. Many are miniature, carved works of art. This category also includes the ojime, the slide or string fastener that was used on the inro cord.

Boxwood, 3 Courtiers, Signed, Masakatsu, 19th Century, 2 ½ In. 3055.00
Boxwood, Boy With Mirror, Signed, 18th Century, 1 ¾ In. 176.00
Boxwood, Dog, 2 Puppies, 2 In. 4113.00
Boxwood, Long-Armed God, Blowing Trumpet, 1 ¾ In. 1293.00
Boxwood, Man With Ball, 19th Century, 1 ½ In. 353.00
Boxwood, Mouse With Chestnut, Signed 1880.00
Boxwood, Rat Catcher With Club, 19th Century, 2 x 2 ½ In. 470.00
Cinnabar, 2 Foo Dogs Playing With Ball, 19th Century. 353.00
Ebony, Officials Post Bell, 18th Century, 1 ½ In. 235.00
Inro, 4 Compartments, Silhouette, Village At Night, Gold Lacquered Bead 6463.00
Inro, Clock, Rosewood Case, Engraved Brass, Silver Netsuke, Dragons, Compass, Sundial. . . . 6463.00
Inro, Tigers By Waterfall, Gold Lacquer, 19th Century. 754.00
Iron, Pavilion, Trees Scene, Gold Inlay, Metal Lid With Hook, 2 In. 235.00
Ivory, 2 Catfish, Gray, Jade Eyes, 2 ½ x 2 ¾ In. . . . . . *illus* 400.00
Ivory, 2 Figures, Carving Buddha, 1 ¾ In. 176.00
Ivory, 2 Figures, With Net, 1 ½ In. 705.00
Ivory, 2 Vegetable Pods, 2 ½ In. 147.00

Nautical, Sextant, Adams London, Brass, Wood Case, 10 x 10 In.
$863.00

Nautical, Ship's Wheel, Walnut, 44 In.
$330.00

Nautical, Stadimeter, Telescopic, Oak Case, U.S. Maritime Commission, 1942
$210.00

TIP

Ivory expands and contracts in heat and cold, so it can crack or craze if the temperature and humidity do not remain moderate.

TIP
Dust ivory with a soft cloth or brush. Buff with a clean woolen cloth.

Netsuke, Ivory, 2 Catfish, Gray, Jade Eyes, 2 ½ x 2 ¾ In. $400.00

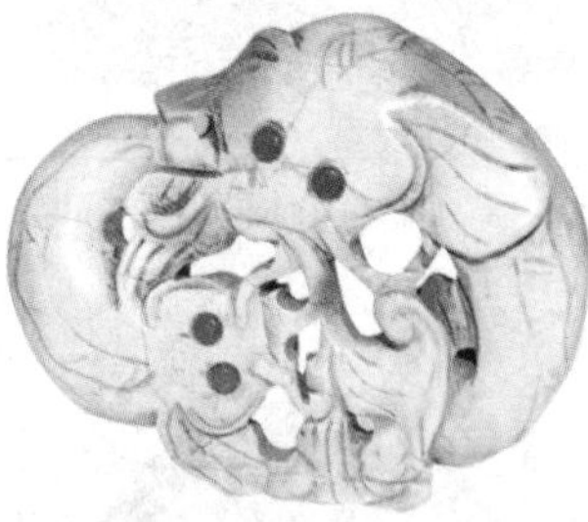

Netsuke, Ivory, Lotus Blossoms, Early 1900s, 2 ½ In. $195.00 $195.00

Newcomb, Bowl, Animal Cracker Band, Incised, MWS, 1910, 2 x 5 ½ In. $9055.00

Newcomb, Sculpture, Organic, Blue, Tan, Signed, 4 ½ x 3 In. $780.00

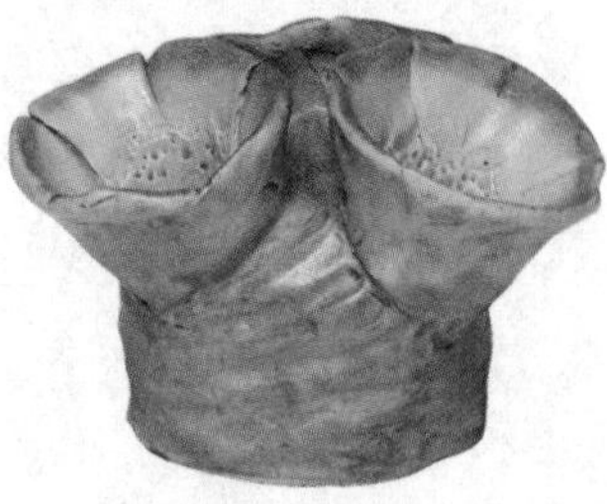

Ivory, 3 Figures, Pounding Rice, Signed, 19th Century 382.00
Ivory, 6 Monkeys, Bug On Fruit, Signed, Mid 19th Century, 2 x 2 In. 200.00
Ivory, Basket, Lacquered Seeds, Nuts, Signed, 19th Century, 1 ½ In. 1293.00
Ivory, Children, Dragon, Octopus, 1 ¾ In. 100.00
Ivory, Chinese Boy, Opening Bag Of Wealth, Signed, 19th Century, 1 ¼ In. 588.00
Ivory, Faces, 2 In. 175.00
Ivory, Figure, Silver Clapper, Multicolored, Signed, 1 ½ In. 1116.00
Ivory, Foo Dog, 1 x 2 In. 175.00
Ivory, God Of Happiness, Bag Of Wealth, Child, 19th Century, 1 In. 176.00
Ivory, God Of Happiness, Dancing With Fan, 19th Century, 2 In. 118.00
Ivory, God Of Happiness, Reclining On Sack, Hand Fan, 19th Century, 1 ½ In. 225.00
Ivory, Horse, Grazing, 1 In. 235.00
Ivory, Lotus Blossoms, Early 1900s, 2 ½ In. . . . . . . *illus* 195.00
Ivory, Man, Agate Drum, 2 In. 150.00
Ivory, Man, Giant Carp, Silver Pouch Chain, 2 In. 470.00
Ivory, Man, Octopus, 2 ½ In. 100.00
Ivory, Man, Rearing Horse, 2 ½ In. 75.00
Ivory, Man Holding Conch Shell, 3 In. 175.00
Ivory, Man Holding Lapis Mask, 2 ¼ In. 175.00
Ivory, Man Holding Mask, Boy, Boxes, 3 ½ In. 125.00
Ivory, Man In Barrel, 2 ½ In. 100.00
Ivory, Man Teaching Child Calligraphy, 1 ½ In. 176.00
Ivory, Men Carving Mask, 1 x 2 In. 100.00
Ivory, Monkey Trainer, Amber Patina, 19th Century, 2 In. 235.00
Ivory, Peasant Woman, Smoking Pipe, Signed, 19th Century, 1 ¼ In. 323.00
Ivory, Rams, Spherical, Early 20th Century, 1 ½ x 1 ¾ In. 176.00
Ivory, Samurai Holding Hawk, Multicolored, Signed, 19th Century 323.00
Ivory, Woman, Child, 3 In. 150.00
Stag Horn, Demon With Bell, 1 ½ In. 294.00
Wood, Mask, Signed, 1 ¾ In. 176.00
Wood, Persimmon, Lotus Pod, Movable Seeds, 19th Century, 1 ¼ In. 294.00
Wood, Woman With Long-Nosed Mask, 19th Century, 1 ½ In. 499.00

NEW HALL Porcelain Manufactory was started at Newhall, Shelton, Staffordshire, England, in 1782. Simple decorated wares were made. Between 1810 and 1825, the factory made a glassy bone porcelain sometimes marked with the factory name. Do not confuse New Hall porcelain with the pieces made by the New Hall Pottery Company, Ltd., a twentieth-century firm.

New Hall

Teapot, Cream Color, Enamel Overglaze, Early 1800s, 4 x 4 In. 650.00
Teapot, Washington Portrait, Seal, Oval Serpentine, Black Sprigs, Vines, c.1790, 6 In. 2032.00

NEW MARTINSVILLE Glass Manufacturing Company was established in 1901 in New Martinsville, West Virginia. It was bought and renamed the Viking Glass Company in 1944. In 1987 Kenneth Dalzell, former president of Fostoria Glass Company, purchased the factory and renamed it Dalzell-Viking. Production ceased in 1998.

Addie, Sugar, Black, 3 ⅛ In. 18.00
Figurine, Baby Bear 36.00
Figurine, Bunny 24.00
Figurine, Chick, Ruby 15.00
Figurine, German Shepherd, 5 ¼ In. 125.00
Figurine, German Shepherd, Ruby, 5 ¼ In. 475.00
Figurine, Wolfhound, 7 In. 170.00
Flame, Candlestick, Meadow Wreath Etch, 3 ½ In. 25.00
Janice, Bowl, Swan, 8 In. 35.00
Janice, Candlestick, Meadow Etch, 5 ¾ In., Pair 40.00
Moondrops, Candlestick, 3-Light, Pair 42.00
Moondrops, Sugar & Creamer, Ruby, Individual 58.00
Moondrops, Tumbler, Whiskey, Handle, Amber, 2 Oz. 16.00
No. 15, Decanter Set, Emerald Green, Tumblers, Tray, 6 Piece 135.00
No. 18, Perfume Bottle, Amber, Dauber Stopper 75.00
No. 18, Perfume Bottle, Clear, Green Stopper 65.00
No. 18, Vanity Set, Puff Box, Bottles, Pink, 3 Piece 165.00
No. 2001, Vanity Set, Blue, Frosted, Tray, Jar, Footed Perfume, 6 In.-Dropper Stopper 155.00
Prelude, Sandwich Server, Handles,13 In. 36.00
Radiance, Cake Plate, Cornflower Etch, Handles, 9 In. 20.00
Radiance, Punch Bowl Underplate, 14 In. 30.00
Radiance, Punch Set, Ladle, Ice Blue, 8 ¼ x 9-In. Bowl, 12 Piece 99.00

adiance, Sugar, Cornflower Etch 10.00
eal, Candlestick, Pair 72.00

EWCOMB Pottery was founded by Ellsworth and William Woodward at Sophie Newcomb ollege, New Orleans, Louisiana, in 1895. The work continued through the 1940s. Pieces of is art pottery are marked with the printed letters *NC* and often have the incised initials of the rtist as well. Most pieces have a matte glaze and incised decoration.

owl, Animal Cracker Band, Incised, MWS, 1910, 2 x 5 ½ In. . . . . *illus* 9055.00
owl, Hammered Copper, 22 x 6 In. 1140.00
owl, Matte Glaze, Low Open Form, 1920, 1 ½ x 6 ¾ In. 1528.00
owl, Matte Glaze, Urn Form, Pink, Blue, 1927, 5 ⅛ x 5 ⅛ In. 2938.00
owl, Morning Glories, Blue, Green, Matte Glaze, 1916, 2 ¾ x 6 In. 1528.00
andlestick, Chamber, Espanol, Handle, Blue, Green, Anna Simpson, 1929, 3 ⅜ In. 4406.00
andlestick, Daisy, Vellum Glaze, Trumpet Foot, Sadie Irvine, 1922, 7 In. 2160.00
andlestick, Dogwood, Blue, Green, Pink, Sadie Irvine, 1925, 9 ¾ In., Pair 10870.00
harger, Blue Crab, Sabina Elliot Wells, 1904, 13 In. 15600.00
reamer, Flowers, Mottled Blue Ground, 4 In. 1610.00
umidor, Blossoms, Sage Green, c.1903, 7 x 5 In. 11750.00
umidor, Jasmine Blossoms, Blue, Green, Yellow Underglaze, 7 ½ x 5 ¼ In. 2350.00
nkwell, Blue Violets, Green Spade Leaves, Cream Ground, 1902, 3 ½ x 4 ½ In. 3120.00
ar, Cover, Landscape, Lucia Jordan, 1907, 7 x 5 In. 9600.00
ardiniere, Blue Irises, Harriet Joor, 1902, 10 x 12 In. 18000.00
oving Cup, Pi Beta Phi Sorority, High Glaze, Henrietta Bailey, 1906, 5 In. 4080.00
ug, Bunnies In The Forest, Signed, Joseph Fortune Meyer, 4 ¼ x 4 ¼ In. 8240.00
itcher, Cherokee Roses, Blue, Green, Anna Frances Simpson, 1927, 7 ¾ In. 3062.00
itcher, Elongated Tulips, Blue & Green On Yellow, 1910, 7 ½ In. 1760.00
itcher, Flower Band, Mottled Blue Ground, 4 In. 1610.00
itcher, Pink Blossoms, 1923, 7 x 5 ½ In. 1800.00
laque, Moonlit Bayou, Hanging, Circular, 1932, 5 In. 3000.00
carf, Table, Trees, Embroidered, Square, Amber, Green, 15 x 15 ¼ In. 7200.00
culpture, Organic, Blue, Tan, Signed, 4 ½ x 3 In. . . . . *illus* 780.00
ankard, Seagull, Green & Brown, Ecru Ground, Loop Handle, c.1945, 3 ⅛ In. 480.00
ile, Rabbit Carrying Hat & Umbrella, Leona Nicholson, 4 ¾ In. Sq. 1680.00
yg, 3 Handles, Medium Blue, Light Blue Ground, 1901, 6 x 7 ½ In. 1800.00
ase, 3 Crayfish, Incised, Painted, 3 ½ x 3 ½ In. 6000.00
ase, Band Of Gladiola, Squat, 1921, 1 ¾ x 3 ¾ In. 600.00
ase, Band Of White Flowers, Stems & Leaves, Blue, Green, H. Bailey, 1923, 6 In. 1645.00
ase, Bayou, Live Oaks, Spanish Moss, 1931, 2 ¼ x 2 ¾ In. 1920.00
ase, Birds, Landscape, Leona Nicholson, 5 x 10 In. 12000.00
ase, Blossoms, Light Blue, Green Leaves, 9 ¼ x 6 In. 7200.00
ase, Blossoms, Tendrils, Blue, Green, Satin Glaze, 4 Handles, 1928, 3 ¾ In. 3525.00
ase, Blue, Pink Roses, A.F. Simpson, 1921, 4 ½ x 2 In. 960.00
ase, Blue Green & Pink Matte, 1929, 8 In. 1998.00
ase, Bougainvillea, 1917, 11 ½ In. 9200.00
ase, Broad Leaves, Buds, Painted, Bulbous, 7 ½ x 4 ½ In. 2160.00
ase, Bud, Flowers In Relief, Blue Green Matte Glaze, 4 In. 1725.00
ase, Candlestick, Pink, Green, Blue, 1915, 7 ¼ In. 2585.00
ase, Cherokee Roses, Baluster, Blue, Green, Sadie Irvine, 1911, 5 ¾ In. 7520.00
ase, Cypress Trees, Landscape, Green, Yellow, Tapered, Alma Mason, 7 ¼ x 3 ½ In. 2300.00
ase, Espanol, Blue, Cream, 7 x 3 ½ In. 6600.00
ase, Espanol, Blue Vellum Glaze, Ribbed, Barrel Shape, A.F. Simpson, 6 In. 4800.00
ase, Freesia, Blue To Mauve, c.1919, 6 x 4 In. 1800.00
ase, Fruiting Branches, Bulbous, Henrietta Bailey, 1918, 8 ½ x 4 ½ In. 2400.00
ase, Fruiting Branches, Sadie Irvine, 1923, 8 ¼ x 7 In. 3480.00
ase, Gray & Brown Glaze, Bulbous, Handles, 6 x 5 In. 360.00
ase, Green & Yellow Matte Glaze, Bulbous, Mark, 4 ½ x 4 In. 288.00
ase, Iris, Green & Blue Vellum Glaze, Bulbous, Footed, Sadie Irvine, 1926, 4 In. 2400.00
ase, Irises, Blue, 3 ½ x 4 In. 960.00
ase, Jasmine, Pink, Blue, Green, Satin Glaze, Sadie Irvine, 1915, 8 ½ In. 2820.00
ase, Jonquil Blossoms In Cream, Green, Blue Ground, Bulbous, 6 ½ x 7 ½ In. 13200.00
ase, Jonquils, Blue, Pink, Matte Glaze, 1922, 4 ¼ x 6 ¾ In. 2468.00
ase, Landscape, Moss Laden Trees, 2 ½ x 5 In. 3600.00
ase, Landscape, Moss Laden Trees, Moon, 6 x 5 In. 4200.00
ase, Landscape, Moss Laden Trees, Moon, Bulbous, c.1932, 6 ½ x 6 ¼ In. 4800.00
ase, Landscape, Moss On Trees, Moon, Tapered, Signed, 5 x 7 In. . . . . 3450.00 to 3600.00
ase, Landscape, Moss On Trees, Shouldered, Green, Yellow, Blue, Sadie Irvine, 7 ½ x 4 In. 6000.00

Newcomb, Vase, Moon & Moss, Baluster, Marked, Sadie Irvine, 6 ½ x 5 In.
$3100.00

Newcomb, Vase, Pine Trees, Blue Green Underglaze, c.1908, 12 ¾ In.
$67000.00

Newcomb, Vase, Trumpet Flowers, Painted & Incised, Glazed, 4 ½ x 8 In.
$6600.00

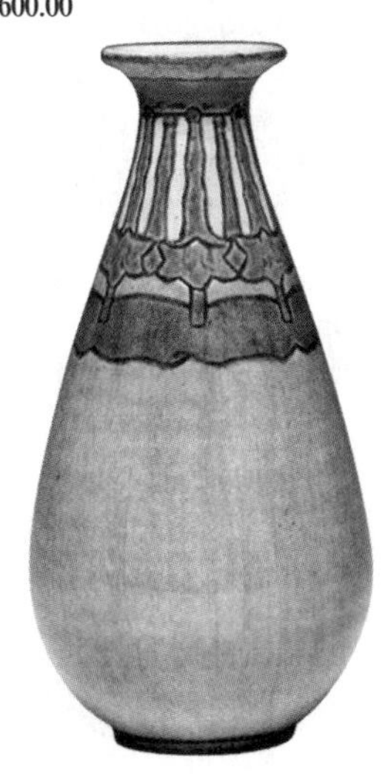

N

TIP

The surface of Niloak marbleized pottery is porous. Oil from your skin, glue residue from sticky labels, and any other type of oil will make permanent marks.

Niloak, Figurine, Squirrel, Ozark Dawn Glaze, Marked, 5¾ In.
$95.00

Nippon, Biscuit Jar, Roses, Gold Trim, 6 x 9 In.
$425.00

Nippon, Humidor, Eagle, Landscape, High Relief, Handles, 6½ x 7 In.
$2500.00

Nippon, Humidor, Raccoon In Tree Trunk, Twig Handles, Marked, 6¼ In.
$1600.00

Vase, Live Oaks, Spanish Moss, Sadie Irvine, 1928, 5½ x 4 In. 3240.0
Vase, Moon & Moss, Baluster, Marked, Sadie Irvine, 6½ x 5 In. *illus* 3100.0
Vase, Moon & Moss, Blue, Green, Satin Glaze, 1922, 29 x 4¾ In. 5581.0
Vase, Moon & Moss, Blue Underglaze, Satin Glaze, c.1920, 11 In.. . . . . 6463.0
Vase, Moon & Moss, Landscape, Green, Blue, Yellow, Marked, 4 x 3½ In.. . . . . 3000.0
Vase, Moon & Moss, Landscape, Blue, Green, Yellow, Tapered, Francis Ford, 7 x 4½ In. 3600.0
Vase, Moon & Moss, Matte Glaze, Anna Frances Simpson, c.1919, 6⅜ In. 3810.0
Vase, Moon & Moss, Vellum Glaze, Bulbous, Aurelia Coralie Arbo, c.1936, 4½ In. 2640.0
Vase, Moon & Moss, Vellum Glaze, Bulbous, Sadie Irvine, 1929, 3⅞ In.. . . . . 3600.0
Vase, Moon & Tall Pine Tree, Blue, Green, Sadie Irvine, 1929, 9 In. 9106.0
Vase, Moonlit Landscape, A.F. Simpson, 1921, 12¾ x 5 In. 5100.0
Vase, Moonlit Landscape, A.F. Simpson, 1930, 6 x 6 In. 9000.0
Vase, Moonlit Landscape, Moss, Oak Trees, A.F. Simpson, 1930, 11 x 5 In. 10200.0
Vase, Moonlit Landscape, Moss, Oak Trees, 1927, 10½ x 4½ In.. . . . . 10800.0
Vase, Moonlit Landscape, Spanish Moss, Oak Trees, 1923, 7¼ x 4¼ In. 3360.0
Vase, Narcissus, Blue, Green, Gourd Form, Marked, Henrietta Bailey, 1914, 8½ In. 3818.0
Vase, Narcissus, Blue Vellum Glaze, Bulbous, Tapered Neck, Sadie Irvine, 1919, 5½ In.. . . . . . 2160.0
Vase, Nicotiana Leaves, Blossoms, Blue, Squat, 4 Handles, 1926, 4¼ x 5¾ In. 840.0
Vase, Nicotiana Leaves, Sadie Irvine, 1922, 7½ x 4 In. 3600.0
Vase, Painted Buds, Leaves, Flaring, 8 x 3½ In. 2040.0
Vase, Paperwhites, Bulbous, Sadie Irvine, 1918, 4½ x 5 In. 1920.0
Vase, Pine Trees, Blue Green Underglaze, c.1908, 12¾ In. . . . . *illus* 67000.0
Vase, Pinecone, Needles, Brown, Green, Mottled Blue Ground, 4¼ In. 2160.0
Vase, Pink & Yellow Blossoms, Large Leaves, Squat, 1924, 4½ x 7¼ In. 1440.0
Vase, Pink Blossoms, Purple Ground, Pear Shape, 1919, 6¼ x 3½ In.. . . . . 2280.0
Vase, Pink Flowers, Blue Ground, Green Vining, Impressed Mark, 2 x 3 In.. . . . . 920.0
Vase, Scuppernong, Signed, Joseph Fortune Meyer, 6¾ x 2¼ In. 4032.0
Vase, Stoneware, Emerald Green, 2 Buttressed Handles, 8¾ x 9 In. 1200.0
Vase, Sunflower Blossom, Yellow, Cream Ground, c.1900, 4½ x 5 In.. 5100.0
Vase, Tall, Narrow, Red, Jade, Marked, c.1900, 10 x 3¼ In. 881.0
Vase, Trefoils, Bulbous, 1920, 8¾ x 4½ In.. . . . . 4800.0
Vase, Trumpet Flowers, Painted & Incised, Glazed, 4½ x 8 In. . . . . *illus* 6600.0
Vase, Trumpet Vine, Blue, White, A.F. Simpson, 1922, 3½ x 2¾ In. 1140.0
Vase, Yellow Blossoms, Bemis Sharp, 1905, 5¼ x 6 In. 2160.0
Vase, Yellow Daffodils, Blue Ground, Squat, 1914, 3¼ x 5¾ In. 1080.0
Vase, Yellow Green Blossoms, Blue Ground, 1930, 5½ x 4 In. 2040.0

NILOAK Pottery (Kaolin spelled backward) was made at the Hyten Brothers Pottery in Benton, Arkansas, between 1910 and 1947. Although the factory did make cast and molded wares, collectors are most interested in the marbleized art pottery line made of colored swirls of clay. It was called Mission Ware. By 1931 the company made castware, and many of these pieces were marked with the name *Hywood*.

Ewer, Cream Glaze, Handle, Bulbous, 6½ In.. . . . . 35.0
Ewer, Lewis Ozark, Handle, 1910, 7 In. 35.0
Figurine, Squirrel, Ozark Dawn Glaze, Marked, 5¾ In.. . . . . *illus* 95.0
Figurine, Woman On Camel, Chinese, 5½ In. 340.0
Pitcher, Brown Gloss Glaze, Handle, 5 In. 22.0
Pitcher, Ozark, Marbleized, Dawn II Glaze, 1910, 5¼ In.. . . . . 50.0
Planter, Deer Jumping Through Grass, Green, 7⅛ x 7 In. 40.0
Vase, Cornucopia, Lewis Ozark, Dawn II, Marbleized, Mauve To Blue, 1910, 7⅛ In.. . . . . 85.0
Vase, Fan, Rose Glaze, Pleated Wing, 2 Ring Pedestal, 5⅛ x 6 In.. . . . . 15.0
Vase, Marbleized, Earth Tones, Round, 4¾ x 6¼ In. 200.0
Vase, Marbleized, Glazed, Bulbous, 3⅝ x 2¼ x 1½ In. 19.0
Vase, Marbleized, Glazed, 1920s, 3½ x 2 x 1½ In. 95.0
Vase, Marbleized, Satin Finish, Browns & Blue, Flared Top, 6½ x 3¾ x 2½ In. 90.0
Vase, Ozark, Dawn II Glaze, Urn Shape, 2 Handles, 1920s, 5 In.. . . . . 75.0
Vase, Ozark, Scalloped Rim, 1920s, 6¼ x 6½ In.. . . . . 45.0
Vase, Seafoam, Bulbous, 7 x 4 In. 49.0

NIPPON porcelain was made in Japan from 1891 to 1921. Nippon is the Japanese word for "Japan." A few firms continued to use the word *Nippon* on ceramics after 1921 as a part of the company name more than as an identification of the country of origin. More pieces marked *Nippon* will be found in the Dragonware, Moriage, and Noritake categories.

Biscuit Jar, Roses, Gold Trim, 6 x 9 In. . . . . *illus* 425.0
Bowl, Raspberry, Footed, 9 In. 95.0
Chocolate Pot, Pink Rose, White, Green Trim, Saucers, Cups, 8½ In., 12 Piece. 100.0

Creamer, Sugar, Cover, Early 20th Century, 2¾ In. 18.00
Dish, Yellow Roses, Gilt, Pink, 2 Handles, Cover, Rose Finial, c.1900, 4 x 8 In. 60.00
Hatpin Holder, Flowers, Cobalt Blue 95.00
Hatpin Holder, Flowers, Gold 60.00
Head Vase, Brown Hair, Flower Dress, Wide Brim Hat, 5⅝ In. 20.00
Humidor, Eagle, Landscape, High Relief, Handles, 6½ x 7 In. .... *illus* 2500.00
Humidor, Raccoon In Tree Trunk, Twig Handles, Marked, 6¼ In. .... *illus* 1600.00
Plate, Flowers, Gold, 9 In. 115.00
Plate, Lion & Lioness On Rocky Ledge & Valley, Blown Out, 10¾ In. 460.00
Plate, Roses, Floral Border, 10½ In. 28.00
Sugar Shaker, Flowers, Gold 45.00
Sugar Shaker, Flowers, Handle 135.00
Tea Set, Teapot, Sugar, Creamer, Cup & Saucer, Set For 6 .... 50.00
Teapot, Geisha Girl, 3 Ladies In Garden, Ball Form, c.1900 .... 185.00
Vase, Applied Roses, Peach, Gilt, 2 Handles, c.1930, 9 x 5 In. 90.00
Vase, Cameo Center, Fired Gold, 2 Handles, c.1940, 12 x 6 In. 82.00
Vase, Cover, Desert Landscape, Camel, Rider, High Relief, Cylindrical, 4¾ x 7½ In. 575.00
Vase, Cover, Flowers, Gold, 2 Handles, 8 x 6 In. 47.00
Vase, Cover, Indian Portrait, High Relief, 5½ x 7 In. 3738.00
Vase, Flower, Pond, Green, White Ground, Handles, 12 In. 58.00
Vase, Flowers, Cobalt Blue, Footed, Handle, 6 In. 55.00
Vase, Flowers, Cobalt Blue, Gold, Handle, 4 In. 30.00
Vase, Flowers, Fired Gold, 2 Handles, c.1930, 9 x 6 x 4 In. 205.00
Vase, Flowers, Ruffled Rim, 2 Handles, c.1910, 13 x 7 In. 100.00
Vase, Framed River Scene, 2 Handles, c.1910, 12 x 5 In. 100.00
Vase, Irises, Handle, 7 In. 165.00
Vase, Mountains, Birds, Blue, Gold Trim, Beading, 2 Handles, Moriage, No. 91, 12 In. 155.00
Vase, Mountains, Lake, Beaded, Gilt, Marked, 9¾ x 6¾ In. .... *illus* 150.00
Vase, Swans, Handle, 9 In. 205.00
Vase, Tapestry, Jeweled, Gilt, Mark, 9½ In. 920.00
Vase, Tapestry, Swan, Buildings, Trees, Light Blue Border, Gold, 5½ In. 66.00

NODDERS, also called nodding figures or pagods, are figures with heads and hands that are attached to wires. Any slight movement causes the parts to move up and down. They were made in many countries during the eighteenth, nineteenth, and twentieth centuries. A few Art Deco designs are also known. Copies are being made. A more recent type of nodder is made of papier-mache or plastic. These often represent sports figures or comic characters. Sports nodders are listed in the Sports category.

Boy, Derby Hat, Dad Said Be A Man, Bisque, Germany, 4 In. 215.00
Brylcreem Kissing Couple, Lego, c.1950, 5½ In. .... *illus* 210.00
Chinese Buddha, Moving Hands, Wagging Tongue, Meissen, Painted. 20160.00
Juggler, Ball Balanced On Head, In Hand, Porcelain, 19th Century 1210.00
Salt & Pepper shakers are listed in the Salt & Pepper category.

NORITAKE porcelain was made in Japan after 1904 by Nippon Toki Kaisha. The best-known Noritake pieces are marked with the M in a wreath for the Morimura Brothers, a New York City distributing company. This mark was used until the early 1950s. There may be some helpful price information in the Nippon category, since prices are comparable. Noritake Azalea is listed in the Azalea category in this book.

Ashtray, Match Holder, Lady In Gondola 175.00
Berry Bowl, Bluebell, 5½ In. 6.00
Berry Bowl, Janice, 5¼ In. 5.45
Biscuit Jar, Cover, Cranes & Flowers, Scalloped Sea Shell Shape, Nippon 125.00
Bowl, Beverly, Oval, 2 Handles 48.00
Bowl, Cereal, Janice, Lug Handles, 7 In. 9.00
Bowl, Cereal, Kilkee 8.00
Bowl, Cereal, Nature's Bounty, 7 In. 15.00
Bowl, Cranberry, Beverly, 5⅛ x 2⅞ In. 48.00
Bowl, Dessert, Buttercup, 5½ In. 9.00
Bowl, Flowers, Oval, Scalloped Rim, Loop Handles, Enamel, 1915, 11 In. 205.00
Bowl, Fruit, c.1910, 8 In. .... *illus* 164.00
Bowl, Hand Painted, Pink & Yellow Roses, Blue Ground, 2 Curled Handles, c.1930 .... 28.00
Bowl, Lineage, Versatone, Oval, 10½ x 5¾ x 2⅛ In. 20.00
Bowl, Nut, Walnut, Purple Ground, 3-Footed, Nippon 29.00
Bowl, Pink & Purple Flowers, Spade Shaped, Handle, Gold Trim, 7 x 7 x 1½ In. 15.00
Bowl, Swan On Lake, 3 Cutout Handles, Painted, 7¼ In. 40.00

Nippon, Vase, Mountains, Lake, Beaded, Gilt, Marked, 9¾ x 6¾ In.
$150.00

TIP
Don't use any type of tape on porcelain or pottery that has overglazed decorations. Gilding and enamels may pull off when the tape is removed. Antiques shops often tape a lid to a bowl; when you buy, ask the dealer to remove the tape to be sure no damage has been done.

Nodder, Brylcreem Kissing Couple, Lego, c.1950, 5½ In.
$210.00

SECURITY TIP
All exterior doors should be made of solid wood or metal. A determined burglar can break through a panel door.

Noritake, Bowl, Fruit, c.1910, 8 In.
$164.00

Noritake, Pin Dish, Mother & Baby Birds On Rim, Art Deco, Green M In Wreath, 1¼ x 4 In.
$88.00

Noritake, Plate, Salad, Bird Over Lake, Painted, 3 Cutout Handles, 7½ In.
$17.00

Bowl, Vegetable, Adelpha, Oval, Handles, 8¾ In. 65.00
Bowl, Vegetable, Adelpha, Round, 10¼ In. 65.00
Bowl, Vegetable, Amorosa, Bouquets Of Flowers, Green & Black Band, Round, 2 Handles 59.00
Bowl, Vegetable, Anita, Round, 2 Handles, Footed, 9 In. 36.00
Bowl, Vegetable, Bancroft, Oval, 10 In. 34.00
Bowl, Vegetable, Beverly, Oval, Handles. 48.00
Bowl, Vegetable, Beverly, 12 In. 65.00
Bowl, Vegetable, Chintz, Oval, 9¾ In. 35.00
Bowl, Vegetable, Croydon, Oval, 10½ x 7½ In. 35.00
Bowl, Vegetable, Edgewood, Pink & Blue Flowers, Gray Scroll, Oval, 10½ In. 45.00
Bowl, Vegetable, Glenwood, Oval, 10½ In. 31.00
Bowl, Vegetable, Lucerne, Oval, 9¾ x 7¼ In. 45.00
Bowl, Vegetable, Polonaise, Oval, 9¾ In. 40.00
Bowl, Vegetable, Roseanne, Oval 22.00
Bowl, Vegetable, Traymore, 12 In. 70.00
Bowl, Vegetable, Vitry, Round, Handles, 9⅞ In. 40.00
Cake Plate, Beverly, 2 Handles, 9¾ In. 48.00
Candlestick, Flowers, Copper Luster, Orange Luster Stem, Green M In Wreath 8½ In. 33.00
Casserole, Cover, Chadwick, Handles, 8¾ In. 45.00
Casserole, Cover, Marguerite, Handles, Cookin' & Server, 8 In. 45.00
Casserole, Cover, Oval, White, Gold Trim 42.00
Casserole, Cover, Up-Sa Daisy, Handles, 8 In. 30.00
Casserole, Cover, Up-Sa Daisy, Handles, 10 In. 49.00
Coffeepot, Petals Plus, 6 Cup, 7½ In. 60.00
Creamer, Asian Song 29.00
Creamer, Boat On Pond, Earth Tone Colors, Gold, Accented Handle 15.00
Creamer, Buttercup 14.00
Creamer, Edgewood, Pink & Blue Flowers, Gray Scrolls, 2⅝ In. 24.00
Creamer, Flowered Transfer, Burnt Sienna Trim, Handle, Nippon, 1⅝ In. 22.00
Creamer, Kilkee 6.00
Creamer, Rosamor 13.00
Creamer, Sunny Side, 3¾ In. 12.00
Cup, Good Times 8.75
Cup, Midnight Majesty 12.00
Cup & Saucer, Blue Orchard 8.00
Cup & Saucer, Kilkee 9.00
Cup & Saucer, Lucerne 25.00
Cup & Saucer, Mardi Gras 8.00
Cup & Saucer, Marguerite 8.00
Cup & Saucer, Oriental, Red, White, Blue, Art Deco, Green M In Wreath 100.00
Cup & Saucer, Rosamor 10.00
Cup & Saucer, Safari 10.00
Dish, 3 Lobes, Floral Medallions, 6¼ In. 28.00
Eggcup, Luster Ware, Green, Pink, Black & White, 2½ In. 18.00
Figurine, Bathing Beauty Lounging Poolside, Tips Of Feet In To Test Warmth 140.00
Figurine, Hen, Painted Face & Waddle, 4¾ x 5¾ In. 175.00
Gravy Boat, Adelpha, Attached Underplate 70.00
Gravy Boat, Asian Song, Underplate 89.00
Gravy Boat, Bancroft, Attached Underplate 40.00
Gravy Boat, Beverly, Underplate 50.00
Gravy Boat, Blue Charm, Attached Underplate, 1984 .... 30.00
Gravy Boat, Cream Color, Gold Trim, Attached Underplate, 1911 .... 45.00
Gravy Boat, Croydon, Attached Underplate, 7½ In. 45.00
Gravy Boat, Freemont, Attached Underplate 35.00
Gravy Boat, Ireland, Edenberry, Underplate 45.00
Gravy Boat, Kilkee 35.00
Gravy Boat, Margaret, Attached Underplate, 9½ In. 33.00
Gravy Boat, Roseberry, Attached Underplate 35.00
Humidor, Tobacco, Silhouettes Of Lady 500.00
Jar, Cover, Blue & Pink Flowers, 2 Handles, Gold Trim, 8½ x 5 In. 38.00
Lemon Server, 2 Baskets Of Fruit, Cream Ground, Gold Rim, Handle, 1935, 5¼ In. 20.00
Lemon Server, Hand Painted, Gold Embellishments, 5⅝ In. 27.00
Mustard, Black & Pearl Luster, Black Trim, 3 Parts, Spoon, 3¼ In. 34.00
Napkin Ring, 3 Women Red Coat, Hat, 2 In., 6 Piece 595.00
Napkin Ring, Flapper Girl, Red Coat, White Fur Trim, Blue Luster, 2 x 1⅝ In. 99.00
Nappy, Yellow Cartouches, Multicolored Flowers, c.1920, 7¼ x 1½ In. 55.00

Pin Dish, Mother & Baby Birds On Rim, Art Deco, Green M In Wreath, 1 ¼ x 4 In. . . . . . *illus* 88.00
Pitcher, Sonoma Trellis, 64 Oz. . . . 40.00
Plate, Bread & Butter, Adelpha, 6 ½ In. . . . 18.00
Plate, Bread & Butter, Bamboo, 6 In. . . . 8.00
Plate, Bread & Butter, Boat On Water, Painted, 6 ¼ In. . . . 25.00
Plate, Bread & Butter, Edgewood, 6 ¼ In. . . . 7.00
Plate, Bread & Butter, Mardi Gras, 6 ¼ In. . . . 6.00
Plate, Bread & Butter, Polonaise, 6 ½ In. . . . 6.00
Plate, Bread & Butter, Ravenna, 6 ¼ In. . . . 8.00
Plate, Bread & Butter, Trees & Cottage In Sunset, Painted, 6 ½ In. . . . 35.00
Plate, Bread & Butter, Up-Sa Daisy, 6 ½ In. . . . 6.00
Plate, Camilla, Gold Banded, 9 ¾ In. . . . 18.00
Plate, Dessert, Buttercup, 7 In. . . . 9.00
Plate, Dinner, Adelpha, 10 In. . . . 29.00
Plate, Dinner, Bancroft, 10 In. . . . 7.50
Plate, Dinner, Barrymore, 10 ½ In. . . . 30.00
Plate, Dinner, Berry Vine, 10 ¾ In. . . . 24.00
Plate, Dinner, Brookhollow, 10 ½ In. . . . 26.00
Plate, Dinner, Buttercups, 10 ½ In. . . . 15.00
Plate, Dinner, Chandon, 10 ½ In. . . . 12.00
Plate, Dinner, Colorwave Blue, 10 ¾ In. . . . 16.00
Plate, Dinner, County Fair, 10 ½ In. . . . 12.00
Plate, Dinner, Edgewood, 10 ¼ In. . . . 24.00
Plate, Dinner, Farentino, 10 ¾ In. . . . 26.00
Plate, Dinner, Firenze, Pink Peonies, Blue & Yellow Blossoms, 10 ½ In. . . . 19.00
Plate, Dinner, Halls Of Ivy, Eggshell, 10 ¾ In. . . . 41.00
Plate, Dinner, Impetuous, 10 ½ In. . . . 26.00
Plate, Dinner, Janice, 10 ½ In. . . . 13.00
Plate, Dinner, Kilkee, 10 ¼ In. . . . 11.00
Plate, Dinner, Mardi Gras, 10 ½ In. . . . 11.00
Plate, Dinner, Marseille, 10 ½ In. . . . 8.00
Plate, Dinner, Medley, 10 ½ In. . . . 12.00
Plate, Dinner, Nature's Bounty, 10 ¼ In. . . . 23.00
Plate, Dinner, Ontario, 10 ½ In. . . . 26.00
Plate, Dinner, Petals Plus, 101/2 In. . . . 14.00 to 23.00
Plate, Dinner, Rosepoint, 10 ¼ In. . . . 13.00
Plate, Dinner, Safari, 10 ½ In. . . . 10.00
Plate, Dinner, Shenandoah, 10 ½ In. . . . 28.00
Plate, Dinner, Sheridan, White On White, Embossed Scrolling, Platinum Trim, 10 ½ In. . . . 20.00
Plate, Dinner, Up-Sa Daisy, 10 ¼ In. . . . 10.00
Plate, Luncheon, Harvard, 8 ½ In. . . . 8.00
Plate, Luncheon, Homecoming, 8 ½ In. . . . 8.00
Plate, Luncheon, Lady With Fan, 7 ½ In. . . . 1350.00
Plate, Salad, Adelpha, 7 ¼ In. . . . 27.00
Plate, Salad, Ardis, 8 ¾ In. . . . 12.00
Plate, Salad, Asian Song, 8 ¼ In. . . . 11.00
Plate, Salad, Bird Over Lake, Painted, 3 Cutout Handles, 7 ½ In. . . . *illus* 17.00
Plate, Salad, Bluebell, 8 In. . . . 7.00
Plate, Salad, Edgewood, 8 ¼ In. . . . 12.00
Plate, Salad, Kilkee, 8 ½ In. . . . 9.00
Plate, Salad, Mardi Gras, 8 ¼ In. . . . 8.00
Plate, Salad, Marseille, 8 ½ In. . . . 8.00
Plate, Salad, Orange Flowers, Green Leaves, Nippon, 7 ½ In. . . . 11.00
Plate, Salad, Safari, 8 In. . . . 4.00 to 7.00
Plate, Salad, Susan Anne, 8 ¼ In. . . . 7.00
Platter, Adelpha, Oval, 11 ¾ In. . . . 95.00
Platter, Adelpha, Oval, 16 x 12 In. . . . 165.00
Platter, Asian Song, Oval, 13½ x 10¼ In. . . . 45.00 to 55.00
Platter, Bancroft, Oval, 11 ¾ In. . . . 49.00
Platter, Beverly, Oval, 11 ½ In. . . . 60.00
Platter, Blue Charm, Oval, Blue & White Daisy, Green Haze, Gray Leaves, 12 In. . . . 25.00
Platter, Bluebell, Oval, 14 In. . . . 75.00
Platter, Buckingham, Oval, 13 In. . . . 30.00
Platter, Chadwick, Oval, 15 ¼ x 11 In. . . . 30.00
Platter, Chelsea, Oval, 13 ¾ In. . . . 30.00
Platter, Croydon, Oval, 13 ¾ x 10 ¼ In. . . . 42.00

TIP
After washing a teapot, dry it as well as possible. Then put a sugar cube in the teapot to absorb the remaining water.

Noritake, Teapot, Peach & White Flowers, Blue Luster, 2 Cup, 4 ½ In. $20.00

TIP
If you use a roller to paint your walls, watch out for tiny droplets that spot furniture and collectibles nearby. The first few days you may be able to get rid of the drops by rubbing them with a cloth dampened with soap and water. Later you may have to use solvents or try to pop the drop off with a fingernail or razor blade.

TIP
Be sure to remove salt and pepper from shakers and dishes after use. Wash, then store.

Norse, Mug, Geometrics, Patinated Copper Glaze, Marked, 5 x 4¾ In.
$160.00

North Dakota School Of Mines, Vase, Multicolored Drip Glaze, Marked, J. Mattson, 2 x 3¼ In.
$175.00

North Dakota School Of Mines, Vase, Pinecones, Brown, Carved, Signed, Marie, 7 x 8 In.
$675.00

Platter, Parkridge, Oval, 14 x 10½ In. 40.00
Platter, Petals Plus, Oval, 13 In. 113.00
Platter, Polonaise, Oval, 13¾ In. 60.00
Platter, Roseanne, Oval, Pink & Tan Leaves, Vines, Gold Trim, 1960, 12⅛ In. 21.00
Platter, Roseanne, Oval, 14 In. 22.00
Platter, Rosepoint, Oval, 13½ x 10¼ In. 30.00
Platter, Selika, Oval, 12 In. 48.00
Platter, Sheridan, Oval, 16 x 11½ In. 55.00
Platter, Vineyard, Oval, 13½ In. 32.00
Platter, Watteau, Oval, 13½ In. 57.00
Relish, Adelpha, 8½ x 4½ In. 55.00
Salt & Pepper, Asian Song 85.00
Salt & Pepper, Kilkee 13.00
Sauce Bowl, Bouquets Of Flowers, China Peach, Ruffled Edges, 5½ In. 20.00
Sauce Bowl, Camilla, 5¼ In. 8.00
Saucer, Edgewood 6.15
Snack Set, Dresden, Shaped Plate, Handle, Cup, 8 Piece 125.00
Soup, Coupe, Up-Sa Daisy 12.00
Soup, Cream, Adelpha, 6¼ In. 36.00
Soup, Cream, Underplate, Revenna, 5½ In. 20.00
Soup, Dish, Bluebell, 7½ In. 7.00
Sugar, Cover, Blue Luster, Black Handle, 5 x 3½ In. 30.00
Sugar, Cover, Chintz 28.00
Sugar, Cover, Rosamor, 6 x 3 In. .... 17.00 to 20.00
Sugar, Cover, Sunny Side, 3½ In. 12.00
Sugar, Cover, Up-Sa Daisy 10.00
Sugar, Cover, Vineyard 12.00
Sugar & Creamer, Ariana 32.00
Sugar & Creamer, Mabel 49.00
Sugar & Creamer, Modjeska 60.00
Sugar & Creamer, Vineyard 42.00
Tea Set, Gold Leaves, Teapot, Creamer, Sugar, 6 Cups & Saucer, c.1900 .... 230.00
Teapot, Chadwick, 6¼ In. 40.00
Teapot, Lady In Garden, Blue Border 225.00
Teapot, Peach & White Flowers, Blue Luster, 2 Cup, 4½ In. .... *illus* 20.00
Teapot, Romance 159.00
Teapot, Tree In Meadow, House & Tree Beside Lake, Handle 110.00
Tray, Nile River At Sunset, Green M In Wreath, 10 In. 75.00
Vase, Flowers, Art Deco, Blue Ground, Urn Shape, c.1920, Miniature, Pair 22.00
Vase, Lake, Trees, Hills, Footed, Handles, Green M In Wreath, 6½ In. 44.00
Vase, Lake, Windmill, Tall Tree, Multicolored, 4½ In. 20.00
Vase, Pink, Blue & Purple Flowers, Gold Luster, Red M In Wreath, 6½ In. 33.00
Wall Pocket, Exotic Bird, Orange Ground, Gold Rim, Green M In Wreath, 8¼ In. 250.00
Wall Pocket, Lady In Garden, Blue Border 350.00
Wall Pocket, Tree In Meadow, Luster, Blue 115.00

NORSE Pottery Company started in Edgerton, Wisconsin, in 1903. In 1904 the company moved to Rockford, Illinois. The company made a black pottery, which resembled early bronze relics of the Scandinavian countries. The firm went out of business in 1913.

Ashtray, Black Matte, Green & Gold Accents, Engraved Designs On Rim, 1¾ x 5 In. 110.00
Ashtray, Engraved, Black Matte, Green, Gilt, c.1903, 1¾ x 5 In. 110.00
Candlestick, Trumpet Shape, Incised Snake Decoration At Base, No. 54, 11 In., Pair 250.00
Mug, Geometrics, Patinated Copper Glaze, Marked, 5 x 4¾ In. .... *illus* 160.00
Vase, Blue Metallic, Verdigris On Rim & Geometric Band At Base, Tapered, 8¾ In. 140.00
Vase, Footed, Broad Bottom, Incised, Copper Colored Glaze, 8 x 11½ In. 300.00
Vase, Geometric, Metallic Finish, 8¾ In. 165.00
Vase, Incised Hieroglyphics, Verdigris, Bulbous, Squat, Flared Rim, Handles, 6 x 9 In. 50.00

NORTH DAKOTA SCHOOL OF MINES was established in 1892 at the University of North Dakota. A ceramic course was included and pieces were made from the clays found in the region. Students at the university made pieces from 1909 to 1949. Although very early pieces were marked *U.N.D.,* most pieces were stamped with the full name of the university.

Bowl, Stylized Designs, Yellow Matte Glaze, c.1929, 6½ x 2 In. 460.00
Pitcher, Handle, Painted Flowers, M. Cable, 5½ x 5¼ In. 345.00

Tile, Incised Fish, Blue, Ivory Glaze, Penelope Thompson, 3 ½ x 3 ½ In. 690.00
Tile, Round, Incised, Painted Design, Penelope Thompson, 4 ½ In. 173.00
Vase, Abstract, Black & Ivory, High Walled, 5 x 5 ¼ In. 1320.00
Vase, Brown Matte Glaze, D. Nasset, Marked, 4 ½ x 4 ¾ In. 1320.00
Vase, Bucking Stallions, Plants, Margaret Cable, Squat, Rolled Sides, 3 x 6 ½ In. 1998.00
Vase, Bulbous, Brown Shaded To Green Matte Glaze, Flared Mouth, 6 In. 223.00
Vase, Bulbous, Carved, Painted Birds, Marie B., 7 x 8 ½ In. 5750.00
Vase, Bulbous, Carved Bird, Blue, 6 ½ x 7 ¼ In. 510.00
Vase, Bulbous, Carved Bird, Blanche Rovelstad, 6 ½ x 7 ¼ In. 633.00
Vase, Bulbous, Carved Calla Lilies, Earth Tones, 6 ½ x 5 ½ In. 960.00
Vase, Bulbous, Carved Pinecone, Signed, Marie, 8 x 7 In. 3738.00
Vase, Bulbous, Carved Sioux Calendar, Julia Mattson, 5 ½ x 7 ¼ In. 403.00
Vase, Bulbous, Cut Back Daffodils, Brown Ground, 8 x 5 ½ In. 3120.00
Vase, Bulbous, Dark Red Matte Glaze, Marked, 1939, 5 ½ In. 294.00
Vase, Bulbous, Fish, Green, Gunmetal Glaze, 8 ½ x 7 In. 6600.00
Vase, Bulbous, Incised, Leaves, Green Matte Glaze, c.1947, 6 ½ x 6 In. 805.00
Vase, Bulbous, Painted Birds & Butterflies, 8 x 6 ¼ In. 390.00
Vase, Bulbous, Painted Figural Design, Julia Mattson, 3 ½ x 3 In. 978.00
Vase, Bulbous, Persian, Jewel Tones, 5 x 5 ½ In. 600.00
Vase, Bulbous, Viking Ships, Brown, Green Ground, 1944, 7 ½ x 5 In. 2040.00
Vase, Carved, Painted, Art Nouveau Design, Flora Huckfield, 5 In. 288.00
Vase, Carved, Pasque Flowers, Signed, Huck, 3 x 4 In. 633.00
Vase, Carved & Painted Flowers, Pink, Green, 3 x 2 In. 420.00
Vase, Carved Daffodil, Brown Matte Glaze, Tobiason, 5 ½ x 8 In. 2300.00
Vase, Cobalt Blue, Carved Leaves, Outlined In Beige, Shouldered, 6 In. 2160.00
Vase, Ducks Flying, Carved, Blue, White, M.S. Davies, 6 ½ x 6 In. .... *illus* 7800.00
Vase, Flared, Carved Flower Design, Signed, C.S. Sorbo, 6 ½ x 5 In. 230.00
Vase, Flower Design, Green Brown Glaze, 1935, 8 x 6 In. 4200.00
Vase, Forest Landscape, Carved, 10 ½ x 6 In. 8400.00
Vase, Low, Carved, Painted Pasque Flower Design, M. Cable, 6 x 3 ½ In. 460.00
Vase, Mountains, Indians, Incised, Green Matte, M. Cable, 5 ¾ x 6 In. .... *illus* 8400.00
Vase, Multicolored Drip Glaze, Marked, J Mattson, 2 x 3 ¼ In. .... *illus* 175.00
Vase, Olive To Brown Glaze, Blue Mark, Penelope Thompson, 8 ½ In. 230.00
Vase, Orange, Incised Design, N.D. Wheat, 5 ¼ In. 575.00
Vase, Pinecones, Brown, Carved, Signed, Marie, 7 x 8 In. .... *illus* 675.00
Vase, Prairie Rose, Green Matte Glaze, 8 ½ x 5 ¾ In. 1320.00
Vase, Shouldered, Carved Birds, 4 x 5 In. 863.00
Vase, Shouldered, Carved Bird, Green To Yellow, 4 x 5 In. 480.00
Vase, Squat, Brown Leaves, Green Ground, 1950, 5 ¼ x 6 ¾ In. 570.00
Vase, Squat, Carved Leaves, Orange, 3 ¾ x 2 ¾ In. 300.00
Vase, Swollen Shape, Carved Unicorn, Signed, Hicks, c.1950, 5 x 8 In. 1035.00
Vase, Tapered, Carved Stylized Design, Signed, Solsen, 4 ½ x 6 ½ In. 316.00
Vase, Tapered, Green Glaze, 1917, 5 x 8 In. 480.00
Vase, Tapered, Painted Flowers, 5 ½ x 9 ½ In. 1495.00

NORTHWOOD glass was made by the H. Northwood Co., founded in Wheeling, West Virginia, in 1901 by Harry Northwood. He worked for the Hobbs-Brockunier and LaBelle firms in the 1880s before operating his own glass plants in Martins Ferry, Ohio, and Ellwood City and Indiana, Pennsylvania. At the Wheeling factory, Harry Northwood and his brother Carl manufactured pressed and blown tableware and novelties in many colors that are collected today as custard, opalescent, goofus, carnival, and stretch glass. Pieces made between 1905 and about 1915 may have an underlined *N* trademark. Harry Northwood died in 1919, and the plant closed in 1925.

Leaf Mold, Pitcher, Water, Amber Body, Red, Yellow Spatter, 8 In. 403.00
Leaf Mold, Salt & Pepper, Yellowine, Yellow, Rose Spatter, 2 ½ In. 132.00
Leaf Umbrella, Pitcher, Water, Rose DuBarry, No. 263, 8 ½ In. .... *illus* 36.00
Leaf Umbrella, Sugar & Creamer, Cover, Cranberry, No. 263 .... *illus* 1028.00

NU-ART *see Imperial category.*

NUTCRACKERS of many types have been used through the centuries. At first the nutcracker was probably strong teeth or a hammer. But by the nineteenth century, many elaborate and ingenious types were made. Levers, screws, and hammer adaptations were the most popular. Because nutcrackers are still useful, they are still being made, some in the old styles.

Bear, Wood, Carved, Tripod Handle, Black Forest, 6 ¼ In. 375.00

North Dakota School Of Mines, Vase, Ducks Flying, Carved, Blue, White, M.S. Davies, 6 ½ x 6 In. $7800.00

North Dakota School Of Mines, Vase, Mountains, Indians, Incised, Green Matte, M. Cable, 5 ¾ x 6 In. $8400.00

Northwood, Leaf Umbrella, Sugar & Creamer, Cover, Cranberry, No. 263 $1028.00

Northwood, Leaf Umbrella, Pitcher, Water, Rose DuBarry, No. 263, 8 ½ In. $36.00

N

Nutcracker, Eagle, Cast Iron, 4¼ x 9½ In.
$75.00

TIP

To dust small, fragile items like flower-decorated figurines, try blowing the dust away with a hand-held hair dryer set on low. For large, sturdy items, cover the end of the vacuum cleaner nozzle with an old nylon stocking, then vacuum.

Occupied Japan, Trinket Box, Baroque Woman, 4½ In.
$65.00

Office Technology, Calculator, Omega, Bamberger, Munich, Germany, 1904
$1054.00

Bear, Wood, Glass Eyes, Black Forest, Swiss, c.1910, 7¼ In.		336.00
Clown, Cast Iron, Painted, Molded Eyes, Ears, Mouth, c.1900, 6 x 5½ In.		840.00
Dog, Black, Iron, Harker Supply Co., 13 In.		275.00
Dog, Brass, Wood Base, c.1900, 11 In.		196.00
Dog, Cast Iron, Harker Supply Co., 13 In.		265.00
Dog, St. Bernard, Cast Iron, c.1915		125.00
Eagle, Cast Iron, 4¼ x 9½ In.	*illus*	75.00
Fish, Brass, c.1885, 7 x 2½ In.		165.00
Gnome, Wood, Carved, Black Forest, 9½ In.		375.00
Grand Old Opry, Dog, Cast Iron, Nashville, Tenn., Nov. 1925, 11 x 6 x 5 In.		56.00
Half Walnut Shape, Metal, Screw-In Crusher, Germany, 3½ x 2½ In.		44.00
Lady's Legs, Brass, 1½ x 5½ In.		55.00
Man, Standing, Wood, Carved, Hands In Pocket, Black Forest, c.1900, 8 In.		295.00
Monkey, Wood, Carved, Black Forest		395.00
Old Woman With Bag & Umbrella, Wood, Carved, Black Forest, 7 x 2 x 4½ In.		250.00
Pliers Type, Nickel Plated, Rope Design Handles, c.1890, 5½ In.		18.00
Punch & Judy, Brass, England, 5 In.		650.00
Santa, Wood, Holding Blue Bag With Stars, 2002, 24 In.		55.00
Soldier, Wood, Musical, Box, 1982, 13 In.		54.00
Squirrel, Cast Iron, 4¼ x 5 x 2 In.		55.00
Squirrel, Wood, Carved, Black Forest		295.00
William Shakespeare, Brass, Reeded Handle		75.00

NYMPHENBURG, *see Royal Nymphenburg.*

OCCUPIED JAPAN was printed on pottery, porcelain, toys, and other goods made during the American occupation of Japan after World War II, from 1945 to 1952. Collectors now search for these pieces. The items were made for export. Ceramic items are listed here. Toys are listed in the Toy category in this book.

Crumb Brush, Oriental Doll, Wood, 10 In.		25.00
Cup & Saucer, Phoenix Bird, Blue & White		16.00
Figurine, Boy With Drum, Bisque, 2⅝ In.		9.00
Figurine, Colonial Couple, Blue Jacket, Red Blouse, 2⅜ In.		8.00
Figurine, Cowboy, Toting Six Gun, Hat Pushed Back On Head, 4¼ In.		39.00
Reindeer, Antlers, Painted Eyes, Celluloid, 6 x 6¾ In.		20.00
Salt & Pepper, Bride & Groom, Tall Hat, Pin Stripe Pants, Flower Bouquet, Blue Ribbon		30.00
Serving Bowl, Cover, Flowers, Teal Green Border, Gold Accents, 10½ x 5½ In.		65.00
Trinket Box, Baroque Woman, 4½ In.	*illus*	65.00
Vase, Woman In Colorful Dress, Satsuma Style, 2 Handles, 4 In.		28.00
Vase, Usabata, Bronze, 2-Part Handles, Inlaid Flowers, c.1952, 10½ In.		118.00

OFFICE TECHNOLOGY includes office equipment and related products, such as adding machines, calculators, and check-writing machines. Typewriters are in their own category in this book.

Adding Machine, 3 Digits, 9 Keys, Release Lever, Velvet Case		585.00
Adding Machine, Curta Type I, Original Box, c.1948		920.00
Bank Punch, Automatic, Check Protector, Williams, c.1885		669.00
Calculating Machine, Doppel-Brunsviga, Twin Spokewheel, Manual, c.1932		392.00
Calculating Machine, Electric, Mecerdes Euklid Model, 8, c.1920		448.00
Calculating Machine, Kuli, All Arithmetical Operations, Wood Case, c.1909		5853.00
Calculating Machine, Madas, Drum, Stepped, Swiss, c.1908		948.00
Calculating Machine, Omega, Art Nouveau, 1904		1054.00
Calculating Machine, Omega, Justin Bamberger, Germany, c.1905, 18 x 5 In.		468.00
Calculator, Omega, Bamberger, Munich, Germany, 1904	*illus*	1054.00
Calculator, Otis King, Model K, Tubular Steel, Chrome, 1950s		150.00
Cipher Machine Case, Wooden, Enigma Type A, Instructions, Germany		4944.00
Quill Pen Cutter, Brass, Ebony Wood, Davis, Leather Covered Case, 4 In.		284.00
Stapler, Arrow Brand, Model S 25-49, Red, Cream Painted Metal, 1940s		27.00
Stapler, Brinco, Wire, c.1902, 5 x 3½ In.		64.00
Telegraph, Messing, Brass Case, Clockwork Spring, Twin Coils, Wood Base, 14 In.		897.00
Telegraph, Morse, M. Hipp, Lacquered Brass, Clockwork Motor, c.1865, 12 x 5½ In.		1589.00
Telegraph, Omnigraph, Morse Code Training Device, Spring Powered, c.1910		310.00
Telegraph, Portable, Siemens Halske, Ink Writer, Voltmeter, Motor, Case, c.1880		2509.00
Time Clock, Oak, International Time Recording Co., c.1906, 62 x 19 x 9 In.		936.00

OHR pottery was made in Biloxi, Mississippi, from 1883 to 1906 by George E. Ohr, a true eccentric. The pottery was made of very thin clay that was twisted, folded, and dented into odd, graceful shapes. Some pieces were lifelike models of hats, animal heads, or even a potato. Others were decorated with folded clay "snakes." Reproductions and reworked pieces are appearing on the market. These have been reglazed, or snakes and other embellishments have been added.

Bank, Bisque Fired, Pouch Shape, 3 ½ x 2 ½ In.		1320.00
Bowl, Brown Mottled Glaze, Stamped, 1880-1900, 2 ⅝ x 2 ⅛ In.		635.00
Bowl, Olive Green Mottled Glaze, White Slag, Stamped, Geo. E. Ohr, Biloxi, 2 ¼ In.		520.00
Chamberstick, Buff Shaded To Terra-Cotta, Unglazed, Loop & Shaped Handle, 5 ¼ In.		1080.00
Cup, Black Olive Green Mottled Glaze, Crimped Sides & Rim, Redware, 1 ¾ In.		520.00
Goblet, Purple, Green, Mottled Glaze, 3 ¾ x 3 ½ In.		3900.00
Hat, Novelty, Gunmetal Glaze, Green Glaze, 2 ¼ x 4 ¾ In.		2040.00
Hat, Speckled Gunmetal Glaze On Amber Ground, Stamped, 3 ¼ x 3 ¼ In.		1920.00
Inkwell, Artist Palette, Brushes, Paint Tubes, Mottled Brown, 7 ½ x 6 ½ In.	*illus*	4190.00
Inkwell, Cottage, Mottled Brown, House Boat, Mottled Olive Green, Stamped, 3 x 7 ½ x 3 ⅞ In.		5600.00
Inkwell, Tent, Mottled Brown, Olive Green, Redware, Incised, Biloxi, 2 ½ x 5 ⅜ x 4 ⅞ In.		2280.00
Mug, Floral Handle, Gunmetal Brown Glaze, Script Signature, 3 ½ x 4 ½ In.		960.00
Mug, Puzzle, Flower Handle, Brown Speckled Glaze, Signed, 6 ¼ x 3 ½ In.		1560.00
Mug, Raspberry, Indigo, Sponged, Glazed, 1896, 4 ½ x 4 ½ In.		5700.00
Teapot, Cobalt Blue Glaze, 5 x 9 In.		4800.00
Teapot, Ear Shape Handle, Serpentine Spout, Green, Brown, 7 ¼ x 8 In.		10800.00
Vase, Asymmetrically Folded Rim, Green & Gunmetal Glaze, Stamped, 4 ¾ x 2 ¾ In.		4800.00
Vase, Bisque, Terra-Cotta, Black Sponge, Incised, 3 x 5 ½ In.	*illus*	3120.00
Vase, Bone White, Unglazed, Squat, Cylindrical Neck, 4 ⅞ In.		1080.00
Vase, Deeply Folded Rim, Gunmetal Glaze, 3 ½ x 3 ½ In.		2520.00
Vase, Flaring, Raspberry, Green, Gunmetal Glaze, 3 ½ x 5 ½ In.		3480.00
Vase, Handle, Multitone Brown Glaze, Sculpted & Applied Interior, 4 x 2 ½ In.		2160.00
Vase, In Body Twist, Brown Speckled Glaze, Black Sponged, 5 ¼ x 3 ½ In.		4500.00
Vase, In Body Twist At Rim, Tapering, Green, Black Gunmetal Glaze, 3 ½ x 4 In.	*illus*	3900.00
Vase, Marbleized Clay, Bisque Fired, Squat, Folded Rim, 3 ¼ x 5 ½ In.		2040.00
Vase, Marbleized Clay, Orange, Tan, 4 x 6 In.		12000.00
Vase, Multitone Mottled Brown Over Metallic Charcoal Glaze, Flared, Footed, 4 In.		5200.00
Vase, Pinched, Incised, Multitone Brown Glaze, 4 x 4 In.		2280.00
Vase, Pinched Top, Green Speckled, Mustard Glaze, 4 x 4 ½ In.	*illus*	6600.00
Vase, Raspberry, Gunmetal Mirrored Glaze, Stamped, Squat, 2 ½ x 3 ¾ In.		3000.00
Vase, Red Clay, Round, Crimped, Narrow Neck & Foot, Signed, c.1900, 3 ¾ In.		2950.00
Vase, Red Clay, Round Body, Narrow Neck, 1906, 3 ¾ In.		2450.00
Vase, Ribbed Body, Pinched Flower Form Rim, Dark Brown Mottled Glaze, 3 ½ x 4 In.		3120.00
Vase, Squat, Twist, Indigo, Plum, Speckled Glaze, 4 x 4 ½ In.		5700.00

OLD IVORY china was made by the Ohme Porcelain Works in Silesia, Germany, a factory working from 1882 to 1928. The china had an ivory matte background and was usually decorated with flowers or fruit. Dinner sets, fish sets, mustache cups, and souvenir pieces were made. Pieces were marked with a crown, the cipher OH, and the word *Silesia*. Some pieces are also marked with the words *Old Ivory*. The pattern numbers appear on the base of many pieces.

Berry Bowl, No. 41, 10 In.	205.00
Berry Set, No. 15, 7 Piece	145.00
Berry Set, No. 16, 6 Piece	45.00
Biscuit Jar, No. 12	750.00
Bowl, Eglantine, Portrait Of Children, Oval, 6 ¾ In.	850.00
Cake Plate, Handle, No. 33, 10 In.	190.00
Cake Plate, Holly, No. 22, 10 In.	185.00
Cake Plate, No. 12, 11 In.	145.00
Cake Plate, No. 15, 11 In.	60.00
Cake Plate, No. 84, 10 In.	45.00
Charger, No. 16, 13 In.	225.00
Chocolate Set, No. 16, 11 Piece	475.00
Chocolate Set, Wreath, No. 19, 19 In.	6300.00
Cup & Saucer, 2 Handles, No. 16	135.00
Dish, Arrowhead Shape, No. 15	195.00
Dish, Eglantine, Oval, 11 ½ In.	115.00
Dish, Mayonnaise, Underplate, No. 32	65.00
Dish, Rectangular, No. 32, 8 In.	40.00
Dish, Rectangular, No. 84, 6 ½ In.	35.00
Mustard, No. 15	110.00

Ohr, Inkwell, Artist Palette, Brushes, Paint Tubes, Mottled Brown, 7 ½ x 6 ½ In.
$4190.00

Ohr, Vase, Bisque, Terra-Cotta, Black Sponge, Incised, 3 x 5 ½ In.
$3120.00

Ohr, Vase, In Body Twist At Rim, Tapering, Green, Black Gunmetal Glaze, 3 ½ x 4 In.
$3900.00

Ohr, Vase, Pinched Top, Green Speckled, Mustard Glaze, 4 x 4 ½ In.
$6600.00

Onion, Knife Rest, Blue Underglaze, Meissen, 19th Century, 3 7/8 In., 8 Piece
$300.00

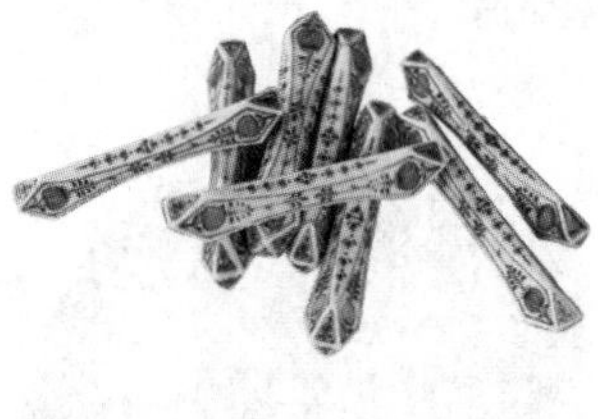

Opalescent, Christmas Snowflake, Pitcher, Cranberry, Ribs, 9 In.
$4400.00

Opalescent, Chrysanthemum Base Swirl, Sugar Shaker, Blue, 4 1/8 In.
$345.00

Opalescent, Coin Spot, Shaker, Cranberry, 9 Panels, Late 19th Century, 4 3/4 In.
$264.00

Nappy, Handle, No. 73 .... 160.00
Pitcher, Milk, No. 84 .... 150.00
Plate, No. 16, 6 1/4 In. 5.00
Plate, No. 16, 8 1/4 In. .... 10.00 to 30.00
Plate, No. 28, 6 In. 15.00
Plate, No. 28, 8 1/2 In. 25.00
Plate, No. 34, 6 In. 20.00
Platter, Eglantine, Oval, Handle, 11 In. 85.00
Porringer, No. 32 .... 30.00
Salt & Pepper, No. 15 .... 45.00
Saltshaker, No. 16 .... 5.00
Soup, Dish, No. 16, 9 1/2 In. 170.00
Sugar, Cover, No. 11 .... 10.00
Sugar & Creamer, Cover, No. 15 .... 60.00
Sugar & Creamer, Cover, No. 28 .... 25.00
Toothpick, No. 16 .... 115.00

OLD PARIS, *see Paris category.*

OLD SLEEPY EYE, *see Sleepy Eye category.*

ONION PATTERN, originally named *bulb pattern,* is a white ware decorated with cobalt blue or pink. Although it is commonly associated with Meissen, other companies made the pattern in the late nineteenth and the twentieth centuries. A rare type is called red bud because there are added red accents on the blue-and-white dishes.

Bowl, Blue, Reticulated, Lacy, Meissen 200.00
Bowl, Cereal, Blue, Cavalier Ironstone 7.50
Canister Set, Blue, Flour, Sugar, Coffee, Tea, Covers, Graduated, Marked, Crossed Swords 165.00
Casserole, Blue, Handles, Vienna Woods, 12 1/2 x 8 In. 18.00
Chop Plate, Blue, Royal China, 11 3/8 In. 30.00
Creamer, Blue, Royal, 3 x 2 In. 11.00
Cup, Tea, Blue & White, Meissen, Pair 58.00
Cup & Saucer, Blue, Cavalier Ironstone 8.00
Cup & Saucer, Blue, Meissen, Early 20th Century, 2 Piece 24.00
Cup & Saucer, Blue, Scio Pottery 10.00
Dessert Stand, 3 Graduated Tiers, Blue & White, Figural Finial, Meissen, 22 In. 1680.00
Dinner Bell, Flow Blue, 5 x 2 1/2 In. 5.00
Dish, Scalloped Shell, Handle, Blue Underglaze, Crossed Swords, 13 In. 207.00
Dish, Sweetmeat, Man Holding Bowl, Underglaze Blue, Meissen, 12 In. 1121.00
Dish, Sweetmeat, Woman Holding Bowl, Underglaze, Blue, Meissen, 3 In. 1003.00
Knife Rest, Blue Underglaze, Meissen, 19th Century, 3 7/8 In., 8 Piece .... *illus* 300.00
Plate, Blue, Japan, 9 1/4 In. 12.00
Plate, Blue, Signed, Crossed Swords, Meissen, 8 1/4 In., 8 Piece 65.00
Plate, Dinner, Blue, Marked, Christina Porcelain, Seltmann Weiden Bavaria W. Germany 25.00
Platter, Crossed Swords Mark, Meissen, 22 1/2 In. 460.00
Platter, Meat, Blue, Metal Bottom, Meissen, 12 1/2 x 9 3/4 In. 165.00
Platter, Meissen, Oval, 12 x 17 In. 263.00
Platter, Scalloped Edges, Crossed Swords Mark, Meissen, 18 1/4 In. 173.00
Relish, 2 Sections, Blue & White, Meissen, 9 1/2 In. .... 94.00 to 117.00
Rolling Pin, Blue & White 45.00
Sugar, Cover, Blue, Handles, Underglaze, Scio Pottery 20.00
Tazza, Pedestal, Blue & White, Blue Crossed Swords, Meissen 280.00
Tea Strainer, Cup With Strainer On Bottom, Marked TK, 1900s, 5 In. 20.00
Tureen, Soup, Footed, Scalloped Shell Handles, Wave Crest Finial, Meissen, 13 1/4 In. 374.00
Tureen, Soup, Stand, Ladle, Blue & White, 2 Handles, Meissen, 10 1/2 x 15 In. 300.00

OPALESCENT GLASS is translucent glass that has the tones of the opal gemstone. It originated in England in the 1870s and is often found in pressed glassware made in Victorian times. Opalescent glass was first made in America in 1897 at the Northwood glassworks in Indiana, Pennsylvania. Some dealers use the terms *opaline* and *opalescent* for any of these translucent wares. More opalescent pieces may be listed in Hobnail, Northwood, Pressed Glass, and other glass categories.

Christmas Snowflake, Pitcher, Cranberry, Ribs, 9 In. .... *illus* 4400.00
Chrysanthemum Base Swirl, Sugar Shaker, Blue, 4 1/8 In. .... *illus* 345.00
Coin Spot, Shaker, Cranberry, 9 Panels, Late 19th Century, 4 3/4 In. .... *illus* 264.00
Corn, Vase, Vaseline, 8 In. .... *illus* 230.00

Opalescent, Corn, Vase, Vaseline, 8 In.
$230.00

Opalescent, Ribbed Lattice, Sugar Shaker, Blue, 4 ½ In.
$217.00

Opalescent, Crisscross, Pitcher, Cranberry, 8 ¾ In.
$3850.00

Opalescent, Stars & Stripes, Pitcher, Cranberry, 8 In.
$4400.00

Opalescent, Daffodil, Sugar Shaker, Blue, 4 ¾ In.
$3850.00

Opalescent, Swirling Maze, Pitcher, Vaseline
$3410.00

TIP
When cleaning mother-of-pearl inlay, use a weak solution of detergent, never an acid.

Opera Glasses, Lemoire, Mother-Of-Pearl, Signed, Case, Original Box, France
$165.00

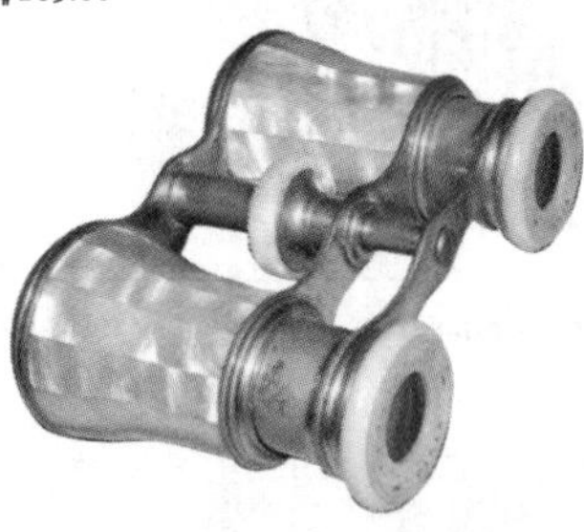

Orphan Annie, Button, Funy Frostys Club, Parisian Nov. Co, 1930s, 1 In.
$253.00

Overbeck, Vase, Stylized Flowers, Green, Maroon, Signed, OBK, 14¼ In.
$57500.00

Crisscross, Pitcher, Cranberry, 8¾ In. . . . . *illus* 3850.00
Daffodil, Sugar Shaker, Blue, 4¾ In. . . . . *illus* 3850.00
Ribbed Lattice, Sugar Shaker, Blue, 4½ In. . . . . *illus* 217.00
Seaweed, Pitcher, Cranberry, Ruffled Edge, 9 In. 518.00
Stars & Stripes, Pitcher, Cranberry, 8 In. . . . . *illus* 4400.00
Swirling Maze, Pitcher, Vaseline . . . . . *illus* 3410.00
Toothpicks are listed in the Toothpick category.

OPALINE, or opal glass, was made in white, green, and other colors. The glass had a matte surface and a lack of transparency. It was often gilded or painted. It was a popular mid-nineteenth-century European glassware.

Plaque, Rectangular, Opaque White, Gypsy Girl, Signed, M.C. Underwood, 15 x 12 In. 863.00

OPERA GLASSES are needed because the stage is a long way from some of the seats at a play or an opera. Mother-of-pearl was a popular decoration on many French glasses.

Bronze, Green Morrow Enamel, Flower Medallions, Gold, Silver, Signed, 4 In. 345.00
C. Dubizy, Cobalt Blue, Enamel Flowers, Beaded, Abalone Eye Cups, Paris, 3 x 4 In. 470.00
Duhme, Brass, Mother-Of-Pearl, Cincinnati, 3 x 4½ x 1¾ In. 120.00
Lemoire, Mother-Of-Pearl, Signed, Case, Original Box, France . . . . . *illus* 165.00
Mother-Of-Pearl, Brass, Leather Case, Late 1800s 95.00
Skyline, Folding, Black, Chrome Trim, Original Red Box, 4¼ x 2½ In. 39.00

ORPHAN ANNIE first appeared in the comics in 1924. The redheaded girl, her dog Sandy, and her friends have been on the radio and are still on the comic pages. A Broadway musical show and a movie in the 1980s made Annie popular again and many toys, dishes, and other memorabilia are being made.

Badge, Decoder, Brass, Ovaltine Premium, c.1935, 1¼ In. 41.00
Badge, Decoder, Speed-O-Meter, Numbers & Letters Around Sides, c.1940 . . . . . 65.00 to 103.00
Belt, Made Of Sunday Funnies Comic Book, Dated 1974, 40 In. 22.00
Book, Better Little Book, Little Orphan Annie Saves Sandy, c.1938 . . . . . 35.00
Book, Big Little Book, Little Orphan Annie, No. 708, c.1933 . . . . . 70.00
Book, Jumbo The Circus Elephant, Pop-Up, 1935 . . . . . 198.00
Book, Little Orphan Annie & Uncle Dan, Cupples & Leon Co., Harold Gray, 1933 . . . . . 41.00
Book, Little Orphan Annie Shipwrecked, 1931 . . . . . 65.00
Book, Radio Orphan Annie Book About Dogs, Wander Co., 1936, 31 Pages 65.00
Book, Secret Society Manual, Radio Premium, c.1937 . . . . . 41.00
Booklet, Radio Orphan Annie's Secret Society, 1936 . . . . . 90.00
Bracelet, Identification Bureau, 6¼ In. 22.00
Button, Funy Frostys Club, Parisian Nov. Co., 1930s, 1 In. . . . . *illus* 253.00
Clicker, Secret Guard, Mysto-Snapper, Red, White, Blue, Tin, Quaker, c.1941, 2½ In. 13.00
Comic Book, Little Orphan Annie Shipwrecked, 1930s 75.00
Costume, Leaping Lizards, Famous Artists Syndicate, 1930s, 36 In., 3 Piece 115.00
Doll, Composition, Red Dress, White Collar, Pantaloons, 10 In. 295.00
Doll, Knickerbocker, Cloth, Little Orphan Annie, Sandy, c.1982, 15 In. 35.00
Game, Little Orphan Annie Shooting Game, Milton Bradley, 1930s, 12 In. 315.00
Lunch Box, Metal, Thermos, c.1981 . . . . . 11.00
Mug, Annie & Sandy Bakelite, Beetleware, 1930s, 2⅝ In. 65.00
Mug, Shake-Up, Ovaltine Premium, Orange Top, Beetleware, 4¾ In. 48.00
Necklace, Heart, Gold Color, Supreme Creations, c.1981, 16-In. Chain 10.00
Nodder, Annie & Sandy, Bisque, 3½-In. Annie, 1-In. Sandy 225.00
Nodder, Painted, Bisque, Germany, 1925, 3½ In. 75.00
Ornament, Annie In Santa Hat, Snowman, 1981 . . . . . 18.00
Pillow, Annie & Sandy, 1940s, 10 In. 75.00
Pin, Cereal Radio Decoder, c.1940 . . . . . 83.00
Ring, Secret Society, Silver Star, Metal, Adjustable, Radio Premium, c.1936 . . . . . 53.00
Ring, Signet, Metal, Adjustable, Stamped Robbins & Co., Radio Premium, ½ In. 40.00
Salt & Pepper, Annie & Sandy 75.00
Sheet Music, Ovaltine Premium, Little Orphan Annie's Song, 1931 . . . . . 28.00
Stove, Green, Electric, Tin Lithograph, 1930s, 8½ x 9⅞ x 5½ In. . . . . 55.00 to 195.00
Toy, Orphan Annie, Seated, 2-Sided, Pull Toy, Painted, Wood, 1930-40, 9½ x 11 In. 633.00
Toy, Sandy, Walker, Suitcase In Mouth, Tin, Windup, Marx, 1931 . . . . . 160.00
Watch, Sundial, Compass, ROA Radio Premium, Booklet, 1938, 1½ In. 36.00
Wristwatch, New Haven, 1935, 4 x 7 x 1 In. 222.00

ORREFORS Glassworks, located in the Swedish province of Smaaland, was established in 1898. The company is still making glass for use on the table or as decorations. There is renewed interest in the glass made in the modern styles of the 1940s and 1950s. In 1990, the company merged with Kosta Boda. Most vases and decorative pieces are signed with the etched name *Orrefors.*

Bowl, Kraka, Blue, Fishnet, 3-Sided, Signed, Sven Palmquist, 3 ¼ x 7 In. 675.00
Figurine, Rabbit, Large Ears, 7 In. 88.00
Vase, Clear, Pillar Shape, Fluted Side, Square Base, 8 ½ x 3 ½ In. 35.00
Vase, Clear Over Smoke, Triangular, Nils Landberg, 1950s, 9 ½ In. 225.00
Vase, Smoke, Nils Landberg, ¾ x 5 In. 300.00

OTT & BREWER Company operated the Etruria Pottery at Trenton, New Jersey, from 1871 to 1892. They started making belleek in 1882. The firm used a variety of marks that incorporated the initials *O & B.*

Jug, Gourd Form, Raised Enamel Cranes In Flight, Gilt Crabstock Handle, 13 In. 148.00
Vase, Pierced, Applied Flower, Leaf, Stamped Crown Mark, 6 ½ x 6 ¾ In. 250.00

OVERBECK pottery was made by four sisters named Overbeck at a pottery in Cambridge City, Indiana. They started in 1911. They made all types of vases, each one-of-a-kind. Small, hand-modeled figurines are the most popular pieces with today's collectors. The factory continued until 1955, when the last of the four sisters died.

Vase, Bulbous, Incised & Painted, Birds, Mauve Matte Glaze, 4 x 5 In. 5100.00
Vase, Elephants, Birds, Russet, Orange Ground, Squat, 3 ½ x 5 ½ In. 10200.00
Vase, Flowers, Carved, Pink & Brown Matte Glaze, Signed, 6 ¼ x 3 ½ In. .... *illus* 4800.00
Vase, Flowers, Red, Yellow & White, Black Matte Ground, 1920, 9 ⅛ In. 2950.00
Vase, Molded Fawns, Painted White, Turquoise Ground, 5 ½ In. 2950.00
Vase, Pink & White Frothy Glaze, 8 ¼ x 6 ½ In. 1200.00
Vase, Shouldered Shape, Carved Flowers, Pink & Brown Matte, 3 ½ x 6 ¼ In. 4800.00
Vase, Stylized Birds, Blossoms, Mustard Glaze, Brown Ground, Barrel, 9 ¼ x 6 In. 15600.00
Vase, Stylized Birds, Flowers, 4 Panels, Cream Slip, Matte Rose, Flared Rim, 6 ¾ In. 5523.00
Vase, Stylized Birds, Green, Brown, Bulbous, 4 ¾ x 5 ¼ In. 5700.00
Vase, Stylized Flowers, Green, Maroon, Signed, OBK, 14 ¼ In. .... *illus* 57500.00

OWENS Pottery was made in Zanesville, Ohio, from 1891 to 1928. The first art pottery was made after 1896. Utopian Ware, Cyrano, Navarre, Feroza, and Henri Deux were made. Pieces were usually marked with a form of the name Owens. About 1907, the firm began to make tile and discontinued the art pottery wares.

Ewer, Utopian, Trefoil, Autumn Leaf, Marked, 10 ½ x 6 ¾ In. .... *illus* 175.00
Jardiniere, Matte Utopian, Cherry Branch Handle, 9 x 10 ½ In. 395.00
Jardiniere, Pedestal, Griffins, Green, 33 x 17 ½ In. .... *illus* 155.00
Mug, Utopian, Hand Painted, Leaves, Cherries, c.1907 .... 165.00
Pitcher, Utopian, 3-Footed, Pansies, Brown, Yellow, 5 ½ In. 106.00
Vase, Indian, Green Matte, Thick Glaze, 5 In. 502.00
Vase, Painted Design, Red, Blue, Green, Signed H. Huebner, 7 x 16 In. 403.00
Vase, Tulip, Green Glaze, Unmarked, 6 ½ x 11 ½ In. 720.00
Vase, Utopian, 2 Handles, c.1891, 6 x 3 ½ In. 165.00
Vase, Utopian, Brown Ware, Underglaze Slip, Fall Leaves, c.1900, 4 ¾ In. 200.00
Vase, Utopian, Pansy, Ruffle Edge, Brown Glaze, Flowers, 7 x 6 In. 175.00
Vase, Utopian, Shouldered, Brown Glaze, Painted Flowers, Applied Silver Overlay, 3 ½ x 5 ½ In. 518.00
Vase, Utopian, Squared, Flowers, Brown, Yellow, 3 ¾ In. 224.00
Vase, Utopian, Twist Form, Clovers, Brown, Yellow, 3 ¾ In. 106.00
Vase, White Glaze, 2 Applied Buttress Handles At Shoulder, Marked, 8 In. 435.00

OYSTER PLATES were popular from the 1880s. Each course at dinner was served in a special dish. The oyster plate had indentations shaped like oysters. Usually six oysters were held on a plate. There is no greater value to a plate with more oysters, although that myth continues to haunt antiques dealers. There are other plates for shellfish, including cockle plates and whelk plates. The appropriately shaped indentations are part of the design of these dishes.

5 Wells, Pink Edge, Sauce Shell, Scallop Edge, Gilded Flowers, 9 In., 12 Piece 2160.00
5 Wells, Blossoms & Gilt Borders, Haviland Limoges Mark Verso, 8 ⅜ In., 8 Piece 431.00
5 Wells, Fish Head, Cobalt Blue Ground, Palissy Style, France, 10 ½ In. 1150.00
5 Wells, George Jones, Majolica, Turquoise, 8 ½ In. 1333.00
5 Wells, Majolica, Blue & White, 3-In. Center, 10 In. 196.00

Overbeck, Vase, Flowers, Carved, Pink & Brown Matte Glaze, Signed, 6 ¼ x 3 ½ In.
$4800.00

Owens, Ewer, Utopian, Trefoil, Autumn Leaf, Marked, 10 ½ x 6 ¾ In.
$175.00

Owens, Jardiniere, Pedestal, Griffins, Green, 33 x 17 ½ In.
$155.00

O

Paden City, Black Forest, Candleholder, Green, Mushroom Style, 3 In., Pair
$110.00

Paden City, Crow's Foot, Cup & Saucer, Ruby
$14.00

Paden City, Figurine, Seahorse, Crystal, 8 ¼ In.
$125.00

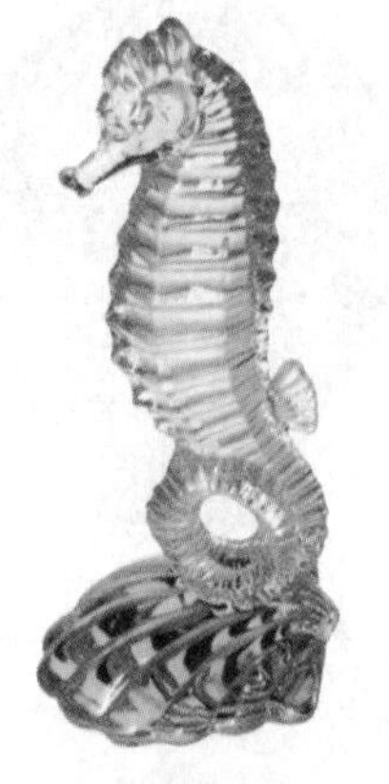

Paden City, Penny, Cordial, Ruby
$18.00

6 Wells, Majolica, Fish, On Seaweed, Turquoise Center, Minton, 11 In. 2300.00
6 Wells, Majolica, Minton . . . . . . 403.00 to 690.00
6 Wells, Majolica, Pink Luster Ground, Moser Style, 10 In. 288.00
6 Wells, Majolica, Sunflower, Yellow Rim, Samuel Lear, 10 In. 1035.00
6 Wells, Pink, White Wells, Cobalt Blue Center, Seaweed Ground, 10 In. . . . . . *illus* 115.00
6 Wells, Turkey, Dark Blue Ground, Haviland, 8 ¾ In. 374.00
Flowers, Gold Gilt, Limoges, 7 ¼ In., 10 Piece 588.00

PADEN CITY Glass Manufacturing Company was established in 1916 at Paden City, West Virginia. The company made over twenty different colors of glass. The firm closed in 1951. Paden City Pottery is not listed here. Some Paden City Pottery may be listed in Dinnerware.

Alexander, Candleholder, 2-Light, c.1930-40, 7 In., Pair 40.00
Alexander, Candy Dish, Ruby, Footed, 9 ½ In. 75.00
Angel, Sandwich Server, Footed,11 In. 88.00
Ardith, Candleholder, 2-Light, Crystal, 1920s, 5 In., Pair 40.00
Ardith, Candy Dish, Cover, Yellow, 2 Sections, Footed, 6 ¼ In. 119.00
Ardith, Candy Dish, Round, Footed, Yellow, 6 In. 279.00
Ardith, Console, Crystal, 13 In. 75.00
Black Forest, Candleholder, Green, Mushroom Style, 3 In., Pair . . . . . . *illus* 110.00
Black Forest, Console, Rolled Edge, Green, 11 ½ In. 150.00
Black Forest, Dish, Mayonnaise, Pink, 6 ½ In. . . . . . . 90.00 to 145.00
Black Forest, Vase, Ebony, Regina Shape, 7 In. 195.00
Black Forest, Vase, Green, Regina Shape, 6 ⅜ In. 175.00
Crow's Foot, Bowl, Nasturtium, Red, 3-Footed, 1930s 185.00
Crow's Foot, Candleholder, Crystal, Mushroom Style, c.1920-30, 2 ¾ In., Pair 30.00
Crow's Foot, Cup & Saucer, Ruby . . . . . . *illus* 14.00
Crow's Foot, Cup & Saucer, Yellow 15.00
Crow's Foot, Soup, Dish, Ruby, Footed 25.00
Crow's Foot, Tumbler, Amber, 4 In. 25.00
Cupid, Candleholder, Pink, Mushroom Style, 5 In., Pair 250.00
Figurine, Pheasant, Blue, 13 ½ In. 238.00
Figurine, Pheasant, Crystal, 13 ½ In. 143.00
Figurine, Pony, Blue 143.00
Figurine, Seahorse, Crystal, 8 ¼ In. . . . . . . *illus* 125.00
Gadroon, Cup, Mulberry 39.00
Gadroon, Plate, Bread & Butter, Mulberry, 6 ⅜ In. 17.00
Gadroon, Plate, Dinner, Mulberry, 9 ½ In. 47.00
Gazebo, Candlestick, Crystal, Old Trim, 6 In., Pair 90.00
Gazebo, Relish, 3 Sections, 1930s, 9 ½ x 7 ½ In. 17.00
Gazebo, Sandwich Server, Center Gooseneck Handle 81.00
Glades, Cocktail, Red, Pinched Waist 28.00
Hostmaster, Sandwich Server, Amber, Cornflower Etch, Handles, 14 In. 400.00
Lela Bird, Candy Dish, Cover, Green, Footed 237.00
Lido, Plate, Salad, 7 ¼ In. 18.00
Lucy, Candleholder, Open Center, 5 ¼ In. 85.00
Marie, Bowl, Pink, Footed, 5 ¼ x 10 ¾ In. 75.00
Maya, Candleholder, 2-Light, 5 ¾ x 8 In. 40.00
Maya, Console, Footed, 12 In. 40.00
Maya, Sandwich Server, Blue, 3-Footed, 13 ¾ In. 45.00
Maya, Serving Dish, 3-Footed, 13 ¾ In. 45.00
Modern Orchid, Berry Bowl, c.1940, 5 ½ In. 6.00
Modern Orchid, Platter, 11 ¾ In. 20.00
Modern Orchid, Platter, 14 In. 29.00
Nasturtium, Platter, 14 x 10 ¾ In. 25.00
Nora Bird, Sugar, Pink, 1930s 52.00
Orchid Etch, Wine, 4 ¼ In. 15.00
Oriental Garden, Ice Tub 60.00
Oriental Garden, Sandwich Server, 2 Handles 40.00
Party Line, Decanter, Pink, 9 ½ In. 125.00
Party Line, Ice Tub, Pink, Handles, 6 ½ In. 42.00
Party Line, Tumbler, Green, Footed, 7 In., 6 Piece 120.00
Party Line, Tumbler, Pink, Footed, 3 In. 14.00
Party Line, Tumbler, Pink, 5 ⅝ In. 15.00
Peacock & Wild Rose, Candleholder, Green, Mushroom Style 55.00
Peacock & Wild Rose, Candleholder, Pink, Mushroom Style, 5 In. 61.00

Peacock & Wild Rose, Compote, Pink, 3 ¼ x 6 ¼ In. 113.00
Peacock & Wild Rose, Console, Pink, 11 In. . . . . 147.00 to 190.00
Peacock & Wild Rose, Dish, Mayonnaise, Pink, Liner 146.00
Peacock & Wild Rose, Ice Tub, Pink 199.00
Peacock & Wild Rose, Plate, Dinner, Pink, 10 In. 135.00
Peacock & Wild Rose, Sandwich Server, Pink, Center Handle, 10 ¾ In. 95.00
Penny, Cocktail, Ruby, Footed, 3 In. 14.00
Penny, Cordial, Ruby . . . . . *illus* 18.00
Penny, Cup & Saucer, Amethyst 15.00
Penny, Dish, Mayonnaise, Amber, Liner, 4 x 8 In. 30.00
Penny, Finger Bowl, 4 ½ In., Pair 46.00
Penny, Sherbet, Cobalt Blue, Footed, 3 ¾ In. 16.00
Utopia, Vase, Flared, Footed, 10 In. 95.00
Vermillion Rose, Creamer 10.00
Vermillion Rose, Cup & Saucer 8.00
Vermillion Rose, Plate, Dessert, 7 ½ In. 4.00
Vermillion Rose, Sugar, Cover, Shell Crest 10.00
Vermillion Rose, Sugar & Creamer 35.00
Willow, Cake Plate, Tab Handles, 12 In. 13.00
Willow, Plate, Dinner, 10 In. 9.00

PAINTINGS listed in this book are not works by major artists but rather decorative paintings on ivory, board, or glass that would be of interest to the average collector. Watercolors on paper are listed under Picture. To learn the value of an oil painting by a listed artist you must contact an expert in that area.

Oil On Board, Cat, Red Tiger, 13 Toes, Grain Painted Pine Frame, c.1850, 10 x 9 In. 36000.00
Oil On Board, Child In White Bonnet, Profile, 17 x 14 In. 3920.00
Oil On Board, City Scene, American School, c.1950, 22 x 28 In. 360.00
Oil On Board, Dog, English Setter, Period Frame, 1823, 10 ⅞ x 12 ⅜ In. 1880.00
Oil On Board, Evangeline Oak St. Martinville, Louisiana, 10 ½ x 18 ¼ In. 1593.00
Oil On Board, Kittens, Climbing Oak Sapling, Gesso Frame, 25 x 11 In. 460.00
Oil On Board, Landscape With Windmill, 15 ¾ x 11 ¾ In. 354.00
Oil On Board, Mountain, River, 19th Century, 9 ¼ x 12 ¼ In. 287.00
Oil On Board, Rocky Coast, 19th Century, 10 ½ x 17 ½ In. 517.00
Oil On Board, Snowy Landscape, Frame, Signed, 1951, 19 ½ x 15 ¾ In. 960.00
Oil On Board, Swamp Scene, Gilt Frame, 18 x 26 ½ In. 4406.00
Oil On Board, Venice Bridge, Frame, 10 x ½ x 13 ¾ In. 1150.00
Oil On Board, View Of The Hudson River At Tarrytown N.Y., Frame, 12 ¼ x 16 In. 558.00
Oil On Board, Village With Mountain Landscape & Waterfalls, 13 ½ x 15 ½ In. 236.00
Oil On Board, Zinnias In Blue Pot, 22 ½ x 15 ½ In. 2937.00
Oil On Canvas, 2 Ladies Sitting On Bench Under Trees, Frame, 38 x 38 In. 45000.00
Oil On Canvas, Arcadian Landscape, Fisherman, 1700s, 29 ½ x 44 ⅜ In. 4113.00
Oil On Canvas, Arts & Crafts, Colorful Landscape, Unsigned, 16 x 12 In. 660.00
Oil On Canvas, Boathouse On River, Harry Stinson, 17 ¾ x 15 ¼ In. 3600.00
Oil On Canvas, Boats Docked In Harbor, James Bonnar, Frame, 20 x 24 In. 5500.00
Oil On Canvas, Boy With Velvet Jacket, Lace Collar, Gilt Frame, 22 x 27 In. 2300.00
Oil On Canvas, Brooklyn Bridge, New York Harbor In Moonlight, 31 ½ x 23 ½ In. 708.00
Oil On Canvas, Canoeing In The Catskills, 1871, 12 ½ x 18 ½ In. 1175.00
Oil On Canvas, Cape Cod House In Spring, 19th Century, 15 x 20 In. 977.00
Oil On Canvas, Cattle In Highland Landscape, British School, Signed, 12 x 20 In. 295.00
Oil On Canvas, Christ, Giltwood Frame, c.1840, 26 ½ x 33 ½ In. 1260.00
Oil On Canvas, Church, Cottage, Frame, c.1830, 15 ½ x 19 ½ In. 2100.00
Oil On Canvas, Coastal Scene, American School, Period Frame, c.1920, 35 x 46 In. 240.00
Oil On Canvas, Countryside Landscape With Cottage & Stream, 20 x 31 ½ In. 1062.00
Oil On Canvas, Duck Hunters, Dogs, Mahogany Frame, 20th Century, 25 x 39 In. 1314.00
Oil On Canvas, Farmhouse, American, Frame, c.1880, 12 x 18 In. 510.00
Oil On Canvas, Farmstead, Lake, Frame, 13 x 20 In. 2703.00
Oil On Canvas, Fawn In Grass, Composition Frame, 22 x 26 In. 201.00
Oil On Canvas, Fisherfolk On Beach, Continental, 18 x 26 In. 353.00
Oil On Canvas, Folk, 10 Kittens, Wood & Gesso Frame, c.1900, 13 ½ x 34 ½ In. 1725.00
Oil On Canvas, Forest Pond, Mount Auburn Cemetery, Pine Frame, 14 x 18 In. 21150.00
Oil On Canvas, French Provincial Town, 18 x 24 In. 384.00
Oil On Canvas, Girl Buying Fruit, Frame, 34 x 26 ½ In. 3290.00
Oil On Canvas, Harbor At St. Ives, Frame, 1908, 10 x 12 In. 8225.00
Oil On Canvas, Harbor Scene, Lighthouse In Sunset, Gesso Frame, 13 ½ x 19 ½ In. 920.00

Painting, Oil On Panel, George Washington, American School, 19th Century, 17 x 13 In.
$825.00

Painting, On Ivory, Woman, Ringlets, Ribbon, Alosandra, Frame, 4 x 4 In.
$275.00

Painting, Reverse On Glass, Lake & Mountains, Figures, Buildings, 24 ¾ x 34 ¾ In.
$3220.00

TIP

A miniature painting should not be washed. Most miniatures are painted on ivory and the paint will wash off.

Pairpoint, Lamp, Exeter Shade, Landscape, Dutch Windmill Band, Bronze Base, 22 ½ x 17 In.
$2703.00

Pairpoint, Lamp, Puffy, Hummingbird, Chrysanthemum, Signed, 21 ¼ In.
$3162.00

Pairpoint, Lamp, Reverse Painted, Ship, Fringe, Bronze Base, 22 ½ x 15 ½ In.
$7500.00

Oil On Canvas, Herdsman, Animals, Ruined Castle, Roman Campagna, Dutch, 21 x 24 In. . . 8519.0

Oil On Canvas, Kitten, Goldfish In Bowl, Frame, 20th Century, 12 x 10 In. . . . 2703.0

Oil On Canvas, Lake Scene, Mountain, Autumn Colors, Gesso Frame, 16 x 22 In. . . . 920.0

Oil On Canvas, Landscape, Farm, 19th Century, 18 x 24 In. . . . 4500.0

Oil On Canvas, Landscape, House, Barn, Pond, Shepherd, Dog, Sheep, 21 x 15 ½ In. . . . 316.0

Oil On Canvas, Landscape, Lake View, 15 ⅞ x 19 ¾ In. . . . 382.0

Oil On Canvas, Landscape Lake Scene, Rowboat, Frame, 29 x 43 In. . . . 200.0

Oil On Canvas, Landscape Lake Scene, Sailboats, Frame, 19th Century, 29 x 43 In. . . . 489.0

Oil On Canvas, Madonna Adoring The Christ Child, 32 x 27 In. . . . 3186.0

Oil On Canvas, Man In Armchair With Pen & Paper, Gesso Frame, 28 x 24 In. . . . 220.0

Oil On Canvas, Man In Night Jacket, Frame, 32 x 26 In. . . . 978.0

Oil On Canvas, Man In Waistcoat, Ruffled Cravat, Gesso Frame, 26 12 x 22 ½ In. . . . 460.0

Oil On Canvas, Military Encampment, Frame, 11 x 17 In. . . . 2070.0

Oil On Canvas, Moses, Bulrushes, On Nile, Arnaldo Nardi, 1800s, 24 x 24 ¼ In. . . . 1645.0

Oil On Canvas, Mother & 2 Boys Under Trees, Frame, c.1888, 62 x 50 In. . . . 5500.0

Oil On Canvas, Native Americans By Waterfall, Giltwood Frame, 22 x 29 In. . . . 440.0

Oil On Canvas, Night Fishing, Dutch School, 19th Century, 25 x 30 In. . . . 1003.0

Oil On Canvas, Nobleman In Parade Armor, 1700s, 30 ⅛ x 25 ½ In. . . . 1200.0

Oil On Canvas, Old Absinthe House, Bourbon Street, c.1947, 24 x 30 In. . . . 4500.0

Oil On Canvas, Pastoral Scene, 19th Century, 28 ¼ x 35 ½ In. . . . 3585.0

Oil On Canvas, Peasant Girl With White Blouse & Red Shawl, France, 24 x 20 In. . . . 2644.0

Oil On Canvas, Plums, Raspberries, 10 x 8 In. . . . 118.0

Oil On Canvas, Queen Mary II Of England, Unsigned, 16 x 12 ¾ In. . . . 1440.0

Oil On Canvas, River Scene, Steamboat Men In Skiff, 19th Century, 12 x 18 In. . . . 805.0

Oil On Canvas, River Scene, Trees, Frame, 12 x 18 In. . . . 1950.0

Oil On Canvas, Sailors In White Caps In Boat, 33 x 42 ½ In. . . . 478.0

Oil On Canvas, Shepherd & Sheep, Frame, 24 x 39 In. . . . 805.0

Oil On Canvas, Spanish Lady In Black, 15 ¾ x 12 In. . . . 826.0

Oil On Canvas, Still Life, 3 Peaches In Grass, 19th Century, 6 ¼ x 8 In. . . . 207.0

Oil On Canvas, Still Life, Fruit, Pitcher, Tumbler, c.1920, 15 x 18 In. . . . 148.0

Oil On Canvas, Still Life, Fruits, 8 ¼ x 11 ½ In. . . . 472.0

Oil On Canvas, Still Life, Grapevine, Marble Top Table, Gilt Gesso Frame, 18 x 21 In. . . . 6463.0

Oil On Canvas, Still Life, Watermelon, Molded Giltwood Frame, 18 x 30 In. . . . 2115.0

Oil On Canvas, Still Life With Peaches, Frame, Giltwood, c.1881, 16 x 20 In. . . . 499.0

Oil On Canvas, The Chase, Hunting Scene, A. Gimello, 19th Century, 38 ¾ x 25 ½ In. . . . 649.0

Oil On Canvas, The Education Of The Virgin, 11 ½ x 9 ¼ In. . . . 3422.0

Oil On Canvas, USS Solace, Naval Hospital Ship, Frame, 15 x 24 In. . . . 4800.0

Oil On Canvas, White Roses On A Table, Eva D. Cowdery, Frame, 22 x 30 In. . . . 880.0

Oil On Canvas, Winter Scene, 2 Men Rabbit Hunting, Gilt Wood Frame, 29 x 34 In. . . . 2070.0

Oil On Canvas, Winter Scene With Stream, Frame, 16 x 14 In. . . . 21850.0

Oil On Masonite, Angel Playing A Horn, Henry Lawrence Faulkner, c.1970, 14 x 10 In. . . . 4200.0

Oil On Panel, Dancing On Village Green, Dutch School, 17th Century, 8 ¼ x 11 In. . . . 1763.0

Oil On Panel, George Washington, American School, 19th Century, 17 x 13 In. . . . *illus* 825.0

Oil On Panel, Group Of Children, Frame, England, 9 x 12 In. . . . 1293.0

Oil On Panel, Madonna & Child, 15 x 11 In. . . . 12980.0

Oil On Panel, Nude, Russian School, 20th Century, 19 ¾ x 15 In. . . . 7670.0

Oil On Panel, Violinist, E. Fichel, 10 ¾ x 8 ½ In. . . . 980.0

Oil On Paper, Board, Moulin With Figures In The Snow, 1888, 7 ¾ x 10 ¾ In. . . . 502.0

Oil On Tin, Horse Drawn Sleigh, Winter Landscape, 19th Century, Frame, 13 x 17 In. . . . 302.0

Oil On Tin, Virgin With Child, 19 x 13 In. . . . 590.0

Oil On Wood, Poetry Of Flowers, Abstract, Frame, D.Y. Ellinger, 9 x 9 In. . . . 187.0

On Ivory, Lady, Blue Dress, Lace, Coiffed Hair, Oval, Signed, Frame, 4 x 3 ⅝ In. . . . 165.0

On Ivory, Woman, Ringlets, Ribbon, Alosandra, Frame, 4 x 4 In. . . . *illus* 275.0

On Ivory, Woman, Tortoiseshell Comb In Hair, Mother-Of-Pearl Case, 3 ¾ In. . . . 316.0

On Ivory, Young Man, Black Formal Clothing, Smith's, No. 2 Milk St., Boston, 4 In. . . . 575.0

Reverse On Glass, Lake & Mountains, Figures, Buildings, 24 ¾ x 34 ¾ In. . . . *illus* 3220.0

Reverse On Glass, Log Cabin, Figures, Animals, Natural Cotton, Frame, 12 x 16 In. . . . 240.0

Reverse On Glass, Pacific Railroad Engine No. 301, Rocky Mountains, 25 x 88 In. . . . 8962.0

PAIRPOINT Manufacturing Company started in 1880 in New Bedford, Massachusetts. It soon joined with the glassworks nearby and made glass, silver-plated pieces, and lamps. Reverse-painted glass shades and molded shades known as "puffies" were part of the production until the 1930s. The company reorganized and changed its name several times but is still working today. Items listed here are glass or glass and metal. Silver-plated pieces are listed under Silver Plate.

Biscuit Jar, Opal, Faceted Mold, Blown, Sailing Ships, Metal Lid, 6 ½ In. . . . 546.0

Biscuit Jar, Opal Body, Gold Stemmed Flowers, Pierced Medallion, Bail Handle, 7 In. 230.00
Bowl, Centerpiece, Cranberry Cut To Clear, Marble & Brass Base, 9 x 11 In. 600.00
Bowl, Centerpiece, Darlington Cutting, Rosaria Rim, Star Cut Foot, 12 In. 635.00
Bowl, Holland Cutting, Flared, 8¾ In. 300.00
Bride's Basket, Opal, Pink Ruffled Rim, Blue Flowers, Gold Scrolling, 9 In. 173.00
Candlestick, Waterford, Clear Foot, Stem, Bobeches, Amethyst Connectors, 10 In., Pair 518.00
Compote, Amethyst, Clear Bubble Ball, Sterling Silver Stem & Foot, 9 x 12 In. 805.00
Compote, Green, Vintage, Control Bubble Stem, 7 In., Pair 450.00
Console Set, Apple Green Cut, Pedestal Bowl, Sterling Base, 3 Piece 450.00
Dresser Box, Green Shaded To Opal, Gold Flowers, Green Stems, Signed, 6½ In. 100.00
Lamp, Exeter Shade, Landscape, Dutch Windmill Band, Bronze Base, 22½ x 17 In. ..... *illus* 2703.00
Lamp, Puffy, Apple Tree, Trunk Base, 21 In. 33925.00
Lamp, Puffy, Devonshire Shade, Flower Garlands, Brass Base, Gothic Arches, 15¼ In. 4750.00
Lamp, Puffy, Garlands, Blossoms, Reverse Painted, 4-Arm Base, 21 In. 4700.00
Lamp, Puffy, Hummingbird, Chrysanthemum, Signed, 21¼ In. .... *illus* 3162.00
Lamp, Puffy, Pansy, 4 Panels, Scalloped, 4-Arm Base, 19 In. 9200.00
Lamp, Puffy, Roma, Red, Green, Yellow, Flowers, Patent, 1907 .... 16960.00
Lamp, Puffy, Roses, Butterflies, Art Nouveau Base, 21 In. 5290.00
Lamp, Puffy, Roses, Butterflies, Boudoir, Signed, Patent, 1907 .... 1522.00
Lamp, Puffy, Venice Shade, Cabbage Rose, Raspberry, Leaves, Buds, 4-Arm, 20 In. 3738.00
Lamp, Puffy, Venice Shade, Red & Pink Roses, White Scrollwork, Brass Base, 20 In. 6600.00
Lamp, Radio, Poppy, Bud, Leaf, Reverse Painted, Silver Plated Base, 11 In. 1610.00
Lamp, Reverse Painted, Autumnal Landscape, Bronze Urn Base, 21 x 15½ In. 3000.00
Lamp, Reverse Painted, Birch Trees & Water, 2-Arm Base, 17½ x 22 In. 3452.00
Lamp, Reverse Painted, Exotic Birds & Flowers, 3-Footed Base, 23 x 18 In. 3900.00
Lamp, Reverse Painted, Flaring Shade, Landscape & Shore, 18 x 23½ In. 2400.00
Lamp, Reverse Painted, La Chinois, Birds On Branch, Flowers, Stamped 1867.00
Lamp, Reverse Painted, Landscape, Woman, Child Walking On Shore, 62 In. 3600.00
Lamp, Reverse Painted, Nautical Scene, Dolphin Base, 20 In. 4025.00
Lamp, Reverse Painted, Nautical Scene, Sailing Ships, Dolphin Base, Bronze, 22 In. 4600.00
Lamp, Reverse Painted, Ship, Fringe, Bronze Base, 22½ x 15½ In. .... *illus* 7500.00
Lamp, Reverse Painted, Wrens, Pink Roses, Leaf Border, Bronze Urn Base, 19 x 24 In. 9200.00
Lamp, Vienna Shade, Olympic Torch & Wreath, Metal Base, 24 In. .... *illus* 2235.00
Paperweight, Mottled Blue Snake, Cane Eyes, Lilac, Blue Orb, Translucent Base, 4 x 3 In. 413.00
Paperweight, Pear, Controlled Air Bubbles, Applied Red Stem, 3 x 2½ In. 40.00
Perfume Bottle, Bulbous, Faceted Rose Stopper, R. Mason, 6⅜ In. 231.00
Pickle Castor, Opal, Crimson & White Mums, Reticulated Basket Holder, 10 In. 345.00
Tankard, Clear, Bubbles, Enameled Vase & Flowers, Black Bands, Bulbous, 5 In. 212.00
Vase, Amethyst, Vintage Cutting, Chalice Shape, Controlled Bubble, Base, 11¾ In. 2000.00
Vase, Cornucopia, Ruby, Controlled Bubble Base, c.1930, 9 In. .... *illus* 95.00
Vase, Emerald Green, Faceted, Metal Mount, Gold Dore, c.1900, 8¾ In. .... *illus* 900.00
Vase, Vaseline, Pedestal Base, Engraved Butterfly & Web, 8¼ In. 550.00

PALMER COX, BROWNIES, *see Brownies category.*

PAPER collectibles, including almanacs, catalogs, children's books, some greeting cards, stock certificates, and other paper ephemera, are listed here. Paper calendars are listed separately in the Calendar category. Paper items may be found in many other sections, such as Christmas and Movie.

Birth Record, Edward Schneider, Lancaster Cocalico Twp., 1818, Verse, Flowers, Illuminated, 22 x 19 In. 165.00
Birth Record, Susanna Brackbill, September 10, 1776, Peafowl, Poem, Frame, 8 x 10 In. 990.00
Birth Record, Watercolor, Ink, 2 Birds, Jerusha Webber, Aug't 23, 1802, N.H., 9 x 7 In. 7050.00
Bookplate, Abraham Grub, Born 1821, June 2, German Verse, Illuminated, 6¾ x 4½ In. 99.00
Bookplate, Flowers, Birds, Verse, Abraham Sussholtz, Pa., March 31, 1836, Frame, 11 x 9 In.. 275.00
Bookplate, Flowers, Red, Green, Maria Jager, Chester Co., Pa., 1797, Frame, 8 x 6 In. 143.00
Bookplate, This Testament Is The Property Of Lydia Getz, Dec. 29, 1829, Flower, Illuminated, 6 x 3 In. 77.00
Broadside, Auction Poster, Public Docks & Slips In New York City, c.1851, 24 x 18½ In. 196.00
Calligraphy Exercise, Property Of Tristam Little, Watercolor, Ink, Frame, c.1826, 8 x 6⅛ In. 1998.00
Catalog, Braxmar Co., Fire & Police Dept Badges, New York, 105 Pages, 6 x 9 In. 110.00
Catalog, Gas Stove Co., Moundsville, W.V., 1920s, 5 Pages 20.00
Catalog, Jim Brown's Bargain Book, Fence & Wire Co., 1936, 140 Pages 25.00
Catalog, Old Town Canoes & Boats, 1943, 8 x 6 In., 42 Pages 50.00
Catalog, Sears, 1984, Wish Book, Masters Of The Universe Toy, 8½ x 11 In. 10.00
Catalog, Sun Rubber Toys, 1961, Color, Price Sheet 15.00
Catalog, Tiffany, Blue Book, 1914, Gilt Tooled Cover, Products, 1914, 4⅜ x 3⅝ In. 390.00

Pairpoint, Lamp, Vienna Shade, Olympic Torch & Wreath, Metal Base, 24 In.
$2235.00

Pairpoint, Vase, Cornucopia, Ruby, Controlled Bubble Base, c.1930, 9 In.
$95.00

Pairpoint, Vase, Emerald Green, Faceted, Metal Mount, Gold Dore, c.1900, 8¾ In.
$900.00

Paper, Die Cut, Children Holding Hands, Embossed, 19th Century, 9 x 13 In.
$265.00

Paperweight, Ayotte, Salamander, Red, Flowers, Signed, 1989, 3⅝ In.
$2250.00

Paperweight, Clichy, Millefiori, Looped, Garlands, 3 In.
$1600.00

Paperweight, Clichy, Millefiori, Pink & White Staves, Footed, 2¾ In.
$4500.00

Cutwork, Scherenschnitte, Temperance Is Wisdom, Eagle, Leaves, Black Paper, c.1835, 8 x 12 In. . . 9400.00
Die Cut, Children Holding Hands, Embossed, 19th Century, 9 x 13 In. . . . . *illus* 265.00
Diploma, Medical, Dr. Valentine Mott Lectures, Dr. Thomas Frye, 1846-48, 16 x 14 In. 175.00
Family Record, Watercolor, Eagle, Banner, Ovals, Heart, Adams, 1804, 12 x 11 In. 19995.00
Family Record, Watercolor, Ink, Hearts, Pineapple, Circles, Mallery, 1824, 15 x 11 In. 1645.00
Fraktur, Birth & Baptism, Elsinger Family, Springfield Township, Ohio, c.1852, 15 x 14 In. . . 144.00
Fraktur, Flowers, Angel, Bird, People, Sussana May, Feb. 24, 1800, Lancaster Co., 4 x 6½ In. . 825.00
Fraktur, German Writing, Eagle, Angels, Birds, Johannes Sollweiler, Frame, 1849, 15 x 13 In. 288.00
Fraktur, Heart, 4 German Words, 3 Flowers, Stem, Frame, 6½ x 4½ In. 230.00
Fraktur, Pen & Ink, Red Watercolor Accents, Pennsylvania Births, 1786, 12 x 7 In. 615.00
Fraktur, Tulips, Hearts, Red, Yellow, Green, 3 Panels, Frame, Penn., 1821, 12¾ x 8 In. 216.00
Fraktur, Tulips, Thistles, Bird, 3 Panels, Frame, Penn, 1826, 13 x 7½ In. 2640.00
Illustration, Newspaper, Memphis Packet Landing, Wood Block Print, Paper, Civil War, 10 x 15 In. . 82.00
Manuscript Page, Indian Mughal, Illuminated, 2-Sided, Gilt Frame, 9¼ x 5 In. 59.00
Marriage Record, Angel, Couple Holding Hands, Watercolor, Ink, 1841, 22 x 17 In. 1410.00
Marriage Record, Black Bride, Groom, Preacher, Cherubs, Frame, 22 x 18 In. 176.00
Menu, Grand Canyon Lodge, Utah Park Systems, Union Pacific, 1929, 4 x 5 In. 45.00
Reward Of Merit, Bird On Flower Branch, Orange, Blue, Yellow, 7½ x 6 In. 495.00
Reward Of Merit, Bird On Tulip Branch, Signed, Nancy Fry, 1826, Frame, 7 x 5½ In. 1210.00
Reward Of Merit, Seaman Paul Jones, Cane, Cloth, Poem, Hand Drawn, 1842 . . . . 578.00
Scrapbook, Victorian, Greeting Card, Trade Cards, Die Cuts, 50 Pages, 1895-1915 . . . . 345.00
Scroll, Botanical, Beet & Its Parts, Linen Back, Black Wood Molding End, France, 58 x 44 In. 720.00
Service Handbook, Harley-Davidson, Repair, 4th Edition, 1977, 180 Pages. 11.00
Stock Certificate, Gustav Stickley, The Craftsman Corp., 1914 . . . . 360.00

PAPER DOLLS were probably inspired by the pantins, or jumping jacks, made in eighteenth-century Europe. By the 1880s, sheets of printed paper dolls and clothes were being made. The first paper doll books were made in the 1920s. Collectors prefer uncut sheets or books or boxed sets of paper dolls. Prices are about half as much if the pages have been cut.

2-Sided Dresses, Hats, Capes, Box, 4½ & 4 In, 15 Piece. 1064.00
Archie Comic Strip, Archie, Betty, Veronica, Jughead, Whitman, 1969, 6 Pages, Uncut. 30.00
Barbie Design-A-Fashion, Mix 'N Match Patterns, Whitman, 1979 . . . . 16.00
Betsy McCall, Dress 'N Play, Sealed, No. 801, 1963, 10 In. 82.00
Betsy McCall Magic Pattern, Coloring Set, 2 10-In. Dolls, Costumes, Pencils, Sharpener, 1964 110.00
Betsy McCall's Fashion Shop, 8-In. Paper Doll, Fabric Outfits, Sequins, Floss, Box, 1959, Uncut 82.00
Betsy McCall's Story Book, Trip To San Francisco, Complete, 1954, Uncut. 192.00
Bewitched, Samantha, Magic Wand, Box, 1965, 14½ In., Uncut. 270.00
Bewitched, Tabatha, Cardboard, Outfit, Wand, Magic Wand Corp., 1966 . . . . 175.00
Charlie's Angels, All 3 Angels, Box, 1977, Uncut. 150.00
Cutout, Postcard, Fairy Tale Dressing Dolls, Cats, Beauty & The Beast, Tuck, Series 3385 . . . . 590.00
Cutout, Postcard, Nursery Rhymes, Baby Bunting, Little Bo Peep, Tuck, Series 3382, 2 Piece . 189.00
Cutout, Postcard Set, Die Cut, Hobby Horse, Tuck Nursery Rhyme, Early 1900s, 7 Piece 307.00
Janet Leigh, Dresses By Janet, 2 Dolls, Leigh-Mor, 1958, 12 x 9 In., 6 Pages, Uncut 65.00
Judy Garland, 3 Dolls, 30 Outfits, Tom Tierney, 1982, Uncut. 13.00
La Petite Elegante, 2-Sided, 17 2-Sided Costumes, Bonnet, Box, c.1860. . . . . 728.00
Mary Poppins, Paper Doll Activity Book, 4 Dolls, Golden Press, 1964, 16 Pages. 35.00
Raggedy Ann, Cutout, 4 Dolls, 6 Sheets Of Clothes, Milton Bradley, Box, 1941 . . . . 75.00
Rock Hudson, 2 Dolls, Universal, Whitman, 1957, 12½ x 10½ In., 8 Pages, Uncut. 193.00
That Girl, Book, Card Stock, 3 Dolls, Saalfield, 1967, 8 x 12 In.. . . . . 121.00
The Waltons, 7 Children, Outfits, Whiteman, 1975, 8 Pages 55.00
Twiggy, Fashion Dresses, Cardboard Punch-Out, Whitman, Minnow Co., 1967. . . . . 55.00
Victorian, Changeable Heads, 6 Torsos, Dresses, Artistic Series 500-A-E, Tuck, 6 x 13 In.. . . . . 118.00

PAPERWEIGHTS must have first appeared along with paper in ancient Egypt. Today's collectors search for every type, from the very expensive French weights of the nineteenth century to the modern artist weights or advertising pieces. The glass tops of the paperweights sometimes have been nicked or scratched, and this type of damage can be removed by polishing. Some serious collectors think this type of repair is an alteration and will not buy a repolished weight; others think it is an acceptable technique of restoration that does not change the value. Baccarat paperweights are listed separately under Baccarat.

Abraham Lincoln, Photograph, Sepia, Multicolored, 2½ x 3¼ In.. . . . . 448.00
Advertising, Segars, Bulldog, Cast Metal, John W. Merriam & Co., 3 x 2 x 1½ In.. . . . . 101.00
Advertising, Segars, Bulldog, Cast Metal, John W. Merriam & Co., 4 x 2 x 3 In. 123.00
Advertising, Tiona Petroleum, Indian, Celluloid, 3½ In. 165.00
Advertising, Yellow Cab, Metal, c.1930, 1 x 2¾ x 1¾ In. 350.00

P

ndrew Byers, Forget-Me-Nots, Roses, Double Bouquet, Signature Cane, 3 3/16 In. 1800.00
votte, Double Pansy Bouquet, Ladybug, Blue, White, Clear Ground, 1988, 3 11/16 In. 1650.00
votte, Ducks On Pond, White Flowers, Moss, Toadstools, Plants, Signed, 1992, 4 In. 1650.00
votte, Red Headed Woodpeckers, Signed, 3 3/4 In. 1450.00
votte, Salamander, Red, Flowers, Signed, 1989, 3 5/8 In. *illus* 2250.00
otte, Thrasher, Brown, On Sumac Branch, Leaves, Berries, Blue Ground, Signed, 1982, 3 1/8 In. 1540.00
ronze, Dragon, Plinth Base, Chinese, 18th Century, 4 In. 2390.00
aithness, Apple, Yellow Interior, Glass, Marked, Scotland, B21687, 2 3/4 In. 22.00
aithness, Nativity Scene, Red, Green, Signed, 3 x 3 1/2 In. 58.00
harles Lotton, Blue Morning Glories, Surface Design, No. 40, Signed, 1977, 2 7/8 In. 660.00
hris Heilman, Crystal Rock Form, Underwater, Seaweed, Signed, 1993, 6 1/2 In. 259.00
ichy, 2-Color Swirl, Green & White Staves, Center Cane, c.1850, 2 7/16 In. 4375.00
ichy, Millefiori, Blue, Pink, White, Yellow Pastry Mold Cane, Star Canes, Garlands, Bull's-Eye, 3 In. 2200.00
ichy, Millefiori, Canes, Edelweiss, Bull's-Eyes, Stars, Crimps, Crosses, Cogs, Rods, 2 7/8 In. 2100.00
ichy, Millefiori, Chequer, 2 7/8 In. 3500.00
ichy, Millefiori, Concentric Circles, Pink & Green Roses, c.1850, 2 1/2 In. 3500.00
ichy, Millefiori, Concentric Circles, Multicolored Flowers, c.1850, 3 3/16 In. 3750.00
ichy, Millefiori, Garlands, Ruby Ground, White & Blue Star Cane, 6 Oval Interlaced 3 In. 2750.00
ichy, Millefiori, Looped, Garlands, 3 In. *illus* 1600.00
ichy, Millefiori, Pink & White Staves, Footed, 2 3/4 In. *illus* 4500.00
ichy, Millefiori, Scrambled, Pink & Purple Roses, 2 11/16 In. *illus* 3000.00
ichy, Spoke, Red & White Center, 5 Clusters, Stardust, Bull's-Eye, Green Ground, 2 3/4 In. 1650.00
ut Glass, Book Shape, Geometric Cut Spine, 4 x 3 In. 175.00
elmo Tarsitano, Snake, Flowers, Leaves, Sandy Ground, Signed, 3 7/16 In. 2465.00
ominick Labino, Round, Green Glass, Trapped Air Bubbles, c.1967, 3 1/2 In. 270.00
gural, Apple Shape, Yellow, Green, Stem, 4 x 3 In. 30.00
gural, Apple, Red, Yellow, Flat Foot, c.1850, 3 x 3 3/4 In. 840.00
aternal, Hexagonal, Blue, Shield, Mosaic Tile Co., 1930s, 3 1/2 In. 55.00
uit, Latticinio Basket, White Double Swirls, 2 3/4 In. 660.00
rover Cleveland, Allen Thurman, Controlled Bubbles, 1888, 2 3/4 In. 418.00
on, Bird, 3 In. 115.00
n D'Onfrio, Men On Raft, Lily Pads, Pond, Brown Speckles, Signed, 1998, 3 3/8 In. 770.00
hn Deacons, Clematis, Blue, Pink, Yellow, Green Leaves, Black Ground, St. Kilda, 2 11/16 In. 187.00
hn Deacons, Peacock Butterfly, Red, Green, White, Black, Signed, 2 7/8 In. 330.00
hn Murphy, Duck, Flying Over Pond, Cattails, Signed, 3 3/4 In. 357.00
aziun, 6-Petal Flower, Yellow & Red, Green Leaves, Speckled Gold, Pedestal, Signed, 2 1/4 In. 345.00
aziun, Crimped Rose, 14 Red Petals, 4 Green Petals, Clear Pedestal, 2 3/4 x 2 In. 660.00
aziun, Pansy, Green Leaves, Stem, Bee, White Ground, 1 5/8 x 2 1/8 In. 935.00
aziun, Snake & Pansy, Heart Petals, Jasper Ground, 2 3/8 In. 938.00 to 1000.00
n Rosenfeld, Honeybees, Flowers, Berries, 3 1/4 In. 700.00
bino, Bird, Burgundy, Signed, 1 3/4 x 4 In. *illus* 120.00
bino, Yellow Flower Center, Hand Blown, 1968, 2 1/2 x 3 In. 85.00
ren Stump, Murrine, 8 Portraits, French Village Center, Inscribed, 1999, 3 3/8 In. 2125.00
ndberg, Butterfly & Clematis, Purple, White, Green Leaves, Signed, Salazar, 1998, 3 In. 359.00
ndberg, Daffodils, Yellow, Green Leaves, Signed, 1983, 2 7/8 In. 770.00
ndberg, Lavender Sweet Pea, Gold Luster, Signed, 3 In. 230.00
ndberg, Moon & Stars, Signed, 1980, 2 3/4 In. 250.00
ndberg, Peach, Fruit, Orange, Yellow, Green Leaves, White & Gilt Base, Signed, 1993, 3 In. 154.00
ndberg, Poinsettia, Gold, Red Ground, Signed, Daniel Salazar, 1997, 3 3/4 In. 330.00
ndberg, Waves, Blue, Green & White Iridescent, Marked, 1976, 2 5/8 In. 115.00
ndberg, World Globe, Blue, Signed, 6 1/2 In. 880.00
cKinley, Roosevelt, 1900, 2 x 4 In. 75.00
cKinley, Photograph, Biography On Back, c.1900 70.00
llville, Horse, White, Blue, Green Grass, Pedestal Base, 4 1/4 x 3 5/8 In. 9900.00
llville, Rose, Pink, Crimped, Green Leaves, Footed, 3 3/8 In. *illus* 2500.00
w England Glass Co., Apple, Rose To Yellow, Round Base, Pontil, 2 5/8 x 2 7/8 In. 825.00
w England Glass Co., Bouquet Of Fruit, Latticinio, 2 15/16 In. *illus* 550.00
w England Glass Co., Flowers & Fruit, Latticinio Ground, 19th Century, 3 1/4 In. 5684.00
w England Glass Co., Millefiori Garland, Pink & White Buttercup, 2 3/4 In. *illus* 2000.00
w England Glass Co., Pears, Red, Yellow, Latticinio Ground, 1 7/8 x 2 5/8 In. 440.00
w England Glass Co., Pears, Vegetables, Leaves, Latticinio Ground, 1 5/8 x 2 In. 121.00
w England Glass Co., Poinsettia, Latticinio Ground, Cobalt Blue Petals, 1 5/8 x 2 3/4 In. 220.00
w England Glass Co., Scramble, Cane, Filigree, Ribbons, 1 1/2 x 2 In. 231.00
ient & Flume, Sky Blue, Millefiori Flower Center, Burgundy Loopings, 2 5/8 In. 141.00
ient & Flume, Sunflower, High Domed, 6 3/4 In. 900.00
irpoint, Swan Top, White, 4 1/2 In. 150.00

Paperweight, Clichy, Millefiori, Scrambled, Pink & Purple Roses, 2 11/16 In.
$3000.00

Paperweight, Labino, Bird, Burgundy, Signed, 1 3/4 x 4 In.
$120.00

Paperweight, Millville, Rose, Pink, Crimped, Green Leaves, Footed, 3 3/8 In.
$2500.00

Paperweight, New England Glass Co., Bouquet Of Fruit, Latticinio, 2 15/16 In.
$550.00

P

Paperweight, New England Glass Co., Millefiori Garland, Pink & White Buttercup, 2¾ In.
$2000.00

Paperweight, St. Louis, Dancing Devil Silhouettes, Concentric Millefiori, 2⅝ In.
$2750.00

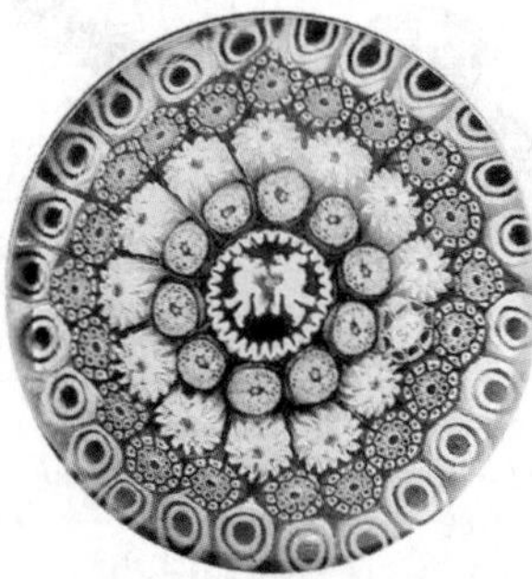

Paperweight, St. Louis, Millefiori, Mushroom & Torsade, SL 1848, 3⅛ In.
$4500.00

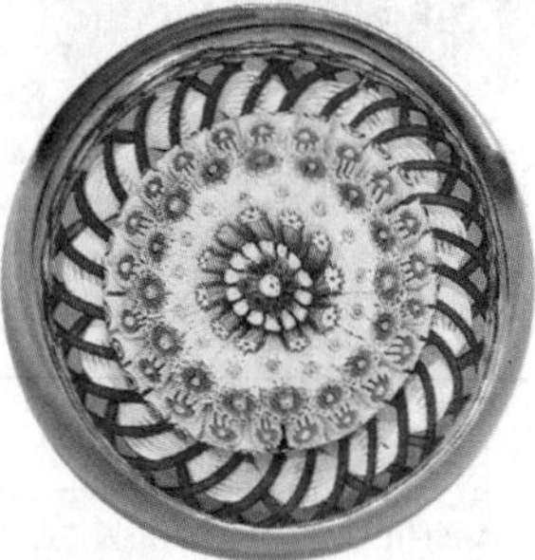

Paperweight, St. Louis, Swirling Filigree, Newel Post, 4⅝ x 3⅞ In.
$700.00

Perthshire, 5-Petal Flower, Multicolored, Green Leaves, Latticinio Base, 2¾ In. 180.0
Pressed Glass, Abraham Lincoln, Bust, Frosted, 1½ x 3¼ In. 96.0
Pressed Glass, Home Sweet Home, Clear, House, Trees, Painted, 3⅝ In. 825.0
R. Hanson, Crocus, 6 Petals, Amethyst, 3 Stamen, 3 Leaves, Faceted, 2⅛ x 1¾ In. 77.0
R. Mason, Tea Rose, 13 Petals, Green Leaves, Cobalt Blue Foot, 2⅞ x 2¾ In. 99.0
Satava, Jellyfish, Gold, Opalescent Tendrils, Signed, 6 In. 374.0
Satava, Jellyfish, Teardrop Body, Gold, Blue Tendrils, Signed, 5 In. 863.0
St. Louis, Apples, Pears, Cherries, Leaves, White Latticinio Basket, 2¾ In. 1500.0
St. Louis, Bouquet, Clematis, Blue, Multicolored Flowers, Signed, 1981, 3⅛ In. 770.0
St. Louis, Bouquet, Faceted, Magnum, Clear Ground, Wood Stand, 3½ x 4⅛ In. 8400.0
St. Louis, Bouquet, Flat, Muslin Ground, Pastry Mold Canes, 19th Century, 2 In. 1450.0
St. Louis, Bouquet, Pyramid Form, Signed, 7½ x 3 In. 5200.0
St. Louis, Bouquet, Torsade, Faceted Overlay, 3⅛ In. 2500.0
St. Louis, Concentric Millefiori, Rondo, 9 Rings, Signed, 1995, 3 In. 1540.0
St. Louis, Concentric Millefiori, Sheep, Faceted Overlay, Signed, 2003, 3⅜ In. 1300.0
St. Louis, Crown, Red & Blue Twists, Alternating Latticinio Rods, Center Cane, 2 15/16 In. 4680.0
St. Louis, Dahlia, Red, Signed, 1996, 3 In. 990.0
St. Louis, Dancing Devil Silhouettes, Concentric Millefiori, 2⅝ In. . . . . *illus* 2750.0
St. Louis, Flower Rim, White Latticinio Ground, 19th Century, 2¾ In. 551.0
St. Louis, Fruit Basket, Latticinio, Signed, 1993, 2⅞ x 4⅛ In. 1540.0
St. Louis, Fruit Bouquet, Latticinio Basket, 2⅞ In. 1450.0
St. Louis, Honeycomb, Red, Signed, 1974, 3 In. 2750.0
St. Louis, Millefiori, Close Packed Canes, Signed, 1981, 2⅞ In. 1320.0
St. Louis, Millefiori, Mushroom & Torsade, SL 1848, 3⅛ In. . . . . *illus* 4500.0
St. Louis, Mushroom Shape Bouquet, Blue & White Latticinio Basket, Marked, 1848, 3 In. . . . 7300.0
St. Louis, Narcissus, White, Blue Ground, Green Leaf, Signature Cane, 1991, 2½ In. 405.0
St. Louis, Pansy, Purple & Yellow Flower, S-Shape Stem, c.1850, 3⅛ In. 2750.0
St. Louis, Ruby Vase, Green, Red, Cane, Crown Base, 6½ In. 2750.0
St. Louis, Swirling Filigree, Newel Post, 4⅝ x 3⅞ In. . . . . *illus* 700.0
St. Louis, Twisted Crown Center, Alternating Coral & Cane, Latticinio Twists, c.1850, 2¾ In. . 3300.0
St. Louis, White Pompon Flower, Swirling Latticinio, 2 9/16 In. . . . . *illus* 2000.0
Stankard, Bouquet, 2 Daisies, 3 Sunflowers, Dark Blue Ground, 1977, 3 3/16 In. 2125.0
Stankard, Male & Female Earth Spirit, Spreading Plant, Signed, 1984, 3⅛ In. 2000.0
Stankard, Meadowreath, Flower, Buds, Dark Blue Ground, 3 In. 1000.0
Stankard, Orchid, 1989, 2¼ x 3 In. 1020.0
Stankard, Orchids, Yellow, Red, Branch, Green Leaves, Clear Ground, 1985, 3 In. 3850.0
Stankard, Oriole, Orange & Black, On Flowering Branch, Signed, 1981, 3⅛ In. 2000.0
Stankard, Pineland Pickerel Weed & Damselfly, Signed, 1999, 3¼ In. . . . . *illus* 3750.0
Stankard, Spider Orchid, Orange & Yellow Flowers, Leaves, Roots, 1980, 3¼ In. 1000.0
Stankard, Trillium, White & Red Petals, Green Leaves, Signed, 2¾ In. 625.0
Stankard, Wasp In Flight, Foxglove, Spray, White Root System, 1980, 3⅛ In. 1500.0
Stankard, Water Lilies, White, Yellow, Green Speckled Lily Pad, Bulb, 1985, 3 In. 3500.0
Stankard, Wild Rose, Pink, White Foxglove, Green Leaves, Clear, Signed, 1978, 3 In. 2000.0
Sulphide, Abraham Lincoln, Bust, Blue & Clear Latticework, 6-Sided, 1½ x 2½ In. 215.0
Sulphide, Abraham Lincoln, Clear, Blue, Hexagonal Faceted, 2½ x 1½ In. 215.0
Sulphide, Deer Running Through Woods, Ruby Base, 19th Century, 3 In. 1624.0
Sulphide, Jenny Lind, Faceted Overlay, Signed, D'Albret, 3⅛ In. 176.0
Theodore Netter, Pig, Glass, Clear, Philadelphia, 7 In. 510.0
Tom Mosser, Pastoral Scene, Painted, Signed, 3¾ In. 165.0
Wendy's, Decade II, Metal, Celluloid 22.0
Whitefriars, Concentric, Millefiori, Central Red & White Cog Cane, 5 Rings, 2⅝ In. 245.0
Whitefriars, Millefiori, Green, White, Multifaceted, Signed, 1971, 3⅛ In. 405.0
Whitefriars, Owl, Picture Cane, Concentric, Millefiori, Faceted, Signed, 1979, 3 In. 660.0
Whitefriars, Paneled Millefiori, Spokes, Multifaceted, Signed, 1973, 3 In. 245.0
Ysart, Blue Parrot, Leafy Branch, Jasper Ground, PY Cane, 3¼ In. 1500.0
Ysart, Millefiori Canes, Latticinio Tubing, Dark Blue Ground, 4⅜ In. 2375.0
Ysart, Pink Flower, Green Leaves, Blue, White & Red Millefiori Garland, Cobalt Blue, PY Cane, 3 In. 880.0

PAPIER-MACHE is made from paper mixed with glue, chalk, and other ingredients, then molded and baked. It becomes very hard and can be painted. Boxes, trays, and furniture were made of papier-mache. Some of the nineteenth-century pieces were decorated with mother-of-pearl. Papier-mache is still being used to make small toys, figures, candy containers, boxes, and other giftwares. Furniture made of papier-mache is listed in the Furniture category.

Box, Black Lacquer, Parcel Gilt, Chinese Scene, Key Fitted, England, 3 x 6 x 4 In. 270.0
Box, Letter, Metallic Gold Design, Lock, 6 x 9 x 2½ In. 40.0

Charger, Painted, Millstream, Signed, B.E. Trippe, American, 16 In. 118.00
Cigar Case, Woman, Blue & Red Dress, Oil Spot, Black, 2 Panels, Oblong, 5 ½ x 3 In. 490.00
Coach, Driver, Prancing Horse, Wood Wheel Platform, c.1875, 12 In. 2352.00
Milliner's Head, Painted, Wood, Hollow, France, 1800s, 14 ½ In. *illus* 2185.00
Skeleton, Articulated, Wire, Tin Strips, Painted Features, Life Size, 58 ½ In. 1920.00
Skeleton, Human, Life Size, c.1900. 1200.00
Tea Caddy, Mother-Of-Pearl Inlay, Footed, England, c.1850, 4 ½ x 8 ½ In. 936.00
Toy, Bulldog, Growler, Head Moves, Glass Eyes, Faux Fur, 1900s, 8 x 12 x 19 In. 2350.00
Tray, Black, Mother-Of-Pearl Inlay, Gilt, Oval, Late 19th Century, 30 x 23 ½ In. *illus* 290.00
Tray, Black Lacquer, Flowers, Birds, Faux Bamboo Stand, Victorian, 19 x 28 x 21 In. 1920.00
Tray, Central Cartouche, Painted, Lake Scene, Castle Ruin, Gilt, 1800s, 31 ¼ In. 546.00
Tray, Chinoiserie, Canted Corners, Buildings, Bridges, Lake, Red Ground, 31 x 21 In. 575.00
Tray, Figures, Village Scene, Gold, Black, Japan, 1800, 24 x 18 ½ x 1 ¼ In. 495.00
Tray, Mother-Of-Pearl, Gilt, Grisaille, Jennens & Bettridge, c.1850, 31 x 24 In. 7500.00
Tray, Painted, Peacocks, Floral Landscape, Regency Faux Bamboo Stand, 20 x 27 In. 735.00
Tray, Raised Shaped Rim, Multicolored, Gilt, Exotic Birds, Trees, 27 x 21 In. 1175.00
Wall Pocket, Gilt, Leaf Carved, Demilune Shape, Berry Cluster Base, 9 ½ x 10 In., Pair. 1020.00
Wall Pocket, Mother-Of-Pearl Pique Inlay, Flowered Needlework, 13 In. 395.00

PARASOL, *see Umbrella category.*

PARIAN is a fine-grained, hard-paste porcelain named for the marble it resembles. It was first made in England in 1846 and gained in favor in the United States about 1860. Figures, tea sets, vases, and other items were made of Parian at many English and American factories.

Bust, Charles Dickens, Stamped, J & T.B., 15 ¾ In. *illus* 133.00
Bust, Daphne, Waisted Round, Socle, Marshall Wood, c.1860, 21 ¼ In. 1175.00
Bust, Edward, Prince Of Wales, Waisted Round Socle, 14 ⅜ In. 499.00
Bust, Gladstone, Waisted Round Socle, 18 In. 705.00
Bust, Ophelia, Waisted Round Socle, 10 ¾ In. 323.00
Bust, Prince Albert, Waisted Round Socle, c.1865, 13 In. 323.00
Bust, Queen Victoria, Waisted Round Socle, c.1865, 13 In. 499.00
Bust, Shakespeare, Early 20th Century, 20 In. 403.00
Bust, Young Girl, Waisted Round Socle, Staffordshire, Late 1800s, 10 ½ In. 147.00
Figurine, Autumn, Standing Figure, Cornucopia Of Fruit, Staffordshire, 1800s, 14 ½ In. 353.00
Figurine, Ceres, Classical, Standing, Column, Wheat, Cornucopia, Flowers, Dove, 12 ½ In. 89.00
Figurine, Greek Slave, Nude, Round Base, 18 ¾ In. 588.00
Figurine, Highland Mary, England, c.1879, 14 In. 176.00
Figurine, Little Girl, Standing, Holding Plate, Dishcloth, 22 In. 235.00
Figurine, Miranda, On Rocky Base, Waves, c.1874, 14 ⅞ In. 529.00
Figurine, Rock Of Ages, Staffordshire, Robinson & Leadbeater, c.1875, 12 ½ In. 235.00
Figurine, Slave, Nude Woman, Bound By Chains, England, c.1860, 19 ¼ In. 1410.00
Figurine, Woman, Holding Dagger, Mask, Turquoise, Gold Trim, 14 In., Pair 1410.00
Figurine, Woman, Seated, Holding Bow, France, Early 19th Century, 9 ¾ In. 460.00
Figurine, Woman, Seated In Chair, Blue, Peach Enamel, Gold Trim, c.1861, 15 ¾ In. 470.00
Group, Grouse, Ribbon Leaf Border, 6 ¼ x 8 In. 58.00
Jug, Gypsy, Figural Camp Scene, 10 In. 148.00
Jug, Tree Shape, Branch Handle, Children On Branches, Brown, Dale Hall, c.1850, 7 ½ In. 384.00
Vase, Purple Bisque, Applied Grape Leaves, Gold Highlights, Handles, 9 In., Pair 35.00

PARIS, Vieux Paris, or Old Paris, is porcelain ware that is known to have been made in Paris in the eighteenth or early nineteenth century. These porcelains have no identifying mark but can be recognized by the whiteness of the porcelain and the lines and decorations. Gold decoration is often used.

Basket, Centerpiece, Gilded, Navette Shape, Mid 19th Century, 11 x 15 In. 1200.00
Basket, Cobalt blue, Gilt, Painted Cherries, Figs, Hexagonal, Scroll Feet, 8 x 8 In., Pair 764.00
Basket, White, Gold, Reticulated, Figural Stem, Eros, Kneeling, Gold Quiver, 10 x 9 In., Pair 1680.00
Desk Set, Inkwell, Bronze Fittings, Flower Closures, White, Blue, c.1890, 5 Piece 325.00
Figurine, Flower Sellers, Dog, Lamb, Parcel Gilt, Gold Anchor, Samson, 13 x 6 In., Pair 660.00
Figurine, Gentleman, Lady, Scrolling Pedestal Base, 18th Century Costume, 19 ¾ In., Pair 649.00
Garniture, Rococo Type, Vining Form, 10 x 16-In. Bowl, 2 19-In. Side Vases 6300.00
Group, Woman On Swing, Children, Blue X Mark, c.1890, 14 x 9 x 6 In. *illus* 489.00
Plaque, Beau Blue Ground, Oblong, Cherubs En Grisaille, 10 ½ x 13 In., Pair 1920.00
Plate, Rose Pompadour Rim, Gilt Flowers, Flower Reserves, Stand, 9 ⅝ In., Pair 206.00
Sauce Bowl, Shell Shape, Tiffany & Co., Gilt Floret, Greek Key Border, 9 In., Pair 59.00

Paperweight, St. Louis, White Pompon Flower, Swirling Latticinio, 2 $\frac{9}{16}$ In.
$2000.00

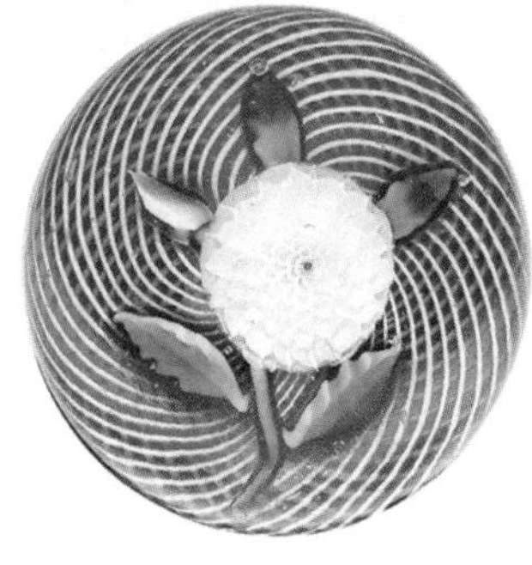

Paperweight, Stankard, Pineland Pickerel Weed & Damselfly, Signed, 1999, 3 ¼ In.
$3750.00

Papier-Mache, Milliner's Head, Painted, Wood, Hollow, France, 1800s, 14 ½ In.
$2185.00

Papier-Mache, Tray, Black, Mother-Of-Pearl Inlay, Gilt, Oval, Late 19th Century, 30 x 23 ½ In.
$290.00

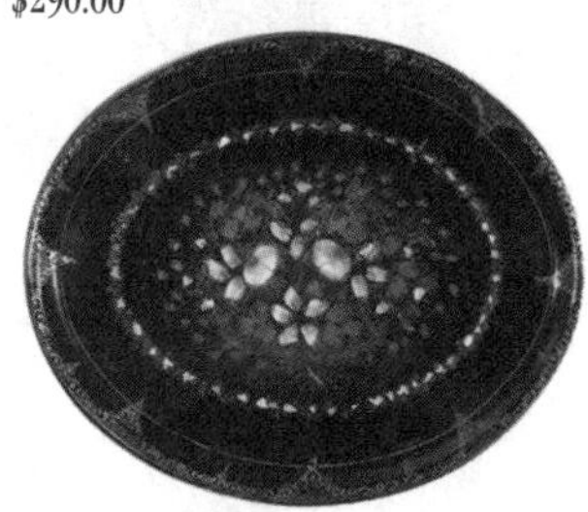

Parian, Bust, Charles Dickens, Stamped, J & T.B., 15¾ In.
$133.00

Paris, Group, Woman On Swing, Children, Blue X Mark, c.1890, 14 x 9 x 6 In.
$489.00

Pate-De-Verre, Vase, Ocean Waves, Green, Handles, Stamped, Decorchemont, 5½ In.
$500.00

Tureen, Canted Corners, Gilt Border, Scrolled Handles, Shell Finial, 19th Century, 10 In. 620.00
Urn, Flowers, Flared, Square Foot, c.1830, 9 In., Pair 445.00
Urn, Gold Leaf, Enamel Decoration, Hand Painted, Scenic, Handles, c.1820, 19 x 12 In. 660.00
Urn, Hand Painted, Square Foot, 19th Century, 11 x 8 In. 715.00
Urn, Medallion, Women Walking In Woods, Gold, Grapes, Leaf Handles, 21 In., Pair 200.00
Vase, Aesthetic, Mantel, Oval, Inverted Ends, Handles, Enameled, Ball Feet, 9⅝ In., Pair 470.00
Vase, Black Matte Glaze, 15 x 8 In. 385.00
Vase, Bluster Shape, Gilt Brass Mounted, Louis XVI Style, Mounted As Lamp, 1800s, 17 x 7 In. 960.00
Vase, Bouquets, Baskets, Vine & Leaf Handles, Gilt, Hand Painted, c.1865, 18 In., Pair 1440.00
Vase, Gilt Porcelain, Swan Handles, 19th Century, 13 In., Pair 1540.00
Vase, Hand Painted, Floral Scenes, 19th Century, 23 x 10 In. 1045.00
Vase, Hand Painted, Flowers, Vine & Leaf Handles, c.1890, 12 In. 220.00
Vase, Hand Painted, Oriental Style, Gilt, 19th Century, 18 x 7½ In. 385.00
Vase, Highland Warrior, Baluster Shape, Pierced Handles, Flowers, 17½ In., Pair 490.00
Vase, Mantel, Flowers, Hand Painted, Gilded, 19th Century, 12 x 9 In. 440.00
Vase, Molded Leaf Handles, Cornflowers, Classical Portrait, Fuchsias, Late 1800s, 16 x 9 In. .. 71.00
Vase, Parisian Figure Under Large Mushroom, c.1880, 15¼ In., Pair 1980.00
Vase, Portrait, Handles, 14 x 10 In. 358.00
Vase, Woman In Flower Wreath, Blue, White, Old Paris, c.1850, 13 In. 70.00

PATE-DE-VERRE is an ancient technique in which glass is made by blending and refining powdered glass of different colors into molds. The process was revived by French glassmakers, especially Galle, around the end of the nineteenth century.

Box, Fish, Square, Signed, Patricia Smith, 2½ x 4½ In. 165.00
Figurine, Alice In Wonderland, 2 Kittens, Edris Eckhardt, c.1981 .... 748.00
Figurine, Alice In Wonderland, Baby Pig, Dutchess, Cheshire Cat, Edris Eckhardt, c.1976. ... 575.00
Figurine, Alice In Wonderland, Walrus & Carpenter, Edris Eckhardt, c.1976 .... 633.00
Figurine, Alice In Wonderland, White Rabbit, Edris Eckhardt, c.1975 .... 748.00
Figurine, Little Miss Muffet, Edris Eckhardt, 5 x 6½ In. 575.00
Inkwell, Green Cylindrical Shape, Leaf Pattern, Orange Rim, Finial Lid, 5¼ In. 3450.00
Paperweight, Mouse, Nut, c.1900, 3½ In. 1416.00
Plaque, Women At Well, Square, Signed, c.1895, 8½ In. 2160.00
Tray, Green, Amber Molded Leaf, Salamander Finial, Butterfly, 8 In. 978.00
Tray, Moth, Mottled Green, Aqua, 5 In. 1652.00
Vase, Ocean Waves, Green, Handles, Stamped, Decorchemont, 5½ In. .... *illus* 500.00

PATENT MODELS were required as part of a patent application for a United States patent until 1880. In 1926 the stored patent models were sold as a group by the U.S. Patent Office, and individual models are now appearing in the marketplace.

Bicycle Lamp, Columbia, Model C, Automatic, Hine-West Mfg. Co., 1899 .... 290.00
Gas Iron, No. 4A, Blue Enameled, Coleman 68.00
Guitar Zither, U.S. Guitar Zither Company, May 29, 1894 .... 225.00
Railroad Track, Brass, 19th Century 285.00
Saltshaker, Canary Glass, Northwood Glass Co., c.1888 .... 110.00
Secretary, Walnut, Bird's-Eye Maple Panels, Eastlake Style, Wooton 40000.00
Sewing Machine, No. 221-1, Portable, Singer, c.1947 .... 446.00
Waffle Iron, No. 1510, Indicator Light, Proctor & Schwartz Electric Co., c.1930 .... 75.00

PATE-SUR-PATE means paste on paste. The design was made by painting layers of slip on the ceramic piece until a relief decoration was formed. The method was developed at the Sevres factory in France about 1850. It became even more famous at the English Minton factory about 1870. It has since been used by many potters to make both pottery and porcelain wares.

Charger, 2 Women Bathers, Flowers, Leaves, Brown, Green, England, 1924, 12 In. 881.00
Charger, 2 Women Bathers, Lilies, Irises, Leaves, Butterfly, England, 1924-51, 12 In. 2115.00
Plaque, Nymphs, Blue Ground, White Slip, Gilt Frame, Solon, c.1860, 4 x 9 In. 12925.00
Plaque, Nymphs, Round, Blue Ground, White Slip, Gilt Frame, c.1860, 6 In., Pair 5581.00

PAUL REVERE POTTERY was made at several locations in and around Boston, Massachusetts, between 1906 and 1942. The pottery was operated as a settlement house program for teenage girls. Many pieces were signed *S.E.G.* for Saturday Evening Girls. The artists concentrated on children's dishes and tiles. Decorations were outlined in black and filled with color.

Bowl, Landscape, Unglazed Outline, Matte, S.E.G., 1924, 4⅞ In. 928.00
Charger, 2 Single-Mast Ships, Mountains, Blue, Clouds, S.E.G., c.1914, 12⅜ In. 16450.00

reamer, 3 Chicks, Blue Band, Ivory Ground, Marked, 1913, 3 In. 735.00

reamer, Flower Border, Blue, Cream Ground, S.E.G., Signed, 1 3/4 In. 206.00

up, Greek Key, Marked, S.E.G., c.1910, 1 7/8 x 4 3/8 In. *illus* 190.00

ar, Cover, Ship Border, Green Glaze Ground, Blue & Brown Band, S.E.G., Signed, 4 1/2 In. 1528.00

itcher, Blue Glaze, Ocher & Brown Interior Drip, Marked, c.1910, 7 In. 294.00

itcher, Ducks, Blue Band, Ivory Ground, S.E.G., Matte, 1915, 3 1/4 In. 348.00

itcher, Flower Petal Border, White, Blue Ground, S.E.G., 1 3/4 In. 206.00

late, Eat Thy Bread In Joy & Thankfulness, House, Landscape, Black, Signed, B.H., 9 In. 1998.00

late, Swan, Navy Blue Rim, Unglazed Outline, Matte, S.E.G., 1919, 8 1/8 In. 377.00

ile, Boston, Charter Street, c.1909, 3 3/4 x 3 3/4 In. 2495.00

ile, Tea, House & Trees, Center Medallion, Brown, Turquoise Glaze, Round, 5 3/4 In. 441.00

ase, Blue Drip Glaze Over Speckled Gray, Bulbous, S.E.G., 7 1/8 In. 353.00

ase, Daffodils, Cylindrical, Tapered, Yellow Glaze, Taupe, Cream, S.E.G., 10 3/8 In. 1998.00

ase, Drip Glaze, Yellow Green, Lavender, S.E.G., 1920, 10 1/2 In. 493.00

ase, Green Matte Glaze, Stand-Up Rim, 3 Square Handles, Arts & Crafts, 9 In. 353.00

ase, Indigo Blue High Glaze, Label, 5 7/8 In. *illus* 150.00

ase, Inverted Rim, Cylindrical, Blue Dripping To Green, 1917, 20 In. 3515.00

ase, Lotus Leaves, Navy Blue Ground, Cylindrical, S.E.G., c.1926, 9 3/4 In. 522.00

all Pocket, Landscape, Blue Glaze, Yellow, Green, Blue, Black, S.E.G., 9 1/2 In. 764.00

EACHBLOW glass was made by several factories beginning in the 1880s. New England eachblow is a one-layer glass shading from red to white. Mt. Washington peachblow shades om pink to bluish-white. Hobbs, Brockunier and Company of Wheeling, West Virginia, made oral glass that they marketed as Peach Blow. It shades from yellow to peach and is lined with hite glass. Reproductions of all types of peachblow have been made. Related pieces may be listed nder Webb Peachblow.

owl, Ruffled, Edge, Glossy, Mt. Washington, 3 7/8 x 8 7/8 In. 810.00

owl, Scalloped Rim, 3 Tapered & Reeded Feet, Mt. Washington, 5 1/2 x 7 1/2 In. *illus* 3300.00

owl, Scalloped Rim, Mt. Washington 2 1/4 x 4 3/4 In. 695.00

elery Vase, Square Scalloped Rim, 6 1/2 In. 520.00

reamer, Applied Reeded Handle, Square Top, Mt. Washington, 4 1/2 In. 720.00

ruet, Bulbous, Reeded Handle, Faceted Amber Stopper, Hobbs, Brockunier, 7 In. 431.00

ruet, Conical, Amber Handle, Faceted Stopper, Hobbs, Brockunier, 7 1/2 In. *illus* 863.00

ruet, Mt. Washington, 4 3/4 x 3 1/2 In. 2040.00

up & Saucer, New England 245.00 to 295.00

ecanter, Twisted & Reeded Amber Handle, Stopper, Glossy, Hobbs, Brockunier. 50.00

inger Bowl, Underplate, Gold Highlights, Crimped & Ruffled Rim, New England, 7 In. 1438.00

oblet, Glossy, New England, 7 1/4 In. 200.00

g, Claret, Reeded Amber Handle & Neck Rigaree, Glossy, Hobbs, Brockunier, 9 1/2 In. 4300.00

g, Claret, Reeded Amber Handle & Neck Rigaree, Hobbs, Brockunier, 9 1/2 In. 2720.00 to 3750.00

itcher, Applied White Handle, Mt. Washington, 3 3/4 In. 1750.00

itcher, Bulbous, Square Mouth, Amber Handle, Hobbs, Brockunier, 8 In. 978.00

itcher, Square Mouth, Amber Handle, Satin, Hobbs, Brockunier, 7 1/2 In. 840.00

itcher, Tankard, Reeded Handle, Hobbs, Brockunier, 10 1/2 In. 7500.00

itcher, White Reeded Handle, Square Rim, New England, 4 1/2 In. 620.00

alt & Pepper, Wheeling, Glossy, Sterling Silver, Lid, Hobbs, Brockunier, 3 In. 575.00

ugar, Loop Handles, Mt. Washington, 5 1/2 In. 700.00

ugar & Creamer, Crimped Rim, Mt. Washington 2100.00

ugar & Creamer, Flowers, Leaves, Gold Enameled, Mt. Washington, 2 3/4 In. 2500.00

ugar & Creamer, Paneled Sides, New England 475.00

othpick, Enameled Daisies, Diamond Quilted, Square Rim, Mt. Washington 600.00

umbler, Mt. Washington, 3 7/8 In. 378.00

se, Baluster, Glossy, Hobbs, Brockunier, 8 1/2 In. 830.00

se, Bud, New England Glass, 8 1/2 In. 530.00

se, Double Gourd, Dimpled, New England, 11 1/4 In. 1400.00

se, Enameled, Flower Branch, Yellow, Blue, White, Bulbous, Square Mouth, Mt. Washington, 8 In. 335.00

se, Enameled Flowers, White, Yellow, Beige Blossoms, Mt. Washington, 8 In. 3105.00 to 4500.00

se, Gourd, Glossy, Hobbs, Brockunier, 7 In. 920.00

se, Gourd, Hobbs, Brockunier, 10 1/2 In. 480.00

se, Gourd, Mt. Washington, 8 x 3 1/2 In. 805.00

se, Jack-In-The-Pulpit, Crimped Rim, Mt. Washington, 12 3/4 In. 2600.00

se, Jack-In-The-Pulpit, Footed, Ruffled Edge, Mt. Washington, 7 1/4 In. 825.00

se, Lily, Gold Enameled Flowers, Vines, Tricornered Rim, Mt. Washington, 10 1/4 In. 2100.00

Paul Revere, Cup, Greek Key, Marked, S.E.G., c.1910, 1 7/8 x 4 3/8 In.
$190.00

Paul Revere, Vase, Indigo Blue High Glaze, Label, 5 7/8 In.
$150.00

Peachblow, Bowl, Scalloped Rim, 3 Tapered & Reeded Feet, Mt. Washington, 5 1/2 x 7 1/2 In.
$3300.00

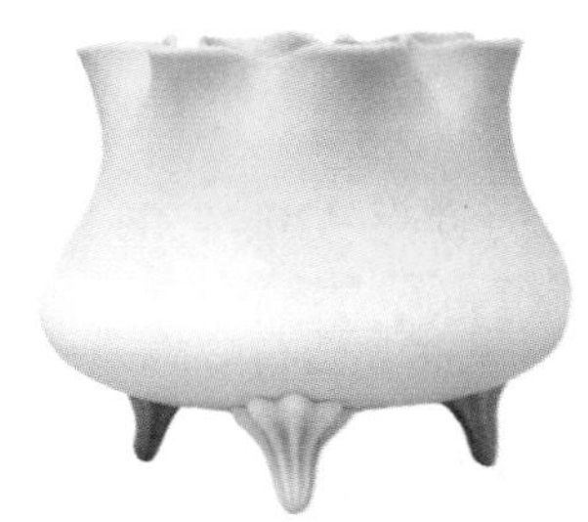

Peachblow, Cruet, Conical Amber Handle, Faceted Stopper, Hobbs, Brockunier, 7 1/2 In.
$863.00

P

Peachblow, Vase, Lily, Tricornered Rim, Footed, New England, 6 In.
$250.00

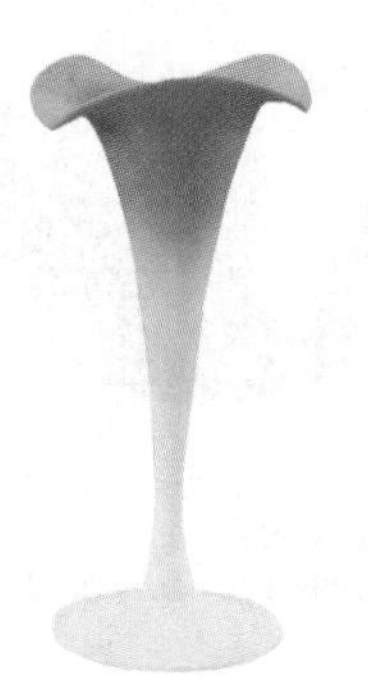

Peanuts, Bank, Linus, Striped Shirt, Holding Blanket, Porcelain, Italy, United Features Syndicate, 1963, 7 In.
$250.00

Peanuts, Button, U Of M, Homecoming, Boil-Illin-Oil, Celluloid, 1960, 2 In.
$69.00

TIP

Some folks who live in areas that flood try to store valuable paper items like stamps or currency in waterproof containers that float. It is probably just as safe to store the papers in boxes on the second or third floor.

Vase, Lily, New England, 10 In. 460.00
Vase, Lily, Tricornered Rim, Footed, New England, 6 In. .... *illus* 250.00
Vase, Morgan, Glossy, Griffin Base, Hobbs, Brockunier, 10 1/8 In. 3750.00
Vase, Morgan, Griffin Base, Hobbs, Brockunier, 10 7/8 In. .... 1350.00 to 2100.00
Vase, Morgan, Griffin Base, Glossy, Hobbs, Brockunier, 10 7/8 In. 1780.00
Vase, Oval, Tapered Neck, Mt. Washington, 8 In. 800.00
Vase, Pinched, New England, 6 1/4 In. 945.00
Vase, Pink To Pale Blue, Scalloped Rim, Peachblow, Mt. Washington, 6 7/8 In. 2300.00
Vase, Queen's Pattern, Double Gourd, Mt. Washington, 8 In. 3450.00
Vase, Shouldered, Glossy, Gold Birds On Stems, Mt. Washington, 9 1/2 In., Pair 460.00
Vase, Stick, 8 1/2 In. 345.00
Vase, Stick, Amber Rigaree Collar, Hobbs, Brockunier, 8 1/4 In. 978.00
Vase, Stick, Bulbous, Base, Hobbs, Brockunier, 6 1/2 x 12 1/2 In., Pair 300.00
Vase, Stick, Gourd Base, New England, 8 1/2 In. 345.00
Vase, Stick, Hobbs, Brockunier, 6 1/4 x 3 1/2 In. 115.00
Vase, Wide Ribs, Scalloped Rim, Mt. Washington, 4 1/4 In. 2300.00

PEANUTS is the title of a comic strip created by cartoonist Charles M. Schulz (1922–2000). The strip, drawn by Schulz from 1950 to 2000, features a group of children, including Charlie Brown and his sister Sally, Lucy Van Pelt and her brother Linus, Peppermint Patty, and Pig Pen, and an imaginative and independent beagle named Snoopy. The Peanuts gang has also been featured in books, television shows, and a Broadway musical.

Bank, Linus, Holding Blanket, Porcelain, Italy, United Features Syndicate, 1963, 7 In. .... *illus* 250.00
Book, A Charlie Brown Christmas, 1st Printing, 1965 .... 28.00
Book, A Charlie Brown Thanksgiving, Scholastic. 4.00
Book, Good Ol' Snoopy, Paperback, 1969 .... 14.00
Book, Snoopy & It Was A Dark & Stormy Night, Charles Schulz, Signed, 1971 .... 450.00
Book, Snoopy & The Red Baron, 1st Edition, United Features Syndicate, Hardcover, 1966. .... 175.00
Bottle, Shampoo, Charlie Brown, Baseball Hat & Glove, Vinyl, Avon, c.1950, 5 3/4 In. 20.00
Button, U Of M, Homecoming, Boil-Illin-Oil, Celluloid, 1960, 2 In. .... *illus* 69.00
Cup, Charlie Brown In Baseball Uniform, Milk Glass, Avon, 1969, 3 1/2 x 2 1/2 In. 18.00
Doll Clothes, Snoopy, Woodstock, Rain Outfit, Vinyl Coat, Cuffed Pockets, Snaps, Let It Rain. 25.00
Figurine, Charlie Brown, Jointed, Porcelain, Red Shirt, Hallmark, 2000. .... 50.00
Figurine, Linus, Sally, Pumpkin Patch, Department 56, 2004, 5 1/4 x 8 In. 69.00
Keychain, Charlie Brown Kicking Football 7.00
Keychain, Lucy & Linus, 1971, 3 x 3 In. 10.00
Lunch Box & Thermos, Charlie Brown On Pitcher's Mound, Metal, Green Band, 1980 .... 60.00
Magnet, Lucy, Baseball Gear, United Features Syndicate, c.1952, 1 3/4 In. 8.00
Movie & Album, Read Along, Great Pumpkin Charlie Brown, c.1978 .... 49.00
Nodder Set, Lucy, Charlie Brown, Snoopy, Box, 4 Piece c.1962, 3 1/2 In. .... *illus* 59.00
Ornament, Charlie Brown & Snoopy, Hallmark, Box, 2000 .... 7.00
Ornament, Charlie Brown By Tree, Red Cord, Marquis Waterford, Box, 2001 .... 45.00
Ornament, Lucy, Porcelain, Hallmark, Box, 2001 .... 29.00
Ornament, Snoopy, Charlie Brown, Lucy, Pig Pen Around Tree, Plays Tannenbaum, 2003 .... 40.00
Paperweight, Snoopy, At Typewriter, Love Letters, Marked, 1966 .... 17.00
Pin, Long Island Newspaper Promotion, c.1963, 2 1/2 In. 75.00
Pin, Snoopy, Sterling, Cheo, Marked 125.00
Pin, Snoopy, With Knapsack, Metal, United Features, 1 1/4 In. 26.00
Play Book, You're A Good Man Charlie Brown, United Artist, 1966 .... 25.00
Ruler, Peanuts In Space, c.1950, 1 5/8 x 12 In. 7.00
Scarf, Peanuts Gang, Multicolored 30.00
Sheet, Peanuts Gang, Flat, Cannon, U.S.A., Twin 14.00
Squeeze Toy, Linus With Blanket, United Features Syndicate, 1952, 4 3/4 In. 9.00
Thermos, Charlie Brown At Bat, Yellow Plastic, Red Cup, c.1950, 8 Oz. .... *illus* 55.00
Thermos, Peanuts Gang, Aladdin 16.00
View-Master, Story Booklet No. 536, c.1966. .... 10.00

PEARL items listed here are made of the natural mother-of-pearl from shells. Such natural pearl has been used to decorate furniture and small utilitarian objects for centuries. The glassware known as mother-of-pearl is listed by that name. Opera glasses made with natural pearl shell are listed under Opera Glasses.

Calling Card Holder, 2 3/4 x 4 In. 219.00
Magnifying Glass, Parasol Handle, Victorian, 16 1/2 In. 117.00

irror Handle, Portrait Of George Washington On Handle, c.1790 .... 450.00
ut Set, Nut Cracker, Picks Sterling Silver, 6 & 7 In., 7 Piece 82.00

EARLWARE is an earthenware made by Josiah Wedgwood in 1779. It was copied by other otters in England. Pearlware is only slightly different in color from creamware and for nany years collectors have confused the terms. Wedgwood pieces are listed in the Wedgwood category in nis book. Most pearlware with mocha designs is listed under Mocha.

Pearl

ust, George Washington, Jacket, Flower Vest, Cravat, Plinth, 8 In. 1912.00
ann, Cup, Blue Scale Ground, Raised Gilding, Flower Scrolls, Handle 140.00
hamber Pot, For A Kiss I'll Hand You This, Transfer, c.1830 .... 305.00
harger, Blue Glaze, Painted Blue Geometric Design, 1780, 14 In. 495.00
offeepot, Cover, England, c.1800, 9 In. 696.00
up, Stylized Star, Leaf Cartouche, Purple Luster, Handle, Child's, c.1810, 1 7/8 x 2 In. 55.00
essert Set, Blue Design, Embossed Leaf, Glaze, 6 Plates, Footed, 8 1/2 In. 80.00
ish, Shell, Fluted Sides, Handle, Scrolls & Flutes, Flowers & Birds, c.1821 .... 160.00
igurine, Andromache Mourning Hector, Staffordshire, c.1825, 9 1/4 In. 120.00
igurine, Cupid, Disguised, Boy, Girl, With Basket, Staffordshire, c.1920, 6 1/2 In., Pair 120.00
igurine, Milkmaid, Cow, Calf, Multicolored, 19th Century, 5 3/4 In. .... *illus* 2468.00
igurine, Youth & Companion, Holding Basket, Staffordshire, c.1820, 6 1/2 In., Pair 240.00
ootbath, Maxstoke Castle, Handles, Blue & White, Transfer, 1820s, 9 x 14 In. 5400.00
roup, Courtship, Couple On Bench, Engagement Ring, Puppy, Staffordshire, 1825, 8 In. 2400.00
ug, Captain Hull, Pike-Be Always Ready, Oval, c.1815, 6 1/2 In. 657.00
ug, Chinese Garden Scene, Handle, Multicolored Glaze, Transfer, c.1830, 3 3/4 In. 225.00
ug, Sunderland, Peace & Plenty, Black Transfer, Enamel, Pink Luster, Early 1800s, 9 In. 575.00
ug, Toy, Milkmaid, Cowbirds & Flowers, Transfer, Handle, c.1835 .... 135.00
lug, Frog, 2 Verses, Black Transfer, Overglaze Enamel, Handle, c.1825 .... 499.00
lug, Mariner's Verse, Frog On Interior, Mid 19th Century, 4 1/4 In. 518.00
lug, Martha, Transfer, Child's, c.1830, 2 3/4 x 2 3/4 In. 700.00
lug, Thomas, Transfer, Child's, c.1830, 2 1/2 x 2 7/8 In. 625.00
epper, Stylized Flowers & Leaves, Blue & White, Transfer, 1830, 4 In. 155.00
itcher, Banded, Handle, Pale Blue Glaze, 7 In. 575.00
itcher, Blue & White, 19th Century, Handle, Horizontal Bands, 4 In. 165.00
itcher, Blue & White, 7 1/2 In. 287.00
itcher, Cherries, Gadrooned Top, Bottom, Twist Handle, Early 1800s, 3 In. 2100.00
itcher, Cream Yellow Glaze, Multicolored Flowered Bouquets, 1800s, 3 In. 85.00
itcher, Ewer, Hand Painted, Handle, Earthenware, 8 1/2 x 5 In. 775.00
itcher, Jug Boy & Dog, Handle, Red, Transfer, Child's, c.1830, 2 x 2 In. 250.00
late, Band Of Hope, Sabbath Breakers, Transfer, Child's, c.1850, 6 1/4 In. 200.00
late, Cottage, Blue Dot, Green Slashes, 8 In. .... *illus* 700.00
late, Doll's, Trellis & Flowers, 1830, 3 1/4 In. 145.00
late, Embossed, Hand Painted Flowers In Center, c.1820, 9 In. 85.00
late, Feather Edge, Vining Border, Serpentine Edge, Yellow Florets, Vines, 8 1/4 In. 374.00
late, Flowers, Blue Feather Edge, Octagonal, 9 1/2 In. 87.00
late, Gleaners, Farm Workers, Cottages, Fruit & Flower Border, Transfer, 1820, 9 1/2 In. 475.00
late, King's Rose, Impressed 8, Early 19th Century, 8 1/4 In. .... *illus* 24.00
late, Leeds Style Painting, Eagle, Shield, Arros, Laurel Branch, 6 1/2 In. 1610.00
late, Shipping Series, Border Depicts Shells & Seaweed, Blue & White, Transfer, 10 In. 550.00
late, Silverlocks & The Bears Letter S, Alphabet Brown, Transfer, Child's, c.1840, 8 3/8 In. 400.00
late, Soup, Eagle, Green Scalloped Feather Edge, Leeds Colors, Early 1800s, 8 1/4 In. 1150.00
latter, Blue Willow, Glazed, c.1840, 6 3/4 x 5 In. 135.00
latter, British Views, Country Scene, Cows, Blue & White, Transfer, 1820s, 11 x 8 1/2 In. 675.00
latter, Feather Edge, Blue Painted Molded Rim, c.1820, 16 3/4 x 13 1/2 In. 300.00
latter, Grapes, Blue & White, Transfer, 1825, 15 In. 950.00
latter, Parkland Scenery, Quatrefoil Frame, Blue & White, Transfer, 18 1/2 In. 1250.00
auceboat, Tower, Glaze, Handle, Ironstone, 7 x 3 In. 111.00
oup, Dish, Fruit & Flowers, Lush Border Of Roses & Leaves, Transfer, 1825, 9 1/2 In. 250.00
ugar, Cover, Exotic Birds, Footed, Handles, c.1835 .... 250.00
ugar, Cover, Handles, Hand Painted, Stylized Flowers, Burgundy & Blue, 8 x 6 In. 250.00
ugar, Cover, Oval, Standing Rim, Fluted, Basket Weave Body, U.S. Seal, c.1800, 5 1/2 In. 269.00
ea Bowl, Blue Band, Hand Painted Chevrons, 18th Century 75.00
eapot, Wood Flower Basket, Impressed Mark, Handle, 1830s 650.00
oby Jug, Multicolored, Seated Figure, Holding Ale Jug, Ralph Wood, 9 3/4 In. .... 940.00 to 1175.00
ureen, Cover, Staffordshire, John Turner, c.1790, 13 1/2 In. 348.00
ase, Rose On Front, Gold Trim On Top & Bottom, 8 In. 8.00

Peanuts, Nodder Set, Lucy, Charlie Brown, Snoopy, Box, 4 Piece c.1962, 3 1/2 In.
$59.00

TIP
Small collectibles can be used as window-shade pulls.

Peanuts, Thermos, Charlie Brown At Bat, Yellow Plastic, Red Cup, c.1950, 8 Oz.
$55.00

Pearlware, Figurine, Milkmaid, Cow, Calf, Multicolored, 19th Century, 5 3/4 In.
$2468.00

Pearlware, Plate, Cottage, Blue Dot, Green Slashes, 8 In.
$700.00

P

Pearlware, Plate,
King's Rose, Impressed 8,
Early 19th Century, 8¼ In.
$24.00

Pencil, Mechanical,
White & Blue Enamel, Calendar,
14K Gold, Early 20th Century, 5¼ In.
$208.00

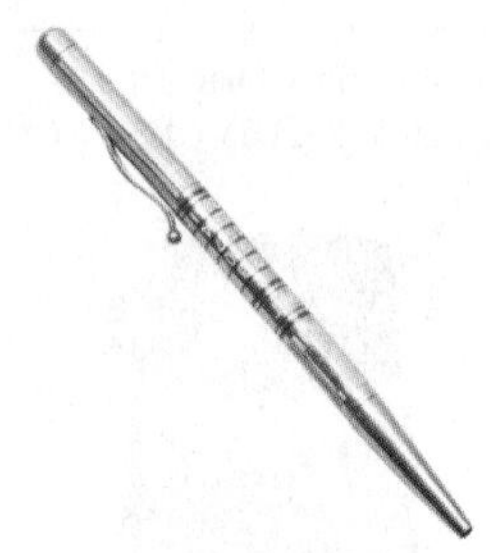

Pencil Sharpener, Automatic,
New York, 1906, 6¾ x 4 In.
$140.00

Pencil Sharpener, Cincinnati Water
Purifier, Stenciled Wood, Iron, 1880s, 10 In.
$770.00

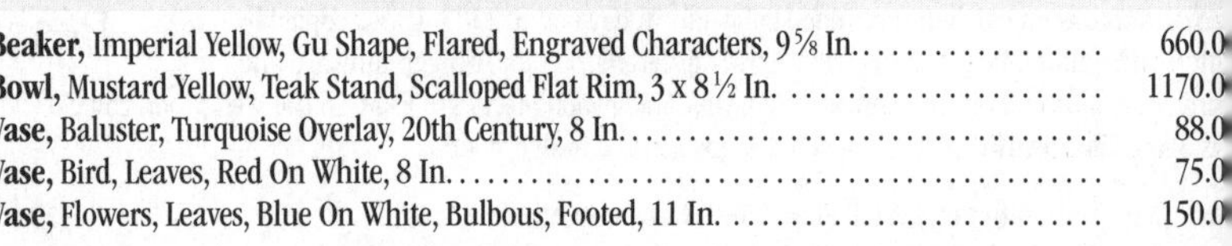

PEKING GLASS is a Chinese cameo glass first made popular in the eighteenth century. The Chinese have continued to make this layered glass in the old manner, and many new pieces are now available that could confuse the average buyer.

Beaker, Imperial Yellow, Gu Shape, Flared, Engraved Characters, 9⅝ In. 660.0
Bowl, Mustard Yellow, Teak Stand, Scalloped Flat Rim, 3 x 8½ In. 1170.0
Vase, Baluster, Turquoise Overlay, 20th Century, 8 In. 88.0
Vase, Bird, Leaves, Red On White, 8 In. 75.0
Vase, Flowers, Leaves, Blue On White, Bulbous, Footed, 11 In. 150.0

PELOTON glass is a European glass with small threads of colored glass rolled onto the surface of clear or colored glass. It is sometimes called spaghetti, or shredded coconut, glass. Most pieces found today were made in the nineteenth century.

Rose Bowl, White, Clear Cased, Melon Ribbed Body, Rigaree Pointed Rim, Kralik, 3¾ In. . . . 316.0

PENS replaced hand-cut quills as writing instruments in 1780, when the first steel pen point was made in England. But it was 100 years before the commercial pen was a common item. The fountain pen was invented in the 1830s but was not made in quantity until the 1880s. All types of old pens are collected. Float pens that feature small objects floating in a liquid as part of the handle are popular with collectors. Advertising pens are listed in the Advertising section of this book.

PEN
Cigar, Dupont Corian, Multicolored, 5¾ x ¾ In. 70.0
Cigar, Maple Burl, 5¾ x ¾ In. 55.0
Dip, Mother-Of-Pearl, Crisscross Pattern, Moore's Maniflex Pen, 6 In. 45.0
Fountain, Brown & Gold Stripes, Gold Band, Parker Vacumatic, c.1930 . . . . . . 295.0
Fountain, Cross, No. 350P, Silver, Box, 1970s 12.0
Fountain, Scripto, Chrome Cap, Red Body, Plastic Cartridge 5.0
Mother-Of-Pearl, Gold Ferule, Velvet & Silk Box, 5½ In. 85.0
Professional Office Service, Wooden Look, Engraved, 5¼ In. 5.0
Waterford, Marquis, Ballpoint, Silver, Gift Box 50.0
Waterman, Ideal, 3V, Fountain, Lever Fill, Marbleized Green, Red, Mother-Of-Pearl Barrel, Cap 100.0

PEN & PENCIL
Cross, Stainless Finish, Original Box. 95.0
Parker 21, Blue Matte Finish, Stainless Steel Cap, Presentation Box, Brochure 119.0
Sterling Silver, Spiral Design, Menorah At Top, Pocket Clip Says Shalom, Globus, Israel 78.0

PENCILS were invented, so it is said, in 1565. The eraser was not added to the pencil until 1858. The automatic pencil was invented in 1863. Collectors today want advertising pencils or automatic pencils of unusual design. Boxes and sharpeners for pencils are also collected. Advertising pencils are listed in the Advertising category. Pencil boxes are listed in the Box category.

PENCIL
Case, 14K Gold, Germany, 20th Century, 3 In. 88.0
Mechanical, Amethyst Seal, Sterling Silver 195.0
Mechanical, Beveled White Opaline Glass Seal, Sterling Silver 195.0
Mechanical, Chatelaine, Amber Glass, Jeweled Wax Seal, Sterling Silver 195.0
Mechanical, Waterman, Sterling Overlay, Art Nouveau, Ideal, 5⅜ In. 245.0
Mechanical, White & Blue Enamel, Calendar, 14K Gold, Early 20th Century, 5¼ In. . . . *illus* 208.0
Mechanical, Walh Eversharp, Silver Plate, 5¾ In. 25.0
Tiffany & Co., Mechanical, Calendar, White, Blue Enamels, 14K Gold, 5¼ In. 187.0

PENCIL SHARPENER
Army Tank, Catalin, Green, Red Circle, White Star 48.0
Automatic, New York, 1906, 6¾ x 4 In. . . . . . *illus* 140.0
Baker's Chocolate Girl, Carrying Tray Of Cups, Reg. U.S. Pat. Office 75.0
Biplane Airplane, Dark Bronze Color, Hong Kong, 3¼ x 3 In. 10.0
Cello, Die Cast Metal, Plastic Strings, Hong Kong, 5¼ In. 9.0
Chicken In Hat, 2⅝ In. 30.0
Cincinnati Water Purifier, Stenciled Wood, Iron, 1880s 10 In. . . . . . *illus* 770.0
Coffee Mill, Red, Gold Eagle, 5½ x 5¾ In. 45.0
Cylindrical, Plastic, Burgundy, Germany, Dux 9207-N 10.0
Desk Top, Red, Blue, Automatic Pencil Sharpener Co. Chicago, Il. 62.0
Domed, Ribbed, Plastic, Green, 4 In. 9.0
Fireplace Hearth, Pot Metal, Brass & Copper Finish, Hong Kong, 3 x 2 x 1 In. 10.0
Globe, Pot Metal, Hong Kong, 3 x 2½ In. 22.0
High Top Boot, Die Cast, Antique Finished No. 13E, Hong Kong, 3¾ In. 9.0

orse & Buggy, Die Cast, Black & Copper Color, 2 ¼ x 4 x 1 ¼ In. 12.00
itten In High Heel Shoe, Ceramic, c.1960, 2 ½ In. 15.00
antern, Hong Kong, c.1970, 3 ¾ In. 4.00
echanical, Roneo, Cast Iron, Table Mount Clamp, 6 ¾ In. 325.00
ilk Bottle, Metal, White, Drink Milk, U.S.A. Keychain 48.00
ummy, Universal Pictures, c.1960, 2 ¾ In. 8.00
ew York Automatic, 1906 .... 132.00
enguin, Celluloid, Made In Japan 125.00
olls-Royce, Metal, Hong Kong 5.00
addle, Copper, 3 ¼ In.. .... 6.00
hip, Plastic, Germany, 2 ½ In. 8.00
lot Machine, Pot Metal, Hong Kong, 2 ½ x 2 In. 10.00
olid Chunk Bakelite, Yellow, Round, c.1920, 1 In. 15.00
tarkist, Charlie The Tuna, Battery 38.00
team Iron, Metal, Gold Tone, 2 ⅛ In. 20.00
tove, Metal, Drawer, Door, Spain, 3 x 2 x 1 In. 13.00
tymie From Our Gang, Derby Hat, Octagonal, Red, 2 In. 144.00
ank, Ribbed Treads, Bakelite, Star 31.00
elephone, Plastic, Hong Kong, c.1960, 1 ¾ In.. .... 5.00
V, Hologram, Cowboy On Horse, Kohner 10.00
.S. Automatic, c.1906 .... 201.00
iolin, Metal, Bronze Patina, Germany 56.00
/all Telephone, Plastic, 3 ¼ In.. .... 10.00

ENNSBURY Pottery worked in Morrisville, Pennsylvania, from 1950 to 1971. Full sets f dinnerware as well as many decorative items were made. Pieces are marked with the ame of the factory.

Pennsbury Pottery

owl, Pretzel, Eagle, American, Holding Shield & Olive Branch, 12 x 8 In. 75.00
owl, Pretzel, Barbershop Quartet, 11 ½ x 8 ½ In. .... 60.00 to 75.00
reamer, Amish Family, Woman & Heart, 2 ½ In. 18.00
reamer, Rooster, Red, 2 ½ In. 20.00
reamer, Rooster, Red, 4 x 3 In. 35.00
reamer, Rooster, Yellow, 4 ½ In. 45.00
ish, Washington Crossing Delaware, Raised, Rotary Club Of Washington Crossing, Pa., Brown, 4 ¾ In. 14.00
igurine, Cardinal, Marked, 6 ¼ In. .... *illus* 180.00
lug, Fisherman, One That Got Away, 5 In. 38.00
laque, B & O Railroad, Veterans, Phil., 1955, 5 ¾ x 7 ¾ In.. .... 65.00
laque, Come In Without Knocking, Go Out The Same Way, 6 In. .... *illus* 25.00
laque, Don't Stand Up While The Room Is In Motion, 6 In. 45.00
laque, Locomotive, Tiger, 1856, Pennsylvania Railroad, 5 ¾ x 8 In. 60.00
laque, Rooster, When The Cock Crows The Night Is All, 4 ¼ In. 30.00
late, Amish Family, Horse & Buggy, Orange Ground, Green Trim, 9 In. 24.00
late, Amish Family, Horse & Buggy, 8 In. 24.00
late, Amish Family, Walking Hand In Hand Down Road, 11 In. 95.00
late, Baltimore & Ohio R.R. 1837, Brown, Black, Yellow, Maroon, Green Trim, 5 ¾ x 8 In. .. 44.00
late, Yuletide, Angel, Marked, Noel Stumar, 1970. .... 15.00
ign, Display, Yellow Bird On Top, 1950-70, 4 ¾ x 5 In. 365.00
ip Tray, Rooster, Yellow, 6 x 8 In.. .... 49.00
ray, Western Atlantic R.R., Marked, 7 ¾ In. .... *illus* 25.00
rivet, Amish Family, Courting In Carriage, No. 1057 .... 45.00
/allpocket, Woman, Marked, 6 ½ In.. .... *illus* 80.00

EPSI-COLA, the drink and the name, was invented in 1898 but was not trademarked until 903. The logo was changed from an elaborate script to the modern block letters in 1963. everal different logos have been used. Until 1951, the words *Pepsi* and *Cola* were separated y 2 dashes. These bottles are called "*double dash.*" In 1951 the modern logo with a single hyphen was ntroduced. All types of advertising memorabilia are collected, and reproductions are being made.

PEPSI-COLA

dvertisement, Come Alive, Lady & Man Drinking Pepsi, 1965, 7 ½ x 5 ½ In. 8.00
dvertisement, Costume Party, Pepsi Makes The Party, 1960, 13 x 10 In.. .... 10.00
dvertisement, Dart Board Game, 1964, 12 x 9 ½ In.. .... 10.00
dvertisement, Man Fishing, Think Young, 1963, 13 x 10 In. 10.00
dvertisement, Think Young Man, 1964, 10 x 13 In., 2 Pages 10.00
dvertisement, Woman & Man, Outdoor Party Scene, 1954, 12 x 9 In. 11.00
shtray, Couple At Bowling Alley, Tin, Round, 5 ½ In.. .... 24.00
ottle, 6-Pack, Carrier, Original Caps, 2 ½ x 2 ¼-In. Bottle 50.00

Pennsbury, Figurine, Cardinal, Marked, 6 ¼ In. $180.00

Pennsbury, Plaque, Come In Without Knocking, Go Out The Same Way, 6 In. $25.00

Pennsbury, Tray, Western Atlantic R.R, Marked, 7 ¾ In. $25.00

Pennsbury, Wallpocket, Woman, Marked, 6 ½ In. $80.00

P

Pepsi-Cola, Radio, Cooler, Blue, Plastic, 1950s, 6½ x 8½ x 5 In. $250.00

Pepsi-Cola, Sign, Refreshing & Satisfying, 5 Cent, Die cut, Tin, c.1940, 29 x 8 In. $450.00

Bottle, Glass, c.1978, Pt., 16 Oz. 10.0
Bottle, Green, Charlottesville, Va., c.1920, 8¼ In. 85.0
Bottle, Light Pink, ABM, Prototype, 7 In. 1300.0
Bottle, New Bern, N.C., June, 1963. 25.0
Bottle, No Return, No Deposit, 10 Oz., 8 In. 12.0
Bottle, Pepsi-Cola Bottling, 1 Clear, Tooled Lip 952.0
Bottle, Sparkling Pepsi-Cola, Garden City, N.Y., 12 Oz., 10 In. 10.0
Bottle, Straight-Sided, Embossed Bottle Cap Logo, No Deposit No Refill, 1960s, 10 Oz. 5.0
Bottle, Stretched, 1970s, 16 Oz., 13½ In. 6.0
Bottle Carrier, Metal, Red, Blue, 1951 38.0
Bottle Carrier, Metal, W.E. Co., Atlanta, 1947 59.0
Bottle Crate, Wood, Yellow, Blue Letters, Cutout Handles, General Bottlers, Inc., 5 x 18 x 12 In. 15.0
Bottle Opener, Drink Pepsi-Cola, 1950s. 18.0
Can, Santa Waving On Water Tube, 1990s, 12 Oz. 5.0
Can, Syrup, Bottle Cap, 1960s, Gal. 35.0
Can, Winter Wonderland, Musical Notes, 1984, 12 Oz. 5.0
Carrier, Wood, 6-Pack, Double Dash, 8¾ x 11½ In. 129.0
Clock, Neon, Pepsi-Cola, Bottle Cap, Marquis Top, Spinner Dial, Cleveland. 1200.0
Clock, Wall, Electric, Double Glass Face, Metal Back, Advertising Products, 1961, 16 x 4 In. 700.0
Goblet, Thumbprint, Red Letters, 1960s, 6¼ x 3¾ In. 3.0
Menu Board, Wooden, Hanging, 1930s, 21½ x 25 In. 253.0
Poster, Counter-Spy, Bottle Cap, 1940s 14.0
Radio, Cooler, Blue, Plastic, 1950s, 6½ x 8½ x 5 In. *illus* 250.0
Score Card, Pepsi & Pete, If You're Gonna Pass, Pass The Pepsi, 1940s, 8 x 4¼ In. 6.0
Sign, Double Dash, Self-Framed, 33 x 25¾ In. 1430.0
Sign, Drink Pepsi-Cola, 5 Cents, Pepsi Pete, Red, White, Blue, Embossed, Tin Litho, c.1930, 3½ x 21 In. 253.0
Sign, Pepsi, Be Sociable, Serve Pepsi, Cardboard, Metal Frame, 29½ x 13 In. 66.0
Sign, Porcelain, Self-Framed, 1940s, 32¼ x 25¼ In. 715.0
Sign, Refreshing & Satisfying, 5 Cent, Die cut, Tin, c.1940, 29 x 8 In. *illus* 450.0
Sign, Say Pepsi Please, Chalkboard, Tin, 19½ x 30 In. 77.0
Straw, Drink Pepsi-Cola, Paper, 10⅜ In., 6 Piece. 15.0
Toy, Car, Model-T, 1912, Die Cast Metal, Red, White, Blue 25.0
Tray, Bigger & Better, Bottle, 1938, 11 x 13 In. 265.0
Tray, Bottle Cap, Red, White, Blue, 12 In. Diam. 50.0
Tray, Delicious & Healthful For 5 Cents, Victorian Woman Holding Glass, Oval, Fabcraft Inc. 27.0
Truck, Tin Friction, 6 Tin Cases, Japan 201.0
Tumbler, Bullwinkle, P.A.T. Ward, 1970s, 5⅛ x 2¼ In. 15.0
Tumbler, Casper The Friendly Ghost, Brockway Glass Co., 6 x 3 In. 20.0
Tumbler, Flared, Etched, 5 In. 15.0
Tumbler, Penguins, 5⅝ In. 5.0
Tumbler, Stained Glass Style, 1970s, 6¼ In. 9.0
Wooden Nickel, 2-Sided, Pepsi-Cola, Mountain Dew, 1½ In. 1.0

PERFUME BOTTLES are made of cut glass, pressed glass, art glass, silver, metal, enamel, and even plastic or porcelain. Although the small bottle to hold perfume was first made before the time of ancient Egypt, it is the nineteenth- and twentieth-century examples that interest today's collector. DeVilbiss Company has made atomizers of all types since 1888 but no longer makes the perfume bottle tops so popular with collectors. These were made from 1920 to 1968. The glass bottle may be by any of many manufacturers even if the atomizer is marked *DeVilbiss*. The word *factice*, which often appears in ads, refers to store display bottles. Glass or porcelain examples may be found under the appropriate name such as Lalique, Czechoslovakia, Glass-Bohemian, etc.

Atomizer, Lavender Glass, Gilt Highlights, Crystal Stem, Disc, Signed, DeVilbiss, 6½ In. 115.0
Cameo Glass, Egg Shape, Citron, Red Over White Lattice, Silver Collar, Ball Stopper, 5 In. 805.0
Cameo Glass, Swan's Head, White Over Yellow, Silver Cap, Marked, RD 11109, 1884, 6 In. 6000.0
Cameo Glass, White Flowers & Leaves, Blue Ground, Silver Cap, 10½ In. 3600.0
Cased Crystal, Pink Orchids, Stopper, Greg Held, Orient & Flume, 7 In. 345.0
Ciro, Bouquet, Blue, Black & Yellow Enamel, c.1932, 3¼ In. 518.0
Ciro, Chevalier, Clear, 4¾ In., 3 In. 125.0
Ciro, Chevalier, Clear, Knights Shoulders & Helmets, 4¾ In. 125.0
Cologne, 8-Sided, Blue, White Flecks, Pinched Waist, Tooled Lip, c.1865, 4⅝ In. *illus* 735.0
Cologne, Chestnut Shape, Blue Molded, Tooled Lip, Pontil, 4 In. 2010.0
Cologne, Cobalt Blue, 8-Sided, Corset Waist, Tooled Lip, c.1865, 4⅝ In. 410.0
Cologne, Cut Glass, Turquoise To Black, Footed, Austria, 19th Century, 7 In. 650.0
Cologne, Glass, Scrolled Acanthus Leaves, Cobalt Blue, Footed, Rolled Lip, Pontil, 5 In. 1320.0
Cologne, Opaque Jade Green, Polished Rim, Molded Neck Rings, Mushroom Stopper, 6½ In., Pair. 99.0

P

TIP

Tin signs and cans will fade from the ultraviolet rays coming in a window or from a fluorescent light. Plexiglass UF-1 or UF-3 will cover the window and keep the rays away from your collection. There are also plastic sleeves to cover fluorescent tubes.

Cologne, Teal Blue, 8-Sided, Pinched Waist, Tooled Lip, 1850-80, 4⅝ In. 735.00
Cologne, Violet Cobalt Blue, 8-Sided, Pinched Waist, Tooled Lip, c.1865, 4¾ In. 410.00
Cologne, Yellow, Squat, Hexagonal, Star Cut Base, Panel Cut Stopper, 4½ x 3¼ In. 303.00
Conical, 3 Block, Printie Pattern, Amethyst, Rolled Mouth, c.1840, 6⅞ In. 2352.00
Cranberry Glass, Engraved Flowers, Gilt Stopper, Victorian, 3¾ In. 104.00
De Vigny, Golliwogg, Original Box, 1950s, 3½ In. 360.00
Des Cologne Des Princes, Sapphire Blue, 12-Sided, Tapered, Label, c.1870, 9½ In. 600.00
DeVilbiss, Blue Frosted, Atomizer, 6½ In. 495.00
DeVilbiss, Blue Over Clear, Atomizer, 6½ In. 195.00
DeVilbiss, Lavender, Atomizer, 4¾ In. 325.00
DeVilbiss, Orange, Atomizer, 6¼ In. 355.00
DeVilbiss, Orange Over Clear, Atomizer, 6¼ In. 250.00
Devon, Torquay, Porcelain, Silver Screw Top, Multicolored, 2½ In. 575.00
Dresden, Figures In Landscape, Flowers, Porcelain, c.1900, 3½ In. 259.00
Elizabeth Arden, My Love, Clear & Frosted Glass, Sealed, 1948, 4 In. 600.00
Enamel, Clear, Hinged Top, Internal Stopper, Russia, 1½ In. 120.00
Enamel, Silver, Gilt, Guilloche, Engine Turned, Norway, 1920s, 5 In. 403.00
Figural, Fox In Hunting Costume, Modern, Enamel, England, 3¼ In. 168.00
Figural, Seated Cat, Continental, Porcelain, Gilt Metal, 3¾ In. 240.00
Glass, Amber, Atomizer, 7¼ In. 250.00
Glass, Hand Blown, Enamel, Stopper, c.1920, 5½ In., Pair 57.00
Glass, Transparent Blue, Atomizer, 6¾ In. 195.00
Hattie Carnegie, Hypnotic, Woman's Head & Shoulder, S-Stopper, 4 In. 645.00
Leaves, Pedestal, Engraved, Crimped Red Rose, Stopper, C. Kaziun, 9 In. 1100.00
Opaline Glass, Brass Cap, Internal Stopper, Horn Shape, England, Victorian, 6 In. 150.00
Opaline Glass, Silver Gilt Overlay, Internal Stopper, 2 In. 288.00
Palmer's Jockey Club, Label Under Glass, Clear, Tooled Lip, Stopper, 8 In. 672.00
Sandwich Glass, Cobalt Blue, Blown, Ribbed, Stopper, 6½ In. 595.00
Sapphire Blue, Ovals & Diamonds, Cut Glass, Silver Lid, 2¾ In. .... *illus* 72.00
Satin Glass, Pink, Ball Stopper, Victorian, Late 19th Century, 5 In. 82.00
Tea Roses, Yellow, White, Applied, Black Applied Geometric Framework, 4¾ In. 4025.00
Vial, Cherub & Flowers, Red Ground, Hinged Silver Gilt Top, France, 3 In. 1035.00
Vial, Continental, Opaline Glass, Gilt Metal Top, 2½ In. 150.00
Vial, Kerr, Silver, Pendant, Dolphin Shape, Renaissance, 3¼ In. 288.00
Vial, Nesting Birds, Blue Ground, Hinged Silver Gilt Top, France, 2¼ In. 540.00
Vial, Stiegel, Seahorse Shape, Applied Cobalt Blue Border, 2½ In. 92.00
Vial, Victorian, Silver Screw Top, Registered 72627, England, 2¼ In. 84.00
Viard, Brass Top, Gilt, Birds, 3 In. 600.00
Viard, Myrurgia, Chypre, Celtic, Clear, Gray Patina, 4¾ In. 633.00

PETERS & REED Pottery Company of Zanesville, Ohio, was founded by John D. Peters and Adam Reed in 1897. Chromal, Landsun, Montene, Pereco, and Persian are some of the art lines that were made. The company, which became Zane Pottery in 1920 and Gonder Pottery in 1941, closed in 1957. Peters & Reed pottery was unmarked.

Bowl, Art, Blue, Squat, 8 In. 50.00
Bowl, Moss Aztec, Acorns & Oak Leaves, Wide Mouth, 8½ In. 140.00
Bowl, Zane Ware, Ruffled Edge, Green Matte, Hand Thrown, 6½ x 3 In. 55.00
Jardiniere, Pedestal, Moss Aztec, Poppies, Buttressed Base, 30 x 15 In. 800.00
Jardiniere, Pereco, Grape Design, 5½ x 6¾ In. 275.00
Jardiniere, Zane Ware, Speckled Cobalt Blue High Glaze, Bulbous, Flared Rim, 8 In. 55.00
Jug, Brown Drip Glaze, Raised Grapes, 5½ In. 90.00
Jug, Handle, Wreath, Lion's Head, Squat, 5 In. 22.00
Mug, Grape Clusters, Leaves, Deep Blue Glaze, Earthy Umber Ground, Twig Handle, 5½ In. 50.00
Tumbler, Metal & Wood Handle, Hostessware, Green, 4⅛ In. 25.00
Vase, Chocolate Glaze, Raised Branches, Bulbous Bottom, Long Neck, 13 In., Pair 200.00
Vase, Chocolate Glaze, Raised Flowers, Cylindrical, Pinched Waist, 7½ In. 40.00
Vase, Chromal, Ethereal Impressions, Landscape Scene, Glazed, 12 x 5½ In. 950.00
Vase, Floral Wreath, Footed, 9½ x 10½ In. .... *illus* 93.00
Vase, Landsun, Farm Scene, Cottage, 7½ x 4 In. 600.00
Vase, Landsun, Trees, Brown Ground, 9½ In. .... *illus* 325.00
Vase, Landsun, Waves, Variegated Browns & Blues, Baluster, 4 In. 125.00
Vase, Marbleized, 9⅛ x 4⅛ In. 195.00
Vase, Matte Blue Glaze, Raised Wisteria Rim, Pinched Waist, 12 In. 130.00
Vase, Moss Aztec, Flowers, Cylindrical, Flared Rim, 8⅞ In. 65.00
Vase, Moss Aztec, Signed, Ferrell, 7⅞ In. .... *illus* 75.00

Perfume Bottle, Cologne, 8-Sided, Blue, White Flecks, Pinched Waist, Tooled Lip, c.1865, 4⅝ In.
$735.00

Perfume Bottle, Sapphire Blue, Ovals & Diamonds, Cut Glass, Silver Lid, 2¾ In.
$72.00

Peters & Reed, Vase, Floral Wreath, Footed, 9½ x 10½ In.
$93.00

P

Peters & Reed, Vase, Landsun, Trees, Brown Ground, 9½ In.
$325.00

Peters & Reed, Vase, Moss Aztec, Signed, Ferrell, 7⅞ In.
$75.00

Pewabic Pottery, Font, Raised Relief, Verdigris, 16 x 10 In.
$644.00

Vase, Mountains, Trees, Road, Cobalt Blue Ground, Oval, 7⅝ In. 382.0
Vase, Pedestal, Moss Aztec, 16½ In. 500.0
Vase, Persian, Brown Matte, 6⅛ x 4⅝ In. 199.0
Vase, Shadow Ware, Tan & Gray Drip Glaze, Bulbous, Tapered Neck, 5 x 5 In. 150.0
Vase, Zane Ware, Ivory, 8 In. 150.0

PETRUS REGOUT, *see Maastricht category.*

PEWABIC POTTERY was founded by Mary Chase Perry Stratton in 1903 in Detroit, Michigan. The company made many types of art pottery, including pieces with matte green glaze and an iridescent crystalline glaze. The company continued working until the death of Mary Stratton in 1961. It was reactivated by Michigan State University in 1968.

PEWABIC

Bowl, Sink, Flower, Blue, Green, 6 x 16½ In. 560.0
Cigarette Box, Bird Sitting On Branch, Blue & Gold, Luster Glaze. 443.0
Dish, Mottled, Multicolored, 6-Sided, Early 20th Century, 2 x 10¾ x 3⅜ In. 575.0
Font, Raised Relief, Verdigris, 16 x 10 In. *illus* 644.0
Tile, Scenic, Oak Frame, 17 In. 198.0
Tile, Scenic, Oak Frame, 32 In. 432.0
Vase, Amber Matte Glaze, Stamped, 10½ x 6¾ In. 1920.0
Vase, Baluster, Flambe Glaze, 20 x 9 In. 7200.0
Vase, Blue, Multicolored, Stand, 14 x 9 In., 2 Piece 6500.0
Vase, Blue Drips, Bulbous, Mid 20th Century, 5 x 4½ In. 1995.0
Vase, Blue Iridescent Glaze, Flared, Hand Thrown, Marked, 3½ In. 520.0
Vase, Dark Blue Luster Glaze, Yellow & Blue Drip Rim, Bulbous, Flared, 10 In. 999.0
Vase, Geometric Decoration, Flambe Matte Glaze, 14½ x 11 In. 4500.0
Vase, Lustered Glaze, Ultramarine Base, Marked, 8 x 8 In. 5400.0
Vase, Orange, Yellow Interior, c.1940, 5¼ x 6 In. 730.0
Vase, Tapered Oval Shape, Green Iridescent Glaze, Label, 9 In. 1380.0

PEWTER is a metal alloy of tin and lead. Some of the pewter made after 1840 has a slightly different composition and is called Britannia metal. This later type of pewter was worked by machine; the earlier pieces were made by hand. In the 1920s pewter came back into fashion and pieces were often marked *Genuine Pewter*. Eighteenth-, nineteenth-, and twentieth-century examples are listed here.

Basin, B. Barnes, Eagle Stamped On Interior, 2⅞ x 10⅜ In. 220.0
Basin, Blakslee Barns, Flared Rim, 6⅝ In. 812.0
Basin, Hammered Bouge, Crowned Monogram, Marked, London, Late 1700s, 18½ In. 1093.0
Basin, Henry Will, Shaped & Rolled Edge, c. 1775, 2⅝ x 12¼ In. 63800.0
Basin, Love, Marked, 11 In. 400.0
Basin, Thomas Melville II, Polished Marked, 2 x 8 In. 500.0
Basin, Townsend & Compton, 2 x 8 In. 55.0
Basin, Townsend & Compton, Hammered, 18th Century, 13 In. 295.0
Basin, Townsend & Compton, London, 2½ x 9¼ In. 110.0
Basin, W. & S. Yale, Meriden, Conn., c.1813, 6⅝ x 1⅝ In. 575.0
Beaker, Bud Terminal Handle, 3½ x 2¾ In. 306.0
Beaker, J.H. Palethorp, Flared, Incised Rings, Philadelphia, 3⅛ In. 696.0
Beaker, James B. Woodbury, Flared, 4 Incised Rings, Philadelphia, 3⅛ In. 290.0
Beaker, James Weekes, Ringed, Flared, Footed, 3¾ In. 1276.0
Beaker, TB & Co., 2 Incised Rings, Marked, 3 In. 255.0
Beaker, Thomas Boardman, Lucius Hart, 3 Horizontal Bands, Flared Base, 4 In., Pair 1856.0
Bowl, J.B. Woodbury, O. Colton, Stepped Foot, 4 x 6 In. 1044.0
Bowl, W. Crossman, W.A. West, Z. Leonard, Taunton, Mass., Lobed, 4 x 6¼ In. 1102.0
Brushpot, London, Stamped, 19th Century, 8 In. 61.0
Candlestick, Freeman Porter, Westbrook, Maine, Turned Stem, Domed Foot, c.1850, 6 In. 812.0
Candlestick, Henry Hopper, New York, Turned & Tapered, 12 In. 1392.0
Candlestick, James Weekes, Turned, Flared Nozzle, Stepped Base, N.Y., c.1825, 7 In., Pair 1508.0
Candlestick, Roswell Gleason, Mass., 8½ In., Pair 1276.0
Candlestick, Rufus Dunham, Turned Stem, Domed Foot, Westbrook, Maine, 6 In., Pair 3248.0
Chalice, Dome Lid, Turned Stem, Ball Knop, Pennsylvania, c.1770, 11⅜ In. 1856.0
Chalice, Israel Trask, Squared Cup, Shaped Domed Foot, Beverly, Mass., 7 In., Pair 2088.0
Chalice, J.C. Heyne, Dome Lid, Ringed Ball Knop, Stepped Foot, 11 x 4½ In. 32480.0
Chalice, Peter Young, Turned & Stepped Stem & Foot, c.1800, 8⅛ In. 7540.0
Chalice, William Calder, Flared Rim, Short Foot, Providence, R.I., 6 In. 812.0
Charger, Beaded Rim, Roses, Crown, 18th Century, 13½ In. 412.0
Charger, Burford & Green, Crested, England, Late 18th Century, 18 In. 1740.0

harger, Lawrence Dyer, London, Mid 17th Century, 20 ¼ In. 460.00
harger, Nathaniel Austin, 15 In. 1740.00
harger, Punched, Scalloped Design Bands, 14 In. 144.00
harger, Richard Collier, Engraved Armorial Shield On Rim, 22 In. 546.00
harger, Samuel Hamlin, 13 In. 870.00
harger, Samuel Hamlin, Marked, 13 ½ In. 375.00
harger, Stamped, ICI On Upper Rim, 15 In. 90.00
offeepot, Boardman & Hart, Polished, Double Bulbous, Ivory Finial, Marked, 11 ½ In. 450.00
offeepot, Dome Lid, Boardman & Co., New York, c.1850, 11 ¾ In. 460.00
offeepot, F. Porter, Westbrook, No. 1, 7 In. 230.00
offeepot, Hinged Lid, Granite, Hinged Cover On Spout, c.1900, 10 In. 105.00
offeepot, Hinged Lid, Wood Finial, 19th Century, 9 x 4 ¾ In. 275.00
offeepot, Lighthouse, Eben Smith, 11 In. 754.00
offeepot, Lighthouse, Westbrook No. 1, Mark, F. Porter, c.1860, 10 ¾ In. 201.00
offeepot, Pear Shape, Sage & Beebe, Marked, 11 In. 300.00
offeepot, Roswell Gleason, Rosewood Handle & Finial, Marked, 10 In. 220.00
ream Pot, Peter Young, Baluster Shape, Shaped Handle, 4 Applied Feet, c.1800, 4 ⅜ In. 13340.00
ream Pot, William, Bulbous, Shaped Edge & Handle, Footed, 4 ⅝ In. 1740.00
ream Pot, William Will, Bulbous, Flared, 4 Knopped Feet, Philadelphia, 4 ¼ In. 5800.00
esk Set, Lift Lid, Divided Side, Removable Sander, Half Round Feet, 4 ¾ x 7 x 1 ¾ In. 115.00
ish, Deep, Blakeslee Barnes, 11 In. 406.00
ish, Deep, Jacob Whittemore, 13 In. 1044.00
ish, Hiram Yale, Banded Edge, Wallingford, Conn., c.1825, 1 ⅜ x 11 ¼ In. 696.00
ish, Hot Water, Lid, Removable Tray, Hinged End Handles, Wood Feet, 7 x 10 x 12 In. 143.00
wer, WMF, Dragonflies, Birds, Water Lilies, Hinged Lid, Marked, 9 ½ In. *illus* 29.00
lagon, Baluster Shape, Spout, Flared Foot, Straight Handle, Shell Thumb Piece, 11 In. 230.00
lagon, Boardman & Co., Strainer Spout, 5-Knuckle Hinge, c.1825, 9 In. 4350.00
lagon, Domed Lid, Boardman & Co., Thumb Latch, Eagle Mark, c.1850, 8 In. 2645.00
lagon, Hiram Yale, 5-Knuckle Hinge, Pedestal Foot, Wallingford, Conn., c.1825, 14 ½ In. 1508.00
lagon, Hunter & Dog, 3-Footed, Pewter Lid, c.1870, Liter, 12 ⅔ In. 490.00
lagon, Tiered Lid, Spherical Thumbpiece, Flared Foot, Continental, c.1771, 12 ½ In. 235.00
lagon, William Calder, 3-Knuckle Hinge, Providence, R.I., 11 In. 1044.00
ug, Boardman, Bulbous, Loop Handle, Lid, Stamped, 8 In. 523.00
ug, Bulbous, Loop Handle, Lid, 10 ½ In. 110.00
amp, Camphene, Acorn Font, Burner, Baluster Shaft, Stepped Base, c.1834, 10 In., Pair 3173.00
amp, Eben Smith, Beverly, Mass., Domed Foot, 9 ¼ x 4 In., Pair 1740.00
amp, Fluid, Glass Font, Baluster Turned Post, Continental, Early 1800s, 14 ½ In. 518.00
amp, Fluid, Lozenge Shape Font, Camphene Burner, Eben Smith, c.1871, 6 ¾ In. 646.00
amp, Fluid, Newell Patent, Cylindrical Font, Embossed Flowers, Dish Base, c.1853, 11 ⅝ In. 1116.00
amp, Kerosene, Grease, 12 In. 50.00
amp, Oil, Ephraim Capen & George Molineux, New York City, 4 ⅛ x 4 In. *illus* 522.00
amp, Oil, F. Porter, Acorn Font, Burning Fluid Burner, No. 2, Westbrook, 1860s, 7 ¾ In. 173.00
amp, Oil, Germany, Glass Reservoir, c.1780 495.00
amp, Oil, Glass Font, 13 ½ In. 72.00
amp, Oil, Removable Glass Bull's-Eye Magnifying Lens, Whale Oil Burner, 8 ½ In. 374.00
amp, Oil, Taunton Britannia, Taunton, Mass., Turned Stem, Footed, 7 x 3 ½ In. 232.00
amp, Whale Oil, Acorn Font, Baluster Shaft, Chapen & Molineux, c.1854, 10 In., Pair 646.00
amp, Whale Oil, Barrel Shape Font, Baluster Shaft, William H. Starr, c.1846, 10 ⅜ In. 382.00
amp, Whale Oil, Cylindrical Font, Early 19th Century, 7 ⅝ In., Pair 499.00
amp, Whale Oil, Cylindrical Font, James Putnam, c.1835, 6 ⅜ In., Pair 646.00
amp, Whale Oil, Cylindrical Font, Ring Handle, Ostrander, c.1854, 7 In., Pair 764.00
amp, Whale Oil, Cylindrical Font, Roswell Gleason, c.1871, 8 ¼ In., Pair 999.00
amp, Whale Oil, Lozenge Shape Font, Leaf & Flower Border Base, c.1871, 8 In., Pair 881.00
amp, Whale Oil, Lozenge Shape Font, Roswell Gleason, c.1871, 10 ¼ In., Pair 5288.00
amp, Whale Oil, Saucer Base, Brass Cap, R. Gleason, 5 ½ In. 413.00
amp, Whale Oil, Smith & Co. Marked, 8 In. 230.00
amp, Whale Oil, Truncated, Cone Shape Font, Roswell Gleason, c.1871, 6 ¾ In., Pair 558.00
leasure, Fillet, England, Qt., 6 ½ In. 51.00
leasure, James Yates, Belly Form, Signed, Birmingham, ½ Pt. 44.00
leasure, Timothy Boardman, Incised Rings, Cylindrical Rim, c.1815, 9 In. 6960.00
leasure, W. Scott, Bulbous, Flat Lid, Embryo Shell Thumbpiece, Marked, 1826, ½ Pt., 4 ¾ In. 148.00
leasure Set, Double Volute Baluster Lidded Shape, Scroll Handle, Bud Terminals, 4 Piece 9200.00
lug, David Melville, Shell Thumb Spot, Newport, R.I., 6 In. 5800.00
lug, Frederick Bassett, 2 Rings, Shaped Handle, c.1775, 4 ⅝ In. 7424.00
lug, Parks Boyd, Horizontal Rings, 4 ½ x 5 In. 14500.00
lug, Robert Palethorp, Jr., Shaped Handle, c.1820, 4 ½ x 5 ½ In. 5510.00

Pewter, Ewer, WMF, Dragonflies, Birds, Water Lilies, Hinged Lid, Marked, 9 ½ In.
$29.00

Pewter, Lamp, Oil, Ephraim Capen & George Molineux, New York City, 4 ⅛ x 4 In.
$522.00

Pewter, Pitcher, Nekrassoff, Beaded Openwork Base, Wood Handle, c.1940, 6 ½ In.
$175.00

Pewter, Porringer, Pierced Handle, American, 5½ In.
$288.00

Pewter, Tankard, Tulip Form, England, Late 18th Century, Qt., 7¾ In.
$420.00

To Sound Like a Pewter Collector, You Must Know These Terms

The eight-inch-plate era lasted from 1750 to 1825 in America. During those years, many undecorated plates measuring eight inches in diameter were made.

The coffeepot era was from 1825 to 1850. Pewter was made in shapes that imitated silver pieces.

Sadware refers to heavy pieces of pewter, like plates and trenchers hammered out of a single sheet of metal.

Hollow ware was cast.

Mug, Samuel Hamlin, Hartford, Conn., Scroll Handle, c.1770, 4⅜ In. 3480.00
Mug, T.D. Boardman & S. Boardman, 2 Handles, c.1850, 6 x 8 In. 3016.00
Mug, Thomas Danforth Boardman, Qt., 6 In. 2784.00
Pitcher, Freeman Porter, Bulbous, Rings, Westbrook, Maine, 6⅝ In. 696.00
Pitcher, George Richardson, Boston, Providence, Bulbous, Stepped Sides, 6½ In. 1508.00
Pitcher, Hinged Lid, Daniel Curtiss, Ball-Topped Domed Finial, c.1840, 8¾ In. 696.00
Pitcher, Nekrassoff, Beaded Openwork Base, Wood Handle, c.1940, 6½ In. *illus* 175.00
Plate, Ashvil Griswold, 8 In. 406.00
Plate, Blakslee Barns, Philadelphia, Eagle Mark, c.1817, 8 In. 201.00
Plate, Brunstrom, Rings, Love, 2 Lovebirds, c.1790, 6 In. 1392.00
Plate, Burford & Green, London, 8⅞ In. 110.00
Plate, Flat Brim, Stag Engraving, Hammered Bouge, Mid 1700s, 9¾ In., 6 Piece 805.00
Plate, G. Lightner, Marked, 7⅞ In. 280.00
Plate, I.B. Finck, J.F. London, 8¾ In. 66.00
Plate, John Skinner, Smooth Rim, Hammered Bouge, Boston, 9⅛ In. 1160.00
Plate, Love, London, Marked, Crowned X, 12 In. 381.00
Plate, Samuel Danforth, Single Reed Brim, Eagle Touchmark, Hallmark, c.1800, 7⅞ In. 382.00
Plate, Samuel Hamlin, Maker's Cartouche, 4 Hallmarks, c.1800, 13½ In. 470.00
Plate, Scalloped, Cast, Continental, Early 20th Century, 9¾ In., 8 Piece 161.00
Plate, Semper Eadem, Boston, Mass., 8⅜ In. 928.00
Plate, T. Danforth II, Molded Edge, Maker's Mark Stamp, c.1780, 6⅛ In. 3712.00
Plate, T. Danforth III, Banded Edge, 7¾ In. 348.00
Plate, Thomas Badger, 8 In. 144.00
Plate, Townsend, Early 17th Century, 8 In. 35.00
Plate, W. Billings, Polished, Marked, 8¼ In. 750.00
Platter, Oval, Beaded Rim, England, 18th Century, 15 x 19¾ In. 231.00
Porringer, Boss Bottom, Crown Handle, Marked WM, Dots Under Handle, c.1800, 4⅝ In. 235.00
Porringer, Coronet Handle, 3⅞ In. Diam. 185.00
Porringer, Elisha Kirk, Tab Handle, Cutout Hole, York, Pa., 2 x 7⅛ In. 1276.00
Porringer, Flowered Handle, Marker's Mark, Figure Of Neptune, Early 1800s, 1¾ x 5 In. 499.00
Porringer, Frederick Bassett, Old English Handle, c.1800, 4⅜ In. 230.00
Porringer, Frederick Bassett, Scrolled Openwork Tab Handle, c.1775, 7⅜ In. 6032.00
Porringer, Hamlin, Flowered Handle, Eagle Mark, c.1801, 5½ In. 805.00
Porringer, IG, Crown Handle, Polished, Marked, Linen Mark, 4⅔ In. 275.00
Porringer, John Bassett, Scrolled Openwork Tab Handle, c.1750, 6¼ In. 17400.00
Porringer, John Will, Scrolled Openwork Tab Handle, N.Y., c.1750, 7⅜ In. 8584.00
Porringer, Pierced Handle, American, 5½ In. *illus* 288.00
Porringer, Richard Lee, Springfield, Vt., c.1815, 3¼ In. 232.00
Porringer, Samuel Green, Jr., Crown Handle, Marked, SG, Boston, 5½ In. 201.00
Porringer, TD & SB, Crown Handle, Polished, Marked, Linen Mark, 5 In. 450.00
Porringer, William Will, Scrolled Openwork Tab Handle, Philadelphia, c.1775, 7½ In. 3248.00
Salt, John Will, Flared, Beaded Edge, Stepped Foot, Philadelphia, c.1775, 2⅜ In., Pair 2088.00
Salt & Pepper, Handle, Clear Plastic Stopper, 2½ In. 36.00
Salt & Pepper, Mushroom Shape 19.00
Sconce, Continental, Double C-Scroll Arm, Cylindrical Socket, 19½ In., Pair 1102.00
Spirit Measure, Marked GR, c.1720, Pt. 495.00
Spoon, John Will, Squared Handle, N.Y., c.1750 6960.00
Spoon, William Bradford, Squared Handle, New York, c.1750, 6⅝ In. 3712.00
Spoon Set, Mark On Handle End, 19th Century, 6⅝ In., 6 Piece 288.00
Stein, Seymour Mann, Detroit Yacht Club, 1973, 16 x 10 In. 60.00
Sugar, Cover, George Richardson, Boston, Providence, 5 x 6½ In. 3712.00
Sugar, Cover, Round, Stepped Rings, Footed, Connecticut, c.1830, 5½ In. 1160.00
Sugar, Cover, T.D. Boardman, L. Hart, Footed, 6 x 8½ In. 1044.00
Sugar, Inverted Bell Shape, Scrolled Handles, Hallmark, Crown Over X, 1700s, 4 x 6¾ In. 345.00
Sugar, Stepped Domed Lid, William Will, Pinched Waist, Footed, 5 In. 3712.00
Syrup, Lid, Sellew & Co. Cincinnati, Marked, 5½ In. 15.50
Tablespoon, Charles Parker, Meriden, Conn., 8 In., Pair 232.00
Tablespoon, Garry I. Mix, Wallingford, Conn., 8¼ In. 174.00
Tablespoon, Robert Palethorpe, Jr., Philadelphia, 8½ In. 290.00
Tankard, Dome Lid, Tulip Shape, Footed, Open Chair Thumblift, c.1800, Qt., 7¾ In. 403.00
Tankard, Hinged Dome Lid, John Will, Shaped Handle & Thumblift, N.Y., 7⅜ In. 23200.00
Tankard, Hinged Lid, J. Brunstrom, Ringed Bands, Beaded Edges, Shaped Handle, 7½ In. 30160.00
Tankard, Hinged Lid, John Will, Engraved, Barrel & Lid, N.Y., c.1750, 7 In. 49880.00
Tankard, Hinged Lid, Joseph Leddel, Sr., Shaped Handle & Thumblift, c.1750, 7 In. 60320.00
Tankard, Hinged Lid, William Kirby, Shaped Handle & Thumblift, New York, c.1780, 7 In. 11600.00
Tankard, Lid, Mason Design, c.1798 132.00

ankard, Semper Eadem, Boston, Mass., 6¾ In. 6960.00
ankard, Tulip Form, England, Late 18th Century, Qt., 7¾ In. .... *illus* 420.00
appit Hen, Lid, Marked, Scotland, 10⅜ In. 175.00
ea Set, Royal Holland, Tray, Coffeepot, Teapot, Sugar, Creamer, c.1950 .... 59.00
eapot, Bailey & Putnam, Gooseneck, Scroll Handle, Black Paint, Stamped, 11 In. 330.00
eapot, Boardman & Hart, Gooseneck, Scroll Handle, Stamped, N.Y., 11½ In. 44.00
eapot, Boardman & Hart, Polished, Marked, 8 In. 325.00
eapot, Charles Yale, Painted Handle, Wafer, Wallingford, c.1824, 8 In. 201.00
eapot, Dome Lid, Bulbous, Ringed, Domed Lid, c.1770, 6⅛ x 8 In. 1160.00
eapot, Dome Lid, J. Brunstrom, Ball Shape, Pinched, Beaded Bands, Lovebirds, 7 x 9 In. 18560.00
eapot, Dome Lid, John Townsend, Treen Handle, Squat Pear Form, 3-Footed, 6 In. 1972.00
eapot, Dome Lid, Scrolled Handle, Cylindrical, 19th Century 402.00
eapot, Dome Lid, William Will, Wooden Handle, Beaded Rings, c.1775, 7 In. .... *illus* 47560.00
eapot, Enamel Body, Flower Bouquets, Individual, 1800s, 5½ x 6½ In. 130.00
eapot, George Richardson, c.1845, 7¾ In. 522.00
eapot, Hiram Yale, 3-Knuckle Hinge, Wallingford, Conn., c.1825, 10¼ x 10 In. 928.00
eapot, Israel Trask, Oval Body, Straight Spout, Beverly, Mass., 5¾ In. 872.00
eapot, Israel Trask, Oval Body, Shaped Spout, Ball Feet, Beverly, Mass., 7 x 10 In. 3840.00
eapot, J. Danforth, Squat, Gooseneck, Scroll Handle, Black Paint, Stamped, 7 In. 66.00
eapot, James Dixon & Sons, Marked, 1 Cup, 4½ In. 78.00
eapot, LL Williams, Gooseneck, Scroll Handle, Philadelphia, Pa., 10½ In. 248.00
eapot, Roswell Gleason, c.1840, 8½ In. 260.00
eapot, Samuel Kilbourn, Hartford, Conn., Bulbous, Flared Foot, 8¾ x 8¼ In. 5104.00
eapot, Smith & Co., Cylindrical, Canted Sides, Scroll Handle, Hallmark, 7½ In. 210.00
eapot, T.D. Boardman, Marked, 9¼ In. 325.00
eapot, Townsend & Compton, Pear Shape, Wood Handle, Bone Finial, c.1784 .... 2450.00
eapot, Undertray, Drum Shape, Wooden Handle, Finials, Engraved, 4½ x 10 In., Pair 460.00
ray, Hammered, Middle Eastern, 21 In. 409.00
ray, Hugo Leven, Waterlily, Dragonfly Handles, c.1898, 11¾ x 18½ In. .... *illus* 3125.00
rophy, Uniformed Male & Female Riding Safeties, 19th Century, 9½ In. 138.00
ase, Figural, Mermaid, 2 Infants, Fishing Net, Dolphin, 13¾ In. 5625.00
ase, Helgi Joennsen, Sculptural, Norway, c.1982, 13 x 9 In. 293.00
ase, Irises, Peonies, Gourd Shape, Inward Flared Lip, Germany, 1885-1910, 21 x 11 In. 460.00
ase, Liberty & Co., Hammered, Original Patina, 5 x 9½ In. 1020.00
ase, Tudric, Heart Shape Leaves, Enamel Over Foil, 7¾ In. .... *illus* 850.00

HOENIX BIRD, or Flying Phoenix, is the name given to a blue-and-white kitchenware opular between 1900 and World War II. A variant is known as Flying Turkey. Most of this innerware was made in Japan for sale in the dime stores in America. It is still being made.

owl, Dessert, Birds, Flowers, Vines, Marked Japan, 5 In. 15.00
up, Bird, Vines 5.00
up & Saucer, Blue & White, Japan, 1930s, 4 Sets 26.00
late, Blue & White, Footed, 7⅛ In. 10.00
ugar & Creamer, Scrolled Vines, Grasses, Round, Loop Handles, Marked Japan 45.00

HOENIX GLASS Company was founded in 1880 in Pennsylvania. The firm made commercial roducts, such as lampshades, bottles, and glassware. Collectors today are interested in the 'Sculptured Artware" made by the company from the 1930s until the mid-1950s. Some ieces of Phoenix glass are very similar to those made by the Consolidated Lamp and Glass Company. hoenix made Reuben Blue, lavender, and yellow pieces. These colors were not used by Consolidated. In 970 Phoenix became a division of Anchor Hocking, then was sold to the Newell Group in 1987. The ompany is still working.

ase, Love Birds, White, Metal Frame, 11 x 9 In. 146.00

PHONOGRAPHS, invented by Thomas Edison in 1877, have been made by many firms. This category also includes other items associated with the phonograph. Jukeboxes and Records are listed in their own categories.

Busy Bee, Cylinder, Box Bottom, Reproducer, Key, Black Conical Gold Band Horn, Box 770.00
Busy Bee, Grand, Disc, Turntable, Red Morning Glory Horn, Case, 11½ In. 529.00
Columbia, AB McDonald, Cylinder, Regular Size & 5-In. Diameter Cylinders 1760.00
Columbia, Graphophone, Model AK, Disc, Brass Bell Horn 770.00
Columbia, Graphophone, Model BI, Disc, Mica Reproducer, Oak Case, Horn, 21 In. 823.00
Edison, A-100, Oak Case, Floor Model, Diamond Disc Unit 165.00
Edison, Amberola, Model VI, Cylinder, Mahogany Case 358.00

TIP
Don't store pewter near cardboard or vinegar. The fumes will cause damage.

Pewter, Teapot, Dome Lid, William Will, Wooden Handle, Beaded Rings, c.1775, 7 In.
$47560.00

Pewter, Tray, Hugo Leven, Waterlily, Dragonfly Handles, c.1898, 11¾ x 18½ In.
$3125.00

Pewter, Vase, Tudric, Heart Shape Leaves, Enamel Over Foil, 7¾ In.
$850.00

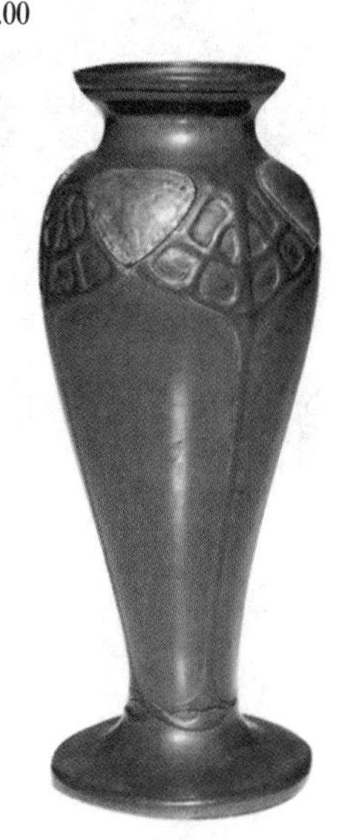

Phonograph, Edison, Fireside, Reproducer, Morning Glory Horn, Oak, 45 Cylinders, 1905, 34 In.
$1600.00

Phonograph, Edison, Standard, Oak Case, Dome Lid, Crane, Flower, Cylinders
$588.00

Phonograph, Fern-O-Grand Co., Baby Grand Piano Form, Mahogany Case, Tapered Legs, 35 In.
$940.00

Edison, Amberola, Model VIII, No. 7500, Oak Case, Internal Horn, 14 In. 411.0
Edison, Concert, Floor Stand, Concert Horn, Perfect Record, c.1899, 15 x 16½ In. 3300.0
Edison, Cylinder, C Reproducer, Crank 605.0
Edison, Diamond Disc, Mahogany, Table, Model B-19, 2 Reproducers 165.0
Edison, Drip Pan, Cylinder, Early Reproducer, Key, Black Conical Horn 880.0
Edison, Fireside, Combination Reproducer, Oak Case, Morning Glory Horn, 1905 .... 1890.0
Edison, Fireside, Model A, Cylinder Unit, Cygnet Horn 578.0
Edison, Fireside, Model B, Soundbox Model, Diamond B, Cygnet Horn, c.1912 .... 2843.0
Edison, Fireside, Reproducer, Morning Glory Horn, Oak, 45 Cylinders, 1905, 34 In. .... *illus* 1600.0
Edison, Home, Model B, Cylinder, Cygnet Horn No. 10, c.1906 .... 1338.0
Edison, Home, Reproducer, Oak Case, Witch's Hat Horn, 41 In. 705.0
Edison, Model, Oak Case, Dome Lid, Crane, Cygnet Horn, 18 x 20½ In. 2585.0
Edison, Standard, Oak Case, Dome Lid, Crane, Flower, Cylinders .... *illus* 588.0
Edison, Triumph, Cylinder, Brass Bell, Witch's Hat Horn, 1903 .... 990.0
Edison, Triumph, Model A, Cylinder, C Reproducer 825.0
Edison Standard, 3 Cylinders, Crank, 13 In. 303.0
Fern-O-Grand Co., Baby Grand Piano Form, Mahogany Case, Tapered Legs, 35 In. .... *illus* 940.0
Gramophone, Anchor, Wood, Collapsible, Kosmophon Soundbox, Swiss 368.0
Gramophone, Coin-Operated, Mammut, Oak Case, Coin Drawer, Tin Horn, Germany 2007.0
Gramophone, Miniature, Gipsy, Completely Collapsible, Leather Bag 414.0
Pathe Coq., Model 25, Cylinder Machine, France, c.1904 .... 569.0
Victor, M Disc, Victrola No. 2 Reproducer, Green Flowered Back 2035.0
Victor, Model Type M, Soundbox, Oak Case, Brass Morning Glory Horn, 12½ In. 940.0
Victor, Model VV-50, Mahogany, Suitcase, Portable, Disc, No. 2 Reproducer 110.0
Victor, Model VV-X, Floor Model, Oak Case, Disc 138.0
Victor, Model VV-XIV, Oak, Floor, Exhibition Reproducer 385.0
Victor, P2 Front Mount Disc, Crank, Brass Bell Horn 2200.0
Victor, Standard, Soundbox, Double Spring Motor, Oak Case, Tin Horn 646.0
Victor Victrola, Mahogany, 43 In. 144.0
Victor VV110, Mahogany 28.0
Victrola, Mahogany, Bowed Case, Double Doors, 50 x 24 In. 605.0
Victrola, Model VV-4-3, Walnut, Floor Model, Orthophonic Reproducer 303.0
Victrola, Model VV-50, Mahogany, Suitcase Model, Victrola, No. 2 Reproducer 88.0
Victrola, Model VV-IV, Table Model, Exhibition Reproducer, Oak Case 132.0
Victrola, Model VV-IX, Table Model, Oak Case, Victrola 2 Reproducer 143.0

PHONOGRAPH NEEDLE CASES of tin are collected today by music and phonograph enthusiasts and advertising addicts. The tins are very small, about 2 inches across, and often have attractive graphic designs lithographed on the top and sides.

Pfanstiehl, Lightweight Crystal Pick Ups, Original Package 5.0

PHOTOGRAPHY items are listed here. The first photograph was a view from a window in France taken in 1826. The commercially successful photograph started with the daguerreotype introduced in 1839. Today all sorts of photographs and photographic equipment are collected. Albums were popular in Victorian times. Cartes de visite, popular after 1854, were mounted on 2½-by-4-inch cardboard. Cabinet cards were introduced in 1866. These were mounted on 4 ¼-by-6½-inch cards. Stereo views are listed under Stereo Card. The cases for daguerreotypes are listed in the Gutta-Percha category. Stereoscopes are listed in their own section.

Album, Albumen Prints, Poetry, Verses, Inscriptions, 1863-74, 8½ x 5½ In. 748.0
Album, Lady Fencer, Flowers, Celluloid, Velvet Back, Gilt Edge, 12 Pages, 10 x 8 x 2 In. 210.0
Albumen Print, Black Laborers In Virginia, A.J. Russell, 19 x 12½ In. 980.0
Albumen Print, Civil War, Officer, N.Y. 12th Regt., 4½ x 3 In. 35.0
Albumen Print, Civil War Regiment In Uniforms, Drummer, Tents, 4½ x 7¾ In. 300.0
Albumen Print, Skulls Of The Cliff Dwellers, W.H. Jackson, 4 x 6½ In. 300.0
Albumen Print, Zouave, Armed Soldier, Marmaduke Myron Haggerty, 6 x 4 In. 153.0
Ambrotype, Abraham Lincoln, Bearded, Inlaid Wood Case, 1860s, 5¼ x 2¾ In. 2988.0
Ambrotype, Antebellum Militiaman, South Carolina, Velvet Liner, ½ Plate 2160.0
Ambrotype, Bearded Man Holding Diploma, 1858, ⅙ Plate 1035.0
Ambrotype, Building In Marysville, Cal., Mounted, ½ Case, ½ Plate 1150.0
Ambrotype, California Frontiersman, Seated 1150.0
Ambrotype, Captain, Federal, Frock Coat, Eagle Buttons, Case, ⅙ Plate 179.0
Ambrotype, Curious Young Man, Ruby, Thermoplastic Case, 1862, ⅑ Plate 155.0
Ambrotype, Gentleman, Double-Breasted Waistcoat, 1850s, ⅙ Plate 239.0
Ambrotype, Gentleman, Octagonal, Thermoplastic Case, 1860s, ⅑ Plate 179.0
Ambrotype, Looking Down Road At Farm, Ruby Glass 391.0

Ambrotype, Man, Apron, Symbols, Metal Frame Border, 4 ¼ x 3 ¼ In. 77.00
Ambrotype, Nautical Man, Smoking Pipe, ⅑ Plate 253.00
Ambrotype, Naval Officer, Sword, ¼ Plate 400.00
Ambrotype, Portrait Of Gentleman, Thermoplastic Case, 1860s, 1/16 Plate 179.00
Ambrotype, Postmortem, Turner Ashby, General Confederate, ⅑ Plate, Leather Case 8365.00
Ambrotype, Professional Gentleman, Thermoplastic Case, 1860s, ⅑ Plate 120.00
Ambrotype, Ruby, Corporal, Federal, Company F, ⅑ Plate, Gutta Percha Case 598.00
Ambrotype, Two Women In Gentlemanly Hats, Gilded Earrings, Pins, ¼ Plate 322.00
Ambrotype, Two Young Women, Seated Beneath Large Painting, 1860s, ⅑ Plate 143.00
Ambrotype, Young Girl, Brass Mat, Temple Facade, 1860s, ¼ Plate 299.00
Baker's Park, Silverton Sultan Mountain, Silver Gelatin, W.H. Jackson, 16 x 20 In. 551.00
Cabinet Card, Colorado Civil War Vet, Seated, GAR Badge Medals, c.1863 .... 230.00
Cabinet Card, Custer's Scout Curley, Mounted 1380.00
Cabinet Card, D.F. Barry & Chief Gall 920.00
Cabinet Card, George Armstrong Custer, In Uniform, April 23, 1876 .... 5463.00
Cabinet Card, George Armstrong Custer, Joseph, Mora, July, 1876 .... 3335.00
Cabinet Card, Joseph, Nez Perce, Military Leader, c.1877 .... 632.00
Cabinet Card, Kiowa Annie, In Hide & Elk Tooth Dress, Hands Behind Head 230.00
Cabinet Card, Kiowa Girls, Dressed, On Horseback 316.00
Cabinet Card, Kiowa Woman, Flower Shawl, Child In Beaded Cradle 316.00
Cabinet Card, Lady Sharpshooter, Mirror, Bo Durtha, Delaware, Ohio .... *illus* 518.00
Cabinet Card, Libbie Custer, Inscribed Herbert Swett, 1870 .... 1150.00
Cabinet Card, Sioux Chief John Grass 460.00
Cabinet Card, Sitting Bull, Command At The Custer Massacre, 1889, 4 ¼ x 6 ½ In. 1715.00
Camera, Atlas, Automatic, Metal, Roussel Trylor 4.5/90 Lens, France, 1945 .... 737.80
Camera, Brownie, No. 2, Model D, Box, 120 Roll Film, c.1933, 5 ¾ x 3 ¼ In. 12.00
Camera, Canon VT, Canon 1.4/50 mm Lens, Japan, 1956 .... 736.00
Camera, Cyclope, Alsaphot, France, 1950 .... 1079.00
Camera, Ducati, Simplex, No. 17610, Etar 3.5/35 mm Lens, Italy, c.1950 .... 417.00
Camera, Ernemann, Tropen-Heag XI, Teak, Brown Bellows, Brass Fittings, Dresden, 1917 .... 1799.00
Camera, Franke & Heidecke, Rolleiflex 3.5, Fplanar, 75 mm Lens, 1960 .... 572.00
Camera, Franke & Heidecke, Rolleiflex T, First Model, Gray Leather, Case, 1958 .... 280.00
Camera, Hill's Cloud 180 Degree, Mahogany, R. & J. Beck Ltd., London, 1923, 6 In. 12756.00
Camera, Horne & Thornthwaite, Wet Plate, Wood, Brass Lens, London, c.1858 .... 1472.00
Camera, Kodak, AG Single Lens, Roll Film, Leather Case, Nagel-Werke 1932 .... 60.00
Camera, Kodak Retina IIC, 35 mm, Leather Case, 20th Century 35.00
Camera, Leica, 72, No. 357174, 1954 .... 20442.00
Camera, Leica, 250 Reporter, FF, No. 135615, 1934 .... 7360.00
Camera, Leica, IIF 35 mm, NR 712305, Elmar 3.5 Lens, Flash, Filter, Manual 450.00
Camera, Leica, IIIC, K-Model, No. 389602 K, 1942 .... *illus* 1472.00
Camera, Leica, M3, No. 1066590, Chrome, Summicron 2.5 mm Lens, 1962 .... 1635.00
Camera, Leica, M4-2, No. 1528547, Gold Plated, Black Snake Covering, 1979 .... 2453.00
Camera, Leitz, Leicaflex, SL2 Model, 1:2/50 Lens, Telephoto Lens, Leather Case 518.00
Camera, Minolta, V3, Rokkor-PF 1.8, 45 mm Lens, Japan, 1960 .... 1390.00
Camera, Movie, Akeley 35 mm, Stand 1708.00
Camera, Movie, Ernemann Kinette, 35 mm, Dresden, Germany, c.1925 .... 818.00
Camera, Movie, Keystone, Model K-8, 8 mm, Manual, Case, Filters, Cap, c.1935 .... 30.00
Camera, Photoret, Pocket Watch Shape, Box, Magic Introduction, N.Y., 1894, 3 In. 1226.00
Camera, Super Kodak Six-20, 1938 .... *illus* 2225.00
Camera, Voigtlander, Prominent, Model 3, 35 mm, Germany, 1957 .... 393.00
Camera, Zeiss Ikon, Hologon, No. R97313, Black, 15 mm Lens 2703.00
Carte De Visite, 39 Union Generals & Others, J.B. Westbrook & Co., c.1866, 2 ½ x 4 In. 896.00
Carte De Visite, Blind Tom, Idiot Savant, Piano Playing Slave 690.00
Carte De Visite, Boston Corbett, Standing By Chair, In Union Blues 837.00
Carte De Visite, Frederick Douglass, Printed Title Line .... *illus* 633.00
Carte De Visite, General U.S. Grant, H.A. Balch's Star Photograph Gallery, 4 x 2 ⅜ In. 70.00
Carte De Visite, Gordon, Escaped Slave, Bull Whipping Scars, c.1863 .... 4025.00
Carte De Visite, Major General Lew Wallace 418.00
Carte De Visite, Masonic, Black Man, C.C. Giers, Nashville, Tenn. 70.00
Carte De Visite, Chester A. Arthur, 4 ½ x 2 ½ In. 30.00
Carte De Visite, Union Civil War Soldier, Theo. Lilienthal, New Orleans, 4 x 2 ½ In. 100.00
Case, Moses Among Bulrushes, Thermoplastic, 1850s, ⅑ Plate 90.00
Daguerreotype, 2 Girls, One Eating Watermelon, Black Americana, 7 x 3 ½ In. 40.00
Daguerreotype, 3 Men In Hats, ⅙ Plate 550.00
Daguerreotype, Andrew Jackson, 19th Century, 1/16 Plate 1434.00
Daguerreotype, Antebellum Virginia House, Greenhouse, ¼ Plate, Leather Case 4600.00

Photography, Cabinet Card,
Lady Sharpshooter, Mirror, Bo Durtha,
Delaware, Ohio
$518.00

Photography, Camera, Leica, IIIC,
K-Model, No. 389602 K, 1942
$1472.00

Photography, Camera,
Super Kodak Six-20, 1938
$2225.00

P

Photography, Carte De Visite, Frederick Douglass, Printed Title Line
$633.00

Photography, Daguerreotype, Woman, Blue Dress, Shawl, Stippled, Scalloped Mat, ½ to ¼ Plate
$460.00

TIP

Never touch the surface of a daguerreotype or an ambrotype. The perspiration will stain the image.

Daguerreotype, Boy, Blue Tinted Coat, Up-Raised Eyes, Leather Case, ⅙ Plate . . . 96.00
Daguerreotype, Boy, Fancy Dress, Reclining, Oval Mat, ¼ Plate . . . 529.00
Daguerreotype, Boy, Plaid Dress, Tinted, ¼ Plate . . . 7320.00
Daguerreotype, California Gold Miner, ⅙ Plate . . . 600.00
Daguerreotype, Display Case, 42 ⅙ Plate, Old Acquaintance, Boston, 1857, 31 x 19 In. . . . 5490.00
Daguerreotype, Elderly Couple, Thermoplastic Case, 1850s, ¼ Plate . . . 299.00
Daguerreotype, Family Of 4, Southworth & Hawes, Frame, Whole Plate . . . 25620.00
Daguerreotype, French Family, Parents, Child, Oval Frame, c.1850, ¼ Plate . . . 229.00
Daguerreotype, Gentleman, Top Hat, Seaside, ⅙ Plate . . . 600.00
Daguerreotype, Girl, Thermoplastic Case, 1850s, ⅑ Plate . . . 102.00
Daguerreotype, John Grover, Father, Child In Arms, Inscription, ⅙ Plate . . . 235.00
Daguerreotype, Little Girl, Seated, Long Curls, Holding Book, Tinted, ⅙ Plate . . . 180.00
Daguerreotype, Man, Lots Of Hair, Oval Mat, Full Case, ⅙ Plate . . . 391.00
Daguerreotype, Man, Lying In Bed, ⅙ Plate . . . 1035.00
Daguerreotype, Man, Quill Pen, Copy, Mat, ⅙ Plate, 2 Piece . . . 1500.00
Daguerreotype, Man, Scar On Upper Lip, Seated, Clutching Vest, ½ Case, ⅙ Plate . . . 36.00
Daguerreotype, Man, Seated, Reverse-Painted, 2 Plates . . . 161.00
Daguerreotype, Mother, 1 Girl, 2 Boys, Leather Case, 1858, ¼ Plate . . . 575.00
Daguerreotype, Mother, Postmortem Child, Gold, Tinted Jewelry, Brown Case, ⅙ Plate . . . 288.00
Daguerreotype, Portrait, Woman, Gilt Mat, Leather Case, ⅙ Plate . . . 29.00
Daguerreotype, Portrait, Woman, Thermoplastic Case, Oval, 1850s, ⅑ Plate . . . 90.00
Daguerreotype, Presidents Up Through Incumbent Zachary Taylor, 6 ½ x 3 ½ In. . . . 2390.00
Daguerreotype, Profile, Man Looking Down, ⅙ Plate . . . 460.00
Daguerreotype, Union Soldier & Wife, Company F Kentucky 108th Infantry, ¼ Plate . . . 6100.00
Daguerreotype, View Of Richmond, Virginia, Frame, c.1850, Whole Plate . . . 7930.00
Daguerreotype, Woman, Blue Dress, Shawl, Stippled, Scalloped Mat, ½ to ¼ Plate . . . *illus* 460.00
Daguerreotype, Woman, Bonnet, Son, ¼ Plate . . . 420.00
Daguerreotype, Woman, Child On Lap, ¼ Plate . . . 173.00
Daguerreotype, Woman, Eyeglasses On Forehead, ¼ Plate, 3 ½ In. . . . 185.00
Daguerreotype, Woman, In Deep Thought, Chin In Hand, Brown Case, ⅙ Plate . . . 156.00
Daguerreotype, Woman & Son, Holding Hands, ⅙ Plate . . . 600.00
Daguerreotype, Woman Wearing Cross, Hair In Ribbons, ⅙ Plate . . . 276.00
Daguerreotype, Young Hunter, Dog, Rifle, Rabbit, ⅙ Plate . . . 2250.00
Daguerreotype, Young Man, Full Suit, Somber Stare, Hexagonal Mat, Gold Foil, ⅙ Plate . . . 36.00
Daguerreotype, Young Woman, Thermoplastic Case, 1850s, ⅑ Plate . . . 90.00
Ferrotype, 2 Stern Wheel Steamboats, Horse, Wagons, W.L. Dugger, 1880s, 6 x 8 In. . . . 1610.00
Flash Pistol, Gutta Percha Grips, Trigger, Brass Bowl, 7 In. . . . 287.00
Magic Lantern, Painted, Tin, Slides, Figure Of Man, 19th Century, 15 In. . . . 110.00
Optical Box, Wood, Multicolored, Round Viewing Window, c.1800, 7 x 23 ½ In. . . . 7475.00
Orotone, Canyon De Chelly, Arts & Crafts Frame, Edward Curtis, 15 x 18 In. . . . 9500.00
Photograph, Apollo Theater, Harlem, Performer On Stage, 1937, 9 ⅛ x 7 ⅛ In. . . . 1035.00
Photograph, Apollo XI Astronauts, Signatures, 10 x 8 In., 3 Piece . . . 978.00
Photograph, Billie Holiday, 1949, 12 ¼ x 9 ¾ In. . . . 863.00
Photograph, Blackfoot Mountain Powwow, Blackfoot Montana, Black & White, c.1910, 20 x 28 In. 4200.00
Photograph, Buffalo Bill, Seated, Holding Rifle, 11 x 14 In. . . . 3738.00
Photograph, Calamity Jane, 1900 . . . 1840.00
Photograph, Canyon Twilight, Aquatint, Harold Lukens Doolittle, Frame, 9 x 11 In. . . . 236.00
Photograph, Doc Carver, Champion Rifle Shot, 1879 . . . 2415.00
Photograph, Dust Storm, Cimarron County, 1936, 19 x 19 In. . . . 2990.00
Photograph, Fighting Cocks, Mat, 8 x 10 In. . . . 506.00
Photograph, Fredericksburg, Stone Wall, A.J. Russell, c.1863, 11 ½ x 14 ¾ In. . . . 2760.00
Photograph, General Sherman & His Generals, Mathew Brady, 13 x 17 In. . . . 1232.00
Photograph, Indian, Crazy Bull, Tinted, Platinum, F.A. Rinehart, c.1899, 7 x 9 In. . . . 590.00
Photograph, Indian, Mrs. Lone Elk, Sioux, F.A. Rinehart, c.1899, 7 x 9 In. . . . 177.00
Photograph, Indian, Papoose White Bull, Platinum, F.A. Rinehart, c.1900, 5 x 9 In. . . . 366.00
Photograph, Indian, Thomas No Water, Sioux, Heyn Photo, c.1899, 7 x 9 In. . . . 531.00
Photograph, Indian, Tree Grave, Crow, F.A. Rinehart, c.1900, 7 ½ x 9 In. . . . 330.00
Photograph, Indian War Troopers, Log Garrison Building, 4 ¾ x 6 ½ In. . . . 33.00
Photograph, Masked Children, Mat, 1903, 8 ¼ x 6 ⅞ In. . . . 299.00
Photograph, Mixed Race Meeting, Black, White Women, Singing In Parlor, 9 x 8 In. . . . 1673.00
Photograph, Orotone, Mirror Lake, Arts & Crafts Frame, Asahel Curtis, 14 x 17 In. . . . 2500.00
Photograph, Orotone, Trail To Paradise, Norman Edson, Frame, 17 x 14 In. . . . 1750.00
Photograph, Pasquale Nava, Italian Sculptor, 1998, 8 ⅛ x 6 ⅜ In. . . . 345.00
Photograph, Pawnee Bill, Buffalo Bill, Wild West Performer, 5 x 7 In. . . . 690.00
Photograph, Plains Indian Chief, c.1890, 8 ¼ x 6 ¼ In. . . . 748.00
Photograph, Red Tomahawk, Lakota Indian Policeman, 6 x 7 In. . . . 2530.00

hotograph, Redwood Giants, Aquatint, Harold Lukens Doolitte, Frame, 12 x 10 In. 177.00
hotograph, Sarah Vaughan, 1950, 12 ¼ x 9 ⅞ In.. .... 863.00
hotograph, Scene From Siegfried Opera, January 15, 1926, 12 x 8 ¼ In. 230.00
hotograph, Sitting Bull, Silver Gelatin, Mounted, 7 ½ x 4 ¾ In. 1610.00
hotograph, Sitting Bull & Family, 9 x 11 ¼ In. 1265.00
hotograph, Where Flowers & Glaciers Meet, Mat Silver Bromide, 18 x 22 In.. .... 300.00
hotograph, Woman Displaying Navajo Blankets, Baskets, Blue Tinted, 5 x 7 In. 236.00
latinum Print, Black Catholic Nun, Holding Pair Of Glasses, Mounted, 11 x 14 In. 980.00
latinum Print, Paul Robeson, Mounted, Doris Ulmann, 11 x 14 In.. .... 956.00
latinum Print, Woman In Field Of Daisies, Mounted, Doris Ulmann, 11 x 14 In. 1470.00
ilver Print, Makah Indian Spinning Yarn, c.1897. .... 800.00
intype, African-American Woman, Seated, Holding Fan, 7 x 10 In. 1315.00
intype, Armed Union Soldier, 1860s, ¼ Plate 598.00
intype, Black Child, Seated On Fringed Stool, 3 ½ x 2 ½ In. 94.00
intype, Black Nanny, White Child, Oval Thermoplastic Frame, ½ Plate, 8 ¼ In.. .... *illus* 1380.00
intype, Civil War, The Holy Family, Thermoplastic Case, 1860s, ½ Plate 359.00
intype, Civil War Soldier, 2 Flags, Gilded, ⅙ Plate 437.00
intype, Dissection, Man In White Laboratory Coat, Holds Skeleton 437.00
intype, Infantryman, Confederate, Armed, Gilt Detail, ½ Case, 2 x 3 ½ In.. .... 478.00
intype, Infantryman, Federal, Armed, Musket, Gutta Percha Case, ⅙ Plate. 263.00
intype, Man, Bearded, In Suit, Full Plate, 8 ½ x 6 ½ In.. .... 11.00
intype, Man In Bowler, Wearing White Suspenders, c.1880, ⅙ Plate. 311.00
intype, Middle Aged Couple, c.1870, ⅑ Plate 120.00
intype, New Orleans Dandy, 1860, ⅑ Plate 143.00
intype, Pennsylvania Soldier, Dandy, Narrow Brim Hat, Composition Case, ⅑ Plate. 403.00
intype, Portrait Of Pugnacious Tyke, Thermoplastic Wall Frame, 1860s, ¼ Plate 239.00
intype, Soldier, Confederate, Clay Pipe, Long Scarf, Gilt Brass Mat, ½ Case, ½ Plate 837.00
intype, Soldier, Federal, Armed, Third Corp Badge, Gutta Percha Case, ⅙ Plate 837.00
intype, Store Front, African-American Men, Women, Children, Ox Cart, 4 x 2 ½ In.. .... 135.00
intype, Union Soldiers, Before Chickamauga, Gilt Brass Frame, ¼ Plate 3345.00
intype, Woman, 2 Daughters, By Fence Of Farmhouse, Pond, 4 x 6 In. 300.00
intype, Young Man In Uniform, Thermoplastic Case, Oval, 1860s, ¹⁄₁₆ Plate 120.00
iewing Case, ⅑ & ¼ Daguerreotype Plates 4255.00

IANO BABY is a collector's term. About 1880, the well-decorated home had a shawl on the iano. Bisque figures of babies were designed to help hold the shawl in place. They range in size om 6 to 18 inches. Most of the figures were made in Germany. Reproductions are being made. ther piano babies may be listed under manufacturers' names.

hild, Seated, Blue & Cream Dress, 11 In. 148.00
rawling, Heubach, 4 ½ In.. .... 135.00
ying On Back, Hat, Bisque, Heubach, 5 In. 135.00
ying On Back, Legs Up, Bisque, Heubach, 8 In. 95.00
itting, Bisque, 5 ½ In.. .... 75.00
itting, Bisque, Germany, 7 ½ x 7 In. 205.00
itting, Bisque, Heubach, 6 ½ In. 225.00
itting, Bisque, Heubach, 8 In. 425.00
itting, Holding Comb, Germany, 7 ½ x 7 In. .... *illus* 135.00
piked Curly Hair, Night Dress, Pink Bows, Holding Fruit, Bisque, 7 ½ In. 173.00

ICKARD China Company was started in 1893 by Wilder Pickard. Hand-painted designs were sed on china purchased from other sources. In the 1930s, the company began to make its wn china wares in Chicago, Illinois. The company now makes many types of porcelains, ncluding a successful line of limited edition collector plates.

owl, Poinsettia, Limoges, 1910, 3 x 6 ⅝ In.. .... 140.00
ake Plate, Flowers, Gold Leaf, 11 In. 495.00
andlestick, Multicolored Cascading Flowers, Leaves, Black Base, 9 ⅛ In. 795.00
harger, Gold Gilded, Stippled Center, Embossed Flowers On Border, Scroll Effect, 13 In. 175.00
ish, Clover, Art Nouveau, 2 Handles, Limoges. 155.00
ish, Rose & Daisy, Gold Leaf, Handle, c.1930, 6 x 4 ¾ In.. .... 35.00
air Receiver, Crocus .... *illus* 275.00
lug, Purple Grapes, Yellow & Rust Brown Ground, Handle 895.00
ut Dish, Leaf Shape, c.1910, 8 ½ In. 325.00
itcher, Cider, Leaves, Berries, Green, White, Gold. 495.00
itcher, Colonial, Cyltic Decoration, Handle, Limoges, c.1910 .... 995.00
itcher, Cornflower Conventional, Light Blue Flowers, Gold Ground, Handle. 1579.00

TIP
If the photograph album you buy smells like plastic, don't use it. The fumes will eventually destroy the pictures.

Photography, Tintype, Black Nanny, White Child, Oval Thermoplastic Frame, ½ Plate, 8 ¼ In.
$1380.00

Piano Baby, Sitting, Holding Comb, Germany, 7 ½ x 7 In.
$135.00

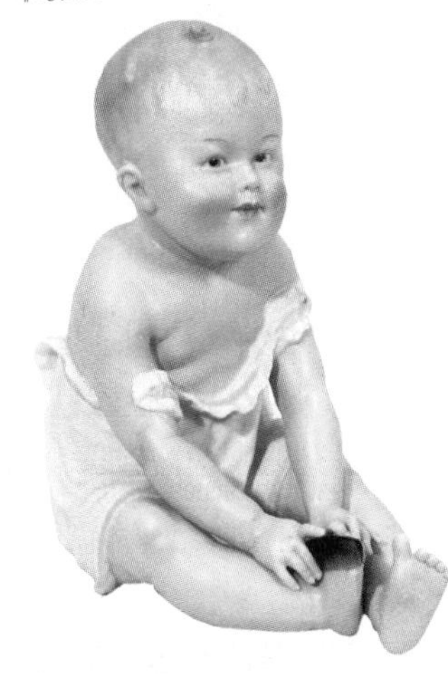

Pickard, Hair Receiver, Crocus
$275.00

P

Displaying Pictures

Decorators now show rooms filled with rows of pictures stacked against the wall, or on special shelves or mantels. Doesn't seem to be a problem that only parts of each picture can be seen!

Picture, Diorama, Winter Scene, Water Mill, In Wooden Bowl, Painted, Mica Fleck
$115.00

Picture, Sand, In Bottle, Paddle Wheeler, Gray Eagle, Flag, Andrew Clemens, c.1885, 9 In.
$29375.00

Picture, Silhouette, Man, Woman, Flower, Hollow Cut, Frame, c.1850, 8½ x 6½ In., Pair
$395.00

Plate, Bavaria, Purple Flowers, 6⅞ In. 80.00
Plate, Bread & Butter, Fleurette, Off-White Ground, Blue Medallion Center, 6¼ In. 15.00
Plate, Cherries, Rust Ground, Gold Border, Limoges, 10 In. 175.00
Plate, Morning Glories, Gold Border, 10 In. 89.00
Plate, Pink Roses, Handles, Limoges, Early 1900s, 10⅝ In. 135.00
Plate, Salad, Regina, Gold Trim, 8¼ In. 35.00
Plate, Twin Poppies, Pink, 8½ In. 195.00
Plate, Violets, Branches & Blossoms, 7½ In. 100.00
Punch Bowl, Peaches, Limoges, 1905 .... 1249.00
Salt & Pepper, Bavaria, Hand Painted, 3¼ x 1⅞ In. 90.00
Sugar, Cover, Rose & Daisy, Gold Encrusted, 2 Handles, No. 511 .... 40.00
Tankard, Grapes, Handle, Limoges, 1932, 12 x 6 In. 795.00
Tankard, Hops In Luster, Green Matte, Handle, 10¾ In. 795.00
Urn, Pink Clover Blossoms, 1896 .... 275.00
Vase, Bud, Gold Rim, Neck & Base, Greek Letter Symbol, 6¾ In. 35.00
Vase, Rose & Daisy, Mini, Gold Encrusted, 3¾ In. 20.00

PICTURES, silhouettes, and other small decorative objects framed to hang on the wall are listed here. Sandpaper pictures are black and white charcoal drawings done on a special sanded paper. Some other types of pictures are listed in the Print and Painting categories.

Bas Relief, Portrait, Ellen Terry, As Marquerite, Spelter, Walnut Frame, 17 x 36 In. 1100.00
Cork, Carved, Landscape, Pagoda, Herons, Glass Box, Black Lacquered Base, 8 In. 2510.00
Diorama, Winter Scene, Water Mill, In Wooden Bowl, Painted, Mica Fleck .... *illus* 115.00
Hair, Wreath, Flowers, Frame, Victorian, c.1850, 9 x 13 In. 82.00
Ink & Graphite On Paper, Cutout, Applied To Paper, Tabby Cat, Seated, Frame, 7 x 8 In. 1880.00
Ink & Pen, Pipe Smoking Rider In Knickers, Frame, c.1896, 13 x 11 In. 28.00
Mourning, Shadowbox, Cabinet Card, Lock Of Hair, Faux Pearl Hatpin, c.1885 .... 800.00
Needlework, 3 Birds On Branches, Cherry Blossom, Frame, Chinese, 53 x 23 In. 1100.00
Needlework, Apple Pickers, Silk, Early 19th Century, England, 11 x 9 In. 550.00
Needlework, Cross-Stitched, Dear Little House, On Linen, Mary Clark, 1929, 15 x 12 In. 490.00
Needlework, Embroidered, Silk, Painted, Shepherdess, Sheep, Cottage, Frame, 13 x 10 In. 3600.00
Needlework, Finding Moses In Rushes, Silk, Frame, 17 x 19 In. 6600.00
Needlework, Fireman's Helmet, Ready, Leaves With Red Berries, Trumpet, Ax, 23 x 11 In. 364.00
Needlework, Girl Feeding Chickens, Painted, Frame, 12 x 9 In. 403.00
Needlework, Little Red Riding Hood, Wolf, Walking In Forest, Early 20th Century, 30 x 46 In. 800.00
Needlework, Silk, Chenille, Peacocks, Flowers, Verse, Mary Ann Pinnock, Aged 8 Years, 1817, Frame, 17 x 13 In. 588.00
Needlework, Woman, Surrounded By Flowers, Plants, Insects, 9¼ x 11½ In. 6325.00
Panel, Eglomise, Garden Setting, Courting Couple, Red Lacquer Frame, Gilt, 32 x 20 In. 323.00
Paper Cutout, Tree, Love Birds, Blue Lined Paper, Green Backing, 7½ x 5½ In. 480.00
Pastel, Landscape, Woman Waving To Man Across Lake, Frame, 19th Century, 15 x 19 In. 110.00
Pastel, On Paper, Couple By Cottage At Sunset, Frame, c.1880, 11 x 17 In. 125.00
Pastel, On Paper, Early Spring Landscape, Colorful, E.T. Hurley, c.1921, 10½ x 13 In. 1320.00
Pastel, On Paper, Portrait, Young Man, Giltwood Frame, c.1840, 22 x 18 In. 646.00
Pastel, On Paper, Still Life With Fruit, Signed, Gilt Frame, 1902, 14 x 17 In. 330.00
Pastel, Still Life, Helen Van Wyk, Frame, c.1980, 22 x 16 In. 390.00
Pastel, Watercolor, Portrait, Man, With Vest, Frock Coat, Oval Frame, c.1800, 9 x 7½ In. 144.00
Pencil, Captain 3-D, Jack Kirby, 17 x 11 In. 1135.00
Pencil, Marilyn Monroe, Jose Gonzalez, c.2002, 14 x 19½ In. 1673.00
Plaque, Gilt Wood, Carved, Filigree, Flower, Chinese Characters, Late 1800s, 22 x 12 In., Pair 249.00
Reverse Painted Glass, Birds, Flowers, George III Gilt Frame, Chinese, c.1770, 31 x 19 In., Pair 25000.00
Sand, In Bottle, Paddle Wheeler, Gray Eagle, Flag, Andrew Clemens, c.1885, 9 In. .... *illus* 29375.00
Scroll, Chinese, Ink & Color, On Paper, Wood End Caps, Figure, Landscape, 76 x 20 In. 316.00
Shadowbox, Fan, Matadors, Flamenco Dancers, Lace, Hatpins, Buttons, 12½ x 10½ In. 28.00
Silhouette, Barrister, Robes, Wig, Gold Details, Rosewood Veneer Frame, 9 x 7 In. 144.00
Silhouette, Boy, Full Length, Bird, Cut Paper, Watercolor, Frame, c.1840, 6 x 5 In. 764.00
Silhouette, Gentleman, Hollow Cut Head, Jacket, Watercolor, Graphite, 3½ x 2¾ In. 382.00
Silhouette, Gentleman, With Top Hat, Master Hankes, Gallery Of Cuttings, 4 x 2¾ In. 529.00
Silhouette, Group Portrait, Watercolor, Ink, On Paper, Auguste Edouart, 15 x 37 In. 14400.00
Silhouette, Lady, Hollow Cut Head, Bodice, Collar Ink Detail, Frame, 5 x 4 In. 705.00
Silhouette, Man, German Text, March 16, 54, Metal Border, Frame, 5 x 4 In. 770.00
Silhouette, Man, John Knowlton, R. Burres, Portsmouth N.H., 1830, 4¾ x 4¼ In. 300.00
Silhouette, Man, Mr. Jewell, West Rindge, N.H., Taken In Jaffrey 1828, 5½ x 4½ In. 300.00
Silhouette, Man, On Ivory, Signed, Dated 1791 .... 650.00
Silhouette, Man, Overcoat, Top Hat, Signed, J. Milne, Frame, 19th Century, 11 x 7¼ In. 115.00
Silhouette, Man, Woman, Flower, Hollow Cut, Frame, c.1850, 8½ x 6½ In., Pair .... *illus* 395.00

Silhouette, Man, Woman, Figured Wood Frame, 19th Century, 2 ¾ In., Pair 646.00
Silhouette, Man's Portrait, Monochromatic Gouache, Sir Robert Wilmot, c.1841, 12 x 9 In. . 316.00
Silhouette, Pen & Ink, Lady, Blue Dress, Black Frame, c.1825, 3 ½ x 3 In. 2160.00
Silhouette, Woman, Lacework Bonnet, Shawl, M. Robt. White, Rosewood Frame, 8 ½ x 7 ½ In. 144.00
Silhouette, Woman, Miss Mary Ann Reece, Hollow Cut, Dec. 19th 1836, Gilt Frame, 7 x 6 In.. 315.00
Silhouette, Young Woman With Letter, Puffy Sleeve Artist, Hollow Cut, c.1831, 5 x 4 In...... 3600.00
Silhouette, Gentlemen, Wearing Top Hat, Cut By Master Hankes, c.1940, 4 x 3 In. 530.00
Theorem, Basket Of Fruit, Giltwood Frame, Margaret Ferguson, Rushville, N.Y., 1835, 12 x 16 In.. 940.00
Theorem, Butterfly & Rose, Watercolor, 19th Century, 17 x 18 In........................ 60.00
Theorem, Chicken In Nest, Velvet, Frame, Wm. Rank, 13 x 15 ⅜ In. 253.00
Theorem, Flower Basket, G.B., France, Frame, 18 x 22 In. 154.00
Theorem, Flowers, Velvet Ground, Gilt Frame, 19th Century, 11 ½ x 11 ½ In................ 385.00
Theorem, Fruit, Bird, Watercolor, On Velvet, Mahogany Frame, 14 ½ x 17 In. 529.00
Theorem, Fruit Basket, 2 Handles, Stitched To Paper Frame, 16 x 18 ½ In.................. 16100.00
Theorem, Fruit Basket, Blue Bird Painted Frame, T.J. Graham, 23 ⅞ x 19 ¾ In. .... *illus* 605.00
Theorem, Watercolor, Ink & Mica, On Paper, Fruit In Footed Compote Bowl, 14 x 18 In. 1800.00
Theorem, Watercolor, On Paper, Still Life, 4 Pieces Of Fruit, Gilt Frame, 7 x 8 ½ In. 345.00
Theorem, Watercolor, On Velvet, Horned Owl, Oak Tree, Sponged Frame, c.1921, 13 x 11 In. . 115.00
Tin, Still Life, Fruit, Silver Centerpiece, Pressed, Lithograph, Frame, Late 19th Century, 25 x 38 In.. *illus* 150.00
Watercolor, Absinthe House, New Orleans, Castleden, George, 1927, 12 x 9 In. 1998.00
Watercolor, American Schoolgirl, Eglomise Glass, Gilt Frame, c.1825 .... 1500.00
Watercolor, Cape Style House, Cherry Blossoms, Spring Landscape, 13 x 19 ¾ In........... 172.00
Watercolor, Coming Home In The Evening, 8 x 9 ¼ In. 705.00
Watercolor, Cottage Scene, Henry Spernon Tozer, Frame, 1933, 10 x 13 ¼ In. 600.00
Watercolor, Easter Sunday, Russian School, 19th Century, 10 x 7 ½ In. 590.00
Watercolor, English Country, Signed, Alwyn Holland, Frame, 11 ½ x 16 ⅛ In. 144.00
Watercolor, Farm Scene, William Corasick, 1940, 13 x 16 In. 240.00
Watercolor, First Street South Boston, Joseph Harry Wheater, 3 ¾ x 5 In................. 1003.00
Watercolor, Forest Landscape, Burt Barnes, Frame, c.1920, 26 x 18 ½ In. 1080.00
Watercolor, Frankfurt Street Scene With Cathedral, Signed, A. Schafer, 18 x 13 ½ In........ 820.00
Watercolor, French Quarter Street, Wayman Adams, 20 x 14 In.......................... 570.00
Watercolor, Girl With Pet Squirrel On String, Gold Frame, Glass, 13 ¾ x 9 ¾ In........... 476.00
Watercolor, Glued Natural Feathers, Birds, Frame, Victorian, 14 x 11 In., 5 Piece 1293.00
Watercolor, Landscape, Edward R. Sitzman, Frame, 3 ¼ x 5 ¼ In........................ 180.00
Watercolor, Landscape, Figures & Distant Village, Raffaele Mainella, 6 ¾ x 12 ¾ In........ 885.00
Watercolor, Landscape, House, Edmund Lewis, Signed, 19th Century, 11 ½ x 25 In. 935.00
Watercolor, Landscape, Polly Nordell, Frame, c.1925, 19 x 16 In. 180.00
Watercolor, Louisiana Scene, Spanish Moss, A.J. Drysdale, Signed, Frame, 20 x 29 ½ In. 2300.00
Watercolor, Low Tide, Armand Jean Heins, 1885, 9 ¼ x 13 ¼ In. 413.00
Watercolor, Maine Shore, Samuel Triscott, c.1900, 9 ½ x 14 In. 780.00
Watercolor, Man With Rooster, William Wind McKim, 1938, 14 x 10 In.................... 480.00
Watercolor, Marsh At Dusk, Charles Partridge Adams, Frame, c.1900, 10 ½ x 15 In......... 4200.00
Watercolor, Memorial, Stylized Willow Tree, Urn Topped Monument, 15 ½ x 20 In. 353.00
Watercolor, Memorial, Woman & Girl Grieving, Urns, Willow, 1829, 16 x 20 In. .... *illus* 4406.00
Watercolor, Mother & Daughter, Hamilton Hamilton, Frame, c.1890, 30 x 15 In. 3900.00
Watercolor, Mourning Scene, Funerary Urn, Weeping Willow, Frame.................... 1725.00
Watercolor, Nantucket Wharf, Fish House, Sailboat, Mat, Frame, 22 ½ x 18 In............. 632.00
Watercolor, New England Harbor Scene, Herbert Gute, Frame, c.1940, 14 x 18 In. 360.00
Watercolor, Niagara Falls, Frame, 20th Century, 12 ¾ x 10 ½ In. 144.00
Watercolor, On Velvet, Flowers, Tan, Blue, Frame, Mid 1800s, 7 x 18 In., Pair .... *illus* 230.00
Watercolor, Paper, Fanciful Landscape, Man & Dog, Formal Clothing, Top Hat, Frame, 18 x 18 In. 978.00
Watercolor, Plate Of Fruit, Frame, 19th Century, 5 x 7 In............................. 2115.00
Watercolor, Portrait, Lady & Gentleman, Frame, Mid 1800s, 6 ½ x 9 In................... 120.00
Watercolor, Redhead Ducks In Flight, Frame, 11 x 15 In. 300.00
Watercolor, Rising Tide, Frame, 24 x 36 In. 999.00
Watercolor, River Landscape, Alexander J. Drysdale, Frame, 9 ½ x 19 ½ In................ 3240.00
Watercolor, Silo With Chickens, Frederic Whitaker, Frame, 1945, 9 ½ x 13 ¼ In............ 330.00
Watercolor, Stencil, On Paper, White Bowl, Strawberries, c.1830, 5 x 6 ¾ In............... 4200.00
Watercolor, Still Life, Basket, Lemons, Grapes, Melons, Frame, 1800s, 11 x 14 In........... 3000.00
Watercolor, Stream In An Autumn Landscape, Raphael Senseman, c.1920, 20 x 30 In. 180.00
Watercolor, Taxco Scene, Carl Pappe, Frame, 1949, 17 ½ x 25 ½ In...................... 450.00
Watercolor, The Abandoned Boat, Rolland Golden, Signed, 22 x 30 In. 1645.00
Watercolor, The Family, Signed, Charles Reinike, 1937, 14 ¼ x 20 ¼ In.................. 7200.00
Watercolor, Venetian Canal Scene, Jaconini, Signed, 12 ¼ x 6 ½ In...................... 106.00
Watercolor, Windmill & Boat Scene, Johannes Carol Leurs, 4 ½ x 6 In. 207.00

Picture, Theorem, Fruit Basket, Blue Bird Painted Frame, T.J. Graham, 23 ⅞ x 19 ¾ In.
$605.00

Picture, Tin, Still Life, Fruit, Silver Centerpiece, Pressed, Lithograph, Frame, Late 19th Century, 25 x 38 In.
$150.00

Picture, Watercolor, Memorial, Woman & Girl Grieving, Urns, Willow, 1829, 16 x 20 In.
$4406.00

Picture, Watercolor, On Velvet, Flowers, Tan, Blue, Frame, Mid 1800s, 7 x 18 In., Pair
$230.00

Pigeon Forge, Figurine Set, Raccoon Family, Signed, Doug Ferguson, 3 Piece
$295.00

Pigeon Forge, Vase, Brown Over Blue Crystalline, 4-Sided, Doug Ferguson, 4⅝ x 8½ In.
$80.00

Pillin, Vase, 2 Women, Holding Flower, Birds, Signed, 11½ In.
$1200.00

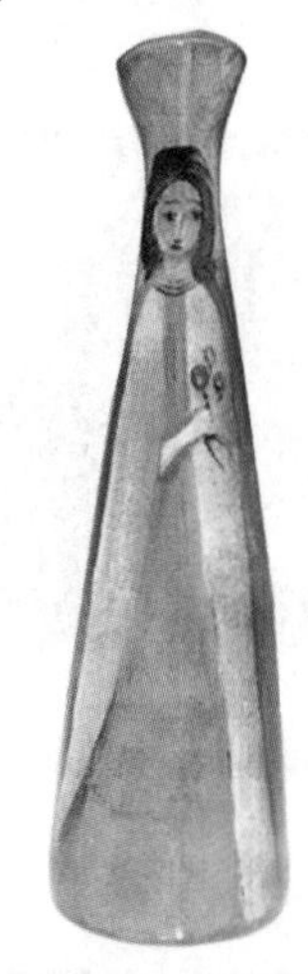

Pillin Pottery

Vases by Polia and William Pillin are now so expensive that fakes are on the market. A real Pillin vase has a different scene on each side. The signature on a real piece should be incised through a black glaze (early pieces) or signed with a blunt-pointed marker on red clay–colored glaze (later pieces).

Watercolor, Woman Holding Book, Bonnet With Blue Ribbon, c.1835, 5 x 4½ In. 1880.00
Watercolor & Gouache On Paper, Birds Of Exotic Plumage, 20 x 26 In. 1410.00
Watercolor & Gouache On Paperboard, Boy With Whip, Horse Pull Toy, Dog, 17 x 14 In. . . 2350.00
Watercolor & Ink, Boy & Dog, Black Tunic, White Collar, Frame, c.1835, 5 x 5 In. 2115.00
Woolie, Wool Work, Flower, Crown, British Empire Flags, Vining, Blue Ground, 11 x 16 In. . . 920.00

PICTURE FRAMES *are listed in this book in the Furniture category under Frame.*

PIERCE, *see Howard Pierce category.*

PIGEON FORGE Pottery was started in Pigeon Forge, Tennessee, in 1946. Red clay found near the pottery was used to make the pieces. Molded or thrown pottery with matte glaze and slip decoration was made. The pottery closed in 2000.

Bowl, Dogwood, Sandy Beige, Turquoise Glazed Interior, 1940s 36.00
Coaster, Swan, Yellow Speckled Glaze, Marked, 2 Piece. 10.00
Creamer, Dogwood Blossom, 3¾ In. 12.00
Creamer, Gray Matte, Glossy Mustard Interior, Handle, 3¾ In. 26.00
Crock, Beige, Flower, Stem, Leaves, Ears, 1940s 45.00
Figurine, Baby Bird, Clear Glaze, 3¼ x 3 x 3 In. 78.00
Figurine, Baby Owl, Brown & White Glaze, 2 x 2 In. 18.00
Figurine, Bear, Black, Satin Matte Glaze, 4 x 3 In.. . . . . 30.00
Figurine, Fledgling, Speckled, Signed, Doug Ferguson, 3¼ x 3 In. 78.00
Figurine, Frog, Lilly Pad, 3½ x 3½ x 3 In. . . . . 55.00 to 60.00
Figurine, Mouse, 2 In. 32.00
Figurine, Owl, Beige, Gold, White, Brown Speckled, 4½ x 5 In. 55.00
Figurine, Owl, Blue, Signed, 2 x 2 In. 20.00
Figurine, Owl, Brown, White Glaze, 2 In. 18.00
Figurine, Owl, Mottled, Gray, 1940s, 4½ x 4½ In. 49.00
Figurine Set, Raccoon Family, Signed, Doug Ferguson, 3 Piece. . . . . *illus* 295.00
Jar, Cover, Dogwood Blossom, 4¼ In. 12.00
Mug, Outline Of Owl, Sandy Beige, Handle, 1940s 20.00
Mug, Outline Of Rooster, Sandy Beige, Handle, 1940s 20.00
Pitcher, Cloverleaf, Pink 45.00
Pitcher, Dogwood Blossoms, Blue Interior, Marked, 1958, 5½ In. 45.00
Vase, Brown Over Blue Crystalline, 4-Sided, Doug Ferguson, 4⅝ x 8½ In. . . . . *illus* 80.00
Vase, Cloverleaf, Soft Buff, Glossy Finish Interior, 2¾ x 5 In. 19.00
Vase, Dogwood Blossom, Bulbous, 3½ In. 9.00
Vase, Unusual Shape, Rich Color, Marked Dusted Tre'sures, 3½ x 3¼ In. 27.00

PILKINGTON Tile and Pottery Company was established in 1892 in England. The company made small pottery wares, like buttons and hatpins, but soon started decorating vases purchased from other potteries. By 1903, the company had discovered an opalescent glaze that became popular on the Lancastrian pottery line. The manufacture of pottery ended in 1937. Pilkington's Tiles Ltd. has worked from 1938 to the present.

Vase, Embossed Jaguars, Floral Ground, Luster, 9¼ x 6½ In. 900.00
Vase, Hand Painted Gray Green Decoration, Royal Lancastrian, 7⅞ x 5¾ In. 120.00
Vase, Leaves & Vines, Royal Lancastrian, Blue, 8⅝ In. 260.00
Vase, Shouldered, Green Mottled & Brown Matte Glaze, 6 x 11 In. 748.00

PILLIN pottery was made by Polia (1909–1992) and William (1910–1985) Pillin, who set up a pottery in Los Angeles in 1948. William shaped, glazed, and fired the clay, and Polia painted the pieces, often with elongated figures of women, children, flowers, birds, fish, and other animals. Pieces are marked with a stylized *Pillin* signature.

Bowl, Birds, Multicolored Patchwork Ground, Curved, 3¾ x 10½ In. 1800.00
Box, Round, Colorful, Horse & Rider, Cover, 4 x 2 In.. . . . . 240.00
Charger, Woman Wearing Head Scarf, Holding Flowers, 10 In. 1995.00
Jardinere, Horses, Women, Painted, Signed, 8½ x 9½ In. 2520.00
Vase, 2 Women, Holding Flower, Birds, Signed, 11½ In.. . . . . *illus* 1200.00
Vase, 3 Women, Birds, Tapered, Wide, Flared Rim, Marked, 5¾ x 5¾ In. . . . . *illus* 730.00
Vase, 3 Women, Squat, Pastel Colors, White Ground, 7 In. 1180.00
Vase, Cylindrical, Colorful, Horses, 4¾ x 5¼ In. 360.00
Vase, Cylindrical, Pastel Horses, 3 x 4 In. 390.00
Vase, Man Riding Stallion, Maiden, Blue, Turquoise, Cylindrical, 7½ In. 999.00
Vase, Women Holding Fish In Nets, Painted, Signed, 14½ x 6¼ In. 2400.00

PINCUSHION DOLLS are not really dolls and often were not even pincushions. Some collectors use the term "half-doll." The top half of each doll was made of porcelain. The edge of the half-doll was made with several small holes for thread, and the doll was stitched to a fabric body with a voluminous skirt. The finished figure was used to cover a hot pot of tea, powder box, pincushion, whiskbroom, or lamp. They were made in sizes from less than an inch to over 9 inches high. Most date from the early 1900s to the 1950s. Collectors often find just the porcelain doll without the fabric skirt.

Woman, Arms In Front, Legs Crossed, Japan, 4 In. 65.00
Woman, Baker's Chocolate, Dutch Style Cap, Holding Tray, 4 In. 575.00
Woman, Composition, Human Hair Wig, Beret, 4 In. 65.00
Woman, Hand On Shoulder, Rose On Chest, Pink Ruffled Blouse, 5 ¾ In. 35.00
Woman, Hands Held Out Front, Blond Updo, Germany, 5 In. 35.00
Woman, Hands Resting On Chin, Lace Dress, Germany, Sitzendofer, 3 ½ In. 165.00
Woman, Holding Fan, Blond Hair, Japan, 2 ¾ In. 45.00
Woman, Holding Head, Blue Satin Cushion, Germany, 1930s, 6 In. 65.00
Woman, Parrot On Arm, Bisque, Swanlike Neck, Platinum Mohair Wig, Goebel, 4 In. 748.00
Woman, Plastic, Scottish, Plaid Dress, Felt Cap, 1960s, 3 ¾ In. 25.00
Woman, With Mask, Art Deco, Nude, Brown Painted Hair, Earrings, Dressel Kister, 5 In. 900.00
Woman's Head, Curly Blond Hair, Blue Eyes, Pouty Lips, 4 In. 42.00
Woman's Head, Earrings, Necklace, Gloves, Germany, 3 ¾ In. 35.00
Woman's Head, Flapper Girl, Hands Resting On Bodice, Green Chemise, 5 In. 55.00
Woman's Head, Flapper Style, Germany, 2 In. 75.00
Woman's Head, Sailor Blouse, Wide Brim Hat, Blond Curl, 4 In. 40.00

PINK SLAG *pieces are listed in this book in the Slag Glass category.*

PIPES have been popular since tobacco was introduced to Europe by Sir Walter Raleigh. Carved wooden, porcelain, ivory, and glass pipes may be listed here.

African Carved Horn, Gourd & Bronze Braiding, c.1900 .... 86.00
Briar, Saint Claude, Carved, c.1890, 9 In. 29.00
Ceramic, Guarani Indian, Paraguay, 5 Lb., c.1450 .... 29.00
Clay, Revolutionary War, Arms Of King George III 110.00
German Wood, Porcelain, 20th Century, 56 In. 117.00
Meerschaum, Bearded Man, Wearing Hat, Amber Stem, c.1930, 6 In. 69.00
Meerschaum, Figural, c.1880, 11 In. 88.00
Meerschaum, Figural, Sultan, Rubies, 19th Century 29.00
Meerschaum, Man On High Wheel, Country Lane, Fence, 6 ½ In. 385.00
Wood, Bark, 4 Sections, England, c.1780 .... 29.00

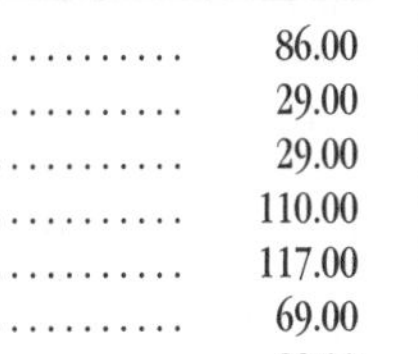

PIRKENHAMMER is a porcelain manufactory started in 1802 by Friedrich Holke and J. G. Lilst. It was located in Bohemia, now Brezova, Czechoslovakia. The company made tablewares usually decorated with views and flowers. Lithophanes were also made. The mark of the crossed hammers is easy to remember as the Pirkenhammer symbol.

Charger, Pink Flowers, Mahogany Stand 175.00

PISGAH FOREST pottery was made in North Carolina beginning in 1926. The pottery was started by Walter B. Stephen, who had been making pottery in that location since 1914. The pottery continued in operation after his death in 1961. The most famous kinds of Pisgah Forest ware are the cameo type with designs made of raised glaze and the turquoise crackle glaze wares.

Mug, Rooster, Blue Matte Glaze, Cameo, 1950s, 3 ¾ In. 495.00
Teapot, Blue Matte Over Glossy White, Wagon Train, Marked WB Stephen, 5 x 9 In. 230.00
Vase, Figures, Cameo, Green Ground, Signed, Stephen, 1959, 13 ½ In. .... *illus* 1600.00

PLANTERS PEANUTS memorabilia is collected. Planters Nut and Chocolate Company was started in Wilkes-Barre, Pennsylvania, in 1906. The Mr. Peanut figure was adopted as a trademark in 1916. National advertising for Planters Peanuts started in 1918. The company was acquired by Standard Brands, Inc., in 1961. Standard Brands merged with Nabisco in 1981. Some of the Mr. Peanut jars and other memorabilia have been reproduced and, of course, new items are being made.

Ad, Lady Eating Sandwich, 12 x 5 ½ In. 10.00
Bank, Plastic, Red, U.S.A. 12.00
Bendor Bank, Yellow, Cocktail Peanut Can, 1950s, 8 x 5 In. 575.00
Blanket, Black & White, Mr. Peanut With Top Hat, 48 x 66 In. 17.00
Blotter, Panel Delivery Truck, Winter Scene. 22.00

Pillin, Vase, 3 Women, Birds, Tapered, Wide, Flared Rim, Marked, 5 ¾ x 5 ¾ In. $730.00

TIP

To clean the stem and bowl of a collectible briar pipe, dip a pipe cleaner in vodka. Push the pipe cleaner through the stem. Use a dry pipe cleaner for any pipe but a briar pipe.

Pisgah Forest, Vase, Figures, Cameo, Green Ground, Signed, Stephen, 1959, 13 ½ In. $1600.00

PLANTERS PEANUTS

Planters Peanuts, Mask, Santa, Celluloid, Red & White Hat, 1940s, 10 x 7 In.
$258.00

Planters Peanuts, Mold, Double Chocolate, Hinged, Metal, 1930s, 7 x 8 In.
$2070.00

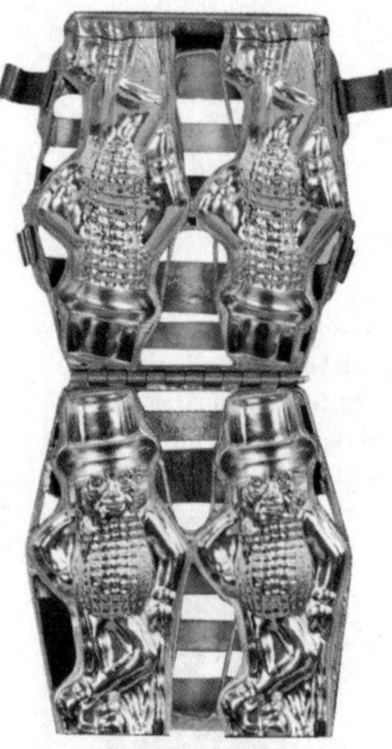

TIP
There is special polish for Lucite and other plastics. It can be found in lamp shops.

Book, Complete World Of Planters, Mr. Peanut, c.1967, 8½ x 11 In. 9.00
Box, Glass, Cocktail, Plastic, 1950s 115.00
Box, Planters Chocolate Peanuts, Mr. Peanut Feeds Mr. Earth, Cardboard, 1930s 1815.00
Box, Planters Chocolate Peanuts, World Goes Nuts, 1930s, 9 x 6 x 3 In. 1730.00 to 1815.00
Box, Wood, Dovetailed, Paper Label, c.1920, 3¾ x 6¾ x 10 In. 300.00
Car, Plastic, Souvenir Of Atlantic Sticker, Blue, 5 In. 460.00
Coaster, Tin, 3½ In. 7.00
Cocktail Glass, Figural, Mr. Peanut Stem, U-Shape Bowl, 1940s, 5 x 2⅝ In. 385.00
Container, Oil, Ali D'Italia, Gal., 1940s, 9 In. 1150.00
Container, Peanut Butter, 25 Lb., 1930s, 9 x 10 In. 402.00
Container, Pennant Brand, 5 Jumbo Peanut Bars, 10 Lb., 1930s, 10½ x 8½ In. 143.00
Costume, Halloween, Children's, Plastic Mask, 2 Sections, 1960s, 10 x 7¼ In. 33.00
Dish, Shell Shape, Mr. Peanut On Top, Bisque, Japan, c.1930, 4 x 3 In. 78.00
Display, Blinker, Light-Up, Box, 1930-40s, 24 In. 5175.00
Display, Mr. Peanut, Cocktail Peanuts Cans, Tiered, Cardboard, 1930s, 18 x 18 In. 2300.00
Display, Peanut Shape, Pressed Board 77.00
Display, Tiered Shelf, Cardboard, Mr. Peanut At Top, 1930s, 18 x 18 In. 2300.00
Doll, Mr. Peanut, Wood, Jointed, Holding Cane, c.1930, 9 In. 190.00
Figure, Mr. Peanut, Inflatable, 2002 K.F. Holdings, 24 In. 16.00
Hand Puppet, Rubber, 1940s, 6 In. 632.00
Jar, Counter Display, Yellow Letters, Embossed, 10 x 5 x 8 In. 125.00
Jar, Figural Mr. Peanut With Cane, Clear, 1930s, 13 x 11 In. 9200.00
Jar, Hexagonal, Mr. Peanut, Cover, Peanut Finial, c.1930, 7¼ In. 125.00
Jar, Lid, 4 Corners, 14 x 8 In. 288.00
Jar, Lid, 5 Lines, Round, 10 x 7 In. 345.00
Jar, Lid, Boy, Winking Decal, Tin, Label, 1930, 10 x 8 In. 1955.00
Jar, Lid, Figural, Barrel, Embossed, 1930s, 12 x 8 In. 403.00
Jar, Lid, Figural, Football, Embossed, 8 x 8 In. 259.00
Jar, Lid, Peanut Finial, Mister Peanut, Barrel Shape, 12 In. 143.00
Jar, Mr. Peanut, 75th Anniversary, 1906-81, 8 In. 9.00 to 15.00
Jar, Mr. Peanut Shape, Pink, 12¾ In. 275.00
Jar, Slant Bottom, Cover, 9 x 5 In. 21.00
Knife & Fork Set, Mr. Peanut Handle, Standing On Peanuts, Carlton Silver. 65.00
Letter Opener, Metal, Cloisonne Porcelain, Inlaid Enamel, c.1920, 9½ In. 440.00
Letter Opener, Peanut Handle, Metal, 9 In. 350.00
Lighter, Peanut Shape, Pulls Apart, Composition, Patina, 2½ In. 100.00 to 175.00
Mask, Halloween, Celluloid, 1940s, 11 x 7 In. 172.00
Mask, Santa, Celluloid, Red & White Hat, 1940s, 10 x 7 In. *illus* 258.00
Mirror, Walnut Frame, c.1980, 17½ x 14½ In. 18.00
Mold, Double Chocolate, Hinged, Metal, 1930s, 7 x 8 In. *illus* 2070.00
Mr. Peanut, Jar, Box, Cast Metal, 1930s, 13 x 11 In. 9200.00
Oil Can, Planter Popcorn Seasoning, 1940s, Gal. 2875.00
Pants, Cotton, Drawstring, Multicolored, c.1970, X-Large 3.00
Pencil, Mechanical, Mr. Peanut, Hands On Hips 35.00
Rack, Planters Peanut Specialties, Z-Shape, Tin Lithograph, 4¾ x 14 x 7¾ In. 1160.00
Roaster Rider, Fiberglass, Mr. Peanut On Top Of Metal Roaster, 1930s, 53 x 33 In. 10350.00
Salt & Pepper, Plastic, Ivory Color, Box 8.00
Sign, Butler, Cardboard, Street Car, 20½ x 10 In. 517.00
Sign, Get Your Mr. Peanut Bank, 25 Cents, Cardboard, Red, Black, White, 22 x 14 In. 187.00
Sign, Maid Cardboard, Street Car, 20½ x 10 In. 517.00
Sign, Peanut Butter, Cardboard, Fine Food For Lent, 11 x 7 In. 853.00
Sign, Plan A Picnic With Planters, Mr. Peanut, Green, White, Cardboard, 22 x 14 In. 187.00
Spreader, Mr. Peanut Handle, Stainless Steel, Chinese, 4¾ In. 14.00
Straw, Mr. Peanut, Green, c.1950 5.00
Tin Lithograph, Pennant Brand, Multicolored, 2 Oz., 3⅝ x 2¾ In. 2640.00
Toy, Car, Plastic, Blue, Atlantic Sticker, 5 In. 460.00
Transistor Radio, Strap, Box, 10 x 5 In. 26.00
Tumbler, Planters Mr. Peanut, Clear Glass, Black & Yellow, 5¼ In. 26.00

PLASTIC objects of all types are being collected. Some pieces are listed in other categories; gutta-percha cases are listed in photography, celluloid in its own category.

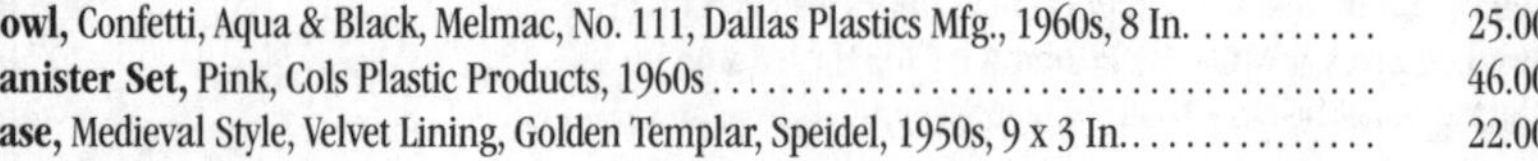

Bowl, Confetti, Aqua & Black, Melmac, No. 111, Dallas Plastics Mfg., 1960s, 8 In. 25.00
Canister Set, Pink, Cols Plastic Products, 1960s 46.00
Case, Medieval Style, Velvet Lining, Golden Templar, Speidel, 1950s, 9 x 3 In. 22.00

P

Clothesline Reel, Lustroware, Red, Retractable 25.00
Coaster Set, Faceted Jewel Rim, Pink, Blue, Amber, Green, Turquoise, 1950s, 6 Piece 34.00
Comb, Art Deco Style, Swirled Pink, Serpentine Shape, Marked France, 4 In., Pair 35.00
Condiment Set, White Tray, Handle, 2 Bowls, Lid, Spoon, Dialene Better Maid, 2 x 3 In. 10.00
Cup, Avalon, Harmony House, Almond Color, 3 ⅛ In., 6 Piece 12.00
Cup, Baby's, 2 Handles, Yellow, Marked Baby, Box 9.00
Figurine, Man & Woman Ballroom Dancers, Bakelite, Oval Wood Base, 21 x 18 In. 82.00
Hair Pick, Rhinestone, Stars, 4 ¾ In. 34.00
Hairpin, 2 Prongs, Faux Diamonds, Horseshoe Shape, Bakelite, 4 In. 35.00
Ice Bucket, Red & White Gingham Check, Marked West Bend, Thermo-Serv, 10 x 8 In. 28.00
Ice Bucket, Thermal Ware, Woven Raffia & Plastic Covering, 1950s, 8 ½ x 7 In. 20.00
Measuring Spoon Set, ML Measurement Marked, Hong Kong 10.00
Measuring Spoon Set, Red, White, Blue, Yellow 12.00
Milk Carton Holder, Red, Handi Holder Cutout, Evlo Plastics, Sandusky, ½ Gal. 15.00
Mug, Amber Gold, Lucite, Glitter, Embedded Plastic Leaves, 1960s, Pair 13.00
Paperweight, Duck Head, Brown, Orange, Bakelite, 5 x 3 ½ x 3 ½ In. 80.00
Picnic Hamper, Art Deco, Leather, Flasks, Bakelite Plates, Cups, Knives, Forks, 21 x 6 In. 300.00
Picture Frame, Nu-Dell Plastics Corp., Chicago, 8 x 10 In. 12.00
Recipe Holder, Marked Royal Product, Made In U.S.A., 1950s, 5 x 5 In. 15.00
Rolling Pin, Tupperware, Screw End To Fill With Water, 1960s, 15 ½ x 2 ¾ In. 15.00
Snack Bowl, Aqua Floral, Hoffman Industries, Sinking Spring, Penn., 1960s 5.00
Sugar & Creamer, Catalina, Pink, Harmony House 13.00
Tieback, Rosettes, Molded, Gold Color, Deco Pattern, Kirsch, Original Package, 2 In., Pair 25.00
Tierack, Hollywood Tie Keeper, Folding, Holds 32, 15 ¼ x 2 ⅛ In. 15.00
Window Candles, Imperial, Patent Nov. 29, 1955, 4 Original Boxes, 9 ¾ x 5 In., 10 Piece 60.00

PLATED AMBERINA was patented June 15, 1886, by Joseph Locke and made by the New England Glass Company. It is similar in color to amberina, but is characterized by a cream colored or chartreuse lining (never white) and small ridges or ribs on the outside.

Bowl, 2 ¾ x 5 ¼ In. 6700.00
Bowl, Ruffled Edge, 3 ¼ x 8 In. .... *illus* 8400.00
Creamer, Applied Amber Handle, 5 ½ In. 16900.00
Creamer, Applied Amber Handle, c.1886, 2 ¾ x 4 ¾ x 3 ¾ In. 10100.00
Cruet, Bulbous, Swirled Neck, Applied Amber Handle & Stopper, 6 ⅞ In. .... *illus* 10500.00
Pitcher, Applied Amber Handle, 7 ½ In. 7900.00
Punch Cup, Applied Amber Handle, Blue Cast Rim, 2 ½ In. 4250.00
Sugar, Applied Pale Amber Handles, 2 x 5 ¼ x 3 ¾ In. 14350.00
Tumbler, 3 3/4 In. .... 2185.00 to 2750.00
Vase, Optic Ribbed, Tricornered Rim, Footed, 8 In. 666.00
Vase, Pinched Waist, Crimped Rim, 4 ¾ In. 18000.00

PLIQUE-A-JOUR is an enameling process. The enamel is laid between thin raised metal lines and heated. The finished piece has transparent enamel held between the thin metal wires. It is different from cloisonne because it is translucent.

Bowl, Japanese, 4 x 1 ¾ In. 53.00
Bowl, Pink Flowers, Green Leaves, Mushroom Pattern, Wood Stand, 2 ½ In. 79.00
Goblet, Red & Blue Flowers, Metal Stem, Hammer, Impressed, 7 ½ In. .... *illus* 7500.00
Lamp, Blue, Flowers, 13 In. 399.00
Snuff Bottle, Pink Flowers, Green Leaves, Green Band, Foot Rim, 3 In. 79.00
Vase, Flowers, Multicolored, Bulbous, 20 In. 699.00

POLITICAL memorabilia of all types, from buttons to banners, is collected. Items related to presidential candidates are the most popular, but collectors also search for material related to state and local offices. Memorabilia related to social causes, minor political parties, and protest movements are also included here. Many reproductions have been made. A jugate is a button with photographs of both the presidential and vice presidential candidates. In this list a button is round, usually with a straight pin or metal tab to secure it to a shirt. A pin is brass, often figural, sometimes attached to a ribbon.

Ad Card, Grover Cleveland, Sulphur Bitters, 6 ½ In. 16.00
Ashtray, Fixin' To Vote For Nixon, Multicolored, Fisherman, Wily Worm, 6 In. 31.00
Ax, Washington's Inaugural, April 30, 1789, 13 x 5 ¼ In. 400.00
Badge, Butler, West, Third Party, Jugate, Frame, 1884, 1 ½ x 1 ¼ In. 311.00
Badge, Charles E. Hughes, Natural Convention, Portrait, Celluloid, 1908, 6 ½ In. 215.00
Badge, Cleveland, Stevenson, Inaugural, Jugate Bronze Medal, 1893 .... 747.00

Plated Amberina, Bowl, Ruffled Edge, 3 ¼ x 8 In. $8400.00

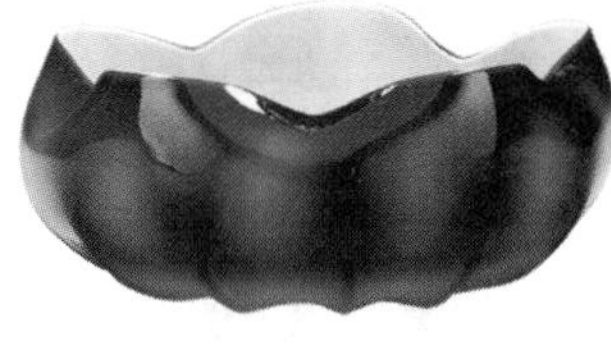

Plated Amberina, Cruet, Bulbous, Swirled Neck, Applied Amber Handle & Stopper, 6 ⅞ In. $10500.00

Plique-A-Jour, Goblet, Red & Blue Flowers, Metal Stem, Hammer, Impressed, 7 ½ In. $7500.00

Political, Badge, McKinley, Brass Hanger, Domed Celluloid, 1896, 1 ¾ In.
$127.00

Political, Badge, Statue Of Liberty, Laminated Cardboard, Peter Max, 1981, 2 x 1 In., 6 Piece
$570.00

Political, Badge, Wilson, Delegate, N.Y., Silvered Brass, Oct. 1st, 1912, 4 In.
$58.00

Badge, Horatio Seymour, White Man's Government, Suspension Loop, 1868 .... 1315.00
Badge, Lincoln, Hamlin, Ferrotype, Brass Shell, 1860 .... 1793.00
Badge, Lincoln, Johnson, 1864 Campaign, Jugate, Eagle Shield 47800.00
Badge, McClellan, Pendleton, Jugate 3675.00
Badge, McKinley, Brass Hanger, Domed Celluloid, 1896, 1 ¾ In. .... *illus* 127.00
Badge, McKinley, Roosevelt, Commercial, Travelers, Celluloid, Ribbon, 1900 .... 430.00
Badge, Police, Made For Eisenhower Inaugural, 1957 .... 1584.00
Badge, Statue Of Liberty, Laminated Cardboard, Peter Max, 1981, 2 x 1 In., 6 Piece .... *illus* 570.00
Badge, Stevenson, Kefauver, Campaign Staff, Oval, 2 ½ In. 568.00
Badge, Theodore Roosevelt, He's Good Enough For Me, Hanging Ribbon, 3 ½ In. 1135.00
Badge, William Jennings Bryan, Ear Of Corn, Celluloid, Ribbon, 2 ⅜ In. 1793.00
Badge, William McKinley, Lithographed, Shield Shape, 3 ½ x 4 In. 717.00
Badge, Wilson, Delegate, N.Y., Silvered Brass, Oct. 1st, 1912, 4 In. .... *illus* 58.00
Ballot, McClellan, Pendleton, 1864 .... 508.00
Ballot Box, Pine, Republican Primaries, Open Bottom, Attached Wastebasket, 1887 .... 633.00
Bandanna, Benjamin Harrison, Protection To Home Industries, Scenic, 22 x 23 ½ In. 442.00
Bandanna, Campaign, Harrison, Morton, Red, White & Blue, 1888, 23 x 23 In. 896.00
Bandanna, Cleveland, Hendricks, Eagles, Cotton, 19 x 20 ½ In. .... *illus* 510.00
Bandanna, FDR, Carry On, 3rd Term, Blue, Red, White, c.1940, 22 x 23 In. 165.00
Bandanna, Garfield, Arthur, Red Ground, Frame, 1880, 21 x 19 In. 335.00
Bandanna, Garfield, People's Choice, Blue, White, Frame, 22 ½ x 24 ¾ In. 201.00
Bandanna, Harrison, Morton, Campaign, Frame, c.1888, 22 ¾ x 23 ¾ In. 165.00
Bandanna, Jimmy Carter, Red Stripe Borders, Blue Stars Center, c.1976, 28 x 28 In. 101.00
Bandanna, Roosevelt, Fairbanks, Right Men In Right Place, 1904, 17 ½ x 15 ¾ In. 1135.00
Bandanna, Roosevelt, Fairbanks, Protection To American Industries, Eagle, 1904, 23 In. 4780.00
Bandanna, Teddy Roosevelt, Bull Moose, Teddy's Hat, Silk, c.1912, 19 x 22 ½ In. 202.00
Bank, Mechanical, Teddy & The Bear, Cap-Firing, Tree Trunk, J.E. Stevens, 1907, 10 In. 2070.00
Bank, Teddy Roosevelt, Bust, Rough Rider, Painted, Silver, Gold, Cast Iron, 5 x 3 ½ In. 294.00
Banner, Bunting, Alf Landon, Frank Knox, Red, White, Blue, 1936, 9 x 3 ½ Ft. 853.00
Banner, Campaign, Cleveland, Hendricks, Cloth, 1884, 25 ½ x 38 In. 4183.00
Banner, Campaign, Garfield, Arthur, Jug, Our Choice, 1880, 26 x 39 In. 4481.00
Banner, Campaign, Winfield Scott Hancock, Red, White & Blue, 1880, 17 x 24 ½ In. .... *illus* 11353.00
Banner, Clay, Frelinghuysen, Whig, Print By N. Currier, 1844, 12 x 16 In. 345.00
Banner, Eisenhower, Stalin, Montgomery, Thanks For The Victory, 24 x 38 In. 657.00
Banner, Elephant Campaigns For Ike, Celluloid, 1952, 1 ¾ In. 678.00
Banner, Grover Cleveland, T. A. Hendricks, Matte, Frame, 1884, 36 x 48 In. 3862.00
Banner, Harrison, Morton, 3 Stars, Red, White, Blue, Pennant Shape, 1888, 8 ½ x 52 In. 538.00
Banner, Henry Clay, Silk, 2 Women, Bald Eagle, 1844, 13 ½ x 19 In. 3049.00
Banner, James A. Garfield, Stars Stenciled, Blue Border, Cloth, Frame, 18 x 23 ½ In. 880.00
Banner, Suffrage, Women's Rights & What Came Of It, c.1881, 21 x 23 In. 598.00
Banner, Willkie, Win With Willkie, 1940 Campaign, 12 In. 94.00
Belt, Hubert Humphrey, Sun, White, Blue, Green, Plastic Discs, Metal Chain 33.00
Belt Buckle, Abraham Lincoln, Beardless, Ferrotype, 1860, 1 ½ x 1 ¾ In. 1315.00
Belt Buckle, Harding, Coolidge, 1920, ¾ x 1 ¼ In. 840.00
Book, Cartoon, Anti-Goldwater, The Goldwater Cartoons, 1964, 44 Pages 35.00
Book, Democratic Convention Campaign, Davis & Bryan Cover, 1924, 352 Pages 105.00
Book, Theodore Roosevelt African Trails, Syndicate Publishing, 1910, 200 Illustrations 58.00
Booklet, Benjamin Harrison, True Blue Republican Campaign Songs, 1892, 32 Pages 110.00
Booklet, Benjamin Harrison Campaign Song For 1892, S. Braindard's Sons & Co. 110.00
Booklet, Life Of General Scott, On Horseback, 32 Pages, 6 x 9 In. 38.00
Booklet, McKinley, Last Speech, Last Words, 12 Pages 42.00
Booklet, The Confederate, Souvenir Published By Walter Tylor, c.1885, 5 x 8 ½ In. 86.00
Bottle, Flask, William Henry Harrison, Aqua, 1840 Campaign, Pt. 7767.00
Bottle, Flask, Zachary Taylor, Cannon, Genl. Taylor Never Surrenders, Aqua, Pt. .... 335.00 to 657.00
Bottle, Flask, Zachary Taylor, George Washington, Bridgeton, N.J., Pt. 359.00
Bowtie, Vote Humphrey, Muskie, Donkey, Red, Clip-On, 1968 .... 35.00
Box, Sewing, Martin Van Buren, Flowers, Hand Painted, Oval, c.1840, 4 x 7 x 11 In. 480.00
Box, Thread, Portrait Under Glass, Andrew Jackson, 1820s, 3 ½ x 5 In. 5378.00
Bracelet, Abraham Lincoln, Locket-Like Centerpiece, 1865, 1 ⅙ x 1 ¹³⁄₁₆ In. 1135.00
Bracelet, Stevenson, Rose, Win With Stevenson, Brass, Enamel, 1 ¾-In. Disc .... *illus* 38.00
Broadside, Democratic Republican Nominations, Andrew Jackson, Engraving, 1832, 17 x 10 In. 9200.00
Broadside, Grant, Wilson, Campaign, Meeting Of Republican Party, 1872, 18 x 23 In. 2271.00
Broadside, Great Suffrage Mass Meeting, 8 ½ x 13 ½ In. 478.00
Broadside, Lincoln, Campaign, Wide Awakes, Thursday Evening, 1860, 13 ¾ x 10 In. 2868.00
Broadside, President Taft, Taft Will Address The Citizens Of Edgewater, 1912, 8 x 11 In. 183.00

Button, Adlai Stevenson, Convention Headquarters, Oval, Celluloid, 1956, 2 ¾ In. 2032.00
Button, Adlai Stevenson, Official Party, Celluloid, 2 In. 388.00
Button, Adlai Stevenson, Official Party, Oval, Celluloid, 2 ¾ In. 478.00
Button, Adlai Stevenson, Vote Democratic & Don't Let Them Take It Away, 2 ¼ In. 717.00
Button, Agnew, Lithograph, Black, Red Lettering, Tab, ⅞ In. 22.00
Button, Alf Landon, Frank Knox, Celluloid, Bastian Brothers, Jugate, 1936, ⅞ In. 146.00
Button, Alfred M. Landon For President, Portrait, Celluloid, ⅞ In. 49.00
Button, Alton B. Parker, Portrait, Pastels, Celluloid, ⅞ In. 40.00
Button, Alton Parker, Henry Davis, Gold Star, Laurel, Baltimore, 1 ¼ In. 956.00
Button, Anti-JFK, Pro-Nixon, 1960, 6 In. 172.00
Button, Baby, I Like Ike On Diaper, Time For A Change, Celluloid, 1952, 1 ¼ In. 249.00
Button, Barry Goldwater, Democratic Lyndon Tree, 3 ½ In. 418.00
Button, Barry Goldwater, Glasses, Celluloid, 1964, 2 ¼ In. 330.00
Button, Barry Goldwater, Without Glasses, Stars & Stripes Border, Celluloid, 4 In. 1065.00
Button, Beer Mug, Anti-Prohibition, No Beer No Work, 1 In. 27.00
Button, Beer Mug, Anti-Prohibition, We Want Beer, Metal, 1 ½ In. 35.00
Button, Betty's Husband For President In '76, Celluloid, 2 ½ In. 11.00
Button, Bobby Kennedy, Civil Rights, Kennedy For Equality, Celluloid, 1 ¼ In. 32.00
Button, Bobby Kennedy, If I Were 21 I'd Vote For Bobby Kennedy, Celluloid, 4 In. 25.00
Button, Bobby Kennedy, I've Got Boston Soul, Caricature, Celluloid, c.1967, 3 ½ In. 1452.00
Button, Bobby Kennedy, Kennedy & Peace, White, Red, Blue, Celluloid, 1968, 1 In. 18.00
Button, Bryan, 16 To 1, William Jennings Bryan, Celluloid, Clock, Bryan, 1 ¼ In. 715.00
Button, Bryan, Diamond Design, Celluloid, 1 ¼ In. 33.00
Button, Bryan, Kern, Rope Bunting, Celluloid, Jugate, 1908, 1 ¼ In. 239.00
Button, Bryan, Kern, Eagle, Celluloid, Jugate, 1908. 287.00
Button, Bryan, Kern, Red, White & Blue, Celluloid, Jugate, 1908, 1 ¼ In. 310.00
Button, Bryan, Kern, Oval, Jugate, 1908, 1 In. 335.00
Button, Bryan, Kern, Cupid's Heart Nouveau, Jugate, 1908, 1 ¼ In. 388.00
Button, Bryan, Kern, BK Flipped, Celluloid, Jugate, 1 ¼ In. 598.00
Button, Bryan, Kern, Clean Sweep For Democracy, Celluloid, Jugate, 1908, 1 ¼ In. 1016.00
Button, Bryan, Kern, Gold Rimmed, Celluloid, Jugate, 1 ¾ In. 1673.00
Button, Bryan, Kern, Jugate, 1 ¾ In. 1912.00
Button, Bryan, Lind, Daly, Coattail, Trigate, Celluloid, 1 ¼ In. 837.00
Button, Bryan, Lithograph, 1 ¼ In. 71.00
Button, Bryan, Stevenson, Sepia, Jugate, Celluloid, 1 ¼ In. 478.00
Button, Bryan, Stevenson, Stevenson-O'Donnell Club, Celluloid, 1 ¼ In. 508.00
Button, Bryan, Stevenson, Elusive Design, Celluloid, 1 ¼ In. 598.00
Button, Bryan, Stevenson, Tammany Star, Celluloid, ⅞ In. 896.00
Button, Bryan, Stevenson, Mechanical, Whistle, Jugate, 1 ⅜ In. 1076.00
Button, Bryan, Stevenson, Celluloid, Jugate, 1 ¼ In. 4481.00
Button, Bush, Alfred E. Neuman Look-Alike, Celluloid, 1 ¾ In. 10.00
Button, Bush, Schulze, Working For You, Celluloid, 3 In. 52.00
Button, Bust The Trust, Figural, Coal Bucket & Shovel, 1 ¼ In. 128.00
Button, Calvin Coolidge, Our President, Deeds Not Words, Portrait, 4 In. 3629.00
Button, Carter, Damn Yankees For Jimmy Carter, Red, Blue, White, Celluloid, 2 ½ In. 38.00
Button, Carter, Jimmy Carter Can Do It, Yellow, Orange, White Dove, Celluloid, 3 In. 14.00
Button, Carter, Just Plains Jimmy, Caricature, Celluloid, 1 ½ In. 19.00
Button, Champs For Ike, 3 ½ In. 202.00
Button, Charles Evans Hughes, Stars & Stripes, Celluloid, Gold Frame, c.1916, 1 ¼ In. 1936.00
Button, Civil Rights, Antiwar, Ying Yang, Dove, Olive Branch, Celluloid, ⅞ In. 14.00
Button, Clint Eastwood, Clint For Mayor, Carmel, Calif., Celluloid, 2 In. 18.00
Button, Clinton, Arsenio Hall, Saxophone, Celluloid, 2 ½ In. 21.00
Button, Clinton, Deadheads For Clinton, Gore In 1996, Grateful Dead Logo, 2 In. 222.00
Button, Clinton, Gore, Celluloid, Bill, Al, White House, 6 In. 25.00
Button, Clinton, Sesame Street, Save Our Jobs, Support Public TV, Celluloid, 3 In. 79.00
Button, Clothing, Hayes & Wheeler, Campaign, Jugate, 1876 598.00
Button, Coolidge, Photograph, ⅞ In. 201.00
Button, Coolidge & Dawes, Square Deal, Celluloid, ⅞ In. 777.00
Button, Cox, Roosevelt, Cloisonne Donkey, Campaign, 1920, 1 In. 388.00
Button, Cox, Roosevelt, St. Louis, Black & White, Photo & Flag, 1920, 1 In. 31460.00
Button, Cox For President, 1 ¼ In. 1930.00
Button, Daley For Mayor, Portrait, Black & White, Celluloid, 1 ¾ In. 124.00
Button, Damn Yankees For Jimmy Carter, Band Of Stars, Celluloid, 1976, 2 In. 95.00
Button, Davis, Nelson, Coattail, Jugate, 1924, ⅞ In. 1554.00
Button, Debs, Hanford, Colorful, Socialist Candidates, Colorful, Jugate, 1904, 1 ¼ In. 1076.00
Button, Debs, Harriman, Social Democratic Party, Celluloid, c.1900, ⅞ In. 3141.00

Political, Bandanna, Cleveland, Hendricks, Eagles, Cotton, 19 x 20 ½ In.
$510.00

Political, Banner, Campaign, Winfield Scott Hancock, Red, White & Blue, 1880, 17 x 24 ½ In.
$11353.00

Political, Bracelet, Stevenson, Rose, Win With Stevenson, Brass, Enamel, 1 ¾-In. Disc
$38.00

P

Political, Button, Ike, January, 1957, Beaver County, Ribbon, 6-In. Ribbon
$115.00

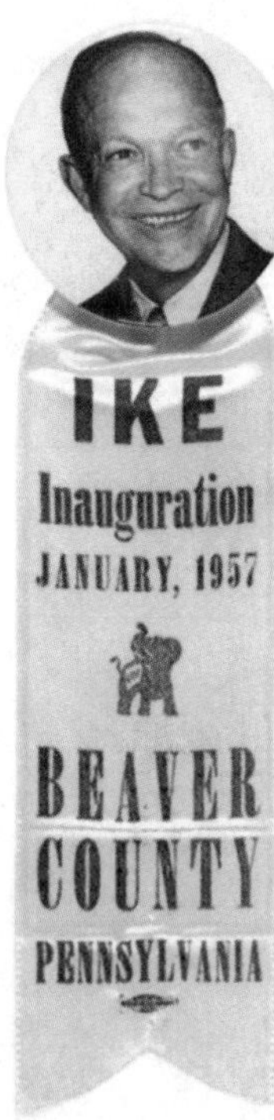

TIP

Condition, size, and small details determine the value of political buttons. To be sure the description is accurate for buying, selling, or insurance, just put the buttons on the glass top of a photocopying machine. Make copies of both the front and the back.

Button, Debs, Seidel Socialist Party, Black & White, Bead Border, c.1912, 1 ¼ In. 1796.00
Button, Dewey, Bricker, White, Blue Jugate, Red Trim, Celluloid, 1944, 1 ¼ In. 434.00
Button, Dewey, Warren, Red, White & Blue, Vote Republican, Celluloid, Jugate, 1948, 9 In.... 191.00
Button, Dick & Pat Go To Bat, Celluloid, 1960, 1 ½ In. 1119.00
Button, Dole, Sinking Ship, Sailing To San Diego, Celluloid, 4 In. 33.00
Button, Drink Goldwater Daily, Yellow Ground, Green Letters, 1964, 1 ½ In. 143.00
Button, Eisenhower, Nixon, Campaign Kick-Off, Sept. 18 1956, Whittier, Calif., 2 ½ In. 363.00
Button, Elephant, McKinley, Figural, Saddle Opens To Jugate, 1896, ⅞ In. 244.00
Button, Enron Employees For Bush, Celluloid, 2 In. 22.00
Button, Eugene Debs, Benjamin Hanford, Shaking Hands, Socialist, Jugate, 1908, ⅞ In. 908.00
Button, Eugene Debs, Shaking Hands Symbol On Border, Celluloid, Back Paper, ⅞ In. 273.00
Button, Eugene V. Debs For President, Portrait, Socialist Party, 1900, ⅞ In. 660.00
Button, FDR, LBJ, Me & Roosevelt For Johnson, Jugate, Lithographed, 2 ¼ In. 896.00
Button, FDR, Photograph, Celluloid, 1 ¼ In. 273.00
Button, For The Love Of Ike, Vote Republican, Red, White, Blue, Celluloid, 6 In. 47.00
Button, Ford, Dole, America's Choice 76, 3 In. 173.00
Button, Ford, Dole, Proud Again, Celluloid, Jugate, 1976, 2 ¼ In. 357.00
Button, Ford, Dole, Spirograph, Celluloid, 1976, 3 In. 133.00
Button, Frank Seidler, American Socialist, For Mayor, Milwaukee, Celluloid, ⅞ In. 97.00
Button, Franklin D. Roosevelt, La Crosse Country, Wisconsin, Celluloid, 1 In. 291.00
Button, Franklin Roosevelt, Profile In Liberty Bell, 2 ¼ In. 53.00
Button, Free Angela Davis, Free The Negro Nations, Celluloid, 1 ¼ In. 22.00
Button, Garret A. Hobart, Memoriam, McKinley's V.P., Died In Office, Celluloid, 1 ¼ In. 68.00
Button, George Washington, G.W., Brass, Dotted Script, Inaugural, 1789, 1 ¼ In. 5975.00
Button, George Washington, Memorial Era, Brass Shank, 1789 .... 1434.00
Button, George Washington, Smaller Size Brass Shank, Inaugural, 1789, 1 ¼ In. 5079.00
Button, Gerald Ford, Robert McClory, Ford Illinois Coattail, Celluloid, Jugate, 2 ¼ In. 484.00
Button, Gold Bug, McKinley, Hobart, Wings Unfold, Metal, Jugate, 1896, 1 ¼ In. 223.00
Button, Goldwater, Go With Goldwater, Mushroom Bomb Explosion, Celluloid, 1 ¼ In. 44.00
Button, Goldwater, I'm A Right-Wing Extremist In Defense Of Liberty, Celluloid, 2 In. 182.00
Button, Goldwater, Let's Bury Goldwater In November, Celluloid, 3 In. 31.00
Button, Gore, Ethnic Council, Celluloid, 4 In. 41.00
Button, Grant, Colfax, Ferrotype, Beveled, Circular, Brass Rim, 1868 .... 568.00
Button, Grass Rooters For Dick, Celluloid, Green, White, c.1960, 3 In. 19.00
Button, Harding For President, Portrait, Celluloid, ⅞ In. 234.00
Button, Harry S. Truman, Black & White, Colorful Flag, Wreath Border, Celluloid, 9 In. 155.00
Button, Harry S. Truman, Cut Off Image Of Tie & Shoulders, Photo, 9 In. 1793.00
Button, Harry S. Truman, For President, Convention, 1948, 9 In. 1016.00
Button, Harry S. Truman, Golden Jubilee, Celluloid, 2 ¼ In. 717.00
Button, Harry S. Truman, Inaugural, 1949, 1 ¾ In. 777.00
Button, Harry S. Truman, Our President, Sitting At Desk, Celluloid, 3 In. 508.00
Button, Harry S. Truman, Photo, Centerpiece As President, 6 In. 4123.00
Button, Harry S. Truman, Portrait, Blue & White, Celluloid, 1 ¼ In. 146.00
Button, Harry S. Truman, Portrait, Facsimile Signature, Celluloid, 1 ¼ In. 176.00
Button, Harvey, Liberty Party, White, Black Lettering, Celluloid, c.1932, ⅞ In. 72.00
Button, Henry Wallace, Progressive Party Candidate, Celluloid, 2 ¼ In. 218.00
Button, Hoover, Anti-Smith, Anti-Catholic, Christian In White House, Celluloid, ⅞ In. 31.00
Button, Hoover, Red & White Stripes, Celluloid, ¾ In. 117.00
Button, Hoover High Hat Club, Enamel, c.1920, 2 In. 1101.00
Button, I Bet On Nixon, Merry Christmas, Celluloid, 1960, 3 In. 420.00
Button, I Like Adlai Better, 20th Congressional District, White, Red Letters, 2 ¼ In. 218.00
Button, I Like Ike, Foil Surface, Embossed Lettering, Peace & Prosperity, 1 ¼ In. 218.00
Button, I Like Ike, Hebrew Letters, 2 ¼ In. 1302.00
Button, If Groundhog Sees His Shadow FDR Will Win, Groundhogs Of Virginia, 2 In. 1345.00
Button, If You Work For A Living How In Hell Can You Vote For Nixon, Celluloid, 2 ½ In. 27.00
Button, Ike, Chinese Lettering, Orange, White, Blue, 2 ½ In. 20.00
Button, Ike, Dick, They're For You, Lithograph, Jugate, 1952, 1 ¼ In. 11.00
Button, Ike, Dick, Jugate, c.1952, 1 ¼ In. 13.00
Button, Ike, Dick, Don't Change Team In The Middle Of The Stream, Celluloid, 1956, 3 In. .. 213.00
Button, Ike, GOP Elephant, Wood, 2 In. 17.00
Button, Ike, January, 1957, Beaver County, Ribbon, 6-In. Ribbon. .... *illus* 115.00
Button, Ike, Labor Likes Ike, Lithograph, Red, White, Blue, ⅞ In. 15.00
Button, Impeach ½ Of LBJ, Antiwar, Green, Red, Celluloid, 1960s, 1 In. 179.00
Button, Inaugural, Truman, Photo, 1949, 3/16 In. 613.00
Button, Jackie Kennedy, David Russell, Limited Edition, Celluloid, 2 ½ In. 90.00
Button, Jimmy Carter For President, In 76, Mirror, Portrait Drawing, 2 ¼ In. 440.00

utton, Joe Louis For Willkie, The Brown Bomber, Celluloid, 1 ½ In. 1097.00
utton, John F. Kennedy, Elect Kennedy President, Celluloid, 2 ¼ In. 263.00
utton, John F. Kennedy, Our Next President, Flag Ground, Celluloid, 1 ¾ In. 287.00
utton, John F. Kennedy, Profile In Courage, Celluloid, 1956, 2 ¼ In. 478.00
utton, John Glenn, For President, Celluloid, c.1984, 2 ¼ In. 19.00
utton, John Glenn, Welcome Back To Earth Glenn, 1st Orbit, Celluloid 14.00
utton, Johnson, Anti-Goldwater, In Your Heart You Know He's Nuts, Celluloid, 2 ½ In. 61.00
utton, Johnson, Going Up With Lyndon, Elevator Theme, Celluloid, 1964, 2 ½ In. 1392.00
utton, Johnson, I Used To Be A Republican, Vote LBJ, Celluloid, 3 ½ In. 30.00
utton, Kennedy, Green, White Letters, 1960, 3 ½ In. 974.00
utton, Kennedy, Republicans For Kennedy, Celluloid, White, Blue Lettering, 1 ¼ In. 94.00
utton, Kennedy For President, White, Celluloid, 1 ¼ In. 152.00
utton, Knox, Hopeful Lithograph, 1936, 1 ⅜ In. 25.00
utton, Labor Youth League, Outlaw The Atom Bomb, Dec. 1949, Celluloid, 1 ½ In. 450.00
utton, Landon, Knox, Sunflower, Celluloid, Jugate, 1936, 1 ¼ In. 4127.00
utton, Lefkowitz, Fino, Gilhooley, United Citizens Committee, Lithograph, ⅞ In. 10.00
utton, Let's Back Ike, Celluloid, 2 In. 16.00
utton, Let's Blitz Grits & Fritz, Pa. State Outline, Ford, Anti-Carter, Mondale, 1 ½ In. 36.00
utton, Life & Freedom, For Sacco & Vanzetti, Lithograph, 1920s, 1 In. 220.00
utton, Little Red Schoolhouse, Celluloid, ⅞ In. 68.00
utton, McGovern, For President, Peter Max, Green, Blue, White, 1 ½ In. 484.00
utton, McGovern, Peace Dove, Blue Ground, White, Red, Celluloid, 1 ½ In. 19.00
utton, McGovern, Shriver, Give Peace A Chance, Blue On White, Celluloid, 1 ½ In. 49.00
utton, McGovern, Think About Children, Celluloid, c.1973, 1 In. 18.00
utton, McGovern, Vermont Autumn Tree, Celluloid, 1972, 2 ¼ In. 660.00
utton, McKinley, Bryan, Eclipse, Celluloid, 1 ¼ In. 2783.00
utton, McKinley, Hobart, Full Dinner Bucket, Blue, Jugate, ⅞ In. 82.00
utton, McKinley, Hobart, Bryan, Sewall, Our Choice, Mechanical, 1 In. 418.00
utton, McKinley, Liberty Bell, 1900 Convention, Philadelphia, 2 ¼ In. 25.00
utton, McKinley, Red Carnation, Celluloid, c.1800, 1 ¼ In. 83.00
utton, McKinley, Roosevelt, Celluloid, Jugate, c.1900, 1 ¼ In. 32.00
utton, McKinley, Roosevelt, Battery, Celluloid, 1888, 1 ¾ In. 359.00
utton, McKinley, Roosevelt, 3 Winners, Celluloid, Trigate, 1 ¼ In. 657.00
utton, McKinley, Roosevelt, First Voters Club, Jugate, ⅞ In. 717.00
utton, McKinley, Roosevelt, Trigate, Minnesota State Republican League, 1 ¼ In. 717.00
utton, McKinley, Roosevelt, Our Choice, Jugate, 1900, 1 ¼ In. 956.00
utton, McKinley, Roosevelt, Riding Horse With Bryan Head, Jugate, 1 ¼ In. 3107.00
utton, McKinley, Roosevelt With Bryan, American Flag, Celluloid, 1 ¾ In. 11950.00
utton, McKinley, TR, Rough Rider, Celluloid, 1 ¼ In. 1132.00
utton, McKinley Patriotism & Prosperity, 2 ¼ In. 1210.00
utton, Mechanical, Theodore Roosevelt, Give Them Hell Boys, Mouth Opens, 1 ¾ x 1 In. 763.00
utton, Missourians For Ford, Yellow, Black Letters, 4 In. 3296.00
utton, MLK, Poor People's Campaign, Washington DC, Black, White, c.1968, 2 ¼ In. 14.00
utton, Mondale, Ferraro, Black, Red, Celluloid, 2 ¼ In. 14.00
utton, Mondale, Will Rogers Never Met Ronald Reagan, Celluloid, 2 In. 11.00
utton, Mothers For Maine, Adlai Stevenson, 1 ¾ In. 315.00
utton, My Friend Ike, Portrait, Black & White Hands Shaking, Lithograph, 1 ¼ In. 84.00
utton, NAACP Freedom Fighters, Black & White Hands Breaking Chains, 1960s, 1 ½ In. 73.00
utton, Neglected Husbands For Nixon, White, Blue & Red Lettering, 1 ½ In. 440.00
utton, Nixon, Ungrateful Dead Thank Nixon, Celluloid, 1 ¼ In. 33.00
utton, Nixon, Would You Buy A Used Car From Him, Celluloid, 1 ¼ In. 35.00
utton, NY Med. Comm., End The War In Vietnam, Dover, Caduceus, Celluloid, 1 ½ In. 32.00
utton, Parker, Davis, Jugate, 1 ¼ In. .... *illus* 82.00
utton, Parker, Davis, Baltimore Badge, Back River, ⅞ In. 98.00
utton, Parker, Davis, White Elephant, Campaign, Celluloid, 1904, 1 ½ In. 418.00
utton, Parker, Davis Gold Star, Alton Parker & Henry Davis, 1 ¼ In. 956.00
utton, President Ford Over Photograph, Flasher, 2 ½ In. 29.00
utton, Profile In Courage, John F. Kennedy, Celluloid, 1956, 2 ¼ In. 581.00
utton, Prohibition, I Am On The Water Wagon Now, White, Black, Celluloid, 1 In. 14.00
utton, Prohibition, Safety First, Vote Dry, Red, Black Umbrella, Yellow, Celluloid, 1 In. 19.00
utton, Project Mercury Friendship 7, John Glenn, February 20, 1962, Celluloid, 1 ¼ In. 163.00
utton, Protest, Peace In Vietnam, Purple, White Lettering, Celluloid, 1 ½ In. 10.00
utton, Protest, Vietnam, Make Love Not War, White, Black, Celluloid, 1 ½ In. 22.00
utton, Protest, Vietnam, Our Boys Are Dying In Vain, Celluloid, c.1967, 1 ½ In. 105.00
utton, Reagan, Hookers For Reagan, Pink Ground, Black Lettering, Celluloid, 4 In. 21.00
utton, Reagan, Mt. St. Helens, We're Still Erupting For You, Washington State, 2 ¼ In. 218.00

TIP
You should not regild, resilver, or repaint political buttons or badges. It lowers the value.

Political, Button, Parker, Davis, Jugate, 1 ¼ In.
$82.00

Political, Button, Teddy Roosevelt, Lincoln, 50th Anniversary, Republican Party, ⅞ In.
$702.00

Political, Button, Thomas Dewey, Get Your Ass Off The Grass It's Dewey, Celluloid, 1 ½ In.
$1195.00

Political, Button, Vietnam Protest, Washington Easter 65, Red, White, 1 ¼ In.
$82.00

Political, Button, William McKinley, Patriotism & Prosperity, Celluloid, 2 ⅛ In.
$717.00

Political, Button, Wilson, Marshall, Carlin, Coattail, Trigate, Celluloid, 1 ¼ In.
$717.00

Button, Reagan, On Steroids, Keep America Strong, Celluloid, c.1984, 3 In. ... 17.0
Button, Reagan, Stay The Course, Schooner, Celluloid, c.1984, 1 ½ In. ... 25.0
Button, Reagan & Bush, Made In Detroit, Convention, Jugate, 1 ¾ In. ... 335.0
Button, Reagan Hood, Rob From The Poor, Give To The Rich, Celluloid, 4 In. ... 91.0
Button, Re-Elect Roosevelt, Celluloid, ⅞ In. ... 21.0
Button, RFK, Kennedy, Litho, Tab, 1968, 1 In. ... 22.0
Button, RFK, Peace Sign, White, Black, Celluloid, c.1968, 1 ¼ In. ... 18.0
Button, Ribbon, Committee, White Celluloid Button, Red Ribbon, Rhinestone Ike, 2 In. ... 21.0
Button, Ribbon, Harding, 19th Amendment, c.1920, 1 ¾ In. ... 989.0
Button, Ribbon, Republican National Convention, Chicago, 1952. ... 29.0
Button, Roosevelt, Fairbanks, Eagle, Stars & Stripes, Jugate, Celluloid, 1904, 1 ¼ In. ... 206.0
Button, Roosevelt, Fairbanks, Lady Liberty, Rough Rider Hat, Jugate, 1904, 1 ¼ In. ... 387.0
Button, Roosevelt, Garner, Celluloid, St. Louis Button Co., Jugate, ⅞ In. ... 1611.0
Button, Roosevelt, Is Worth My Buck, Celluloid, Red Border, ⅞ In. ... 68.0
Button, Roosevelt, Picture Of Rose, Letters, VELT, Rebus, Celluloid, 1904, ⅞ In. ... 567.0
Button, Roosevelt, Watch Willkie Wilt, Celluloid, ⅞ In. ... 16.0
Button, Roosevelt & Garner, Blue Filigree, Celluloid, Jugate, 1 ¼ In. ... 3346.0
Button, Roosevelt & Garner, Hello, Good Luck From Missouri Friends, 2 ¼ In. ... 3585.0
Button, Roosevelt & White House, Baltimore Badge, 1904, 1 ¼ In. ... 443.0
Button, Send Batman To Vietnam, Uncommon Cello, 1 ¼ In. ... 86.0
Button, Shovel, Bucket Of Coal, Bust The Trust, 1902, 1 ¼ In. ... 440.0
Button, Smith, Robinson, Celluloid, Jugate, 1928, 1 ¼ In. ... 1330.0
Button, Spanish American War, Maine, Great Western Back Paper, Celluloid, 1 ½ In. ... 28.0
Button, Stevenson, Crossed Legs, Hole In Shoe Sole, Celluloid, 4 In. ... 16.0
Button, Stevenson, Humphrey, Red, White, Blue Ground, Photo Of Both, Celluloid, 3 In. ... 278.0
Button, Stevenson, Humphrey, Celluloid, Red, White & Blue, Photo Of Both, 3 In. ... 280.0
Button, Stevenson, Kefauver, The Winning Team, Cloverleaf, Celluloid, 3 In. ... 311.0
Button, Stevenson, Kefauver, Four-Leaf Clover, Jugate, 1956, 2 ¼ In. ... 388.0
Button, Stevenson, Kefauver, Winning Team, Oval, Celluloid, Jugate 1956, 2 ¾ In. ... 986.0
Button, Stevenson, Nix-On Ike, White, Red Lettering, Celluloid, 2 In. ... 35.0
Button, Stevenson, Sparkamn, Vote Straight Democrat, Jugate, 1952, 4 In. ... 253.0
Button, Stevenson, Switched To Stevenson, Lithograph, White, Blue Lettering, ⅞ In. ... 10.0
Button, Support Johnson & Civil Rights, Lithograph, 3 In. ... 2796.0
Button, Taft, Liberty Cap, Celluloid, ⅞ In. ... 41.0
Button, Taft, Oval, Whitehead & Hoag Back Paper, ⅞ In. ... 42.0
Button, Taft, Portrait, Stars & Stripes, Celluloid, W.F. Miller, 1 ¼ In. ... 447.0
Button, Taft, Sherman, Sepia, Celluloid, Jugate, ⅞ In. ... 13.0
Button, Taft, Sherman, Pastels, Celluloid, Jugate, 1 ¼ In. ... 60.0
Button, Taft, Smile Of Prosperity, Portrait, Celluloid, 1908, ⅞ In. ... 990.0
Button, Teddy Roosevelt, Figural, 2 Teddy Bears, 1 ¼ In. ... 132.0
Button, Teddy Roosevelt, I Feel Like A Bull Moose, Cartoon, Hassan Back Paper, ⅞ In. ... 61.0
Button, Teddy Roosevelt, In Front Of Capitol, Baltimore Badge, Celluloid, 1904, 1 ¼ In. ... 666.0
Button, Teddy Roosevelt, Lincoln, 50th Anniversary, Republican Party, ⅞ In. ... *illus* 702.0
Button, Teddy Roosevelt, Portrait, Stars & Stripes Border, 1912, 1 ¼ In. ... 818.0
Button, Teddy Roosevelt, Rough Rider, Portrait, Celluloid, 1 ¼ In. ... 439.0
Button, Teddy Roosevelt, Stand Pat, Hand Holding Cards, 5 Aces, Celluloid, ⅞ In. ... 400.0
Button, Teddy Roosevelt, Teddy Bear, Button, ¾ In. ... 40.0
Button, Teddy Roosevelt, The Winner, 2 ⅛ In. ... 747.0
Button, Theodore Roosevelt, Booker T. Washington, Equality, Celluloid, 1 ¾ In. ... 7319.0
Button, Theodore Roosevelt, Coattail, Celluloid, Trigate, 1904, ⅞ In. ... 4481.0
Button, Theodore Roosevelt, Rough Rider, Portrait, Stars & Stripes, Celluloid, 2 ⅛ In. ... 853.0
Button, Theodore Roosevelt, Standing, For Vice President, Celluloid, 1 ¼ In. ... 2032.0
Button, Theodore Roosevelt, Zig Zag Candy, Political, Advertising, 1 ¼ In. ... 1793.0
Button, Thomas Dewey, Get Your Ass Off The Grass It's Dewey, Celluloid, 1 ½ In. ... *illus* 1195.0
Button, To Hell With Hitler, 3 ½ In. ... 95.0
Button, Truman, 8 Ball, Lithograph, Green Duck Co., ⅞ In. ... 13.0
Button, Truman, All 48 In '48, Young Democrats, White, Red, Celluloid, 1 ¼ In. ... 146.0
Button, Truman, Barkley, Flag Ground, Jugate, 3 ½ In. ... 263.0
Button, Truman, Barkley, Celluloid, American Flag, Jugate, 3 In. ... 436.0
Button, Truman, Barkley, Black & White, Oval Portraits, Jugate, 1948, 1 ¼ In. ... 448.0
Button, Truman, Barkley, Black Star, Jugate, 1 ¼ In. ... 538.0
Button, Truman, Blue, White Letters, Celluloid, ⅞ In. ... 249.0
Button, Truman, Stars & Stripes, Celluloid, 1 ¼ In. ... 118.0
Button, Truman For Senator, Portrait, Blue & White Border, ⅞ In. ... 400.0
Button, Truman Photograph, Red, White & Blue Ribbon, Plastic Donkey, 1 ¼ In. ... 48.0
Button, United Christian Party, Sword, Cross, Star, Celluloid, c.1900, ⅞ In. ... 413.0
Button, Vietnam, Draft Beer Not Students, Celluloid, 1 ¾ In. ... 25.

P

Button, Vietnam, End The War, Black, Red Lettering, Celluloid, 1½ In. 25.00
Button, Vietnam Protest, Washington Easter 65, Red, White, 1¼ In. .... *illus* 82.00
Button, Vote Ford, Dole, Steelman, Coattail, Elephant Kicking Donkey, 2¼ In. 307.00
Button, Vote Truman & Barkley In '48, Blue, White, Lithograph, ⅞ In. 143.00
Button, Votes For Women, 12 Stars, Ehrman Back Paper, Yellow, Blue, Celluloid, 1 In. 297.00
Button, Votes For Women, Shield Shape, Stars & Stripes, Lithograph, 1⅜ In. 825.00
Button, W. Wilson, Watchful Waiting Wins, Celluloid, Whitehead & Hoag, ⅝ In. 27.00
Button, W.J. Bryan, Free Silver, 16 To 1, Portrait In Daisy, 1896, ⅞ In. 204.00
Button, W.J. Bryan, I Vote For Bryan & The Old Republic, Portrait, Sepia, 1¼ In. 676.00
Button, W.J. Bryan, No Cross Of Gold, No Crown Of Thorns, Celluloid, 1896, ⅞ In. 427.00
Button, Wallace, KKK Hood, Cartoon, White, Black, Celluloid, c.1968, 1¼ In. 25.00
Button, Wallace, Progressive, Olivier Printing Co., Celluloid, c.1948, 1 In. 61.00
Button, War Bond, Phil. Badge Back Paper, Eagle, Flags, Celluloid, 1940s, 1 In. 20.00
Button, War In Europe, Peace In America, God Bless Wilson, Celluloid, 1916, ⅞ In. 25.00
Button, Warren G. Harding, For President, Smiling, 1920, 1¼ In. 508.00
Button, Warren Harding, Coattail, Celluloid, Cuyahoga County, 1¼ In. 440.00
Button, We Want Truman, White, Blue Letters, Celluloid, 1¼ In. 262.00
Button, Wendell Willkie, Brass Hanging Loop, 9 In. 478.00
Button, What Should William Howard Taft Do, Caricature, 1¼ In. 495.00
Button, William Jennings Bryan, 16 To 1 Clockface, Celluloid, 1¼ In. 239.00
Button, William Jennings Bryan, 16 To 1 Daisy, Celluloid, Whitehead & Hoag, ⅞ In. 65.00
Button, William Jennings Bryan, Ear Of Corn, Oval, Celluloid, 2½ x ½ In. 1320.00
Button, William Jennings Bryan, Laurel Wreath, Multicolored, Celluloid, 1¼ In. 478.00
Button, William Jennings Bryan, Multicolored, Ehrman Design, Celluloid, 1¼ In. 2868.00
Button, William Jennings Bryan, Novel Cartoon, Celluloid, 1¾ In. 1554.00
Button, William Jennings Bryan, Ribbon Flag, Celluloid, 1908, 1¾ x 3¾ In. 837.00
Button, William Jennings Bryan, Wishbone, Celluloid, 1908, 2⅛ In. 388.00
Button, William McKinley, Cartoon, Viewing New Courthouse, Celluloid, 1¼ In. 657.00
Button, William McKinley, Colonies, Celluloid, 1¼ In. 478.00
Button, William McKinley, Count Me For, Full Color, Celluloid, 1¼ In. 2629.00
Button, William McKinley, Front Porch, White Ground, Celluloid, 1½ In. 568.00
Button, William McKinley, Keep The Philippines, Celluloid, ⅞ In. 263.00
Button, William McKinley, Knapsack, Campaign, Celluloid, 1¼ In. 335.00
Button, William McKinley, Patriotism & Prosperity, Celluloid, 2⅛ In. .... *illus* 717.00
Button, Willkie, Elephant, Wood, Blue, Red, White, Pinback, 3 In. 85.00
Button, Willkie, Rotten Eggs With Roosevelt, Omelets With Willkie, Yellow, 1¼ In. 35.00
Button, Willkie Worker, Stars & Stripes Borders, Celluloid, ⅞ In. 125.00
Button, Wilson, Marshall, Carlin, Coattail, Trigate, Celluloid, 1¼ In. .... *illus* 717.00
Button, Wilson, Marshall, Celluloid, Jugate, ⅞ In. 16.00
Button, Wilson, Metal Braid Border, Whitehead & Hoag Back Paper, Celluloid, 1¼ In. 40.00
Button, Women's Freedom League, Votes For Women, Green, Gold, White, 1½ In. 1331.00
Button, Woodrow Wilson, For President 1912, Portrait, Whitehead & Hoag, 1¼ In. 182.00
Button, Woodrow Wilson, Win With Wilson, Portrait, Pastel Colors, Bastian Brothers, 1¼ In. 55.00
Calendar, Franklin D. Roosevelt, Complement Of Burlington, Vt. Grocery, 1934 .... 98.00
Candy Wrapper, Tilden, Hendricks, Colorful, 1876, 5⅛ x 4⅛ In. 448.00
Canteen, Daughter Of Confederacy, Thread For Hanging, Celluloid, 1900, 2⅜ In. 657.00
Canteen, Lincoln, Grant, Cork Top, Gold Ribbon, 2-Sided, 1¾ In. 1560.00
Cap, Liberty, 1¼ In. 853.00
Card, Drawn By 4-Year Old John Kennedy Jr., Dec. 9, 1964, Blue, Red, Yellow Crayons 430.00
Cartoon, End Of War, Hand Colored, Lithographed, The First Day Of May 508.00
Certificate, Your County Thanks You, 11/11/42, 8½ x 11 In. 24.00
Change Holder, Stevenson, Donkey, Flower Form, Orange, Hard Plastic, c.1952, ½ x 3 In. 72.00
Charger, Abraham Lincoln, Delft, Signed, Van Durn, Frame, 20 In. Diam. 657.00
Cigar Cutter, Lamp Lighter, James G. Blaine, 12½ x 7 In. 2022.00
Clock, Animated, FDR, Man Of The Hour, Bronze Luster, Windup, 1933, 5 x 10 x 15 In. 1012.00
Coin Purse, Bryan, Stevenson, ⅞ In. 777.00
Coin Purse, McKinley, Roosevelt, ⅞ In. 1315.00
Compact, Al Smith, Our Next President, Celluloid, 1928, 2⅜ In. .... *illus* 538.00
Creamer, William Henry Harrison, Flags, Log Cabin, Copper Luster, 1840 .... 3049.00
Cup, Teddy Roosevelt, Bust, Shields, Flags, Soldiers, Tin, American Can Co., 2 x 3 In. 717.00
Cup, Teddy Roosevelt, Portrait, Tin, 3½ In. 717.00
Cup, William Henry Harrison, Blue Over Copper Luster, Flags, 1840 .... 6991.00
Dinner Pail, Bryan, Celluloid, 1900, 1¼ In. 720.00
Dinner Pail, McKinley, Glass, Wood Grip, Removable Tin Cup, 1900, 5½ In. 506.00
Dinner Pail, McKinley, Roosevelt, Glass, Clear, Iron Wire Handle, Wood Grip, 3¾ In. 1315.00
Dinner Pail, McKinley, Roosevelt, 4 More Years Of Full Dinner Pail, Glass, Bail Handle, 1900, 4 In... 1315.00

Political, Compact, Al Smith, Our Next President, Celluloid, 1928, 2⅜ In.
$538.00

Political, Drum, Parade, William Henry Harrison, 1840, 19½ x 23 In.
$2271.00

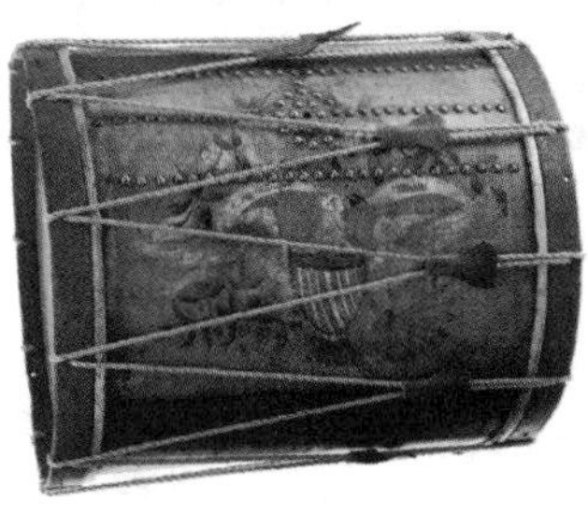

Political, Flag, U.S. Grant, Cotton, 7 x 5¼ In.
$4288.00

POLITICAL

Political, Goblet, Wine, Dorflinger Engraved, Lincoln White House Stemware Service, 1861
$18560.00

Political, License Plate Attachment, America Needs Roosevelt, Portrait, 1940, 9 ¾ In.
$150.00

Political, Medal, Lincoln, Hamlin, Campaign, White Metal, 1860
$1315.00

Dinner Program, JFK's Birthday, At Nation Guard Armory Washington, D.C., 1961 .... 176.00
Display, McKinley, Roosevelt, Republican Club Sepia, Jugate, 3 ½ In. 777.00
Drum, Campaign For Grover Cleveland, Stars On Sides, 36 x 18 In. 1150.00
Drum, Parade, Suffragette, Washington, D.C., March, 1913, 12 x 6 In. 55.00
Drum, Parade, William Henry Harrison, 1840, 19 ½ x 23 In. .... *illus* 2271.00
Envelope, Debs, Seidel, Campaign, Socialist Ticket, This Is Our Year, 1912................ 568.00
Fan, Goldwater, DuPage County Republicans, Paper, Wood, 1964, 8 ¾ In.................. 17.00
Fan, Landon Campaign, Cardboard, Alfred Mossman Landon, 1936, 7 x 14 In. 100.00
Fan, Zachary Taylor, Cannons, Bayonets, Flags, 8 ½ x 16 In.. .... 2291.00
Ferrotype, Lincoln, Hamlin, Uniface, Beaded Brass Rim, 1860 .... 3884.00
Figurine, Black Bisque Cat, Tail In Air, Ruffled Fur, I Want My Vote, 5 In.. .... 1793.00
Figurine, Lincoln For The Defense, Abraham Lincoln, Bisque, 9 ½ In. 95.00
Figurine, Win With Barry, Goldwater, Vinyl, Remco, 1964, 5 x 7 x 3 ½ In.. .... 107.00
Figurine, Women's Suffrage, Woman, Holding Umbrella, Purse, Hand Painted, Porcelain, 4 ½ In. . 1912.00
Flag, Eisenhower, Nixon, Elephant, Blue, White, Wooden Flagstaff, 1950s, 6 In. 22.00
Flag, Fairbanks, Celluloid, Keystone Badge Co., 1 ¼ In. 2483.00
Flag, U.S. Grant, Cotton, 7 x 5 ¼ In. .... *illus* 4288.00
Flag, United States, 33 Stars, Single Sided Print, Wood Frame, 8 ¼ x 6 In.. .... 2629.00
Flue Cover, Al Smith, For President, Blue, Yellow, 8 In. Diam. 88.00
Flyer, Let Money Talk, Labor's Non Partisan League For Roosevelt, 4 x 8 In. 6.00
Goblet, Wine, Dorflinger Engraved, Lincoln White House Stemware Service, 1861...... *illus* 18560.00
Handkerchief, Cleveland-Stevenson, Public Office Is A Public Trust, c.1892, 19 x 19 In. 145.00
Handkerchief, Silk, McKinley, Hobart 1896, Protection-Prosperity-Money, 5 x 7 In. 75.00
Hat, LBJ, Plastic, Western Stetson Style, 1964, 12 x 15 In. 46.00
Invitation, Dinner, George Washington, Engraved, 4 ⅝ x 2 ¾ In.. .... 1253.00
Invitation, Tickets, Kennedy, Johnson Inauguration, January 20, 1961 .... 173.00
Invitation, Ulysses S. Grant, Inaugural, 1873, 8 x 10 In. 837.00
Label, Cigar Box, Abraham Lincoln Portrait, Carved, Wood, 4 ¼ x 10 ½ In.. .... 120.00
Label, Cigar Box, Baltimore 1912 Democratic Convention Candidate 329.00
Label, Cigar Box, Cleveland & Stevenson, 1892 Democratic Candidates, 6 x 8 In.. .... 173.00
Label, Cigar Box, Franklin Pierce, American Flags, c.1890, 6 ¼ x 10 In. 115.00
Label, Cigar Box, Los Angeles Herald, Teddy Roosevelt, c.1904, 4 ½ x 4 ¾ In. 230.00
Letter, Harry Truman, County Judge, Jackson County, Missouri, 1932, 8 ½ x 11 In. 149.00
License Plate, Alf Landon, Picture, Sunflowers, Landon For President, c.1936, 6 ½ In....... 230.00
License Plate, Hee Haw We're Coming Back, Elephant Works While Mule Kicks, 1932 ...... 189.00
License Plate, I Like Ike, Round, Metal, Red, Glitter, White Lettering, 6 In. 95.00
License Plate, Ike, Nixon, Inaugural, White Ground, 1957, 12 In.. .... 121.00
License Plate, Want Prosperity, Repeal 18th Amendment, Metal, Black, White, 14 In....... 179.00
License Plate Attachment, America Needs Roosevelt, Portrait, 1940, 9 ¾ In. .... *illus* 150.00
License Plate Attachment, Davis For President, Green, Yellow, 1924, 3 x 12 In. 294.00
License Plate Attachment, From Sidewalks Of New York To White House, Al Smith, 10 In. .. 152.00
License Plate Attachment, Goldwater, White, Red, Metal, 6 x 12 In. 30.00
License Plate Attachment, Great Race Of 68, George Wallace, Tortoise & Hare, 12 In. 51.00
License Plate Attachment, Hoover For President, Yellow, Oval, Metal, 5 ¾ In. 44.00
License Plate Attachment, Hoover, Curtis, Elephant Shape, Rubber, 1928, 6 ½ x 8 In. 270.00
License Plate Attachment, Ike, Yellow, Blue, Metal, 8 In. 63.00
License Plate Attachment, LaFollette For President, Green, White, Metal, 12 In. 424.00
License Plate Attachment, Landon, Knox, Yellow, Metal, 1936, 11 ½ In.. .... 114.00
License Plate Attachment, Our Choice, Hoover, Curtis, Yellow, Metal, 15 In. 188.00
License Plate Attachment, Re-Elect Roosevelt, Uncle Sam, 1936, 3 ½ x 5 ½ In. 180.00
License Plate Attachment, Repeal 18th Amendment, Orange, Blue, Metal, 10 In. 109.00
License Plate Attachment, Roosevelt, Garner, Happy Days, Aluminum, 1936, 5 x 6 In...... 294.00
License Plate Attachment, Roosevelt, Green, White, Metal, 12 In. 133.00
License Plate Attachment, Roosevelt Humanitarian, Indiana State Comm., Metal, 9 ½ In. . 373.00
License Plate Attachment, Stevenson For President, Green, White, 4 ¼ x 11 ½ In.. .... 196.00
License Plate Attachment, The World Needs Dewey & Warren, Aluminum, 1948, 3 x 10 In.. 108.00
License Plate Attachment, Victory In '64, Goldwater, Yellow, Black, Metal, 12 In. 55.00
License Plate Attachment, Want Prosperity?, Repeal The 18th Amendment, Metal, 14 In. .. 212.00
License Plate Attachment, Wendell Willkie For President, Wood & Metal, 1940........... 145.00
License Plate Attachment, Willkie, Elephant, Reflecting Metal Corp., 1940, 4 ¼ x 9 In. 215.00
License Plate Attachment, Win With Willkie, Red, White, Blue, 1940, 4 ¾ x 9 ¾ In.. ...... 120.00
Match Holder, Theodore Roosevelt, Aluminum, Marked, Acme-Die, 2 x 4 ¼ x 2 In.. .... 191.00
Matchbook, Lady Bird Special, Airplane 182.00
Medal, Andrew Jackson, Gold, 1833. .... 2032.00
Medal, FDR, Inaugural, Bronze, High Relief Profile Of Roosevelt, 1933, 3 In.. .... 460.00
Medal, Hayes, Stickpin, Gilt Brass, 1876 .... 533.00
Medal, Landon, Sunflower, Painted, ⅞ In. 30.00

edal, Lincoln, Hamlin, Campaign, White Metal, 1860 . . . *illus* 1315.00
edal, Seymour Sim, Blue Star Ferrotype, 1868 . . . 396.00
edallion, George Washington, Portrait, Wedgwood, Jasper, Oval, 4 x 4 ½ In. . . . 657.00
edallion, Nixon, Wedgwood, Limited Edition, 1969 . . . 85.00
irror, Hoover Iowa Coattail, Hoover, Charles Curtis, Celluloid, 1932, 2 ⅛ In. . . . 275.00
irror, Theodore Roosevelt, Photo, Bust Image, Lithograph, Celluloid, 2 ¼ In. . . . 353.00
irror, Zachary Taylor, Pewter, Raised Profile, Embossed, 1840s, 3 In. . . . 581.00
ug, Memorial, Garfield, Image & Date Of Birth, Pressed Glass, 1881, 2 ¼ In. . . . 100.00
ug, Modification, Man Tripping Over Barrel Of Beer, 1933, 4 ¼ In. . . . 51.00
ug, Nixon, Figural, Ears Like Elephant, Profile, By Rumph, 1971, 5 ¼ In. . . . 90.00
usic Cover, FDR, Campaign Song, One With Roosevelt, Written By Louis Greaser . . . 27.00
eedlework, William Henry Harrison, Alphabet, Cabin, Tree, 1841, 17 ¼ x 8 ½ In. . . . 1195.00
yster Plate, 6 Wells, Rutherford B. Hayes, White House China, Turkey, Haviland, c.1880, 8 ¾ In. . . 1438.00
endant, George Washington, Memorial Silhouette, 1 ¾ In. . . . 598.00
ennant, Harry Truman For President, Blue, White, 25 In. . . . 109.00
ennant, JFK The Man For The 60s, Blue Vertical Strip, Red Ground, 28 In.. . . . 140.00
ennant, Landon, Portrait In Sunflower, Brown, Gold Ink, Cloth, 1936, 5 x 11 In. . . . 180.00
ennant, Landon Motor Corps, 1936, 11 ½ In. . . . 95.00
ennant, Roosevelt, Johnson, Bull Moose, Blue, White, 1912, 24 ½ In. . . . 853.00
ennant, Socialist Party, Eugene Debs, Emil Seidel, Felt, 19 In.. . . . 1914.00
ennant, Truman, Dewey, Matched Pair For 1948, Rolled Stiff Paper, 5 x 40 In. . . . 95.00
ennant, Vote For Al Smith, 17 ½ In. . . . 91.00
ennant, Votes For New Jersey Women, Felt, 17 x 7 ½ In. . . . 1315.00
ennant, Votes For Women, Clarion Statue Of Suffragist, Felt, 34 x 12 In. . . . 1315.00
ennant, Votes For Women, Suffrage Party, 1909, 25 In. . . . *illus* 1554.00
ennant, Votes For Women, Yellow, Felt, Ink, Frame, 7 ½ x 17 ¼ In. . . . 776.00
in, Gold Bug, McKinley & Hobart On Wings, Mechanical, 1896, 1 ¼ In.. . . . 201.00
itcher, Campaign, William Henry Harrison, Yellowware, Paneled, 1840, 12 x 10 In. . . . 32200.00
itcher, Copper Luster, Bust Of Andrew Jackson On Each Side, 6 In. . . . 5079.00
itcher, Cornwallis Surrender, Copper Luster, Black Transfer, England, 4 ¾ In. . . . *illus* 219.00
itcher, George Washington Apotheosis, Black Transfer, Oval Image, c.1800, 11 x 11 In. . . . 4522.00
itcher, Ironstone, Cleveland, Thurman, Multicolored Flowers, White Ground, 5 In.. . . . 311.00
itcher, Water, William Henry Harrison, Our Country's Hope, Cabin, 1840, 7 ½ x 11 In. . . . 5530.00
itcher, William Henry Harrison, Yellowware, Transfer, 1840, 11 ½ x 10 In. . . . *illus* 32200.00
laque, Hanging Wall, Henry Clay, Wire Loop, 1848, 4 ¾ x 5 ¾ In. . . . 508.00
laque, Re-Elect Franklin D. Roosevelt, 1936, 4 x 6 In.. . . . 230.00
laque, Theodore Roosevelt, Bust, One Hundred Per Cent American, Bronze, 9 x 6 In. . . . 796.00
late, Lincoln, White House China, Purple & Gilt Border, Haviland, c.1864, 9 ⅜ In. . . . 11750.00
late, Polk, White House China, Gilt Scroll Medallion, Shield, Banner, 1845, 10 In.. . . . 3055.00
late, Ronald Reagan, White House China, 12 In.. . . . 717.00
late, Teddy Roosevelt, Portrait, L.P.E., Weller, 1904, 4 ½ In.. . . . 119.00
laying Cards, Bush, Dukakis, Pictures George, Barbara, Mike, Kitty, Full Deck . . . 30.00
laying Cards, Votes For Women, Woman, Rising Sun, 52 Cards, 3 ¾ x 2 ½ In. . . . 956.00
ocket Knife, Smith & Robinson, Portraits, Flag, Shield, Eagle, Donkey, 3 ½ In. . . . 299.00
ortrait, Abraham Lincoln, Miniature On Ivory, Black Lacquer Frame, 4 x 5 In. . . . 2271.00
ostcard, Bryan, Let The People Rule, Tokam Process Co., 1908, 3 ½ x 5 ½ In. . . . 59.00
ostcard, Bryan-Taft, 2 Bills, Columbia Holding Bills, 1908, 3 ½ x 5 ½ In. . . . 68.00
ostcard, Debs, Hanford, Campaign, 1908. . . . 777.00
ostcard, Debs, Seidel, Political, Socialist Presidential Ticket, 1912 . . . 418.00
ostcard, Eugene V. Debs, Campaign, Postmarked, 1908 . . . 215.00
ostcard, Eugene V. Debs, Classic Convict, Socialist Party For President, 1920 . . . 777.00
ostcard, Eugene V. Debs, Portrait, c.1908. . . . 149.00
ostcard, Eugene V. Debs, Real Photo, 1910 . . . 131.00
ostcard, JFK Assassination Scene . . . 17.00
ostcard, Schoolgirls With Banner, Suffrage, Britain, c.1910. . . . *illus* 236.00
ostcard, Stevenson As Illinois Governor, 1949, 3 ½ x 5 ½ In. . . . 172.00
ostcard, Theodore Roosevelt, Big Stick, c.1902, 3 ½ x 11 In. . . . 158.00
ostcard, Willkie Headquarters, Real Photo By Wolfe, 3 ½ x 5 ½ In. . . . 129.00
oster, Adlai Stevenson, Labor Committee, Which Will Be Safer For You, 1952, 21 x 26 In. . . . 3107.00
oster, Bob Kennedy, All Chicago Welcomes, DNC Convention, c.1968, 14 x 22 In. . . . 360.00
oster, Concert, Bobby Kennedy, Los Angeles, Psychedelic, Orange, Black, May 24, 1968. . . . 285.00
oster, Cox, Roosevelt, Matt, Frame, 1920, 15 ½ x 18 ½ In.. . . . 1315.00
oster, Dwight Eisenhower, I'm Pulling For Ike, Man On Tractor, 1952, 23 x 11 ¼ In. . . . 777.00
oster, Franklin D. Roosevelt, Lehman, New York Re-Election, 1930, 14 x 21 In. . . . 258.00
oster, Harry Truman, Matt, Frame, 1934, 13 x 10 In. . . . 1434.00
oster, James Montgomery Flagg, Uncle Sam Wants FDR, Cardboard, 1944, 3 x 3 In. . . . 380.00
oster, Kennedy, Johnson, Campaign, Two Great Democrats, 1960, 21 ½ x 13 ¼ In.. . . . 60.00

Political, Pennant, Votes For Women, Suffrage Party, 1909, 25 In.
$1554.00

Political, Pitcher, Cornwallis Surrender, Copper Luster, Black Transfer, England, 4 ¾ In.
$219.00

Political, Pitcher, William Henry Harrison, Yellowware, Transfer, 1840, 11 ½ x 10 In.
$32200.00

Political, Postcard, Schoolgirls With Banner, Suffrage, Britain, c.1910
$236.00

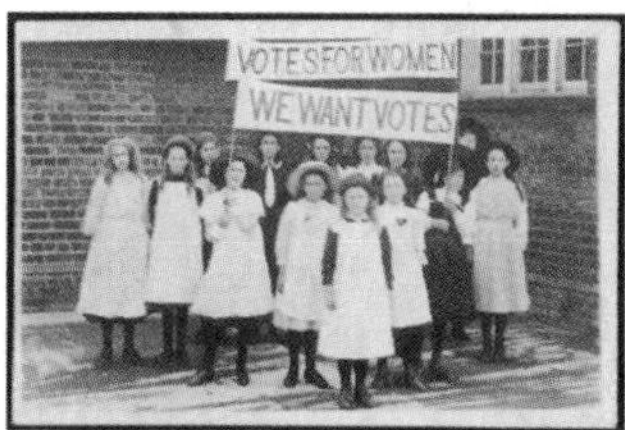

Political, Scale, Harrison, Cleveland, Bisque, Wood, Metal, c.1888, 5½ In.
$86.00

Political, Stickpin, Bryan, Skeleton, 16 To 1 Is Dead, Portrait, c.1896
$850.00

Political, Toy, JFK, Rocker, Musical, Windup, Vinyl, Cloth, Wood, Kamar, Box, 11 In.
$424.00

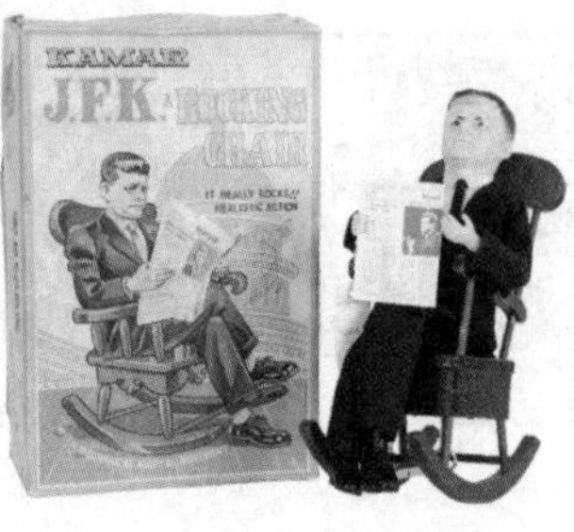

Poster, Kennedy For President, Frame, 29 x 20 In. 72.0
Poster, Re-Election, Franklin D. Roosevelt, New York Governor, 1930, 14 x 21 In. 385.0
Poster, Roosevelt, Lehman, American Labor Party, 28 x 37 In. 448.0
Poster, Teddy Roosevelt, Colored, Mat, Frame, 1904, 20½ x 26 In. 1253.0
Poster, Theodore Roosevelt, First In War, First In Peace, Frame 637.0
Poster, Vote For Dewey, Kill The Klan, 1948, 28 x 40 In. 2000.0
Poster, Wendell L. Willkie, For President, Photograph, c.1940, 14¼ x 19¼ In. 145.0
Print, William Henry Harrison, Farmers, 22¼ x 15½ In. 777.0
Program, Dinner, Electors Of U.S., January 19, 1937, FDR & Garner, 6 x 9¾ In. 30.0
Quilt, Garfield, Arthur, Hancock, English Campaign, Picture Ribbons, 1880. 14340.0
Reflector, Roosevelt, Yellow, Glass Cover, Mirror Back, 10¾ In. 262.0
Ribbon, Abraham Lincoln, Wide Awake, Portrait, 1860 Campaign 1554.0
Ribbon, Abraham Lincoln Mourning, Nation Mourns, Died April 15, 1865, 25 x 5 In. 368.0
Ribbon, Bell, Everett Ferrotype, Crossed Cannon Hanger, 1860, 2 x 6¾ In. 2032.0
Ribbon, Campaign, Harrison, Tyler, Dated Virginia 1840, Silk, 2 x 6 In. 177.0
Ribbon, Charles E. Hughes, Campaign, Red, White & Blue, Portrait, 8 In. 508.0
Ribbon, Garfield, Arthur, Black On Dark Blue, Portrait, 1880, 1⅝ x 5½ In. 255.0
Ribbon, Henry Clay, Silk, Whig Symbol, Coon Poking Rooster, 1844, 2¾ x 7 In. 598.0
Ribbon, Henry Clay, Whig National Convention, 1844, 3½ x 9½ In. 418.0
Ribbon, Honest Old Abe, Lincoln, Hamlin, Abe's Photo, Silk, 1860, 2⅛ x 6¾ In. 2772.0
Ribbon, Honorable James K. Polk, Silk, 7 In. 31460.0
Ribbon, Hughes, Fairbanks, Oil Cloths, Colorful, 7¼ In. 508.0
Ribbon, Jackson, Van Buren, Jefferson In Center, Polk, Dallas, Silk, 1844, 2¾ x 7 In. 1673.0
Ribbon, James Buchanan, Campaign, Light Green, Silk, 1856, 2 x 7 In. 717.0
Ribbon, Lincoln, Hamlin, Free Homes For The People, Silk, 1860, 2¼ x 7 In. 1673.0
Ribbon, Lincoln, Hamlin, Silk Campaign, Oval Salt Prints, Yellow, 1860, 2 x 8 In. 15535.0
Ribbon, Lincoln, Hamlin, Wide Awakes, 1860 Campaign, White Silk, 2½ x 7 In. 2151.0
Ribbon, Millard Fillmore, Blue, Campaign, Silk, 1856, 2½ x 7¼ In. 837.0
Ribbon, National Convention, North Carolina Delegate, People's Party, 1896, 3 x 9 In. 717.0
Ribbon, President Jackson, Our Welcome Guest, Silk, 1833, 4⅛ x 1½ In. 3049.0
Ribbon, Roosevelt, Wallace, For Freedom & Humanity, Black, White, c.1940, 5½ In. 33.0
Ribbon, T. Roosevelt, Red, White, Blue, Bull Moose Pin At Center, Celluloid, ⅞ In. 42.0
Ribbon, William Henry Harrison, 1840 Connecticut Convention, 2½ x 7¼ In. 263.0
Ribbon, William Henry Harrison, Georgia, New England Convention, 1840, 3 x 7 In. 263.0
Ribbon Badge, Eisenhower, Northumberland Country, 1953, 4 In. 115.0
Sash, Silk, William Henry Harrison, Military Uniform, Log Cabin, Cider Barrel, 22 x 3 In. 777.0
Scale, Harrison, Cleveland, Bisque, Wood, Metal, c.1888, 5½ In. *illus* 86.0
Seashell, Bryan, Kern For President, 1908, 3 In. 145.0
Sheet Music, Harry Truman, I'm Just Wild About Harry, 4 Pages, 9 x 12 In. 73.0
Sheet Music, McKinley Campaign Songs, Lyrics, c.1896, 5 x 7 In., 32 Pages 86.0
Snuffbox, Daniel Webster, Round, Celluloid, c.1836, 3½ In. 909.0
Snuffbox, George Washington, Silver, Hinged Cover, Relief Vine, Berries, 2¼ x 1 In. 1554.0
Snuffbox, Martin Van Buren, Papier-Mache, 3¼ In. 5079.0
Snuffbox, Zachary Taylor, In Uniform, Black Lacquer Halves, 3⅜ In. 968.0
Song Book, Benjamin Harrison, 32 Pages, Rue Lue Republican Songs For 1892, 10 Cent. 110.0
Sticker, Dewey & Bricker, Red, White, Blue, 5 In. 9.0
Sticker, Stick With Ike, For Peace & Prosperity, Red, White, Blue, 4¾ x 6¼ In. 5.0
Stickpin, Bryan, Skeleton, 16 To 1 Is Dead, Portrait, c.1896. *illus* 850.0
Stickpin, McKinley, 1900 Convention, Celluloid, ⅞ In. 30.0
Stickpin, McKinley, Photograph, Cloth Flag, Celluloid, 1¼ In. 88.0
Stickpin, William McKinley, Pinwheel, Mechanical, Sepia, Red, White, Blue Paint, 1⅛ In. 120.0
Stud, Barrel, We Want Beer, Anti-Prohibition, 1 In. 15.0
Stud, Bull Moose, ⅞ In. 37.0
Stud, Cox, Rooster, I Will Crow In November, Embossed, ⅞ In. 17.0
Stud, FDR, Profile, ⅞ In. 61.0
Stud, Hoover, Owl, Enamel, Who? Who?, ⅞ In. 72.0
Stud, McKinley, Hobart, Figural Elephant Head, Stars, Metal, Enamel, 1896, ⅞ In. 59.0
Stud, Safari Elephant, Metal, 1¼ In. 49.0
Stud, Taft, 4-Leaf Clover, Enamel, ⅞ In. 58.0
Stud, Teddy Roosevelt, Bull Moose, ⅞ In. 15.0
Tankard, McKinley, Bryan, 2-Sided, Sepia, 2 Handles, 1896, 5 x 6 In. 389.0
Tea Service, W.H. Harrison, Columbia Star, Ridgway, 1840, Service For 6 2875.0
Thread Holder, Sarah's Suffrage Victory Campaign Fund, Tin, Celluloid, 1½ x 4½ In. 1315.0
Ticket, 1937 Inauguration Ceremonies, East Platform 20.0
Ticket, Coolidge, Dawes, Republican, 1924, Whole Ticket, 1¾ In. 2079.0
Ticket, JFK Acceptance Speech, Democratic National Convention, 1960, 3 x 5 In. 45.0
Tie, Brooks, Green, Dewey, Warren, Elephant, GOP, Green, Coattail, 1948 80.0
Tie, I Like Ike, 5-Star Design, Purple 30.0

P

ile, Abraham Lincoln, Bust, J.G. & J.F. Low Art Tile Works, Chelsea, 1885, 6 x 4½ In. 459.00
ile, Lincoln, Photographic, 1909, 9 x 6 In. 201.00
intype, Abraham Lincoln, 5 Dollar Bill Portrait, 1/16 Plate 717.00
intype, Ulysses S. Grant, Mounted In Embossed CDV, 2¼ x 4 In. 508.00
oby Mug, William McKinley, Holding Money & McKinley Bill, 9 x 4½ In. 1434.00
oken, Abraham Lincoln, White Metal, Campaign, 1864 . . . . 191.00
oken, Hartford Wide Awakes, Silver Plated, Yellow Metal, 1869. . . . . 179.00
op Hat, Zachary Taylor Portrait Inside, 7 x 10 x 12 In. 1355.00
orch, Campaign, Parade Rifle, Wood, Replica Of Civil War Musket, c.1880, 5 In. 487.00
oy, JFK, Rocker, Musical, Windup, Vinyl, Cloth, Wood, Kamar, Box, 11 In. . . . . *illus* 424.00
oy, Ulysses S. Grant, Jiggler, Movable Head, Arms, Legs, Wood Cup, Glass, 3 In. Diam. 1290.00
ray, Teddy Roosevelt, Scenic, Roses, Meek Co., Coshocton, Ohio, c.1903, 16½ In. 363.00
ray, Tin, Lithograph, Wm. McKinley, c.1896, 13 x 16 In. 235.00
ray, William Henry Harrison, Log Cabin, Farmer, Flower Border, 1840, 14 x 20 In.. . . . . 3355.00
ray, William McKinley, c.1896, 13¼ x 16¼ In.. . . . . 235.00
mbrella, McKinley, Roosevelt, Campaign, 1900. . . . . 717.00
mbrella, Votes For Women, Oregon, Yellow, White, 35 x 50 In.. . . . . 6572.00
oting Box, Renaissance Revival, Walnut, Pedestal Shape, 36½ x 30 In. 495.00
'alking Stick, William Jennings Bryan, Portrait, Silver Dimpled Ball, Wood, 32 In.. . . . . 508.00
'all Display, Presidents Of The United States, 10 Presidents, 1943, 30 x 42 In. 230.00
'all Plaque, Jugate 2-Sided, Hoover, Curtis, Cardboard, 7 x 7½ x 25 In. 304.00
'atch, Lincoln On Obverse, Washington On Reverse, Convex Covers, Gold Frame, 1866. . . . . 478.00
'atch Fob, Debs, Seidel, Socialist Party, Celluloid, Leather, 1912, 1¼ In.. . . . . 4676.00
'atch Fob, Teddy Roosevelt, Brass, Square, c.1904, 2¼ In. 20.00
'heel Barrow, Campaign, Majorities Must Rule, New Hampshire, Cameo, 1800s. 10350.00
'ristwatch, Franklin D. Roosevelt, Inaugural 538.00

OMONA glass is a clear glass with a soft amber border decorated with pale blue or rose-colored owers and leaves. The colors are very, very pale. The background of the glass is covered with a etwork of fine lines. It was made from 1885 to 1888 by the New England Glass Company. First rind was made from April 1885 to June 1886. It was made by cutting a wax surface on the glass, en dipping it in acid. Second grind was a less expensive method of acid etching that was developed later.

itcher, Midwest, Red, Blue Flowers, 8 In. 86.00

ONTYPOOL, *see Tole category.*

OOLE POTTERY was founded by Jesse Carter in 1873 in Poole, England, and has operated nder various names since then. The pottery operated as Carter & Co. for several years and stablished Carter, Stabler & Adams as a subsidiary in 1921. The company specialized in tiles, rchitectural ceramics, and garden ornaments. Tableware, bookends, candelabra, figures, vases, and ther items have also been made. The name Poole Pottery Ltd. was taken in 1963. The company went ankrupt in 2003 but is in business today with new owners.

owl, Cross, Orange & Burgundy, Scalloped Rim, Delphis, Signed, 4 x 11 In. 225.00
ish, Delphis, Orange, Green, Red Ground, Marked, 5¾ In.. . . . . *illus* 29.00
ish, Galaxy, Splotches, Shiny Flame Glaze, 10½ In. 81.00
ggcup, Marked, 1¾ x 1¾ In.. . . . . 20.00
igurine, Bearded Tit On Pinecone, 5 In. . . . . *illus* 31.00
igurine, Fawn, Lying Down, Marked, 5¼ In. 90.00
igurine, Otter, Holding Fish, Blue Green Glaze, Marked, 5 x 3 In. 23.00
oast Rack, Stamped, 2⅛ x 6½ x 2⅞ In. 15.00
ase, Floral, Multicolored, Marked, 8½ In.. . . . . 198.00
ase, Flowers, 4-Sided, Late 1950s, 8½ In. 90.00
ase, Orange Textured Glaze, Marked, 1921-50, 4½ In. 40.00

OPEYE was introduced to the Thimble Theatre comic strip in 1929. The character became a vorite of readers. In 1932, an animated cartoon featuring Popeye was made by Paramount udios. The cartoon series continued and became even more popular when it was shown on levision starting in the 1950s. The full-length movie with Robin Williams as Popeye was made in 1980. FS stands for King Features Syndicate, the distributor of the comic strip.

ank, Daily Dime, Tin Lithograph, 1956, 2½ In.. . . . . 103.00
ank, Dime Register, Locks At First Dime, 1929, 2½ x 2½ In. 89.00
ank, Knock Out, Bluto, Tin, 3½ x 5 In.. . . . . *illus* 201.00
ook, Pop-Up, Hag Of The Seven Seas, Pleasure Books, 1935. . . . . *illus* 86.00
ubble Set, 2 Pipes, Tray, Bubble Solution, Transogram, Box, 1936 . . . . 121.00
ap, Sailor, Chin Strap, Popeye On Front & Top, K.F.S., Child's. 109.00
omic Book, No. 25, Overstreet, 1942. . . . . 448.00

Poole, Dish, Delphis, Orange, Green, Red Ground, Marked, 5¾ In. $29.00

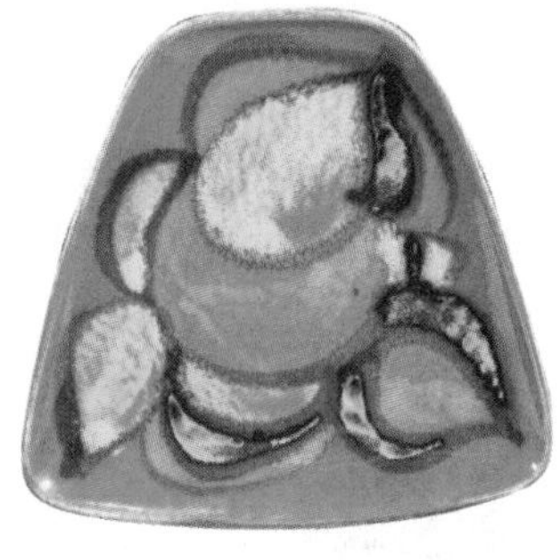

Poole, Figurine, Bearded Tit On Pinecone, 5 In. $31.00

Popeye, Bank, Knock Out, Bluto, Tin, 3½ x 5 In. $201.00

P

Popeye, Book, Pop-Up, Hag Of The Seven Seas, Pleasure Books, 1935
$86.00

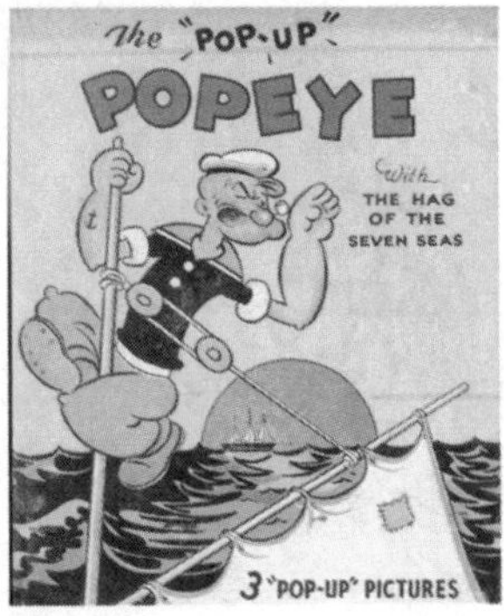

Popeye, Toy, Popeye, Paper On Wood, Pull Toy, Fisher-Price, 1937, 11 In.
$920.00

Popeye, Toy, Popeye, Parrot On Wheelbarrow, Tin, Windup, Chein, 8 ½ In.
$725.00

P

TIP

To keep tin toys from rusting further, try this: Rinse the metal, scrub, dry, then coat with a thin layer of petroleum jelly.

Doll, Popeye, Cloth, Stuffed, Rubber, 1979, 16 In. 85.0
Doll, Swee'pea, Original Tag, King Features Syndicate, 10 In.. .... 57.0
Doorstop, Popeye, No Pipe, Cast Iron, Hubley, c.1920, 9 x 4 ½ In. 1840.0
Doorstop, Popeye, Removable Pipe, Cast Iron, Hubley, c.1929, 9 x 4 ½ In. 6900.0
Eggcup, Popeye & Olive Oyl Dancing, Porcelain, Hand Painted, 1930s, 2 ¼ In.. .... 65.0
Figure, Popeye, Composition, Wood, c.1933, 15 In. 1100.0
Figure, Popeye, Wood, Jointed, Painted, King, Chein, c.1932, 10 ¾ In. 634.0
Game, Menu, King Features Syndicate, 1935, 23 x 14 In. 287.0
Game, Ring Toss, Popeye & Olive Oyl Targets, Rosebud Art Co., Box, 1937, 10 x 15 In. 167.0
Lamp, Popeye, Next To Lamppost, Pipe, Shade, Pot Metal, 1935, 16 In. 328.0
Marble, Blue, Yellow & White, ⅝ In. 45.0
Mug, Popeye, Olive Oyl, Brutus, Wimpy & Swee'pea, Plastic, 1971, 3 ½ x 2 ¾ In.. .... 14.0
Paperweight, Wimpy, Full Figure, Painted, Cast Iron, Hubley, 3 ¼ In.. .... 201.0
Pencil Jar, Popeye, Olive Oyl, Wimpy & Swee'pea, Hand Painted 15.0
Pencil Sharpener, Popeye Flexing Muscles, Butterscotch, Catalin, 1929 .... 82.0
Pencil Sharpener, Popeye Holding Pencil, Bakelite, Green, King Features, 1929, 1 ¾ In. 85.0
Pin, Jeep, Good Luck, Horseshoe, Enamel, Silvered Brass, c.1936, 1 ⅛ In. 115.0
Pin, Kellogg Pep, 1 ¼ In. 30.0
Pin, Popeye, Running, Blue & White Sailor Suit, Enamel, 1930, 1 ¼ In. 82.0
Plate, Happy Birthday Popeye, 50th Anniversary, 1980, 8 ½ In. 22.0
Puppet, Olive Oyl, 1957, 9 In. 49.0
Puzzle, Taking Out Bad Guy, 1945, 13 ½ x 21 ¼ In. 50.0
Smoking Stand, Popeye, Figural, Wood, Painted, Glass Ashtray, Cigarette Holders, 35 In. 220.0
Smoking Stand, Popeye, Pipe, Wood, Metal Ashtray, Hampstead Body Corp., 29 In. 248.0
Soap, Popeye, Olive Oyl, Wimpy, Kerk Guild Inc., 5 In., 3 Piece 144.0
Teapot, Popeye Blowing Smoke From Pipe, Figural, Porcelain, Paul Cardew, 7 In.. .... 100.0
Toothbrush Holder, Popeye The Sailor, Bisque, King Features Syndicate, 1932, 5 In. 115.0
Toy, Bag Puncher, Floor Bag, Tin Lithograph, Windup, J. Chein, 7 ½ In. .... 725.00 to 1103.0
Toy, Charm, Wimpy, Reading Paper, Celluloid, 1 In. 25.0
Toy, Olive Oyl, Squeaks, Pop-Up, Squeaks, Composition, Tin, Wire, Linemar, 7 In. 230.0
Toy, Patrol Motorcycle, White Rubber Tires, Cast Iron, Hubley, 1918, 8 ½ In.. .... 4025.0
Toy, Popeye, Aeroplane, Pilot, Tin Lithograph, Windup, Marx, 8 In. .... 977.00 to 1395.0
Toy, Popeye, Bag Puncher, Overhead Bag, Tin, Windup, Chein, 1932, 9 ½ In. .... 2875.00 to 3162.0
Toy, Popeye, Barrel Walker, Tin Lithograph, Windup, Chein, 1930s, 7 In. .... 300.00 to 550.0
Toy, Popeye, Boat, S.S. Popeye, Die Cut, Wood, Paper Lithograph, Pull Toy, 15 ½ In.. .... 250.0
Toy, Popeye, Boxer, Shadow, Tin Lithograph, Windup, Chein, 7 ½ In. 1103.0
Toy, Popeye, Dippy Dumper, Tin Lithograph, Celluloid, Windup, Marx, 9 In.. .... 575.0
Toy, Popeye, Drummer, Chein, Tin, 7 In. 1017.0
Toy, Popeye, Lantern, Tin, Glass, Battery Operated, Linemar, 7 ½ In. 431.0
Toy, Popeye, Paper On Wood, Pull Toy, Fisher-Price, 1937, 11 In. .... *illus* 920.0
Toy, Popeye, Parrot Cages, Carrying, Tin Lithograph, Marx, Box, 8 ¼ In. .... 403.00 to 448.0
Toy, Popeye, Parrot On Wheelbarrow, Tin, Windup, Chein, 8 ½ In. .... *illus* 725.0
Toy, Popeye, Roller Skater, Holding Spinach Can, Tin, Windup, Linemar, 6 ½ In.. .... 650.00 to 1610.0
Toy, Popeye, Rowboat, Tin Lithograph, Battery Operated, Linemar, 10 In. .... 1150.00 to 1840.0
Toy, Popeye, Rowboat, Oars On Bench, Red, Pressed Steel, Windup, Hoge Mfg., 14 In. 1265.0
Toy, Popeye, Tricycle, Bell, Tin, Celluloid, Windup, Linemar, 4 In. 345.0
Toy, Popeye, Tumbling, Tin, Linemar, Windup, 4 ½ In. 1413.0
Toy, Popeye, Turns Head, Arm Holding Pipe Raises, Pipe Lights, Blows Smoke, Tin, 9 In. 1702.0
Toy, Popeye, Unicyclist, Fat Tire, Tin, Windup, Linemar, 5 ½ In. 575.0
Toy, Popeye, Waddler, Name On Hat, Tin, Windup, Chein, 6 In.. .... 523.0
Toy, Popeye & Mean Man, Fighters, Celluloid, Tin, Windup, Linemar, 6 In. 862.0
Toy, Popeye & Olive Oyl, Dancing On Roof, Tin, Windup, Marx, 9 ½ In. .... 575.00 to 863.0
Toy, Popeye & Olive Oyl, Handcar, Pull Toy, Stretchy, Linemar, 8 In.. .... 517.0
Toy, Popeye & Olive Oyl, Handcar, Tin Lithograph, Windup, Louis Marx, Box, 7 ½ In. 863.0
Toy, Popeye Smoking, On Spinach Can, Tin, Battery, Linemar, 1950s, 9 In. 1670.0
Toy, Spinach Eater, Bangs Top Of Can, Pull Toy, Fisher-Price, 1939, 9 x 10 In. 518.0
Toy, Spinach Motorcycle, Moveable Arms, Cast Iron, Hubley, 1930s, 5 ½ In. .... 403.00 to 675.0
Toy, Truck, Popeye Transit Co., Tin, Friction, Linemar, 13 In. 571.0

PORCELAIN factories that are well known are listed in this book under the factory name. This category and the two following list pieces made by the less well-known factories. Porcelain-Contemporary lists pieces made by artists working after 1975. Porcelain-Midcentury includes pieces made from the 1940s to the 1980s.

Ashtray, Cigarette Holder, Frog Lid, Guillot, France, 7 x 8 ½ In. .... *illus* 110.0

Ashtray, Shmoo, Painted, Glass Dish Insert, 1940s, 4½ In. 175.00
Basket, Scalloped Rim, Openwork Basket Weave, Enamel, Gold, Vine, Flowers, 10⅝ In. 382.00
Beaker, Cicada, Shou Characters, Underglaze, Chinese, 19th Century, 11 In. 881.00
Biscuit Jar, Demi, Shaped Swing Handle, Painted Flowers, Continental, c.1900, 6¾ x 6 In. 59.00
Bottle, Mallet, Blue & White, Chinese, 19th Century, 14 In. 542.00
Bottle, Rose Water, Checkered, Underglaze, Imari Palette, Flowers, Chinese, 8½ In. 353.00
Bottle, Rose Water, Flowers, Blue & White, Chinese, 7½ In. 764.00
Bowl, Blue & White, Flower Scroll, Chinese, 18th Century, 8 In. 411.00
Bowl, Dragons, Clouds, Blue De Hui, Chinese, 19th Century, 7¼ In. 264.00
Bowl, Dragons, Molded, Scrolling, Globular, Blue Glaze, Chinese, 19th Century, 11 In. 823.00
Bowl, Flowers, Sepia, Yellow Ground, Chinese, 20th Century, 4 In., Pair 2703.00
Bowl, Green Jade, Flared Lip, Translucent Stone, Chinese, 2¾ x 70½ In. 600.00
Bowl, Jaune, Dead Bird, Cemetery, Flowers, Handles, 16 x 15 In. 2880.00
Bowl, Kakiemon, Flower, Figural, Japan, 6 In. 354.00
Bowl, Latticework, Girl With Flowers In Hand, Germany, 8½ In. 95.00
Bowl, Lid, Blue & White, Scrolling Lotus, Mid 19th Century, 10½ x 12½ In. 518.00
Bowl, Lute Player, Lady, Putto Scattering Flowers, Ormolu, Tripodal, 8½ x 15 In. 2400.00
Bowl, Penang Pattern, Scenic, Man Fishing, Garden, Pagoda, 2 x 10¾ In., 6 Piece 210.00
Bowl, Prunus, Sepia, Iron Red, Chinese, 19th Century, 7¾ In. 235.00
Bowl, Scholars, Blue & White, Hexagonal, Indented Corners, Chinese, 7½ In. 2938.00
Bowl, Scrolling Ling Chih, Blue, White, 7½ In., Pair 1763.00
Bowl, Sevres Style, Flowers, Bronze Mount, Blue Ground, c.1880, 17½ In. .... *illus* 800.00
Bowl, Stylized Flowers, Chinese, c.1840, 3 x 8 In. 23.00
Bowl, Vegetable, White Ground, Blue Trim, Flowers, Cover, 9 In. 117.00
Bowl, Women By Stream, Chinese, 4 x 15 In. 702.00
Bowl Set, Green Dragons, Cloudy Sky, Red Stamped Character Mark, 7½ In., 25 Piece 374.00
Breakfast Set, Capo-Di-Monte Style, Gilt, Relief Decoration, Classical Figures, 6 Piece 600.00
Brush Holder, Blue & White, Octagonal, Calligraphy, Birds, Flowers, 6 x 6 In. 212.00
Brush Holder, Dogs, Landscape, White, Chinese, 19th Century, 5¾ In. 1175.00
Brushpot, Birds, Lotus, Green, White Glaze, Chinese, Early 20th Century, 6 In. 382.00
Bust, Bisque, Girl Holding Bird's Nest, France, c.1880, 20½ In. 502.00
Bust, Woman, Head Cocked To Shoulder, Fallen Bodice, Bisque, France, 13 In. 1175.00
Cake Plate, Flower, Hand Painted, Pierced Handles, RS Prussia, c.1910, 10 In. 71.00
Cake Plate, Square, Multicolored, Gilt Border, Pansy Center, England, 9¼ x 9¼ In. 353.00
Candlestick, 3 Spiraling Sides, Painted Figures & Flowers, Gold Highlights, 7½ In. 207.00
Casket, Vienna Style, Bronze Mounted, Classical Busts, Cobalt Blue Ground, 14 x 16 In. 1293.00
Centerpiece, Neoclassical, 3 Ladies Holding Basket On Heads, 20 x 10 In. 260.00
Charger, Blue & White, Birds In Conifer Interior, Mt. Fuji, Japan, 18¼ In. 230.00
Charger, Fairy Tale Scene, Cyrillic Signature, Kuznetsov, Russia, c.1890, 12 In. .... *illus* 2200.00
Charger, Kang His Style, Enameled Dragon, Gray, Blue Ground, 11½ In. 207.00
Charger, Plate, Blue Flowers & Geometric Design, 14 & 9¾ In., 3 Piece 117.00
Charger, Round, Scenic, Hunting Dogs On Point, Arzberg, 12 In. 175.00
Charger, Scene Of Russian Fairy Tale, Raised Gilt Rim, c.1890, 12 In. 2596.00
Charger, Sevres Style, Royal Portrait Medallions, Blue, Gilt Ground, Frame, 41 x 30 In. 2300.00
Charger, Village Scene, Japan, c.1900, 18 In. 697.00
Clock, White, Blue Flowers, Enamel Face, Gold Highlights, 9 x 7 In. 47.00
Coffeepot, Tavern Scene, Blue Ground, France, 12 In. 263.00
Compote, Beaded Flower Bouquet, Almond Shape, 19th Century, 14 In., Pair 138.00
Compote, Sevres Style, Rose Pompadour, Portrait, Gilt Framed Reserves, 4 x 8 In., Pair 180.00
Cooler, Fruit, Flower Sprays, Pink Ground, Handles, Butterfly Finial, Squat, 11 In., Pair 705.00
Cup & Saucer, Gilt, Enamel, Flowers, Harp, Tucker, Early 1800s, 2¾ x 5¾ In., 10 Piece 1800.00
Cup & Saucer, Tandem Tricycle Riders, c.1890 .... 220.00
Curio, Forest Scene, Germany, 19th Century, 20 x 14½ x 6 In. 2047.00
Cuspidor, Pink, White Roses, Ruffled Rim, Stamped, BDB, Karlsbad, 7 x 6 x 7 In. 160.00
Cuspidor, White Ground, Blue Rings, 19th Century, 5½ x 8 In. 205.00
Decanter, Chinoiserie, Cobalt Blue, Gilt, Depicting Pagoda, Birds, Figures, 7 In., Pair 259.00
Decanter, Sake, Flowers, Grass, Fence, Blue, Green Enamel, Cylindrical, 5½ In. 1175.00
Demitasse Set, Gold Sprigged, Viennese, Enamel, c.1850, 6 In., 14 Piece 118.00
Desk Altar, Madonna & Child, Gothic Triptych Pierced Gilt Brass Frame, 3⅝ x 2 In. 230.00
Dish, Kakieman Imari Style, Partridge, Flowers, Bow Leaf Shape, 10¼ In. 259.00
Dish, Kraak Style, Peony, Flower Panels, Fishscale, Swastika, Chinese, 1800s, 8 In., Pair 259.00
Dish, Scalloped, Flowers, Harcourt, 4½ In. 35.00
Dish, Sweetmeat, Cover, 4 Parts, Chinese, Early 20th Century, 8 x 7½ In. 112.00
Easter Egg, Gilt, Wildflowers, Green Ground, Russia, 19th Century, 4½ In. 1121.00
Easter Egg, Imperial, Painted, Christ Blessing The Children, 19th Century, 2½ In. 1003.00

Porcelain, Ashtray, Cigarette Holder, Frog Lid, Guillot, France, 7 x 8½ In.
$110.00

Porcelain, Bowl, Sevres Style, Flowers, Bronze Mount, Blue Ground, c.1880, 17½ In.
$800.00

Porcelain, Charger, Fairy Tale Scene, Cyrillic Signature, Kuznetsov, Russia, c.1890, 12 In.
$2200.00

Porcelain, Figurine, Girl, Arms Crossed, Marked, Lenci PE, 1937, 11⅝ In.
$800.00

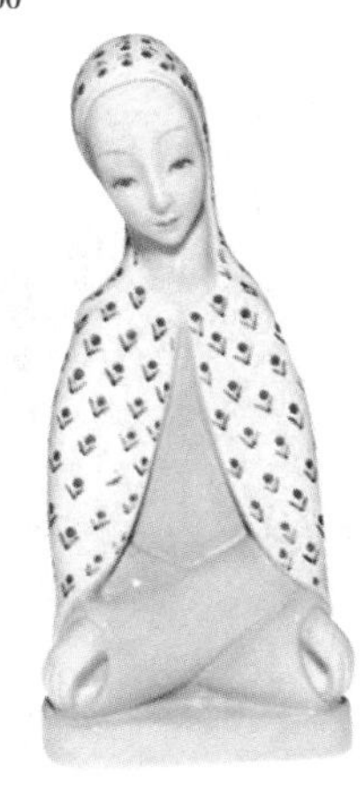

Porcelain, Plate, Gray Design, White Ground, Peter Behrens, c.1901, 7¾ In.
$4375.00

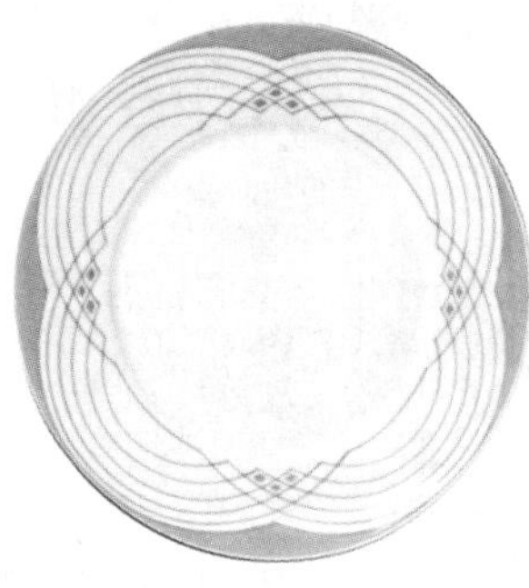

Porcelain, Urn, Yellow, Applied Gold, Marked, Trenton, 7¾ x 8½ In.
$10.00

Porcelain, Vase, Cherry Blossoms, Gray, Pink, Makuzu Kozan, c.1914, 9½ In.
$1100.00

Easter Egg, Painted, 3 Bouquets Of Wildflowers, Blue Ground, Silk Ribbon, Russia, 4 In. 826.00
Easter Egg, Painted, Roses, Blue Ground, Russia, 19th Century, 5 In. 1298.00
Easter Egg, Painted, Wildflowers, Blue Ground, Russia, 19th Century, 4 In. 649.00
Ewer, Gilt Leaves, Scroll Handle, Pear Shape, France, c.1890, 10 x 4¼ In. 149.00
Ewer, Wine, Fish, Leaves, Red, Blue, Green Underglaze, Signed Kakei, Japan, 1800, 8½ In. 764.00
Figurine, 18th Century Man Riding Goat, Rectangular Base, Germany, c.1900, 9½ In. 358.00
Figurine, 2 Children, Puppet, Germany, c.1885, 5 In. 308.00
Figurine, Boy Seated On Basket, Holding Posy, 5½ In. 266.00
Figurine, Chickadee Family, Bisque, 7¾ x 11½ x 8½ In. 264.00
Figurine, Dancer, Girl On Knee, Leg Extended, Yellow, Gray Dress, 10¾ In. 235.00
Figurine, Dog, Collie, Brown Spotted, Gold Collar, Lock, Flower Base, 4 x 5 In., Pair 489.00
Figurine, Dog, Pekingese, Standing, Gray, White, Denmark, 19th Century, 15 In. 1076.00
Figurine, Flora, Barefoot Maiden, Classical Drapery, Meissen Style c.1880, 14 In. 353.00
Figurine, Game Birds, Square Gilt Base, Nymphenburg, Early 1900s, 5½ In., Pair 207.00
Figurine, Girl, Arms Crossed, Marked, Lenci PE, 1937, 11⅝ In. .... *illus* 800.00
Figurine, Girl With Goose, Germany, 7 x 6 In. 88.00
Figurine, Holiday Mice, Bronn, 9 x 8 x 9 In. 175.00
Figurine, Man, Woman Dancers, Germany, c.1920, 7 In., Pair 59.00
Figurine, Man On Lipizzaner Stallion, 10½ x 8 In. 235.00
Figurine, Monkey With Peach, Chinese, 19th Century, 6½ In. 176.00
Figurine, Napoleon On Horseback, Gilt, Germany, 10½ x 9½ In. 146.00
Figurine, Napoleon On Rearing Horse, Austria, 15½ x 11 In. 263.00
Figurine, Noble Woman Next To Table, Marble Base, Gilt Bronze, 14 x 7½ In. 2467.00
Figurine, Seated Lady, Blue & White, Ermine Trimmed Cape, Germany, 7¾ In. 293.00
Figurine, Serving Boy, Standing By Tree Trunk, Holding Jug, Grapes, Germany, 6¼ In. 382.00
Figurine, Sheep Shearer, Rococo Style, Sitzendorf, 5 x 8 In. 150.00
Figurine, Water Bird, Perched On Leafy Branch, c.1750, 4¾ In., Pair 3900.00
Figurine, Woman, 18th-Century Dress, Germany, 9¼ In. 502.00
Figurine, Woman, Reclining On Arm, 18th Century Costume, 8 In. 263.00
Fishbowl, Iron Red, Gilt, Wooden Base, Chinese, 15 x 18 In., Pair 189.00
Flask, Regimental, Matr. Kahlmann, S.M.S. Hessen, 1903-06, ¼ Liter 328.00
Garniture Set, Blue, White, Beaker Shape, Cover, Lotus, Chinese, 12 x 13 In., 5 Piece 1920.00
Garniture Set, Urns, Candelabrum, 4-Light, Cover, Blue & White, 18 x 19 In., 3 Piece 468.00
Ginger Jar, Blue, White, Double Happiness Characters, Leaves, Squat, 9¼ In., Pair 150.00
Ginger Jar, Chinese Blue, White, 19th Century, 9½ In. 192.00
Ginger Jar, Flat Lid, Yellow, Globular, 9½ In., Pair 1440.00
Group, Courting Couple, Attendant, Oval Base, Germany, 19th Century, 8 In. 382.00
Group, Diana, The Huntress, Cherub, Dog, Germany, c.1800, 7 In. 266.00
Group, Exotic Birds, Red, Early 20th Century, 6½ In., Pair 88.00
Group, Gondola, Musician, Oarsman, Child, Painted, Early 1900s, 10½ x 18½ In. 230.00
Group, Leopards, Signed, Etha Richter, Germany, 17 In. 7344.00
Group, Napoleon With Daughter, Germany, Early 1900s, 7 x 8½ In. 59.00
Group, Sevres Style, Biscuit, Venus Having Crown The Beauty, 15 x 13 In. 295.00
Group, Shepherdess, Seated On Swing, 2 Putti, Boy, Lute Player, 14½ x 9½ In. 489.00
Group, Women Awakening Cupid, 13 In. 3068.00
Group, Courting Scene, Meissen Style, 6 x 6 In. 220.00
Hat Stand, Birds, Flowers, Bamboo Shaped, Multicolored, Yellow Ground, 10 In., Pair 235.00
Holy Water Font, Hand Painted, Bronze, Onyx, Oval Plaque, 8 In. 354.00
Jar, Apothecary, Flowers, 5 x 4 In. 22.00
Jar, Birds, Flowers, Baluster, Blue Underglaze, Chinese, 12 In. 1410.00
Jar, Child Riding Kylin, Garden, Blue Underglaze, Oval, Chinese, 19th Century, 8½ In. 1763.00
Jar, Clouds, Phoenix, Blue, White, Korea, 19th Century, 5½ In. 1763.00
Jar, Cover, Blue, White, Scrolls, Copper Mounted Rims, Chinese, 18th Century, 9 In. 470.00
Jar, Cover, Hardwood, Woman, Children, Blue & White, Blue Underglaze, Chinese, 12½ In. 7344.00
Jar, Cover, Phoenix, Peony Scrolls, Blue & White, Blue Underglaze, Chinese, 14 In. 705.00
Jar, Cover, Women, Landscape, Square, Blue Underglaze, Chinese, 19th Century, 8 In., Pair 382.00
Jar, Dome Lid, Finial, Birds, Plants, Multicolored, Baluster, 28 x 15 In., Pair 4112.00
Jar, Landscapes, Sepia, Red, Ribbed, Robin's Egg Ground, Chinese, 20th Century, 5 In. 470.00
Jar, Pomegranates, Butterflies, Blue, Gilt, Baluster, Chinese, 20th Century, 10½ In. 129.00
Jar, Storage, Blue Underglaze, Globular, Buddha's Hand, Korea, 10 In. 940.00
Jar, Wood Cover, Blue & White, Prunus, Crackle Ice Ground, Chinese, 1800s, 9½ In. 212.00
Jardiniere, Flowers, Birds, Multicolored, Japan, 13 x 17½ In. 323.00
Jardiniere, Flowers, Yellow Ground, Chinese, 5½ x 8 In., Pair 236.00
Jardiniere, Underglazed Blue, Yellow, Branches, Chinese, 7 x 7 x 7 In., Pair 1020.00
Jewelry Box, Blue, Gilt, Multicolored Flowers, Egg Shape, 8 x 7½ x 11½ In. 325.00

Panel, Mountain Landscape, Vertical Characters, Wood Frame, Gilt Liner, 46 x 21 In. 1955.00
Perfume Vial, 2 Blue Willow Plates, Silver Screw Cap, c.1850, 2 ¼ In. 546.00
Perfume Vial, Bird's Egg, Silver Chicken Head Screw Cap, 2 ½ In. 863.00
Pitcher, Enameled, Gilt Rim & Foot, Tucker, Early 1800s, 6 In., Pair 1800.00
Pitcher, Gilt, Enameled, Flowers, Marked, Tucker, Early 1800s, 7 ½ In., Pair 7800.00
Pitcher, Gilt, Enameled, Flowers, Marked B, Tucker, Early 1800s, 7 ¼ In. 2540.00
Pitcher, Gilt, Enameled, Flowers, Marked W, Tucker, Early 1800s, 8 ½ In. 1800.00
Pitcher, Gilt, Enameled, Flowers, Reeded Base, Tucker, Early 1800s, 9 ⅜ In. 1800.00
Pitcher, Gilt, Porcelain, Flowers, Tucker, 1800s, 9 ¼ In. 3840.00
Pitcher, Iris Pattern, L.E. & S., c.1890, 11 In. 205.00
Pitcher, Presentation, Arms Of New Jersey, Hon. David O. Watkins, c.1898, 9 ¼ In. 840.00
Pitcher, Tucker, Painted Birds, Gilt Highlights, Early 1800s, 9 ¼ In. 3105.00
Pitcher, Washbasin, Demi, Painted Flowers, c.1900, 12 ½ x 16 In. 94.00
Planter, Blue & White, Conifers, Flowering Trees, Geometric, Chinese, 12 x 18 In. 259.00
Planter, Dragons, Crashing Waves, Octagonal, Blue Underglaze, Chinese, 14 In., Pair 1293.00
Planter, Enameled, Scenic, Flower & Geometric Borders, Late 1900s, 9 x 11 In. 146.00
Plaque, Abraham Lincoln, Bust, White, c.1890, 6 ¾ In. Diam. 90.00
Plaque, Birds On Flowering Branches, Longmore, Marked, Oval, c.1889, 8 In. Diam. 165.00
Plaque, Biscuit, Low Relief, Court Lady In Pavilion, Attendants, Chinese, 17 x 11 In. 443.00
Plaque, Child Leaning On Stump, 2-Tone, A. Freche, France, 1800s, 11 x 7 ¾ In. 173.00
Plaque, Courting Scene, Soft Paste, 8 ½ x 6 In., Pair 193.00
Plaque, Gilt Frame, Fruit, Oval, 23 ½ In., Pair 1645.00
Plaque, Harem Dancer, Painted, Linen Texture, Germany, c.1910, 19 x 11 In. 3910.00
Plaque, Man Covering Woman's Eyes, Winged Cherub Looks On, Painted, 7 x 10 In. 2070.00
Plaque, Parian Figure Group, Giltwood Frame, Germany, 19 ¾ x 15 ⅜ In. 3055.00
Plaque, Portrait, Old Man, Long White Hair, Beard, Oval, 10 ½ In. 440.00
Plaque, Scenic, Painted, Neoclassical Mausoleum, Striegauer, Frame, 13 x 12 In. 764.00
Plaque, Sevres Style, Hand Painted, Gilt, Cupid & Venus, 29 x 18 In. 1035.00
Plaque, Young Maiden Drawing Water, Mid 19th Century, 21 ¼ x 10 ½ x 3 In. 4113.00
Plate, Apple Green, Flower Head, Scrolling Leaves, Chinese, Early 20th Century, 9 In. 177.00
Plate, Classic Beauty In Garden, Roses, Leaf Gilt, Cobalt Blue Border, Cherubs, 9 In. 207.00
Plate, Cobalt Blue, Yellow, Gilt Border, Botanical Reserve, England, 9 ½ In., Pair 118.00
Plate, Dessert, Apple Green, Gilt Gadrooned Border, Floral Center, c.1850, 9 In. 353.00
Plate, Dessert, Rose Border, Monogram BC, Jacob Petit, Presentation Note, 10 Piece 480.00
Plate, Diana Bathing, Viennese, Hand Painted, c.1920, 9 ½ In. 59.00
Plate, Dinner, Blue Borders, Monogram, Flower Garlands, France, 10 In., 12 Piece 354.00
Plate, Gilt, Enamel, Landscape, Maiden, Cupid, Floral Garlands, c.1910, 9 In., Pair 459.00
Plate, Gold Rim, Faberge Egg Design Center, 10 In., 3 Piece 146.00
Plate, Gray Design, White Ground, Peter Behrens, c.1901, 7 ¾ In. *illus* 4375.00
Plate, Multicolored, Flowers, Chinese, 19th Century, 1 ½ x 9 In. 292.00
Plate, Orange Banded Rims, c.1825, 9 ½ In., Pair 2350.00
Plate, Reticulated Border, Medallion, Classical Figure, Lavender, Gilt, 9 In., 8 Piece 288.00
Plate Set, Artichoke, Fianco White Pattern, Richard Ginori, 9 In., 8 Piece 94.00
Plate Set, Botanical Center, Green & Gilt Leafy Border, c.1860, 6 Piece 529.00
Plate Set, Dessert, Coalport, Ruby, Scrolling Gilt Border, Rims, 9 In., 6 Piece 531.00
Plate Set, Gilt, Leaf Scrolling, Yellow Border, White Ground, Cauldon, 10 In., 12 Piece 264.00
Plate Set, Regency, Heart Design, Iron Red, Gilt, England, c.1810, 9 ¼ In., 5 Piece 176.00
Plate Set, Strawberry Leaves, Berries, Buds, Flower Sprays, Longton Hall, 8 In., 3 Piece 2700.00
Platter, Armorial, Parcel Gilt, Mint Green, England, 18 ¼ x 15 ¾ In. 570.00
Platter, Courtyard, Trees, Birds, Geometric & Flower Borders, Chinese, 1800s, 17 In. 748.00
Platter, Gilded, Greek Key Border, Red & Green Leaf Ground, Reserves, 9 x 7 In. 411.00
Platter, Pink Rim, Peach, 2 Handles, c.1900, 14 In. 117.00
Platter, Turkey, Enoch Woods, 13 ¾ x 21 In. 94.00
Relish Tray, Silesia, Cream, Yellow Roses, 20th Century, 11 In. 35.00
Salt & Pepper, Gilt, Autumn Currants, Trailing Leaves 95.00
Saucer, Iron Red, Gold, Battle Scene, Monogram, Chinese, c.1815, 4 ¾ In. 280.00
Spitter, Flowers, Hand Painted, Gilt, Handle, Spout, 6 x 4 x 3 In. 50.00
Stirrup Cup, Fox Head, Early 20th Century, 5 In. 58.00
Teapot Stand, George III, Botanical Decoration, Cobalt, Gilt, 7 ¾ x 6 ¼ In. 323.00
Tureen, Tray, Cover, Blue & Tan Leaf & Scroll Design, Chinese, 10 ½ x 14 In. 146.00
Tureen, Yellow Glazed Basket, Cover, Hen Setting On Nest Of Eggs, Russia, 7 ½ In. 529.00
Umbrella Stand, Blue, White, 5 Holes, Stylized Blue, Leaf, Scrolled Supports, Japan, 23 x 13 In. 1700.00
Urn, 22K Gold Decorations, 2 Handles, Lemieux, c.1930, 13 ½ In. 35.00
Urn, Court Scenes, Gilt Borders, Magenta Ground, Transfer Panels, c.1880, 18 In., Pair 633.00
Urn, Cover, Multicolored Flowers, Gilt, 2 Rams Head Handles, Germany, 22 In., Pair 388.00

Crossed Swords
Crossed swords are a mark used by the eighteenth-century Meissen pottery in Germany, but crossed swords have been used by dozens of other companies since then. Check in a book of pottery marks to learn more.

Porcelain, Vase, Flowers, Green, Cameo, Mercier, 14 In.
$350.00

Porcelain-Contemporary, Plate Set, Conchylorium, 3 Different Shells, Piero Fornasetti, 9 ½ In., 6 Piece
$840.00

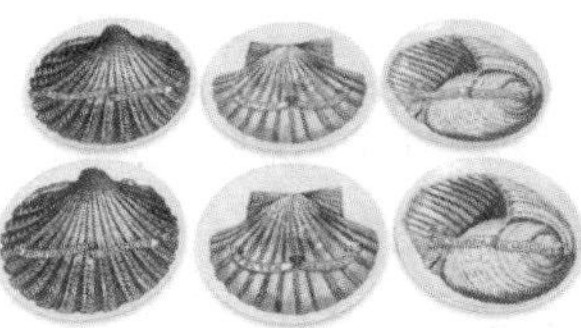

P

Postcard, 2 Fashionable Women, No. 906, Wiener Werkstatte
$531.00

Postcard, Brooklyn Bridge, Fold-Out, Die Cut
$59.00

TIP
Clean dirty postcards with a piece of white bread. Be sure to cut the crust off first.

Postcard, Cats, Our Club, Louis Wain
$130.00

Postcard, Cigarettes Job, Alphonse Mucha, c.1911
$318.00

Urn, Covered, Footed, 2 Gilt Angular Handles, Cobalt Blue, Figural, c.1900, 10½ In. 531.00
Urn, French Style, Handles, Scenic Reserve, Marble Base, c.1910, 52 In. 4680.00
Urn, Gilt Bronze, Warriors & Courtiers, 26 x 20 In., Pair 2450.00
Urn, Mantel, Flowers, Gilt Base & Rim, c.1920, 11½ x 8½ In., Pair 1053.00
Urn, Painted, Flowers, Gilt Highlights, Gilt Bronze Mount, France, 12½ In., Pair 288.00
Urn, Pedestal, Cover, Allegorical Groups, Gilt Decoration, 1800s, 8 In., Pair 1175.00
Urn, Sevres Style, Blue & Gilt Ground, Classical Scene Reserves, 19 x 15 In., Pair 2702.00
Urn, Sevres Style, Champleve Mounted, Romantic Couple, 23 x 8 In. 823.00
Urn, Victorian Lady, Church, Riverbank, Turquoise, Gold Trim, Jacob Petit, 6 In. 353.00
Urn, Yellow, Applied Gold, Marked, Trenton, 7¾ x 8½ In. *illus* 10.00
Vase, 2 Women At Table, Flying Birds, Oval, Waisted Neck, Japan, 9½ In. 413.00
Vase, Baluster, 2 Loop Handles, Flowers, Allegorical Scene, Gilt, c.1900, 10 In. 59.00
Vase, Baluster, Birds, Flowers, 19th Century, Japan, 18½ In. 124.00
Vase, Baluster, Multicolored, Buddhist Lion Head Handles, Birds, Plants, 15½ In. 3120.00
Vase, Birds, Flowers, Blue Underglaze, Seto Ware, Japan, 19th Century, 16 In., Pair 764.00
Vase, Black, Gold Flowers, Cylindrical, Japan, 12 In. 35.00
Vase, Blue, Gold Trim, Ruffled Rim & Base, Germany, 10 x 7 In. 351.00
Vase, Blue & White, Foo Dog Decoration, Chinese, 19th Century, 19¾ In., Pair 3540.00
Vase, Blue & White, Gathered Neck, Gilt Edges, Germany, 10 x 7 In. 351.00
Vase, Blue & White, Hirado, Dragon Form Handles, Landscape, Japan, 14 In., Pair 780.00
Vase, Blue & White, Ku Form, Cranes, Clouds, Center Knop, Lotus, Chinese, 31¼ In. 489.00
Vase, Bud, Japanese, Green Ground, Flowers, Pink, White, 3¾ x 2¼ In. 468.00
Vase, Bud, Raised Scrolls, Flowers, White Ground, Blue, Gilt, Double Handles, 5 x 3 In. 125.00
Vase, Bulbous, Incised Flowers, Yellow, Chinese, 18th Century, 13¾ In. 1075.00
Vase, Bulbous, River Scene, Blue Ground, Crown Devon, c.1930, 7½ x 4 In. 41.00
Vase, Bulbous, Turquoise & Blue Crackle Glaze, Lachenal, 5 x 5½ In. 240.00
Vase, Cherry Blossoms, Gray, Pink, Makuzu Kozan, c.1914, 9½ In. *illus* 1100.00
Vase, Cherry Blossoms, Gray & Rose, Makuzu Kozan, Japan, c.1914 1298.00
Vase, Chinese, Black Glaze, Mei Ping, Art Deco Style, Elongated, 12 In. 150.00
Vase, Chinese, Crushed Strawberry Glaze, Sang De Boeuf, Bottle Shape, 19th Century, 13 In. 1528.00
Vase, Chinese, Flambe, Milky Purple Streaks, 19th Century, 38¼ In. 646.00
Vase, Circular Reserve, Figural Scene, Flower-Form Neck, 2 Handles, Footed, 13 In. 118.00
Vase, Clair-De-Lune, Baluster Shape, Waisted Neck, Jade, 18th Century, 8½ In. 531.00
Vase, Continental, Bulbous, Green, Gilt Framed Medallion, Fishing Scene, 13 In. 206.00
Vase, Cover, Flowers, 2 Handles, Floral Reserves, Basket Weave Neck, c.1835, 15 In., Pair 2500.00
Vase, Cover, Mandarin Palette, Oval, Figural, Foo Dog Finial, Chinese, c.1795, Pair 5310.00
Vase, Double Gourd, Lotus Petals, Green, White Glaze, 10½ In. 1410.00
Vase, Enamel, Gilt Decorated, Egg Shape, Open Fan, Japan, Late 1800s, 8¼ In. 235.00
Vase, Famille Noir, Dragons, Flowers, Squat Globular Body, Elongated Neck, 35 In. 330.00
Vase, Family In Pine Grove, Sepia Enamel, Chinese, 20th Century, 13 In. 1116.00
Vase, Figural, Art Nouveau, Maiden Gathering Grapes, France, 28 x 7 x 7 In. 153.00
Vase, Fired Gold, Flowers, Japan, 27 x 12 In. 150.00
Vase, Fired Gold, Flowers, Pink, 19th Century, 4 In. 35.00
Vase, Flambe, Baluster Shape, Chinese, 19th Century, 13 In. 944.00
Vase, Flowers, Green, Cameo, Mercier, 14 In. *illus* 350.00
Vase, Foo Dogs, Red, Chinese, Early 20th Century, 18 In., Pair 118.00
Vase, Fukugawa, Dragon, Phoenix, Yellow Ground, Japan, 5 In., Pair 531.00
Vase, Garniture, Classical Figures, Black Matte, Ground, Amphora Form, 9 In., Pair 840.00
Vase, Garniture, Franco Bohemian, Rococo Style, Mulberry, Floral Reserve, 20 In., Pair 1140.00
Vase, Gilt, Multicolored, Flare, Floral Handles, Center Portrait, 21 x 12 In., Pair 1058.00
Vase, Landscapes, Blue Overglaze, Enameled, Kakiemon Ware, Japan, c.1920, 11½ In. 999.00
Vase, Lidded Spiral Shape, Chinese Style, Painted Bouquets, Gilt, Early 1900s, 13½ In. 374.00
Vase, Loop Handles, River Scene, Swans, Japan, c.1910, 11 x 5½ In. 40.00
Vase, Oxblood, Glazed, Mounted As Lamp, Everted Rim, Wood Base, Top, Chinese, 27 In. 2160.00
Vase, Oxblood Glaze, Flared Lip Rim, Chinese, 18th Century, 7 In. 720.00
Vase, Parcel Gilt, Raised Enamel, Portrait, Maiden, Wagner, Una Gitana, Gilt, 6 In. 1880.00
Vase, Peaches On Vine, White Ground, Bulbous, Japan, 8 In. 351.00
Vase, Poppy Shaped Handles, Robin's Egg Blue Glaze, Chinese, 19th Century, 9 In. 1410.00
Vase, Portrait, Profile Of Woman, Gilt Highlights, Iridescent Ground, 12 In. 207.00
Vase, Portrait, Young Woman, Pink & Gold Rose Swags, Blue Ribbons, 1938, 12 In. 148.00
Vase, Russian Blue Glass, Trophy, 2 Handles, Gilt, c.1850, 19 In. 2340.00
Vase, Sang De Bouef, Baluster Shape, Chinese, 15½ In. 398.00
Vase, Sang De Boeuf, Baluster Shape, Wood Stand, Chinese, c.1910, 32 In. 460.00
Vase, Silver Flowers, Silver Mounted Foot & Rim, Maroon Ground, 10½ In. 236.00
Vase, Turquoise Crystalline Glaze, Adelaide Robineau, 2¾ x 5 In. 4800.00

ase, White, Gold, Caryatid Handles, France, 13 In. 189.00
ase, White Glaze, Bottle Shape, Korea, 19th Century, 10 In. 561.00
ase, Spill, Gilt, Enameled, Trumpet Shape, Flowers, Tucker, Early 1800s, 5 ⅜ In. 2640.00

ORCELAIN-CONTEMPORARY lists pieces made by artists working after 1975.

igurine, White Tiger, Fleur Cowles, c.1987, 6 x 12 ½ x 7 ¼ In. 146.00
late Set, Conchylorium, 3 Different Shells, Piero Fornasetti, 9 ½ In., 6 Piece *illus* 840.00
rn, Cover, Crimson, Gold Highlights, Medallions, Lion Cabochons, Mottahedeh, 12 In., Pair 384.00
ase, Atelier, Glazed, Carl Harry Stalhane, 8 ½ x 7 ½ In. 960.00

ORCELAIN-MIDCENTURY includes pieces made from the 1940s to about 1975.

late Set, Lotus & Bat, Shou Decoration, Red Stamped Mark, 9 In., 12 Piece 201.00
azza, Chinaman Supports, Mottahedeh, 17 ½ x 8 ½ In., 4 Piece 3760.00
ase, Bottle, Black Matte, Raised White Rectangles, Raymor, 12 In. 225.00
ase, Swimming Fish, Nils Thorssen, Cylindrical, Extended Neck, 12 ¼ In. 290.00

OSTCARDS were first legally permitted in Austria on October 1, 1869. The United States assed postal regulations allowing the card in 1872. Most of the picture postcards collected oday date after 1910. The amount of postage can help to date a card. The rates are: 1872 (1 ent), 1917 (2 cents), 1919 (1 cent), 1925 (2 cents), 1928 (1 cent), 1952 (2 cents), 1958 (3 cents), 1963 4 cents), 1968 (5 cents), 1971 (6 cents), 1973 (8 cents), 1975 (7 cents), 1976 (9 cents), 1978 (10 cents), larch 1981 (12 cents), November 1981 (13 cents), 1985 (14 cents), 1988 (15 cents), 1991 (19 cents), 995 (20 cents), 2001 (21 cents), 2002 (23 cents), 2006 (24 cents), 2007 (26 cents). While most ostcards sell for low prices, a small number bring high prices. Some of these are listed here.

Fashionable Women, No. 906, Wiener Werkstatte *illus* 531.00
Girls, Fur Trimmed Coats Under Umbrella, Germany, 1910. 14.00
oston, Massachusetts, Old State House, Wagons, People, Street Lights, Statues, 1905 6.00
ristol Steel Fishing Rods, Oliver Kemp, Honeyman Hardware Co., 5 ½ x 3 ½ In. 146.00
rooklyn Bridge, Fold-Out, Die Cut *illus* 59.00
udapest Exposition, Drawings, Buildings, c.1896, 9 Piece 118.00
ull Durham Tobacco, Alaskan Gold Miner, c.1913, 3 ¾ x 5 ½ In. 101.00
ambridge Glass Co., No. 2, Cambridge, Ohio 15.00
ambridge Glass Co., No. 3, Cambridge, Ohio 10.00
ase Motor Cars, Barney Oldfield, Giving Joe Tinker Driving Lesson, c.1910, 5 x 3 In. 250.00
ats, Our Club, Louis Wain *illus* 130.00
ats, Three Blind Mice, Louis Wain, Early 20th Century 153.00
herokee Indians, 2 Braves In Dance Regalia, Headdresses, 1950s, 5 ½ x 3 In. 15.00
hildren Sitting In Homemade Airplane, Photo, Mid 20th Century 94.00
igarettes Job, Alphonse Mucha, c.1911 *illus* 318.00
reme-De-Menthe, Drinking Series, Schmucker, Detroit Publishing, Early 1900s 106.00
lectric Car Interior View, Photo, Bruce, Minneapolis, c.1907 189.00
appy Easter, Woman, Red Dress, Easter Egg Basket, Art Nouveau, E.R. Wien, c.1909 30.00
ndanthren, Tessuti Colorati, A Sorgiani *illus* 95.00
nternational Girls, Italy, Schmucker *illus* 24.00
a Dame Aux Camelias, Sarah Bernhardt, Alphonse Mucha, Editions Cinos, c.1898 378.00
lartini, Drinking Series, Schmucker, Detroit Publishing, Early 1900s 47.00
liddletown High School, Middletown, N.Y. 7.00
lount Fuji, Trees, Birds, Boats, c.1905 24.00
otre Dame, Paris, c.1899 75.00
ilot Pens, Camel Caravan Against Yellow Sky, Red Sun, Japan, Early 1900s *illus* 83.00
lastic, Stamped, Postmark Nov. 26 1915, Hamburg, Germany 8.00
easide Trailer Park, Pacific Ocean, 1960s 12.00
et, Acropolis, Type 2, Raphael Kirchner, Enamel-Like Panels, 7 364.00
et, American & Foreign Buildings, Hold-To-Light, Early 20th Century, 28 201.00
et, Au Serail, Languishing Ladies, Gold Border, Raphael Kirchner, 6 248.00
et, Bears, Doing Chores, Days Of The Week, William S. Heal, c.1907, 7 47.00
et, Boy Scouts, Series 9950, Scouts As Owl, Tiger, Eagle, Bear, Tucks, Early 1900s, 4 502.00
et, Cats, Months Of The Year, French Titles, Boulanger, Early 20th Century, 12 413.00
et, Cutout Animals, Salmon Series, Early 20th Century, 10 1652.00
et, Elegant Ladies, Russian Back, Signed, Philip Boileau, Early 1900s, 3 83.00
et, Elves & Fairies, Outhwaite, Early 20th Century, 4 106.00
et, Fantasy, Skull Head Illustrations, Blaesi & Bell, c.1905, 6 153.00
et, Fashion, Evelyn Nesbit, Hand Tinted, c.1902, 4 201.00
et, Flowers, Seasons, 4 Ages Of Man, Alphonse Mucha, F. Champenois, 12 944.00

TIP
When buying postcards, remember—usually the larger the city the lower the value of the card. The smaller the city the higher the value of the card because fewer cards were made.

Postcard, Indanthren, Tessuti Colorati, A Sorgiani
$95.00

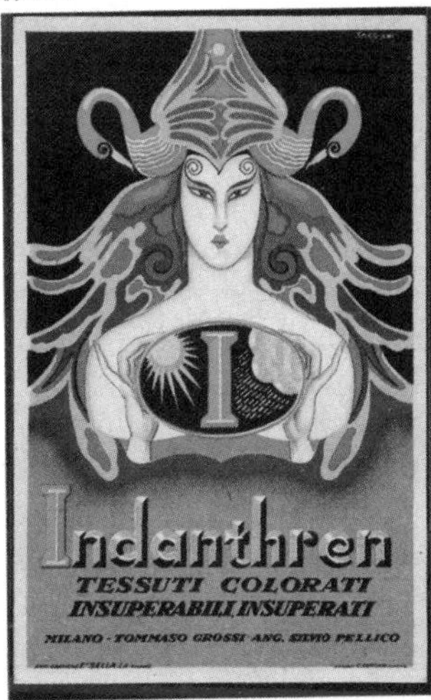

Postcard, International Girls, Italy, Schmucker
$24.00

P

Postcard, Pilot Pens, Camel Caravan Against Yellow Sky, Red Sun, Japan, Early 1900s
$83.00

Propaganda Posters
During World War I, posters were used for propaganda purposes and to recruit soldiers. The most famous example is James Montgomery Flagg's 1917 "I Want You" poster that shows Uncle Sam pointing his finger at you.

Poster, Ville De Nice, Henri Toulouse-Lautrec, Signed, Frame, c.1954, 29 x 19 In.
$370.00

Set, Girls With Beige Border, Raphael Kirchner, M.M. Vienne, c.1901, 10 . . . . . 885.0
Set, Glamour, Lovely Ladies, Flowers, C.C. Company, Series 57, Early 1900s, 10 . . . . . 71.0
Set, Infants, Children, Bessie Pease Gutmann, Early 20th Century, 9 . . . . . 71.0
Set, Les Grandes Femmes, Stylized Women, Floral Border, Henri Meunier, 12 . . . . . 590.0
Set, Love Flowers, Raphael Kirchner, Theo. Stroefer, c.1903, 6 . . . . . 342.0
Set, Pierrot, Chiostri, Bellerini & Frantini, Series 167, Early 20th Century, 6 . . . . . 35.0
Set, Pierrot, Sofia Chiostri, Bellerini & Fratini, Series 31, Complete Set, 4 . . . . . 103.0
Set, Scantily Clad Women, Calderara, Metlicovitz, Signed, Italy, Early 1900s, 12 . . . . . 165.0
Set, Scene, Shell Border, Early 20th Century, 34 . . . . . 201.0
Set, St. Patrick's Day, Winsch, 3 Schmucker Silk Inserts, 3 Booklet Style, 6 . . . . . 84.0
Set, State Belles, Tucks, Series 2669, Early 20th Century, 45 . . . . . 212.0
Set, Street Flowers, Raphael Kirchner, Back & Schmitt, c.1899, 6 . . . . . 649.0
Set, Suffrage, Parade, Washington D.C., Sepia Tone, Leet Bros., c.1913, 6 . . . . . 248.0
Set, Thanksgiving, Booklet Cards, Winsch, Schmucker, 1912-13, 6 . . . . . 248.0
Set, Tropical Moonlight, Blue, Gray, Black, Gouache, Early 20th Century, 12 . . . . . 165.0
Set, Vignettes, Women, Couples, Bertiglia, Santino, Signed, Italy, Early 1900s, 12 . . . . . 118.0
Set, Women Draped In Flags, National Flag Series Number 80, Early 20th Century, 15 . . . . . 59.0
Set, Krampus, Devil Heads & Silhouette, Red Background, Early 1900s, 3 . . . . . 165.0
Set, Le Mois, Month, Alphonse Mucha, Champenois, 4th Series, France, 12 . . . . . 1534.0
Set, Novelty, Real Hair, Blond, Brunette, Gypsy-Esque, Early 20th Century, 3 . . . . . 130.0
Slavia, Alphonse Mucha, Late 19th Century 330.0
St. Mary's French Hospital, Lewiston, Maine 7.0
St. Patrick's Day, Erin Go Bragh, Silk Vignette, Winsch, Schmucker, Early 1900s, 4 . . . . . 118.0
Suffrage, Schoolgirls With Banners, Real Photo, England, c.1910 . . . . . 236.0
Suffrage, Women Marching In Parade, San Francisco, c.1909 . . . . . 71.0
Vin Fiz, Grape Drink, c.1912 . . . . . 826.0
Waverley Cycles, Alphonse Mucha, Art Nouveau, c.1898 . . . . . 4956.0
Women's Rights, Miss Gordon Holmes, Acton Business & Professional Clubs, c.1906 . . . . . 35.0

POSTERS have informed the public about news and entertainment events since ancient times. Nineteenth-century advertising and theatrical posters and twentieth-century movie and war posters are of special interest today. The price is determined by the artist, the condition, and the rarity. Other posters may be listed under Movie, Political, and World War I and II.

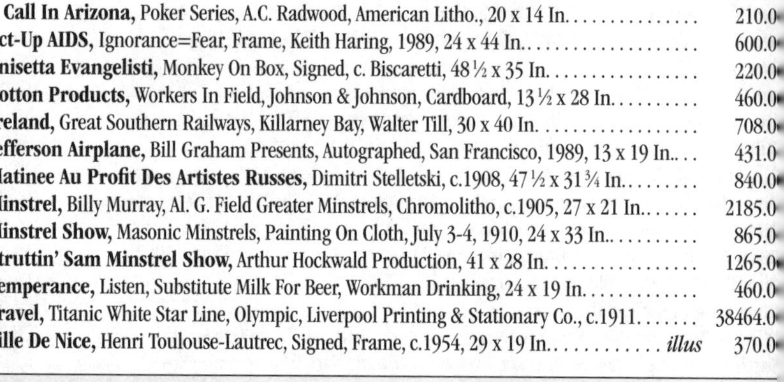

A Call In Arizona, Poker Series, A.C. Radwood, American Litho., 20 x 14 In. 210.0
Act-Up AIDS, Ignorance=Fear, Frame, Keith Haring, 1989, 24 x 44 In. 600.0
Anisetta Evangelisti, Monkey On Box, Signed, c. Biscaretti, 48 ½ x 35 In. 220.0
Cotton Products, Workers In Field, Johnson & Johnson, Cardboard, 13 ½ x 28 In. 460.0
Ireland, Great Southern Railways, Killarney Bay, Walter Till, 30 x 40 In. 708.0
Jefferson Airplane, Bill Graham Presents, Autographed, San Francisco, 1989, 13 x 19 In. 431.0
Matinee Au Profit Des Artistes Russes, Dimitri Stelletski, c.1908, 47 ½ x 31 ¾ In. 840.0
Minstrel, Billy Murray, Al. G. Field Greater Minstrels, Chromolitho, c.1905, 27 x 21 In. 2185.0
Minstrel Show, Masonic Minstrels, Painting On Cloth, July 3-4, 1910, 24 x 33 In. 865.0
Struttin' Sam Minstrel Show, Arthur Hockwald Production, 41 x 28 In. 1265.0
Temperance, Listen, Substitute Milk For Beer, Workman Drinking, 24 x 19 In. 460.0
Travel, Titanic White Star Line, Olympic, Liverpool Printing & Stationary Co., c.1911 . . . . . 38464.0
Ville De Nice, Henri Toulouse-Lautrec, Signed, Frame, c.1954, 29 x 19 In. . . . . . *illus* 370.0

POTLIDS are just that, lids for pots. Transfer-printed potlids had their heyday from the 1840s to the early 1900s. The English Staffordshire potteries made ceramic containers with decorative lids for bear's grease, shrimp or meat paste, cold cream, and toothpaste. Printed advertising and pictures of historical events, portraits of famous people, or scenic views were designed in black and white or color. Reproductions have been made.

A.M. Cole, Cold Cream, Nevada, 1878, 2 ¾ In. 840.0
American Dentifrice, CJ Peacock DDS, American Eagle, Embossed, Red, White, 3 In. 1050.0
Bazin's Premium Shaving Cream, Lavender, 3 ½ In. 90.0
Bear's Grease, Perfumer, Bear, 120 Chestnut St., Philadelphia 305.0
Charcoal Tooth Paste, Bazin Perfumer, 3 ¾ In. 532.0
Cherry Toothpaste, Queen Profile, 3 ¼ In. 123.0
Children Feeding Chickens, Victorian Scene, 5 Colors, Pratt, 1870, 4 In. 360.0
Formodenta, For The Teeth, Caswell Hazard & Co., New York & Newport, R.I., 2 In. 715.0
H. P. Wakelee Druggist, Bear's Grease, 3 ¼ In. 2240.0
Jules Hauel Perfumer, Purple, 3 ½ In. 308.0
Lyman's Cherry Toothpaste, Blue, White, Canada, 3 In. 305.0
Saponaceous Shaving Compound, HP & WC Taylor's, 1851, 3 ¼ In. 280.0

P

POTTERY and porcelain are different. Pottery is opaque; you can't see through it. Porcelain is translucent. If you hold a porcelain dish in front of a strong light, you will see the light through the dish. Porcelain is colder to the touch. Pottery is softer and easier to break and will stain more easily because it is porous. Porcelain is thinner, lighter, and more durable. Majolica, faience, and stoneware are all pottery. Additional pieces of pottery are listed in this book in the categories Pottery-Art, Pottery-Contemporary, Pottery-Midcentury, and under the factory name. For information about pottery makers and marks, see *Kovels' Dictionary of Marks—Pottery & Porcelain: 1650–1850* and *Kovels' New Dictionary of Marks—Pottery & Porcelain: 1850 to the Present.*

Beaker, Andreas Hofer, Tiroler, Etched, c.1909, 1/4 Liter 92.00
Bowl, Acoma Pueblo, Hand Painted, 2 1/2 x 5 1/2 In. 88.00
Bowl, Village, Blue Sky, Painted, c.1900, 5 x 9 In. 70.00
Cigarette Holder, Barbershop Quartet, 4 Different Faces, c.1930, 5 In., 4 Piece 350.00
Crock, Lug Handles, Henry Lowndes, 1841, 9 3/4 In. 11500.00
Crock, Redware, Manganese Glaze, Handle, Urn Shape, 9 1/2 In. 431.00
Cup, 2 Handles, Bulbous, Cream, Wavy Lines, Dot Border, Slipware, c.1720, 5 1/2 In. 5625.00
Cuspidor, Concave Panels, Scroll Design, Rockingham Glaze 44.00
Cuspidor, Diamond Design, Bennington Style Flint Enamel Glaze, 8 In. 33.00
Dish, Bird, Cobalt & Gilt Border, Shell Shape, Chelsea Style, Earthenware, 1 x 9 x 6 In. 144.00
Ewer, Garniture, Gilt Bronze Mounted, Drip Glaze, Renaissance Style, c.1880, 8 x 3 In., Pair . 96.00
Figurine, Boar, Amber Glaze, 4 1/2 In. 294.00
Figurine, Cat, Seated, Oval Base, Brown Glaze, England, 19th Century, 12 In. 1195.00
Figurine, Dog, Spaniel, Tooled Fur, Gold Base, Gothic Arches, Black, Gold, 11 x 12 In. 1035.00
Figurine, Dog, Terrier, Seated, Brown & White Glaze, Logan Pottery, Ohio, 9 In. 173.00
Figurine, Dog, Yellow, Oval Base, Marked, Souvenir 1877, F.M. King Co., 1897, 7 In. 173.00
Figurine, Fisherman, Oriental, Mud, Clay, 8 1/2 In. 45.00
Figurine, Foo Dog, Seated, Blanc-De-Chine, Glazed, Asian, 23 In. 236.00
Figurine, Squirrel, On Branch, Eating Nut, Brown, Yellow, Olive Paint, 8 1/2 In. 1495.00
Figurine, Trident, Military Spear Finial, Green Glaze, 3 In., Pair 360.00
Figurine, Woodsman, Oriental, Mud, Clay, 9 1/4 In. 55.00
Food Mold, French Provincial, Leaves, Handles, Footed, Oval, Early 1900s, 7 x 13 In. 240.00
Food Mold, Provincial, Lamb, Chocolate Glaze, Late 19th Century, 7 1/2 x 11 In. 210.00
Jar, Confit, Provincial, Green Glaze, 2 Handles, France, 4 3/4 x 9 1/2 In., 6 Piece 324.00
Jar, Oatmeal Glaze White Clay, Rim Brown Drip Glaze, Earthenware, 1800s, 7 3/8 In. 705.00
Jar, Storage, Birds, Blue & White, Bulbous, Everted Rim, Underglaze Blue, 10 In., Pair 684.00
Jug, Rye, Helmet, Brown, Cream, Max Fruhauf & Co., 3 In. 146.00
Jug, Whiskey, McKenna, Inscribed, The Best Made In Ky., 3 1/4 In. 123.00
Lion, Yellow Clay, Running Brown Glaze, Oval Base, Late 19th Century, 19 In. 1380.00
Mold, Dessert, French Provincial, Handles, Oval, Ribbed, Footed, 6 x 12 In. 450.00
Mold, Dessert, French Provincial, Oblong, 8 Compartments, c.1910, 19 x 10 In. 660.00
Pitcher, Gothic Panels, Embossed, Salt Glaze, Charles Meigh, c.1850, 10 1/2 In. .... *illus* 350.00
Pitcher, Hunters, Hound Handle, Greatbach Mold, Vance F. Co., Late 1800s, 11 3/4 In. 259.00
Pitcher, Oak Leaves, Acorns, Hunters, Brown, Molded, Hound Handle, c.1845, 9 1/4 In. 588.00
Pitcher, Rooster, St. Clement, 11 1/2 In. 146.00
Planter, Saucer, Copper Luster, Lion's Head, Ring Handles, Relief, 1800s, 5 3/8 In., Pair 176.00
Plaque, Marked M. W. G. Rhenania Sei's Panier, 1887, 9 3/4 In. 345.00
Plate, Flower, Graffito, Mumbauer, Penn., 11 3/4 In. 34000.00
Soup, Coupe, Mottled Green Glaze, Emile Decoeur, Stamped ED, 4 1/2 In. 1000.00
Storage Jar, Brown Glazed, Globular Shape, Waisted Foot, China, 5 1/2 In. 150.00
Teapot, Double Chamber, Turnspout, Blue, Gold Luster Bands, c.1930, 7 In. 41.00
Water Jug, Decagon Shape, Blue & White, 19th Century, 13 x 8 In. 263.00

POTTERY-ART Art pottery was first made in America in Cincinnati, Ohio, during the 1870s. The pieces were hand thrown and hand decorated. The art pottery tradition continued until the 1930s when studio potters began making the more artistic wares. American, English, and Continental art pottery by less well-known makers is listed here. Most makers listed in *Kovels' American Art Pottery,* such as Arequipa, Ohr, Rookwood, Roseville, and Weller, are listed in their own categories in this book. More recent pottery is listed under the name of the maker or in another pottery category.

Bowl, Shell Shape, Brown Clay, Turquoise Interior, Galloway, 18 In. 144.00
Box, Cover, Mermaid, Ivory & Blue Glaze, Art Nouveau, 3 3/4 x 3 3/4 In. 300.00
Cachepot, Shields, Embossed, Red, Blue, Black, Dalpayrat, 3 7/8 In. .... *illus* 400.00
Cachepot, Theodore Deck, Multicolored Enamel, Blue Ground, Faience, 7 1/4 In. 823.00
Charger, 4 Blue Nude Art Deco Women, Metallic Glaze, Impressed BACS, 10 In. 826.00
Ewer, Pergamon, Flowers, Gouda High Glaze, Marked, Ernst Wahliss, 6 3/8 In. .... *illus* 130.00
Figurine, Cat, Russian Siberian, Keramos, c.1920, 12 1/2 x 10 1/2 In. 425.00
Figurine, Flower Frog, Nude, White High Glaze, Coifed Hair, Plinth, 23 In. 224.00

TIP

If you want to preserve a poster, have it framed under glass with acid-free mounting, or roll and tie it loosely for safe storage. Plexiglas sheets filter out ultraviolet light and may be substituted for glass in a frame.

Pottery, Pitcher, Gothic Panels, Embossed, Salt Glaze, Charles Meigh, c.1850, 10 1/2 In. $350.00

Pottery-Art, Cachepot, Shields, Embossed, Red, Blue, Black, Dalpayrat, 3 7/8 In. $400.00

TIP

If you are using glue to fix an antique, work in a room that is about 70° F. Glue will not work well if it's too hot or too cold.

Pottery-Art, Ewer, Pergamon, Flowers, Gouda High Glaze, Marked, Ernst Wahliss, 6 3/8 In.
$130.00

Pottery-Art, Jardiniere, Flowers, Art Nouveau, Slip, Tube Lining, Marked, Wardle, 6 5/8 In.
$130.00

Pottery-Art, Jug, Mushroom, Luster Glaze, Marked, Paul Daschel, 6 5/8 In.
$700.00

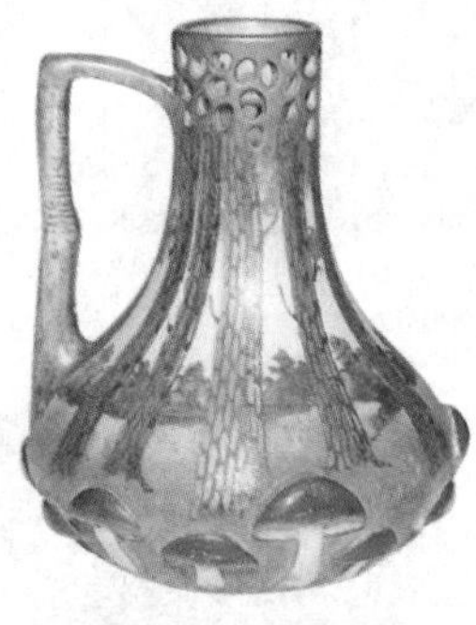

Pottery-Art, Incised Fish, Flared, Footed, Child's, Brannam Barum, 1903, 3 1/2 In.
$177.00

Figurine, Fountain, Seated Frog, Turquoise Glaze, 12 x 13 In. 440.00
Jardiniere, Flowers, Art Nouveau, Slip, Tube Lining, Marked, Wardle, 6 5/8 In. *illus* 130.00
Jardiniere, Turquoise Glaze, Handles, Early 20th Century, 8 1/2 x 12 In. 117.00
Jug, Mushroom, Luster Glaze, Marked, Paul Daschel, 6 5/8 In. *illus* 700.00
Mug, Incised Fish, Flared, Footed, Child's, Brannam Barum, 1903, 3 1/2 In *illus* 177.00
Mug, Tree, Cattails, Sun, Marked, Vance, Avon Works, 5 1/4 In. *illus* 85.00
Paperweight, Scarab, Egyptian Characters, Blue & Tan Crystalline Glaze, Rambervillers, 1 x 3 In. 236.00
Pitcher, Duckling, Running, Petal Border, Cream, Green, 7 1/4 In. 173.00
Pot, Squat, Geometric, Huastec, Mexican, 20th Century 75.00
Teapot, Turquoise, Metallic Glaze, Round, Angular Handle, Art Deco, Rambervillers, 6 In. *illus* 325.00
Tile, Sea Horse, Underwater Vegetation, Incised & Painted, 4 In. 150.00
Vase, 2 Nude Men, Flowers, Carved, Blue Gray Crackle Glaze, Rene Buthaud, 11 In. 881.00
Vase, 4 Handles, Multicolored Glaze, Signed, Denbac, 5 x 9 1/2 In. 230.00
Vase, 4 Sculptured Fish Feet, Flaring, Austria, 6 x 6 In. 840.00
Vase, 4-Sided, Red & Blue Glaze, Dalpayrat, No. 303, 8 1/3 In. 1140.00
Vase, 6 Art Nouveau Protruding Faces, Brown, Tan, Swollen Shape, Larroux, 20 In. 4720.00
Vase, African People, Leaves, Blue, Black, Rene Buthaud, c.1900, 15 x 10 In. 6000.00
Vase, Baluster Bodies, Gilded Leaves, Enamel, Green Glaze, Ribbed Ground, 8 In., Pair 118.00
Vase, Bamboo, Crane, Green High Gloss, Bretby, Tooth & Co., c.1900, 11 In. 118.00
Vase, Bird, Landscape, Painted, Raised Design, Shouldered, Signed EH, 6 x 9 1/2 In. 144.00
Vase, Birds, Oval, Charles Catteau, Belgium, 11 In. 3840.00
Vase, Blue, Red, Yellow Matte Glaze, Organic Form, Handles, Baudin, 7 x 4 3/4 In. 490.00
Vase, Blue Gloss, Triple Disc, Art Deco, Trenton Potteries, 8 1/2 x 8 7/8 In. *illus* 173.00
Vase, Bottle Shape, Mottled Red & Green Matte Glaze, Signed, Dalpayrat, 8 1/2 x 5 In. 1900.00
Vase, Brown, Blue, White Abstract, Marked, Herman Kahler, 3 1/2 In. *illus* 140.00
Vase, Brown, Red, Acoma Pueblo, 7 x 4 In. 175.00
Vase, Brown Dripped Crystalline Matte Glaze, 2 Long Looped Handles, Denbac, 8 1/4 In. 130.00
Vase, Bulbous, 3 Handles, Tan, Brown, Blue Crystalline Glaze, Signed, Greber, 6 x 4 In. 230.00
Vase, Bulbous, Green Swirl, Carved Horizontal Ribs, Signed, Arabia, 9 x 12 3/4 In. 230.00
Vase, Bulbous, Incised, Turquoise High Glaze, Herbert Sanders, 5 1/2 x 7 1/2 In. 633.00
Vase, Bulbous, Red & Turquoise Glaze, No. 63, Dalpayrat, 2 3/4 x 5 In. 450.00
Vase, Bulbous, Turquoise Glaze, Applied Metal Foot, Signed, Lachenal, 5 1/2 x 7 In. 29.00
Vase, Church, Grove Of Trees, Hilton, 4 1/2 In. 633.00
Vase, Cloisonne Flowers, Bats, Blue Metallic Ground, Tapered, Montieres, 1917, 7 In. 1416.00
Vase, Cloisonne Panel, Wheat, Metallic Luster Glaze, Tapered, Montieres, 13 In., Pair 3540.00
Vase, Cloisonne Seaweed, 3 Fish, Metallic Glaze, Oval, Tapered, Montieres, 6 1/2 In. 1416.00
Vase, Double Gourd, Applied Spiral, Max Lauger, c.1899, 8 1/4 In. *illus* 7500.00
Vase, Eggplant, Flared, Inward Rolled Rim, Auguste Delaherche, 3 1/8 In. 236.00
Vase, Faux Wood Grain, Brown Glaze, Applied Handles, Bretby, 4 1/4 x 10 1/2 In. 518.00
Vase, Fish, Flambe, Bernard Moore, 10 In. 983.00
Vase, Flowers, Birds, Applied Twisted Fish, Shaped Rim, Brannam Barum, 1900, 21 In. 1416.00
Vase, Geometric, Orange Matte Glaze, Broad Form, Marked, Z48, Valentien, 5 1/2 x 7 In. 3600.00
Vase, Grapes, Cream Crackle Glaze, Metallic Colors, Jean Barol, 12 5/8 In. *illus* 1200.00
Vase, Green & Brown Glaze, Squat, Tapered, 4 Loop Handles, A. Delaherche, 2 5/8 In. 354.00
Vase, Green Drip Glaze, Brown Streaks, Bulbous, Christopher Dresser, c.1880, 5 3/4 In. 176.00
Vase, Hand Thrown Blue Glaze, White Drip, Pointu, 7 1/4 x 7 1/4 In. 360.00
Vase, Incised Fish, Clam, Plants, Blue & Green Glaze, Wavy Rim, Baron Barnstaple, 5 In. 236.00
Vase, Incised Trees, Bands Of Green Leaves, Swollen Neck, Handles, Wardle, 10 In. 265.00
Vase, Inlaid Geometric, Flaring, Hammered Copper, Linossier, 7 1/4 x 5 1/4 In. 1440.00
Vase, Iridescent Blue, Gathered At Neck, Applied White Spider, 4 Handles, 9 1/2 In. 294.00
Vase, Leaves, 2 Handles, Brown, Metallic Red Glaze, Desmant, 9 x 13 1/2 In. 420.00
Vase, Light Blue Crystals, Mustard Ground, Shouldered, Pierrefonds, 9 3/4 In. 472.00
Vase, Lobster, Seaweed, Metallic Luster Glaze, 2 Handles, Montieres, 10 In. 1416.00
Vase, Maroon, Blue & Green Matte Glaze, Bottle Shape, Dalpayrat, 6 7/8 In. 1770.00
Vase, Mottled Green Glaze, Ruffled Rim, Egg Shape, Frank Reuss Kelley, c.1930, 7 1/2 In. 764.00
Vase, Multicolored, Gilt, Peacock, High Shouldered, Reflected Sun, c.1900 949.00
Vase, Organic, Shouldered, Incised, Marked, Rhead, 6 1/4 x 4 In. *illus* 25000.00
Vase, Pastel Fish, Daisies, Cream Luster Glaze, Tapered, St. Lukas, Utrecht, 6 In. 705.00
Vase, Poppies, Art Nouveau, Green Ground, Bulbous, Squat, Pauline Pottery, 6 x 10 In. 529.00
Vase, Purple Poppies, Marked, Morris Ware, 6 1/2 In. *illus* 850.00
Vase, Red, Gray & Blue Mottled Glaze, Tapered Organic Shape, Dalpayrat, 4 In. 502.00
Vase, Red, Green & Gray Glaze, Gray To White Base, Cylindrical, Dalpayrat, 5 1/2 In. 708.00
Vase, Reflective Ebony, Shiny Gold Angular Patterns, Black Matte Ground, 8 In. 885.00
Vase, Tall Narrow Barrel Form, Glaze, Signed, H. Sim, Henri Simmen, 1920s, 8 In. 188.00
Vase, Turquoise Glaze, Rhombic Shape, Muncie, c.1930, 4 1/2 In. 351.00
Vase, Variegated Brown Crystalline Glaze, Bronze Swag Mounts, Pinched, Denbac, 8 In. 71.00

ottery-Art, Mug, Tree, Cattails, Sun, larked, Vance, Avon Works, 5 ¼ In.
85.00

ottery-Art, Teapot, Turquoise, letallic Glaze, Round, Angular Handle, Art eco, Rambervillers, 6 In.
325.00

ottery-Art, Vase, Blue Gloss, Triple Disc, rt Deco, Trenton Potteries, 8 ½ x 8 ⅞ In.
173.00

ottery-Art, Vase, Brown, Blue, White bstract, Marked, Herman Kahler, 3 ½ In.
140.00

Pottery-Art, Vase, Double Gourd, Applied Spiral, Max Lauger, c.1899, 8 ¼ In.
$7500.00

Pottery-Art, Vase, Grapes, Cream Crackle Glaze, Metallic Colors, Jean Barol, 12 ⅝ In.
$1200.00

Pottery-Art, Vase, Organic, Shouldered, Incised, Marked, Rhead, 6 ¼ x 4 In.
$25000.00

Pottery-Art, Vase, Purple Poppies, Marked, Morris Ware, 6 ½ In.
$850.00

Pottery-Midcentury, Bowl, Effigy, 3 Egyptian Figures, Brayton Laguna, 12 ¾ x 11 ½ In., 2 Piece
$153.00

Art Pottery

The term "art pottery" as it is used today by collectors includes handmade pottery and ceramics, including commercial florist lines, of companies that made art pottery from 1870 to about 1930. Sometimes it includes the work of studio potters from the 1920s through the 1940s.

Art pottery at first was hand thrown and hand decorated. Many of the art potteries started as one-man or one-woman operations and grew into large commercial factories.

Pottery-Midcentury, Figurine, Rabbit, Green Glaze, Impressed, Sylvac, 10 ⅔ In.
$36.00

Pottery-Midcentury, Figurine, Walrus & Carpenter, Signed, Edris Eckhardt, 1930s, 6 ½ In.
$1290.00

Pottery-Midcentury, Jar, Cover, Lines, Gray Glaze, Incised, CB, 9 x 7 ½ In.
$715.00

Pottery-Midcentury, Vase, Blue Matte Glaze, Handles, Art Deco, Marked, American Art Clay, 8⅜ In.
$345.00

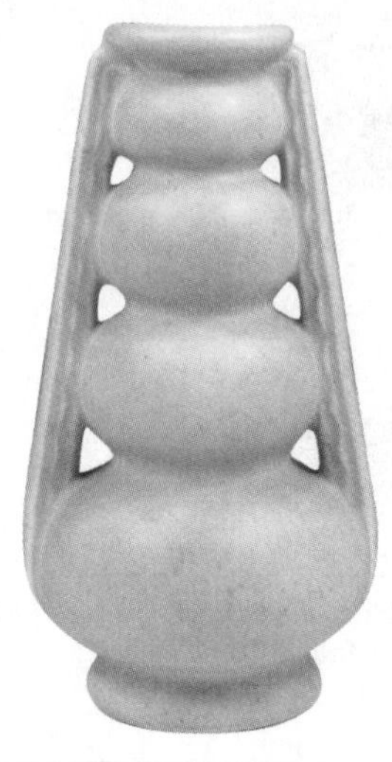

Pottery-Midcentury, Vase, Feelie, Forest Green, Black Striations, Marked, R. Cabat, 2¾ x 2½ In.
$595.00

Pottery-Midcentury, Vase, Flowers, Leaves, Bursley Ware, Marked, Charlotte Rhead, 6 x 5 In.
$135.00

ase, Victorian Maiden, Blue Gown, Trees, Raised Gold Vine & Birds On Neck, France, 7 In. . . 823.00
ase, Yellow Art Deco Flowers, Crackle Glaze, Blue & Red Metallic Ground, J. Barol, 6 In. 944.00

OTTERY-CONTEMPORARY lists pieces made by artists working after 1975.

owl, Brown, Orange, Marked, 1977, 12 In. 360.00
owl, Glazed Stoneware, Carved Concentric Lines, Clyde Burt, 6 x 4 In. 300.00
owl, Mottled Microcrystalline Copper, Blue, Green, Stoneware, M. Grotell, 6 x 9 In. 1080.00
owl, Painted Tomato, Ken Ferguson, 14 x 3 In. 960.00
owl, Pastel Rings, Joseph Panacci, Dated, 1986, 13 In. 126.00
owl, Shallow, Glazed Stoneware, Carved Concentric Lines, Clyde Burt, 14 x 3¼ In. 420.00
lowerpot, Women, Fluted Neck, Green & White Glaze, Bjorn Wiinblad, 21 x 20 In. 717.00
ar, Cover, Dolphins, Kayo O'Young, Dated, 1993, 7½ In. 198.00
ar, Cover, Gray Glaze, Carved Abstract Design, Clyde Burt, 8 x 11 In. 2520.00
amp, Marked, Harlan House, 1975, 18½ In. 126.00
lanter, Maggie May, Whimsical Woman, Bjorn Wiinblad, c.1979, 62 x 20 In. 10157.00
late, Oval, Multicolored, c.1980, 2⅛ x 19⅜ x 10⅝ In. 1200.00
eapot, Bugs, Brown Ground, Bamboo Handle, Joseph Panacci, 8 In. 126.00
eapot, Pink, Off-White, Matte, Marked, Sasaki, 1980s 75.00
ase, Stoneware, White Glaze, Wax-Resist, Relief, Clyde Burt, 4 x 24 In. 2160.00

OTTERY-MIDCENTURY includes pieces made from the 1940s to about 1975.

shtray, Round, Deeply Incised Marks Around Edges, Yellow & Green Niches 200.00
owl, Blue, Brown Hare's Fur Glaze, Hemispherical, Natzler, 2 x 4½ In. 3120.00
owl, Effigy, 3 Egyptian Figures, Brayton Laguna, 12¾ x 11½ In., 2 Piece . . . . . *illus* 153.00
owl, Finger Marks, Turquoise Blue, Otto Natzler, c.1965, 4¼ x 5¾ In. 2400.00
owl, Flaring, Uranium Volcanic Glaze, Stoneware, Natzler, 2½ x 5¾ In. 6600.00
owl, Green, Turquoise, Brown Mottled, Semimatte, Stoneware, Natzler, 5 x 8 In. 1680.00
owl, Red-Orange Crater Glaze, Signed, Otto Natzler, c.1956, 1½ x 5½ In. 5100.00
owl, Royal Lancastrian, Flower Trim, Red, 14 In. 184.00
owl, Shearwater, Blue Glaze, 3⅜ x 8 In. 147.00
asserole, Cover, Flowers, Red Earthenware, C.B., c.1963, 6 x 10½ In. 1800.00
harger, Sea Horse, Cobalt Blue Rim, Catalina, 12⅜ In. 823.00
igurine, Horse, Head Down, Saddle, On Base, Marked, Carl Walters, c.1925, 8 x 10 In. 2640.00
igurine, Penguin, Blue, Aldo Londi, Raymor Bitossi, Italy, 6 In., Pair 300.00
igurine, Rabbit, Green Glaze, Impressed, Sylvac, 10⅔ In. . . . . *illus* 36.00
igurine, Walrus & Carpenter, Signed, Edris Eckhardt, 1930s, 6½ In. . . . . *illus* 1290.00
ar, Cover, Lines, Gray Glaze, Incised, CB, 9 x 7½ In. . . . . *illus* 715.00
itcher, Tetes, Black & White, Picasso, 5¼ In. 2340.00
itcher, Water, Bird Shape, Marked, Picasso, Madoura, 9 x 9¾ In. 5100.00
lanter, Fused, 3 Pots, 6 Legs, David Cressey, c.1963, 18 x 36 x 16 In. 6000.00
laque, Lute, Multicolored, No. 46 & 47, Harris Strong, 36 x 9 In., Pair 400.00
laque, Playing Card, King On Horseback, Queen Playing Lute, Harris Strong, 13 x 8 In., Pair 595.00
laque, Rooster On Weathervane, Multicolored, Wood Mount, 16 x 24 In., Pair 675.00
alt & Pepper, Green Plaid Handle, Blue Ridge, 2¾ In. 28.00
trawberry Pot, Runny Green & Brown Glaze, North Carolina, Mid 1900s, 13½ In, Pair . . . 259.00
ase, Blue & Green Wax-Resist, Relief Glaze, Incised, Cabat, Stoneware, 4 In. 660.00
ase, Blue Matte Glaze, Blue Highlights, Cylindrical, California Faience, 6⅛ In. 353.00
ase, Blue Matte Glaze, Handles, Art Deco, Marked, American Art Clay, 8⅜ In. . . . . *illus* 345.00
ase, Bottle Shape, Black Matte, White & Black Rectangles, Marked, Raymor Bitossi, 12 In. . . 225.00
ase, Bowl, Gray & Brown Crystalline Glaze, Natzler, 4½ x 9½ In. 5875.00
ase, Bulbous, Orange Matte Glaze, Royal Lancaster, England, 9 In. 175.00
ase, Colorful Figures, White Ground, Fantoni, c.1957, 8½ x 20 In. 2040.00
ase, Feelie, Brown Clay, Green & Brown Glaze, Cabat, 3 x 3 In. . . . . 480.00 to 660.00
ase, Feelie, Forest Green, Black Striations, Marked, R. Cabat, 2¾ x 2½ In. . . . . *illus* 595.00
ase, Flowers, Leaves, Bursley Ware, Marked, Charlotte Rhead, 6 x 5 In. . . . . *illus* 135.00
ase, Globe, Brown Gloss, Matte, 5 In. 150.00
ase, Green Matte Glaze, Turquoise Crystals, Signed, Cabat, 3½ x 2½ In. . . . . *illus* 1080.00
ase, Gunmetal Glaze, Stoneware, Gourd Shape, Natzler, 10½ x 7½ In. 9600.00
ase, Mottled Blue High Glaze Over Red Clay, Flared, Natzler, 7¾ In. 9145.00
ase, Owl, Face, Edition Picasso, Marked, Madoura, 9½ In. . . . . *illus* 5250.00
ase, Pastel Glazes, Burst Bubbles, Fantoni, 12 x 20½ In. 1440.00
ase, Red Lava Glaze, Black Swirls, 4-Sided, Impressed, Raymor, W. Germany, 6½ In. 125.00
ase, Square, Yellow & Green Glaze, Carved, Fantoni, 14¼ In. 420.00
ase, Striated Copper Crystalline Glaze, Yellow Ground, Baluster Shape, Catalina, 6 In. 823.00
ase, Westward Ho, Oxen, Wagon, Speckled Brown Glaze, 1953, 13½ In. 1725.00
Wind Chime, Barrel Shape, Protruding Holes, Otto Natzler, c.1962, 18 x 6 In. 10200.00

Pottery-Midcentury, Vase, Green Matte Glaze, Turquoise Crystals, Signed, Cabat, 3½ x 2½ In.
$1080.00

Pottery-Midcentury, Vase, Owl, Face, Edition Picasso, Marked, Madoura, 9½ In.
$5250.00

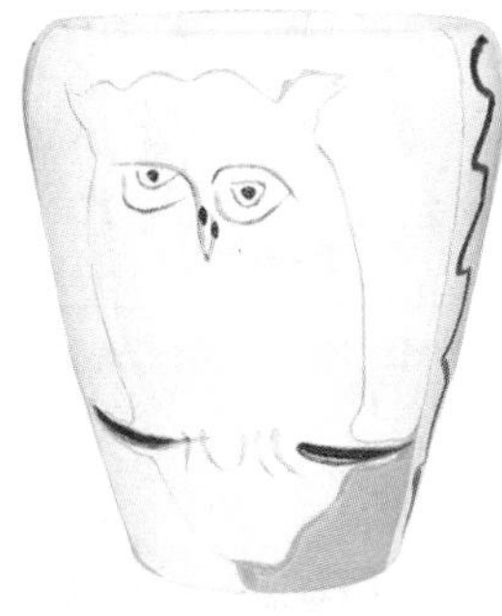

TIP

Go to antiques shows early; there may be plenty of antiques left at the end of the show, but the dealers are tired and not as eager to talk to the customers.

Powder Flask, Copper, Crossed Rifles, Vines, Leaves, Violin Shape
$173.00

Powder Flask, U.S. Navy, Anchor, Stimpson O.H.P., Brass, 1845, 9 In.
$370.00

Pratt, Pitcher, Men, Hand Painted, Embossed, c.1780
$300.00

Pressed Glass, Actress, Vase, HMS Pinafore, Frosted, 9 x 4½ In.
$234.00

POWDER FLASKS AND POWDER HORNS were made to hold the gunpowder used in antique firearms. The early examples were made of horn or wood; later ones were of copper or brass.

POWDER FLASK

Brass, 7¾ x 3 In. 125.00
Brass, Copper, Italy, 1884 .... 215.00
Brass, Dog Chasing Deer, 9 In. 143.00
Brass, Navy, Fouled Anchor, Marked, Stimpson O.H.P. 1845, 9¼ In. 374.00
Camels, Copper Spout, Steel Lugs, Rings, Mid Eastern, c.1800s 201.00
Copper, 2 Hands Shaking, Stars, Eagle, Shield Spears, Swords, Bugle 95.00
Copper, Crossed Rifles, Vines, Leaves, Violin Shape .... *illus* 173.00
U.S. Navy, Anchor, Stimpson O.H.P., Brass, 1845, 9 In. .... *illus* 370.00

POWDER HORN

Animal, Wood Bottom, Wooden Peg, 1900s, 8 In. 35.00
Bone, Scrimshaw, 3 Pierced Openings, 6 In. 345.00
Brass Armorial Crest Of Stag, Inscribed, 1767 .... 195.00
Burlwood, Etched Brass, Trefoil Mounts, Spherical, 19th Century, 5½ In. 264.00
Carved, John Moore, St. Augustine, Wood Cap, 1771, 12¼ In. 1150.00
Carved, Sailing Ships, Fort, Lighthouse, American Flags, Wood Cap, Leather Strap, 15 In. 575.00
Engraved, 2 Mast Ship, Banner, Fox, Wood Plug, Early 19th Century 330.00
Engraved, Deer, Flowers, Pinwheel, Forts, Wood Plug, 18th Century 4125.00
Engraved, Unicorn, Lion Coat Of Arms, Cityscape, Philadelphia, 1700s, 11 In. 8400.00
Relief Carved Bands, Engraved, Landscape, Birds, Trees, Peacocks, Stags, 8¾ In. 1175.00

PRATT ware means two different things. It was an early Staffordshire pottery, cream-colored with colored decorations, made by Felix Pratt during the late eighteenth century. There was also Pratt ware made with transfer designs during the mid-nineteenth century in Fenton, England. Reproductions of the transfer-printed Pratt are being made.

Figure, Rabbit, White, Black Spots, Green Brown Base, 2¼ In. 359.00
Figurine, Woman, Bird, Wearing Hat, Holding Horn, Early 1800s, 7 In. 150.00
Group, Teacher, 4 Students, Brick Arch, Vines, Marble Columns, Transfer, c.1815, 6 In. 1116.00
Pitcher, Men, Hand Painted, Embossed, c.1780 .... *illus* 300.00
Vase, Spill, Shepherd Boy Seated On Tree, Sheep, Dog, c.1925, 5¾ In. 160.00

PRESSED GLASS was first made in the United States in the 1820s after the invention of glass pressing machines. Hundreds of patterns of pressed glass were made in complete table settings. Although the Boston and Sandwich Works was the most famous of the pressed glass factories, there were about sixteen other factories making pressed glass from 1830 to 1850, and still more from 1850 to 1900, when pressed glass reached its greatest popularity. It is now being widely reproduced. The pattern names used in this listing are based on the information in the book *Pressed Glass in America* by John and Elizabeth Welker. There may be pieces of pressed glass listed in this book in other categories, such as Lamp, Ruby, Sandwich, and Souvenir.

1000-Eye pattern is listed here as Thousand Eye.
Acanthus pattern is listed here as Ribbed Palm.
Actress, Goblet, 6½ In. 95.00
Actress, Vase, HMS Pinafore, Frosted, 9 x 4½ In. .... *illus* 234.00
Almond Thumbprint, Tumbler, Polished Table Ring, 3¾ x 3 In. 35.00
Argus, Goblet, 5 Rows, 6 In. 55.00
Argus, Tumbler, Whiskey, Tapered, Applied Handle, 2¾ x 3 In. 88.00
Artichoke, Cake Stand, Ribbed Stem, 6 x 10½ In. .... *illus* 157.00
Artichoke, Compote, Frosted, 8¾ In. 99.00
Ashburton, Ale, 6-Sided Stem, 6⅜ x 3 In. 55.00
Atlanta, Tumbler, Lion, Engraved, Helen, 1897, 3¾ In. 132.00
Bar & Diamond pattern is listed here as Kokomo.
Barberry, Compote, Cover, Shell Finial, 8½ In. Diam. .... *illus* 225.00
Barred Ovals, Pitcher, 9¾ In. 77.00
Beaded Circle, Tumbler, Whiskey, Applied Handle, 3 x 2½ In. 121.00
Bellflower, Champagne, 5 In. 110.00
Bellflower, Compote, 2 Vines, 8-Sided Stem, Wafer, 8¾ x 8⅞ In. 383.00
Bellflower, Creamer, Applied Handle, 36 Rays, Footed, 6¾ In. 110.00
Bellflower, Decanter, 6 Cut Panels, 3 Rows, Pontil, Stopper, 13 In., Qt. 467.00
Bellflower, Pitcher, Applied Handle, 9¼ x 4½ In. 385.00
Bellflower, Table Set, Butter, Sugar, Creamer, 3 Piece 220.00

P

Bellflower, Tumbler, Ribbed To Rim, Table Ring, 3 ½ x 3 ⅛ In. . . . 132.00
Bellflower, Tumbler, Whiskey, Applied Handle, Left Facing Vine, 2 ⅞ x 2 ½ In. . . . 1100.00
Bellflower & Loops, Goblet, 5 ⅝ In. . . . 99.00
Belmont 100, Butter, Cover, Pedestal Base, 8 x 8 In. . . . 100.00
Bird & Strawberry, Berry Set, 3-Footed, 7 Piece . . . 88.00
Bird & Strawberry, Compote, Cover, 7 x 4 ⅝ In., Pair . . . 187.00
Bird & Strawberry, Tumbler, Stained, 4 ⅝ x 3 In., Pair. . . . *illus* 143.00
Bleeding Heart, Pitcher, Applied Handle, Impressed Fan, 8 ¾ x 4 ½ In. . . . 248.00
Bleeding Heart, Salt, Oval, 1 ½ In. . . . 88.00
Block & Fan, Biscuit Jar, Cover, 7 ½ In. . . . 25.00
Bluebird pattern is listed here as Bird & Strawberry.
Bowtie, Bowl, Orange, Wafer Stem, 10 x 10 ⅜ In. . . . *illus* 169.00
Bradford Blackberry, Tumbler, 3 ¾ In. . . . 55.00
Bradford Grape pattern is listed here as Bradford Blackberry.
Brilliant, Goblet, 6 ⅛ In. . . . 35.00
Bucket pattern is listed here as Oaken Bucket.
Bugler, Ale, Pontil, 6 ⅛ x 3 In. . . . 132.00
Bull's-Eye, Creamer . . . 290.00
Bull's-Eye, Goblet, Lobular, 5 ⅞ In. . . . 22.00
Bull's-Eye, Tumbler, Jelly, Polished Pontil, 5 ⅜ In. . . . 354.00
Bull's-Eye & Fleur-De-Lis, Ale, 6 ¼ x 3 In. . . . 605.00
Bull's-Eye & Fleur-De-Lis, Butter, Cover, Handles, 4 ½ x 6 ⅜ In. . . . 99.00
Bull's-Eye & Fleur-De-Lis, Decanter, Bar Lip, Pontil, Qt., 10 ⅞ In. . . . 110.00
Bull's-Eye & Fleur-De-Lis, Goblet, 6 ⅜ In. . . . *illus* 109.00
Bull's-Eye & Fleur-De-Lis, Vase, Scalloped Rim, Wafer, 6-Sided Stem, 9 ¾ x 5 In. . . . 110.00
Bull's-Eye & Fleur-De-Lis, Vase, Wafer, 6-Sided Stem, 9 ½ x 4 ¾ In. . . . 440.00
Bull's-Eye & Rosette, Tumbler, Whiskey, 3 In. . . . 121.00 to 275.00
Bull's-Eye & Wishbone, Goblet, 5 In. . . . 55.00
Bull's-Eye & Wishbone, Goblet, 6 In. . . . 110.00 to 190.00
Bull's-Eye With Diamond Point, Goblet, 6 ¾ In. . . . *illus* 104.00
Bull's-Eye With Diamond Point, Sugar, Cover, Pontil, 9 x 4 ⅜ In. . . . 106.00
Bull's-Eye With Diamond Point, Tumbler, Whiskey, 3 ¼ In. . . . 200.00
Button, Vase, Amber Stain, Scalloped Rim, Footed, 7 ¾ x 4 In. . . . *illus* 129.00
Candlewick, see the Imperial pattern called Candlewick, listed in this book in the Imperial Glass category.
Champion, Butter, Cover, Gold Trim, 5 ¼ In. . . . 33.00
Chilson, Goblet, Polished Pontil, 6 ¾ In. . . . 143.00
Classic, Bowl, Cover, Log Feet, 8 ¾ x 9 ½ In. . . . 66.00
Classic, Bowl, Footed, 4 ¼ x 7 ½ In. . . . 75.00
Classic, Creamer, Log Feet, 5 ½ x 3 ½ In. . . . *illus* 72.00
Classic, Goblet, 6 In. . . . 77.00
Classic, Pitcher, Log Feet, 10 x 5 ½ In. . . . 165.00
Classic, Butter, Cover, Footed, 6 ¾ In. . . . 176.00
Colonial, Compote, Sweetmeat, Cobalt Blue, 6-Sided Base, 1840-60, 4 ¼ x 5 In. . . . *illus* 460.00
Colonial, Cruet . . . 26.00
Colonial Way, Goblet, Polished Pontil, 6 In. . . . 132.00
Columbian Coin, Goblet, 6 In. . . . 66.00
Columbian Coin, Saltshaker, Gold Trim, 2 ¾ In. . . . *illus* 48.00
Columbian Coin, Toothpick, 2 ⅞ x 1 ⅞ In. . . . 48.00
Comet, Diamond Point, Tumbler, Rayed Base, Pontil, 3 ⅞ x 3 ⅜ In. . . . 22.00
Comet, Goblet, 6 In. . . . 154.00 to 165.00
Comet, Tumbler, Pontil, 3 ½ x 3 ¼ In. . . . 385.00
Compact pattern is listed here as Snail.
Cosmos pattern is listed in this book as its own category.
Croesus, Creamer, Amethyst, Gold Trim, 3 x 2 In. . . . *illus* 152.00
Cube with Fan pattern is listed here as Pineapple & Fan.
Daisy & Button, Pitcher, Amber, Air Twist Handle, 8 ¾ In. . . . 77.00
Deer & Doe With Lily Of The Valley, Goblet, 6 In. . . . 143.00 to 310.00
Deer & Dog, Goblet, 6 ¼ In. . . . 66.00
Diamond Quilted, Creamer, Green, Red Stain, 6-Sided Foot, c.1870, 5 In. . . . *illus* 60.00
Diamond Thumbprint, Champagne, 5 ⅜ In. . . . 467.00
Diamond Thumbprint, Goblet, 6 ¾ In. . . . 1430.00
Diamond Thumbprint, Tumbler, Pontil, 3 ¾ x 3 ⅜ In. . . . 143.00
Divided Heart, Goblet, 6 ⅛ In. . . . 99.00
Dog, Compote, Cover, Pedestal Base, Frosted, 14 ½ x 8 ¾ In. . . . 132.00
Dog With Rabbit In Hole, Pitcher, 9 x 4 ½ In. . . . 165.00

Pressed Glass, Artichoke, Cake Stand, Ribbed Stem, 6 x 10 ½ In. $157.00

Pressed Glass, Barberry, Compote, Cover, Shell Finial, 8 ½ In. Diam. $225.00

Pressed Glass, Bird & Strawberry, Tumbler, Stained, 4 ⅝ x 3 In., Pair $143.00

Pressed Glass, Bowtie, Bowl, Orange, Wafer Stem, 10 x 10 ⅜ In. $169.00

P

Pressed Glass, Bull's-Eye & Fleur-De-Lis, Goblet, 6 3/8 In.
$109.00

Pressed Glass, Bull's-Eye With Diamond Point, Goblet, 6 3/4 In.
$104.00

Pressed Glass, Button, Vase, Amber Stain, Scalloped Rim, Footed, 7 3/4 x 4 In.
$129.00

Pressed Glass, Classic, Creamer, Log Feet, 5 1/2 x 3 1/2 In.
$72.00

Doric pattern is listed here as Feather.
Double Wedding Ring pattern is listed here as Wedding Ring.
Draped Window, Goblet, 5 3/4 In. 1045.00
Drum & Eagle, Mug 35.00
Duncan Block, Cruet, Ruby Stain, 5 1/2 x 3 1/2 In. . . . . *illus* 169.00
Earl pattern is listed here as Spirea Band.
Early Moon & Star, Compote, Flared Scalloped Rim, Wafer, Plain Foot, 8 x 9 1/4 In. 99.00
Early Moon & Star, Compote, Scalloped Rim, Wafer, Plain Foot, 8 x 8 In. 248.00
Early Thumbprint, Ale, 4 Rows, 7 x 2 3/4 In. 143.00
Early Thumbprint, Compote, Cover, 7 Rows, Scalloped Rim, Wafer Stem, 14 x 9 In. 2124.00
Early Thumbprint, Compote, Cover, 7 Rows, Scalloped Rim, Wafer Stem, 18 x 12 In. 3575.00
Early Thumbprint, Decanter, 4 Rows, Bar Lip, Neck Ring, Metal Pour Stopper, Qt., 12 In. 220.00
Early Thumbprint, Decanter, 4 Rows, Bar Lip, Neck Ring, 6 3/4 x 2 1/2 In. 605.00
Early Thumbprint, Goblet, 6 1/4 In. 77.00
Early Thumbprint, Inkwell, Bull's-Eye Center, 20 Rays, Hinged Lid, 2 3/4 x 3 3/8 In. 198.00
Early Thumbprint, Nappy, 3 Rows, Scalloped Rim, Pedestal Foot, 5 1/2 x 8 1/4 In. 77.00
Early Thumbprint, Pitcher, 4 Rows, Applied Handle, Pontil, 8 1/8 In. 385.00
Early Thumbprint, Tumbler, Flip, 4 Rows, Pontil, 6 7/8 x 5 1/2 In. 605.00
Early Thumbprint, Tumbler, Whiskey, 3 Rows, Tapered, Pontil, 3 3/8 x 3 In. 110.00
Elk & Doe, Goblet, 6 In. 143.00
Elk Medallion, Goblet, 6 1/8 In. 99.00
Ellrose, Compote, Amber Stain, Vaseline, 7 x 11 In. . . . . *illus* 1760.00
Excelsior, Ale, 6 1/4 x 2 3/4 In. 66.00
Excelsior, Vase, Scallop & Point Rim, 6-Sided Stem, Pontil, 7 1/2 x 5 In. 95.00
Expanded Diamonds, Salt, Cobalt Blue, Sloping Foot, 3 x 2 1/2 x 2 In. 176.00
Feather, Pitcher, Green, 8 1/4 x 5 In. . . . . *illus* 332.00
Feather, Tumbler, Green, 4 x 2 3/4 In. 154.00
Fine Cut & Feather pattern is listed here as Feather.
Fine Rib, Tumbler, Tapered, 3 1/2 x 3 In. 55.00
Fine Rib With Cut Ovals, Goblet, 2 Rows, Pontil, 6 1/4 In. 357.00
Fine Rib With Cut Ovals, Tumbler, 3 Rows, Table Ring, 3 1/2 x 3 In. 715.00
Flower Band, Goblet, 6 1/4 In. 220.00
Flower Band, Goblet, Frosted, 6 1/4 In. 176.00
Flower Medallion, Goblet, 6 1/4 In. 77.00
Flower Medallion, Sugar, Cover, Short Stem, 6-Sided Finial, 7 1/2 x 4 In. 33.00
Flying Robin pattern is listed here as Hummingbird.
Forget-Me-Not, Goblet, Paneled, Amethyst, 5 7/8 In. 165.00
Frog & Spider, Goblet, 6 1/8 In. 495.00
Frosted Chick, Compote, Cover, 12 1/2 x 7 In. 50.00
Frosted Crane pattern is listed here as Frosted Stork.
Frosted Leaf, Goblet, 5 3/4 In. 33.00
Frosted Leaf, Spooner, 5 x 3 3/8 In. 110.00
Frosted Leaf, Sugar, Cover, Short Stem, 6-Sided Finial, 7 1/2 x 4 In. 33.00
Frosted Leaf, Wine, 3 7/8 In. 88.00
Frosted Lion, Compote, Scalloped Foot, 1875, 7 1/4 x 8 In. . . . . 66.00 to 75.00
Frosted Lion, Creamer, Footed, 6 1/2 x 6 In. 70.00
Frosted Lion, Jar, Cover, 7 x 3 1/2 In. 42.00
Frosted Lion, Pitcher, Footed, 6 5/8 In. 115.00
Frosted Lion, Spooner, Scalloped Rim, 5 5/8 x 4 7/8 In. 50.00
Frosted Lion, Sugar, Cover, Finial, Footed, 8 1/2 x 5 1/4 In. 80.00
Frosted patterns may also be listed under the name of main pattern.
Frosted Stork, Compote, Footed, 7 1/2 x 8 1/4 In. 55.00
Frosted Stork, Goblet, 5 3/4 In. 44.00
Frosted Stork, Goblet, 6 1/4 In. 99.00
Garfield Drape, Cake Stand, Pedestal Base, 6 1/2 x 11 In. 88.00
Garfield Drape, Goblet, Rope Border, 6 1/4 In. 110.00
Garfield Drape, Pitcher, Applied Handle, Feather, 10 In. 176.00
Georgian, Compote, Jelly, 3 1/2 x 5 1/2 In. 24.99
Good Luck pattern is listed here as Horseshoe.
Gothic, Tumbler, Pontil, 3 1/2 x 3 1/4 In. 385.00
Gothic Arch & Loop, Compote, Flint, 5 1/4 x 8 In. 22.00
Gothic Arch Printie Panel & Loop, Celery Vase, Canary Yellow, c.1860, 10 1/4 In. . . . . *illus* 990.00
Grape, see also the related pattern Magnet & Grape.
Hamilton, Tumbler, Frosted Leaf, Pontil, 3 3/8 x 3 1/8 In. 66.00
Hamilton, Wine, 4 7/8 In. . . . . *illus* 60.00

P

Item		Price
Hawaiian Pineapple, Tumbler, 3¾ x 3⅛ In.		110.00
Heart & Thumbprint, Bottle, Water, 8¼ x 5¼ In.		154.00
Heart & Thumbprint, Goblet, Ruby Stain, 5⅞ In.	*illus*	3046.00
Heart In Panel, Tumbler, 6 Panels.		99.00
Hearts of Loch Laven pattern is listed here as Shuttle.		
Hexagonal Block, Tumbler, 3 Rows, Table Ring, 4 x 3⅜ In.		88.00
Hobnail pattern is in this book as its own category.		
Holly, Tumbler, Footed, 4¾ In.		176.00
Honeycomb, Tumbler, Whiskey, Amber, Scalloped Rim, Footed, 2⅛ x 2½ In.		99.00
Horn Of Plenty, Cologne, Embossed, H.E. Swan, 11 x 2½ In.		358.00
Horn Of Plenty, Compote, Scalloped Rim, Ribbed, Stem, Wafer, 8 x 8 In.		413.00
Horn Of Plenty, Creamer, Applied Handle, Scalloped Foot, 5¼ In.		110.00
Horn Of Plenty, Dish, Sweetmeat, Cover, 6-Lobed Stem, Wafer, 6-Sided Finial, 8 x 6 In.		358.00
Horn Of Plenty, Salt, Scalloped Rim, Oval, 1¼ x 2⅜ x 3⅛ In.		55.00
Horn Of Plenty, Sugar & Creamer, Domed Cover, Applied Handle, Scalloped		154.00
Horn Of Plenty, Tumbler, Jelly, Pontil, 4⅞ x 2⅜ In.		1416.00 to 1770.00
Horn Of Plenty, Tumbler, Whiskey, Applied Handle, Pontil, 3 x 2⅝ In., 3 Piece		385.00
Horn Of Plenty, Vase, Scalloped Rim, Faceted Knop, Wafer Stem, 8¾ x 4¾ In.		176.00
Horseshoe, Cake Stand, Wafer Stem, 10 x 12¼ In.		330.00
Hummingbird, Goblet, Blue, 6 In., Pair.		120.00
Hummingbird, Waste Bowl, 2¾ x 4⅝ In.		33.00
Icicle With Chain Band, Goblet, 6⅛ In.	*illus*	72.00
Iconoclast, Goblet, 6¼ In.		88.00
Indiana Swirl pattern is listed here as Feather.		
Inverted Fern, Tumbler, 3½ x 3⅛ In.		143.00
Jumbo, Spoon Rack, Canton Glass Co., 11 x 6 In.	*illus*	556.00
King's 500, Whiskey Jug, Engraved, Applied Handle, 8½ In.		385.00
King's Crown, Salt, 1¾ In.		121.00
Kokomo, Spooner, c.1901, 4¾ In.		28.00
Lacy, Salt, Acorn Medallion, Pedestal Base, 3¼ In.		33.00
Lacy, Salt, Amber Clambroth, Reeded Oval Base, c.1850, 1¾ x 2 x 3½ In.	*illus*	475.00
Lacy, Salt, Beaded Chain, Pedestal Base, 2½ In.		33.00
Lacy, Salt, Beaded Scroll & Flower Basket, Footed, Cover, 3 x 3 In.		1276.00
Lacy, Salt, Hexagon, Star, 14-Point Star Base, 1 x 1½ In.		10.00
Lacy, Salt, Jacob's Ladder, Turned Down Top, Pedestal Base, 2¾ In.		33.00
Lacy, Salt, Pittsburgh Steamboat, Sapphire Blue, 1⅝ x 1⅞ x 3⅝ In.		1100.00
Lattice & Oval Panels, Tumbler, Rayed, Base, Table Ring, 3⅝ x 3¼ In.		59.00
Leaf & Dart, Salt, Cover, Footed, 4 x ½ In.		198.00
Lee, Goblet, 6¾ In.		176.00
Lee, Wine, Pontil, 4¾ In.		110.00
Liberty Bell, Bread Tray, 13¼ In.		47.00
Lily Of The Valley, Pitcher, Applied Handle, 9¼ In.		220.00
Lily Of The Valley, Salt, 2¾ In.		33.00
Lincoln Drape, Dish, Sweetmeat, Cover, Wafer, 7½ x 6 In.	*illus*	145.00
Lincoln Drape, Jug, Molasses, Applied Handle, Tin Lid, 6½ In.		163.00
Lincoln Drape & Tassel, Goblet, 6 In.		220.00
Little Infant Samuel, Epergne, Tree Of Life Bowl, Hobbs, 18½ In.		275.00
Log Cabin, Creamer, 4¾ x 2½ In.		77.00
Log Cabin, Pickle Castor, Central Glass Co., 6¾ x 2½ x 3 In.		265.00
Loop & Star, Sugar, Cover, 6-Sided Stem, Pontil, 8½ In.		132.00
Magnet & Grape, Goblet, Frosted Leaf, 4 In.		66.00
Magnet & Grape, Tumbler, Frosted Leaf, 3½ x 3 In.		110.00
Magpies & Frog, Goblet, Etched, 6⅛ In.		275.00
Master Argus, Goblet, 6 In.		44.00
Melon, Butter, Cover, 5½ x 5½ In.		71.00
Menagerie, Spooner, Fish Shape, Amber, 3½ x 2 x 2 In.	*illus*	64.00
Millard, Table Set, Butter, Sugar, Creamer, Spooner, Amber Stain.	*illus*	250.00
Minerva, Cake Stand, Pedestal Base, 6½ x 9 In.		55.00
Monkey, Celery Vase, 6¾ x 3¾ In.		265.00
Monkey, Celery Vase, Fiery Opalescent, 6¾ x 3¾ In.		523.00
Monkey, Jam Jar, No Cover, Fiery Opalescent, 4¾ x 3¼ In.		495.00
Monkey, Spooner.	*illus*	80.00
Monkey, Sugar, Cover Only, Fiery Opalescent, 3 x 3½ In.		385.00
Monkey, Table Set, Butter, Sugar, Creamer, Fiery Opalescent, 3 Piece		2420.00
Monkey, Waste Bowl, Fiery Opalescent, 2⅜ x 4⅞ In.		77.00
Moon & Star, Creamer, Medial Rib, Applied Handle, Pontil, 5½ In.		217.00
Moon & Star, Sugar, Cover, Acorn Finial, Pontil, 6½ x 4½ In.		108.00

Pressed Glass, Colonial, Compote, Sweetmeat, Cobalt Blue, 6-Sided Base, 1840-60, 4¼ x 5 In.
$460.00

Pressed Glass, Columbian Coin, Saltshaker, Gold Trim, 2¾ In.
$48.00

TIP

Dishwasher detergents are not kind to nineteenth-century pressed glass and other old glassware. We are using some Moon & Star pattern sauce dishes and noticed a few are showing wear on the flat part of the bottom. The marks are not scratches, but seem to be rough spots on the original sheen. Now the bottoms look dull.

P

Pressed Glass, Croesus, Creamer, Amethyst, Gold Trim, 3 x 2 In.
$152.00

Pressed Glass, Diamond Quilted, Creamer, Green, Red Stain, 6-Sided Foot, c.1870, 5 In.
$60.00

Pressed Glass, Duncan Block, Cruet, Ruby Stain, 5 ½ x 3 ½ In.
$169.00

Pressed Glass, Ellrose, Compote, Amber Stain, Vaseline, 7 x 11 In.
$1760.00

Moon & Star, Tumbler, Rayed Base, 3 ⅜ x 3 ⅛ In. 121.00
Moon & Stork pattern is listed here as Ostrich Looking At The Moon.
Morning Glory, Bowl, Footed, 9-Sided Stem, Wafer, 4 x 6 ¾ In. 115.00
Morning Glory, Goblet, 6 In.. . . . . . 660.00
New England Pineapple, Champagne, 5 ¼ In., 4 Piece 265.00
New England Pineapple, Compote, Scalloped Rim, Dome Foot, 9 ⅛ x 10 ¾ In. 88.00
New England Pineapple, Decanter, Stopper, Pt., 11 ¼ In. . . . . . . 201.00 to 302.00
New England Pineapple, Goblet, 6 ¼ In., 6 Piece 357.00
New England Pineapple, Lacy, Salt, Pedestal Base, 2 ¾ In. 22.00
New England Pineapple, Pitcher, Applied Handle, Table Ring, 8 ¼ In. 715.00
New England Pineapple, Sugar, Cover, 6-Sided Knop, 8 ½ x 5 In. 130.00
New England Pineapple, Table Set, Butter, Sugar, Creamer, Spooner, Handle, 4 Piece 220.00
New England Pineapple, Tumbler, Pontil, 3 ¾ In., 4 Piece 330.00
New England Pineapple, Tumbler, Whiskey, Applied Handle, Pontil, 3 x 2 ¾ In.. . . . . . 85.00
Niagara Falls, Tray, Scalloped Edge, Shell Handles, 16 In. 638.00
Oaken Bucket, Pitcher, Amethyst, 8 ¼ x 5 ⅛ In. . . . . . . *illus* 154.00
One-Thousand Eye pattern is listed here as Thousand Eye.
Ostrich Looking At The Moon, Goblet, 5 ⅝ In.. . . . . . 143.00 to 303.00
Oval With Long Bars, Goblet, 6 $\frac{9}{16}$ In.. . . . . . 55.00
Owl & Possum, Goblet, 6 In.. . . . . . 248.00
Owl pattern is listed here as Bull's-Eye with Diamond Point.
Peacock Eye, Salt, Clear, Sawtooth Rim, Bull's-Eye Scallop Foot, 2 ¾ x 2 ⅝ In. 165.00
Peacock Eye, Salt, Lavender Blue, Opalescent To Opaque, Pedestal, 2 ⅛ x 3 ¼ In. 99.00
Petticoat, Pitcher, Vaseline, Gold Trim, 10 ½ x 3 ⅞ In.. . . . . . *illus* 109.00
Pheasant, Bowl, Cover, Frosted, 8 ½ x 8 ⅝ In. 132.00
Pigs In Corn, Goblet, Right Bent Husk, 5 ¾ In. 247.00
Pillar, Ale, 6 x 2 ¾ In. 88.00
Pinafore pattern is listed here as Actress.
Pineapple & Fan, Spooner, 4 ⅝ x ¾ In. 30.00
Pointed Thumbprint pattern is listed here as Almond Thumbprint.
Polar Bear, Goblet, Flared Rim, 6 In. 187.00
Polar Bear, Pitcher, 9 ⅞ In.. . . . . . 408.00
Prayer Rug pattern is listed here as Horseshoe.
Prism & Thumbprint, Goblet, 6 ⅜ In.. . . . . . 121.00
Rebecca At The Well, Compote, Frosted, Ribbon, 12 ¾ x 10 ¼ In. . . . . . . *illus* 169.00
Rhode Island, Goblet, 5 ¾ In.. . . . . . 209.00
Ribbed Ivy, Tumbler, 3 ½ x 3 ½ x 3 ⅛ In. 110.00
Ribbed Palm, Salt, Pedestal Base, 2 ⅞ In. 22.00
Rope & Thumbprint, Pitcher, Vaseline, 8 ½ In. 176.00
Sandwich Star, Decanter, Bar Lip, Metal Pour Spout, Pontil, ½ Pt., 9 ⅛ In. 176.00
Sandwich Star, Goblet, Pontil, 6 ½ In.. . . . . . 715.00
Sandwich Star, Wine, Pontil, 4 ½ In. 143.00
Scarab, Goblet, Rayed Foot, 6 ⅜ In. 121.00
Scroll, Salt, Pedestal Base, 2 ½ In.. . . . . . 33.00
Shell & Tassel, Bride's Basket, Silver Plated Frame, James W. Tufts, 9 ⅝ In. 118.00
Shell & Tassel, Oyster Plate, 3 ¾ x 9 ¾ In. 358.00
Shell & Tassel, Saltshaker, 2 ¾ In. 88.00
Shrine, Salt, Mold Blown, 3 ½ In. 35.00
Shuttle, Cake Stand, 6 ½ x 10 In. 132.00
Snail, Syrup, 5 ¼ x 3 ½ In.. . . . . . 132.00
Spanish Coin pattern is listed here as Columbian Coin.
Spiked Argus, Jelly Glass, 6-Sided Knop, Rayed Base, 5 ⅝ x 2 ⅜ In. 154.00
Squirrel, Table Set, Butter, Sugar, Creamer, Spooner, 4 Piece 440.00
Star & Bars, Salt, Train Car Shape, 1 ⅞ x 2 x 3 ¾ In. 77.00
Star & Circle, Goblet, 6 In. 77.00
Star & Punty pattern is listed here as Moon & Star.
Stedman, Tumbler, 3 ⅝ x 3 ¼ In. 124.00
Stippled Pepper, Salt, Pedestal Base, 3 In.. . . . . . 44.00
Stippled Scroll pattern is listed here as Scroll.
Stippled Swag, Salt, Pedestal Base, 2 ¼ In. 11.00
Stork Looking at the Moon pattern is listed here as Ostrich Looking At The Moon.
Swan, Compote, Cover, Netted, 11 ½ x 8 ½ In. 143.00
Swan, Pitcher, Netted, 9 ½ x 5 In. 121.00
Swan, Plate, 6 ⅞ In. 33.00
Swan & Rushes, Goblet, 6-Panel Stem, 6 ¼ In.. . . . . . 248.00
Swan With Flowers, Pitcher, 7 ¾ x 4 In. 303.00

Pressed Glass, Feather, Pitcher, Green, 8 ¼ x 5 In.
$332.00

Pressed Glass, Icicle With Chain Band, Goblet, 6 ⅛ In.
$72.00

Pressed Glass, Menagerie, Spooner, Fish Shape, Amber, 3 ½ x 2 x 2 In.
$64.00

Pressed Glass, Gothic Arch Printie Panel & Loop, Celery Vase, Canary Yellow, c.1860, 10 ¼ In.
$990.00

Pressed Glass, Jumbo, Spoon Rack, Canton Glass Co., 11 x 6 In.
$556.00

Pressed Glass, Millard, Table Set, Butter, Sugar, Creamer, Spooner, Amber StaIn.
$250.00

Pressed Glass, Hamilton, Wine, 4 ⅞ In.
$60.00

Pressed Glass, Lacy, Salt, Amber Clambroth, Reeded Oval Base, c.1850, 1 ¾ x 2 x 3 ½ In.
$475.00

Pressed Glass, Monkey Spooner
$80.00

Pressed Glass, Heart & Thumbprint, Goblet, Ruby Stain, 5 ⅞ In.
$3046.00

Pressed Glass, Lincoln Drape, Dish, Sweetmeat, Cover, Wafer, 7 ½ x 6 In.
$145.00

Pressed Glass, Oaken Bucket, Pitcher, Amethyst, 8 ¼ x 5 ⅛ In.
$154.00

Pressed Glass, Petticoat, Pitcher, Vaseline, Gold Trim, 10 ½ x 3 ⅞ In.
$109.00

Pressed Glass, Rebecca At The Well, Compote, Frosted, Ribbon, 12 ¾ x 10 ¼ In.
$169.00

Pressed Glass, Thousand Eye, Cake Stand, Blue, Scalloped Rim, 6 ½ x 10 In.
$121.00

Pressed Glass, Wedding Ring, Goblet, 6 ¼ In.
$60.00

Teardrop & Tassel, Pitcher, Emerald Green, 8 ½ x 4 ½ In. 385.00
Tennessee, Tumbler, 4 x 2 ¾ In. 154.00
Texas, Wine, Stippled Panels, 4 ⅛ In. 106.00
Thousand Eye, Cake Stand, Blue, Scalloped Rim, 6 ½ x 10 In. *illus* 121.00
Three Face, Bowl, Low Foot, 5 ½ x 6 In. 531.00
Three Face, Champagne, 5 ½ In. 188.00
Three Face, Compote, Cover, Oval, 13 ½ x 9 In. 2860.00
Three Face, Goblet, 6 ¼ In. 71.00
Three Face, Pitcher, Milk, 1 Qt., 8 ¼ x 3 ¾ In. 2090.00
Three Face, Spooner, Pedestal Base, 6 ½ x 3 ¾ In. 154.00
Three Graces, see the related pattern Three Face.
Three Sisters pattern is listed here as Three Face.
Thumbprint, Ale, Plain Stem, 6 ½ x 2 ¾ In. 99.00
Thumbprint, Compote, Spherical, Scalloped Rim, Cover, 18 In. 3575.00
Trilby, Goblet, 5 ¾ In. 176.00
Tulip & Oval, Vase, Spill, 8 Panels, 5 ⅞ x 2 ⅞ In. 121.00
Tulip With Sawtooth, Bowl, Flared Rim, Footed, Wafer, 5 ½ x 9 In. 295.00
Tulip With Sawtooth, Champagne, 5 In., 6 Piece 325.00
Tulip With Sawtooth, Goblet, 6 ½ In. 70.00 to 110.00
Tulip With Sawtooth, Wine, 4 ⅜ In., 6 Piece 142.00
Two Owls, Butter, Cover, Pedestal Base, 7 ½ x 6 In. 187.00
Two Owls, Sugar, Cover, 9 x 4 ½ In. 120.00
U.S. Coin, Tumbler, 3 ¾ x 2 ¾ In. 154.00
Valentine pattern is listed here as Trilby.
Waffle, Tumbler, Pontil, 3 ½ x 3 ⅛ In. 132.00
Waffle & Thumbprint, Goblet, Faceted Knop, Pontil, 6 ¼ In. 110.00
Washington, Bowl, Cover, Low Foot, Wafer, 6 ⅝ x 6 ⅛ In. 143.00
Washington, Celery Vase, 6-Sided Stem, 8 ¼ x 4 ¼ In. 27.00
Washington, Goblet, 6 In. 55.00
Wedding Ring, Goblet, 6 ¼ In. *illus* 60.00
Westward Ho, Bowl, Cover, Footed, Oval, 11 ¾ x 5 ½ x 8 ¾ In. 220.00
Westward Ho, Compote, Cover, Oval, c.1879, 9 ½ x 6 ¾ x 4 In. 175.00
Westward Ho, Compote, Cover, 11 x 6 In. 132.00
Westward Ho, Relish, Deer Handles, 1 ¼ x 5 ½ x 10 In. 55.00
Westward Ho, Sauce, Footed. 25.00
Wooden Pail pattern is listed here as Oaken Bucket.
Worcester, Ale, Pontil, 5 ¼ x 3 ⅜ In. 165.00
Worcester, Pitcher, Applied Handle, Scalloped Rim, 8-Sided Stem, Pontil, 8 ¼ In. 440.00
Wyoming, Pitcher, Enigma, 9 ½ x 4 ½ In. 88.00
Yoked Loop, Tumbler, 18-Rayed Base, 3 ⅝ x 3 ¼ In. 110.00

PRINT, in this listing, means any of many printed images produced on paper by one of the more common methods, such as lithography. The prints listed here are of interest primarily to the antiques collector, not the fine arts collector. Many of these prints were originally part of books. Other prints will be found in the Advertising, Currier & Ives, Movie, and Poster categories.

Audubon bird prints were originally issued as part of books printed from 1826 to 1854. They were issued in two sheet sizes, 26 ½ inches by 39 ½ inches and 11 inches by 7 inches. The quadrupeds were issued in 28-by-22-Inch prints. Later editions of the Audubon books were done in many sizes, and reprints of the books in the original size were also made. The words *after John James Audubon* appear on all of the prints, including the originals, because the pictures were made as copies of Audubon's original oil paintings. The bird pictures have been so popular they have been copied in myriad sizes by both old and new printing methods. This list includes originals and later copies because Audubon prints of all ages are sold in antiques shops.

J.W.Audubon

Audubon, American Green-Winged Teal, R. Havell, Frame, 25 ⅜ x 37 ½ In. 8400.00
Audubon, Baltimore Oriole, R. Havell, Frame, 1825, 39 x 26 In. 7200.00
Audubon, Bay-Breasted Warbler, No. 14, Hand Colored Engraving, 38 x 25 ¼ In. 2820.00
Audubon, Black Vulture, 24 x 37 ¾ In. 1250.00
Audubon, Black Warrior, Hand Colored, Aquatint Engraving, Frame, c.1830, 48 x 34 In. 5750.00
Audubon, Black Warrior, R. Havell, Mat, Frame, 1830, 39 ⅞ x 26 ½ In. 5100.00
Audubon, Brant Goose, R. Havell, 1837, 25 ⅜ x 38 ¼ In. 3900.00
Audubon, Canada Lynx, J.T. Bowen, Frame, c.1860, 21 ½ x 27 $^{1}/_{16}$ In. 12000.00
Audubon, Cardinal Grosbeak, R. Havell, Frame, 1833, 38 x 26 ½ In. 9000.00
Audubon, Carolina Turtle Dove, Amsterdam Edition, Burl Frame, 30 x 23 In. 708.00
Audubon, Cougar, J.T. Bowen, 1846, 21 ¾ x 27 ½ In. 7200.00
Audubon, Field Sparrow, R. Havell, Frame, 1832, 37 ½ x 25 ½ In. 3000.00

P

Audubon, Louisiana Tanager, R. Havell, Mat, Frame, 1837, 38 1/8 x 26 1/16 In. 7800.00
Audubon, Polar Hare, J.T. Bowen, 1844, 21 5/8 x 26 3/4 In.. .... 7800.00
Audubon, Prairie Wolf, 6 5/8 x 10 3/8 In. 3000.00
Audubon, Red-Tailed Hawk, 38 x 25 1/8 In. 4000.00
Audubon, Red-Breasted Nuthatch, Robert Havell, Frame, 19 3/8 x 12 1/2 In. 316.00
Audubon, Scaup Duck, R. Havell, Frame, 1834, 25 3/8 x 37 3/8 In. 5400.00
Audubon, Sharp-Tailed Finch, R. Havell, 1832, 37 1/2 x 25 1/2 In.. .... 4200.00
Audubon, Sharp-Tailed Grouse, R. Havell, Frame, 1837, 25 3/8 x 37 5/8 In. 5100.00
Audubon, Spotted Grouse, R. Havell, Mat, Frame, 1833, 25 3/4 x 38 3/8 In.. .... 6000.00
Audubon, Stanley Hawk, Hand Colored, Aquatint Engraving, Frame, c.1828, 48 x 34 In. 5463.00
Audubon, Tell-Tale Goodwit Or Snipe, R. Havell, Frame, 1836, 25 1/2 x 37 5/8 In. 5100.00
Audubon, Tropic Bird, R. Havell, Mat, Frame, 1835, 25 x 38 In.. .... 7800.00
Benton, Thomas Hart, Cradling Wheat, Lithograph, Frame, c.1939, 9 1/2 x 12 In.. .... 4200.00
Bishop, Richard E., Ducks In Flight, Etched, Signed, Frame, c.1940, 7 3/4 x 5 3/8 In.. .... 502.00
Bishop, Richard Evett, Wood Duck, Inscribed, Black Stick Frame, 10 1/2 x 9 In.. .... 672.00
Cappiello, Leonetto, Reglisse Sanguinede, Lithograph, Glazed, Mat, Frame, 51 x 36 In. 2040.00
Cheret, Jules, Exposition Universelle Des Arts Incoherents, Frame, 48 x 34 In.. .... 2040.00
Cheret, Jules, Folies Bergere, L'Arc En Ciel, Lithograph, Glazed, Mat, Frame, 49 x 34 In.. .... 2640.00
Collins, F., Mount Vernon, Lithograph, Gilt Frame, 19th Century, 20 x 24 In.. .... 220.00
Currier, View On The Harlem River, N.Y., High Bridge, c.1852, 21 x 27 3/8 In. 1645.00
Dawn, R. Atkinson Fox, Frame, 10 x 18 In.. .... 99.00
Denton, Fisherman Playing A Bass, Signed, Mat, Frame, c.1889, 18 1/2 x 24 1/2 In.. .... 1232.00
Glorious Vista, R. Atkinson Fox, Frame, 17 x 30 In. 44.00
Gorman, R.C., Navajo Woman With Jar Kneeling At River, Lithograph, Frame, 30 x 38 In.. ... 1100.00
Gould, John & Elizabeth, Red-Breasted Toucan, Lithograph, c.1835, 22 x 15 In. 1380.00
Gould & Richter, Toucans, Chromolithograph, Frame, 19th Century, 20 x 14 In., Pair 780.00
Havell, 3-Toed Woodpecker, After Audubon, c.1832, 34 x 25 1/4 In. 2880.00
Havell, American Goldfinch, After Audubon, Frame, c.1834, 37 1/2 x 24 5/8 In. 10200.00
Havell, Baltimore Oriole, Hand Colored, Frame, c.1824, 37 x 25 In. 9375.00
Havell, Bank Swallow, Violet Green Swallow, After Audubon, c.1837, 38 x 25 3/16 In. 2040.00
Havell, Ivory Gull, After Audubon, c.1836, 24 5/8 x 39 In.. .... 3120.00
Havell, Orchard Oriole, After Audubon, Frame, c.1833, 37 3/4 x 25 In. 10200.00
Humphries, Butterfly & Moth, Lithograph, Hand Colored, London, c.1880, 10 x 8 In., 6 Piece 805.00
Hurd, Peter, Watering Tank, Lithograph, Black & White, Frame, 15 1/4 x 19 1/4 In. 86.00

Icart prints were made by Louis Icart, who worked in Paris from 1907 as an employee of a postcard company. He then started printing magazines and fashion brochures. About 1910 he created a series of etchings of fashionably dressed women and he continued to make similar etchings until he died in 1950. He is well known as a printmaker, painter, and illustrator. Original etchings are much more expensive than the later photographic copies.

Icart, La Lettre, Woman, Walking, Handing Letter Back, Frame, 21 x 17 In.. .... 88.00
Icart, Madame Butterfly, Signed, 1927, 20 x 13 1/4 In.. .... *illus* 850.00
Inger, C., George Washington, Triumphal Entry, Nov. 25 1783, Lithograph, 45 x 32 In.. ...... 1725.00

Jacoulet prints were designed by Paul Jacoulet (1902–1960), a Frenchman who spent most of his life in Japan. He was a master of Japanese woodblock print technique. Subjects included life in Japan, the South Seas, Korea, and China. His prints were sold by subscription and issued in series. Each series had a distinctive seal, such as a sparrow or butterfly. Most Jacoulet prints are approximately 15 x 10 inches.

Jacoulet, Le Reveil, 20 1/2 x 17 In. .... *illus* 720.00
Jacoulet, Man Seated Wearing Yellow Costume, Bird Design, 15 x 11 In. .... *illus* 650.00

Japanese woodblock prints are listed as follows: Print, Japanese, name of artist, title or description, type, and size. Dealers use the following terms: Tate-e is a vertical composition. Yoko-e is a horizontal composition. The words Aiban (13 by 9 inches), Chuban (10 by 7 ½ inches), Hosoban (13 by 6 inches), Koban (7 by 4 inches), Nagaban (20 x 9 inches), Oban (15 by 10 inches), Shikishiban (8 x 9 inches), and Tanzaku (15 x 5 inches) denote approximate size. Modern versions of some of these prints have been made. Other woodblock prints that are not Japanese are listed under Print, Woodblock.

Japanese, Hiroshige, View Of The Tokaido Road, 8 1/2 x 13 1/4 In.. .... 720.00
Japanese, Hiroshige, Village With Figures On Path, 8 3/4 x 13 3/4 In. 390.00
Japanese, Kawano Kaoru, Girl, Signed, 14 1/2 x 8 1/4 In.. .... *illus* 80.00
Japanese, Saito Kiyoshi, Daitoko-Ji Garden, Color, Signed, Red Seal, 20 1/2 x 14 1/2 In. 767.00
Japanese, Shinsui Ito, Woman Penciling Her Eyebrows, Signed, c.1928, 11 x 15 In. 1770.00
Japanese, Yazawa Genetsu, Cherry Blossoms In Vase, Ink & Color On Paper, Frame, 10 x 9 In. 177.00
Kavin, Zena, Victims Of Misfortune & Folly, Lithograph, Frame, c.1935, 12 x 15 1/4 In.. .... 390.00

Print, Icart, Madame Butterfly, Signed, 1927, 20 x 13 1/4 In.
$850.00

Print, Jacoulet, Le Reveil, 20 1/2 x 17 In.
$720.00

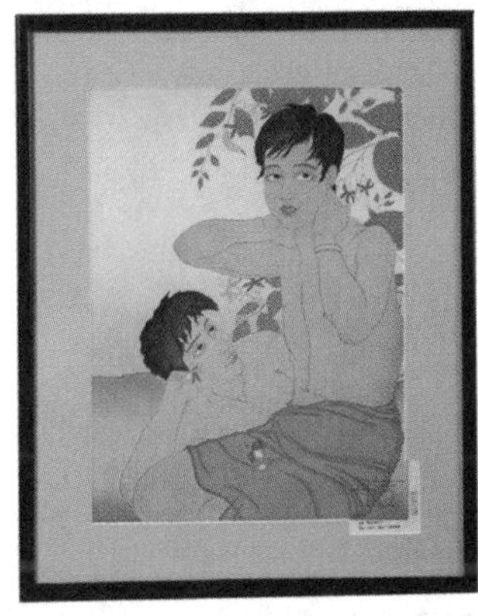

Print, Jacoulet, Man Seated Wearing Yellow Costume, Bird Design, 15 x 11 In.
$650.00

P

Print, Japanese, Kawano Kaoru, Girl, Signed, 14 ½ x 8 ¼ In.
$80.00

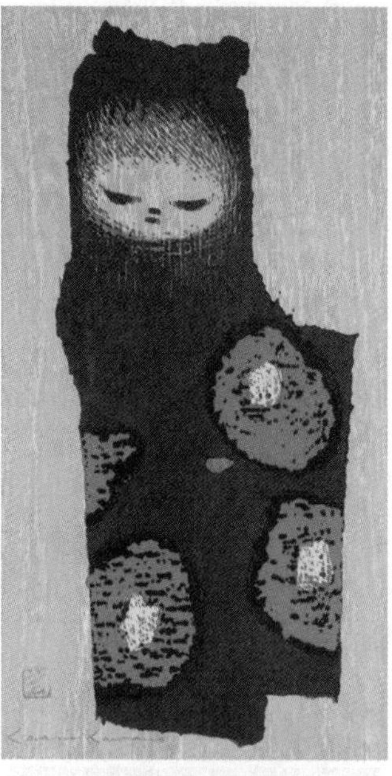

Print, Kurz & Allison, Siege Of Vicksburg, 1888, 21 x 28 In.
$465.00

Print, Parrish, Girl In Mountain, Frame, 21 x 15 In.
$175.00

Kemp, Oliver, Silent Places, Hunter By Lake, Lithograph, c.1915, 18 x 14 In. 146.00
Kurz & Allison, Battle Of Antietam, Color, Mat, 1862, 20 ½ x 27 ¼ In.. . . . . 1035.00
Kurz & Allison, Battle Of Atlanta, Color, Mat, 1864, 22 x 28 ¼ In. 690.00
Kurz & Allison, Battle Of Bull Run, Color, Mat, 1889, 21 ⅞ x 27 ⅜ In.. . . . . 460.00
Kurz & Allison, Battle Of Chancellorsville, Color, Mat, 1889, 22 ¼ x 28 ¼ In.. . . . . 373.00
Kurz & Allison, Battle Of Cold Harbor, Color, Mat, 1888, 20 x 26 In. 1725.00
Kurz & Allison, Battle Of Lookout Mountain, Color, Mat, 1889, 21 x 28 In. 431.00
Kurz & Allison, Battle Of Missionary Ridge, Color, Mat, 1886, 22 x 28 In.. . . . . 2185.00
Kurz & Allison, Battle Of Pea Ridge, Arkansas, Color, Mat, 1889, 22 ½ x 28 ¼ In. 230.00
Kurz & Allison, Battle Of Resaca, Color, Mat, 1864, 22 x 28 In. 1840.00
Kurz & Allison, Battle Of The Wilderness, Color, Mat, 1887, 22 x 28 In. 1955.00
Kurz & Allison, Siege Of Vicksburg, 1888, 21 x 28 In. . . . . *illus* 465.00
Lear, Edward, Barnard's Parakeet, Lithograph, Hand Colored, c.1832, 21 ¼ x 14 ¾ In. 2875.00
Lear, Edward, Red-Capped Parakeet, Female, Lithograph, c.1832, 21 x 15 In.. . . . . 805.00
Lear, Edward, Rose-Ringed Parakeet, Lithograph, Hand Colored, c.1832, 21 x 15 In.. . . . . 1035.00
McKinn, William Wind, Bighorn Ram, Lithograph, c.1945, 12 x 9 In.. 240.00
Moran, Thomas, Grand Canyon Of Arizona On The Santa Fe, Chromolithograph, c.1912, 44 x 35 In. 1416.00

Nutting prints are now popular with collectors. Wallace Nutting is known for his pictures, furniture, and books. Nutting prints are actually hand-colored photographs issued from 1900 to 1941. There are over 10,000 different titles. Wallace Nutting furniture is listed in the Furniture category.

Nutting, Among Saffron Sails, Signed, Original Mat, Frame, c.1915, 14 x 17 In. 385.00
Nutting, Arlington Hills, Signed, Original Mat, Frame, c.1905, 20 x 10 In. 770.00
Nutting, By A Cottage Door, Signed, Original Mat, Frame, c.1915, 13 x 16 In.. . . . . 2090.00
Nutting, Castle, Signed, Original Mat, Frame, c.1915, 9 x 7 In. 209.00
Nutting, Climbing The Fence, Signed, Original Mat, Frame, c.1930, 11 x 9 In.. . . . . 303.00
Nutting, Dell Dale Road, Signed, Original Mat, Frame, c.1915, 16 x 13 In.. . . . . 88.00
Nutting, Four O'Clock, Signed, Original Mat, Frame, c.1910, 14 x 17 In.. . . . . 770.00
Nutting, From The Pool's Edge, Signed, Original Mat, Frame, 13 x 16 In.. . . . . 358.00
Nutting, Genial Stream, Signed, Original Mat, Frame, 21 x 12 In.. . . . . 660.00
Nutting, Gloucester Peter, Signed, Original Mat, Frame, c.1905, 12 x 15 In.. . . . . 4290.00
Nutting, Going For The Doctor, Signed, Original Mat, Frame, c.1915, 17 x 14 In.. . . . . 605.00
Nutting, Jar Of Posies, Frame, c.1930, 8 x 10 In. 330.00
Nutting, Sweetness Of June, Signed, Original Mat, Frame, c.1915, 12 x 9 In. 198.00
Nutting, Three Chums, Signed, Original Mat, Mahogany Frame, c.1915, 14 x 11 In.. . . . . 176.00
Nutting, Valley Forge Headquarters, Signed, Original Mat, Frame, c.1915, 12 x 10 In.. . . . . . . 468.00
Nutting, Watching For Papa, Frame, Original Mat, c.1915, 14 x 17 In.. . . . . 440.00
Nutting, Willow By The Tower, Signed, Original Mat, Frame, c.1905, 16 x 14 In. 440.00
Nutting, Wisteria Gate, Signed, Original Mat, Frame, c.1915, 10 x 16 In. 248.00
Nuyttens, Josef Pierre, Man-O'-War, Portrait, Etched, Signed, Frame, 10 x 11 ⅝ In.. . . . . 260.00

Parrish prints are wanted by collectors. Maxfield Frederick Parrish was an illustrator who lived from 1870 to 1966. He is best known as a designer of magazine covers, posters, calendars, and advertisements.

Parrish, Bower Of Paradise, 2 Women, Swan, Multicolored, Frame, 13 ½ x 21 ½ In. 86.00
Parrish, Daybreak, Frame, 17 ½ x 29 ½ In. 173.00
Parrish, Girl In Mountain, Frame, 21 x 15 In. . . . . *illus* 175.00
Parrish, Stars, Gilt Frame, 19 ½ x 11 ½ In. 180.00
Picasso, Imaginary Portraits, No. 13, Lithograph, Signed, 1969, 21 x 19 In.. . . . . 3885.00
Rockwell, Norman, Aviary, Signed, Mat, Frame, 28 x 27 In.. . . . . 258.00
Ruscha, Ed, Sailing Ship, Spattered Blue Spots, Lithograph, Signed, 36 x 27 In. 4800.00
Sandzen, Birger, White Trumpets, Stone, Black & White, Lithograph, c.1935, 25 x 29 In. 750.00
Weik, John, View Of Boston, July 4, 1870, Lithograph, c.1871, 32 x 43 In.. . . . . 235.00
Wengenroth, Stow, Owl In Pine Tree, Lithograph, Signed, 10 ½ x 15 ¾ In.. . . . . 767.00
Wood, Grant, Fruits, Hand Colored, Lithograph, Signed, c.1939, 7 x 10 In.. . . . . 2124.00

Woodblock prints that are not in the Japanese tradition are listed here. Most were made in England and the United States during the Arts and Crafts period. Japanese woodblock prints are listed under Print, Japanese.

Woodblock, Baumann, Gustave, Road To Town, Original Frame, 9 ½ x 11 In.. . . . . 5100.00
Woodblock, Baumann, Gustave, Spring, New Mexico, No. 49 Of 120, Signed, 11 x 12 In. 9000.00
Woodblock, Baumann, Gustave, Corn Dance, Santa Clara, Signed, 7 ½ x 6 In.. . . . . *illus* 13200.00
Woodblock, Baumann, Gustave, Grandma Battin's Garden, Signed, 14 x 14 In. 13200.00
Woodblock, Church Rancho De Taos, No. 32, Frame, 11 ½ x 9 ½ In.. 9000.00

Woodblock, Dean, Frank, Pines & Evening Sky, Frame, 11 ¼ x 6 ¾ In. 330.00
Woodblock, Geritz, Franz, Death Valley, Mat, Frame, 9 x 12 In. 900.00
Woodblock, Hyde, Helen, Child & Butterflies, Mat, Frame, 7 ½ x 2 ¾ In. 270.00
Woodblock, Landscape Of Haystacks, Arts & Crafts, Rice Paper, 9 ½ x 12 ¾ In. 3900.00
Woodblock, Lum, Bertha, Asia, Signed, Frame, 14 ½ x 7 ½ In. .... *illus* 1200.00
Woodblock, Rotky, Carl, Cathedral, Frame, 7 x 8 ½ In. 390.00
Woodblock, Rotky, Carl, River, Hillside, Frame, 10 ½ x 8 ½ In. 420.00
Woodblock, Rotky, Carl, Village, Frame, 6 x 8 ½ In. 420.00

PURINTON POTTERY COMPANY was incorporated in Wellsville, Ohio, in 1936. The company moved to Shippenville, Pennsylvania, in 1941 and made a variety of hand-painted ceramic wares. By the 1950s Purinton was making dinnerware, souvenirs, cookie jars, and florist wares. The pottery closed in 1959.

Apple, Cookie Jar, 10 x 6 In. .... 65.00 to 79.00
Apple, Creamer, Cover, 5 ½ In. 20.00
Apple, Grease Jar, Red, Brown & Yellow Apple, 5 ½ In. 95.00
Apple, Jug, Kent, 1 Pint. 35.00
Apple, Lazy Susan. 15.00
Apple, Plate, Dinner, 9 ¾ In. 20.00
Apple, Salt & Pepper, 2 ¾ In. 12.50
Apple, Salt & Pepper, Jug Shape, 2 ½ In. 14.00
Apple, Saltshaker, Jug Shape, Red, Brown & Yellow Apple, 2 ½ In. 6.00
Apple, Sugar & Creamer .... 23.00 to 40.00
Apple, Teapot, 2 Cup, 4 In. 12.00
Apple, Teapot, Red, Brown & Yellow Apple, 6 Cup, 6 ½ In. 85.00
Blue Pansy, Ivy Basket, Handle, 6 ¼ x 6 In. 113.00
Fruit, Bottle, Oil, 9 ½ In. 32.00
Fruit, Canister Set, Flour, Sugar, Coffee, Tea, Wooden Revolving Base, 10 In., 5 Piece 125.00
Fruit, Canister Set, Pie Shape, 4 Piece. 65.00
Fruit, Grease Jar, Cover, Apple & Pear, 5 ½ In. 25.00
Fruit, Jug, Dutch, Apple & Pear, Pastel Color, 4 ½ x 5 ½ In. 12.00
Fruit, Jug, Dutch, Apple & Pear, Pastel Color, 6 ½ x 9 In. 40.00
Fruit, Jug, Kent, Apple & Pear, Pastel, Pt. 30.00
Fruit, Jug, Dutch, Beige, Red Apple & Yellow Pears, 6 ½ In. 45.00
Fruit, Mug, Juice, 2 ¾ In. 30.00
Fruit, Pitcher, Apple & Pear, Dark Colors, 2 Green Leaves, 4 ½ x 5 ¾ In. 30.00
Fruit, Salt & Pepper, Apple & Pear, Cork Stopper, 4 x 2 In. 21.00
Fruit, Sugar & Creamer, Apple & Pear, Green Leaf .... 10.00 to 25.00
Fruit, Teapot, Apple & Pear, Green Leaf, 6 Cup, 6 In. .... 50.00 to 55.00
Fruit, Tumbler, 12 Oz., 5 In. 13.00
Fruit, Tumbler, Water, 5 In. 35.00
Half Blossom, Vase, 5 In. 12.00
Heather Plaid, Plate, Dinner, 9 ¾ In. 20.00
Heather Plaid, Salt & Pepper, Pour 'N Shake, 4 ¼ In. 50.00
Heather Plaid, Saltshaker, Jug Shape 20.00
Heather Plaid, Saucer, 5 ½ In. 5.00
Intaglio, Beer Mug, Brown, 16 Oz. 14.00
Intaglio, Cup & Saucer, Brown 16.00
Intaglio, Plate, Bread & Butter, Brown, 6 ¾ In. .... 6.50 to 10.00
Intaglio, Plate, Chop, Oval, Brown, 12 In. 32.00
Intaglio, Plate, Dinner, Brown, 9 ¾ In. 20.00
Intaglio, Platter, Meat, Brown, 11 In. 45.00
Intaglio, Roll Tray, Rectangular, Brown, 11 In. 29.00
Intaglio, Snack Set, Brown 13.00
Intaglio, Sugar, Cover, Brown 33.00
Intaglio, Sugar & Creamer, Brown 45.00
Intaglio, Teapot, Brown, 6 Cup 95.00
Ivy, Biscuit Jar, Cover, Red Blossom, 7 ½ In. 50.00
Ivy, Creamer, Red Blossom 13.00
Ivy, Honey Jug, Red Blossom, 6 ½ In. 35.00
Ivy, Jug, Kent, Yellow Blossom, Pt. 32.00
Ivy, Pitcher, Dutch Jug, Red Blossom, 5 ½ x 8 ¼ In. 45.00
Ivy, Pitcher, Red Blossom, 4 ½ In. 27.00
Ivy, Pitcher, Red Blossom, 5 ½ In. .... 35.00 to 45.00
Ivy, Teapot, Red Blossom, 6 Cup. 75.00

Protecting Paper
Did you know that the Declaration of Independence is stored at a constant temperature in an inert helium atmosphere? Too bad we can't all afford to protect our paper valuables with helium.

Print, Woodblock, Baumann, Gustave, Corn Dance, Santa Clara, Signed, 7 ½ x 6 In.
$13200.00

Print, Woodblock, Lum, Bertha, Asia, Signed, Frame, 14 ½ x 7 ½ In.
$1200.00

TIP
Don't frame a good print in a clip frame. There should be air space between the paper and the glass.

Purse, Beaded, Miser, Edwardian, 3¼ In.
$58.00

Purse, Mesh, 14K Gold, Sapphire, Seed Pearl, Watch, Longines, Coin Purse, Tiffany, 10 In.
$4780.00

Purse, Mesh, 14K Gold, Sapphire Cabochons, 7¾ x 4¼ In.
$1912.00

Purse, Mesh, Yellow Metal, Rhinestones, Chain, France, c.1920, 6 x 4⅝ In.
$389.00

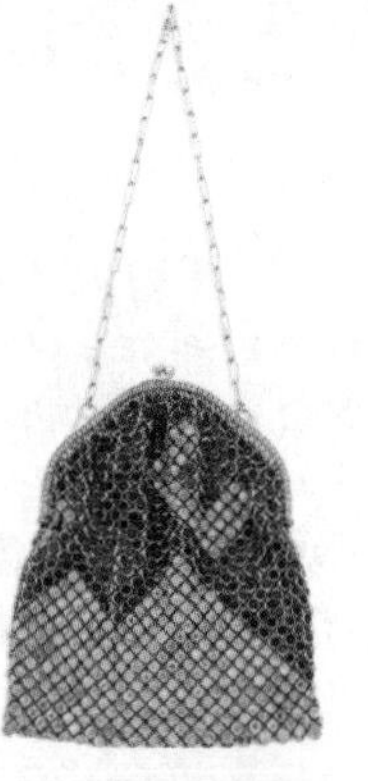

Ming Tree, Teapot, 2 Cup 40.00
Morning Glory, Honey Jug, 6½ In. 40.00
Mountain Rose, Planter Basket, 6¼ x 6 In. 45.00
Mountain Rose, Teapot, 2 Cup . . . . 25.00 to 40.00
Normandy Plaid, Sugar 10.00
Pennsylvania Dutch, Hostess Platter 35.00
Plaid, Plate, Dinner, 9¾ In. 8.50
Seafoam, Plate, Dinner, 10 In. 25.00
Shooting Star, Honey Jug, 6¼ In. 35.00
Shooting Star, Vase, 5 In. . . . . 18.00 to 95.00
Sunny, Jardiniere, Yellow Flower, 5 In. 30.00

PURSES have been recognizable since the eighteenth century, when leather and needlework purses were preferred. Beaded purses became popular in the nineteenth century, went out of style, but are again in use. Mesh purses date from the 1880s and are still being made. How to carry a handkerchief and lipstick is a problem today for every woman, including the Queen of England.

Alligator, Beige, Rigid Form, Goldtone Hardware, Charles Jourdan, 6⅝ x 7 x 2½ In. 764.00
Basket, Dyed White Oak Splint, 2 Arched Handles, Carved Rim Notches, 11 x 4 x 9 In. 66.00
Basket, Nantucket, Carved Ivory, Swing Handle, Jose Formoso Reyes, 1973, 10 In. 3290.00
Basket, Nantucket, Ivory, Whale, Jose Formoso, Signed, Wood Handle, 7 x 11 In. 2468.00
Beaded, Miser, Edwardian, 3¼ In. . . . . *illus* 58.00
Carnival Glass Beaded, Clutch, 2-Sided Vanity Mirror, 9¼ x 4¼ In. 150.00
Carpetbag, Autumn Tones, Blue Highlights, Leather Bottom, Coxackie 650.00
Carpetbag, Rose Tapestry, Double Hand Straps 45.00
Chrome, Change, Piano Hinge, Blue Silk Lining, Chatelaine, 1920s, 2½ x 1¾ In. 20.00
Coin, Mesh, Enameled, Art Deco, 7-Point Van Dyke Fringe, Whiting & Davis, c.1920 . . . . 245.00
Coin, Silver, Hammered, James Blake Co., 20th Century, 2¾ x 3¾ In. 94.00
Dyed, Embroidered, Ribbon, Ring Closure, Reinforced Bottom, Arts & Crafts, 6½ x 8 In. 180.00
Evening Bag, Silver, Trapezoid Shape, Engraved Owls, Green Stones, Russia, 1917, 8 In. 645.00
Faux Leather, Black, Lunch Box Shape, Roll Top, Embossed, Snakeskin, 7¾ x 5 In. 40.00
Leather, Brass, Enameled Lion's Head, Drawstring, Wine Color, Shoulder Strap, Gucci 325.00
Leather, Enamel Panels, Romantic Scene, Sterling Silver Rim, Austria, c.1910 . . . . 1495.00
Leather, Kelly, Brown, Gilt Metal Hardware, Lock & Key Sheath, Hermes, 9 x 11 In. 2160.00
Leather, Matte, Kelly, Navy Blue, Gold Tone Trim, Buttons, Scalloped Edge 42.00
Lucite, Clutch, Gray, Embedded Silver & Black Sparkles, Gold Plated Clasp, 9¼ x 1⅜ In. 80.00
Lucite, Gray & Clear, Charles Kahn, 7½ x 5 x 4 In. 245.00
Lucite, Oval, Clear, Chrysanthemum Sides, Clear Handle, Wilardy, 1940s, 9 x 9 In. 200.00
Mesh, 14K Gold, Sapphire, Seed Pearl, Watch, Longines, Coin Purse, Tiffany, 10 In. . . . . *illus* 4780.00
Mesh, 14K Gold, Sapphire Cabochons, 7¾ x 4¼ In. . . . . *illus* 1912.00
Mesh, 14K Yellow Gold, Cabochon Sapphire Clasp, Side Handle, Fringe, 15 In. 1450.00
Mesh, Charlie Chaplin, Ivory, Black, Shoulder Strap, Whiting & Davis, 5¾ x 3 In. 1125.00
Mesh, Sterling Silver, Repousse Floral Frame, Teardrop Bead Dangles, 6 In. 475.00
Mesh, Yellow Metal, Rhinestones, Chain, France, c.1920, 6 x 4⅝ In. . . . . *illus* 389.00
Mesh, Silver, Shaped Frame, Pierced, Engraved, Fruiting Grapevines, Link Chain Handle, 6 In. 88.00
Metal, Austrian Crystals, Cabochon, Signed, Judith Leiber, 4½ x 5 x 1½ In. . . . . *illus* 4183.00
Metal, Flowers, Austrian Crystals, Chain Strap, Signed, Judith Leiber, 5⅞ x 3½ In. . . . . *illus* 4183.00
Metal, Mouse, Yellow, Austrian Crystals, Strap, Signed, Judith Leiber, 5 x 4¼ x 3 In. . . . . *illus* 3346.00
Oil On Wood, Bakelite Handle, Brass Mounts, 6¾ x 8¼ x 4⅞ In. 999.00
Plastic, 2 Compartments, Cameo Latch, Handle, Goldcrest, 7¼ x 4¾ In. 45.00
Plastic, Black Plastic Beads, Matching Handle, 7 x 8¼ In. 32.00
Plastic, Clear, Gold Tone Frame, Chain, Round Faux Opals, 8½ x 7 In. 32.00
Plastic, Woven, Shell Collage, Lucite Handles, Trim, Gold Lace, Prince Charming 65.00
Rattan, Nantucket, Cherry Lid, Scrimshaw Whale & Ship, Leather Strap, c.1950 . . . . 500.00
Satin, Embroidered, Tiger's-Eye Stones, Brass Frame, Shoulder Strap, Judith Leiber 1710.00
Silk, Austrian Crystals, Signed, Judith Leiber, 6½ x 6½ In. . . . . *illus* 3585.00
Silk, Black, Austrian Crystal, Quartz, Onyx, Signed, Judith Leiber, 8 x 6 x 2½ In. . . . . . . *illus* 2629.00
Silk, Flowers, Beaded, Austrian Crystal, Shell, Signed, Judith Leiber, 6½ x 4½ In. . . . . . . *illus* 1315.00
Silk, Gilt Woven, Flower, Green Jade C-Shape Handle, 9½ x 7¼ In. 862.00
Silk On Linen, Pocketbook, Vines, Sarah Mendenhall, Late 18th Century, 4½ In. . . . . . *illus* 710.00
Silver, Flowers, Scrolls, Ribbons Of Flowers, Geometric Lines, 3½ x 2¾ In. 115.00
Silver, Scroll Decoration, Lid, Flower & Scroll Grille, Picture, Birth Of Venus, 4½ x 3 In. 690.00
Snakeskin, Camel Color, Brown Trim, Shoulder Strap, Judith Leiber, 1970s, 15 x 14 In. 615.00
Taffeta, Black, Tiffany Sterling Silver Frame, Faux Amethyst, Marked Tiffany & Co., 6 In. 1095.00
Western Saddle Style, Strap 55.00

Purse, Metal, Austrian Crystals, Cabochon, Signed, Judith Leiber, 4 ½ x 5 x 1 ½ In.
$4183.00

Purse, Metal, Flowers, Austrian Crystals, Chain Strap, Signed, Judith Leiber, 5 ⅞ x 3 ½ In.
$4183.00

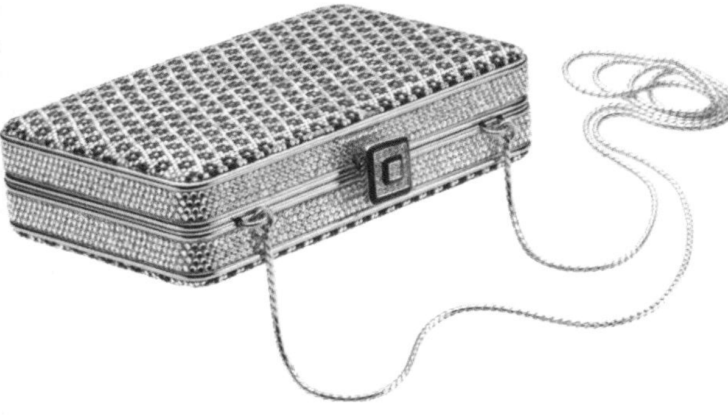

Purse, Metal, Mouse, Yellow, Austrian Crystals, Strap, Signed, Judith Leiber, 5 x 4 ¼ x 3 In.
$3346.00

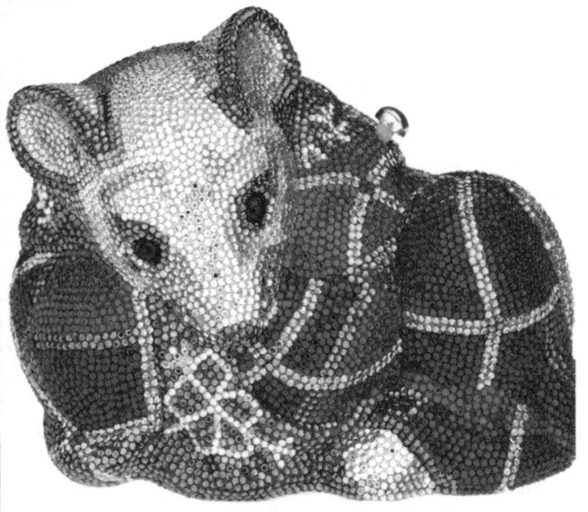

Purse, Silk, Austrian Crystals, Signed, Judith Leiber, 6 ½ x 6 ½ In.
$3585.00

Purse, Silk, Black, Austrian Crystal, Quartz, Onyx, Signed, Judith Leiber, 8 x 6 x 2 ½ In.
$2629.00

Purse, Silk, Flowers, Beaded, Austrian Crystal, Shell, Signed, Judith Leiber, 6 ½ x 4 ½ In.
$1315.00

Purse, Silk On Linen, Pocketbook, Vines, Sarah Mendenhall, Late 18th Century, 4 ½ In.
$710.00

Quezal

Quezal, Vase, Flower Shape, Green & White Pulled, Iridescent Gold, Signed, 5 x 6 In.
$1950.00

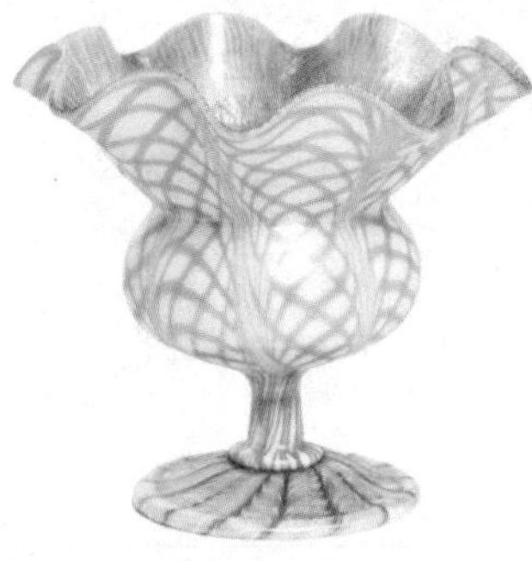

Quezal, Vase, Lincoln Drape, Gold, Opal, Signed, 6 ½ In.
$4700.00

Quezal, Vase, Gold Feather, Opal Ground, Green Striped, 7 ¼ In.
$6600.00

QUEZAL glass was made from 1901 to 1924 at the Queens, New York, company started by Martin Bach, Sr. Other glassware by other firms, such as Loetz, Steuben, and Tiffany, resembles this gold-colored iridescent glass. Martin Bach died in 1921. His son-in-law, Conrad Vahlsing, Jr., went to work at the Lustre Art Company about 1920. Bach's son, Martin Bach, Jr., worked at the Durand Art Glass division of the Vineland Flint Glass Works after 1924.

Bowl, Centerpiece, Marigold, Iridescent White, Footed, Signed, 10 In. 300.00
Candle, Lamp, Candlestick, Diamond Quilted Shade, Scalloped Rims, 18 In., Pair 1380.00
Compote, Butterscotch Luster, Calcite Interior, Flared, 4 ⅜ x 10 In. 235.00
Compote, Sweet Pea, Opal, Green Pulled Feather, Scalloped Rim, Signed, 5 In. 1610.00
Cordial, Iridescent Gold Luster, Conical Bowl, Signed, 3 ½ In. 144.00
Lamp, Boudoir, Bonnet Shape Shade, Iridescent Gold Pulled Ribbon, Signed, 7 x 5 In. 230.00
Lamp, Ceiling, Iridescent Pulled Feather, Opal & Gold Luster Interior, 7 ¼ x 34 In. 4600.00
Lamp, Iridescent Gold Ribbed Bell Shape Shade, Emeralite Base, 16 In. 288.00
Lamp, Pulled Feather Shade, Iridescent Gold, White, Bronze Base, 3-Footed, 22 In. 3600.00
Lamp, Stalactite, Bullet Shade, Iridescent White, Feathering, Gold, c.1920, 9 x 3 ¼ In. 2000.00
Salt, Iridescent Gold, Blue & Pink Highlights, Ribbed, Flared & Ruffled Rim, 1 ¼ In. 460.00
Salt, Iridescent Gold, Ribbed, Signed, 1901-25, 2 ½ In. 294.00
Salt, Iridescent Gold, Ribbed, Rolled Rim, Signed, 3 ¾ In. 175.00
Sconce, 5-Lily, Iridescent Gold, Patinated, Metal, 19 ½ In., Pair 8813.00
Shade, Bell, Hooked Feather, Iridescent Gold Interior, Ruffled Edge, Signed, 5 ¾ In. 323.00
Shade, Blue, Iridescent Gold, Pulled Feather, 5 ¼ In. 575.00
Shade, Gold Zipper, Opal, 2 ¾ x 1 ¾ In. 345.00
Shade, Green & Iridescent Gold Hooked Feather, Opal, Gold Luster Interior, 3 In. 690.00
Shade, Green Pulled Feather, Iridescent Gold, 5 In. 173.00
Shade, Hooked Feather, Iridescent Blue, 12 In. 2500.00
Shade, Hurricane, White, Gold Pulled Feather, Gold Interior, 3-Fitter Rim, 7 x 6 In. 1500.00
Shade, Iridescent Gold, White Pulled Zipper, Signed, 5 ½ In. 345.00
Shade, Iridescent Gold Heart & Vines, Opal, Gold Luster Interior, 5 x 2 ¼ In. 575.00
Shade, Iridescent Gold Luster, Purple Highlights, Ribbed, Flared, 5 ½ x 7 ½ In. 460.00
Shade, King Tut, Gold Zipper Edge, Opal, 3 ¼ x 5 In., Pair 1035.00
Shade, King Tut, Swirls, Iridescent Gold, 6 x 2 ¼ In. 460.00
Shade, King Tut, Yellow, Blown Into, Bronze Open Basket, 4 ½ x 3 ⅛ In. 2155.00
Shade, Lily, Iridescent Gold, Green Pulled Feather, Opal Interior, 4 ½ x 1 ½ In. 460.00
Shade, Lily, Pulled Green Feather, White, Gold, Signed, 6 x 4 ½ In., Pair 345.00
Shade, Opal, Gold Pulled Feather, Signed, 5 ½ In. 201.00
Shade, Tulip Shape, Ribbed, Iridescent Gold, Red, 5 ½ x 4 ¼ In. 288.00
Shade, White Ground, Gold Pulled Hearts, Signed, 5 x 3 ½ In. 351.00
Shade, White Pulled Waves, Iridescent Gold, Ribbed, 5 ½ x 2 ¼ In. 518.00
Shade, Yellow, Gold & Green Pulled Feather, Opal Interior, 6 x 2 ¼ In. 180.00
Shade, Yellow Zipper, Opal, 4 x 2 ¼ In., Pair 978.00
Tumbler, Iridescent Gold, Pinched Waist, Controlled Threading, Signed, 4 In. 345.00
Vase, Agate, Gray, Green, Amber, Shouldered, 4 ½ In. 2588.00
Vase, Agate, Green, Brown & Yellow Bands, Slightly Flared Rim, 5 ½ In. .... 1440.00 to 1560.00
Vase, Flower Shape, Green & White Pulled, Iridescent Gold, Signed, 5 x 6 In. .... *illus* 1950.00
Vase, Flower Shape, Green Pulled Feather, Opal Ground, Tricornered Rim, 7 ¾ In. 2645.00
Vase, Flower Shape, Green Pulled Feather, Rolled Scalloped Rim, 9 ¼ In. 4313.00
Vase, Flower Shape, Green Pulled Feathers, Iridescent Gold, Pinched Waist, 6 ½ In. 3838.00
Vase, Flower Shape, Green Pulled Feathers, Knopped Stem, Scalloped Bowl, 10 In. 12075.00
Vase, Flower Shape, Iridescent Gold, Green, White Pulled Design, Signed, 6 x 5 In. 2040.00
Vase, Flower Shape, Iridescent Gold, Ribbed Foot, Knopped Stem, 6-Petal Ruffled Rim, 9 In. 4600.00
Vase, Flower Shape, Pulled Feathers, Gold Interior, Stretched, Ruffled Rim, 6 ¾ In. 2875.00
Vase, Gold, Bulbous, Elongated Neck, Silver Overlay, Art Nouveau Flowers, Signed, 7 In. 1920.00
Vase, Gold Feather, Opal Ground, Green Striped, 7 ¼ In. .... *illus* 6600.00
Vase, Gold Luster, White Pulled Feather, Melon Ribbed, 6 ¼ In. 920.00
Vase, Golden Orange, Tubular, Iridescent Amber Spread Foot, 10 ¼ In. 294.00
Vase, Green, White, Gold, Pulled Feather, Flared, Ruffled Rim, Footed, Signed, 8 ¾ In. 1700.00
Vase, Green & White Pulled Feather, Signed, 7 ½ In. 1725.00
Vase, Green Hooked, Iridescent Yellow Outline, Cream Ground, Squat, 3 x 4 ⅛ In. 1560.00
Vase, Green Hooked, Silvery Iridescent Fishnet, Green, Cream Ground, 6 ¼ In. 920.00
Vase, Green Hooked Feather, Iridescent Gold Tips, Cream Ground, 7 x 7 In. 4600.00
Vase, Green Pulled Feather, Iridescent Gold, Applied Reeded Tendril, 7 In. 4200.00
Vase, Green Pulled Feathers Tipped In Gold, Tricornered Rim, 7 In. 2070.00
Vase, Iridescent Gold, Applied Serpent, Signed, 5 ¼ In. 4000.00
Vase, Iridescent Gold, Blue, Green & Pink Highlights, Ribbed, Ruffled Rim, 3 In. 403.00
Vase, Iridescent Gold, Fishnet At Top, Ruffled Rim, Green Pulled Feather Foot, 8 In. 2588.00
Vase, Iridescent Gold, Green, Opal Pulled Feather, Shouldered, Signed, 6 In. 3048.00

Vase, Iridescent Gold, Green, Blue, Spiral Looped White Bands, Signed, 6 In. 4300.00
Vase, Iridescent Gold, Pulled Vines, Blue Gray Leaves, Shouldered, 10 In. 235.00
Vase, Iridescent Gold, Purple, Blue, Flared Rim, 8 In. 300.00
Vase, Iridescent Gold, Purple, Blue, Silver Flower Overlay, Shoulder, 7 ½ In. 2640.00
Vase, Iridescent Gold, Ribbed, Scalloped Pinched Rim, Signed, 2 ¼ In. 275.00
Vase, Iridescent Green, Blue To Gold Hooked Feather, Oval, 4 ½ In. 6613.00
Vase, Jack-In-The-Pulpit, Green Pulled Feather, Gold Stretched Edge, 8 ½ In.. .... 4200.00
Vase, Jack-In-The-Pulpit, Iridescent Gold Luster, Bulbous Base, Signed, 9 ½ In. 920.00
Vase, Jack-In-The-Pulpit, Opal, Elephant Ear, Green, Gold Pulled Feathers, 9 In. 3163.00
Vase, Jack-In-The-Pulpit, Pulled Feather, Iridescent Gold, Onionskin Edge, 9 In. 2875.00
Vase, King Tut, Iridescent Gold, Ivory, Bulbous, Elongated Neck, 9 ¼ In. 1058.00
Vase, Lincoln Drape, Gold, Opal, Signed, 6 ½ In. .... *illus* 4700.00
Vase, Platinum Iridescent Heart & Vines, Iridescent Ground, Bulbous, 5 ½ In. 3450.00
Vase, Stick, Iridescent Blue, Bulbous Base, Knopped Stem, 5 ½ In. 345.00
Vase, Stick Innovations, Swirled, Bulbous Base, Ruffled Edge, Signed, 7 In. 3450.00
Vase, Trumpet, Bright Gold, Footed, Signed, 8 ½ In.. .... 460.00
Vase, Trumpet, Green, Silver Overlay, Flowers, Signed, 14 In. 690.00
Vase, Trumpet, Iridescent Gold, Purple, Folded Rim, 4 ½ In.. .... 345.00

QUILTS have been made since the seventeenth century. Early textiles were very precious and every scrap was saved to be reused. A quilt is a combination of fabrics joined to a filler and a backing by small stitched designs known as quilting. An appliqued quilt has pieces stitched to the top of a large piece of background fabric. A patchwork, or pieced, quilt is made of many small pieces stitched together. Embroidery can be added to either type.

48 Squares, Pre 1950 Textiles, Silk, Cotton, Wool, Rayon & Boucle, 23 x 29 In. 150.00
Amish, Bar, Cotton, Red, Blue, Orange, Yellow, Tan, White, Blue, c.1900, 86 x 86 In. 575.00
Amish, Bar, Purple, Pink, Black, Green, Blue, Gold, Blue Back, Hand Tied, 70 x 75 ½ In.. .... 115.00
Amish, Bear's Paw, Black, Blue, Lattice, Border, Amanda Herchberger, 45 x 34 In. 288.00
Amish, Diamond Block, 9 Patch, Purple Border, Black Ground, 70 x 81 In. 550.00
Amish, Patchwork, 9 Patch Variation, Wool, Rayon, Flannel, Green, Blue, 71 x 81 In. 173.00
Amish, Patchwork, Double 4 Patch, c.1950, 48 x 80 In. 248.00
Amish, Patchwork, Roman Bars, Wool, Cotton, 20th Century, 84 x 94 In. 413.00
Amish, Patchwork, Triple Irish Chain, Amish, Early 20th Century, 88 x 88 In. 230.00
Appliqued, 9 Blocks, Red, Green Floral Wreaths, Sawtooth Border, Binding, 91 x 91 In. 1725.00
Appliqued, Campaign, Bust Of Garfield, Flags, Shields, Multicolored, Cotton, 70 x 72 In. 2530.00
Appliqued, Compasses, Gold Embroidery, Multicolored Bars, Wool, Cotton, 67 x 77 In.. ...... 1725.00
Appliqued, Diamond, Swag Border, 19th Century, 34 x 35 In. 5850.00
Appliqued, Flags, Flowers, Queen Of Rosary, Velvet, Embroidered, c.1905, 62 x 72 In. 550.00
Appliqued, Floral Wreath, Cockscomb Corners, 19th Century, 106 x 108 In.. .... 1980.00
Appliqued, Flower Basket, Flower Vines, White Ground, Scalloped Border, 89 x 76 In. 230.00
Appliqued, Flowers, Leaves, Multicolored, Yellow Binding, c.1920, 82 x 82 In. 250.00
Appliqued, Grape Clusters, Hand Sewn, Multicolored, Vining Border, 78 x 78 In.. .... 546.00
Appliqued, Green Leaves, Natural Ground, Green Border, 64 x 89 In. 259.00
Appliqued, Green Wreaths, Border, Red Stylized Flowers, White Ground, 90 x 84 In. 44.00
Appliqued, Hawaiian, Yellow Leaves, Wine Red Ground, Cotton, c.1950, 75 ½ x 86 In.. ...... 978.00
Appliqued, Nursery Design, Early 20th Century, 62 x 42 In. 118.00
Appliqued, Potted Flower Vines, 6 Flower Medallions, Red, Yellow, Blue, 93 x 73 In. 316.00
Appliqued, Princess Feather, Cotton, c.1850, 80 x 80 In. .... *illus* 570.00
Appliqued, Princess Feather, Red, Gray Green, Double Star, Print Back, 86 x 84 In.. .... 546.00
Appliqued, Princess Feather, Red, Green, Flowers & Bead Border, 77 x 95 In. 546.00
Appliqued, Princess Feather Variation, 4 Blocks, Red, White, Sawtooth Border, 72 x 75 In. ... 635.00
Appliqued, Red & Green Flowers, Vine, Crosshatch & Rayed Stitches, 81 x 80 In.. .... 345.00
Appliqued, Red & Green Oak Leaves, Stars, Berries, White Ground, 98 x 82 In. 198.00
Appliqued, Red Flower Center, Green & Red Flowers, Leaf & Flower Border, 84 x 80 In.. ..... 44.00
Appliqued, Rose Of Sharon, Red, Green, Yellow Reverse Applique Centers, 78 x 80 In.. ...... 431.00
Appliqued, Rose Sampler, 20 Blocks, Diagonal Line, Cotton, Wool, 68 x 83 In.. .... 748.00
Appliqued, Roses, Tulips, Sawtooth & Vine Border, 92 x 90 In. 99.00
Appliqued, Star Of Bethlehem, 76 x 80 In. 7500.00
Appliqued, Sunbonnet Babies, 20 Blocks, Blue, White, 72 x 84 In.. .... 275.00
Appliqued, Tulip, 16 Blocks, Red & Orange, Green Stems & Leaves, White Ground, 78 x 79 In. 230.00
Appliqued, Tulip, White Ground, Quilted Pinwheels, Plumes, c.1850, 80 x 84 In.. .... 558.00
Appliqued, Tulips, 8 Alternating Rows, Medallions, Grapes & Vines Border, 1870, 84 x 87 In. . 3450.00
Appliqued, Whig Rose, Red, Tan, Natural Ground, Tan Binding, Cotton, c.1840, 72 x 75 In. . . 690.00
Appliqued, Wild Poppies, Natural Ground, 98 x 98 In.. .... 978.00
Crazy, Birds, Flowers, Insects, Dog, Embroidered, Late 1800s, 74 x 80 In. 150.00
Crazy, Patchwork, Diamond, Embroidered, Goldenrod, Black & Gold Design, 63 x 59 In. 3565.00

Quilt, Appliqued, Princess Feather, Cotton, c.1850, 80 x 80 In.
$570.00

Quilt, Patchwork, Double 9 Patch, Cotton, Late 19th Century, 77 x 78 In.
$403.00

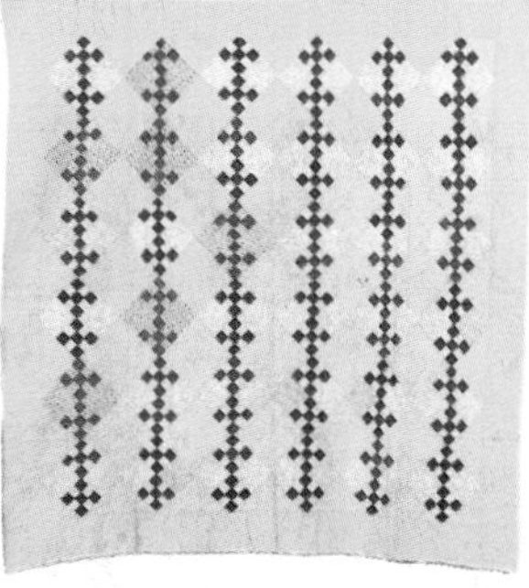

Quilt, Patchwork, Double Irish Chain, Diamond & Concentric Circle, 76 x 78 In.
$290.00

Quilt, Patchwork, Grandmother's Flower Garden, 6-Sided Printed Blocks, c.1880, 78 x 83 In.
$345.00

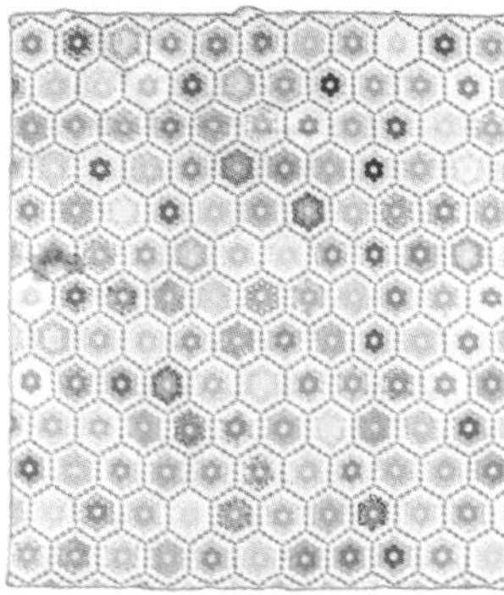

Quilt, Patchwork, Log Cabin, Early 20th Century, 80 x 80 In. $310.00

Quilt, Patchwork, Mariner's Compass, Embroidery, Wool, Cotton, c.1878, 67 x 77 In. $1725.00

Quilt, Patchwork & Appliqued, Blazing Star, Feather Border, c.1850, 90 x 90 In. $805.00

Quilt Trim

Black buttonhole stitching outlining an appliqué on a quilt was popular from 1925 to 1950. Earlier quilts sometimes had tan or white buttonhole trim for the appliqué.

Crazy, Patchwork, Embroidered, Silk, Velvet, Satin Border, 19th Century, 56 x 78 In. 478.00
Crazy, Patchwork, Fan, Embroidered, Brown, Wool, Flannel, Silk, 72 x 76 In. 1440.00
Crazy, Patchwork, Velvet, Anchor, Artist Palette, Horse Shoe, Silk, Border, 1884, 66 x 67 In. . . . 777.00
Mennonite, Bar, Green & Black Print, Orange Print, Alternating Stripes, 88 x 77 In. 518.00
Mennonite, Patchwork, Drunkard's Path, Black & Purple, Wool, c.1890, 68 x 80 In. 413.00
Mennonite, Patchwork, Mosaic, Diagonal Rows, Purple, Black, Wool, c.1870, 67 x 70 In. 468.00
Patchwork, 4 Patch, Reversible, Cross Hatching, Scallops, 18 ½ x 36 In. 247.00
Patchwork, 8-Point Star, Red, Green, Yellow Star & Border, Brown Ground, 84 In. 2530.00
Patchwork, 8-Point Stars, Diagonal Lattice, Banded Border, 108 x 92 In. 1276.00
Patchwork, Alternating Diamonds, Red & White, White Baskets, c.1880, 70 x 80 In. 252.00
Patchwork, Barn Raising, Wool, Cotton, 82 x 82 In. 460.00
Patchwork, Basket, Brown, Orange Calico, 69 x 82 In. 168.00
Patchwork, Carpenter's Wheel, Red, Orange, Cotton, Lebanon, 1885, 85 x 84 In. 7050.00
Patchwork, Diamond In A Square, Flower Head, Leaf, 80 x 80 In. 6000.00
Patchwork, Double 9 Patch, Cotton, Late 19th Century, 77 x 78 In. . . . . *illus* 403.00
Patchwork, Double Irish Chain, Diamond & Concentric Circle, 76 x 78 In. . . . . *illus* 290.00
Patchwork, Drunkard's Path, Red, Black Dots, Blue Flower Ground, 75 x 84 In. 303.00
Patchwork, Fan, Geometric Center, Embroidered, Black Sateen, Green, 63 x 71 In. 259.00
Patchwork, Feathered Star, 9 Blocks, Cotton, Scalloped Quilting, 83 x 86 In. 978.00
Patchwork, Flowers, Stylized, Red, Blue, Green, Green Border, c.1880, 88 x 88 In. 375.00
Patchwork, Flying Geese, Brown & White Calico, White Border, c.1880, 76 x 76 In. 460.00
Patchwork, Goose On The Pond, Blue & White, Calico, Shell Pattern, 70 ½ x 74 In. 632.00
Patchwork, Grandmother's Flower Garden, 6-Sided Printed Blocks, c.1880, 78 x 83 In. . *illus* 345.00
Patchwork, Lady Of The Lake, Red & Yellow, 66 x 78 In. 518.00
Patchwork, LeMoyne Star, Dress Prints, Double Border, Muslin Back, 68 x 76 In. 460.00
Patchwork, Log Cabin, 19th Century, 62 x 76 In. 495.00
Patchwork, Log Cabin, Burgundy Border, Late 19th Century, 65 x 65 In. 353.00
Patchwork, Log Cabin, Early 20th Century, 80 x 80 In. . . . . *illus* 310.00
Patchwork, Log Cabin, Graduating Diamonds, c.1880-90, 62 x 54 In. 550.00
Patchwork, Mariner's Compass, Embroidery, Wool, Cotton, c.1878, 67 x 77 In. . . . . *illus* 1725.00
Patchwork, Monkey Wrench Pattern, Calico, Cotton, 78 x 80 In. 230.00
Patchwork, Ocean Waves, Cheddar, Prussian Blue & White, 66 x 83 In. 748.00
Patchwork, Ocean Waves, Indigo Blue, White, 19th Century, 72 x 81 In. 633.00
Patchwork, Odd Fellows, Dress Prints, Sawtooth Inner Border, Mid 1800s, 90 x 78 In. 633.00
Patchwork, Ohio Star, Dress Prints, Homespun Back, Early 1800s, 102 x 108 In. 690.00
Patchwork, Patriotic, Red, White, Blue, V For Victory, Cotton, 84 x 74 In. 3000.00
Patchwork, Pinwheel, Shell, Heart, Line, Prints, Solid Cotton, 77 x 78 In. 403.00
Patchwork, Printed Cotton, Chintz, Dewindt, Michigan, c.1853, 90 x 90 In. 2585.00
Patchwork, Sawtooth Round, Red & Green, Striped Border, Cotton, 66 x 80 In. 374.00
Patchwork, Schoolhouse, Red, White, Late 19th Century, 72 x 74 In. 500.00
Patchwork, Star, Orange & Red, Blue Ground, Late 19th Century, 84 x 82 In. 345.00
Patchwork, Star, Variation, Multicolored, 19th Century, 83 ½ x 81 ½ In. 1293.00
Patchwork, Stars, Blocks, Bars, Wool, 44 x 34 In. 12870.00
Patchwork, Sunburst, 20 Blocks, Set On Diamond, Blue & White Binding, 82 x 103 In. 403.00
Patchwork, Sunburst, Variation, Cotton, Red, Sage, Natural Ground, c.1890, 66 x 84 In. 345.00
Patchwork, Trapunto Star, Cotton, Prints, Solids, Stars, Blues, 1930s, 71 x 72 In. 1035.00
Patchwork, Tree Of Life, Wreaths, Rising Sun, Yellow, Green, Red Ground, 75 x 78 In. 1870.00
Patchwork, Trip Around The World, Solids, Prints, Striped Border, Cotton, 76 x 75 In. 1380.00
Patchwork, Zigzag, Red, Gold, Green, Borders, Binding, Cotton, 1900s, 82 x 80 In. 646.00
Patchwork & Appliqued, 4 Flowerpots, Late 19th Century, 76 x 74 ½ In. 8225.00
Patchwork & Appliqued, Blazing Star, Feather Border, c.1850, 90 x 90 In. . . . . *illus* 805.00
Patchwork & Appliqued, Vases, Green, White, Roses, Teal Lattice, Muslin Back, 100 x 100 In. 316.00

HR. Quimper

QUIMPER pottery has a long history. Tin-glazed, hand-painted pottery has been made in Quimper, France, since the late seventeenth century. The earliest firm, founded in 1685 by Jean Baptiste Bousquet, was known as HB Quimper. Another firm, founded in 1772 by Francois Eloury, was known as Porquier. The third firm, founded by Guillaume Dumaine in 1778, was known as HR or Henriot Quimper. All three firms made similar pottery decorated with designs of Breton peasants and sea and flower motifs. The Eloury (Porquier) and Dumaine (Henriot) firms merged in 1913. Bousquet (HB) merged with the others in 1968. The group was sold to a United States family in 1984. The American holding company is Quimper Faience Inc., located in Stonington, Connecticut. The French firm has been called *Societe Nouvelle des Faienceries de Quimper HB Henriot* since March 1984.

Basket, Footed, Handle, c.1968, 11 ½ x 9 ¾ x 4 ¾ In. 600.00
Bowl, Handles, Petit Breton, Flowers, 7 In. 125.00
Bowl, Mustard Yellow Glossy Glaze, 1928, 10 ½ x 3 ¾ In. 385.00
Bowl, Petit Breton, Yellow Glaze, 4 ¼ x 2 ½ In. 38.00

Bowl, Salad, Blue, Cranberry & Orange, Girl Frolicking In Meadow, c.1930, 9⅜ In. 375.00
Bowl, Vegetable, Round, Navy Blue & Burgundy Designs, 11½ x 3 In. 87.00
Box, Sweetmeat, Footed, Rich Colors, Town Symbols, c.1925, 4½ x 6½ x 5 In. 755.00
Butter, Breton Bagpipe, Rich Colors, c.1900, 2½ x 8¼ x 10½ In. 1295.00
Butter, Raised Wheat Handle, Ribbon Rimming The Lid, Wild Flowers, 1920s, 4 x 9 In. 965.00
Butter Tray, Mistral Blue, Octagon 50.00
Candleholder, Round Base, Colorful, 9¾ In., Pair 225.00
Charger, Broderie, Father & Son, c.1930, 12 In. 1875.00
Chest, Jewelry, Cover, Bombay, Painting Of Woman On Top, 4 x 4½ x 6 In. 149.00
Dish, Fish Shape, Woman In Center, 1930, 10 x 4½ In. 210.00
Dish, Oval, Ravier Carrying Basket Of Eggs, Scalloped Edge, Handles, 9¾ x 5½ In. 160.00
Flask, Perfume, Pipe Smoker On Front, Flowers On Reverse, 1930s 345.00
Jardiniere, Boat Shape, Breton On Side, Flowers On Reverse, 1930s, 6 x 3 x 2 In. 225.00
Jardiniere, Flowers, Handles .... *illus* 530.00
Jardiniere, White Ground, Flowers, Birds, Signed, France, 1800s, 13 In. 1200.00
Oyster Plate, Fouillen, Shell Shaped, Starfish Center, 1930s, 9 In. 500.00
Planter Pot, Breton, Trees, 7 x 8½ In. 125.00
Plate, 4 Cobalt Blue Flowers, Cream Ground, Octagonal, c.1925, 9 In. 125.00
Plate, Breton, Flowers, c.1880, 8¼ In. 285.00
Plate, Fouillen Musician In Center, Rich Border, Detailed Center Panel, 1930s, 8 In. 120.00
Plate, Ovington, Ridged Edge, Rich Decor Border, Breton In Center, 8½ In. 340.00
Plate, Petite Breton Woman With Basket, Scalloped Edge, 1890s, 9¼ In. 385.00
Platter, Croisille, Oval, 12½ x 8½ In. 125.00
Platter, Man & Woman Holding Hands, Tree, Oval, c.1900, 10 x 13 In. 785.00
Platter, Wreaths Of Roses, Draped Blue Bows, Octagonal, 11¾ x 8¾ In. 225.00
Salt, Double, Breton Couple, Handle, 7 x 5½ In. 200.00
Salt, Painted Flowers, White Ground, 1900s, 2 x ¾ In. 45.00
Sugar, Cover, France Paneled, Yellow, Flowers & Garlands, 1930s, 6 x 6½ x 4 In. 175.00
Sugar, Cover, Man On One Side, Woman On Reverse Side 90.00
Swan, 3½-In. Opening, 8 x 7 In. 285.00
Teapot, Handle, Petit Breton, 1900s 300.00
Trivet, Ivoire Corbeille, Cut Corners, 1930s, 10 x 1 In. 150.00
Vase, Art Nouveau, 3 Handles Connecting The Top & Bottom, 5¾ In. 185.00
Vase, Binou, 2 Dancers, Crest On Reverse, Riche Border, Gorse & Heather Designs, 7 In. 465.00
Vase, Bud, Horn Shaped, Bretonne Holding Flower, 19th Century, 5 In. 66.00
Vase, Bulbous, Painted, Black & White, Tan Ground, Signed, HB, 6 x 9½ In. 805.00
Vase, Dolphin Tail Arms, 2 Musicians, Flowered Bouquet, 13 x 9½ In. 895.00
Vase, Petit Breton, Vibrant Colors, Glossy, 5½ In. 125.00
Vase, Squat, Blue Neck, 2 Handles, Orange & Red Details, 5 In. 290.00
Vase, Stained Glass Panels, Unusual Shape, c.1930, 12 x 9½ In. 3165.00
Wall Plaque, Young Couple, Leaf Border, 16 In. 50.00
Wall Pocket, Geometric Décor, Flowers, Man Smoking Pipe, 10 x 7 x 3 In. 475.00

RADFORD pottery was made by Alfred Radford in Broadway, Virginia; Tiffin and Zanesville, Ohio; and Clarksburg, West Virginia, from 1891 until 1912. Jasperware, Ruko, Thera, Radura, and Velvety Art Ware were made. The jasperware resembles the famous Wedgwood ware of the same name. Another pottery named Radford worked in England and is not included here.

RADURA.

Cup & Saucer, Chintz, Roses & Lavender Flowers, Gold Rim 38.00
Jardiniere, Pedestal, Birds, Flowers, 3 Handles, Majolica, Marked, 41½ In. .... *illus* 950.00
Vase, Jasperware, Cameo Angels, Eagles, Applied Brown Volcanic Glaze, 9⅜ In. 176.00
Vase, Lincoln & Eagle, Volcanic Glaze, Jasperware, Marked, 7 In. .... *illus* 170.00

RADIO broadcast receiving sets were first sold in New York City in 1910. They were used to pick up the experimental broadcasts of the day. The first commercial radios were made by Westinghouse Company for listeners of the experimental shows on KDKA Pittsburgh in 1920. Collectors today are interested in all early radios, especially those made of Bakelite plastic or decorated with blue mirrors. Figural advertising radios and transistor radios are also collected.

Atwater Kent, Model 10C, Breadboard, Part Number 4700, 1924 .... 1320.00
Crosley, Model 706, Showbox, 1928 .... 550.00
Delco, Push Button, Pink, White, Light-Up, Belmont Co., 1947 .... 630.00
Detrola, Super Pee-Wee, Red, White, c.1938 .... 1600.00
Dewald, Catalin Model A-301, Bakelite, 1946, 6½ x 9½ In. 1035.00
E.H. Scott Philharmonic, c.1930, Floor Model 8000.00
Edison, Model R5, Floor Model 242.00
Emerson, Model Bt-245, Tombstone Shape, Catalin, Red Marble, 1939, 10 In. 4245.00

Quimper, Jardiniere, Flowers, Handles
$530.00

Radford, Jardiniere, Pedestal, Birds, Flowers, 3 Handles, Majolica, Marked, 41½ In.
$950.00

Radford, Vase, Lincoln & Eagle, Volcanic Glaze, Jasperware, Marked, 7 In.
$170.00

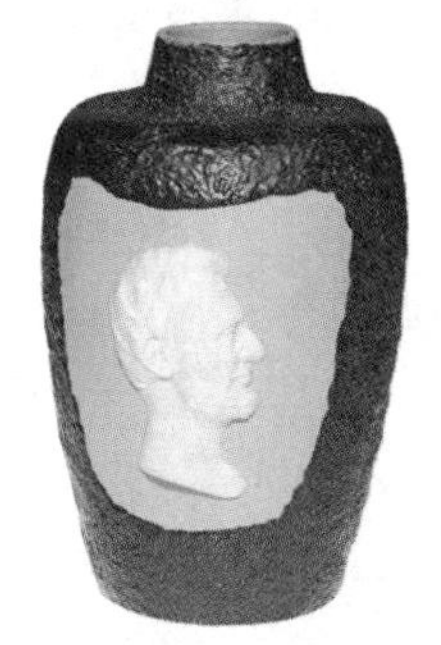

Radio, Fada, Bullet, Bakelite, 10½ In.
$600.00

R

Railroad, Badge, Baltimore & Ohio Railroad Co., Celluloid, Metal, c.1930, 2 In.
$28.00

Railroad, Lantern, Switch, Chicago Minneapolis St. Paul Railroad, 19 In.
$345.00

Railroad, Plate, Baltimore & Ohio Railroad, Shell Border, E. Wood & Sons, 10 ⅛ In.
$950.00

TIP

"Never invest your money in anything that eats or needs repainting." Wise words from Billy Rose, a successful showman and art collector.

Fada, Bullet, Bakelite, 10 ½ In. ... *illus* 600.00
Gloritone, Model 26, Cathedral, 1931 ... 165.00
McIntosh, Model 240, Tube Amplifier, 1950-60 ... 1600.00
Philco, 20B, Cathedral, 1930 ... 231.00
Radiola, No. 516, Plastic, 1942 ... 65.00
RCA Radiola, Model 18, 1927, Wood ... 75.00
RCA Victor, Oriental, 8 x 10 In. ... 201.00
Sentinel, Bakelite, 7 ½ x 11 In. ... 403.00
Stewart Warner, Model 300, Wood, 1925, Table Model ... 125.00
Transistor, Sony, Model TR-63, Yellow, Red Dial, Leather Case, 1957, 5 x 3 In. ... 780.00
Zenith, Model 16-A-63, Stratosphere, Console, 16 Tubes, c.1936 ... 24150.00
Zenith, Transistor, Royal 1000, Trans Oceanic Shortwave, Original Box ... 55.00

RAILROAD enthusiasts collect any train memorabilia. Everything is wanted, from oilcans to whole train cars. The Chessie system has a store that sells many reproductions of their old dinnerware and uniforms.

Badge, Baltimore & Ohio Railroad Co., Celluloid, Metal, c.1930, 2 In. ... *illus* 28.00
Baggage Cart, Iron, Oak Planks, Georgia Railroad Station, 18 x 72 x 36 In. ... 150.00
Lantern, Switch, Chicago Minneapolis St. Paul Railroad, 19 In. ... *illus* 345.00
Lock, Key, B & O, Brass, Heart Shape, Dayton Mfg. Co. ... 100.00
Lock, Key, B & O, Brass, Marked, Signal Dept, Cumberland Div., Yale & Towne Mfg. ... 75.00
Lock, Key, Brass, Heart Shape, Fraim Co. ... 85.00
Lock, Key, CRI & PRR, Brass, Heart Shape, Hansel Mfg. Co. ... 75.00
Lock, Key, N & W ... 70.00
Lock, Key, Yale, Peanut Shape, Steel, Brass, WMRY Co. ... 75.00
Lock, Switch, Key, Amtrak ... 40.00
Lock, Switch, Key, B & O RR, Marked, RT, 1944 ... 60.00
Lock, Switch, Key, B & O, Marked, 1969 ... 65.00
Lock, Yale, Brass, Marked, P & R ... 65.00
Mirror, Frisco Line Railroad, There Is Something To See, Celluloid, 2 In. ... 70.00
Plate, Baltimore & Ohio Railroad, Blue Transfer, Shell Border, Staffordshire, 9 In. ... 805.00
Plate, Baltimore & Ohio Railroad, Shell Border, E. Wood & Sons, 10 ⅛ In. ... *illus* 950.00
Plate, Baltimore & Ohio Railroad, Shell Border, Blue, Staffordshire, 1830s, 10 ⅛ In. ... 978.00
Rug, Hooked, Baltimore & Ohio 1830, Wool, Hazel Walker, 1957, 24 x 36 In. ... *illus* 790.00
Sign, Hudson & Manhattan Railroad Co., N.Y. & N.J., Porcelain, 22 x 25 In. ... 495.00
Sign, L. & S.W.R., Beware Of Trains, Cast Iron, Rounded Corners, 16 ½ x 26 In. ... 258.00

RAZORS were used in ancient Egypt and subsequently wherever shaving was in fashion. The metal razor used in America until about 1870 was made in Sheffield, England. After 1870, machine-made hollow-ground razors were made in Germany or America. Plastic or bone handles were popular. The razor was often sold in a set of seven, one for each day of the week. The set was often kept by the barber who shaved the well-to-do man each day in the shop.

Arnold Fountain Safety Razor Co., Fountain, Looks Like Pen, c.1911 ... 325.00
Gem Micromatic, Straight, Brass, 1930s, 3 ½ In. ... 24.00
Keen Kutter, Woman, Scrolls, Embossed, Aluminum, Metal, 6 ¼ x ⅞ In. ... 77.00
Rolls, Whetter On Side, Razor On Other, Nickel Plated Case, Felt Lined, 2 ¾ x 6 In. ... 85.00
Schick, Cream Handle, Plastic Case, Blades, Metal Head, 4 ¾ In. ... 38.00
Schick, Injection, Repeating Blade, Goldtone Head, Beige Bakelite Handle, 1940s ... 18.00
Shavemaster, Sunbeam, Model R, Brown Bakelite, Cloth Covered Cord, c.1937 ... 60.00
Star, Tin Case, Kampfe Brothers ... 90.00
Straight, Transparent, Orange Celluloid Handle, Torrey Razor Co. ... 32.00
Straight, Worcester Razor Co., Box ... 23.00
Strap, Keen Kutter, No. 15C ... 20.00
Strap, Keen Kutter, No. K5 ... 23.00
Strap, Keen Kutter, No. K8 ... 45.00
Strap, Winchester, No. 8373 ... 95.00
Valet, Goldtone Finish, 1937 ... 25.00
Valet, Straight, 20th Century, Auto Stop Razor Co. ... 18.00
Wilkinson, Sword, 7 Day, 7 Blades, Chrome Art Deco Case ... 125.00

REAMERS, or juice squeezers, have been known since 1767, although most of those collected today date from the twentieth century. Figural reamers are among the most prized.

Aluminum, Hand Held, Hole, Hanging, Foley ... 6.00
Aluminum, Handle, Foley ... 25.00

Aluminum, Lemon, Handle, Griswold, A703 160.00
Ceramic, Clown, Japan, 7 ½ In. *illus* 191.00
Glass, Checkerboard Pattern, Swirled Center, Handle, Hazel Atlas, 8 ½ x 4 In. 18.00
Glass, Citrus, Loop Handle, 6 x 4 In. 15.00
Glass, Crisscross, Cobalt Blue, Loop Handle, Hazel Atlas, 7 ¾ In. 315.00
Glass, Crisscross, Loop Handle, Twisted Cone, Footed, Hazel Atlas 23.00
Glass, Delphite Blue, Jeannette Glass Co., 1930s *illus* 88.00
Glass, Fry Glass, Tab Handle, Opalescent Pearl, 1930s, 6 ½ x 8 In. 30.00
Glass, Green, Handle, 8 x 2 ⅜ In. 25.00
Glass, Green, Tab Handle, Hazel Atlas, 5 ¼ In. 25.00
Glass, Jade Green, Embossed Sunkist, McKee Glass, c.1940, 8 In. *illus* 55.00
Glass, Lemon, Aqua Tint, Elongated, Germany 30.00
Glass, Lemon, Green, Tab Handle, Hazel Atlas 30.00
Glass, Lemon, Jadite, Jeannette Glass Co., 7 ¼ x 5 ¼ In. 24.00
Glass, Milk Glass, Loop Handle, McKee Glass Co. 9.00
Glass, Milk Glass, Sunkist, Opalescent, Swirls, Loop Handle 35.00
Glass, Orange, Hocking, Green, Loop Handle 20.00
Glass, Orange, Ribbed Sides, Looped Handle, Footed, Hocking 16.00
Glass, Orange, Vertical Ribbing, Tab Handle, 8 x 1 ⅝ In. 10.00
Glass, Stoneware, Blue & White, Blue Design, Loop Handle, Germany, 7 ½ x 5 In. 65.00
Glass, Vaseline, Tab Handle, 5 ½ In. 22.00
Lemon, Wood, Hand Held, c.1820 185.00
Pottery, Child's Face, Japan, 3 In. 195.00
Pottery, Citrus Face, Pink, Japan, 1940s, 5 ¼ In. 175.00
Pottery, Citrus Fruit, England, 1940s, 3 ½ In. 165.00
Pottery, Clown, Japan, 1940s, 5 ½ In. 185.00
Pottery, Duck, Japan, 2 ½ In. 145.00
Sunkist, Milk Glass, 3 ½ x 8 x 5 ½ In. 29.00

RECORDS have changed size and shape through the years. The cylinder-shaped phonograph record for use with the early Edison models was made about 1889. Disc records were first made by 1894, the double-sided disc by 1904. High-fidelity records were first issued in 1944, the first vinyl disc in 1946, the first stereo record in 1958. The 78 RPM became the standard in 1926 but was discontinued in 1957. In 1932, the first 33 ⅓ RPM was made but was not sold commercially until 1948. In 1949, the 45 RPM was introduced. Compact discs became available in the U.S. in 1982 and many companies began phasing out the production of phonograph records.

Barbra Streisand, Christmas Album, 1967 20.00
Bobby Darin, Mack The Knife, ATCO, 45 RPM, 1959 45.00
Dinah Washington, Original Queen Of Soul, Mercury Records, LP, 2 Records 24.00
Frank Sinatra, September Of My Years, Reprise Records, LP, 1965 16.00
Herman's Hermits, Best Of Album, MGM Records, 33 RPM, 1960s 25.00
Jimmy Durante, September Song, Warner Bros. Records, LP, c.1963 15.00
Marilyn Monroe, Recordings, Sealed, Radiola, Nude Photo, LP, 1979 60.00
Oscar Levant, Moonlight Sonata, Menuetto, Columbia Records, 78 RPM, 1945 23.00
Restless, Go Giants Go, Football Novelty, Sutra Records, 45 RPM, 1987 12.00
Roy Orbison, Greatest Hits, Red, Hua Sheng Record, 33 RPM, 1970s 45.00
Strawberry Shortcake, Picture Dish, American Greetings, 45 RPM, 1982 13.00
Terry Stafford, The Suspicion Record, Ace Label, Mono LP 15.00
Tommy Dorsey, Greatest Band, 20th Century Fox Records, LP, c.1973, 2 Records 15.00
Yogi Bear & Huckleberry Hound, Fairy Tales, 33 ⅓ RPM, 1977 9.00

RED WING Pottery of Red Wing, Minnesota, was a firm started in 1878. The company first made utilitarian pottery, including stoneware jugs and canning jars. In the 1920s art pottery was introduced. Many dinner sets and vases were made before the company closed in 1967. Rumrill pottery made by the Red Wing Pottery for George Rumrill is listed in its own category. For more information, see *Kovels' Depression Glass & Dinnerware Price List*.

Advertising, Bean Pot, Compliments Of Borgerding Lumber Co., Park Rapids, Minn. 75.00
Advertising, Bean Pot, Compliments Of Farmers Co-Operative Elevator Co., Norwood 75.00
Advertising, Bean Pot, Compliments Of Sanitary Meat Market, Herman, Minn. 85.00
Advertising, Bean Pot, Saffron, Compliments Of Wecota Farmer's Elevator Co. 40.00
Advertising, Bed Warmer, Goodwill's Bed & Foot Warmer & Water Carrier 125.00
Advertising, Bowl, It Pays To Mix With Al. Bailey, Dows, Ia., Sponge Panel, 7 In. 105.00
Advertising, Bowl, It Pays To Trade At Hansen's Get The Habit, Sponge Panel, 6 In. 155.00
Advertising, Casserole, Open, Henry's Market, Chamberlain, S. Dakota, 8 In. 55.00
Advertising, Crock, 5 Lb., Riceland Creamery Gilt Edge Butter Association 105.00

Railroad, Rug, Hooked, Baltimore & Ohio 1830, Wool, Hazel Walker, 1957, 24 x 36 In.
$790.00

Reamer, Ceramic, Clown, Japan, 7 ½ In.
$191.00

Reamer, Glass, Delphite Blue, Jeannette Glass Co., 1930s
$88.00

Reamer, Glass, Jade Green, Embossed Sunkist, McKee Glass, c.1940, 8 In.
$55.00

78 Records
Old 78 records were made of shellac. Vinyl 78s were introduced around 1951. The records that followed are all vinyl.

R

Red Wing, Cookie Jar,
Dutch Girl, Blue, c.1950, 11 In.
$100.00

Red Wing, Jardiniere, Vine & Flowers,
Marked, 9 ½ x 8 In.
$70.00

Red Wing, Stoneware, Vase,
Panels Of Wooded Scenery,
Union, Marked, 9 ⅝ x 4 ⅞ In.
$130.00

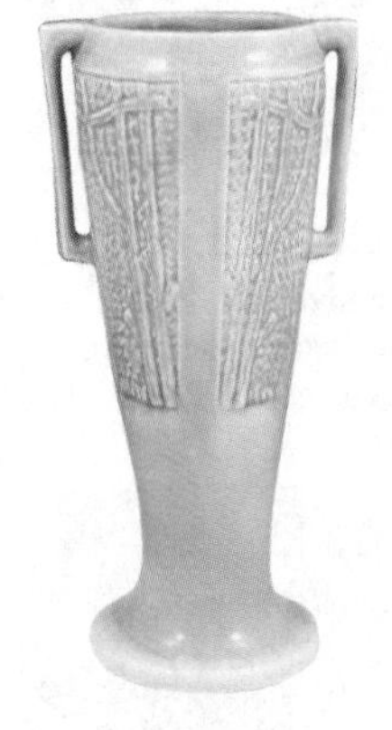

Red Wing, Vase, Nokomis,
Green Glaze, Handles, Marked, 8 ¼ In.
$800.00

Advertising, Crock, Bill's Beans, Lb. 100.00
Advertising, Crock, Butter, Enjoy Kennedy Creamery Butter, 2 Lb. 80.00
Advertising, Crock, Butter, Gasser Co., 3 Lb. 55.00
Advertising, Crock, Butter, M. Wolff & Sons, Chicago, Gal. 3250.00
Advertising, Crock, Butter, Minnesota Stoneware Co., 3 Lb. 15.00
Advertising, Crock, Butter, Pure Farm Products Co., Chicago, 10 Lb. 110.00
Advertising, Crock, Butter, Sunberg Bros., Groceries & Meats, 5 Lb. 375.00
Advertising, Crock, Drier's Broadway Maid Quality Butter, Yankton, S.D., 2 Lb. 165.00
Advertising, Crock, Eureka Bazaar Co., Where Cash Is King, Eureka, S.D., Gal. 550.00
Advertising, Crock, Goodhue County Co-Operative Company, 5 Lb. 400.00
Advertising, Crock, J. B. Andrews, General Merchandise Volga, S.D., 10 Lb. 450.00
Advertising, Crock, Lakeside Dairy, Madison, S.D., 3 Lb. 95.00
Advertising, Crock, Modern Dairy Company, La Crosse, Wisconsin 105.00
Advertising, Crock, Return To North Star Creamery, Kenyon, Minn, 10 Lb. 400.00
Advertising, Crock, S.S. Collins Fancy Table Butter, 2 Lb. 80.00
Advertising, Crock, White & Mather Fancy Butter & Whipping Cream, Black 55.00
Advertising, Crock, White & Mather Fancy Butter & Whipping Cream, Blue 195.00
Advertising, Jug, Beehive, Colfax Sanitarium, Colfax, Ia., 5 Gal. 450.00
Advertising, Jug, Beehive, From Grand Hotel, Mineral Springs, 5 Gal. 1000.00
Advertising, Jug, Beehive, Fry's Hotel & Mineral Springs, Colfax, Ia, 5 Gal. 800.00
Advertising, Jug, California Wine House St. Cloud, Minn., 2 Gal 200.00
Advertising, Jug, Henry Fischer Grape Wines, Bail Handle, Gal. 225.00
Advertising, Jug, Jonas F. Brown & Co., Wines & Liquors, 2 Gal. 125.00
Advertising, Jug, Jonas F. Brown & Co., Wines & Liquors, Gal. 95.00
Advertising, Mug, West End Commercial Club, St. Paul June 21-26, 1909 . . . . . 165.00
Advertising, Pail, Butter, Compliments Of Schroeder-Schultz Co., Blue, White 160.00
Cookie Jar, Dutch Girl, Blue, c.1950, 11 In. . . . . . *illus* 100.00
Jardiniere, Vine & Flowers, Marked, 9 ½ x 8 In. . . . . . *illus* 70.00
Lexington Rose, Casserole, Cover, Handle, S-Shaped Finial, 8 ½ In. 35.00
Stoneware, Ashtray, Donkey, Aqua 155.00
Stoneware, Ashtray, Scottie Dog, Maroon 325.00
Stoneware, Bean Pot, Bail Handle 2.00
Stoneware, Bowl, Gray Line, 4 In. 275.00
Stoneware, Bowl, Gray Line, 11 In. 300.00
Stoneware, Bowl, Gray Line, 5 In. 350.00
Stoneware, Churn, Birch Leaves, Ski Oval, 5 Gal. . . . . . 95.00 to 245.00
Stoneware, Churn, Butter, Lid, Birch Leaves, Ski Oval, 5 Gal. 225.00
Stoneware, Churn, Butterfly, Salt Glaze, 6 Gal. 900.00
Stoneware, Churn, Cover, Wing & Oval, 6 Gal. 250.00
Stoneware, Crock, 6-Sided, Bung Hole, Wing & Oval, 15 Gal. 600.00
Stoneware, Crock, Bail Handle, Wing & Oval, 10 Gal. 85.00
Stoneware, Crock, Bail Handle, Wing & Oval, 12 Gal. 115.00
Stoneware, Crock, Bail Handle, Wing & Oval, 15 Gal. . . . . . 110.00 to 315.00
Stoneware, Crock, Butter, 5 Lb. 10.00
Stoneware, Crock, Butter, 10 Lb. . . . . . 30.00 to 35.00
Stoneware, Crock, Butter, Greek Key, Blue, White 30.00
Stoneware, Crock, Butter, Lid, Bird On Branch, Salt Glaze, 6 Gal. 3550.00
Stoneware, Crock, Elephant Ear, Salt Glaze, Union Oval, 5 Gal. 2400.00
Stoneware, Crock, Elephant Ears & Union Oval, 3 Gal. 45.00
Stoneware, Crock, Wing & Oval, 5 Gal. 115.00
Stoneware, Jar, Applesauce, Wing & Oval, 3 Gal. 200.00
Stoneware, Jar, Applesauce, Wing & Oval, 5 Gal. 200.00
Stoneware, Jar, Draining, Wing, 5 Gal. 125.00
Stoneware, Jug, Beehive, Birch Leaves, Union Oval, 3 Gal. 215.00
Stoneware, Jug, Beehive, Wing & Union Oval, 5 Gal., 4 In. 250.00
Stoneware, Jug, Shoulder, Wing & Oval, 5 Gal. 50.00
Stoneware, Pitcher, Windmill & Bush, Blue, White 65.00
Stoneware, Vase, Panels Of Wooded Scenery, Union, Marked, 9 ⅝ x 4 ⅞ In. . . . . . *illus* 130.00
Stoneware, Water Cooler, Lid, 5 Gal. 275.00
Stoneware, Water Cooler, Lid, Paul Stationary Co., 14 In. 590.00
Town & Country, Bowl, Dusk Blue, Comma, 6 In. 14.00
Town & Country, Bowl, Gunmetal, Comma 19.00
Town & Country, Creamer, Peach 46.00
Town & Country, Cup & Saucer, Rust 22.00
Town & Country, Mixing Bowl, Chartreuse, Large 125.00

Town & Country, Mixing Bowl, Rust, Large 100.00
Town & Country, Mug, Gunmetal 110.00
Town & Country, Mug, Rust 74.00
Town & Country, Pitcher, Peach, 2 Qt. 160.00
Town & Country, Plate, Bread & Butter, Rust 9.00
Town & Country, Plate, Dinner, Peach 33.00
Town & Country, Plate, Salad, Sand, 8 In. 26.00
Town & Country, Relish, Dusk Blue 22.00
Town & Country, Relish, Gunmetal, 7 In. 22.00
Town & Country, Relish, Rust 16.00
Town & Country, Syrup, Chartreuse 125.00
Vase, 2 Birds On Branches, Gray Glaze, Marked, 10 In. 55.00
Vase, Green, Brown Band, Incised Scrolling, Textured Center, 22 In., Pair 826.00
Vase, Green & Brown Marbleized Glaze, Bulbous, Squat, Arched Handles, 2½ x 3½ In. 71.00
Vase, Nokomis, Green Glaze, Handles, Marked, 8¼ In. .... *illus* 800.00

REDWARE is a hard, red stoneware that originated in the late 1600s and continues to be made. The term is also used to describe any common clay pottery that is reddish in color. Redware molds are listed in Kitchen.

Bank, Apple Form, 2⅝ In. 165.00
Bank, Bulbous, Finial, Side Slot, Pumpkin Glaze, Mottled, C.B. March, 1864, 5 x 3 In. 3960.00
Bank, Coggle & Stamped Flower Band, Orange Glaze, Brown Drip, Finial, 5½ x 4 In. 468.00
Bank, Piggy, Marbleized Swirls, Multicolored, 7 In. 392.00
Bank, Round, Tapered Base, Finial, Bands, Kate Clark, Born March 9, 1865, 6½ x 4 In. 825.00
Bank, Savings, Empire Dresser Shape, Yellow Clay Accents, 6¾ x 4 In. 403.00
Bean Pot, Dome Lid, Orange, Black, Tulips, Birds, Lines, C-Shape Handle, Sgraffito, 6 x 7 In. 2640.00
Bell, Hand, Brown Mottled Glaze, Incised Line, Russell Stahl, 1976, 5⅝ In. 385.00
Birdhouse, Green Glaze, Incised Line, Finial Top, Albert Hodge, Newtown, N.C., 8¾ In. 88.00
Birdhouse, Painted, Light Blue, Dome Top, Incised Spiral Band, Round Openings, 9 x 6 In. .. 143.00
Bowl, Cover, Blue Glaze, L.S. Stahl, July 6, 1939, 5⅝ x 5½ In. 132.00
Bowl, Daisies, Tulips, Yellow, Green, Black, Scalloped Rim, 19th Century, 6½ In. .... *illus* 29500.00
Bowl, Flowerpot, German Verse, Scalloped Edge, Sgraffito, Breininger, 11½ x 8¾ In. 358.00
Bowl, Green, Yellow Squiggle Lines, 8¼ In. 99.00
Bowl, Green Glaze, Spout, Thomas Stahl, Aug. 21, 1942, 1⅞ x 5⅝ In. 121.00
Bowl, Green Mottled Interior Glaze, Stahl, 1⅜ x 5⅛ In. 55.00
Bowl, Orange Glaze, Yellow & Green Wiggled Slip Band, 3¾ x 12¾ In. 770.00
Bowl, Orange Ground, Black Sponge Band, 3½ x 11 In. 66.00
Bowl, Slip Decorated, Flared, Tapered, Orange, Yellow, Green, Black Drip, 2½ x 8½ In. 2750.00
Butter Print, Brick Form, Whet Sheaves, Jay E. Boeshore, Fredericksburg, Pa., 2 x 4 x 2¼ In. 770.00
Butter Print, Pineapple, Yellow & Green Under Glaze, R.R. Stahl, 3/15/48, 4 In. Diam. 88.00
Cake Pan, Scalloped Rim, Center Post, Orange, Black Manganese Drip Band, 2½ x 7 In. 44.00
Charger, Coggled Rim, 4 Wavy Lines, Yellow Slip, 13½ In. 467.00
Charger, Coggled Rim, Tulips, Yellow, Mottled Highlights, Sgraffito, 2¾ x 12½ In. 4125.00
Charger, Yellow Slip, Wavy Squiggle Lines, c.1830, 13½ In. 578.00
Colander, Brown Glaze, Black Spatter, Applied Ear Shape Handles, 4¼ x 6 In. 22.00
Colander, Orange Glaze, Flared Rim, C-Shape Handles, Holes In Side & Bottom, 6 x 9 In. 77.00
Creamer, Applied Handle, Running Brown & Cream Glaze, c.1800, 6¼ In. 2070.00
Creamer, Baluster Form, C-Shape Handle, Yellow, Green Glaze, 3¾ x 3 In. 88.00
Crock, Apple Butter, Bulbous, Incised Band, Handle, Orange, Green, Brown Spatter, 6 x 6 In. .. 55.00
Crock, Elongated Neck, Tab Handles, Edward W. Farrar, 9¾ In. 10500.00
Crock, Incised Shoulder Wavy Line, Oval, Manganese Glaze, Burnt Orange, 8 In. 115.00
Crock, Round, Flared Base, Dark Brown Mottled Glaze, 1⅝ x 2 In. 22.00
Crock, Tooled Top Rim, Straight Sided, Handles, 1800s, 7 x 7⅞ In. 375.00
Cup, Dark Brown Glaze, Flared Rim, C-Shape Handle, Incised Line Band, 3¼ In. 66.00
Cup, Tapered, Round Base, Dark Orange, 2¾ x 3½ In. 44.00
Cup, Yellow, Green & Brown Drip Glaze, 2¾ x 3⅜ In. 44.00
Cuspidor, Flower Form, Orange Glaze, Mottled Drip, John Bell Waynesburg, 4¾ x 8½ In. *illus* 8525.00
Cuspidor, Orange & Black Alkaline Glaze, c.1830, 4 x 8 In. 187.00
Cuspidor, Round, Concave, Waste Opening, Brown Mottled Glaze, 1¼ x 3½ In. 77.00
Custard, Round, Tapered, Incised Rim Banding, Green & Orange Glaze, 2 x 3¼ In. 44.00
Dish, Game Pie, Bird, Flowering Tree, Green Glaze, Crimped Edge, Oval, Handles, 7 x 11 In. .. 201.00
Dish, Loaf, Combed Slip, Early 19th Century, 14¾ x 18¾ In. 5288.00
Figurine, Bird, Orange Glaze, Black & White Marble Highlights, 3¼ x 3½ x 1½ In. 55.00
Figurine, Dog, Spaniel, Seated, Glazed, Miniature, 3½ In. 1380.00

Redware, Bowl, Daisies, Tulips, Yellow, Green, Black, Scalloped Rim, 19th Century, 6½ In.
$29500.00

Redware, Cuspidor, Flower Form, Orange Glaze, Mottled Drip, John Bell Waynesburg, 4¾ x 8½ In.
$8525.00

Redware, Figurine, Lion, Yellow Slip, Brown, 19th Century, 6 x 7 x 4 In.
$288.00

Redware, Inkstand, Dog, Lions, Arched Panels, Brown Glaze, Drip, 19th Century, 5 x 7 x 3 In.
$357.00

Redware, Jar, Cover, Fox, Coleslaw Mane, Late 19th Century, 10 ½ In.
$2200.00

Redware, Jar, Cover, Orange, Mottled Black Drip Glaze, Incised Band, 9 ½ x 5 In.
$198.00

Redware, Pitcher, Yellow, Green & Brown Mottled Glaze, Shenandoah, 7 x 4 In.
$2530.00

Figurine, Lion, Reclining, Smiling, Molded Form, Brown Glaze, Black Spatter, 4 x 9 x 3 In. . . 3190.00
Figurine, Lion, Yellow Slip, Brown, 19th Century, 6 x 7 x 4 In. . . . *illus* 288.00
Figurine, Rooster, Tan, Brown Drip Glaze, Folded Form, Round Base, 4¾ x 2½ x 2 In. . . . 523.00
Figurine, Sheep, Brown Mottled Drip, Rectangular Base, 1800s, 5½ x 5½ x 2½ In. . . . 523.00
Flask, Dark Brown Alkaline Glaze, Footed, Inscribed, J A, c.1830, 6 In. . . . 248.00
Flask, Oval, Round Rim, Dark Brown Glaze, Black Streaks, 7 x 4 x 2½ In. . . . 132.00
Flowerpot, Banded, Orange, Green, Attached Tray, W. Smith, Womelsdorf, Pa., 5 x 6 In. . . . 1756.00
Flowerpot, Banded Rim, Incised, Orange, Yellow Highlights, Attached Tray, 3¾ x 4½ In. . . . 385.00
Flowerpot, Basket Shape, Rope Twist Handle, Coggled Rim, Attached Tray, 1824, 5 x 8 In. . . . 460.00
Flowerpot, Black Paint, Flared Sides, Crimped Rim, Attached Tray, 5 x 9 In. . . . 110.00
Flowerpot, Brown Mottled Glaze, Applied Base, Incised Band, Flared, W. Smith, 4 x 5 In. . . . 715.00
Flowerpot, Grain Paint, Flared & Crimped Beaded Mold Banding, Round Base, 3 x 8 In. . . . 66.00
Flowerpot, Light Orange Glaze, Brown Sponge Band, 5½ x 6½ In. . . . 132.00
Flowerpot, Red Paint, Green Band, Crimped Rim, Attached Tray, 3½ x 7½ In. . . . 154.00
Flowerpot, Saucer, Green Glazed, Mass., Early 19th Century, 5⅞ x 5½ In. . . . 235.00
Flowerpot, Tray, Collared Rim, Manganese Sponging, c.1899, 5 x 4½ In. . . . 575.00
Flowerpot, Tray, Orange Glaze, Black Sponge Band, Crimped, Flared Rim, 6 x 8 In. . . . 132.00
Inkstand, Dog, Ball Finials, Serrated Edges, Scalloped Front, Brown Glaze, 5 x 7 x 4 In. . . . 330.00
Inkstand, Dog, Lions, Arched Panels, Brown Glaze, Drip, 19th Century, 5 x 7 x 3 In. . . . *illus* 357.00
Inkwell, Raised Opening, Coggled Rim, Brown Glaze, 2½ x 3¼ In. . . . 44.00
Inkwell, Yellow Slip, Lead Glaze, Incised S. Halsey, Sparta 1824. . . . 9200.00
Jar, Barrel Shape, Lug Handles, Incised Zigzag Band, c.1830, 9½ In. . . . 267.00
Jar, Bulbous, Flared Rim, Ear Handles, Wavy & Straight Incised Band, 8¾ x 8 In. . . . 248.00
Jar, Bulbous, Flared, Incised Band, Ear Handles, Brown, Black Mottled Drip, 10 x 8 In. . . . 176.00
Jar, Cover, Fox, Coleslaw Mane, Late 19th Century, 10½ In. . . . *illus* 2200.00
Jar, Cover, Green Copper Oxide Glaze, 18th Century, 10½ In. . . . 29375.00
Jar, Cover, Orange, Black Sponge, Mottled, Incised Band, Rope Form Handles, 7¼ x 7 In. . . . 770.00
Jar, Cover, Orange, Brown Glaze, Brown Spots, Cylindrical, Flat Finial, 6¾ In. . . . 258.00
Jar, Cover, Orange, Mottled Black Drip Glaze, Incised Band, 9½ x 5 In. . . . *illus* 198.00
Jar, Cover, Oval, Mottled Rust, Green Glaze, Incised Shoulder Lines, Early 1800s, 9¼ In. . . . 881.00
Jar, Lapped Over Loop Handles, Oval, Brown Manganese Glaze, c.1820, 8⅛ In. . . . 353.00
Jar, Light Green Glaze, Dark Green Drapery Swags, 3 Rings To Shoulder, Oval, 9 In. . . . 115.00
Jar, Olive Green & Red Applied Glaze, New York State, c.1830, ½ Gal., 8½ In. . . . 66.00
Jar, Orange Mottled Glaze, Yellow & Green Line, Slip Decorated, Flat Handles, 11 x 10 In. . . . 3300.00
Jar, Oval, Incised Bands, Red Glaze, Applied Handles, 3 Gal., 14¼ In. . . . 144.00
Jar, Wheel Thrown, Black & White Slip Design, Orange Ground, 9 x 14 In. . . . 115.00
Jug, Brown Shiny Glaze, Black Base, C-Shape Handle, Incised Band, Bulbous, 5½ x 5 In. . . . 44.00
Jug, Bulbous, Brown Glaze, Black Drip, Round Rim, Applied C-Shape Handle, 4 x 4 In. . . . 187.00
Jug, Bulbous, Flared Rim, C-Shape Handle, Green Glaze, Yellow Highlights, 6¾ x 4 In. . . . 660.00
Jug, Bulbous, Green Glaze, Tooled Line, 3 Raised Ribs, Handle, 19th Century, 6¼ In. . . . 350.00
Jug, Bulbous, Orange Glaze, Mottled, Applied C-Shape Handle, Berks Co., 6 x 5½ In. . . . 770.00
Jug, Egg Shape, Loop Handle, Dark Brown Spots, Speckled Ground, 6½ In. . . . 290.00
Jug, Field, 2 Spouts, Strap Handle, 3 Incised Shoulder Lines, Green, Brown Glaze, 6⅝ In. . . . 1528.00
Jug, Olive Green Applied Glaze, c.1830, 11 In. . . . 303.00
Jug, Streaky Green Glaze, Applied Handle, Small Mouth, Footed, 7 In. . . . 518.00
Jug, Yellow Slip Unicorn, Tulips, Leaves, Verse, Only A Maiden Pure, Van Duren, 1985, 13 In. . . 468.00
Loaf Pan, Coggled Wheel Edge, Squiggle Lines, Dot's, L.B. Breininger, 1979, 4 x 20 x 13 In. . . 154.00
Loaf Pan, Rectangular, Yellow Slip Decoration, Christmas, Late 1800s, 13 x 10½ In. . . . 863.00
Loaf Pan, Yellow Slip Design, Running Deer, Signed, Label, 13 x 16 In. . . . 230.00
Loaf Pan, Yellow Slip Seaweed, 2½ x 11½ In. . . . 413.00
Mold, Cake, Scalloped Rim, Spiral Center Post, Orange & Green Mottled Glaze, 3 x 9¼ In. . . . 33.00
Mold, Cake, Scalloped Rim, Spiral Center Post, Orange Glaze, Black Drip, 3 x 8¼ In. . . . 33.00
Mold, Cake, Scalloped Rim, Spiral Center Post, Orange, Green Mottled Glaze, Spots, 3 x 8 In. . 22.00
Mold, Cake, Tapered, Conical Center Post, Incised Bands, Orange Glaze, 3¾ x 7½ In. . . . 209.00
Mold, Cake, Yellow Scalloped Rim, Spiral Center Post, Orange Glaze, 3½ x 9½ In. . . . 66.00
Mold, Gelatin, Grape Bunch Form, Orange Glaze, 3-Footed, 3¼ x 11¼ x 6½ In. . . . 55.00
Mold, Turk's Head, Tobacco Spit Decoration, John Bell, Waynesboro, 5½ x 9½ In. . . . 1995.00
Mug, Embossed Fish, Rosettes, Hobnail, Manganese Polka Dots, Orange Ground, JCS, 5 In. . . 99.00
Mug, Tapered, C-Shape Handle, Incised Bands, Brown Mottled Glaze, 4½ x 5 In. . . . 330.00
Pie Plate, Brown Spots, Orange Ground, Slip Decorated, 8 In. . . . 384.00
Pie Plate, Coggled Rim, Yellow Slip Decoration, 9½ In. . . . 259.00
Pie Plate, Wavy Lines, Yellow Slip, Coggled Rim, 11¼ In. . . . 406.00
Pie Plate, Yellow Slip Wavy Line, Coggled Rim, 8 In. . . . 288.00
Pitcher, Brown Glaze, Sponge, Flared Rim, Applied C-Shape Handle, 6½ x 6 In. . . . 77.00
Pitcher, Bulbous, Coggled Band, Sgraffito, Orange, Black Spatter, J. Medinger, 6½ x 5 In. . . . 1980.00

R

Pitcher, Bulbous, C-Shape Handle, Orange & Green, Brown Spatter & Drip Glaze, 3 x 2 ¼ In.	303.00
Pitcher, Bulbous, Flared Rim, Incised Band, Orange, Black Sponge, 9 x 6 In.	385.00
Pitcher, Coggled Band, Bulbous, Orange, Green, Mottled Brown, Flared Rim, 8 x 5 In.	330.00
Pitcher, Daubed Manganese Glaze, Tooled Lines, Applied Strap Handle, c.1800, 9 ½ In.	201.00
Pitcher, Glazed Interior, Rim, Applied Handle, Pinched Pour Spout, 1800s, 9 x 6 In.	50.00
Pitcher, Impressed 2, Flare Rim, Tooled Spout, Applied Strap Handle, 2 Gal., 13 ¼ In.	173.00
Pitcher, Manganese Glaze, Incised, Applied Handle, 5 ¼ In.	179.00
Pitcher, Orange, Black Spatter Drip, Flared Rim, Bulbous, Sgraffito, 6 ¾ x 5 ½ In.	2420.00
Pitcher, Owl Form, Manganese Polka Dots, Orange Glaze, Marked, JCS, 5 ½ In.	121.00
Pitcher, Running Glazes, Cream, Green, Applied Strap Handle, Late 1800s, 7 ¾ In.	230.00
Pitcher, Textured Surface, Albany Glaze, Cold Beer, Dexter Pottery, 1926, 7 In.	575.00
Pitcher, Yellow, Green & Brown Mottled Glaze, Shenandoah, 7 x 4 In. *illus*	2530.00
Pitcher & Washbowl, Shenandoah River, Multi-Glazed, J. Eberly & Co., Strasburg, Va.	29900.00
Plate, 3 Musical Notes, Yellow Slip, 8 ½ In.	121.00
Plate, Coggled Rim, 3 Wavy Lines, Orange, Yellow Slip, 9 ½ In.	523.00
Plate, Coggled Rim, Band, Eagle, Shield, Liberty, Yellow, Green, Brown, Sgraffito, 7 ¾ In.	550.00
Plate, Coggled Rim, Band, Tulips, Yellow, Green, Brown Highlights, Sgraffito, 8 In.	2310.00
Plate, Coggled Rim, Diamond, Spiral Ends, Yellow Slip, Dark Orange Ground, 8 ¼ In.	1320.00
Plate, Coggled Rim, Eagle & Shield, Yellow Glaze, Green Highlights, Sgraffito, 8 ¾ In.	550.00
Plate, Coggled Rim, Orange Glaze, 3 Yellow Wavy Zigzag Lines, 9 ¼ In.	1100.00
Plate, Coggled Rim, Orange Glaze, 3 Lines, 9 ¼ In. *illus*	220.00
Plate, Coggled Rim, Pumpkin Glaze, 3 Yellow Wavy Lines, Slip Decorated, 7 In.	220.00
Plate, Coggled Rim, Slip Decorated, Orange, 3 Wavy Lines, 11 In.	715.00 to 1320.00
Plate, Coggled Rim, Slip Decorated, Orange, 3 Wavy Lines, Stylized Flowers, 9 In.	550.00
Plate, Coggled Rim, Slip Decorated, Orange, 3 Yellow Wavy Lines, 12 ¼ In.	605.00
Plate, Coggled Rim, Slip Decorated, Orange, Brown Spatter, 3 Yellow Wavy Lines, 10 In.	1430.00
Plate, Coggled Rim, Slip Decorated, Orange, Brown, Yellow, Grapes, 8 ¾ In.	1870.00
Plate, Coggled Rim, Slip Decorated, Orange, Triangle Design, Leaves, 7 ½ In.	2310.00
Plate, Coggled Rim, Yellow Slip Design, c.1850, 11 In.	209.00
Plate, Coggled Wheel Rim, Orange Glaze, 5 Yellow Wavy Lines, Slip Decorated, 11 In.	523.00
Plate, Orange Glaze, Black Mottled Highlights, Tapered, 12 ½ In.	220.00
Plate, Sgraffito Military Man, Tulips, Multicolored Slip, Yellow Band, 12 In.	2200.00
Plate, Slip Decorated, Coggled Rim, Black Slip, Red Ground, 7 ½ In.	177.00
Plate, Slip Decorated, Coggled Rim, Yellow Wavy Line, X-Shape Slip, 1800s, 13 ¾ In.	646.00
Plate, Slip Decorated, Orange, Yellow, Green, Black Tulip Form, Dryville, 8 In.	2640.00
Plate, Slip Decorated, Tapered, 8-Sided, Raised Geometrics, 3 Yellow Wavy Lines, 5 ½ In.	1980.00
Plate, Yellow Slip Decoration, Round, 7 In.	881.00
Porringer, Pour Spout, Reeded Shape Handle, Brown Glaze	88.00
Pot, Green & Orange Peppery Alkaline Glaze, 5 In.	358.00
Preserve Jar, Lid, Mustard & Orange Glaze, c.1820, 9 In.	578.00
Puzzle Jug, Sgraffito Decoration, Yellow Glaze, Green Mottling, Tulips, Birds, c.1827, 8 In.	1763.00
Shaving Mug, Applied Cup To Side, Reeded, C-Shape Handle, Brown, Black Glaze, 3 ¾ x 4 In.	132.00
Shaving Mug, Round, Flared, Cup, Serrated, Handle, Orange Glaze, Mottled, 4 x 5 In.	330.00
Teapot, Cover, Molded, Gooseneck Spout, Rectangular Base, Philadelphia, 6 x 11 x 5 In.	990.00
Toby, Footed, Strap Handle, Incised Facial Features, 3 ¼ x 2 ½ In.	575.00
Vase, Abraham Lincoln, Bust, Eagle, Wreath, Victorian Style, Footed, 5 In.	490.00
Vase, Bulbous, Slip Decorated, Tulips, Vines, Orange, Green, Yellow, Handles, 11 x 9 In.	2200.00
Vase, Coggled Band, Flared Rim, Bulbous, Orange, Mottled Black Highlights, 7 x 5 In.	880.00
Vase, Coggled Rim & Band, Flared Rim, Green, Orange, Black, C-Shape Handles, 11 x 7 In.	1045.00
Vase, Coggled Rim & Band, Orange, Green, Black, Bulbous, C-Shape Handles, 11 x 9 In.	1320.00
Vase, Crane & Dragon Design, Large Opening, Unglazed, 3 ¾ x 7 ¼ In.	101.00
Vase, Painted Design, 3 Human Heads Form Base, 9 ¼ In.	403.00
Vase, Rosette, Banner, Flowers, Yellow, Green Drip, Orange Band, 2 Handles, 20 x 14 In.	770.00
Washboard, Green Paint, c.1880, 13 In.	798.00
Whistle, Bird, Conical Base, Branches, Smaller Birds, Yellow Slip, Late 1800s, 9 In.	115.00
Whistle, Bird, Seated, Fantail, Orange, Black & White Highlights, 2 ½ x 4 ½ x 2 In.	33.00
Whistle, Bird, Stylized Stump, 4 Birds, White, Brown Drip, Shenandoah Valley, 10 x 8 In.	665.00
Whistle, Dog, Coleslaw Mane, Tail, c.1870, 2 ¾ In. *illus*	6000.00

REGOUT, *see Maastricht category.*

RICHARD was the mark used on acid-etched cameo glass vases, bowls, night-lights, and lamps made by the Austrian company Loetz after 1918. The pieces were very similar to the French cameo glasswares made by Daum, Galle, and others.

Vase, 4 Flamingos Wading In Lake, Tree, Green, Pink, Sulfur Yellow, Squat Base, 5 In.	650.00

Redware, Plate, Coggled Rim, Orange Glaze, 3 Lines, 9 ¼ In.
$220.00

Redware, Whistle, Dog, Coleslaw Mane, Tail, c.1870, 2 ¾ In.
$6000.00

TIP
In case of a major theft, keep careful records. You may be able to deduct part of the uninsured loss from your income tax.

Richard, Vase, Riverscape, Trees, Sunset Orange, Brown, Cameo, 8 ½ In.
$325.00

Ridgway, Pitcher, Oriental Scene, Green, Marked, Late 19th Century, 7 In.
$50.00

Ridgway, Tureen, Balmoral, Pink, Blue Flowers, Gold Trim, 8 x 13 x 8 In.
$33.00

Riviera, Green, Sugar & Creamer
$8.00

Riviera, Mauve Blue, Teapot, Cover
$105.00

Riviera, Yellow, Casserole, Cover, 10 ½ x 7 In.
$62.00

Vase, Footed, Cylindrical, Mottled Green, Purple Wisteria, Cameo, Signed, 14 In. 604.00

Vase, Orange, Riverscape, Village, Trees, Cameo, 8 ½ In. 383.00

Vase, Pink Glass, Green Art Deco Flowers, Reverse Pinched Waist, Cameo, 9 In. 460.00

Vase, Riverscape, Trees, Sunset Orange, Brown, Cameo, 8 ½ In. .... *illus* 325.00

Vase, Yellow Glass, Brown Pine Needle Branches, Cameo, Signed, 10 ¾ In. 460.00

RIDGWAY pottery has been made in the Staffordshire district in England since 1808 by a series of companies with the name Ridgway. The transfer-design dinner sets are the most widely known product. Other pieces of Ridgway may be listed under Flow Blue.

Dessert Service, Gray & Yellow Border, Botanical Center, Gilt Detail, c.1840, 16 In. 1351.00

Pitcher, Oriental Scene, Green, Marked, Late 19th Century, 7 In. .... *illus* 50.00

Plate, City Hall, N.Y., Beauties Of America, Medallion Border, Blue, c.1820, 9 ¾ In. 143.00

Plate, Coaching Days, Amber To Green, 10 In. 22.00

Platter, Alms House N.Y., Beauties Of America, Rose, Leaf Border, c.1820, 16 ⅝ In. 1195.00

Platter, Capitol At Washington, Beauties Of America, Rose, Leaf Border, Blue, c.1820, 20 ½ In. .. 2032.00

Platter, Exchange Charleston, Rose, Leaf Border, Blue, Early 19th Century, 6 ¾ In. 657.00

Tea Set, Chintz, Blue & White, Stoke-On-Trent, Staffordshire, c.1890, Child's, 12 Piece 475.00

Tray, Bank Savannah, Medallion & Rose Border, Blue, 7 ⅛ In. 508.00

Tureen, Balmoral, Pink, Blue Flowers, Gold Trim, 8 x 13 x 8 In. .... *illus* 33.00

Tureen, Cover, Columbian Star, Oct. 28th, 1840, Log Cabin, 8-Sided, Blue, c.1840, 11 x 14 In. 837.00

RIVIERA dinnerware was made by the Homer Laughlin Co. of Newell, West Virginia, from 1938 to 1950. The pattern was similar in coloring and in mood to Fiesta and Harlequin. The Riviera plates and cup handles were square. For more information, see *Kovels' Depression Glass & Dinnerware Price List*.

Green, Bowl, 8 ¼ In. 10.00

Green, Bowl, Fruit, 5 ½ In. 14.00

Green, Soup, Dish, 8 In. 27.00

Green, Cup 10.00

Green, Plate, 6 In. 8.00

Green, Plate, Dinner, 9 In. 20.00

Green, Platter, 11 In. 20.00

Green, Shaker 10.00

Green, Sugar & Creamer .... *illus* 8.00

Green, Tumbler 75.00

Ivory, Platter, 11 In. 20.00

Ivory, Platter, 15 In. 31.00

Ivory, Sugar 15.00

Mauve Blue, Bowl, Fruit, 5 ½ In. 14.00

Mauve Blue, Bowl, Vegetable, 8 ¼ In. 18.00

Mauve Blue, Casserole 119.00

Mauve Blue, Plate, 6 In. 9.00

Mauve Blue, Plate, Dinner, 9 In. 13.50

Mauve Blue, Teapot, Cover .... *illus* 105.00

Mauve Blue, Tumbler 75.00

Red, Baker, 9 In. .... 20.00 to 24.00

Red, Berry Bowl, 5 ¼ In., 4 Piece 32.00

Red, Bowl, Oatmeal, 6 In. 33.00

Red, Butter, ½ Lb. 115.00

Red, Casserole, Cover 80.00

Red, Shaker 10.00

Yellow, Butter, ½ Lb. 129.00

Yellow, Casserole, Cover, 10 ½ x 7 In. .... *illus* 62.00

Yellow, Casserole, No Cover 60.00

Yellow, Creamer 13.00

Yellow, Plate, Salad, 7 In. 14.50

Yellow, Teapot, Cover 170.00

Yellow, Tumbler 55.00

ROBLIN Art Pottery was founded in 1898 by Alexander W. Robertson and Linna Irelan in San Francisco, California. The pottery closed in 1906. The firm made faience with green, tan, dull blue, or gray glazes. Decorations were usually animal shapes. Some red clay pieces were made.

Vase, Bisque, Tooled Design At Top, Cylindrical, Carved Stepped Foot, 2 ½ x 1 ½ In. 200.00

ROCKINGHAM, in the United States, is a pottery with a brown glaze that resembles ortoiseshell. It was made from 1840 to 1900 by many American potteries. Mottled brown Rockingham wares were first made in England at the Rockingham factory. Other types of eramics were also made by the English firm. Related pieces may be listed in the Bennington category.

ook Flask, Amber, Glaze, 5⅝ In. 374.00
uspidor, Hexagonal, 19th Century, 3½ x 6 In. 58.00
igurine, Dog, Spaniel, Seated, Free-Standing Front Legs, 10¼ In. 460.00
lask, Mermaid, Curled Tail, 8 In. 150.00
rame, Embossed Ornamentation, Bead & Rope Rim, Oval, 19th Century, 10 x 8 In. 302.00
rame, Little Girl, Lithograph, Glazed, Oval, Mid 19th Century, 10 x 8¼ In. 147.00
itcher, Begging Dogs, Tricornered Hat, Lid, c.1850, 11¼ In. 201.00
itcher, Carved, Brown Mottled Glaze, 8 In. 59.00
itcher, Dog, Seated, Ribbon, Bow, Late 1800s, 9 In. 144.00
itcher, Embossed Grapevine, 19th Century, 9¼ x 7½ In. 302.00
itcher, Grapes, Wide Mouth, Applied Handle, 9 In. 110.00
itcher, Hunting Scenes, Molded Grapevines, Hound Handle, 11 In. 210.00
itcher, Hunting Scenes, Molded, Acorn Branches, Squirrel Handle, Mid 1800s, 9 In. 173.00
itcher, Hunting Scenes, Molded, Grapevines, Hound Handle, 1852, 8¾ In. 510.00
itcher, Mask Spout, Paneled, Running Brown Glaze, Green Traces, 9 In. 115.00
itcher, Peacocks, 8 In. 100.00

ROGERS, *see John Rogers category.*

ROOKWOOD pottery was made in Cincinnati, Ohio, from 1880 to 1960. All of this art pottery s marked, most with the famous flame mark. The R is reversed and placed back to back with he letter P. Flames surround the letters. After 1900, a Roman numeral was added to the mark o indicate the year. The company went bankrupt in 1941. For several years various owners tried to evive the pottery, but by 1967 it was out of business. The name and some of the molds were bought by a ollector in 1984. The molds were kept in his basement until 2006 when a group of investors bought hem and revived the pottery. The Rookwood Pottery Co. currently makes fireplaces, tiles, and bookends n old designs and special items for limited edition vases and steins for Christmas.

shtray, Clown, Yellow Suit, Sitting On Corner, Sallie Toohey, 4 x 6 x 6 In. 460.00
shtray, Nude, Brown Shell, Mottled, 4½ In. 138.00
shtray, Owl Center, Brown Matte Glaze, 1936, 5⅝ In. Diam. 210.00
shtray, Rook, Figural, Blue & Tan Matte Glaze, McDonald, 1929, 4 In. 1175.00
shtray, Rook, Green, Glazed, 1946, 4¼ x 7¼ In. 210.00
shtray, Rook, Ivory Matte Glaze, 1948, 4 In. 150.00
shtray, Rook, Olive Green, 1942 . . . . . . 80.00
asket, Lion's Head Feet, Butterflies, A.R. Valentien, Stamped, 1882, 9¾ x 20 In. 540.00
ookends, Basket Of Flowers, Multicolored Matte Glaze, 1929, 6 In. 600.00
ookends, Basket Of Flowers, Pink & Green Matte Glaze, c.1929, 6 x 5 In. 144.00
ookends, Double Reader, Crystalline Blue Matte Glaze, 1922, 7 In. 850.00
ookends, Dutch Children, Brick Wall, Tulips, c.1928, 5¾ In. 431.00
ookends, Eagle & Book, Ombroso Glaze, William McDonald, c.1922, 7½ x 7 In. 863.00
ookends, Egyptian, Maiden Kneeling, Brown Matte Glaze, 1921, 5½ In. 705.00
ookends, Elephant, Raised Trunk, Bisque, 1937, 7 In. 210.00
ookends, Elephant, Variegated Brown Matte Glaze, 1923, 5 In. 200.00
ookends, Hippopotamus, Ivory Matte Glaze, 1933, 4 x 6½ In. 3200.00
ookends, Ladybug On Sunflower, Red, Black, Yellow, Green, 1936, 3¾ In. 9650.00
ookends, Lion, Blue & Tan Matte Glaze, Abel, 1928, 6½ In. 725.00
ookends, Lotus Blossoms, Green, Yellow, Ivory, 3¾ x 6 In. 353.00
ookends, Man-O-War, Wine Madder Glaze, 1958, 6½ In. 579.00
ookends, Oak Tree, 1928, 5½ x 5½ In. . . . . . *illus* 1020.00
ookends, Owl, Green Glaze, Book Base, William McDonald, 1925, 6⅝ In. 529.00
ookends, Owl, Turquoise, Sand-Filled Base, 5¾ In. 132.00
ookends, Panther, Reclining, Brown High Glaze, c.1947 . . . . . . 361.00
ookends, Penguin, Ivory Matte Glaze, 1927-28, 5⅞ In. 1195.00
ookends, Polar Bear, Ivory Matte Glaze, 1934 . . . . . . 975.00
ookends, Rook, Large, Green Matte Glaze, 1929, 6 In. 2235.00
ookends, Rook, Open Book Base, Blue Matte Glaze, c.1929, 6½ x 6½ In. . . . . . *illus* 863.00
ookends, Seated Ladies, Fancy Dress, Matte Glaze, 7 In. 489.00
ookends, Ship, Black, Yellow, Green, Brown, 1924, 5¼ x 5½ In. 632.00
ookends, Ship, Full Sail, Brown Yellow Glaze, McDonald, 1926, 5½ In. 350.00
ookends, Sphinx, Green Frogskin Glaze, 1929, 7 In. 3410.00
ookends, St. Francis, Brown, Gray, Flesh Tone, 1945 . . . . . . 412.00

Rookwood, Bookends, Oak Tree, 1928, 5½ x 5½ In.
$1020.00

Rookwood, Bookends, Rook, Open Book Base, Blue Matte Glaze, c.1929, 6½ x 6½ In.
$863.00

Rookwood, Candleholder, Elephant, Trunk Raised, Green Matte Glaze, Pink, 1929, 4 In.
$170.00

Rookwood, Flower Frog, Frog On 5 Lily Pads, Black Glossy High Glaze, 1926, 3¾ In.
$420.00

R

Rookwood, Paperweight, Rooster, Multicolored, McDonald, 1946, 5 In. $430.00

Rookwood, Pitcher, Yellow Roses, Silver Pomegranate Overlay, 1890, 8 ¼ x 10 ½ In. $4800.00

Rookwood, Plaque, Landscape, Vellum Glaze, Lorinda Epply, Frame, 1912, 8 x 10 In. $1920.00

Rookwood, Plaque, Windmills, Landscape, Vellum, Fred Rothenbusch, 1894, 9 x 15 In. $2520.00

Bookends, Water Lilies, Ivory Matte Glaze, 1939, 3 ½ x 5 ¼ In. 395.0
Bowl, Blue Leaves, Turquoise, Green, Three Legs, Sallie Coyne, 1922, 5 ¾ x 11 In. 780.0
Bowl, Blue Matte Glaze, 3 Handles, 1917, 3 ¼ x 10 In. 350.0
Bowl, Flowers On Rim, Black Opal, Lorinda Epply, 3 ½ x 8 In. 225.0
Bowl, Green, Rose Blush, Incised, Albert Pons, 1908, 3 x 6 ½ In. 235.0
Bowl, Incised Wave Band, Matte Green, Z Line, 1902, 2 ⅝ x 7 ¼ In. 176.0
Bowl, Organic Designs, Yellow & Green Matte Glaze, 1921, 3 x 7 In. 350.0
Bowl, Red Weeds, Squat, William Hentschel, 1920, 3 x 5 ¼ In. 600.0
Candleholder, 3 Fish Holding Aperture, High Blue Glaze, 3 ½ In., Pair 165.0
Candleholder, Dragon, Claws Grasping Candlecup, Blue, Brown Matte, 1926, 3 In. 849.0
Candleholder, Egyptian Maidens Hold Candlecup, Brown Matte, 1921, 11 In., Pair 590.0
Candleholder, Elephant, Trunk Raised, Green Matte Glaze, Pink, 1929, 4 In. *illus* 170.0
Candlestick, Cameo Glaze, Ed Abel, c.1891, 6 In. 345.0
Candlestick, Twisted, Blue Matte Glaze, Handles, Arts & Crafts, c.1913 215.0
Chamberstick, Pink & Green Matte Glaze, c.1920, 6 x 3 ½ In. 86.0
Creamer, Flowering Branches, Green, Adeliza Drake Sehon, 1896, 3 ¼ In. 559.0
Ewer, Autumn Maple Leaves, Dark Amber Ground, 1898, 5 ⅜ In. 324.0
Ewer, Cherry Blossom, Tiger Eye Glaze, A.M. Valentien, c.1889, 5 x 12 In. 575.0
Ewer, Flowering Branches, Extended Neck, Pinched Spout, Loop Handle, 1888, 6 In. 174.0
Ewer, Jasmine, White Clay, 1893, 9 ⅞ In. 472.0
Ewer, Red Clover, Standard Glaze, Ruffled Rim, Fred Rothenbusch, 1902, 5 ⅜ In. 323.0
Ewer, Rose Bough Bearing Leaves, Thorns & Rose Hips, 1892, 7 ½ In. 501.0
Ewer, Yellow Flowers, Standard Glaze, Adeliza Sehon, 1888, 10 ½ In. 176.0
Ewer, Yellow Flowers, Standard Glaze, Irene Bishop, c.1901, 7 In. 316.0
Ewer, Yellow Flowers, Trifold Rim, Squat, Brown To Umber, 6 In. 546.0
Figurine, Ballerina, Head Back, Chest Out, Gray, 5 In. 950.0
Figurine, Ballerina, Head Back, Ivory Matte Glaze, Louise Abel, 1934, 8 ⅛ In. 1480.0
Figurine, Cat, Seated, Bisque, White, Abel, 1946, 6 ¾ In. 155.0
Figurine, Dachshund, Ivory Matte Glaze, Abel, 1939, 3 x 5 In. 615.0
Figurine, Frog, Wide Open Mouth, Green Matte Glaze, Marked, 1944 345.0
Figurine, Honey Bear, Nubian Black Glaze, Louise Abel, 1948, 4 In. 715.0
Figurine, Rooster, Brown Glossy Glaze, 5 ¼ x 2 ½ x 3 ¼ In. 154.0
Figurine, Seated Nude Female, 1929, 4 In. 377.0
Figurine, Spanish Dancer, Red Dress, Doing Tango, 1945, 8 In. 177.0
Flower Frog, Frog On 5 Lily Pads, Black Glossy High Glaze, 1926, 3 ¾ In. *illus* 420.0
Flower Frog, Nude Nymph, Frog, Ivory Matte Glaze, 1931, 5 ¼ In. 230.0
Flower Holder, Lotus, Glossy Shades Of Green, Pink, Purple & Brown, 1927 383.0
Flower Holder, Mushroom Girl, Cream High Glaze, Porcelain, 1916, 6 In. 425.0
Humidor, Green Glaze, Molded Panels, Flattened Knob Finial, Pink Interior, 1929, 4 In. 213.
Humidor, Man Lighting Pipe, Painted, Standard Glaze, c.1903, 5 ½ x 5 ½ In. 518.0
Inkwell, Red Oak Leaves, Harriet Wilcox, 1902, 2 x 4 ¼ In. 180.0
Jar, Potpourri, Bird On Branch, Cameo, Cover, 7 ½ x 6 In. 840.0
Jardiniere, Magnolia Branches, Multicolored Ground, Spherical, 1889, 5 ½ In. 319.0
Jug, Devil, Playing Lute, Cats, Singing, Dancing, Climbing Trees, 1884, 7 ¾ x 5 ¼ In. 2400.0
Jug, Ear Of Corn, Standard Glaze, Flame Stopper, Sallie Coyne, 1898, 7 In. 353.0
Jug, Owl & Bat, Full Moon, Green Ground, Nicholas J. Hirschfeld, c.1880, 3 x 2 In. 660.0
Jug, Peach Sky, Black Swallows, Caramel, 1883, 9 In. 475.0
Lamp Base, Tulips, Leaves, Ivory Brown Ground, Egg Shape, 1950, 13 In. 522.
Mug, Otto Von Bismarck, Portrait, Standard Glaze, 3 Handles, 1901, 6 In. 960.0
Paperweight, 2 Geese, Ivory, 4 ¼ In. 353.0
Paperweight, Cat, Nubian Black Glaze, Shirayamadani, 1958, 2 ¾ In. 965.
Paperweight, Cat, Seated, Black Matte Glaze, 1922, 5 ½ In. 1290.
Paperweight, Cat, Seated, Rust High Glaze, 1965, 4 ½ In. 460.
Paperweight, Cocker Spaniel, Wine Madder Glaze, 1952, 4 In. 323.0
Paperweight, Donkey, Ivory Matte Glaze, 1941, 6 In. 472.0
Paperweight, Duck, Aventurine Glaze, 1964, 2 ½ In. 72.
Paperweight, Easter Lily, Ivory Matte Glaze, Shirayamadani, 1934 1175.
Paperweight, Elephant, Clowns, Nubian Black Glaze, McDonald, 1922, 3 ¾ In. 435.
Paperweight, Elephant, Dark Yellow Matte Glaze, 1929, 3 In. 382.
Paperweight, Elephant, Seated, Nubian Black Glaze, Marked, 1934, 4 In. 345.
Paperweight, Foo Dog, Seated, Base, Green Matte Glaze, 3 ¾ In. 460.
Paperweight, Frog, Seated, Base, Green Matte Glaze, 1906, 3 ¼ x 4 ½ In. 1300.
Paperweight, Fruit Basket, Multicolored, Sallie Toohey, 1928, 3 ½ In. 365.
Paperweight, Gazelle, Brown & White Glaze, K. Brown, Impressed, 1935 345.
Paperweight, Goose, Ivory Matte Glaze, 1933, 5 In. 944.
Paperweight, Lamb, Cirrus Glaze, Virginia Scalf, 1959, 5 In. 380.

R

aperweight, Mandarin Duck, Ivory Matte Glaze, 1933, 2 ¼ x 3 In. 325.00
aperweight, Monkey, Seated, Holding Knees, Brown, 1965, 3 ¾ In. 323.00
aperweight, Monkey, Seated, Wine Madder Glaze, 1948, 4 ⅞ In. 890.00
aperweight, Penguin, Ivory Matte Glaze, 1934, 5 In. 826.00
aperweight, Potter At The Wheel, Green Matte Glaze, 12-Sided, 1935 228.00
aperweight, Rabbit, Ivory Matte Glaze, 1930, 3 ⅛ In. 354.00
aperweight, Rabbit, Ivory Matte Glaze, 1953, 3 In. 695.00
aperweight, Rabbit, Wine Madder Glaze, 1945, 3 In. 402.00
aperweight, Rook, Blue Matte Glaze, Crystals, 1931, 3 In. 520.00
aperweight, Rook, Green & Brown Matte Glaze, c.1930, 4 x 3 In. 489.00
aperweight, Rooster, Coromandel Glaze, McDonald, 1936, 5 In. 320.00
aperweight, Rooster, Multicolored, McDonald, 1946, 5 In. *illus* 430.00
aperweight, Squirrel, Eating Nut, Chestnut Brown Matte Glaze, Toohey, 1925 460.00
aperweight, Turtle, Green Matte Glaze, Crystals, 1965, 2 ⅛ x 4 ¼ In. 485.00
aperweight, Woodpecker, Blue & White Matte Glaze, Abel, 1931, 4 ½ In. 849.00
encil Holder, Art Deco, Dark Blue Crystalline Matte Glaze, 1931, 3 In. 515.00
in Tray, Frog Perched On One Side, Green Glaze, 1906, 1 ⅛ x 4 In. 472.00
in Tray, Ivory Matte Glaze, 1951, 1 ¾ x 4 ½ In. 200.00
in Tray, Owl, Green Matte Glaze, 6 ¾ In. 645.00
itcher, Aquatic Plants, Dark Brown Ground, Glaze, Bulbous, 1901, 7 ⅜ In. 232.00
itcher, Blue Flowers, Footed, Harriet Wilcox, 1887, 9 x 5 In. 540.00
itcher, Clover Stems, Leaf Tip Border, Silver Overlay Handle, Egg Shape, 1892, 8 In. 1276.00
itcher, Dandelion Leaves, Stippled Blue Ground, Purple Glaze, 1910, 6 ¼ x 5 ¾ In. 840.00
itcher, Indian Portrait, Standard Glaze, Marie Rauchfuss, c.1897, 4 ¾ In. 2760.00
itcher, Leaf & Berry, Standard Glaze, Handle, Carl Schmidt, 1898, 3 ½ x 4 ½ In. 345.00
itcher, Rose, White, 1888, 6 ¼ x 4 In. 360.00
itcher, Rose Spray, Leaf Tips, Silver Overlay, Bulbous, Extended Neck, 1892, 9 ¼ In. 928.00
itcher, Yellow Roses, Silver Pomegranate Overlay, 1890, 8 ¼ x 10 ½ In. *illus* 4800.00
laque, Autumn Landscape, Original Frame, 1912, 8 ¼ x 10 ½ In. 4800.00
laque, Autumn Landscape, Trees, Lake, Vellum Glaze, E.T. Hurley, 8 ¾ x 11 ¾ In. 9400.00
laque, Boats, Anchored In Venice Harbor, Vellum Glaze, V, Frame, 1916, 9 ½ x 12 In. 5758.00
laque, Coastline, Lorinda Epply, 1912, 7 ½ x 5 ½ In. 4200.00
laque, Early Autumn, Landscape, Vellum Glaze, Ed Diers, Frame, 10 x 8 In. 5175.00
laque, Fence-Lined Path, Vellum Glaze, Frame, Carl Schmidt, c.1915, 7 x 9 In. 5175.00
laque, Landscape, Vellum Glaze, Lorinda Epply, Frame, 1912, 8 x 10 In. *illus* 19200.00
laque, Landscape, Vellum Glaze, Oak Frame, Fred Rothenbusch, 1918, 9 x 12 In. 6800.00
laque, Landscape, Vellum, 1916, 8 ½ x 11 In. 6600.00
laque, Landscape, Trees, Stream, Vellum, Painted Oak Frame, 1947, 9 x 12 In. 6000.00
laque, Mountain Lake At Dusk, Vellum Glaze, Oak Frame, Fred Rothenbusch, 1912, 5 x 7 In. 2880.00
laque, Quiet Stream, Vellum Glaze, Frame, Carl Schmidt, c.1916, 8 x 6 In. 4025.00
laque, River Bend, Cloudy Sky, Vellum, Frame, 1916, 7 ½ x 9 ½ In. 2520.00
laque, River Bend, Trees, Blue, Celadon, Frame, 1900, 5 ½ x 7 ¼ In. 4200.00
laque, River Landscape, Earthenware, Edward Diers, c.1900, 6 ⅞ x 8 ¾ In. 3600.00
laque, River Landscape, Frame, Lenore Asbury, 1917, 9 x 12 ½ In. 6000.00
laque, Snow-Covered Alpine Landscape, Vellum, Frame, 1913, 8 ½ x 10 ¾ In. 5400.00
laque, Snowy Landscape, Original Frame, Sallie Coyne, 9 ¼ x 12 ¼ In. 10800.00
laque, Snowy Mountain Landscape, Vellum, Frame, 1914, 5 x 8 In. 2760.00
laque, Venetian Moonlight, Vellum Glaze, E.T. Hurley, Frame, 5 ½ x 8 ½ In. 4888.00
laque, Windmills, Landscape, Vellum, Fred Rothenbusch, 1894, 9 x 15 In. *illus* 25200.00
laque, Winter Landscape, Vellum Glaze, Elizabeth McDermott, c.1918, 5 x 8 ½ In. 3738.00
laque, Winter Sunset, Vellum Glaze, Painted, Sallie Coyne, Frame, 9 x 5 In. 3738.00
late, Butterfly, Plants, Blue, Green Ground, c.1886 190.00
owder Box, Spanish Woman Holding Fan, Glazed Tan Ground, 1918, 8 In. 235.00
conce, Trees, McIntosh Roses, Mottled Dark Blue Porcelain High Glaze, 1916, 8 In. 575.00
culpture, Head, Child, Ivory & Green Matte Glaze, A.M. Valentein, c.1904, 3 x 2 In. 460.00
tein, George Weidmann Brewing Co., Inc., Pewter Lid, ½ Liter 297.00
eapot, Blue Matte Glaze, Squat, Shaped Handle, 1921, 3 ¾ x 8 In. *illus* 294.00
ile, Elephant, Light Blue Matte Glaze, 1921, 3 ½ In. 470.00
ile, Faience, Griffin, Dark Blue & Brown Glaze, Oak Frame, 12 In. 2280.00
ile, Geometric, Brown On Blue Matte Ground, Impressed Mark, Oak Frame, 8 In. 375.00
ile, Lake, Trees, Mountains, Oak Frame, c.1904, 12 In., 2 Piece 11400.00
ile, Landscape, Blue, Green, Oak Frame, 12 In. 4000.00
ile, Parrot, Yellow Beak, Pink, Purple Green, Yellow, Blue Matte Foliage, 1930, 5 In. 315.00
ile, Rookwood Pottery Building, Gates, Black, Pale Green High Glaze Ground, 5 In. 290.00
ile, Ship, 3-Mast, Light Blue, Red, Blue, Green, Tan, Faience, Frame, 8 In. 765.00
ile, Tulips, Leaves, Yellow, Green, Blue Ground, Faience, 6 In. 400.00

Revised Rookwood Mark
The Rookwood Pottery went out of business in the 1960s, and the molds and name were purchased in 1984. A new version of the RP flame mark is used. The Roman numerals for the entire year are used instead of just the last numerals. 1908 is VIII, 2008 is MMVIII.

Rookwood, Teapot, Blue Matte Glaze, Squat, Shaped Handle, 1921, 3 ¾ x 8 In.
$294.00

Rookwood, Vase, Clematis Vines, Green, Yellow, Kataro Shirayamadani, 1922, 11 In.
$6150.00

Rookwood, Vase, Crocus, Iris Glaze, Carl Schmidt, 1911, 9½ In.
$3900.00

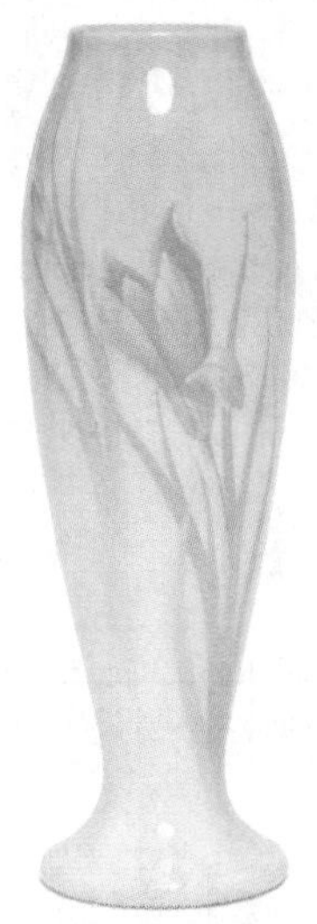

Rookwood, Vase, Elephants, Flowers, Elizabeth Barrett, 1944, 6½ x 5½ In.
$2760.00

Rookwood, Vase, Elephants, Landscape, Jens Jensen, 1948, 11¾ x 8½ In.
$6000.00

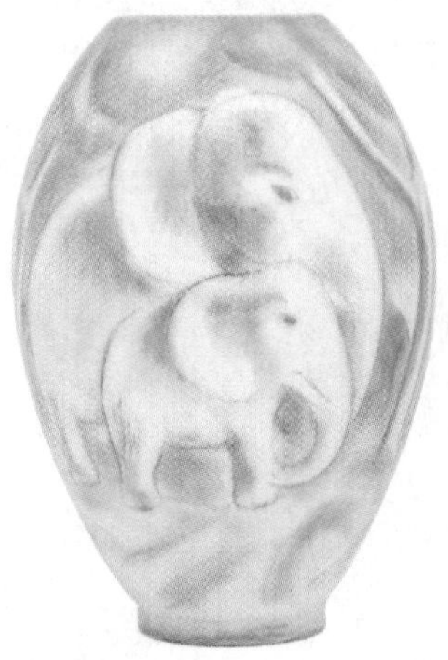

Tile, Urn, Garland, White, Blue Ground, Faience, 11¾ x 4½ In. 479.0
Tray, Flower, Leaves, Blue Crystalline Matte Glaze, Leaf Shape, 6½ In. 215.0
Tray, Leaf Shape, Brown Matte Glaze, c.1909, 6½ In. 58.0
Tray, Swan, White Matte Glaze, 1929, 2¼ x 5¾ In. 165.0
Trivet, 2 Birds Perched On Flowering Tree, Blue, Pink, Frame, 1913, 5⅝ In. 1500.0
Trivet, 3 Geese, Matte Glaze, Oak Frame, 5½ In. 720.0
Trivet, Blue Rook, White Lattice, Frame, 5½ In. 360.0
Trivet, Geometric, Pink, Blue, Purple, Oak Frame, 1922, 6 In. 500.0
Trivet, Rook, Latticework Ground, Blue & White Matte Glaze, 5⅝ x 5⅝ In. 410.0
Urn, Classical Scene, Indigo Matte Glaze, Embossed, 1929, 13 x 9 In. 1140.0
Urn, Garden, Terra-Cotta, Italian Renaissance, Blue Engobe, Stand, 43 x 26 In. 3900.0
Urn, Plums, Peach Ground, Wax, 1930, 13¾ x 9½ In. 1140.0
Vase, 2 Carousel Horses, Wax Matte Glaze, Bulbous, Wide Rim, 4½ In. 470.0
Vase, 2 Handles, William Hentschel, 1921, 3¼ x 5½ In. 360.0
Vase, 3 Jonquils, Deep Blue Ground, 1903, 9½ In. 3586.0
Vase, 3 Swallows Dipping, Clouds, Glaze, Cylindrical, Flared, 1907, 9⅝ In. 3712.0
Vase, Apple Blossoms, Pale Shading, Cylindrical Flared, 1913, 9¼ In. 522.0
Vase, Aqua Blue Matte Glaze, Flowers, Baluster, 20th Century, 4¾ x 3¾ In. 165.0
Vase, Autumn Landscape, Ed Diers, 1925, 8¾ x 4¾ In. 3600.0
Vase, Band Of Cherry Blossoms On Shoulder, Vellum Glaze, Bulbous, E.T. Hurley, 4 In. 1645.0
Vase, Bands Of White Roses, Blue Vellum Glaze, Oval, F. Rothenbusch, 1922, 5⅝ In. 441.0
Vase, Beads, Leaves, Dusty Rose To Green Glaze, Bulbous, 3½ x 4¼ In. 143.0
Vase, Berries, Red, Green Leaves, Tapered, K. Shirayamadani, 1900, 13⅝ In. 3290.0
Vase, Bird, Black, Indian, Sioux, Portrait, c.1900, 11 x 10½ In. 9775.0
Vase, Birds, High Glaze, S. Toohey, 11 In. 863.0
Vase, Blossoms, Art Deco Dark Brown, Orange Ground, 6½ x 5 In. 900.0
Vase, Blossoms, Blue & Green, Ivory Butterfat Glaze, Bottle Shape, 1928, 15 x 8 In. 3900.0
Vase, Blossoms, Blue & Red, Purple Ground, Wax, 1925, 5½ x 7 In. 900.0
Vase, Blossoms, Blue, Blue & Purple Butterfat Ground, Carved, 1913, 7 x 3 In. 1440.0
Vase, Blossoms, Deep Red & Blue, Squat, Wax, 1922, 2½ x 6½ In. 840.0
Vase, Blossoms, Golden, 2 Handles, Kataro Shirayamadani, 1890, 13 x 12½ In. 540.0
Vase, Blossoms, Pink & Purple, Wax, 1932, 4¾ x 4½ In. 660.0
Vase, Blossoms, Pink, Leaves, Shaded Ground, Tapered, 1912, 8 x 4¼ In. 420.0
Vase, Blossoms, Triangular, Full Height Stems, Green Matte Glaze, 9½ x 4¼ In. 1800.0
Vase, Blossoms, White, Orange, Leaves, Gray Ground, 1919, 5 x 7 In. 1920.0
Vase, Blue Birds In Flight, Pink, Sand, Kate Curry, 1918, 8½ x 5 In. 720.0
Vase, Blue Fruit, Green Leaves, Butterfat Mustard Ground, 1915, 6 x 6¼ In. 1020.0
Vase, Boats, Harbor, Venice, Blue, White, Vellum Glaze, Carl Schmidt, 1920, 11 In. 5875.0
Vase, Bottle Shape, Linear Wave Band, Matte Brown Glaze, 1912, 6 In. 294.0
Vase, Branch, Blossoms, Barbotine, 1885, 13½ x 8 In. 720.0
Vase, Branch, Cherry Blossoms, Pink Blue Ground, Cylindrical, 1905, 7⅞ In. 319.0
Vase, Branch, Hydrangea, Flame Mark, Lorinda Epply, 14¼ x 8½ In. 5640.0
Vase, Branches, Apple Blossoms, Vellum, 1918, 9¾ x 6 In. 1200.0
Vase, Branches, Pink Flowers, Leaves, Yellow, 2 Handles, 1927, 6¼ x 4¼ In. 780.0
Vase, Brown Leaves, Stippled Brown & Green Ground, Squat, Flared, J. Jensen, 1930, 5 In. 470.0
Vase, Brown Matte Glaze, Dark Highlights, 1917, 90½ In. 531.0
Vase, Bud, Blossoms, Green Ground, Incised, Glaze, 1903, 6⅝ In. 638.0
Vase, Bud, Branches, White Cherry Blossoms, Rose Ground, 1923, 6 x 2¾ In. 780.0
Vase, Bud, Dark Purple High Glaze, Squat Base, Elongated Neck, 7 In. 141.0
Vase, Bud, Triple Cylinder, Green Matte Frogskin Glaze, Art Deco, 1930, 7⅜ In. 353.0
Vase, Butterscotch Glaze, Stepped, Bulbous, Squat, Flared Rim, Blue Interior, 1933, 4 In. 213.0
Vase, Cactus, Carved, Charles Todd, c.1912, 3¾ x 4½ In. 575.0
Vase, Camellias, Wax, 1924, 8¾ x 4¾ In. 1680.0
Vase, Cherries, Ripe Red, Brown Underglaze, 7 In. 825.0
Vase, Cherry Blossoms, Leaves, Purple, Blue Ground, Wax, 1940, 5½ x 3½ In. 1440.0
Vase, Cherry Blossoms, Painted, Vellum Glaze, E.T. Hurley, c.1914, 4 x 7¾ In. 460.0
Vase, Cherry Blossoms, Raspberry Pink Ground, 1922, 7½ x 3 In. 4200.0
Vase, Cherry Blossoms, Vellum, Pink Matte Glaze, Bulbous, 1925, 5½ In. 558.0
Vase, Chrysanthemums, Blue Ground, Painted, 1918, 8¾ x 6¾ In. 10800.0
Vase, Clematis Blossoms, Porcelain Faceted, Elizabeth Barrett, 1944, 7 x 5 In. 1200.0
Vase, Clematis Vines, Green, Yellow, Kataro Shirayamadani, 1922, 11 In. . . . . *illus* 6150.0
Vase, Clover, Standard Glaze, A.D. Sehon, c.1898, 5½ In. 345.0
Vase, Cornflowers, Buds, Leaves, Multicolored Ground, Egg Shape, 1900, 5 In. 406.0
Vase, Cosmos, Pink & Red Blue Ground, Vellum, 1927, 7¼ x 3¾ In. 1140.0
Vase, Crescent, Purple Iris, Silver Molded Iris, Iris Glaze, 1900, 4½ x 4 In. 7200.0
Vase, Crocus, Blue, Painted, Iris Glaze, Carl Schmidt, c.1908, 9¾ In. 3738.0
Vase, Crocus, Iris Glaze, Carl Schmidt, 1911, 9½ In. . . . . *illus* 3900.0

ase, Crocus, Leaves, Impressed, Cylindrical, 1908, 8 7/8 In. . . . 754.00
ase, Crocus, Leaves, Multicolored Ground, Egg Shape, 1906, 6 1/4 In. . . . 319.00
ase, Crocus, Painted, Iris Glaze, Carl Schmidt, c.1911, 9 1/2 In. . . . 3738.00
ase, Cyclamen, White, Pink, Iris Glaze, Lenore Asbury, 8 5/8 In. . . . 1528.00
ase, Daffodil, Glaze, 1895, 7 x 12 In. . . . 240.00
ase, Daisies, Molded, Green Glaze, Globe Shape, 1931, 4 1/2 In. . . . 200.00
ase, Daisies, Pastel Ground, Vellum, 1926, 6 3/4 x 3 In. . . . 720.00
ase, Daisies, Pink Tint, Baluster, Flared Rim, Sallie Coyne, 1924, 9 1/2 In. . . . 3290.00
ase, Daisy Stems, Brown & Gold Ground, Bulbous, 1903, 6 3/4 In. . . . 261.00
ase, Daisy Stems, Olive Green & Gold Ground, Cylindrical, Flared, 1905, 6 3/4 In. . . . 174.00
ase, Daisy Stems, Pale Shaded Ground, Cylindrical, 1912, 7 In. . . . 464.00
ase, Dogwood Blossoms, Blue Green & Pink Ground, Egg Shape, 1914, 6 1/4 In. . . . 464.00
ase, Dogwood Blossoms, Brown Green Ground, Circular Base, Handle, 1894, 7 1/2 In. . . . 116.00
ase, Dogwood Blossoms, Pink Ground, 1917, 9 1/4 x 7 1/4 In. . . . 600.00
ase, Dragonflies, Cream, Vellum, 1904, 7 x 5 1/2 In. . . . 9000.00
ase, Drip Design, Matte Glaze, Shouldered, Jens Jensen, c.1930, 6 x 6 3/4 In. . . . 518.00
ase, Easter Lily, Pink & Green Glaze, 1917, 5 1/2 x 9 1/2 In. . . . 330.00
ase, Elephants, Flowers, Elizabeth Barrett, 1944, 6 1/2 x 5 1/2 In. . . . *illus* 2760.00
ase, Elephants, Landscape, Jens Jensen, 1948, 11 3/4 x 8 1/2 In. . . . *illus* 6000.00
ase, Evening Scene, Trees Along River, Blue Hills, Marked, 1916, 9 In. . . . 1121.00
ase, Exotic Birds, Trees, Lorinda Epply, 1927, 8 1/4 x 6 1/2 In. . . . 2640.00
ase, Exotic Birds, Wooded Landscape, Flowering Tree, Cylindrical, c.1916, 11 x 5 In. . . . 1955.00
ase, Fish, Amber, Yellow Ground, Painted, Barrel, 1930, 8 x 6 1/4 In. . . . 4500.00
ase, Fish, Jens Jensen, 1934, 5 x 4 1/2 In. . . . *illus* 1560.00
ase, Fish, Swimming, Sea Green, Cylindrical, 1905, 10 1/4 x 4 In. . . . 1320.00
ase, Fish, Underwater Plants, Painted, Porcelain Glaze, Hurley, c.1944, 8 x 7 1/2 In. . . . 14900.00
ase, Fish, Underwater Vegetation, E.T. Hurley, 1944, 7 x 8 In. . . . *illus* 15600.00
ase, Flaring Rim, Vellum Glaze, Flowers, Bulbous, Fred Rothenbusch, c.1831, 5 In. . . . 863.00
ase, Flitting Butterflies, Threaded Bands, Blue To Ivory, Bulbous, 1946, 4 1/2 In. . . . 174.00
ase, Flower, Yellow, Brown Stamen, Leaves, Ivory Ground, Egg Shape, 1944, 6 7/8 In. . . . 232.00
ase, Flowers, Blue & Red, Green Leaves, Blue Ground, Baluster, S. Toohey, 9 5/8 In. . . . 705.00
ase, Flowers, Blue, Black & Green, 1930, 5 1/4 In. . . . 295.00
ase, Flowers, Blue, Vellum, 1925, 8 1/4 x 4 1/2 In. . . . 2040.00
ase, Flowers, Brown & Mint Ground, Matte, 1929, 5 1/2 x 5 1/2 In. . . . 780.00
ase, Flowers, Brown Matte Ground, Elizabeth Barrett, 1925, 5 1/4 In. . . . 489.00
ase, Flowers, Geometric, Aqua Blue, 20th Century, 6 1/4 x 6 3/4 In. . . . 253.00
ase, Flowers, Green, Pink Ground, Vellum Glaze, Van Horne, c.1912, 5 1/2 x 3 In. . . . 374.00
ase, Flowers, Incised, Painted, Purple Glaze, 1912, 5 x 10 In. . . . 1140.00
ase, Flowers, Indigo, Ivory Ground, Squat, William Hentschel, 1931, 4 x 4 1/2 In. . . . 840.00
ase, Flowers, Ivory Glaze, Swollen, Elizabeth Barrett, 1930, 3 In. . . . 470.00
ase, Flowers, Jewel, Bulbous, Arthur Conant, 1921, 7 x 4 1/2 In. . . . *illus* 3150.00
ase, Flowers, Maroon, Green Blades, Butter Yellow Ground, 1930, 9 5/8 In. . . . 348.00
ase, Flowers, Multicolored, Matte Glaze, 1921, 5 x 13 1/4 In. . . . 1560.00
ase, Flowers, Ocher, Blue, White, Pink Matte Glaze, 1924, 8 7/8 In. . . . 999.00
ase, Flowers, Orange, Standard Glaze, Silver Overlay, Helen Pabodie Stuntz, c.1895, 8 In. . . . 2875.00
ase, Flowers, Painted, French Red Glaze, Tapered, Sara Sax, c.1920, 7 3/4 In. . . . 1150.00
ase, Flowers, Painted, Iris Glaze, Sara Sax, c.1911, 3 1/2 x 9 3/4 In. . . . 633.00
ase, Flowers, Painted, Turquoise Glaze, C.J. McLaughlin, c.1916, 4 1/2 x 6 In. . . . 288.00
ase, Flowers, Raised, Blue Matte Glaze, 1931, 7 x 5 1/2 In. . . . 420.00
ase, Flowers, White, Blue Matte Glaze, Oval, Flame Mark, c.1934, 5 In. . . . 546.00
ase, Flowers, Yellow & Brown, Leaves, Yellow Ground, Wax, 1932, 5 1/2 x 6 In. . . . 840.00
ase, Flowers, Yellow, Green Stems, Brown Ground, Bottle Form, c.1903, 6 In. . . . 225.00
ase, Flowers, Yellow, Ivory Ground, 1954, 3 1/2 In. . . . 354.00
ase, Flowers, Yellow, Twigs, Brown, Olive, 1891, 7 3/4 In. . . . 529.00
ase, Flowers & Leaves, Vellum Glaze, Yellow Ground, E. Barrett, 1926, 17 1/2 In. . . . 3120.00
ase, Flowers At Shoulder, Red & Purple Glaze, 1921, 3 1/2 x 5 In. . . . 540.00
ase, Flowers Garland, Band Of Fruit, 1928, 11 1/2 In. . . . 383.00
ase, Flowers On Shoulder, Ombroso Glaze, Squat, W. Hentschel, 1915, 4 3/4 x 8 In. . . . 2585.00
ase, Fruit, Branches, Silver Overlay Glaze, Silver Cover, 1894, 4 3/4 x 4 In. . . . 3360.00
ase, Fruit, Wreath, Yellow, Amber, Purple Ground, 1919, 9 1/2 x 4 1/2 In. . . . 1020.00
ase, Fuchsia, Vellum Glaze, Painted, Harriett Wilcox, c.1925, 7 1/2 x 14 3/4 In. . . . 6325.00
ase, Full Moon Over Lake, Vellum, Sallie Coyne, 1913, 7 1/2 x 3 1/2 In. . . . 1320.00
ase, Geese Amid Rushes, White Geese, Yellow Ground, 1937, 4 3/4 In. . . . 265.00
ase, Geometric, Gray & Tan Glaze, 1925, 3 x 6 In. . . . 210.00
ase, Geometric, Gray, Brown, Butterfat Glaze, Flared, Porcelain, 1943, 5 x 5 1/2 In. . . . 840.00
ase, Geometric, Green & Brown Glaze, 3 Handles, 1905, 8 1/2 x 6 3/4 In. . . . 330.00
ase, Geometric, Green & Red Matte Glaze, 1911, 4 1/2 x 9 1/2 In. . . . 374.00 to 390.00

Rookwood, Vase, Fish, Jens Jensen, 1934, 5 x 4 1/2 In.
$1560.00

Rookwood, Vase, Fish, Underwater Vegetation, E.T. Hurley, 1944, 7 x 8 In.
$15600.00

Rookwood, Vase, Flowers, Jewel, Bulbous, Arthur Conant, 1921, 7 x 4 1/2 In.
$3150.00

R

Rookwood, Vase, Irises, Vellum Glaze, Carl Schmidt, 1923, 7 In.
$3000.00

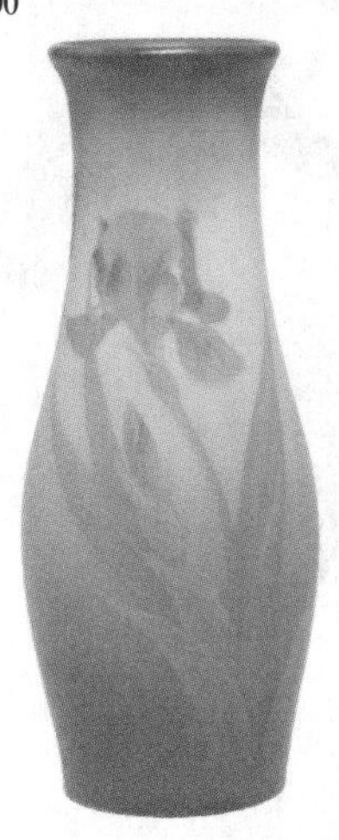

Rookwood, Vase, Sea Horses, Underwater Vegetation, E.T. Hurley, 1944, 6 x 4 In.
$3240.00

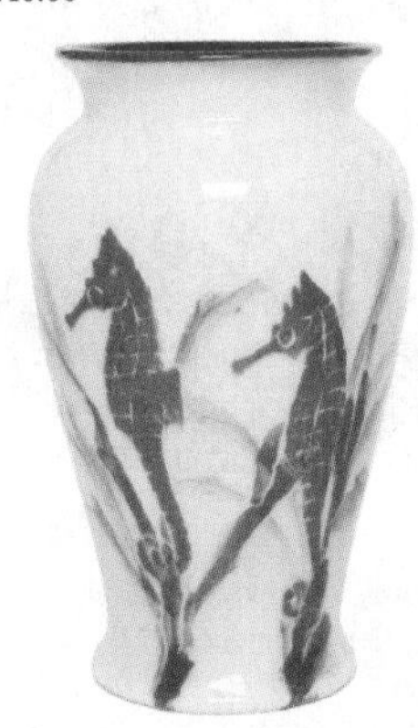

TIP

If a white powder forms on a piece made of lead or glasses or pottery decorated with a lead glaze, immediately remove the piece from your house. The powder is poisonous. Consult an expert conservator if the piece is valuable and should be saved. Do the ecologically correct thing if you must dispose of the piece.

Vase, Geometric Panels, Red, Blue, Tan, Matte Glaze, Janet Harris, c.1930, 5¼ In. 863.00
Vase, Geometrics, Rose Matte Glaze, Yellow, Navy, Tapered, Cylindrical, C. Todd, 8½ In. 529.00
Vase, Geraniums, Standard Glaze, 3 Handles, E.T. Hurley, c.1900, 6½ x 5½ In. 374.00
Vase, Glossy Maroon, Lined In Black, 1924, 9¼ In. 265.00
Vase, Golden Yellow Glaze, Flowers, Incised Stems, Asian, 8⅛ In. 118.00
Vase, Goldenrod, Multicolored, Glaze, Tapered, 1891, 12 In. 348.00
Vase, Grapevine, Blue & Green Matte Glaze, 1905, 4 x 8 In. 840.00
Vase, Grapevines, Leaves, Rooks, Green, Ginger, Pressed Shells, Geometrics, A.R.V., 20 In. 8050.00
Vase, Green Matte Glaze, Tapered, Flared Yellow Rim, 1926, 6 x 11 In. 390.00
Vase, Green Matte Glaze, Yellow Rim, Tapered, Flared, 1926, 11¾ x 6 In. 390.00
Vase, Hawthorn Branches, Vellum Glaze, Shouldered, Bulbous, E.T. Hurley, 1942, 5 In. 1175.00
Vase, Hollyhocks, White, Green Leaves, Iris Glaze, Incised, Lenore Asbury, 1910, 12 In. 10575.00
Vase, Hydrangea, Standard Glaze, Albert R. Valentien, 1891, 12½ x 11½ In. 2640.00
Vase, Incised, Painted, Matte Glaze, Charles Todd, c.1919, 22 In. 1955.00
Vase, Incised, Painted, Multicolored Matte Glaze, c.1922, 22 In. 3335.00
Vase, Indian Woman & Baby, Standard Glaze, 2 Handles, Grace Young, 1900, 9 In. 30680.00
Vase, Iris, Blue, Leaves, Tan To Green, Vellum, Cylindrical, 9 In. 834.00
Vase, Iris, Mistletoe, Laura Lindeman, 1903, 5¾ x 3¼ In. 780.00
Vase, Irises, Golden Matte Lip, c.1885, 8 In. 538.00
Vase, Irises, Painted, Vellum Glaze, Carl Schmidt, c.1911, 8¾ In. 1380.00
Vase, Irises, Vellum Glaze, Carl Schmidt, 1923, 7 In. .... *illus* 3000.00
Vase, Ivory Matte Glaze, 3 Lobes, Flared Out Rim, 1931, 4½ In. 118.00
Vase, Japanese Maples, Landscape, Turquoise Blue, 1924, 4 x 5⅓ In. 3304.00
Vase, Jewel, Flowers, Leaves, Ivory Ground, Cylindrical, 1933, 6 In. 348.00
Vase, Jewel, Leaping Gazelle, Flowering Stems, Cylindrical, Tapered, 8½ In. 522.00
Vase, Jewel, Magnolia Blossoms, Blue Ground, Brown Glaze, 1945, 8½ In. 696.00
Vase, Jewel, Magnolia Blossoms, Speckled Blue Ground, Cylindrical, 1933, 7⅛ In. 551.00
Vase, Jewel Porcelain Glaze, Flared, Sara Sax, c.1921, 5¾ x 5¼ In. 1150.00
Vase, Jewel Porcelain Glaze, Flowers, Bulbous, Arthur Conant, c.1921, 4½ x 7 In. 2990.00
Vase, Jonquils, Leaves, Blue To Green Ground, Cylindrical, Flared, 1904, 10½ In. 1508.00
Vase, Jonquils, Yellow, Standard Glaze, Shouldered, Anna Marie Valentien, 8 In. 825.00
Vase, Lake, Deep Colors, Vellum, Lorinda Epply, 1916, 11 x 5½ In. 2520.00
Vase, Lake, Vellum, Ed Diers, 1919, 9¼ x 5¼ In. 2040.00
Vase, Lake, Vellum, Fred Rothenbusch, 1921, 8¾ x 4 In. 2520.00
Vase, Lake, Vellum, Sallie Coyne, 1920, 8 x 3½ In. 2040.00
Vase, Lake, Vellum, Sallie Coyne, 1921, 7¾ x 3½ In. 1920.00
Vase, Lamp, Birds In Magnolia Tree, Blue, Brown, Ivory, Loretta Holtkamp, 12 In. 264.00
Vase, Landscape, Dark Trees, Pink Sky, Lenore Asbury, 1917, 10½ In. 3990.00
Vase, Landscape, Misty, Vellum, Ed Diers, 1909, 9¾ x 4¾ In. 1440.00
Vase, Landscape, Oval, Lenore Asbury, c.1915, 9¼ x 3¼ In. 1080.00
Vase, Landscape, Painted, Vellum Glaze, E.T. Hurley, c.1921, 12 In. 4925.00
Vase, Landscape, Snow, Misty, Vellum, Pinched Waist, 1923, 8¾ x 5 In. 3900.00
Vase, Landscape, Snow, Vessel Beneath, Pink To Blue Sky, 1911, 7 In. 2006.00
Vase, Landscape, Water, Black Top, Kataro Shirayamadani, 1910, 10¾ x 5¼ In. 3750.00
Vase, Leaf, Pink & Green Glaze, Vertical, 1922, 3 x 7 In. 240.00
Vase, Leaf, Raised, Purple, Brown Matte Glaze, Elizabeth Barrett, c.1927, 12¼ In. 805.00
Vase, Leaf & Berry, 3 Panels, Blue & Green Matte, 1920, 7 In. 395.00
Vase, Leaf & Berry, Sea Green Glaze, Painted, Bulbous, Sallie Coyne, c.1902, 7½ In. 2530.00
Vase, Leaf & Berry, Vellum Glaze, Swollen Shape, Fred Rothenbusch, c.1928, 6¾ In. 863.00
Vase, Leaf & Berry Vines, Blue Matte Glaze, Round, Charles Todd, 1913, 3¾ In. 558.00
Vase, Leafy Stems, Pale Green Ground, Egg Shape, 1946, 6¼ In. 319.00
Vase, Leaves, Beige, Carmel Ground, Squat, William Hentschel, 1931, 4 x 4¾ In. 1440.00
Vase, Leaves, Beige, Yellow Ground, Squat, William Hentschel, 3¾ x 5¼ In. 1320.00
Vase, Leaves, Berries, Olive Green Ground, Squat, 1926, 5 x 7 In. 1440.00
Vase, Leaves, Embossed, Dusty Rose To Green Matte Glaze, 5¼ x 3¾ In. 121.00
Vase, Leaves, Standard Glaze, Squat, Irene Bishop, 1899, 3 In. 264.00
Vase, Leaves, White Mint Green Ground, 1929, 7 x 5½ In. 2280.00
Vase, Light Blue, Squat, 2 Handles, c.1922, 3¾ x 5½ In. 292.00
Vase, Lilies, Matte Glaze, Painted, Bulbous, Kataro Shirayamadani, c.1926, 6 x 6½ In. 3450.00
Vase, Lilies On White Band, Pink Ground, Vellum Glaze, Swollen Shape, 7¾ In. 1175.00
Vase, Magnolia Branches, Blossoms, Buds, Blue Ivory Ground, Egg Shape, 1950, 16 In. 464.00
Vase, Magnolias, Maroon, Brown Branches, 1946, 9½ In. 413.00
Vase, Maple Leaves, Bulbous, Janet Harris, 1929, 7½ x 6½ In. 660.00
Vase, Maroon Glaze, Interior Black, 1925, 12 In. 295.00
Vase, Men On Horses, Turquoise, Bulbous, c.1950, 5¾ x 3½ In. 292.00

R

Vase, Mistletoe, Green, Carved, Iris Glaze, Matt Daly, 1901, 8 3/8 In. 3055.00
Vase, Moderne, Ridged, William Hentschel, 1926, 7 x 5 1/2 In. 840.00
Vase, Molded Floral Band, Dark Blue Matte Glaze, Cylindrical, Folded-In Rim, 6 1/4 In. 235.00
Vase, Molded Floral Band, Frogskin Glaze, Cylindrical, Folded-In Rim, 6 1/2 In. 264.00
Vase, Molded Wave Band, Matte Green, Z Glaze, Swollen Shape, 1904, 5 3/4 In. 588.00
Vase, Moonlit Lake, Pinched Waist, Vellum, E.T. Hurley, 1910, 8 3/4 x 4 3/4 In. 2640.00
Vase, Moonlit Lake, Vellum, Sallie Coyne, 1908, 8 x 4 1/4 In. 2400.00
Vase, Morning Glories, Aquamarine Ground, Jewel Porcelain, 1920, 9 1/2 x 5 In. 600.00
Vase, Mottled Navy Blue & Gray, 1929, 7 In. 796.00
Vase, Mountain Landscape, Fred Rothenbusch, 1924, 11 x 5 In. 960.00
Vase, Mushrooms, Iris Glaze, Shouldered, 1902, 6 x 9 3/4 In. 1140.00
Vase, Native American Design On Shoulder, Purple Drip Glaze, A. Munson, 1901, 3 In. 588.00
Vase, Oak Leaves, Raspberry Ground, Bulbous, 1904, 5 1/4 x 5 In. 960.00
Vase, Orchids, Purple, Green Ground, Matte, 1901, 12 1/4 x 4 1/2 In. 7800.00
Vase, Palm Fronds, Standard Glaze, Bulbous, Elongated Neck, Matt Daly, 15 In. 823.00
Vase, Palm Fronds, Standard Glaze, Matt Daly, 1898, 20 1/2 x 10 In. 3480.00
Vase, Palm Trees, Sailboats, Vellum Glaze, Shouldered, Sara Sax, c.1909, 4 x 6 1/2 In. 2415.00
Vase, Pansy Stems, Multicolored, Glaze, Baluster, Extended Neck, 1901, 9 1/8 In. 290.00
Vase, Peony Blossoms, Stems, Leaves, Pink To Green Ground, Egg Shape, 1936, 5 1/2 In. 406.00
Vase, Perched Bird, Flowering Leaves, Jewel, Ivory Ground, Baluster, 1928, 7 1/2 In. 348.00
Vase, Pine Cone, Pine Needles, Bulbous, 1922, 8 x 10 In. 1920.00
Vase, Pink Lotus Blossoms, Lavender Leaves, Pinched Waist, Porcelain, 1924, 10 x 6 In. 2040.00
Vase, Poppies, Brown, Howard Altman, 1904, 8 3/4 x 5 In. 780.00
Vase, Poppies, High Relief, Turquoise Matte Glaze, Flared, c.1921, 11 In. 431.00
Vase, Poppies, Silver Overlay Glaze, Silver Cover, 1898, 9 x 4 In. 3240.00
Vase, Poppy Stems, Multicolored, Cylindrical, Tapered, 1941, 6 3/4 In. 870.00
Vase, Purple Trillium, Iris Glaze, 1902, 8 1/4 x 4 In. 2040.00
Vase, Raised & Painted Circles, Hi-Glaze, Loretta Holtkamp, c.1951, 7 1/4 In. 518.00
Vase, Rook Flying Under Pine Branch, Iris Glaze, 1906, 7 1/4 x 4 1/4 In. 330.00
Vase, Rose, Brown, Yellow, Green, Oval, Cylindrical Neck, Flared, 8 In. 770.00
Vase, Rose, Painted, Iris Glaze, Fred Rothenbusch, c.1909, 9 1/4 In. 2875.00
Vase, Rose Stems, Thorny, Pink, Blue, Green & Ivory Ground, Cylindrical, 1913, 14 In. 928.00
Vase, Roses, Pink, A.R. Valentien, 15 x 8 In. 8400.00
Vase, Roses, Pink, Vellum, 1906, 8 x 5 In. 840.00
Vase, Roses, Yellow, Bottle Shape, 1891, 12 x 7 In. 660.00
Vase, Sea Horses, Underwater Vegetation, E.T. Hurley, 1944, 6 x 4 In. .... *illus* 3240.00
Vase, Seated Lemurs, Celadon Ground, Tapered, Bulbous, 1945, 6 1/4 In. 435.00
Vase, Sioux Indian, Green Ground, 13 In. 15525.00
Vase, Small Islands, Pine Trees, Lake, Sunset, Vellum, 1908, 8 x 4 1/2 In. 3240.00
Vase, Tall Pines, Mountain Landscape, Sara Sax, 1909, 9 1/2 x 4 1/2 In. 9000.00
Vase, Thistle, Blue, Green To Blush Glaze, Cylindrical, Tapered, 1909, 7 1/4 In. 881.00
Vase, Thistle, Carved, Matte Glaze, Marianne Mitchell, c.1905, 4 In. 288.00
Vase, Thistles, Standard Glaze, Bulbous, Flared Rim, Amelia Sprague, 1894, 6 1/2 In. 1058.00
Vase, Trees, Lake, Blue Matte Glaze, Vellum, Lenore Asbury, c.1915, 9 1/2 x 4 1/2 In. 3750.00
Vase, Trees, Pond, Rolling Hills, Cream Ground, 1913, 10 1/8 In. 1415.00
Vase, Trees, Silhouetted In Fog, Vellum Snow Glaze, E.T. Hurley, 1908, 8 1/2 In. 4230.00
Vase, Trillium Flowers, Purple, Leaves, Lavender To Green Ground, 1901, 9 In. 1888.00
Vase, Trumpet Flowers, Pink, Pale Blue To Green Ground, 1901, 6 In. 649.00
Vase, Tulips, Leaves, Ivory Ground, Glaze, Cylindrical, 1938, 11 1/2 In. 232.00
Vase, Tulips, Red, Cream Ground, Green Leaves, 1942, 6 In. 944.00
Vase, Tulips, Red, Mint Green Ground, Wax, 1929, 9 x 3 3/4 In. 1020.00
Vase, Tulips On Pink To Lavender Ground, Marked, 9 3/4 In. 708.00
Vase, Vellum, Winter Landscape, Pink & Yellow Sunset, Cylindrical, 1910, 10 3/4 In. 4800.00
Vase, Violets, Purple, Pink, Cream & Green Vellum, K. Shirayamadani, 1939, 6 5/8 In. 2235.00
Vase, Violets, Silver Overlay, Bulbous, A.R. Valentien, 1893, 11 3/4 x 7 1/2 In. 1440.00
Vase, White Flowers & Stems Around Top, Black Opal, 1927, 5 1/4 In. 944.00
Vase, White Leaves, Turquoise Ground, 1929, 9 1/4 x 7 In. 1320.00
Vase, Wild Rose, Lavender & Sea Green Ground, Bulbous, Tapered, 1926, 7 5/8 In. 812.00
Vase, Wild Rose, Red Matte, Harriet Wilcox, 1904, 6 1/2 In. .... *illus* 3950.00
Vase, Wild Roses, Buds, Leafy Stems, Ivory Ground, Tapered, 1914, 7 1/4 In. 232.00
Vase, Wild Roses, Painted, Iris Glaze, Marianne Mitchell, c.1904, 7 1/2 In. 690.00
Vase, Women, Blue, David Seyler, 1937, 7 x 7 In. .... *illus* 5100.00
Vase, Yellow Matte, 1928, 6 x 2 1/2 In. 351.00
Vase, Yellow Matte Glaze, Incised Swirled Green Lines, 2 Handles, c.1913, 8 1/4 In. 1035.00
Wall Pocket, Greek Key Border, Pink & Green Matte Glaze, 1909, 11 In. 705.00
Wall Pocket, Overlapping Shells, Blue Matte Glaze, Cone Shape, Scroll Handles, 7 In. 294.00

TIP
If you move a table, cabinet, or stand, take everything off it first. We once broke a Buffalo Pottery pitcher because we forgot it was out of sight on a shelf beneath a table we moved.

Rookwood, Vase, Wild Rose, Red Matte, Harriet Wilcox, 1904, 6 1/2 In.
$3950.00

Rookwood, Vase, Women, Blue, David Seyler, 1937, 7 x 7 In.
$5100.00

Rorstrand, Candleholder, Girls Holding Hands, Marked, 10 x 8½ In.
$150.00

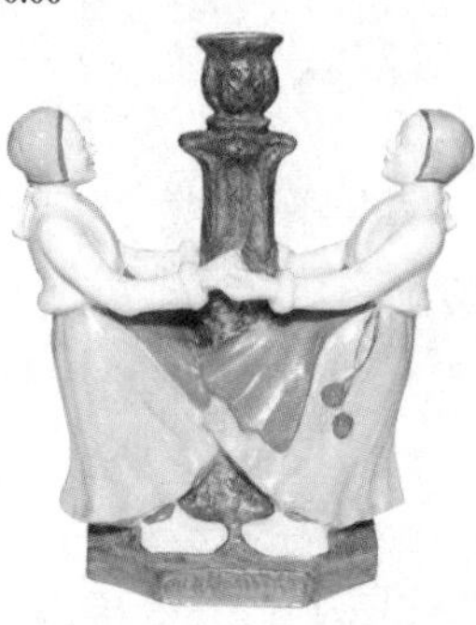

Rose Mandarin, Charger, Women, Gilt Hair, Butterflies, Late 19th Century, 15 In.
$575.00

Rose Mandarin, Jug, Cider, Ribbed, Twist Handle, Foo Dog Finial, c.1850, 8½ In.
$1350.00

Rose Mandarin, Mug, Court, Figures On Terrace, c.1800, 6¼ In.
$880.00

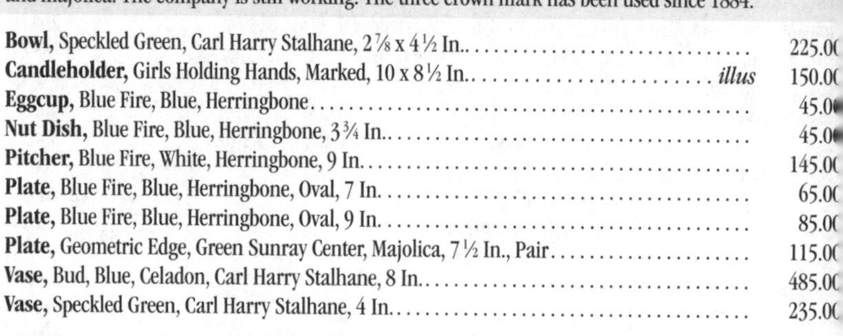

RORSTRAND was established near Stockholm, Sweden, in 1726. By the nineteenth century Rorstrand was making English-style earthenware, bone china, porcelain, ironstone china, and majolica. The company is still working. The three crown mark has been used since 1884.

Bowl, Speckled Green, Carl Harry Stalhane, 2⅞ x 4½ In. 225.0
Candleholder, Girls Holding Hands, Marked, 10 x 8½ In. . . . . . *illus* 150.0
Eggcup, Blue Fire, Blue, Herringbone 45.0
Nut Dish, Blue Fire, Blue, Herringbone, 3¾ In. 45.0
Pitcher, Blue Fire, White, Herringbone, 9 In. 145.0
Plate, Blue Fire, Blue, Herringbone, Oval, 7 In. 65.0
Plate, Blue Fire, Blue, Herringbone, Oval, 9 In. 85.0
Plate, Geometric Edge, Green Sunray Center, Majolica, 7½ In., Pair 115.0
Vase, Bud, Blue, Celadon, Carl Harry Stalhane, 8 In. 485.0
Vase, Speckled Green, Carl Harry Stalhane, 4 In. 235.0

ROSALINE, *see Steuben category.*

ROSE BOWLS were popular during the 1880s. Rose petals were kept in the open bowl to add fragrance to a room, a popular idea in a time of limited personal hygiene. The glass bowls were made with crimped tops, which kept the petals inside. Many types of Victorian art glass were made into rose bowls.

Pink To White, Globular, Ruffled Rim, 3 In. 29.00

ROSE CANTON china is similar to Rose Mandarin and Rose Medallion, except no people or birds are pictured in the decoration. It was made in China during the nineteenth and twentieth centuries in greens, pinks, and other colors.

Bowl, Flowers, Birds, Flower & Butterfly Medallion, Panels, 12 x 9 In. 240.00
Bowl, Flowers, Fruit, Birds, Floral Medallion, Panels, 10 x 8 In. 240.00
Sauceboat, Underplate, Flowers, Birds, Insects, Shaped Rim, Split Strap Handles, 8 In. 270.00
Vase, Pear Shape, Flared Lip Rim, 17½ In., Pair 1080.00

ROSE MANDARIN china is similar to Rose Canton and Rose Medallion. If the panels in the design picture only people and not birds, it is Rose Mandarin.

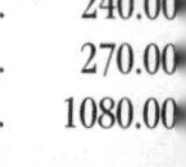

Bowl, Courtyard, People, Red & Black Ground, Multicolored Enamel, Gilt, 4½ x 10 In. 940.00
Charger, Women, Gilt Hair, Butterflies, Late 19th Century, 15 In. . . . . . *illus* 575.00
Charger, Women, Flowers, Alternating Panels, 15 x 2¼ In. 575.00
Cup, 5 Mandarin Figures 55.00
Cup & Saucer, c.1840, 2½ x 4 In. 295.00
Jug, Cider, Ribbed, Twist Handle, Foo Dog Finial, c.1850, 8½ In. . . . . . *illus* 1350.00
Mug, Court, Figures On Terrace, c.1800, 6¼ In. . . . . . *illus* 880.00
Mug, Garden, Transfer Print, 4 x 4 In. 38.00
Plate, c.1930, 8½ In. 32.00
Plate, Dinner, c.1820, 10 In. 750.00
Platter, Well & Tree, Monogram, Chinese, 19th Century, 19 In. 2360.00
Punch Bowl, 14 In. 895.00
Soap Dish, Lucky Bats, Lid, Late 19th Century, 5 x 6 x 3½ In. . . . . . *illus* 195.00
Teapot, Cover, Globular, Dragon Spout, Diapered, 5½ In. 390.00
Tureen, Cover, Animal Mask Handles, Gilt Finial, c.1780, 11 In. 2478.00
Vase, People, Flowers, 14 x 6¾ In. 1100.00

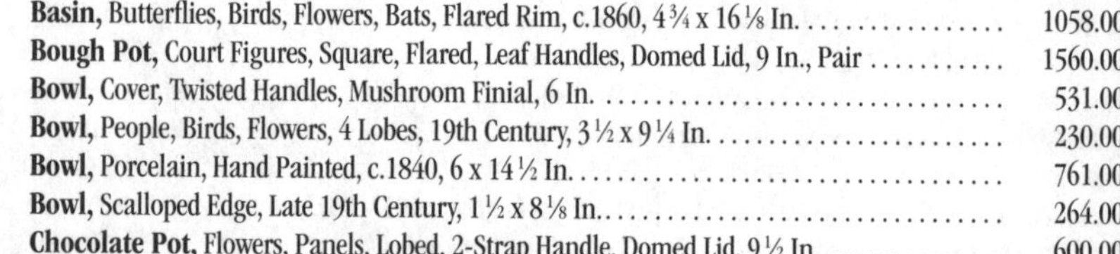

ROSE MEDALLION china was made in China during the nineteenth and twentieth centuries. It is a distinctive design with four or more panels of decoration around a central medallion that includes a bird or a peony. The panels show birds and people. The background is a design of tree peonies and leaves. Pieces are colored in greens, pinks, and other colors. It is similar to Rose Canton and Rose Mandarin.

Basin, Butterflies, Birds, Flowers, Bats, Flared Rim, c.1860, 4¾ x 16⅛ In. 1058.00
Bough Pot, Court Figures, Square, Flared, Leaf Handles, Domed Lid, 9 In., Pair 1560.00
Bowl, Cover, Twisted Handles, Mushroom Finial, 6 In. 531.00
Bowl, People, Birds, Flowers, 4 Lobes, 19th Century, 3½ x 9¼ In. 230.00
Bowl, Porcelain, Hand Painted, c.1840, 6 x 14½ In. 761.00
Bowl, Scalloped Edge, Late 19th Century, 1½ x 8⅛ In. 264.00
Chocolate Pot, Flowers, Panels, Lobed, 2-Strap Handle, Domed Lid, 9½ In. 600.00
Cup & Saucer, Roses, Light & Dark Pink, Hand Painted 49.00

Dish, Court Figures, Multicolored Enameled, Reserves, Oval, 9 x 7 & 11 x 9 In., 2 Piece 173.00
Dish, Cover, Late 19th Century, 4 3/4 x 8 1/4 In., Pair 353.00
Plate, 19th Century, 13 1/2 In. 588.00
Plate, Dessert, Birds, Flowers, People, Rose, Green, Panels, 6 1/4 In., 7 Piece 112.00
Platter, Well & Tree, Celadon, Oval 19 1/4 x 15 1/4 In. 176.00
Punch Bowl, Alternating Reserves, 1800s, 15 In. 1080.00
Punch Bowl, c.1840, 14 1/2 In. 977.00
Punch Bowl, Figures, Flowers, Bird Panels, 6 1/2 x 16 In. 1380.00
Punch Bowl, Panels, People, Birds, Peonies, Trellis Border, 15 1/2 In. 6600.00
Punch Bowl, People, Birds, Flowers, Multicolored, White Ground, 6 x 15 In. 1155.00
Punch Bowl, People, Gilt Scrolls, 18th Century, 15 3/4 In. 2271.00
Punch Bowl, People In Garden Pavilion, Enamel, 15 3/4 In. 1500.00
Punch Bowl, Petal Shape Reserve Panels, 15 In. 2040.00
Soup, Dish, Bird & Flower Medallion & Panels, Wide Rim, 7 1/2 In., Pair 210.00
Sugar & Creamer, Enameled, Figures, Flowers, Panels 300.00
Sugar & Creamer, People, Reserve Panels, Flowers, 19th Century 240.00
Vase, Floor, Foo Dog Handles, 17 1/2 x 9 In. 400.00
Vase, Ku-Form, Late 19th Century, 13 1/4 In. 558.00
Vase, Lion Head Ring Handles, Flared Neck, 24 1/2 In. 3360.00
Vase, People, Flowers, Reserve Panels, Elongated Neck, 14 In. 960.00
Water Bottle, Basin, Cover, 1800s, 16 1/2-In. Bottle, 6 x 18 1/2-In. Basin 1763.00

ROSE O'NEILL, *see Kewpie category*

ROSE TAPESTRY porcelain was made by the Royal Bayreuth factory of Tettau, Germany, during the late nineteenth century. The surface of the porcelain was pressed against a coarse fabric while it was still damp, and the impressions remained on the finished porcelain. It looks and feels like a textured cloth. Very skillful reproductions are being made that even include a variation of the Royal Bayreuth mark, so be careful when buying.

Creamer, Marked, Gobelin Ware, Royal Bayreuth, 3 1/2 In. 120.00
Creamer, Royal Bayreuth, 3 5/8 In. 295.00
Dresser Box, 3 Gilt Feet, Round, Royal Bayreuth, 4 1/2 x 2 1/2 In. 395.00
Toothpick, Pink & Yellow Roses, 1900s, 2 3/4 In. 79.00
Tray, Green Ground, Royal Bayreuth, 7 3/4 x 4 3/4 In. 250.00
Tray, Vanity, Pink Roses 50.00
Vase, Woman Holding Pink Shawl, Royal Bayreuth, 8 In. 300.00
Vase, Woman With Muff, Royal Bayreuth, 4 In. 160.00

ROSENTHAL porcelain was made at the factory established in Selb, Bavaria, in 1880. The factory is still making fine-quality tablewares and figurines. A series of Christmas plates was made from 1910. Other limited edition plates have been made since 1971. In 1998 Rosenthal was acquired by the Waterford Wedgwood Group.

Bowl, Cobalt Blue, Gold Wheat, Square, 9 In. 255.00
Bowl, Courtship, Oval, 13 1/4 x 3 In. 125.00
Bowl, Fruit Cobalt Blue, Gold Wheat, 5 1/4 In. 25.00
Bowl, Moliere, Flowers, Pink & Green, Gray & Maroon Trim, Ivory Ground, 3-Footed 85.00
Bowl, Salad, Regina, 9 x 5 1/4 In. 45.00
Bowl, Vegetable, Bettina, Round, Gold Trim, Annette, 9 x 3 1/4 In. 40.00
Bowl, Vegetable, Cover, Pompadour, Courtship, Handles, 7 x 11 1/2 In. 85.00
Box, Collar Button, Apple Blossom, Gold Accents, 2 1/2 x 1 1/2 In. 125.00
Candlestick, Blue, Green, Blue Glaze, Netter, 7 x 4 In., Pair 120.00
Candlestick, Paisleys, Green, Egyptian Blue Glaze, Stamped, Italy, Signed, 7 x 4 In., Pair 120.00
Charger, Bavarian Woman, Portrait, Green Border, Scalloped Rim, 10 In. 165.00
Coffeepot, Maria, 10 3/4 x 5 1/2 In. 45.00
Coffeepot, Mini, Sansoucci, 9 In., 3 Cup 100.00
Coffeepot, Piemonte, Flowers, Emilio Pucci, 9 1/2 In. 135.00
Creamer, Geisha, Gold Trim, 2 3/8 x 4 5/8 In. 22.00
Creamer, Maria, Handle, 5 1/2 In. 25.00
Dish, Cover, Bettina, Blue & Pink Flowers, 6 1/2 In. 50.00
Dresser Box, Applied Leaf, Blue, Green, Yellow, Netter, 8 x 4 x 2 In. 160.00
Figurine, Bird, Green & Orange Glaze, Netter, 8 In. 85.00
Figurine, Bird, Paisley, Ocher, Green, Burnt Orange, Incised, Marked, 8 In. 85.00
Figurine, Boy & Goat, c.1941, 7 1/2 In. 295.00
Figurine, Butterfly, Marked, 2 In. ..... *illus* 40.00

Rose Mandarin, Soap Dish, Lucky Bats, Lid, Late 19th Century, 5 x 6 x 3 1/2 In.
$195.00

Rosenthal, Figurine, Butterfly, Marked, 2 In.
$40.00

Rosenthal, Figurine, Duckling, Marked, 7 3/4 In.
$60.00

Rosenthal, Figurine, Woodpecker, Marked, 8 1/2 In.
$90.00

Roseville, Apple Blossom, Wall Pocket, Pink, Marked, 8⅜ x 5⅞ In.
$142.00

Roseville, Cherry Blossom, Vase, Brown, Beige, Handles, 5⅛ x 5½ In.
$160.00

Roseville, Clematis, Tea Set, Teapot, Sugar, Creamer, 7⅛-In. Teapot
$132.00

Roseville, Crystallis, Vase, Yellow, Ivory Crystalline Glaze, 14 x 7 In.
$4400.00

Figurine, Doe & Fawn, Kunstabteiluns, Selb., 6 In. . . . . 85.00 to 176.00
Figurine, Duckling, Marked, 7¾ In. . . . . *illus* 60.00
Figurine, Little Girl, Eating Porridge, Bird Perched On Bowl, 1930s, 4½ x 3¼ In. 195.00
Figurine, Nymph, Seminude, Blond, Blue Skirt, Art Deco Style, 1900s, 8 In. 235.00
Figurine, Rabbit, Brown, Himmelstoss 225.00
Figurine, Scottie, Fur Detail, 7 In. 395.00
Figurine, Woman On Bench, Poodle, Art Deco, c.1930, 5¾ x 7 x 5⅛ In. 625.00
Figurine, Woodpecker, Marked, 8½ In. . . . . *illus* 90.00
Gravy Boat, Quince, 4½ x 4⅛ x 3½ In. 28.00
Gravy Boat, Underplate, Chrysanthemums, Purple, Yellow, Green Leaves, 1956. . . . . 65.00
Jardiniere, Poppies, Multicolored, Green Leaves, 1918, 7¾ x 4½ In. 219.00
Plate, Nasturtium, Art Nouveau, 1940, 9 In. 120.00
Plate, Phoenix Bird, Ivory, Flowers, Gold Trim, Square, Cut Corners, 8 x 8 In. 45.00
Plate, Salad, Continental, 7½ In. 22.00
Platter, Annette, Gold Trim, 15 x 8¾ In. 45.00
Platter, Antoinette Pompadour, Oval, 12¾ In. 100.00
Sandwich Server, Footed, 1900s, 9½ In. 175.00
Soup, Dish, Hillside, Flowered Rim, Gold Trim, 8⅛ x 1½ In. 22.00
Sugar, Cover, Ceres, Gray Trim, 2⅞ x 3½ In. 26.00
Teacup, Forget-Me-Nots, Blue, Green, Red Details, Gold Trim, 1922, 2½ x 3½ In. 42.00
Teapot, Lid, White, 20th Century, 8 In. 35.00
Teapot, Pompadour, 11¼ x 7½ In. 475.00
Teapot, Studio Line, Orange Design, White Ground. 175.00
Tureen, Cover, Antoinette Pompadour 170.00
Tureen, Cover, Blue, Gray, Gold Design, Ring Handle, Raymond Loewy, 4½ x 11 In. 225.00
Tureen, Cover, Continental, Shower Of Gold, Marked, Raymond Loewy, 4½ x 11 In. 225.00
Vase, Black Crosshatch, Rough White Ground, Round, Netter, 6½ In. 135.00
Vase, Blue Green, Craquelure, Gilt Rim, Bulbous, Germany, 8 In. 150.00
Vase, Crosshatch, Round, Black & White, Netter, 6½ In. 135.00
Vase, Fiery Orange Glaze, Footed, Netter, 1950s, 10½ x 5 In. 200.00
Vase, Studio, Grooved Wave Form, Crystal, 10½ x 12 In. 250.00
Vase, White, Bisque, Signed, 12 x 17 In. 293.00

ROSEVILLE Pottery Company was organized in Roseville, Ohio, in 1890. Another plant was opened in Zanesville, Ohio, in 1898. Many types of pottery were made until 1954. Early wares include Sgraffito, Olympic, and Rozane. Later lines were often made with molded decorations, especially flowers and fruit. Most pieces are marked *Roseville*. Many reproductions made in China have been offered for sale the past few years.

Roseville U.S.A.

Apple Blossom, Vase, Mauve, c.1948, 7 In. 145.00
Apple Blossom, Wall Pocket, Pink, Marked, 8⅜ x 5⅞ In. . . . . *illus* 142.00
Aztec, Vase, Swags, Blossoms, Blue Gray Ground, Squeezebag, 11¼ x 4¾ In. 390.00
Baneda, Jardiniere, Orange Blossom Border, Blue Green, Bulbous, c.1933, 8 x 11 In. 764.00
Baneda, Lamp Base, Yellow Flowers, Leaves, Green Blue Ground, Bulbous, 10 In. 960.00
Baneda, Vase, Blue, Handles, 15 In. 3105.00
Baneda, Vase, Green Matte Glaze, Bulbous, 10¼ x 8 In. 1320.00
Baneda, Vase, Mottled Green, Footed, Marked, 16 In. 30.00
Bank, Eagle Head, 3 In. 350.00
Bank, Pig, Standing, Blue Gray Sponge, Cream Ground, Early 1900s, 2 x 3½ In. 125.00
Bittersweet, Wall Pocket, Yellow, Brown, 7¼ In. 325.00
Blackberry, Vase, Green, 2 Handles, 6½ x 10¼ In. 1020.00
Bleeding Heart, Candlestick, Blue, Handles, c.1940, 4½ In., Pair 250.00
Bleeding Heart, Candlestick, c.1940 . . . . 250.00
Bushberry, Basket, Blue, Green Handle, 12, 12 x 12¼ In. 266.00
Carnelian I, Vase, Mottled Pink Matte Glaze, Bulbous, Handles, 8½ x 10 In. 520.00
Carnelian II, Bowl, Red & Green Drip Glaze, Flared, 2 Loop Handles, Footed, 3 x 9 In. 705.00
Cherry Blossom, Vase, Brown, Beige, Handles, 5⅛ x 5½ In. . . . . *illus* 160.00
Chloron, Bowl, Cherub Faces, Green Matte Glaze, 8 x 3½ In. 360.00
Chloron, Vase, Raised Flowers, Green Matte Glaze, 9 x 15 In. 1800.00
Clematis, Tea Set, Teapot, Sugar, Creamer, 7⅛-In. Teapot . . . . *illus* 132.00
Clematis, Teapot, Brown, Yellow, 1940s, 7½ x 11½ In. 325.00
Columbine, Vase, Applied Flowers, Cinnamon To Green Ground, 2 Handles, 9½ In. 118.00
Corinthian, Wall Pocket, 5 x 8 In. 374.00
Cornelian, Toothbrush Holder, Sponged, Early 1900s. 100.00
Cosmos, Vase, Green Frieze Flowers, 2 Handles, 3½ In. 106.00
Creamware, Creamer, Sunbonnet, 3½ x 4 In. 112.00

Crystalis, Vase, Frothy Mustard Matte, Glaze, 29 x 12 In.		2400.00
Crystalis, Vase, Tall Neck, Squat Base, Golden Crystalline Glaze, 25 x 13½ In.		4200.00
Crystallis, Vase, Yellow, Ivory Crystalline Glaze, 14 x 7 In.	*illus*	4400.00
Dahlrose, Wall Pocket, 2 Handles, 8 x 6¾ In.		350.00
Della Robbia, Vase, Apricot, Yellow, Blue Blossoms, Celadon Ground, 16 x 4 In.		21600.00
Della Robbia, Vase, Celadon Penguins, Trees, Blue Gray, EL, 8¼ x 4½ In.		2760.00
Della Robbia, Vase, Concentric Rings, Incised Daisies, Blue Ground, 8½ x 6½ In.		11400.00
Della Robbia, Vase, Daisies, Green Ground, 10½ x 8 In.		13200.00
Della Robbia, Vase, Lavender Tulips, Blue & Green Leaves On Celadon, 7¾ x 7 In.		6600.00
Della Robbia, Vase, Peach Gardenias, Blue Gray, Reticulated Rim, WM, 10 x 7 In.		6000.00
Donatello, Bowl, Cream, Fawn, Beige, Rolled Edge, c.1915, 3½ x 7¾ In.		50.00
Donatello, Compote, Green, Beige, Cream, Footed, c.1915, 5¾ x 7½ In.		125.00
Earlam, Vase, 2 Handles, 5½ In.		189.00
Egypto, Basket, Green Matte Glaze, Oval, 6½ In.		382.00
Egypto, Vase, Embossed Medallions, Green Matte Glaze, Marked, 12½ x 3½ In.		1080.00
Egypto, Vase, Green Matte Glaze, Footed, 8½ x 4 In.		660.00
Falline, Vase, Blue, 1930s, 7⅛ In.		435.00
Falline, Vase, Blue, Green, Brown, Yellow, Double Handles, 5 x 6¼ In.		690.00
Falline, Vase, Double Handle, Brown, 6½ x 7¼ In.		633.00
Falline, Vase, Pea Pod, Multicolored, c.1930, 6¼ In.		558.00
Ferella, Bowl, Brown, Built-In Flower Frog, 3¾ x 9¼ In.		531.00
Ferella, Flowerpot, Brown, Green & Cream Flowers, 5⅛ In.		708.00
Ferella, Vase, Brown, Flared Rim, 5 In.		472.00
Ferella, Wall Pocket, Brown, Green & Cream Flowers, 6½ x 6½ In.		1062.00
Flowers, Jardiniere, Pedestal, 13 x 28 In.		900.00
Foxglove, Ewer, Blue, Footed, 10 x 5½ In.		325.00
Foxglove, Tray, Green Shade To Pink, Leaf Form, 6¾ x 7½ In.		165.00
Foxglove, Vase, Cornucopia, Green, Pink, c.1942, 6 In., Pair		225.00
Freesia, Candleholder, Green, 2 In., Pair		145.00
Freesia, Ewer, Cream Flowers, Green Stems, Blue Ground, 16 In.		342.00
Freesia, Jardiniere, Brown, Yellow, White, Handles, 5 In.		250.00
Freesia, Vase, Flared, 2 Low Handles, c.1940, 6 In.		149.00
Freesia, Vase, Handles, Marked, 7¼ x 5⅞ In.	*illus*	52.00
Fuchsia, Vase, 2 Handles, c.1940, 9 In.		118.00
Fuchsia, Vase, Green, Brown, 2 Handles, 3½ x 4¾ In.		99.00
Fujiyama, Vase, Incised & Painted Poppies, c.1906, 10⅝ In.		1416.00
Fujiyama, Vase, Twisted, Blue Poppies, Blue, Tan & Green Designs At Rim, 9 x 3 In.		2280.00
Futura, Bowl, 6-Sided, Footed, c.1928, 4 x 8 x 6 In.		350.00
Futura, Planter, Blue, Beige Interior, Mottled Green Feet, 4 x 5 In.		1265.00
Futura, Vase, 4 Bulbs On Base, 12¼ x 4½ In.	*illus*	485.00
Futura, Vase, 4-Ball Base, Brown, Beige, Milky Overglaze, 12¼ In.		767.00
Futura, Vase, Balloon, 4-Footed, Base, c.1928, 8 x 6¾ x 6½ In.		1400.00
Futura, Vase, Beehive, 8¼ In.		1121.00
Futura, Vase, Beige, Green, 10 In.		2185.00
Futura, Vase, Bulbous, Balloon, Open Legs, 8 x 6 In.		2300.00
Futura, Vase, c.1928, 7 In.		250.00
Futura, Vase, Handles, c.1928, 7 In.		250.00
Futura, Vase, Telescopic, Urn Form, 7¼ x 4⅝ In.	*illus*	190.00
Gardenia, Wall Pocket, Silver Haze, Gray, 8½ In.		266.00
Hexagon, Vase, Brown, Bulbous, 7 x 4½ In.		316.00
Hexagon, Vase, Brown, Footed, 7½ x 5½ In.		259.00
Hexagon, Wall Pocket, Brown, 8½ x 4 In.		403.00
Imperial I, Vase, Green Matte Glaze, Handles, 8 In.		118.00
Imperial II, Vase, Green & Purple Matte Glaze, 4 x 5¼ In.		230.00
Imperial II, Vase, Green Matte Glaze, Flared, Ribbed, 8 In.		316.00
Imperial II, Vase, Mottled Blue & Yellow Glaze, Ribbed, Oval, 11¼ x 6½ In.		840.00
Imperial II, Vase, Streaked Gold & Brown Glaze, 8¼ In.		224.00
Imperial II, Vase, Yellow & Purple Drip Glaze, 6 In.		325.00
Imperial II, Vase, Yellow & Purple Glaze, Ribbed, 6 x 6 In.		316.00
Iris, Console, White, Yellow, Brown Ground, Handles, 3 x 10 In.		170.00
Ixia, Vase, Pale Green To Aqua Ground, Art Deco Handles, c.1937, 6 x 4 In.		165.00
Juvenile, Bowl, Duck, Orange Band, c.1920, 6 In.		88.00
Juvenile, Candlestick, Sunbonnet Girl, c.1920, 7 In.		383.00
Juvenile, Chamber Pot, Chicks, No Lid, c.1920, 7 In.		60.00
Juvenile, Chamber Pot, Lid, Chicks, c.1920, 6 In.		147.00

Roseville, Freesia, Vase, Handles, Marked, 7¼ x 5⅞ In. $52.00

Roseville, Futura, Vase, 4 Bulbs On Base, 12¼ x 4½ In. $485.00

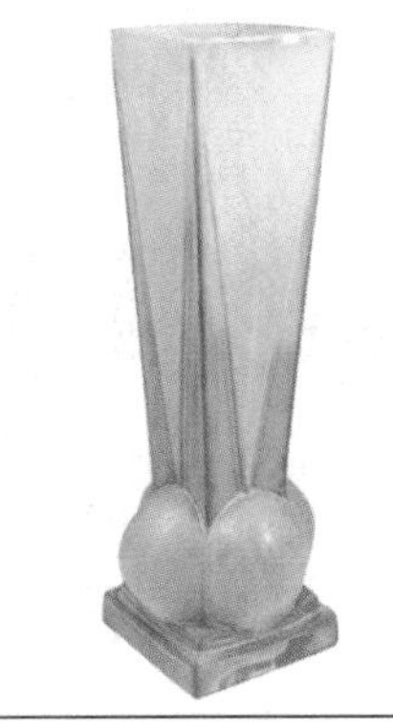

Roseville, Futura, Vase, Telescopic, Urn Form, 7¼ x 4⅝ In. $190.00

Roseville, Juvenile, Dish, Feeding, Rabbit, Rolled Edge, Baby's Plate, 6½ In. $135.00

R

Roseville, Luffa, Jardiniere, Handles, 4 x 6 In.
$93.00

Roseville, Magnolia, Ewer, Brown, Marked, 10⅛ x 7½ In.
$64.00

Roseville, Persian, Jardiniere, Leaves, Berries, Blue Rim, 4⅞ x 6½ In.
$155.00

Roseville, Pine Cone, Rose Bowl, Footed, Marked, 6½ x 7½ In.
$150.00

Juvenile, Creamer, Bear, Brown, c.1920, 3¾ In. 147.00
Juvenile, Creamer, Dog, c.1920, 3¾ In. 35.00
Juvenile, Cup & Saucer, Sunbonnet Girl, Stamped, RV, c.1920, 5 In. 118.00
Juvenile, Custard Cup, Chicks, c.1920, 2¾ In. 118.00
Juvenile, Dish, Feeding, Rabbit, Rolled Edge, Baby's Plate, 6½ In. . . . . *illus* 135.00
Juvenile, Eggcup, Bunny Head, c.1920, 2¾ In. 560.00
Juvenile, Eggcup, Chicks, c.1920, 3¾ In. 147.00
Juvenile, Eggcup, Rabbit, c.1920, 3½ In. 147.00
Juvenile, Mug, Chicks, c.1920, 3 In. 177.00
Juvenile, Mug, Dog, c.1920, 2¾ In. 236.00
Juvenile, Mug, Duck, c.1920, 3 In. 147.00
Juvenile, Mug, Rabbit, c.1920, 2¾ In. 147.00
Juvenile, Plate, Chick, Green Rim, Stamped, RV, c.1920, 7½ In. 88.00
Juvenile, Plate, Duck, Orange Rim, Stamped, RV, c.1920, 7½ In. . . . . 88.00 to 118.00
Juvenile, Plate, Rabbits, Blue Rim, Stamped, RV, c.1920, 7½ In. 177.00
Juvenile, Plate, Sunbonnet Girl, Red Rim, Stamped, RV, c.1920, 7½ In. 118.00
Juvenile, Tumbler, Rabbit, c.1920, 4 In. 265.00
Luffa, Jardiniere, Handles, 4 x 6 In. . . . . *illus* 93.00
Luffa, Wall Pocket, Brown, 8¼ In. 649.00
Magnolia, Cookie Jar, Caramel & Green, 2 Handles, 11 In. 248.00
Magnolia, Cornucopia, Blue, Footed, 1943 . . . . . 350.00
Magnolia, Ewer, Applied Flowers, Peach, Cream, Blue Ground, Handle, 16 In. 266.00
Magnolia, Ewer, Brown, Marked, 10⅛ x 7½ In. . . . . *illus* 64.00
Mara, Vase, Green & Pink Glaze, Chloron Form, Squat, 2 Handles, 5½ In. 353.00
Ming Tree, Basket, Green Ground, 8¼ In. 120.00
Mock Orange, Ewer, 7 In. 175.00
Monticello, Vase, Double Handles, Aqua To Brown, 5½ x 8¼ In. 546.00
Monticello, Vase, Green Ivory, Handles, Bulbous, Short Neck, 7 In. 377.00
Monticello, Vase, Turquoise, Cinnamon Band, Cream & Peach, 2 Handles, 5 In. 271.00
Morning Glory, Vase, Ivory, Handles, 1935, 10 In. 675.00
Morning Glory, Vase, Ivory, Squat, Handles, 1935, 4 In. 300.00
Mostique, Bowl, Yellow Ground, Green Interior, c.1916, 3 x 8½ In. 195.00
Mostique, Jardiniere, Handles, 10 In. 195.00
Mostique, Vase, 2 Handles, 8¼ In. 94.00
Mostique, Wall Pocket, Gray, Scottish Rose Design, 9⅞ In. 295.00
Open Book, Bookends 225.00
Pauleo, Lamp, Brown, Mica 10-Panel Shade, 17¼ In. 4700.00
Pauleo, Vase, 3 Sets Of Trees, Oval, Elongated Neck, Flared Rim, 15 In. 940.00
Pauleo, Vase, Black & Green Mottled Glaze, 21 x 11 In. 2040.00
Pauleo, Vase, Mottled Fuchsia, Oval, 9¼ In. 382.00
Peony, Vase, Yellow, Handles, Footed, 8 In. 200.00
Persian, Jardiniere, Leaves, Berries, Blue Rim, 4⅞ x 6½ In. . . . . *illus* 155.00
Pine Cone, Ashtray, Green, 1¼ x 4¾ x 4 In. 200.00
Pine Cone, Console, Green, 2 Handles, 7 x 16 In. 295.00
Pine Cone, Jardiniere, Green, Twig Handles, 1931, 3 x 5½ In. 229.00
Pine Cone, Pitcher, Blue, Handle, Impressed, 7½ In. 295.00
Pine Cone, Pitcher, Brown, Branch Handle Terminals, 7½ In. 232.00
Pine Cone, Rose Bowl, Footed, Marked, 6½ x 7½ In. . . . . *illus* 150.00
Pine Cone, Vase, 6 In. 195.00
Pine Cone, Vase, Brown, Urn Form, 15¼ x 11 In. 1440.00
Pine Cone, Vase, Mottled Green, 10 In. 1380.00
Pine Cone, Vase, Pillow, Brown, 8 In. 413.00
Primrose, Vase, Blue, Handles, Footed, 9 In. 275.00
Rosecroft, Vase, Hexagon, Green Matte Glaze, 5⅛ In. 266.00
Rozane, Bowl, Flowers, Swirled Body, Green Glaze, c.1905, 6¼ In. 443.00
Rozane, Bowl, Yellow & Lavender Roses, Blue Stippled Ground, 1917, 7¾ In. 186.00
Rozane, Vase, Horse Portrait, Brown Glaze, Broad Shouldered, Signed, Steele, 16 In. 4600.00
Rozane Royal, Vase, Grapes, Bulbous, 2 Curled Handles, Josephine Imlay, 11⅜ In. 1175.00
Rozane Royal, Vase, Woodbine, Lavender, White, Green, 15½ In. 411.00
Russco, Lamp Base, Mottled Orange Green Glaze, 10½ In. 480.00
Russco, Vase, Brown, Tan, Flared, Double Handles, 4 x 8½ In. 201.00
Silhouette, Vase, Dusty Rose, Swing, Pedestal, 1952, 6 In. 135.00
Silhouette, Vase, Nude Female In Panel, Brown, Orange, 7⅜ In. 325.00
Snowberry, Bowl, Blue, Beige, Leaf Form, Handle, 1940s, 12 In. 150.00
Snowberry, Vase, Fan, Pink, Marked, 6½ x 7 In. . . . . *illus* 52.00

Snowberry, Vase, Green, Marked, 7 3/8 x 3 1/2 In. . . . . *illus* 42.00
Sunflower, Vase, Egg Shape, 10 1/4 x 6 1/4 In. 1440.00
Sunflower, Wall Pocket, 7 1/4 x 6 In. 840.00
Travel Scene, Jardiniere, Cow, 8 1/2 x 9 3/4 In. 780.00
Umbrella Stand, Green Matte, Brown, Florentine Design, 2 Handles, 20 In. 575.00
Velmoss, Vase, 10 In. 1350.00
Velmoss, Vase, Green, Flared Rim, 8 In. 1528.00
Velmoss, Vase, Vertical Leaves, Green & Brown Matte Glaze, Bulbous, 7 x 10 In. 720.00
Velmoss, Vase, Vertical Leaves, Green & Yellow Matte Glaze, 6 x 5 1/2 In. 460.00
Velmoss II, Vase, Blue, Orange, 2 Handles, 6 1/8 In. 224.00
Vista, Basket, Blue & Green Matte Glaze, Foot Ring, Handle, 8 In. 1062.00
Vista, Vase, Palm Trees, Tapered, Ringed Top, Flared Foot, 15 x 6 1/2 In. 364.00
White Rose, Jardiniere, Pedestal, 8 & 16 7/8 In. 206.00
Wincraft, Console, Yellow, Teal, Brown, Footed, 1948, 4 3/4 x 15 1/4 In. 100.00
Wincraft, Vase, Dogwood, Mottled Blue & Green Ground, Double Handles, 7 x 14 In. 431.00
Windsor, Vase, Brown Squat, 2 Handles, 7 x 9 1/2 In. 780.00
Zephyr Lily, Basket, Hanging Chain, Brown Glaze, 6 In. 121.00
Zephyr Lily, Console, Brown Glaze, Handles, Marked, 15 In. 121.00
Zephyr Lily, Console, Brown Glaze, Marked, Handles, 13 3/4 In. 187.00
Zephyr Lily, Console, Round, Brown Glaze, Marked, 11 1/8 In. 121.00
Zephyr Lily, Cookie Jar, Brown Glaze, 10 1/4 In. 495.00
Zephyr Lily, Ewer, Brown Glaze, 15 1/2 In. 247.00
Zephyr Lily, Ewer, Brown Glaze, Marked, 6 In. 82.00
Zephyr Lily, Ewer, Brown Glaze, Marked, 10 1/2 In. 220.00
Zephyr Lily, Ewer, Brown Glaze, Marked, 22-6, 6 In. 88.00
Zephyr Lily, Flowerpot, Green, Marked, 5 1/8 x 6 In. . . . . *illus* 29.00
Zephyr Lily, Flowerpot, Undertray, Brown Glaze, Marked, 5 1/4 In. 232.00
Zephyr Lily, Rose Bowl, Brown Glaze, Marked, 6 1/4 In. 121.00
Zephyr Lily, Teapot, Brown Glaze, Marked, 7 In. 165.00
Zephyr Lily, Vase, Blue Ground, Yellow Flowers, Lower Handles, c.1946, 7 In. 160.00
Zephyr Lily, Vase, Brown Glaze, Handles, Marked, 8 3/8 In. 176.00
Zephyr Lily, Vase, Brown Glaze, Marked, 18 3/4 In. 660.00
Zephyr Lily, Vase, Flared, Handles, Footed, 12 3/8 In. 309.00

ROWLAND & MARSELLUS Company is part of a mark that appears on historical Staffordshire dating from the late nineteenth and early twentieth centuries. Rowland & Marsellus is the mark used by an American importing company in New York City. The company worked from 1893 to about 1937. Some of the pieces may have been made by the British Anchor Pottery Co. of Longton, England, for export to a New York firm. Many American views were made. Of special interest to collectors are the plates with rolled edges, usually blue and white.

Cup & Saucer, Blue & White 105.00
Pitcher, American Pilgrims, Plymouth Rock, Mayflower, 5 1/2 In. 132.00
Plate, Beauty Spots Of California, 6 Oval Medallion Scenes, Blue & White, 10 In. 137.00
Plate, Harrisburg, Pa., 4 Views, Blue & White, 10 In. 65.00
Plate, Portraits Of William Howard Taft & James S. Sherman, Blue, c.1900, 10 In. 100.00

ROY ROGERS was born in 1911 in Cincinnati, Ohio. In the 1930s, he made a living as a singer; in 1935, his group started work at a Los Angeles radio station. He appeared in his first movie in 1937. From 1952 to 1957, he made 101 television shows. The other stars in the show were his wife, Dale Evans, his horse, Trigger, and his dog, Bullet. Roy Rogers memorabilia is collected, including items from the Roy Rogers restaurants.

Bank, Roy Rogers On Trigger, Ceramic, Glazed, 7 1/2 In. 98.00
Bolo Tie, Display Card, Plastic, Putnam Products, 1950s, 11 In. 125.00
Box, For Kilgore Cap Gun, 1940s 455.00
Cap Pistol, Holster, c.1950 . . . . . 350.00
Clock, Alarm, Desert Sand, Roy & Trigger Go Up & Down, Box, c.1951 . . . . . 230.00
Comic Book, Dale Evans, No. 2, DC 1948 . . . . . 262.00
Comic Book, Dale Evans, No. 8, DC 1949 . . . . . 603.00
Comic Book, Dale Evans, No. 14, Mile High Pedigree, DC, 1950 . . . . . 487.00
Hat, Quick Shooter, Black Wool Felt, Silk Band, Cap Gun, Instructions, Ideal, Box 337.00
Holster Set, Guns, Horse Head Grips, Leather Studded Holster, Kilgore, Box 623.00
Lunch Box, Roy Rogers, Dale Evans, Double Bar Ranch, Metal, American Thermos 255.00
Pen, Roy, Trigger, Ballpoint, Brown Plastic, Chrome Cap & Clip, 5 1/4 In. 171.00
Pencil, Lead, Unused, 7 1/2 In. 10.00

Roseville, Snowberry, Vase, Fan, Pink, Marked, 6 1/2 x 7 In. $52.00

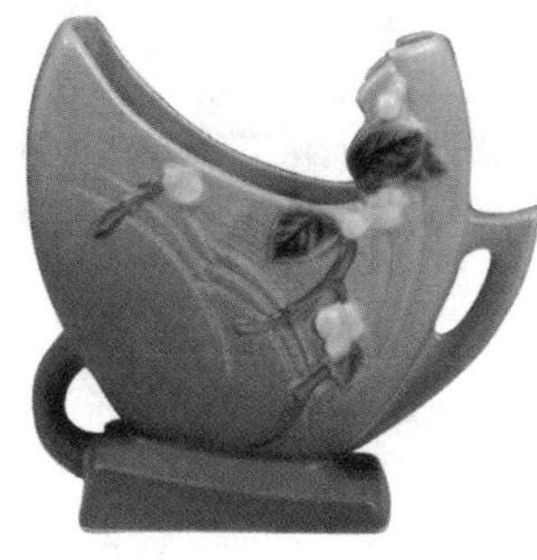

Roseville, Snowberry, Vase, Green, Marked, 7 3/8 x 3 1/2 In. $42.00

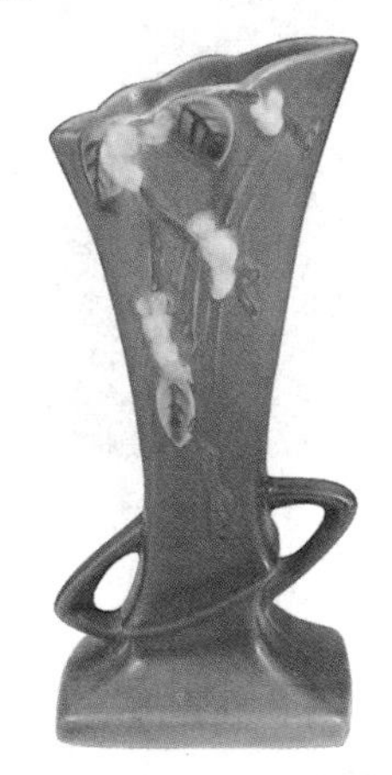

Roseville, Zephyr Lily, Flowerpot, Green, Marked, 5 1/8 x 6 In. $29.00

TIP
Never leave your house keys on your key chain when an attendant parks your car.

Spurs, Child's, Kilgore 125.00
Toy, Figure, Trigger, Chain Reins, 1963 190.00

ROYAL BAYREUTH is the name of a factory that was founded in Tettau, Bavaria, in 1794. It has continued to modern times. The marks have changed through the years. A stylized crest, the name *Royal Bayreuth*, and the word *Bavaria* appear in slightly different forms from 1870 to about 1919. Later dishes may include the words *U.S. Zone,* the year of the issue, or the word *Germany* instead of *Bavaria*. Related pieces may be found listed in the Rose Tapestry, Sand Babies, Snow Babies, and Sunbonnet Babies categories.

Ashtray, Lobster Claw, Souvenir From Cafe Dreyfus, Boston, Mass., Blue Mark, 6 ½ In. 99.00
Bowl, 2 Swans, Leaf, Blossom Mold, 10 ½ In. 150.00
Bowl, Rose Tapestry, Green, Yellow, Red, Mark, 10 ¼ In. 690.00
Creamer, 2 Polar Bears, Arctic Scene, Marked, 4 In. 305.00
Creamer, Apple, 4 ¼ In. 60.00
Creamer, Coachman, Red, 4 ¼ In. 60.00
Creamer, Pig, Red, 4 ¼ In. 75.00
Creamer, Robin, Blue Mark, Bavaria, 5 In. 595.00
Creamer, Rooster, Gray, 4 ¼ In. 175.00
Mustard, Lobster Cover, Spoon, Blue Mark, 4 ¼ In. 176.00
Pitcher, Elk, Blue Mark, Bavaria, 7 ¼ In. *illus* 795.00
Pitcher, Monkey, Green, 5 In. *illus* 265.00
Pitcher, Polar Bear, Pinched Waist, Light Blue Ground, 7 ½ In. 1500.00
Pitcher, Yellow, Apple, Lemonade, Stamped, 7 ½ x 10 In. *illus* 590.00
Relish, Holly, Green, Red Berries, Leaf Shape, Marked, 8 ¼ In. 187.00
Sugar, Cover, Lobster, Blue Mark, 3 ¾ In. 88.00
Sugar, Rooster, Black, Brown, Red Crest, 5 ½ In. 250.00
Sugar & Creamer, Cottage, Waterfall, Tapestry Pinch Spout, 5 In. 70.00
Sugar & Creamer, Lobster, Marked *illus* 138.00
Tray, Pen, Hunter & Dog, Green, c.1900, 8 ½ In. 106.00
Vase, Brown Bear, Teardrop Shape, 3 ½ In. 400.00
Vase, Desert Nomad, Baluster, Blue Mark, Signed, c.1900, 5 In. 48.00
Vase, Flowers, Ivory, Cutout Rim, Footed, Signed, 7 In. 245.00
Vase, Lovebirds, Tricornered Top, 5 ½ In. 80.00
Vase, Woman Picking Wheat, 3 Chickens, 6 ¾ In. *illus* 125.00

ROYAL BONN is the nineteenth- and twentieth-century trade name used by Franz Anton Mehlem, who had a pottery in Bonn, Germany, from 1836 to 1931. Porcelain and earthenware were made. The factory was purchased by Villeroy & Boch in 1921 and closed in 1931. Many marks were used, most including the name *Bonn*, the initials *FM*, and a crown.

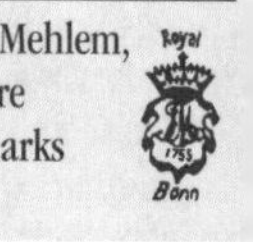

Clock, Ansonia, Bouquet, White Porcelain Dial, Germany, 16 ⅝ In. *illus* 1100.00
Clock, Ansonia, China, Painted, c.1900, 13 In. 358.00
Clock, Ansonia, La Chartres, c.1905, 11 In. 550.00
Clock, Ansonia, La Vendee, Painted Flowers, 8-Day, c.1904, 15 In. 468.00
Clock, Ansonia, Porcelain, Lavender 1895.00
Vase, Flowers, Ivory Matte Ground, Pear Shape, Flower-Form Neck, c.1920, 21 In. 207.00
Vase, Poppies, Handles, Franz Ant. Mehlem, 8 x 10 ¾ In. 86.00
Vase, Woman, Pastoral Scene, Flower Border, 2-Sided, 10 ⅜ In. 177.00

ROYAL COPENHAGEN porcelain and pottery have been made in Denmark since 1775. The Christmas plate series started in 1908. The figurines with pale blue and gray glazes have remained popular in this century and are still being made. Many other old and new style porcelains are made today.

Bowl, Salad, Flora Danica, Flowers, White Ground, 9 ⅝ In. 1416.00
Box, Butterfly Cover, Purple, Pink, Marked, 3 ½ x 5 x 2 ¼ In. 60.00
Coffeepot, Blue Flowers, White Ground, 10 In. 150.00
Dish, Chrysanthemum, White, c.1930, 9 In. 60.00
Dish, Fish, Embossed, Faience, Square, Nils Thorsson, 6 ¾ In. 135.00
Dish, Modern Art, Blue, Cream, Brown, Pottery, 1 ½ x 10 In. 70.00
Figurine, Birds, 5 x 4 In. 59.00
Figurine, Boy, With Umbrella, c.1956, 6 ½ In. 85.00 to 88.00
Figurine, Cat, Curled In Ball, Marked, 4 ½ In. *illus* 61.00
Figurine, Elephant, Mottled Brown, Porcelain, Kyhn, 3 ¾ x 5 In. 60.00
Figurine, Ermine, On Log, Hand Painted, Marked, Dahl Jensen, 5 In. *illus* 161.00
Figurine, Reindeer, White, Wood Stand, 1921, 12 x 17 In. 450.00

Royal Bayreuth, Pitcher, Elk, Blue Mark, Bavaria, 7 ¼ In. $795.00

Royal Bayreuth, Pitcher, Monkey, Green, 5 In. $265.00

Royal Bayreuth, Pitcher, Yellow, Apple, Lemonade, Stamped, 7 ½ x 10 In. $590.00

Stock Certificates

Old stock certificates can be worth money, even if the company seems to have disappeared. Try to trace the stocks through the secretary of state in the state where the stock was issued. Check in the unclaimed property division of the state to see if stock owners may have money coming. There are also companies that will do this type of search for a fee.

Royal Bayreuth, Sugar & Creamer, Lobster, Marked
$138.00

Royal Bayreuth, Vase, Woman Picking Wheat, 3 Chickens, 6 ¾ In.
$125.00

Royal Bonn, Clock, Ansonia, Bouquet,
White Porcelain Dial, Germany, 16 ⅝ In.
$1100.00

Royal Copenhagen, Figurine, Cat, Curled In Ball, Marked, 4 ½ In.
$61.00

Royal Copenhagen, Figurine, Ermine, On Log, Hand Painted,
Marked, Dahl Jensen, 5 In.
$161.00

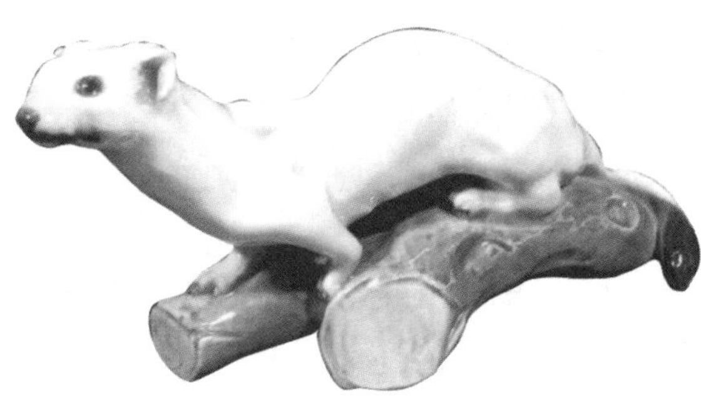

Royal Copenhagen, Group, Sonderjylland,
2 Women, Man, Marked, 13 In.
$3800.00

Royal Copenhagen, Plate, Christmas, 1966, Blackbird At Christmas Time, 7 In.
$55.00

Royal Copenhagen, Plate, Christmas, 1971, Hare In Winter, 7 In.
$32.00

Royal Copley, Planter, Cat With Yarn, 1950s, 8 In.
$40.00

Royal Copley, Planter, Dog At Mailbox, 8 x 8 ¼ In.
$34.00

Group, Sonderjylland, 2 Women, Man, Marked, 13 In. *illus* 3800.00
Plate, Blue Fluted, Half Lace, 8 ¾ In. 47.00 to 59.00
Plate, Christmas, 1913, Spire Of Frederik's Church, Copenhagen, 7 In. 200.00
Plate, Christmas, 1914, Sparrow's In Tree At Church, 7 In. 200.00
Plate, Christmas, 1922, 3 Singing Angels, 7 In. 80.00
Plate, Christmas, 1926, View Of Christianshavns Canal, Copenhagen, 7 In. 85.00
Plate, Christmas, 1927, Ship's Boy At Tiller On Christmas Night, 7 In. 135.00
Plate, Christmas, 1936, Roskilde Cathedral, 7 In. 250.00
Plate, Christmas, 1947, Good Shepherd, 7 In. 600.00
Plate, Christmas, 1950, Boeslunde Church, Zealand, 7 In. 350.00
Plate, Christmas, 1962, Little Mermaid At Wintertime, 7 In. 190.00
Plate, Christmas, 1965, Little Skaters, 7 In. 60.00
Plate, Christmas, 1966, Blackbird At Christmas Time, 7 In. *illus* 55.00
Plate, Christmas, 1968, Last Umiak, 7 In. 46.00
Plate, Christmas, 1969, Old Farmyard, 7 In. 30.00
Plate, Christmas, 1971, Hare In Winter, 7 In. *illus* 32.00
Plate, Christmas, 1972, In The Desert, 7 In. 33.00
Plate, Christmas, 1973, Going Home For Christmas, 7 In. 20.00
Plate, Christmas, 1974, Winter Twilight, 7 In. 52.00
Plate, Christmas, 1975, Queen's Christmas Residence, 7 In. 32.00
Plate, Christmas, 1976, Viback Water Mill, 7 In. 32.00
Plate, Christmas, 1977, Immervad Bridge, 7 In. 32.00
Plate, Christmas, 1978, Greenland Scenery, 7 In. 37.00
Plate, Christmas, 1984, Jingle Bells, 7 In. 47.00
Plate, Christmas, 1988, Christmas Eve In Copenhagen, 7 In. 70.00
Plate, Mother's Day, 1971, American Mother, 6 In. 11.00
Plate, Mother's Day, 1972, Mother & 5 Children, 6 In. 65.00
Plate, Mother's Day, 1973, Danish Mother, 6 In. 35.00
Plate, Mother's Day, 1974, Eskimo Dogs, 6 In. 18.00
Plate, Mother's Day, 1982, Birds, 6 In. 25.00
Plate, Troubadour & Maiden, Arrows Around Rim, Porcelain, 10 x 10 ¼ In. 75.00 to 80.00
Platter, Flora Danica, Flowers, Pierced Edge, 13 In. 1652.00
Platter, Flora Danica, Flowers, Round, 15 ¼ In. 2360.00
Platter, Flora Danica, Oval, Marked, 15 ¾ In. 2500.00
Sandwich Server, Flora Danica, Sawtooth Border, Gilt, Handle, Marked, 1 x 8 ½ In. 840.00
Sculpture, Girl With Braids, Embraced By Merman In Sea, 22 ¼ In. 705.00
Vase, Bronze Cover, Ball Finial, Green, Brown Blotches, Wave Mark, 1935, 8 In. 3500.00
Vase, Brown, Gray Flambe Glaze, Cone Shape, Tapered, Axel Salto, 10 ½ x 5 In. 7200.00
Vase, Budding, Gray, Olive Crystalline Glaze, Stoneware, 5 ¾ x 6 ½ In. 6600.00
Vase, Budding, Gray, Olive Matte Glaze, Stoneware, A. Salto, 7 x 5 ½ In. 3600.00
Vase, Church, Bulbous, Porcelain, c.1950, 9 x 7 In. 125.00
Vase, Colonial Man, Woman, Rose, Green Ivy, Cupids, 11 ¼ In., Pair 288.00
Vase, Ship, Water, Buildings, Signed, PO, 6 ½ In. 55.00
Vase, Tree, Embossed, Black, Mahogany Glaze, Round, A. Salto, 7 ¾ x 7 ¾ In. 3600.00
Vase, White Daffodil, Leaves, Hand Painted, Porcelain, c.1950, 12 ½ In. 175.00
Wine Cooler, Flora Danica, Applied Flowers, Gilt Handles, Marked, 6 ½ x 10 ¾ In. 3000.00

ROYAL COPLEY china was made by the Spaulding China Company of Sebring, Ohio, from 1939 to 1960. The figural planters and the small figurines, especially those with Art Deco designs, are of great collector interest.

Bank, Pig, Pink, Blue, Gold Trim, 4 ⅝ In. 32.00
Figurine, Cat, Black & White Pink Bow, 8 In. 35.00
Figurine, Cockatoo, On Stump, Pink, 7 In., Pair 45.00
Figurine, Hen, 6 In. 85.00
Figurine, Mallard Duckling, 5 ½ In. 15.00
Figurine, Parakeets, Teal, Pink, Tan, 7 ¼ In. 38.00
Figurine, Pheasant, 6 ½ In. 16.00
Figurine, Rooster, Yellow, Green, Tan, Red, Black, 7 In. 30.00
Pitcher, Bouquet, Pink, Yellow, Blue, 6 x 4 ½ In. 25.00
Pitcher, Pharaoh, Headdress, c.1925, 6 In. 375.00
Pitcher, Roses, Marked, 6 In. 20.00
Planter, Balinese Girl, Blackamoor, 1950s, 8 ¼ x 4 In. 45.00
Planter, Cat, Brown, 8 In. 98.00
Planter, Cat With Yarn, 1950s, 8 In. *illus* 40.00
Planter, Cocker Spaniel, Tan, Brown, 8 In. 32.00

Planter, Deer & Fawn, Marked, 9 ½ x 5 ½ In. 30.00
Planter, Dog, Foot Raised, 7 ½ In. 35.00
Planter, Dog At Mailbox, 8 x 8 ¼ In. *illus* 34.00
Planter, Elf & Stump, 6 x 5 ¾ In. 40.00
Planter, Girl, Seated, Head Resting On Arms, Pink Hat, Blue Jeans 25.00
Planter, Oriental Girl, 1942-57, 6 In. 25.00
Planter, Siamese Cat, 6 ¼ In. 25.00
Planter, Springer Spaniel, Marked, 1950s, 5 ½ In. 27.00
Vase, Bud, Parrot, c.1940-50, 5 x 3 ¾ In. *illus* 17.00
Vase, Deer & Fawn, Beige Footed, 1948-57, 6 ½ In. 40.00
Vase, Ivy, Footed, 7 ⅛ In. 9.00
Wall Pocket, Apple, Red & Yellow, Green Leaves, 6 x 5 ¾ In. 18.00
Wall Pocket, Cocker Spaniel, 5 In. 38.00
Wall Pocket, Farmer Boy Going Fishing, 6 ½ In. 38.00
Wall Pocket, Flamingos, 6 ⅞ x 4 ⅞ In., Pair 133.00
Wall Pocket, Girl Leaning On Fence Post, 6 ¼ In. *illus* 21.00
Wall Pocket, Oriental Girl, Straw Hat, Ruby Kimono, 7 ¼ In. 65.00
Wall Pocket, Pigtail, Girl, Marked, 6 ¾ x 4 ½ In. 9.00 to 28.00
Wall Pocket, Rooster, 1948-57, 6 ½ In. 38.00

ROYAL CROWN DERBY Company, Ltd., was established in England in 1890. There is a complex family tree that includes the Derby, Crown Derby, and Royal Crown Derby porcelains. The Royal Crown Derby mark includes the name and a crown. The words *Made in England* were used after 1921. The company is now a part of Royal Doulton Tableware Ltd.

Candlestick, Red Aves, Orange Birds, Flowers, Leaves, Gilt, 10 ½ In., Pair 285.00
Cup & Saucer, Imari 59.00
Dessert Tray, Imari Decoration, 10 ⅞ x 9 ½ In. 170.00
Dish, Blue Starburst, Gold Trim, c.1850, 7 ½ In. 234.00
Dish, White Ground, Floral Medallions & Band, c.1850, 7 ½ In. 234.00
Figurine, Savannah Leopard, On Rock, Box, Certificate, 1999, 5 ½ x 6 ⅝ In. 750.00
Figurine, Swan, White, Gray, Sitting On Base, Box, 1996-99, 3 ¾ x 5 ⅜ In. 156.00
Paperweight, Bakewell Duck, Green Head, Box, Certificate 1500.00
Paperweight, Blue Tit With Chicks, 4 x 5 ¾ x 3 ½ In. 82.00
Paperweight, Dragon Of Happiness, Stand, Box, Certificate, 1999, 3 ¾ In. 260.00
Paperweight, Fawn, Box, 1996, 5 ½ In. 384.00
Paperweight, Fox, Blue, Box 240.00
Paperweight, Honey Bear, Box, 1994, 4 ⅛ In. 132.00
Paperweight, Imperial Panda, Box, Certificate, 1998 369.00
Paperweight, Madagascan Tortoise, Box, Certificate, 2000 234.00
Paperweight, Mole, 1995, 2 In. 480.00
Paperweight, Mulberry Hall Frog, Box, 1998 780.00
Paperweight, Pheasant, Red, Box, 1983-98, 3 ½ In. 96.00
Paperweight, Queensland Koala, Box, 2001 86.00
Paperweight, Queensland Koala, Box, Certificate, 2001 432.00
Paperweight, Savannah Leopard, Box, Certificate, 1999, 5 ⅛ x 6 ⅝ In. 900.00
Paperweight, Seahorse, Box, 1991-94, 3 ⅞ In. 480.00
Paperweight, Unicorn, White, Laying On Grass, Box, 1999, 5 ⅛ In. 510.00
Paperweight, Woodland Pheasant, 1999 108.00
Plate, Dessert, Red Exotic Birds, 8 ¼ In., 12 Piece 406.00
Platter, Imari Decoration, Oval, 15 x 12 In. 510.00
Salt & Pepper, Flowers, 3 ¾ x 2 ½ In. 575.00
Spoon, Porcelain Handle, 5 ¾ In., 6 Piece 126.00
Tureen, Soup, Platter, c.1920, 15 x 11 x 10 In. 825.00

ROYAL DOULTON is the name used on Doulton and Company pottery made from 1902 to the present. Doulton and Company of England was founded in 1853. Pieces made before 1902 are listed in this book under Doulton. Royal Doulton collectors search for the out-of-production figurines, character jugs, vases, and series wares. Some vases and animal figurines were made with a special red glaze called flambe. Sung and Chang glazed pieces are rare. The multicolored glaze is very thick and looks as if it were dropped on the clay. Royal Doulton was acquired by the Waterford Wedgwood Group in 2005.

Animal, Cat, Siamese, Seated, DA 127, 1990-94, 9 In. 41.00
Animal, Dog, Alsatian Ch. Benign Of Picardy, HN 1116, 6 In. 59.00
Animal, Dog, Black Labrador, Box, DA 13, 2004-Present 35.00
Animal, Dog, Bulldog, Standing, HN 1044, 3 ¼ In. 156.00

Royal Copley, Vase, Bud, Parrot, c.1940-50, 5 x 3 ¾ In.
$17.00

Royal Copley, Wall Pocket, Girl Leaning On Fence Post, 6 ¼ In.
$21.00

Royal Doulton, Animal, Dog, Cocker Spaniel, Lying In Basket, HN 2585, 1941-85, 2 x 3 ¾ In.
$25.00

Royal Doulton, Bowl, Lotus Blossom, Cracked Chang, Glaze, Signed, Noke, Nixon, 3 x 6 ¾ In.
$1000.00

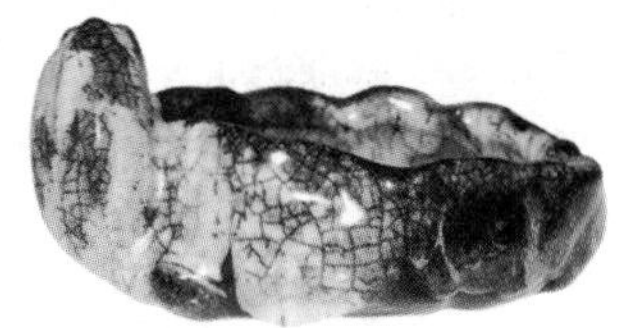

R

Royal Doulton, Character Jug, Falconer, D 6533, 1960-91, Large $69.00

Royal Doulton, Character Jug, Neptune, D 6548, 1960-73, Large $80.00

Character Jugs

Royal Doulton started making character jugs in 1934. Early jugs were three-dimensional portraits of famous English characters of history, literature, and song. By the 1980s, movie, television, and political figures from many countries were included. The jugs had figural handles: Long John Silver's handle was a parrot, Clark Gable's was a movie camera. A few rarities like the Granny with no teeth (the common jug has one tooth) or the red-headed Clown have sold for thousands of dollars each.

R

Animal, Dog, Cocker Spaniel With Pheasant, HN 1001, 6 ½ In. . . . 260.00
Animal, Dog, English Foxhound, HN 1026, 5 In. . . . 432.00
Animal, Dog, Fox Terrier, Seated, Marble Calendar Base, K 8, 1931-77, 2 ½ In. . . . 168.00
Animal, Dog, Pointer, HN 2624, 5 ½ x 11 ½ In. . . . 336.00
Animal, Dog, Running With Ball, HN 1097, 2 In. . . . 47.00
Animal, Dog, Cocker Spaniel, Lying In Basket, HN 2585, 1941-85, 2 x 3 ¾ In. . . . *illus* 25.00
Animal, Dog, English Setter, With Pheasant, HN 2529, 1939-85, 10 ½ In. . . . 292.00
Animal, Duck, Mallard Drake, Flambe, HN 2547, 1959-62, 5 ½ In. . . . 110.00
Animal, Elephant, Trunk In Salute, Flambe, HN 489. . . . 460.00
Animal, Fox, Seated, Flambe, HN 147B, 1912-96, 4 ½ In. . . . 144.00
Animal, Hare, Crouching, Flambe, HN 2592, 1941-68, 2 ¾ In. . . . 106.00
Animal, Horse, Ideal Pony For Nervous Child, Thelwell, NT 10, Box, 2003, 5 ¼ In. . . . 83.00
Animal, Horse, Shetland Pony, Gloss Gray, DA 185, 5 ¼ In. . . . 59.00
Animal, Lamb, Matte Ivory, HN 2505, 1 ½ In. . . . 156.00
Animal, Merely A Minor, Grassy Base, HN 2571, 6 In. . . . 312.00
Animal, Pelican, Beak Down, HN 295, 6 ¼ In. . . . 600.00
Animal, Polar Bear, Seated, HN 121, 3 ¾ In. . . . 450.00
Bookends, Holmes & Watson . . . 300.00
Bowl, Flow Blue, Lily, Stylized Flowers, Leaves, Art Nouveau, 5 x 16 In. . . . 295.00
Bowl, Flowers, Enameled Overlay, Blue Ground, Green Mark, c.1910, 5 x 16 In. . . . 82.00
Bowl, Golfers Series Ware, Footed, D 3395, 8 In. . . . 390.00
Bowl, Lotus Blossom, Cracked Chang, Glaze, Signed, Noke, Nixon, 3 x 6 ¾ In. . . . *illus* 1000.00
Box, Roses, Round, Cover, Finial, Hand Painted, 4 In. . . . 330.00
Bunnykins, Teapot, DB 6010, 1939-45, 4 ¾ In. . . . 1320.00

Royal Doulton Character Jugs depict the head and shoulders of the subject. They are made in four sizes: large, 5¼ to 7 inches; small, 3¼ to 4 inches; miniature, 2¼ to 2½ inches; and tiny, 1¼ inches. Toby jugs portray a seated, full figure.

Character Jug, Aramis, D 6441, 1956-91, Large . . . 59.00
Character Jug, Aramis, D 6829, 1988, Large . . . 216.00
Character Jug, 'Arry, D 6235, 1947-60, Small . . . 80.00
Character Jug, Athos, D 6827, 1988, Large . . . 168.00
Character Jug, Beefeater, D 6251, 1947-53, Miniature . . . 80.00
Character Jug, Bootmaker, D 6572, 1963-83, Large . . . 168.00
Character Jug, Captain Cuttle, D 5842, 1938-48. . . . 132.00
Character Jug, Dick Turpin, D 5485, 1935-60, Large . . . 83.00
Character Jug, Dick Whittington, D 6375, 1953-60, Large . . . 216.00 to 264.00
Character Jug, Falconer, D 6533, 1960-91, Large . . . *illus* 69.00
Character Jug, Field Marshal Smuts, D 6198, 1946-48, Large . . . 1320.00
Character Jug, Gondolier, D 6595, 1964-69, Miniature . . . 96.00
Character Jug, Gulliver, D 6566, 1962-67, Miniature . . . 192.00
Character Jug, Henry Cooper, D 7050, 1996, Small . . . 159.00
Character Jug, Henry V, D 6671, 1982-84, Large . . . 510.00
Character Jug, Henry VIII, D 6648, 1979-91, Miniature . . . 135.00
Character Jug, Huckleberry Finn, D 7177, 2002, Small . . . 84.00
Character Jug, Izaak Walton, D 6404, 1953-82, Large . . . 83.00
Character Jug, Jarge, D 6288, 1950-60, Large . . . 132.00
Character Jug, Johann Strauss II, D 7097, 1998-2001, Large . . . 103.00
Character Jug, John Barleycorn, D 5327, 1939-60, Large . . . 1260.00
Character Jug, John Barleycorn, D 6041, 1939-60, Miniature . . . 76.00
Character Jug, John Doulton, D 6656, 1980-82, Small . . . 36.00
Character Jug, M. Quaker, D 6738, 1985, Large . . . 234.00
Character Jug, Mad Hatter, D 6606, 1965-83, Miniature . . . 85.00
Character Jug, Marley's Ghost, D 7142, 1999, Large . . . 1260.00
Character Jug, Mr. Micawber, D 7040, 1996, Large . . . 49.00
Character Jug, Mr. Pickwick, D 5839, 1938-48 . . . 142.00
Character Jug, Neptune, D 6548, 1960-73, Large . . . *illus* 80.00
Character Jug, Old Charley, D 6046, 1939-83, Miniature . . . 48.00
Character Jug, Old Salt, D 6551, 1961-2001, Large . . . 58.00
Character Jug, Pearly King, D 6760, 1987-91, Large . . . 106.00
Character Jug, Porthos, D 6828, 1988, Large . . . 120.00
Character Jug, Punch & Judy Man, D 6596, 1964-69, Miniature . . . 288.00
Character Jug, Queen Mary I, D 7188, 2004, Large . . . 106.00
Character Jug, Robin Hood, D 6534, 1960-92, Small . . . 58.00
Character Jug, Santa Claus, D 6668, 1981, Large . . . 77.00
Character Jug, Santa Claus, D 6706, 1984-91, Miniature . . . 59.00

Character Jug, Santa With Elf, D 7243, Small. 98.00
Character Jug, Santa With Snowman, D 7238, 2004, Large. 98.00
Character Jug, Sir Henry Doulton, Two Handles, D 7054, 1997, Large 216.00
Character Jug, Tam O'Shanter, D 6632, 1973-80, Large. 125.00
Character Jug, The Viking, D 6502, 1959-75, Small. 71.00
Character Jug, The Yachtsman, D 6820, 1988-91, Large 108.00
Character Jug, Toby Philpotts, D 6043, 1939-69, Miniature. 48.00
Character Jug, Tony Weller, D 5531, 1936-42, Extra Large 164.00
Character Jug, Walrus & Carpenter, D 6600, 1965-80, Large. 75.00
Character Jug, Wilbur Wright, D 7179, 2003, Large 264.00
Display, Toilet Bowl, White, Early 1900s, 5 x 4 x 3 ½ In. 170.00
Figurine, A' Courting, HN 2004, 1947-53, 7 ¼ In. 146.00
Figurine, A Winters Morn, HN 4622, 2004, 8 ¾ In.. . . . . 94.00
Figurine, Adrienne, HN 2304, 1964-91, 7 ½ In. 106.00
Figurine, Afternoon Tea, HN 1747, 1935-82, 5 ¾ In. 322.00
Figurine, An Old King, HN 2134, 1954-92, 10 ¾ In.. . . . . 205.00
Figurine, Autumn, HN 2087, 1952-59, 7 ¼ In.. . . . . 94.00
Figurine, Autumn Breezes, HN 1911, 1939-76, 7 ½ In.. . . . . 70.00 to 94.00
Figurine, Autumn Breezes, HN 1934, 1940, 7 ½ In.. . . . . 59.00
Figurine, Autumn Breezes, HN 3736, 1997-98, 7 ½ In. 65.00
Figurine, Balloon Clown, HN 2894, 1986-92, 9 ¼ In. 312.00
Figurine, Balloon Man, HN 1954, 1940-Present, 7 ¼ In. . . . . 164.00 to 234.00
Figurine, Balloon Seller, HN 583, 1923-49, 9 In.. . . . . 354.00
Figurine, Balloons, HN 3187, 1998, 9 ¼ In.. . . . . 180.00
Figurine, Bedtime Story, HN 2059, 1950-96, 4 ¾ In.. . . . . 146.00 to 158.00
Figurine, Belle, HN 3703, 1996, 9 In.. . . . . 88.00
Figurine, Biddy Penny Farthing, HN 1843, 1938-Present, 9 In. 160.00
Figurine, Blossom, Mother, HN 1667, 1934-49, 6 ¾ In.. . . . . 840.00
Figurine, Bon Appetit, Matte, HN 2444, 1972-76, 6 In. 94.00
Figurine, Bonnie Lassie, HN 1626, 1934-53, 5 ¼ In. 432.00
Figurine, Bride, HN 1588, 1933-38, 8 ¾ In. 336.00
Figurine, Bride, HN 1600, 1933-49, 8 ¾ In. 760.00
Figurine, Bride, HN 1762, 1936-49, 8 ¾ In. 761.00
Figurine, Bunnykins, Arabian Nights, Box, DB 315. . . . . 59.00
Figurine, Bunnykins, Bath Night, DB 241, 2001 . . . . 59.00
Figurine, Bunnykins, Betsy Ross, DB 313, 2004. . . . . 48.00
Figurine, Bunnykins, Boy Skater, DB 187, 1998, 4 ¼ In.. . . . . 36.00
Figurine, Bunnykins, Cavalier, DB 179, 1998, 4 ½ In.. . . . . 60.00
Figurine, Bunnykins, Clarinet, Box, DB 184, 1999, 5 In.. . . . . 59.00
Figurine, Bunnykins, Cowboy, Box, DB 201, 4 ½ In. 59.00
Figurine, Bunnykins, Daisie Spring Time, DB 7, 1972-83, 3 ½ In. 84.00
Figurine, Bunnykins, Day Trip, Box, DB 260, 3 ½ In.. . . . . 59.00
Figurine, Bunnykins, Digger, DB 248, 2001, 5 ½ In. 108.00
Figurine, Bunnykins, Drummer, Box, DB 250, 2002 . . . . 59.00
Figurine, Bunnykins, England Athlete, DB 216, 2000, 5 ½ In. 60.00
Figurine, Bunnykins, Guardsman, DB 127, 1992, 4 ½ In. . . . . 235.00 to 240.00
Figurine, Bunnykins, Ice Cream, DB 82, 1990-93, 4 ½ In. . . . . *illus* 47.00
Figurine, Bunnykins, Ice Hockey, DB 282, 2003, 4 ¾ In. . . . . *illus* 59.00
Figurine, Bunnykins, Joker, Box, DB 171, 1997, 5 In. 71.00
Figurine, Bunnykins, Juggler, DB 164, 1996, 4 ½ In.. . . . . 96.00
Figurine, Bunnykins, Little Bo-Peep, DB 220, 2003, 4 ½ In. 36.00
Figurine, Bunnykins, Master Potter, DB 131, 1992-93, 3 ¾ In.. . . . . 132.00
Figurine, Bunnykins, Merry Christmas Tableau, DB 194, 1999, 5 ½ x 7 ¼ In.. . . . . 200.00
Figurine, Bunnykins, Mexican, Box, DB 316, 2004, 4 ½ In. 59.00
Figurine, Bunnykins, Milkman, DB 125, 1992, 4 1/2 In. . . . . 288.00 to 384.00
Figurine, Bunnykins, Minstrel, DB 211, 2000, 4 ½ In.. . . . . 48.00
Figurine, Bunnykins, Mr. Bunnybeat Strumming, DB 16, 1982-88, 4 ½ In.. . . . . 65.00
Figurine, Bunnykins, Mr. Bunnykins, Autumn Days, DB 5, 1972-82, 4 In.. . . . . 72.00
Figurine, Bunnykins, Old Balloon Seller, Box, DB 217, 2000, 4 In.. . . . . 156.00
Figurine, Bunnykins, Parisian, Box, DB 317, 4 ½ In.. . . . . 59.00
Figurine, Bunnykins, Ringmaster, Box, DB 165. . . . . 123.00
Figurine, Bunnykins, Rise & Shine, DB 11, 1973-88, 3 ¾ In. 60.00
Figurine, Bunnykins, Saxophone, Box, DB 186, 1999, 5 In. 59.00
Figurine, Bunnykins, Scotsman, DB 180, 1998, 5 In. 65.00
Figurine, Bunnykins, Susan As Queen Of The May, DB 83, 1990-91, 4 In.. . . . . 71.00
Figurine, Bunnykins, Sydney, DB 195, 1999, 5 In.. . . . . 83.00

Royal Doulton, Figurine, Bunnykins, Ice Cream, DB 82, 1990-93, 4 ½ In. $47.00

Royal Doulton, Figurine, Bunnykins, Ice Hockey, DB 282, 2003, 4 ¾ In. $59.00

Royal Doulton, Figurine, Elyse, HN 2474, 1986-99, 5 ¾ In. $106.00

Royal Doulton, Figurine, Janet, HN 1916, 1939-49, 5 ¼ In. $50.00

Royal Doulton Marks
Royal Doulton collectors can easily identify character jugs and figurines made before 1984. That year the words "hand made" and "hand decorated" were added above the lion and crown mark, in the shape of an arch.

Royal Doulton, Figurine, Jester, HN 2016, 1949, 10 In.
$95.00

Royal Doulton, Figurine, Master, HN 2325, 1967-92, 6 ¼ In.
$88.00

Figurine, Bunnykins, Town Crier, Box, DB 259, 2002, 4 ½ In. 71.00
Figurine, Bunnykins, Umpire, Box, DB 360, 1997, 5 In. 180.00
Figurine, Bunnykins, Welsh Lady, Box, DB 172, 1997, 5 In. 71.00
Figurine, Bunnykins, Wicket Keeper, DB 150, 1995, 3 ½ In. 103.00
Figurine, Bunnykins, Wizard, DB 168, 1997, 5 In. 142.00
Figurine, Bunny's Bedtime, HN 3370, 1991, 6 In. 108.00
Figurine, Butterfly, HN 720, 1925-40, 6 ½ In. 2520.00
Figurine, Calumet, HN 2068, 1950-53, 6 ¼ In. 401.00
Figurine, Captain Hook, HN 3636, 1993-96, 9 ¼ In. 235.00
Figurine, Caroline, HN 4785, 2005, 8 ½ In. 94.00
Figurine, Carpet Seller, HN 1464, 1929, 9 ¼ In. 176.00
Figurine, Catherine Of Aragon, HN 3233, 1990, 6 ½ In. 261.00
Figurine, Catherine Parr, HN 3450, 1992, 6 ¼ In. 392.00
Figurine, Charley's Aunt, HN 35, 1913-36, 7 In. 432.00
Figurine, Chloe, M 9, 1932-45, 2 ¾ In. 100.00
Figurine, Christopher Columbus, HN 3392, 1992, 12 In. 510.00 to 614.00
Figurine, Clock Maker, HN 2279, 1961-75, 7 In. 110.00
Figurine, Clown, HN 2890, 1979-88, 9 In. 216.00
Figurine, Cobbler, Box, HN 1706, 1935-69, 8 ¼ In. 198.00
Figurine, Country Maid, HN 3163, 1988-91, 8 ¼ In. 235.00
Figurine, Cowboy, Snowman, DS 6, 1986-92, 5 In. 142.00
Figurine, Craftsman, HN 2284, 1991-65, 6 In. 288.00
Figurine, Cruella De Ville, HN 3839, 1997, 8 In. 130.00
Figurine, Cyrano De Bergerac, HN 3751, 1995-96, 8 ½ In. 130.00
Figurine, Darling, HN 1372, 1930-38, 7 ¾ In. 1260.00
Figurine, D'Artagnan, HN 3638, 1993-96, 9 In. 235.00
Figurine, Deborah, Box, HN 3644, 1995, 7 ½ In. 59.00 to 75.00
Figurine, Doctor, HN 4286, 2001-02, 9 ¼ In. 112.00
Figurine, Easter Parade, HN 4628, 2005, 9 In. 83.00
Figurine, Eeyore Nose To The Ground, Box, WP 25, 2000, Large 84.00
Figurine, Elaine, HN 2791, 1980-2000, 7 ½ In. 83.00
Figurine, Elyse, HN 2474, 1986-99, 5 ¾ In. *illus* 106.00
Figurine, Fairy, HN 1396, 1930-38, 2 ½ In. 600.00
Figurine, Farmer's Boy, HN 2520, 1938-60, 8 ½ In. 2040.00 to 2160.00
Figurine, Favourite, HN 2249, 1960-90, 7 ¾ In. 145.00
Figurine, Female Study, HN 606, 1924-36, 5 In. 192.00
Figurine, Fleurette, HN 1587, 1933-49, 6 ½ In. 336.00
Figurine, Foaming Quart, HN 2162, 1955-92, 6 In. 142.00
Figurine, Fortune Teller, HN 2159, 1955-67, 6 ½ In. 390.00
Figurine, Fragrance, HN 2334, 1966-95, 7 ¼ In. 50.00
Figurine, Geisha, Flambe, HN 3229, 1989, 9 ½ In. 205.00
Figurine, Genie, HN 2989, 1983-90, 9 ¾ In. 94.00 to 204.00
Figurine, Geraldine, HN 2348, 1972-76, 7 ¼ In. 71.00
Figurine, Going Sledding, Christopher, Pooh, Base, Box, WP 34. 72.00
Figurine, Granny's Heritage, HN 1874, 1938-49, 7 In. 585.00
Figurine, Happy Anniversary, HN 3097, 1987-93, 6 ½ In. 120.00
Figurine, Happy Birthday, HN 4215, 2000, 8 ¾ In. 70.00
Figurine, Harp, HN 2482, 1973, 8 ¾ In. 450.00
Figurine, Henry VIII, HN 3458, 1994, 9 ¼ In. 449.00
Figurine, Hilary, HN 2335, 1967-81, 7 ¼ In. 88.00
Figurine, His Master's Voice, Nipper, Wood Base, 2000, 6 ¼ x 12 In. 662.00
Figurine, Jack Point, HN 3920, 1996, 17 In. 2040.00
Figurine, Janet, HN 1652, 1934-49, 6 ½ In. 312.00
Figurine, Janet, HN 1916, 1939-49, 5 ¼ In. *illus* 50.00
Figurine, Janice, HN 2165, 1955-65, 7 ¼ In. 187.00
Figurine, Jennifer, HN 3447, 1994, 7 ¼ In. 171.00
Figurine, Jessica, HN 3850, 1997, 9 ½ In. 58.00
Figurine, Jester, HN 2016, 1949-97, 10 In. *illus* 95.00
Figurine, Jovial Monk, HN 2144, 1954-76, 7 ¾ In. 105.00
Figurine, Kimberley, HN 3379, 1992-97, 8 ½ In. 70.00
Figurine, Lady Charming, HN 1948, 1940-73, 8 In. 146.00
Figurine, Lady Jester, HN 1222, 1927-38, 7 In. 2520.00
Figurine, Lady Pamela, HN 2718, 1974-81, 8 ½ In. 82.00
Figurine, Lambing Time, HN 1890, 1938-81, 9 ¼ In. 70.00 to 134.00
Figurine, Last Waltz, HN 2315, 1967-93, 7 ¾ In. 71.00
Figurine, Little Boy Blue, HN 2062, 1950-73, 5 ½ In. 108.00 to 132.00

gurine, Long John Silver, HN 2204, 1957-65, 9 In. 240.00
gurine, Loretta, HN 2337, 1966-81, 7 ¾ In. 106.00
gurine, Lydia, HN 1908, 1939-95, 4 ¾ In. 106.00
gurine, Margaret, HN 1989, 1947-59, 7 ½ In. 293.00
gurine, Margaret, HN 2397, 1982-99, 7 ½ In. 110.00
gurine, Marguerite, HN 1946, 1940-49, 8 In. 351.00
gurine, Marie, HN 1417, 1930-49, 4 ¾ In. 146.00
gurine, Mary Queen Of Scots, HN 3142, 1989, 9 In. 432.00
gurine, Mask, HN 733, 1925-38, 6 ¾ In. 2100.00
gurine, Mask Seller, HN 2103, 1953-95, 8 ½ In. 122.00
gurine, Master, HN 2325, 1967-92, 6 ¼ In. *illus* 88.00
gurine, Mendicant, HN 1365, 1929-69, 8 In. 146.00
gurine, Michele, HN 2234, 1967-93, 7 In. 88.00
gurine, Mirabel, HN 1743, 1935-49, 7 ¾ In. *illus* 702.00
gurine, Miranda, HN 3037, 1987-908 ½ In. 82.00
gurine, Miss Muffet, HN 1936, 1940-67, 5 ½ In. 130.00
gurine, Mr. Pickwick, Box, HN 2099, 1952-67, 7 ½ In. 186.00
gurine, Mrs. Crustybread, Brambly Hedge, DBH 15, 1987, 3 ½ In. 132.00
gurine, My First Figurine, HN 3424, 1993-98, 4 ¼ In. 71.00
gurine, My Love, HN 2339, 1969-96, 6 ¼ In. 82.00
gurine, Nadine, HN 1886, 1938-49, 7 ¾ In. 760.00
gurine, Newsboy, HN 2244, 1959-65, 8 ½ In. 330.00
gurine, Ninette, HN 2379, 1971-97, 7 ½ In. 118.00
gurine, Old Balloon Seller, HN 1315, 1929-98, 7 14½ In. 176.00
gurine, Old Mother Hubbard, HN 2314, 1964-75, 8 In. 200.00
gurine, Omar Khayyam, HN 2247, 1965-83, 6 ¼ In. 175.00
gurine, Orange Lady, HN 1759, 1936-75, 8 ¾ In. 117.00 to 183.00
gurine, Orange Vendor, HN 1966, 1941-49, 6 ¼ In. 410.00
gurine, Paige, HN 4767, 2005, 8 ¼ In. 83.00
gurine, Paisley Shawl, HN 1987, 1946-59, 8 ¼ In. 117.00
gurine, Paisley Shawl, HN 1988, 1946-75, 6 ½ In. 117.00
gurine, Paisley Shawl, M 4, 1932-45, 4 In. 100.00
gurine, Penny's Worth, HN 2408, 1986-90, 7 In. 171.00
gurine, Pooh Began To Eat, Box, WP 28, 2000, 3 ¾ In. 72.00
gurine, Potter, HN 1493, 1932-92, 7 In. 351.00
gurine, Pretty Polly, HN 2768, 1984-86, 6 In. 192.00
gurine, Proposal, Man, HN 725, 1925-38, 5 ½ In. 480.00
gurine, Prudence, HN 1883, 1938-49, 6 ¾ In. 468.00
gurine, Quality Street, HN 1211A, 1926-36, 7 ¼ In. 630.00
gurine, Queen Anne, Box, HN 3141, 1988, 9 In. 159.00
gurine, Queen Elizabeth II Coronation, HN 4476. 350.00
gurine, Rachel, HN 2936, 1985-97, 7 ½ In. 94.00
gurine, Rag Doll Seller, HN 2944, 1983-95, 7 In. 353.00
gurine, Rebecca, HN 2805, 1980-96, 7 ¼ In. 83.00
gurine, Red Red Rose, HN 3994, 1997, 9 In. 108.00
gurine, Rhapsody, HN 2267, 1961-73, 6 ¾ In. 70.00
gurine, Ritz Bell Boy, HN 2772, 1989-93, 8 In. 188.00
gurine, Rose, HN 1416, 1930-49, 4 ½ In. 146.00
gurine, Rosebud, HN 1983, 1945-52, 7 ½ In. 351.00
gurine, Sandra, HN 2275, 1969-97, 7 ¾ In. 147.00
gurine, Schoolmarm, HN 2223, 1958-81, 6 ¾ In. 156.00
gurine, Secret Thoughts, HN 2382, 1971-88, 6 ¼ In. 147.00
gurine, Sharon, HN 3603, 1994, 8 ¾ In. 83.00
gurine, Shepherd, HN 1975, 1945-75, 8 ½ In. 135.00 to 146.00
gurine, Snowman, Adventure Begins, Box 228.00
gurine, Snowman, Dancing In The Snow, Box 204.00
gurine, Snowman, Journey Ends, Box 282.00
gurine, Snowman, Skiing, DS 21 392.00
gurine, Southern Belle, HN 2229, 1958-97, 7 ½ In. 82.00 to 94.00
gurine, Spring, HN 2085, 1952-59, 7 ¾ In. 198.00
gurine, Spring Morning, HN 1923, 1940-49, 7 ½ In. 468.00
gurine, Stop Press, HN 2683, 1977-81, 7 ½ In. 171.00
gurine, Summer's Darling, HN 4401, 2001, 4 ¼ In. 85.00
gurine, Sunday Best, HN 2206, 1979-84, 7 ½ In. 84.00 to 117.00
gurine, Sweet & Twenty, HN 1298, 1928-69, 5 ¾ In. 205.00

Royal Doulton, Figurine, Mirabel, HN 1743, 1935-49, 7 ¾ In. $702.00

Royal Doulton, Toby Jug, Happy John, D 6031, 1939-91, Large $35.00

Royal Doulton, Vase, Flambe, Sung, Marked, Charles Noke, 6 In. $750.00

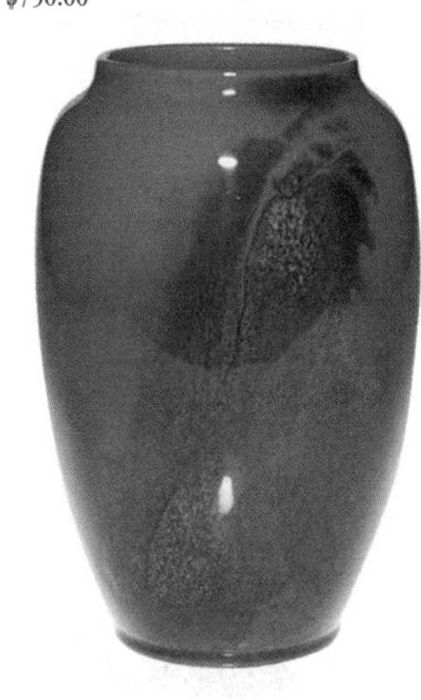

TIP

If a capital letter A is printed next to the usual Royal Doulton mark, it means the piece was made between about 1939 and 1955.

Royal Doulton, Vase, Fruit, Incised, Winnie Bowstead, c.1928, 10½ In.
$130.00

Royal Doulton, Vase, Cabbage Roses, Minnie Webb, c.1923, 6¾ In.
$130.00

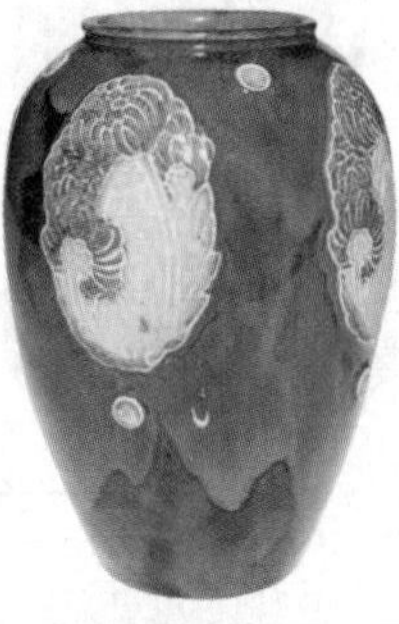

Royal Doulton, Vase, Tapestry, Enameled White & Blue Flowers, 1914, 11¾ In.
$489.00

R

Figurine, Taking Things Easy, HN 2680, 1987-96, 6¾ In. 282.0
Figurine, Teatime, HN 2255, 1972-95, 7½ In. . . . . 90.00 to 145.0
Figurine, This Little Pig, HN 1793, 1936-95, 4 In. 120.0
Figurine, Tinsmith, HN 2146, 1962-67, 6½ In. 235.0
Figurine, Toinette, HN1940, 1940-49, 7 In. 1287.0
Figurine, Top O' The Hill, HN 1833, 1937-71, 7 In. 75.0
Figurine, Top O' The Hill, HN 1834, 1937-2004, 7 In. . . . . 88.00 to 118.0
Figurine, Top O' The Hill, HN 1849, 1938-75, 7 1/4 In. . . . . 117.00 to 134.0
Figurine, Toymaker, HN 2250, 1959-73, 6 In. 360.0
Figurine, Treasure Island, HN 2243, 1962-75, 4¾ In. 168.0
Figurine, Tumbler, HN 3183, 1989-91, 9 In. 61.0
Figurine, Uriah Heep, HN 2101, 1952-67, 7½ In. 235.0
Figurine, Vanity, HN 2475, 1973-92, 5¼ In. 88.0
Figurine, Victoria, HN 2471, 1973-2000, 6 1/2 In. . . . . 70.00 to 118.0
Figurine, Wales, Ladies Of The British Isles, HN 3630, 1995-98, 8½ In. 377.0
Figurine, Wedding Morn, HN 3853, 1996-99, 8 In. . . . . 82.00 to 120.0
Figurine, When I Was Young, HN 3457, 1994-2000, 5½ In. 216.0
Figurine, Wilfred Entertains, Brambly Hedge, DBH 23, 1990-95, 3¼ In. 72.0
Figurine, Will He, Won't He, HN 3275, 1990-94, 9 In. 216.0
Figurine, Wintertime, HN 4826, 2005, 9 In. 83.0
Figurine, Wizard, HN 3722, 1994-96, 10 In. 223.0
Figurine, Wizard Of Oz Set, Certificate, Box, 4 Piece . . . . 390.00 to 401.0
Flask, Whiskey, Huntsman, 6¾ In. 144.0
Jardiniere, Wild Horses, Hannah Barlow, 6½ In. 1320.0
Lamp Base, Art Deco, 3 Tiers, Lambeth, 14 In. 180.0
Pitcher, Coaching Days, E 3804, 7½ x 5½ In. 146.0
Pitcher, Dickens Ware, Pegotty, 5 In. 70.0
Pitcher, Dog In Field, Hunting Series Ware, 6 In. 125.0
Pitcher, Sairey Gamp, D 6015, 1939-42, 7 In. 35.0
Plate, Bookworm, Series Ware, D 3889, 10½ In. 480.0
Plate, Fish, Multicolored, Raised Gold Border, 9¼ In., 12 Piece 1880.0
Teapot, Child On Donkey, Gypies Series Ware, 5½ In. 168.0
Tobacco Jar, Cover, Leaf, Branches, Brown, Caramel Glaze, 3¾ In. 147.0
Toby Jug, Alderman Mace The Mayor, D 6766, 1987-91, 4 In. 60.0
Toby Jug, Happy John, D 6031, 1939-91, Large . . . . *illus* 35.0
Toby Jug, Happy John, D 6070, 1939-91, Small 48.0
Toby Jug, Honest Measure, D 6108, 1939-91, Small 175.0
Toby Jug, Miss Nostrum The Nurse, D 6700, 1983-91, Small 47.0
Toby Jug, Old Charlie, D 6030, 1939-60, Large 212.0
Toby Jug, Winston Churchill, D 6171, 1940-41, Large . . . . 70.00 to 83.0
Urn, Roses, Pink, Hand Painted, 2 Handles, 6 In. 600.0
Vase, Cavalier, Brown, Hand Painted, 9½ In. 228.0
Vase, Deer, Flambe, Blue, White, Bulbous, 11½ In. 288.0
Vase, Deer In Woods, Blue Slip, c.1900, 21 In. 443.0
Vase, Embossed Mums, Rouge Flambe, Silver Overlay, Cylindrical, 16 In. 1800.0
Vase, Flambe, Sung, Marked, Charles Noke, 6 In. . . . . *illus* 750.0
Vase, Flambe, Veined, Bulbous, Globular, Elongated Neck, 10¼ In. 108.0
Vase, Fruit, Incised, Winnie Bowstead, c.1928, 10½ In. . . . . *illus* 130.0
Vase, Fruit, Leaves, Cobalt Blue, Bulbous, Tapered, 1930s, 9¾ In. 384.0
Vase, Hunter In Woods, Flambe, Egg Shape, No. 1617, 13½ In. 99.0
Vase, Incised Crocus Flowers, Mottled Green & Brown, c.1936, 9⅜ In. 767.0
Vase, Lady Walking In Snow, Blue & White, 31 In. 213.0
Vase, Monks, 2 Handles, 6 In. 59.0
Vase, Monks, Observing Raven, Gray, Blue Band, 8¾ In. 180.0
Vase, Mountain Scene, Gold Painted, Leaf Molded Rim, Foot, 8 In. 353.0
Vase, Multicolored, Fruit, Flowers, Embossed, Egg Shape, 10½ In. 116.0
Vase, Oriental Landscape, Flambe, 18 In. 390.0
Vase, Cabbage Roses, Minnie Webb, c.1923, 6¾ In. . . . . *illus* 130.0
Vase, Roses, Yellow, Pink, 2 Handles, 4 In. 432.0
Vase, Rouge, Flambe, No. 7306, 6 In. 885.0
Vase, Scrolling Leaves, 14 In. 720.0
Vase, Stick, Embossed Tulips, Rouge, Flambe, Silver Collar, Rim, Bulbous Base, 16 In. 550.0
Vase, Tapestry, Enameled White & Blue Flowers, 1914, 11¾ In. . . . . *illus* 489.0
Vase, Van Riebeeck Portrait, Delft Style, Blue & White, 20 In. 166.0
Vase, Woman & Girl, Blue, White, 8¾ In. 360.0

ROYAL DUX is the more common name for the Duxer Porzellanmanufaktur, which was founded by E. Eichler in Dux, Bohemia (now Duchov, Czech Republic), in 1860. By the turn of the century, the firm specialized in porcelain statuary and busts of Art Nouveau–style maidens, large porcelain figures, and ornate vases with three-dimensional figures climbing on the sides. The firm is still in business.

Basket, Cherubs, Grapes, Leaves, Embossed, c.1900, 7 In. . . . *illus* 100.00
Centerpiece, Women, Lily Pad Dishes, Gilt, Marked, 13 ½ In. . . . *illus* 640.00
Dish, Standing Woman, String Instrument, Oval, Art Nouveau, 14 In. . . . 529.00
Figurine, Boy, 2 Oxen, 14 In. . . . 230.00
Figurine, Hunting Dogs, Glossy, 14 In. . . . 65.00
Figurine, Man, Goat, 27 In. . . . 600.00
Figurine, Man, Woman With Baskets, 10 In., Pair. . . . 525.00
Figurine, Water Nymph, Rising From Water, Water Lilies In Hair, Earthenware, 1900s, 21 In. 2703.00
Group, 2 Classical Maidens, Painted, Pink Triangle Mark, 1900s, 20 ½ In. . . . 142.00
Umbrella Stand, Bearded & Robed Oriental Male Figure, 37 In. . . . 649.00
Umbrella Stand, Figural Turkey, Large Flower, 28 ¾ In. . . . 2360.00
Vase, Girl & Lamb, Tree, Pink Triangle Mark . . . 275.00
Vase, Girl With Pitcher, Pink Triangle Mark, Signed, Daebrich . . . 385.00

ROYAL FLEMISH glass was made during the late 1880s in New Bedford, Massachusetts, by the Mt. Washington Glass Works. It is a colored satin glass decorated with dark colors and raised gold designs. The glass was patented in 1894. It was supposed to resemble stained glass windows.

Biscuit Jar, Crimson Frosted, Gilt Stems, Flowers, Butterfly, Melon Ribbed, 7 In. . . . 690.00
Biscuit Jar, Guba Ducks, Gold Enamel Sun, Silver Plated Rim, Handle, Cover, 6 ½ In. . . . 5750.00
Cracker Jar, Gold, Gray Panels, Rose Mums, Blue Leafy Stems, 8 In. . . . 1600.00
Ewer, Medallion, Lion, Banner, Eagle Shield, Bulbous, 12 ½ In. . . . 3500.00
Ewer, Raised Gold Panels, Twisted Rope Handle, 10 In. . . . 2645.00
Shaker, Fig Shape, Pale Chartreuse, Bark Texture, Blue Enamel Asters, 2 ½ In. . . . 264.00
Vase, Earth Tone Panels, Gold Griffin, Dragon, Bulbous, 11 ¼ In. . . . 4600.00
Vase, Enameled, Griffin, Medallion, Panels, Frosted Long Neck, 11 In. . . . 2300.00
Vase, Roman Medallions, Raised Gold Panels, Earth Tone, Scrolled Handles, 9 ½ In. . . . 2750.00
Vase, Stick, Bulbous Base, Gold Earth Tone Panels, Flowers, 12 ½ In. . . . 2530.00
Vase, Stick, Stylized Flowers, Handles, Cupped Mouth, Bulbous Base, 9 In. . . . 2875.00
Vase, Stick Shape, Frosted Panels, Gold Mums, Red, Purple, 11 ¾ In. . . . 2588.00
Vase, Stylized Dragon, Earthtone Panels, Ring Collar, 10 ½ In. . . . 3750.00

ROYAL HAEGER, *see Haeger category.*

ROYAL HICKMAN designed pottery, glass, silver, aluminum, furniture, lamps, and other items. From 1938 to 1944 and again from the 1950s to 1969, he worked for Haeger Potteries. Mr. Hickman operated his own pottery in Tampa, Florida, during the 1940s. He moved to California and worked for Vernon Potteries. The last years of his life he lived in Guadalajara, Mexico, and continued designing for Royal Haeger. Pieces made in his pottery listed here are marked *Royal Hickman* or *Hickman*.

Bowl, Oxblood Glaze, Blue Drip, 8 x 2 ¾ x 3 ½ In. . . . 50.00
Console, High Gloss Plum, Green Accents, Shaped & Flared Rim, 1940s . . . 32.00
Planter, Crystalline Drip Glaze, Green, Brass Stand, c.1936 . . . *illus* 48.00
Planter, Green, White Drip, Flared, Cylindrical Foot, 5 ½ x 10 ¾ In. . . . 76.00
Planter, Petty Crystal Glaze, Turquoise, Beige, Bulbous Sides, 8 x 3 ½ In. . . . 75.00
Tray, Leaf, Aluminum, Bruce Fox, 15 x 11 In. . . . 75.00
Vase, Bottle Shape, Petty Crystal Glaze, Rose, Blue, 11 In. . . . 150.00
Vase, Green Agate Glaze, Fluted, c.1944, 11 ½ x 4 ¾ In. . . . 42.00
Vase, Petty Crystal Glaze, Blue, Oval, 4 ½ In. . . . 75.00
Vase, Petty Crystal Glaze, Bulbous, Cylindrical Neck, 8 In. . . . 250.00
Vase, Petty Crystal Glaze, Lavender, Blue & Pink, Bulbous, Cylindrical Neck, 8 In. . . . 175.00
Vase, Swan, Mauve Agate, c.1940, 10 ½ In. . . . *illus* 100.00

ROYAL NYMPHENBURG is the modern name for the Nymphenburg porcelain factory, which was established at Neudeck-ob-der-Au, Germany, in 1753 and moved to Nymphenburg in 1761. The company is still in existence. Marks include a checkered shield topped by a crown, a crowned *CT* with the year, and a contemporary shield mark on reproductions of eighteenth-century porcelain.

Bowl, Chestnut, Oval, Early 20th Century, 3 x 8 x 9 In., Pair. . . . 351.00

Royal Dux, Basket, Cherubs, Grapes, Leaves, Embossed, c.1900, 7 In.
$100.00

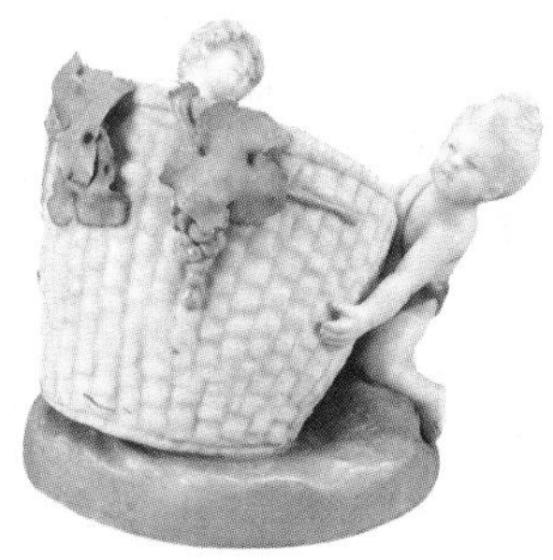

Royal Dux, Centerpiece, Women, Lily Pad Dishes, Gilt, Marked, 13 ½ In.
$640.00

Royal Hickman, Planter, Crystalline Drip Glaze, Green, Brass Stand, c.1936
$48.00

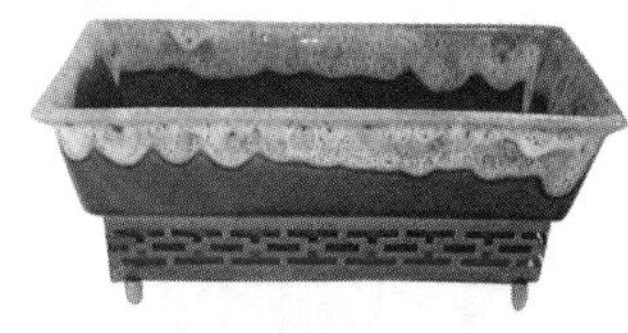

Royal Hickman, Vase, Swan, Mauve Agate, c.1940, 10 ½ In.
$100.00

Royal Nymphenburg, Plate, Fish, Green, Purple, Handle, Hermann Gradl, c.1899, 9½ In.
$1375.00

Royal Worchester, Coffeepot, Fruit, 10 In.
$318.00

Royal Worcester, Vase, Flowers, Ivory Ground, Marked, 5 In.
$132.00

Royal Worcester, Vase, Tusk Shape, Flowers, Antler Style Handle, Marked, 11 In.
$250.00

Figurine, Reclining Puma, c.1925, 5¾ x 16 x 5¾ In. 351.00
Plate, Fish, Green, Purple, Handle, Hermann Gradl, c.1899, 9½ In. . . . . *illus* 1375.00

ROYAL OAK *pieces are listed in the Northwood category by that pattern name.*

ROYAL RUDOLSTADT, *see Rudolstadt category.*

ROYAL VIENNA, *see Beehive category.*

ROYAL WORCESTER is a name used by collectors. Worcester porcelains were made in Worcester, England, from about 1751. The firm went through many different periods and name changes. It became the Worcester Royal Porcelain Company, Ltd., in 1862. Today collectors call the porcelains made after 1862 "Royal Worcester." In 1976, the firm merged with W. T. Copeland to become Royal Worcester Spode. Some early products of the factory are listed under Worcester.

Biscuit Jar, Flowers, Branches, Gray, Brown, c.1889, 7 In. 465.00
Bowl, Basket Weave & Grape Leaf, Reticulated Rim, Square, 3 x 7 In., Pair. 270.00
Bowl, Fruit, 4 x 11 In. 351.00
Coffeepot, Fruit, 10 In. . . . . *illus* 318.00
Creamer, Flowers, Multicolored, Gilt Handle, Rim, c.1890, 4 In. 60.00
Ewer, Flower Sprays, Handle, Griffin Mask, Enameled, Lobed Oval, c.1887, 14⅝ In. 264.00
Figurine, Argenteuil, Gilt Bronze, 6½ x 14½ In. 176.00
Figurine, Blond Woman, Blue Dress, White Cap, F.G. Doughty, 6 In. 117.00
Figurine, Boy, With Parakeet, 6½ In. 117.00
Figurine, Calico Cat, 6 In. 205.00
Figurine, Canvasback Duck, 17 In. 468.00
Figurine, Cecelia, Victorian Ladies, 1972, 8 In. 146.00
Figurine, Elaine, Victorian Ladies, 1970, 6 In. 205.00
Figurine, Elf Owl & Saguaro, Wood Base, 14 In. 1062.00
Figurine, Galloping Dartmoor Ponies, Doris Lindner, 17 x 18 In. 878.00
Figurine, Madelaine, Van Roychevelt, c.1967, 8 In. 117.00
Figurine, Moorhen Chick On Water Lily Pads, D. Doughty, 3 x 12 In. 450.00
Figurine, Passionflower, Van Roychevelt, 1960, 5 x 10 In. 702.00
Figurine, Queen Elizabeth, The Queen Mother, 9 In. 176.00
Figurine, Ring Neck Pheasant Hen, 12 x 11 In. 468.00
Figurine, Robin In Autumn Woods, D. Doughty, 7½ x 7 In. 200.00
Figurine, Royal Canadian Mounted Police, 1966, 13 In. 995.00
Figurine, Saturday's Girl, 1982, 11 In. 88.00
Figurine, Spanish Hog & Sergeant-Major, Wood Base, 1956, 12 In. 550.00
Figurine, Squirrel Fish, Wood Base, 1961, 10 In. 550.00
Figurine, Swordfish, 11 In. 235.00
Incense Burner, Dome Cover, Bell Shape, Elephant Masks, Japanesque, 1873, 6¼ In. Diam.. 3500.00
Jug, Flowers, Blush Ground, 6 In. 98.00
Perfume Bottle, Victoria, Silver Jubilee, 1887, 3 In. 96.00
Pitcher, Figural, Fish, Pike, Fish Handle, 12 In. 978.00
Pitcher, Flowers, Gilt, Curved Spout, c.1888, 6 In. 82.00
Pitcher, Maple Leaves, Twig Handle, Purple Mark, 8 In. 115.00
Plaque, Gundog Holding Game Bird, Hand Painted, Gilt Frame, 9 x 7 In. 682.00
Plate, Venice Lagoon, c.1917, 9⅛ In. 558.00
Potpourri, Cover, Globular, Pierced, Flowers, Scrolled Handles, 10¾ In. 441.00
Ramekin, Cover, Evesham, 6 Piece 94.00
Teakettle, Flower Panels, Aesthetic, Bail Handle, 9 In. 2990.00
Teapot, Turquoise, Oriental, Cobalt Blue Dragon Handle, Square, Majolica, 8 In. 5750.00
Vase, Bird Feet Holding Orange Vase, Beaded, 7 In. 325.00
Vase, Bulbous, Salamander Climbing Around Vase, 7 In. 460.00
Vase, Cover, Raised Ferns, Enameled Flowers, Scrolled Handles, 15 In. 767.00
Vase, Egg Shape, Long Neck, Beaded, c.1919, 7 x 4 In. 11950.00
Vase, Egg Shape, Roses, 4 In. 144.00
Vase, Flower Sprays, Ivory Ground, Tall Tapered Neck, 16 x 7½ In. 360.00
Vase, Flowers, Ivory Ground, Marked, 5 In. . . . . *illus* 132.00
Vase, Flowers, Ivory, Gilt, Handles, 8¼ In. 384.00
Vase, Flowers, Women's Masks, Bulbous, Slender Neck, Loop Handles, 1970, 11 In. 115.00
Vase, Fruit, Gilt Base, Rim, Handles, 9½ In. 370.00
Vase, Leaves, Ivory, Gilt, 6¾ In. 204.00
Vase, Lighthouse, Dolphin Head Handles, 2-Tone Gilt, c.1890, 18 In. 2832.00
Vase, Tusk Shape, Flowers, Antler Style Handle, Marked, 11 In. . . . . *illus* 250.00

ROYCROFT products were made by the Roycrofter community of East Aurora, New York, in the late nineteenth and early twentieth centuries. The community was founded by Elbert Hubbard, famous philosopher, writer, and artist. The workshops owned by the community made furniture, metalware, leatherwork, embroidery, and jewelry. A printshop produced many signs, books, and the magazines that promoted the sayings of Elbert Hubbard. Furniture by the Roycroft community is listed in the Furniture category.

Bell, Copper, Hammered, 1¾ x 3¼ In. 210.00
Bookends, Copper, Hammered, Arched, Marked, 4 x 3½ In. .... *illus* 150.00
Bookends, Copper, Hammered, Trees In Field Of Blossoms, 6½ x 4 In. 7800.00
Bookends, Leather Wrapped, Tooled Designs, 6 x 5¼ In. 780.00
Bowl, Bronze, Hammered, Scalloped Rim, Footed, c.1920, 2 x 9½ In. 150.00
Bowl, Copper, Hammered, Footed, Patina, Marked, 4 x 10½ In. 1080.00
Bowl, Copper, Hammered, Patina, 5½ x 1½ In. 390.00
Bowl, Copper, Hammered, Patina, Marked, 4¼ x 2½ In. 288.00
Box, Copper, Hammered, Tooled Design, Patina, 2 x 7 In. .... *illus* 490.00
Box, Copper, Tooled Design, 7 x 2 In. 510.00
Candlestick, Copper, Hammered, 4 Riveted Bands, Dark Patina, 11½ x 12 In., Pair 2640.00
Candlestick, Copper, Hammered, Patina, 3¼ x 6½ In., Pair 780.00
Candlestick, Copper, Patina, Orb & Cross, Marked, 15 In., Pair 5700.00
Chandelier, 3-Light, Copper, Hammered, Dark Patina, 31 x 17 In. 7200.00
Compote, Copper, Hammered, Patina, 5½ x 4 In. 300.00
Frame, Bronze Textured Metal, 12 x 10 In. 450.00
Lamp, Candlestick, Copper, Hammered, Rope Twist Base, Lace Shade, 15 x 8 In. 1020.00
Lamp, Copper, Hammered, Mica Panels, c.1920, 13 x 7⅛ In. 2880.00
Lamp, Desk, Copper, Hammered, Helmet Shade, Patina, 17 x 7 In. 960.00
Sconce, Cylindrical Shade, Green, Purple Hanging, Leaded Glass, 18 x 5 In. 7800.00
Sconce, Cylindrical Shade, Green, Purple, Leaded Glass, 8½ x 5 x 6¼ In. 9600.00
Shade, Flared, Green, Purple, Leaded Slag Glass, 6 x 18 In. 10800.00
Tray, Copper, Double Hammered, 8-Sided, Handles, Patina, Marked, 17 In. .... *illus* 480.00
Tray, Copper, Hammered, 8-Sided, 2 Handles, 17 In. 480.00
Tray, Copper, Hammered, Metal Overlay, Marked, 8 In. 420.00
Vase, Copper, Hammered, Brass Patina, Flared, 4 x 9 In. 316.00
Vase, Copper, Hammered, Cylindrical, 7 In. 1020.00
Vase, Copper, Hammered, Dogwood, Etched, Cylindrical, 7 x 2½ In. 2040.00
Vase, Copper, Hammered, Patina, Squat, Marked, 6½ x 4½ In. 431.00
Vase, Copper, Hammered, Patina, Tapered, 2½ x 4 In. 480.00
Vase, Copper, Hammered, Patina, Tapered, 4½ x 5 In. 330.00
Vase, Copper, Hammered, Patina, Tapered, Crimped Rim, 3 x 5 In. 360.00
Vase, Copper, Hammered, Silver Overlay, Cylindrical, Marked, 6 x 3 In. 960.00
Vase, Copper, Hammered, Stamped, 21 x 8 In. 6000.00
Vase, Copper, Hammered, Tooled Flowers, Green Band, Marked, 2½ x 5 In. 330.00
Vase, Copper, Hammered, Tooled Flowers, Green Band, Patina, Cylindrical, 5 x 2½ In. 330.00

ROZANE, *see Roseville category.*

ROZENBURG worked at The Hague, Holland, from 1890 to 1914. The most important pieces were earthenware made in the early twentieth century with pale-colored Art Nouveau designs.

Cup & Saucer, Flowers & Bird, Marked, Cup 2¼ In. 1800.00
Vase, 2 Birds, Flowers, Green, Blue, Brown, Glossy Glaze, 2 Handles, Footed, 8½ In. 529.00
Vase, 2 Birds In Flower Setting, Art Nouveau Manner, 19½ In. 4838.00
Vase, Vining Flowers, Crazing To Interior, 11⅜ In. 472.00
Vase, Yellow Lizard, Stylized Flowers, Eggshell, 4 Swollen Sides, Black Bee Mark, 3 In. 295.00

RRP, or RRP Roseville, is the mark used by the firm of Robinson-Ransbottom. It is not a mark of the more famous Roseville Pottery. The Ransbottom brothers started a pottery in 1900 in Ironspot, Ohio. In 1920, they merged with the Robinson Clay Product Company of Akron, Ohio, to become Robinson-Ransbottom. The factory is still working.

Cookie Jar, Cow Jumped Over The Moon, 9⅞ In. .... *illus* 83.00
Cookie Jar, Hi Diddle Diddle, 9¾ In. 60.00
Cookie Jar, Hootie Owl, 9½ In. 15.00
Cookie Jar, Peter, Peter, Pumpkin Eater, 8¾ In. 50.00
Cookie Jar, Sheriff Pig, Gold Trim, 12 In. 60.00
Figurine, Gnome, Open Bottom, 11 In. .... *illus* 40.00

Roycroft, Bookends, Copper, Hammered, Arched, Marked, 4 x 3½ In. $150.00

Roycroft, Box, Copper, Hammered, Tooled Design, Patina, 2 x 7 In. $490.00

Roycroft, Tray, Copper, Double Hammered, 8-Sided, Handles, Patina, Marked, 17 In. $480.00

TIP

Never polish Arts & Crafts copper or pewter. Even if the green patina on a piece of Heinz Art is damaged, it is better than a cleaned piece. Original finish is important.

RRP, Cookie Jar, Cow Jumped Over The Moon, 9 7/8 In.
$83.00

RRP, Figurine, Gnome, Open Bottom, 11 In.
$40.00

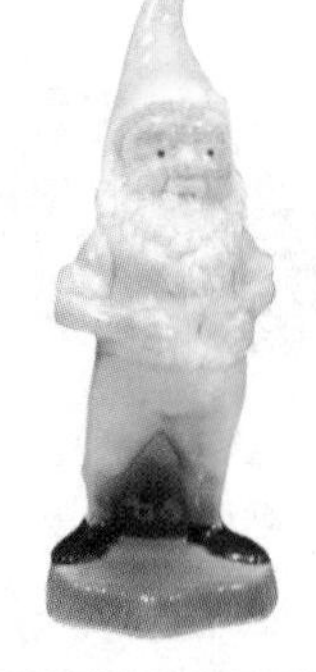

RS Germany, Toothpick, 3 Handles, Hand Painted, Peachy & Pink Roses, Gold Accents
$65.00

RS Poland, Vase, 2 Ostriches, Leaf Silhouette, 5 In.
$235.00

Mixing Bowl, Blue Sponge, White Ground, 2 ½ Qt., 9 In. 75.00
Planter, Sun, Moon, Stars, Brown Shaded To Green, Marked, 6 x 5 In. 18.00

RS GERMANY is part of the wording in marks used by the Tillowitz, Germany, factory of Reinhold Schlegelmilch from 1914 until about 1945. The porcelain was sold decorated and undecorated. The Schlegelmilch families made porcelains marked in many ways. See also ES Germany, RS Poland, RS Prussia, RS Silesia, RS Suhl, and RS Tillowitz.

Basket, Bird & Flowers, Handle, 4 ¼ x 5 ¼ In. 125.00
Bowl, Deeply Scalloped, Hand Painted, Pink & Yellow Roses, 1900s, 6 In. 60.00
Bowl, Footed, Oval, 2 Handles, Straw Flowers, 7 ¾ x 6 In. 100.00
Bowl, Hand Painted, Pheasants, Game Birds, Vivid Colors, Handle, 7 In. 100.00
Bowl, Poppy & Wisteria Blossoms, 3 Ball Feet, Color Tinted, 5 ¼ x 2 ½ In. 25.00
Bowl, Underplate, Pink Rose, White, Tiffany Satin, Leaf Mold, 9 ¼ In. 240.00
Bowl, Yellow Rose, Cobalt Blue, Gold Stencil, 10 In. 60.00
Cake Plate, Art Nouveau, c.1900, 10 In. 145.00
Cake Plate, Peach Flowers, Gold Rim, Green Fading Ground, 2 Handles, 9 ¾ In. 46.00
Cake Plate, Yellow Rose, Cobalt Blue, 2 Handles, 10 ½ In. 55.00
Chocolate Set, Pot, Cups & Saucers, Stylized Yellow Iris, White, 9 In. 140.00
Chocolate Set, White Flower, Pot, Cups & Saucers, Sugar & Creamer, Light Cream 175.00
Creamer, Molded Details, Soft Violet Flowers, Cream Centers, Gold Trim, Handle, 1920 .... 50.00
Creamer, White Water Lily, Scalloped Rim, Fluted Sides, Handle, 3 ⅜ x 4 In. 29.00
Plate, Pink Roses, Gold & Mauve Borders, Iridescent Finish, 8 ¼ In. 45.00
Sugar & Creamer, Chinese Pheasant, Green 75.00
Sugar & Creamer, Pink Flower, Light Green, Gold Trim 35.00
Teapot, Hand Painted, Garlands Of Pink & Burgundy Roses, Gold Accents 250.00
Teapot, Lid, Handle, Art Nouveau, c.1900, 11 In. 175.00
Toothpick, 3 Handles, Hand Painted, Peachy & Pink Roses, Gold Accents. .... *illus* 65.00
Tray, Dresser, Oval, Red & Pink Roses, 2 Handles, Gold Rim, 10 ¾ x 7 ⅜ In. 38.00
Tray, Oriental Pheasants, Wooded Stream, 2 Handles, 11 ½ x 7 In. 425.00
Tray, Serving, Breasted Pheasant, Red, Blue, Cream, Green, Brown, 15 ¼ x 5 ¼ In. 225.00

RS POLAND (German) is a mark used by the Reinhold Schlegelmilch factory at Tillowitz from about 1946 to 1956. After 1956, the factory made porcelain marked *PT Poland*. This is one of many of the RS marks used. See also ES Germany, RS Germany, RS Prussia, RS Silesia, RS Suhl, and RS Tillowitz.

Dresser Set, Flowers, Ring Tree, Pin Tray, Candlestick, Hair Receiver, Tray, 5 Piece 295.00
Vase, 2 Ostriches, Leaf Silhouette, 5 In. .... *illus* 235.00
Vase, Swedish Scenes, Blue, White, 4 Medallions, Satin, 7 ¼ In. 300.00

RS PRUSSIA appears in several marks used on porcelain before 1917. Reinhold Schlegelmilch started his porcelain works in Suhl, Germany, in 1869. See also ES Germany, RS Germany, RS Poland, RS Silesia, RS Suhl, and RS Tillowitz.

Biscuit Jar, Cover, Swan, Bluebird, 2 Handles, 5 x 9 In. 200.00
Biscuit Jar, Point & Clover Mold, White, Pink Rose, White, 7 ¼ In. 175.00
Boot, Blown Floral Mold, Embossed Flowers, Gilt Detail, 5 In. 145.00
Bowl, Carnation Mold, Pink Rose, White, Peach, Lavender, Satin, 11 ½ In. 350.00
Bowl, Carnation Mold, Poppy, Pink, White, Peach, Lavender, Satin, 9 ¼ In. .... *illus* 150.00
Bowl, Carnation Mold, Rose, Pink, White, Green, Yellow, 7 In. 140.00
Bowl, Daffodil Mold, Yellow, Pink Rose, White Center, Cobalt Blue Border, 10 ½ In. 320.00
Bowl, Flower, Pierced Handle, Light To Dark Lavender, 11 ¾ In. 210.00
Bowl, Flower Mold, Wildflower, White, Blue, 10 ¼ In. 25.00
Bowl, Fruit, Iridescent Luster Finish, Scalloped Edges, 10 ¼ In. 270.00
Bowl, Hand Painted, House With Tree, 2 Handles, 7 In. 125.00
Bowl, Leaf Mold, Pink Rose, Yellow, Pierced Edge, 10 ¼ In. 225.00
Bowl, Leaf Mold, White Poppy, White, Green, Satin, 10 ¼ In. 160.00
Bowl, Lettuce Mold, Pearl Luster, 9 In. 80.00
Bowl, Lily Mold, Flowers, Gold Stencils, 10 In. 1200.00
Bowl, Lily Mold, Huntress Scene, Cream, Green, Footed, 10 ½ In. 475.00
Bowl, Madam Recamier Portrait, Green Ground, Bronze, Tiffany Swirl Domes, 10 ½ In. 375.00
Bowl, Masted Schooner, 10 ¾ In. 300.00
Bowl, Mill Scene, Brown, 9 3/4 In. .... 160.00 to 225.00
Bowl, Oblong, Iris & Roses, Gold Edges, 12 ¾ x 8 ¼ In. 275.00
Bowl, Puff Mold, Pink Rose, White, Lavender, Footed, 9 ½ In. 50.00
Bowl, Red, White Roses Growing Out Of Urn, Marked, c.1900, 8 In. 236.00

R

Bowl, Reticulated, Beige Ground, White Snowballs, Gold Highlights, 7 In. 110.00
Bowl, Rose, Acorn Mold, White, Gold Stencil, Satin, 10 ¼ In. 150.00
Bowl, Rose, Pink, Cream Center, Light Blue, Heavy Gold Border, 10 ½ In. 200.00
Bowl, Rose, Pink, White, Green Luster Border, Cream Center, 10 ¾ In. 200.00
Bowl, Swan & Blue Bird Scene, Cream, Blue, 9 In. 120.00
Bowl, Tiffany, Lady Watering Flowers In Center, 10 ½ In. 999.00
Bowl, Turkey, Bluebird, Evergreen Scene, Tapestry, 10 ¾ In. 450.00
Bowl, Water Lily, Cream, Green, 10 ¼ In. 100.00
Bowl, Yellow, Gold, Woodland Church, c.1900, 10 In. 265.00
Bowl, Yellow Rose, 6-Sided, Cream Center, Cobalt Blue Border, Gold Highlights, 10 ¾ In. 90.00
Bread Bowl, Medallion Mold, Old Man In The Mountain, 13 In. 190.00
Cake Plate, Carnation Mold, Pink Rose, White, Lavender, 2 Handles, Satin, 10 In. 120.00
Cake Plate, Castle, Brown, 2 Handles, 11 In. 200.00
Cake Plate, Medallion Mold, Old Man In The Mountain, 2 Handles, 11 ¼ In. 230.00
Cake Plate, Pink Carnations, c.1900, 9 ½ In. 146.00
Cake Plate, Poppy, Carnation, 2 Handles, Pink, Yellow, 10 In. 85.00
Cake Plate, Water Lily, Light Blue, Cream, Gold Stencil Border, 2 Handles, 10 ¼ In. 80.00
Celery Tray, Flower, Portrait Medallions, Potocka, Recamier, Gold Tapestry, 14 In. 610.00
Celery Tray, Medallion Mold, Old Man In The Mountain, 12 ¼ In. 120.00
Celery Tray, Red Star, Pink & Green Flowers, Gilt Highlights, 12 In. 146.00
Celery Tray, Swag & Tassel Mold, Pink Rose, Cream, Green Luster, Cobalt Blue, 13 In. 150.00
Celery Tray, Swallows, 2 Handles, Medallions, Applied Decal, 12 ¼ x 6 In. 480.00
Chamberstick, Rose, White, Green, Pink, Handle, 5 ¼ In. 90.00
Charger, Hand Painted, Portrait, Brown Haired Woman, 11 ½ In. 275.00
Chocolate Pot, Castle, Brown, 9 ½ In. 850.00
Chocolate Pot, Footed, Poppies, Cover, 8 x 7 In. 129.00
Chocolate Pot, Lid, Handle, Gold Rim, 10 ½ In. 510.00
Chocolate Pot, Scalloped Rim, Footed, White Ground, Flowers, c.1900, 10 In. 118.00
Chocolate Set, Flower, 6 Cups & Saucers, Tiffany Satin 575.00
Chocolate Set, Icicle Mold, Water Lily, Pot, 5 Cups, Saucers, 9 In. 600.00
Creamer, Pink Roses, White Ground, Petal Footed 29.00
Cup & Saucer, Plate, Stylized Swan, Satin, 7 ½ In. 60.00
Dish, Pink & Red Roses, Buds, Gold Accents, Green Piecrust Edge, 9 ½ x 4 ¾ In. 65.00
Dish, Yellow, Purple, Red Roses, 2 Handles, Marked, c.1900, 4 ¼ In. 177.00
Dresser Box, Cover, Water Lily, Green, 3-Footed, 4 x 6 ½ In. 80.00
Ewer, Ornate Handle, Cream Ground, Portrait Of Tillie, 7 In. 750.00
Ferner, Double Cottage, Brown, 4-Footed, 6 ½ In. 125.00
Ferner, Pink & White Roses, Cream Ground, Flat Scalloped Base, 1920, 6 ½ x 3 ½ In. 295.00
Hair Receiver, Turquoise, Pink Roses, c.1890, 2 x 5 ½ x 6 In. 322.00
Hatpin Holder, 6-Footed, 6-Sided, Embossed Decorations, Dainty Flowers 100.00
Nappy, Steeple Mold, Stylized Flower, Rosebud, Handle, Cobalt Blue, 6 ½ In. 55.00
Pitcher, Cider, Medallion Mold, Water Lily, Cream, Green, 6 ¼ In. 250.00
Pitcher, Hand Painted, Yellow & Peach Roses, Gold Trim, Handle, 4 In. 75.00
Pitcher, Lemonade, Carnation Mold, Rose, Daisy, Pink, 8 ¾ In. 280.00
Pitcher, Lemonade, Stylized Flower, Cobalt Blue, 10 ¼ In. 210.00
Pitcher, Pink & Yellow Roses, Gilt, Stippled, Late 19th Century, 13 ⅜ In. *illus* 392.00
Pitcher, Yellow Roses, Gilt, Stippled, Late 19th Century, 13 ⅜ In. *illus* 363.00
Plaque, Wall, Pheasant, Evergreen, Luster Finish, 8 ¾ In. 125.00
Plate, Hand Painted, Flowers, Reticulated, 1900s, 8 ½ In. 65.00
Plate, Mill Scene, Green, Gold Stencil, 8 ½ In. 170.00
Plate, Portrait Of Mademoiselle DuBoise, 4-Leaf Clovers, Tall Flowers, 1890s, 10 In. 235.00
Plate, Ribbons & Jewel Mold, Dice Thrower, Gold, Opal Jewels, 8 ½ In. 950.00
Plate, Stylized Water Lily, Cobalt Blue, Gold Highlight, Steeple Mold, 12 In. 260.00
Powder Box, Cover, Pink Rose, Green, Lavender, Orange, Luster Finish, 4 In. 60.00
Relish, Castle, Brown, 9 ¼ In. 170.00
Relish, Cover, Hand Painted, Spoon, Handle, 3 x 3 In. 125.00
Relish, Iris, Pink & Yellow Roses, Gold Trim, 9 ½ In. 77.00
Relish, Medallion Mold, Old Man In The Mountain, 8 In. 140.00
Relish, Melon Eaters, Green Tone, 9 ½ In. 120.00
Relish, Mill Scene, Pierced Handle, 10 ½ x 5 ⅛ In. 175.00
Relish, Wild Flower, Pink, Yellow, 9 ½ In. 50.00
Sugar, Cover, Summer, Satin, Gilt, Marked, Late 19th Century, 4 ½ In. *illus* 157.00
Sugar & Creamer, Carnation Mold, Fall Season, Peach, Lavender, Satin 575.00
Sugar & Creamer, Lily, Cream, Green, Pink, Yellow Rose 125.00
Sugar & Creamer, Summer Season, Yellow, Green 520.00
Tankard, Iris, Stipple Flower Mold, Cobalt Blue, Handle, 1910 3900.00
Tankard, Spring Portrait, Cottage Scene, Bright Colors, Handle, 13 In. 3040.00

RS Prussia, Bowl, Carnation Mold, Poppy, Pink, White, Peach, Lavender, Satin, 9 ¼ In.
$150.00

RS Prussia, Pitcher, Pink & Yellow Roses, Gilt, Stippled, Late 19th Century, 13 ⅜ In.
$392.00

RS Prussia, Pitcher, Yellow Roses, Gilt, Stippled, Late 19th Century, 13 ⅜ In.
$363.00

RS Prussia, Sugar, Cover, Summer, Satin, Gilt, Marked, Late 19th Century, 4 ½ In.
$157.00

RS Suhl, Plate, LeBrun Portrait, Brown Ground, Maroon Border, Gold Stencil, 11 ¼ In.
$325.00

Rubina, Vase, Inverted Thumbprint, Birds, Flowers, James Tufts Quadruple Frame, 8 In.
$278.00

Rubina Verde, Pitcher, Petal Felt, 4 ½ In.
$145.00

Tea Set, Castle, Pot, Creamer & Sugar, 3 Piece 410.00
Tea Set, Poppy, Pot, Creamer & Sugar, Green, Lavender, Cream, 3 Piece 160.00
Tea Set, Snowball & Rose, Teapot, Sugar & Creamer, White, Green, 3 Piece 300.00
Teapot, Lid, Pink Roses, White Hydrangea, Magenta & Yellow Ground, Footed 144.00
Tray, 2 Handles, Green, Pastoral Windmill, Marked, 10 In. 236.00
Tray, Dresser, Carnation Mold, Pink Poppy, White, Lavender, Satin, 11 ½ In. 150.00
Tray, Dresser, Rose, Yellow, Pink, Green, 11 ¾ In. 100.00
Tray, Dresser, Art Nouveau, Gold Accents, 11 x 7 In. 600.00
Vase, Blue & Pinks, Gold Rim, Roses, Handle, 10 ½ x 5 ¾ In. 69.00
Vase, Cottage Scene, Teardrop Shape, Brown, 2 Handles, 6 ½ In. 150.00
Vase, Courtly Lady Feeding Chickens, 2 Handles, 20th Century, 9 In. 767.00
Vase, Gold Dots, Pink & Yellow Roses On Wide Bands, 4 ½ In. 450.00
Vase, Melon Eaters, Shaded Mountains, 5 In. 675.00
Vase, Mill Scene, 2 Handles, Green, Gold Stencil, 7 In. 270.00
Vase, Pink Roses, Gilded Double Handles, c.1900, 10 ½ In. 495.00
Vase, Poppy, Pink, 3 Handles, 3-Footed, Brown, Yellow, Green, 4 ¼ In. 180.00
Vase, Portrait Of Art Nouveau Woman, Iridescent, 2 Gold Handles, 1890s, 10 In. 325.00
Vase, Purple Clematis In Center, 2 Ornate Handles, 11 ¾ In. 695.00
Vase, Woman With Fan In Center, 2 Handles, Multicolored, 7 ½ In. 900.00
Vase, Yellow Rose, Skirted, 2 Handles, Dark Green, Yellow, 11 In. 80.00

RS SILESIA appears on porcelain made at the Reinhold Schlegelmilch factory in Tillowitz, Germany, from the 1920s to the 1940s. The Schlegelmilch families made porcelains marked in many ways. See also ES Germany, RS Germany, RS Poland, RS Prussia, RS Suhl, and RS Tillowitz.

Candlestick, 3 Panels, Fruit, Gold Frames, Marbled Finish, Cream Ground, Dwarf, Pair 60.00
Plate, Cream Ground, Daisies, Pink, Yellow Centers, Gold Trimmed, 8 ½ In. 15.00
Plate, Side, 3 Panels, Fruit, Gold Frames, Marbled Finish, 8 ½ In. 19.00
Plate, White Roses, Green & Cream Ground, Gold Stenciling, Gold Rim, 1930s, 8 ½ In. 38.00
Tray, Roses & Elaborate Designs, Ivory Ground, 6 ¼ In. 75.00

RS SUHL is a mark used by the Reinhold Schlegelmilch factory in Suhl, Germany, between 1900 and 1917. The Schlegelmilch families made porcelains in many places. See also ES Germany, RS Germany, RS Poland, RS Prussia, RS Silesia, and RS Tillowitz.

Bowl, Melon Eaters, Red Ground, Fancy Crimp Mold, 7 ⅜ In. 399.00
Bowl, Portrait Of Napoleon, Deep & Light Maroon, Heavy Gold, 7 ½ In. 350.00
Celery Tray, Flowers, Dogwood & Pine, Scalloped, Cream Ground, 16 In. 175.00
Dispenser, White Ground, Teal Blue Highlights, Flowers, Roses, Handle, 1900s 119.00
Plate, LeBrun Portrait, Brown Ground, Maroon Border, Gold Stencil, 11 ¼ In. .... *illus* 325.00
Sugar, Cover, Classical Courting Scene, White, Green, 4-Footed, 7 In. 30.00
Vase, Melon Eaters, Green Ground, Red Border, Bowling Pin Shape, 7 In. 180.00

RS TILLOWITZ was marked on porcelain by the Reinhold Schlegelmilch factory at Tillowitz from the 1920s to the 1940s. Table services and ornamental pieces were made. See also ES Germany, RS Germany, RS Poland, RS Prussia, RS Silesia, and RS Suhl.

Bowl, Vegetable, Hand Painted, Poppies, Orange Leaves, Green Centers, Gold Trim, 6 In. 75.00
Cake Plate, Flowers, Soft Ground, Shades Of Green & Cream 45.00
Celery Tray, Fuchsias, Cream & Peach, Beige Ground, 2 Open Handles, 10 ½ In. 125.00
Celery Tray, Hand Painted, Blue Wreath, Ivory Flowers, Stems, Gold Trim Border, 7 In. 65.00
Chocolate Pot, Hand Painted, Gold Trim, Apple Blossoms, Handle, 9 ¾ In. 225.00
Plate, Roses, Pastel Pinks, Creamy Whites, Gold Border, 8 ½ In. 42.00
Powder Jar, Cover, Melon Eaters, Gold Trim, Shadow Flowers, 4 x 3 In. 350.00
Sugar, Cover, Yellow Flowers, Gold Trim, 2 Handles 25.00
Teapot, Lid, Art Nouveau, Handle, c.1900, 11 In. 175.00

RUBINA is a glassware that shades from red to clear. It was first made by George Duncan and Sons of Pittsburgh, Pennsylvania, about 1885. This coloring was used on many types of glassware. The pressed glass patterns of Royal Ivy and Royal Oak are listed under Northwood.

Vase, Inverted Thumbprint, Birds, Flowers, James Tufts Quadruple Frame, 8 In. .... *illus* 278.00

RUBINA VERDE is a Victorian glassware that was shaded from red to green. It was first made by Hobbs, Brockunier and Company of Wheeling, West Virginia, about 1890.

Pitcher, Petal Felt, 4 ½ In. .... *illus* 145.00
Sugar Shaker, White, Enameled, Dogwood Blossoms, 5 ½ In. 1208.00

:UBY GLASS is the dark red color of a ruby, the precious gemstone. It was a popular Victorian olor that never went completely out of style. The glass was shaped by many different processes) make many different types of ruby glass. There was a revival of interest in the 1940s when iodern-shaped ruby table glassware became fashionable. Sometimes the red color is added to clear lass by a process called flashing or staining. Flashed glass is clear glass dipped in a colored glass, then ressed or cut. Stained glass has color painted on a clear glass. Then it is refired so the stain fuses with ie glass. Pieces of glass colored in this way are indicated by the word *stained* in the description. Related ems may be found in other categories, such as Cranberry Glass, Pressed Glass, and Souvenir.

ecanter, Ball Stopper, Applied Neck Rings, 14 In. 35.00
umbler, Cameo Of Woman & Bird, 4¾ In. 1900.00

:UDOLSTADT was a faience factory in the Thuringia region of Germany from 1720 to about 791. In 1854, Ernst Bohne began working in the area. From about 1887 to 1918, the New York nd Rudolstadt Pottery made decorated porcelain marked with the RW and crown familiar to ollectors. This porcelain was imported by Lewis Straus and Sons of New York, which later ecame Nathan Straus and Sons. The word *Royal* was included in their import mark. Collectors often all it "Royal Rudolstadt." Most pieces found today were made in the late nineteenth or early twentieth entury. Additional pieces may be listed in the Kewpie category.

owl, Fruit, White & Yellow Roses, Cream Ground, Gold Trim, F. Hahn, 6 In. 33.00
owl, Pink Roses, Reticulated, Embossed Border, Gold Trim, Oval, c.1910, 3 x 13 x 9 In. 68.00
owl, Roses, 2½ x 9¾ In. 65.00
ake Plate, Red Roses, Gold Scalloped Rim, Handles, c.1900, 11¼ In. 265.00
andelabra, 2-Light, Girl, Tree Branches, Art Nouveau, Marked, 10¼ x 10¾ In. 185.00
andelabrum, 2-Light, Rose, Marked, Karl Ens, c.1913-39, Pair 45.00
elery Tray, White & Yellow Roses, Cream Ground, Gold Trim, Signed, F. Hahn, 12 x 5½ In. 65.00
reamer, Flower, Flow Blue, Gilt, Marked, 4 In. 38.00
wer, Flowers, Cream Ground, Gold Trim, Marked, 10½ In. 215.00
wer, Flowers, Gold Trim, Scroll Handle, Marked, 10½ x 3½ In. 220.00
wer, Peach, Blue Ferns, Bird, Gold Trim, Bulbous, Marked, RW, 10 In. 120.00
igurine, Dog, German Shepherd, Alsatian, Signed, Karl ENS, 5¾ x 8 x 4 In. 325.00
igurine, Gypsy Children, Catching Coins, Ernst Bohne, 7½ In. 275.00
igurine, Man & Woman Walking Home, Carrying Produce, Stamped, N, 1800s, 3 x 4 In. 125.00
igurine, Woman, Scarf Wrap Headpiece, Green, Beige, 14 In. 500.00
air Receiver, Flowers, Multicolored, Gilt, 4¼ In. 45.00
lanter, Girl, Holding Basket, Wall, Fountain, Marked, 10 x 5½ In. 425.00
late, Bread & Butter, White & Yellow Roses, Cream Ground, Gold Trim, F. Hahn, 6 In. 36.00
late, Dessert, White & Yellow Roses, Cream Ground, Gold Trim, Signed, F. Hahn, 8 In. 40.00
late, Pink Roses, Gilt, 8¾ In. 43.00
late, Roses, Signed, 8½ In. 60.00
late, Roses, Yellow & White Ground, Gold Trim, Marked, 8¼ In. 10.00
aucer, White & Yellow Roses, Cream Ground, Gold Trim, Signed, F. Hahn, 5 In. 18.00
ugar, Flowers, Blue & Orange, Gold Trim, Handles, Marked 10.00
ugar & Creamer, Violets, Gold Trim, Marked 95.00
oast Holder, Blue Flowers, 4-Slice, Ring Handle, Gilt, 1906, 3½ x 8 x 4⅜ In. 135.00
ase, Boy & Girl Climbing Corners, Pillar Shape, Blue Mark, 10 In. 165.00
ase, Flowers, Orange, Blue, Pink, Cream Ground, Gilt, 9½ x 3¾ In. 85.00
ase, Mums, Yellow, Pink, Blue, Gold Outline, Handles, Ruffled Base, 10 In. 120.00
ase, Pink Flowers, Green Leaves, Gold Dots, Handles, Marked, c.1887-1918, 8½ In. 175.00
ase, Purple Lilies, Burgundy & Green Leaves, Gilt, Handles, Marked, 7¼ In. 125.00

:UGS have been used in the American home since the seventeenth century. The oriental rug f that time was often used on a table, not on the floor. Rag rugs, hooked rugs, and braided ugs were made by housewives from scraps of material.

badeh, Flowers, Birds, Stepped Medallion, Brick Red Field, Wool, 6 Ft. 6 In. x 10 Ft. 2 In. 990.00
fshar, Dark Blue Abrash Ground, Burgundy & Dark Blue Borders, 5 Ft. 3 In. x 8 Ft. 1150.00
fshar, Spandrels, Blue Ground, Ivory Border, Red Border, 3 Ft. 9 In. x 5 Ft. 8 In. 374.00
gra, Rosettes, Palmettes, Flowers, Rust, Sea Foam Green, Camel, 8 Ft. 10 In. x 12 Ft. 2530.00
ngora, Prayer, Multicolored, Red Field, Niche, Border, Turkey, c.1890, 4 Ft. x 6 Ft. 7 In. 1265.00
pplique, Horse, Trotting, Black, Gray Wool Field, Green Cut Velvet Border, 39 x 27 In. 288.00
ubusson, Cream, Blue Ground, Classical Motifs, Urns, Fluted Vase, 12 Ft. x 19 Ft. 8225.00
ubusson, Pink Flowers, Cream Field, Flower Border, Wool, 6 Ft. 7 In. x 8 Ft. 4 In. 161.00
akhtiari, Cartouche, Orange Field, Ivory Border, 5 Ft. 3 In. x 6 Ft. 9 In. 633.00
akhtiari, Center Medallion, Blue, Red Field, Ivory Borders, 1900s, 9 Ft. x 11 Ft. 13800.00
akhtiari, Flowers, Blue Field, 5 Ft. 4 In. x 9 Ft. 9 In. 805.00

Rug, Braided, Oval, 13 x 10 In.
$132.00

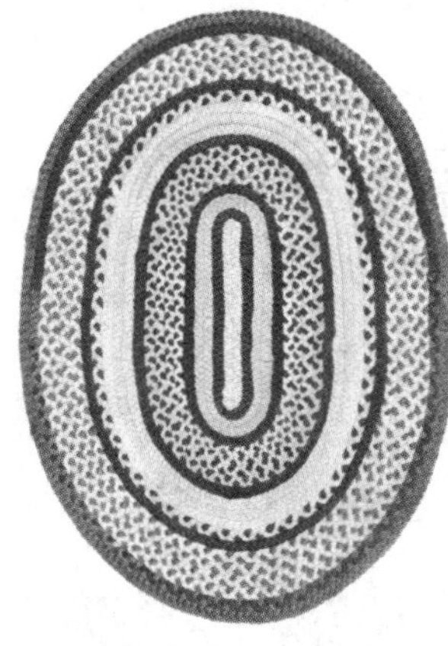

Rug, Chinese, Center Medallion, Blue Ground, Late 19th Century, 6 Ft. 4 In. x 4 Ft.
$795.00

Embroidered Rugs

Embroidered rugs were made by many of the "well-to-do" American women of the early nineteenth century. Woolen yarn was stitched on a heavy material, with the stitching covering the entire surface of the rug. Early embroidered rugs are very rare. Modern embroidered rugs are being made today.

Rug, Chinese, Round Medallion, Flowers, Gold & Blue Borders, c.1950, 3 Ft. x 2 Ft.
$495.00

Rug, Drugget, Honeycomb Pattern, Oatmeal, Green, Gustav Stickley, 36 x 19 In.
$360.00

R

Orientals on the Wall

There is a modern safe way to hang an antique Oriental rug on the wall. Put a strip of 2-inch-wide Velcro on a strip of wood. Mount the wood on the wall. Hang the rug directly on the Velcro. The rug will stay in place and can be pulled loose to be cleaned.

Bakhtiari, Tree & Flowers, Diagonal Grid, Ivory Highlights, 7 Ft. 7 In. x 10 Ft. 9 In. 230.00
Belouch, Center Panel, Diagonals, Floral & Geometric Borders, 3 Ft. 3 In. x 5 Ft. 5 In. 230.00
Bidjar, 6-Sided Center Medallion, Allover Flower Design, Red, 10 Ft. 8 In. x 7 Ft. 10 In. 230.00
Bidjar, Center Medallion, Corner Blocks, Red, Blue, Geometric, c.1910, 5 Ft. x 6 Ft. 7 In. 575.00
Bidjar, Central Medallion, Crimson Ground, 7 Ft. 3 In. x 11 Ft. 9 In. 862.00
Bidjar, Flowers, Blue, Tan, Ivory, Salmon Border, 10 Ft. x 12 Ft. 6 In. 920.00
Bidjar, Flowers, Ivory Ground, Mid 20th Century, 3 Ft. 5 In. x 4 Ft. 9 In. 354.00
Bokhara, Geometric, Salmon Field, Navy Blue, West Turkestan, 10 Ft. 5 In. x 12 Ft. 440.00
Bokhara, Rust, 3 Rows, Octagonal, Diamond Shaped Medallions, 8 Ft. 4 x 10 Ft. 1210.00
Boteh Rows, Ivory Field, c.1900, 4 Ft. 3 In. x 6 Ft. 7 In. 1456.00
Braided, Bright Multicolored, Oval, Runner, 20½ In. x 23 Ft. 132.00
Braided, Brown, Pumpkin, Green, Blue, Red, Oval, 9 Ft. 4 In. x 12 Ft. 3 In. 650.00
Braided, Oval, 13 x 10 In. .... *illus* 132.00
Caucasian, 3 Medallions, Blue Field, Runner, c.1950, 3 Ft. 2 In. x 6 Ft. 11 In. 540.00
Caucasian, Alternating X & Geometric Medallions, Olive, Runner, 4 Ft. x 16 Ft. 1840.00
Caucasian, Center Medallion, Blue, Stepped Ivory Corners, 4 Ft. 5 In. x 6 Ft. 3 In. 345.00
Caucasian, Center Panel, Diagonal Banding, Multiple Borders, Ivory, 4 Ft. x 8 Ft. 518.00
Caucasian, Center Panel, Medallions, Blue, Ivory Border, 4 Ft. 4 In. x 6 Ft. 1610.00
Caucasian, Medallions, Red, Geometric & Floral Borders, 6 Ft. 10 In. x 11 Ft. 8 In. 920.00
Caucasian, Prayer, Guls, Ivory, Floral & Geometric Borders, 3 Ft. x 5 Ft. 4 In. 1380.00
Caucasian, Prayer, Repeating Diagonal Bands, Blue, Floral Borders, 4 Ft. x 4 Ft. 2530.00
Caucasian, Shirvan, Diamond, Geometric, Red, Blue, Tan, c.1910, 4 Ft. 9 In. x 11 Ft. 1800.00
Caucasian, Star & Lattice, Yellow Ground, Geometric Borders, 3 Ft. 5 In. x 8 Ft. 9 In. 518.00
Caucasian, Tree, Salmon Field, Geometric Borders, Runner, 2 Ft. 11 In. x 11 Ft. 5 In. 633.00
Causasian, Navy Blue Field, Runner, c.1910, 3 Ft. 8 x 7 Ft. 8 In. 605.00
Chinese, Art Deco, Flowers, Dragons, Gold & Blue, Red, c.1940, 8 Ft. 9 In. x 11 Ft. 9 In. 1200.00
Chinese, Birds, Flowers, Blue Field, Multiple Ivory & Rose Borders, 12 Ft. x 17 Ft. 2 In. 748.00
Chinese, Blossoming Tree With Bird, Red Field, 3 Ft. x 4 Ft. 10 In. 570.00
Chinese, Center Medallion, Blue Ground, Late 19th Century, 6 Ft. 4 In. x 4 Ft. .... *illus* 795.00
Chinese, Flowers, Bat, Dragon, Fish, Gray Field, Red Border, c.1930, 9 Ft. x 12 Ft. 1440.00
Chinese, Flowers, Birds, Blue, Yellow, 9 Ft. 2 In. x 11 Ft. 7 In. 600.00
Chinese, Flowers, Pagoda, Blue Field, Corner Butterflies, c.1960, 9 Ft. x 11 Ft. 6 In. 230.00
Chinese, Flowers, Rose, Green, Ivory, Slate Blue Field, c.1915, 12 Ft. x 18 Ft. 770.00
Chinese, Pagodas, Landscape, Ivory Field, Early 1900s, 5 Ft. 4 In. x 7 Ft. 9 In. 690.00
Chinese, Round Medallion, Flowers, Gold & Blue Borders, c.1950, 3 Ft. x 2 Ft. .... *illus* 495.00
Chinese, Trees, Birds, Peacocks, Chickens, Medallion Border, 11 Ft. 3 In. x 14 Ft. 3 In. 4500.00
Drugget, Honeycomb Pattern, Oatmeal, Green, Gustav Stickley, 36 x 19 In. .... *illus* 360.00
Erivan, Purple Medallions, Center Blue Field, Snowflake, Animals, 3 Ft. x 5 Ft. 4 In. 546.00
Flower, Red, White, Blue, Wool, 1970s, 69 In. .... *illus* 240.00
Gharajeh, Gabled Medallions, Hooked Bars, Flowers, Ivory, 2 Ft. 5 In. x 8 Ft. 6 In. 700.00
Gorevan, Spandrels, Red Ground, Blue Border, 9 Ft. x 11 Ft. 6 In. 2530.00
Gravan, 13 Hooked Medallions, Blue, Flower Border, 3 Ft. x 12 Ft. 8 In. 1000.00
Hamadan, 3 Columns Of Flowers, Dark Brown Ground, Runner, 9 Ft. x 2 Ft. 9 In. 633.00
Hamadan, 3 Medallions, Midnight Blue Ground, 1930s, 4 Ft. 10 In. x 2 Ft. 6 In. 295.00
Hamadan, Center Diamond, Blue Field, Serrated Borders, 3 Ft. 6 In. x 4 Ft. 9 In. 288.00
Hamadan, Center Medallion, Red Field, 4 Ft. 2 In. x 6 Ft. 6 In. 403.00
Hamadan, Center Panel, Allover Designs, Blue Field, Runner, 3 Ft. 3 In. x 9 Ft. 3 In. 431.00
Hamadan, Fine Weave, Central Medallion, Red Ground, c.1940, 2 Ft. x 2 Ft. 11 In. 180.00
Hamadan, Flowers, Blue Ground, Red Border, c.1930, 3 Ft. 7 In. x 5 Ft. 8 In. 150.00
Hamadan, Flowers, Central Medallion, Red Ground, c.1940, 2 Ft. 1 In. x 3 Ft. 2 In. 150.00
Hamadan, Flowers, Dark Blue Ground, Red Border, c.1920, 3 Ft. 8 In. x 7 Ft. 2 In. 360.00
Hamadan, Flowers, Red Ground, Blue Border, 5 Ft. x 6 Ft. 8 In. 1380.00
Hamadan, Ivory, Blue Field, Salmon Border, 4 Ft. 1 In. x 5 Ft. 10 In. 374.00
Hamadan, Ivory, Center Medallion, Boteh Rows, Salmon, Blue Corners, 3 Ft. 8 In. x 6 Ft. 230.00
Hand-Knotted, Purple, Orange, Fuschia, Off-White, Wool, 1960s, 8 Ft. 8 In. x 6 Ft. .... *illus* 600.00
Herati, Multicolored, Navy Field, Boteh & Flower Borders, 3 Ft. 7 In. x 5 Ft. 10 In. 175.00
Hereke, Center Medallion, Flowers, Pink, Silk, Fringe, c.1950, 2 Ft. x 3 Ft. 403.00
Heriz, 14 Medallions, Flowers, Geometric Design, Red Field, c.1930, 8 Ft. x 10 Ft. 8 In. 2128.00
Heriz, Allover Design, Red, Blue, Ivory, Green, Black Border, c.1900, 10 Ft. x 6 Ft. 7 In. 1380.00
Heriz, Blue, Diamond Lobed Medallion, Red Field, c.1920, 8 Ft. 8 In. x 11 Ft. 10 In. 4144.00
Heriz, Blue Medallion & Border, Red, Ivory Border, 9 Ft. 10 In. x 13 Ft. 6 In. 12650.00
Heriz, Center Medallion, Red, Blue, Ivory, Early 20th Century, 12 Ft. 2 In. x 9 Ft. 4 In. 240.00
Heriz, Central Flower Medallion, Flowers, Multicolored, Red, 7 Ft. 9 In. x 22 Ft. 6 In. 2475.00
Heriz, Central Medallion, Midnight Blue Field, Runner, c.1920, 10 Ft. 6 In. x 14 In. 1540.00
Heriz, Dark Blue Border, Central Medallion, Flowers, Geometric, 12 Ft. x 8 Ft. 3 In. 5405.00
Heriz, Flowers, Ivory Spandrels, Red Ground, Blue Borders, 9 Ft. 5 In. x 12 Ft. 7 In. 1840.00

Heriz, Flowers, Red, Blue, Cream, c.1920, 8 Ft. 5 In. x 4 Ft. 10 In. . . . . 1440.00 to 1560.00
Heriz, Gabled Medallion, Burnt Umber Field, 6 Ft. 2 In. x 9 Ft. 1035.00
Heriz, Gabled Square Medallion, Geometric, Flowers, Multicolored, Knotted, 9 x 12 Ft. 1200.00
Heriz, Geometric Border, Flowers, Medallion, 10 Ft. 7 In. x 7 Ft. 3 In. 1495.00
Heriz, Medallion, Geometric, Ivory, Slate Blue, Black, Camel, c.1930, 7 Ft. 6 In. x 9 Ft. 1344.00
Heriz, Medallion, Red/rose Ground, Blue Border, Wool, 20th Century, 15 Ft. 6 In. x 10 Ft. 836.00
Heriz, Red, White, Black, c.1940, 11 Ft. 4 In. x 8 Ft. 2 In. 400.00
Heriz, Red Field, Blue Borders, 9 x 12 Ft. 1265.00
Heriz, Red Medallion, Spandrels, Green, Cream, Wool, Cotton, 6 Ft. 7 In. x 9 Ft. 4 In. 3220.00
Hooked, 2 Flowers, Cream, Tan, Gray, Pink, Black Striated Ground, Wool, Cotton, 6 x 53 In. . 230.00
Hooked, 2 Geese, Flying Over Pine Trees, Grenfell Mission, Labrador, 17 x 24 In. 173.00
Hooked, 2 Horse Heads, Mounted, 19th Century, 26 x 35 In. 358.00
Hooked, 2 Roosters, Brown, Red, Orange, Gray, Marbleized Ground, 33 x 55 In. 14400.00
Hooked, 2 Roosters, Flowers, Multicolored, Diamond Border, c.1900, 30 x 47 In. 476.00
Hooked, 2-Masted Schooner Under Sail, Multicolored, 29 x 40 In. 126.00
Hooked, 3 Kittens, Ball Red Yarn, Braided Border, Wool, Oval, c.1910, 25 x 40 In. 633.00
Hooked, 3 Tulips, Red, Yellow, Orange, Green Leaves, Gray, Checkered Border, 31 x 34 In. . . . 546.00
Hooked, 4 Oak Leaves, A M Initial, Square Borders, 26 x 30 In. 385.00
Hooked, Abstract Puzzle Shapes, Apple, Truck, Wool, Burlap, 38 x 33 In., Pair 863.00
Hooked, Airplane, Red, Gray Oval Field, Green Field, Striped Corners, 24 x 36 In. 130.00
Hooked, Art Nouveau, Yellow, Green, Rose, Flowers, Spandrels, 36 x 66 In. 1525.00
Hooked, B & O, Engine, Passenger Coach, Wool, Hazel Walker, c.1957, 24 x 36 In. 805.00
Hooked, Barn Hex Sign, 3 Circles, Gray Ground, 20 x 55 In. 110.00
Hooked, Basket, Salmon, Flower, Circle, Square Border, Wool, Cotton, 1863, 31 x 52 In. 5580.00
Hooked, Birds, Flower Basket, Undulating Border, Wool, Burlap, 31 x 55 In. 270.00
Hooked, Black Cat, Orange Eyes, Kitten, Striped, Wool, Knit, 14 x 11 ½ In. 431.00
Hooked, Blue, Purple, Orange Flowers, Green Leaves, Blue Urn, Wool, 24 x 18 In. 489.00
Hooked, Cat, Gray, 4 Tulips, Green Ground, 21 ½ x 40 In. 1045.00
Hooked, Cat, Gray, On Platform, Scrolled Leaves, Gray Ground, Brown Border, 20 x 38 In. . . . 660.00
Hooked, Cat, On Oval Rug, Cream, Blue, Gray, Cotton, Denim, Knit Stocking, 41 x 31 In. 920.00
Hooked, Cat, Wearing Bow, 14 x 11 In. 28.00
Hooked, Centennial, Monk's Cloth, Felt Backing, c.1876, 33 x 47 In. 1700.00
Hooked, Center Flower Panel, Taupe Field, Grape & Leaf Border, 44 x 118 In. 1120.00
Hooked, Central Flower, Vines, Black, Mottled Border, 19th Century, 46 x 35 In. 252.00
Hooked, Central Star, Red, Blue, Frame, 38 x 38 In. 176.00
Hooked, Clamshell Pattern, Greens, Browns, Plum, Wine, Border, 1900, 68 x 37 In. 1950.00
Hooked, Clock Face, 4:00, Multicolored, 27 x 29 In. 650.00
Hooked, Concentric Rings, Black, Gray, Blue, Green, Clipped Loops, Wool, 49 x 36 In. 316.00
Hooked, Conestoga Wagon, 6 Horses, Mill Scene, Frame, 27 ½ x 50 ½ In. 154.00
Hooked, Cottage, Trees In Garden, Sky Worked In Strips, Black, 1925, 52 x 36 In. 255.00
Hooked, Couple, Silhouette, Landscape, Trees, Red Flowers, Black Border, 24 x 46 In. 144.00
Hooked, Cow Pull Toy, Red Border, 28 x 16 ½ In. 1495.00
Hooked, Cupid's Lament, Wool, Early 20th Century, 37 x 50 ½ In. 1058.00
Hooked, Dog, Collie, Brown, White, Pine Trees, Gold, Black, Crocheted Edge, 26 x 43 In. 242.00
Hooked, Dog, German Shepherd, Black Lab, Tan, Black, Pink, Blue Border, 24 x 36 In. 115.00
Hooked, Dog, Labrador Retriever, Black, Geese Flying, Nighttime, Trees, Grenfell, 26 x 38 In. . 1560.00
Hooked, Dog, Lying Down, Black, Red Ears, Cotton, Wool, c.1899, 27 ¾ x 40 In. 1920.00
Hooked, Dog, Rover, Short Hair, Gray, Red Collar, White Bird, Swans, Fringed, Wool, 25 x 48 In. 360.00
Hooked, Dog, Scottie, Gray, Rose Vine Border, Wool, Cotton, c.1930, 22 x 35 In. . . . . *illus* 460.00
Hooked, Dog Sled, 5 Brown Dogs, Beige Ground, Grenfell, 1930s, 26 x 40 In. 2465.00
Hooked, Eagle, 13 Red Stars, Navy Ground, Wool, On Burlap, 24 x 37 In. 1380.00
Hooked, Eagle, Spread Wing, Cotton, Wool, GBC 1953, 65 x 48 In. . . . . *illus* 547.00
Hooked, Elephant, Striped Ground, Gray, Black, Maroon, Tan, Green, 32 x 38 In. 575.00
Hooked, Elk, Landscape, Tan, Red, Gold, Black, Cotton, Burlap, 24 x 38 In. 173.00
Hooked, Elk, Standing, Landscape, Red Scrolls, Wood Frame, 30 x 54 In. 230.00
Hooked, Ewe, White, Flowers, Landscape, Sky, Blue, Blue & Tan Border, 24 x 35 In. 288.00
Hooked, Farmhouse, People, Dog, Mottled Border, Barbara Merry, 1900s, 32 x 61 In. 550.00
Hooked, Flower Basket, c.1920, 31 x 38 In. 116.00
Hooked, Flowerpot, Geometric & Flower Border, Burlap Backing, 29 x 39 ½ In. 77.00
Hooked, Flowers, Birds, Multicolored, 96 x 48 In. 2300.00
Hooked, Flowers, c.1920, 25 x 36 In. 55.00
Hooked, Flowers, Circles, Red, Green, Brown, Pink, Burlap Backing, 23 x 35 ½ In. 55.00
Hooked, Flowers, Flowers In Center, c.1880, 30 x 54 In. 5200.00
Hooked, Flowers, Green Border, Oval, 13 x 8 ½ In. 55.00
Hooked, Flowers, Green Leaves, Scalloped Inner Border, Oval, 108 x 79 In. 2030.00
Hooked, Flowers, Leafy Border, Early 20th Century, 74 x 49 In. 518.00

Rug, Flower, Red, White, Blue, Wool, 1970s, 69 In.
$240.00

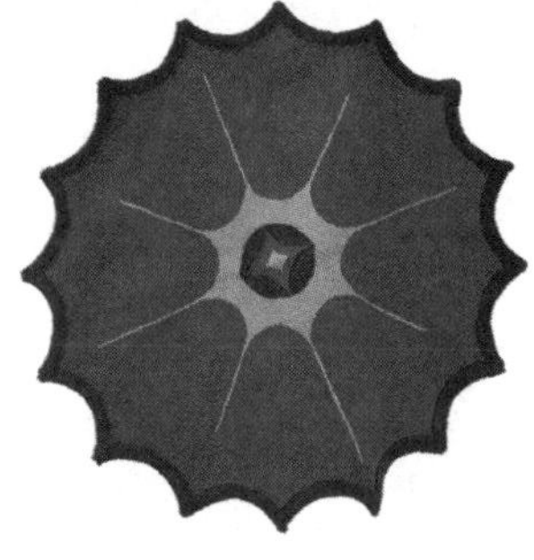

Rug, Hand-Knotted, Purple, Orange, Fuschia, Off-White, Wool, 1960s, 8 Ft. 8 In. x 6 Ft.
$600.00

Rug, Hooked, Dog, Scottie, Gray, Rose Vine Border, Wool, Cotton, c.1930, 22 x 35 In.
$460.00

Rug, Hooked, Eagle, Spread Wing, Cotton, Wool, GBC 1953, 65 x 48 In.
$547.00

R

TIP
Try not to vacuum rugs with fringe. The vacuum "eats" corners, damaged edge bindings, and edges and tears fringe.

Rug, Hooked, Legend, Children Will Play, 4 Seasons Round, Muted, 35 x 52 In. $11400.00

Rug, Hooked, Man, 3 Dogs, Buildings, Grenfell, Early 20th Century, 14 x 18 In. $605.00

Rug, Hooked, Pony, Purple, Stars, Tulips, c.1920-40, 24 x 40 In. $375.00

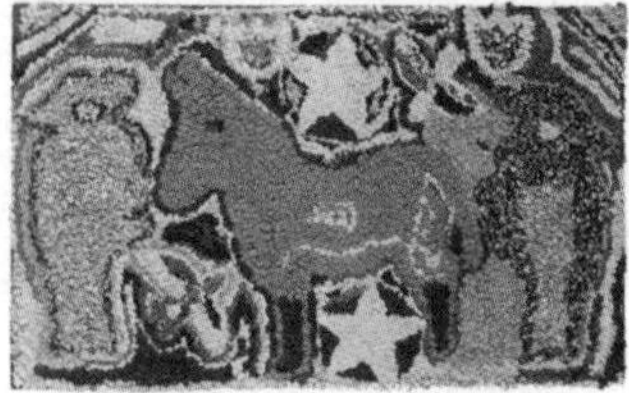

TIP
Don't dry clean a rag rug. It should be carefully washed.

Hooked, Flowers, Red, Yellow, Peach, Purple, Gray, Black Squiggle Ground, 57 x 56 In. 460.00
Hooked, Flowers, Striped Diamond Center, Multicolored Wool, Burlap, 30 x 56 In. 180.00
Hooked, Flowers, Vase, Strawberry Bowl, Hummingbird, Wool, Burlap, 36 x 49 In. 230.00 to 510.00
Hooked, Flowers, Vines, Multicolored, Burlap Back, 19th Century, 46 x 35 In. 225.00
Hooked, Folk Art, Barnyard Animals, Robins, Striated Ground, Wool, 31 x 37 In.. . . . . 720.00
Hooked, Folk Art, Flowers, Blue Ground, Scroll Top, Variegated Border, 40 x 35 In. 200.00
Hooked, Fox, Brown Orange, Rabbit, White, Green Tree, White Ground, 26 x 38½ In. 210.00
Hooked, Geometric, Argyle Pattern, Multicolored, Stripe Borders, Cubes, 7 x 9 Ft. 10200.00
Hooked, Geometric, Squares, Triangles, Multicolored, c.1850, 32 x 55 In.. . . . . 588.00
Hooked, Geometric, Wool, Early 20th Century, 32 x 62 In. 588.00
Hooked, Geometric Design, Square & Triangle Border, Multicolored, c.1850, 32 x 48 In.. . . . . 525.00
Hooked, Geometric Squares, Multicolored, Brown & Red Border, 23½ x 40 In. 248.00
Hooked, Gothic Medallion, Gray, Blue, Black, Mounted, Wool, On Canvas, 45 x 31 In.. . . . . . . 230.00
Hooked, Grenfell, Fishing Village, 17 x 24 In. 1035.00
Hooked, Grenfell, Flying Tern, 10 x 10 In. 259.00
Hooked, Grenfell, Gulls, 17 x 19 In. 575.00
Hooked, Grenfell, Polar Bears, 11 x 14 In.. . . . . 259.00
Hooked, Grenfell, Seal Hunt, 15 x 11 In. 403.00
Hooked, Grenfell, Tern In Flight, 11 x 10 In.. . . . . 345.00
Hooked, Grenfell, Village Church, 14 x 18 In. 1035.00
Hooked, Homeward Bound, Ship Flying American Flag, 1930s, 34 x 66 In.. . . . . 2116.00
Hooked, Horse, Running, Scrolled Border, Brown, Green, Cream, Wool, 33 x 60 In.. . . . . 475.00
Hooked, Horse, Sleigh & Rider, Landscape, Pumpkin Sky, Bare Trees, Wool, 29 x 48 In. 805.00
Hooked, Horse, Striated Ground, Blue Sawtooth Border, Wool, 1900s, 25 x 36 In. 489.00
Hooked, Horse, Trotting, Cotton, Wool, Early 20th Century, 30¾ x 39 In.. . . . . 5400.00
Hooked, Horse Heads, Bob, Bonnie, Blue Ribbon, Wool, Bill Gorringe, 1967, 24 x 36 In.. . . . . 115.00
Hooked, House, 5 Chickens, 2 Geese, Blues, Browns, Wool, Cotton, Frame, 24 x 41 In.. . . . . . . 4994.00
Hooked, House, Tree, Well Sweep, Flowers, Dog, Cat, Wool, Cotton, Mounted, 25 x 38 In. 1293.00
Hooked, House & Barn, Leaf Border Along Top, 38 x 60 In. 963.00
Hooked, Houses, Christmas Trees, Beige, Striped Border, 20th Century, 24 x 40 In. 1410.00
Hooked, In God We Trust Center, Spiral, Flowers, Initials L.B., 1898, 39 x 40 In. 990.00
Hooked, Indian, Shooting Oversized Gray Deer, Pink Antlers, Landscape, 20 x 39 In. 2520.00
Hooked, Knit Stockings, Horse-Drawn Coach, Purple, Striated Border, Wool, 27 x 54 In.. . . . . 115.00
Hooked, Landscape, Amish Man, In Buggy With Horse, Ohio, 32 x 60 In.. . . . . 2450.00
Hooked, Landscape, House, Red Rooster, Striped Border, 20th Century, 36 x 37 In. 225.00
Hooked, Leaping Stag, Red Tongue, Button Eye, Flowers, Embroidery, Border, 19 x 37 In.. . . . 1380.00
Hooked, Legend, Children Will Play, 4 Seasons Round, Muted, 35 x 52 In. . . . . *illus* 11400.00
Hooked, Leopard, Flowers, Multicolored, Butterscotch, Flowered Border, 33 x 59 In.. . . . . 580.00
Hooked, Lion, Reclining, Leaf Border, Frame, Frost, Biddeford, Maine, 20 x 60½ In.. . . . . 895.00
Hooked, Lion & Palm, Flowers, Landscape, Striped Border, Wool, Burlap, 35 x 57 In. 1265.00
Hooked, Lions, Deer, Rabbits, Birds, Butterflies, Trees, Flowers, PH 93, 29 x 107 In.. . . . . 770.00
Hooked, Lobster, Swordfish, Clams, Blue Ground, 1940s, 30 x 43 In.. . . . . 775.00
Hooked, Mallard Duck, Flying, Oak Leaf Clusters, 24 x 36 In. 460.00
Hooked, Man, 3 Dogs, Buildings, Grenfell, Early 20th Century, 14 x 18 In.. . . . . *illus* 605.00
Hooked, Mother Cat, Kittens, Checked Floor, Leaf Borders, Frost Pattern, No. 39, 51 x 28 In.. . 518.00
Hooked, Paisley, Reds, Blues, Greens, Tan, Wool, 28 x 53 In.. . . . . 403.00
Hooked, Polka Dots, Abstract Border, Cotton, Wool, Early 1900s, 33 x 64½ In.. . . . . 3840.00
Hooked, Pony, Purple, Stars, Tulips, c.1920-40, 24 x 40 In. . . . . *illus* 375.00
Hooked, Quebec Center, Variegated Block Border, 16 x 32½ In.. . . . . 11.00
Hooked, Red Design, Black Ground, Flowers, Blue Bird Corners, Wool, Burlap, 39 x 25 In.. . . . 230.00
Hooked, Red Flowers, Scalloped Oval, Leaf Border, Wool, On Canvas, 34 x 68 In.. . . . . 173.00
Hooked, Roosters, Flowers, Diamond Border, c.1900, 30 x 47 In.. . . . . 425.00
Hooked, Schoolhouse, Multicolored, 60 x 27 In.. . . . . 4950.00
Hooked, Seat Cover, Log Cabin, Campfire, 14 x 15½ In.. . . . . 44.00
Hooked, Ship, Bluenose, Under Sail, Flying Flags, Clouds, c.1920, 29 x 38 In. 250.00
Hooked, Spread-Wing Eagle, Clipped Corners, Cotton, Wool, Burlap Back, 65 x 45 In.. . . . . . . 546.00
Hooked, Stockings, Houses, Blue Sky, Multicolored Stripes, Wool, Cotton, 30 x 45 In. 374.00
Hooked, Striated Center, Red, Tan, Gray, Green, Diamond Border, Wool, Burlap, 79 x 42 In.. . 345.00
Hooked, Swan, White, Red, Tan, White, Blue, Blue, Stripe Border, Wool, 45 x 33 In.. . . . . 900.00
Hooked, Tulips, Red, White, Gray, Black Ground, 30 x 45 In.. . . . . 66.00
Hooked, Winter Homestead, Border, Block Corners, Barbara E. Merry, 24 x 36 In.. . . . . 500.00
Hooked, Winter Scene, Flower Border, c.1910, 90 x 108 In.. . . . . 9500.00
Indo-Persian, Pale Salmon Field, Dark Blue Borders, 4 Ft. x 5 Ft. 9 In. 690.00
Isfahan, Center Medallion, Blue, Ivory, Amber, Olive Field, Woven Silk, 9 x 12 Ft. 1035.00
Isfahan, Center Rosette, Blue, Medallions, Square Border, 1900s, 10 Ft. x 6 Ft. 8 In. 460.00
Isfahan, Flowers, Vines, Ivory Field, 7 Ft. 2 In. x 10 Ft. 1 In.. . . . . 4370.00

arabagh, Prayer, Diagonal Diamond Bands, Black, Barber Pole Border, 3 Ft. x 4 Ft. 518.00
araghasli, Serrated Center Diamond, Pendants, Corner & Border, 4 Ft. x 5 Ft. 8 In. 633.00
araja, Center Medallion, Mid 20th Century, 9 Ft. 11 In. x 13 Ft. 7 In. .... *illus* 4830.00
ashan, Allover Vine & Flower, Amber Field, Blue Ground, 9 Ft. 11 In. x 13 Ft. 7 In. 1035.00
ashan, Flowers, Burgundy Field, 9 Ft. 10 In. x 22 Ft. 1 In. 20700.00
ashan, Flowers, Diamond Medallion, Blue, Scalloped Edge, 10 Ft. 6 In. x 18 Ft. 10000.00
ashan, Flowers, Red Field, Blue Weft, Early 1900s, 8 Ft. 8 In. x 11 Ft. 8 In. 2070.00
ashan, Flowers, Scrolled, Burgundy Ground, c.1920, 10 Ft. 1 In. x 13 Ft. 7 In. 1298.00
ashan, Medallion, Ivory, Amber, Blue Accents, Blue Field, 10 Ft. 1 In. x 13 Ft. 7 In. 690.00
azak, Caucasus, Multicolor Medallion, Brick Ground, c.1860, 5 Ft. 7 In. x 4 Ft. 2390.00
azak, Caucasus Rosettes, 1920s, 3 Ft. 2 In. x 5 Ft. 4 In. 767.00
azak, Geometric, Wing Style, Medallions, Crescents, Green, Burgundy, 9 Ft. x 11 Ft. 1150.00
azak, Hook & Flowers, Blue, Red, Ivory & Green, 7 Ft. 10 In. x 5 Ft. .... *illus* 920.00
azak, Prayer, Repeating Diamond Medallions, Hook Borders, 3 Ft. 8 In. x 4 Ft. 9 In. 1265.00
azak, Red, Blue, Blue Green, Camel Borders, 4 Ft. 5 In. x 6 Ft. 10 In. 1725.00
azak, Square Blue Center Panel, Birds, Multiple Geometric Borders, 3 Ft. x 3 Ft. 9 In. 316.00
erman, Concentric Flower Medallions, Yellow Spandrels, Blue Field, 9 Ft. x 12 Ft. 1500.00
erman, Palace, Beige Ground, Celadon Border, Wool, Cotton, 24 Ft. 6 In. x 14 Ft. 3 In. 3738.00
horsan, Red Medallion, Birds, Corner Blocks, Blue Ground, 8 Ft. 6 In. x 10 Ft. 7 In. 1200.00
uba, Ivory, Cinnamon, Indigo Field, 1930, 5 Ft. 2 In. x 8 Ft. 3 In. 1200.00
urdish, 4 Medallions, Caucasian Style, Diagonal Internal Borders, 3 Ft. 6 In. x 6 Ft. 546.00
urdish, Rosettes, Hand Woven, 1920s, 4 Ft. 11 In. x 3 Ft. 5 In. 531.00
urdish Kazak, Geometric, Navy Field, c.1920, 3 Ft. 10 In. x 6 Ft. 6 In. 900.00
avar Kerman, Flower Medallion, Multiple Borders, 9 Ft. 5 In. x 7 Ft. 8190.00
avar Kerman, Medallion, Ivory, Vine, Leaf Border, Rabbits, 4 Ft. 5 In. x 6 Ft. 6 In. 1840.00
lian, Flower, Blue, Tan, Fuchsia Ground, Fringed, c.1880, 9 x 11 Ft. 1800.00
lihan, Flowers, Red Field, c.1920, 3 Ft. 5 In. x 4 Ft. 8 In. 480.00
ahal, 3 Center Medallions, Coral Field, 10 Ft. 1 In. x 13 Ft. 6 In. 1150.00
ahal, Allover Flower, Deep Blue Ground, Early 20th Century, 14 Ft. 6 In. x 9 Ft. 10 In. 1035.00
ahal, Flowers, Brick Red Ground, Hand Woven, 1940s, 8 Ft. 6 In. x 11 Ft. 9 In. 3304.00
ahal, Geometric, Flower, Ivory Field, Serrated Borders, 8 Ft. 8 In. x 12 Ft. 5 In. 748.00
alayer, Center Medallion, Blue Field, Brick Red Borders, 10 Ft. 9 In. x 13 Ft. 8 In. 2300.00
alayer, Center Medallion, Blue Ground, Red Border, 13 Ft. 8 In. x 10 Ft. 9 In. .... *illus* 2295.00
alayer, Center Medallion, Border, Green, Blue, Ivory, Salmon Field, 5 Ft. x 6 Ft. 1093.00
alayer, Diamond Lattice, Camel Field, Runner, 3 Ft. 3 In. x 16 Ft. 2 In. 633.00
alayer Hamadan, Rosettes, Midnight Blue Ground, 5 Ft. 4 In. x 6 Ft. 7 In. 2006.00
eshed, Flower Medallion, Serrated Palmettes, Vines, Multicolored, 9 Ft. 5 In. x 13 Ft. 3025.00
ohajram Sarank, Flowers, Navy & Tan, Red Ground, c.1910, 4 Ft. x 6 Ft. 6 In. 1080.00
ahavand, Tree Of Life, Brown Ground, Red & Blue Borders, 3 Ft. 6 In. x 9 Ft. 3 In. 345.00
ain, Flowers, Vines, Central Medallion, Scalloped Corner, Ivory, 6 Ft. x 10 Ft. 4 In. 1093.00
ain, Hand Woven, Part Silk, Scrolling Design, 1950s, 4 Ft. 11 In. x 7 Ft. 8 In. 826.00
orthwest Persian, Trees, Blue Field, Salmon Border, 5 Ft. 11 In. x 13 Ft. 6 In. 2530.00
riental, Sarouk, Burgundy Ground, Midnight Blue Border, 3 Ft. 11 In. x 6 Ft. 3 In. 460.00
ushak, Center Medallion, Bittersweet, Gold, Lattice, Geometric, Wool, Angora, 10 Ft. x 15 Ft. 6325.00
ushak, Center Medallion, Gold, Blue, Geometric Border, 12 Ft. 3 In. x 14 Ft. 7 In. 9775.00
ushak, Flowers, Geometric, Ivory Field, Turkey, 15 Ft. 5 In. x 14 Ft. 9 In. 1840.00
enny, Concentric Discs, Multicolored Fabric, Hexagonal, Wool, Cotton, 26 x 90 In. 2838.00
ersian, 5 Medallions, Ivory, Rosette Border, Wool, 12 Ft. x 17 Ft. 5 In. 9440.00
ersian, Allover Design, Blue Ground, Finely Knotted, c.1950, 10 Ft. x 14 Ft. 4 In. 1534.00
rsian, Allover Flower Design, Blue Spandrels, Medallion, Red, 8 Ft. 8 In. x 11 Ft. 5 In. 1116.00
ersian, Animals, Birds, Flowers, Chocolate, Camel Ground, Silk, 4 Ft. 5 In. x 7 Ft. 999.00
ersian, Brick Red, Geometric Medallion, 20th Century, 4 Ft. 5 In. x 6 Ft. 11 In. 198.00
ersian, Brick Red Field, Geometric Medallions, 20th Century, 2 Ft. 6 In. x 10 Ft. 3 In. 143.00
ersian, Center Panel, Winged & Flower Designs, 4 Ft. 4 In. x 6 Ft. 4 In. 748.00
ersian, Flower Center Medallion, Multicolored, Ivory Field, 8 Ft. 2 In. x 10 Ft. 5 In. 935.00
ersian, Flower Medallion, Flower Border, 20th Century, 4 Ft. 4 In. x 6 Ft. 11 In. 132.00
rsian, Flower Medallions, Multicolored, 8 Ft. 9 In. x 12 Ft. 10 In. 192.00
rsian, Flowers, Blue & Red Ground, c.1920, 3 Ft. 7 In. x 6 Ft. 3 In. 150.00
rsian, Flowers, Blue Ground, Blue Border, 8 Ft. 6 In. x 11 Ft. 6 In. 633.00
ersian, Flowers, Burgundy Ground, Hand Woven, 1940s, 12 Ft. 6 In. x 22 Ft. 2 In. 17700.00
rsian, Flowers, Central Medallion, Red Ground, c.1940, 3 Ft. 6 In. x 5 Ft. 210.00
rsian, Flowers, Green, Blue Highlights, Blue Field, 6 Ft. 7 In. x 20 Ft. 7 In. 2415.00
rsian, Flowers, Multicolored, Central Medallion, c.1910, 2 Ft. 6 In. x 3 Ft. 10 In. 420.00
rsian, Flowers, Olive Ground, 9 x 14 Ft. 245.00
ersian, Flowers, Red Ground, c.1930, 3 Ft. 5 In. x 5 Ft. 6 In. 150.00
ersian, Flowers, Vines, Ivory, Burgundy Field, Blue Border, 9 Ft. 11 In. x 13 Ft. 863.00

TIP
Oriental rugs should be vacuumed once a week and have an expert cleaning and mothproofing once a year, if in a heavy traffic area.

Rug, Karaja, Center Medallion, Mid 20th Century, 9 Ft. 11 In. x 13 Ft. 7 In. $4830.00

Rug, Kazak, Hook & Flowers, Blue, Red, Ivory & Green, 7 Ft. 10 In. x 5 Ft. $920.00

TIP
If your guests spill tomato sauce or ketchup on the carpet, sprinkle salt on the stain. Sweep up the salt and repeat over and over until the stain is gone.

Rug, Malayer, Center Medallion, Blue Ground, Red Border, 13 Ft. 8 In. x 10 Ft. 9 In. $2295.00

TIP
If you get gum on your Oriental rug or carpet, freeze it with an ice cube in a plastic bag, then scrape it off with a plastic credit card.

Persian, Flowers, Wheat-Colored Ground, Crimson Border, 8 Ft. 8 In. x 11 Ft. 8 In. 4012.0
Persian, Leopard, Red Field, Multicolored Geometric Border, 3 Ft. 8 In. x 5 Ft. 253.0
Persian, Lobed Diamond Medallion, Flowers, Vines, Spandrels, Red, 9 Ft. 6 In. x 13 Ft. 1500.0
Persian, Medallion, Vines, Flowers, Multicolored, Ivory, Wool, 8 Ft. 7 In. x 121 Ft. 1980.0
Persian, Northwest, Flowers, Blue Gray Ground, 1920s, 3 x 4 Ft. 767.0
Persian, Rosette Medallions, Palmettes, Scrolling Arabesques, 8 Ft. 2 In. x 11 Ft. 2 In. 1250.0
Persian, Scrolling Vines, Flowers, Multicolored, Navy Field, Vine Border, 8 Ft. x 12 Ft. 935.0
Persian, Tribal, Blue, Red, Tan, c.1920, 3 Ft. 9 In. x 6 Ft. 8 In. 180.0
Prayer, Crimson Ground, Blue Scroll Flower Border, 3 Ft. 7 In. x 5 Ft. 6 In. 1400.0
Quashkai, Serrated Diamond Center Panel, Geometric Borders, 4 Ft. 10 In. x 4 Ft. 3 In. 546.0
Sarouk, Allover Design, Crimson Ground, Hand Woven, 1930s, 5 Ft. 2 In. x 3 Ft. 4 In. 472.0
Sarouk, Allover Flowers, Red Ground, Fringe, c.1910, 13 Ft. 3 In. x 10 Ft. 2 In. 1035.0
Sarouk, Allover Flowers, Red Ground, Runner, c.1910, 11 Ft. 1 In. x 2 Ft. 8 In. 403.0
Sarouk, Blue Border, Ivory Ground, Hand Woven, 1940s, 6 Ft. 6 In. x 9 Ft. 6 In. 1062.0
Sarouk, Blue Center Medallion, Pendants, Brick Red Field, 4 Ft. 2 In. x 6 Ft. 7 In. 978.0
Sarouk, Blue Flowering Vines, Red Field, 3 Ft. 6 In. x 5 Ft. 1 In. 431.0
Sarouk, Blue Ground, Burgundy Border, 4 Ft. 1 In. x 6 Ft. 6 In. 546.0
Sarouk, Center Medallion, Burgundy Field, 4 Ft. 5 In. x 6 Ft. 10 In., Pair 2530.0
Sarouk, Central 8-Lobbed Medallion, Cobalt Blue Ground, c.1880, 9 Ft. x 15 Ft. 6 In. 1003.0
Sarouk, Central Medallion, Flowers, Leaves, Rust, Blue Border, 10 Ft. 8 In. x 14 Ft. 4700.0
Sarouk, Flower Bouquets, Burgundy Field, 10 Ft. 6 In. x 18 Ft. 10 In. 1093.0
Sarouk, Flower Bouquets, Dark Burgundy Field, 11 Ft. 6 In. x 16 Ft. 5750.0
Sarouk, Flowers, Blue Field, 4 Ft. 2 In. x 6 Ft. 8 In. 489.0
Sarouk, Flowers, Border, Red, Blue, Amber, Green, 8 Ft. 9 In. x 17 Ft. 5 In. 504.0
Sarouk, Flowers, Crimson Ground, Hand Woven, 8 Ft. 6 In. x 12 Ft. 2242.0
Sarouk, Flowers, Multicolored, Crimson Ground, c.1920, 8 Ft. 8 In. x 11 Ft. 10 In. 1180.0
Sarouk, Flowers, Palmettes, Multicolored, 8 x 12 Ft. 1250.0
Sarouk, Flowers, Salmon Field, 1930s, 9 Ft. x 11 Ft. 9 In. 1035.0
Sarouk, Multicolored Flowers, Crimson Ground, 1920s, 5 Ft. 4 In. x 3 Ft. 7 In. . . . . 1062.
Sarouk, Red Center Medallion, Blue Field, Ivory, 4 Ft. 1 In. x 6 Ft. 2 In. . . . . 633.
Senneh, 3 Serrated Diamond Medallions, Brick Red Field, 4 Ft. 1 In. x 6 Ft. 2 In. . . . . 1035.
Senneh, Flowers, Red & Cream, Navy Ground, c.1910, 4 x 6 Ft. . . . . 2160.
Senneh, Geometric, Blue Field, Runner, 3 Ft. 9 In. x 15 Ft. 2 In. . . . . 230.
Senneh Kurd, Boteh Design, 1930s, 4 Ft. 7 In. x 3 Ft. 2 In. . . . . 561.
Serab, Central Medallion, Chevron Field, Blue, Orange, Wool, Cotton, 3 Ft. x 6 Ft. 9 In. . . . . . . 863.
Serab, Serrated Geometric, Ivory Field, Camel Border, Runner, 2 Ft. 11 In. x 14 Ft. 2 In. . . . . . 690.
Serapi, Central Medallion, Flowers, Red, Teal, 8 Ft. 10 In. x 10 Ft. . . . . 4113.
Serapi, Central Medallion, Tangerine, Ivory Vines, 9 Ft. 2 In. x 12 Ft. 7 In. . . . . 1840.
Serapi, Dark Blue Medallion, Ivory Spandrels, Red Border, 9 Ft. 7 In. x 12 Ft. . . . . 18400.
Serapi, Flowers, Red, Blue, Carmel Ground, 13 Ft. 2 In. x 16 Ft. 4 In. 9400.
Serapi, Medallion, Allover Flowers, Red, Camel Ground, 9 Ft. 9 In. x 12 Ft. 5 In. . . . . 4113.
Serapi, Medallion, Spandrels, Red, Camel Ground, Flower Borders, 7 Ft. x 10 Ft. . . . . 5405.
Serapi, Peshawar, Brick Medallion, Ivory Ground, 9 Ft. x 12 Ft. 4 In. . . . . 2640.
Sherivan, Geometric, Cream, Red, Blue, Multiple Borders, c.1910, 4 Ft. 5 In. x 7 Ft. 3 In. . . . . 600.
Shiraz, 3 Medallions, Red, Blue, Ivory, 3-Line Border, c.1950, 5 Ft. 9 In. x 3 Ft. 8 In. . . . . 288.
Shiraz, Central Medallion, Red Field, c.1970, 4 Ft. 4 In. x 7 Ft. 4 In. . . . . 270.
Shiraz, Spandrels, Blue Ground, Red Border, 3 Ft. 5 In. x 11 Ft. 9 In. 374.
Soumak, Blue Designs, Burnt Orange Ground, Black Border, 7 x 9 Ft. 431.
Soumak, Flat Woven, Burgundy, Green, Blue, Black, Gold Azerbaijan, 7 Ft. x 12 Ft. 7 In. . . . . 230.
Sultanabad, Cartouches, Flowers, Mustard, Blue Ground, 13 Ft. 2 In. x 20 Ft. 7 In. . . . . 8813.
Sultanabad, Center Medallion, Pendants, Blue, Salmon, Ivory, 8 Ft. 10 In. x 10 Ft. . . . . 546.
Sultanabad, Flowers, Red Central Field, Blue Border, 13 Ft. 4 In. x 19 Ft. 5 In. . . . . 10575.
Sumac, 3 Center Medallions, Red Field, Hook Outer Border, 5 Ft. 1 In. x 6 Ft. . . . . 1265.
Sumac, Flower Vase, Geometric, Bird Corners, Embroidered, Olive, 3 Ft. 6 In. x 5 Ft. 3 In. . . . 489.
Tabriz, 2 Noblemen Seated, Attendants, Musicians, Hand Woven, c.1870, 4 Ft. x 6 Ft. . . . . 4248.
Tabriz, 48 Brown Pictorial Medallions, Ivory, Embroidered, Olive, 6 Ft. 5 In. x 9 Ft. . . . . 280.
Tabriz, Allover Flower & Vines, Brown, Ivory, 3 Borders, c.1910, 8 Ft. 5 In. x 12 Ft. . . . . 805.
Tabriz, Blue, Rose, Natural Field, 13 Ft. 8 In. x 9 Ft. 9 In. . . . . 575.
Tabriz, Flowers, Indigo Medallion, Deep Red Field, 1970, 9 Ft. 7 In. x 12 Ft. 10 In. . . . . 660.
Tabriz, Palace, Ivory Ground, 3 Ft. 1 In. x 3 Ft. 11 In. . . . . 59.
Tabriz, Red & Blue Medallion, Red & Blue Field, Red, c.1910, 11 Ft. 8 In. x 9 Ft. . . . . 460.
Tabriz, Ruby Red Medallion, Ivory Spandrels, 1970, 6 Ft. 7 In. x 9 Ft. 10 In. . . . . 360.
Turkeman, Hatchley Geometric, Red Field, Low Pile, c.1930, 4 Ft. 6 In. x 6 Ft. 1 In. . . . . 390.
Turkish, Central Medallion, Red Field, c.1940, 1 Ft. 10 In. x 3 Ft. 4 In. . . . . 600.
Turkish, Flowers, Blue Field, Red Border, c.1950, 3 Ft. 3 In. x 5 Ft. 9 In. . . . . 420.
Turkish, Geometric Medallions, Earth Tones, 20th Century, 2 Ft. 10 In. x 9 Ft. 6 In. . . . . 121.

Villiam Morris, Flowers, Amber, Dark Plum, Black Field, 9 Ft. 1 In. x 12 Ft. 1 In. 660.00
Villiam Morris, Flowers, Jade Green Ground, 6 Ft. x 9 Ft. 3 In. 960.00
Villiam Morris, Flowers, Jewel Tones, 8 Ft. 10 In. x 11 Ft. 9 In. 1560.00
Villiam Morris, Flowers, Jewel Tones, Pale Celadon Field, 5 Ft. x 6 Ft. 10 In. 480.00
Villiam Morris, Flowers, Midnight Blue Ground, Cream Border, 8 x 10 Ft. 510.00
Villiam Morris, Flowers, Olive Green Ground, 10 Ft. x 13 Ft. 9 In. 1560.00
Villiam Morris, Flowers, Vine, Jewel Tones, 8 Ft. 2 In. x 10 Ft. 840.00
Vilton, Persian Patter, Purple Field, c.1920, 4 Ft. 2 In. x 7 Ft. 1 In. 112.00
Vool, Bands Of Diamond Shapes, Pink, 19th Century, 8 Ft. 11 In. x 5 Ft. 8 In. 478.00
Vool, Embroidered Geometric, Woven, Red, 20th Century, 8 Ft. 4 In. x 5 Ft. 478.00
Vool, Geometric, Pink, Design, Bird Border, 20th Century, 9 Ft. 10 In. x 6 Ft. 478.00
Voolwork, Oval Flower Medallion, Multicolored, Burlap Backing, 4 x 5 Ft. 200.00

UMRILL Pottery was designed by George Rumrill of Little Rock, Arkansas. From 1933 to 938, it was produced by the Red Wing Pottery of Red Wing, Minnesota. In January 1938, roduction was transferred to the Shawnee Pottery in Zanesville, Ohio. It was moved again in December f 1938 to Florence Pottery Company in Mt. Gilead, Ohio, where Rumrill ware continued to be manufacured until the pottery burned in 1941. It was then produced by Gonder Ceramic Arts in South Zanesville ntil early 1943.

RumRill

ase, 3 Leaf Design, Blue, 7 In. 43.00
ase, Blue, 5 ¼ In. 33.00
ase, Blue, 7 ½ In. 11.00
ase, Blue, Handles, 7 ⅜ In. 27.00
ase, Blue, Ribs, 6 In. 32.00

USKIN is a British art pottery of the twentieth century. The Ruskin Pottery was started by Villiam Howson Taylor, and his name was used as the mark until about 1899. The factory, at Vest Smethwick, Birmingham, England, stopped making new pie ces in 1933 but continued o glaze and sell the remaining wares until 1935. The art pottery is noted for its exceptional glazes.

RUSKIN POTTERY WEST SMETHWICK

owl, Blue, Mottled Cream, 20th Century, 2 x 6 In. 66.00
in, Porcelain, Silver, Lozenge Shape, Art Nouveau, Marked, 1 ¼ In. *illus* 80.00
ase, Cloudy Flambe, Footed, Marked, c.1910, 12 ½ In. 2160.00
ase, Cream & Green Crystalline Glaze, 6-Sided, W. Howson Taylor, 4 ⅝ In. *illus* 325.00
ase, Mottled Gray, Bulbous Bottom, Cylindrical Neck, Flared Rim, 1927, 12 In. 424.00
ase, Shouldered, Yellow Luster Glaze, Mark, 5 x 9 ½ In. 86.00

USSEL WRIGHT designed dinnerwares in modern shapes for many companies. Iroquois hina Company, Harker China Company, Steubenville Pottery, and Justin Tharaud and Sons nade dishes marked *Russel Wright*. The Steubenville wares, first made in 1938, are the most ommon today. Wright was a designer of domestic and industrial wares, including furniture, aluminum, adios, interiors, and glassware. Dinnerwares and other pieces by Wright are listed here. For more nformation, see *Kovels' Depression Glass & Dinnerware Price List*.

Russel Wright MFG. BY STEUBENVILLE

merican Modern, Bowl, Salad, Granite Gray, 8 In. 95.00
merican Modern, Bowl, Salad, Seafoam Blue, 8 In. 125.00
merican Modern, Bowl, Vegetable, Black Chutney 40.00
merican Modern, Bowl, Vegetable, Divided, Chartreuse 150.00
merican Modern, Bowl, Vegetable, Divided, Coral 84.00
merican Modern, Bowl, Vegetable, Seafoam Blue 34.00
merican Modern, Butter, Cover, Granite Gray *illus* 32.00
merican Modern, Casserole, Cover, Stick Handle, Chartreuse, 4 x 8 ¼ In. 51.00
merican Modern, Celery Dish, Black Chutney 45.00
merican Modern, Celery Dish, Coral 32.00
merican Modern, Celery Plate, Chartreuse 50.00
merican Modern, Celery Plate, Granite Gray, 10 In. 40.00
merican Modern, Chop Plate, Square, Seafoam Blue, 12 ½ In. 55.00
merican Modern, Coaster, Coral 29.00
merican Modern, Coaster, Seafoam Blue 29.00
merican Modern, Coaster, White 39.00
merican Modern, Coffeepot, Granite Gray, 8 In. *illus* 45.00
merican Modern, Creamer, Black Chutney 20.00
merican Modern, Creamer, Handle, Granite Gray 9.00
merican Modern, Creamer, White 55.00
merican Modern, Cup & Saucer, After Dinner, Coral *illus* 20.00
merican Modern, Cup & Saucer, After Dinner, Seafoam 28.00

TIP
For a quick shine on a silver belt buckle or large pin, try rubbing it on your dark-colored carpet.

Ruskin, Pin, Porcelain, Silver, Lozenge Shape, Art Nouveau, Marked, 1 ¼ In.
$80.00

Ruskin, Vase, Cream & Green Crystalline Glaze, 6-Sided, W. Howson Taylor, 4 ⅝ In.
$325.00

Russel Wright, American Modern, Butter, Cover, Granite Gray
$32.00

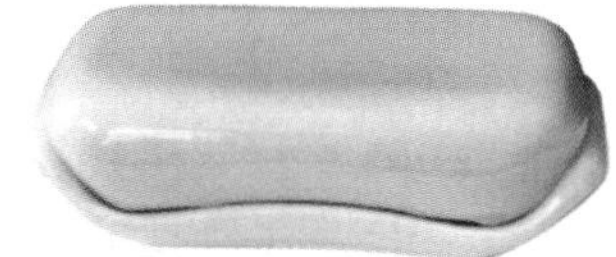

R

Russel Wright, American Modern, Coffeepot, Granite Gray, 8 In.
$45.00

TIP

Some tips on what to take to a flea market: a flashlight, especially if you go early-bird; a mirror with a handle you can use to examine the bottom of a piece of furniture; pre-wet tissues that can be used to wash your hands or a dirty find; a roadmap of the area in case you get lost; reference books like Kovels' Antiques & Collectibles Price Guide *and dictionaries of marks to keep in the car if you need to look something up; bubble wrap or an old blanket to protect fragile pieces on the drive home; and bungee cords to keep the trunk shut. Of course, you already have a shopping bag, money, sunscreen, magnet, tape measure, pencil and paper, and a cell phone. Take a camera, too, if you don't have a camera phone.*

American Modern, Cup & Saucer, Chartreuse 15.0
American Modern, Dish, Pickle, Oval, Chartreuse 25.0
American Modern, Fork & Spoon, Chartreuse 68.0
American Modern, Gravy Boat, Underplate, Granite Gray *illus* 45.0
American Modern, Pitcher, Bean Brown, 11 In. 93.0
American Modern, Pitcher, Black Chutney 60.0
American Modern, Pitcher, Brown,11 In. 93.0
American Modern, Pitcher, Cover, Chartreuse, 7 ½ In. *illus* 299.0
American Modern, Pitcher, Coral, 11 In. 90.0
American Modern, Pitcher, Granite Gray,11 In. 65.0
American Modern, Plate, Bread & Butter, Chartreuse, 6 ¼ In. 5.0
American Modern, Plate, Dinner, Chartreuse, 10 In. 15.0
American Modern, Plate, Dinner, Coral, 10 In. 11.0
American Modern, Plate, Dinner,Chartreuse,10 In. 15.0
American Modern, Plate, Hostess, Cup Holder, Black Chutney 115.0
American Modern, Plate, Hostess, Cup Holder, Cedar Green 185.0
American Modern, Plate, Hostess, Cup Holder, Chartreuse 82.0
American Modern, Plate, Hostess, Cup Holder, Granite Gray 115.0
American Modern, Plate, Salad, Bean Brown, 8 In. 26.0
American Modern, Plate, Salad, Coral, 8 In. 24.0
American Modern, Platter, Square, Granite Gray 29.0
American Modern, Salt & Pepper, Granite, Gray 15.0
American Modern, Saltshaker, Cedar Green 45.0
American Modern, Sauceboat, Black Chutney 52.0
American Modern, Spoon, Salad, Granite Gray 59.0
American Modern, Spoon, Salad, Seafoam Blue 35.0
American Modern, Spoon, White 66.0
American Modern, Teapot, Child's, Pink Salmon Speckle 20.0
American Modern, Teapot, Coral 115.0
American Modern, Teapot, Seafoam Blue 55.0
American Modern, Tumbler, Black Chutney 88.0
American Modern, Tumbler, Chartreuse 66.0
American Modern, Tumbler, Coral 60.0
Casual, Platter, Ivy Green, Sterling China, 13 ¼ x 9 ¼ In. 25.0
Clock, Meadow Green, General Electric *illus* 75.0
Eclipse, Shot Glass, Blue & Gold, 2 ⅛ In. *illus* 35.0
Imperial Flair, Bowl, Bowl, Smoke, 5 In. 300.0
Imperial Flair, Bowl, Pink, 5 In. 300.0
Imperial Flair, Plate, Chartreuse, 8 ¼ In. 225.0
Imperial Flair, Plate, Clear, 8 ¼ In. 225.0
Imperial Flair, Plate, Green, 8 ½ In. 225.0
Imperial Flair, Plate, Smoke, 8 ¼ In. 225.0
Imperial Flair, Tumbler, Chartreuse, 3 In. 200.0
Imperial Flair, Tumbler, Chartreuse, 4 ¾ In. 225.0
Imperial Flair, Tumbler, Clear, 3 In. 200.0
Imperial Flair, Tumbler, Clear, 4 ½ In. 225.0
Imperial Flair, Tumbler, Hemlock Green, 11 Oz. 280.0
Imperial Flair, Tumbler, Iced Tea, Chartreuse, 14 Oz. 90.0
Imperial Flair, Tumbler, Iced Tea, Clear 90.0
Imperial Flair, Tumbler, Juice, Chartreuse, 6 Oz. 45.0
Imperial Flair, Tumbler, Juice, Clear, 6 Oz. 65.0
Imperial Flair, Tumbler, Juice, Pink, 6 Oz. 100.0
Imperial Flair, Tumbler, Light Blue, Ground Bottom, 11 Oz. 125.0
Imperial Flair, Tumbler, Smoke, 4 ½ In. 225.0
Imperial Pinch, Tumbler, Iced Tea, Aqua, 14 Oz. 45.0
Imperial Pinch, Tumbler, Iced Tea, Pink, Frosted, 14 Oz. 125.0
Imperial Pinch, Tumbler, Iced Tea, Smoke, 14 Oz. 40.0
Imperial Pinch, Tumbler, Iced Tea, Smoke, Frosted, 14 Oz 125.0
Imperial Pinch, Tumbler, Iced Tea, Verde, 14 Oz. 35.0
Imperial Pinch, Tumbler, Juice, Aqua, 6 Oz. 100.0
Imperial Pinch, Tumbler, Juice, Pink, Frosted 100.0
Imperial Pinch, Tumbler, Juice, Smoke, 6 Oz 30.00 to 35.0
Imperial Pinch, Tumbler, Juice, Verde, 6 Oz 30.0
Imperial Twist, Old Fashioned Glass, Clear, 3 In. 160.0
Imperial Twist, Tumbler, Iced Tea, Clear, 6 In. 150.0
Imperial Twist, Tumbler, Juice, Clear, 6 Oz 100.0

Imperial Twist, Tumbler, Water Glass, Clear, 11 Oz . . . 125.00
Iroquois Casual, Ashtray, Promotional, Holiday, White, 1952 . . . 575.00
Iroquois Casual, Ashtray, Promotional, Ice Blue, 8 In. . . . 125.00
Iroquois Casual, Ashtray, Promotional, White, 8 In. . . . 700.00
Iroquois Casual, Bowl, Cereal, Aqua . . . 60.00 to 85.00
Iroquois Casual, Bowl, Cereal, Avocado Yellow, 5 In. . . . 15.00
Iroquois Casual, Bowl, Cereal, Cantaloupe, 5 In. . . . 35.00 to 45.00
Iroquois Casual, Bowl, Cereal, Charcoal, 5 In. . . . 30.00
Iroquois Casual, Bowl, Cereal, Cover, Lemon Yellow . . . 28.00
Iroquois Casual, Bowl, Cereal, Cover, Oyster . . . 90.00
Iroquois Casual, Bowl, Cereal, Ice Blue, 5 In. . . . 15.00
Iroquois Casual, Bowl, Cereal, Lemon Yellow, 5 In. . . . 25.00
Iroquois Casual, Bowl, Cereal, Lettuce Green, 5 In. . . . 10.00 to 26.00
Iroquois Casual, Bowl, Cereal, Nutmeg Brown, 15 In. . . . 11.00 to 30.00
Iroquois Casual, Bowl, Cereal, Oyster, 5 In. . . . 25.00
Iroquois Casual, Bowl, Cereal, Parsley Green, 5 In. . . . 11.00
Iroquois Casual, Bowl, Cereal, Pink Sherbet, 5 In. . . . 7.00 to 18.00
Iroquois Casual, Bowl, Cereal, Ripe Apricot, 5 In. . . . 12.00 to 18.00
Iroquois Casual, Bowl, Cereal, White . . . 12.00 to 25.00
Iroquois Casual, Bowl, Fruit, Avocado Yellow, 5 3/4 In. . . . 8.00
Iroquois Casual, Bowl, Fruit, Cantaloupe, 5 3/4 In. . . . 34.00 to 65.00
Iroquois Casual, Bowl, Fruit, Ice Blue, 5 3/4 In. . . . 18.00
Iroquois Casual, Bowl, Fruit, Lemon Yellow, 5 3/4 In. . . . 28.00
Iroquois Casual, Bowl, Fruit, Lemon Yellow, Raindrop, 5 3/4 In. . . . 30.00
Iroquois Casual, Bowl, Fruit, Mustard Gold, 5 3/4 In. . . . 30.00
Iroquois Casual, Bowl, Fruit, Nutmeg Brown, 5 3/4 In. . . . 15.00 to 35.00
Iroquois Casual, Bowl, Fruit, Oyster, 5 3/4 In. . . . 25.00
Iroquois Casual, Bowl, Fruit, Pink Sherbet, 5 3/4 In. . . . 20.00
Iroquois Casual, Bowl, Fruit, Ripe Apricot, 5 3/4 In. . . . 15.00 to 18.00
Iroquois Casual, Bowl, Fruit, White, 5 3/4 In. . . . 20.00
Iroquois Casual, Bowl, Fruit, White, Raindrop, 5 3/4 In. . . . 65.00
Iroquois Casual, Bowl, Gumbo, Avocado Yellow, 21 Oz. . . . 52.00
Iroquois Casual, Bowl, Gumbo, Ice Blue, 21 Oz. . . . 52.00
Iroquois Casual, Bowl, Gumbo, Ripe Apricot, 21 Oz . . . 40.00 to 60.00
Iroquois Casual, Bowl, Gumbo, White, 21 Oz. . . . 40.00 to 115.00
Iroquois Casual, Bowl, Serving, Parsley Green, 8 In. . . . 46.00
Iroquois Casual, Bowl, Serving, White, 8 In. . . . 38.00
Iroquois Casual, Bowl, Vegetable, Divided, Avocado Yellow . . . 65.00
Iroquois Casual, Bowl, Vegetable, Divided, Charcoal . . . 65.00
Iroquois Casual, Bowl, Vegetable, Divided, Cover, Cantaloupe . . . 325.00
Iroquois Casual, Bowl, Vegetable, Divided, Cover, Lemon Yellow . . . 125.00
Iroquois Casual, Bowl, Vegetable, Divided, Cover, Lemon Yellow, Raindrop . . . 80.00 to 180.00
Iroquois Casual, Bowl, Vegetable, Divided, Cover, Nutmeg Brown . . . 95.00
Iroquois Casual, Bowl, Vegetable, Divided, Cover, Oyster . . . 150.00
Iroquois Casual, Bowl, Vegetable, Divided, Cover, Pink Sherbet . . . 95.00
Iroquois Casual, Bowl, Vegetable, Divided, Cover, Ripe Apricot, 10 In. . . . 35.00 to 65.00
Iroquois Casual, Bowl, Vegetable, Divided, Cover, White . . . 100.00
Iroquois Casual, Bowl, Vegetable, Divided, Cover, White, Raindrop . . . 225.00
Iroquois Casual, Bowl, Vegetable, Divided, Lemon Yellow . . . 40.00
Iroquois Casual, Bowl, Vegetable, Divided, Oyster, 10 In. . . . 75.00
Iroquois Casual, Bowl, Vegetable, Divided, Parsley Green . . . 65.00
Iroquois Casual, Bowl, Vegetable, Divided, Ripe Apricot . . . 30.00
Iroquois Casual, Bowl, Vegetable, Divided, White, Raindrop . . . 150.00
Iroquois Casual, Bowl, Vegetable, Open, Ice Blue, 10 In. . . . *illus* 45.00
Iroquois Casual, Bowl, Vegetable, Open, Pink Sherbet, 8 In. . . . 25.00 to 40.00
Iroquois Casual, Bowl, Vegetable, Open, Ripe Apricot, 8 In. . . . 38.00
Iroquois Casual, Bowl, Vegetable, Open, White, 8 In. . . . 90.00
Iroquois Casual, Bowl, Vegetable, Oyster, 8 In. . . . 95.00
Iroquois Casual, Bowl Lid, Cereal, Avocado, Yellow . . . 22.00
Iroquois Casual, Bowl Lid, Cereal, Charcoal . . . 18.00
Iroquois Casual, Bowl, Serving, Avocado Yellow, 10 In. . . . 30.00
Iroquois Casual, Butter Dish, Cover, Lemon Yellow, 1/2 Lb. . . . 90.00
Iroquois Casual, Butter Dish, Cover, Lettuce Green, 1/2 Lb. . . . 180.00
Iroquois Casual, Butter Dish, Cover, Charcoal, 1/2 Lb. . . . *illus* 85.00
Iroquois Casual, Butter Dish, Cover, Parsley Green, 1/4 Lb. . . . 350.00
Iroquois Casual, Butter Dish, Cover, Pink Sherbet, 1/2 Lb. . . . 100.00

Russel Wright, American Modern, Cup & Saucer, After Dinner, Coral
$20.00

Russel Wright, American Modern, Gravy Boat, Underplate, Granite Gray
$45.00

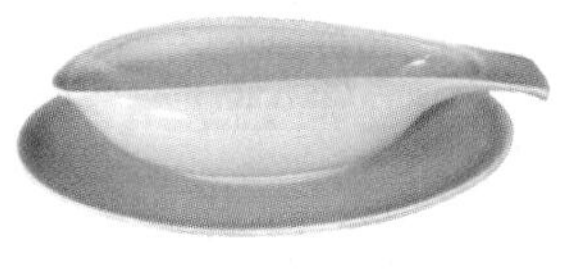

Russel Wright, American Modern, Pitcher, Cover, Chartreuse, 7 1/2 In.
$299.00

Russel Wright, Clock, Meadow Green, General Electric.
$75.00

Russel Wright, Eclipse, Shot Glass, Blue & Gold, 2 ⅛ In. $35.00

Russel Wright, Iroquois Casual, Bowl, Vegetable, Open, Ice Blue, 10 In. $45.00

Russel Wright, Iroquois Casual, Butter Dish, Cover, Charcoal, ½ Lb. $85.00

TIP

Be careful loading the dishwasher. Metal utensils that touch ceramic dishes may leave marks on the china. Dishes can also show black marks if rubbed against a stainless steel sink. The marks can be removed with a wet sponge and a bit of silver polish or other mild abrasive.

Iroquois Casual, Butter Dish, Cover, Ripe Apricot, ½ Lb. 125.00
Iroquois Casual, Butter Dish, Cover, White, ½ Lb. 150.00
Iroquois Casual, Carafe, Cantaloupe 2250.00
Iroquois Casual, Carafe, Charcoal .... 425.00 to 475.00
Iroquois Casual, Carafe, Lemon Yellow 375.00
Iroquois Casual, Carafe, Lettuce Green .... 500.00 to 575.00
Iroquois Casual, Carafe, Parsley Green 500.00
Iroquois Casual, Carafe, Pink Sherbet .... 100.00 to 200.00
Iroquois Casual, Carafe, White .... 325.00 to 400.00
Iroquois Casual, Casserole, Cover, Avocado Yellow, 2 Qt. .... 35.00 to 60.00
Iroquois Casual, Casserole, Cover, Avocado Yellow, 4 Qt. 225.00
Iroquois Casual, Casserole, Cover, Charcoal, 2 Qt. 150.00
Iroquois Casual, Casserole, Cover, Charcoal, 4 Qt. 650.00
Iroquois Casual, Casserole, Cover, Ice Blue, 2 Qt. 125.00
Iroquois Casual, Casserole, Cover, Ice Blue, 4 Qt. 350.00
Iroquois Casual, Casserole, Cover, Lemon Yellow, 2 Qt. 75.00
Iroquois Casual, Casserole, Cover, Lemon Yellow, Raindrop, 2 Qt. 225.00
Iroquois Casual, Casserole, Cover, Lettuce Green, 4 Qt. 700.00
Iroquois Casual, Casserole, Cover, Nutmeg Brown, 2 Qt. .... 70.00 to 200.00
Iroquois Casual, Casserole, Cover, Nutmeg Brown, 4 Qt. 265.00
Iroquois Casual, Casserole, Cover, Oyster, 4 Qt. 2000.00
Iroquois Casual, Casserole, Cover, Parsley Green, 2 Qt. 150.00
Iroquois Casual, Casserole, Cover, Parsley Green, 4 Qt. 750.00
Iroquois Casual, Casserole, Cover, Pink Sherbet, 2 Qt. 150.00
Iroquois Casual, Casserole, Cover, Pink Sherbet, 4 Qt. 300.00
Iroquois Casual, Casserole, Cover, White, 4 Qt. 575.00
Iroquois Casual, Casserole, Cover, White, Raindrop, 2 Qt. 200.00
Iroquois Casual, Casserole, Knob Cover, Lettuce Green, 2 Qt. 100.00
Iroquois Casual, Casserole, Knob Cover, White, 2 Qt. 125.00
Iroquois Casual, Casserole, Pinch Cover, Lettuce Green, 2 Qt. 150.00
Iroquois Casual, Casserole, Pinch Cover, White, 2 Qt. 125.00
Iroquois Casual, Chop Plate, Avocado Yellow, 13 ⅞ In. 65.00
Iroquois Casual, Chop Plate, Charcoal, 13 ⅞ In. 175.00
Iroquois Casual, Chop Plate, Lemon Yellow, 13 ⅞ In. 125.00
Iroquois Casual, Chop Plate, White, 13 ⅞ In. 150.00
Iroquois Casual, Coffeepot, Cover, Ice Blue 180.00
Iroquois Casual, Coffeepot, Cover, Lemon Yellow, Raindrop 500.00
Iroquois Casual, Coffeepot, Cover, Nutmeg Brown .... 375.00 to 580.00
Iroquois Casual, Coffeepot, Cover, Oyster .... 350.00 to 375.00
Iroquois Casual, Coffeepot, Cover, White, Raindrop 425.00
Iroquois Casual, Creamer, Avocado Yellow, 2 ¼ In. 15.00
Iroquois Casual, Creamer, Cantaloupe 85.00
Iroquois Casual, Creamer, Charcoal 125.00
Iroquois Casual, Creamer, Lemon Yellow .... 24.00 to 40.00
Iroquois Casual, Creamer, Nutmeg Brown 35.00
Iroquois Casual, Creamer, Oyster, Stack .... *illus* 12.00
Iroquois Casual, Creamer, Pink Sherbet .... 8.00 to 30.00
Iroquois Casual, Creamer, Redesigned, White 45.00
Iroquois Casual, Creamer, Ripe Apricot 35.00
Iroquois Casual, Cup, Coffee, Avocado Yellow 18.00
Iroquois Casual, Cup, Coffee, Parsley Green 20.00
Iroquois Casual, Cup, Lemon Yellow, Raindrop 15.00
Iroquois Casual, Cup, Tea, Avocado Yellow 5.00
Iroquois Casual, Cup, Tea, Cantaloupe 15.00
Iroquois Casual, Cup, Tea, Charcoal 7.00
Iroquois Casual, Cup, Tea, Ice Blue 7.00
Iroquois Casual, Cup, Tea, Nutmeg Brown 5.00
Iroquois Casual, Cup, Tea, Pink Sherbet 5.00
Iroquois Casual, Cup, Tea, Ripe Apricot 7.00
Iroquois Casual, Cup, Tea, White 10.00
Iroquois Casual, Cup & Saucer, After Dinner, Oyster 750.00
Iroquois Casual, Cup & Saucer, After Dinner, White 375.00
Iroquois Casual, Cup & Saucer, Avocado Yellow 15.00
Iroquois Casual, Cup & Saucer, Charcoal .... 18.00 to 25.00
Iroquois Casual, Cup & Saucer, Lettuce Green 20.00

Iroquois Casual, Cup & Saucer, Nutmeg Brown . . . 15.00
Iroquois Casual, Cup & Saucer, Oyster . . . 35.00
Iroquois Casual, Cup & Saucer, Parsley Green . . . 480.00
Iroquois Casual, Cup & Saucer, Ripe Apricot . . . 15.00
Iroquois Casual, Cup & Saucer, White . . . 25.00
Iroquois Casual, Dutch Oven, Cover, Charcoal, 6 Qt. . . . 1000.00
Iroquois Casual, Dutch Oven, Cover, Ice Blue, 6 Qt. . . . 425.00
Iroquois Casual, Dutch Oven, Cover, Lettuce Green, 6 Qt. . . . 925.00
Iroquois Casual, Dutch Oven, Cover, Pink Sherbet, 6 Qt. . . . 750.00
Iroquois Casual, Dutch Oven, Cover, White, 6 Qt. . . . 800.00
Iroquois Casual, Fry Pan, Cover, Lemon Yellow . . . 400.00
Iroquois Casual, Fry Pan, Lettuce Green . . . 500.00
Iroquois Casual, Fry Pan, White . . . 325.00
Iroquois Casual, Gravy Boat, Underplate, Ice Blue, 3 Piece . . . 84.00
Iroquois Casual, Gravy Boat, Underplate, Ice Blue . . . 40.00
Iroquois Casual, Mug, Pink Sherbet . . . *illus* 95.00
Iroquois Casual, Mug, Ice Blue . . . 95.00
Iroquois Casual, Mug, Lettuce Green . . . 130.00
Iroquois Casual, Pitcher, Cover, White . . . 225.00
Iroquois Casual, Pitcher, No Cover, White . . . 150.00
Iroquois Casual, Plate, Bread & Butter, Avocado Yellow, 6 ½ In. . . . 6.00
Iroquois Casual, Plate, Bread & Butter, Charcoal, 6 ½ In. . . . 10.00
Iroquois Casual, Plate, Bread & Butter, Oyster, 6 ½ In. . . . 15.00
Iroquois Casual, Plate, Bread & Butter, Parsley Green, 6 ½ In. . . . 8.00
Iroquois Casual, Plate, Bread & Butter, Ripe Apricot, 6 ½ In. . . . 8.00
Iroquois Casual, Plate, Dinner, Charcoal, 10 In. . . . 14.00
Iroquois Casual, Plate, Dinner, Lettuce Green, 10 In. . . . 11.00
Iroquois Casual, Plate, Dinner, Nutmeg Brown.10 In. . . . 9.00
Iroquois Casual, Plate, Dinner, Oyster, 10 In. . . . 60.00
Iroquois Casual, Plate, Dinner, Pink Sherbet, 10 In. . . . 9.00 to 12.00
Iroquois Casual, Plate, Dinner, Ripe Apricot, 10 In. . . . 15.00
Iroquois Casual, Plate, Dinner, White, 10 In. . . . 18.00
Iroquois Casual, Plate, Luncheon, Oyster, 9 ½ In. . . . 22.00 to 30.00
Iroquois Casual, Plate, Salad, Lemon Yellow, 9 ½ In. . . . 11.00
Iroquois Casual, Plate, Salad, Oyster, 7 ½ In. . . . 19.00
Iroquois Casual, Plate, Salad, Parsley Green, 7 ½ In. . . . 12.00
Iroquois Casual, Plate, Salad, White, 7 ½ In. . . . 18.00
Iroquois Casual, Platter, Oval, Avocado Yellow, 14 ½ In. . . . 16.00
Iroquois Casual, Platter, Oval, Lettuce Green, 12 ¾ In. . . . 40.00
Iroquois Casual, Platter, Oval, Nutmeg Brown, 12 ¾ In. . . . 30.00
Iroquois Casual, Platter, Oval, Parsley Green, 12 ¾ In. . . . 40.00
Iroquois Casual, Platter, Oval, White, 12 ¾ In. . . . 40.00
Iroquois Casual, Platter, Oval, White, 15 In. . . . 100.00
Iroquois Casual, Platter, Oval, White, Individual, 10 In. . . . 100.00
Iroquois Casual, Salt & Pepper, Stacking, Ice Blue . . . 30.00
Iroquois Casual, Salt & Pepper, Stacking, Nutmeg Brown . . . 30.00
Iroquois Casual, Shaker Top, Stacking, Lettuce Green . . . 13.00
Iroquois Casual, Soup, Dish, Deep, Aqua . . . 160.00
Iroquois Casual, Soup, Dish, Deep, Brick Red, 11 ½ Oz. . . . 225.00
Iroquois Casual, Soup, Dish, Deep, Cantaloupe . . . 95.00
Iroquois Casual, Soup, Dish, Deep, Charcoal . . . 55.00
Iroquois Casual, Soup, Dish, Deep, Ice Blue, 11 ½ Oz . . . 40.00 to 48.00
Iroquois Casual, Soup, Dish, Deep, Lemon Yellow, 11 ½ Oz. . . . 55.00 to 60.00
Iroquois Casual, Soup, Dish, Deep, Lettuce Green, 11 ½ Oz. . . . 70.00 to 75.00
Iroquois Casual, Soup, Dish, Deep, Nutmeg Brown, 11 ½ Oz. . . . 40.00 to 45.00
Iroquois Casual, Soup, Dish, Deep, Oyster, 11 ½ Oz . . . 75.00
Iroquois Casual, Soup, Dish, Deep, Pink Sherbet, 11 ½ Oz . . . 45.00
Iroquois Casual, Soup, Dish, Deep, Ripe Apricot, 11 ½ Oz. . . . 42.00 to 45.00
Iroquois Casual, Soup, Dish, Deep, White, 11 ½ Oz. . . . 75.00 to 85.00
Iroquois Casual, Soup, Dish, Deep, White, Raindrop, 11 ½ Oz . . . 140.00
Iroquois Casual, Sugar, Lettuce Green . . . 45.00
Iroquois Casual, Sugar, Stacking, Ripe Apricot . . . 25.00
Iroquois Casual, Sugar & Creamer, Cantaloupe . . . 225.00
Iroquois Casual, Sugar & Creamer, Stacking, Charcoal . . . 75.00
Iroquois Casual, Sugar & Creamer, Stacking, Nutmeg Brown . . . 28.00 to 75.00
Iroquois Casual, Sugar & Creamer, Stacking, Parsley Green . . . 80.00

TIP
Don't use a repaired plate for food. It could be a health hazard.

Russel Wright, Iroquois Casual, Creamer, Oyster, Stack
$12.00

Russel Wright, Iroquois Casual, Mug, Pink Sherbet
$95.00

Soup Bowls
A soup bowl holds soup, but some dinner sets have many types of soup bowls. A cream soup (round, two-handled shallow bowl) held cream of tomato or other creamy soups. A bouillon cup (small, about 5 inches round, with handles) held clear soup. A coupe soup is a shallow pottery bowl about 7 inches in diameter.

Iroquois Casual, Sugar & Creamer, Stacking, Pink Sherbet 30.00
Iroquois Casual, Sugar & Creamer, Stacking, White 50.00
Iroquois Casual, Sugar & Creamer, Stacking, Yellow, Raindrop 375.00
Iroquois Casual, Teapot, Lid, Ripe Apricot 70.00
Philodendron, Platter, Pink Sherbet, Black Oval 58.00
Vase, Broad Shape, Mottled Brown & Tan Glaze, c.1950, 10 x 8 ½ In. 240.00
Vase, Bulbous, Spouted Shape, Yellow Glaze, c.1950, 7 ½ x 9 In. 1140.00
White Clover, Sugar, Cover, Meadow Green, Golden Spice, Harkerware 145.00

SABINO glass was made in the 1920s and 1930s in Paris, France. Founded by Marius-Ernest Sabino (1878–1961), the firm was noted for Art Deco lamps, vases, figurines, and animals in clear, colored, and opalescent glass. Production stopped during World War II but resumed in the 1960s with the manufacture of nude figurines and small opalescent glass animals. The new pieces are a slightly different color and can be recognized.

Vase, Frolicking Water Nymphs, Gray Green, Frosted, 9 In. 413.00
Vase, Grove Of Trees In Bloom, Amber, Frosted, Flared, 7 ¾ In. 646.00
Vase, Trees In Bloom, Amber, Frosted, Marked, 7 ¾ In. *illus* 550.00

SALOPIAN ware was made by the Caughley factory of England during the eighteenth century. The early pieces were blue and white with some colored decorations. Another ware referred to as Salopian is a late nineteenth-century tableware decorated with color transfers.

Cup & Saucer, Blue, White, Pagoda Transfer, Fluted, Gilded Rims, c.1790, 2 x 2 In. 175.00
Cup & Saucer, Multicolored, Milk Boy, Handleless Cup, 5 In. *illus* 170.00
Ewer, Chinese Scene, Underglaze Transfer, Pearlware Glaze, 5 ½ In. 350.00
Plate, Blue & White, Oriental Scene, 1800s, 9 ¾ In. 235.00

SALT AND PEPPER SHAKERS in matched sets were first used in the nineteenth century. Collectors are primarily interested in figural examples made after World War I. Huggers are pairs of shakers that appear to embrace each other. Many salt and pepper shakers are listed in other categories and can be located through the index at the back of this book.

Aerial Tramway, Metal, Franconia Notch, New Hampshire, 2 ⅝ In. 24.00
Amish Couple, Cast Iron, 1940s 19.00
Angel, Cream, Pink, Gold, Japan, 3 ½ In. 25.00
Aunt Jemima & Uncle Mose, Painted, 3 ¼ In. 39.00
Avon, Cylindrical, Bulbous Top, c.1980, 4 In. 6.00
Baby Chicken, Yellow, Brown, Green Accent, Japan, 3 ½ In. 12.00
Banana & Pineapple, 2 ⅛ In. 8.00
Bar Set, Salt Girl With Corkscrew, Pepper Boy With Bottle Opener, 4 x 3 ¾ In. 12.00
Bird, Rose Tree Chintz, Royal Patrician, Bone China, Rubber Stopper, 2 ½ In. 32.00
Bird House, Hanging From Tree, Silver Plate, Dodinger, 5 x 4 In. 33.00
Black Cat, Green Eyes, Red Bows, Redware, Old Painted, Shafford, 1950s, 4 In. 20.00
Bongo Dog, Japan, 3 In. 25.00
Brass, Bulbous, Leaf Design, Tulip Openings, 3 Lion Feet, 3 ¾ x 2 In. 75.00
Cactus, Jadite, Summit Art Glass Co., 3 In. 28.00
Chefs, Woman, Man, Germany, 3 In. *illus* 35.00
Chicks In A Basket 22.00
Cobalt Blue, Metal Basket Holder, 8 x 8 In. 22.00
Colonel Sanders, KFC, Figural, Hard Plastic, Black Base For Pepper, 4 ¼ In. 35.00
Compatibles, Pyrex, Spring Blossom Green 20.00
Cone Shape, Yellow, Plastic, Black Handle, 3 ½ In. 12.00
Copper, Brass, Handle, 3 ½ x 2 ½ In. 30.00
Corn, Anthropomorphic, Blue Eyes, Red Mouth, Brown Suit, 3 ½ In. 5.00
Cow & Calf, Cork Stopper 16.00
Dog, Chintz Painted *illus* 22.00
Donkey & Cart, Boxed Flowers In Cart Are Shakers, Japan, 3 ¾ x 3 In. 15.00
Figural, Gavel, Plastic, 3 ¾ x 2 ½ In. 8.00
Flower, Bud Pepper, Leaves & Yellow Center Salt, Pink, Yellow, Green, 3 x 4 In. 12.00
Fort Pit Special Beer, Beer Bottle Shape, 2 ⅞ In. 10.00
Fox Man & Woman, Cork Stopper 35.00
Garlic Bulb, Red Onion, Original Box, 4 x 3 In. 13.00
Gay 90's Man & Woman's Heads, Pink Hat, Green Dress, Yellow Hat, Blue Tie, 4 ¾ In. 12.00
Glass, Basket Weave, 6 In. 35.00
Green Tomato, Green Pepper, Plastic, 1 ½ & 2 In. 6.00
Humpty Dumpty, Marked Japan, c.1925, 3 ¾ x 2 ¼ In. 40.00

TIP

Tired of scrubbing and scrubbing glass to remove marks from masking tape and labels? Get commercial hand cleaner, pat some on the stain, and let it stay for 30 minutes. Then rub it off with a cloth and wash the glass.

Sabino, Vase, Trees In Bloom, Amber, Frosted, Marked, 7 ¾ In. $550.00

TIP

If you are having your antiques moved in a van to a new home, watch out for damage. Check the antiques as they are unloaded. Sweep the inside of the moving van and save any small pieces of veneer or wood that might have chipped off your furniture.

S

daho Potato, Spud King, Victoria Ceramic, Japan, 1950s ... 39.00
Kissing Angels, White & Yellow Gowns, Gold Trim, Napco, 3½ In. ... 12.00
Kitchen Stove, Old Fashioned, Black, Gold Trim, Japan, 4½ x 2½ In. ... 45.00
Lady's Head, Wide Eyed Expression, Japan, c.1985 ... 38.00
LuRay, Bulbous, Surf Green, 4 In. ... 23.00
Maid & Chef, 1950s, Japan, 3 In. ... 19.00
Mammy & Cook, 3 In. ... 33.00
Max & Ray, Camel Cigarettes, Plastic, 1993, 4½ In. ... 35.00
Milk Bottle, Country Fresh, Cow, Wire Carrier, 1½ x 4 In. ... 4.00
Moon & Stars, Green, L.E. Smith, 1970s, 4 x 1¾ In. ... 18.00
Mother Gorilla & Baby, Early 1940s ... 35.00
Mouse, Acrylic, Plastic Plug ... 4.00
Mushroom, Wood, Marked, GC, Denmark ... 75.00
Onion & Corn, Japan, 5½ In. ... 24.00
Outhouse, I'm Fulla S, I'm Fulla P, 2 x 2½ In. ... 14.00
Penguins, Willie & Millie, Plastic, F & F Mold & Dye Works, 1950s, 3¼ In. ... 15.00
Pillar, Flowers, Footed, Opal Glass, Embossed Mark, Homan Caddy, 5½ In. ... 115.00
Pink Roses, Coin Spot, Cranberry, Cylindrical, Wilcox Caddy, 5 In. ... 201.00
Plastic, Clear Body, Red Top, V.A. Kasin Molded Prods., 3¼ x 1¼ In. ... 11.00
Poodle, Black Collar, White Polka Dots, Red & Yellow ... 45.00
RCA Nipper Dog, Tilted Head ... 26.00
Red, Pillar Shape, Bakelite, 3¾ In. ... 30.00
Red Plastic Cap, Carrier Basket, Rubber Coated Wire, 6 x 4½ In. ... 13.00
Rooster & Hen, Nodder, Center Condiment Holder, Japan, c.1950 ... 45.00
Rosewood, Copper, Cylindrical, Marked, SAAP, Denmark, 8 In. ... 135.00
Salty & Peppy, Happy Chefs, Red & White Hats, Wood, Japan, 4½ In. ... 25.00
Scottie Dog, Art Deco, Silver Tone, 7¼ In. ... 125.00
Scottie Dog, Tam-O'-Shanter ... 12.00
Sea Captain, Ceramic, Japan, 4¼ In. ... 15.00
Seal, Umbrella, Painted, Yellow, White, Red Bowtie, 3½ x 2 & 2½ x 1¾ In. ... 32.00
Single Shaker, Red, Salt Out Top, Pepper Out Bottom, Plastic, 3 x 2 In. ... 6.00
Smiley Face, Have A Happy Day, Green ... 14.00
Soda Bottle, Glass, Plastic, Vess, 1950s ... 28.00
Sourdough Jake & Burro, Kelvin, 1960s ... 25.00
Spice Of Life, Corning, Gemco, 3½ In. ... 12.00
Sweet Violets, Bell Shape, Norcrest, 3½ x 2¼ In. ... 17.00
Toaster, Toast, Ceramic, Painted, 3 x 3¼ In. ... 12.00
Toby Jug, Art Deco, 1930s, 2⅝ In. ... 24.00
Tomato, Red Pepper, Red, Green, Plastic, 1¾ In. ... 6.00
Torii Gateway, Sterling Silver ... 129.00
Ultramarine, Jeannette Glass Co., c.1950 ... 71.00
Vegetables, Smiling Faces, Red, Turquoise Face ... 17.00
Whiskey Keg, On Brick Wall, Redware, 4 x 2 x 2½ In. ... 15.00
Windmill, Blue, White, Plastic, Tray, 3 Piece ... *illus* 18.00
Windmill, Wood, 2¼ In. ... 8.00
Wood, Signed, Dan Droz Designs, Lauffer, 6 In. ... 85.00

SALT GLAZE has a grayish white surface with a texture like an orange peel. It is a method of decoration that has been used since the eighteenth century. Salt-glazed pieces are still being made.

Beer Glass, Pilsner, Gerzit, Germany, Dortmunder Union Export, Gold Seals, 9 x 3⅜ In. ... 9.00
Bowl, Wire Handle, Medium Blue Glaze Top Rim, 10¼ x 4⅞ In. ... 109.00
Crock, Blue, 3¾ x 5½ In. ... 125.00
Crock, Blue, Stoneware, Germany, 2½ x 3 In. ... 50.00
Crock, Demuths Snuff, F.H. Cowden, c.1870, 9½ x 6½ In. ... 260.00
Crock, Redware, Brown Glaze, Red Swirl, 6½ x 5½ In. ... 50.00
Crock Planter, Embossed Roses, Ribbed Band, Yellow Green, 1900s, 7½ x 6 In. ... 40.00
Ginger Jar, Sgrafitto, 1970s, 9 x 6½ In. ... 65.00
Jar, Storage, Drippy Glaze, Lid, Signed, Stuempfle, 14 In. ... 495.00
Jug, Brown, Imprinted 5, Beehive Shape, 1800s, 15¾ In. ... 245.00
Jug, Cobalt Blue, Handle, Westerwald, 5¼ In. ... 12.00
Jug, Cobalt Blue Flower Stem, Egg Shape, Loop Handle, 12¼ In. ... 267.00
Jug, Incised Flowers, Geometric Designs, Blue, Gray, Pewter Hinge, Westerwald, 14 In. ... 319.00
Jug, Pewter Lid, No. 604, Blue, Gray, Merkelbach Hohr Grenzhausen, 1970s, 9 x 8 In. ... 175.00
Jug, Tavern, Blue Slip, Germany, c.1861, 14 In. ... 329.00

Salopian, Cup & Saucer, Multicolored, Milk Boy, Handleless Cup, 5 In.
$170.00

Salt & Pepper, Chefs, Woman, Man, Germany, 3 In.
$35.00

Salt & Pepper, Dog, Chintz Painted
$22.00

TIP
Black lights can detect repairs to antiques that are invisible to the eye, but be sure you use a longwave black light. A shortwave black light could injure your eyes or skin.

S

Salt & Pepper, Windmill, Blue, White, Plastic, Tray, 3 Piece
$18.00

Sampler, Verse, Butterflies, Flowers, Birds, Building, Animals, Vine, Born August 8, 1824, Frame, 16 x 17 In.
$2588.00

Sampler, Verse, Castle, Flowers, Trees, Ribbon Border, Frame, 19 x 16 In.
$165.00

TIP

Store needlework, samplers, and other small fabric pieces flat in a drawer. Line the drawer with acid-free tissue paper from an art supplies store.

Jug, White, 10½ x 8 In. 48.00
Jug, Young Girl, Instructed By Older Woman, c.1870, 8½ In. 285.00
Jug Lamp Base, Pinched Handles, 1800s, 14½ x 7 In. 225.00
Mixing Bowl, Blue & White, 2½ x 5 In. 145.00
Mixing Bowl, Blue & White, Blue Rim, Swirl Pattern, 3¾ x 9 In. 185.00
Pitcher, Cherry Pattern, Stoneware, 8½ x 5½ In. 75.00
Pitcher, Flowers, Cobalt Blue, 10½ In. 65.00
Pitcher, Left-Handed, Cobalt Blue, 2½ x 2½ In., 2 Piece 21.00
Pitcher, Monkeys & Vines, Blue & Gray, 11½ In. 201.00
Pitcher, Raised Ribbed, Medium Blue, 4½ x 3¼ In. 60.00
Pitcher, White, Dogs On The Hunt, Minton, 20th Century 50.00
Platter, White, Press Molded, Basket Weave, Dot & Diaper, Star Patterns, 1700s, 17 In. 975.00
Rose Bowl, Applied Roses, Petals, Handles, 4½ x 5 In. 75.00
Salt, Pink High Gloss, Germany, 1¾ x 1 In., 6 Piece 24.00
Salt Box, Apricot, Honeycomb, Blue & White, Early 1900s, 6¼ x 5¾ In. 150.00
Salt Crock, Blackberry Pattern, Blue & White, Handing, 6 x 6 In. 140.00
Teapot, Oval, Serpentine, Blue Outline, U.S. Seal, Female, Castleford, c.1810, 9 In. 657.00
Teapot, Pewter Lid, Morning Glories, Twig Finial, Early 1800s 295.00
Vase, Blue Shrimp Design, 9⅛ x 4½ In. 44.00
Vase, Bulbous, 4 Light Green Rings, 5 In. 40.00
Vase, Leaf Design, Brown, Tan, Taupe, 8 x 2½ In. 42.00
Vase, Rough Glaze, Squat, Delft Blue Flowers, Black Interior Glaze, 5 x 19 In. 49.00
Whistle, Bird In Nest, 2¾ x 2¼ In. 30.00

ABCDE

SAMPLERS were made in America from the early 1700s. The best examples were made from 1790 to 1840. Long, narrow samplers are usually older than square ones. Early samplers just had stitching or alphabets. The later examples had numerals, borders, and pictorial decorations. Those with mottoes are mid-Victorian. A revival of interest in the 1930s produced simpler samplers, usually with mottoes.

3 Alphabets, Numbers, Blue, Brown, Frame, S.E. Robinson Aged 11, 1840s, 12 x 12 In. 440.00
Adam & Eve, Angels, Animals, Urns, Heart, Ada Williamson, Wool On Linen, 1875, 12 x 18 In. 403.00
Adam & Eve, Silk, Wool, Martha Smallman Aged 11 Years, March 1848, 12 x 8 In. 8225.00
Adam & Eve, Trees, Castle, Flowers, Susanna Bridges, 1781, Bird's-Eye Frame, 15 x 18 In. 403.00
Alphabet, Alabama, Caroline Day, Aged 7, 1840, Greek Key Border, 11 x 15 In. 2700.00
Alphabet, Ann Cotton, 13 Years Old, Devon, England, Black Silk, Wool, 1843, 9 x 6¾ In. 403.00
Alphabet, Baskets, Flower Grapes, Grapevine Border, Elvira Piper, 1826, 17½ x 17 In. 780.00
Alphabet, Bird, Tree, Lion, House, Flower, Mid 19th Century, 25½ x 17¼ In. 121.00
Alphabet, Black Man, Flower Basket, Table, Chairs, H.G., 1827, Silk, Wool, 11 x 10 In. 294.00
Alphabet, Floral Sprays, Geometric Border, Susan Hodgkins, 12¾ x 10 In. 1265.00
Alphabet, Flower Baskets, Strawberries, Leaf Border, Inscribed FWL, c.1836, 17 x 17 In. 805.00
Alphabet, Flower Letter, Dove, Man, Woman, Cat, Dog, Wreaths, 1862, 27 x 19 In. 275.00
Alphabet, Flower Vine Border, Frame, c.1848, 19¼ x 10 In. 412.00
Alphabet, House, Birds, Flowers, Lorenda Ruth Sanford, Aged 15, 1820, 18 x 21 In. 863.00
Alphabet, Numbers, Adam & Eve, Flowers, Wreaths, Silk, On Linen, c.1851, 12 x 12 In. 374.00
Alphabet, Numbers, Amelia Burrhomer, Frame, 1887, 34 x 22 In. 1195.00
Alphabet, Numbers, Awake My Soul & Rouse, Silk On Linen, Frame, 1834, 18 x 17½ In. 8050.00
Alphabet, Numbers, Flowers, Leaves, Abigail H. Stodder, Aged 8 Years, 1811, Frame, 11 x 9 In. 353.00
Alphabet, Numbers, Flowers, Loretto Osage Mission, Wool On Linen, 20 x 19 In. 2645.00
Alphabet, Numbers, Flowers, Tree, Flower Border, Hannah Walker, 1831, Frame, 12 x 8 In. 460.00
Alphabet, Numbers, Verse, Songbirds, Floral Border, Mary Pile, 1808, Frame, 16 x 12 In. 2320.00
Alphabet, Numbers, Verse, Loretto Academy, Silk, Linen, Frame, c.1834, 18 x 17 In. 8050.00
Alphabet, Pious Verse, House, Widow's Walk, 24 x 20½ In. 7200.00
Alphabet, Stylized Vine, House, Mean Oswald, 1808, Silk, Linen, Frame, 16½ x 23 In. 960.00
Alphabet, Verse, Figures, Trees, Birds, November 30th, 1833, Frame, 24 x 20 In. 1998.00
Alphabet, Verse, Flowering Vine, Sawtooth Border, Elizabeth Hobart, Aged 12, 1829, Frame, 19 x 16 In. 999.00
Alphabet, Verse, Flowers, Birds, Diamonds, Aged 10, c.1835, Frame, 18 x 18 In. 1295.00
Alphabet, Verse, Flowers, Trees, Aged 13, Silk, Linen, c.1760, Frame, 17 x 11 In. 1645.00
Alphabet, Verse, Flower Pots, Strawberry Vine, AE 12 Yrs., Frame, 17 x 17½ In. 881.00
Alphabet, Verse, Fruit Vines, Ruth C. Risbrough, Aged 9 Years, Boston, Frame, 24 x 19 In. 1058.00
Alphabet, Verse, Grass, Tree, Flower Border, Born May 11, 1808, Aged 10, 20 x 14 In. 4312.00
Alphabet, Verse, House, Trees, Birds, Harriot Parker, Aged 10, 1808, Frame, 24 x 20½ In. 7200.00
Alphabet, Verse, Houses, Trees, Mary Jane Tibbets, Aged 13 Years, 1840, Frame, 17 x 16 In. 1410.00
Alphabet, Verse, Love To Enemies, Flowers, Ann Walker, Aged 11 Years, 1832, 18 x 15 In. 403.00
Alphabet, Village Scene, Vine Border, c.1860, 18 x 18 In. 644.00
Alphabets, Fringe, Susanna Harr, 1824, Frame, 13 x 8¼ In. 248.00

lphabets, House, Trees, Birds, Amanda Fuller, 1827, Frame, 16 x 12 ½ In. 275.00
lphabets, Number, Birds, Baskets, Mary Robinson, Silk, Linen, 1820, 12 ½ x 16 In. 660.00
phabets, Sarah Jane Bunce, Aged 10 Years, Jan. 1834, Silk, Linen, Frame, 17 x 17 In. 588.00
lphabets, Verse, Flower Baskets, Diamond Border, Harriet Tanner, 1835, 17 x 17 In. 575.00
lphabets, Verses, Trees, Butterfly, Martha Elliott, Silk, Wool, 1783, Frame, 16 x 12 In. 690.00
lowers, Deer, Floral Border, 10 Years Old, Silk, Linen, c.1840, Frame, 18 x 17 In. 518.00
lowers, Geometric Borders, Aged 13, 1834, Silk, Linen, Frame, 16 x 17 In. 558.00
heep, Dogs, Trees, Urn, Flowers, Mary Todd, Born April 2, 1792, 1802, 22 x 18 In. 2013.00
hip, Figures, Dog, Church, Fait A Lille, June 16, 1817, Silk, Wool, 13 ¾ x 14 In. 546.00
erse, Adam & Eve, House, Church, Age 16, 1844, Silk, Linen, Frame, 23 x 21 In. 633.00
erse, Adam & Eve, Serpent Tree, Birds, Flower Urns, 1835, Frame, 20 ¾ x 18 ¼ In. 1293.00
erse, Adam & Eve, Vine Border, Margaret White, 1839, Frame, 16 x 16 In. 780.00
erse, Alphabet, Flowering Vine, Mary M. Case, Age 11, 1828, Chelsea, Vermont, 14 x 18 In. . . 2938.00
erse, Alphabet, Hearts, Bird, Initials, Frame, Emily Wells, Silk, Linen, 1830, 9 x 7 ½ In. 460.00
erse, Alphabet, Vine Border, Flower Basket, Gold Frame, 12 ¼ x 12 ½ In. 288.00
erse, Animals, Flower Urns, Buildings, Birds, Age 11, Linen, 1836, Frame, 18 x 18 In. 495.00
erse, Animals, Flowers, Black, Brown, Green, Frame, 1800s, 14 ½ x 12 ½ In. 220.00
erse, Baskets Of Flowers, Quaker, Eliza T. Slack's Work, 1822, Attleborough, 26 x 22 In. 1093.00
erse, Birds, Urns, Baskets, Bordered, McClung, 1825, 17 x 13 ½ In. 345.00
erse, Butterflies, Flowers, Birds, Building, Animals, Vine, Born August 8, 1824, Frame, 16 x 17 In. *illus* 2588.00
erse, Castle, Flowers, Trees, Ribbon Border, Frame, 19 x 16 In. . . . . . . *illus* 165.00
erse, Cat, Butterflies, Trees, Strawberry Vine Border, Mary Crisel, Age 12, 1823, 18 x 14 In. . . 2640.00
erse, Flower Basket, Birds, Trees, Flower Vine Border, 1836, Frame, 14 ½ x 13 In. 230.00
erse, Flower Border, J Garrison, April 3, 1939, Frame, 16 ¾ In. . . . . . . *illus* 219.00
erse, Flowers, Leaves, Animals, Vine Borders, Aged 10, Early 1800s, 16 x 14 In. 460.00
erse, Flowers, Vines, Ann Hansel 1856, Silk & Wool, Linen, Frame, 16 x 13 In. 823.00
erse, Girl With Parasol, House, Tree, Lebanon, Pa., Age 9, 1820, Frame, 18 ½ x 14 ¾ In. 51000.00
erse, House, Trees, Potted Flowers, Peacock, Vining, Mary Calahan, 1838, Frame, 20 x 22 In. 940.00
erse, Ode To May, Love All, Trust Few, Do Wrong To None, Ann, Early 1800s, Frame, 10 x 8 In. 323.00
erse, On Truth, Mary Ann Venner, December 20, 1806, Frame, 15 ¼ x 13 In. 489.00
erse, Pine Trees, Fruit, Flower Baskets, Birds, Vine Border, Aged 12 Years, 1851, Frame, 16 x 12 In. . 881.00
erse, Quaker, Floral Motif, Vining Oval, Mary Warner Allen, 1824, Frame, 13 ½ x 18 In. 1528.00
erse, Resting Sheep, Peacock, 8-Point Star, Bird Nest, 1862, 12 x 13 In. 690.00
erses, Leaf Border, Bird's-Eye Maple Frame, Gilt Liner, 30 x 24 In. 748.00
erses, Sarah Ann Barrington, St. Mary's Academy, 1838, 21 x 17 In. 747.00
irtue, Butterflies, T, Birds, 9 Year Old Mary Cox, 1798, Silk, Linen, 16 x 16 In. 865.00

AMSON and Company, a French firm specializing in the reproduction of collectible wares of nany countries and periods, was founded in Paris in the early nineteenth century. Chelsea, Meissen, amille Verte, and Chinese Export porcelain are some of the wares that have been reproduced by he company. The firm uses a variety of marks on the reproductions. It is still in operation.

ish, Leaf Shape, Lemons, Leaf Handle, c.1900, 9 In., Pair 390.00
late, American Eagle, Red & Cobalt Blue Band, 12 Dinner, 12 Soup 2640.00
late, Dinner, American Eagle, Red & Cobalt Blue Band, 12 Piece 1200.00
late, Gilt, Great Seal Of The United States, Blue, Gilt Bands, Chinese Export Style, 10 In. . . . 118.00
alt, Oriental Figure, Bowl In Hand, Flowers, Marked, 2 In. . . . . . . *illus* 50.00
ea Canister, Gold Leaves, Red Birds, Cover, 6 In., Pair 444.00
ase, Cover, Armorial, Bell Shape, Gilt Crown, Flowers, Handles, Famille Rose, 12 x 8 In. 288.00

ANDWICH GLASS is any of the myriad types of glass made by the Boston and Sandwich Glass Vorks in Sandwich, Massachusetts, between 1825 and 1888. It is often very difficult to be sure vhether a piece was really made at the Sandwich factory because so many types were made there nd similar pieces were made at other glass factories. Additional pieces may be listed under ressed Glass and in related categories.

owl, Cover, Arch & Thistle, Clear, 5 ½4 x 7 x 4 ½ In. 605.00
owl, Daisy & Acanthus Leaf Scroll, Clear, Shaped Rim, 11-Petal Center, 2 x 10 In. 66.00
owl, Daisy & Peacock Eye, Translucent Milky Cobalt Blue, Scalloped, 1 x 6 In. 468.00
owl, Fiery, Opalescent, Folded Rim, 1840, 4 ½ x 14 ¾ In. 2240.00
owl, Lyre, Cinquefoil, Translucent Cobalt Blue, Scalloped Rim, 2 x 5 x 7 In. 253.00
andlestick, Amethyst, Hexagonal, Wafer, 1840, 9 In. 575.00
andlestick, Canary, Hexagonal, 7 ½ In., Pair 380.00
andlestick, Clambroth, Blue Socket, Octagonal, 8 ½ In., Pair 615.00
andlestick, Dolphin, Canary, Petal Socket, Wafer, c.1860, 10 ¼ In., Pair. . . . . . . *illus* 350.00

Sampler, Verse, Flower Border, J Garrison, April 3, 1939, Frame, 16 ¾ In.
$219.00

Samson, Salt, Oriental Figure, Bowl In Hand, Flowers, Marked, 2 In.
$50.00

Sandwich Glass, Candlestick, Dolphin, Canary, Petal Socket, Wafer, c.1860, 10 ¼ In., Pair
$350.00

Sandwich Glass, Candlestick, Petal & Column, Blue Alabaster, Wafer, c.1860, 9 ¼ In.
$1010.00

Sandwich Glass, Cologne, Apple Green, Cut Panels, Lily Stopper, Pontil, 1845-70, 6¾ In.
$385.00

Sandwich Glass, Cologne, Cranberry Cut To Clear, Diamond, 8 Panels, c.1870, 6½ In.
$400.00

Sandwich Glass, Cologne, Star & Punty, Amethyst, 6-Sided Stopper, Pontil, c.1850, 7 In.
$4150.00

Sandwich Glass, Dish, Pekingese Cover, Basket Base, Milk Glass, 4¾ In.
$633.00

Candlestick, Petal & Column, Blue Alabaster, Wafer, c.1860, 9¼ In. . . . . . *illus* 1010.00
Celery Vase, Horn Of Plenty, Clear, 9 In., 4 Piece 489.00
Cologne, Amethyst, Waisted, 8 Panels, Rolled Lip, Blown, 4½ In. 55.00
Cologne, Amethyst, Waisted, Neck Rings, Angular Shoulder, Spire Stopper, 8½ In. 385.00
Cologne, Apple Green, Cut Panels, Lily Stopper, Pontil, 1845-70, 6¾ In. . . . . . *illus* 385.00
Cologne, Boston & Cobalt Blue, Melon Ribbed, Orange 144.00
Cologne, Canary, Flared Lip, Stopper, 1860-70, 8 In. 123.00
Cologne, Canary, Star & Punty, Hexagonal, 7¼ In. 358.00
Cologne, Cranberry Cut To Clear, Diamond, 8 Panels, c.1870, 6½ In. . . . . . *illus* 400.00
Cologne, Peacock Blue, 10 Panels, Applied Lip, 4⅛ x 1 In. 99.00
Cologne, Ruby Cut To Clear, Cut Grapes & Leaves, Facet-Cut Neck, Ring, 7⅜ x 5 In. 187.00
Cologne, Star & Punty, Amethyst, 6-Sided Stopper, Pontil, c.1850, 7 In. . . . . . *illus* 4150.00
Compote, Cover, Horn Of Plenty, 6 In., Pair 259.00
Compote, Hairpin, Clear, 4 x 8½ In. 13200.00
Compote, Hairpin, Clear, 5 x 10½ In. 24200.00
Compote, Peacock Eye, Clear, Hexagonal Base, 6½ x 10¾ In. 2590.00
Compote, Princess Feather & Baskets Of Flowers, Amethyst, 6 x 9 x 10 In. 4400.00
Compote, Princess Feather & Baskets Of Flowers, Canary, 6 x 10 x 9 In. 47000.00
Creamer, Cobalt Blue To White To Clear, Cut Ovals, Trefoils, 4½ In. 160.00
Curtain Pin, Rosette, Beaded Petals, Canary, Shaped Rim, 4½ In., Pair 33.00
Curtain Pin, Rosette, Central Star, Opalescent, 5 In., Pair 66.00
Decanter, Horn Of Plenty, Clear Stopper, 8½ In., Pair 460.00
Decanter, Starburst & Diamond, Clear Ribbed, Blown Stopper, 10 x 4½ In. 448.00
Decanter, Starburst & Diamond Point, Emerald Green, Ribbed, Stopper, 10 In. 400.00
Dish, Bull's-Eye, Medallion, Clear, 11⅛ In., Pair 4100.00
Dish, Cover, Princess Feather Medallions, Grapevine Border, 5¼ x 11 x 8¾ In. 2390.00
Dish, Gothic Arch & Heart, Clear, Dome Cover, 4½ x 7 In. 1430.00
Dish, Hen Cover, Medium Blue, Straw Rim, Draped Sides, Waffle Base, 1870, 7 In. 2750.00
Dish, Open Chain Border, Clear, Peacock Eye, Handles, 2 x 9 x 12 In. 2420.00
Dish, Pekingese Cover, Basket Base, Milk Glass, 4¾ In. . . . . . *illus* 633.00
Dish, Sheaf Of Wheat & Strawberry Diamond, Clear, Oval, 2 x 5 x 7⅛ In. 303.00
Dish, Swan Cover, Nesting, Clear, 7½ In. 66.00
Ewer, Clear, Waisted, High Handle, 6-Pointed Star Base, 2½ In. 330.00
Ewer, Violet Blue, Waisted, High Thorn Handle, 2⅝ In. 165.00
Inkwell, Clear, Blown, Annulated Rings, Pressed Hexagonal Base, 7¼ In. 258.00
Lamp, Amethyst, Octagonal, Square, 1840-60, 9 In. 840.00
Lamp, Fluid, Acanthus Leaf, Clambroth, Starch Blue, Wafer, c.1850, 11 In. . . . . . *illus* 1090.00
Lamp, Kerosene, Dark Cranberry To Clear, Allover Cane Cut, 8 In. 550.00
Lamp, Kerosene, Green, Ribbed, Blown Molded, Eaton, c.1870, 11½ In. . . . . . *illus* 5100.00
Lamp, Oil, Blown Glass, Pressed Cup Plate Base, Cup Plate, 6⅜ x 3¼ In. 646.00
Lamp, Oil, Blown Glass, Pressed Cup Plate Base, Cup Plate, c.1835, 7½ In. 705.00
Lamp, Whale Oil, Flint, Free Blown Font, Wafer, Columnar Stem, c.1840, 8¾ In. 200.00
Lamp, Whale Oil, Flint, Free Blown, Pressed Foot, Linear Pattern, 7¾ In. 325.00
Lamp, Whale Oil, Loop Pattern, Blue, Octagonal Standard, c.1865, 8½ In. 2585.00
Lamp, Whale Oil, Pressed Glass, 3 Printie Block Pattern, Peacock Blue, c.1860, 11 In. 2938.00
Nappy, Princess Feather Medallion, Clear, 14-Petal Rosette Base, 2 x 10 In. 110.00
Nappy, Princess Feather Medallion, Peacock Eye, Clear, 13-Point Star Base, 2 x 12 In. 413.00
Paperweight, Cross Flower, Jasper Ground, 3 In. 1100.00
Paperweight, Pansy, Multicolored, c.1870, 2⅝ In. 870.00
Paperweight, Poinsettia, Clear Ground, c.1870, 3⅛ In. 667.00
Paperweight, Poinsettia, Red, Double, Blue & White Jasper Ground, 2¾ In. 1100.00
Paperweight, Poinsettia, Red, Blue, White Jasper, 2 x 3 In. 375.00
Plate, Roman Rosette, Fiery Opalescent, 9¼ In. 3530.00
Platter, Hearts, Fans, Diamonds, Canary, 1⅞ x 2⅝ In. 143.00
Pomade Jar, Bear, Amethyst, 3¾ In. 170.00
Pomade Jar, Bear, Collared, Black, 3¾ In. 258.00
Pomade Jar, Bear, Muzzled, Starch Blue, Marked, J. Hauel & Co., Philada, c.1865, 4½ In. *illus* 3000.00
Salt, Basket Of Flowers, Clear, 1⅞ In. 77.00
Salt, Basket Of Flowers, Electric Blue, 4-Footed, 2¼ x 1⅞ x 3⅛ In. 55.00
Salt, Basket Of Flowers, Moonstone, 4-Footed, 2 x 1⅞ x 3 In. 88.00
Salt, Beaded Scroll, Basket Of Flowers, Opaque Blue White, 1⅞ x 1⅞ x 3⅛ In. 1980.00
Salt, Cadmus, Ships & Eagles, 1¾ x 3 In. 467.00
Salt, Chariot, Opaque, Powder Blue, Rosette Medallion Base, 1¾ x 2⅛ x 2⅞ In. 1210.00
Salt, Eagle, Clear, Octagonal, Scalloped Rim, 1½ x 2⅞ x 3⅞ In. 209.00
Salt, Eagle, Constitution, Willow Tree, Clear, 2 In. 99.00

Salt, Eagle, Empire Sofa, 2 ¼ x 4 In. ... 99.00
Salt, Eagle, Octagonal, Clear, 1 ½ In. ... 121.00
Salt, Eagle, Scrolled, 2 x 3 ¼ In. ... 121.00
Salt, Eagle & Shield, Clear, Flared, Scallop Rim, 1 ⅛ x 3 x 4 In. ... 66.00
Salt, Eagle & Shield, Opalescent, 4-Footed, 2 ⅛ x 2 x 3 ¼ In. ... 176.00
Salt, Gothic Arch, Heart, Clear, 1 ¾ In. ... 165.00
Salt, Gothic Arch, Large Arches, Clear, 1 ⅝ In. ... 99.00
Salt, H. Clay, Steam Locomotive, Clear, Hairpin Ends, 1 ⅝ x 2 x 3 In. ... 154.00
Salt, Heart & Arch, Clear, Rope Ring, Pedestal, 2 x 3 ¼ In. ... 99.00
Salt, Lafayet, Cobalt Blue, 1830-45, 3 ⅝ In. ... 2100.00
Salt, Lafayet Steamboat, Blue, Opalescent, 1 ⅝ x 1 ⅞ x 3 ⅝ In. ... 1760.00
Salt, Lyre, Clear, 1 ¾ In. ... 154.00
Salt, Lyre, Opaque Mottled Blue, 1 ⅞ x 2 x 3 ⅛ In. ... 121.00
Salt, Mount Vernon, Pink Tint, 1 ¾ x 2 ⅛ x 2 ⅞ In. ... 22.00
Salt, Oblong, Octagon, Wheat Sheaf, 1 ⅝ In. ... 143.00
Salt, Oblong, Swags, Bull's-Eyes, Clear, 1 ¾ In. ... 187.00
Salt, Oval, Cornucopia, Rayed Base, Clear, 1 ⅜ In. ... 110.00
Salt, Peacock Eye, Clear, Oval, Rope Table Ring, 1½ x 3 x 3⅞ In. ... 110.00 to 220.00
Salt, Round Pedestal, 1 ¾ In. ... 110.00
Salt, Shell, 4-Footed, Clear, 1 ⅝ In. ... 77.00
Salt, Shell, Pedestal, Clear, 1 ⅝ In. ... 88.00
Salt, Stag Horn, Medium Amber, 1 ¾ In. ... 154.00
Salt, Strawberry Diamond, 16-Petal Base, Clear, 1 ⅞ In. ... 44.00
Salt, Strawberry Diamond, 16-Point Star Base, Clear, 1 ⅞ In. ... 55.00
Salt, Strawberry Diamond, 16-Point Star In Octagon, Clear, 1 ⅞ In. ... 88.00
Salt, Strawberry Diamond, Waffle Diamond, Cut Corner, Clear, 1 ⅞ In. ... 77.00
Salt, Strawberry Diamond, Waffle Diamond Base, Clear, 2 In. ... 88.00
Salt Loop, Fiery Opalescent, Pedestal, Flint, c.1860, 2 ¼ In. ... 55.00
Spoon Holder, Translucent Starch Blue, Rings, Footed, 1 ¾ x 1 ⅜ In. ... 88.00
Sugar, Cover, Acanthus Leaf, Shield, Blossom Finial, Clear, 5 ¾ In. ... 115.00
Sugar, Cover, Baskets Of Flowers, Eagle, Shields, Footed, Clear, 5 ⅞ In. ... 2200.00
Sugar, Cover, Gothic Arch, Clambroth, 5 ½ In. ... 895.00
Sugar, Cover, Gothic Arch, Canary, Footed, 5 ½ In. ... 1040.00
Sugar, Cover, Gothic Arch, Fiery Opalescent, 6 ¼ In. ... 4500.00
Sweetheart Lamp, Heart Design, Burner, c.1850, 10 ¾ In. ... 300.00
Toothpick, Cover, Alabaster, Clambroth, Handles, Ribbed Finial, 3 ⅞ x 2 ¼ In. ... 110.00
Toothpick, Cover, Translucent Blue, Handles, Ribbed Finial, 3 ⅞ In. ... 413.00
Tray, U.S.F. Constitution, Hearts, Stars, Rectangular, Clear 1 x 5 x 7 In. ... 1870.00
Tumbler, 9 Panels, Amethyst, Toy, 1 ¾ In. ... 112.00
Tumbler, 9 Panels, Canary, Toy, 1 ½ In. ... 112.00
Tumbler, 9 Panels, Teal, Toy, 1 ½ In. ... 112.00
Tumbler, Lemonade, Canary, 9 Panels, Handle, Toy, 1 ½ In. ... 90.00
Tumbler, Lemonade, Cranberry Threading, Pontil, c.1885, 5 ½ In. ... *illus* 85.00
Tumbler, Prism, Blue Opalescent, Toy, 1¾ In. ... 78.00 to 134.00
Tumbler, Whiskey, 6 Panels, Lime Green, 2 In. ... 22.00 to 78.00
Tumbler, Whiskey, 6 Panels, Cobalt Blue, Pontil, 2 In. ... 34.00
Tumbler, Whiskey, 6 Panels, Sapphire, 1 ½ In. ... 34.00
Tumbler, Whiskey, 6 Panels, Electric Blue, 2 ½ In. ... 45.00
Tumbler, Whiskey, 6 Panels, Moss Green, Smooth Base, 2 ¼ In. ... 78.00
Tumbler, Whiskey, 6 Panels, Orange Amber, 2 ½ In. ... 78.00
Tumbler, Whiskey, 8 Panels, Cobalt Blue, 3 ¼ In. ... 56.00
Tumbler, Whiskey, Diamond Faceted, Lime Green, Handle, 4 In. ... 336.00
Tureen, Cover, Fans, Lilies, Scrolls, Stars, Diamonds, Blue, Toy, 2 x 3 In. ... 165.00 to 220.00
Tureen, Cover, Opaque White, Fans, Lilies, Scrolls, Stars, Diamonds, Toy, 2 x 3 In. ... 1210.00
Vase, 3 Printie Block, Amethyst, White Striations, Footed, 10 In. ... 1690.00
Vase, Bigler, Canary, Fluted Rim, Octagonal Base, Bigler, 11 ⅛ x 4 ½ In. ... 715.00
Vase, Loop, Blue, Fluted Rim, Hexagonal Base, 10 ⅞ x 4 ⅝ In. ... 660.00
Vase, Three Printie Block, Opalescent, Footed, 10 ¼ In. ... 4700.00
Vase, Trumpet, Amethyst, Blown, Footed, Rolled Rim, 10 In. ... 1380.00
Vase, Tulip, Amethyst, Panels, Octagonal Base, 10 x 5 ⅛ In., Pair ... 6600.00
Vase, Tulip, Blue Violet, Panels, Octagonal Base, 10 ¼ x 5 ½ In., Pair ... 9900.00
Vase, Tulip, Canary, Footed, 10 In., Pair ... 7100.00
Vase, Tulip, Canary Yellow, Octagonal Base, c.1845, 10 In. ... 2128.00
Vase, Tulip, Emerald Green, Panels, Octagonal Base, Wafer Stem, 10 ⅛ x 5 ⅛ In. ... 8250.00
Vase, Tulip, Teal, Panels, 8-Sided Base, 1845-65, 10 x 4 ⅞ In. ... *illus* 2400.00

Sandwich Glass, Lamp, Fluid, Acanthus Leaf, Clambroth, Starch Blue, Wafer, c.1850, 11 In.
$1090.00

Sandwich Glass, Lamp, Kerosene, Green, Ribbed, Blown Molded, Eaton, c.1870, 11 ½ In.
$5100.00

Sandwich Glass, Pomade Jar, Bear, Muzzled, Starch Blue, Marked, J. Hauel & Co., Philada, c.1865, 4 ½ In.
$3000.00

Sandwich Glass, Tumbler, Lemonade, Cranberry Threading, Pontil, c.1885, 5 ½ In.
$85.00

Sandwich Glass, Vase, Tulip, Teal, Panels, 8-Sided Base, 1845-65, 10 x 4 7/8 In.
$2400.00

Sarreguemines, Pitcher, Figural, Dog Begging, 9 In.
$316.00

Sascha Brastoff, Bowl, Village Scene, Crescent Shape, Marked, 5 ¼ x 7 ¼ In.
$35.00

TIP

Don't store ceramic dishes or figurines for long periods of time in old newspaper wrappings. The ink can make indelible stains on china.

SARREGUEMINES is the name of a French town that is used as part of a china mark. Utzschneider and Company, a porcelain factory, made ceramics in Sarreguemines, Lorraine, France, from about 1775. Transfer-printed wares and majolica were made in the nineteenth century. The nineteenth-century pieces, most often found today, usually have colorful transfer-printed decorations showing peasants in local costumes.

Bowl, Boat Shape, Masks On Each Side, Blue Ground, 14 ½ In. 230.00
Butter Chip, Holdcroft, Flower Shape 138.00
Dessert Service, Majolica, Fraises Et Fleurs, Plates, Compotes, 9 ¾ & 4 ½ In., 14 Piece 2040.00
Ewer, Shouldered, Handle, Brown & Gold Crystalline Glaze, 4 x 12 In. 460.00
Oyster Plate, 6 Wells, Majolica, Plates, Compotes, 14 Piece 115.00
Pitcher, Double Face, 8 ¾ In. 230.00
Pitcher, Figural, Dog Begging, 9 In. .... *illus* 316.00
Pitcher, Figural, Face, John Bull, 6 ½ In. 288.00
Plaque, Game, Cobalt Blue, 3 Quail, Wheat, Leaves, 23 In. 1438.00
Plate Set, Strawberry, Turquoise Ground, 8 In., 6 Piece 748.00
Stein, Stoneware, Ram Handle, Relief, Marked 2718, Pewter Lid, ½ Liter 460.00
Vase, Gilt Bird On Branch, Mottled Violet Ground, Drilled For Lamp, 17 x 13 In. 150.00
Vase, Water Lily Flowers, Brown Ground, Blue Base, 9 In., Pair 288.00

SASCHA BRASTOFF made decorative accessories, ceramics, enamels on copper, and plastics of his own design. He headed a factory, Sascha Brastoff of California, Inc., in West Los Angeles, from 1953 until about 1973. He died in 1993. Pieces signed with the signature *Sascha Brastoff* were his work and are the most expensive. Other pieces marked *Sascha B.* or with a stamped mark were made by others in his company.

Ashtray, Abstract, Light Brown Crackle, Gray Highlights, No. 3, Marked, 5 ½ x 5 ½ In. 55.00
Ashtray, Alaska Series, Walrus 70.00
Ashtray, Americana, Flowers, Glossy Black Glaze, 9 In. 64.00
Ashtray, Bird Eggs, On Nest, Chi-Chi, 13 ½ In. 40.00
Ashtray, Bird King, Chi-Chi 40.00
Ashtray, Citrus, 13 ½ x 5 In. 30.00
Ashtray, Freeform, Jewels, Bird, Gray Ground, Marked, 15 x 7 In. 50.00
Ashtray, Freeform, Turquoise Crackle, Gold Accents, Signed, 3 In. 13.00
Ashtray, Houses, Square, Signed, 8 In. 42.00
Ashtray, Jewel Bird, Signed, c.1947-62, 1 ½ x 8 ½ x 6 In. 85.00
Ashtray, Mushrooms, Copper, Signed, 5 In. 30.00
Ashtray, Persian Design, Irregular Shape, Signed, 5 ½ x 7 In. 28.00
Ashtray, Rooftops, Enamel, Copper, Round, 10 ½ x 7 ¾ In. 150.00
Ashtray, Rooftops, White, Gray, Copper, Marked, 10 ½ x 7 ¾ In. 50.00
Ashtray, Rooster, Stamped, 4 ¼ x 3 In. 15.00
Ashtray, Star Steed, Enamel, Copper, 8 ½ In. 170.00
Ashtray, Stylized Flowers, White, Blue, Green, Signed, c.1960, 4 ⅛ In. 20.00
Ashtray, Turbaned Man, Mottled Gray Matte, Signed, 7 ½ x 7 ½ In. 125.00
Ballet Dancer's Foot & Hand, Gold Tip, Ruffled Rim, Pottery, Marked, 5 ½ In. 150.00
Bowl, Candy, Lid, Turbaned Man, Legs Crossed, Upraised Arms, Mottled Gray Matte Ground, 5 ¾ In. 150.00
Bowl, Enamel On Copper, Mottled Gray Matte, Signed, 3 ¼ x 8 In. 60.00
Bowl, Village Scene, Crescent Shape, Marked, 5 ¼ x 7 ¼ In. .... *illus* 35.00
Charger, Abstract Design, Brown, Gold, Glass Cabochons, Signed, 17 ¾ In. 165.00
Charger, Flowers, Jewels, Turbaned Man, Legs Crossed, Upraised Arms, Mottled Gray Matte, 5 ¾ In. 35.00
Cigarette Holder, Pipe Form, Jewels Bird, Signed, 1947-62, 4 ½ x 4 ¼ x 2 ½ In. 49.00
Dish, Abstract, Brown, Yellow, White Ground, Marked, 8 x 8 In. 45.00
Dish, Aztec, Marked, 7 In. 45.00
Dish, Bird, Black, Mauve, Gold, Black Ground, Dots, 6 x 6 In. 42.00
Dish, Free-Form, Circle Center, 7 x 6 ½ In. 35.00
Dish, Free-Form, Flowers, Black Ground, 9 ½ x 5 ½ In. 95.00
Dish, Rooftops, Oval, 7 In. 50.00
Figurine, Bird, Orange, Marked, 6 ½ In. 75.00
Jar, Igloo, Green Ground, Mountains, 3-Footed, Oval, 1950s 28.00
Lighter, Leaves, Blue, Gold Highlights, Green Ground, 3 ½ In. 47.00
Pipe, Purple Flowers, Marked, 4 ¾ In. .... *illus* 25.00
Pitcher, Surf Ballet, White, Gold, Pottery, 10 x 8 In. 30.00
Plate, Flower Border & Center, Gold, Signed, 10 ⅞ In. 200.00
Plate, Flowers, Mottled Gray Ground, Signed, 10 ⅞ In. 200.00
Plate, Free-Form, Citrus, Yellow, Blue, Gold, Black Leaves, 10 ½ In. 45.00
Plate, Gold Concentric Circles, Ivory Ground, Signed, 10 ⅞ In. 200.00

Plate, Gold Design, Ivory Ground, Signed, 10⅞ In. 200.00

Plate, Gold Design Border, Signed, 10⅞ In. 200.00

Plate, Gold Flower Border, Ivory Ground, Signed, 10⅞ In. 200.00

Plate, Gold Flowers, Ivory Textured Ground, Signed, 10⅞ In. 200.00

Plate, Ivory Ground, Gold Concentric Circles, Signed, 10⅞ In. 200.00

Platter, Alaska Series, Seal, Gray, Taupe, White, Blue Sky, 1973, 14 x 8 In. 125.00

Sugar & Creamer, Alaska Series, Eskimo, 1965 94.00

Sugar & Creamer, Surf Ballet, White, Gold 30.00

Tankard, Green Ground, Design, Brochure, Signed, 4¾ In. 45.00

Tankard, Lid, Surf Ballet, White, Gold, 15¼ In. 30.00

Tea Set, Gray Smoke Tree, 3 Piece 175.00

Vase, Alaska Series, Eskimo Head, Signed, 8 In. 45.00

Vase, Alaska Series, Igloos, Blue, White Ground, Signed, 7¾ In. 19.00

Vase, Craquelure, Rooster Mark, 10 In. 125.00

Vase, Fish, Stylized, Metallic Gold, Silver Glaze, 17⅜ In. 150.00

Vase, Mayan-Aztec, Gold, White Matte, No. 082, Marked, 8 In. 75.00

Vase, Pagoda, Pottery, Signed, 5⅝ x 3⅞ In. 44.00

Vase, Ballet Dancer's Foot & Hand, Gold, Black, Sunfish Form, 3-Footed, Signed, 2½ x 10 x 8½ In. 40.00

SATIN GLASS is a late-nineteenth-century art glass. It has a dull finish that is caused by hydrofluoric acid vapor treatment. Satin glass was made in many colors and sometimes has applied decorations. Satin glass is also listed by factory name, such as Webb, or in the Mother-of-Pearl category in this book.

Biscuit Jar, Cranberry, White, Basket Weave, Flowers, Silver Plated Lid, Handle, 10¾ In. 1010.00

Bowl, Cranberry, Diamond Quilted, Clear Glass Rim & Feet, Marked, Patent, 5 In. 685.00

Bowl, Flower Branches, Diamond Quilted, Pink Over Ivory, Lobed, Ruffled Edge, 4¾ x 10 In. 550.00

Bowl, Pink Diamond Quilted, Scalloped Rim, 3 Clear Feet, Patent, 5 x 8 x 5¾ In. 230.00

Bowl, White Over Pink, Leaves, 7¾ x 10 In. 1521.00

Dish, Blue Diamond Quilted, Scalloped Rim, 3 Clear Feet, Patent, 3¾ x 7¾ x 7 In. 250.00

Lamp, Pink, Inverted Style, Ribbed Shade, Melon Rib Base, Brass Fittings, Foot, 18 In. 480.00

Pitcher, Yellow To Amber, Swirled Ribs, Frosted & Reeded Handle, 7½ In. 245.00

Powder Jar, Cover, Light Green, Woman's Head Finial, 3-Footed, 4¾ x 4¾ In. 30.00

Vase, Apricot To Chartreuse, Diamond Quilted, Bulbous, Tapered Neck, 13 In. 945.00

Vase, Cranberry, Amber, Swirled Ribs, Gourd Shape, Marked, Patent, c.1880, 10 In. 2950.00

Vase, Peach Shaded To Yellow, Ruffled Edge, Tapered Foot Ring, 5 In. 150.00

SATSUMA is a Japanese pottery with a distinctive creamy beige crackled glaze. Most of the pieces were decorated with blue, red, green, orange, or gold. Almost all Satsuma found today was made after 1860, especially during the Meiji Period, 1868–1912. During World War I, Americans could not buy undecorated European porcelains. Women who liked to make hand-painted porcelains at home began to decorate plain Satsuma. These pieces are known today as "American Satsuma."

Bowl, 2 Panels, Figures, 5-Scalloped Rim, Multicolored, Gilt, c.1850, 2 x 5 In. 250.00

Bowl, 3 Reserves, Figures, Gilt, Earthenware, Late 19th Century, 3 x 4¼ In. 50.00

Bowl, Phoenix, Dragons, Storm Clouds, Signed, 19th Century, 6¾ In., Pair 588.00

Bowl, Tea, Hundred Rakan, Jewel Borders, Indented Sides, Signed, 1800, 5 In. *illus* 235.00

Box, Cover, Seal Paste, Round Body, Multicolored Enamel, Gilt, Japan, c.1912, 2½ In. 180.00

Censer, Birds, Silver Cover, Cylindrical, Diamond Shape Handles, 4¾ In. 1763.00

Censer, Warriors, Courtiers, Animal Form Feet, Foo Dog Finial, 40 In. 3408.00

Censer, Women, Flower Reserves, Brocade, Double Walled, 19th Century, 6 In. 4406.00

Charger, Women, Cobalt Blue Back, Borders, Signed, Kinkozan, 1868-1911, 14 In. 9400.00

Dish, Peacock, Flowering Plum & Peonies, Gilt, Red Cartouche, Fan Shape, 2 x 16½ x 11 In. 690.00

Ewer, Dragon Shape Spout, Handle, 9½ In. 767.00

Ewer, Wine, Dragons, Buddhist Saints, Dragon Handle, Spout, 19th Century, 8½ In. 470.00

Incense Burner, Seated Buddha, Moriage, Nippon, Gold, 6 x 4 In. 44.00

Jar, Cover, Hundred Poets, Cobalt Blue Ground, Hexagonal, 19th Century, 12 In. 235.00

Jar, Lid, Torii Gate, Shimazu Mon, Crest, Red & Gilt, Crackled, 1900s, 11½ In., Pair 173.00

Model, Boat, Earthenware, Signed, 17 In. 2596.00

Oyster Plate, 6 Wells, 9 In. 1380.00

Plate, 2 Men, Moriage, 10½ In. 100.00

Plate, Birds, Wisteria, Impressed, Kinkozan, 19th Century, 8¾ In. 294.00

Tea Set, Warriors, Teapot, Creamer, Sugar, 6 Cups, Saucers, 15 Piece 264.00

Temple Jar, Cover, Court Scenes, Foo Dog Handles, Multicolored Enamel, 28 In. 230.00

Vase, Artisans, Flower Border, Gilt, Multicolored, Early 1900s, 2¼ In. 2530.00

Vase, Bamboo, Flowers, Peacock, Blue, Disk Shape, Signed, Echi-Den, 9 In. *illus* 675.00

Vase, Birds & Flowers, 4¾ In. 118.00

Sascha Brastoff, Pipe, Purple Flowers, Marked, 4¾ In.
$25.00

Satsuma, Bowl, Tea, Hundred Rakan, Jewel Borders, Indented Sides, Signed, 1800s, 5 In.
$235.00

Satsuma, Vase, Bamboo, Flowers, Peacock, Blue, Disk Shape, Signed, Echi-Den, 9 In.
$675.00

TIP

If there are raised applied decorations on your art glass, be careful when cleaning it. Gold or silver accents, painted enamel decoration, and beads must be kept in fine condition to maintain the value.

Satsuma, Vase, Water Mills, Gilt, Marked, 6 1/4 In., Pair.
$135.00

Scale, Balance, Butter, Wood Pans, Rope, 19th Century, 29 x 22 In.
$325.00

Scale, Balance, Micrometer, Brass, Chrome, Marble, Late 1880s, 15 x 12 In.
$500.00

Schafer & Vater, Bottle Set, Baker, Face Cups, Tray, 6 Piece
$350.00

Vase, Cobalt Blue & Olive Glaze, Ivory Lid, Paper Label, 19th Century, 3 1/2 In. 144.00
Vase, Flowers, 35 Figures, Brocade Panels, Flared Rim, 3 1/2 In.. . . . . 1560.00
Vase, Flowers, Fired Gold, 2 Handles, c.1880, 25 In. 117.00
Vase, Lady, Young Girl, Catching Fireflies, Black, Gilt Mark, Early 1900s, 14 1/4 In. 86.00
Vase, Roosters, Ducks, Flowering Plants, Gilt Phoenixes, Cobalt Blue Ground, 16 In. 9988.00
Vase, Scholars, Children, Geometric, Ribbon Tassels, Panels, 19th Century. 196.00
Vase, Water Mills, Gilt, Marked, 6 1/4 In., Pair.. . . . . *illus* 135.00
Vase, Woman, Colorful Dress, 2 Handles, Moriage, 4 In. 28.00

SATURDAY EVENING GIRLS, *see Paul Revere Pottery category.*

SCALES have been made to weigh everything from babies to gold. Collectors search for all types. Most popular are small gold dust scales and special grocery scales.

Balance, Apothecary, Brass, Cast Iron, c.1900, 32 x 26 In. 146.00
Balance, Apothecary, Brass, Counter Weights, Wood Case, Trays, c.1880, 20 x 14 In. 330.00
Balance, Apothecary, Brass, Weight Set, c.1880, 20 x 14 In. 234.00
Balance, Brass, 2 Pans, Urn Supports, 20th Century, 56 1/2 x 45 In. 620.00
Balance, Brass, Cast Iron, c.1900, 32 x 26 In. 270.00
Balance, Brass, Wrought Iron, Avery's Class C, Weights, 34 x 28 x 12 In.. . . . . 200.00
Balance, Butter, Wood Pans, Rope, 19th Century, 29 x 22 In.. . . . . *illus* 325.00
Balance, Mahogany, Christian Becker, Brass Knife Edge Pivots, Weights, 18 x 16 In. 250.00
Balance, Mahogany, Fisher Scientific, Glass Knife Edge Pivots, Weights, 16 x 16 In. 175.00
Balance, Micrometer, Brass, Chrome, Marble, Late 1880s, 15 x 12 In. . . . . *illus* 500.00
Balance, Pocket, Brass, Hanging, Germany, 50 Lb., 10 In. 20.00
Balance, Pocket, Coin, Brass Pans, Steel Arm, Leather Case, 8 1/4 In. 176.00
Balance, W. & T. Avery Ltd., Birmingham, Brass, Mahogany Drawer Base, 27 x 20 In. 1006.00
Candy, Howe Mfg., Brass Scoop, Late 19th Century, 19 In.. . . . . 245.00
Dayton Scale Co., White Painted, 30 x 19 In. 55.00
Pan, Brass, Owl Finial, Weight Set, Greece, 3 1/2 x 2 In.. . . . . 198.00
Penny, Columbia Weighing Machine Co., 1 Cent, c.1920 . . . . 110.00
Postage, Brass, Oak Base, 3 Weights, 3 1/2 x 7 x 4 In. 140.00
Postage, Brass, Victorian, Flowers, 6 Weights, England, Late 1800s 559.00
Postage, Brass, Weights, England, 3 1/2 x 7 In. 53.00
Postage, Cast Iron Open Frame, American Scale Mfg. Co., Patd. 1882, 8 In. 264.00
Postage, Gilt Design, Brass Pans, Green Onyx Base, 10 1/2 In. 264.00
Postage, Gilt Metal, Brass, Steel Hanging Hook, Leather Case, England, c.1860, 5 In. 4481.00
Postage, Steel, Ohio Valley, Wheeling, W.Va., 1940s, 3 In. 35.00
Salters, No. 11, Green Painted Steel, Brass Dial, 7 In. 295.00
Weighing, Porcelain, Blue Delft Style, 2 Brass Pans, Max Weight 5 Kg, 10 x 15 In.. . . . . 137.00

SCHAFER & VATER, makers of small ceramic items, are best known for their amusing figurals. The factory was located in Volkstedt-Rudolstadt, Germany, from 1890 to 1962. Some pieces are marked with the crown and R mark, but many are unmarked.

Bottle, Figural, Rabbit, Porcelain, Marked 9 1/2 In.. . . . . 552.00
Bottle, Fire Water, Fireman Holding Hose, Early 1900s 282.00
Bottle, Girl, Long Stem Glass, Rose, Early 1900s 228.00
Bottle, Man & Dog, Old Scotch, Early 1900s. 345.00
Bottle, Monk, Music Box, Early 1900s. 585.00
Bottle, September Morn, Porcelain, Marked, 6 1/2 In. 403.00
Bottle Set, Baker, Face Cups, Tray, 6 Piece . . . . *illus* 350.00
Box, Cover, Buddha, Pagoda, Dragons, Early 1900s 185.00
Box, Cover, Girls Face, Woman, Blue, Cameo, Jasperware, 3 1/2 x 3 3/4 In.. . . . . 85.00
Box, Figures, Blue, White, Jasperware, Signed, c.1900, 5 In. 195.00
Candlestick, Cameo, Marked 170.00
Creamer, Black Boy, Long Fingernails, Early 1900s, 3 1/2 In. 125.00
Creamer, Girl With Keys, Marked, Early 1900s, 3 1/2 In. . . . . *illus* 138.00
Creamer, Pharaoh, Jasperware, c.1925, 3 1/2 x 4 In. . . . . *illus* 375.00
Dish, Monkey On Donkey, 4 1/4 x 6 3/8 x 3 3/4 In. 225.00
Dresser Box, Oriental Man Smoking Pipe, On Elephant, Early 1900s 180.00
Figurine, Cockatoos, 1962. . . . . 250.00
Figurine, Man, Tenor Singer, Early 1900s 385.00
Figurine, Scotsman, Waiting For Tide, 1900s. 245.00
Figurine, Woman, With Basket, Marked, 4 3/4 In. 104.00

Hatpin Holder, Egyptian Queen, Jewels, Scrolls, Pink, Jasperware, 5 ¾ In. 165.00
Jar, Cover, Child Playing Pan Flute, Green, Bronze, Cameo, Jasperware 140.00
Jar, Dresser, Fairy Playing Violin, Harp, Sage, White, Round, Jasperware, Early 1900s 150.00
Jar, Dresser, Woman, Grecian Robe, Bird, Sage Green, Jasperware 150.00
Match Holder, Gnome, Early 1900s 275.00
Match Holder, Toothpick, Golfer, Early 1900s, 3 ⅝ x 2 ¼ In. 165.00
Pitcher, Pierrot, Playing Mandolin, Wide Mouth, Marked 175.00
Teapot, Woman, Reclining, Cornucopia, Bird, Sage Green, Jasperware 400.00
Tray, Pin, Woman, Dragonfly 249.00
Vase, Bird, White, Snow, Branches, Early 1900s 92.00

SCHNEIDER Glassworks was founded in 1917 at Epinay-sur-Seine, France, by Charles and Ernest Schneider. Art glass was made between 1917 and 1930. The company still produces clear crystal glass. See also the Le Verre Français category.

Bowl, Centerpiece, Pink, Amethyst Mottled, 9 ½ In. 115.00
Compote, Mottled Raspberry Pink, Bubbles, Signed, 3 ¾ In. .... *illus* 225.00
Compote, Red, Art Deco, Wrought Iron Foot, 7 x 5 In. 500.00
Compote, Sunset Orange Shaded To Pink, 2 ¼ x 7 ¾ In. 235.00
Console Set, Yellow, Orange Compote, Amethyst Foot, 2 Cylindrical Vases, 14 & 17 In. 6038.00
Ewer, Yellow Striated Glass, Green & Brown Rim, Bird Beak Spout, Snake Handle, 13 In. 748.00
Inkwell, Mottled Amethyst To Crimson, Blue Jewel Finial, 3 Sections, Signed, 7 In. 920.00
Pitcher, Mottled Orange & Rust, Black Handle, Pedestal Base, 15 ¾ In. 1035.00
Tray, Amber, Fern Fronds, Cameo, Art Deco, Round, 14 In. 176.00
Vase, Amethyst, Mottled Red Rim, Yellow Spattering, 15 In. 920.00
Vase, Mottled, Amethyst, Crimson Foil Spangle, Footed, 7 ½ In. 301.00
Vase, Mottled Pink Shaded To Orange & Rust, Bulbous, Cupped Rim, Signed, 8 In. 441.00
Vase, Prunts, Enameled, Gold Foil, Signed, 13 In. .... *illus* 1300.00
Vase, Red Flowers, 3 Vines, Mottled Citron Yellow, Iron Red, Signed, 18 In. .... *illus* 2235.00
Vase, Red Tango Body, Blue Inclusions, Urn Shape, Signed, 11 ½ In. 1150.00

SCIENTIFIC INSTRUMENTS of all kinds are included in this category. Other categories such as Barometer, Binoculars, Dental, Medical, Nautical, and Thermometer may also price scientific apparatus.

Chronometer, Alexander Cairn, Brass Mount, Mahogany, 54-Hour, 4 In. 2233.00
Compass, Pocket, 32-Point Rose, Steel Needle, Brass Hub, 18th Century, 2 ¼ In. 176.00
Compass, Pocket, Floating Paper Dial, Roman Chapter Ring, Fruitwood Case, 2 In. 323.00
Compass, Pocket, Paper Card, 32-Point Rose, Steel Needle, 19th Century, 2 ¾ In. 118.00
Compass, Pocket, Pendant Loop, Enamel Dial, Jeweled Pivot, 1 ½ In. 5079.00
Compass, Surveyor's, 4-In. Dial, Richard Pattern, New York, 11 ½ In. 660.00
Compass, Surveyor's, Benjamin Pike, Brass, Mahogany Case, 14 ½ In. 470.00
Compass, Surveyor's, C.T. Amsler, Brass, Mahogany Case, Label, 12 In. 646.00
Compass, Surveyor's, Christopher Hurtin, Brass, 13 In. 2468.00
Compass, Surveyor's, Vernier, Jacob's Staff, Meneeley & Oothout, 16 In. 7260.00
Compass, Theodolite, Elliott Bros., Brass, Silvered Scales, c.1880, 11 In. 434.00
Compass, Surveyor's, Whitehurst Derby, Blue Needle, Fruitwood Case, c.1780 .... 418.00
Cutting Machine, For Typesetting, Cast Iron, c.1915, 17 x 14 x 6 In. 167.00
Drafting Set, Pens, Ivory Handle, Dividers, Compass Insert, Leather Case, 7 In. 147.00
Electrostatic Machine, Foil Strips, Leyden Jars, Hand Crank, Wilmshurst, 10 x 7 In. 345.00
Galvanometer, Max Kohl, Wood Case, 18 ½ In. 301.00
Graphometer, Le Febvre, Fixed Sights, Engraved, Signed, c.1720 .... 8362.00
Hot Air Engine, Balance Machine, Cast Iron Base, Frame, 4 ¾ x 11 In. 753.00
Level, Surveyor's, W. & L.E. Gurley, Mahogany Case, Label, 11 ½ In. 235.00
Level Tester, Lacquered Brass, Bubble Levels, c.1850, 28 In. 207.00
Magnifying Glass, Ivory Handle, Chinese, 20th Century, 9 ¾ In. 526.00
Micrometer, Digital, J.T. Slocomb, Providence, 4 ½ In. 176.00
Microscope, Bausch & Lomb, Binocular, Oak Case, c.1910, 13 In. .... *illus* 100.00
Microscope, Binocular, Henry Crouch, Mahogany Case, 14 ½ In. 1058.00
Microscope, Brass, 2 Lenses, Thumb Operated, Wood Box, 12 x 12 In. 896.00
Microscope, Brass, Ivory Handle, 6 Lenses, Fish Skin Case, 3 ½ In. 896.00
Microscope, Brass, Lenses, Stand, 4 Ivory Slides, Wood Box, 4 In. 1316.00
Microscope, Cast Brass, Cast Iron Base, Wooden Case, Drawer, 1900s, 10 In. 259.00
Microscope, Compound, Leitz, Brass, Walnut Case, 11 ½ In. 323.00
Microscope, Culpeper, Brass, Monocular, Mirror, Mahogany Base, c.1820 .... 3103.00
Microscope, Murray & Heath, London, Folding, Lacquered Brass Draw Tube, 9 In. 264.00

Schafer & Vater, Creamer, Girl With Keys, Marked, Early 1900s, 3 ½ In.
$138.00

Schafer & Vater, Creamer, Pharaoh, Jasperware, c.1925, 3 ½ x 4 In.
$375.00

Schneider, Compote, Mottled Raspberry Pink, Bubbles, Signed, 3 ¾ In.
$225.00

Schneider, Vase, Prunts, Enameled, Gold Foil, Signed, 13 In.
$1300.00

S

Schneider, Vase, Red Flowers, 3 Vines, Mottled Citron Yellow, Iron Red, Signed, 18 In.
$2235.00

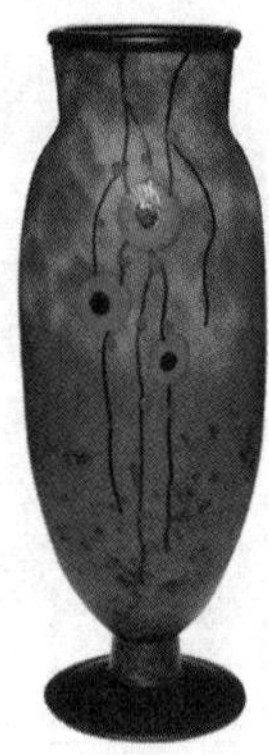

Scientific Instrument, Microscope, Bausch & Lomb, Binocular, Oak Case, c.1910, 13 In.
$100.00

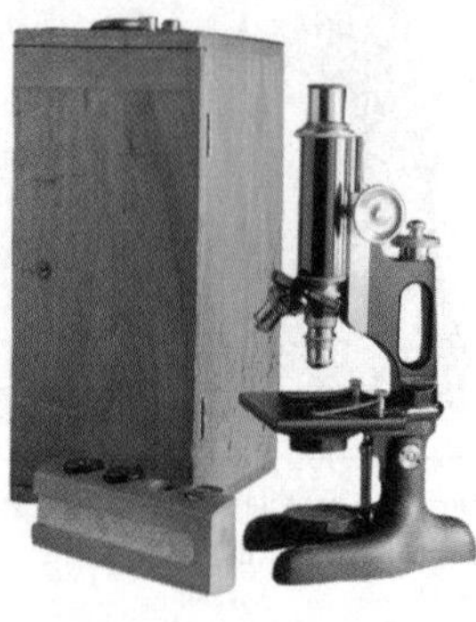

Scientific Instrument, Planetarium, Orrery, Brass, Ivory Spheres, Wood Base, c.1850, 14 In.
$5000.00

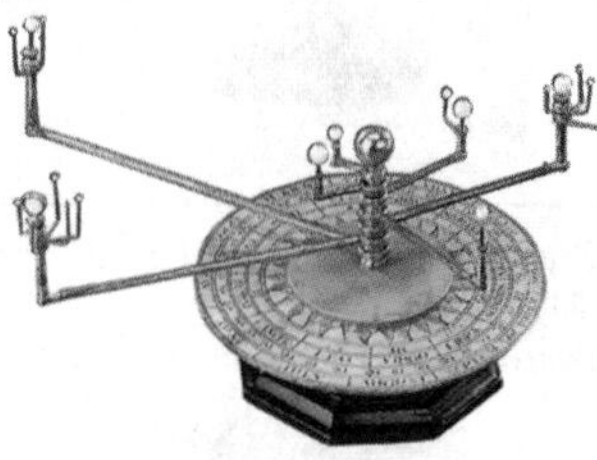

Microscope, Student Drum, J.H. Steward, 406 Strand, London, 7 In. 206.00
Odometer, Wittmann, Lacquered Brass Case, Cast Iron Wheel, Signed, 40 In. 1422.00
Opthalmascope, Brass Mount, Ivory Handle, Leather Box, 7 ½ In. 9560.00
Picture Binocular, Binoca, Japan, Bakelite, White, Gold, Opera Glasses, 1950 843.00
Planetarium, Orrery, Brass, Ivory Spheres, Wood Base, c.1850, 14 In. *illus* 5000.00
Sand Glass, Pillar Shape, Mahogany Stand, 3 Barley Twist Columns, 15 In. 2988.00
Slide Rule, Keuffel & Esser Co., Oak, c.1900, 20 In. 130.00
Spyglass, 8 Draw, Brass, Tortoiseshell Grip, Dust Cover, England, 31 In. 508.00
Spyglass, Pull Draw, Brass, Mahogany, Fish Skin Case, 15 In. 2510.00
Steam Engine, Horizontal, Fixed Brass Cylinder, 2-In. Flywheel, 17 In. 552.00
Steam Engine, Vertical, Fire Tube Boiler, Cast Iron Base, 7 x 19 In. 753.00
Stock Ticker, Western Union, Edison Universal Type 3A, 10 x 9 In. *illus* 13800.00
Telegraph Operator's Training Board, Oak, Patd. 1895, 11 ¼ In. 118.00
Telescope, 2 Draw, Mahogany, Twisted Twine Rings, 14-In. Tube, 2 ½ In. 294.00
Telescope, 3 Draw, Paper Card, Dust Slides, c.1780, 12 ½ In. 759.00
Telescope, Bardou, Brass, Oak Tripod, Celestial, Terrestrial, France, 60 In. 2875.00
Telescope, Bardou & Sons, Single Draw, Tripod, U.S. Navy 2511, Paris, 31 In. 470.00
Telescope, Brass, 2 Lens, Dust Cover, Wood Tripod, 58 x 38 In. 4780.00
Telescope, Brass, 4 Draw, Lacquered Brass, Wooden Tube, c.1820, 12 In. 301.00
Telescope, Brass, Portable, Screw Dust Cap, Rotating Tripod, 7 x 11 In. 508.00
Telescope, Brass, Portable, Tripod, 12 x 20 In. 508.00
Telescope, Dollond, 3 Draw, Lacquered Brass, Mahogany, c.1820, 14 ½ In. 241.00
Telescope, E. Krauss, Brass, Spotting, 3 Power, Leather Case, Marked 1610.00
Telescope, J.H. Steward, 2 Draw, Refracting, Brass, 3 ½ In. 4249.00
Telescope, Lawrence & Mayo, 3 Draw, Brass, Hinged Cap, Compass, 34 In. 345.00
Telescope, R.J. Hopgood, London, Oak, Brass, Tripod Base, 1916, 16 x 27 In. 480.00
Telescope, Spotting, Cast Brass, Rack Gear, 17 x 31 In. 502.00
Telescope, Tube, Dollond, London, 2 Draw, Refracting, Mahogany, 138 In. 4994.00
Telescope, Voigtlander & Son, Telephoto Collinear No. 4, 3 Draw, 31 In. 262.00
Telescope, Widdifield & Co., Boston, Single Draw, Tapered, Mahogany, 48 In. 294.00
Transit, Surveyor's, A. Lietz, Solar Attachment, Aluminum Upgrade, c.1900 595.00
Transit, Surveyor's, Holbern, London, ESCC Surveyor's Dept., Mahogany Tripod Base, 56 In. 2040.00
Transit, Surveyor's, Keuffel & Esser, No. 5127, c.1912 495.00
Transit Level, Brass, Spirit Level, Tripod, 2 Stadia Rods, Case, c.1874, 9 ¾ x 58 In. 460.00

SCRIMSHAW is bone or ivory or whale's teeth carved by sailors and others for entertainment during the sailing-ship days. Some scrimshaw was carved as early as 1800. There are modern scrimshanders making pieces today on bone, ivory, or plastic. Other pieces may be found in the Ivory and Nautical categories.

Basket, Knitting, Whalebone, Maple, Baluster Spokes, Ebony Compass Inlay, 4 x 7 In. 14400.00
Basket, Pierced, Carved, Scalloped Base, Inlaid Silver, Whale Ivory Sides, 6-Sided 33000.00
Bedstead, Doll's, Tall Post, Whalebone, Ivory, Scalloped Headboard, c.1850, 10 x 8 In. 7200.00
Box, Sewing, Panbone, Engraved, Fitted Lid, Damask Pincushion, 1800s, 2 x 7 In. 18000.00
Figurine, Eskimo In Kayak, Wood Paddle & Harpoon, 13 ½ In. 303.00
Group, Hunting Scene With Walrus, 5 In. 138.00
Hair Comb, Corkscrew Type Design, 4 x 5 ½ In. 49.00
Lake Scene, Wood Base, 7 ½ In. 263.00
Measuring Stick, Bone, Inscribed AB, Alton Ellsworth Barker, c.1815, 35 ⅝ In. 1175.00
Pie Crimper, Figural, Whale Ivory, Baleen, Swimming Eel, 19th Century, 9¼ In. 1430.00
Pie Crimper, Figural, Whale's Tooth, Ivory, Seahorse, c.1850, 4 ¾ In. 8800.00
Pie Crimper, Ivory, Heart Shaped Cutout, 6 ¼ In. 695.00
Pie Crimper, Whale Ivory, 5-Point Star, Crescent Moons, c.1870, 6 ½ In. 880.00
Plaque, Ivory, Bust Portrait, Commdr Stephen Decatur, Frame, Square, 5 In. 1315.00
Swordfish Bill, Circular Design, 26 In. 489.00
Walrus Tusk, Animals, Human Figures, Structures, Hanging Hole, 20th Century, 14 In. 330.00
Whale's Tooth, Eagle, Outstretched Wings, 1978, 6 In. 478.00
Whale's Tooth, Engraved, Bust Of Man, Duck, Inscribed, W.Y., c.1850, 6 ⅜ In. 529.00
Whale's Tooth, Engraved, Woman In Profile, Elaborate Hair, 4 ¼ x 2 ¼ In. 896.00
Whale's Tooth, Engraving Of Woman, Oval Wood Base, 4 ¼ x 2 ¼ In. 800.00
Whale's Tooth, Ship's Figurehead, Woman, Eagle Tip, 1973, 6 In. 448.00
Whale's Tooth, Whaler, Bookend Mounted, 8 In., Pair 2988.00
Whale's Tooth, Whaling Scene, Etched, 2-Sided, Signed, 20th Century, 6 ½ In. 354.00
Whale's Tooth, Woman, Seated, Eagle, American Shield & Arrows, 3-Masted Ship, 7 In. 568.00
Whale's Tooth, Woman Pirate, Hands On Sword, Holding Flag Pole, Pistols, 5 ½ In. 6600.00

TIP

When looking at scrimshaw, check the large hole in the tooth. Reproductions are brown, dyed to look old. Real teeth have clean root cavities.

SEBASTIAN MINIATURES were first made by Prescott W. Baston in 1938 in Marblehead, Massachusetts. More than 400 different designs have been made, and collectors search for the out-of-production models. The mark may say *Copr. P.W. Baston U.S.A.*, or *P. W. Baston, U.S.A.*, or *Prescott W. Baston*. Sometimes a paper label was used.

Abe Lincoln, 3 In. 45.00
Amish Folk, 3 In. 60.00
Aunt Betsy Trotwood, 3 In. 48.00
Aunt Polly, 3 In. 15.00
Bob Cratchit & Tiny Tim, 3½ In. 23.00
Boy & Pelican, 3 In. 20.00
Colonial Bell Ringer, 3⅛ In. 89.00
Colonial Glassblower, 2⅞ In. .... 30.00 to 49.00
Colonial Watchman, 3⅛ In. 65.00
Coronado & Senora, 3¼ In. 21.00
Cowhand, 3½ In. 24.00
Cranberry Picker, 1⅞ In. 18.00
Donald McKay, 3½ In. 20.00
Drummer Boy, 3½ In. 21.00
Family Reads Aloud, 2⅝ In. .... 12.00 to 21.00
Farmer, 3 In. 40.00
Games In Springtime, 4 In. 15.00
Gibson Girl, Gibson Girl At Home, c.1960, 3 In. 24.00
Ichabod Crane, 3¼ In. 19.99
In The Candy Store, 3 In. 25.00
John Alden, 2⅕ In. 40.00
Lobsterman, 3 In. 8.00
Mr. Obocell, 4½ In. 40.00
Old Covered Bridge, 2¾ In. 29.00
Parade Rest, 4⅛ In. 21.00
Patrick Henry, 3 In. 60.00
Plate, The Candy Store, 6 In. 19.99
Rip Van Winkle, 3 In. 22.00
Rub A Dub Dub, 4 In. 34.00
Sailing Days, 3⅝ In. 19.00
School Days Boy, 3 In. .... 39.00 to 52.00
School Days Girl, 3½ In. 20.00
Scrooge, 3 In. 49.00
Self Portrait, 4¼ In. 29.99
The First Kite, 3½ In. 20.00
The Pilgrims, 3⅜ In. 22.00
The Shoemaker, 2½ In. 20.00
Uncle Sam, 4¼ In. 35.00
Will Rogers, 3½ In. 68.00
Williamsburg Couple, 3⅛ In. 24.00

SEG, *see Paul Revere Pottery category.*

SEVRES porcelain has been made in Sevres, France, since 1769. Many copies of the famous ware have been made. The name originally referred to the works of the Royal Porcelain factory. The name now includes any of the wares made in the town of Sevres, France. The entwined lines with a center letter used as the mark is one of the most forged marks in antiques. Be very careful to identify Sevres by quality, not just by mark.

Bird, Standing, Frosted Crystal, 9 x 4 In. 146.00
Bowl, Bronze Mounts, Blue, Flowers, Cherubs, Monogram, Handles, Footed, 6¾ x 9 In. 720.00
Bowl, Red Berry Laurel Wreath, Garlands, 1766, 8¾ In. 2160.00
Bowl Set, Painted Borders, Blue Morning Glories, Gilt, 8¾ In., 12 Piece. 920.00
Breakfast Set, Multicolored, Gilt, Rococo Style, Celeste Ground, Medallions, c.1846. .... 1531.00
Cabaret Service, Birds In Branches, Blue, Pink, Tray, Cups, Saucers, Sugar, Cover, 7 Piece .. 2160.00
Compote, Marbleized Cobalt Blue, Parcel Gilt Foot, 1899, 8¼ x 10¾ In. 600.00
Compote, Roses, Pink, Marked, c.1900, 10¾ In. 198.00
Cup & Saucer, Cupid Reclining, Clutching Grapes, c.1770, 6⅛ In. 4800.00
Dresser Box, Blue, Gilt Foliage, Romantic Couple, Flowered Interior, 8 x 12 x 6 In. 1292.00
Dresser Box, Maiden, Cherub Holding Mirror, Flowers, Gold, Oval, Callet, 3 x 7 x 5 In. 518.00
Figurine, Allegory Of Fire, 4 Small Children Around Campfire, 7 In. 354.00
Figurine, Leda & The Swan, Biscuit Porcelain, c.1909, 14½ x 15¼ In. 1998.00

TIP
There are many ecologically sound products made for care and repair of antiques. Look at the labels. Our ancestors cleaned pewter with wood ashes and oil. Be sure to dispose of paint thinners, harsh chemical cleaners, and other dangerous products in the approved manner. Don't just dump them in the sewer.

Scientific Instrument, Stock Ticker, Western Union, Edison Universal Type 3A, 10 x 9 In. $13800.00

Sevres, Urn, Girl Seated In Garden, Gold Scrolls, Aqua Luster, Ormolu Mounts, 6½ In. $375.00

S

TIP
Try not to immerse figurines in water. Many have small holes in the bottom that will let water get inside. It is difficult to remove the water and it may drip out and stain a wooden table or the figurine.

Figurine, Man, 2 Women, Oval Base, 10 ½ x 9 x 5 ½ In. 896.00
Figurine, Man, Lady, Servant, Oval Base, 10 ½ x 9 x 5 ½ In. 800.00
Jardiniere, Louis XVI Style, Kingwood, Bronze, Quatrefoil Shape, Tole Liner, 8 x 14 In. 235.00
Planter, Bulb, Cobalt Blue, Gilt, Footed, Ladies On Bench, Signed, c.1750. 920.00
Plaque, Coved Molded, Ebonized Frame, c.1640, 5 ½ x 6 ⅜ In. 4700.00
Plate, Cobalt Blue, Gilt Anthemion Border, 19th Century, 9 ¼ In., 6 Piece 764.00
Plate, Multicolored, Gilt, Court Figures, Magenta Border, Gilt Filigree, 9 ½ In., 6 Piece 674.00
Plate, Portrait, Hand Painted, Gilt Trim Border, 9 ½ In., Pair 330.00
Plate Set, 11 French Royalty Portraits, Each Signed, Transfer Print, Marked, 9 ½ In. 374.00
Potpourri, Gilt Bronze Mounts, Spherical, Cover, c.1846, 7 In. 764.00
Stein, Knight, Character, Blue, White, Gold, Pink, Inlaid Lid, Marked, 1 Liter 1121.00
Urn, Cover, Cobalt Blue Ground, 2 Handles, Baluster, 2 Painted Reserves, 26 ½ In. 944.00
Urn, Cover, Men On Horseback, Scenic, 30 In., Pair 2351.00
Urn, Girl Seated In Garden, Gold Scrolls, Aqua Luster, Ormolu Mounts, 6 ½ In. *illus* 375.00
Urn, Painted Mythological Scene, Dome Lid, Handles, Ormolu Mounts, Signed, c.1920 5280.00
Urn, U-Shape Body, Painted, 2 Reserves, Courting Couple, Landscape, 18 ½ In., Pair 2006.00
Vase, Cobalt Blue Ground, Campana Form, c.1820, 10 ¼ In., Pair 3600.00
Vase, Iris, Baluster Shape, E. Granger, 11 In. 510.00
Vase, Monumental Shape, Mottled Blue, Green & Brown Glaze, 15 x 17 ½ In. 1200.00
Vase, Multicolored Enamel, Gold Leaf, Art Nouveau, Baluster Shape, Wisteria, 6 x 3 ½ In. 960.00
Vase, Sterling Silver Overlay, Mottled Blue Glaze, Art Nouveau, 13 ¾ In. 2115.00
Vase, Woman Walking Home With Baskets, Snow, Handles, D'Eaubonne, 8 ½ In. 472.00

SEWER TILE figures were made by workers at the sewer tile and pipe factories in the Ohio area during the late nineteenth and early twentieth centuries. Figurines, small vases, and cemetery vases were favored. Often the finished vase was a piece of the original pipe with added decorations and markings. All types of sewer tile work are now considered folk art by collectors.

Bank, Pig, Mottled Green Salt Glaze, Red Clay, c.1900, 9 In. *illus* 460.00
Bank, Pig, Seated, Long Eyelashes, 9 In. 460.00
Birdhouse, Mushroom Shape, Mottled Yellow Glaze, Tooled Perch, 8 ½ In. 489.00
Chimney Cap, Fluted Column, Square Base, Scalloped Rim, 12 x 12 x 28 ½ In. 259.00
Chimney Cap, Paneled, Serrated Top, Resembles A Crown, Glazed, 14 x 37 ½ In. 403.00
Doorstop, Chicken, Painted, c.1900, 8 In. 1155.00
Figure, Cat, Mottled Yellow Glaze, Red Clay, c.1900, 8 In. *illus* 546.00
Figure, Cat, Seated, Incised Lines, Yellow Mottled Glaze, c.1900, 8 In. 546.00
Figure, Dog, Boston Terrier, Signed, Louie Staley, 1944, 8 ¾ In. 575.00
Figure, Dog, Collie, Early 20th Century, 12 x 11 In. 920.00
Figure, Dog, Flat Head, Early 20th Century, 11 ¼ In. 805.00
Figure, Dog, Flat Head, Seated, Tooled Collar, Early 20th Century, 11 ¼ In. 978.00
Figure, Dog, Seated, Incised Details, Free-Standing Front Legs, Brown Glaze, 10 In. 2875.00
Figure, Dog, Spaniel, Seated, Contrasting Eyes, Tag, Signed, Roy Blind, 8 ¾ In. 173.00
Figure, Dog, Spaniel, Cardboard Base, Rhinestone Collar, Superior Clay Corp., 1920s, 10 ½ In. 403.00
Figure, Dog, Spaniel, Mottled Brown Matte Glaze, 13 x 13 ½ In. 978.00
Figure, Lion, Molded, Tooled, Yellow Clay, Unglazed, Bob Taley, c.1941, 15 x 8 In. 403.00
Figure, Lion, Reclining, Oval Base, Molded, Hand Tooled, Unglazed, 15 x 10 In. 690.00
Figure, Owl, Horned, Perched On Branch, 14 ½ In. 288.00
Figure, Lion, Rectangular Base, Zoar, Ohio, 1920s, 9 x 6 ¾ In. 145.00
Inkwell, Coleslaw, Scalloped Top, Tooled Accents, Footed, c.1900, 3 ½ In. 110.00
Jar, Cover, Tree Stump Shape, Dog Finial, 7 In. 115.00
Pedestal, Trefoil Base, Lion Heads, Foliage, 14 ½ x 34 In. 230.00
Planter, Bulbous Feet, Corners, Stippled, Cambria Clay, 15 x 10 x 12 In. 259.00
Plaque, Eagle, Inscribed E.J.E., Edward J. Ellwood, 5 In. 115.00
Umbrella Stand, Glazed, Applied Ornaments, Fish, 10 x 23 In. 575.00
Umbrella Stand, Tree Stump Shape, Tooled Bark, Applied Vines, 8 x 20 In. 201.00

Sewer Tile, Bank, Pig, Mottled Green Salt Glaze, Red Clay, c.1900, 9 In.
$460.00

Sewer Tile, Figure, Cat, Mottled Yellow Glaze, Red Clay, c.1900, 8 In.
$546.00

SEWING equipment of all types is collected, from sewing birds that held the cloth to tape measures, needle books, and old wooden spools. Sewing machines are included here. Needlework pictures are listed in the Picture category.

Awl, Seated Monkey Finial, Metal, 5 In. 330.00
Basket, Wicker, Scrolled Decoration, 4 Legs, c.1900, 31 In. 147.00
Bird, Embroidered Pincushion, Satin Wood, Clamp, 6 x 2 In. 295.00
Bird, Maple, Victorian, 6 x 3 In. 295.00
Bird, Metal, Heart Cutout Screw, Brown Paint, Spring Clamp, 4 ½ In. 77.00
Bird, Tin, Cast Iron Base, 1860s, 5 In. 110.00

TIP
A hair dryer set for cool can be used to blow the dust off very ornate pieces of porcelain.

S

Box, Birch, Satinwood, Inlaid Diamond Shapes, Cutout Handle, Lift-Out Box, 10½ x 15 In... 345.00
Box, Black Lacquer, Fitted Interior, Drawer, Paw Feet, 6½ x 14½ x 10½ In. 480.00
Box, Black Lacquer, Tray, Drawer, Figures, Drop Handles, Hinged Lid, Chinese, 6 x 15 x 11 In. 978.00
Box, Black Lacquer, Tray, Drawer, Dragon's Head Feet, Hinged Lid, Chinese, 6 x 13 x 10 In... 863.00
Box, Blond Wood, c.1950, 6 x 11½ x 10¼ In. 25.00
Box, Coffin Shape, Mahogany, Inlay, Pincushion, Cushion Stretcher, Stand, 33 x 11 x 7 In. 1380.00
Box, Decoupage, Ebonized, Gilt Stenciled, 19th Century, 5 x 13 x 8½ In. 823.00
Box, Lacquer, Coffin Shape, Brass Bail Handles, Drawer, Lift Top, Chinese, 14 x 11 x 6 In. 252.00
Box, Mahogany, Domed Lid, Brass Handle, Lock, Key, Tray, 14 In. 650.00
Box, Mahogany, Fitted Interior, Swing-Out Mirror, Hidden Drawers, 19th Century, 14 In. 495.00
Box, Mahogany, Tray, Edwardian, 16¾ x 11 In. 118.00
Box, Papier-Mache, Mother-Of-Pearl Inlay, Divided Interior, England, 9 x 11 In. 695.00
Box, Pine, Shelves, Spool Holder, Drawer, Crest, Circles, Red, Black, 9 x 8 x 5 In. 935.00
Box, Poplar, Fruitwood Veneer, Dovetailed Drawer, Iron Clamp, Cloth Pincushion, 5 In. 431.00
Box, Rosewood, Mahogany, Maple Panels, Cherry Pinwheel, 19th Century, 6 x 13 In. 450.00
Box, Rosewood, Mahogany, Maple, Cherry Pinwheel, Brass Hinges, Octagonal, 6 x 13 In. 504.00
Box, Sandalwood, Palace Animals, Leaves, Ivory Inlay, Marquetry, Anglo Indian, 5 x 8 x 12 In. 147.00
Box, Woven, Padded Top, Handle, Plastic Insert, 8 x 11 x 7½ In. 23.00
Cabinet, Lift Top, Spool Hooks, Tray, Drawers, Brass Pulls, 1940, 25 In. 220.00
Cabinet, Lift Top, Victorian, Walnut, Pincushion, c.1880, 36 x 15 x 15 In. 1995.00
Cabinet, Louis XV Style, Pigeonholes, Drawers, Cabriole Legs, 25 In. 575.00
Cabinet, Martha Washington, Mahogany, Drawer, Tray, c.1930, 27 x 30 x 13 In. 295.00
Cabinet, Renaissance Revival, Walnut, Tile Inset, c.1870, 30 x 23 In. 3450.00
Cabinet, Spool, see also the Advertising category under Cabinet, Spool.
Cabinet, Spool, Curly Maple, Cage Shape, 12 Removable Spindles, Pincushion, Ohio, 8 x 7 In. 546.00
Cabinet, Spool, Mahogany, Timbles, Pullout Drawers, 22 In. 279.00
Cabinet, Spool, Oak, 12 Drawers, c.1910, 36 In. 220.00
Cabinet, Spool, Walnut, 6 Drawers, Recessed Panels, Brass Pulls, 25 x 22 x 19 In. 672.00
Cabinet, Spool, Walnut, Porcelain Pulls, 2 Drawers, c.1880, 8½ x 21 x 14 In. 193.00
Case, Thimble, Corozo Palm Tree Nut, Silver Thimble, Stanhope Lens, England, 1897 275.00
Chest, Bowfront, Mahogany, Inlay, Hinged Top, Lift-Out Tray, Drawers, 11 x 13 In. 2350.00
Clamp, Painted, Flower Basket, Green, Blue, Red, Gilt Ground, Pincushion, 5 In. 201.00
Clamp, Reel, Wood, Late 19th Century, 10 In. 143.00
Clamp, Wood, Box Shape, Grain Painted, Steel Table Clamp, Pincushion, Zoar, 5¾ In. 230.00
Darner, Ebonized Wood, Sterling Silver Rococo Handle, Faceted Amethyst Glass Finial, 6 In. 60.00
Dress Form, Maple Bentwood Bottom, Papier-Mache Torso, c.1800s, 58 x 15 In. 5320.00
Etui, Case, Sloped Top, Needles 565.00
Kit, Gold, Thimble, Scissors, Bodkin, Stiletto, Reeds, Ivory Case, Mid 1800s, France, 4¼ x 2½ In. 1090.00
Kit, Gold, Vinaigrette, Scissors, Needle Case, Thimble, Pasteboard Case, France, 1888, 5 x 2½ In. 415.00
Kit, Scissors, Thimbles, Notions, Leather Case 4995.00
Lamp, Lacemaker's, Blown Glass, Maple, 4 Balls, 10 x 11 In. 2415.00
Machine, Bradbury & Co. Ltd., Oldham, Lift-Top Panel, Iron Base, 38 x 30 x 16 In. 115.00
Machine, Ideal, Treadle, Oak Top, Cast Iron, 31 x 18 x 10 In. 1320.00
Machine, Little Comfort, Improved Hand Sewing Machine In The Box, Smith & Egge 295.00
Machine, Oller, Stockholm, Sweden, c.1865 *illus* 1724.00
Machine, Shaw & Clark, Paw Foot Style, Ketchum's Patent, Painted, Decorated, 1860s 1295.00
Machine, Singer, Featherweight, Side Shelf, Lift-Out Tray, Attachments, 11½ In. 196.00
Machine, Singer, Featherweight, Accessory Tray, Buttonholer, Manual, 10 x 15 x 7 In. *illus* 485.00
Machine, Singer, Featherweight, Carrying Case, Accessory Tray, Box, 14 x 13 In. 489.00
Machine, Singer, Featherweight 221, Black, c.1954 525.00
Machine, Singer, Featherweight 221, Booklet, Attachments, c.1948 475.00
Machine, Singer, Featherweight 221, Centennial, Black, Case, 1948-50 350.00
Machine, Singer, Featherweight 221, Chrome Wheel, Scroll Faceplate, Attachments, 1940 425.00
Machine, Singer, Tabletop, Electric, Dome Lid, 12 x 17 x 8 In. 10.00
Machine, Treadle, Oak Top, Cast Iron, Child's, Ideal, 31 x 18 x 10 In. 1320.00
Machine, Wood, Cast Iron, Germany, 20 x 26½ In. *illus* 3000.00
Needle Case, Brass, Diamond Shape, Butterfly, Leaf Cover, Hirsch & Stern, Birmingham, 3 In. 675.00
Needle Case, Brass, England, 2¼ x ⅝ In. 65.00
Needle Case, Copper, Paper Insert, 6 Needles 30.00
Needle Case, Felt, Mitten, Embroidered, 2⅜ In. 10.00
Needle Case, Gold, Emery, Berry Shape, 1½ In. 95.00
Needle Case, Ivory, 1880s, 4½ In. 125.00
Needle Case, Ivory, Pea Pod, Victorian, England, 3⅞ In. 235.00
Needle Case, Leather, Book Form, Mexico, 2¾ x 3½ In. 18.00
Needle Case, Mahogany, Friction Fit Lid, Needles, England, 5 x ¾ In. 12.00
Needle Case, Metal Lion, Birds, Flowers, German Coins, Sections, 9 Needles, Germany, 2½ In. 45.00

Sewing, Machine, Oller, Stockholm, Sweden, c.1865
$1724.00

Sewing, Machine, Singer, Featherweight, Accessory Tray, Buttonholer, Manual, 10 x 15 x 7 In.
$485.00

Sewing, Machine, Wood, Cast Iron, Germany, 20 x 26½ In.
$3000.00

Sewing, Pincushion, Peach, Velvet, Early 19th Century, 3½ In.
$940.00

S

Sewing, Tape Measure, Edison Mazda Lamps, His Only Rival, Blue, Yellow, c.1930, 1¾ In. $67.00

TIP

A freezer can get rid of moths, silverfish, or mold, but it must be a freezer that goes to –4°F; most refrigerator freezers do not set that low. Roll or fold the infested fabric and put it in a heavy, clear freezer bag. Remove as much air as possible from the bag before you seal it with duct tape. (Some other tapes become loose if frozen.) Put the package into the freezer for at least 48 hours. Don't peek. Remove it and thaw it completely before you open it. Remove the fabric, then vacuum it inside and out to remove dead pests and dirt.

Needle Case, Plastic, Sunbonnet Sue, Yellow, Pink, Blue, 1920s, 4¾ In. 12.00
Needle Case, Silver Plate, Cobalt Blue Glass Liner, Victorian, 2¼ x 1¼ In. 62.00
Needle Case, Sterling Silver, Owl, Sitting On Branch, ½ x 3¼ In. 32.00
Needle Case, Sterling Silver, Rabbit, Running, Toby Jug Character, 3¼ In. 68.00
Needle Case, Sterling Silver, Woman, 3 In. 345.00
Needle Case, Vegetable Ivory, 2-Sided, 3½ In. 150.00
Niddy Noddy, 1842, 18½ In. 297.00
Pattern, Barbie Teen Fashion, 1969, 11½ In. 12.00
Pattern, Simplicity No. 7951, Evening Gown, Ruffled Stole, Size 12, 34, 1968 .... 22.00
Pattern, Vogue, Pullover Dress, Albert Nipon, Size 12 .... 15.00
Pincushion, Barrel, Tartan Fabric, Scotland, 1950s, 2½ In. 12.00
Pincushion, Blue Cloth Cushion, Wood, Screw Clamp, 7½ x 4 In. 88.00
Pincushion, Butterfly, Glass Bead Pin Eyes, Early 19th Century, 4¼ x 5 In. 2350.00
Pincushion, Canoe, Gold Metal, Velvet, Victorian, 4¼ x 1½ In. 98.00
Pincushion, Carrot, Strawberry, Velvet, Early 19th Century, 1⅝ x 5¾ In. 1058.00
Pincushion, Carrot, Velvet, Early 19th Century, 13 In. 1175.00
Pincushion, Dog Banging Drum, Japan, 3 x 2 In. 15.00
Pincushion, Hat, Crocheted, 5½ In. 12.00
Pincushion, Maple, Turned, Cloth Top, Varnished, 4½ x 2¼ In. 44.00
Pincushion, Mixed Wood, Turned, Screw Clamps, 7 x 1½ In. 55.00
Pincushion, Peach, Velvet, Early 19th Century, 3½ In. .... *illus* 940.00
Pincushion, Pedestal, Turned, Felt Top, Flat Base, Turned Feet, Painted, 4 x 3 x 3 In. 715.00
Pincushion, Pig, Sterling Silver, England, 1⅓ x ⅝ In. 47.00
Pincushion, Puzzle Ball, Pin, Green Cloth, Yellow Ribbon, Mennonite, 3½ In. 22.00
Pincushion, Roses, Leaves, Milk Glass, Velvet, 4¼ In. 45.00
Pincushion, Shoe, Brass, Blue Velvet, Pins, Hatpin, Seed Pearl 55.00
Pincushion, Shoe, Onion, Blue, 7¼ x 2¼ In. 30.00
Pincushion, Strawberry, Velvet, Green Wool Felt Leaves, Red, White Silk Ribbon, 4 In. 1175.00
Pincushion, Tomato, Pull Out Tape Measure, 2¾ In. 25.00
Pincushion, Tomato, Red, 3¼ In. 10.00
Pincushion, Wood, 3 Tiers, Painted Bands, Wire Spool Holders, 3-Footed, 6½ x 4⅓ In. 550.00
Pincushion, Wood, Painted Bands, Green & White Cushion, Screw Clamp, 5½ x 3¼ In. 248.00
Pincushion, Wood Heart, Star, Photo In Cutout, Victorian Shoe, Gilt, 4¾ x 11½ x 10 In. 22.00
Pincushion Dolls are listed in their own category.
Ruler, Folding, Brown, 24 In. 15.00
Scissors, Crane Shape, 4⅛ In. 15.00
Spool Cabinets are listed here or in the Advertising category under Cabinet, Spool.
Spoolholder, 3-Tier, Cushion, Red, Yellow, Green, Salmon, Footed, 5¾ x 4 In. 1210.00
Swift, Brass Shaft, Embossed, Turned & Footed Base, Victorian, 19th Century, 23 In. 55.00
Tape Measure, 2 Women, Arkin Girls, Model Hairdos, Celluloid, Germany West Zone, 1 7/16 In. 65.00
Tape Measure, Apple, Red, Locking, Plastic, Leaf Turn Stem 21.00
Tape Measure, Barrel, Vegetable Ivory, Rewind Peg, c.1875, 1⅛ In. 85.00
Tape Measure, Climax Dental Supply, 1⅜ In. 38.00
Tape Measure, Clown Head, Celluloid, Painted Cream, Black Hat, c.1900 .... 295.00
Tape Measure, Dairypak Butler, Inc., Zippo 25.00
Tape Measure, Edison Mazda Lamps, His Only Rival, Blue, Yellow, c.1930, 1¾ In. .... *illus* 67.00
Tape Measure, Flamingo, Plastic, Beach Scene, Retracting, Cloth, 1⅓ x ½ In. 10.00
Tape Measure, Flower Basket, Celluloid, Japan, 1¾ x 1¼ In. 135.00
Tape Measure, Lady Bug, Cloth, Celluloid, Flowers In Bowl 245.00
Tape Measure, Mammy, Googly Eyes, Brown Dress, Apron, Scarf, Cast Metal, 4½ In. 413.00
Tape Measure, Miami, Fla., Metal, Retracting, Cloth, Germany, 1½ x ½ In. 24.00
Tape Measure, Rose, Metal, Retracting, Inches, Centimeters, 1950s, 1½ x ½ In. 15.00
Tape Measure, Singing Tower, Lake Wales, Fla., Metal, Retracting, Germany, 1½ x ½ In. 35.00
Tape Measure, Sterling Silver, Crank Handle, Embossed Case, Cloth, 1 x 1 In. 86.00
Tape Measure, Vegetable Ivory, Carved, Pierced, 19th Century 54.00
Tatting Shuttle, Abalone, 2⅛ In. 22.00
Thimble, Oriole, Porcelain, 1979, 1⅛ In. 10.00
Thimble, Petite Point, Austria 25.00
Thimble, Porcelain, Bisque, Woman, Flowing Hair, Rose Bow, c.1938, 2 In. 35.00
Thimble, Porcelain, Canadian Flag, Niagara Falls, England 14.00
Thimble, Sterling Silver, Size 8, ¾ x 9/16 In. 15.00
Thread, Spool, Forest Green, 3½ In. 15.00
Thread Winder, Ivory, Mother-Of-Pearl, 1840-60 .... 135.00
Thread Winder, Mother-Of-Pearl, 8 Petals, Flower, Chinese Man, 1¾ x 3⅙ In. 135.00
Work Box, Painted, Leaves, Handle, Knob Feet, Lid, England, c.1820, 7 x 8 x 6 In. 1462.00
Yarn Winder, Maple, Pine, Black & Red Paint, Finial Top, Platform, 5 Legs, 41 x 27 In. 90.00

'arn Winder, Mixed Wood, Wood Gears, Heart Cutout Finial, Splayed Legs, 31 In. 22.00
arn Winder, Painted Green, Homespun Yarn, New England, c.1780 650.00
arn Winder, Salmon Paint, Black Stripes, 3 Legs, Clicking Mechanism, N.H., 42 In. 288.00
arn Winder, Squirrel Cage, Mixed Wood, Blue & Red Paint, 39 In. 22.00

HAKER items are characterized by simplicity, functionalism, and orderliness. There were nany Shaker communities in America from the eighteenth century to the present day. The eligious order made furniture, small wooden pieces, and packaged medicines, herbs, and jellies) sell to "outsiders." Other useful objects were made for use by members of the community. Shaker urniture is listed in this book in the Furniture category.

pple Sorter, Poplar, 7 Holes, Harvard, Mass., c.1850, 7 x 25 x 7½ In. 450.00
asket, Berry, Cut Staves, Tin Bands, Mt. Lebanon, N.Y., 4½ x 6 In. 480.00
asket, Carrier, Maple, Pine, Hoop Handle, Nailed, Applied Rim, c.1855, 10 x 14 In. 468.00
asket, Drying, Splint, Black Ash, Open Weave, Square, c.1835, 24 In. 878.00
asket, Splint, Black Ash, Single Wrapped Rim, Carved Handles, c.1850, 13 x 24 In. 702.00
asket, Wool, Black Ash, Splint, Side Handles, Wrapped Rim, Convex Bottom, 12 x 23 In. 468.00
asket, Cheese, Black Ash, Open Weave, Double Wrapped Rim, Mt. Lebanon, c.1881, 9 x 24 In. 410.00
onnet, Straw, Blue Silk Liner, Ribbon, Size 13, 9½ x 12 x 6½ In. 290.00
onnet, Woven, Splint, Natural, Brown, Pleated Back, 10 In. *illus* 290.00
owl, Tiger Maple, Iron Band, Flared Rim, c.1840, 9 x 28 In. 819.00
ox, 2-Finger, Oval, Copper Tacks, 5½ x 2⅛ In. 978.00
ox, 2-Finger, Oval, Fingers Facing Left, 3 x 8½ x 6 In. 470.00
ox, 2-Finger, Oval, Green Paint, Copper Tacks, c.1890, 2 x 5 In. *illus* 955.00
ox, 2-Finger, Oval, Lid, Copper Tacks, 1800s, 6 x 8¾ x 3⅝ In. 489.00
ox, 2-Finger, Oval, WXC Carved At Top, 3½ x 11 x 8½ In. 120.00
ox, 3-Finger, Maple, Pine, Copper Tacks, Lid, Fabric Pincushion, 2 x 3 In. 1755.00
ox, 3-Finger, Maple, Pine, Painted, Copper Tacks, Canterbury, N.H., c.1835, 1 x 3¼ In. 15210.00
ox, 3-Finger, Oval, Copper Tacks, Early 1900s, 12 x 5½ In. 144.00
ox, 3-Finger, Oval, 1½ x 4 x 2½ In. 510.00
ox, 3-Finger, Oval, 4 x 10½ x 7 In. 290.00
ox, 4-Finger, Oval, Lid, Copper Tacks, 1800s, 9¾ x 13½ In. 546.00
ox, 4-Finger, Oval, Maple, Pine, Green Paint, Enfield, N.H., c.1840, 3¾ x 9¼ In. 3510.00
ox, 4-Finger, Oak, Pine, Maple, Yellow Paint, Leaf Decoration, 4¾ x 11 In. 940.00
ox, 5-Finger, Maple, Pine, Copper Tacks, Canterbury, c.1840, 1¾ x 2⅞ In. 7605.00
ox, 5-Finger, Oval, Bent Maple, Copper Tacks, Pine Cover, Paint, 5¾ x 9 x 13 In. 6463.00
ox, 6-Finger, Oval, Lid, Maple, Pine, Red Stain, c.1840, 6½ x 14¾ In. 936.00
ox, 12-Finger, Oval, Bonnet, Ash, Pine, Iron Tacks, Wooden Pegged, 19 x 14 x 11 In. 585.00
ox, Desk, Pine, Painted, Breadboard Slant Lid, Interior Well, Nailed, c.1840, 7 x 15 x 11 In. 4914.00
ox, Double Lid, Dovetailed, Handle, Hancock, Mass., 8½ x 16½ x 9 In. 950.00
ox, Harvard Type, Oval, Green Paint, 6¼ x 2⅝ In. 374.00
ox, Harvard Type, Oval, Opposing Fingers, Copper Tacks, Red Paint, 5 x 2 In. 690.00
ox, Hat, Round, Pine, Maple, Overlap, Nailed, Handmade Tacks, New Lebanon, c.1840, 17 In. 350.00
ox, Sewing, Stepped, Wood, 3 Drawers, Finials, Footed, 9 x 9 x 6½ In. 275.00
ox, Spit, 3-Finger, Copper Tacks, New Lebanon, 1800s, 10½ x 4½ In. 1380.00
ox, Spit, 3-Finger, Round, 3½ x 9 In. 475.00
ox, Spit, Round, Yellow Paint, Lapped Sides, Copper Tacks, c.1850, 3⅜ x 14¼ In. 940.00
ox, Storage, 4-Finger, Oval, Maple, Pine Lid, Copper Tacks, Impressed 3, 4¾ x 12¼ In. 588.00
rush & Dustpan, Maple & Horsehair, String-Tied Brush, Maple & Tin Pan, 15½ In. 468.00
ucket, Cover, Tapered, Metal Bands, Bail Handle, Diamond Handle Hinges, 10 x 9 In. 440.00
ucket, Cut Staves, Tin Bands, Marked, Enfield, Ct., c.1860, 3½ x 4½ In. 410.00
ucket, Lid, Pine, Iron Bands, Yellow Paint, Iron Bail, Birch Handle, Canterbury, c.1845, 10½ In. 936.00
ucket, Pine, Painted, Steel Bail, Iron Bands, Birch Handle, Canterbury, 18 x 11¼ In. 5265.00
ucket, Pine, Red, White Interior, Black Bail Plates, Swing Handle, Mt. Lebanon, c.1860, 12 In. 1872.00
ucket, Pine Staves, Carved Ash Swing Handle, 2 Iron Wraps, Black Paint, 15 In. 5265.00
ucket, Sap, Slats, Mustard Paint, Marked, NF Shakers Enfield, N.H., 11½ x 12 In. 475.00
utter Churn, Pine, Ash, Oak, Chamfered Lid, Piggen Handle, Wrapped, c.1840, 45½ In. 1170.00
arrier, 3-Finger, Oval, Wooden, Maple Sides, Copper Tacks, Pine Bottom, 9¼ In. 3290.00
arrier, 4-Finger, Maple, Pine, Swing Handle, Tacks, Needlecase, Pincushion, 7 x 9 In. 1170.00
arrier, 4-Finger, Pine, Maple, Painted, Double-Hinged Lid, Fixed Handle, c.1840, 15 In. 2340.00
arrier, Herb, 3-Finger, Oval, Patina, Fixed Handle, No Lid, 9 x 13 x 9½ In. 1400.00
arrier, Rectangular, Cherry, Pine, Sectioned, Dovetailed, Initials, c.1840, 14½ In. 1521.00
arrier, Rectangular, Wood, Nailed Construction, Swing Handle, Copper Tacks, 8 x 7 x 10 In. 323.00
arrier, Round, Maple, Hickory, Pine, Red Stain, Handle, c.1850, 10½ x 12 In. 690.00
arrier, Round, Wood, Red Stained, Lap Seam Construction, Maple Sides, 10½ x 12 In. 382.00
loak, Gray Wool, Blue Label, Dorothy, Hart & Shepard, Canterbury, N.H. 760.00

TIP

A two-finger Shaker box really has three. Two are on the bottom, one is on the lid.

Shaker, Bonnet, Woven, Splint, Natural, Brown, Pleated Back, 10 In.
$290.00

Shaker, Box, 2-Finger, Oval, Green Paint, Copper Tacks, c.1890, 2 x 5 In.
$955.00

Shaker, Cloak, Wool, Red, Late 19th Century, 47 In.
$415.00

Shaving Mug, Occupational, Artist Palette, O.N. Falk, Marked, D & C
$161.00

Shaving Mug, Occupational, Bartender, Bar Scene, Art Maas, Limoges, France
$230.00

Shaving Mug, Occupational, Chef, Kitchen Scene, Richard Mell
$3450.00

Shaving Mug, Occupational, Furniture Dealer, Engelb Feige
$805.00

Cloak, Wool, Red, Late 19th Century, 47 In. . . . *illus* 415.00
Cloak, Wool Broadcloth, Red, Shoulder Cape, Pleated Back, Hood, Pinked Seams, 47 In. . . . 431.00
Clothespins & Holder, 18 Maple Clothespins, Turned & Carved, Round, 3 ½ x 4 In. . . . 819.00
Dipper, Oak, Turned Handle, Peg & Nail, Patina, 7 x 5 ¼ In. . . . 187.00
Door, Pine, 6 Raised Panels, Painted, Dairy, Canaan, N.Y., c.1835, 88 ½ x 53 ½ In. . . . 2106.00
Drying Rack, Herb, White Paint, 25 x 25 In. . . . 580.00
Garment Hanger, Wood, 4 Tiers, Signed, E.B., M.C. Allen, 1903, 20 x 15 In. . . . 730.00
Hanger, 5 Bars, Pine, Hardwoods, Natural Patina, Label, New Lebanon, 13 x 17 In. . . . 1287.00
Hanger, Pine, Poplar, Vertical Post, 5 Hangers, Nailed Tacks, Signed, Ann B, 64, 25 ¼ In. . . . 5850.00
Hanger, Pine, Round Top, 3 Bars, Hole For Hanging, Pegrail, 23 In. . . . 3159.00
Measure, Tailor's, Maple, Hand Numbered, c.1840, 36 In. . . . 4972.00
Measuring Cups, Nested, Pine, Ash, Oak, Sabbathday Lake, 12 In. To 3 ¾ In., 5 Piece . . . 1287.00
Pincushion, Tomato, Velvet, Maple, Adjustable, Barrel Clamp, Table Top, c.1860, 12 In. . . . 819.00
Postcard, Photo, Last Of The Shakers, Group Of Women, Harvard, Mass. . . . 248.00
Scoop, Wood, 19th Century, 13 ½ x 5 ½ In. . . . 225.00
Shovel, Grain, Walnut, Enfield, N.H., c.1850, 36 In. . . . 585.00
Shovel, Wood, 36 x 12 ½ In. . . . 120.00
Sieve, Winnowing, Open Weave Basket, Oak Sides, Stamped AP, c.1850, 21 ½ In. . . . 410.00
Spinning Wheel, Maple, Quartered Oak, Stamped SRAL, Samuel Ring, Alfred, c.1860, 34 In. 702.00
Spinning Wheel, Oak, Flax, Signed, T. Thompson, 35 x 22 x 35 In. . . . 175.00
Spinning Wheel, Walking Wool, Birch, Oak & Maple, Alfred, 1800s, 59 x 46 In. . . . 925.00
Spinning Wheel, Walking Wool, Bone Collar, Stamped, Canterbury, N.H., 57 x 75 In. . . . 819.00
Spinning Wheel, Walking Wool, Stamped JH, 57 ½ x 70 x 45 ½ In. . . . 410.00
Spool Holder, Walnut, 2 Tiers, 14 Spools, 3-Footed, 5 x 3 ¾ In. . . . 1872.00
Stand, Flax Hatchel, 30 x 18 x 18 In. . . . 120.00
Swift, Yellow Wash, Mixed Wood, Maple, Metal Rivets, Tin Washers, c.1850, 23 In. . . . 518.00
Tool, Rule, Maple, Hand Numbered 1 Through 11, ⅛ Increments, Shaker, Stamped 1834 . . . 858.00
Tray, Pine, Arched Ends, Cutout Handles, Dovetailed, Painted, 6 x 18 x 11 In. . . . 7020.00
Tray, Pine, Tin Divider, Yellow Paint, Initials, S.W., New Lebanon, c.1840, 9 ¾ x 6 ½ x 2 In. . . . 702.00
Tray, Walnut, Red Wash, Dovetailed Sides, Sloping Front, Cutout Handles, 24 x 16 In. . . . 2340.00
Washtub, Pine, Iron Bands, 2 Handle Holes, New Lebanon, c.1820, 21 x 29 In. . . . 1287.00
Window Jack, Tiger Maple, Drilled On 4 Sides, Adjustable, L-Shape Hanger, 19 ½ In. . . . 205.00
Wood Box, Pine, Dovetailed, Hinged Lid, 2-Section Interior, Brass Knob, Enfield, c.1840, 22 x 33 In. 760.00
Yarn Winder, Cherry, 4 Arms, Pegged, Mortised, Snake Leg Tripod Base, Enfield, c.1820. . . . 1521.00
Yarn Winder, Maple, Oak, Red Stain, Stamped, BB, 40 ½ x 21 x 26 In. . . . 510.00
Yarn Winder, Oak, Maple, Clock Reel, 6 Arms, 4 Legs, Label, Canterbury, c.1840, 43 In. . . . 936.00
Yarn Winder, Pine, Maple, Paint, Clock Face, 40 Increments Skeins, c.1840, 39 In. . . . 7605.00

SHAVING MUGS were popular from 1860 to 1900. Many types were made, including occupational mugs featuring pictures of men's jobs. There were scuttle mugs, silver-plated mugs, glass-lined mugs, and others.

Flowers, Leaves, Cobalt Blue, Brush Holder, Incised Bands, Flared Top, Stoneware, 4 In. . . . 990.00
Fraternal, Egyptian Cat, Concatenated Order of Hoo-Hoo, 3 ½ In. . . . 1495.00
Fraternal, Elk, Custard Glass, Silver Plate, Oval Top, 3 ½ In. . . . 156.00
Fraternal, Locomotive & Tender, Engineer, Masonic Cross, Robert Blair, Germany, 3 ⅝ In. . . . 156.00
Fraternal, Sons Of America & Order Of Red Men, R.A. Richards, 3 ⅞ In. . . . 173.00
Fraternal, Surveyor, Transit On Tripod, Masonic Symbol, Harry L. Clark, 3 ⅝ In. . . . 1140.00
Occupational, Artist Palette, O.N. Falk, Marked, D & C . . . *illus* 161.00
Occupational, Bartender, Bar Scene, Art Maas, Limoges, France . . . *illus* 230.00
Occupational, Baseball Catcher, Wm. Branigan, T & V Limoges, France, c.1900, 3 ½ In. . . . 4600.00
Occupational, Baseball Player, Jedium Adams, International Royal China, c.1910, 3 ½ In. . . 1265.00
Occupational, Beer Brewers, Patron Saint Of Beer, W.R. Scurlock, 3 ⅝ In. . . . 510.00
Occupational, Bicycle, John De St. Legier, Porcelain, 1885-1910, 3 ⅝ In. . . . 460.00
Occupational, Bicycle Shop J. Lagacy, 3 ½ In. . . . 4600.00
Occupational, Billiard Players, Edward Hocker, Germany, 1925, 3 ½ In. . . . 978.00
Occupational, Blacksmiths, Anvil, Jacob Lotz, Koken Barber's Supply, St. Louis, c.1900, 3 ⅝ In. 489.00
Occupational, Bottle Capper, Raffaele Brucci, 1913, 3 ½ In. . . . 2300.00
Occupational, Boxcar & Caboose, J.C. Broocrir, Porcelain, 3 ⅝ In. . . . 230.00
Occupational, Boxer, J. Morrell, Ironstone, K.T. & K. China, 1895-1925, 3 ½ In. . . . 1840.00
Occupational, Boxing, John L. Sullivan World's Champion Heavyweight, 1909, 3 ⅞ In. . . . 1150.00
Occupational, Brick Mason, In Shop, J.J. Bittinger, Heimerdinger, Louisville, Ky., 3 ⅞ In. . . . 230.00
Occupational, Bugle Boy, Wm. Thompson, J & C Bavaria, 3 ⅝ In. . . . 3450.00
Occupational, Builder, House, G.W. Hess, 3 ½ In. . . . 1093.00
Occupational, Butcher, Steer Head, Chas. T. Dress, T & V Limoges, France, 3 ¾ In. . . . 99.00
Occupational, Butcher, Bull's Head, Tools, J. Berlinsky, Porcelain, 1875-1925, 3 ⅞ In. . . . 149.00

Occupational, Caboose, Buck, De Vry, B.S. Co. Evansville, Ind., 4 In. 44.00
Occupational, Car, Upholstered Bench Seat, F. M. Tewksbury, 3 ½ In. 1265.00
Occupational, Cattleman, Steer, J.F. Wilson, 3 ½ In. 259.00
Occupational, Chauffeur, Driving Red Convertible, A. De Paolo, Porcelain, c.1920, 3 ⅝ In. .. 1380.00
Occupational, Chef, Kitchen Scene, Richard Mell. .... *illus* 3450.00
Occupational, Cigar Roller & Press, S.A. Ingham, Porcelain, 1885-1920, 3 ⅝ In. 633.00
Occupational, Coal Miner, Swing Pick, Joe Borhs, Limoges, France, 1890-1920, 3 ½ In. 1610.00
Occupational, Dentist, Examining Patient, F.C. Blosser, Porcelain, 1880-1920, 3 ⅝ In. 1020.00
Occupational, Dentist, Patient In Chair, Dr. T.J. Holland, T & V Limoges, France, 3 ⅝ In. 450.00
Occupational, Electrical Lineman, On Pole, J.J. Boyle, Heckel Bros., Kansas City, Mo., 3 ½ In. 2645.00
Occupational, Ferryboat, Crossing River, Jas. A Krager, T & V France, 3 ⅞ In. 1725.00
Occupational, Fire Chief, Firemen, Fire, Joseph Johnson, Felda China, Germany, 3 ½ In. 1380.00
Occupational, Fireman, Jos. McCrystal, Horse Drawn Pumper, Hand Painted, 3 ¾ In. 350.00
Occupational, Fireman, White, Gold, New York Fire Department, 1909, 3 ⅝ In. 1232.00
Occupational, Fireman, Fire Hose Wagon, Geo. W. Gray, CFH/GDM, France, 3 ½ In. 570.00
Occupational, Florist, Greenhouse, P.F. Ammann, St. Louis, 3 ⅝ In. 1840.00
Occupational, Flour Mill Operator, H. Rump, St. Louis, Mark, 1880-1925, 3 ½ In. 230.00
Occupational, Fruit Salesman, Bananas, Oranges, O.V. Smith, 3 ⅝ In. 403.00
Occupational, Furnace Maker, Tool, G.D. Bonnell, 3 ½ In. 115.00
Occupational, Furniture Dealer, Engelb Feige .... *illus* 805.00
Occupational, Glassblower, G.J. Staieg, 3 ½ In. 2016.00
Occupational, Greyhound, Dick Claire, H.D. Ragan, 3 ½ In. 374.00
Occupational, Groceries, Provisions, Horse Drawn Wagon, J.H. Mullin, KFM, Germany, 3 ⅞ In. 546.00
Occupational, Horse Jockey, Jack Foster, Marked, T & V Limoges, France. .... *illus* 460.00
Occupational, House Painters, H.F. Steckman, T & V Limoges, 3 ⅝ In. 1430.00
Occupational, Human Skull, Scuttle, Porcelain, 1875-1925, 3 ⅝ In. 403.00
Occupational, Ice Wagon, Horse Drawn, John Wentink, Porcelain, c.1900, 3 ⅞ In. 1150.00
Occupational, Ice Wagon, Horse Drawn, Proprietor, Geo. W. Davis, C.F.M., c.1895, 3 ⅝ In. ... 567.00
Occupational, Indian Motorcycle, H.R. Nowlen, P. Eisemann, T & V Limoges, France, 3 ⅞ In. 6900.00
Occupational, Lawn Mower, Samuel Mommo, Roma-Bros., B.S., 1927, 3 ⅝ In. 1495.00
Occupational, Lighthouse Keeper, Joseph Wachmeyer .... *illus* 2530.00
Occupational, Livery Man, Washing Wheels, G.F. Holden, H & C, 3 ⅞ In. 690.00
Occupational, Livery Stable, John Montgomery, Devry B.S. Co., Evansville, In., 3 ⅞ In. 330.00
Occupational, Locomotive, William K. Furner, Gilt Trim, 3 ⅝ In. 130.00
Occupational, Loom Operator, Pedals & Shuttles, Joseph Whitaker, Inscribed, 5084, 3 ⅝ In. . 1150.00
Occupational, Lucky Spots, Scuttle, Porcelain, Marked, Grandenburg, 3 ½ In. 80.00
Occupational, Man, Delivery Wagon, Express, C.J. Redmond, c.1890, 3 ⅝ In. 345.00
Occupational, Man, Driving Race Car, Seeley J. Benedict, Felda China, Germany 9487.00
Occupational, Man, Horse-Drawn Bologna Wagon, A. Marx, c.1890, 3 ⅝ In. 805.00
Occupational, Man, Horse-Drawn Hearse, James Cunningham, T & V France, 3 ⅞ In. 1150.00
Occupational, Man, Horse-Drawn Ice Wagon, Robert Green, Gilt Trim, 3 ½ In. 190.00
Occupational, Man, Horse-Drawn Omnibus, Montgomery C. Savage, D & C Limoges, 3 ⅝ In. 978.00
Occupational, Man, Mule-Drawn Wagon, D.J. Zartman, P. Eisemann, 3 ½ In. 260.00
Occupational, Man, Running, T-Shirt, High Socks, James Smith, T & V, 3 ⅝ In. 2070.00
Occupational, Man, On Trapeze, C.C. Mathews, Porcelain, 1890-1920, 3 ⅞ In. 2645.00
Occupational, Men, Boilermaker, J.C. Stamm, Elite, France, 1890-1900, 3 ½ In. 920.00
Occupational, Men, Working In Front Of Brick Oven, H.L. Reiter, 3 ⅝ In. .... *illus* 295.00
Occupational, Miner, With Pick Ax, Shovel, Lantern, James D. Farley, 3 ⅞ In. .... *illus* 1300.00
Occupational, Motorcycle, O.M. Squires, Marked, Germany, 1901-20, 3 ½ In. 5750.00
Occupational, Painters, On Scaffold, George Peterson, T & V Limoges, France, 3 ⅝ In. 1150.00
Occupational, Parlor Set, 2 Chairs, Couch, Wm. Alsen, D & C Limoges, c.1890, 3 ⅝ In. 403.00
Occupational, Pharmacist, Preparing Prescription, Weatherford, Koken, B.S. Co., 3 ⅞ In. ... 978.00
Occupational, Playwright, Idiots Delight, R.E.S., Germany, 1936, 3 ⅝ In. 1725.00
Occupational, Plumber, Repairing Pipe, C.H. Bottsch, J & C Bavaria, 3 ⅞ In. 575.00
Occupational, Plumber Working On Sink, W.N. Corcoran, 3 ⅝ In. .... *illus* 965.00
Occupational, Pocket Watch, Gold, Jno. F. Ernst, H & C, 3 ⅞ In. 567.00
Occupational, Polo Players, Chas. Newman, Royal China International, 1900-30, 3 ½ In. ... 1380.00
Occupational, Printer, Selecting Blocks, C.R. Barber, Limoges, France, 3 ⅝ In. 431.00
Occupational, Reaper, Horse Drawn, Lewis W. Hemke, D & C, France, 1875-1910, 3 ⅞ In. ... 920.00
Occupational, Saddle, J.P. Kuhl Manf., Cottonwood Falls, Kan., Porcelain, c.1900, 3 ⅞ In. ... 2990.00
Occupational, Sailboat, Timothy Sullivan, T & V Limoges, France, 1891-1907, 4 In. 863.00
Occupational, Seafood Restaurant, Jim Sheirr, Royal China International, c.1900, 3 ½ In. .. 2645.00
Occupational, Secretary, At His Desk, Lewis G. Woods, T & V Limoges, France, 3 ⅝ In. 403.00
Occupational, Shoe Salesman, Woman, D.G. Wilett, T & V Limoges, France, 3 ½ In. 748.00
Occupational, Skull & Crossbones, Dr. D.N. Shippee, J & C Bavaria, 1875-1925, 3 ⅞ In. 978.00

Shaving Mug, Occupational, Horse Jockey, Jack Foster, Marked, T & V Limoges, France
$460.00

Shaving Mug, Occupational, Lighthouse Keeper, Joseph Wachmeyer
$2530.00

Shaving Mug, Occupational, Men, Working In Front Of Brick Oven, H.L. Reiter, 3 ⅝ In.
$295.00

Shaving Mug, Occupational, Miner, With Pick Ax, Shovel, Lantern, James D. Farley, 3 ⅞ In.
$1300.00

Shaving Mug, Occupational, Plumber Working On Sink, W.N. Corcoran, 3⅝ In.
$965.00

Shaving Mug, Occupational, Skull & Crossbones, Dr. F.W. Delmage, 3⅝ In.
$570.00

Shaving Mug, Occupational, Stove, B.A. Hoffner, Gilt Tim, Marked, CFH/GDM, 3⅞ In.
$489.00

Shaving Mug, Occupational, Undertaker, Hearse, O.S. Wilson, V&D Austria, 3¾ In.
$1112.00

Occupational, Skull & Crossbones, Dr. F.W. Delmage, 3⅝ In. . . . . *illus* 570.00
Occupational, Stained Glass Artist, In Shop, George C. Clark, J & C, Bavaria, 3½ In. 3738.00
Occupational, Steam Tractor, Red Wheels, G. Karmstatter, Koken B.S. Co., St. Louis, 3⅝ In. . 2530.00
Occupational, Steamboat, O.O. Hickerson, T & V Limoges, France, 3⅞ In. 1610.00
Occupational, Stove, B.A. Hoffner, Gilt Tim, Marked, CFH/GDM, 3⅞ In.. . . . . *illus* 489.00
Occupational, Tailor, Frank Graute, Beringhaus Co., Cincinnati, Oh.. . . . . 431.00
Occupational, Tandem Tricycle, W. Shern, Porcelain, 1880-1910, 3⅝ In. 1035.00
Occupational, Taxi Driver, 2 Rear Passengers, Palace Taxi Co., Germany, 1921, 3¾ In. 2850.00
Occupational, Teeth, Upper Set, A.R. Ames Dentist, Gilt Trim, T & V France, 3⅝ In. 390.00
Occupational, Telegraph Operator, Behind Counter, William Olsen, R.S., 3⅞ In. 1495.00
Occupational, Tobacconist, Robt Kenyon 345.00
Occupational, Train, Crossing Cantilever Bridge, J.J. Whitworth 1495.00
Occupational, Trolley Operator, Electric, F.W. Goyt, France, 1890-1920, 3½ In.. . . . . 360.00
Occupational, Truck Driver, Freight Delivery, Tony Sira, Felda China, Germany, c.1920, 3⅞ In. 431.00
Occupational, Typewriter, Albert C. Manning, Ransom & Randolph Co., Limoges, France . . . 805.00
Occupational, U.S. Mail Truck Driver, Warren Stailey, Marked, H.B., 1927 . . . . . 5750.00
Occupational, Undertaker, Hearse, O.S. Wilson, V&D Austria, 3¾ In. . . . . *illus* 1112.00
Occupational, Violin, Crossed Bow, C.O. McAllister 184.00
Occupational, Wallpaper Hanger, W.A. Kramer, Waite Barber Supplies 690.00
Patriotic, Grand Army Of The Republic, 88th Pa. Infantry, Medal, J.W. Davis, 3½ In. 461.00
Photograph, Man, Gilt Leaf Design, Frank D. Mowen 345.00
Spanish-American War Veteran, Medal, Wm. C. Miller, Adjt. Gen., 1902 . . . . . 748.00
U.S. Flag, 22 Stars, Waving In Breeze, J. Heitahrends, T & V France 120.00

SHAWNEE POTTERY was started in Zanesville, Ohio, in 1937. The company made vases, novelty ware, flowerpots, planters, lamps, and cookie jars. Three dinnerware lines were made: Corn, Lobster Ware, and Valencia (a solid color line). White Corn pattern utility pieces were made in 1945. Corn King was made from 1946 to 1954; Corn Queen, with darker green leaves and lighter colored corn, from 1954 to 1961. Shawnee produced pottery for George Rumrill during the late 1930s. The company closed in 1961.

Shawnee USA

Ball Jug, Sunflower, Tilt Ball, Marked, 7½ In. 55.00
Butter Dish, Corn King 129.00
Butter Dish, Corn King 150.00
Casserole, Cover, Corn King, 4½ In.. . . . . 100.00
Casserole, Cover, Corn King, 11 In. . . . . 40.00 to 75.00
Casserole, Sundial, Pink, Black, 11 In.. . . . . 35.00
Casserole, Valencia, Turquoise, 7½ In. 32.00
Cookie Jar, Dutch Boy, Happy Jack, Petit Point Flowers, Gold Trim, 1940s, 12 In.. . . . . 195.00
Cookie Jar, Dutch Tulip 145.00
Cookie Jar, Muggsy, 11 In.. . . . . 650.00
Cookie Jar, Owl, Plain, 11½ x 12 In. 185.00
Cookie Jar, Pennsylvania Dutch, Cork, Ivory, Burgundy, 8¼ In. 135.00
Cookie Jar, Pennsylvania Dutch Jug, Heart, Flowers, Marked, 8 In. 135.00
Cookie Jar, Puss 'N Boots, Gold Trim, 10¼ In. 449.00
Cookie Jar, Smiley Pig, Cream, Green Scarf, Shamrocks, 1939-44, 11 In. . . . . 250.00 to 275.00
Corn Holder, Corn King, 8½ In.. . . . . 68.00
Creamer, Corn King . . . . . 55.00 to 110.00
Creamer, Elephant, Plain, 4¼ In. . . . . 20.00 to 45.00
Creamer, Puss 'N Boots, 4¾ In. . . . . 29.00 to 77.00
Creamer, Smiley Pig, Clover Bud, Gold Trim, 4¾ In. 165.00
Creamer, Smiley Pig, Peach Flower, 4¾ x 4 In. 47.00
Dish, Corn King, Fruit, 6 In.. . . . . 75.00
Dish, Corn Queen, 9 In. 68.00
Ewer, Green, No, 1067, Small. 15.00
Figurine, Chinese Boy, 5 In.. . . . . 18.00
Figurine, Dog, Terrier, 7½ In. 45.00
Figurine, Dutch Girl, Green, Yellow, Orange, 4½ In. 14.00
Figurine, Parrot, 3½ In. 32.00
Lamp Base, Moor, Heads, 8 In., Pair 195.00
Mixing Bowl, Corn King, 6½ In.. . . . . 35.00
Mixing Bowl, Snowflake, Aqua, 7 In.. . . . . 30.00 to 34.00
Pie Bird, 5 In.. . . . . 65.00
Pitcher, Bo-Peep, Lavender, Green, 7½ In. . . . . 84.00 to 125.00
Pitcher, Bo-Peep, Lavender & Green, 1940s, 8 In. 84.00
Pitcher, Bo-Peep, Red, Yellow, Blue, Marked, 7½ In.. . . . . 138.00

S

Pitcher, Chanticleer, 7½ In. 124.00 to 150.00
Pitcher, Corn King 81.00 to 95.00
Planter, Basket Weave, Mauve Glaze, 5½ x 3½ In. 8.00
Planter, Boy At Stump, 6½ In. 12.00
Planter, Bridge, 5 x 9¼ In. 29.00
Planter, Butterfly, 4 x 2 In. 13.00
Planter, Classic Jardinere, 5½ In. 12.00
Planter, Covered Wagon, 4½ x 5¼ In. 13.00
Planter, Doe & Fawn, 6 x 7 In. 30.00
Planter, Dog, Spaniel, 4½ In. 10.00
Planter, Dutch Boy & Girl At Wishing Well, 5½ x 8½ x 3 In. 35.00 to 45.00
Planter, Elf On Boot, 5½ x 6 In. 20.00
Planter, Fawn & Stump 22.00
Planter, Gazelle, 10 In. 27.00
Planter, Girl With Basket, 6¼ In. 28.00
Planter, Gnomes & Log, 3½ x 8 In. 48.00
Planter, Gourd, 11½ In. 13.00
Planter, Old Mill & Pond, Green, 6 x 7 In. 20.00 to 25.00
Planter, Oriental Man, Carrying Basket, 4 In. 22.00
Planter, Pixie, Seated, Gold, Green, Mauve, 4 In. 15.00
Planter, Prancing Pony, Red, 7½ In. 48.00
Planter, Rooster, 6½ In. 45.00
Planter, Sea Foam Green, Ruffles, 13½ x 4 In. 20.00
Planter, Sitting Pony, Cream, Tan Glaze, 6 In. 18.00
Planter, Wheelbarrow, Blue Flowers, 1⅞ In. 14.00
Planter, Wood Grain Texture, White Matte, Green Matte Interior, 3½ x 15 x 5 In. 13.00
Plate, Corn King, 10 In. 15.00 to 32.00
Salt & Pepper, Bo-Peep & Sailor Boy, 3½ In. 25.00
Salt & Pepper, Boy Blue, Bo Peep, 3½ In. 30.00
Salt & Pepper, Corn King, Label *illus* 34.00
Salt & Pepper, Corn King, 3½ In. 25.00
Salt & Pepper, Corn King, 5¼ In. 40.00 to 69.00
Salt & Pepper, Cottage, 3½ x 2¾ In. 325.00
Salt & Pepper, Dutch Boy & Girl, 5 In. 55.00
Salt & Pepper, Fruit, 2¾ In. 38.00
Salt & Pepper, Jack & Jill, 2¾ In. 85.00
Salt & Pepper, Milk Can 28.00
Salt & Pepper, Muggsy, Cobalt Blue Eyes, Ribbon, 3½ In. 50.00
Salt & Pepper, Owl, 3¼ In. 15.00
Salt & Pepper, Smiley & Winnie Pig, Clover, 5 In. *illus* 84.00
Salt & Pepper, Wheelbarrow, 2 In. 14.00
Shaker, Rooster, Chanticleer, 5 In. 14.00
Shaker, Smiley & Winnie Pig, Range, Red Neckerchief, Suspenders, 5½ In. 60.00
Spoon Holder, Corn King, 7¼ x 5¼ In. 27.00
Teapot, Corn, 6½ x 9 In. 73.00
Teapot, Embossed Rose, Ivory, 6½ In. 36.00
Teapot, Granny Ann, Green Apron, Shawl, Burgundy & Yellow Trim, 8½ In. 115.00 to 221.00
Teapot, Granny Ann, Lavender Apron, Green Trim, 1940-59, 8½ In. 95.00 to 139.00
Teapot, Sunflower, c.1940-50, 7 x 9½ In. 55.00
Teapot, Tom, The Piper's Son, 7 In. 125.00 to 181.00
Vase, Bamboo, 6 In. 29.00
Vase, Bud, Chantilly, White, Green, 10 In. 22.00
Vase, Burlap, 9 In. 20.00
Vase, Cornucopia, Blue, Marked, 6 In., Pair 35.00
Vase, Doe, Shadowbox, Gray, White, 9 x 5 In. 60.00
Vase, Fawn & Stump 30.00
Vase, Leaf, Green, Gold Trim, 9 In. 35.00
Vase, Peach, 2 Handles, 8 x 5½ In. 30.00
Vase, Ruffled, Jade Green, White 24.00
Vase, Sorcery, Lavender, Cameo Splatter White, 4½ In. 30.00
Vase, Swirl, Gold Fleck, Cream Interior, Ruffled Rim, 6 x 5 In. 20.00
Wall Pocket, Antelope, 6 x 5 In. 33.00
Wall Pocket, Bluebirds At Birdhouse, 6 x 5 x 2¾ In. 26.00
Wall Pocket, Flowers, Green Wash, c.1930-40, 7 x 3 In., Pair 147.00
Wall Pocket, Wheat, 5 In. 35.00

TIP
Most shaving mug reproductions are imaginative copies of old mugs that would not fool a serious collector. There is often no space for the owner's name. Some examples are marked "Brandenburg." Copies include designs such as Currier and Ives prints, a hearse drawn by horses, and trade names such as Peddler, Fireman, or Painter.

Shawnee, Salt & Pepper, Corn King, Label
$34.00

Shawnee, Salt & Pepper, Smiley & Winnie Pig, Clover, 5 In.
$84.00

TIP
Restoring and reusing old things is the purest form of recycling.

Shearwater, Bowl, Duck Design, 3 ½ x 10 In.
$ 9400.00

Shearwater, Vase, Pelicans, Mottled Blue & Turquoise Glaze, 7 x 6 In.
$6600.00

Shelley, Coffeepot, Cup & Saucer, Marked
$40.00

Music From the Movies
Watch out for reprints of old movie sheet music. Music before the 1960s was about 50 cents a copy. Now it is almost $3.00. The reprints are usually made to be sold in a store, not to fool the collector, so the price will be shown.

SHEARWATER pottery is a family business started by Mr. and Mrs. G.W. Anderson, Sr., and their three sons. The local Ocean Springs, Mississippi, clays were used to make the wares in the 1930s. The company is still in business.

Bowl, Blue, Green Glaze, Wide Flared, c.1935, 9 ½ In. 504.00
Bowl, Blue Rain, Low Form, Brown Streaks On Bottom, 1880, 9 In. 645.00
Bowl, Duck Design, 3 ½ x 10 In. .... *illus* 9400.00
Bowl, Footed, Green Mottled Glaze, Low Open Body, Mark, Late 1900s, 3 x 8 In. 206.00
Bowl, Fruit, Flowers, Vines, Green, Brown Glaze, c.1940, 5 ¼ x 6 ¾ In. 4113.00
Teapot, Bulbous, Mottled Turquoise Glaze, 9 ½ x 5 ½ In. 540.00
Vase, Alkaline Blue Glaze, Everted Lip, Waisted Baluster, c.1931, 9 ¾ In. 720.00
Vase, Bronze Glaze, Cylindrical, Pinched Lip Rim, c.1929, 9 In. 648.00
Vase, Earth, Sea & Sky, Green & Tan Glaze, Relief Panels, Signed, c.1950, 12 In. 1165.00
Vase, Pelicans, Mottled Blue & Turquoise Glaze, 7 x 6 In. .... *illus* 6600.00

SHEET MUSIC from the past centuries is now collected. The favorites are examples with covers featuring artistic or historic pictures. Early sheet music covers were lithographed, but by the 1900s photographic reproductions were used. The early music was larger than more recent sheets, and you must watch out for examples that were trimmed to fit in a twentieth-century piano bench.

Ben Hur March, Chariot Race On Cover, E.T. Paull, 1922, 9 x 12 In. 40.00
Buttons & Bows, From Movie Paleface, Bob Hope, Jane Russell, 1948 .... 55.00
Chariot Race Or Ben Hur March, E.T. Paull, Chariot Race On Cover, 1922, 9 x 12 In. 40.00
My One & Only Highland Fling, Ira Gershwin & Harry Warren, 1949 .... 25.00
Ophelia Rag, James Scott, Little Girl On Cover, 1910, 9 x 12 In. 45.00
Over There, George M. Cohan, 1918, Soldiers Singing 40.00
Rum & Coca-Cola, Jerri Sullivan, 1944 .... 10.00
The Flashlight, March, E.T. Paull, Lighthouse On Cover, 1909, 9 x 12 In. 50.00

SHEFFIELD *items are listed in the Silver Plate and Silver-English categories.*

SHELLEY first appeared on English ceramics about 1912. The Foley China Works started in England in 1860. Joseph Ball Shelley joined the company in 1862 and became a partner in 1872. Percy Shelley joined the firm in 1881. The company went through a series of name changes and in 1910 the then Foley China Company became Shelley China. In 1929 it became Shelley Potteries. The company was acquired in 1966 by Allied English Potteries, then merged with the Doulton group in 1971. The name Shelley was put into use again in 1980. A trio is the name for a cup, saucer, and cake plate set.

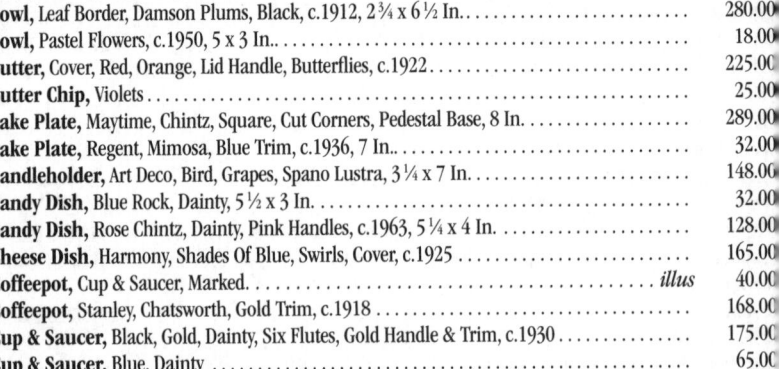

Bowl, Centerpiece, Orange Red Deco Ground, Enamel Cranes, White & Yellow 110.00
Bowl, Leaf Border, Damson Plums, Black, c.1912, 2 ¾ x 6 ½ In. 280.00
Bowl, Pastel Flowers, c.1950, 5 x 3 In. 18.00
Butter, Cover, Red, Orange, Lid Handle, Butterflies, c.1922 .... 225.00
Butter Chip, Violets 25.00
Cake Plate, Maytime, Chintz, Square, Cut Corners, Pedestal Base, 8 In. 289.00
Cake Plate, Regent, Mimosa, Blue Trim, c.1936, 7 In. 32.00
Candleholder, Art Deco, Bird, Grapes, Spano Lustra, 3 ¼ x 7 In. 148.00
Candy Dish, Blue Rock, Dainty, 5 ½ x 3 In. 32.00
Candy Dish, Rose Chintz, Dainty, Pink Handles, c.1963, 5 ¼ x 4 In. 128.00
Cheese Dish, Harmony, Shades Of Blue, Swirls, Cover, c.1925 .... 165.00
Coffeepot, Cup & Saucer, Marked .... *illus* 40.00
Coffeepot, Stanley, Chatsworth, Gold Trim, c.1918 .... 168.00
Cup & Saucer, Black, Gold, Dainty, Six Flutes, Gold Handle & Trim, c.1930 .... 175.00
Cup & Saucer, Blue, Dainty 65.00
Cup & Saucer, Blue Rock 35.00
Cup & Saucer, Blue Rock, Pale Blue Trim, Dainty, Fluted Rim 79.00
Cup & Saucer, Canterbury, 3 x 1 ½ In. 125.00
Cup & Saucer, Charm, Blue Flowers, Gilt Trim 50.00
Cup & Saucer, Deep Blue Flowers, Dainty 82.00
Cup & Saucer, Footed, Oleander, Multicolored Gold Edges, c.1940 .... 225.00
Cup & Saucer, Footed, Oleander, Rock Garden, Chintz, Black Ground 240.00
Cup & Saucer, Footed, Oleander, Stocks, Laurel, Pink Ribbon Border, c.1940 .... 215.00
Cup & Saucer, Gainsborough, Applied Roses, Green & Black 62.00
Cup & Saucer, Gainsborough, Roses, Tulips, Pink Trim 62.00
Cup & Saucer, Green Charm, Canterbury, 3 x 1 ½ In. 100.00
Cup & Saucer, Heather, Landscape, Richmond, Green Handle, Gold Trim 88.00
Cup & Saucer, Maytime, Chintz, Green Trim 125.00
Cup & Saucer, Melody, Chintz, Crested, Gold Trim, c.1940 .... 188.00

p & Saucer, Melody, Chintz, Gold Trim	120.00
p & Saucer, Melody, Chintz, Mint Green, Oleander Shape	72.00
p & Saucer, Oleander, Flower Bouquets, Gold Trim	115.00
p & Saucer, Pink Daisy, Dainty, c.1940	161.00
p & Saucer, Pink Handle, Pink & Green Leaves, Scalloped Rims, Gold Trim, 2 ½ In.	75.00
p & Saucer, Primrose, Ripon Shape, Gold Trim	110.00
p & Saucer, Primrose, White, Flowers Inside Cup, Gold Trim, Oleander, Footed	100.00
p & Saucer, Queen Anne, Gray & Black Swirled Lines, Pink Handle	74.00
p & Saucer, Rose Pansy Forget-Me-Not, Blue Trim, Dainty, Fluted Rim	80.00
p & Saucer, Roses & Red Daisy, Pink Trim, Dainty, Fluted Rim	62.00
p & Saucer, Thistles, Stems, Leaves, Pink Handle, Dainty, Six Flutes	115.00
sh, Dog, 3 x 6 ¾ In.	225.00
sh, Shamrock, Fluted, 5 ¾ In.	80.00
gcup, White, Gold Trim, Dainty, 1 ⅞ In.	25.00
ffin Dish, Harmony, Yellow, Orange, Light Brown, Swirls, Cover, c.1925	255.00
ffineer, Lily Of The Valley, White, Green, Dainty, 7 x 4 In.	220.00
cher, Melody, Chintz, Green Bottom & Trim, c.1945, 6 ½ x 5 ½ In.	248.00
ite, Blue, Dainty, 6 In.	20.00
ite, Dinner, Blue, Dainty, c.1925	39.00
ite, Landscape, Flowers, Trees, Rounded Corners, 6 ¾ In.	65.00
ite, Salad, Naples, Multicolored Balls, Avon Shape, c.1964	28.00
ite, Semi-Scalloped Edges, Multicolored Flowers, Sheraton, 6 In.	15.00
ite, Summer Glory, Gold Trim, 8 In.	150.00
ite, Wildflowers, Multicolored, 7 In.	25.00
ucer, Daisies, Twigs, Lace, Gold Trim, Lily, c.1890, 5 ½ In.	20.00
gar, Blue Glorious Devon, Cambridge, Landscape, Gold Trim, c.1940	78.00
gar & Creamer, Fluted Sides, Pink Trim & Handle	58.00
gar & Creamer, Royalty, Pink Rose & Bud	41.00
gar & Creamer, Rural Scene, Primroses, Fence, Blue Trim, c.1925	68.00
up, Lid, Chelsea, Flowers, Multicolored Lid, c.1920	125.00
pot, Gainsborough, Laurel, Wreath Of Leaves, Cover, c.1945	228.00
pot, Lid, Roses, Yellow, Dainty, c.1945, 6 ½ x 10 ½ In.	388.00
o, Bailey's Dogwood, Windsor, c.1962	118.00
o, Campanula, Fluted, Lavender, Dainty, c.1955	205.00
o, Campanula, Purple Flowers, Leaves, Stems, Buds, Fluted, Scalloped, Dainty	125.00
o, Fluted, Scalloped, Rose Pansy Forget-Me-Not	110.00
o, Melody, Chintz, Richmond, Green Ground	135.00 to 155.00
o, Melody, Chintz, Semi-Scalloped	135.00
o, Queen Anne, Black & Gray Swirls, Pink Trim & Interior	158.00
o, Queen Anne, Blue Iris, c.1927	190.00
o, Wallflower, Oxford, c.1933	125.00
e, Bulbous, Carnations, Black Ground, c.1918	72.00
e, Orange, Red, Fruit, Ribbons, c.1920	53.00
e, Violets, Leaves, Urn, Marked, 4 ½ In.	53.00

RLEY TEMPLE, the famous movie star, was born in 1928. She made her first movie in 2. Thousands of items picturing Shirley have been and still are being made. Shirley Temple s were first made in 1934 by Ideal Toy Company. Millions of Shirley Temple cobalt blue glass es were made by Hazel Atlas Glass Company and U.S. Glass Company from 1934 to 1942. They were n away as premiums for Wheaties and Bisquick. A bowl, mug, and pitcher were made as a breakfast Some pieces were decorated with the picture of a very young Shirley, others used a picture of Shirley er 1936 *Captain January* costume. Although collectors refer to a cobalt creamer, it is actually the inch-high milk pitcher from the breakfast set. Many of these items are being reproduced today.

k, Now I Am Eight, c.1937	131.00
l, Capt. January, Vinyl, Jointed Shoulders & Hips, Rooted Hair, Box, c.1958	247.00
l, Composition, Sleep Eyes, Mohair Wig, NRA Label, Ideal, c.1934, 20 In.	235.00
l, Composition, Sleep Eyes, Open Mouth, Mohair Curls, Coat, Hat, Box, 1939, 22 In.	1980.00
l, Composition, World's Darling Pin, Ideal, 1930s, 21 In. *illus*	2280.00
l, Vinyl, Jointed Shoulders, Hips, White Dress, Red Ribbon Trim, Hat, c.1958, 12 In.	83.00
l, Vinyl, Jointed Shoulders, Hips, Blue & White Dress, Suspenders, Box, c.1958, 12 In.	192.00
l, Vinyl, Jointed Shoulders & Hips, Blue & White Dress, Ideal, c.1958, 12 In.	82.00
l Clothes, Heidi Costume, Ideal, Unopened Package, 1974, Fits 16-In. Doll. *illus*	60.00
l Clothes, Rebecca Of Sunnybrook Farm, Ideal, Unopened Package, 1974, Fits 16-In. Doll	11.00
p, 2 Figures, Red Bow, Blue Bow, Painted Hair, Kerk Guild, Box, 5 In., 2 Piece	115.00

TIP

Wash doll clothes, handkerchiefs, and other small textiles in a kitchen salad washer. Put the water, detergent or soap, and textiles in the washer, spin the handle, empty, rinse, spin.

Shirley Temple, Doll, Composition, World's Darling Pin, Ideal, 1930s, 21 In.
$2280.00

Shirley Temple, Doll Clothes, Heidi Costume, Ideal, Unopened Package, 1974, Fits 16-In. Doll
$60.00

Silver Flatware Sterling, Medallion, Server, Gorham, 10 In. $510.00

Silver Flatware Sterling, Salad Servers, Black Plastic, Gio Ponti Diamond Pattern, Reed & Barton, 13 x 2½ In. $890.00

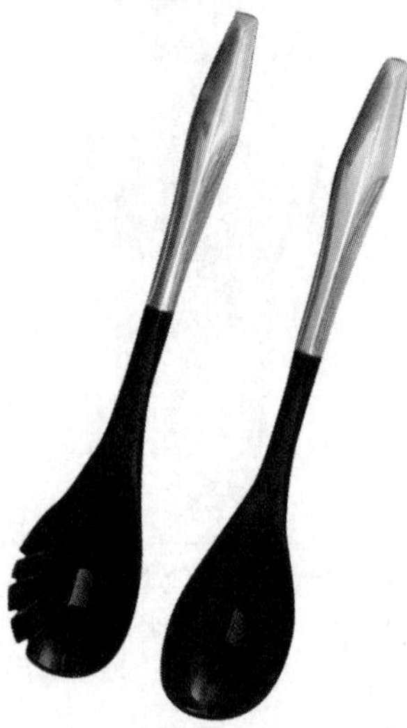

Silver Plate, Basket, Roses, Repousse, Pairpoint, c.1900, 8 x 9¾ In. $60.00

SHRINER, *see Fraternal category.*

SILVER DEPOSIT glass was first made during the late nineteenth century. Solid sterling silver is applied to the glass by a chemical method so that a cutout design of silver metal appears against a clear or colored glass. It is sometimes called silver overlay.

Cake Plate, Pedestal, Silver Band & Rim, Pedestal .... 65.
Candy Dish, 3 Legs, Scalloped Edge, Clear, 6⅝ x 2½ In. .... 15.
Pitcher, Flowers, Applied Handle, Oval .... 75.
Salt & Pepper, White, Porcelain, Flowers, Chrome, Irice, 2¼ x 1¾ In. .... 24.
Tray, Fleur-De-Lis, Center Handle .... 25.
Vase, Blue Glass, Art Nouveau, Diamond Quilted, Blue, Bulbous, Square Rim, 8¼ In. .... 460.
Vase, Emerald Green, Venice Scene, Bulbous, 6¼ x 2¾ In. .... 15.

SILVER FLATWARE includes many of the current and out-of-production silver and silver-plated flatware patterns made in the past eighty years. Other silver is listed under Silver-American, Silver-English, etc. Most silver flatware sets that are missing a few pieces can be completed through the help of one of the many silver matching services that advertise in many of the national publications.

SILVER FLATWARE PLATED

Adam, Carving Fork, Community, c.1917, 11½ In. 27
Adam, Fork, Monogram, Community, c.1917, 8⅜ In. 17
Adam, Jelly Server, Community, c.1917, 6⅛ In. 11
Adam, Knife, Community, c.1917, 9⅞ In. 8
Adam, Spoon, Community, c.1917, 6 In. 5
Berkeley Square, Spoon, Box, Community, c.1935, 12 Piece 68
Bouquet, Tablespoon, Embassy, c.1939, 8¼ In. 9
Bride, Sugar Shell, International, 6 In. 11
Champlain, Sauce Ladle, Monogram, Wm. Rogers, c.1912, 7 In. 14
Cotillion, Baby Spoon, Straight Handle, Stratford, c.1932, 4¼ In. 10
Daffodil, Baby Spoon, Rogers, c.1950, 5¼ In. 13
Daffodil, Pie Server, Cut Out In Center, Rogers, 1847 45
Doric, Cold Meat Fork, Rogers & Hamilton, c.1909, 8¼ In. 23
First Colony, Cake Server, Pierced Handle, Oneida, 1975 25
Flower, Serving Spoon, Wm. Rogers & Son, c.1906 36
Holly, Gravy Ladle, Lakeside, 1904 110
Jasmine, Baby Spoon, Oneida, c.1958, 5¾ In. 13
King Cedric, Jelly Knife, Community Plate, Oneida Silver Co., c.1933 17
La France, Serving Fork, Wm. Rogers & Son, c.1920, 8⅜ In. 11
Lady Esther, Salad Fork, Queen Esther, 5⅞ In., 6 Piece 50
Lorne, Ice Tongs, Rogers, 1847, 8 In. 125
Old Colony, Ladle, Rogers Bros. International, c.1911, 9¼ In. 18
Pearl, Dinner Fork, Reed & Barton, c.1898, 7½ In. 23
Romance, Salad Fork, Holmes & Edwards, International Silver, c.1925, 6¼ In. 4
Rosalie, Sugar Spoon, Shell Shape Bowl, Royal Plate Co., c.1905, 6 In. 8
Silver Flowers, Dessert Server, Oneida, c.1960, 9⅜ In. 14
Victoria, Cream Ladle, William Rogers & Sons, 1895 55
Vineyard, Cold Meat Fork, Monogram, Williams Bros. Mfg. Co., c.1906, 8¼ In. 15

SILVER FLATWARE STERLING

Acorn, Pie Server, Elongated Blade, Georg Jensen, Post 1945, 10½ In. 176
Acorn, Seafood Pick, Georg Jensen, 1950s, 10 In., Set Of 6 645
Anthemion Medallion, Ice Cream Server, Krider & Biddle, Engraved, 9½ In. 360
Antique Engraved, Teaspoon, Frank M. Whiting, Case, 6 In., 6 Piece 36
Arts & Crafts, Spoon, Hammered, Whiting Division, Gorham, 7½ In. 585
Bird's Nest, Cream Ladle, Gorham, c.1865, 6¼ In. 1793
Blossom, Marrow Scoop, Georg Jensen, 7½ In. 585
Blossom, Pastry Server, Georg Jensen, 9½ In. 35
Blossom, Pickle Fork, Georg Jensen, 5¼ In. 32
Burgundy, Egg Spoon, Reed & Barton, 6 In. 5
Burgundy, Pie Knife, Heavily Scrolled Handle, Reed & Barton 22
Buttercup, Fork, Monogram, Gorham, 6⅞ In. 3
Cactus, Pastry Server, Georg Jensen, 8¾ In. 23
Chantilly, Fruit Spoon, Gorham, 5¾ In. 2
Chrysanthemum, Ice Cream Set, Slicer Blade, Spoons, Gorham, 13 Piece 127
Colonial, Master Salt Spoon, Gorham, c.1885, 3½ In. 5
Dauphin, Pickle Fork, Gilt Tines, W.B. Durgin, Co., c.1890, 8¾ In. 44

S

'ontainbleau, Ladle, Gilt Bowl, Bright Cut Engraving, Gorham, 12 ½ In. 460.00
'rancis I, Cake Breaker 250.00
'rancis I, Dinner Set, Reed & Barton, Fitted Chest, 161 Piece 6300.00
;eorge III, Spoon, Frank M. Whiting, c.1891, 3 ⅝ In. 43.00
Ielena I, Carving Set, Frank M Whiting & Co., 10-In. Fork, 14-In. Knife 72.00
Ioroscope, Youth Spoon, Cancer, Engraved Crab & No. 69 On Stem 95.00
apanese, Ice Cream Slice, Gorham, c.1880, 11 ¾ In. 1315.00
Kings Court, Salad Set, Vermeil, F.M. Whiting, 9-In. Fork, 8 ⅜-In. Spoon 535.00
.ady Baltimore, 6 Forks, 6 Spoons, Whiting, c.1910, 12 Piece 123.00
.ancaster, Ice Cream Slice, Gorham, 20th Century 125.00
ily, Fork, Embossed Lilies, Frank M. Whiting, c.1915, 4 ½ In. 18.00
ouis XIV, Sugar Sifter, Engraved, Monogram, Towle, 6 ½ In. 95.00
ove Disarmed, Serving Fork & Spoon, Salad, Reed & Barton, 10 In. 865.00
ove Disarmed, Serving Pieces, Fish Slice, Salad Servers, Meat Fork, Reed & Barton 900.00
Iadam Jumel, Citrus Spoon, Monogram, Whiting Mfg., c.1911, 5 ⅞ In. 40.00
Iargaret Old, Teaspoon, Monogram, International Silver Co., 12 Piece 106.00
Iedallion, Macaroni Server, Gorham, 10 In. 518.00
Iedallion, Sauce Ladle, Gilt Bowl, Wood & Hughes, Marked, c.1882, 7 ½ In. 358.00
Iedallion, Server, Gorham, 10 In. .... *illus* 510.00
Iedici, Asparagus Server, Scalloped Edge Flowers, Gorham, c.1883, 9 ¾ In. 986.00
.ightingale, Fish Set, Gorham, c.1885, 2 Piece 695.00
Iightingale, Ice Cream Set, Slicer Blade & Spoons, Gorham, 13 Piece 1275.00
Iightingale, Oyster Soup Ladle, Gorham, 12 In. 425.00
Old Maryland Engraved, Olive Fork, S. Kirk & Sons, 1970s, 6 In. 50.00
Orleans, Fork Set, Strawberry, F.M. Whiting, 5 In., 6 Piece 225.00
'arallel, Ladle, Winged, Georg Jensen, 1945, 12 ½ In. 470.00
'arallel, Marrow Scoop, Georg Jensen, c.1930, 7 In. 111.00
'ointed Antique, Brandy Spoon, Reed & Barton, 4 ¾ In., Set Of 6 .... 225.00
'ortland, Ladle, Gorham, c.1904, 4 In. 49.00
'yramid, Salad Serving Set, Georg Jensen, Harald Nilsen, Felt Pouches, c.1926 .... 390.00
'yramid, Tomato Server, Georg Jensen, c.1927, 7 ½ In. 351.00
Queen Bess, Pie Server, Oneida, 1946, 9 ½ In. 55.00
Repousse, Bonbon Spoon, Embossed Bowl Of Berries & Fruit, S. Kirk 95.00
Repousse, Serving Fork, 5 Tine, S. Kirk, c.1890, 9 ¼ In. 195.00
Repousse, Tomato Server, Pierced, S. Kirk, c.1890, 7 ½ In. 105.00
Rococo, Punch Ladle, Detailed Engraved Flowers, Dominick & Haff 650.00
alad Servers, Black Plastic, Gio Ponti Diamond Pattern, Reed & Barton, 13 x 2 ½ In. . . *illus* 890.00
ilver Flute, Service For 8, Towle, Lined Box 1100.00
potswood, Salad Set, Gorham, 2 Piece 279.00
potswood, Spoon Set, Ice Cream, Gorham, 4 ⅞ In., 6 Piece 256.00
rianon Pierced, Ice Serving Spoon, Gilt Bowl, Dominick & Haff, c.1888, 9 In. 329.00
ersailles, Punch Ladle, Gorham, Early 20th Century, 11 In. 382.00
ersailles, Sugar Shell, Gorham, c.1888, 5 In. 143.00
Vashington, Berry Spoon, Wallace, 8 ½ In. 95.00
Vedgwood, Bouillon Ladle, International, 6 ¼ In. 125.00

ILVER PLATE is not solid silver. It is a ware made of a metal, such as nickel or copper, hat is covered with a thin coating of silver. The letters *EPNS* are often found on merican and English silver-plated wares. Sheffield is a term with two meanings. Sometimes it refers to terling silver made in the town of Sheffield, England. Sometimes it refers to an old form of plated silver.

shtray, Golf, Open Ball Sits Atop 3 Golf Club Feet, 5 x 3 ½ In., Pair 30.00
asket, Aesthetic, Oval Handle, Flower Sprays, Rogers Smith & Co., c.1880, 15 ½ In. 207.00
asket, Bail Handle, Ribbed, 4-Footed, c.1890, 10 x 9 In. 70.00
asket, Roses, Repousse, Pairpoint, c.1900, 8 x 9 ¾ In. .... *illus* 60.00
iscuit Box, Flower & Ivy Design, Twig Frame, 8 ½ x 8 ½ x 5 ½ In. 450.00
iscuit Box, Greyhound, Beaded Border, 4 Winged Paw Feet, 8 ½ x 9 ½ x 8 In. 805.00
onbon, Flower Design, Pierced Cutouts, Art Nouveau, Community, 8 In. 32.00
ottle Wagon, Wood Base Coasters, 6 Spoke Wheels, Ivory Pull, England, 3 ⅞ x 18 In. 968.00
owl, Center, Reticulated, Oval, Spreading Foot, Sheffield, 1800s, 13 ½ In. 390.00
owl, Vegetable, Electroplated, Cover, Early 20th Century, 3 ¾ x 12 In. 29.00
owl, Vegetable, George V, Reeded Rim, Handles, Legs, Swags, Paw Feet, 7 x 13 In. 270.00
utter, Cover, Footed, Handle, Simpson, Hall, Miller, Late 19th Century, 13 x 7 ½ In. . . . . *illus* 195.00
ake Basket, Basket Weave, Pierced, Putto, Square, Hinged Handle, 4 Paw Feet, J. Tufts, 8 In. 240.00
andelabra are listed in the Candelabrum category.

Silver Plate, Butter, Cover, Footed, Handle, Simpson, Hall, Miller, Late 19th Century, 13 x 7 ½ In.
$195.00

Silver Plate, Egg Stand, Edwardian, Gilt Interior, 6 Cup, Early 20th Century, 8 x 7 In.
$269.00

Silver Plate, Grape Stand, Scissors, Bird Finial, 3 Bun Feet, CG&CO., 8 ¾ x 8 In.
$420.00

S

Silver Plate, Hot Water Urn, Scroll Handles, c.1880, 20¾ In.
$480.00

Silver Plate, Tea Set, Hammered, Poole Silver Co., Sheffield Hallmark, 6 Piece
$72.00

Silver Plate, Tea Set, Scroll & Flowers, Bud Finial, Bigelow Bros. & Kennard, c.1845
$920.00

Silver Plate, Tray, Meat, Cover, Acanthus & Berry, Old Sheffield, Marked, W.W., 12 x 20 x 15 In.
$403.00

Candlesticks are listed in their own category.
Carving Set, Art Nouveau, Wallace, c.1900, 3 Piece . . . 59.00
Centerpiece, Pedestal, 2 Attached Shell Form Dishes, Urn Trumpet Glass Vase, 21 In. . . . 489.00
Chafing Dish, Cover, James Dickson, Rococo, Claw Feet, c.1825, 10 x 14 x 9 In. . . . 292.00
Coaster, On Copper, Round, Gadroon Body, Flowers, Sheffield, 5 In. . . . 59.00
Cocktail Shaker, Lighthouse Shape, 14 x 5 In. . . . 460.00
Coffee Urn, Bulbous Body, Repousse Hunting Scene, Bacchic Mask Handles, 18 x 13 In. . . . 1800.00
Coffeepot, Pear Shape, Wood Handle, Hinged Cover, Finial, Pairpoint, 9½ x 8 In. . . . 88.00
Compote, 2 Handles, Footed, c.1854 . . . 650.00
Compote, Figural, Victorian, Cased, Pink & White Ruffled Dish, Late 1800s, 19 x 12 In. . . . 702.00
Compote, Handle, Simpson, Hall & Miller, Game Bird Design, 12 x 12 In. . . . 94.00
Compote, S.F. Co., 2 Tiers, Reticulated Edge, Center Handle, 14 x 13 In. . . . 176.00
Cover, Meat, Oval Dome, Gadroon Border, Old Sheffield, 11 x 20 x 14 In. . . . 400.00
Cover, Meat, Tray, Lobed, Acanthus & Berry Handle, Acanthus Border, Sheffield, 12 x 20 In. . . . 345.00
Dish, Entree, Regency, Cover, 2 Handles, Scroll Supports, Lion Finial, 15 x 24 In. . . . 2644.00
Dish, Preserve, On Stand, Victorian, Satin, Blue Rim, Flowers, c.1890, 4¾ x 6¼ In. . . . 82.00
Egg Stand, 6 Cup, Rectangular, 6-Footed, Central Loop Handle, Ball Feet, 5¾ In. . . . 89.00
Egg Stand, Edwardian, Gilt Interior, 6 Cup, Early 20th Century, 8 x 7 In. . . . *illus* 269.00
Epergne, Sweetmeat, Oval Cut Glass Bowl, Footed Stand, 4 Scroll Branches, 11 x 21 In. . . . 1770.00
Epergne, Tree Shape, 5 Branches, 3 Seated Stags, Mirror Plateau, 25 x 24½ In. . . . 2045.00
Ewer, Neoclassical, Arched Handle, Figures, Raised Decoration, 23¾ In. . . . 644.00
Ewer, Wine, Aesthetic, Oval Body, Spreading Round Foot, Sunflowers, c.1880, 10 In. . . . 118.00
Frame, Cherub On Winged Wheel, Flowers, c.1890, 14 In. . . . 660.00
Fruit Set, Victorian, Cased, Mother-Of-Pearl, Benetfink & Co., London, 16 Piece . . . 660.00
Fruit Spoon, Embossed Bowl, Fruit & Fiddle, Shell Shape Stem, English Sheffield . . . 95.00
Grape Stand, Scissors, Bird Finial, 3 Bun Feet, CG&CO., 8¾ x 8 In. . . . *illus* 420.00
Hot Water Urn, Engraved Flowers, Monogrammed, 13½ In. . . . 230.00
Hot Water Urn, Scroll Handles, c.1880, 20¾ In. . . . *illus* 480.00
Hot Water Urn, Sheffield, Oval, Gadroon Rim, Girdle, Lion Mask Handles, 17½ In. . . . 235.00
Inkstand, Ball Feet, Edwardian, c.1900, 10½ In. . . . 348.00
Inkwell, Dome Top Trunk, Lion Masks, 19th Century, 5 x 2¼ x 3¼ In. . . . 165.00
Jardiniere, Christofle, Oval, 4-Footed, 5 x 10½ x 16¼ In. . . . 1287.00
Knife Rest, Dogs, Goats, Cast Joined By Center Bar, 1¼ x 3½ In., 8 Piece . . . 209.00
Lazy Susan, Central Shaped Well, 4 Sections, Glass Liners, Scrolling Border, 21 In. . . . 142.00
Master Salt, Figural, Napoleon III, Putti, Fowl, Water Jug, Gold Wash, 6½ In., 4 Piece . . . 4888.00
Mirror, Dressing, Rococo Style, Pierced, Repousse, Late 19th Century, 24 x 18 In. . . . 708.00
Mirror, Pedestal, Sheffield, 2 x 12 In. . . . 117.00
Napkin Rings are listed in their own category.
Nutcracker, Decorated Handles, Man's Smiling Face, In Costume, Rogers Bros. . . . 43.00
Pickle Fork, Reed & Barton, Flowers Tied With Bow, 5⅜ In. . . . 14.00
Pitcher, Water, 2 Goblets, Stand, Victorian, Electroplate, c.1860, 22 In. . . . 351.00
Plate, Dinner, Gadroon, Bead Border, Cross Keys, Crown, England, 11 In., 8 Piece . . . 1293.00
Plate Set, Sheffield, Fluted, Gadroon Border, Crab Crest, 12 Piece, 9½ In. . . . 4800.00
Plate Warmer, Wicker Handles, Tapering Legs, Pad Feet, Asprey & Co., 13 x 11 In. . . . 3120.00
Plateau, Elkington, Vintage Design, Round, Cast Grapevine Rim, c.1885, 2¼ x 15½ In. . . . 411.00
Plateau, Regency, Circular Mirror, Lobed Border, Paw Feet, 2½ x 25½ In., Pair . . . 1680.00
Plateau, Round, Gadroon Rim, Acanthus, Rococo Scroll, 18½ x 3 In. . . . 1560.00
Platter, Dome Cover, Oval, Flared Rim, Applied Lobsters, Italy, 7½ x 33 x 17¾ In. . . . 1725.00
Platter, Meat, Christofle, Early 20th Century, Reeded Rim, 23¾ In. . . . 206.00
Platter, Meat, George III, Sheffield, Oval, Gadroon Rim, Crest, c.1800, 21 x 16 In. . . . 353.00
Platter, Round, Openwork Rim, Scrolling Acanthus, Masks, 1800s, 24 x 2¾ In. . . . 1080.00
Punch Bowl Set, Ladle, Tray, 9 x 16 & 19 In. . . . 193.00
Salt, Green Liner, c.1870-75, 2 In. . . . 66.00
Salt & Pepper, Cobalt Blue Liner, Fretwork Design, 3¾ x 1½ In. . . . 38.00
Salt & Pepper, Toy Soldier Shapes, 1 Gold Plate Top, 1 Silver Plate Top, Godinger, 4 In. . . . 40.00
Saltshaker, Handle, Footed, Dome Screw Cover, 4¼ In. . . . 38.00
Salver, Georgian Style, Molded, Beaded Rim, Rocaille Engraved, 12½ In., Pair . . . 176.00
Salver, Piecrust Rim, Shells, Armorial, Scroll Feet, England, 1⅜ x 10¼ In. . . . 86.00
Salver, Round, Floral Shell & Scroll Rim, Footed, Cresswick, 14¾ In. . . . 600.00
Salver, Round, Pierced, Cast Border, Allegorical Masks, 1900s, 16 In. . . . 561.00
Serving Spoon, Flower, Wm Rogers & Son, c.1906 . . . 36.00
Soup Ladle, Family Crest, Crown, Engraved B, E. Kayser Berndorf, c.1910, 16⅛ In. . . . 75.00
Spoon, Souvenir, see Souvenir category.
Tea & Coffee Set, Art Deco, 12 Vertical Panels, Round Foot, Rosewood Handle, 4 Piece . . . 360.00
Tea & Coffee Set, Victorian, Reed & Barton, Wilcox Tray, 6 Piece . . . 325.00
Tea Set, Hammered, Poole Silver Co., Sheffield Hallmark, 6 Piece . . . *illus* 72.00

ea Set, Meriden, Engraved, c.1900, 3 Piece 176.00
ea Set, Scroll & Flowers, Bud Finial, Bigelow Bros. & Kennard, c.1845 *illus* 920.00
ea Trolley, Edwardian, Box Stretchers, Detachable Tray, Pierced, 31 x 34 In. 10200.00
ea Urn, Cover, Finial, 4 Ball Feet, 2 Handles, Sheffield, c.1790, 22½ In. 480.00
ea Urn, Edwardian, Oval, Acanthus Scroll Mounted Milk Glass Handles, 15 x 12 In. 240.00
ea Urn, Sheffield, Egyptian Style, Applied Decoration, Animal Mask Handles, 17 x 11 In. 646.00
eakettle, Stand, Melon Shape, Turned Wood Handle, Hinged Lid, Melon Finial, 12 In. 235.00
eapot, Domed Lid, Dragon Finial, Squat Bulbous Body, Wood Handle, 7 x 10 x 5 In. 459.00
eapot, Ribbed, Wooden Handle, Finial, 4¾ x 6 In. 900.00
oothpick, Cat, Swag, Flower Rimmed, Urn Shape, 4 x 2½ x 3½ In. 224.00
oothpick, Penny Farthing, c.1884, 5½ In. 143.00
ray, 2 Handles, Animal Paw Feet, Pierced Curved Gallery, Gadroon, 2⅝ x 28 In. 470.00
ray, 2 Open Handles, Scrolls, Flowers Leaves, Gorham, No. 0805, 29¾ x 21⅝ In. 881.00
ray, Applied Grapevine, Meriden Britannia, Rounded Rectangular, 30 x 17 In. 1020.00
ray, English, Gallery, 2 Handles, 5½ x 26½ x 16½ In. 1763.00
ray, Flowers, Scrolls, Menorah Mark, Ellis-Barker Silver Co., Birmingham, Eng., 16⅜ In. 143.00
ray, Gadroon Rims, Pierced Gallery, 2 Handles, Faux Tortoise Shell Inlay, 38 x 24 In. 826.00
ray, Grape & Leaf, Flower & Scroll Interior, 4 Grape & Leaf Feet, 2½ x 17 In. 84.00
ray, Meat, Cover, Acanthus & Berry, Old Sheffield, Marked, W.W., 12 x 20 x 15 In. *illus* 403.00
ray, Meat, Cover, Egg & Dart Border, Family Crests, Oval, c.1880, 16 x 26 x 20 In. *illus* 695.00
ray, Oval, Crest & Motto, Handles, 4-Footed, 27¾ x 18 In. 823.00
ray, Oval, Rococo Scrolls, Flower Cartouches, 27½ x 17½ In. 480.00
ray, Oval, Shaped, Cutout Heart Handles, Pierced Scrollwork, c.1840, 27 x 16 In. 112.00
ray, Round, Webster, Crown, 12 & 15 In., 2 Piece 146.00
ray, Rounded Rectangular, Handles, Shell, Floral, Vine & Berry Border, 27 x 17 In. 288.00
ray, Serving, Continental, Rococo Style, Scroll & Acanthus Rim, Handles, 27 In. 240.00
ray, Serving, Stepped Border, Scroll & Shell Rim, Cast Handles, 30 In. 189.00
ray, Sheffield, Cutout Rim, 11 x 16 In. 82.00
ray, Sheffield, Hand Chased, Footed, Galleried, England, 17 x 24 In. 263.00
ray, Sheffield, Mirror, Ball Feet, c.1900, 2½ x 12 x 15 In. 292.00
ray, Sheffield, On Copper, Tin Coating, Footed, 2 Handles, Applied Flowers, 1800s 531.00
ray, Tea, Gadroon, Shell, Handles, 4-Footed, England, 1½ In. 690.00
rophy, Chalice Shape, Safety Rider, 19th Century, 7½ In. 55.00
rophy, France, Marble Base, c.1896, 14¼ In. 690.00
rophy, Pierpoint Mfg. Co., 19th Century, 6¾ In. 303.00
ureen, Baltimore, Oval, Gadroon Rim, Footed, Domed Cover, Gorham, 10 x 13 In. 1200.00
ureen, Bell Form Cover, Fluted, Flared Rim, Handle, Artichoke Knop, 13 x 17 In. 978.00
ureen, Cover, Sheffield, Oval, Gadroon Borders, Loop Handles, Finial, 16⅛ In. 2400.00
ureen, Empire, American, 19th Century, 12 x 12 In. 88.00
ureen, Sauce, Oval Bombe, Cauliflower Finial, Reeded Handles, Paw Feet, 5 x 7 In., Pair 499.00
ase, Grape & Leaf Design, Footed, Sheffield, England, 12 x 5 In. 40.00
ase, Josef Hoffmann, Circular Foot, Marked, c.1908, 7¾ In. 9000.00
/arming Dish, Cover, Tree & Well, Oval, Handles, Scroll Supports, Panels, 15 x 26 In. 1175.00
/arming Plate, Hinged Lid, Scroll Handles, Old Sheffield, c.1825, 11 x 9 In. *illus* 400.00
/arming Stand, Domed Cover, Round Reserve, 4-Footed, Lion Finial, 22 x 16 In. 1062.00
'atch Holder, Monkey Holding Pot, Sitting Under Palm Tree, Bronze Tone Wash, Boston 525.00
/hiskey Flask, Fish Shape, Towle, Marked, 6 In. 168.00
/ine Coaster, George III, Sheffield, Gadroon Rim, Wood Base, c.1785, 6¼ In., Pair 529.00
/ine Coaster, Round Lobed Body, Gadroon Rim, Wood Bottom, 5⅜ In., 4 Piece 325.00
'ine Cooler, Campana, Gadroon Rim, Oak Leaf Handles, Liner, Sheffield, 10 In., Pair 3360.00
/ine Cooler, Crested, Raised On Four Supports, 10¾ x 12 In., Pair 1645.00
/ine Cooler, Footed, Handles, Lobed Body, Cylindrical Bottle Holder, 9¼ In., Pair 1003.00
/ine Cooler, Regency, Banded, Lion Mask, Drop Ring Handles, Liner, 8 x 8 In., Pair 2937.00
'ine Cooler, Round, Bulbous, Fluted At Base, Let In Shield, Old Sheffield, 7 x 9 In., Pair 489.00
ine Cooler, Sheffield, 4 Acanthus Legs, Hoop Handles, 1829, 8½ In., Pair 3600.00
/ine Cooler, Tapered, Pail, Applied Reeded Bands, Ring Handles, Rogers, 8 In., Pair 1534.00

ILVER, SHEFFIELD, *see Silver Plate; Silver-English categories.*

ILVER-AMERICAN. American silver is listed here. Coin and sterling silver are included. lost of the sterling silver listed in this book is subdivided by country. There are also other ieces of silver and silver plate listed under special categories, such as Candelabrum, Napkin ing, Silver Flatware, Silver Plate, Silver-Sterling, and Tiffany Silver. For information about makers and arks, see *Kovels' American Silver Marks: 1650 to the Present.*

asket, Applied Leaves, Scroll Border, Round, Coin, Gelston & Co., 10 x 13 In. *illus* 1150.00
asket, Boat Shape, Grape Cluster, Leaf, Vine, Swing Handle, c.1870, 7 x 6 x 5¼ In. 1912.00

Silver Plate, Tray, Meat, Cover, Egg & Dart Border, Family Crests, Oval, c.1880, 16 x 26 x 20 In.
$695.00

Silver Plate, Warming Plate, Hinged Lid, Scroll Handles, Old Sheffield, c.1825, 11 x 9 In.
$400.00

Silver-American, Basket, Applied Leaves, Scroll Border, Round, Coin, Gelston & Co., 10 x 13 In.
$1150.00

Silver-American, Coffee Set, Engraved Panels, Pedestal Base, Watson, 9¾ In., 4 Piece
$495.00

S

Silver-American, Dish, Cover, Repousse, Serpentine Edge, Coin, Allcock & Allen, c.1815, 4 ½ x 7 In. $960.00

Silver-American, Gravy Set, Arts & Crafts, Hammered, Bowl, Plate, Ladle, Frank Smith Silver Co., 3 x 4 In. $415.00

Silver-American, Julep Cup, Beaded Lip, Coin, Fletcher & Bennett, Louisville, Ky., c.1850 $633.00

TIP

Be sure to rinse a piece of silver until all of the polish is removed. If some remains in the crevices, it will continue to react and may lead to corrosion. A toothpick or toothbrush will help you get the polish out of crevices.

S

Basket, Round, Bead Border, Engraved Initials, William F. Ladd, c.1830, 13 In. 1440.00
Basket, Vertical Ribs, Ogee Flared Rim, Ball Tompkins & Black, 12 ½ In. 999.00
Beaker, Applied Rim, Foot, Engraved, A. Metcalfe Steele, c.1854, 3 ½ In. 300.00
Beaker, Cylindrical, Applied Bands, Joseph Lawrence Stephens, c.1820, 3 In. 9600.00
Berry Set, Twist Handle, Engraved Design, Shell Bow Spoon, Bailey & Co., c.1855. 200.00
Berry Spoon, Repousse, Leaf, Gilt Bowl, Gorham, c.1870, 9 ½ In. 359.00
Berry Spoon, Shaped Bowl, Repousse, c.1868-96, 9 In. 287.00
Bonbon Scoop, Gilt, Shell, Wave Terminal, Stem, Pierced Bowl, c.1900, 10 ¾ In. 418.00
Bonbon Scoop, Pierced Bowl, Ribbon, Scroll, Ivory Leaf Handle, Gorham, c.1890, 5 In. 478.00
Bonbon Spoon, Openwork Handle, Ribbon Stem, Reticulated Bowl, 9 In. 388.00
Bonbon Spoon, Sunflower, Leaf Form Terminal, Flower, Leaf Bowl, c.1870, 6 ½ In. 597.00
Bowl, 3-Footed, Repousse Border, c.1903, 2 ½ x 5 In. 179.00
Bowl, Applied Leaf & Bird Decorations, Copper Dragonfly, Gorham, 5 In. 1912.00
Bowl, Applied Roses, Scalloped Rim, Monogram, 12 In. 489.00
Bowl, Art Nouveau, Repousse, Bulbous Sides, Shreve, Crump & Low, 8 In. 881.00
Bowl, Arthur Stone, 1937, 3 ½ x 7 In. 205.00
Bowl, Arts & Crafts, Hammered, Lotus Shape, Cellini Craft, 2 x 9 In. 224.00
Bowl, Blossom, Irregular Rim, Hammered, Gilt, G. W. Shiebler, c.1880, 5 ½ In. 1015.00
Bowl, Center, Footed, Richard Woods & Co., c.1925, 5 ½ x 9 In. 292.00
Bowl, Center, Spreading Foot, Scrolls, Masks, William B. Kerr & Co., 9 ¾ In. 294.00
Bowl, Centerpiece, Oval, Round Pedestal, Flowers, Ram's Heads, Gorham, c.1888, 13 In. 2640.00
Bowl, Cover, Woodside Sterling Co., Jensen Style, Early 20th Century, 6 In. 382.00
Bowl, Dominick & Haff, Early 20th Century, 2 ¼ x 8 In., Pair 293.00
Bowl, Elliptical Shape, 4 S-Scroll Supports, Alfredo Sciarrotta, c.1940, 13 ¾ In. 812.00
Bowl, Embossed Flowers, Cattails, Sterling, Simpson, Hall & Miller, 6 In. 50.00
Bowl, Flared Rim, Hammered, Pedestal Base, Dodge, c.1929, 2 ½ x 7 ½ In. 1150.00
Bowl, Flower Band, Gadroon Border, Embossed, John Wanamaker, 9 ⅛ In. 66.00
Bowl, Francis I, Reed & Barton, c.1956, 4 ½ x 8 In. 780.00
Bowl, Francis I, Reed & Barton, 1907, 11 ½ In. 1135.00
Bowl, Fruit, Floral Embossed Edge, Kirk & Sons, 10 x 2 In. 250.00
Bowl, Fruit, Lobed Body, Flower Repousse, 8 ¼ In. 403.00
Bowl, Fruit Shape, Textured, Leaves, Stem, Crab, Gorham, c.1888, 2 x 6 x 4 In., Pair. 1792.00
Bowl, Horn Style Handles, Geometric Band, Ruffled Rim, Shiebler & Co., 4 ½ In. 3835.00
Bowl, Impressed Marks, No. 839, Randahl, 8 x 2 In. 240.00
Bowl, Japanese Style, Mixed Metal, 3-Footed, Hammered, Birds, Flowers, c.1882, 8 ¾ In. 5838.00
Bowl, Mixed Metal, Round, 3 Ball Feet, Hammered, Applied Fish, Crab, Whiting, c.1890, 7 In. 2880.00
Bowl, Monogram, No. 127, Spaulding & Gorham, 9 ½ x 2 In. 270.00
Bowl, On Stand, Round, Engraved Scroll Border, Monogram, Eoff & Phyfe, c.1844, 5 ¾ In. 360.00
Bowl, Openwork, Scroll Border, Looping Openwork, Whiting, 2 x 10 ½ In. 144.00
Bowl, Oyster Shell Shape, Raised Shell Feet, Gorham, c.1890, 1 ¼ x 5 x 2 ½ In. 567.00
Bowl, Pierced, Boat Shape, Floral Border, 4-Footed, Gorham, 2 ¾ x 7 ½ In. 269.00
Bowl, Presentation, Spreading Foot, Molded Edges, Engraved, Gorham, c.1935, 9 ¾ In. 245.00
Bowl, Repousse, Fern Fronds, Flowers, Drop Ring Handles, Footed, Square 11 ½ In. 7475.00
Bowl, Repousse Flower Border, Scrolling Rim, Reed & Barton, 12 ¾ x 10 ¼ In. 502.00
Bowl, Revere Style, E.G. Webster & Son, 4 ½ x 9 In. 295.00
Bowl, Scalloped Flower Repousse Rim, Oval, Monogram, 7 ½ In. 173.00
Bowl, Scalloped Rim, Acanthus, Scrolls, Gold Washed, Gorham, 9 ⅜ In. 441.00
Bowl, Towle, 5 x 6 ¾ In. 88.00
Bowl, Trimmed With Strawberry Clusters, c.1900, 3 ½ x 12 ¼ In. 418.00
Bowl, Underplate, Family Crest, Alphabet Borders, Gorham, 1902, 8 x 5 In. 1150.00
Bowl, Vegetable, Open, Oval, Reeded Rim, Monogram, Towle, 9 In., Pair. 235.00
Bowl, Vegetable, Windsor, Ogee Rim, Lobed Sides, Divided, Reed & Barton, 11 ½ In. 235.00
Box, Tobacco, Embossed Inscription, Solace, Gorham, 3 ½ In. 58.00
Brandy Spoon, Pointed Antique, Reed & Barton, 4 ¾ In., Set Of 6 225.00
Bread Tray, Flower Repousse Border, 12 In. 748.00
Bread Tray, Francis I, Monogram, Inscribed, Reed & Barton, c.1957, 2 x 12 x 8 In. 537.00
Bread Tray, Francis I, Reed & Barton, c.1907, 11 ¾ x 7 ½ In. 420.00
Bread Tray, Repousse Flower Border, Oval, Reed & Barton, 11 ¾ In. 354.00
Bread Tray, Stradivari, Wallace, 5 ½ x 10 In. 176.00
Butter, Cover, Waisted Base, Scrolled Handles, Flower, J.R. Wendt, c.1880, 5 x 7 x 6 In. 1912.00
Butter Knife, Bird's Nest, Gorham, c.1865, 8 In. 1434.00
Butter Knife, Master, Banded Stem, Dot Pattern, Cow, Shaped Blade, c.1860, 8 In. 1195.00
Caddy Spoon, Hammered, Brass Butterfly On Handle, c.1880, 4 In. 521.00
Cake Knife, Applied Wave, Flower Handle, Japanese Style Flower, c.1880, 10 In. 836.00
Cake Plate, Cutout, Initials FBY In Center, Gorham, c.1913, 1 ½ x 11 In. 175.00

Cake Plate, Husk Swags, Reeded, Flared Foot, 11 In.. . . . 206.00
Cake Plate, Openwork, Floral & Scroll, Pedestal Base, George A. Henckel & Co., 12 In. . . . 460.00
Cake Plate, Reticulated, Renaissance Revival, J.E. Caldwell & Co., 11 In. . . . 411.00
Cake Server, Beaded Edges, Etched With A Fish, c.1895, 7¼ In. . . . 209.00
Candelabra are listed in the Candelabrum category.
Candlesnuffer, 10 In. . . . 41.00
Candlesticks are listed in their own category.
Cann, Cup, Baluster Shape, Stepped Foot, C-Scroll Handle, W. Holmes, Boston, 5¼ In. . . . 3738.00
Card Case, Open Scroll Work, Dragon, Peacock, Late 1800s, 4 x 2 In.. . . . 70.00
Card Case, Rectangular, Flowers, Mirror, Leather Lined, Chain, Pad, Pencil, c.19003 x 2 In. . . . 239.00
Carving Set, Mandarin Pattern, Whiting Division, Gorham, c.1920, 3 Piece . . . 70.00
Centerpiece, Boat Shape, Serpentine Rim, Handles, Chrysanthemum, Leaf, 8 x 23 In. . . . 3450.00
Centerpiece, Undulating Sides, Base, Decorated Knop, Reed & Barton, 1929, 6 x 12 x 10 In. . . . 403.00
Centerpiece, Urn, c.1940, 11½ x 12½ In. . . . 643.00
Chalice, Gold, Diamond, Swag & Leaf, Jenkins & Jenkins, c.1915, 9 In. . . . 7170.00
Cheese Scoop, Faceted Stem, Oval Terminal, Mouse At Base, c.1880, 8½ In. . . . 598.00
Cheese Scoop, Flared Stem, Shaped Terminal, Cow's Head, Gilt, c.1850 . . . 777.00
Cheese Scoop, Twist Stem, Handle, Embossed Cat, Mouse, Whiting Mfg., c.1880, 8¾ In. . . . 897.00
Claret Jug, Ball Shape, Cylindrical Neck, Reed & Barton, 1899, 14½ In.. . . . 1175.00
Claret Jug, Figural, Duck, Glass Body, Engraved Feathers, Enameled Eyes, c.1900, 12 In. . . . 3750.00
Cocktail Fork Set, Overture Pattern, National, 6 In., 12 Piece. . . . 176.00
Coffee Set, Creamer, Sugar, Cover, Flowers, Leaves, Handles, Gorham, 8½ In. . . . 1410.00
Coffee Set, Engraved Panels, Pedestal Base, Watson, 9¾ In., 4 Piece . . . *illus* 495.00
Coffee Set, Repousse, Floral Band, Pedestal Base Pot, Stieff Co., c.1941, 3 Piece. . . . 1840.00
Coffee Urn, Vase Shape, Engraved, Detachable Burner, Krider & Biddle, c.1865, 16 In. . . . 2640.00
Coffeepot, Baluster Shape, Domed Foot, Scroll Spout, Gorham, c.1925, 32 In.. . . . 10200.00
Coffeepot, Creamer, Queen Anne Style, Sterling, Ebonized Handle, 10⅝ & 5¼ In. . . . 323.00
Coffeepot, Hinged Lid, Urn Knop, Wood Handle, Swan's Neck, Federal, 14 x 12¾ In.. . . . 1725.00
Coffeepot, Turkish Style, Baluster, Repousse, Applied Leaves, Gorham, c.1891, 9¼ In. . . . 3840.00
Communion Plate, Dome Lid, Flower & Ball Knop, Presentation Inscription, 1815, 7 x 10 In. . . . 881.00
Compote, Cupid, Flower Garland, Reticulated Dome Base, Clam Shell, 8 In. . . . 502.00
Compote, Footed, Floral Handles, Column Feet, Gorham, 2¼ x 9 x 5¼ In. . . . 402.00
Compote, Francis I, Inscribed, Reed & Barton, 1907, 4¾ x 8 In., Pair. . . . 956.00
Compote, Graff, Washbourne & Dunn, Scrolled Rim, c.1930, 4¾ x 10½ In. . . . 321.00
Compote, Pedestal, Gorham, c.1970, 4½ x 10 In. . . . 293.00
Compote, Plate, Bowl, Francis I, Holloware, Reed & Barton, c.1948 . . . 1265.00
Compote, Schmitz, Moore & Co., c.1920, 3½ x 8¾ In. . . . 146.00
Cream Ladle, Bird's Nest, Gilt Bowl, c.1865, 6¼ In. . . . 1793.00
Cream Ladle, Faceted, Beaded Shaft, Bucket Shaped Gilt Bowl, c.1866, 6¾ In. . . . 538.00
Creamer, Bigelow Bros. & Kennard, Boston, c.1850. . . . 96.00
Creamer, Flower, Acanthus Spout, C-Scroll Handle, 2¼ x 3¾ x 2¾ In. . . . 52.00
Creamer, Pear Shape, Scroll Handle, Molded Foot, c.1750, 3⅜ In. . . . 1200.00
Cruet Stand, Leaf Scrolled Handle, 6 Bottles, Stoppers, 15 x 8 In. . . . 420.00
Cup, Cylindrical, Rounded Base, Lewis Fueter, c.1780, 1⅝ In. . . . 960.00
Cup, New Orleans, Hollow Cast Scroll Handle, c.1860, 3½ In. . . . 2468.00
Cup & Saucer, Palmette Border, Gadroon, D-Shape Handle, Gorham, c.1875, 2½ In. . . . 358.00
Cup Set, Punch, Orange Shape, Branch Handles, Leaves, Gorham, c.1886, 2 In., 12 Piece . . . 4182.00
Demitasse Set, Pot, Creamer, Sugar, Bulbous, Gorham, 9 In., 3 Piece . . . 1763.00
Demitasse Spoon, Vine Stems, Leaf, Fruit, Flower Shaped, c.1880, 6 Piece . . . 155.00
Demitasse Spoon, Wave Handle, Medallion, Gorham, Marked, 3¾ In., 4 Piece. . . . 179.00
Desk Tray, Art Nouveau, Gorham, Harold Perry Erskine, Pond, Fish, 10½ In. . . . 3408.00
Dish, Cover, Repousse, Serpentine Edge, Coin, Allcock & Allen, c.1815, 4½ x 7 In.. . . . *illus* 960.00
Dish, Cover, Vegetable, Hexagonal, Monogram, Wreath Mark, Watson, c.1929 . . . 184.00
Dish, Footed, Flared, Demilune, Lion Form Feet, Triangular Base, Gorham, 2⅞ In.. . . . 264.00
Dish, Scroll Rim, J. E. Caldwell & Co., 2½ x 8 x 10¾ In.. . . . 154.00
Dish, Sweetmeat, Reticulated, Teardrop Shape, S-Scroll, Howard, c.1900, 3¾ x 9¾ In. . . . 264.00
Dish, Wallace, Mid 20th Century, 1¼ x 9¼ In.. . . . 60.00
Dresser Set, Repousse, Hand Mirror, Comb, Hairbrush, c.1890, 12 In., 3 Piece . . . 179.00
Dust Pan, Tulip Trim, Reed & Barton, c.1900, 2 x 8¾ x 7½ In.. . . . 388.00
Egg Set, Parcel Gilt, Cracked Egg Shape, Chicken Feet, Gorham, c.1872, 24 Piece . . . 5400.00
Epergne, Footed, Repousse, 10 In.. . . . 403.00
Ewer, Baluster Shape, Pedestal Foot, Chased, Roses, Scrolls, Sullivan & Co., c.1940, 14 In. . . . 1200.00
Ewer, Classical Baluster Shape, Leafy Scroll Handle, Shell Spout, Coin, 13 x 7 In. . . . 4313.00
Ewer, Flower Repousse, Rams Head Handle, Andrew Ellicott Warner, 16 In. . . . 4887.00
Ewer, Grapevines, Clusters, Domed Foot, S.L. Hellman, 1936, 13¾ x 5½ In.. . . . 1560.00
Ewer, Repousse, Grape Cluster, Vine, Handles, Baluster Form, c.1870, 15¾ In. . . . 7170.00

Silver-American, Ladle, Fiddle & Thread Handle, Coin, Duhme, c.1850, 11½ In.
$288.00

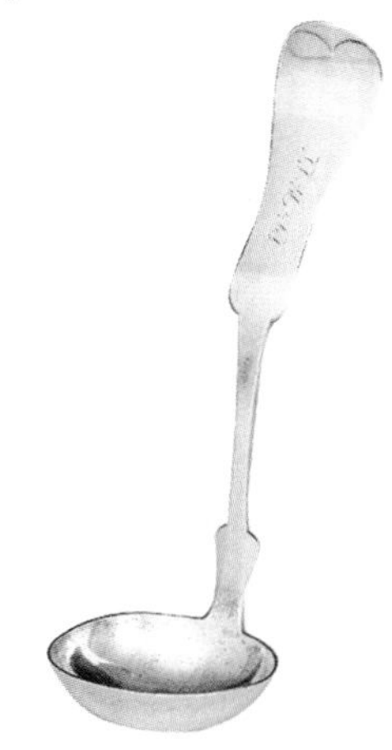

Silver-American, Ladle, Shell, Twisted Shank, Monogram, Coin, Duhme & Co., 10¾ In.
$288.00

TIP

Never put silverware and stainless-steel flatware in the dishwasher basket together. The stainless can damage the silver.

Silver-American, Pepper Shaker, Cover, Molded Borders, Scroll Handle, J. Blowers, c.1740, 4 In.
$7800.00

Silver-American, Pitcher, Baltimore Rose, Schofield, 9 ¼ In.
$1980.00

Silver-American, Pitcher, Flowers, Repousse, Cartouche, MLP, Ball, Black & Co., c.1851, 10 ¾ In.
$2100.00

Silver-American, Pitcher, Lobed, Repousse, Monogram, Coin, Ball, Tompkins & Black, c.1850, 10 In.
$840.00

Silver-American, Pitcher, Morning Glories, Scalloped Rim, Marked, Bailey & Co., 11 ¼ In.
$1400.00

S

Fish Slice, Coin Silver, Pierced Scimitar Blade, Mother-Of-Pearl Handle, c.1846, 12 In. 245.00
Fish Slice, Duhme & Co., Wafer Tray, Twist Shank, Engraved Handle, 12 ¼ In. 345.00
Fish Slice, Twig & Leaf, Pierced Gilt Blade, Etched Leaf, Scroll, c.1860-70, 12 In. 1553.00
Flask, Baluster Shape, Chased, Waterscape, Hammered, William B. Durgin, c.1880, 4 In. 2400.00
Fork Set, Fiddle Handle, Rounded Fins, William I. Tenney, c.1852, 7 ½ In., 12 Piece 805.00
Fork Set, Seafood, Parcel Gilt, Animal Shaped Terminals, Shiebler, c.1880, 6 In., 6 Piece 1320.00
Fork Set, Viola, Monogram, Wood & Hughes, 7 ⅛ In., 12 Piece 176.00
Frame, Lunaria, Green Velvet Mat, Easel Stand, Art Nouveau, 8 ⅝ x 7 ⅝ In. 881.00
Glove Stretcher, Kirk 12.00
Goblet, Deep Octagonal Paneled, Scroll Cartouches, Flowers, c.1853, 6 ⅝ In., Pair 1116.00
Goblet, New Orleans, Lake Scene, c.1840, 5 ¼ In. 2468.00
Goblet, Rolled Reeded Lip, Gilt Interior, Monogram, International, 6 ½ In., 6 Piece 518.00
Goblet, Water, Celestis, Monogram, Dunkirk Silversmith, 6 ¼ In., 6 Piece 1140.00
Goblet Set, York Pattern, Chalice Shape, Chicago Silver Co., 5 ¼ In., 6 Piece 489.00
Gravy Boat, Arthur Stone, c.1937, 3 ½ x 7 In. 205.00
Gravy Boat, Flower Repousse, Engraved Handle, Hoof Feet, 8 In. 748.00
Gravy Boat, Gadroon Rim, 3-Footed, Leaf Capped, Double Scroll Handle, 7 ¼ In. 4500.00
Gravy Boat, Tray, Monogram, Inscribed, Reed & Barton, 1907, 5 ½ x 10 x 6 In. 4481.00
Gravy Boat, Underplate, Royal Danish, International, 9 In. 263.00
Gravy Set, Arts & Crafts, Hammered, Bowl, Plate, Ladle, Frank Smith Silver Co., 3 x 4 In. *illus* 415.00
Hand Mirror, Girl's Head, Flower Border, 20th Century, 11 x 5 In. 538.00
Hot Water Urn, Chased, Repousse, Applied Handles, Lion's Heads, Calvert, 17 In. 3450.00
Hot Water Urn, Male Masks, Scrolls, Palmette, Drop Loops Handles, Globular, c.1870 ..... 4481.00
Ice Cream Server, Flower Handle, Engraved Blade, Gorham, 11 ¼ In. 161.00
Ice Cream Slice, Gilt Blade, Etched, Gorham, c.1880, 11 ¾ In. 1314.00
Ice Cream Slice, Halberd Shape, Stippled Ground, 11 ¾ In. 956.00
Jar, Cover, Flower Repousse, Baluster Shape, 4 ½ In. 546.00
Jelly Slice, Chamfered, Emperor Head Terminal, Gilt Blade, c.1870, 9 ½ In. 478.00
Jewelry Box, Motorboat, Velvet Covered Seat, Man's, c.1920, 2 x 10 x 2 In. 1075.00
Jewelry Box, Woods & Chatellier, c.1900, 4 x 10 ½ x 6 In. 600.00
Jug, Claret, Baluster, Cartouche Flowers, Bailey & Co., 10 ½ In. 1725.00
Julep Cup, Beaded Lip, Coin, Fletcher & Bennett, Louisville, Ky., c.1850 ..... *illus* 633.00
Julep Cup, Coin, Applied Beaded Lip 630.00
Julep Cup, Coin, Applied Flower Rings, 2 ¾ In. 230.00
Julep Cup, Coin, Applied Rings, Cylinder, Stamped, 3 ⅞ In. 460.00
Julep Cup, Flared Lip, Applied Rim, Beading, Banded Foot, 3 In. 1093.00
Julep Cup, Presidential, Johnson, Kennedy, Mark J. Scearce, 4 Piece 1035.00
Julep Cup, Tapered, Cylindrical, Monogram, International, 3 ¾ In., 8 Piece 1057.00
Kettle, Aesthetic, Copper, Squat Oval Body, Reeded Dome Lid, Gorham, 11 ¾ In. 764.00
Kettle, Hot Water, Stand, Repousse Bird, Flowers, Chinese Figure Finial, S. Kirk, 9 In. 3248.00
Knife, Macaroni, Oval Thread Handle, Scimitar Shape, Ball Black & Co., c.1856, 10 In. 295.00
Ladle, Downturned Fiddle Handle, Coin, Anthony Rasch, 12 ½ In. 940.00
Ladle, Engraved, Monogram, Herman Duhme, Cincinnati, 11 In. 240.00
Ladle, Fiddle & Thread Handle, Coin, Duhme, c.1850, 11 ½ In. ..... *illus* 288.00
Ladle, Fiddle Handle, Oval Bowl, Monogram, Enoch Sullivan, 12 In. 2990.00
Ladle, Fiddle Handle, Pointed Fins, 1820, 12 ¼ In. 4140.00
Ladle, Fiddle Handle, Tipt Back, Oval Bowl, Scottish Hallmark, 13 ½ In. 230.00
Ladle, Fiddlehead, Downcurved Handle, 1851, 13 ¼ In. 2464.00
Ladle, Flower Bud & Leaves, Downcurved Fiddle Tipped Handle, c.1810, 15 ¼ In. 1348.00
Ladle, Leaf, Lily-Of-The-Valley Stem, Gold Washed, Pointed, Gorham, 8 ¾ In. 705.00
Ladle, Monogram, William R. Evans, Cincinnati, Mid 19th Century, 11 ½ In. 259.00
Ladle, Oval Bowl, Cut Floral Decoration, Twisted Handle, Duhme & Co., 11 In. 374.00
Ladle, Shell, Twisted Shank, Monogram, Coin, LBJ, 10 ¾ In. 288.00
Ladle, Shell, Twisted Shank, Monogram, Coin, Duhme & Co., 10 ¾ In. ..... *illus* 288.00
Ladle, Shell Bowl, Twisted Shank, 10 ¾ In. 288.00
Ladle, Stew, Coin, Scovil & Co., 8 ¾ In. 138.00
Letter Opener, Cased Wood, Polo Player Over Pumpkin Handle, 12 ¼ In. 230.00
Letter Opener, Curved Ivory Blade, Gorham, c.1880, 9 ½ In. 836.00
Loving Cup, Baluster Shape, Dolphin Handles, Feet, Mermaids, Gorham, c.1902, 10 In. 96000.00
Loving Cup, Trophy, Girdle Band, Ear Handles, Heart Shape Terminals, c.1901, 7 In. 1645.00
Mirror, Table, Reed & Barton, c.1900, 13 In. 870.00
Muffineer, Glass, Leaf, Wreath, Domed Base, Embossed, W. B. Durgin Co., c.1890, 8 ½ In. 836.00
Mug, Baluster, Circular Foot, C-Scroll Handle, Garret Eoff, c.1800, 5 ¼ In. 1044.00
Mug, Bright Cut Floral & Scroll, Hazel 1887-1888, Knowles, 3 x 2 ½ In. 200.00
Mug, C-Handle, Floral Border, Knowles, Inscribed Henry G. Dill, c.1882, 3 ½ x 4 ½ In. 288.00
Mug, Cylindrical, Engine Turned Design, Floral Cartouche, c.1862, 4 In. 345.00

Silver-American, Platter, Well & Tree, Gadroon & Flower Border, 4-Footed, Gorham, 2 x 24 x 17 In.
$1600.00

Silver-American, Soup Ladle, Fluted Bowl, Leaf Handle, c.1860, 13 ¾ In.
$1314.00

TIP

Experts say you should never put silverware in a dishwasher for several reasons: Eventually the oxidation (black highlights) will disappear, hollow-handled knives are filled with a material that will melt, and if the silver touches stainless steel it will get black spots. Be safe. Wash silver by hand.

TIP
When storing silver in an attic, remember that 97° F or more will melt the filler in some candlesticks. Heat speeds corrosion.

Silver-American, Spoon, Washington Bust, Kings Pattern, Coin, T. Harland
$1150.00

Grapefruit Spoons
"I wish they had a left-handed grapefruit spoon," said the lefty struggling to loosen the sections from the grapefruit half she was eating for breakfast. The comment made us wonder. A grapefruit spoon looks like a pointed teaspoon with serrated edges on the bowl. A right-handed spoon has serrated edges on one side—the wrong side for a person eating with the left hand. We checked. The grapefruit or citrus spoon was introduced in the 1890s. It was silver or silver plated. The bowl was pointed but not serrated, so it was good for right- and left-handed diners. The serrated spoon was a twentieth-century improvement.

Mug, Mixed Metal, Hammered, Gold Bee, Dragonfly, Copper Grass, Gorham, c.1879, 4 In. 3360.00
Mug, Presentation, Vine & Grape Leaf Scrolling, 19th Century, 4 In. 540.00
Napkin Rings are listed in their own category.
Nut Pick Set, Looped Twig Handle, Pendant Shield, Squirrel, c.1900-20, 5 ¼ In., 3 Piece 167.00
Nut Set, Francis I, Reed & Barton, 3 In., 12 Piece 597.00
Nut Set, Swan Shape, Gorham, 8 x 6 In., 3 ¾ In., 2 ½ In., 7 Piece 2464.00
Nut Spoon, Cylindrical, Beaded Bands, Domed Terminal, Pierced Flower Hood, c.1890, 9 In.. 597.00
Olive Fork, Spoon, Aesthetic, Leaf & Berry, Twig Stem, Monogram, Gorham 521.00
Olive Pick, Branch Form Stem, Cast Olive, Leaf Terminal, Gorham, c.1880, 4 In., Pair 388.00
Olive Spoon, Pierced Serrated Edge, Coin, Adolphe Himmel, c.1877, 10 ¾ In. 176.00
Oyster Spoon, Barbed Twig Stem, Shell Bowl, Gorham, c.1880, 5 ¾ In., Pair 311.00
Pepper Castor, Salt Cellar, Mixed Metal, Hammered, Applied Fish, Grass, Gorham, c.1880... 2160.00
Pepper Shaker, Cover, Molded Borders, Scroll Handle, J. Blowers, c.1740, 4 In. .... *illus* 7800.00
Pickle Fork, Hand Holding Leaf & Berries Tip, Gorham, c.1870, 7 In. 568.00
Pickle Fork, Terminal, Hand Holding Leaf With Berries, c.1865-80, 7 In. 567.00
Pickle Fork-Spoon, Twist Stem, Gilt Pierced Shaped Bowl, Gorham, 9 In. 358.00
Pie Server, Arts & Crafts, Blossom Handle, Hammered Finish, Randahl, 9 ¾ In. 345.00
Pitcher, Baltimore Rose, Schofield, 9 ¼ In. .... *illus* 1980.00
Pitcher, Classical Revival, Gorham, Short Spout, Scrolled Handle, Early 1900s, 10 In. 881.00
Pitcher, Coin Silver, C Handle, Thumbpiece, Helmet Shape Spout, c.1854, 10 x 9 In. 1150.00
Pitcher, Cover, New Orleans, c.1860, 7 ⅛ In. 4800.00
Pitcher, Edgeworth Pattern, Monogram, 1927, 8 In. 960.00
Pitcher, Flowers, Repousse, Cartouche, MLP, Ball, Black & Co., c.1851, 10 ¾ In. .... *illus* 2100.00
Pitcher, Helmet Shape, Oval Tapering Body, Rolled Beaded Borders, Coin, 7 ½ x 4 In. 403.00
Pitcher, Lobed, Repousse, Monogram, Coin, Ball, Tompkins & Black, c.1850, 10 In. .... *illus* 840.00
Pitcher, Milk, Baluster Shape, Beaded Collar, Ear Handle, Coin, c.1851, 8 In. 489.00
Pitcher, Morning Glories, Scalloped Rim, Marked, Bailey & Co., 11 ¼ In. .... *illus* 1400.00
Pitcher, Pear Shape, Repousse Oak Branches, Leaves, Acorns, 9 ¼ x 6 x 10 In. 7920.00
Pitcher, Pear Shape, Spiral, Fluted, Spout, Double Scroll Handle, 12 x 6 x 10 In. 1320.00
Pitcher, Rose Repousse, 7 ½ In. 2588.00
Pitcher, Urn Shape, Wide Spout, Footed, Monogram, Gorham, 7 ¾ In. 295.00
Pitcher, Water, Baluster, Hammered, Dragonflies, Lily Pads, Dominick & Haff, 8 ½ In. 13200.00
Pitcher, Water, Baluster Shape, Exotic Scenes, Flowers, c.1907, S. Kirk & Co., 8 In. 2880.00
Pitcher, Water, Baluster Shape, Stepped Base, Thistles, W. Thompson, c.1831, 12 ¾ In. 3360.00
Pitcher, Water, Ear Handle, Oval, S. Kirk & Co., 1925-32, 7 ¾ In. 353.00
Pitcher, Water, Fisher Silversmith, Inc., 20th Century, 10 ¼ In. 353.00
Pitcher, Water, Francis I, Monogram, Inscribed, Reed & Barton, 1907, 11 In. 5975.00
Pitcher, Water, Oval, Waisted Neck, Acanthus, Handle, 10 ¼ x 6 x 9 ¼ In. 510.00
Pitcher, Water, Oval Form, Circular Base, Floral Band, Gorham, 9 x 9 x 6 In. 1175.00
Pitcher, Water, Repousse, Chased Cherry Blossoms, Gorham, c.1914, 8 ½ In. 1135.00
Pitcher, Water, Royal Danish, International, 8 In. 263.00
Plate, Applied Die Rolled Border, Acanthus, Hayden & Gregg, c.1846, 9 In. 3220.00
Plate, Francis I, Monogram, Reed & Barton, 1907, 11 ½ In. 836.00
Plate, Reticulated, Floral Trim, c.1900, 12 In. 269.00
Plate Set, Bread, Castle Pattern, Late 19th Century, S. Kirk & Sons, 24 Piece 2990.00
Plate Set, Bread & Butter, 6 With Beaded Edge, 4 Plain, Monogram, Gorham, 10 Piece 470.00
Plate Set, Bread & Butter, Gadroon Rim, Monogram, Gorham, 6 In., 12 Piece 384.00
Plate Set, Bread & Butter, Reeded Borders, International, 6 ⅛ In., 10 Piece 411.00
Plate Set, Dessert, Chased Border, Monogram, Gorham, c.1917, 9 ¼ In., 12 Piece 4688.00
Plate Set, Dinner, Round, Shell & Leaf, Oval & Leaf Rim, Watson Co., 11 In., 12 Piece 10200.00
Plate Set, Flute Pierced Rim, Paterae, Towle, 6 In., 12 Piece 470.00
Plate Set, Francis I, 15 Dinner, 14 Bread, Reed & Barton, 10 ½ & 7 In. 26400.00
Platter, Acanthus, Berries, Husk Border, Oval, Gorham, 1928, 18 ⅜ In. 999.00
Platter, Acanthus Edge, Historic Homes, Recessed Plateau, 20 x 14 ¾ In. 1140.00
Platter, Gorham, Monogram, 10 In., 8 Piece 1003.00
Platter, Pierced Flowers, Monogram, Wallace, 17 In. 413.00
Platter, Scalloped, Shell, Leaf Cast Rim, Gorham, 20 ½ In. 719.00
Platter, Well & Tree, Gadroon & Flower Border, 4-Footed, Gorham, 2 x 24 x 17 In. .... *illus* 1600.00
Porringer, Francis I, Monogram, Reed & Barton, 1907, 2 x 6 ¼ x 4 ¾ In. 239.00
Porringer, Gorham, c.1936, 6 ¾ In. 47.00
Porringer, Keyhole Handle, Signed, TKE, Boston, c.1805 .... 5000.00
Porringer, S. Kirk & Son, 6 In. 88.00
Poultry Shears, Francis I, Stainless Steel, Reed & Barton, 1907, 10 ¾ In. 119.00
Punch Bowl, Grapevine Rim, Footed, 1895, 11 ⅜ In. 1528.00
Punch Ladle, Oval, Beveled Fins, Twisted Shank, Engraved Handle, Coin, 11 ½ In. 267.00
Punch Ladle, Oval Bowl, Rounded, Beveled Fins, Twisted Shank, 11 ½ In. 207.00

Punch Ladle, Ruffled Edge, 20th Century, 11 In. 118.00
Punch Ladle, Shell, Sharp Fins, Coin, 11 In. 196.00
Punch Ladle, Shell Bowl, Sharp Fins, Cut Decorations, 11 In. 196.00
Punch Ladle, Thumb Handle, Asa Blanchard, Lexington, c.1820, 12 In. 1320.00
Punch Ladle, Twisted Stem, Draped Female, Flared Bowl, Medallion, c.1860, 14 In. 1553.00
Punch Ladle, Twisted Stem, Stag's Head, Flower, Fluted, Gilt, Coin, c.1855, 13 ¼ In. 1015.00
Ramekin, Porcelain, Long Handle, Watson Co., Mid 20th Century, 6 In., 12 Piece 527.00
Ruler, Scroll & Shell Decoration To Upper Edge, c.1900, 10 In. 287.00
Salad Servers, Gilt Bowl, Tines, Engraved Monogram, Whiting & Co., 9 ¾ In. 353.00
Salad Servers, Gold Washed Embossed Flowers, Gorham, 10 In. 225.00
Salt, Beaded Rim, Footed, Coin, 1 ⅞ In., Pair 59.00
Salt, Bucket Shape, Flower, Loop Handles, Butterflies, c.1869, 2 x 4 x 3 In., Pair 508.00
Salt, Cobalt Blue Liner, 4-Footed, c.1850-60, 2 In. 66.00
Salt & Pepper, Alvin, 4 In. 39.00
Salt & Pepper, Francis I, Gilt Tops, Reed & Barton, 1907, 4 ¾ In. 418.00
Salt & Pepper, Strasbourg, Gorham, 4 ½ In. 43.00
Salt, Bird's Nest Shape, Bird On Edge, Plain Base, Gilt Interior, 2 In., Pair 1135.00
Salver, Arabesques Band, Wrigglework Patera, Gorham, 1871, 12 ⅛ x 9 In. 210.00
Salver, Copper, Stylized Fish, Kelp, Sailboat, Gorham, c.1901, 17 ⅛ In. 5581.00
Salver, Flower Acanthus Scrolls, Grapevine, Cluster Edge, 4 Cast Feet, 16 ½ In. 420.00
Salver, Grape Clusters, Acanthus Scrolls, Trellis Ground, 14 ¼ In. 240.00
Sardine Fork, Rope Wrapped Shaft, Winged Lion, Pierced Tines, G.W. Shiebler, c.1890, 7 In. 478.00
Sauceboat, Brandy, Underplate, Francis I, Reed & Barton, 2 ½ In. 388.00
Sauceboat, Spoon, Oval, Pedestal Foot, Leaf Borders, Loop Handle, Gorham, c.1870, 9 ½ In. .. 1320.00
Sauceboat, Stand, Reed & Barton, c.1946, 5 x 5 ½ In. 94.00
Scoop, Lily Of The Valley On Leaf, Gilt Shaped, Wood & Hughes, c.1870, 8 In. 388.00
Server, Seafood, Aesthetic, Figural, Double Tined, Shell Shape Spoon, Gorham, 11 In. 3408.00
Server, Twist Stem, Classical Medallion End, c.1860, 12 ½ In. 418.00
Server, Wirework Stem, Cast Cupid Terminal, Gilt Bowl, Tines, c.1870, 11 ½ In. 776.00
Serving Fork, Medallion, Twist Stem, Stylized Flower, Gilt Bowl, Tines, c.1863, 12 In. 777.00
Serving Fork, Snail Shell, Wave Edged Shaft, Gilt Tines, Water, Flower, c.1870, 11 In. 1314.00
Serving Spoon, Cat Tail Terminal, Shaped Bowl, Etched, G.E. Sharp, c.1870, 11 In. 1434.00
Serving Spoon, Grecian, Ribbed Gilt Bowls, Coin, Gorham, 9 In., Pair 263.00
Serving Spoon, Scrolled Bud Finial, 8 In. 420.00
Side Dish, Cover, Oval, Shaped Border, Lid, Gorham, 10 ½ x 7 ½ In. 295.00
Soup Ladle, Fluted Bowl, Leaf Handle, c.1860, 13 ¾ In. .... *illus* 1314.00
Soup Ladle, Oval, Flowers, Twist Handle, Coin, 11 ½ In. 374.00
Soup Ladle, Oval, Upturned Fiddle, Thread Handle, Beveled, Coin, c.1850, 11 ½ In. 288.00
Soup Ladle, Oval, Upturned Fiddle, Upturned Fiddle, Thread Handle, Sharp Fins, Coin, c.1850, 13 In. 330.00
Soup Ladle, Thread & Leaf Terminal, Engraved, Hayden & Gregg, c.1843, 13 ½ In. 1020.00
Soup Spoon, Dotted Oval Handle, Federal, 8 In. 173.00
Soup Tureen, Oval, Scroll Feet, Rococo, Chased, William Forbes, c.1851, 16 In. 12000.00
Spoon, Barbed Twig Stem, Oyster Shell Bowl, Gilt, Gorham, c.1880, 5 ¾ In., Pair 597.00
Spoon, Coin, Pointed End Handle, Dove, Olive Branch, Vogler, 5 ½ In. 1265.00
Spoon, Long Handle, Kalo, No. H201, 13 ¾ In. 360.00
Spoon, Olive, Gilt, Branch Shape Stem, Pierced Leaf Shape Bowl, Gorham, c.1880, 11 ⅝ In. .. 660.00
Spoon, Olive, Spear, Crescent, Star, Cylindrical, Gilt Spear, Gorham, c.1870, 10 In. 597.00
Spoon, Pointed End Handle, Dove & Olive Branch, Vogler, c.1820, 5 ¼ In. 1610.00
Spoon, Reeded, Flowerhead Terminal, Pointed Bowl, 11 ½ In. 147.00
Spoon, Thread & Fiddle Handle, Rounded Fin, Monogram, Charleston, 13 In., 2 Piece 1495.00
Spoon, Washington Bust, Kings Pattern, Coin, T. Harland .... *illus* 1150.00
Spoon Set, Demitasse, Gold Washed, Basse Taille Enamel, Watson, 12 Piece 176.00
Spoon Set, Shell Bowl, Gilt Wash, Twist Stem, Coin, Bailey & Co., 5 ½ In., 13 Piece 431.00
Spurs, Woman's, Round Boot Guard, Leather Strap, 7 ¾ In., Pair 460.00
Stand, Footed, Dominick & Haff, c.1900, 3 ½ x 11 In. 150.00
Stirrer, Lemonade, Twist Stem, Flower Bordered Handle, Dominick & Haff, 13 ¼ In. 227.00
Straw Spoon Set, Gorham, 8 ¼ In., 8 Piece 205.00
Stuffing Spoon, Engraved Scroll Tip, Monogram, George B. Sharp, c.1870, 13 In. 2032.00
Sugar, Bulbous, 2 Handles, Strap & Leaves, Circular Foot, Open, 3 ¾ x 6 ½ In. 1920.00
Sugar, Castle Pattern, Cover, Engraved Crest, S. Kirk & Son, c.1860, 9 In. 1200.00
Sugar, Cover, Paneled Oval Shape, Urn Finial, Coin, J. Richardson, 6 x 8 ½ In. 1380.00
Sugar, Cover, Tennessee, Reeded, Domed Lid, Floral Finial, Footed Form, 8 ¼ In. 2938.00
Sugar & Creamer, Cylindrical, Footed, Monogram, JLL, Watson, 6 ¾ In. 143.00
Sugar & Creamer, Round Body, Flaring Lip, 4 Lion & Hoof Feet, Becht & Hartl. 266.00
Sugar Shell, Gilt, Bundle Stem, Bird, Ball Terminal, Flower, c.1860, 6 ¼ In. .... *illus* 334.00
Sugar Tongs, Hammered, Feather Engraved, Claw Tips, G.W. Schiebler, c.1880, 3 In. 179.00

Silver-American, Sugar Shell, Gilt, Bundle Stem, Bird, Ball Terminal, Flower, c.1860, 6 ¼ In.
$334.00

Silver-American, Tea Infuser, Squash Form, Vine, Gorham, Late 19th Century, 3 ¼ x 1 ¾ In.
$1200.00

Silver-American, Tea Set, Teapot, Tray, Sugar, Creamer, Ivory Accents, EMR, Marked, Lebolt, 4 Piece
$2400.00

Silver-American, Tea Strainer, Spoon, Repousse Border, Vine Handle, Ritter & Sullivan, 7 ½ & 8 ½ In.
$748.00

TIP
Do not wrap silver in aluminum foil, newspaper, or plastic wrap. Never use rubber bands.

Silver-American, Tureen, Terrapin Shape, Cover, Shell Handle, Gilt Interior, Gorham, 2 x 5 x 3 In.
$4900.00

Silver-Continental, Letter Rack, Flowers, Figures, Panel, Pierced, 3¾ In.
$47.00

Silver-Continental, Plate, 2 Cherubs, Rabbit, Acanthus Scrolls, Cartouches, 1895, 9¼ In.
$254.00

Silver-Continental, Tray, Art Nouveau, Flowers, Early 20th Century, 5½ x 9½ In.
$200.00

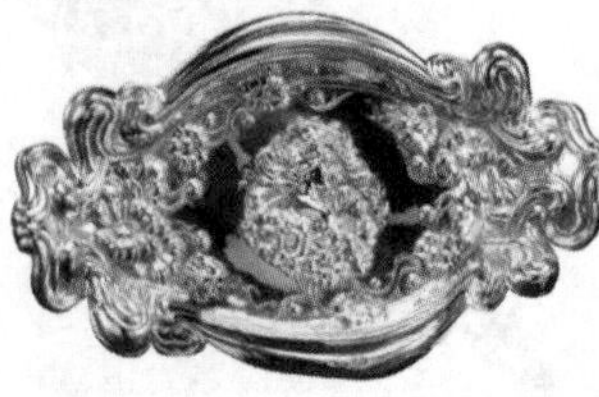

Tablespoon, Bright Cut, Engraved Initials, William Wilson & Son, 8⅜ In. 74.00
Tankard, Dome Lid, Flared, Cylindrical Bowl, Ram's Head, S-Scroll Handle, 6 x 4 In. 1610.00
Tea & Coffee Set, Berry Finials, Monogram, Bigelow Bros. & Kennard, 9 In., 4 Piece 1320.00
Tea & Coffee Set, Medallion, Gorham, c.1865, 6 Piece 3818.00
Tea & Coffee Set, Reeded Sides, Ivory Handle Insulators, 5 Piece 4025.00
Tea & Coffee Set, Tray, Hampton Court, Reed & Barton, 1900s, 7 Piece 5400.00
Tea & Coffee Set, Vase Shape, Oval Base, Chased, Gorham, c.1907, 12 In., 6 Piece 4560.00
Tea Caddy, Cover, Bulbous, Flowers, Leaves, Leafy Handles, Ring Foot, 7 In. 2880.00
Tea Caddy, Egyptian Style, Enamel, Sunflowers, Lotus, Vase Shape, Shiebler, c.1890, 7 In. 14400.00
Tea Caddy, Oval, Flat Chased, Hinged Cover, 18th Century, 5¼ x 4⅞ In. 2938.00
Tea Infuser, Hinged Lid, Golf Club Shape, 20th Century, 6½ In. 59.00
Tea Infuser, Squash Form, Vine, Gorham, Late 19th Century, 3¼ x 1¾ In. .... *illus* 1200.00
Tea Set, C-Scroll Handles, Stepped Base, Monogram, S. Kirk & Son, 7 Piece 1725.00
Tea Set, Garlands, Beaded, Hexagonal Body & Foot, Redlich & Co., N.Y., 5 Piece 1508.00
Tea Set, Gorham, Coffeepot, Teapot, Creamer, Sugar 1521.00
Tea Set, Kettle, Warming Stand, Pot, Sugar, Cover, Waste Pail, 5 Piece 1035.00
Tea Set, Leafy Bands, Lobed, Stepped Foot, Coin, Baldwin Gardiner, 10-In. Teapot, 3 Piece 3450.00
Tea Set, Pear Form, Ball Finial, Wood Handle, Monogram, Gorham, 1941, 6 Piece 1495.00
Tea Set, Round, Flower Repousse, C Handle, Bun Finial, Whiting, 3 Piece 920.00
Tea Set, Silver & Copper, Hammered Finish, Bird, Butterfly, Flowers, Gorham, 1902 .... 5100.00
Tea Set, Teapot, Creamer, Sugar, Kettle, Lampstand, Whiting Mfg. Co., c.1885, 5 Piece 10200.00
Tea Set, Teapot, Sugar, Waste, Kettle, Lampstand, Samuel Kirk, c.1830, 15½ In. 5938.00
Tea Set, Teapot, Tray, Sugar, Creamer, Ivory Accents, EMR, Marked, Lebolt, 4 Piece. .... *illus* 2400.00
Tea Strainer, Hollowware, Engraved, Initials, Reed & Barton, c.1894, 7 In. 68.00
Tea Strainer, Pierced Clover, Leaf, Berry Stem, Flower, Howard & Co., c.1870, 8 In. 311.00
Tea Strainer, Spoon, Repousse Border, Vine Handle, Ritter & Sullivan, 7½ & 8½ In. .... *illus* 748.00
Tea Tray, Oval, Tab Feet, Greek Key Border, Mask Handles, Gorham, c.1868, 26 In. 4560.00
Teapot, Flower & Fruit Bands, Footed, J. Crawford, Marked, 9½ x 11½ In. 522.00
Teapot, Oval, Stepped Foot, Fluted, Scroll Spout, Wood Handle, Joseph Hall, c.1810, 11 In. 1020.00
Teapot, Repousse, Gorham 1150.00
Teaspoon, Coin, Duhme & Co., Mid 19th Century, 5¾ In., 10 Piece 146.00
Teaspoon, Fiddle Tipt, Monogram, Hotchkiss & Schreuder, 12 Piece 60.00
Tomato Server, Cattail & Butterfly Tip, Engraved, Krider Mark, c.1870, 9¾ In. 598.00
Toothpick Holder, Francis I, Reed & Barton, 1907, 2¼ x 3½ In. 95.00
Toothpick Holder Set, Francis I, Reed & Barton, 2¼ x 3½ In., 4 Piece 418.00
Tray, Acanthus Scrolls, Trellis Ground, Grapevine, Cluster, 35 x 24½ In. 1140.00
Tray, Black Starr & Frost, Scroll & Husk Wreath, Early 20th Century, 18 In. 1410.00
Tray, Cutout Shaped Handles, Monogram, Reed & Barton, 25 x 17 In. 1232.00
Tray, Flower Repousse Border, Acanthus Border, Oval, 14 In. 805.00
Tray, Medici, Reed & Barton, 14 In. 118.00
Tray, No. 2201, Oval, Fisher, 20th Century, 7 x 9 In. 82.00
Tray, Open Handles, Monogram, Gorham, 1¼ x 22¼ x 16 In. 880.00
Tray, Oval, Scroll Feet, Incised Border, Floral Scroll Surface, 11⅜ In. 568.00
Tray, Pierced Border, J. E. Caldwell, 20th Century, 12 In. 235.00
Tray, Rose Bouquet Patter, Fishern, 16 In. 322.00
Tray, Scalloped Edge, Marked, Kalo, 10¾ In. 660.00
Trophy, Golf, Chalice Shape, C-Scroll Handles, Redlich & Co., c.1919, 10 x 9 In. 288.00
Trophy, Horse, Goblet Shape, Our Cherrycote, Ritz Purse, c.1931, 7½ In. 1265.00
Trophy Cup, Urn Shape, Engraved, Troop Officer's Course, Kirk & Son, c.1929, 13 In. 649.00
Tumbler, Tapered, Reeded Top & Bottom Rim, E. Kinsey, c.1861, 3½ In., Pair 649.00
Tureen, Terrapin Shape, Cover, Shell Handle, Gilt Interior, Gorham, 2 x 5 x 3 In. .... *illus* 4900.00
Tweezers, Woman Shaped Handle, Art Nouveau, c.1910, 6¼ In. 107.00
Urn, Cover, Classical Revival, Durgin, Cobalt Blue Glass, Early 1900s, 11 In. 235.00
Vase, Bud, Francis I, Reed & Barton, 1907, 6 In. 597.00
Vase, Bud, Trumpet Flared Edge, Roses, Acanthus Leaves, Stieff, 10¼ In. 920.00
Vase, Chrysanthemum, Trumpet, Flared Base, 4 Scrolled Feet, C-Form Handles, 14 In. 4200.00
Vase, Embossed Flowering Medallion, Cylindrical, Sterling, 6¼ In. 150.00
Vase, Trophy, Sterling, Trumpet Form, Domed, Trumpet Foot, 1929, 18½ In. 411.00
Vase, Trumpet, Applied Cherubs, Scroll Band, Gorham, c.1860, 6¾ In. 546.00
Vase, Trumpet, Watson Company, 17 x 9 In. 760.00
Vase, Trumpet Shape, Swag & Acanthus, Black Starr & Frost, Late 1800s, 10 x 5 In. 920.00
Waiter, Stuart, Round, Shaped Rim, Monogram, Gorham, c.1929, 12¼ In. 295.00
Whistle & Rattle, Mermaid, Blowing & Trumpet, Bells, Moons, c.1805, 4½ x 28 In. 1998.00
Wine, Chased Ivy Vine, Berries, Punch Work, R. & W. Wilson, c.1850, 6½ In., Pair 940.00
Wine Coaster, Magnum Size, Flared Rim, Scrollwork, Howard & Co., 8¾ x 2 In., Pair 1140.00

SILVER-ASIAN

Box, Cigar, Repousse Scene, Tiger, Dragon, Hinged Lid, 2 3/4 x 9 1/4 In.. 150.00

SILVER-AUSTRIAN

Bowl, Alpaca, Handles, Josef Hoffmann, c.1925-31, 7 1/2 x 11 In.. 38400.00
Pitcher, Water, Jugenstil Style, 7 7/8 In. 695.00
Soup, Coupe, Hammered, Josef Hoffmann, c.1915, 3 5/8 x 10 3/8 In. 18000.00

SILVER-CANADIAN

Box, Cover, Circular, Poul Petersen, c.1935, 5 1/2 In. 510.00
Tea & Coffee Set, Urn Shape, Spreading Foot, Scroll Handle, c.1945, 4 Piece. 551.00
Toast Rack, 6-Slice, Henry Birks & Sons, 1898, 5 1/2 In.. 324.00

SILVER-CHINESE

Trophy, Leaves, Birds, Landscapes, Ewer Shape, Paw Feet, 15 3/4 In. 5100.00
Tureen, Cover, Embossed, Peonies, Chrysanthemums, Leaves, Birds, 13 3/4 In. 4800.00

SILVER-CONTINENTAL

Beaker, Tapered Cylinder, Rolled Rim, Engraved Cartouche, c.1760, 4 In. 575.00
Box, Enamel, Flower Border, Germany, 3 3/8 In.. 441.00
Box, Enamel, Reveling Courtiers, Flower Border, Hinged Lid, 3 3/8 In.. 441.00
Box, Oval, 19th Century, 1985-89 588.00
Box, Oval, Hinged Lid, 19th Century, 5 3/4 x 4 7/8 In.. 588.00
Chocolate Pot, Dome Lid, Pear Shape, Fluted Spout, Flower Knop, 9 In. 1265.00
Cigarette Box, Dome Lid, Inset Coin, Gilt Surround, Cedar Lining, 2 x 7 In. 360.00
Creamer, Figural, Cow, Standing, Bee On Hind Quarter, 934, Netherlands, 4 In. 643.00
Figurine, Dog, Pointing In Rushes, Mid 20th Century, 3 1/4 In. 325.00
Figurine, Duck, Standing, Red Glass Eyes, 9 x 6 1/2 In., Pair 633.00
Ladle, Ebonized Wood Handle, 16 x 2 3/4 In. 144.00
Letter Rack, Flowers, Figures, Panel, Pierced, 3 3/4 In. *illus* 47.00
Milk Jug, Dome Lid, Crabstock Handle, Chased, Embossed, Paw Feet, 5 In.. 206.00
Pill Box, Figural, Pig, 2 x 3 3/4 In. 275.00
Plate, 2 Cherubs, Rabbit, Acanthus Scrolls, Cartouches, 1895, 9 1/4 In. *illus* 254.00
Plate, Repousse, Chased, Embossed, Cavorting Putti, Pierced Rim, 9 In. 294.00
Plate, Serving, Round, Ribbon, Thread Border, Openwork, Early 1900s, 11 In.. 259.00
Sauceboat, Ladle, Green Glass Eyes, Spiral Twist Handle, 4 1/2 x 2 3/4 In., Pair 863.00
Teapot, Oval Body, Leaf & Dart Border, Swan's Head Spout, Wood Handle, 12 In.. 1840.00
Tray, Art Nouveau, Flowers, Early 20th Century, 5 1/2 x 9 1/2 In. *illus* 200.00
Tray, Guilloche Reticulated Gallery, 20th Century, 19 1/4 In. 881.00

SILVER-DANISH

Beaker, Pendant Grapes On Base, Marked, Georg Jensen, 4 In.. *illus* 1495.00
Bowl, Center, Reticulated Base, Georg Jensen, Marked, c.1926, 11 1/4 In. 22800.00
Bowl, Center, Ribbed Rim, Georg Jensen, c.1945, 4 x 8 1/2 In.. 1053.00
Bowl, Flared Rim, Leaf, Ball Stem, Circular Foot, Georg Jensen, 4 In. 1058.00
Chafing Dish, Georg Jensen, c.1956, 11 1/2 In. 27000.00
Cheese Scoop, Georg Jensen, c.1945, 7 1/8 In. 147.00
Cigarette Box, Georg Jensen, Hinged Cover, Removable Wood Lining, 2 x 5 3/4 x 4 In. 2376.00
Dish, Black Lanyard Wrapped Handle, Footed, Marked, 3 x 6 In. 85.00
Dish, Georg Jensen, Octagon, 3 1/2 In. 360.00
Gravy Boat, Stand, 9 In., 2 Piece 230.00
Gravy Ladle, Shell Tip, Hans Hansen, c.1950, 6 1/2 In. 70.00
Master Salt Spoon, Meka, 2 1/4 In. 22.00
Olive Fork, 2 Tines, Folded-Back Handle, Georg Jensen, 4 7/8 In.. 36.00
Pick, Shellfish, Stylized Prawn Handle, Marked, Georg Jensen, 7 1/4 In., 4 Piece. 150.00
Pitcher, Bulbous, Cylindrical, Hammered, Blossom Handle, G. Jensen, 11 3/8 In.. 9400.00
Pitcher, C.C. Hermann, c.1950, 6 In.. 702.00
Salt, Embossed Serpentine, Bead Rim, Hammered, Oval, Georg Jensen, 2 3/4 In., Pair. 235.00
Sauceboat, Georg Jensen, Swirled Handle, c.1938, 5 1/2 In., Pair. 7200.00
Tazza, Grapes, Georg Jensen, c.1940, 7 1/2 In.. *illus* 2000.00
Tea & Coffee Set, Blossom Pattern, Ivory Handle, Georg Jensen, c.1925, 4 Piece 9600.00
Tea Set, Jensen Blossom Style, Teapot, Cream Jug, Sugar, Cover, Georg Jensen, c.1945. 4200.00
Tray, Oval, Buds At Intervals, c.1945, 11 1/2 x 8 In. 1225.00

SILVER-DUTCH

Sailboat, Miniature, c.1916, 4 3/4 In. 174.00
Tea Caddy, Oval Lid, Flat Leaf Shoulders, Rectangular, 19th Century, 4 1/4 In.. 470.00
Tray, Rectangular, 4 Claw & Ball Feet, Pierced Gallery, Handles, 19 3/4 In. 4130.00

TIP
You might be able to remove salt spots from your silver-plated saltshakers with olive oil. Rub it on the spots, let stand a few days, then wipe it off.

Silver-Danish, Beaker, Pendant Grapes On Base, Marked, Georg Jensen, 4 In.
$1495.00

Silver-Danish, Tazza, Grapes, Georg Jensen, c.1940, 7 1/2 In.
$2000.00

TIP
Never use lemon-scented dishwashing detergent to wash silver. It leaves spots.

Silver-English, Basket, Embossed Flowers, Swing Handle, Pierced, 1900, 8 In. $145.00

Silver-English, Basket, Openwork, Flower & Putti, Handle, Burrage Davenport, London, 1778, 10 ½ x 10 x 13 In. $1695.00

Silver-English, Bowl, Celtic Knots, Repousse, Marked, Birmingham, 1902, 4 x 6 In. $2990.00

Silver-English, Cup, Scroll Cartouche, Fluted Body, Scroll Handles, John King, London, 1769, 4 x 6 In. $400.00

SILVER-ENGLISH. English sterling silver is marked with a series of four or five small hallmarks. The standing lion mark is the most commonly seen sterling quality mark. The other marks indicate the city of origin, the maker, and the year of manufacture. These dates can be verified in many good books on silver.

Basket, Embossed Flowers, Swing Handle, Pierced, 1900, 8 In.. *illus* 145.00
Basket, Fruit, Oval, Gadroon Sides, Stag Handles, George III, 3 ½ x 5 ¾ In.. 4224.00
Basket, Openwork, Flower & Putti, Handle, Burrage Davenport, London, 1778, 10 ½ x 10 x 13 In.. *illus* 1695.00
Basket, Openwork Sides, Hinged Handle, Scroll & Floral Rim, George III, 4 ½ x 5 ¾ In. 546.00
Basting Spoon, Oval, Engraved, Family Crest, Dragon's Head, William Sumner, 12 In.. 173.00
Biscuit Box, Flower Relief, Footed Frame, Round, Hinged Double Slop Cover, 9 ½ In. 649.00
Biscuit Box, Hinged Cover, Reeded Borders, Applied Drop Handles, 5 In. 1140.00
Bonbon, Shell Shape, Reticulated, Dolphins, George V, c.1916, 4 ½ In., Pair. 1410.00
Bonbon Spoon, Openwork Rocaille, Wrigglework, Edwardian, c.1901, 8 ⅜ In., Pair 176.00
Bowl, 3-Footed, Henry Holland, 1874, 5 ½ In. 270.00
Bowl, Celtic Knots, Repousse, Marked, Birmingham, 1902, 4 x 6 In.. *illus* 2990.00
Bowl, Footed, George III, Leaf Tip Rim, Paterae Band, Leaves, Husk Legs, 5 x 4 ½ In., Pair 646.00
Bowl, Oval, Scalloped Rim, Pedestal, Gadroon Border, Repousse, c.1898, 4 ½ x 10 ½ In. 633.00
Bowl, Scalloped Rim, Shell, Flower Repousse, Punch Work Ground, 1897, 5 ⅜ x 10 ½ x 5 ¾ In. 690.00
Bowl, Scroll & Flower Repousse, Gadroon & Shell Border, Scalloped, Pedestal, Sheffield, 15 x 10 In., Pair 4300.00
Bowl, Vegetable, Cover, Beaded, Border, Divider, F.T. Boone, 10 ¼ In. 3120.00
Bowl, Vegetable, Cover, Domed, Ring Handle, Wooden Handle, Victorian, 5 ¼ x 10 In.. 180.00
Box, Repousse, Cover, Mythological Scene, Square, Victorian, 4 ¼ x 1 ½ x 3 ½ In.. 266.00
Brandy Saucepan, Hinged Lid, Acorn Finial, Wood Handle, George III, 4 ½ x 8 ½ In.. 978.00
Brazier, Ring, 3 Scroll Legs, Family Crest, Thomas Cooke II, George III, 1724, 2 ¾ x 5 In.. 978.00
Caddy Spoon, Shell Bowl, Oval Handle, George Smith & William Fearn, 1792, 3 In. 345.00
Cake Basket, Boat Shape, Leaf, Flute Pierced, Swing Handle, George III, 4 x 4 ½ In. 1093.00
Cake Basket, Pierced, Leaf Panels, Trellis, Swing Handle, George II, 1759, 14 ¼ In.. 6600.00
Candelabra are listed in the Candelabrum category.
Candlesticks are listed in their own category.
Castor, Footed, Pierced Domed Cover, Flame Finial, George III, 1773, 5 ⅛ In.. 177.00
Castor, Octagonal Body, Georgian Style, Crichton Brothers, 1900s, 4 ¼ In., Pair. 144.00
Castor, Urn Shape, Reeded Border, Square Pedestal Base, George III, 1804, 6 ¾ In. 690.00
Chafing Dish, Cover, Leaf Case Rims, Reeded Handles, Fruitwood Ball Feet, 13 ¼ In. 106.00
Chafing Dish, Cover, Oval, Branch Handles, William IV, 10 x 11 x 14 In., Pair. 1003.00
Chocolate Pot, Dome Cover, Cylindrical, Hinged Urn Finial, E. Pocock, 1736, 9 ⅛ In.. 5760.00
Claret Jug, Hinged Lid, Oval, Shield Armorial, Loop Handle, George III, 1785, 14 ½ In.. 2415.00
Coffeepot, Armorial, Pear Shape, Footed, Fluted Spout, Handle, George III, 1761, 10 ¼ In. 1495.00
Coffeepot, Baluster, Dome Lid, Benjamin Gignac, George II, c.1751, 10 ⅜ In. 1116.00
Coffeepot, Baluster, Fluted, Lid, Ball Finial, Beaded Edge, Wooden Handle, 10 In. 896.00
Coffeepot, Dome Lid, Pear Shape, Fruitwood Handle, George III, 1787, 11 ⅝ In. 3525.00
Coffeepot, George III, Square Pedestal Base, Peter & William Bateman, c.1808, 10 In. 823.00
Coffeepot, Hinged Cover, Baluster, Leaf Capped Spout, Scroll Handle, George III, 10 ½ In. 1121.00
Coffeepot, Oval, Border, Shaped Skirt, Wooden Handle, 1897, 9 ¼ x 9 ¼ In. 374.00
Coffeepot, Queen Anne Style, Lighthouse Shape, Engraved, George V, c.1933, 8 ½ In. 294.00
Coffeepot, Rococo, Flowers, Trellis Ground, S-Scroll Handle, George III, 10 ½ x 4 ¼ In. 924.00
Coffeepot, Tapered Cylinder, Triple Scroll Handle, Cast Finial, George II, 9 In.. 1495.00
Compote, E.S. Barnsley & Co., 1911, 6 ¾ In. 348.00
Coronation Medallion, King Charles II Of England, King On Throne, Dated 1661. 595.00
Cream Jug, Footed, Classical Shape, Handle, Square Base, 6 x 4 In. 336.00
Creamer, Helmet Shape, Reeded Loop Handle, Trumpet Foot, George III, 1788, 6 In. 353.00
Creamer, Helmet Shape, Trumpet Foot, Hester Bateman, George III, c.1787, 5 ⅝ In. 294.00
Creamer, Mark, Baluster, Ogee Rim, Serpentine Handle, George III, c.1767, 4 In. 264.00
Creamer, Paw Feet, Harps, Scrolls, Acorns, George III, Ireland, 1814, 4 ½ In. 323.00
Creamer, Pear Shape, 3 Shaped Feet, George II, c.1757, 4 ¼ In.. 649.00
Cruet Frame, Engraved Swag, Openwork Border, Oval, 4 Ball & Claw Feet, London, 1785, 9 x 6 In. 295.00
Cruet Frame, Oval, Center Post, Loop Handle, Openwork, Swags, George III, c.1788, 9 x 7 In. 259.00
Cup, Beaker Form, C-Scroll Handles, 1910, 6 ½ x 8 ¼ In. 403.00
Cup, Cover, Gilt, Swags, Armorials, 2 Handles, George III, 1772, 16 ¾ x 14 ½ In.. 8330.00
Cup, Greek Revival, Parcel Gilt Electroplate, Elkington Mason & Co., c.1850, 8 ¼ In.. 410.00
Cup, Reeded Lip, Dolphin Stems, Circular Foot, George IV, 1824, 3 ⅝ x 2 ¼ In., Pair 201.00
Cup, Repousse, Flower, Fruit, Leaves, Handles, Dome Foot, George III, 1810, 8 x 11 In. 1265.00
Cup, Round, Engraved, Block Letters, Samuel Wood, London, 2 ½ x 3 In., Pair. 1700.00
Cup, Scroll Cartouche, Fluted Body, Scroll Handles, John King, London, 1769, 4 x 6 In.. *illus* 400.00
Dish, Cover, Regency, Rectangular, Fluted Gadroon Rims, Shells, 11 ⅞ In., Pair. 4320.00
Dish, Entree, Bell Form Cover, Ring Drop Handle, George III, 1803, 6 ⅛ x 9 ¼ In. 1495.00

Dish, Entree, Cover, Ivory Finial, Handles, Crest, Crown, Motto, George III, 9 ¾ In. 1062.00
Dish, Entree, Cover, Rectangular, Twist-Off Ring Handle, George III, 1816, Pair 2990.00
Dish, Entree, Cover, Removable Handle, George III, 1816-17, Pair 4700.00
Dish, Entree, Oval, Gadroon Borders, Edward VII, 5 ¼ x 11 ¼ In. 518.00
Dish Cross, X-Shape, Star Arm Terminals, Shell Feet, Reeded Border, George III, 3 x 11 In. ... 2070.00
Dish Set, Quatrefoil, Georgian Style, Gadroon Rims, Fluted Grips, 1878, 8 ⅝ In., 4 Piece 5400.00
Epergne, Swirled Oval Basket, 8 Arms, Cartouche, London, 1765, 13 x 24 In. .... *illus* 27000.00
Fish Set, Grapes, Leaves, Hallmarks, Plated Blades, Tines, Box, 10 x 7 In., 12 Piece 375.00
Fish Slice, Downturned Fiddle End, George III, c.1812, 17 In. 176.00
Fish Slice, Ivory, Scimitar Shape Blade, Bateman & Co., George III, c.1800, 12 In. 270.00
Flask, Rectangular, Ribbed, c.1930, 8 ¾ In. 191.00
Fork Set, Hanoverian, Chawner, George Smith, Unicorn Crest, George III, 7 ½ In., 6 Piece ... 316.00
Frame, Art Nouveau, E. Mander & Sons, c.1902, 6 ¼ x 5 ¼ In. 231.00
Goblet, Bulbous Body, Repousse, Domed Foot, Presentation, George III, 7 ¼ x 4 In. 540.00
Goblet, Campana, Grapevine & Acanthus Bands, Flared, Footed, Paul Storr, 8 In. 6600.00
Goblet, Coconut, Silver Mounted, Victorian, 1872, 7 ¾ x 3 ⅝ In. 748.00
Goblet, Urn Shape Bowl, Knight's Helmet, Crossed Arrows, George III, 1816, 6 ¼ In., Pair 2070.00
Goblet Set, Sheffield, Repousse, Gilt, Waisted Stem, Round Foot, 7 ¾ x 3 ¾ In., 12 Piece 1680.00
Grape Scissors, Flowers, Ribbon, Wreath, 1785, 6 ½ In. 620.00
Gravy Boat, Gadroon Rim, Handle, Paw Feet, Oval, George III, 1819, 7 ¼ In. 4994.00
Horn Beaker, Tapering, Cylindrical, Mounted, Banded Silver Rim, Cartouche, 5 x 3 In. 432.00
Hot Water Urn, 2 Handles, 17 ½ x 11 In. 1293.00
Ice Cream Server, George III, 1814 .... 345.00
Jewel Casket, Dressing Table Shape, Beveled Mirror, Edwardian, c.1904, 6 x 5 In. 529.00
Jug, Hot Milk, Baroque Style, Pear Shape, Wood Handle, Knop, 1932, 6 ½ x 7 In. 575.00
Kettle, Dome Cover, Lampstand, Pear Shape, Swing Handle, George III, 1767, 16 In. 4200.00
Kettle, On Stand, Bulbous, Gooseneck Spout, Dome Lid, George III, c.1754, 14 In. 3120.00
Kettle, Warming Stand, Hinged Lid, Raised Handles, Wood Urn Knop, 1886, 11 x 8 In. 288.00
Knife Set, Gilt, Fern Pattern, Chawner & Company, Victorian, 8 ½ In., 14 Piece 150.00
Ladle, Rounded Upturned Tipt Handle, Shell Shape Bowl, George III, c.1771, 14 In. 288.00
Lobster Pick, Elizabeth II, Scoop On Opposite End, Engraved Lobster, Sheffield, 7 ⅜ In. 411.00
Marrow Scoop, George III, 8 ¼ In. 358.00
Marrow Scoop, Oval Bowl, Rattail Back, Thomas Spackman, Early 1700s, 8 ½ In. 460.00
Mirror, Hand Held, Angel's Heads, Embossed, Edwardian, 11 ¼ x 6 ¼ In. 285.00
Mirror, Rectangular, Pierced Border, Figures, Dragons, Monsters, Easel, 1890, 25 ½ In. 3600.00
Muffineer, Urn Finial, Domed Foot, George II, 1749, 7 In. 475.00
Mug, Baluster Stem, Vertical Fluting, Chased, Monogram, Victorian, c.1891, 3 ¾ In. 147.00
Mug, Cylindrical, Flared Rim, Scrolled Handle, Gilt Interior, Victorian, 3 ¾ In. 150.00
Mug, Queen Anne Britannia Standard, Heavy Gauge, Reeded Foot, c.1709, 4 In. 823.00
Mug, Tapered Cylinder, Grapevine Rim, Foot, George III, c.1811, 3 ½ In. 720.00
Mustard Pot, Flat Lid, Cobalt Blue Glass Liner, George III, 1802, 2 ¾ In. 294.00
Napkin Rings are listed in their own category.
Nutmeg Grater, Half-Cylindrical, Chained Monkey Crest, c. 1765, 3 ⅜ In. 5100.00
Nutmeg Grater, Lid, Crest, Navette, George III, 1795, 2 In. 646.00
Page Turner, Repousse Handle, Tortoiseshell, Initial MPH, c.1902, 16 x 1 ½ In. 550.00
Pitcher, Pear Shape, C.J. Vander Ltd., London, 1940, 8 ¾ In. .... *illus* 840.00
Pitcher, Scroll Handle, Gadroon Border, Swirl Flower, Shell, George III, 4 ¾ x 5 ¼ In. 489.00
Pitcher, Swirl Flowers, Scroll, Shell Cartouche, George III, 1763, 3 ½ x 4 ¼ x 2 ½ In. 403.00
Pitcher, Water, Pear Shape, Footed, Double Scroll Handle, Bracket Spout, 4 Pt., 8 ½ In. 518.00
Place Setting, Knife, Fork, Spoon, Cup, Triangular Case, Youth, 1858-59, 4 Piece 558.00
Plate, Domed Meat Cover, Gadroon Border, Leaf Handle, Monogram, 13 ¾ In. 295.00
Plate, Gadroon Border, Edward Wakelin, George II, c.1759, 9 ½ In., Pair 1725.00
Platter, Circular, Gadroon Border, Shells, Leaves, George IV, 12 ⅝ In., Pair 4800.00
Platter, Domed Cover, Oval, Water Reservoir, Acanthus Scrolls, Edwardian, 11 x 18 x 14 In. .. 1080.00
Platter, Meat, Oval, Ogee Gadroon Rim, Motto, Coat Of Arms, George III, 18 ⅜ In. 1528.00
Platter, Meat, Oval, Gadroon Rim, William IV, 1831, 20 ⅜ In. 5040.00
Platter, Meat, Shaped Oval, Gadroon Rim, George III, 20 In. 9600.00
Platter, Meat, Shaped Oval, Gadroon Rim, Shells, P. Storr, George III, 15 ⅛ In. 6000.00
Platter, Oval, Hunt & Roskell, Gadrooned Rim, George V, 18 In., Pair 1880.00
Platter, Strainer, William Fountain, Motto, Coat Of Arms, George III, 17 ¾ In. 1116.00
Platter Set, Graduated, William K. Reid, Gadrooned Rim, William IV, 13 x 15 In., 4 Piece ... 5875.00
Punch Bowl, Hemispherical, Molded Rim, Domed Foot, George III, 6 x 9 In. 3696.00
Punch Bowl, Tray, Ladle, Scalloped Rim, Cherub Heads, Lion Mask, 3 Piece 6000.00
Punch Ladle, S-Form Handle, Monogram, George III, 1763, 12 ½ In. 288.00
Punch Set, Flower Pattern, Barker & Ellis, 14 Piece 4700.00

Silver-English, Epergne, Swirled Oval Basket, 8 Arms, Cartouche, London, 1765, 13 x 24 In. $27000.00

Silver-English, Pitcher, Pear Shape, C.J. Vander Ltd., London, 1940, 8 ¾ In. $840.00

Silver-English, Salver, Cartouche, Family Crest, Border, 3 Scroll Feet, George II, 6 In. $725.00

Silver-English, Saucepan, Brandy, Inscribed, E&A, 1732, 3 x 6 x 3 In. $795.00

Silver-English, Spoon, Apostle, Bearded Figure, Knife, Flying Bird, George Smith, 1780, 7 ⅛ In.
$294.00

Silver-English, Sugar, God Grant Grace Crest, Mappin & Webb, London, 1901, 4 In.
$58.00

Silver-English, Tongs, King's Pattern, George III, 1834, 6 In.
$127.00

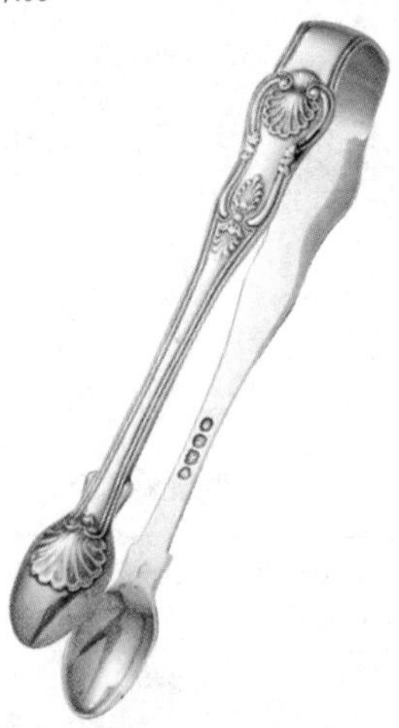

TIP
Eighteenth- and nineteenth-century Irish silver is more valuable than English because it is rarer.

Punch Strainer, Round Bowl, 2 Scroll Handles, London, George II, 1759, 11 x 4 In. 840.00
Rose Bowl, Round Body, Spreading Foot, Double Scroll Handles, c.1905, 6 ¼ In. 944.00
Salt, Cutout Design, Cobalt Blue Liner, 4-Footed, c.1830-40, Sheffield, 2 In. 33.00
Salt, Glass Liner, Scooped Rim, 4-Footed, Georgian, c.1796, 2 ¼ In. 132.00
Salt, Octagonal, Inward Sloping Sides, Oval Well, Stepped Base George I3 In., Pair 575.00
Salt, Oval, Hoof Footed, Chased, John Sanders, George II, c.1733, 2 ¾ In., Pair 147.00
Salt, Reeded Borders, Openwork, Fleur-De-Lis, Scroll Feet, Bateman, 2 x 3 ¼ In., Pair 230.00
Salt Cellar, Oblong, Gilt, Stepped Feet, Engraved Crest, George III, 2 ¼ In., Pair 316.00
Salt Set, Openwork, Ball & Claw Feet, Blue Glass Liners, George III, 2 x 3 ¼ In., 5 Piece 805.00
Salt Set, Shell, Gadroon, Lion Head, Lion's Paw Feet, George IV, 1825, 4 Piece 805.00
Salver, 3 Ball & Claw Feet, Serpentine Rim, Gadroon Edge, George III, 13 ¾ In. 1534.00
Salver, Beaded Edge, Spiral Reeded Border, Shell Scroll Feet, 1884, 1 ½ x 12 In. 403.00
Salver, Cartouche, Family Crest, Border, 3 Scroll Feet, George II, 6 In. .... *illus* 725.00
Salver, Circular, 4 Panel Feet, Reeded, Beaded Rim, George III, 18 In. 3300.00
Salver, Circular, Molded Border, Gadroon Rim, Leaf Mantle, 4 Pad Feet, 1774, 15 ¾ In. 3900.00
Salver, Flared, Stepped Serpentine Rim, 4-Footed, George V, 14 ¼ In. 1298.00
Salver, Flower Wreath, Rococo Rim, 3-Footed, 1767, 1 x 8 In. 840.00
Salver, Gadroon Rim, 4-Footed, Center Crest, 15 ½ In. 4900.00
Salver, Gadroon Rim, Embossed Flowers, Ball & Claw Feet, W. Tweedie, George III, 1772, 13 ¾ In.. 3900.00
Salver, Hexagonal, Gadroon Rim, Flower, Acanthus Border, 3-Footed, 12 In. 324.00
Salver, Leafy Shell & Gadroon Border, Ball & Claw Feet, Crest, George II, 14 ½ In. 4370.00
Salver, Round, Scroll Feet, Chippendale Border, Cartouche, Crest, George II, 6 ¼ In. 748.00
Salver, Round, Scroll Feet, Rectangular Reserve, George III, c.1800, 8 In. 259.00
Salver, Scroll & Shell Edge, Pad Feet, Engraved Crest, George III, c.1772, 7 In. 748.00
Salver, Scroll Rim, Feet, Shells, Leaf, Carrington, Victorian, 1897, 19 ¾ In. 2700.00
Salver, Scrollwork Edge, Pad Feet, Monogram, George II, c.1757, 10 ¾ In. 1093.00
Salver, Shaped Rim, Leaves, Center Wreath Cartouche, 1796, 7 ¼ x 5 ¼ x 1 In. 504.00
Sauce Ladle, Armorial, Fiddle, Ram On Knight's Helmet, Victorian, 1838, 7 In., Pair 144.00
Sauce Ladle, Feather Edge, Georgian, c.1804 .... 98.00
Sauceboat, Double Ogee Rim, Leaf, C-Scroll Handle, George III, c.1764, 5 ⅜ In. 999.00
Sauceboat, Oval, Pedestal, Shaped Rim, Handle, P. Archambo, George II, 1700s, 7 ¼ In. 7200.00
Sauceboat, Oval, Scroll Handle, 3 Shell Feet, George II, 1754, 4 ½ x 8 ½ x 4 ¼ In. 1495.00
Sauceboat, Rococo Style, Double Scroll Handle, George IV, c.1828, 3 In. 180.00
Sauceboat, Walker & Hall, 6 ½ In., Pair 270.00
Saucepan, Brandy, Inscribed, E&A, 1732, 3 x 6 x 3 In. .... *illus* 795.00
Saucepan, Flared, Reeded Rim, Foot, Fruitwood Handle, George III, 1791, 2 ½ In. 323.00
Skewer, Crown, Monogram, Victorian, 1862, 12 In. 201.00
Skewer, Meat, Thomas Wallis II, Jonathan Hayne, George III, 12 In. 230.00
Skewer, Shell Terminal, Bright Cut Monogram, George III, c.1781, 13 ½ In. 323.00
Snuffer, Loop Handle, Crossed Branches, Acorn, Oak Leaf, George III, 1802, 6 ½ In., Pair.... 518.00
Soup Ladle, Fluted Bowl, Crest Of Knight On Handle, George III, 1765, 13 In. 650.00
Spoon, Apostle, Bearded Figure, Knife, Flying Bird, George Smith, 1780, 7 ⅛ In. .... *illus* 294.00
Strainer, Engraved Phoenix, Scroll Handle, Hanging Hook, George III, 4 ¼ In. 510.00
Strainer, Openwork Handles, Monogram, George III, c.1802, 3 ⅛ In. 230.00
Strainer Spoon, George III, Oval Bowl, Central Divider, Downturned Handle, 12 In. 460.00
Stuffing Spoon, Coffin Shape Stem, Engraved, George III, 1813, 12 In. 176.00
Sugar, 2 Handles, Repousse Flowers, Matted Ground, Pedestal Base, 1825, 4 ⅜ In. 354.00
Sugar, God Grant Grace Crest, Mappin & Webb, London, 1901, 4 In. .... *illus* 58.00
Sugar, Urn Shape, Repousse, Classical Masks, Acanthus, George III, 8 x 3 ¾ In. 2640.00
Sugar & Creamer, 2 Handles, Flower Panels, Victorian, 4 ½ x 7 ¾ & 4 ½ x 6 ¼ In. 345.00
Sugar & Creamer, Oblong, Fluted, Ball Feet, Engraved, George III, 1807-08, 4 In. 382.00
Sugar Nips, Rococo Style, Shell Ends, Georgian, 5 In. 230.00
Sugar Tongs, Bright Cut Engraving, Monogram, Hallmark, c.1770, 7 ½ In. 112.00
Tablespoon, Gold Wash Bowl, George III, 9 In., Pair. 176.00
Tankard, Banded, William Shaw, London, c.1762, 7 ¾ In. 4350.00
Tankard, Domed Cover, Engraved Ship, Baluster Form, Reeded Band, George II, 1768, 8 ¼ In.. 7800.00
Tankard, Flower Repousse, Openwork Scroll Thumb Piece, George III, 8 ½ x 4 ¾ In. 3575.00
Tankard, Scroll Handle, Baluster, Gilt Interior, George III, 4 ¾ In. 836.00
Tazza, Lobed Border, Engraved, Armorial, Ringed Stem, George IV, 3 ¾ x 10 In. 863.00
Tea & Coffee Set, Creamer, Sugar, Handles, Victorian, 1851-52, 4 Piece 2468.00
Tea & Coffee Set, Lids, Wood Knop, 2 Pots, Creamer, Sugar, Waste Pail, 6 Piece. 2300.00
Tea & Coffee Set, Pear Shape, Ribbon Tied Flower Swags, c.1848, 5 Piece 1175.00
Tea Caddy, Cover, Finial, Footed, Thomas Bradbury, 1898, 4 ¾ In. 990.00
Tea Caddy, Cylindrical, Fluted, Lid, Hinged, Ball Finial, 3 Ball Feet, c.1806, 7 In. 1225.00
Tea Caddy Set, Mahogany Box, Rectangular, Rococo Cartouche, 5 ¼ In., 3 Piece 4600.00
Teapot, Flat Lid, Cylindrical, Beaded, Upraised Spout, Ivory Handle, Victorian, 1869, 3 ¼ In. . 259.00
Teapot, Hinged Lid, Boat, Swan's Neck Spout, Wood Handle, George III, 1801, 6 ⅜ x 12 In.... 374.00

Teapot, Hinged Lid, Oval, Scroll, Ivory Finial, Wood Handle, Marked, B.M., London, 1785, 5 x 10 In. 805.00
Teapot, Oval, Carved Wood Handle, Finial, Beaded, Hallmark, Georgian, 6 x 11 In. 3000.00
Teapot, Oval, Paneled Body, Tapering Spout, Wooden Handle, George III, 5 ½ x 10 ½ In. 1495.00
Teapot, Paneled, Grapevine, Band Of Leaves, Ebony Handle, George III, 11 ⅝ In. 6000.00
Teapot, Repousse, Paw Feet, Squatty, 1817, 6 x 12 x 6 In. 468.00
Teapot, Scrolled Flowers, Oval Cartouche, George III, 11 ½ x 5 x 3 ¾ In. 560.00
Teapot, Spherical, Engraved, Swan's Head Spout, C-Scroll Handle, Victorian, 1879, 6 ¼ In. 460.00
Teapot, Stand, Wood Handle, Knop, 4-Footed, George III, 1782, 5 ⅝ x 10 ¾ In. 748.00
Teapot Stand, Oval, Bright Cut Engraving, Scalloped Rim, Charles Fox, George III, 7 ¼ In. 323.00
Toddy, Ladle, Baleen Handle, Hester Bateman, London, 1788, 14 In. 232.00
Tongs, King's Pattern, George III, 1834, 6 In. *illus* 127.00
Tray, Butler's, Gadroon Rim, Handles, Shells, Women Heads, 19 x 29 In. 3136.00
Tray, Gadroon Border, Two Gadroon Handles, George IV, 1820, 25 x 14 ¼ In. 3335.00
Tray, Ogee Molded Rim, C-Scrolls, Leaves, Flower Heads, Victorian, 1854, 26 In. 7050.00
Tray, Oval, 2 Scroll Handles, Scalloped Border, Fruit & Flowers, Engraved Crest, 28 x 17 In. 2990.00
Tray, Oval, Embossed Gadroon, Shell & Scroll, Handles, George V, 29 ½ x 18 ¾ In. 510.00
Tray, Oval, Plated, Pierced Gallery, Arabesques, Handles, Victorian, 24 ¾ x 18 ½ In. 1440.00
Tray, Snuffer, Navette Shape, Flared Ends, Bateman, George III, Late 1700s, 10 x 3 ¾ In. 1920.00
Tray, Tea, Handles, Oval, Reeded, Leaf Border, Flower Sprigs, Gothic Arches, 30 ¼ In. 3360.00
Trophy Cup, Lid, Oval Finial, Pear Shape, Handles, George V, 1914, 16 In. 3819.00
Tureen, Bulbous, Oval, Acanthus, Oak Cluster Handles, William IV, 11 x 16 ½ x 9 ¾ In. 1560.00
Tureen, Round, Domed Lid, Reeded Handle, Motto, Coat Of Arms, George III, 12 ½ In. 7638.00
Vase, Fleur-De-Lis, Pellets, Flaring Cylindrical, Chased, Charles II, 1675, 6 In. 6600.00
Vase, Inverted Pear, Rococo, Flower Spray, George III, 1761, 7 ¾ In. 1920.00
Vase, Scalloped Rim, Stokes & Ireland, 8 In. 198.00
Vase, Waisted, Snake Feet, Double Handles, Art Nouveau Style, Rex Silver, 9 x 4 In., Pair. 1140.00
Vinaigrette, Hinged Lid, Gilt Pierced Work Grill, Leafy Scroll, George IV, 2 x 1 In. 240.00
Vinaigrette, Rounded Rectangular, Hinged Cover, Victorian, 2 ⅛ x 1 ¼ In. 264.00
Waiter, Duke & Duchess, Square, Incurved Angles, Engraved, George III, 1727, 6 ½ In. 1800.00
Waiter, Shaped Molded Border, Crested Center, 3-Footed, George II, 1737, 7 In., Pair. 3000.00
Wine Coaster, Ball & Claw Feet, George III, 1767, 3 x 5 ½ In. 975.00
Wine Coaster, Beaded Edge, Open Fretwork, Wooden Base, 19th Century, 4 ⅜ In. 353.00
Wine Coaster, Reticulated Sides, Ball & Claw Feet, George III, 2 ⅜ x 5 ½ In. 975.00
Wine Coaster, Scalloped Rim, Beaded Border, Openwork, George III, c.1786, 1 ¾ x 5 In. 805.00
Wine Coaster, Scroll Rim, Wood Insert, c.1900, 6 ½ In., Pair. 299.00
Wine Cooler, Barrel, Reeded Band, Scroll Handles, Removable Ring, c.1794, 8 In. 9187.00
Wine Cooler, Handles, Campana Shape, Repousse, William IV, c.1831, 8 In. 1298.00
Wine Cooler, Handles, Sheffield Liners, Crest, Paul Storr, London, 1795, 8 x 7 In., Pair. *illus* 12400.00
Wine Cooler, Oak Leaf, Acorn Border, Acanthus Leaf Border At Waist, William IV, 9 ¾ In. 2242.00
Wine Funnel, Clip, Hester Bateman, 1784, 5 x 3 ¼ In. *illus* 1200.00
Wine Funnel, Fluted Curved Spout, Strainer, Shell Thumb Rest, George IV, 6 In. 1016.00

SILVER-FRENCH

Box, Circular, Cover, Leafy Borders, Gilt Interior, 1 ⅜ x 3 ⅜ In. 480.00
Centerpiece, Gothic Style, Carnelian Cabochons, Flared Handles, c.1840, 18 In. 3900.00
Chalice, Provincial, Strapwork Leaf & Dart, Trumpet Foot, Double Knop, 9 x 5 In. 1020.00
Chocolate Pot, Cylindrical, Leaf Band, Pineapple Finial, D-Shape Ivory Handle, c.1900, 6 ¾ In. 1195.00
Coffeepot, Swirl & Wave, Acanthus Spout, Berry Finial, Wood Handle, 8 x 7 ¾ x 5 In. *illus* 910.00
Creamer, Swirl Fluted, Pear Shape, Handle Scroll, c.1770, 6 ⅝ In. 480.00
Cup, Tea, Saucer, Spoon, Applied Floral Decoration, Gilt Interior, Ring Handles 259.00
Dish, Meat, Engraved Cipher, Shaped Rim, Molded Border, 17 ¾ x 11 ¾ In. 823.00
Ewer, Shaped Spout, S-Shape Handle, Abel Etienne Giroux, 1st Empire, 10 ½ In. 1920.00
Fish Slice, Scimitar Shape Blade, Engraved, Wrigglework Banding, 14 ¾ In. 780.00
Monstrance, Provincial, Gilt Copper, Cherubim, Wheat, Napoleon III, 24 x 12 In. 3600.00
Salt, Trencher, Gadrooned, Bowed Sides, Stepped Bases, c.1698, 1 ¼ x 3 In. 1495.00
Soup, Coupe, Glazed Ceramic Inside, Green Leaves, M. Dufrene, c.1912, 4 x 14 In. 1440.00
Spoon Set, Rounded Handle, Threaded, Monogram, Louis XVIII, 5 ½ In., 6 Piece 489.00
Teapot, Figural, Rooster, Open Beak Spout, Feather Wings, Feather Handle, 3 x 7 In. 2242.00
Teapot, Oval, Floral Mouthed Arched Wooden Handle, Swan Finial, Napoleonic, 6 x 9 In. 1440.00
Tray, Metal, Jean Despres, c.1950, ⅞ x 18 ⅝ x 15 In. 15600.00
Wine Taster, Chased Grapevines, Coiled Serpent Handle, Marc Parrod, 3 ½ In. 390.00
Wine Taster, Gadroon, Ring & Thumbpiece, Francois-Hubert Martin, 3 In. 450.00
Wine Taster, Lilleois Style, Round, Threaded Rim, Ring Handle, 4 ½ x 5 ¾ In. 360.00

SILVER-GERMAN

Bowl, Art Deco, 2 Handles, c.1930, 15 ½ In. 630.00
Bowl, Oval, Flared Rim, Cornucopia, Musical Instruments, Handles, 6 ¼ x 17 ½ In. 2304.00
Box, Circular, c.1900, 3 ½ In. 174.00

Silver-English, Wine Cooler, Handles, Sheffield Liners, Crest, Paul Storr, London, 1795, 8 x 7 In., Pair
$12400.00

Silver-English, Wine Funnel, Clip, Hester Bateman, 1784, 5 x 3 ¼ In.
$1200.00

Silver-French, Coffeepot, Swirl & Wave, Acanthus Spout, Berry Finial, Wood Handle, 8 x 7 ¾ x 5 In.
$910.00

TIP

Keeping the windows closed and controlling the humidity in the house will help retard tarnish on silver.

Silver-Irish, Basket, Pierced Bands, Swing Handle, Gust'v's Byrne, Dublin, 1818, 15 In.
$2530.00

Silver-Irish, Basting Spoon, Cut & Star, Cartouche, Dublin, 1810, 13 ½ In.
$840.00

Silver-Irish, Creamer, Rococo Style, Dublin, 1877, 6 In.
$630.00

Silver-Japanese, Bowl, Iris, Relief, 6 x 10 In.
$4600.00

Cake Knife, Applied Star Of David, Steel Blade, Hebrew Inscription, c.1885, 11 ½ In. 420.00
Chalice, Bruckmann & Sohne Heilbronn, c.1911, 7 ½ In. 1989.00
Chalice, Gilt, Continental, Tapered Bowl, Chased, Scroll Rib Stem, 7 ½ In. 881.00
Chalice, Presentation, Bruckmann & Sohne, c.1900, 8 In. 1638.00
Chalice, Presentation, c.1863, 7 ¾ In. 702.00
Cup, Figural, Squirrel Eating Nut On Tree Trunk, Detachable Head, c.1800, 10 In. 4182.00
Decanter, Lid, Blue Glass, Square, Round Neck, Stopper, Openwork, 5 ½ x 3 ¾ In. 662.00
Figure, Cockerel, Fighting Stance, Raised Claw, Mid 1900s, 7 ¾ In. 1298.00
Figure, Knight, Full Armor, Jousting, Gem Set Mounted, Parcel Gilt, 12 In., Pair 9600.00
Figure, Knight, Holding Standard, Shield, Plinth, 23 ½ In. 3600.00
Ice Bucket, Handle, Scallop Base, c.1930, 9 ¼ In. 480.00
Salt, Cutout Design, 3-Footed, No Liner, Augsburg, c.1736, 2 In. 165.00
Spoon, Apostle, Figural Terminal, Openwork Gothic Style Arch, Cherub, 7 ⅜ In., Pair 176.00
Spoon Set, Demitasse, Gilt, Shield Handles, Faces, Fleur-De-Lis, Scrolling, 5 ¼ In., 12 Piece 115.00
Tray, Cartouche Shape, Flower, Scroll & Fruit Border, Scroll Handles, c.1890, 34 x 26 In. 3200.00
Vase, Spill, Jugendstil Style, Flower Shape, Stylized Iris, Wirework Stamen, 12 ¾ In. 558.00
Wine Cooler, Acanthus Leaves, Ram's Head Handles 3575.00

SILVER-INDIAN
Desk Box, Damascened, Patinated Steel, Portrait Miniatures, Moghul Style, 2 x 11 ½ In. 270.00
Wine Cooler, Tapering, Cylindrical, Cartouches, Tree Of Life Motif, 10 ¼ x 13 ½ In. 660.00

SILVER-IRISH
Basket, Pierced Bands, Swing Handle, Gust'v's Byrne, Dublin, 1818, 15 In. . . . . *illus* 2530.00
Basting Spoon, Cut & Star, Cartouche, Dublin, 1810, 13 ½ In. . . . . *illus* 840.00
Basting Spoon, George III, Bright Cut, Star, Open Cartouche, John Power, c.1810, 13 ½ In. 805.00
Basting Spoon, Hanoverian Pattern, James Douglas, 1749, 15 In. 1800.00
Box, Bougie, Domed Cover, Drum Form, Swivel Cap, 1800, 2 ⅝ In. 1800.00
Butter, Cover, Oval Tub, Pierced, Edward Boyce, Dublin, c.1775, 6 ⅛ In. 16800.00
Coffeepot, Repousse, Baluster, Gooseneck Spout, Scroll Handle, R. Smith, Dublin, 11 In. 1265.00
Creamer, Ewer Shape, Classical Women, Winged Victory, Man, J. Fray, 1839, 4 ¼ In. 1320.00
Creamer, Helmet Shape, Flat Chased, Rococo, Double Scroll Handle, 4 ¼ In. 2400.00
Creamer, Helmet Shape, Molded Girdle, Wave Rim, Dublin, 1750, 5 In. 1440.00
Creamer, Rococo Style, Dublin, 1877, 6 In. . . . . *illus* 630.00
Cup, Caudle, George III, Reeded Girdle, Serpentine Handles, Flat Leaf, c.1773, 5 ½ In. 1175.00
Ladle, Oval Handle, Bright Cut Engraving, Round Shell Bowl, Crest, George III, 13 In. 1035.00
Sauceboat, Armorial, Tripod, Gadroon Rim, Flower, Leaf, George III, c.1770, 5 x 7 ½ In. 1380.00
Sauceboat, Band Of Quilting, Crest, 3 Shell, Scroll Supports, John Lloyd, Dublin, 1777, 9 In. 4500.00
Sauceboat, Rococo, Dolphin, Cow, Figures, Paw Supports, Williamson, Dublin, c.1765, 9 In. 5100.00
Sauceboat, Tapered Spout, Beaded Rim, Handle, 3 Legs, Pad Feet, George III, 1819, 4 In. 529.00
Serving Slice, Spade Shaped, Engraved, Pierced Trefoil, 14 ⅝ In. 3600.00
Spoon Set, Oval Handle, Family Crest, Monogram, Dublin Makers, Late 1700s, 18 Piece 805.00
Teapot, Bachelor, Banded Oval, Fluted Spout, Daniel Eagan, 1801, 5 In. 2700.00
Tongs, William IV, Edward Power, 1835, 6 ¾ In. 150.00

SILVER-ISRAELI
Open Salt, Reticulated Rim, Twisted Silver Rope, 3-Footed, 1 ¼ x 2 In. 58.00
Wine Coaster, Openwork, Grape & Vine Leaf Pattern, 5 x 2 ⅜ In. 200.00

SILVER-ITALIAN
Bowl, Flower Form, Original Case, Buccellati, Milan, 7 In. 960.00
Centerpiece, Duck On Water Lilies, Blossoms Form Candleholder, 13 x 10 x 6 . . . . 14430.00
Dish, 3 Stylized Acanthus Leaves, Joined At Stem, Buccellati, Milan, 8 In. 1560.00
Dish, Apple Shape, Gianmaria Cuccellati, Milan, Case, 5 ⅜ x 5 In. 450.00
Figure, Horse, Prancing, Green Marble Base, 8 ¼ x 10 In. 633.00
Salver, Circular, Molded Border, 3 Openwork Shells, Scroll Feet, c.1825, 17 ½ In. 3900.00
Tea Set, Signed Tutunzi, Roma, c.1900, 5 Piece 1760.00
Wine Cooler, Tapering Cylindrical, Serpentine Paneled Sides, 2 Handles, 7 x 8 In. 1122.00

SILVER-JAPANESE
Bowl, Enamel, Flowers, Dragonfly, Bird, Octagonal, Carved Wood Base, 8 ½ In. 8400.00
Bowl, Iris, Leaves, Scalloped Rim, Bamboo Shaped Legs, 6 ⅛ x 7 ¼ In. 2300.00
Bowl, Iris, Relief, 6 x 10 In. . . . . *illus* 4600.00
Container, 3-Footed, Silver Liner, Leafy Vines, Wisteria Pods, Cover, 5 In. 2832.00
Creamer, Bulbous, Arched Handle, Applied Crayfish, Etched Reeds, 3 ⅛ In. 3120.00
Tea & Coffee Set, Urn Shape, Urn Finial, Monogram, 12 ½ In. Coffeepot, 5 Piece 920.00

SILVER-MEXICAN
Bowl, Danish Style, Triangular, Flared Corners, 1 ¼ x 7 ¼ x 7 ½ In. 115.00
Bowl, Fruit, Repousse, Footed, Vertically Lobed, Garlands, Trumpet Foot, 6 x 9 In. 353.00

Bowl, Lotus Form, Petals, Domed Foot, Oval, 10¼ In. 353.00
Bowl, Trophy, Sanborns, 3¾ x 8 In. 205.00
Cocktail Shaker, Engraved, Flower Band, Monogram, Marked Mac'el, 12¼ In. 950.00
Coffee Set, Dogwood, Tray, Waste Bowl, Open Sugar, Sanborns, 9½ In., 4 Piece 600.00
Dish, Shell Form, Scroll Stand, Sanborns, c.1950, 7 In., Pair 540.00
Pitcher, Lobed Bottom, Turquoise Stone-Clad Parrot Handle, Castillo, 11½ In. 764.00
Pitcher, Maciel, 11½ In. 353.00
Pitcher, Water, Dolphin Handle, Stippled Shoulder, Leaf Band, 1900s, 8½ In. 118.00
Pitcher, Water, Faceted Body, Sanborns, Marked 925, c.1950, 10 In. 660.00
Punch Set, Bowl, Ladle, 12 Cups, Tray, 7¾ x 13 In.-Bowl, 15 Piece *illus* 2400.00
Salad Servers, Rosewood, Tersine, Mid 20th Century, 10½ In. *illus* 165.00
Salt & Pepper, Glass, Floral Filigree 50.00
Serving Set, Entwined Snakes, Turquoise, Lapis Lazuli, Los Castillo Plateado, 12 x 3 In. *illus* 480.00
Tray, Serving, 2 Handles, Serpentine Gadrooned Edge, Shaped Feet, 32 In. 1293.00
Vase, Hammered, Applied Lizards, Turquoise, Los Castillo Taxco, 12½ x 10 In. *illus* 2500.00

SILVER-NORWEGIAN

Salt & Pepper, Guilloche Enamel 69.00
Spoon, Child's, Bear Fox & Hare Handle, David Anderson, 5¾ In. 180.00

SILVER-PERUVIAN

Box, Symbolic Carving, 1¼ x 4 In. 351.00
Charger, Handles, Hammered Body, Stepped Serpentine Rim, 1940s, 17 In. 767.00

SILVER-PORTUGUESE

Coffer, Tortoiseshell, Domed Top, Rectangular, 6½ x 9 x 5 In. 3360.00
Pot, Cover, Swag & Ribbon, Strawberry Finial, 4 Scroll Feet, Marked, P. Titulo, 5 x 6 In. 525.00
Toothpick Holder, Molded Native American, Feathered Headdress, 11½ In. 4200.00
Urn, Sugar, Cover, Waisted Oval, Chased, Embossed, Flat Leaf Bands, 5¾ In. 558.00

SILVER-RUSSIAN. Russian silver is marked with the Cyrillic, or Russian, alphabet. The numbers 84, 88, or 91 indicate the silver content. Russian silver may be higher or lower than sterling standard. Other marks indicate maker, assayer, or city of manufacture. Many pieces of silver made in Russia are decorated with enamel. Faberge pieces are listed in their own category.

Belt Buckle, Interlocking Cartouche Shape, Niello Decor, Lady's, 1800s, 29 In. 690.00
Box, Hinged Cover, Chased & Nielloed, Geometric, 1908, 3¼ In. 1298.00
Box, Melon Form, 4 Strut Feet, Attached Handles, Hinged Top, 1917, 5¼ x 9 In. 1770.00
Box, Niello, Scene, Moscow, 1874, 2¼ x 4¼ In. 705.00
Cigarette Case, Applied Gold Monogram, 1917, 4¼ In. 2124.00
Cigarette Case, Cloisonne Enamel, Bird Amongst Flowers, Beaded Border, 1917, 4¼ In. 1652.00
Cigarette Case, Cloisonne Enamel, Scrolling Leaves, Geometric Designs, 1917, 4½ In. 1298.00
Cigarette Case, Hinged Cover, Repousse Blacksmithing Scene, 1917, 4½ In. 2360.00
Cigarette Case, Hinged Cover, Repousse Eagle Atop Laurel Wreath, 1917, 4½ In. 1121.00
Cigarette Case, Hinged Cover, Repousse Prince Ivan & Firebird, 1917, 4½ In. 1416.00
Coffeepot, Flared, Crosshatched Rondels, Swan's Neck, S-Scroll Handle, 6⅞ In. 662.00
Creamer, Cloisonne Enameled, Ball Feet, Handle, 1890, 2¾ In. 1770.00
Creamer, Embossed, Reeded, Leaf Tip Bands, Ivory Handle, Nicholas I, 1832, 6 In. 764.00
Creamer, Rosehead Band, Lobed, Wood Handle, Oval, Nicholas I, 1835, 4½ In. 441.00
Cup, Cover, Cylindrical, 3 Ball Feet, Flattened Domed Lid, Leaf Finial, 5⅛ In. 529.00
Cup, Demitasse, 6 Panels, Shaded Enamel Bird, Scrolling Leaves, 1908, 3¼ In. 3068.00
Cup, Troika Scene, Beaded Rim, Interior Gilt, Red Lacquered, Handle, 1917, 2¾ In. 5428.00
Eggcup, Tiered Trumpet Base, 20th Century, 2¼ In., Pair 705.00
Figurine, Rabbit, Garnet Eyes, Chased Fur, 2 x 4 x 2⅜ In. 662.00
Frame, Enamel, Tea Glass, Leaves, Trefoil Cloisonne, Angular Handle, c.1908, 3½ In. 2468.00
Kovsh, Boat Shape, Straight Handle, Gilt Interior, c.1894, 6¾ In. 1592.00
Kovsh, Enameled Scrolling Flowers, Geometric Designs, Hook Handle, 1917, 4½ In. 7080.00
Kovsh, Flowers, Scrolls, Enamel, Gilt, Pierced Border, Impressed, 88, 2 x 7 In. *illus* 14000.00
Kovsh, Gilt, Enamel, Flowers, Scrolling Leaves, c.1900 18375.00
Kovsh, Shaded Enamel Flower, Beaded Border, 3 x 4½ x 2¾ In. 5290.00
Ladle, Fiddle Type Handle, Oval Bowl, Gilt Interior, 1856, 12⅜ In. 323.00
Ladle, Gold Washed Bowl, Monogram, 13¼ In. 294.00
Ladle, Turned Round Bowl, Engraved Long Handle, Vine Attachment, c.1854, 11½ In. 431.00
Lamp, Icon, Scrolling Flowers, 3 Suspension Chains, Silver Smoke Bell, 27 In. 2832.00
Pitcher, Lid, Copper Overlay, Art Nouveau, c.1910, 14 In. 2750.00
Plate, Presentation, Gold Washed, Enamel, Geometric Cloisonne, c.1882, 8 In. 3055.00
Purse, Coin, Enamel, Scroll Cloisonne, Faille Lining, 1908-17, 2¾ In. 588.00
Salt Box, Hinged Cover, Loaf Of Bread Modeled, Gilt Interior, 1860, 10 Oz., 4 In. 3600.00
Salt Set, Gilt, Champleve Enamel, Gustave Klingert, Bombe, Flowers, Box, 1⅝ In., 6 Piece 2813.00

Silver-Mexican, Punch Set, Bowl, Ladle, 12 Cups, Tray, 7¾ x 13 In.-Bowl, 15 Piece
$2400.00

Silver-Mexican, Salad Servers, Rosewood, Tersine, Mid 20th Century, 10½ In.
$165.00

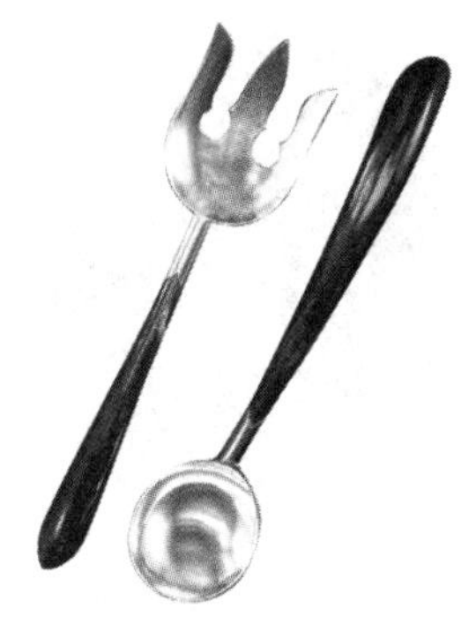

Silver-Mexican, Serving Set, Entwined Snakes, Turquoise, Lapis Lazuli, Los Castillo Plateado, 12 x 3 In.
$480.00

Silver-Mexican, Vase, Hammered, Applied Lizards, Turquoise, Los Castillo Taxco, 12½ x 10 In.
$2500.00

SILVER-RUSSIAN

Silver-Russian, Kovsh, Flowers, Scrolls, Enamel, Gilt, Pierced Border, Impressed, 88, 2 x 7 In.
$14000.00

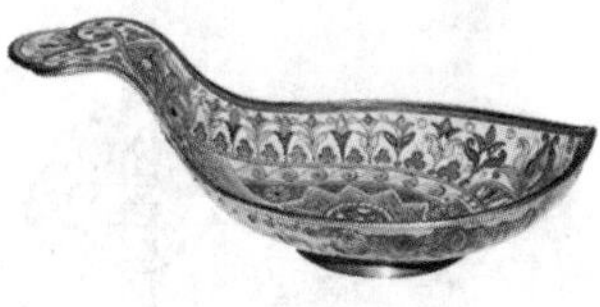

Silver-Russian, Scent Bottle, Green Enamel, Snowflake Design, Cyrillic Signature, c.1908-17, 1 In.
$3800.00

Silver-Sterling, Bowl, Flower Shape, Embossed, Stamped, Blair & Crawford, 2½ x 10 In.
$248.00

TIP

Use your silver often and wash it to keep it clean. Polish it as seldom as possible. Silver polish removes a small bit of silver each time it is used.

Samovar, Cover, Egg Shape, Bun Feet, Handles, Spout, Carved Ivory, 1917, 14½ In. 24780.00
Scent Bottle, Green Enamel, Snowflake Design, Cyrillic Signature, c.1908-17, 1 In. . . . . *illus* 3800.00
Spice Tower, Bell, Bird, 4 Bells Hanging, Domed Base, Grapevine Feet, 11 In. 1175.00
Spoon, Gold Washed, Stylized Leaves, Oval, 1908-17, 5½ In. 94.00
Spoon Set, Boxed, Enamel, Twisted Stem, Oval Bowl, c.1917, 4⅛ In., 12 Piece 5581.00
Spoon Set, Enamel, Oval Bowl, Enameled Back, Handle, Gilt Finish, 4¼ In., 8 Piece 1150.00
Sugar, Cover, Enamel, Pear Shape, Ear Handles, Lid Handle, 5⅛ In. 9988.00
Teaspoon Set, Enamel, Gold Washed, Leaves, Demilune, Navette, 5¼ In., 4 Piece. 470.00
Tray, 2 Handles, Rectangular, Molded Rim, Shells, Acanthus, Rocaille, 25⅝ In. 4800.00
Vase, Trumpet, Vine Wrapped Around Base, Footed, 1911, 17 In. 1750.00

SILVER-SCOTTISH

Decanter Label, Scotch, Silver Chain, 2⅝ x 1½ In. 45.00
Snuff Mull, Mounted Horn, Curved, Hinged Lid, Applied Thistle, Monogram, 3¼ In. 323.00
Sugar & Creamer, Eagle Head Handle, George III, 1810, 4½ x 6 & 4⅜ x 8 In. 345.00

SILVER-SOUTH AMERICAN

Crucifix, 19th Century, 5¾ In. 246.00

SILVER-SPANISH

Bowl, Colonial, Lobed, Chased Base, Patera, Swags, Leaf Handles, 5⅛ In., Pair 88.00

SILVER-STERLING. Sterling silver is made with 925 parts silver out of 1,000 parts of metal. The word *sterling* is a quality guarantee used in the United States after about 1860. The word was used much earlier in England and Ireland. Pieces listed here are not identified by country. Other pieces of sterling quality silver are listed under Silver-American, Silver-English, etc.

Andirons, Column Shaft, Lemon Finials, Cabriole Legs, c.1900, Miniature, 2⅝ In. 441.00
Beaker, Pereisner Silver Co., Cylindrical, Flared Rim, 5¼ x 3 In., 12 Piece. 540.00
Bowl, Arts & Crafts, Round, Hammered Finish, Handles, Kuhler, Peru, 2¾ x 18 In. 690.00
Bowl, Center, Ornate Pierced Border, 5¼ x 12 In. 920.00
Bowl, Center, Underplate, Pedestal Shape, Scalloped Rim, Openwork, 6¾ x 8¼ In. 920.00
Bowl, Circular, Square Base, Architectural Design, 3½ x 6½ In. 1495.00
Bowl, Flower Shape, Embossed, Stamped, Blair & Crawford, 2½ x 10 In. . . . . *illus* 248.00
Bowl, Lobed, Hand Wrought, Marked, Randahl, 5 In. . . . . *illus* 250.00
Bowl, Lobed Sides, Floral Sprays, Leaves, Vines, c.1905, 3¼ x 13 In. 705.00
Bowl, Oval, Dove, Ribbons, Acanthus, Putto, 2¾ x 10½ In. 240.00
Bowl, Oval, Scroll Border, Openwork Body, Marked, 2 x 10 x 8 In. . . . . *illus* 140.00
Bowl, Pedestal, Chrysanthemum, Wooden Storage Box, c.1919, 8 x 10 In. 13800.00
Bowl, Presentation, Circular Medallion, American Indian, 1918, 2½ x 5 In. 4200.00
Bowl, Round, Paneled Sides, Openwork Border, Engraved Wreath, 9¾ In. 144.00
Bowl, Round, Scalloped Rim, Chased, Flower, Matte Ground, Gilt, 4½ x 10½ In. 679.00
Bowl, Vegetable, Classical Pattern, Cover, c.1915, 11½ In. 1092.00
Bowl, Vegetable, Warren D. Perry, c.1939, 13½ In., Pair 760.00
Box, Enamel, Singing Bird, Key, Rooster On Lid, 3¾ x 2½ In. 12075.00
Bread Basket, Reticulated 431.00
Bread Tray, Banded Rim, c.1930, 6 x 13 In. 117.00
Caddy Spoon, Eagle Wing, Eagle Head Handle, Feather Design Bowl, c.1839. . . . . 2459.00
Cake Basket, Hemispherical, Scalloped Pierced Edge, Handle, 7 In. 431.00
Candelabra are listed in the Candelabrum category.
Candlesticks are listed in their own category.
Castor, Cockayne, Wings Hinged, Paste Eyes, Neresheimer, 17th Century Style, 7 x 3 In. 720.00
Chalice, Cover, Footed, Seated Satyr, Floral Repousse, 13½ x 5 In. 1200.00
Chocolate Pot, Classical Urn Shape, Angular Wooden Handle, 1940s, 9½ In. 384.00
Cigarette Case, Art Deco, Enameled. 374.00
Clothes Brush, L Pierre Mfg. Co., c.1940, 3½ In., Pair. 23.00
Cocktail Forks, Twisted Round Handles, Owl & Shell Decoration, 6 In., 12 Piece 288.00
Cocktail Shaker, 10¼ In. 413.00
Coffee Set, Coffeepot, Sugar, Cover, Creamer, Coventry, 10½ In. 489.00
Coffee Set, Gothic Revival, Applied Beaded Borders, Lion & Ring Handles, 9½ In. 1955.00
Compote, Flared Rim, Reeded Stem, Spherules, Grapes, c.1945, 7⅜ In. 3173.00
Compote, Fruit & Flowers, Repousse, Marked, Loring Andrews Co., 9 x 12 In. . . . . *illus* 2300.00
Compote, Quaker, Open Work Pedestal, Cast Scrolling Leaves, 12 In. 413.00
Creamer, Cow, Hinged Bee Lid, c.1907, 5 x 3½ In. 1320.00
Cruet, Art Nouveau, Stopper, 6 In. 146.00
Decanter, Stopper, Overlay, Leaves, Applied Sterling Overlay Handle, 13½ In. 885.00
Decanter Set, Overlay, Bottle Shape, Shield Above Fence, 6 Cordials, Fitted Case 144.00
Demitasse Set, Coffeepot, Sugar, Creamer, Queen Anne Style, 3 Piece. 431.00
Dish, Cover, Branch Shape Handle, Engraved, Stag Head Crest, c.1840, 4 x 10 In. 600.00

Dish, Entree, Repousse, Oval, Floral Decoration, Acanthus Border, c.1916, 4½ x 11 In. 2645.00
Epergne, Flower Relief, Paw Feet, Movable Arms, Glass Bowls, c.1805, 13 In. 16100.00
Ewer, Cranberry & Yellow Overlay, 11 In. 1404.00
Ewer, Vase Shape, Pedestal Base, Grapes, Vines, Branch Handle, c.1890, 17 In. 2629.00
Flask, Embossed, 5½ x 3 In. .... 176.00 to 323.00
Flask, Repousse, Oval, Round Neck, Screw Top Lid, Flowers, c.1898, 6½ x 3¼ In. 575.00
Frame, Photograph, Edwardian, Square, Circular Aperture, 9½ In. 132.00
Gaucho Stirrups, Leather Hangers, Engraved Flowers. 248.00
Grape Scissors, Scrolled Handles, c.1910, 6 In. 205.00
Gravy Boat, Georgian Style, Ogee Rim, Flying Flat Leaf Loop Handle, 4¾ x 8 In., Pair 294.00
Gravy Boat, Tray, Warren D. Perry, c.1939 .... 234.00
Gravy Boat, Undertray, Flared Scalloped Top, Loop Handle, 3 Cabriole Legs 168.00
Ice Tongs, S. Kirk & Son, Shell Grips, Monogram, 6½ In. 83.00
Julep Cup, Cartier, Tapering, Reeded Rim, Foot, Monogram, 3¾ x 3 In., 10 Piece 3360.00
Kettle, Panel Form, Engraved Flowers, Hinged Lid, Ivory Finial, 11 x 9 In. 1400.00
Kettle, Stand, Bullet Shape Teapot, Spiral Gadrooning, Gooseneck Spout, 9 x 6 In. 450.00
Kettle, Stand, Oval, Bands Of Floral Swags, Wooden Handle, Crichton Bros., 13 In. 977.00
Ladle, Arabesque Style, Pointed Oval Bowl, Bright Cut Decoration, 1800s, 13 In. 403.00
Lighter Case, Turquoise, 1 x 2¾ In. 90.00
Manicure Set, Scissors, Crystal Bottles, Buffer, c.1927, 8 x 4⅔ In. 242.00
Master Salt, Glass Insert, Filigree Work, 1 x 2 In. 25.00
Master Salt Spoon, 2½ In. 2.00
Nail Buffer, Apple Green Enamel, Art Deco Pattern, Chamois, c.1933, 5½ In. 47.00
Napkin Rings are listed in their own category.
Open Salt, S.C.S. Co., c.1930, 1¼ In., 9 Piece 176.00
Pitcher, Ecclesiastical, Paneled Sides, Squared Handles, Flat Lid, Cross Finial, 6 1/12 In. 201.00
Pitcher, Presentation, Scrolling, Repousse. 1495.00
Pitcher, Royal Danish, Four Pint, No. E 84, 8 In. 263.00
Pitcher, Water, Faceted Baluster Shape, Stepped Foot, Leaves & Shells, c.1840, 8½ In. 1920.00
Pitcher, Water, Hammered, Urn Shape, Applied Handle, Footed, 11 x 5 In. 475.00
Pitcher, Water, Helmet Top, Lion's Head Handle, Band Of Spearheads, 13 In. 2185.00
Plate Set, Bread & Butter, Reeded Border, Monogram, 1900s, 6⅛ In., 12 Piece 613.00
Platter, Round, Pierced, Engraved Rim, Applied Cast Grapevine Border, 19 In. 2280.00
Platter, Warren D. Perry, c.1939, 13 x 18 In. 761.00
Platter, Well & Tree, Oval, Gadroon & Floral Border, Scroll Feet, c.1874, 24 x 16¾ In. 1840.00
Potpourri, Bulbous, Footed, Hinged Lid, Birds, Flowering Branches, c.1908, 5 x 4 In. 660.00
Punch Bowl, Art Nouveau, Bulbous Sides, Cast Scrollwork, c.1900, 7½ x 13½ In. 2938.00
Punch Bowl, Swan Shape, 10 Cups, Looped & Bowed Head Handles, 10½ x 19 In. 2875.00
Rose Bowl, Repousse, Marked Yokohama, 3½ x 7½ In. 165.00
Salad Set, Fork, Spoon, Repousse, Floral Handles, Loring Andrews Co., 10 & 10¼ In. 230.00
Salt, Robin's-Egg Blue Liner, Oval, c.1880, 1⅛ In. 77.00
Salt & Pepper, Art Deco, Gold Washed Top, 2¼ In. 38.00
Salt & Pepper, Art Deco Style, 1½ In. 24.00
Salt & Pepper, Crystal, Jacob's Ladder Variation 50.00
Salt & Pepper, Eames Ear, Box 54.00
Salver, John Carter, c.1775, 11¾ In. 1638.00
Salver, Scalloped Edge, Etched Design, c.1771, 12¼ In. 1287.00
Serving Spoon, Art Nouveau, Woman, Child, Pierced, Chased Handle, 10⅛ In. 236.00
Serving Spoon, Engraved Figure, Middle Eastern Man, Scimitar, Hallmarks, 10 In. 225.00
Shovel, Cut Engraving, Square Bowl, Marked, Kitts & Werne, 10¾ In. .... *illus* 230.00
Spoon, Souvenir, see Souvenir category.
Spurs, Horse Head Shank, Brass Rowels, Applied Feathers, Horsehair Straps, 6 In. 518.00
Spurs, Pinwheels, Shaped Chap Guard, Tooled Leather Straps, 6½ In. 690.00
Sugar & Creamer, Floral Repousse, Horse Head Crest, Claw Foot Base, c.1866 .... 300.00
Sugar Castor, Faceted Bulbous, Pierced Cover, Monogram, c.1905, 8½ In. 354.00
Sugar Tongs, Figural, Monk, Marked, Germany, 4 In. 550.00
Tea & Coffee Set, Vase Shape Coffeepot, Tray, 26½ In., c.1907, 7 Piece. 5875.00
Tea Caddy, Urn Shape, Vertical, Flower Band, Dot Borders, 4¾ x 3½ x 2¾ In. 112.00
Tea Set, Oval, Palmette Band, Paw Feet, Strawberry Band, c.1820, 3 Piece 2880.00
Toddy Ladle, Crested, Applied Beaded Rim, Twist Whalebone Handle, c.1800, 13¼ In. 235.00
Tray, Pen, Rounded Ends, Angles, c.1905, 9 x 3 In. 265.00
Tureen, Dragon Handles, Flowers, Relief, Hallmarked, 16 x 8 In. 13800.00
Wine Cistern, Oval, Acanthus Scroll Feet, Engraved Arms, Lion Crest, 8 x 16 In. 4700.00

SILVER-SWEDISH

Serving Bowl, Cherub Musicians, Pomegranates, Beaded Rim, c. 1929, 13⅝ In. 206.00

Silver-Sterling, Bowl, Lobed, Hand Wrought, Marked, Randahl, 5 In.
$250.00

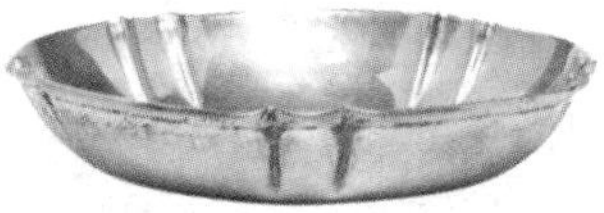

Silver-Sterling, Bowl, Oval, Scroll Border, Openwork Body, Marked, 2 x 10 x 8 In.
$140.00

Silver-Sterling, Compote, Fruit & Flowers, Repousse, Marked, Loring Andrews Co., 9 x 12 In.
$2300.00

Silver-Sterling, Shovel, Cut Engraving, Square Bowl, Marked, Kitts & Werne, 10¾ In.
$230.00

Slag Glass, Purple, Butter, Cover, Cow, Greener & Co., 7 ¾ In.
$600.00

Slag Glass, Purple, Obelisk, Monument Style, 7 ¾ x 3 ½ In.
$103.00

Sleepy Eye, Stein, Blue & White, Teepees, Campfire, Indian Head, c.1900, 7 ¾ x 4 ⅜ In.
$240.00

Sleepy Eye, Vase, Cattails & Dragonflies, Salt Glaze, Early 20th Century, 8 ½ x 4 In.
$180.00

SINCLAIRE cut glass was made by H.P. Sinclaire and Company of Corning, New York, between 1904 and 1929. He cut glass made at other factories until 1920. Pieces were made of crystal as well as amber, blue, green, or ruby glass. Only a small percentage of Sinclaire glass is marked with the S in a wreath.

Compote, Mirror Black, White Lip Wrap, 12 In. 345.00
Console Set, Celeste Blue, Optic Ribbed Bowl, Rolled Rim, 2 Trumpet Vases, 12 & 8 In. 288.00
Cruet, Hobstar Band, Intaglio, Triple Notched Handle, Stopper, 7 In. 350.00
Finger Bowl, Water Lily, Marked, 4 ½ In. 120.00
Pitcher, Cider, Hobstar, Squares, Daisy Border, Marked, 6 ½ In. 450.00
Plate, Assyrian, 6 ¼ In. 525.00
Plate, Bengal, Signed, 10 In. 1600.00
Teapot, Flute Cut Panels, Greek Key & Ivy Border, 5 x 9 In. 700.00
Vase, Black, Intaglio, Chinese Dragon, Clouds, Whitelip Wrap, Oval, Signed, 9 In. 518.00
Vase, Mirror Black, Intaglio Dragons, Cylindrical, 16 ½ In. 2500.00

SKIING, *see Sports category.*

SLAG GLASS resembles a marble cake. It can be streaked with different colors. There were many types made from about 1880. Caramel slag is the incorrect name for Chocolate glass. Pink slag was an American product made by Harry Bastow and Thomas E.A. Dugan at Indiana, Pennsylvania, about 1900. Purple and blue slag were made in American and English factories in the 1880s. Red slag is a very late Victorian and twentieth-century glass. Other colors are known but are of less importance to the collector. New versions of chocolate glass and colored slag glass are being made.

Caramel Slag is listed in the Imperial Glass category.
Pink, Tumbler, Inverted Fan & Feather, Dugan, 3 ¾ In. 144.00
Pink, Water Set, Inverted Fan & Feather, Dugan, 8-In. Pitcher, 4 Piece 633.00
Purple, Butter, Cover, Cow, Greener & Co., 7 ¾ In. *illus* 600.00
Purple, Obelisk, Monument Style, 7 ¾ x 3 ½ In. *illus* 103.00

SLEEPY EYE collectors look for anything bearing the image of the nineteenth-century Indian chief with the drooping eyelid. The Sleepy Eye Milling Co., Sleepy Eye, Minnesota, used his portrait in advertising from 1883 to 1921. It offered many premiums, including stoneware and pottery steins, crocks, bowls, mugs, and pitchers, all decorated with the famous profile of the Indian. The popular pottery was made by Western Stoneware, Weir Pottery Company, and other companies long after the flour mill went out of business in 1921. Reproductions of the pitchers are being made today. The original pitchers came in only five sizes: 4 inches, 5¼ inches, 6½ inches, 8 inches, and 9 inches. The Sleepy Eye image was also used by companies unrelated to the flour mill.

Crock, Butter, Blue & Gray, Old Sleepy Eye, Village Scene, 6 In. 375.00
Crock, Butter, Indian, Teepees & Trees, Blue & Gray Salt Glaze, Relief, c.1890, 4 ¾ In. 248.00
Crock, Indian One Side, Teepee Other, Weir Pottery, c.1914, 5 x 6 ⅜ In. 270.00
Crock, Salt, Indian Head, 21st Annual Sleepy Eye Collectors Convention, c.1996, 5 In. 30.00
Mug, Indian On One Side, Teepee Other, Stoneware. 69.00
Pitcher, Blue, Indian Head, 8 In. 43.00
Pitcher, Blue, Indian One Side, Teepee Other, Monmouth Pottery, 8 ¾ x 6 ¾ In. 76.00
Pitcher, Blue & White, Old Sleepy Eye, No. 2, 5 In. 320.00
Pitcher, Blue & White, Old Sleepy Eye, No. 3, 6 In. 390.00
Pitcher, Blue & White, Old Sleepy Eye, No. 4, 8 In. 280.00
Pitcher, Blue & White, Old Sleepy Eye, No. 5, 9 In. 390.00
Pitcher, Blue Rim, Blue & White, Old Sleepy Eye, No. 4, 8 In. 350.00
Pitcher, Indian Profile, Landscape, Teepees, Blue, Cream Ground, 8 ½ x 8 In. 173.00
Plate, Souvenir, Blue Bird, Roses, 7 ½ In. 150.00
Postcard, Old Sleepy Eye Flour, Indian Picture, c.1904. 82.00
Salt, Stoneware, Indian Head, Blue & Gray 376.00
Sign, Sleepy Eye Flour, Embossed, Tin, Wood Frame, 20 x 24 In. 44000.00
Sign, Sleepy Eye Mills, Paper, Indian Picture, Minn., 16 In. 11.00
Stein, Blue, Embossed, Indian On One Side, Teepee, 7 ½ x 4 ⅜ In. 279.00
Stein, Blue & White, Teepees, Campfire, Indian Head, c.1900, 7 ¾ x 4 ⅜ In. *illus* 240.00
Stein, Flemish Blue Gray, Indian Head Handle, 4 ¼ In. 475.00
Stein, Old Sleepy Eye, Indian, Blue & Gray, 7 ½ x 4 ¼ In. 475.00
Stein, Western Stoneware, 1979. 355.00
Toothpick Holder, Black Slag Glass, Indian Chief, Banner, Arrowhead, 2 ½ x 2 In. 11.00
Vase, Cattails & Dragonflies, Salt Glaze, Early 20th Century, 8 ½ x 4 In. *illus* 180.00
Vase, Indian, Cat O' Nine Tails, Cobalt Blue, 8 ½ x 4 In. *illus* 259.00
Vase, Indian Chief, Old Sleepy Eye, Blue, Gray, Embossed, Old Sleepy Eye, Early 20th Century, 8 ½ In. 295.00

Vase, Old Sleepy Eye, Cattails, Blue, White, 8 ½ In. 375.00
Vase, Old Sleepy Eye, Indian Chief, Blue & Gray Glaze, 20th Century, 8 ½ In. 295.00

SLOT MACHINES *are included in the Coin-Operated Machine category.*

SMITH BROTHERS glass was made after 1878. Alfred and Harry Smith had worked for the Mt. Washington Glass Company in New Bedford, Massachusetts, for seven years before going into their own shop. They made many pieces with enamel decoration.

Smith Bros. Co.

Atomizer, Opal, Wisteria Blossoms On Vine, Gold Trim, 6 ½ In. 529.00
Biscuit Jar, Daisies, Leaves, Rectangular, Diagonal Swirl, Marked, 7 ½ In. 201.00
Vase, Blue, Melon Ribbed, Gold Scrolling Flowers, Mold-Blown Rim, 9 In. 345.00
Vase, Opal, Heron In Reeds, Double Ring, Gold Trim, c.1885, 8 In. 80.00

SNOW BABIES, made from bisque and spattered with glitter sand, were first manufactured in 1864 by Hertwig and Company of Thuringia. Other German and Japanese companies copied the Hertwig designs. Originally, Snow Babies were made of candy and used as Christmas decorations. There are also Snow Babies tablewares made by Royal Bayreuth. Copies of the small Snow Babies figurines are being made today and can easily confuse the collector.

Figurine, Bisque, Holding Copper Wire Staffs, 4 ¼ In., Pair . . . . *illus* 265.00
Figurine, On Sled, Marked, Germany, 3 In. 40.00

SNUFF BOTTLES *are listed in the Bottle category.*

SNUFFBOXES held snuff. Taking snuff was popular long before cigarettes became available. The gentleman or lady would take a small pinch of the ground tobacco or snuff in the fingers, then sniff it and sneeze. Snuffboxes were made of many materials, including gold, silver, enameled metal, and wood. Most snuffboxes date from the late eighteenth or early nineteenth centuries.

18K Gold, Engraved Flowers, Leaves, Matte Interior, Hinged, Leon Tournan, 3 x 2 In. 1553.00
Bone, Book Shape, Hinged Lid, Tulips, Flowering Plants, Tools, Red, Yellow, 1828, 2 x 3 In. . . 646.00
Bronze, Woman, Tourmalines, Scrolls, Enamel, Gilt, France, c.1880, 1 x 2 ½ In. . . . . . *illus* 450.00
Coquilla Nut, Basket Shape, Double Flap, Swing Handle, Silver Hinges, 5 x 1 ¾ In. 1750.00
Coquilla Nut, Clamshell Shape, Artemis, Quiver, Dog, Flowers, 1800s, 2 ¾ x ¼ In. 250.00
Coquilla Nut, Clamshell Shape, Cherubs, Eagle, Demon, Ivory Teeth, 3 x 4 In. 2100.00
Coquilla Nut, Flask Shape, Hunting Weapons, Animal Head, Rabbit Foot, 3 ½ x 1 ¾ In. . . . 1850.00
Coquilla Nut, Scipion Ship, 79 Gun, Lift Lid, Silver Hinge, 5 x 1 ½ In. 1900.00
Enamel, Gold, Rectangular, Ivy Leaves, Translucent Blue Ground, France, 3 ¼ In. 3600.00
Enamel, Hobby Horse, 1 ½ x 1 In. 220.00
Enamel, Portrait Of Young Woman, 20-Pin Tourmaline, Raised Acanthus Scrolls, 2 In. 531.00
Horn, Washington Profile Medallion, Friction Fit Lid, Gilt, c.1815, 3 ¼ x 1 In. 1495.00
Horn, Carved, 19th Century, 1 ¼ x 2 ½ In. 59.00
Louis XV, Black Lacquer, Gilded Flowers, Octagonal, Genillon, France, 1753, 2 ⅜ In. 1800.00
Papier-Mache, Black Lacquered, Victorian Bar Scene, Hunters, Round, c.1860, 6 In. 7170.00
Papier-Mache, Man With Dog, England, 19th Century, ¾ x 2 ⅞ In. 235.00
Papier-Mache, Older Man, Stobwasser Style, Germany, 19th Century, 1 ½ x 4 ¾ In. . . . *illus* 115.00
Silver, C. Parker, c.1850, ⅝ x 3 ¼ In. 147.00
Silver, Cowry Shell, Flush Hinged Cover, John Moore, Dublin, c.1740, 3 ¼ In. 3900.00

SOAPSTONE is a mineral that was used for foot warmers or griddles because of its heat-retaining properties. Soapstone was carved into figurines and bowls in many countries in the nineteenth and twentieth centuries. Most of the soapstone seen today is from China or Japan. It is still being carved in the old styles.

Box, Flowers, Carved, Brass Mounts, Foo Dog Finial, Chinese, ¾ x 3 ½ x 6 ½ In. 235.00
Figurine, Buddhist Saint, Seated, On Rocky Outcrop, Chinese, 18th Century, 7 In. 2938.00
Figurine, Bull, Yellow, Dark Brown, Chinese, Early 20th Century, 10 In. 118.00
Figurine, Hand Carved, Oriental, Early 20th Century, 6 x 6 ½ In. 44.00
Figurine, Immortal, Chinese, 19th Century, 3 ½ In. 2703.00
Figurine, Lion, Carved, 7 x 12 In. 75.00

SOFT PASTE is a name for a type of pottery. Although it looks very much like porcelain, it is a chemically different material. Most of the soft-paste wares were made in the early nineteenth century. Other pieces may be listed under Gaudy Dutch or Leeds.

Bowl, Landscape, Cover, Apple Finial, France, c.1759 . . . . 2500.00

Sleepy Eye, Vase, Indian, Cat O' Nine Tails, Cobalt Blue, 8 ½ x 4 In. $259.00

Snow Babies, Figurine, Bisque, Holding Copper Wire Staffs, 4 ¼ In., Pair $265.00

Snuffbox, Bronze, Woman, Tourmalines, Scrolls, Enamel, Gilt, France, c.1880, 1 x 2 ½ In. $450.00

Snuffbox, Papier-Mache, Older Man, Stobwasser Style, Germany, 19th Century, 1 ½ x 4 ¾ In. $115.00

S

Souvenir, Handkerchief, Denver, Colorado, Round, 13 ½ In.
$15.00

Souvenir, Plate, Indiana, Hoosier State, Marked, Nautilus, 10 In.
$10.00

TIP

Want to clean a copper-colored souvenir building or other small copper-coated piece? Soak it in a shallow bowl in the juice of one lemon or two tablespoons of vinegar and enough water to cover the souvenir. Leave it only about five minutes. Dry. Repeat if necessary. The acid of the lemon or vinegar chemically removes the oxide that is darkening the piece. But too much soaking may harm the copper coloring.

S

Bowl, Woman, Cupid, Hearts, 19th Century, 8 In. 225.00
Cake Plate, Flowers, Scalloped Shape, Scrolled Border, Gold Trim 62.00
Cup & Saucer, Green & Black Curly Cues, Sprigs, Bavaria, c.1800 .... 65.00
Cup & Saucer, Mother Playing With Child, Black, White, c.1800 .... 120.00
Cup & Saucer, Purple, Silver Luster, 19th Century 140.00
Pitcher, Banded, Pale Blue Glaze, Pearlware, 9 In. 575.00
Pitcher, Milk, Fruit Design, C-Handle, Bulbous, c.1856, 7 In. 295.00
Plate, Flower Trim, Central Basket, 18th Century, 6 ½ In. 26.00
Plate, Flowers, Leaves, Multicolored Scalloped Rim, c.1800, 9 In. 40.00
Plate, Flowers, Multicolored Scalloped Rim, Beading, W. Adams & Sons, c.1879, 9 In. 48.00
Saucer, Flowers, Lavender & Blue Trim, c.1780 .... 26.00
Tankard, Strawberry Design, St. Cloud Pottery, France, c.1766 .... 225.00
Teapot, Queen's Rose, Strawberry, Flowers, Vines, 7 ½ In. 176.00
Urn, Bird Scene, c.1780, 21 In. 2500.00
Wine Strainer, Flowers, Ribbed Neck, c.1800, 5 ½ In. 350.00

SOUVENIRS of a trip—what could be more fun? Our ancestors enjoyed the same thing and souvenirs were made for almost every location. Most of the souvenir pottery and porcelain pieces of the nineteenth century were made in England or Germany, even if the picture showed a North American scene. In the twentieth century, the souvenir china business seems to have gone to the manufacturers in Japan, Taiwan, Hong Kong, England, and America. Another popular souvenir item is the souvenir spoon, made of sterling or silver plate. These are usually made in the country pictured on the spoon. Related pieces may be found in the Coronation and World's Fair categories.

Bottle Opener, Can Punch, Ocean City, Parrot, Cast Iron, John Wright Co., 5 In. 165.00
Bowl, Bagnell Dam, Missouri, Reticulated Border, Gold Rim, Japan 17.00
Bowl, Salem, Massachusetts, First Church, Reticulated, Porcelain, Oval, Germany 40.00
Button, Wright Brothers, Home Celebration, Dayton, Ohio, Celluloid, c.1909, ⅞ In. 294.00
Corkscrew, Bottle Opener, New Orleans, Goldtone, Jeweled 9.00
Creamer, West Virginia, Red, Paden City, 4 ¼ In. 15.00
Cup, Nashville Music City U.S.A., Guitar Handle, Red Guitar, Music Notes 7.00
Cup, Niagara Falls, Maroon Band, Flowers, Vines, 24K Gold, 2 ¼ In. 28.00
Dish, Atlantic City, N.J., Casinos, Slot Machine, Cards, Dice, Fluted Edge, 5 In. 7.00
Dish, Map Of St. Lawrence Seaway, Porcelain, Alfred Meakin, 1959, 5 In. 30.00
Glass, Florida, Flamingo, Poinsetta, Frosted, Multicolored 7 In. 15.00
Glass, Kansas Sunflower State, Map, Oil Well, Barn, Wagon, Prairie, Frosted 6.00
Glass, Weeki Wachee Florida, Mermaids, Brown, Metal Bands, Handle, 5 ¼ In. 15.00
Handkerchief, California, Map, Blue, Pink, White 18.00
Handkerchief, Denver, Colorado, Round, 13 ½ In. .... *illus* 15.00
Letter Opener, Miami Beach, Alligator Handle, Bronze, 1930s, 6 In. 15.00
Mirror, Lake Placid Olympics, Winter Games, 1980, 3 In. 10.00
Paperweight, St. Peter's, Rome, Micro Mosaic, Octagonal Onyx Base, 3 In. 4000.00
Pillow Cover, Coney Island, Ferris Wheel, Sunken Gardens, Boardwalk, 1930s, 20 x 20 In. 85.00
Pillow Sham, Missouri, Indians, Log Cabin, Pine Cones, Mountains, Deer, Fringe 18.00
Pin, 7th Annual Reunion Baer Family, Kutztown Park, Aug. 4, 1906, Celluloid, 2 In. 147.00
Pincushion, U.S. Capitol, White House, Occupied Japan, 3 In. 30.00
Pipe, Hershey Park, Pa., Flowers, Glass, Hand Painted 20.00
Plate, Carlsbad Caverns National Park, N.m., Hall Of Giants, Flow Blue, Flowers, 10 In. 40.00
Plate, Chicago, Skyline View, Blue, White, 9 In. 20.00
Plate, Florida, Palm Trees, Flamingos, Heart Shape, Heart Cutout Border, Black, 7 In. 28.00
Plate, Heidelberg United Church Of Christ, Marion, Pa., 10 In. 10.00
Plate, Indiana, Hoosier State, Marked, Nautilus, 10 In. .... *illus* 10.00
Plate, Mitchell's World's Only Corn Palace, Gold Luster Rim 30.00
Plate, National Apple Museum, Biglerville, Pa., 9 ¼ In. 10.00
Plate, Old Faithful Geyser, Yellowstone National Park, Flow Blue, 10 In. 40.00
Plate, Old Log Church, Protestant Methodist, Blairs Valley, Pa., 1844-1972, 9 ¼ In. 14.00
Plate, Shenandoah Caverns, Virginia, Cardross Castle, 9 ¼ In. 10.00
Plate, Smokey Mountains, Mount Leconte, Indians, Bears, Ironstone China, 9 In. 28.00
Plate, Tuscarora Summit Inn, McConnellsburg, Pa., 9 ⅜ In. 65.00
Plate, Tuscarora Summit Inn, Summit, Pa., 8 ½ In. 45.00
Plate, Washington D.C., U.S. Capitol, Jefferson Memorial, White House, 7 ½ In. 15.00
Ring, Olympics, Swimming, Berlin, Summer, Participant's, 9K Gold, 1936, Size 9 .... 1016.00
Salt & Pepper, California, Map, Prospector, Gold Letter, Red, Clear Plastic, 2 x 3 In. 12.00
Salt & Pepper, Fairbanks, Alaska, Fighting Roosters, Brown, White Slag, 2 ¾ In. 12.00
Salt & Pepper, Figural, Teapot, South Carolina, Silver Plate, 2 ½ In. 16.00
Salt & Pepper, Hawaii, Pineapple Shape, Brown, Holder, Stopper, 5 x 4 ½ In. 18.00

alt & Pepper, Maine, Seagull, Come Fly With Me, Up Turned Wings, Plastic Stopper 17.00
alt & Pepper, South Carolina, Footed Teapot Shape, Silver Plate, 2 ½ In. 16.00
poon, Australia, Koala & Baby Bear, Gilt Enamel, Scrolling Raised Pattern, 1900s, 5 In. 95.00
poon, Chicago, Sterling, 4 x ¾ In. 25.00
poon, Denmark, Crest, Sterling Silver, c.1937, 4 ⅛ In. 40.00
poon, Jacksonville, Florida, Alligator, Sterling Silver, 5 In. 39.00
poon, Mount Rushmore, Black Hills S.D., 4 Presidents, Sterling Silver 59.00
poon, Mount Vernon, Martha & George Washington, Sterling Silver, c.1759 20.00
poon, Napoli, Landscape, Bay, Mt. Vesuvius, Shield Handle, Enameled Bowl, 8 In. 294.00
poon, Oslo, Norway, Sterling Silver 13.00
poon, San Juan Mission, Capistrano, California, 4 ½ In. 16.00
poon, St. Petersburg, Russia, Gilt Enamel, Heraldic, Scrolling, Cyrillic Letters, 5 In. 75.00
poon, Stockbridge Massachusetts, Indian Chief, Corn Stalks, Sterling Silver, 4 ¼ In. 44.00
poon, Vancouver, Canadian Maple Leaf, Sterling Silver, 3 ¾ x ¾ In. 25.00
tatue Of Liberty, Enlightening The World, Metal, Wood, 1885, 7 In. 657.00
ugar, Garden Of The Gods, Colorado, Cover, Finial, 3 In. 16.00
ea Towel, Atlantic City N.J., Sunbathers, Airplanes, Golders, Multicolored, 28 x 16 In. 32.00
ea Towel, Tower Bridge London River, c.1960, 31 x 20 In. 12.00
hermometer, New Orleans, Frame, c.1940 16.00
oothpick Holder, Santa Fe Depot, Kiowa Kansas, Railroad Tracks, Cobalt Blue 43.00
oothpick Holder, Shoot The Chutes, Dreamland, Coney Island, 1900, 3 ¾ In. 125.00
oothpick Holder, Shoot The Chutes, Dreamland, Coney Island, 1900s, 2 In. 125.00
ray, Miami Beach Florida, Oranges, Palm Trees, Flamingos, Masonite, 17 x 11 In. 16.00
ray, New York City, Pot Metal, c.1950 20.00
ray, Osborne House, England, 3-In. Reverse Painting On Glass *illus* 395.00
ase, Wangerooge, Germany, Cylindrical, Coat Of Arms, Flowers, Gold Glaze, c.1970 20.00

PANGLE GLASS is multicolored glass made from odds and ends of colored glass rods. It includes netallic flakes of mica covered with gold, silver, nickel, or copper. Spangle glass is usually ased with a thin layer of clear glass over the multicolored layer. Similar glass is listed in the 'asa Murrhina category.

owl, Yellow, Pink Interior, Gold Flecks, Frosted, Footed, 3 ½ x 5 ¾ In. 180.00
ruet, Blue & White, Gold Aventurine, Bulbous, Tricornered Rim, 6 In. 460.00
itcher, Pink, Mica Flecks, 19th Century, 8 In. 146.00

PANISH LACE *is listed in the Opalescent category as Opaline Brocade.*

PATTER GLASS is a multicolored glass made from many small pieces of different colored lass. It is sometimes called End-of-Day glass. It is still being made.

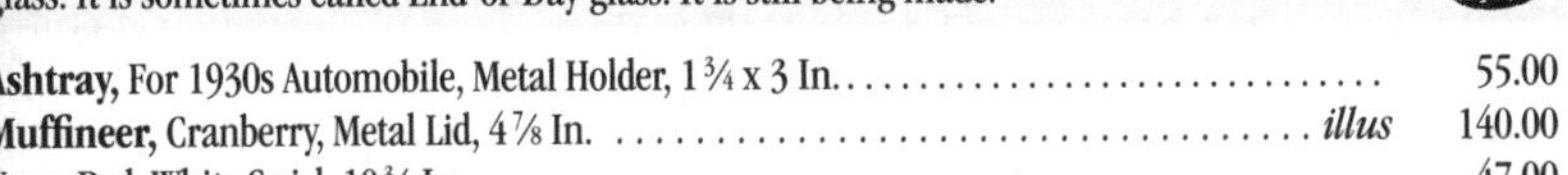

shtray, For 1930s Automobile, Metal Holder, 1 ¾ x 3 In. 55.00
Iuffineer, Cranberry, Metal Lid, 4 ⅞ In. *illus* 140.00
ase, Red, White Swirl, 10 ¾ In. 47.00

PATTERWARE and spongeware are terms that have changed in meaning in recent years, ausing much confusion for collectors. Some say that *spatterware* is the term used by mericans, *sponged ware* or *spongeware* by the English. Spatterware is creamware or soft paste innerware decorated with colored spatter designs. The earliest pieces were made in the late eighteenth entury, but most of the spatterware found today was made from about 1800 to 1850. Early spatterware vas made in the Staffordshire district of England for sale in America. Collectors also use the word *batterware* to refer to kitchen crockery with added spatter made in America during the late nineteenth nd early twentieth centuries. Spongeware is very similar to spatterware in appearance. Designs were pplied to ceramics by daubing the color on with a sponge or cloth. Many collectors do not differentiate etween spongeware and spatterware and use the names interchangeably. Modern pottery is being made o resemble old spongeware, but careful examination will show it is new.

Bowl, Peafowl, Blue, Yellow, Green, Full Red Spatter, Footed, 2 ⅜ x 4 ⅜ In. 248.00
Bowl, Rose, Red, Green Leaves, Blue Spatter On Side, 2 ¾ x 4 ¼ In. 198.00
hamber Pot, Blue, Center Band, Applied Loop Handle, 5 ¼ x 9 ¼ In. 55.00
reamer, 2 Men In Raft, Blue Spatter, Helmet Form, 2-Sided, 4 ½ In. 3080.00
reamer, Blue, White, Band, 4 In. 144.00
reamer, Cluster Of Buds, Red Spatter, 4 ¾ In. 472.00
reamer, Dahlia, Red & Blue, Green Sprigs, Purple Spatter, Helmet Form, 4 ½ In. 522.00
Creamer, Peafowl, Blue, Yellow, Red, Full Green Spatter, Bulbous, 3 ⅜ In. 605.00
Creamer, Peafowl, Blue, Yellow, Red, Brown Spatter, Helmut Form, 2-Sided, 5 In. 1045.00
Creamer, Rainbow, Red, Blue, Bulbous, 4 ¼ In. 275.00

Souvenir, Tray, Osborne House, England, 3-In. Reverse Painting On Glass
$395.00

Spatter Glass, Muffineer, Cranberry, Metal Lid, 4 ⅞ In.
$140.00

Spatterware, Creamer, Thistle, Yellow, Red Flower, 3 ½ In.
$500.00

Spatterware, Cup & Saucer, Morning Glory, Red, Blue, Black, Green, 19th Century
$960.00

TIP
Put foam or paper plates between the china plates stacked for storage.

SPATTERWARE

Spatterware, Cup & Saucer, Peafowl, Green, Handleless
$130.00

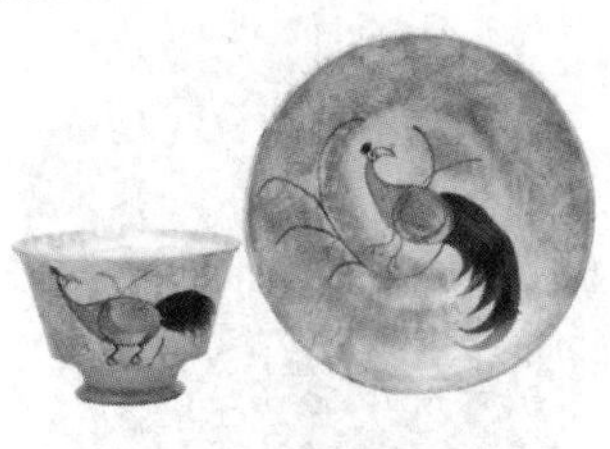

Spatterware, Cup & Saucer, School House, Red, Handleless
$3000.00

Spatterware, Plate, Clover, Red, Green, 9 5/8 In.
$5000.00

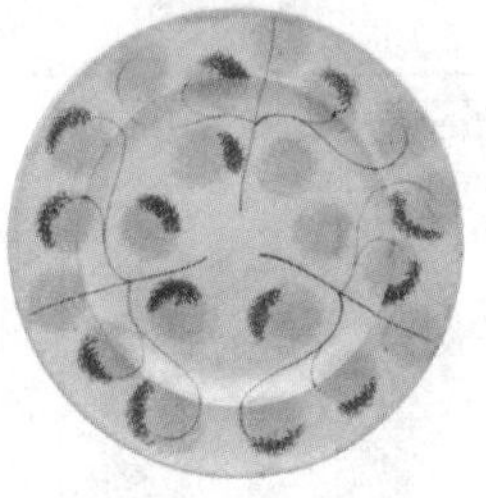

Spatterware, Plate, Fort, Blue, Paneled, Early 19th Century, 7 In.
$300.00

Spatterware, Plate, School House, Red, Green Tree, Blue House
$950.00

Creamer, Thistle, Yellow, Red Flower, 3 1/2 In. . . . . *illus* 500.00
Creamer, Tulip, Blue, White, Red, Green, Blue Spatter, Paneled, Footed, 5 3/4 In. 275.00
Cup & Saucer, 2 Men In Raft, Red Spatter, Handleless, Child's 3080.00
Cup & Saucer, Berry Wreath, Purple Spatter, Handleless, 2 1/2 x 5 3/4 In. 531.00
Cup & Saucer, Deer, Peafowl, Blue & Green, Red Spatter, Handleless, 2 1/2 x 5 3/4 In. 295.00
Cup & Saucer, Exotic Bird, Blue, Yellow, Red, Green Spatter, Child's 1210.00
Cup & Saucer, Memorial Tulip, Full Blue Spatter, Handleless 550.00
Cup & Saucer, Morning Glory, Red, London Shape, 1855. . . . . 905.00
Cup & Saucer, Morning Glory, Red, Blue, Black, Green, 19th Century . . . . . *illus* 960.00
Cup & Saucer, Peafowl, Blue, Yellow, Red, Full Green Spatter, Handleless. 468.00
Cup & Saucer, Peafowl, Green, Handleless . . . . . *illus* 130.00
Cup & Saucer, Peafowl, On Bar, Yellow, Blue, Green, Red, Full Green Spatter, Handleless 1540.00
Cup & Saucer, Peafowl, Red, Brown & Green, Blue Spatter, Handleless, 2 3/4 x 6 In. 295.00
Cup & Saucer, Purple & Black Rainbow, Bull's-Eye Spatter, Handleless, 2 3/4 x 5 1/2 In. 826.00
Cup & Saucer, Rainbow, Red, Green, Handleless. 330.00
Cup & Saucer, Red, Green, Yellow Border, Handleless. 2860.00
Cup & Saucer, Red & Green Thistle, Yellow, Handleless, Mid 1800s, Miniature. 1840.00
Cup & Saucer, Red Spatter, Handleless 708.00
Cup & Saucer, Rose, Red, Green Leaves, Blue Border, Handleless 176.00
Cup & Saucer, Rose, Red, Green Leaves, Red & Green Rings, Handleless 165.00
Cup & Saucer, Rose & Bud, Rainbow, Red, Blue, Green, Handleless, Child's. 935.00
Cup & Saucer, School House, Red, Handleless . . . . . *illus* 3000.00
Cup & Saucer, School House, Red, Yellow Roof, Blue Spatter, Handleless 1870.00
Cup & Saucer, Star, Red, Blue, Green, Red Border, 6-Sided, Handleless. 1540.00
Cup & Saucer, Thistle, Yellow Spatter, Handleless, 2 1/2 x 6 In. 502.00
Cup & Saucer, Tulip, Red, Green Leaves, Red Border, Handleless. 275.00
Cup & Saucer, Yellow & Purple Spatter, 2 1/2 x 6 In. 59.00
Cuspidor, Blue, White, 7 1/2 In. 58.00
Cuspidor, Blue & White, Blue Accent Band, 4 1/2 In., Pair 176.00
Footbath, Yellow Ground, Brown, Ocher, Handles, Stoneware, 9 x 20 x 12 In. 1760.00
Mixing Bowl, Blue, Center Band, 5 1/2 x 11 1/4 In. 77.00
Mug, Rabbits In Field, Red, Blue & Green Flowers, Stick Blossoms, 5 3/8 In. 1265.00
Mustard Pot, Cover, Peafowl, Blue, Yellow, Brown, Green Spatter, Handle, 2 1/2 In. 1650.00
Pitcher, Blue, Center Band, Applied Loop Handle, 11 1/4 In. 88.00
Pitcher, Blue, Smoke Ring Design, Tapered, Applied Handle, 9 In. 605.00
Pitcher, Blue, White, 7 In. 259.00
Pitcher, Blue, White, 9 In. . . . . 200.00 to 460.00
Pitcher, Blue, White, Band, 8 In. 230.00
Pitcher, Brown, Peacock, 8 1/4 In. 55.00
Pitcher, Mauve & Black Spatter Stripes, 6 Panels, c.1820, 6 3/8 In. 1410.00
Pitcher, Primrose, Bud, Red, Yellow, Green Leaves, Blue Spatter, Paneled, 10 1/4 In. 385.00
Pitcher, Red & Green, Cover, Applied Handle, 8 In. 885.00
Pitcher, Rose, Red, Green Leaves, Blue Spatter, Paneled, 2-Sided, 6 1/2 In. 198.00
Pitcher, Rose, Red, Green Leaves, Blue Spatter, Paneled, 12 3/8 In. 275.00
Pitcher, Rose, Red, Under Spout, Green Leaves, Blue Spatter, Paneled, 7 1/2 In. 330.00
Pitcher, Salt Glaze, c.1850, 5 In. 90.00
Plate, 3 Acorns, Brown, Teal Caps, Green Leaves, Purple Spatter, Paneled, 10 1/2 In. 2090.00
Plate, 6-Point Star, Blue, Green, Red, Blue Spatter, Paneled, 9 1/2 In. 385.00
Plate, 6-Point Star, Red, Blue, Green, Sunburst Border, Blue Spatter, Paneled, 8 1/2 In. 440.00
Plate, 6-Point Star, Red, Green, Yellow, Blue Spatter, Paneled, 9 1/2 In. 303.00
Plate, Blue & Red Dahlia Center, Blue Spatter, 8 1/2 In. 826.00
Plate, Bull's-Eye, Rainbow, Purple, Blue, 9 1/2 In. 220.00
Plate, Bull's-Eye, Rainbow, Red, Green, 9 1/2 In. 1430.00
Plate, Clover, Red, Green, 9 5/8 In. . . . . *illus* 5000.00
Plate, Cup & Saucer, Pinwheel, Rainbow, Green, Yellow, Red, Brown, Handleless, Child's 5500.00
Plate, Double Rose, Red, Flower, Blue, Green Leaves, Blue Border, 10 3/8 In. 605.00
Plate, Fort, Blue, Paneled, Early 19th Century, 7 In. . . . . *illus* 300.00
Plate, Peafowl, Blue, Yellow, Red, Full Green Spatter, Paneled, 8 1/4 In. 770.00
Plate, Peafowl, Green, Red, Yellow, Full Blue Spatter, Paneled, 9 3/8 In. 187.00
Plate, Peafowl, On Branch, Blue, Yellow, Red, Blue Ground, 9 3/8 In. 330.00
Plate, Peafowl, On Branch, Blue, Yellow, Green, Red Ground, 9 3/8 In. 358.00
Plate, Peafowl, Purple, Green & Yellow, Red Spatter, 8 In. 413.00
Plate, Primrose Center, Blue Spatter, 8 1/2 In. 236.00
Plate, Rabbitware, Rabbits Golfing, Thistle & Rose Border, 9 1/4 In. 825.00
Plate, Rose, Red, Blue Bud, Green Leaves, Blue Border, Paneled, 8 1/2 In. 209.00
Plate, Rose, Red, Green Leaves, Blue Spatter, Paneled, 10 3/4 In. 66.00

S

late, Rose, Red, Green Leaves, Mulberry Spatter, Paneled 770.00
late, Rose Center, Green & Red Spatter, 8 ½ In. 413.00
late, School House, Red, Green Tree, Blue House.......... *illus* 950.00
late, Thistle, Red, Green, Yellow Border, Paneled, 9 ¾ In. 5225.00
late, Thumbprint, Blue & Red, 9 ½ In. 708.00
late, Tulip, Red, White, Blue, Green Leaves, Blue Border, Paneled, 9 ¼ In.. .... 578.00
late, Tulip, Red, Yellow, Green Leaves, Blue Sponge Border, 9 In. 176.00
late, Wagon Wheel, Rainbow, Red, Green, 8 ¼ In. 550.00
late, Soup, Rainbow, Green, Blue, Red Bands, 10 ½ In. 3300.00
latter, Purple, Blue, Mottled, 7 ⅜ x 10 ⅛ In.. .... 1430.00
latter, White Starburst Center, Blue, Scalloped, Octagonal, 10 ½ x 13 ¾ In. 230.00
ugar, Cluster Of Buds, Blue, 3 ½ x 4 ½ In.. .... 59.00
ugar, Cover, Purple & Blue Vertical, Rainbow Spatter, 3 ½ In.. .... 649.00
ugar, Cover, Rose, Red, Green Leaves, Bulbous, 2-Sided, 5 ¾ In. 88.00
ugar, Cover, Tulip, Rosette Finial, Blue Sponge, Bulbous, 4 ½ In. 275.00
ugar, Flower, Leaves, Yellow, Bulbous, 5 x 4 In. 3850.00
ugar & Creamer, Rainbow, Black, Yellow, Bulbous 3300.00
eapot, Black & Yellow, Bulbous, Table Ring, 5 ¼ x 5 ¼ In.. .... 3575.00
eapot, Blue & Red Tulips, Paneled, c.1850, 8 ½ In. 345.00
eapot, Red, Blue, Green, 6 ¾ In. .... *illus* 800.00
eapot, Spread Winged Eagle, American Shield, Pink, Baluster, Paneled, 6 In.. .... 418.00
/ashbowl, Cottage, Blue, 19th Century, 13 ½ In. 920.00
/ashbowl, Pitcher, Peafowl, Blue, Phillips, Longport, 12 ¼ x 4 & 10 In.. .... 518.00
/ashbowl, Rainbow, Red, Blue Interior Stripes, Crisscross Center, Paneled, 14 x 4 In. 230.00

PELTER is a synonym for a zinc alloy. Figurines, candlesticks, and other pieces were made f spelter and given a bronze or painted finish. The metal has been used since about the 1860s) make statues, tablewares, and lamps that resemble bronze. Spelter is soft and breaks easily.) test for spelter, scratch the base of the piece. Bronze is solid; spelter will show a silvery scratch.

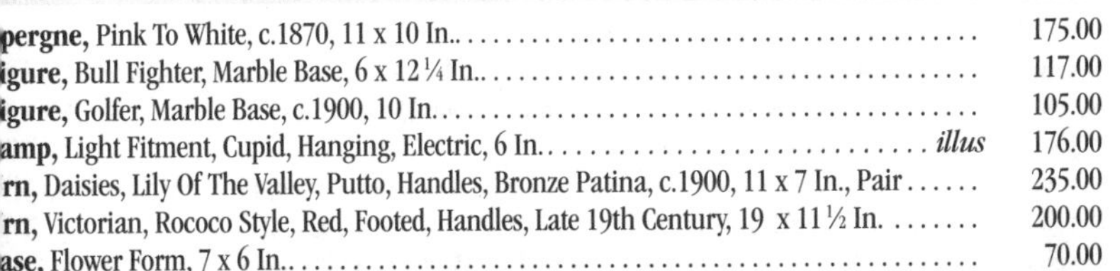

pergne, Pink To White, c.1870, 11 x 10 In.. .... 175.00
igure, Bull Fighter, Marble Base, 6 x 12 ¼ In.. .... 117.00
igure, Golfer, Marble Base, c.1900, 10 In. 105.00
amp, Light Fitment, Cupid, Hanging, Electric, 6 In. .... *illus* 176.00
rn, Daisies, Lily Of The Valley, Putto, Handles, Bronze Patina, c.1900, 11 x 7 In., Pair 235.00
rn, Victorian, Rococo Style, Red, Footed, Handles, Late 19th Century, 19 x 11 ½ In. 200.00
ase, Flower Form, 7 x 6 In.. .... 70.00

PINNING WHEELS in the corner have been symbols of earlier times for the past 100 years. lthough spinning wheels date back to medieval days, the ones found today are rarely more ıan 200 years old. Because the style of the spinning wheel changed very little, it is often impossible) place an exact date on a wheel.

larked MJDM, 1872, 33 ½ x 34 In. .... *illus* 370.00
lixed Wood, Bulb-Turned Blunt Arrow Feet, D. Klein, 50 x 26 x 22 ½ In.. .... 88.00
lixed Wood, Turned Spindles, Legs, Stamped, D. Shelly, 47 ½ In. 209.00
lodel, 15 In.. .... 27.00
/alnut, 37 In.. .... *illus* 200.00

PODE pottery, porcelain, and bone china were made by the Stoke-on-Trent factory of England ounded by Josiah Spode about 1770. The firm became Copeland and Garrett from 1833 to 1847, ıen W.T. Copeland or W.T. Copeland and Sons until 1976. It then became Royal Worcester pode Ltd. The word *Spode* appears on many pieces made by the factories. Most collectors include all ıe wares under the more familiar name of Spode. Porcelains are listed in this book by the name that ppears on the piece. Related pieces may be listed under Copeland, Copeland Spode, and Royal Worcester.

omport, Blue & Gilt Banded, Marked, 19th Century, 14 In. 450.00
ureen, Sauce, Cover, Stand, Gold Trim, 19th Century, 9 ½ In., Pair 600.00
ureen, Soup, Tapered Oval, Grotesque Lion Mask Handles, Artichoke Finials, 14 In. 1058.00

PORTS equipment, sporting goods, brochures, and related items are listed here. Items are sted by sport. Other categories of interest are Bicycle, Card, Fishing, Sword, Toy, and Trap. entucky Derby glasses are listed in the Decorated Tumblers category.

aseball, Award, Bob Gibson, St. Louis Cardinals, MVP, Glass, 1968. .... 1837.00
aseball, Award, Cal Ripken Jr., Baltimore Orioles, MVP, Glass, 1983. .... 2222.00
aseball, Award, Jackie Robinson, Brooklyn Dodgers, MVP, Glass, 1949 .... 2510.00
aseball, Award, Lou Gehrig, New York Yankees, MVP, Glass, 1936. .... 2760.00

Spatterware, Teapot, Red, Blue, Green, 6 ¾ In.
$800.00

Spelter, Lamp, Light Fitment, Cupid, Hanging, Electric, 6 In.
$176.00

Spinning Wheel, Marked MJDM, 1872, 33 ½ x 34 In.
$370.00

Spinning Wheel, Walnut, 37 In.
$200.00

S

Sports, Baseball, Figure, Babe Ruth, Hartland, Tag, Box, 1958, 8 In.
$1000.00

Sports, Baseball, Matchbook, Honus Wagner, Baseball Records Inside, c.1940, 3⅜ x 4 In.
$253.00

Sports, Baseball, Model, Willie Mays, Aurora, Sealed, Box, 1966
$460.00

Sports, Baseball, Sheet Music, I Love Mickey Mantle, 45 RPM Record, 1956, 12 x 8 In.
$115.00

Baseball, Ball, Autographed, 1951 New York Giants N.L. Champions. 262.0
Baseball, Ball, Autographed, Babe Ruth . . . . . 4652.00 to 45000.0
Baseball, Ball, Autographed, Babe Ruth, 1931. . . . . 5316.0
Baseball, Ball, Autographed, Babe Ruth, Lou Gehrig, 1931 . . . . . 10575.0
Baseball, Ball, Autographed, Babe Ruth, Official American League Ball, 1930s 5676.0
Baseball, Ball, Autographed, Barry Bonds 2001 Home Run, No. 70. . . . . 14400.0
Baseball, Ball, Autographed, Boston Red Sox, 2004 World Champions 858.0
Baseball, Ball, Autographed, Connie Mack. 1789.0
Baseball, Ball, Autographed, Cy Young, Official League Ball, c.1950 . . . . . 1793.0
Baseball, Ball, Autographed, Derek Jeter 1008.0
Baseball, Ball, Autographed, Grover Cleveland Alexander, Official League Ball, c.1930 . . . . . 9560.0
Baseball, Ball, Autographed, Jackie Robinson 7050.0
Baseball, Ball, Autographed, Joe DiMaggio 1645.0
Baseball, Ball, Autographed, Josh Beckett, Florida Marlins, 2003 World Series. 386.0
Baseball, Ball, Autographed, Los Angeles Dodgers, 1966 World Champions 752.0
Baseball, Ball, Autographed, Mantle, Larsen, Berra, c.1956 . . . . . 1434.0
Baseball, Ball, Autographed, Mickey Mantle 592.0
Baseball, Ball, Autographed, Mickey Mantle & Roger Maris, Blue Ink. 3191.0
Baseball, Ball, Autographed, New York Yankees, 1954. . . . . 777.0
Baseball, Ball, Autographed, New York Yankees, 1956. . . . . 1170.0
Baseball, Ball, Autographed, New York Yankees, 1976. . . . . 290.0
Baseball, Ball, Autographed, Pie Traynor, 1930. . . . . 940.0
Baseball, Ball, Autographed, President Harry Truman 6194.0
Baseball, Ball, Autographed, Roberto Clemente, 1960s. 896.0
Baseball, Ball, Autographed, Roberto Clemente, 2000th Hit Game Ball, 1966. . . . . 4350.0
Baseball, Ball, Autographed, Ted Williams. 145.0
Baseball, Ball, Autographed, Ty Cobb, Dated June 19, 1954 . . . . . 3720.0
Baseball, Bat, Autographed, Babe Ruth, Hillerich & Bradsby, 1923 . . . . . 51500.0
Baseball, Bat, Autographed, Barry Bonds, Pittsburgh Pirates, Game Used, 1991-92. . . . . 1289.0
Baseball, Bat, Autographed, Brooks Robinson, 1971-79 . . . . . 1293.0
Baseball, Bat, Autographed, Duke Snider, Brooklyn Dodgers, N.L. All-Star, Game Used, 1955 . 5316.0
Baseball, Bat, Autographed, Frank Thomas, Chicago White Sox, Home Run No. 7, 1996. . . . . 1037.0
Baseball, Bat, Autographed, Joe DiMaggio, 1941 . . . . . 2233.0
Baseball, Bat, Autographed, Rocky Colavito, Kansas City Athletics, Game Used, 1964 . . . . . 643.0
Baseball, Bat, Hall Of Fame Edition, 1975 Class, No. 225, 36 In. 115.0
Baseball, Book, Babe Ruth Story, Soft Cover, Autographed, 1948, 8¼ x 10¾ In. 3204.0
Baseball, Book, Player's Pocket Companion, Rules Of Game, 1860, 3¾ x 5½ In. 8963.0
Baseball, Button, Baltimore Orioles, I'm A Bird Watcher At WBAL-TV 11, Celluloid, 1¾ In. . . 31.0
Baseball, Button, Chicago Cubs Team, 1929 . . . . . 940.0
Baseball, Button, Mickey Mantle, 1950s, 1¾ In. 95.0
Baseball, Button, Salute To Roger Maris, 61st Home Run, 1961, 3½ In.. . . . . 900.0
Baseball, Button, St. Louis Browns, American League Champions, Celluloid, 1944, 2 In. 61.0
Baseball, Button, Willie Mays, Ball & Glove Hanging Charms, 1950s, 1¾ In.. . . . . 300.0
Baseball, Cap, Autographed, Willie Mays, New York Giants, Game Used, 1954 . . . . . 7074.0
Baseball, Cap, Spud Chandler, 1940s 1058.0
Baseball, Catcher's Vest, Apron Style, Leather Straps, c.1890 . . . . . 478.0
Baseball, Chair, Clubhouse, Jeff Kent, L.A. Dodgers, Used, Autographed, 2006. . . . . 1160.0
Baseball, Cufflinks, New York Yankees, 1958 World Champions, Jack Lang 4472.0
Baseball, Equipment Trunk, New York Yankees, c. 1930, 41 x 19 x 24 In. 1998.0
Baseball, Figure, Babe Ruth, Hartland, Tag, Box, 1958, 8 In. . . . . *illus* 1000.0
Baseball, Game, Pitch-N-Hit, Mickey Mantle & Roger Maris, c.1962 . . . . . 705.0
Baseball, Glove, Catcher's Mitt, Johnny Bench, Game Used, 1970s. 8963.0
Baseball, Glove, Fielder's, Luis Tiant, Game Used, 1969-70. . . . . 1348.0
Baseball, Glove, Jon Matlack, New York Mets, Autographed, Game Used, c.1974. . . . . 612.0
Baseball, Glove, Red Rolfe, New York Yankees, 1930s 4407.0
Baseball, Glove, Tommy Henrich, N.Y. Yankees, Rawlings Metal, 1940s. 1763.0
Baseball, Hat, Barry Bonds, San Francisco, Game Worn, c.2001 . . . . . 657.0
Baseball, Jersey, Andy Carey, Yankees, Game Worn, 1955 . . . . . 1673.0
Baseball, Jersey, Boston Braves, c.1950. . . . . 1175.0
Baseball, Jersey, Detroit Tigers, Flannel, c.1923-25 . . . . . 4994.0
Baseball, Jersey, Dutch Reuther, New York Yankees, 1927. . . . . 34800.0
Baseball, Jersey, Ernie Banks, Chicago Cubs, 1969 . . . . . 425.0
Baseball, Jersey, Gerry McNamara, Syracuse, Autographed, 2004 . . . . . 161.0
Baseball, Jersey, Gil Coan, Washington Senators, 1949-50 . . . . . 1528.0
Baseball, Jersey, Joe DiMaggio, Autographed 566.0

Baseball, Jersey, Luke Appling, Chicago White Sox, Autographed, 1947 .... 4700.00
Baseball, Jersey, Mickey Mantle, New York Yankees, Late 1970s 2772.00
Baseball, Jersey, Mickey Mantle, New York Yankees, Autographed, 1956 .... 4994.00
Baseball, Jersey, Negro League, Multi-Autographed, 1980s 2629.00
Baseball, Jersey, Sammy Sosa, Chicago Cubs, Autographed 317.00
Baseball, Lighter, Dodgers Stadium, 1962, 1 ¾ x 2 ⅛ In. 190.00
Baseball, Magazine Page, Thurman Munson, Autographed, 1975, 8 ¼ x 10 ¾ In. 518.00
Baseball, Matchbook, Honus Wagner, Baseball Records Inside, c.1940, 3 ⅜ x 4 In. ...... *illus* 253.00
Baseball, Model, Willie Mays, Aurora, Sealed, Box, 1966 .... *illus* 460.00
Baseball, Necklace, New York Yankees Pendant, 1996 World Series Championship 8077.00
Baseball, Nodder, Mickey Mantle, Cartoon Box, 1966 .... 940.00
Baseball, Nodder, Roger Maris, Box, 1961-63 .... 940.00
Baseball, Pencil Clip, Cleveland Indians, c.1949, 1 ¾ In. 115.00
Baseball, Pennant, Baltimore Orioles, 1966 World Series, Felt, Orange Ground, 29 In. 115.00
Baseball, Pennant, Detroit Tigers, A.L. Championship, Cane, 23 x 52 In. 837.00
Baseball, Pennant, St. Louis Cardinals, 1926, 23 In. 777.00
Baseball, Photograph, Billy Martin, New York Yankees, Autographed, 8 x 10 In. 240.00
Baseball, Photograph, Derek Jeter, The Dive, Autographed, Silver Ink, 16 x 20 In. 396.00
Baseball, Photograph, Elston Howard, New York Yankees, Autographed, 8 x 10 In. 180.00
Baseball, Photograph, Hank Greenberg, Black & White, Autographed, 8 x 10 In. 559.00
Baseball, Photograph, John McGraw, Pacific & Atlantic, Autographed, 7 ½ x 9 ½ In. 2868.00
Baseball, Photograph, Mantle, Maris, Autographed, 1960s, 7 ½ x 9 ½ In. 2032.00
Baseball, Photograph, Mickey Mantle, Autographed, Long Signature, 8 x 10 In. 323.00
Baseball, Photograph, Mickey Mantle, Autographed, 40 x 54 In. 4183.00
Baseball, Plaque, Baltimore Orioles, Colts, c.1960, 10 x 12 In. 95.00
Baseball, Postcard, Photograph, Jimmie Foxx, Autographed, 1930, 3 ⅜ x 5 ⅜ In. 1216.00
Baseball, Press Pin, All-Star Game, Chicago, 1947 .... 568.00
Baseball, Press Pin, Boston Braves, 1948 World Series 538.00
Baseball, Press Pin, Chicago Cubs, 1929 World Series 1195.00
Baseball, Press Pin, New York Yankees, 1936 World Series 777.00
Baseball, Press Pin, Pittsburgh Pirates, 1938 World Series Phantom 508.00
Baseball, Press Pin, St. Louis Cardinals, 1934 World Series 956.00
Baseball, Program, 1919 World Series, Golden Jubilee, Cincinnati Reds, 1869-1919 .... 1475.00
Baseball, Radio, Roger Maris & Mickey Mantle, Wood Case, White, Box, 1960s 790.00
Baseball, Ring, Detroit Tigers, World Championship, 1984 .... 5316.00
Baseball, Ring, Jim Catfish Hunter, Yankees, 1978 World Series 37200.00
Baseball, Scoreboard, Squirt, Baseball Boys, 2-Sided, 16 x 32 In. 120.00
Baseball, Scorecard, Hank Aaron Bat & Ball, Ideal, Embossed, 1972, 34 x 36 In. 86.00
Baseball, Sheet Music, I Love Mickey Mantle, 45 RPM Record, 1956, 12 x 8 In. .... *illus* 115.00
Baseball, Uniform, Cal Ripken Jr., Baltimore Orioles, Game Worn, 1985 .... 7170.00
Baseball, Vendor's Box, Baby Ruth, Red, Yellow Ground, 1930s, 10 ½ x 16 x 7 In. 1650.00
Baseball, Vest, Felipe Alou, Oakland A's, 1970 .... 940.00
Baseball, Watch, Attributed To Nap Lajoie, 1910 .... 1112.00
Baseball, Watch & Charm, Paul Krichell, New York Yankees, 1923 World Series 3819.00
Basketball, Arena Seats, Dual, Boston Garden, Celtics, Bruins, 1928 .... 1348.00
Basketball, Ball, Autographed, Wilt Chamberlain & Kareem Abdul Jabbar 761.00
Basketball, Ball, Autographed, NBA All-Star Team, 1995 .... 1793.00
Basketball, Jersey, Gail Goodrich, Phoenix, 1968 .... 7200.00
Basketball, Jersey, Kevin McHale, Boston Celtics, Game Worn, Autographed, 1992-93 .... 1254.00
Basketball, Jersey, LeBron James, Cleveland Cavaliers, Rookie, 2003-04 .... 4673.00
Basketball, Jersey, LeBron James, High School, Game Worn, 2001-02 .... 8365.00
Basketball, Jersey, Magic Johnson, Los Angeles Lakers, Game Worn, Autographed 2970.00
Basketball, Lithograph, Michael Jordan, Autographed, 26 x 33 In. 1554.00
Basketball, Parquet Flooring, Green, White, Celtics, Boston Garden, 1946-49, 17 x 36 In. 896.00
Basketball, Poster, Michael Jordan, Rare Air, Autographed 624.00
Basketball, Poster, Michael Jordan, Wings By Nike 1969.00
Basketball, Shoes, Allen Iverson, 2004 Olympics, Autographed 566.00
Basketball, Shoes, Julius Erving, All Star, Converse, Autographed, 1976 .... 1562.00
Basketball, Shoes, Michael Jordan, Chicago Bulls, Game Worn, Autographed, 1995-96 .... 3300.00
Boxing, Book, Louis, Dempsey, Picture Story, Ted Carroll, 1947, 8 ½ x 11 ½ In. .... *illus* 185.00
Boxing, Cap, Muhammad Ali Fan Club, Rubber Logo, Adjustable Band, Black, Gold Letters, 1970s 172.00
Boxing, Gloves, Muhammad Ali, Red, Everlast, Autographed 759.99
Boxing, Photograph, Jack Dempsey, 7 ½ x 9 ½ In. 92.00
Boxing, Photograph, Jake LaMotta, Raging Bull, Autographed, 8 x 10 In. 86.00
Boxing, Trophy, Cassius Clay, Kentucky Golden Gloves, 1958, 20 In. 7768.00
Boxing, Button, Muhammad Ali, Float Like A Butterfly, Sting Like A Bee, Celluloid, 1978, ⅞ In. 44.00

Sports, Boxing, Book, Louis, Dempsey, Picture Story, Ted Carroll, 1947, 8 ½ x 11 ½ In.
$185.00

Sports, Football, Button, Rockne Of Notre Dame, 1 ¾ In.
$196.00

Sports, Football, Nodder, Baltimore Colts, 1960s, 7 In.
$133.00

Sports, Pool, Ball Rack, Oak, National Billiard Table Co., c.1890, 31 x 22 In.
$1118.00

Sports, Pool, Cue Rack, Oak, Holds 14 Cues, National Billiard Table Co., c.1890, 61 x 36 In.
$6400.00

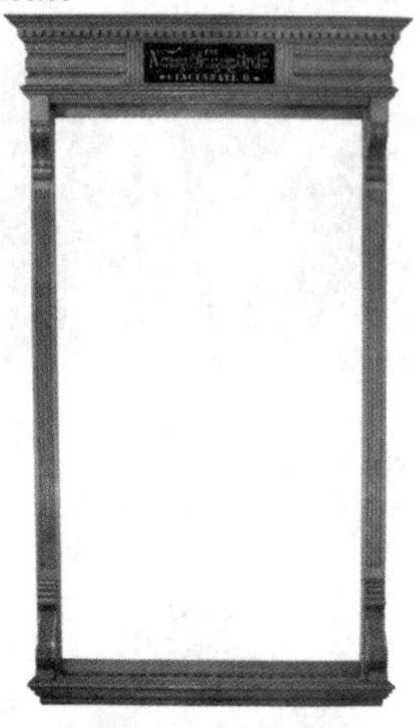

Sports, Pool, Table, Walnut, Rosewood Veneer, Inlaid Ivory, Brunswick, c.1885, 4 x 8 Ft.
$13000.00

Sports Photographs

Sports collectors pay high prices for original prints or studio portraits of players. These were developed, often by the photographer, from the original film used to shoot the picture. Many are marked on the back with a date and the name of the publication that first printed the photo or the name of the news agency that employed the photographer. Sports photographers to look for include George Brace, George Burns, Charles Conlon, Nat Fein, Carl Horner, Lewis Van Oeyen, Arthur Rickerby, Robert Riger, and Paul Thompson.

Football, Ashtray, Baltimore Colts, H-Shape, Stadium, Brown & White, Seiko Co., 1960 ..... 172.00
Football, Ball, Autographed, 1963 Pro Bowl 1554.00
Football, Ball, Autographed, Baltimore Colts, 1968 ..... 657.00
Football, Ball, Autographed, Baltimore Colts, White, c.1971-72 ..... 390.00
Football, Ball, Autographed, Johnny Unitas, Wilson Official, Silver Ink 684.00
Football, Ball, Autographed, Kansas City Chiefs, 1965 ..... 478.00
Football, Ball, Autographed, New York Giants, 1952 ..... 436.00
Football, Ball, Autographed, Washington Redskins, Brown & White, 1986 ..... 180.00
Football, Button, Rockne Of Notre Dame, 1 3/4 In. ..... *illus* 196.00
Football, Cleats, Jerry Rice, San Francisco 49ers, Autographed, 1999 ..... 288.00
Football, Helmet, Anthony Carter, Michigan, Game Used, Autographed, 1980s 565.00
Football, Helmet, Elijah Pitts, Green Bay Packers, Game Used, Mid-1960s 1673.00
Football, Helmet, Jim Otto, Oakland Raiders, Game Used, Autographed, 1978 ..... 944.00
Football, Helmet, Jim Swink, Dallas Texans, Game Used, 1960 ..... 3107.00
Football, Helmet, Joe Montana, Notre Dame, Game Used, Autographed, 1970s 657.00
Football, Helmet, Lawrence Taylor, New York Giants, 1980s 7768.00
Football, Helmet, Leather, Executioner, 1920s 6463.00
Football, Helmet, New York Giants, XXV Super Bowl, Autographed, 1990 ..... 598.00
Football, Helmet, New York Jets, Autographed, 1969 ..... 624.00
Football, Helmet, Notre Dame, Black Leather, Cross Stripes, Bubble Ear, 1950s 837.00
Football, Helmet, Notre Dame, Leather, Dog Ear, 1920s 2868.00
Football, Helmet, Rubberized Face Mask, Spalding 385.00
Football, Helmet, Terry Bradshaw, Pittsburgh Steelers, Game Used, c.1979 ..... 6573.00
Football, Helmet, Travis Williams, Green Bay Packers, Game Used, 1960s 1315.00
Football, Jersey, Terrell Owens, San Francisco, Game Worn, 2003 ..... 568.00
Football, Jersey, Tom Mitchell, Baltimore Colts, 1970 World Champions 1109.00
Football, Jersey, Walter Payton, Chicago Bears, Game Worn, c.1986 ..... 4183.00
Football, Nodder, Baltimore Colts, 1960s, 7 In. ..... *illus* 133.00
Football, Pendant, Pittsburgh Steelers, 1974 World Champions, 10K Gold, Stone 1793.00
Football, Pennant, Green Bay Packers, World Champions, Felt, 1960s, 29 In. 58.00
Football, Pennant, New York Giants, Felt, Black & Gold, 1950s, 28 In. 86.00
Football, Press Pin, 1947 NFL Championship 566.00
Football, Stadium Blanket, Baltimore Colts, Wool, Navy, White, Pendleton, 1950s, 40 x 60 In. 175.00
Football, Wristwatch, Joe Namath, Presentation, Engraved, Leather, 1968 ..... 657.00
Golf, Bag, Arnold Palmer, Tournament Used, 1970s 5228.00
Golf, Bag, Ben Hogan, Leather, Red, White, Blue, 1970s 3346.00
Golf, Bag, Louis Vuitton, Brown Canvas, Tan Leather Trim, 33 1/2 x 7 In. 368.00
Golf, Bag, Payne Stewart, Tournament Used, 1980s 837.00
Golf, Ball, Feather, Central Band, Pole Caps, Leather, c.1840, 3 Piece 4375.00
Golf, Ball, Gutta Percha, Orange, Machine Cut, c.1890 ..... 1500.00
Golf, Ball, Rubber Core, Bramble, Red, Henley Telegraph Works, c.1911 ..... 1625.00
Golf, Club, Brassie, Convex Sole, Sheepskin Grip, Willie Dunn, c.1890 ..... 1250.00
Golf, Club, Driver, Sheepskin Grip, Clan Golf Club Co., c.1891 ..... 375.00
Golf, Club, Iron, Hickory Shaft, Leather Grip, Spalding, c.1897 ..... 1250.00
Golf, Club, Iron, Hickory Shaft, Sheepskin Grip, J. Gray, c.1880, 39 In. 1200.00
Golf, Club, Putter, Adjustable, Leather Grip, Nickel Plated, Ed Fitzjohn, c.1917 ..... 3125.00
Golf, Club, Putter, Ben Hogan, Tournament Used, 1940s 20315.00
Golf, Club, Sheepskin Grip, Musselburgh & Royal Blackheath, c.1860 ..... 7500.00
Golf, Club, Track Iron, Sheepskin Grip, c.1840 ..... 3750.00
Golf, Club, Wedge, Right Hand, Wilson, 37 In. 6.00
Golf, Club, Wedge, Triple Duty, Wilson, Leather Reminder Grip, 37 In. 6.00
Golf, Head Cover, Ben Hogan, Leather, Pair 896.00
Golf, Money Clip, Ben Hogan, USGA, Sterling Silver, 1940s 2940.00
Golf, Shag Bag, Balls, Ben Hogan, 1960s 1195.00
Hockey, Glove, Wayne Gretzky, Left Hand, Game Used, 1993-94 ..... 2271.00
Hockey, Jersey, Henri Richard, Montreal Canadiens, Game Worn, 1968 ..... 16800.00
Hockey, Program, N.Y. Americans Vs N.Y. Rangers, Madison Square Garden, 1928, 4 Pages ... 316.00
Hockey, Puck, Phil Esposito, Boston Bruins, Goal, Autographed, Dated, Dec. 16, 1973 ..... 319.00
Hockey, Skates, Bobby Orr, Game Used, 1970 ..... 6573.00
Hockey, Stick, Bobby Orr, Game Used, Autographed, c.1970 ..... 717.00
Hockey, Stick, Brian Leetch, New York Rangers, Game Used, Autographed, c.2002 ..... 900.00
Hockey, Stick, Wayne Gretzky, Game Used, Autographed, 1990 ..... 1554.00
Horseback Racing, Belt, Eddie Arcaro, Hickok Award, Leather, Decade Of Sports, 1950-60 .. 2032.00
Horseback Riding, Bit, Silver, Openwork, Bird, Marked 800, Mexico, c.1950, 8 1/4 In. 460.00
Horseback Riding, Bridle, Reins, Horsehair, Flag Motif, Tassels, 6 Ft. 1035.00
Horseback Riding, Bridle, Reins, Horsehair, Silver Mounted Bit, Tassels, 7 Ft. 949.00
Horseback Riding, Halter, Lead, Horsehair, Braided, 3 Color, 10 Ft. 8 In. 259.00

Horseback Riding, Horse Bridle, Braided Horsehair, Horse & Dog Heads, Glass Buttons, 26 x 43 In. . 1495.00
Horseback Riding, Lariat, Horsehair, Woven, 33 Ft. 978.00
Hunting, Turkey Call, Walnut, Narrow Box Form, Hinged Lid, 20th Century, 3 x 8 x 1 In. 121.00
Pool, Ball Rack, Oak, National Billiard Table Co., c.1890, 31 x 22 In. *illus* 1118.00
Pool, Cue Ball, Ivory, Brunswick Balke, Box, 2 ½ x 8 x 3 ¼ In., 3 Piece 330.00
Pool, Cue Rack, Oak, Holds 14 Cues, National Billiard Table Co., c.1890, 61 x 36 In. *illus* 6400.00
Pool, Table, Veneer, Ebonized Legs, Lafe Keafer, Balke Collander Model, 34 x 109 In. 4070.00
Pool, Table, Walnut, Rosewood Veneer, Inlaid Ivory, Brunswick, c.1885, 4 x 8 Ft. *illus* 13000.00
Skating, Ice Skates, Tiger Maple, Iron Runners, Leather Straps, 4 ¾ x 12 x 2 ⅜ In. 1430.00
Skating, Ice Skates, Woman's Figure, White, Bauer Canadian Club, 1960s, Size 7 25.00
Skating, Roller Skates, Vineyard, Wood, Leather Bindings, 1880-82, Size 10 ½. 265.00

STAFFORDSHIRE, England, has been a district making pottery and porcelain since the 1700s. Hundreds of kilns are still working in the area. Thousands of types of pottery and porcelain have been made in the many factories that worked and still work in the area. Some of the most famous factories have been listed separately, such as Adams, Davenport, Ridgway, Rowland & Marsellus, Royal Doulton, Royal Worcester, Spode, Wedgwood, and others. Some Staffordshire pieces are listed under categories like Fairing, Flow Blue, Mulberry, Shaving Mug, etc.

Bowl, Blue, Beaded Rim, Brighton Beach, Water, Boat Scene, 3 x 11 ½ In. 1045.00
Bowl, Blue, White, Pittsfield Elm, 8 ¾ In. 431.00
Bowl, Footed, Bunker Hill, Green, 5 ¾ x 10 ¼ In. 191.00
Bowl, Fruit, Jessups Landing Near Hudson River, Black, Clews, c.1830, 5 ¾ x 10 In. 1554.00
Bowl, Fruit, Reticulated, Oblong, Baluster, Pierced Rim, Blue 4481.00
Bowl, Vegetable, Arms Of Virginia, Oval, Footed, Handles, Mayer, c.1830, 4 ½ x 12 In. 7170.00
Bowl, Vegetable, Cover, Square, Cut Corners, Boston State House, 9 x 5 In. 239.00
Bowl, Vegetable, Cover, Landing Of Gen. LaFayette, Blue, Clews, c.1830, 6 ¼ x 12 ½ In. 1434.00
Bowl, Vegetable, Dome Lid, Passsamaquoddy Bay, Green, 7 x 12 In. 717.00
Box, Pomade, Cylindrical, Cattle, Rustic Scenes, Blue, 2 ½ In. 448.00
Box, Pomade, Round, Washington Crossing The Delaware, Lavender, 3 ½ In. 2390.00
Chamber Pot, Floral Border, Blue, 19th Century, 8 ½ In. 2988.00
Charger, Boston State House, Flower Vine Border, Blue, 12 ½ In. 239.00
Coffeepot, Egg Shape, Domed Lid, Molded Spout, Pink, 12 In. 418.00
Coffeepot, Green, White, Columbia, Octagonal, 9 ½ In. 57.00
Coffeepot, Lafayette At Franklin's Tomb, Baluster, Dome Lid, Enoch Wood & Sons, 10 In. 2151.00
Coffeepot, Octagonal, Lavender Flowers, No. 20, 19th Century, 11 ¾ x 6 In. 198.00
Compote, Footed, Flaring, Baluster, 2 Handles, New York City Hall, Blue, 10 In. 2390.00
Creamer, Baluster Paneled, Eagle, Blue, c.1830, 6 In. 329.00
Creamer, Washington At Tomb, Flower & Leaf Border, Historic Blue, Enoch Wood & Sons, c.1835, 6 In. 448.00
Creamer, Welcome Lafayette The Nation's Guest, Blue, Clews, c.1830, 4 In. *illus* 3107.00
Dinner Service, Argos, Greek Style Geometrical, Green, Black, Gold, 1800s, 27 Piece 177.00
Dish, Entree, Blue, White, Landscape, Flowers, 2 Handles, Cover, 5 x 8 ½ In. 172.00
Dish, Hen On Nest Cover, Multicolored, 19th Century, 7 x 9 In. 467.00
Dish, Hen On Nest Cover, Painted, 3 ¾ x 4 x 3 In. 325.00
Figurine, Aunt Chloe, Gilt, Holding Purse, 19th Century, 8 ½ In. 896.00
Figurine, Ben Franklin, Enamel, Gilt, Holding Hat & Book, 19th Century, 15 In. 777.00
Figurine, Benjamin Franklin, Blue Coat, Holding Paper, c.1830, 10 In. 1035.00
Figurine, Boar Hunter, Plumed Hat, Foot On Dead Boar, 19 In. 384.00
Figurine, Boy Wearing Top Hat, Holding Horn, Floral Arch, Dog, c.1825, 6 ½ In. 120.00
Figurine, Caernarvon Castle, Multicolored, Modeled, Turret Spills, Mid 1800s, 7 In. 206.00
Figurine, Children On High Wheel & Tandem, c.1880, 2 ¾ In. 165.00
Figurine, Children With Rabbit, Gold Trimmed Base, 19th Century, 6 ½ In. 99.00
Figurine, Cow, Calf, On Grassy Knoll, Stream, Bocage Trim, Multicolored, 6 In., Pair 431.00
Figurine, Deer, Bocage, Red Speckled, Earthenware, 19th Century, 6 In. 558.00
Figurine, Deer, Lying Down, c.1800, 5 x 3 ¾ In. 264.00
Figurine, Dog, Dalmatian, Gold Collar, 3 ½ In., Pair 171.00
Figurine, Dog, Greyhound, Seated, Collar, 7 ½ In., Pair 508.00
Figurine, Dog, Hound, Lying Down, c.1800, 4 x 6 ½ In. 588.00
Figurine, Dog, Hounds, Red Spotted, Seated, Gilt Collar, Chain, 8 ¼ x 7 ⅞ In., Pair 345.00
Figurine, Dog, King Charles Spaniel, White, c.1850, 13 In., Pair 411.00
Figurine, Dog, Poodle, Seated, 19th Century, 4 ¾ x 4 ¾ In. 235.00
Figurine, Dog, Spaniel, 19th Century, 10 ½ In., Pair 529.00
Figurine, Dog, Spaniel, Rust, Gold, 5 In., Pair 81.00
Figurine, Dog, Spaniel, Rust, Gold, 7 ½ In., Pair 173.00
Figurine, Dog, Spaniel, Seated, White, Gold Trim, 10 x 17 ½ x 5 In, Pair. 196.00
Figurine, Dog, Spaniel, Orange, White, c.1900, 11 x 8 ¾ In., Pair 263.00

Staffordshire, Creamer, Welcome Lafayette The Nation's Guest, Blue, Clews, c.1830, 4 In.
$3107.00

Staffordshire, Figurine, Scottish Lass, Early 19th Century, 8 ¼ In.
$180.00

Staffordshire, Figurine, Zebra, Flat Back, Green Base, 4 ¾ In., Pair
$244.00

TIP

Store your signed baseball in a container designed for display, keep it away from light, and don't handle it. Another option is to store it in a sock and put it in your drawer. Do not shellac the ball or paint it with clear nail polish or glue. That lowers the value.

S

Staffordshire, Mug, With All Thy Soul, Pink Luster Border, 2 ⅝ In.
$225.00

Staffordshire, Pitcher, New York Insane Asylum, Almshouse, Blue, Clews, c.1830, 6 ¼ In.
$508.00

Staffordshire, Plate, Boston State House, Flower Vine Border, Blue, John Rogers & Son, 9 ½ In.
$131.00

Staffordshire Colors

Blue Staffordshire patterns were the earliest, with both black and blue transfer designs used during the eighteenth century. Pink, green, or brown transfer designs were used about 1830, and the combination of several colors began about 1850.

Figurine, Dog, Spaniel, Multicolored, 4 In. . . . 288.00
Figurine, Dog, Spaniel, Seated, 7 In., Pair . . . 485.00
Figurine, Dog, Spaniel, White, Black Muzzles, Gilt Chain, Late 19th Century, 13 ⅜ In., Pair . . 316.00
Figurine, Dog, Whippet, Rabbit In Mouth, Straddling Tree Trunk, 11 ¼ x 9 ½ In., Pair . . . 173.00
Figurine, Dog, Whippet, Seated, Gilt Base, 8¼ x 2 ⅔ x 4¾ In. . . . 187.00 to 235.00
Figurine, Dog, White, 14 In., Pair . . . 234.00
Figurine, Duke & Duchess Of Cambridge, On Horseback, Multicolored, 13 ¼ In., Pair . . . 764.00
Figurine, Gardener, Walton, c.1800, 5 ⅝ x 2 ¾ In. . . . 147.00
Figurine, Gardeners, Boy, Girl, 19th Century, 5 ½ In., Pair . . . 510.00
Figurine, George Washington, Long Coat, Britches, Holding Hat, 19th Century, 15 In. . . . 1076.00
Figurine, Giuseppe Garibaldi, Sampson Smith, Multicolored, c.1864, 14 ½ In. . . . 764.00
Figurine, Giuseppe Garibaldi, Standing Next To Pedestal, Scroll, 18 ½ In. . . . 230.00
Figurine, Hunter, Deer, Lamp Mounted, 13 x 6 ½ In. . . . 411.00
Figurine, King John Signing Magna Carta, Seated Inside Tent, Mid 1800s, 12 ¾ In. . . . 384.00
Figurine, Lamb, Lying Down, Green Base, Blue Trim, Floral Bocage, c.1800, 4 ½ In. . . . 180.00
Figurine, Lion, Glass Eyes, Early 20th Century, 10 x 13 In., Pair . . . 220.00
Figurine, Lion, On Base, c.1870, 10 x 11 In. . . . 750.00
Figurine, Lion, Paw Raised On Ball, Base, 19th Century, 12 In., Pair . . . 10200.00
Figurine, Little Red Riding Hood, 19th Century, 10 ¼ In. . . . 234.00
Figurine, Scottish Hunter, 15 x 5 ¾ In. . . . 529.00
Figurine, Scottish Lass, Early 19th Century, 8 ¼ In. . . . *illus* 180.00
Figurine, Scottish Man & Woman, 14 x 9 In. . . . 60.00
Figurine, Tiger Over Man, Glazed, 5 x 6 In. . . . 117.00
Figurine, Tom King On Horseback, c.1880, 9 In. . . . 80.00
Figurine, Uncle Tom, Seated, Eva Seated On His Lap, 9 In. . . . 690.00
Figurine, Uncle Tom & Eva, Multicolored Enamel, Mid 1800s, 11 In. . . . 235.00
Figurine, Well-Dressed Women, Riding Horse Sidesaddle, 1800s, 9 & 9 ½ In., Pair . . . 234.00
Figurine, William Shakespeare, Red Coat, Leaning On Square Plinth, 1800s, 8 In. . . . 470.00
Figurine, Woman, 19th Century, 7 ½ x 2 ¾ In. . . . 94.00
Figurine, Woman, Long Robe Leaning On Dolphin, Winged Cupid, c.1825, 7 ½ In. . . . 150.00
Figurine, Zebra, Black & Green Enamel, Mid 1800s, 6 ⅛ & 6 ½ In., Pair . . . 323.00
Figurine, Zebra, Flat Back, Green Base, 4 ¾ In., Pair . . . *illus* 244.00
Flask, Hudson, Hudson River, Purple Transfer, Clews, 1829-36, 9 ½ In. . . . 3107.00
Group, Boy, Cow, c.1850, 6 ¾ x 6 In. . . . 353.00
Group, Prince & Princess Of Wales, Denmark, c.1860, 15 ½ In. . . . 176.00
Group, Spaniel, Pup, 19th Century, 8 x 6 ¼ In. . . . 294.00
Group, Virgin Mary & Child, c.1825, 9 ¾ x 5 ½ In. . . . 323.00
Incense Burner, Cottage Form, 4 ¼ x 3 ½ In. . . . 294.00
Jug, Mask, Man With Beard, Protrusions, Yellow Glaze, Transfer Printed, 4 ¾ In. . . . 232.00
Jug, Scenic Blue Transfer, Footed, Angular Handle, 1800s, 6 In. . . . 213.00
Ladle, Soup, Bank, Rose & Leaf Medallion Border, Blue, 11 In. . . . 4183.00
Ladle, Vignette From American Views, Light Blue, 12 In. . . . 388.00
Lady's Boot, Trees, Blue, White, 9 In. . . . 50.00
Mug, 2 Handles, Boston State House, Flower Vine Border, Blue, 6 In. . . . 2032.00
Mug, Eagle Holding Banner, Canary, Sepia, 19th Century, 2 ½ In. . . . 956.00
Mug, Maritime Scene, Shell Border, Dark Blue, 3 ¾ x 3 ¾ In. . . . 715.00
Mug, With All Thy Soul, Pink Luster Border, 2 ⅝ In. . . . *illus* 225.00
Pitcher, Lafayette At Franklin's Tomb, Blue, Enoch Wood & Sons, 1819-46, 9 ¼ In. . . . 837.00
Pitcher, Landing Of Gen. Lafayette At Castle Garden, Clews, c.1830, 8 ¾ In. . . . 657.00
Pitcher, New York Insane Asylum, Almshouse, Blue, Clews, c.1830, 6 ¼ In. . . . *illus* 508.00
Pitcher, Paneled Baluster, Battle Scene, Purple, 12 In. . . . 2749.00
Pitcher, States Design, English Castle, Historic Blue, Blauster, Clews, 9 ¼ In. . . . 956.00
Pitcher, Welcome Lafayette The Nation's Guest, Blue, Oval, Clews, c.1825, 9 In. . . . 538.00
Pitcher & Basin, Flower Filled Urn, Blue Transfer, c.1825, 9 ¾-In. Pitcher . . . 1028.00
Plate, America & Independence, States Border, Scalloped Edge, Blue, 10 ½ In. . . . 230.00
Plate, American Museum, Acorn & Oak Leaf Border, Blue, 7 ½ In. . . . 448.00
Plate, Arms Of New York, Flower Border, Blue, Thomas Mayer, c.1830, 10 In. . . . 657.00
Plate, Arriving At Plymouth, Blue, 6 ½ In. . . . 230.00
Plate, Bird Pattern, Dark Blue, 9 In., Pair . . . 201.00
Plate, Birds, Country Homes, Dark Blue, 19th Century, 10 In. . . . 209.00
Plate, Boston State House, Blue, 9 ½ In. . . . 431.00
Plate, Boston State House, Flower Border, Blue, 10 In. . . . 72.00
Plate, Boston State House, Flower Vine Border, Blue, John Rogers & Son, 9 ½ In. . . . *illus* 131.00
Plate, British Scene, Cobalt Blue, 10 In. . . . 144.00
Plate, Commodore MacDonnough's Victory, Shell Border, Blue, 9 ⅛ In. . . . 575.00
Plate, Commodore MacDonnough's Victory, Shell Border, Blue, 10 In. . . . 345.00 to 518.00

'late, Dam & Water Works, Philadelphia, Flower Border, Blue, 9¾ In. .... 345.00 to 690.00
late, Dinner, Moral Maxim, Black Transfer, Clews, c.1825, 10½ In. 155.00
late, Doctor Syntax Turned Nurse, Blue, White, Clews, c.1825, 7⅞ In. 70.00
'late, Dog & Boy With Broom, Blue & White, 19th Century, 10 In. 67.00
'late, Figures In Pavilion, Flower Reserves, Cranberry Transfer, 9¼ In., 10 Piece 288.00
'late, Historical, Nahant Hotel Near Boston, Eagle Border, Blue, c.1829, 8½ In. 288.00
'late, Landing Of Gen. Lafayette At Castle Garden, Blue, Clews, c.1830, 10 In. 215.00
'late, Luncheon, City Hotel, Acorn & Leaf Border, Blue, c.1825, 8½ In. 179.00
'late, Medallions, 2 Portraits, City Hotel, N.Y., Stevenson & Williams, c.1825, 8½ In. 14340.00
late, Medallions, 4 Portraits, Niagara Sheep Shearing, Stevenson, 1808-29, 10¼ In. 9560.00
late, Medallions, 4 Portraits, Park Theater, N.Y., Blue, Stevenson & Williams, c.1820, 10 In. .. 8356.00
late, Mother & Child, 9¾ In. 40.00
'late, Near Hudson, Hudson River, Pink Transfer, 1829-36, 9 In. 448.00
'late, Officer On White Horse, Green, 9¼ In. 329.00
late, Shell Pattern, Dark Blue, Joseph Stubbs, Longport, 7½ In., Pair 300.00
late, Soup, Writtle Lodge, Essex, Flowers & Leaf Border, Blue, A. Stevenson, 10¼ In. 110.00
late, Texian Campaigne, Black Transfer, Anthony Shaw, 8¼ In. 375.00
late, Toddy, Arms Of South Carolina, Blue, Mayer, c.1830, 5¾ In. 500.00
late, Tomb Of Washington, Blue, White, 10 In. 460.00
late, Water Hen, c.1890, 5 In. 80.00
late, Soup, 2 Hunters, Dogs, Cottage, Trees, Shrubs, Scalloped Edge, Blue, Clews, 10⅜ In. .. 176.00
late, Soup, Fishing Scene, Village, Castle Ruins, Scroll & Leaf Border, Blue, Clews, 10 In. 154.00
latter, All Souls College Scene, Blue, White, Footed, Coffin Shape, 3 x 21 x 16 In. 615.00
latter, Arms Of Delaware, Flower Border, Blue, Thomas Mayer, c.1830, 17 In. 14340.00
latter, Arms Of Georgia, Flower Border, Blue, Thomas Mayer, c.1830, 7½ In. 2510.00
latter, Arms Of Pennsylvania, Flower Border, Blue, Thomas Mayer, c.1830, 20¾ In. 17925.00
latter, Brancepeth Castle, Grapevine, Enoch Wood & Sons, c.1820, 19 x 14 In. .... *illus* 450.00
latter, Cape Coast Castle, Gold Coast Africa, Enoch Wood, 16¼ In. 400.00
latter, Castle Garden Battery, N.Y., Shell Border, Blue, Enoch Wood & Sons, 20½ In. 3884.00
latter, Chinese Flowers, Octagonal, Blue & White, Ironstone, 20½ x 13¾ In. 720.00
latter, Chinoiserie, Oval, Blue, 19th Century, 20½ In. 246.00
latter, Deaf & Dumb Asylum, Rose & Leaf Border, Blue, Octagonal, 14¾ In. 1076.00
latter, Geneva, Hunting Party, Greyhounds, Castle, Lake, Blue, Octagonal, 1820, 15 In. 195.00
latter, Landing Of Gen. Lafayette At Castle Garden, N.Y., Blue, c.1830, 17 In. 1195.00
latter, Leopard & Antelope, Passion Flower Border, Blue, 18½ x 14 In. 1495.00
latter, Little Falls At Luzerne, Hudson River, Brown, Clews, 1829-36, 18 In. 717.00
latter, Oval, Boston State House, Shaped Edge, Eagle, Scroll & Flower Border, 14 In. 1912.00
latter, Palestine, Red Transfer, Scalloped Rim, 13 x 10½ In. 485.00
latter, Penitentiary In Allegheny, Purple, Clews, c.1830, 15½ In. 1554.00
latter, Pittsburgh, Pa., Light Blue, Clews, 1829-36, 19¾ In. 1793.00
latter, Sandusky, Rose & Scroll Border, Mismarked Detroit, Blue, Early 1800s, 16¼ In. 4780.00
latter, Scenic, Dark Blue, Riley's Semi China, 21 x 16½ In. 863.00
latter, States Design, Custom House, Blue, Clews, 1829-36, 19½ In. 3585.00
latter, Sydenham, Blue & White, Francis Morley, Ashworth, c.1860, 15 In. 234.00
latter, Woman On Porch, Clementson, Sydenham, 19th Century, 18 In. 147.00
unch Bowl, Capitol At Washington, Transfer, Blue, Scalloped Edge, Footed, 5 x 12 In. 7150.00
alt & Pepper, Finlandia, Blue & White 28.00
auceboat, Eagle, Scroll & Flower Border, 5 In. 388.00
erving Dish, Dark Blue, Flower & Fruit Border, Flower Form Finial, 6 x 8 x 9 In. 143.00
lop Bucket, View Of Hudson, Urn Shape, Ribbed, Light Blue, c.1844, 12 In. 598.00
oap Dish, Landing Of General Lafayette, 3 Compartments, Cover, 8¾ In. 3712.00
tand, Ink Pen, Figural, Reclining Dog, 3½ x 4¾ In. 206.00
tand, Pen, Figural, 2 Women, 4 x 3¾ In. 147.00
trainer, St. Lawrence, Purple, 13 In. 359.00
ugar, Cover, Gentleman's Cabin, Boston, Black Transfer, 7½ x 7 In. 160.00
ugar, Cover, Landscape, Blue, White 345.00
ugar & Creamer, Bird Pattern, Dark Blue 115.00
ugar & Creamer, Eagle Over Panel, Dark Blue, Davenport 300.00
azza, Boston State House, Flower Vine Border, Blue, 10½ x 2¾ In. 359.00
ea Bowl, Saucer, Bird, On Branch, Blue Transfer, Pink Luster Rim, Early 1800s, 2½ In. 59.00
a Set, Punch & Judy, Allerton & Son, Child's, 11 Piece 205.00
apot, Cover, Boston Views, Oblong, C-Scroll Handle, Medium Blue 837.00
apot, Cover, Washington At Tomb, Blue, Enoch Wood, 8¾ In. 400.00
apot, Franklin's Tomb, Blue, White, 7¾ In. 632.00
apot, Washington At Tomb, Blue, Enoch Wood & Sons, 1819-46, 6½ In. 657.00
by Jugs are listed in their own category.

Staffordshire, Platter, Brancepeth Castle, Grapevine, Enoch Wood & Sons, c.1820, 19 x 14 In.
$450.00

Staffordshire, Tureen, Sauce, Cover, Eagles, River Schuylkill, Blue, 6 In.
$837.00

Staffordshire, Vase, Spaniel, Flat Back, Gilt, 13¼ In.
$80.00

TIP

The material used to make repairs is warmer to the touch than the porcelain. Feel the surface of a figurine to see if there are unseen repairs.

Stangl, Bird, Allen Hummingbird, No. 3634, Marked, 3¾ In.
$40.00

Stangl, Bird, Cerulean Warbler, No. 3456, Marked, 4½ In.
$30.00

Stangl, Bird, Cockatoo, No. 3584, Marked, 12⅛ In.
$210.00

Stangl, Bird, Lovebirds, No. 3404, Marked, 5¼ In.
$150.00

Tureen, Cover, Green, Flowers, 9¾ x 12¾ In. 180.0
Tureen, Cover, Hollywell Cottage Cavan, Blue, White, 9 x 13¼ In. 977.0
Tureen, Cover, Rural Scene, Dark Blue, Fruit Finial, Undertray, Ladle, 6 x 8 In., 3 Piece 495.0
Tureen, Dome Cover, Platter, Blue, Iron Red, Flower Border, Gilt, Footed, 9 & 17 In. 148.0
Tureen, Sauce, Cover, Eagles, River Schuylkill, Blue, 6 In. *illus* 837.0
Tureen, Soup, Cover, Flower & Leaf, Handles, 11 x 13¼ x 9 In. 144.0
Vase, Cover, Enameled, Bleu Celeste, Bird Reserves, 6¼ In., Pair 2640.0
Vase, Cover, Garniture, Bleu Celeste, Fisherman, Brass Mounted, Flowers, 18 x 7 In. 2160.0
Vase, Spaniel, Flat Back, Gilt, 13¼ In. *illus* 80.0
Vase, Spill, Church Form, Raised Flower Vines, 19th Century, 9 x 7 In. 176.00 to 230.0
Vase, Spill, Church Shape, 19th Century, 8⅞ x 7 In. 146.0
Vase, Spill, Deer, Snake Wrapped Around Body, Yellow Green Mottled Base, 7 In. 140.0
Vase, Spill, Group, 19th Century, 7½ x 5½ In. 147.0
Vase, Spill, Yellow Glaze, Transfer Printed, Flowers, Flared, Spread Foot, 5½ In. 348.0
Vase, Spill, Zebra, Snake Wrapped Around Body, Green Mottled Base, 7½ In. 180.0
Washbowl, Battle Scene, Purple, 14½ In. 1554.0
Washbowl, Boston State House, Flower & Leaf Border, Blue, 12½ In. 777.0
Washbowl, Lafayette At Franklin's Tomb, Blue, Enoch Wood & Sons, c.1830, 10¾ In. 956.0
Washbowl, Landing Of Gen. Lafayette At Castle Garden, Blue, Clews, 1829-36, 12 In. 1016.0
Washbowl, Lawrence Mansion, Leaf & Vine Border, Molded Edge, Blue, 13 In. 3884.0
Washbowl, States Design, White House, Washington, Scalloped Edge, Clews, c.1830, 12 In. 1076.0
Waste Bowl, Blue, Baltimore Court House, Henshall Williamson & Co., 5⅝ In. 2500.0

STANGL Pottery traces its history back to the Fulper Pottery of New Jersey. In 1910, Johann Martin Stangl started working at Fulper. He left to work at Haeger Pottery from 1915 to 1920. Stangl returned to Fulper Pottery in 1920, became president in 1926, and changed the company name t Stangl Pottery in 1929. Stangl acquired the firm in 1930. The pottery is known for dinnerware and a lin of bird figurines. Martin Stangl died in 1972 and the pottery was sold to Frank Wheaton, Jr., of Wheaton Industries. Production continued until 1978, when Pfaltzgraff Pottery purchased the right to the Stangl trademark and the remaining inventory was liquidated. A single bird figurine is identified by a number Figurines made up of two birds are identified by a number followed by the letter *D* indicating Double.

Ashtray, Mallard Duck, Oval, c.1958 24.0
Ashtray, Pheasant, c.1950 51.0
Bird, Allen Hummingbird, No. 3634, Marked, 3¾ In. *illus* 40.0
Bird, Audubon Warblers, Double, No. 3756, 8 In. 176.0
Bird, Bird Of Paradise, No. 3408, 5½ In. 44.0
Bird, Blue Jay With Leaf, No. 3716, 10½ In. 470.0
Bird, Broadbill Hummingbird, No. 3629, 4½ In. 55.0
Bird, Canary, Right Facing, No. 3746, 6¼ In. 66.0
Bird, Cerulean Warbler, No. 3456, Marked, 4½ In. *illus* 30.0
Bird, Chestnut Backed Chickadee, No. 3811, 5 In. 55.0
Bird, Cockatoo, Double, No. 3405D, Open Base, 9½ In. 94.0
Bird, Cockatoo, No. 3580, 8⅝ In. 94.0
Bird, Cockatoo, No. 3584, Marked, 12⅛ In. *illus* 210.0
Bird, Golden Crowned Kinglets, No. 3853, 5¼ In. 302.0
Bird, Goldfinches, 4 Birds Seated On Branch, No. 3635, 4¼ x 11½ In. 106.0
Bird, Gray Cardinal, No. 3596, 5 In. 78.0
Bird, Hen Pheasant, No. 3491, 6½ In. 118.0
Bird, Indigo Bunting, No. 3589, 3¼ In. 60.00 to 85.0
Bird, Kentucky Warbler, No. 3598, 3½ In. 30.00 to 48.0
Bird, Key West Quail Dove, No. 3454, 9¼ In. 118.0
Bird, Lovebirds, No. 3404, Marked, 5¼ In. *illus* 150.0
Bird, Passenger Pigeon, No. 3450, 9 x 18 In. 529.0
Bird, Red-Faced Warbler, No. 3594, 2⅞ x 4 In. *illus* 24.0
Bird, Redstarts, Double, No. 3490, 9 In. 71.0
Bird, Running Duck, No. 3432, 5 In. 264.0
Bird, Scarlet Tanager, Double, No. 3750D, 7½ In. 176.0
Bird, Scissortail Flycatcher, No. 3757, 11 In. 413.0
Bird, Turkey, No. 3275, 3⅜ x 4¼ In. *illus* 240.0
Bird, Western Bluebird, No. 3815, 7 In. 165.0
Bird, White Wing Crossbills, Double, No. 3754, 9 In. 176.0
Bird, Wren, No. 3401, 3½ In. 55.0
Cigarette Box, Fluted, Gold, c.1965, 5¾ x 4½ In. 30.0
Dish, Jade Green, Divided, c.1930 22.0
Golden Blossom, Pitcher, Brown Trim, Yellow, c.1964, Qt., 5 In. 48.0

olden Blossom, Plate, 10 In. 10.00
olden Harvest, Chop Plate, c.1953, 14½ In. 35.00
olden Harvest, Pitcher, 6½ x 9 In. 40.00
amp Base, Love Bird Sitting On Branch, Tan Clay, No. 1023, 8½ In. 142.00
itcher, Blue Daisy, Cylindrical, c.1940, 6¼ In. 45.00
lanter, Swan, Antique Gold, c.1960, 3¼ x 3½ In. 20.00
abbit, Natural Colors, 2⅛ x 3½ In. *illus* 150.00
alt & Pepper, Angel's Head Is Salt, Winged Shoulders Is Pepper, Ross Ware, c.1940 55.00
ign, Stangl Birds, Red, Blue, Yellow, Green, 5⅜ x 6 In. 660.00
erra Rose, Planter, Cosmos, Glaze, 7⅝ x 7¾ In. 55.00
erra Rose, Vase, 2 Handles, c.1940, 6 In. 33.00
erra Rose, Vase, Rope Handles, Oval, Ruffled, 5 x 9½ In. 120.00
histle, Bread Plate, c.1951, 6¼ In. 3.00
histle, Cup, c.1951, 3¾ In. 5.00 to 6.50
histle, Trinket Box, c.1950, No. 3844 50.00
own & Country, Soup, Dish, Blue, Spongeware, c.1974, 6¾ In. 36.00
rinidad, Tidbit, Flowers, Central Handle, 10 In. 48.00
ase, Antique Gold, 22K, Long Neck, 9½ In. 55.00
ase, Antique Gold, c.1957, 6½ In. 30.00
ase, Sea Green Matte Glaze, 2 Handles, Ribbed Neck, 7 In. 49.00
ase, Stoneware, Salt Glaze, Flared Rim, Marked, Stangl Stoneware, c.1940, Qt., 8 In. 110.00
hite Dogwood, Cup, 2⅝ In. 12.00
ild Rose, Bowl, Vegetable, Divided, c.1955, 10½ In. 40.00

TAR TREK AND STAR WARS collectibles are included here. The original *Star Trek* television ries ran from 1966 through 1969. The series spawned an animated series, three sequels, and prequel, which is still in production. The first *Star Trek* movie was released in 1979 and nine thers followed, the most recent in 2002. The movie *Star Wars* opened in 1977. Sequels were released in 980 and 1983; prequels in 1999, 2002, and 2005. Other science fiction and fantasy collectibles can be und under Batman, Buck Rogers, Captain Marvel, Flash Gordon, Movie, Superman, and Toy.

TAR TREK

alendar, Ballantine Books, 1976, 13 x 24 In. 50.00
omic Book, No. 8, The Youth Trap, September 1970 18.00
omic Book, Volume 2, Golden Press, 1976, 224 Pages 34.00
igure, B'Etor, Box, 1994, 4½ In. 13.00
igure, Borg, Accessories, Playmates, Box, 1997, 6 In. 9.00
igure, Guinan, Swivel Body, Box, 1993, 2½ x 5 In. 30.00
igure, Lore, Moving Arms & Legs, 1993, 2¼ x 4½ In. 25.00
igure, Lt. Tasha Yar, c.1988, 1¼ x 3½ In. 30.00
igure, Lursa, Box, 1994, 4½ In. 4.00
ug, Frosted Glass, Gold Decals, 1994 10.00
ug, Sulu, Hamilton Collection 1966, 1983 Paramount Pictures Corp. 15.00
usic Box, No. 931284, Star Trek Theme, Paramount, 1991, 8 x 6 x 2 In. 50.00
rnament, Romulan Warbird, Hallmark, 1995 23.00
rnament, The Voyager, Hallmark, 1996 10.00
late, Best Of Both Worlds, Gold Trim, Hamilton Collection 45.00
uzzle, Journey To Undiscovered Country, 1000 Pieces, 24 x 30 In. 25.00
rading Card, Times Arrow, Mounted, c.1990 20.00
ravel Set, Wallet, Captain's Cologne, Soap, Box 20.00

TAR WARS

owl, Decal, Not For Microwave, Dishwasher Safe, 5½ In. 4.00
utton, Star Wars, R2-D2, C-3PO, Factors Etc. Inc., 1977, 3 In. *illus* 54.00
omic Book, Star Duel, Marvel, No. 15, 1978 10.00
gure, Bespin Security Guard, Weapon, No. TO1207, Kenner, 1980, 3¾ In. 13.00
gure, Imperial Commander, Weapon, No. TO1259, Kenner, 1980, 3¾ In. 13.00
gure, Jawa With Gonk Droid, Posable, Commtech Chip, Hasbro, Box, 1999 9.00
gure, Lobot, No. TO1247, Kenner, 1978, 3½ In. 13.00
gure, Luke Skywalker, X-Wing Fighter, Power Of The Force Toy Line, Box, c. 1998 72.00
gure, Queen Amidala, Hallmark, No. QXI4187, Box, 1999, 4½ In. 15.00
odel Kit, Millennium Falcon, Original Box, c.1979 74.00
ug, Chewbacca, Ceramic, Applause, c.1997, 5 In. 18.00
ug, Han Solo, Lucas Productions, c.1996 15.00
ster, 20th Century Fox, 1977, 27 x 41 In. 123.00
ster, Chewbacca, No. 4, 1977, 10 x 34 In. 15.00
ster, Darth Vader, No. 5, 1977, 10 x 34 In. 15.00

Stangl, Bird, Red-Faced Warbler, No. 3594, 2⅞ x 4 In.
$24.00

Stangl, Bird, Turkey, No. 3275, 3⅜ x 4¼ In.
$240.00

Stangl, Rabbit, Natural Colors, 2⅛ x 3½ In.
$150.00

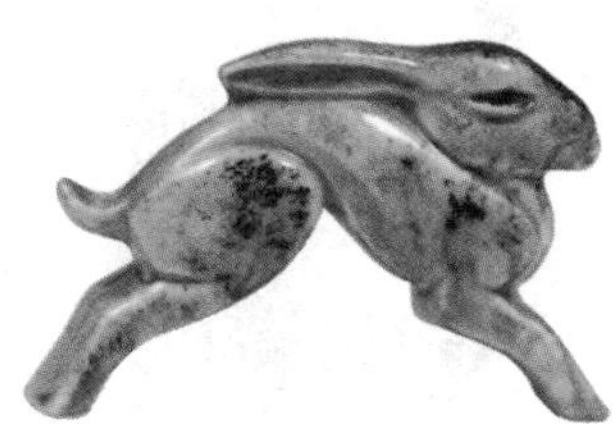

Star Wars, Button, Star Wars, R2-D2, C-3PO, Factors Etc. Inc., 1977, 3 In.
$54.00

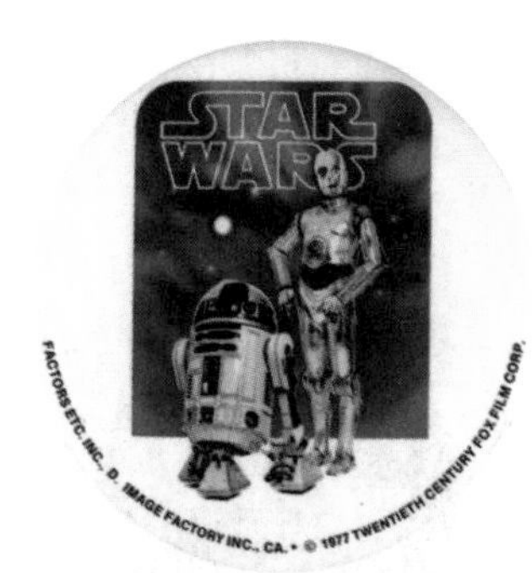

Stein, Character, Bismarck Radish, Porcelain, Marked, Musterschutz, Schierholz, ½ Liter
$288.00

Stein, Character, Munich Child, Pottery, Painted Face, Inlaid Lid, J. Reinemann, ½ Liter
$242.00

Stein, Character, Rabbit, Porcelain, Inlaid Lid, RPM, c.1950, ½ Liter
$136.00

Toy, C-3PO, Plastic, Jointed, 1978, 12 In. 110.00
Toy, Tripod Laser Canon, No. 93450, Kenner, Box, 1982. 9.00

STEINS have been used by beer and ale drinkers for over 500 years. They have been made of ivory, porcelain, stoneware, faience, silver, pewter, wood, or glass in sizes up to nine gallons. Although some were made by Mettlach, Meissen, Capo-di-Monte, and other famous factories, most were made by less important German potteries. The words *Geschutz* or *Musterschutz* on a stein are the German words for "patented" or "registered design," not company names. Steins are still being made in the old styles. Lithophane steins may be found in the Lithophane category.

Character, Acorn, Porcelain, Inlaid Lid, E. Bohne & Sohne, ½ Liter 1034.00
Character, Alligator, Wraparound, Porcelain, E. Bohne & Sohne, ½ Liter 633.00
Character, Alpine Man, Porcelain, Marked, Musterschutz, Schierholz, ½ Liter 1150.00
Character, Artillery Shell, Stoneware, Pewter Lid, Marked, No. 2385, 1914, ½ Liter 242.00
Character, Baby, Flowers, Pink Bows, Porcelain, Head Is Lid, ½ Liter 1495.00
Character, Bag Of Coffee, Kathreiners Kneipp, Malz, Porcelain, Schierholz, ½ Liter 4715.00
Character, Barbell, Pottery, Marked 1227, Lid, 1 Liter 313.00
Character, Barmaid, Hands Behind Head, Porcelain, Schierholz, ½ Liter 1955.00
Character, Barmaid Lisl, Stoneware, Inlaid Lid, Marked, J. Reinemann, ½ Liter 431.00
Character, Barrel, Man's Head Finial, Porcelain, ½ Liter 184.00
Character, Bismarck Radish, Porcelain, Marked, Musterschutz, Schierholz, ½ Liter *illus* 288.00
Character, Bison, Porcelain, Inlaid, Marked, E. Bohne & Sohne, ½ Liter 1995.00
Character, Bock, Porcelain, Inlaid Lid, Schierholz, ½ Liter 725.00
Character, Bowling Pin, Porcelain, Inlaid Lid, Schierholz, ½ Liter 193.00
Character, Bustle Lady, Umbrella, Stoneware, Pewter Lid, Hauber & Reuther, ½ Liter 891.00
Character, Bustle Lady, Wood, Pewter Overlay, ½ Liter 1438.00
Character, Cat, Stoneware, Inlaid Lid, Marked Gerz 030, ¼ Liter 116.00
Character, Devil, Porcelain, E. Bohne & Sohne, 4 ½ In. 212.00
Character, Dice, Pottery, Pewter Strap, Marked, 1781, ½ Liter 311.00
Character, Drunken Monkey, Blue, White, Porcelain, Schierholz, ½ Liter 1323.00
Character, Fat Man's Face, Stoneware, Pewter Lid, Sarreguimines, P. Jung, 1907, 2 Liter 805.00
Character, Fireman, Stoneware, Purple Salt Glaze, Marked, 750, ½ Liter 460.00
Character, Frauenkirche Tower, Porcelain, Marked, Martin Pauson, ½ Liter 546.00
Character, Frauenkirche Tower, Porcelain, Marked, Martin Pauson, 1 Liter 633.00
Character, Frog, Porcelain, Lid, Schierholz, ½ Liter 920.00
Character, Gentleman Dog, Porcelain, Schierholz, ½ Liter 1634.00
Character, Goat, Porcelain, Marked, Musterschutz, Schierholz, ½ Liter 403.00
Character, Happy Radish, Porcelain, Inlaid Lid, Schierholz, ½ Liter 217.00
Character, Happy Radish, Porcelain, Inlaid Lid, Musterschutz, ½ Liter 403.00
Character, Hobo, Hand In Pockets, Porcelain, E. Bohne & Sohne, ½ Liter 2875.00
Character, Hunter, Pottery, Marked 422, Lid, ½ Liter 266.00
Character, Indian, Porcelain, Inlaid Lid, E. Bohne & Sohne, ¼ Liter 469.00
Character, Indian, Porcelain, E. Bohne & Sohne, ½ Liter 575.00
Character, Iron Maiden, Stoneware, Purple Salt Glaze, Marked, T.W., ½ Liter 299.00
Character, Ludwig II, Porcelain, Schierholz, ½ Liter 2128.00
Character, Man With Derby, Pottery, Marked, 764, Deisinger, ½ Liter 719.00
Character, Monk, Nun, Porcelain, Inlaid Lid, ½ Liter, Pair 173.00
Character, Monk, Porcelain, Inlaid Lid, Marked, Full Bee, Goebel, ½ Liter 284.00
Character, Monkey, Porcelain, Inlaid Lid, Schierholz, ½ Liter 497.00
Character, Munchen, Stoneware, Transfer, Enamel, Relief Pewter Lid, ½ Liter 160.00
Character, Munich Child, Holding Radishes, Porcelain, Marked, Jos. M. Mayer, ½ Liter 115.00
Character, Munich Child, Holding Stein & Radish, Pottery, Porcelain, Inlaid Lid, ½ Liter 375.00
Character, Munich Child, On Barrel, Porcelain, Schierholz, ¼ Liter 431.00
Character, Munich Child, On Barrel, Porcelain, Musterschutz, Schierholz, ½ Liter 633.00
Character, Munich Child, On Barrel, Porcelain, Inlaid Lid, Schierholz, ½ Liter 920.00
Character, Munich Child, Porcelain, Inlaid Lid, 5 ½ In., ¼ Liter 121.00
Character, Munich Child, Porcelain, Marked, Jos. M. Mayer, 14¾ In., 3 Liter 1610.00
Character, Munich Child, Pottery, Painted Face, Inlaid Lid, J. Reinemann, ½ Liter *illus* 242.00
Character, Munich Child, Stoneware, Transfer, Enamel, Pewter Lid, ½ Liter 180.00
Character, Munich Child, Stoneware, Lid, Franz Ringer, ½ Liter 604.00
Character, Nun, Blue & Purple Salt Glaze, Stoneware, Marked, HR 60, ½ Liter 288.00
Character, Nurnberger Trichter, Porcelain, Marked, Musterschutz, Schierholz, ½ Liter 776.00
Character, Owl, Porcelain, E. Bohne & Sohne, ½ Liter 2530.00
Character, Owl, Pottery, Inlaid Lid, 2 Liter 265.00
Character, Owl, Stoneware, Inlaid Lid, ½ Liter 435.00
Character, Owl, Wood, Glass Eyes, Initials HB, ½ Liter 345.00

haracter, Pig With Target, Pottery, Inlaid Lid, Marked J.M., 1116 .... 490.00
haracter, Poodle, Porcelain, Marked Schierholz, ½ Liter 213.00
haracter, Rabbit, Porcelain, Inlaid Lid, RPM, c.1950, ½ Liter .... *illus* 136.00
haracter, Rich Man, Pottery, Inlaid Lid, Marked MW GR, ½ Liter 161.00
haracter, Rich Man, Stoneware, Inlaid Lid, M & W GR., ½ Liter 209.00
haracter, Rooster, Porcelain, Lid, Schierholz, ½ Liter 230.00
haracter, Sad Radish, Porcelain, Inlaid Lid, Schierholz, ½ Liter .... 362.00 to 453.00
haracter, Sailor, S.M.S. Deutschland, Pottery, Marked, 1821, ½ Liter 1323.00
haracter, Sea Captain, Holding Pipe, Porcelain, Musterschutz, Schierholz, ½ Liter 1006.00
haracter, Seated Ram, Porcelain, Marked Musterschutz, ½ Liter 460.00
haracter, Skull, Porcelain, E. Bohne & Sohne, ½ Liter 489.00
haracter, Skull, Snake Handle, Porcelain, Marked, 695, ½ Liter 633.00
haracter, Skull On Book, Porcelain, Inlaid Lid, Marked E. Bohne & Sohne, ¼ Liter 259.00
haracter, Sleepy Hunter, Porcelain, Bauer, ½ Liter 891.00
haracter, Smiling Mikado, Pottery, Verse, Marked, 1081, ½ Liter 489.00
haracter, Smoking Pig, Marked, Musterschutz, Schierholz, ¼ Liter 403.00
haracter, Snowman, Holding Cane, Porcelain, Marked, Musterschutz, Schierholz, ½ Liter .. 1783.00
haracter, Soccer Ball, Pottery, Rochlitz Sporthaus Charlottenburg, ½ Liter 468.00
haracter, Soldier, Porcelain, Marked Musterschutz, ½ Liter 891.00
haracter, Student Fox, Porcelain, Inlaid Lid, ½ Liter .... 345.00 to 423.00
haracter, Target Lady, Porcelain, Marked, Geschutzt, Schierholz, ½ Liter 1783.00
haracter, Trumpeter Of Sackingen, Pottery, Inlaid Lid, Deisinger, ⅓ Liter 623.00
haracter, Umbrella Men, Porcelain, Pewter Lid, Schierholz, ½ Liter 604.00
haracter, Von Moltke, Porcelain, Lid, Schierholz, ½ Liter .... 230.00 to 242.00
haracter, Wendelstein, Stoneware, Inlaid Lid, Martin Pauson, ½ Liter 472.00
haracter, Wilhelm I, Pottery, Marked, 13, Marzi & Remy, ½ Liter 863.00
haracter, Wilhelm II, Porcelain, Lid, Schierholz, ½ Liter 943.00
haracter, Woman On Stump, Stoneware, Inlaid Lid, ½ Liter 357.00
haracter, Zugspitze, Stoneware, Inlaid Lid, Martin Pauson, ½ Liter 472.00
ience, Birnkrug, Flower, Pewter Lid, Late 1700s, ⅓ Liter, 6 ½ In. 483.00
ience, Birth Of Christ, Pewter Lid, Footring, Gmunden, c.1800, 1 ¼ Liter, 10 ⅔ In. 2300.00
ience, Blue, White, Bierre, Hand Painted, Pewter Lid, c.1850, 1 Liter 213.00
ience, Floral, Pewter Lid & Footring, c.1900, 1 Liter, 11 ¼ In. 311.00
ience, Frankfurt, Flowers, Multicolored Enamel, Pewter, Footring, 1700s, ½ Liter 460.00
ience, Freiburg, Pewter Lid & Foot Ring, c.1920, 1 Liter, 9 ½ In. 217.00
ience, Hanau, Building, Pewter Lid & Footring, Late 1700s, ½ Liter .... *illus* 518.00
ience, Hanau, Pewter Lid & Footring, Mid 1700s, ¼ Liter, 6 In. 299.00
ience, Magdeburg, Enamel, Man, Goat, Pewter Lid & Footring, Late 1700s, 1 Liter 776.00
ience, S. Bernardus, Enamel, Pewter Lid & Footring, Marked, Florsheim, 1 Liter, 8 ⅓ In. ... 6325.00
ience, Schrezenheim, Enamel, Flowers, Multicolor, Pewter Lid & Footring, Late 1700s, 1 Liter, 9 ½ In. 345.00
ience, Thuringen, Enamel, Pewter Lid, c.1790, 1 Liter, 10 ⅛ In. 575.00
ience, Thuringen, Pewter Lid, Footring, Late 1700s, 1 Liter, 10 In. 1117.00
ience, Thuringen, Stag & Dog, Pewter Lid, c.1760, 1 Liter, 9 ½ In. 489.00
ass, Blown, Amber, Flowers, Enamel, Pewter Lid, 2 Liter 36.00
ass, Blown, Amber, Enamel, Blue Handle, Mary Gregory Type, Glass Inlaid Lid, ¼ Liter 58.00
ass, Blown, Amber, Young Boy, Enamel, Pewter Lid, ½ Liter 81.00
ass, Blown, Amber, Man & Woman, Enamel, Verse, Pewter Lid, ½ Liter 173.00
ass, Blown, Amber, Munich Child, Enamel, Pewter Lid, ½ Liter 182.00
ass, Blown, Amber, Man Carrying Turkey On Tray, Enamel, Ribbed, Pewter Lid, ½ Liter 193.00
ass, Blown, Amber, Woman, Enamel, Pewter Lid, ½ Liter 193.00
ass, Blown, Amber, Children, Enamel, Pewter Lid & Footring, ½ Liter 311.00
ass, Blown, Amber Flashed, Engraved, Stag, Does, Clear, Inlaid, Pewter Footring, c.1890, 2 Liter. 1840.00
ass, Blown, Art Nouveau, Gambrinus, Enamel, Relief Pewter Lid, ½ Liter 288.00
ass, Blown, Art Nouveau Silver Plated Mounts, Lid, W.F.M., ½ Liter 196.00
ass, Blown, Blue, Wheel Engraved, Lion & Shield, Pewter Lid, Footring, c.1850, ½ Liter 434.00
ass, Blown, Cherubs, Flashed, Wheel Engraved, Woman On Inlaid Lid, c.1850, ½ Liter. 1323.00
ass, Blown, Clear, Red Stain, Inlaid Lid, Engraved Stag, c.1850, ½ Liter 140.00
ass, Blown, Columns, Blue On Clear Overlay, Clear Lid, c.1880, ½ Liter 1898.00
ass, Blown, Crackle, Bumps Sticking Out, Porcelain, Inlaid Lid Of Woman, ½ Liter 350.00
ass, Blown, Cranberry, Pewter Lid, Handle, Base, ½ Liter .... *illus* 253.00
ass, Blown, Cranberry, Munich Child, Pewter Lid & Overlay, ½ Liter 403.00
ass, Blown, Crosses, Red On Clear Overlay, Flower Gilt Lid, c.1850, 1 Liter 2300.00
ass, Blown, Cut, Man With 2 Horses, Porcelain Inlaid Lid, c.1850, ½ Liter 265.00
ass, Blown, Cut, Bronze Tschako Helmet Finial, Silver Lid, ½ Liter 1553.00
ass, Blown, Dead Stag & Bird, Blue On Clear, Wheel Engraved, Inlaid Lid, c.1850, ½ Liter .. 2645.00
ass, Blown, Deutsches Bundesschiessen, 1912, Enamel, Relief Pewter Lid, F. Ringer, ½ Liter 403.00

The Simpsons
The Simpsons animated TV series has spawned a quantity of collectibles, and because the series is thriving, more collectibles will appear. The show is now seen in more than sixty countries and is one of the most successful animated television series ever created. Looks like a promising collectibles field.

Stein, Faience, Hanau, Building, Pewter Lid & Footring, Late 1700s, ½ Liter
$518.00

Stein, Glass, Blown, Cranberry, Pewter Lid, Handle, Base, ½ Liter
$253.00

S

Stein, Glass, Blown, Milk Glass, Blue Glass Design, Pewter Lid, Late 1600s, 1 Liter, 9 In.
$7188.00

Stein, Occupational, Bierfuhrer, Transfer, Pewter Lid, ½ Liter
$242.00

Stein, Porcelain, Schutzengesellschaft Oberlauterbach, Transfer, Pewter Lid, ½ Liter
$345.00

Glass, Blown, Engraved, Wheat, 25th Anniversary Berlin Street Car Dept., 1913, ½ Liter 230.0
Glass, Blown, Faceted, Wheel Engraved, Flowers, Pewter Lid, Mid 1800s, ½ Liter........... 138.0
Glass, Blown, Faceted Copper Wire Inside, Pewter Lid, Aktien-Gesellschaft Dresden, ½ Liter .. 374.0
Glass, Blown, Faceted Flashed, Wheel Engraved, Meinem Freunde, Cherubs, Inlaid Lid, ½ Liter 332.0
Glass, Blown, Farmer, Wheel Engraved, Pewter Lid, Footring, Brass Inlay, Mid 1800s, 1 Liter . 1121.0
Glass, Blown, Flowers, Aus Freundschaft, Enamel, Blue, Pewter Lid, Mid 1800s, ½ Liter...... 253.0
Glass, Blown, Horse In Field, Wheel Engraved, Footed, Pewter Lid, ½ Liter 242.0
Glass, Blown, Leaves, Glucklich, Cobalt Blue, Enamel, Stag, Relief Pewter Lid, c.1850, 1 Liter. 345.0
Glass, Blown, Liebend Hoffe, Cobalt Blue, Enamel, Pewter Lid, c.1850, ⅛ Liter 115.0
Glass, Blown, Lion Attacking Stag, Wheel Engraved, Faceted, Inlaid Lid, ½ Liter............ 546.0
Glass, Blown, Man With Balloons, Enamel, Dog, Pewter Lid, ½ Liter 150.0
Glass, Blown, Man With Stein, On Barrel, Wheel Engraved, Pewter Lid, Mid 1800s, ½ Liter ... 374.0
Glass, Blown, Milk Glass, Flower Baskets, Enamel, Birds, Verse, Pewter Lid, c.1800, ½ Liter ... 217.0
Glass, Blown, Milk Glass, Flowers, Enamel, Pewter Lid, ½ Liter......................... 489.0
Glass, Blown, Milk Glass, Flowers, Columns, Enamel, Pewter Lid, Footring, 1810, 1 Liter 949.0
Glass, Blown, Milk Glass, Chinese Man, Pipe, Enamel, Flowers, Bands, Pewter Lid, 1792, ⅓ Liter 1121.0
Glass, Blown, Milk Glass, Hunting Accident, Enamel, Pewter Lid, Footring, c.1850, ½ Liter ... 2530.0
Glass, Blown, Milk Glass, Blue Glass Design, Pewter Lid, Late 1600s, 1 Liter, 9 In.. ...... *illus* 7188.0
Glass, Blown, Opaline, Blue & White, Enamel, Gilt, Silver Lid, c.1850, ½ Liter............. 2013.0
Glass, Blown, Pink, White Overlay, Enamel Flowers, Scrolls, Inlaid Lid, c.1850, ¼ Liter 1495.0
Glass, Blown, Pink On White, Enamel, Glass Inlaid Lid, ⅓ Liter 265.0
Glass, Blown, Red, Clear Overlay, Woman, Porcelain Inlaid Lid, ½ Liter 345.0
Glass, Blown, Ruby Flashed, Wheel Engraved, Wartburg, Glass Inlaid Lid, 1 Liter 242.0
Glass, Blown, Ruby Flashed, Flared, Wheel Engraved, Stag & Doe, Glass Inlaid Lid, c.1850, ½ Liter . 403.0
Glass, Blown, Ruby Flashed, Faceted, Handle, c.1850, ½ Liter......................... 863.0
Glass, Blown, Schutzengesellschaft Michaelschuch, 1908, Enamel, Pewter Lid, ½ Liter ...... 201.
Glass, Blown, Stag & Doe, Yellow Flashed, Wheel Engraved, Inlaid Lid, c.1850, ½ Liter ...... 1006.
Glass, Blown, Student Association, Enamel, Faceted, Pewter Lid, 1921, ½ Liter............ 350.
Glass, Blown, Student Association, Ckeruskia Sei's Panier, Enamel, Pewter Lid, 1911, ½ Liter. 374.
Glass, Blown, Student Association, Timbria Sei's Panier, Enamel, Pewter Lid, 1899, ½ Liter .. 575.
Glass, Blown, Student Association, Armenia Sei's Panier, Enamel, Pewter Lid, 1902, ½ Liter .. 633.
Glass, Blown, Uranium, Enamel, Mary Gregory, Inlaid Lid, ¼ Liter .... 127.
Glass, Blown, Uranium, Green, Enamel, Boy Standing By Fence, Inlaid Lid, c.1890, 1 Liter... 2645.
Glass, Blown, Waidmann's Heil, Rifle, Horn, Animals, Stag Thumblift, Pewter Lid, ½ Liter ... 265.
Glass, Blown, White On Clear, Wheel Engraved, Porcelain Inlaid Lid, c.1850, ½ Liter........ 863.
Glass, Blown, Woman, Holding Leaves, Engraved, Pewter Lid, Bird Thumblift, c.1800, ½ Liter 1380.
Glass, Blown Milk Glass Enamel, Warriors, Glass Inlaid Lid, ½ Liter .... 276.
Glass, Cut, Hobnail, Swag, Hound Dog Finial, Applied Handle, Pewter Lid, 6 In............. 384.
Glass, Cut, Porcelain Inlaid Lid, Angels, ½ Liter...................................... 311.
Glass, Mold Blown, Enamel Flowers, Green Inlaid Lid, ½ Liter .... 81.
Glass, Mold Blown, Gilded, Coins, Finial Ground, Glass Inlaid Lid, 2 ½ Liter............... 283.
Glass, Pressed, Porcelain Inlaid Lid, McAvoy's Kloster-Brau, ½ Liter..................... 86.
Metal, Relief, Silver Plated, Lid, Ball Feet, Denmark, ½ Liter.......................... 224.
Mettlach steins are listed in the Mettlach category.
Military, German, Austrian Soldiers, Stoneware, Enamel, Eagles, Tree, Pewter Lid, ½ Liter ... 242.
Military, Iron Cross, Stoneware, Pewter Lid, ½ In...................................... 76.
Military, Pottery, Reiter Regiment, Relief Helmet, Pewter Lid, 1920s, ½ Liter .... 282.
Military, Regensburg Scene, Stoneware, Pewter Lid, ½ Liter............................ 248.
Military, Streif Batl., Stoneware, 1919, Pewter Lid, ½ Liter .... 403.
Occupational, Bierfuhrer, Transfer, Pewter Lid, ½ Liter .... *illus* 242.
Occupational, Cheese Maker, Porcelain, Schweizer, Transfer, Enamel, Pewter Lid, ½ Liter ... 250.
Occupational, Gerber, Leather Tanner, Pottery, Enamel, Transfer, Metal Lid, ½ Liter........ 163.
Occupational, Hufbeschlagkurs, Wurzburg, Porcelain, Enamel, Pewter Lid, 1937, ½ Liter... 338.
Occupational, Kaser, Porcelain, Pewter Lid, ½ Liter................................... 282.
Occupational, Kaserei, Cheese Maker, Porcelain, Enamel, Pewter Lid, ½ Liter............. 362.
Occupational, Landmann, Farmer, Horses Pulling Plow, Porcelain, Enamel, Pewter Lid, ½ Liter . 160.
Occupational, Maler, Glass, Mold Blown, Porcelain Inlaid Lid, ½ Liter.................. 127.
Occupational, Mason, Steinhauer, Porcelain, Transfer & Enamel, Pewter Lid, ½ Liter ...... 518.
Occupational, Okonomie, Farmer, Porcelain, Enamel, Pewter Lid, ½ Liter .... 167.
Occupational, Okonomie, Farmer, Konrad Mayerhofer, Porcelain, Enamel, Pewter Lid, ½ Liter 200.
Occupational, Rennsport, Jockey, Transfer, Pewter Lid, ½ Liter .... 460.
Occupational, Schlosser, Metal Worker, Porcelain, Enamel, Pewter Lid, ½ Liter .... 302.
Occupational, Schreiner, Porcelain, Transfer, Enamel, Pewter Lid, ½ Liter .... 437.
Occupational, Schuster, Shoemaker, Transfer, Pewter Lid, ½ Liter .... 518.
Occupational, Socialist Traveling Carpenter, Porcelain, Enamel, Pewter Lid, ½ Liter .... 431.
Occupational, Steinmetz, Stonecutter, Porcelain, Transfer, Enamel, Pewter Lid, ½ Liter..... 690.

lympia, Pilsen Brewing Co., Glass, Pewter Handle, Lid, Porcelain Insert, 7 x 5 In. 88.00
ewter, 14 Applied Copper Coins On Body & Lid, c.1800, 10 ⅛ In., 1 Liter 891.00
ewter, Eagle, Pewter Lid, English Verse, Relief, Pewter Lid, ½ Liter 181.00
ewter, Eagle, Relief, Pewter Lid, ½ Liter 170.00
ewter, Engraved, Pewter Lid, c.1858, 1 ½ Liter 207.00
ewter, Pillow Fight, Barth Munchen, 1871, ½ Liter 604.00
ewter, Seymour Mann, c.1973, 16 x 10 In. 12.00
orcelain, Barmaid, Blacksmith School, Pewter Lid, Base, ½ Liter 230.00
orcelain, Beethoven, Relief, Hand Painted, Pewter Lid, ½ Liter 431.00
orcelain, Dresden, Bees, Flowers, Butterflies, Hand Painted, Silver Lid, ⅓ Liter 891.00
orcelain, Enamel, Royal Vienna Style, 4 Nude Women, Pewter Lid, c.1908, 1 Liter, 12 In. ... 1328.00
orcelain, Faust, Hand Painted, Transfer, Inlaid Lid, ½ Liter 311.00
orcelain, Hand Painted, Marked HR, Hauber & Reuther, Pewter Lid, ½ Liter 242.00
orcelain, Hand Painted, Silver Lid, Theodore P. Starr, Ceramic Art Co., c.1898, ½ Liter 518.00
orcelain, Hunters, Dog, Carved Horn On Pewter Lid, Horn Thumblift, Enamel, ½ Liter 374.00
orcelain, Munich Child, Gruss Aus Munchen, Pewter Lid, Transfer, ½ Liter 104.00
orcelain, Postbote, Postman, Transfer, Enamel, Pewter Lid, ½ Liter 489.00
orcelain, Schutzengesellschaft Oberlauterbach, Transfer, Pewter Lid, ½ Liter .... *illus* 345.00
orcelain, Staatl Hufbeschlagkurs, Mannheim, 1928, Pewter Lid, ½ Liter 299.00
ottery, Babies, Relief, Marked, 1276, Pewter Lid, ½ Liter 98.00
ottery, Dog, Hand Painted, Pewter Lid, ½ Liter 265.00
ottery, Engraved Flowers, Pewter Lid, ½ In. 109.00
ottery, Etched, Marked HR, 414, Pewter Lid, Hauber & Reuther, ½ Liter 115.00
ottery, Hand Painted, Pewter Lid, Marked Royal Bonn, Delft, 2 ½ Liter 489.00
ottery, Hotel Savoy, Seattle, Relief, Marked 5339, ½ Liter 115.00
ottery, Monkeys, Inlaid Lid, ½ In. 357.00
ottery, Third Reich, Garnison Kindau Bodensee, Relief Helmet, Swastika, ½ Liter 518.00
ottery, Third Reich, Muchen, Preisschiessen, Relief Helmet, Swastika, 1937, ½ Liter 460.00
ottery, Third Reich, Weihnachts Feier, Pewter Lid, 1935, ½ Liter 719.00
ottery, Trumpeter, Relief, Marked 200, Pewter Lid, ½ Liter 92.00
ottery, Warriors, Relief, Marked 40, Pewter Lid, 1 Liter 161.00
egimental, Roster, 1 Comp., Bayr. Inft. Regt. Nr. 7, Bayreuth, 1909-11, ½ Liter 518.00
egimental, Roster, 1 Comp., 2 Bayr. Jager Batl., Aschaffenburg 1912-14, ½ Liter 828.00
egimental, Roster, 1 Comp., Jager Batl. Nr. 12, Freiberg, 1904-06, 2 Scenes, ½ Liter 1898.00
egimental, Roster, 8 Comp., Bayr. Inft. Regt. Nr. 21, Sulzbach, 1912-14, ½ Liter 633.00
egimental, Roster, 11 Comp., Bayr. Inft. Regt. Nr. 5, Bamberg, 4 Scenes, Hans Graf, 1904-06, ½ Liter 453.00
egimental, Roster, 11 Comp., Bayr. Inft. Regt. Nr. 142, Mulhausen, 1911-13, ½ Liter, ... 863.00
egimental, Roster, 12 Comp., Bayr. Inft. Regt. Nr. 20, Lindau, 1912-14, ½ Liter 748.00
egimental, Roster, Backer-Abteil. D. 8 Armee Corps, Ehrenbreitstein, 1911-13, 4 Scenes, 1 Liter 1495.00
egimental, Roster, Chevauleger Otto Kaltenberger, Finial, Porcelain, ½ Liter 460.00
egimental, Roster, Dragoner Seidel, 2 Scenes, Porcelain, 1905-08, ½ Liter 754.00
egimental, Roster, Fahrer Elsalzer, Porcelain, Enamel Copper Lid, 1893-95, ½ Liter 631.00
egimental, Roster, Gefr. Keller, 2 Scenes, Porcelain, 1902-05, ½ Liter 492.00
egimental, Roster, Gefreiter Werscher, 2 Scenes, Porcelain, 1902-04, ½ Liter 748.00
egimental, Roster, Geftr. Neubert, 2 Scenes, Porcelain, 1903-05, ½ Liter 644.00
egimental, Roster, Joh. Martin Emtmann, Porcelain, ½ Liter, 10 In. 328.00
egimental, Roster, Johannes Kemper, Porcelain, ½ Liter, 11 ½ In. 270.00
egimental, Roster, Karl Bollack, 2 Scenes, Porcelain, 1900-03, ½ Liter 604.00
egimental, Roster, Konrad Rollmann, Screw-Off Lid, ½ Liter 1122.00
egimental, Roster, L. Bayerisches Luftschiffer-Bataillon, ½ Liter, 10 In. .... *illus* 138.00
egimental, Roster, Martin Knaisch, 2 Scenes, Porcelain, 1900-02, ½ Liter 544.00
egimental, Roster, Masch. Gew. Komp., Jager Batl. Nr. 12, Freiberg, 1904-06, 2 Scenes, ½ Liter 3910.00
egimental, Roster, Masch. Gewehr Komp., Inft. Regt. 56, Wesel, 1907-09, 2 Scenes, ½ Liter . 891.00
egimental, Roster, Matthaus Vilsmeier, 4 Scenes, Porcelain, 1901-03, ½ Liter 285.00
egimental, Roster, Oberjager Heinrich Ebert, 2 Scenes, Porcelain, 1902-04, ½ Liter 483.00
egimental, Roster, Pionier Versuchs Kompagnie, Berlin, 1908-10, 2 Scenes, ½ Liter ... *illus* 1038.00
egimental, Roster, Porcelain, Feftr. Res. Narr, Porcelain, ½ Liter 374.00
egimental, Roster, Pottery, Reservist Echardt, ½ Liter 518.00
egimental, Roster, Remigi Reutemann, Porcelain, Relief Leaves, ½ Liter 276.00
egimental, Roster, Res. Malakowsky, 2 Scenes, Porcelain, 1900-03, ½ Liter 1148.00
egimental, Roster, Res. Seim, 4 Scenes, Porcelain, 1894-96, ½ Liter 362.00
egimental, Roster, Reserv. Zink, Porcelain, ½ Liter 138.00
egimental, Roster, Reservist Arbogast, Lithophane, Porcelain, ½ Liter 242.00
egimental, Roster, Reservist Ernenwein, 4 Scenes, Pottery, 1909-11, ½ Liter 1148.00
egimental, Roster, Reservist Fingens, 4 Scenes, Pottery, 1909-11, ½ Liter 1148.00
egimental, Roster, Reservist Hornist Herr, Porcelain, ½ Liter 546.00

Stein, Regimental, Roster,
L. Bayerisches Luftschiffer-Bataillon,
½ Liter, 10 In.
$138.00

Stein, Regimental, Roster,
Pionier Versuchs Kompagnie, Berlin,
1908-10, 2 Scenes, ½ Liter
$1038.00

Missing Lids

Many beer steins seem to be missing their metal lids. In 1916, Germany needed metal for the war effort and citizens had to sell items made of gold, silver, brass, bronze, copper, and pewter to the government. The pewter steins and lids were melted for the war effort.

S

Stein, Regimental, Roster, S.M.S. Thuringen, 1911-14, 2 Scenes, Pottery, 1 Liter
$1783.00

Stein, Stoneware, Blue Salt Glaze, Art Nouveau, Relief, Marked, 1655, ½ Liter
$460.00

Stereo Card, Empire State Building, NYC, Aerial View, Keystone View Company
$64.00

TIP
Don't store old paint rags. They may ignite spontaneously.

Regimental, Roster, Reservist Lohmana, Porcelain, ½ Liter 1553.0
Regimental, Roster, Reservist Plessmann, Pottery, 1 Liter 546.0
Regimental, Roster, Reservist Semmelhaack, Pottery, ½ Liter 265.0
Regimental, Roster, S.M.S. Danzig, 2 Scenes, Stoneware, ½ Liter 1148.0
Regimental, Roster, S.M.S. Oldenburg, Wilhelmshaven, 1913-19, 4 Scenes, Pottery, 1 Liter . . 1955.0
Regimental, Roster, S.M.S. Thuringen, 1911-14, 2 Scenes, Pottery, 1 Liter . . . . . *illus* 1783.0
Regimental, Roster, Schutze Haberstroh, 4 Scenes, Porcelain, 1909-11, ½ Liter 1328.0
Regimental, Roster, Unteroffz. Scherer, Porcelain, ½ Liter 288.0
Stoneware, 2 Men & Clock, Art Nouveau, Transfer, Enamel, Pewter Lid, ½ Liter 127.0
Stoneware, Apostles, Blue Salt Glaze, Relief, M.W.G., Creussen Style, Pewter Lid, 1 Liter 173.0
Stoneware, Arnet Family Crest 1935, Transfer, Enamel, Pewter Lid, ½ Liter 115.0
Stoneware, Art Nouveau, Relief Birds, Blue Salt Glaze, Pewter Lid, ½ Liter 115.0
Stoneware, Blue Salt Glaze, Art Nouveau, Relief, Marked, 1655, ½ Liter . . . . *illus* 460.0
Stoneware, Blue Salt Glaze, Gruss Aus Munchen, Relief, Marked 818, 1 Liter 230.0
Stoneware, Blue Salt Glaze, Relief, Pewter Lid, White's, Utica, ½ Liter 92.0
Stoneware, Deutsches Bundesschiessen Muchen 1927, Officieller Festkrug, Enamel, Pewter Lid, 1 Liter 359.0
Stoneware, Deutsches Turnfest, Munchen, Transfer, Enamel, Pewter Lid, 1923, 1 Liter 339.0
Stoneware, Deutsches Turnfest Munchen 1923, Transfer, Enamel, Vater Jahn, ½ Liter 329.0
Stoneware, Etched, Marked Girmscheid 938, Stoneware Lid, 1 Liter 138.0
Stoneware, Gerbertshausen 1940, Transfer, Enamel, Crossed Rifles & Targets, 1 Liter 370.0
Stoneware, Kranken-Unterstutzungsverein, Transfer, Enamel, Pewter Lid, 1 Liter 345.0
Stoneware, Muchen Kgl. Hofbrauhaus, Transfer, Enameled, Relief Pewter Lid, ½ Liter 150.0
Stoneware, Prince Of Pilsen, Relief, Pewter Lid, White's, Utica, New York, 1 Liter 190.0
Stoneware, Siegburg Style, Relief, Pewter Lid, Late 1800s, 2 Liter 253.0
Stoneware, Ski Heil 1932, Transfer, Enamel, Pewter Lid, 1 Liter 196.0
Stoneware, Thewalt, Alchemist, Relief, Marked 536, Pewter Lid, ½ Liter 127.0
Stoneware, Third Reich, Erganzungs Komp. Lufen, Relief Helmet, Swastika, ½ Liter 834.0
Stoneware, Third Reich, Komp., I.R. 42, Hof, Pewter Lid, Relief Helmet, Swastika, ½ Liter . . . 299.0
Stoneware, Third Reich, Kriegs Weihnachten, Relief Jager Cap, Pewter Lid, 1940, ½ Liter . . . 207.0
Stoneware, Third Reich, Zur Nationalen Erhebung Deutschland, Heil Hitler, 1933, ½ Liter . . 665.0
Stoneware, Transfer, Enamel, Schwabingerbrau, Relief Pewter Lid, ½ Liter 173.0
Stoneware, Westerwald, Engraved, Relief, Deer & Flowers, Pewter Lid, c.1800, ½ Liter, 8 In. . . 604.0
Stoneware, Westerwald, Incised, Applied Relief, Blue Salt Glaze, Pewter Lid, c.1750, ½ Liter. . 265.0
Wood, Burl, Carved Names, c.1900, 1 ½ Liter 288.0
Wood, Daubenkrug, Pewter, Inlaid Deer, Pewter Lid, c.1800, ¾ Liter, 6 ½ In. 489.0
Wood, Lid, Leaves, Relief, Norway, c.1850, 1 Liter 1449.0
Wood, Stag & Dog Pewter Inlay, Pewter Lid, Sweden, Late 1800s, 9 In., 1 Liter 575.0

STEREO CARDS that were made for stereoscope viewers became popular after 1840. Two almost identical pictures were mounted on a stiff cardboard backing so that, when viewed through a stereoscope, a three-dimensional picture could be seen. Value is determined by maker and by subject. These cards were made in quantity through the 1930s.

A Hurried Toilet, No. 83, Griffith & Griffith 8.0
Battle Of Gettysburg, July 31863, No. 802, William H. Rau, c.1887 . . . . 65.0
Bride In Bedroom, Women Putting Veil On Her Head 15.0
Cuban Farmer In Havana, Strohmeyer & Wyman, New York, c.1899, 7 x 3 ½ In. 20.0
Don't Dolly Look Like Me, Black Girl, Blond Doll, Keystone View, No. 9644, c.1899 . . . . 55.0
Empire State Building, NYC, Aerial View, Keystone View Company. . . . . *illus* 64.0
Fontana Medina, Naples, No. 577, Conrad 19.0
Franklin Street, Rumford, Maine, Lee Abbot View Company. 31.0
Girls Praying By Bed, No. 9450, Keystone View Company 18.0
Indian Men In Blankets By Water, Taos, New Mexico, Keystone View Company 24.0
Indian Squaw Making Pottery, Oraibi, Arizona 24.0
Iroquois Indians, Tercentenary Pageant, Quebec, Canada, c.1905. . . . . 65.0
Mother Sewing Britches With Boy In Them, Griffith & Griffith . . . . 7.
Muslim Pilgrims, Jerusalem, Mohammedan Tomb Of Moses, B.W. Kilburn, 7 x 3 ½ In. . . . . . 26.
Niagara-Dixon Crossing Niagara On Highwire, George Barker, c.1890, 7 x 3 ½ In. . . . . . 16.
Orange Blossoms, Los Angeles, California, Keystone, c.1897. . . . . 8.
Smoking Behind The Barn, No. 10572, Keystone View Company . . . . 7.
U.S. Cruiser Brooklyn, Hampton Roads, Virginia, No. 9071, Keystone Co.. . . . . 25.
Underwood, Battleship Texas, Battle Of Santiago, Strohmeyer & Wyman, c.1898 . . . . 8.
Underwood, Christmas Tree, Santa Claus, Strohmeyer & Wyman, c.1898 . . . . 26.
Western, Cowboys, Horses, Winchester Rifle, 1873 Colt Handguns, Keystone . . . . 11.
White Star Docks, New York, Mounted, 3 ½ x 7 Inches . . . . 44.

S

STEREOSCOPES were used for viewing stereo cards. The hand viewer was invented by Oliver Wendell Holmes, although more complicated table models were used before his was produced in 1859. Do not confuse the stereoscope with the stereopticon, a magic lantern that used glass slides.

Burl, Walnut, Vistascope, Griffith & Griffith, Viewing Card, c.1896, 12 In. 395.00
Express Newness Stereo, Murer & Duroni, Milan, Italy, Leather Covered Wood, c.1900 .... 337.00
Gibbons Traveling Stereo Card Viewer 150.00
H.C. White Company, Embossed Medallion, Silver Etching, c.1900 .... 125.00
Holmes-Pattern Tramp Art, Reeded Walnut Hood & Sides 353.00
Metal, Bakelite, No. 50, Keystone, 12¾ x 7 In., 9 Cards 655.00
Murray & Heath, London, Walnut Case, Metal Pillar, Gilded Cherub Base, c.1870, 16 In. 3204.00
Pattberg Type, Double Serpentine Arm, Rosewood Veneer, Patd. 1881, 13 In. 294.00
Rosenfield, Drop Card, Oak, c.1905, 68 x 17 In. .... *illus* 6407.00
S.W. Harts, 2 Positions, Wooden Case, Carved Recesses, Painted, 1871, 40 x 12 In. 7015.00
Stereo Reflex, No. 212134, Ernemann, Dresden, Germany, 1913 .... 490.00

STERLING SILVER, *see Silver-Sterling category.*

STEUBEN glass was made at the Steuben Glass Works of Corning, New York. The factory, founded by Frederick Carder and T.G. Hawkes, Sr., was purchased by the Corning Glass Company. Corning continued to make glass called Steuben. Many types of art glass were made at Steuben. The firm is still making exceptional quality glass but it is clear, modern-style glass. Additional pieces may be found in the Aurene, Cluthra, and Perfume Bottle categories.

Ashtray, Clear, 2¼ x 8 In. 47.00
Basket, Green, Handles, 4 x 8 In. 160.00
Bottle, Bath Salt, Rectangular, Optic Swirl, Gold Ruby, Signed, 5 In. 200.00
Bowl, Amethyst, Optic Ribbed, Rolled Rim, 3 Applied Clear Feet, 8½ In. 230.00
Bowl, Blue, Clear, Intarsia, Signed, c.1930, 2¾ x 5⅛ In. 14400.00
Bowl, Calcite, Blue Aurene Interior, Oval, Footed, 8½ In. 275.00
Bowl, Centerpiece, Amber, Swirling, Celeste Blue Foot, Mica Flecks, 11¾ x 5¼ In. 230.00
Bowl, Centerpiece, Calcite, Scalloped Rim, Blue Aurene Interior, 3 x 12 In. 403.00
Bowl, Centerpiece, Citron Yellow, Flared, Tapered Base, 4½ x 10 In. 100.00
Bowl, Centerpiece, Grotesque, Ivrene, Footed, 7 In. 230.00
Bowl, Centerpiece, Ivrene, Optic Ribbed, Elongated Shell Shape, 14 In. 460.00
Bowl, Cobalt Blue, Footed, 2 x 10¼ In. 345.00
Bowl, Green Jade, Alabaster, 2¾ x 6 In. 275.00
Bowl, Green Jade, Hexagonal, Ribbed, Alabaster Foot, 10 x 6 In. .... *illus* 600.00
Bowl, Green Jade, Iridescent, White Opalescent Striations, 6 In. 300.00
Bowl, Green Jade, Rolled Rim, 8½ In. 259.00
Bowl, Grotesque, Amethyst, Elongated, 12 In. 288.00
Bowl, Grotesque, Dark Blue Jade, 12 x 7½ In. .... *illus* 4500.00
Bowl, Grotesque, Green To Clear, 5 x 8 In. 633.00
Bowl, Grotesque, Wisteria, Shaded, 4-Sided, 5½ In. 920.00
Bowl, Millefiori, Multicolored, 6 x 3¼ In. 1220.00
Bowl, Plum Jade, Medallions, Flower Scrolls, Oval, Cupped Rim, 8½ In. 4500.00
Bowl, Silveria, Amethyst, Diamond Shape, Signed, 10 In. 1035.00
Candlestick, Amethyst, c.1925, 17⅛ In., Pair 7200.00
Candlestick, Blown, Opalescent, 2¼ x 4¾ In., Pair 322.00
Candlestick, Cintra, Green Jade, Pale Rose Cup, 8¼ In., Pair 5500.00
Candlestick, Diamond Optic, Swirled Pomona Green Foot, Green Tadpole Prunts, 12 In. 115.00
Candlestick, Ivory, Urn Shape, Flared Rolled Rim, 3¾ In., Pair 230.00
Candlestick, Pomona Green, Amber Cup, Flared Bobeche, Saucer Foot, 12 In., Pair 690.00
Candlestick, Selenium Red Cup, Clear Stems, Engraved Flowers, 7 In. 375.00
Candlestick, Spanish Green, Twisted Stem, Spread Foot, 4¾ x 12 In., Pair 575.00
Candlestick, Topaz, Baluster Stem, Pair, 10 In. 400.00
Candlestick, Topaz, Hollow Ribbed Stem, Pedestal Foot, 12 In. 230.00
Candy Dish, Cover, Pink, Pear Finial, Blue Rim & Stem, 4½ x 7½ In. 1200.00
Chandelier, 3-Light, Brown Aurene Shades, Gold Iridescent Border, 28 In. 3048.00
Cologne, Oriental Orchid, Rectangular, Amethyst Opalescent Stripes, Petal Stopper, 5½ In. 8625.00
Compote, Amethyst, Ribbed, Spool Stem, Rolled Rim, 3⅛ x 7½ In. .... *illus* 130.00
Compote, Aquamarine, Cover, Urn Shape, Pear Finial, 10 In. 920.00
Compote, Blue, Calcite, Blue Aurene Interior, Amethyst Highlights, 6 In. 350.00
Compote, Bristol Yellow, Black Edges, Spread Foot, 22⅛ x 3¾ In. 295.00
Compote, Calcite, Gold Aurene Interior, 6 In. 259.00
Compote, Cintra, Orange, Turquoise Cabochons, Turquoise Rim, 7 In. 2875.00

Stereoscope, Rosenfield, Drop Card, Oak, c.1905, 68 x 17 In. $6407.00

Steuben, Bowl, Green Jade, Hexagonal, Ribbed, Alabaster Foot, 10 x 6 In. $600.00

Steuben, Bowl, Grotesque, Dark Blue Jade, 12 x 7½ In. $4500.00

S

TIP

Stains on porcelains can be removed by soaking in a mixture of 2 tablespoons denture cleaner in 1 quart tepid water.

TIP
Cruet tops for American glass pieces are almost always cut or pressed, not blown.

Steuben, Compote, Amethyst, Ribbed, Spool Stem, Rolled Rim, 3⅛ x 7½ In.
$130.00

Steuben, Lamp, Acid Cutback, Corinta, Blue Aurene, Alabaster, 25 x 8 In.
$3000.00

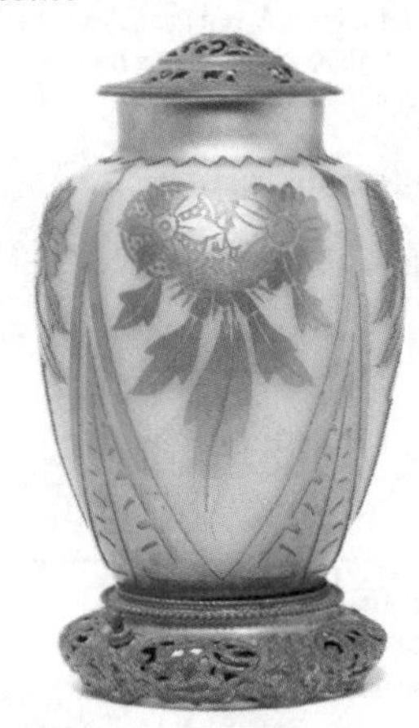

Steuben, Lamp, Acid Cutback, Grape, Black, Purple, Claw Feet, 32 x 8 In.
$2520.00

Compote, Cover, Marina Blue, Hollow Stem, Clear Finial, 9 x 8½ In. 575.00
Compote, Green Jade, Alabaster Foot, Signed, 6½ In. 575.00
Compote, Ivory Jade, Black Jade Foot, Signed, 3 In. 400.00
Compote, Rosaline, Twisted Alabaster Stem, 6½ In., Pair 748.00
Compote, Spanish Green, Signed, 10¾ In. 58.00
Console, Amber, Iridescent, 10 In. 590.00
Console Set, Cintra, Green, 13½-In. Bowl, 3-In. Candleholder, Signed, 3 Piece 235.00
Dish, Clear Engraved Flowers, 8½ In. 150.00
Dish, Green Jade, Alabaster, 2¾ x 6 In. 205.00
Dish, Olive, Clear, 5½ In. .... 115.00 to 146.00
Figurine, Apple Of Eden, Inset Bubbles, 18K Gold Leaves, Worm, John Huston, 3 x 5 In. 1840.00
Figurine, Fish, 10½ In. 50.00
Figurine, Koala Bear, Seated, 6 In. 288.00
Figurine, Pineapple, 7½ In. 409.00
Figurine, Polar Bear, Box, c.1950, 5 x 8 In. 525.00
Figurine, Seal, Balancing Ball, 7 x 6 In. 760.00
Figurine, Toadstool, 18K Gold Butterfly On Top, 3½ In. 725.00
Figurine, Unicorn's Head, Box, 7⅛ In. 1400.00
Figurine, Water Birds In Flight, Mounted On Clear Wave, 3 Piece, 10 x 10 In. 1725.00
Finger Bowl, Underplate, Citron Yellow, Ribs, 5 & 6½ In. 345.00
Finger Bowl, Yellow Jade, 6 In. 431.00
Flower Frog, Bonsai Tree Shape, Clear, 3 In. 59.00
Goblet, Cranberry Cut To Clear, Pheasant, Stemmed Leaves, 5 In. 115.00
Goblet, Engraved Rampant Lion, 3½ x 5¼ In., 6 Piece 230.00
Goblet, Green, Hollow Stem, 3¼ x 7¾ In., Pair 115.00
Goblet, Oriental Jade Green & Opalescent Bowl, Clear Twisted Stem & Foot, 5⅞ In. 382.00
Goblet, Oriental Poppy, Pink, Opalescent Bowl, Green Stem, Foot, 6 In. 805.00
Goblet, Oriental Poppy, Pink, Twisted Green Opalescent Stem, 8 In., Pair 750.00
Goblet, Rosaline Alabaster, Twisted Stem, 6¼ In. 145.00
Jar, Cover, Oriental Orchid, Amethyst, Opalescent Stripes, Oval, 2¾ In. 5000.00
Jar, Cover, Wisteria, Egg Shape Melon Ribbed, Teardrop Finial, 4 In. 690.00
Jar, Marmalade, Topaz, Red & Green Pear Finial, Disk Base, 6½ In. 690.00
Lamp, Acid Cutback, Corinta, Blue Aurene, Alabaster, 25 x 8 In. .... *illus* 3000.00
Lamp, Acid Cutback, Grape, Black, Purple, Claw Feet, 32 x 8 In. .... *illus* 2520.00
Lamp, Acid Cutback, Tropic, Black, Alabaster, 29 x 9 In. .... *illus* 2840.00
Lamp, Blue, Urn Shape, Opal Shade, Black Marble Base, 16 In. 850.00
Lamp, Brown Aurene Shade, White Intarsia Border, Bronze Handel Base, 55 In. 4313.00
Lamp, Ceiling, Domed, Calcite, Etched Band, Swags, Ribbon, Center Star, 10 In. 345.00
Lamp, Luminor, Internal Bubbles, Black Light Box Base, Teardrop, 10 In. 748.00
Lamp, Opal, Pulled Green & Gold Aurene, Notched Foot, 13½ x 9 In. 3105.00
Lamp, Pilgrim Flask Shape, Green, Gold Aurene Ginkgo, Swan Base, 28 In. 2070.00
Lamp Base, Acid Cutback, Yellow Cintra, Scrolling Berries, Cylindrical, 30 In. 2415.00
Lamp Base, Black Amethyst, Bulbous, Brass Scrolled Foot, 11 In. 588.00
Lamp Base, Quartz Alabaster Urn Shape, Branches & Leaves, Metal Mountings, 24 In. 2645.00
Nappy, Amber, Pomona Green, Shell Shape, Leaf Handle, Signed, 6¼ In. 403.00
Paperweight, Pear, Signed, 3½ x 2½ In. 82.00
Perfume Bottle, Aqua Marine, Melon Ribbed, Flame Stopper, 4½ In. 330.00
Perfume Bottle, Blue Jade, Alabaster Foot, Teardrop Stopper, 8 In. 900.00
Perfume Bottle, Bristol Yellow, Black Threading, Stopper, 5¼ In. 180.00
Perfume Bottle, Clear, Black Reeding, Ball Shape, Black Button Stopper, 3½ In., Pair 558.00
Perfume Bottle, Flemish Blue, Footed, Optic Ribbed, Teardrop Stopper, 10 In. 950.00
Perfume Bottle, Green Jade, Melon Ribbed, Alabaster Teardrop Stopper, 5 In. 633.00
Perfume Bottle, Green Threading, Stopper, 10 In. 360.00
Perfume Bottle, Oriental Orchid, Amethyst, Opalescent Stripes, Stopper, 5 In. 6565.00
Perfume Bottle, Rosaline, Alabaster Foot, 11 In. 540.00
Perfume Bottle, Rose DuBarry, Faceted, Stopper, 4½ In. 960.00
Perfume Bottle, Wisteria, Blue, Dabber, 4½ In. 1020.00
Plaque, Amber, Kneeling Woman, Grape Arboretum Border, Signed, 9 In. 1725.00
Plate, Amethyst, 8½ In., 10 Piece 403.00
Plate, Blue, 8½ In. 518.00
Plate, Rouge Flambe, Opaque Red, Orange, 8½ In. 4000.00
Platter, Clear, Mollusks, Sea Life, Red Leather-Lined Case, Signed, 10 In. 345.00
Sculpture, Moby Dick, Signed, Sidney Waugh, Box, 8 x 11½ In. .... *illus* 15600.00
Shade, Blue, Calcite, Gold Aurene, Pulled Feather, Ivrene, 5¼ x 5 In., 4 Piece 3623.00
Shade, Calcite, Applied Ribs, Pulled Gold Aurene, 6 In., Pair 604.00

S

Shade, Calcite, Etched, 3 Women In Gossamer Gowns, 4 ½ In., Pair 374.00
Shade, Frosted, Intaglio Flowers, Leaves, Stems, 4 ¾ x 2 ¼ In. 173.00
Shade, Green, Melon Ribbed, Opal Interior, 3 ¾ x 2 ¼ In. 805.00
Shade, Opal, Gold Aurene Swag, Squat Bell Shape, Signed, 4 ½ In. 288.00
Shade, Opal, Green Feathers Tipped In Gold Aurene, Squat, Ruffled Rim, 5 ½ In. 403.00
Sherbet, Oriental Poppy, Pink, Opalescent Stem & Foot, 6 ¼ In. 288.00
Sherbet, Ruby Cut To Clear, Cordova Pattern, 3 In. 345.00
Sherbet, Underplate, Amethyst Cut To Clear, Wheat, Signed, 8 ½ In. 200.00
Sherbet, Underplate, Blue Jade, Alabaster Stem, 4 ¼ In. 633.00
Sherbet, Underplate, Yellow Jade, 3 ¾-In. Sherbet 529.00
Shrimp Icer, Alabaster Twisted Stem, Insert, 6 ½ In., 4 Piece 600.00
Sugar, Aquamarine, Celeste Blue Handles, Footed, 2 ⅞ In. 212.00
Toothpick, Rosa, Cut Circles, Swags, Signed, 2 ½ In. 489.00
Tumbler, Selenium Red, Etched Grape Vine Band, Signed, 5 ¼ In., Pair 748.00
Urn, Ivrene, Ovoid, M-Shaped Handles, Footed, 10 ⅝ In. 940.00
Urn, Rose Quartz, Applied Vines, Leaves, Frosted Handles, Signed, 11 In. 3600.00
Vase, Acid Cutback, Bat Pattern, Double Gourd Shape, Alabaster, 9 ½ In. 2750.00
Vase, Acid Cutback, Belgrade Pattern, Green Jade, Mirror Black, Oval, Flared Rim, 9 ½ In. 7638.00
Vase, Acid Cutback, Bird Pattern, Green Jade, Alabaster, Footed Urn Shape, 9 In. 1668.00
Vase, Acid Cutback, Carved Pattern, Green Alabaster, 7 In. 1437.00
Vase, Acid Cutback, Chambored Pattern, Gold Ruby, Green Cintra, 12 In. 12075.00
Vase, Acid Cutback, Dragon Pattern, Green Jade, Alabaster, 10 In. 4830.00
Vase, Acid Cutback, Florida Pattern, Mirror Black, Alabaster, 14 ½ In. 7680.00
Vase, Acid Cutback, Flowers, Black, Green Jade, 7 x 7 In. 420.00
Vase, Acid Cutback, Japanese Pattern, Green, Alabaster, Oval, Rolled Inverted Rim, 7 ¼ In. 690.00
Vase, Acid Cutback, Rostrand Pattern, Rose Quartz, 16 In. 5175.00
Vase, Acid Cutback, Stylized Mums, Jade Green, Shouldered, 12 ½ In. 633.00
Vase, Acid Cutback, Teasel Pattern, Black, Green Jade, 6 ⅛ In. *illus* 1000.00
Vase, Acid Cutback, Valeria Pattern, Green Jade, Alabaster, 10 In. 1500.00
Vase, Alabaster, Mirror Black Handles, Lip Wrap, Signed, 8 ¼ In., Pair 2875.00
Vase, Alabaster, Mirror Black Lip Wrap, Flared Rim, 6 In. 633.00
Vase, Amber, Lion's Mask Cabochons, Rectangular, 9 ½ In. 374.00
Vase, Amethyst, Egg Shape, Pulled Applied Tadpole, Signed, 15 In. 575.00
Vase, Amethyst, Optic Ribbed, Footed, Ring Handles, 12 In. 805.00
Vase, Amethyst, Twisted, Ruffled Edge, 8 x 6 ½ In. 120.00
Vase, Black, Flared, Ruffled Edge, Footed, 6 ¼ x 8 ½ In. 820.00
Vase, Blue Cut To Clear, Punties & Panels, Flared, 7 x 8 In. 3240.00
Vase, Bristol Yellow, Black Threading, Diamond Optic, 8 ½ In. 250.00 to 460.00
Vase, Bud, Rosaline, Baluster, Alabaster Foot, Signed, 6 In. 345.00
Vase, Cintra, Purple, Bulbous, 9 x 10 ½ In. 1800.00
Vase, Cintra, White To Lime Green, Oval Clear Foot, Star Burst Top, 10 ½ In. 805.00
Vase, Clear, Diamond Quilted, Ruby Reeding On Top, Flared, 8 x 7 In. 235.00
Vase, Clear, Donald Pollard, Original Box, Cloth Bag, 10 ¾ In. 748.00
Vase, Clear, Optic Diamond, Blue Reeding Band At Top, Flared, 6 ¾ In. 382.00
Vase, Clear, Ribbed, 3 Celeste Blue Rings, Applied Blue Dots, Bulbous, 7 x 8 In. 290.00
Vase, Clear Crackle, 2 Applied Green Lion's Head Medallions, Rectangular, 5 ½ x 9 In. 290.00
Vase, Cobalt Blue, Bulbous, Footed, 7 x 5 ½ In. 190.00
Vase, Cornucopia, Amber, Ruffled Edge, Celeste Blue Cupped Base, 8 In. 411.00
Vase, Cornucopia, Ivrene, Footed, Scalloped Rim, Shape No. 6119, 6 In. 345.00
Vase, Cover, Topaz, Ribbed, Green Foot & Finial, 9 ½ x 4 In. 315.00
Vase, Fan, Pale Pink, Celadon Foot, 10 ¾ In. 510.00
Vase, Florentia, Frosted, Silver Mica, Striated Green Leaves, 7 In. 6900.00
Vase, Flower Shape, Ivrene, Ribbed, Flared, Ruffled Edge, 6 ¾ In. 411.00
Vase, Gold, Calcite, Pinched Waist, Ruffled Edge, 9 In. 275.00
Vase, Green Jade, Alabaster Handles, 12 x 7 ½ In. 1725.00
Vase, Green Jade, Opalescent Stripes, Baluster, 6 In. 2250.00
Vase, Green Jade, Ribbed, Flared Rim, 4 ⅞ In. 345.00
Vase, Green Jade, Urn Shape, Optic Rubbed, Signed, 5 In. 403.00
Vase, Grostesque, Ivory, Scalloped Rim, Signed, 6 In. 173.00
Vase, Iridescent Amber, Silvery Blue Top, Double Gourd, Wide Mouth, 15 ¼ In. 1416.00
Vase, Ivory, Ribbed, Footed, 9 In. 173.00
Vase, Light Blue Jade, Mat-Su-No-Ke Leaves & Vines, Bulbous, Ribbed, 5 x 8 ½ In. 840.00
Vase, Millefiori, Flowers, Branches, Brown, Pink, Blue Aurene, c.1910, 5 In. 5400.00
Vase, Oriental Poppy, Pink Opalescent Stripes, Oval, 7 In. 3565.00

TIP

Forged glass signatures, including Steuben, Quezal, and Tiffany, are appearing on newer glass. This has been true for years. Do not trust a signature. Be sure the glass is the proper shape and type to have been produced by the original factory. Some fake marks are written with a diamond-tipped drill; some are acid-stamped. All look real.

Steuben, Lamp, Acid Cutback, Tropic, Black, Alabaster, 29 x 9 In.
$2840.00

Steuben, Sculpture, Moby Dick, Signed, Sidney Waugh, Box, 8 x 11 ½ In.
$15600.00

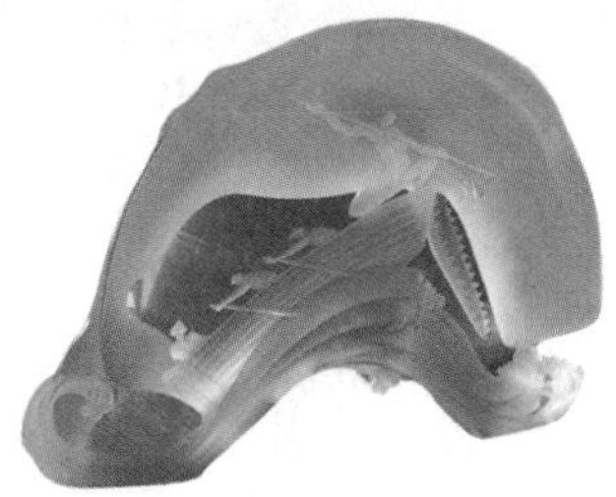

TIP
Never stack cups or bowls inside each other.

Steuben, Vase, Acid Cutback, Teasel Pattern, Black, Green Jade, 6 ⅛ In.
$1000.00

Stevens & William, Vase, Pompeian Swirl, Cranberry Shaded To Purple, c.1890, 8 In.
$850.00

TIP
If you hear crickets in the house, spray with insect killer. Crickets eat wool, as well as old rugs, silks, and paper.

Vase, Oriental Poppy, Pink Opalescent Stripes, Oval, Shouldered, Rolled Rim, 6 x 5 In. 2645.00
Vase, Rosaline, Applied Alabaster Handles, Foot, Flared Rim, 10 x 5 ¾ In. 660.00
Vase, Rose Quartz, Handles, 12 In. 4600.00
Vase, Selenium Red, Urn Shape, Footed, Optic Ribbed, 8 In. 403.00
Vase, Tree Trunk, 3-Prong, Bristol Yellow, Disc Foot, 6 ½ In. 748.00
Vase, Tree Trunk, 3-Prong, Clear, Scalloped Base, Signed, 6 In. 633.00
Vase, Tree Trunk, 3-Prong, Clear, Signed, 6 In. 175.00
Vase, Tree Trunk, 3-Prong, Ivory, Disc Foot, 6 ½ In. 575.00
Vase, Trumpet, Calcite, Blue Aurene Interior, 7 In. 767.00
Vase, Trumpet, Clear, Green Threading, Engraved Flowers, 12 ½ In. 250.00
Vase, Trumpet, Clear To Green, Footed, 10 In. 288.00
Vase, Trumpet, Green Florentina, Footed, 13 In. 10950.00
Vase, Trumpet, Red Flambe, Optic Ribbed, Wide Rim, 5 ½ In. 805.00
Vase, White Aurene Flowers, Urn Shape, Signed, 7 ⅜ In. 15600.00
Vase, Yellow Jade, Ginger Jar Shape, Carved Wooden Cover, 10 In. 5175.00
Wine, Cut Leaf, 5¼ In., 6 Piece .... 374.00 to 410.00
Wine, Green Jade, Twisted Stem, Alabaster Footed, 5 ½ In. 518.00
Wine, Oriental Jade, Green & Opalescent Twisted Stem, 7 In., Pair 575.00
Wine, Oriental Poppy, Pink Opalescent Bowl, Green Stem, Foot, 6 ¼ In. 575.00

STEVENGRAPHS are woven pictures made like fancy ribbons. They were manufactured by Thomas Stevens of Coventry, England, and became popular in 1862. Most are marked *Woven in silk by Thomas Stevens* or were mounted on a cardboard that tells the story of the Stevengraph. Other similar ribbon pictures have been made in England and Germany.

Bookmark, Centennial, 1776-1876, American Symbols, Silk, 7 ¾ In. 61.00
Bookmark, Flowers, Monogram T, Silk, Marked, 10 In. 66.00
Bookmark, My Brother, Silk, Marked, 7 x 1 ½ In. 13.00
Bookmark, Nevada's Admission To Union, 36-Star Flag, Silk, c.1864, 1 ½ x 2 In. 18.00
Bookmark, Star Spangled Banner, Silk, Warner Mfg., 10 ½ x 2 ½ In. 60.00
Picture, Called To The Rescue, Heroism At Sea, Lifeboat, Rowers, Silk, Frame, 5 x 8 In. 490.00
Picture, Lady Godiva Procession, Silk, 6 x 2 In. 130.00
Picture, LaFayette Nous Voici, Gun Boat, Eagle & Shield, Frame, 7 ½ x 6 In. 145.00
Picture, The Death, Fox Hunting, Silk, 6 x 2 In. 208.00

STEVENS & WILLIAMS of Stourbridge, England, made many types of glass, including layered, etched, cameo, and art glass, between the 1830s and 1930s. Some pieces are signed *S & W*. Many pieces are decorated with flowers, leaves, and other designs based on nature.

Basket, Pink, Twisted Amber Handle, Gold Aventine, Egg Shape, Ruffled Rim, 7 In. 86.00
Bowl, Amber, Pulled Zipper Design, 6 In. 60.00
Bowl, Satin, Yellow, Pink, White, Ruffled Edge, Northwood, 9 In. 530.00
Goblet, Rosaline Bowl, Alabaster Stem & Foot, 6 ⅜ In., Pair 212.00
Plate, Engraved Vintage, Blue To Orange To Clear, 7 ¾ In. 800.00
Syllabub, Yellow, Pink & White Swirls, Melon Ribbed, Cover, Frosted Thorn Finial, 14 In. 430.00
Vase, Amethyst To Clear, Grape Clusters, Leaves, Cut Rim, Footed, 6 In. 690.00
Vase, Blossoming Canterbury Bells, Butterflies, Apricot & White, 12 ¼ In. 6903.00
Vase, Bud, Yellow Jade, Alabaster Foot, 8 In. 115.00
Vase, Champagne & White, Scroll & Blossoms, Urn Shape, Cameo, 1885, 3 ¼ In. 5868.00
Vase, Citron, Flowers, Half Moon Border, Cameo, 5 ½ In. 2415.00
Vase, Flower & Acorns, Blue Satin, Pinched Rim, 4 ½ In. 345.00
Vase, Green, Acorns, Oak Leaves, Gold & Silver, Textured, 4 ¼ x 5 ½ In. 1657.00
Vase, Osiris, Pull-Up, Yellow, Crimson Ribbons, Teal Inside, Oval, Northwood, 6 In. 2415.00
Vase, Pompeian Swirl, Bottle Shape, Blue Shaded To Cranberry, White Interior, c.1880, 8 In. 1800.00
Vase, Pompeian Swirl, Cranberry Shaded To Purple, c.1890, 8 In. .... *illus* 850.00
Vase, Pompeian Swirl, Zipper, Brown, Pink Interior, Tricornered, 7 In. 920.00
Vase, Prussian Blue, Flowering Branch, Gourd Shape, 12 In. 8050.00
Vase, Red Flowers & Leaves, Ivory Ground, Oval, Flared Rim, Cameo, Marked, 8 ⅛ In. 2900.00
Vase, Shaded Rose Flowers, Leaves, Stems, Rings, Frosted, Cameo, 9 In. 4000.00
Vase, Silveria, Melon Ribbed, Green Threading, Ruffled Edge, 4 ¾ x 5 ¼ In. 1438.00
Vase, Stick, Pompeian Swirl, Bulbous Base, Cranberry Shading, c.1890, 8 In. .... 590.00 to 1003.00
Vase, Stick, Pompeian Swirl, Chartreuse To Blue, White Interior, Satin, Bulbous Base, 9 In. 1450.00
Vase, Topaz, Jeweled, Pulled Zipper, Oval, Ruffled Edge, 7 In. 748.00
Vase, Trumpet Blossoms, Autumn Colors, Baluster, Etched Ground, 11 ½ In. .... *illus* 3176.00
Vase, White Over Red, Wild Flowers, Grass, Egg Shape, Cameo, 7 ½ In. 5523.00
Vase, Yellow & White, Apple Blossoms, Buds, Double Gourd, 12 In. 4004.00

STIEGEL TYPE glass is listed here. It is almost impossible to be sure a piece was actually made by Stiegel, so the knowing collector refers to this glass as "Stiegel type." Henry William Stiegel, a colorful immigrant to the colonies, started his first factory in Pennsylvania in 1763. He remained in business until 1774. Glassware was made in a style popular in Europe at that time and was similar to the glass of many other makers. It was made of clear or colored glass and was decorated with enamel colors, mold blown designs, or etching.

Cologne, Enameled, Urn & Flower, Flowers, Leaves, Pewter Cap, Collar, 6 In. 495.00
Creamer, Diamond, Cobalt Blue, Bulbous, Broken Pontil With Comet Tail, 3 ¼ In. 440.00
Creamer, Paneled Ribs, Cobalt Blue, Applied Loop Handle, Pontil, 5 In. 413.00
Salt, Blue, Footed, Flint, Pontil, 3 ¼ In. . . . . *illus* 100.00
Salt, Diamond, Cobalt Blue, Footed, Broken Pontil With Comet Tail, 3 In. 413.00
Salt, Diamond, Footed, Petal Form Base, Broken Pontil, 3 In. 303.00
Tumbler, Enameled, Bird, Flowers, Leaves, Broken Pontil, 3 ⅛ In. 550.00
Tumbler, Engraved, 2 Birds, Sunburst, Flint, Pontil, 3 ¾ In. . . . . *illus* 300.00

STONE includes those articles made of stones, coral, shells, and some other natural materials not listed elsewhere in this book. Micro mosaics (small decorative designs made by setting pieces of stone into a pattern), urns, vases, and other pieces made of natural stone are listed here. Stoneware is pottery and is listed in the Stoneware category. Alabaster, Jade, Malachite, Marble, and Soapstone are in their own categories.

Amethyst, Geode, Brazilian, 12 ½ x 12 In. 234.00
Basin, Polished Rim & Exterior, Chisel Marks, 1900s, Chinese, 18 ½ x 27 ½ In. 489.00
Beaker, Derbyshire Spar, Vase Shape, Flared Rim, Gilt Bronze Base, 4-Footed, 7 In. 3120.00
Bench, Scroll Shape, Carved Sides, Dragon, Flaming Pearl, Gray, Chinese, 12 x 25 In., Pair . . 1062.00
Finial, Pelican In Her Piety, Limestone, White, Mid 1800s, 11 ½ In. 5040.00
Garden Bouquet, Urn Base, 39 x 24 In., Pair 2400.00
Head, Black Man, Carved, Black & Paint Traces, Tool Marks, 15 In. 805.00
Plaque, Slate, Relief Carved, Couple Dressed As Indians, Willows, 19th Century, 10 x 7 In. . . . 3300.00
Sculpture, Apple Blossoms, Rose Quartz, Japan, 13 ½ x 10 ½ In. 105.00
Sculpture, Aztec Head, Plaited Hair, Plugs In Ears, Meso-American, 5 ½ x 5 x 5 ½ In. 550.00
Sculpture, Cat, Lying Down, Central America, 5 ½ x 7 ½ In. 345.00
Sculpture, Eagle, Cast, Rockwork Base, 20th Century, 33 x 10 ½ In., Pair. 245.00
Sculpture, Holding Staff, Black, 10 ¾ In. 708.00
Sculpture, Horse, Recumbent, Rose Quartz, Rosewood Stand, Cloud Design, Chinese, 5 In. . . 150.00
Sculpture, Hotei, Lapis, Chinese, Mid 20th Century, 1 ½ x 1 ¾ In. 118.00
Sculpture, Hotei, Seated, Rose Quartz, Carved, 3 x 4 ½ x 4 In. . . . . *illus* 180.00
Sculpture, Lion, Seated, Male & Female, Wax Export Seals, Drum Base, 13 In., Pair. 518.00
Sculpture, Mermaid, Merbaby On Tail, Sandstone, Popeye Reed, 16 In. 3565.00
Sculpture, Mythological, Lapis, Carved, Chinese, Mid 20th Century, 2 x 4 In. 118.00
Sculpture, Owl, Tool Marks, 22 ½ In. 1955.00
Sculpture, Pharaoh Head, Oval Crown, Cobra Uraeus, Egyptian, 4 ¾ In. 2360.00
Sculpture, Rabbit, Charles Francois Quest, Inscribed, 5 ¾ x 8 x 4 In. 690.00
Sculpture, Spinach Jade, Carved, Double Leaf, Chinese, 6 ⅞ In. 590.00
Sculpture, Woman, Bowl Of Fruit, Lapis, Carved, 2 In. 118.00
Sculpture, Woman, Lapis, Carved, Chinese, Mid 20th Century, 3 In. 118.00
Sculpture, Woman, Seated, Lapis, Carved, Mid 20th Century, 2 ½ x 3 In. 118.00
Statue, American Indian Chief, Jackson County Sandstone, Popeye Reed, 50 In. 6900.00
Statue, Indian, Holding Ax, Carved, Popeye Reed, 51 In. 15400.00
Statue, Woman's Bust, Tapered Column Base, Limestone, Late 1800s, 55 x 12 In. 1955.00
Teapot, Spinach Jade, Silver Mounted, 5 ¼ In. 266.00
Urn, Gray, Globular, Carved, Flowers, Mythical Beasts, Cartouche, Chinese, 16 x 20 In., Pair . 920.00

STONEWARE is a coarse, glazed, and fired potter's ceramic that is used to make crocks, jugs, bowls, etc. It is often decorated with cobalt blue decorations. In the nineteenth and early twentieth centuries, potters often decorated crocks with blue numbers indicating the size of the container. A *2* meant 2 gallons. Stoneware is still being made. American stoneware is listed here.

Basket, Tea, Celadon Glaze, Ken Ferguson, 11 ½ x 10 In. 1440.00
Batter Bowl, Blue, Gal., 5 x 11 In. 167.00
Batter Jar, Tulip, Cobalt Blue, Spout, Wire Bail Handle, F.H. Cowden, 8 ½ In. . . . . *illus* 990.00
Batter Pail, Slip Blue Running Bird, Bail Handle, White's, Utica, c.1865, 4 Qt., 8 ½ In. 440.00
Batter Pail, Tin Lid, Spitting Flower, Blue Accent, Evan R. Jones, c.1870, 1 ½ Gal., 10 In. 688.00
Batter Pail, Yellow Flowers, Albany Glaze, Earthenware, Gallery Rim, Handles, 4 x 3 In. 44.00
Bedpan, Brushed Design, Cobalt Blue, Handle, 3 ½ x 13 In. 715.00
Bottle, B. Whitcombe Sarsaparilla Beer, Salt Glaze, c.1855, 10 In. . . . . *illus* 250.00

Stevens & William, Vase, Trumpet Blossoms, Autumn Colors, Baluster, Etched Ground, 11 ½ In.
$3176.00

Stiegel Type, Salt, Blue, Footed, Flint, Pontil, 3 ¼ In.
$100.00

Stiegel Type, Tumbler, Engraved, 2 Birds, Sunburst, Flint, Pontil, 3 ¾ In.
$300.00

Stone, Sculpture, Hotei, Seated, Rose Quartz, Carved, 3 x 4 ½ x 4 In.
$180.00

Stoneware, Batter Jar, Tulip, Cobalt Blue, Spout, Wire Bail Handle, F.H. Cowden, 8 ½ In.
$990.00

Stoneware, Bottle, B. Whitcombe Sarsaparilla Beer, Salt Glaze, c.1855, 10 In.
$250.00

Stoneware, Crock, Bird, Stylized, On Branch, Blue, Applied Ear Handles, White's Utica, 9 ¼ In.
$413.00

Bottle, Beer, John N. Cushing, Gray, Cobalt Blue Slip Cone & Mouth, 10 In. 504.00

Bottle, Durfee's Knickerbocker Root Beer, Gray, Cobalt Blue Accent, 12-Sided, 10 In. 157.00

Bottle, Impressed, L. Beard & Co. Root Beer, Brown, Albany Glazed Shoulder, 10 ½ In. 168.00

Bottle, Impressed, Robinson's Superior Root Beer, Gray, Cobalt Blue Letters, 9 ¼ In. 112.00

Bottle, Impressed, Smith & Snow's, White Root Beer, Tan, Blue, Pat'd July 17, 1863, 10 In. 235.00

Bottle, Impressed, Vincent & Hathaway White Root Beer, Cream, Salt Glaze, 9 ⅞ In. 56.00

Bottle, Impressed, Watts Root Beer, Gray, Cobalt Blue Slip Mouth, Salt Glaze, 9 ⅜ In. 157.00

Bottle, J. Lewis & Co., Root Beer, Salt Glaze, Cream, Cobalt Blue Accents, 10 ¼ In. 78.00

Bottle, Punch'ong, Pear Shape, Incised Fish Decoration, Korea, 7 ½ In. 590.00

Bowl, Anagama Fired, Indigo, Gray, Rust Volcanic Glaze, c.1996, 3 x 10 ½ In. 3120.00

Bowl, Brown Mottled Glaze, Ikebana, 10 x 15 In. 35.00

Bowl, Wreaths, Stylized Leaves, Brown, Indigo, Label, Harrison McIntosh, 3 ¼ x 6 In. 1140.00

Box, Tobacco, Cover, Cottage, c.1830, 4 ½ x 4 x 6 In. 529.00

Canister, 3 Flowers, Leaves, Cobalt Blue, 9 In. 275.00

Canister Set, Blue & White Salt Glaze, Basket Weave, 2 Lids, Sugar, Coffee, Tea, 5 ¾ In. 220.00

Charger, Partially Glazed, Etched, Abstract Design, Robert Turner, 4 x 16 In. 7200.00

Churn, Bird, Branch, Cobalt Blue, Bulbous, Ear Handles, S. Hart, Fulton, 5 Gal., 16 ¾ In. 1760.00

Churn, Blue Slip Decoration, C.J. Merrill, Ear Handles, 3 Gal., 16 In. 144.00

Churn, Brown Glaze, Blue Decoration, Dog Ear Handles, 4 Gal., 15 x 9 In. 175.00

Churn, Double Flower, John Burger, Rochester, c.1865, 5 Gal., 18 In. 2530.00

Churn, Leaves, Handles, Salt Glaze, Wooden Dasher, Handle, 5 Gal., 17 x 9 In. 302.00

Churn, Medium Olive Alkaline Glaze, Lanier Meaders, 14 ¼ In. 489.00

Cream Pot, Flower, Buds, Leaves, Blue Mark, Lehman & Co., N.Y., c.1870, 2 Gal., 10 In. 523.00

Crock, 2 Drooping Flowers, Cobalt Blue, Cylindrical, Applied Ear Handles, 12 ¼ In. 165.00

Crock, 3 Birds On Branches, Cobalt Blue, Lug Handles, West Troy, N.Y. Pottery, 5 Gal. 1410.00

Crock, 5-Petal Flower, Blue, Ear Handles, Burger & Lang, Rochester, N.Y., 4 Gal., 11 ½ In., . . . 88.00

Crock, 5-Petal Flower, Leaves, Drooping Flowers, Cobalt Blue, 2-Sided, 8 ½ In. 220.00

Crock, Antler Design, Stylized, M. Woordruff, Cortland, c.1870, 3 Gal., 11 In. 77.00

Crock, Bell Flower, Drooping, Blue, Bulbous, Ear Handles, Cowden & Wilcox, 2 Gal., 10 ½ In. 220.00

Crock, Bennace & Sutherland, Applied Handles, Cobalt Blue Decoration, Oval, 12 In. 259.00

Crock, Bird, Cobalt Blue, 2 Handles, 13 ¼ x 9 ¼ In. 625.00

Crock, Bird, Cobalt Blue, Salt Glaze, Nathan Clark & Co., c.1848, 3 Gal., 12 ½ In. 6600.00

Crock, Bird, Cobalt Blue, Underwood, 1 ½ Gal. 375.00

Crock, Bird, Hunter, Flat Rim, Salt Glaze, 19th Century, Gal., 9 ½ x 5 ¾ In. 825.00

Crock, Bird, Marked, S. Skinner & Co., Picton CW, For Canada West, c.1860, 6 Gal. 3850.00

Crock, Bird, On Stylized Branch, Brown Glaze, Geo. W. Miller, Strasburg, Va., Gal., 8 ¼ In. . . . 99.00

Crock, Bird, Stylized, On Branch, Blue, Applied Ear Handles, White's Utica, 9 ¼ In. . . . . *illus* 413.00

Crock, Bird On Branch, Cobalt Blue, Ottman Bro's, Fort Edward, N.Y., c.1885, 4 Gal. 529.00

Crock, Bird On Branch, Cobalt Blue, Stamped, 4 Gal., 11 x 12 In. 978.00

Crock, Bird On Plume, Haxstun & Co., Fort Edward, c.1870, 4 Gal., 11 In. 358.00

Crock, Bird On Stump, Cobalt Blue, Ear Handles, Cowden & Wilcox, 6 Gal., 12 ½ x 13 ¼ In. . . 3575.00

Crock, Blue Design, Signed, S.H. Sonner Strasburg, Va., Gal. 250.00

Crock, Blue Double Flower, N.A. White & Son, Utica, c.1870, 3 Gal., 10 In. 110.00

Crock, Blue Flowers, Salt Glaze Finish, Late 19th Century, 5 Gal., 16 In. 1180.00

Crock, Brushed Cobalt Blue Leaf Design, 3, J. Swank & Co., Penn., 11 ½ x 12 In. 316.00

Crock, Brushed Cobalt Blue Leaves, Handles, Swank & Co., Johnstown, 4 x 12 x 13 In. 863.00

Crock, Brushed Cobalt Blue Tulip, Leaf Band, Impressed 2, Late 19th Century, 12 In. 230.00

Crock, Brushed Flower, Peacock Tail Leaves, Blue, Roberts, Birmingham, 11 x 11 In. 460.00

Crock, Brushed Vining Flower, Blue, Applied Handles, Ballard & Bros., 9 ½ x 12 In. 316.00

Crock, Buckeye Pottery, 6 Gal. 90.00

Crock, Butter, 3 Brushed Blue Stripes, Snake In Lake, Western Penn., c.1850, Qt., 5 In. 303.00

Crock, Butter, Cobalt Hearts, Salt Glaze, Tulips, Lid, 4 ½ x 7 In. 805.00

Crock, Butter, Cover, Tulips, Blue, Salt Glaze, Incised Bands, Late 1800s, 4 ½ x 7 In. . . . . *illus* 690.00

Crock, Butter, Flowers & Leaves, Banded, Cobalt Blue, Wreath, Applied Handles, 6 x 11 In. . . . 330.00

Crock, Butter, Macomb, 6 Gal. 120.00

Crock, C.I. Grabill Grocer, Tea & Coffee Dealer, Blue & White Bands, 6 ½ In. 303.00

Crock, Cake, Clovers, Handles, 19th Century, 4 ¾ x 9 ¼ In. 198.00

Crock, Cake, Cover, Flowers, Leaves, Cobalt Blue, Applied Ear Handles, 6 ½ x 11 In. 605.00

Crock, Cake, Flowers & Leaves, Cobalt Blue, Ear Handles, John Bell, Pa., Lid, 6 x 9 In. 1650.00

Crock, Chicken Pecking Corn, Adam Caire, Pokeepsie, c.1880, 3 Gal., 10 In. 495.00

Crock, Chicken Pecking Corn, Blue, New York State, c.1870, 2 Gal., 9 ½ In. 468.00

Crock, Cobalt Blue, Ear Handles, 1840-65, 8 ½ In. 168.00

Crock, Cobalt Blue, Flowers, Handles, Oval, 19th Century, 4 Gal. 495.00

Crock, Cobalt Blue, Trumpeter Flower, 3, J. Burger Jr., Rochester, N.Y., 11 ¼ x 10 In. 230.00

Crock, Cobalt Blue Design, Jas. Hamilton, 9 ½ In. . . . . *illus* 248.00

S

Crock, Cover, Cobalt Blue Bands, Pewter Lion Finial, George Sal, Heyde, c.1820, Pt. 1500.00
Crock, Cow, Standing, Blue Mark, Gardiner Maine Stoneware, c.1880, 3 Gal., 10 In. 165.00
Crock, Deer, Cobalt Blue, 2 Gal., 9 x 10 In. 16250.00
Crock, Dotted, Bull's-Eye Leaf, Ottman Bro's & Co., Ft. Edward, c.1870, 4 Gal., 11½ In. 605.00
Crock, Dotted Bird, S. Hart, Fulton, c.1875, 2 Gal., 9 In. 198.00
Crock, Dotted Flower, Blue Mark, Wme Warner, West Troy, c.1850, 2 Gal., 10 In. 330.00
Crock, Double Flower, Blue Mark, J. Burger Jr., Rochester, c.1885, 3 Gal., 10 In. 165.00
Crock, Double Flower, Blue Mark, J.C. Waelde, North Bay, c.1855, 4 Gal., 11 In. 209.00
Crock, Double Handles, Cobalt Blue Highlights, Oval, S. Purdy, Ohio, c.1820, 16 In. 345.00
Crock, Double Tulip, Leaf, Cobalt Blue, Ear Handles, D.P. Shenfleder, Reading, Pa., 3 Gal. 1100.00
Crock, Drooping Flowers, Cobalt Blue Band, Penn., c.1880, 2¾ In. 1045.00
Crock, Fan Shaped Flower, Cobalt Blue, Applied Handles, c.1850, 10½ x 9 In. 403.00
Crock, Flower, Brushed Blue, Oval, S.S. Perry, Troy, c.1830, Gal., 9 In. 385.00
Crock, Flower, Cobalt Blue, Lug Handles, Ballard & Brothers, Burlington, Vt., 13 In. 499.00
Crock, Flower Sprays, Banded, Cobalt Blue, 3, Applied Ear Handles, 3 Gal., 13 In. 99.00
Crock, Flower Sprays, Cobalt Blue, Turned Upper Rings, Applied Handles, 3 Gal., 11 In. 1100.00
Crock, Flower Sprigs, Cobalt Blue, Applied Ear Handles, 5 Gal., 15½ In. 77.00
Crock, Flowers, Cobalt Blue, Backward 1, Marked, Shenfelder, Reading, Pa. 425.00
Crock, Flowers, Cobalt Blue, Ear Handles, Cylindrical, P. Herrmann, 3 Gal., 13¾ In. 187.00
Crock, Flowers, Cobalt Blue, Impressed Label, A.E. Smith & Sons, 12 In. 86.00
Crock, Flowers, Cobalt Blue, Incised, Bangor Stoneware Company, 3 Gal. 263.00
Crock, Flowers, Cobalt Blue, Straight-Sided, Handles, c.1850, 3 Gal., 12½ x 9 In. 4125.00
Crock, Flowers, Cobalt Blue, Tab Handles, R. Butt, c.1835, 5 Gal. 8050.00
Crock, Flowers, Leaves, Cobalt Blue, Bulbous, Applied Ear Handles, 4 Gal., 13 x 9 In. 66.00
Crock, Flowers, Leaves, Cobalt Blue, Handle, 2 Gal., 14 In. 161.00
Crock, Flowers, Leaves, Cobalt Blue, Molded Rim, Applied Ear Handles, 3 Gal., 13 In. 165.00
Crock, Flowers, Leaves, Cobalt Blue, 2-Sided, Bulbous, Applied Handles, 8 Gal., 16½ In. 385.00
Crock, Flowers & Leaves, Stylized, Cobalt Blue, Ear Handles, White's Utica, 2 Gal., 10 In. 132.00
Crock, Grape Clusters, Flowers, Cobalt Blue, Ear Handles, Cowden & Wilcox, 2 Gal., 11 In. 1760.00
Crock, Green Brown Slip Glaze, Signed, J. Fisher, Lyons, N.Y., 2 Handles, 1½ Gal. 265.00
Crock, Hamilton & Jones, Cobalt Blue, Greensboro, Pa., 1½ Gal., 9⅜ In. 165.00
Crock, House, Palm Trees, Cobalt Blue, Lug Handles, R.O. Wittemore, Havana, N.Y., 4 Gal. 2350.00
Crock, John Jamison, 68 N. Water St., Phila., Blue Script, 7 In. 935.00
Crock, John Jamison, Water & Market Sts., Phila., Blue Script, Handles, 7¼ In. 358.00
Crock, Leaf, Blue, Ear Handles, W.H. Lehew & Co., Strasburg, Va., 1½ Gal., 6 x 9 In. 165.00
Crock, Leaves, Cobalt Blue, Turned Molded Top, 2¾ In. 2310.00
Crock, Manganese Decoration, Salt Glaze, 19th Century, Gal., 9¾ x 6¾ In. 154.00
Crock, Maple Leaf, Western, Early 20th Century, 5 Gal., 13 In. 47.00
Crock, Oval, Drooping Flower, E.W. Farrington & Co., Elmira, c.1890, 2 Gal., 9½ In. 248.00
Crock, Parrot, Plumes, F.B. Norton & Co., Worcester, c.1870, 3 Gal., 10½ In. 908.00
Crock, Pinwheel Flower, Oval, Somerset Potters' Works, c.1870, 3 Gal., 11 In. 110.00
Crock, Quail, Cattails, Cobalt Blue, Salt Glazed, John Burger, c.1860, 5 Gal., 13 In. 6000.00
Crock, Ribbed Oak Leaf, John Burger, Rochester, c.1865, 5 Gal., 13 In. 743.00
Crock, Ribbed Orchid, N.A. White & Son, Utica, c.1870, 5 Gal., 12 In. 770.00
Crock, Rooster, 5, Sunburst, Cobalt Blue, Applied Ear Handles, 5 Gal., 12¾ In. 88.00
Crock, Rows, A.P. Donaghho, Parkersburg, Salt Glazed, 16 In. 805.00
Crock, Running Bird, White's, Utica, c.1865, 2 Gal., 9½ In. 275.00
Crock, Scrolled Flowers, Birds, Cobalt Blue, 19th Century, 7¾ x 10¼ In. 69.00
Crock, Slip Blue, New York State, c.1860, 1½ Gal., 8 In. 88.00
Crock, Swan On Water, Cobalt Blue, Ear Handles, Cowden & Wilcox, 2 Gal., 11¼ In. 2200.00
Crock, Thistle Flower, Leaves, Cobalt Blue, Applied Ear Handles, 2 Gal., 9½ In. 154.00
Crock, Tulips, Cobalt Blue, Ear Handles, D.P. Shenfelder, Reading, Pa., 3 Gal., 11½ In. 275.00
Crock, Tulips, Cobalt Blue, Ear Handles, John Bell, Waynesboro, Pa., 6 Gal., 16½ In. 4400.00
Crock, Underwood, Cobalt Blue Bird, 2 Gal., 9 x 9½ In. 425.00
Crock, Urn Of Flowers, Cobalt Blue, Leaf Clusters, Applied Handles, 4 Gal., 15 In. 3850.00
Crock, Wreath, Blue, Ear Handles, Evan R. Jones, Pittston, Pa., 1887, 2 Gal., 9½ In. 1320.00
Cuspidor, Flower & Leaf Band, Cobalt Blue, 5 x 10 In. *illus* 143.00
Cuspidor, Leaf Band, Cobalt Blue, Signed, 4¼ x 8¼ In. 165.00
Dish, Yellow Stripes, Coggled Rim, Lead Glaze, 19th Century, 2 x 12 x 17 In. 550.00
Figurine, Camel, Gray, Green, Chinese, 13 In. 531.00
Figurine, Goddess, Blue Robes, Japan, 20th Century, 24 In. 118.00
Figurine, Lion, Lying Down, Cast, England, 23 x 38 x 15 In., Pair 3456.00
Figurine, Rooster, Surface Detail, Orange & Green Mottled Glaze, 14 In. 431.00
Figurine, Frog, Molded, On Maple Leaf, Orange Matte Glaze, John Crosley, c.1903, 8½ x 3½ In. 374.00
Figurine, Pillow, Reclining Cat, Raised Haunches, Black Glaze, Exposed Base, Chinese, 5 x 9¾ In. 120.00
Flask, Flower Blossom, Cobalt Blue, Flattened Egg Shape, 6¾ In. 8225.00

Stoneware, Crock, Butter, Cover, Tulips, Blue, Salt Glaze, Incised Bands, Late 1800s, 4½ x 7 In.
$690.00

Stoneware, Crock, Cobalt Blue Design, Jas. Hamilton, 9½ In.
$248.00

Stoneware, Cuspidor, Cobalt Blue, Flower & Leaf Band, 5 x 10 In.
$143.00

Stoneware, Flowerpot, Sunflower, Blue, Crimped Applied Collar, c.1860, 8¾ x 10⅝ In.
$9000.00

Stoneware, Jar, Flower & Leaf Band, Cobalt Blue, R.C.R., 10 In.
$303.00

Stoneware, Jar, Flowers, Cobalt Blue, Slip, West Troy N.Y. Pottery, c.1865, 12 x 9 In., 3 Gal.
$270.00

TIP
Hot air rises. Be careful what you display on high shelves in rooms with very high ceilings. The temperature at the ceiling could be over 80 degrees, and wax dolls or crèche figures could melt. Some plastic purses will deteriorate quickly if kept in a hot location.

S

Flowerpot, 2 Flowers, Cobalt Blue, Attached Saucer, 5¼ x 6⅜ In. 121.0
Flowerpot, Hanging, Cobalt Blue Swags, Crimped Bands, Center Drop, 7 x 10¾ In. 6710.0
Flowerpot, Sunflower, Blue, Crimped Applied Collar, c.1860, 8¾ x 10⅝ In. . . . . *illus* 9000.0
Humidor, Seascape Design, Diamond Pattern, Blue, Relief, Bristol Glaze, 7½ In. 88.0
Jar, 4 Incised Dots, Medium Olive, Alkaline Glaze, Applied Handles, Edgefield, 16 In. 4750.0
Jar, Alkaline Mottled Glossy To Olive Matte Glaze, Blue Highlights, N.C., 15¾ In. 81.0
Jar, Arts & Crafts Style, Green Mottled Glaze, 2 Angular Handles, Early 1900s, 23½ In. 633.0
Jar, Bird, 3, Cobalt Blue, Handles, Late 1800s, 3 Gal., 12 x 9 In. 748.0
Jar, Bird, Cobalt Blue, 3 Gal., 13½ x 10 In. 325.0
Jar, Canning, 3 Blue Stripes, Western Penn., c.1850, Qt., 6 In. . . . . 187.00 to 248.0
Jar, Canning, Blue Accent Line, A. Conrad, New Geneva, c.1875, Gal., 9½ In. 110.0
Jar, Canning, Blue Stencil, 4 Stripes, Jas. Hamilton & Co., c.1870, 2 Gal., 11½ In. 220.0
Jar, Canning, Cobalt Blue, Stripes, Wax Groove Rim, Black Interior, Pt., 5 x 3 In. 522.0
Jar, Canning, Mason, Union, Zinc Lid, Red Wing, Minn., Pat. Jan 24, 1899, 7 In. 154.0
Jar, Canning, Mason, Union, Zinc Lid, Red Wing, Minn., Pat. Jan 24, 1899, 8½ x 6 In. 176.0
Jar, Canning, Mason, Zinc Lid, Red Wing, Minn., Jan. 24, 1899, 11 x 3½ In. 715.0
Jar, Canning, Salt Glaze, 4 Stripes, Wax Groove Rim, 19th Century, Gal., 10 x 5 In. 209.0
Jar, Canning, Stenciled Blue Name, Jas. Hamilton & Co., c.1870, ½ Gal., 8 In. 121.0
Jar, Canning, Stenciled Oak Leaf, Shoulder Stripe, c.1850, ½ Gal., 8½ In. 303.0
Jar, Cobalt Blue Decoration, Brushed, Applied Lunate Handles, 18 x 11 In. 1495.0
Jar, Cover, Brown, Cowden & Wilcox, 6½ In. 45.0
Jar, Eagle, Federal Shield, Freehand Designs, Cobalt Blue, 1800s, 12 Gal. 2185.0
Jar, Flower, Cobalt Blue, Salt Glazed, Nathan Clark, Lug Handles, c.1830, 14 In. 705.0
Jar, Flower & Leaf Band, Cobalt Blue, R.C.R., 10 In. . . . . *illus* 303.0
Jar, Flowers, Blue Shaped Sides, Applied Handles, 3 Gal., 12 x 10 In. 125.0
Jar, Flowers, Cobalt Blue, Slip, West Troy N.Y. Pottery, c.1865, 12 x 9 In., 3 Gal. . . . . *illus* 270.0
Jar, Flowers, Leaves, Cobalt Blue, Molded Top, 3 In. 2420.0
Jar, Flowers, White Slip Glaze, Brown Band, Baluster Shape, Straight Neck, Chinese, 24 In. . . 540.0
Jar, Grain, Gray, Cylindrical Body, Horizontal Ribs, Round Opening, 7¾ In. 120.0
Jar, Leaf & Scroll Design, Cobalt Blue, Lug Handles, L.W. Fenton, Vermont, c.1825, 11 In. 176.0
Jar, Leaf Design, Cobalt Blue, Bulbous, 5¼ In. 605.0
Jar, Leaves, Cobalt Blue, Brushed, Cylindrical, Turned Molded Lip, 9 In. 160.0
Jar, Lid, Brown Mottled Matte Glaze, Spherical, Daniel Rhodes, 1973, 6½ x 7½ In. 360.0
Jar, Lid, Impressed, Oregon, 5 On Lid, Brown Alkaline Glaze, c.1870, 5 In. 88.0
Jar, Mottled & Runny Olive Alkaline Glaze, Oval, 4 Applied Handles, JCM, 19 In. 15000.0
Jar, Olive To Brown Alkaline Glaze, Handles, Edgefield, 2 Gal., 11¾ In. 2150.0
Jar, Opaque Green Glaze, Tapered Baluster Shape, Rolled Lip, Chinese, 24 x 21 In. 660.0
Jar, Oval, Cobalt Blue Decoration, Applied Strap Handles, Mid 1800s, 10 Gal., 19½ In. 4313.0
Jar, Oval, Cobalt Blue X, Leaves, Applied Strap Handles, Mid 1800s, 10 Gal., 20 In. 489.0
Jar, Screw Lid, Pewter Collar, Embossed, Continental, 10 In. 83.0
Jar, Snuff, Cobalt Blue, Demuth's Snuff, Lancaster, Pa., 7 In. 303.0
Jar, Snuff, Cover, Bell Shape, Albany Glazed Interior, 10 x 5 In. 88.0
Jar, Snuff, Cover, Flowers, Cobalt Blue, H.C. Demuth, Lancaster, Pa., Gal.8¼ In. 1540.0
Jar, Snuff, Demuth's Snuff, Lancaster, 1770, F.H. Cowden, Harrisburg, Pa., 9½ In. 1980.0
Jar, Squat, Impressed Drape & Tassel Design, Open Handles, c.1805 . . . . 5865.00
Jar, Tree Of Life, Cobalt Blue Design, Handles, Hudson Valley, N.Y., c.1810, 10 In. 385.00
Jar, Tulip Design, Oval, John Bell, Waynesboro, 4 Gal. 3910.00
Jar, Wide-Mount, Coggled Band, Open Loop Handle, c.1805, 9 In. 2115.00
Jar, Canning, Blue Plume, Blue Mark, New York Stoneware, c.1870, 2 Gal., 11 In. 110.00
Jar, Canning, Bud Flower, Blue Accents, John Burger, Rochester, c.1865, 2 Gal., 11 In. 440.00
Jar, Canning, Draped Flower Repeat, Kiln Drip, c.1850, Gal., 10½ In. 99.00
Jar, Canning, Eneix & Frankenberry, New Geneva, c.1877, Gal., 10 In. 358.00
Jar, Canning, Flower, Brushed, Blue Accents, Cowden & Wilcox, c.1870, Gal., 9½ In. 413.00
Jar, Canning, Flower, Petal Design, Brushed Blue, c.1850, Gal., 10 In. 176.00
Jar, Canning, Lid, Brushed Plume, Blue Mark, Lyons, c.1850, Gal., 9½ In. 275.00
Jar, Canning, Tornado, Slip Blue, Burger & Co., Rochester, c.1877, 2 Gal., 11 In. 440.00
Jug, Alkaline Glaze, Thomas Richie, North Carolina, c.1909, 11¾ In. 978.00
Jug, Antler Design, Blue Mark, G. Heiser, Buffalo, c.1838, Gal., 11 In. 413.00
Jug, Aschembach & Miller, 400 No. 3 Rd St., Philada., Blue Script, 11¼ In. 385.00
Jug, Batter, Flower, Blue, 4 Gal., 14¾ In. 167.00
Jug, Batter, Tulip, Cobalt Blue, Wreath Band, Bail Handle, Wood Grip, F.H. Cowden, 8½ In. . . 990.00
Jug, Bellarmine, Bearded Face, 3 Medallions, Portraits, Germany, 17th Century, 8¼ In. 1116.00
Jug, Bird, Cobalt Blue, W.A. Lewis, Leesville, N.Y., 4 Gal. 575.00
Jug, Bird, Long Neck, On Stump, Blue, Cowden & Wilcox, Harrisburg, Pa., 3 Gal., 15½ In. . . . 6050.00
Jug, Bird, Scrolling Branch, Blue, Straight Side, Loop Handle, Gal., 11½ x 7 In. 95.00
Jug, Bird & Plume, A.B. Wheeler & Co., Boston, c.1870, Gal., 10½ In. 550.00

ug, Bird On Branch, Blue, P.J. Fitzgerald & Bro., Troy, N.Y., 2 Gal. 489.00
ug, Bird On Branch, Cobalt Blue, New York, 2 Gal., 14¼ In. 358.00
ug, Bird On Branch, Incised, Blue Slip, West Troy, Gal, 11½ x 7 In. 225.00
ug, Bird On Branch, Leaves, Cobalt Blue, Salt Glaze, 1800s, 3 Gal., 14½ In. 19200.00
ug, Bird On Sprig, Blue Slip, New York Stoneware Co., 3 Gal., 16 In. 805.00
ug, Bird On Stump, Holding Grapes In Beak, Cobalt Blue, Cowden & Wilcox, 3 Gal. 4950.00
ug, Bluebird, Cobalt Blue, Floral Branch, Seymour & Bosworth, Hartford, Ct., 15½ In. 375.00
ug, Bolen & Byrne Co., Spirit Merchants, Philadelphia, Pa., Blue Script, 11 In. 495.00
ug, Brown, White, C.A. Dorsheimer, Wholesale Liquor Dealer, Lancaster, Pa., 11 In. 880.00
ug, Brown Mottled, Glossy Glaze, Marguerite Wildenhain, 10 x 9 In. 660.00
ug, California Cough Balm, Price 10 Cents, 2-Tone, Stencil, 3¼ In. 242.00
ug, Chas. A Grove, 15 Centre Square, Lancaster, Pa., Blue Script, 9½ In. 715.00
ug, Chas. A. Grove, 15 Centre Square, Lancaster, Pa., Cobalt Blue, 11½ In. 880.00
ug, Chas. Seitz, 492 Rhode Island St., Blue Script, Buffalo, c.1880, 10 In. 143.00
ug, Closed Tulip, Leaves, Cobalt Blue, Cowden & Wilcox, Harrisburg, Pa., Gal., 10¾ In. 523.00
ug, Cobalt Blue, Global, Flower Stamped, c.1800, 14½ In. 1763.00
ug, Cobalt Blue, Stripes, Flared Lip, 19th Century, 2 Gal., 15 In. 187.00
ug, Cobalt Blue Highlights, Stedman & Seymour, New Haven, 11½ In. 130.00
ug, Compliments Of J.J. Rennie, Annadale, Minn., 2-Tone, 3 In. 176.00
ug, Compliments Of L. Wieber, Marty, Minn., 2-Tone, 3 In. 176.00
ug, Daniel Goodale, Incised Blue Flower, Oval, Strap Handle, c.1830, 2 Gal., 12½ In. 999.00
ug, Dean Foster & Co., Boston, Dotted, Stylized Flower, Boston, c.1870, 5 Gal., 19 In. 275.00
ug, Dotted Bird, Flowering Branch, Red Tint, Edmands & Co., c.1870, 2 Gal., 13 In. 275.00
ug, Double Tulip, Leaves, Cobalt Blue, 5 In. 8525.00
ug, Double Tulips, Dotted Outlines, Cobalt Blue, 2 Applied Handles, 22 In. 575.00
ug, Exotic Bird, Cobalt Blue, On Stump, Applied Handle, White's, Utica, 14½ In. 805.00
ug, Face, Grotesque, Dark Green Ash Glaze, Stone Teeth, Redware Face, Lanier Meaders, 9 In. 4025.00
ug, Face, Jagged Ceramic Teeth, Glossy Brown Glaze, Louis D. Brown, 8 x 6½ In. 201.00
ug, Face, Marie Rogers, Ga., 20th Century, 6 In. 35.00
ug, Face, Marked, Reggie Meaders, c.1993, ½ Gal. 165.00
ug, Face, Olive Glaze, Blue Eyes, Incised, Lanier Meaders, 10 x 8 x 8 In. *illus* 1490.00
ug, Face, Reggie Meaders, Ceramic Eyes, Teeth, Olive Gloss Glaze, 9 x 7 In. 633.00
ug, Face, Rock Teeth, Applied Eyes, Signed, Lanier Meaders, 9¾ In. *illus* 1159.00
ug, Floral Spray, Cobalt Blue, Molded Handle, Lewis & Cady, Fairfax, Vt., c.1860, 14 In. 382.00
ug, Flower, Blue Accent On Handle, E.S. Fox, Athens, c.1840, 2 Gal., 13 In. 523.00
ug, Flower, Cobalt Blue, Applied Strap Handle, A.O. Whittlemore, 2 Gal., 12 In. 144.00
ug, Flower, Cobalt Blue, Date 1863, A.O. Whittemore, Havana, N.Y., 13½ In. 450.00
ug, Flower, Cobalt Blue, Oval, Daubed Handle Terminals, c.1820, 12⅛ In. 764.00
ug, Flower, Cobalt Blue, Oval, Daubed Handle Terminals, Early 1800s, 10⅝ In. 764.00
ug, Flower, Leaves, Cobalt Blue, Fulper Bros., Flemington, N.J., 2 Gal., 13¾ In. 121.00
ug, Flower, Leaves, Cobalt Blue, Ear Handles, White's, Utica, 2 Gal., 14 In. 187.00
ug, Flower, Slip Decorated, Handle, Stamped F. Stetzenmeyer, Rochester, N.Y., 2 Gal. 2875.00
ug, Flowers, 3 Gal., 15½ x 9½ In. 375.00
ug, Flowers, 3 Gal., 16½ x 9½ In. 250.00
ug, Flowers, Cobalt Blue, 19th Century, 2 Gal., 13 In. 1320.00
ug, Flowers, Cobalt Blue, Leaves, J.W. Cowden, Harrisburg, Pa., c.1861, 3 Gal., 16 In. 4950.00
ug, Flowers, Cobalt Blue, Slip Trailed, Pulled Handle, White's, Utica, 13½ x 8½ In. 207.00
ug, Flowers, Cobalt Blue, Strap Handle, R.O. Wittemore, Havana, N.Y., c.1870, 5 Gal. 353.00
ug, Flowers, Leaves, Blue, C. Hadle & Co., Union Pottery, Newark, N.J., 4 Gal., 17½ In. 55.00
ug, Goodwinn & Webster, Oval, 15¼ In. 82.00
ug, Hawthorn Pottery Co., Hawthorn, Pa., Marked, Gal. 45.00
ug, Insect, Double 3, Slip Blue, Geddes, N.Y., c.1870, 3 Gal., 15 In. 165.00
ug, J.B. Caire & Co., Pokeepsie, N.Y., Bullet Head Form, Tan, Salt Glaze, Handle, Gal., 10 In. 235.00
ug, John Hortin, 142 N. Queen St., Lancaster, Pa., Blue Script, 9½ In. 3575.00
ug, Leaf, Brushed, Cobalt Blue, Ear Handles, Bulbous, Gilson & Co., Reading, Pa., 13 In. 715.00
ug, Leaf, Cobalt Blue, Applied Strap Handle, A.K. Ballard, Vt., 14 In. 144.00
ug, Leaf, Cobalt Blue, Applied Handle, Felix P. Morway, Worcester, Mass., 13 In. 230.00
ug, Leaf Design, c.1900, 2 Gal., 12½ In. 748.00
ug, Louis Mai, 433 Straight St., Patterson, N.J., Cobalt Blue, 11¼ In. 198.00
ug, Louis Zapp & Co., Pure Winds & Liquors, Louisville, Ky., Brown, Gal. 269.00
ug, Milk, Cylinder Spout, Metal Bail Handle, Southern Stoneware Pottery, 9 In. 171.00
ug, Morgan & Van Winckle, Incised Cobalt Blue Flower, Leaf, Oval, 3 Gal.,15¼ In. 558.00
ug, Mottled & Runny Olive Alkaline Glaze, Edgefield, Mid 19th Century, 15 In. 3720.00
ug, Open Winged Sparrow, Multicolor, Oval, Loop Handle, 19th Century, 2¼ In. 300.00
ug, Oval, Bird On Leaf, Blue, Handle, Mark, I. Seymour & Co., Troy, c.1825, Gal., 11 In. 2200.00
ug, Oval, Brushed Flower, Blue Mark, H. & G. Nash, Utica, c.1832, 2 Gal., 13 In. 358.00

Stoneware Face Jugs

Face jugs are dark jugs with distorted faces, crooked teeth, and big eyes. Older face jugs, pieces with alkaline glaze, and jars with cobalt decorations—animals, plants, or people—sell for the highest prices.

Stoneware, Jug, Face, Olive Glaze, Blue Eyes, Incised, Lanier Meaders, 10 x 8 x 8 In.
$1490.00

Stoneware, Jug, Face, Rock Teeth, Applied Eyes, Signed, Lanier Meaders, 9¾ In.
$1159.00

S

STONEWARE

Stoneware, Mortar, Flower Band, Dots On Rim, Cobalt Blue, Base, 5⅝ In. $6435.00

Stoneware, Pitcher, 10 Flower Heads, Cobalt Blue, Salt Glaze, Late 1800s, Baltimore, 10 In. $847.00

Stoneware, Pitcher, Blue, Sponge, Smoke Rings, 9 In. $605.00

S

Jug, Oval, Brushed Flower, Blue Wash, C. Boynton & Co., Troy, c.1825, 13½ In. 413.00
Jug, Oval, Filled Bird On Branch, Blue, Incised, R. Weaver, Ohio, c.1845, 4 Gal., 8 In.. . . . . 578.00
Jug, Oval, Flowers, Cobalt Blue, Lyman & Clark, Gardiner, 13 In. 1380.00
Jug, Oval, Stylized Leaf, Cobalt Blue, Applied Handle, 14¾ In. 374.00
Jug, Oval, Tulip, Cobalt Blue, Impressed T. Crafts & Co., Applied Strap Handle, 12½ In.. . . . . . 489.00
Jug, Oval, Tulip, Cobalt Blue, Salt Glazed Exterior, 3 Gal., c.1825, 14¾ In. 1410.00
Jug, Peacock, Cobalt Blue, Pulled Handle, L. Seymour, Troy, Impressed, 3 Gal. 3819.00
Jug, Peter Herman Stoneware, Baltimore, Md., Signed, Handle, c.1860, 2 Gal. 150.00
Jug, Pheasant On Stump, Cobalt Blue, Salt Glaze, West Troy N.Y. Pottery, 1800s, 5 Gal. 11400.00
Jug, Ribbed Bull's Eye Flower, Fort Edward Pottery Co., c.1860, 4 Gal., 17 In. 495.00
Jug, Singing Bird, A. Cohen, Brooklyn, c.1870, 2 Gal., 13½ In. 688.00
Jug, Sparrow Holding Letter, Multicolored, Oval, Loop Handle, 19th Century, 2¼ In. 336.00
Jug, Spitting Tulip, Cobalt Blue, Applied Handle, Moyer, Harrisburg, Pa., c.1859, Gal., 11 In.. . 935.00
Jug, Spitting Tulip, Cobalt Blue, Ear Handles, Cowden & Wilcox, Gal., 10¼ In.. . . . . 330.00
Jug, Spitting Tulip, Cobalt Blue, H.B. Pfaltzgraf, York, Pa., Gal., 11½ In. 440.00
Jug, Stripe & Feather, Cobalt Blue, 19th Century, Qt., 7½ x 4½ In.. . . . . 330.00
Jug, Stylized Flower, Cobalt Blue, Strap Handle, Channeled Top, 19th Century, 4 Gal. 550.00
Jug, Tulip, Blue, Stenciled, S. Johnston & Son, Beaver, Pa., 2 Gal., 14¼ In. 1265.00
Jug, Tulip, Leaves, Cobalt Blue, M & T Miller, Newport, Pa., 2 Gal., 14 In. 1650.00
Jug, Tulips, Cobalt Blue, Ribbed Leaves, 2, Applied Handle, Cortland, N.Y., 13½ In. 489.00
Jug, Whiskey, Compliments Of I.W. Harper, Nelson County Kentucky, 2-Tone, 3 In.. . . . . 66.00
Jug, Whiskey, Old 1869 Rye, Distilled, Little Brown Jug, Red Brown Glaze, Qt. 395.00
Keg, Wine, Pinwheel, Cobalt Blue, Incised, Salt Glaze, Molded Bands, 18½ In. 7200.00
Keg, Wine, Sprigged Knights, Coat Of Arms, Lions, Grapevines, 15 In. 118.00
Measure, Bristol Glaze, Blue Stencil, J.I. Prentiss & Co., Buffalo, c.1900, 6½ In. 99.00
Milk Pail, Leaf Design, Cobalt Blue, Brushed, Pour Spout, 4¼ x 12 In.. . . . . 358.00
Milk Pan, Flower & Leaf, Cobalt Blue, Pour Spout, 3½ x 10¼ In. 198.00
Milk Pan, Salt Glaze, 2 Handles, Pour Spout, 19th Century, Gal., 4½ x 11¾ In. 231.00
Mortar, Flower Band, Dots On Rim, Cobalt Blue, Base, 5⅝ In.. . . . . *illus* 6435.00
Mug, Brown Albany Slip Glaze, Scribed, 1st Triennial, c.1905, 3¾ In. 121.00
Mug, Cobalt Blue Design, Barrel Form, Applied Handle, 4 In. 1150.00
Pedestal, Molded, Ram's Heads, Wolf Heads, Garlands, Blue, Metal Top Plate, 31 x 15 In.. . . . 235.00
Pitcher, 2 Flowers, Cobalt Blue, Applied Handle, 8½ In. 605.00
Pitcher, 5 Flower Sprays, Cobalt Blue, Turned Rings, Shenfelder, Reading, Pa., Gal., 11 In. . . 2860.00
Pitcher, 10 Flower Heads, Cobalt Blue, Salt Glaze, Late 1800s, Baltimore, 10 In.. . . . . *illus* 847.00
Pitcher, Baluster, Paneled, Seal Of U.S.A., Glazed, 19th Century, 8 In. 418.00
Pitcher, Blue, Sponge, Smoke Rings, 9 In. . . . . *illus* 605.00
Pitcher, Brushed Plume, Lyons, c.1855, Gal., 10½ In.. . . . . 385.00
Pitcher, Chain Links, Ferns, Cobalt Blue, H.C. Smith, Alexa. D.C., 2 Gal., 13½ In. 11500.00
Pitcher, Cobalt Blue, Bulbous Base, L-Shape Handle, Sponged, 9 In. 77.00
Pitcher, Cobalt Blue Decoration, Handle, 4¼ In.. . . . . 7020.00
Pitcher, Cylindrical, Sgraffito, Manganese Glaze, Molded Rim, 5½ In. 179.00
Pitcher, Flower Sprays, Cobalt Blue, D.P. Shenfelder, Gal, 11 In.. *illus* 2860.00
Pitcher, Flowers, Blue, White & Green, Impressed Base, BB Craig, Vale, N.C., 16 In. 748.00
Pitcher, Flowers, Leaves, Cobalt Blue, Applied Ribbed Handle, Squat, 6 In. 9350.00
Pitcher, Flowers, Leaves, Cobalt Blue, Bulbous, 11 In.. . . . . 990.00
Pitcher, Grapes, Vine, Runny Alkaline Glaze, Highlights, Harold Hewell, 14½ In. 104.00
Pitcher, Poppy, Cobalt Blue, Applied Strap Handle, Whites, Binghamton, 9½ In. 288.00
Pitcher, Salt Glaze, Flower Heads, Ribbed Handle, Flanking Spout, Gal., 10 x 4¾ In. 770.00
Pitcher, Smoke Ring, Cobalt Blue, Tapered, Applied Loop Handle, Sponged, 9¼ In. 121.00
Pitcher, Spirit Of 76, Blue, Gray, High Relief, Bunker Hill, Baron Von Steuben, 8½ In. 431.00
Pitcher, Spitting Tulip, Leaves, Cobalt Blue, Irvine Pottery, Newville, Pa., 2 Gal., 13 In. 1430.00
Pitcher, Uncle Tom's Cabin, Slave Auction, Escape, Ridgway & Abington, 1853, 7 In. 508.00
Pitcher, White, Blue Glaze, Windmill, 7 In. 58.00
Pitcher, Wreath, Cobalt Blue, Bulbous, Incised, P.M. Tommey, For Beer Only, 8¾ In.. . . . . 5500.00
Planter, David Cressey, Arc Texture, No. 4047/R, c.1970, 24 x 22 In.. 4200.00
Planter, Sombrero, Iron Stand, John Follis, Rex Goode, c.1949, 29 In. 5400.00
Plate, Birds, Incised, Mottled Green, Martz, 10 x 6 In. 75.00
Plate, Fish, Glazed, c.1957, 3 x 10½ In. 390.00
Plate, Sugar Cane, Tea Dust Glaze Ground, Shoji Hamada, 10¾ In. 3900.00
Presentation Piece, Blue Stencil, L.D. Stoneburner, Bristol Glaze, c.1900, 20 In. 7425.00
Punch Bowl, Art Nouveau, Salt Glaze, Relief, Lid, Reinhold Merkelbach, 4 Liter, 11 In. 212.00
Sculpture, Torso, Daniel Rhodes, Marked, 50 x 20 x 14 In. 6600.00
Syrup, Bull's-Eye Leaf, New York Stoneware Co., Fort Edward, c.1870, 2 Gal., 14 In. 275.00
Tea Bowl, Brown Glaze, Black Details, Hare's Fur Pattern, 4½ In.. . . . . 510.00

ea Bowl, Oil Spot Glaze, Conical Shape, Straight Foot, Black Glaze, Chinese, 5 In. 390.00
eapot, Fish Handle, Glazed, Bronzed, Signed, Tim Mather, 11 x 12 In. 840.00
eapot, Green, Chinese, Early 20th Century, 7 ½ In. 89.00
ureen, Winged, Deep Green Matte, Mottled Glaze, Karen Karnes, 8 x 21 In. 5100.00
rn, On Stand, White, Smear Glaze, Gadroon Border, Entwined Handles, 20 x 22 In. 881.00
ase, Canyon, Mottled Red, Amber Matte, Funnel Shaped, R. Turner, 9 ½ x 8 ½ In. 9000.00
ase, Cylinder, Characters, Gridded Band, Hexagons, Gray, Celadon Glaze, 6 In. 1121.00
ase, Cylindrical, Tortoiseshell Glaze, Axel Salto, Marked, 6 x 2 ¾ In. 3000.00
ase, Embossed Deer, Amber, Brown Matte Glaze, Gourd Shape, Keramis, 12 x 7 ½ In. 1830.00
ase, Gilt Relief, Dragons, Antiques, Blue Ground, Chinese, 19th Century, 14 ¼ In. 1410.00
ase, Glazed, Mottled Red, Amber, Blue Matte, Funnel Shape, R. Turner, 10 ½ x 8 ½ In. 4800.00
ase, Glazed, Mottled Red, Amber Matte, Funnel Shape, Signed, R. Turner, 9 x 8 ¼ In. 5700.00
ase, Globe, Purple Glaze, Deeply Carved Surface, Marianne Westmann, 5 ½ In. 120.00
ase, Indigo, Amber, Double Gourd, Toshiko Takaezu, 21 ½ x 9 In. 6600.00
ase, Matte Tortoiseshell Glaze, Axel Salto, Marked, c.1935, 2 ½ x 3 ¾ In. 1560.00
ase, Oak Leaves & Acorns, Salt Glaze, 3 ¼ x 3 ¼ In. 8400.00
ase, People, Holding Fish, Gun Metal Brown Glaze, Coupe Shape, 13 ¼ x 9 In. 4800.00
ase, Relief Molded Dragon, Blue Glaze, Japan, Late 19th Century, 36 In. 940.00
ase, Ribbed, Glazed, Brown, Semimatte, Signed, Turner, 4 x 5 In. 1800.00
ase, Runny Cobalt Blue Glaze, 3 Looped Handles, Auman Pottery, 4 ½ x 8 In. 748.00
ase, Salt Glaze, Controlled-Drip Cobalt Blue Glaze, C.R. Auman Pottery, N.C., 7 ½ In. 3680.00
ase, Shakespearian Scenes, 4-Sided, Faience, 1932, 14 ½ x 7 In. 7800.00
ase, Slab Built Glaze, Faceted Form, Copper, Gunmetal, Leathery, 29 ¼ x 11 In. 360.00
ase, Sponged Folk Art, Amber, Green Luster Glaze, B. Woodman, Marked, 5 x 30 In. 5400.00
Vater Cooler, 6 Gal., 2 Handles, Bird On Branch, Satterlee & Mory, c.1869 . . . . 3950.00
Vater Cooler, Barrel Shape, Incised Rings, Leaves, Wingender, 13 In. 719.00
Vater Cooler, Flowers, Cobalt Blue, Applied Handles, Strainer, Lid, 4, 25 In., 2 Piece 1980.00
Vater Cooler, Incised Rum Inscription, Open Handles, Pheasant, New York, 16 ½ In. 5463.00
Vater Cooler, Maple Leaf Stamp, Cold Drink, Western Stoneware Co., 12 x 11 In. . . . . . *illus* 425.00
Vater Cooler, Shenandoah Valley, Eagle, Liberty 1853, 3 Gal., 13 In. 5380.00
Vater Cooler, Whiskey, Green Bands, Barrel Form, 14 In. 77.00
Vater Cooler, White, Raised Blue Flowers & Letters, Ice Water, Metal Spigot, 3 Gal., 16 In. . . . 336.00
Vater Filter, Leadless Glaze, Robb Moore & Neill, Floral Garland, Spigot, 26 x 10 ½ In. 540.00

Stoneware, Pitcher, Flower Sprays, Cobalt Blue, D.P. Shenfelder, Gal, 11 In.
$2860.00

Stoneware, Water Cooler, Maple Leaf Stamp, Cold Drink, Western Stoneware Co., 12 x 11 In.
$425.00

TORE fixtures, cases, cutters, and other items that have no advertising as part of the decoration re listed here. Most items found in an old store are listed in the Advertising category in this book.

Bin, Grain, Pine, Slant Front Lid, Mustard Paint, Cut Nail Construction, 37 x 37 In. 920.00
Bin, Grain, Poplar, Dovetailed Case, Hinged Lids, Divided Interior, Mid 1800s, 24 x 60 In. 489.00
Bin, Meal, Poplar, Blue Paint, Hinged Top, Divided Interior, 19th Century, 32 x 56 In. 748.00
Bin, Seed, Poplar, Black Paint, Cutout Feet, Slant Lift Lid, Divided Interior, 14 x 6 ¾ In. 489.00
Cabinet, Dispensing, Walnut, 7 Drawers, Stepped Base, Lock, c.1900, 16 x 13 In. 364.00
Cabinet, Notions, Walnut, Best Made Geoff's Drygoods, Counter, 1800s, 9 x 25 In. 264.00
Cabinet, Ribbon, Oak, A.N. Russell & Sons, Ilion, N.Y., 38 x 25 ½ x 30 In. . . . . *illus* 1700.00
Cabinet, Seed, Grain, Oak, Glass Front Slots, 9 Drawers, 38 x 22 ½ x 33 ¾ In. 1045.00
Cabinet, Self-Weighing Shot Case, Oak, Vandergrift Mfg. Co., 1881, 18 x 31 x 11 In. . . . . *illus* 6400.00
Case, Display, Glass, Metal, Counter, 34 ½ x 5 x 9 In. 77.00
Case, Oak, Glass, 8-Sided, Revolving, 4 Shelves, J. Schumm, 44 x 22 In. . . . . *illus* 2300.00
Case, Oak, Glass, Shelves, 31 ¾ x 24 ½ In. 495.00
Case, Oak, Glass, Vertical, 64 ¼ x 21 ½ In. 1210.00
Case, Ribbon, Oak, 8 Drawers, 25 x 27 x 18 In. 413.00
Case, Walnut, Glass, German Silver, Claes & Lehnbeuter, St. Louis, 98 In. . . . . *illus* 5800.00
Case, Display, Carved Rosewood, Glass Top, Sides, Chinese, 31 x 19 In. 275.00
Case, Display, Country, Oak, Mirrored Rear Doors, c.1910, 45 x 9 In. 400.00
Case, Display, Ice Cream, 10 Cents, 50 Cents, 2 Glass Shelves, Copper, Jewels. 495.00
Case, Display, Ice Cream Cone, Chocolate, Pink, Beige, Papier-Mache, 60 In. 295.00
Case, Display, Jewelry, White Wile & Warner Rings, Key Wind, Revolves, 18 x 21 In. 2090.00
Case, Display, Knife, Winchester, Wood, Slanted Glass, 19 ½ x 22 ½ In. 316.00
Case, Display, Mahogany, Spilt Glass, Tabletop, Slanted Top, Rear Doors, 88 ½ x 23 In. 403.00
Case, Display, Oak, Frame, Mirror Sliding Doors, New England Cabinet Works, 49 x 34 In. . . . 250.00
Case, Display, Oak, Glass, Cash Drawer, Lock, Counter, 20 ½ x 20 ½ x 13 ½ In. 560.00
Case, Display, Oak, Glass, Shelves, 24 x 20 ½ x 19 ½ In. 385.00
Case, Display, Oak, Glass Sides, Rear Hinged Door, Jos. Knittel, c.1900, 30 x 32 In. 450.00
Case, Display, Pugh Auger Bit, Pugh Hardware Corp., Philadelphia, Penn., 22 In. 248.00
Cigar Cutter, Town Crier, Metal, Pull-Down Hand, Japanned, Counter, 7 ½ x 5 In. 198.00

SECURITY TIP
Going away for the weekend? If you have a car at home, park it at the back of the driveway and lock it. It makes it look as if someone is home and it blocks easy access to a back door.

STORE

Store, Cabinet, Ribbon, Oak, A.N. Russell & Sons, Ilion, N.Y., 38 x 25 ½ x 30 In.
$1700.00

Store, Cabinet, Self-Weighing Shot Case, Oak, Vandergrift Mfg. Co., 1881, 18 x 31 x 11 In.
$6400.00

Store, Case, Oak, Glass, 8-Sided, Revolving, 4 Shelves, J. Schumm, 44 x 22 In.
$2300.00

Cigar Cutter & Lighter, Elephant, Red Glass, Iron, 11 x 10 In. . . . *illus* 3390.00
Dispenser, Stamp, Side Crank, Light Globe, Glass Top Panels, c.1919, 27 x 12 In. . . . 168.00
Dispenser, Straw, Green Glass, Nickel Over Brass Cover, Metal Insert, 11 ¼ In. . . . 1125.00
Display Rack, 15 Candy Jars, Glass, Metal . . . *illus* 1600.00
Door Screen, Dry Goods, Wire Mesh, Green, Gilt Paint, 30 x 37 In. . . . 58.00
Micro Mosaic, Coliseum, Grand Tour, Ruins, Figures, Ebonized Frame, 19 x 15 In. . . . 21150.00
Seed Counter, 2 Parts, 39 x 22 x 32 In. . . . 275.00
Sign, Apothecary, Red Glass Lenses, Gold Paint, Sheet Copper, Early 1900s, 35 x 23 In. . . . 1725.00
Sign, Boot Maker, Boot, Wood, Carved, Gilt, Late 19th Century . . . 2585.00
Sign, Boot Maker, Boot Shape, Black, Green Paint, Wood, Wrought Iron . . . 2645.00
Sign, Boot Shape, Guaranteed Waterproof, Black Paint, Metal, c.1920, 12 ¼ In. . . . 495.00
Sign, Crab, Silhouette, Red Paint, Cutout, Sheet Metal, Iron Post . . . 518.00
Sign, Dentist, Gold Paint, Wood, Carved, Chain, 9 x 15 ½ In. . . . 2243.00
Sign, Hardware, 2-Sided, Hanging, 8 x 48 In. . . . 55.00
Sign, Ice Cream Bowl, Strawberry, Embossed, Enamel, Die Cut, 26 x 35 In. . . . 110.00
Sign, Jewelry, Watches, Clocks, Iron, Tin, Pocket Watch, 2-Sided, Late 1800s, 25 x 20 In. . *illus* 1800.00
Sign, Locksmith, Key, Figural, Gold, Black, Wood . . . 2875.00
Sign, Meat Market, White, Black Letters, Wood, 10 ½ x 48 In. . . . 1645.00
Sign, No Admittance, Cobalt Blue, White, Porcelain, 4 x 18 In. . . . 60.00
Sign, Palm Reader, Hand, Figural, Tin, Metal Ribbed Cuff, Early 1900s . . . 1080.00
Sign, Pawnbroker, Black Paint, 3 Wood Balls, Wrought Iron, Trefoil Frame, 38 In. . . . 431.00
Sign, Popsicle, Red, Black, Yellow, Embossed, Tin Lithograph . . . 303.00
Sign, Root Beer Float, Embossed, Enamel, Die Cut, Tin, 24 x 9 In. . . . 110.00
Sign, Watch Maker, Pocket Watch Shape, Zinc Face, Cast Iron Rim, Painted, 16 In. . . . 1035.00
Strawholder, Glass, Purple, Metal Lid, Original Straws, 14 In. . . . *illus* 230.00
Strawholder, Green, Pressed Glass, Metal Base, Metal Lid, Lift-Up Rod, 12 x 4 ⅝ In. . . . 330.00
Tobacco Cutter, Horse, Prancing, Tail Handle, Iron, Hardwood Base, 7 ½ x 17 x 8 In. . . . 201.00
Tobacco Cutter, Iron, Enterprise Champion Tobacco, 1885 . . . 35.00
Tobacco Cutter, Wrought Iron, Sheet Tin, Wood Case, 39 In. . . . 248.00

STORE, COFFEE GRINDERS *are listed in their own category.*

STOVES have been used in America for heating since the eighteenth century and for cooking since the nineteenth century. Most types of wood, coal, gas, kerosene, and even some electric stoves are collected.

Atlanta Stove Works, Cast Iron, 2-Eye, Coal, 23 x 22 x 16 In. . . . 90.00
Birmingham Stove & Range Co., Red Mountain T, Cast Iron, Porcelain, 56 x 35 x 22 In. . . 275.00
Franklin Anchor, No. 216, Iron, Tile Medallions, Footed, c.1888, 42 x 34 x 26 In. . . . *illus* 535.00
Franklin Heater Stove, Columbus 99, Cast Iron, 22 x 22 x 24 In. . . . 175.00
Montgomery Ward, K38-2 Anchor, 21 ¾ x 20 ¾ x 19 In. . . . *illus* 28.00
Parlor, Osage Model, Broice Beach & Co., St. Louis, Pat. 1875, 17 x 24 x 13 In. . . . 81.00
Parlor, Round, Royal Oak, No. 16, 52 x 25 In. . . . *illus* 60.00
Plate, Iron, Curved, Cow Heads Facing Away, Corn Ears, Black Paint, 20 x 11 In. . . . 86.00

SULPHIDES are cameos of unglazed white porcelain encased in transparent glass. The technique was patented in 1819 in France and has been used ever since for paperweights, decanters, tumblers, marbles, and other type of glassware. Paperweights and Marbles are listed in their own categories.

Pitcher, Classical Figures, Cut Cross Hatching, Serrated Edge, England, 7 x 8 In. . . . *illus* 7800.00

SUMIDA is a Japanese pottery that was made from about 1895 to 1941. Pieces are usually everyday objects—vases, jardinieres, bowls, teapots, and decorative tiles. Most pieces have a very heavy orange-red, blue, brown, black, green, purple, or off-white glaze, with raised three-dimensional figures as decorations. The unglazed part is painted red, green, black, or orange. Sumida is sometimes mistakenly called *Sumida gawa*, but true Sumida gawa is a softer pottery made in the early 1800s.

Bowl, Applied Blossoms & Branches, Coiled Base, 7 x 7 In. . . . 375.00
Pilgrim's Bottle, Red Matte Glaze, 9 x 7 ½ In. . . . 475.00
Pitcher, Buddhist Figures, c.1915, 12 ½ In. . . . 1850.00
Pitcher, Buddhist Figures, c.1920, 12 ½ x 5 In. . . . 1850.00
Vase, Black, Cream, Blue, Applied Figures, Bearded Men, Children, 12 x 12 In. . . . 1835.00
Vase, Boys, 9 ½ x 5 In. . . . 300.00
Vase, Children, Orange Ground, Black Drip Glaze, Inoue Ryosai, c.1890, 9 ¾ In. . . . 595.00
Vase, Mother, Children, Peach Of Immortality, Man, Elephants, Ribbed, Red, 12 In., Pair . . . 1680.00
Vase, Red, Turquoise, Black, Gathered Neck, Ribbed, 32 Applied Monkeys, 18 ¼ In. . . . 4113.00

S

Store, Case, Walnut, Glass, German Silver, Claes & Lehnbeuter, St. Louis, 98 In.
$5800.00

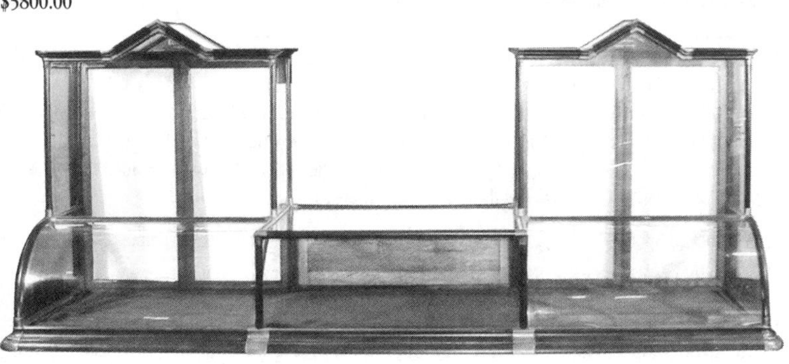

Stove, Franklin Anchor, No. 216, Iron, Tile Medallions, Footed, c.1888, 42 x 34 x 26 In.
$535.00

Store, Cigar Cutter & Lighter, Elephant, Red Glass, Iron, 11 x 10 In.
$3390.00

Store, Sign, Jewelry, Watches, Clocks, Iron, Tin, Pocket Watch, 2-Sided, Late 1800s, 25 x 20 In.
$1800.00

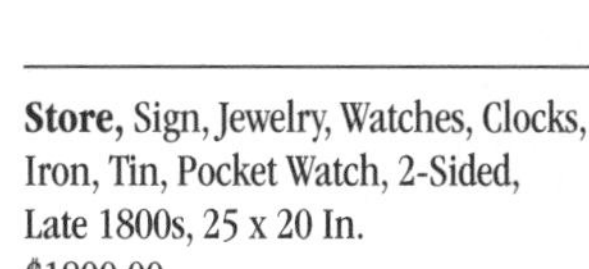

Stove, Montgomery Ward, K38-2 Anchor, 21¾ x 20¾ x 19 In.
$28.00

Store, Display Rack, 15 Candy Jars, Glass, Metal
$1600.00

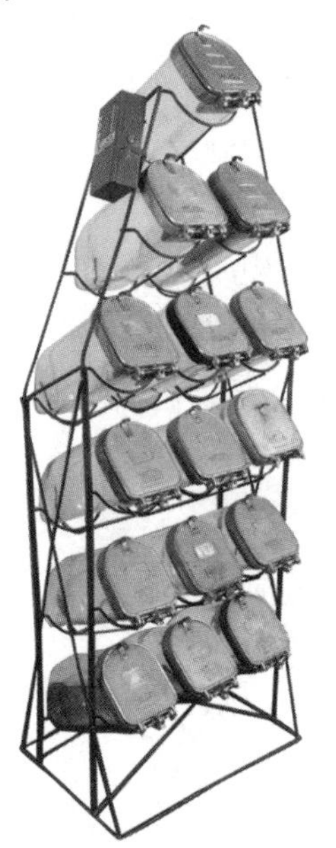

Store, Strawholder, Glass, Purple, Metal Lid, Original Straws, 14 In.
$230.00

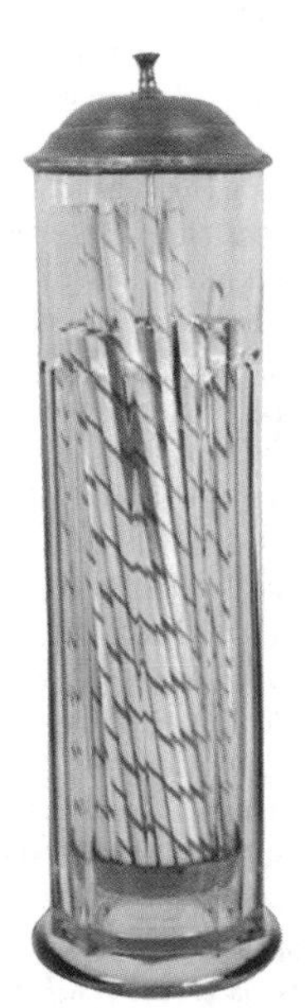

Stove, Parlor, Round, Royal Oak, No. 16, 52 x 25 In.
$60.00

S

Sulphide, Pitcher, Classical Figures, Cut Cross Hatching, Serrated Edge, England, 7 x 8 In.
$7800.00

Sunderland, Bowl, Iron Bridge, Masonic, Script, Northumberland, Elijah Quilter, 12 In.
$942.00

Sunderland, Jug, Peace & Plenty, Pearlware, Black Transfer, Early 19th Century, 9 In.
$575.00

Superman, Badge, Superman American, Junior Defense League, Brass, 1941, 1 ⅛ In.
$86.00

Vase, Red Ground, Brown Overlay, Applied Robed Figure, 12 In., Pair 400.00
Vase, Red Orange, Marbleized Black Drip, Children In Relief, 1890 .... 595.00

SUNBONNET BABIES were first introduced in 1900 in the book *The Sunbonnet Babies*. The stories were by Eulalie Osgood Grover, illustrated by Bertha Corbett. The children's faces were completely hidden by the sunbonnets. The children had been pictured in black and white before this time, but the color pictures in the book were immediately successful. The Royal Bayreuth China Company made a full line of children's dishes decorated with the Sunbonnet Babies. Some Sunbonnet Babies plates have been reproduced, but they are clearly marked.

Creamer, Pinched Spout 65.00
Pitcher, 5 ¼ In. 75.00
Plate, Friday, Sweeping, 1 ⅛ In. 39.00
Plate, Friday, Sweeping, 6 In. 98.00
Plate, Friday, Sweeping, 7¼ In. .... 175.00 to 200.00
Plate, Monday, Washing, 7 ¼ In. 200.00
Plate, Saturday, Baking, 7 ¼ In. 200.00
Plate, Sunday, Fishing, 1 ⅛ In. 39.00
Plate, Sunday, Fishing, 7 ¼ In. 199.00
Plate, Thursday, Scrubbing, 1 ⅛ In. 35.00
Plate, Thursday, Scrubbing, 7 ¼ In. 225.00
Plate, Tuesday, Ironing, 1 ⅛ In. 39.00
Plate, Wednesday, Mending, 1 ⅛ In. 40.00
Plate, Wednesday, Mending, 7 ¼ In. 189.00
Tablecloth, Appliqued, Hand Embroidered, 34 x 34 In. 22.00

SUNDERLAND luster is a name given to a special type of pink luster made by Leeds, Newcastle, and other English firms during the nineteenth century. The luster glaze is metallic and glossy and appears to have bubbles in it. Other pieces of luster are listed in the Luster category.

Bowl, Iron Bridge, Masonic, Script, Northumberland, Elijah Quilter, 12 In. .... *illus* 942.00
Creamer, 4 In. 109.00
Jug, Bridge On Front, Verse On Back, 5 In. 170.00
Jug, Peace & Plenty, Pearlware, Black Transfer, Early 19th Century, 9 In. .... *illus* 575.00
Mug, Ship, Strap Handle, 4 ¾ In. 345.00
Mug, West View Of Cast Iron Bridge At Sunderland, Sailor's Tear Verse, 5 In. 299.00
Pitcher, Black Transfers, Ship, Sailor's Verse, Wreath, 5 ¾ In. 201.00
Pitcher, View Of Iron Bridge Over The Wear, 6 ½ In. 633.00

SUPERMAN was created by two seventeen-year-olds in 1938. The first issue of *Action* comics had the strip. Superman remains popular and became the hero of a radio show in 1940, cartoons in the 1940s, a television series, and several major movies.

Action Figure, Arms & Legs Move, Jointed Knees, D.C., 4 ¾ In. 10.00
Badge, Superman American, Junior Defense League, Brass, 1941, 1 ⅛ In. .... *illus* 86.00
Bank, Dime Register, Superman Breaking Out Of Chains, Tin, 8-Sided, 2 ½ In. 173.00
Carton, Orange Flavored Drink, 2 Qt. 30.00
Cookie Jar, Escaping From Chains, Warner Bros., D.C. Comics, c.1997, 12 x 9 ¼ In. 65.00
Cookie Jar, Superman In Phone Booth, California Originals, c.1978 .... 449.00
Figure, Lead, Warner Bros., Limited Edition, 5 In. 35.00
Figure, Painted Plaster, Carnival, c.1940, 15 In. 288.00
Figure, Porcelain, Vinyl Cape, Box, 10 ½ In. 460.00
Figure, Rubber, Ben Cooper, National Periodical Publications, c.1973, 7 In. 44.00
Game, Board, News Reporting, Box, c.1954 .... 209.00
Milk Cap, Roberts Dairy, Omaha, Neb., No. 10, I Pledge To Keep My Mind & Body Clean. 54.00
Ornament, 50th Anniversary, Action Comics & Hallmark, c.1998, Miniature 16.00
Ornament, Phone Booth, Light & Motion, Hallmark, Box, 1995, 5 ½ In. 30.00
Ornament, Schooldays Lunch Box, Hallmark, 1998 .... 28.00
Pencil, Mechanical, Brass Tip, c.1940, 5 In. 316.00
Pocket Watch, Superman Looking Over Buildings, Glass Bezel, Nickel Plated, 2 In. 316.00
Puzzle, Frame Tray, Golden, 1989, 14 ½ x 11 ½ In. 15.00
Salt & Pepper, Ceramic, Tin Lunch Box Holder, Black, White, Vandor, 6 x 4 In., 3 Piece 20.00
Toy, Plane, Superman Rolls Over Plane, Tin Lithograph, Windup, Marx, 5 ¾ In. 1150.00
Valentine, Mechanical, 1940 .... 95.00
Watch, Metropolis, Daily Planet, Brass Finish, Shield Shape Box 221.00
Wristwatch, Leather Band, Fossil, Man's, c.1993 .... 100.00
Yo-Yo, Faster Than A Speeding Bullet, Duncan, 1978 .... 25.00

SUSIE COOPER began as a designer in 1925 working for the English firm A.E. Gray & Company. In 1932 she formed Susie Cooper Pottery, Ltd. In 1950 it became Susie Cooper China, Ltd., and the company made china and earthenware. In 1966 it was acquired by Josiah Wedgwood & Sons, Ltd. The name Susie Cooper appears with the company names on many pieces of ceramics.

Bell, Flowers, Leaves, Silver Luster, 4 ¼ In. 81.00
Bowl, Vegetable, Wedgwood, Flower Band, 2 ½ x 9 ¾ x 7 ¾ In. 38.00
Casserole, Cover, 5 In. 95.00
Chop Plate, Endon, 8 ¾ In. 38.00
Coffee Set, Glen Mist, 12 Piece 106.00
Creamer, Wedgwood, Flower Band, 2 ¾ In. 20.00
Cup & Saucer, Endon . . . . . *illus* 46.00
Cup & Saucer, Flowers, Pink Interior. 30.00
Dish, Cover, Dusty Rose, Beige Ground, Colorway 21, 1930s 65.00
Jug, Hand Painted, Marked, 5 ¼ In.. . . . . *illus* 73.00
Plate, Art Deco, Flower Spray, 1930s, 10 In. 23.00
Plate, Bread & Butter, Endon, 6 ¾ In. 20.00
Plate, Bread & Butter, Wedgwood, Flower Band, 6 ½ In. 17.00
Plate, Dinner, Wedding Band, Burgundy, Gray, No. 1, 10 In. 21.00
Plate, Dinner, Wedding Band, Gray, Burgundy, No. 2, 10 In. 15.00
Plate, Dinner, Wedgwood, Flower Band, 10 ½ In. 22.00
Plate, Salad, Endon, 8 In. 28.00
Platter, Wedgwood, Flower Band, 13 ¼ x 10 ½ In. 45.00
Saucer, Art Deco, Yellow Swirl, Pink 28.00
Saucer, Corn Poppy 15.00
Soup & Saucer, Endon, Ribbed, Liner, Handles. 68.00
Sugar & Creamer, White 22.00
Tea Set, Art Deco, Red & Gray Bands, Marked, 3 Piece . . . . . *illus* 121.00

SWASTIKA KERAMOS is a line of art pottery made from 1906 to 1908 by the Owen China Company of Minerva, Ohio. Many pieces were made with an iridescent glaze.

Vase, Flower, Gold Iridescent, 7 ¾ In. . . . . *illus* 170.00
Vase, Trees, Clouds, Shades Of Gold, Red Flowers, 3 Buttressed Handles, 7 ¼ In. 529.00

SWORDS of all types that are of interest to collectors are listed here. The military dress sword with elaborate handle is probably the most wanted. A *tsuba* is a hand guard fitted to a Japanese sword between the handle and the blade. Be sure to display swords in a safe way, out of reach of children.

Ceremonial, Cast Brass Hilt, Eagles, Twisted Brass Wire, Sharkskin Handle, 39 In. 200.00
Ceremonial, Diplomat's, Napoleon III, Steel, Gilt Bronze, Mother-Of-Pearl, 35 ¼ In. 1080.00
Ceremonial, Diplomat's, Steel, Gilt Bronze, Mother-Of-Pearl, Prussia, 1800s, 38 In. 1140.00
Cutlass, U.S. Navy, Brass Guard, Leather Scabbard, Mid 19th Century, 31 ½ In. 1840.00
Field Officer's, Brass Guard, Scabbard, Presentation, Capt. George G. Steel, c.1895, 34 In. 489.00
Officer's, England, Lion's Head Pommel, Roped Grip, Leather Sheath, c.1810 . . . . . 650.00
Officer's, U.S. Naval, Brass Guard, Engraved, Early 20th Century, 35 In. 345.00
Parade, U.S. Officer's, Pettibone, Brass Guard, Engraved Blade, 19th Century, 31 ½ In., Pair . 316.00
Presentation, U.S. Officer's, Horstmann & Sons, To Colonel Robert Sewell, c.1864, 32 In. 3680.00
Rapier, Steel, Reed Carved Wood Grip, Straight Quillons, Basket Hilt, Latin Motto, 39 In. 646.00

SYRACUSE is a trademark used by the Onondaga Pottery of Syracuse, New York. The company was established in 1871. It is still working. The name became the Syracuse China Company in 1966. It is known for fine dinnerware and restaurant china.

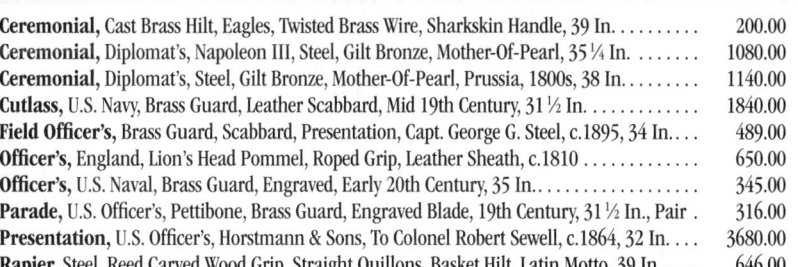

Advertising, Platter, U.S. Army Medical Department, Econo Rim, Oval, 13 ¼ x 10 ⅝ In. 55.00
Artint, Creamer, Econo Rim, Orange, Tan 14.00
Blue Willow, Plate, Bread & Butter, 5 ½ In. 6.00
Cadet, Gravy Boat, Marked, 9 ½ In.. . . . . *illus* 12.00
Captain's Table, Platter, Oval, 13 In. 20.00
Cardinal, Platter, Oval, 11 ⅜ x 9 ¼ In. 20.00
Concord Rose, Bowl, Vegetable, Divided, Oval, 10 In. 24.00
Concord Rose, Cup & Saucer 4.00
Concord Rose, Plate, Bread, 6 ¼ In.. . . . . 4.00
Concord Rose, Plate, Dinner, 10 In.. . . . . 5.00
Concord Rose, Platter, Oval, 12 ½ x 11 ¼ In.. . . . . 9.00
Concord Rose, Saucer, 5 ¾ In. 2.00
Coralbel, Platter, Platinum Trim, 12 In.. . . . . 30.00

Susie Cooper, Cup & Saucer, Endon
$46.00

Susie Cooper, Jug, Hand Painted, Marked, 5 ¼ In.
$73.00

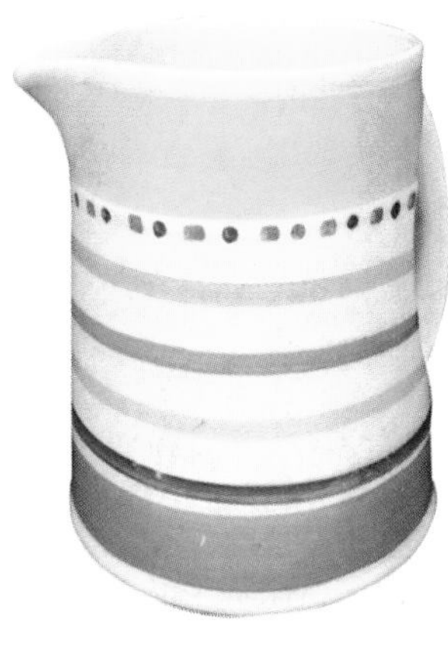

Susie Cooper, Tea Set, Art Deco, Red & Gray Bands, Marked, 3 Piece
$121.00

Swastika Keramos, Vase, Flower, Gold Iridescent, 7 ¾ In.
$170.00

S

Syracuse, Cadet, Gravy Boat, Marked, 9½ In.
$12.00

Syracuse, Wayside, Plate, Salad, 8⅛ In.
$8.00

Tea Caddy, Mahogany, Satinwood, Brass Ball Feet, Regency, Early 19th Century, 6 x 5 x 8 In.
$453.00

Tea Caddy, Porcelain, Flower Medallion, Monogram, Gilt, c.1790, 5 x 3 In.
$225.00

Dogwood, Cup & Saucer, 10-In. Dinner Plate, 3 Piece 15.00
Dogwood, Cup & Saucer, Demitasse 20.00
Harvest Gold, Platter, Oval, 11½ x 10 In. 24.00
Juno, Casserole, Handles, Footed, 12 x 7 In. 25.00
Madame Butterfly, Bowl, Dessert, 1¼ x 5 In. 8.00
Madame Butterfly, Bowl, Vegetable, Oval, 10⅜ In. 50.00
Madame Butterfly, Cup & Saucer 35.00
Madame Butterfly, Plate, Dinner, 9¾ In. 18.00
Madame Butterfly, Platter, 12 In. 35.00
Madame Butterfly, Sugar, Cover, Stamped, 1952, 3⅛ In. 35.00
Mayfair, Plate, Dinner, 9 In. 12.00
Mayfair, Plate, Salad, 8 In. 10.00
Mesa Grande, Plate, Salad, 8¼ In.. .... 3.00
Radcliffe, Bowl, Cover, Federal Shape, Footed, 9 In. 75.00
Strawberry Hill, Mug, Blue, 4 Piece 60.00
Wayside, Plate, Salad, 8⅛ In.. .... *illus* 8.00
Webster, Cup 20.00
Webster, Cup & Saucer, Mustard 28.00
Webster, Plate, Dinner, 9¾ In. 25.00
Webster, Soup, Dish, 8⅞ In. 28.00
Windswept, Bowl, Vegetable, 8 In. 18.00
Windswept, Bowl, Vegetable, Divided, Oval, 9¾ In.. .... 25.00
Windswept, Sugar & Creamer 25.00
Woodbine, Bowl, Vegetable, Divided, Oval, 9¾ In.. .... 26.00
Woodbine, Butter, Brown, Aqua 20.00
Woodbine, Gravy 26.00
Woodridge, Platter, Oval, 1½ x 12½ In. 10.00

TAPESTRY, PORCELAIN, *see Rose Tapestry category.*

TEA CADDY is the name for a small box made to hold tea leaves. In the eighteenth century, tea was very expensive and it was stored under lock and key. The first tea caddies were made with locks. By the nineteenth century, tea was more plentiful and the tea caddy was larger. Often there were two sections, one for green tea, one for black tea.

Burl, Rectangular, Marquetry Border, Seashell, Bone Grips, Silver Bail Handle, 10 In.. .... 2640.00
Burl, Tunbridge, Marquetry Border, 2 Compartments, 5 x 8 In. 510.00
Burl Yew Wood, String Inlay, Drop Handles, Brass Ball Feet, 6 x 13 x 5 In. 517.00
Coromandel, Lock, Marked, England, 1910-20, 6¼ x 12½ In. 695.00
Edwardian, Nickel Edge, Rosewood, 3 Compartments, Regency Style, Suede Cover, 6 x 9¾ In.. 600.00
Elm, Burl, Canted Corners, Patera String Inlay, Star, George III, c.1800, 4 x 5 x 4 In.. .... 780.00
Fruitwood, Apple Shape, Carved Segments, Inset Stem, 5 In.. .... 4313.00
Fruitwood, Apple Shape, Cut Steel, Silver Lining, George III, 4 In. 1998.00
Fruitwood, Pear Shape, Hinged Lid, Metal Lock Plate, George III, 6¾ In. 1955.00
Fruitwood, Turned, Apple Shape, Varnish, 4¼ x 3¾ In.. .... 660.00
Hardwood Inlay, Dome Lid, Oval Medallions, Recesses, 6⅛ x 8 x 4¾ In.. .... 2530.00
Lacquer, Black, Gilt Floral Sprays, Scroll Border, Chinese, 6 x 11 x 8 In. 1140.00
Lacquer, Black, Gilt Mandarin Garden Decoration, 2 Compartments, 4 x 9 x 4½ In.. .... 1140.00
Lacquer, Black, Gilt Mandarin Garden Decoration, Octagonal, Winged Paw Feet, 9 x 6 In.... 960.00
Lacquer, Black, Hinged Lid, 2 Compartments, Dragon-Headed Feet, Chinese, 6 x 10 x 7 In. .. 633.00
Lacquer, Black, Pewter Sections, Gilded, 4 x 8¼ x 6¼ In. 1200.00
Lacquer, Maroon, Hinged Lid, 2 Compartments, Metal Mounted, France, 4¾ x 8 x 4 In.. .... 3220.00
Lacquer, Maroon, Hinged Lid, Boat Shape, Gilt Flower Heads, 4-Footed, 7 x 5¼ x 3½ In.. .... 748.00
Lacquer, Maroon, Hinged Lid, Quatrefoil, Dragon-Headed Feet, Chinese, 4¾ x 7½ In. 2070.00
Lacquer, Octagonal, Figures, Chinese, 4½ x 7¾ In. 764.00
Lacquer, Rectangular, Black & Gold, Canted Corners, Carved Feet, Pewter Inserts, 9 In. 1508.00
Lacquer, Tin, Bird In Tree, 5 In. 150.00
Lacquer, Black, Chinese Pavilions, 2 Colors, Gilded, Green Accent, 7 x 9 In. 2040.00
Lacquer, Black, Gilt Dragon's Head Feet, 5 x 9 x 7 In. 1715.00
Lacquer, Black, Mandarin's Garden, Gilded, Pewter Inserts, 8 x 5½ In. 660.00
Lid, Porcelain, Blue & White, New Castle Upon Tyne, 19th Century, 8 In.. .... 176.00
Mahogany, 3 Compartments, Banded, Sarcophagus Shape, Georgian, 7½ x 13 In. 850.00
Mahogany, 3 Sections, Brass Applied Feet, Handle, Chippendale, c.1775, 7 x 10 x 5½ In. 420.00
Mahogany, Brass Bail Handle, Escutcheon, George III, 6 x 3 x 4 In. 632.00
Mahogany, Brass Ogee, Ebony Lined, Chippendale, c.1775, 7 x 10 x 5 In. 375.00
Mahogany, Burl Veneer, Coffin Shape, Inlaid Parquetry, 2 Sections, 1800, 6 x 12 x 8 In. 840.00

ahogany, Carved, Brass, Handles, Bowl Well, George VI, 6 x 15 In. 480.00
ahogany, Coffin Shape, Inlaid Corner, Beveled, Brass Escutcheon, c.1820, 6 x 11 In. 644.00
ahogany, Concave Lid, England, 19th Century, 4¾ x 5 x 3½ In. 264.00
ahogany, Curly, Hinged Lid, Coffin Shape, 3 Compartments, Handles, Ball Feet, 6 x 13 x 5 In. 518.00
ahogany, Ebony, Satinwood Inlay, Crossbanded Front, Top, England, 5 x 9 x 5 In. 316.00
ahogany, Hinged Lid, Molded Top, Bracket Base, Chippendale, 1700s, 6 x 9 x 5 In. 360.00
ahogany, Inlaid, 3 Tin Lidded Interior Compartments, Bracket Feet, 7¾ x 11½ In. 1035.00
ahogany, Inlaid, Bracket Feet, Blob Top 1035.00
ahogany, Inlaid, Hinged Lid, Bird, Shield Escutcheon, c.1800, 5 x 5¼ x 5 In. 403.00
ahogany, Inlaid Shell Lid, Georgian, 7¼ x 4½ In. 705.00
ahogany, Lift Lid, Molded Edge, Rococo Brass Bail Handle, 5½ x 9½ x 5½ In. 575.00
ahogany, Marquetry Inlay, Hinged Lid, 3 Cans, George III Style, 7 x 10¼ x 6½ In. 3105.00
ahogany, Satinwood, Brass Ball Feet, 2 Compartments, 5 x 5 x 8 In. 412.00
ahogany, Satinwood, Brass Ball Feet, Regency, Early 19th Century, 6 x 5 x 8 In. ...... *illus* 453.00
ahogany, Satinwood, Regency, England, c.1830, 5¼ x 7¼ x 4¼ In. 529.00
ahogany, Tin Inserts, Velvet Ling, Bail Handle, Regency, c.1800, 5½ x 13 In. 345.00
ahogany, White Pine, Brass Feet, Laurel Wreath, Chippendale, c.1770, 7 x 9 x 6 In. 550.00
ahogany, Wood Inlay, Geometric Design, England, c.1810, 5½ x 8 In. 1053.00
ahogany Veneer, Banded Inlay, Pine, Ivory Escutcheon, Brass Handle, 10 x 5½ In. 374.00
ahogany Veneer, Flame Graining, Lid, Chevron Inlay, 2 Compartments, 1800s, 12 x 6 In. . 489.00
aple, Curly, Oval, Inlaid Blossom, Engraved Details, Flower Garland, 4¾ x 5⅝ In. 1175.00
ulticolored Enamels, Puce Diapering, 11½ x 14 In. 219.00
ak, Silvered Brass Mounted, Sarcophagus Shape, Victorian, 5 x 7 In. 588.00
apier-Mache, Gilt, Mother-Of-Pearl, Black Lacquer, Flowers, c.1850, 4 x 9 In. 411.00
ear Shape, Silver Foil Lined, Key Hole Escutcheon, England, 1800s, 6 x 5 In. 3190.00
ewter, Oval, Scalloped Sides, Oval Knob Finial, F & C, Britannia, 4¾ x 5 x 3½ In. 2610.00
ewter, Oval, Shield, Floral Bands, Domed Lid, Urn Finial, 4⅜ x 4½ x 3 In. 2436.00
orcelain, Blue & White, Quail, Grasshopper, Peonies, Gilt, Chinese Export, 1800s, 5 In. 259.00
orcelain, Hexagonal, Blue, White, 5 Gilin, Artemisia Leaf Mark, c.1900, 6 x 5 In. 374.00
orcelain, Blue & White, Riverscape, Ribs, c.1820, 4½ In., Pair 384.00
orcelain, Flower Medallion, Monogram, Gilt, c.1790, 5 x 3 In. .... *illus* 225.00
osewood, 4 Lined Compartments, Hinged Lids, Cut Glass Canisters, 10 x 20 In. 489.00
osewood, Brass Inlay, Coffin Shape, 7¾ x 13 x 7 In. .... *illus* 200.00
osewood, Marquetry, Inlaid Instruments & Bowl Of Fruit, Restauration, 8 x 5 In. 840.00
osewood, Satinwood, Victorian, c.1850, 3 x 8¼ x 6 In. 147.00
atinwood, Patera Inlay, Oval, 5½ x 8 x 4½ In. 862.00
ilver, Cylindrical Lid, Chased, Embossed, Grotesque Scrolls, c.1891, 5¾ In. 294.00
ilver, Decanter Shape, 5-Sided, Flattened Top, 4⅝ x 3¼ In. 234.00
ortoiseshell, Blond, Bone Inlay, 2 Compartments, Bombe, 4 Silver Ball Feet, 6 x 8 x 4 In. .. 4080.00
ortoiseshell, Carved Fluted Sunburst, Silver & Rose Brass Finial & Ball Feet, 7 x 7 In. 5760.00
ortoiseshell, Chocolate, Rectangular, Serpentine Front, Caramel Ivory Bun Feet, 4 x 5 In.. 3600.00
ortoiseshell, Dome Lid, Borders, Molding, Silver Wire, 2 Interior Compartments, 5½ x 7 In. 1265.00
ortoiseshell, Honey Tone, Silver Wire Inlay, Brass Ball Feet, Lidded Compartments, 4½ x 9¾ In.. 1495.00
ortoiseshell, Serpentine, Ivory Interior, Regency, Monogram, c.1820, 4 x 5½ In. 2128.00
ortoiseshell Veneer, Ivory, Double, c.1800, 5½ x 8¼ x 5 In. 2468.00
ortoiseshell Veneer, Ivory, Knob Finial, 18th Century, 5¾ x 5 x 3¾ In. 2468.00
ortoiseshell Veneer, Sunburst Fluting Panel, Silver Fillets, Ivory, Regency, 7½ x 5 In...... 1880.00
alnut, Burl, Coffin Shape, Fitted Interior, Crystal Jar, Georgian Style, 7½ x 12 In. 443.00
ood, Marquetry, Checkerboard Pattern, 3 Compartments, Rectangular, Oval Handle, 6 x 12 x 6 In. 720.00
ood, Marquetry, Flower Garlands, Bone Escutcheon, Oval, 6 x 3¼ In. 2400.00
ood, Marquetry, Penwork, Flower Sprays, Teardrop Escutcheon, Oval, Paktong, 5 x 6 In.... 780.00
ood, Quillwork, Tin Liner, Regency, Early 19th Century, 7½ In. .... *illus* 2415.00
ood, Veneer, Hinged Lid, Inlaid Shells, Compartments, 5 x 7¼ x 4⅜ In. 1135.00

EA LEAF IRONSTONE dishes are named for their decorations. There was a superstition that was lucky if a whole tea leaf unfolded at the bottom of your cup. This idea was translated to the pattern of dishes known as "tea leaf." By 1850 at least twelve English factories were aking this pattern, and by the 1870s it was a popular pattern in many countries. The tea leaf as always a luster glaze on early wares, although now some pieces are made with a brown tea leaf. There e many variations of tea leaf designs, such as Teaberry, Pepper Leaf, and Gold Leaf. The designs were sed on many different white ironstone shapes, such as Bamboo, Lily of the Valley, Empress, and Cumbow.

aker, Chelsea, Johnson Bros. 45.00
owl, Square, 8½ x 8½ In. 40.00
owl, Vegetable, Cover, Bamboo, 7 x 9½ x 3½ In. .... *illus* 25.00
owl, Vegetable, Cover, Sunburst, Wilkinson 55.00

1876
The Colonial Revival started with the patriotism kindled by the 1876 Centennial Exhibition in Philadelphia. The old styles popular in the days of George Washington represented the security and standards of the founders of the country.

Tea Caddy, Rosewood, Brass Inlay, Coffin Shape, 7¾ x 13 x 7 In.
$200.00

Tea Caddy, Wood, Quillwork, Tin Liner, Regency, Early 19th Century, 7½ In.
$2415.00

TIP
To clean tortoiseshell, rub it with a mixture of jeweler's rouge and olive oil.

T

TEA LEAF IRONSTONE

Tea Leaf Ironstone, Bowl, Vegetable, Cover, Bamboo, 7 x 9½ x 3½ In.
$25.00

Tea Leaf Ironstone, Pitcher, Shaw, 6⅜ In.
$100.00

Tea Leaf Ironstone, Sugar, Cover, Shaw, A.J. Wilkinson
$20.00

Teco, Vase, 4 Buttressed Handles, Impressed, 9 In.
$2900.00

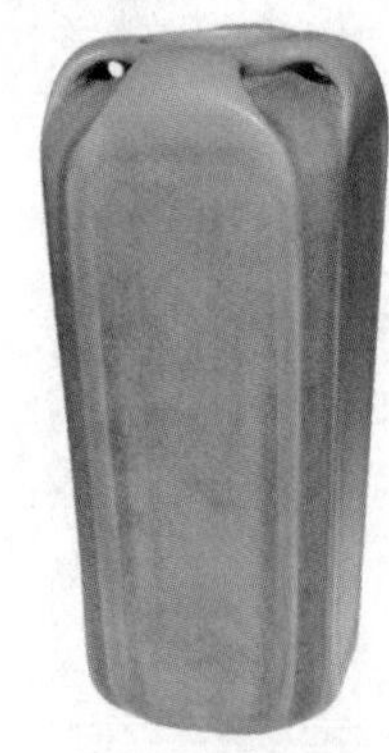

T

Bowl, Vegetable, Cover, Peerless, Edwards 100.00
Brush Box, Lily Of The Valley, Shaw 550.00
Butter, Bamboo, Grindley, 3 Piece 50.00
Butter Chip 12.00
Cake Plate, Daisy 'N Chain, Wilkinson 170.00
Cake Plate, Empress, Adams 160.00
Casserole, Cover 100.00
Chamber Pot, Cable, Shaw 80.00
Coffeepot, Favorite, Grindley 120.00
Creamer, Bamboo, Meakin 45.00
Creamer, Basket Weave, Shaw 290.00
Creamer, Blanket Stitch, Alcock 150.00
Cup & Saucer, Daisy 'N Chain, Wilkinson 40.00
Cup & Saucer, Scroll, Walley 50.00
Dish, Pickle, Rosetta, Johnson Bros. 220.00
Eggcup, Empress, Adams 160.00
Ewer, Hawthorn, Wilkinson 145.00
Gravy Boat, Dangling Tulips, John Farrell 270.00
Gravy Boat, Empress, Adams 80.00
Mug, Hanging Leaves, Sayres 90.00
Nappy, Fishhook, Meakin, 4 Piece 25.00
Pitcher, Lenoir 15.00
Pitcher, Maidenhair Fern, Wilkinson 70.00
Pitcher, Moss Rose, Fishhook, Meakin 150.00
Pitcher, Niagara Fan, Shaw 280.00
Pitcher, Shaw, 6⅜ In. .... *illus* 100.00
Plate, 9¾ In. 25.00
Plate, Bread, 6¾ In. 30.00
Plate, Meakin, 8½ In., 6 Piece 40.00
Plate, Salad, 8 In. 100.00
Platter, 14 In. 65.00
Platter, Oval, Wilkinson 25.00
Platter, Scalloped, 12 In. 40.00
Salad, 9 In. 30.00
Sauceboat, 8⅛ In. 100.00
Shaving Mug, Sonata, Shaw 1100.00
Soap, Dish 25.00
Soap, Dish, Bamboo, Meakin, 3 Piece 90.00
Soup, Dish, Cover, Strainer 125.00
Sugar, Cover, Shaw, A.J. Wilkinson .... *illus* 20.00
Sugar & Creamer, Fishhook, Meakin 100.00
Teapot, Bamboo 100.00
Teapot, Bamboo, Meakin 75.00
Teapot, Ginger Jar, Thos. Elsmore 60.00
Toothbrush Holder 70.00

TECO is the mark used on the art pottery line made by the American Terra Cotta and Ceramic Company of Terra Cotta and Chicago, Illinois. The company was an offshoot of the firm founded by William D. Gates in 1881. The Teco line was first made in 1885 but was not sold commercially until 1902. It continued in production until 1922. Over 500 designs were made in a variety of colors, shapes, and glazes. The company closed in 1930.

Bowl, Bulbous, Green Matte Glaze, Charcoal Highlights, 2½ x 8½ In. 1080.0
Bowl, Flat, Fruiting Wreath, Green Matte Glaze, 2¼ x 9½ In. 840.0
Bowl, Green Matte Glaze, 9 x 2 In. 600.0
Bowl, Rolled Out Rim, Green Matte Glaze, Charcoal Highlights, William Gates, 2⅜ x 6⅜ In. 382.0
Chamberstick, Angular Handles, Green Matte Glaze, Gray Highlights, 2¼ x 5 In., Pair 585.0
Lamp Base, Buttressed Handles, Green Matte Glaze, Double Gourd, 13¼ x 10½ In. 4200.0
Planter, No. 506, Green Matte Glaze, Applied Design, 12 x 21 In. 1800.0
Vase, 3 Buttressed Handles, Green Matte Glaze, Charcoal Highlights, 15⅞ In. 5875.0
Vase, 4 Buttressed Handles, Green Matte Glaze, Charcoal Highlights, 2½ x 6½ In. 1610.0
Vase, 4 Buttressed Handles, Green Matte Glaze, Charcoal Highlights, 7¼ In. 1116.0
Vase, 4 Buttressed Handles, Green Matte Glaze, Impressed Mark, Gates, 5¾ x 3 In. 1200.0
Vase, 4 Buttressed Handles, Impressed, 9 In. .... *illus* 2900.0
Vase, 4 Buttressed Handles Loop Out Of Body & Reconnect At Rim, 9 In. 3422.0
Vase, 4 Footed, Floral, Ultramarine Matte Glaze, Stamped, 18½ x 7½ In. 7800.0

Vase, 4 Handles, Gourd Shape, Green Matte Glaze . . . 2587.00
Vase, Aventurine, Marked, 15 x 6½ In. . . . 3900.00
Vase, Beaker Shape, 4 Buttressed Handles, Green Matte Glaze, Stamped, 7¾ x 6 In. . . . 3600.00
Vase, Bulbous, Flared, Tapered Concave Neck, Green Matte Glaze, Silver Highlights, 4¼ In. . . 353.00
Vase, Buttressed Handles, Bottle Shape, Green Matte Glaze, 9¼ x 4 In. . . . 1560.00
Vase, Columbine, Leaves, Molded, Green Matte Glaze, Silver Luster, Flared Rim, 8 In. . . . 264.00
Vase, Folded Leaves, Green Matte Glaze, Stamped, 11½ x 4½ In. . . . 9600.00
Vase, Gourd Shape, Green Matte Glaze, Stamped, 10 x 7 In. . . . 3900.00
Vase, Green Matte Glaze, Bulbous, 9½ x 4¾ In. . . . 1560.00
Vase, Handle, Bulbous, Green Matte Glaze, 5 x 4 In. . . . 540.00
Vase, No. 50, Bulbous, Long Neck, Green Matte Glaze, 4½ x 5½ In. . . . 660.00
Vase, No. 52, Squat, Green Matte Glaze, 4½ x 4½ In. . . . 720.00
Vase, No. 60 A, Mottled Blue & Gray Glaze, 4 x 8½ In. . . . 720.00
Vase, No. 64 B, Blue Matte Glaze, 4½ x 11 In. . . . 900.00
Vase, No. 78, Footed, Green Matte Glaze, No. 78, 5 x 3 In. . . . 600.00
Vase, No. 89, Green Matte Glaze, Charcoal Highlights, 5 x 12 In. . . . 1680.00
Vase, No. 151, Folded Leaves & Buds, Green Matte, 5½ x 11 In. . . . 10200.00
Vase, No. 182, Organic, Green Matte, 8 x 16½ In. . . . 4800.00
Vase, No. 184, Tapered, 4-Sided, Green Matte Glaze, 4 x 9 In. . . . 2520.00
Vase, No. 252, Cream Glaze, 6½ x 11¾ In. . . . 2160.00
Vase, No. 283, Cream Glaze, 2 Handles, 5 x 9 In. . . . 1080.00
Vase, No. 284, Green Matte Glaze, Charcoal Highlights, 5 x 11 In. . . . 3360.00
Vase, No. 297, 2 Handles, Mottled Green Glaze, 8½ x 5½ In., Pair . . . 1680.00
Vase, No. 363, Green Matte Glaze, 4 x 5 In. . . . 780.00
Vase, No. 418, 4 Handles, Green Matte Glaze, Charcoal Highlights, 6½ x 11 In. . . . 9600.00
Vase, No. 429, Cream Glaze, 4 x 9 In. . . . 660.00
Vase, Reticulated Handles, Leaves, Flaring Neck, Green Matte Glaze, 11½ x 4¼ In. . . . 12000.00
Vase, Shouldered, Green Matte Glaze, W.D. Gates, 4 x 4½ In. . . . 316.00
Vase, Tall Gourd Shape, Green Matte Glaze, Stamped, 16¾ x 8 In. . . . 3900.00
Vase, Tulip Shape, Green Matte Glaze, Stamped, 12½ x 6 In. . . . 6000.00
Wall Pocket, No. 443, Geometric, Green Matte Glaze, 6½ x 6½ In., Pair . . . 1440.00

TEDDY BEARS were named for a president of the United States. The first teddy bear was a cuddly toy said to be inspired by a hunting trip made by Teddy Roosevelt in 1902. Morris and Rose Michtom started selling their stuffed bears as "teddy bears" and the name stayed. The Michtoms founded the Ideal Novelty and Toy Company. The German version of the teddy bear was made about the same time by the Steiff Company. There are many types of teddy bears and all are collected. The old ones are being reproduced. Other bears are listed in the Toy section.

Growler, Mohair, Blond, Glass Eyes, Leather Pads, Germany, Early 20th Century, 11 In. . . . 200.00
Hermann Co., Growler, Mohair, Gold, Jointed, Glass Eyes, Swivel Head, 1930s, 12 In. . . . 175.00
Ideal, Mohair, Gold, Glass Eyes, Jointed, Hump, 1910, 20 In. . . . 470.00
Ideal, Mohair, Gold, Straw Stuffed, Swivel Head, Glass Eyes, 1920s, 23 In. . . . 175.00
Merrythought, Golden, Jointed, 18 In. . . . *illus* 29.00
Mohair, Floss Nose, Jointed, Shoebutton Eyes, Felt Pads, 20th Century, 20 In. . . . 77.00
Mohair, Gold, Football Shaped Body, Hump, Jointed, Glass Eyes, 1910, 20 In. . . . 470.00
Mohair, Gold, Swivel Joints, Shaved Muzzle, Button Eyes, Excelsior Stuffed, 23 In. . . . 2938.00
Mohair, White, Stitched Nose, Mouth, Glass Eyes, Felt Pads, Ribbon, 1900s, 15 In. . . . 220.00
Roosevelt, Laughing, Mohair, Gold, Glass Eyes, Teeth, Squeeze Stomach, 1908, 20 In. . . . 2235.00
Slight Hump, Jointed Arms, Legs, Glass Eyes, Early 20th Century, 21½ In. . . . 345.00
Steiff, Apricot, Shoebutton Eyes, Pewter Ear Button, Swivel Neck, Pre 1940, 14 In. . . . 2520.00
Steiff, Beige, Shoebutton Eyes, Black Stitched Nose, Mouth, Pre 1940, 12 In. . . . 978.00
Steiff, Beige, Swivel Neck, Black Stitched Nose, Mouth, Shoebutton Eyes, Pre 1940, 12 In. . . . 2300.00
Steiff, Mohair, Apricot, 1906-10, 45 In. . . . 35460.00
Steiff, Mohair, Jointed, Stitched Nose, Mouth, Shoebutton Eyes, Button In Ear, c.1910, 17 In. . . *illus* 5000.00
Steiff, Mohair, Blank Ear Buttons, c.1905 . . . 1725.00
Steiff, Mohair, Blond, Button Eyes, Embroidered Nose, Mouth, Claws, 16 In. . . . 3525.00
Steiff, Mohair, Blond, Embroidered, Jointed, Button Eyes, Button In Ear, c.1907, 14 In. . . *illus* 3450.00
Steiff, Mohair, Cinnamon, Embroidered Nose, Mouth, Claws, Button Eyes, 16 In. . . . 5288.00
Steiff, Mohair, Cinnamon, Embroidered Nose, Mouth, Claws, Excelsior Stuffed, 9½ In. . . . 2350.00
Steiff, Mohair, Dark Golden, Embroidered Nose, Mouth, Claws, c.1920, 9 In. . . . 2350.00
Steiff, Mohair, Stitched Mouth, Nose, Claws, Shoebutton Eyes, Bowtie, c.1907, 15 In. . . . 1840.00
Steiff, Mohair, White, Stitched Mouth, Nose, Paw Pads, Button In Ear, c.1907, 16 In. . . . 3162.00
White, Stitched Nose, Mouth & Paws, Jointed, Swivel Head, Glass Eyes, c.1930, 16 In. . . . 840.00
Wool, Floss Nose, Shoebutton Eyes, Felt Pad, Stuffed With Shavings, Fully Jointed, 15 In. . . . 100.00

Stuffed Teddy Bears
Early teddy bears were stuffed with straw, kapok, or excelsior. Modern bears have polyester stuffing and nylon or plastic parts.

Teddy Bear, Merrythought, Golden, Jointed, 18 In.
$29.00

Teddy Bear, Steiff, Mohair, Jointed, Stitched Nose, Mouth, Shoebutton Eyes, Button In Ear, c.1910, 17 In.
$5000.00

Teddy Bear, Steiff, Mohair, Blond, Embroidered, Jointed, Button Eyes, Button In Ear, c.1907, 14 In.
$3450.00

T

Telephone, Bakelite, Ivory, No. 164-50.
$369.00

Telephone, Deckert & Homolka, No. 11430, Budapest, Hungary, c.1905
$5141.00

Telephone, Grammont, Type 10, No. 15077, Wood, Stone, France, c.1917
$1085.00

Telephone, Kellogg, Wall, Oak, Ringer, c.1900, 10 ½ In.
$94.00

TELEPHONES are wanted by collectors if the phones are old enough or unusual enough. The first telephone may have been made in Havana, Cuba, in 1849, but it was not patented. The first publicly demonstrated phone was used in Frankfurt, Germany, in 1860. The phone made by Alexander Graham Bell was shown at the Centennial Exhibition in Philadelphia in 1876, but it was not until 1877 that the first private phones were installed. Collectors today want all types of old phones, phone parts, and advertising. Even recent figural phones are popular.

Bakelite, Ivory, No. 164-50. . . . . *illus* 369.00
Deckert & Homolka, No. 11430, Budapest, Hungary, c.1905. . . . . *illus* 5141.00
Donut, Oak Bell Box, Western Electric, 9 x 6 ½ In. . . . . 358.00 to 485.00
Elektrisk Bureau, Tin Lithograph Case, Cast Iron Base, Decorated, Norway, 1897 . . . . . 1552.00
Grammer, Oak, Horn, 48 In. 737.00
Grammont, Type 10, No. 15077, Wood, Stone, France, c.1917 . . . . . *illus* 1085.00
Henry Dreyfuss Model No. 302, Bakelite & Metal, c.1937, 5 ½ In. 2850.00
Kellogg, Wall, Oak, Ringer, c.1900, 10 ½ In. . . . . *illus* 94.00
L.M. Ericsson, Desk Type, 13 Connection Clamps, Lighting Conductor, c.1910. . . . . 585.00
L.M. Ericsson, Desk Type, Rigid Mouthpiece, Spoon Shape Hearing Device 1003.00
Sign, Bell System Connections, Public Telephone, 2-Sided, Flange, c.1925, 18 x 20 In. 170.00
Signal Box, Police, Auxiliary, Oak Case, Gamewell, 15 x 11 In. 1650.00
Stromberg Carlson, No. 1224, Black, Rotary Dial, c.1940. . . . . 45.00
Wall, Conical Grip Handset, Battery Case, Royal Coat Of Arms, c.1920. . . . . 502.00
Western Electric, Wall, No. 1317-P, Oak Case, 1895, 20 In. 565.00

TEPLITZ refers to art pottery manufactured by a number of companies in the Teplitz-Turn area of Bohemia during the late nineteenth and early twentieth centuries. Two of these companies were the Alexandra Works and the Amphora Porcelain Works, run by Reissner, Stellmacher, and Kessel. Ernst Wahliss, connected with the RS & K wares, started his own factory after 1900.

Basket, Hydrangeas, Leaf & Vine, Amphora, Signed, 7 In. 77.00
Ewer, Bird Head, Multicolored, Incised, Amphora, 10 ¼ In. . . . . *illus* 170.00
Ewer, Peacock Head Rim, Incised Wings, Blue Slip, Tail Handle, Amphora, 10 In. 200.00
Pitcher, Applied Fruit & Leaves, Green Matte Luster, Amphora, 11 ½ In. . . . . *illus* 200.00
Vase, Applied Grape Decoration, Basket Shape, 2 Handles, Amphora, 10 x 13 ½ In. 1380.00
Vase, Applied Pinecones, Maroon Matte Ground, Tapered, Swollen Rim, Amphora, 15 In. 588.00
Vase, Bird & Flower, 4 Handles, Gilt, Impressed, Amphora, 7 x 9 ½ In. . . . . *illus* 150.00
Vase, Brown, Green & Blue Matte, Organic, Handle, Amphora, 5 ½ x 6 ½ In. 720.00
Vase, Embossed Leaves, Faux Jewels, Gold Trim, Flattened Rim, Amphora, 10 ½ In. 236.00
Vase, Fairy Tale Princess, Urn Form, Gilt Handles, Ball Feet, Amphora, c.1905, 10 In. 5700.00
Vase, Forest, Tree Trunks, Flowers, Lavender, Tan, Gold Trim, Tapered, Amphora, 6 In. 264.00
Vase, Lotus Leaves Under Arched Handles, Gold, Green, Swollen Rim, Amphora, 6 In. 529.00
Vase, Organic Shape, 3 Twisting Handles, Amphora, 3 ½ x 6 In. 720.00
Vase, Painted, Female Portrait, Tapered, Signed, Amphora, 4 x 9 In. 5175.00
Vase, Poppies, Fired-On Gold, Reissner & Kessel Amphora, 5 ¾ In. 141.00
Vase, Portrait Of Woman, Chrysanthemums In Hair, Double Gourd, Amphora, 3 x 5 In. 670.00
Vase, Portrait Of Woman, Double Gourd, Amphora, 4 ½ x 6 In. 1080.00
Vase, Round, Green Mottled, Red Iridescent Glaze, Raised Panels, Amphora, 1900s, 6 ¾ In. . . 1035.00
Vase, Tree Trunks, Opalescent Leaves, Red Berries, Paul Dachsel, 6 In. 764.00
Vase, Woman, Painted, Tapered, Signed, Amphora, 9 x 4 In. . . . . *illus* 5400.00
Vase, Woman, Water, Sunset, Signed, Turn Teplitz Bohemia, 8 x 4 In. . . . . *illus* 6600.00

TERRA-COTTA is a special type of pottery. It ranges from pale orange to dark reddish-brown in color. The color comes from the clay, which is fired but not always glazed in the finished piece.

Bowl, Studio Pottery, Textured, Green Glaze Interior, Irregular Shape, 6 x 6 In. 160.00
Bust, Dorine, Maid Of Orleans, Waisted Round Socle, Leopold Harze, c.1880, 20 ¼ In. 764.00
Bust, Smiling Chinese Man, Chin-Fan Han Yang, Susse Frers, Early 1900s, 9 In. 374.00
Casserole, Lid, Underplate, Rabbits, Cabbage, 6 x 9 In., 3 Piece . . . . . *illus* 415.00
Cassoulet, French Provincial, Gloss Burnt Orange Interior Glaze, 1900s, 8 x 14 ½ In. 390.00
Crock, Cover, Yellow Glaze, Circular, 2 Handles, 13 In x 12 In. 363.00
Figurine, Camel, Burial, Turned Head, Open Mouth, Chinese, 17 ¼ x 13 ½ In. 2160.00
Figurine, Camel, Kneeling, Burial Encrustation, Unglazed, Chinese, 3 ¾ x 5 ½ In. 612.00
Figurine, Camel, Kneeling, Incised Details, Chinese, 2 ¼ x 3 ¾ In. 360.00
Figurine, Camel, Standing, Tang Style, Maroon, Orange, Chinese, 23 ½ In. 502.00
Figurine, Chick & Cracked Egg, Green, Yellow, Majolica Style, Incised, 390, 3 ¼ In. 66.00

Teplitz, Ewer, Bird Head, Multicolored, Incised, Amphora, 10¼ In.
$170.00

Teplitz, Pitcher, Applied Fruit & Leaves, Green Matte Luster, Amphora, 11½ In.
$200.00

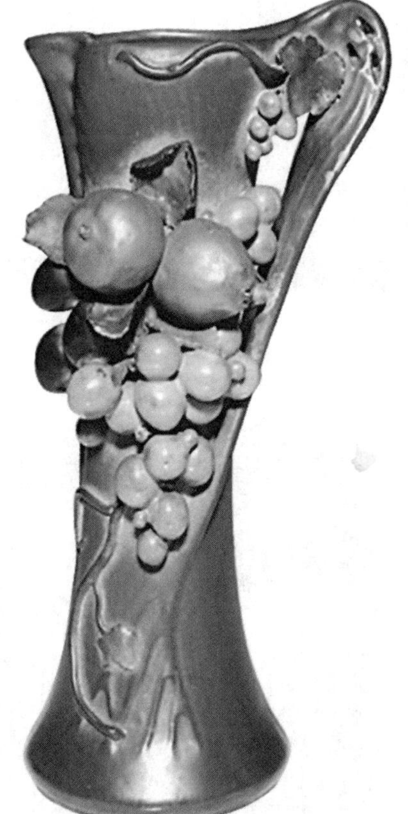

Teplitz, Vase, Bird & Flower, 4 Handles, Gilt, Impressed, Amphora, 7 x 9½ In.
$150.00

Teplitz, Vase, Woman, Painted, Tapered, Signed, Amphora, 9 x 4 In.
$5400.00

Teplitz, Vase, Woman, Water, Sunset, Signed, Turn Teplitz Bohemia, 8 x 4 In.
$6600.00

Terra-Cotta, Casserole, Lid, Underplate, Rabbits, Cabbage, 6 x 9 In., 3 Piece
$415.00

Textile, Bell Pull, Red, Ocher, Embossed, Gilt, Lacquer, Brass, Stenciled, England, c.1890, 38 In.
$110.00

Textile, Fabric, Taliesin Line, 6 Samples, Marked, Frank Lloyd Wright, 44 x 22 In.
$640.00

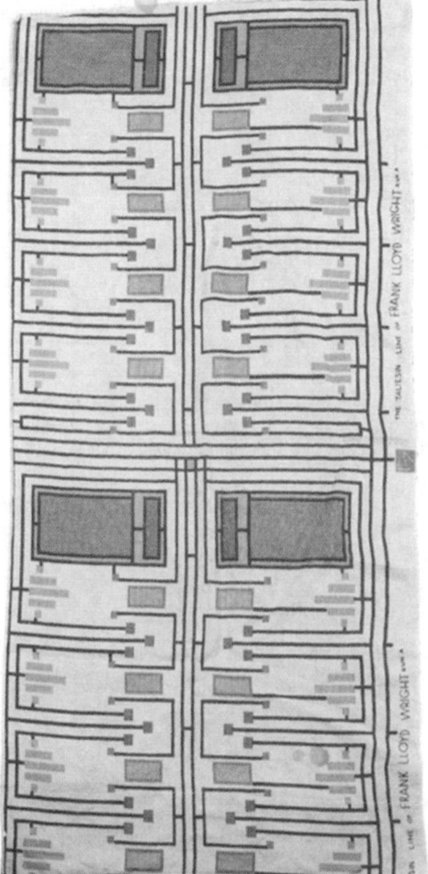

Textile, Needlework, Boats, Arts & Crafts Frame, 11 x 6 In.
$720.00

Textile, Needlework, Dog, On Pillow, Frame, 17 x 23 In.
$990.00

Textile, Needlework, Sailor's Farewell, Silk, Chinese, Late 19th Century, 10½ x 20½ In.
$2300.00

'igurine, Deity, 5 Leaf Crown, Collar, Long Sanghati, Cambodia, 20th Century, 21 x 27 In. . . 173.00
'igurine, Dog, Standing, Han Style, Brown, Red, Chinese, 24¾ In. . . . 354.00
'igurine, Female Sphinxes, Plaster Pedestals, France, 19th Century, 65 x 38 x 18 In. . . . 7500.00
'igurine, Flower Sellers, Multicolored, Late 19th Century, 22½ x 6½ In., Pair . . . 2938.00
'igurine, Groom, Burial, Tunic, Boots, Cap, Chinese, 12 In. . . . 300.00
'igurine, Head Of Alexander, Wood Base, 19th Century, 11 In. . . . 480.00
'igurine, Loka Pala, Burial, Posed On Bullock, Full Armor, Helmet, Chinese, 19½ In. . . . 1080.00
'igurine, Man Playing Accordion, Sitting, c.1927, 24¾ x 13½ x 13 In. . . . 19200.00
'igurine, Musician With Drum, Domed Hat, Degraded Glaze, Chinese, 14½ x 11 In. . . . 1140.00
'igurine, Musician With Horn, Domed Hat, Degraded Glaze, Chinese, 13¾ x 11 In. . . . 1140.00
'igurine, Student, Beer Stein, Pipe, Marked J.M., 6987, 7½ In. . . . 604.00
'igurine, Tomb Guardian, Burial, Tunic, Armor, Helmet, Black, Red Paint, Chinese, 25 In. . . 2040.00
'igurine, Warrior, Armor, Helmet, Raised Hand, Shield, Breastplate, Chinese, 21½ In. . . . 6300.00
'igurine, Woman, Carrying Jug, Infant, Louis-Charles Leve, France, 1828-88, 25 In. . . . 1872.00
'ountainhead, Sea Nymph, Cattail Crown, Holding Stylized Dolphin, Mouth Spout, 36 In. . . 5280.00
'arden Seat, Tasseled, Upholstered Look, Pink, White, Italy, 15 In. . . . 159.00
ar, Storage, Provincial, Old Ivory, Glazed Buff, France, 13½ In. . . . 420.00
ar, Storage, Provincial, Old Ivory, Glazed Buff, France, 15 In. . . . 420.00
ar, Storage, Rounded Lip, 4 Handles, Applied Rope Swag, 40 x 24 In. . . . 2880.00
ar, Storage, Rounded Lip, Ocher Glaze, Oval, 34 x 23 In. . . . 2880.00
ardiniere, Dragon In Cloud, 19th Century, 11 x 15 In. . . . 330.00
Aixing Bowl, Partially Glazed, 2 Handles, Lip, 19th Century, 9 x 20 In. . . . 858.00
'live Jar, Provincial, Unglazed Bulbous Body, Footed Base, 20½ x 17 In. . . . 582.00
'itcher, Pillow Shape, c.1978, 17¼ In. . . . 9000.00
'lanter, Liberty, Circular, Architectural, Column Base, 14 x 31½ In. . . . 780.00
'laque, Beaux Arts Revival Style, Heraldic Crest, Round Rim, 24 x 24 In. . . . 900.00
'laque, Della Robbia Style, Madonna & Child, Gold Mosaic, Fruit Border, 40 x 12 In. . . . 2875.00
'laque, Troubadour Style, Polychrome Glaze, Vertical, Shield, c.1875, 21 x 16 In. . . . 1800.00
'obacco Jar, Boy On Log, Marked J.M., 3355, 8 In. . . . 507.00
'obacco Jar, Elephant, Marked, 7¾ In. . . . 150.00
'obacco Jar, Fat Man, Marked J.M., 6¼ In. . . . 604.00
'obacco Jar, Gnome On Log, Marked, 9 In. . . . 242.00
obacco Jar, Gypsy, Marked J.M., 10¼ In. . . . 604.00
obacco Jar, Man With Wheel Barrow, Marked S & S, 9 In. . . . 776.00
obacco Jar, Monk, Marked J.M., 10¼ In. . . . 569.00
ub, Green Glaze, 4 Applied Loop Handles, France, 24¼ x 27 In. . . . 720.00
Jrn, Cover, Han Style, 4 Serpents Handle, Roosters, Gray, Buff, 21½ In. . . . 354.00
Jrn, Cover, Han Style, Bird Finials, Scenic Panels, Animals, Dragons, 24 In., Pair . . . 826.00
Jrn, Figures, Female Figural Handles, 20th Century, 19¼ x 17 In., Pair . . . 300.00
Jrn, Garden, Cover, Ball Finials, Painted, France, 22 x 14 In., Pair . . . 1020.00
Jrn, Palace, Painted Scenic Panels, Anthemion & Arabesque, Stand, 65 In., Pair . . . 1093.00
'ase, Black Matte, 2 Handles, Greek Key Borders, Bas Relief Figural Friezes, 32 In. . . . 480.00
'ase, Blue & White Glaze, Craquelure Ground, Fish Frieze, 12½ x 15½ In. . . . 1528.00
'ase, Cover, Louis XVI Style, Buff, Ribbed, Pyriform, France, 32 In., Pair . . . 600.00
'ase, Neoclassical, Germany, c.1840, 11 In., Pair . . . 445.00
'ase, Painted, White Matte, France, 34 x 13½ In., Pair . . . 1680.00
'ase, Striped, Glazed, Paolo Cosenza, 5¾ In. . . . 70.00

EXTILES listed here include many types of printed fabrics and table and household linens. ome other textiles will be found under Clothing, Coverlet, Rug, Quilt, etc.

Bag, 2-Sided, Hooked Mats, Sailing Ship, Striped Sky, Silk, Rayon, Grenfell, 10 x 11 In. . . . 201.00
Banquet Cloth, 12 Napkins, Damask, Ivory, Birds, Vines, Monogram, c.1900, 88 x 108 In. . . . 115.00
Banquet Cloth, 12 Napkins, Linen, Lace, Fairies, Maidens, Birds, Flowers, 73 x 134 In. . . . 4313.00
Banquet Cloth, Point De Venise, Tan Thread, Flowers, Baskets, c.1893, 71 x 182. . . . 3048.00
Bedspread, Marseilles, Floral Medallion, Corner Cartouches, White, c.1920, 88 x 96 In. . . . 180.00
Bell Pull, Needlepoint, Bird, Dog, Victorian, Brass Ring, 82 x 3½ In. . . . 150.00
Bell Pull, Red, Ocher, Embossed, Gilt, Lacquer, Brass, Stenciled, England, c.1890, 38 In.. *illus* 110.00
Blanket, Chief Joseph Pattern, Multicolored Wool, Pendleton, 1960s, 74 x 60 In. . . . 90.00
Blanket, Homespun, Multicolored, Stripe Design, Black Ground, 19th Century . . . 165.00
Blanket, Navajo, Wedge Weave, Eye Dazzler, Multicolored, Late 1800s, 57 x 77 In. . . . 17250.00
Blanket, Pendleton, Chief Joseph Pattern, Wool, Gray, White, 64 x 80 In. . . . 104.00
Blanket, Pendleton, Wool, Red, Multicolored, 68 x 66 In. . . . 207.00
Blanket, Trapper Point, Red Wool, Black Stripe, Eaton, Early 1900s, 76 x 58 In. . . . 225.00
Embroidery, Chinese Export, Silk, Reclining Lion, Lioness, Early 1900s, 22 x 15 In. . . . 470.00

Textile, Needlework, Temperance, Woman, Reverse Painted Black Glass, Frame, 13 x 11 In.
$467.00

Pillowcase, Embroidered Egyptian, Dyed, Arts & Crafts, 16½ x 19½ In.
$390.00

Candlewick Bedspreads

Candlewick bedspreads made in the 1920s and '30s were often handmade as part of a cottage industry. Many were sold from clotheslines strung in front of homes on traveled roads in the South. Sewing machines could do tufting by the 1930s, so factories started making chenille spreads. By the 1940s many designs and colors were offered. Most desirable are the handmade candlewick spreads, easy to spot because of irregularities in the design. But even factory-made spreads are popular today, selling, in mint condition, for over $125 each.

T

Textile, Roundel, Battenburg Lace, Flowers, Frame, 19th Century, 8 In.
$20.00

Textile, Tapestry, Woman, With Basket, Wool, Evelyn Ackerman, Era Industries, 48 x 19 In.
$270.00

TIP

Never wash a colored textile without talking to an expert. Most of the old colors run.

Embroidery, Landscape, Figures Seated On Lawn, Silk, Chenille, Painted, 21 x 29 In. 7500.00
Fabric, Crewelwork, Repeating Flower & Leaf Motif, Muslin, 4 Ft. 2 In. x 52 Ft. 1840.00
Fabric, Taliesin Line, 6 Samples, Marked, Frank Lloyd Wright, 44 x 22 In. *illus* 640.00
Flag, American, 13 Stars, Wool, Early 20th Century, 15 x 21¾ In. 382.00
Flag, American, 21 Stars, Muslin, Great Luminary, War Stripe, c.1818, 57 x 104 In. 20000.00
Flag, American, 34 Stars, 1 Row 6 Stars, 4 Rows 7 Stars, Printed Linen, 28 x 33 In. 1800.00
Flag, American, 34 Stars, 5-Point Pattern, 1860, 50 x 74 In. 7650.00
Flag, American, 36 Stars, Great Star Pattern, Linen, Machine Sewn, c.1867, 43 x 65 In. 1610.00
Flag, American, 38 Stars, Linen, Stenciled, Wood Frame, Gilt Liner, c.1877, 17 x 26 In. 588.00
Flag, American, 39 Stars, Cotton, Frame, c.1889, 33 x 25 In. 480.00
Flag, American, 42 Stars, Stitched Field, Weighted Corners, c.1890, 58 x 105 In. 125.00
Flag, American, 45 Stars, c.1896, 6 x 12 Ft. 100.00
Flag, Confederate, 11 Stars, 1st National, Linen, Blue, 2 Red, 1 White Bars, 16 x 19½ In. 4183.00
Mattress Cover, Blue & White Checked, Cotton, 54 x 66 In. 22.00
Mattress Cover, Blue & White Checked, Cotton, 74 x 58 In. 33.00
Mattress Cover, Blue & White Checked, Cotton, Sewn Edges, 51 x 64 In. 33.00
Mattress Cover, Blue & White Checked, Cotton, Button Closures, 62 x 70 In. 44.00
Mattress Cover, Blue & White Checked, Cotton, Bone Button Closures, 56 x 66 In. 77.00
Mattress Cover, Brown & White Checked, Cotton, Child's, 35 x 29 In. 154.00
Mattress Cover, Dark Blue & White Checked, Cotton, String Ties, 58 x 74 In. 154.00
Mattress Cover, Dark Blue & White Checked, Tan Bottom, Tape Loom Ties, Linen, 72 x 58 In. 44.00
Mattress Cover, Red, White & Blue, Cotton, 49 x 64 In. 77.00
Needlework, 2 Women Mourning, Willow Tree, Tomb, In Memory Of, Frame, 1818, 26 x 24 In. 5500.00
Needlework, Boats, Arts & Crafts Frame, 11 x 6 In. *illus* 720.00
Needlework, Bouquet, Wool Yarn, Tent Stitch, Mahogany Frame, c.1780, 18¾ x 17 In. 705.00
Needlework, Boy On Boneshaker, 19th Century, 12 x 12 In. 132.00
Needlework, Crested Exotic Birds, Silk Ground, Black Frame, Gilt Liner, 16¼ x 10 In. 201.00
Needlework, Dog, On Pillow, Frame, 17 x 23 In. *illus* 990.00
Needlework, Eagle, Silk, Metallic Threads, Shield, Flags, Banner, 1900s, 20 x 22 In. 546.00
Needlework, Emblem Of America, Silk, Watercolor, Liberty With Flag, Frame, 14 x 10 In. 3055.00
Needlework, Embroidered Peacock Perched In Tree, Arts & Crafts, 17 x 31 In. 900.00
Needlework, Flowerpot, Tulips, Leaf Border, Hannah Battye, Frame, 1841, 25 x 20 In. 605.00
Needlework, Memorial, George Washington, Painted, Silk, Chenille, c.1805, 15 x 20 In. 11700.00
Needlework, Memorial, Nantucket Quaker, Silk, Linen, Lucretia Starbuck, c.1812, 6 x 5 In. 863.00
Needlework, Mother Reading To Child, Woman, Harp, Silk, Painted Faces, 18 x 20 In. 1763.00
Needlework, Parrot, Branch, Red, Yellow, Green, Brown, Geometric Border, Frame, 18 x 15 In. 132.00
Needlework, Ruins, Pastoral Landscape, Figures, Farm Animals, Wool, Canvas, 21 x 25 In. 115.00
Needlework, Sailor's Farewell, Silk, Chinese, Late 19th Century, 10½ x 20½ In. *illus* 2300.00
Needlework, Shepherdess Against Tree, Sheep, Painted Face, Arms, Feet, Silk, 13 x 11 In. 253.00
Needlework, Silk, Chenille, Basket Of Flowers, Lititz, Penn., Frame, 1816, 19 x 22 In. 1410.00
Needlework, Silk, Chinese, Flowers, Frame, 10 x 8 In. 138.00
Needlework, Temperance, Woman, Reverse Painted Black Glass, Frame, 13 x 11 In. *illus* 467.00
Needlework, Young Botanist, Girl Watering Flowers, Ink, Wool, On Paper, 13 x 13 In. 1200.00
Panel, 100 Birds, Mother-Of-Pearl, Rosewood Frame, Glazed, Chinese, 31 x 18 In. 2468.00
Panel, Embroidered, Birds, Glazed, Frame, Chinese, 19th Century, 20 x 16 In. 3173.00
Panel, Embroidered, Geometric, Multicolored, Dark Blue, Tibet, 20th Century, 104 x 55 In. 176.00
Panel, Embroidered, Green Silk, Gold Thread, Dragons, Chinese, 1800s, 10 Ft. x 3 Ft. 8 In. 708.00
Panel, Kesi Silk, Birds, Flowers, Chinese, 36 x 21 In. 1652.00
Panel, Landscape, Ruins, Yellow & Red Leaves, Velvet Bordered Frame, 44 x 48 In. 1058.00
Panel, Needlework, Medieval Figures, Black Ground, 5 Ft. 4 In. x 7 Ft. 7 In. 690.00
Panel, Spanish American War, Red & White, Cotton, Regimental Seal, Frame, 32 x 31 In. 250.00
Panel, Tapestry, Franco-Belgian, Verdure, Goose, Eagle, Sylvan Pond, 85 x 76 In. 3840.00
Pillow, Embroidered Pinecones, Vibrant Colors, Arts & Crafts, 15½ x 14½ In. 330.00
Pillow, Normandy Lace, Embroidery, Silk Flowers, 9½ x 9½ In. 325.00
Pillow, Tapestry, Aubusson, Tasseled Edge, Bronze Dupioni Silk, 22 x 22 In. 420.00
Pillow, Tapestry, Dogs, Puppy, Silk, 22 x 22 In. 420.00
Pillow, Tapestry, Gold Silk Ground, Gold Silk Welting, France, 18 x 18 In., Pair 900.00
Pillow, Tapestry, Millefiori, Spiraled, Blue, Taupe, Ivory Cord, Velvet Back, 17 x 17 In., Pair 210.00
Pillow Cover, Flowers, Leaves, Geometrics, Needlework, Applique, Anna Greider, 30 x 16½ In. 132.00
Pillowcase, Embroidered Egyptian, Dyed, Arts & Crafts, 16½ x 19½ In. *illus* 390.00
Pillowcase, Red Embroidery, Flowers & Date, 1810. 145.00
Prayer Cloth, Embroidered, Gold Thread, Black Ground, Islamic, 15½ x 22 In. 529.00
Robe Fragment, Opposing Dragons, Embroidered, Metallic Threads, Chinese, 52 x 91 In. 1495.00
Roundel, Battenburg Lace, Flowers, Frame, 19th Century, 8 In. *illus* 20.00
Stumpwork On Silk, Girl Sitting On Bench In Woods, Frame, 18th Century, 8½ x 7 In. 526.00
Table Runner, Felt, Embroidered Poppy, Fringed Ends, Arts & Crafts, 83 x 16 In. 420.00

Table Runner, Marriage, Embroidered, Red, Flowers, Hearts, Birds, Bride & Groom, 1786 . . . 850.00
Table Runner, Pinecones, Green Ground, Contemporary, 3 x 10 Ft. . . . 900.00
Tablecloth, Embroidered, Flowers, Multicolored, Belgium, 54 x 72 In. . . . 132.00
Tablecloth, Round, Embroidered Grapevine, Jewels, Lace Border, Arts & Crafts, 58 In. . . . 300.00
Tapestry, Armed Horsemen, Forest, Distant Town, Wool, Brown, Green, 57 x 57 In. . . . 2468.00
Tapestry, Aubusson, Courting Couple, Girl Fishing, Metallic Ribbon Trim, 80 ½ x 75 In. . . . 4406.00
Tapestry, Circus, Maguey Jute Fiber, Hand Woven, Signed, A. Calder, 1975, 84 x 56 In. . . . 3000.00
Tapestry, Courting Couples In Garden, Wool, Fringe, Flemish, 83 x 93 In. . . . 588.00
Tapestry, Crucifixion, Cornucopia, Flower Urn, Scroll Borders, Wool, Flemish, 112 x 132 In. . 15275.00
Tapestry, Enthroned, King, Soldier, Fruit, Flower Borders, Cherub, 57 x 55 In. . . . 6463.00
Tapestry, Franco Flemish, Armored Figure, Garden, Late 1600s, 84 x 53 In. . . . 6600.00
Tapestry, Gobelin Style, Wool, 3 Drinkers In Tavern, Flower Borders, 1900s, 60 x 81 In. . . . 1116.00
Tapestry, Landscape, Mill, Flowing Stream, Flower Border, Mid 1800s, 80 x 60 In. . . . 1064.00
Tapestry, Landscape, Pastoral, Shepherd, Shepherdess, Continental, 39 x 39 In. . . . 735.00
Tapestry, Landscape, Wooded, Garden Folly, Fountain, Wool, Belgium, 81 ¼ x 48 In. . . . 3408.00
Tapestry, Moses, Defending 7 Daughters, Gilt Gesso Frame, 19th Century, 46 x 44 In. . . . 1998.00
Tapestry, Multicolored, Leaves, Cartouche, Continental, Early 1900s, 53 x 54 In. . . . 176.00
Tapestry, Needlework, Forest Landscape, Swans, Castle, 71 ¾ x 107 In. . . . 764.00
Tapestry, Panel, Aubusson Style, 19th Century, 34 x 74 In. . . . 690.00
Tapestry, Pyramid, Maguey Jute Fiber, Hand Woven, 1975, A. Calder, 72 x 96 In. . . . 7200.00
Tapestry, Shepherd, By Tree, Blue, Tan, Brown, Belgium, 18th Century, 27 x 65 In. . . . 900.00
Tapestry, Turquoise, Maguey Jute Fiber, Hand Woven, 1975, Signed, A. Calder, 56 x 84 In. . . . 7200.00
Tapestry, Woman, With Basket, Wool, Evelyn Ackerman, Era Industries, 48 x 19 In. . . . *illus* 270.00
Tieback, Tassels, Silk, Cream, Light Blue, Green, Knotted, Twisted, 26 In., 24 Piece . . . 300.00
Towel, Flowerpots, Geometrics, Red, Blue, Needlework, Fringed Ends, 1838, 45 x 18 In. . . . 330.00
Towel, Show, Linen, Alphabet, Flower, Birds, Sarah Ann Kline, 1842, 68 x 20 In. . . . 470.00
Wall Hanging, Arts & Crafts, Copper, Hammered, Embossed Ship, Patina, 17 In. . . . 480.00
Wall Hanging, Embroidered, Dragons, Flaming Pearls, Clouds, Chinese, 127 x 48 In., Pair . . 5060.00
Wall Hanging, Poppies, Intertwined Stems, Embroidered Linen, Arts & Crafts, 41 x 29 In. . . . 900.00
Yardage, Crewelwork, Butterflies, Stylized 2-Tone Pink Blossoms, Vines, 6 Yds. . . . 354.00

THERMOMETER is a name that comes from the Greek word for heat. The thermometer was invented in 1731 to measure the temperature of either water or air. All kinds of thermometers are collected, but those with advertising messages are the most popular.

7 Up, Fresh Up With, You Like It, It Likes You, Bottle, White, Porcelain . . . 220.00
7 Up, Green, Blue, Pink, Yellow, Red, Ohio Thermometer, 12 In. Diam . . . 110.00
7 Up, Likes You, Glass Face, Metal Back, 1940-50s, 12 In. . . . 146.00
7 Up, Quality Drink, Green, Red, 10 In. Diam. . . . 120.00
A.C. Daniels Dog & Cat Medicines, White, Black, Wood, 21 ¼ x 5 In. . . . 525.00
Aard-Vark Shop, Taxidermist Supplies, 7 In. Diam. . . . 210.00
B-1 Lemon Lime, More Zip In Every Sip, Blue, White, Metal, 16 In. . . . 90.00
Biltrite Heels & Soles, Embossed, Enamel, Tin, 5 ½ x 13 In. . . . 112.00
Brass, Rococo Style, Cherub Crest, Easel Back, Bradley & Hubbard, 13 ½ In. . . . 120.00
Brass, White Glass Scales, Easel Back, 19th Century, 12 ½ In. . . . 92.00
Dr Pepper, Metal, Glass Dome, 12 In. . . . 152.00
Dr. Daniels' Veterinary Medicine, Wood, 23 x 6 In. . . . 325.00
Drink Hires Root Beer, Brown, 12 In. Diam. . . . 80.00
Ex-Lax, Chocolated Laxative, Keep Regular, Porcelain, 8 x 36 In. . . . 213.00
Franklin Fire Insurance Company, Paper Dial, c.1920, 9 x 1 ½ In. . . . 149.00
Frostie, Old Fashioned, Cold Brewed, Root Beer, Tin, Glass Dome, c.1960, 12 In. . . . *illus* 243.00
Girl, Wood, Carved, 1930-40, 20 In. . . . *illus* 275.00
Grads Cigarettes, Burgundy, White, Porcelain, 8 x 39 In. . . . 123.00
Hills Bros. Tea & Coffee, Man Drinking, Red, Yellow, Black, Porcelain, 21 x 9 In. . . . 700.00
Hires Root Beer, Glass Face, 1960s, 12 In. . . . 101.00
Hooker Bros. Ice Cream, The Taste Tells Why, Children, Wood, 14 ¼ x 4 In. . . . 550.00
Ken-L-Ration, Feed Your Dog, Tin, 1940-50, 27 x 7 ½ In. . . . *illus* 200.00
Kirk's Jap Rose Soap, Black, Yellow, White, Porcelainc.1915, 7 x 27 In. . . . 258.00
Leesville, Louisiana, Plastic, Key Shape, Compass, c.1958 . . . 10.00
Magic Chips, Deep Fat Frying, Enamel & Wood, Reads From 0-650 F. . . . 30.00
Mail Pouch Tobacco, Treat Yourself To The Best, Blue, Red, White, Yellow, Tin, 38 In. . . . 88.00
Merck & Co, Storage Of Fine Chemicals, Wood, 15 x 4 In. . . . 358.00
Moxie, Bottle, Frank Archer Image, Tin, 9 ¾ x 25 ½ In. . . . 1020.00
Peters Shoes, Weatherbird, Solid Leather Footwear, Red, Black, Porcelain, 27 x 7 In. . . . 415.00
Sprenger Beer Co., On Draught, In Bottles, White, Red, Black, Metal, Red Alcohol, 39 x 8 In. . 358.00
Tom's Roasted Peanuts, Red, White, Blue, Yellow, Metal, 16 x 6 In. . . . 100.00
Triple XXX Root Beer, Tin, 1940s, 27 x 7 In. . . . *illus* 259.00

Thermometer, Frostie, Old Fashioned, Cold Brewed, Root Beer, Tin, Glass Dome, c.1960, 12 In.
$243.00

Thermometer, Girl, Wood, Carved, 1930-40, 20 In.
$275.00

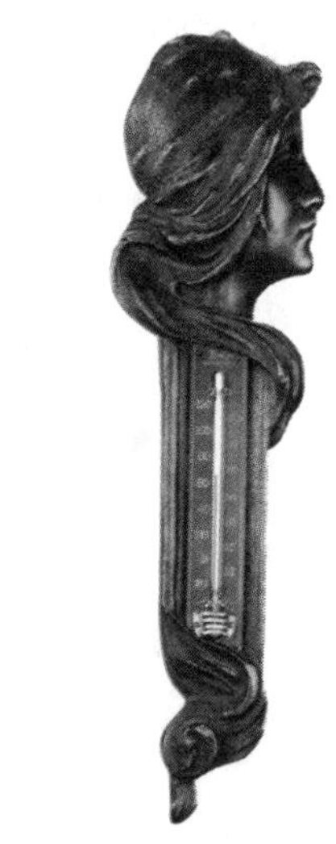

Thermometer, Ken-L-Ration, Feed Your Dog, Tin, 1940-50, 27 x 7 ½ In.
$200.00

T

Thermometer, Triple XXX Root Beer, Tin, 1940s, 27 x 7 In.
$259.00

Tiffany, Candlestick, Flower Form, Bronze, Gold Dore, Signed, 8 x 5 In.
$3850.00

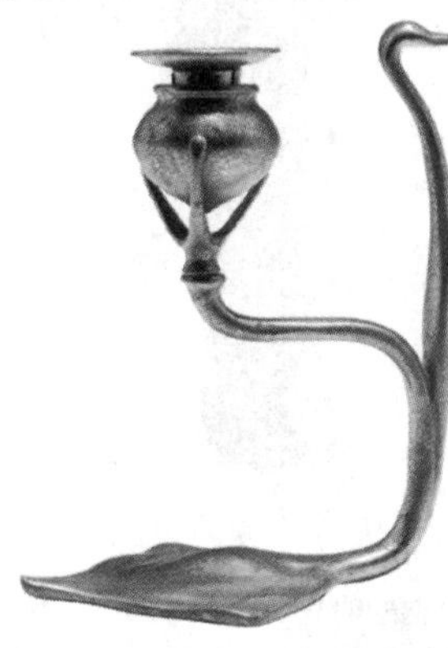

Tiffany, Frame, Pine Needle, Green Slag Glass, Bronze, Marked, 9 ½ x 7 ¾ In.
$2470.00

Woman, Robed, On Pedestal, Figural, Cast, Green Marble Base, Marked, F.R, 5 ½ In. 86.00
Woman Finial, Footed, Brass, 9 ½ In. 103.00

TIFFANY is a name that appears on items made by Louis Comfort Tiffany, the American glass designer who worked from about 1879 to 1933. His work included iridescent glass, Art Nouveau styles of design, and original contemporary styles. He was also noted for stained glass windows, unusual lamps, bronze work, pottery, and silver. Other types of Tiffany are listed under Tiffany Glass, Tiffany Gold, Tiffany Pottery, or Tiffany Silver. The famous Tiffany lamps are listed in this section. Tiffany jewelry is listed in the Jewelry and Wristwatch categories. Some Tiffany Studio desk sets have matching clocks. They are listed here. Clocks made by Tiffany & Co. are listed in the Clock category. Reproductions of some types of Tiffany are being made.

Louis C. Tiffany

Ashtray, Match Holder, American Indian, Black, Red Highlights, 3 ½ x 6 ¼ In. 550.00
Ashtray, Match Holder, Pine Needle, Green Slag Glass, Bronze, Patina, 4 ½ x 5 In. 700.00
Ashtray, Pine Needle, Green Slag Glass, Bronze, Dark Patina, 4 ½ x 5 ½ In. 700.00
Ashtray, Tortoiseshell Insert, Bronze, Gold Dore, Favrile, 5 In. 690.00
Ashtray, Tree Stump, Copper, Brass, Hinged, Insert, Signed, 5 ¼ x 5 ¾ In. 66.00
Ashtray Set, Nesting, Graduate, Bronze, Gold Dore, 4 ½ In., 4 Piece 350.00
Basket, Blue, Green & Yellow, Bronze, Pedestal Base, Enamel, Gold Dore, Handle, 5 ¼ In. 450.00
Bill File, Pine Needle, Green Slag Glass, Bronze, Dark Patina, 7 ½ x 3 ½ In. 1500.00
Bill File, Venetian, Bronze, Gold Dore, 7 x 3 ½ In. 2000.00
Blotter, Abalone, Bronze, Gold Dore, 2 ¾ x 5 ¾ In. 650.00
Blotter, Adam, Bronze, Gold Dore, 2 x 19 In., Pair 350.00
Blotter, American Indian, Bronze, Dark Patina, 3 x 5 ½ In. 350.00
Blotter, American Indian, Knob Handle, Dark Patina, 3 x 5 ½ In. 350.00
Blotter, Graduate, Bronze, Gold Dore, Marked, 5 ½ x 2 ¾ x 1 ½ In. 350.00
Blotter, Pine Needle, Green Slag Glass, Handle, Bronze Beading, Patina, 6 ¾ x 3 x 2 In. 650.00
Blotter Ends, American Indian, Bronze, Dark Patina, 2 x 19 In., Pair 400.00
Blotter Ends, Grapevine, Bronze, Dark Patina, 2 x 19 In., Pair 650.00
Blotter Ends, Modeled, Bronze, Gold Dore, 19 ½ In., Pair 177.00
Blotter Ends, Pine Needle, Bronze, 19 ¼ In., Pair 266.00
Blotter Ends, Zodiac, Copper, Brass, Signed, 2 x 19 ¼ In., Pair 450.00
Book Rack, Grapevine, Bronze, Gold Dore, 14 In. 4600.00
Bookends, Abalone, Leaf & Line, Bronze, Gold Dore, 5 x 5 ½ In. 3000.00
Bookends, Buddha, Arched Top, Ribbed Ridge, Bronze, Gold Dore, 6 x 5 In. 950.00
Bookends, Graduate, Gold Dore, Marked, 6 In. 1500.00
Bookends, Grapevine, Amber Slag Glass, Bronze, Gold Dore, Marked, 5 ½ In. 2500.00
Bookends, Modeled, Greek Key, Bronze, Gold Dore, 6 x 4 ½ In. 1500.00
Bookends, Peacock, Portal, Bronze, Gold Dore, 6 x 4 ½ In. 2000.00
Bookends, Venetian, Bronze, No. 1683, 4 ¾ x 5 ¼ x 6 ¼ In. 2040.00
Bowl, Bronze, Gold Dore, 4 ¼ In. 390.00
Bowl, Centerpiece, Enameled, Green Blue, Flared, Favrile, 4 ½ x 8 In. 2500.00
Box, American Indian, Bronze, Gold Dore, 3 x 8 x 5 In. 3000.00
Box, Art Deco, Enameled, Geometric, Bronze, Carved, Patina, 6¼ x 2½ In. . . . . . . 2280.00 to 5700.00
Box, Bronze, Cut Half Moons, Ribs, Raised Centers, 6 Gold Glass Panels, 6-Sided, 2 x 6 In. 4500.00
Box, Card, Hinged Cover, Pine Needle, Green Slag Glass, Bronze, Patina, 4 x 3 x 2 In. 2500.00
Box, Double X, Enameled, Gold Dore Patina, Bronze, Gold Dore Patina, 4 ½ x 2 In. 4500.00
Box, Grapevine, Green Slag Glass, Bronze, 4 ¼ x 1 ½ In. 840.00
Box, Grapevine, Green Slag Glass, Bronze Beading, Dark Patina, 4 ½ x 3 x 1 ¾ In. 850.00
Box, Handkerchief, Grapevine, Green Slag Glass, Bronze, Dark Patina, 7 x 2 ½ In. 3500.00
Box, Hinged Cover, Abalone, Bronze, Gold Dore, 1 x 5 ¼ x 3 ½ In. 2500.00
Box, Hinged Cover, Abalone Discs, Leaf & Line, Bronze, 5 ¼ x 3 ½ x 1 In. 2500.00
Box, Hinged Cover, Bookmark, Bronze, Gold Dore, 1 ¼ x 5 x 3 In. 1200.00
Box, Hinged Cover, Grapevine, Green Slag Glass, Bronze, Patina, Ball Feet, 2 x 6 x 4 In. 1500.00
Box, Hinged Cover, Grapevine, Green Slag Glass, Bronze, 3 ½ x 9 ½ x 6 ½ In. 2115.00
Box, Hinged Cover, Zodiac, Bronze, Gold Dore, 2 x 4 ½ x 3 In. 750.00
Box, Letter, Sterling Silver, Favrile Glass Insert, 2 x 9 x 4 In. 3300.00
Box, Pine Needle, Caramel Slag Glass, Bronze, Ball Feet, 4 x 1 ¼ In. 600.00
Box, Pine Needle, Carmel Slag Glass, Dark Bronze Patina, 3 ¾ x 5 ½ In. 960.00
Box, Pine Needle, Slag Glass, Triple Beading, Bronze, 4 ½ x 3 In. 748.00
Box, Stamp, Abalone, 3 Sections, Bronze, Gold Dore, 1 ½ x 4 x 2 ¼ In. 850.00
Box, Stamp, Bookmark, Palm Leaves, Bronze, Gold Dore, 2 ½ x 2 ⅛ In. 920.00
Box, Stamp, Hinged Cover, Bookmark, Bronze, Gold Dore, 1 ½ x 2 ½ x 2 In. 950.00
Box, Stamp, Hinged Cover, Zodiac, Bronze, Gold Dore, 3 Sections, 1 x 3 ¾ x 2 ¼ In. 600.00
Box, Zodiac, Bronze, Patina, 6 x 2 ½ In. 1680.00
Calendar, Adam, Bronze, Gold Dore, Easel Back, Perpetual, 6 x 6 ½ In. 1200.00

T

alendar, American Indian, Bronze, Dark Patina, 6 x 7 ½ In. 1500.00
alendar, Bookmark, Bronze, Gold Dore, 5 ¾ x 4 ½ In. 4370.00
alendar, Grapevine, Green Slag Glass, Bronze, Perpetual, 6 ½ x 7 ½ In. 1380.00
andelabrum, 3-Light, 4 Wide-Ribbed Legs, Paw Feet, Dore Bronze, 11 ⅜ In. 1933.00
andelabrum, 4-Light, Stick Body, Oval Base, Bronze, Dark Patina, 15 x 14 In. 7500.00
andelabrum, 5-Light, Silver Plate, Removable Branches, 4-Footed, 14 ¾ In., Pair 3585.00
andlestick, 6-Leaf Cup, Stick, Bronze, Teardrop Base, 10 x 5 In., Pair 4000.00
andlestick, Bobeches, Bronze, Gold Dore, Padded Base, 17 In., Pair 2875.00 to 4888.00
andlestick, Flower Form, Bronze, Footed, 5 ¾ In. 175.00
andlestick, Flower Form, Bronze, Gold Dore, Signed, 8 x 5 In. *illus* 3850.00
andlestick, Flower Form, Green Glass Cup, 20 In. 2280.00
andlestick, Green, Pineapple Stem, Platform, Bronze, Green, Brown Patina, 14 In. 4600.00
andlestick, Green Glass Cup, Bronze, Patina, 3-Footed, Favrile, 12 In. 2400.00
andlestick, Green Jewels, Bronze, Patina, 5-Footed, 11 ½ In. 13200.00
andlestick, Reticulated Glass Cup, 3 Curving Legs, Triangular Base, Bronze, 14 In. 8050.00
anister, Sailboat, Bronze, Gold Dore, Cover, 3 ½ In. 450.00
hamberstick, Purple Enamel, Bronze, Gold Dore, 3 ½ x 4 In., Pair 2500.00
handelier, 13-Light, Turtleback Tile, Favrile Glass, Bronze, c.1916, 24 x 21 ¼ In. 180000.00
handelier, Grapes Shade, Leaded Glass, Bronze, c.1905, 28 In. 312000.00
handelier, Leaded Glass, Turtleback Tile, Prisms, Yellow, Green, Bronze, c.1910, 13 ¾ In. 33000.00
handelier, Leaded Glass, Turtleback Tile, Yellow, Orange, Gems, Bronze, c.1910, 19 In. 34800.00
handelier, Leaded Glass, Turtleback Tile, Multicolored, 6 Chains, Bronze, c.1910, 27 x 17 In. 51000.00
harger, Floral Embossed Edge, Mother-Of-Pearl Inlay, Bronze, Gold Dore, 14 In. 100.00
hest, Hinged Cover, Dore Finish, Bronze, Textured, Gold Dore, 5 ¾ x 3 ½ x 2 ¾ In. 1500.00
igarette Box, Bookmark, Bronze, Gold Dore, 4 ½ x 2 ¼ In. 600.00
igarette Box, Bookmark, Bronze, Gold Dore, Cedar Lining, 3 ⅜ x 4 ½ In. 3220.00
lock, Bookmark, Cathedral, Bronze, Gold Dore, 5 ¾ In. 6613.00
lock, Desk, Art Deco, Red Enamel, Bronze, Brass Wash, 5 ½ x 5 ¾ x 4 In. 8400.00
lock, Spanish, Cut Corners, Bronze, 2 ¾ x 3 ¾ x ¼ In. 8400.00
ompote, Abalone Band, Bronze, Silver Dore, 3 x 7 In. 288.00
ompote, Border Of Flowers, Roundels, Geometric Line, Center Well, Bronze, 10 x 3 In. 1500.00
ompote, Design Border, Raised Foot, Favrile, Impressed, Louis C. Tiffany Furnaces, Inc., 2 ⅝ x 6 In. 206.00
ompote, Enameled, Wreath Of Flowers Encircling Foot, Bronze, Gold Dore, 9 x 8 ¼ In. 1495.00
ompote, Flower Heads, Berry Panels, Artichoke Pedestal, Gold Dore, 4 ¾ In. 348.00
ompote, Raised Flowers, Red Enameled Centers, Lines, Bronze, Gold Dore, 3 x 10 In. 1500.00
esk Set, Pine Needle, Slag Glass, Bronze, Letter Rack, Pen Tray, Inkwell, c.1910, 3 Piece 1375.00
esk Set, Zodiac, Inkwell, Blotter, Stamp Box, 3 Piece 1380.00
ish, Arrowhead Fern, Bronze, Patina, c.1905, 3 x 12 In. 55000.00
ish, Gold Favrile, Ribbed Body, Scalloped Rim, Marked, 8 ½ In. 575.00
ame, Abalone, Mother-Of-Pearl, Bronze, Gold Dore, Oval Opening, c.1910, 10 x 6 In. 6600.00
ame, Adam, Band Of Swags On Bottom, Bronze, Gold Dore, Signed, 12 x 9 In. 3000.00
ame, Chinese, Bronze, Gold Dore, Easel Back, Marked, 7 ¼ x 8 ¾ In. 1500.00
ame, Grapevine, Amber Slag Glass, Bronze, Patina, Oval Opening, 10 x 8 In. 7200.00
ame, Grapevine, Amber Slag Glass, Bronze, Patina, 2 Openings, 9 ⅓ x 7 ¾ In. 10200.00
ame, Grapevine, Green, Slag Glass, Bronze, Brown Patina, 8 x 9 ½ In. 3950.00
ame, Grapevine, Green Slag Glass, Bronze, 7 ½ x 9 In. 1080.00
ame, Grapevine, Green Slag Glass, Bronze, Dark Patina, 7 ½ x 6 ½ In. 3000.00
ame, Grapevine, Slag Glass, Bronze, Gold Dore, Easel Back, 14 x 12 In. 4500.00
ame, Grapevine, Slag Glass, Bronze, Oval Opening, 6 ½ x 7 In. 5750.00
ame, Oak Leaf, Green Slag Glass, Bronze, Dark Patina, Easel Back, 9 ¼ x 7 ¾ In. 3500.00
ame, Pine Needle, Amber Slag Glass, Bronze, Patina, 9 ⅓ x 7 ⅞ In. 5400.00
ame, Pine Needle, Green Slag Glass, Bronze, Marked, 9 ½ x 7 ¾ In. *illus* 2470.00
ame, Pine Needle, Green Slag Glass, Brown Patina, 2 Openings, 4 x 5 ¾ In. 8050.00
ame, Zodiac, Bronze, Gold Dore, 11 x 9 In. 1550.00 to 2000.00
ame, Zodiac, Bronze, Gold Dore, Easel Back, 8 x 7 In. 2500.00
ame, Zodiac, Bronze, Patina, 14 ¼ x 12 ¼ In. 3600.00
umidor, Cigar, Grapevine, Green Slag Glass, Bronze, Cedar Lined, 6 ½ x 9 In. 2703.00
umidor, Pine Needle, Grapevine, Metal, 2 Covers, Green Glass, Patina, 7 In. 8050.00
kwell, Abalone, Glass Insert, Bronze, 8-Sided, Patina, Signed, 3 x 3 ½ In. 520.00
kwell, Art Nouveau, Bronze, Gold Dore, Curved Tray, Swirls, Glass Insert, 3 x 8 x 5 In. 2500.00
kwell, Bronze, Zodiac, Original Patina, 4 x 2 In. 540.00
kwell, Chinese, 2 Wells, Bronze, Gold Dore, 5 ½ In. 384.00
kwell, Etched Metal & Glass, Grapevine, Marked, c.1920, 4 In. 510.00
kwell, Grapevine, Amber Glass Insert, Bronze, Footed, Marked, 3 In. 316.00
kwell, Grapevine, Caramel Slag Glass, Bronze, Brown Patina, 6 In. 834.00
kwell, Grapevine, Caramel Slag Glass, Bronze, Square, 3 x 3 ⅛ In. 483.00

Tiffany, Inkwell, Pine Needle, Green Slag Glass, Bronze, 3 x 3 ¼ In.
$530.00

Tiffany, Inkwell, Zodiac, Bronze, 3 ⅜ x 6 ⅜ In.
$295.00

Tiffany, Lamp, Desk, Abalone, Bronze, Signed, 9 x 7 In.
$3750.00

Tiffany Lamps
Since about 1970, the phrase "Tiffany Lamp" has been misused. You see it in ads and stores to describe modern lamps with stained glass shades. A true Tiffany lamp was made by Louis Comfort Tiffany at his studio from 1891 to 1928.

T

Tiffany, Lamp, Desk, Damascene, Green Iridescent, Bronze, Marked, c.1900, 14 x 7 In.
$3400.00

Tiffany, Lamp, Linenfold Shade, Green, Bronze Inverted Mushroom Base, 19 x 13 In.
$29600.00

TIP

Don't use bleaching cleansing powders or disinfectant floor-washing products that contain chlorine in a room that has bronze figures on display. Chlorine harms bronzes.

Inkwell, Grapevine, Green Slag Glass, Bronze, 2 Wells, 5 ¾ x 3 ¼ In. . . . 3220.00
Inkwell, Grapevine, Green Slag Glass, Bronze, Ball Feet, 4-Sided, Signed, 3 ½ x 4 In. . . . 425.00
Inkwell, Hinged Cover, Abalone, Bronze, Gold Dore, 8-Sided, 3 ½ x 3 ½ In. . . . 850.00
Inkwell, Hinged Cover, Adam, Glass Insert, Bronze, Gold Dore, 2 ½ x 4 x 3 In. . . . 750.00
Inkwell, Hinged Cover, American Indian, Glass Insert, Bronze, 3 x 5 ½ In. . . . 950.00
Inkwell, Hinged Cover, Bookmark, Glass Insert, 8-Sided, Bronze, Gold Dore, 2½ x 3 In. . 750.00 to 1200.00
Inkwell, Hinged Cover, Graduate, Bronze, Gold Dore, 4 x 2 In. . . . 550.00
Inkwell, Hinged Cover, Grapevine, Green Slag Glass, Bronze, Dark Patina, 7 In. . . . 3000.00
Inkwell, Hinged Cover, Modeled, Glass Insert, Bronze, Gold Dore, Cone Shape, 3 In. . . . 750.00
Inkwell, Hinged Cover, Venetian, 2 Wells, Bronze, Gold Dore, 2 x 5 x 3 In. . . . 1500.00
Inkwell, Hinged Cover, Zodiac, Clear Glass Insert, Bronze, 1 ⅞ x 4 In. . . . 295.00
Inkwell, Hinged Cover, Zodiac, Bronze, Gold Dore, 4 x 6 ½ In. . . . 950.00
Inkwell, Hinged Cover, Zodiac, Bronze, Gold Dore, 8-Sided, 2 x 4 In. . . . 550.00
Inkwell, Pine Needle, Bronze, 3 ½ In. . . . 580.00
Inkwell, Pine Needle, Green Slag Glass, Bronze, 3 x 3 ¼ In. . . . *illus* 530.00
Inkwell, Pine Needle, Green Slag Glass, Bronze, Dark Patina, 4-Footed, 4 x 3 ½ In. . . . 950.00
Inkwell, Pine Needle, Slag Glass, Bronze, Round, 7 In. . . . 898.00
Inkwell, Venetian, Double, Bronze, Gold Dore, 2 x 5 x 3 In. . . . 1500.00
Inkwell, Zodiac, Bronze, 3 ⅜ x 6 ⅜ In. . . . *illus* 295.00
Jewelry Box, Cover, Posts, Arches, Squares, Chain Link Design, Bronze, Patina, 8 x 3 ¾ In. . . 4000.00
Jewelry Box, Grapevine, Slag Glass, Bronze, Beaded, Velvet Tray, 9 x 6 In. . . . 6900.00
Jewelry Box, Pine Needle, Green Slag Glass, Bronze, Brown Patina, 9 ¼ x 6 ½ In. . . . 3220.00
Lamp, 2-Light, Ribbed Bell Shades, Ruffled Rims, Adjustable, Bronze, Brown Patina, 26 In. . . 9200.00
Lamp, Acorn Shade, Green, Yellow, Slag Glass, 3 Supports, One Socket, 21 x 14 In. . . . 13200.00
Lamp, Bamboo Shade, Leaded Glass, Bronze Bamboo Base, c.1910, 22 x 16 In. . . . 133000.00
Lamp, Black-Eyed Susan Shade, Leaded Glass, Urn In Tripod Base, 22 In. . . . 34500.00
Lamp, Butterscotch Carved Damascene Shade, Harp Base, c.1920, 57 In. . . . 12000.00
Lamp, Candle, Tulip Shade, Bamboo, Bronze, Brown Patina, Green Highlights, 15 In. . . . 8625.00
Lamp, Cone Shade, Amber Slag Glass, 4-Socket Base, Gold Finish, 25 x 20 ½ In. . . . 12000.00
Lamp, Damascene Shade, Gold Iridescent, Blue, Purple, Bronze, Base, 16 In. . . . 1265.00
Lamp, Damascene Shade, Organic Bronze, Base, Root Feet, Signed, 54 In. . . . 11400.00
Lamp, Desk, 2-Light, Bronze Base, Favrile, c.1910, 20 In. . . . 2530.00 to 5250.00
Lamp, Desk, Abalone, Bronze, Signed, 9 x 7 In. . . . *illus* 3750.00
Lamp, Desk, Damascene Bell Shade, Favrile, 7 x 12 In. . . . 4130.00 to 7475.00
Lamp, Desk, Damascene, Green Iridescent, Bronze, Marked, c.1900, 14 x 7 In. . . . *illus* 3400.00
Lamp, Desk, Grapevine, Green Glass, Blown Into Bronze Openwork, Harp Base, 6 ¼ In. . . . 7415.00
Lamp, Desk, Heraldic, Red Enamel, Silvered Bronze, c.1920, 12 ¼ In. . . . 4800.00
Lamp, Desk, Pulled Feather, Bell Shape Shade, Harp Base, Bronze, Gold Dore, Favrile, 12 In. . 2760.00
Lamp, Desk, Zodiac, 2-Light, Bronze, Cylinder, Brown Patina, 14 In. . . . 3565.00
Lamp, Desk, Zodiac, Turtleback, Adjustable, Hexagon Base, Bronze, 14 ¾ In. . . . 10800.00
Lamp, Dogwood Border Shade, Leaded Glass, Bronze, c.1910, 28 x 20 ½ In. . . . 48000.00
Lamp, Dogwood Shade, Leaded Glass, 14 x 18 ½ In. . . . 34500.00
Lamp, Dragonfly Shade, Leaded Glass, Bronze Globular Base, c.1910, 19 ¾ x 17 In. . . . 145000.00
Lamp, Dragonfly Shade, Leaded Glass, Bronze Mushroom Base, c.1910, 18 x 14 In. . . . 109000.00
Lamp, Fabrique, Gold, Leaded Glass, Bronze Base, Patina, Favrile, c.1913, 19 ¼ In. . . . 12000.00
Lamp, Flower, Shade, Leaded Glass, Magenta Iridescent, Blue, Purple, 8 Panels, 15 In. . . . 1783.00
Lamp, Geometric Shade, Leaded Glass, Bronze, c.1910, 60 x 22 In. . . . 57600.00
Lamp, Greek Key Shade, Leaded Glass, Bronze, c.1910, 20 ½ x 16 In. . . . 26400.00
Lamp, Hanging, Iridescent Shade, Leaf Swirled, Favrile, c.1910, 14 In. . . . 27600.00
Lamp, Hanging, Leaded Glass, Silvered Bronze, c.1910, 12 In. . . . 9600.00
Lamp, Leaf & Vine Shade, Leaded Glass, Bronze, c.1910, 22 x 16 In. . . . 13200.00
Lamp, Leaf & Vine Shade, Leaded Glass, Green, Bronze Base, Stamped, c.1910, 29 In. . . . 20000.00
Lamp, Lily, 3-Light, Gold Iridescent, Bronze, Gold Dore, 12 ¾ In. . . . 7500.00
Lamp, Lily, 3-Light, Green Pulled Feathers, Opalescent Ground, Bronze, 21 In. . . . 6900.00
Lamp, Lily, 3-Light, Piano, Gold Iridescent Ribbed, 8 ½ In. . . . 8050.00
Lamp, Lily, 6-Light, Gold Iridescent, Bronze Base, Patina, Favrile, c.1910, 20 In. . . . 12000.00
Lamp, Lily, 12-Light, Gold Iridescent, Bronze Base, Patina, Favrile, c.1910, 18 ¼ In. . . . 42000.00
Lamp, Linenfold Shade, Bronze, Gold Dore, Favrile, c.1920, 22 ½ x 19 ½ In. . . . 168000.00
Lamp, Linenfold Shade, Green, Bronze Inverted Mushroom Base, 19 x 13 In. . . . *illus* 29600.00
Lamp, Lotus Bell Shade, Leaded Glass, Green, White, Bronze Arms, 15 x 21 In. . . . 43125.00
Lamp, Mosque Shade, Green Feather, Gold Iridescent, Ivory Opalescent, Bronze, Gold Dore, 8 In. 5500.00
Lamp, Mushroom Shade, Green, Bronze, Favrile, c.1910, 58 x 12 In. . . . 14400.00
Lamp, Nasturtium Domed Shade, Leaded Slag Glass, Footed, Library Steps Base, 21 In. . . . 162150.00
Lamp, Nautilus Shell Shade, Iridescent, Patina, 13 In. . . . 8050.00
Lamp, Oak Leaf, Shade, Leaded Glass, Bronze, Gold Dore, c.1910, 22 ½ x 17 ¾ In. . . . 22800.00
Lamp, Oak Leaf & Acorn, Shade, Leaded Glass, Bronze, Green Patina, 26 x 18 In. . . . 36000.00

mp, Peacock, Shade, Leaded Glass, Bronze, Green Teardrop Protrusions, c.1905, 22 ½ x 16 In. 156000.00
mp, Poinsettia Shade, Domed, Red & Wine Flowers, Jeweled Centers, Signed, 16 In........ 46000.00
mp, Poinsettia Shade, Slag Glass, Acanthus Urn Base, Bronze, c.1910, 20 x 16 In......... 4950.00
mp, Pomegranate Shade, Leaded Glass, Bronze, c.1910, 21½ x 16 In. .... 16450.00 to 27600.00
mp, Poppy Shade, Leaded Glass, Bronze, c.1910, 24 x 20 In.......................... 24000.00
mp, Poppy Shade, Leaded Glass, Red, Yellow, Green, Gilt Bronze, c.1920, 62 x 20 In....... 72000.00
mp, Poppy Shade, Leaded Glass, Glass Ball & Bronze Base, c.1905, 27 x 21 In............ 313000.00
mp, Poppy Shade, Cone, Leaded Glass, Twisted Lily Stem Base, c.1910, 25 x 20 ¾ In....... 169000.00
mp, Spiderweb Shade, Leaded Glass, Bronze, Baluster, Marked, Favrile, 19 In............ 14400.00
mp, Swirling Leaf Shade, Leaded Glass, Bronze, 25 ½ x 18 In......................... 26400.00
mp, Trumpet Creeper Shade, Bronze Base, c.1905, 26 ¼ x 18 ¾ In..................... 421000.00
mp, Tulip Shade, Leaded Glass, Bronze, c.1910, 25 ½ x 16 In.......................... 114000.00
mp, Vine Border Shade, Leaded Glass, Green, Yellow, Bronze, Patina, c.1910, 17 x 10 In.... 9000.00
mp, Vine Border Shade, Leaded Glass, Green, Red, Bronze, Patina, c.1910, 21 x 16 In...... 18000.00
mp, Weight-Balance, Raised Leaf Design, Bronze Shade Base, 16 In.................... 6500.00
mp, Wisteria Shade, Leaded Glass, Pierced Bronze Base, c.1905, 26 x 18 In.............. 881000.00
mp, Zodiac, Gold Pulled Feather Shade, Harp Base, Bronze, Signed, 18 In............... 5500.00
tter Holder, Abalone, Sections, Bronze, Gold Dore, 5 ¼ In........................... 1500.00
tter Holder, American Indian, Bronze, Dark Patina, Sections, 5 ¾ x 11 x 2 ¾ In.......... 1500.00
tter Holder, Bookmark, Bronze, Gold Dore, Sections, Signed, 5 ½ x 9 In................ 1500.00
tter Holder, Graduate, Bronze, Gold Dore, Sections, Marked, 5 ¼ x 9 ½ x 2 ¾ In.......... 850.00
tter Holder, Grapevine, Green Slag Glass, Bronze, Sections, Signed, 6 ½ x 10 In...... *illus* 1400.00
tter Holder, Pine Needle, Green Slag Glass, Bronze, Dark Patina, 6 x 10 x 2 In........... 1500.00
tter Holder, Venetian, Bronze, Gold Dore, Sections, 6 x 10 x 2 ¾ In.................... 1800.00
tter Holder, Venetian, Bronze, Gold Dore, 4 ½ x 6 ¼ In............................ 2000.00
tter Holder, Zodiac, Bronze, Gold Dore, Sections, Signed, 4 ½ x 6 In.................. 1200.00
tter Opener, Adam, Bronze, Gold Dore, Curved Handle, Signed, 9 In.................. 600.00
tter Opener, Bookmark, Bronze, Gold Dore, Signed, 10 In.................. 750.00 to 950.00
tter Opener, Grapevine, Amber Slag Glass, Bronze, Gold Dore, Signed, 9 ¼ In........... 750.00
tter Opener, Grapevine, Green Slag Glass, Bronze, Dark Patina, Signed, 9 ½ In.......... 950.00
tter Opener, Ninth Century, Bronze, Gold Dore, Signed, 10 In....................... 950.00
tter Opener, Pine Needle, Amber Slag Glass, Bronze, Gold Dore, Signed, 9 ¼ In.......... 750.00
tter Opener, Venetian, Bronze, Gold Dore, 10½ In........................ 750.00 to 950.00
gnifying Glass, Abalone, Bronze, Gold Dore, 8¾ x 4 In................... 1175.00 to 2000.00
gnifying Glass, American Indian, Bronze, Gold Dore, 8 ½ x 4 In.................... 1500.00
gnifying Glass, Graduate, Bronze, Gold Dore, 8 ½ x 4 In.......................... 1500.00
gnifying Glass, Grapevine, Bronze, Gold Dore, 8 ¾ x 3 ½ In........................ 1800.00
gnifying Glass, Ninth Century, Bronze, Gold Dore, 8¾ x 4 In....................... 2500.00
gnifying Glass, Venetian, Bronze, Gold Dore, 9 x 4 In............................ 1500.00
gnifying Glass, Zodiac, Bronze, Dark Patina, 8 ¾ x 4 In.......................... 1500.00
tch Safe, Zodiac, Bronze, Gold Dore, ¾ x 1 ¾ x 2 ½ In............................ 450.00
rror, Hand, Grapevine, Amber Slag Glass, Bronze, Bevel Edge, 11 ½ x 7 ½ In............. 2500.00
tepad Holder, Bookmark, Bronze, Gold Dore, 7 ½ x 4½ In.......................... 950.00
tepad Holder, Graduate, Bronze, Gold Dore, 7 ½ x 4½ In........................... 450.00
tepad Holder, Zodiac, Bronze, Gold Dore, 2 x 6 x 4 In............................. 1200.00
per Clip, American Indian, Bronze, Gold Dore, 2 ¾ x 4 In.......................... 650.00
per Clip, Bookmark, Bronze, Gold Dore, 2 ½ x 3 ¼ In............................. 750.00
per Clip, Grapevine, Green Slag Glass, Bronze, Dark Patina, 3 ¼ x 2 ½ In.............. 650.00
per Clip, Pine Needle, Amber Glass, Bronze, Gold Dore, 2 ½ x 3 ¾ In.................. 650.00
per Clip, Pine Needle, Green Slag Glass, Bronze, Patina, 2 ½ x 4 In.................. 780.00
per Clip, Zodiac, Bronze, Gold Dore, 2 ½ x 4 In.............................. *illus* 400.00
per Holder, Grapevine, Green Slag Glass, Bronze, 6 x 10 In......................... 805.00
per Holder, Pine Needle, Green Slag Glass, Bronze, 12 ½ x 9 ½ In.................... 2530.00
per Holder, Zodiac, 3 Tiers, Patina, 8 x 12 In.................................. 460.00
perweight, Bulldog, Bronze, Patina, Signed, 2 ¼ x 1 In....................... *illus* 665.00
perweight, Grapevine, Green Slag Glass, Bronze, Dark Patina, Raised Knob, 3 ½ In...... 650.00
perweight, Lion, Reclining, Bronze, Gold Dore, c.1910, 7 In........................ 2900.00
perweight, Zodiac, Bronze, 3 ½ x 2 ¼ In.. 2875.00
n Brush, Abalone, Bronze, Gold Dore, 8-Sided, 2 x 2 ¼ In.......................... 650.00
n Brush, Bookmark, Bronze, Gold Dore, 2 x 2 ¼ In................................ 750.00
n Brush, Venetian, Bronze, Gold Dore, 8-Sided, 2 ½ x 2 ¾ In....................... 850.00
n Tray, American Indian, Bronze, Dark Patina, 4 x 11 In........................... 450.00
n Tray, Graduate, Bronze, Gold Dore, Sections, 4 Ball Feet, 4 x 10 In................ 350.00
n Tray, Grapevine, Green Glass, Bronze, Dark Patina, Ball Feet, 9½ x 3½ In.... 309.00 to 550.00
n Tray, Zodiac, Bronze, Patina, 3 ¼ x 10 In................................ *illus* 180.00
n Tray, Zodiac, Bronze, Patina, 9 ½ x 3 In...................................... 120.00

Tiffany, Letter Holder, Grapevine, Green Slag Glass, Bronze, Sections, Signed, 6 ½ x 10 In.
$1400.00

Tiffany, Paper Clip, Zodiac, Bronze, Gold Dore, 2 ½ x 4 In.
$400.00

Tiffany, Paperweight, Bulldog, Bronze, Patina, Signed, 2 ¼ x 1 In.
$665.00

Tiffany, Pen Tray, Zodiac, Bronze, Patina, 3 ¼ x 10 In.
$180.00

TIP

Outdoor lights help prevent crimes, but install them high enough so they are difficult to unscrew.

T

Tiffany Glass, Bowl, Gold Iridescent, Green, Blue, Scalloped Rim, Footed, Favrile, 4 x 6 1/4 In.
$260.00

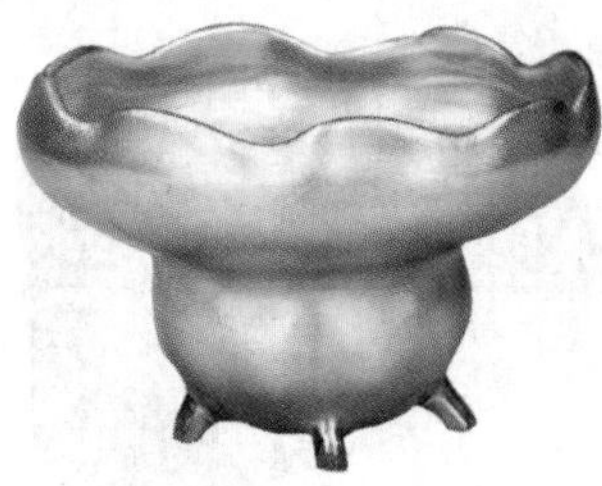

Tiffany Glass, Finger Bowl, Underplate, Blue Iridescent, Rippled Rim, Favrile, c.1900, 2 3/4 x 6 In.
$1554.00

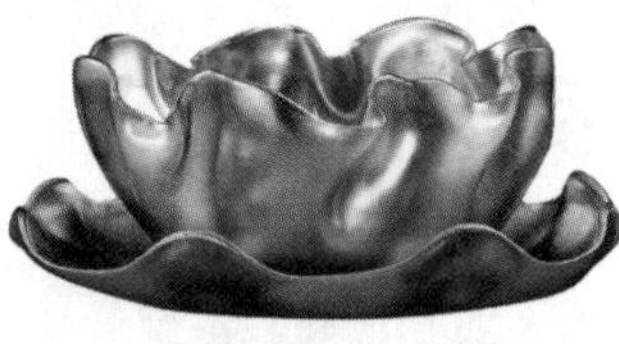

Tiffany Glass, Finger Bowl, Underplate, Gold Iridescent, Ruffled Edge, Favrile, Signed, 3 1/2 x 6 In.
$425.00

Tiffany Glass, Goblet, Wisteria, Pink, Purple, Opal, Ribbed, Engraved, 7 1/4 In.
$1000.00

Plate, Bronze, Decorated Border, c.1907, 8 7/8 In. .... 235.
Postage Scale, Bookmark, Bronze, Gold Dore, 3 1/4 x 3 x 1 1/2 In. .... 2500.
Postage Scale, Grapevine, Green Slag Glass, Bronze, Dark Patina, 3 x 2 x 3 In. .... 2000.
Postage Scale, Pine Needle, Green Slag Glass, Bronze, Dark Patina, 3 x 2 x 3 In. .... 2000.
Postage Scale, Venetian, Bronze, Gold Dore, 3 1/4 x 1 3/4 x 3 In. .... 2500.
Sconce, 2-Light, Favrile Glass, Bronze, c.1910, 3, 15 1/2 x 12 1/4 x 6 1/4 In. .... 24000.
Sconce, Lily, 4-Light, Gold Iridescent, Bronze, Gold Dore, Favrile, c.1910, Pair .... 27000.
Sconce, Tulip, 2-Light, Yellow, Red, Bronze, Patina, Favrile, c.1910, 16 x 9 x 9 In., Pair .... 18000.
Shade, Mesh, Embossed Maple Leaf Band, 16 x 7 3/4 In. .... 201.
Stringholder, Bookmark, Hexagon, Bright Gold Patina, Cover, 3 In. .... 3105.
Tazza, Bronze, Gold Iridescent, Enameled Heart-Shaped Rim, Raised Platform Base, 6 In. .... 3500.
Tea Screen, 3 Sections, Red, White, Green, Violet Swirls, Bronze, Ball Feet, 7 x 12 In. .... 4500.
Thermometer, Pine Needle, Green Slag Glass, Bronze, Dark Patina, 8 1/2 x 4 In. .... 3500.
Thermometer, Zodiac, Bronze, Dark Patina, 8 x 4 In. .... 2000.
Tray, Abalone, Bronze, Gold Dore, 12 In. Diam. .... 1200.
Tray, Bird Of Paradise, Bronze, Dark Patina, Enameled, Border, 8 In. .... 3000.
Tray, Bronze, Gold Dore, Raised Border, 9 In. .... 250.
Tray, Bronze, Gold Dore, Raised Geometric Border, 12 In. .... 350.
Tray, Bronze, Raised Gold Dore Well, Red, Green Enameled Flowers, Leaves, 10 x 6 In. .... 1500.
Tray, Enameled Dogwood, Leaves, Bronze, Openwork Border, 11In. .... 2070.
Vase, Blue, Pulled Design, Favrile, 3 x 4 1/2 In. .... 3240.
Vase, Creamy Opal, Gold, Green Pulled Feather, Oval, 3 In. .... 863.
Vase, Flower Leaves, Clear, Intaglio Carved, c.1910, 5 In. .... 24000.
Vase, Flower Shape, Bronze, Gold Dore, Raised Rib, Saucer Foot, Favrile, 21 1/2 In. .... 2300.
Vase, Flower Shape, Paperweight, Leaves, c.1910, 5 In. .... 6600.
Vase, Gold, Bulging Chain Crimps, Favrile, Signed, c.1901, 6 1/2 In. .... 2013.
Vase, Trumpet, Bronze, Gold Dore, Turquoise Enamel On Foot, Favrile, 11 In. .... 1000.

TIFFANY GLASS

Basket, Amethyst Pastel, Enameled Handle, Bronze Basket, Glass Dish, Signed, 5 1/2 In. .... 1333.
Bonbon, Scalloped Rim, Marigold Iridescent, Marked, c.1908, 6 In. .... 230.
Bowl, Blue, Oval Ribbed, Rolled Rim, Favrile, Signed, 7 In. .... 748.
Bowl, Blue, Ribbed, Scalloped Rim, Butterfly, Flowering Branch, Favrile, Signed, 9 In. .... 2588.
Bowl, Blue, Squat, Everted Rim, Favrile, Signed, 6 1/2 In. .... 460.
Bowl, Blue Pastel, Onionskin Edge, Blue & Opalescent Bands, Signed, 9 In. .... 978.
Bowl, Centerpiece, Blue Iridescent, Flared & Flattened Rim, Favrile, 3 x 11 1/2 In. .... 3000.
Bowl, Centerpiece, Gold, Green Leaves, Tendrils, Double Flower Frog, Favrile, 4 x 11 In. .... 3120.
Bowl, Centerpiece, Gold, Leaves, Vines, Rainbow Iridescent, Favrile, 12 x 3 3/4 In. .... 2300.
Bowl, Floral, Underplate, Blue Iridescent, Purple, Green, Gold, Red Highlights, Favrile, 11 1/2 In. 4000.
Bowl, Gold, Optic Ribbed, Scalloped Rim, Favrile, 6 1/4 In. .... 575.
Bowl, Gold, Ribbed, Iridescent Highlights, Pinched Scalloped Rim, 7 1/2 In. .... 863.
Bowl, Gold Favrile, Optic Ribbed, Rolled Rim, 4 1/4 In. .... 259.
Bowl, Gold Iridescent, 10 Ribs, Flared Rim, 3 5/8 x 9 1/2 In. .... 705.
Bowl, Gold Iridescent, Crimped Rim, Signed, 2 3/4 In. .... 200.
Bowl, Gold Iridescent, Gold & Purple Highlights, Favrile, 7 In. .... 561.
Bowl, Gold Iridescent, Green, Blue, Scalloped Rim, Footed, Favrile, 4 x 6 1/4 In. .... *illus* 260.
Bowl, Gold Iridescent, Pinched, Scalloped Rim, Favrile, Signed, 2 1/4 x 4 1/2 In. .... 330.
Bowl, Ice Blue Pastel Rim, Snowflake, Opalescent Bands, Footed, Favrile, 2 In. .... 604.
Bowl, Iridescent Blue Over White Petals, Flat Rim, Favrile, Signed, 2 1/2 x 8 1/2 In. .... 1600.
Bowl, Yellow Over White, Opalescent, Snowflake, 7 3/4 In. .... 374.
Box, Cover, Silver, Blue Iridescent, Favrile, 3 1/2 x 6 x 2 1/4 In. .... 2875.
Box, Hinged Cover, Half Moons, Ribs, Raised Center, Hexagonal, Favrile, 6 x 2 In. .... 4500.
Cake Plate, Butterscotch To Honey, Laurel Leaf Border, Signed, 5 x 10 In. .... 1035.
Candlestick, Cobalt Blue, Purple, Magenta Iridescent, 5 1/4 In. .... 1610.
Candlestick, Damascene, Bulbous, Sterling Stem, 9 1/2 In., Pair .... 6613.
Candlestick, Gold, Rainbow Iridescent, Twisted Stem, Favrile, 5 In., Pair .... 1035.
Candlestick, Gold, Ribbed, Button Pontil, Favrile, Signed, 5 In. .... 411.
Candlestick, Gold Iridescent, Twisted, Scalloped Rim, Favrile, Signed, 5 1/4 x 3 3/4 In. 520
Candlestick, Green Iridescent, Yellow, Pink, Tapered, Ribbed, Favrile, Signed, 1826, 12 In. 3200
Candlestick, Opalescent, Stretched Rims, Laurel Leaf, Foot, Favrile, 4 In., Pair .... 1725.
Candlestick, Yellow, Opalescent Snowflake, Twisted Stem, Banded Foot, 12 In. 2530
Ceiling Light, Flowers, Intaglio, Green Vines, Opalescent, Oval, Enameled, Bronze, c.1921, 10 1/2 In. 21600
Champagne, White Opalescent, Star, Clear Stem, 7 1/4 x 4 1/4 In. 978
Compote, Alabaster Foot, Stem, Acanthus Leaves, Blue Onionskin Edge, 4 In. .... 978.
Compote, Amber Optic Rib, Iridescent Green, Onionskin Edge, Green Pedestal, 8 In. 715
Compote, Amethyst Pastel, Onionskin Border, Opalescent Leaf, Paper Label, 6 In. 690

T

ompote, Blue, Bulbous Rolled Rim, Ribbed, Favrile, c.1919, 6 ¼ In. 2415.00
ompote, Blue, Swirling Optic Ribbed, Scalloped Rim, Favrile, Signed, 4 In. 2300.00
ompote, Blue Green Pastel, Opalescent Diamonds & Rim, Clear Base, 2 ¼ x 5 ¼ In. 950.00
ompote, Blue Iridescent, Applied Foot, Cupped Bowl, Favrile, 2 ¼ x 4 ¼ In. 748.00
ompote, Blue Iridescent, Pedestal Base, 4 ½ x 8 In. 3000.00
ompote, Bulbous Flower, 5-Point Onionskin Rim, Pulled Feather, Footed, Favrile, 5 In. 1668.00
ompote, Butterscotch, Scalloped Rim, Applied Saucer Foot, Favrile, 3 ¾ x 6 In. 690.00
ompote, Gold, Onionskin Edge, Favrile, 6 In. 550.00
ompote, Gold, Onionskin Edge, Favarile, Marked, c.1905, 5 In. 1150.00
ompote, Gold, Optic Ribbed, Scalloped Rim, Favrile, 3 ¼ x 6 In. 403.00
ompote, Gold Iridescent, Flat Onionskin Rim, Applied Saucer Foot, Favrile, 2 ¾ x 8 In. 780.00
ompote, Gold Iridescent, Intaglio Leaves & Vines, Onionskin Edge, 4 ½ x 5 ½ In. 2200.00
ompote, Green, Pulled Feather, Opalescent, Gold Iridescent, Favrile, 4 ¼ x 5 ¼ In. 1668.00
ompote, Green Pastel, Amber Foot, Green Onionskin Edge, Signed, 7 ½ In. 805.00
ompote, Green Pastel, Opalescent Bands, Low Footed, Favrile, Signed, 2 ¼ In. 518.00
ompote, Iridescent Pink Over Stars & Diamonds, Clear Stem, Favrile, Signed, 6 In. 2400.00
ompote, Optic Ribbed, Onion Skin Edge, Favrile, Signed, 3 In. 805.00
ompote, Pastel, Yellow Iridescent, Onionskin Edge, White Stars, Favrile, 5 x 7 In. 633.00
ompote, Pastel Amethyst, Onionskin Edge, Marked, 4 In. 1438.00
ompote, Pastel Pink, Onionskin Edge, Diamond Quilted, 8 In. 863.00
ompote, Silver, Gold Iridescent, Onionskin Edge, Purple Interior, 5 ¼ x 7 In. 2645.00
ompote, Yellow Pastel, Oval, Iridescent Yellow, Opalescent, Signed, 5 In. 690.00
rdial, Gold, Barrel Shape, Pigtail Prunts, Favrile, Signed, 2 ½ In. 259.00
rdial, Gold, Favrile, Signed, 4 ¼ In., Pair 403.00
rdial, Gold Favrile Glass, Pinch Sided, Signed, c.1900, 3 In. 144.00
ecanter, Gold Iridescent, Blue To Purple To Red, Favrile, 9 ¼ In. 2300.00
ecanter, Gold Iridescent, Genie Bottle Shape, Favrile, Stopper, Signed, 8 In. 2200.00
ecanter, Verre-De-Soie, Pulled Waves, Rainbow Highlights, 8 In. 825.00
nger Bowl, Gold, Underplate, Swirling Prunts, Favrile, Signed, c.1900, 6 In. 690.00
nger Bowl, Gold Iridescent, Ribbed, Scalloped Rim, 2 ¾ x 5 In. 345.00
nger Bowl, Millefiori, Green Leaves, Vines, 4 x 2 ¼ In. 9789.00
nger Bowl, Underplate, Blue Iridescent, Rippled Rim, Favrile, c.1900, 2 ¾ x 6 In. *illus* 1554.00
nger Bowl, Underplate, Gold, Ribbed Body, Scalloped Rims, Favrile, Signed, 6 ½ In. 518.00
nger Bowl, Underplate, Gold Favrile, Blue Highlights, Signed, 6 In. 345.00
nger Bowl, Underplate, Gold Iridescent, Ruffled Edge, Favrile, Signed, 3 ½ x 6 In. *illus* 425.00
nger Bowl, Underplate, Gold Iridescent, Pulled Prunts, Favrile, 6 & 3 In. 518.00
nger Bowl, Underplate, Queen, Gold, Scalloped Rim, Favrile, 6 x 3 In. 920.00
nger Bowl, Water Lily Shape, Gold Iridescent, Ruffled Rim, 4 ½ In. 442.00
ame, Gold To Green To Red Iridescent Insets, Favrile, 10 ½ x 7 In. 7475.00
blet, Gold Iridescent, Favrile, 5 ¾ In. 250.00
blet, Gold Iridescent, Pigtail Prunts, Pinched Stem, 3 ¾ In. 412.00
blet, Pink Pastel, Pinched Bowl, Opalescent Bands, Ribbed, Green Stem, 7 ¾ In. 863.00
blet, Topaz, Vertical Lines Of Ruby Dots, Topaz Stem & Foot, 7 ¾ In. 1020.00
blet, Wisteria, Pink, Purple, Opal, Ribbed, Engraved, 7 ¼ In. *illus* 1000.00
blet, Wisteria Bowl, Ribbed, 10 Opal Petals, Opal Cupped Foot, Favrile, 7 ¼ In. 1175.00
midor, Cover, Carved Flower, Silver, Blue Iridescent, Favrile, 7 ¼ In. 2875.00
r, Cover, Gold Iridescent, Rim, Handle, Signed, 3 ½ x 2 ¾ In. 2000.00
r, Cover, Gold Iridescent, Sunburst, Favrile, 7 ½ x 4 In. 1800.00
mp, Candle, Blue Iridescent, Ribbed, Swirled, Flared, Base, Favrile, 5 ¼ In. 530.00
mp, Candle, Gold, Scalloped Shade, Pulled Leaf, Twist Base, 12 ¼ In. 1495.00
mp, Candle, Honeycomb Shade, Swirled Ribs, Gold Iridescent, Pink, Platinum, 12 In. 1840.00
mp, Candle, Iridescent Gold Twist Stem, Amber Chimney, Favrile, Signed, 13 In. 1093.00
mp, Candle, Opal Shade, Gold Favrile, Twisted Stem, Ruffled Edge, 16 In. 1265.00
mp, Candle, Purple, Blue, Rainbow Iridescent, Gold Favrile, 5 ½ In. 863.00
mp, Candle, Ruffled Shade, Peacock Blue Iridescent, Twisted, Ribbed, Favrile, 14 In. 6000.00
mp Base, Baluster Shape, Green Matte Glass, Iridescent Blue, Silvered Collar, 11 x 23 In. 2760.00
ving Cup, Gold Iridescent, Green Leaf, Vine, 3 Handles, Favrile, 5 In. 2200.00
ppy, Gold Favrile, Footed, Triangular, Everted Rim, Applied Looping Holder, 5 In. 403.00
nament, Gold Iridescent, Round, Favrile, 2 In. 325.00
rfait, Amethyst, Opalescent Bands, Favrile, Signed, 5 ¼ In. 550.00
rfait, Yellow Opalescent, Bands, Marked, 5 In. 259.00
rfume Bottle, Trailing Vines, Engraved, Favrile, 4 ¼ In. 5463.00
tcher, Gold Favrile, Red Hues, Signed, 2 ½ In. 345.00
ate, Blue Iridescent, Stretched Pattern, Scalloped Border, 6 ¾ In. 531.00
ate, Green Pastel, Optic Ribbed, Opalescent Band, Onionskin Edge, 8 ¼ In. 403.00
ate, Opalescent, Sea Foam, Alternating Bands, 11 In. 450.00

Tiffany Glass, Shade, Gold Damascene, Dome Shape, Favrile, Signed, 5 x 10 In. $9600.00

Tiffany Glass, Shade, Green Damascene, Dome Shape, Favrile, Signed, 5 x 10 In. $12000.00

Tiffany Glass, Vase, Blue, Green Iridescent, Favrile, Signed, 8 x 4 ½ In. $1450.00

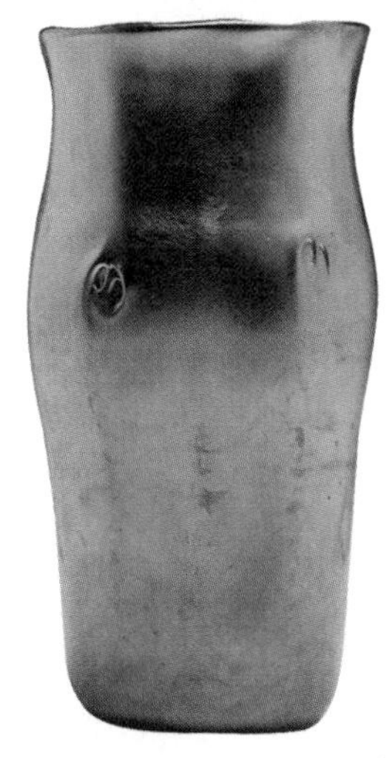

TIP

It is said creativity comes from a messy, cluttered environment. It inspires ideas. Remember that the next time you rearrange your collectibles.

T

TIFFANY GLASS

Tiffany Glass, Vase, Flower Shape, White, Green Leaves, Gold Interior, 4 ⅝ In.
$1500.00

Tiffany Glass, Vase, Flower Shape, White, Pink, Clear Stem, Favrile, Signed, 9 ¼ In.
$1075.00

TIP
Tell your heirs about your collection. Inventory items by category, and include what you paid. Then list names and addresses of people who might want to buy your collection or dealers you trust. Consider donating to a museum or charity.

T

Plate, Pink Pastel, Optic Ribs, Opalescent Bands, Onionskin Edge, Favrile, Signed, 8 In. 403.0
Punch Cup, Gold, Purple, Applied Handle, Favrile, 2 ¼ In. 288.0
Salt, Blue, Ruffled Edge, Favrile, Signed, 3 In. 374.0
Salt, Blue, Squat, Side Handles, Favrile, 1 In., Pair 850.0
Salt, Gold Iridescent, 8 Applied Stemmed Leaf Pods, Paneled, Flared Rim, 1 x 2 In. 940.0
Salt, Gold Iridescent, Blue Highlights, Pulled Twists, Round, Favrile, 1 x 2 In. 375.0
Salt, Gold Iridescent, Ruffled Rim, Favrile, 1 x 2 ½ In. 200.0
Salt, Gold Iridescent, Silver Blue Highlights, Bulbous, Flared Rim, 4-Footed, Favrile, 1 ½ x 2 In. 250.0
Salt, Silver To Purple Iridescent, Blue, Ruffled Edge, 1 x 4 In. 920.0
Scent Bottle, Pulled Leaf, White Ground, Gold Iridescent, Stopper, 11 ½ In. 58.0
Seal, Gold Iridescent, Violet, Blue Highlights, 3 Scarabs, Beaded Base, Favrile, 1 ¾ In. 750.0
Shade, 3 Paneled Sides, Gold Iridescent, Favrile, 2 ⅜ In. 898.0
Shade, Bullet, Green Pulled Feather, Gold Iridescent, Clambroth Ground, 8 x 3 ¼ In. 4715.0
Shade, Candle, Lamp, Linenfold, Green, 5 ½ x 4 ½ In. 518.0
Shade, Candle Lamp, Gold Iridescent, Purple, Red, Onionskin Edge, 7 ¼ In. 3738.0
Shade, Gold Damascene, Dome Shape, Favrile, Signed, 5 x 10 In. . . . . *illus* 9600.0
Shade, Gold Iridescent, Hooked Feather, Green Opalescent Ground, 5 ¾ x 2 ¼ In. 1560.0
Shade, Green Damascene, Dome Shape, Favrile, Signed, 5 x 10 In. . . . . *illus* 12000.0
Shade, Lily, Ribbed, Gold Iridescence, Red, Blue Highlights, Flared Ruffled Rim, 5 In. 2703.0
Shade, Purple, Blue, Green, Iridescent, Diamond Quilted, 4 ½ In. 1725.0
Shade, Stalactite, Green, Hooked Feather, Gold Trim, Opalescent Ground, 13 In. 3450.0
Soup, Coupe, Flower Shape, Green Pulled Feather, Gold Luster Interior, Favrile, 4 x 5 In. 2280.0
Soup, Coupe, Gold Favrile, Footed, Scalloped Rim, Signed, c.1908, 4 In. 575.0
Tile, Favrile, Red, Green, Yellow, 3 x 3 In. 180.0
Tile, Religious Theme, Multicolored, Mosaic Set In Plaster, Signed, c.1910, 16 x 12 In. 10200.0
Vase, Agate, Favrile, 4 ¼ In. 3600.0
Vase, Amber, Green Pulled Feather, Opalescent, Translucent Foot, Favrile, 10 ½ In. 6000.0
Vase, Applied Chain Design, Gold Overtones, Pinched, Pontil, c.1912, 3 ½ In. 1898.0
Vase, Black, Iridescent Blue Pulled Feathers, c.1900, 3 ½ In. 2415.0
Vase, Blue, Baluster, Favrile, 10 ¼ x 8 In. 2400.0
Vase, Blue, Flared Rim, Base, Favrile, c.1919, 8 In. 2340.0
Vase, Blue, Gold Luster, 3 In. 5400.0
Vase, Blue, Green Iridescent, Favrile, Signed, 8 x 4 ½ In. . . . . *illus* 1450.0
Vase, Blue, Pinch Sides, Ribs, Oval, Ruffled Rolled Rim, Signed, Favrile, c.1919, 4 In. 900.0
Vase, Blue, Purple & Green Iridescence, Favrile, 4 x 10 ¾ In. 1800.0
Vase, Blue, Purple Iridescent, 8 Applied Tendrils, 4 In. 540.0
Vase, Blue Iridescent, Pulled Drape, Favrile, Signed, 10 ½ In. 1600.0
Vase, Blue Iridescent, Swirled Hooked Feather, Squat Shoulders, Favrile, c.1897, 4 In. 1035.0
Vase, Blue Over Red, Swirl, Ribbed, Favrile, Signed, N-3578, 11 In. 700.0
Vase, Brilliant Green, White Neck, Bottle Shape, Favrile, Signed, 11 In. 3360.0
Vase, Bud, Ribbed, Rolled Rim, Bronze, Gold Dore Base, 10 ½ In. 633.0
Vase, Calla Lily Shape, Translucent Amber To Opal, Pulled Feathers, Iridescent, 12 In. 4250.0
Vase, Cobalt Blue, Shaded, Indigo & Gold Handkerchief Pattern, Bulbous, 6 In. 3175.0
Vase, Colorful Iridescence, Gold, Bulbous, Swirling Ribs, Favrile, 4 ½ x 4 ½ In. 620.0
Vase, Crimson, Caramel Pulled Feathers, Oval Base, Elongated Neck, 8 In. 4700.0
Vase, Cypriote, Gold Iridescent, Bubbled, Pinched, Favrile, 5 In. 3738.0
Vase, Cypriote, Red, Blue Opalescent Flashes, Bulbous, 8 ¼ In. 3910.0
Vase, Cypriote, Textured, c.1910, 6 ⅜ In. 16800.0
Vase, Egyptian, Blue, Elongated Neck, Favrile, 6 In. 1150.0
Vase, Egyptian, Rainbow Iridescent, Gold Favrile, 3 ¾ In. 633.0
Vase, Flower Shape, Amber To Green, Paper Label, c.1895, 9 ¾ In. 5100.0
Vase, Flower Shape, Chartreuse Pulled Feather, Opal White Ground, 5 In. 1610.0
Vase, Flower Shape, Gold, Ribbed Foot, Knopped Stem, Bulbous Rim, Favrile, 9 In. 800.0
Vase, Flower Shape, Gold, Footed, Scalloped Rim, Favrile, c.1909, 4 ½ In. 950.0
Vase, Flower Shape, Gold, Optic Ribbed Body, Everted Scalloped Rim, Favrile, c.1905, 9 In. . . . 1150.0
Vase, Flower Shape, Gold, Optic Ribbed Body, Everted Rim, Favrile, Signed, c.1913, 11 In. . . . 1265.0
Vase, Flower Shape, Gold Favrile, Quadrafoil Rim, 4-Footed, Bulbous, c.1905, 2 ¾ In. 403.0
Vase, Flower Shape, Gold Iridescent, Folded Rim, Pedestal Base, Favrile, 4 x 5 In. 1800.0
Vase, Flower Shape, Gold Iridescent, 5-Fold Flared Rim, Favrile, 4 In. 1800.0
Vase, Flower Shape, Green, Pulled Feather, Opalescent Clambroth Ground, 12 In. 10350.0
Vase, Flower Shape, Green Iridescent, Lilies, Bulbous Base, Spreading Rim, c.1903, 15 In. . . . 690.0
Vase, Flower Shape, Green Pulled Feathers, Opal Ground, Gold Iridescent, Foot, 15 In. 9200.0
Vase, Flower Shape, Green Pulled Hearts, Vines, 9 ½ In. 259.0
Vase, Flower Shape, Green Stem, Clear, Marked, c.1905, 11 ¾ In. 12000.0
Vase, Flower Shape, Opalescent, Ribs, Gold Iridescent, Favrile, 12 ¼ In. 7475.0
Vase, Flower Shape, Opalescent, Pulled Green Leaves, Favrile, c.1905, 11 ¾ In. 12000.0

Vase, Flower Shape, Rainbow Iridescent, Copper To Orange, 4¾ In. 1495.00
Vase, Flower Shape, Rainbow Iridescent, Gold, Favrile, 4¼ x 6 In. 978.00
Vase, Flower Shape, White, Green Leaves, Gold Interior, 4⅝ In. *illus* 1500.00
Vase, Flower Shape, White, Pink, Clear Stem, Favrile, Signed, 9¼ In. *illus* 1075.00
Vase, Flower Shape, White Opalescent, Striated Feathering, Favrile, c.1906, 9½ In. 5705.00
Vase, Flower Shape, White Top, Green Pulled Leaves, Flared, Ruffled Rim, Gold Foot, 5 In. 1765.00
Vase, Flower Shape, Yellow Ground, Pulled Feather, Gold, Opalescent, Bronze Holder, 17 In. 6900.00
Vase, Gold, Bulbous, Favrile, 3¾ In. 150.00
Vase, Gold, Footed, Shouldered, Tapered Flaring Rim, Favrile, c.1911, 13 In. 3680.00
Vase, Gold, Platinum & Purple Iridescent, Footed, Favrile, Signed, 1½ x 2½ In. 340.00
Vase, Gold, Purple, Green Iridescent, Swollen Stem, Broad Bowl, Favrile, Signed, 9 x 6 In. 1420.00
Vase, Gold Favrile, Pinched Pigtail Prunts, Signed, c.1905, 3 In. 518.00
Vase, Gold Favrile, Ribbed Lobed Body, Inverted Rim, Signed, c.1900, 3½ In. 403.00
Vase, Gold Iridescent, 4 Pinched Sides, Flared Rim, 2¾ In. 265.00
Vase, Gold Iridescent, Bulbous, Handles, Favrile, Signed, 4 In. *illus* 1300.00
Vase, Gold Iridescent, Green Translucent Ground, Scalloped Rim, 2½ In. 2300.00
Vase, Gold Iridescent, Millefiori Flowers, Green Leaves, Favrile, c.1905, 7 In. 6600.00
Vase, Gold Iridescent, Pulled Feather, Frosted White Ground, Streaks, 14 In. 1035.00
Vase, Gold Iridescent, Pulled Waves, Translucent Green Ground, 3½ In. 920.00
Vase, Gold Iridescent, Raised Zipper Design, Blue, Violet, Pink, Bulbous, Favrile, 4 In. 1800.00
Vase, Gold Iridescent, Ruffled Rim, Footed, Favrile, Signed, 3¼ x 4½ In. 520.00
Vase, Gold Iridescent, Wavy Ribbon, Green, Blue Iridescent, 8 In. 1840.00
Vase, Gold Pulled Feather, Pale Yellow Ground, Favrile, 9½ x 4 In. 1560.00
Vase, Grapes, Vines, Leaves, Intaglio Carved, Pinched Waist, Gold, Favrile, 5½ In. 2760.00
Vase, Green, Blue, Gold Damascene, Oval, Square Mouth, Favrile, 3¼ In. 1955.00
Vase, Green, Gold Pulled Feather, Opal Rim, Pontil, Oval, Favrile, c.1901, 6 In. 2415.00
Vase, Green, Silver, Caramel Hooked Feather, Squat, Shouldered, Favrile, 2 In. 1300.00
Vase, Green, Yellow, Pastel, Morning Glory Blossom Rim, Signed, 10½ In. *illus* 1770.00
Vase, Green Feathers, Gold Iridescent Ground, Favrile, 2¼ In. 1323.00
Vase, Green Heart, Vines, White Centers, Gold Ground, Blue, Green & Red Flashes, 6¼ In. 2358.00
Vase, Green Hearts, Vines, White Millefiori, Gold, Favrile, Shoulder, Oval, c.1908, 4¼ In. 2300.00
Vase, Green Hearts & Vines, Gold Iridescent Ground, Flower Form, 6 In. 2640.00
Vase, Green Iridescent, Gold Pulled Feather, Button Pontil, Double Gourd Shape, 6 In. 2875.00
Vase, Green Pulled & Hooked Feather, Platinum Iridescent Outline, 3 In. 1265.00
Vase, Iridescent Gold, Green Hooked Feather, Handles, Pot Shape, c.1907, 2 In. 800.00
Vase, Iridescent Gold & Pink, Flared, Favrile, Marked, 4 In. 495.00
Vase, Jack-In-The-Pulpit, Golf, Favrile, Bulbous, Optic Ribbed Foot, c.1903, 15 In. 1725.00
Vase, Lustered Agate, Favrile, 3¼ In. 2280.00
Vase, Millefiori, Gourd Shape, Favrile, Signed, c.1905, 7 In. 6600.00
Vase, Nasturtium, Green Leaves, Signed, 10 In. *illus* 1093.00
Vase, Opal, Gold Iridescent, Hooked Feathers, Squat, Oval, Handles, Favrile, 1919, 4 In. 650.00
Vase, Opal, Green Pulled Leaves, Gold Highlights, Oval Gourd, Favrile, 5½ In. 1035.00
Vase, Opal, Iridescent Green Pulled Feathers, Brown Tip, Gourd Shape, Favrile, 3¼ In. 1200.00
Vase, Orange & Lime Green Ground, Handles, Favrile, 2¾ x 3¼ In. 2520.00
Vase, Paperweight, Aquamarine, Sea Plants, Flowers, Favrile, Marked, 3¾ In. 13000.00
Vase, Paperweight, Intaglio, Translucent Amber, Green Leaves, 13½ In. 6500.00
Vase, Peacock Blue, Favrile, 10 In. 1440.00
Vase, Pulled Green & White Feathers, Favrile, Signed, 2¼ In. *illus* 1050.00
Vase, Pulled Ribbons, Corset Shape, Wave Pattern, 13¼ In. 920.00
Vase, Purple, Agate Swirl, 4 In. 1080.00
Vase, Red, Baluster, Favrile, c.1919, 9¾ In. 9600.00
Vase, Red, Bulbous, 4 Iridescent Gold Pulled Feathers, Favrile, Signed, 3 In. 4600.00
Vase, Reverse Trumpet, Gold Iridescent, Stalagmite Leaves, Favrile, 8 In. 900.00
Vase, Ribs, Gold, Bulbous, Shouldered, Button Pontil, Favrile, 4¼ In. 1000.00
Vase, Silver, Blue Iridescent, Applied Fluted Handles, Baluster, 9½ In. 3738.00
Vase, Stick, Turquoise, Enamel, Bronze, Signed, 12 In. 1020.00
Vase, Trumpet, Blue Iridescent, Ribbed, Bronze Foot, 18¼ In. 2185.00
Vase, Trumpet, Carved Flowers, Shades Of Green, 15 In. 4720.00
Vase, Trumpet, Gold Favrile, Flared Rim, Blue Overtones, Signed, c.1917, 18 In. 2530.00
Vase, Trumpet, Gold Iridescent, Blue, Ribs, Rolled Rim, Bronze Base, Gold Dore, 17¾ In. 4025.00
Vase, Trumpet, Gold Iridescent, Green Vine, Flared, Ribbed Foot, Favrile, 9⅝ In. 1410.00
Vase, Trumpet, Gold Iridescent, Opal, Pulled Feathers, Favrile, c.1915, 6 In. 800.00
Vase, Trumpet, Gold Iridescent, Optic Ribbed Base, Knopped Stem, Favrile, 1916 1210.00
Vase, Trumpet, Gold Iridescent, Pulled Feathers, Opal, Bronze Base, Patina, c.1905, 12 In. 3000.00
Vase, Trumpet, Raspberry, Stretched, Opalescent, Clear Applied Knop, Foot, 9 In. 1610.00
Vase, Trumpet, Ribs, Onionskin Edge, Purple On Gold Foot, 10 In. 1035.00

Tiffany Glass, Vase, Gold Iridescent, Bulbous, Handles, Favrile, Signed, 4 In.
$1300.00

Tiffany Glass, Vase, Green, Yellow, Pastel, Morning Glory Blossom Rim, Signed, 10½ In.
$1770.00

Tiffany Glass, Vase, Nasturtium, Green Leaves, Signed, 10 In.
$1093.00

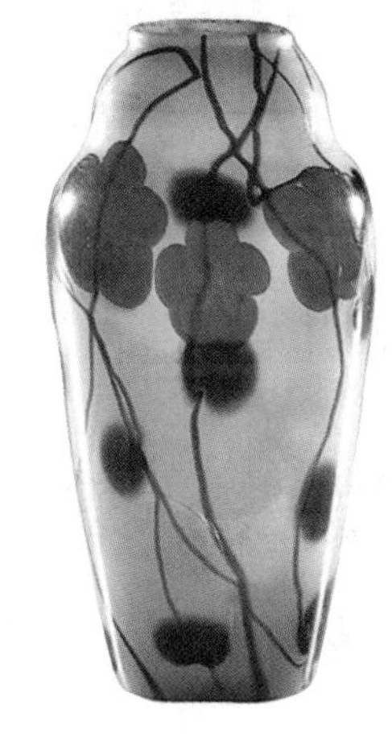

Tiffany Glass, Vase, Pulled Green & White Feathers, Favrile, Signed, 2¼ In.
$1050.00

T

Tiffany Pottery, Vase, Artichoke, White Glaze, Bisque, Favrile, c.1910, 6 In.
$3600.00

Tiffany Pottery, Vase, Green Matte, Amber & Brown Mottled Glaze, 16 x 8½ In.
$4200.00

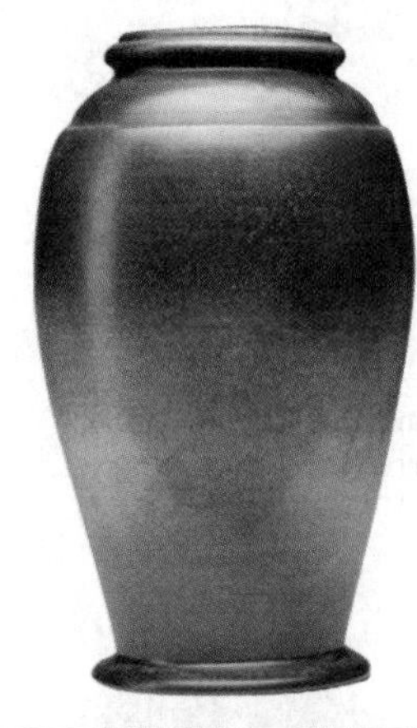

Tiffany Silver, Bowl, Acanthus & Drape Border, Scalloped Base, c.1884, 2¾ x 8½ In.
$725.00

Tiffany Silver, Incense Burner, Leaves, Gourd Form, Marked, 2½ In.
$480.00

Vase, Tulip Shape, Citron Iridescent, Pulled Feathers, Red, Amber, Ribbed Base, 9½ In. 5750.00
Vase, Turquoise, Olive Green Applied Rim, Favrile, 6½ In. 1725.00
Wine, Lavender, White Opalescent Ribbing, Clear Stem, Foot, 8¼ In. 1725.00
Wine, Moonstone Opalescent, Clear Stem, Foot, 4¼ In. 633.00
Wine, Pastel, Light Purple, Feathers, White Opalescent, 6¼ In. 748.00
Wine, Raspberry, Pale Opalescent Stripes & Rim, 4-Part Stem, Favrile, 9 In. 1380.00

TIFFANY GOLD
Pill Box, Flattened Rectangular Body, Basket Weave, Ribbed, 14K Gold, 2 In. 840.00

TIFFANY POTTERY
Vase, Artichoke, White Glaze, Bisque, Favrile, c.1910, 6 In. *illus* 3600.00
Vase, Cherry Blossoms, White Matte Glaze, Burst Bubbles, 7 x 3½ In. 960.00
Vase, Chestnut Branches, Ivory Ground, Blue & Green Glaze, Porcelain, 9 x 6½ In. 5400.00
Vase, Cobalt & Gray Crystalline Glaze, Bottle Shape, 11 x 8 In. 1920.00
Vase, Dogwood Blossoms, White Bisque Surface, Green Glazed Interior, 9 x 14 In. 5700.00
Vase, Green Matte, Amber & Brown Mottled Glaze, 16 x 8½ In. *illus* 4200.00
Vase, Verdigris Crystalline Glaze, Bronze Rim, Bottle Shape, 12¼ x 5½ In. 2040.00
Vase, White Bisque, Leaves, Amber Glazed, 4½ x 2¾ In. 780.00

TIFFANY SILVER
Asparagus Dish, Liner, Scroll Feet, Flared Rim, Beaded Border, c.1907, 13 In. 2400.00
Asparagus Tongs, Wave Edge, Marked, c.1884, 7½ In. 1076.00
Baby Cup, c.1911, 2¾ In. 199.00
Berry Spoon, Pierced Handle, Kidney Shaped Bowl, c.1890, 9½ In. 448.00
Bonbon Spoon, 3 Women, Singing, Playing Harp, Art Nouveau, Gilt Bowl, 9¼ In. 431.00
Bowl, Acanthus & Drape Border, Scalloped Base, c.1884, 2¾ x 8½ In. *illus* 725.00
Bowl, Art Deco Tomato, Ring Foot, Fruit Bands, 1943-45, 3⅝ x 9⅜ In. 1020.00
Bowl, Centerpiece, Repousse, Scrolling Vines, Footed, c.1902, 4 x 9 In. 1521.00
Bowl, Embossed, 4 Seasons, Ice Skating Cherubs, c.1902, 5⅜ In. 646.00
Bowl, Flared Edge, Embossed, Chased Flowers, Scrolls, c.1900, 26½ In. 32200.00
Bowl, Fruit, Graduated Hexagon, Reeded Rim, c.1938, 9⅛ In. 323.00
Bowl, Fruit, Shells, C-Scroll Cartouches, Scalloped Rim, 1907-39, 11¾ In. 382.00
Bowl, Ice, Pinecone, Bombe Shape, 10¾ In. 7200.00
Bowl, Queen Anne, Wide Rim, Low Foot, 10⅛ In. 470.00
Bowl, Scalloped & Reeded Border, Monogram, c.1911, 2¾ x 12 In. 460.00
Bowl, Shallow, Trailing Bluebell Rim, c.1891, 7¾ In., Pair 885.00
Bowl, Shaped Edge, c.1925, 2½ x 12 In. 646.00
Box, Stamp, Hinged Cover, Wooden Interior, 3 Sections, 1⅞ x 7⅛ In. 590.00
Bread Basket, Reticulated, Oval, Trefoil, Panel Piercing, c.1938, 11 In., Pair 999.00
Bread Tray, Oval, Flower, c.1900, 12 In. 1050.00
Caddy Spoon, Pierced Flower, Leaf Stem, Shaped Gilt Bowl, c.1900, 5½ In. 448.00
Cake Knife, Palm Pattern, Engraved, Aesthetic Motifs, c.1880, 11¼ In. 353.00
Cake Plate, Everted Rim, Trefoil Shaped Leaves, 1907-38, 10½ In. 999.00
Candlestick, Cannon-Shaped, Tapered Shaft, Knop Ring, Trumpet Foot, 13 In., Pair 3360.00
Child's Set, Porringer, Bowl, Stands, Mug, Napkin Ring, Musicians, Case, c.1887, 6 Piece 10625.00
Christening Set, Ring Handled Spoon, Fork, Food Pusher, Napkin Ring, 3 Piece 150.00
Cigar Lighter, Round Base, Guilloche Border, Satyr Head Bracket, c.1860, 10½ In. 13750.00
Cocktail Shaker, Jigger Top, Openwork Strainer, c.1946, 3 Pt., 10¾ In. 1495.00
Coffee Set, Scalloped Base, Scroll Border, Monogram, Gilt Wash, c.1905, 3 Piece 1840.00
Coffeepot, Demitasse, Ball Finial, Tapered, Ear Handle, Acanthus Band, 7⅝ In. 705.00
Coffeepot, Demitasse, Repousse, Angular Handle, Ball Lid, Flowers, c.1890, 8½ In. 1528.00
Compote, Openwork, Scroll & Shell Border, Lattice & Flowers, c.1902, 2¾ x 9 In. 1035.00
Compote, Scroll & Shell Borders, Flowers, Openwork, c.1893, 5 x 9 In., Pair 2645.00
Cruet Set, Yachting Trophy, Entwined Rope Frame, c.1860, 12 In., 7 Piece 9360.00
Crumber, Scalloped Edge, Persian, c.1872, 14 In. 836.00
Cup, Lobed Handle, Infant Revelers Band, Child's, 1875-91, 3½ In. 646.00
Cup, Presentation, Roses, Scrolls, Engraved, Owl Masks, 3 Handles, c.1901, 16 In. 15000.00
Dish, Cover, Acanthus Leaf & Pineapple Handles & Feet, 7 x 13 In. 2645.00
Dish, Entree, Cover, Chrysanthemum, c.1985, 11 In., Pair 9600.00
Dish, Entree, Oval, Floral Repousse Band, Acanthus Handle, Monogram, 5 x 11 In. 3220.00
Fish Fork Set, Wave Over Edge, Splayed Tines, c.1884, 6¼ In., 6 Piece 956.00
Flask, Rectangular, Engraved Script Monogram, 1½ Pt., 7¾ In. 1293.00
Flask, Sloping Shoulders, Twist-Off Hinged Stopper, 8 x 4½ x 2¼ In. 489.00
Fork Set, Dessert, Persian, c.1891, 7 In., 15 Piece 600.00
Frame, Desk, Stylized Engraved Flowers, Scroll, 6⅕ In. 756.00
Frame, Leaf Wrapped, Reeded Border, Oak Leaves, Scrolls, c.1895, 15¾ In. 5100.00

T

Frame, Stylized Flowers Engraved On Sides, c.1900, 8 x 10 In. 675.00
Gravy Boat, Scrolled Handle, Oval, 1907-38, 4½ In. 264.00
Ice Bucket, Banded, Scroll Handles, 4¾ x 10½ x 5½ In. 1314.00
Ice Cream Fork, Renaissance Pattern, Monogram, c.1907, 5½ In., 12 Piece 1840.00
Incense Burner, Leaves, Gourd Form, Marked, 2½ In. *illus* 480.00
Jardiniere, Gilt, Oval, Fluted Supports, Flowers, Roses, Vines, c.1900, 11½ In., Pair 15600.00
Knife, Butter, Chrysanthemum, Individual, 6 Piece 450.00
Knife, Dinner, Lap Over Edge, Animals & Sea Creatures, c.1890, 10½ In., 12 Piece 8750.00
Knife, Fruit, Pocket, Shaped, Hammered, Gilt Blade, Pick, c.1873-91, 2¾ In. 179.00
Ladle, Soup, Saratoga Pattern, 12¾ In. 950.00
Loving Cup, Buffalo Driving Club, Shaped Handles, 1899, 9¼ x 9½ In. 1880.00
Mustard Pot, Spoon, Aesthetic, Baluster Shape, Rosettes, c.1874, 4½ In. 2400.00
Nutmeg Grater, Melon Shape, c.1902, 1¾ x 1¾ In. 2530.00
Pitcher, Urn Shape, Spreading Foot, Ivy, Leaves, 9¾ In. 2572.00
Pitcher, Wisteria Band, Hanging Around Shoulder, 5 Pt., 9½ In. 2990.00
Plate, Molded Rim, Angled Gadroons, Acanthus Border, c.1920, 11 In., 12 Piece 17500.00
Porringer, Queen Anne, c.1947, 7⅝ In. 176.00
Punch Bowl, Cover, Ladle, Paw Feet, Monogram, c.1920, 19¼ x 15½ In. 46000.00
Punch Ladle, Japanese Pattern, Oblong Bowl, Crimped Edge, 12 In. 1116.00
Salad Set, Medallion Pattern, 11 In., 2 Piece 1575.00
Saltshaker, Cylindrical, 2 In. 70.00
Salver, Ivy Vine Wreath, Embossed Rim, Oval Beaded Feet, 1854-70, 10¼ In. 823.00
Salver, Scalloped Low Rim, Engraved, Presentation Inscription, c.1987, 12 In. 646.00
Scoop, Stepped, Short Handle, 5½ In. 125.00
Spoon, Bonbon, Holly Pattern, Gilt Bowl, Marked, 1907-47, 3¾ In. 145.00
Sugar Sifter, Chrysanthemum, Pierced, Gilt, c.1880, 7 In. 507.00
Sugar Sifter, Vine Pattern, Gilt Bowl, Monogram, c.1891, 7¼ In. 690.00
Sugar Sifter, Wave Edge Pattern, Oval Shell-Shaped Bowl, Reticulated 498.00
Tankard, Lid, Trophy, C-Scroll, Flowerhead Cartouche, Flared Foot, 7⅞ In. 2233.00
Tea & Coffee Set, Lids, Berry Finials, Stand, Pinecone Finial, Griffin, 9¾ In., 6 Piece 9400.00
Tea & Coffee Set, Oval, Pad Feet, Chased Flowers, Scrolls, c.1907, 11¾ In. 5760.00
Tea & Coffee Set, Oval Body, Oak Leaves, Ivory Finials, Monogram c.1906, 7 Piece 11875.00
Tea & Coffee Set, Tray, Engraved Geometric Panels, Festoons, Lattice, c.1915, 6 Piece 13750.00
Tea & Coffee Set, Tray, Gold Handles, 5 Piece 8190.00
Tea Caddy, Basket Shape, Beaded Borders, Engraved Palmettes, c.1870, 6 In. 4200.00
Tea Set, Flowers, Marked, c.1900, 6 Piece *illus* 3400.00
Tea Set, Repousse, Pear Shape, Milk Jug, Waste Bowl, Sugar, c.1853, 4 Piece 4994.00
Tea Set, Urn Shape, Dome Top, Urn Finial, Wood Handle, Monogram, 7 Piece 7480.00
Teapot, Blue Enamel Ground, Flowers, Leaves, Globular, Round Foot, c.1879, 7½ In. 9000.00
Teapot, Round, Squat, Chased Acanthus, Scroll Handle, Ivory, c.1891, 9½ In. 1920.00
Tray, 6-Lobed Flower, Monogram, c.1907-47, 1 x 10 In. 597.00
Tray, Oval, Cast Wave Border, Marked, c.1880, 16 x 11½ In. 2990.00
Tray, Oval, Footed, Chippendale Style, Marked, 12 x 9½ In. 862.00
Tray, Oval, Shell & Leaf Rim, Marked, c.1882, 17 x 12 In. 3286.00
Tray, Serpentine Leaf Handles, Leaf Tip Cast Edge, c.1916, 30 In. 4113.00
Vase, Mixed Metal, Baluster Shape, Chinese Fretwork, Hammered, c.1891, 8½ In. 33600.00
Vase, Red, Yellow, Green Enamel Tulip, Bud, Square, 10 In. 1560.00
Vase, Scroll Handles, Swan Heads, 2 Bands, c.1930, 14⅞ In. 2700.00
Waffle Knife, Chrysanthemum, Pierced Blade, c.1880, 8¾ In. 1135.00
Watch Holder, Ribbed Columns, Finial 3450.00
Water Kettle, Urn, Swing Handle, Stand, R Monogram, 1918, 13 In. *illus* 1300.00

TIFFIN Glass Company of Tiffin, Ohio, was a subsidiary of the United States Glass Co. of Pittsburgh, Pennsylvania, in 1892. The U.S. Glass Co. went bankrupt in 1963, and the Tiffin plant employees purchased the building and the inventory. They continued running it from 1963 to 1966, when it was sold to Continental Can Company. In 1969, it was sold to Interpace, and in 1980, it was closed. The black satin glass, made from 1923 to 1926, and the stemware of the last twenty years are the best-known products.

Amberina, Vase, Flower Arranger, 1920s 100.00
Classic, Console Set, Bowl, Candlesticks, Black Satin, 3 Piece 210.00
Classic, Goblet, 10 Oz. 40.00
Classic, Vase, Sand Carved, Copen Blue, Signed, Billie Kay, 10 In. 265.00
Dancing Girl, Powder Jar, Pink, Frosted 185.00
Fuchsia, Cordial, 1 Oz. 8.00
Jungle, Decanter Set, Bird On Bar, Metal Holder, Marked, 11-In. Decanter, 6 Piece *illus* 45.00

Tiffany Silver, Tea Set, Flowers, Marked, c.1900, 6 Piece
$3400.00

Tiffany Silver, Water Kettle, Urn, Swing Handle, Stand, R Monogram, 1918, 13 In.
$1300.00

Tiffin, Jungle, Decanter Set, Bird On Bar, Metal Holder, Marked, 11-In. Decanter, 6 Piece
$45.00

Tiffin, Killarney, Iced Tea, Forest Green, 6 ½ In.
$20.00

Tiffin, Poppy, Vase, Black Amethyst, Red, Green, 5 ¼ x 6 ½ In.
$40.00

Tile, Elizabethan Style Man & Woman, Green Glaze, Kensington, 6 In., Pair
$325.00

Tile, Fruit Basket, Multicolored, Signed, Empire, 6 In.
$150.00

Tile, King Playing Instrument, Terra-Cotta, Marked, F. Ruth, 6 x 7 In.
$62.00

Killarney, Iced Tea, Forest Green, 6 ½ In. . . . *illus* 20.00
Milady, Vanity Set, Sky Blue, 3 Piece . . . 144.00
Modern, Vase, Velva Blue, Footed, 1930s, 11 In. . . . 150.00
Poppy, Vase, Black Amethyst, Red, Green, 5 ¼ x 6 ½ In. . . . *illus* 40.00

TILES have been used in most countries of the world as a sturdy building material for floors, roofs, fireplace surrounds, and surface toppings. The cuerda seca (dry cord) technique of decoration uses a greasy pigment to separate different glaze colors during firing. In cuenca (raised line) decorated tiles, the design is impressed, leaving ridges that separate the glaze colors. Many of the American tiles are listed in this book under the factory name.

2 Women On Balcony, Man Reaching Up, Hauber & Reuther, 7 ⅔ x 5 In. . . . 207.00
3 Women, Cubist, 4 Tiles, Frame, Harris Strong, 12 x 12 In. . . . 450.00
Apartment Buildings, Central Park Scene, Harris Strong, Frame, 6 In., Pair . . . 250.00
Arts & Crafts, Coastline Scene, Stamped, Frame, 7 ½ x 3 ¾ In. . . . 1920.00
Arts & Crafts, Rocky Mountain Road, Stamped, Frame, 12 x 4 In. . . . 1440.00
Black Crow Flying Through Snowy Forest, Flint Faience, 2 Tiles, Frame, 18 x 9 In. . . . 8850.00
Blue, Flower Urn, Rearing Horses, Boy, Cows, Wood Frame, 1800s, 20 x 14 ½ In. . . . 1150.00
Bottles, Black, Red, Yellow, Blue, White, Brown, Keramik Weber & Koln, Italy, 16 In. . . . 125.00
Elizabethan Style Man & Woman, Green Glaze, Kensington, 6 In., Pair . . . *illus* 325.00
Farmer Sowing Seeds, Signed, 12 ¼ x 6 In. . . . 960.00
Floor, Encaustic, Multicolored Matte Glaze, Villeroy & Boch, c.1880, 6 ⅝ x 6 ⅝ In. . . . 225.00
Flowers, Chocolate Brown, 6 x 6 In. . . . 59.00 to 165.00
Flowers, White, Orange, 12 x 10 In. . . . 146.00
Fruit Basket, Multicolored, Signed, Empire, 6 In. . . . *illus* 150.00
King Playing Instrument, Terra-Cotta, Marked, F. Ruth, 6 x 7 In. . . . *illus* 62.00
Men On Horseback, Turquoise, Black Faience, Islamic, 10 In. . . . 354.00
Mochaware, Slip Marbled, Dark Brown, White, c.1790, 5 x 5 In. . . . 239.00
Moravian, White, Blue, 3 ⅞ In. . . . *illus* 25.00
Panel, Glazed, Horses & Riders, c.1962, 32 x 46 In., 70 Piece . . . 2868.00
Pillow, Brown Majolica Glaze, Malibu Potteries, c.1930, ⅞ In. . . . 50.00
Temple, Flowering Peony, Leaf, Bird, Ocher, Green, Blue, Frame, Chinese, 11 ½ x 27 In. . . . 1080.00
Urn & Flower Design, Brown, Tan, Signed, England, 6 x 6 In. . . . 176.00

TINWARE containers for household use have been made in America since the seventeenth century. The first tin utensils were brought from Europe, but by 1798, tin plate was imported and local tinsmiths made the wares. Painted tin is called tole and is listed separately. Some tin kitchen items may be found listed under Kitchen. The lithographed tin containers used to hold food and tobacco are listed in the Advertising category under Tin.

Bed Warmer, Walnut, Punched Heart Design, Turned Columns, Wire Bail Handle, 6 x 9 x 7 In. 143.00
Bowl, Cobalt Blue, Yellow, Brown Lead Glaze, Flowers, Geometric, Ring Foot, 4 x 15 In. . . . 59.00
Cage, Squirrel, House Shape, Rotating, Sliding Tray, Window, Cupola, Flag, 29 x 28 In. . . . 316.00
Candle Lamp, 2-Light, Rectangular Pan, Cone Base, 29 x 7 In. . . . 425.00
Candle Mold, 20 Tube, Wood, Footed, Metal Strap Hinges, Mechanical, 28 x 16 x 7 In. . . . 1980.00
Candlestand, Cone Base, Drip Pan, 19th Century, 36 x 6 In., Pair . . . 110.00
Coffeepot, Dome Lid, Gooseneck, C-Shape Handle, Flower Finial, Footed Base, 11 x 7 In. . . . 330.00
Coffeepot, Dome Lid, Heart Cutout On Spout, Brass Finial, Ear Shape Handle, Footed, 10 x 5 In. 248.00
Fish Horn, Conical, Flared Bell & Mouthpiece, Wire Hanger, 44 x 4 In. . . . 303.00
Lamp Filler, Braced Spout, Mid 19th Century, 5 ½ x 3 ½ In. . . . 154.00
Mold, Candle, 12 Tube, Applied C-Shape Handle, 10 ½ x 8 ¼ x 5 ¾ In. . . . 66.00
Mold, Candle, 12 Tube, Applied C-Shape Handle, 9 ¾ x 11 ¾ x 5 ½ In. . . . 66.00
Mold, Candle, 12 Tube, C-Shape Handle, Rectangular Reservoir, Wire Hanger, 8 x 8 x 5 In. . . 121.00
Mold, Candle, 24 Tube, Bench Style, Dovetailed Frame, 19th Century, 18 x 22 In. . . . 1955.00
Mold, Candle, 24 Tube, Bootjack Case, Wrought Hook, Wood Handle, 24 x 9 x 14 In. . . . 2420.00
Mold, Candle, 24 Tube, Wood, 19th Century, 18 x 22 x 7 In. . . . *illus* 1900.00
Mold, Candle, Tube, C-Shape Handle, Rectangular Reservoir, Arch Base, 11 ¼ x 7 x 5 In. . . . 176.00
Punched Panel, Frame, 19th Century, 30 x 36 In. . . . 110.00
Sconce, 3-Sided, Rectangular Base, Candle, 7 x 3 ⅜ x 2 In. . . . 220.00
Sconce, 8-Convex Designs, Round, U-Shape Strap, Crimped-Edge Drip Pan, 13 x 9 In. . . . 518.00
Sconce, Oval Reflector, Inset Mirror, Candle, 15 ¼ x 8 x 4 In., Pair . . . 330.00
Sconce, Pie Crimped Edge, Oval, U-Shape Support, Crimped-Edge Drip Pan, 14 x 13 x 9 In. . 287.00
Sconce, Rayed Reflector, Star, Curved, Shallow Bowl, Crimped-Edge Drip Pan, S-Strap, 13 x 9 In. 1265.00
Trunk, Dome Top, Painted, Tulips, Flowers, Black Ground, J.M. Whitcher, 7 x 10 In. . . . 9988.00
Wine Tester, Cylindrical, Conical Terminals, Ring Handles, 29 ½ In. . . . 99.00

TOBACCO CUTTERS *may be listed in either the Advertising or Store categories.*

OBACCO JAR collectors search for those made in odd shapes and colors. Because tobacco eeds special conditions of humidity and air, it has been stored in special containers since the ighteenth century.

corn Finial, Brass, England, c.1760, 3 ¼ In. 550.00
ustrian Soldier, Terra-Cotta, Marked, J.M. 3738, 12 In. 424.00
ear, With Walking Stick, Black Forest, Carved, Wood, Humidor 1654.00
lack Forest, Bear, Holding Hat, Glass Eyes, Wood, Swiss, c.1900, 13 ½ In. 920.00
ust Of Man, Iron, England, Humidor, c.1880, 5 x 4 ⅛ In. 259.00
igar Holder, Brass, Monkey Bathing, Helmet, Humidor, Early 1900s, 6 x 10 ½ In. 588.00
og, Begging, Terra-Cotta, Marked, W & C 264, 12 ½ In. 253.00
og Finial, Ribbed, Cast Iron, Crowley & Pearson, Humidor, 5 ½ In. 86.00
og Head, Black, White Glaze, Terra-Cotta, 5 ⅔ In. 92.00
ouis Adolphe Thiers, Terra-Cotta, Marked, B.B. 141, 9 ¾ In. 495.00
ewter, Sheffield, c.1800 .... 58.00
oldier, Face, Side-Glancing Eyes, 5 ½ In. 94.00
alnut, Owl, Glass Eyes, Humidor, Regency Style, 19th Century, 13 x 6 In. 2585.00

OBY JUG is the name of a very special form of pitcher. It is shaped like the full figure of a man r woman. A pitcher that shows just the top half of a person is not correctly called a toby. More xamples of toby jugs can be found under Royal Doulton and other factory names.

dmiral David Beatty, Holds Bullet Shell, Royal Staffordshire, c.1917, 10 ½ In. 784.00
dmiral John Jellicoe, Painted, Multicolored, Royal Staffordshire, c.1915-20, 10 In. 1232.00
lan, Holding Jug, Wooden Branch Handle, Staffordshire, c.1860, 5 ¼ In. 225.00
lan, Seated, Holding Ale Jug, Green Matte, England, 5 ½ In. 55.00
lan, Tricornered Hat, 18th Century Clothes, England, 9 In. 59.00
lan In Vest, Hat, Rockingham Glaze, England, 19th Century, 13 x 7 In. .... *illus* 2040.00
lr. Pickwick, 5 ½ In. 45.00
unch & Judy, Hand Painted, Gilt, Staffordshire, 19th Century, 12 In., Pair .... *illus* 538.00
quire, Seated, England, 1930s, 14 x 6 In. 295.00
riah Heep, Seated, England, Staffordshire, 1980, 6 In. 49.00
oman, Hand Painted, 2 ¾ In. 22.00

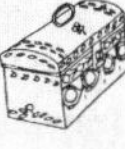

OLE is painted tin. It is sometimes called *japanned ware*, *pontypool*, or toleware. Most ineteenth-century tole is painted with an orange-red or black background and multicolored ecorations. Many recent versions of toleware are made and sold. Related items may be listed 1 the Tinware category.

ox, Document, Dome Top, Flowers, Japanned Black, 6 ½ x 9 ½ x 5 ½ In. 99.00
ox, Document, Dome Top, Flowers, Yellow, Orange, Green, Japanned, Wire Pull, 4 x 9 x 4 ½ In. 121.00
ox, Document, Dome Top, Green, Ring Handle, Tin Hasp, Stenciled Flower Basket, 10 x 6 In. 201.00
ox, Document, Dome Top, Honey Brown, Flowers, Swag, Japanned, 5 x 8 x 4 In. 385.00
ox, Document, Flowers, Leaves, Late 19th Century, 5 x 9 x 5 In. .... *illus* 240.00
ox, Document, Flowers, Yellow Line, Wire Ring, Japanned Black, 5 ¾ x 9 x 5 In. 198.00
ox, Document, Flowers & Leaf Design, Black Ground, 5 ½ x 8 ¾ In. 230.00
ox, Dome Top, Brown, White, Japanned, Flower Band, Tin Clasp, 3 ⅞ x 4 ¼ x 3 In. 248.00
ox, Mug, Flower Band, Japanned Black, C-Shape Handle, 4 ½ x 3 ¼ In. 55.00
ox, Wall, Hanging, Pinwheel, Flower Band, Cutout Sides, Crimped Edge, 7 ½ x 5 x 1 ½ In. .. 143.00
achepot, French, Grape Leaf, Scalloped Rim, 19th Century, 4 ½ x 8 ½ x 12 ¾ In. 294.00
anister, Covered, Vivid Flowers, Black Ground, 5 ¼ x 4 In. 354.00
anister, Dome Top, Flowers, Landscape, Gold Stencil, Japanned Black, 17 ½ x 11 In. 440.00
anister, Dome Top, Flowers, Yellow Leaves, Japanned Black, Wire Ring Pull, 8 x 10 x 7 In. .. 77.00
anister, Flowers, Hinged Lid, Wire Ring, Japanned Black, 6 x 7 In. 33.00
anister, Flowers, Hinged Lid, Wire Ring, Japanned Black, 9 x 8 ¾ In. 33.00
anister, Lid, Black, Flowers, Yellow Band, Japanned, Wire Pull, 6 ¾ x 5 ¾ In. 275.00
anister, Stylized Flowers, Orange, Yellow, Japanned Black, 6 ¾ In. 132.00
anister, Yellow Stylized Flowers, Japanned Black, Oval, 8 x 10 x 7 In. .... *illus* 77.00
oal Hod, Rust, Gold, Elliptical, Mask, Carrier, Handles, Pontypool, 19 x 18 In. 3360.00
oal Scuttle, Cast Iron, Gilt Design, Hinged Lid, Removable Liner, Wheels, 14 x 24 In. 940.00
oal Scuttle, Victorian, 18th Century 425.00
offeepot, Dome Lid, Black, Flowers, Yellow Band, Gooseneck, Flared Base, 12 x 9 x 6 In. ... 660.00
offeepot, Dome Lid, Flowers, Crimson Ground, Gooseneck, Flared Base, 10 ½ x 6 In. 413.00
offeepot, Flowers, Tulips & Fruit, Black Ground, Conical, Side Handle, 10 ½ In. 531.00
offeepot, Fruit, Signed, Peter Omper, 9-5-76, 14 In. .... *illus* 165.00
offeepot, Fruit & Flowers, Black Ground, Applied C-Scroll Handle, Conical Spout, 9 x 6 In. .. 3068.00
offeepot, Red & Yellow Flowers, Lid Guard, Flanged Base, c.1790, 10 ½ In. .... *illus* 945.00

Tile, Moravian, White, Blue, 3 ⅞ In. $25.00

Tinware, Mold, Candle, 24 Tube, Wood, 19th Century, 18 x 22 x 7 In. $1900.00

Toby Jug, Man In Vest, Hat, Rockingham Glaze, England, 19th Century, 13 x 7 In. $2040.00

Toby Jug, Punch & Judy, Hand Painted, Gilt, Staffordshire, 19th Century, 12 In., Pair $538.00

T

Tole, Box, Document, Flowers, Leaves, Late 19th Century, 5 x 9 x 5 In.
$240.00

Tole, Canister, Yellow Stylized Flowers, Japanned Black, Oval, 8 x 10 x 7 In.
$77.00

Tole, Coffeepot, Fruit, Signed, Peter Omper, 9-5-76, 14 In.
$165.00

Tole, Coffeepot, Red & Yellow Flowers, Lid Guard, Flanged Base, c.1790, 10½ In.
$945.00

T

Creamer, Lid, Stylized Ball Design, C-Shape Handle, Pour Spout, 4¼ x 4½ x 3 In. 248.0
Footbath, Black, Chinese Garden Decoration, Oval, Gilt Brass Handles, 8 x 19 x 14 In. 2280.0
Jardiniere, Empire, Reticulated Edge, Handles, Paw Feet, 20th Century, 7 x 13 x 8 In. 1058.0
Lamp, Green, Gold, Removable Shades, 19th Century, 11 In. .... *illus* 600.0
Lamp, Oil, Red, Square Weighted Base, Triangular Reservoir, C-Shape Handle, 8 x 3 In. 303.0
Mug, Flower Sprays, Crimson Ground, Tapered Sides, Black, 5¾ x 4 In. 110.0
Pitcher, Lid, Painted, New York Or Philadelphia, c.1830, 4¼ In. 535.0
Sander, Flower Band, Pierced, Concave Top, Cylindrical, Japanned Black, 2¾ x 3 In. 88.0
Sconce, Candle, Black, Red, Yellow, Green Stylized Design, Flared, 8½ x 2 x 1½ In. 358.0
Shaker, Dome Lid, Orange, Stylized Red & Green Band, Tin Ring Handle, 2¾ x 1⅝ In. 88.0
Sugar, Dome Lid, Flower Band, Ring Pull, Black, 4¼ x 4½ In. 66.0
Sugar, Dome Lid, Footed Base, Fruits & Flowers, 3½ x 4 In. 797.0
Tazza, Multicolored, Blue Outlined Flowers, Ring Foot, Italy, 2½ x 14¾ In. 207.0
Tea Caddy, Double, Red, Gold, Hinged Lid, Corn Finial, Ball Feet, Early 1800s, 8 x 12 In. 1440.0
Tea Caddy, Flower Band, Oval, Lid, Black, 4¼ In. 121.0
Tea Caddy, Lid, Crimson Red Ground, Stylized Design, 4¼ x 3½ x 2¾ In. 1045.0
Teapot, Hinged Lid, Black With Red & Yellow Flowers, Globe Form, 1865, 5½ In. 325.0
Teapot, Red, Gold, Oval, Gilded Leaf Bands, Urn Finial, Wood Handle, c.1810, 7 In. 2100.0
Teapot, Urn Form, Red & Black Marbled Surface, Gilt Greek Key Border, c.1820, 9½ In. 499.0
Tray, Black, 2 Chinese Figures With Umbrella, Gilt & Multicolored, 23 x 29 In. 617.0
Tray, Black, Stylized Flower Border, Crystallized Bottom, 12½ x 7⅞ x 2½ In. 715.0
Tray, Chippendale Style, Flowers, 2 Parrots, Scalloped, Multicolored, 24 x 18 x 1 In. 110.0
Tray, Cows, Gilt Flowers & Scrolled Border, 19th Century, 2 x 9½ x 12 In. 176.0
Tray, Eagle, Shield Breasted, Clipped Corners, Canted Sides, Early 1800s, 12 x 8½ In. 115.0
Tray, Flower Band, Black, 8-Sided, Tapered Sides, 1 x 17½ x 12 In. 77.0
Tray, Flower Band, Tapered Sides, Oval, Cutout Handles, Crystallized Bottom, 3 x 13 x 7 In. .. 66.0
Tray, Flowers, Crystallized Center, 8-Sided, 12¼ x 8⅝ In. 300.0
Tray, Flowers, S-Band & Line Design, Cutout Handles, Black Ground, 8-Sided, 17 x 12 In. ... 303.0
Tray, Flowers, Yellow Leaf Band, Black, Oval, 4 x 12¼ x 8 In. 358.0
Tray, Fox Hunter On Horse Back, Hounds, 22 x 27 In. 303.0
Tray, Fruit & Flower, Deep Center, 14 x 8 In. 55.0
Tray, Landscape, Red Ground, Gilt Leaves, England, c.1800, 32½ x 25 In. .... *illus* 3400.0
Tray, Oval, Restauration, Parcel Gilt, Red, Neoclassical, Gilt Border, Flowers, 30 x 22 In. 960.0
Tray, Painted, Victorian, Central Cartouche, Figures In 18th Century Costume, 18 x 32 In. ... 1116.0
Tray, Stand, Claret, Boy, Bird's Nest, Cornucopia, Leaf Scrolls, Lyres, Oval, 20 x 26 x 21 In. ... 570.0
Tray, Stand, Panoramic Village View, Green Ground, Handles, France, 1800s, 19 x 30 In. 805.0
Tray, Stand, Yellow, 8 French Scenes, River Goddess, Cornucopia, 19½ x 30 In. 863.0
Tray, Table, Hydrangeas, Parcel Gilt, Black Enamel, Cabriole Legs, England, 18 x 13 x 10 In. . 3600.0
Tray, Woman Holding Umbrella, Dog, Flowers, Landscape, Red Ground, 35 x 77 x 20 In. 193.0
Umbrella Stand, Hand Painted, 27 x 12 In. 145.0

TOM MIX was born in 1880 and died in 1940. He was the hero of over 100 silent movies from 1910 to 1929, and 25 sound films from 1929 to 1935. There was a Ralston Tom Mix radio show from 1933 to 1950, but the original Tom Mix was not in the show. Tom Mix comics were published from 1942 to 1953.

Book, Rides To The Rescue, L.A. Ranch, Stephen Sleginger, c.1939, 3½ x 2½ In. 33.0
Bowl, Ralston Purina Straight Shooter, Premium, c.1982 .... 9.0
Bracelet, Ralston Straight Shooters, Cereal Premium, St. Louis Mo., 1½ x 6¼ In. 45.0
Comic, On The Santa Fe Trail, Sagebrush Sam, Chicle Gum Miniature, 8 Pages, 2¼ x 2¾ In. 230.0
Comic, Tom Mix Western, Vol. 5, No. 28, 1950 .... 33.0
Comic, With Tony At The Bar-Diamond Ranch, No. 5, 2¼ x 2¾ In. 26.0
Comic Strip, Straight Shooters, Ralston 8.0
Decoder, Pinback, Instructions, Mailer, 1946, 5 Piece 66.0
Letterhead, Envelope, Wild West Circus, Color, c.1935, 8½ x 11 In. 58.0
Lobby Card, No Man's Gold, Tom Mix & Tony The Wonder Horse, 1926, 11 x 14 In. 48.0
Mirror, Pocket, Yankiboy Play Clothes, Bastain Bros., 2 In. 10.5
Pendant, Gold Ore, Ralston 16.0
Pistol, Wood, Ralston Straight Shooters, 9 In. 35.0
Ring, Look Around Mirror, Brass, 1945 .... 26.0
Whistle, Signal, Arrowhead, Instructions 29.0
Wristwatch, 50th Anniversary, Box 50.0

TOOLS of all sorts are listed here, but most are related to industry. Other tools may be found listed under Iron, Kitchen, Tinware, and Wooden.

Angle Divider, Stanley, No. 30 .... 125.00 to 130.0
Anvil, Cast Iron, 8 x 18 In. 90.0

I, Buttonhole Cutter, Turned Wood Handle, Iron, Stamped, 5 ¾ x 1 In. 715.00
Battle, Viking Style, Case Iron Head, Oak Wood Handle, 33 In. 392.00 to 560.00
Camper's, Double Bit, Marble's, No. 15 350.00
Camper's, Marble's, No. 10 150.00
Cooper's, D. Hofman 103.00
Goosewing, Marked, Carl Aug & Tillmanns 375.00
Goosewing Blade, 13 In. *illus* 100.00
Mortise, McKinnon Bros., Marked 110.00
Safety, Marble's, No. 6 140.00
Sheath, Marble's, No. 9 200.00
Broad, Offset Handle, L. Fenn, Connecticut, c.1850, 12-In. Blade, 29 In. 77.00
e Gauge, Adjustable, 27 In. 275.00
ach, Sailmaker's, Oak, 10 Holes, Canvas Bag, Mallets, 19th Century, 16 x 79 x 15 In. 2970.00
ach Rule, Brown & Sharpe Mfg. Co., 6 x 72 In. 193.00
vel, Brass Body, Rosewood, St. Johnsbury Tool Company, c.1879, 9 In. 605.00
vel, Bronze Body, Detroit, Mich., 19th Century, c.1884, 10 In. 132.00
vel, Sliding T, Rosewood, Brass, St. Johnsbury, 15 In. 1210.00
el, Stanley, No. 25, 12 In. *illus* 46.00
vel, Steel Body, St. Johnsbury Tool Company, June 14, 1870, 6 In. 440.00
vel, Wedge Lock, Multipurpose, Bissel's Patent, May 23, 1880, 11 ½ In. 121.00
ck Plane, No. 6, Cast Bronze, L.A. Hamm, Malden, Mass., 4 ¼ In. 358.00
ck Plane, Stanley, Shoe Buckle, 7 In. 605.00
w Torch, Solder Iron, New Marvel, Patent Pending, 20 ½ In. 66.00
ok Press, Cast Iron, 12 x 12 In. 145.00
ok Press, Dolphin Supports, Cast Iron, Painted, Late 19th Century, 14 In. *illus* 300.00
x, Butterfly Core, Scalloped Edge, G. Wahler, 9 ½ In. 644.00
ace, Bit, Armourers, Cage Head, Harp Pattern, Dark Patina, 17 In. 165.00
ace, Iron, Nordic Type, Hand Forged, Washer Cutter, 10 In., 2 Piece 165.00
ace, Piano Maker's, Rosewood, Turned Silver Fittings, Germany, 10 In. 468.00
ace, Scottish, Jellinghaus & Company, 11 ½ In. 110.00
ace, Wagon Maker's, Hull & Leister, Hand Forged, 16 ½ In. 83.00
ace, Whimble, Rosewood Handle, Knob, Nickel Plating, Lacquer, Millers Falls Co. *illus* 193.00
ace, Winchester, No. 3523, 10 In. 35.00
ass, Corner, J.F. Corry, New York, Patent June 25, 1861, 10 In. 688.00
oom Vise, Pine, Maple, Mortise, Pinned, Legs, c.1840, 51 x 30 In. 585.00
iper, Carpenter's, Stanley, No. 13, 2-Fold, 6 In. 65.00
iper, Carpenter's, Stanley, No. 136 ½, 1 Ft. 65.00
iper, Decorative Filed Pattern At Joint & Finial, 19th Century, 13 In. 72.00
iper, Ivory, German Silver Tips, Belcher Bros., 3 ½ In. *illus* 468.00
iper, Log, Copper, Brass, Stamped, Wm. Greenlief, 28 x 61 In. 18000.00
iper, Log, Marked F.M. Greenleaf, Mass., c.1900 3960.00
iper, Sliding, Smith's Patent, R.H. Brown & Company, March 11, 1890, 4 ¼ In. 303.00
rier, Figured Wood, 2 Compartments, Divider, Pierced Handle, 7 x 33 x 9 In. 173.00
est, Piano Maker's, Mahogany, Oak, Hinged, Drawers, 43 In. 468.00
est, Pine, Painted, Occupational Scene, Dovetailed, Fitted Interior, 1800s, 36 x 20 In. 1250.00
est, Woodworker, Painted, Scenic, Maine, 36 x 19 ½ In. 3200.00
isel, Corner, Marked, James Swan, 1 ½ In. 125.00
isel, Crank Neck, D.R. Barton & Company, 3-In., Width, Bevel Edge, 22 ½ In. 297.00
isel, Lathe Type, Paring, D.R. Barton & Company, Rochester, N.Y., 21 ¾ In., Pair 187.00
isel, Socket, Framing, Union, Hardware Co., Torrington, Conn., 16 In. *illus* 85.00
isel Set, Tang Type, D.R. Barton & Company, Applewood Handles, 1 ¼, 1 ½, 1 ¾ In., 3 Piece 248.00
mp, Flooring, Hatch's Patent, Dexter, Maine, Patent May 27, 1884, 48 In. 154.00
nb, Wool, Carved, Wood 22.00
nbination, Koeth's Interchangeable, Luther Grinder Mfg. Company, 11 ¾ In. 248.00
nbination, Odd Jobs, Green Box, Stanley, No. 1, Patent January 25, 1887, 4 In. 605.00
k Cutter Set, Brass, Sharpening Tool, 9 In. 231.00
n Planter, Patent, Paper Label, 1850s 75.00
anberry Rake, Ash Handle, Metal Tines, 43 In. 172.00
rling Iron, Applied Finger Ring, Double Burner, Reservoir Base, 4 x 6 ¼ In. 110.00
rling Iron, Applied Finger Ring, Double Burner, Reservoir Base, 9 ½ In. 110.00
ll, Breast, Cast Bronze, 12 In. 275.00
ll, Breast, Drill Bit, Hand Crank, Ayres High Speed, Patented June 1868 175.00
ll, Egg Beater Style, Painted, 10 In. 45.00
ll, Push, Hand, Bits, Box, Millers Falls 143.00

Tole, Lamp, Green, Gold, Removable Shades, 19th Century, 11 In. $600.00

Tole, Tray, Landscape, Red Ground, Gilt Leaves, England, c.1800, 32 ½ x 25 In. $3400.00

Tool, Ax, Goosewing Blade, 13 In. $100.00

Tool, Bevel, Stanley, No. 25, 12 In. $46.00

T

Tool, Book Press, Dolphin Supports, Cast Iron, Painted, Late 19th Century, 14 In.
$300.00

Tool, Brace, Whimble, Rosewood Handle, Knob, Nickel Plating, Lacquer, Millers Falls Co.
$193.00

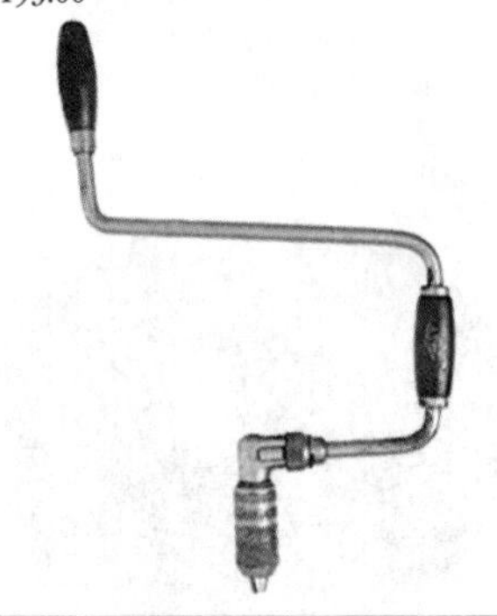

Tool, Caliper, Ivory, German Silver Tips, Belcher Bros., 3½ In.
$468.00

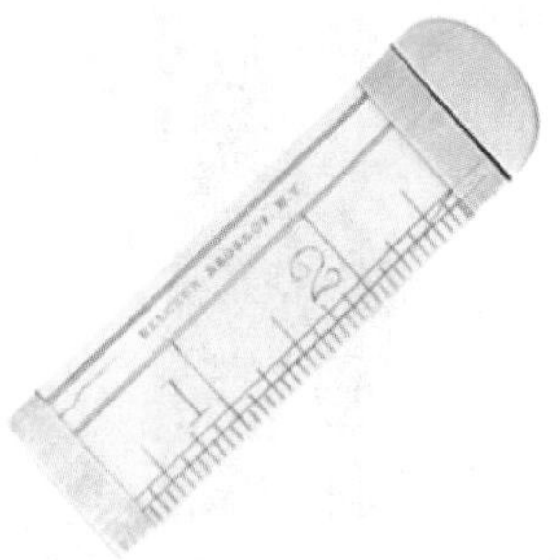

Tool, Chisel, Socket, Framing, Union, Hardware Co., Torrington, Conn., 16 In.
$85.00

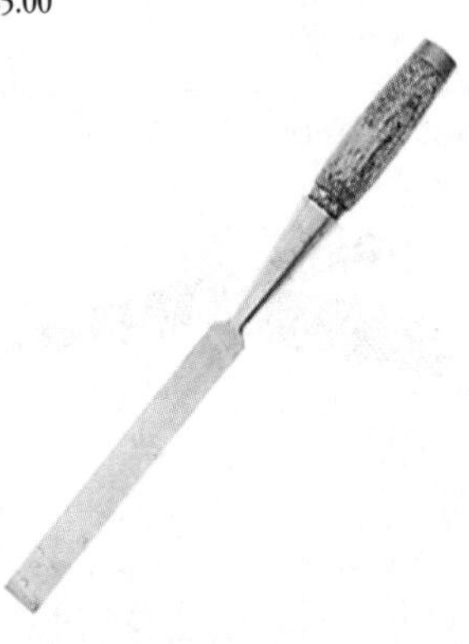

Drill, Push, Rosewood Handle, Goodell Bros. Co, Greenfield, Mass., 10 In. *illus* 35
Drill, Reciprocating, Auto, Black Japanning, Best Tool Company, Boston, c.1895, 10 In. 853
Froe, Grafting, Orchardist's, D.R. Barton & Co., 11½ In. 138
Gauge, Butt, Winchester Co., Cast Iron, Patented February 28, 1911 44
Gauge, Draw, J. Crawford, Rosewood, Brass, Newark, N.J., 5½ In. 121
Gauge, Marking, C.R. Macy, Brass Bound, Maple, Solid Cast, 10½ In. 193
Gauge, Marking, Combination, John Nester, Portland, Ore., c.1867, 12 In. 146
Gauge, Marking, H.F. Sisson, Cam Lock, Patented December 27, 1870, 7½ In. 352
Gauge, Marking, Mortise, Rosewood, M.M. Brainard, Green River, 8 In. 138
Gauge, Marking, Stanley, No. 66, Rosewood, Oval Head, c.1873, 6 In. 85
Glue Pot, Ladle, Copper, Heat Chamber, c.1870 154
Gouge, Figural Chip Carved Handle, 18th Century, 10 In. 77
Gouge Set, Millwright's, D.R. Barton & Company, 22½ In., 7 Piece 363
Grinding Stone, Sandstone, Square Hole Cutout, 5½ x 24 In. 11
Grinding Wheel, Granite, 4½ x 30 In. 450
Hacksaw, Bissell Mfg. Company, Chicago, 20 In., 3 Piece 132
Hacksaw, Double Handle, Blade By P.S. Stubs, 20½ In. 44
Hacksaw, P.S. Stubs, No. 14, Lancashire, Mahogany Handle 165
Hammer, Claw, No. 6022, Winchester 200
Hammer, Patternmaker's, Rounded Octagonal Poll, Oval Head, 11 In. 121
Handcuffs, Keyhole, Engraved, Peerless Handcuff Co., c.1925 150
Hatchel, Flax, Wood Base, Iron, Tin Edge, Anno 1793 PB, Cover, 7½ x 15 x 4 In. *illus* 390
Hatchet, Double Bevel, No. 2, C. Hammond 44
Ice Pick, Winchester, No. 9501, Nickel Plated 35.00 to 96
Jarvis, Wheelwright's, Fruitwood, S. Sawyer, 10 In. 77
Knife, Hay, Russell Kellogg, Patented July 20, 1875 248
Lathe, Watchmaker's, Hand Crank, Iron Stand, 18 In. 330
Level, Inclinometer, Pendulum Type, Brass Face Dial, 28 In. 385
Level, Spirit, E.L. Barnes, Boston, 30 In. 660
Level, Spirit, John Kendall, Black Walnut, New Lebanon, 19th Century, 36 In. 935
Level, Stanley, No. 98, Brass Bound, Rosewood, Pinned Rails, 6 In. 495
Level, Stratton Brothers, No. 1, Brass Bound, Mahogany, Greenfield, 24 In. 127
Mallet Hawsing, Shipwright's, Essex, Mass., 19th Century, 33 In. 198
Mold, Brick, 2 Compartments, Wood, Mortar & Tenon Joints, 18th Century 350
Monkey Wrench, Adjustable, Coe's, 4⅝ In. 150
Monkey Wrench, Bicycle Type, Frank Mossberg Co., No. 1, Side Adjusting 33
Paper Punch, Keen Kutter, No. 50 35
Paper Punch, Keen Kutter, No. 65 35
Pin Vise, Bellamy's Patent, 6 In. 50
Pipe Threader, Keen Kutter, 2 Cutters, No. 2 35
Pipe Threader, Keen Kutter, 4 Cutters, No. 1 85
Pitchfork, Hardwood, Wrought Iron, 10 Tines, France, Early 20th Century, 41 In. 60
Plane, Beveling, Crown Molding, J. Fisher, 18th Century, 22 In. 2750
Plane, Block, Ohio Tool Co., Adjustable, Columbus, Oh 72
Plane, Block, Stanley, No. 15, 7 In. 45
Plane, Block, Stanley, No. 18, Knuckle Cap, 6 In. 18
Plane, Block, Stanley, No. 203, High Angle, 5½ In. 65
Plane, Block, Stanley, Shoe Buckle, 7 In. 605
Plane, Buck Bros., Tiger Maple, c.1900, 25 In. 269
Plane, Bull-Nose Rabbet, Stanley, No. 90A, Original Box & Label, 4 In. 8750
Plane, Chamfer, Adjustable, Brass Plate, Side Stop, London, 22 In. 99
Plane, Circular, Stanley, No. 13, Adjustable, Black Japanning, 10 In. 176
Plane, Combination, Babson & Repplier, 4 Cutting Irons, Mayo's Patent Jan. 1, 1872 3300
Plane, Combination, Stanley, No. 46, 6 Blades, 10 x 7 In. 232
Plane, Combination, Stanley, No. 54, Light Duty, c.1940, 7½ In. 605
Plane, Combination, Stanley, No. A45, Aluminum, 11½ In. 2090
Plane, Compass, Stanley, No. 113, Solid Adjuster Wheel 150
Plane, Crown Molding, Handles, 11½ In. 248
Plane, Fiberboard, Stanley, No. 194, 8½ In. 75
Plane, Filletster, Silcock Patent, 12 In. 3960
Plane, Fore, Fruitwood, Carved, Incised Bell Flower, Continental, 28½ In. 605
Plane, Jack, Stanley, No. 5½, 15 In. 65
Plane, Jack, Stanley, No. 605¼, Bedrock, Black Japanning, 11½ In. 413
Plane, Jointer, Buck Brothers, Rosewood, Razee Type, 20 In. 121

Plane, Jointer, J. Metcalf, Wood, Winthrop, Maine, 19th Century, 27 In. 154.00
Plane, Jointer, Lakeside 24, No. 8 .... 83.00
Plane, Jointer, Razee, J. Bradford, Shipwright's, 30 In. 220.00
Plane, Jointer, Shipwright's, Buck Brothers, Live Oak, Swirled Grain, 34 In. 66.00
Plane, Jointer, Stanley, No. 7, Rosewood Handle, 22 In. 85.00
Plane, Jointer, Stanley, No. 8, Rosewood Handle & Knob, Cast Iron, 24 In. .... 75.00 to 93.00
Plane, Jointer, Stanley, No. 33, Eagle Imprint, Black Japanning, Lacquer, 28 In. 248.00
Plane, Jointer, Stanley, No. 607, Bed Rock, 22 In. 154.00
Plane, Miter, Piano Maker's, Lucien Brandt, Rosewood Wedge, Dovetail, 7¾ In. 1430.00
Plane, Miter, Piano Maker's, Vertical Post Adjustment, Bailey Lever, Mahogany, 9 In. 1320.00
Plane, Molding, Astragal, I. Nicholson, Yellow Birch, Wrentham, Mass., 9¾ In. 2970.00
Plane, Molding, Complex, Handle, 2 Squares, 14 In. 22.00
Plane, Molding, Complex, T.J. McMaster & Co., Fruitwood, Bevel Pattern, 9½ In. 55.00
Plane, Molding, Door Profile, W. Harris., 18th Century, New London, Conn., 10 In. 153.00
Plane, Molding, E.W. Carpenter, Double Iron, Dovetailed, Brass Faced, Covers, 7 In. 231.00
Plane, Molding, Fixed Sash, Douglass, New York, 9½ In. 132.00
Plane, Molding, Gothic Bead, F. Dallicker, Iron, Single, Douglas, Penn., 9½ In. 385.00
Plane, Molding, Gothic Bead, W.W. Williams, Single Iron, 9½ In. 495.00
Plane, Molding, Halving, J. Nicholson, Yellow Birch, Wrentham, Mass., 9¾ In. 187.00
Plane, Molding, Handle, Complex, A. Wheaton, c.1820, 12¼ In. 1375.00
Plane, Molding, Hollowing, Bead, Yellow Birch, Rehoboth, Mass., 10 In., 2 Piece 105.00
Plane, Molding, Oar Maker's, E.W. Carpenter, Handle, 14½ In. 154.00
Plane, Molding, Ogee Cornice, George Burnbam Jr., Amherst, Mass., 4½ In. Edge 176.00
Plane, Molding, Ovolo, C. Tobey, Cove & Astragal, Hudson, N.Y., 9½ In. 275.00
Plane, Molding, Ovolo, D.R. Barton & Co., Greece, 2½ x 9½ In. 94.00
Plane, Plow, E.W. Carpenter, Screw Arm, No Handle, Fruitwood Arms, Lancaster, 13 In. 231.00
Plane, Plow, Huntington, Screw Arm, No Handle, Angled Joints, Oswego, N.Y., 9½ In. 77.00
Plane, Plow, J. Gibson, Screw Lock Arm, UR Imprint, 1820s, 9 In. 209.00
Plane, Plow, P.B. Rider, Boxwood, Patinated, Gold, Red Handle, Knob, c.1839, 10 In. 385.00
Plane, Plow, Rosewood, Handle, Boxwood Arms, Nuts, Ivory Tips, 12 In. 935.00
Plane, Plow, S. Cumings, Screw Lock Arm, Providence, 9 In. 121.00
Plane, Plow, Shelton & Osborn Mfg., Macassar Ebony, Boxwood Arms, Conn., 1800s 1760.00
Plane, Plow, Stanley, No. 44, Miller Patent, Cutting Irons, 9 In. 3630.00
Plane, Plow, William Ward, Boxwood, Handle, Round Imprint, N.Y., 10½ In. 121.00
Plane, Rabbet, Carriage Maker, Stanley, No. 10½, 9 In. 303.00
Plane, Rabbet, Edward Preston & Sons, Gunmetal, Bullnose, Ebony Wedge, 3¾ In. 203.00
Plane, Rabbet, Keen Kutter, E.C. Simmons Hardware, No. K 192, 10½ In. .... *illus* 203.00
Plane, Raising, Israel White, Adjustable Panel, Philadelphia, 14 In. 165.00
Plane, Router, Cast Iron, Sargent & Co., No. 73, 3 In. .... *illus* 165.00
Plane, Sash, Round, Fruitwood, Double Iron, Steep Compass Sole, 7¾ In. 358.00
Plane, Scraper, Cabinet, Stanley, No. 83, 9½ In. 100.00
Plane, Scrub, Stanley, No. 40½, 10½ In. 95.00
Plane, Smoothing, O.R. Chaplin, No. 0, Patent, 4⅞ In. 7700.00
Plane, Smoothing, Stanley, No. 1, 5½ In. 1000.00
Plane, Smoothing, Stanley, No. 2, 1930s, 7 In. 198.00
Plane, Spill, Mahogany, 7½ In. 154.00
Plane, Splint, Basket Maker's, Maple, Brass, 5½ In. 358.00
Plane, Tongue & Groove, Stanley, No. 48, 10½ In. 75.00
Plane, Tongue & Groove, Union Plane Co., Hinged Wooden Case, New Britain, 12 In., Pair 149.00
Plane, Topping, A. Heald & Son, Milford, 13 In. 88.00
Plane, Transitional, Patented January 16, 1855, Pittsburgh, 8 In. 121.00
Plane, Violin, Nickel Plated Bronze, 4½ In. 143.00
Plane, Weather Strip, Rabbet, Stanley, No. 378, Includes Rods, Cutter & 3 Depth Stops, Box 275.00
Pliers, Parallel, Nickel Plated, Spring Action, 10 In. 165.00
Pliers, Winchester, No. 2106, 6 In. 40.00
Pliers, Winchester, No. 2109, 10 In. 30.00
Pliers, Winchester, No. 2495, 5½ In. 45.00
Pliers, Winchester, No. 2499, 10 In. .... *illus* 95.00
Plow, Field, Bronze, Horse Drawn, Vulcan Steel Beam, Salesman's Sample, c.1888, 13 x 6 In. 1150.00
Plumb & Level, Davis & Cook, No. 10, Mahogany, Nickel Plating, 16 In. 550.00
Plumb & Level, Stratton Brothers, No. 10, Rosewood, Side Vial 193.00
Plumb Bob, Millwright's, Nickel Plated, Integral Reel, 7¼ In. 248.00
Radio Kit, Yankee, No. 106, North Brothers Mfg., Drill, Accessories, 10 In. 176.00
Ripsaw, Disston & Sons, Etching, Extra Large Teeth, 29 In. 143.00

Tool, Drill, Push, Rosewood Handle, Goodell Bros. Co, Greenfield, Mass., 10 In.
$35.00

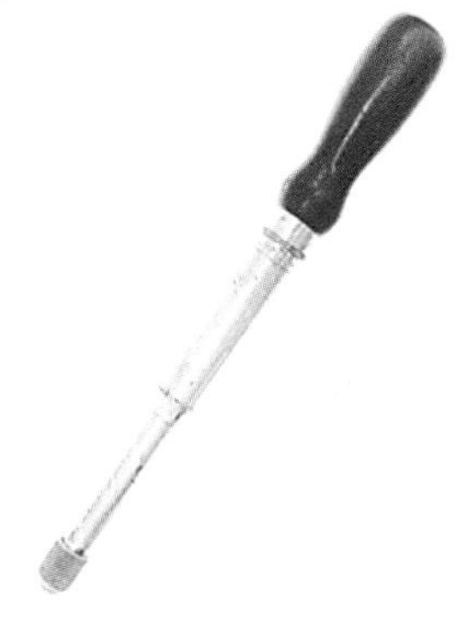

Tool, Hatchel, Flax, Wood Base, Iron, Tin Edge, Anno 1793 PB, Cover, 7½ x 15 x 4 In.
$390.00

Tool, Plane, Rabbet, Keen Kutter, E.C. Simmons Hardware, No. K 192, 10½ In.
$203.00

Tool, Plane, Router, Cast Iron, Sargent & Co., No. 73, 3 In.
$165.00

T

Tool, Pliers, Winchester, No. 2499, 10 In.
$95.00

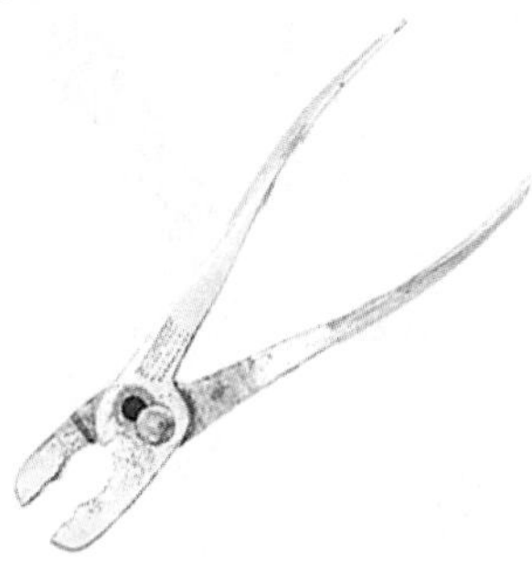

Tool, Seed Stripper, Metal, Cutout Handle, R.C. King, Carlisle, Ky., c.1890, 17 x 10 In.
$145.00

Stanley Tools
Before 1920 there were two companies using the Stanley name. Stanley's Bolt Manufactory in New Britain, Connecticut, was founded in 1843 by brothers Frederick and William Stanley. The company was incorporated in 1852 as The Stanley Works. Augustus, Timothy, and Gad Stanley and Thomas Conklin founded A. Stanley & Company in New Britain in 1854. After mergers they became The Stanley Works in 1920. It is now The Stanley Tools Division of The Stanley Works in New Britain, Connecticut.

Router, Double Pistol, Coachmaker's, Live Oak, Inlaid Steel Bands, 17 In. 77.00
Router, Double Pistol, Mockridge & Francis, Newark, 19 In. 165.00
Rule, Architect's, Stanley, No. 53 ½, Beveled Interior, 4-Fold, 2 Ft. 65.00
Rule, Calculation, Cordage, Kerby & Brothet, N.Y., 6 In. 358.00
Rule, Combination, Gentleman's, Leather Case, 6 ½ In. 633.00
Rule, Folding, Carpenter's, Stanley, No. 18, 2-Fold, 2 Ft. 25.00
Rule, Folding, Carpenter's, Stanley, No. 65, 4-Fold., 1 Ft. 121.00
Rule, Folding, Carpenter's, Stanley, No. 86, Ivory, German Silver, 4-Fold, 2 Ft. 231.00
Rule, Folding, Carpenter's, Stanley, No. 90, 4-Fold, Brass Joint, 1 Ft. 154.00
Rule, Folding, H. Chapin, Arch Tips, Union Factory, 24 In. 193.00
Rule, Folding, Winchester, No. 9568, 2 Ft. 75.00
Rule, Hat Measure, Robert Cushman & Company, 5 In. 50.00
Rule, Paktong, Rosewood, 2-Fold, England, c.1740 .... 350.00
Rule, Pocket, Folding, Ivory, Hand Scribed Numbers, Shagreen Case, c.1740 .... 350.00
Rule, Rod, Wantage, Stanley, No. 44, 16 ½ In. 88.00
Rule, Rolling Parallel, James W. Queen & Co., Rosewood, Brass, 18 In. 99.00
Rule, Square Level, Davis Level & Tool Company, Springfield, Mass., 4 In. 303.00
Ruler, School, Stanley, No. 34 ¼, Boxwood, Marked, 12 In. 25.00
Sander, Brass, Cylindrical, Turned Rims, Pierced Top, Square Stone Quill Holder, 3 In. 174.00
Saw, Coping, Trojan, 2 Boxes Of Blades, Cutters, Original Box 35.00
Saw, Coping, Winchester, No. 3501 .... 50.00
Saw, Crosscut, Keen Kutter, No. 300 .... 55.00
Saw, Dovetail, Disston & Sons, Brass Back, For Hammacher Schlemmer & Co., 13 In. 193.00
Saw, Dovetail, Hoe & Company, Brass Back, New York, c.1850, 14 ½ In. 578.00
Saw, Firewood, 29-In. Diam. Blade, 48 x 40 x 48 In. 55.00
Saw, Hand, Crosscut, 26-In. Blade Saw, Henry Disston & Sons, 29 In. 88.00
Saw, Hand, Winchester, No. 40, Old Trusty 240.00
Saw, Metal Working, George A. Deacon, Laminated Handle, c.1878, 11 ½ In. 39.00
Saw, Rip, E.C. Atkins Co., 5-Point, No. 51, Carved Applewood Handle, 26 In. 55.00
Scissor Sharpener, Loveland's Patent, c.1858, 3 ¾ In. 220.00
Scissors, Winchester, No. 9012, 7 In. 60.00
Scissors, Winchester, No. 9029, 6 In. 60.00
Scoop, Cranberry, Wood, Screen, Stand, Marked Bullock Co., 20 ½ x 19 ½ In. 750.00
Screwdriver, Pocket, Winchester, No. 7160 .... 45.00 to 50.00
Seed Stripper, Metal, Cutout Handle, R.C. King, Carlisle, Ky., c.1890, 17 x 10 In. .... *illus* 145.00
Sieve, Gold Panner's, Bellow Type Action 121.00
Slick, Provost & Williams, Newark, Turned Oak Handle, c.1874, 3 x 22 In. 248.00
Slick, T Handle, Blade, 4 In. 165.00
Spoke Wrench, Johnson, Adjustable, c.1899, 3 ½ In. 50.00
Spokeshave, Cooper's, Manning Hollis, Cast Iron, N.H., c.1886, 17 ½ In. 121.00
Spokeshave, John Booth & Son, Applewood, Philadelphia, 11 In. 50.00
Spokeshave, Stanley, No. 84, Razor Edge, Boxwood, 11 ½ In. 66.00
Square, Bevel, Combination Try, Stanley, No. 24, Center Find 95.00
Square, Bevel, Davis Level & Tool Co., Center Find, Marshall Patent, 4-In. Base 95.00
Square, Carpenter's, Maple, Hand Stamped Numbers, Lap & Peg, 1854, 36 In. & 24 In. 819.00
Square, Combination, L.S. Starrett Company, No. 439, Japanned, Athol, 18 In. 248.00
Square, Combination, Sawyer Tool Company, 12-In. Blade, Cast Iron Head, 12 In. 275.00
Square, Miter, Stanley, Type 1, c.1870, 12 In. 85.00
Square, Universal, Marshall's Patent, Painted, Pinstriping, L.L. Davis, c.1877, 4 ½ In. 99.00
T Bevel, Sliding, Antique Star Tool Co., Rosewood Handle, 10 In. 115.00
T Bevel, Sliding, Winchester, No. 9756 .... 40.00
T Bevel, Sliding, Winchester, No. 9758 .... 45.00
Tack Puller, Draughtsman's, Wm. Schollhorn & Company, New Haven, Conn., 5 ½ In. 94.00
Tape Measure, Lufkin Rule Co., Embossed, Art Deco, 6 In. 154.00
Tape Measure, Stanley, No. 556, Pull-Push, Art Deco Script, 72 In. 110.00
Tool Handle, Aiken's Patent, Original Tools, 4 ½ In. 72.00
Traveler, Wheelwright's, Machined Bronze Gears, 11 In. 358.00
Try Square, Henry Disston & Sons, Cast Iron 28.00
Try Square, Patternmaker's, Oval Handle Cutout, Goodell-Pratt, 10 In. 248.00
Try Square, Steel Handle, Winchester, No. 9728 .... 75.00
Trying Plane, Boxwood, Carved, Human Faces, Continental, c.1750, 22 In. 110.00
Vise, Bookbinders, Dolphin Head, Painted, 19th Century, 18 In. 550.00
Vise, Hand, Pollard's Patent, August 10, 1875, 6 In. 28.00
Vise, Screw, Colton's Patent, Homer, N.Y., c.1885, 3 ¼ In. 165.00

'ine Cork Press, Cast Iron, Baldwin, c.1900, 11 x 3 In. 345.00
/orkbench, Cabinet Maker's, Head & Tail Vises, 96 In. 1320.00
/rench, Alligator, Combination, Elgin, Holder 105.00
/rench, Nut, Coe's, Key Lock, Adjustable, 36 In. 150.00
'rench, Pipe, Keen Kutter, Steel, 18 In. 50.00
'rench, Pipe, No. 1032, 10 In. 85.00
'rench, Pipe, Winchester, 1922, 6 x 12 In. 140.00
/rench, Pipe, Winchester, No. 1001, Wood Handle, 6 In. 110.00
/rench, Pipe, Winchester, No. 1006, Wood Handle 20.00
/rench, Searls Mfg. Co., Cast Iron 152.00
'rench, Self-Adjusting, Cleveland Wrench Co., 10 In. 50.00

OOTHBRUSH HOLDERS were part of every bowl and pitcher set in the late nineteenth entury. Most were oblong covered dishes. About 1920, manufacturers started to make children's othbrush holders shaped like animals or cartoon characters. A few modern toothbrush olders are still being made.

ear, Brown, Curved Arms, Ceramic, 5 ½ In. 115.00
lack Chef, Holding Bananas, Pineapple, Porcelain, 4 ½ x 3 In. 77.00
onzo, Green, Bisque, Glazed, c.1930s, 6 In. 275.00
oy, Playing Flute, Striped Pants, Porcelain, Japan, 4 ¼ x 2 ½ In. 65.00
at, Reclining, Blue Luster, Old Japan, 3 x 4 In. 40.00
lown, Spotted Costume, Holding 2 Balls, Porcelain, 1930s, 5 In. 95.00
utch Boy, California Figurine, Co., 1940s, 6 ½ In. 45.00
utch Girl, California Pottery, 7 In. 45.00
ld King Cole, Hanging, Japan, 5 ¼ In. 113.00
irate, Big Boots, Skull & Crossbones Cap, Porcelain, 5 ¼ x 2 ¼ In. 168.00
owder Puff Girl, Seated, Bisque, Embossed, G.B. Corp., 5 x 2 x 2 ¼ In. 50.00
keezix, Tin, Marked, U.S.A. King, Box, 6 In. *illus* 173.00
oldier Boy, Sash, Red Shirt, Black Hat, Japan, 6 In. 168.00

OOTHPICK HOLDERS are sometimes called "*toothpicks*" by collectors. The variously shaped ontainers used to hold small wooden toothpicks are made of glass, china, or metal. Most of e toothpick holders are Victorian. Additional items may be found in other categories, such as isque, Silver Plate, Slag Glass, etc.

tlas 10.00
oy, Red & Green Outfit, Japan, 2 x 4 ¼ In. 73.00
uckingham 30.00
uzz Star 20.00
olonial 15.00
oney Island, Top Hat Shape, Germany, c.1900, 2 In. 124.00
elaware 20.00
ureka 20.00
ashion 20.00
aelic 15.00
athered Knot 15.00
nome, Ceramic, Japan, 2 ¾ In. *illus* 18.00
nverted Strawberry 35.00
owa 20.00
lardi Gras 15.00
layflower 20.00
louse, On Ear Of Corn, Portugal, 4 In. 748.00
ew Hampshire 15.00
'aneled Cherry, 2 ½ x 1 ¾ In. 36.00
ennsylvania 20.00
'ig, With Barrel, Seated On Flat Car Of Train, Amber Glass, 3 ½ x 5 ⅜ In. 260.00
'yramids 15.00
teared Playful Cat, Swag & Flowers, Silver Plate, Victorian 200.00
tepeat-S, Amber, 2 ½ In. *illus* 30.00
calloped Base, 2 ⅝ x 2 ¼ In. 24.00
tar In Bull's-Eye 15.00
easel 25.00
humbnail 20.00
oltec 20.00

Toothbrush Holder, Skeezix, Tin, Marked, U.S.A. King, Box, 6 In.
$173.00

Toothpick, Gnome, Ceramic, Japan, 2 ¾ In.
$18.00

Toothpick, Repeat-S, Amber, 2 ½ In.
$30.00

TIP
Check wall-hung and glass shelves regularly to be sure they have not loosened or bent.

Torquay, Vase, Stylized Leaves, Green, 4 Spouts, Marked, Longpark, 6⅔ In.
$15.00

Tortoiseshell, Inkstand, Rust, Mother-Of-Pearl Inlay, Blue Bottles, Late 1800s, 4 x 9 x 6 In.
$1500.00

TIP

To restore the sheen to a tortoiseshell box, rub it with a cloth dipped in lemon juice and salt. Rinse it with cold water, dry. Sometimes rubbing yogurt on the shell will help.

Tulip Top, Bulbous, Alexandrite, 2 ½ In. 850.0
Woodpecker, Sits On The End Of Branch, Yellow, Plastic, ¼ x 4 ½ In. 15.0

TORQUAY is the name given to ceramics by several potteries working near Torquay, England, from 1870 until 1962. Until about 1900, the potteries used local red clay to make classical-style art pottery vases and figurines. Then they turned to making souvenir wares. Items were dipped in colored slip and decorated with painted slip and sgraffito designs. They often had mottoe or proverbs, and scenes of cottages, ships, birds, or flowers. The Scandy design was a symmetrical arrangement of brushstrokes and spots done in colored slips. Potteries included Watcombe Pottery (1870–1962); Torquay Terra-Cotta Company (1875–1905); Aller Vale (1881–1924); Torquay Pottery (1908–1940); and Longpark (1883–1957).

TORQUA

Perfume Bottle, Tan, Turquoise & Gold Drips, Silver Screw Top, c.1888, 2 ½ In. 500.0
Vase, Incised Gold Script, Gold & Lands May Be Lost, Flowers, 3 Handles, 6 ¼ In. 30.0
Vase, Stylized Leaves, Green, 4 Spouts, Marked, Longpark, 6⅔ In. .... *illus* 15.0

TORTOISESHELL is the shell of the tortoise. It has been used as inlay and to make small decorative objects since the seventeenth century. Some species of tortoise are now on the endangered species list, and old or new objects made from these shells cannot be sold legally.

Box, Dressing Table, Serpentine Edge, Bone Lip, Velvet Lining, Ivory Bun Feet, 2 x 5 In. 540.0
Box, Dressing Table, Velvet Lined, Bone Bun Feet, Early 1900s, 1 ½ x 5 In. .... 720.00 to 840.0
Box, Horn, Silver Inlay, 19th Century, England, 1 x 3 ¼ In. 353.0
Box, Leather, Brass, Victorian, England, 19th Century, 2 x 3 In. 235.0
Box, Ring, Sterling Silver Mounted, Green Satin Padded, 1 ¼ x 4 ¼ In. 510.0
Box, Tea, Block Front, Inlaid Nickel Silver Wire, Brass, Bun Feet, England, 5 x 6 x 4 In. 1440.0
Box, Tea, Georgian, Silver, Gilt, Brass Mounted, 3 Sections, Paw Feet, 8 x 12 ½ x 6 In. 5760.0
Box, Veneer, Mid 19th Century, England, 1 ¼ x 2 ¾ x 1 ½ In. 294.0
Case, Calling Card, Ivory, England, 2 ½ x 3 ½ In. 529.0
Case, Match Safe, Calling Card Case, Lady's, Man's, 2 & 3 ½ & 4 In., 3 Piece 480.0
Case, Spectacles, Victorian, England, 19th Century, 3 x 5 ⅞ In. 235.0
Cigar Holder, Cherubs, Black, 3 Gold Rings, Removable End, Painted, Lacquer, Tube Shape, 6 In. 345.0
Inkstand, Rust, Mother-Of-Pearl Inlay, Blue Bottles, Late 1800s, 4 x 9 x 6 In. .... *illus* 1500.0
Vanity Set, Mirror, Comb, 4 ¾ x 3 ½ x 1 ¼ In. 365.0

TOY collectors have special clubs, magazines, and shows. Toys are designed to entice children, and today they have attracted new interest among adults who are still children at heart. All types of toys are collected. Tin toys, iron toys, battery-operated toys, and many others are collected by specialists. Dolls, Games, Teddy Bears, and Bicycles are listed in their own categories. Other toys may be found under company or celebrity names.

3 Stooges, Flying Cane, Extends, Plastic, Empire Plastics, Original Card, 1959, 25 In. 115.0
Acrobat, Man, Porcelain Head, Wood, Jointed, Painted Features, Schoenhut, 7 ¾ In. 690.0
Acrobatic Marvel, Monkey On High Wire, Rocks Back & Forth, Tin, Marx, 13 In. 173.0
Acrobats, Man, Bisque, Woman, Composition, Wood, Schoenhut, 7 ½ In. .... *illus* 400.0
Aeroplane, Sparkling, Brown, White, Green, Tin Litho, Marx, Box, 18-In. Wingspan 896.0
Aeroplane Whirler, Chein, 11 In. 625.0
Airplane, Aero, Windup, Tin, U.S. Zone, Germany, 5 In. 110.0
Airplane, Aqua, Navy Pontoon, Working Propeller, Linemar, Tin, 13 In. 407.0
Airplane, Army Scout, Pressed Steel, Green, Orange, Steelcraft, 1930, 22 In. 287.0
Airplane, Biplane, Die Cast, Yellow, Red, Tootsietoy 99.0
Airplane, Biplane, Model, Sopwith Camel, Wingtip Color Striping, England 145.0
Airplane, Boeing 377 Stratocruiser, Northwest, 4 Engine, Advances, Prop Turns, 1949, 14 In. 904.0
Airplane, Boeing B-50 Superfortress, Prop Spins, Yonezawa, Tin, 19 In. 632.0
Airplane, Bomber, Tin, Friction, Japan, 1950s, 19-In. Wingspan 295.0
Airplane, Cessna 210, Tail Marker 10785, Crank Operated, Advances, Prop Turns, Tin, 21 In. 153.0
Airplane, Cessna 310L, Advances, Prop Turns, Wing Marking N6717X, Tin, 24 ½ In. 461.0
Airplane, China Clipper, 4 Brass Propellers, Red Wings, Black, White, Steel, Wyandotte, 9 x 13 In. 187.0
Airplane, DC-7 American Airlines, Prop Turns, Plane Advances, Linemar, Tin, 18 ½ In. 181.0
Airplane, Douglas, TWA, Die Cast, Red & Silver 110.0
Airplane, Ford Trimotor, Red, Rubber Tires, Arcade, 4 In. 225.0
Airplane, Friendship, 3 Motors, Iron, Nickel, Rubber, Hubley, 13 In. .... *illus* 3650.0
Airplane, Grumman F9F-5 Panther, Folding Wing, Crank, 3 Plastic Missiles, Tin, 12 In. 438.0
Airplane, Grumman F9F-8 Cougar, Rocking Motion, Lighted Wing Guns, 10 ½ In. 237.0
Airplane, JEP Monocoupe, Pilot, Tin Lithograph, Clockwork, France, 16 In. .... *illus* 895.0
Airplane, Jet, Boeing 2707 SST Supersonic, Stop & Go Action, Engine Noise, Swing Wings, 13 In. 181.0
Airplane, Jet, Plastic, Blue, Yellow, Red, Nosco, c.1954, 9 In. 85.0

Airplane, Lindy, Gray, Pull Toy, Hubley, 13 ¼ In. . . . 977.00
Airplane, Lindy, Spirit Of St. Louis, Cast Iron, Propeller Spins, Hubley, 1930s, 13 In. . . . 3105.00
Airplane, Lockheed Electra, Advances, Stop & Go Action, Illuminated Propeller Action, 14 In. 237.00
Airplane, Lockheed P-38, Silver, Tootsietoy, 5 In. . . . 150.00
Airplane, Lockheed Super G Constellation, Advances, Prop Turns, Door Opens, Tin, 20 In. . . . 525.00
Airplane, Metal, Hard Plastic, Battery Operated, Japan, 10-In. Wingspan . . . 110.00
Airplane, Metal, Hard Plastic, Battery Operated, Japan, 1960s, 13 In. . . . 195.00
Airplane, Monocoupe, Nickel Propeller, Wheels, Struts, Arcade 8 ½-In. Wingspan . . . 1500.00
Airplane, Monoplane, Lindy, Blue, Hubley, 4 ½ In. . . . 350.00
Airplane, Monoplane, Lucky Boy, Silver, Dent, 5 In. . . . 350.00
Airplane, Navy Fighter, Advances, Prop Turns, Tin, Bandai, 14 ¼ In. . . . 1414.00
Airplane, Pan American, Stratocruiser, Tootsietoy . . . 165.00
Airplane, Rollover, Tin Lithograph, Marx, 6-In Wingspan, 5 ½ In. . . . 167.00
Airplane, Seaplane, Amphibian, Die Cast, Silver, Red, Tootsietoy . . . 154.00
Airplane, Spiral, Spring, Wood, Penny, Einfalt, Germany, 6 ½ In. . . . *illus* 675.00
Airplane, Spirit Of St. Louis, Prop Turns As Plane Advances, Tin, 12 ¼ In. . . . 345.00
Airplane, Spitfire, Advances, Prop Turns, Royal Air Force, Lincoln International, 9 ¾ In. . . . 224.00
Airplane, Transport, Army, Die Cast, Camouflage, Tootsietoy . . . 198.00
Airplane, Transport, Tin, Friction, 4 Motors, Marx, Box . . . 518.00
Airplane, Twin Engine Transport, Pressed Steel, 2-Tone, Wood Wheels, 13 In. . . . 96.00
Airplane, Windup, Tin Lithograph, Marx, Box, 18-In. Wingspan . . . 956.00
Airport, Hangar, 2 Airplanes, Tootsietoy, Box, 8 x 11 ¾ In. . . . *illus* 810.00
Airship, Silver, Nickel Wheels, Dent, 4 ½ In. . . . 150.00
Airship, U.S.N. Los Angeles, Tootsietoy, 5 In. . . . 195.00
Alabama Coon Jigger, Dances On Box, Windup, Lehmann, 1910 . . . 485.00
Alley Alligator, Rubber, Battery Operated, Box, Marx, 18 In. . . . 450.00
Alvin's Harmonica, Plush, Windup, Plays Music . . . 150.00
Ambulance, Accessories, Buddy L, 1956 . . . 495.00
Ambulance, Chevrolet, Back Windows, Japan, 1950s, 9 ½ In. . . . 175.00
Ambulance, Open-Front Cab, Enclosed Body, Pressed Steel, Sturditoy, 1925, 26 In. . . . 1035.00
Ambulance, White, Tootsietoy. . . . 250.00
Ambulance, White, Wyandotte, 11 In. . . . 250.00
Amos 'N' Andy, Amos, Walking, Moving Eyes, Windup, Marx, 1930 . . . 535.00 to 595.00
Arnold, Acrobatic Cycle, Man In Hoop, Windup, Tin Lithograph, Box, 14 In. . . . 1980.00
Astronaut, Walking, Lighted Walkie-Talkie, Beeping Sound, Tin, Nomura Rosko, 13 In. . . . 848.00
Atomic Energy Laboratory, U-238, A.C. Gilbert, Case, 1950s . . . *illus* 3250.00
Baby In Highchair, Tin Lithograph, Meier, Germany, 2 ¾ In. . . . 173.00
Badge, Child's G-Men, 1930s, 1 ¾ In. . . . 18.00
Badge, Muleskinner, Post's Raisin Bran Premium, Tin, 1950s, 2 ½ In. . . . 12.00
Badge Set, Sheriff, Policeman, Fire Chief, Cowboy, 20th Century Novelty Casting Co., 1952 . . 30.00
Ball, Rolling, Windup, Roll-Mops, Lehmann, 1929 . . . 150.00
Balloon Vendor, Box With Toys, Eyes Move, Arm Moves, Monkeys Swing, Tin, 6 ½ In. . . . 424.00
Balloon Vendor, Moves Back & Forth, Rings Bell, Battery Operated, Frankonia, Box, 1961, 11 In. 155.00
Barber Bear, Black, Battery Operated, Linemar, Box, 9 ½ In. . . . 695.00
Barn, Yellow, Red Roof, Silver Cupolas, Slide Lid Doors, Stalls Inside, Wood, 15 x 19 x 9 In. . . 825.00
Barney Google, Riding Sparkplug, Windup, Tin, Nifty, Germany, c.1923, 8 In. . . . 717.00 to 805.00
Bat, Eric The Bat, Stuffed, Original Tag, Button In Ear, Beige, Black Wings, Steiff . . . 315.00
Bear, Acrobat, Somersaults, Burlap, Dressed, Factory Clothes, Bing, 9 In. . . . 920.00
Bear, Barber, Baby, Kicks Feet, Barber Cuts Hair, Battery Operated, Tin, Plush, Nomura, Box, 10 In. . 370.00
Bear, Barber, Battery Operated, Japan, Box, 7 In. . . . *illus* 288.00
Bear, Barney, Drummer Boy, Battery Operated, Tin, Plush, Alps . . . 295.00
Bear, Blacksmith, 6 Actions, Battery Operated, Mixed Material, 9 In. . . . 295.00
Bear, Blacksmith, Battery Operated, Eyes & Fire Light-Up, Hammer, Anvil, Bell, Japan, 9 In. . . 173.00
Bear, Cubby The Reading Bear, Tin, Fur, Cloth, Windup, Alps, Box, 7 In. . . . 145.00
Bear, Golfer, Attached Net, Tin, Windup, Japan, T.P.S., Box, 4 x 5 In. . . . 230.00
Bear, Mad, Lead Feet, Dances With Staff, Glass Eyes, Windup, Tin Nose, Mouth, Japan. . . . 150.00
Bear, Panda, Plush Fur, Glass Eyes, Stitched Nose, Down Turned Snout, Gruff, 1880, 24 In. . . 350.00
Bear, Performing, Windup, Gunthermann, Germany, c.1910, 5 In. . . . 322.00
Bear, Polar, White, Wood, Jointed, Glass Eyes, Leather Ears, Rope Tail, Schoenhut, 8 ¼ In. . . . 690.00
Bear, Trainer, Lever, Painted, Distler, Germany, 2 ⅞ In. . . . 2587.00
Bear, Washing Clothes, Bubbles, Battery Operated, Tin, Yonezawa, Box, 8 In. . . . 304.00
Bears are also listed in the Teddy Bears category.
Bed, Doll's, Chestnut, Head, Foot Boards, Linens, Bed Cover, France, c.1850 . . . 840.00
Bed, Doll's, Folding Accordion Style, Fener & Co., Patented November 11, 1873, 10 x 8 In. . . . 450.00
Bell Ringer, Baby Quieter, J. & E. Stevens Of Connecticut, c.1890 . . . 1053.00

Toy, Acrobats, Man, Bisque, Woman, Composition, Wood, Schoenhut, 7 ½ In.
$400.00

Toy, Airplane, Friendship, 3 Motors, Iron, Nickel, Rubber, Hubley, 13 In.
$3650.00

Toy, Airplane, JEP Monocoupe, Pilot, Tin Lithograph, Clockwork, France, 16 In.
$895.00

Toy, Airplane, Spiral, Spring, Wood, Penny, Einfalt, Germany, 6 ½ In.
$675.00

Toy, Airport, Hangar, 2 Airplanes, Tootsietoy, Box, 8 x 11¾ In.
$810.00

Toy, Atomic Energy Laboratory, U-238, A.C. Gilbert, Case, 1950s
$3250.00

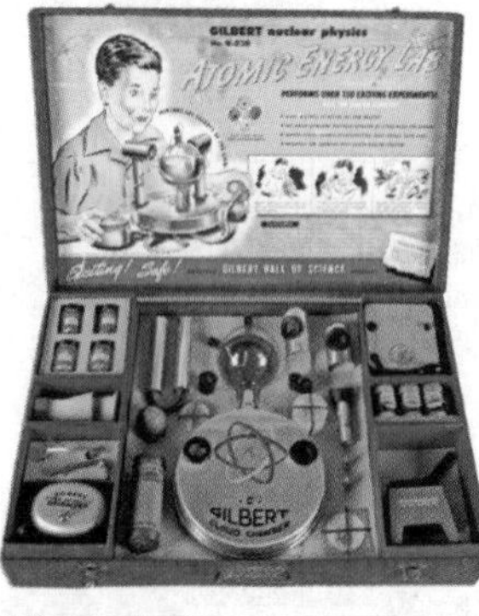

Toy, Bear, Barber, Battery Operated, Japan, Box, 7 In.
$288.00

Toy, Black Dancing Couple, Wire Supports, Wood, Backdrop, 1800s, 10½ In.
$1900.00

Bell Ringer, Harold Lloyd, Squeeze Mechanism, 1930s, 6 In. 195.00
Bell Ringer, Monkey Chariot, Pull, Monkey Pounds Bell, Kyser & Rex, c.1895 2808.00
Bell Ringer, Teddy Bear, Riding 3-Wheeled Vehicle, Cast Iron, Watrous Co., 1905, 4 In. 385.00
Bell Toy, 2 Horses, Gong Bell Of Connecticut, c.1875, 6 In. 761.00
Betty The Dancing Doll, Windup, Lindstrom, 1920s 350.00
Bicycles that are large enough to ride are listed in their own category.
Big League Hockey Player, Skates, Moves Stick, Tin, Windup, T.P.S., Box, 5¾ In. 491.00
Bike, Kid Special, Pull, Windup, 3 Wheels, B & R, USA, 1920, 6 In. 475.00
Billiards Player, Hits Balls Into Pockets, Windup, Tin Lithograph, Kico, Germany, 6¼ In. 374.00
Binoculars, Compass Between Eye Lenses, Leather Case, West Germany, 1950, 6 x 5 In. 45.00
Bird, In Cage, Moves Up & Down, Windup, Tin, Gunthermann, 1900, 9 x 6 In. 450.00
Black Dancing Couple, Wire Supports, Wood, Backdrop, 1800s, 10½ In. *illus* 1900.00
Black Drummer, Tin, Windup, Marx, c.1920 575.00
Black Man Carrying Suitcases, Red Cap, Windup, Marx, c.1930 650.00
Blacksmith, 2 Blacksmiths Hitting Anvil, Lever, Tin Lithograph, 5⅜ In. 1035.00
Blimp, Los Angeles, Silver Paint, Wheels, Cast Iron, Kenton, 10½ In. *illus* 520.00
Boat, Aircraft Carrier, Tin Lithograph, Friction, Cragstan, 1950s, 9 In. 125.00
Boat, Battleship, 8 Movable Turrets, 4 Stacks, Clockwork, Bing, c.1920, 24 In. 2880.00
Boat, Cabin Cruiser, Princess Pat, Windup, Tin, Chein, Box, 15 In. 98.00
Boat, Cruiser, Marcella, Steel, Orkin Co., Partial Box, 18 In. *illus* 1800.00
Boat, Flywheel Drive, Germany, c.1915, 7 In. 175.00 to 185.00
Boat, Gun, Steel, Painted, 2 Deck Guns, Smoke Stack, Friction, 10 In. 147.00
Boat, Ocean Liner, 2 Stacks, Die Cut Lifeboats, Wheels, Tin, Painted, Germany, 5 In. 345.00
Boat, Ocean Liner, Windup, Germany, CKO, 1930, 13 In. 295.00
Boat, Ocean Queen, SSS, Japan, 1950s, 10 In. 195.00
Boat, Peggy Jane Motorboat, Tin, Windup, Chein, Box, 14 In. 98.00
Boat, Sea Queen, Tin, Crank, Japan, 1950s, 10 In. 110.00
Boat, Speedboat, Dolphin, Plastic, Wood, Battery, K & O, Box, c.1955, 3 x 16 x 7 In. *illus* 315.00
Boat, Speedboat, Tin, Windup, USA Chein, 7 In. 95.00
Boat, Swinging, Tin, Windup, Technofix, Germany, 6 x 10 In. 165.00
Boat, Thunder Jet, Battery Operated, Remote, Japan, 1950s, 9½ In. 175.00
Boat, Torpedo, Bow, Stern Guns, Original Flag, Marusan, Tin, 11½ In. 283.00
Boat, Tug, Wood, Cass, Box, 8 In. 55.00
Boat, U.S. Navy, Cast Metal, Silver, Red, Box, Tootsietoy Navy 5700, 15 x 10 x 2 In. 470.00
Boat, Warship, Tin Lithograph, Windup, Marx, Box, 1940. 385.00
Boat, Wooden, Green, Burgundy, Fog Horn, Life Preserver, Battery Operated, Japan, 17¼ In. 259.00
Boat, Speedboat, Battery Operated, Dolphin, Plastic Hull, Wood Deck, Seats, 1960s, 3 x 16 In. 316.00
Boat, Speedboat, Boucher, Polly-Wog, Steam Hot Air Outboard Motor, Green, Aluminum, 23 In. 7188.00
Boat, Speedboat, Hornby Condor, Tin Plate, Windup, Meccano, 1950s, 3 x 18½ In. 489.00
Boat, Speedboat, Penguin, Plastic, Windup, 1950s, 6½ In. 75.00
Boat, Speedboat, Tin, Crank, Japan, c.1950, 9½ In. 175.00
Bomber, U.S. Navy, Die Cast, Green, Silver, Tootsietoy 219.00
Boy, Bitten On Seat By Dog, Celluloid, Windup, Occupied Japan 285.00
Boy, Carrying Suitcase, Tin, Windup, Occupied Japan 120.00
Boy Fiddler, Painted Metal Head, Hands, Feet, Violin, Bow, Felt Suit, Bliss, 5 In. 323.00
Boy On 3-Wheel Velocipede, Mechanical, Windup, Arthur Allen, 9 x 12 In. 2016.00
Boy On Bicycle, Windup, Tin Lithograph, 8¾ In. 116.00
Boy On Rocking Horse, Dressed In Soldier Suit, Blowing Trumpet, Tin, Meier, Germany, 2½ In. 1093.00
Boy On Scooter, Tin, Windup, U.S. Zone, Germany, Box, 3½ In. 132.00
Boy On Sled, Universal Theater, Tin Lithograph, Georg Levy, Germany, 2½ In. 230.00
Boys Pointing At Box, Lean Forward, Tin, Fischer, Germany, 4¼ In. 747.00
Bronco, Ride On, 30½ x 26½ In. 99.00
Bronco Bucks Cowboy, Wild West, Windup, Lehmann, Patent Date 1906 535.00
Bruno Accordion Bear, Plays Accordion, Eyes Light, Battery Operated, Remote Control, Japan, 10 In. 121.00
Bucket Loader, Swivel Chute, Doepke, 1946, 18 In. 525.00
Bucking Bronco, Tin, Windup, Lehmann, Germany, DRGM, 6 In. *illus* 275.00
Buffalo, Glass Eyes, Carved Fur, Leather Horns, Rope Tail, Wood, Schoenhut, 8 In. 978.00
Bump Ball, Instruction Book, Milton Bradley, Box, c.1968 35.00
Bunk Bed, Doll's, Wood, White Paint, Ladder, Betsy McCall, Box, Late 1950s 275.00
Bunny, Happy, Advances, Car Shakes, Bunny Jumps Out Of Seat, Tin, 1957, 5¾ In. 164.00
Bunny, Happy, Fold-Up Car, Tin, Friction, Japan, 6 In. 85.00
Bunny On Cart, Easter Basket, Wheels, Wood, Fisher-Price, c.1930, 3 x 3 x 1 In. 475.00
Burger Chef, Dog Flips Burgers, Rocks, Sniffs, Burner Lights, Battery Operated, Yonezawa, Box, 9 In. 128.00
Burro, Jointed, Glass Eyes, Gray, Leather Harness, Ears, Rope Tail, Wood, Schoenhut, 8 In. 259.00
Bus, Blue, Beige, Seats, Rear Entrance, Friction, 13 In. 115.00
Bus, Bonnet, Lithographed, Roof Rack, Driver, Passengers, Black Woman In Rear, 14½ In. 2486.00

Bus, Cast Iron, Kilgore, 8 In. 325.00
Bus, Cast Iron, Orange, Dent, 8 ½ In. 450.00
Bus, Coach, Green, Disc Wheels, Buddy L, c.1927, 28 In. 823.00
Bus, Coast To Coast, Tin Lithograph, Clockwork, Marx, 10 In. 935.00
Bus, Double-Decker, 3 Figures, Green, Gold Trim, Arcade, 8 In. 650.00
Bus, Double-Decker, Chicago Motor Coach, Iron, Tin, Rubber, Arcade, 13 In. .... *illus* 790.00
Bus, Double-Decker, Electric Omnibus, Die Cut Figures On Deck, Tin, Meier, Germany, 3 In. .. 1725.00
Bus, Double-Decker, Green Paint, Red & Gold Trim, Staircase To Top, Hubley, 11 ¾ In. 460.00
Bus, Double-Decker, Tin Lithograph, Friction Working, Kimi, 6 ½ In. 225.00
Bus, Double-Decker, Tin Lithograph, Windup, Wells, 6 ¾ In. 121.00
Bus, Driver, Cast Iron, Fageol, 10 ½ In. 173.00
Bus, Excursion, Lithographed Wheels, Hayashi, Tin, Prewar, 6 ¾ In. 2091.00
Bus, Greyhound, Blue, White, Cast Iron, 2 x 7 x 2 In. 88.00
Bus, Greyhound, Blue, White, Rear Lights, Windup, Buddy L, 15 In. 345.00
Bus, Greyhound, Cast Iron, Arcade, 9 In. 575.00
Bus, Greyhound, Century Of Progress, Pulled By GMC Tractor, 1933, 7 ½ In. 235.00
Bus, Greyhound, Century Of Progress, Pulled By GMC Tractor, 1933, 11 ½ In. 325.00
Bus, Greyhound, Century Of Progress, Pulled By GMC Tractor, 1933, 14 ½ In. 375.00
Bus, Greyhound, Pressed Steel, Battery Operated, Buddy L, Box, 16 ½ In. .... *illus* 425.00
Bus, Greyhound, Scenic Cruiser, Tootsietoy, Box 250.00
Bus, Greyhound, Super Coach, Arcade, c.1937, 9 In. 325.00
Bus, Greyhound, White, Blue, Silver 75.00
Bus, Greyhound Cruiser Coach, Arcade, c.1941, 9 In. .... 450.00 to 475.00
Bus, Greyhound Lines, GMC, Arcade, 10 In. 295.00
Bus, Inter-City, Pressed Steel, 13 Windows, 10 Seats, Steelcraft, 1930, 24 ½ In. 920.00
Bus, Inter-State, Green, Yellow, White Tires, Windup, Tin Lithograph, Strauss, 6 x 10 ½ In. 490.00
Bus, Jack Rabbit, Wood, Holgate, 12 In. 95.00
Bus, Jackie Gleason Honeymooners, Tin, Wolverine, 14 ⅛ In. 440.00
Bus, Lithograph Of Passengers, Maroon, Blue, Battery Operated, Tin, 13 In. 115.00
Bus, Los Angeles Inter City, Red, Steelcraft, 23 ½ In. 495.00
Bus, Mobile Post Office, Tin, Friction, Japan, c.1950, 6 In. 95.00
Bus, New York World's Fair, Greyhound Line, Arcade, 6 ½ In. 250.00
Bus, Oh Boy, Kiddie Metal Toys, 1926, 19 In. 995.00
Bus, Pressed Metal, White Cab, Blue Body, 1941 .... 350.00
Bus, Routemaster, 289, Red, Dinky 70.00
Bus, San Francisco, Nickel Plated Radiator, Steelcraft, 1941, 21 In. 1725.00
Bus, School, Tin, Battery Operated, Japan, 1950s, 6 ½ In. 110.00
Bus, School, Tin, Japan, 1950s, 10 In. 110.00
Bus, Tin, Battery Operated, France, 1950s, 11 ¼ In. 295.00
Bus, Tin, Driver, Windup, Germany, Nifty 201.00
Bus, Tin, Painted, Clockwork, Green, Minic, Box 775.00
Bus, Twin Coach, Cast Iron, Kenton, 8 ½ In. 275.00
Bus, Upton Shore Line Cannon Ball Express, Yellow, Red, Black, 9 ½ In. 295.00
Bus, Yellow Coach, Green, Gold Trim, Arcade, 14 In. 3250.00
Busy Lizzie, Woman Sweeping, Dress, Windup, Tin Lithograph, Germany, 7 In. 717.00
Buttercup & Spareribs, Animated, Platform, Pull Toy, Nifty Co., 1920s .... 750.00 to 850.00
Caboose, Railroad, Pressed Steel, Buddy L, c.1928, 19 In. 690.00
Cage, Parrots, Celluloid, Windup, Bells, Revolving Balls, Box, 1930s 195.00
Calliope, 4 Horses, Royal Circus, Blue, Gold, Cast Iron, Hubley, 24 In. .... *illus* 1725.00
Calypso Joe, Walker, Eyes Light-Up, Plays Drum, Battery Operated, Tin, Cloth, Linemar, 11 In. 144.00
Camel, Bactrian, Jointed, Wood, Rope Tail, Glass Eyes, Schoenhut, 7 In. .... *illus* 680.00
Camel, Dromedary, Wood, Jointed, Painted Eyes, Rope Tail, Leather Ears, 8 ½ In. 201.00
Canary Cage, Canary Pecks Forward, Red, Blue, Yellow, Lever, Meier, Germany, 3 ½ In. 173.00
Candy Cart, Monkey Pedals, Cart Advances, Bell Rings, Ohta, Tin, 5 ½ In. 186.00
Cannon, Big Bang, Carbide, 105 mm, Box, 1950s, 17 In. 95.00
Cannon, Wood, 15 In. 165.00
Cap Gun, Bulldog, Cast Iron, Pat 1923, 6 In. 11.00
Cap Gun, Monkey With Coconut, 4 x 4 In. 230.00
Cap Gun, Spy, Cast Iron, Nickel Plate, Kilgore, 1936, 2 x 4 ½ x ¾ In. 40.00
Captain Hook, Raises Gun In Air & Fires, Smokes, Battery Operated, Marusan, Box, 9 In. 581.00
Car, 2 Door, Tin, Windup, Germany, 1920s, 6 In. 695.00
Car, Airflow, Coupe, Iron, Nickel, Rubber & Wood Tires, Dent, 6 In. .... *illus* 1800.00
Car, Andy Gump, Crank, License Plates, Figure, 7 ½ In. 840.00
Car, Andy Gump, Red, Green, Iron, Arcade, 7 In. .... *illus* 4313.00
Car, Armored, Back Door Key, Tin, Friction, Japan, 1958, 8 ½ In. 145.00
Car, Armored, Die Cast, Tootsietoy 77.00

Toy, Blimp, Los Angeles, Silver Paint, Wheels, Cast Iron, Kenton, 10 ½ In.
$520.00

Toy, Boat, Cruiser, Marcella, Steel, Orkin Co., Partial Box, 18 In.
$1800.00

Toy, Boat, Speedboat, Dolphin, Plastic, Wood, Battery, K & O, Box, c.1955, 3 x 16 x 7 In.
$315.00

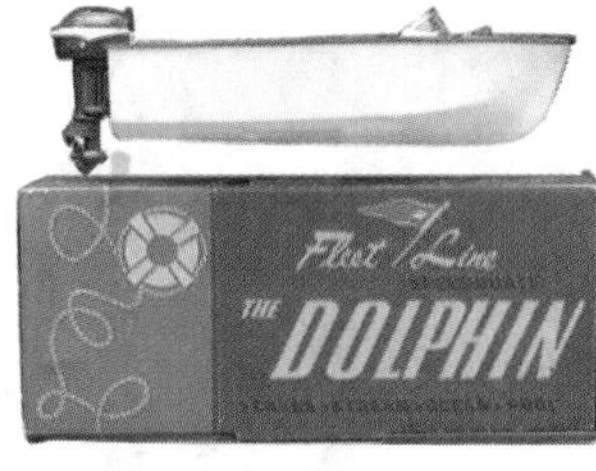

Toy, Bucking Bronco, Tin, Windup, Lehmann, Germany, DRGM, 6 In.
$275.00

Toy, Bus, Double-Decker, Chicago Motor Coach, Iron, Tin, Rubber, Arcade, 13 In.
$790.00

T

Toy, Bus, Greyhound, Pressed Steel, Battery Operated, Buddy L, Box, 16 ½ In. $425.00

Toy, Calliope, 4 Horses, Royal Circus, Blue, Gold, Cast Iron, Hubley, 24 In. $1725.00

Toy, Camel, Bactrian, Jointed, Wood, Rope Tail, Glass Eyes, Schoenhut, 7 In. $680.00

Toy, Car, Airflow, Coupe, Iron, Nickel, Rubber & Wood Tires, Dent, 6 In. $1800.00

Toy, Car, Andy Gump, Red, Green, Iron, Arcade, 7 In. $4313.00

Car, Army, Gun, Metal, Windup, Tippco, Germany, 1937, 7 ½ In., 2 Piece . . . 495.00
Car, Atom, Driver, Dark Helmeted, Open Wheel, Chrome Trim, Rubber Tire Skins, 16 In. . . . 4012.00
Car, Austin Healey, Driver, Windshield, Yellow, No. 103, 1957, 3 ½ In. . . . 55.00
Car, Beverly Hillbillies, 5 Figures, Accessories, Plastic, Windup, Ideal, Box, 1963, 22 In. . . . 437.00
Car, Boat, Gun, Hillclimber, Wheels, Dark, Light Green, Schiebel, 1920s, 10 ½ In. . . . 140.00
Car, Buick, 1927 Model, Sedan, Driver, Cast Iron, Arcade, 8 ¼ In. . . . 3450.00
Car, Buick, Cast Iron, Blue, Black, Rubber Tires, Arcade, c.1930, 8 ¾ In. . . . 1552.00
Car, Buick, LeSabre, Concept, Light Green, Tin, Yonezawa, 1950s, 8 In. . . . 578.00
Car, Buick, Riviera, 2 Door, Hardtop, Removable Roof, Doors Open, Operable Windows, 11 In. 315.00
Car, Buick, Tin, Friction, Japan, c.1950, 12 In. . . . 375.00
Car, Bumper, Clown, Windup, Pressed Steel, 11 ¼ x 9 In. . . . 385.00
Car, Bumper, Pop-Up Clown, Tin, Friction, Box, 7 In. . . . 110.00
Car, Cabrio Super, Driver, Lever, Tin, Kellerman, Germany, Box, 9 In. . . . *illus* 425.00
Car, Cadillac, Coupe, Tin, Friction, Japan, 1950s, 8 In. . . . 95.00
Car, Cadillac, Red, White, Japan, c.1961, 12 In. . . . 285.00
Car, Cadillac Coupe, Die Cast, Red & Tan, Tootsietoy . . . 88.00
Car, Cadillac Coupe 1929 Model, Driver, Windup, Marx, 12 In. . . . 475.00
Car, Chevrolet, 1932 Model, Roadster, Metal, Hubley, 1950s . . . 50.00
Car, Chevrolet, 1954 Model, Hood Ornament, Friction, Linemar, 11 In. . . . 725.00
Car, Chevrolet, Camaro, Advances, Bump & Go, Light Blinks, Engine Noise, 1960s, 13 In. . . . 181.00
Car, Chevrolet, Corvair, 1959 Model, Telephone Truck, Japan, 8 In. . . . 175.00
Car, Chevrolet, Fire Chief, Battery Operated, Light, Japan, 1963, 14 In. . . . 145.00
Car, Chevrolet, Impala, 1963 Model, News, CBS, Tin, Friction, Japan, Ichiko, 8 In. . . . 120.00
Car, Chevrolet, Station Wagon, 4 Door, Tin Lithograph, 1958, 8 ¼ In. . . . 86.00
Car, Chevrolet, Station Wagon, Tin, Friction, Japan, 1957, 9 ½ In. . . . 175.00
Car, Chitty Chitty Bang Bang, Flip-Out Wings, Metal, Plastic, Corgi Toys, Box, 1967, 5 ½ In. . *illus* 316.00
Car, Chrysler, 2 Door, Hardtop, 2-Tone, Irco, Tin, 1955, 8 ½ In. . . . 277.00
Car, Chrysler, Airflow Sedan, Green, Hubley, 6 ½ In. . . . 425.00
Car, Chrysler, Tin, Friction, Japan, 1950s, 8 ½ In. . . . 195.00
Car, Chrysler, V8, Blue, Yonezawa, c.1953, 9 In. . . . 225.00
Car, Circus, Clown, Tin, Friction, Pop-Up Clown, Cragstan Star, 6 ¾ In. . . . 99.00
Car, Circus, Elephant, Tin, Friction, Cragstan, Japan, 7 ½ x 7 In. . . . 330.00
Car, Circus, Merry Ball Blower, Tin, Windup, Box, 5 In. . . . 55.00
Car, Citroen, Tin, Friction, Daya, Japan, 1950s, 8 ½ In. . . . 195.00
Car, Convertible, Woman Driver, Windup, Occupied Japan, 4 ¾ In. . . . 145.00
Car, Convertible, Yellow, Windup, U.S. Zone, Germany, c.1948 . . . 187.00
Car, Coo Coo, Tin, Windup, Marx, 8 In. . . . 403.00
Car, Cougar, Tin, Battery Operated, Asakusa, Japan, 15 In. . . . 345.00
Car, Coupe, Electric, Battery Operated, Motor, Pressed Steel, Marx, 1930s, 15 ¼ In. . . . 715.00
Car, Coupe, Fire Chief, Siren, Metal, Rubber Tires, Metal, 14 In. . . . 56.00
Car, Coupe, Metal, Cream, Windup, Arnold, Occupied Germany, 10 In. . . . 196.00
Car, Coupe, Red, White, Rubber Tires, Hubley, 1930s, 4 ½ In. . . . 110.00
Car, Coupe, Rumble Seat, Red, A.C. Williams, 5 In. . . . 250.00
Car, Coupe, Tin, Windup, Marx, USA, 1920s, 9 In. . . . 295.00
Car, Coupe, Tin Lithograph, Windup, Marx, 8 In. . . . 425.00
Car, DeSoto, Airflow, Coupe, Rose, Hubley, 4 ½ In. . . . 500.00
Car, Dodgem, Peter Pan Series, Tin, Windup, England, Box, 4 ⅜ x 3 In. . . . 303.00
Car, Donkey, Driver, Metal, Windup, Marx, 10 In. . . . 195.00
Car, Doodle Bug, Blue, Tootsietoy, 4 In. . . . 135.00
Car, Edsel, Station Wagon, Cream, Lavender, Tin, Friction, Japan, 10 In. . . . 575.00
Car, Ferrari, Metal, Battery Operated, Moves Up, Shakes, Japan, 11 In. . . . 475.00
Car, Ferrari, Super America, Friction, Bandai, Japan, 1960s, 11 ½ In. . . . *illus* 445.00
Car, Fire Chief, Battery Operated, 1950s, 10 In. . . . 295.00
Car, Fire Chief, Bell, Tin, Pull Toy, 1940s, 8 In. . . . 185.00
Car, Fire Chief, Bell, Tin, Red, Pull Toy, T. Cohn, 9 In. . . . 250.00
Car, Fire Chief, Big Lupor, Tin, Friction, USA, 1950, 10 ½ In. . . . 145.00
Car, Fire Chief, Windup, Marx, USA, 1950s, 8 In. . . . 120.00
Car, Flivver Coupe, Buddy L, No. 210-B, c.1924, 11 In. . . . 2500.00
Car, Ford, 1936 Model, Cast Iron, A.C. Williams, 9 In. . . . 1000.00
Car, Ford, 1957 Model, Tin, Friction, Japan, 12 In. . . . 375.00
Car, Ford, Bronco, Fire Chief, Red, Pressed Steel, Ny-Lint, 11 In. . . . 235.00
Car, Ford, Cast Iron, A.C. Williams, 1936, 4 In. . . . 1000.00
Car, Ford, Falcon, Station Wagon, Woodgrain Trim, Opening Rear Door & Window, 1962, 9 In. 158.00
Car, Ford, Flower Delivery Wagon, Tailgate Opens, Rear Window, Wheel Covers, 1956, 12 In. . 277.00
Car, Ford, Forward, Reverse, Battery Operated, Japan, 7 ½ In. . . . 95.00
Car, Ford, Model A, Sedan, 4 Door, Red, A.C. Williams, 4 ½ In. . . . 325.00 to 375.00

T

ar, Ford, Model T, Sedan, Black, Red, Lever Action, Side Lamps, 6 ½ In. 55.00
ar, Ford, Model T, Roadster, Phaeton, Blue, Beige, Friction, Folding Windshield, 9 ½ In. 75.00
ar, Ford, Model T, Tin, Japan, 7 x 3 x 4 In. 125.00
ar, Ford, Model T, 4 Door, Black, Gold Stripe, 5 In. 450.00
ar, Ford, Model T, Touring, Black, Arcade, 6 ½ In. 450.00
ar, Ford, Model T, Sedan, 4 Door, Black Gold Stripe, Arcade, 5 In. 475.00
ar, Ford, Model T, Sedan, Center Door, Black, 6 ½ In. 575.00
ar, Ford, Model T, Sedan, Driver, Center Door, Black, 6 ½ In. 575.00
ar, Ford, Model T, Sedan, Center Door, Black, Gold Stripe, Arcade, 6 ½ In. 650.00
ar, Ford, Model T, Touring, Black, Arcade, 6 ½ In. 650.00
ar, Ford, Mustang, Mach I, Battery Operated, White, Tavio, 10 ½ In. 110.00
ar, Ford, Phaeton, Touring, Issemayer, Chauffeur, Passenger, Germany, c.1912 . . . . 5558.00
ar, Ford, Model T, Touring, Black, Arcade, 6 ½ In. 575.00
ar, Garage Car, Metal, 2 Doors Open, Germany, 1920s, 6 ½ In. 695.00
ar, Gerard Coupe, Windup, Electric Headlights, Pressed Steel, 15 In. 325.00
ar, Hand, Tom & Dick, Japan, 1950s, 5 In. 75.00
ar, Happy Clown, Battery Operated, 6 ½ x 6 In. 77.00
ar, Hot Rod, Tin, Friction, Japan, 1950s, 8 In. 155.00
ar, Isetta, Tin, Friction, Japan, 1950s, 7 In. 225.00
ar, Jaguar, Coupe, Blue, Red, Japan, 7 ½ In. 115.00
ar, Jaguar, Die Cast, K.K. Sakura, Japan, 5 In. 48.00
ar, Jaguar, Friction, Waving Driver, Tin Lithograph, Late 1950s, 7 ¼ In. 115.00
ar, Jaguar, Hubley, Box, 7 ½ In. 75.00
ar, Jaguar, Plastic, Remote Control, Bandai, 12 In. 125.00
ar, Jaguar, Plastic, Windup, Minic, 5 ¾ In. 65.00
ar, Jaguar, Push Toy, Steering, Plastic, Empire, 9 In. 50.00
ar, Jaguar, Saloon, Plastic, Empire, 9 In. 65.00
ar, Jaguar, Stunt, Battery Operated, TM, Japan, 1960s, 9 ½ In. 120.00
ar, Jaguar, Tin, Friction, Driver, Japan, 1950s, 7 ½ In. 195.00
ar, Jaguar, Tin, Friction, Hubcaps, Japan, 1950, 9 ½ In. 225.00
ar, Jaguar, Tin, Friction, Japan, 8 In. 145.00
ar, Jaguar XK 150 Convertible, Lithographed Interior, Wheel Covers, Tin, Bendai, 10 In. 224.00
ar, Jalopy, Friction, Driver, Linemar, c.1950, 5 In. 115.00
ar, Jalopy, Limping Lizzie, Driver, Windup, Marx, Box, 1930s, 7 In. 495.00
ar, Jalopy, Rollover, Windup, 2 Riders, Tin Lithograph, Marx, 4 ½ x 5 ½ In. 120.00
ar, Jet Race T14, Open Wheel Racer, Advances, Siren, Tin, Nomura, 12 In. 424.00
ar, Jet Race Y53, Advances, Siren, Spark, Tin, Yonezawa, 12 In. 356.00
ar, Karl Bub Saloon, Black, Brown, Gold Pinstripe, c.1910, 12 ½ In. 2595.00
ar, Krazy, Clown, Tin Lithograph, Windup, Strauss, 7 In. 440.00
ar, LaSalle, Land Cruiser, Wyandotte, 1936-39, 15 In. 495.00
ar, Limousine, Dark Red Paint, Flywheel Drive, Republic, 1932, 12 In. 225.00
ar, Lincoln Continental III, 2 Door, Hardtop, Tin Lithograph, 1959, 11 In. 443.00
ar, Lincoln Slush, Coupe, Tan, 4 ½ In. 75.00
ar, Lincoln XL-500 Sundeck, Convertible, Concept, Red, Plastic Dome, Tin, 1950s, 7 In. 514.00
ar, Mercedes-Benz, Racer, Tin, Painted, Clockwork, Marklin, 10 ¾ In. 550.00
ar, Mercedes-Benz 220, Convertible, Plastic Hood Ornament, Rin, 1960, 8 In. 294.00
ar, MGA, 1600 MKII Rally, Right Hand Drive, Tin, Bandai, 1960s, 8 In. 181.00
ar, MGA, Convertible, 2 Door, Lithographed Interior, Wheel Covers, Tin, Terai, 9 ½ In. 153.00
ar, Milton Berle, Red Hat, Tin Lithograph, Windup, Marx, Box, 5 ½ In. 260.00
ar, Milton Berle, Yellow Hat, Tin Lithograph, Windup, Marx, Box, c.1950, 5 ½ In. 374.00
ar, Moxie, Pull Toy, Blue, Tin, c.1920, 8 ¾ In. 4675.00
ar, Moxiemobile, Tin Lithograph, c.1917, 8 ½ x 6 ½ In. 2500.00
ar, Mystery Police, Buick, Advances, Roof Light, Siren, Tin, Komoda, 8 In. 113.00
ar, Nash Metropolitan, Blue, Die Cast, Tootsietoy, 2 ½ In. 175.00
ar, OHO, Driver, Tin Lithograph, Clockwork, Lehmann, Germany, 4 In. . . . . *illus* 455.00
ar, Old Jalopy, Marx, 1930s, 7 In. 125.00
ar, Old Jalopy, Tin Driver, Friction, 1950s, 5 In. 110.00
ar, Oldsmobile, 1956 Model, Tin, Battery, Japan, 7 In. 175.00
ar, Oldsmobile, Battery Operated, Japan, 1960s, 15 ½ In. 295.00
ar, Oldsmobile, Super 88, Tin Bumpers, Tin Lithograph Trim, Nakamura, 7 In. 198.00
ar, Packard, Convertible, Die Cast, Tin Lithograph, White Wood Wheels, Hubley, c.1940, 5 ½ In. . 165.00
ar, Peter Rabbit, Eccentric, Built-In Key, Plastic, Tin Lithograph Front, 1950s, 6 x 8 In. 589.00
ar, Photographer, Man Turns Steering Wheel, Woman Turns Camera, Battery, 13 In. 195.00
ar, Pierce-Arrow, Sedan, 1935, 7 In. 980.00
ar, Plymouth, Coupe, Red, Pink, Japan, 1958, 7 In. 165.00
ar, Plymouth, Station Wagon, RAI TV, Box, 12 ¼ In. 1430.00

Toy, Car, Cabrio Super, Driver, Lever, Tin, Kellerman, Germany, Box, 9 In.
$425.00

Toy, Car, Chitty Chitty Bang Bang, Flip-Out Wings, Metal, Plastic, Corgi Toys, Box, 1967, 5 ½ In.
$316.00

Toy, Car, Ferrari, Super America, Friction, Bandai, Japan, 1960s, 11 ½ In.
$445.00

Toy, Car, OHO, Driver, Tin Lithograph, Clockwork, Lehmann, Germany, 4 In.
$455.00

T

Toy, Car, Station Wagon, Doors Open, Maroon, Tan, Wood, Buddy L, 18 ½ In.
$720.00

Toy, Car, Subaru, 260, Tin, Friction, Bandai, Japan, Box, 1959, 8 In.
$1400.00

Toy, Car Set, Bus, Track, Windup, Tippco, U.S. Zone, Germany, Box
$518.00

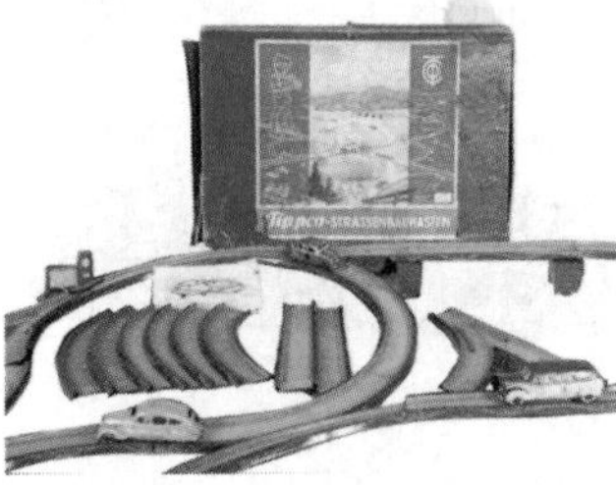

Toy, Carousel, Figures, Children, Tin, Windup, Chein, 9 ¾ In.
$260.00

Car, Police, Chevrolet, Tin, Battery Operated, Japan, c.1962, 14 In. 295.0
Car, Police, Dark Blue, Friction, U.S. Zone, Germany, Arnold, 1940s, 10 In. 175.0
Car, Police, Mercury, Tin, Friction, Japan, 1958, 11 ½ In. 475.0
Car, Pontiac, Blue, Tin, Friction, Ichiko Japan, c.1958, 14 In. 295.0
Car, Pontiac, Driver, Cream, Blue, Japan, 1950s, 14 In. 275.0
Car, Pontiac, Red, Tin, Friction, Ichiko Japan, c.1950, 14 In. 375.0
Car, Pontiac, Safari, Blue, Off-White, Working Tailgate, Tootsietoy, Die Cast, 1956, 7 In. 265.0
Car, Pontiac, Sedan, Tin, Friction, Japan, 1960s, 8 ¼ In. 145.0
Car, Pontiac, Trans Am, Black, Kitt, Knight Rider, Lights, Action, Battery Operated, Box, 17 In. 125.0
Car, Porsche 356, Plastic, Green, Interior, Motor, Rear Opens, c.1955, 8 In. 265.0
Car, Pressed Steel, U.S.A., 1930s, 8 ½ In. 145.0
Car, Racing, Aluminum, Windup, U.S.A., c.1930, 9 In. 95.0
Car, Racing, Buffalo Silver Bullet, Tin, Driver, 26 In. 403.0
Car, Racing, Captain Campbell's Bluebird, England, Box, 11 In. 4400.0
Car, Racing, Gas Engine, Thimble Drome, Cox, 8 ½ In. 675.0
Car, Racing, Golden Arrow, Clockwork, Kingsbury, 19 ¾ In. 175.00 to 935.0
Car, Racing, Green, Cast Iron, Champion, 9 In. 425.0
Car, Racing, Green, Die Cast, Hubley, 7 In. 48.0
Car, Racing, Hard Plastic, Metal, Friction, Sanders, U.S.A., 7 ¼ In. 75.0
Car, Racing, Hot Rod, Driver, Hard Plastic, Aurorail, U.S.A., 1950s, 8 ½ In. 55.0
Car, Racing, Hot Rod, Flashlight, Driver, Tin, Friction, Battery Operated, Japan, 1950s, 7 ½ In. 195.0
Car, Racing, Hot Rod, Tin, Battery Operated, Japan, TN, 1950s, 7 In. 145.0
Car, Racing, Mercedes, Tin, Friction, 1950s, 10 In. 275.0
Car, Racing, Mercedes, Tin, Friction, Noise, Linemar, Japan, 1950s, 9 In. 225.0
Car, Racing, MG, White, Doepke, 1955, 15 ½ In. 295.0
Car, Racing, Midget, Tin, Windup, Marx, U.S.A., c.1950, 7 In. 875.0
Car, Racing, Miller Indy 500, White Tires, Red Hubs, Lincoln, 4 In. 150.0
Car, Racing, No. 5, Midget, Yellow & Black, Marx, 5 In. 175.0
Car, Racing, No. 7, Plastic, Windup, Marx, U.S.A., 1950s, 6 ½ In. 110.0
Car, Racing, No. 8, Plastic, Windup, Driver, Blue, Yellow, Red, Nosco, 9 ½ In. 175.0
Car, Racing, No. 52, Tin, Windup, Wood Wheels, 1950s 110.0
Car, Racing, Plastic, Tin, Rubber Powered, Box, 4 ½ In. 38.0
Car, Racing, Plastic, Yellow, Red, Pagco, 11 In. 165.0
Car, Racing, Pressed Steel, Windup, Driver, C.I.J., France, 15 In. 715.0
Car, Racing, Rally Monte Carlo, Tin, Windup, Germany, 8 ½ x 8 ⅞ In. 220.0
Car, Racing, Red, Cast Aluminum, Gas Powered, Ohlson & Rice, 10 In. 875.0
Car, Racing, Red, Silver, Auburn, Rubber, 1940s, 10 ½ In. 95.0
Car, Racing, Roadster, Rumble Seat, Driver, Blue, Kilgore, 6 ¼ In. 400.0
Car, Racing, Silver Bullet, Tin, Windup, RSA Spain, 10 ⅝ In. 275.0
Car, Racing, Speed, Bluebird, Die Cast, 1935 Western Models, No. 542, Box, 7 ⅞ In. 88.0
Car, Racing, Speed, Craig Breedlove's Spirit Of America Land, Windup, Parachute, Decals, 20 In. 523.0
Car, Racing, Tin, Battery Operated, Lights, TN, Japan, 11 In. 295.0
Car, Racing, Tin, Friction, Champion, Japan, ATC, 1950s, 8 ½ In. 175.0
Car, Racing, Tin, Windup, Argentina, 1950s, 8 In. 145.0
Car, Racing, Tin, Windup, England, 1930s, 12 ½ In. 475.0
Car, Racing, Tin, Windup, England, 1940s, 8 ½ In. 145.0
Car, Racing, Tin, Windup, Marx U.S.A, c.1948, 12 In. 145.0
Car, Racing, Tin, Windup, Marx, U.S.A., 1950s, 5 In. 110.0
Car, Racing, Tin, Windup, No. 3, Lupor, U.S.A., 1950s, 12 In. 145.0
Car, Racing, Tin, Windup, No. 27, Marx, U.S.A., 12 In. 145.0
Car, Racing, White, Blue, Coaster, Cast Aluminum, Thimble Drome, c.1950, 10 In. 295.0
Car, Racing, Yellow, ACL Plastic, White Driver, Black Wheels, 4 In. 20.0
Car, Railway Express, Battery Operated, Ride'em, Cor-Cor, 24 x 9 ½ In. 150.0
Car, Rambler, Station Wagon, Die Cast, Tootsietoy 242.0
Car, Rambler, Tin, Friction, Japan, c.1960, 8 ¼ In. 110.0
Car, Roadster, Cast Aluminum, Chrome Like Finish, Faith Mfg. Co., 1930s, 11 In. 500.0
Car, Roadster, Cast Iron, A.C. Williams, c.1932, 3 ⅝ In. 145.0
Car, Roadster, Cast Iron, Nickel Trim, Thomas Kilgore, 10 ½ In. 220.0
Car, Roadster, Model MG, British Racing Green, Doepke, Mid 20th Century, 15 In. 420.0
Car, Roadster, No. 370, Yellow, Black, Sidemount Spares, Hubley, 5 In. 375.0
Car, Roadster, Red, Cream, Cast Iron, Kilgore, 4 In. 165.0
Car, Roadster, Sport, Driver, Rumble Seat, Blue, Kilgore, 6 ¼ In. 350.0
Car, Rolls-Royce, Tin, Hood Ornament, Spring Bumpers, Breaks, Headlamps, Driver, 20 In. 3600.0
Car, Sedan, Driver, Bing, Germany, c.1925, 8 In. 1872.0
Car, Sedan, Graham, 6 Wheels, Tootsietoy 65.0
Car, Sedan, Vindex, Forest Green, Cast Iron Spoked Nickel Plated Wheels, 5 ½ In. 1093.0

ar, Shanghai Isetta, Brown, Cream, Chinese, 1960s, 8 In. 185.00
ar, Space Car, SP-1, Robot Head, Sparks, Tin, Friction, Usagiya, 6 ½ In. 316.00
ar, Sports Motor, Rubber Tire Skins, Open Wheel Racer, Tin, Yonezawa, 11 ½ In. 736.00
ar, Station Wagon, Doors Open, Maroon, Tan, Wood, Buddy L, 18 ½ In. *illus* 720.00
ar, Station Wagon, No. 234, Red, White, Fisher-Price, Box, c.1960, 13 In. 345.00
ar, Station Wagon, Pontiac, Blue, Yellow, Triumph, Box, 1946, 7 In. 150.00
ar, Studebaker, Roadster, Red, Hubley, 7 In. 575.00
ar, Stutz, Cast Iron, Kilgore, 10 ¼ In. 1150.00
ar, Subaru, 260, Tin, Friction, Bandai, Japan, Box, 1959, 8 In. *illus* 1400.00
ar, Tin, 2 Lights, Battery Operated, Japan, 1950s, 10 In. 275.00
ar, Tin, Battery Operated, Japan, c.1950, 7 In. 55.00
ar, Tin, Windup, Garage, Japan, 1950s, 5 In. 145.00
ar, Tin, Windup, Marx, U.S.A., 1920. 375.00
ar, Toyota 2000, GT, Tin, Friction, Japan, 1960s, 14 In. 275.00
ar, Traffic, Indian, Orange, Hubley, c.1931, 4 ¾ In. 375.00
ar, UHU, Driver, Tin, Windup, Lehmann, 1907 2350.00
ar, Valiant, Tin, Friction, Japan, 1960s, 9 ¼ In. 245.00
ar, Volkswagen, Black, Orange, Tin, Battery Operated, Taiyo, 9 ½ In. 135.00
ar, Wagon, Light Blue, Pressed Steel, Wood Wheels, Deco Style, Wyandotte, c.1940, 4 In. 125.00
ar, Whoopy Cowboy, Characters On Wheels, Marx, c.1932, 8 In. 650.00
ar, Yellow Cab, No. 2, Arcade, 8 In. 1200.00
ar Set, Bus, Track, Windup, Tippco, U.S. Zone, Germany, Box. *illus* 518.00
arnival Round-A-Bout, Passengers In Seats, Suspended By Wires, Circular Motion, 1900s, 14 In. 675.00
arousel, 2 Swans, Canopied Carousel, Spins, Crank, Tin Lithograph, Germany, 2 ¾ In. 490.00
arousel, 4 Horses, Flag, Gunthermann, 6 ¾ In. 875.00
arousel, Cardboard Horses & Riders, Hand Crank, Lamps, Tin, Germany, c.1910, 17 In. 690.00
arousel, Figures, Children, Tin, Windup, Chein, 9 ¾ In. *illus* 260.00
arousel, Horse, Mahogany, Carved, Painted, Left Leg Raised, Glass Eyes, c.1890, 16 x 16 x 5 In. 7200.00
arousel, Music Box, Riders, Mattel, Box, 9 x 9 ½ In. 121.00
arousel, Swans, Airplanes, Windup, Wyandotte, c.1930 325.00
arousel, Wood, Painted, Windup, Cutout Riders, Cloth Umbrella Top, 15 x 19 ½ In. 230.00
arriage, Baby, Charlotte Doll, Metal, Painted, Rock & Graner, Germany, 3 ½ In. 546.00
arriage, Horses, Metal, Black, Gold Stenciling, Double Facing Seats, Folding Shades, 39 In. 10640.00
arriage, Horses, Wood, Leather Covered, Upholstered Seat, Floor, Spoke Wheels, 27 In. 2352.00
arriage, Round, Bentwood Frame, Casters, Suspended Saddle Seat, Early 1900s, 18 x 27 In. 23.00
arriage, Tin, Spoke Wheels, Curved Handles, Wood Handgrip, Sunshade, Stenciled, 8 In. 2128.00
arriage, Wicker, Metal Wheels, Undercarriage, Turned Wood Handle, 29 x 32 x 13 ½ In. 33.00
arriage, Wood Frame, Painted, Canvas Lift Top, Seat, Spoke Wheels, Child's, 1880 303.00
art, Horse Drawn, Baltimore Dray, Painted, Tin, Wheel Under Dray, 2 Wheels, Label, 23 In. 881.00
art, Horse Drawn, Driver, Cast Iron, Carpenter, 10 In. 115.00
art, Horse Drawn, Passenger, Red, Figures, Cast Iron, Carpenter, 14 In. 1380.00
art, Ice Cream, Vendor Riding, Tin, Celluloid, Windup, Occupied Japan, 10 In. 110.00
art, Maple, Bent Bamboo, Rickshaw Style, 2 Seats, Handle Bars, Spoke Wheels, 14 In. 336.00
art, Mule Drawn, Coal, Dent, 13 ½ In. 695.00
art, Red, White, Cast Iron, 9 ½ In. 29.00
art, Wood, Black Paint, Metal Bands, Pull, 23 x 62 x 22 In. 220.00
asey The Cop, Tin, Windup, 9 In. 978.00
ash Register, Pressed Steel, Buddy L, Yellow, Red, 11 x 9 In. 29.00
at, Circus, Wood, Jointed, Glass Eyes, Leather Tail, Schoenhut, 9 In. 1265.00
at, Felix, Irish Mail, Squeak, Steiff, 9 ½ In. 10350.00
at, Felix, Jointed Wood Body, Rubber Head, K. E. S. Co., 9 In. 425.00
at, Felix, On Scooter, Yellow, Green Wheels, Tin Lithograph, Windup, Nifty, 7 ½ In. 747.00
at, Felix, Pull Toy, Tin, Felix Goes Up & Down, Pull Toy, Pat Sullivan, Nifty, 8 In. 1610.00
at, Mouth Open, Stuffed, Fur, Wheels In Paws, c.1889, 10 x 17 In. 100.00
at, Watching Bird In Cage, Folk Art, Animated, Hand Crank, Painted, 10 x 12 In. 690.00
hariot, Horse Drawn, Fallows, 1880s, 7 ½ In. 475.00
harleston Trio, Windup, Tin Lithograph, Marx, 1921, 9 In. 495.00
harm, Dwarf, Celluloid, ¾ In. 22.00
harm, Hula Girl, Silver, Movable Hips & Legs, ¾ In. 25.00
harm, Keewie, White, Celluloid, ¾ In. 22.00
harm, Kewpie, Red, Celluloid, ⅞ In. 21.00
harm, Monkey, Celluloid, Brown, 1 ¼ In. 21.00
hest, Blanket, Molded Lid, Dovetailed, Turned Feet, Tan, Brown Highlights, 9 x 18 x 8 In. 1650.00
hest, Blanket, Molded Lid, Porcelain Escutcheon, Turned Feet, Putty Designs, 16 x 23 x 13 In. 4675.00
hest, Doll's, Burled Walnut, Ball Feet, 5 Drawers, Bone Drawer Pulls, 1940, 10 In. 728.00

Toy, Chicken, Composition, Squeak, 4 ½ In.
$143.00

Toy, Child, In Stroller, Tin Lithograph, Penny, Distler, Germany, 3 ½ In.
$325.00

Toy, Circus Set, Humpty Dumpty, Side Show Panels, Schoenhut, 28 x 42 In.
$13000.00

Toy, Clown, 2-Part Head, Jointed, Wood, Body, Schoenhut, 8 ¼ In.
$72.00

Toy, Clown, Clownie, PVC Head, Glass Eyes, Mohair Wig, Jointed Felt Body, Tag, Steiff, 17 In.
$120.00

Toy, Clown, Holding Suitcase, Tin, Windup, Schuco, 4 ½ In.
$397.00

Toy, Clown, On Pig, Tin Lithograph, Penny, Gustav, Fischer, Germany, 3 ¼ In.
$1900.00

Toy, Curiscope, Optical Illusion, 3 Discs, c.1895
$1231.00

Chest, Doll's, Federal, 2 Over 3 Drawers, Split Columns, Lancaster Co., Pa., 12 x 9 ½ x 6 In. ... 550.0
Chicken, Composition, Squeak, 4 ½ In. ... *illus* 143.0
Chicken, Lays Colored Eggs When Pressed, Yellow, Plastic, 3 ¾ x 3 ¾ In. ... 20.0
Chicken Eater, Wood, Paper, Mechanical, c.1890 ... 1035.0
Child, In Stroller, Tin Lithograph, Penny, Distler, Germany, 3 ½ In. ... *illus* 325.0
Chinese Boy, Roly Poly, Papier-Mache, 4 In. ... 95.0
Chompy The Beetle, Advances, Chewing Action, Sound, Marx, Tin, 5 ½ In. ... 258.0
Circus, Wagon, Fisher-Price, No. 156, c.1942, 12 In. ... 403.0
Circus, Wagon, J.B. Thomas Combined Shows, Red, Yellow Letters, Signed, J.W. Taggert, 12 x 17 x 7 In. 1995.0
Circus, Wagon, Overland, Caged Bear, Cast Iron, Driver, Rear Rider, c.1900, 14 x 6 x 4 In. ... 138.0
Circus, Wagon, Overland, Horses, 9 Figures, Kenton, 1940s, 15 In. ... 1050.0
Circus Cage Wagon, Blue, Gold, Horses, Elephants In Cage, Hubley, Cast Iron, 16 In. ... 920.0
Circus Parade, Wagon, Wood, Paper, 9 Animals, Fisher-Price, 1932, 15 In. ... 66.0
Circus Set, Barnum & Bailey, Wagon, Animals, Elephant, Tin, Windup, Linstrom, 18 ½ In. ... 1155.0
Circus Set, Beton Circus, Animals, Wild West Figures, Box, Early 1950s ... 159.0
Circus Set, Humpty Dumpty, Side Show Panels, Schoenhut, 28 x 42 In. ... *illus* 13000.0
Circus Trailer, Cab Pulls Trailer, Gate Opens, Animals Slide Out By Turning Crank, Tin, 11 In. 192.0
Clicker, Circus Elephant, Plays The Cymbal, Moves His Head & Tail, Tin, 2 ½ In. ... 141.0
Clicker, Clown Playing Banjo, Eyes Move, Body Moves, Tin, 5 In. ... 141.0
Clicker, PEZ, Girl Hands PEZ To Child, Tin, c.1955, 3 ½ In. ... 700.0
Clicker, Stork, Tips Hat, Opens Beak Revealing Baby, Tin, 2 ¾ In. ... 226.0
Clock, Red Roses, Blue Ground, Pendulum, Tin Lithograph, Meier, Germany, 6 ¾ In. ... 230.0
Clock, Teddy Bear, Beating Drum, Wood Face, Head Moves, 1920s-30s ... 285.0
Clown, 2-Part Head, Jointed, Wood, Body, Schoenhut, 8 ¼ In. ... *illus* 72.0
Clown, 3 Musicians On Bench, Windup, Plink-Plink Mechanism, Gunthermann, 9 ½ In. ... 4675.0
Clown, Acrobat, Motorcycle, Tin, Windup, 6 ⅜ In. ... 468.0
Clown, Acrobat, Motorcycle, Tin, Windup, England, 5 ⅜ In. ... 358.0
Clown, Acrobat, Tin, Cloth, Windup, Crosses Hand Over Hand, Germany, 8 ½ In. ... 1430.0
Clown, Advances With Pedaling Motion, Arms Go Back & Forth, Tin, 5 ½ In. ... 678.0
Clown, Ball Blowing, Waves Arms, Ball Floats, Battery Operated, Nomura, Box, 10 ½ In. ... 184.0
Clown, Banjo Player, Mechanical, Tin, Germany, 5 ¾ In. ... 33.0
Clown, Car, Unique Artie, Crazy, Jumps, Tin, Windup, Unique Art, Box, 10 In. ... 425.0
Clown, Celluloid Head, Cloth, Gund, 1940s, 19 In. ... 65.0
Clown, Circus, Roller Skating, Tin, Battery Operated, Remote Control, T.P.S., Box, 6 In. ... 805.0
Clown, Circus, Walking, Tin, Cloth, Box, 10 ½ In. ... 220.0
Clown, Cirko, Cyclist, Windup, Marx, Box, 9 x 9 ½ In. ... 3950.0
Clown, Clownie, PVC Head, Glass Eyes, Mohair Wig, Jointed Felt Body, Tag, Steiff, 17 In. . *illus* 120.0
Clown, Dozo, Sweeping, Battery Operated, Nomura, Box, 14 In. ... 275.0
Clown, Handstand On Barrel, Tin Plate, Windup, 8 ¼ In. ... 523.0
Clown, Happy, Upper Body & Head Move As He Opens & Closes Eyes, Tin, 6 In. ... 113.0
Clown, Happy Fiddler, Battery Operated, Cragstan, Box, 10 ¼ In. ... 248.0
Clown, Happy Fiddler, Plays Violin, Moves Back & Forth, Battery Operated, Alps, Box, 10 In. ... 193.0
Clown, Happy 'N Sad, Plays Accordion, Battery Operated Remote Control, Yonezawa, Box, 10 In. 115.0
Clown, Holding Suitcase, Tin, Windup, Schuco, 4 ½ In. ... *illus* 397.0
Clown, In Barrel, Chein, 7 ½ In. ... 440.0
Clown, In Hoop, Windup, Gunthermann, 4 ¾ In. ... 1320.0
Clown, Juggling, Tin, Windup, Box, 8 ½ In. ... 605.0
Clown, Magic Man, Puffs Smoke, Tin, Fabric, Battery Operated, Remote, Marusan, Box, 12 In. 395.0
Clown, Mechanical, Roller Skates, Japan, 5 ½ In. ... 120.0
Clown, Motorcycle, Sidecar, Tin, Windup, 3 ⅜ In. ... 358.0
Clown, Moves Up & Down, Japan, 1950s, 7 In. ... 275.0
Clown, Musical, Battery Operated, Nomura, 9 ½ In. ... 121.0
Clown, On Donkey, Tin Plate, Windup, 8 ½ In. ... 880.0
Clown, On Horse, Bounces Up & Down, Wheels, Germany, 1900, 8 In. ... 475.0
Clown, On Motorcycle, England, 7 ½ In. ... 523.0
Clown, On Pig, Riding Backward, Wheels, Tin, Gustav Fischer, 3 ¼ In. ... 1955.0
Clown, On Pig, Tin Lithograph, Penny, Gustav, Fischer, Germany, 3 ¼ In. ... *illus* 1900.0
Clown, On Tricycle, Tin, Windup, Swirl Wheel, Technofix, U.S. Zone, Germany, 5 x 5 ½ In. ... 1045.0
Clown, Pinky, Juggling, Tin, Cloth, Battery Operated, Alps, Box, 10 In. ... 281.0
Clown, Playing Guitar, Tin Lithograph, Windup, Distler, Germany, 8 ¼ In. ... 747.0
Clown, Playing Saxophone, Tin Lithograph, Windup, Distler, Germany, 8 In. ... 836.0
Clown, Riding Circus Horse, Celluloid, Metal, Windup, Japan, Box, 7 x 7 In. ... 221.0
Clown, Riding On Clown, Tin Windup, Germany, 6 x 5 ½ In. ... 1870.0
Clown, Riding Unicycle, Around Big Top, Painted, Tin, Cardboard, Metal, Windup, 5 x 9 In. ... 520.0
Clown, Roly Poly, Composition, Schoenhut, 1920s, 5 ½ In. ... 150.0
Clown, Roly Poly, On Ball, Papier-Mache, Pressed Cardboard, 9 ½ In. ... 248.0

Clown, Roly Poly, On Ball, Tin, Germany, 7¾ In.... 605.00
Clown, Seesaw, Propeller, Tin, Windup, England, Stoddard Acorn Toy Co., 7¾ x 10 In.... 468.00
Clown, Skating, Schuco, Germany, 8¼ In.... 358.00
Clown, Spinning Star Wheel, Gunthermann, 9⅛ In.... 1870.00
Clown, Tin Plate, Celluloid, Windup, 6 In.... 148.00
Clown, Tricycling, Box, 12 In.... 248.00
Clown, Tumbling Tim, Push Stick, Fisher-Price, No. 166, 1939, 27¾ In.... 385.00
Clown, Violinist, Dancing Dog, Tin, Windup, Sound, Painted, Gunthermann, 9 In.... 3575.00
Clown, Wood, Jointed, Painted Features, 2-Part Head, Original Costume, Schoenhut, 9 In.... 173.00
Clown & Lion, Battery Operated, 8¾ x 5¾ x 13 In.... 385.00
Clown Acrobat, Revolves, Green Base, Tin Lithograph, 3½ In.... 633.00
Clowns, Walking, Gyroscope Operated, Tin Plate, 8¼ x 5 In.... 468.00
Coach, Coronation, Horses, Queen Elizabeth, Box, c.1953, 5 In.... 50.00
Combat Soldier, Turns, Fires Rifle, Tin, Plastic, Windup, Nomura, Box, 6 In.... 201.00
Comical Clara, Wiggles, Eyes Pop, Polka Dot Dress, Tin, Windup, T.P.S., Japan, Box, 5 In.... 173.00 to 425.00
Construction Set, Tin, Painted, Booklet, Bilt-E-Z, c.1924, 10 x 7 x 1½ In.... 147.00
Cow, 4 Wheels, Mooing Mechanism, Pull Toy, Steiff, Mid 20th Century.... 590.00
Cow, Brown, White, Wood, Jointed, Painted Eyes, Leather Ears, Horns, Bell, Rope Tail, Schoenhut, 9 In. 259.00
Cowboy, Gallop, In Cart, Pulled By Zebra, Windup, Lehmann, 1954.... 350.00
Cradle, Doll's, Pine, Scalloped Edge, Red & Green, Flowers, 5 x 8¾ x 5½ In.... 275.00
Cradle, Doll's, Rocking, Walnut, Roundels, Spool Turnings & Finials, 21 x 30 In.... 1331.00
Crane, Crank Operates Bucket, Chein, 9 In.... 295.00
Crane, Magnetic, Lever-Operated Crane With Magnet, Bandai, Box, 16 In.... 170.00
Crying Baby & Dog, Celluloid, Windup, 6 In.... 167.00
Cupboard, Step Back, 2 Doors, Serpentine Bottom, Bracket Feet, Paint, 28 x 16 x 11 In.... 1650.00
Curiscope, Optical Illusion, 3 Discs, c.1895.... *illus* 1231.00
Cyclist, Kiddy, Windup, Tin Lithograph, Unique Art Mfg., 8⅝ In.... 110.00
Dagwood Aeroplane, Tin Lithograph, Windup, Marx, 11½-In. Wingspan.... 1553.00
Dagwood The Driver, Windup, Tin Lithograph, Marx, Box, 6 x 8 In.... 2695.00
Dan Dare, Pilot Of The Future, Crescent Toys, Box, 7 Piece Set.... 3055.00
Dancing Couple, Celluloid, Windup, Occupied Japan, 4½ In.... 125.00
Dancing Mouse, Baby Mouse, Mother Dances & Lifts Baby Up & Down, 4¼ In.... 119.00
Diorama, Doll Hospital, Interior Setting, Pine Box, Gilt Style Decals, Front Glass, 27 x 18 In.... 2588.00
Diorama, General Store, Country Store Items, Bisque Head Doll, 4½ In., 31 x 10½ In.... 173.00
Dog, Bulldog, Brown, Painted Features, Collar, Leather Ears, Tail, Wood, Schoenhut, 6 In.... 1035.00
Dog, Bulldog, Jointed, White & Black, Leather Ears, Tail, Collar, Wood, Schoenhut, 6 In.... 920.00
Dog, Bulldog, Movable Head, Studded Collar, Papier-Mache, 19 In.... 1392.00
Dog, Bulldog, Papier-Mache, Glass Eyes, Head Moves, Barks, Wheels, Pull Toy, 13½ x 26 In. 919.00
Dog, Bulldog, Papier-Mache, Bristle Collar, Articulated Jaw, Castors, Chain, France, c.1900, 14 In.. 2390.00
Dog, Dalmation, Leather Collar, Button In Ear, Steiff, 13 In.... *illus* 920.00
Dog, Flippo, Tin, Windup, Linemar, Japan, 1950s, 4 In.... 95.00
Dog, French Bulldog, Bully, Mohair Bag, Plush, Horsehair Neck, Stieff, 1930s, 4 x 10 x 12 In.. 5462.00
Dog, Gaylord, Barks, Walks, Plastic, Battery Operated, Box, Ideal, 25 In.... 86.00
Dog, In Dog House, Moves In & Out, Crank, 2⅝ In.... 747.00
Dog, Poodle, White, Wood, Jointed, Fur, Glass Eyes, Rope Tail, Schoenhut, 8 In.... 144.00 to 173.00
Dog, Rollover, Gunthermann, Germany, 1920-25.... *illus* 234.00
Dog, Scottie, Black, Red, Marx, Box, 13 In.... 395.00
Dollhouse, 2 Story, Paper On Wood, Front Porch, Bay Windows, 23 x 21¼ In.... 705.00
Dollhouse, 2 Story, Paper On Wood, Glass, Furniture, 2 Figures, 19 x 12 x 8 In.... *illus* 1200.00
Dollhouse, 3 Story, Clapboard Siding, Glass Windows, Furniture, 1900, 27 x 42 x 16 In.. *illus* 1000.00
Dollhouse, 4 Rooms, Furniture, Composition Board & Wood, Schoenhut, 24 x 24½ In.. *illus* 450.00
Dollhouse, 4 Rooms, Mustard Paint, Olive Trim, 2 Chimneys, Glass Windows, 41 x 23 In.... 288.00
Dollhouse, 6 Rooms, French Villa, Doorbell, Mansard Roof, Christian Hacker, 28 x 30 In.... 3105.00
Dollhouse, 6 Rooms, Front Opens, Closet, Wallpaper, Porches, Gottschalk, 31 x 37 In.... 8050.00
Dollhouse, Horse Stable, Hayloft, Shed, Wood, Accessories, Gottschalk, c.1910, 26 x 10 In.... 585.00
Dollhouse, Lithograph On Wood, Glassine Windows, Lace Curtains, Dormer, Bliss, 15 In.... 610.00
Dollhouse, Log Cabin, Wood, 1940-65, 27 x 21 x 19 In.... 295.00
Dollhouse, Queen Anne Cottage, Red Roof, Porch, Balcony, Bliss, 1911, 24 x 18 x 12 In.... 2115.00
Dollhouse, Seaside Cottage, Paper Lithograph, 6 Columns, 3 Rooms, Bliss, 23 x 18 In.... 2070.00
Dollhouse Furniture, Armoire, Dresser, Mirror, Secretary, Chest, Fire Screen, Germany, 1885 7616.00
Dollhouse Furniture, Bedroom, Bathroom, Cast Iron, Kilgore, 1930s, 7 Piece.... 118.00
Dollhouse Furniture, Mirror Set, Overmantel, Chippendale, 2 Convex, c.1920, 4 Piece.... 2875.00
Dollhouse Furniture, Radio, Gramophone, Metal, Wood Stand, Crank Wind, Tin.... 106.00
Dollhouse Furniture, Rocker, Baby Bed, High Chair, Stroller, Cradle, Carriage, Metal, 6 Piece 224.00
Dolls are listed in their own category.

Toy, Dog, Dalmation, Leather Collar, Button In Ear, Steiff, 13 In.
$920.00

Button in Ear
The Steiff "Button in Ear" trademark was first used in 1905.

Toy, Dog, Rollover, Gunthermann, Germany, 1920-25
$234.00

Toy, Dollhouse, 2 Story, Paper On Wood, Glass, Furniture, 2 Figures, 19 x 12 x 8 In.
$1200.00

T

Toy, Dollhouse, 3 Story, Clapboard Siding, Glass Windows, Furniture, 1900, 27 x 42 x 16 In.
$1000.00

Toy, Dollhouse, 4 Rooms, Furniture, Composition Board & Wood, Schoenhut, 24 x 24½ In.
$450.00

Toy, Drummer Boy, Windup, Tin Lithograph, Louis Marx, 8 In.
$405.00

Toy, Elephant, Jointed Wood Body, Glass Eyes, Leather Ears, Schoenhut, 10½ In.
$725.00

Dolly Seamstress, Head Turns, Material Moves, Tin, Vinyl, Battery Operated, Nomura, Box, 8 In. 356.00
Donkey, Mechanical, Papier-Mache, Bisque Man, 3 Wheels, Tin Base, Vichy, c.1875, 16 x 14 In. 5264.00
Donkey, Wood, Papier-Mache, Hide Cover, Horsehair, Wicker Seat, Pull Toy, 1885, 22 x 22 In. 2352.00
Donkey & Cart, Driver, Cast Iron, Dent, 1906, 13½ In. 695.00
Dray, Driver, Horse, Pratt & Letchworth, 12 In. 550.00
Dresser, Doll's, Mirror, Walnut, Burled Veneers, 4 Drawers, c.1880, 29 In. 1456.00
Drum, Circus, Tin, Cloth, Chein, 11 In. 55.00
Drummer Boy, Walks, Beats Drum, Tin, Windup, Marx, 1938, 9 In. 360.00
Drummer Boy, Windup, Tin Lithograph, Louis Marx, 8 In. *illus* 405.00
Drunkard, Painted, Burlap, Champagne Bottle, Cup, Windup, Mechanical, c.1900, 7¾ In. 429.00
Dry Sink, Door, Drawer, Cutout Bracket Feet, Grain Paint, 16 x 21 x 10 In. 4125.00
Duck, Daisy, Jolly Drumming, Cragstan Melody Band, Battery Operated, Alps, Box, 10 In. 130.00
Duck, Mallard, Tin Lithograph, Flywheel On 3 Wheels, Pull Toy, 7½ In. 116.00
Duck, Mallard On Wheels, Velvet Head, Felt Body, Tin Wheels, Squeak, Steiff, c.1920, 10 In. 118.00
Duck, Quack Quack, Mama Duck Pulling Cart, 3 Babies, Windup, Tin Litho, Lehmann, 2¾ x 7 In. 385.00
Dump Car, Bonnet, Lever-Operated Bed, Tin, Mitsuhashi, 8¾ In. 153.00
Dutch Oven, Griswold, No. 0, 568, No Trivet 800.00
Electromobile G-Men Car, Hood-Mounted Machine Gun, Roof Light, Headlights, 8¼ In. 316.00
Electromobile Taxi, Green & Yellow, Runs Forward & Reverse, Headlights, Tin, 8¼ In. 305.00
Electromobile Taxi, Tan & Red, Runs Forward & Reverse, Headlights, Tin, 8¼ In. 362.00
Elephant, Circus, Windup, Tin Lithograph, U.S. Zone, Germany, 1950s, 9 In. 275.00
Elephant, Circus, Wood, Jointed, Glass Eyes, Woven Blanket, Headdress, Schoenhut, 10½ In. 748.00
Elephant, Gray, Jointed, Wood, Glass Eyes, Leather Tusks, Ears, Headdress, Schoenhut, 9¾ In. 115.00
Elephant, Gray, Jointed, Wood, Glass Eyes, Leather Ears, Headdress, Schoenhut, 8 In. 546.00
Elephant, Jointed Wood Body, Glass Eyes, Leather Ears, Schoenhut, 10½ In. *illus* 725.00
Elephant, Jolly Daddy, Walks, Smokes Pipe, Battery Operated, Marusan, Box, 9 In. 156.00
Elephant, Jumbo, Bubble Blowing, Tin, Plush, Battery Operated, Yonezawa, Box, 7½ x 7¼ In. 110.00
Elephant, Man Rider, Platform, Pull Toy, Hall & Stafford, c.1880, 9 In. 702.00
Elephant, Papier-Mache, Felt Cover, Painted, Squeak, Pull Toy, 10½ x 15 In. 696.00
Elephant, Pulling Cart, Head Nods, Tin, Painted, Fischer, Germany, 5 In. 201.00
Elephant, Ride On, Iron Wheels, Button Eyes, Felt Tusks, Iron Frame, Steiff, 22 x 19 In. 575.00
Elephant & Zebra, Seesaw, Rocks As Elephant & Zebra Play The Drum, Hishimo, Tin, 7 In. 622.00
Elsie's Dairy Truck, Bottles, Mallets, Bells, Fisher-Price, 1948, 10 In. *illus* 288.00
End Loader, Scoop, Wood Wheels, Cast Aluminum, Hubley, 10½ In. 66.00
Erector Set, No. 7½, Truck, Box, 21½ x 8¼ In. 248.00
Eric The Bat, Stuffed, Beige With Black Wings, Tag, Button In Ear, Steiff, 5½ In. 315.00
Felix The Cat, Ball Shaped Head, Segmented Arms & Legs, Wood, 8 In. 350.00
Felix The Cat, Wood, Jointed, Leather Ears, Schoenhut, Copyright 1922, 8 In. 382.00
Ferris Wheel, 6 Cars, Figures, Red, Iron, Mechanical, Hubley, 17 In. *illus* 2300.00
Ferris Wheel, Clockwork, Tin, Iron, Hubley, 17 In. 1320.00
Ferris Wheel, Tin, Windup, Musical, W. Germany, c.1955, 9¾ In. 164.00
Ferris Wheel, Tin Lithograph, Figure, Windup, Painted, Kellerman, 17¾ In. 495.00
Ferris Wheel, Tin Lithograph, Windup, 4 Cars, Chein, 1930s, 16½ In. 358.00
Ferris Wheel, Tin Lithograph, Windup, Built-In Key, 1930s, 16 In. 443.00
Ferris Wheel, Tin Lithograph, Windup, 12¾ In. 468.00
Fiddle, Box, Coffin Style Box, Black Paint, 18½ x 5¾ In. 29.00
Field Hospital Tent, Doctor Treating Patients, White, Red, Tin Lithograph, Meier, Germany, 4 In. 345.00
Figure, Chris Colt, Movable Arms, 1961, 7⅜ In. 153.00
Figure Set, McDonald's McDonaldland, On Card, 1976, 7 In., 7 Piece 324.00
Fire House, Wood, Red Brick Sides, c.1900, 7¼ x 6½ x 8 In. 22.00
Fire Pumper, 2 Horses, Driver, Cast Iron, c.1900, 11 In. 90.00
Fire Pumper, 2 Horses, Driver, Cast Iron, c.1900, 18½ In. 672.00
Fire Pumper, 3 Horses, Cast Iron, c.1900, 18½ In. 112.00
Fire Pumper, 3 Horses, Driver, Cast Iron, c.1900, 11½ In. 78.00
Fire Pumper, Automotive, Driver, Red, Gold, Cast Iron, 8 In. 345.00
Fire Pumper, Driver, Cast Iron, Red, Gold, Black Paint, 20th Century, 8¼ In. 188.00
Fire Pumper, Driver, Figures, Painted, Iron, Dent, 10½ In. *illus* 345.00
Fire Pumper, Driver, Rider, Cast Iron, Painted Green, Spoke Wheels, 6½ x 10¾ x 6½ In. 165.00
Fire Pumper, Driver, Tin, Wood, Windup, 6¼ x 9½ In. 187.00
Fire Pumper, Horses, Driver, Cast Iron, c.1900, 18 In. 258.00
Fire Pumper, No. 5, Pressed Steel, Hose Reel, Hoses, Ladder, Red, Tonka, 17 In. 201.00
Fire Pumper, Red, Ahrens-Fox, Hubley, 7½ In. 175.00
Fire Pumper, Red, Box, Hubley, 7½ In. 225.00
Fire Pumper, Steam, Red, Silver, Nickel Grille, Drivers, Boiler, Hubley, 8½ In. 375.00
Fire Pumper, Texaco, Buddy L, 1962 295.00
Fire Pumper, Texaco Fire Chief, Painted Steel, Chrome Accessories, Trim, Box, Buddy L, 24½ In. 146.00

Fire Pumper, Upright Engine, Iron, Brass, Burner, Red, Yellow Painted, 1885, 12 x 17 x 6 In. 2860.00
Fire Station, Red, Green, Embossed, Pressed Steel, Keystone, 8 In.. *illus* 400.00
Fire Steamer, Horse Drawn, Wood, Black, Silver, Side Hoses, Gauges, No. 22, 24 In. 173.00
Fire Truck, Advances, Siren, Tin, Marx, 14 ¼ In. 124.00
Fire Truck, Aerial Ladder, Headlights, Steel Grill, Spoke Tires, Pull Along, Buddy L, 29 In. 1380.00
Fire Truck, Aerial Ladder, Pressed Steel, White Rubber Tires, Kingsbury, 35 In. 978.00
Fire Truck, Chemical Hose, 1914 Model T, c.1977, Box, 7 ½ In. 22.00
Fire Truck, Friction, Argentina, 1950s, 12 In. 275.00
Fire Truck, Hook & Ladder, 2 Riders, Steel, Cast Iron, 19 In. 348.00
Fire Truck, Hook & Ladder, 3 Firemen, Arcade, c.1934, 16 In. 950.00
Fire Truck, Hook & Ladder, Eagle, Side Shield, Cast Iron, Painted, 33 In. 928.00
Fire Truck, Hook & Ladder, Hubley, 20 In. 761.00
Fire Truck, Hook & Ladder, Pressed Steel, Red, Box, c.1952, 33 ½ In. 585.00
Fire Truck, Hook & Ladder, Red Painted, Steel, Open Cab, Rubber Tires, Kingsbury, 34 ½ In.. 823.00
Fire Truck, Ladder, Aerial, Hydraulic, Buddy L, 39 In.. 3500.00
Fire Truck, Ladder, Diamond T, Nickel Grille, Ladders, Red, Hubley, 6 ½ In. 250.00
Fire Truck, Ladder, Die Cast, Red, Yellow, Tootsietoy, 1927, 3 ½ In. 85.00
Fire Truck, Ladder, Driver, Dog, Silver, Red, Hubley, 5 In. 350.00
Fire Truck, Ladder, Hose, Nozzle, Pressed Steel, Decals, Tonka, 17 In. 144.00
Fire Truck, Ladder, No. 3, Pressed Steel, Smith-Miller, Lights, Bumper, 36 In. 316.00
Fire Truck, Ladder, Pressed Steel, Decals, Tonka, 32 In. 201.00
Fire Truck, Ladder, Red, Silver, Nickel Grill, Drivers, Ladders, Hubley, 8 ½ In.. 375.00
Fire Truck, Ladder, Tin Lithograph, 5 Embossed Firemen, c.1940, 5 ¼ In. 55.00
Fire Truck, Patrol, Driver, 5 Firemen, Hubley, c.1915, 15 In. 4680.00
Fire Truck, Patrol, Figures, Red, Kenton, 7 In.. 375.00
Fire Truck, Pumper, Motorized, Cast Iron, 6 In. 45.00
Fire Truck, Pumper, Motorized, Driver, c.1910, 6 ½ In.. 45.00
Fire Truck, Red, Tin, Plastic Cab, Battery Operated, Ladders, Box, Yonezawa, 12 In. 150.00
Fire Truck, Sit On Ride, Pressed Steel, Wyandotte, 30 In. 58.00
Fire Truck, Wyandotte Fire Dept., Decals, Light, Red, c.1940, 30 In. 110.00
Fire Wagon, Hook & Ladder, 2 Horses, Cast Iron, Ladders, 2 Drivers, c.1890, 9 x 27 x 4 In. 990.00
Fire Wagon, Hook & Ladder, 2 Horses, Gong Bell, 2 Firemen, Hubley, 1910, 24 In.. 825.00
Fire Wagon, Hook & Ladder, Yellow, 2 Horses, 2 Firemen, Phoenix, 1880s, 26 In.. 1295.00
Fire Wagon, Horse, Driver, Fire Chief, Painted, Iron, Wilkins, 13 ¾ In. *illus* 3900.00
Fire Wagon, Horse Drawn, Driver, Cast Iron, c.1910, 12 In. 784.00
Fire Wagon, Horse Drawn, Fire Chief, Wilkins, 5 x 12 In. 210.00
Fire Wagon, Horse Drawn, Ladders, Tin, Steel, Blue, Bell, Yellow Iron Wheels, Wilkins, 27 In. 518.00
Fire Wagon, Ladder, 2 Wood Ladders, 2 Horses, 2 Firemen, Cast Iron, c.1900, 24 In. 784.00
Fire Wagon, Ladder, 3 Horses, Cast Iron, c.1900, 17 In. 56.00
Fire Wagon, Pumper, 3 Horses, Driver, Hubley, 1906, 15 In. 595.00
Fire Wagon, Pumper, Phoenix, 2 Articulated Horses, Driver, Ives, 1890, 19 In.. 1350.00
Fire Wagon, Hose Reel, Cast Iron, Horse, c.1900, 13 ½ In. 560.00
Fire Wagon, Hose Reel, Cast Iron, Horse, Driver, c.1900, 11 ½ In. 308.00
Fire Wagon, Hose Reel, Cast Iron, Horse, Driver, c.1900, 14 ½ In. 478.00
Fire Wagon, Pumper, Driver, 2 Horses Gallop, Bell Rings, Iron, Ten, Steel, Wood, 17 In. 685.00
Fire Wagon, Pumper, Horse Drawn, Iron, Painted, American Eagle, 21 In.. 1044.00
Fire Wagon, Pumper, White Horse, Ringing Bell, Horses Gallop, Iron, Tin, Steel, Wood, 17 In. 750.00
Fire Wagon, Pumper, Yellow Gold, 3-Horse Team, Driver, Cast Iron, Wilkins, 22 In. 748.00
Fireman, Climbing, Yellow Ladder, Plastic, Tin Lithograph, Windup, Marx, Box, 21 In.. 403.00
Flintstones, Dino-The-Dinosaur, Hops, Purple, Tin, Windup, Marx, 3 ½ In. 260.00
Flintstones, Dino-The-Dinosaur, Opens Mouth, Walks, Tin, Windup, Linemar, 5 ½ In. 166.00
Flintstones, Dino-The-Dinosaur, Purple, Windup, Tin Lithograph, Linemar, Box, 1961, 5 In.. 353.00
Flintstones, Hoppy, Rubbles Family Pet, Tin, Windup, Marx, Box, 4 In.. 259.00
Flip The Frog, Bisque, Japan, 1930s, 5 In. 195.00
Flying Horse Race, Tin Plate, Plunger Operated, 6 ¾ In. 132.00
Flying Saucer, Astronauts, Red, Tin, Battery, K.O., Japan, Box, 7 In.. *illus* 155.00
Folk Dancers, Male, Painted Tin Face, Female, Celluloid, Schuco, Germany, 5 & 3 ¾ In. 110.00
Folk Dancers, Man & Woman, Tin, Celluloid, Windup, Schuco, Germany, 5-In. Man, 3¾-In. Woman 110.00
Ford, Hot Rod, Car, Racing, Flat Head Motor, 2 Caps, Japan, 1950, 8 In. 295.00
Fort Set, Trees, Bushes, Towers, Buildings, 10 Soldiers, Officers, Flag Bearer, 6 x 17 ¾ x 14 In. 88.00
Fox The Magician, Rabbit Appears & Disappears, Mixed Material, Nomura, 6 ½ In. 175.00
Fox The Magician, Windup, Tin, Fabric, Plush, Box, 6 ½ In. 475.00
Freddie Fireplug, Wood, Take-A-Part, Red, White, Blue, Doepke, Box, 1957, 6 In. 150.00
Freight Station, Tin, Marx, 1950s, 26 In. 65.00
Funny Dancer, Pan Gee, Jointed Figure Dances, Tin, 10 In.. 384.00
G.I. Joe, Bouncing Jeep, Tin Lithograph, Windup, Unique Art Mfg., 6 ½ In. 115.00

Toy, Elsie's Dairy Truck, Bottles, Mallets, Bells, Fisher-Price, 1948, 10 In.
$288.00

Toy, Ferris Wheel, 6 Cars, Figures, Red, Iron, Mechanical, Hubley, 17 In.
$2300.00

Toy, Fire Pumper, Driver, Figures, Painted, Iron, Dent, 10 ½ In.
$345.00

Toy, Fire Station, Red, Green, Embossed, Pressed Steel, Keystone, 8 In.
$400.00

TIP

Don't repaint old metal toys. It lowers the value.

T

Toy, Fire Wagon, Horse, Driver, Fire Chief, Painted, Iron, Wilkins, 13 3/4 In.
$3900.00

Toy, Flying Saucer, Astronauts, Red, Tin, Battery, K.O., Japan, Box, 7 In.
$155.00

Toy, Giraffe, Painted, Wood, Rope Tail, Wire Cage, Schoenhut, 10 1/2 In.
$850.00

Toy, Girl, Skipping Rope, Die Cut, Paper, Mechanical, Penny Toy, 4 3/8 In.
$465.00

Gabby Goose, Scarf, No. 120, Pull, Fisher-Price, c.1936, 9 In. 518.00
Games are listed in their own category.
Garage, Cardboard, Box, Built-Rite, c.1936, 7 x 7 In. 75.00
Gas Pump, Crank, U.S.A., 1930s, 9 In. 275.00
Gas Pump, Red, Gold, Arcade, 4 1/2 In. 275.00
Gas Pump, Tin, Chein, USA, 1930s, 9 In. 375.00
Gas Station, Esso, Tin, Army Car, Japan, 3 In. 145.00
Gas Station Garage, Tin Lithograph, Japan, Prewar, 3 3/4 In. 316.00
George Washington Bridge, Greyhound Bus, Tin Litho, Windup, Fritz Bueschel, N.J., 25 In. 748.00
Giraffe, Circus, Wood, Painted, Wire Metal Cage, Painted Gold, Schoenhut, 10 1/2 In. 863.00
Giraffe, Lofty Lizzy, Fisher-Price, 1931, 9 In. 400.00
Giraffe, Painted, Wood, Rope Tail, Wire Cage, Schoenhut, 10 1/2 In. . . . . *illus* 850.00
Giraffe, Wood, Ball-Jointed, Crackle Black & Yellow Paint, Marked Oakland, 1950s, 14 In. . . . 150.00
Girl, Skipping Rope, Die Cut, Paper, Mechanical, Penny Toy, 4 3/8 In. . . . . *illus* 465.00
Girl & Chicken, Leans Forward, Lever, Tin Lithograph, Meier, Germany, Penny Toy, 3 7/8 In. . . 863.00
Gnomes Sawing Log, Tin Lithograph, Fischer, Germany, 4 1/4 In. 489.00
Goat, Hide Cover, Leather Ears, Pulls Cart, Papier-Mache, Metal, 2 Wheels, 18 In. 4256.00
Goat, On Platform, Gold Paint, Wheels, Germany, 2 3/4 In. 260.00
Go-Cart, Driver, Metal, Battery Operated, Japan, 1950s, 10 In. 175.00
Godzilla, Tin, Windup, Linemar, 8 In. . . . . *illus* 155.00
Golfer, Man, Full Figure, Wood, Golf Club In Hand Ratchet, Long Handle, Schoenhut, 27 In. . 230.00
Golfer, Woman, Full Figure, Wood, Golf Club In Hand Ratchet, Long Handle, Schoenhut, 27 In. 288.00
Good Time Charlie, Drinks, Smokes, Nods Head, Moves Foot, Battery Operated, Illfelder, Box, 12 1/2 In. 150.00
Goose, Nodder, Painted, Tin, Germany, 4 In. 144.00
Goose, Red Goose Shoes, Pecks, Bobs Up & Down, Windup, 1924, 4 x 9 In. 920.00
Grader, Adams, Yellow, Doepke, 1949, 26 In. 295.00
Grandpa's New Car, Advances, Car Shakes, Moving Hat, Driver Jumps From Seat, Tin, 5 3/4 In. 175.00
Great Son Of Garloo, Walker, Plastic, Windup, Marx, Box, 5 3/4 In. 345.00
Greyhound Super Coach, Arcade, 1937, 9 In. 375.00
Grocery Store, Cast Iron, Blue Paint, Silver, Dayton, 4 1/8 In. 59.00
Grocery Store, Wood, Windows, Spice Drawers, Table, Stairs, Dog, France, 24 x 13 x 12 In. . . 4480.00
Gumby, Cowboy, Holding Gun, Rifle, Bends, Hong Kong, 1950-60, 5 In. 5.00
Gun, Sure-Shot Machine Gun, Sparks, Rat-Tat-Tat Sound, Tin, Crank, T. Cohn, Box, 21 In. . . 121.00
Gun, Tom Corbett's Space Cadet Official Pistol, Tin Lithograph, Marx, Box, 10 In. 858.00
Handcar, Hoky Poky, Windup, Metal, U.S.A., c.1950, 7 In. 275.00
Handcar, Tin, Windup, U.S.A. Girard, c.1920, 6 In. . . . . 175.00 to 253.00
Hang Tag, Buddy L, c.1925, 1 5/8 x 1 5/8 In. 288.00
Hansom Cab, Lithograph, Painted, Tin, Windup, Pink, 5 1/2 In. 1100.00
Happy Hooligan, Walker, Tin, Windup, Chein, 1930s, 6 In. 525.00
Happy Hooligan Comic Strip Character, Lithographed Paper On Wood, Movable Arms, 14 In. 110.00
Happy Jack, Die Cut Figure, Black Minstrel, Crank, Moves Leg, Tin, 6 1/4 In. 396.00
Happy Joe, Peg Leg, Dances, Crank, Tin, 3 5/8 In. 546.00
Harold Lloyd, Happy Face To Sad Face When Bell Rings, Tin, Germany, 6 1/4 In. 311.00
Helicopter, Circus Clowns, Tin, Windup, Japan, 1950s, 6 In. 95.00
Helicopter, Metal, Battery Operated, Japan, 1950s, 10 In. 110.00
Hey-Hey Chicken Snatcher, Tin Lithograph, Windup, Marx, April 13, 1926, 8 In. 1016.00
Hippopotamus, Brown, Wood, Jointed, Tusks, Glass Eyes, Leather Ears, Schoenhut, 9 1/2 In. . . 115.00
Hippopotamus, Wood, Jointed, Brown, Glass Eyes, Leather Tail, Ears, Schoenhut, 9 1/4 In. . . . 633.00
Hobbyhorse, Dappled Black & White, Glass Eyes, Saddle, Stirrups, Platform Base, 28 x 35 x 14 In. . 130.00
Hobo, Accordion Player, Battery Operated, Box, 10 1/2 x 11 1/4 In. 330.00
Hobo, Tumbling, Einfalt, 4 7/16 In. 688.00
Hoky & Poky, Clown Hand Car, Wyandotte, 6 x 5 1/2 In. 330.00
Horse, Carved Muzzle, Hooves, Mohair, Pull Toy, 19th Century, 23 In. 413.00
Horse, Cloth Body, Tack Eyes, Horsehair Tail, Victorian, Wheels, Pull Toy, 20 x 20 In. 330.00
Horse, Dapple Painted, Wood, Leather Harness, Platform, Tin Wheels, c.1890, 11 x 12 x 4 3/4 In. 100.00
Horse, Hide, Glass Eyes, Horsehair Mane, Tail, Pull, 19th Century, 13 In. . . . . *illus* 460.00
Horse, Jockey, Tin, Platform, Iron Wheels, Pull Toy, 2 Parts, c.1870, 8 x 12 x 3 In. 1430.00
Horse, On Wheels, Brown Paint, Black Mane, Straw Tail, Leather Saddle, 15 In. 595.00
Horse, Painted, Leather Bridle, Real Hair Mane, Carved, Wood, Nova Scotia, 9 In. 683.00
Horse, Papier-Mache, Wood Legs, Base, Tin Wheels, Horsehair Tail & Mane, Germany, 8 3/4 x 7 1/2 In. . 110.00
Horse, Rocking, Carriage Cradle, 28 In. 248.00
Horse, Rocking, Original Paint, Crandall New York, 42-In. Rockers, c.1860, 23-In. Horse 995.00
Horse, Rocking, Painted, Horsehair Mane, Tail, Saddle, c.1850, 27 x 46 In. . . . . *illus* 1265.00
Horse, Rocking, Platform, Dappled, Leather & Corduroy Saddle, 1800s, 25 x 35 In. 180.00
Horse, Rocking, White, Black Sponge, Wood, Red Base, Mane, Tail, 29 x 37 x 13 In. 385.00
Horse, Rocking, White, Gray Sponge, Wood, Metal Stirrups, Leather, Platform Base, 42 x 51 x 17 In. 385.00

Horse, Rocking, White Paint, Saddle, 19th Century, 24 x 49 In. 275.00
Horse, Rocking, Wood, Crackled White Paint, Gesso Ground, Horsehair Tail, 40 x 30½ In.... 345.00
Horse, Rocking, Wood, Tack, Faux Leather, Felt Saddle, Braided Horsehair, Base, 34 x 40 In. . 805.00
Horse & Carriage, Papier-Mache, 6 Dolls, Wood Legs, Painted Feathers, Germany, 6 In. 2576.00
Horse & Carriage, Passengers Looking Out Windows, Tin, Meier, Germany, 4½ In. 373.00
Horse & Wagon, 2 Horses, Iron, Tin Canopy, Paper Lithograph, Kenton, 8½ x 20 x 4¾ In. .. 2310.00
Horse & Wagon, Aerial, 2 Horses, Driver, Wilkins, 44 In. 6435.00
Horse & Wagon, Dapple Gray Horse, Hay, Meier, Germany, 5¼ In. 201.00
Horse & Wagon, Dapple Gray Horse, Yellow, Red Wheels, Tin, Fischer, Germany, 4 In. 104.00
Horse & Wagon, Driver, Iron, Green Painted, Sand & Gravel, c.1920, 15 x 3½ x 5 In.. ...... 224.00
Horse & Wagon, Driver, Tin, Painted, Georg Fischer, 4¾ In. 173.00
Horse & Wagon, Dump, Horses, Driver, Rubber Wheels, Cast Iron, 13 In.. .... 350.00
Horse Race, Riding Motion, Bell Rings, Tin, Celluloid, Windup, Japan, Box, 7 In. 150.00
Horse Team, Platform Base, Iron Wheels, Hide Cover, Glass Eyes, Horsehair Mane, Pull Toy, 13 In. 460.00
Hot Air Balloon, Jupiter, Figure, Tin Lithograph, Lehmann, Germany, Box, 5 In.. ...... *illus* 2300.00
Humphrey Mobile, Outhouse, Driver, Tin Lithograph, Wyandotte, 8¼ x 7¼ In.... 203.00 to 431.00
Ice Box, Oak, Knickerbocker, 37 x 23 x 15 In. 413.00
Ice Cream Vendor, Good Flavor, Tin, Celluloid, Windup, Japan, Box, 4 In.. .... 195.00
Ice Cream Vendor On Scooter, Courtland, Mechanical, Tin, 6 x 3½ x 4¼ In.. .... 155.00
Indian Baby, Roly Poly, Papier-Mache, 4 In. 95.00
ackie The Horn Pipe Dancer, Tin, Windup, Strauss, 8 In.. .... 403.00
azzbo Jim, Box, Unique Art, 9¾ In.. .... 900.00
azzbo Jim, Dancer On The Roof, Keywind, Ferdinand Strauss Co., c.1921 .... 517.00
eep, Air Force, Pressed Steel, Dark Blue, White, Tonka, Box, 10 In. 250.00
eep, Army, Die Cast, Tootsietoy, Box 66.00
eep, Gumby, Metal, Japan, 1959, 10 In. 195.00
eep, Jumpin', Advances, Good Gloss, Tin, c.1947, 5½ In. 277.00
eep, Jumpin', Crazy Car, Tin, Windup, Marx, Box, 6 In. 188.00
eep, Police, Pressed Steel, Plastic Top, Black, White, Tonka, Box, 10 In. 265.00
eep, Surrey, Green, Side Spare Tire, Tonka, 1963, 10 In.. .... 495.00
eep, Surrey, Pink, Tonka, 1962, 10 In. 125.00
eep, Willys, Battery, Headlights, Trailer, Pressed Steel, Marx, 1950s, 22 In. 150.00
eep, Willys, Lithograph Wheels, Blue, Marx, Box, 13 In.. .... 325.00
eepster, Pressed Steel, Blue, White Plastic Top, Interior, Tonka, 13 In. 275.00
enny, Balking Mule, Clown Driver, Windup, Strauss, 9½ In.. .... 285.00 to 450.00
et Launching Station, Navy, Turn Crank, Lever To Launch, Fires Missiles, Tin, 9½ In.. .... 1469.00
igger, Carved, Glass Eyes, Late 19th Century, 20 x 20 In. 690.00
igger, Carved, Hand Painted, Glass Eyes, 20 x 20 In.. .... 288.00
igger, Dixie Danny, Moving Arms & Legs, Wood, Early 20th Century 575.00
oe Penner & Duck Goo Goo, Walker, Hat Flips Up, Down, Tin, Windup, Marx, 1934, 8½ In. 978.00
oe Penner & Ducks, Walker, Tin, Windup, Louis Marx, 7⅝ In. 1093.00
olly Cyclist, Rides Bike, Rings Bell, Tin, Celluloid, Windup, Kuramochi, Box, 5½ In.. ...... 210.00
uggling Clown, Tin, Cloth, Windup, Composition, Alps, 11½ In. 413.00
umping Jack, Jumps & Beats Drum, Pull String, Tin Lithograph, Germany, 4 3/16 In. 288.00
Kaleidoscope, Ship's-Wheel Shape, Paper Cylindrical Tube, Brass, Wood Base, 14 x 10 In.... 784.00
Kamerun, Ostrich Walking, Friction, Black Man Seated In Bin, Lehmann, 6½ In. 720.00
Kangaroo, Mohair, With Joey, Glass Eyes, Black Stitched Nose, Jointed, Steiff, 1960s, 39 x 76 In. . 374.00
Keystone Kop, Roly Poly, Papier-Mache, 4 In. 125.00
Kid Sampson, Heavy Hitter, Tin Lithograph, Windup, B & RT, Patent 1921, 9 In.. .... 796.00
Kiddy Television, Windup, Picture Changes On Screen, Chrome Trim, Tin, 5¼ In.. .... 288.00
King Racer, Yellow, Black, Tin, Windup, Marx, 1925, 8½ In. 333.00
Kitchen, Wood, Oak Floors, Fireplace Mantel, Stove, Cupboards, Pots, Pans, 39 x 20 x 11 In. . 1792.00
Knockout Champs, Boxers Move Around Ring, Celluloid, Metal, Windup, Marx, Box, 1930s . 625.00
Komical Kop, Crazy Car, Drivers Head Spins, Tin, Windup, Marx, 1930, 7 In.. .... 310.00
ady, Victorian, Walking, Wheels, Tin, Germany, c.1880, 3½ In.. .... 316.00
ady With Umbrella & Opera Glasses, Tin Windup, Arm Lifts To Face, Germany, 9 In. 2588.00
ester The Jester, Windup, Tin, Cloth, Alps, 9 In. 33.00
i'l Abner Dogpatch Band, Tin Lithograph, Windup, Unique Art, c.1945....... 489.00 to 695.00
imousine, Chauffeur, Tin, Windup, England Chad Valley, 1960, 9 In. 375.00
imousine, Flywheel Drive, Red, Republic, 1930, 12 In. 225.00
imousine, Lincoln C., Slush Streamline, Red, Rubber Tires, 4 In. 135.00
imousine, Opening Rear Doors, Tin, Bing, 6 In. 311.00
imousine, Red, Blue, Electric Head Lamps, Clockwork, Chauffer, Lehmann, 11 In. 3680.00
incoln Tunnel, Cars, Traffic Cop, Tin Lithograph, Windup, Unique Art, 24 In.. .... 115.00
ion, Brown, Carved Mane, Wood, Jointed, Painted Eyes, Rope Tail, Schoenhut, 7¼ In.. ...... 115.00

Toy, Godzilla, Tin, Windup, Linemar, 8 In.
$155.00

Toy, Horse, Hide, Glass Eyes, Horsehair Mane, Tail, Pull, 19th Century, 13 In.
$460.00

Toy, Horse, Rocking, Painted, Horsehair Mane, Tail, Saddle, c.1850, 27 x 46 In.
$1265.00

Toy, Hot Air Balloon, Jupiter, Figure, Tin Lithograph, Lehmann, Germany, Box, 5 In.
$2300.00

T

Toy, Mary & Lamb, Wood, Desk, Storybook, Schoenhut, 8 ¼ In.
$525.00

Toy, Merry-Go-Round, 3 Levels, Mechanical, Wood, Cloth, Stoudt, Germany, 19 x 13 In.
$10250.00

Toy, Merry-Go-Round, 6 Carts, Figures, Tin, Windup, Germany, Box
$575.00

Toy, Motorcycle, Hillclimber, Driver, Blue, Iron, Hubley, 6 ½ In.
$259.00

Lion, Circus, Battery Operated, 2-Sided, Carpet, Wand, Box, 10 In. 523.00
Lion, Circus, Magic Action, Tin, Plush, Battery Operated, Rock Valley, Box, 10 In. . 215.00 to 575.00
Lion, Wood, Jointed, Glass Eyes, Carved Mane, Open Mouth, Teeth, Rope Tail, Schoenhut, 8 In. 288.00
Lion Tamer, Wood, Jointed, Composition Head, Red Hoop, Fez, Schoenhut, 8 In. 518.00
Loader, Green, Swivel Chute, Doepke, 1947, 18 In. 275.00
Locomotive, Cast Iron, Painted Wood, 19th Century, 10 ¼ x 15 In. 1528.00
Locomotive, Hillclimber, Flywheel Drive, Red, Gold, Dayton, 1912, 16 In. 245.00
Locomotive, Windup, Tin Plate, Germany, 7 In. 77.00
Log Cabin, Wood, Gilt, Red Painted Roof & Chimney, 15 x 20 x 14 In. 132.00
Loop The Loop, No. 30, Tin, Windup, Wolverine, Box, 19 In. 468.00
Lucky Monkey Cycle, Advances With Pedaling Motion, Umbrella Spins, Bell Rings, 6 In. ... 362.00
Machine Gun, Big Dick, Spring & Crank Operated, Cast Iron, Wood, c.1915, 18 In. 142.00
Maggie & Jiggs, Moves, Swings Rolling Pin & Umbrella, Tin, Windup, Nifty, 7 In. 1093.00
Mail Car, Double, Irish, 2 Riders, Lithograph, Windup, Bing, 12 In. 1955.00
Main Street, 6 Moving Vehicles, Traffic Cop, Bridges, Buildings, Marx, 1929, 24 In. 625.00
Main Street Bridge, Buildings, Cars, Traffic Cop, Tin Lithograph, Windup, Box, Marx, 24 In. 632.00
Major Tooty, Plays Drum, Blows Whistle, Moves, Battery Operated, Alps, Box, 14 In. 150.00
Mammy, Walker, Red Dress, White Apron, Cap, Tin, Windup, Lindstrom, 7 ¾ In. 287.00
Man On Flying Trapeze, Mechanical, Tin, Windup, Box, 8 ⅞ In. 110.00
Man Pushing Yellow Wheelbarrow, Smoking Pipe, Georg Levy, Germany, 3 In. 230.00
Marionette Theater, Celluloid Clowns Dance, Canopy, Toyland, Japan, Box, 10 ½ x 10 In. ... 550.00
Mary & Her Little Lamb, Moves In Circle, Tin, Celluloid, Windup, Kuramochi, Box, 6 ½ In. . 540.00
Mary & Lamb, Wood, Desk, Storybook, Schoenhut, 8 ¼ In. .... *illus* 525.00
Mary's Lamb, Huboid, No. 105, Pull Toy, Hubley, Box, c.1946, 4 ½ In. 85.00
Mego Man, Yoneya, Red Face, Moving Arms & Legs, Wheels Turn, Bells Ring, Tin, 6 ¾ In. ... 384.00
Merry-Go-Round, 3 Levels, Mechanical, Wood, Cloth, Stoudt, Germany, 19 x 13 In. ... *illus* 10250.00
Merry-Go-Round, 6 Carts, Figures, Tin, Windup, Germany, Box .... *illus* 575.00
Merry-Go-Round, Playland, Tin, Windup, J. Chein & Co., Box, 10 In. 575.00
Mexicali Pete, Moves Body, Plays Drums, Battery Operated, Alps, Box, 12 In. .... 115.00 to 175.00
Minstrel, Woman Playing Banjo, Man With Top Hat, Clockwork, Germany, 7 ½ In. 7800.00
Miss Friday, Typist, Battery Operated, Tin, Vinyl Head, Box, 7½ x 8½ In. .... 220.00 to 268.00
Model, Whale Boat, Moby Dick, Harpoon Gun, Wood, Battery Operated, Japan, 15 ½ In. 403.00
Model Kit, Archies Car, Aurora, No. 582-200, 1971 .... 204.00
Model Kit, Boat, 3-Masted, Wood, Gunboat, Folk Art, Display Case, Cannons, c.1900 .... 500.00
Model Set, Noah's Ark Animals, 12 Paper Animals, Cardboard Box 4541.00
Monkey, Affen, No. 48, Brown Felt, Orange Ball, Steiff, c.1893, 9 ½ In. 4025.00
Monkey, Boxing, Arms Swing, Plush, Tin, Windup, M.M., Japan, Box, 7 ½ In. 92.00
Monkey, Circus, Wood, Jointed, Standing, Painted Features, Schoenhut, 8 In. 288.00
Monkey, Playing Guitar, Occupied Japan, 8 In. 150.00
Monkey, Tin Face, Windup, Japan, 1950s, 5 In. 75.00
Monkey, Trumpet Playing, Rings Bell, Scratches At Fly, Battery Operated, Alps, Box, 9 ½ In. .. 127.00
Monkey Batter, Vibrates, Turns Head, Raises & Lowers Bat, Rubber Tail, Tin, 7 ½ In. 390.00
Monkey Cyclist, Pedaling Motion, Rings Bell, Eyes Pop In & Out, Tin, Bandai, 4 ¾ In. 311.00
Monkey Trio, 2 Drummers, Violinist, Clockwork, Schuco, 4 ¼ In. 235.00
Monkeys, Tin, Windup, Wyandotte, U.S.A., 10 In. 295.00
Monoplane, Air Ford, Blue, Hubley, 3 ¾ In. 275.00
Monoplane, Lucky Boy, Silver, 5 In. 350.00
Moon Creature, Opens & Closes Mouth, Moves, Tin, Windup, Marx, Box, 5½ In. . 167.00 to 201.00
Moon Explorer, Crank Operated, Advances, Sways, Antenna Spins, Tin, Yoshiya, 7 In. 524.00
Moon Express, Fins & Blades Rotate, Tin, Plastic, Battery Operated, T.P.S., Box, 14 ½ In. 391.00
Moon Flight, Battery Operated, Tin, Plastic, Germany, 18 ⅛ x 4 ½ In. 770.00
Moon Mullins, Handcar, Kayo, Tin Lithograph, Windup, Louis Marx, 6 In. ...... 403.00 to 450.00
Motorcycle, Circus, Rider, Tin, Windup, 6 In. 198.00
Motorcycle, Clown, Acrobat, Tin, Friction, 6 ¼ In. 385.00
Motorcycle, Cop, Cast Iron, Red Paint, Black Wheels, Marked, Made In U.S.A., 4 ¼ In. 88.00
Motorcycle, Cop, Sidecar, Driver, Rider, Red, Blue, Hubley, 4 In. 225.00
Motorcycle, Driver, Headlight, Orange, Tan, Gray, Red, Tin, Meier, Germany, 4 In. 1093.00
Motorcycle, Driver, Speed Boy, Marx, 4 In. 245.00
Motorcycle, Driver, Tin, Fiction, Rubber Wheel, Japan, 1950s, 4 In. 75.00
Motorcycle, Engineering, Advances, Engine Noise, Working Headlight, Tin, Chinese, 9 ¾ In. .. 85.00
Motorcycle, Harley-Davidson, Sidecar, Driver, Passenger, Hubley, 1930s, 8 ½ x 5 In. 896.00
Motorcycle, Hillclimber, Driver, Blue, Iron, Hubley, 6 ½ In. .... *illus* 259.00
Motorcycle, MAC700, Mechanical, Windup, Tin Lithograph, Arnold, 7 ½ x 4 ½ In. 428.00
Motorcycle, Painted, Champion, 1930, 7 In. 59.00
Motorcycle, Police, Blue, Rubber Tires, Driver, Champion, 7 ¼ In. 475.00
Motorcycle, Police, Mechanical, Tin Lithograph, Marx, 5 ½ x 8 ½ In. 897.00

ɔtorcycle, Police Squad, Driver, Sidecar, Moves, Siren, Sparks, Tin, Windup, Marx, Box, 1950, 8 In. . . 1036.00
ɔtorcycle, Police Squad, Sidecar, Yellow, Tin Lithograph, Clockwork, 8 ½ In. 288.00
ɔtorcycle, Policeman, Graphics, Friction, Rubber Tires, Tin Lithograph, Japan, 8 ¼ In. 633.00
ɔtorcycle, Policeman, Red, Lithographed Siren, Tin, Blue Uniform, Marx, 8 In. 288.00
ɔtorcycle, Policeman, Tin Lithographed, Graphics, Clockwork, 8 ½ In. 690.00
ɔtorcycle, Policeman, Yellow, Tin Lithograph, Siren, Clockwork, Marx, 8 ½ In. 144.00
ɔtorcycle, Policeman Rides In Circles, Siren Sounds, Tin, Marx, 8 ½ In. 412.00
ɔtorcycle, Race Driver, Tin Lithograph, Clockwork, Germany, Technoflex, 7 ¼ In. 201.00
otorcycle, Racing, Tandem, Tin Lithograph, Kellerman, Germany, 5 ¾ In. . . . . *illus* 1560.00
ɔtorcycle, Red, Orange, Runs In Circles, Tin, Technofix, 7 In. 486.00
ɔtorcycle, Sidecar, Cast Iron, Nickel Wheels, Rider, Kilgore, 6 In. 518.00
ɔtorcycle, Sidecar, Red, Blue, Driver, Passenger, Hubley, 4 In. 250.00
otorcycle, Soldier, Tin Lithograph, Camouflage, Clockwork, Germany, 7 ½ In. 316.00
otorcycle, Stunt, Tin Lithograph, Windup, 1930s, 12 ¼ x 3 ½ In. 523.00
ɔtorcycle, Tin, Windup, Rider, Technofix, France, 1960s, 7 ½ In. 195.00
ɔtorcycle, Tin Lithograph, Windup, Marx, 8 In. 302.00
otorcycle & Sidecar, Driver, Cast Iron, Hubley, 9 In. 115.00
otorcycle With Cop, Hubley, 4 ½ In. 145.00
ouse Trap, Mouse, Tin, Painted, Meier, Germany, 4 ⅛ In. 546.00
ɔving Van, Driver, Cast Iron, Nickel Wheels, Stenciled, 13 In. 4313.00
oxiemobile, Tin Lithograph, c.1917, 8 ½ x 6 ½ In. 1495.00
: Fox, Magician, Bubble Blower, Battery Operated, Tin, Cloth, Box, Yonezawa, 9 ½ In. 303.00
: Machine, Moving Parts, Plastic, Windup, Box, 21 In. 115.00
ıg, Doll's, Rudolstadt, Stick Figures, Golliwogs, c.1914, 2 In. 18.00
le, Go'n Back, Windup, Fisher-Price, 1932, 8 x 10 In. 275.00
ısic Box, Kalliope, Wood, Handle Crank, Stop, Start Lever, 34 Discs, 8 In. 4928.00
ısical Circus Horse, Horse Pulling Musical Wheel, Tin, Marx, Box, 4 ½ x 10 In. 419.00
ıtoscope, Charlie Chaplin Reels, Tin, Wood, Int'l. Mutoscope Reel Co., N.Y., 73 In. 8430.00
ınny, Baby Stork, Tin Lithograph, Penny, Meier, Germany, 4 In. . . . . *illus* 1360.00
ah's Ark, 50 Animals, Tin Lithograph, Lead, Hudson Scott Co., England, 13 ½ In. . . . . *illus* 1500.00
ah's Ark, House Form, Wheeled Platform, Animals, Angels, Detached Roof, Pull Toy, 7 x 11 In. 2151.00
ah's Ark, Pine, Painted, Multicolored, 110 Painted Animal Pairs, 4 People, c.1900, 19 ½ x 6 In. 1495.00
ah's Ark, Stencil Painted, Floral Band, Flocked Roof, 29 Wood Animals, 13 x 6 In. 460.00
ah's Ark, Wood, Ramp, Lift-Off Roof, Blue, White, Animals, Noah, Wife, Peter Mar, Box, 22 In. 600.00
ah's Ark, Wood Model, Storage Bay, Stair Case, 46 Animal Figures, 13 x 25 In. 3466.00
dder, Cart Pulled By Mule, Rubber Neck, Painted, Iron, Kenton, 6 In. . . . . *illus* 518.00
dder, Dobie Gillis, Composition, Japan, c.1960, 8 In. 345.00
tty Mad Indian, Plays Drums, Yells, Battery Operated, Marx, Box, 11 ½ In. 140.00
tty Nibbs, Native, Holds Platter, Catches Nut In Mouth, Tin, Battery, Box, Linemar, 12 ½ In. . 805.00
topus, Battery Operated, Alps, 9 ½ x 19 ½ In. 330.00
topus Ride, Cars, Riders, Raise & Lower, Ride Turns, Tin, 7 In. 226.00
Sleepy Head Rip, Bird Spins & Peeps, Sleeps, Tin, Battery Operated, Yonezawa, Box, 9 In. 288.00
ınibus, Tin, Painted, Issmayer, Germany, 4 ⅝ In. 747.00
phan Annie, Sandy, Wood, Pull, Trixy Toys, 7 In. 150.00
car Mayer Wienermobile, Moving Figure, Plastic, 1950s, 10 In. 140.00
wald The Lucky Rabbit, Celluloid, Wood Hands & Feet, c. 1928, 6 ¾ In. 113.00
il, Duck Pond, Duck Driving Express Truck, Handle, Tin Lithograph, Chein, 4 x 3 ⅝ x 3 ¾ In. 635.00
il, Shovel, Eagles, Shield, Ohio Art, Tin, Bail Handle, 6 In. 175.00
nda, Stuffed, Long Fur, White Glass Eyes, Gruff Looking, 1880, 24 In. 350.00
n-Gee, Funny Dancer, Tin Lithograph, Windup, C.E. Carter Co., 10 ¼ In. 298.00
ıcock, Windup, Tin Lithograph, 9 ½ In. 348.00
lal Car, Airplane, Curtis Hawk, American National, 49 In. 12100.00
lal Car, Airplane, Pressed Steel, Wood, Rubber, Keystone, 28-In. Wingspan . . . . *illus* 465.00
lal Car, Lincoln, Steelcraft, c.1930, 38 In. 1495.00
lal Car, Pressed Steel, c.1960, 36 In. 201.00
lal Car, Roadster, White Paint, Spring Suspension, Hand Brake, 1920s, 50 In. 1058.00
lal Car, Steelcraft, Windshield, Rubber Tires, Headlights, Red, 45 In. 3737.00
lal Car, Tin Lizzy, Pressed Steel, Garton, 32 In. . . . . *illus* 633.00
lal Car, Truck, Sit N Ride Koaster, Steel, Paint, Keystone, 24 In. . . . . *illus* 690.00
lal Car, Wood Spoke Wheels, Green, Iron Steering Wheel, Pedals, Early 1900s, 32 x 57 In. . 1840.00
ıguin, Tin, Windup, Japan, 1950s, 5 In. 95.00
er Rabbit, Handcar, Basket, Yellow, Pressed Steel, Composition, Windup, Lionel, 10 In. . . . 489.00
's Grocery Store, Wood, Wallpaper Lined, Candy Bottles, 15 ½ x 21 In. 143.00
onograph, Crank Handle, Painted, Meier, Germany, 3 ⅝ In. 230.00
ıno, Baby Grand, 3 Turned Legs, Marked, Schoenhut, 16 x 10 x 15 In. 90.00
ıno, Baby Grand, Die Cast, White, Bench, Tootsietoy, Box, 2 Piece 330.00

Toy, Motorcycle, Racing, Tandem, Tin Lithograph, Kellerman, Germany, 5 ¾ In. $1560.00

Toy, Nanny, Baby Stork, Tin Lithograph, Penny, Meier, Germany, 4 In. $1360.00

Toy, Noah's Ark, 50 Animals, Tin Lithograph, Lead, Hudson Scott Co., England, 13 ½ In. $1500.00

Toy, Nodder, Cart Pulled By Mule, Rubber Neck, Painted, Iron, Kenton, 6 In. $518.00

TIP

If your heavy cast-iron toy has rubber tires, display it on a partial stand so there is no pressure on the tires.

TIP
If you are having a piece restored, get a written estimate first.

Toy, Pedal Car, Airplane, Pressed Steel, Wood, Rubber, Keystone, 28-In. Wingspan
$465.00

Toy, Pedal Car, Tin Lizzy, Pressed Steel, Garton, 32 In.
$633.00

Toy, Pedal Car, Truck, Sit N Ride Koaster, Steel, Paint, Keystone, 24 In.
$690.00

Pedal Cars
Important pedal car makers include American National, Garton, Gendron, Kirk-Latty, Murray-Ohio (Steelcraft), and Toledo Metal Wheel Company.

Piano, Interior Xylophone, Label, Schoenhut, 26 ½ x 24 x 18 In. . . . . 431.
Piano Player, Windup, Human Hair, Felt Jacket, Pants, Tin, Painted, France, 5 ¼ x 5 In. . . . . 757.
Pig, Push Pull, Wood, Carved, Painted, Glass Inset Eyes, Platform Base, 4 Wheels, 12 x 30 In.. 2468.
Pinky Lee Xylophone, Emenee, 1950s, 14 In.. . . . . 45.
Play Golf, No. 110, Tin Lithograph, Windup, Strauss, 7 x 12 x 7 In.. . . . . 717.
Player, Jazz Saxophone, Black Figure, Facial Expression, Arms & Legs Move, 6 ½ In.. . . . . 367.
Playing Mice, 2 Mice Race Down Spiral Rod, Lehmann, 1926, 14 In.. . . . . 125.
Playland Whip, 4 Cars Whip Around, Spring Mounted, Heads Move, Bell Rings, Tin, 20 In. . . 1130.
Pony Phaeton, Driver, Brown Horse, Pulling Buggy, Cast Iron, Pratt & Lechtworth, 1885, 17 In. 1495.
Pool Player, Shoots Ball In Holes, Painted, Tin, Windup, Germany, 6 x 10 ¾ In. . . . . 956.
Popcorn Vendor, Battery Operated, Cranstan, Box, 7 ¼ x 8 ½ In. . . . . 330.
Porky Pig, Cowpuncher, Tin, Windup, Spins Lasso, Marx, 1949, 8 In. . . . . 235.00 to 250.
Porter, Pushing Luggage Cart, Tin Lithograph, Georg Levy, Germany, 2 ¾ In. . . . . 260.
Porter, Walking, Red Cap, Head Moves, Walks, Tin, Windup, Marx, 1930s, 8 In. . . . . 363.
Porter, Walking, Red Cap & Suit, Luggage, Head Bobs, Tin Lithograph, Windup, Marx, Box . . 836.
Postman, Pushing Delivery Cart, Tin, Painted, Fischer, Germany, 2 ⅞ In.. . . . . 460.
Powerful Katrina, Windup, Tin Lithograph, Fontaine Fox, Germany, 1923, 5 In. . . . . 490.
Private Garage, Cardboard, Box, Go With, Built-Rite, 1936, 7 x 7 In.. . . . . 75.
Rabbit, Pushing Cart With Basket, Meier, Germany, c.1890, 3 ¼ In.. . . . . 546.
Rabbit, Roly Poly, Red, White Yellow Striped Bottom, Tin Lithograph, Chein, 6 ¼ In.. . . . . 575.
Rabbits Sawing Egg, Tin Lithograph, Fischer, Germany, 4 ⅛ In.. . . . . 1840.
Railroad, Talking Railroad Station, Tin Lithograph, Box, Louis Marx, 3 ½ x 23 ½ x 11 In. . . . 143.
Range, Electric, Black, White, Porcelain, Nickel Trim, Empire, Early 1900s, 16 ½ In.. . . . . 118.
Range Rider, Brown Horse, Marx, Box, 11 ⅜ x 9 ½ In. . . . . 605.
Range Rider, Rocks, Cowboy Rider Spins His Lariat, Jointed Arm Moves, Tin, c.1946, 9 In.. . . 475.
Red Ranger, Ride 'Em Cowboy, Tin, Windup, Wyandotte, Box, 6 ½ x 7 In. . . . . 165.
Refrigerator, GE, Nickel-Plated Cube Tray, Iron, Green Paint, 7 In.. . . . . *illus* 201.
Rhinoceros, Wood, Jointed, Glass Eyes, Carved Mouth, Horn, Leather Ears, Schoenhut, 9 In.. 374.
Ring, Capt. Midnight Mystic Sun God, Ovaltine Premium, 1946. . . . . 575.
Ring, Magni Glow, Writing, Sky King, 1949 . . . . 150.
Ringmaster, Jointed, Wood Body, Bisque Head, Schoenhut, 7 ¼ In. . . . . *illus* 546.
Road Grader, Caterpillar, Die Cast, Tootsietoy, Box. . . . . 77.
Road Roller, Diesel, Cast Aluminum, Orange, Hubley, c.1950, 10 In. . . . . 55.
Road Roller, Huber, Olive Green, Gold Trim, Nickel Wheels, Hubley, 7 ¾ In.. 845
Road Roller, Pistons, Green, Pull Toy, Buddy L, 18 In. . . . . 1840.
Robot, Adding Machine, Answer Game, Eyes Blink, Tin, Ischida, Japan, 14 In. . . . . *illus* 1254.
Robot, Advances, Moving Arms, Lighted Head, Space Sound, Head Spin, Tin, Alps, 9 In. . . . . . 1356.
Robot, Attacking Martian, Walking, Chest Door Open, Fires Guns, Tin, Horikawa, 11 In.. 300
Robot, Calculating, Answer Game, Adding Machine, Blinking Eyes, c.1963, 14 In.. . . . . 1254.
Robot, Driving Robot, Lucky, Mouth Opens & Closes, Swings, Tin, Windup, Yonezawa, 11 In. . 267.
Robot, Gettsuko Kamen, Walker, Rubber Head, Tin, Windup, Bullmark, Japan, Box, 9 ¼ In. *illus* 500
Robot, Lost In Space, Lights, Claw Hands, Plastic, Battery Operated, Remco, Box, 12 In. 368.00 to 495
Robot, Lost In Space, Tin, Windup, Box, 10 In. . . . . 150.
Robot, Mighty Robot, Green, Walker, Sparks, Tin Lithograph, Windup, Noguchi, Japan, 5 ½ In. 144.
Robot, Mr. Atomic, Tin, Bullet-Shaped Dome, 4-Wheels, Battery Operated, Yonezawa, 9 In.. . . 823
Robot, Mr. Robot, Head Lights, Interior Spins, Tin, Plastic, Battery Operated, Yonezawa, 11 In. 604
Robot, Mr. Sandman, Non-Powered, Painted Tin & Wood, Take Apart, Wolverine, 11 ½ In. . . . 678
Robot, Musical Drummer Robot, Walks, Lights Flash, Tin, Battery Operated, Nomura, Box, 8 In. 4313
Robot, Non Stop Robot, Bump & Go, Lights, Tin, Battery Operated, Masudaya, Box, 15 In. . . . 4600
Robot, Piston Action, Walks, Lights Up, Tin, Plastic, Rubber, Remote Control, Nomura, Box, 8 In. 1266
Robot, Planet, Walker, Tin, Windup, Rubber, Japan, 9 In.. . . . . *illus* 210
Robot, Silver, Red Highlights, Walking Motion, Sparking Chest, Tin, Strenco, 7 ¼ In. . . . . . . 580.
Robot, Skirted, Mystery Action, Head Lights, Interior Spins, Tin, Yonezawa, 11 In.. . . . . 322.
Robot, Swinging Baby Robot, Mouth Opens & Closes, Tin, Windup, Yonezawa, Box, 11 In. 460.00 to 595
Robot, Windup, Tin, Sparks, Yoshiya, Japan, 1950s, 7 In. 125
Robot Commando, The Amazing Mike Controlled Robot, Plastic, Ideal Toy, 1961, 16 In.. . . . 1155
Robot Tractor, Tin, Battery Operated, Nomura, 9 ¾ In. 935
Rocket, Space Rocket, Robot Driver, No. 7, Moves Arms, Tin, Friction, Yonezawa, Box, 4 ¾ In. 690
Rocket Army Truck, Metal, Friction, Japan, c.1950, 11 In. 125
Rocket Ranger, Truck Advances, Siren, Gun Turret Turns, Firing Sound, Tin, Marusan, 6 In. 961
Rocking Clown, On Pig, Tin Plate, Windup, Germany, 1920s, 4 ⅞ x 4 ¾ In.. 1650
Rodeo Joe, Cowboy, Riding Tractor, Tin Lithograph, Windup, Unique Art Mfg., 7 In.. 173
Rodeo Joe, Crazy Car, Windup, Tin Lithograph, Unique Art Co., c.1930, 9 ½ x 8 x 4 In. 160
Roller Coaster, 2 Cars, Tin, Windup, Chein, 18 ½ In. . . . . *illus* 260
Roller Coaster, 2 Cars, Tin, Windup, Chein, Box, 1950s, 19 In. 345
Roller Coaster, Big Eight, Tin, Windup, Grand Huit, Box, 11 In. 578

ɔller Coaster, Coney Island, Box, 46 x 16 In. . . . 633.00
ɔller Coaster, Embossed, Windup Lithographed Cars, Germany, Box, 3 & 39 x 21 x 12 In. . . 770.00
ɔller Coaster, Tin, Windup, Wolverine, 21 In. . . . 154.00
ɔokie Cop, Moves In Circle, Siren, Tin, Windup, Marx, 1950, 8½ In. . . . 173.00
ɔokie Pilot, Head Moves, Crazy Car Motion, Tin, Windup, Marx, 1930s, 7 In. . . . 363.00
ɔoster, Squeak, Painted, Molded Wood Composition, Wire Legs, Nest, Germany, c.1880, 6 In. 411.00
ɔund-About, Clockwork, Gunthermann, Tin Figures, Germany, c.1910, 12 x 3½ In. . . . 2400.00
ıtellite Moon Radio, Hard Plastic, Education Electronics U.S.A., 1950s, 3 In. . . . 125.00
enicruiser, Greyhound, Tootsietoy, 7 In. . . . 225.00
:ooter, Chief, Shooting Star, Mid 1900s, 33 x 39 In. . . . 50.00
ooter, Vespa, Driver, Tin Litho, Plastic, Clockwork, HWN, U.S. Zone, Germany . . . *illus* 465.00
a Lion, Circus, Performing, Wood, Jointed, Leather Flippers, Ball, Stand, Schoenhut, 8½ In. 259.00
cretary, Doll's, Cherry Wood, Slant Front, Drawers, Key, 15 x 13 In. . . . 1232.00
rvice Station, Arcade Service, Green, Red, Wood, 6½ x 12 In. . . . *illus* 210.00
rvice Station, Tin Lithograph, Wood Pumps, Hoses, Nozzles, Meters, Gibbs, c.1920. . . . 985.00
ːrvice Station Playset, Cardboard, Figures, 2 Die Cast Tootsietoy, Parker Bros., 1961 . . . 150.00
wing Kit, Junior Miss, Doll, Pre-Cut Patterns, Supplies, Instructions, Box, 1950s . . . 82.00
wing Machine, Casige, Fancy Fitted, Gold & Green Vines & Leaves . . . 225.00 to 450.00
wing Machine, Casige, Little Red Riding Hood, Storybook. . . . 245.00
wing Machine, Iron, Black Painted, Gold, Brown, Wheel Spokes, Needle, Germany, c.1900 448.00
wing Machine, Little Mother, Tin, 8 x 8 In. . . . 155.00
wing Machine, No. 20, Singer & Co., Child's. . . . 138.00
wing Machine, Sew-O-Matic Sr., Straco, Metal Base, Gears, Plastic, England. . . . 35.00
wing Machine, Singer, Model 20, Hand Crank, Black, Gilt, Wood Base, Glass Cover, 7 In. . . 382.00
wing Machine, Tin, Black Painted, Gold Scrolls, Wheel, Needle, c.1890, 4 In. . . . 2128.00
wing Machine, Tin, Black Painted, Turning Handle, Needle, Germany, 4½ In. . . . 392.00
wing Machine, Wood Frame, Cast Iron Wheels & Treadle, 2 Drawers, c.1875, 31 In. . . . 690.00
ıed, Freight, Tin, Boom, Hook, Marklin, 1920s, 8 x 9 x 12 In. . . . 690.00
ıeep, Cotton Fur, Composition, Wood, Base, Wheels, Pull, 8 x 8¾ x 3¼ In. . . . 468.00
ıooting Gallery, Posse, 5 Jesse Jones Targets, Tin, Plastic, Windup, Wyandotte, 14 In. . . . 75.00
ıutter-Bug, Photographer, Turns Head, Lifts Camera, Lights, Box, Nomura, Japan, 1950s, 8 In. 472.00
nging Bird, Flaps Wings, Moves Head, Sings, Plastic Feet, Tin, 8 In. . . . 73.00
:ating Chef, Black, Holds Platter In Hand, Tin, Windup, T.P.S., Box, 6¼ In. . . . 893.00 to 1470.00
i Jumper, Sun Valley, Wolverine, 26 In. . . . 250.00
ip Rope, Tin, Windup, Japan, 1950s . . . 125.00
ittles Set, Rabbit, Papier-Mache, Wood Platform, 7 Piece, 12 x 10 In. . . . *illus* 1200.00
yhawk Flyer, Instructions, Marx, Box, c.1930, 20 In. . . . 500.00
ed, Bentwood, Lake Scene, Painted, Early 20th Century, 36 In. . . . *illus* 265.00
ed, Black Beauty, Black Paint, Gilt Striping, Iron Clad Runners, 1880, 40 In. . . . 385.00
ed, Black Beauty, Iron Runners & Tips, Painted, Wood, Early 1900s, 41 In. . . . 288.00
ed, Cradle Style, Iron Runners, Rail, Upholstered, Wood, Painted, Late 1800s, 50 In. . . . 518.00
ed, Flexible Flyer, 1935, 52 In. . . . 210.00
ed, Flowers, Red & Blue Paint, Wood, Iron Runners, Fabric Liner, 13½ In. . . . 288.00
ed, Galloping Horse, Wood, Iron, Painted, Early 20th Century, 34 In. . . . 431.00
ed, Gooseneck, Dragon Head Terminals, Wood, c.1920, 35 In. . . . 546.00
ed, Gooseneck Tips, Iron Mounts, Painted, Yellow, Black, Wood, c.1900, 40 In. . . . 403.00
ed, Iron, Wood, Painted, Galloping Horse, Early 20th Century, 34 In. . . . 546.00
ed, Lake Scene, Wood, Iron, Painted, Early 20th Century, 32 In. . . . 115.00 to 200.00
ed, Leaves, Green, Gold Stripes, Red, Wood, Sheet Iron, c.1890, 36 x 11 In. . . . *illus* 330.00
ed, Orange, Cream, Blue, Side Handles, Wood Runners, Metal Blades, 40 x 14¾ In. . . . 99.00
d, Ornate, Scrolled Iron Mounts, Old Paint, Wood, c.1900, 42 In. . . . 633.00
ed, Painted, Alphonse & Louis, Early 20th Century, 37 In. . . . 201.00
ed, Pansy Center, Painted, Red, Metal Bell, Wood, 15½ x 35 x 15 In. . . . 198.00
ed, Running Horse, Red, Black Trim, Iron Runners, c.1890, 36 x 11 In. . . . 935.00
d, Sailing Ship & Columbus, Painted, Wood, c.1920, 37 In. . . . 288.00
ed, Shield Shape Platform, Mixed Wood, Sheet Iron, Wood Runners, 36½ x 11 In. . . . 330.00
ed, Shield Shape Platform, Pine, Flower Sprays, Wrought, Cast Iron, Runners, 32 x 12 In. . . 316.00
ed, Ship Scene, Applied Shaped Side Rails, Iron Runners, 1890, 46 x 13½ In. . . . 660.00
d, Ship Scene, Applied Shaped Side Rails, Iron Runners, 1890, 48 x 12 In. . . . 1100.00
eping Baby Bear, Alarm Rings, Bear Rises, Yawns, Stretches, Battery Operated, Linemar, 9 In. . 158.00
eigh, Doll's, Upholstery, Brass Trim Runners, Handle, 22 In. . . . 225.00
eigh, Painted, Red, Blue Pinstripes, Bentwood Runners, Iron Rim, Wood, 21 x 34 x 12 In. . . 230.00
eigh, Pony, Bentwood Fronts, Scrolled Iron Mounts, c.1915, 31 x 56 x 22 In. . . . 920.00
igh, Prancing Horse, Woman Driver, Hubley, 1906 . . . 1050.00
eigh, Swan Heads, Red, Handle, 30 x 17 In. . . . 173.00
eigh, Yellow Pinstripes, Pink Interior, Wood, E.I. Wright, 1855, 65 In. . . . 375.00

Legos
You can combine six eight-stud Lego blocks of the same color 102,981,500 different ways. It is estimated that over 203 billion Lego parts have been made since 1949.

Toy, Refrigerator, GE, Nickel Plated Cube Tray, Iron, Green Paint, 7 In.
$201.00

Toy, Ringmaster, Jointed, Wood Body, Bisque Head, Schoenhut, 7¼ In.
$546.00

Toy, Robot, Adding Machine, Answer Game, Eyes Blink, Tin, Ischida, Japan, 14 In.
$1254.00

T

Toy, Robot, Gettsuko Kamen, Walker, Rubber Head, Tin, Windup, Bullmark, Japan, Box, 9 ¼ In.
$500.00

Toy, Robot, Planet, Walker, Tin, Windup, Rubber, Japan, 9 In.
$210.00

Toy, Roller Coaster, 2 Cars, Tin, Windup, Chein, 18 ½ In.
$260.00

Toy, Scooter, Vespa, Driver, Tin Litho, Plastic, Clockwork, HWN, U.S. Zone, Germany
$465.00

Smiling Sam, Carnival Man, Alps, Tin, Cloth Windup, Box, 9 In. 99.0
Smitty Scooter, Boy On Scooter, Tin, Windup, Marx, 1932, 8 In. 978.0
Smitty Scooter, Marx, Tin, Windup, Famous Artist's Syndicate, Marked, 8 In. 1955.0
Snowman, Holding Broom, Floating Snowball, Battery Operated, Box, 1960s 215.0
Snowmobile, Metal, Battery Operated, Japan, 1950s, 8 In. 295.0
Snowmobile, Rubber, Plastic, Metal, Battery Operated, Decal, Polaris, Box, 12 ½ x 5 ½ In. . . . 66.0
Sojourner Truth, Hits Podium, Head Turns, Speaks, Windup, E.R. Ives & Co., 1880s, 11 x 4 x 5 In. . . 7170.0
Soldier, Composition, Painted, Green Wood Base, Germany, 5 ¼ In. 489.0
Soldier, Crawling, Advances, Crawling Motion, Tin, Ohio Art, 9 ½ In. 175.0
Soldier Set, Abyssinian Tribesmen, No. 1425, Britains, Box, 7 Piece 115.0
Soldier Set, Australian Infantry, Mustache, No. 2030, Britains, Box, 5 Piece. 143.0
Soldier Set, Band Of Highland Pipers, Britains, Box, 20 Piece 2400.0
Soldier Set, British Infantry, No. 1612, Gas Masks, Throwing Grenades, Britains, Box, 8 Piece 115.0
Soldier Set, Cape Town Highlanders, No. 1901, Britains, Box, 8 Piece. 172.0
Soldier Set, City Imperial Volunteers, No. 104, Britains, Box, 10 Piece 1575.0
Soldier Set, Coldstream Guards At Ease, No. 314, Britains, 5 Piece 145.0
Soldier Set, Confederate Infantry, No. 2060, Britains, Box, 7 Piece 143.0
Soldier Set, Cuirassiers, No. 138, Britains, Box, 5 Piece 86.0
Soldier Set, Devonshire Regiment, No. 110, Britains, c.1910, 8 Piece 800.0
Soldier Set, Dublin Fusiliers In Khaki, No. 109, Britains, Box, 8 Piece 650.0
Soldier Set, East Yorkshire, No. 113, Britains, c.1901, 8 Piece 2375.0
Soldier Set, German Infantry, No. 432, Britains, Box, 8 Piece 172.0
Soldier Set, Greek Evzones, Britains, 4 Piece. 85.0
Soldier Set, Heyde Highlanders, 9 Piece. 165.0
Soldier Set, Indian Infantry, No. 1892, Britains, 8 Piece. 265.0
Soldier Set, Indian Infantry, No. 1892, Britains, Box, 8 Piece 345.0
Soldier Set, Musketeers, Louis XIII, 17th Century, 8 Piece 155.0
Soldier Set, New Zealand Infantry, No. 1542, Britains, Box, 8 Piece. 201.0
Soldier Set, No. 1631, Canadian Governor General's Horse Guard, London, c.1940, 5 Piece. . 112.0
Soldier Set, Royal Sussex Regiment, No. 36, Britains, Box, 8 Piece 143.0
Soldier Set, Spanish Infantry, No. 92, Britains, 8 Piece. 345.0
Soldier Set, Svea Lifeguards, No. 2035, Britains, Box, 8 Piece 172.0
Soldier Set, U.S. Marine Corp Band, No. 2014, Britains, Box, 21 Piece 5200.0
Soldier Set, U.S. Marine Corp Color Guard, No. 2101, Britains, Box, 5 Piece. 201.0
Somstepa Coon Jigger, Dances, Tin Lithograph, Windup, Marx, 8 In. 673.0
Space Control Car, Volkswagen, Convertible, Astronaut Driver, Noise, Nomura, 13 In. 6780.0
Space Explorer, Bump & Go, Green Driver, Tin, Plastic, Windup, Yoshiya, Box, 6 In. 397.0
Space Pistol, Tom Corbett Space Cadet, Tin Lithograph, 10 In., Marx, Box, 10 In. 888.0
Space Rocket Racer No. 1877, Rubber Tires, Cast Iron, Hubley, 7 x 2 x 3 In. 180.0
Space Scout, S-17, Light-Up, Battery Operated, Tin, Japan, Box, 10 In. . . . . . *illus* 978.0
Sparkler, Cat, Felix, Germany, 5 ½ In. 690.0
Sparkler, Harold Lloyd, Bell Rings, Tin Lithograph, Germany, 5 ½ In. 345.0
Stagecoach, Overland, Tin, Battery Operated, Ichita Of Japan, 18 In. 155.0
Stake Truck, Pressed Steel, Doors Open, Buddy L, 1930s, 24 In. 12000.0
Stake Wagon, Wood Barrels, Horses, Driver, Cast Iron, 17 In. 920.0
Steam, Copper Tank, Pump, Wheel, Electric Cord, 5 x 6 ½ In. 50.0
Steam, Holding Tank, Glass Level, 5 x 9 ½ In. 94.0
Steam, Platform, Building, Smokestack, 8 x 11 In. 138.0
Steam, Platform, Wheel & Pump, Paint Original Paint, Germany, 7 x 7 ½ In. 66.0
Steam, Swing Toy, Tin Plate, Germany, 10 In. 303.0
Steam Engine, Dual Piston, Catwalks, Mamometer Gage, Governor, Whistle, Germany, 6 x 12 In. . 1320.0
Steam Pumper, Red, Nickel Wheels, A.C. Williams, 5 In. 275.0
Steam Roller, Boycraft, Black, Red, Pressed Steel, Decals, 11 ½ x 16 ½ x 7 ½ In. 44.0
Steam Shovel, Mack Chassis, Driver, Hubley, 10 In. 230.0
Steam Shovel, Mounted On Truck, Cast Iron, General, Hubley, 10 In. 450.0
Stepin Tom, Wood Sturdui, Jointed, c.1930, 13 In. 173.0
Steve Canyon Scarf & Goggles, Rock Industries, Original Card, 14 ½ x 7 ½ In. 132.0
Stool, Doll's, Windsor, Painted, Stenciled Horse & Carriage, 3 ½ x 5 ¾ In. 690.0
Stove, Charm, Nickel Plated Iron, Grey Iron Casting Co., 5 In. . . . . . *illus* 115.0
Stove, Charter Oak, Cast Iron, 1880, 12 x 14 ½ In. 600.0
Stove, Charter Oak, Cast Iron, Pat. Hot Air Flue, No. 103, 1880, 13 ¾ x 20 x 12 In. 1300.0
Stove, Charter Oak, Cast Iron, Pat. Hot Air Flue, No. 503, 1880, 12 x 14 ½ In. 1600.0
Stove, Charter Oak, No. 503, Cast Iron, Filey's Pat., June 1867, 25 x 15 x 12 In. 825.0
Stove, Cherub On Warming Shelf, 6 Burners, Cast Iron, 17 x 14 ½ In. 1150.0
Stove, Cloverleaf Top, Side, Front Oven Doors, Warming Plate, Kettles, Cast Iron, 13 x 7 x 7 In. 784.0
Stove, Grey Iron Casting Co., Range, Charm, Cast Iron, Nickel Plate, Shelf, 5 In. 104.0

tove, Karr Range Co., Bellville, Ill., Copperclad, Footed, 21 x 12 ½ x 8 ½ In. 2600.00
tove, Majestic Jr., Cast Iron, Nickel, Black Paint, Salesman's Sample, 31 x 24 x 16 In. 6612.00
tove, Marklin, Simulated Porcelain, Turn Of The Century, 22 x 21 In. 575.00
tove, Quick Meal, Cast Iron, 26 x 16 In. 3500.00
tove, Range, Bird, Cast Iron, Embossed Legs, Nickel Top Plate, Black, 10 ½ In. 201.00
tove, Range, Hubley, Eagle, Cast Iron, Nickel Plate, Back Shelf, 18 ½ In. 920.00
tove, Range, Marvel, Cast Iron, Electroplated, Pots & Pans, Kenton, 19 ½ In. 316.00
tove, Range, T. Southard, Little Eva, Cast Iron, Embossed, Black, 3-Footed, 14 In. 230.00
tove, Range, Union, Cast Iron, Embossed, 9 In. 201.00
treet Sweeper, Tin, Friction, Lifting Brushes, Orange, Japan, 7 In. 155.00
treetcar, Tin Lithograph, Painted, Clockwork, Orobr, 8 ½ In. 187.00
tubborn Donkey, Pulling Cart With Clown, Tin, Windup, Lehmann, 8 In. 173.00
ubmarine, Metal, Windup, Wolverine, 13 In. 245.00
ulky, Pedal, Solid Wheels, White Horse, Mobo, 35 x 21 ½ In. 132.00
ulky & Rider, Cast Iron, Wilkins, 8 In. 259.00
uper Susie, Bear Rings Up Groceries, Battery Operated, Linemar, Box, 8 In. 374.00
urrey, 2 Seats, Driver, Woman, Horse, Shimmer, 1900, 13 ¼ & 5 In. 695.00
weeping Katinka, Waddles, Tin, Windup, Lindstrom, Box, 8 In. .... *illus* 270.00
weeping Mammy, Tin, Windup, Lindstrom, Box, 8 In. .... 345.00 to 525.00
weeping Mammy, Tin Lithograph, Windup, Lindstrom, 1950s, 7 In. 175.00
wimming Tarzan, Holds Knife In Mouth, Swims, Tin, Celluloid, Marusan, Box, 7 In. 285.00
wing, 2 Bears Swinging, Tin, Windup, Japan, 1950s, 6 In. 175.00
witchboard Operator, Moves, Lights Flash, Tin, Vinyl, Battery Operated, Linemar, Box, 1950s, 8 In. . 920.00
alking Clown, Tin, Windup, Germany, 6 ¾ In. 248.00
ank, Camouflage, Cast Iron Arcade, 8 In. 201.00
ank, Casper Ghost, Green, Tin, Windup, Linemar, 4 In. 242.00
ank, Combat, Recoiling Cannon, Clockwork, Marx, Box, 9 ¾ In. .... *illus* 115.00
ank, Radar, Battery Operated, Tin Lithograph, Plastic Dome, Japan, 1950s, 8 In. 230.00
ank, U.S. Army, Tin, Windup, Rubber Treads, Recoiling Gun, Marx No. 392, c.1952, 9 In. ... 145.00
anker, Courtland, Metal, Windup, USA, 1950s, 12 ½ In. 145.00
arzan Clicker, Fights With Gorilla, Upper Bodies Move When Clicker Is Operated, Tin, 3 In. 198.00
axi, 4 Door, Orange, Black, Rear Spare, Friction, c.1925, 9 ½ In. 75.00
axi, American Yellow Cab Co., Windup, Driver, Lenox 530, Germany, 1920s, 7 In. 475.00
axi, Amos 'N' Andy, Fresh Air, Clockwork, Tin Lithograph, Marx, 1930s, 8 In. .... 517.00 to 940.00
axi, Brown & Red, Tin Lithograph, Battery, Japan, Box, 8 In. .... *illus* 345.00
axi, Tin, Windup, Strauss, Box, 8 In. 978.00
axi, Yellow, Arcade, 8 In. 750.00
axi, Yellow, Driver, Windup, Strauss, 8 In. 575.00
axi, Yellow, Windup, Mohawk, 7 In. 275.00
axi, Yellow Cab, Tin Lithograph, Windup, Lenox No. 530, 4 ¾ x 3 ¼ In. 450.00
axi, Yellow Cab Co., Driver, Orange, Black, Iron, Nickel, 9 In. .... *illus* 425.00
eakettle, Colonial, Griswold, No. 0, 567 .... 225.00
ddy Bears are also listed in the Teddy Bear category.
eddy Tootor, Fisher-Price, 1939 .... *illus* 288.00
heater, Pollock's, Wood, Celluloid, Audience, Orchestra Pit, Lift Curtain, 13 x 13 In. 392.00
hresher, McCormick-Deering, Cast Iron, Painted, Arcade, Early 20th Century, 10 ½ In. 265.00
iger, Walker, Mixed Material, Windup, Marx, Esso, Box, 8 In. 325.00
iger, Walking, Esso, Marx, Box, 8 In. 325.00
ightrope Walker, Arnold Lucky, Tin, Composition, Windup, Box, 14 ¾ In. 880.00
nkling Trolley, Tin, Battery Operated, Broadway, Japan, 12 In. 115.00
boggan, Tin, Windup, Coaster, Box, 22 x 11 ½ In. 176.00
mbo The Alabama Coon Jigger, Tin, Windup, Strauss, 9 ¾ In. 796.00
ol Chest, Saws, Planes, Screwdriver, Hammer, Wood, Boycroft, 17 ¼ x 7 In. 330.00
onerville Trolley, Bisque, Japan, 1920s, 3 ½ In. 225.00
onerville Trolley, Cracker Jack Size, Tin, Germany, 1922. .... 725.00
onerville Trolley, Tin, Windup, Fontaine Fox, c.1922, 7 In. .... *illus* 845.00
op, Brownies, Movie Top, 17 Brownies, c.1900, 4 ½ In. 172.00
op, Clown, Tin Lithograph, Chein, 9 ¾ In. 66.00
op, Spinning, Celluloid, Geo. D. Fisher Optical Co., St. Louis, Parisian Novelty Co., 1 ¼ In. .. 125.00
ouchdown Pete, Runs With Ball, Tin, Windup, Linemar, 5 ½ In. 250.00
ower, Spiral, Tin, Windup, CKO, Germany, 9 ⅝ x 5 ⅛ In. 242.00
ractor, Driver, Cast Iron, Original Tires, Red Paint, Farmall, 7 In. 330.00
ractor, Driver, John Deere, Green Paint, Marked, Ertl, U.S.A., 7 ½ In. 88.00
ractor, Farm, Allis Chalmers, Arcade, Red, 3 ¼ In. 275.00
ractor, Ford, Farm, Red, Tootsietoy, 5 In. 135.00
ractor, Highboy, Copper Color, Lithographed Driver, Climbing, Tin, 8 ¼ In. 96.00

Toy, Service Station, Arcade Service, Green, Red, Wood, 6 ½ x 12 In.
$210.00

Toy, Skittles Set, Rabbit, Papier-Mache, Wood Platform, 7 Piece, 12 x 10 In.
$1200.00

Toy, Sled, Bentwood, Lake Scene, Painted, Early 20th Century, 36 In.
$265.00

Toy, Sled, Leaves, Green, Gold Stripes, Red, Wood, Sheet Iron, c.1890, 36 x 11 In.
$330.00

T

TIP
Remove the batteries from a stored toy.

Toy, Space Scout, S-17, Light-Up, Battery Operated, Tin, Japan, Box, 10 In.
$978.00

Toy, Stove, Charm, Nickel Plated Iron, Grey Iron Casting Co., 5 In.
$115.00

Toy, Sweeping Katinka, Waddles, Tin, Windup, Lindstrom, Box, 8 In.
$270.00

Tractor, Mechanical, Lithographed Driver, Rubber Front Tires, Tin, Marx, c.1940, 5½ In. 113.00
Tractor, Painted, Steam, 9 In. 180.00
Tractor, Queen Of Campus, 3 Figures, Tin, Windup, Marx, USA, 6 In. 195.00
Tractor, Space Controlled, Steers, Engine Lights, Pistons Move, Bulldozer Advances, 12 In. 622.00
Tractor, Steam Engine, Scale Model, J. Newton, Rugby, England, c.1941, 18 In. 2970.00
Tractor, Tin, Friction, Japan, c.1950 .... 65.00
Tractor, Yellow & Green, Plastic Driver, Advances, Rubber Treads, Tin, 8¼ In. 130.00
Traffic Cop, British, Celluloid, Movable Arms, 4½ In. 55.00
Trailer, Circus, Car, Tin, Friction, American, Box, 11¼ In. 358.00
Trailer, Coupe & Camper, Windup, Lincoln Zephyr, Pressed Steel, Kingsbury, 1939, 23 In. 402.00
Train Accessory, American Flyer, Switch Tower, Pressed Steel, 9¼ x 12 In. .... *illus* 620.00
Train Accessory, Lionel, Standard Gauge No. 71, 12 Tin Telegraph Poles, Box, 8½ In. 259.00
Train Accessory, Station, American Flyer O Gauge, Box, 8 x 12 x 7½ In. 518.00
Train Accessory, Waiting Room, City, No. 124, Tin, Lionel, Prewar, 9 x 10 x 14 In. 259.00
Train Accessory, Water Tower, Tin, Bing, Germany, 1930s, 9 In. 125.00
Train Car, Bing, Handcar, 2 Figures, Tin, Windup, O Gauge, 4½ In. .... *illus* 460.00
Train Car, Buddy L, Boxcar, Railroad, Sliding Doors, Decals, Pressed Steel, 22 In. 460.00
Train Car, Buddy L, Cattle Car, Sliding Doors, Decals, Pressed Steel, c.1928, 22 In. 863.00
Train Car, Buddy L, Dump Car, Railroad, Side Chains, Couplers, Pressed Steel, c.1928, 12 In. 4025.00
Train Car, Buddy L, Tanker, Red, Pressed Steel, c.1928, 19 In. 805.00
Train Car, Buddy L, Tanker, Yellow, Pressed Steel, c.1928, 19 In. 1150.00
Train Car, Dayton, Locomotive, Hillclimber, Flywheel Drive, 1912, 16 In. 245.00
Train Car, Distler, Locomotive, Red, Black, Gold, Tin Lithograph, 2⅝ In. 115.00
Train Car, Lionel, Tender, No. 6, NYC & HRRR, No. 4351 .... 120.00
Train Car, Locomotive, Tender, Painted Steel, Brass, Inscribed, 82 In. 5975.00
Train Car, Locomotive, Union, Painted, Tin, Iron, Clockwork, 10½ In. .... *illus* 1025.00
Train Car, Marklin, Locomotive, Doors Open, Brown, 1 Gauge, Electric, 12 In. .... *illus* 1390.00
Train Car, Zephyr, No. 0117, Blue, 2¼ In. 35.00
Train Set, American Flyer, O Gauge, Passenger Set, Box, 3 Piece .... *illus* 305.00
Train Set, Ives, Meteor, Painted, Tin, Box, 16 In., 3 Piece. .... *illus* 725.00
Train Set, Lionel, Girl's, Pastel, Engine, Tender, Box Car & Hopper, Gondola, Caboose, Transformer. .. 6900.00
Train Set, Lionel, Streamliner, O Gauge, 1071e, Box, 4 Piece. .... *illus* 415.00
Tram Car, Horse Drawn, Tin Lithograph, Gold Trim On Wheels, Pull Toy, 13 In. 1650.00
Tricycle, Pressed Steel, Red, Flare Fender, 22 x 17 In. 144.00
Trolley, Bi-Directional Seats, Rolled Steel, Painted, Clockwork, 10 x 16 In. 525.00
Trolley, Friction, Pressed Steel, Pay As You Enter On Sides, 23 In. 230.00
Trolley, Hillclimber, Dayton, Summer, Friction, c.1910, 15 In. 410.00
Trolley, Orange, Metal, Embossed, Friction, Ichiko, Japan, 1960, 9 In. 75.00
Trolley, People In Windows, Red, Green, Tin Litho, Mechanical, Marx, Box, 2¾ x 9 x 3 In. ... 1077.00
Trolley, Pressed Steel, Kingsbury, USA, 1920s, 9 In. 295.00
Trolley, Pressed Steel, Kingsbury, USA, 1920s, 14 In. 375.00
Trolley, Tin, Friction, Japan, 1953, 6 In. 95.00
Trolley, Tin, Push, Chein, USA, 1930s, 8½ In. 175.00
Trolley, Union Pacific R.R., Iridescent Copper, Merriam Co., 9 In. 750.00
Trolley, Yellow, Metal, Embossed, Friction, Ichiko, Japan, 1960s, 14 In. 95.00
Truck, 2 Nodding Cows, Tin, Friction, Japan, 1950s, 8 In. 245.00
Truck, Airmail, Mack, Tootsietoy, c.1931 .... 175.00
Truck, Animal, Tiger Goes In & Out, Tin, Friction, Japan, 1950s, 10 In. 145.00
Truck, Army, Tin, Friction, 1920s, U.S.A., Marx, 5½ In. 175.00
Truck, Army, Troop Carrier, Pressed Steel, Plastic Canopy, Olive, Tonka, 14 In. 285.00
Truck, Army Cannon, Tin, Chein USA, 1920s, 8 In. 225.00
Truck, Bell Telephone, Shovels, Ladder, Tools, Hubley, 1920s, 9½ In. 460.00
Truck, Big Show Circus, Lion & Lion Tamer, Windup, Mechanical, Strauss, 1920s 675.00
Truck, Bingo's Circus, Tin, Windup, England, 1940s, 9½ In. 295.00
Truck, Bond Bread, Pressed Steel, Tonka, 12 In. .... *illus* 1380.00
Truck, Bread, Red, White, Sun, 6¼ In. 65.00
Truck, Cannon, Bullets, Windup, Kingsbury, 16 In. 195.00
Truck, Car Carrier, 3 Austin Cars, A.C. Williams, 12½ In. 650.00
Truck, Car Carrier, 3 Austin Cars, Arcade, 14 In. 850.00
Truck, Car Carrier, Green, Red, Cast Iron, Arcade, 15 In. 595.00
Truck, Car Carrier, Mack, 31928 Buicks, Tootsietoy, 8½ In. 325.00
Truck, Car Carrier, Tonka, Box, 1963 .... 495.00
Truck, Cattle, Mack, Die Cast, Tootsietoy 143.00
Truck, Cattle, Tonka, 1955. .... 295.00
Truck, Cattle Carrier, Tin, Friction, Cows, Japan, 1950s, 8 In. 195.00
Truck, Cement, Mack, Red, Yellow, Tootsietoy 65.00
Truck, Cement Mixer, Cast Iron, Motor, Orange, Silver Hopper, Jaeger, 7 In. 294.00

uck, Cement Mixer, Pressed Steel, Buddy L, 18 x 17 In.. *illus* 2300.00
uck, Cement Mixer, Pressed Steel, Spins When Pushed, Emmets, 19 In.. 1265.00
uck, Cement Mixer, Yellow, Turbine, Tonka, 1970, 14 In.. 110.00
uck, Circus, 4 Animals, Tin, Friction, Namura, Box, 10 In. 330.00
uck, Circus, American National, Pressed Steel, Animal Decals, 25 In.. 978.00
uck, Circus, Big Show, Windup, Flat Front, Strauss, 9 ¼ In.. 495.00
uck, Circus, Buddy L, 1962, 17 In.. 495.00
uck, Circus, Tin, Friction, Box, 9 ½ In. 413.00
uck, City Delivery, Steelcraft, Pressed Steel, 22 ½ In. 468.00
uck, Coal, High Lift, Red, Arcade, 10 In. 1250.00
uck, Coal, Mack, High Lift, Red, Arcade, 10 In.. 1250.00
uck, Coal, Mack Bulldog, Black Rubber Tires, Dual Rear Wheels, Arcade, 1930s, 10 In.. 920.00
uck, Corvair, Standard Drug, White, 8 In.. 40.00
uck, Delivery, Bakery, Die Cast, Maroon, Tootsietoy 121.00
uck, Delivery, Blue, McLean Decals, Die Cast, Tootsietoy 710.00
uck, Delivery, Panel, Tonka, 1954-57, 12 In.. 475.00
uck, Delivery, Pressed Steel, Tonka, 16 In.. 230.00
uck, Delivery, Rubber Tires, Orange, Green, Gilt, Silver Trim, Clockwork, Kingsbury, 24 In.. 1610.00
uck, Delivery, Sportsman, Tan, Tonka, 13 In.. 426.00
uck, Diamond T, Red, Nickel Grille, Stakes, Hubley, 7 In. 295.00
uck, Digger, Mack, Panama, Green, Red, Iron, Pivots, Nickel, Hubley, 13 In. *illus* 1620.00
uck, Dodge Van, Panel, Die Cast, Tin Bottom, Tootsietoy 44.00
uck, Driver, AHA, Painted, Lehmann, c.1910 *illus* 1170.00
uck, Dump, Big Mike, Desalle Contemporary, Box, 14 ½ In. 675.00
uck, Dump, Blue Diamond Service, Pressed Steel, Hydraulic, Smith-Miller, 19 In. 575.00
uck, Dump, Cast Iron, Arcade, 10 ½ In.. 475.00
uck, Dump, Cast Iron, Hydraulic Pump, Driver, Arcade, 12 In.. 95.00
uck, Dump, Chevrolet, 1957, Pressed Steel, Tan & Cream, Rubber Tires, Marx, 17 ½ In. 285.00
uck, Dump, Diamond Service, Pressed Steel, Smith-Miller, 19 In. 690.00
uck, Dump, Ford, Model T, Red, Green, Nickel Wheels, Arcade, 6 In.. 500.00
uck, Dump, Gray, Red, Rubber Tires, Cast Iron, Hubley, 8 In. 575.00
uck, Dump, Green, Doepke, 1950, 27 In.. 225.00
uck, Dump, High Lift, Toyland Const. Co., Windup, Structo, 1951, 12 ½ In.. 95.00
uck, Dump, High Lift, Windup, Structo, 1951, 12 ½ In.. 95.00
uck, Dump, Hydraulic, Yellow, Structo, c.1961, 18 In. 55.00
uck, Dump, International Harvester, Fixed Bed, Rubber Tires, Crank, Arcade, 1920s, 11 In. 86.00
uck, Dump, International Harvester, Red Baby, 11 In.. 750.00
uck, Dump, International K5, Die Cast, Tootsietoy, 6 In. 44.00
uck, Dump, Mack, Blue Diamond, Smith-Miller, 19 In.. 690.00
uck, Dump, Mack, Cast Iron, Hydraulic Pump, Driver, Arcade, 12 In.. 650.00
uck, Dump, Mack, Red, Blue, Nickel Wheels, Champion, 4¾ In. 175.00 to 225.00
uck, Dump, Mack, Spring Tab On Cab Roof, Painted Blue, Arcade, 12 In. 863.00
uck, Dump, Orange, 1950, 27 In.. 175.00
uck, Dump, Press Steel, Tri-Ang, England, 1930s, 11 ½ In. 110.00
uck, Dump, Red, Green, Tonka, 1955, 13 In. 195.00
uck, Dump, Red, Pressed Steel, Steelcraft Diamond, 20 In.. 259.00
uck, Dump, Tin, Blue, Red, Chein, 9 In. 110.00
uck, Dump, Tin, Windup, Courtland, U.S.A., 1950s, 8 In.. 110.00
uck, Dump, Turner, Lincoln Front End, C-Type Cab Roof, Pressed Steel, 1930, 30 In.. 632.00
uck, Dump, Yellow, Wooldridge, Doepke, 1946, 25 In. 225.00
uck, Eaton's Of Canada, Black, Red, Japan, 1960s, 10 In. 85.00
uck, Electromage Crane, Trailer, 3 Sections Of Pipe, Magnet On Boom, Tin, Excelo, 13 In.. 537.00
uck, Express, Driver, Red, 5 In.. 275.00
uck, Express, Painted Steel, Composition Tires, Green Open Body, Buddy L, 1930s, 24 In.. 235.00
uck, Express Line Van, Pressed Steel, Black, Buddy L, 26 In. 633.00
uck, Farmer's Market, Tin, Friction, Linemar, Japan, 1940, 4 ½ In.. 75.00
uck, Ferris Wheel, Tin, Friction, Nomura, Japan, Box, 8 ½ In.. 385.00
uck, Flat Bed, Foden F.G., Mechanical, Schakleton Toys, Box, 12 In. *illus* 725.00
uck, Foden Army, No. 668, Die Cast, Dinky Toys, Box *illus* 66.00
uck, Ford, 1 Ton, No. 212, Buddy L, c.1927, 14 ¼ In. 4500.00
uck, Ford, 1936 Model, Panel, Yellow, Black, Rubber Wheels, 33 In.. 45.00
uck, Ford, Koin Panel, 2-Tone Blue, 8 ½ In. 165.00
uck, Ford, Koin Panel, Red, 8 ½ In. 85.00
uck, Ford, Koin Window, 2-Tone Green, 8 ½ In. 165.00
uck, Ford, Model T, Red, Nickel Wheels, Arcade, 7 In.. 475.00
uck, Ford, Pickup, Japan, 1956, 12 In.. 375.00
uck, Ford, Stake, Cast Iron, Blue, Arcade, 1935, 4 ½ In. 750.00

Toy, Tank, Combat, Recoiling Cannon, Clockwork, Marx, Box, 9 ¾ In.
$115.00

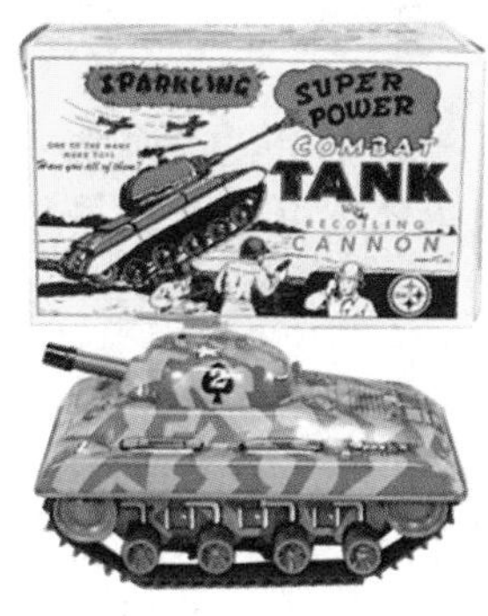

Toy, Taxi, Brown & Red, Tin Lithograph, Battery, Japan, Box, 8 In.
$345.00

Toy, Taxi, Yellow Cab Co., Driver, Orange, Black, Iron, Nickel, 9 In.
$425.00

Toy, Teddy Tootor, Fisher-Price, 1939
$288.00

T

TIP
Old metal toy trucks were made of iron or tin, not brass or aluminum, the metals favored by some reproductions.

Toy, Toonerville Trolley, Tin, Windup, Fontaine Fox, c.1922, 7 In.
$845.00

Toy, Train Accessory, American Flyer, Switch Tower, Pressed Steel, 9 ¼ x 12 In.
$620.00

Toy, Train Car, Bing, Handcar, 2 Figures, Tin, Windup, O Gauge, 4 ½ In.
$460.00

Truck, Ford, Union Freightways, Semi, Red, Die Cast, Ralstoy, c.1950, 8 In. 165.0
Truck, Freight Transport, Opening Rear Door, Tin, Yamaichi, 14 In. 220.0
Truck, Frosty Bar, Tin Lithograph, Japan, Ice Cream Bar Decals, c.1950, 7 ½ In. 295.0
Truck, GMC, Nursery, Buddy L, 1959 495.0
Truck, Golden Apples, Green, White, 6 ¼ In. 65.0
Truck, Grain Hauler, Trailer, Tin, Friction, Japan, 10 In. 95.0
Truck, Hauler, Express, Tin, Courtland, 1948 95.0
Truck, Heinz Pickle, Pressed Steel, Metalcraft, 12 In. *illus* 316.0
Truck, High Side, Stake, Blue, Rubber Tires, Champion, 7 ½ In. 650.0
Truck, Horse, Open Door, Horse Comes Out, Tin, Friction, Japan, 1950, 10 In. 175.0
Truck, Ice, Mack, Blue, Driver, Cast Iron, Arcade, 8 In. 316.0
Truck, Ice Cream, Howard Johnson, Daiya, Japan, 1950s, 8 In. 175.0
Truck, Ice Cream, Tin, Friction, Japan, 1950s, 8 ¼ In. 195.0
Truck, Ice Cream, Tin, Friction, Japan, 1960, 8 ¼ In. 175.0
Truck, International Harvester, Driver, Red, Cast Iron, Arcade, 10 In. 403.0
Truck, Ladder, Kelmet Big Boy, Pressed Steel, Wood Ladders, 34 In. 920.0
Truck, Livestock, Tin, Friction, Japan, 1950s, 13 In., 2 Piece 95.0
Truck, Livestock Transporter, Tin, Friction, Japan, c.1950, 16 In. 145.0
Truck, Log, Mack, Red, Tootsietoy, Box, 9 In. 225.0
Truck, Log, Orange, Hubley, 7 ½ In. 275.0
Truck, Log, Pressed Steel, Logs, Red, Tonka, 16 In. 230.0
Truck, Logger, Red, Tootsietoy, Box, 9 In. 275.0
Truck, Lumber, Pressed Steel, Mud Flaps, Tonka, c.1950, 17 In. 345.0
Truck, Mail, Model A, Ford, Light Green, Tootsietoy, 2 ½ In. 140.0
Truck, Mail, Tin, Front Crank, Driver, Gibbs, 8 In. 490.0
Truck, Merry-Go-Round, Tin, Battery Operated, Tin, Nomura, Box, 8 In. 495.0
Truck, Metro Daily News, Green, 5 In. 115.0
Truck, Military, Camouflage, 2 Soldiers Pulls Artillery Piece On Wheels, Windup, 7 In. 275.0
Truck, Milk, Borden's, Hino, 2 Door, Delivery, Hayashi, Tin, 8 ¼ In. 186.0
Truck, Milk, M & K, Tin, Friction, Japan, 1950s, 11 In., 2 Piece 95.0
Truck, Milk & Cream, White, Hubley, 3 ¾ In. 450.0
Truck, Minute Maid, Pressed Steel, Decals, Tonka, c.1950s, 14 In. 288.0
Truck, Motor Express, 2 Parts, Red, Silver Tractor, Green Trailer, Hubley, 9 In. 750.0
Truck, Moving Van, Allied, Pressed Steel, Decals On Sides, Box, 24 In. 345.0
Truck, Oil, Junior, Tin, Chein, USA, 1920s, 8 ½ In. 195.0
Truck, P.I.E., Fred Thompson, Pressed Steel, Smith-Miller, 1980s, 38 In. 747.0
Truck, Panama Digger, Cast Iron, Rubber Tires, Back Scoop, Figures, Hubley, 13 In. 3738.0
Truck, Panel, Green, Tin, Japan, c.1952, 5 In. 85.0
Truck, Panel, Nickel Grill, Green, Kenton, c.1928, 3 ½ In. 211.0
Truck, Pepsi, Plastic, White, Wood Wheels, Decals, 3 Cases, Marx, 7 ½ In. 95.0
Truck, Pickup, Light Blue, Buddy L, 1958 295.0
Truck, Pickup, Metallic Blue, Tonka, 1955, 13 In. 175.0
Truck, Post Office, Ford, Tin, Painted, Clockwork, King Edward Decal, Minic, Prewar 154.0
Truck, Postal, Volkswagen, Plastic, Yellow, Black Trim, Driver, Wiking, 4 In. 335.0
Truck, Poultry, Ford, '57, Die Cast, 3 Plastic Crates, 15 Birds, Hubley, 10 In. 245.0
Truck, Power Construction, Runs Forward & Reverse, Boom Raises & Lowers, Tin, 13 In. 195.0
Truck, Pressed Steel, Black, Green, Metalcraft, 11 In. 144.0
Truck, RCA, NBC Mobile TV, Camera, Battery Operated, Box, 9 x 6 ¼ In. 1430.0
Truck, Rescue Squad, Tonka, 1956-57, 12 In. 350.0
Truck, Road Roller, Pressed Steel, Paint, Keystone, 20 In. *illus* 201.0
Truck, Safeway, Van Semi, Tin, Plastic Trim, White, Box, Shudo Shoji, 12 ½ In. 165.0
Truck, Scoop Dump, Pressed Steel, Yellow, Blue, Structo, 23 In. 385.0
Truck, Searchlight, Army, Tin, Windup, Tippco, Germany, 1937, 10 In. 495.0
Truck, Searchlight, Hollywood, Mack, Pressed Steel, Smith-Miller, 18 In. 1092.0
Truck, Seesaw, Elephants, Tin, Friction, Box, 8 ¼ In. 495.0
Truck, Semitrailer, Smith-Miller Pacific Intermountain Express, Red Cab, 1950s, 24 x 9 In. 263.0
Truck, Shovel, Green, Red, Rubber Tires, Hubley, 10 ½ In. 950.0
Truck, Shovel, Hubley, 8 ½ In. 575.0
Truck, Side Dump, Tin, 2-Piece, Lupor, USA, 1950s, 8 ½ In. 145.0
Truck, Silver Streak, Polished Aluminum, GMC, Smith-Miller, 1951, 24 In. 225.0
Truck, Slush Cast, Bronze Plated, GMC, 1948-53, 7 In. 125.0
Truck, Sportsman's, Back Tailgate, Chains, Tonka, Box, 1960, 13 In. 348.0
Truck, Stake, Cast Iron, Blue, Door Decal, 8 Barrels, Arcade, 6 In. 350.0
Truck, Stake, Red, Blue, Pressed Steel Wheels, Marx, 1940s, 20 In. 150.0
Truck, Stake, Red, Green, Wood Wheels, Wyandotte, 1938, 16 In. 195.0
Truck, State Highway, Pressed Steel, Tailgate, Mud Flaps, Snow Plows, Tonka, c.1950, 13 In. 403.0
Truck, Strawbridge & Clothier, Hand Erbel, Box, 8 In. 7800.0

Toy Trains

The easiest trains to sell are the O gauge trains of the 1950s, not the larger trains of earlier years.

Toy, Train Car, Locomotive, Union, Painted, Tin, Iron, Clockwork, 10½ In.
$1025.00

Toy, Train Car, Marklin, Locomotive, Doors Open, Brown, 1 Gauge, Electric, 12 In.
$1390.00

Toy, Train Set, American Flyer, O Gauge, Passenger Set, Box, 3 Piece
$305.00

Toy, Train Set, Ives, Meteor, Painted, Tin, Box, 16 In., 3 Piece
$725.00

Toy, Train Set, Lionel, Streamliner, O Gauge, 1071e, Box, 4 Piece
$415.00

Toy, Truck, Bond Bread, Pressed Steel, Tonka, 12 In.
$1380.00

Toy, Truck, Cement Mixer, Pressed Steel, Buddy L, 18 x 17 In.
$2300.00

Toy, Truck, Digger, Mack, Panama, Green, Red, Iron, Pivots, Nickel, Hubley, 13 In.
$1620.00

Toy, Truck, Driver, AHA, Painted, Lehmann, c.1910
$1170.00

Toy, Truck, Flat Bed, Foden F.G., Mechanical, Schakleton Toys, Box, 12 In.
$725.00

Toy, Truck, Foden Army, No. 668, Die Cast, Dinky Toys, Box
$66.00

Dinky
DIE CAST TOYS
Foden
Army Truck
Dinky
Foden Army Truck

Toy, Truck, Heinz Pickle, Pressed Steel, Metalcraft, 12 In.
$316.00

Toy, Truck, Road Roller, Pressed Steel, Paint, Keystone, 20 In.
$201.00

Toy, Truck, Tanker, Esso Motor Oil, Tin, Battery Operated, Citroen, Box, 13½ In.
$398.00

Tonka Trucks
If you made a line of all the Tonka trucks made in the last fifty years, it would stretch from Los Angeles to Pawtucket, Rhode Island.

Toy, Truck, Tanker, Gasoline, Mack, Driver, Green, Cast Iron, Tin, Arcade, 13 In.
$863.00

Toy, Truck, Tanker, Gasoline, Red, Yellow, Windup, Marx Toys, Box, 14 ½ In.
$575.00

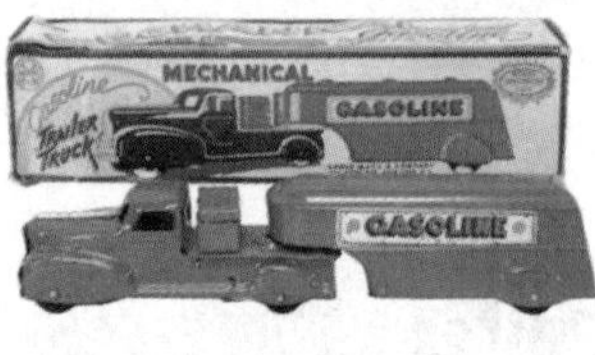

Toy, Truck, Tanker, Mack, Sinclair, Green, Chrome Catwalk, 19 In.
$695.00

Toy, Wagon, Royal Circus, 2 Horses, Rhino, Red, Gold, Iron, Hubley, 16 In.
$2875.00

Truck, Swiss Ice Cream, 2-Tone Blue, 6 ¼ In. . . . 115.00
Truck, Tank, Open Front, Tank Body, Filler Cap, GMC, Pressed Steel, Steelcraft, 1925, 26 In. . . 575.00
Truck, Tanker, Esso Motor Oil, Tin, Battery Operated, Citroen, Box, 13 ½ In. . . . *illus* 398.00
Truck, Tanker, Gas & Oil, Red, Wyandotte, 10 ½ In. . . . 250.00
Truck, Tanker, Gasoline, Dodge, Tin, Friction, Japan, 1957, 9 In. . . . 95.00
Truck, Tanker, Gasoline, International, Tin, Windup, Mettoy, England, 8 ½ In. . . . 225.00
Truck, Tanker, Gasoline, Mack, Driver, Green, Cast Iron, Tin, Arcade, 13 In. . . . *illus* 863.00
Truck, Tanker, Gasoline, Mack, Green, Driver, Rubber Tires, Arcade Cast Iron, Tin, 13 In. . . . 863.00
Truck, Tanker, Gasoline, Mobilgas, Japan, 1950s, 8 ½ In. . . . 75.00
Truck, Tanker, Gasoline, Red, Yellow, Windup, Marx Toys, Box, 14 ½ In. . . . *illus* 575.00
Truck, Tanker, Gasoline, Shell, 10 Wheels, Tin, Harusame, 11 ¼ In. . . . 130.00
Truck, Tanker, Gasoline, Shell, Tin, Friction, Japan, 1950s, 4 In. . . . 75.00
Truck, Tanker, Gasoline, Texaco, Cast Iron, Red, Kenton, 9 ½ In. . . . 1575.00
Truck, Tanker, Gasoline, Texaco, Pressed Steel, Plastic Wheels, Buddy L, 1960s, 24 In. . . . 115.00
Truck, Tanker, Mack, Service Distr. Co., Plastic, Battery Operated, 12 ½ In. . . . 1650.00
Truck, Tanker, Mack, Sinclair, Green, Chrome Catwalk, 19 In. . . . *illus* 695.00
Truck, Tanker, Oil, Gas, Rear Door, Red, Wyandotte, 10 ½ In. . . . 175.00
Truck, Tanker, Oil, Pure, Pressed Steel, Electric Headlights, Metalcraft, 1936, 15 In. . . . 517.00
Truck, Tanker, Pemex Oil, Die Cast, Decals, Ford, Mexico, Tootsietoy . . . 44.00
Truck, Tanker, Silver & Red Paint, White Rubber Tires, Iron, Marked, Made In U.S.A., 5 ½ In. 88.00
Truck, Tanker, Water, White Fire, Tonka, 1958 . . . 595.00
Truck, Television, Cameramen Turn, Truck Advances, Images Projected On Screen, 11 ½ In. . 1131.00
Truck, Thunderbird Van Lines, Tin, Friction, Japan, 1950s, 10 In. . . . 95.00
Truck, Timber, Tin, Painted, Clockwork, Postwar, Minic, Box . . . 286.00
Truck, Tin, Windup, Red, Walt Beach Toys, Camden, N.J., 4 x 6 x 3 In. . . . 70.00
Truck, Tow, Austin, Red, 4 ½ In. . . . 325.00
Truck, Tow, Buddy L, 1951 . . . 395.00
Truck, Tow, Fix It, Blue, Buddy L, Box, c.1961 . . . 295.00
Truck, Tow, Lincoln Zephyr, Die Cast, Clockwork, Tootsietoy . . . 660.00
Truck, Tow, Tin, Windup, England, 1940s, 12 In. . . . 475.00
Truck, Tow, Tonka, 1956, 12 In. . . . 350.00
Truck, Tow, Tow Hook, Decal On Sides, Smith-Miller, 16 In. . . . 401.00
Truck, Tow, Yellow, Cast Iron, Plated Boom, Hubley, 6 In. . . . 165.00
Truck, U.S. Army, Non Powered, Canvas Top, Marked US Army 5th Division, Tin, 16 ¼ In. . . . 283.00
Truck, U.S. Mail, Buddy L, Box, 1966 . . . 295.00
Truck, U.S. Mail, Ford, Die Cast, Tootsietoy . . . 30.00
Truck, U.S. One Gama, Metal, Windup, 2 Door, Guide Wheels, 9 In. . . . 175.00
Truck, Volkswagen, Vanagon, Buddy L, Box, 1966 . . . 295.00
Truck, Wheaton, White, Metal, Tonka, 1965 . . . 595.00
Truck, World Circus, Tin, Friction, Japan, 1950s, 5 In. . . . 225.00
Truck, Wreck Truck, Buddy L, Painted, Pressed Steel, Light On Roof, Battery Operated, 15 In. 127.00
Truck, Wrigley's, Die Cast, Decal, Tootsietoy . . . 121.00
Tumbling Monkey, Flips Between 2 Chairs, Tin, Windup, Marx, Box, 4 ½ In. . . . 190.00
Turtle, Wood, Carved, Black Paint, White Spots, Head & Tail Move, 1 ½ x 6 ½ x 2 In. . . . 88.00
Tut-Tut, Man In Car, Blowing Horn, Windup, Lehmann, 1903 . . . 860.00 to 950.00
Typewriter, Berwin Gold, Tin, 5 x 10 In. . . . 135.00
Typewriter, Junior Dial, Tin Lithograph, Marx, 1930s, 8 x 11 x 7 In. . . . 45.00
Typewriter, Simplex, No. 300, Instructions, Box . . . 55.00
Typewriter, Tom Thumb, Case Top, Western Stamping Co., c.1955-60 . . . 50.00
Typewriter, Tom Thumb, Red Orange, Metal, Case . . . 75.00
Uncle Wiggily's Crazy Car, Marx, Box, 1930, 7 In. . . . 1080.00
Unique Artie, Clown, Driving Car, Cat On Hood, Windup, Tin Lithograph, Unique Art Mfg., 7 In. . 230.00
Violinist, Man Plays, Head Moves Side To Side, Tin, 5 ¼ In. . . . 153.00
Waffle Iron, Griswold, No. 0, 406/407, Base No. 408 . . . 1900.00
Wagon, Art Deco, Pressed Steel, Arrow Flight, Electric Headlight, c.1930, 47 x 19 In. . . . 316.00
Wagon, Bear, Seal, Pull Toy, Germany, 1910, 10 In. . . . 575.00
Wagon, Cast Iron, Pull Handle, Rubber Tires, Champion, 8 In. . . . 58.00
Wagon, Conestoga, White Horse, Merriam Mfg. Co., c.1875, 11 In. . . . 351.00
Wagon, Confectionery, Horse Drawn, Driver, c.1875, 14 In. . . . 4972.00
Wagon, Deco Style, Pressed Steel, Wood Wheels, Yellow, Wyandotte, 1930s, 4 In. . . 85.00 to 125.00
Wagon, Dump, Contractor's, Man, Arcade, 1908, 14 In. . . . 650.00
Wagon, Goat, Driver, Tin, Windup, Germany, 1880, 9 In. . . . 875.00
Wagon, Hose Reel, Horse Drawn, Driver, Cast Iron, 21 In. . . . 259.00
Wagon, Ice, Cast Iron, Hubley, 15 In. . . . 144.00
Wagon, Ice, Die Cast, Non Eccentric, Kayo, Tootsietoy . . . 231.00
Wagon, Ice, Horse Drawn, Tin Lithograph, Mid 20th Century, 13 ½ In. . . . 148.00
Wagon, Milk, Horse Drawn, Tin, Windup, Marx, 1950s, 10 In. . . . 245.00

'agon, Milk, Horse Drawn, Driver, Kenton, 13 In.. 475.00
'agon, Phoenix Ladder, Japanned White Horse, Foot Patrol, Iron, Accessories, Ives, c. 1900, 26 In. 575.00
'agon, Police Patrol, 2 Horses, Gong Bell, 7 Figures, Harris, 1903, 19½ In.. 1250.00
'agon, Royal Circus, 2 Horses, Rhino, Red, Gold, Iron, Hubley, 16 In. *illus* 2875.00
agon, Sand & Gravel, 2 Horses, Driver, Iron, Kenton, 15 In.. *illus* 230.00
'agon, Sunnyside Farm, Yellow, Black Stencil, Wheels, Wood, Smith Toy Co., 1800s, 10 x 26 In. 300.00
agon, Wood, Horse Drawn, Pull Toy, Fisher-Price, Box, 1951, 16 In.. *illus* 316.00
'agon, Wood, Orange, Pull Toy, 13 x 36 x 16 In.. 336.00
agon, Wood, Spoke Wheels, 42 x 26 In. 403.00
'arehouse, Paper Lithograph, Roof, Working Elevator, Glass Windows, 1900s, 21 x 11½ In. 288.00
'ater Tower, American-LaFrance, Open Front Cab, Pressed Steel, Sturditoy, 1925, 33 In. 977.00
'estern Play-Time Set, Wagons, Horses, Figures, Tin, Plastic, Archer Plastics, Box, 48 Piece 98.00
heelbarrow, Katrinka, Jimmy, Tin, Windup, Nifty, 1925 2400.00
'heelbarrow, Stencil Decoration, Squirrels, PMC Logo, No. 2, Paris Mfg. Co., 39 In. 288.00
'histling Kooky Spooky Tree, Walker, Moves Arms, Leaves, Tin, Battery Operated, Marx, 14 In. 697.00
'ild Mule Jack, Cast Iron, Gold Paint, Pull Toy, c.1900, 8½ In. 212.00
'olf, Wood, Jointed, Brown, Painted Eyes, Open Mouth, Long Tail, Schoenhut, 8½ In. 690.00
ylophone, Topo Gigio Xylofono, Plays London Bridge, Tin, Rubber, Battery Operated, Box, 10 In. 718.00
ebu, Wood, Jointed, Brown, Black Humpback, Leather Horns, Rope Tail, Schoenhut, 8½ In.. 690.00
eppelin, 4 Propellers, 2 Gondolas, Die Cut Passengers, Tin Litho, Meier, Germany, 4½ In. 920.00
eppelin, Die Cast, USN Los Angeles, Tootsietoy. 176.00
eppelin, Transatlantic, Windup, Silver, Marx, Box, String, 10 In. 500.00
ig Zag, Riders Sit & Rock Back & Forth, Toy Advances, Tin, 5 In. 1469.00

RAMP ART is a form of folk art made since the Civil War. It is usually made from chip-arved cigar boxes. Examples range from small boxes and picture frames to full-sized pieces f furniture.

ox, Chip Carved, Multitiered Lid, Base, Sides, Applied Acorn Shape, 6¼ x 10 x 6 In.. 132.00
ox, Chip Carved, Porcelain Pull, Multitiered, Hinged Lid, Brown Stain, 7¼ x 10 x 7 In.. 154.00
ox, Chip Carved, Tiered, Velvet Panels, Lion's Head Pulls, Wallpaper, 5¾ x 11 x 6¾ In.. 99.00
ox, Wedding, Applied Velvet Panels, Brass Ornaments, 10½ In. 295.00
athedral, Tower Clock, Steeples 2600.00
hest, 4 Drawers, Split Baluster Turned Columns, Footed, Maine, c.1850, 20 x 20 x 13 In. 173.00
hurch, Wood, Linoleum, Mirrors, 59½ x 27½ x 29 In. *illus* 440.00
orkscrew, Threaded Brass Bullet Casing, 4 In. 35.00
resser, Pine, Mirror, Chip Carved Drawers, Crest, c.1930, Child's, 28 x 17 In. 1320.00
rame, Chip Carved, 3 Tiers, Corner Blocks & Diamonds, House Shape, 10¾ x 8½ In. 99.00
rame, Chip Carved, 4 & 5 Tiers, Stylized Tulips, c.1890, 21 x 18 In.. *illus* 605.00
rame, Chip Carved, 5 Tiers, Sides, Corner Blocks, 10 x 8½ In. 22.00
rame, Chip Carved, 6 Tiers, Applied Ornaments, Silver, March 3, 1932, 12 x 12 In. 4400.00
rame, Chip Carved, Applied Rondels, Hearts, 16½ x 21 In.. 144.00
rame, Chip Carved, Oak, Pinwheels, Quarter Fans, 11 x 7 In.. 316.00
rame, Crown Of Thorns, Late 19th Century, 23 x 28 In. 395.00
rame, Mirror, Chip Carved Edges, Diamonds & Hearts, Cut Glass Stones, 5¼ In. 220.00
ocker, Twig, Chip Carved, Miniature, 10½ In.. 144.00
'all Pocket, Vines, Hearts, Applied Comb Box, Early 20th Century, 17 x 11 In. *illus* 485.00

RAPS for animals may be handmade. One of the most unusual is the mousetrap made so at when the mouse entered the trap, it was hit on the head with a mallet. Other traps were ommercially manufactured and often are marked with the name of the manufacturer. any traps were designed to be as humane as possible, and they would trap the live animal so it could e released in the woods.

nimal, Oneida Victor, No. 2, Animal Trap Co., 14½ x 7 In.. 66.00
nt, Lilly's, Yellow, Red, Tin, F.C. Sturtevant Co. 14.00
nt, Tin, Black Flag, Side Perforations 14.00
ear, Iron, Hand Forged, 13-In. Jaws, 40 In.. 468.00
ee, Blown Glass, Topper, French, 20th Century, 10½ x 10 In., Pair. 525.00
el, Basket, Splint, Oak, Cone Shape, Interior Funnel, 29 x 9 In. 132.00
y, Clockwork, Brass Automation Movement, Wire Case, Mid 20th Century, 9½ In. 59.00
y, Glass, Hand Blown, Amethyst, 3-Footed, Mid 19th Century, Pair. 198.00
innow, Hinged Lid, c.1900, 15 x 9 In.. 75.00
ouse, Cardboard, Wood Finish 15.00
ouse, Choker, Wooden, Victor Animal Trap Co., 4 x 4 In. 45.00
ouse, McGill's, Wood, Pre Scent Baited 18.00
at, Wood, Metal Spring, 7½ x 6¼ In. 40.00

Toy, Wagon, Sand & Gravel, 2 Horses, Driver, Iron, Kenton, 15 In.
$230.00

Toy, Wagon, Wood, Horse Drawn, Pull Toy, Fisher-Price, Box, 1951, 16 In.
$316.00

Tramp Art, Church, Wood, Linoleum, Mirrors, 59½ x 27½ x 29 In.
$440.00

Tramp Art, Frame, Chip Carved, 4 & 5 Tiers, Stylized Tulips, c.1890, 21 x 18 In.
$605.00

T

Tramp art, Wall Pocket, Vines, Hearts, Applied Comb Box, Early 20th Century, 17 x 11 In. $485.00

Trunk, Dome Top, Pine, Iron Mounts, Europe, 19th Century, 23 x 42 x 20 In. $60.00

Trunk, Leather, Brass Tacks, Handles, 18¾ x 42 x 21 In. $350.00

TIP

If you are storing a large closed container like a trunk for a long time, put a piece of charcoal in it to absorb odors.

TREEN, *see Wooden category.*

TRENCH ART is a form of folk art made by soldiers. Metal casings from bullets and mortar shells were cut and decorated to form useful objects, such as vases.

Ashtray, Large Caliber Shell, Marked U.S., 5 Lbs. 6 Oz., Brass Anchor, c.1944, 6¼ In. 47.0
Ashtray, Mortar Shell 6.0
Bracelet, German Artillery Shell, Sweetheart, Iron Cross, 2½ In. 165.0
Buckle, Brass, American Flag, 1⅞ x 1¼ In. 11.0
Lamp, American Artillery Shell, 74 mm, Wood, 3 Tie, Painted, 1st Inf. Div., 25 In. 148.0
Lamp, German Artillery Shell, 75 mm, Projectile, Maple Base, Punched Initials, 37 In. 93.0
Lamp, Table, Shell, 30 mm, Green Helmet Can Shade, Wooden Base, 1940s 33.0
Letter Opener, Brass, Argonne, Meuse-Argonne Offensive, Armistice, c.1918, 8½ In. 17.5
Letter Opener, Dagger Sword, Nude Woman, World War II, 11 In. 22.0
Light, Bullet, Brass, Granite Base Mounted, World War II, 8¼ x 3 In. 125.0
Lighter, Brass, Book Shape, Hinged, Bottom Pulls Out, S.S. Oxfordshire, 1¼ x 2 In. 50.0
Lighter, Dog, Peeing On German Pickelhaube Helmet, Versa Dog With Red Cross Harness . . . 281.0
Lighter, Shell, 50 Caliber, c.1940 . . . . 128.0
Lighter, Tank, World War I, Great Britain, 2 In. 654.0
Matchbox Holder, Brass, Beaten Picklehaube Helmet, c.1918 . . . . 19.0
Needle Case, Bullet & Shell, Brass, Copper Cross, England, 2¾ x ½ In. 25.0
Paperweight, Pencil Holder, 20 mm Hollow Brass Shells, 20 mm Aluminum Cartridge, 6 x 4 In. 15.0
Pill Box, Silver Coin, 1915 Italian 2 Lire, Marked 800 Italy, c.1918, ¼ In. 30.0
Salt & Pepper, Japanese 25 mm Projectiles, Drilled Holes, Brass Shoulders, Painted 46.0
Shot Glass, Shell Casing, World War II, 6 Piece 200.0
Snuff Box, Brass, J Tatley On Lid, World War I, England, 2½ x 2 In. 33.0
Vase, Brass Shell, Swaged Top, Corrugated Lip, Copper Band, 1918, 6½ In. 18.0
Vase, Shell Case, Marked Febr. 1917, 9⅛ In. 86.0

TRIVETS are now used to hold hot dishes. Most trivets of the late nineteenth and early twentieth centuries were made to hold hot irons. Iron or brass reproductions are being made of many of the old styles.

Brass, George Washington, Virginia Metalcrafters 12.0
Brass, Wrought Iron, Riveted, Turned Maple Handle, Penny Feet, 7½ In. 81.0
Bronze, Hen, Marked, Hagenauer, 13¾ In. 540.0
Cast Iron, Circle, Around Star, Serrated Edge, 3-Footed, Cast Iron, 5½ In. 33.0
Cast Iron, Open Hearts, Diamonds, Serrated Edge, Etched Line, 3-Footed, 2 x 8 x 5 In. 187.0
Cast Iron, Tailor's, Dover 24.0
Enamel, On Copper, Circles, Triangles, Ceramic, Metal Caddy, Signed, Wheeling 2, 6 In. 65.0
Fireplace, Wrought Iron, Round, Pot Handle, Adjustable Holder, 3-Footed, 5 x 25 In. 288.0
Iron, 4 Hearts, Scrolls, 29 x 18 In. 165.0
Iron, Classic, Griswold . . . . 30.00 to 35.0
Iron, Footed, Rosenbaum Mfg. Co., 10¼ x 6 In. 20.0
Iron, Heart Shape, Rattail Terminal, 3-Footed, 11 In. 187.0
Iron, Hearth, 4-Point Star Design, Cabriole Legs, Penny Feet, 1700s, 13¾ In. 588.0
Iron, Hearth, Round, 3-Footed, 5½ In. 66.0
Iron, Leaf Shape, Marked, Christopher Dresser, c.1890, 9 In. 102.0
Iron, Magic, 4-Footed, Handle, Streeter's 12.0
Iron, Native American Figure, Multicolored, 5 x 5 x 1 In. 35.0
Iron, Old Lace, Griswold, No. 1739 . . . . 70.0
Iron, Tailor's, 3-Footed, Koenig 12.0
Iron, Tailor's, Spade Shape, 10 x 6½ In. 12.0
Iron, Wavy Bars, 4-Footed, 14½ In. 110.0
Mosaic, 3 Mod Flowers, Orange, Pearl Gray Abstract Oval Tiles, 1960s 7.0
Royal Chrome, 1960s 12.0

TRUNKS of many types were made. The nineteenth-century sea chest was often handmade of unpainted wood. Brass-fitted camphorwood chests were brought back from the Orient. Leather-covered trunks were popular from the late eighteenth to mid-nineteenth centuries. By 1895, trunks were covered with canvas or decorated sheet metal. Embossed metal coverings were used from 1870 to 1910. By 1925, trunks were covered with vulcanized fiber or undecorated metal. Suitcases are listed here.

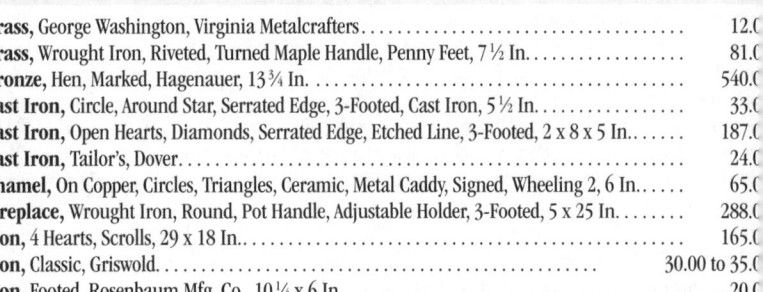

Arts & Crafts, Oak, Dome Top, Peg & Through Tenon, Footed, 29 x 36 x 23 In. 725.0
Arts & Crafts, Flat Top, Paneled Sides, Handles, Footed, 21 x 44 x 22 In. 980.0
Camphorwood, Lift Top, Brass Trim, 19th Century, 18 x 38 x 20½ In. 345.0
Dome Top, Painted, Blue, White Borders, Birds, Dots, Flowers, Early 1800s, 10 x 16 In. 705.0

Dome Top, Painted, Flower Border, 19th Century, 13 x 35 x 17 ¼ In.. . . . . 1175.00
Dome Top, Pine, Iron Mounts, Europe, 19th Century, 23 x 42 x 20 In. . . . . *illus* 60.00
Dome Top, Pine, Lift Top, Interior Till, Iron Mounts, Green Paint, 1800s, 23 x 42 In. 58.00
Dome Top, Pine, Painted, Black, Red Borders, Yellow, Blue, c.1830, 12 x 24 In. 11750.00
Dome Top, Pine, Painted, Martha Cahoon, New England, Early 19th Century 999.00
Dome Top, Pine, Yellow, Red, Black Graining, 10 x 24 In. 1035.00
Dome Top, Tin, Painted Flowers, 19th Century, 7 ⅜ x 10 x 6 ½ In.. . . . . 4406.00
Dome Top, Tin, Wire Handle, Red Flowers, Leaves, Black Ground, 7 x 10 x 6 In. 4406.00
Dome Top, Tooled Leather, Wrought Iron, 2-Headed Eagle, Early 1900s, 21 x 38 In. 944.00
Indian, Dome Top, Brass, Iron Mounted, Lift Top, Locks, Animal, Flower Decor, 40 x 55 In. . . 173.00
Lacquered, Multicolored, Japanese Export, Stand, 18th Century, 33 x 35 In. 881.00
Leather, Brass Tacks, Handles, 18 ¾ x 42 x 21 In. . . . . *illus* 350.00
Louis Vuitton, Suitcase, Leather Trim, Handle, c.1940, 18 x 18 x 7 In. 430.00
Pine, Grain Painted, Transfer, Boston Buildings, Faneuil Hall, Early 1800s, 12 x 30 In. 529.00
Steamer, Leather Strap Corners, Brass Locks, Tacks, c.1900, 23 x 32 ½ x 20 In. 6720.00
Suitcase, Bamboo, Rectangular, Chinese, 19th Century, 12 x 34 ½ x 24 In. 178.00
Tin, Grain Painted, Hinged Lid, Brass Latch, Early 1900s, 10 ¼ x 14 x 10 ¼ In.. . . . . 118.00
Wedding, Walnut, Multicolored, Flower Vase, Mongolia, 17 x 17 In., Pair 1534.00

TUTHILL Cut Glass Company of Middletown, New York, worked from 1902 to 1923. Of special interest are the finely cut pieces of stemware and tableware.

Bowl, Stars, Stripes, Sawtooth, Scalloped Rim, 8 ¼ In. 200.00

TYPEWRITER collectors divide typewriters into two main classifications: the index machine, which has a pointer and a dial for letter selection, and the keyboard machine, most commonly seen today. The first successful typewriter was made by Sholes and Glidden in 1874.

Commercial Visible, No. 6, Wasp Waist, Case, c.1898. . . . . 4682.00
Corona, Standard, Animal Pictures On Keypads, Case, Child's . . . . . *illus* 70500.00
Hammond Multiplex, 2-Row Keyboard, Oak Bentwood Case . . . . . *illus* 235.00
Nippon, 2380 Characters, Spare Ribbon, Japan, c.1958 . . . . . 1087.00
Olympia, Manual, Portable, Case, Germany 18.00
Peoples, Typewheel Cover, c.1893 . . . . . 1034.00
Remington, Gold Letters, Canada, Early 1900s, 11 x 13 x 14 In. 120.00
Royal, Quiet De Luxe, Portable, Case, 1950s. 23.00
Smith Corona, Silent Super, Blue, Pica Type, Metal, Plastic Case, 11 ½ x 12 In.. . . . . 16.00
Smith Corona, Sterling, Portable, Case, 1940s 67.00
Underwood, Leader, Basket Shift, 1940s 103.00
Underwood, Portable, White Glass Keys, Glossy Black Finish. 66.00
Underwood, Portable, White Keys, Gold & Red Decals, Case, Brush, 1940s. 74.00
Woodstock, Standard, Model 5N, c.1923 . . . . . 10.00
Writing Ball, 54 Typebars, No. 97, Malling-Hansen, Case, 1867. . . . . *illus* 79930.00

TYPEWRITER RIBBON TINS are now being collected. The lithographed tin containers have been used since the 1870s. Most popular with collectors are tins with pictorial graphics.

Allied, Bird Flying, Allied Carbon & Ribbon Mfg. Co. 34.00
Carnation, Miller, 2 ⅝ In. 15.00
Carter's, Ideal, Nylon, Royal No. 10, 1950s, 2 ½ In. 8.00
Carter's, Midnight, Round, Black Ground, White Stars, Carter Ink Co. 12.00
Carter's, Valiant, Woman's Silhouette 12.00
Columbia, Square, 2 ½ In.. . . . . 10.00
Elk, Sealed, Cellophane Wrap, Miller, Bryant, Pierce Co. 10.00
Hallmark, Cameron Mfg., Dallas, Tex., 2 ½ In. 20.00
Herald Square, No. 3, Square, 2 Packs 20.00
Keelox, Burroughs, 2 x 1 ¼ In. 16.00
Keelox, Gold 12.00
Keelox, Round, Red, White 18.00
Keelox, Royal, No. 10, Square 12.00
M & M, Mittag & Volger Inc., Park Ridge, N.J. 8.00
Tagger, 2 ½ In. 12.00
Thorobred, Round, Red Ground, Gold, White, Underwood Corp.. . . . . 20.00
Type Bar, LC Smith Corona Typewriters, Square 14.00
Underwood, 1 ⅝ In.. . . . . 12.00
Vogue, Green & Blue Flowers, Art Deco, 2 ½ In. 13.00
Webster Star Brand, Hinged Lid, Boston, Mass. 18.00

TIP
Display groups of at least three of your collectibles to get decorating impact.

Corona, Standard, Animal Pictures On Keypads, Case, Child's
$70500.00

Hammond Multiplex, 2-Row Keyboard, Oak Bentwood Case
$235.00

Typewriter, Writing Ball, 54 Typebars, No. 97, Malling-Hansen, Case, 1867
$79930.00

TIP
Don't turn on the porch light if you will be gone for a long time. It tells everyone that you are away. Install a photocell light that automatically turns on at dusk, off at daylight, or you can install a gas light.

Val St. Lambert, Vase, Blue Chameleon On Branch, Green Ground, Cameo, 4⅝ In. $1180.00

Val St. Lambert, Wine, Colored Bowl, Clear Stem, 8 x 3½ In., 24 Piece $2900.00

TIP
Store parasols and umbrellas closed.

UHL pottery was made in Evansville, Indiana, in 1854. The pottery moved to Huntingburg, Indiana, in 1908. Stoneware and glazed pottery were made until the mid-1940s.

Batter Jug, Blue, White Interior, Handle, 5 x 8 In. 19.00
Churn, Blue Huntington Acorn Stamp, 3 Gal. 250.00
Cookie Jar, Ransburg, Orange, White Glaze, Tan Clay, 9¾ In. 65.00
Figurine, Dog, Cocker Spaniel, Miniature, Blue, 1⅝ x 2⅛ In. 99.00
Jug, Sandstone, Handle, No. 125, 1940s, 10¼ In. 20.00
Pitcher, Globe Shape, Blue, Multicolored Flowers, Ransburg, 3-Footed, 6 x 7¾ In. 65.00

UMBRELLA collectors like rain or shine. The first known umbrella was owned by King Louis XIII of France in 1637. The earliest umbrellas were sunshades, not designed to be used in the rain. The umbrella was embellished and redesigned many times. In 1852, the fluted steel rib style was developed, and it has remained the most useful style.

Asian, Brown Paper, Wood Spokes, Hand Painted Flowers, 24½ In. 25.00
Bakelite Handle, Black Ground, Blue, Red, 24 In. 60.00
Bakelite Handle, Red Plaid, Multicolored, Bakelite Spoke Holders, 1940s, 22 x ½ In. 95.00
Ball End, Engraved, 12K Gold Handle, France, Reigning Beauty, P.K. & Co., Balto, 12 In. 200.00
Bamboo, Paper, Blue, Pink Flowers, Japan, 1940s, 32 In. 82.00
Black Wood Handle, Dark Blue, Chrome Tip, Silver Plated, Squirrels, Acorns, Leaves, 34 In. 85.00
Bone Handle, 8 Ribs, Gold Tone Trim, Metal, 54 In. 99.00
Brass Handle, Engraved, Metal Shaft, Black, 10 Ribs, Nylon, 1940-50s, 36 x 24 In. 65.00
Carved Handle, Bamboo, Purple Fabric, Flowers, Pink Threading, 25½ In. 30.00
Clear Vinyl, Green, Plastic Flowers On Interior Spokes, Stitching Twisted On Handle, 29 In. 25.00
Lace Over Ivory Nylon, Metal Ribs, Shaft, Painted, Handle, Tassel, 1950s, 25½ In. 50.00
Lucite Handle, Jacquard Weave, Orange, Straw Yellow, 16-Gore 55.00
Lucite Handle, Jacquard Weave, Orange, Yellow, Tan, White, Haas-Jordan, 25½ In. 55.00
Niello Handle, Silver, Russia, 19th Century, 9 x 38 In. 250.00
Parasol, Handle, Ivory, Tigers Intertwined In Teeth, Paws & Fur 995.00
Parasol, Victorian, Black Lace, Ivory, Ivory Handle, Shaft, Knop, 1800s, 22½ In. 175.00
Red Handle, Woven Plaid, Multicolored, 10-Gore, 18½ In. 25.00
Red Plastic Handle, Plaid, Royal Blue, Kelly Green, Orange, Yellow, Black, Japan, 26 In. 25.00
Wood Handle, Asian, Heavy Paper, Bamboo, Wood Handle, Flower Design, 30 x 50 In. 45.00
Wood Handle, Bamboo, Paper, Metal Cap, Green, Orange, Tan Flower, Asia 45.00
Wood Handle, Bamboo, Paper, Metal Cap, Japanese Dragon, Red, Yellow, Black, 31 x 24 In. 50.00
Wood Handle, Black, 1920-30s, 32 In. 60.00
Wood Handle, Parasol, Nylon, Red, White, Blue, 8-Gore, 34 x 46 In. 27.00
Wood Handle, Print, Children Playing, Floating Alphabet Letters, Painted, Child's, 18 In. 45.00
Wood Handle, Red White & Blue, Nylon, Made In USA, 34 In. 27.00
Yellow Plastic Handle, Purple, Black, Blue, Geometric, Brophey Co., c.1940, 23 In. 75.00

UNION PORCELAIN WORKS was established at Greenpoint, New York, in 1848 by Charles Cartlidge. The company went through a series of ownership changes and finally closed in the early 1900s. The company made a fine quality white porcelain that was often decorated in clear, bright colors.

Oyster Plate, 6 Wells, Sea Life, Crab, Fish, Shells, Seaweed, 9½ In. 805.00
Pitcher, Uncle Sam, King Gambrinus, Walrus Spout, Polar Bear Handle, Light Blue, 9¾ In. 8963.00
Vase, Historical Vignettes, George Washington, Buffalo Handles, 12¾ x 10 In. 19200.00

UNIVERSITY CITY POTTERY, of University, Missouri, worked from 1909 to 1915. Well-known artists, including Taxile Doat, Adelaide Alsop Robineau, and Frederick Hurten Rhead, worked there.

Vase, Stylized Trees, Green Matte Glaze, Frederick Rhead, 9 x 5 In. 5100.00

UNIVERSITY OF NORTH DAKOTA, *see North Dakota School of Mines category.*

VAL ST. LAMBERT Cristalleries of Belgium was founded by Messieurs Kemlin and Lelievre in 1825. The company is still in operation. All types of table glassware and decorative glassware have been made. Pieces are often decorated with cut designs.

Bowl, Scalloped Edge, Flowered Center, 3¾ x 10 In. 58.00
Candy Dish, Cover, Green, Cut To Clear, Oval, Art Deco Flowers, 6½ In. 230.00
Knife Rest, Embossed Pillar, 1¼ x 3½ In. 68.00
Paperweight, Unicorn, Abstract Shaped, 4 x 5 x 1½ In. 117.00
Pitcher, Milk, Diamond Cut, Applied Handle, 5¾ x 4¼ In. 65.00

Sauce Bowl, Smooth Interior, Ribbed, Tricornered, 1 5/8 x 4 7/8 In. 39.00
Vase, Blue Chameleon On Branch, Green Ground, Cameo, 4 5/8 In. .... *illus* 1180.00
Vase, Campagna Shape, Square Base, 7 1/4 x 6 3/4 In. 395.00
Vase, Flowers, Leaves, Vines, Brown, Olive Green, Brown Ground, Cameo, 7 1/2 In. 201.00
Vase, Tulip Shape, Engraved Iris, Signed, 16 1/2 In. 700.00
Vase, Twisting Stylized Floral Cutting, 7 3/4 x 6 1/2 In. 175.00
Wine, Colored Bowl, Clear Stem, 8 x 3 1/2 In., 24 Piece .... *illus* 2900.00

VALLERYSTHAL Glassworks was founded in 1836 in Lorraine, France. In 1854, the firm became Klenglin et Cie. It made table and decorative glass, opaline, cameo, and art glass. A line of covered, pressed glass animal dishes was made in the nineteenth century. The firm is still working.

Basket, Opaque Blue Basket Weave, Handles, Marked, c.1900, 2 1/4 x 4 In. 22.00
Dish, Argonaut Shell, 3 Dolphin Feet, Opaque Blue, 6 1/2 x 5 1/2 In. 175.00
Dish, Dog On Rug Cover, Amber, Marked, 5 x 5 x 4 In. .... 150.00 to 250.00
Dish, Dog On Rug Cover, Opaque Blue, Marked, 5 x 5 x 4 In. .... 195.00 to 250.00
Dish, Duck, Swimming, Amber, 5 In. 55.00
Dish, Fish, Milk Glass, Signed, Late 1880s, 7 1/2 In. 225.00
Dish, Hen On Nest Cover, Milk Glass, 1880, 5 In. 37.00
Dish, Mouse On Toadstool Cover, Opaque Ivory, Signed, 6 In. .... *illus* 633.00
Salt, Duck, Gray & Fiery Opalescent, c.1890 .... 29.00
Vase, Grapes & Leaves, Ruby Red, Enameled Dragonfly, Gold Streaks, 4 x 6 1/2 In. 3450.00
Vase, Mottled Yellow, Red Flowers, Insects, Blue, Gold Foot, Cameo, 7 In. 2013.00

VAN BRIGGLE pottery was started by Artus Van Briggle in Colorado Springs, Colorado, after 1901. Van Briggle had been a decorator at Rookwood Pottery of Cincinnati, Ohio. He died in 1904 and his wife took over managing the pottery. The wares usually had modeled relief decorations and a soft, dull glaze. The pottery is still working and still making some of the original designs.

Bookends, Peacock, Mountain Craig Brown, Felt Bottom, 4 3/4 x 5 1/2 In. 325.00
Console, Blue To Aqua, Scalloped & Rolled Rim, c.1920, 2 3/4 x 14 In. 175.00
Figurine, Bunny, Purple Over Blue Matte, Marked, 2 3/4 In. .... *illus* 87.00
Jardiniere, Rustic Bark, Pink Matte Glaze, 1914, 3 1/2 x 9 3/4 In. 150.00
Lamp, Owl, Persian Rose Glaze, Yellow Glass Eyes, 9 1/2 x 4 1/2 In. 600.00
Lamp, Woman At The Well, 14 In., Pair 450.00
Mug, Eagle, Black Crystalline Glaze, 1907, 4 1/2 In. 529.00
Mug, Fraternity, Kappa Epsilon, Feathered Green Matte Glaze, 1908, 6 3/4 x 5 In. 840.00
Paperweight, Figural, Horned Toad, Amber, Green, 1 1/4 x 4 1/2 In. 1140.00
Tea Set, 2-Tone Blue Matte Glaze, Rattan Handle On Teapot, Teapot 4 1/4 In., 3 Piece 411.00
Teapot, Cover, Rattan Handle, Green To Brown Glaze, 4 1/8 In. 153.00
Tile, Incised, Painted Landscape, Oak Frame, Treed Scene, 6 In. 2760.00
Vase, Arts & Crafts, Green Matte, c.1920, 6 x 2 1/2 In. 395.00
Vase, Blossoms, Frothy Green Matte Glaze, Chocolate Brown Clay, 6 1/4 x 4 In. 1440.00
Vase, Bowl, Squat, Gray Matte, Paneled Flowers, c.1906, 2 1/2 x 6 In. 600.00
Vase, Bud, Green To Blue, c.1950, 8 1/4 In. 53.00
Vase, Bud, Trillium, Lime Green Glaze, 6 1/2 x 3 In. 1920.00
Vase, Bulbous, 2 Handles, Turquoise, c.1905, 6 1/2 x 7 1/2 In. 795.00
Vase, Bulbous, Art Nouveau, Spiderwort, c.1920, 4 x 4 3/4 In. 225.00
Vase, Bulbous, Flowers, Branches, Rose Glaze, Blue Blush, Handles, Marked, 9 1/2 In. 147.00
Vase, Bulbous, Full Height Leaves, Blue Matte Glaze, 1917, 4 1/2 x 3 1/2 In. 540.00
Vase, Bulbous, Maroon & Green Glaze, 1905, 4 1/2 x 5 1/2 In. 960.00
Vase, Bulbous, Raised Calla Lily, Turquoise Glaze, Blue Highlights, 10 3/8 In. 207.00
Vase, Bulbous, Raised Flower, Maroon & Blue Matte, c.1920, 7 x 8 1/2 In. 720.00
Vase, Bulbous, Spade Leaf Flowers, Red Brown Matte Glaze, 1912, 2 1/4 In. 499.00
Vase, Bulbous, Tobacco Leaves, Green & Brown Matte Glaze, 4 1/2 x 4 3/4 In. 1680.00
Vase, Charcoal Matte Glaze, Shouldered, Incised Mark, c.1902, 10 1/2 x 6 1/2 In. 2880.00
Vase, Cream Matte, Frosted, Mottled, Yellow Rim, c.1906, 9 1/2 x 4 1/2 In. 2295.00
Vase, Crocuses, Blue Matte Glaze, 1908, 5 1/4 x 3 3/4 In. 1200.00
Vase, Dragonfly, Mulberry, c.1920, 7 x 3 1/4 In. 345.00
Vase, Flared, Blossoms, Yellow, Pearl Gray Glaze, 9 1/2 x 4 1/2 In. 1320.00
Vase, Flared, Egret, Turquoise Ground, 1930s, 16 3/4 In. 384.00
Vase, Flared, Morning Glories, Frothy Green Glaze, 8 x 6 In. 1440.00
Vase, Flared Cylindrical, Stylized Tulip, Rose Glaze, Blue Relief, Early 1900s, 17 In. 353.00
Vase, Flared Shape, Green Matte Glaze, Incised Marks, c.1905, 4 1/2 x 4 In. 518.00
Vase, Flowers, Maroon & Blue Matte Glaze, 12 x 10 1/2 In. 3000.00
Vase, Flowers, Petals, Branches, Leaves, Rose Glaze, Blue Blush, Handles, 9 1/2 In. 147.00
Vase, Gathered Neck, c.1914, 4 1/4 x 3 1/2 In. 395.00

Vallerysthal, Dish,
Mouse On Toadstool Cover,
Opaque Ivory, Signed, 6 In.
$633.00

Van Briggle, Figurine, Bunny,
Purple Over Blue Matte,
Marked, 2 3/4 In.
$87.00

Van Briggle Marks

Van Briggle pottery has been made since 1901. Pieces are usually marked "AA" and "Colorado Springs," sometimes in abbreviated form. "Original," used after 1920, means the piece was turned on a wheel, not made in a mold. "Hand carved" was used on pieces with carved, not molded decorations. "Hand decorated" was used for slip decorated pieces. None of these marks add extra value.

Vasa Murrhina, Vase, Red, Blue, White Marbling, Silver Mica Chips, c.1890, 5½ In., Pair
$240.00

Vasart, Lamp, Sapphire Blue, Millefiori Confetti, Mottled White, Tooled Rim, 10⅜ In.
$250.00

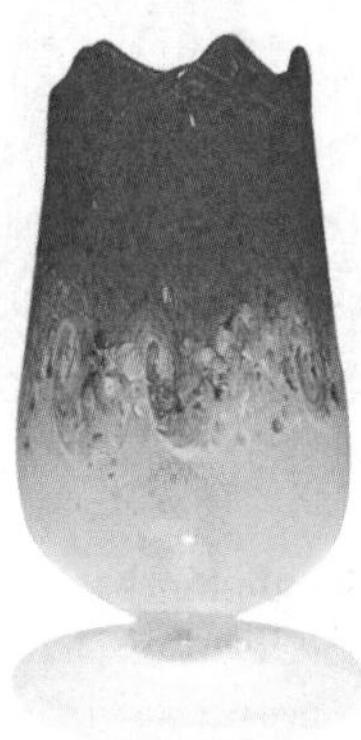

Vaseline Glass, Fish Bowl, Wrought Iron Floor Stand, c.1930, 44 x 14 In.
$258.00

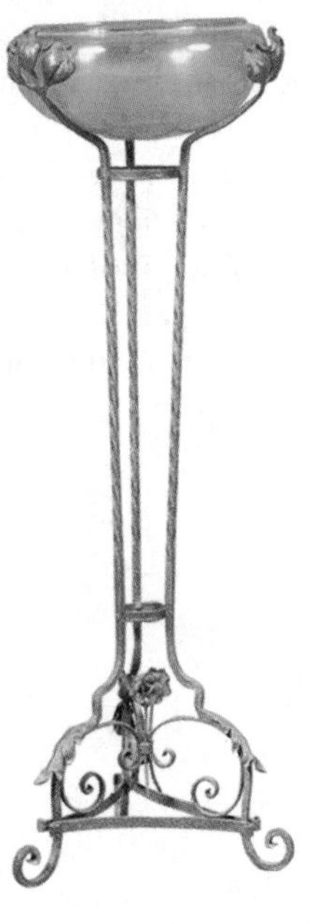

Vase, Geese, Green Matte, Chartreuse Glaze, 1903, 6¼ x 5½ In. 7800.00
Vase, Geometric Design, Maroon & Blue Matte Glaze, Handles, c.1925, 15 x 8 In. 600.00
Vase, Green Matte, 2 Handles, 11¼ x 10½ In. 1095.00
Vase, Green Matte, Flower Panels, Arts & Crafts c.1907, 4½ x 5 In. 995.00
Vase, Green Matte Glaze, 1902, 4¼ x 3 In. 1320.00
Vase, Green Peacock Feathers, Purple Ground, Footed Base, 13 x 4¼ In. 42000.00
Vase, Herons, Blue, 17 In. 351.00
Vase, Large Shouldered Form, Charcoal Matte Glaze, Marked, 1902, 6½ In. 2880.00
Vase, Leaf, Flower, Mulberry Glaze, Arts & Crafts, c.1920, 3¼ x 3 In. 245.00
Vase, Leathery Blue Green Glaze, 1905, 9¾ x 4¼ In. 1320.00
Vase, Lorelei, Rose Glaze, Blue Blush, Impressed, 10½ In. 470.00
Vase, Lotus Blossoms, Mottled Glossy Turquoise Glaze, 2¾ x 2¾ In. 300.00
Vase, Molded Design, Maroon & Blue Matte Glaze, 2 Handles, c.1925, 7 x 7½ In. 316.00
Vase, Molded Leaves, Green, Mountain Craig Brown Matte, Handles, 1920s, 8½ In. 353.00
Vase, Moth, Mulberry & Blue Glaze, c.1920, 3 x 3½ In. 100.00
Vase, Mountain Craig Brown, c.1920, 2½ x 3¼ In. 195.00
Vase, Mountain Craig Brown, c.1920, 3¼ x 6½ In. 295.00
Vase, Nautilus, Turquoise Glazed, Blue Highlights, Monogram, 5⅝ x 17 In. 207.00
Vase, Olive Green Matte, 2 Handles, c.1903, 11 x 4½ In. 1095.00
Vase, Overlapping Leaves, Brown To Green Matte Glaze, 1920, 5 In. 294.00
Vase, Poppies, Pod, Blue Matte, c.1902, 8 x 3¾ In. 16900.00
Vase, Poppy Pods, Robin's-Egg Blue Glaze, Brown Clay, 9½ x 4¾ In. 4200.00
Vase, Raised Organic Design, Cream, Light Blue Matte Glaze, c.1904, 5½ In. 1560.00
Vase, Round, Brown, Green, Leafy Footed Base, 1916, 3 x 3½ In. 390.00
Vase, Shouldered Shape, Raised Poppy, Blue & Green Glaze, 1916, 3½ x 7½ In. 600.00
Vase, Squat, Organic At Neck, Brown & Pink Glaze, Incised, 1912, 4 x 4¾ In. 660.00
Vase, Stylized Daffodil, Maroon & Blue Matte, Shape No. 133, c.1920, 4½ x 13 In. 520.00
Vase, Stylized Flowers, Blue Matte, Shape No. 661, 3 x 7 In. 360.00
Vase, Stylized Leaves, c.1907, 6¾ x 2¾ In. 1895.00
Vase, Swollen Neck, Poppies, Green To Brown Matte Crystalline Glaze, 7¼ In. 1998.00
Vase, Tapered, Dragonflies, Green & Purple Glaze, 9¾ x 4¾ In. 1080.00
Vase, Tapered, Yucca, Yellow & Green Glaze, 1903, 12½ x 5 In. 2760.00
Vase, Trefoils, Green Matte Glaze, 1907-11, 7½ x 3½ In. 1020.00
Vase, Trefoils, Indigo & Green Glaze, 2 Handles, 1903, 12¼ x 5¼ In. 2160.00
Vase, Vertical Ribbing, c.1920, 17¼ x 6¼ In. 550.00

VASA MURRHINA is the name of a glassware made by the Vasa Murrhina Art Glass Company of Sandwich, Massachusetts, about 1884. The glassware was transparent and was embedded with small pieces of colored glass and metallic flakes. The mica flakes were coated with silver, gold, copper, or nickel. Some of the pieces were cased. The same type of glass was made in England. Collectors often confuse Vasa Murrhina glass with aventurine, spatter, or spangle glass. There is uncertainty about what actually was made by the Vasa Murrhina factory. Related pieces may be listed under Spangle Glass.

Pitcher, Water, Bulbous, Cranberry, White Spatter, Silver Mica, 8½ In. 173.00
Vase, Red, Blue, White Marbling, Silver Mica Chips, c.1890, 5½ In., Pair .... *illus* 240.00
Water Set, Mottled Red, White, Silver, Melon Ribbed, 5 Piece 518.00

VASART glass was made in Scotland. Salvador Ysart and his sons Vincent and Augustine started the Ysart Brothers Glass factory in Perth, Scotland, in 1946. They called the glass *Vasart*, using the initial of each man's first name and the last part of Ysart. The company name became Vasart Glass Ltd. in 1956. The glass is marked with the acid-etched name *Vasart* in script or, after 1956, with a paper label. The company was renamed Strathearn Glass in 1965. Stuart Glass bought the company in 1980 and all of the Vasart lines were discontinued. The company's paperweights are the products best known to collectors today.

Vasart

Lamp, Sapphire Blue, Millefiori Confetti, Mottled White, Tooled Rim, 10⅜ In. .... *illus* 250.00

VASELINE GLASS is a greenish-yellow glassware resembling petroleum jelly. Pressed glass of the 1870s was often made of vaseline-colored glass. Some vaseline glass is still being made in old and new styles. Additional pieces of vaseline glass may also be listed under Pressed Glass in this book.

Basket, Opalescent, Ruffled Pink Rim, Twisted Branch Handle, 9 In. 230.00
Cordial, Panel Optic Bowl, c.1950, 4¼ x 3 In., 4 Piece 30.00
Cruet, Petticoat, Gold Paint, Stopper, Handle, c.1901 .... 350.00
Fish Bowl, Black Glass Base, 1920-30, 12 x 12 In., 2 Piece 795.00
Fish Bowl, Wrought Iron Floor Stand, c.1930, 44 x 14 In. .... *illus* 258.00

itcher, Rolled Rim, 20th Century, 9 ¼ In. 47.00
orte Plate, Opalescent, Handle, c.1940, 9 ½ x 4 In. 48.00

ENETIAN GLASS, *see Glass-Venetian category.*

ENINI GLASS *is listed in the Glass-Venetian category.*

ERLYS glass was made in Rouen, France, by the Société Holophane Français, a company hat started in 1920. It was made in Newark, Ohio, from 1935 to 1951. The art glass is ither blown or molded. The American glass is signed with a diamond-point-scratched name, but the rench pieces are marked with a molded signature. The designs resemble those used by Lalique.

shtray, Swallow, Frosted, 4 ¾ x 3 ⅝ In. 35.00
owl, Birds & Dragonflies, Frosted, Signed, 2 ¼ x 11 ¾ In. .... *illus* 76.00
owl, Centerpiece, Birds & Bees, Satin Frosted, 2 $\frac{5}{16}$ x 11 ½ In. 165.00
owl, Lovebirds, Fan Shape, Footed, Frosted, Signed, 1935-51, 6 ½ x 4 ¾ In. 95.00
owl, Pinecone, Frosted, 6 In. .... 20.00 to 45.00
owl, Tassel, Frosted, Signed, 12 In. 450.00
owl, Thistle, Frosted, 1935-51, 8 ½ In. 50.00
owl, Water Lilies, French Opalescent, Signed, 13 ¾ In. 289.00
harger, Lotus Blossoms, Leaves, Frosted, Signed, 14 In. 120.00
late, Girl, Ewe & Lamb, Frosted Image, 13 In. 29.00
ase, Lovebirds, Fan Shape, Frosted, 4 ¼ x 6 ½ In. 105.00
ase, Mandarin, Frosted, c.1935-51, 9 x 5 In. 425.00

ERNON KILNS was the name used by Vernon Potteries, Ltd. The company, which started in 931 in Vernon, California, made dinnerware and figurines until it went out of business in 958. The molds were bought by Metlox, which continued to make some patterns. Collectors search for e brightly colored dinnerware and the pieces designed by Rockwell Kent, Walt Disney, and Don landing. For more information, see *Kovels' Depression Glass & Dinnerware Price List.*

rcadia, Platter, 12 In. 22.00
rcadia, Sugar, Cover, Handles 13.00
arkwood, Pitcher & Tumbler Set, 2-Qt. Pitcher, 9 Tumblers 59.00
everly, Teapot, 10 In. 64.00
its Of The Old Northwest, Plate, Log Jam, 8 ½ In. .... *illus* 125.00
lack Americana, Plate, Bits Of The Old South, Cypress Swamp, 1940s, 8 ½ In. 34.00
lack Americana, Plate, Southern Mansion, 1940s, 8 ½ In. 34.00
lack Americana, Platter, Bits Of The Old South, Slavery Scenes, 14 In. 98.00
luebird, Planter, Aqua, 5 ½ x 7 ½ x 6 ½ In. 19.00
rown Eyed Susan, Plate, Bread & Butter, 6 ½ In. 8.00
rown Eyed Susan, Salt & Pepper 18.00
asual California, Creamer, Brown 15.00
asual California, Creamer, Yellow 15.00
entral Park, Bowl, Divided 30.00
hintz, Bowl, Vegetable, 9 In. 35.00
hintz, Chop Plate, 12 ½ In. 40.00
hintz, Chop Plate, 13 ¾ In. 60.00
hintz, Creamer, 1940s 20.00
hintz, Cup & Saucer, After Dinner .... *illus* 40.00
hintz, Plate, Bread & Butter, 6 ½ In. 10.00
hintz, Plate, Salad, 7 ½ In. 12.00
ommemorative, Plate, General Douglas MacArthur, 10 ½ In. 29.00
ommemorative, Plate, Gibraltar Of The South, Vicksburg, Miss., Blue, White, 10 In. 75.00
ommemorative, Plate, Mount Rainier, Paradise Lodge, Washington State, 10 In. 64.00
ommemorative, Plate, Veiled Prophet, St. Louis, c.1940, 10 ⅜ In. .... 25.00 to 30.00
ommemorative, Plate, Will Rogers, 1935, 10 ½ In. 37.00
oronado, Coffee Server, Bakelite Handle 39.00
esert Bloom, Bowl, Oval, Scalloped Edge 26.00
esert Bloom, Coffeepot, Lid, 10 ½ In. 85.00
esert Bloom, Gravy, Underplate 42.00
olores, Plate, Dinner, 10 ½ In. 12.00
arly California, Bowl, Blue, Oval, 9 ¾ In. 14.00
arly California, Platter, Light Blue, 12 In. 35.00
arly California, Salt & Pepper 15.00
arly California, Shaker, Dark Blue 15.00
ayety, Sugar & Creamer 28.00

Verlys, Bowl, Birds & Dragonflies, Frosted, Signed, 2 ¼ x 11 ¾ In.
$76.00

Vernon Kilns, Bits Of The Old Northwest, Plate, Log Jam, 8 ½ In.
$125.00

Vernon Kilns, Chintz, Cup & Saucer, After Dinner
$40.00

Vernon Kilns, Gingham, Pitcher, Qt.
$40.00

VERNON KILNS

Vernon Kilns, Homespun, Bowl, Vegetable, Divided, Oval, 2 x 6¾ x 11¾ In. $22.00

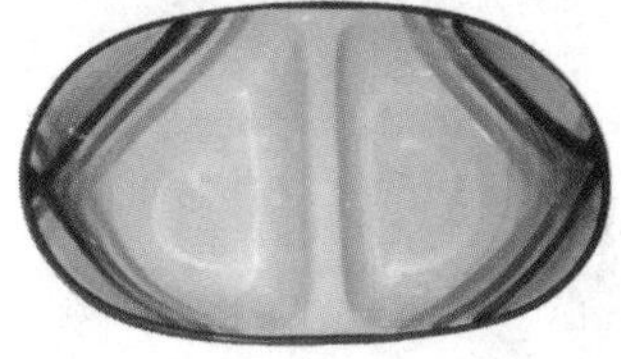

Vernon Kilns, May Flower, Plate, Dinner, 10½ In. $27.00

Vernon Kilns, Organdie, Creamer, 3 In. $13.00

Vernon Kilns Plaid Patterns

Gingham (1949 to 1958), green and yellow plaid with a dark green border.
Homespun (1948 to 1958), cinnamon, green, and yellow.
Organdie (1940s and '50s), brown and yellow.
Tam O'Shanter (1949 to 1958), rust, chartreuse, and dark green.
Tweed (1950 to 1955), yellow and gray blue.

Gingham, Bowl, Cereal, Deep . . . 20.00

Gingham, Bowl, Vegetable, 8⅞ In. . . . 25.00

Gingham, Butter, Cover . . . 55.00

Gingham, Pitcher, Qt. . . . *illus* 40.00

Gingham, Plate, Bread & Butter, 6½ In. . . . 5.00

Gingham, Plate, Dinner, 10½ In. . . . 18.00

Gingham, Plate, Salad, 7½ In. . . . 12.00

Gingham, Plate, Luncheon, 9¾ In. . . . 9.00

Gingham, Platter, 14 In. . . . 25.00

Gingham, Sugar & Creamer . . . 35.00

Gingham, Tumbler, 1950s, 14 Oz. . . . 22.00

Hawaiian, Tumbler Set, Lei Lani, 5½ In., 6 Piece . . . 695.00

Heavenly Days, Pitcher, 6¼ x 5¾ In. . . . 7.00

Heyday, Cup & Saucer . . . 10.00

Heyday, Plate, Bread & Butter, 6 In. . . . 8.00

Hibiscus, Bowl, Chowder, Lug Handles . . . 24.00

Hibiscus, Bowl, Vegetable, Oval . . . 28.00

Hibiscus, Gravy Boat, Attached Underplate . . . 45.00

Homespun, Bowl, 2⅜ x 9 In. . . . 19.00

Homespun, Bowl, Vegetable, Divided, Oval, 2 x 6¾ x 11¾ In. . . . *illus* 22.00

Homespun, Casserole, Cover, 8 x 11 In. . . . 45.00

Homespun, Chop Plate, 12 In. . . . 18.00 to 28.00

Homespun, Cup & Saucer . . . 8.00

Homespun, Gravy Boat . . . 22.00

Homespun, Plate, Dessert, 6⅜ In. . . . 7.00

Homespun, Platter, Oval, 10 x ¼ In. . . . 25.00

Homespun, Platter, Round, 12¼ In. . . . 26.00

Homespun, Salt & Pepper . . . 8.00

Homespun, Sugar, Cover . . . 17.00

Linda, Bowl, Fruit, 5⅝ In. . . . 10.00

Linda, Chop Plate, 12¼ In. . . . 32.00

Linda, Cup & Saucer . . . 17.00

Linda, Plate, Dinner, 9⅝ In. . . . 18.00

May Flower, Bowl, Vegetable, Oval . . . 30.00

May Flower, Bowl Set, Chowder, Lug Handles, 7⅜ In., 4 Piece . . . 90.00

May Flower, Cup & Saucer . . . 15.00

May Flower, Plate, Bread & Butter, 6½ In. . . . 15.00

May Flower, Plate, Dinner, 10½ In. . . . *illus* 27.00

May Flower, Plate, Luncheon, 9⅜ In. . . . 9.00

May Flower, Platter, Oval, 13½ In. . . . 30.00

May Flower, Saucer . . . 8.00

Modern California, Chop Plate, 13 In. . . . 49.00

Modern California, Tray, Purple, Oval . . . 37.00

Monterey, Plate, Bread & Butter, 6½ In. . . . 9.00

Monterey, Plate, Dinner, 10¼ In. . . . 15.00

Monterey, Plate, Luncheon, 9⅜ In. . . . 13.00

Monterey, Platter, Oval, 13¾ x 10⅜ In. . . . 35.00

Organdie, Bowl, Divided, 10½ In. . . . 28.00

Organdie, Bowl, Vegetable, 2¼ x 9 In. . . . 35.00

Organdie, Butter, Cover, 2⅝ x 7¼ x 3½ In. . . . 35.00

Organdie, Chop Plate, 12 In. . . . 30.00

Organdie, Coffeepot, 8⅜ In. . . . 65.00

Organdie, Creamer, 2⅞ x 3⅝ In. . . . 7.00 to 12.00

Organdie, Creamer, 3 In. . . . *illus* 13.00

Organdie, Cup & Saucer . . . 8.00

Organdie, Mixing Bowl, 9 In. . . . 45.00

Organdie, Plate, Dinner, 10½ In. . . . 7.00

Organdie, Plate, Luncheon, 9⅝ In. . . . 7.00

Organdie, Salt & Pepper . . . 15.00

Organdie, Sugar, Cover, 4¼ x 3½ In. . . . 18.00

Poppy Trails, Teapot, Pepper Tree, 7 In. . . . 55.00

Porthole, Plate, Dinner, Marine Series, 10½ In. . . . 225.00

Raffia, Bowl, Vegetable, Cover, 10¾ In. . . . 52.00

Raffia, Butter, Cover . . . 35.00

Raffia, Plate, Bread & Butter, 6 In. . . . 4.00

Raffia, Plate, Dinner, 10⅛ In. . . . 10.00

Rio Chico, Cup & Saucer.... 18.00
Rosedale, Soup, Dish, 8 ½ In.... 12.00
Sherwood, Carafe, 2 Qt.... 38.00
Sherwood, Relish, 12 ½ x 7 In.... 25.00
Sierra Madre, Charger, 12 ½ In.... 12.00
Souvenir, Ashtray, Alaska, Maroon, White, 5 ¾ In.... 10.00
Souvenir, Ashtray, Alaska, Snow, Icebergs, Walrus, Red Transfer, 5 ½ In.... 15.00
Souvenir, Ashtray, Arizona, Maroon, White, Round, 5 ½ In.... 7.00
Souvenir, Ashtray, Kentucky, 5 ¾ In.... 16.00
Souvenir, Ashtray, Montana, 5 ¾ In.... 10.00
Souvenir, Ashtray, Nebraska, Maroon, White, 5 ¾ In.... 10.00
Souvenir, Ashtray, Oklahoma, Maroon, White, 5 ¾ In.... 10.00
Souvenir, Ashtray, Utah, 5 ¾ In.... 10.00
Souvenir, Plate, 48th National Convention Of Postmasters, Oct. 12-16, 1952, 10 ½ In.... 18.00
Souvenir, Plate, Alaska, Husky Dog, 10 ½ In.... *illus* 35.00
Souvenir, Plate, Carlsbad Caverns, 10 ½ In.... *illus* 35.00
Souvenir, Plate, Carlsbad Caverns, Whites City, New Mexico, 10 ½ In.... 12.00
Souvenir, Plate, Charleston, South Carolina, 1930s, 10 ½ In.... 33.00
Souvenir, Plate, Colorado, Red Transfer, Grand Lake, Pikes Peak.... 25.00
Souvenir, Plate, Colorado Springs, States, Cities, Colleges, 10 ½ In.... 24.00
Souvenir, Plate, Delaware, 10 ½ In.... 36.00
Souvenir, Plate, Dwight, Illinois, 10 ½ In.... 15.00
Souvenir, Plate, Fort Benning, Ga., 10 ¼ In.... 38.00
Souvenir, Plate, Illinois, 10 ½ In.... 37.00
Souvenir, Plate, Jacksonville, Florida, 10 ½ In.... 16.00
Souvenir, Plate, Kentucky, Maroon Transfer, Sites, Man-O-War, 10 ⅜ In.... 24.00
Souvenir, Plate, New Mexico, 10 ½ In.... 35.00
Souvenir, Plate, North Carolina, 10 ½ In.... *illus* 33.00
Souvenir, Plate, Our West, First Edition, 1942, 10 ½ In.... 48.00
Souvenir, Plate, Palm Springs, 1950s, 10 ½ In.... 38.00
Souvenir, Plate, Pennsylvania Turnpike, 10 ½ In.... 35.00
Souvenir, Plate, Savannah, Georgia, 10½ In.... 20.00 to 38.00
Souvenir, Plate, South Dakota, Mt. Rushmore, 10 ½ In.... 45.00
Souvenir, Plate, St. Augustine, 10 ½ In.... 15.00
Souvenir, Plate, St. Louis, Missouri, 10 ½ In.... 16.00
Souvenir, Plate, Statue Of Liberty, Bedloe Island, 10 In.... 33.00 to 40.00
Souvenir, Plate, Tennessee, 10 In.... 15.00
Souvenir, Plate, University Of Washington, 10 ½ In.... 12.00
Souvenir, Plate, Vicksburg, Mississippi, Gibraltar Of The South, 10 In.... 75.00
Souvenir, Plate, Wisconsin, 10 ½ In.... 10.00
Tam O'Shanter, Cup & Saucer.... 10.00
Tam O'Shanter, Saucer.... 5.00
Trade Winds, Plate, Bread & Butter, 6 In.... 6.00
Trade Winds, Platter, Oval, 13 ½ In.... 27.00
Trailing Rose, Platter, Round, 12 ¼ In.... 45.00
Tweed, Sugar.... 15.00
Woodleaf, Gravy Boat, Attached Underplate.... 30.00

VERRE DE SOIE glass was first made by Frederick Carder at the Steuben Glass Works from about 1905 to 1930. It is an iridescent glass of soft white or very, very pale green. The name means "*glass of silk*," and it does resemble silk. Other factories have made verre de soie, and some of the English examples were made of different colors. Verre de soie is an art glass and is not related to the iridescent, pressed, white carnival glass mistakenly called by its name. Related pieces may be found in the Steuben category.

Basket, Coupe Shape, Triangular Handle, Berry Prunts, Steuben, 12 In.... 345.00
Basket, Ruffled Edge, Berry Buttons, Arched Handle, Steuben, 10 In.... 382.00
Bowl, Floral, Coupe, 4 Pinch Sides, Cupped Rim, 6 In.... 230.00
Bowl, Iridescent, Red, Green, Gold, Flared Rim, Steuben, 11 ½ In.... 230.00
Bowl, Marina Blue Rim & Feet, Signed, Steuben, 9 In.... 405.00
Candlestick, Pink Lip Wrap, Bobeche With Shield, Flower Etching, 10 ½ In.... 863.00
Cologne, Intaglio Flowers, Raised Bands, Shouldered, Hawkes, 5 ½ In.... 546.00
Lemonade Set, Applied Green Threading, Steuben, 9 x 10 In.... 805.00
Loving Cup, Blue Threading, Applied Handles, c.1900, 6 In.... *illus* 200.00
Perfume Bottle, Blue Dabber, Steuben, 4 ½ In.... 316.00

TIP

The water for your dishwasher should be set at over 120 degrees to help prevent the spread of disease, but it should be under 140 degrees to avoid unnecessary stress and damage on old dishes.

Vernon Kilns, Souvenir, Plate, Alaska, Husky Dog, 10 ½ In.
$35.00

Vernon Kilns, Souvenir, Plate, Carlsbad Caverns, 10 ½ In.
$35.00

Vernon Kilns, Souvenir, Plate, North Carolina, 10 ½ In.
$33.00

Verre De Soie, Loving Cup, Blue Threading, Applied Handles, c.1900, 6 In.
$200.00

Vienna Art, Plate, Independence Beer, Topless Woman, Tin, 1905, 10 In.
$350.00

Villeroy Boch, Vase, Boy Climbing, Roses, Applied, Ewer Form, Marked, c.1842-60, 13 In.
$165.00

TIP

Quick cure for a leaking flower vase: Coat the outside and inside with clear silicone household glue. Coat again if it still leaks.

Perfume Bottle, Blue Jade Dabber, Steuben, 4½ In. 374.00
Perfume Bottle, Cone, Elongated Amber Stopper, Steuben, 7 In. 288.00
Perfume Bottle, Fig Shape, Blue Jade Flame Stopper, Steuben, 3 In. 470.00
Perfume Bottle, Glass, Black Stopper, Steuben, 3 In. 390.00
Perfume Bottle, Light Amethyst Stopper, Steuben, 7 In. 300.00
Perfume Bottle, Melon Ribbed, Green Jade Stopper, Steuben, 4½ In. 575.00
Sherbet, Flared Rim, Steuben, 3¾ x 3¾ In., 6 Piece 288.00
Vase, Applied Green Jade, Marked, 12 In. 345.00
Vase, Ribbed, Applied Light Blue Jade Threading & Prunts, Flared, 10 In. 999.00
Vase, Tapered Optic Ribbed Body, Ruffled Rim, Gold Ruby Threading, Steuben, 4 In. 144.00
Vase, Urn Shape, Footed, Rose Lip Wrap, 7 In. 518.00

VIENNA, *see Beehive category.*

VIENNA ART plates are round metal serving trays produced at the turn of the century. The designs, copied from Royal Vienna porcelain plates, usually featured a portrait of a woman encircled by a wide, ornate border. Many were used as advertising or promotional items and were produced in Coshocton, Ohio, by J. F. Meeks Tuscarora Advertising Co. and H.D. Beach's Standard Advertising Co.

VIENNA ART PLATES PAT. FEB. 21ST 1905

Face Mask, Keramos, Marked, 5¾ x 5¼ In. 25.00
Plate, Goddess, In Garden, Birds, c.1900, 10 In. 25.00
Plate, Goddess Artemis, Cupids In Forest, c.1900, 10 In. 39.00
Plate, Independence Beer, Topless Woman, Tin, 1905, 10 In. .... *illus* 350.00
Plate, Jno. T. Barbee Co. Distillers, Louisville Ky., Girls, Log Cabin, c.1906, 10 In. 575.00
Vase, Double Handles, Birds, Blue & Green, c.1914, 15 x 6 In. 225.00

VILLEROY & BOCH Pottery of Mettlach was founded in 1836. The firm made many types of wares, including the famous Mettlach steins. Collectors can be confused because although Villeroy & Boch made most of its pieces in the city of Mettlach, Germany, they also had factories in other locations. The dating code impressed on the bottom of most pieces makes it possible to determine the age of the piece. Additional items, including steins and earthenware pieces marked with the famous castle mark or the word *Mettlach*, may be found in the Mettlach category.

Charger, Mettlach Castle Scene, Scalloped Rim, Marked, Dec 187-B, 18 In. 275.00
Figurine, Bird, Beak Behind Wing, White, 7¾ In. 345.00
Medallion, Woman, Children, Man, Cherub, Green, White, Marked, J.B., 2¾ In., Pair 276.00
Plaque, Hannover, Hand Painted, Gold Rim, Dresden, 12 In. 115.00
Plate, Die Heilige Familie, 1977, 11½ In. 99.00
Salt Container, Blue Onion, 9½ In. 70.00
Tile, Cavalier, On Branch, Hand Painted, Wood Frame, Dresden, 11½ x 7½ In. 87.00
Tray, Fish, On Basket, 25 In. 173.00
Tray, Woman, Blossoming From Flower, Holding Stein, Verse, Frame, Handles, 11 x 17 In. 144.00
Tray, Woman, Blossoming From Flower, Verse, Vines, Hand Painted, Wood Frame, Dresden, 14 x 21 In. 366.00
Vase, Art Deco Shape, Flaring, 8-Sided, Turquoise Glaze, 6 x 9 In. 230.00
Vase, Blue Crystalline Drip Glaze, Cream Ground, Bulbous, c.1928-45, 5 In. 264.00
Vase, Boy Climbing, Roses, Applied, Ewer Form, Marked, c.1842-60, 13 In. .... *illus* 165.00
Vase, Gray Masks, Dancing Dwarf, Blue Ground, Urn Form, Incised, c.1900, 12 In., Pair 71.00

VOLKMAR pottery was made by Charles Volkmar of New York from 1879 to about 1911. He was associated with several firms, including the Volkmar Ceramic Company, Volkmar and Cory, and Charles Volkmar and Son. He was hired by Durant Kilns of Bedford Village, New York, in 1910 to oversee production. Volkmar bought the business and after 1930 only the Volkmar name was used as a mark. Volkmar had been a painter, and his designs often look like oil paintings drawn on pottery.

VOLKMAR Corona N.Y

Bowl, Persian Blue Glaze, Flared Rim, Circular Foot, Durant Kilns, 3¾ x 10⅛ In. 353.00
Bowl, Persian Blue Glaze, Flared Rim, Incised, Durant, Leon Volkmar, 1918, 4 x 10 In. 353.00
Bowl, White Glaze, Pink Blush, Lobed Rim, Durant Kilns, c.1912, 2¼ x 5 In. 118.00
Bowl, White Glaze, Sang De Boeuf Interior, Blue Spots, Leon Volkmar, c.1915, 2 x 4 In. 59.00
Classical, Vase, Iron Spot Glaze, Recessed Foot, Leon Volkmar, Durant Kilns, 1919, 12 In. 1175.00
Jar, Cover, Sang De Bouef Glaze, Bulbous, Earthenware, Durant Kilns, 1923, 4½ In. 1058.00
Plate, Egyptian Blue Crackle Glaze, Leon Volkmar, Durant Kilns, 1915, 7 In. 176.00
Vase, Apple Green Glaze, Oriental Form, Marked, Leon Volkmar, 1930, 7¾ In. 1175.00
Vase, Cobalt Blue, Bulbous, Hammered Surface, Incised V, Leon Volkmar, c.1920, 12 In. 2350.00
Vase, Platter, Yellow Crackle Glaze, Cut Corners, Press Mold, 11½ x 7¾ In. 147.00
Vase, Sang De Boeuf Glaze, Bulbous, Raised Foot, Leon Volkmar, c.1920, 5¾ In. 353.00
Vase, Volcanic Gray Glaze, Oval, Slight Rim, Footed, Leon Volkmar, c.1923, 7⅜ In. 382.00

VOLKSTEDT was a soft-paste porcelain factory started in 1760 by Georg Heinrich Macheleid at Volkstedt, Thuringia. Volkstedt-Rudolstadt was a porcelain factory started at Volkstedt-Rudolstadt by Beyer and Bock in 1890. Most pieces seen in shops today are from the later factory.

Candelabrum, 2-Light, Rose Decor, Green Glaze, c.1919, Pair . . . 45.00
Clock, Oval Glass Dome, Wood Base, c.1860, 12 ½ x 7 In. . . . 1295.00
Cup & Saucer, Pansy Pattern, Purple, Yellow, White, Gold Trim, c.1905 . . . 38.00
Figurine, Anthony & Cleopatra, Early 20th Century, 13 x 12 x 8 ½ In. . . . 2500.00
Figurine, Ballerina, Dresden Lace, 6 In. . . . 225.00
Figurine, Coach & 2 Horses, Driver, Woman Passenger, 5 ½ x 10 x 3 ½ In. . . . 395.00
Figurine, Courting Couple, Cream Colors, Browns & Gold Accents, c.1877, 6 x 4 ½ x 3 In. . . . 325.00
Figurine, Dog, Fox Terrier, 4 ½ In. . . . 350.00
Figurine, Dog, German Shepherd, Laying Down, 5 In. . . . 325.00
Figurine, Dog, Sealyham Terrier, Intaglio Eyes, 3 ½ x 7 In. . . . 175.00
Figurine, Lace Male Dancer No. 1481, Base, 4 In. . . . 85.00
Figurine, Man In Fancy Dress, Lace Jabot & Cuffs, c.1907, 4 ½ In. . . . 195.00
Figurine, Man With Harp, Woman With Flowing Robe, c.1787, 8 In. . . . 600.00
Figurine, Woman Sitting With Birdcage, Art Deco, 10 x 10 x 4 ½ In. . . . 850.00
Figurine, Woman With Apron, c.1787, 14 ½ In. . . . 945.00
Potpourri Jar, Putto Handles, Rocailles, Flowers, Signed . . . 649.00
Vase, Flowers, Ram Handles, Gilt, Bronze, Early 20th Century, 10 In., Pair . . . *illus* 630.00

WADE pottery is made by the Wade Group of Potteries started in 1810 near Burslem, England. Several potteries merged to become George Wade & Son, Ltd. early in the twentieth century, and other potteries have been added through the years. The best known Wade pieces are the small figurines given away with Red Rose Tea and other promotional items. The Disney figures are listed in this book in the Disneyana category.

Barrel, Cask, Port, 5 ½ In. . . . 15.00
Barrel, Cask, Scotch, 4 ¾ In. . . . 15.00
Creamer, Rose, Apple Blossoms, Copper Luster, 3 ⅞ x 4 In. . . . 45.00
Decanter, Bell's Scotch Whisky, 9 ¾ In. . . . 18.00
Figurine, Andy Pandy, Certificate, Box, 5 ⅛ In. . . . 71.00
Figurine, Beaver, Brown, Red Rose Tea Premium, 1 In. . . . 5.00
Figurine, Camel, Tan, Red Rose Tea Premium, 1 ½ In. . . . 5.00
Figurine, Cocker Spaniel, Red Rose Tea Premium, 1 ⅜ In. . . . 6.00
Figurine, Custard Pie Clown, Blue, Red Rose Tea Premium, 1 ½ In. . . . 5.00
Figurine, Elephant, Blue-Gray, Red Rose Tea Premium, 1 ½ In. . . . 5.00
Figurine, Giraffe, Tan, Red Rose Tea Premium, 1 ¼ In. . . . 5.00
Figurine, Gorilla, Brown, Red Rose Tea Premium, 1 ¼ In. . . . 5.00
Figurine, Huckleberry Hound, Certificate, Box, 1 ¼ In. . . . 94.00
Figurine, Human Cannonball, Blue Gray, Red Rose Tea Premium, 1 ¼ In. . . . 5.00
Figurine, Koala Bear, Tan, Red Rose Tea Premium, 1 In. . . . 5.00
Figurine, Leopard, Tan, Red Rose Tea Premium, 1 In. . . . 5.00
Figurine, Monkey, In Tree, Brown, Red Rose Tea Premium, 1 ½ In. . . . 5.00
Figurine, Orangutan, Brown, Red Rose Tea Premium, 1 In. . . . 5.00
Figurine, Owl, Tan, Brown, Red Rose Tea Premium, 1 ½ In. . . . 5.00
Figurine, Panda, Limited Edition, Certificate, Box, 2 ¾ In. . . . *illus* 103.00
Figurine, Pine Martin, Tan, Red Rose Tea Premium, 1 ½ In. . . . 5.00
Figurine, Polar Bear, Red Rose Tea Premium, 1 In. . . . 5.00
Figurine, Rabbit, Brown, Red Rose Tea Premium, 1 ¼ In. . . . 5.00
Figurine, Raccoon, Brown, Red Rose Tea Premium, 1 In. . . . 5.00
Figurine, Rhino, Gray, Red Rose Tea Premium, 1 In. . . . 5.00
Figurine, Squirrel, Red Rose Tea Premium, 1 ¼ In. . . . 6.00
Figurine, Strongman, Sand, Red Rose Tea Premium, 1 ½ In. . . . 5.00
Figurine, Tiger, Tan, Red Rose Tea Premium, 1 In. . . . 5.00
Figurine, Tom & Jerry, Marked, 3 ½ -In. Tom, 2 Piece . . . *illus* 221.00
Figurine, Zebra, Gray, Red Rose Tea Premium, 1 ⅜ In. . . . 5.00
Figurine Set, Goldilocks & 3 Bears, 4 Piece . . . 12.00
Gravy Boat, Underplate, Bramble, 2 ⅝ In. . . . 17.00
Mug, Irish Jaunting, Marked, 4 ¼ In. . . . 15.00
Pitcher, Copper Luster, 1950s, 6 ½ In. . . . 43.00
Pitcher, Hamlet Cigars, 5 In. . . . 19.00
Pitcher, Johnny Walker, Red Label, 7 ⅝ In. . . . 275.00
Pitcher, Seagram's 100 Pipers, 7 In. . . . 16.00
Pitcher, Teachers Scotch Whisky, 4 ¾ In. . . . 16.00
Plate, Dinner, Hedgerow, Flowers, 10 In. . . . 9.00

Volkstedt, Vase, Flowers, Ram Handles, Gilt, Bronze, Early 20th Century, 10 In., Pair
$630.00

TIP
Dental wax (ask your orthodontist about it) is a good adhesive to keep figurines on shelves, or lids on teapots.

Wade, Figurine, Panda, Limited Edition, Certificate, Box, 2 ¾ In.
$103.00

Wade, Figurine, Tom & Jerry, Marked, 3 ½-In. Tom, 2 Piece
$221.00

Wall Pocket, Teapot, 3½ x 6½ In. $15.00

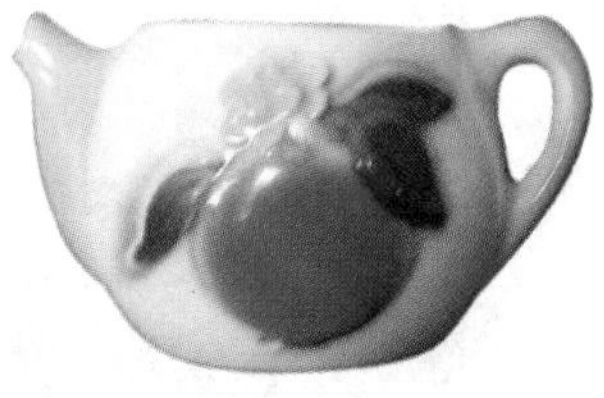

Warwick, Vase, Portrait, Woman, Holding Roses, Brown Glaze, Handles, 10½ In. $66.00

TIP

Clean the plastic crystal of a vintage watch with silver polish. If you accidentally drop a vintage watch in water, take it to a professional jeweler immediately. If you can't do that, take the back off the watch and dry it with a hair dryer set on low.

Saucer, Hedgerow, Fluted Rim, 5⅝ In. 1.00
Sugar & Creamer, Bramble, Gold Trim, 3½-In. Creamer 24.00
Sugar & Creamer, Cover, Bramble, Gold Trim, 5-In. Creamer 29.00
Toby Jug, Charrington Ale, 7¼ In. 79.00
Trinket Box, Treasure Chest, 1961, 1½ x 3⅝ In. 18.00

WAHPETON POTTERY, *see Rosemeade category.*

WALL POCKETS were popular in the 1930s. They were made by many American and European factories. Glass, pottery, porcelain, majolica, chalkware, and metal wall pockets can be found in many fanciful shapes.

Bird, Majolica Style, Brown, Multicolored Glaze, Japan, 6¾ In. 40.00
Duck, Mallard, Flying, Multicolored, Flower, Porcelain, 3¾ x 6 x 2 In. 18.00
Fish, Dolphin, Pink, Luster, 1950s, 8¾ x 5½ In. 33.00
Flower, Blue, Orange, Black Wash, Japan, 6 x 2 In. 25.00
Hull, Picture Frame, Lavender, Oval, Scrolls, Marked, 611, 8½ In. 22.00
Jean & Sady, D131 & D130, 1950s 122.00
Pine, Stenciled, Berkshire Hills Housatonic Railroad, Early 1900s, 6⅜ x 11 In. 264.00
Red Riding Hood, Flowers, Gold, 8½ In. 75.00
Rose, Leaves, 6 x 5 In. 29.00
Swan, Rose & Flowers, 5 x 3¾ In. 8.00
Teapot, 3½ x 6½ In. .... *illus* 15.00
Trellis, Pot, Blue Rose, Pottery, 6 x 2⅜ x 6⅞ In. 16.00
Wood, Paint Decorated, Early 19th Century, 7⅜ x 4⅝ In. 29375.00
Wood, Rack, Painted Black, Cherries, Green Leaves, 15 x 10½ x 3 In. 38.00

WALLACE NUTTING *photographs are listed under Print, Nutting. His reproduction furniture is listed under Furniture.*

WALRATH was a potter who worked in New York City; Rochester, New York; and at the Newcomb Pottery in New Orleans, Louisiana. Frederick Walrath died in 1920. Pieces listed here are from his Rochester period.

Walrath Pottery

Bowl, Crouching Nude Flower Frog, Green Matte Glaze, Signed, 5¾ x 7¼ In. 441.00
Bowl, Footed, Blue Matte Glaze, Signed, 7 x 1¾ In. 115.00
Cider Set, Cherries, Green & Brown Ground, Incised, 6½ x 8 In. 4994.00
Flower Frog, Figural, Swan, White, Bed Of Greenery, Signed, 4⅛ x 3⅛ In. 245.00
Paperweight, Sleeping Nude, Art Nouveau, Impressed, 4½ x 2⅝ In. 850.00
Vase, Broad Footed, Olive Green Matte Glaze, Mark, 7 x 3 In. .... 1200.00 to 1700.00
Vase, Green, Leafy Stems, Pink Blossoms, Cylindrical, c.1910, 8 In. 6264.00
Vase, Landscape, Matte Painted, 6¼ x 4½ In. 3000.00
Vase, Lemon Tree Branch, ¾ In. 2200.00
Vase, Orange, Speckled Green, 6 In. 4486.00
Vase, Orange Water Lilies, Green Lily Pads, Green Matte Glaze, 7¼ x 4½ In. 5288.00
Vase, Pink Blossoms, Green Leaves, Green Mottled Matte Glaze, 8¾ x 4½ In. 8225.00
Vase, Stylized Water Lilies, Matte Painted, 7 x 4½ In. 6000.00
Vase, Trees, Brown Trunks, Green Leaves, Dark Green Ground, Incised, 6¾ x 4½ In. 4994.00

WALT DISNEY, *see Disneyana category.*

WALTER, *see A. Walter category.*

WARWICK china was made in Wheeling, West Virginia, in a pottery working from 1887 to 1951. Many pieces were made with hand painted or decal decorations. The most familiar Warwick has a shaded brown background. The name *Warwick* is part of the mark and sometimes the mysterious word *IOGA* is also included.

Bowl, Cereal, Rust, Blue, Green, Vine Border, 6 In. 6.00
Bowl, Cereal, Sunflower, 6 In. 8.00
Bowl, Fruit, Lochs Of Scotland, Blue Flower Border, Scalloped Edge, 5 In. 13.00
Bowl, Indian Tree, Oval, Marked, 1940, 1¾ x 7 x 5¼ In. 12.00
Bowl, Sunflower, 2½ x 8½ In. 40.00
Bowl, Vegetable, Cover, Gold Garland, Pink Roses, White, Handles, 1940s, 5 x 11 In. 40.00
Casserole, Cover, Purple Flowers, Green Leaves, Gold Trim, 1887, 10½ x 7 In. 255.00
Celery Dish, Purple Flowers, Gold Trim, c.1950, 12¼ In. 20.00
Chocolate Set, Pink & White Flowers, Gold Trim, Transfer, 9½-In. Pot, 5 Piece 135.00
Chop Plate, Regency, Gold Trim, Tab Handles, 10¾ In. 35.00

reamer, Restaurant Ware, White, Indian Tree, Liggetts United Drug Co. 5.00
reamer, Restaurant Ware, White, Geometric 12.00
reamer, Restaurant Ware, White Ground, Geometric, Straight Sides, 1940s 12.00
up, Lochs Of Scotland, Blue, 2 3/4 x 4 1/2 In. 13.00
up & Saucer, Cherries, Green Leaves 50.00
up & Saucer, Regency, Gold Trim 24.00
up & Saucer, Restaurant Ware, Tan, Red & Black Line 8.00
ravy Boat, Blue Flowers, Gold Trim, Marked, 4 3/4 x 8 1/2 In. 10.00
rill Plate, Restaurant Ware, White, Tudor Rose, Blue, 1928 .... 25.00
itcher, Lemonade, Handle, Flow Blue, Early 1900s 94.00
late, Dessert, Pheasant, Rust & Black Border, 7 In. 8.00
late, Dessert, Tulip, Red, Black, Red Trim, Stamped, E.B. Adams, 7 In. 8.00
late, Dinner, Flowers, 22K Gold Trim, 10 1/2 In. 36.00
late, Dinner, Loch Otch, Blue, 10 In. 26.00
late, Dinner, Lochs Of Scotland, Blue Flower Border, Scalloped Edge, 10 In. 25.00
late, Dinner, Restaurant Ware, Green Trim, GH Monogram, 10 In. 10.00
late, Dinner, Spring Flowers, Gold Trim, 10 In. 18.00
late, Dinner, Sunflower, 10 In. 10.00
late, Luncheon, Flower Border, Blue, Tan, 1936, 9 In. 19.00
late, Luncheon, Garland, Pink Roses, Gold Trim, 9 1/4 In. 18.00
late, Monk, Reading Fashion Page, 10 In. 25.00
late, Salad, Regency, Gold Trim, 8 3/4 In. 20.00
late, Tennis, 1908, 10 1/4 In. 245.00
latter, Lochs Of Scotland, Flowers, Blue, Oval, 14 x 11 In. 80.00
latter, Regency, Gold Trim, Tab Handles, 11 In. 35.00
atter, Regency, White, Gold Trim, Scalloped Edge, Tab Handles, 13 In. 453.00
atter, Restaurant Ware, White, Brown Flowers, 11 3/4 In. 12.00
atter, Stylized Brown Flowers, White, 1947, 11 3/4 In. 12.00
ucer, Ironstone, Flowered Border, Blue, Rose, 6 In. 4.00
ucer, Neo Classic, Blue, Gold Trim, Scalloped Edge 8.00
aving Mug, Pink Roses, Transfer, Gold Trim, c.1880, 4 1/2 x 5 In. 24.00
ap Dish, Pink & Yellow Flowers, Brown, Round 15.00
igar, Cover, Gold Coin Bands, Handles 37.00
igar, Cover, Green Flowers, Early 1900s 65.00
apot, Lochs Of Scotland, Pastoral Scene, Blue & White, 7 x 9 In. 120.00
ivet, Triumphal Car, Blue, Gold Trim, Marked, 7 1/4 In. 55.00
se, Portrait, Handles, Signed, IOGA, 10 5/16 x 5 7/8 In. 375.00
se, Portrait, Woman, Holding Roses, Brown Glaze, Handles, 10 1/2 In. .... *illus* 66.00
se, Portrait, Woman, Cylindrical, Handles, Signed, IOGA, 10 1/2 x 5 1/2 In. 215.00
se, Portrait, Woman, Urn, Brown To Red-Brown, White, Handles, c.1800, 10 x 5 In. 275.00
se, Verona, Poinsettias, Umber Shaded To Red, Handles, Signed, IOGA, c.1880, 11 3/4 In. 180.00

ATCH pockets held the pocket watch that was important in Victorian times because it was not til World War I that the wristwatch was used. All types of watches are collected: silver, gold, or ated. Watches are listed here by company name or by style. Wristwatches are a separate category.

Jewel, Sidewinder, Duel Second Hand, Chain, Pocket 250.00
rbie, Silver Luster Case, Fixed Loop, 1964, 1 1/4 In. .... *illus* 70.00
llodes, White Enamel Dial, Roman Numbers, Case, Maiden Picking Blossoms, 14K 1058.00
rtier, Travel, Silver, Gilt, Arabic Numerals, Movado Movement, 1 3/4 x 1 In. 1293.00
ronograph, Hunting Case, 14K Yellow Gold, Swiss, c.1910 .... 2880.00
dley, 14K, Goldtone Dial, Arabic Numeral Indicators, Masonic Symbols, Pocket, 14K 2585.00
Koehn, Open Face, 29 Jewel, 8 Adjustments, 18K Gold, 18 Size, Box 1400.00
gin, Father Time, 21 Jewel, Gold Case, Enamel Arabic Dial, Pocket 288.00
gin, Hunting Case, 14K Gold, Size 18 .... *illus* 600.00
gin, Veritas, 21 Jewel, Enameled, Arabic Dial, Pocket 316.00
gin, Woman's, 14K Tricolor Gold, Diamond, Hunting Case, Flowers, Leaves, Bird, Pocket 705.00
Samuels, 18K Tricolor, Floral & C-Scroll Repousse, 1831, Pocket 1116.00
lay Fils & Stahl, Pendant, Diamond, Enamel, Platinum, 18K Gold, Chain, c.1900, 19 1/2 In. 5019.00
belin, 18K Pink Gold, Pendant With Pin, Rubies, Diamonds, Swiss, c.1940 .... 500.00
din, Paris, 18K Gold, Enamel Dial, Portrait Of 18th Century Lady, Pastes, Pocket 825.00
milton, 21 Jewel, 10K Rolled Gold Plate, Enamel Arabic Dial, Pocket 259.00
milton, No. 946, Dial Size 18, 23 Jewel, Pocket 1320.00
inois, 21 Jewel, A. Lincoln, Gold Filled, Enamel, Arabic Dial, Pocket 173.00
inois, 21 Jewel, Gold Case, Enamel Arabic Dial, Pocket 259.00
perial, Empress Maria Feodorovna On Face, Russia, c.1896, Pocket, 2 1/4 In. 4956.00
perial, Portrait Of Czar Alexander III, Russia, 19th Century, Pocket, 2 In. 2242.00

Watch, Barbie, Silver Luster Case, Fixed Loop, 1964, 1 1/4 In.
$70.00

Watch, Elgin, Hunting Case, 14K Gold, Size 18
$600.00

Watches
Collectible watches range from expensive Cartier women's watches and Rolex watches that tell the time, day, date, month, and moon phase to inexpensive novelty and fashion watches, like Mickey Mouse watches, introduced in 1933, and Swatch watches, first sold in 1983.

W

Watch, J.E. Caldwell & Co., 14K Gold, Porcelain Face, Inscribed, Dec. 25th, 1903, 1¾ x 1 In.
$145.00

Watch, Rockford, 18-S, Porcelain Dial, Jewel Movement, Coin, c.1880
$125.00

Watch Fobs, Advertising, Hires Root Beer, Gold Tone, Ugly Kid, Leather Strap
$58.00

J.E. Caldwell & Co., 14K Gold, Porcelain Face, Inscribed, Dec. 25th, 1903, 1¾ x 1 In. . . . *illus* 145.00
J.E. Caldwell & Co., Pendant, Porcelain Face, Nickel Alloy Case, Swiss, 2¾ In. 144.00
Jeff Arnold, Gun In Hand Dial, Ingersoll, 1953, Pocket 281.00
Locomotive, Open Face, Blue & White Porcelain Face, Man On Safety, Pocket 55.00
Lucien Piccard, Woman's, Diamonds, 14K Gold 374.00
Moulinie & Le Grandroy, Hunt Case, Diamond, Black Enamel, c.1885, 1¼ In. 2760.00
Open Face, Key Wind, Engraved Face, Lakeside Scene, 18K Yellow Gold, c.1840, 2 In. 725.00
Open Face, Safety Riders, Leafy Case, c.1890, 2¾ In. 66.00
Ovida Watch Co., Platinum, Diamond, Sapphire, Black Ribbon Band 1058.00
P.S. Bartlett Waltham, Coin Silver Case, Key, Civil War Era, Pocket, 2¼ In. 115.00
Patek Philippe, Open Face, Hinged, Enamel, Silver Dial, 18K Gold, c.1924, Pocket 1960.00
Patek Philippe, Open Face, Screw Back Case, White Enamel Dial, 15½ In. 1800.00
Patek Philippe, Open Face, Subsidiary Seconds, 20 Jewel, Case, Pocket, 18K Gold 3600.00
Patek Philippe, Open Face, White Enamel Dial, Roman Numerals, 18K, Fitted Box, c.1905 . . 2468.00
Patek Philippe, Open Face, Woman's, Enamel, Pendant, Henry Bohm Co., 18K Gold 7638.00
Paul Burhe, Imperial, Russia, Enameled Double Headed Eagle, c.1900, Pocket, 1¾ In. 7080.00
Perret & Fils, 18K Gold, 5-Minute Repeating, Roman Numerals, No. 46835, Pocket 3290.00
Platinum, Ivorytone Dial, Bezel & Lugs Set With, Diamonds, 14K Gold 2938.00
Rectangular Shutter, Sterling Case, Black Enamel, 15 Jewel, c.1925 . . . . 650.00
Rockford, 18-S, Porcelain Dial, Jewel Movement, Coin, c.1880 . . . . *illus* 125.00
South Bend, 21 Jewel, Gold Case, Enamel Arabic Dial, Pocket 144.00
Tiffany, Open Face, Cigar Cutter, Pen Knife, Chain, Pocket 403.00
Tiffany & Co., Goldtone Dial, Black Enamel Bezel, 14K, Pocket 529.00
Waltham, Hunter Case, 14K Gold, Sweep Second Hand 625.00
Waltham, Vanguard, 21 Jewel, Gold Case, Enamel Arabic Dial, Pocket 230.00
Waltham, Woman's, 14K, Gold, White Enamel Dial, Arabic Numbers, 15 Jewel, Case, Pocket . 705.00
Waltham Watch Co., Gold, Chain, Slide, 1913, Pocket 99.00
Whiteside & Blank, Pendant, 18K Gold, Guilloche Case, 14K Gold Chain, Swiss, 20 In. 2703.00
Zimmermann, Open Face, Key Wind, Split Plate Movement, Pin Set, 18K Gold, 1881, Pocket. 2040.00

WATCH FOBS were worn on watch chains. They were popular during Victorian times and after. Many styles, especially advertising designs, are still made today.

Advertising, Dead Shot Powder, Am Badge Co., Pewter, 1⅜ In. 58.00
Advertising, Gold Dust Wash Powder, 2 Black Boys In Tub, Celluloid, Brass, ⅞ x ¼ In. 80.00
Advertising, Hires Root Beer, Gold Tone, Ugly Kid, Leather Strap . . . . *illus* 58.00
Agate, 10K Rose Gold, Late 19th Century 110.00
Knight On Horseback, Gold, Sterling Silver, 1⅞ x 13⅜ In. 224.00
National Sportsman, Raised Moose, 1½ In. 25.00

WATERFORD type glass resembles the famous glass made from 1783 to 1851 in the Waterford Glass Works in Ireland. It is a clear glass that was often decorated by cutting. Modern glass is being made again in Waterford, Ireland, and is marketed under the name Waterford. Waterford merged with Wedgwood in 1986 to form the Waterford Wedgwood Group.

Bowl, Centerpiece, Astragal Border, Diamond Crosshatch, 7½ x 12 In. 201.00
Celery Vase, Diamond Point Band, Late 18th Century, 8¾ In. . . . . *illus* 265.00
Clock, 8-Sided, 2¾ x 1¼ In. 90.00
Compote, Lismore, 4½ x 6¼ In. 105.00
Cross, Celtic Style, 9½ x 6 In. 117.00
Decanter, Allover Diamond, Ball Stopper, Signed, 10 x 8 In. 88.00
Decanter, Ball Stopper, 11 In. 88.00
Decanter, Colleen, 11 In. 205.00
Goblet, Trumpet, Tapered Panels, Stems, 7 & 6½ In., 24 Piece 978.00
Ice Bucket, Lismore, 7 x 7 In. 100.00
Tumbler, Highball, Sheila, 4⅝ In., 12 Piece 646.00
Vase, Marquis, Signed, 15 x 7 In. 70.00

WATT family members bought the Globe pottery of Crooksville, Ohio, in 1922. They made pottery mixing bowls and tableware of the type made by Globe. In 1935 they changed the production and made the pieces with the freehand decorations that are popular with collectors today. Apple, Starflower, Rooster, Tulip, and Autumn Foliage are the best-known patterns. Pansy, also called Rio Rose, was the earliest pattern. Apple, the most popular pattern, can be dated from the leaves. Originally, the apples had three leaves; after 1958 two leaves were used. The plant closed in 1965. For more information, see *Kovels' Depression Glass & Dinnerware Price List.*

American Red Bud, Mixing Bowl, No. 5, 5 In. 45.00

W

nimal Dish, Purina Mink Chow, Checkerboard, 1 x 9 In. 50.00
pple, Bowl, Spaghetti, No. 39, 14¾ In. 175.00
pple, Casserole, Cover, No. 601, 8½ In. 90.00
pple, Casserole, Cover, 3-Leaf, No. 54, 6 x 8½ In. 140.00
pple, Casserole, Cover, 3-Leaf, Tab Handles, No. 18, 3¾ x 5 In. *illus* 175.00
pple, Casserole, Cover, Tab Handles, Individual, No. 18, 4½ x 6¼ In. 225.00
pple, Creamer, 2-Leaf, No. 62, 4¼ In. 90.00
pple, Creamer, Pelican Rapids, Minn., No. 62, 4¼ In. 60.00
pple, Ice Bucket, No. 59, 7 x 7½ In. 185.00
pple, Mixing Bowl, 2-Leaf, No. 65, 5¾ x 8⅞ In. 95.00
pple, Mixing Bowl, 3-Leaf, No. 64, 4¾ x 7¾ In. 100.00
pple, Mixing Bowl, It Pays To Mix With Rieke's Produce, Gaylord, Minn., No. 5, 5 In. 120.00
pple, Mixing Bowl, No. 5, 2¾ x 5 In. 100.00
pple, Mixing Bowl, No. 6, 3½ x 6 In. 55.00 to 85.00
pple, Mixing Bowl, No. 7, 4 x 7 In. *illus* 85.00
pple, Mixing Bowl, No. 8, 4½ x 8 In. 98.00
pple, Mixing Bowl, No. 9, 5 x 9 In. 175.00
pple, Mixing Bowl, Ribbed, No. 4, 2 x 4 In. 95.00
pple, Mixing Bowl, Ribbed, No. 5, 2½ x 5 In. 90.00
pple, Mixing Bowl, Ribbed, No. 6, 3¼ x 6¼ In. 95.00
pple, Mixing Bowl, Ribbed, No. 7, 3¾ x 7¾ In. 110.00
pple, Pie Plate, Annadale Hardware, Annadale, Minn., No. 33, 9¼ In. 65.00
pple, Pie Plate, Farmer's Co-Op Elev. Darwin, Minn., No. 33, 9¼ In. 55.00
pple, Pitcher, 3-Leaf, No. 15, 5¼ x 3 In. 42.00
pple, Pitcher, 3-Leaf, Ice Lip, No. 17, 8 In. 80.00
pple, Pitcher, Compliments Of Lankin Farmers Union, Lankin, N.D., No. 15, 5½ In. 45.00
pple, Pitcher, Compliments Of Pine City Mill, No. 15, 5½ In. 45.00
pple, Pitcher, Compliments Of St. Joe Co-Op Elevator Co., No. 15, 5½ In. 30.00
pple, Pitcher, Fairfax Co-Op Creamery Co., Fairfax, Minn., No. 15, 5½ In. 55.00
pple, Pitcher, Fulda Co-Op Creamery Assn., No. 15, 5½ In. 40.00
pple, Pitcher, Millers Feed Mill Of Cadot, Wis., No. 15, 5½ In. 139.00
pple, Pitcher, Mobile Heat Marion Gas & Oil, No. 16, 6½ In. 55.00
pple, Pitcher, Nelson Impl. & Chevrolet, Elwood R. Nelson, Milnor, N. Dakota, 5½ In. 40.00
pple, Pitcher, No. 15, 5½ In. 45.00 to 165.00
ple, Pitcher, No. 17, 8¼ In. 200.00
ple, Sugar, No. 98, 4¼ In. 70.00
tumn Foliage, Pitcher, No. 16, 6½ In. 85.00
tumn Foliage, Sugar, Meyer's Dairy Grade A Milk, No. 98, 4¼ In. 65.00
sket Weave, Mixing Bowl, Blue, No. 5, 3 x 5 In. 20.00
rolina Blue, Salt & Pepper, Hourglass, Box, 4½ In. 60.00
mond, Cookie Jar, Apple & Pear, No. 36. 50.00
e-N-Bake, Bowl, Brown Spray Bands, 6 x 10 In. 35.00
tch-N-Queen, Mixing Bowl, No. 9, 6 x 9 In. 48.00
oon & Stars, Casserole, Cover, Salmon, 8¾ In. 35.00
ne Loops, Casserole, Cover, 8 In. 35.00
ne Loops, Pie Plate, No. 8, 8 In. 15.00
en Ware, Mixing Bowl, Brown Stripes, No. 10, 5¾ x 10½ In. 95.00
nsy, Bowl, Rio Rose, No. 5, 6 In. 22.00
nsy, Casserole, Cover, Rio Rose, No. 8, 8¾ In. 110.00
nsy, Casserole, Cover, Stick Handle, Individual, No. 18, 3¾ x 5 In. 33.00
nsy, Casserole, French Handle, Raised, Individual, 5 In. 145.00
nsy, Plate, Snack, Bullseye, 11¼ In. *illus* 50.00
o Rose, see Pansy
oster, Bean Pot, Batman Grain, No. 76, 6½ In. 600.00
oster, Bowl, Ice Bucket, No. 59, 7 x 7½ In. 55.00
oster, Pitcher, No. 15, 5½ In. 85.00 to 135.00
oster, Pitcher, No. 16, 6½ In. 75.00
oster, Sugar, Sac City Carroll Calrinda, No. 98, 4¼ In. 115.00
arflower, Baker, Cover, Becker Lumber Co., Caledonia, Minn. 30.00
arflower, Bowl, Interstate Lumber Co., No. 9 25.00
arflower, Bowl, No. 8, 4 x 8 In. 65.00
arflower, Casserole, Cover, No. 54, 6 x 8½ In. 245.00
arflower, Grease Jar, Renville Co-Op Creamery, Renville, Minn., No. 1, 5 In. 375.00
arflower, Mixing Bowl, No. 5, 2¾ x 5¼ In. 45.00
arflower, Mixing Bowl, No. 6, 5 In. 38.00
arflower, Pitcher, 1960 Random Lake Co-Op, No. 15, 5½ In. 30.00

Waterford, Celery Vase, Diamond Point Band, Late 18th Century, 8¾ In. $265.00

Watt, Apple, Casserole, Cover, 3-Leaf, Tab Handles, No. 18, 3¾ x 5 In. $175.00

Watt, Apple, Mixing Bowl, No. 7, 4 x 7 In. $85.00

Watt, Pansy, Plate, Snack, Bullseye, 11¼ In. $50.00

W

Starflower, Pitcher, Caven Elevator, Franklin, Minn., No. 15, 5 ½ In. 35.0
Starflower, Pitcher, Christmas 1954, Wilmar, Minn., No. 15, 5 ½ In. 85.0
Starflower, Pitcher, Compliments Of Hills Co-Op Creamery, Hills, Minn., No. 16, 6 ½ In. 150.0
Starflower, Pitcher, Compliments Of Johnson Grain Company, No. 15, 5 ½ In. 85.0
Starflower, Pitcher, Ice Lip, No. 17, 8 In. 165.0
Starflower, Pitcher, No. 15, 5 ½ In. 25.0
Starflower, Pitcher, No. 16, 6½ In. .... 35.00 to 85.0
Starflower, Pitcher, Thanks For Your Confidence & Loyalty Gienapp Hatchery, 15 In. 65.0
Tulip, Bowl, No. 65, 5 ¾ x 8 ½ In. 190.0
Tulip, Creamer, No. 62, 4 ¼ In. 75.0
Tulip, Mixing Bowl, No. 64, 5 x 7½ In. .... 35.00 to 175.0
Tulip, Pitcher, Ice Lip, No. 17, 8 In. 105.0
Tulip, Pitcher, No. 15, 5 ½ In. 375.0
Tulip, Pitcher, No. 16, 6 ½ In. 75.0

WAVE CREST glass is an opaque white glassware manufactured by the Pairpoint Manufacturing Company of New Bedford, Massachusetts, and some French factories. It was decorated by the C.F. Monroe Company of Meriden, Connecticut. The glass was painted in pastel colors and decorated with flowers. The name Wave Crest was used after 1898.

WAVE CREST WARE

Biscuit Jar, Blue Blossoms, Branches, Metal, Cover, Bail, c.1900, 4 x 7 ½ In. .... *illus* 293.0
Biscuit Jar, Cream, Blue, White, Flowers, Silver-Plated Cover, Bail, Bird Finial, 7 ½ In. 100.0
Biscuit Jar, Pink, White, Yellow Rose, Silver Plated Cover, Bail, 8 In. 125.0
Biscuit Jar, Scroll Mold, Blue, White, Pink Flowers, Silver Plated Cover, Bail, 7 In. 400.0
Biscuit Jar, White, Blue Flowers, Mauve, Gray Stems, Egg Shape, Swirl Cover, 7 In. 374.0
Bowl, Diamond, Mold, Enameled Flowers, Brass Liner, c.1900, 3 ½ x 6 ½ In. 263.0
Bowl, Flowering Branches, Blue, White, Square, Brass Liner, c.1900, 3 ½ x 6 ½ In. 263.0
Box, Collar, Flowers, Gischol & Spenler 1995.0
Box, Collars & Cuffs, Flowers, Egg Crate Mold 1995.0
Box, Collars & Cuffs, Flower Mold, Blue, White, Round, 4 x 7 ½ In. 100.0
Box, Collars & Cuffs, Flower Sprays, Brass Feet, Round, Hinged Cover, 7 ¾ x 7 In. 690.0
Call Bell, Embossed, 4-Footed, c.1890, 4 In. .... *illus* 250.0
Dresser Box, Baroque, Shell Mold, c.1890, 3 In. .... *illus* 83.0
Dresser Box, Baroque Shell Mold, Pink & White Flowers, 7 ½ In. 259.0
Dresser Box, Blue, Enameled Tapestry, Flowers, Round, Hinged Cover, 3 ½ x 7 In. 700.0
Dresser Box, Blue Around Red Flowers, Oval, 4 In. 288.0
Dresser Box, Egg Crate Mold, Opal Glass, Blue Medallions, 4-Footed, 6 In. 748.0
Dresser Box, Egg Crate Mold, White, Blue, Flowers, Hinged Cover, 3 ½ x 7 In. 650.0
Dresser Box, Leaf Branch Mold, White, Pink, Blue Flowers, Hinged Cover, 5 ½ x 7 In. .... 300.
Dresser Box, Octagonal, Powder Blue, Red Mum Medallion, 4 Metal Feet, 5 ½ In. .... 288.
Dresser Box, Pink, Yellow Pansy, Green Ground, Egg Shape, Signed, 4 In. 374.0
Dresser Box, Puff Mold, Yellow, Lavender Enamel, Round, Hinged Cover, 3 ½ x 7 In. 275.0
Dresser Box, Scroll, Mold, Pansy, Blue, Pink, Maroon, Round, 4 In. .... 118.
Dresser Box, Swirl Mold, Purple, Blue Pansies, Gold Lined Panels, 7 In. .... 518.
Dresser Box, Yellow Flower Cover, Blue, 4 ½ In. 403.0
Ewer, Courting Scene, Melon Ribbed, Brown, Embossed Gilt Metal Spout, Base, 15 In. 110.0
Fernery, Round, Scroll Mold, Enameled Fern, 4 x 7 In. .... 150.
Fernery, Yellow, White, Gilt Metal Feet, 4 ¾ x 7 In. .... 275.
Jardiniere, Blue, Dark Green, Pink Rose, 7 ½ x 9 In. .... 250.
Jardiniere, Clematis Blossoms, Green Ground, Angels Around Rim, 7 ½ x 9 In. .... 294.
Jardiniere, Scroll Mold, Pink, Green, White Flowers, Embossed Feet, 8 ½ x 8 In. .... 600.
Jewelry Box, Cobalt Blue, Embossed, Hinged Cover, Zinnia, 2 ¾ x 4 ½ In. .... 550.
Jewelry Box, Cream, Blue, Pink Flower, Round, Hinged Cover, Metal Base, 6 x 5 In. .... 850.
Jewelry Box, Flower Mold, White, Pink, Blue Lattice, Round, Hinged Cover, 7 In. .... 250.
Jewelry Box, Flowers, Egg & Band Borders, Brass Rim, Marked, 5 ¼ x 8 In. .... 630.
Jewelry Box, Green, White, Pink Flowers, Hinged Clock Cover, Beveled Glass, 4 x 5 In. .... 1600.
Jewelry Box, Round, Molded, Hinged Cover, c.1900, 3 ½ x 5 ½ In. .... 293.
Jewelry Box, Shell Mold, Blue, White, Flowers, Round, Hinged Cover, 2 ¾ x 4 In. .... 250.
Jewelry Box, Swirl Mold, Hinges, Cream, Yellow Flowers, 4 ½ x 6 In. .... 175.
Jewelry Box, Swirl Mold, Pink Blossoms, White Enamel, Hinged Cover, 3 ½ x 5 ½ In. .... 293.
Jewelry Box, Swirl Mold, Pink Flowers, Round, Hinged Cover, 5 In. .... 175.
Jewelry Box, Yellow & White, Round Swirl, Mold Hinge, Enamel, 4 ¼ In. .... 90.
Letter Box, Raised Scroll, Flowers, Enameled, Painted, Brass Rim, Footed, 5 x 7 ¼ x 4 ¼ In. .... 210.
Letter Holder, Egg Crate Mold, Cream, Blue, Pink, Flowers, 4 x 6 In. .... *illus* 300.
Letter Holder, Puffy Mold, Flowers, Enameled, Hand Painted, Brass Rim, 4 x 6 In. .... 315.
Letter Holder, Scroll Mold, Blue, Pink Flowers, Embossed Lion's Head Feet, 5 x 6 ½ In. .... 275.

Wave Crest, Biscuit Jar, Blue Blossoms, Branches, Metal, Cover, Bail, c.1900, 4 x 7 ½ In.
$293.00

Wave Crest, Call Bell, Embossed, 4-Footed, c.1890, 4 In.
$250.00

Wave Crest, Dresser Box, Baroque, Shell Mold, c.1890, 3 In.
$83.00

Wave Crest, Letter Holder, Egg Crate Mold, Cream, Blue, Pink, Flowers, 4 x 6 In.
$300.00

Pin Dish, Green, Blue Flowers, Oval, 4 In. 100.00
Pin Dish, Swirl Mold, Blue, Pink, Daisy, Round, 3 In. 50.00
Pin Dish, Swirl Mold, Blue, Multicolored Flowers, Round, 5 ½ In. 125.00
Pin Dish, Swirl Mold, Blue, Pink, Daisies, Round, Gilt Metal Handles, 3 ½ x 8 In. 200.00
Sugar & Creamer, Swirl Mold, White, Pink Flowers, Silver Plated Rims, Handles, Cover 125.00
Sugar Shaker, Cream, Pink, Blue Flower, 5 In. 175.00
Tobacco Jar, Yellow, White, Blue Flowers, 5 In. 750.00
Toothpick, White, Flowers, Metal Footed, 2¼ In. .... 200.00 to 325.00
Vase, Barrel Shape, Crimson, Green, Flowers, 4-Footed, Handles, 11 In. 1093.00
Vase, Blue Blossoms, Brown & White Highlights, Gilt Metal Mounts, 8¼ In., Pair. 820.00 to 1320.00
Vase, Cream & Yellow Chrysanthemums, 12 In. 2587.00
Vase, Maiden On Gargoyle Dolphin, Molded Waves, Gold Trim, Ormolu Base, 13 In. 4465.00
Vase, Scroll Mold, Pink, White, Yellow Flowers, 9 ½ In. 325.00
Vase, Sea Foam Mold, Blue, White, Flowers, Metal Footed Base, 6 In. 250.00

WEAPONS listed here include instruments of combat other than guns, knives, rifles, or swords. Firearms are not listed in this book. Knives and Swords are listed in their own categories.

Bayonet, French Sword Style, For Gras Infantry Rifle, Brass Pommel, 20 ⅝ In. 145.00
Boomerang, Mulga Wood, Aboriginal, c.1930, 28 ½ In. 145.00
Spear, Wood, Melanesian, 45 In. 68.00

WEATHER VANES were used in seventeenth-century Boston. The direction of the wind was an indication of coming weather, important to the seafaring and farming communities. By the mid-nineteenth century, commercial weather vanes were made of metal. Today's collectors often consider weather vanes to be examples of folk art, even though they may not have been handmade.

Airplane, Sheet Copper Over Wood, Wood Propeller, Weathered, 17 In. 546.00
Arrow, Copper, Applied Verdigris Patina, Bullet Holes, Cast Iron Directionals, 65 In. 374.00
Arrow, Copper, Cast Iron Directional Signs, Hammered Tail Feathers, 14 ½ In. 545.00
Arrow, Iron, Wood Painted Column, c.1900, 45 In. 2390.00
Arrow, Wrought Iron, Scrolls, Iron Tail, Black Metal Stand, Late 1800s, 14 x 34 In. 823.00
Arrow, Zinc, Copper, Stand, 37 x 28 In. 374.00
Automobile, Driver, 2-Sided, Lead Cast, Cast Iron Arrow, 30 In. 546.00
Banner, Cutout C, Pointing Hand, Flower, Directionals, Copper, J.W. Fiske Co., N.Y., 65 In. 8225.00
Banner, Pointing Hand Directional, Sheet Iron, Cast Bronze, Painted, 15 ¾ x 35 ½ In. 2115.00
Banner, Sheet Iron, Cutout, Riveted Spearheads, Painted, Stand, c.1864, 25 x 33 In. 823.00
Bull, Copper, Full-Bodied, Cast Head, 26 In. 5750.00
Carved Rooster, White Paint, 22 x 30 In. 3480.00
Civil War Soldier, On Horse, Sheet Metal, Old Paint 1850.00
Codfish, Gold Paint, 32 In. 4950.00
Cow, Copper, Flattened, Gilt, 15 x 15 ¼ In. 1528.00
Cow, Copper, Zinc, Molded, Paint, Gilt, Cooperstown, 1800s, 42 x 61 In. .... *illus* 628000.00
Cow, Copper, Zinc, Paint, Molded, Full-Bodied, Metal Stand, c.1890, 16 ½ x 30 In. 6469.00
Cow, Copper, Zinc Head & Horns, Verdigris, Cushing & White, Waltham, Mass., 18 x 28 In. .. 25850.00
Cow, Full-Bodied, L.W. Cushing & Sons, c.1883, 35 In. 27500.00
Cow, Lightning Rod, Star Finial, Hand Blown Glass Ball, c.1880 .... 1595.00
Cow, Softwood, Tin Ears, Strap Metal Supports, Red Paint, 24 x 36 In. 413.00
Deer, Running, Sheet Metal, 23 x 17 In. 55.00
Dog, Setter, Full-Body, Molded, Flattened, Copper, Gilt, Verdigris, c.1890, 15 x 35 In. 44063.00
Dog, Tin, Wrought Iron Directionals & Base, Scrolls, 31 x 23 In. 1200.00
Donkey, Gilt, 30 In. 4950.00
Dove, Tan Flower In Mouth, Sheet Metal, Gray Paint, 24 x 29 ¾ In. 2420.00
Duck, Flying, Copper 358.00
Eagle, Full-Bodied, Spread Wings, Ball With Arrow Directional, Copper, 25 x 20 In. 1150.00
Eagle, Full-Bodied, Stylized Feathers, On Globe, Copper, Zinc Head, 22 x 16 In. 5463.00
Eagle, Gilt Copper, Zinc, Stand, Early 20th Century, 17 ½ x 17 In. 3055.00
Eagle, On Ball, Copper, 21 x 43 In. 385.00
Eagle, Painted Red, Wrought Back Bracing, Riveted Sheet Iron, Early 1900s, 23 x 37 In. 633.00
Eagle, Spread Wings, On Ball, Directional Arrow, Copper, 10 x 9 ¾ In. 1725.00
Eagle, Spread Wings, Pressed Copper, Hollow, Patina, 14 ½ x 24 In. 121.00
Eagle, Standing On Ball, Wings Up, Ready For Flight, Copper, 21 x 12 x 15 In. 1870.00
Eagle, Tin, Red, Gray, Green, Brackets, Signed, D.Y. Ellinger, 14 ½ x 20 In. 154.00
Fireman, Arrow Directional, Tinned Sheet Iron, Stand, Painted Red, 30 x 34 In. 1410.00
Fish, Cod, J. Howard & Company, Bridgewater, Mass., 25 In. 24000.00
Fish, Copper, Gilt, 8 x 20 In. 5510.00

Weather Vane, Cow, Copper, Zinc, Molded, Paint, Gilt, Cooperstown, 1800s, 42 x 61 In.
$628000.00

Weather Vane, Fish, Sheet Iron, White Paint, Wooden Finial, Late 19th Century, 31 ½ x 40 In.
$748.00

Weather Vane, Horses, Fire Pumper, Welded, Cast Iron, 26 x 23 ½ In.
$250.00

W

Weather Vane, Indian, Massasoit, Copper, Molded, Harris & Co., c.1878, 32 x 31½ In.
$180000.00

Weather Vane, Rooster, Crowing, Cast Zinc, Red & White Paint, Wood Stand, 1900s, 23 x 18 In.
$575.00

Weather Vane, Stag, Copper, Molded, Metal Stand, Mid 20th Century, 29 In.
$3737.00

Fish, Copper, Verdigris Patina, Full-Bodied, 25½ In. 1725.00
Fish, Sheet Iron, White Paint, Wooden Finial, Late 19th Century, 31½ x 40 In. .... *illus* 748.00
Fish, Wood, Metal, Carved, Painted, Early 20th Century, 14 x 32 In. 2800.00
Fish, Wood & Tin, Painted, Screw-Head Eyes, 26½ In. 600.00
Flag, American, 16 Stars, Iron, Pine, Carved, Cannon Base, Late 1800s, 79 x 28 In. 8400.00
Geese, Flying, Sheet Metal, 47 In. 93.00
Geometric Design, Pierced, Copper On Iron, 24½ x 41½ In. 575.00
Heart Cutouts, Sheet Metal, Copper Ball, Turned Wood Base, White Paint, 39 x 24 In. 303.00
Horse, Cast Iron, Metal Stand, 13¼ x 28½ In. 1265.00
Horse, Copper, Wrought Iron, 63 In. 292.00
Horse, Galloping, Copper, Cast Iron Head, Marked J. Harris & Son, Boston, 28 In. 8900.00
Horse, Jockey, Copper, Cast Iron, Painted, Green, 20th Century, 25 x 57¾ In. 8813.00
Horse, Jockey, Molded Sheet Copper, Cast Iron, Verdigris, c.1885, 19 x 31 In. 15275.00
Horse, Molded Copper, Cast Zinc, Verdigris, Mounted, c.1900, 35 x 41 In. 4994.00
Horse, Rider, Trotting, Molded, Gilt Copper & Zinc, Verdigris, Stand, 1800s, 17 x 30 In. 39000.00
Horse, Running, Blackhawk, Copper, Gilt, Molded, J. Harris, Late 1800s, 20 x 26 In. 7200.00
Horse, Running, Cast Iron, Ethan Allen, Oxidation, 19th Century, 17 x 30 In. 2200.00
Horse, Running, Cast Zinc Head, Verdigris Patina, Repaired Bullet Holes 6900.00
Horse, Running, Copper, 30 In. 2013.00
Horse, Running, Copper, Cast Iron, c.1852, 16¾ x 28 In. 4348.00
Horse, Running, Copper, Cast Iron Directional, 26 In. 690.00
Horse, Running, Copper, Full-Bodied, Zinc Head, Fiske, New York, c.1870, 31 x 18½ In. 1495.00
Horse, Running, Copper, Hollow, Iron Base, 17 x 28¾ In. 1500.00
Horse, Running, Copper, Hollow, Iron Base, Patina, 20th Century, 17 x 28¾ In. 1680.00
Horse, Running, Copper, Zinc Head, Gilt, Ethan Allen By Fiske, 26½ In. 6038.00
Horse, Running, Full-Bodied, Copper, Flattened Tail, Bullet Holes, c.1870, 39 x 25 In. 12650.00
Horse, Running, Gilt Copper, Flat, Rod Mounted, Metal Tripod Stand, c.1900, 27 x 25 In. 2938.00
Horse, Running, Molded Sheet Copper, Mounted, Ball, Directional, c.1885, 47 x 32 In. 3819.00
Horse, Running, Pine, Carved, Red Paint, Custom Metal Stand, c.1900, 16 x 33 In. 325.00
Horse, Running, Sheet Copper, Zinc Head, Embossed, Gilt Traces, Metal Stand, 19 x 28 In. 12925.00
Horse, Standing, Lexington, Copper, Flattened, Yellow Sizing, Verdigris, 28 x 32 In. 25850.00
Horse, Standing, On Arrow, Hollow Body, 47 In. 2950.00
Horse, Standing, Zinc, Copper, Painted Mustard, Stand, Late 1800s, 31½ x 31 In. 4994.00
Horse, Sulky, Driver, Copper, Iron, Late 19th Century, 20 x 32 In. 8813.00
Horse, Sulky, Driver, Copper, Wire Wheels & Reins, Directional Post, 29 In. 403.00
Horse, Trotting, Black Hawk, Copper, Painted White, 18¾ x 24½ In. 6463.00
Horse, Trotting, Copper, Dexter, Late 19th Century 550.00
Horse, Trotting, Metal, Blue Base, Verdigris, Early 20th Century, 30 In. 578.00
Horse, Trotting, Molded, Copper, Zinc Ears, Verdigris, Base, J.W. Fiske & Co., c.1890, 18 x 30 In. 7200.00
Horse, Trotting, Molded Sheet Copper, Flat, Iron Rod, Directional, 18 x 57 In. 1528.00
Horse, White Paint, Full-Bodied, Dexter 2970.00
Horses, Fire Pumper, Welded, Cast Iron, 26 x 23½ In. .... *illus* 250.00
Hunter, Holding Shot Gun, On Canoe, Copper, 30½ x 40 In. 7200.00
Indian, Copper, Flat, Arrow In One Hand, Bow In Other, 32 In. 6612.00
Indian, Massasoit, Copper, Molded, Harris & Co., c.1878, 32 x 31½ In. .... *illus* 180000.00
Indian, On Horseback, Sheet Copper, Brown Patina, Verdigris, Early 1900s, 20 x 22 In. 235.00
Leafy Scrolls, Sheet Copper, Halbert, Ball Finial, Terminals, Gold Paint, 28 x 37 In. 940.00
Man, Blowing Trumpet, Wearing Hat, Outstretched, Wood, Iron Rod, 47 x 39 In. 3055.00
Man, Holding Shotgun, Standing On Capsized Canoe, Copper, Late 1800s, 30½ x 40 In. 7200.00
Man In The Moon, Sunburst, Verdigris Patinated, Galvanized Metal, Wrought Iron, 89 In. 2400.00
Peacock, Copper, Silhouette, Arrowhead, Verdigris, 15½ x 30 In. 2415.00
Pigeon, Ball & Arrow, Copper & Zinc, Full-Bodied, Outstretched Wings, c.1875, 29 x 34 In. 1410.00
Quill Pen, Copper, Gilt, Verdigris, Stand, 2 Balls, Black Plinth, c.1890, 26¾ x 24 In. 4405.00
Ram, Copper, Molded, Gilt, L.W. Cushing & Son, Late 1800s, 27 x 34 In. 60000.00
Ram, Wood, Painted Yellow, Iron Tack Eyes & Sheet Horns, Mounted On Bar, 35 In. 1410.00
Rooster, Copper, 22 In. 3738.00
Rooster, Copper, Cast Feet, Mahogany Base, 28 x 27 In. 10200.00
Rooster, Copper, Gilt, 19th Century, 21 x 24 In. 4406.00
Rooster, Copper, Molded, Swelled Body, Cast Feet, Mahogany Base, c.1890, 28 x 27 In. 10200.00
Rooster, Copper, Tin Tail, Comb & Wattle, Old Gilt, Full-Bodied, 31 In. 11213.00
Rooster, Copper, Tin Tail, Verdigris Patina, Old Paint, Full-Bodied, Cushing, c.1890, 45 In. 3910.00
Rooster, Copper, Zinc, White Comb, Wattle, Legs, Ball, Gilt, Stand, c.1890, 30 x 23 In. 4406.00
Rooster, Crowing, Cast Zinc, Red & White Paint, Wood Stand, 1900s, 23 x 18 In. .... *illus* 575.00
Rooster, Hamburg, Full-Bodied, Molded Copper, L.W. Cushing, 1800s, 27 x 28 In. 15275.00
Rooster, Metal, 19th Century, 17½ In. 1295.00
Rooster, Tin, Limestone Base, 60 x 23½ In. 936.00

Sailing Ship, Applied Verdigris Patina, Cast Iron Directionals, Mid 1900s, 78 In. 374.00
Ship, Sheet Metal, Wood Base, 30 x 32 In. 460.00
Sloop, Central Mast Holding 2 Sails, Top Flag, Rudder, Copper, Gilt, Metal Stand, 1800s, 30 x 35 In. 3450.00
Spear Heads, Sheet Iron, Black, American, 1864, 25 x 32 In. 775.00
Stag, Copper, Molded, Metal Stand, Mid 20th Century, 29 In. *illus* 3737.00
Stag, Leaping, Copper, Molded, Gilt, Late 19th Century, 24 x 31 In. 17400.00
Stag, Running, Gilt Copper, Cast Head, 26 x 26 In. 7475.00
Steer, Copper, Gilt, Cushing & White, 20 x 33 In. 13340.00
Swordfish, Wood, 29 ½ x 29 ½ In. 345.00
Whale, Copper, Molded, Applied Small Fins, Tail, Verdigris, 1900s, 38 In. 748.00
Witch, Salem Halloween, Flying Bat, Sheet Iron, 24 x 43 In. 3480.00

WEBB glass was made by Thomas Webb & Sons of Ambelcot, England. Many types of art and cameo glass were made by them during the Victorian era. Production ceased by 1991 and the factory was demolished in 1995. Webb Burmese and Webb Peachblow are special colored glasswares of the Victorian era. They are listed at the end of this section. Glassware that is not Burmese or Peachblow is included here.

Webb

Biscuit Jar, Mother-Of-Pearl, Rose, Pinched Side, Moire, Gold Flowers, Lid, 6 ½ In. 2185.00
Bottle, Pilgrim, Scrolled White Floral Medallion, Crimson Ground, 3 Layer, Cameo, 7 In. 15515.00
Bowl, Basket Weave, Butterscotch, Blue, Tricornered, Silver Plate, Footed Holder, 9 ½ In. 400.00
Bowl, Emerald Green, White, Vines, Tendrils, Blossoms, Pods, Crimped Rim, Cameo, 2 x 5 In. 4487.00
Bowl, Raisin Ground, Blue & White, Fleur-De-Lis, Rosettes, Cameo, Woodall, 2 x 5 In. 15575.00
Bowl, White Flowers & Leaves, Green Ground, Ruffled Rim, Signed, Cameo, 2 ½ x 6 In. 4710.00
Charger, Roses, White, Applied Butterflies, Insects, 10 ¾ In. 8338.00
Condiment Set, Yellow Satin, Gingko, Butterflies, Shaker, Mustard, Salt, Caddy, 5 In. 750.00
Ewer, White, Blue Overlay, Cameo, Stopper, 11 ½ x 6 In. *illus* 1900.00
Flask, Frosted Red, Flower Stem, Cameo, Silver Flip Cap, 5 ½ In. 2070.00
Inkwell, Red & White Fuchsias, Frosted Ground, Silver Lid, Signed, 6 In. 3200.00
Perfume Bottle, Flowers, Lemon Ground, Cameo, Lay Down, Silver Screw Cap, 6 In. 960.00
Perfume Bottle, Flowers, White Over Ruby, Butterfly, Silver Gilt Stopper, 3 ¼ In. 1920.00
Perfume Bottle, Palms, Bamboo, White Over Pale Blue, Cameo, Silver Cap, Stopper, 4 In. 2588.00
Perfume Bottle, Swan's Head, White, Red, Cameo, Laydown, Silver Cap, Case, 9 ¼ In. 18000.00
Perfume Bottle, Swan's Head, White Over Blue, Cameo, Laydown, Sterling Cap, 5 ¾ In. 6700.00
Perfume Bottle, Teardrop Shape, Red Body, Gold Enameled Flowers, 6 In. 575.00
Perfume Bottle, White Bamboo, Red Ground, Cameo, Silver Cap, Marked, 1887, 7 In. 1800.00
Perfume Bottle, White Flowers & Leaves, Apricot, Cameo, Silver Cap, 1884, 10 ¾ In. 3800.00
Pitcher, Alexandrite, Amber To Fuchsia To Blue, Waves, Oval, Crimped Rim, 5 ½ In. 1955.00
Pitcher, Pink Cased, Egg Shape, Oval Rim, Camphor Handle, 8 In. 201.00
Pitcher, Yellow, Pink Interior, Egg Shape, Pinched Square Rim, 7 ½ In. 115.00
Rose Bowl, Enameled Flower Blossoms & Leaves, Crimped Rim, 3 x 3 In. 518.00
Rose Bowl, Yellow, Red Over White, Raspberry Branch, Egg Shape, Cameo, 3 ½ In. 978.00
Scent Bottle, Citron, White, Palms, Butterflies, Globular, Cameo, Silver Cap, 3 In. 1116.00
Scent Bottle, Red, White Flowering Branches, Laydown, Cameo, Sterling Silver Cap, 7 In. 2115.00
Serving Spoon & Fork, White Over Blue, Blossoms, Cameo, Gorham Silver, 12 In. 1840.00
Vase, Amethyst Cut To Clear Bull's-Eyes, Swags & Vines, Swollen Neck, Footed, 5 ⅞ In. 71.00
Vase, Amethyst, Tulips, Chipped Ice Ground, Cameo, 6 ¼ x 8 ½ In. 575.00
Vase, Arabesque, Flowers & Scrolls, Lavender, Olive, White, Cameo, Marked, 5 ⅞ In. 49000.00
Vase, Arabesque, Red Ground, Cameo, Marked, 10 In. 39000.00
Vase, Berry Sprigs, Blue, Cameo, Marked, 3 ½ In. *illus* 325.00
Vase, Blue, White, Scroll & Flowers, Bellflower, Bead, Petal Border, Cameo, Marked, 8 In. 22500.00
Vase, Bud, White Flowers, Blue Ground, Bulbous, Base, Cameo, 8 ½ In. 3900.00
Vase, Citron, Bulbous, Overlaid In White, Trumpet Blossoms & Buds, 3 Bumblebees, 14 In. 8284.00
Vase, Citron, Leafy Stemmed Flower, Butterfly, Cameo, 9 ½ In. 748.00
Vase, Citron, White Wildflower Blossoms, Footed, Cameo, Signed, 10 ¼ In. 1093.00
Vase, Copper Metallic, Cobalt Blue, Holly & Berries, Scroll Ground, 6 ¾ In. *illus* 4833.00
Vase, Cranberry Iris, Textured Ground, Pinched Waist, Cameo, 6 In. 266.00
Vase, Flora, Amethyst & Clear, Classical Female, Flowers, Clouds, Borders, c.1901, 7 ¼ In. 64975.00
Vase, Flower Garlands, Butterflies, Gold, Pink, White, Cameo, Marked, 8 In. 30100.00
Vase, Flowers, Leaves, Butterfly, Blue Ground, Cameo, 4 ¼ In. 1150.00
Vase, Flowers, Leaves, Sand Dollar, Clear Blue Ground, Cameo, 4 ¾ In. 2300.00
Vase, Flowers, Leaves, White, Blue, Cameo, 6 ¾ In. 6900.00
Vase, Flowers, Pink, White, Yellow Ground, Cameo, 3 ¾ In. 518.00
Vase, Flowers, Pink & White, Yellow Ground, Cameo, 1 ½ x 3 In. 720.00
Vase, Frosted Red, Cockle Shells, Butterflies, Oval, Shouldered, Cameo, 7 In. 4313.00
Vase, Fruit, Leaves, White, Purple, Blue Ground, Cameo, 8 ¾ In. 4600.00

Webb, Ewer, White, Blue Overlay, Cameo, Stopper, 11 ½ x 6 In.
$1900.00

Webb, Vase, Berry Sprigs, Blue, Cameo, Marked, 3 ½ In.
$325.00

Webb, Vase, Copper Metallic, Cobalt Blue, Holly & Berries, Scroll Ground, 6 ¾ In.
$4833.00

Webb, Vase, Raspberry, White, Flowers, 2 White Borders, Bulbous, Cameo, 4 ¼ In.
$967.00

Webb, Vase, Rubina, Marked, 8 ⅛ In.
$60.00

Webb Burmese, Epergne, Crimped Edge, Brass Holder, Clarke's Patent Fairy Lamps, 11 ½ In.
$2233.00

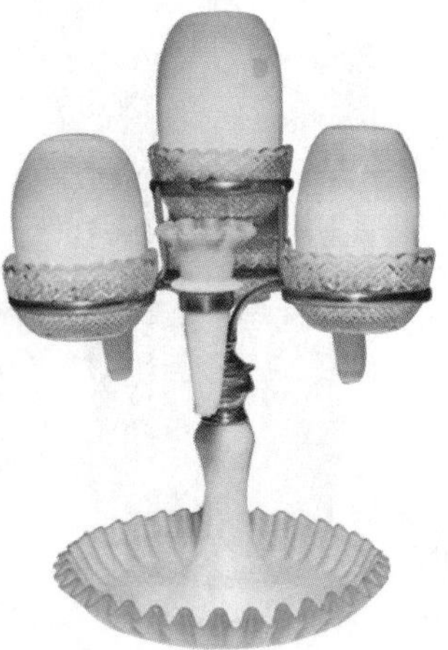

Vase, Green Satin, Opal Cased, Gold Stem Flower, Butterfly, Bulbous, 5 ½ In. 173.00
Vase, Hat Shape, Black Cut To Clear, Punty & Fan, 2 x 7 In. 100.00
Vase, Ivory, Cascading Branches, 6 Insects, Shouldered, Cameo, 4 ¼ In. 345.00
Vase, Ivory, Ginkgo Branches, Gourd Shape, Cameo, Signed, 6 In. 690.00
Vase, Ivory, Swags, Tassels, Bows, Brown Patina, Raised Rim, Oval, Cameo, 5 In. 2761.00
Vase, Lily Pad, Wide Mouth, Raised Round Foot, Marked, 30 In. 353.00
Vase, Opaque Flowers, Butterfly, Crimson Ground, Tapered Oval, Cameo, 5 ½ In. 1265.00
Vase, Pink Floral Vines, Frosted Ground, Pink Scroll Handles, Footed, Cameo, 4 ⅛ In., Pair... 3525.00
Vase, Pond Flowers, Crab, Frog, Butterfly, Gray & Salmon, White Ground, Cameo, 6 In. 2818.00
Vase, Prussian Blue, Rampant Dueling Dragons, Oval, Cameo, c.1889, 6 In. 32200.00
Vase, Raisins, Stemmed Flowers, Holly Border, Baluster Shape, Cameo, 3 ¼ In. 7480.00
Vase, Raspberry, White, Flowers, 2 White Borders, Bulbous, Cameo, 4 ¼ In. .... *illus* 967.00
Vase, Red Over Yellow, Berry Clusters, Leafy Branches, Cameo, 6 ¼ In. 4142.00
Vase, Rubina, Marked, 8 ⅛ In. .... *illus* 60.00
Vase, Ruby, Gold Cascading Flowers, Shouldered, 13 In., Pair 207.00
Vase, Stick, Prussian Blue, Leafy Morning Glories, Bulbous Base, Cameo, 10 In. 2990.00
Vase, Stick, White Berries, Leaves, Orange Brown, Bulbous, Cameo, Marked, 6 ¾ In. 3450.00
Vase, Sunflower, Grasses, Double White Bands On Top, Green, Cameo, 8 ⅞ In. 3452.00
Vase, White, Flowers & Leaves, Citron Ground, Bulbous, Cameo, 7 In. 540.00
Vase, White, Sunflowers, Leaves, Butterfly, Citron Ground, Cameo, 5 In. 805.00
Vase, White & Pink Flowers, Gold & Rose, Bulbous, Flared Rim, Cameo, Marked, 6 In. 2500.00
Vase, White Over Red Blossoms & Leaves, Citron Ground, Cameo, 5 ¼ In. 2875.00
Vase, White Shells, Sea Plants, Red, Scalloped Rim, Bulbous, Footed, Cameo, 7 x 4 In. 13200.00
Vase, White To Light Blue Leaves & Branches, Azure Blue Ground, Cameo, 7 ½ In. 3450.00
Vase, Yellow, Passion Flower, Butterfly, 5 In. 863.00
Vase, Yellow Over Red, Double Gourd, Amber Elephant Handles, 6 ¼ In. 173.00

WEBB BURMESE is a colored Victorian glass made by Thomas Webb & Sons of Stourbridge, England, from 1886.

Bowl, Rose, Prunus, Hexagonal Mouth, 4 In. 125.00
Epergne, Crimped Edge, Brass Holder, Clarke's Patent Fairy Lamps, 11 ½ In. .... *illus* 2233.00
Fairy Lamp, Domed Shade, Double Crystal Insert, Footed Base, Marked, 6 In. 2300.00
Jam Jar, Cylindrical, Bed Berries, Gilt Branches, Butterfly, Stamped, 4 ½ In. 546.00
Perfume Bottle, Gold Leafy Branches, Berries, Oval, Sterling Silver Cap, 3 ½ In. 805.00
Sugar & Creamer, Red Berries, Leafy Vines, Oval, Satin, Silver Plated Caddy, 7 In. 1800.00
Tumbler, Sprigs Of Leaves, Applied Blueberries, Diamond Quilted, 2 ⅞ In. 708.00
Vase, Bud, Footed, Star Shape, Everted Rim, 4 In. 100.00
Vase, Ivy, Leaves, Melon Ribbed, 3 ½ In. 345.00
Vase, Lavender Vine, Blue Flowers, Hexagonal Rim, Globular, 3 ¼ In. 443.00
Vase, Melon Ribbed, c.1890, 4 ¼ In. .... *illus* 350.00
Vase, Oak Leaves, Acorns, Stick, Ruffled Rim, Bulbous Base, 8 ½ In. 4313.00
Vase, Pink, Brown Seashells, Gold Branches, Egg Shape, 3 ½ In. 288.00
Vase, Pouch, Pinched Sides, Scalloped Rim, 3 ½ In. 259.00
Vase, Prunus Blossoms, Ruffled Edge, Footed, 4 In., Pair 374.00

WEBB PEACHBLOW is a colored Victorian glass made by Thomas Webb & Sons of Stourbridge, England, from 1885.

Biscuit Jar, Songs Birds On Branches, Oval, 6 In. 175.00
Bride's Bowl, White & Yellow Flowers, Melon, Ribbed, Gold Rim, 5 ⅜ x 10 In. 1298.00
Vase, Bulbous, 9 ½ In. 230.00
Vase, Cameo Butterfly, Inverted Rim, 9 ¼ In. 4025.00
Vase, Flowers, Gold & Platinum Vines, 5 In. .... *illus* 176.00
Vase, Hibiscus Blossoms, Butterfly, Bulbous, 4 ¾ In. 1880.00
Vase, Hobnail, Ruffled Edge, Amber Petal Feet, Satin, 6 In. 200.00

WEDGWOOD, one of the world's most successful potteries, was founded by Josiah Wedgwood, who was considered a cripple by his brother and was forbidden to work at the family business. The pottery was established in England in 1759. A large variety of wares has been made, including the well-known jasperware, basalt, creamware, and even a limited amount of porcelain. There are two kinds of jasperware. One is made from two colors of clay, the other is made from one color of clay with a color dip to create the contrast in design. The firm is still in business. Other Wedgwood pieces may be listed under Flow Blue, Majolica, Tea Leaf Ironstone, or in other porcelain categories. In 1986 Wedgwood and Waterford Crystal merged to form the Waterford Wedgwood Group.

WEDGWOOD

Barber Bottle, Cover, Jasperware, White Ground, Lilac, Green, Late 1800s, 10 In. 2350.00

arber Bottle, Cover, Victoria Ware, Blue Ground, Horned Bacchus Head, 10¾ In. 1116.00

iggin, Cover, Caneware, Smear Glaze, Orange Peel Ground, Arabesques, 6¾ In. 353.00

iscuit Barrel, Hinged Pewter Lid, Jasper Dip, Green, Raised Gold Design, 5½ In. 499.00

iscuit Barrel, Jasper Dip, Dice Ware, Green, Yellow, White, c.1870, 5¾ In. 940.00

iscuit Barrel, Jasper Dip, Green, White, Lilac, Silver Plated Rim, 5½ In. 353.00

iscuit Barrel, Jasper Dip, Green, Yellow, Silver Plated Rim, c.1882, 5 In. 353.00

iscuit Barrel, Jasper Dip, Silver Plated Rim, Late 1800s, 6 In. 999.00

iscuit Barrel, Majolica, Hexagonal, Green Ground, Flowers, c.1868, 6⅛ In. 176.00

iscuit Jar, Cover, Jasper Dip, Black, Egyptian Design, 1900s, 6¼ In. 1058.00

iscuit Jar, Cover, Jasper Dip, Crimson, White Figures, Oak Leaves, c.1920, 6⅜ In. 999.00

iscuit Jar, Cover, Jasper Dip, Tricolor, Black Ground, Classical Relief Figures, 5⅝ In. 1116.00

iscuit Jar, Cover, Jasper Dip, Yellow, Black Relief, Festoons, Silver Plate, Rim, 5¾ In. 264.00

iscuit Jar, White, Blue Ground, Figures, Metal Lid & Handle, 5 x 6 In. 89.00

ough Pot, Cover, Terra-Cotta, White, Brown Slip, Scrollwork, c.1785, 6¼ In. 881.00

owl, Black Basalt, Multifaceted Border Panels, Keith Murray, c.1935, 9¼ In. 646.00

owl, Butterfly Luster, Mottled Purple, Blue Exterior, Gilt, Mother-Of-Pearl, 8¼ In. 558.00

owl, Butterfly Luster, Octagonal, Oriental Motif, Mother-Of-Pearl Inside, c.1920, 8 In. 764.00

owl, Copper Luster, Cane Glazed, Multicolor Enamel Flowers, Millicent Taplin, 9 In. 118.00

owl, Dragon Luster, Gilt Dragon, Blue Luster Ground, Marked, 8 In. 1610.00

owl, Dragon Luster, Imperial, Gold Gilt Rain Dragons, Blue, Round, Marked, 5 In. 500.00

owl, Dragon Luster, Mottled Blue, Gold Gilt, Pearlescent Interior, 3⅛ In. 230.00

owl, Dragon Luster, Mottled Blue, Mother-Of-Pearl, 3 Jewels, c.1920, 7 In. 999.00

owl, Dragon Luster, Octagonal, Gilded Dragons, Mottled Blue, 7¼ In. 441.00

owl, Earthenware, Footed, Multicolor Enamel, Millicent Taplin, c.1925, 9 In. 382.00

owl, Fairyland Luster, Black Ground, Poplar Tree, Elves In Bell Branch, 9¼ In. 2990.00 to 5175.00

owl, Fairyland Luster, Imperial, Woodland Bridge, River Picnic, c.1920, 8 In. 5581.00

owl, Fairyland Luster, Lahore, Black Ground, Yellow, Warriors, Elephants, c.1920, 8 In. 3290.00

owl, Fairyland Luster, Octagonal, Castle On Road, Fairy In Cage, 9 In. 2875.00 to 5175.00

owl, Fairyland Luster, Octagonal, Cobalt Blue, Cream Interior, 4 x 7¾ In. 325.00

owl, Fairyland Luster, Octagonal, Woodland Elves, Fiddler In Tree, Blue Ground, 8 In. 6325.00

owl, Fairyland Luster, Thumbelina Medallion, Lily Pads, Marked, 9¾ In. 2875.00

owl, Fairyland Luster, Willow, Midnight Luster, Japanese Lantern, Marked, 9 In. 2760.00

owl, Jasper Dip, Black, Classical Relief, 3-Footed, Late 1800s, 6 In. 441.00

owl, Jasperware, Dancing Hours, White, Black, 9¾ In. 231.00

owl, Luster, Emerald Green, Mythical Creatures, Bai-Fuku Riding Feng Birds, Marked, 4 In. 230.00

owl, Luster, Octagonal, Fruit, Mottled Blue Exterior, Orange, Red Interior, 8⅛ In. 646.00

owl, Mariposa, Footed, 3 x 4½ In. 15.00

owl, Potpourri, Cover, Muses Bearing Gifts, c.1900, 9 x 6 In. 215.00

owl, Powder Blue, Multicolored, Butterflies, Mottled Inside, c.1915, 6¼ In. 176.00

owl, Salad, Jasper Dip, Yellow, Black Relief, Lion, Masks, c.1930, 8⅜ In. 881.00

owl, Salad, Servers, Queen's Ware, Multicolored Chickens, c.1863, 10¼ In. 353.00

ox, Jasperware, Black, Square, Leaf Border, 4 In. 64.00

oth Set, Queen's Ware, Multicolor Enamel, Insects, Flowers, c.1878, 9¾ In. 235.00

ıst, Eisenhower, Black Basalt, Box 83.00

ıst, Milton, Waisted Round Pedestal, Carrara, Mid 19th Century, 14¼ In. 823.00

ıst, Robert Stephenson, Waisted Round Pedestal, 1860, 14¾ In. 441.00

ıst, Shakespeare, Black Basalt, Waisted Pedestal, 19th Century, 12¼ In. 646.00

ıst, Venus, Black Basalt, Waisted Pedestal, 19th Century, 13 In. 1410.00

itter, Willow, Child's, Gaudy Willow Finish, 5 x 2½ In. 230.00

itter Chip, Green, Leaf Shape 115.00

itter Chip, Majolica, Sunflower 104.00

itter Chip, Mottled, Cobalt Blue & Brown 81.00

chepot, Jasper Dip, Tricolor, Light Blue Ground, Muses, Framed Medallions, 7 In., Pair 1645.00

nopic Jar, Cover, Jasperware, Black, Terra-Cotta Bands, Hieroglyphs, c.1977, 9½ In. 1763.00

arger, Earthenware, Multicolored Enamel, Flowers, Monogram, c.1913, 16¼ In. 1645.00

arger, Majolica, Multicolored, Enameled, Nymph On Sea Serpent, Birds, Dolphins, 15 In. 754.00

eese Dish, Cover, Jasper Dip, Dark Blue, White Barnyard Animals, 12¾ In. 823.00

eese Keeper, Dark Blue, Circular, 6½ x 11½ In. 146.00

ffee Set, Queen's Ware, Yellow Ground, Green Band, Copper Luster, c.1925, 11 Piece 646.00

mpote, Majolica, Dolphin, Reticulated Border, Cobalt Blue, 7 x 9¼ In. 230.00

mpote, Queen's Ware, Pink Ground Border, Landscape, Emile Lessore, c.1870, 9 In. 588.00

mpote, Stand, Nautilus Shell, Pink, Cream, Red, Green Coral, c.1874, 10¾ In. *illus* 999.00

eam Jug, Jasperware, White Body, Lilac Medallions, Green, 2¾ In. 646.00

eam Jug, Queen's Ware, Black Tea Party Transfer, Pear Shape, Late 1700s, 5½ In. 294.00

eamer, Majolica, Mr. Punch, Turquoise, 4½ In. 1208.00

ocus Pot, Tray, Black Basalt, Hedgehog, Pierced Body, Mid 1800s, 9 In. 1175.00

Webb Burmese, Vase, Melon Ribbed, c.1890, 4¼ In.
$350.00

Webb Peachblow, Vase, Flowers, Gold & Platinum Vines, 5 In.
$176.00

Wedgwood, Compote, Stand, Nautilus Shell, Pink, Cream, Red, Green Coral, c.1874, 10¾ In.
$999.00

Wedgwood

The real Wedgwood company run by Josiah Wedgwood is spelled WEDGWOOD. Another English company took advantage of the name by using the mark WEDGEWOOD.

TIP

We once pulled some of the silver plating from a Sheffield candlestick when we removed the cellophane tape that held a Christmas decoration to the candlestick. A friend pulled some of the glaze from a plate when she pulled masking tape off the plate. Don't use anything with a strong glue on an antique surface.

Wedgwood, Jug, Jasper Dip, Crimson, Etruscan, White Relief, c.1915, 6 ⅛ In.
$1293.00

Wedgwood, Pie Dish, Cover, Chick Finial, Majolica, Oval, Brown Ground, c.1872, 9 In.
$2233.00

Cup, Fairyland Luster, Melba, Leapfrogging Elves, Mother-Of-Pearl, 4 ¾ In. 2585.0
Cup & Saucer, Jasper Dip, Dice Ware, Black, Yellow, White, 5 ¼ In. 1645.0
Cup & Saucer, Tea, Jasper Dip, Crimson, White Classical Design, c.1915, 5 ½ In. 1880.0
Cuspidor, Black Basalt, Dice Banding, Mid 1800s, 5 In. 529.0
Dinner Service, Columbia Sage, Green Porcelain, 59 Piece 761.0
Dish, Cover, Finial, Caneware, Game Birds, Grape Clusters, c.1815, 6 x 10 x 7 In.. . . . . 269.0
Dish, Cover, Majolica, Rectangular, Flower Urns, Scallops, c.1884, 8 ⅜ In.. . . . . 558.0
Dish, Earthenware, Silver Luster, Brown Enamel, c.1923, 18 In.. . . . . 1645.0
Dish, Majolica, Game, Lovebirds, Flowers, Ribbons, Bows, Winged Griffin Ends, 12 In. 2300.0
Dish, Majolica, Game, Rabbit, Fence, Leaves, Branches, Crossed Guns On Cover, 9 In. 4025.0
Dish, Molded Dome Cover, Divided, Queen's Ware, Pierced, 9 ¾ In. 881.0
Dish, Pickle, Majolica, Argenta, Heart Shape, 6 ¾ In.. . . . . 150.0
Dish, Queen's Ware, Oval, Cut Corners, Multicolored Enamel, Etruria Volunteers, 10 In.. . . . . 764.0
Dish, Sweetmeat, Imperial Queen's Ware, Pierced Trellis, Shell Shape, c.1875, 8 In., Pair 881.0
Figurine, Crane, Pierced Rock Base, Black Basalt, Glass Eyes, c.1915, 6 ¼ In.. . . . . 441.0
Figurine, Egret, Pierced Rock Base, Black Basalt, 20th Century, 7 ¼ In. 235.0
Figurine, Elephant, Black Basalt, Glass Eyes, Ernest Light, c.1915, 3 ⅜ In. 382.0
Figurine, Raven, Black Basalt, On Base, Glass Eyes, Ernest Light, c.1915, 4 ¼ In.. . . . . 470.0
Figurine, Sea Lion, Celadon Glaze, Rocky Base, John Skeaping, c.1927, 6 ¾ In.. . . . . 294.0
Figurine, Sleeping Boy, Black Basalt, 5 Boys From Fiammingo, 1800s, 5 ¼ In.. . . . . 323.0
Figurine, Sphinx, Seated, Black Basalt, Raised Rectangular Base, 1800s, 6 In., Pair 1410.0
Figurine, Sphinx, Seated, Egyptian Motif Base, Basalt, 8 ¼ In.. . . . . 1800.0
Figurine, Vultures, Black Basalt, Perched Birds, Glass Eyes, 20th Century, 5 ⅜ In. 1645.0
Fish Platter, Majolica, Oval, Scalloped Edge, Multicolored, c.1880, 25 In. 2938.0
Flowerpot, Biscuit, Black Slip, Vertical Fluting, Bead Border, 1700s, 4 In.. . . . . 411.0
Hot Water Pot, Cover, Caneware, Egyptian, Applied Relief, Hieroglyphs, 8 ½ In.. . . . . 4113.0
Ice Bucket, Creamware, Sepia Grapevine Border, Tapered, Shaped Handles, 9 In. 717.0
Inkstand, Rosso Antico, Black Basalt, Oil Lamp Shape, Attached Oval Tray, 7 In.. . . . . 646.0
Jar, Cover, Foo Dog Finial, Blue & White, 19th Century, 10 ½ In., 2 Piece 380.0
Jar, Jasperware, Reticulated Ferns, Pictorials Of Romanesque Life, Marked, 3 ½ In. 173.0
Jardiniere, Jasper Dip, Lilac, Muses, Vine Festoons, Late 1800s, 7 ¾ In.. . . . . 881.0
Jardiniere, Jasper Dip, Yellow, White Relief, c.1900, 7 In.. . . . . 999.0
Jardiniere, Jasperware, White, Lilac, Green, Late 1800s, 5 In. 1058.0
Jardiniere, Stand, Jasper Dip, Crimson, Classical Relief, Floral Band, 4 ¼ In.. . . . . 2233.0
Jardiniere, Stand, Jasper Dip, Green, Yellow, White, 19th Century, 9 In. 264.0
Jardiniere, Stand, Redware, Enamel, Gilded, Ring Handles, Incised, 1800s, 6 In.. . . . . 558.0
Jug, Caterer, Majolica, Multicolored, Medallions, Verse, c.1865, 9 ⅜ In. 353.0
Jug, Ivory Glaze, Multicolored Enamel, Punch, Toby, Pewter Lid, c.1880, 7 ¾ In. 470.0
Jug, Jasper Dip, Crimson, Etruscan, White Relief, c.1915, 6 ⅛ In. *illus* 1293.0
Jug, Majolica, Blue Ground, Bird & Fan, Birds, Prunus, c.1884, 7 ¼ In.. . . . . 323.0
Jug, Rosso Antico, Club, Multicolored, Enameled, Gilt Flowers, c.1830, 7 ¼ In.. . . . . 470.0
Jug, Stoneware, White, Smear Glaze, Gothic, Hexagonal, Blue Relief, Muses, c.1830, 8 In.. . . . 411.0
Jug, Veronese Ware, Globular, Ribbed Neck, Blue Ground, Silver Luster, c.1930, 6 In.. . . . . 118.0
Letter Box, Mounted Ormolu, Light Blue Jasper Medallions, 6 ¾ In. 411.0
Medallion, Blue Jasper, Portrait, Empress Catherine Of Russia, Oval, Frame, 4 In. 4700.0
Medallion, Jasper Dip, Black, Wood Frame, Wedgwood & Bentley, c.1780, 1 ½ In., Pair 499.0
Mold, Queen's Ware, Oval, Scalloped Border, Incised Flower Basket, 1700s, 11 In. 235.0
Mug, Hops Cider, Vine Handle, 4 ¼ In.. . . . . 115.0
Mug, Jasper Dip, Light Blue, White Palmettes, Verse, c.1900, 5 ¼ In.. 881.0
Mug, Jasper Dip, Olive Green, White Vines, Verse, c.1920, 5 ¼ In. 441.0
Mug, Town Crier, 7 In. 165.0
Oil Lamp, Inkstand, Rosso Antico, Applied Black Band, Scrolled Handle, 5 ⅜ In. 441.0
Orange Bowl, Domed Cover, Queen's Ware, Scrollwork, Elongated Piercing, 12 In.. . . . . 470.0
Oyster Plate, 6 Wells, Chrysanthemum, Burgundy, Yellow, 9 In. 2013.0
Oyster Plate, 6 Wells, Majolica, Shell & Waves, Green Ground, Multicolored Wells, 7 In. 374.0
Perfume, Jasperware, Light Blue, Lilac, White, Silver Cover, Oval, 3 ¼ In. 1058.0
Pie Dish, Cover, Caneware, Hare Finial, Oval, Molded, c.1872, 9 ⅜ In.. 499.0
Pie Dish, Cover, Caneware, Oval, Molded, Vines, Early 1800s, 11 In. 353.0
Pie Dish, Cover, Caneware, Oval, Oval Platter, Acanthus, Early 1800s, 14 In. 353.0
Pie Dish, Cover, Chick Finial, Majolica, Oval, Brown Ground, c.1872, 9 In.. . . . . *illus* 2233.0
Pin, Butterfly Luster, Oval, Multicolored Enamel, Mother-Of-Pearl, Silver, c.1920, 2 In.. . . . . . . 294.
Pitcher, Black Basalt, Upright Dolphin Form, c.1855, 8 ¼ In.. . . . . 720.
Pitcher, Cobalt Blue & Ivy Band, 8 In. . . . . 92.
Pitcher, Majolica, Bird & Fan, 6 ¼ In.. . . . . 17.
Pitcher, Majolica, Bird & Fan, Turquoise Interior, England, 19th Century, 7 ½ In.. . . . . 132.
Pitcher, Majolica, Primrose, Brown, Cobalt Blue Handle, 5 In. 489

Pitcher, Pewter Lid, Rockingham, Glazed, Ribbed Panels, Gilt, c.1875, 7 ½ In. 646.00
Planter, Tile, Iron Mounted, Square, Blue Transfer, Late 1800s, 7 ½ In. 264.00
Plaque, Dancing Woman, Ebonized Frame, 6 x 18 In. 478.00
Plaque, Jasper Dip, Black, Round, Cupid Sharpening Arrows, Wood Frame, 5 ¾ In. 353.00
Plaque, Jasper Dip, Green, The Choice Of Hercules, 6 x 16 ½ In. 529.00
Plaque, Jasperware, Black, Applied White Bacchanalian Boys, 19th Century, 22 ½ In. 823.00
Plaque, Jasperware, Hercules In The Garden Of Hesperides, 6 x 15 ¾ In. 340.00
Plaque, Jasperware, Oval, Tricolor, Cupid, Psyche, Hymen, Bert Bentley, 3 ¾ In., Pair 646.00
Plaque, Jasperware, Portrait, General LaFayette, Profile, 4 ¼ In. 777.00
Plaque, Jasperware, Romanesque Woman, Gilt Matte, Walnut Frame, 15 ½ x 13 In. 115.00
Plaque, Queen's Ware, Multicolored Enamel, Peace, French Inscription, c.1919, 15 In. 588.00
Plaque, Redware, Portrait, William Shakespeare, Oval, Mahogany Frame, 4 ½ x 5 In. 1645.00
Plate, Christmas, 1969, Windsor Castle, Box, 8 In. 60.00
Plate, Christmas, 1970, Jasperware, Blue, 8 In. 18.00
Plate, Christmas, 1972, Jasperware, Blue, 8 In. 41.00
Plate, Christmas, 1975, Jasperware, Blue, 8 In. 41.00
Plate, Cromer, Pink Ground, Yellow Flower Spray Center, 10 ½ In. 708.00
Plate, Etruria, Mass Clipper Ships, Black Transfer, White Ground, Flags, 5 Piece 385.00
Plate, Fish, Luster, Gold Gilt Fish, Fishnet, Marked, 9 In. 35.00
Plate, Green Border, Flower Spray, 10 ¾ In., 8 Piece 148.00
Plate, Jasper Dip, Black, Classical Design, Ribbon, Vine Band, Mid 1800s, 8 ¾ In. 1175.00
Plate, Majolica, Oriental Flower, Pink Border, Mottled, 8 ¼ In. 104.00
Plate, Majolica, Shell & Waves, Mottled Ground, 8 ¾ In. 92.00
Plate, Majolica, Stork, In Marsh, Reticulated Border, 9 In. 489.00
Plate, Queen's Ware, Multicolored, Orange Rim, Emile Lessore, c.1863, 9 In., 12 Piece 1645.00
Plate, Service, White Center, Blue & White Floral Rim, c.1930, 10 ¾ In., 12 Piece 234.00
Plate Set, Green Glaze, 8 In., 6 Piece 117.00
Platter, Landscape, 5 Cows, Blue, 16 x 18 In. 795.00
Platter, Majolica, Bird & Fan, 13 ½ In. 633.00
Platter, Majolica, Butterfly, Flowers, Argenta, 12 In. 104.00
Platter, Pearlware, Blue Shell Edge, c.1775, 18 In. 435.00
Platter, Sepia, Cream Glaze, Impressed Mark, 14 ½ In. 23.00
Pot, Malfrey, Cover, Luster, Landscape, 9 ½ In. 560.00
Pot, Malfrey, Fairyland Luster, Flame Ground, Willow, Lighthouse, 7 ½ In., Pair 1880.00
Potpourri Vase, Cover, Basalt, Vine, Berries Festoons, 3 Dolphins, Triangular Base, 16 In. 9988.00
Potpourri Vase, Cover, Birds, Flowers, Globular, Upturned Loop Handles, 11 In. 1058.00
Potpourri Vase, Cover, Caneware, Smear Glaze, Acorn Finial, Loop Handles, 11 In. 1293.00
Potpourri Vase, Cover, Jasper Dip, Dark Blue, Applied Leaf Relief, 6 In. 353.00
Potpourri Vase, Cover, Jasper Dip, Dark Blue, Loop Handles, Pierced Dome, 7 In. 411.00
Potpourri Vase, Cover, Pearlware, Green Ground, Flowers, Loop Handles, 15 ¾ In. 705.00
Potpourri Vase, Cover, Rosso Antico, Globular, Loop Handles, c.1830, 9 ¼ In. 646.00
Potpourri Vase, Cover, Stoneware, Fluting, Terra-Cotta, Pearl Glaze, 1700s, 5 ¾ In. 529.00
Potpourri Vase, Crater, Cover, Stoneware, White Smear Glazed, Pierced, c.1820, 13 In. 588.00
Potpourri Vase, Jasperware, Light Blue, Pierced Grid Cover, Scalloped Rim, 7 In. 823.00
Powder Box, Cover, Textured Brown & White Glaze, Mid 1900s, 5 In. 235.00
Tea Bowl, Saucer, Jasper Dip, Green, Polished Rim, White Classical Figures, 5 In. 1058.00
Tea Canister, Cover, Jasperware, White, Bottle Shape, Applied Green Design, 5 ½ In. 705.00
Tea Set, Jasperware, Black Dip Ground, White, Yellow, 3 Piece *illus* 5875.00
Tea Set, Liberty, Multicolored Transfers, Allied Flags, Gilt Rims, c.1918, 25 In. 588.00
Tea Set, Queen's Ware, Multicolored Landscape, Globular Pot, c.1870, 4 Piece 881.00
Teakettle, Cobalt Blue, Vine Handle, Ferns On Spout, Stand, 7 In. 805.00
Teapot, Cover, Queen's Ware, Black Tea Party Transfer, Globular, 4 ½ In. 764.00
Teapot, Cover, Queen's Ware, Strawberries, Globular, Molded Spout, c.1770, 5 ½ In. 1528.00
Teapot, Cover, Rosso Antico, Egyptian, Applied Black Hieroglyphs, 1800s, 4 ¼ In. 1175.00
Teapot, Jasperware, Primrose, Cream, 3 ½ In. 70.00
Tobacco Jar, Dome Cover, Jasper Dip, Tricolor, Lilac Medallions, White Figures, 5 ½ In. 588.00
Tray, Fairyland Luster, Mottled Blue, Green Ground, Lily, Garden Of Paradise, 11 In. 4025.00
Tray, Fairyland Luster, Mottled Green, Lily, Jumping Faun, Flying Geese, c.1920, 9 In. 2703.00
Tray, Fairyland Luster, Mottled Purple, Blue, Lily, Flying Geese, 13 In. 8225.00
Tray, Ice Cream, Earthenware, Multicolored, Elks, Deer, Icicle Rim, Handles, 16 In. 646.00
Tray, Majolica, Corn, Poppy, Wheat, Basket Weave, 13 In. 316.00
Tray, Serving, Majolica, Tiered Leaf Shape, Yellow, Brown, c.1866, 16 In. 353.00
Urn, Cover, Black, Basalt, Gilt Garland & Flowers, Cover, c.1880, 8 ¼ In. 7170.00
Urn, Cover, Blue & White, Loop Handles, Pedestal Base, c.1885, 12 ½ In., Pair 1762.00
Urn, Cover, Caneware, Pierced Disc Cover, Scrolled Handles, Vines, 8 ⅜ In. 764.00
Urn, Jasperware, Light Blue, 2 Handles, Cover, c.1976, 12 ½ In. 209.00

Wedgwood, Tea Set, Jasperware, Black Dip Ground, White, Yellow, 3 Piece
$5875.00

Wedgwood, Vase, Cover, Fairyland Luster, Ghostly Woods, Pale Blue Sky, c.1920, 15 ½ In.
$37600.00

Wedgwood, Wall Pocket, Majolica, Bird, Nest, Oak Tree, Stamped, c.1900, 9 In.
$80.00

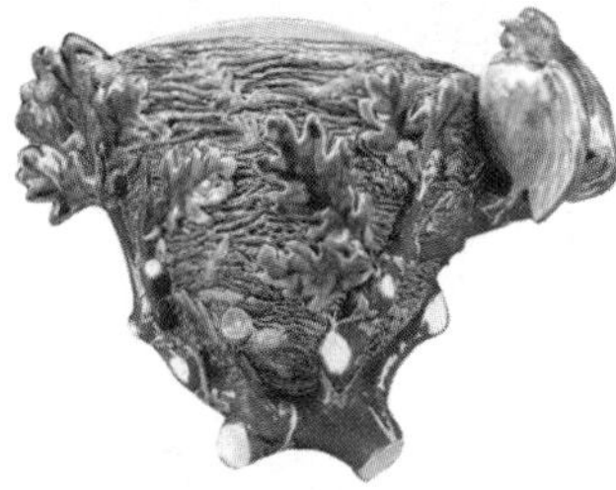

Retired Plates

When a limited edition figurine or plate is "retired," it is no longer made and will never be made again. When the figurine or plate is "suspended," it is not currently in production but may be at a later date.

Weller, Aurelian, Vase, Roses, Multicolored, H.S. Mitchell, 40 x 20 In.
$9000.00

Weller, Blue Drapery, Vase, 7¾ In.
$47.00

Weller, Coppertone, Vase, Frog Holding Lotus Flower, Marked, 4 x 4½ In.
$155.00

Urn, Majolica, Putti, Cobalt Blue, 11 x 10 In. 1380.00
Vase, Auro Basalt, Raised Slip Leaves, Fruit, Enameled, c.1885, 9 In. 2350.00
Vase, Black Basalt, Multicolored, c.1900, 9¼ In., Pair 3055.00
Vase, Black Basalt, Trumpet, Molded, Leafy Vining, Early 1900s, 11½ In., Pair 470.00
Vase, Blue, Gilt, Coiling Dragon, Scrolled Leaf Borders,1915, 13½ In., Pair. 558.00
Vase, Bone China, Double Gourd Shape, Imari Colors, Flowers, 4⅜ In., Pair 206.00
Vase, Butterfly Luster, Gold Gilt, Mottled Pearlescent Ground, 8 In. 288.00
Vase, Butterfly Luster, Red Ground, Gold Gilt, 9¼ In.. . . . . . 660.00
Vase, Cane Glaze, Flared Rim, Multicolored Enamel, c.1930, 8 In. 353.00
Vase, Cane Glaze, Pink & Green Enamel, Flowers, c.1930, 8 In. 176.00
Vase, Cover, Black Basalt, Swags, Palmette Rim, Wedgwood & Bentley, c.1775, 8 In., Pair 1880.00
Vase, Cover, Black Basalt, Tripod, Egyptian Design, Goat Heads, Hoof Feet, 9¼ In. 4113.00
Vase, Cover, Cream Ground Band, Gilt, Leaves, Brown Enamel, Late 1800s, 9¾ In.. . . . . . 646.00
Vase, Cover, Fairyland Luster, Candlemas, c.1920, 11¼ In. 3819.00
Vase, Cover, Fairyland Luster, Ghostly Woods, Pale Blue Sky, c.1920, 15½ In. . . . . . *illus* 37600.00
Vase, Cover, Jasper Dip, Olive Green, Loop Handles, c.1925, 10¼ In.. . . . . . 588.00
Vase, Cover, Jasper Dip, Tricolor, Handles, Bronze Mounts, Lilac Medallions, Cupids, 15 In.. . . . . . 2103.00
Vase, Cover, Jasper Dip, White, Green, Yellow, 9 In.. . . . . . 558.00
Vase, Cover, Jasperware, Tripod, White, Green, Lilac, Early 1800s, 8⅝ In. 1998.00
Vase, Cover, Porphyry, White Terra-Cotta, Speckle Glaze, Wedgwood & Bentley, 10½ In.. . . . . . 1645.00
Vase, Cover, Powder Blue, Gilt, Enameled, c.1915, 9¼ In. 470.00
Vase, Cover, Victoria Ware, Gilt Trim, Iron Red, Teal Ground, Festoons, c.1880, 10 In. 382.00
Vase, Daventry Luster, Oriental Figures, Landscape, Flowers, c.1920, 8½ In. 881.00
Vase, Dragon Luster, Gold Gilt Dragons, Orange Luster Ground, Marked, 6 In. 345.00
Vase, Dragon Luster, Mottle Blue, Wine Exterior, Gilt Dragon, Mother-Of-Pearl, 5 In.. . . . . . 206.00
Vase, Dragon Luster, Tapered Rim, Foot, Mottled Blue, Coiled Dragon, c.1920, 11 In.. . . . . . 676.00
Vase, Earthenware, Ivory Glaze, Bottle Shape, Gilt, Flowers, c.1885, 14¼ In.. . . . . . 294.00
Vase, Earthenware, Red Matte Ground, Mid 1900s, 5¾ In. 646.00
Vase, Earthenware, Teal Ground, Silver Luster, Leaves, c.1930, 14 In. 588.00
Vase, Fairyland Luster, Candlemas, 4 Panels Of Candles, Queen's Head, Marked, 7 In. 920.00
Vase, Fairyland Luster, Candlemas, Cover, Queen's Head, Fairies, Marked, 8½ In.. . . . . . 1080.00
Vase, Fairyland Luster, Candlemas, Faces, Fairies Hanging From Bellrope, 7 In.. . . . . . 3450.00
Vase, Fairyland Luster, Willow, Oriental Buildings, Bridges, Boats, Marked, 8 In. 1610.00
Vase, Globular, Gray Blue Ground, Silver Luster, c.1930, 11 In. 3173.00
Vase, Hispano-Moresque, Cane Glaze, Pink Luster, 1925, 4½ In. 382.00
Vase, Jasper Dip, Blue, Drum Base, Scrolled Handles, Trophy Drops, Figures, 19 In., Pair 8225.00
Vase, Jasper Dip, Brown, Medallions, Laurel Swags, Bacchus Head Masks, 9¾ In.. . . . . . 2468.00
Vase, Jasper Dip, Bulbous, Light Blue, Lilac, White, 5⅜ In. 1763.00
Vase, Jasper Dip, Dark Blue, Portland, Man In Phrygia Cap, 1800s, 10 In.. . . . . . 2115.00
Vase, Jasper Dip, Lilac, Blue Ground, Torches, c.1800, 7 In. 999.00
Vase, Jasperware, 2 Handles, 19th Century, 8 In. 508.00
Vase, Jasperware, Black, Fish, 8¼ In., Pair 216.00
Vase, Jasperware, Black, White Classical Relief, Figure, Phrygian Cap, 1800s, 10 In. 1880.00
Vase, Jasperware, Tricolor, Diced Flower, 5½ In.. . . . . . 369.00
Vase, Marsden Art Ware, Slip, Scrolled Leaves, Brown Ground, c.1885, 14¼ In. 2115.00
Vase, Queen's Ware, Gilded Scroll Handles, Multicolored, c.1863, 8 In. 1116.00
Vase, Trumpet, Yellow Ground, Black Transfer Temple, c.1915, 9½ In., Pair 382.00
Vase, Victoria Ware, Blue Ground, Gilded Florets, Festoons, c.1885, 5¼ In. 646.00
Vestal Lamp, Jasperware, White, Oval, Carved Fluting, Bellflower, 1900s, 8½ In., Pair 10575.00
Wall Pocket, Majolica, Bird, Nest, Oak Tree, Stamped, c.1900, 9 In. . . . . . *illus* 80.00
Waste Bowl, Majolica, Coral, Turquoise, 6 In. 127.00

WELLER pottery was first made in 1872 in Fultonham, Ohio. The firm moved to Zanesville, Ohio, in 1882. Artwares were introduced in 1893. Hundreds of lines of pottery were produced, including Louwelsa, Eocean, Dickens Ware, and Sicardo, before the pottery closed in 1948.

LOUWELSA WELLER

Art Nouveau, Vase, Lily Pads, Lotus Flowers, Frog, Tan & Green Glaze, 3¾ In. 1416.00
Athens, Vase, Nymphs, Seahorses, Swags, 2 Panels, Green Ground, 9¾ In. 1888.00
Aurelian, Vase, Monk, Singing, Playing Mandolin, Flared Rim, 19 In. 944.00
Aurelian, Vase, Roses, Multicolored, H.S. Mitchell, 40 x 20 In. . . . . . *illus* 9000.00
Blue Drapery, Vase, 7¾ In. . . . . . *illus* 47.00
Bo Marblo, Vase, Camel Brown Swirls, Tapered, Rolled Rim, 6⅜ In. 235.00
Bo Marblo, Vase, Veins, Tan, Gold Amber, Bulbous, Flared Rim, 4½ In.. . . . . . 223.00
Brighton, Figurine, Parrot, Multicolored, 12½ In. 561.00
Burnt Wood, Vase, Battle Scene, 7 x 4¾ In.. . . . . . 300.00
Burnt Wood, Vase, Children Playing, Carved, 5 x 6¼ In. 316.00

Burnt Wood, Vase, Magi On Camels, Brown, Tan, Tapered, Flared Rim, 16 In. 705.00
Camelot, Jardiniere, Stylized Peacock Feathers, White, Yellow Matte Ground, 9 In. 354.00
Cameo Jewell, Vase, Fiddlehead Ferns, Embossed Band Of Birds, Purple Ground, 13 x 7 In. 3600.00
Cameo Jewell, Vase, Fruit Leaves, Ribbed, Buttressed Handles, 11 1/2 x 6 1/2 In. 4500.00
Coppertone, Bowl, Mottled, Green, Over Brown, Leaves, Flower Medallion, 3 x 12 1/2 In. 499.00
Coppertone, Console Set, Bowl, Candlesticks, Double Handles, 4 1/2 x 7 1/2-In. Bowl 259.00
Coppertone, Jardiniere, Fish, Frog, 7 1/2 x 7 1/2 In. 1800.00
Coppertone, Pitcher, Fish Handle, 7 3/4 x 7 1/2 In. 2520.00
Coppertone, Sprinkler, Frog, 10 1/4 x 10 1/4 In. 2760.00
Coppertone, Urn, Frog Climbing, 5 1/2 x 6 1/2 In. 1440.00
Coppertone, Vase, Double Bud, Jumping Fish, 8 x 7 In. 3900.00
Coppertone, Vase, Frog Holding Lotus Flower, Marked, 4 x 4 1/2 In. *illus* 155.00
Coppertone, Vase, Frog Perched At Rim, No. 29, 7 x 7 1/2 In. 1062.00
Coppertone, Vase, Oil Jar Shape, Flared, Handles, Ribbed, 4-Footed Stand, 26 In. 3600.00
Delta, Vase, Poppies, Blue Shaded To Green, Swollen Form, 12 In. 708.00
Dickens Ware, Dragon, Purple, Blue Gray Glaze, Stamped, 9 3/4 x 4 1/2 In. 6600.00
Dickens Ware, Ewer, American Indian, Stamped, 11 x 5 1/2 In. 840.00
Dickens Ware, Jardiniere, Fish, Green, Pink, Cobalt Blue Ground, Bulbous, 9 1/2 x 12 In. 1534.00
Dickens Ware, Vase, American Indian, Headdress, Yellow To Brown Ground, 11 1/2 In. 345.00
Dickens Ware, Vase, Canterbury Pilgrimage, 11 Pilgrims, Horse, Bulbous, Dunlavy, 17 In. 5750.00
Dickens Ware, Vase, Cavalier, Plumed Hat, 10 7/8 In. 443.00
Dickens Ware, Vase, Dombey & Son, Incised, Marked, 11 5/8 In. *illus* 397.00
Dickens Ware, Vase, Pickwick Papers, Portrait, Applied Medallions, 7 1/2 x 7 1/2 In. 748.00
Dresden, Vase, Dutch Scene, 16 x 4 1/2 In. 510.00
Eocean, Vase, Daisies, 7 3/8 In. 142.00
Eocean, Vase, Daisies, Matte Glaze, Oval, 10 1/4 x 3 In. 420.00
Eocean, Vase, Milkweed, Lavender, Green Leaves, Oval, Tapered, 8 1/2 In. 411.00
Eocean, Vase, Purple & Yellow Irises, 17 1/2 x 7 1/4 In. 1920.00
Eocean, Vase, Daisy Stems, Green, Ivory Ground, 8-Sided, Impressed, 9 5/8 In. 232.00
Etched Floral, Vase, Grapevines, Leaves, Fruit, Swollen Arm, 13 1/4 In. 1175.00
Fleron, Vase, Hand Thrown, Green, Handles, Ruffled Rim, Marked, 9 1/2 In. 200.00
Floretta, Vase, Pink Strawberries, Marked, 5 x 5 In. *illus* 60.00
Fru Russet, Vase, Green Glaze, Handles, 8 x 5 1/4 In. 450.00
Garden Ornament, Chicken, Matte, Glossy Eyes, 12 x 10 In. 2645.00
Garden Ornament, Gnome, Seated, Brown Jacket, Blue Pants, 14 1/2 x 10 In. 3186.00
Garden Ornament, Monkey, Brown Matte Glaze 2242.00
Garden Ornament, Pelican, 19 3/4 In. 5192.00
Garden Ornament, Squirrel, Holding Nut, Marked, Late 1920s, 11 3/4 In. 1045.00
Glendale, Flower Frog, Marked, 2 1/8 x 5 1/8 In. *illus* 31.00
Hudson, Jardiniere, Purple Nasturtiums, Green Leaves, 6 5/8 In. 142.00
Hudson, Vase, 2 Birds, Trumpet Creeper Vine, Blue Ground, Mae Timberlake, 13 1/4 In. 5170.00
Hudson, Vase, Apple Blossoms, White Crimson, Flared, 9 In. 325.00
Hudson, Vase, Blue Irises, Frosted Matte, Marked, 9 x 4 1/2 In. 2280.00
Hudson, Vase, Blue Lilacs, Green & Pink Ground, 13 1/4 In. 354.00
Hudson, Vase, Classical Woman, Fountain, Cylindrical, Tapered, E. Pickens, 13 In. 9988.00
Hudson, Vase, Delphinia, Blue, Pink, Urn Form, Handles, Mae Timberlake, 7 7/8 In. 558.00
Hudson, Vase, Dogwood Flower, Blue Shaded To Cream, Sarah Timberlake, 13 7/8 In. 1770.00
Hudson, Vase, Irises, Green Ground, Baluster, Signed, Hester P. Hudson, 15 3/8 In. 3173.00
Hudson, Vase, Irises, Stamped, 9 1/4 x 4 In. 900.00
Hudson, Vase, Lily Of The Valley, Blue, Green, 7 1/8 In. 443.00
Hudson, Vase, Lily Of The Valley, White, Green To Blue Ground, 1920s, 8 3/4 In. 580.00
Hudson, Vase, Nasturtium Blossoms, 12 3/4 x 4 3/4 In. 1080.00
Hudson, Vase, Poppy, Brown, Handles, 9 3/4 x 12 In. *illus* 2575.00
Hudson, Vase, Roses, Green, Blue, Handles, 5 7/8 In. 384.00
Hudson, Vase, Roses, Pink & Yellow, Swollen Footed, Sarah Timberlake, 7 3/4 In. 294.00
Hudson, Vase, Saguaro Cactus Flowers, Red, Yellow, Green, Blue, Square Handles, 6 In. 1770.00
Hudson, Vase, Trillium, Red & Blue Ground, Baluster, 8 1/2 In. 384.00
Hudson, Vase, Violets, Green & Pink Ground, 7 3/4 In. 384.00
Hudson, Vase, White Roses, Gray Ground, Bulbous, Cylindrical Neck, 6 1/4 In. 235.00
Jap Birdimal, Jardiniere, Pedestal, Landscape, House, Blue Ground, 13 x 31 In. 690.00
Jap Birdimal, Vase, 5 Blue Fish, Yellow Fins, Bubbles, Green Ground, Bottle Form, 6 In. 2350.00
Jap Birdimal, Vase, Bird In Flight, Green Ground, Signed VMH, 3 1/4 x 6 3/4 In. 633.00
Jap Birdimal, Vase, Duck, Wearing Blue Bonnet, Trees, 5 1/8 In. 885.00
Jap Birdimal, Vase, Geisha, Cat, Trees, Squeezebag, Double Handles, Rhead, 8 x 10 In. 3738.00
Jap Birdimal, Vase, Geisha, Cat, Trees, Handles, Marked, 10 x 8 In. *illus* 3900.00

Weller, Dickens Ware, Vase, Dombey & Son, Incised, Marked, 11 5/8 In.
$397.00

Weller, Floretta, Vase, Pink Strawberries, Marked, 5 x 5 In.
$60.00

Weller, Glendale, Flower Frog, Marked, 2 1/8 x 5 1/8 In.
$31.00

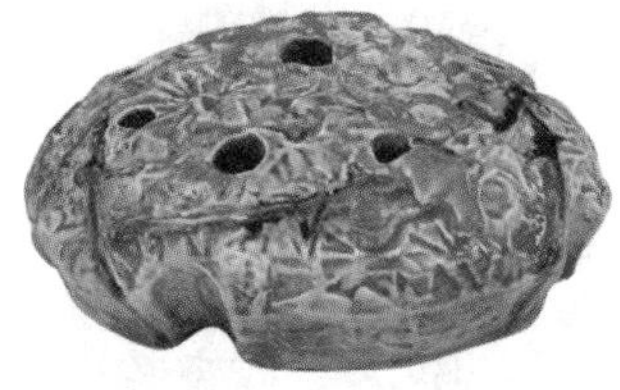

Weller, Hudson, Vase, Poppy, Brown, Handles, 9 3/4 x 12 In.
$2575.00

Weller, Jap Birdimal, Vase, Geisha, Cat, Trees, Handles, Marked, 10 x 8 In.
$3900.00

Jap Birdimal, Vase, Geisha, Green, Yellow, Brown Ground, 7 ½ In. 1770.0
Jap Birdimal, Vase, Woman, Casual Dress, 7 ¾ In. 885.0
Jardiniere, Pedestal, Burgundy, Brown Glossy Glaze, 27 ¾ x 10 ¾ In. 353.0
Jardiniere, Pedestal, Leaves, Green Matte Glaze, Embossed, 31 ½ In. 325.0
Knifewood, Jardiniere, Daisies, Butterflies, 7 ¾ x 8 ½ In. 600.0
Knifewood, Vase, Owls, Squirrels, Birds On Branches, 7 In. 720.0
Knifewood, Vase, Owls In Trees, Crescent Moons, Oval, 8 x 4 ¼ In. 900.0
Knifewood, Vase, Peacock, Trees, Ivory Textured Ground, Black Rim, 11 ¾ In. 147.0
Knifewood, Vase, Peacocks, Roses, Pinched Waist, 11 x 4 ¾ In. 1200.0
Knifewood, Vase, Peacocks In Trees, Ivory Textured Ground, Black Rims, 11 ¾ In. 147.0
Knifewood, Vase, Squirrels, Branches, Oval, 11 x 5 ¼ In. 2280.0
Lamar, Vase, Palm Trees, Water, Mountains, Red Luster Glaze, 8 ½ In. 472.0
LaSa, Vase, Metallic Glaze, 8 In. 750.0
LaSa, Vase, Metallic Glaze, 13 ½ In. 1200.0
Louwelsa, Ewer, Vine, Leaves, Blueberries, Signed, 13 ½ In. 115.0
Louwelsa, Jug, Cherry, Diamond Form, Loop Handle, 4 ¾ In. 94.0
Louwelsa, Jug, Raspberries On Leaves, Handle, 6 In. 118.0
Louwelsa, Mug, Berries, Marked, 5 ¾ x 6 In. *illus* 220.0
Louwelsa, Vase, Bearded Old Man, Anthony Dunlavy, 11 ½ In. 944.0
Louwelsa, Vase, Blue, Geranium, Marked, 3 ½ x 6 ½ In. 575.0
Louwelsa, Vase, Blue, Tapered, Flowers, Impressed Mark, 8 ½ In. 863.0
Louwelsa, Vase, Davy Crockett, Coonskin Cap, 12 In. 1495.0
Louwelsa, Vase, Dog, Bulbous, Lisabeth Blake, 10 ½ In. 590.0
Louwelsa, Vase, Flowers, Green, Brown Glaze, Cylindrical, Shouldered, 7 In. 100.0
Louwelsa, Vase, Iris, Brown Glaze, 4-Sided, Signed, 9 x 5 ½ In. 316.0
Louwelsa, Vase, Jonquil, Marked, 8 ⅞ In. 130.0
Louwelsa, Vase, Pillow, Fish, Brown Glaze, Eugene Roberts, 10 x 10 In. 748.0
Matte Ware, Bowl, Hollies, Blue, Red, Green Glaze, 6 ½ In. 2360.0
Matte Ware, Vase, Grapes, Flowers, Blue, Green, Double Gourd Form, Handles, 4 In. 1175.0
Matte Ware, Vase, Hollies, Green & Red Glaze, Handles, 4 ¾ In. 1534.0
Minerva, Pedestal, Orange, Brown Matte Ground, 24 In. 1888.0
Muskota, Figurine, Elephant, Brown, Ivory Matte Glaze, 10 ¼ x 15 In. 708.0
Rhead Faience, Vase, 4 Geishas, No. 503, 6 ½ In. 1416.0
Rhead Faience, Vase, Geisha With Umbrella Under Canopy Of Trees, Swollen, 9 ¼ In. 4230.0
Sicardo, Vase, Chrysanthemum, Iridescent, 8 x 15 ½ In. 4800.0
Sicardo, Vase, Daisies, 5 ½ x 3 In. 720.0
Sicardo, Vase, Flowers, Multicolored, Metallic Glaze, 4-Sided, 4 ½ In. 345.0
Sicardo, Vase, Grapevine, 25 ¼ x 9 In. 5100.0
Sicardo, Vase, Leaves, Berries, Blue, Purple, Green, Blue, Metallic Luster, Signed, 18 In. 4113.0
Sicardo, Vase, Morning Glory, Marked, 7 x 6 ½ In. *illus* 3200.0
Sicardo, Vase, Star Form, Indented Sides, Iridescent Metallic Glaze, Signed, 6 x 4 ¼ In. 748.0
Sicardo, Vase, Stylized Art Nouveau Flowers, Maroon, Green, Metallic Luster, 15 In. 3995.0
Sicardo, Vase, Stylized Flowers, Blue & Green Iridescent Metallic Luster, Oval, 4 ⅝ In. 470.0
Sicardo, Vase, Stylized Flowers, Tapered, Twisted Form, J. Sicard, 8 ⅝ In. 1763.0
Sicardo, Vase, Twisted Form, Ruffled Rim, c.1905, 5 In. 700.0
Silvertone, Basket, Green Matte Glaze, 8 ¾ x 7 ¼ In. 180.0
Silvertone, Vase, Roses, Red, Multicolor Ground, Handles, 8 In. 259.0
Tray, Fox, Full Body, Oval, 7 In. 978.0
Tulips, Jardiniere, Etched, Pink Matte Glaze, 8 x 10 ½ In. 1080.0
Tutone, Vase, Plants, Berries, 3-Sided, Maroon Ground, 11 ⅝ In. 413.0
Warwick, Pitcher, 3-Footed, 3 ⅞ x 7 ⅝ In. 275.0
Woodcraft, Bowl, Squirrel, Marked, 5 ¾ x 10 ¾ In. *illus* 345.0
Woodcraft, Planter, Impressed, 5 ¾ In. 495.0
Woodcraft, Vase, Owl, On Apple Tree Branch, 15 ¾ x 6 ½ In. 2040.0
Woodcraft, Vase, Relief Foxes, Cylindrical, Marked, 7 ½ x 4 ¼ In. 230.0
Woodcraft, Vase, Tree Form, Climbing Squirrel, Owl, 18 x 7 ½ In. 1080.0
Woodcraft, Vase, Tree Trunk, Owl, Brown Glaze, c.1900-25, 13 ½ In. 470.0
Woodcraft, Wall Pocket, Owl, 11 ½ In. 575.0
Zona, Dish, Candy, Apple, Twig Handle, 6 ¼ In. 295.0

Weller, Louwelsa, Mug, Berries, Marked, 5 ¾ x 6 In.
$220.00

Weller, Sicardo, Vase, Morning Glory, Marked, 7 x 6 ½ In.
$3200.00

Weller, Woodcraft, Bowl, Squirrel, Marked, 5 ¾ x 10 ¾ In.
$345.00

WEMYSS ware was made by Robert Heron in Kirkaldy, Scotland, from 1850 to 1929. It is a colorful peasant-type pottery that is occasionally found in the United States.

Figurine, Pig, Red Roses, Early 20th Century, 16 In. 1440.0
Figurine, Piglet, Sleeping, Pink Cabbage Roses, c.1900, 6 ½ In. *illus* 16739.0

W

WESTMORELAND GLASS was made by the Westmoreland Glass Company of Grapeville, Pennsylvania, from 1890 to 1984. They made clear and colored glass of many varieties, such as milk glass, pressed glass, and slag glass.

Animal, Dish, Cat Cover, Lacy Base, Vaseline, Applied Glass Eyes, Marked, 8 In. . . . . *illus* 518.00
Animal, Dish, Swan Cover, Raised Wing, Black, Marked, 9¾ In. . . . . *illus* 345.00
Animal, Dish, Hen On Nest Cover, Basket Weave Base, 7½ In. 55.00
Animal, Dish, Lamb Cover, Purple Slag Glass, 4 x 5½ In. 80.00
Animal, Dish, Lovebirds Cover, Amber Slag, 6 In. 85.00
Animal, Dish, Lovebirds Cover, Green Mist Satin, 6 In. 55.00
Animal, Dish, Robin On Twig Nest Cover, Green Mist, 6¼ x 5½ x 5 In. 42.00
Animal, Dish, Rooster Cover, 8½ x 7 x 4 In. 34.00
Ball & Swirl, Vase, Lilac Amethyst, Footed, Flared, 1973, 9½ In. 65.00
Beaded Grape, Box, Cover, Milk Glass, 5½ x 3¾ In. 25.00
Beaded Grape, Dish, Honey, Cover, Milk Glass, 4-Sided, Footed, 5 x 4 In. 35.00
Bookend, Owl, Pink Satin, Rhinestone Eyes, Paper Label, 6 In. . . . . *illus* 230.00
Della Robbia, Console Set, Candlesticks, 6-In. Compote, 3 Piece 95.00
Della Robbia, Plate, Luncheon, Crystal Luster, 9 In. 40.00
Della Robbia, Platter, 14 In. 38.00
Dolphin, Candlestick, Milk Glass, 9 In., Pair 85.00
Dolphin, Compote, Shell Bowl, Milk Glass, 9 In. 45.00
Doric, Compote, Dark Blue Mist, Scalloped Rim, 4⅞ x 5¼ In. 38.00
Drinking Troubadours, Mug, Decal, Brown Ground, c.1910, 4¾ In. 90.00
English Hobnail, Candy Dish, Cover, Milk Glass, 3-Footed, 5½ x 6 In. 55.00
English Hobnail, Dish, Pickle, Milk Glass, Sawtooth Edge, 8 In. 20.00
English Hobnail, Salt, Green, Footed, 2 x 3 In. 15.00
English Hobnail, Toothpick, Top Hat, Milk Glass, 2½ x 3¾ In. 7.00
English Hobnail, Vase, Fan, Amber, 5 x 6¼ In. 18.00
Figurine, Owl, Milk Glass, Glass Eyes, 5 In. . . . . 27.00 to 35.00
Figurine, Owl On Books, Green Satin, 4 In. 12.00
Figurine, Pig, Milk Glass, Hollow, 3¼ In. 25.00
Figurine, Pig, Satin, Hollow, 3¼ In. 19.00
Forget-Me-Not, Bowl, Vegetable, 11 In. 48.00
Forget-Me-Not, Tidbit, Center Handle, Green Satin, c.1930, 4¾ x 11 In. 54.00
Lace & Dewdrop, Pitcher, Amber Scalloped Rim & Foot, 1970s, 7½ In. 24.00
Maple Leaf, Rose Bowl, Milk Glass, Crimped Rim, 6 x 8 In. 34.00
No. 60, Ivy Ring, Black Milk Glass, 12 In. 125.00
Old Quilt, Compote, Milk Glass, 5¼ x 7½ In. 17.00
Owl, Toothpick, Milk Glass, 3 In. 25.00
Paneled Grape, Banana Boat, Milk Glass, Footed, 9 x 12 In. 80.00
Paneled Grape, Basket, Oval, Split Handle, Scalloped Edge, 4 x 6½ In. 38.00
Paneled Grape, Basket, Purple Slag Glass, 6½ x 4 x 4 In. 55.00
Paneled Grape, Bowl, Cover, Pedestal Base, Milk Glass, 9 In. 60.00
Paneled Grape, Bowl, Fruit, Pink, 2⅞ x 10½ In. 80.00
Paneled Grape, Cheese Dish, Cover, Milk Glass, 7 x 4¼ In. 45.00
Paneled Grape, Dresser Set, 2 Bottles, Box, Tray, Milk Glass, 4 Piece 198.00
Paneled Grape, Perfume Bottle, Milk Glass Trim, Gold, Stopper, 6¼ In. 55.00
Paneled Grape, Pitcher, Footed, Milk Glass, 8 In. 35.00
Paneled Grape, Pitcher, Milk Glass, 9 x 4½ In. 20.00
Paneled Grape, Sugar, Cover, Ruby Stain, Gold Trim, Marked, 6¾ In. 40.00
Paneled Grape, Vase, Bud, Milk Glass, Marked, 11 In. 18.00
Paneled Grape, Vase, Laurel Green, Scalloped Rim, Footed, 9¼ In. 65.00
Ring & Petal, Bowl, Milk Glass, Crimped Rim, Footed, 4¾ x 7 In. 40.00
Ring & Petal, Candlestick, Milk Glass, 3½ In., Pair 32.00
Ring & Petal, Candlestick, Milk Glass, 5 In., Pair 37.00
Ring & Petal, Tray, Milk Glass, 8¾ x 14 In. 125.00
Roses & Bows, Basket, Milk Glass, 9 x 3½ x 6 In. 125.00
Roses & Bows, Basket, Pansy, Milk Glass, 4¾ x 3⅝ In. 30.00
Roses & Bows, Candlestick, Milk Glass, Gold Trim, 4½ In., Pair 65.00
Roses & Bows, Candy Dish, Crystal Mist Satin, 4 In. 40.00
Roses & Bows, Compote, Cover, Milk Glass, 6¾ x 4¾ x 5 In. . . . . 45.00 to 55.00
Roses & Bows, Perfume Bottle, Stopper, Milk Glass, 6¼ In. 98.00
Roses & Bows, Wedding Bowl, Cover, Milk Glass, 5 x 10 In. 75.00
Simplicity Scroll, Toothpick, Milk Glass, Brown Paint, c.1890-1910, 2¼ In. 25.00
Swan, Toothpick, Scalloped Edge, Milk Glass, 1960s, 2½ In. 20.00
Thousand Eye, Bowl, Ruffled Edge, 9¾ x 12 In. 63.00

Wemyss, Figurine, Piglet, Sleeping, Pink Cabbage Roses, c.1900, 6½ In.
$16739.00

Westmoreland, Animal, Dish, Cat Cover, Lacy Base, Vaseline, Applied Glass Eyes, Marked, 8 In.
$518.00

Westmoreland, Animal, Dish, Swan Cover, Raised Wing, Black, Marked, 9¾ In.
$345.00

Westmoreland, Bookend, Owl, Pink Satin, Rhinestone Eyes, Paper Label, 6 In.
$230.00

Wheatley, Lamp, 3 Sculpted Heads, Green Matte Glaze, Etched Shade, Marked, 21 x 14 In.
$1750.00

Wheatley, Umbrella Stand, Figures, Gold Paint, Embossed, 6-Sided, Signed, 21 ⅜ In.
$200.00

Wheatley, Vase, Thistles, Applied, Green Matte Glaze, 11 In.
$1700.00

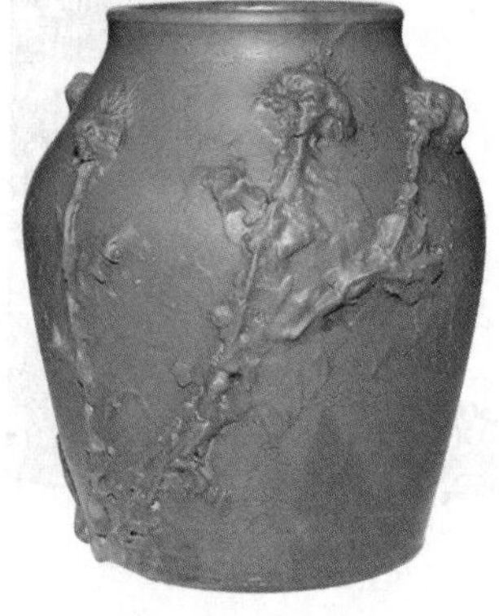

Thousand Eye, Candlestick, 5 In., Pair 44.00
Thousand Eye, Plate, 13 ½ In. 38.00
Thousand Eye, Sugar & Creamer, Handles 44.00
Zodiac, Dish, Ruby Stain, Gold Stars, Dividers, 1940-50, 9 In. 30.00
Zodiac, Plate, Sagittarius, Boy, Bow & Arrow, Stars, Blue Mist, Lacy Edge, 5 ½ In. 24.00

WHEATLEY Pottery was established in 1880. Thomas J. Wheatley had worked in Cincinnati, Ohio, with the founders of the art pottery movement, including M. Louise McLaughlin of the Rookwood Pottery. Wheatley Pottery was purchased by the Cambridge Tile Manufacturing Company in 1927.

Jardiniere, Green Variegated Glaze, 4 Loop Handles, 4 Buttressed Feet, 12 In. 129.00
Lamp, 3 Sculpted Heads, Green Matte Glaze, Etched Shade, Marked, 21 x 14 In. . . . . . *illus* 1750.00
Lamp Base, 3 Buttressed Feet, Full Height Leaves, Buds, Brown Glaze, 12 ½ x 10 In. 1560.00
Lamp Base, Buttressed Feet, Leaf & Bud, Green Matte Glaze, 10 x 8 ½ In. 1680.00
Mug, Pretzel Shaped Handle, Thick Green Glaze, 7 ¼ In.. . . . . . 142.00
Pitcher, Molded Bunches Of Grapes Hanging From Vines, Feathery Green Glaze, 8 In. 295.00
Planter, Flower Medallions, Green Matte Glaze, Round Rolled, Rim, 12 x 21 In. 764.00
Pot, Applied Thistles In Relief Encircling, Dark Green Glaze, 11 x 10 In.. . . . . . 2006.00
Tile, Suit Of Armor, Shield, Brown & Green, Frame, 8 In. 240.00
Umbrella Stand, Figures, Gold Paint, Embossed, 6-Sided, Signed, 21 ⅜ In. . . . . . *illus* 200.00
Vase, Applied Thistle, Green Matte Glaze, 11 ½ x 10 ¼ In. 780.00
Vase, Bulbous, White Flowers, Multitoned Blue Ground, 7 x 11 In.. . . . . . 86.00
Vase, Floor, Green Crackle Drip Glaze, Unglazed Clay, 16 x 30 In.. . . . . . 3600.00
Vase, Frothy Green Matte Glaze, Bulbous Bottom, Flared, 4 Buttressed Feet, 12 ½ In. 2115.00
Vase, Scarabs, Leaves, Thick Green Matte Glaze, Bulbous, 8 ⅛ In.. . . . . . 2938.00
Vase, Shoulder, Painted, Cherry Blossom, Signed, c.1880, 5 ½ x 8 In.. . . . . . 259.00
Vase, Thick Organic Green Matte Glaze, Bulbous, 4 Buttressed Feet, 11 In. 2938.00
Vase, Thistles, Applied, Green Matte Glaze, 11 In.. . . . . . *illus* 1700.00

WHIELDON was an English potter who worked alone and with Josiah Wedgwood in eighteenth-century England. Whieldon made many pieces in natural shapes, like cauliflowers or cabbages and is almost always unmarked. Do not confuse it with F. Winkle & Co. that made a dinnerware pattern marked *Whieldon Ware.*

Creamer, Green, Yellow, Brown Mottled Glaze, Footed, 5 In.. . . . . . *illus* 800.00
Loving Cup, N. Dame D'Orval, 4 In. . . . . . *illus* 26.00

WILLETS Manufacturing Company of Trenton, New Jersey, began work in 1879. The company made belleek in the late 1880s and 1890s in shapes similar to those used by the Irish Belleek factory. They stopped working about 1912. A variety of marks were used, all including the name Willets.

Bowl, Ruffled Edge, Handles, Entwined Snakes, Belleek, 9 ¼ x 4 ¼ In. 479.00
Cup & Saucer, Shell, Iridescent Pearl Dainty, Gold Handle & Trim 65.00
Hatpin Holder, Sterling Silver Overlay, 4 ⅞ In. . . . . . *illus* 120.00
Pitcher, Belleek, Marked, c.1880, 6 ⅜ x 8 ¼ In.. . . . . . 125.00
Pitcher, Grape Clusters, Leaves, Green To Yellow Ground, Tapered, Belleek, 14 ¾ In. 115.00
Plate, Grapes, Marked, Belleek, 9 ¼ In. 125.00
Platter, Flowers, Blue, 17 ¼ x 12 ¼ In.. . . . . . 35.00
Punch Bowl, Pink Flowers, Green Stems, Muted Ground, Belleek, 7 ⅝ x 10 ¼ In.. . . . . . 118.00
Salt Cellar, Marked, Belleek 22.00
Tankard, Handle, Renaissance Scene, Belleek, 20th Century 275.00
Vase, Bouquet Of Roses, Pink White, Greenery, Vines, Belleek, 14 ½ In. 2750.00
Vase, Bulbous, Daffodils, Belleek, c.1905, 10 In.. . . . . . 684.00
Vase, Crimson Pink, Tea Roses, Gold Rim, Belleek, 8 In. 399.00
Vase, Landscape Scene, Blue, Green, Brown, Marked, Belleek, 16 ¼ In. 1645.00
Vase, Roses, Gilded Lip, c.1879, 14 ½ In. 1100.00
Vase, Roses, Leaves, Thorns, Pink, White, Belleek, 15 ¾ In. 995.00
Vase, Squat, Roses, Marked, Belleek, 5 ¾ x 7 In. 975.00

WILLOW pattern has been made in England since 1780. The pattern has been copied by factories in many countries, including Germany, Japan, and the United States. It is still being made. Willow was named for a pattern that pictures a bridge, birds, willow trees, and a Chinese landscape. Most pieces are blue and white.

Bowl, Cereal, Scio, 6 ⅝ In. 8.00
Bowl, Vegetable, Cover, 8 ⅜ x 10 ¼ In. 45.00
Bowl, Vegetable, Cover, Mandarin, Scroll & Flower Border 425.00

Bowl, Vegetable, Cover, Round, 7 ½ x 2 ¾ In. 13.00
Butter, Cover, England, Round, 1920s, 7 In. 155.00
Cheese Dish, Cover, Multicolored, c.1906, 6 x 8 In. 250.00
Coaster, Yorkshire Relish, 4 ⅛ In. 70.00
Compote, 8 ½ In. 165.00
Creamer, Handle, 4 ⅝ x 3 x 3 ⅝ In. 40.00
Cup, Scio, 4 ¼ x 2 ⅞ In. 6.00
Cuspidor, Antique Brush, c.1916, 5 ¼ x 7 ½ In. 95.00
Goblet, 1880s 110.00
Gravy Boat, Attached Underplate, 1927 275.00
Jardiniere, Multicolored, Hexagonal, c.1910, 8 ⅜ x 8 ¼ In. 395.00
Lamp, Kerosene, 1940s 155.00
Lamp, Oil, Miniature 450.00
Pitcher, c.1891, 7 ¼ x 4 ¾ In. 150.00
Pitcher, Milk Jug, Japan, 4 ¾ x 5 In. 30.00
Plate, Bread & Butter, 6 In. 6.00
Plate, Bread & Butter, Herringbone Border, Boat, Trees, 3 Men, 2 Birds, Myott, c.1920, 6 In. 16.00
Plate, Herringbone Border, Boat, Bridge, 3 Men, Birds, Myott, c.1920, 9 ¾ In. 32.00
Plate, Scinde, 2 Temples, Figure Crossing Bridge, Weeping Cherry Tree, 1846, 8 ⅝ In. 175.00
Platter, Blue & White Transferware, 15 ½ x 12 In. 120.00
Platter, Churchill, Round, 12 ½ In. 20.00
Serving Dish, Cover 375.00
Soup, Cream, 2 Handles, 2 ¼ x 3 ¼ In. 20.00
Sugar, 2 Handles, 4 ¾ x 3 x 3 ¼ In. 45.00
Teapot, Lid, Crosshatch Handle, 6 ¾ In. 75.00

WINDOW glass that was stained and beveled was popular for houses during the late nineteenth and early twentieth centuries. The old windows became popular with collectors in the 1970s; today, old and new examples are seen.

Decorative, Double Starburst, Geometric Fretwork, Wood Frame, 1800s, 28 x 41 In. 168.00
Enameled, Spanish Provincial, Scenes Of Christ's Life, Hexagonal, 17 x 19 In. 1440.00
Fan Shape, Loops & Triangles, Iron Floral & Leaf Decoration, Frame, 1800s, 27 x 61 In. 896.00
Leaded, Balustrade, Column, Flower Vase, Arts & Crafts, Frame, 70 ¾ x 29 In. 1920.00
Leaded, Beveled, Transom Sash, Fleur-De-Lis, 15 ¾ x 36 In. 470.00
Leaded, Circular, 8 Lobed Panels, Flowers, Center Panel, Cabochon, 84 ½ In. 3585.00
Leaded, Frank Lloyd Wright, From Avery Coonley Playhouse, c.1916, 31 ¾ x 14 ½ In. 21250.00
Leaded, Hand Drawn, Colored Panels, Scholars, Skeletons, 12 ¼ x 10 ½ In. 345.00
Leaded, Hand Painted, Alchemist Experimenting, Sparking Elements, 10 x 8 In. 403.00
Leaded, Multicolored Enamel, Seated Crowned Man, 18 ⅝ x 18 ⅝ In. 1150.00
Leaded, Portrait, Bust, Nobleman, Fur Wrap, Landscape, Shadowbox, 19 x 15 In. 400.00
Leaded, Stained, Christ, 22 x 21 In. 235.00
Leaded, Stained, Jeweled, Third Street Studios, 32 x 86 In. 16800.00
Panel, Rectangular, Multicolored, Latin America, 36 x 32 In., Pair 118.00
Skylight, Domed, Flowers, Circles, Acid Cut, Oak Frame, Arts & Crafts, 42 x 31 x 7 In. 1900.00
Stained, Amethyst, Beveled Border Panel, Iron Frame, 1900s, 37 x 27 In. *illus* 125.00
Stained, Art Deco, Wood Frame, Double Pane, Stylized Sunburst, 26 x 48 ½ In. 450.00
Stained, Center Medallion, Center Panel, Iridescent Blue, Green, Purple, 36 x 30 In. 920.00
Stained, Flowers, Pastel Shades, Arched Top, 102 x 41 In. *illus* 1140.00
Stained, Medallion, Blue, Green, Purple, Amber Double Shell Glass Tile, 35 x 30 In. *illus* 895.00
Stained, Mosaic, Figure Holding Child, Wood Frame, 36 ¼ x 75 In. 6110.00
Stained, Multicolored Flowers, Leaves, Amber Border, Green, Pink Slag, 30 x 36 In. 224.00
Stained, Panels, Beveled Mirrors, c.1900, 15 x 15 In., Pair 275.00
Stained, Slag Leaded, Wood Frame, Leaves In Landscape, 49 ⅞ x 20 x 4 ¾ In. 588.00
Stained, Windmill, Rocks, Water, Sky, Clouds, Arts & Crafts, 28 x 21 In. 340.00

WOOD CARVINGS and wooden pieces are listed separately in this book. Many of the wood carvings are figurines or statues. There are also wooden pieces found in other categories, such as Kitchen.

Abe Lincoln, Railsplitter, Holding Ax, Pine, 20th Century, 19 ¾ In. 6000.00
Abraham Lincoln, Standing, Painted, Holding Book & Cane, c.1885, 22 In. 4113.00
Angel's Wing, Beechwood, Bronze Finished Wrought Steel Stand, Black Finish, 26 In. 96.00
Apostles, St. James, St. John, 3-Quarter Round, Gilt Wood, 23 In. 531.00
Bacchus, Holding Grapes, Crossed Legs, Pine, c.1700, 60 In. 7767.00
Bear, c.1920, 75 x 34 In. 4025.00
Beaver, Side View, Standing On Rock, 42 In. 4125.00
Bird, Blue Heron, Metal Legs, Feet, Wooden Stump Base, 47 ¾ x 16 x 10 In. 840.00

Whieldon, Creamer, Green, Yellow, Brown Mottled Glaze, Footed, 5 In.
$800.00

Whieldon, Loving Cup, N. Dame D'Orval, 4 In.
$26.00

Willets, Hatpin Holder, Sterling Silver Overlay, 4⅞ In.
$120.00

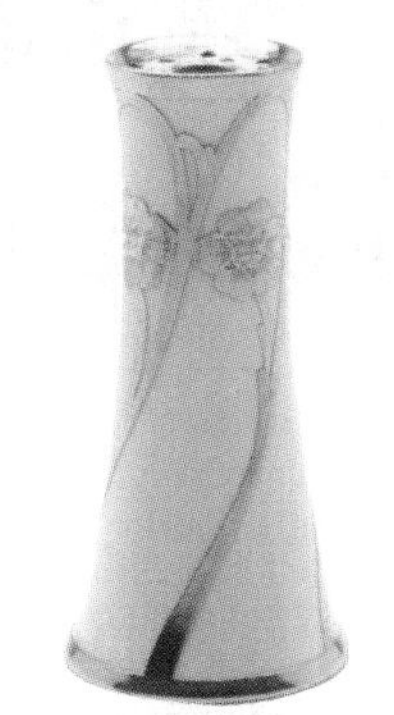

Window, Stained, Amethyst, Beveled Border Panel, Iron Frame, 1900s, 37 x 27 In.
$125.00

TIP
Don't store wooden bowls and other pieces on their sides. This can cause them to warp.

Window, Stained, Flowers, Pastel Shades, Arched Top, 102 x 41 In.
$1140.00

Window, Stained, Medallion, Blue, Green, Purple, Amber Double Shell Glass Tile, 35 x 30 In.
$895.00

Bird, On Branch, Cypress Wood, Frame, c.1860, 9 ½ x 12 ½ In. 616.00
Blackamoor, Holding Flame Finials, Multicolored, 40 ½ In., Pair 2640.00
Blackamoor, Multicolored, Holding Pillow On Head, Glass Eyes, 46 x 16 In. 2160.00
Blue Bird, Painted, Wire Legs, On Branch, Early 1900s, 10 ¾ In. 86.00
Buddha, Chinese, 22 In. 1416.00
Buddha, Happy, Chinese, 37 x 14 In. 585.00
Buddha, Lacquered, Gilt, Seated In Dhyanasana, Bhumisparsa, Asia, 16 ¼ In. 403.00
Buddha, Lacquered, Japan, 16 ½ In. 5015.00
Buddhist Monk, Seated, Votive, Painted, Gilt Detail, Chinese, 1700s, 23 In. 2640.00
Bust, Abraham Lincoln, Black, Base, Signed, Leo Cherne, 7 x 10 ½ In. 191.00
Bust, Man In Anguish, O. Flath, 20th Century, 15 x 11 In. 94.00
Bust, Man With Beard, 13 ½ In. 115.00
Bust, Victorian Woman, 14 In. 70.00
Bust, Virgin Mary, Walnut Plinth, France, 19th Century, 12 ½ In. 649.00
Butler, Black, Carved, Painted, Wooden Plinth, New Orleans, c.1910, 26 ½ In. 881.00
Canister, Cover, Painted, Strawberries, Stylized Flowers, Lehnware, 5 ½ In. 1998.00
Cat, Burl Root, Painted Blue Green, Stand, c.1910, 12 x 39 In. 4700.00
Cherub Head, Gilt Wings, Carved, Wood, 5 ⅜ x 6 In. 132.00
Chinese Man, On Horseback, 19th Century, 26 x 24 In. 205.00
Chinese Man, Standing On Plinth, Holding Vial, Multicolored, 63 In. 9200.00
Cow & Calf, Brown, Standing On Grass Base, White Daisies, Painted, 12 ½ x 12 ½ In. 115.00
Crocodile, Inset Cowrie Shell Eyes, Geometric Border, Toothy Grin, 19 In. 288.00
Cross, Leafy Arms, Acanthus Leaf Pedestal, Octagonal Plinth, 20 ¾ In. 450.00
Crucifix, White Corpus, Loincloth, Rocky Base, Serpent, Bark Covered Base, 27 x 10 In. 510.00
Crucifix Base, Beechwood, Louis XV, Scroll Feet, Cartouche Shape, 11 x 12 In. 480.00
Curlew, Eskimo, Relief Wing, Extended, Dropped Tail, Wood, c.1880s, 14 x 11 In. 33600.00
Deer, Antlers, Softwood, Red Paint, Dark Varnish, Base, 7 x 3 x 6 In. 550.00
Dog, Boxer, 8 ¼ In. 22.00
Dog, Greyhound, Seated, Glass Eyes, Padlock Collar, Black Forest, 44 In., Pair 11950.00
Duck, In Flight, Painted, 19 x 29 ½ In. 259.00
Eagle, Glass Eyes, Driftwood Perch, Oak Platform, c.1990, 22 In. 880.00
Eagle, Holding U.S. Shield & Banner, Don't Give Up The Ship, Painted, 9 x 26 In. 5290.00
Eagle, On Globe, Gold Over Yellow Paint, Faux Marble Plinth, Early 1800s, 70 In. 8050.00
Eagle, Perched On Globe, Carved, Gilt, c.1860, 39 x 44 In. 10000.00
Eagle, Spread Wings, Bellamy Style, Gilt, Patina, c.1900, 8 x 20 ¾ In. 650.00
Eagle, Spread Wings, Carved, Gilt, 31 x 26 In. 1495.00
Eagle, Spread Wings, Gesso, Gilding, Mirror Crest, Gold Paint, Wood Stand, 6 In. 316.00
Eagle, Spread Wings, Oak, Gilt, c.1860, 15 x 25 In. 400.00
Eggcup, Flowers, Leaves, Orange Ground, Turned, Poplar, Footed, Pa., 3 x 2 ½ In. 165.00
Elephant, Standing, Lowered Trunk, Beaded Necklace, India, 8 ½ x 9 ½ In. 210.00
Family, 3 Figures, Rectangular Base, Swivel Arms, Painted, 6 ½ x 6 x 2 ¼ In. 55.00
Fish, Salmon, Painted, 19th Century, 22 ½ Lb., 42 ½ x 11 In. 2200.00
Gnome, Multicolored Glass Eyes, Germany, 26 In. 550.00
Griffen, Flat Head, Mahogany, c.1920, 19 x 12 In. 165.00
Guan Yu, Inlaid Eyes, Brass Wire, 20th Century, 35 ½ In. 4416.00
Gull, Painted, Round Base, 9 In. 144.00
Halberdier, 17th Century Period Attire, Plumed Hat, Spiked Halberd, 25 In. 413.00
Hawk, Glass Eyes, Driftwood Perch, Walnut Base, 16 x 30 ½ In. 990.00
Hawk, Red Shouldered, Painted, Glass Eyes, Driftwood, Richard Koeditz, 15 x 23 In. 840.00
Horse, Wagon, Pine, Whittled, Base, 19th Century, 10 ¼ x 10 In., 2 Piece 540.00
Hourglass, Blown Glass Bulb, Treen, Stand, Early 19th Century, 6 In. 1528.00
Leg, Beechwood, Painted Shoe, 14 In. 173.00
Madonna, Child, Germany, 41 In. .... 585.00 to 819.00
Madonna, Flowing Hair, Robes, Germany, Signed, 19 ½ In. .... *illus* 325.00
Man, Baule, Hands On Knees, Palm Out, Headdress, Cowry Shell, Africa, 17 In. 5288.00
Man, Baule, Hands To Abdomen, Tripartite Coiffure, Africa, 16 In. 940.00
Man, San Juan Nepomuceno, Multicolored, Glass Eyes, Spain, 48 ½ x 17 x 12 In. 5288.00
Man, Songye, Hands To Abdomen, Stylized Face, Africa, 10 ¾ In. 5875.00
Man, Thermometer, Bavarian, Black Forest, Swiss, 7 ½ x 4 In. 236.00
Man & Woman, Abstract, Lovers, Mabel Hutchinson, c.1968, 24 x 10 x 11 In. 4200.00
Man & Woman, Man Holding Pipe, Woman Knitting, Painted, 8 x 3 x 3 In., Pair 220.00
Man Playing Accordion, Man Holding Top Hat, Painted, 6 ½ x 2 ⅜ x 2 ⅜ In., Pair 209.00
Mannequin, Jointed, England, 19th Century, 15 ½ In. 1950.00
Man's Head, Pine, Painted, Black Metal Base, c.1870, 16 In. 20400.00
Maria & Anna, Painted, Germany, 17th Century, 16 x 8 x 5 In. 448.00
Mask, Antelope, Banana, Oval, Prominent Nose, 4 Projecting Horns, Africa, 17 In. 558.00

Mask, Chokwe, Pierced Mouth, Pointed Teeth, Coffee Bean Eyes, Africa, 9 In. 353.00
Match Striker, Bear, Brass Ashtray, 5 ½ In. . . . . *illus* 36.00
Monk, Red Lacquer, Burma, 20 In. 177.00
Mythical Beast, ½ Dog, ½ Fish, Plinth Base, Painted Fish Scale, India, 9 x 7 In. 150.00
Nurse, Barefoot, Shoes In Hand, Medical Box, Broad Hat, Chinese, 8 ½ In. 1195.00
Ornament, Pineapple Leaf, Black Brown, Mounted, Late 1800s, 8 x 9 In., Pair 1800.00
Panel, Arts & Crafts, Wood, Carved Peacock, Brown & Green Stain, 19 x 7 ¾ In. 480.00
Panel, Girl On Chair, Green Dress, Marquetry, Veneer, Bird's-Eye Maple, 17 ½ x 11 In. 225.00
Parrot, Painted, Red, Green, Blue, Yellow Head, Wood Base, Late 1800s, 13 In. 1380.00
Plaque, American Eagle, Shield, Painted, Pine, 21 x 47 In.. . . . . 7200.00
Plaque, American Eagle, Shield, Painted, Pine, 24 x 27 In.. . . . . 18000.00
Plaque, Dog's Head, Walnut, Glass Eyes, Oval, Henry Leach, Late 1800s, 9 x 8 In. 1150.00
Plaque, Dragon, Ruyi Fungus, Square 6 In.. . . . . 2151.00
Plaque, Eagle, Relief Carved, Gilt, Spread Wings, c.1900, 5 ⅝ x 25 ¼ In. 499.00
Plaque, Eagle, Spread Wings, 2 American Flags Under Wings, Painted, Pine, 21 x 47 In.. . . . . 7200.00
Plaque, Eagle, Spread Wings, Shield Body, Holding Arrows & Olive Branch, 17 x 38 In.. . . . . . 8000.00
Plaque, Oak, Bas Relief, Green Man, Garden Mythology, Gryphons, 44 x 28 In. 400.00
Plaque, Village, Church, Town Building, 2 Houses, Trees, 1800s, 11 ½ x 17 ¾ In. 316.00
Policeman, Bobby's Hat & Billy Club, Gesso, 20th Century, Life-Size 805.00
Poseidon & His Attendants, Dolphin, Ebonized Relief, Frame, 9 ¾ x 21 In. 1020.00
Praying Man, On Lotus, Woman In Robes, Oriental, 1800s, 5 ½ x 6 In., 2 Piece. 115.00
Putto, Child's Head, Applied Wings, White Paint, Black, Softwood, 11 ½ x 37 ½ In. 825.00
Putto, Winged Head, Giltwood, Continental, Early 19th Century, 10 x 9 In.. . . . . 300.00
Putto, Winged Head, Giltwood, Provincial Baroque, Late 18th Century, 16 x 14 In. 450.00
Queen Mother Of West, Bearing Peaches, 19th Century, 24 In. 502.00
Rooster, Treen Head, Fantail, Varnish, Nyor Penns, Germany, 6 ½ x 6 ¼ x 1 ¾ In. 198.00
St. Christopher, Carrying Infant Christ, 20th Century, 25 In. 206.00
St. George Slaying Dragon, Germany, 20th Century, 28 In. 502.00
Statue, Christ, On Cloud Globe, Arms Outstretched, Multicolored, 26 x 15 ½ In.. . . . . 224.00
Statue, Saint, Dominican Friar, Hooded Monk's Robe, Detached Halo, Italy, 29 In. 600.00
Stump, Walnut, G.A.R., Crossed Sabers, Eagle, Flag, c.1887, 27 x 14 In. 14000.00
Sunburst, Altar, Giltwood, Cloud Center, Gilded Finish, Italy, Early 1800s, 38 In.. . . . . 1320.00
Sunburst, Altar, Giltwood, Gilded Finish, Weathered, Italy, Early 1800s, 43 ½ In.. . . . . 2160.00
Tree, 9 Birds, Folk Art, Log Base, 20th Century, 51 ½ x 18 In. 1200.00
Virgin Mary, Carved Folds, Germany, 19th Century, 32 ½ In. 649.00
Virgin Mary, Flowing Hair, Robes, c.1920, 19 ½ In.. . . . . 383.00
Wild Boar, Walking, Walnut, Black Forest, 5 ½ x 5 ½ In.. . . . . 470.00
William Tell & Son, Rockery Base, Shields, 23 x 12 In. 1880.00
Woman, African, Elongated, Dogon, Tellum, 30 ¾ x 5 ¼ x 5 ¾ In.. . . . . 89.00
Woman, Carrying Basket Of Fruit, Painted, Multicolored Dress, 14 ¾ x 7 x 5 In. 84.00
Woman, On Horseback, Dogon, 35 x 17 x 19 In. 165.00
Woman, Smiling, White Coat, Hat, Muff, Shoes, Walnut, Painted, 12 In.. . . . . 1293.00
Woman, Yombe, Seated, Hands To Breasts, Glass Eyes, Filed Teeth, Africa, 23 ½ In. 1880.00

WOODEN wares were used in all parts of the home. Wood was used for many containers and tools. Small wooden pieces are called treenware in England, but the term *woodenware* is more common in the United States. Additional pieces may be found in the Advertising, Kitchen, and Tool categories.

Basket, Root Wood, Loop Handle, 20th Century, 6 ½ x 11 ¼ In.. . . . . 582.00
Book Press, Mahogany, Drawer, Acorn Finial, String Border Inlay, c.1910, 21 x 17 x 11 In. . . 750.00
Book Press, Turned Screws, Bone Finial Ends, Inlaid Star, Borders, Footed 412.00
Bookshelf, Cutout Shapes, Through Tenon, Arched Ends, Arts & Crafts, 7 ¼ x 24 x 7 In.. . . . . . 265.00
Bootjack, Oak, Folding, Framed, Peal & Co., 20th Century, 32 x 16 In. 88.00
Bootjack, Round, Gray Paint, Square Nails, 21 x 5 In. 33.00
Bowl, 2 Bears, Seated, Holding Bowl In Center, Glass Eyes, Swiss, c.1910, 8 ⅛ x 19 In. 2128.00
Bowl, Ash Burl, Yellow Paint, Hand Hewn, Tab Handles, Painted, 5 x 20 In. 1150.00
Bowl, Bird's-Eye Maple, Burl, 4 x 14 ¾ In.. . . . . 2310.00
Bowl, Burl, Almond Shape, Loose Figure, 12 ¾ x 15 ¾ In. 1265.00
Bowl, Burl, Carved, 13 ½ x 4 In.. . . . . 2013.00
Bowl, Burl, Carved Rim Handles, Scrubbed Interior, 16 ¼ In. 11500.00
Bowl, Burl, Early 19th Century, 4 ⅛ x 10 ⅞ In. 1116.00
Bowl, Burl, Flared, Short Turned Foot, 3 ⅜ x 8 In. 431.00
Bowl, Burl, Oval, Carved Tab Handles, Footed, Early 19th Century, 5 x 21 26 In. 1320.00
Bowl, Burl, Rim Handles, 19th Century, 16 ¾ x 5 ½ In. 7475.00
Bowl, Burl, Turned, Molded Rim, Woodlands, 6 ½ x 20 ¼ In.. . . . . 3600.00
Bowl, Burl, Turned, Scrubbed Surface, 15 ¾ x 6 ¼ In. 2115.00

Wood Carving, Madonna, Flowing Hair, Robes, Germany, Signed, 19 ½ In.
$325.00

Wood Carving, Match Striker, Bear, Brass Ashtray, 5 ½ In.
$36.00

Wooden, Bowl, Treen, Burl, Late 18th Century, 6 ¼ x 15 In.
$1452.00

Wooden, Jar, Cover, Maple, Wire Handle, Peaseware, c.1880, 6 ½ In.
$425.00

W

TIP
When cleaning dolls or furniture or other wooden pieces, use the foam from a mixture of one tablespoon soap to one quart water. Whip the mixture with a beater and clean with the foam.

Wooden, Mold, Candle, 24 Pewter Tubes, Marked, W. Webb, 1800s, 18 x 21 x 6 In. $1150.00

Wooden, Stand, Decanter, Bear Hiking, 3 Cordials, Black Forest, c.1900, 15 In. $1534.00

TIP
Wooden items should be kept off a sunny windowsill. Direct sunlight will harm wood finishes.

Bowl, Burl, Wide Turned Outside Rim, 4¾ x 13 In. 2070.00
Bowl, Deep, Round, Medial Incised Line Design, Treen, c.1820, 3⅝ x 5¾ In. 881.00
Bowl, Flared, Blue Paint, Amish, 21 In. 1093.00
Bowl, Fruit, Treen, Satin Finished, Pitch Pine, Footed, Flared Lip, Early 1900s, 14 In. 210.00
Bowl, Fruit Drying, Fruitwood, Scroll Carved, Provincial, 8 x 36 In. 1800.00
Bowl, Maple, Burl, Flared, Footed, 3 x 5½ In. 550.00
Bowl, Maple, Burl, Molded Rim, Patina, Woodlands, 5¼ x 16 In. 2040.00
Bowl, Maple, Treen, Lathe Turned, Incised Rings, 19th Century, 4 x 9¼ In. 259.00
Bowl, Oblong, Natural Finish, Red Bottom, 4¾ x 23 x 9 In. 258.00
Bowl, Oval, 2 Handles, Light Red Paint, 5½ x 24 x 15 In. 201.00
Bowl, Oval, Red Stain, Carved On Bottom, MP, 1872, 4 x 9¾ x 13¼ In. 804.00
Bowl, Painted Blue, 19th Century, 4¾ x 15¼ In. 411.00
Bowl, Pine, Raised Band, Green Paint, Treen, 2¼ x 9¾ In. 110.00
Bowl, Shenandoah Community Workers, 8 x 21¾ In. 431.00
Bowl, Tiger Maple, Bird's-Eye, 19th Century, 13½ In. 350.00
Bowl, Treen, Burl, Late 18th Century, 6¼ x 15 In. *illus* 1452.00
Bowl, Treen, Red Paint, Deep, 4½ x 13¾ In. 403.00
Bowl, Treen, Ribs, Flat Rim, Round, 5 x 26 In. 115.00
Bowl, Treen, Windsor Green Paint, 19th Century, 2½ x 10¾ In. 345.00
Bowl, Tulipwood, Collared Rim, Tapered Foot, 7½ x 21 In. 287.00
Bowl, Turned, Checked, Flared Rim, 2½ x 5½ In. 55.00
Bowl, Turned, Cuban Mahogany, James Prestini, c.1936, 2½ x 11½ In. 3300.00
Bowl, Turned, Gray Paint, 2¾ x 8½ In. 523.00
Bowl, Turned, Gray Paint, 3 x 12 In. 330.00
Bowl, Turned, Maple, Incised Band, 8¼ x 23½ In. 275.00
Bowl, Turned, Mexican Mahogany, James Prestini, c.1936, 2¾ x 8 In. 2160.00
Bowl, Turned, Ribbed, Carved Lip, Medium Gray Paint, 7½ x 19½ In. 1323.00
Bowl, Turned, Shaped Rim, Gray Paint, Hanging Hole, 19½ x 6¼ In. 345.00
Bowl, Turned, Siamese Teak, Signed, Arthur Espenet, c.1960, 3¾ x 11½ In. 2700.00
Bowl, Turned, Worn Blue Paint, Early 20th Century, 18 x 5½ In. 546.00
Bowl, Walnut, Carved, Wharton Esherick, 1962, 2½ x 11½ x 6¼ In. 9000.00
Bowl, Walnut, Hand Turned, Rude Osolnik, 10 x 2½ In. 840.00
Bowl, Walnut, Oblong, Natural Finish, Patina, 4¾ x 20¾ x 11¾ In. 173.00
Bowl, White Oak, Burl, 2 Handles At Base, 9 x 27 In. 489.00
Brush Holder, Amorphous, Chinese, 4⅝ In. 118.00
Brush Holder, Rosewood, Figural Decoration, Chinese, 6¾ x 6¼ In. 236.00
Bucket, Bentwood Handle, Metal Bands, Slat, 12 In. 66.00
Bucket, Blue Paint, Copper Bands, White Interior, Rope Handle, 8¾ x 11 In. 248.00
Bucket, Carved From Log, 10 In. 55.00
Bucket, Cover, Blue, Turned Wood, Raised Band, Rope & Wood Handle, 3¼ x 2½ In. 198.00
Bucket, Georgian, Mahogany, Brass Handle, Mounts, Side Opening, Slot, Britain, Late 1700s, 22 In. 2100.00
Bucket, Kindling, Brassbound, Liner, Multicolored, George IV, 14 x 14 x 11 In. 900.00
Bucket, Oak, Brass Band, Flat Side, Handle, 13 In. 570.00
Bucket, Pine, 2 Metal Bands, Wire Bail, Wood Handle, Grain Painted, 1800s, 6 x 7½ In. 100.00
Bucket, Poplar Lid, Pine, Green Paint, Marked, S.Z., 14 x 9½ In. 99.00
Bucket, Sugar, Banded, Bail Handle, A. Tyler, Marked, Cover, 12¼ x 11¾ In. 357.00
Bucket, Sugar, Painted, Stave Construction, Staple Bentwood Bands, Handle, 10 x 10 In. 144.00
Bucket, Swing Handle, Ash Bands, Slate Gray, 19th Century, 13½ x 13 In., Pair 770.00
Canteen, Leather Strap, Stopper, c.1870, 8 In. 303.00
Carrier, Bentwood, Lid, Bail Handle, Diamond Shape Escutcheons, 12 x 6 In. 978.00
Carrier, Interior Trays, Walnut, Cut Nail, Splayed Sides, Handle Cutout, 6 x 15 x 12 In. 431.00
Carrier, Pine, Green, Blue Paint, Name Plaque, Eagle, Shield, Lift-Out Tray, 20 x 7 In. 201.00
Coffee Container, Pine, Painted, Stenciled Panels, Hinged Cover, 33 x 21 x 16 In. 561.00
Compote, Peaseware, Maple, Treen, 19th Century, 4¾ x 7½ In. 633.00
Compote, Provincial, Round, Tapered, Late 19th Century, 14 x 20 In. 240.00
Container, Sponge Decorated, Vinegar Grain, Tobacco Leaf Pattern, 1800s, 6 x 6½ In. 999.00
Cup, Saffron, Cover, Painted, Strawberries, Pink Ground, Lehnware, 4 In. 1763.00
Cup, Saffron, Painted, Blue & Red Pansies, Salmon Ground, Lehnware, 3 In. 345.00
Cup, Saffron, Pansies, Salmon Ground, Strawberries On Lid, Lehnware, c.1876, 4¾ In. 3276.00
Cup, Saffron, Poplar, Treen, Thistle Design, Painted, Footed, Lid, 4¾ x 2½ In. 990.00
Cup, Thistle, Salmon Ground, Yellow Interior, Footed, 3 x 2½ In. 302.00
Eggcup, Strawberry Decoration, Salmon, Blue, Green, Yellow, Lehnware, c.1858 3172.00
Feeding Trough, Rough Hewn, Rectangular, Handles, Continental, 13 x 14 x 50 In. 648.00
Firkin, 3-Finger Joints, Red Finish, Cover, A.J. Sprague So. Hingham, Mass., 12 x 11 In. 230.00
Firkin, 3-Finger Joints, Slat Side, Swing Handle, Gray Over Red Paint, 9¾ x 9¾ In. 230.00
Firkin, Cover, Pine, Staves, Bands, Blue Paint, Handle, 9¾ x 10¼ In. 187.00
Firkin, Cover, Pine, Staves, Bands, Green Paint, Handle, Mrs. Reiff, 11 x 12 In. 330.00

irkin, Cover, Pine, Staves, Bands, Paint, Handle, E. Vinson, Weymouth, Mass., 11 x 11 In. . . . 412.00
irkin, Cover, Pine, Staves, Bands, Tacks, Light Green Paint, Handle, 9¾ x 9½ In. 440.00
irkin, Cover, Pine, Staves, Bands, Tacks, Light Green Paint, Handle, 11¾ x 12 In. 358.00
irkin, Cover, Pine, Staves, Bands, Tacks, Red Paint, Handle, 14 x 14¾ In. 605.00
irkin, Gray Paint, Lap Joints, Swing Handle, 10 x 9 In. 115.00
irkin, Pine, Green Paint, Staves, Bands, Tapered Lap Joints, Handle, 9 x 9½ In. 413.00
irkin, Pine, Wood Staves, Tapered Lap Joints, Bail Handle, Gray Paint, 6½ x 6¾ In.. . . . . 330.00
irkin, Pine Staves, Maple Lapped Hoops, Handle, Cover Impressed CH, 1800s, 2½ In. 441.00
irkin, Poplar, Wood Staves, Tapered Joint Bands, Handle, Green Paint, 9¼ In. 495.00
irkin, Swing Handle, 19th Century, 13 In. 94.00
rape Hod, Bentwood, Oval, Banded, Rod Divider, England, Late 1800s, 26 x 26 In. 840.00
oly Water, Font, Black Forest, Well & Cross Shape, 13 x 8 In.. . . . . 351.00
oly Water, Font, Crucifix, Bird, Flowers, Black Forest, Germany, 13 x 8 x 4 In.. . . . . 230.00
ar, Cover, Maple, Wire Handle, Peaseware, c.1880, 6½ In. . . . . *illus* 425.00
ar, Peaseware, Maple, Treen, Wire Bale Handle, Flattened Ball Finial, 6½ In.. . . . . 431.00
eg, Rum, Flower In Circle, Hearts, Double Loop Handle, Iron Bands, Late 1700s, 7 x 8 In. . . 230.00
amp Base, Oak, Woodsman Beside A Tree, Circular Carved Base, Germany, 16 In. 295.00
azy Susan, Mahogany, Rope Twist Inlaid Edge, Dutch, 3½ x 21½ In. 2160.00
azy Susan, Mahogany, Rotates, Short Pedestal, Dish Base, 4⅝ x 24½ In. 546.00
etter Opener, Bald Eagle, Pine, Painted, Glass Eye, Black Metal Stand, 8¾ In.. . . . . 230.00
iquor Case, Oak, Tumbler, Wine Glass, Funnel, Decanters, 12 x 17, 13 Piece 690.00
Mold, Candle, 24 Pewter Tubes, Marked, W. Webb, 1800s, 18 x 21 x 6 In. . . . . *illus* 1150.00
Pail, Mahogany, Brass Mounted, Swing Handle, Cylindrical, George III, 17 14 x 16 In. 2300.00
Pail, Mahogany, Peat, 2 Bands, Swing Handle, Cylindrical, George III, 16¾ x 14 In. 978.00
Piggin, Blue Paint, 11 x 6 In.. . . . . 960.00
Piggin, White Paint, Metal Band, 12½ x 8 In. 44.00
Pipe Holder, Bear, Black Forest, Basket On Back, 7 x 6¼ x 10 In. 936.00
Pitcher, Oil, Boat Shape, Low Relief, Circles, Geometric Pillar Rows, India, 2½ x 4 In. 48.00
Platter, Provincial, Hardwood, Round, Raised Edge, Late 19th Century, 17 In.. . . . . 360.00
Propeller, Airplane, Erco Compreg, Brass Tips, 73 In.. . . . . 529.00
Propeller, Airplane, Flottorp, No. 18709, 8-Bolt Hub, 80 In.. . . . . 411.00
Propeller, Airplane, Sensenich Brothers, No. 9580, 6-Bolt Hub, Copper Blades, 69 In.. . . . . 235.00
Shelf, Mountain Goat, Head, Leaves, Stained, 12½ x 10 x 5 In. 99.00
Spoon, Wedding, Man On Handle, 6¼ In.. . . . . 66.00
Spoon, Wedding, Openwork Handle, Norwegian, 7¾ In.. . . . . 55.00
Staff, Shango, Yoruba, Woman Kneeling, Ax Shape Headdress, Africa, 17 In.. . . . . 2115.00
Stamp, Wallpaper, Heart Shape, 2 Center Hearts, Serrated Border, Handle, 7½ x 7 In.. . . . . 550.00
Stand, Decanter, Bear Hiking, 3 Cordials, Black Forest, c.1900, 15 In. . . . . *illus* 1534.00
Storage Jar, Hollowed-Out Palm Trunk, Pyriform, 40½ x 27 In.. . . . . 864.00
Tankard, Barrel Form, Cover, c.19th Century, 10 In.. . . . . 88.00
Tray, Cutlery, Georgian, Mahogany, Brass Handle, Binding Straps, 7¼ x 15½ In.. . . . . 1293.00
Tray, Mahogany, Brass Handles, 18 x 27 In.. . . . . 59.00
Tray, Poplar, Red Paint, Splayed Sides, Dovetailed, Turned Feet, 4½ x 11 x 11 In.. . . . . 440.00
Tray, Poplar, Tapered Sides, 3 x 8 x 7¾ In.. . . . . 468.00
Tray, Serving, G. Nelson, Walnut, Square, Raised Lip, Herman Miller, 15 x 15 In.. . . . . 360.00
Tray, Utensil, Mixed Wood Sides, Scalloped Handle, 5 x 14½ x 9½ In.. . . . . 88.00
Tray, Utensil, Poplar, Yellow Paint, Brown Grain, Blue Interior, Center Handle, 5 x 12 x 8½ In.. 209.00
Trencher, Blue Paint, Carved Rim Handles, Scrubbed Inside, 10¾ x 20½ In.. . . . . 805.00
Trencher, French Provincial, Waxed, Maize Ears, 18 x 9½ In.. . . . . 120.00
Trencher, Gray Paint, Oblong, 19th Century, 4½ x 19 x 14 In.. . . . . 230.00
Trencher, Hardwood, Green Paint, Oblong, 3½ x 20¼ x 10¼ In.. . . . . 144.00
Trencher, Poplar, Red Paint, Carved, Oval, Tapered, 4¾ x 20 x 12¾ In.. . . . . 143.00
Trencher, Pouring Spout, Hand Carved, 2 x 10 x 5 In.. . . . . 275.00
Trencher, White Paint, Oblong, 19th Century, 4¾ x 24¾ x 11¼ In.. . . . . 173.00
Tub, Painted, Stave & Lapped Band Construction, Round, Integral Handle, 10¼ x 14 In. 176.00
Watch Hutch, Pipe Rack, Cherry, Man's Bust, Columns, c.1880, 22½ x 10 In. . . . . *illus* 5000.00
Watch Hutch, Walnut, Tall Case Form, Removable Lid, c.1880, 16 x 5 x 5 In.. . . . . *illus* 345.00
Watch Safe, Vase, Flower Finial, 4 Treen, Finials, Arches, Columns, 16 x 10⅝ x 3⅝ In.. . . . . . 358.00
Wheel, Cart, Convex, Axel Opening, Iron Rim, Mounted, Chinese, 36 x 28 In.. . . . . 420.00

WORCESTER porcelains were made in Worcester, England, from 1751. The firm went through many name changes and eventually, in 1862, became The Royal Worcester Porcelain Company Ltd. Collectors often refer to Dr. Wall, Barr, Flight, and other names that indicate time periods or artists at the factory. It became part of Royal Worcester Spode Ltd. in 1976. Related pieces may be found in the Royal Worcester category.

Basket, Pearlware, Center Flower Spray, Raised Flower Heads, Reticulated, 6½ In., Pair 598.00

Wooden, Watch Hutch, Pipe Rack, Cherry, Man's Bust, Columns, c.1880, 22½ x 10 In.
$5000.00

Wooden, Watch Hutch, Walnut, Tall Case Form, Removable Lid, c.1880, 16 x 5 x 5 In.
$345.00

Worcester, Vase, Hand Holding Urn, Painted, Gilt, Marked, 5¾ In.
$247.00

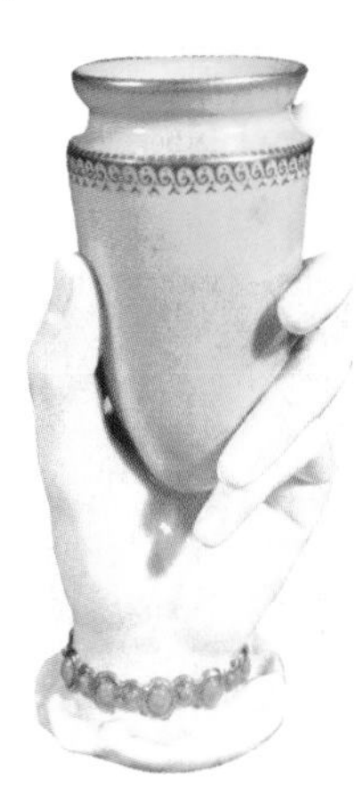

W

World War I, Pin, Welcome Home Our Heroes, 77th Div., Pershing, 1¼ In.
$115.00

World War I, Poster, Soldier With Gun Rooster Coin, France, Frame, 50 x 36 In.
$50.00

World War II, Jacket, Gunner's, Leather, Fleece Liner, Army Air Forces Insignia, 36R, Aero Leather Co.
$288.00

World War II, Pencil Sharpener, Remember Pearl Harbor, Plastic, Soldier, Rifle, ⅞ x 1 In.
$95.00

Bough Pot, Japan Pattern, Cover, Finial, c.1800, 6¾ In. 690.00
Bough Pot, Paneled, Scenic, Gold Trim, c.1800, 9 In., Pair 3000.00
Bowl, Hop Trellis, c.1775, 6½ In. 870.00
Bowl, Royal Lily, Gold Rim, 18th Century, 6½ In. 198.00
Candlestick, Column Form, Square Base, Raised Flower Swag, 1955, 10½ In. 295.00
Cup & Saucer, Butterflies, c.1810, 5¼ In. 360.00
Cup & Saucer, Hop Trellis, c.1775, 5¼ In. 870.00
Figurine, Joy & Sorrow, Colored Parian, 19th Century, 10 In., Pair 780.00
Pitcher, Imari Decoration, Multicolored, Spiral Ribbed, Shaped Handle, c.1800, 7 x 5 In. 1050.00
Sauceboat, Blue Flowers, Crescent Mark, c.1760, 6¼ In. 118.00
Serving Dish, Scalloped Borders, Square, Marked, 8¼ In., Pair 575.00
Stand, Condiment, Scenic, Hand Painted, c.1800, 6 In. 236.00
Sugar, County Scene, Gold Trim, Cover, 18th Century, 5 In. 630.00
Tea Set, Gilt Vermicelli, Rust Dots, Grainger Wood & Co., c.1810, 26 Piece 1880.00
Tray, Revolving, Scalloped, Purple Rim, Leaves, Pedestal Foot, 1880, 19¾ x 4¼ In. 354.00
Tureen, Lid, Purple Flowers, Leaves, Gilt, Flower Finial, Marked, FBB, 5¾ x 9 x 8 In. 795.00
Urn, Chamberlain, Bouquets, Grapevine Handles, Footed, Black Crown, 11¾ x 13½ In. 4900.00
Vase, Hand Holding Urn, Painted, Gilt, Marked, 5¾ In. *illus* 247.00

WORLD WAR I and World War II souvenirs are collected today. Be careful not to store anything that includes live ammunition. Your local police will tell you how to dispose of the explosives. See also Sword and Trench Art.

WORLD WAR I

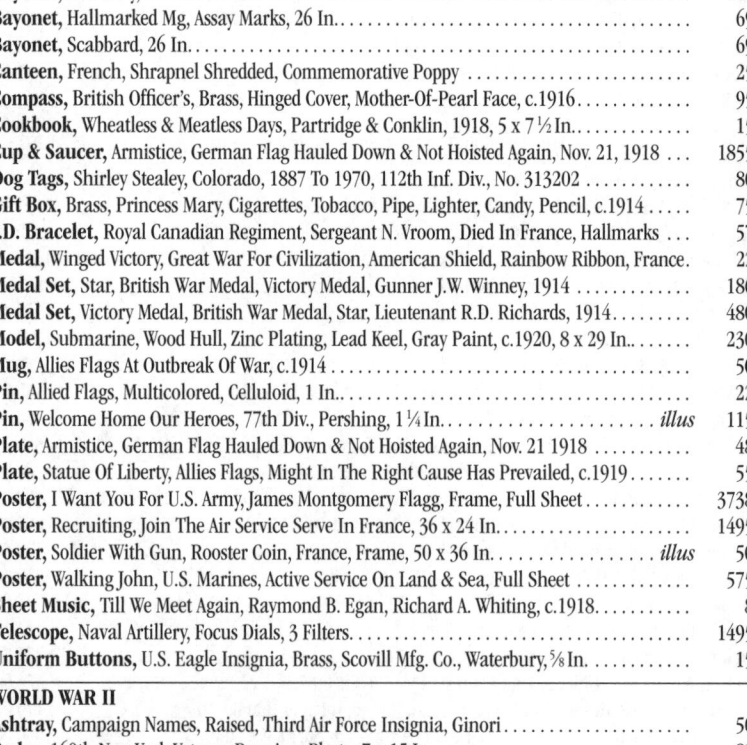

Badge, 1897 Buffalo, New York Gar Encampment, 2½ x 1½ In. 45.00
Badge, 1904 1st New York Light Artillery Reunion 142.00
Badge, Pilot, Prussian Army, Silver Tone Metal, 2¾ In. 500.00
Bayonet, Germany, 20¼ In. 144.00
Bayonet, Hallmarked Mg, Assay Marks, 26 In. 69.00
Bayonet, Scabbard, 26 In. 69.00
Canteen, French, Shrapnel Shredded, Commemorative Poppy 25.00
Compass, British Officer's, Brass, Hinged Cover, Mother-Of-Pearl Face, c.1916 95.00
Cookbook, Wheatless & Meatless Days, Partridge & Conklin, 1918, 5 x 7½ In. 15.50
Cup & Saucer, Armistice, German Flag Hauled Down & Not Hoisted Again, Nov. 21, 1918 1855.00
Dog Tags, Shirley Stealey, Colorado, 1887 To 1970, 112th Inf. Div., No. 313202 80.00
Gift Box, Brass, Princess Mary, Cigarettes, Tobacco, Pipe, Lighter, Candy, Pencil, c.1914 75.00
I.D. Bracelet, Royal Canadian Regiment, Sergeant N. Vroom, Died In France, Hallmarks 57.00
Medal, Winged Victory, Great War For Civilization, American Shield, Rainbow Ribbon, France. 22.00
Medal Set, Star, British War Medal, Victory Medal, Gunner J.W. Winney, 1914 186.00
Medal Set, Victory Medal, British War Medal, Star, Lieutenant R.D. Richards, 1914 480.00
Model, Submarine, Wood Hull, Zinc Plating, Lead Keel, Gray Paint, c.1920, 8 x 29 In. 230.00
Mug, Allies Flags At Outbreak Of War, c.1914 50.00
Pin, Allied Flags, Multicolored, Celluloid, 1 In. 22.00
Pin, Welcome Home Our Heroes, 77th Div., Pershing, 1¼ In. *illus* 115.00
Plate, Armistice, German Flag Hauled Down & Not Hoisted Again, Nov. 21 1918 48.00
Plate, Statue Of Liberty, Allies Flags, Might In The Right Cause Has Prevailed, c.1919 55.00
Poster, I Want You For U.S. Army, James Montgomery Flagg, Frame, Full Sheet 3738.00
Poster, Recruiting, Join The Air Service Serve In France, 36 x 24 In. 1495.00
Poster, Soldier With Gun, Rooster Coin, France, Frame, 50 x 36 In. *illus* 50.00
Poster, Walking John, U.S. Marines, Active Service On Land & Sea, Full Sheet 575.00
Sheet Music, Till We Meet Again, Raymond B. Egan, Richard A. Whiting, c.1918 8.00
Telescope, Naval Artillery, Focus Dials, 3 Filters 1495.00
Uniform Buttons, U.S. Eagle Insignia, Brass, Scovill Mfg. Co., Waterbury, ⅝ In. 15.00

WORLD WAR II

Ashtray, Campaign Names, Raised, Third Air Force Insignia, Ginori 50.00
Badge, 160th New York Veteran Reunion, Photo, 7 x 15 In. 89.00
Badge, National Savings Effort, Lend To Defend, Red, St. George, 1½ x 1¼ In. 18.00
Badge, War Effort Savings, Lend To Defend, Red Enamel, St. George & Dragon, 2 In. 18.00
Card, Valentine, Patriotic, Wishes, Son, For Blessings Day By Day, c.1943, 5¼ x 4¼ In. 8.00
Cup & Saucer, Paragon Patriotic Series, Marked Britain Shall Triumph, c.1941 75.00
Cup & Saucer, Paragon Patriotic Series, Marked Canada, For Right & Liberty, c.1941 65.00
Envelope, Patriotic, Aviation, Mail Delivered To Parachutist, High-Ho! Letter For, 9 x 4 In. 8.00
Flag, Japanese, Silk, 27 x 40 In. 350.00
Hat, U.S. Navy, Wool, U.S. Navy On Front, Ribbon Band, Side Bow 20.00
Jacket, Gunner's, Leather, Fleece Liner, Army Air Forces Insignia, 36R, Aero Leather Co. *illus* 288.00
Magazine Ad, Black-Out Curtains, Ways To Help War Effort, 1942, 10¼ x 14 In. 5.00

Medal, Star, Bronze, 6 Months Overseas Service, 3 Sept. 1939 To 2 Sept. 1945, Britain....... 10.00
Pencil Sharpener, Remember Pearl Harbor, Plastic, Soldier, Rifle, ⅞ x 1 In.......... *illus* 95.00
Pillow Cover, U.S. Army, Ft. Benning, Airplanes, Tank, Soldiers, Poem, 16 x 16 In.......... 18.00
Pin, German Artillery, 2 ½ In.. 75.00
Pin, War Bonds, Kilroy Was Here, White, Red, Celluloid, 1 ¼ In. 15.00
Pin, We Protest Hitler's Persecution Of Jews, Late 1930s, 1 ¼ In. *illus* 316.00
Plaque, Homefront Wood Working Kit, USA War Enemies Images, 1945, 6 x 4 ¾ In. 12.00
Plate, British Coat Of Arms, Bundles For Britain, White Border, Steubenville, 8 Piece 125.00
Pocket Watch, British Military, Swiss 15 Jewel, Stem Wind, White Metalloid, Dial 250.00
Postcard, US Military Propaganda, Hitler, Royal Flush, Slam The Axis, D.R. & Co, 1943 20.00
Poster, News Map, April 30 1945, 2-Sided, Maps, War Details, United Nations, 35 x 47 In. 54.00
Poster, U.S. War Bonds, Statue Of Liberty, Text In Italian, 1943, 22 x 28 In. 115.00
Ration Book, Office Of Price Administration, Issued To Enes W. Cole, Partially Used. 24.00
Sweater, U.S. Navy, Wool, Turtleneck, Black, Red Cross, Pocohontas Chapter, c.1943. 75.00
Sword, Japanese Officer's, Shin-Gunto, Cherry Blossom, Inscriptions, Scabbard, 40 In. 1150.00
Tag, Navy Mothers Clubs Of America, Inc., Sailor, Die Cut, String, 3 ¾ In. *illus* 23.00
Teapot, War Against Hitlerism, Crown Ducal, Replaces Aluminum, c.1939 220.00

WORLD'S FAIR souvenirs from all of the fairs are collected. The first fair was the Great Exhibition of 1851 in London. Some other important exhibitions and fairs include Philadelphia, 1876 (Centennial); Chicago, 1893 (World's Columbian); Buffalo, 1901 (Pan-American); St. Louis, 1904 (Louisiana Purchase); Portland, (Lewis & Clark Centennial Exposition) 1905; San Francisco, 1915 (Panama-Pacific); Philadelphia, 1926 (Sesquicentennial); Chicago, 1933 (Century of Progress); Cleveland, 1936 (Great Lakes); San Francisco, 1939 (Golden Gate International); New York, 1939 (World of Tomorrow); Seattle, 1962 (Century 21); New York, 1964; Montreal, 1967; New Orleans, 1984; Tsukuba, Japan, 1985; Vancouver, B.C., 1986; Brisbane, Australia, 1988; Seville, Spain, 1992; Genoa, Italy, 1992; Seoul, South Korea, 1993; Lisbon, Portugal, 1998; Hanover, Germany, 2000; and Aichi, Japan, 2005. Memorabilia of fairs include directories, pictures, fabrics, ceramics, etc. Memorabilia from other similar celebrations may be listed in the Souvenir category.

Apron, 1939, New York, Bib Style, Map Of Fair, Trylon & Perisphere Border 29.00
Ashtray, 1933, Chicago, Enamel 175.00
Ashtray, 1939, New York, Ballantine Beer Inn, Blue, Purity, Body, Flavor, 5 x 5 In. 63.00
Ashtray, 1964, New York, Federal Pavilion, Thailand, Spain, Unisphere, 4 In.. 12.00
Ashtray, 1964, New York, Pottery, 4 In. 12.00
Ball, 1964, New York, Inflatable, Plastic, See-Through, Boy & Girl, Original Package 15.50
Bank, 1893, Chicago, My Expenses To Chicago, Ball Shape, Pottery, 5 ¼ In. 1650.00
Barber Bottle, 1933, Chicago, Tree Stump, Figural, 12 In.. 259.00
Bell, 1893, Chicago, Columbia Exposition, Frosted Twist Handle, 4 ¼ In.. 200.00
Bell, 1982, Knoxville, Tennessee, 3 ½ In. 10.00
Blanket, 1933, Chicago, Century Of Progress, Rust, Beige, Hall Of Science, 62 x 72 In. 137.00
Bone Dish, 1904, St. Louis, Palace Of Varied Industries, Porcelain, 6 ½ x 4 In. 42.00
Book, 1964, New York, Official Souvenir 19.00
Bottle, 1939, New York, Bulbous, White Glass, 6 In.. 18.00
Bowl, 1964, New York, Molded Wood, Unisphere, 11 ½ x 10 ¼ In. 22.00
Butter Dish, 1964, New York, Plastic 35.00
Button, 1893, Chicago, I'm From Chicago, Green Duck Co., Celluloid, 1 ¼ In. 10.00
Button, 1904, St. Louis, Metal 24.00
Button, 1933, Chicago, I Was There, Green, Red, White, ¾ In. 21.00
Can Opener, 1962, Seattle 15.00
Card Table, 1939, New York 125.00
Change Holder, 1964, New York, Vinyl, Triangular, Orange, Children With Balloons. 30.00
Cigar Case, 1904, St. Louis, Aluminum, Brass Clasp, Holds 3 Cigars 50.00
Coaster, 1939, New York, Tin Lithograph, Various Exhibition Building, 8 Piece 23.00
Coloring Book, 1964, New York 65.00
Compact, 1934, Chicago, Can Style, Silver Gray Lid, Stainless Steel Edge, Clasp, 3 In. 26.00
Compact, 1934, Chicago, Red Powder, Silvered Inside Cover, 1 ¾ x 1 ½ In. 42.00
Cup, 1915, San Francisco, Panama-Pacific Exhibition, Small Handle, Wagner Ware 1000.00
Earrings, 1962, Seattle, Pinch Style, Space Needle, Box 80.00
Envelope, 1964, New York, Preprinted, 5 Cent Stamp, 6 ½ In.. 9.00
Goblet, 1876, Philadelphia, Centennial, 6 ¼ In. 26.00
Handkerchief, 1876, Philadelphia Centennial Exhibition, 26 x 22 In.. *illus* 330.00
Handkerchief, 1939, New York, Communications Exhibit 29.00
Handkerchief, 1939, New York, Hall Of Metals 29.00
Hat, Taxi Driver's, 1939, New York. 195.00
Hotpad, 1933, Chicago, Themes Of The Fair, Federal Building Center, 6 x 8 In. 12.50
Jacket, 1939, New York, Guide's Uniform, Blue, Bakelite Trylon & Perisphere Buttons 130.00

World War II, Pin, We Protest Hitler's Persecution Of Jews, Late 1930s, 1 ¼ In.
$316.00

World War II, Tag, Navy Mothers Clubs Of America, Inc., Sailor, Die Cut, String, 3 ¾ In.
$23.00

World's Fair, Handkerchief, 1876, Philadelphia Centennial Exhibition, 26 x 22 In.
$330.00

World's Fair, Jacket, 1964, New York, Greyhound At The World's Fair, Brass Buttons
$173.00

W

World's Fair, Lantern, 1934, Chicago, Century Of Progress, Glass, Brass, 5½ x 3 In.
$316.00

World's Fair, Pitcher, 1939, New York, Porcelien Trademark, Dec., 4½ x 8 x 7 In.
$345.00

World's Fair, Radio, 1939, New York, Trylon & Perisphere, Wood, Composition, 6 x 9 x 7 In.
$1391.00

World's Fair, Sticker, 1939, New York, Bakelite Exhibit, Hall Of Industrial Science, 1½ x 2¼ In.
$107.00

World's Fair, Stickpin, 1905, Portland, Miss Liberty, Mason & Hamlin, Celluloid, ⅞ x 1 In.
$125.00

Jacket, 1964, New York, Greyhound At The World's Fair, Brass Buttons . . . . *illus* 173.00
Key, 1933, Chicago, 8½ In. 34.00
Keychain, Rabbit's Foot, 1939, New York, Not Lucky For The Rabbit, Trylon Perisphere 34.00
Knife, 1982, Knoxville, Surgical Steel, Brass Handle, Raised Images, Box, 5¾ In. 20.00
Lantern, 1934, Chicago, Century Of Progress, Glass, Brass, 5½ x 3 In. . . . . *illus* 316.00
Letter Opener, 1933, Chicago, Planet, Century Of Progress, Brass, Copper, 7½ In. 35.00
License Plate, 1940, New York, 2 Piece 133.00
License Plate Tag, 1933, Chicago, Century Of Progress, Metal, Eagle, U.S. Flag, 5 x 3 In. 54.00
Life Magazine, 1964, New York. 35.00
Lighter, 1939, New York, Silent Flame, Black Bakelite, Trylon & Perisphere, 3 x 3 In. 237.00
Magazine, 1964, New York, Life Magazine, Opening Day, May 1 1964, 112 Pages. 6.00
Map, 1934, Chicago, Century Of Progress, Pure Oil Pathfinder, Rand McNally, Chicago. 10.00
Map, 1962, Seattle, Touring 36.00
Match Safe, 1901, Pan American Exposition, Nickel Plated, 3 x 1½ x ¼ In. 275.00
Match Safe, 1904, St. Louis. 95.00
Membership Certificate, 1904, St. Louis, Fraternal Building, Sisseton Agency, 17 x 14 In. . . 130.00
Mug, 1967, Montreal, Glass, Gold Trim, Blue, 2¾ In. 12.00
Mystery Coin, 1933, Chicago, Accordion Style Fold-Out Pavilion Photos, ½ In. 22.00
Necktie, 1962, Seattle, Space Needle, Monorail 20.00
Pen, 1962, Seattle, Hardwood, Space Needle Shape, Evergreen Company Inc. 16.50
Pennant, 1933, Chicago, Buildings, Red Felt Band, Orange Trim, Tassels, 29 x 11 In. 20.00
Pennant, 1933, Chicago, Hall Of Science, 28 In. 25.00
Pennant, 1964, New York, Unisphere, 26 In. 16.00
Pin, 1901, Buffalo, Image Of Buffalo, I Am Next, Lithograph, Baldwin & Gleason, 2 In. 123.00
Pin, 1939, New York, Airplane, Twin-Engine, Flight 1939, 1½ x 1½ In. 24.00
Pin, 1939, New York, American Jubilee, ¾ In. 19.00
Pin, 1939, New York, Mother-Of-Pearl, Theme Building, Swirled Petals, 1 In. 35.00
Pincushion, 1893, Chicago, High Heel Shoe, 4¼ In. 30.00
Pitcher, 1939, New York, Porcelien Trademark, Dec., 4½ x 8 x 7 In. . . . . *illus* 345.00
Placemat, 1962, Seattle, Space Tower, Paper, 14 x 9¾ In. 5.00
Plaque, 1904, St. Louis, Louisiana Purchase, Uncle Sam, Bag Of Gold, 5½ x 7 In. 616.00
Plaque, 1964, New York, Globe, Peace Through Understanding, Ceramic, 4¾ x 7 In. 28.00
Plate, 1893, Chicago, Metal, Reverse Painted Glass, Administration Building, 5¼ In. 48.00
Plate, 1893, Chicago, Santa Maria Clipper Ship, Smith Brothers, Libbey Glass, 7½ In. 264.00
Plate, 1904, St. Louis, Tin, Advertising, Flowers, Compliments Of A.J. Child & Son 34.00
Plate, 1939, New York, Raised Design, Potter, Homer Laughlin, 7 In. . . . . 45.00 to 154.00
Plate, 1962, Seattle, Hanging, 8 In. 15.00
Plate, 1964, New York, Green, 9 In. 20.99
Plate, 1982, Knoxville, Tennessee 6.00
Playing Cards, 1904, St. Louis, Varied Images, Samuel Cupples Envelope Co., 54 Piece 152.00
Playing Cards, 1934, Chicago 45.00
Pocket Knife, 1933, Chicago, 2 Blades, Brass, Enameled, Pavilion Images, 3⅜ In. 63.00
Pocket Knife, 1982, Knoxville, Tennessee, 3¼ In. 35.00
Postcard, 1933, Chicago, Century Of Progress, Oriental Village, 5½ x 3½ In. 13.00
Postcard, 1939, New York, Du Pont Building. 8.99
Postcard, 1939, New York, Florida Building. 4.75
Postcard, 1939, New York, General Motors 6.99
Postcard, 1939, New York, Information Booth 3.00
Postcard, 1939, New York, Music Hall, Linen. 7.99
Postcard, 1939, New York, Railroad Building, Linen. 7.99
Postcard, 1939, New York, Star Pylon. 5.00
Purse, 1964, New York, Vinyl, White, Snap, Strap, Unisphere, Children, 7 x 5½ In. 45.00
Puzzle, 1964, New York, Greyhound Bus. 25.00
Radio, 1939, New York, Trylon & Perisphere, Wood, Composition, 6 x 9 x 7 In. . . . . *illus* 1391.00
Rain Bonnet, 1964, New York, Box. 15.00
Record, 1939, New York, Remington Rand Hall, Trylon & Perisphere, Lew Lehr. 45.00
Ribbon, 1876, Philadelphia, Centennial, Exhibition Buildings, Silk, Frame, 11 x 6 In. 590.00
Salad Server, 1964, New York, Ceramic, Wood, Spoon, Fork, 11 In., Set 50.00
Salt & Pepper, 1939, New York, 3½ In. 27.00
Scarf, 1964, New York, Unisphere U.S. Steel, 26 In. 85.00
Sewing Kit, 1939, New York, 17 Spools. 15.00
Sewing Needle Book, 1933, Chicago, 4½ x 6½ In. 15.00
Shoe, 1904, St. Louis, Palace Of Mines & Metallurgy, Porcelain, Gold Trim, Miniature 30.00
Sign, 1939, New York, Swifts Premium Frankfurts, Frame, Plexiglas, 66 x 36 In. 1840.00
Souvenir Folder, 1964, New York, Flash Cards 6.00
Spoon, 1933, Chicago, Fort Dearborn End, Century Of Progress Stem, 6 In. 17.00

W

Spoon, 1934, Chicago, A Century Of Progress, Gold & Green Duck Co. 20.00
Spoon, 1939, New York, Theme Building, 6 In. 30.00
Stein, 1901, Buffalo, Pan-American Exposition, 5 ¾ In. 117.00
Sticker, 1939, New York, Bakelite Exhibit, Hall Of Industrial Science, 1 ½ x 2 ¼ In. ...... *illus* 107.00
Stickpin, 1905, Portland, Miss Liberty, Mason & Hamlin, Celluloid, ⅞ x 1 In. .... *illus* 125.00
Tee Shirt, 1964, New York, White, Avenue Of Flags Scene, Unisphere, Cotton, XL 16-18...... 40.00
Thermometer, 1939, New York, Sphere & Trylon, 1939 .... 27.00
Ticket, 1893, Chicago, Good Only On Chicago Day, October 9th, Child's Admission 46.00
Ticket Book, 1939, New York.................. 19.00
Tie Clip, 1939, New York, 2 ½ In.................. 24.00
Tip Tray, 1904, St. Louis, Alphonse & Gaston 95.00
Toy, Bus, 1939, New York, Greyhound Line, Cast Iron, Arcade, 6 ½ In. 225.00
Toy, Wagon, 1933, Chicago, Blue, Radio Flyer, Radio Steel & Mfg. Co., 4 ½ In.................. 375.00
Trade Card, 1901, Buffalo, Pan-American Exposition, Heinz.................. 20.00
Tray, 1939, New York, Enameled, Blue, White, Trylon & Perisphere, Chinese, 4 In.......... 30.00
Tray, 1964, New York, 16 x 22 In.................. 39.00
Tray, 1967, Montreal, Pavilion Of The U.S., Globe On Blue Sky, 7 x 5 In.................. 15.00
Tumbler, 1904, St. Louis, Palace Of Arts, Blue Ground, Gilt Accents, Germany, 3 ¾ In........ 38.00
Tumbler, 1904, St. Louis, Porcelain, Gilt Bands, Louisiana Purchase, 3 ¾ In. 42.00
Tumbler, 1904, St. Louis, Black & White Fair Scenes, White, Gilt Bands, 3 ¾ In.................. 51.00
Tumbler, 1964, New York, Kodak Pavilion, Yellow, White, 5 ½ In.................. 35.00
Vase, 1940, New York, Blue Jasperware Type, 5 In.................. 85.00
View-Master Reel, 1964, New York, Sawyer, 5 Packs, 3 Reels In Each, 21 Pictures 161.00
Wallet, 1964, New York, Vinyl, Orange, Unisphere, Children With Balloons.................. 42.00
Wrapping Paper, 1964, New York, 12 Ft. x 20 In. 27.00

WPA is the abbreviation for Works Progress Administration, a program created by executive order in 1935 to provide jobs for millions of unemployed Americans. Artists were hired to create murals, paintings, drawings, and sculptures for public buildings. Pieces are marked WPA and may have the artist's name on them.

Booklet, New Orleans City Guide, American Guide Series Map, Houghton Mifflin, 1938 ..... 75.00
Doll, Book, Little Black Sambo, Cloth, Painted Face, 23 In.................. 2135.00
Model, Outhouse, Wood, Lost WPA Worker, Skeleton Interior, Occupied Sign, 2 x 3 x 5 In..... 255.00
Pocket Kit, Fold-Out Ashtray, Metal, Property Of U.S. Government 15.00
Poster, Pennsylvania Game Commission, Winter Feeding, Game, Corn Shocks, 14 x 11 In. .. 38.00
Print, End Of The Line San Francisco, Silkscreen, Trolley, Man On Bench, 12 ½ x 14 In...... 50.00
Puerto Rico, Guide To Island Of Boriquen, American Guide Series, c.1940 .... 142.00
Tag, Brass, No. 7733 .... 15.00

WRISTWATCHES came into use during World War I. Wristwatches are listed here by manufacturer or as advertising or character watches. Wristwatches may also be listed in other categories. Pocket watches are listed in the Watch category.

Argentina, Woman's, Silvertone Dial, Diamond Melee Cover, 18K Gold, 7 In.................. 1175.00
Baume & Mercier, 18K Gold, White Dial, Abstract & Roman Numerals, Leather Strap...... 823.00
Bertolucci, Pulchra, Leather Band, 18K Gold 2390.00
Bueche Girod, Woman's, Stirrup Bracelet, 18K Gold, Blue Enamel, Foldover Clasp......... 1593.00
Bulgari, Woman's, Black Dial, Link, Stainless Steel Band, 18K Gold, 6 ¾ In.................. 940.00
Bulgari, Black Hexagonal Dial, Flexible Clip Bracelet, 18K Gold 2115.00
Cartier, 18K Gold, Stepped Bezel, White Dial, Roman Numerals, Black Leather Strap 1998.00
Cartier, Ceinture, Stepped Octagonal Case, White Dial, Roman Numerals, 18K Gold........ 1440.00
Cartier, Woman's, Panthere, Ivorytone Dial, Roman Numerals, Quartz Movement 4406.00
Character, Barbie, Dial, Barbie & Ken, Heartbeat Second Hand, Bradley, 1960.................. 950.00
Character, Laurel & Hardy, Pendant, On Chair, Dirty Time Co., 1970 .... 335.00
Chaumet, Woman's, Mother-Of-Pearl Dial, Diamonds, 18K White Gold, Diamond Buckle ... 999.00
Chronograph, 18K Gold, Breitling Premier.................. 3025.00
Chronograph, Pasha, Ivory Dial, 18K Gold Dial, No. 1032, Cartier, Box 4113.00
Citroen, 14K Gold, Diamond, Snake Link Band, Retro, Paul Ditisheim, 5 ⅝ In. 823.00
Concord, Woman's, Cut Diamond Melee, Brickwork Band, 18K Gold, 6 ½ In.................. 1410.00
Corum, 18K Gold, Coppertone Textured Dial, Roman Numerals, Shaped Bezel, 21 Jewel..... 499.00
Corum, Woman's, Bracelet, Diamond, Gold Covered Dial, 18K Gold, Pave Set 2390.00
Croton W. Co., Platinum, Diamond, 17 Jewels, Swiss, 1920s 2500.00
Ebel, Woman's, Goldtone Dial, 17 Jewel, Textured Bracelet, Diamond Melee, 18K Gold 823.00
Ernie Keebler, Quartz, Box, 1970s, 1-In. Face, 9-In. Band.................. *illus* 86.00
Eterna, Woman's, Jewel Movement, White Gold, 18K Gold, White Gold Mesh Band 1170.00
Hamilton, Diamonds, White Gold, Alligator Strap, 19 Jewel, Signed, 8 ⅞ In.......... *illus* 567.00

Wristwatch, Ernie Keebler, Quartz, Box, 1970s, 1-In. Face, 9-In. Band
$86.00

Wristwatch, Hamilton, Diamonds, White Gold, Alligator Strap, 19 Jewel, Signed, 8 ⅞ In.
$567.00

Wristwatch, International Watch Co., Diamonds, Rubies, 14K Gold, 17 Jewel, c.1940, 6 ½ In.
$1793.00

Wristwatch, Lucien Piccard, 14K White Gold, Roman Numerals, 17 Jewel, Signed, 7 ¼ In.
$418.00

W

Wristwatch, Vacheron & Constantin, Diamond, Platinum, 18K Gold, 16 Jewel, c.1918, 6 In.
$2868.00

Wristwatch, Vacheron & Constantin, Platinine, Enameled Bezel, Crocodile Strap, c.1920, 9 In.
$3346.00

Yellowware, Bowl, Rockingham Glaze, 2 ½ x 8 ¾ In.
$55.00

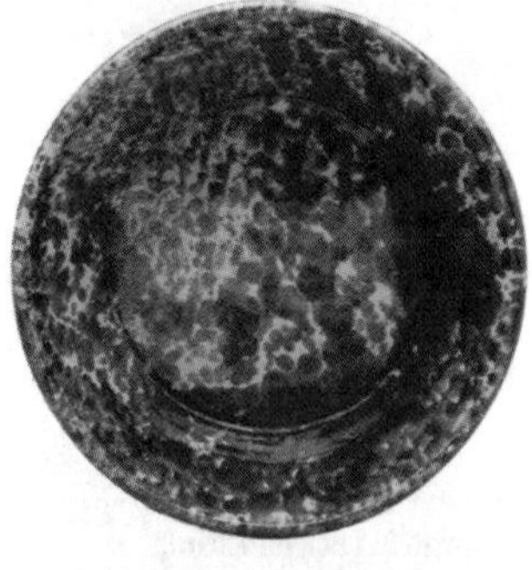

Yellowware, Sugar, Seaweed, Blue, 19th Century, 4 ¼ In.
$1093.00

Hamilton, Platinum Case, 54 Round Single-Cut Diamonds, 7 ½ In. 978.00
Hamilton, Woman's, Bracelet, Diamond, Platinum, 17 Jewel, Art Deco, 6 ½ In. 1016.00
International Watch Co., Diamonds, Rubies, 14K Gold, 17 Jewel, c.1940, 6 ½ In. . . . . . *illus* 1793.00
Invicta, Diamond, Stainless Steel, 17 Jewel, Leather Band, 18K Gold, Swiss 657.00
Jules Jurgensen, Round, Second Hand, Black Leather Strap, 14K Gold 336.00
Lady Hamilton, 32 Full Cut & 44 Single Cut Diamonds, 14K White Gold, 6 ½ In. 460.00
LeCoultre, Memovox, 14K Gold, 17 Jewel, Automatic, Date, Alarm, Mesh, c.1950 . . . . . . 1195.00
LeCoultre, Silvertone Dial, Abstract Numerals, Day, Month, 18K Gold, No. 335583 . . . . . . 1763.00
Longines, Woman's, Silvertone Metal Dial, 17 Jewel, Wind Movement, 18K Gold 940.00
Lucien Piccard, 14K White Gold, Roman Numerals, 17 Jewel, Signed, 7 ¼ In. . . . . . *illus* 418.00
Lucien Piccard, Woman's, Seed Pearls, Sapphires, 14K Gold, 17 Jewel, Ivory Dial 646.00
Mary Marvel, Chrome Case, Leather Band, Marvel Importing, Box, 1948 . . . . . . 374.00
Movado, 14K Gold, Ivorytone Dial, Roman Numerals, Square Bezel, 17 Jewel 558.00
Omega, 14K Gold, Diamonds, Mesh Band, 20th Century, 6 ½ In. 187.00
Omega, De Ville, Automatic, Textured Case, 24 Jewel, 2 Adjustments, 18K Gold 1680.00
Omega, De Ville, Emerald Shaped Case, Bronze Face, Faceted Crystal, 18K Gold, 6 ⅞ In. 1140.00
Omega, Man's, Seamaster, Goldtone Dial, Date Aperture, Brickwork Bracelet, 14K 881.00
Omega, Mesh Band, Case, 14K Gold, 7 x ⅞ In. 784.00
Omega, Woman's, Diamonds, 14K Gold Mesh Strap, 6 ⅞ In. 940.00
Patek Philippe, Calatrava, 18K Gold, Ivorytone Dial, 18 Jewel, Crocodile Strap, c.1945 . . . . . . 5288.00
Patek Philippe, Ivorytone Metal Dial, 18 Jewel, 18K Gold, c.1965 . . . . . . 3173.00
Patek Philippe, Silvertone Dial, Abstract Numbers, Sloping Lugs, 18K Gold 5875.00
Patek Philippe, White Gold Dial, 18 Jewel, Green Leather Band, 18K Gold 4113.00
Patek Philippe, Woman's, Goldtone, Metal Dial, Abstract Numbers, Size 7 ¼ 1763.00
Piaget, 18K Yellow Gold Case, Textured Band, 32 Diamonds, Sapphires, 6 x 1 In. 920.00
Piaget, Polo, Goldtone Dial, Quartz Movement, 18K Gold, 7 ⅞ In. 2938.00
Piaget, Woman's, Textured Strap, Oval Dial, Diamonds, 18K Gold, 6 ½ In. 2400.00
Rolex, 18K Gold, Diamond, Perpetual Date, Pearlmaster Bracelet, Oysterlock Clasp 9988.00
Rolex, Datejust Diamond Bezel, Stainless, Gold Band, 1989 . . . . . . 3520.00
Rolex, Gold, Silver Dial, Gold Markers, Oyster Perpetual, 14K Gold Case, c.1950 . . . . . . 1955.00
Rolex, Goldtone Butterfly Dial, Manual Wind Movement, Black Crocodile Band, 9K Gold 764.00
Rolex, Oyster Perpetual, Bubble Back, Goldtone Dial, Leather Strap, 18K Gold, 1938 . . . . . . 5288.00
Rolex, Oyster Perpetual, Datejust, Stainless Steel, Baton Numerals, Date, 1985 . . . . . . 1175.00
Rolex, Oyster Perpetual, Goldtone Dial, Diamond Numbers, Jubilee Band, 18K Gold 5581.00
Rolex, Pink Gold, Leather Strap, 17 Jewel, Secondary Dial, 14K Gold, c.1938 . . . . . . 1440.00
Rolex, Precision, Stainless Steel, Silvertone Dial, Baton Numerals, Oyster Band 999.00
Rolex, Silver & Goldtone Dial, Integral Lugs, Leather Band, Stainless Steel, 1930s 940.00
Rolex, Woman's, Flat Woven, Belt Style, Snakeskin Strap, 18K Gold 3520.00
Rolex, Woman's, Ivorytone Dial, 17 Jewel, Black Leather Strap, 18K Gold 940.00
Rolex, Woman's, Model 290921, Round Head, Mesh Band, 14K Gold 550.00
Rolex, Woman's, Oyster Perpetual Date, Auto Wind, Stainless Steel Case, c.1999 . . . . . . 1620.00
Rolex, Woman's, Round, 9K Gold Bracelet, 14K Gold, 7 x ⅝ In. 880.00
Rolex, Woman's, Tudor Princess, Self Wind, Date, Link Band, 7 ½ x ⅞ In. 1540.00
Tiffany & Co., White Enamel Dial, 17 Jewel, Sapphires, Diamond Melee, 14K Gold 1410.00
Vacheron & Constantin, Diamond, Platinum, 18K Gold, 16 Jewel, c.1918, 6 In. . . . . . *illus* 2868.00
Vacheron & Constantin, Platinine, Enameled Bezel, Crocodile Strap, c.1920, 9 In. . . . . . *illus* 3346.00
Waltham, Woman's, Hunter Case, Windup, Stag In Landscape, 14K Gold 252.00
Wegelin, Ivorytone Dial, Frosted Crystal, Diamonds, Gold Mesh Band 2468.00

YELLOWWARE is a heavy earthenware made of a yellowish clay. It varies in color from light yellow to orange-yellow. Many nineteenth- and twentieth-century kitchen bowls and jugs were made of yellowware. It was made in England and in the United States. Another form of pottery that is sometimes classed as yellowware is listed in this book in the Mocha category.

Baking Dish, Green & Brown Sponge Decorated, Lobed Cover, 20th Century, 4 x 8 In. 100.00
Bottle, Figural, Mermaid, Brown Glaze Highlights, 7 In. 224.00
Bowl, 11 ½ In. 38.00
Bowl, Brown & White Slip Trailed Bands, Late 19th Century, 7 x 15 In. 334.00
Bowl, Rockingham Glaze, 2 ½ x 8 ¾ In. . . . . . *illus* 55.00
Bowl, Sugar, Cover, Wide Slip Band, Blue Seaweed, 4 ¼ In. 1092.00
Cann, Slip Decorated, Footed Base, Incised Lines, Brown & Wavy Bands, 3 ¼ x 3 ½ In. 863.00
Foot Warmer, Cask Form, Rosette Button Handles, Lyre & Leaf Opening, 6 ½ x 11 x 7 In. 11.00
Jug, Pottery, Amber Brown Glaze, Applied Decoration, Applied Handle, 11 In. 148.00
Mixing Bowl, Dark Green Seaweed, White Bands, 19th Century, 4 ½ x 9 ½ In. 440.00
Mug, Cobalt Blue Design, 3 In. 187.00
Pig, Seated On Base With Freestanding Front Legs, Rockingham Glaze, 1880s, 48 x 54 In. 920.00

Pitcher, Mottled Ground, Green & Brown Slip Flowers, Flared Rim, 1812, 6 x 4½ In. 770.00
Rolling Pin, Pine Handles, 20th Century, 3¼ x 15 In. 412.00
Salt, Footed, Blue Seaweed, White Band, 19th Century, 2 x 2¾ In. 357.00
Sugar, Seaweed, Blue, 19th Century, 4¼ In. .... *illus* 1093.00
Washbasin, Pitcher, Banded, Gresley Ware, T.G. Green & Co., Early 1900s, 10 x 14 In. 441.00
Washboard, Blue Sponge, c.1880, 11½ x 11 In. 550.00

ZANESVILLE Art Pottery was founded in 1900 by David Schmidt in Zanesville, Ohio. The firm made faience umbrella stands, jardinieres, and pedestals. The company closed in 1962. Many pieces are marked with just the words *La Moro.*

LA MORO

Bowl, Delph, Blue, Footed, 10¼ x 5½ In. 65.00
Bowl, White Gloss, 8-Sided, Art, 6⅛ In. 60.00
Candleholder, Rose, Gloss, Marked Sesquicentennial Phila, Pa., 1926, 7 In. 95.00
Casserole, 1940s, 2¼ x 4½ In. 28.00
Ice Bucket, White, High Gloss, 7 In. 85.00
Jardiniere, Grapevine, Yellow, 16½ x 17 In. .... *illus* 270.00
Jardiniere, Tan, Homespun, No. 1005, 5⅞ In. 50.00
Lamp, Drip, Blue & Black, 7 In. 100.00
Vase, Aqua, 1930s, 6½ In. 34.00
Vase, Aqua, 7 x 4 In. 24.00
Vase, Aqua, Gloss Glazed, No. 858, 6 x 6 In. 34.00
Vase, Arts & Crafts, Lavender Matte, 7 In. 125.00
Vase, Blue Gloss, 4 In. 38.00
Vase, Bud, Aqua, c.1951, 6 x 3½ In. 28.00
Vase, Homespun, Cylinder, Concentric Rings, 1960, 10 x 4 In. 48.00
Vase, Homespun Gold, 1960s, 10 In. 48.00
Vase, Leaf In Relief, Matte Finish, 8 In. 165.00
Vase, Neptune, 2 Handles, 6 In. 100.00
Vase, Pillow, Aqua, 1930s, 5¾ In. 36.00
Vase, Pink, Gloss, 2 Handles, 5⅛ In. 60.00
Vase, Planter, Aqua, Black Speckles, 7 x 4 In. 24.00
Vase, Seacrest Green, Flat, Stubby Side Handles, 6 x 4⅝ In. 32.00

ZSOLNAY pottery was made in Hungary after 1862 and was characterized by Persian, Art Nouveau, or Hungarian motifs. A series of new Zsolnay figurines with green-gold luster finish is available in many shops today. Early Zsolnay was not marked, but by 1878 the tower trademark was used.

ZSOLNAY PÉCS 5 TJM

Bowl, Boat Shape, Two Crimson Red Parrots, Marbleized Gold Glaze, 6½ x 15 In. 3000.00
Ewer, Pierced Body & Handle, Red Enamel, Yellow Ground, Marked, 9½ In. 1265.00
Figure, Maiden With Pitcher, Luster Glaze, 11 x 4½ In. 1200.00
Figure, Owl, On Book, Blue, Gold, Art Nouveau, 1840-1900, 11¼ x 8¼ In. 100.00
Figure, Owl, Red Glaze, 13½ x 5½ In. 1080.00
Figure, Peacock, Iridescent Pink, Purple, Gold, 3¾ In. 90.00
Jardiniere, Weeds & Cattails, Luster Glaze, 8¼ x 12 In. 11400.00
Tile, Organic Design, Brown Mottled Ground, Metallic Glaze, 6 In. .... *illus* 960.00
Vase, Art Deco, Panels Of Birds Of Paradise, Luster Glaze, 6¾ x 8¼ In. 5400.00
Vase, Broad Shape, Ribbed, Limoges Style Flower Design, 15 x 14 In. 1035.00
Vase, Bud, Iridescent, Early 20th Century, 5½ In. 71.00
Vase, Bud, Iridescent, Stamped, Early 20th Century, 5½ In. 140.00
Vase, Daisies, Green, 3 Spouts, Eosin Glaze, Marked, 8⅛ In. .... *illus* 1900.00
Vase, Deeply Crackled Exterior, Rust Red Luster Glaze, Brown Lined, 5⅜ In. 354.00
Vase, Geraniums Marked Hungary, 8¾ x 5¾ In. 5400.00
Vase, Labrador Glaze, Swollen Shape, 12¾ In. 323.00
Vase, Red, Textured, High Waisted, 1840-1900, 11 x 3¾ In. 50.00
Vase, Stylized Flowers, Red, Gold, White Ground, Eosin, Marked, 14⅛ In. .... *illus* 3500.00
Vase, Trees, Crows, Embossed, Eosin Glaze, Scrolled-Out Handles, 6¾ In. 2468.00
Vase, Tulip, Shape, Luster Glazes, Stamped, 14 x 5½ In. 14400.00
Vase, Waisted, Sculpted Figures Above Waves, Iridescent Green Glaze, 5 x 6 In. 6000.00

Zanesville, Jardiniere, Grapevine, Yellow, 16½ x 17 In.
$270.00

Zsolnay, Tile, Organic Design, Brown Mottled Ground, Metallic Glaze, 6 In.
$960.00

Zsolnay, Vase, Daisies, Green, 3 Spouts, Eosin Glaze, Marked, 8⅛ In.
$1900.00

Zsolnay, Vase, Stylized Flowers, Red, Gold, White Ground, Eosin, Marked, 14⅛ In.
$3500.00

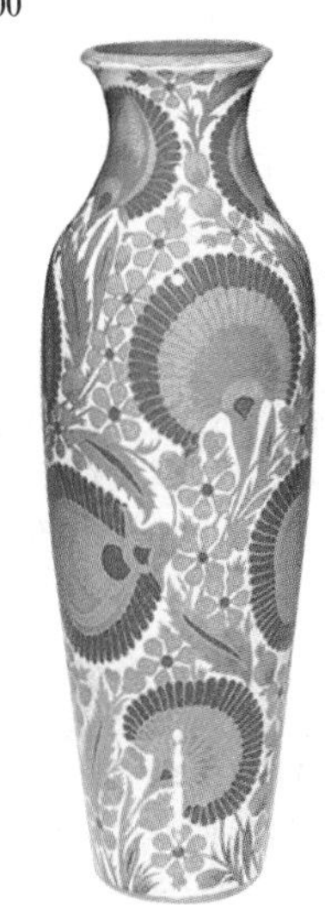

INDEX

This index is computer-generated, making it as complete and accurate as possible. References in uppercase type are category listings. Those in lowercase letters refer to additional pages where pieces can be found. There is also an internal cross-referencing system used in the main part of the book, so if you look for a Kewpie doll in the Doll category, you will be told it is in its own category. There is additional information at the end of many paragraphs about where to find prices of pieces similar to yours.

D

E

M

N

T

U

V

W

Y

Z

Picture Credits

Alderfer Auction Co. 142-147, 162, 208, 213, 215-219, 235, 252, 264, 308, 335, 382, 397, 405, 408, 442, 468, 521, 550, 579, 606, 625, 642, 699, 716-718, 734, 745, 762
Allard Auctions 377
Auction Team Köln 156, 212, 413, 484, 511, 614, 617, 665, 684, 716, 725, 735
Be-Hold 512
Belhorn Auction Services 2-3, 40, 51, 95-96, 100-101, 126, 138, 160, 165-166, 182, 228, 254, 346, 350-352, 365-367, 403, 408, 410, 414, 432-433, 441, 450-451, 454, 459-460, 478-479, 482, 489, 498, 503, 505-506, 516-517, 531-532, 539-540, 560, 573-577, 579, 581-582, 584-585, 590, 610-611, 658-659, 675, 677, 679, 685, 700-701, 737, 747, 756-758, 771
Bertoia Auctions 2, 6, 24, 34-35, 37, 42, 44, 53, 95, 98, 113-114, 119, 123, 128-129, 133, 135, 145, 154-155, 196, 208-209, 210-211, 218, 220-221, 240, 331, 334, 351, 365, 369, 384, 448-449, 530, 677, 683, 709-733
Brunk Auctions 19, 39-40, 42, 51-52, 83-86, 97, 108, 110-112, 116, 123, 131, 147, 149, 161, 170, 174, 181, 185, 222, 233, 237-239, 255, 260-265, 267-269, 273-274, 276, 279-280, 282-287, 289-293, 296, 298, 300-303, 305-306, 311-319, 321-324, 330, 333-334, 339, 350, 353, 357, 370-371, 375, 378, 380, 396, 402, 406, 408, 410, 413, 415-416, 419-420, 433, 440, 455, 465-466, 468-469, 475, 491, 507, 519, 542, 555-556, 586, 588, 593-594, 597-598, 615, 617, 626-630, 632-633, 635, 637-639, 641, 645, 647, 673, 677, 681, 694, 697-698, 701-702, 711, 727, 734, 746, 762
Cincinnati Art Galleries 1-2, 21, 22, 27-28, 33, 50, 90, 93, 119, 137-138, 175-176, 179, 185-186, 222-223, 233, 254, 329, 338, 341-343, 345, 347-348, 354, 357, 387, 389, 403-404, 417-419, 423, 425, 429, 432, 436-437, 439-440, 446-448, 457, 459-460, 462-463, 467, 471, 476, 488, 492, 495, 506, 509, 516, 519, 531-533, 537-539, 541, 554, 557, 560, 563, 565, 567, 572, 579, 581, 585-586, 599, 604, 613-615, 644, 666, 668, 682, 685, 690, 694, 696-697, 700, 736, 738, 751-753, 760, 771
Conestoga Auction Co. 25, 49, 83, 87, 96, 111, 115, 123, 127, 164, 167, 180, 184, 217-218, 241, 243, 258-259, 282, 290, 305, 308, 310, 314, 319, 326, 336, 339, 356, 384, 386, 406-407, 410, 412, 419, 427-428, 430, 458, 501, 515, 561-563, 593, 605-606, 632, 644, 649-651, 656, 669-672, 674-675, 687, 702, 715, 761, 770
Cowan's Auctions 40, 45, 54-55, 61-62, 83-84, 86, 89, 107, 110-112, 116, 126, 130, 132, 136, 148, 157, 164, 167, 169, 184-185, 236-238, 241, 243, 251-252, 256, 259, 266, 275-276, 281, 283, 288, 290-292, 294, 297, 299-300, 304-307, 309, 315, 322, 326-328, 334-335, 337, 346, 371, 383, 409-411, 414, 426-428, 430, 433, 442-443, 451, 453, 456, 457-458, 468, 470, 486, 497-498, 508, 511-513, 515, 525, 542, 545, 555-556, 561, 572, 595, 608, 616, 620-622, 628, 630-632, 634, 638, 640, 642, 645-647, 649-650, 655, 657, 671-672, 678, 681, 686, 701-703, 721, 727, 735, 737, 750, 759, 765-766, 770
DuMouchelles 23, 42, 48, 51-52, 91, 453, 463, 480, 506, 513, 583-585, 588, 748
Eastbourne Auction Rooms 28, 44, 46-49, 90, 115, 119, 126, 137-138, 147, 150-151, 158, 161, 163, 167, 185, 226-227, 252, 272, 344-347, 382, 387, 389, 393-394, 396-397, 400, 417, 442, 497, 507, 529, 540, 552, 579, 587-588, 599, 607, 612, 624, 636, 638, 640, 651, 655, 657, 678-679, 683-684, 701, 708, 716, 731, 743, 761, 763, 765
Garth's Auctions 92, 123, 127, 151, 169, 242, 272, 274, 276, 281, 297, 304, 322, 339, 375-377, 381, 386, 392-395, 397, 400, 409, 415, 434, 443, 458, 474-476, 491, 514, 549-550, 558-559, 572-573, 596, 611, 619, 733-734, 749, 763-764
Glass Works Auctions 33, 54, 56-81, 113, 234-236, 338-339, 382, 449, 485, 505, 621, 622, 670, 691, 749
Green Valley Auctions 39, 87, 90, 105, 120-121, 124-125, 166-168, 171, 254, 259-260, 265, 277-278, 282, 284, 287, 291, 304, 310, 313, 320, 323, 330, 339, 346, 349, 378, 392, 397, 425, 439, 457, 467, 476, 483, 486-487, 501-502, 514, 542-549, 591-592, 596, 607-610, 612, 628, 636, 646, 673-674, 677, 679-680, 702, 705-706, 733, 739, 763, 765
Hake's Americana & Collectibles 9, 10, 12, 29, 34, 88, 116-117, 136, 141, 152, 157, 177, 180, 209, 252, 364, 405, 437, 449, 466, 479, 488, 500, 520-524, 528, 558, 618, 652-653, 659, 678, 689, 713, 745, 766-769
Heritage Auction Galleries 158-159, 178, 337, 390-391, 395, 397-400, 521-527, 552-553, 633, 635-636, 694, 738, 769-770
Hewletts Antiques 102-104, 107
Jackson's International Auctioneers & Appraisers 8, 19, 23, 27, 30-31, 44, 47, 53, 90-93, 97, 99-100, 108, 118-119, 121-122, 134, 136, 149-151, 159, 163, 167, 186, 224, 226, 273, 275-276, 289-292, 295, 301, 305, 308, 313, 315-316, 318, 324, 327, 335, 340-341, 352, 368-370, 372, 375-377, 387, 390, 392, 395-396, 398-399, 422, 424, 426, 434-435, 445, 447, 449, 455, 463, 465, 493, 498-499, 510, 527-528, 531, 534-537, 543, 549-550, 560, 564, 587, 614, 637, 644, 647, 651, 668, 684, 688, 692, 699, 704, 738, 742, 747-748, 753, 755, 763-764
L.H. Selman 32, 494-497
Lang's Sporting Collectables 238-240
Live Free or Die Antique Tool Auctions 703-706
McMasters Harris Auction Co. 625
Morphy Auctions 3-9, 11-19, 21, 24-25, 28-29, 53, 67-68, 79, 82, 94-95, 99, 113-114, 124, 127-128, 133-135, 139-141, 145-146, 152-157, 208, 210-211, 220, 307, 332, 335, 352, 403, 414, 422, 424, 438, 444-445, 472-473, 475, 484, 500, 504, 518, 529-530, 542, 551, 557, 612, 617, 642, 652, 677, 689-690, 707, 710-712, 714, 719, 722-725, 728-729, 731-733, 742, 746, 766
Neal Auction Co. 25, 43, 446, 477, 624
New Orleans Auctions Galleries 20, 26, 43, 48, 84, 88-89, 146, 149, 155, 196, 224, 227, 255, 257-272, 275-281, 283, 288-289, 291, 293, 295-296, 297, 300-306, 310, 312, 316, 320-321, 323-325, 328, 330, 333, 337, 390, 396-398, 405, 474, 477, 491, 497, 515, 627, 636, 641-643, 669, 680, 686, 708, 743, 761
Norman C. Heckler & Co. 81
Northeast Auctions 182-183, 507, 509, 526
Pook & Pook 39, 47, 111, 137, 143-144, 221, 277, 289, 332, 443, 469, 492, 553, 557, 561-563, 572, 643, 671, 674, 686, 703, 767
Rago Arts and Auction Center 26, 183, 224, 418, 485, 554-566, 624, 698
Rich Penn Auctions 3-5, 7-8, 11, 19, 38, 142, 152-153, 287, 384, 402, 409, 502, 653, 654, 676-677, 748
RSL Auction Co. 34-38, 117, 717, 731
Ruby Lane 20, 22, 31, 41, 98, 100, 102-104, 106-107, 109, 132, 160, 163, 184, 187-206, 223-225, 228-232, 240, 243-244, 246-251, 253, 348-349, 354-356, 359-364, 371, 373-374, 390, 393, 401-403, 414, 431, 454, 461, 464, 471, 478, 480-481, 484, 488, 490, 493, 500-501, 513, 516, 529, 559, 578, 580-581, 583, 587, 592, 599-603, 605, 606, 612-613, 623, 626, 648-649, 664, 680, 682, 699-700, 707, 739-741, 744, 747
Samuel T. Freeman & Co. 655-657
Skinner, Inc. 25-26, 41, 45, 91, 94, 131, 169, 181, 183, 212, 250, 385, 409, 428, 501, 510, 514-515, 611, 617, 640, 669, 735, 751-755
Sloans & Kenyon 130-131, 387-388
Sotheby's 89, 184, 309, 337, 339, 388, 412, 415, 452, 509, 532, 539, 588, 596, 632, 698, 749-750, 759
Stein Auction Co. 660-664
Strawser Auction 94, 230-232, 441-442, 564, 610, 623
Tom Harris Auctions 28, 43, 47, 49, 61, 88, 120-122, 125, 132, 142-143, 145, 170, 176-177, 212-215, 219, 228, 353, 358, 362-364, 368, 404, 406, 422-424, 434, 440, 456-457, 478, 487, 502, 505, 558, 560, 564, 578-579, 590, 647, 649, 651, 685, 742, 744
Treadway Gallery 27, 50, 85, 93, 101, 110, 112, 148, 161-162, 177-178, 207, 237-239, 255-257, 263, 268, 269-273, 275, 278, 285, 297-299, 303, 307, 309-318, 321, 324-327, 329, 344-345, 354, 360, 372-373, 379, 381, 390-392, 397-399, 418-421, 423, 427, 436-438, 446, 459-460, 476-478, 482-483, 485, 489, 517, 533, 536, 539-541, 551, 554, 565-571, 574, 589, 594-595, 626, 635, 643, 645, 665-667, 678, 685-688, 690-698, 736, 751, 756, 758, 760, 771
Trocadero.com 244-247, 490, 679
Woody Auction Co. 170-174, 591-592

HOW TO GET ANTIQUE PRICING INFORMATION THAT CHANGES MONTHLY

Some markets are more volatile than others.
Auctions, trends, and collections impact prices in some categories dramatically.

If you're a dealer or a collector who NEEDS to know what is happening, SUBSCRIBE NOW to our award-winning monthly newsletter, *Kovels on Antiques and Collectibles.*

This is THE SOURCE that helps COLLECTORS and DEALERS keep up with the fast-changing world of antiques and collectibles.

- Learn about auction prices at the latest sales and auctions
- Spot tomorrow's emerging trends so you can cash in TODAY
- Discover the true value of dozens of collectibles as prices change month to month
- Find out how to avoid fakes and frauds and what is being faked right now!
- Accurately assess the quality of antiques and collectibles every month

For a FREE sample copy of the newsletter, just fill in your name and address on the back of this form and mail it to:

Kovels on Antiques and Collectibles
P.O. Box 420349
Palm Coast, Florida 32142-9656

The Kovels (collectors for more than 40 years, syndicated columnists, authors of 95 books, and stars of the show "Flea Market Finds with the Kovels" on HGTV) will clue you in so you can identify treasures that might be disguised as trash. Become part of the community of more informed, successful collectors.

Don't wait! Mail the form on the back of this page now, and we'll rush you a FREE issue of Kovels.

SUBSCRIBE NOW

to our award-winning monthly newsletter, *Kovels on Antiques and Collectibles.*

Mail this form now, and we'll send you a FREE issue of Kovels.

◯ YES! Please send me a FREE sample of *Kovels on Antiques and Collectibles* newsletter!

Name ______________________________ 08KPL

Address ______________________________

City ______________________________

State ______________________ Zip ____________

Email ______________________________

Mail to:

Kovels on Antiques and Collectibles
P.O. Box 420349
Palm Coast, Florida 32142-9656

Or call **800-829-9158**

Kovels on Antiques and Collectibles can be previewed at **www.Kovels.com**